Oxford Student's Dictionary of Current English

A S Hornby
Christina Ruse

Second Edition
by Christina Ruse

WESTMINSTER AES
QUINTIN KYNASTON CENTRE
MARLBOROUGH HILL
LONDON NW8 0NL

Oxford University Press

Oxford University Press,
Great Clarendon Street, Oxford OX2 6DP

Oxford New York
Athens Auckland Bangkok Bogota Bombay
Buenos Aires Calcutta Cape Town Dar es Salaam
Delhi Florence Hong Kong Istanbul Karachi
Kuala Lumpur Madras Madrid Melbourne
Mexico City Nairobi Paris Singapore Taipei
Tokyo Toronto

and associated companies in
Berlin Ibadan

OXFORD and OXFORD ENGLISH
are trademarks of Oxford University Press

ISBN 0 19 431122 8
© Oxford University Press, 1978, 1988

First published 1978 (reprinted fifteen times)
Second edition 1988
Eleventh impression 1997

No unauthorized photocopying

All rights reserved. No part of this publication may be
reproduced, stored in a retrieval system, or transmitted,
in any form or by any means, electronic, mechanical,
photocopying, recording or otherwise, without the prior
permission of Oxford University Press.

This book is sold subject to the condition that it shall
not, by way of trade or otherwise, be lent, re-sold, hired
out or otherwise circulated without the publisher's prior
consent in any form of binding or cover other than that
in which it is published and without a similar condition
including this condition being imposed on the
subsequent purchaser.

This book includes some words which are or are
asserted to be proprietary names. The presence or
absence of such assertions should not be regarded as
affecting the legal status of any proprietary name or
trademark.

Typeset in Great Britain by
Interactive Sciences Ltd, Gloucester

Printed in Great Britain by
Caledonian International Book Manufacturing Ltd

A, Nadt

Contents

Preface

The first edition of this dictionary was adapted from the *Oxford Advanced Learner's Dictionary*, Third Edition. During the period of its preparation and for some years before that, I had the very good luck to work with A S Hornby. I am deeply grateful for that experience since he gave me my interest and skills as a reference compiler and left me with a firm commitment to prepare material which provides all the necessary information in a form that is easy to find and use.

This new text has been completely rewritten and redesigned and takes into account current awareness of intermediate problems. Many dictionaries prepared for this level are simply shortened versions of more advanced ones. My experience in the classroom and in the field of reference research has shown me that intermediate-level students need *more* help with their English than advanced-level students, not less. This text has been built up from my own identification of intermediate-level students' special needs, and I would like to thank the many students and teachers in Britain and overseas who have provided information, ideas, criticisms and encouragement.

Oxford, 1988   Christina Ruse

What this dictionary can tell you about English

Spelling

For detailed information, read Appendices 1 and 2.

gorg·eous /'gɔːdʒəs/ *adj* **1** richly coloured; magnificent: *a gorgeous sunset*. **2** (*informal*) giving pleasure and satisfaction: *gorgeous weather; a gorgeous dress*.
gorg·eous·ly *adv*

> headword

bur·glar /'bɜːglə(r)/ *nc* a person who breaks into a house etc at night in order to steal.
'**burglar alarm** *nc* a device used to warn of burglars.

> derivative

> compound

> For an explanation of these words, read pages F7–8.

NASA /'næsə/ *acronym* National Aeronautics and Space Administration (the US government department for space exploration).

mkt *written abbr* (*commerce*) market.

> abbreviations are given in the main text of the dictionary with full information

col·our[1] (*US* = **col·or**) /'kʌlə(r)/ *n* **1** *nu* (also

> American spelling

fer·til·ize (also **-ise**) /'fɜːtɪlaɪz/ *vt* **1** to make

> correct alternative spelling

mys·tery /'mɪstərɪ/ *n* (*pl* **-ies**) **1** *nc* something of

> plural form

ba·sis /'beɪsɪs/ *nc* (*pl* **bases** /-siːz/) **1** the basic

> an irregular plural

ad·mit /əd'mɪt/ *v* (**-tt-**) **1** *vt,vi* **admit (sth; to**

> the last letter is doubled before you add *-ed* or *-ing*

eat /iːt/ *v* (*pt* **ate** /et/, *pp* **eaten** /'iːtn/) **1** *vi* to

> irregular verb forms

un·hap·py /ˌʌn'hæpɪ/ *adj* (**-ier, -iest**) not happy.

> comparative and superlative forms

Meaning

bake /beɪk/ *v* **1** *vt,vi* (of fish, vegetables, cakes etc) to cook, be cooked, by dry heat in an oven: *bake bread/potatoes/apples*.

> a simple explanation

al·so /'ɔːlsəʊ/ *adv* **1** in addition: *I love chips and I also like peas. Also, I like tomatoes. I can also hold a spider*.

> examples of how the word is used in sentences

how /haʊ/ *adv* . . .

3 in what state of health (when referring to a person): *How's your mother?* Ⓝ *'How'* always refers to health. When asking about a person's character, appearance etc use *What is . . . like?* as in *What's your new teacher like?*

> a full note, with examples, on a common error when this word is used in sentences

Grammar

hov·er·craft /ˈhɒvəkrɑːft/ *nc* a vehicle that

nail² /neɪl/ *vt* **1** to fasten, join etc (something)

parts of speech — for an explanation of *vt* and *vi* or *nc* and *nu*, read pages F14–16

EEC /ˌiː iː ˈsiː/ *abbr* (the —) the European Economic Community. ⇨ the Common Market.

'*the*' is always used before '*EEC*'

con·sist /kənˈsɪst/ *vi* (*no passive*) Ⓝ Not used in the continuous tenses, e.g. '*is/was -ing*'. **1 consist**

'I am consisting. . .', 'It has been consisting. . .' etc are not possible

ill¹ /ɪl/ *adj* **1** (*pred*) in poor health: *He's very ill. Unwashed fruit can make you seriously ill. She's been ill with measles. Does society care about those who are mentally ill?* Compare well¹(1). **be taken/fall ill** to become ill. **2** (*attrib*) bad: *She suffers from ill health. The ill effects of the weather are obvious. He's noted for his ill manners.* Compare good¹(1). Ⓝ '*Worse*' can be used as a comparative form of '*ill*', as in *He was very ill yesterday but today he's worse.*

this meaning of '*ill*' is used after a verb. . .

this meaning of '*ill*' is used before a noun — for detailed information, read pages F17–18

con·trary¹ /ˈkɒntrərɪ/ *adj* (*pred*) **contrary to sth** opposite to something: *What you have done is*

de·pend·ence /dɪˈpendəns/ *nu* **dependence (on sb/sth) 1** the state of being supported by

edge² /edʒ/ *v* **1** *vt* **edge sth (with sth)** to

shows that a particular preposition is used after the word

press² /pres/ *v*
press ahead (with sth) to continue (an activity) using a determined effort: *press ahead with urgent reforms.*
press down on sb to be a heavy burden: *The new taxes pressed down on everyone.*
press (sb) for sth to demand (from a person) action, a decision etc often and strongly: *press for a new enquiry.* **be pressed for sth** to have (almost) too little of something: *be pressed for time/money/space.*
press on (with sth) = press ahead (with sth).

the uses of verbs with an adverb or preposition are listed at the end of the entry for the verb — for detailed information, read pages F14–15

Usage

min·ute¹ /maɪˈnjuːt/ *adj* (*no comp*, but *the minutest* can be used for emphasis) **1** very small: *minute particles of dust.* **2** giving small details; careful and exact: *the minutest details.*

the special use of the superlative

cost¹ /kɒst/ *n* **1** *nc,nu* the amount of money (to be) paid for something: *the cost of repairs/of renting a flat/of learning to drive; without regard to cost* (= without considering how much money would be needed). Ⓝ '*Cost*' is used when referring to an amount to be paid (e.g. for building, repairs, paying fees etc) which involves paying people for labour, materials, rent, meals etc. '*Price*' is used when referring to payment to be paid when buying individual things as in shops. '*Cost*' is also used for general expenses such as running a car, living expenses etc.

a simple explanation of a common difficulty with choosing between two words that have similar meanings

orate /ɔː'reɪt/ *vi* (*formal*) to speak in public.

fiv·er /'faɪvə(r)/ *nc* (*informal*) a £5 note.

'data bank/base *nc* (*computers*) a collection of information ready for processing in a computer.

car·ni·vore /'kɑːnɪvɔː(r)/ *nc* (*science*) an animal that eats meat. Compare herbivore, insectivore, omnivore.

pro·tag·on·ist /prə'tægənɪst/ *nc* (*literature*) the main character in a drama or novel. Compare antagonist(2).

> words that are used in particular situations are labelled

econ·omi·cal /ˌiːkə'nɒmɪkl/ *adj* careful in using money, time, supplies etc: *an economical system for heating water.* Opp uneconomical.

grave[1] /greɪv/ *adj* (**—r, —st**) serious; very sad and disappointing: *grave news.* ⇨ gravity(2).

real /rɪəl/ *adj* existing in fact; not imagined or artificial: *Was it a real man you saw or a ghost? Things that happen in real life are sometimes stranger than in stories. Who is the real manager of the business? Tell me the real* (= true) *reason for your anger.* Compare genuine, unreal.

fa·mous /'feɪməs/ *adj* known widely; having fame: *a famous scientist.* Compare infamous.

> references to opposites, related words and words that are often confused

Spoken English

read·er /'riːdə(r)/ *nc* **1** a person who reads, esp

'day-long *adj, adv* (lasting) for the whole day.
ˌday-re'turn *nc* (also *attrib*) a ticket to travel to a place and back on the same day.

> special symbols show how each word is spoken, and the marks , and ' show stress — for detailed information, read page F20

May /meɪ/ *n* (also *attrib*) the fifth month of the year, with 31 days: *He came on 6 May.* Ⓝ *'6 May'* is spoken as *'May the sixth'* or *'the sixth of May'.*

> a note on special problems when saying a written sentence or phrase

Make the best use of your dictionary

These notes will show you how to use this dictionary. Read all of this section so that you know the ways in which this dictionary can help you.

You can use this dictionary to find a spelling or meaning of a word but you can also use it to increase your vocabulary, learn English grammar and improve your ability to form many kinds of sentences.

Find the word you need

If you have any problems with the spelling of the word, read Appendix 1 at the back of this dictionary.

Use the word in the top corner of each page (called a *running head*) to find the page that has the word you are looking for.

For example, **brand** is on page 75:

bow	74

low bow.
bow³ /baʊ/ *nc* (often *pl*) the front end of a boat or ship.
bow⁴ /baʊ/ *v* **1** *vi* to bend the head or body forward (as a greeting etc): *They bowed low.* **bow and scrape** to behave with too much respect in order to get a person's favour. **2** *vt* to bend (⸱ head) forward: *They bowed their heads in pr*

75	bread

disgrace. **6** a piece of burning wood (in a fire).
brand² /brænd/ *vt* **1** to mark (cattle, goods etc) with a brand¹(3). **2** (*fig*) to give (a person) a bad name: *She has been branded as a thief.*

bread /bred/ *nu* **1** (also *attrib*) a kind of food made by mixing flour with water and yeast and

The running heads show the words that are included in pages 74–75 of the dictionary.

A single word

The word you are looking for is in **thick black letters.** It is put into the dictionary in one of three ways:

☐ A word such as *bottle, happy, run, through* has a complete entry in the dictionary with numbered meanings and examples. It is in **thick black letters** and is called a *headword*:

hap·py /'hæpɪ/ *adj* (**-ier, -iest**) **1** feeling or expressing pleasure, contentment, satisfaction etc: *a happy face/child. Their marriage has been a happy one.*

headword

If a word is used in two or more grammatical forms (e.g. as a *noun* and a *verb*, or as an *adj*, *adv* and *pron*), each form is given a separate entry in alphabetical order (e.g. the *noun* entry comes before the *verb* entry) and the headwords are numbered:

bottle¹ /'bɒtl/ *nc* **1** a container with a narrow neck, used for liquids: *a wine bottle; a bottle of* (= filled with) *wine.* **2** as much as a bottle holds: *Mary drinks two bottles of milk a day.*
bottle² /'bɒtl/ *vt* **1** to put, store, (something) in bottles: *bottle fruit.* **2 bottle sth up** (*fig*) to be unable or unwilling to express feelings, anger.

numbered headwords

If a word has two or more completely different meanings, each meaning is given a separate entry and the headwords are numbered:

> **grate¹** /greɪt/ *nc* (a metal frame for holding coal etc in) a fireplace.
> **grate²** /greɪt/ *n sing* a harsh noise made by scraping (esp metals): *the grate of a door on its hinges.*
> **grate³** /greɪt/ *v* **1** *vt* to rub (esp food) into small pieces: *grate cheese.* **2** *vi* **grate (on sth)** to make a harsh noise by rubbing: *The gate grates on its hinges.* **3** *vi* **grate (on sb)** (*fig*) to have an irritating effect (on a person): *His bad manners grated on everyone.*

numbered headwords

☐ A word such as *happily, laziness, rearrangement* is formed by adding *-ly, -ness, -ment* etc to a word. This changes the grammatical form (e.g. *happy* (adjective) becomes *happily* (adverb)) but the meaning is almost the same. A word of this kind is called a *derivative* and it is in **thick black letters** at the end of the entry for the main word (e.g. **happy**):

> **hap·py** /ˈhæpɪ/ *adj*
> **hap·pily** /-əlɪ/ *adv*
> **hap·pi·ness** *nu*

derivatives in alphabetical order

☐ A word such as *air letter, face-cloth, haircut* is formed by joining two words together. It can be written as two words, as one word with a hyphen or as a single word. This new word has a different meaning from the meaning of the words that form each part. A word of this kind is called a *compound* and it is in **thick black letters** at the end of the entry for the word that forms the first part:

> **face¹** /feɪs/ *nc*
> **'face-ache** *nc* (*fig; derog*) an annoying person.
> **'face-cloth** *nc* a small square towel used for washing the face and hands.
> **'face-cream** *nu* a kind of cream for cleaning and softening the face.
> **face·less** *adj* (*fig*) unknown to the public: *the faceless leaders of commerce and industry.*
> **'face-lift** *nc* (**a**) a form of surgery to make the face look younger. (**b**) (*fig*) an improvement to the appearance (of a building etc).
> **'face-powder** *nu* cosmetic powder for the face.
> **'face-saving** *adj* ⇨ face¹(2).

compounds in alphabetical order

A group of words

The word you are looking for may be part of a group of words, e.g. *check on a person/something, be in good hands, hold one's tongue, the man in the street, first of all,* and these are in **thick black sloping letters.** There are many kinds of groups but it will help you to remember that they are usually one of three kinds:

☐ A group of words such as *check on a person/something, be in good hands, hold one's tongue* is a verb with a special meaning. The meaning is not the same as the meaning for a verb (e.g. *check, be, hold*) that forms part of the group. There are two kinds of groups like these:

a verb followed by a word like *about, down, in, on, up* (e.g. *check on a person/something*). This is in **thick black sloping letters** in the entry for the verb. If there are more than two of these in an entry, they are put at the end of the entry for the verb:

check² /tʃek/ *v* **1** *vt,vi* to examine (something) in order to learn whether it is correct: *check the bill; check the time.* ⇨ check on sb/sth. **2** *vt* to cause (an emotion, feeling etc) to stop: *He couldn't check his anger.* ⇨ unchecked. **3** *vt,vi* (*chess*) to call, make, a check(4).
check in (at sth) to arrive and register at a hotel, airport. Hence **'check-in** *nc* a place at an airport etc where one checks in for a flight.
check sb/sth off to mark a person, item etc as correct, present, dealt with etc using a list: *check off their names.* ⇨ checklist.
check on sb/sth to examine, confirm, something, a person's health etc: *check on the score; check on the baby; check on a candidate.*
check out (of sth) to pay the bill, return keys etc and leave (a hotel). **check sb/sth out** (*informal*) = check on sb/sth. ⇨ also check-out.
check sb/sth over (*informal*) = check on sb/sth.
check through sth to check(1) a list or series (to find errors, identify one item, person etc).
check up (on sb/sth) = check on sb/sth. ⇨ also check-up.

in alphabetical order (*'on'* comes before *'out'*, *'over'* etc)

a verb with a noun like *hand, tongue* in the group (e.g. *be in good hands, hold one's tongue*). This is in **thick black sloping letters** in the entry for the noun. It is put at the end of the meaning of the noun that is nearest to the meaning of the group (e.g. **hold one's tongue** is at the end of **tongue**, meaning **1**):

tongue /tʌŋ/ *n* **1** *nc* the movable organ in the mouth, used in talking, tasting, licking etc: *A white layer on your tongue can be a sign that you are ill.* **have a rough tongue** to have a habit of being rude or bad-tempered. **on the tip of one's tongue** ⇨ tip¹(1). **have one's tongue in one's cheek** to say something that one does not intend to be taken seriously. **have lost one's tongue** to be too shy to speak. **have a sharp tongue** to be easily angered, critical etc. **hold one's tongue** to be silent, stop talking. **put one's tongue out (at sb)** to do this as a rude sign. **2** *nc,nu* (also *attrib*) an animal's

in alphabetical order (*'have'* comes before *'hold'* etc)

☐ A group of words such as *the man in the street* has a special meaning. The meaning is not the same as the meanings for the separate words that form the group. This is in **thick black sloping letters** in the entry for the first main word, usually a noun (e.g. *man*). It is put at the end of the meaning that is nearest to the meaning of the group (e.g. **the man in the street** is at the end of **man¹**, meaning **1**):

man¹ /mæn/ *n* (*pl* **men** /men/) **1** *nc* (often used in combinations) an **adult male human being**: *a post-man/clergyman. There's a man at the door.* **man and boy** from boyhood onwards: *He has worked for the firm, man and boy, for thirty years.* **the man in the street** a person regarded as representing the interests and opinions of ordinary people. **a man of the world** a person with wide experience of business and society. **2** (usually *pl;*

in alphabetical order (*'street'* comes after *'boy'* and before *'world'*)

Because it is often very difficult to know where to find a group like this in the dictionary, there are references (using ⇨) to send you to the right place:

boy /bɔɪ/ *nc* **1** a male person up to the age of 17 or 18. ⇨ boyish. **jobs for the boys** (*informal*) appointing one's own supporters, the people one likes etc to (senior) jobs. **man and boy** ⇨ man¹(1). **2** a son: *He has two boys and one girl.*

Look at the entry for **man¹**.

☐ A group of words such as *first of all* has a special meaning. It is in **thick black sloping letters** in the entry for the first main word (e.g. *first*). It is put at the end of the meaning that is nearest to the meaning of the group (e.g. **first of all** is at the end of **first²**, meaning **1**):

first² /fɜːst/ *adv* **1** before any other or others: *I saw her first. What will do you first? First, I'd like to thank my wife.* Compare last²(1), next²(1). **first of all** (used for emphasis): *First of all we must rescue the children.* **first and foremost** (used for emphasis) before anything else: *First and foremost you must check that the electricity is off.* **2** for the first time: *I first met her in Paris*

in alphabetical order (*'all'* comes before *'foremost'*)

Because it is often very difficult to know where to find a group like this in the dictionary, there are references (using ⇨) to send you to the right place:

all³ /ɔːl/ *pron, nu* . . .   **first/last/ second of all** ⇨ first²(1), last²(1), second². **2**

Look at the entry for **first²** meaning **1**.

Look inside the front cover of the dictionary. There is a chart that has the information about how to find the word you need.

Find the meaning you need

You have found the word you need but you need the right meaning or use:

Each meaning in a main entry begins with a thick black number, **1, 2, 3** etc (called a *definition number*). The meanings are organized so that the one used most often and in most situations comes first. The last meanings are ones that are less used, more formal or used in special situations like science or a particular sport. Read each numbered meaning until you find the one you need.

If you are still not sure about which meaning to choose, read all the examples that follow the meanings. These will help you to understand the meanings better.

pros·pect¹ /ˈprɒspekt/ *n* **1** *nc,nu* (an example of) an expectation or hope: *I see no/little/not much prospect of his recovery. There are good prospects for me if I accept the job.* **2** *nc* a wide view over land or sea. **3** *nc* something that is likely: *We must face the prospect of higher bus fares.* **4** *nc* a person who is likely to be successful, to buy one's goods etc: *He's a good prospect for the gold medal.*

definition number, meaning, examples

Some entries have information about when the word is used (e.g. *formal, informal; science, sport*) to help you choose the right meaning or use of a word.

Choose the word you need

You have found the word you were looking for but you are not sure that it is the word you need:

First, you must read the entry carefully because you may find information that will make you sure.

You may be given a reference to another entry for a word that is used in similar ways. For example, at **every** you are asked to compare the use of *all*:

every /ˈevrɪ/ *adj* or *det* **1** each one (of a group) with no exception: *I've read every book she's written/every one of her books. Every single one of my answers was wrong. Every word he said is true. I try to do my exercises every day.* Ⓝ *'Every'* is used with a singular noun and verb. Compare: all¹(1),

Compare the meaning and use of *'all'*.

If you look at **all¹**, you will find information to help you choose between *every* and *all*:

all¹ /ɔːl/ *adj* or *det* . . .   **1**
(used with pl nouns) the whole number of: *All students need a good dictionary.* Ⓝ *'All'* and *'every'* can have the same meaning but *'all'* is used with a plural noun, as in *All towns have a post office*, and *'every'* is used with a singular noun, as in *Every town has a post office.* Similarly, in the negative, *'not all'* is used with a plural noun and *'not every'* with a singular noun, as in *Not all towns have/Not every town has a hospital.* Compare both¹, each¹, every.

an explanation of the differences between *'all'* and *'every'* and how each word is used in a sentence

You may be given a reference to the entry for another word that is often confused with the word you have found. For example, at **continuous** you are asked to compare '*continual*':

> **con·tin·u·ous** /kən'tɪnjʊəs/ *adj* going on without
> stopping: *a continuous struggle for human rights*.
> Compare continual.

Look at the meaning and use of '*continual*'.

When you have read the meanings and examples for both words, you can decide which one to choose.

You may be given the more usual word as the explanation but only if that word is very easy:

> **com·mence** /kə'mens/ *vt* (*formal*) to begin (the
> more usual word). **(N)** For a comparison of *com-*
> *mence, begin* and *start*, ⇨ the *note* at begin(1).

'*Commence*' means '*begin*' and '*begin*' is used much more often. Look at **begin** for detailed information.

Write the word you have chosen

The biggest problems when you write a word in a sentence are spelling and grammar.

Spelling

There is information in **thick black letters** about spelling the forms of a word when it is used in sentences:

> **tom·ato** /tə'mɑːtəʊ/ *nc* (*pl* **—es**) (also *attrib*) (a

how to spell the plural form of a noun

> **sink²** /sɪŋk/ *v* (*pt* **sank** /sæŋk/ or **sunk** /sʌŋk/, *pp*
> **sunk**) **1** *vt,vi* (to cause a person, ship etc) to go

how to spell the different forms of a verb

> **dear¹** /dɪə(r)/ *adj* (**—er, —est**) **1** (*attrib*) loved;

how to spell the different forms of an adjective

> **rub²** /rʌb/ *v* (**-bb-**) **1** *vt,vi* to move (something)
>
> **big** /bɪg/ *adj* (**—ger, —gest**) **1** more than aver-

doubling the last letter of a verb or adjective

For details about spelling forms of verbs, look at the section on spelling in Appendix 2 at the back of this dictionary.

For details about spelling forms of other words, look at Appendix 1 at the back of this dictionary.

Word-division

There is one special problem when you write words. Near the end of a line of writing you may find that you do not have enough room to write the next word. The best thing to do is to begin that word on the next line.

Sometimes, especially if you are typing, you may want to divide the word at the end of a line and put part of it on the next line. This is called *word-division*. The places where a word can be divided are shown in the head-word using a thick black dot:

every·body   ex·amine   ex·cla·ma·tion

You can divide the word at a place where there is a · by putting the part before the · at the end of a line and adding a hyphen (e.g. *every-*) and then putting the part after the · at the beginning of the next line (e.g. *body*). Always divide a *compound* at the place where the two words that form it are joined:

eye-shadow   love-letter   ring-leader

Grammar

There is a great deal of information about grammar in this dictionary. To help you make the most use of it, there are no codes, no difficult labels and no complicated abbreviations. Here is an explanation of how grammar is described for verbs, nouns and adjectives.

Verbs

We have most difficulty with verbs. This dictionary gives detailed information that is easy to learn and use.

Look at Appendix 2 at the back of the dictionary where there is a chart that shows all the verb tenses and their passive forms. This chart will help you to identify the tenses and choose the one you need. If you are not sure about which tense to use, look at the entry for the tense (e.g. **past perfect**) in the dictionary.

Under the chart there is useful information about particular verbs and sentences.

There is also a section in Appendix 2 on spelling verb forms (e.g. **-d**, **-ed** and **-ied**) and doubling last letters (e.g. *dragged, beginning*). These forms are also given in **thick black letters** at the entry for the verb in the dictionary:

mar·ry /'mærɪ/ *v* (*pt,pp* **-ied**) **1** *vt,vi* to take (a	The past forms are '*married*'.
trav·el² /'trævl/ *v* (**-ll-**, *US* **-l-**) **1** *vt,vi* to make	In British English the final letter is doubled in the past tenses and the *-ing* form.

At the end of Appendix 2, there is a complete list of verbs with irregular forms. These forms are also given at the entry for the verb in the dictionary:

sing¹ /sɪŋ/ *v* (*pt* **sang** /sæŋ/, *pp* **sung** /sʌŋ/) **1**	irregular forms for the past tense (e.g. I *sang*) and the past participle (e.g. I have *sung*)

When you look at the entry for a verb, you will see *vt* or *vi* or *vt,vi*.

vt means that the verb (or a particular meaning of the verb if *vt* follows a definition number) is always followed by a noun or a noun phrase (e.g. *I broke the cup*). This is called a *transitive verb*. You cannot use a verb or meaning of a verb that is marked *vt* unless you use a noun or a noun phrase after it (e.g. *I sold my bike*, not 'I sold.').

vi means that the verb (or a particular meaning of the verb if *vi* follows a definition number) cannot be used before a noun or a noun phrase (e.g. *I laughed* or *I laughed at her*, not 'I laughed her dress.') This is called an *intransitive verb*.

vt,vi means that the verb can be used with a noun or a noun phrase (e.g. *I burned the wood*) or without a noun or a noun phrase (e.g. *It burned easily*).

Other special difficulties when using a particular verb are given at the entry in the dictionary:

seem /si:m/ *vi* Ⓝ Not used in continuous tenses, e.g. *is/was -ing.* to have or give the impression or appearance of being or doing; appear to be: *You seem tired. There seems to be no one here. What*

'It is seeming', 'He was seeming' etc are not possible. Use a tense that does not have *-ing* such as 'It seems all right', 'He seemed to be working'.

If the verb is used with a particular group of words, this is given in **thick black sloping letters** in the entry for the verb:

re·cover /rɪ'kʌvə(r)/ *v* **1** *vt* to get back (something lost etc); get back the use of (something): *recover what was lost; recover consciousness* (i.e. after fainting); *recover one's sight/hearing.* **2** *vi* **recover (from sth)** **(a)** to become well again: *He is slowly recovering (from his illness).* **(b)** to get back to a former position of strength, wealth etc: *Has the country recovered from the effects of the war yet?*

'Recover' is used on its own or with 'from something' as shown in the example. No other addition (e.g. 'in something', 'to something' etc) is possible.

re·ly /rɪ'laɪ/ *vi* (*pt,pp* **-ied**) **rely on sb/sth** **1** to depend on (a person, thing): *We rely on that bus to get to the shops.* **2** to trust (a person, thing) with confidence: *He can always be relied on for help.*

'Rely' is always used with 'on a person' or 'on something'. 'I rely.' is not possible.

( ) round some words in the group shows that these words can be used with the verb or you can leave them out (e.g. *Will he recover?* and *Will he recover from his illness?* are both possible). If there are no ( ), you must use all the words in the group (e.g. *You can rely on me*, not 'You can rely.').

/ in a group of words shows that you have a choice. **Rely on sb/sth** means that *You can rely on me* and *You can rely on this dictionary* are both possible.

Sometimes you will find ( ) and / used in the same group:

res·cue² /'reskju:/ *vt* **rescue sb/sth (from sb/ sth)** to save (a person, thing) (from danger, disaster, attack, being held prisoner etc): *rescuing a child (from drowning); rescue a business by lending money.*

The following choices are possible:
rescue a person,
rescue something,
rescue a person from another person,
rescue a person from something,
rescue something from a person,
rescue something from something.

This use of ( ) and / is the same in every entry (for nouns, adjectives etc as well as verbs) and every part of an entry (in explanations, examples, idioms etc).

If you remember these easy rules about the use of ( ) and /, you can often use a verb in many ways in sentences and you will quickly increase your use of English.

Nouns

There is a section in Appendix 1 on spelling noun forms (e.g. **-s**, **-es**, and **-ies**).

All *-ies* forms and irregular plural forms are given in **thick black letters** at the entries for nouns in the dictionary:

fly¹ /flaɪ/ *nc* (*pl* **flies**) a kind of two-winged insect

one fly, two flies

child /tʃaɪld/ *nc* (*pl* **children** /'tʃɪldrən/) **1** a

one child, two children

When you look at the entry for a noun, you will see *nc* or *nu* or *nc,nu*.

nc means that the noun (or a particular meaning of the noun if *nc* follows a definition number) can be used with *a/an/one* and in the plural. This is called a *countable noun*.

nu means that the nouns (or a particular meaning of the noun if *nu* follows a definition number) cannot be used with *a/an/one* and cannot be used in the plural. This is called an *uncountable noun*.

house¹ /haʊs/ *nc* (*pl* **—s** /'haʊzɪz/) **1** a building for people to live in: *New houses are going up everywhere.*

'A house', 'the house', 'two houses' etc are possible.

in·for·ma·tion /ˌɪnfə'meɪʃn/ *nu* news, facts or knowledge given: *That's a useful piece/bit of information.*

Only *'information'* and *'the information'* are possible.

pa·per¹ /'peɪpə(r)/ *n* **1** *nu* (also *attrib*) a substance in the form of sheets, used for writing, printing, drawing, wrapping, packing etc: *a sheet of paper; a paper bag.* **2** *nc* = newspaper: *the evening papers.* **3** (*pl*) documents showing who a

Only *'paper'* and *'the paper'* are possible with this meaning.

'A paper', 'two papers' etc are possible with this meaning.

nc,nu means that the noun (or a particular meaning of the noun if *nc,nu* follows a definition number) can be used in the singular (with or without *a/an/one*) and in the plural:

mar·riage /'mærɪdʒ/ *n* **1** *nc,nu* (an instance of) a legal union of a man and woman as husband and wife; the state of being married: *Do you believe in marriage?* (= Do you think people should marry?) *A marriage has been arranged between Jane and Tom.* **a broken marriage** one that has

'Marriage' can be used in either way, as shown by the examples.

Some nouns are always plural:

par·ticu·lars /pə'tɪkjʊləz/ *n pl* details: *We need*

'Particulars' is always used with a plural verb, e.g. *are*.

Some nouns are always singular:

man·ner /'mænə(r)/ *n* **1** *nc* a way in which something is done or happens: *Do it in this manner.* **2** *n sing* a person's way of behaving towards others: *I don't like his manner.* **3** (*pl*) social behaviour:

'a manner', *'his manner'* etc but no plural

Some nouns are used with *the* (e.g. *the police*) and this is shown by (the —) at the entry for the noun:

po·lice¹ /pə'liːs/ *n pl* (the —) an official group of

You must use *'the police'* and not *'a police'* or *'police'*.

Other nouns are the names of unique things, e.g. the planet 'Earth', and these are marked *n*:

earth¹ /ɜːθ/ *n* **1** *n* (often E-) the planet on which

There is only one.

Some nouns are always used with a capital letter (e.g. *Highness*) or are often used with a capital letter (e.g. *Parliament*). These are shown at the entry in the dictionary:

high·ness /'haɪnɪs/ *n* **1** *nu* the state or quality of being high. **2** *nc* (H-) a title used of and to a royal person: *His/Her/Your Royal Highness.*

Only *'Highness'* is possible with this meaning.

par·lia·ment /'pɑːləmənt/ *nc* (also P-) a

'Parliament' is also used.

If the noun is used with a particular group of words, this is given in **thick black sloping letters** in the entry for the noun:

lec·ture¹ /'lektʃə(r)/ *nc* **lecture (about/on sth)** a talk for the purpose of teaching: *a course of philosophy lectures.*

The following choices are possible:
a lecture,
a lecture about something,
a lecture on something

give sb a lecture to tell a person off or state one's disapproval.

All the words in the group must be used.

( ) round some words in a group, e.g. **get (hold of) the wrong end of the stick**, shows that these words can be used with the noun or you can leave them out (e.g. *He got the wrong end of the stick* is also possible). If there are no ( ), you must use all the words in a group (e.g. *I gave him a lecture*) and you cannot change any (e.g. 'I wrote him a lecture' or 'I gave the lecture' are not possible with this meaning of *lecture*).

/ in a group of words shows that you have a choice (e.g. *lecture (about/on sth)* means that *a lecture about something* and *a lecture on something* are both possible).

Sometimes you will see ( ) and / used in the same group as shown here (and so *listen to a lecture* is also possible).

Adjectives

There is a section in Appendix 1 on spelling comparative and superlative forms (e.g. *-r*, *-st*; *-er*, *-est*; *-ier*, *-iest*). These forms are given in **thick black letters** in the entry for the adjective in the dictionary:

fine¹ /faɪn/ *adj* (**—r**, **—st**) **1** (of weather) bright;	*finer, finest*
great /ɡreɪt/ *adj* (**—er**, **—est**) **1** well above aver-	*greater, greatest*
hap·py /'hæpɪ/ *adj* (**-ier**, **-iest**) **1** feeling or	*happier, happiest*

Unusual comparative and superlative forms are also shown in **thick black letters**:

good¹ /ɡʊd/ *adj* (**better** /'betə(r)/, **best** /best/)	irregular forms
fat¹ /fæt/ *adj* (**—ter**, **—test**) **1** having much	*fatter, fattest*

Some adjectives have (*no comp*) which means that they cannot be used as a comparative or superlative (i.e. *-r, -st* etc and *more . . ., most . . .* are not possible).

equal¹ /'iːkwəl/ *adj* **1** (*no comp*) being the same in size, amount, number, degree, value etc: *equal pay for equal work; equal opportunity; divide it into two equal parts; two boys of equal height.* **2**	'Equal' used with this meaning has no comparative or superlative.

In English we can use most adjectives before a noun or after a verb (e.g. 'It's a *red* ball' or 'The ball is *red*'). But when you look at an entry for an adjective, you will sometimes see (*attrib*) or (*pred*).

(*attrib*) means that the adjective (or a particular meaning of the adjective if (*attrib*) follows a definition number) can only be used before a noun (e.g. *advance* in *an advance warning*). This is called an *attributive* position.

Another common use of (*attrib*) is to show that a noun (e.g. *family*) is often used as an attributive (e.g. *a family discussion* = a discussion between members of a family):

ad·vance¹ /əd'vɑːns/ adj (attrib) **1** done before or earlier: an advance payment/booking/warning. **2** sent before others: an advance copy/guard.

attributive adjective (with examples)

fam·ily /'fæmlɪ/ n (pl -ies) **1** nc (also attrib) parents and children: How many families live in that house? I enjoy family life. Ⓝ 'Family' is used

a noun that can also be used as an attributive (with examples)

(pred) means that the adjective (or a particular meaning of the adjective if (pred) follows a definition number) can only be used after a verb (e.g. awake in He is awake). This is called a predicative position:

awake¹ /ə'weɪk/ adj (pred) not asleep; having woken: He was lying awake thinking about her.

predicative adjective (with an example)

Problems when using a word

If you have problems when using a word, look at the entry for the word in the dictionary. Where you see Ⓝ there are notes to help you.

few¹ /fjuː/ adj or det . . .
　　Ⓝ 'Few' is used to refer to 'a small number of', as in few animals/clocks. 'A little' is used to refer to 'a small amount of', as in a little bread/time/kindness. ⇨ the note at less¹. **fewer . . . than . . .**

explains the difference between 'few' and 'a little'

about² /ə'baʊt/ prep . . .
　　Ⓝ 'A book about wild animals' gives general information but 'a book on economics' suggests that it is a serious, academic work. **2** through-

explains different uses of 'about' and 'on'

'active (voice) n (gram) . . .
　　Ⓝ In general, the active voice is more effective because it is more direct and emphatic than the passive voice, but the passive voice is especially useful when referring to the action or event and not the performer, as in The winning goal was scored in the final minutes of the match. Compare passive (voice).

explains a common problem about style

ad·di·tion /ə'dɪʃn/ n . . .
　　3 in addition (adv) as an added person or thing: We have one spare bed but we need another in addition. Ⓝ 'As well' is also possible. **in**

suggests another way of saying the same thing so that you can increase your vocabulary

ago /ə'gəʊ/ adv . . .
　　Ⓝ 'Ago' is always used with a past tense and is always placed after the expression of time, as in a month ago. 'Ago' refers to when an event or situation happened, as in He died in London three years ago. 'For' refers to the length of time an event or situation lasted or lasts, as in He lived in London for three years. 'Since' refers to the time when an event or situation began, as in We've lived in London since last year. Compare before.

how to use 'ago' in a sentence and how to choose between 'ago', 'for' and 'since'

meat /miːt/ *nu* **1** the flesh of animals used as food. Ⓝ *'Meat'* usually refers to cattle, sheep etc (*red meat*) but is also used for chickens, ducks etc (*white meat*) and sometimes the flesh of fish. **2** (*fig*) useful or

more detailed information to increase your vocabulary

must² /məst *strong form:* mʌst/ *auxiliary verb* Ⓝ *'Must'* is a *modal auxiliary verb* used with another verb to express obligation. *'Must'* has no infinitive or imperative form and no participles. *'Must'* is always followed by an infinitive without *'to'*. Compare

a summary of the features of this special kind of verb

little¹ /'lɪtl/ *adj or det* . . . **3** (*attrib*) small in size: *my little finger/toe; a little fish in a big pond. He's a little man with a big heart. What a horrible little mind you have!* Ⓝ The comparative and superlative forms are *'littler'* and *'littlest'* but they are rarely used. *'Small'* is also possible but is used to refer to physical size only, as in *a small room/box/town/space. 'Little'* is preferred when expressing an emotional idea with the size, as in *He has a nasty little temper. I can afford only a little present.* Com-

Many dictionaries tell you *'little'* = *'small'*. This is not true for all meanings and you are told when *'small'* can be used to mean 'little'.

lay² /leɪ/ *v* (*pt,pp* **laid** /leɪd/) Ⓝ . . . Be careful because *'to lay'* may be mistaken for the past tense of the verb *'to lie'* (which is also *'lay'*, as in *I lay down on the bed*). *'To lay'* always has a direct object, as in *lay your coat over a chair; lay an egg; lay a table* but *'to lie'* never has a direct object. Compare: *We were laying a carpet on the floor* and *We were lying on the grass looking at the stars.* **1** *vt* to put (some-

explains a common mistake

all² /ɔːl/ *adv* . . . **1** in every way; completely; entirely: *They were dressed all in black.* Ⓝ *'All'* is used for emphasis and can often be omitted without changing the meaning. Be careful because the meaning of the sentence depends on the position of *'all'.* Compare *We all sat alone* (= Each one of us sat alone) and *We sat all alone* (= A group of us sat together but without others). *all at once* ⇨

explains how the position of a word in a sentence decides the meaning of the sentence

There is also information in entries about opposites and you are told where to find information about words with similar or related meanings:

hap·py /'hæpɪ/ *adj* (**-ier, -iest**) **1** feeling or expressing pleasure, contentment, satisfaction etc: *a happy face/child. Their marriage has been a happy one.* Opp unhappy.

The opposite is *'unhappy'*.

easy¹ /'iːzɪ/ *adj* . . . **6** (*informal*) willing to agree, let others decide etc: *I don't mind where we go—I'm easy. She's very easy to get on with.* Compare difficult(2).

'Difficult' is not an exact opposite and the meanings and examples will show this.

es·tate /ɪ'steɪt/ *n* **1** *nc* a piece of property in the form of land, esp in the country: *He owns large estates in Scotland.* ⇨ council/housing/industrial/real estate. **2** *nu* (*legal*) a person's whole property.

Look at *'council estate'*, *'housing estate'*, *'industrial estate'* and *'real estate'* for special uses.

like⁴ /laɪk/ *prep* . . .
    4 in that manner; in the same way as: *Don't talk to me like that! She was acting like an idiot.* ⇨ anything(1,5), clockwork, crazy, hell, mad(2), shot(1), wildfire.

When you look at these entries you will find *'like'* used in special idioms, e.g. *like anything.*

Say the word you have chosen

Each word has a phonetic spelling immediately after the ordinary spelling:

broth·er /'brʌðə(r)/ *nc* **1** a son of the same

phonetic spelling showing you how to say *'brother'*

Phonetic spelling is a way of writing so that one symbol (e.g. i:) *always* represents only one sound (e.g. *-ee-* in *feet* or *-ea-* in *seat*). Look inside the back cover of the dictionary. If you learn the symbols you will be able to say the words in the dictionary.

When a word has more than one syllable (e.g. *forget*) one syllable is said more strongly than the other (e.g. *forGET*). This is called *stress* and the syllable which is stressed has a mark ' before it (e.g. **for'get**):

for·get /fə'get/ *vt,vi* (*pt* **forgot** /fə'gɒt/, *pp* **for-**

The phonetic spelling shows you how to say *'forget'*. Notice that you are also shown how to say *'forgot'*.

In longer words, other syllables may also be said strongly but this stress is not as strong as the one marked '. This weaker stress has a mark ˌ before it (e.g. ˌ**under'stand**):

under·stand /ˌʌndə'stænd/ *v* (*pt,pp* **-stood**

You must say *un-* with stress and *-stand* with stronger stress.

The marks ' and ˌ are very useful when you need to say compounds (e.g. **'story-book**, when the first part is stressed, and ˌ**strong-'willed**, when the second part is stressed):

ˌ**dead 'heat** *nc* a race in which competitors finish at exactly the same time.

This shows that you must stress the second part.

'dead·line *nc* a date fixed for completing a task.

You must stress the first part.

Aa

A, a /eɪ/ (pl **A's, a's** /eɪz/) the first letter of the English alphabet.

A symbol (electricity) ampere(s).

AA /ˌeɪ 'eɪ/ abbr **1** (the —) Automobile Association: join the AA. **2** Alcoholics Anonymous.

AAA /ˌeɪ eɪ 'eɪ/ abbr (the —) (GB) Amateur Athletics Association.

A1 /ˌeɪ 'wʌn/ (a) (of ships) first class. (b) (informal) excellent: feeling A1 (= feeling very fit and healthy).

a /ə strong form: eɪ/, **an** /ən strong form: æn/ indefinite article or det Ⓝ 'A' is used before a consonant, but not if the initial sound is a vowel, as in an hour. 'An' is used before a vowel, but not if the initial sound is a consonant, as in a university. 'A' or 'an' is only used with a singular countable noun. Compare the². **1 (a)** one (but no particular one): a book; an apple. A healthy child is a happy one. Let's go to a Chinese restaurant. She's got a cold/an earache. Have you a pen (pl = any pens)? I have a pen (pl = some pens). **(b)** one (not yet known or named): We saw a good film on TV last night. I'm still waiting for a decision. **2** (used when speaking or writing about number, quantity, groups etc): a lot of money; a few books; a little more; half a dozen; costing a hundred pounds; a quarter of an hour; a spoonful of sugar; a friend of mine (= one of my friends); a knife and fork. ⇨ the note at and(1). **3** one portion or quantity of: a steak; a slice of bread; a piece of cake. Can I have a tea (= a cup of tea) and two coffees (= two cups of coffee), please? **4** each: 60 miles an hour; twice a week; 50p a metre. Compare the²(8). **5** (used when speaking or writing about a person's profession, hobby, qualifications etc): She wants to be a brain surgeon. He has a BA in history/an IQ of 130. She's an MP. He's a good chess player/a boring speaker. A botanist is a person who studies plants. **6** (used to explain meaning or use): A thermometer is an instrument for measuring temperature. A spider is not an insect. **7** one example of: Is this a useful dictionary? Toyota is a Japanese make of car. What a lovely day! **8** one like: He thinks he's a Romeo and that she's a Juliet. Ⓝ 'A/an' comes before any attributive adjective, as in a big, red ball, but some words can be placed before 'a/an', as in such a lovely smile; rather a sad story.

aback /ə'bæk/ adv **be taken aback (at/by sth)** to be suddenly surprised or upset (by something): He was taken aback at the news/by the high cost of the repairs.

aba·cus /'æbəkəs/ nc (pl **—es** or **-ci** /'æbəsaɪ/) a frame with beads or balls sliding on rods, for learning to count or (still in East Asia) for calculating.

aban·don¹ /ə'bændən/ nu careless behaviour without worrying about the result or effect: dancing with gay abandon.

aban·don² /ə'bændən/ vt **1** to go away from (a person, place etc), not intending to return: He abandoned his wife and child. The order was given

to abandon ship. **2** to stop doing (something): They abandoned the game because of rain.

aban·don·ed /ə'bændənd/ adj left or deserted (esp for ever): an abandoned car/wife.

aban·don·ment nu

abash·ed /ə'bæʃt/ adj (formal) very embarrassed or ashamed. Opp unabashed.

abate /ə'beɪt/ v (formal) **1** vt,vi (to cause winds, storms, floods, pain etc) to become less: The ship sailed when the storm abated. **2** vt to bring (a condition etc) to an end: We must abate pollution in our big cities.

abate·ment nu

ab·at·toir /'æbətwɑː(r)/ nc a slaughterhouse (for cattle etc).

ab·bess /'æbes/ nc a woman (Mother Superior) at the head of a convent or nunnery.

ab·bey /'æbɪ/ nc (pl **—s**) **1** a building in which monks or nuns live as a community in the service of God. **2** such a community.

ab·bot /'æbət/ nc a man (Father Superior) at the head of an abbey or monastery.

abbr, abbrev abbr abbreviation.

ab·brevi·ate /ə'briːvɪeɪt/ vt to shorten (a word, title etc): We can abbreviate January to Jan/Doctor to Dr.

ab·brevi·ation /əˌbriːvɪ'eɪʃn/ nc **1** a shortened form of a word, e.g. approx; etc; mm; Sept; Tues (usually not spoken as written but as the original full word). **2 (a)** the first letters of a group of words, e.g. BA; MP; USA (usually spoken as separate letters: /ˌbiː 'eɪ/; /ˌem 'piː/; /ˌjuː es 'eɪ/). **(b)** (also called acronym) the first letters of a group of words spoken as a new word, e.g. NATO /'neɪtəʊ/; UNESCO /juː'neskəʊ/. Ⓝ In modern written style full stops are not used in most abbreviations.

ABC /ˌeɪ biː 'siː/ nu the alphabet. **as easy as ABC** ⇨ easy(1).

ab·di·cate /'æbdɪkeɪt/ vt,vi to give up (a throne, a high office, control or responsibility): King Edward VIII abdicated in 1936.

ab·di·ca·tion /ˌæbdɪ'keɪʃn/ nc,nu

ab·do·men /'æbdəmen/ nc (science) **1** the part of the body that includes the stomach and bowels. **2** the last (back part) of the three divisions of an insect, spider, crab etc.

ab·domi·nal /æb'dɒmɪnl/ adj (attrib) in, of, for, the abdomen: abdominal pains.

ab·duct /æb'dʌkt/ vt to take or lead away (a person) unlawfully, esp by force. Compare kidnap.

ab·duc·tion /æb'dʌkʃn/ nc,nu

ab·er·ra·tion /ˌæbə'reɪʃn/ n **1** nc an instance of forgetting for a short time: a mental aberration. **2** nu a departure from what is usual, expected or right: stealing chocolate in a moment of aberration.

abet /ə'bet/ vt (-tt-) **abet sb (in sth)** (legal) to help or encourage (a person) (in vice, crime). **aid and abet sb** ⇨ aid²(1).

abey·ance /ə'beɪəns/ nu (formal) **1 in abeyance** (of a rule, condition etc) temporarily not in force or in use. **2 fall/go into abeyance** (of a custom, law etc) to become no longer in use (for a period of time).

ab·hor /əb'hɔː(r)/ vt (-rr-) (formal) to think of (something) with hatred and disgust: I abhor cruelty to both children and animals.

ab·hor·rence /əb'hɒrəns/ nu (formal) the feeling of disgust or extreme hatred.

ab·hor·rent /əb'hɒrənt/ adj (usually pred) **abhorrent (to sb)** (formal) causing a person to be shocked, disgusted: Torture is abhorrent to him.

abide /ə'baɪd/ v 1 vi **abide by sth** (no passive; formal) to obey (a rule); to remain faithful to (an agreement): abide by a decision/promise. 2 vt **cannot/can't/couldn't abide sb/sth** cannot/could not tolerate, hate(d), (a person, thing): She can't abide that man/watching horror films.

abid·ing /ə'baɪdɪŋ/ adj (usually attrib; formal) continuing for a very long time: an abiding trust in a doctor's advice.

abil·ity /ə'bɪlətɪ/ n (pl **-ies**) 1 nc,nu (an instance of) the capacity, skill or power needed to do something physical or mental: a remarkable ability to recall names/dates; showing great ability as a political leader. **to the best of one's ability.** ⇨ best³(3). 2 (pl) talents (the more usual word): a woman of many abilities.

abiot·ic /ˌeɪbaɪ'ɒtɪk/ adj (science) without life: Pebbles and sand are abiotic (parts of this beach).

ab·ject /'æbdʒekt/ adj (usually attrib; formal) 1 (of conditions) poor; miserable: living in abject poverty. 2 (derog) (of a person, behaviour) thought to be worthless because cowardly or undignified: an abject liar; an abject apology.
ab·ject·ly adv

ablaze /ə'bleɪz/ adj (pred), adv 1 on fire: The house was (set) ablaze in a few minutes. 2 (fig) shining; bright: The streets were ablaze with lights.

able /'eɪbl/ adj (**—r, —st**) 1 clever; capable; having or showing knowledge, skill: an able lawyer/ speech; the ablest/most able man I know. ⇨ ably. 2 **be able to (do sth)** to have the power, means or opportunity: She wasn't able to (finish the exam). Will you be able to come? Compare can²(1,2).
,able-'bodied adj physically healthy.

ab·lu·tions /ə'blu:ʃnz/ n pl 1 a place for washing in a camp or on a ship. 2 a ceremonial washing of the hands or the body as an act of religion.

ably /'eɪblɪ/ adv in a skilful way.

ab·nor·mal /ˌæb'nɔ:ml/ adj different from what is normal, usual or expected: abnormal temperatures/conditions. Compare subnormal.
ab·nor·mal·ly /-məlɪ/ adv

ab·nor·mal·ity /ˌæbnɔ:'mælətɪ/ nc (pl **-ies**) a thing or part that is abnormal: physical abnormalities.

aboard /ə'bɔ:d/ adv, prep on, in, onto or into a ship, plane, or (US) a train or coach: It's time to go aboard. All aboard! Welcome aboard!

abode /ə'bəʊd/ nc **of/with no fixed abode** (legal) having no permanent home.

abol·ish /ə'bɒlɪʃ/ vt to put an end to (a law, an old custom, war etc).

abol·ition /ˌæbə'lɪʃn/ nu the act of abolishing something or being abolished: the abolition of nuclear weapons.

abom·in·able /ə'bɒmɪnəbl/ adj 1 causing disgust because bad: Their prison conditions are abominable. 2 (informal) unpleasant; bad: abominable weather/food.
abom·in·ably /-əblɪ/ adv: behave abominably.

abom·in·ation /ə,bɒmɪ'neɪʃn/ n (formal) 1 nu extreme hatred and disgust. 2 nc something that causes great hatred and disgust: Poverty is an abomination.

abo·rig·inal /ˌæbə'rɪdʒɪnl/ adj (of people, living creatures etc) belonging to, existing in, a region from earliest times, or from the time when the region was first known.

Abo·rig·ine /ˌæbə'rɪdʒənɪ/ nc 1 an inhabitant of Australia before the arrival of European settlers. 2 any language spoken by such a person.

abort /ə'bɔ:t/ v 1 vt,vi (to cause a person) to end a pregnancy before the foetus is fully developed. 2 vt to cancel, stop, end, (an activity): abort a space mission (e.g. because of mechanical problems).

abor·tion /ə'bɔ:ʃn/ nc,nu 1 (an act of causing) the removal of the foetus from the womb before it is fully developed: a legal or an illegal abortion. **have an abortion** to experience one. 2 (informal) a failure of a project or activity: The meeting was a total abortion because of all the noise.
abor·tion·ist /-ʃənɪst/ nc (a) a person who carries out an abortion. (b) a person who favours and supports legal abortion.

abort·ive /ə'bɔ:tɪv/ adj unsuccessful: an abortive attempt to reach agreement.
abort·ive·ly adv

abound /ə'baʊnd/ vi **abound in/with sth** to have a great number or quantity of something: The river abounds with fish.

about¹ /ə'baʊt/ adv Ⓝ For uses with verbs such as bring, come etc, ⇨ the verb entries. 1 approximately; a little more or less than: for about 3 miles; from about 4 to 6 years old; in about 3 weeks; about 50 competitors; about as high as that tree; about the best example; about the same age. 2 a little before or after: on about 6 May; at about 10 o'clock. 3 near; close: Is anyone about? There was no-one about. 4 in all directions: The children were running about in the field. 5 in all places and positions: There were books lying about on the floor. 6 (of a person after illness etc) living, acting, normally. **be out and about** ⇨ be out. **be up (and about)** ⇨ be up(a). 7 (informal) (used to show irony, impatience, anger etc): Isn't it about time you behaved properly? I've had (just) about all I can take of your rudeness.

about² /ə'baʊt/ prep Ⓝ For uses with verbs such as go, get etc, ⇨ the verb entries. 1 with reference to; on the subject of: He's worried about the exams. They often quarrel about money. What do you know about him? Tell me all about it! What is the story about? Ⓝ 'A book about wild animals' gives general information but 'a book on economics' suggests that it is a serious, academic work. 2 throughout; in every direction: walking about the streets; travelling about Europe. 3 near to: I dropped the key somewhere about here. 4 **be about to +** verb to be ready to, be going to, do something: He was about to close the door when the phone rang. As I was (just) about to say, the café is open. 5 **How/What about . . . ?** (used to make a suggestion, to ask for information or to get an opinion): How about having eggs for breakfast? What about the cost of petrol? 6 occupied with: And while you're about it (= doing that), can you make one for me, too?

above¹ /ə'bʌv/ adv 1 at a higher point; overhead;

on high: *My bedroom is above. A voice from above shouted a welcome.* **2** more: *costing £10 and above.* **3** (also *attrib*) earlier (in a book, article etc): *As I quoted/mentioned above, the author died in France. The above quotation is from 'Hamlet'.*

a,bove-'board *adj* (*pred*), *adv* fair(ly); without deceiving: *The activities of the committee were (legal and) above-board.*

a,bove-'mentioned/-'named *adj* (*attrib*) mentioned/named earlier in this book etc.

above² /ə'bʌv/ *prep* **1** higher than; on top of: *The water came above our knees. The sun rose above the horizon. Put the picture 30 cm above the sofa.* Ⓝ *'Above'* and *'over'* can be used to mean *'higher than'*. *'Above'* is used if one thing is not directly on top of another, as in *'the trees above the farmhouse.'* *'Over'* is used if one thing covers another, as in *'the cloth over the food'* or if one thing crosses another, as in *'while the plane flew over the Sahara.'* **above ground** ⇨ ground¹(1). Opp below²(1). **2** more than in quantity, age, value, mass etc: *above-average temperatures; above the age of 21; not if it is above £20 in price.* Ⓝ *'Over'* is more usual with numbers, as in *over 50 members; over 21 (years of age).* Opp below²(2). Compare under. **3** louder (than another noise): *We couldn't hear the speaker above the shouting.* **4** higher in rank, position etc: *A colonel is above a major. Who is above you in the department?* Opp below²(3). **above oneself** conceited. **5** too good, respected etc for: *be above stealing/suspicion.* **6** showing more desire, enthusiasm, than: *I put happiness above wealth.* **above all (else)** more than anything or anybody: *Above all, I love Mozart. I prefer watching TV above all else.* **over and above** ⇨ over⁴(10). **7** farther from the sea: *the areas of London above Tower Bridge.* Opp below²(4). **8** (*music*) (of a note, voice etc) higher in tone than. Opp below²(5).

ab·ra·sion /ə'breɪʒn/ *nc* an injury where the skin has been worn or scraped away: *an abrasion of the skin.*

ab·ras·ive¹ /ə'breɪsɪv/ *adj* **1** causing an abrasion. **2** (*fig; derog*) making a person angry or annoyed because unpleasant and severe: *an abrasive voice/personality.*

ab·ras·ive² /ə'breɪsɪv/ *nc,nu* a substance (e.g. *emery*) used for rubbing or grinding down surfaces.

abreast /ə'brest/ *adv* (of people, ships etc) side by side and facing the same way: *walking three abreast; tankers in line abreast.* **be/keep abreast (of sb/sth)** to be/keep up to date (with a person, thing): *keep abreast of the news.*

abridge /ə'brɪdʒ/ *vt* to make (a report, story) shorter, esp by using fewer words: *an abridged edition of 'David Copperfield'.*

abridge·ment, abridg·ment *nc,nu*

abroad /ə'brɔːd/ *adv* **1** in or to a foreign country or countries; away from one's own country: *be/go/live/travel abroad.* **2** (*dated*) (of information etc) being circulated everywhere: *There's a rumour abroad that* (= People are saying that) *the arts centre will close.*

abrupt /ə'brʌpt/ *adj* **1** (*attrib*) unexpected and sudden: *The road is full of abrupt turns.* **2** (*derog*) (of speech, writing, behaviour) bad-tempered

and unfriendly: *sound abrupt on the telephone.*
abrupt·ly *adv*
abrupt·ness *nu*

ab·scess /'æbses/ *nc* a collection of thick yellowish-white liquid (called *pus*) formed in a diseased part of the body: *abscesses on the gums.*

ab·scond /əb'skɒnd/ *vi* **abscond (from sth) (with sb/sth)** to go away suddenly, secretly and aware of having done wrong: *abscond from the meeting with the society's funds.*

ab·sence /'æbsəns/ *n* **1** *nu* the state of being away: *In the absence of the manager* (= While he is away), *Mr Green is in control. He met her during his absence in America* (= while he was there). Compare presence(1). **leave of absence** ⇨ leave¹(2). **2** *nc* an occasion or period of being away: *after an absence of three months.* **3** *nu* the state of being without something: *in the absence of definite information.*

ab·sent¹ /'æbsənt/ *adj* **1** **absent (from sth)** not present (at a place): *absent from school/work. This is a time to think of absent friends.* **2** not giving a person, thing, one's attention: *He looked at me in an absent way but did not hear what I was saying.*

,absent-'minded *adj* giving all one's attention to something so that one does not notice, hear etc.

,absent-'minded·ly *adv*

ab·sent² /əb'sent/ *v reflex* **absent oneself (from sth)** (*formal*) to stay away (from something): *She absented herself from the meeting.*

ab·sen·tee /,æbsən'tiː/ *nc* (also *attrib*) a person who is absent, e.g. who lives away from her or his property.

ab·so·lute /'æbsəluːt/ *adj* **1** (*attrib*) complete; perfect: *absolute trust/honesty/truth.* **2** having complete authority or power: *An absolute ruler need not ask anyone for permission to do anything.* **3** (*attrib*) certain; undoubted: *It is an absolute fact. Do you have absolute proof of his guilt?*

,absolute con'struction *nc* (*gram*) a part of a sentence grammatically independent of the main clause, such as 'In all probability' in *In all probability I shall not be able to come.*

,absolute ma'jority *nc* one that is more than 50% (e.g. of votes in an election).

,absolute 'zero *n* the lowest temperature theoretically possible, = −273·15°C.

ab·so·lute·ly /'æbsəluːtlɪ/ *adv* **1** completely: *It's absolutely impossible. You're absolutely right.* **2** unconditionally: *He refused absolutely.* **3** /,æbsə'luːtlɪ/ (*informal*) (used in answer to a question or as a comment) I agree; certainly: *'Don't you agree that he was rude?'—'Absolutely!'*

ab·so·lu·tion /,æbsə'luːʃn/ *nu* forgiveness for sinning, given by a priest.

ab·solve /əb'zɒlv/ *vt* **absolve sb (from sth)** (*formal*) to release a person (from sin, guilt, a promise, duty etc): *I absolve you from all blame/from your vows.*

ab·sorb /əb'zɔːb/ *vt* **1** to take in (e.g. liquid, heat, light): *Plants absorb moisture from the soil.* **2** (*fig*) to gain (knowledge etc): *The clever boy absorbed all the knowledge his teachers could give him.* **3** to use up a great deal of the attention or interest of (a person): *He is completely absorbed in his work.* ⇨ absorbing.

ab·sorb·ent /əb'zɔːbənt/ adj able to absorb liquid: absorbent cotton wool.

ab·sorb·ing /əb'zɔːbɪŋ/ adj (of a story, film, book etc) very interesting.

ab·sorp·tion /əb'zɔːpʃn/ nu 1 the state of using a great deal of attention, time etc: Complete absorption in sport interfered with his studies. 2 (tech) the process of taking in liquid, heat etc.

ab·stain /əb'steɪn/ vi **abstain (from (doing) sth)** to refuse to drink, take part in etc, something: His doctor told him to abstain from beer and wine. At the last election he abstained (from voting).

ab·stain·er nc a person who abstains.

ab·stemi·ous /əb'stiːmɪəs/ adj taking only a little (food or drink).

ab·stemi·ous·ly adv
ab·stemi·ous·ness nu

ab·sten·tion /əb'stenʃn/ n 1 nu the refusal to act etc (esp not using one's vote at an election). 2 nc instance of this: There were six votes for, three against and two abstentions.

ab·sti·nence /'æbstɪnəns/ nu the state, act, of avoiding e.g. food, enjoyment or esp alcoholic drink.

ab·stract¹ /'æbstrækt/ adj thought of separately from facts, objects or particular examples, often as ideal rather than real: A flower is beautiful but beauty itself is abstract.

ab·stract² /'æbstrækt/ nu the ideal or general nature of something rather than its real or outer form. **in the abstract** regarded in a general or theoretical way.

abstract 'art nu art which does not represent an object, scene etc in its true, normal or usual form.

abstract 'noun nc (gram) one referring to an idea, quality or state, such as length, goodness, freedom, poverty. Compare concrete noun.

ab·stract³ /'æbstrækt/ nc a short account, e.g. of the main points of a book, speech etc. Compare summary².

ab·stract⁴ /əb'strækt/ vt **abstract sth (from sth)** to take something out; separate something (from another): abstract metal from ore; abstract the main events in the story.

ab·stract·ed /əb'stræktɪd/ adj thinking or worrying about something. Compare distracted.

ab·stract·ed·ly adv

ab·strac·tion /əb'strækʃn/ n (formal) 1 nu the state of being abstracted: in a moment of abstraction. 2 nc an idea of a quality (e.g. truth, beauty) separate from actual examples: Don't lose yourself in abstractions (= Be realistic).

ab·struse /əb'struːs/ adj (formal) using words with a meaning that is difficult to understand.

ab·struse·ly adv
ab·struse·ness nu

ab·surd /əb'sɜːd/ adj unreasonable; foolish; ridiculous: What an absurd suggestion! Don't be absurd!

ab·surd·ity nc,nu
ab·surd·ly adv

abun·dance /ə'bʌndəns/ nu 1 a large amount: food and drink in abundance. 2 **an abundance of sth** more than enough of something: an abundance of good things.

abun·dant /ə'bʌndənt/ adj (usually attrib) more than enough; plentiful: We have abundant proof of his guilt.

abuse¹ /ə'bjuːs/ n 1 nc,nu (an instance of) unfair or immoral use: abuse of power; an abuse of trust. 2 nu angry or insulting language: abuse from an enemy; shower abuse on somebody. 3 nc,nu (an instance of) harmful use: The record-player suffered a lot of abuse.

abuse² /ə'bjuːz/ vt 1 to use (something) unfairly or immorally: Don't abuse the confidence they have placed in you. 2 (formal) to say severe, cruel or unjust things to or about (a person).

abus·ive /ə'bjuːsɪv/ adj angry and insulting: abusive language.

abus·ive·ly adv

abys·mal /ə'bɪzməl/ adj (esp fig and informal) (of something bad) extreme; extremely bad: abysmal ignorance/weather.

abys·mal·ly /-məlɪ/ adv: an abysmally small wage increase.

abyss /ə'bɪs/ nc (pl —es) (formal) 1 a hole so deep as to appear bottomless. 2 (fig) the lowest level: the abyss of despair.

a/c abbr (commerce) account.

AC /,eɪ'siː/ abbr (electricity) alternating current.

aca·dem·ic¹ /,ækə'demɪk/ adj 1 (attrib) (of teaching, studying, schools, colleges etc) scholarly, literary or classical (contrasted with technical or scientific): academic subjects; the academic year. 2 not practical: The question is academic (= is of no practical importance).

academic 'dress nu formal clothes worn by university teachers and students, including a gown, hood and cap.

academic 'freedom nu the freedom to teach and to discuss issues without outside, e.g. Government, interference.

aca·demi·cal·ly /-klɪ/ adv

aca·dem·ic² /,ækə'demɪk/ nc a teacher, graduate student etc at a university etc.

aca·dem·ician /ə,kædə'mɪʃn/ nc a member of an academy.

acad·emy /ə'kædəmɪ/ nc (pl -ies) (A- in names) an institute for higher learning, usually for a special purpose: a naval/military academy; the Royal Academy of Music.

ACAS /'eɪkæs/ acronym (GB) Advisory, Conciliation, and Arbitration Service (a government department to help settle industrial disputes).

ac·cede /æk'siːd/ vi **accede (to sth)** (formal) to agree (to a request etc).

ac·cel·er·ate /ək'seləreɪt/ vi 1 (of a driver) to increase speed: She accelerated and passed the bus in front. 2 vt to cause (something) to occur faster or happen earlier: Fertilizers accelerate the growth of plants. 3 vi (of a process) to become faster, increase quickly: Hostilities are accelerating.

ac·cel·er·ation /ək,selə'reɪʃn/ nu the act, rate, of increasing speed.

ac·cel·er·ator /ək'seləreɪtə(r)/ nc 1 a device, e.g. the pedal in a car, used for controlling speed. 2 (physics) a device for increasing the speed of atomic particles. 3 (chem) a substance for increasing the speed of a chemical reaction.

ac·cent¹ /'æksənt/ n 1 nc an individual, local or national way of pronouncing: speaking English with a foreign accent. 2 nc a mark or symbol used in writing and printing to show a vowel sound or syllabic stress. ⇨ acute accent, circumflex, grave³. **3** nc an emphasis when speaking (using stress or intonation): *In the word 'today', the accent is on the second syllable.* **4** nu (*informal*) the emphasis given to one aspect of a display, performance etc: *At this year's Motor Show the accent is on sports cars.*

ac·cent² /æk'sent/ vt to put emphasis on (a syllable or word).

ac·cen·tu·ate /ək'sentʃʊeɪt/ vt to give more emphasis or importance to (something): *The lines in her dress accentuate her height.*

ac·cept /ək'sept/ vt **1** to take, receive, (something given): *accept a gift/prize.* **2** to agree to take (something offered): *accept an invitation/a job.* **3** to approve of, agree to, (something): *He accepted the judges' decision. I accept that change is necessary.*

ac·cept·able /-əbl/ adj satisfactory; welcome: *Is this proposal acceptable to you?* Opp unacceptable.

ac·cept·ance /ək'septəns/ n **1** nu the act of taking or receiving something offered. **2** nc,nu a positive reply to an invitation or offer. **3** nu approval (the usual word): *There was complete acceptance of the plan.*

ac·cept·ed /ək'septɪd/ adj generally agreed to be true: *an accepted fact.*

ac·cess¹ /'ækses/ n **access (to sth) 1** n sing the way in (to a place): *The only access (to the house) is across the field. There is easy access to the shops.* **gain access (to sb/sth)** (to be given permission) to talk (to a person), use (a set of information etc): *How did you gain access to the manager/the files/my office?* **2** nu the opportunity, means etc to obtain, reach, use, something: *Students must have access to good books.*

'access road nc a road leading to a motorway or other main road.

ac·cess·ible /ək'sesəbl/ adj able to be reached, visited easily etc: *an accessible hospital/manager.* Opp inaccessible.

ac·cessi·bil·ity /ək,sesə'bɪlətɪ/ nu

ac·cess² /'ækses/ vt (*computers*) to select (information) from a storage system.

'access time nu the time needed to select an amount of information from a storage system.

ac·cess·ary /ək'sesərɪ/ nc ⇨ accessory(2).

ac·ces·sion /æk'seʃn/ n **accession (to sth) 1** nu the act of obtaining power etc: *the Queen's accession to the throne.* **2** nc (*formal*) an addition: *recent accessions to the school library.*

ac·cess·ory /ək'sesərɪ/ nc (pl -ies) **1** (usually pl) something that is extra, helpful or useful but not an essential part: *the accessories of a bicycle* (e.g. the lamp, a pump). **2** (also accessary) (*legal*) a person who helps in or knows about a crime.

ac·ci·dence /'æksɪdəns/ nu (*gram*) the part of grammar concerning the variable form of words to make tenses, case, number etc.

ac·ci·dent /'æksɪdənt/ n **1** nc something that happens unexpectedly and often without an obvious cause, usually something unfortunate and undesirable: *She had an accident with a knife. He was killed in a car accident.* **Accidents will happen** (*saying*) Some unfortunate events must be accepted as inevitable. **2** nu **by accident** not expected or planned: *We met by accident.*

'accident-prone adj (of a person) often having accidents.

ac·ci·den·tal /,æksɪ'dentl/ adj happening unexpectedly and not planned: *an accidental meeting with a friend. The scientific discovery was accidental.*

ac·ci·den·tal·ly /-təlɪ/ adv

ac·claim¹ /ə'kleɪm/ nu (*formal*) approval (the more usual word): *The film received great critical acclaim.*

ac·claim² /ə'kleɪm/ vt (*formal*) **1** to welcome (a person, thing) with shouts of approval: *acclaim the winner of a race.* **2** to state (something) with enthusiasm: *acclaim him as a great actor.*

ac·cla·ma·tion /,æklə'meɪʃn/ nu (or n(pl)) (*formal*) enthusiastic shouts of praise and approval.

ac·cli·mat·ize (also **-ise**) /ə'klaɪmətaɪz/ vt,vi (often *reflex*) **1** to get (oneself, animals, plants etc) used to a new climate. **2** (*fig*) to get (oneself, a person) used to a new environment, new conditions etc: *You will soon become acclimatized (to this cold weather).*

ac·cli·mat·iz·ation (also **-is·ation**) /ə,klaɪmə-taɪ'zeɪʃn/ nu

ac·col·ade /'ækəleɪd/ nc a show of great praise or approval.

ac·com·mo·date /ə'kɒmədeɪt/ vt **1** to have, provide, lodging or space for (people): *This hotel can accommodate 600 guests.* **2** (*formal*) to adapt, change, (a plan etc) so that it fits with something else: *My plans can accommodate you. Eating arrangements on airliners must accommodate vegetarians.*

ac·com·mo·dat·ing /ə'kɒmədeɪtɪŋ/ adj willing to do things to please others; easy to live, work, reach an agreement, with.

ac·com·mo·da·tion /ə,kɒmə'deɪʃn/ nu a place to stay or live: *Accommodation was difficult to find during the Olympic Games.*

ac·com·pani·ment /ə'kʌmpənɪmənt/ nc **1** something that naturally or often goes with another thing: *Disease is often an accompaniment of famine.* **2** (*music*) (usually) the instrumental part to go with a voice, choir or solo instrument: *a song with piano accompaniment.*

ac·com·pan·ist /ə'kʌmpənɪst/ nc a person who plays music for a singer or another musician.

ac·com·pany /ə'kʌmpənɪ/ vt (pt,pp **-ied**) **1** to go with (a person): *She usually accompanies the doctor on his rounds.* **2** to do something or occur at the same time as (something): *A fever is often accompanied by a headache.* **3** (*music*) to play, sing, an accompaniment(2) to (a singer, player).

ac·com·plice /ə'kʌmplɪs/ nc a helper or companion (in doing something illegal): *an accomplice in a bank robbery.*

ac·com·plish /ə'kʌmplɪʃ/ vt to do or finish (something) successfully: *accomplish a task.*

ac·com·plish·ed adj well-trained; skilled: *an accomplished dancer.*

ac·com·plish·ment /ə'kʌmplɪʃmənt/ n (*formal*) **1** nu successful achievement: *the accomplishment of their aims.* **2** nc something well done or successfully completed.

ac·cord¹ /ə'kɔːd/ nu (*formal*) **of one's own accord** without being asked or forced; willingly. **in/out of accord (with sb/sth)** agreeing/not agreeing (with a person, thing). **with one**

accord with everyone agreeing.

ac·cord² /ə'kɔːd/ *v* (*formal*) **1** *vi* **accord with sth** to be in agreement or harmony with something: *His description does not accord with mine.* **2** *vt* to give (a person) a greeting etc: *He was accorded a warm welcome.*

ac·cord·ance /ə'kɔːdəns/ *nu* **in accordance with sth** (*formal*) in agreement with something: *in accordance with your wishes/the regulations.*

ac·cord·ing /ə'kɔːdɪŋ/ *prep* **according to sth** **1** on the authority of: *According to the Bible, God created the world in six days.* **2** in relation to size, age etc: *He will be punished according to the seriousness of his crime.* **3** using (an agreed method): *The books are arranged on the shelves according to subject.*

ac·cord·ing·ly *adv* for that reason or to suit the occasion: *She told me Princess Diana was coming so I dressed accordingly.* .

ac·cord·ion /ə'kɔːdɪən/ *nc* (also *attrib*) a portable musical instrument with a box of air, metal reeds and a keyboard: *an accordion player.*

ac·cost /ə'kɒst/ *vt* to go up to (a person) and speak to her or him first, esp a stranger in a public place: *I was accosted by a beggar.*

ac·count¹ /ə'kaʊnt/ *n* **1** *nc* a written or spoken report or description: *Don't always believe newspaper accounts of political events.* **by/from all accounts** according to everybody, all reports etc. **2** *nc* an explanation of behaviour. **give a good/poor** etc **account of oneself** to act in a way that brings credit/discredit: *Bob gave a good account of himself at his interview.* **3** *nu* reason; basis: *Don't miss the concert on my account* (= because of me). **on account of** (*prep*) because of: *The game was cancelled on account of the rain.* ⇨ the *note* at because of. **on no account; not on any account** not for any reason: *Don't on any account leave the baby alone in the house.* **4** *nu* importance; consideration: *It's of little account to me whether you stay or not.* **take sth into account; take account of sth** to take it into consideration, pay attention to it: *The judge took her previous good behaviour into account when deciding a punishment.* **take no account of sth** to pay no attention to it when deciding something. **5** *nu* (*formal*) advantage. **put/turn sth to good account** to use money, experience, ability etc to one's advantage. **6** *nc* (*commerce*) a business arrangement or relationship, e.g. between a bank and a client, a shop and a customer: *I have an account with Lloyds Bank* (= keep my money with this bank). *We have an account at Marks and Spencers* (= have an arrangement to use credit facilities). *Please charge these goods to my parents' account.* **on account** on credit. **open an account; open a bank/building society** etc **account** to start to keep money with a bank etc. ⇨ also bank, current, deposit, joint and savings account. **7** *nc* (*commerce*) the money deposited at a bank, building society etc: *My account will be worth nothing after this holiday!* **8** *nc* (*commerce*) a statement of money (to be) paid or received: *I receive my telephone account every three months.* **settle/square accounts (with sb)** (a) to pay what is owed. (b) (*fig*) to get one's revenge. **9** *nc* (*bookkeeping*) a list of debits and credits relating

to particular expenses, income etc: *a trading account; a profit-and-loss account.*

ac·count² /ə'kaʊnt/ *vt* **account for sb/sth** **1** to be an explanation of (something): *His illness accounts for his absence. Ah, that accounts for it! Have these expenses been accounted for?* (i.e. been explained?) ⇨ unaccounted for. ⇨ also taste¹(4). **2** to give an explanation of (money spent). **3** be responsible for killing, defeating etc (people): *The flood accounted for forty people.*

ac·count·able /ə'kaʊntəbl/ *adj* responsible: *A mental patient is not accountable for his actions.* Opp unaccountable.

ac·count·an·cy /ə'kaʊntənsɪ/ *nu* the profession of an accountant. ⇨ chartered accountant.

ac·count·ant /ə'kaʊntənt/ *nc* (*GB*) a person whose profession is to keep and examine business accounts.

ac·crue /ə'kruː/ *vi* (esp of money) to increase by growth or development: *While your money is in the savings bank, interest is accruing.*

acct *abbr* account.

ac·cu·mu·late /ə'kjuːmjʊleɪt/ *vt,vi* (to cause something) to become greater in number or quantity: *Dust soon accumulates if the rooms are not swept.*

ac·cu·mu·la·tion /ə,kjuːmjʊ'leɪʃn/ *nc,nu* (an instance of) the process of collecting something: *an accumulation of books/rubbish.*

ac·cu·mu·la·tive /ə'kjuːmjʊlətɪv/ *adj* growing by being added to: *accumulative interest on a savings account.*

ac·cu·racy /'ækjərəsɪ/ *nu* exactness; precision.

ac·cu·rate /'ækjərət/ *adj* **1** free from error: *Clocks in airports should be accurate.* **2** careful and exact: *be accurate in one's work/in what one says.*

ac·cur·ate·ly *adv*

ac·cu·sa·tion /,ækjʊ'zeɪʃn/ *n* **1** *nu* the act of accusing or being accused. **2** *nc* a charge of doing something wrong or illegal: *bring an accusation (of theft) against a person.*

ac·cu·sa·tive /ə'kjuːzətɪv/ *nc* (*gram*) (also *accusative form*) the form of a word when it is the object in a sentence. Compare nominative.

ac,cusative 'case *nc* (*gram*) = objective case.

ac,cusative 'pronoun *nc* (*gram*) the form of a pronoun when it is the object in a sentence, as in 'They like *me*', 'I hate *him*'. Compare nominative pronoun.

ac·cuse /ə'kjuːz/ *vt* **accuse sb (of sth)** to say that (a person) has done wrong, has broken the law, is to be blamed (for something wrong): *accuse him of theft; be accused of stealing.*

ac·cused *nc* (*pl* —) (the —) (*legal*) the person charged in a criminal case.

ac·cuser *nc* a person who accuses a person.

ac·cus·ing·ly /ə'kjuːzɪŋlɪ/ *adv* in an accusing manner: *He pointed accusingly at me.*

ac·cus·tom /ə'kʌstəm/ *v reflex* (often *passive*) to make oneself used to (something) by experience, practice; *accustom oneself to cold weather. This is not the kind of treatment I'm accustomed to* (= not the kind I usually receive.)

ac·cus·tomed *adj* (*attrib*) usual: *in his accustomed seat.*

ace /eɪs/ *nc* **1** the one on dice, playing-cards etc; card so marked: *the ace of spades.* **2** (*informal*) a person who is the best or an expert. **3** (*tennis*) a winning serve. **4** *within an ace of sth* only just escaping something bad or unlucky: *within an ace of death/of being killed.*

ache¹ /eɪk/ *nc* a dull continuous pain: *I have a headache. I suffer from headaches.* Ⓝ *'Ache'* is only combined with *back, belly, ear, face, head, heart, stomach, tummy* and *tooth*. For others, use *'a pain in my leg'* etc.

ache² /eɪk/ *vi* **1** to have a continuous dull pain: *My head aches/is aching.* **2** *ache for/to do sth* to want (to do) something very much: *He was aching for freedom/to go.*

achieve /ə'tʃiːv/ *vt* **1** to complete (something) successfully; get (something) done: *He will never achieve anything* (= will not do anything successfully). **2** to gain or reach (something) by effort: *achieve success/distinction in public life.*

achiev·able /-əbl/ *adj*

achieve·ment /ə'tʃiːvmənt/ *n* **1** *nu* the act or process of achieving: *the achievement of one's aims.* **2** *nc* something done successfully, with effort and skill: *She won a Nobel Prize for her scientific achievements.*

acid¹ /'æsɪd/ *adj* **1** (also *acidic* /ə'sɪdɪk/) containing an acid substance and esp sour or sharp to the taste: *A lemon is an acid fruit. Vinegar has an acid taste.* **2** (*attrib; fig*) sarcastic: *an acid wit; acid remarks.*

,acid 'rain *nu* rain containing acid substances that kill trees, fish etc.

acid² /'æsɪd/ *nc,nu* (*chem*) any of a group of substances that contain hydrogen and are able to dissolve metals and form salts: *Some acids burn holes in wood and cloth.*

'acid test *nc* (*fig*) a test that proves the value of something, e.g. a person's ability.

acid·ity /ə'sɪdətɪ/ *nu* the state or quality of containing acid.

ac·knowl·edge /ək'nɒlɪdʒ/ *vt* **1** to admit the truth, existence or reality of (something): *He refused to acknowledge defeat/that he was defeated.* **2** to report that one has received (something): *acknowledge (receipt of) a letter.* **3** to show that one recognizes (a person) by giving a greeting, a smile, a nod of the head etc: *I met her in town but she didn't even acknowledge my wave.* **4** to show one's appreciation of something: *We must acknowledge her contribution to the success of the project.* **5** to admit, show, the use of (a person's work): *The author should acknowledge his colleagues' help in his book.*

ac·knowl·edge·ment, **ac·knowl·edg·ment** /ək'nɒlɪdʒmənt/ *n* **1** *nu* the act of acknowledging: *We are sending you a gift in acknowledgement of your kindness.* **2** *nc* something given or done to acknowledge something: *We have had no acknowledgement of our letter* (i.e. no reply). **3** *nc* a statement about the use of another person's work: *a list of acknowledgements.*

acne /'æknɪ/ *nu* a skin infection (common among young people) in which there are spots on the face and neck.

acorn /'eɪkɔːn/ *nc* a seed or fruit of the oak tree.

acous·tic /ə'kuːstɪk/ *adj* (*tech*) **1** of sound, the science of sound and the sense of hearing. **2** (of musical instruments) not electric: *an acoustic guitar.*

acous·tics *n* (**a**) *nu* the scientific study of sound. (**b**) *n pl* the design of a hall etc, that makes it good, poor etc for hearing music or speeches: *The acoustics of the new concert hall are excellent.*

ac·quaint /ə'kweɪnt/ *vt* **1** *acquaint sb/oneself with sth* (*formal*) to show, make known, something; learn about something: *acquaint oneself/become acquainted/make oneself acquainted with one's new duties.* **2** *be acquainted (with sb)* to have met a person: *We are not acquainted.*

ac·quaint·ance /ə'kweɪntəns/ *n* **1** *nc* a person who one knows but not as well as a friend: *I can't ask him—he's only an acquaintance.* *make sb's acquaintance* to get to know a person, e.g. by being introduced. **2** *nu* knowledge or information gained through general experience, but not organized learning.

ac·qui·esce /,ækwɪ'es/ *vi* *acquiesce (in sth)* (*formal*) to agree, accept, something without argument: *She refused to acquiesce in the reorganization of the committee.*

ac·qui·es·cence /-'esns/ *nc,nu*

ac·qui·es·cent /-'esnt/ *adj*

ac·quire /ə'kwaɪə(r)/ *vt* to get or gain (something) by work, skill or ability, by one's own efforts or behaviour: *acquire a good knowledge of English/a reputation for dishonesty.* *an acquired taste* ⇨ taste¹(4).

ac·qui·si·tion /,ækwɪ'zɪʃn/ *n* **1** *nu* (*formal*) (the act of) gaining or collecting: *He devotes his time to the acquisition of knowledge.* **2** *nc* a person or thing obtained: *Mr Brown will be a valuable acquisition to* (= a valuable new member of) *the teaching staff of our school.*

ac·quis·itive /ə'kwɪzətɪv/ *adj* enjoying, in the habit of, buying or collecting more and more things.

ac·quis·itive·ness *nu*

ac·quit /ə'kwɪt/ *vt* (**-tt-**) *acquit sb (of/on sth)* to give a legal decision that a person is not guilty (of an offence).

ac·quit·tal /ə'kwɪtl/ *nc,nu* (an example of) the judgement that a person is not guilty: *He won his acquittal on a legal technicality.*

acre /'eɪkə(r)/ *nc* a measure of land, about 4000 square metres. ⇨ hectare.

acre·age /'eɪkərɪdʒ/ *nu* an area of land measured in acres.

ac·rid /'ækrɪd/ *adj* (*derog*) (of smell or taste) unpleasantly sharp; bitter.

ac·ri·moni·ous /,ækrɪ'məʊnɪəs/ *adj* (*formal*) (of arguments etc) showing hate, bitterness and disappointment.

ac·ri·mony /'ækrɪmənɪ/ *nu* (*formal*) hate, bitterness and disappointment shown in one's language, manner.

ac·ro·bat /'ækrəbæt/ *nc* a person who can do clever or unusual physical or gymnastic acts, e.g. on a trapeze.

ac·ro·bat·ic /,ækrə'bætɪk/ *adj* of or like an acrobat.

ac·ro·bat·ics *nu*

ac·ro·nym /'ækrənɪm/ *nc* a word formed from the (usually first) letters of other words, e.g. *NATO.*

across¹ /ə'krɒs/ *adv* from one side to the other: *Can you swim across? The river is a mile across* (= wide).

across² /ə'krɒs/ prep (N) For uses with verbs such as come, get, put etc, ⇨ the verb entries. **1** from one side to another side of: walk across the street; draw a line across a sheet of paper. (N) 'Over' can also be used, but 'across' is more usual for movement to the other side of a flat area, as in across the sea. 'Over' is used for movement to the other side of something tall, as in over a mountain. 'Across' is more usual for movement on land and water, as in across the fields; across the river, and 'over' is more usual for movement in the air, as in over the forest; over the ocean. 'Through' is used for movement to the other side of something with things on all sides or along something deep and narrow, as in through a town; through a valley. **2** on the other side of: I live across the street. (N) 'Over' can also be used, as in My house is across/over the bridge. Soon he will be across/over the border. **3** so as to cross each other or form a cross: He sat with his arms across his chest.

across-the-board /ə,krɒs ðə 'bɔːd/ adj (attrib) including all groups, members etc in a business or industry: an across-the-board wage increase.

act¹ /ækt/ nc **1** something done: That was a kind act/an act of kindness. (N) 'Deed' can also be used but is more formal. **act of God** a harmful event (e.g. a flood) caused by natural forces. **in the act of** while: I photographed them in the act of trying to steal my car. **2** a main division of a play or opera. ⇨ one-act play. **3** a short performance in a longer programme: a comic act. **get in on the act** (informal) to join an activity in order to gain part of the profit, publicity etc. **put on an act** (informal) (a) to behave in an exaggerated or artificial way in order to impress. (b) to behave in a way that deceives. ⇨ act²(5). **4** a performer or group in an act(3): They are a popular act. **5** (also A-) a law made by a government; legal document: an Act of Parliament.

act² /ækt/ v **1** vi to do something: We must act now or it will be too late. **2** vi,vt to take (a part) in a play, film etc: act (the part of) James Bond in 'Goldfinger'. **3** vi to do one's professional or official duty: The police refused to act. Did the chairperson act correctly? **4** vi (of a machine etc) to do what is expected: The brakes wouldn't act properly. **5** vi to behave in an exaggerated or inappropriate way (to impress or deceive): She's only acting to get your sympathy. **act one's age.** ⇨ age¹(1). **act the fool** ⇨ fool².

act as sb to do the duties of another person: act as an interpreter.

act for sb to represent another person: Who is acting for the defence? Will you act for me at the meeting?

act on sth (a) to respond to something by doing something: act on a suggestion/her advice. (b) to have an effect on something: Acids act on metals. Antibiotics act on bacteria.

act on behalf of sb = act for sb.

act sth out to express an emotion, fear etc through unconscious behaviour.

act up (informal) to cause problems; misbehave: My car/son is acting up again.

act upon sth (formal) = act on sth.

act·ing¹ /'æktɪŋ/ adj (attrib) doing the duties of another person for a limited time: the acting Manager/Headteacher.

act·ing² /'æktɪŋ/ nu (the art of) performing in a play for the theatre, cinema, TV etc: She did a lot of acting while she was at college.

ac·tion /'ækʃn/ n **1** nu the process of doing things, using energy, influence etc: The time has come for action rather than discussion. **in action** doing something (esp as a particular or good example): We saw the Brazilian team in action at the World Games. **be out of action** to be not working (e.g. because broken). **put sth out of action** to make something unfit for use. **2** nc something done: We shall judge you by your actions, not by your promises. (N) 'Act' or 'deed' can also be used. **3** nc a way in which a machine, musical instrument etc works. **4** nc (the —) (in drama, literature) the series of main events in the plot: The action takes place in Spain. **5** nc (legal) a charge or other process in a law court. **bring an action against sb** to try to get a judgement in a law court. **take legal action (against sb/sth)** to use legal processes (against a person, business etc). **6** nc,nu (mil) (an instance of) fighting between armed forces. **killed in action** killed while fighting in a war.

'action painting nc,nu a form of abstract painting in which paint is splashed, dribbled etc.

,action 'replay nc a repeat of a short incident (in a sporting event etc) on television.

ac·ti·vate /'æktɪveɪt/ vt to cause (an effect) to operate: Break the glass to activate the alarm.

ac·tive /'æktɪv/ adj doing things; able to do things; in the habit of doing things: He's over 90 and not very active. Mount Vesuvius is an active volcano (= is one that erupts). Opp inactive. **under (active) consideration** ⇨ consideration(1). **on active service** ⇨ service¹(1).

,active 'verb nc (gram) a verb describing an action and not a state, such as to push; to laugh; to think.

'active (voice) n (gram) (a) (the —) the form of a sentence etc containing a transitive verb in which the subject is performing the action or causing the event, as in John scored a goal. We love chips. Her song ended the performance. (b) a verbal phrase, such as He is driving, that does not contain be + past participle. Compare He was being driven. (N) In general, the active voice is more effective because it is more direct and emphatic than the passive voice, but the passive voice is especially useful when referring to the action or event and not the performer, as in The winning goal was scored in the final minutes of the match. Compare passive (voice).

ac·tive·ly adv

ac·tiv·ist /'æktɪvɪst/ nc a person taking an active part, esp in politics.

ac·tiv·ity /æk'tɪvətɪ/ n (pl -ies) **1** nu the state of being active: When a man is over 70, his time of full activity is usually past. **2** nc a particular act, deed, hobby etc (to be) done; My numerous activities leave me little leisure.

ac·tor /'æktə(r)/ nc a person who acts on the stage or TV, or in films. ⇨ actress.

ac·tress /'æktrɪs/ nc a woman who acts on the stage or TV, or in films.

ac·tual /'æktʃʊəl/ adj (attrib) existing in fact; real: Can you give me the actual figures (= not an estimate or a guess). **in (actual) fact** ⇨ fact(4).

⇨ actually(1).

ac·tu·al·ity /ˌæktʃʊˈælətɪ/ nu (formal) actual existence; reality.

ac·tu·al·ly /ˈæktʃʊlɪ/ adv **1** really; as a real fact: Tell me what actually happened. Do ghosts actually exist? **2** (used to show mild emphasis): He looks honest, but actually he's a thief. **3** strange or surprising as it may seem: He not only ran in the race; he actually won it!

acu·men /ˈækjʊmen/ nu the ability to understand quickly and clearly: business acumen.

acu·punc·ture /ˈækjʊpʌŋktʃə(r)/ nu (med) the practice of putting small needles into the skin, e.g. to relieve pain and as a local anaesthetic.

acute /əˈkjuːt/ adj (—r, —st) **1** (of sensations) very strong: acute pain. **2** (of a disease) coming quickly to a crisis: the acute stage of the disease (= when the disease is most severe). Compare chronic. **3** (of a difficulty, problem) very serious: an acute need for financial aid.

a,cute 'accent nc a mark over a vowel ('), as over e in café.

a,cute 'angle nc an angle of less than 90°.

acute·ly adv

acute·ness nu

ad /æd/ nc (informal) = advertisement.

AD /ˌeɪˈdiː/ abbr (Latin: Anno Domini 'in the year of our Lord') (used to number a year after the supposed year of Jesus Christ's birth): in AD 250. Ⓝ 'AD' is only used when contrasting the year with the time before the birth of Jesus Christ, e.g. from 55 BC to AD 120, and for the years up to 1000. Compare BC.

ad·age /ˈædɪdʒ/ nc a familiar and wise saying, e.g. 'Beauty is only skin deep'.

Adam /ˈædəm/ n not know sb from Adam to have no idea who a person is.

,Adam's 'apple nc the part that projects at the front of the throat, esp in men.

ada·mant /ˈædəmənt/ adj (usually pred) refusing to give in: On this point I am adamant (= Nothing can change my decision).

adapt /əˈdæpt/ vi,vt to make (something) suitable for a new use, need, situation etc: I'll need time to adapt to the English climate. Novels are often adapted for the stage, television and radio.

adapt·able /əˈdæptəbl/ adj able to adapt or be adapted: An adaptable person is willing to change her or his style of living to suit new circumstances.

adapta·bil·ity /əˌdæptəˈbɪlətɪ/ nu

ad·ap·ta·tion /ˌædæpˈteɪʃn/ n **1** nu the state of being adapted. **2** nc something made by adapting: an adaptation (of a novel) for the stage/for television.

adap·ter (also **adap·tor**) /əˈdæptə(r)/ nc **1** a device used to connect one or more electrical plugs to a socket. **2** a person who rewrites a literary work, e.g. for younger readers or as a play.

add /æd/ v **1** vt to say (something more); continue by saying (something): 'And don't be late', he added. **2** vt,vi to join, unite, put (one thing, amount to another): If you add 5 and/to 12 you get 17.

add in sth to include something: When the water is boiling, add in the sugar.

add on sth to put more, another etc on: You must add on 50p for postage.

add to sth (a) to increase something: This extra

expense only adds to our problems. **(b)** to join something extra, new etc in order to increase the size, capability: add a second bathroom to a house. Another printer has been added to our computer system.

add sth together to combine two or more things: add together the electricity and water costs.

(not) add up (informal) to make (no) sense: Her explanation didn't add up. **add sth up** to find the total of something: add up the number of applicants; use a calculator to add them up. **add up (to sth) (a)** to amount to a total when combined: The various costs add up to £30. **(b)** (informal) to mean or indicate something: It all adds up to the fact that you had no intention of marrying her.

add. abbr address.

ad·den·dum /əˈdendəm/ nc (pl **-da** /-də/) something (omitted) in writing, a speech etc that is to be added.

ad·der /ˈædə(r)/ nc (also **viper**) a kind of small poisonous snake, common in Europe.

ad·dict¹ /ˈædɪkt/ nc a person who is addicted to something harmful: drug addicts.

ad·dict² /əˈdɪkt/ vt **be/become addicted to sth** to drink, smoke etc something without being able to stop wanting to: He is addicted to alcohol/smoking/drugs.

ad·dic·tion /əˈdɪkʃn/ nc,nu (an instance of) being addicted: drug addiction.

ad·dic·tive /əˈdɪktɪv/ adj causing addiction: addictive drugs.

ad·di·tion /əˈdɪʃn/ n **1** nu the process, result, of adding: The sign + stands for addition. **2** nc a person or thing added or joined: He will be a useful addition to the staff of the school (= a useful new teacher). **3** in addition (adv) as an added person or thing: We have one spare bed but we need another in addition. Ⓝ 'As well' is also possible. **in addition to** (prep) (used in positive statements and in questions) (formal) as a person or thing added to: We'll need passports in addition to other documents. Ⓝ For a comparison of in addition (to), besides and as well (as), ⇨ the notes at besides¹(1) and besides²(1,2).

ad·di·tion·al /əˈdɪʃənl/ adj extra; added: additional charges; problems additional to the usual ones.

ad·di·tion·al·ly /-əlɪ/ adv

ad·di·tive /ˈædɪtɪv/ nc a substance added in small amounts for a particular purpose: food additives (e.g. to add colour).

addr. abbr address.

ad·dress¹ /əˈdres/ nc **1** a statement of where a person lives, works etc and where letters etc may be delivered: What's your home/business address? **2** a formal speech or talk (to an audience); speak to (a person), using a title: Mr Green will now address the meeting. Don't address me as 'Colonel'; I'm only a major. **3** (computers) a code used to find a piece of stored information.

ad·dress² /əˈdres/ vt **1** to write the name and address(1) on (a letter etc). **2** to make a speech to (an audience); speak to (a person), using a title: Mr Green will now address the meeting. Don't address me as 'Colonel'; I'm only a major. **3** **address sth to sb** (formal) to speak or write a remark, complaint etc to a person: Please address your comments to the chair(person).

ad·en·oids /ˈædɪnɔɪdz/ n pl the soft growth between the back of the nose and the throat, sometimes making breathing difficult.

adept /'ædept/ *adj* (*pred*) **adept (at/in sth)** expert; skilled: *He's adept in photography/at playing chess.*

ad·e·qua·cy /'ædɪkwəsɪ/ *nu* (*formal*) the state of being adequate: *He often doubts his adequacy as a husband and father.*

ad·e·quate /'ædɪkwət/ *adj* satisfactory; sufficient (but not more): *Are you getting adequate payment for the work you're doing?* Compare **inadequate**.
　ad·e·quate·ly *adv*

ad·here /əd'hɪə(r)/ *vi* **adhere (to sth)** (*formal*) **1** to stick (to something): *Glue is used to make one surface adhere to another.* **2** to support (something) firmly: *adhere to an opinion/a political party.*
　ad·her·ence /-əns/ *nu*

ad·her·ent /əd'hɪərənt/ *nc* (*formal*) a supporter (of an opinion, a political party): *The idea is gaining more adherents.*

ad·he·sion /əd'hi:ʒn/ *nu* (*formal*) the condition of being or becoming attached or united.

ad·he·sive /əd'hi:sɪv/ *adj, nc,nu* (a substance, e.g. glue, that is) able to stick or join: *adhesive tape/plaster.*

adieu /ə'dju:/ *int, nc* (*pl* **—s** or **—x** /ə'dju:z/) (*formal*) goodbye: *The cast of the play bid her adieu.*

adj *abbr* adjective.

ad·jac·ent¹ /ə'dʒeɪsnt/ *adj* **adjacent (to sb/ sth)** **1** next (to a person, thing); near (to a person, thing) but not necessarily touching: *the adjacent room; the restaurant adjacent to the cinema.* **2** sharing a boundary or side: *adjacent countries; adjacent angles.*

ad·jac·ent² /ə'dʒeɪsnt/ *nc* (*maths*) the side between a particular angle and the right angle in a right-angled triangle.

ad·jec·tiv·al /ˌædʒɪk'taɪvl/ *adj* (*gram*) of or like an adjective: *an adjectival phrase.*
　ˌadjecˌtival 'clause *nc* (*gram*) a clause acting as an adjective, such as 'that you lent me yesterday' in *Here's the pen that you lent me yesterday.* Compare **adverbial clause**.

ad·jec·tive /'ædʒɪktɪv/ *nc* (*gram*) a word giving information about a noun or pronoun, such as *blue, forgotten, crooked, amazing, great, miserable, aflame,* as in *a blue sky, forgotten dreams, crooked paths, amazing beauty, great hope, miserable news, The ship was aflame.* Ⓝ The grammatical term for the process of giving information in this way is 'modify'. Adjectives are words that modify nouns and pronouns. Some adjectives can be used with 'the' as nouns, as in *the blind, the French, the best, the young, the cheapest.* Other adjectives can be used as nouns in informal conversation, as in *'A cup of coffee, please'—'Black or white?'* When several adjectives are listed together before a noun, the order is: first purpose, as in *a garden chair,* then what it is made of, as in *a plastic garden chair,* then its colour, as in *a white, plastic garden chair,* and finally size, age etc, as in *a small, old, white, plastic garden chair.* ⇨ the *note* at **and**(1). ⇨ also the *note* at **adverb.** For particular types of adjectives, ⇨ **attributive, comparative¹**(3), **demonstrative adjective, predicative, superlative¹**(2).

ad·join /ə'dʒɔɪn/ *vt,vi* to be next to (something): *The two houses adjoin.*

ad·journ /ə'dʒɜːn/ *v* **1** *vt,vi* (*formal*) to stop, e.g. discussion at (a meeting etc) for a short time: *The meeting was adjourned for a week.* **2** *vi* (*legal*) (of a court) to stop working at the end of a session.
　ad·journ·ment *nc,nu*

ad·ju·di·cate /ə'dʒuːdɪkeɪt/ *vt,vi* **adjudicate (on sth)** (*formal*) (of a judge, referee etc) to give a judgment or decision (about something): *adjudicate at a flower show; adjudicate on a disagreement during a music competition.*
　ad·ju·di·ca·tion /ə,dʒuːdɪ'keɪʃn/ *nc,nu*
　ad·ju·di·ca·tor /-tə(r)/ *nc* (*formal*) a person who judges a competition.

ad·junct /'ædʒʌŋkt/ *nc* (*gram*) a part of a sentence that is not the subject or predicate (and can be omitted without making the sentence ungrammatical), such as 'with the red hair' in *The boy with the red hair fell off his bike.*

ad·just /ə'dʒʌst/ *vt,vi* to put (something) right; change (something) in order to make it suitable for new conditions or use: *adjust a watch. Please adjust the level of sound. It takes time to adjust/get adjusted (to the heat).*
　ˌwell-a'djusted *adj* getting on well with other people.
　adjust·able /-əbl/ *adj* that can be adjusted: *The lamp is adjustable.*
　ad·just·ment *nc,nu*

ad lib /ˌæd 'lɪb/ *adv, adj* (*informal*) spoken or performed without practising or preparing.

ad-lib /ˌæd 'lɪb/ *vi* (**-bb-**) (*informal*) to say or do something without preparation (because of a sudden need).

Adm. *abbr* Admiral.

admin. /'ædmɪn/ *abbr* administration.

ad·min·is·ter /əd'mɪnɪstə(r)/ *v* **1** *vt* to control, manage, govern, (a country, a business, the law etc). **2** *vt,vi* **administer (sth) (to sb/sth)** to give (organized help, medicine etc): *administer drugs/food to starving populations; administer to the needs of the injured.*

ad·min·is·tra·tion /əd,mɪnɪ'streɪʃn/ *nu* **1** *nu* the control or management of the affairs of a government, business or organization. **2** *nu* the controlled distribution of food, drugs, aid etc. **3** *nc* a group of people who control an institution.

ad·min·is·tra·tive /əd'mɪnɪstrətɪv/ *adj* of the management of business or government affairs: *He shows no administrative ability.*

ad·min·is·tra·tor /əd'mɪnɪstreɪtə(r)/ *nc* a person who administers or organizes something.

ad·mir·able /'ædmərəbl/ *adj* deserving respect and praise: *an admirable performance.*
　ad·mir·ably /-əblɪ/ *adv*

ad·miral /'ædmərəl/ *nc* (abbr **Adm.**) an officer in command of a country's warships, or of a fleet or squadron.

Ad·mir·al·ty /'ædmərəltɪ/ *n* (the —) the branch of government which controls the Navy.

ad·mir·ation /ˌædmə'reɪʃn/ *nu* a feeling of approval, satisfaction, respect: *She speaks English so well that her friends are filled with admiration. He won admiration for his efforts.*

ad·mire /əd'maɪə(r)/ *vt* **1** to show or express approval or liking for (a person, thing): *She admired his painting.* **2** to have a high opinion of (something): *admiring Britain's legal system.*
　ad·mir·ing *adj* (*attrib*) showing or feeling admiration: *an admiring audience.*

ad·mir·ing·ly /ədv

ad·mis·si·ble /əd'mɪsəbl/ *adj* (*legal*) that can be used as proof in a law court: *admissible evidence*. Opp inadmissible.

ad·mis·sion /əd'mɪʃn/ *n* **1** *nc,nu* (an instance of) being allowed to enter a club, disco, hospital, museum etc: *No admission to people under 16 years of age*. **2** *nc* a fee or condition for entry: *Right of admission reserved* (= The owner can refuse to allow badly-behaved people to enter). **3** *nc* a statement confessing or acknowledging that one has done wrong: *an admission of guilt*.

ad·mit /əd'mɪt/ *v* (-tt-) **1** *vt,vi* **admit (sth; to sth; that . . .)** to acknowledge something as true or valid; confess: *I admit my mistake/that I was wrong. He admitted his guilt/that he was guilty. I admit to feeling ashamed of my behaviour*. **2** *vt* to allow (a person) to enter; to let (a person) in: *The secretary admitted me into his office*. **3** *vt* (*formal*) to have enough room for (people): *The new stadium can admit 120 000 people*.

ad·mit·tance /əd'mɪtəns/ *nu* (the act of) being allowed to enter: *No admittance except on business*.

ad·mit·ted·ly /əd'mɪtɪdlɪ/ *adv* by general agreement; as is agreed: *Admittedly, he has not misbehaved before*.

ad·mon·ish /əd'mɒnɪʃ/ *vt* (*formal*) to give a mild warning to (a person) or show disapproval: *The teacher admonished the boys for being lazy*.

ad nau·seam /ˌæd 'nɔːsɪəm/ *adv* (*informal*) causing (great) annoyance, esp because of continuing for too long: *His lecture went on ad nauseam*.

ado /ə'duː/ *nu* fuss: *Without more/much/further ado, he signed the agreement*.

ado·les·cence /ˌædə'lesns/ *nu* the period between childhood and maturity.

ado·les·cent /ˌædə'lesnt/ *adj, nc* (a person) growing up (aged about 12 to 18).

adopt /ə'dɒpt/ *vt* **1** to take (a child) into one's family as a son or daughter, with the legal responsibilities of a parent: *adopt an orphan*. Compare foster(2). **2** to choose and use (one method, plan) instead of another; take and use (an idea or custom etc): *Management has adopted her plan to increase profitability. European dress has been adopted by people in many parts of the world*. **3** to accept (a suggestion, plan): *Congress adopted the new measures*.

adop·tion /ə'dɒpʃn/ *n* **1** *nc,nu* the act of adopting or being adopted: *the country of his adoption*. **2** *nu* the act of using something after approval: *The adoption of this plan will mean employing another 20 people*.

adop·tive /ə'dɒptɪv/ *adj* (*attrib*) taken by adoption: *his adoptive parents*.

ador·able /ə'dɔːrəbl/ *adj* deserving to be greatly appreciated and loved: *an adorable child; an adorable little cottage*.

ador·ably /-əblɪ/ *adv*

ador·ation /ˌædə'reɪʃn/ *nu* great love: *his adoration for Jane*.

adore /ə'dɔː(r)/ *vt* **1** to love (a person) greatly: *I adore you*. **2** (*informal*) to like (something) very much: *The baby adores being tickled*.

adorer *nc* a person who adores another person.

ador·ing *adj* (*attrib*) showing great love: *adoring looks*.

ador·ing·ly *adv*

adorn /ə'dɔːn/ *vt* **adorn sb/sth (with sth)** (*formal*) to add ornament(s) or decorations to a person, room etc (using jewels etc).

adorn·ment *nc,nu*

ad·renal /ə'driːnl/ *adj* (*attrib; anat*) of or near the kidneys: *adrenal glands*.

ad·rena·lin /ə'drenəlɪn/ *nu* the chemical substance in the body that makes the heart beat faster etc, produced by anger, fear, excitement etc: *His adrenalin rose as he entered the examination hall*.

adrift /ə'drɪft/ *adj* (*pred*), *adv* **1** (of ships, boats) not under control, not tied or anchored: *The canoe was cut adrift from its moorings*. **2** (*informal*) without any purpose or direction: *She was adrift in London after she graduated*.

adu·la·tion /ˌædjʊ'leɪʃn/ *nu* (*formal*) (the giving of) too much praise or respect, esp to win favour.

adult /'ædʌlt/ *nc* **1** (also *attrib*) a person or animal grown to full size and strength: *adult education classes*. **2** (*legal*) a person old enough to vote, marry etc.

adult·hood /'ædʌlthʊd/ *nu* the period or state of being adult.

adul·ter·er /ə'dʌltərə(r)/ *nc* a man who commits adultery.

adul·ter·ess /ə'dʌltərɪs/ *nc* a woman who commits adultery.

adul·ter·ous /ə'dʌltərəs/ *adj* (guilty) of adultery.

adul·tery /ə'dʌltərɪ/ *nc,nu* (*pl* -ies) (an instance of) voluntary sexual intercourse of a married person with a person to whom he or she is not married.

adv *abbr* adverb.

ad·vance¹ /əd'vɑːns/ *adj* (*attrib*) **1** done before or earlier: *an advance payment/booking/warning*. **2** sent before others: *an advance copy/guard*.

ad·vance² /əd'vɑːns/ *n* **1** *nc,nu* **advance (on sth)** forward movement; progress or spread: *the advance of desert regions on grassland; the enemy's advance on the cities*. **make advances (to/towards sb)** to make romantic suggestions (towards a girl etc). **2** *nc* (usually *pl*) a stage of progress: *Science has made great advances during the last fifty years*. **3** **in advance** before: *send luggage/book tickets/pay rent in advance*.

ad·vance³ /əd'vɑːns/ *v* **1** *vt,vi* (to cause soldiers etc) to move forward: *Our troops have advanced two miles*. **2** *vi* to make progress: *Has civilization advanced during this century?* **3** *vi* (*formal*) (of costs, values, prices) to increase: *House prices continue to advance*. **4** *vt* (*formal*) to bring (an event etc) forward to an earlier date: *The* (*date of the*) *meeting was advanced from 10 June to 3 June. Such actions are unlikely to advance your promotion*.

ad·vance·ment *nu* (esp) the progress of a plan, a career.

ad·vanced /əd'vɑːnst/ *adj* **1** far on in life: *be advanced in years* (= very old); *advanced civilizations*. **2** having made much progress; at a higher standard: *advanced courses of study*. Compare elementary.

ad·van·tage /əd'vɑːntɪdʒ/ *n* **1** *nc* something useful, helpful or likely to bring success, esp in competition with others: *the advantages of a good edu-cation.* **have/gain/score/win an advantage (over sb)** to have etc a better position or oppor-tunity: *Tom's university education gave him an advantage over the other canditates.* Opp disad-vantage. **2** *nu* benefit; profit: *There's no advan-tage in lying if she knows the truth already.* **take advantage of sb** to use her or him unfairly, play a trick on her or him: *Don't take advantage of your little brother.* **take (full) advantage of sth** to use (something) profitably, for one's own benefit: *He always takes full advantage of every oppor-tunity to see her.* **be/prove to sb's advantage** to be profitable or helpful to a person. **3** *n sing* (*tennis* etc) a point scored after deuce.

ad·van·tage·ous /ˌædvən'teɪdʒəs/ *adj* profit-able; useful; helpful. Opp disadvantageous.
ad·van·tage·ous·ly *adv*

advent /'ædvənt/ *n* **1** *nc* **the advent of sth** the arrival of an important event etc: *Since the advent of computers, there have been great changes in industry.* **2** *n sing* (A-) the coming of Christ; the period (with four Sundays) before Christmas Day.

ad·ven·ture /əd'ventʃə(r)/ *n* **1** *nc* a strange or unusual event, esp an exciting or dangerous jour-ney or activity: *The explorer told the boys about his adventures in the Arctic.* **2** *nu* danger, excite-ment, e.g. in travel and exploration: *He's always looking for adventure.*

ad·ven·turer *nc* a daring or adventurous per-son.

ad·ven·tur·ess /-ɪs/ *nc* a female adventurer.

ad·ven·tur·ous /əd'ventʃərəs/ *adj* **1** fond of, eager for, adventure: *feeling adventurous.* **2** full of danger and excitement: *an adventurous jour-ney.*

ad·verb /'ædvɜːb/ *nc* (*gram*) a word (**a**) giving information (how, when, where) about a verb, such as *happily, today, well,* as in *smile happily, come today, feel well*; (**b**) giving information about adjectives or other adverbs, such as *very, really,* as in *walk very fast, really dirty clothes.* Ⓝ The grammatical term for the process of giving infor-mation in this way is 'modify'. *Adverbs* are words that modify verbs and also adjectives and other adverbs. Many adjectives become adverbs by adding *-ly,* such as *quietly, nicely,* but be careful because some words ending in *-ly* are always adjectives, such as *lovely, ugly.* Other words can be either an adjective or an adverb, such as *early, only, well.* Be careful because the meaning of the sentence can depend on the pos-ition of the adjective or adverb. Compare *'Only* I wore a hat' (= I was the only person) and 'I wore *only* a hat' (= A hat was the only thing I wore). ⇨ the *note* at adjective.

ad·verb·ial /æd'vɜːbɪəl/ *adj* (*gram*) of or like an adverb: *an adverbial phrase.*

ad,verbial 'clause *nc* (*gram*) a clause acting as an adverb, such as 'when I've finished my coffee' in *I'll come when I've finished my coffee.* Com-pare adjectival clause.

ad,verbial 'particle *nc* (*gram*) a word used as part of a multi-word verb to change the meaning of the verb, such as *away, off, out, through, up,* as in *throw away the box, tell her off, go out, fall through, get up to something.* Ⓝ Many words can be adverbial particles and prepositions, such as *in, off, down.* Adverbial particles are used with intransi-

tive verbs, as in *'The lights went out'. 'Stand up!'* Adverbial particles can also be used with some transitive verbs, as in *'Put your books away/Put away your books.' 'Put them away.'* Be careful because when the object is a noun, the adverbial particle can be placed before or after the object, as in *give the books out/give out the books* or *make an excuse up/ make up an excuse,* but when the object is a pronoun, the adverbial particle always comes after the object, as in *give them out* or *I made it up.* Prepositions are used with transitive verbs and are always used before the object, as in *'sit on the grass', 'walk up the stairs'.* Some multi-word verbs have an adverbial particle and a preposition, such as *'put up with'* (verb + adver-bial particle + prep) as in *I won't put up with your rudeness.* For the meanings of particular multi-word verbs, ⇨ the *verb* entries.
ad·verb·ial·ly *adv*

ad·ver·sary /'ædvəsərɪ/ *nc* (*pl* **-ies**) (*formal*) an enemy; opponent (in a contest).

ad·verse /'ædvɜːs/ *adj* (*attrib*) unhelpful or hurt-ful: *adverse weather conditions.*
ad·verse·ly *adv*

ad·ver·sity /əd'vɜːsətɪ/ *nc,nu* (*pl* **-ies**) (an instance of) bad luck, trouble: *Try to be patient/ cheerful in times of adversity.*

ad·vert /'ædvɜːt/ *nc* (*GB informal*) = advertise-ment.

ad·ver·tise /'ædvətaɪz/ *vt,vi* to make (some-thing) known to people by notices in newspapers, announcements on TV etc: *advertise in the news-paper for a typist.*

ad·ver·tiser *nc* a person, business, that adver-tises.

ad·vert·ise·ment /əd'vɜːtɪsmənt/ *nc* an announcement (in the press, on TV etc) of some-thing for sale, wanted etc.

ad·vice /əd'vaɪs/ *nu* opinion about what to do, how to behave: *You won't get well unless you fol-low your doctor's advice.* **(give sb) a piece/a word/a few words of advice** (to give) an opinion about what to do etc.

ad·vis·able /əd'vaɪzəbl/ *adj* sensible; to be recommended: *Do you think it advisable to wait?* Opp inadvisable.

ad·vise /əd'vaɪz/ *vt* **1** to give advice to (a person); recommend (something): *What do you advise me to do? She can advise you on a suitable career. The doctor advised a complete rest.* **2** (*commerce*) to inform, notify, (a person, business): *Please advise us when the goods are ready.*

ad·viser *nc* a person who gives advice, esp one who is regularly consulted: *an adviser to the Government.* Compare consultant.

ad·vis·ory /əd'vaɪzərɪ/ *adj* (*attrib*) giving advice; having the power to advise: *an advisory com-mittee.*

ad·vo·cate¹ /'ædvəkət/ *nc* a person who speaks in favour of a person or idea: *an advocate of equal opportunities for men and women.*

ad·vo·cate² /'ædvəkeɪt/ *vt* to support (the usual word): *Do you advocate euthanasia?*

aer·ate /'eəreɪt/ *vt* to let or put air into (some-thing): *aerate the soil by digging.*

aer·ial¹ /'eərɪəl/ *adj* (*attrib*) existing in, moving through, from, the air: *an aerial photograph.*

aer·ial² /'eərɪəl/ *nc* (also called *antenna*) a part of a radio or TV system which receives or sends out

aero·bics /eə'rəʊbɪks/ nu (also attrib) a method of physical exercise with music: aerobics classes.

aero·dy·nam·ic /ˌeərəʊdaɪ'næmɪk/ adj allowing air to flow over or round easily: an aerodynamic design of a car.

aero·dy·nami·cal·ly /-klɪ/ adv

aero·plane /'eərəpleɪn/ nc an aircraft with one or more engines.

aero·sol /'eərəsɒl/ nc a container for spraying a mist of scent, paint etc.

aes·thet·ic (also **es·thet·ic**) /ˌiːs'θetɪk/ adj showing appreciation of beauty in music, painting, nature etc.

aes·thet·ics (also **es-**) /ˌiːs'θetɪks/ nu the philosophy or study of the principles of beauty.

afar /ə'fɑː(r)/ adv (literary) far off or far away. **from afar** from a distance.

af·fable /'æfəbl/ adj (formal) polite and friendly: an affable person; be affable to everybody.

af·fably /-əblɪ/ adv

af·fair /ə'feə(r)/ nc **1** something (to be) done or thought about: That's my affair, not yours (= is important to, affects, me and not you). **2** happening: The plane crash was a terrible affair. **3** a relationship between two people: a love affair. **have an affair (with sb)** to have a sexual relationship. **4** (pl) business of any kind: A prime minister is kept busy with affairs of state (= the business of government). **state of affairs** ⇨ state²(1).

af·fect /ə'fekt/ vt **1** to influence or change (the condition of something), esp in a harmful way: The cold climate affected his health. His left lung is affected (e.g. by cancer). Compare effect². **2** (usually passive) to produce sad, grateful etc feelings in (a person): He was greatly affected by the news.

af·fec·ted /ə'fektɪd/ adj not natural or genuine (often in order to make oneself seem superior): affected manners/speech.

af·fec·ta·tion /ˌæfek'teɪʃn/ nc,nu (a kind of) behaviour, style (of speaking), that is not natural or genuine: The affectations in the way she speaks (e.g. her vocabulary, accent) annoy me.

af·fec·tion /ə'fekʃn/ nu a kindly and loving feeling: Every mother has affection for/feels affection toward her children.

af·fec·tion·ate /ə'fekʃənət/ adj showing affection: an affectionate daughter/father.

af·fec·tion·ately adv **Yours affectionately** (dated) (formula used to end a letter, e.g. from a man to his sister).

af·fi·da·vit /ˌæfɪ'deɪvɪt/ nc (legal) a written statement, made on oath, (to be) used as legal proof or evidence: swear/make/take an affidavit.

af·fili·ate /ə'fɪlɪeɪt/ vt,vi (of a society or an institution, or a member) to join officially: The College is affiliated to the University.

af·fili·ation /əˌfɪlɪ'eɪʃn/ nc,nu

af·fin·ity /ə'fɪnətɪ/ nc (pl **-ies**) **1** affinity (between/with sth) a close connection, relation, similarity: an affinity between English and German; the affinity of some religions with living peacefully. **2** affinity for/to sb (formal) a strong emotional attraction to a person: She feels a strong affinity for him.

af·firm /ə'fɜːm/ vt to say or write (that something is true, correct etc): affirm the truth of a statement/affirm that it is true.

af·firm·ation /ˌæfə'meɪʃn/ nc,nu

af·firm·ative /ə'fɜːmətɪv/ adj, nc (gram) (of) a statement expressing 'yes', agreement etc or one that is true, real etc, as in The answer is (in the) affirmative. (= is 'Yes'). Compare negative¹(1).

af·fix¹ /'æfɪks/ nc a suffix or prefix, e.g. -ly, -able, un-, co-.

af·fix² /ə'fɪks/ vt (formal) to fix or attach (something) (the usual words): affix a stamp to a document.

af·flict /ə'flɪkt/ vt (usually passive) to cause bodily or mental harm to (a person, animal, plant): be afflicted with rheumatism.

af·flic·tion /ə'flɪkʃn/ nc something causing suffering: the afflictions of old age (e.g. deafness, blindness).

af·flu·ence /'æfluəns/ nu wealth.

af·flu·ent /'æfluənt/ adj (of people) rich.

af·ford /ə'fɔːd/ vt (usually with can/could, be able to) to spare or find enough money or time for (something): We can't afford a holiday. I can't afford to neglect my work.

af·front /ə'frʌnt/ nc a deliberate insult or act of disrespect: an affront to his pride.

afield /ə'fiːld/ adv **far/further afield** far away from home; to or at a distance: in India and countries even further afield.

aflame /ə'fleɪm/ adj (pred; poetic) on fire.

afloat /ə'fləʊt/ adj (pred) **1** floating; carried along on air or water: The ship crashed on the rocks and we couldn't get it afloat again. **2** at sea; on board ship: life afloat (= the life of a sailor). **3** (of a business) making enough profit.

afoot /ə'fʊt/ adj (pred) in progress or operation; being prepared: There's a scheme afoot to improve the roads.

afore·said /ə'fɔːsed/ adj (legal) said or written before: the aforesaid remarks.

afraid /ə'freɪd/ adj (pred) **1** frightened: She's afraid to ask you/of the dark/that you'll be angry. There's nothing to be afraid of. **2** doubtful or anxious about what may happen: I was afraid of hurting his feelings/that I might hurt his feelings. **3** **be afraid** (a polite way of saying or writing something that may be unwelcome): I'm afraid we shall be late again. 'Is he here?'—'I'm afraid not' (= no). 'Is it broken?'—'I'm afraid so' (= yes).

afresh /ə'freʃ/ adv again; in a new way: Let's start afresh.

af·ter¹ /'ɑːftə(r)/ adv later in time or order: He fell ill on Monday and died three days after (later is more usual). Soon after (afterwards is more usual), he went to live in Wales. Compare before.

af·ter² /'ɑːftə(r)/ conj (subord) at or during a time later than: I arrived after he (had) left. Ⓝ 'After' cannot be followed by a future tense. Compare before.

af·ter³ /'ɑːftə(r)/ prep Ⓝ For uses with verbs such as ask, look, take, ⇨ the verb entries. **1** following in time; later than: after dinner/dark/two o'clock. **after that** then; next. **2** next in order to; following in order or position: 'Against' comes after 'again' in a dictionary. Shut the door after you. **3** noun + **after** + noun repeatedly; very often: day after day; one after the other. **4** as a result of: I shall never speak to him again after what he has *said about me.* **5** in spite of: *After all my care, it was broken.* **after all** in spite of all that was done, happened etc: *He died after all.* **6** searching for: *The police are after my brother.*

af·ter-effect /'ɑːftər ɪfekt/ *nc* an unpleasant result, e.g. a delayed effect of a drug.

af·ter·life /'ɑːftəlaɪf/ *nc* (the —) the life that some people think comes after death.

af·ter·math /'ɑːftəmæθ/ *nc* (the —) the result (of a war, famine or other bad event): *Misery is usually the aftermath of war.*

after·noon /ˌɑːftəˈnuːn/ *nc* (also *attrib*) the period between morning and evening: *in/during the afternoon; this/yesterday/tomorrow afternoon; on Sunday afternoon; an afternoon sleep.*

af·ter·thought /'ɑːftəθɔːt/ *nc* an idea, suggestion etc that one thinks about when it is (almost) too late.

after·wards /'ɑːftəwədz/ *adv* after; later: *We talked and afterwards went to a disco.*

again /əˈgen/ *adv* **1** once more; a second time: *If you fail the first time, try again. I'll never see her again* (= not even once more). **again and again** very often; many times. **as many/much again** (= the same quantity once more). **(every) now and (then) again** ⇨ now¹(1). **time and (time) again** ⇨ time¹(4). **2** to or in the original condition, possible etc: *You'll soon be well again. He was glad to be home again.* **3 then/there again** (used to indicate more thought or a possible change of opinion): *Then again, I'm not really sure.* **Come again?** (*informal*) What did you say?

against /əˈgenst/ *prep* Ⓝ For uses with verbs such as *go, set* etc, ⇨ the *verb* entries. **1** by the side of (and touching): *He was leaning against the door. Put the piano against the wall.* **2** in contact with (and with strong force): *Stop pushing against me! The rain was beating against the window.* **3** in disagreement with: *I'm against smoking in restaurants. John is against the idea. It's a march against nuclear weapons. Parking on the pavement is against the law.* **4** in opposition to: *We'll have to play against Morocco Swallows in the next round.* **5** in the opposite direction to: *We sailed against the wind.* **6** in order to prevent (the harmful effect of): *an injection against measles; be insured against fire and flood.* **7** having a harmful or unfavourable effect; to the disadvantage of: *Will her physical disability work against her at the interview?* **8** in contrast to: *The flowers will look better against a white background.* **as against** which is in contrast to: *I earned £100 as against £70 last week.*

age¹ /eɪdʒ/ *n* **1** *nc* the length of time a person has lived or a thing has existed: *What's his age?* ('How old is he?' is more usual.) *He's 18 years of age.* ('He's 18 years old' is more usual.) *Their ages are 4, 7 and 9.* ⇨ **age of consent**. **over age** no longer young enough: *He won't be allowed a child's fare as he's over age.* **under age** not old enough. **act one's age** to behave sensibly (as an adult does). **come of age** to become legally old enough to vote, drive, have a bank account etc. **look one's age** to look as old as one is. ⇨ middle age, old age. **2** *nu* later part of life (contrasted with *youth*): *His back was bent with age.* **3** *nc* (often A-) an important or long period of time, with special

characteristics or events: *the electronic age.* ⇨ also Dark Ages, Middle Ages, Stone Age. **4** (*pl*) (*informal*) a very long time: *We've been waiting (for) ages (and ages).*

'age-bracket *nc* a period of life between two ages, e.g. between 20 and 30.

'age-group *nc* people of the same age.

'age limit *nc* a minimum or maximum age at which a person can take part in an activity, become a member etc.

ˌage of con'sent *nc* (the —) the legal age when a person can marry, have sexual intercourse etc.

'age-old *adj* (*attrib*) known, practised etc for a long time: *age-old customs/ceremonies.*

age² /eɪdʒ/ *vt,vi* (*pres p* **ageing** or **aging**, *pp* **aged** /eɪdʒd/) (to cause a person) to grow old: *He's ag(e)ing fast. Prison has aged him.*

age·less *adj* always appearing to be young.

aged¹ /eɪdʒd/ *adj* (used before a number) having the age of: *a boy aged ten.*

aged² /'eɪdʒɪd/ *adj, n* (the —) (the) very old: *the poor and the aged; an aged professor.*

age·ing (also **ag·ing**) /'eɪdʒɪŋ/ *nu* the process of growing old.

agen·cy /'eɪdʒənsɪ/ *nc* (*pl* **-ies**) a business, place of business, of an agent(1): *He found a job through an employment agency.*

agen·da /əˈdʒendə/ *nc* (*pl* **—s**) (a list of) things to be done or discussed, e.g. by a committee: *the next item on the agenda.*

agent /'eɪdʒənt/ *nc* **1** a person or business that represents, or that manages or arranges the affairs of, another or others: *a house-agent* (= a person who buys, sells, lets and rents houses); *an insurance agent* (= a person who sells insurance). ⇨ secret agent. **2** (*science*) a substance having an effect: *Rain and frost are natural agents that wear away rocks.*

ag·gra·vate /'ægrəveɪt/ *v* **1** *vt* to make (something) worse or more serious: *aggravate an illness/offence.* **2** *vt,vi* (*informal*) to make (a person) annoyed or angry: *How aggravating!*

ag·gra·va·tion /ˌægrəˈveɪʃn/ *nu*

ag·gre·gate /'ægrɪgət/ *nc* the total obtained by adding amounts together.

ag·gres·sion /əˈgreʃn/ *n* **1** *nc,nu* an action that may begin a quarrel or war: *It was difficult to decide which country was guilty of aggression.* **2** *nu* hostile behaviour.

ag·gres·sive /əˈgresɪv/ *adj* **1** (*derog*) attacking or quarrelling without a reason: *an aggressive man.* **2** to be used for attacking: *aggressive weapons.* **3** not afraid of opposition and able to argue powerfully: *A salesperson has to be aggressive if he or she wants to succeed.*

ag·gres·ive·ly *adv*

ag·gres·ive·ness *nu*

ag·gres·sor /əˈgresə(r)/ *nc* a country, person, deliberately attacking another.

ag·grieved /əˈgriːvd/ *adj* (*formal*) feeling great sadness (esp because of unfair treatment): *be aggrieved (at not being promoted).*

aghast /əˈgɑːst/ *adj* (*pred*) filled with fear or surprise; shocked: *He stood aghast at the terrible sight.*

agile /'ædʒaɪl/ *adj* moving, acting, quickly and easily: *an agile child/mind.*

agil·ity /əˈdʒɪlətɪ/ *nu*

ag·ing /'eɪdʒɪŋ/ *nu* = ageing.

agi·tate /'ædʒɪteɪt/ *v* **1** *vt* to move or shake (a liquid). **2** *vt* to cause anxiety to (a person): *He was agitated about his wife's health.* **3** *vi* **agitate against/for sth** to argue publicly against or in favour of, take part in a campaign against or for something: *agitating for higher wages; agitating against higher taxes.*

agi·tated *adj* very worried.

agi·ta·tion /,ædʒɪ'teɪʃn/ *nu* (*formal*) **1** the act of moving or shaking (of a liquid). **2** anxiety: *She was in a state of agitation.* **3** **agitation (against/for sth)** the act of arguing or working (against or for something): *agitation against the government for lower water rates.*

agi·ta·tor /'ædʒɪteɪtə(r)/ *nc* (usually *derog*) a person who causes unrest in order to get political or social change.

aglow /ə'gləʊ/ *adj* (*pred*) bright with colour: *The sky was aglow with the setting sun.*

ag·nos·tic /æg'nɒstɪk/ *adj, nc* (of a) person who believes that nothing can be known about the existence of God.

ag·nos·ti·cism /æg'nɒstɪsɪzəm/ *nu*

ago /ə'gəʊ/ *adv* (used to show a length of time measured back to a point in the past); before now: *The train left a few minutes ago/not long ago/a long time ago. It is six years ago that he died.* Ⓝ *'Ago'* is always used with a past tense and is always placed after the expression of time, as in *a month ago. 'Ago'* refers to when an event or situation happened, as in *He died in London three years ago. 'For'* refers to the length of time an event or situation lasted or lasts, as in *He lived in London for three years. 'Since'* refers to the time when an event or situation began, as in *We've lived in London since last year.* Compare before.

agog /ə'gɒg/ *adj* (*pred*) full of interest; excited: *agog for news/to hear the news.*

ag·on·iz·ing (also **-is·ing**) /'ægənaɪzɪŋ/ *adj* causing, showing, great pain or anxiety: *an agonizing decision.*

ag·ony /'ægənɪ/ *n* (*sing*, or *pl* **-ies**) great pain or anxiety: *She looked on in agony at her child's suffering. We suffered agonies.*

agora·phobia /,ægərə'fəʊbɪə/ *nu* extreme fear of (crossing) open spaces.

agrar·ian /ə'greərɪən/ *adj* (*formal*) of land (esp farmland) or land ownership: *agrarian policies.*

agree /ə'griː/ *v* **1** *vi* to say 'Yes': *I asked him to help and he agreed. She has agreed to come.* **2** *vi* to have, decide to have, the same opinion: *We agreed to start early/that we must start early. Are we agreed?* ⇨ agree about/on sth. **agree to differ** to decide to stop trying to convince each other. **3** *vt* to admit (something): *I agree that I am to blame.* **4** *vi* to be happy together; get on well with one another: *That young couple will never agree.* **5** *vt* to accept or approve (an account, plan etc): *The Manager has agreed your expenses.*

agree about sth to have the same opinion about something: *They can never agree about anything.*

agree (on sth) (to decide) to have the same opinion: *We agreed on an early start/on starting early.*

agree with sb (a) to have the same opinion as a person: *I agree with you that he is clever.* (b) (used

with negatives or in questions) to be right or appropriate for a person's health, character etc: *Does living on a farm agree with him? This climate/Too much heat doesn't agree with me.*

agree with sth (a) to be the same as something: *This bill does not agree with your original estimate.* (b) (*gram*) (of adjectives, nouns etc) to have the same form (number, gender etc) as another word or words in the same sentence: *In 'He plays' and 'They play', the verb agrees with the subject.*

agree·able /ə'griːəbl/ *adj* **1** pleasant (the usual word): *She has an agreeable voice.* Compare disagreeable. **2** (*formal*) ready to agree: *Are you agreeable (to the proposal)?*

agree·ably /-əblɪ/ *adv* pleasantly: *I was agreeably surprised.*

agree·ment /ə'griːmənt/ *n* **1** *nc* an arrangement or understanding (spoken or written) made by two or more people, governments etc: *sign an agreement.* **arrive at/come to/reach an agreement (with sb)** to decide to have the same opinion. **break an agreement** to fail to keep to what has been agreed. **make an agreement** to agree(2). **2** *nu* **be in agreement (with sb) (on sth); with sth** to have the same opinion(s) (as a person) (about something): *We are in agreement on that point. I'm quite in agreement with what you say.* **3** *nu* (*gram*) (of the relationship between a subject and a verb or a pronoun and its antecedent(3)) the fact of having the same number, gender, person etc, as in '*War is unnecessary*', '*Children learn skills which they can use later on*'.

ag·ri·cul·tural /,ægrɪ'kʌltʃərəl/ *adj* of farming: *agricultural machinery.*

ag·ri·cul·ture /'ægrɪkʌltʃə(r)/ *nu* the science or practice of farming.

aground /ə'graʊnd/ *adv, adj* (*pred*) (of ships) touching the bottom in shallow water: *The ship went aground.*

ah /ɑː/ *int* (used to express surprise, pity etc): *Ah, you've come! Ah, it's raining!*

aha /ɑː'hɑː/ *int* (used to express triumph, satisfaction etc): *Aha, I knew I was right!*

ahead /ə'hed/ *adj* (*pred*), *adv* **1 ahead (of sb/sth)** (a) in front, in advance, (of a person, thing): *She was ahead of me in the queue. I'll go on ahead and tell them you're coming. The period ahead will not be easy.* ⇨ go ahead. (b) having more success (than a person, thing): *In this business, it's not easy to keep ahead of the competition.* ⇨ get ahead. **2** into the future: *plan/think ahead.* ⇨ look ahead.

ahem /ə'hem/ *int* (usual spelling form of) (the noise made when clearing the throat or to get a person's attention).

aid¹ /eɪd/ *n* **1** *nu* help (esp money, advice, medical assistance): *financial/international/technical aid. The Red Cross came to the aid of the refugees.* **in aid of sth** in order to be used for something: *What is the collection in aid of?* ⇨ first aid. **2** *nc* a person or thing that helps: *teaching aids. He is a great aid to his community.* ⇨ hearing aid, visual aids.

aid² /eɪd/ *vt* **1** to help (a person, business etc) by giving money, advice etc: *These maps will aid you on your journey. The World Bank aids developing* *countries*. **aid and abet sb** (*legal*) to help a person to do something illegal. **2** to help the progress of (recovery from illness, pain etc): *A long holiday will aid your recovery*.

AIDS /eɪdz/ *acronym* Acquired Immune Deficiency Syndrome (a very dangerous disease passed into the blood through sexual intercourse, syringe needles already used by an infected person etc).

ail /eɪl/ *vi* (*old use*) to be ill: *The children are always ailing*.

ail·ing /'eɪlɪŋ/ *adj* becoming poorer or worse: *an ailing business*.

ail·ment /'eɪlmənt/ *nc* (*dated*) an illness.

aim¹ /eɪm/ *n* **1** *nu* the act of directing (a gun, remark etc): *Take careful aim at the target*. **2** *nc* a purpose; objective: *He has only one aim in life—to make a fortune before he is fifty*.

aim·less *adj* having no purpose or ambition.

aim·less·ly *adv* in no particular direction; without a purpose or reason etc: *changing aimlessly from one job to another*.

aim² /eɪm/ *v* **1** *vi, vt* to point (a gun etc) towards a person etc: *He aimed (his gun) at the lion. He aimed for the target but hit the tree*. **2** *vt* to direct (e.g. a blow): *Tom aimed a heavy book at his brother's head*. **3** *vt* (*fig*) to direct (e.g. a remark, criticism): *My remarks were not aimed at you*. **4** *vi* **aim at/to do sth** to have something as a plan or intention: *Harry aims to win the London Marathon. What career are you aiming at?*

ain't /eɪnt/ (*incorrect*) short form of *are/is/am not* and *have/has not*, as in *I ain't going. We ain't got any*.

air¹ /eə(r)/ *n* **1** *nu* the mixture of gases that surrounds the earth and which we breathe: *Let's go out and enjoy the fresh air*. **in the air** (a) uncertain: *My plans are still in the air*. (b) (of opinions etc) passing from one person to another: *There are rumours in the air that he's resigned*. **in the open air** outside (a building). **into thin air** leaving no evidence of existing: *She's vanished into thin air*. **on/off the air** being/not being broadcast on radio or TV. **up in the air** (*informal*) = in the air (a). **clear the air** (*fig*) to reduce suspicion, doubt, fear etc by giving facts etc. **live on air** to survive without eating. **walk on air** to feel pleased and proud. ⇨ also hot air. **2** *by air* in a plane: *travel/send a letter by air*. **3** *nc* an appearance, quality, feeling etc (of a kind mentioned): *He has an air of importance. There was an air of fear in the crowd*. **airs and graces** exaggerated ways of behaving in order to impress people. **give oneself/put on airs** to behave in an unnatural way in the hope of impressing people. **4** *nc* (*music*) a simple tune.

'air·bed *nc* a mattress inflated with air.

'air·borne *adj* (a) being carried, transported, by air: *airborne diseases/seeds*. (b) (of a plane) in flight.

'air·brush *nc* an apparatus for spraying paint.

'air·bus *nc* a kind of large airliner.

,air·con'ditioned *adj* (of a room etc) supplied with air that is cleaned and kept at a certain temperature: *an air-conditioned room*.

'air-conditioner *nc* a machine used to make a room etc air-conditioned.

,air-con'ditioning *nu* the process of producing

an air-conditioned building etc.

,air-'cooled *adj* cooled by a current of air: *an air-cooled engine*.

'air·craft *nc* (*pl* —) plane(s).

,air·craft-carrier *nc* a ship with a deck for aircraft to take off and land.

'air·crew *nc* the crew of a plane.

'air duct *nc* a device, e.g. in a plane, for directing a flow of air for the comfort of passengers.

'air·field *nc* an area of land for (esp military) aircraft.

'air force *nc* the military forces of a country that fight in or from the air.

'air hostess *nc* a woman who help passengers in an airliner.

'air letter *nc* a sheet of paper (to be) folded and sent without an envelope by airmail.

'air·lift *nc* a large-scale transport of people or supplies by air, esp in an emergency.

'air·line *nc* (a business company owning) a regular service of aircraft for passengers and cargo.

'air·liner *nc* a plane for passengers.

'air·lock *nc* (a) a blockage in a pipe etc caused by air. (b) a compartment (in a submarine, spacecraft etc) used to enter a place that has more air pressure than outside.

'air·mail *nu* mail (to be) carried by air.

'air·plane *nc* (*US*) = aeroplane.

'air·port *nc* a place for passengers and airliners.

'air raid *nc* an attack by aircraft.

'air·ship *nc* an aircraft having a large bag filled with gas to make it float and an engine to move it.

'air·space *nc* the part of the earth's atmosphere above a country: *We shall not allow violation of our airspace by foreign aircraft*.

'air speed *nc* the speed of an aircraft relative to the air through which it is moving.

'air·strip *nc* a piece of land for planes, esp during war or in an emergency.

'air terminal *nc* (a) building(s) in a town or city centre for passengers etc travelling to or from an airport. (b) building(s) in an airport for passengers arriving and leaving by air.

'air·tight *adj* not allowing air to enter or escape.

,air-to-'air *adj* (*attrib*) (of missiles) fired from one aircraft to hit another.

,air-to-'ground *adj* (*attrib*) (of missiles) fired from an aircraft to hit a target on the ground.

'air·waves *n pl* (*informal*) radio frequencies.

'air·worthy *adj* safe to fly (in).

air² /eə(r)/ *vt* **1** to put (clothing etc) into the open air or into a warm place to make it dry: *The blankets need to be aired*. **2** to let fresh air into (a room etc). **3** (*fig*) to let others know (one's opinions, troubles etc): *He likes to air his views*.

air·ing /'eərɪŋ/ *n sing* **give sth an airing** (a) to expose it to the fresh air. (b) (*fig*) to discuss it.

'airing-cupboard *nc* a warm cupboard in which to store sheets, towels etc.

air·less /'eəlɪs/ *adj* not having (enough) fresh air: *an airless room*.

airy /'eərɪ/ *adj* (-ier, -iest) having plenty of fresh air moving through it: *an airy room*.

aisle /aɪl/ *nc* **1** a main passage in a church. **2** a main passage in a theatre, cinema etc.

aitch /eɪtʃ/ *nc* the letter H. **drop one's aitches** to fail to sound /h/ at the beginning of a word, e.g. by a saying /æt/ for *hat*.

ajar /ə'dʒɑ:(r)/ adj (pred) (of a door) slightly open.

akin /ə'kɪn/ adj **akin to sth** (literary) similar to something: Pity is often akin to love.

à la carte /ˌɑː lɑː 'kɑːt/ adj, adv (Fr) ordered as separate items from the menu: an à la carte meal; eat à la carte.

à la mode /ˌɑː lɑː 'məʊd/ adj, adv (Fr) fashionable; fashionably: an à la mode coat; dress à la mode.

alarm[1] /ə'lɑːm/ n **1** nc (a sound or signal giving) a warning of danger: give/raise the alarm. **a false alarm** a warning (esp a mistaken one) of something bad that does not happen. **2** nc an apparatus used to give a warning sound: a fire-alarm. **3** nu fear and anxiety caused by the expectation of danger: He jumped up in alarm.

alarm[2] /ə'lɑːm/ vt to give a warning or feeling of danger or worry to (a person): Everybody was alarmed at/by the news.

a'larm clock nc a clock that can ring at a fixed time.

alarm·ing adj causing fear or anxiety.

alarm·ist /-ɪst/ nc (a) a person who is easily alarmed. (b) (derog) a person who often alarms others.

alas /ə'læs/ int (used to express sorrow or regret): He tried to rescue her but alas he was too late.

al·ba·tross /'ælbətrɒs/ nc a very large, white seabird.

al·bino /ˌælbiːnəʊ/ nc (pl —s) an animal or person born without natural colouring matter in the skin, and hair (which is white) and the eyes (which are pink).

al·bum /'ælbəm/ nc **1** a book used for collecting photographs, postage stamps etc. **2** a long-playing record by the same musician(s), singer(s), composer(s) etc.

al·bu·men /'ælbjʊmən/ nu the white of an egg.

al·co·hol /'ælkəhɒl/ nu (the pure, colourless liquid as present in) such drinks as beer, wine, brandy, whisky.

al·co·hol·ic /ˌælkə'hɒlɪk/ adj containing, caused by, alcohol: alcoholic drinks/poisoning. □ nc a person whose desire for drink is so great that her or his health is affected.

al·co·hol·ism /'ælkəhɒlɪzəm/ nu the physical effect, illness, of having too much alcoholic drink.

al·cove /'ælkəʊv/ nc a part of a wall set back from the rest, often with a bed or seats.

ale /eɪl/ nc,nu (a portion of) a kind of light-coloured beer.

alert[1] /ə'lɜːt/ adj fully awake and ready to act, speak etc: be alert in answering questions; be alert to danger.

alert[2] /ə'lɜːt/ n **on the alert** ready to act, attack etc: Firemen must be on the alert for fires.

alert[3] /ə'lɜːt/ vt to warn (a person) quickly; make (a person) aware: be alerted to the dangers of smoking/the changes in the syllabus.

al·fres·co /æl'freskəʊ/ adj, adv (of meals) in the open air: lunching alfresco; alfresco meals.

al·gae /'ældʒiː/ n pl (sing **alga** /'ælgə/) green water plants with a very simple structure.

al·gebra /'ældʒɪbrə/ nu (maths) the branch of mathematics in which signs and letters are used to represent quantities, as in $2a + 3a = 5a$.

al·ge·braic /ˌældʒɪ'breɪɪk/ adj

alias /'eɪlɪəs/ adv also called: Rosie Border alias Theresa Green. □ nc (pl —es) a name which a person, esp a criminal, uses to hide her or his own.

alibi /'ælɪbaɪ/ nc (pl —s) **1** (legal) a statement to the police etc that one was in another place at the time of an act, esp a crime: The accused man was able to establish an alibi by proving that he was at a party when the money was stolen. **2** (informal) an excuse (for failure etc).

alien[1] /'eɪlɪən/ adj **1** belonging to, coming from, a foreign country: an alien environment; alien vegetation (= plants which do not occur naturally). **2** (pred) **alien (to sb/sth)** the opposite to, different from, a person, thing, (in character, behaviour): Cruelty is alien to her/to her personality.

alien[2] /'eɪlɪən/ nc a person who is not a citizen of the country in which he or she is living: An Englishman is an alien in the United States.

alien·ate /'eɪlɪəneɪt/ vt **1** to cause (a person) to become unfriendly or indifferent (by unpopular or unpleasant actions): The Prime Minister's policy alienated many of her followers. **2** **alienate sb (from sb/sth)** to cause a person to feel strange or less able: New technology has alienated many people. Parents often feel alienated from their children.

alien·ation /ˌeɪlɪə'neɪʃn/ nu (esp) the mental state of feeling or being different from other people, without friends.

alight[1] /ə'laɪt/ adj (pred) on fire; lit; burning: The sticks were damp and wouldn't catch alight.

alight[2] /ə'laɪt/ vi (formal) **1** **alight (from sth)** to get down (from a horse, plane etc). **2** **alight on sth** to discover something by accident: alight on a new cure for cancer.

align /ə'laɪn/ v **1** vt,vi (to cause things, people) to be arranged in a straight line: Can you align the green spots in the pattern? **2** vi,v reflex to agree with (and join) others: They aligned (themselves) with us.

align·ment /ə'laɪnmənt/ nc,nu **1** (an) arrangement in a straight line: The desks are in alignment/ out of alignment. **2** an agreement to join and work together.

alike /ə'laɪk/ adj (pred) like one another: The two sisters are very much alike. □ adv in the same way: We treat everybody alike.

ali·men·tary /ˌælɪ'mentrɪ/ adj (science) of food and digestion.

ali,mentary ca'nal nc (the —) (anat) the parts of the body through which food passes (from the mouth to the anus) and is digested.

ali·mony /'ælɪmənɪ/ nu the money (to be) paid by one person to another by a judge's order, after a legal separation or divorce.

alive /ə'laɪv/ adj (pred) **1** living: Who's the greatest man alive? **2** in existence; active: The issue of air-pollution should be kept alive by the press and TV. **alive and well** (informal) active and lively (often suggesting that this is unexpected): They're alive and well and living in China. **alive to sth** aware of something: He is fully alive to the dangers of the situation. **alive with sth** full of living or moving things: The lake was alive with fish.

al·kali /'ælkəlaɪ/ nc (pl —s) (chem) a soluble substance (such as soda, potash, ammonia) that combines with acids to form salts. Compare acid.

al·ka·line /'ælkəlaın/ adj

all¹ /ɔːl/ adj or det Ⓝ For uses with nouns such as cost, ear, means, thing etc, ⇨ the noun entries. **1** (used with pl nouns) the whole number of: All students need a good dictionary. Ⓝ 'All' and 'every' can have the same meaning but 'all' is used with a plural noun, as in All towns have a post office, and 'every' is used with a singular noun, as in Every town has a post office. Similarly, in the negative, 'not all' is used with a plural noun and 'not every' with a singular noun, as in Not all towns have/Not every town has a hospital. Compare both¹, each¹, every. **all kinds/sorts/types of** many varieties of: That shop sells all kinds of cheese. **by all accounts** ⇨ account¹(1). **2 (a)** (used with sing nouns) the whole of; every part of: We swam all day. Ⓝ Compare: We swam every day (= each day of the week). **all manner of** many different kinds of: She wears all manner of styles. **(b)** (used with uncountable nouns) the whole amount or extent of: All hope is lost. She likes all poetry. All stealing is wrong. He spent all his time in Europe. Ⓝ 'All' and 'the whole' can have the same meaning, as in She spent all her life alone/the whole of her life alone, but 'all' is usually used with uncountable nouns, as in He ate all the food, and 'the whole' is used with singular countable nouns, as in He ate the whole meal. **(c) all the/that/my/six** etc the whole number, amount or extent of: They walked all the way. I've spent all my money. Please return all six copies. Ⓝ 'All' can be used before another determiner, such as the, this, her, a number etc. It is called a predeterminer when it is used in this way, as in all these trees, all three books. 'Every' cannot be used before another determiner except numbers, as in They stopped every hundred miles. 'Whole' cannot be used before a determiner. Compare: I ran all the way and I ran the whole way. **all the best** (informal) (used as a friendly remark when leaving a person or when ending a letter) good luck. **all the time** ⇨ time¹(2). **3** any: It's beyond all doubt. He gave up all idea of winning.

all² /ɔːl/ adv Ⓝ For uses with verbs such as cap, depend, end etc ⇨ the verb entries. **1** in every way; completely; entirely: They were dressed all in black. Ⓝ 'All' is used for emphasis and can often be omitted without changing the meaning. Be careful because the meaning of the sentence depends on the position of 'all'. Compare We all sat alone (= Each one of us sat alone) and We sat all alone (= A group of us sat together but without others). **all at once** ⇨ once¹(4). **(all) by herself/himself** etc = all alone. **all right (a)** (adj (pred)) satisfactory: Is my work all right? **(b)** (adj (pred)) well: Are you feeling all right? **(c)** (adv) well enough: Does this bike go all right? **(d)** (used to express agreement, approval etc): All right, I'll come. It's all right if you don't come. 'Will you?'—'All right.' **all the same** nevertheless: He didn't promise; all the same, I expected him to come. **be all the same to sb** ⇨ same³. **be all set (to + verb)** ⇨ set¹(5). **all square** ⇨ square¹(6). **all there** (informal) mentally aware; sane: He behaves very strangely—is he all there? **all told** = altogether. **2 all the + comp** much, so much the . . . -er: You'll be all the better for a holiday/the richer for that experience. If you haven't seen her for a year, that's all

the more reason to see her now. **all too + adj/adv** much more: all too easily/often/quickly/soon. **not (all) that . . .** ⇨ not(1).

all alone (a) not in the company of others: He lives all alone. **(b)** without the help of others: I did it all alone. **(c)** lonely: I feel all alone without you here.

all along (a) for the whole length of: There are trees all along the road. **(b)** (informal) for the whole period of time: But I knew that all along! **all but** (formal) almost: She was all but drowned. ⇨ also be all very well but at all³(4).

all for (informal) strongly in favour of: I'm all for accepting the offer.

all in (informal) without any more energy or strength; exhausted: She was all in at the end of the squash match.

all-in adj (attrib) inclusive of everything: an all-in price. **all in** ⇨ all³(1).

all of a sudden ⇨ sudden².

all out (informal) using all possible strength, ability, effort etc: He was going all out.

all-out adj (attrib): He was making an all-out effort to win.

all over (a) in every part of: He's travelled all over Europe. **(b)** at an end: It's/The show's all over—please leave. **all over the place** ⇨ place¹(1).

all round (a) in all respects; in every way: All round, it's a good school. Ⓝ 'All together' is also possible. **(b)** in every part of: We walked all round the museum. **(c)** to, for, each person: Is there enough food to go all round? ⇨ all-round below.

all³ /ɔːl/ pron, nu **1** everything or everybody: They were all broken. Take it/them all. We all want to go. All is lost. What's it all about? We all want some. Are they all here? We don't all speak Polish. You will all need your passports. That's all for the moment. All that you say is true. They are all ready to leave. (Compare: already as in They have left already.) At last the family is all together. All together now (= Everybody together), shout! (Compare: altogether as in There are five in our family altogether.) Compare both², each³. **all but** everything, everybody, except: I got all but two questions right. **all else** (formal) everything apart from that: All else has been destroyed. If all else fails, use an axe. **all of** the whole quantity of; every one in the group of: I've lost all of my pens. He's eaten all of it. This affects all of us. Not all of the students work hard. Are all of you ready? **all or nothing** (of a commitment, effort etc) completely or not even a little: My coach demands all or nothing of the team (= He or she expects us to try very hard or leave). **be all very well but** (informal) to seem sensible or understandable but (it is not because): It's all very well for you to complain but I'm the person who is paying. Jogging is all very well but you must be healthy. **first/last/second of all** ⇨ first²(1), last²(1), second². **2** (used as a noun) everything: He gave his all (= tried as hard as he could). **3** (in games, sport) the same score for both teams or players: four all; (tennis) love (i.e. 0) all. **4** (uses with prepositions) **above all (else)** ⇨ above²(2). **after all** ⇨ after³(5). **not as/so + adj/adv + as all that** not to that extent: It's not as easy as all that (= as it appears). I managed but not so easily as all that.

(not) at all (not) in the least; (not) even a little: *She's not at all suitable. Are you at all worried? I'll come if at all possible.* **not at all** (a) (used for emphasis) not even a little: *We weren't at all worried.* (b) (used as a polite reply to a person thanking you): *'Thanks a lot.'—'Not at all.'* **away from it all** away from the usual routine, daily responsibilities, pressure etc: *Let's go camping and get away from it all.* **in all** as the total: *We were 15 in all.* **all in all** considering all the facts: *All in all it's been a successful conference.*

all- /ɔːl/ *prefix* completely: *an all-red uniform; an all-British expedition.*

,all-'clear *nc* a signal that danger has passed: *She gave the all-clear and we opened the door.*

,all-e'lectric *adj* having only electrical equipment: *an all-electric kitchen.*

,all 'found *adj* including all the costs: *Our estimate is £100 all found.*

,all-im'portant *adj* (*attrib*) more important than anything else; vital: *This is an all-important opportunity.*

,all-'in ⇨ *all in* at all² (3).

,all-in'clusive *adj* including everything: *all-inclusive prices.*

,all-'out ⇨ *all out* at all²(3).

,all-'powerful *adj* (*attrib*) too strong to challenge: *I resigned when I realized his all-powerful position.*

,all-'purpose *adj* (*attrib*) having several uses: *an all-purpose knife.*

,all-'round *adj* (*attrib*) having various abilities: *an all-round athlete.*

,all-'rounder *nc* a person with many and various abilities.

,all-'star *adj* (*attrib*) with many famous actors: *an all-star cast.*

,all-'time *adj* (*attrib*) best, worst etc experienced: *Sales have reached an all-time high/low.*

Al·lah /ˈælə/ *n* the name of God among Muslims.

al·lay /əˈleɪ/ *vt* (*formal*) to make (fears, doubt) less strong.

al·le·ga·tion /ˌælɪˈɡeɪʃn/ *nc* an accusing statement, esp one made without proof: *You have made serious allegations but can you prove them?*

al·lege /əˈledʒ/ *vt* to state or write (something) as a reason or excuse, in support of a claim or in denial of a charge: *Are you alleging that you saw the accused man?*

al·leg·ed·ly /-ɪdlɪ/ *adv*: *It's allegedly true.*

al·le·giance /əˈliːdʒəns/ *nu* duty, support, loyalty, (to a ruler or government): *They must take an oath of allegiance to the Queen.*

al·le·gori·cal /ˌælɪˈɡɒrɪkl/ *adj* of, using, allegory.

al·le·gory /ˈælɪɡərɪ/ *nc* (*pl* **-ies**) a story or description in which characters symbolize ideas such as patience, purity and truth (usually to teach a moral lesson).

al·ler·gic /əˈlɜːdʒɪk/ *adj* (usually *pred*) *allergic (to sth)* having an allergy (to a substance etc).

al·ler·gy /ˈælədʒɪ/ *nc* (*pl* **-ies**) *allergy to sth* (*med*) a condition of being affected by particular foods, fur, insect stings etc.

al·levi·ate /əˈliːvɪeɪt/ *vt* to make (pain, suffering) less or easier to bear.

al·levi·ation /əˌliːvɪˈeɪʃn/ *nu*

al·ley /ˈælɪ/ *nc* (*pl* **—s**) a narrow passage or street.

⇨ also **blind alley.**

al·li·ance /əˈlaɪəns/ *n* **1** *nu* the state of association or connection: *They are working in alliance with us.* **2** *nc* a union, agreement, e.g. between states (by treaty): *They entered into an alliance with other Asian countries.* ⇨ **ally.**

al·lied /ˈælaɪd/ *adj* connected (by similar qualities): *allied methods of production.* **be allied to sth** (of things) to be connected: *English is allied to German.* ⇨ **ally².**

al·li·ga·tor /ˈælɪɡeɪtə(r)/ *nc* a reptile like a crocodile but with a shorter head.

al·li·ter·ation /əˌlɪtəˈreɪʃn/ *nu* the repetition of the first sound or letter in a succession of words, e.g. *safe and sound; through thick and thin.*

al·lit·er·ative /əˈlɪtərətɪv/ *adj*

al·lo·cate /ˈæləkeɪt/ *vt* *allocate sth (to sb) (for sth)* to give or have something as a share (for a purpose): *allocate hotels to the tourists for the holiday.*

al·lo·ca·tion /ˌæləˈkeɪʃn/ *nc,nu*

al·lot /əˈlɒt/ *vt* (**-tt-**) to give out (to each person, group) a part or share etc of (something): *to allot various tasks to the committee; Can we do it within the time allotted (to) us?*

al·lot·ment *nc* a part or share, esp (in GB) of a small area of land rented as a vegetable garden.

al·low /əˈlaʊ/ *vt* **1** to give permission to (a person) (to do something): *My father allowed me to go swimming. Dogs are not allowed (to come) in here.* Ⓝ *'Allow'* is more formal than *'let'. 'Allow'* is used with an object and an infinitive verb with *'to'*, as in *allow Mike to go home. 'Let'* is used with an object and an infinitive verb without *'to'*, as in *let Mike go home. 'Let'* has no passive form; use *'allow'*, as in *be allowed to go home. 'Permit'* is more formal than *allow.* **2** to give permission for a person or thing to have, provide, (things, money, time etc) for: *How many cakes are we allowed? You are allowed £30 as expenses. Allow 10 minutes to each candidate.* **allow for sth** to think about something when forming an opinion or deciding: *You'll need an hour to get to the station allowing for traffic delays.*

al·low·able /-əbl/ *adj* that is or can be allowed (by law, the rules etc).

al·low·ance /əˈlaʊəns/ *n* **1** *nc* a sum of money, amount, (regularly) allowed. **2** *make allowances for sb/sth* to allow for a person's age, lack of experience etc when deciding, forming an opinion etc: *We must make allowances for his youth.*

al·loy /ˈælɔɪ/ *nc,nu* a mixture of metals, esp a metal of low value mixed with a metal of higher value: *Steel is an alloy.*

all right /ˌɔːl ˈraɪt/ *adv* ⇨ all²(1).

al·lude /əˈluːd/ *vi* *allude to sth* (*formal*) to mention (the more usual word): *I was alluding to a newspaper article on the subject.*

al·lur·ing /əˈlʊərɪŋ/ *adj* attractive (the usual word): *an alluring smile.*

al·lu·sion /əˈluːʒn/ *nc* (*literature*) an indirect reference (often by using a figure of speech) to another famous event or person: *Hardy's novels are full of classical allusions. 'Herculean strength' is an allusion to Hercules, a Greek hero noted for his great strength.*

al·lus·ive /əˈluːsɪv/ *adj* containing allusions.

al·luv·ial /ə'lu:vɪəl/ *adj* (*attrib; tech*) made of sand, earth etc left by rivers or floods: *alluvial soil.*

al·ly¹ /'ælaɪ/ *nc* (*pl* **-ies**) a person, state etc giving help or support to another.

al·ly² /ə'laɪ/ *vt, v reflex, vi* (*pt,pp* **-ied**) **ally (oneself) to/with sb/sth** (to cause a person, oneself, a family) to become united by treaty, marriage etc: *Britain is allied with the United States.*

al·ma·nac /'ɔ:lmənæk/ *nc* a book of months and days, with information about the sun, moon, tides, historical facts etc.

Al·mighty /ɔ:l'maɪtɪ/ *n* (the —) God.

al·mond /'ɑ:mənd/ *nc* (also *attrib*) (a long, flat nut inside) a hard seed of a kind of tree similar to the peach and plum: *an almond flavour.*

al·most /'ɔ:lməʊst/ *adv* very nearly: *He slipped and almost fell. They're almost the same size. It's almost time to go. Those flowers look almost real. I'm almost certain he did it. She says almost nothing of importance.* (N) *'Almost'* and *'nearly'* can have the same meaning but *'almost'* suggests that something is very near or accurate, as in *99 is almost 100* and *2.50 is nearly 3 o'clock. 'Almost'* can be used to refer to progress other than in time or space, as in *be almost sure,* but *'nearly'* cannot. *'Almost'* can be used with *never, none, no-one, nothing* etc, but *'nearly'* cannot. Compare *hardly.*

alms /ɑ:mz/ *n pl* (*dated*) money, food etc given to the poor.

aloft /ə'lɒft/ *adj* (*pred*), *adv* high up in the air (esp at the top of a ship): *go aloft to look for land.*

alone /ə'ləʊn/ *adj* (*pred*), *adv* **1** without other people: *He lives alone. I shall be alone at the station.* ⇨ **all alone** or **all².** (N) *'Alone'* does not mean *'lonely'* except in the expression *all alone.* **2** without the help of other people: *You can't do the job alone.* **go it alone** (*informal*) to do something without help. **3** *n/pron* + **alone** and no other person or thing: *He alone knows what happened. Birds alone have feathers.* **4** **be alone in doing sth/that** to be the only person: *Am I alone in believing you?* **leave sb/sth alone** ⇨ leave²(11). **let alone** ⇨ let³(1).

along¹ /ə'lɒŋ/ *adv* (N) For uses with verbs such as *come, get, go,* ⇨ the *verb* entries. **1** (of movement on a long, flat surface) forward: *We were driving along very happily.* (N) *'Along'* refers to where and in what direction the movement is. *'On'* is used when referring to continuous or more movement, as in *Go on until you reach the garage.* **2** into a more advanced state: *Your garden is coming along well.* **3** (used to refer to movement) here; there: *I'll be along in a minute.* (N) *'Along'* refers to movement in any direction to get here or there, as in *come along to my party,* but *across, down, up* etc are used when referring to a particular direction, as in *Come up* (i.e. upstairs) *to my office.* **4** with a person: *Please bring your girlfriend along.*

along² /ə'lɒŋ/ *prep* **1** from one end to the other end (of a section) of: *We were driving along the motorway.* (N) *'Along'* refers to movement on a long, flat surface, as in *go along the path. 'Through'* refers to movement from one side to the other of a wide area, as in *go through London on a train. 'Through'* is also used with words referring to activity, period of time etc meaning *'during',* as in *sleep through the journey/the night.* **2** at a position on the length of: *The restaurant is along this street. Let's stop along the way for lunch.*

along·side /ə,lɒŋ'saɪd/ *adv, prep* close to (and in line with) the side of: *driving alongside a lorry.*

aloof /ə'lu:f/ *adj, adv* (often *derog*) (of a person) not able or willing to show feelings or take part (because nervous, arrogant etc): *She's difficult to know because she's so aloof.*

aloof·ness *nu*

aloud /ə'laʊd/ *adv* in a voice powerful enough to be heard, not in a whisper: *He called aloud for help.* (N) *'Out loud'* can also be used. **read/think aloud** to read/think in a spoken voice, not silently.

al·pha /'ælfə/ *n* the first letter (A, α) in the Greek alphabet.

'alpha particle/ray *nc* (*science*) a kind of atomic radiation.

al·pha·bet /'ælfəbet/ *nc* (usually —) the letters used in writing a language, arranged in order: *the Greek alphabet.*

al·pha·beti·cal /,ælfə'betɪkl/ *adj* in the order of the alphabet: *The words in a dictionary are in alphabetical order.*

al·pha·beti·cal·ly /-klɪ/ *adv*

al·ready /ɔ:l'redɪ/ *adv* (N) *'Already'* is mainly used to show emphasis and can be omitted without changing the meaning. **1** by this/that time: *The postman has already been/has been already. They had already left when I arrived.* **2** before now, previously: *I've already been there/been there already and I don't want to go again.* Compare *before¹.* **3** (showing surprise) as early as this: *You're not leaving us already, are you?* (N) *'Already'* is used when something has or might have happened, as in *She has already left. She may have already left.* It is placed near the verb or, for emphasis, at the end of a sentence, as in *Don't tell me she's left already! 'Still'* is used when something is continuing to happen and is placed near the verb, as *She's still here. Is she still here? 'Yet'* is used when something is expected but has not happened. It is only used in negative sentences and questions and is usually placed at the end, as in *She hasn't left yet. Has she left yet? 'All ready'* cannot be used. It means *'everyone/everything + prepared',* as in *They are all ready to leave.* ⇨ all³(1).

al·so /'ɔ:lsəʊ/ *adv* **1** in addition: *I love chips and I also like peas. Also, I like tomatoes. I can also hold a spider.* (N) *'Also'* is placed near the verb, as in *I would also like to go. 'As well'* and *'too'* can be placed at the end of a clause etc, as in *I would like to go on a trip to India as well/too. 'Also'* is preferred when referring to the verb, as in *I can also swim* (in addition to doing other activities) and *'too'* is preferred when referring to the subject, as in *I, too, can swim* (in addition to other people). *'Also', 'as well'* and *'too'* cannot be used in negative sentences. Use *not . . . either/neither . . . nor,* as in *I don't want to go either.* **not only . . . but also** ⇨ not(1). **2** (used as a *conj*) and in addition: *Bring a pen and pencil, also a calculator.*

also-ran /'ɔ:lsəʊ ræn/ *nc* (*informal; derog*) a person who has tried (a career etc) but failed to do well.

al·tar /'ɔ:ltə(r)/ *nc* a raised place (table or platform) used in religious services (as in Christian churches).

al·ter /'ɔːltə(r)/ *vt,vi* (to cause a person, thing) to become different, change in character, appearance etc: *These clothes are too large; they must be altered. He has altered a great deal since I last saw him.*

alter·ation /ˌɔːltə'reɪʃn/ *n* **1** *nu* the process of becoming different. **2** *nc* an act of changing; the result of changing: *Alterations to the house will cost a lot of money.*

al·ter·nate¹ /ɔːl'tɜːnət/ *adj* (of two kinds of things) first one and then the other: *Tom and Harry do the work on alternate days* (e.g. Tom on Monday, Harry on Tuesday etc).

al,ternate 'angles *n pl* (maths) two angles on opposite sides of a line crossing two other lines.

al·ter·nate·ly *adv*

al·ter·nate² /'ɔːltəneɪt/ *vt,vi* (to cause two things) to occur by turns, one after the other: *She alternates boiled eggs with fried eggs for breakfast.*

alternate between sth and sth to change from one state etc to the other and then back to the first: *He alternates so easily between happiness and sadness.*

,alternating 'current *nc* (electricity) a current that changes direction at regular intervals. ⇨ direct current.

al·ter·na·tive¹ /ɔːl'tɜːnətɪv/ *adj* (of two or more things) that may be used, chosen etc in place of the other or others: *There are alternative answers to your question.*

al·ter·na·tive·ly *adv* as a choice: *a fine of £50 or alternatively six weeks' imprisonment.*

al·ter·na·tive² /ɔːl'tɜːnətɪv/ *nc* a choice between two or more things: *You have the alternative of working hard and succeeding or of not working and being unsuccessful. You have no alternative but to work. I was given three alternatives.*

al·though /ɔːl'ðəʊ/ *conj* **1** regardless of the fact that: *Although he was younger, he won the race. She went out although it was raining.* **2** but continuing to be: *He is hard working although poor.* **3** apart from the fact that: *I believe her although she may be lying.* Ⓝ *'Though'* can also be used but it is less formal. *'Even'* can be used with *'though'* for emphasis, as in *I trust him even though he's been in prison, but not with 'although.'*

al·ti·meter /'æltɪmiːtə(r)/ *nc* (tech) an instrument that measures height above sea-level.

al·ti·tude /'æltɪtjuːd/ *nc* **1** (tech) the height of an object above sea-level. **2** (maths) a distance between the base and the highest point of a figure.

al·to /'æltəʊ/ *nc* (pl —s) (a musical part for) a person having the highest adult male singing voice or the lowest female singing voice (above tenor).

al·to·gether /ˌɔːltə'geðə(r)/ *adv* **1** entirely; completely: *I don't altogether agree with him.* **2** with everything included: *You owe me £10 altogether.* **3** having considered everything: *Altogether, it was a horrible day.* Ⓝ *'All together'* cannot be used for *'altogether.'* It means *'everyone/ everything in the same place or at the same time'*, as in *Are the suitcases all together? The children arrived all together.*

al·tru·ism /'æltruːɪzəm. *nu* the quality of considering the well-being and happiness of others before yourself.

al·tru·ist /'æltruːɪst/ *nc* a person who is altruistic.

al·tru·is·tic /ˌæltruː'ɪstɪk/ *adj* showing altruism: *altruistic behaviour.*

al·tru·is·ti·cal·ly /-klɪ/ *adv*

alu·min·ium /ˌæljuː'mɪnɪəm/ (US = alumi·num /ə'luːmɪnəm/) *nu* a light, silver-coloured metal, used to make saucepans etc.

al·ways /'ɔːlweɪz/ *adv* **1** at all times; without exception: *The sun always rises in the east. I have always liked you. Why are you always late for work? I almost/nearly always arrive at work on time. 'Do you have milk in your coffee?'—'Not always.'* **2** all the time; for ever: *I'll remember you always.* **3** again and again: *He's always asking me for money.* Ⓝ *'Always'* is usually placed near the verb and cannot be used at the beginning of a sentence unless it is imperative, as in *Always tell the truth. 'Ever'* meaning *'at any (single) time'* is used in questions, as in *Are you ever late for work?*, or in sentences with *'if'*, as in *Ask me if you ever need advice. 'Always'* can be used with *almost, nearly* etc, but *'ever'* cannot. Compare never.

am¹ /əm *strong form:* æm; *after 'I':* -m/ ⇨ be¹.

am² /ˌeɪ 'em/ *abbr* (Latin: *ante meridiem*) before noon: *7.30 am.*

amal·ga·mate /ə'mælgəmeɪt/ *vi,vt* (to cause businesses, societies, groups of people) to join together.

amal·ga·ma·tion /əˌmælgə'meɪʃn/ *nc*

amass /ə'mæs/ *vt* to collect (a great deal of money, power): *amass a fortune/riches.*

ama·teur /'æmətə(r)/ *nc* (also *attrib*) **1** a person who acts in drama, performs music etc, for pleasure only and not professionally: *an amateur photographer.* **2** a person who plays a game, takes part in sports, without receiving payment: *an amateur tennis-player.* Compare professional¹(2).

ama·teur·ish /'æmətərɪʃ/ *adj* (derog) without skill: *an amateurish performance.*

amaze /ə'meɪz/ *vt* (usually *passive*) to fill (a person) with great surprise or wonder: *I was amazed at the news/amazed to hear that he'd won.*

amaz·ing *adj: How amazing!*

amaz·ing·ly *adv: He's doing amazingly well.*

amaze·ment /ə'meɪzmənt/ *nu* great surprise: *I heard with amazement that he'd won.*

am·bas·sa·dor /æm'bæsədə(r)/ *nc* (also A-) an official representing the Government of her or his country in a foreign country: *the British Ambassador to Greece.*

am·bas·sa·dor·ial /æmˌbæsə'dɔːrɪəl/ *adj*

am·ber /'æmbə(r)/ *nu* (also *adj*) **1** a hard, clear yellowish-brown gum used for making ornaments etc. **2** its colour.

am·bi·dex·trous /ˌæmbɪ'dekstrəs/ (also **-ter·ous**) /-tərəs/ *adj* able to use the left hand and the right equally well.

am·bi·ence /'æmbɪəns/ *nu* (formal) the general character or quality in a place; atmosphere (the more usual word): *a hotel with a friendly ambience.*

am·bi·gu·ity /ˌæmbɪ'gjuːətɪ/ *n* (pl **-ies**) **1** *nc* an expression of an idea so that more than one meaning is possible. **2** *nu* the state of being ambiguous.

am·bigu·ous /æm'bɪgjʊəs/ *adj* having more than one interpretation: *'I don't like the make-up of the women's team'* is ambiguous.

am·bigu·ous·ly *adv*

am·bi·tion /æm'bɪʃn/ *n* **1** *nu* a strong desire to be successful: *Those with ambition usually work hard.* **2** *nc* a particular desire of this kind: *He has great ambitions.*

am·bi·tious /æm'bɪʃəs/ *adj* **1** having a strong desire for success: *an ambitious woman; be ambitious to succeed in life.* **2** showing or needing strong desire, great effort etc: *ambitious plans; an ambitious attempt.*

am·bi·tious·ly *adv*

am·biva·lent /æm'bɪvələnt/ *adj* (*formal*) having two opposing opinions, opinions: *I'm ambivalent about whether to go or not.*

amble /'æmbl/ *nc* a slow, gentle, rate of walking. □ *vi* **amble (about)** to move without hurrying.

am·bu·lance /'æmbjʊləns/ *nc* a vehicle designed for carrying people who are ill or injured to a hospital.

am·bush /'æmbʊʃ/ *nc,nu* (the place of) a surprise attack: *be attacked from an ambush; wait in ambush* (= wait to attack). □ *vt* to attack (a group, place) suddenly from a hidden place.

ameli·or·ate /ə'miːlɪəreɪt/ *vt,vi* (*formal*) (to cause a condition etc) to become better; improve (the usual word): *ameliorate the economic situation.*

amen /ɑː'men/ *int* (used at the end of a prayer or hymn and meaning 'May it be so').

amen·able /ə'miːnəbl/ *adj* (of a person) willing to be guided or controlled: *be amenable to kindness/advice/reason.*

amend /ə'mend/ *vt* to improve (something) by changing the words, adding information etc: *He amended his speech to include recent economic statistics.* Compare emend.

amend·ment *nc,nu*: *amendments to the constitution.*

amends /ə'mendz/ *n pl* **make amends (to sb) (for sth)** to give (a person) something, apologize (for injury, loss, bad behaviour): *make amends to a friend for being unkind.*

amen·ity /ə'miːnəti/ *n* (*pl* **-ies**) (usually *pl*) the things, conditions, that make life easy or pleasant: *a town with many amenities* (e.g. a park, a public library, playing fields).

am·ethyst /'æmɪθɪst/ *nc* a precious stone which is purple or violet.

ami·able /'eɪmɪəbl/ *adj* (*formal*) likeable: *I found him a most amiable person.*

amic·able /'æmɪkəbl/ *adj* friendly: *We settled our quarrel in an amicable way.*

amic·ably /-əblɪ/ *adv*

amid /ə'mɪd/ (also **amidst**) /ə'mɪdst/ *prep* (*literary*) among, in the middle of: *There was suddenly calm amid the chaos.*

amir (also **emir**) /ə'mɪə(r)/ *n* the title used by some Muslim rulers.

amiss /ə'mɪs/ *adj, adv* (*dated*) wrong(ly); out of order: *There's not much amiss with it.* **take sth amiss** to become (too) angry or upset: *Don't take it amiss if I show you your errors.*

am·me·ter /'æmɪtə(r)/ *nc* (*tech*) an instrument that measures electric current.

am·mo·nia /ə'məʊnɪə/ *nu* (*chem*) a kind of colourless gas (NH_3) with a strong smell, used to make explosives, fertilizers etc.

am·mu·ni·tion /ˌæmjʊ'nɪʃn/ *nu* **1** military stores, esp of explosives (for weapons). **2** (*fig*)

information, evidence, (to use in an argument etc): *That gives me the ammunition I need for tomorrow's debate.*

am·nesia /æm'niːzɪə/ *nu* (*med*) (a part or total) loss of memory.

am·nes·ty /'æmnəstɪ/ *nc* (*pl* **-ies**) a general pardon, esp for political offences: *The rebels returned home under an amnesty.*

amoe·ba /ə'miːbə/ *nc* (*pl* **—s** or **—e** /-biː/) a very small kind of animal, consisting of one cell.

amoe·bic /ə'miːbɪk/ *adj* of, concerning, caused by, amoebas: *amoebic dysentery.*

amok /ə'mɒk/ (also **amuck**) /ə'mʌk/ *adv* **run amok/amuck** to run about wildly (esp with a desire to kill people).

among /ə'mʌŋ/ (also **amongst** /ə'mʌŋst/) *prep* Ⓝ 'Amongst' is dated but is sometimes used before a vowel, as in *amongst ourselves*. **1** surrounded by, in the middle of, (more than two): *It was hidden among the flowers. They were standing among the crowd.* Ⓝ 'Among' is only used with plurals and collectives. 'In' can also be used, as in *a hotel in the trees; be in a group of tourists.* 'Between' is used to refer to two only, as in *the border between France and Spain; standing between my parents.* **2** (of more than two) giving each a portion (when dividing, sharing etc): *Please divide the cake among the children. You must distribute them equally among the four of us.* Ⓝ 'Between' is used for two only, as in *share it between both of us.* ⇨ between²(3). **3** (of more than two) including each one (when fighting, talking, sorting etc): *There was a quarrel among the members. We were gossiping among/amongst ourselves. If you search among the books you'll find it.* Ⓝ 'Between' is used for two, as in *a debate between the manager and her assistant.* It is also used when referring to a list longer than two, as in *a choice between fruit, cheese and ice-cream.* ⇨ between²(4). **4** one of, some of, (many or a group): *I was among several candidates who were interviewed. Among/amongst other things, I have problems with English grammar. There is a lot of experience among his staff. Are they among the best singers? It is not among the poorer nations.* **from among** ⇨ from(8).

amoral /ˌeɪ'mɒrəl/ *adj* (of behaviour, a person) not showing an interest in being bad or good. Compare moral¹, immoral.

am·or·ous /'æmərəs/ *adj* showing a feeling of love (esp sexual): *amorous looks.*

am·or·ous·ly *adv*

amor·phous /ə'mɔːfəs/ *adj* **1** (*science*) not crystallized: *amorphous rocks.* **2** (*fig*) with no definite or agreed form: *amorphous plans to reorganize.*

amount¹ /ə'maʊnt/ *nc* a total sum; quantity: *He owed me £100 but could pay only half that amount* (= could pay only £50). *A large amount of money is spent on tobacco every year.*

amount² /ə'maʊnt/ *vi* **amount to sth** to add up to, be equal to, something: *The costs amount to £5000. Riding on a bus without paying the fare amounts to* (= is the same thing as) *stealing.*

amp(s) /æmp(s)/ *abbr* (*electricity*) ampere(s).

am·pere /'æmpeə(r)/ *nc* (abbr **amp**, symbol A) (*electricity*) a unit for measuring electric current.

am·pheta·mine /æm'fetəmiːn/ *nc* (*med*) a kind of drug used to stimulate the nervous system.

am·phib·ian /æm'fɪbɪən/ *nc* **1** an animal able to

live both on land and in water: *A frog is an amphibian.* **2** a plane designed to land on and take off from both land and water. **3** a vehicle able to move in water and on land.

am·phibi·ous /æm'fɪbɪəs/ *adj* adapted for both land and water: *Frogs are amphibious.*

am·phi·theatre (*US* = **-ter**) /'æmfɪθɪətə(r)/ *nc* a round building with rows of seats round an open space, used for sports and amusements.

ample /'æmpl/ *adj* (**—r, —st**) **1** with plenty of space: *There's ample room for the children and their toys.* **2** enough: *£5 will be ample for my needs.* Compare scanty.

am·ply /'æmplɪ/ *adv*

am·pli·fy /'æmplɪfaɪ/ *vt* (*pt,pp* **-ied**) **1** to increase the strength of (sound) using electricity: *an amplified guitar.* **2 amplify (on) sth** (*formal*) to make a report etc larger or fuller, esp by giving more information: *Today I shall amplify on yesterday's lecture.*

am·pli·fi·ca·tion /ˌæmplɪfɪ'keɪʃn/ *nu*

am·pli·fier /'æmplɪfaɪə(r)/ *nc* an electrical appliance used for making sound louder.

am·pu·tate /'æmpjuteɪt/ *vt* (*med*) to cut off (e.g. an arm, a leg) by surgery.

am·pu·ta·tion /ˌæmpju'teɪʃn/ *nc,nu*

amuck /ə'mʌk/ *adv* = amok.

amuse /ə'mjuːz/ *vt* **1** to make (a person) laugh or smile: *His funny stories amused all of us.* **2** to make time pass pleasantly for (a person): *amusing the baby with toys.*

amuse·ment /ə'mjuːzmənt/ *n* **1** *nu* the state of being amused: *To the great amusement of everybody, the actor's beard fell off.* **2** *nc* something organized or built to make time pass pleasantly: *There are plenty of amusements here—cinemas, theatres, football matches etc.*

amus·ing /ə'mjuːzɪŋ/ *adj* causing laughter or smiles: *an amusing story/storyteller.*

an /ən *strong form:* æn/ ⇨ a.

anach·ron·ism /ə'nækrənɪzəm/ *nc* something out of date either now or in a description of past events: *In the sentence 'Julius Caesar looked at his watch and picked up the telephone' there are two anachronisms. Is the House of Lords an anachronism?*

anach·ron·is·tic /ˌænækrə'nɪstɪk/ *adj*

anae·mia (*US* = **ane·mia**) /ə'niːmɪə/ *nu* (*med*) the condition of having poor blood, which makes a person pale and weak.

anae·mic (*US* = **ane·mic**) /ə'niːmɪk/ *adj* unhealthy because of anaemia; pale.

an·aes·thesia (*US* = **an·es·**) /ˌænɪs'θiːzɪə/ *nu* (*med*) the state of being unable to feel pain, heat etc.

an·aes·thet·ic (*US* = **an·es·**) /ˌænɪs'θetɪk/ *nc* (*med*) a substance that removes the feeling of pain, consciousness etc: *be given an anaesthetic.* ⇨ general/local anaesthetic.

an·aes·the·tize (also **-tise**) (*US* = **anes-**) /ə'niːsθətaɪz/ *vt* (*med*) to make (a person, animal) unable to feel pain etc.

an·aes·the·tist (*US* = **an·es·**) /ə'niːsθətɪst/ *nc* a person trained to use anaesthetics.

ana·gram /'ænəgræm/ *nc* a word made by changing the order of the letters in another word: *'Decimal' is an anagram of 'medical'.*

anal /'eɪnl/ *adj* (*anat*) of the anus.

an·al·gesic /ˌænæl'dʒiːzɪk/ *nc* a substance, e.g an ointment, which takes away pain.

ana·log com·pu·ter /ˌænəlɒg ˌkəm'pjuːtə(r)/ *nc* a computer using different strengths of electricity for numbers. Compare digital computer.

ana·log·ous /ə'næləgəs/ *adj* **analogous (to/ with sth)** similar: *The two processes are not analogous (to/with each other).*

ana·logue (*US* = **-log**) /'ænəlɒg/ *nc* **1** (*literature*) a word in one language with the same origin as a word in another language: *'Table' is an analogue of the Latin word 'tabula'.* **2** a product that is similar to another: *a meat analogue* (= an artificial substitute for meat, of soya beans).

ana·logy /ə'nælədʒɪ/ *n* (*pl* **-ies**) **1** *nc* a similarity in some aspects: *The teacher drew an analogy between the human heart and a pump.* **2** *nu* the process of reasoning between similar examples: *argue by/from analogy.*

ana·lyse (*US* = **-lyze**) /'ænəlaɪz/ *vt* **1** to examine (a thing) carefully in order to learn something about it: *If we analyse water, we find that it is made up of two parts of hydrogen and one part of oxygen. The leader tried to analyse the causes of our failure.* **2** (*gram*) to divide (a sentence) into its grammatical parts. **3** = psychoanalyse.

ana·ly·sis /ə'næləsɪs/ *n* (*pl* **-ses** /-siːz/) **1** *nu* (e.g. of a book, character, situation) separation into parts possibly with comment and judgement: *the critical analysis of literary texts.* **2** *nc* an instance of this; a statement of the result of doing this. **3** = psychoanalysis.

ana·lyst /'ænəlɪst/ *nc* **1** a scientist who makes (esp chemical) analyses: *a food analyst.* **2** = psychoanalyst.

ana·lyt·ic /ˌænə'lɪtɪk/, **-ical** /-kl/ *adj* of or using analysis.

ana·lyti·cal·ly /-klɪ/ *adv*

ana·phora /ə'næfərə/ *nu* **1** (*gram*) the use of (esp) a pronoun to avoid repetition of a noun or phrase, e.g. 'it' in 'I found a cheap camera and I bought it'. **2** (*literature*) the style of writing in which a word or phrase is repeated at the beginning of two or more lines of verse or sentences (for emphasis), as in 'Gone is the winter; Gone is the cold . . .'.

an·arch·ic /ə'nɑːkɪk/ *adj* supporting anarchism.

an·arch·ism /'ænəkɪzəm/ *nu* the political theory that organized government and laws are undesirable.

an·arch·ist /'ænəkɪst/ *nc* a person who believes in anarchism.

an·archy /'ænəkɪ/ *nu* **1** the absence of organized government. **2** disorder: *There was anarchy among students.*

anas·trophe /ə'næstrəfɪ/ *nu* (*literature*) the reversal of the usual order of the parts of a sentence for poetic effect, as in 'To London I came'.

anat *abbr* anatomy.

anath·ema /ə'næθəmə/ *nc* (*pl* **—s**) (*formal*) something that is hated very much: *Violence is an anathema to them.*

anat·omy /ə'nætəmɪ/ *nu* (the scientific study of) the structure of animal bodies.

ana·tomi·cal /ˌænə'tɒmɪkl/ *adj*

anat·om·ist /-ɪst/ *nc* an expert in, student of, anatomy.

an·ces·tor /'ænsestə(r)/ *nc* a person earlier than

a grandparent who is a direct relative: *My ances-tors came from Africa.*

an·ces·tral /æn'sestrəl/ *adj* (*attrib*) belonging to, from, ancestors: *his ancestral home.*

an·ces·try /'ænsestrɪ/ *nc* (*pl* **-ies**) a person's group of direct relatives.

an·chor /'æŋkə(r)/ *nc* a heavy piece of iron used for keeping a ship fixed to the sea bottom. *drop anchor* to cause an anchor to go down into the sea. □ *vt,vi* (to cause a ship) to be fixed with an anchor: *to anchor off Japan.*

an·chovy /'æntʃəvɪ/ *nc* (*pl* **-ies**) (also *attrib*) a small fish of the herring family with a strong taste: *anchovy paste.*

an·cient /'eɪnʃənt/ *adj* **1** (*attrib*) belonging to times long ago: *ancient Rome and Greece.* **2** very old: *an ancient-looking hat.*

,ancient 'history *nu* the period up to AD 476, when the Western Roman Empire was destroyed.

,ancient 'world *n* (the —) the region and civili-zations (esp of the Greeks and Romans) known during ancient history.

an·cil·lary /æn'sɪlərɪ/ *adj* (*formal*) **1** secondary (the usual word): *ancillary roads.* **2** additional (to a larger one): *ancillary industries.*

and /ənd *strong form:* ænd/ *conj* (*coord*) **1** in addition; also: *Spain and the rest of Europe; pets and their owners; a boy and a girl; five hundred and sixty-two; one pound and twenty pence.* Ⓝ When the phrase etc has more than two adjectives, nouns etc, '*and*' is put in front of the last one only, as in *red, white and blue; men, women and children; slowly, quietly and carefully; a pen, a pencil and a cal-culator; the sun, the moon and the stars.* When the adjectives, nouns etc are members of a well-known group, *a, the, some* etc are not given at the end, as in *a knife and fork; the men and women; a table and chairs.* Sometimes *a/the* are not given in order to avoid repetition, as in *to the left and right* (not 'the right'). When a group of adjectives are put in front of the noun and describe similar 'qualities' (e.g. colour, behaviour), '*and*' is used, as in *a black and white dog; a kind and polite person.* '*And*' is not used when the adjectives describe different 'qualities', as in *a big, red ball.* Some special expressions with '*and*' have an order that cannot be changed, as in *each and every; flesh and blood; forgive and forget; a knife, fork and spoon; left, right and centre.* Other expressions can be changed, as in *day and night* (or *night and day*) *clean and fresh; boys and girls.* **and all** in addition to other things: *He stole my bag, camera and all.* **and all that** (*informal*) also other similar quali-ties: *It was interesting and all that, but I didn't like it.* **and/or** (used in official documents) both or either: *shares and/or securities.* **and so on** ⇨ so²(6). **2** as a result; so: *I was tired and I fell asleep. It was cheap and I bought it.* **3** afterwards: *He cooked the meal and ate it. I opened the door and switched on the light.* **4** (used to replace an *if*-clause) if you, they etc do: *Help me and I'll reward you.* (= If you help me, I'll . . .). *Work hard and you'll pass the exam.* Ⓝ '*And*' is some-times replaced by a comma to show obligation, as in *Love me, love my dog* (= If you love me, you must also love my dog). **5** (*maths*) together with as a total: *4 and 4 are/make 8.* **6** (used in repetition for emphasis): *for ages and ages; walk miles and miles; get better and better; go on and on and on.* **7**

in order to: *Let's go and find out. Come and see for yourself.* **8** (*informal*) (used to replace a *to*-infinitive): *Please try and come.*

an·ec·dote /'ænɪkdəʊt/ *nc* a short, interesting story about a person or event.

anemia, anemic = anaemia, anaemic.

an·emom·eter /,ænə'mɒmɪtə(r)/ *nc* (*tech*) an instrument for measuring the strength (and direc-tion) of winds.

anem·one /ə'nemənɪ/ *nc* **1** a kind of woodland flower, usually white, pale-blue or dark red. **2** = sea anemone.

an·es·thesia = anaesthesia.

anew /ə'njuː/ *adv* (*literary*) in a new or different way: *Let's start anew.*

an·gel /'eɪndʒəl/ *nc* **1** (in Christian belief) a mes-senger from God (usually shown as a human being in white with wings). **2** (*fig*) a kind, helpful etc person.

an·gel·ic /æn'dʒelɪk/ *adj* like an angel.

an·ger /'æŋgə(r)/ *nu* the strong feeling that comes after being insulted, wronged or because of cruelty and injustice (and makes a person want to quarrel or fight): *I was filled with anger after he crashed my car.* □ *vt* to make (a person) angry: *He is easily angered.*

angle¹ /'æŋgl/ *nc* **1** a space between two lines or surfaces that meet: *an acute/obtuse/right angle.* **2** (*fig*) an attitude or opinion: *What angle are you using in the story?*

angle² /'æŋgl/ *vt* **1** to turn (something) on an angle(1): *angle a telescope towards the sea.* **2** (*fig*) to use a particular attitude in (a report etc), esp to gain an advantage.

angle³ /'æŋgl/ *vi* **1** to fish with a rod and line. **2** *angle for sth* (*fig*) to use tricks, hints etc in order to get something: *He was angling for an invitation to the party.*

ang·ler /'æŋglə(r)/ *nc* a person who fishes with a rod and line. Compare fisherman.

Ang·li·can /'æŋglɪkən/ *nc, adj* (a member) of the Church of England.

ang·li·cize (also **-ise**) /'æŋglɪzaɪz/ *vt* to make (a word etc) English or like English: *anglicize a French word.*

an·gry /'æŋgrɪ/ *adj* (**-ier, -iest**) **1** *angry (with sb/at sth)* filled with, showing, anger (because of a person, thing): *angry parents; an angry dog. Don't be angry with me. He was angry at being kept waiting.* **2** (*fig*) (of the sea, sky etc) showing bad weather.

an·gri·ly *adv*

an·guish /'æŋgwɪʃ/ *nu* great mental suffering: *She was filled with anguish/was in anguish until she knew he was safe.*

an·guish·ed *adj* (usually *attrib*) expressing great mental suffering: *anguished looks.*

an·gu·lar /'æŋgjʊlə(r)/ *adj* **1** (*attrib*) having angles or sharp corners. **2** (of a person) thin and bony.

ani·mal /'ænɪml/ *nc* **1** (also *attrib*) a living thing that can feel and move about: *animal skins/behaviour. Men, horses, birds, flies, fish, snakes are all animals.* **2** any animal other than man: *Do you love animals?*

'animal kingdom *n* (the —) all animal life.

ani·mate /'ænɪmət/ *adj* (*tech*) having life: *Plants are animate.* Opp inanimate(1).

ani·mated /'ænɪmeɪtɪd/ adj **1** lively, enthusiastic: *There was an animated discussion.* **2** designed to move as if having life: *an animated cartoon/film.*

ani·ma·tion /ˌænɪˈmeɪʃn/ nu

ani·mos·ity /ˌænɪˈmɒsətɪ/ nc,nu (pl **-ies**) (formal) (an instance of) strong, active hatred: *animosity among/between them; show animosity to/towards her for hitting the boy.*

ankle /ˈæŋkl/ nc **1** the joint connecting the foot with the leg. **2** the thin part of the leg above this joint.

an·nals /ˈænəlz/ n pl the year by year records of historic events or discoveries, esp of an academic society.

an·nex /əˈneks/ vt **1** to take possession of (a region, country) (usually by force): *Syria was annexed to the Roman Empire.* **2** to add or join (something) (as another part): *annex statistics to a report.*

an·nexe (also **an·nex**) /ˈæneks/ nc a smaller building added to, or situated near, a larger one; *a hotel annexe.*

an·ni·hi·late /əˈnaɪəleɪt/ vt to destroy (a group, community) completely: *The village was annihilated by the disease.*

an·ni·hi·la·tion /əˌnaɪəˈleɪʃn/ nu

an·ni·ver·sary /ˌænɪˈvɜːsərɪ/ nc (pl **-ies**) (a celebration on) a day when something happened on the same day a year, or many years, before: *my wedding anniversary; the anniversary of Shakespeare's birth.*

an·no·tate /ˈænəteɪt/ vt to add notes to (a book etc) explaining difficulties etc: *an annotated text/version.*

an·no·ta·tion /ˌænəˈteɪʃn/ nc,nu

an·nounce /əˈnaʊns/ vt **1** to make (something) known (to other people): *David announced (to his friends) that he was getting married.* **2** to say that (a person) is about to enter, speak, play music etc.

an·nounce·ment nc

an·nouncer nc (esp) a person who introduces a speaker, singer etc on the radio or TV.

an·noy /əˈnɔɪ/ vt,vi to make (a person) bad-tempered: *Do stop annoying me!*

an·noy·ing adj making a person bad-tempered: *The annoying thing is that I could have done it.*

an·noy·ance /əˈnɔɪəns/ n **1** nu the state of being annoyed: *with a look of annoyance.* **2** nc something that annoys: *This delay is an annoyance.*

an·nual¹ /ˈænjʊəl/ adj (attrib) **1** coming, happening, every year: *an annual exhibition.* **2** of one year: *his annual income.*

an·nual·ly adv

an·nual² /ˈænjʊəl/ nc **1** a book etc that appears with the same title but with new contents every year. **2** a plant that lives for one year or less. Compare perennial(3).

an·nu·ity /əˈnjuːɪtɪ/ nc (pl **-ies**) a sum of money paid yearly during a person's lifetime.

an·nul /əˈnʌl/ vt (**-ll-**) to cause (a marriage agreement, a law etc) to exist no longer.

an·nul·ment nc,nu

an·ode /ˈænəʊd/ nc (electricity) a part (called a *terminal*) of a battery etc where electricity enters. Compare cathode.

anoint /əˈnɔɪnt/ vt to put oil or ointment on (a person) as a religious ceremony: *anoint him with oil.*

an·oint·ment nc,nu

anom·al·ous /əˈnɒmələs/ adj (formal) different in some way from what is usual.

a,nomalous 'verb nc (gram) a verb that forms questions and negatives without the verb 'do', e.g. *must, ought.*

anom·aly /əˈnɒməlɪ/ nc (pl **-ies**) a person, thing, different from the usual type: *A bird that cannot fly is an anomaly.*

anon /əˈnɒn/ (used in footnotes etc) short for 'by an anonymous author'.

anon·ym·ity /ˌænəˈnɪmɪtɪ/ nu the state of being anonymous.

anony·mous /əˈnɒnɪməs/ adj without a name, esp deliberately: *an anonymous poem; an anonymous gift.*

anony·mous·ly adv: *The book was published anonymously.*

an·or·ak /ˈænəræk/ nc a thick jacket with a hood, worn to keep out rain, wind and cold. Compare cagoule.

ano·rec·tic /ˌænəˈrektɪk/ (also **ano·rex·ic** /-ˈreksɪk/) adj nc (of) a person suffering from anorexia.

ano·rexia /ˌænəˈreksɪə/ nu (also *anorexia nervosa* /nɜːˈvəʊsə/) a mental illness that makes a person refuse to eat.

an·oth·er¹ /əˈnʌðə(r)/ adj or det (pl **other**) Ⓝ 'Another' cannot be used with uncountable nouns. **1** an additional: *Have another cup of coffee. I'd like another slice of bread. Can I have another one? He left after another few days/six weeks. I won't say another word about it* (= will not talk about it any more). *They won't do another thing for you* (=refuse to help you any more). **2** a different: *I'll come another day. She didn't like it so she took another one.* **3** any other: *I'd never steal another man's girlfriend.* **4** a similar: *She plays like another Navratilova.*

an·oth·er² /əˈnʌðə(r)/ pron (pl **others**) **1** an additional one: *You have this ticket and I'll buy another. Would you like another (of these cakes)? For one thing* (= reason) *he's too old and for another* (= an additional reason) *he's too fat.* **one another; one with another** ⇨ one³(1). **2** a different one: *You use a blue pen and I'll choose another. That's one way to do it but there is another* (pl = there are others).

A.N.Other /ˌeɪ en ˈʌðə(r)/ nc (informal) an unnamed person.

an·swer¹ /ˈɑːnsə(r)/ nc **1** something said or written after a question, request, a letter asking for something etc: *Have you had an answer to your letter?* **in answer to sth** as a reply to it: *in answer to your letter.* **a straight answer** an honest and frank answer. **2** a result of working with numbers etc: *The answer to 3 × 17 is 51.*

an·swer² /ˈɑːnsə(r)/ vt,vi **1** to say, write or do (something) in return or reply: *'I arrived at six o'clock', he answered. Have you answered his letter? Why don't you answer (him)?* **answer to the name of sb** ⇨ name¹(1). **answer the door** to open the door when a person has knocked or rung the bell. **answer the (tele)phone** to pick up the receiver when the telephone has rung. **2** to say or write (something) as a solution: *I can only answer two questions in this exam paper*.

answer sb back to give a rude reply, esp when told one has done wrong.

answer for sb/sth (a) to be responsible for a person, thing: *I can't answer for his brother/his safety*. (b) to be punished for something: *If the police catch you, you'll have a lot to answer for*.

answer to sb (for sth) to be responsible and deserve punishment from a person (for bad behaviour): *If you hurt her you'll have to answer to me*.

an·swer·able /ˈɑːnsrəbl/ *adj* **answerable (to sb) (for sth)** responsible: *A mental patient is not answerable for her or his actions*.

ant /ænt/ *nc* a kind of small, very active insect, living in organized groups.

an·tag·on·ism /ænˈtægənɪzəm/ *nc,nu* (an instance of) opposition involving fighting or hatred: *antagonism between the two men; feel a strong antagonism for/toward a person*.

an·tag·on·ist /ænˈtægənɪst/ *nc* **1** an opponent (the usual word). **2** (*literature*) a main character who hates or opposes the hero or heroine: *In 'Othello', Iago is the antagonist*. Compare protagonist.

an·tag·on·is·tic /æn,tægəˈnɪstɪk/ *adj* (*formal*) **antagonistic to/towards sb/sth** feeling hatred for a person; opposing a person, idea.
an·tag·on·is·ti·cal·ly /-klɪ/ *adv*

an·tag·on·ize (also **-ise**) /ænˈtægənaɪz/ *vt* **1** to cause (a person) to become an enemy. **2** (*fig*) to annoy (a person): *I advise you not to antagonize him*.

ant·arc·tic /ænˈtɑːktɪk/ *adj* of the very cold region in the south of the earth.
An,tarctic 'Circle *n* (the —) the line of latitude 66½°S.

ante·ced·ent /æntɪˈsiːdənt/ *nc* **1** an event or situation happening before. **2** (*pl*) ancestors (the usual word). **3** (*gram*) a noun or noun clause to which a following relative pronoun or relative clause is linked, such as 'the pop group' in 'That's the pop group which you like so much'.

ante·date /æntɪˈdeɪt/ *vt* to come before (something) in history or time: *This event antedates the arrival of Columbus by several centuries*.

ante·di·lu·vian /æntɪdɪˈluːvɪən/ *adj* (*fig*) very old-fashioned; very out of date.

ante·lope /ˈæntɪləʊp/ *nc* a kind of animal like a deer, that can run very fast.

ante·natal /æntɪˈneɪtl/ *adj* existing or occurring before birth: *antenatal clinics* (i.e. for pregnant women).

an·ten·na /ænˈtenə/ *nc* (*pl —e* /-niː/) **1** one of a pair of long, narrow organs on the heads of insects, shellfish etc, used as a feeler. **2** = aerial².

an·them /ˈænθəm/ *nc* a formal song of loyalty. ⇨ national anthem.

an·thol·ogy /ænˈθɒlədʒɪ/ *nc* (*pl -ies*) a collection of poems or pieces of prose by one or more authors, often on a single subject or theme: *an anthology of modern American poetry*.

an·thro·po·logi·cal /æn θrəpəˈlɒdʒɪkl/ *adj* of anthropology.

an·thro·pol·ogist /æn θrəˈpɒlədʒɪst/ *nc* an expert in, student of, anthropology.

an·thro·pol·ogy /æn θrəˈpɒlədʒɪ/ *nu* the science of human beings, esp of the beginnings, development, customs and beliefs of humanity.

an·thro·po·mor·phism /æn θrəpəˈmɔːfɪzəm/ *nu* (*literature*) the act of giving human form or character to a god or animal: *'Mickey Mouse' is an example of anthropomorphism*.
an·thro·po·mor·phic /-fɪk/ *adj*

anti·bi·ot·ic /æntɪbaɪˈɒtɪk/ *adj, nc* (of) a substance (e.g. *penicillin*) produced by very small fungi, able to destroy bacteria.

anti·body /ˈæntɪbɒdɪ/ *nc* (*pl -ies*) a substance in the blood which destroys harmful bacteria etc.

an·tici·pate /ænˈtɪsɪpeɪt/ *vt* **1** to expect (a particular event, result etc): *We don't anticipate much trouble*. **2** to do (something) before another person does it: *anticipate a scientific discovery*. **3** to see (what needs doing, what is likely to happen etc) and do what is necessary: *He tries to anticipate all my needs* (= to act before I mention them).

an·tici·pa·tion /æn,tɪsɪˈpeɪʃn/ *nu* the act of anticipating. **in anticipation (of sth)** (*formal*) before (the expected event): *Thanking you in anticipation* (= in advance and expecting you to reply).

an·tici·pa·tory /æntɪsɪˈpeɪtərɪ/ *adj* occurring, placed, done, before the usual or normal time or order.
,antici,patory 'object *nc* (*gram*) = preparatory object.
,antici,patory 'subject *nc* (*gram*) = preparatory subject.

anti·climax /æntɪˈklaɪmæks/ *nc* a sudden change from something exciting or important to something much less exciting or important (causing disappointment).

anti·clock·wise /æntɪˈklɒkwaɪz/ *adj, adv* in the direction opposite to the movements of the hands of a clock. Opp clockwise.

an·tics /ˈæntɪks/ *n pl* unusual behaviour or activity, e.g. of a child or clown.

anti·cyc·lone /æntɪˈsaɪkləʊn/ *nc* (*tech*) an area in which atmospheric pressure is high giving calm weather. Compare depression(4).

anti·dote /ˈæntɪdəʊt/ *nc* a medicine used to prevent a poison or disease from having an effect: *an antidote against/for/to snakebite*.

anti·freeze /ˈæntɪfriːz/ *nu* a substance put in water to prevent it from freezing, used in the radiator of a vehicle.

anti·hero /ˈæntɪ hɪərəʊ/ *nc* (*pl -es*) (*literature*) a leading character who does not have the traditional characteristics of a hero, such as courage and dignity.

anti·nov·el /ˈæntɪ nɒvl/ *nc* (*literature*) a novel that has no obvious plot and no development of the characters: *Virginia Woolf's 'The Waves' is an example of an anti-novel*.

an·tipa·thy /ænˈtɪpəθɪ/ *nc,nu* (*pl -ies*) (an instance or example of) strong dislike: *antipathy among the team; feel a strong antipathy to/towards a place/against a person*.

an·ti·phra·sis /ænˈtɪfrəsɪs/ *nu* (*literature*) the deliberate use of a word or phrase to put across the opposite opinion, idea etc: *In Shakespeare's 'Julius Caesar', Antony uses antiphrasis when he calls Brutus 'honourable'*.

an·tipo·des /ænˈtɪpədiːz/ *n pl* (the —) Australia

and New Zealand.

anti·quated /ˈæntɪkweɪtɪd/ adj (derog) old and out of date: antiquated ideas.

an·tique /ænˈtiːk/ adj, nc (of) an object (e.g. furniture, a work of art) that is very old and valuable.

an·tiqui·ty /ænˈtɪkwətɪ/ n (pl -ies) (formal) 1 nu ancient times. 2 (pl) buildings, ruins, works of art, from ancient times: The museum is full of Greek and Roman antiquities.

anti·sep·tic /ˌæntɪˈseptɪk/ adj, nc (of) a chemical substance able to prevent disease, esp by destroying germs.

anti·so·cial /ˌæntɪˈsəʊʃl/ adj (derog) 1 not willing to be with other people: He's too antisocial to enjoy travelling. 2 causing harm or annoyance to other people: It is antisocial to play music loudly on the beach. Compare unsocial.

anti·stat·ic /ˌæntɪˈstætɪk/ adj (tech) able to reduce the effects of static electricity.

an·tith·esis /ænˈtɪθəsɪs/ nc,nu (pl -eses /-əsiːz/) 1 the direct opposite: The antithesis of good is evil. 2 (literature) a technique in which opposite or contrasting ideas etc are put together for emphasis or dramatic effect, as in 'Give me liberty or give me death'.

an·to·nym /ˈæntənɪm/ nc a word that is contrary in meaning to another: 'Hot' is the antonym of 'cold'. Compare synonym.

anti·tox·in /ˌæntɪˈtoksɪn/ nc (med) a substance able to reduce the effects of poison.

anus /ˈeɪnəs/ nc (pl —es) (anat) the opening at the end of the alimentary canal, through which solid waste matter leaves the body.

an·vil /ˈænvɪl/ nc an iron block on which heated metal is hammered into shape.

anx·iety /æŋˈzaɪətɪ/ n (pl -ies) 1 nu fear and uncertainty about the future: We waited with anxiety for news of her safe arrival. 2 nc an instance of such a feeling: All these anxieties made him look pale and tired. 3 nc a strong wish: In his anxiety to please his employers he neglected his family.

anx·ious /ˈæŋkʃəs/ adj 1 **anxious (about/for sb/sth)** feeling anxiety; troubled: I am very anxious about my son's health/for my son. 2 causing anxiety: We have had an anxious time. 3 **anxious for sth/to do sth/that . . .** strongly wishing: He was anxious to meet you. We were anxious that help should be sent.

any¹ /ˈenɪ/ adj or det 1 every: Any child can do it. It's true, as any intelligent person knows. ⇨ anybody. Compare some¹(2). 2 (used of more than two) it does not matter which: You can wear any shoes with that dress. Take any record you like. Please buy any fruit that looks fresh. I can come any day except Friday. Ⓝ Use 'either' for two, as in Take either of the two records. I can come either Monday or Tuesday. Compare some¹(1). **any one** the one (person or thing) which: We'll send you any one record from the list that you choose. Compare anyone. **in any case** ⇨ case¹(1). **in any event** ⇨ event(3). **at any rate** ⇨ rate¹(4). 3 (a) even one: Are there any cakes left? He hasn't any idea. We haven't any more left. Isn't there any way you can help him? (b) an amount or quantity of: Have you any bread? He did it without any help. She hasn't any appetite. Ⓝ 'Any' is used in questions

and after 'not'. Use 'some' in positive statements, as in I have some bread. Use 'no' in positive statements meaning 'not any', as in He has no idea. She has no appetite. 'Without' meaning 'with no' uses 'any', as in without any difficulty. (c) (used with barely, hardly etc) very nearly no or none: We had barely any time to warn them. There were hardly any people at the meeting. Ⓝ 'Almost no time', 'almost no-one/nothing' are more usual. 4 (used with verbs such as avoid, prevent etc) every possibility of: We took a taxi to avoid any delay. 5 (informal) a, an: It hasn't any handle.

any² /ˈenɪ/ adv Ⓝ 'Any' is used with comparatives. 1 to even a little extent: Is he feeling any better? We can't go any further. You don't look any different in that photograph. Is the new map any good? Ⓝ 'Any' is used in questions and after 'not'. 'Some' cannot be used. Use 'no' in positive statements meaning 'not any', as in We can go no further. It's no good. **any more** (also **anymore**) any longer; still: I don't love you any more. She doesn't come anymore. Ⓝ 'Any more' used as an adverb is often written 'anymore', but it is two words when it means 'even one more', as in Do you have any more? 2 (used with if): If I were any richer, I'd buy a yacht. If it's any good, buy it.

any³ /ˈenɪ/ pron 1 each one: Any of them could do it. 2 it does not matter which: Please take any that you like. 3 (a) even one: Are there any left? I don't want any. (b) an amount or quantity: 'Can I have some bread?'—'No, there isn't any.' 'Do you have the money?'—'I came without any.' Ⓝ 'Any' is used after 'not' and 'without' and in questions. Use 'some' in positive statements. **hardly any** very nearly none: We've sold hardly any. Ⓝ 'Almost none' is more usual. ⇨ anybody(4), anything(4).

any·body /ˈenɪbɒdɪ/ (also **any·one** /ˈenɪwʌn/) pron 1 a person but no particular or known one: Is anybody there? We didn't meet anybody we knew. I wouldn't marry just anybody! Ⓝ 'Anybody/anyone' is used in questions and after 'not'. 'Somebody/someone' can also be used in questions, as in Is somebody there?, but not after 'not'. Use 'nobody/no-one' in positive statements meaning 'not anybody', as in We met no-one we knew. 2 (used with if): If anybody telephones me, tell them I'm out. Ⓝ 'Somebody/someone' can also be used. 3 it does not matter who: Anybody will tell you where to park your car. Won't anybody come with me to complain? Who will win the competition is anybody's guess (= no-one can be certain). Ⓝ 'Somebody/someone' cannot be used. **anybody/anyone else** any other person or people in addition: Does anybody else know the answer? Anybody else who needs tickets must tell me. 4 **hardly anybody/anyone** very nearly no-one: Hardly anybody likes his paintings.

any·how /ˈenɪhaʊ/ adv = anyway.

any·more /ˌenɪˈmɔː(r)/ adv ⇨ any²(1).

any·one /ˈenɪwʌn/ pron = anybody.

any·thing /ˈenɪθɪŋ/ pron 1 an event or object but no particular or known one: Has anything unusual happened? We didn't notice anything in particular. Did you have anything to do with the quarrel? Ⓝ 'Anything' is used in questions and after 'not'. 'Something' can also be used in questions, as in Has something unusual happened?, but not after *'not'*. Use *'nothing'* in positive statements meaning *'not anything'*, as in *We noticed nothing in particular.* ⇨ 5 below.

like anything using as much effort as possible: *She ran like anything but she missed the bus.* ⇨ 5 below. **2** (used with *if*): *If anything happens to her, I'll blame you.* **3** it does not matter what: *He'll do anything to save his marriage. Anything will do. Don't say anything!* Ⓝ *'Something'* cannot be used. ⇨ also **easy¹**(1). **anything else** any thing or things in addition: *Would you like to buy anything else? Is there anything else in the box?* **4 hardly anything** very nearly nothing: *You've eaten hardly anything all day.* Ⓝ *'Almost nothing'* is more usual. **5** (used as an *adv*) **anything but** not at all: *She's anything but sad.* **anything like** in any way: *He isn't anything like his father/as brave.*

any·way /'enɪweɪ/ (also **any·how** /'enɪhaʊ/) *adv* **1** (a) whatever happens: *It's too late now, anyway. Anyway, I'll still love you.* (b) although that happened: *I forgot my umbrella but anyway it was too windy. Anyway, I did try to help him.* Ⓝ Compare: *Is there any way* (= even one way) *I can help?* **2** as an added reason: *It's expensive and anyway I don't like it.* ⇨ the *note* at **besides¹**(2). **3** (used when not sure about something): *He lived in Paris or Rome—anyway it was one of the European capitals.* **4** (used after a pause or a period talking or writing about a different topic): *Anyway, as I was saying, we must decide what to do.*

any·where /'enɪweə(r)/ *adv* **1** at, to, no particular or known place: *Have you seen my handbag anywhere? Are we going anywhere in particular? I haven't anywhere to keep a car.* Ⓝ *'Anywhere'* is used in questions and after *'not'*. *'Somewhere'* can be used in questions, as in *Is there somewhere we can go?* but not after *'not'*. Use *'nowhere'* in positive statements meaning *'not anywhere'*, as in *My bag is nowhere to be found.* **2** (used with *if*) a particular place: *If there's anywhere you'd like to go, tell me.* **3** it does not matter which place: *We'll live anywhere you like. I'm not going anywhere without you.* Ⓝ *'Somewhere'* cannot be used. **anywhere else** to any place in addition or as an alternative: *Is there anywhere else you'd prefer to live?*

a.o.b. *abbr* any other business.

aor·ta /eɪ'ɔːtə/ *nc* (*pl* —**s**) (*anat*) the main blood-vessel carrying blood from the left side of the heart.

apart /ə'pɑːt/ *adv* Ⓝ For uses with verbs such as *come, pull, take, tell*, ⇨ the *verb* entries. **1** separated by a (mentioned) distance: *The cities are 100 kilometres apart. The two angles are 3 cm apart. How far apart are the two houses?* **wide apart** separated by a big distance: *standing with legs wide apart.* **2** into separate parts: *It came/fell apart in my hands. Can you take an engine apart?* **3** not taking a thing or person into account: *These problems apart, I think I can win.* **apart from** (*prep*) not including: *There are 30 people apart from the two leaders. Apart from that silly mistake, you did very well.* Compare **besides²**.

apart·heid /ə'pɑːtheɪt/ *nu* (*S Africa*) the policy that separates ethnic groups and has given political, economic and social control to people of European origin.

apart·ment /ə'pɑːtmənt/ *nc* (*esp US*) a set of rooms as a place to live, esp one of several in one tall building. Ⓝ *'Flat'* in GB.

apa·thet·ic /ˌæpə'θetɪk/ *adj* (*formal*) showing or having no interest, energy etc.

apa·thy /'æpəθɪ/ *nu* the state of having no wish to act and no enthusiasm.

ape¹ /eɪp/ *nc* **1** a kind of large hairy animal, similar to a human. **2** (*derog*) a clumsy person.

ape² /eɪp/ *vt* to make fun of (a person) by copying her or his behaviour.

aperi·tif /ə'perətɪf/ *nc* an alcoholic drink (e.g. *sherry*) taken before a meal.

ap·er·ture /'æpətʃʊə(r)/ *nc* an opening, esp one that admits light into a camera.

apex /'eɪpeks/ *nc* (*pl* —**es** or **apices** /'eɪpɪsiːz/) the top or highest point: *the apex of a triangle/his career.*

aphor·ism /'æfərɪzəm/ *nc* (*literature*) a short statement expressing a general truth (usually from a known literary work): *'Hell is other people' is an aphorism from Sartre's 'Huis Clos'.* ⇨ **proverb**.

apiece /ə'piːs/ *adv* each: *They cost £1 apiece.*

apoca·lypse /ə'pɒkəlɪps/ *nc* an extremely violent event of great importance as in a war.

apo·gee /'æpədʒiː/ *nc* (*tech*) the highest point, e.g. the greatest distance between the earth and a satellite.

apol·iti·cal /ˌeɪpə'lɪtɪkl/ *adj* (of a person) having no political interest or belief.

apolo·get·ic /əˌpɒlə'dʒetɪk/ *adj* expressing regret for doing wrong or not doing something: *He was apologetic for arriving late.*

apolo·geti·cal·ly /-klɪ/ *adv*

apolo·gize (also **-ise**) /ə'pɒlədʒaɪz/ *vi* **apologize** (*to sb*) (*for sth*) to say one is sorry (for doing wrong or not doing something): *You must apologize to your sister for being so rude. I apologize* (= I'm sorry).

apol·ogy /ə'pɒlədʒɪ/ *nc* (*pl* **-ies**) a statement of being sorry (for doing wrong or not doing something): *make one's apologies* (*to a friend*) (*for being late*).

apostle /ə'pɒsl/ *nc* (often A-) one of the twelve men chosen by Jesus to spread his teaching.

apos·tol·ic /ˌæpə'stɒlɪk/ *adj* (*attrib*) **1** of the apostles. **2** of the Pope.

apos·trophe /ə'pɒstrəfɪ/ *nc* the punctuation mark ('), a raised comma. Ⓝ It is used (a) to show possession, as in *Paul's watch; teachers' materials*; (b) to show omission of letters in contractions, as in *I've; o'clock; '86*; (c) to show the plural of dates, letters etc, as in *in the 1980's; two c's in 'occur'*; (d) for the possessive, as in *boy's; boys'*.

ap·pal (*US* also **ap·pall**) /ə'pɔːl/ *vt* (**-ll-**) to shock (a person) greatly: *They were appalled at the news.*

ap·pal·ling *adj*: *appalling news.*

ap·par·atus /ˌæpə'reɪtəs/ *nc* (*pl* —**es**) a set of tools, instruments or equipment put together for a purpose: *climbing apparatuses; an electrical apparatus.*

ap·par·el /ə'pærəl/ *nu* (*old use; literary*) clothes.

ap·par·ent /ə'pærənt/ *adj* **1** (*pred*) **apparent** (*to sb*) easily seen or understood (by a person): *It was apparent to all of us.* **2** not necessarily true or genuine: *the apparent cause but not the real one.*

ap·par·ent·ly *adv*

ap·par·ition /ˌæpəˈrɪʃn/ *nc* a ghost or the spirit of a dead person being seen.

ap·peal¹ /əˈpiːl/ *n* **1** *nc* a serious and determined request: *an appeal for money to feed the poor.* **2** *nu* an effect of asking for sympathy and help: *with a look of appeal on her thin face.* **3** *nu* (the power of) producing feelings of interest, pleasure etc: *His music has no appeal for me/has lost its appeal.* **4** *nc* a request to a referee or umpire to make a decision or to a higher official to change it. **5** *nc* (*legal*) an act of asking a higher court to change a decision made in a lower court.

ap·peal² /əˈpiːl/ *vi* **1** *appeal (to sb) (for sth)* to make a serious and determined request: *The famine victims appealed to the United Nations for help. The police are appealing for calm.* **2** *appeal (to sb)* to produce feelings of interest, pleasure etc: *Does a holiday in Athens appeal to you?* **3** (*sport*) *appeal (against sth)* to ask a higher official to change the decision of a referee or umpire. *appeal (for sth)* to ask a referee or umpire to make a favourable decision: *The players appealed for a penalty.* **4** (*legal*) to ask a higher court to change a decision made in a lower court.

ap·peal·ing /əˈpiːlɪŋ/ *adj* **1** (*attrib*) producing feelings of sympathy and wanting to help: *an appealing look.* **2** attractive and interesting: *an appealing smile/idea.* Opp unappealing.

ap·peal·ing·ly *adv*

ap·pear /əˈpɪː(r)/ *vi* **1** to come into view, become visible: *When we reached the top of the hill, the town appeared below us.* **2** to appear: *He promised to come at 4 but didn't appear until 6.* **3** to give the impression of being (but not necessarily a true or genuine one): *Is she as poor as she appears?* **4** (**a**) (of an actor, singer etc) to come before the public and perform: *He has appeared in every large concert hall in Europe.* (**b**) (of a book) to be published: *When will your new novel appear?* **5** (*legal*) to be present: *The defendant failed to appear before the court.* **appear for sb** (*legal*) to represent a person as a barrister, solicitor etc in a law court.

ap·pear·ance /əˈpɪərəns/ *nc* **1** an act of appearing: *make one's first appearance* (of an actor, singer etc, appear for the first time). **put in an appearance** to attend for a short time (a party, meeting etc). **2** the form, quality etc which can be seen; what a thing or person seems to be: *The child had the appearance of being half starved.* **keep up appearances** to continue to seem happy, rich etc, esp after a bad experience, loss of money etc. **3** a way of dressing: *have an untidy/ smart appearance.*

ap·pease /əˈpiːz/ *vt* (*formal*) to make (a person) less angry, calm: *I sent flowers to appease him after being late.*

ap·pease·ment *nu*

ap·pend /əˈpend/ *vt* **append sth (to sth)** (*formal*) to add something in writing; to add something at the end: *append a signature to a document.*

ap·pend·age /əˈpendɪdʒ/ *nc* (*formal*) something added to, joining to, forming a part of, a larger thing.

ap·pen·di·ci·tis /əˌpendɪˈsaɪtɪs/ *nu* the diseased condition of the appendix².

ap·pen·dix¹ /əˈpendɪks/ *nc* (*pl* **-dices** /-dɪsiːz/) something added, esp at the end of a book.

ap·pen·dix² /əˈpendɪks/ *nc* (*pl* **—es** or **-dices** /-dɪsiːz/) (*anat*) the short, thin tube attached to the bowel.

ap·pe·tite /ˈæpɪtaɪt/ *nc,nu* **1** a physical desire for food: *The long walk gave him a good appetite.* **2** (*fig*) a desire: *He had no appetite for the fight.*

ap·pe·tizer /ˈæpɪtaɪzə(r)/ *nc* a drink (usually alcoholic) or food (small and attractive) taken before a meal to encourage an appetite.

ap·pe·tiz·ing *adj* encouraging the appetite: *an appetizing smell from the kitchen.* Opp unappetizing.

ap·plaud /əˈplɔːd/ *vi,vt* **1** to show approval of (an actor, speaker, winner etc) by clapping the hands: *The audience applauded (the singer) for five minutes. He was loudly applauded.* **2** to express approval of (something): *I applaud your decision/ courage.*

ap·plause /əˈplɔːz/ *nu* the act of showing approval by clapping the hands.

apple /ˈæpl/ *nc* (a tree with) a round fruit with firm juicy flesh and a thin (green, red or yellow) skin. **the apple of one's eye** a person or thing particularly loved. ⇨ also Adam's apple.

ap·pli·ance /əˈplaɪəns/ *nc* a piece of equipment (often mechanical) for a particular purpose: *electrical appliances; household appliances such as a washing-machine.*

ap·pli·cable /ˈæplɪkəbl/ *adj* **applicable (to sb/ sth)** that is relevant or concerns: *Is the rule applicable to me/this situation?* Opp inapplicable.

ap·pli·cant /ˈæplɪkənt/ *nc* a person who asks for something (esp a job) in writing.

ap·pli·ca·tion /ˌæplɪˈkeɪʃn/ *n* **1** *nc,nu* (an act of) making a request (esp in writing): *A sample will be sent on application. I made an application to the manager for an interview.* **2** *nc,nu* (an act of putting on) a substance such as antiseptic cream: *He suggests an application of this cream to small cuts only. This application is for burns and cuts.* **3** *nc,nu* (putting something to) a special or practical use: *The application of computers has revolutionized industrial processes. This machine has several applications.* **4** *nu* (*formal*) continuous effort: *If you show application in your studies you will succeed.*

appli·cation form *nc* a paper asking for information to be used when asking for a job, membership etc.

ap·plied /əˈplaɪd/ *adj* (*attrib*) put to practical use: *applied mathematics.*

ap,plied ˈscience *nc* a scientific study put to practical use: *Engineering is an applied science.*

ap·ply /əˈplaɪ/ *v* (*pt,pp* **-ied**) **1** *vi* **apply (to sb) (for sth)** to ask formally in writing: *apply to the manager for a job.* **2** *vt* to make practical use of (a substance, method, effort etc): *apply paint to a wall; apply ice to a bruise. He applied his new invention to teaching and it worked. Apply plenty of fertilizer. Please apply yourself/your mind to your studies.* **3** *vi* **apply (to sb)** to be relevant: *What I have said does not apply to you.* **Ⓝ** Not used with the continuous tenses (e.g. *be/was + -ing*). **4** *vt* to put (something) into operation: *We intend to apply economic sanctions.*

ap·point /əˈpɔɪnt/ *vt* **1** to choose (a person,

group) for a job, responsibility: *They appointed Mr White (to be) manager. We must appoint a committee.* **2** to arrange or decide (a place, time etc): *The time appointed for the meeting was 8.30pm.*

ap·point·ment /ə'pɔɪntmənt/ *n* **1** *nc,nu* (an act of) agreeing to a time and place to meet. **by appointment** at an agreed time and place. **make an appointment (for sth)** to arrange one (for a particular day, for a reason etc): *make an appointment for Thursday/for my son to see his doctor.* **2** *nc* a meeting at an agreed time and place: *She has an appointment with her manager at five o'clock.* **break an appointment** to fail to arrive at it. **keep an appointment** to arrive at it. **3** *nc* a particular job or position: *We were pleased at the appointment of Susan as deputy manager/at her appointment to the board of directors.*

ap·prais·al /ə'preɪzl/ *nc* an opinion or judgement of how good, valuable etc a person or thing is.

ap·praise /ə'preɪz/ *vt* (*formal*) to judge the value, worth, quality of (something): *a report appraising her work.*

ap·preci·able /ə'priːʃəbl/ *adj* (*formal*) that can be seen or felt: *an appreciable change in the temperature.*

ap·preci·ably /-əblɪ/ *adv*

ap·preci·ate /ə'priːʃɪeɪt/ *v* **1** *vt* to value (a person, thing) highly: *We all appreciate a holiday.* **2** *vt* to understand (something): *I appreciate that you were trying to help.* **3** *vi* (of land, goods, etc) to increase in value: *The house has appreciated greatly since the new motorway was built.* Opp depreciate.

ap·preci·ation /ə,priːʃɪ'eɪʃn/ *nc,nu* approval.

ap·preci·ative /ə'priːʃɪətɪv/ *adj* showing gratitude or enjoyment: *an appreciative audience.* Opp unappreciative.

ap·pre·hend /,æprɪ'hend/ *vt* (*legal*) to arrest (a person): *apprehend a thief.*

ap·pre·hen·sion /,æprɪ'henʃn/ *n* **1** *nu* (also *pl*) fear and worry: *feel apprehension/apprehensions about the future/for her safety.* **2** *nc,nu* (*legal*) (an act of) arresting a person: *the apprehension of a thief.*

ap·pre·hen·sive /,æprɪ'hensɪv/ *adj* (*formal*) worried: *be apprehensive for his safety.*

ap·pren·tice /ə'prentɪs/ *nc* a learner of a trade who has agreed to work for a number of years for a small amount of money in return for being taught. □ *vt* to send (a person) as an apprentice: *The boy was apprenticed to a carpenter.*

ap·pren·tice·ship /-ʃɪp/ *nc,nu* (time of) being an apprentice.

appro /'æprəʊ/ *abbr* **on appro** (*informal*) on approval: *bought on appro.* ⇨ approval.

ap·proach¹ /ə'prəʊtʃ/ *n* **1** *nc* (also *attrib*) a way of entering or getting near: *All the approaches/approach roads to the Houses of Parliament were filled with demonstrators.* **2** *nc* a method of doing something: *a new approach to studying literature. What approach will you use?* **3** *nu* the act of coming nearer: *the approach of winter/of an anniversary/of the enemy.*

ap·proach² /ə'prəʊtʃ/ *v* **1** *vi* to come near(er): *As winter approached, the weather became colder.*

2 *vt* **approach sb (about sth)** to go to a person with a request or offer: *When is the best time to approach him about an increase in salary?* **3** *vt* (*formal*) to use a particular method of doing (something): *How can we approach the problem of economic decline?*

ap·proach·able /ə'prəʊtʃəbl/ *adj* **1** (of a person) easy to discuss a problem with, ask for help etc. Opp unapproachable. **2** (*pred*) (of a place) easy to get to.

ap·pro·pri·ate¹ /ə'prəʊprɪət/ *adj* correct for the occasion or purpose: *That dress is not appropriate for a formal wedding. Write in a style appropriate to your subject.* Opp inappropriate.

ap·pro·pri·ate·ly *adv*

ap·pro·pri·ate² /ə'prəʊprɪeɪt/ *vt* (*formal*) **1** to put (an amount) on one side for a special purpose: *£80 000 has been appropriated for the new building.* **2** to take and use (something) as one's own: *He often appropriates my ideas.*

ap·pro·pri·ation /ə,prəʊprɪ'eɪʃn/ *nc,nu*

ap·pro·val /ə'pruːvl/ *nc,nu* (an act of) feeling, showing or saying, that one is satisfied, that something is right, that one agrees: *Your plans have my approval. Does what I have done meet with your approval?* **on approval** (of something bought) to be returned if not the correct size, colour, contents etc, with no loss of payment. ⇨ appro.

ap·prove /ə'pruːv/ *v* **1** *vi* **approve (of sb/sth)** to think of a thing, person as suitable for the occasion or purpose: *Her father will never approve (of you/of the marriage).* Opp disapprove. **2** *vt* to agree to (something) as correct: *The minutes (of the meeting) were read and approved. Our expenses have been approved.*

ap·prov·ing·ly *adv*: *He wrote approvingly about their engagement.* Opp disapprovingly.

approx. *abbr* approximately.

ap·proxi·mate¹ /ə'prɒksɪmət/ *adj* almost accurate: *The approximate speed was 30 miles an hour.* Compare exact¹(1).

ap·proxi·mate·ly *adv*: *It's approximately six o'clock.*

ap·proxi·mate² /ə'prɒksɪmeɪt/ *vi* **approximate to sth** (*formal*) to be close to something (esp in quality or number): *His description approximated to the truth but there were a few errors.*

ap·proxi·ma·tion /ə,prɒksɪ'meɪʃn/ *nc,nu*

Apr written *abbr* April.

après-ski /,æpreɪ 'skiː/ *adj* (*attrib*), *nu* (*Fr*) (of) the evening period after skiing: *après-ski clothes.*

apri·cot /'eɪprɪkɒt/ *n* (also *attrib*) **1** *nc* (a kind of tree with) a round, yellow or orange fruit with soft flesh and a large seed. **2** *nu* the colour of this fruit when ripe.

April /'eɪprəl/ *n* (also *attrib*) the fourth month of the year, with 30 days: *April showers. Our course finishes on 16 April.* (N) *'16 April'* is spoken as *'April the sixteenth'* or *'the sixteenth of April'.*

April 'fool *nc* a person who has a practical joke played on her or him on *All Fools' Day* (1 April).

apron /'eɪprən/ *nc* a loose covering worn round the front part of the body to keep clothes clean.

'apron stage *nc* (in some theatres) a part of the front of a stage extending into the audience.

apt /æpt/ *adj* (**—er, —est**) **1** correct for the occasion or situation: *an apt remark.* Opp inapt. **2**

(*pred*) **apt to do sth** having a tendency to do something: *He's a clever boy but apt to be lazy.*

apt·ly *adv* suitably: *aptly named.*

apt·ness *nu*

ap·ti·tude /'æptɪtjuːd/ *nc,nu* (an example of) natural or acquired ability: *He shows an aptitude for languages.*

'**aptitude test** *nc* an examination to find a person's level of natural ability.

aqua·lung /'ækwəlʌŋ/ *nc* a set of breathing equipment (mask, cylinder(s)) used for underwater swimming.

aquar·ium /ə'kweərɪəm/ *nc* (*pl* —s or -**ria** /-rɪə/) (a building for) a glass container for living fish and water plants.

Aquar·ius /ə'kweərɪəs/ *n* the Water Carrier, the eleventh sign of the zodiac.

aquat·ic /ə'kwætɪk/ *adj* **1** (of plants, animals etc) growing or living in or near water. **2** (of sports) taking place on or in water, e.g. rowing, swimming.

Arab·ic nu·meral /ˌærəbɪk 'njuːmərəl/ *nc* any of the signs 0, 1, 2, 3 etc used to write numbers.

ar·able /'ærəbl/ *adj* (*tech*) (of land) suitable for growing plants for food.

ar·bit·rary /'ɑːbɪtrərɪ/ *adj* **1** decided by personal opinion and not because of a rule or for a reason: *an arbitrary choice.* **2** (*attrib*) showing unlimited power without taking account of other opinion etc: *an arbitrary decision against the workers.*

ar·bi·trate /'ɑːbɪtreɪt/ *vt,vi* to settle a dispute (between two opposite sides, opinions etc) by acting as the chosen judge(s): *Mr Smith has been asked to arbitrate (between the employers and their workers).*

ar·bi·tra·tion /ˌɑːbɪ'treɪʃn/ *nu* the settlement of a dispute by the decision of a person or group chosen and accepted as judges: *The Union agreed to (go to) arbitration for a settlement of their claims.*

ar·bi·tra·tor /'ɑːbɪtreɪtə(r)/ *nc* a person appointed by two opposite sides to settle a dispute.

arc /ɑːk/ *nc* (*tech*) a part of the edge of a circle or other curved line.

ar·cade /ɑː'keɪd/ *nc* a covered passage, usually with an arched roof, e.g. with shops along one or both sides: *a shopping arcade.*

arch[1] /ɑːtʃ/ *nc* **1** a curved part over a door, bridge, gate etc. **2** a large building with a curved top over an opening, usually as a monument: *a triumphal arch.* **3** anything in the shape of an arch, e.g. the curved part under the foot.

arch[2] /ɑːtʃ/ *vt,vi* to form (something) into an arch: *The cat arched its back when it saw the dog. The trees arch over the river.*

ar·chaeo·logi·cal (also and *US* **ar·cheo-**) /ˌɑːkɪə'lɒdʒɪkl/ *adj* of archaeology.

ar·chae·ol·ogist (also and *US* **ar·che·ol-**) /ˌɑːkɪ'ɒlədʒɪst/ *nc* an expert in, student of, archaeology.

ar·chae·ol·ogy (also and *US* **ar·che·ol-**) /ˌɑːkɪ'ɒlədʒɪ/ *nu* the study of ancient things, esp the buried remains of prehistoric times.

ar·chaic /ɑː'keɪɪk/ *adj* **1** (of languages, words) not now used. **2** of ancient times.

ar·cha·ism /'ɑːkeɪɪzəm/ *nc* an archaic word or expression.

arch·angel /ˌɑːk'eɪndʒəl/ *nc* an angel of the highest rank.

arch·bishop /ˌɑːtʃ'bɪʃəp/ *nc* (in Christian churches) a senior bishop who governs a province.

arch·bishop·ric *nc* the position or province of an archbishop.

arch·er /'ɑːtʃə(r)/ *nc* a person who shoots arrows with a bow.

arch·ery /'ɑːtʃərɪ/ *nu* (the sport of) shooting with a bow and arrows.

arche·type /'ɑːkɪtaɪp/ *nc* (esp of a person) a perfect example (of a certain character).

archi·pel·ago /ˌɑːkɪ'peləgəʊ/ *nc* (*pl* —s or —es) (a region of sea with) a group of islands.

archi·tect /'ɑːkɪtekt/ *nc* a person who designs (and supervises the construction of) buildings etc.

archi·tec·tural /ˌɑːkɪ'tektʃərəl/ *adj* of architecture: *the architectural beauties of a city.*

archi·tec·ture /'ɑːkɪtektʃə(r)/ *nu* the art and science of building; style of building(s): *Elizabethan architecture.*

ar·chives /'ɑːkaɪvz/ *n pl* (a place for keeping) public or government records, esp for historical reasons.

arch·way /'ɑːtʃweɪ/ *nc* a way under an arch(1,2).

arc·tic /'ɑːktɪk/ *adj* of the very cold region in the north of the earth: *the Arctic Ocean; arctic weather* (esp (*fig*) = very cold weather).

ˌArctic '**Circle** *n* (the —) the line of latitude 66$\frac{1}{2}$°N.

ar·dent /'ɑːdənt/ *adj* (usually *attrib*) very enthusiastic: *ardent supporters.*

ar·dent·ly *adv*

ar·dour (*US* = **ar·dor**) /'ɑːdə(r)/ *nu* (*formal*) enthusiasm (the more usual word).

ar·du·ous /'ɑːdjʊəs/ *adj* needing and using much energy and thought: *an arduous job/training schedule.*

ar·du·ous·ly *adv*

are /ə(r) *strong form*: ɑː(r)/ ⇨ be.

area /'eərɪə/ *nc* **1** a piece of land, section of a building etc used for a particular activity: *a parking/picnic area; the reception/dining area of a hotel.* **2** a large piece of land with a particular characteristic: *tropical/desert areas.* **3** the size of a flat surface: *We measure area by multiplying length by width. The area of my bedroom is 12 square metres. England is 84 000 square kilometres in area. The area of a triangle is half the base times the height. How do we find the area of a circle?* Compare volume(3). **4** an extent of an activity, division of study, interest etc: *areas of disagreement; related scientific areas of study; problem areas in learning English.* **5** a part (of): *certain areas of the body.*

ˌ**area code** *nc* (*telephoning*) a number to be used as a code when calling a different region of a country.

arena /ə'riːnə/ *nc* (*pl* —s) **1** the central part of a stadium used for sport and games. **2** (*fig*) any scene of competition or struggle: *the political arena.*

aren't /ɑːnt/ *v* **1** = are not: *They aren't coming. Aren't they allowed in?* **2** (*GB informal*; used in questions only) short for am not: *Aren't I allowed in? I'm next, aren't I?* Ⓝ '*I aren't*' is not possible.

ar·gu·able /'ɑːgjʊəbl/ *adj* able to be supported

with reasons: *It is arguable that he'll fail.* Opp **unarguable.**

ar·gu·ably /-əblɪ/ *adv*

argue /'ɑːgjuː/ *v* (*pt,pp —d*) **1** *vi* to talk about a decision, what is to happen, a meaning etc and express a different opinion: *We were arguing in a friendly way. Don't argue (with me)—my decision is final!* **2** *vi,vt* to give organized reasons in support of or against (something): *'We could stay another week,' she argued, 'but we need more money and the banks are closed.' He argued that unemployment is a necessary evil. The lawyers have been arguing (the case) for hours.*

  argue about sth to express a different opinion: *They argued (with each other/with the manager) about who should pay for the broken window.*

  argue against sth (**a**) to give organized reasons against a plan, an appointment, an award etc: *argue against giving them more money/her promotion.* (**b**) (of information, evidence etc) to indicate the strong possibility of the opposite: *The statistics argue against the idea that children are healthier.*

  argue for sth (**a**) to give organized reasons in favour of something: *argue for the plan to ban smoking.* (**b**) (*formal*) to indicate the strong possibility of something: *The results argue for the benefits to one's health.*

  argue over sth = argue about sth.

ar·gu·ment /'ɑːgjumənt/ *n* **1** *nc* a (serious) disagreement: *endless arguments about money; an argument with the referee.* **2** *nc,nu* (**a**) discussion giving reasons for agreeing or disagreeing: *arguments against/for government policy. It is beyond argument* (= is certain) *that he did it.*

ar·gu·men·ta·tive /ˌɑːgjuˈmentətɪv/ *adj* (*derog*) often expressing disagreement.

aria /'ɑːrɪə/ *nc* (*pl —s*) a song for one voice in an opera etc.

arid /'ærɪd/ *adj* (*tech*) (of land, climate) having not enough rain to grow plants etc.

Aries /'eərɪːz/ *n* the Ram, the first sign of the zodiac.

arise /əˈraɪz/ *vi* (*pt* **arose** /əˈrəʊz/, *pp* **arisen** /əˈrɪzn/) **1** to come into existence; be noticed: *A new difficulty has arisen.* **2** **arise from sth** to result from something: *Serious effects may arise from your mistakes.* **3** (*old use*) to get up; stand up. (N) *'Rise'* is now used.

ar·is·toc·racy /ˌærɪˈstɒkrəsɪ/ *n* (*pl* **-ies**) **1** *nc,nu* (a country with) government by people of the highest social class. **2** *nc* the social class from which these people come (e.g. *dukes, earls, lords*).

ar·is·to·crat /'ærɪstəkræt/ *nc* a member of the aristocracy.

ar·is·to·cra·tic /ˌærɪstəˈkrætɪk/ *adj* of, like, the aristocracy: *with an aristocratic walk.*

ar·is·to·crati·cal·ly /-klɪ/ *adv*

arith·me·tic /əˈrɪθmətɪk/ *nu* the science of numbers; working with numbers.

arith,metic pro'gression *nc* (*maths*) a series of numbers etc in which each differs from the next by the same amount, such as 2, 5, 8, 11 etc. Compare geometric progression.

arith·meti·cal /ˌærɪθˈmetɪkl/ *adj*

arm¹ /ɑːm/ *nc* **1** either of the two upper limbs of the human body, from the shoulder to the hand:

She was carrying a child in her arms. **arm in arm** with the arm of one person round the arm of another: *standing/walking arm in arm.* **with open arms** with friendliness and enthusiasm: *He welcomed us with open arms.* **chance one's arm** to try to achieve something with a strong possibility of failure: *I'll chance my arm and invest my money in the steel industry.* **fold one's arms** to cross them in front of one's chest. **keep sb at arm's length** to keep a person at a distance (esp to avoid being too friendly): *It is best to keep your rival at arm's length.* **twist sb's arm** to try (in a friendly or unfriendly way) to make a person agree. **2** a sleeve: *The arms of this coat are too long.* **3** anything shaped like or suggesting an arm: *the arms of a chair; the arm of a record-player* (= the long part holding the needle). **4** **the long arm of the law** the authority and power (of various related sections) of the police, law courts etc. **5** (*mil*) a division of a country's armed forces: *the infantry/air arm.*

'arm·chair *nc* a chair with supports for the arms.

'arm·ful /-fʊl/ *nc* as much as one arm or both arms can hold: *an armful of books.*

'arm·hole *nc* a hole (in a shirt, jacket etc) through which the arm is put.

'arm·pit *nc* the part under the arm near the shoulder.

arm² /ɑːm/ *vt* **1** to give weapons and armour to (a soldier, ship etc): *a warship armed against nuclear attack/with nuclear weapons.* Compare disarm(1,2). **2** to provide (a person, group etc) with (information, evidence, clothes, medicine etc): *She came to the meeting armed with all the facts. He arrived armed (with blankets) against the cold weather.*

,armed 'forces/'services *n pl* (the —) the military forces, i.e. the army, navy and air force.

ar·ma·dil·lo /ˌɑːməˈdɪləʊ/ *nc* (*pl —s*) a small animal of S America with a shell of bony plates, able to roll itself into a ball when attacked.

ar·ma·ment /'ɑːməmənt/ *n* **1** (usually *pl*) military forces and their weapons. **2** *nu* the process of equipping military forces.

ar·mis·tice /'ɑːmɪstɪs/ *nc* an agreement during a war or battle to stop fighting for a time.

ar·mour (*US* = **ar·mor**) /'ɑːmə(r)/ *nu* **1** the protective covering of metal or leather, worn in fighting: *a suit of armour.* **2** a metal covering for warships, tanks, vehicles etc.

ar·moured *adj* (*attrib*) protected with armour(2): *an armoured car.*

ar·moury /'ɑːmərɪ/ *nc* a place where weapons are kept.

arms /ɑːmz/ *n pl* **1** weapons: *The soldiers had plenty of arms and ammunition.* **be up in arms (about/over sth)** (to be ready) to argue angrily. **bear arms** to carry weapons. **lay down one's arms** to stop fighting. **present arms** (*mil*) to put one's rifle etc into a forward position as a salute. **rise up in arms (against sb/sth)** to begin to fight. **take up arms (against sb/sth)** to prepare to fight with weapons. **2** ⇨ coat of arms.

'arms-race *nc* (the —) the competition among nations for military strength.

ar·my /'ɑːmɪ/ *nc* (*pl* **-ies**) **1** (often the —) the military forces of a country organized for fighting on land: *be in the army.* **2** a large number or group: *an army of workmen/officials/ants.*

aroma /ə'rəʊmə/ *nc* (*pl* —**s**) a strong pleasing smell: *the aroma of roses/apple blossom/cooking.*

aro·mat·ic /ˌærə'mætɪk/ *adj* having an aroma: *aromatic herbs.*

arose /ə'rəʊz/ *pt* of arise.

around[1] /ə'raʊnd/ *adverbial particle* Ⓝ For uses with verbs such as *be, fool, play, shop* etc, ⇨ the *verb* entries. *'Round'* is now more usual in *GB* but *'around'* is used more often in *US*. **1** moving in a circle or curve to face the opposite way: *She turned around and saw me.* **2** (esp when repeated) moving in a complete circle: *The wheels went around and around but nothing happened. All this worry makes my head go around and around.* **3** (so as to be) in a circle: *The children gathered around.* **4** from one (place, point, person etc) to another: *Please pass these papers around.* **5** in every direction; in many different places: *The children were running around in the playground. He's going around telling lies about me.* **6 around about** = round about. **7** near; close by: *I'll be around if you need me.* Ⓝ *'Round'* is not possible.

around[2] /ə'raʊnd/ *prep* Ⓝ *'Round'* is now more usual in *GB* but *'around'* is used more often in *US*. **1** (of position) so as to be on all sides of: *sitting around the table; had a scarf around his neck.* **2** (of movement) in a path changing direction: *The shop is just around the corner.* **3** in every direction in or on; in many different places in or on: *You mustn't leave your clothes lying around the floor.* Ⓝ *'About'* can also be used. **4** near (in number or time): *There were around 50 visitors. Come at around 6 o'clock. He was born around 1960.* Ⓝ *'Round'* is not possible. *'About'* can also be used. **5** near; close to: *I left my glasses around here somewhere.* Ⓝ *'Round'* is not possible.

arouse /ə'raʊz/ *vt* **1** to cause (an emotion, opinion etc) to exist: *behaviour that might arouse suspicion.* **2** to cause (a person) to become active, interested.

arr. *abbr* arrival; arrives.

ar·range /ə'reɪndʒ/ *vt* **1** to put (things) in good order: *She's good at arranging flowers.* **2** to make (plans) in advance; see to the details of (something): *I have arranged to meet her at ten o'clock. I've arranged that you can have the car. I've arranged a car for you. The meeting arranged for tomorrow has been postponed.* **3 arrange sth (for sth)** (*music*) to adapt a piece of music (for an instrument, orchestra): *arrange a piece of music for the violin.*

ar·range·ment /ə'reɪndʒmənt/ *n* **1** *nc,nu* (the act of) arranging: *a new arrangement of the furniture in our new house; a beautiful flower arrangement.* **2** *nc,nu* an agreed plan: *an arrangement about when to meet; an arrangement to meet at 6 o'clock. We have an arrangement for cashing our cheques at this bank.* **come to an arrangement** to agree a method: *come to an arrangement about repaying the money.* **3** (*pl*) preparations. **make arrangements (for sb/sth)** to plan, arrange, something: *Have you made arrangements for your journey to Scotland?* **4** *nc* (*music*) an adaptation (of a piece of music): *an arrangement for the piano; an orchestral arrangement.*

ar·ray /ə'reɪ/ *nc* **1** a splendid collection, display etc: *an impressive array of carpets/medals.* **2** (*literary*) clothes: *in military/academic array.*

ar·rears /ə'rɪəz/ *n pl* **1** money that is owing and that ought to have been paid: *arrears of rent.* **be in/fall into arrears (with sth)** to be late in paying debts. **2** work that is still waiting to be done.

ar·rest[1] /ə'rest/ *nc,nu* (an act of) arresting a thief etc: *The police made several arrests.* **under arrest** made a prisoner: *She was placed/put under arrest. You're under arrest.*

ar·rest[2] /ə'rest/ *vt* **1** to seize (a person) by the authority of the law: *The police arrested the thief and put him in prison.* **2** to put a stop to (a process or movement): *Poor food arrests the growth of children.*

ar·ri·val /ə'raɪvl/ *n* **1** *nc,nu* (an act of) arriving: *waiting for the arrival of news.* **to await arrival** (on a letter, parcel etc) to be kept until the person arrives. **2** *nc* a person or thing that arrives: *new arrivals in the hotel; the latest arrivals in clothes shops. We met at 'Arrivals' in the airport. The new arrival* (= The newborn child) *is a boy.*

ar·rive /ə'raɪv/ *vi* **1** to reach a place, esp the end of a journey: *arrive home. What time did you arrive?* **2** to come; happen: *At last the day arrived. Her baby arrived* (= was born) *yesterday.* **arrive at sth** to reach a building, place, position in a discussion etc: *arrive at the hotel/a decision/a satisfactory agreement.* **3** (*modern use*) to establish one's reputation: *The publicity he received proved he'd arrived.*

ar·ro·gance /'ærəgəns/ *nu* arrogant behaviour, manner: *She's full of arrogance.*

ar·ro·gant /'ærəgənt/ *adj* (*derog*) behaving in a proud, superior way; (of behaviour etc) showing too much pride in oneself and too little thought for others: *speak in an arrogant tone.*

ar·ro·gant·ly *adv*

ar·row /'ærəʊ/ *nc* **1** a thin, pointed stick (to be) shot from a bow. **2** a mark or sign (→) used to show direction or position, e.g. on a map or a road sign.

ar·senal /'ɑːsənl/ *nc* (*mil*) a government building where weapons and ammunition are made or stored. ⇨ armoury.

ar·senic /'ɑːsnɪk/ *nu* (*chem*) a chemical element (symbol As) that is a strong poison.

ar·son /'ɑːsn/ *nu* (*legal*) the act of deliberately starting a dangerous fire.

art /ɑːt/ *n* **1** *nu* (also *attrib*) the creation or expression of what is beautiful, esp in visual form; great skill or ability in such expression: *the art of the Renaissance; children's art; an art gallery.* ⇨ fine art; work of art. **2** *nc* a skill in which imagination and personality are important: *Cooking/Making people happy is an art.* ⇨ arts. **3** *nc,nu* (an example of) using (dishonest and) clever ways (to get or achieve something): *her art in persuading us all to believe her.* ⇨ also black art.

'art gallery *nc* a building for the display of paintings, sculpture etc.

'art school *nc* a college where painting, sculpture etc are taught.

ar·te·fact /'ɑːtɪfækt/ *nc* something made by a person, e.g. a tool or work of art.

ar·ter·ial /ɑː'tɪərɪəl/ *adj* (*attrib; anat*) of or like an artery: *arterial blood.*

ar·tery /'ɑːtərɪ/ *nc* (*pl* **-ies**) **1** one of the tubes carrying blood from the heart to all parts of the body. Compare vein(1). **2** a main road, river etc.

art·ful /'ɑːtfəl/ adj (often derog) clever at getting what one wants. ⇨ art (3).
art·ful·ly /-fəlɪ/ adv
art·ful·ness nu

arth·rit·ic /ɑːˈθrɪtɪk/ adj of, suffering from, arthritis.

arth·ri·tis /ˌɑːˈθraɪtɪs/ nu painful inflammation of a joint or joints.

ar·thro·pod /'ɑːθrəpɒd/ nc (science) any animal of a group having jointed legs, a segmented body and a hard external skeleton, such as a crab, spider, beetle or centipede.

ar·ti·choke /'ɑːtɪtʃəʊk/ nc **1** globe artichoke a kind of plant with a head of thick, leaf-like scales, used as a vegetable. **2** Jerusalem artichoke a kind of plant with white roots, used as a vegetable.

ar·ticle /'ɑːtɪkl/ nc **1** a particular or separate thing: articles of clothing; toilet articles (e.g. soap, toothpaste). **2** a piece of writing, complete in itself, as in a newspaper or magazine. **3** (gram): definite article, 'the'; indefinite article, 'a', 'an'. ⇨ determiner.

ar·ticu·late¹ /ɑːˈtɪkjʊlət/ adj **1** (of a person) able to put thoughts and feelings into clear speech. Opp inarticulate. **2** (of speech) in which the separate sounds and words are clear.
ar·ticu·late·ly adv

ar·ticu·late² /ɑːˈtɪkjʊleɪt/ vt,vi (formal) to speak, say (something) (clearly).

ar·ticu·lated /ɑːˈtɪkjʊleɪtɪd/ adj having joints that allow movement.
ar,ticulated 'vehicle nc one having articulated parts, e.g. a lorry with a trailer.

ar·ticu·la·tion /ɑːˌtɪkjʊˈleɪʃn/ nu (formal) the production of speech sounds: The speaker's ideas were good but his articulation was poor.

ar·ti·fact /'ɑːtɪfækt/ nc = artefact.

ar·ti·fi·cial /ˌɑːtɪˈfɪʃl/ adj not natural or real; made by humans: artificial flowers/teeth/light.
,arti,ficial ,respi'ration nu the method of attempting to force air into the lungs, e.g. of a person nearly drowned.
ar·ti·fi·cial·ly /-ʃəlɪ/ adv

ar·til·lery /ɑːˈtɪlərɪ/ nu (mil) (a part of an army using) big guns (on wheels etc).

ar·ti·san /ˌɑːtɪˈzæn/ nc a skilled workman in an industry or trade, using her or his hands.

art·ist /'ɑːtɪst/ nc a person who practises one of the fine arts, esp painting.

art·iste /ɑːˈtiːst/ nc a professional singer, actor, dancer etc.

ar·tis·tic /ɑːˈtɪstɪk/ adj done with, showing, skill and good judgement, of beauty, colour, shape. Opp inartistic.
ar·tis·ti·cal·ly /-klɪ/ adv

art·ist·ry /'ɑːtɪstrɪ/ nu (formal) artistic skill and good judgement.

arts /ɑːts/ nu (often the —; also attrib) the academic subjects, areas of study, in which imagination and personal appreciation are more important than exact measurement and calculation: study arts/the arts/arts subjects such as history, literature, languages and philosophy. Compare humanities, science. ⇨ also Bachelor/ Master of Arts.

arty /'ɑːtɪ/ adj (-ier, -iest) (informal; derog) pretending or falsely claiming to be artistic.

as¹ /əz strong form: æz/ adv, prep **1** (used in comparisons) **(a)** as + adj/adv (+ as sb/sth) equally: She's as lazy as me. I'm twice as rich as you. You're not as rich (as me). He's just as rich (= owns exactly the same amount of money) as you. She's not nearly as rich as you (= is much poorer than you). Ⓝ 'As' can be used in positive and negative statements. 'So' is only possible with 'not', as in I'm not so tall as you. ⇨ also same¹(1). **(b)** (as) + adj/adv + as sb/sth (used in well-known phrases meaning 'extremely'): He's as brave as a lion. Its as easy as ABC. She tiptoed upstairs as quietly as a mouse. Ⓝ The first 'as' can be omitted, as in He's brave as a lion. **(c)** (used with many/much, few/little etc expressing amount, extent etc): as many as 40 students; not as much as 2 metres/£100; as few as two applicants; as little as three days/£30; as early/late as 6 o'clock. **(d)** as + adj/adv + as not equally: The buses are late as often as not. It's as likely as not that he'll be late. **2** (used with verbs such as regard, imagine, treat etc expressing similarity to): Many people think of him as a fool. I can imagine you as a union leader. I refuse to be treated as a child. I was always considered as (being) a good swimmer. **3** in the character, profession, function, of: He was loved as a husband and a father. As their leader, she made the decision. He used my favourite vase as a bird bath! Why is he dressed as a woman? She is acting as their representative. He's employed as a musician. Did you see Roger Moore as James Bond? **4 as against** ⇨ against(8).

as² /əz strong form: æz/ conj (subord) **1** (used in comparisons) **(a)** as + adj/adv + as ... equally: She's as lazy as I am. They worked as hard as we did. Ⓝ 'As' can be used in positive and negative statements. 'So' is only possible with 'not', as in She's not so lazy as I am. Compare than. **(b)** (used with many/much, few/little etc expressing amount, extent etc): There are not as many members as we used to have. I gave as much help as I could. **as many/much again** ⇨ again(1). **2** (used of events or situations happening at the same time) at the moment; during the period: I noticed him as he entered the room. As the sun was rising, the birds began to sing. As the tree grew, its leaves turned brown. I knew her as a girl. Think of us as we are crossing the Himalayas. Ⓝ 'When' and 'while' can also be used, especially if the background situation has existed before a shorter event happens, as in When/While she was shopping, she suddenly remembered her dentist appointment. 'When' is preferred if the event happened during a short moment as in I woke up when the door closed. 'While' is preferred if the situation existed over a long period, as in I met him while I was living in Paris. 'While' is also preferred if two long events or situations happen at the same time, as in While I was at the disco, my brother was studying. 'As' is preferred if two short events or situations happen at the same time, as in As I stepped into the bath, the telephone rang. 'As' is also preferred if two closely related situations develop at the same time, as in As the baby became hungrier, it cried more loudly. **just as** at the same moment: The telephone rang just as I was getting into the bath. Ⓝ 'While' is not possible. 'Just when' is possible but it is not as usual. **as and when** (*informal*) (used to emphasize an exact moment): *I'll deal with those problems as and when they arise.* **3** for the reason that: *As he wasn't ready, we left without him. I must hurry as I have another appointment. As she has the fastest time, let her enter for the race.* Ⓝ *'Because'* can also be used, as in *Because he wasn't ready, we left without him. 'Because'* is preferred if the reason is very important, as in *I'm resigning because I'm not appreciated. 'Since'* can also be used, as in *Since she has the fastest time, let her enter for the race. 'Since'* is preferred if the reason is a general one that is already known, as in *Since cooking destroys vitamins, we should eat raw vegetables.* **4** in spite of the extent to which: *Old as he was, he jumped over the gate. Much as I like you, I won't marry you.* Ⓝ Compare: *Although he was old, . . . ; Although I like you, . . .* **5** for example: *Adjectives are used with nouns and pronouns, as in 'red faces' and 'You're beautiful'.* **such as** ⇨ such¹(1). **6** (used to avoid repetition) in the same way that: *He's tall, as is his father.* **7** in the way which: *Don't do as I do, do as I tell you. Leave it as it is.* **8** (used as a *relative pron*) which fact, topic etc: *Kenya, (as you all know, is in Africa. As I was saying, jazz has its roots in Africa.*

as far as ⇨ far²(3).

as for /ˌæz fə(r)/ with reference to (a new but related subject): *I can speak Spanish and Japanese but as for English, it's very difficult. As for you, I never want to speak to you again.*

as from from (a certain date or time): *We'll be living in Rome as from July (US = as of).*

as good as ⇨ good¹(14).

as if/though (a) (*informal*) (used with verbs such as *appear, look, seem*) probable that: *It seems as if they'll be late again.* **(b)** (followed by a *pt*) as the case would be if: *He behaves as if/though he knew nothing about it.* Ⓝ *'It isn't as if'* suggests that the opposite of what follows is true, as in *It isn't as if we were rich* (= We are not rich). **as if to** + *verb* in a way that suggests: *She opened her mouth as if to say something.*

as it is/was (a) already: *I mustn't have another coffee—I'm late as it is.* **(b)** under the existing conditions: *He fell in the race, though as it was he wouldn't have won.*

as long as ⇨ long²(1).

as a matter of fact ⇨ fact(4).

as much ⇨ much³.

as of (esp *US*) from (a certain date or time): *Your salary will be increased as of 1 April.*

as of now (*informal*) from this moment: *As of now, you are the sales director.*

as per ⇨ per.

as regards ⇨ regard²(3).

as a rule ⇨ rule¹(2).

as soon as ⇨ soon(2).

as though = as if.

as to (used when arguing or discussing) with reference to: *As to visiting China, I still haven't decided.*

as usual ⇨ usual.

as well ⇨ well²(5).

as a whole ⇨ whole²(2).

as yet ⇨ yet(2).

ASA /ˌeɪ es ˈeɪ/ *abbr* **1** (*photography*) (used to indicate film speed, using a method developed in USA). ⇨ DIN. **2** (the —) (*GB*) Amateur Swimming Association.

as·bes·tos /æzˈbestəs/ *nu* (also *attrib*) a soft, grey substance that used to be made into fireproof material: *asbestos walls.*

as·cend /əˈsend/ *vt,vi* (*formal*) **1** to go or come up (a mountain etc): *They ascended the mountain from the south. We watched the mists ascending from the valley.* ⇨ ascent. **2 ascend the throne** to become king or queen.

As·cen·sion /əˈsenʃn/ *n* (the —) (*Christianity*) the departure of Jesus from the earth.

as·cent /əˈsent/ *nc* an act of going or coming up: *The ascent of the mountain was not difficult.* ⇨ ascend.

as·cer·tain /ˌæsəˈteɪn/ *vt* (*formal*) to find out (something) (in order to be certain): *ascertain the facts; ascertain that the stick was the murder weapon; ascertain what really happened.*

as·cer·tain·able /-əbl/ *adj*

as·cetic /əˈsetɪk/ *adj, nc* (of) a person who (often for religious reasons) leads a very simple life without pleasures.

as·cribe /əˈskraɪb/ *vt* **ascribe sth to sb/sth** (*formal*) to consider something to be caused or done by a person, thing: *He ascribed his failure to bad luck.*

asep·tic /eɪˈseptɪk/ *adj* (*med*) (of wounds etc) free from infection (disease germs). Opp septic.

asex·ual /eɪˈsekʃʊəl/ *adj* (*science*) without sex or sex organs: *Mushrooms have asexual reproduction.*

ash¹ /æʃ/ *nu* **1** the powder that is left after something has burnt: *Don't drop cigarette ash on the carpet.* **2** (*pl*) the burnt (= *cremated*) remains of a human body.

'ash·tray *nc* a small dish for tobacco ash.

ash² /æʃ/ *nc,nu* (the hard wood of) a kind of forest-tree with silver-grey bark.

'ash-key *nc* a winged seed of the ash.

ashamed /əˈʃeɪmd/ *adj* (*pred*) **ashamed (of sb/sth/oneself)** feeling shame: *You should be ashamed of yourself/of your behaviour/of what you have done.*

ash·en /ˈæʃn/ *adj* (*formal*) of (the colour of) ashes; pale: *His face turned ashen at the news.*

ashore /əˈʃɔː(r)/ *adv, adj* (*pred*) on, on to, the shore. **go ashore** to leave a ship to go on land.

aside¹ /əˈsaɪd/ *adv* **1** on or to one side: *Step aside and let the cyclist pass. Please put this money aside* (= keep it) *for the telephone bill.* **2** out of hearing: *She took me aside to explain.* **3 aside from** (*prep*) (esp *US*) = apart from.

aside² /əˈsaɪd/ *nc* (*drama*) a remark made by a character in a play that is heard by the audience but not by other characters.

as·in·ine /ˈæsɪnaɪn/ *adj* (*informal; derog*) (of a person, remark) very stupid.

ask /ɑːsk/ *v* **1** *vt,vi* to call to (a person) for an answer to or about (something): *'What's your name?' he asked. Ask that man the time. I'll ask (him) how to get there. They asked me a question about my education. Didn't you ask him who he is? If you don't know, please ask. I telephoned to ask if you can be ready by 8 o'clock.* **2** *vt* to invite (a person): *She has asked me to her party. Did he ask you to dinner?* **3** *vt,vi* to make a request to (a person): *Can I ask you a favour—would you hold* *this for me? They've asked us to be quiet. He asked for a deposit. If you need something, you have only to ask. We're asking £80 000 for the house. Isn't that asking a great deal? I think you're asking too much. It's asking a lot to expect her to walk from the station.* ⇨ **asking.**

ask about sb/sth to request information about a person's health, a business's success etc.

ask after sb to inquire about a person's health, general news etc.

ask around to request help, information etc from friends, neighbours etc: *We asked around but our cat was never found.*

ask (for) sth to request something: *ask (for) advice from a solicitor.* **be asking for trouble** ⇨ **trouble¹(1).**

ask sb in to invite a person into one's home.

ask sth of sb (*formal*) to request help, information etc from a person: *Can I ask another question of you? He'll never ask anything of her again.*

ask sb out (to sth) to invite a person out (to a disco, restaurant etc): *Paul's asked me out (to dinner) on Friday.*

ask sb over to invite a person to visit one's home: *Let's ask the neighbours over to a meal soon.*

askew /ə'skju:/ *adv, adj* (*pred*) not in the straight or usual (level) position: *have a hat on askew.*

ask·ing /'ɑ:skɪŋ/ *n* **for the asking**: *It's yours for the asking* (= You have only to ask for it and it will be given to you).

'asking price *nc* (the —) the price asked by the seller of a house etc.

asleep /ə'sli:p/ *adj* (*pred*), *adv* **1** in a state of sleep: *He has been asleep since 9 o'clock.* Ⓝ 'Sleeping' can also be used, as in *She's sleeping.* 'Sleeping' can be used before the noun, as in *a sleeping baby*, but 'asleep' cannot. Compare **awake.** **fast/sound asleep** in a deep sleep. **fall asleep** to go to sleep. **2** (of the arms or legs) without feeling (as when under pressure); numb.

as·para·gus /ə'spærəgəs/ *nu* a kind of plant with long, green shoots, eaten as a vegetable.

as·pect /'æspekt/ *nc* **1** a side (usually the front) that faces a particular direction: *a house with a southern aspect.* **2** (*fig*) a particular part of an idea etc: *study every aspect of a subject* (= study it thoroughly). **3** a particular look or appearance (of a person or thing): *a man with a serious aspect.*

as·per·sions /ə'spɜ:ʃnz/ *n pl* **cast aspersions (on sb/sth)** to say false things about a person, a person's character etc.

as·phalt /'æsfælt/ *nu* a black, sticky substance used for making road surfaces.

as·phyxi·ate /əs'fɪksɪeɪt/ *vt* to cause (a person) to die or be very ill by stopping enough air from entering the lungs: *The men in the coalmine were asphyxiated when the tunnel collapsed.*

as·phyxi·ation /əs,fɪksɪ'eɪʃn/ *nu*

as·pic /'æspɪk/ *nu* clear meat jelly: *chicken in aspic.*

as·pir·ant /'æspɪrənt/ *nc* (*formal*) a person who is ambitious for personal success, fame etc: *an aspirant to high office.*

as·pir·ate¹ /'æspərət/ *nc* (*tech*) the sound of 'h'; sound with an 'h' in it.

as·pir·ate² /'æspəreɪt/ *vt* (*tech*) to make (an 'h' sound): *The 'h' in 'honour' is not aspirated.*

as·pir·ation /,æspə'reɪʃn/ *nc,nu* (often *pl*) ambition: *the aspirations of young people.*

as·pire /ə'spaɪə(r)/ *vi* **aspire to (do) sth** (*formal*) to be ambitious: *aspire to become an author/ to a gold medal.*

ass /æs/ *nc* **1** a small animal like a horse with long ears. **2** (*fig; derog*) a stupid person: *He made an ass of himself.*

as·sail /ə'seɪl/ *vt* (*formal*) to attack (a person) (the usual word): *assail a speaker with questions/ insults.*

as·sail·ant /-ənt/ *nc* an attacker (the usual word).

as·sas·sin /ə'sæsɪn/ *nc* a person (employed by others) who kills a person.

as·sas·sin·ate /ə'sæsɪneɪt/ *vt* to kill (a person, esp a politician, ruler), esp for political reasons.

as·sas·sin·ation /ə,sæsɪ'neɪʃn/ *nc,nu*

as·sault /ə'sɔ:lt/ *vt, nc* (to make) a sudden and violent attack: *They made an assault on the enemy's positions.* **assault and battery** (*legal*) the act of beating or hitting a person.

as·semble /ə'sembl/ *v* **1** *vt, vi* (to cause people) to gather together: *The pupils assembled/were assembled in the school hall.* **2** *vt* to put together (the parts of) (something): *assemble a car.*

as·sem·bly /ə'semblɪ/ *nc* (*pl* **-ies**) (A- in names) a group of people who have come together for a particular purpose: *the Legislative Assembly.*

as'sembly line *nc* a place in a factory where parts of a machine, vehicle etc move along slowly while being fixed together.

as·sent /ə'sent/ *nc* an official agreement (e.g. to a proposal, a bill passed by Parliament): *by common assent* (= everybody agreeing). □ *vi* **assent to sth** (*formal*) to agree officially to something.

as·sert /ə'sɜ:t/ *vt* **1** to justify (something) by using evidence or firm behaviour: *assert one's rights.* **2** to state (something) firmly: *assert one's innocence/that one is innocent.*

as·ser·tion /ə'sɜ:ʃn/ *nc,nu* (an act, example, of) stating something firmly: *make an assertion that one is innocent.*

as·ser·tive /ə'sɜ:tɪv/ *adj* having or showing a great deal of confidence: *speaking in an assertive tone.*

as·sert·ive·ly *adv*

as·sess /ə'ses/ *vt* **assess sth (at sth)** **1** to decide or fix e.g. a tax or a fine, or the value of property etc (at an amount): *Damages were assessed at £500.* **2** (*fig*) to judge the value of something: *assess a speech at its true worth.*

as·sess·ment *nc,nu*

as·ses·sor /ə'sesə(r)/ *nc* a person who assesses property, income taxes etc.

as·set /'æset/ *nc* **1** (usually *pl*) anything owned by a person, business etc that has money value and that may be sold to pay debts. Compare liability(2,3). **2** a valuable or useful quality or skill: *Good health is a great asset.*

as·sign /ə'saɪn/ *vt* (*formal*) **1** to give (something) for use or as a share or part in: *Those rooms have been assigned to us.* **2** to decide (a time, place, reason etc): *Has a day been assigned for the trial? Can one assign a cause to these events?* **3** to give (a person) an amount of work etc to be done: *The supervisor assigned us various jobs in the factory.* **4** (*legal*) to transfer (property, rights etc) to another person or business.

as·sign·ment *nc,nu* (esp) a piece of work assigned(3) to a person.

as·simi·late /ə'sɪmɪleɪt/ *vt* (*formal*) **1** to allow (people) to become part of another social group or state: *The USA has assimilated people from many countries.* **2** to learn (facts etc) thoroughly. **3** to absorb (food) into the body (after digestion): *We assimilate some foods more easily than others.*
as·simi·la·tion /ə,sɪmɪ'leɪʃn/ *nu*

as·sist /ə'sɪst/ *vt,vi* **1** to help (the usual word): *Can I assist you* (*with filling in those application forms*)? *We have been assisting in the search for the children. I need you to assist me with these boxes.* **2** to work or act as an assistant to (a person).

as·sist·ance /ə'sɪstəns/ *nu* help and support: *give assistance* (*to a person*).

as·sist·ant /ə'sɪstənt/ *nc* (also *attrib*) a person who helps another (esp as a deputy or as a junior worker): *the assistant manager; a classroom assistant.* ⇨ shop assistant.

Assoc. *written abbr* Associate; Association.

as·so·ci·ate¹ /ə'səʊʃɪət/ *nc* (also *attrib*) **1** a person joined with others in work, business or crime: *a business associate.* **2** a person given certain limited rights in a society, alliance etc: *an associate member.*

as·so·ci·ate² /ə'səʊʃɪeɪt/ *v* **1** *vt* **associate sb/ sth (with sth)** to think of a person, idea etc as connected (with something): *Health and happiness are associated. We associate springtime with apple blossom.* **2** *vi* **associate with sb** to be often in the company of a person: *Don't associate with dishonest boys.*

as·so·ci·ation /ə,səʊsɪ'eɪʃn/ *n* **1** *nc* (A- in names) a group of people joined together for some common purpose: *the Automobile Association.* **2** *nu* **association (with sb/sth)** the state of connecting or being connected (with a person, thing): *I benefited so much from my association with him/from our association. Our company is working in association with* (= together with) *an Italian company.*
As,sociation 'football *nu* (*formal*) ⇨ football.

as·so·nance /'æsənəns/ *nu* (*literature*) the similarity of sound between one word and another because they have the same vowel (as in *speak* and *feet*) or the same consonant (as in *chief* and *child*). ⇨ consonance(2).

as·sort·ed /ə'sɔːtɪd/ *adj* (*attrib*) of various sorts; mixed: *a pound of assorted chocolates.*

as·sort·ment /ə'sɔːtmənt/ *nc* a collection of different examples or types: *This shop has an assortment of goods to choose from.*

Asst *written abbr* assistant.

as·sume /ə'sjuːm/ *vt* **1** to believe (something) before there is proof: *You must assume him to be innocent/that he is innocent.* **2** to begin having authority or control etc over (something): *assume office* (i.e. begin to govern). **3** (*formal*) to take for oneself (something not genuine or sincere): *assume an academic qualification.*
as·sumed *adj* (*attrib*) not genuine: *He registered at the hotel under an assumed name.*
as·sum·ing *conj* if: *I'll be there, assuming* (*that*) *it doesn't rain.*

as·sump·tion /ə'sʌmpʃn/ *nc* **1** something

regarded as true or likely to happen but not proved: *Their assumption that the famine would end was soon proved wrong. I am going on the assumption that dad will buy the bike.* **2** (*formal*) an act of taking authority, control: *a year after her assumption of office.*

as·sur·ance /ə'ʃʊərəns/ *n* **1** *nc* a statement (e.g. a promise) made to give confidence: *He gave me a definite assurance that the repairs would be finished by Friday.* **2** *nu* (often *self-assurance*) belief and trust in one's own ability or powers: *He answered all the questions with assurance.*

as·sure /ə'ʃʊə(r)/ *vt* to say something to (a person) positively, with confidence: *I can assure you of our full support. I assure you* (*that*) *flying is perfectly safe.*
as·sured *adj* confident: *an assured tone.*
as·sur·ed·ly /ə'ʃʊərɪdlɪ/ *adv* confidently.

as·ter·isk /'æstərɪsk/ *nc* the mark *, used to call attention to something, to show that letters are omitted etc.

as·ter·oid /'æstərɔɪd/ *nc* any of many small planets between Mars and Jupiter.

asth·ma /'æsmə/ *nu* a serious chest disease making breathing difficult.
asth·mat·ic /,æs'mætɪk/ *adj*

as·tig·ma·tism /ə'stɪgmətɪzəm/ *nu* (*tech*) (faulty vision caused by) the lens of the eye having the wrong shape.

astir /ə'stɜː(r)/ *adv, adj* (*pred*) (*formal*) in a state of excitement: *The whole village was astir with the news that the Queen was coming.*

as·ton·ish /ə'stɒnɪʃ/ *vt* (usually *passive*) to surprise (a person) greatly: *The news astonished everybody.*
as·ton·ish·ing *adj* very surprising: *That's astonishing news.*
as·ton·ish·ment /ə'stɒnɪʃmənt/ *nu* great surprise: *I heard to my astonishment that he'd won! He looked at me in astonishment.*

as·tound /ə'staʊnd/ *vt* (usually *passive*) to surprise (a person) greatly: *I'm astounded!*

as·tral /'æstrəl/ *adj* of, from, the stars.

astray /ə'streɪ/ *adv, adj* (*pred*) out of, off, the right path, esp (*fig*) into doing wrong. **go astray** to become lost: *Your letter seems to have gone astray.* **lead sb astray** to encourage a person to live dishonestly or immorally.

astride /ə'straɪd/ *adv, prep* with one leg on each side (of): *sitting astride his father's knee.*

as·trin·gent /ə'strɪndʒənt/ *adj, nc* (of) a substance that makes the skin tight or contracts blood vessels to stop bleeding.

as·trol·oger /ə'strɒlədʒə(r)/ *nc* an expert in, student of, astrology.

as·tro·logi·cal /,æstrə'lɒdʒɪkl/ *adj* of astrology.

as·tro·logy /ə'strɒlədʒɪ/ *nu* the science or art of observing the positions of the stars in the belief that they influence human affairs.

as·tro·naut /'æstrənɔːt/ *nc* a person who travels in a spacecraft.

as·tron·om·er /ə'strɒnəmə(r)/ *nc* an expert in, student of, astronomy.

as·tro·nomi·cal /,æstrə'nɒmɪkl/ *adj* **1** of the study of astronomy. **2** (*informal*) enormous: *an astronomical salary.*

as·tron·omy /ə'strɒnəmɪ/ *nu* the scientific study of the sun, moon, stars and planets.

as·tute /ə'stjuːt/ *adj* quick at seeing how to gain an advantage: *an astute lawyer/businesswoman*.
as·tute·ly *adv*

asy·lum /ə'saɪləm/ *n* **1** *nc,nu* (a place of) refuge or safety. **2** *nu* protection from cruel treatment etc: *ask for political asylum.* **3** *nc* (formerly) institution where mentally ill people were cared for (now called a *mental hospital*).

asym·met·ric (also **asym·met·ri·cal**) /ˌeɪsɪ'metrɪk(l)/ *adj* (*no comp*) not symmetric.

at /ət *strong form:* æt/ *prep* Ⓝ For uses with verbs such as *get, go, guess* etc, ⇨ the *verb* entries. **1** (expressing position or location): *at a hotel; at a disco; at the station; at the office; at the theatre; at the supermarket; at the doctor's; at the top of the stairs; at the end of the road; at home; at school; at work; at church; at sea; at Boots the chemist; at Edinburgh University; at a small seaside town called Lynton.* Ⓝ 'At' and 'in' are used in expressions of position or location. 'At' is used to refer to a particular location, as in *at a party, at the corner of the street.* 'In' is used to refer to a location inside an area such as a box, room, forest, town, country etc, as in *in the corner, in the bedroom; in the countryside, in Japan, in Europe.* 'At' can be used with the name of a town only if it is small or if the reason for being there is not important, as in *We had lunch at Keele, a village near the motorway. The train stops at Stratford.* 'In' is used with the name of a large town or city or with a small town if the reason for being there is important, as in *We spent three days in London. I live in Stratford.* 'At' cannot be used for countries, continents etc. **at a distance** ⇨ distance. **at cross-purposes** ⇨ cross-purposes. **at heart** ⇨ heart(2). **at large** ⇨ large³. **2** (a) (expressing a point in time or order): *at 2 o'clock; at midnight; at about 6.30; at night; at the weekend; at Christmas; at present; at any moment; at any time; at one time or another; at regular intervals; at short notice; at first sight; at first; at last; at the last minute; at the third attempt; at the beginning/the end.* Ⓝ 'At', 'in' and 'on' are all used in expressions of time. 'At' is used with exact time, as in *at 5'clock, at dawn, at the first opportunity,* and with public holidays, as in *at Easter.* 'In' is used with longer periods such as months, seasons, years, as in *in April, in winter, in 1980, in modern times,* and with parts of the day, as in *in the morning.* 'In' is also used to refer to when something will happen or how long it takes, as in *I'll be there in a few minutes. It will be ready in an hour.* 'On' is used with exact dates, as in *on 21 May,* with the days of the week, as in *on Monday, on Sunday evening,* and also with days celebrating a special occasion, as in *on my birthday, on her wedding day, on their anniversary.* Compare by²(11,12). **(not) at all** ⇨ all³(4). **at times; at all times** ⇨ time¹(4). **(b)** (expressing a point in a lifetime): *at 13 (years of age); at birth/death; at the height of her career.* **3** (used with superlatives expressing quantity, occasion, state etc): *at least; at (the) most; at best/worst; at its ripest; at their poorest.* **4** (expressing a rate of doing something): *drive at 30mph; type at 120 words a minute; go at full speed.* Compare by²(13). **5** (expressing cost): *buy it at £10 and sell it at £25.* Ⓝ 'For' is now more usual in everyday conversation, as in *I bought it for £20.* In commercial use, 'at' is more usual and the symbol @ is used to mean 'for . . . each', as in *5 packets @ £5.* ⇨

also expense(1). **6** (expressing movement or direction towards): *throw a stone at a window; wave at the train driver; shout at a thief; look at a photograph; smile at a camera; arrive at a decision.* **7** (expressing an activity, occupation, condition etc): *at work* (= working) *on a new design; at play* (= playing) *in the park; at peace; at war.* **8** (used after adjectives expressing ability): *good at English; skilled at carpentry; terrible at football.* **9** (expressing the cause of an emotion): *annoyed at his silly behaviour; shocked at the news; surprised at the result.* Ⓝ 'By' can also be used.

ate /et/ *pt* of eat.

athe·ism /'eɪθɪɪzəm/ *nu* the belief that there is no God.

athe·ist /'eɪθɪɪst/ *nc* a person who believes that there is no God.
athe·is·tic /ˌeɪθɪ'ɪstɪk/ *adj*

ath·lete /'æθliːt/ *nc* a person trained for competing in physical exercises and outdoor games, e.g. a person who is good at running, jumping, swimming etc.

ath·let·ic /æθ'letɪk/ *adj* **1** (*attrib*) of, for, athletes: *athletic clothing; an athletic diet.* **2** physically strong and well-balanced: *an athletic/ athletic-looking young man.*
ath·let·ics *nu* (also *attrib*) the practice of physical exercises and sports, esp competitions in running, jumping etc: *an athletics track.*

atishoo /ə'tɪʃuː/ *int* (the spelling form used to indicate a sneeze).

at·las /'ætləs/ *nc* a book of maps.

at·mos·phere /'ætməsfɪə(r)/ *nc* **1** (the —) the mixture of gases surrounding the earth. **2** air in any place such as a room: *a smoky atmosphere.* **3** the general feeling produced by a place, conditions etc: *the atmosphere of a big city.* **4** (*literature*) the mood or feeling produced by the effect a piece of writing has on the reader.
at·mos·pher·ic /ˌætməs'ferɪk/ *adj*
at·mos·pher·ics /ˌætməs'ferɪks/ *n pl* noises from radios, caused by electrical disturbances (e.g. lightning) in the air.

atoll /'ætɒl/ *nc* a ring of coral reef(s) round a lagoon.

atom /'ætəm/ *nc* **1** (*science*) the smallest unit of a chemical element: *A molecule of water (H_2O) is made up of two atoms of hydrogen and one atom of oxygen.* ⇨ electron, neutron, nucleus(1), proton. **2** (*fig*) a very small bit: *There's not an atom of truth* (= no truth at all) *in what he said.*

atom·ic /ə'tɒmɪk/ *adj* of an atom, or atoms.
a,tomic 'bomb *nc* a bomb which uses atomic energy.
a,tomic 'energy *nu* = nuclear energy.
a,tomic 'mass *nc* (*science*) the ratio between the average mass of an atom and half the mass of an atom of an element called carbon 12.
a,tomic 'number *nc* (*science*) the number of positive charges in the nucleus of an atom.
a,tomic 'pile *nc* = nuclear reactor.

atone /ə'təʊn/ *vi* **atone (for sth)** (*formal*) to make repayment (for doing wrong): *How can I atone for hurting your feelings?*
atone·ment *nu*

atro·cious /ə'trəʊʃəs/ *adj* **1** (*derog*) very wicked or cruel: *an atrocious crime.* **2** (*informal*) very

bad: *an atrocious dinner; atrocious weather*.
atro·cious·ly *adv*

atroc·ity /ə'trɒsətɪ/ *nc,nu* (*pl* **-ies**) (an act of) extreme wickedness or cruelty: *Shooting prisoners of war is an atrocity*.

at·tach /ə'tætʃ/ *vt* **1** to fasten or join (something) (to another): *attach labels to the luggage; a house with a garage attached. Do you attach much importance to what he says?* **2** *be attached to sb/sth* to be fond of a person, house, sport etc: *She is very attached to her young brother*. **3** to join (an organization) as a member for a short time: *I am attached to the European delegation*.

at·taché /ə'tæʃeɪ/ *nc* a person who is attached to the staff of an ambassador: *the cultural/military/press attaché*.

attaché case /ə'tæʃɪ keɪs/ *nc* a small, flat, rectangular case for documents.

at·tach·ment /ə'tætʃmənt/ *n* **1** *nu* the act of joining or being joined. **2** *nc* something that is attached: *an attachment for an electric drill*. **3** *nc* a warm liking (for a person): *have an attachment for her*.

at·tack¹ /ə'tæk/ *nc* **1** a violent attempt to hurt or defeat: *make an attack on the enemy*. **2** a sudden beginning (of a pain, illness etc): *an attack of asthma; a heart attack*. **3** a continuous harmful effect: *an attack of dry rot in the roof*. **4** a piece of hostile criticism in speech or writing: *a strong attack against/on the government*. **5** (in sports and games) an offensive move: *an attack on the goal/ his backhand/the knights*.

at·tack² /ə'tæk/ *v* **1** *vt,vi* to make a violent attempt to hurt or defeat (a person, army etc): *to attack the enemy*. **2** *vt* (of pain, illness etc) to affect (a person, part of the body etc) (suddenly and) violently: *a disease that attacks children*. **3** *vt* to damage or harm (something) continuously: *Rust attacks metals. Alcohol attacks the liver*. **4** *vt* to criticize (a person, plan etc) severely: *to attack the government's economic policy*. **5** *vt,vi* (in sports and games) to make an offensive move in order to win: *to attack the goal/the defenders*.

at·tacker *nc* a person who attacks.

at·tain /ə'teɪn/ *vt* (*formal*) to achieve (the usual word): *attain one's hopes*.

at·tain·able /-əbl/ *adj* that can be attained. Opp unattainable.

at·tain·ment *nc,nu*

at·tempt¹ /ə'tempt/ *nc* an effort to do something: *He will make an attempt on the Olympic record. They made no attempt to escape. We were successful in our attempt at winning the championship/to rescue the survivors*.

at·tempt² /ə'tempt/ *vt* to make an effort (to do something): *The prisoners attempted to escape but failed*. Ⓝ *'Try'* can also be used and is less formal.

at·tend /ə'tend/ *v* **1** *vt* to go to (a meeting etc); be present at (a gathering): *attend college/church/a meeting*. **2** *vi* **attend (to sth)** to give care and thought (to something): *attend to one's work. You're not attending* (= not listening, not paying attention). **3** *vt* (*formal*) to be of service to, look after, (a person): *Which doctor is attending you?*

at·tend·ance /ə'tendəns/ *n* **1** *nu* the state being present: *The boy was given a prize for regular attendance* (= for attending school regularly). **2** *nc* (used with adjectives) a number of people

present: *There was a large/poor attendance at the meeting*. **3** *nu* **in attendance** looking after or seeing to people: *The doctor is no longer in attendance*. ⇨ tend¹

at·tend·ant /ə'tendənt/ *nc* a person who looks after another person or a place: *an attendant in an art gallery*.

at·ten·tion /ə'tenʃn/ *nu* **1** the act of directing one's thoughts by looking and listening: *Give me your full attention*. **attract attention** (of behaviour, beauty etc) to cause a person to look or listen (and respond): *He shouted to attract attention*. **bring/call/draw sb's attention to sth** to direct a person's thoughts to something deliberately: *Let me draw your attention to the regulations*. **come to the attention of sb/sth** to be noticed by a person, group: *She has come to the attention of the social services*. **pay attention (to sb/sth)** to look and listen carefully (to): *Pay attention (to me/what you're doing)*. **2** particular and detailed care or treatment: *Children need a lot of care and attention. This old house has had no attention for years*. **3** (*mil*) the position in which a soldier etc stands straight and still.

at·tent·ive /ə'tentɪv/ *adj* looking and listening carefully: *an attentive audience*. Opp inattentive.
at·tent·ive·ly *adv*: *listen attentively*.

at·test /ə'test/ *vt,vi* **attest (to) sth** (*formal*) to be or give clear proof of something: *achievements which attest to his determination*.

at·tic /'ætɪk/ *nc* a space inside the roof of a house: *two small rooms in the attic*.

at·tire /ə'taɪə(r)/ *nu* (*literary*) clothes.

at·ti·tude /'ætɪtjuːd/ *nc* **1** a way of feeling, thinking or behaving: *What is your attitude towards this problem?* (= What do you think about it and what would you do?) **2** a way of placing or holding the body: *He stood there in a threatening attitude*.

at·tract /ə'trækt/ *v* **1** *vt* to cause a feeling of pleasure, liking etc in (a person): *I'm very attracted to her/by her beauty*. Opp repel(2). **2** *vt* to cause a person, animal, thing to be noticed by (a person, animal): *Male birds are colourful in order to attract female birds*. **3** *vt,vi* (to cause a person, animal, thing) to move towards a person, thing: *Light attracts moths. Dirt attracts disease. Magnets attract metals. Like poles* (= Similar poles¹(2) of a magnet) *repel and unlike poles* (= opposite poles¹(2)) *attract*. Opp repel(1).

at·trac·tion /ə'trækʃn/ *n* **1** *nu* the strong feeling of being pulled towards: *He cannot resist the attraction of the sea on a hot day/of a pretty girl*. **2** *nc* something which attracts: *the attractions of a big city*, (e.g. concerts, cinemas, large shops). **3** *nu* (*physics*) the tendency of bodies to attract each other. Opp repulsion(2).

at·trac·tive /ə'træktɪv/ *adj* having the power to cause pleasure, liking etc: *a most attractive girl; attractive prices*. Opp unattractive.
at·trac·tive·ly *adv*

attrib *abbr* (*gram*) attributive.

at·tribute¹ /'ætrɪbjuːt/ *nc* a quality considered to belong naturally or necessarily to a person or thing: *A sense of humour is an essential attribute for happiness in life*.

at·tribute² /ə'trɪbjuːt/ *vt* **attribute sth to sb/ sth 1** to consider something as being the result of, as coming from a person, thing: *He attributes* *his success to hard work.* **2** to consider a person as the author etc of something: *Shakespeare's plays have sometimes been attributed to other writers.*

at·tribu·tive /ə'trɪbjʊtɪv/ *adj* (*gram*) (of adjectives) placed before the noun, as in 'a *burnt* hamburger.' Ⓝ Marked (*attrib*) in this dictionary. Compare predicative.

at·tune /ə'tjuːn/ *vt* (usually *passive*) to cause (a person) to become used to something: *It is not easy for many Europeans to become attuned to Chinese music.*

a·typi·cal /ˌeɪ'tɪpɪkl/ *adj* (*tech*) not typical; not the usual or normal type: *atypical behaviour.*

au·ber·gine /'əʊbəʒiːn/ *nc* (also *eggplant*) a white fruit with a purple skin, used as a vegetable.

au·burn /'ɔːbən/ *adj* (usually of hair) reddish-brown.

auc·tion /'ɔːkʃn/ *nc,nu* a public meeting at which goods are sold to the person offering the most money. **by auction** in an auction: *The house will be sold by auction.* □ *vt* **auction sth (off)** to sell something by auction.

auc·tion·eer /ˌɔːkʃə'nɪə(r)/ *nc* a person in charge of an auction.

au·da·cious /ɔː'deɪʃəs/ *adj* (*formal; often derog*) daring (esp in a rude way).
au·da·cious·ly *adv*

au·dac·ity /ɔː'dæsətɪ/ *nu* bold rudeness: *He had the audacity to ask me for a loan!*

au·dible /'ɔːdəbl/ *adj* loud enough to be heard: *The speaker was scarcely audible.* Opp inaudible.
au·dibly /-əblɪ/ *adv*

au·di·ence /'ɔːdɪəns/ *nc* **1** a gathering to see a play, hear a speaker, singer etc: *There was a large audience at the pop concert. This audience is a big one.* **2** people watching, reading etc: *Television has an audience of several million. His book has reached a wide* (= large and varied) *audience.* **3** a formal interview given by an important person: *The Pope granted him an audience.*

au·dio-vis·ual /ˌɔːdɪəʊ 'vɪʒʊəl/ *adj* of, using, sound and sight: *audio-visual aids* (i.e. teaching aids such as tapes and video).

au·dit /'ɔːdɪt/ *nc* an official examination of accounts to see that they are correct and organized. □ *vt* to examine (accounts) officially.

aud·ition /ɔː'dɪʃn/ *nc* a test given to a musician, singer or actor wishing to take part in a performance. □ *vt* to give an audition to (a person).

audi·tor /'ɔːdɪtə(r)/ *nc* a person who audits accounts.

audi·tor·ium /ˌɔːdɪ'tɔːrɪəm/ *nc* (*pl* —**s**) a part of a building in which an audience sits.

audi·tory /'ɔːdɪtrɪ/ *adj* (*attrib*) (*tech*) of the sense of hearing: *the auditory nerve.*

Aug *abbr* August.

aug·ment /ɔːg'ment/ *vt,vi* (*formal*) (to cause an income, group etc) to become larger or better: *augment one's income by writing short stories.*

au·gur /'ɔːgə(r)/ *vi* **augur ill/well for sb/sth** (*formal*) to be a sign that something will develop badly/well: *Their quarrels augur ill for their marriage.*

au·gust /ɔː'gʌst/ *adj* (*formal*) causing feelings of respect or awe: *an august professor.*

Au·gust /'ɔːgəst/ *n* (also *attrib*) the eighth month, with 31 days: *the August holidays. They're coming on 2 August.* Ⓝ '2 August' is spoken as

'August the second' or 'the second of August'.

aunt /ɑːnt/ *nc* **1** a sister of one's father or mother. **2** the wife of one's uncle.

aun·tie /'ɑːntɪ/ *nc* (*informal*) aunt.

au pair /ˌəʊ'peə(r)/ *adj, nc* (*Fr*) (in GB) (of) a young woman from overseas who, in return for light household duties, receives board and lodging, and facilities for study.

au·ra /'ɔːrə/ *nc* (*pl* —**s**) a feeling surrounding a person or object thought to be the cause of it: *There seemed to be an aura of holiness about the Indian saint.*

au·ral /'ɔːrəl/ *adj* (*attrib*) relating to hearing or the ears: *aural comprehension; an aural surgeon.* Compare oral.

au re·voir /ˌəʊ rə'vwɑː(r)/ *int* (*Fr*) till we meet again; goodbye.

aur·icle /'ɔːrɪkl/ *nc* (*anat*) **1** the external part of the ear. **2** either of the two upper cavities of the heart.

aus·pices /'ɔːspɪsɪz/ *n pl* **under the auspices of sth** helped and encouraged by something: *a conference held under the auspices of the British Council.*

aus·pi·cious /ɔː'spɪʃəs/ *adj* showing signs of future success. Opp inauspicious.
aus·pi·cious·ly *adv*

aus·tere /ɔː'stɪə(r)/ *adj* **1** (of a person, behaviour) severely moral and strict. **2** (of a way of living or of places, styles) simple and plain; without ornament or comfort.
aus·tere·ly *adv*
aus·ter·ity /ɔː'sterətɪ/ *nu*

au·then·tic /ɔː'θentɪk/ *adj* genuine; known to be true: *an authentic signature.* Opp unauthentic.
au·then·ti·cal·ly /-klɪ/ *adv*

au·then·ti·cate /ɔː'θentɪkeɪt/ *vt* (*formal*) to prove beyond doubt the origin etc of (something): *authenticate a signature.*
au·then·ti·ca·tion /ɔːˌθentɪ'keɪʃn/ *nu*

au·then·tic·ity /ˌɔːθen'tɪsətɪ/ *nu* the quality of being genuine: *feel confident about the authenticity of a signature.*

au·thor /'ɔːθə(r)/ *nc* a writer of a book, play etc: *Dickens is his favourite author.*

au·thor·ess /'ɔːθərɪs/ *nc* a woman author.

au·thor·i·tar·ian /ɔːˌθɒrɪ'teərɪən/ *adj* (often *derog*) favouring the power of authority more than personal freedom of choice. □ *nc* a supporter of this principle.

au·thori·ta·tive /ɔː'θɒrɪtətɪv/ *adj* **1** having or showing authority: *in an authoritative manner.* **2** that can be trusted because from a reliable source: *an authoritative report.*
au·thori·tat·ive·ly *adv*

au·thor·ity /ɔː'θɒrətɪ/ *n* (*pl* -**ies**) **1** *nu* the (legal) power or right to control, give orders and make others obey: *Who is in authority here? Only the treasurer has authority to make payments.* **2** *nc* a person or (*pl*) group of people having authority(1): *the health authorities.* **3** *nc* a person, book etc supplying reliable and detailed information or evidence: *She is a leading authority on the nerve structure of the housefly.*

au·thor·ize (also -**ise**) /'ɔːθəraɪz/ *vt* **1** to give (legal) power to or right of control to (a person): *I have authorized him to act for me while I am abroad.* **2** to give permission for (something):

The Finance Committee authorized the spending of £100 000 on a new sports ground.

au·thor·iz·ation (also **-is·ation**) /ˌɔːθəraɪ-ˈzeɪʃn/ *nu*

au·thor·ship /ˈɔːθəʃɪp/ *nu* (the person responsible for) the origin of a book etc: *Nothing is known of the authorship of the book.*

au·to·bio·graphi·cal /ˌɔːtəˌbaɪəˈɡræfɪkl/ *adj* (consisting) of autobiography.

au·to·bi·ogra·phy /ˌɔːtəʊˌbaɪˈɒɡrəfɪ/ *n* (*pl* **-ies**) **1** *nc* a story of a person's life written by herself or himself. **2** *nu* the art and practice of this sort of writing.

au·toc·racy /ɔːˈtɒkrəsɪ/ *n* (*pl* **-ies**) **1** *nu* government by a ruler who has unlimited power. **2** *nc* (a country with) a government having unlimited power.

au·to·crat /ˈɔːtəkræt/ *nc* **1** a ruler with unlimited power. **2** (*informal; derog*) a person who gives orders without considering the wishes of others.

au·to·crat·ic /ˌɔːtəˈkrætɪk/ *adj*
au·to·crati·cal·ly /-klɪ/ *adv*

au·to·graph /ˈɔːtəɡrɑːf/ *nc* a person's signature. □ *vt* to write one's name on or in (something): *a book autographed by the author.*

au·to·mated /ˈɔːtəmeɪtɪd/ *adj* using automation: *an automated manufacturing process.*

au·to·mat·ic /ˌɔːtəˈmætɪk/ *adj* **1** (of a machine etc) able to work or be operated without attention: *an automatic washing-machine; the automatic renewal of an insurance policy each year.* **2** (of an action) done without thought; unconscious: *Breathing is automatic.*

au·to·mati·cal·ly /-klɪ/ *adv*

au·to·ma·tion /ˌɔːtəˈmeɪʃn/ *nu* the use of machines needing little or no attention in industry.

au·to·mo·bile /ˈɔːtəməbiːl/ *nc* (esp *US*) = motor car.

au·ton·omous /ɔːˈtɒnəməs/ *adj* (of states) self-governing.

au·ton·omy /ɔːˈtɒnəmɪ/ *nu* self-government.

au·top·sy /ˈɔːtɒpsɪ/ *nc* (*pl* **-ies**) (*med*) an examination of a body (by cutting it open) to learn the cause of death.

au·tumn /ˈɔːtəm/ *nc* (also *attrib*) the season of the year between summer and winter: *autumn weather; during/in autumn.* (*US* = *fall*).

au·tum·nal /ɔːˈtʌmnəl/ *adj* of autumn.

aux·ili·ary /ɔːɡˈzɪlɪərɪ/ *adj* giving additional help or support: *auxiliary staff/textbooks.*

au‚xiliary 'verb *nc* (*gram*) a verb (*be*, *do* or *have*) used with another verb to make tenses, to form the passive etc, as in *I am waiting*, *It was sold yesterday*, *Does he need it? I've waited an hour.* ⇨ also modal auxiliary verb. Ⓝ An '*auxiliary verb*' is sometimes used on its own in short answers, as in '*You look well*'—'*Yes, I am*', after '*so*' and '*neither/ nor*', as in *She hates spinach and so do I*, and to avoid repeating the main verb, as in '*Please brush your teeth*'—'*I have*'.

AV /ˌeɪ ˈviː/ *abbr* audio-visual.

Av. *abbr* Avenue.

avail¹ /əˈveɪl/ *nu* (*formal*) **of no/little avail** not helpful; not effective: *His intervention was of little avail.* **to no avail** without result; unsuccessfully: *We pulled him out of the river and tried to revive him, but to no avail.*

avail² /əˈveɪl/ *v reflex* **avail oneself of sth** (*formal*) to make use of, take advantage of, something: *You should avail yourself of every opportunity to practise speaking English.*

avail·able /əˈveɪləbl/ *adj* that may be used, seen or obtained: *There were no tickets available for Friday's performance.* Opp unavailable.

avail·abil·ity /əˌveɪləˈbɪlətɪ/ *nu*

ava·lanche /ˈævəlɑːnʃ/ *nc* **1** a large mass of snow and ice sliding down a mountain side. **2** (*fig*) a large amount: *an avalanche of words/letters/ questions.*

avant-garde /ˌævɒŋˈɡɑːd/ *adj* (*Fr*) of, produced by, a person using the latest or most original ideas (in art, drama, literature etc): *Writing with innovations in technique or ideas is avant-garde.*

av·ar·ice /ˈævərɪs/ *nu* (*formal*) greed (the usual word).

av·ar·icious /ˌævəˈrɪʃəs/ *adj* (*formal; derog*) greedy.

av·ar·icious·ly *adv*

Ave. *abbr* Avenue.

avenge /əˈvendʒ/ *vt* (often *reflex*) (*formal*) to get or take revenge for (oneself) for (something): *avenge an insult. He avenged himself on the murderers for his daughter's death.*

av·enue /ˈævənjuː/ *nc* **1** a road with trees on each side, esp a private road to a large country house. **2** (A- in names) a wide street with buildings on one or both sides. **3** (*fig*) a way to achieve something: *avenues to success/promotion.*

av·er·age¹ /ˈævərɪdʒ/ *adj* **1** (*attrib*) found by making an average: *The average age of the boys in this class is fifteen.* **2** (often *derog*) of the ordinary or usual standard: *boys of average ability.*

av·er·age² /ˈævərɪdʒ/ *nc* **1** the result of adding several quantities together and dividing the total by the number of quantities: *The average of 2, 3 and 10 is 5.* Compare mean³(2). **on average** taking the average over a period: *We sleep six hours a night on average.* **2** a standard or level regarded as ordinary or usual: *Tom's work at school is above/below (the) average.*

av·er·age³ /ˈævərɪdʒ/ *vt* **1** to find the average of (quantities): *If you average 7, 14 and 6, you get 9.* **2** to amount to (an amount mentioned) as an average: *averaging 200 miles a day in the car. My expenses average (out at) £20 a month.*

averse /əˈvɜːs/ *adj* (*pred*) **averse to sth** (*formal*) opposed to something: *He is averse to hard work.*

aver·sion /əˈvɜːʃn/ *n* **1** *nc,nu* a strong dislike: *He has a strong aversion to getting up early.* **2** *nc* something or a person that is disliked: *That's my pet aversion* (something I specially dislike).

avert /əˈvɜːt/ *vt* (*formal*) **1** to turn away (one's eyes etc): *avert one's eyes/gaze from a terrible spectacle.* **2** to prevent, avoid, (something): *avert an accident.*

avi·ary /ˈeɪvɪərɪ/ *nc* (*pl* **-ies**) a place for keeping birds, e.g. in a zoo.

avi·ation /ˌeɪvɪˈeɪʃn/ *nu* (the industry, science, of) flying aircraft.

avid /ˈævɪd/ *adj* (*formal*) eager, keen: *be avid for fame/applause; an avid bridge player.*

avid·ly *adv*

avo·cado /ˌævəˈkɑːdəʊ/ *nc* (*pl* **-s**) (also *attrib*) a pear-shaped tropical fruit with a **tough green**

skin: *avocado green; avocado soup*.

avoid /ə'vɔɪd/ *vt* to keep away from (something): *Try to avoid danger*.

avoid·able /-əbl/ *adj* that can be avoided. Opp unavoidable.

avoid·ance /-əns/ *nu* the act of avoiding something.

avoir·du·pois /ˌævədə'pɔɪz/ *nu* the system of weights used, before metrication, in most English-speaking countries (1 pound = 16 ounces), used for all goods except precious metals and stones, and medicines.

avow /ə'vaʊ/ *vt* (*formal*) to declare (something) openly: *He avowed that he was not a thief*.

avow·al /ə'vaʊəl/ *nc,nu* (an instance of a) free and open confession.

await /ə'weɪt/ *vt* **1** (of a person) to wait for (something): *I await your instructions*. **2** to be waiting for (a person): *Death awaits all men*. Ⓝ *'Await' is always transitive, but 'wait' is usually intransitive*.

awake¹ /ə'weɪk/ *adj* (*pred*) not asleep; having woken: *He was lying awake thinking about her*. **awake to sth** fully aware of it: *be awake to danger*. **wide awake** ⇨ wide²(1).

awake² /ə'weɪk/ *vi* (*pt* **awoke** /ə'wəʊk/, *pp* **awoken** /ə'wəʊkən/) to wake up (which is more usual): *She awoke to find the children had gone*.

awak·en /ə'weɪkən/ *vi* (*formal*) = wake up.

awak·en·ing /ə'weɪknɪŋ/ *nc* an act of becoming aware, of realizing, esp something unpleasant: *It was a rude awakening to arrive at work and be told that he was to be dismissed*.

award¹ /ə'wɔːd/ *nc* **1** something given as the result of an official decision, e.g. a prize in a competition. **2** a decision made by a judge: *an award for damages*.

award² /ə'wɔːd/ *vt* to give or grant (something) (by official decision): *He was awarded the first prize*.

aware /ə'weə(r)/ *adj* (*pred*) **aware (of sth/ that . . .)** having knowledge of, conscious of, something: *We are fully aware of the facts*.

aware·ness *nu*

away¹ /ə'weɪ/ *adj* **1 away (from sth)** (*pred*) not present at something: *away from school*. **2** (*pred*) having begun: *They were up and away before dawn*. **3** (*attrib*) (*sport*) played on the opponent's ground: *an away match*. Compare home¹(3).

away² /ə'weɪ/ *adverbial particle* Ⓝ For uses with verbs such as *come, do, get, go etc*, ⇨ the *verb* entries. **1 away (from sb/sth)** to or at a distance (from the person, place etc): *Please keep away (from the fire). They ran away (from the police). The sea is five miles away*. **away from it all** ⇨ all³(4). **far and away** ⇨ far²(2). **2** in or to the usual place: *Tidy your room and put your clothes away*. **3** with the result of gradually being gone, less, weaker etc: *boil away; die away; give away*. **4** continuously: *working away; chatting away*. **5** without delay: *right/straight away* (= immediately). **6 away with sb/sth** (used in exclamations without a verb): *Away with them!* (= Take them away!)

awe /ɔː/ *nu* a feeling of amazement, fear and respect: *We looked up at the pyramids filled with awe at the achievement of the ancient Egyptians*. ⇨ overawe.

'awe-inspiring *adj* causing awe: *Mount Everest is an awe-inspiring sight*.

'awe·some /-səm/ *adj* causing awe.

'awe-struck *adj* (*pred*) filled with awe.

aw·ful /'ɔːfəl/ *adj* **1** terrible; dreadful: *He died an awful death*. **2** (*informal*) very bad; extreme of its kind: *What an awful nuisance! Why this awful hurry? What awful handwriting/weather!*

aw·ful·ly /'ɔːflɪ/ *adv* very (much): *It has been awfully hot this week. I'm awfully sorry/pleased. Thanks awfully*.

awhile /ə'waɪl/ *adv* (*literary*) for a short time.

awk·ward /'ɔːkwəd/ *adj* **1** (of living things) clumsy; having little skill: *Some animals are awkward on land but able to move easily in the water*. **2** (of an object, place etc) not well designed for use; causing inconvenience, embarrassment or difficulty: *This is an awkward corner—there have been several road accidents here. 6 o'clock in the morning is an awkward time to come*. **an awkward customer** ⇨ customer(2). **an awkward silence** ⇨ silence¹(2).

awk·ward·ly *adv*

awk·ward·ness *nu*

awn·ing /'ɔːnɪŋ/ *nc* a covering against rain or sun, e.g. over a boat.

awoke /ə'wəʊk/ *pt* of awake².

awoken /ə'wəʊkən/ *pp* of awake².

axe¹ /æks/ *nc* (*pl* **axes** /'æksɪz/) a tool with a metal blade on a long handle, used for cutting down trees or splitting wood. **have an axe to grind** (*fig*) to have a special reason for wanting something to happen.

axe² /æks/ (*vt*) (often *passive*) to reduce (e.g. jobs, services): *His grant has been axed*.

ax·iom /'æksɪəm/ *nc* a true statement that is obvious, such as 'All humans are mortal'.

axio·mat·ic /ˌæksɪə'mætɪk/ *adj*

axis /'æksɪs/ *nc* (*pl* **axes** /'æksiːz/) **1** an imaginary line round which a turning object spins: *the earth's axis*. **2** a line that divides a figure into two symmetrical parts, e.g. the diameter of a circle. **3** (*maths*) a horizontal or vertical line used as a fixed reference in a graph: *the X and Y axes*.

axle /'æksl/ *nc* a bar or rod on which a pair of wheels turn.

ay (also **aye**) /aɪ/ *int* (*Scot; regional*) yes. □ *n* (*pl*) the people supporting a proposal: *The ays/ ayes have it* (= Those in favour are in the majority).

az·ure /'æʒə(r)/ *adj, nu* (*poetic*) bright blue (colour): *an azure sky*.

Bb

B, b /biː/ (*pl* **B's, b's** /biːz/) the second letter of the English alphabet.

b. *abbr* born.

B /biː/ *symbol* (used on) a pencil with a soft lead which produces a thick, dark line (also 2B, 3B etc on pencils with softer lead). Compare H, HB.

BA /ˌbiː'eɪ/ *abbr* **1** British Airways: *We'll fly BA to Delhi*. **2** Bachelor of Arts: *U.R. Bright, BA (Hons)*.

b. and b. (also **B & B**) /ˌbiː ənd 'biː/ *abbr* bed and breakfast. ⇨ bed¹(1).

baa /baː/ *nc, vi* (to make) a cry of a sheep or lamb.

babble¹ /'bæbl/ *nu* **1** talk that is difficult to understand (e.g. of a baby, people at a party). **2** the sound of water in a small river.

babble² /'bæbl/ *vi* **1** to talk quickly or unclearly so that it is difficult to understand (e.g. like a baby). **2** to make the sound of water in a small river: *a babbling stream*.

babe /beɪb/ *nc* **1** (*literary*) a baby. **2** (*US sl*) a girl or young woman.

ba·boon /bə'buːn/ *nc* a kind of large monkey of Africa and S Asia.

baby /'beɪbɪ/ *nc* (*pl* **-ies**) (also *attrib*) a very young child: *She has a baby boy/girl. Which of you is the baby* (= the youngest member) *of the family?*

baby 'grand *nc* a small grand piano.

baby·hood *nu* the state, period, of being a baby.

baby·ish *adj* (*derog*) of, like, a baby: *babyish behaviour.*

baby-minder *nc* a woman paid to look after a baby for long periods (e.g. while the mother is out working). Hence **baby-mind** *vi*

baby-sit·ter *nc* a person paid to look after a baby for a short time (e.g. while the parents are at the cinema). Hence **baby-sit** *vi* (**-tt-**).

bach·elor /'bætʃələ(r)/ *nc* **1** an unmarried man. Compare spinster. **2** (used as an *adj* (*attrib*)) of, suitable for, an unmarried person: *bachelor flats.*

Bachelor of 'Arts/'Science *nc* (*abbr* BA, BSc) (a person who has taken) the first university degree.

ba·cil·lus /bə'sɪləs/ *nc* (*pl* **bacilli** /-laɪ/) (*tech*) a kind of long bacteria, one of which causes disease.

back¹ /bæk/ *adj* (*attrib*) **1** of the part that is opposite or behind the front: *the back door; back teeth.* **2** earlier in time: *a back issue/number of a magazine.* **3** from an earlier agreed time: *back pay.* ⇨ back²(6).

back² /bæk/ *adverbial particle* Ⓝ For uses with verbs such as *come, get, go, put, set, take* etc, ⇨ the *verb* entries. **1** to or at the rear; away from the front: *Keep back from the flames! Stand back! Sit back in your seats.* **back and forth** away (from the front) and then in the opposite direction many times: *travel back and forth between home and work every day.* **back to front** (a) with the back part at the front: *You've got your sweater on back to front.* (b) confused: *Your ideas about the savings schemes are back to front.* **2** to, into, an earlier position: *You can go but be back soon. Please put the books back. She didn't need it so she gave it back* (again). Ⓝ *'Back again'* refers to an activity or movement opposite to an earlier one, as in *give it and take it back again, go and come back again. 'Again' can be omitted without changing the meaning. If the verb already refers to an activity or movement opposite to an earlier one, such as exchange, reappear, return, then back cannot be used, but again* (meaning 'once more') can, as in *The flowers will reappear again next year.* **3** in an earlier position (order or time): *back in chapter one; back in my student days/in 1985.* **4** in return: *Don't answer me back! Can I pay you back next week? Please call me back* (= telephone me) *tomorrow.* Ⓝ Be careful because the position of *'back'* can change the meaning of the sentence. Compare: *I'll call back later* (= I'll telephone you later) and *Please call me back* (= Please telephone me). **get/have one's own back (on sb)** ⇨ own². **5** (of time) in the past: *a few weeks back.* Ⓝ *'Ago'* is also possible, as in *a few weeks ago.* **6** (uses as an *adj* or *adv particle* in compounds):

back·bite *vi* to say things to damage a person's reputation.

back·chat *nu* (*informal*) (an exchange of) rude remarks.

back·'date *vt* to date (something) from an earlier agreed time: *backdate a wage increase.* ⇨ back¹(3).

back-door *adj* (*attrib*) (*fig*) dishonest: *back-door methods.*

back 'door *nc* the door at the back of a building. **through the back door** (*fig*) dishonestly.

back·'fire *vi* (a) (of a vehicle) to make a loud noise in the exhaust system or engine, of gas exploding. (b) (*fig*) (of a plan etc) to be unsuccessful and have an unpleasant result.

back·hand *nc* (*tennis* etc) a stroke with the back of the hand to the front.

back·'handed *adj* (*attrib*) not genuine: *a backhanded compliment.*

back·lash *n sing* a strong and unpleasant reaction (to a political or social condition).

back 'light *nc* (of a bike, car etc) a light at the back.

back·log *nc* work to be done but not yet dealt with.

back number *nc* (a) an earlier issue. ⇨ back¹(2). (b) (*fig; derog*) an old-fashioned person, method, machine etc.

back pay *nu* wages owed over a period of time.

back·pedal *vi* (a) (on a bicycle etc) to pedal backwards. (b) (*fig*) to reverse an earlier decision, promise, opinion etc.

back 'seat *nc* (of a vehicle) a seat behind the driver. **take a back seat** (*fig*) to stay deliberately in the background (during a discussion etc).

back·'stage *adj, adv* (*theatre*) in, to, the part behind the stage: *go backstage to meet the cast.*

back·track *vi* (*fig*) (a) to go back the way one came. (b) = back-pedal(b).

back·water¹ *adj* (*attrib*) old-fashioned: *backwater business methods.*

back·water² *nc* (*fig*) a place that is not affected by social or economic progress etc.

back·'yard *nc* a small area or garden behind a small house.

back³ /bæk/ *nc* **1** (of a person or animal) the part of the body behind the chest and stomach and between the neck and the top of the legs: *If you lie on your back you can look up at the sky. He sat on the horse's back.* **(flat) on one's back** (*fig*) ill and in bed. **be glad to see the back of sb** to be pleased when he or she has gone away. **do sth/say sth/go behind sb's back** to do or say something that is harmful or critical without her or his knowledge. **get/put sb's back up** to make her or him angry. **have/with one's back to the wall** (during an argument etc) to have/ having difficulty defending oneself, one's opinions etc. **put one's back into sth** to work very hard at it. **put one's back out** to injure one's back by accidentally moving a bone out of position. **turn one's back on sb** (a) to turn round rudely (and walk away). (b) (fig) to refuse to help her or him. **2** the part of any object, building, area, person, vehicle etc that is furthest from the front or from view: *at the back of a house/tennis court/queue/theatre/book/newspaper; in the back of a car/cupboard/drawer; on the back of a cheque/door; on the back of a motorbike* (i.e. as a passenger). **at the back of one's mind** vaguely in one's thoughts but not consciously aware. **the back of beyond** a place, area, very far away (and with very few people). **3** the part of a chair etc on which a person's back rests when sitting.

'**back·ache** *nc,nu* a pain in the back(1).

'**back·bone** *nc* (a) the long series of bones in the back(1). (b) (fig) strength of character: *He has no backbone.*

'**back·breaking** *adj* (attrib) (of work) exhausting.

'**back·pack** *vi, nc* (to have a walking holiday with) a bag carried on one's back used for clothes, sleeping-bag, food etc.

,**back·'side** *nc* the part of the body on which a person sits.

'**back·stroke** *nu* a style of swimming on one's back.

back⁴ /bæk/ *v* **1** *vt,vi* (to cause oneself, a vehicle etc) to move backwards: *backing (a car) down a narrow street.* **2** *vt* to give encouragement, money etc to (a person, business, idea, scheme); state one's agreement with (a person, opinion etc): *back a team/a friend in a contest; back a business with £10 000; back a colleague/his opinion at a meeting.* ⇨ back sb/sth up. **3** *vt* to accompany (a singer or musician) by playing music: *She has backed several famous pop singers.* **4** *vt* to put behind (something) as a lining or background: *curtains backed with cotton; green meadows backed by mountains.* **5** *vt* to put money on (a horse, person, team etc) to win: *to back the favourite/Liverpool (to win).*

back away (from sb/sth) to move away (from a person, thing) because of fear or dislike: *The crowd backed away as the body was uncovered.*

back down to withdraw an accusation, give up a claim etc: *The quarrel will never end until one of them backs down.*

back (sth) into sb/sth (a) to move (a vehicle) backwards into a person, thing: *back into a parking space.* (b) to move backwards and accidentally touch a person, thing: *I backed into her as I stepped off the bus.*

back off (a) to move backwards to avoid something. (b) (informal; imperative) Don't come so close!

back on/onto sth to have the back facing towards something: *the houses back onto a park.*

back out (of sth) to withdraw (from a promise, agreement etc): *You can't back out (of your promise) now that profits are low.*

back (sth) up to move (a vehicle) backwards: *The lorry was backing up when it hit a lamp-post.*

back sb/sth up to support a person, an opinion etc with encouragement, statistics, money, ability etc: *Thanks for backing me up at the meeting. We'll need expensive advertising to back up the new product.*

back·ground /'bækgraʊnd/ *nc* **1** the part of a view, picture etc that is at the back or behind the main objects, people etc. **in the background** deliberately away from being clearly seen or heard: *stay/keep in the background.* **2** (fig) a person's experiences, education etc (which helped to form her or his character): *her family/school/Italian background; a simple/poor background; a background of poverty/affluence.* **3** information for understanding, identifying or describing a situation: *the political/economic background.* **4** (also *attrib*) the general condition, sound etc: *background heating/lighting/music.*

back·ing /'bækɪŋ/ *n* **1** *nc,nu* (a group of people giving) support for opinions etc: *The new president has a large backing.* **2** *nu* music played for a pop singer. **3** *nc* material used to form the back of something else: *cloth with a backing of rubber.*

back·ward /'bækwəd/ *adj* **1** (attrib) towards the back or beginning: *a backward glance.* **a backward step** (esp *fig*) an action that stops or reverses progress. **2** making, having made, less than normal or expected progress (intellectually, economically etc): *a backward child; backward-looking* (= not using or encouraging progressive ideas) *policies/politicians.*

back·wards /'bækwədz/ (also **back·ward**) *adv* **1** away from one's front: *glance/look/stretch backwards.* ⇨ also lean³. Opp forwards. **2** (in a forward direction and) with the back or end first: *walk/drive backwards.* **3** in reverse order: *spell a word backwards; have a dress on backwards* (= with the back part at the front). ⇨ back to front at back²(1). **backwards and forwards** first in one direction (towards) and then the opposite (away from): *travelling backwards and forwards between home and school.* **know sth backwards** to know the words of a song, instructions etc very well. **4** (of health, culture, economy etc) in, into, a worse or less progressive state: *go backwards.*

ba·con /'beɪkən/ *nu* salted or smoked meat from the back or sides of a pig.

bac·teria /bæk'tɪərɪə/ *npl* (*sing* **bac·terium** /-rɪəm/) (tech) (kinds of) very small living things, many of which cause disease or help dead animals and plants to decay.

bac·ter·ial /bæk'tɪərɪəl/ *adj* of bacteria: *bacterial diseases.*

bad¹ /bæd/ *adj* (comp **worse;** superl **worst**) Ⓝ '*Good*' can mean the opposite of '*bad*', but only in definitions 1 to 6. **1** not pleasant or enjoyable: *bad news/weather/breath/manners; a bad dream; bad language* (= swearwords). ⇨ also name¹(1), temper¹. **2** of poor quality: *bad English/eyesight; a bad driver/actor/loser; a bad accent/memory/TV programme / performance / example / impression.* **be bad at sth** to show little or no ability: *be bad at maths/drawing.* **go from bad to worse** to become increasingly worse. **not bad** (used to express surprise) quite good: *This meal's really not bad!* **not (so) bad** (informal) only a little bad: *The weather's not so bad.* **not half bad** (informal) very good: *This book is not half bad!* **3** not suitable: *bad light/soil/conditions.* **4** (*no comp*) worthless: *a bad cheque.* ⇨ debt(1). **5** (of a person, behaviour) wicked: *bad thoughts; a bad boy. It's bad to steal.* **feel bad (about sth)** to be very sorry (about something): *I feel bad about being unable to help.* **6 bad for sb/sth** harmful to a person, thing: *Sugar is bad for you/your teeth/health/figure.* **7** (of an unpleasant experience) serious; extreme: *a bad headache/cold/mistake/accident.* **8** (*no comp*) (of parts of the body) in pain; injured: *a bad leg/finger.* **be in a bad way (a)** to be very ill. **(b)** to be in great difficulty. **9** (*no comp*) (of food) not fit to be eaten: *bad eggs/meat/fish/milk.* **go bad** to become unfit to be eaten. **10** (*informal*) unfortunate: *It's too bad I can't join you.* (used as a noun) *take the bad with the good* (= the bad fortune with the good fortune). ⇨ bad luck below.

,bad 'luck *nu* (used to show sympathy): *You missed the prize by one vote—what bad luck!*

,bad-'mannered *adj* behaving badly.

,bad-'tempered *adj* easily made angry.

bad·ness *nu* the quality of being bad(1): *the badness of the weather.*

bad² /bæd/ *n* ⇨ bad¹(10).

bade /bæd/ *pt* of bid³.

badge /bædʒ/ *nc* something (usually a design on cloth or a metal brooch) worn to show a person's occupation, rank etc or membership of a society.

badger¹ /'bædʒə(r)/ *nc* a kind of dark-grey furry animal living underground and going about at night.

badger² /'bædʒə(r)/ *vt* to worry or annoy (a person) with questions, requests etc: *Tom has been badgering his uncle to buy him a camera.*

bad·ly /'bædlɪ/ *adv* (*comp* **worse**; *superl* **worst**) Ⓝ *'Badly'* is always placed after the verb (and its direct object), as in *I cook (fish) badly,* or before a past participle, as in *This meal is badly cooked.* When *'badly + past participle'* is placed before the noun, a hyphen is used, as in *a badly-cooked meal.* *'Well'* can mean the opposite of *'badly',* but not in definitions 1 and 7. **1** (of unpleasant experiences) seriously; extremely: *aching badly; badly injured.* **badly off** extremely poor. **2** (of actions) done using little or no ability or effort: *badly built/made/judged/dressed; sing/write badly; speak English badly.* **3** not satisfactorily or well: *do badly in the exam; sleep badly.* **4** not suitably: *badly lit/situated.* **5** naughtily; wickedly: *behave badly; a badly-behaved girl.* **6** cruelly: *treat her badly.* **7** (of failure etc) by a very large amount: *lose badly; be badly beaten.* **need/want sth badly** to need/want it very much: *I need this job badly.*

bad·min·ton /'bædmɪntən/ *nu* an indoor game for two or four players who use rackets to hit a *shuttlecock* across a high net.

baffle /'bæfl/ *vt* to be too difficult for (a person) to do, understand etc: *One of the examination questions baffled me completely.*

bag¹ /bæg/ *nc* **1** a container made of paper, cloth, leather, plastic etc with an opening at the top, used for carrying things: *a paper bag; a travelling-bag; a handbag.* **2** (*pl*) **bags of sth** (*informal*) plenty of something: *There's bags of room. He has bags of money.*

bag² /bæg/ *v* (-gg-) **1** *vt* **bag sth (up)** to put something into a bag or bags: *to bag (up) wheat.* **2** *vt* to kill or catch (animals, esp for food): *They bagged nothing except a couple of rabbits.* **3** *vt* (*dated informal*) to take (somebody else's prop-

erty etc without permission, but not intending to steal): *Who's bagged my matches?* **4** *vi* to hang loosely: *trousers that bag at the knees.*

bag·gage /'bægɪdʒ/ *nu* luggage (the usual word).

bag·gy /'bægɪ/ *adj* (**-ier, -iest**) hanging loosely: *baggy trousers.*

bag·pipes /'bægpaɪps/ *n pl* (the —) a musical instrument with air stored in a bag held under one arm and pressed out through pipes to produce music.

bail¹ /beɪl/ *nu* a sum of money kept by a law court so that a person can be out of prison until her or his trial. **go bail for sb** to pay her or his bail. **jump (one's) bail** to fail to appear at a trial after bail has been paid. □ *vt* **bail sb out** to obtain her or his freedom by payment of bail.

bail² /beɪl/ *nc* (*cricket*) either of the two cross-pieces on the three stumps of a wicket.

bail³ /beɪl/ *vt,vi* **bail (sth) (out)** to throw water out of a boat using buckets etc: *bailing water (out).*

bail·iff /'beɪlɪf/ *nc* **1** a law officer (who takes goods etc from a person who owes money). **2** (*dated*) a landowner's agent or manager.

bait¹ /beɪt/ *nu* **1** food, or an imitation, used to attract fish or animals. **2** (*fig*) anything that attracts or tempts a person: *use low prices as bait.*

bait² /beɪt/ *vt* **1** to put food, real or imitation, on (a hook), in (a trap) to catch fish etc: *bait a hook with a worm.* **2** to make (a person) angry by using cruel or insulting remarks.

bake /beɪk/ *v* **1** *vt,vi* (of fish, vegetables, cakes etc) to cook, be cooked, by dry heat in an oven: *bake bread/potatoes/apples.* Compare roast³. **2** *vt* (to cause something) to become hard by heating: *The sun baked the ground hard.* **3** *vi* (*fig*) to become (too) warm: *We are baking in the sun.*

ba·ker /'beɪkə(r)/ *nc* a person, business, that bakes bread, cakes etc.

,baker's 'dozen *nc* (*informal*) thirteen.

ba·kery /'beɪkərɪ/ *nc* (*pl* **-ies**) a place where bread, cakes etc are made (and sold).

ba·king /'beɪkɪŋ/ *adj* (*attrib*) **1** (of temperature) very hot: *We had baking (hot) weather.* **2** used to bake food: *a baking-dish.*

'baking-powder *nu* a mixture used to produce air in bread, cakes etc.

bal·ance¹ /'bæləns/ *n* **1** *nc* a scientific instrument used for measuring mass (*weight*). **2** *nu* the condition existing when two opposite forces are equal: *the balance of power* (⇨ below). **in the balance** (of a result, decision) uncertain. **on balance** considering all the information etc (and deciding): *On balance it's a good story.* **3** *nu* the physical condition of standing without difficulty: *A gymnast needs a good sense of balance.* **keep/lose one's balance** to remain steady/become unsteady: *Babies learn to keep their balance when walking.* **4** *nu* the mental condition of thinking, deciding etc without difficulty: *She did it while her balance of mind was disturbed.* **5** *nc* (*accounts*) the difference between two sides of an account: *a negative balance* (= money is owed); *a positive balance* (= profit). **6** *nc* (the —) **(a)** an amount of money owed after part has been paid: *a deposit of £100 and the balance to be paid over two years.* **(b)** an amount left after some has been used: *the balance of my holiday.* Ⓝ *'Remainder'* or *'rest'* can also be used. ⇨ **imbalance. 7** *nu* (in art, literature, architecture etc) the state of order and equality in pattern, design, composition etc: *These trees give balance to the picture. There is a poor balance of major events during the action of the play.*

,balance of 'payments *nc* (*finance*) the difference between money brought into and taken out of a country.

,balance of 'power *nc* (*politics*) the deliberate organization of political and military strength between countries so that no individual country or group can threaten others.

,balance of 'trade *nc* (*finance*) the difference between the cost of imports and exports.

'balance sheet *nc* (*accounts*) a written statement showing income and costs. ⇨ balance¹(5).

bal·ance² /'bæləns/ *v* **1** *vi* to be in a state of balance(3): *balancing on a narrow ledge.* **2** *vt* to keep, put, (something) in a state of balance(3): *balance a book on your head.* **3** *vt* **balance sth against/with sth** to compare two explanations, ideas, opinions etc in order to decide the truth, the best etc: *balance going to the concert against/ with buying the record.* **4** *vt* (*accounts*) to find the difference between two sides of (an account) and record it: *balance the accounts/books.* **balance (each other) (out) (a)** (of both sides of an account) to be equal: *These books do not balance (out).* **(b)** to be equal: *Their experience and our enthusiasm balance each other (out).*

bal·anced /'bælənsd/ *adj* **1** (of a person's mental state) normal and healthy: *a balanced state of mind; a well-balanced person.* Opp unbalanced. **2** (usually *attrib*) (of a meal, way of living etc) with the correct amount and variety needed for good health: *a balanced diet/routine of work, rest and play.* **3** (*accounts*) (of both sides of an account) equal: *balanced accounts.*

bal·cony /'bælkənɪ/ *nc* (*pl* **-ies**) **1** (the —) the area with seats for people at the top of a theatre, cinema etc. **2** a platform (with a wall or rail) built on an outside wall of an upstairs room.

bald /bɔːld/ *adj* (**—er**, **—est**) **1** (of a man) having no or not much hair on the head. **2** (of an animal) hairless; (of a bird) without feathers. **3** (*fig*) without extra details, careful phrasing or exciting information: *a bald statement of the facts.*

bald·ness *nu*

bald·ly /'bɔːldlɪ/ *adv* (of a way of saying something) plainly (and often cruelly): *To put it baldly, you're useless!*

bale¹ /beɪl/ *nc* a heap of material pressed together and tied with rope or wire: *bales of cloth.* □*vt* to make (something) into bales.

bale² /beɪl/ *vi* **bale out (of sth)** to jump with a parachute (from an aircraft).

balk (also **baulk**) /bɔːk/ *v* **1** *vt* to get in the way of (a person, thing) deliberately: *balk a person's plans* (= prevent her or him from carrying them out). **2** *vi* **balk at sth** to hesitate because of something: *Her mother balked at the fees for the college.*

ball¹ /bɔːl/ *nc* **1** a round object used in games: *a football/tennis-ball/cricket-ball.* **be on the ball** to be alert, competent (in what one is doing). **keep/start the ball rolling** to continue/start the conversation, activity etc. **play ball (with sb)** (*informal*) (*fig*) to cooperate: *The manage-*

ment refused to play ball. **2** an amount of something gathered or rolled into a round mass: *a ball of wool/string: a snowball; a meatball.* **3** a round part: *the ball of the foot* (= near the bottom of the big toe).

ball² /bɔːl/ *nc* **1** a formal social gathering for dancing. **2 have a ball** (*informal*) to enjoy oneself a lot.

'ball-dress *nc* a woman's long dress to be worn at balls.

'ball·room *nc* a large room for dancing.

bal·lad /'bæləd/ *nc* (*literature*) a form of poetry for speaking or singing that tells a story.

bal·lade /bæ'lɑːd/ *nc* **1** (*literature*) a form of poetry with three verses (*stanzas*) followed by an explanatory verse, each ending with the same line. **2** (*music*) a composition (usually for the guitar or the piano) with a romantic theme.

bal·last /'bæləst/ *nu* heavy material (e.g. rock, iron, sand) put into a ship to keep it steady or used to make a road or a railway.

bal·ler·ina /,bælə'riːnə/ *nc* a woman ballet-dancer (esp who takes the main classical role).

bal·let /'bæleɪ/ *n* (also *attrib*) **1** *nc* (an example of) a dramatic performance by dancers to music: *ballet music.* **2** *nu* the art of performing ballet: *study at the Royal Ballet School.* **3** (the —) the profession, art, a company, of ballet-dancers.

'ballet-dancer *nc* a person who dances in ballets.

bal·lis·tics /bə'lɪstɪks/ *nu* the scientific study of bullets, rockets etc moving through air.

bal·loon /bə'luːn/ *nc* **1** a bag filled with air or with gas lighter than air. ⇨ hot-air balloon. **2** (in a cartoon etc) an outline for speech.

bal·loon·ist *nc* a person who flies in a hot-air balloon.

bal·loon² /bə'luːn/ *vi* **balloon (out)** to become round like a balloon: *with her sleeves ballooning (out) in the wind.*

bal·lot¹ /'bælət/ *n* **1** *nc* a piece of paper used to vote in secret. **2** *nc,nu* (an act of) voting in secret: *Let's put it to the ballot.* **3** *nc* the number of votes recorded.

'ballot-box *nc* a box used in a ballot.

'ballot-paper *nc* a ballot(1).

bal·lot² /'bælət/ *vi* to have a ballot(2).

ball·point /'bɔːlpɔɪnt/ *nc* (also *ballpoint pen*) a pen with a small ball in place of a nib which rolls ink onto paper.

balm /bɑːm/ *nu* an oil with a pleasant smell, used for soothing pain or healing.

balmy *adj* (**-ier**, **-iest**) (of air) soft and warm.

bal·us·ter /'bæləstə(r)/ *nc* one of the upright posts supporting a handrail.

bal·us·trade /,bælə'streɪd/ *nc* a row of stone or wooden banisters with a bar on top, built round a balcony etc.

bam·boo /,bæm'buː/ *nc,nu* (*pl* **—s**) (also *attrib*) a kind of tall plant of the grass family, with hard, hollow, jointed stems: *bamboo furniture.*

bam·boozle /bæm'buːzl/ *vt* (*informal*) to cheat, trick (a person): *bamboozling him into doing it/ out of it.*

ban¹ /bæn/ *nc* an official order that something must not be done: *a ban on smoking.*

ban² /bæn/ *vt* (**-nn-**) to order officially that (something) must not be done, said etc: *Advertising* *cigarettes should be banned.*

ba·nal /bə'nɑ:l/ *adj* without interest: *banal remarks.*

ba·na·na /bə'nɑ:nə/ *nc* (also *attrib*) a long, curved, thick-skinned (yellow when ripe) tropical fruit.

band¹ /bænd/ *nc* **1** a flat, thin piece of material used to fasten things or to strengthen something: *put a rubber band round the papers; a box with metal bands round it.* **2** a flat, thin piece of cloth forming part of an item of clothing: a *waistband/hat-band.* **3** a flat, thin area round or across something which is a different colour etc: *a band of white round her dress; a band of cloud across the sky.* **4** a group or series with the same value, number, ability, quality etc: *be placed in the senior band.* **5** (*radio*) a range of sound frequencies: *the long/medium/short waveband.*

band² /bænd/ *nc* **1** a group of musicians who play jazz, pop music etc: *a dance/jazz band.* **2** a group of musicians who play the same kinds of instruments: *a brass/steel band.* **3** an organized group of people for a particular purpose: *a band of robbers/protesters.*

'band·stand *nc* an outside platform with a roof where a band²(1,2) plays: *the bandstand in the park.*

'band·wagon *nc jump on the bandwagon* to do something because other people are doing it or because success is almost certain.

band³ /bænd/ *vi band together* to join together for a particular purpose: *banding together in protest.*

ban·dage /'bændɪdʒ/ *nc* a long, thin piece of material used for binding round a wound or injury. □ *vt* to wrap (a part of the body, a wound) in a bandage.

ban·dit /'bændɪt/ *nc* an armed robber, esp one who attacks travellers.

ban·dy¹ /'bændɪ/ *adj* (-ier, -iest) (of the legs) curving outwards at the knees.

ban·dy² /'bændɪ/ *vt bandy words (with sb)* (*dated*) to quarrel. *have one's name bandied about* to be talked about in an unfavourable way.

bang¹ /bæŋ/ *adv* **1** *go bang* to explode with a loud noise. **2** (used with another adv or a prep) *bang in the middle (of sth)* exactly in the middle. *bang on sth* (*informal*) exactly at; at the exact time: *bang on 6 o'clock/on time.*

bang² /bæŋ/ *nc* **1** a sudden violent blow: *He fell and got a nasty bang on the head.* **2** a short loud noise: *He always shuts the door with a bang.*

bang³ /bæŋ/ *v* **1** *vt* to hit (something) with force: *She banged her toe on the step. He banged his fist on the table/banged in the nail with a hammer.* **2** *vt,vi* (to cause a door, lid etc) to close with a loud noise: *The door banged shut. Don't bang the lid down.* **3** *vi bang about sth* to make many loud noises (as when angry, clumsy etc): *She banged about the room. bang at sth* to make a series of loud hits: *banging at the door.*

bang·er /'bæŋə(r)/ *nc* (*sl*) **1** a sausage. **2** a noisy firework. **3** an old, worn-out car.

bangle /'bæŋgl/ *nc* a band worn round the arm or ankle as jewellery.

ban·ish /'bænɪʃ/ *vt* **1** to send (a person) away, esp out of a city, country etc as a punishment: *He was*

banished from the city. **2** to put (thoughts) out of one's mind: *banish any idea of losing.*

ban·ish·ment *nu*

ban·is·ters /'bænɪstəz/ *n pl* posts with a piece across the top on the outer edge of a staircase.

ban·jo /bæn'dʒəʊ/ *nc* (*pl* —**s** or —**es**) a kind of stringed musical instrument with a round body.

bank¹ /bæŋk/ *nc* **1** a business for keeping money which is paid out when its customers write cheques: *have money in the bank.* ⇨ run¹(6). **2** a place for storing blood etc for medical use: *a blood bank.*

'bank account *nc* an arrangement for keeping money in a bank.

'bank balance *nc* (a statement of) the amount remaining or owed in a bank account.

'bank card *nc* a plastic card with which a customer can use her or his bank account at a machine outside a bank.

'bank clerk *nc* a person who serves customers in a bank.

'bank draft *nc* an order sent from one bank to another for issuing money to a customer.

,bank 'holiday *nc* a day (except Sundays) when banks are closed by law.

'bank·note *nc* a piece of paper money .

'bank robber *nc* a person who steals money from a bank.

bank² /bæŋk/ *nc* **1** the land along each side of a river, lake etc. **2** an area of sloping land forming a border or division: *There were flowers growing on the banks on each side of the country lanes.* **3** a mass of cloud, snow etc: *The sun went down behind a bank of clouds.* ⇨ sandbank.

bank³ /bæŋk/ *v* **1** *vt* to put (money) in a bank¹(1). **2** *vi bank with sth* to have a bank account with a particular bank: *Who do you bank with?* **3** *vt bank on sth* (*informal*) to depend on something: *Can I bank on your cooperation?*

bank⁴ /bæŋk/ *v* **1** *vt bank sth up* to form something into a heap: *bank up the snow/(wood in) the fire.* **2** *vi* (of a car, plane) to travel with one side higher than the other (e.g. round a corner).

bank·er /'bæŋkə(r)/ *nc* a person who manages or owns a bank¹(1).

,banker's 'order *nc* an instruction for a bank to pay money at regular intervals (e.g. to pay off a house loan).

bank·ing /'bæŋkɪŋ/ *nu* **1** the business of keeping a bank¹(1): *Banking hours are 9 am to 3.30 pm.* **2** the act of using a bank¹(1): *Where do you do your banking?*

bank·rupt¹ /'bæŋkrʌpt/ *adj* **1** unable to pay one's debts. **2** (*fig*) completely without: *He was bankrupt of ideas.*

bank·rupt² /'bæŋkrʌpt/ *nc* (*legal*) a person judged by a law court to be unable to pay her or his debts.

bank·rupt³ /'bæŋkrʌpt/ *vt* to make (a person, business) bankrupt.

bank·rupt·cy /'bæŋkrəpsɪ/ *nc,nu* (*pl* -**ies**) (an instance of) being bankrupt.

ban·ner /'bænə(r)/ *nc* a piece of cloth with a written announcement, usually fixed to two poles, e.g. carried in political demonstrations.

banns /bænz/ *n pl* (the —) a public announcement in church that two people are to be married: *put up/publish the banns.*

ban·quet /'bæŋkwɪt/ *nc* a formal and grand meal at which speeches are made: *a wedding banquet*.

ban·tam /'bæntəm/ *nc* (also *attrib*) **1** a kind of small chicken. **2** a boxer weighing between 112 and 118 lb (51 and 53·5 kg).

ban·ter /'bæntə(r)/ *nu* amusing and gentle teasing. □ *vt,vi* to tease (a person), talk, in a playful way.

bao·bab /'beɪəbæb/ *nc* (also *attrib*) a kind of tree of tropical Africa with a trunk that grows to an enormous size.

bap·tism /'bæptɪzəm/ *nc,nu* (an instance of) the Christian ceremony of touching a person with, or putting a person in, water, to show that he or she is accepted as a member of the Church.
bap·tis·mal /bæp'tɪzməl/ *adj*

Bap·tist /'bæptɪst/ *nc* a Christian who believes that baptism should happen when a person is old enough to understand the meaning of the ceremony.

bap·tize (also **-ise**) /bæp'taɪz/ *vt* to give baptism to (a person): *He had been baptized a Roman Catholic*.

bar¹ /bɑ:(r)/ *nc* **1** a (long, narrow) piece of hard material: *an iron bar; a bar of chocolate/soap; the bars of an electric fire. Gymnasts exercise on the high bar/the parallel bars.* ⇨ crossbar. **2** a length of metal or wood across a window, door etc (e.g. in a prison). **behind bars** (*informal*) in prison. **3** (*fig*) something that is an obstacle or barrier: *Poor eyesight is a bar to becoming a pilot.* **4** a room, counter, where alcoholic drinks are sold: *the hotel/saloon bar.* **5** a small café where hot drinks and snacks are served: *a coffee/sandwich/snack bar.* **6** a long heap of sand where a river joins the sea across the entrance to a bay. **7** a long, thin area of colour, light etc: *a bar of red across the sky.* **8** (*legal*) the area in a law court for the judges and barristers separated from the general public. **be called to the Bar** to become a barrister. **9** (*music*) (**a**) a vertical line drawn to divide written notes into groups (beats of the same value). (**b**) the group of beats (to be) repeated to create rhythm: *four beats to the bar.*
'bar·maid *nc* a woman who works in a bar(4).
'bar·man *nc* a man who works in a bar(4).

bar² /bɑ:(r)/ *vt* (**-rr-**) **1** to fasten (a door, gate etc) with a bar or bars¹(2). **2** to keep (oneself, a person) in or out: *He barred himself in* (= fastened doors, windows, etc so that no-one could enter the building). **3** to form a barrier or obstacle across (a route): *The fallen tree was barring the way.* **4** to ban (a person): *bar a person from a competition* (= order that he or she shall not take part).

bar³ /bɑ:(r)/ *prep* except: *We all went bar Mary who was ill.* **bar none** without any exceptions. **bar one** except one. ⇨ shouting.

barb /bɑ:b/ *nc* a curving point of an arrow, spear, fish-hook etc.
barb·ed *adj* having a barb or barbs: *barbed wire* (= wire with short, sharp points at intervals).

bar·bar·ian /bɑ:'beərɪən/ *nc* (*derog*) an uncultured person.

bar·bar·ic /bɑ:'bærɪk/ *adj* (*derog*) cruel, uncultured: *barbaric ideas/punishments/behaviour.*
bar·bar·i·cal·ly *adv*

bar·bar·ity /bɑ:'bærətɪ/ *nc,nu* (*pl* **-ies**) (an

instance of) extreme cruelty: *the barbarities of modern warfare* (e.g. bombing cities).

bar·bar·ous /'bɑ:bərəs/ *adj* (*derog*) extremely cruel: *barbarous weapons.*
bar·bar·ous·ly *adv*

bar·be·cue¹ /'bɑ:bɪkju:/ *nc* **1** a social occasion at which food is cooked over a fire outdoors. **2** a structure used to cook outdoors.

bar·be·cue² /'bɑ:bɪkju:/ *vt* to cook (meat, fish etc) over a fire outdoors.

bar·ber /'bɑ:bə(r)/ *nc* a person who cuts men's hair (now called a *men's hairdresser*).

bar·bitu·rate /bɑ:'bɪtjʊrət/ *nc,nu* (*med*) a (kind of) drug used to calm a person's nerves and to cause sleep.

bard /bɑ:d/ *nc* (*literary*) a poet: *the Bard of Avon* (= William Shakespeare).

bare¹ /beə(r)/ *adj* (**—r, —st**) **1** without clothing, covering, protection or decoration: *bare floors* (= without carpets etc); *a bare hillside* (= without shrubs or trees); *in his bare skin* (= naked). **2** (*attrib; no comp*) not more than: *the bare necessities of life* (= things needed just to keep alive); *earn a bare living* (= only just enough money to live on); *approved by a bare majority* (= a very small one).
'bare·back *adv* (of a horse) ridden without a saddle: *ride bareback.*
'bare·faced *adj* (*attrib*) shameless; undisguised: *a barefaced lie. It's barefaced robbery to ask £25 for such an old bicycle!*
'bare·foot *adj,adv* without shoes and socks: *be/go/walk barefoot; barefoot children.*
,bare·'footed *adj* with bare feet.
,bare·'headed *adj* not wearing a hat.
,bare in'finitive *nc* (*gram*) the infinitive form of a verb without *to*, as in 'I can *swim*'.

bare² /beə(r)/ *vt* to uncover, show, (something): *bare one's head* (= take one's hat off). **bare one's heart (to sb)** ⇨ heart(2). **bare one's teeth** ⇨ tooth(1).

bare·ly /'beəlɪ/ *adv* only a very little: *We barely had time to catch the train. There was barely any food left.* Compare hardly(1), just²(4), scarcely.

bar·gain¹ /'bɑ:gən/ *nc* **1** an agreement to buy, sell or exchange something (often made after discussion). **a good/bad bargain** one that favours/does not favour oneself. **into the bargain** as well; in addition: *She lost her handbag and her cheque book into the bargain.* **drive a hard bargain** to try to obtain a business agreement very favourable to oneself. **make/strike a bargain with sb** to reach agreement. **2** (also *attrib*) something offered, sold or bought cheap: *a bargain basement* (= the section of a shop where goods are offered at reduced prices); *a bargain price* (= a low one).

bar·gain² /'bɑ:gən/ *v* **1** *vi* to talk in order to reach an agreement (about buying or selling, doing a piece of work etc): *We bargained with the farmer for permission to camp on his land.* **2** *vt* **bargain sth away** to give up something in return for something of less value: *bargain away rights which took many years to achieve.* **3** *vi* **bargain for sth** to be ready or willing to accept something: *He got more than he bargained for when he married her* (= (*informal*) was unpleasantly surprised).

barge[1] /bɑːdʒ/ *nc* a long flat-bottomed boat for rivers and canals.

barge[2] /bɑːdʒ/ *vi* (*informal*) **1** to move roughly or carelessly (esp among other people): *Stop barging (into the queue).* **2 barge in; barge into sth** to interrupt rudely: *Stop barging into our private conversation! Stop barging in!*

bari·tone /'bærɪtəʊn/ *nc* (a man with) a voice between tenor and bass.

bark[1] /bɑːk/ *nu* the outer covering of a tree.

bark[2] /bɑːk/ *nc* the sound made by dogs. *her/his* **bark is worse than her/his bite** a person is not as angry and dangerous as he/she pretends to be.

bark[3] /bɑːk/ *v* **1** *vi* **bark (at sb/sth)** (of dogs) to give a bark or barks: *The dog barks at strangers.* **bark up the wrong tree** (*fig*) to be angry with, accuse, the wrong person. **2** *vt* **bark sth (out)** to say something in a fierce, loud voice: *The officer barked (out) his orders.*

bar·ley /'bɑːlɪ/ *nu* a cereal plant and its seed (called *grain*), used for food and for making beer and whisky.

bar·my /'bɑːmɪ/ *adj* (**-ier, -iest**) (*informal; derog*) mad; foolish.

barn /bɑːn/ *nc* a covered building used for storing hay, grain etc on a farm.

'barn dance *nc* a kind of country dance.

'barn·yard *nc* = farmyard.

bar·nacle /'bɑːnəkl/ *nc* a kind of small sea animal that fastens itself to rocks, the bottoms of ships etc.

ba·rom·eter /bə'rɒmɪtə(r)/ *nc* (*tech*) an instrument for measuring the pressure of the atmosphere, used for forecasting the weather and measuring height above sea-level.

baro·met·ric /ˌbærə'metrɪk/ *adj*

bar·on /'bærən/ *nc* **1** (B- in names) (*GB*) a member of the aristocracy with the lowest rank of peer. **2** a great industrial leader: *oil barons.*

bar·on·ess /'bærənɪs/ *nc* (B- in names) a baron's wife or a woman who is a baron in her own right.

bar·on·et /'bærənɪt/ *nc* (abbr Bart) a member of the aristocracy with the lowest hereditary title.

bar·rack /'bærək/ *vi,vt* to shout and laugh rudely at (a speaker) during a meeting.

bar·racks /'bærəks/ *n pl* a large building or buildings for soldiers to live in.

bar·rage /'bærɑːʒ/ *nc* **1** an obstacle built across a river to store water for irrigation. ⇨ dam[2]. **2** (*mil*) continuous gunfire. **3** (*fig*) continuous questions etc: *a barrage of questions/requests.*

bar·rel /'bærəl/ *nc* **1** a round container, made of curved strips of wood: *a beer barrel.* **2** the amount a barrel can hold: *a barrel of beer.* **3** the long metal tube of a rifle etc: *the barrel of a gun.*

bar·ren /'bærən/ *adj* **1** (of a woman, female animal) unable to have young ones. **2** (of land) not able to produce crops. **3** (of a plant, tree) not producing fruit or seeds. **4** (*fig*) having no result; useless: *a barren discussion.*

bar·ri·cade /ˌbærɪ'keɪd/ *nc* a barrier of objects (e.g. sacks of sand) put in front of something as a defence. □ *vt, v reflex* to make a barricade across (a street, doorway etc); make a barricade for (oneself, people): *They barricaded themselves in.*

bar·rier /'bærɪə(r)/ *nc* **1** something (e.g. a gate, bar, objects) that prevents or controls progress or

movement: *Show your ticket at the barrier* (e.g. in a railway station). **2** a limit or boundary: *the sound barrier.* **3** (*fig*) obstruction: *Poverty should not be a barrier to educational progress.*

bar·ring /'bɑːrɪŋ/ *prep* unless there is/are: *We'll arrive by 4 o'clock barring unforeseen problems.*

bar·ris·ter /'bærɪstə(r)/ *nc* (not *US*) a lawyer who has the right to speak and argue in higher law courts. Compare solicitor.

bar·row /'bærəʊ/ *nc* **1** = wheelbarrow. **2** a small cart with two wheels, pulled or pushed by hand, e.g. one used to sell fruit.

bar·ter /'bɑːtə(r)/ *vt,vi* to exchange (goods, property etc) (for other goods etc): *barter wheat for machinery;* (*fig*) *barter away one's rights/freedom* (i.e. make a bad or foolish bargain).

bar·ter·er *nc* a person who barters.

base[1] /beɪs/ *adj* (**—r, —st**) **1** (*derog*) (of a person, behaviour, thought) dishonourable; immoral: *act from base motives.* ⇨ debase. **2** of inferior quality: *use base materials to construct a cheap building.*

ˌbase 'metal *nc,nu* any non-precious metal such as copper, tin, lead.

base[2] /beɪs/ *nc* **1** the lowest part of anything, esp the part on which it rests or is supported: *the base of a pillar.* **2** any position to begin a process of action, thinking etc: *use the statistics as a base for proving the product's value.* **3** (also *attrib*) a place where armed forces, expeditions etc are controlled, have their stores etc: *a base camp* (e.g. for an expedition). **4** a substance into which others are mixed: *We'll boil these bones as a base for the soup.* **5** (*maths*) a line or surface on which a figure stands or can stand: *BC is the base of the triangle ABC.* **6** (*maths*) a number (usually 10) which is the starting-point for a numerical system: *Computers use a numeral system with base 2, which is 0 and 1.* **7** (*chem*) a substance which combines with an acid to form a salt.

'base rate *nc* the lowest amount of interest charged by a bank when lending money.

base·less *adj* having no cause or reason: *baseless fears.* Ⓝ *'Groundless'* is more usual.

base[3] /beɪs/ *vt* **1 base sb/sth at a place** to put a person, army etc in a place as the controlling or main centre: *The navy is based at Portsmouth.* **2 base sth on sth** to use something as a basis for something: *Direct taxation is usually based on income.*

base·ball /'beɪsbɔːl/ *nu* an outdoor game played with a bat and ball, by two teams of nine players each, on a large, diamond-shaped field.

base·ment /'beɪsmənt/ *nc* the lowest part of a building, partly or wholly below ground level.

bases /'beɪsiːz/ *n* **1** *pl* of basis. **2** *pl* of base[2].

bash /bæʃ/ *nc* (*informal*) a strong blow or knock: *I gave him a bash on the nose.* **have a bash at sth** (*informal*) to try to do (something) successfully. □ *vt* (*informal*) to hit (a person, thing) with force (so as to break or injure it): *bash in the lid of a box; bash him on the head with a stick; bash one's head in the dark.*

bash·ful /'bæʃfəl/ *adj* shy (the usual word).

bash·ful·ly /-fəlɪ/ *adv*

ba·sic /'beɪsɪk/ *adj* forming, of, the main, most important or useful part: *basic needs/necessities* (e.g. food, sleep and exercise).

ba·si·cal·ly /-klɪ/ *adv* concerning everything that is basic: *Basically she does the work but she's very slow.*

BASIC /'beɪsɪk/ *acronym* Beginners' All-purpose Symbolic Instruction Code (the computer language used in most home computers).

ba·sics /'beɪsɪks/ *n pl* the most basic or simplest parts: *I don't understand even the basics of computer technology.* **get down to basics** to start from the beginning (e.g. when studying).

ba·sin /'beɪsn/ *nc* **1** = wash-basin. **2** a bowl used for preparing or serving food. **3** as much as a basin holds. **4** a deep pool at the base of a waterfall, a deep part of a harbour etc. **5** (*geog*) an area of land with a river and its tributaries: *the Thames basin.*

ba·sis /'beɪsɪs/ *nc* (*pl* **bases** /-siːz/) **1** the basic substance used to make, develop, build, measure etc something: *What is the basis of this soup?* **2** (*fig*) a foundation: *arguments that have a firm basis* (= that are easily supported by facts). *On the basis of our sales figures* (= From what these show), *we may make a profit next year.*

bask /bɑːsk/ *vi* (usually **bask in sth**) **1** to relax and enjoy warmth and light: *sitting in the garden, basking in the sunshine.* **2** (*fig*) to enjoy (approval, success etc): *basking in her approval.*

bas·ket /'bɑːskɪt/ *nc* **1** a container made of materials that bend and twist easily: *a shopping basket; a waste-paper basket.* ⇨ also egg¹(2). **2** as much as a basket holds: *They ate a basket of plums.*

bas·ket·ball /'bɑːskɪtbɔːl/ *nu* an indoor game played by two teams of five players who try to throw a large ball into high baskets fixed at each end of the court.

bass¹ /beɪs/ *adj* deep-sounding; low in tone. □ *nc* a singer or instrument with the lowest notes.

bass² /bæs/ *nc* (*pl* unchanged) a kind of fish used as food, caught in rivers, lakes and in the sea.

bas·soon /bə'suːn/ *nc* a wooden musical wind-instrument with double reeds giving low notes.

bas·tard /'bɑːstəd/ *nc* **1** (also *attrib; dated*) a person whose parents are not married when he or she is born: *a bastard child.* **2** (*vulgar; derog*) a ruthless, insensitive person: *He's a real bastard, leaving his wife in that way.* **3** (*slang*) (used without abuse): *Harry, you old bastard! Fancy meeting you here!* **4** (*slang*) an unfortunate person: *Poor bastard! He's been sacked and he won't find another job very easily.* **5** (*slang*) something that is annoying, very bad etc: *This is a bastard of an essay.*

baste¹ /beɪst/ *vt* to sew (cloth) with long stitches.

baste² /beɪst/ *vt* to pour fat, juices etc over (meat) while it is cooking.

bat¹ /bæt/ *nc* a small animal like a mouse with large wings, that flies at night and feeds on fruit and insects.

bat² /bæt/ *nc* a shaped wooden stick for hitting the ball in games, e.g. in cricket and table tennis. **do sth off one's own bat** (*fig*) to do it without help.

bat³ /bæt/ *vt,vi* (**-tt-**) to use a bat²: *He batted the ball over the fence.* ⇨ batsman.

batch /bætʃ/ *nc* a number of people or things receiving attention as a group: *a batch of letters to be answered; cakes baked in batches of twenty.*

bath¹ /bɑːθ/ *n* (*pl* **-s** /bɑːðz/) **1** a large, oblong container for a person to sit or lie in and wash the whole body. **2** *nc* an act of washing the body by sitting or lying in water: *I'll have a hot bath and go to bed.* **3** *nu* water for a bath: *Your bath is ready.* **4** (*pl*) (a building with) a large indoor swimming pool.

'bath-mat *nc* a small mat placed at the side of a bath.

'bath·room *nc* a room in which there is a bath.

'bath-tub *nc* = bath(1).

bath² /bɑːθ/ *v* **1** *vi* to have a bath(1). **2** *vt* to give (a person or animal) a bath(1): *bath the baby.*

bathe¹ /beɪð/ *nc* an act of swimming etc in the sea, a river: *Let's go for a bathe!*

bathe² /beɪð/ *v* **1** *vi* to go into the sea, a river, lake etc for sport, swimming etc: *They're bathing in the river.* **2** *vt* to soak, put, (something) in water: *The doctor told him to bathe his eyes twice a day.* **be bathed in sth** to be made wet or bright all over because of something: *Her face was bathed in tears/sunlight.* ⇨ also sunbathe.

bath·er /'beɪðə(r)/ *nc* a person who bathes(1).

bath·ing /'beɪðɪŋ/ *nu* the act or practice of going into the sea to swim etc: *The bathing here is safe.*

'bathing-costume *nc* a one-piece article of clothing worn by women and girls for swimming.

ba·thos /'beɪθɒs/ *nu* (*literature*) the sudden change from something interesting, noble etc to something ridiculous or insincere (often deliberately for humorous effect).

ba·tik /bə'tiːk, 'bætɪk/ *n* (also *attrib*) **1** *nu* a method of printing designs on cloth by waxing areas not to be dyed. **2** *nc* a piece of cloth dyed in this way.

bat·man /'bætmən/ *nc* (*pl* **-men**) (*GB mil*) an army officer's personal servant.

bat·on /'bætɒn/ *nc* a short, thin stick as used by the conductor of an orchestra.

bats /bæts/ *adj* (*sl; derog*) mad; eccentric.

bats·man /'bætsmən/ *nc* (*pl* **-men**) **1** (*cricket*) a player who bats. **2** a person who guides aircraft moving on the ground in an airport.

bat·tal·ion /bə'tælɪən/ *nc* (*mil*) an army unit made up of several companies and forming part of a regiment or brigade.

bat·ten /'bætn/ *nc* a long wooden board as used to keep other boards in place. □ *vt* **batten sth down** to make something secure using battens.

bat·ter¹ /'bætə(r)/ *nu* a mixture of flour, eggs, milk etc used for cooking.

bat·ter² /'bætə(r)/ *vt* to strike (something, a person) hard and often: *Let's batter the door down.*

bat·ter·ed /'bætəd/ *adj* of a person or thing having been hit hard and often: *a battered baby; a badly-battered old car.*

bat·tery /'bætərɪ/ *n* (*pl* **-ies**) **1** *nc* an apparatus for storing and producing electricity: *This radio uses four small batteries.* **2** *nc* (also *attrib*) series of boxes etc in which hens are kept for laying eggs or for fattening: *battery hens.* **3** *nu* the act of hitting a person hard. ⇨ assault.

'battery-charger *nc* a device for putting electricity into a battery(1).

,battery-'operated *adj* needing batteries to work: *a battery-operated calculator.*

battle¹ /'bætl/ *nc* **1** a fight between organized and armed forces. **2** (*fig*) any struggle: *the battle*

be	Present participle **being** /'biːɪŋ/; past participle **been** /biːn/

Positive statements	**Negative statements**	**Questions***

Present tense forms:

I **am** /æm/, I'**m** /aɪm/	I am not, I'm not	am I? aren't I?
you **are** /ɑː(r)/, you'**re** /jʊə(r)/	you are not, you're not, you **aren't** /ɑːnt/	are you? aren't you?
he/she/it **is** /ɪz/, he'**s**/she'**s**/it'**s**† /hiːz, ʃiːz, ɪts/	he/she/it is not, he's/she's/it's not, he/she/it **isn't** /'ɪznt/	is he/she/it? isn't he/she/it?
we **are** /ɑː(r)/, we'**re** /wɪə(r)/	we are not, we're not, we **aren't**	are we? aren't we?
you **are** /ɑː(r)/, you'**re** /jʊə(r)/	you are not, you're not, you **aren't**	are you? aren't you?
they **are** /ɑː(r)/, they'**re** /ðeə(r)/	they are not, they're not, they **aren't**	are they? aren't they?

Past tense forms:

I **was** /wəz, wɒz/	I was not, I **wasn't** /'wɒznt/	was I? wasn't I?
you **were** /wə(r), wɜː(r)/	you were not, you **weren't** /wɜːnt/	were you? weren't you?
he/she/it **was**	he/she/it was not, he/she/it **wasn't**	was he/she/it? wasn't he/she/it?
we/you/they **were**	we/you/they were not, we/you/they **weren't**	were we/you/they? weren't we/you/they?

The other tenses of *'be'* are formed in the same way as those of other verbs, as in *will be late, is being kind, was being friendly, have been there.*

* The negative question forms *am I not? was he not?* etc are also correct but are more formal.

† Be careful, because *he's, she's, it's* can mean either *he is, she is, it is* or *he has, she has, it has.*

---

of life.

'**battle-cruiser** *nc* (*mil*) a large, fast cruiser with heavy guns and lighter armour than a battleship.

'**battle·field/ground** *nc* a place where a battle is or was fought.

'**battle·ship** *nc* (*mil*) a kind of large warship, with big guns and heavy armour.

battle² /'bætl/ *vi* to struggle: *battling with the wind/against poverty.*

battle·ments /'bætlmənts/ *n pl* the low wall round a tower or castle with openings through which to shoot.

bat·ty /'bæti/ *adj* (**-ier, -iest**) (*sl; derog*) mad; eccentric.

bauble /'bɔːbl/ *nc* an attractive and cheap jewel.

baulk /bɔːk/ *v* = balk.

baux·ite /'bɔːksaɪt/ *nu* the clay-like substance from which aluminium is obtained.

baw·dy /'bɔːdɪ/ *adj* (**-ier, -iest**) (*derog*) (of talk, a person) using rude language, subjects etc to laugh at etc: *bawdy talk/jokes.*

bawl /bɔːl/ *vt,vi* to shout or cry (something) loudly: *The frightened child bawled for help.*

bay¹ /beɪ/ *nc* (B- in names) a part of the sea or of a large lake, enclosed by a wide curve of the shore: *Hudson Bay.*

bay² /beɪ/ *nc* **1** an extension of part of a room beyond the line of one or two of its walls. **2** a building in a school etc for those who are ill or injured: *the sick-bay.* **3** a place for putting something in a building: *a parking-bay* (i.e. for a car). **4** a compartment in a warehouse etc for storing things: *Please clear No. 3 Bay to make room for new stock.*

bay³ /beɪ/ *nc* (also *attrib*) a kind of tree with leaves

that are used in cooking: *a bay tree; bay leaves.*

bay⁴ /beɪ/ *nu* **keep/hold sb at bay** to keep an enemy etc from being successful.

bay⁵ /beɪ/ *vi* (esp of large dogs) to bark with a deep note.

bay·onet /'beɪənɪt/ *nc* a blade like a dagger, fixed to a rifle. □ *vt* to stab (a person) with a bayonet.

ba·zaar /bə'zɑː(r)/ *nc* **1** a place where there is a sale of goods for charity. **2** (in Eastern countries) that part of a town where the markets and shopping streets are.

ba·zoo·ka /bə'zuːkə/ *nc* (*pl* **—s**) (*mil*) a portable weapon for firing armour-piercing rockets.

BBC /ˌbiː biː 'siː/ *abbr* (the —) (*GB*) British Broadcasting Corporation.

BC /ˌbiː 'siː/ *abbr* before Christ: *Julius Caesar conquered Britain in 44 BC.* Compare AD.

be¹ /bɪ *strong form:* biː/ *auxiliary verb* Ⓝ *'Be'* as an auxiliary verb is used with another verb to form tenses and the passive. **1** (used with the present participle of another verb to form the continuous tenses): *They are eating. I'm not moving in next week. Where were you living? I'll be wearing a blue coat. Wasn't she working here? He is going to write a letter.* **2** (used with the past participle of a transitive verb to form the passive): *The house is being built/was being built/will be built/has been built.* **3** (used with *to* + verb) (**a**) to show intention or a plan: *They are/were to marry in June. Are we to have dinner here?* Ⓝ In newspapers etc (the form of) *'be'* is often omitted, as in *Prince Charles to visit Spain.* (**b**) to show an order or obligation: *These doors are to* (= must) *be kept locked. You're not to* (= must not) *come home late. He's to* (= should/ought to) *be congratulated.*

(c) to show permission: *They're not to* (=not allowed to) *make too much noise.* (d) to show result, destiny etc (esp when already known to the speaker): *They were never to meet again. If they were to phone us, I'd be pleased.* Ⓝ *'I were'* can also be used with *if*, as in *If I were to agree, would you also go?* **4** (used in conversation) (a) (joined to the end of a statement to form a question): *It's Monday, isn't it? I'm early, aren't I? You weren't the thief, were you? Mary isn't old enough, is she?* Ⓝ The short addition is always negative (e.g. *isn't*) if the verb in the statement is positive (e.g. *is*) and it is positive (e.g. *are*) if the verb in the statement is negative (e.g. *aren't*). Statements with *neither, no, nobody, nothing* etc are considered to be negative and the short addition is always positive, as in *Nobody was hurt, were they? Neither of us is to blame, are we?* (b) (used to make a short question): *'I'm the greatest.'—'Are you?' 'It was Ben who did it.'—'Was it?' 'We aren't rich.'—'Aren't you?'* Ⓝ If the statement is positive, the question is also positive. If the statement is negative, the question is also negative. Statements with *neither, no, nobody* etc are considered to be negative. (c) (used to give a short answer showing agreement or disagreement): *'This is my book.'—'No, it isn't.' 'Is he your boyfriend?'—'Yes, he is.' 'Is that your husband over there?'—'Yes, it is.'* Ⓝ *'Be'* is used in (a), (b) and (c) only when *'be'* is used in the main statement. Compare: *can², do², have¹, may, might², must², should, will²,* would.

be² /bɪ *strong form:* biː/ *vi* Ⓝ *'Be'* as an intransitive cannot be used in the continuous tenses, e.g. *is/was -ing,* except in 4 below. **1** (used to show existence): *I think, therefore I am. To be or not to be . . . for the time being* ⇨ *time¹(2).* **there is/was** etc there exists/existed: *There's a fly in my soup. There are some chips in the oven. Are there any eggs left? Isn't there a train to Athens? Yes, there is. No, there isn't.* Ⓝ The subject is always the noun which comes after *'be'.* If the noun is plural, *'be'* must also have a plural form. **2** (used with a noun or pronoun to show identity): *Today is Monday. Weren't you world champion once? I'm a liar. Who is it? What are those black things? Which is the best? I'm the one who did it. 4 and 9 is 13. Four nines are thirty-six. I want to be* (= become) *a brain surgeon.* **-to-be** (used to describe a person who will have the mentioned relationship, position etc): *She's a bride-/mother-to-be/the manager-to-be.* **3** (used to describe a physical or mental condition, age, colour, mass, price, size, time etc): *She's tall/happy. He's 16 years old. We're blue with cold. It's 6 o'clock. That's 20 kilometres wide. How much are they? They're £10 each. Aren't I lucky? It's not fair!* **4** (used in the continuous tenses to show a person's behaviour or continuous activity): *She's being very silly. I was being unkind. Who was being a silly boy? Being* (= Because she was) *late, she took a taxi.* Ⓝ *'Being'* cannot be used to describe a condition that is permanent (e.g. size, colour etc) or exists for a long time (e.g. age, physical state etc). ⇨ 3 above. **5** (used with adverbs and prepositions to show position in space and time): *She's in the bedroom/at the office/on television/over there. The meeting will be in here on Tuesday at 5 o'clock. Kenya is in Africa. When is your birthday? Where are my keys?* **6** (used with a posses-

sive pronoun to show possession): *That's mine. It's not yours. This is John's.* **7** (used in perfect tenses only) to visit; to go to: *Have you ever been to Paris?—Yes, I've been there. I will have been six times after this next visit. Have you been to see 'Star Wars'? Has the doctor been?* (*informal* = Has the doctor come to visit?) **8** (used to give an order): *Be careful! Do be quiet! Don't be late! Don't be an idiot!* Ⓝ *'Do'* can be used to add force to an order which is positive and can be omitted without changing the meaning. *'Don't'* is used to order a person not to do something.

be about (a) to be present (but without knowing where exactly): *She's somewhere about.* (b) to be available: *There are many good singers about.* **be (about) the size of it** ⇨ *size¹(1).*

be above sth to be too important, superior, good etc to do something bad: *They're not above taking bribes. He's above suspicion.*

be after sth to wish to have, try to obtain, something: *You two are after the same job.*

be against sth to disapprove of something: *I'm against smoking in cinemas.*

be along to come to a place (not far away): *I'll be along in a minute.*

be around (a) = be about(a,b). (b) (*informal*) to be active (and famous): *The Rolling Stones have been around a long time.*

be 'at it (*informal*) to be very busy: *I've been at it all day and I'm tired.*

be away to be absent from home (on holiday): *They're away for the weekend.*

be well away (*informal*) to be very drunk.

be back to return: *I'll be back by 6 o'clock.*

be behind (sb/sth) (a) to be late: *I'm behind with the rent.* (b) to be the reason for (something): *What's behind her bad temper?* (c) to be less important, successful (than another): *She's behind other players in the competition.*

be below sb/sth to be less important, usual etc than a person, thing: *He's below me in the office. The sales figures are below average.*

be beyond sb to be too difficult, academic etc for a person to understand: *This computer is beyond me.* **be beyond sth** to be too old, ill etc: *It's beyond repair.* ⇨ *joke¹.*

be down (sth) (a) to have been reduced: *House prices are down.* (b) (also **be down an amount**) to be without (an amount of money etc): *I'm £5 down compared to last month's savings.* (c) (*informal*) to be sad: *She's been down ever since her father died.* **be down (for sth)** to be written on a list (to give money, to do a duty etc): *You're down for Friday/for £20.* **be down on sb** (*informal*) (a) to be critical of a person: *They'll be down on you for making a bad speech.* (b) to demand money, revenge from a person: *The bank will be down on him to pay the loan.* **be down and out** to be extremely poor (and without a home). **be down to sth** to have nothing left except something: *I'm down to my last penny.*

be (all) for sth to support (strongly) something: *He's all for saving on petrol by cycling.*

be in (a) to be in fashion: *Pink shirts are in.* (b) to be picked, cut etc: *All the wheat is in.* (c) (of the sea) to have come up onto the beach. (d) (in games) to be batting: *The Indians have been in all day.* **be all in** to be exhausted. **be in for sth** to be a competitor for something: *Coe is in for the 5000 metres. I'm in for the supervisor's job.* **be in on sth (a)** to know about something: *She's in on our plans.* **(b)** to have a share in something: *We want to be in on the new salary scheme.*

be into sth (*informal*) to find pleasure in something: *I'm not into horror films.*

be off (a) (of food) to be unfit to eat: *This fish is off.* **(b)** (of water, electricity etc) to be disconnected. **(c)** (of food in a restaurant etc) to be unavailable: *Apple pie is off today.* **(d)** to be cancelled: *The wedding is definitely off.* **(e)** to leave; begin to race: *It's time we were off. The horses are off.* **be well off** to be rich.

be on (a) (of water, electricity etc) to be connected. **(b)** (of food in a restaurant etc) to be available. **(c)** to be going to happen: *The match is still on although it's raining.* **(d)** to be shown, performed: *What's on (TV)?* **not be on** (*informal*) to be unacceptable, not allowed, (because impossible): *A 20-per-cent wage increase is not on.* **be on about sth** to speak continuously (and boringly) about something: *What's he on about now?* **be on at sb** to find fault with a person continually: *He's always on at me to cut my hair.* **be on to sb/sth** (*informal*) to know, be aware of, a person, her or his faults etc.

be out (a) to be away from home. **(b)** to be released from school, work, prison etc. **(c)** to be out of fashion: *Grey suits are out.* **(d)** to have flowers: *The roses will be out soon.* **(e)** to be unconscious. **(f)** to be no longer lit: *The fire's out.* **(g)** to be inaccurate: *Your estimate is out (by £1000).* **(h)** to be removed from government: *The Liberals are out.* **(i)** to be on strike: *The miners are out.* **(j)** to have been announced: *The exam results are out.* **(k)** (of the sea) to have gone away from the beach. **(l)** (in games, competitions) to be defeated. **be out and about** to be outside and active (e.g. after an illness). **be out at a place** to be away from home and at a place: *They're out at the disco.* **be out for sth** to be determined to get something: *She's out for success.* **be out of sth (a)** to have left something or a place: *Are you out of bed? She's out of town.* **(b)** to have none left of something: *We're out of ice-cream.* **(c)** to be without a job etc: *He's been out of work for months.* ⇨ also action(1), fashion¹(1), focus¹(2), order¹(1).

be outside sth to be something a person does not understand, has not experienced, cannot control etc: *That topic is outside my own area of study.*

be over (a) to be at an end: *The waiting is over.* **(b)** to come, go, to a person's home: *We'll be over later.* **be (all) over** to be (completely) finished: *The game's all over.* **be all over sth (a)** to be known by people in a place: *Their engagement was all over the office.* **(b)** to be present everywhere in a place: *His clothes were all over the floor.* **be over and done with** = be all over.

be through (a) (*informal*) (of a relationship) to be at an end: *We're through.* **(b)** (*telephoning*) to be connected. **be through with sb/sth** to be tired of (and so ready to abandon) a person, activity etc: *I'm through with (listening to) you.*

be up (a) to be out of bed (and active): *I'm up at 7 o'clock each morning. She was up (and about) early this morning.* **(b)** to have increased in price:

Bus fares are up. **(c)** (of time) to have expired: *Your time is up.* **(d)** (of the sun, moon) to be visible. **be up and about** = be up(a). **be up for sth** to be a candidate for something: *You're up for promotion.* **be up to sb** to be a person's responsibility, choice: *You could do well—it's up to you.* **be up to sth (a)** to have reached something: *The water's up to my knees. Is this dictionary up to standard?* **(b)** (*informal*) to be busy doing something: *What has he been up to now?*

be with sb (a) to support a person: *Are you with us or against us?* **(b)** to be in the company of a friend (esp a romantic one): *Are you with that boy over there?* **(c)** to help a person (e.g. in a shop): *I'll be with you in a moment, sir.* **(d)** (*informal*) to understand a person: *Are you with me or shall I explain again?* **be with it** (*informal*) to be completely up to date with the latest fashions, ideas etc.

beach /biːtʃ/ *nc* (B- in names) a part of a shore covered with sand or pebbles. □ *vt* to push or pull (a boat) onto the beach.

'beach ball *nc* a large lightweight ball used for games on the beach.

'beach·wear *nu* (*commerce*) clothes used for sunbathing, swimming etc.

bea·con /'biːkən/ *nc* a light on a hill or mountain, or on the coast etc to give warning of danger to planes, ships etc.

bead /biːd/ *nc* **1** a small ball of coloured glass etc with a hole through it for a string or wire. **2** (*fig*) a drop of liquid: *beads of sweat.*

beady /'biːdɪ/ *adj* (-ier, -iest) (of eyes) small, round and bright.

beak /biːk/ *nc* the hard, horny mouth of a bird.

beak·er /'biːkə(r)/ *nc* **1** a tall drinking cup (of plastic), usually without a handle. **2** as much as a beaker holds. **3** (*science*) a similar glass vessel used by scientists etc.

beam¹ /biːm/ *nc* **1** a long piece of wood etc used in building etc. **2** a ray or line of light (e.g. from a lamp or the sun). **3** (*fig*) a bright look or smile showing happiness etc: *with a beam of delight.* **4** a radio signal used to direct planes.

beam² /biːm/ *v* **1** *vi* (of the sun etc) to send out light (and heat). **2** *vi* (*fig*) to smile happily and cheerfully: *beaming with happiness.* **3** *vt* to send (a radio or TV signal) in a particular direction: *The football match was beamed from Britain to South America.*

bean /biːn/ *nc* **1** (any of several plants with) a seed in a long container (*pod*) (all used as vegetables): *runner beans; French beans; soya beans.* **2** a seed of other plants similar in shape: *coffee beans.* **full of beans** very happy and active. **spill the beans** to make a secret known.

bear¹ /beə(r)/ *nc* a kind of large, heavy animal with thick fur. ⇨ polar bear, teddy bear.

bear² /beə(r)/ *v* (*pt* **bore** /bɔːr/, *pp* **borne** /bɔːn/) **1** *vt* to give birth to (a child or young animal): *She has borne him six children.* Ⓝ The past participle is 'born' in the passive, as in *I was born in 1965.* **2** *vt, vi* (of trees etc) to produce fruit: *bearing (berries) throughout the autumn; fruit-bearing trees.* **bear fruit** ⇨ fruit¹(4). **3** *vt* (*formal*) to carry (something) from one place to another: *bearing a heavy suitcase; bear gifts; water-borne diseases.* ⇨ airborne. **4** *vt* to support, accept, (the cost, weight, blame etc): *I'll bear your weight while you climb up. Why have I borne all the costs of repair? Responsibility for breakages will be borne by everyone.* **5** *vt* to hold (something) in one's mind; feel (something): *I bear no hatred towards you. She bears you no ill-will. Do you bear grudges?* **bear sb/sth in mind** ⇨ mind¹(1). **6** *vt* **(a)** *can/could bear sth* to be able to tolerate something: *Can you bear the pain? I could bear the isolation for a week but not longer.* ⇨ bearable. **(b)** *cannot/can't bear sb/sth* to be unable to tolerate (something); hate (a person, thing) very much: *I can't bear English winters. She can't bear him/spiders/eating olives.* ⇨ unbearable. Ⓝ *'Can/could'* is also used with the verbs *abide, endure, put up with, stand* with the same meaning. **grin and bear it** ⇨ grin². **7** *vt* to possess (something); *They have borne the scars of war/the signs of poverty for decades. What you say bears no relationship to the truth. He bears the name of a famous family. Does this contract bear your signature?* ⇨ also witness¹(4). **8** *vt* to be worthy of (being done): *That remark doesn't bear repeating.* **9** *vi* to turn slightly (in the direction mentioned) while travelling: *bear left/right.*

bear sth away (*formal*) to take, carry, something away: *bear away the first prize.*

bear down (on sb) to move towards a person (as if) to attack: *Photographers bore down on her as she was leaving the airport.*

bear sth off ⇨ bear sth away.

bear on sth to affect, concern, something: *This issue bears on everyone's health.* **bring sth to bear on sb (to do sth)** to use something to (try to) force a person (to act): *Pressure was brought to bear on him to agree.*

bear sb/sth out to confirm, support, a person, idea etc: *The evidence bears him out/bears out his account of what happened.*

bear up (against/under/to sth) to remain strong (while experiencing bad fortune, illness etc): *How will she bear up against the shock/under the pain/ to the news of his death?*

bear with sb/sth to tolerate a person, situation etc; be patient with a person, condition etc: *Can you bear with his untidiness if you marry him? Bear with me while I explain it to the others.*

bear·able /'beərəbl/ *adj* that can be tolerated. ⇨ bear²(6). Opp unbearable.

beard /bɪəd/ *nc* a mass of hair on the lower part of a man's face (excluding the moustache). **beard·ed** *adj* having a beard.

bear·er /'beərə(r)/ *nc* (*formal*) **1** a person who brings a letter or message: *I'm the bearer of good news.* **2** a person who helps to carry a coffin to a grave, who carries a stretcher, flag etc.

bear·ing /'beərɪŋ/ *n* **1** *nu* the way a person stands, walks etc: *a man of military bearing.* **2** *nu* or *sing* **bearing on sth** a connection with something: *What he said has no/not much bearing on the subject.* **3** *nu* the possibility of being tolerated: *His conduct was beyond (all) bearing.* ⇨ bear²(6), bearable. **4** *nc* (*tech*) a (compass) direction: *take a compass bearing on a lighthouse.* **find/lose one's bearings** to find/lose one's position, confidence etc.

beast /bi:st/ *nc* **1** a four-footed animal Ⓝ *'Animal'* is the usual word. **beast of burden** an animal, such as a horse, which carries heavy loads. **2** (*informal; derog*) a cruel or disgusting person. ⇨ bestial.

beast·ly *adj* (*informal*) (of weather, behaviour etc) unpleasant: *What beastly weather!*

beat¹ /bi:t/ *adj* (*pred; no comp*) (*informal*) (of a person) exhausted: *We're beat! dead beat* completely exhausted.

beat² /bi:t/ *nc* **1** one hit or stroke, or a sound of several: *We heard the beat of a drum. His heartbeats were getting weaker.* **2** (the —) the regular stress marking rhythm in music or poetry. **3** a regular route of a police officer.

beat³ /bi:t/ *v* (*pt* —, *pp* —**en** /'bi:tn/) **1** *vt,vi* to hit (something) several times (as if) with a stick: *beat a carpet; beat at/against/on the door in anger. The rain was beating against the window.* **beat about the bush** ⇨ bush(2). **beat it** (*sl; usually imperative*) to go away. **2** *vt* to punish (a person) by hitting many times: *He was beaten severely and sent to bed.* ⇨ beat sb up. **3** *vt* to hit (something) with a tool and change the shape: *I beat it flat with a hammer.* **4** *vt* (*cooking*) to mix (food) thoroughly with a spoon, fork or whisk using fast movements: *beating eggs.* **5** *vi,vt* to move (something) with a regular rhythm: *My heart was beating fast. I could see the bird beating its wings high in the sky.* **6** *vt* to do better than (a person, situation, score etc): *I beat her at tennis/in the exam/race. Let's beat the rush-hour traffic by leaving very early.* **beat the record** ⇨ record²(6). **beat sb to it** to arrive, achieve something, before another person. **7** *vt* to be too difficult for (a person): *This crossword has beaten me. It beats me how they manage on so little money. The cyclists were beaten by the steep mountains/the bad weather.*

beat sth back to force it to go back, stop its progress: *beat back a fire.*

beat sb/sth down to force or persuade a person to reduce a price; force a price to be reduced: *I beat her/the price down to £30.* **beat down (on sb)** (of the sun's light, heat, rain etc) to affect a person strongly: *The sun beat down (on us) as we climbed the rocks.*

beat sth in to destroy a door, lid etc by hitting it (with a hammer etc): *He beat in the windows to rescue the child from the fire.*

beat off sb/sth to force a person, an attack etc to go away: *beat off an attacker/a cold.*

beat sth out **(a)** to remove something by hitting it (with a hammer): *beat out a dent in a car.* **(b)** to stop (a fire) from burning by hitting it: *beat out the flames with one's coat.* **(c)** (*music*) to produce (a rhythm) by beating(5): *beat out a rhythm on the drum.*

beat sb up (*informal*) to hurt a person severely by fighting: *Do that again and I'll beat you up.*

beat·en /'bi:tn/ *adj* (*no comp*) **1** (of a person, a record) defeated: *a beaten man* (e.g. one who has lost a legal or personal battle). **2** (*attrib*) shaped by beating: *beaten gold.* **3** (of a path) worn by use: *a well-beaten path.* **off the beaten track** **(a)** in or to a place not visited by many people. **(b)** unusual: *wearing clothes that are off the beaten track.*

beat·er /'bi:tə(r)/ *nc* a cooking utensil used for beating (⇨ beat³(4)): *an egg-beater.*

beat·ing /'bi:tɪŋ/ *nc* (esp) a punishment by hitting many times: *give him a good beating*.

beau·ti·cian /bjuːˈtɪʃn/ *nc* a trained person who works in a beauty salon.

beau·ti·ful /ˈbjuːtɪfəl/ *adj* giving pleasure or delight to the mind or senses: *a beautiful face/flower/voice; beautiful weather/music*. Compare ugly.

beau·ti·ful·ly /-flɪ/ *adv* in a beautiful manner: *She plays the piano beautifully*.

beau·ti·fy /ˈbjuːtɪfaɪ/ *vt* (*pt,pp* **-ied**) to make (a person, a room etc) beautiful (for a special occasion).

beau·ty /ˈbjuːtɪ/ *n* (*pl* **-ies**) **1** *nu* the attractive qualities that give pleasure to the senses (esp the eye and ear) or to the mind or the intellect: *the beauty of the mountains/Mozart's symphonies/Renoir's art/Keats' poetry*. **2** *nc* a person, thing, characteristic etc that is beautiful or particularly good: *Isn't she a beauty! Look at this horse—isn't it a beauty!*

'beauty parlour *nc* = beauty salon.

'beauty queen *nc* a girl chosen as the most beautiful in a contest.

'beauty salon *nc* a place where women have treatment (of the figure, skin, hair etc) to become more beautiful (*US* = beauty shop).

'beauty spot *nc* a place with beautiful scenery.

bea·ver /ˈbiːvə(r)/ *nc,nu* (the fur of) a kind of animal that lives on land and in water and makes dams across rivers.

be·came *pt* of become.

be·cause /bɪˈkɒz, -ˈkəz/ **1** *conj* (*subord*) for the reason that (the fact is the cause of the action): *Because it was raining, we took a taxi. I'm telephoning because I'm going to be late.* Ⓝ For a comparison of 'as', 'because' and 'since', ⇨ as²(3). 'So' is also possible but the order of the sentence is changed, as in It was raining so we took a taxi. It is not possible to use more than one of these conjunctions (e.g. because and so) together in the same sentence. **2** *because of* (*prep*) (used before a noun or pronoun) the fact that is the reason for the action is/was: *Because of her age she paid only half the fare. I can't come because of another commitment. I'm annoyed because of that letter.* Ⓝ 'On account of' and 'owing to' are also possible. Compare be due to at due¹(4).

beck·on /ˈbekən/ *vt,vi* to call (a person) by a movement of the hand or arm, e.g. to show that he or she must come nearer or follow.

be·come /bɪˈkʌm/ *v* (*pt* **became** /bɪˈkeɪm/, *pp* —) **1** *vt* (used with a noun or adj) to develop or grow into (a person, thing); to be (the kind mentioned) as a result, after a period of time, after training etc: *She became a brain surgeon. Caterpillars become butterflies. Acids become neutral when they are mixed with alkalis. He's become famous. It's becoming very expensive to travel by train.* Ⓝ 'Become' is used with an adjective to describe the subject (a person or thing) of the statement, as She became rich; Exams are becoming more and more difficult. The verbs 'get' and 'go' are used in the same way and are less formal than become, as in He gets angry when he's tired; She's going grey with worry. Compare also come(6). **2** *vt* (no *passive*; rarely used in continuous tenses; usually *negative*) (*formal*) (of clothes, behaviour etc) to be suitable or correct for: *Swearing does not become you.*

Those shoes do not become a girl of your age. ⇨ becoming(2). **3** *become of sb/sth* (**a**) (suggesting the possibility of an unhappy, harmful, evil etc result) to happen to (a person or thing) as a result: *What will become of her children if she dies?* (**b**) (used to ask where a person or thing is etc after a long time has passed): *Do you know what became of my old bicycle? I don't know what became of her.*

be·com·ing /bɪˈkʌmɪŋ/ *adj* (*formal*) **1** attractive: *a becoming smile/dress*. **2** (of clothes, behaviour) suitable or correct: *Her dress/bad language is not at all becoming*. Opp unbecoming.

be·com·ing·ly *adv: smile becomingly*.

bed¹ /bed/ *nc* **1** a piece of furniture used for sleeping: *be asleep in bed; make your bed; fall out of bed; jump into/out of bed; go to bed at midnight; put/send her to bed; a wooden bed; a single bed* (= for one person); *a double bed* (= for two people); *twin beds* (= two identical single beds); *sit on the bed; put it next to the bed*. Ⓝ 'A' is not used before 'bed' with such prepositions as in, into, out of, to which refer to a person using a bed, as in be ill in bed, get into bed, jump out of bed, go willingly to bed, but 'a' must be used before an adjective, as in sleep in a soft bed; ask for a double bed. 'The' is used before 'bed' when referring to the position of a person or object in relation to a bed, as in It's near the bed/at the foot of the bed/under the bed. 'The' is also used with certain verbs in special expressions, as in make the bed. ⇨ also air-bed. **bed and breakfast** (abbr b. and b., B & B) (in a hotel, house) a room to use as a paying guest with breakfast provided. **change the bed** to put clean sheets etc on it. **make the bed** to tidy the sheets, blankets etc after it has been used. **strip the bed** to take off the (used) sheets etc. Ⓝ Possessive pronouns can also be used, as in change/make/strip your bed. **2** an area of a garden etc for (particular) flowers: *a flower bed; a rose bed, a bed of tulips*. **3** (the —) the floor (of a river, the sea etc): *on the bed of the ocean; the sea bed*. **4** a (bottom) horizontal division under the ground, a building etc: *a bed of concrete/clay*.

'bed·clothes *n pl* sheets, blankets etc for a bed.

'bed·pan *nc* a container for urine etc as used by a patient in hospital.

'bed·rid·den *adj* kept in bed because of illness, weakness or old age.

'bed·roll *nc* a sleeping bag or blanket rolled up and carried, e.g. by a camper.

'bed·room *nc* a room for sleeping in.

'bed·side *nc* (also *attrib*) the side of a (esp a sick person's) bed: *a bedside table. Dr Green has a good bedside manner* (= knows how to give her or his patients confidence etc).

'bed·sitter (also **bed·sit** (*informal*)) *nc* a room used (e.g. by students) for both living in and sleeping in.

'bed·sore *nc* a painful area on the skin caused by lying in bed for a long time.

'bed·spread *nc* a covering that is put over a bed during the day.

'bed·time *nu* the time for going to bed: *His usual bedtime is 11 o'clock*.

bed² /bed/ *v* (**-dd-**) **1** *vt,vi* **bed (sb) down** to put (a person), get, into a temporary bed: *bed down (a visitor) on the sofa*. **2** *vt* **bed sth (out)** to plant (seedlings etc): *He was bedding out young cabbage plants.* **3** *vt* to place or fix (something) under the surface: *The nail bedded itself in* (= went deep into) *the pipe.*

bed·ding /'bedɪŋ/ *nu* **1** = bedclothes. **2** straw etc for animals to sleep on.

be·deck·ed /bɪ'dekt/ *adj* **bedecked with sth** decorated with flowers, jewels etc.

be·dev·il·led /bɪ'devld/ (*US* = **-vil·ed**) *adj* (*pred*) (of a situation etc) affected or troubled (by something bad): *The issue is bedevilled by Smith's refusal to cooperate with us.*

bed·lam /'bedləm/ *nc,nu* (a scene of) noisy confusion: *There was bedlam in the classroom.*

be·drag·gled /bɪ'drægld/ *adj* made wet or dirty: *bedraggled clothes/children.*

bee /biː/ *nc* a kind of small flying insect that makes honey and can sting. **have a bee in one's bonnet (about sth)** to be obsessed by an idea. **make a bee-line for sb/sth** to go quickly towards a person, thing by the shortest way.

'bee·hive *nc* ⇨ hive.

beech /biːtʃ/ *nc,nu* (also *attrib*) (the wood of) a kind of tree with a smooth bark and dark-green or reddish-brown leaves: *beech forests.*

beef /biːf/ *nu* (also *attrib*) the flesh of an ox, bull or cow, used as meat: *beef stew.*

'beef·burger *nc* a flat piece of minced beef, to be grilled or fried.

'beef·steak *nc* a thick slice of beef for grilling or frying.

beefy /'biːfɪ/ *adj* (**-ier, -iest**) (of a person) big and strong.

been /biːn/ *pp* of be. ⇨ esp be²(7).

beep /biːp/ *nc* a repeated signal or note (as made by a car horn, electronic timer etc).

beer /bɪə(r)/ *nc,nu* (a kind, portion, of) alcoholic drink made from malt, special plants (*hops*) and yeast.

beery *adj* like beer in taste or smell.

bees·wax /'biːzwæks/ *nu* wax made by bees, as used for polishing wood.

beetle /'biːtl/ *nc* a kind of insect with hard, shiny wing-covers.

beet·root /'biːtruːt/ *nc,nu* (also *attrib*) (a) red beet used as a vegetable: *beetroot soup.*

be·fore¹ /bɪ'fɔː(r)/ *adv* (used to refer to a point of time in the past) at an earlier time: *I've seen that film before. Haven't we met before? You should have told me before. I'd have written before but I was ill.* Ⓝ 'Before' is always placed after the verb. 'Already' can have a similar meaning (⇨ already(2)) and can be placed after or in front of the verb, as in *He's already seen it.* 'Already' cannot be used when 'before' means 'before now', as in *I found a ring I'd lost three years before.* ⇨ also ago.

be·fore² /bɪ'fɔː(r)/ *conj* (*subord*) **1** earlier than the time when: *Do it now before you forget. Before taking off the cover, disconnect the electricity.* Ⓝ 'Will' is not usually used in the 'before' clause. **2** with more desire, interest etc than: *I'll resign before I let her insult me again. You should think twice before giving up your job.* Ⓝ 'Rather than' is also possible but the structure of the sentence changes, as in *I'll resign rather than let her insult me again.*

be·fore³ /bɪ'fɔː(r)/ *prep* **1** earlier than: *He finished before me. The day before yesterday* (= two

days ago); *the year before last* (= two years ago). Ⓝ The past perfect tense (*had* + *pp*) has a special use with 'before' to refer to an action not completed or done at the time, as in *She walked away before I'd finished explaining.* **before dark** ⇨ dark²(1). **a little before** a short time before: *a little before midnight.* Ⓝ Compare *soon after midnight.* **before long** soon: *We'll meet again before long.* **2** (more) towards the beginning (of a list, order, queue etc): *B comes before C. That woman is before you* (e.g. when waiting to be served in a shop). Ⓝ 'Ahead of' and 'in front of' are also possible. **3** still to happen to: *You have your whole life before you.* **4** facing towards (a person): *standing before the judge/head teacher.* **5** showing more desire, enthusiasm, than: *Would you put marriage for love before marriage for money?* Compare above²(6), preference(1).

be·fore·hand /bɪ'fɔːhænd/ *adv* earlier; before something happens: *I knew we'd be late so I phoned the hotel beforehand.*

be·friend /bɪ'frend/ *vt* (*formal*) to be a friend to (esp a person who needs help).

beg /beg/ *v* (**-gg-**) **1** *vt* to ask (a person) with sincere and strong feeling: *I beg you not to take any risks. He begged me to forgive him.* **I beg your pardon** (used as a polite way to show one is sorry, did not hear etc). **2** *vi,vt* to ask for (money, food, help etc) because one is very poor, helpless etc: *She sits outside the station begging* (*for money*). *He begs food and clothes from strangers.*

be·gan /bɪ'gæn/ *pt* of begin.

beg·gar /'begə(r)/ *nc* a person who lives by begging(2). **beggars can't be choosers** (*saying*) people asking for help must take whatever is offered them.

be·gin /bɪ'gɪn/ *vi,vt* (*pt* **began** /bɪ'gæn/, *pp* **begun** /bɪ'gʌn/) **1** to take the first action, do the first part: *begin to play/playing the piano. The meeting/show/interview begins at/will begin at 10 o'clock. Let's begin by looking at page 15. Your journey begins at Heathrow Airport. I began with soup and then had steak. I couldn't begin to* (= I am not able to) *explain what happened.* Ⓝ 'Start' can also be used but 'begin' is preferred if the situation is more formal, as in *begin to conduct an orchestra/write a book/speak to an audience.* 'Begin' is not possible when 'start' is used with machinery, as in *start an engine,* or with business, as in *start a company.* 'Commence' is a formal alternative to 'begin'. **2** to show the first sign(s) of something: *He's beginning to get cold. She began to weaken. Summer is beginning at last!* Ⓝ 'Start' is also possible but is not as usual. **3 to begin with** the first reason is: *He can't come; to begin with he's too young and also he has no money.*

be·gin·ner /bɪ'gɪnə(r)/ *nc* a person who is learning and has only a little experience.

be·ginner's luck *nu* early success or good fortune that is by chance and not because of effort, experience etc.

be·gin·ning /bɪ'gɪnɪŋ/ *nc,nu* the starting-point: *I've read the book from beginning to end.*

be·guile /bɪ'gaɪl/ *vt* (*formal*) to cheat, deceive (a person): *They were beguiled into signing the contract.*

be·gun /bɪ'gʌn/ *pp* of begin.

be·half /bɪ'hɑːf/ *n* **on behalf of sb; on sb's**

behalf (speaking, doing something) for another person or group: *On behalf of my colleagues and myself, I'd like to thank you for coming.*

be·have /bɪˈheɪv/ *v* **1** *vi* to act: conduct oneself in the way mentioned: *behave badly/well towards her.* **2** *vi, v reflex* to be polite, well-mannered: *I told my son to behave (himself).* **3** *vi* (of machines etc and how well/badly they work): *How's your new car behaving?*

,badly-/,well-be'haved *adj* (of a person, esp a child) (not) polite, well-mannered.

be·hav·iour (*US* = **-ior**) /bɪˈheɪvɪə(r)/ *nu* the (good or bad) way a person behaves; treatment shown towards others: *His behaviour towards me shows that he doesn't like me. Tom won a prize for good behaviour.* **be on one's best behaviour** to take great care to behave well.

be·head /bɪˈhed/ *vt* to cut off the head of (a person) as a punishment.

be·held /bɪˈheld/ *pt,pp* of behold.

be·hind¹ /bɪˈhaɪnd/ *adv* **1** in, to, a position at or further back: *Be careful—there's a bus behind. Look behind before you turn right. The second runner was a long way behind.* ⇨ go behind. **2** in a place where a person or something is or was: *You've left your watch behind in the swimming pool. The manager asked us to remain/stay behind* (= stay after others have gone) *after work.* **leave sb/sth behind** ⇨ leave². **3** **behind in/with sth** late dealing with something: *be/fall behind with the rent/payments.* ⇨ behindhand.

be·hind² /bɪˈhaɪnd/ *nc* the part of the body on which one sits: *He fell on his behind.* Ⓝ *'Backside', 'bottom', 'buttocks' are also possible.*

be·hind³ /bɪˈhaɪnd/ *prep* **1** in, to, a position at the back of: *a path behind the house; run behind a tree. The sun went behind a cloud. What was the reason behind that decision?* **do sth/say sth/go behind sb's back** ⇨ back³(1). **behind the scenes** ⇨ scene(6). **2** not having made the same progress, developed as quickly, as: *She's far behind the others in her class. Population growth keeps that country behind its neighbours.* **3** later in time than: *The meeting is running behind schedule.* **4** in the past: *Your exams will soon be behind you.* **5** in support of: *Apply for the job—I'm certain the director is behind you/your application.*

be·hind·hand /bɪˈhaɪndhænd/ *adv* (*formal*) late (in paying): *be behindhand with the rent.* ⇨ behind¹(3).

be·hold /bɪˈhəʊld/ *vt* (*pt,pp* **beheld** /bɪˈheld/) (*old* or *literary use*) to look at (a person, thing).

beige /beɪʒ/ *adj, n* light-brown (colour).

be·ing /ˈbiːɪŋ/ *n* **1** *nu* existence. **come into being** to begin to exist: *When did the law come into being?* **2** *nc* a living person: *Men, women and children are human beings.*

be·lated /bɪˈleɪtɪd/ *adj* coming very late or too late: *a belated apology.*

belch¹ /beltʃ/ *nc* an act or sound of belching.

belch² /beltʃ/ *vt,vi* **1** to send out (gas) from the stomach noisily through the mouth. **2** (of a volcano, factory chimney etc) to send out (smoke etc).

bel·fry /ˈbelfrɪ/ *nc* (*pl* **-ies**) a (church) tower in which bells hang.

be·lief /bɪˈliːf/ *n* **1** *nu* **belief (in sb/sth)** the feeling that something exists or is true, that a person

is honest, will be successful etc: *I haven't much belief in his honesty. I lost my belief in* (= trust in) *doctors after my child died in hospital.* **to the best of my belief** ⇨ best³(3). **2** *nc* something accepted as true or real (esp as part of a religion): *the beliefs of the Christian Church.*

be·lieve /bɪˈliːv/ *vt* **1** to feel sure of the truth of (something, that a person is honest etc): *I believe you/what you have said. I believe what that man says. They believed that he was insane.* **believe in sth** (a) to feel sure of the existence of something: *believe in God.* (b) to feel sure of the value or worth of something: *He believes in getting plenty of exercise.* **2** **make believe (that sth)** to pretend (something): *The boys made believe that they were explorers in Africa.* ⇨ make-believe.

be·liever *nc* a person who believes, esp in a religious faith.

be·little /bɪˈlɪtl/ *vt* to cause (a person, achievement etc) to seem unimportant or of small value: *Don't belittle yourself by cheating in the exam.*

bell /bel/ *nc* a metal object shaped like a cup that makes a ringing sound when hit. ⇨ sound¹(1). **ring a bell** (*fig; informal*) to recall to one's memory something almost forgotten.

belle /bel/ *nc* an attractive woman.

belles-lettres /ˌbel ˈletrə/ *nu* (*Fr*) (*literature*) written works (esp essays, poetry) valued because of the style or artistic quality and not the factual contents.

bel·li·cose /ˈbelɪkəʊs/ *adj* (*formal*) willing, anxious, to fight.

bel·liger·en·cy /bɪˈlɪdʒərənsɪ/ *nu* (*formal*) the state of being anxious to fight.

bel·liger·ent /bɪˈlɪdʒərənt/ *adj* (appearing) anxious to fight: *a belligerent speech/politician.*

bel·low /ˈbeləʊ/ *v* **1** *vi* to make a loud, deep noise (like a bull): *He bellowed even before the dentist had started.* **2** *vi,vt* **bellow (sth) (out)** to sing, shout, (something) loudly or angrily: *They bellowed (out) a drinking song.*

bel·lows /ˈbeləʊz/ *n pl* (also *a pair of bellows*) an apparatus for blowing or forcing air into something, e.g. a fire, an organ in a church.

bel·ly /ˈbelɪ/ *nc* (*pl* **-ies**) **1** (*informal*) the part of the body which includes the stomach and the bowels: *I've a pain in my belly.* **2** a round, curved part: *the belly of a ship/plane.*

'belly·ache *vi* (*informal*) to complain without a good reason.

'belly-button *nc* (*informal*) = navel.

'belly-landing *nc* a landing of a plane without its undercarriage in position.

'belly-laugh *vi, nc* (to make) a loud, coarse laugh.

belly·ful /-fʊl/ *nc* (*informal*) (more than) enough: *He's had his bellyful of your criticism.*

be·long /bɪˈlɒŋ/ *vi* Ⓝ *'Belong' cannot be used in the continuous tenses, e.g. is/was -ing.* **1** **belong to sb/sth** (a) to be the property of a person, organization etc: *These books belong to me.* (b) to be a member of, be connected with, an organization, set etc: *Which union do you belong to? To which union do you belong?* **2** **belong (with sth/together)** to be a (natural, attractive, essential etc) part (of something): *That sock belongs with this one. Those curtains don't belong with the car-*

pet. They don't belong together. **3** to have a right or proper place: *Does it belong here?*

be·long·ings /bɪˈlɒŋɪŋz/ *n pl* personal possessions such as clothes, furniture (but not land, buildings etc): *Take all your belongings with you when you leave the aircraft. Does your insurance policy cover your household belongings?*

be·loved /bɪˈlʌvd/ *nc, adj* (a person who is) greatly loved: *He was beloved by all.*

be·low[1] /bɪˈləʊ/ *adv* **1** at, to, a lower point or level: *My office is immediately below. We heard voices coming from below.* **down below** in a lower part of a building, ship etc. **here below** here on Earth. Ⓝ *'Under'* is not possible. Compare above. **2** later (in a book, article etc): *See the illustration below on page 20.* Opp above[1](3).

be·low[2] /bɪˈləʊ/ *prep* **1** lower than: *Skirts are below the knee this year. The water is below sea-level. The switch is 30cm below the top of the door.* Ⓝ *'Below'* is used when there is a space between the two areas or objects. *'Under'* is used when contact between the edges or surfaces is possible, as in *under the cushion, under my feet.* *'Under'* is also used when referring to a general low position, as in *under the sun, under the ground.* **below ground** ⇨ ground[1](1). ⇨ also belt(1). Opp above[2](1). **2** less than in quantity, age, price, weight etc: *below average temperatures; below the age of 18; below £10 in price.* Ⓝ *'Under'* is also possible, as in *under the age of 18, under £10, under 120kg.* Opp above[2](2) ⇨ over[4](10), under[2](3). **3** lower in rank, position etc: *A captain is below a major. Who is below you at work?* Ⓝ *'Under'* is not possible because it has a different meaning ('controlled, managed, ruled, by') as in *She's under me* (= my assistant) *in the office.* Compare *'the staff below her* (= those having a lower rank or grade) *in the school'* and *'the staff under her* (= those she has control over) *in the school'.* Opp above[2](4). **4** nearer the sea than: *the areas of London below Waterloo Bridge.* Ⓝ Compare *the boats under London Bridge.* Opp above[2](7). **5** (*music*) (of a note, voice etc) lower in tone than. Opp above[2](8).

belt[1] /belt/ *nc* **1** a band of cloth, leather etc worn round the waist. **below the belt** unfair: *That unpleasant remark was below the belt.* **2** a circular strap, used to drive machinery: *a fan-belt* (in the engine of a car). **3** any long and wide area: *a belt of trees.* ⇨ green belt.

belt[2] /belt/ *v* **1** **belt (sth) up** (a) *vt* to fasten (something) with a belt(1): *Belt up your coat.* (b) *vi* (*fig*) (*sl*) to be quiet: *Why don't you belt up!* **2** *vt* to fit (a coat, etc) with a belt(1). **3** *vi* (*informal*) to drive very fast: *We were belting along/down the motorway.*

bench /bentʃ/ *nc* **1** a long seat of wood or stone, e.g. in a public park. **2** a long table at which a carpenter etc works. **3** (the —) (*legal*) judges; magistrates.

'bench mark *nc* a standard or reference point used in measuring (e.g. grades in an exam, efficiency of computers etc).

'bench seat *nc* (in a car) a seat across the width of the car.

bend[1] /bend/ *nc* a curve or turn: *a sharp bend in the road.* **be/go round the bend** (*sl*) to be/ become mad.

bend[2] /bend/ *v* (*pt,pp* **bent** /bent/) **1** *vt,vi* (to

cause something) to form a curve or angle: *Bend the end of the wire up/down/back. Her head was bent over her book.* **bend a rule** ⇨ rule[1](1). **2** *vi* (often **bend down**) to become curved (downwards): *The branches were bending (down) with the weight of the fruit. Can you bend down and touch your toes without bending your knees?* **3** *vi* to change direction: *The road bends to the left here.* **4** *vi* **bend (to sb/sth)** to agree to obey: *bend to her wishes. He'll never bend* (= never agree). **5** **be bent on doing sth** to be determined to do it: *He is bent on learning English.*

be·neath /bɪˈniːθ/ *adv, prep* **1** (*old or literary use*) below, underneath. **2** not worthy of: *His accusations are beneath contempt* (= should be ignored).

ben·edic·tion /ˌbenɪˈdɪkʃn/ *nc* a religious blessing.

ben·efac·tor /ˈbenɪfæktə(r)/ *nc* a person who gives money to charity.

ben·efac·tress /ˈbenɪfæktrɪs/ *nc* a woman who gives money to charity.

ben·efi·cial /ˌbenɪˈfɪʃl/ *adj* (*formal*) having a healthy, helpful, productive etc effect: *Fresh air and good food are beneficial to one's health.*

ben·efi·ci·ary /ˌbenɪˈfɪʃəri/ *nc* (*pl* **-ies**) (*legal*) a person who receives money, property etc, esp from a person when he or she dies.

bene·fit[1] /ˈbenɪfɪt/ *n* **1** *nu* good effect; profit: *Did you get much benefit from your holiday? The money is to be used for the benefit of the poor* (= to help poor people). **give sb the benefit of the doubt** to assume that he or she is innocent because there is not enough evidence of guilt. **2** *nc* an advantage; a good effect: *the benefits of a good education.* **3** *nc* money given to a person by a government or an insurance company: *unemployment/sickness benefit.*

bene·fit[2] /ˈbenɪfɪt/ *vi, vt* to receive an advantage; to have a good effect on (a person): *They benefited/are benefiting from a holiday by the sea.*

ben·ev·ol·ence /bɪˈnevələns/ *nu* (*formal*) the wish to do good (by giving money): *His benevolence allowed many poor boys to attend college.*

ben·ev·ol·ent /bɪˈnevələnt/ *adj* (*formal*) showing benevolence: *a benevolent pop star giving a concert in aid of famine victims.*

ben·ev·ol·ent·ly *adv*

be·nign /bɪˈnaɪn/ *adj* **1** (*formal*) (of a person) kind and gentle. **2** (of soil, climate) mild. **3** (of a tumour) not dangerous to life. Compare malignant.

bent[1] /bent/ *adj* (*sl*) **1** dishonest: *a bent policeman.* **2** (*dated*) homosexual.

bent[2] /bent/ *nc* **bent (for sth)** an ability and interest: *She has a bent for music.*

bent[3] /bent/ *pt,pp* of bend[2]. **bent on** ⇨ bend[2](5).

be·queath /bɪˈkwiːð/ *vt* **bequeath sth (to sb)** to arrange (by making a will) to give property etc (to a person) after one's death: *He has bequeathed me his gold watch.*

be·quest /bɪˈkwest/ *nc* an amount of money, property etc that is bequeathed: *He left bequests of money to all his staff.*

be·reaved /bɪˈriːvd/ *adj* (*pred*) not having a husband, wife, child etc because he or she has died: *a bereaved mother.*

be·reave·ment *nc,nu*

be·reft /bɪˈreft/ *adj* *(pred)* **bereft of sth** *(formal)* without luck, happiness etc: *He was bereft of hope.*

be·ret /ˈbereɪ/ *nc* a flat, round cap of felt or cloth, as worn by soldiers.

ber·ry /ˈberɪ/ *nc* *(pl* **-ies)** a small, soft fruit with seeds: *a strawberry; blackberries/raspberries.*

ber·serk /bəˈzɜːk/ *adj* **send sb/go berserk** make a person/become uncontrollably wild: *He went completely berserk.*

berth¹ /bɜːθ/ *nc* **1** a sleeping-place in a train, ship etc. **2** a place where a ship can be tied up.

berth² /bɜːθ/ *vi,vt* (to cause a ship) to come into a harbour etc and be tied up.

be·seech /bɪˈsiːtʃ/ *vt* *(pt,pp* **besought** /bɪˈsɔːt/) *(old or literary use)* to ask (a person) earnestly or urgently: *Spare his life, I beseech you.*

be·set /bɪˈset/ *vt* *(pt,pp* **beset)** **(-tt-)** (usually *passive)* to attack, cause trouble for, (a person, business etc) in several ways: *a job beset with difficulties. She was beset by doubts.*

be·side /bɪˈsaɪd/ *prep* **1** at, by, the side of: *the trees beside the river. He was sitting beside (= next to) me in the meeting.* Ⓝ *'By', meaning 'next to', is also possible.* **2** compared to: *These sales figures seem very good beside the original budget.* **be beside the point** ⇨ point¹(7). **3 be beside oneself (with sth)** have lost all self-control (because of anger, excitement etc): *She was beside herself with joy/anger at the news.*

be·sides¹ /bɪˈsaɪdz/ *adv* **1** as an added person or thing: *They may look poor but they both have good jobs and rich parents besides.* Ⓝ *'As well' and 'in addition' are more usual.* **2** as an added reason: *It's too far to walk and besides it's raining.* Ⓝ *'Besides' is one of several words such as 'also', 'anyway', 'moreover', used to introduce another (often more important) reason.*

be·sides² /bɪˈsaɪdz/ *prep* **1** (used in positive statements) as an added person or thing to: *I have another sister besides Jane. Besides milk and cheese, we need vegetables. Besides swimming, she enjoys tennis and netball.* Ⓝ *'As well as' is also possible. 'In addition to' is possible but is more formal. 'Apart from' and 'except (for)' have a different meaning. 'Besides' includes another person or thing in the statement. 'Apart from' or 'except (for)' excludes another person or thing. Compare: Besides potatoes, we need carrots, onions and tomatoes (i.e. we need all of them) and We need all of them apart from/except (for) carrots (i.e. but not carrots).* **2** (used in questions and negative statements not including the person or thing mentioned (because he/she/it is already included or known): *I haven't any relatives besides my brother. Who saw the accident besides you?* Ⓝ *'Apart from' is also possible and is more usual. 'As well as' is not possible. 'In addition to' is only possible in questions. 'Except (for)' is only possible in negative statements.*

be·siege /bɪˈsiːdʒ/ *vt* **1** to surround (a place) with armed forces: *Troy was besieged by the Greeks for ten years.* **2** *(fig)* to surround (a person): *He was besieged by his fans.* **besiege sb (with sth)** to attack a person (with many questions, requests etc): *The pop singer was besieged with requests for her autograph.*

be·sieger *nc* a person who besieges a place, per-

son.

be·sot·ted /bɪˈsɒtɪd/ *adj* (usually *pred)* behaving stupidly (because of alcohol, love etc): *I'm besotted (with love for her).*

be·sought /bɪˈsɔːt/ *pt,pp* of beseech.

be·spat·ter·ed /bɪˈspætəd/ *adj* (usually *pred)* covered with (large drops etc of): *bespattered with mud.*

be·spec·tacled /bɪˈspektəkld/ *adj* *(formal)* wearing spectacles.

best¹ /best/ *adj* *(superl* of good) **1** most superior in quality (of a group): *This is the best film I've ever seen. Does France produce the best cheese in the world? This is the best price* (= the cheapest) *available. What is your best offer? He's produced the best record by far/by far the best record* (= a much more superior record than others). ⇨ also foot¹(1). **2** most suitable (of a choice): *This is the best medicine. The best thing to do is to rest. The best way to go is along the motorway.* **the next best thing** ⇨ thing(3). **3** most liked (of a group): *Literature is my best subject. Paul is my best friend.* Compare worst¹. **4 the best part of sth** almost all of it: *the best part of an hour/£1/a mile.* ⇨ better¹(4).

,best 'man *nc* the man who helps a bridegroom at a wedding. Compare bridesmaid.

,best·'seller *nc* a book, record, tape etc that is sold in large quantities.

best² /best/ *adv* *(superl* of well) **1** in a way that is superior (to others): *Bob did best in the exam. This particular tool does the job best. This pen isn't ideal but you must try (to do) your best/do the best you can* (= make your best effort) *with it.* **2** to the greatest extent: *I like Paul best. Which colour suits me best? He enjoys playing rugby best. This is the best-equipped car on the market.* **3 be best at sth** to be most skilled at something: *Which sport are you best at?* Compare worst².

best³ /best/ *pron, nu* (not used with *a)* **1** (the —) the most superior person, thing, part, quality etc of a group: *They're all good at football but Peter is the best. Her exam results were the best. We're the best of friends* (= like each other very much). **2** the greatest effort: *Her best wasn't enough to break the world record. We'll try our very best* (= will make the greatest possible effort). *The competition brought out the best in him* (= encouraged him to make his greatest effort). Compare worst³. **3** (phrases using *best)* **All the best** (formula used to end a letter to a friend or to say goodbye) I wish you happiness, health etc. **at best** which is the most hopeful possibility: *We won't finish the work until Friday at best.* **at her/ its/our etc best** in the best condition: *The garden is at its best in summer.* **at the best of times** when conditions are most favourable: *Even at the best of times we manage only ten hours of work a day.* **to the best of one's ability** (done) as well as possible. **to the best of my belief/knowledge** in my opinion (although I may be wrong). **with the best of intentions; with the best will in the world** wishing to be as helpful as possible: *With the best will in the world he couldn't finish the job today.* **do one's (level) best (to** + *verb)* to make every effort (to do something successfully): *I did my level best to persuade him.* **have the best of**

both worlds to enjoy the benefits, advantages, of two opposite possibilities. **look one's best** to appear as smart or attractive as possible: *He looks his best in a suit.* **make the best of it/things/a bad job** to do all one can and be satisfied because conditions are not very good.

bes·tial /'bestɪəl/ *adj* (*derog*) (of a person's behaviour) extremely cruel. ⇨ beast(2).

be·stow /bɪ'stəʊ/ *vt* **bestow sth on sb** (*formal*) to give an honour, title etc to a person.
be·stow·al *nc,nu*

bet¹ /bet/ *nc* **1** an agreement to risk money etc on an event of which the result is doubtful: *make a bet; win/lose a bet.* **2** the money etc offered: *to place a £1 bet.*

bet² /bet/ *v* (*pt,pp* — or occasionally **—ted**; **-tt-**) **1** *vt,vi* to risk (money) on a race or an event of which the result is doubtful: *He bet me £5 that he could win.* **2** *vt* (*informal*) to be certain about (something): *I bet (you anything)* (= am absolutely certain) *that I pass the exam.*

be·tray /bɪ'treɪ/ *vt* **1** to be an enemy to (one's country etc): *She betrayed her country by selling important information to the enemy.* **2** to behave without loyalty or honesty towards (a person, a person's feelings): *You've betrayed my trust in you.* **3** to allow (a secret) to become known, either by accident or on purpose. **4** to make (something) known: *His accent betrayed the fact that he was a foreigner.*
be·tray·al /bɪ'treɪəl/ *nc,nu* (an act of) betraying.
be·tray·er *nc* a person who betrays.

be·troth·ed /bɪ'trəʊðd/ *adj* (*literary*) engaged to be married.
be·troth·al /-ðl/ *nc* an engagement to marry.

bet·ter¹ /'betə(r)/ *adj* (*comp* of good) **1** superior in quality (to others): *This is a better programme than the one I saw last night. Their prices are much better* (= much cheaper) *than ours. She's made an even better record* (i.e. this achievement is surprising etc because her last one was very good). **better luck next time** (used to show sympathy) I hope you are more successful, lucky etc when you try again. **have seen better days** to have not been as poor, unlucky etc as now. **2** more suitable: *This is a better car for long journeys. This cure is better for colds than flu. It's better to let them know you are coming than to arrive unexpectedly.* **better late than never** (used as an excuse (often ironically) for arriving, deciding, finishing late). **3** (*pred*) (of health) **(a)** improving: *He's feeling so much better today.* **(b)** fully recovered: *I'm better now, thanks. She's completely/quite better.* **4 the better part of sth** more than half of it: *the better part of an hour/ £5/100 kilometres.* ⇨ best¹(4).

bet·ter² /'betə(r)/ *adv* (*comp* of well) **1** in a superior way (to others): *I'd write better if I had a suitable pen. A computer can do the job better than you. She did better in the interview than she'd hoped. I work better with music playing. This tool works better on wood than stone.* **be better off** to have more money, happiness etc. **be better off without sb** to be happier without an unkind etc person as a husband, wife, friend: *You'll be better off without him.* Compare worse²(1). **2** to a greater extent: *I like Mary better (than Jane). Which curtains suit this room better, those ones or*

these? *I enjoy tennis better than cricket.* **3 be/get better** to be/become healthy after an illness: *I hope you get better soon.* **know better** to be more intelligent, responsible etc: *You should know better (than to play with lighted matches).* **4 had better** + *verb* without 'to' (showing duty or obligation) ought to: *We'd better hurry or we'll miss the train. I'd better not tell her, it would only worry her. Hadn't you better take an umbrella?* **5 better at sth** more skilled at something: *He's better/getting better at selling the product than designing it.*

bet·ter³ /'betə(r)/ *nu* **1** (the —) the more superior, useful (of two): *He's the better of the two finalists. This is the better of the two.* **be all the better for sth** to benefit very much from something: *You'll be all the better for a good holiday.* **get the better of sb/sth** to defeat her/him/it: *I got the better of her in the semifinals.* **for the better** producing an improvement (in behaviour, conditions etc): *Moving house was a change for the better.* **for better or (for) worse** whether the result is good or bad: *I married you for better or worse.* **2** (*pl*) people who are socially superior: *Is it necessary to respect one's betters?*

bet·ter⁴ /'betə(r)/ *vt* (often *reflex*) to improve (on something): *I hope you can better your performance in the competition/exam/World Games. She hopes to better herself* (= earn more etc) *in the Civil Service.*

be·tween¹ /bɪ'twiːn/ *adv* **1 (in) between (a)** in, into, the middle (of two points in space, time, quantity etc): *We went to the museum in the morning and the theatre in the afternoon, with a quick lunch (in) between.* **(b)** at various intervals inside: *There were blue spots with white lines (in) between.* **2 few and far between** ⇨ few¹(2).

be·tween² /bɪ'twiːn/ *prep* **1** in the middle of (two points in space, time, order, distance, temperature, price etc): *Paraguay is situated between Brazil and Argentina. Come between 6 and 7 o'clock. An MA is between a BA and a PhD. The price will be somewhere between £10 and £15.* Ⓝ For a comparison of 'between' and 'among', ⇨ the note at among(1). **2** to and from: *travelling between Europe and America; flying between Paris, Rome and Madrid.* Ⓝ More than two points are possible. **3** giving each (of two) a portion (when sharing or dividing): *She divided the money between both of us.* Compare among(2). **4** including each one (when fighting, talking, sorting etc): *quarrelling between my parents; an agreement between the parties.* Ⓝ 'Among' is used for more than two, as in *searching among the flowers* but 'between' is now often used for more than two, as in *peace talks between the nuclear powers.* Compare among(3). **between you and me/you, me and the gatepost/ourselves** to be known only by the two of us. **5** showing choice of one and not the other: *choosing between right and wrong; distinguish between the best and the worst; decide between staying and going.* Ⓝ The use of 'or' in the middle of the two choices is not possible. Use 'and'. **6** involving both or all: *We bought the car between us. They carried all the equipment between them.* Ⓝ More than two people etc are possible.

bev·el /'bevl/ *nc* a sloping edge. □ *vt* (**-ll-**, *US* = **-l-**) to make a sloping edge on (something).

big

bev·er·age /'bevərɪdʒ/ nc any sort of drink except water, e.g. milk, tea, wine, beer.

be·ware /bɪ'weə(r)/ vi **beware (of sb/sth)** (usually *imperative* as a warning) to be very careful about a (bad) person, thing etc: *Beware of the dog! Beware of pickpockets.*

be·wil·der /bɪ'wɪldə(r)/ vt to confuse (a person): *bewildered by the crowds and traffic in the city.*
be·wil·der·ing adj
be·wil·der·ment nu

be·witch /bɪ'wɪtʃ/ vt **1** to cause a (bad) effect on (a person) using magic: *In the story she is bewitched by the wizard.* **2** to attract, delight, (a person) as if by magic: *She bewitched the audience with her dancing.*
be·witch·ing adj: *a bewitching smile.*
be·witch·ing·ly adv

be·yond[1] /bɪ'jɒnd/ adv at, to, a distance farther on or away: *We can visit India, Thailand and the countries beyond.*

be·yond[2] /bɪ'jɒnd/ prep **1** at, on, to, the farther side of: *The house is beyond the bridge.* **2** farther than the limits of: *My bike is beyond repair. This maths problem is beyond me/my capabilities* (= I can't understand, solve it). *The apples are beyond my reach* (= too high). **3** (used in negative statements and questions) not including the person or thing mentioned: *We were not able to help beyond keeping her warm.* Ⓝ *'Apart from' is more usual.* **4** (of time) later than: *Don't stay out beyond 6 o'clock.* Ⓝ *'After' is more usual.*

b/f abbr (*bookkeeping*) brought forward.

bi·as[1] /'baɪəs/ nc (pl **-es**) **1** a particular attitude, preference, (without having full knowledge): *He has a strong bias towards/against the plan* (= is in favour of it/opposed to it). *She shows a bias towards scientific subjects rather than arts.* **2** *cut sth on the bias* cut diagonally across cloth.

bi·as[2] /'baɪəs/ vt (pt,pp **-ed**) to influence (something) unfairly: *They biased the application forms in favour of richer families.*
biased, biassed adj favouring one side unfairly: *a biased report/opinion. The judge was not biased.*

bib /bɪb/ nc **1** a piece of cloth etc tied under a child's chin. **2** the upper part of an apron.

Bible /'baɪbl/ n (the —) the sacred writings of the Jews and the Christians.
bib·li·cal /'bɪblɪkl/ adj (also B-) of, contained in, the Bible: *biblical references.*

bib·li·ogra·pher /ˌbɪblɪ'ɒɡrəfə(r)/ nc a person who writes or studies bibliographies.
bib·lio·graphi·cal /ˌbɪblɪə'ɡræfɪkl/ adj of, concerning, a bibliography.
bib·li·ogra·phy /ˌbɪblɪ'ɒɡrəfɪ/ nc (pl **-ies**) a list of books and writings of one author or about one subject.

bi·cam·er·al /baɪ'kæmrəl/ adj (of a legislative assembly) having two separate groups of members, e.g. the Senate and the House of Representatives in USA.

bi·cen·ten·ary /ˌbaɪsen'tiːnərɪ/ nc (pl **-ies**) (the celebration of the) 200th anniversary of an event.
bi·cen·ten·nial /ˌbaɪsen'tenɪəl/ adj **1** of a 200th anniversary: *the bicentennial celebrations in the USA in 1976.* **2** lasting for 200 years. □ nc (*US*) a 200th anniversary.

bi·ceps /'baɪseps/ nc (pl **—**) (*anat*) the large muscle in the front part of the upper arm.

bi·cycle /'baɪsɪkl/ nc a machine with two wheels moved by using pedals. □ vi (*formal*) to cycle (the more usual word).

bid[1] /bɪd/ nc **1** (at an auction) an offer of a price: *Are there no bids for this very fine painting?* **2** (in card games, esp bridge) a statement of the number of tricks a player proposes to win: *a bid of two hearts.* **3** *make a bid for sth* (*informal*) to try to achieve something: *make a bid for freedom* (i.e. by escaping).

bid[2] /bɪd/ vt,vi (pt,pp **—; -dd-**) **1** (at an auction) to make an offer of a price: *What am I bid for this painting?* **2** (in card games) to make a bid(2): *I bid two hearts.* ⇨ outbid.

bid[3] /bɪd/ vt (pt **bade** /bæd/ or—, pp **—den** /'bɪdn/ or —; **-dd-**) (*old use*) **1** to order (a person) (to do something): *He bade me (to) come in.* **2** to say (something) (to a person) as a greeting etc: *He had bidden me good morning.*
bid·der /'bɪdə(r)/ nc a person who makes a bid(1,2).
bid·ding /'bɪdɪŋ/ nu **1** *do sb's bidding* (*formal*) to do what he or she commands. **2** an act of offering a price at an auction sale: *Bidding was slow/brisk.* **3** the making of a bid(2).

bi·det /'biːdeɪ/ nc (*Fr*) a small, low bath used for washing the genitals etc.

bi·en·ni·al /baɪ'enɪəl/ adj **1** lasting for two years. **2** happening every alternate year.

bier /bɪə(r)/ nc a movable stand for a coffin or a dead body.

bi·fo·cal /ˌbaɪ'fəʊkl/ adj (esp of lenses in spectacles) designed for both distant and near vision.
bi·focals /ˌbaɪ'fəʊklz/ n pl spectacles with bifocal lenses.

big /bɪg/ adj (**—ger**, **—gest**) **1** more than average or usual in size, mass, amount, strength etc: *a big house/man/salary/push/effort. This shirt is too big/far too big/much too big for me. Your trousers are a bigger size than mine. I'm no bigger than* (= the same size as) *you. This supermarket is the biggest in the country.* Ⓝ *'Large' is also possible but is more formal. 'Great' is not possible because it has a different meaning.* ⇨ *the note in 3 below, but 'great' meaning 'a lot of' is possible with uncountable nouns, as in great care/generosity, and also with words meaning quantity or size as in a great amount/size/ degree/quantity. 'Big' is also possible with these words but is very informal.* Compare little[1](3), small[1]. *great big* ⇨ great(6). **2** (*informal*) elder: *my big brother/sister.* Ⓝ *'Large' and 'great' are not possible.* Compare little[1](6). **3** of more than average importance: *a big decision/occasion/moment/ mistake/nation/success.* Ⓝ *'Large' is not possible. 'Great' is possible but is preferred for very important situations, as in a great occasion; a great moment in history, or to mean 'famous' or 'special' as in a great man/painting/victory.* Opp small(3). **4** ambitious: *have big ideas; do things in a big way* (e.g. to impress); (used as an adv): *to talk/think big* (sl; to describe, have, ambitious plans). Ⓝ *'Large' and 'great' are not possible.* **5** successful; popular: *He's a big star. She's big in the retail business.* Ⓝ *'Large' and 'great' are not possible.* ⇨ *the note in 3 above.* **6** generous: *It was big of you to say such kind things about me. Let's give this young singer a big hand* (= applaud loudly). Ⓝ *'Large' and 'great' are not* possible.

,Big 'Brother *nc* a person, organization, having complete power and control.

,big 'business *n* (a) *nu* powerful financial or business organizations. (b) *nc* (*informal*) a very important concern.

,big 'game *nu* large animals, such as elephant, lion, rhinoceros.

'big·head *nc* (*informal; derog*) a conceited person.

,big·'headed *adj* (*derog*) conceited.

,big·'hearted *adj* kind and generous.

'big-mouth *nc* (*sl; derog*) a person who often tells secrets.

'big noise/shot/wig *nc* (*sl*) a successful, powerful, person (in business).

'big time *nu* (the —) (*sl*) the most successful level in show business: *to hit the big time*.

,big 'top *nc* (the —) a large tent used for a circus.

big·am·ist /'bɪgəmɪst/ *nc* a person who is guilty of bigamy.

big·am·ous /'bɪgəməs/ *adj* of, involving, bigamy.

big·amy /'bɪgəmɪ/ *nu* having two wives or husbands living (a crime among Christians). Compare monogamy, polygamy.

bight /baɪt/ *nc* (the sea inside) a long curve in a coastline.

big·ot /'bɪgət/ *nc* (*derog*) a person with a strong opinion or belief and who thinks other ideas are wrong.

big·ot·ed *adj* (*derog*) intolerant of other people's opinions.

bike /baɪk/ *nc* (*informal*) = bicycle.

bi·ki·ni /bɪ'ki:nɪ/ *nc* (*pl* —**s**) a two-piece garment (bra and briefs) worn by girls and women for swimming and sun-bathing.

bi·lat·er·al /ˌbaɪ'lætərəl/ *adj* **1** of, on, with, two sides. **2** (*legal*) (of an agreement etc) made between two (people, governments).

bile /baɪl/ *nu* the brownish-yellow bitter liquid produced by the liver to help in digesting food.

bilge /bɪldʒ/ *nu* **1** the dirty water that collects in the bottom of a ship. **2** (*sl; derog*) foolish talk or writing.

bil·har·zia /ˌbɪl'hɑ:zɪə/ *nu* a kind of tropical disease caused by parasites in the blood.

bi·lin·gual /ˌbaɪ'lɪŋgwəl/ *adj* **1** able to speak two languages. **2** using, concerning, two languages. ⇨ monolingual.

bil·ious /'bɪlɪəs/ *adj* feeling sick, because of too much bile: *a bilious attack; feel bilious.*

bill¹ /bɪl/ *nc* a horny part of the mouth of some birds. □ *vi* **bill and coo** (of doves and (*fig*) of two people) to exchange caresses.

bill² /bɪl/ *nc* **1** a written statement of charges for goods delivered or services given: *There are some bills to pay/to be paid.* **foot the bill** (to agree) to pay the expenses. **2** a written or printed notice, poster etc. **fill the bill** to be, do, all that is required or expected. **3** (*legal*) a proposed law to be discussed by a parliament (called an *Act* when passed). **4** a certificate: *bill of entry* (= one from Customs to show final clearance of goods); *a clean bill of health* (i.e. certifying that a person is healthy). **5** (*US*) a banknote: *a ten-dollar bill.*

,bill of 'lading *nc* (*commerce*) a document listing goods to be shipped overseas.

bill³ /bɪl/ *vt* **1** to make (something) known, announce in a poster, programme: *Olivier was billed to appear as Lear.* **2 bill sb (for sth)** to give or send a bill²(1) to a person (for something).

bil·let /'bɪlɪt/ *vt, nc* (to provide) a place (usually a private house) where soldiers are boarded and lodged.

bil·liards /'bɪlɪədz/ *nu* an indoor game played with balls and long tapering sticks (called *cues*) on an oblong, cloth-covered table.

bil·lion /'bɪlɪən/ *adj or det, nc* **1** (*GB*) one million millions or 10^{12}. **2** (*Fr, US*) one thousand millions or 10^9.

bil·low /'bɪləʊ/ *nc* (*literary*) a large wave. □ *vi* to rise like waves: *The flames billowed over the roof.*

bil·lowy *adj* like large waves.

billy-goat /'bɪlɪ gəʊt/ *nc* a male goat. Compare nanny-goat.

bin /bɪn/ *nc* a large rigid container, usually with a lid: *a bread-bin; a litter-bin; a dustbin.*

bi·nary /'baɪnərɪ/ *adj* (*tech*) of, involving, a pair or pairs.

,binary 'code *nc* (*computers*) a method of storing information with each letter, number etc represented by a set of values using two alternatives (negative and positive).

,binary 'scale *nc* (the —) (*maths*) a number system with only two digits, 0 and 1, in which $1 = 1$, $10 = 2$, $11 = 3$, $100 = 4$, $101 = 5$ etc.

bind¹ /baɪnd/ *n sing* (*informal*) a difficult, irritating situation or condition: *Having to work overtime is a bind.*

bind² /baɪnd/ *vt* (*pt, pp* **bound** /baʊnd/) **1** to tie or fasten (something) with rope etc: *They bound his legs (together) so that he couldn't escape.* **2** (*fig; often as pp*) to link (people, ideas etc) closely: *We are bound to him by gratitude/by a close friendship.* **3** to strengthen the edge of (something) with tape etc: *bind the cuffs of a jacket with leather.* **4** to wrap cloth etc round (something): *bind a wound.* **5** to cause (a person) (by legal agreement, a promise etc) to agree to a certain course of action: *bind him to secrecy* (= make him promise to keep a secret). *This agreement is legally binding* (= It would be illegal to break it). ⇨ bound¹ for special uses of the *pp*. **6** to fasten (sheets of paper) into a cover: *a book bound in leather.*

bind·ing /'baɪndɪŋ/ *n* **1** *nc* a book cover. **2** *nu* cloth etc for protecting an edge or seam (on clothes etc).

binge /bɪndʒ/ *nc* (*informal*) a social occasion of drinking and eating too much.

bin·ocu·lars /bɪ'nɒkjʊləz/ *n pl* (also *a pair of binoculars*) an instrument with lenses for both eyes, making distant objects seem nearer.

bi·no·mi·al /baɪ'nəʊmɪəl/ *adj, nc* (*maths*) (of) an expression having two terms, e.g. $2x + y$.

bio·chem·is·try /ˌbaɪəʊ'kemɪstrɪ/ *nu* the scientific study of the chemistry of animals and plants.

bio·de·grad·able /ˌbaɪəʊdɪ'greɪdəbl/ *adj* (of materials such as packaging) able to rot and be destroyed by natural means: *Plastics are not biodegradable.*

bi·ogra·pher /baɪ'ɒgrəfə(r)/ *nc* a person who writes a biography.

bio·graph·ic /ˌbaɪə'græfɪk/ *adj* of biography.

bi·ogra·phy /baɪ'ɒgrəfɪ/ *n* (*pl* **-ies**) **1** *nc* a person's life history written by another. **2** *nu* literature dealing with the life history of people.

biol *abbr* biology.

bio·logi·cal /ˌbaɪə'lɒdʒɪkl/ *adj* of biology.

bio·logical 'warfare *nu* the deliberate use of germs etc to spread disease in a war.

bi·ol·ogist /baɪ'ɒlədʒɪst/ *nc* a student of, expert in, biology.

bi·ol·ogy /baɪ'ɒlədʒɪ/ *nu* the scientific study of the physical life of animals and plants.

bi·on·ic /baɪ'ɒnɪk/ *adj* of bionics (and, in stories, having exceptional physique because of electronic transplants).

bi·on·ics /baɪ'ɒnɪks/ *nu* the scientific study of the way the brain works and its application to electronic development.

bio·phys·ics /ˌbaɪəʊ'fɪzɪks/ *nu* the scientific study of the relationship of physics to biology.

bio·rhythm /'baɪəʊrɪðəm/ *nc* (an organized chart with) a pattern of mental, emotional or physical activity affecting each person's (way of) life.

bio·sphere /'baɪəʊsfɪə(r)/ *n* (the —) (*tech*) the area of the atmosphere and ground containing living things.

bi·ped /'baɪped/ *nc* (*tech*) a two-footed animal, e.g. a man or a bird.

birch /bɜːtʃ/ *nc,nu* (also *attrib*) (the wood of) a kind of forest tree with a smooth bark and thin branches.

bird /bɜːd/ *nc* **1** a creature with feathers, usually able to fly: *a blackbird.* **birds of a feather** (*fig*) people with the same interests. **a bird in the hand is worth two in the bush** (*saying*) be content with the little one has because it is better than anything one has not or cannot have. **kill two birds with one stone** to achieve two aims at the same time. **2** (*sl*) a woman, esp a girlfriend.

,bird of 'prey *nc* a bird that kills small animals for food.

'bird·cage *nc* a cage for birds.

,bird's-eye 'view *nc* (**a**) a wide view seen from high up. (**b**) (*fig*) a general survey without details.

'bird·song *nu* the musical cry of a bird.

'bird-watcher *nc* a person who studies the habits of birds.

biro /'baɪrəʊ/ *nc* (*P*) a kind of ballpoint pen.

birth /bɜːθ/ *n* **1** *nc,nu* (the process, time, of) being born: *The baby weighed seven pounds at birth* (i.e. when it was born). **give birth to sb** to produce a child. **2** *nc,nu* (*fig*) the process of coming into existence: *the birth of a new political party.* **3** *nu* family origin: *She is Russian by birth and British by marriage.*

'birth control *nu* (any method of) preventing an unwanted pregnancy.

'birth·day *nc* (also *attrib*) (an anniversary of) the day of one's birth: *a birthday present/card. What would you like for your birthday?*

'birthday suit *nc* (*humorous*) the state of being naked: *seen in his birthday suit.*

'birth·mark *nc* a mark on the body at birth.

'birth·place *nc* the house or district in which one was born.

'birth·rate *nc* the numbers of births in one year for every 1000 individuals.

bis·cuit /'bɪskɪt/ *nc* a flat, thin, crisp cake of many kinds, sweetened or unsweetened.

bi·sect /baɪ'sekt/ *vt* (*tech*) to cut or divide (something) into two (usually equal parts).

bi·sec·tion /ˌbaɪ'sekʃn/ *nu*

bish·op /'bɪʃəp/ *nc* **1** a Christian clergyman of high rank who organizes the work of the Church in a city or district. **2** a chess piece.

bish·op·ric /-rɪk/ *nc* = diocese.

bi·son /'baɪsn/ *nc* (*pl* —) a wild ox (*US = buffalo*).

bis·tro /'biːstrəʊ/ *nc* (*pl* —s) a small café, restaurant or nightclub.

bit¹ /bɪt/ *nc* **1** (a part of) a tool used for boring or drilling holes. **2** a piece for the mouth (metal bar) forming part of a horse's bridle.

bit² /bɪt/ *nc* **1** a small piece (of anything): *He ate every bit* (= all) *his dinner.* **a bit** a short time: *Let's wait a bit.* **a bit . . .** a little . . . : *She's feeling a bit tired.* ⇨ off²(4). **a bit of a . . .** to a small degree: *He's a bit of a coward.* **not a bit** not at all; not in the least: *She's not a bit sorry. He doesn't care a bit.* **bit by bit** slowly, gradually: *She's improving bit by bit.* **every bit as good** etc as equally good etc. **come/fall to bits** to break into small pieces. **cut/pull/tear sth to bits** to cause it to become small pieces. **2** (*computers*) a binary digit (0 or 1).

bit³ /bɪt/ *pt* of bite².

bitch¹ /bɪtʃ/ *nc* **1** a female dog, wolf or fox. Compare dog(2). **2** (*sl; derog*) spiteful woman or girl.

bitch² /bɪtʃ/ *vi* (*sl*) to speak spitefully to or about a person.

bite¹ /baɪt/ *nc* **1** an act of biting. ⇨ bark². **2** an injury resulting from a bite or sting: *His face was covered with insect bites.* **3** a piece cut off by biting: *I haven't had a bite since morning.* **4** an act, result, of catching a fish on a hook: *He'd been fishing all morning but hadn't had a bite.* **5** a sharp feeling: *There's a bite in the air this morning.*

bite² /baɪt/ *vt,vi* (*pt* **bit** /bɪt/, *pp* **bitten** /'bɪtn/) **1** to attack, cut into, (something) with the teeth: *The dog bit me in the leg. It's OK, my dog won't bite.* **bite off more than one can chew** to attempt too much. **bite the dust** ⇨ dust¹. **bite sb's head off** ⇨ head¹(1). **bite one's lip** ⇨ lip(1). **2** (of insects) to sting (a person). **3** (of fish) to accept (the bait): *The fish wouldn't bite.* **4** to cause a sharp pain to (the body): *His fingers were bitten by the frost/were frost-bitten.*

bit·ing /'baɪtɪŋ/ *adj* (*attrib*) **1** causing a sharp, cold feeling: *a biting wind.* **2** (*fig*) severe and painful: *biting criticism.*

bit·ten /'bɪtn/ *pp* of bite².

bit·ter¹ /'bɪtə(r)/ *adj* **1** tasting sharp (and sometimes unpleasant): *Beer, olives and unripe fruit taste bitter.* Opp sweet¹(1). Compare sour¹(1). **2** unpleasant and causing anger or sorrow: *bitter disappointments/memories.* **3** (*attrib*) filled with, caused by, envy, hate or disappointment: *bitter quarrels/enemies.* **4** extremely sharp and cold: *a bitter wind. The weather was bitter.* **5 to the bitter end** until all that is possible has been tried, done.

bit·ter·ly *adv*: *He's bitterly disappointed.*

bit·ter·ness *nu*

bit·ter² /'bɪtə(r)/ *nu* a kind of beer: *a pint of bitter.*

bit·tern /'bɪtɜːn/ *nc* any of many kinds of wading birds that live on marshes.

bit·ty /'bɪtɪ/ adj (-ier, -iest) (informal; derog) made up of many small, disorganized parts: a bitty report/speech.

bitu·men /'bɪtʃʊmən/ nu the black, sticky substance (from petroleum) used for making roads etc.

bi·valve /'baɪvælv/ nc (tech) a water animal with a hinged double shell, e.g. an oyster, a mussel.

bi·week·ly /ˌbaɪˈwiːklɪ/ adj 1 occurring two times a week. 2 happening every two weeks.

bi·zarre /bɪˈzɑː(r)/ adj very strange to look at, to have occurred etc: a bizarre experience.

bk written abbr book.

blab /blæb/ vi (-bb-) (informal) 1 to talk foolishly. 2 to tell a secret.

black¹ /blæk/ adj (—er, —est) 1 without colour or light: as black as coal/ink/night; wearing a black dress; the black pieces in chess; a black (= bruised) eye. Compare white¹. **be black and blue** to have many bruises. **in black and white** written down. 2 (of the body, clothes etc) very dirty: Your face is black! 3 (no comp) without milk or cream: black coffee/tea. 4 without hope, employment etc: a black future; black regions with many social problems. 5 (of feelings, behaviour etc) very evil, angry: a black look/mood. 6 (no comp) (GB) (of jobs, materials, in a factory during a strike) not to be done, moved etc. 7 (also B-) (of a person) having a dark brown skin colour.

,**black 'art/'magic** nu the kind used for evil purposes.

'**black·ball** vt to prevent (a person) from being elected a member of a club by voting against him at a secret ballot.

'**black belt** nc (a holder of) the highest grades in judo.

'**black·berry** nc (also attrib) a kind of small berry, black when ripe, growing wild on bushes (called brambles): blackberry pie.

'**black·bird** nc a common European songbird.

'**black·board** nc a board used in schools for writing and drawing on with chalk.

,**black 'comedy** nu (literature) a type of drama using the idea that people live in an environment beyond their control so that moral values are unimportant, often with a tragic result.

'**black·cur·rant** nc (also attrib) a kind of European currant with black fruit: blackcurrant jam.

'**black·guard** /'blægɑːd/ nc (dated) a person who behaves dishonourably.

'**black·head** nc a spot on the skin, the top being black.

,**black 'humour** nu (literature) humour using cruelty or immorality (often as part of black comedy).

,**black 'ice** nu ice on a road surface which is invisible and dangerous to drive on.

'**black·leg** nc (informal) a person who works when other workers are on strike. ⇨ black¹(6).

'**black·list** vt, nc (to put a person on) a list of those who are disapproved of, to be avoided etc.

,**black 'magic** nu = black art.

'**black·mail** vt, nu (to force a person to make) a payment of money for not making known something to harm her or his character.

'**black·mailer** nc a person who blackmails.

,**black 'mark** nc a sign of disapproval.

,**black 'market** nc (the —) the unlawful buying and selling of goods, currencies etc.

'**black·out** nc (a) a loss of consciousness for a short time. (b) a period when a TV broadcast is stopped during a strike or when windows etc are covered to prevent light from entering, people observing etc. ⇨ also black³(3,4).

,**black 'pudding** nu a kind of dark sausage.

black² /blæk/ n 1 nu the colour of the print on this page: dressed in black. 2 **be in the black** to have money in one's account; have made a profit. 3 nc (also B-) a person who has a dark brown skin colour.

black³ /blæk/ v 1 vt to make (something) black in colour: black one's boots. 2 vt (GB) to refuse to work with (materials, a company etc) especially during a strike: The shipworkers blacked the imports in support of the miners. 3 vi **black out** to lose consciousness for a short time. 4 vt **black sth out** (a) to stop a TV broadcast using strike action. (b) to give an official order that news etc must not be made known. (c) to cover windows etc to prevent light from entering, people observing etc. ⇨ blackout above.

black·en /'blækən/ vt, vi 1 (to cause something) to become black. 2 (fig) to say harmful things about (a person's character etc): blacken her reputation.

black·smith /'blæksmɪθ/ nc a person who makes and repairs things made of iron, esp horseshoes.

blad·der /'blædə(r)/ nc 1 (anat) a bag of skin in which urine collects in human and animal bodies. ⇨ also gall-bladder. 2 a bag of rubber etc that can be filled with air, e.g. in a football.

blade /bleɪd/ nc 1 a sharp cutting part of a knife etc. 2 = razor blade. 3 the flat wide end of an oar, propeller etc. 4 a flat, long, narrow leaf, esp of grass.

blame¹ /bleɪm/ nu responsibility for failure, bad behaviour etc. **lay/put the blame (for sth) on sb** to accuse her or him (of something): Don't put all the blame on her—you also helped to steal it.

blame² /bleɪm/ vt **blame sb (for sth); blame sth on sb** to accuse a person of being responsible (for failure, bad behaviour etc): It's no good blaming your teacher for failing the exam. She blamed her accident on the other driver.

blame·less adj free from blame; innocent.

blame·less·ly adv

blame·worthy adv deserving to be blamed.

blanch /blɑːntʃ/ v 1 vt (to cause nuts) to become pale or white, e.g. by taking off the skin of almonds. 2 vi to become pale with fear etc.

bland /blænd/ adj (—er, —est) (of food) with very little taste.

bland·ness nu

blank¹ /blæŋk/ adj (no comp) 1 (of paper) with nothing written or drawn on it: a blank sheet of paper. 2 (of a facial expression) without interest or understanding: There was a blank look on his face. **go blank** to be unable to remember something: I/My mind went blank.

blank·ly adv

blank² /blæŋk/ nc 1 a space left empty or to be filled (in an application form etc). **draw a blank** (fig) to search and find nothing. 2 an empty mind: His mind/memory was a complete blank (=

he could remember nothing). **3** a cartridge without a bullet.

,blank 'cartridge *nc* = blank²(3).

,blank 'cheque *nc* a signed one but with no amount of money stated.

blan·ket¹ /'blæŋkɪt/ *nc* **1** a thick woollen covering as used on beds. **2** *(fig)* a covering or layer: *a blanket of snow.* ⇨ also wet blanket.

blan·ket² /'blæŋkɪt/ *vt* (usually *passive*) to cause (something) to be thickly covered (with something): *The valley was blanketed with fog.*

blank verse /,blæŋk 'vɜːs/ *nu (literature)* unrhymed verse (usually with 10 syllables in each line) used in poetry and drama: *Many speeches in Shakespeare's plays are written in blank verse.*

blare /bleə(r)/ *nu* a loud, rough sound or noise (as of trumpets or horns). □ *vt,vi* **blare (sth) (out)** to produce (something using) loud, rough sounds: *The trumpets were blaring. The police blared out a warning.*

blasé /'blɑːzeɪ/ *adj* without enthusiasm or interest: *She was blasé about her money/success.*

blas·pheme /blæs'fiːm/ *vi* to speak in an irreverent way about God and sacred things: *blaspheme against the name of God.*

blas·phemer *nc* a person who blasphemes.

blas·phem·ous /'blæsfəməs/ *adj* **(a)** (of a person) using blasphemy. **(b)** (of language) containing blasphemy.

blas·phem·ous·ly *adv*

blas·phemy /'blæsfəmɪ/ *nc,nu* (an instance of) irreverent talk about God and sacred things.

blast¹ /blɑːst/ *nc* **1** a strong, sudden movement: *A blast of hot air came from the oven.* **2** a strong rush of air or gas after an explosion: *Thousands of windows were broken by the bomb-blast.* **at full blast** *(informal)* with maximum sound, speed etc: *He plays his radio at full blast.* **3** a sound made by a wind instrument: *The policeman blew a blast on his whistle.*

'blast-furnace *nc* one used for melting iron ore by forcing heated air into it.

blast² /blɑːst/ *v* **1** *vt* to break (rock etc) using explosives. **2** *vt (fig)* to cause (hopes etc) to be destroyed: *His hopes were blasted when she married John.* **3** *vi* **blast off** (of spacecraft etc) to leave the ground and rise.

'blast-off *nc* (the time of) a launching of a spacecraft. ⇨ blast²(3).

blast³ /blɑːst/ *int* (used to show anger): *Blast you/it!*

blast·ed *adj (attrib): What a blasted nuisance!*

bla·tant /'bleɪtənt/ *adj* (of bad behaviour, telling a lie etc) obvious and without caring; without regret: *a blatant abuse of my trust; a blatant lie.*

bla·tant·ly *adv: blatantly ignoring the law.*

blaze¹ /bleɪz/ *n* **1** *n sing* (usually the —) the bright flames of a fire: *We could see the blaze of a fire through the window. It took the firemen two hours to put out the blaze.* ⇨ ablaze. **2** *nc* a glow (of colour); a bright light: *The red tulips made a blaze of colour in the garden.* **3** *nc* a violent outburst: *in a blaze of anger.* **4** *(pl)* **like blazes** with maximum effort: *work/run like blazes.*

blaze² /bleɪz/ *vi* **1** to burn with bright flames: *When the firemen arrived the whole building was blazing.* ⇨ ablaze. **2** to be bright with colour or light: *The sun blazed down on us.* **3** **blaze with**

sth to have very strong feelings of anger etc: *He was blazing with anger/indignation.*

blaz·ing *adj*

blaze³ /bleɪz/ *vt* **blaze a trail** *(fig)* to be first to do something and show others how to do it.

blaze⁴ /bleɪz/ *vt* to make (something) known far and wide: *blazing the news (abroad).*

blaz·er /'bleɪzə(r)/ *nc* a loose-fitting jacket (often in the colours of a school, team etc).

Bldgs *abbr* Buildings.

bleach /bliːtʃ/ *nu* a chemical used for bleaching. □ *vt,vi* (to cause something) to become white (by chemical action or sunlight): *bleach linen; bones of animals bleaching on the desert sand.*

bleak /bliːk/ *adj* **(—er, —est) 1** (of the weather, a region, cold and miserable: *a bleak hillside.* **2** *(fig)* sad and hopeless: *bleak prospects. The future looks bleak.*

bleak·ly *adv*

bleary /'blɪərɪ/ *adj* (-ier, -iest) (of eyes) tired and so not able to see well.

,bleary-'eyed /,blɪərɪ'aɪd/ *adj* having tired and weak vision.

bleat /bliːt/ *vi, nc* (to make) a cry of a sheep, goat or calf.

bleed /bliːd/ *v (pt,pp bled /bled/)* **1** *vi* to lose blood: *If you cut your finger it will bleed.* **2** *vi (poetic)* to feel great sadness: *Our hearts bleed for homeless people during this cold winter.* **3** *vt (informal)* to force (a person) to pay money: *The blackmailers bled him for £500.*

bleep /bliːp/ *nc, vi* (to make) a short, high-pitched signal (e.g. in a hospital to call a doctor).

blem·ish /'blemɪʃ/ *vt, nc* (to produce) a mark etc that spoils the beauty or perfection: *blemishes in fruit/cloth/the skin. Stealing sweets is the one blemish on his character.*

blend¹ /blend/ *nc* a mixture (of sorts of one thing, different foods etc): *a new blend of coffee. The sauce is a blend of milk, flour and cheese.*

blend² /blend/ *v* **1** *vt* to mix together (sorts of one thing, different foods etc): *Now blend the eggs with the butter.* **2** *vi* to form a mixture: *Oil does not blend with water.* **3** *vi* to go well together: *How well their voices blend! These two colours blend well.*

blend·er *nc* an electric appliance used for mixing foods to make sauces, soups etc.

bless /bles/ *vt (pt,pp blessed, blest /blest/)* **1** to ask God's favour for (a person): *The Pope blessed the children.* **2** to make (food, a building etc) sacred or holy: *bread blessed at the altar.* **3** **be blessed with sth** to be fortunate in having something: *May you always be blessed with good health.* **4** **Bless you!** (said to a person who has sneezed).

bles·sed /'blesɪd/ *adj* **1** (B-) holy, sacred: *the Blessed Virgin* (= the mother of Jesus). **2** favoured by God: *Blessed are those who help the poor.*

bless·ing /'blesɪŋ/ *nc* **1** (a prayer for) the favour of God. **2** something that one is glad of, that brings comfort or happiness: *What a blessing it is you didn't get caught in the storm yesterday!* **a blessing in disguise** something that seemed unfortunate but that is seen later to be fortunate.

blest /blest/ *pt,pp* of bless.

blew /bluː/ *pt* of blow².

blight¹ /blaɪt/ n **1** nu a kind of plant disease. **2** nc a bad influence: *a blight on his hopes.*

blight² /blaɪt/ vt (usually *passive*) to be a bad influence on (hopes etc): *His hopes were blighted.*

blind¹ /blaɪnd/ adj (*no comp*) **1** without the power to see: *as blind as a bat* (= completely blind). *I'm almost blind without sunglasses. Tom helped the blind man across the road.* **turn a blind eye (to sth)** to pretend not to see it. **2** (*pred*) **blind to sth** unaware of or unable to understand something well: *Mothers are sometimes blind to the faults of their children.* **3** (*attrib*) thoughtless; uncontrolled: *In his blind haste he almost ran into the river.*

,blind 'alley nc (**a**) a narrow street closed at one end. (**b**) (*fig*) a career etc with no opportunity for progress.

,blind 'corner nc one that makes it difficult to see where one is going.

,blind 'date nc a social meeting between two people who have not met before.

,blind 'drunk adj very drunk.

'blind spot nc (*fig*) something one does not seem able to understand or know in spite of having information.

blind·ly adv

blind·ness nu

blind² /blaɪnd/ n pl (the —) blind people.

blind³ /blaɪnd/ nc a roll of cloth pulled down to cover a window: *pull down/lower/draw up/raise the blinds.*

blind⁴ /blaɪnd/ vt **1** to make (a person, animal) blind. **2** (*fig*) to take away the power of judgement (a person): *His feelings for her blinded him to her faults.*

blind·fold /'blaɪndfəʊld/ vt, nc (to cover the eyes of a person with) a piece of cloth.

blind·ing /'blaɪndɪŋ/ adj (*attrib*) making seeing difficult because very bright: *a blinding light.*

blink¹ /blɪŋk/ nc **1** one act of blinking. **2 on the blink** (*informal*) (of machines, equipment) developing faults: *My kettle is on the blink.*

blink² /blɪŋk/ v **1** vt, vi to shut and open (the eyes) quickly: *blink the eyes; blink away a tear.* **2** vi (of a light) to come on and go off: *We saw the lighthouse blinking on the horizon.*

blink·ers /'blɪŋkəz/ n pl leather squares used to prevent a horse from seeing sideways.

blip /blɪp/ nc **1** a short sound as from electronic equipment. **2** a spot of light on a radar screen.

bliss /blɪs/ nu perfect happiness; great joy.

bliss·ful /-fəl/ adj: *a blissful marriage.*

bliss·fully /-fəlɪ/ adv: *blissfully happy.*

blis·ter¹ /'blɪstə(r)/ nc **1** a small swelling under the skin filled with liquid (caused by rubbing, burning etc): *These shoes have given me blisters.* **2** any similar swelling on a painted surface etc.

blis·ter² /'blɪstə(r)/ vt, vi (to cause something) to develop a blister.

blitz /blɪts/ nc **1** a rapid, violent attack (esp from the air). **2 blitz (on sth)** (*fig*) a sudden strong effort (with a problem, or a commercial market etc): *a blitz on drug users/smoking; a sales blitz on Europe.*

bliz·zard /'blɪzəd/ nc a violent and heavy snowstorm.

bloat·ed /'bləʊtɪd/ adj fat and large in an unhealthy way: *a bloated face; feel bloated with*

food.

blob /blɒb/ nc a drop of liquid, e.g. paint, colour: *blobs of cream on the cake.* □ vt (**-bb-**) to make blobs with (paint etc).

bloc /blɒk/ nc a group of political parties, states etc with a special interest: *the Soviet bloc.* **en bloc** /ˌɑːn 'blɒk/ (*adv*) (*Fr*) as a group: *We went en bloc to complain to the principal.*

block¹ /blɒk/ nc **1** a large, solid piece of wood, stone etc: *Are there ice blocks in the orange juice?* ⇨ also starting-block. **2** a large building with different sections (e.g. flats, shops etc): *a block of flats; a modern office block.* **3** (also *attrib*) a group (of seats, members, travellers etc) as one unit: *sitting in a block; a block booking for seats in a theatre/for people to go on an organized holiday; a block vote by the women.* **4** (*computers*) a section of information considered as one unit. **5** an object etc that makes movement difficult or impossible: *a block in the pipe.* ⇨ blockage, road-block. **6** (*fig*) anything that makes progress or an activity difficult or impossible: *His broken leg has been a block to his career as an actor.*

,block 'capitals/'letters nu a writing style with each letter separate and in capitals: *Write your name in block capitals, e.g.* BOB SMITH.

block² /blɒk/ vt **1** to make movement along (something) difficult or impossible: *All roads were blocked by the heavy snowfall.* **2** to make progress or activity in (something) difficult or impossible: *The accountant has blocked our request for more money.*

block sth in (**a**) to fill something to make a solid block(1). (**b**) to begin a plan, report etc by putting in sections of information, buildings, statistics etc.

block sth off to put up a barrier to make progress difficult: *block off a road.*

block sth out = block sth in(b).

block·ade /blɒ'keɪd/ nc the surrounding of a place, e.g. by armies or warships, to stop goods or people from entering or leaving. **run the blockade** to get through it. □ vt to make a blockade of (a place).

block·age /'blɒkɪdʒ/ nc something that blocks: *There's a blockage in the drain-pipe.*

block·head /'blɒkhed/ nc (*derog*) a stupid person.

bloke /bləʊk/ nc (*GB sl*) a man.

blond /blɒnd/ nc, adj (a person) having fair skin and yellow hair.

blonde /blɒnd/ nc, adj (a woman who is) blond.

blood /blʌd/ nu **1** the red liquid flowing through the body. ⇨ cold-blooded, hot-blooded, warm-blooded. **bad blood between sb and sb** anger and hatred between: *His promotion to manager caused bad blood between them.* **in cold blood** cruelly and showing no mercy: *The escaped prisoner killed the old woman in cold blood.* **in one's blood** a natural part of a person's character, personality etc: *I love listening to music—it's in my blood.* **make one's blood boil** to make one very angry: *Racial prejudice makes my blood boil.* **make one's blood run cold** to make one very afraid and shocked: *Hearing someone trying to open the window made my blood run cold.* **shed blood** (**a**) to bleed. (**b**) to injure a person so that he or she bleeds (and dies).

⇨ bloodshed. **2** family relationship: *They are of the same blood* (= are relatives). **one's (own) flesh and blood** one's relatives. **blood is thicker than water** (*saying*) one's family is more important than other people. **run in one's blood** to be typical of a person's family: *The Churchills have been politicians for generations—it runs in their blood.*

'**blood bank** *nc* a place for storing blood for medical use.

'**blood-bath** *nc* an act of killing many people, esp civilians, e.g. in a political revolution.

'**blood count** *nc* (the counting of) the number of red and white corpuscles in a certain volume of blood.

'**blood-curdling** *adj* (*attrib*) producing feelings of horror: *blood-curdling screams.*

'**blood-donor** *nc* a person who gives blood for medical use.

'**blood feud** *nc* a serious quarrel between families.

'**blood group/type** *nc* any of several classes of human blood.

'**blood heat** *nu* the normal temperature of human blood (about 98·5°F or 37°C).

'**blood orange** *nc* one with red colour in the fruit.

'**blood-poisoning** *nu* an infection caused when poisonous germs enter the blood.

'**blood pressure** *nc,nu* the force of the blood in the arteries measured in relation to the heartbeat.

,**blood-'red** *adj* having the colour of blood.

'**blood relation** *nc* one related by family, not by marriage.

'**blood·shed** *nu* killing or wounding people.

'**blood·shot** *adj* (of the white of the eyes) red.

'**blood sports** *n pl* outdoor sports in which animals or birds are killed for pleasure.

'**blood·stream** *nc* the flow of blood, system of blood vessels, in the body.

'**blood·thirsty** *adj* (**-ier, -iest**) (*derog*) very cruel and taking pleasure in killing.

'**blood transfusion** *nc* a transfer of blood (originally taken) from the veins of one person to another person who is ill.

'**blood-vessel** *nc* a tube (called a *vein* or *artery*) through which blood flows in the body.

blood·less *adj* without people being killed: *a bloodless coup.*

bloody¹ /'blʌdɪ/ *adj* (**-ier, -iest**) (usually *attrib*) **1** bleeding; covered with blood: *a bloody nose.* **2** with much bloodshed: *a bloody battle.*

bloody² /'blʌdɪ/ *adj* (*attrib*), *adv* (*vulgar*) (used to give emphasis, either bad or good, but often with no meaning): *He's a bloody nuisance. What a bloody shame! You're a bloody fool/genius! Not bloody likely!* (= Certainly not!)

bloody-minded /,blʌdɪ 'maɪndɪd/ *adj* (*sl*) (*derog*) unwilling to cooperate or agree.

bloom¹ /bluːm/ *n* **1** *nc* a flower, esp of a plant admired mainly for its flowers (e.g. a rose): *The daffodils are in full bloom now.* **2** *n sing* (*literary*) (the time of) greatest beauty or perfection: *She was in the bloom of youth.*

bloom² /bluːm/ *vi* **1** to be in flower: *The roses have been blooming all summer.* **2** (*fig*) (of a person) to be in full health and beauty: *She's blooming after her holiday.*

blos·som¹ /'blɒsəm/ *n* **1** *nc* a flower, esp of a fruit-tree. **2** *nu* a mass of flowers on a bush or tree: *The apple trees are in blossom.*

blos·som² /'blɒsəm/ *vi* **1** to open into flowers: *The cherry trees will blossom next month.* **2** to develop: *He blossomed* (*out*) *as a first-rate athlete.*

blot¹ /blɒt/ *nc* **1** a mark, stain etc that spoils something: *a blot of ink/oil on his trousers.* **2** anything that spoils (a view, a person's character etc): *a blot on her character/good name.* **a blot on the landscape** (e.g. an ugly building).

blot² /blɒt/ *vt* (**-tt-**) **1** to make a blot(1) on (something). **2** to dry (something) using a special kind of paper that absorbs liquid: *blotting* (*up*) *the mess on the kitchen floor; blotting ink after writing.* **3** **blot sth out** to cover, hide, (something) from view: *The clouds have blotted out the sun.*

'**blot·ter** *nc* a piece of blotting-paper.

'**blotting-paper** *nu* a kind of absorbent paper used to dry wet ink after writing.

blotch /blɒtʃ/ *nc* a large mark (esp on the skin): *blotches of sunburn.*

blouse /blaʊz/ *nc* an article of clothing from neck to waist, for women and girls.

blow¹ /bləʊ/ *nc* **1** a hard stroke (given with the hand, a stick etc): *He struck his enemy a heavy blow on the head.* **come to blows** to fight. **strike a blow for sth** to perform a single act of support for something; struggle for something: *strike a blow for freedom.* **2** a shock; disaster: *His wife's death was a great blow to him.* **soften the blow** to make the shock (e.g. of bad news) easier to bear: *The doctor softened the blow by choosing his words carefully.* **3** an instance of blowing(4): *Give your nose a good blow.*

blow² /bləʊ/ *v* (*pt* **blew** /bluː/, *pp* **blown** /bləʊn/) **1** *vi* (of wind, air etc) to move with a strong force: *The cold wind blew. Warm air was blowing round the room. The storm blew across the sea. The winds blowing from the north will bring rain.* **blow hot and cold** (of a person) to be very sure or willing and then very uncertain or unwilling. **2** *vt* (of wind, air etc) to cause (something) to move: *The wind blew my hat off. The hurricane blew huge trees into the sea. The* (*air from the*) *fan was blowing her hair dry. The seeds were blown all over the garden.* **3** *vi* (of an object) to move (as if) by wind or air: *The door blew open/shut. My papers were blowing across the room.* **4** *vt* to send a strong movement of air across, into, through etc (something): *blow into a bag* (e.g. to find out whether you have been drinking alcohol)*; blow on food* (i.e. to cool it)*; blow one's fingers* (i.e. to warm them in cold weather)*; blow one's nose* (i.e. to clear it). **blow (sb) a kiss** ⇨ kiss. **5** *vt* to produce (something) by blowing air in: *blow bubbles; blow glass* (= blow air into hot glass to make a vase etc). **6** *vt,vi* (to cause something) to be destroyed because of air pressure, explosives etc: *The thieves blew the safe. The volcano blew* (= erupted). *The bomb blew away the concrete wall.* ⇨ blow (sth) down. **be blown to bits/pieces** to be completely destroyed in an explosion. **blow one's mind** ⇨ mind¹(2). **blow one's top** ⇨ top³(1). **7** *vt* to produce sound by means of air blown into or through (something): *blow a whistle/horn. The trumpets blew.* **blow one's own trumpet** ⇨ trumpet[1](1). **8** *vi* to breathe deeply and with difficulty: *He was puffing and blowing as he climbed the stairs.* **9** *vt, vi* (to cause an electrical connection) to break because the current is too strong: *All the fuses blew and the lights went out. You've blown the lights.* **10** *vt* (*informal*) to spend (a lot of money) without caring: *She blew £100 on a leather coat.* **11** *vt* (*imperative*) (expressing annoyance or indifference) *Blow it/you!*

blow (sth) down (to cause something) to fall down, be destroyed: *The storm has blown down our tent.*

blow into sth (a) ⇨ 4 above. (b) to enter a room etc suddenly and noisily: *You can't just blow into my office when you want to! Guess who's blown into town—Mick Jagger!*

blow off (*sl*) to send air out of one's anus; fart.

blow out (a) (of a flame, candle) to go out because of wind. (b) (of a tyre etc) to burst. Hence **'blow-out** *nc*. **blow sth out** to put out a flame etc by blowing(4): *She blew out the candles.* **blow one's brains out** ⇨ brain[1](1).

blow over (*informal*) (of a scandal, critical gossip) to become unimportant, uninteresting: *The news of their divorce will soon blow over.*

blow up (a) (of a storm etc) to increase in strength. (b) (of a quarrel etc) to come into existence: *Our family arguments seem to blow up over nothing.* (c) (*informal*) to lose one's self-control because of anger: *When he sees his damaged car he'll blow up.* (d) to be destroyed by explosives: *As the train crossed the bridge it blew up.* **blow sb up** (*informal*) to be very angry with her or him. **blow sth up** (a) to blow(4) into it and make it larger: *blow up a balloon/tyre.* (b) to make (a photograph) larger: *blow up a photo.* Hence **blow-up** *nc*. (c) to destroy something using explosives: *blow up a train.* (d) (*informal*) to exaggerate news etc: *The quarrel between them was blown up in the newspapers.*

blow-out /'bləʊ aʊt/ *nc* **1** ⇨ blow out(b). **2** a blowing(9) of an electric fuse. **3** (*sl*) a big, expensive meal.

blown /bləʊn/ *pp* of blow[2].

blow-up /'bləʊ ʌp/ *nc* ⇨ blow sth up(b).

blub·ber /'blʌbə(r)/ *nu* the fat of whales and other sea animals from which oil is obtained.

bludg·eon /'blʌdʒən/ *vt* **1** to hit (a person) with a stick: *He had been bludgeoned to death.* **2** (fig) to bully (a person) (into doing something).

blue[1] /blu:/ *adj* (**—r, —st**) **1** having, of, the colour blue: *a blue dress; a dark blue car. His face was blue with cold.* ⇨ bluish. **once in a blue moon** very rarely. **2** (*no comp*) (*politics*) opposed to sudden change or large social reforms. **3** (*informal*) sad and miserable: *feel blue.*

,blue-'blooded *adj* of aristocratic birth.

,blue 'cheese *nu* kind(s) with a blue mould.

,blue-'collar *adj* (*attrib*) of a worker in a factory etc. Compare white-collar.

'blue-eyed *adj* (a) having blue eyes. (b) (*attrib; fig*) favourite: *He's mummy's blue-eyed boy!*

,blue 'film *nc* an obscene film.

,blue 'joke *nc* an obscene joke.

'blue-print *nc* (a) a photographic print, white on blue paper, usually for building plans. (b) (*fig*) any plan, scheme.

'blue·stock·ing *adj, nc* (of) a woman con-

sidered to have superior literary tastes and intellectual interests.

blue[2] /blu:/ *n* **1** *nu* the colour of the sky on a clear day: *dark/light blue.* **2** (the —) the sky. **out of the blue** unexpected(ly): *They arrived out of the blue.* **a bolt from the blue** ⇨ bolt[2](3).

blue[3] /blu:/ *vt* (*informal*) to spend (a lot of money) without caring: *He blued £300 on a new guitar.*

blues /blu:z/ *n pl* (the —) **1** (*informal*) the state of feeling sad and miserable: *suffering from the blues because he's left me.* **2** (dances, songs, for) a style of sad, sentimental music with a slow rhythm originally of Blacks in the southern USA.

bluff[1] /blʌf/ *adj* (**—er, —est**) (of a person, behaviour) rough but honest and kind.

bluff[2] /blʌf/ *nc* **1** a steep side of a cliff etc. **2** an instance of bluffing. **call sb's bluff** to challenge her or him to carry out a threat.

bluff[3] /blʌf/ *vi, vt* to deceive (a person) by pretending to know more, be stronger, tell the truth etc but hoping not to be challenged. **bluff it out** to survive a situation by bluffing.

blu·ish /'blu:ɪʃ/ *adj* a little blue in colour: *a bluish-green sea.*

blun·der[1] /'blʌndə(r)/ *nc* a foolish mistake.

blun·der[2] /'blʌndə(r)/ *vi* **1** to move about uncertainly as if blind: *blunder into a wall.* **2** to make a foolish mistake: *Our leaders have blundered again.*

blunt[1] /blʌnt/ *adj* (**—er, —est**) **1** without a point or sharp edge: *a blunt knife/needle.* **2** (of a person, statement) honest and not trying to be polite: *He's a blunt man.*

blunt·ly *adv:* to speak bluntly (in a blunt(2) way).

blunt·ness *nu:* bluntness in speaking.

blunt[2] /blʌnt/ *vt* to make (something) blunt: *If you cut stone with a knife, you'll blunt the edge.*

blur[1] /blɜː(r)/ *nc* a view, sight, image, that is unclear and difficult to identify: *If you see only a blur when you read, you need glasses.*

blur[2] /blɜː(r)/ *vt, vi* (**-rr-**) (to cause something) to become unclear: *Tears blurred her eyes. The writing was blurred.*

blurt /blɜːt/ *vt* **blurt sth out** to tell e.g. a secret suddenly and without deciding to.

blush[1] /blʌʃ/ *nc* a reddening of the face (e.g. because of shame, nervousness etc): *She turned round to hide her blushes.*

blush[2] /blʌʃ/ *vi* to become red in the face (because of shame, nervousness etc): *He blushed as he walked onto the stage.*

blus·ter[1] /'blʌstə(r)/ *nu* **1** the noise of strong wind or waves. **2** noisy and threatening talk or behaviour.

blus·tery *adj* (of the weather, the sea) rough and windy.

blus·ter[2] /'blʌstə(r)/ *vi* **1** (of the wind, waves) to be noisy and violent. **2** (of a person) to act, speak, in a noisy, threatening way (often to hide fear).

BMA /ˌbiː em 'eɪ/ *abbr* (the —) British Medical Association.

BO /ˌbiː 'əʊ/ *abbr* body odour.

boa /'bəʊə/ *nc* (also **'boa-constrictor**) a kind of large non-poisonous snake that kills by crushing its prey.

boar /bɔː(r)/ *nc* **1** a wild male pig. **2** a male domestic pig kept for breeding.

board¹ /bɔ:d/ *n* **1** *nc* a long thin and flat piece of wood, with square edges, used in building: *a floor board*. **2** *nc* a thin flat piece of wood etc in any shape, used for a particular purpose: *a notice-board; a black-board; a cheese-board; an ironing-board*. **3** *nu* a kind of flat material as used in packaging, building, books etc: *cardboard; plaster-board*. **4** *nc* a piece of wood or board(3) with a pattern on it, used for playing games (called *board-games*) such as chess. **5** *nc* (also B-) a group of people who control a business, a government department etc: *a board of directors; the Board of Trade*. ⇨ **across-the-board**. **6** *nu* (the cost of) meals provided (e.g. as part of an arrangement for working as a nurse, working in a hotel etc): *board and lodging £50 a week; a salary of £30 a week and/plus board and lodging*. ⇨ bed¹(1). **7** (uses in phrases) **on board** on, onto, into, a ship, plane etc: *He's on board. We'll be going on board the spacecraft at 10 o'clock*. **go by the board** (*informal*) to be completely abandoned: *Good manners went by the board during the argument*. **sweep the board** to win all the prizes in a competition: *Germany swept the board in the international championships*. ⇨ also above-board, overboard.

board·ing *nu* **(a)** a structure of boards(1). **(b)** providing or receiving of board(6).

'board·room *nc* a room used for directors of a business to meet.

board² /bɔ:d/ *v* **1** *vt* **board sth in/over/up** to cover, fill in, something with boards(1)2: *board up/in a window*. **2** *vt* to go onto, into, (a passenger vehicle etc): *board a bus/train/plane/ship*. **3** *vi* to allow passengers to enter (a plane, ship etc): *The British Airways flight to Tokyo is boarding at Gate 20*. **4** *vt,vi* (to allow a person) to live in a rented room with meals provided: *They board students for extra income. We are boarding with a very nice family*.

board·er *nc* **(a)** a person who boards(4). **(b)** a boy or girl who lives at school during the term.

'boarding-card/-pass *nc* a pass for getting on a plane or ship.

'boarding-house *nc* a private house with rooms for rent.

'boarding-school *nc* one at which pupils live.

boast¹ /bəʊst/ *nc* **1** a statement, speech, that one is or can do better, is richer etc than others: *We're tired of her boasts about her beauty*. **2** a reason for feeling proud that is justified: *a remarkable boast that there is no more tuberculosis in the village*.

boast² /bəʊst/ *v* **1** *vt,vi* **boast (about/of sth) (that . . .)** to say that one can do better, is richer etc than others: *He boasts about/of being/boasts that he is the best tennis-player in the town*. **2** *vt* to possess (something) with pride: *Our school boasts a fine swimming-pool*.

boast·ful /-fəl/ *adj* (usually *derog*) (of a person) fond of making boasts(1).

boat /bəʊt/ *nc* a small open vessel for travelling on water, esp the kind moved with oars (a *rowing boat*), sails (a *sailing boat*), engines (a *motor-boat*): *We crossed the river by boat*. ⇨ also ferry-boat, houseboat, lifeboat. **be (all) in the same boat** (*fig*) to have the same dangers to face. **miss the boat** (*fig*) to be too late to use an opportunity. **rock the boat** ⇨ rock³.

'boat·house *nc* a building in which boats are stored.

'boat people *n pl* (the —) the refugees from Vietnam who left their country (1980s) in small boats.

'boat-train *nc* a train that takes people to or from a boat.

boat·swain /'bəʊsn/ *nc* a senior seaman on a ship.

bob /bɒb/ *vi* **(-bb-)**, *nc* (to make) a quick movement up and down.

bob·bin /'bɒbɪn/ *nc* a small spool for thread, wire etc in a machine.

bob·by /'bɒbɪ/ *nc* (*pl* -ies) (*GB dated informal*) a policeman.

bob·sleigh /'bɒbsleɪ/ (also **bob·sled** /'bɒbsled/) *vi, nc* (to ride in) a sleigh for two or more people, used to race outdoors over frozen snow.

bode /bəʊd/ *vi* **bode ill/well for sb/sth** (*formal*) to suggest, be a sign of, failure/success: *His idle habits bode ill for his future*.

bod·ice /'bɒdɪs/ *nc* a close-fitting part of a woman's dress from the shoulders to the waist.

bod·ily¹ /'bɒdəlɪ/ *adj* (*attrib*) physical: *bodily assault*.

bod·ily² /'bɒdəlɪ/ *adv* **1** as a whole or in one piece: *The shed was transported bodily to the end of the garden*. **2** in person: *The missing child suddenly appeared bodily in the mist*.

body /'bɒdɪ/ *nc* (*pl* -ies) **1** the whole physical structure of a person or animal: *We wear clothes to keep our bodies warm*. ⇨ also anybody, everybody, nobody, somebody **2** a dead body: *His body was brought back to England for burial*. **3** the body of a person or animal without the head, arms and legs: *She had a scar on her leg and one on her body*. **4** the main part of a structure: *the body of a car*. **5** a group of people who do something together or who are united in some way: *Large bodies of unemployed people marched through the streets demanding work*. **in a body** all together: *The staff resigned in a body*. **6** an amount, quantity, collection: *A lake is a body of water. We have a large body of evidence*. **7** a piece: *a foreign body* (e.g. dirt, a piece of wood) *in a wound; the heavenly bodies* (= the sun, moon and stars).

'body·guard *nc* a man or men guarding an important person.

'body-snatcher *nc* a person who steals corpses from graves.

'body·work *nu* the body(4) (of a vehicle).

bog¹ /bɒg/ *nc,nu* (an area of) soft, wet ground.

bog·gy *adj* **(-ier, -iest)** (of land) soft and wet.

bog² /bɒg/ *vt* **(-gg-)** **bog oneself/sb down** (usually *passive*) to cause oneself, a person, to become stuck and unable to make progress: *The bus was bogged down in the mud. Don't get bogged down in too many facts*.

bo·gey (also **bo·gy**) /'bəʊgɪ/ *nc* (*pl* -ies) (in stories) an evil spirit.

boggle /'bɒgl/ *vi* **boggle (at sth)** to be alarmed (and unwilling): *The mind/imagination boggles (at the idea)*.

bo·gus /'bəʊgəs/ *adj* (no *comp*) not genuine.

boil¹ /bɔɪl/ *nc* a hard, painful and poisoned swelling under the skin.

boil² /bɔɪl/ *nu* the temperature at which water boils(1). **bring sth to the boil** to heat it until it boils. **come to the boil** (a) (of a liquid) to begin to boil. (b) (*fig*) (of a difficulty) to reach a crisis.

boil³ /bɔɪl/ *v* **1** *vt,vi* (to cause water or other liquid, also the vessel that contains it) to reach the temperature at which it changes to gas and bubbles: *Put the egg in when the water boils. The kettle's boiling.* **boil dry** (of a pan, kettle etc) to boil until all the liquid in it has changed to gas: *The pan has boiled dry.* **2** *vt,vi* to cook (something) in boiling water: *Please boil my egg for three minutes. The potatoes are boiling and will be ready soon.* **3** *vi* (*fig*) to become angry: *He was boiling with anger.* ⇨ blood(1). **4** *vi* (*fig*) (of the sea) to make very big waves because of bad weather. **5** *vi* (of a person) to feel very hot because of the sun's heat etc: *I'm boiling in this thick jacket.*

boil away (a) to continue to boil: *The kettle was boiling away but no-one saw it.* (b) to boil until nothing remains: *The water had all boiled away and the kettle was empty.* ⇨ boil dry at boil³(1).

boil down to sth (*informal*) (of an idea, problem, statement) to have something as the most important or significant issue: *The problem boils down to who will pay for the tickets.*

boil over (a) to boil and flow over the side: *The milk had boiled over.* (b) (*fig*) (of a person) to lose self-control and become angry.

boil up (*informal*) (of a quarrel, crisis) to develop, get worse.

boil·er /'bɔɪlə(r)/ *nc* a metal container in which water etc is heated, e.g. for supplying hot water.

'boiler-suit *nc* a pair of overalls worn for dirty work.

boil·ing /'bɔɪlɪŋ/ *adj* (*no comp*) (of water etc) at a temperature when bubbles form.

'boiling hot *adj* (*boiling-hot* when *attrib*) (*informal*) very hot: *a boiling-hot day.*

'boiling-point *nc* (a) the temperature at which a liquid boils(1). (b) (*fig*) the point after which a person is very angry.

bois·ter·ous /'bɔɪstərəs/ *adj* (of a person, behaviour) noisy and cheerful.

bold /bəʊld/ *adj* (—**er**, —**est**) **1** (of a person, behaviour) without fear; showing no fear: **2** (of a person) without shame or respect: *She asked me, as bold as brass, to lend her £5.* ⇨ also front¹(4). **3** clearly marked and easy to see: *the bold outline of a mountain.*

bold·ly *adv*
bold·ness *nu*

bol·lard /'bɒləd/ *nc* a short post as used to tie up a ship or on a road for directing traffic.

bol·ster¹ /'bəʊlstə(r)/ *nc* a long pillow.

bol·ster² /'bəʊlstə(r)/ *vt* **bolster sb/sth (up)** to give necessary encouragement or support to a person, theory etc: *She'll need bolstering up if you want her to win the race.*

bolt¹ /bəʊlt/ *adv* (only in) **bolt upright** suddenly and completely upright: *sit bolt upright.*

bolt² /bəʊlt/ *nc* **1** a metal fastening for a door or window, consisting of a sliding bar and a hole into which it fits. ⇨ bolt⁴. **2** a metal pin with a head at one end and a thread (as on a screw) at the other, used with a nut for holding things together. **3** a discharge of lightning. ⇨ thunder-bolt. **a bolt from the blue** a surprising result, instance of good or bad luck etc.

bolt³ /bəʊlt/ *nc* an act of running away. **make a bolt for it** to run away (esp to escape). ⇨ bolt⁵(2).

bolt⁴ /bəʊlt/ *vt* to fasten (something) with a bolt²(1): *bolt the doors.*

bolt⁵ /bəʊlt/ *v* **1** *vi* (esp of a horse) to run off out of control. **2** *vi* to run away quickly: *As soon as I came downstairs the burglar bolted through the back door.* **3** *vt* to swallow (food) quickly: *We bolted (down) a little food and hurried on.*

bomb /bɒm/ *vt,vi, nc* (to attack (a place etc) with) a hollow metal container filled either with explosive or with tear gas etc. **go like a bomb** (*GB sl*) to be very efficient, successful etc: *My new car/ The concert went like a bomb.*

bomb·er *nc* a plane used for bombing.

'bomb·shell *n sing* (*fig*) something that causes great surprise or shock.

bom·bard /bɒm'bɑːd/ *vt* **bombard sb/sth (with sth)** **1** to attack a person, building etc (using big guns). **2** (*fig*) to attack a speaker etc (with many questions, requests, complaints etc).

bom·bard·ment *nc,nu*

bond /bɒnd/ *nc* **1** an agreement that a person must keep to, esp one that has force in law; the document containing such an agreement. **2** (usually *fig*) something that joins or unites: *the bond(s) of affection.* **3** a printed paper from a government or a corporation acknowledging that money has been lent to it and will be paid back with interest.

bone¹ /bəʊn/ *nc* one of the parts that make up the framework of an animal's body: *There are 212 named bones in the human body. This fish has a lot of bones in it.* **(as) dry as a bone** (a) = bone-dry. (b) very thirsty. **chilled to the bone** feeling very cold. **feel in one's bones (that . . .)** feel certain (that . . .). **have a bone to pick with sb** to have something to argue or complain about. **make no bones about it/doing sth** to do it without hesitating or objecting.

,bone-'dry *adj* (*no comp*) completely dry.

,bone-'idle/-'lazy *adj* (*no comp*) (*derog*) very lazy.

bone² /bəʊn/ *vt* to take bones out of (a chicken, fish etc) when preparing food.

bon·fire /'bɒnfaɪə(r)/ *nc* a large fire made out of doors either to celebrate some event or to burn rubbish etc.

bon·kers /'bɒŋkəz/ *adj* (*pred*) (*sl; derog*) (of a person) mad.

bon·net /'bɒnɪt/ *nc* **1** a close-fitting hat tied under the chin, as worn by babies. **2** (*GB*) the protective lid over the engine of a vehicle (*US* = hood).

bon·ny /'bɒnɪ/ *adj* (-**ier**, -**iest**) happy and looking healthy: *a bonny baby.*

bo·nus /'bəʊnəs/ *nc* (*pl* —**es**) a payment in addition to what is usual, necessary or expected, e.g. an extra payment to workers. ⇨ no-claims bonus.

bo·ny /'bəʊnɪ/ *adj* (-**ier**, -**iest**) **1** (of food) having many bones: *a bony fish.* **2** having big or obvious bones: *bony fingers.*

boo /buː/ *int* **1** the sound made to show disapproval or contempt. **2** an exclamation used to surprise or startle.

boo² /bu:/ *vt,vi* to make boos at (a person etc): *The speaker was booed off the platform.*

boob¹ /bu:b/ *vi, nc* (*informal*) (to make) a silly mistake.

'**booby prize** /'bu:bɪ praɪz/ *nc* a prize given as a joke, e.g. to the person who is last in a race etc.

boob² /bu:b/ *nc* (*sl*) a woman's breast.

booby-trap /'bu:bɪ træp/ *nc* an object that looks harmless but will kill or injure when picked up or interfered with.

book¹ /buk/ *nc* **1** a number of printed sheets of paper fastened together in a cover: *a long book* (= one with many pages); *a thin book* (= one with few pages). *be (like) an open book* (of a person, a facial expression, a subject for study etc) to be easy to understand, interpret. **2** a literary work that would fill such a set of sheets: *write a book.* **3** a number of sheets, without writing, fastened together: *a notebook; an exercise book.* **4** (*pl*) business accounts, records etc: *The firm has full order books* (= has many orders for goods). *be in sb's good/bad/black books* to have/fail to have her or his favour or approval. *close the books* to balance the accounts. *cook the books* to make deliberately incorrect entries in business accounts. **5** a book(1) with rules and regulations. *do sth by the book* to keep strictly to the rules. *throw the book at sb* (of the police, a judge) to charge a person with every offence possible. **6** (B-) a main division of the Bible: *the Book of Genesis.*

'**book·case** *nc* a piece of furniture with shelves for books.

'**book·club** *nc* an organization that sells books at a discount to members.

'**book-ends** *n pl* a pair of ornaments etc used to keep a row of books upright.

'**book·keeper** *nc* a person who keeps accounts, e.g. of a business.

'**book·keeping** *nu* (the profession of) keeping (business) accounts.

'**book·maker** *nc* (also (*informal*) *bookie*) a person, business, that takes bets on horse-races etc.

'**book·mark** *nc* something put in a book to show where the reader is.

'**book·seller** *nc* a person, business, that sells books.

'**book·shop** *nc* a shop selling books.

'**book·stall** *nc* a kiosk etc at which books, newspapers etc are sold, e.g. in a station.

'**book token** *nc* a receipt (on an attractive card) exchangeable for a book at the value stated.

'**book·worm** *nc* (*fig*) a person who is very fond of reading.

book² /buk/ *v* **1** *vt,vi* to order (and pay for) (a place on a course of study, (a ticket for) a seat in a theatre or bus etc). **2** *vt,vi* to reserve (places) in a restaurant, hotel etc. *fully booked* with no more seats, places, available. **3** *vt* (of the police) to charge (a person) with a legal offence: *I was booked for speeding.* **4** *vt* to make an arrangement with (a person) to speak at a meeting etc. **5** *vt* to reserve (a room, building etc) for a special purpose: *book a hall for a meeting; book space for an exhibition.*

book in (at sth) to arrive and register (at a hotel etc). *book sb in* to register a client at a hotel etc.

book sb/oneself out to record in a notebook that a person/oneself will not be in for a meal etc.

book up to reserve places (on a train, in a hotel etc): *It is best to book up during the summer.*

booked up with no more seats, rooms, places, available (in a theatre, restaurant, train, hotel etc): *I'm sorry but we're completely/fully booked up next week.*

bookie /'bukɪ/ *nc* (*informal*) = bookmaker.

book·ing /'bukɪŋ/ *nc,nu* (an instance of) reserving seats, rooms, places (in a theatre, restaurant, train, hotel etc) *Bookings are up/down on* (= have increased/decreased compared to) *last year.*

'**book·ing-clerk** *nc* a person who sells tickets, e.g. at a railway station.

'**book·ing-office** *nc* an office where tickets are sold (for travel, the theatre etc).

book·let /'buklɪt/ *nc* a thin book.

boom¹ /bu:m/ *nc* **1** a long pole used to keep the bottom of a sail stretched out. **2** a long movable arm for a microphone.

boom² /bu:m/ *nc* a loud, deep sound: *the boom of supersonic aircraft.*

boom³ /bu:m/ *vi, nc* (to experience) a sudden increase in trade activity, esp a time when money is being made quickly.

boom⁴ /bu:m/ *v* **1** *vi* *boom (out)* (of big guns etc) to make deep, hollow sounds. **2** *vt* *boom sth (out)* to say something in a loud deep voice: *booming out instructions.*

boom·er·ang¹ /'bu:məræŋ/ *nc* a curved stick of wood, which returns to the thrower if it does not hit anything.

boom·er·ang² /'bu:məræŋ/ *vi* (*fig*) (of plans etc) to be unsuccessful and harm the originator.

boon /bu:n/ *nc* (usually *sing*) something that causes pleasure, enjoyment: *Parks are a great boon to people in big cities.*

boor /buə(r)/ *nc* (*derog*) an ill-mannered person. **boor·ish** *adj*

boost /bu:st/ *vt, nc* **1** (to cause) an increase in the value, reputation, strength, of (something): *Seeing him boosted my morale.* **2** (to cause) an increase in the performance of a car engine.

boo·ster /'bu:stə(r)/ *nc* **1** something that encourages a person, activity etc. **2** another dose of vaccine to strengthen the effect of an earlier dose: *a booster dose.*

'**booster rocket** *nc* a rocket used to give speed at the start of a spacecraft's journey.

boot¹ /bu:t/ *nc* **1** an outer covering for the foot and ankle, made of leather or rubber: *a pair of boots. get the boot* (*sl*) to be dismissed from a job. *give sb the boot* (*sl*) to dismiss a person from her or his job. *lick sb's boots* (*informal*) to behave without self-respect and be too willing and obedient in order to please her or him. **2** (*GB*) a place for luggage at the back of a car or coach (*US = trunk*).

'**boot·lace** *nc* a piece of string or leather used for tying a boot.

boot² /bu:t/ *vt* **1** to kick (a person). **2** *boot sb out* (*sl*) to dismiss a person from her or his job suddenly and without pity.

boo·tee /'bu:ti/ *nc* a baby's knitted boot.

booth /bu:ð/ *nc* **1** a covered shelter where goods are sold at a market or a fair. **2** an enclosure for a public telephone: *a phone booth.* **3** = polling booth.

boo·ty /'buːtɪ/ *nu* things taken by robbers or captured from the enemy in war.

booze /buːz/ *vi, nu* (*informal*) (to drink a lot of) alcoholic drinks.

'**booze-up** *nc* (*sl*) a period of boozing.

booz·er /'buːzə(r)/ *nc* (*GB sl*) **1** a person who often has (too much) alcoholic drink. **2** a pub.

bor·der¹ /'bɔːdə(r)/ *nc* **1** an edge; the part near the edge: *We camped on the border of a lake. There is a border of flowers round the lawn.* **2** (land near) the line dividing two states or countries: *The criminal escaped over the border.*

bor·der² /'bɔːdə(r)/ *vt* **1** to put or be an edge to (something): *Our garden is bordered by a stream.* **2 border on sth** (**a**) to be next to something: *My land borders on yours.* (**b**) (*fig*) to be almost the same as something: *The proposal borders on the absurd.*

'**border-line** *nc* a line that marks a boundary. *a* **borderline case** one that is doubtful, e.g. a person who may or may not pass an examination.

bore¹ /bɔː(r)/ *nc* **1** (*derog*) a person who people find uninteresting and tiring. **2** a task, duty etc that is uninteresting: *Washing up is a bore.*

bore² /bɔː(r)/ *nc* (*tech*) the measurement across a pipe, gun barrel etc.

bore³ /bɔː(r)/ *vt* to make (a person) lose interest and feel tired (because of uninteresting, unimaginative talk): *His stories about his achievements bored us. Am I boring you?* **bore sb to death** to bore her or him extremely. ⇨ **boring**.

bore·dom /-dəm/ *nu* the state of being bored.

bore⁴ /bɔː(r)/ *vt,vi* to make (a narrow, round, deep hole): *boring a hole in wood/a tunnel through a mountain.*

bore⁵ /bɔː(r)/ *pt* of **bear²**.

bor·ing /'bɔːrɪŋ/ *adj* (*derog*) (of talk, behaviour, work etc) causing a person to lose interest and feel tired: *a boring speaker/job.* ⇨ **bore³**.

born /bɔːn/ *pp* of **bear²**(1) (*passive*) **1 be born** to come into the world by birth: *I was born in 1970.* ⇨ **bear²**(1). **born and bred** from birth and throughout childhood (usually suggesting pride): *He's Australian born and bred.* **2** (*attrib*) having the qualities stated (as if) from birth: *a born leader/poet.*

'**born-again** *adj* (*attrib*) (*informal*) having new religious faith as an adult: *a born-again Christian.*

borne /bɔːn/ *pp* of **bear²**.

bor·ough /'bʌrə/ *nc* (in England) a (part of a) town that elects an MP or a local government council.

bor·row /'bɒrəʊ/ *v* **1** *vt,vi* to take (something) (from a person) and use it on the understanding that it is to be returned: *I've borrowed this bike from Tom. It's best not to borrow. May I borrow your pen?* Compare lend(1). **2** *vt* to take and use (another person's ideas, methods etc).

bor·row·er *nc* a person who borrows.

bos'n /'bəʊsn/ *nc* = boatswain.

bos·om /'bʊzəm/ *nc* (*old use*) a woman's breasts or the part of a dress covering this. *a* **bosom friend** a friend who is loved greatly.

boss¹ /bɒs/ *nc* (*informal*) a person (at work) who controls or gives orders: *Who's the boss in this house?*

boss² /bɒs/ *vt* **boss sb (about/around)** to order a person (esp in a bossy way) to do something.

bos·sy /'bɒsɪ/ *adj* (**-ier, -iest**) (*derog*) taking too much pleasure in giving orders.

bo·sun /'bəʊsn/ *nc* = boatswain.

bo·tan·ical /bə'tænɪkl/ *adj* of botany: *botanical gardens.*

bot·an·ist /'bɒtənɪst/ *nc* a student of, expert in, botany.

bot·any /'bɒtənɪ/ *nu* the scientific study of the structure and distribution of plants.

botch /bɒtʃ/ *nc* an example of poor, careless work: *She's made a botch of repairing her coat.* □ *vt* **botch sth (up)** to do something, e.g. repairing, building, arranging or reporting, poorly and carelessly: *Don't let him paint the car—he'll botch it up.*

both¹ /bəʊθ/ *adj* or *det* (of two people, things etc) the one and also the other: *I want both books. Both ideas are good. I saw him on both occasions. There are trees on both sides of the street. Both players have the same score.* Ⓝ 'Both' is used with a plural verb, as in *Both parents have visited the school.* 'Neither' means 'not the one and not the other' and is used with a singular verb, as in *Neither parent has visited the school.* Compare all¹, each¹, every. **both the/these/her** *etc* . . . the two of them: *I drove both my parents to the airport. Both the children like ice-cream.* Ⓝ 'Both' can be used before another determiner such as *the, those, her* etc. It is called a *predeterminer* when it is used in this way, as in *both those teams, both his hands.* **want it/can't have it both ways** (*informal*) to want to/cannot support the two sides in an argument, benefit from two opposite possibilities etc.

both² /bəʊθ/ *pron, n* **1** (of two people, things etc) the two; not only the one: *I need both/both of them/them both. They're both coming. We've both been to Rome. Both of us have been to Paris. Both of you/You are both invited. Both of the lungs are infected.* Ⓝ 'Both' is used with a plural verb. 'Neither' means 'not one or the other' and is used with a singular verb, as in *Neither is satisfactory, Neither of us has won.* 'Both' cannot be used in front of personal pronouns such as *us, you, them.* Use 'both of' as in *Both of us arrived late.* ⇨ both/these/her . . . at both¹. Compare all³, each³. **2** (used as a *conj*) **both** . . . **and** . . . (used for emphasis) . . . and in addition . . . : *She's both young and healthy. They have both the skill and the opportunity. He both cooks and entertains well.* Ⓝ Use similar structures (e.g. two related adjectives, two nouns with *the*, two similar phrases) in this construction. A sentence with different structures such as *She both cooks well and has several children* is considered to be bad style. Be careful because the position of 'both' in the sentence can change the meaning. Compare: *We are against both his hairstyle and his clothes* (= We oppose the two aspects of his appearance) and *We are both against his hairstyle and his clothes* (= The two of us oppose his appearance). 'Both . . . as well as . . .' and 'both . . . and . . . as well' are not possible because 'as well (as)' includes the meaning of 'the one with the other' and so 'both' becomes unnecessary.

both·er¹ /'bɒðə(r)/ *n* **1** *nc* a person, thing, that causes trouble, worry or annoyance: *Having to go out in this rain to buy bread is such a bother! His teenage son is quite a bother to him.* **2** *nu* trouble;

inconvenience: *Please don't put yourself to any bother—I can take a bus.*

'bother·some /-səm/ *adj* (*derog*) annoying; causing trouble.

both·er² /'bɒðə(r)/ *v* **1** *vt* to cause trouble, worry, pain etc to (a person): *Is something bothering you? My bad back has been bothering me all week.* **2** *vt* to annoy (a person) by asking many questions, requests etc: *Don't bother me with such things when I'm busy.* **3** *vi* to take the time or trouble: *Don't bother about/with the washing-up/Don't bother to wash up—I'll do it later. I can't be bothered to read all this computer printout.*

bottle¹ /'bɒtl/ *nc* **1** a container with a narrow neck, used for liquids: *a wine bottle; a bottle of* (= filled with) *wine*. **2** as much as a bottle holds: *Mary drinks two bottles of milk a day.*

bottle² /'bɒtl/ *vt* **1** to put, store, (something) in bottles: *bottle fruit.* **2 bottle sth up** (*fig*) to be unable or unwilling to express feelings, anger.

'bottle-fed *adj* (of a child) given milk from a bottle, not from its mother's breast.

bottle-'green *adj, nu* (of) a kind of dark green.

'bottle-neck *nc* (**a**) a place, e.g. a narrower length of road, where traffic slows down. (**b**) that part of a manufacturing process etc where production slows down.

bot·tom /'bɒtəm/ *nc* **1** the lowest position or part: *the bottom of the ladder/stairs/bag. We were glad to reach the bottom of the mountain.* Opp top³(1). **2** the part farthest from the front or more important part: *at the bottom of the garden.* **3** the land under the sea, a lake, river etc: *The ship went to the bottom.* **4** (*informal*) the part of the body on which a person sits: *Put cream on the baby's bottom.* **5** (also *attrib*) in the lowest, last, position: *Put it on the bottom shelf.* Opp top¹(2). **from the bottom of my heart** with genuine and deep feeling. **come bottom** to get the lowest mark in an exam etc. **get to the bottom of sth** to find out the truth about it.

bot·tom·less *adj* very deep: *a bottomless pit.*

bough /baʊ/ *nc* a large branch growing from the trunk of a tree.

bought /bɔːt/ *pt,pp* of buy².

boul·der /'bəʊldə(r)/ *nc* a large piece of rock or stone.

bounce¹ /baʊns/ *nc,nu* an act, the action, of bouncing: *a bed with plenty of bounce.*

bounce² /baʊns/ *v* **1** *vi,vt* (to cause a ball) to move away or back when sent against something hard: *The ball bounced over the wall. She was bouncing a ball.* **2** *vi* to move up and down (on a bed etc): *The boy was bouncing (up and down) on the bed.* **3** *vi* (*informal*) (of a cheque) to be returned by a bank because there is no money in the account.

bounce back (*informal*) to recover quickly (from a disappointment, failure etc): *She/The economy soon bounced back.*

bounce in/out; bounce into/out of sth to come in/go out noisily (and often angrily): *She bounced out (of the room) and slammed the door.*

bounc·ing /'baʊnsɪŋ/ *adj* (*attrib*) (of babies) big and healthy: *a bouncing boy.*

bound¹ /baʊnd/ *adj* (*pt,pp* of bind²) **1** fastened with ropes etc (as a prisoner): *a bound captive/dog.* **2** (*pred; fig*) forced to stay (in a place, job

etc): *He's bound to the job because there is no other choice.* ⇨ fogbound. **3 bound by sth** compelled by the law, a promise, custom etc: *She was bound by social convention to marry young.*⇨ duty-bound. **4** (*pred*) **bound to do sth** certain; destined: *He's bound to win/come/succeed.* **5 bound up in sb/sth** very busy with and interested in: *She's bound up in her work and has no time for holidays. He's so bound up in her that he's neglecting his studies. You're too bound up in yourself.* **6 bound up with sth** closely connected with: *The state of the economy is bound up with the country's political future.*

bound² /baʊnd/ *nc* a jumping movement upward or forward: *at one bound.* **by leaps and bounds** ⇨ leap¹(2). □ *vi* to move or run using jumping movements: *His dog came bounding to meet him.*

bound³ /baʊnd/ *vt* (usually *passive; formal*) to mark the limits of, be the boundary of, (a place): *England is bounded to the north by Scotland.*

bound·ary /'baʊndrɪ/ *nc* (*pl* -ies) **1** an imaginary line between areas, countries, surfaces etc: *This stream forms a boundary between my land and his.* **2** the limit (of knowledge etc): *the present boundaries of applied physics.* **3** (*cricket*) the line round the edge of the field or a hit beyond it.

bound·less /'baʊndlɪs/ *adj* (*fig*) without limits: *his boundless generosity.*

bounds /baʊndz/ *n pl* **1** limits: *It is beyond the bounds of human knowledge.* **2 out of bounds (to sb)** (*adj* (*pred*)) (of an area) not allowed to be visited (by): *This military area is out of bounds (to tourists).*

boun·te·ous /'baʊntɪəs/ *adj* (*formal*) providing plenty; abundant: *a bounteous harvest.*

boun·ti·ful /'baʊntɪfəl/ *adj* = bounteous.

boun·ty /'baʊntɪ/ *n* (*pl* -ies) **1** *nu* (*formal*) generosity in giving: *show bounty towards poor populations.* **2** *nc* a payment offered (usually by a government) to encourage something (e.g. to kill dangerous animals).

bou·quet /bʊ'keɪ/ *nc* **1** a bunch of flowers (to be) carried in the hand. **2** the perfume of wine.

bour·geois /'bʊəʒwɑː/ *adj, nc* **1** (of) a person who owns property or engages in trade. **2** (*derog*) (of) a person too concerned with material prosperity and social status.

bour·geoisie /ˌbʊəʒwɑː'ziː/ *nu* (the —) bourgeois(1) people in a society.

bout /baʊt/ *nc* **1** a period of exercise, work or other activity: *a wrestling bout; a bout of drinking.* **2** a short period (of illness): *a bout of flu.*

bou·tique /buː'tiːk/ *nc* a small shop selling articles (clothes, cosmetics, shoes, jewellery etc) of the latest fashion.

bov·ine /'bəʊvaɪn/ *adj* (*tech*) of, like, an ox.

bow¹ /bəʊ/ *nc* **1** a knot made with a loop or loops; a shoelace, ribbon etc tied in this way. **2** a piece of wood curved by a tight string, used for shooting arrows. **3** a rod of wood with horse-hair stretched from end to end, used for playing the violin, cello etc.

bow-'legged *adj* with the legs curved outwards at the knees.

bow 'tie *nc* one made into a bow(1).

bow² /baʊ/ *nc* an act of bending the head or bending the body forward (as a greeting etc): *make a* *low bow.*

bow³ /bau/ *nc* (often *pl*) the front end of a boat or ship.

bow⁴ /bau/ *v* **1** *vi* to bend the head or body forward (as a greeting etc): *They bowed low.* **bow and scrape** to behave with too much respect in order to get a person's favour. **2** *vt* to bend (the head) forward: *They bowed their heads in prayer.* **bow to sb/sth** to agree with a person, opinion etc. **3** *vt* (*usually passive*) to bend (something): *The branches were bowed (down) with the weight of the snow.*

bow·els /ˈbauəlz/ *n pl* **1** the part of the inside of the body below the stomach where food is digested and waste matter is carried out. **2** (*fig*) the lowest and innermost part: *in the bowels of a building.*

bowl¹ /baul/ *nc* **1** a deep, round, hollow dish: *a salad-/sugar-bowl.* **2** as much as a bowl holds: *She ate three bowls of rice.* **3** something shaped like a bowl: *the bowl of a spoon/pipe.*

bowl² /baul/ *vi,vt* **1** (*cricket*) to send a ball from one's hand to the batsman. **2** to play bowls.
bowl along (*informal*) (of a car etc) to move at a regular, quick speed.
bowl sb out (*cricket*) to hit a batsman's wicket or leg so that he or she is out of the match.
bowl sb over (a) to knock a person over: *The cyclist bowled me over as he came round the corner.* **(b)** (*fig*) to make a strong impression on a person: *He was bowled over by the wonderful news.*

bowl·er¹ /ˈbaulə(r)/ *nc* (*cricket*) a person who bowls.

bowl·er² /ˈbaulə(r)/ *nc* (also **bowler hat**) a kind of hard, rounded, black hat.

bowls /baulz/ *nu* a game in which a large ball is rolled across grass.

bow-wow /ˌbau ˈwau/ *int* an imitation of a dog's bark □ /ˈbau wau/ *nc* a young child's word for a dog.

box¹ /bɒks/ *nc* **1** a container with straight sides, usually with a lid, used for holding solids: *a box of matches; a tool-box.* **2** as much as a box holds. **3** (the —) (*informal*) a television set: *There's nothing on the box tonight?* **4** a compartment with seats for several people in a theatre, concert hall etc. **5** a compartment in a law court for the purpose mentioned: *a jury-box; a witness-box.* **6** any compartment for a purpose mentioned: *a telephone-box; a horse-box.* ⇨ also Christmas box, letter box, money-box, pillar-box.
'box number *nc* **(a)** a number used in a newspaper advertisement as an address to which answers may be sent (and forwarded from the newspaper office). **(b)** (*PO Box No.*) a postal number used as an address.
'box-office *nc* the office for booking seats in a theatre, cinema etc.

box² /bɒks/ *vt* **1** to put (something) into a box. **2** **box sb in** to prevent a person from passing oneself (in a race etc). **box sb/sth up** (*usually passive*) **(a)** to keep a person, thing, in a small space: *I've been boxed up in this small flat all evening and I must go out for a walk.* **(b)** to keep a fear, problem etc secret and tell no-one: *She'd kept her true feelings about him boxed up for years.*

box³ /bɒks/ *vt,vi* to fight (a person) with the fists

or with padded gloves as a sport. **box sb's ears** to give her or him a blow with the open hand on the ears.

box·er /ˈbɒksə(r)/ *nc* **1** a person who boxes as a sport. **2** a kind of bulldog.

box·ing /ˈbɒksɪŋ/ *nu* the sport of fighting while wearing padded gloves.
'boxing-glove *nc* a padded glove for use in boxing.
'boxing-match *nc* a fight between two boxers.

Box·ing Day /ˈbɒksɪŋ deɪ/ *n* the first weekday after Christmas Day.

boy /bɔɪ/ *nc* **1** a male person up to the age of 17 or 18. ⇨ boyish. **jobs for the boys** (*informal*) appointing one's own supporters, the people one likes etc to (senior) jobs. **man and boy** ⇨ man¹(1). **2** a son: *He has two boys and one girl.*
'boy-friend *nc* a girl's or woman's special male friend.
'boy-hood *nc* the time when one is or was a boy.

boy·cott /ˈbɔɪkɒt/ *vt* to refuse to have anything to do with, trade with, (a person, business firm, country etc) for a reason. □ *nc* an instance of boycotting: *a political boycott.*

boy·ish /ˈbɔɪɪʃ/ *adj* **1** (esp of a woman's hair, clothes, behaviour) like a boy. **2** (*derog*) (of an older boy or man) childish.

bra /brɑː/ *nc* (*informal*) a woman's close-fitting article of clothing for the breasts.

B. Phil /ˌbiː ˈfɪl/ *abbr* Bachelor of Philosophy.

BR /ˌbiː ˈɑː(r)/ *abbr* British Rail: *I work for BR.*

brace¹ /breɪs/ *nc* **1** something used to hold, tighten or support, e.g. the walls of a building or (*pl*) the teeth. **2** (*pl*) (*GB*) straps worn over the shoulders, used to keep trousers up.

brace² /breɪs/ *v* **1** *vt* to give support to (something): *Her teeth have been braced to straighten them.* **2** *v reflex* to prepare oneself (for bad news, bad weather, a difficult activity etc): *He braced himself to hear the doctor's news.*

brace·let /ˈbreɪslɪt/ *nc* a band or chain of metal etc worn on the wrist or arm as an ornament.

brac·ing /ˈbreɪsɪŋ/ *adj* (of air, wind, exercise) making one feel active and healthy: *a bracing climate/walk.*

brack·en /ˈbrækən/ *nu* a kind of large fern that grows on hillsides.

brack·et¹ /ˈbrækɪt/ *nc* **1** a support on a wall for a shelf etc. **2** (*usually pl*) = parenthesis. Ⓝ The signs [ ] (*square brackets*) have the same use as ( ). **3** a particular section or group with the same qualities: *an age bracket; an income bracket* (e.g. of incomes between £8 000 and £10 000).

brack·et² /ˈbrækɪt/ *vt* **1** to use brackets(1) to fix (a shelf to a wall etc). **2** **bracket sth off** to put words etc inside brackets(2). **3** **bracket sb/sth (together)** to put a person, thing etc in the same group: *bracket together poverty and disease.*

brack·ish /ˈbrækɪʃ/ *adj* (of water) a little salty.

brag /bræg/ *vi* (**-gg-**) to say that one can do better, is richer etc than others: *He brags about/of being clever/that he is cleverer.* Ⓝ 'Boast' is also possible.

brag·gart /ˈbrægət/ *nc* (*derog*) a person who brags.

braid /breɪd/ *n* **1** *nu* silk, linen etc woven into a band, used for edging or decorating cloth or clothes: *gold/silver braid.* **2** *nc* (*US*) = plait.

Braille /breɪl/ n a system of writing for blind people, using raised dots which they read by touch.

brain¹ /breɪn/ n **1** nc (the —) the soft grey matter in the head, centre of the nervous system and of thought and emotion: *The human brain is a complex organ.* ⇨ cerebral. **blow sb's/one's brains out** to kill a person, oneself by shooting at the head. **2** n sing the mind: *I can't keep telephone numbers in my brain.* **have sth on the brain** (informal) to be always thinking about it. **3** (pl) (informal) intelligence: *That girl has brains. Use your brains!* **pick sb's brains** to learn and use her or his ideas. **4** (pl) an animal's brain eaten as food: *sheep's brains.* **5** nc a very clever person: *He's the brain of the college.*

'**brain-child** nc an original idea etc produced by a person or group.

'**brain drain** nc a movement of trained technical and scientific personnel from one country to another (because of better opportunities etc).

'**brain·storm** nc a mental upset with uncontrolled emotion and often violence.

'**brain-teaser** nc a difficult problem.

'**brain-washing** nu the process of forcing a person to reject old beliefs and accept new ones by using extreme mental pressure.

'**brain·wave** nc (informal) a sudden inspiration or intelligent idea.

'**brain·less** adj (fig; derog) stupid.

'**brainy** adj (-ier, -iest) intelligent.

brain² /breɪn/ vt (informal) to hit (a person) hard on the head.

braise /breɪz/ vt to cook (meat) slowly, first in fat and then in a little water: *braised beef/chicken.*

brake¹ /breɪk/ nc **1** an apparatus for reducing speed or stopping motion, e.g. of a bicycle, vehicle etc. *the foot/hand brake.* **2** act as a brake on sth; put the brakes on sth** to (try to) prevent something or control it.

'**brake-light** nc a light at the back of a vehicle that goes on when the brakes are used.

brake² /breɪk/ vi to use a brake: *The driver braked suddenly.*

bramble /'bræmbl/ nc,nu (also attrib) a wild bush with long prickly stems producing blackberries.

bran /bræn/ nu the outer covering (husks) of grain (wheat, rye etc) separated from flour.

branch¹ /brɑːntʃ/ nc **1** a part of a tree growing out from the trunk or a bough: *He climbed up the tree and hid among the branches.* ⇨ root¹(1). **2** a main division of a river, road, railway, mountain range etc. **3** a separate part of a business, family, subject of knowledge etc: *The bank has branches in all parts of the country.*

branch² /brɑːntʃ/ vi to send out, divide into, branches(1,2): *The road branches here.*

branch off (of a driver, car, road, train etc) to leave a main route and take a smaller one.

branch out (of a person, business etc) to expand in a new direction, open new departments or lines of activity.

brand¹ /brænd/ nc **1** a trademark or tradename: *famous brands.* **2** a particular kind of goods with such a mark: *an excellent brand of coffee.* **3** an identifying design (to be) burned on the skin of animals. **4** (also branding-iron) the shaped metal used to make a brand(3). **5** (fig) a mark of guilt or

disgrace. **6** a piece of burning wood (in a fire).

brand² /brænd/ vt **1** to mark (cattle, goods etc) with a brand¹(3). **2** (fig) to give (a person) a bad name: *She has been branded as a thief.*

bran·dish /'brændɪʃ/ vt to wave (a weapon) about (as a threat etc): *brandishing a sword.*

brand-new /,brænd 'njuː/ adj (no comp) completely new: *a brand-new dress. Is it brand-new?*

bran·dy /'brændɪ/ nc,nu (pl -ies) (a portion of) a kind of strong alcoholic drink: *Two brandies, please.*

brash /bræʃ/ adj (informal; derog) **1** (esp of a young person) rude and not showing respect. **2** (of an inexperienced person) doing things without enough thought, knowledge.

brass /brɑːs/ n (also attrib) **1** nu a bright yellow metal made by mixing copper and zinc: *brass knobs.* **get down to brass tacks** to consider the most important facts only. **2** nu things made of brass, e.g. ornaments. **3** (the —) musical instruments made of brass. ⇨ also top brass.

,**brass 'band** nc a group of musicians with brass instruments.

brass·ière /'bræzɪə(r)/ nc (always shortened to) bra.

brassy /'brɑːsɪ/ adj (-ier, -iest) **1** like brass(1) in colour. **2** (derog) producing a loud, unattractive sound.

brat /bræt/ nc (derog) a badly behaved child.

bra·va·do /brə'vɑːdəʊ/ nc,nu (pl —es or —s) (an instance of) a display of boldness or courage: *She said it out of bravado.*

brave¹ /breɪv/ adj (—r, —st) **1** ready to face danger, pain or suffering; having no fear: *as brave as a lion* (= very brave). **2** needing or showing courage: *a brave act.*

brave·ly adv

brave² /breɪv/ vt to meet (danger, pain etc) with courage: *braving a storm; braving criticism.*

brav·ery /'breɪvərɪ/ nu courage.

bra·vo /,brɑː'vəʊ/ int Well done! Excellent!

brawl /brɔːl/ vi, nc (to take part in) a noisy quarrel or fight.

brawl·er nc a person who brawls.

brawn /brɔːn/ nu **1** physical strength: *You need brawn to lift that.* **2** meat (esp pork) cut up, spiced, pickled and compressed.

brawny adj (-ier, -iest) physically strong.

bray¹ /breɪ/ nc **1** the cry of an ass. **2** the loud sound of, or like, a trumpet.

bray² /breɪ/ vi to make a bray.

bra·zen /'breɪzn/ adj (often brazen-faced) (derog) (of a bad person, bad behaviour) without shame: *a brazen liar/lie.*

bra·zier /'breɪzɪə(r)/ nc an open metal container for a coal fire.

breach¹ /briːtʃ/ nc **1** an act of breaking (a rule, duty, agreement etc). **breach of the peace** an act of fighting in a public place, e.g. the streets. **breach of promise** a breaking of an agreement to marry. **2** an opening, e.g. made in a defensive wall etc: *The waves made a breach in the sea wall.* **step into/fill the breach** to replace a person who is unable to do something.

breach² /briːtʃ/ vt to make an opening in (a defensive wall etc).

bread /bred/ nu **1** (also attrib) a kind of food made by mixing flour with water and yeast and baking it in an oven: *brown/white/wholemeal bread; a loaf/slice/piece of bread; bread rolls.* **2** (*sl*) money.

,**bread and 'butter** *nu* (**a**) slice(s) of bread spread with butter. (**b**) (*sl*) enough money to live: *earn one's bread and butter by writing.*

'**bread·board** *nc* a wooden board on which bread is sliced.

'**bread·crumb** *nc* a tiny bit of bread.

'**bread·fruit** *nc* (a tree with) a starchy fruit, grown in the South Sea Islands and W Africa.

'**bread-knife** *nc* one for slicing bread.

'**bread·line** *n sing* a line of people waiting for food given as charity or relief. *on the breadline* very poor.

'**bread·winner** *nc* (*informal*) a person who works to provide money for a family.

breadth /'bretθ/ *nc,nu* (*formal*) **1** a distance or measurement from side to side: *It's ten metres in breadth.* **2** (*fig*) a range of thought or expression (esp in art, music, or in knowledge of a subject).

break¹ /breɪk/ **1** *nc* (an instance, act, of) a division, opening, made by breaking(1,2,3,11): *a break in the chain/electricity/skin/clouds.* **2** *nc* an interruption or pause (in an activity): *a break in the conversation; a break from the usual routine; a lunch-/coffee-/tea-break; an hour's break for lunch; a weekend break by the sea.* *without a break* without a pause for rest, food etc: *She's been working six hours without a break.* **3** *nc* an escape (from a prison etc): *a successful break by several prisoners; a gaol break.* *make a break for it/for freedom* to (try to) escape. **4** *nc* (*informal*) an opportunity (good or bad): *a lucky/unlucky break.* *give sb a break* to give a person a chance to do better, try again etc. **5** *nc* a sudden change (in the weather): *a break in the hot weather.* **6** *nu* the time when daylight begins: *at break of day; at daybreak.* **7** *nc* (*literature*) a pause in a line of poetry (also called a *caesura*).

break² /breɪk/ *v* (*pt* **broke** /brəʊk/, *pp* **broken** /'brəʊkən/) **1** *Svt,vi* (to cause something hard and rigid) to separate into many pieces because of a fall, hit etc: *The ball broke my glasses. This vase has broken. The heat has broken the dish. The windscreen broke into pieces. How did this chair get broken?* ⇨ **broken. 2** *vt,vi* (to cause something) to separate into two pieces because of strain, weight etc: *If you pull too hard you'll break the rope. As I bent down I felt the elastic break. He pulled my collar and broke my necklace. Stop it—you're breaking my arm! He broke a rose from the bush and gave it to me.* ⇨ also neck¹(1). **3** *vt,vi* (to cause a surface or thin rigid material) to have a long division (but not separate pieces): *The glass in the bedroom window has been broken. The blister broke and water came out. The skin was broken round the injury.* **4** *vt,vi* (to cause a machine, instrument etc) to become damaged and not work: *Who's broken my calculator? The traffic lights have broken.* ⇨ heart(2). **5** *vt* to use force to make (a route, way in or out etc): *break a new trail through a forest; break open a box/door/safe.* ⇨ break sth down, break into/through sth. *breaking and entering* illegally entering a building (to commit a crime). **6** *vt,vi* to force (a person, animal) to obey; become controllable: *The authorities will never break her spirit/will.*

Will he break under questioning/torture? **7** *vt* to defeat (something): *The government broke the strike by refusing to negotiate. She's broken the world record* (= achieved a better one). ⇨ code¹(4), habit(1). **8** *vt* to make (a person, business) very poor and unable to continue working: *High taxes are breaking me/my company.* *break even* to make neither a profit nor a loss. **9** *vt* to fail to keep (an agreement, law etc): *break the law/the rules/the regulations; break a promise/an appointment; break a contract/treaty; break one's word.* Compare keep²(4). **10** *vt,vi* to interrupt (an activity, state): *break a journey/one's sleep; break for lunch; break a slimming diet by eating chocolate; break one's silence by making a statement.* ⇨ fall¹(1). **11** *vi* (of two or more people or things) to separate: *The players broke and ran to their positions. The boxers were asked to break. The clouds broke and the sun came out. The waves broke over the rocks. The enemy's lines broke under our gunfire.* **12** *vt* to divide (one group, set etc): *The referee broke the two wrestlers. Don't break the set (of china/books/stamps) by selling one. Can I pay you tomorrow because I don't want to break this £5 note?* **13** *vi* (*racing*) to go faster (suddenly): *Coe broke when he was 200 metres from the tape.* **14** *vi* (of daylight, bad weather) to begin: *Day-light/dawn/day broke early. The storm broke and the children ran into the house.* ⇨ daybreak. **15** *vi* (of any kind of weather) to come to an end: *The heatwave/cold weather is breaking at last.* **16** *vi* (of news) to become known: *The news/story of her death broke last night and was in all the newspapers this morning.* **17** *vi* (of a male voice) to become deeper when a boy is about 12 to 15.

break (sb/sth) apart to separate (a lock, fighters) into two: *He broke the padlock/the two boys apart.*

break away (from sb/sth) (**a**) (of a prisoner etc) to escape (from the police etc) (**b**) (of a person) to separate oneself (from a group, family, particular belief etc): *She's broken away from the socialists in order to form a new party.* (**c**) (of a country, state, political party) to separate (from a larger group) and become independent. Hence '**break·away** *adj* (*attrib*): *a breakaway party.*

break back (*tennis*) to win a game against service(8) after one's opponent has done so.

break down (**a**) (of an engine, instrument, machine) to stop working (because of a fault): *My car broke down on the motorway.* (**b**) (of negotiations, communications) to become too difficult and stop: *Talks between the two governments have broken down.* (**c**) (*chem*) (of living things) to separate into its parts: *When a leaf decays, it breaks down and becomes part of the soil.* (**d**) (of a person's health) to become weak(er): *He's breaking down under the strain.* (**e**) (of a person) to lose self-control (and cry, collapse etc): *She broke down when she heard the sad news.* *break sth down* (**a**) to knock, hit, a building etc to the ground: *break down a door/wall.* (**b**) to be successful in opposing suspicion, opposition etc: *The President broke down all resistance to his plans.* (**c**) to defeat a person's shyness, unwillingness etc: *A good teacher can break down a child's reluctance to cooperate.* (**d**) to produce a detailed analysis of something: *My results have been* *broken down into three categories.* (**e**) (*chem*) to separate a living thing into parts: *Enzymes in the stomach help to break down food into a soluble form.* ⇨ breakdown.

break even ⇨ break²(8).

break in (**a**) to enter a building using force: *Thieves broke in while we were on holiday.* Hence '**break-in** *nc*. (**b**) to interrupt a conversation. **break sb in** (*informal*) to train a new employee. **break sth in** (**a**) to make new shoes, a new computer etc work well by using it. (**b**) **break in a horse** to make it obedient and accept riders. **break in on sth** to interrupt a person's thought, conversation etc.

break into sth (**a**) to enter a building using force: *Burglars broke into the shop last night.* (**b**) to occupy time: *These extra duties break into my leisure time too much.* (**c**) (of a person or animal) to change to a faster pace suddenly: *The man broke into a run. The horse broke into a gallop.* (**d**) to begin a song, a cry, a laugh suddenly: *break into song/tears/laughter.* (**e**) to begin to use reserve supplies: *break into savings/reserves/stores.* (**f**) to use a banknote to buy something worth less than the note: *break into a £5 note to buy a stamp.*

break off (**a**) to become separated: *The handle has broken off.* (**b**) to stop talking: *He broke off in the middle of a sentence.* (**c**) to stop (doing something) for a short time: *Let's break off for half an hour.* **break sth off** (**a**) to cause something to become separated: *She broke off all the dead flowers.* (**b**) to end negotiations, an engagement to marry etc: *They have broken off talks with the unions. Their engagement has been broken off. We've broken off diplomatic relations.*

break out (of a disease, violent action) to begin suddenly: *Cholera/War has broken out.* Hence '**out·break** *nc*. **break out (of sth)** to escape (from prison etc): *Several prisoners are breaking out of the gaol.* Hence '**break·out** *nc*. **break out in sth** (**a**) to be covered with spots etc suddenly: *Her mouth broke out in cold sores.* (**b**) to begin a rage, tears etc suddenly: *He broke out in tears/in a temper/in a sweat.*

break through (sth) (**a**) to force a way through (something): *We broke through (their defences/the barbed wire).* (**b**) (of the sun) to appear through (clouds etc): *The sun is trying to break through.* (**c**) to make new and important discoveries: *The scientists hope to have broken through by this time next year.* Hence '**break·through** *nc*: *several exciting breakthroughs in cancer research.*

break up (**a**) (of people in groups) to separate: *Before the party had broken up, fighting began.* (**b**) (of a marriage, love affair) to come to an end: *Their marriage has broken up.* Hence '**break·up** *nc*: *He's been depressed since the breakup of their relationship.* (**c**) (of a person) to collapse (mentally or physically): *She was on the point of breaking up under the pressure.* (**d**) (of a ship etc) to come to pieces (in a storm etc): *The little boat broke up on the rocks.* **break sth up** (**a**) to cause a group to separate: *to break up a group of demonstrators.* (**b**) to destroy a friendship etc: *He broke up their marriage.* **break sth up (into sth)** (**a**) to divide something (into pieces): *We can break up this box into firewood.* (**b**) to divide a

sentence, problem, land etc (into sections): *Sentences can be broken up into clauses. The field is being broken up into building plots.*

break with sb to end a friendship etc with a person: *Paul has broken with Mary.* **break with sth** to end an association, connection, with something: *Let's break with tradition and have a cheese pie next Christmas.*

break·able /'breɪkəbl/ *adj* easily broken. Opp unbreakable.

break·age /'breɪkɪdʒ/ *nc* **1** an act of something breaking. **2** a place in, part of, something that has been broken. **3** (*pl*) broken articles: *The hotel allows £500 a year for breakages.*

break·away /'breɪkəweɪ/ *adj* (*attrib*) ⇨ break away (from sb/sth). □ *n* (an instance of) a group separating from a larger one.

break·dance /'breɪkdɑːns/ *vi* to dance (esp in a public place) to highly rhythmic popular music using free physical movement including spinning on one's back.

'**break·dancing** *nu*

break·down /'breɪkdaʊn/ *nc* **1** a failure (of an engine, machine etc). **2** an end to negotiations, communication etc: *a breakdown in talks between the heads of state.* **3** a failure of mental or physical health: *a nervous breakdown.* **4** a separation (of a report, statistics etc) into sections: *breakdowns of expenses.*

break·er /'breɪkə(r)/ *nc* a large wave breaking against a rock etc.

break·fast /'brekfəst/ *vi, nc* (to have) the first meal of the day: *An English breakfast usually includes fried eggs, bacon, sausages and tomatoes. A Continental breakfast includes fruit juice, bread and jam, and coffee.*

break-in /'breɪk ɪn/ *nc* ⇨ break in(a).

break·neck /'breɪknek/ *adj* (*attrib*) **at break·neck speed** at a dangerously fast speed.

break·out /'breɪkaʊt/ *nc* ⇨ break out (of sth).

break·through /'breɪkθruː/ *nc* **1** a way forced through (barbed wire, defences etc). **2** ⇨ break through (sth)(c).

break·up /'breɪkʌp/ *nc* ⇨ break up(b).

break·water /'breɪkwɔːtə(r)/ *nc* a structure built out into the sea to make the water in a harbour calm.

bream /briːm/ *nc* (*pl* —) **1** a kind of freshwater fish. **2** (*also sea-bream*) a salt-water variety of this fish.

breast /brest/ *n* **1** *nc* either of the parts of a woman's body producing milk. **2** *n sing* (*literary*) the upper front part of the human body: *a troubled breast* (= a sad, anxious etc feeling). **make a clean breast of sth** to confess everything one has done wrong. **3** *nu* the part of an animal corresponding to the human breast: *breast of lamb.*

'**breast·bone** *nc* the bone in the front of the chest supporting the ribs (also called *sternum*).

'**breast pocket** *nc* a small pocket in the top of the front of a jacket, shirt etc.

'**breast·stroke** *nu* (*swimming*) a stroke in which the arms are brought from in front of the head to the sides of the body while facing towards the water.

breath /breθ/ *n* **1** *nu* air taken into and sent out of the lungs. **2** *nc* a single act of taking in and send-

ing out air: *take a deep breath* (= fill the lungs with air). *in the same breath* (of two opposite statements, actions) said, done, at almost the same time. *out of breath* unable to breathe easily (because of running etc). *catch one's breath* to breathe in suddenly (because of pain, fear etc). *get one's breath back* (to rest in order) to return to one's usual way of breathing (after running etc). *hold one's breath* to stop breathing for a moment (because of fear, excitement etc). *take sb's breath away* (of great beauty, a great painting, building etc) to amaze a person. Hence '**breath-taking** *adj.* *waste one's breath* to talk, try to persuade, but without success. **3** *nc* a small movement (of air etc): *There wasn't a breath of air/wind.* **4** *nc* (*fig*) a small suggestion: *not a breath of suspicion/scandal.*
breath·less *adj* out of breath.
breath·less·ly *adv*
breath·alyser /'breθəlaɪzə(r)/ *nc* a bag containing chemicals (into which a person breathes) to test the alcoholic content of a person's breath.
breathe /bri:ð/ *v* **1** *vi* to take air into the lungs and send it out again: *breathing in/out. He's still breathing* (= is still alive). **2** *vt* to say (something) quietly: *Don't breathe a word of this* (= Keep it secret).
breath·er *n sing* a short period for exercise in the fresh air: *take/go for a breather.*
breath·tak·ing /'breθteɪkɪŋ/ *adj* ⇨ breath(2).
bred /bred/ *pt,pp* of breed². ⇨ well-bred.
breeches /'brɪtʃɪz/ *n pl* (also *a pair of breeches*) an article of clothing fitting round the waist and below the knees.
breed¹ /bri:d/ *n* a variety (of an animal): *a breed of cattle/dog.*
breed² /bri:d/ *v* (*pt,pp* **bred** /bred/) **1** *vt* to keep (animals etc) in order to produce young, esp by selection of parents: *breed horses/cattle.* ⇨ also well-bred. **2** *vi* to give birth to young: *Rabbits breed quickly.* **3** *vt* to be the cause of (something): *Dirt breeds disease.*
breed·er *nc* a person who breeds animals.
breed·ing *nu* (**a**) (also *attrib*) (used in verbal senses of breed²(1)): *the breeding of horses; the breeding season for birds.* (**b**) knowledge of how to behave well because of upbringing: *a man of good breeding.*
breeze¹ /bri:z/ *nc,nu* a gentle wind. *a stiff breeze* a fairly strong wind.
breezy *adj* (**-ier, -iest**) pleasantly windy: *breezy weather.*
breeze² /bri:z/ *vi* **breeze in/out** (*informal*) to come in/go out happily or unexpectedly: *What's the idea—breezing into my office without knocking?*
breth·ren /'breðrən/ *n pl* (*old use*) brothers. ⇨ brother(4).
brev·ity /'brevətɪ/ *nu* the shortness (of statements, human life and other non-material things).
brew¹ /bru:/ *nc* the result of brewing(1): *a strong brew (of tea).*
brew² /bru:/ *vt,vi* **1** *vt* **brew (up) sth** to prepare tea etc. **2** *vi* (of tea etc) to be made and becoming strong. **3** *vi* (*fig*) to develop: *A storm is brewing. There's trouble brewing between them.* **4** *vt* to make (beer).

brew·ery /'bru:ərɪ/ *nc* (*pl* **-ies**) a place where beer is made.
bri·ar /'braɪə(r)/ *nc* = brier.
bribe¹ /braɪb/ *nc* something given, offered or promised in order to influence or persuade a person (often to do something wrong): *offer/take bribes.*
bri·bery *nu* the giving, taking, of bribes.
bribe² /braɪb/ *vt* to offer, give, a bribe to (a person): *bribe a judge/witness.*
bric·à·brac /'brɪk ə bræk/ *nu* old china, ornaments etc of little value.
brick¹ /brɪk/ *nc* **1** (also *attrib*) a usually rectangular block of baked clay used for building: *a brick wall. drop a brick* (*informal*) to do or say something indiscreet. **2** something like a brick(1) in shape: *an ice-cream brick.*
'**brick·layer** *nc* a worker who builds with bricks.
'**brick·work** *nu* a structure made of bricks.
brick² /brɪk/ *vt* **brick sth in/up** to fill in an opening with bricks: *brick in a window.*
bri·dal /'braɪdl/ *adj* of a bride or wedding.
bride /braɪd/ *nc* a woman on her wedding-day; a newly married woman.
bride·groom /'braɪdgrʊm/ *nc* a man on his wedding-day; a newly married man.
brides·maid /'braɪdzmeɪd/ *nc* a girl or young unmarried woman attending a bride at her wedding. Compare best man.
bridge¹ /brɪdʒ/ *nc* **1** a structure providing a way over a road, river, railway etc. **2** (*fig*) any method or means of connecting ideas, people, needs etc: *act as a bridge between those involved in the argument. burn one's bridges* to commit oneself to doing something without the possibility of changing one's mind. **3** a platform over and across the deck of a ship for the use of the captain and officers. **4** the upper, bony part of the nose. **5** a movable part over which the strings of a violin etc are stretched.
bridge² /brɪdʒ/ *nu* a kind of card-game in which two players play to win a certain number of tricks against another two players.
bridge³ /brɪdʒ/ *vt* **1** to build a bridge over (a road, river etc). **2** (*fig*) to connect (ideas etc) or fill (a space etc): *Can you speak for ten minutes to bridge the gap before the next speaker?*
'**bridging loan** *nc* a loan (from a bank) to cover a period of time, e.g. between the purchase of one house and the sale of another.
bridle¹ /'braɪdl/ *nc* that part of a horse's harness that goes on its head, including the metal bit for the mouth, the straps and the reins.
bridle² /'braɪdl/ *v* **1** *vt* to put a bridle on (a horse). **2** *vi* to show strong anger (because of injustice, rudeness etc): *I bridled at her cruel remarks.*
brief¹ /bri:f/ *adj* (**—er, —est**) (of time, events, writing, speaking) lasting only for a short time: *a brief moment/reply. in brief* using a few words.
brief·ly *adv*
brief² /bri:f/ *nc* **1** (*legal*) a summary of the facts of a law case prepared for a barrister. *hold a/no brief for sb* to argue in support/not be prepared to support a person. **2** a piece of information, advice etc given in advance, e.g. to sales staff about new products.
brief³ /bri:f/ *vt* **1** to give a brief(1) to (a barrister). **2** to give information, advice etc to (a salesper-

son, soldiers etc).

brief·case /'bri:fkeɪs/ *nc* a flat case used e.g. by a business executive for papers etc.

briefs /bri:fs/ *n pl* (also *a pair of briefs*) women's pants without legs, held in position by an elastic waistband.

bri·er (also **bri·ar**) /'braɪə(r)/ *nc* a bush with thorns, esp the wild rose.

Brig. *abbr* Brigadier.

brig·ade /brɪ'geɪd/ *nc* **1** (*mil*) a group of soldiers forming part of an army division. **2** an organized body of people in uniform with special duties: *the fire-brigade*.

briga·dier /brɪgə'dɪə(r)/ *nc* an officer commanding a brigade(1).

brig·and /'brɪgənd/ *nc* = bandit.

bright /braɪt/ *adj* (**—er**, **—est**) **1** giving out or reflecting a lot of light: *Sunshine is bright. The leaves on the trees are bright green in spring.* **bright and early** very early in the day. **2** (usually *attrib*) (of a face, expression) cheerful and happy: *bright faces; a bright smile.* **3** clever: *as bright as a button* (= very clever). *A bright child learns quickly.* **4** showing good possibilities: *a bright future; bright prospects.*

bright·ly *adv*

bright·ness *nu*

bright·en /'braɪtn/ *vt,vi* (to cause something) to become brighter, lighter or more cheerful etc: *These flowers brighten* (*up*) *the classroom. The sky is brightening.*

bril·liance /'brɪlɪəns/ *nu* **1** the state of being very bright(1). **2** great intelligence.

bril·liant /'brɪlɪənt/ *adj* **1** very bright(1): *a week of brilliant sunshine.* **2** very clever or impressive: *a brilliant scientist/teacher; a brilliant idea.*

bril·liant·ly *adv*

brim¹ /brɪm/ *nc* **1** the top edge of a cup, bowl, glass etc: *full to the brim.* **2** the edge of a hat that turns out.

brim² /brɪm/ *vi* (**-mm-**) **brim over 1** to be so full that some spills over the top. **2** (*fig*) to show great happiness etc: *brimming over with joy.*

bring /brɪŋ/ *vt* (*pt,pp* **brought** /brɔːt/) **1** to cause (a person, thing) to come by carrying or coming with: *May I bring my dog? He's bringing his children to see the play. Is she bringing her mother with her? Would you kindly bring my son a warm coat? I've brought the map for you. He brought me a cup of coffee. Dad, I'm bringing my boyfriend home to meet you.* Compare fetch(1), send(1), take²(2). **2** to cause (something) to happen (as a result): *The warm weather brought birds to breed on the island. The sad news brought pain to her family. Chopping onions brings tears to my eyes.* Ⓝ For uses of *'bring'* with nouns such as *attention, boil, home, mind* etc, ⇨ the noun entries. **3** (usually *reflex*) to persuade or force (oneself or others): *I couldn't bring myself to do it/to trust her. Can't you bring yourself to forgive him?* **4** to sell something for (an amount): *That bike ought to bring £30.* **5** (*legal*) to start (a lawsuit etc). Ⓝ For uses of *'bring'* with nouns such as *action, charge, trial*, ⇨ the noun entries.

bring sth about to cause something to happen: *Will the new government bring about urgent economic reforms?*

bring sb along to help and encourage a stu-

dent, athlete etc. **bring sth along** to help a plant to grow: *The sunshine will bring the tomatoes along.* **bring sb/sth along (to sth)** to come with a person or thing (to an event): *Please bring your parents along to the meeting.*

bring sb/sth back to return with a person or thing: *Please bring my bike back tomorrow. I'll bring your sister back at 7 o'clock. He's gone and nothing will bring him back.* **bring sth back (a)** to reintroduce something: *Will the government bring back hanging?* **(b)** to cause something to be remembered: *The sight of the airport brought back memories of my first visit.* **bring sb back to life** to make a person conscious, healthier etc: *The doctor failed to bring the drowned man back to life.*

bring sb/sth before sth to present a person, thing, for discussion, judgement: *She'll bring the issue before the city council. He was brought before the court and found guilty.*

bring sth down (a) to cause the defeat of a group: *The scandal brought down the government.* **(b)** to cause prices, costs etc to be reduced: *Overseas competition will bring down the price of local produce.* **(c)** to cause aircraft, birds, to be destroyed in the air: *Their guns brought down three of our planes. The hunters brought down two ducks.* **(d)** to cause an opposing player to fall over: *He deliberately brought me down as I aimed at the goal.* **(e)** to transfer numbers from one column to another when calculating. **bring sb down to earth** ⇨ earth¹(2).

bring sth forward (a) to change a meeting time to an earlier date or time: *The meeting has been brought forward to 10 o'clock.* **(b)** to cause something to be discussed or considered: *The director hopes the new managers will bring forward fresh ideas for organizing the factory.* **(c)** (*business*) to ask for correspondence to be seen again at a later date: *Please bring this letter forward in two weeks.* **(d)** (*pp; abbr* b/f) (*bookkeeping*) to record the total amount at the bottom of the previous page on the top of the next one.

bring sb in (a) to bring a person into a police station for questioning, charging etc. **(b)** to give a person a part in a plan, scheme: *They've brought in computer experts to advise on a new system for calculating profits.* **bring sth in (a)** to produce an amount as profit or income: *Overtime can bring in as much as £50 a week.* **(b)** to cause something to become noticed and adopted: *bring in a new fashion.* **(c)** (of a government) to introduce legislation: *bring in tax reforms.* **(d)** to pick and gather crops, fruit etc: *bring in a good harvest.* ⇨ also verdict(1). **bring sb in on sth** to allow a person to have a share in a plan, scheme etc.

bring sth into sth Ⓝ For uses with nouns such as *being, fashion, focus, play, use, world* etc, ⇨ the noun entries.

bring sth off to manage to do something successfully: *It wasn't an easy record to achieve but she brought it off.*

bring sb/sth on = bring sb/sth along. **bring sth on** to cause an effect as a result: *The rain brought on his cold. The famine was brought on by the drought.*

bring sb out (a) to help a person to lose shyness: *His success as an athlete has helped to bring* *him out.* (**b**) to cause a person to take part in a strike: *The union has brought out the miners.*

bring sth out (**a**) to produce and make a product available for sale: *New personal computers are brought out almost daily.* (**b**) to produce an effect, as a result: *The challenge of a high mountain brings out the best in her as a mountaineer.* (**c**) to show something as a result: *The enlargement has brought out the detail in the photograph.* (**d**) to help a plant to flower: *The warm sunshine has brought out the roses.* (**e**) to make an intended meaning clear: *The meaning of the poem is clearly brought out in this particular verse.* **bring sb out in sth** to cause a person to have spots, a rash etc: *Chocolate brings him out in spots.*

bring sb over to cause (and accompany) a person to come from abroad: *She brought her mother over from Chile to see the grandchildren.*

bring sb round (**a**) to help a person to regain consciousness: *The doctor brought her round.* (**b**) to persuade a person to agree with one's opinion etc: *He was not happy with the plan but we were able to bring him round.* (**c**) to invite and accompany a person on a visit (to a home, office etc nearby): *If your wife is free do bring her round on Friday.*

bring sb through to help a person to survive and recover: *Only her husband's careful nursing brought her through.*

bring sb/sth to sth Ⓝ For uses with nouns such as *attention, end, halt, life* etc, ⇨ the noun entries.

bring sb together to help two opposing individuals or groups to end a quarrel: *The loss of their only son brought the parents together again.*

bring sb/sth under control ⇨ control¹(1).
bring sth under sth to include something in a category: *The issues to consider must be brought under three main headings.*

bring sb up to care for a person and give moral and social training during childhood: *She has brought up five children. I was brought up in France.* Hence '**up·bring·ing** *nu.* Ⓝ *'Bring up'* is not the same as *'educate'*, which means 'give intellectual and cultural training to (usually in a school etc)'.

bring sth up (**a**) to cause something to be discussed or considered: *The chairman brought up the problem of fund-raising.* (**b**) (*informal*) to cause food to return to the mouth from the stomach: *He keeps on bringing up his milk.* ⇨ also rear¹(2) **bring sb/sth up to sth** to cause a person, study, to achieve a satisfactory standard: *His maths needs to be brought up to the same level as the others.* **bring sb/sth up to date.** ⇨ date²(2).

brink /brɪŋk/ *nc* **1** an upper edge of a steep place, a sharp slope etc. **2** the edge (of water, esp when deep): *He stood shivering on the brink, hesitating to dive into the water.* **3** (*fig*) the start of something unknown, dangerous or exciting: *on the brink of disaster/an exciting discovery.*

bri·quette /brɪˈket/ *nc* a small shaped piece of coal, charcoal etc used as fuel.

brisk /brɪsk/ *adj* (**—er, —est**) (of movement, activity) quick and lively: *a brisk walk. Trade is brisk.*

brisk·ly *adv*

bristle¹ /'brɪsl/ *nc* one of the short stiff hairs on an animal, in a brush etc: *a toothbrush with stiff bristles.*

bristle² /'brɪsl/ *vi* **1** (of hair) to stand up, rise on end: *The dog was angry and its hair bristled.* **2** (*fig*) to show anger because of injustice: *bristling with anger.*

Brit *abbr* (*informal* /brɪt/) Britain; (**a**) British (person): *She's a Brit.*

Brit·ish /'brɪtɪʃ/ *nc* (the —; also *adj*) (of) (the people of) Great Britain: *The British are Europeans. Do you like British cooking/weather?*

brittle /'brɪtl/ *adj* (e.g. of ice, glass) hard but easily broken.

broach /brəʊtʃ/ *vt* to begin a discussion of (a topic): *broach the subject of a pay rise.*

broad¹ /brɔːd/ *adj* (**—er, —est**) **1** having a large breadth or width: *a broad road/valley/leaf; broad shoulders; a broad back/chest.* Opp narrow¹(1). **2** covering a large area: *a broad desert/field.* Ⓝ *'Wide'* is also possible, as in *a wide motorway/river/ mountain range. 'Wide'* is preferred when describing the physical distance separating the sides or edges of something, as in *a wide gap, wide eyes, wide trousers/sleeves. 'Broad'* is preferred when referring to a large area, as in *a broad back, the broad spread of a tree's branches. 'Broad'* cannot be used with *'open'* but *'wide'* can, as in *with his mouth wide open/open wide.* **3** (*fig*) covering a large range: *broad support.* Opp narrow¹(4). Ⓝ *'Wide'* is not possible. **4** (*pred*) from one side to the other: *a river 50 metres broad.* Ⓝ *'Wide'* is possible and is less formal than *broad.* **5** general and not detailed: *a broad outline of the plans; in the broadest sense of the word; be in broad agreement.* Ⓝ *'Wide'* is not possible. ⇨ broadly. **6** (of the mind, opinions, ideas) liberal; tolerant: *broad political views; a broad attitude to young offenders; having a broad mind.* ⇨ broad-minded. Ⓝ *'Wide'* is not possible. Compare: *a broad view* (i.e. a tolerant opinion) and *a wide view* (i.e. with a large area visible). Opp narrow¹(5). **7** having a large range of opportunities: *broad career opportunities in the civil service.* Ⓝ *'Wide'* is not possible. **8** obvious, clear: *give a broad hint; make broad distinctions between good and bad influences.* **9** (of accent when speaking) obvious and strong: *speaking with a broad Scottish accent.* **10** (of humour, jokes) indecent. **11** **in broad daylight** ⇨ daylight(1).

,**broad-'minded** *adj* liberal and tolerant: *broad-minded parents.* Opp narrow-minded.

broad² /brɔːd/ *nc* the wide part: *the broad of the back.*

broad·cast /'brɔːdkɑːst/ *vt,vi* (*pt,pp* **broadcast**) to send out (speech, music etc) by radio or TV: *broadcast a speech/a concert.* □ *nc* something broadcast: *a radio/TV broadcast; a live broadcast* (= one that has not been recorded).

broad·cast·er *nc* a person who speaks etc on the radio or TV.

broad·ly /'brɔːdlɪ/ *adv* (esp) **broadly speaking** speaking in a general way without giving details.

broad·side /'brɔːdsaɪd/ *nc* **1** the whole of a ship's side above the water. **2** (*fig*) a strong spoken or written attack against a person or group.

bro·cade /brəˈkeɪd/ *nc,nu* (a kind of) cloth richly ornamented with designs (e.g. in gold or silver thread).

broc·coli /'brɒkəlɪ/ *nc,nu* (*pl* —) a vegetable with many white or purple heads of flowers like small cauliflowers.

bro·chure /'brəʊʃʊə(r)/ *nc* an illustrated pamphlet, esp as an advertisement: *travel/holiday brochures*.

brogue[1] /brəʊg/ *nc* (also *a pair of brogues*) a strong leather shoe for country wear.

brogue[2] /brəʊg/ *nc* a regional way of speaking, esp the Irish way of speaking English.

broil /brɔɪl/ *vt* (esp *US*) = grill[1](1).

broke /brəʊk/ **1** *pt* of break[2]. **2** *adj* (*pred*) (*informal*) without any money: *be/go broke*. ⇨ flat[1](10), stony-broke.

bro·ken /'brəʊkən/ **1** *pp* of break[2]. **2** *adj* (**a**) caused to be in two or more pieces after a fall or hit: *a broken window/leg*. (**b**) (of a machine etc) damaged and not working: *a broken clock*. (**c**) (of an agreement etc) not kept: *a broken promise*. **a broken home** a family in which the parents are separated or divorced. **a broken marriage** one which has ended in separation or divorce.

,**broken 'English** *nu* imperfect English.

,**broken-'hearted** *adj* feeling great sadness.

,**broken 'sleep** *nc,nu* interrupted sleep e.g. because of noise.

bro·ker /'brəʊkə(r)/ *nc* (also *stockbroker*) a person, business, that buys and sells (business shares etc) for others.

brol·ly /'brɒlɪ/ *nc* (*pl* **-ies**) (*dated informal*) = umbrella.

bron·chi /'brɒŋkaɪ/ *n pl* (*sing* **bronchus** /-kəs/) (*anat*) the two main branches into which the windpipe divides before entering the lungs (also called *bronchial tubes*).

bron·chi·al /'brɒŋkɪəl/ *adj* of or affecting the bronchi: *bronchial asthma*.

bron·chi·tis /brɒŋ'kaɪtɪs/ *nu* an illness with inflammation of the bronchi.

bronze[1] /brɒnz/ *n* **1** *nu* (also *attrib*) a metal made of a mixture of copper and tin: *a bronze statue*. **2** *nu* (also *adj*) its golden-brown colour. **3** *nc* a work of art made of bronze: *Benin bronzes*.

'**Bronze Age** *n* (the —) the period in history when people used tools and weapons made of bronze (between the Stone Age and the Iron Age).

,**bronze 'medal** *nc* a prize for third place in a sporting contest.

bronze[2] /brɒnz/ *vt,vi* (to cause something) to become bronze in colour: *faces bronzed by the sun and wind*.

brooch /brəʊtʃ/ *nc* an ornament with a pin for fastening on clothes.

brood[1] /bru:d/ *nc* all the young birds hatched at one time in a nest.

brood[2] /bru:d/ *vi* **1** (of a bird) to sit on eggs to hatch them. **2** (*fig*) to think about problems etc for a long time: *brooding over/on his misfortunes*.

broody /'bru:dɪ/ *adj* (**-ier, -iest**) **1** (of a hen) wanting to brood(1). **2** (*informal*) (of a woman) feeling the desire to have children.

brook[1] /brʊk/ *nc* a small stream.

brook[2] /brʊk/ *vt* (*formal*) to tolerate (something): *He will not brook interference.* ℕ Usually used in the negative or in questions.

broom /bru:m/ *nc* a brush on a long handle, used for sweeping.

Bros *abbr* (*informal* /brɒs/) (*commerce*) Brothers: *Moss Bros*.

broth /brɒθ/ *nu* water in which meat has been boiled (flavoured and thickened with vegetables etc and served as soup).

broth·el /'brɒθl/ *nc* a house at which prostitutes may be visited.

broth·er /'brʌðə(r)/ *nc* **1** a son of the same parents as another person. **2** (also *attrib*) a person united to others by membership of the same society, profession etc: *brother officers* (i.e. in the same regiment). **3** a member of a socialist organization, trade union etc. **4** (*pl* **—s** or **brethren** /'breðrən/) a member of a religious society. **5** (*pl*; *commerce*) (abbr Bros) a business owned by sons of the same family: *Smith Bros*.

'**brother·hood** *n* (**a**) *nu* the close feeling (as if) of brother for brother. (**b**) *nc* (the members of) an association of men with the same interests and aims, esp a religious or socialist organization.

'**brother-in-law** /'brʌðər ɪn lɔ:/ *nc* (*pl* **—s-in-law**) (**a**) a brother of one's husband or wife. (**b**) the husband of one's sister.

'**brother·ly** *adj*: *brotherly affection*.

brought /brɔ:t/ *pt,pp* of bring.

brow /braʊ/ *nc* **1** (usually *pl*; also *eye·brow*) an arch of hair above the eye. **2** the forehead. ⇨ highbrow, lowbrow. **3** the top of a steep slope: *the brow of a hill*.

brow·beat /'braʊbi:t/ *vt* (*pt* **browbeat**, *pp* **browbeaten** /-bi:tn/) to bully (a person): *a browbeaten little woman*.

brown[1] /braʊn/ *adj, n* (**—er, —est**) (having) the colour of coffee, suntan etc: *as brown as a berry* (= very suntanned).

brown[2] /braʊn/ *vt,vi* **1** (to cause something) to become brown: *brown potatoes in the oven; browning my legs in the sun*. **2 browned off** (*informal*) very irritated and bored.

,**brown 'bread** *nu* bread made with wholemeal flour.

,**brown 'rice** *nu* rice which has still its brown covering on each grain.

,**brown 'sugar** *nu* sugar that is not (or only a little) refined.

browse[1] /braʊz/ *nc* an act of browsing(2): *have a good browse in the library*.

browse[2] /braʊz/ *vi* **1** to feed as animals do (on grass etc): *cattle browsing in the fields*. **2** to read parts of a book, newspaper etc without any serious purpose: *browsing through a magazine*.

bruise[1] /bru:z/ *nc* an injury made by a blow or knock to the body or to a fruit, so that the skin is blue etc but not broken: *He was covered with bruises after falling off his bicycle*.

bruise[2] /bru:z/ *v* **1** *vt* to cause a bruise to (a person, fruit etc): *Pack the peaches carefully so that they won't be bruised*. **2** *vi* to show the effects of a blow or knock: *A child's flesh bruises easily*.

brunch /brʌntʃ/ *nc,nu* a late morning meal instead of breakfast and lunch.

bru·nette /bru:'net/ *nc* a woman with light skin and dark-brown hair.

brunt /brʌnt/ *nc* **bear the brunt of sth** to suffer the main strain, hardship, of an attack, criticism, anger etc.

brush[1] /brʌʃ/ *nc* **1** an implement with bristles, hair etc, used for scrubbing, sweeping cleaning (e.g. *toothbrush, nail-brush*), for tidying the hair (*hairbrush*) or used by painters and artists (*paint brush*). **2** (the act of) using a brush: *He gave his clothes a good brush.*

brush² /brʌʃ/ *nc* (*informal*) a short encounter (with the police, an enemy etc).

brush³ /brʌʃ/ *vt,vi* **1** to clean, sweep, tidy etc (something) with a brush: *brush your teeth/hair/ shoes.* **2** to touch (a person) when passing: *He brushed past me/against me rudely.*

brush sth aside (a) to defeat an enemy, defences etc easily. **(b)** to treat difficulty, opposition etc as if it is not important: *The supervisor brushed aside the complaints of the staff.*

brush sth away (a) to remove something (as if) with a brush: *He brushed away a fly from his nose.* **(b)** = brush sth aside(b).

brush sb down (*informal*) to speak angrily to a child, a student etc. **brush sth down** to clean a jacket, coat etc with a brush.

brush sb off (*sl*) to end a relationship with a person quickly and rudely: *I tried to be kind but he brushed me off.* Hence **'brush-off** *nc* (*informal*) a rude rejection. **brush sth off** to remove dust, mud, hair etc with a brush.

brush up (on) sth to practise or study a language, a subject at school etc in preparation for an exam, interview etc: *I'm brushing up my Spanish because we are going to Madrid.*

brush-off /'brʌʃɒf/ *nc* ⇨ brush sb off.

brusque /bruːsk/ *adj* (*derog*) (of speech or behaviour) rough, impolite and abrupt.
  brusque·ly *adv*
  brusque·ness *nu*

brus·sels sprout /ˌbrʌsl 'spraʊt/ *nc* (often B-; also *sprout*) a green vegetable with buds growing on the stem; one of the buds.

bru·tal /'bruːtl/ *adj* (*derog*) cruel and very unkind.
  bru·tal·ly /-əlɪ/ *adv*

bru·tal·ity /bruː'tælətɪ/ *n* (*pl* -ies) **1** *nu* great cruelty. **2** *nc* a cruel act.

brute¹ /bruːt/ *adj* (*attrib*) showing the strength of a large animal: *brute force.*

brute² /bruːt/ *nc* **1** a large animal except a human: *The poor brutes spend all their lives in zoos.* **2** (*derog*) a cruel and strong person: *That brute beats his children.*

brut·ish /'bruːtɪʃ/ *adj* (*derog*) of or like a brute(2).
  brut·ish·ly *adv*: *behave brutishly.*

BSc /ˌbiː es 'siː/ *abbr* Bachelor of Science: *Ms Penny Wise BSc.*

BST /ˌbiː es 'tiː/ *abbr* British Summer Time.

bubble¹ /'bʌbl/ *nc* **1** a ball formed of liquid and containing air or gas, e.g. one that forms in boiling water: *soap bubbles.* **2** an air-filled cavity in a solidified liquid, e.g. glass.

'bubble gum *nu* chewing-gum which can be blown into bubbles.

ˌbubble and 'squeak *nu* a dish of boiled potato and cabbage which are fried together.

bub·bly /'bʌblɪ/ *adj* (-ier, -iest) full of bubbles. □ *nu* (*informal*) = champagne.

bubble² /'bʌbl/ *vi* **1** to produce, make the sound of, bubbles: *The soup is bubbling (away) on the cooker.* **2 bubble over** (of liquids) to produce bubbles when boiling so that the liquid rises over the top of the pan. **bubble over (with sth)** (*fig*) to show great happiness very clearly: *She was bubbling over with joy.*

buck¹ /bʌk/ *nc* a male of a deer, hare or rabbit. Compare doe.

buck² /bʌk/ *nc* (*sl*) US dollar.

buck³ /bʌk/ *n* **pass the buck (to sb)** (*sl*) to shift the responsibility (to a person).

buck⁴ /bʌk/ *v* **1** *vi* (of a horse) to jump up with the four feet together and the back arched. **2** *vt* to throw (a rider) to the ground by doing this. **3** *vi* **buck up** (*sl*) to hurry up: *Buck up or you'll miss the bus.* **4** *vt* **buck (sb) up** (to cause oneself, a person) to become more cheerful and energetic: *The good news bucked us all up.* **buck up your ideas** to behave better, be more responsible.

buck·et¹ /'bʌkɪt/ *nc* **1** a container with a handle, used for holding or carrying water etc. **kick the bucket** (*sl*) to die. **2** as much as a bucket can hold: *a bucket of water.*

'bucket·ful /-fʊl/ *nc* = bucket(2).

'bucket seat *nc* a seat (e.g. in a car) with a curved back.

'bucket shop *nc* a place selling bucket tickets.

'bucket ticket *nc* a cheap reservation on a plane often without all the usual facilities and protection.

buck·et² /'bʌkɪt/ *vi* **bucket (down)** (of rain) to come down heavily.

buckle¹ /'bʌkl/ *nc* a fastener with one or more spikes made to go through a hole in a belt etc.

buckle² /'bʌkl/ *v* **1** *vt,vi* (to cause shoes etc) to be fastened with a buckle: *buckle (up) one's shoes/ belt.* **2** *vi* (of metal etc) to bend, become twisted, because of heat, strain etc: *The door of my car was buckled in the accident.* **3** *vi* **buckle down (to sth)** to begin work, study etc seriously: *Buckle down or you'll fail the exam.*

bu·col·ic /bjuː'kɒlɪk/ *adj* (*literature*) (of poetry etc) concerning the countryside and the people who live outside the towns.

bud /bʌd/ *vi* (**-dd-**), *nc* (to produce) a leaf or flower at the beginning of its growth. **in bud** having buds or sending out buds: *The trees are in bud.* **nip sth in the bud** (*fig*) to put an end to e.g. a plot while it is beginning.

bud·ding *adj* (*attrib; fig*) beginning to develop: *a budding lawyer/poet.*

Bud·dhism /'bʊdɪzəm/ *n* the religion founded by Gautama /'gaʊtəmə/ or Siddartha /sɪ'dɑːtə/ Buddha /'bʊdə/ (teacher) in N India, in about the 6th century BC.

Bud·dhist /'bʊdɪst/ *nc* a person believing in Buddhism.

bud·dy /'bʌdɪ/ *nc* (*pl* -ies) (*sl*) friend.

budge /bʌdʒ/ *vt,vi* (usually with *can't, couldn't* or with *won't, wouldn't*) **1** (to cause a person, thing) to move very little: *We couldn't budge the piano.* **2** (*fig*) (to cause a person) to change a decision or attitude: *The committee refuses to budge on this issue.*

bud·geri·gar /'bʌdʒərɪɡɑː(r)/ *nc* a kind of small Australian bird, often a pet in Britain.

budget¹ /'bʌdʒɪt/ *nc* **1** an estimate of future income and expenditure, esp (the B-) that made by the Chancellor of the Exchequer: *a school/ family budget; a production/sales budget.* **2** the money involved in a budget: *a budget of £50 a* *week for food.*

budget² /'bʌdʒɪt/ *vt* **budget for sth** to allow or arrange money for something: *budget for the coming year.*

buff¹ /bʌf/ *adj, nu* dull yellow (colour).

buff² /bʌf/ *nc* (*informal*) a person with much knowledge and interest in something: *a wine buff.*

buff³ /bʌf/ *vt* to polish (metal) with a soft leather cloth.

buf·falo /'bʌfələu/ *nc* (*pl* —**s**) **1** a kind of long-horned black ox. **2** a N American bison.

buf·fer /'bʌfə(r)/ *nc* (usually *pl*) an apparatus for reducing the effect of a collision, e.g. on a railway engine.

'buffer ˌstate *nc* a small nation between much more powerful ones who oppose each other.

buf·fet¹ /'bʊfeɪ/ *nc* **1** a place where food and drink may be bought and eaten, e.g. in a train station. **2** a table from which (usually cold) food is served.

buf·fet² /'bʌfɪt/ *vt* to hit (something) with force: *The ships were buffeted about by the storm.*

buf·foon /bə'fuːn/ *nc* (*dated*) a fool.

bug¹ /bʌg/ *nc* **1** a small blood-sucking insect in dirty houses and beds. **2** (esp US) any small insect. **3** (*informal*) a germ; virus infection: *You've got the Asian flu bug.* **4** (*sl*) an error, e.g. in a computer program. **5** an electronic device etc for listening secretly to conversations etc. **6** (*informal*) a strong desire to do something: *She's always dancing—she's really got the bug!*

bug² /bʌg/ *vt* (**-gg-**) **1** (*informal*) to use electronic devices in (a room etc) in order to listen secretly to conversations. **2** (*sl*) to annoy (a person): *That man really bugs me.*

bugle /'bjuːgl/ *nc* a musical instrument of copper or brass, used for military signals.

bugler *nc* a person who plays a bugle.

build¹ /bɪld/ *nu* (of a person) the general size, shape and strength: *having a powerful/weak build.*

build² /bɪld/ *vt, vi* (*pt, pp* **built** /bɪlt/) **1** to make (something) by putting parts, materials etc together: *build a house/road/bridge. She's building shelves for her books. It's built of/out of wood. This shed looks well built. It's a well-built school but the sports centre is badly built/built badly.* Ⓝ 'Make' is also possible but only when referring to how something is built, as in made of/out of stone, badly made, or when referring to small constructions, as in make a box/model aeroplane/shelf (i.e. not buildings, bridges, roads etc). **2** to start and develop (a business, computer program, reputation, wealth etc): *He's built that company from nothing. She's built her reputation at the hospital by hard work.*

build sth in (**a**) to make and fix a piece of furniture in a house: *build in a wardrobe.* (**b**) to include something in the design (and manufacture), the cost etc: *build in an electronic flashlight; build in an opportunity to analyze sales in Italy when designing the computer program; build in the travel costs.* (**c**) to make a permanent addition to a contract etc: *build in a clause about selling rights.* Hence **'built-in** *adj* (*attrib*): *a built-in cupboard/flash/safety clause.*

build on to extend an existing building: *There's space at the side to build on.* **build sth on** to add something extra to a building: *build on a garage.*

build on sth to use a good start to develop a business, trade, reputation etc: *build on last year's success/a previous good performance.*

build sth on sth to use information, evidence etc to defend, prepare, an idea, reputation, lawsuit etc: *He built his reputation on reliability. I've very little evidence to build my case on.*

build up (**a**) (of traffic, debts, work etc) to increase in quantity. (**b**) (of pressure, pain, strain etc) to increase in strength: *Tension in South America is building up.* Hence **'build·up** *nc: a buildup of traffic/pressure.* **build sb up** (**a**) to improve the health, strength, of a person: *Fresh milk will soon build you up.* (**b**) (*informal*) to praise a person to others (often too much): *Don't build me up too much before I meet her.* Hence **'build·up** *nc: be given a terrific buildup in the newspapers.* **build sth up** (**a**) to improve strength, fitness etc: *Jogging builds up stamina.* (**b**) (*only passive*) to cover land with buildings. Hence **'built-up** *adj* (*attrib*): *What's the speed limit in built-up areas?* (**c**) to develop a business, reputation, funds etc: *She's building up a strong business. She's building up her savings for a trip to Peru.* **build sth up into sth** to put parts together to make a whole: *He's built up his books into an excellent library.*

build·er /'bɪldə(r)/ *nc* **1** a person, business, that builds and repairs houses, hotels etc. **2** (*fig*) a person who develops and controls businesses: *an empire builder* (= a controller of many powerful businesses).

build·ing /'bɪldɪŋ/ *n* **1** *nc* a house or similar structure: *Houses, schools, churches, factories and sheds are all buildings.* **2** *nu* (art of) constructing houses etc: *building materials.*

'building society *nc* an organization for making loans to people who wish to buy a house, using money from other people's savings.

build·up /'bɪldʌp/ *nc* ⇨ build up, build sb up.

built /bɪlt/ *pt, pp* of build².

built-in /'bɪlt ɪn/ *adj* ⇨ build sth in.

built-up /'bɪlt ʌp/ *adj* ⇨ build sth up(b).

bulb /bʌlb/ *nc* **1** a round, thick root of some plants. **2** anything like a bulb in shape, e.g. the glass case for an electric light: *a light-bulb.*

bul·bous /'bʌlbəs/ *adj* of, having, like, growing from, a bulb(1).

bulge¹ /bʌldʒ/ *nc* **1** a swelling or outward curve. **2** (*fig*) an increase in volume or numbers: *a bulge in membership/births.*

bulge² /bʌldʒ/ *vi* to swell or curve outwards beyond the usual size: *bulging pockets/eyes. His pockets were bulging with apples.*

bulk /bʌlk/ *nu* a large quantity, volume, size etc. **in bulk** in large amounts: *buy in bulk.* **the bulk of sth** the larger part or number of something: *He left the bulk of his property to his brother.*

bulky *adj* (**-ier, -iest**) taking up much space and difficult to move or carry.

bull¹ /bʊl/ *nc* **1** the male of any cattle, kept for breeding. **a bull in a china shop** a person who is rough and clumsy where skill and care are needed. **take the bull by the horns** to try to deal with a difficulty boldly instead of trying to escape from it. **2** a male of the whale, elephant and other large animals. Compare cow.

'bull·dog *nc* a powerful breed of dog, with a

short neck, noted for its courage.

'bull·doze *vt* (**a**) to remove (earth), flatten (obstacles), using a bulldozer. (**b**) (*fig*) to force (a person) into doing something by using physical strength or threats.

'bull·dozer *nc* a powerful tractor with a wide blade in front, used for moving earth etc.

'bull market *nc* (*finance*) the situation when prices are rising. ⇨ bullish.

'bull's-eye *nc* the centre of a target (for archers, gunners etc).

bull² /bʊl/ *nu* (*sl*) nonsense.

bull³ /bʊl/ *nc* an official order from the Pope.

bul·let /'bʊlɪt/ *nc* a shaped piece of lead (to be) fired from a rifle or revolver.

'bullet-proof *adj* (no *comp*) able to stop bullets: *a bullet-proof jacket.*

bul·letin /'bʊlətɪn/ *nc* **1** an official statement of news: *The doctors issued bulletins twice a day.* **2** a printed sheet of paper with official announcements.

bul·lion /'bʊlɪən/ *nu* gold or silver in bars.

bul·lish /'bʊlɪʃ/ *adj* (*finance*) describing a situation when prices are rising.

bul·lock /'bʊlək/ *nc* a castrated bull.

bul·ly¹ /'bʊlɪ/ *nc* (*pl* -ies) (*derog*) a person who uses her or his strength or power to frighten or hurt others.

bul·ly² /'bʊlɪ/ *vt* (*pt,pp* -ied) to behave like a bully towards (a person). **bully sb into doing sth** to be a bully and force a person to do something.

bul·wark /'bʊlwək/ *nc* **1** a strong wall built against attack. **2** (*fig*) something that defends or protects: *Law is the bulwark of society.*

bum¹ /bʌm/ *nc* (*informal*) the part of the body on which a person sits.

bum² /bʌm/ *nc* (*sl; derog*) a beggar or often lazy person. □ *vi* (-mm-) **bum around** to wander about doing nothing. **bum off sb** (*sl*) to ask a person for money, food, without intending to return it.

bumble-bee /'bʌmbl biː/ *nc* a kind of large hairy bee.

bump¹ /bʌmp/ *adv* (*informal*) suddenly and violently: *The child went bump into the wall.*

bump² /bʌmp/ *nc* **1** (a sound made by) a hit or knock: *I heard a bump downstairs.* **2** a swelling on the skin made by a hit or knock: *a bump on the head.* **3** a similar swelling, e.g. on a road.

bumpy *adj* (-ier, -iest) (of a road etc) with many bumps: *a bumpy road/journey/flight.*

bump³ /bʌmp/ *v* **1** *vt,vi* to hit or knock (something) violently: *The room was dark and I bumped my head on the door. The child ran round the corner and bumped into me.* **2** *vi* (of a car etc) to move (as if) over bumps(3): *The old bus bumped along/down the mountain road.*

bump into sb (*informal*) to meet an old friend etc by chance (after a long time): *I bumped into an old schoolfriend I hadn't seen for twenty years.*

bump sb off (*informal*) to kill a person.

bump sth up (*informal*) to increase a price, marks, salary etc (suddenly): *A dock strike bumped up the price of imports. A good essay could bump up your English marks.*

bum·per¹ /'bʌmpə(r)/ *adj* (*attrib*) unusually large or abundant: *a bumper harvest.*

bum·per² /'bʌmpə(r)/ *nc* a bar on a vehicle (front and back) to reduce the effect of a collision.

bump·kin /'bʌmpkɪn/ *nc* (*derog*) a clumsy, uncultured person, esp from the country.

bump·tious /'bʌmpʃəs/ *adj* (*formal; derog*) conceited: *bumptious officials.*

bun /bʌn/ *nc* **1** a kind of small round, sweet cake. **2** a twisted knot of hair above the back of the neck.

bunch¹ /bʌntʃ/ *nc* **1** a collection of the same fruit etc growing together: *a bunch of grapes/bananas.* **2** a collection of things of the same sort placed or fastened together: *a bunch of flowers/keys.*

bunch² /bʌntʃ/ *vi,vt* **bunch (sb/sth) together/up** (to cause people, things) to form into a bunch(2): *They bunched the children together inside the tent. They were bunched up to keep warm.*

bundle¹ /'bʌndl/ *nc* a number of things fastened, tied or wrapped together: *a bundle of toys. The books were tied up in bundles of twenty.* **be a bundle of nerves** to feel extremely frightened.

bundle² /'bʌndl/ *vt* **1** **bundle sth (up)** to make things into a bundle: *bundling up old clothes.* **2** to put (things) away in a confused heap: *We bundled everything into a drawer.* **3** to put (a person) somewhere in a hurried and rough way: *They bundled him into a taxi.*

bung¹ /bʌŋ/ *nc* a stopper for closing a hole in a cask or barrel.

bung² /bʌŋ/ *vt* **1** to put a bung into (something). **2 be bunged up** (**a**) (of the nose) to be blocked with mucus. (**b**) (of drains) to be blocked with dirt.

bun·ga·low /'bʌŋgələʊ/ *nc* a small house with only one storey.

bungle /'bʌŋgl/ *vt* to do (a piece of work) badly and clumsily.

bun·ion /'bʌnɪən/ *nc* a swelling on the large joint of the big toe.

bunk¹ /bʌŋk/ *nc* **1** a narrow bed fixed on the wall, e.g. in a ship. **2** one of two narrow beds built one above the other, usually for children.

bunk² /bʌŋk/ *n sing* **do a bunk** (*sl*) to run away.

bunk³ /bʌŋk/ *vt* **bunk off sth** (*sl*) to stay away from school, work etc without permission.

bunk·er /'bʌŋkə(r)/ *nc* **1** the part of a ship where coal or fuel oil is stored. **2** a sandy hollow on a golf-course. **3** (*mil*) an underground shelter.

bun·ny /'bʌnɪ/ *nc* (*pl* -ies) (a child's word for) a rabbit.

bun·sen burner /ˌbʌnsn 'bɜːnə(r)/ *nc* (also B-) a burner using gas mixed with air (used in science laboratories).

buoy¹ /bɔɪ/ *nc* a floating object, anchored to the bottom of the sea used to guide ships, to indicate reefs, submerged wrecks etc.

buoy² /bɔɪ/ *vt* **buoy sth (up) 1** to keep a boat etc afloat. **2** (*fig*) to keep hopes, ambitions etc strong and positive: *His spirits were buoyed up by her friendliness.*

buoy·an·cy /'bɔɪənsɪ/ *nu* **1** the power to float or keep things floating. **2** (*fig*) the feeling of being cheerful, having courage. **3** (*fig*) (of the stock market) the tendency of prices to rise.

buoy·ant /'bɔɪənt/ *adj* **1** able to float or to keep things floating. **2** (*fig*) cheerful: *a buoyant personality.* **3** (*fig*) (of the stock market) maintaining high prices.

buoy·ant·ly adv

BUPA /'buːpə/ acronym British United Provident Association (an organization for private medical care).

burble /'bɜːbl/ vi to make a gentle murmuring or bubbling sound: burbling with happiness.

bur·den¹ /'bɜːdn/ nc **1** a heavy load. ⇨ beast(1). **2** (fig) something difficult to bear: the burden of taxation on industry. **3** an obligation to show proof: The burden of proof rests with him.

bur·den² /'bɜːdn/ vt **1** to put a burden(1) on: a burdened donkey. **2** (fig) to make (a person) bear responsibility, difficulties: be burdened (down) with many duties/financial problems; a mind burdened with useless knowledge. Compare unburden.

bur·den·some /-səm/ adj difficult to bear.

bu·reau /'bjʊərəʊ/ nc (pl —**x** /-rəʊz/) **1** a writing desk with drawers. **2** (often B-) a business, government department etc supplying information: a travel bureau; the Information Bureau.

bu·reau de change /ˌbjʊərəʊ də 'ʃɑːndʒ/ nc (pl **bureaux de change**) (Fr) a place where foreign currency can be bought or sold.

bu·reauc·racy /bjʊə'rɒkrəsɪ/ n **1** nu government by paid officials not elected by the people who keep their positions whatever political party is in power. **2** nc this system of government; the officials as a group.

bu·reau·crat /'bjʊərəkræt/ nc (often derog) an official who works in a government department, esp who obeys the rules without exercising much judgement.

bu·reau·crat·ic /ˌbjʊərə'krætɪk/ adj (often derog) of or like a bureaucrat (and obeying rules too much).

bu·reau·crati·cal·ly /-klɪ/ adv

bur·glar /'bɜːglə(r)/ nc a person who breaks into a house etc at night in order to steal.

'**burglar alarm** nc a device used to warn of burglars.

'**burglar-proof** adj made so that burglars cannot break in: a burglar-proof office.

bur·glary /'bɜːglərɪ/ n (pl **-ies**) nc,nu (an instance of) the crime of breaking into a house by night to steal.

burgle /'bɜːgl/ vt,vi to break into (a building) and commit burglary.

bur·ial /'berɪəl/ nc,nu (an instance of) burying.

'**burial-ground** nc a cemetery.

bur·ly /'bɜːlɪ/ adj (**-ier**, **-iest**) (of a person) big and strong.

burn¹ /bɜːn/ nc an injury, mark, made by fire, heat or acid: He died of the burns he received in the fire.

burn² /bɜːn/ v (pt,pp **burnt** /bɜːnt/ or (esp with intransitive uses) —**ed**) **1** vi to be on fire: The fire burned all night. The forest was burning. Quickly—the toast is burning. **2** vt to use (fuel) for heat or light: burn wood/coal/oil; an oil-burning stove; burn a candle. **3** vt to damage, destroy, (something) by fire, heat or acid: burn the rubbish; burn one's clothes; burn the food/a saucepan. **burn one's bridges** ⇨ bridge¹(2). **burn (sth) to the ground** (to cause it) to be destroyed completely. **4** vt to make (a hole, mark etc) by (using) heat, fire or acid: burn a hole in the

carpet. **5** vt, v reflex to injure (oneself) by fire, heat or acid: I've burnt my feet on the sand. **burn one's fingers** ⇨ finger¹. **6** vt,vi (to cause one's skin) to be suntanned (too much and too quickly): My skin burns easily. Her back is badly burnt. Be careful—this African sun burns skin very quickly. **7** vi to suffer a high temperature (because of ill health): He's burning with fever. **8** vi (fig) to have a strong feeling (of anger, hate, love etc): She burned (with desire) to see her children again. **9** vt to produce a strong, hot taste in (something): This curry burns my mouth.

burn away (**a**) to be on fire: The fire is burning away brightly. (**b**) to become reduced, completely used up, by burning: Half the oil had burned away in the furnace.

burn (sth) down (to cause a building etc) to be destroyed in a fire: The school burnt down. Who has burnt the fence down?

burn for sth (fig) to wish very much for something: burn for the opportunity to play for England.

burn sth off to remove paint etc by burning.

burn out (**a**) (of a fire) to burn until no fuel is left. (**b**) (of a space rocket) to use up all the available fuel. (**c**) ⇨ burn (oneself) out. **burn sth out** (usually passive) to destroy something by fire, an electrical fault etc: The house was completely burnt out. **burn (itself) out** = burn out(a). **burn (oneself) out** (informal) to destroy one's health by working too hard, drinking too much etc.

burn up (**a**) (of a fire etc) to become stronger: Put more wood on the fire and make it burn up. (**b**) (of a spacecraft, meteor etc) to enter the atmosphere and be completely destroyed by heat. **burn sth up** to get rid of something by burning: burn up all the garden rubbish.

burn with sth ⇨ burn²(8).

burn·er /'bɜːnə(r)/ nc (a part of) a stove, furnace etc producing flames: an oil/gas-burner.

burn·ing /'bɜːnɪŋ/ adj (attrib) (of feelings etc) extreme: a burning desire/thirst.

bur·nish /'bɜːnɪʃ/ vt,vi to polish (metal) (as if) by rubbing.

burnt /bɜːnt/ pt,pp of burn².

burp /bɜːp/ vi, nc (sl) = belch.

burr /bɜː(r)/ nc a continuous low sound made by parts of machines that turn quickly.

bur·row /'bʌrəʊ/ nc a hole made in the ground (by rabbits etc). □ vi,vt to make a burrow.

bur·sar /'bɜːsə(r)/ nc **1** a treasurer (esp of a college). **2** (a student with) a scholarship or grant: British Council bursars in Great Britain.

bur·sary nc (pl **-ies**) (**a**) the office of a bursar. (**b**) a scholarship (the usual word).

burst¹ /bɜːst/ nc **1** a bursting explosion: the burst of a bomb; a burst in the water main. **2** a brief, strong effort: a burst of energy/speed. **3** an outbreak: a burst of applause.

burst² /bɜːst/ v (pt,pp **burst**) **1** vt,vi (to cause a bomb, tyre, balloon etc) to break or explode. **2** vt,vi (to cause river banks, a dam, an abscess, a boil) to break outwards. **3** vi (of a flower, leaf) to open suddenly. **4** vi to make a way in or through suddenly or by force: He burst into the room. The sun burst through the clouds.

burst in to appear, enter, suddenly: She burst in

and found me reading what she had written.

burst in (on sth) to interrupt a conversation with excitement.

burst into sth (a) to begin suddenly to cry, laugh, sing etc: *burst into tears/laughter/song.* **(b)** to display blossom, flowers etc suddenly: *burst into flower.* **(c)** to appear suddenly: *burst into view.* **burst into flames** to be suddenly on fire.

burst (sth) out to say or declare something (suddenly): *burst out a warning.* ⇨ **outburst**. **burst out crying/laughing** to begin to cry/laugh (suddenly). **burst out (of sth)** to leave a place suddenly: *He burst out of the room in anger.*

burst with sth to show a great deal of something: *bursting with energy/impatience/wealth/happiness/enthusiasm.*

bury /'berɪ/ *vt* (*pt,pp* **-ied**) **1** to place (a dead body) in the ground, in a grave or in the sea. **2** (of a clergyman) to perform the burial service for (a dead person). **3** to put (something) underground, cover with earth, leaves etc: *buried treasure.* **4** to hide (something) from view: *She buried her face in her hands.* **5 bury oneself in sth** to be completely occupied with something: *He buried himself in his studies/book/work.*

bus /bʌs/ *nc* (*pl* **—es**) a public passenger vehicle that travels a fixed route along the roads and takes people on and sets them down: *Shall we walk or go by bus? miss the bus* (*sl*) to be too late to use an opportunity. □ *vi,vt* (**-ss-**) to go, take (a person), by bus.

'bus-stop *nc* a stopping place for buses.

bush /buʃ/ *n* **1** *nc* a low-growing plant with many woody stems coming up from the root: *a rose-bush.* **2** *nu* (often the **—**) wild, uncultivated land in Africa and Australia. **beat about the bush** (usually in the negative) to talk about something without mentioning it directly: *Say what you mean—don't beat about the bush.*

bushy /'buʃɪ/ *adj* (**-ier, -iest**) **1** covered with bushes. **2** growing thickly: *bushy eyebrows.*

busier, busiest ⇨ busy.

busi·ly /'bɪzəlɪ/ *adv* in a busy way: *busily engaged in working.*

busi·ness /'bɪznɪs/ *n* **1** *nu* the activity of buying and selling as a way of earning money: *We do not do much business with them.* **on business** for the purpose of doing business: *Are you here on business or for pleasure?* **2** *nc* a commercial organization such as a factory, company etc: *He is the manager of three different businesses.* **3** *nu* or sing a task, duty: *It is a teacher's business to help pupils.* **be none of your/her** etc **business** to be nothing to do with you/her etc. **get down to business** to start the work that must be done. **go about one's business** to occupy oneself with one's personal tasks: *During the crisis we tried to go about our business in the usual way.* **mean business** (*informal*) to be serious, determined (to act, not just talk). **mind one's own business** to attend to one's own duties and not interfere with those of others.

'business hours *n pl* the time in the day when a shop etc is open to customers.

'busi·ness·like *adj* using, showing, care, organization etc.

'busi·ness·man/woman *nc* a person owning or working for a business(2) (not a lawyer, doctor

etc).

'business studies *nu* the scientific study (at a university etc) of how to control, manage a business(2).

busk /bʌsk/ *vi* to entertain people for tips, e.g. singing to queues outside cinemas.

busk·er *nc* a person who busks.

bust¹ /bʌst/ *adj* (*pred*) (*sl*) **1** (esp **go bust**) (of a business) no longer operating because of having no more money. **2** (of a machine etc) broken: *My zip is bust.*

bust² /bʌst/ *nc* **1** the head and shoulders of a person in stone etc. **2** a woman's breast. **3** the measurement round a woman's chest and back.

bustle /'bʌsl/ *vt,vi* (to cause people) to move quickly and excitedly: *Everyone was bustling about/in and out.* □ *nu* excited activity: *the bustle of city streets.*

busy¹ /'bɪzɪ/ *adj* (**-ier, -iest**) **1** having a lot of work to do: *The doctor is a busy man.* ⇨ busily. **2** full of activity: *a busy day.* **3** (of places) filled with active people, traffic etc: *The shops are busy before Christmas.* **4** (of a telephone line) in use.

'busy·body *nc* (*pl* **-ies**) a person who interferes although help is not wanted.

busy² /'bɪzɪ/ *v reflex* (*pt,pp* **-ied**) **busy oneself (with sth)** to keep busy, occupy oneself doing something: *He busied himself with all sorts of little tasks.*

but¹ /bʌt/ *adv* only (now the usual word): *We can but try. He's but a boy.* **all but** almost: *She all but accused me of lying.*

but² /bət *strong form:* bʌt/ *conj* **1** (*coord*) **(a)** as an alternative: *Tom can't come but his brother will.* **(b)** (showing the opposite to what is or was expected): *He's poor but he's honest. She left her bag on the train but she didn't worry.* **(c)** (showing the opposite condition, effect or result): *My mother speaks Chinese but I don't.* **but then** on the other hand: *Their parties are too noisy, but then I like the music they play.* **2** (*subord*) (*formal*) (used after a negative) without the result or effect that: *I could not choose but go* (= I had no choice).

but³ /bət *strong form:* bʌt/ *prep* **1 (a)** (used with *all, everybody, everything, nobody, nothing* etc) other than: *I know everyone but that tall woman. We've been everywhere but Scandinavia. You do nothing but watch TV.* **(b)** (used with *who, where* etc in questions) other than: *Who but she would go camping in the rain? Where but Austria can you buy good chocolate?* Ⓝ *'Except'* is also possible and is more usual. **2 the last/next but one/two** etc the first, second etc after the last/next: *I was last but one in the queue. He was next but two on the list.* **3 but for sb/sth** without a person, thing: *But for you, he'd have drowned. We'd have been unable to buy the house but for her generosity.*

butch·er¹ /'butʃə(r)/ *nc* **1** a person, business, that kills, cuts up and sells animals for food. **2** (*derog*) a person who kills savagely and needlessly.

butch·er² /'butʃə(r)/ *vt* **1** to prepare (meat) for selling as food. **2** to kill (people, animals) violently, esp with a knife.

butch·ery *nu* (esp) the cruel killing of people.

but·ler /'bʌtlə(r)/ *nc* the head of staff in a rich

household.

butt¹ /bʌt/ nc **1** a large cask for wine or ale. **2** a large barrel for storing rainwater.

butt² /bʌt/ nc **1** the thicker, larger end (esp of a fishing-rod or rifle). **2** the unburned end of a smoked cigar or cigarette.

butt³ /bʌt/ nc a person who is a target for ridicule, jokes etc: *He is the butt of the whole school.*

butt⁴ /bʌt/ v **1** vt to push (a person) with the head (as a goat does): *butt a man in the stomach.* **2** vi **butt in** (*informal*) to force oneself into the conversation or company of others.

but·ter¹ /'bʌtə(r)/ nu **1** a yellow fatty food substance made from milk, used on bread, in cooking etc. **2** a food substance similar to butter, made from other materials: *peanut butter.*

'**but·ter·cup** nc a kind of wild yellow flower.

'**but·ter·fin·gers** nc (*derog*) a person unable to hold or catch things well.

but·ter² /'bʌtə(r)/ vt **1** to spread, cook with, butter: *buttered toast.* **2 butter sb up** to praise a person in order to gain something.

but·ter·fly /'bʌtəflaɪ/ nc (pl **-ies**) **1** an insect with large, often colourful, wings. **2** (pl) a feeling of fear, nervousness: *I've got butterflies (in my stomach).*

but·tocks /'bʌtəks/ n pl the part of the body on which a person sits: *a smack on the buttocks.*

but·ton¹ /'bʌtn/ nc **1** a small, usually round, object used for fastening articles of clothing, or sewn on as an ornament. **2** a small, round object, esp one that, when pushed, makes an electrical contact, e.g. for a bell: *press the button.*

but·ton² /'bʌtn/ vt **button sth (up)** to fasten clothes etc with a button or buttons: *button (up) one's coat.*

but·ton·hole¹ /'bʌtnhəʊl/ nc **1** a hole through which a button is passed. **2** a flower in the lapel of a jacket or coat.

but·ton·hole² /'bʌtnhəʊl/ vt to speak to (a person) and make her or him listen.

but·tress /'bʌtrɪs/ nc **1** a support built against a wall. **2** (*fig*) something that supports: *the buttress of a business.*

bux·om /'bʌksəm/ adj (of a woman) large and healthy-looking.

buy¹ /baɪ/ nc something that is obtained in return for money: *a good buy; the best buy.*

buy² /baɪ/ vt (pt,pp **bought** /bɔːt/) **1** to get (something) in return for money: *I bought it for £10. Can I buy your old bike from you? Money can't buy happiness.* **buy (extra etc) time** (*informal*) to talk, delay one's response etc in order to get more time to avoid a crisis, disaster etc: *He was able to buy some more time to pay off his debts.* **2** (*fig*) (usually *passive*) to obtain (something) at a sacrifice: *Victory was dearly bought* (= many people died). **3 buy it** (*sl*) to be killed (in a war).

buy in sth to buy supplies (and avoid a shortage): *buy in coal for the winter.*

buy into sth to buy shares (and control) in a business.

buy sb off (*informal*) to pay a person so that he or she will not act against one's interests: *Are you trying to buy me off with this gold watch?*

buy sb/sth out to buy (a person's shares in) a business.

buy sth up to buy all of something: *They've bought up all this land for building.*

buy·er /'baɪə(r)/ nc **1** a person who buys articles on sale. **2** a person who chooses articles to be sold in a shop.

buzz¹ /bʌz/ nc **1** the sound made by bees and other insects when flying. **2** a similar sound of an electric bell etc.

buzz² /bʌz/ v **1** vi to make a humming sound (as of bees or an electric bell). **2** vt to call (a person) by using an electric bell. **3** vi (of the ears) to be filled with a buzzing noise: *My ears buzz.* **4** vi to move quickly or excitedly: *buzz about/around; buzzing along the road.* **buzz off** (*sl*) go away.

buz·zer nc an electrical bell that produces a buzzing sound.

buz·zard /'bʌzəd/ nc a kind of falcon.

by¹ /baɪ/ adv particle Ⓝ For uses with *verbs* such as *call, come, get, go, put, stand* etc, ⇨ the *verb* entries. **1** at a short distance: *We live close by.* Ⓝ '*Near*' has a similar meaning but is used to refer to a position at a very short distance, as in *Don't come near or I'll scream.* '*Near*' can be used with *too, very* etc, as *It's too/very near,* but '*by*' cannot. ⇨ *near by* at near². **2** past: *He hurried/drove/walked by.* **3** in reserve: *It has been kept/put by.* **4 by and by** later (on): *By and by the old man returned to the beach.* **5 by and large** in general: *By and large I like her songs but not the ones on her new record.*

by² /baɪ/ prep Ⓝ For uses with verbs such as *come, go, stand* etc, ⇨ the *verb* entries. **1** at, to, the side of: *Come and sit by me/by my side. We live by* (= a short distance from) *the sea.* Ⓝ '*Near*' is also possible but is preferred to show a closer position, as in *Don't go near the edge of the cliff.* (**all**) **by herself/myself** etc (**a**) alone: *He was all by himself* (= completely alone). (**b**) without any help: *I carried it by myself.* **2** past: *She ran by me.* **3** using a route across, along, through etc: *Come in by the side entrance. We came by the motorway. They travelled by way of* (= passing through) *Athens.* **4** (used to show the way of travelling): *go by air/land/sea.* **5** (used to show the kind of transport used): *travel by bus/car/bike/train/plane/foot.* Ⓝ '*On a/the*' is also possible but is used particularly to refer to the state of being in or on a vehicle etc as in *I first saw him on a bus. We met on the train.* Note the use of '*a/the*' with '*on*' but not with '*by*'. **6** (of the method used in an activity etc) using: *works by electricity; designed by computers; being made by robots; pay by cheque; hold it by the handle; took him by the arm. We'll be able to see by the moon. I need glasses to read by.* **by ear** ⇨ ear¹(2). **by heart** ⇨ heart(2). Ⓝ '*With*' is used when referring to the instrument used and to answer questions using *how,* as in *I opened it with a coin.* **7** (used to show responsibility for writing, creating etc something): *a play by Chekhov; a record by Louis Armstrong; a programme by the BBC; government by the people.* **8** (used after a passive to show the person, thing, causing the action etc): *She was prevented by her mother from going to the party. It can be distinguished by its large ears.* **9** (used to show how a person, thing, is known etc): *I recognized him by his jacket. Please call me by my first name.* **10** (used before -ing forms to show method): *I got the job by pretending I was 18. He earns a living by painting.* **11** during: *by day/*

night; by daylight. **12** at or before: *I need it by 4
o'clock/by the weekend. By the time I arrived,
he'd gone.* Ⓝ Compare *'till/until'*, which are used
when referring to a continuous state during a period
of time, as in *I'll stay until Friday/next week.* Compare also *up to* sth(c). **13** (used in phrases of time,
length, mass etc to show rate): *paid by the hour;
sold by the metre; packaged by the kilo; come in
two by two* (= pairs); *watch the experiment day by
day* (= each day). **14** (expressing the cause of an
emotion): *surprised by his anger; annoyed by her
refusal; amazed by their success.* Ⓝ '*At*' is also
possible. **15** (*maths*) (**a**) (showing dimensions):
The room is 10 by 12 metres in area. (**b**) (when calculating): *multiply/divide by 8; 12 by 2 equals 24.*
16 to the extent of: *cheaper by £10; shorter by 5
cm; missed me by a mile.* **by far** ⇨ far²(3). **by
degrees** ⇨ degree(4). **17** according to: *By my
watch it's 2 o'clock. He's Australian by birth. The
match was played by international rules.* Ⓝ For
expressions such as *by accident/chance/mistake/
rights* etc, ⇨ the noun entries. **by all means; by
means of** ⇨ means(1). **17 by the way** (*informal*) (used to mention news, a message etc suddenly remembered): *By the way, did you know
Jean is in Delhi?*

bye-bye /ˌbaɪ ˈbaɪ/ *int* (*informal*) goodbye.

by·elec·tion /ˈbaɪ ɪlekʃn/ *nc* an election made
necessary by the death or resignation of a member during the life of Parliament. Compare
general election.

by·gone /ˈbaɪɡɒn/ *adj* (*attrib*) past: *in bygone
days* (= in the past). □ *n* (*pl*) **let bygones be
bygones** to forgive and forget the past.

by·law (also **bye-law**) /ˈbaɪ lɔː/ *nc* a law or regulation made by a local authority (e.g. a city council or railway company).

by·pass¹ /ˈbaɪpɑːs/ *nc* a wide road passing round
a town or village.

by·pass² /ˈbaɪpɑːs/ *vt* **1** to travel around (a
place) on a bypass. **2** to provide (a place) with a
bypass. **3** (*fig*) to avoid taking (a person) into
account: *They bypassed Mike and gave Peter the
job.*

by·prod·uct /ˈbaɪ prɒdʌkt/ *nc* a substance
obtained during the manufacture of another substance.

by·stand·er /ˈbaɪstændə(r)/ *nc* a person standing near but not taking part in an event or activity.

byte /baɪt/ *nc* (*computers*) **1** a group of (usually 8)
binary numbers used to code a unit of infor-
mation. **2** the storage space in a memory (1K =
1024 bytes).

by·word /ˈbaɪwɜːd/ *nc* **byword (for sth)** a person, place etc regarded and spoken of as a notable
example (of a (bad) quality).

Cc

C, c /siː/ (*pl* **C's, c's** /siːz/) the third letter of the
English alphabet.

C, c. *abbr/symbol* **1** cent(s). **2** century. **3** cubic. **4**
(C) Centigrade. **5** (*Latin: circa*) (of dates)
approximately: *born c. 1650.*

Ⓒ *abbr* copyright.

ca. *abbr* (*Latin: circa*) (of dates) approximately:
born ca. 1650.

CA /ˌsiː ˈeɪ/ *abbr* Chartered Accountant.

cab /kæb/ *nc* **1** (also *taxi-cab*) = taxi: *Shall we go
by bus or take a cab?* **2** the part of a railway
engine, bus, lorry etc for the driver.

cab·aret /ˈkæbəreɪ/ *nc,nu* (an) entertainment
(songs, dancing etc) provided in a restaurant etc
while guests are dining or drinking.

cab·bage /ˈkæbɪdʒ/ *nc,nu* (also *attrib*) (a kind of)
vegetable with a round head of green or red
leaves: *cabbage leaves.*

cab·in /ˈkæbɪn/ *nc* **1** a small house with one
room, usually made of wood: *a log cabin.* **2** a
small room on a ship where a passenger lives and
sleeps. **3** the area in a plane where passengers sit.
'cabin cruiser *nc* a kind of motorboat with a
cabin(2).

cabi·net /ˈkæbɪnɪt/ *nc* **1** a piece of furniture with
drawers or shelves for storing or displaying
things: *a medicine cabinet; a filing cabinet* (i.e. for
storing letters, documents). **2** a container for a
music centre, TV, sewing-machine etc. **3** (C-)
(also *attrib*) a group of men and women chosen by
the head of the government (the prime minister)
to be responsible for government administration
and policy: *a Cabinet Minister.*

cable¹ /ˈkeɪbl/ *n* **1** *nc,nu* (a length of) thick,
strong rope (or wire), used on ships, bridges etc.
2 *nc* a tube of electricity or telephone wires put
under the ground and the sea. **3** *nc* a telegram.
'cable-car/railway *nc* one moving up a steep
slope, worked by a cable(1).

cable² /ˈkeɪbl/ *vt,vi* to send (a person) a telegram.
'cable·gram *nc* a telegram.

ca·cao /kəˈkaʊ/ *nc* (a seed of) a tropical tree from
which cocoa and chocolate are made.

cackle¹ /ˈkækl/ *n* **1** *nu* the noise made by a hen
after laying an egg. **2** *nc* a loud laugh.

cackle² /ˈkækl/ to make a cackle(1,2).

cac·tus /ˈkæktəs/ *nc* (*pl* **—es** or **cacti** /ˈkæktaɪ/)
(any kind of) plant from hot, dry climates, with a
fleshy stem, often covered with prickles.

ca·dence /ˈkeɪdəns/ *nc,nu* (*literature*) the stress,
emphasis, rhythm etc of the voice when reading
poetry or prose: *Some poetry has no regular pattern in the verse lines and uses cadence to provide
rhythm.*

ca·det /kəˈdet/ *nc* **1** a student at a naval, military
or air force college. **2** a young person training for
a profession: *police cadets.*

cadge /kædʒ/ *vt,vi* (*informal*) to (try to) get
(something) by begging: *He's always cadging
sweets off me.*
cadger *nc* (usually *derog*) a person who cadges.

cae·sar·ean /sɪˈzeərɪən/ *nc* (often C-; also *attrib*)
a delivery of a child by cutting the walls of the
abdomen and uterus: *a Caesarean section.*

cae·sura /sɪˈzjʊərə/ *nc* (*pl* **—s**) (*literature*) a pause
in the rhythmic pattern of a line of verse because
of meaning or punctuation.

café /ˈkæfeɪ/ *nc* **1** (in Europe) a place where
people can drink coffee, beer, wine,
spirits etc **2** (in GB) a small, usually self-service,
restaurant where meals, drinks (but not alcoholic
drinks) can be bought.

cafe·teria /ˌkæfəˈtɪərɪə/ *nc* = café(2), esp in a

hospital, school etc. ⇨ canteen(1).

caf·feine (also **caf·fein**) /'kæfi:n/ *nu* a substance in coffee, tea etc that causes a person to be more awake, feel more energetic etc (and often used in medicines). ⇨ decaffeinated.

caf·tan /'kæftæn/ *nc* 1 a long tunic with a cord at the waist, worn by men in the Near East. 2 a woman's loosely hanging dress.

cage¹ /keɪdʒ/ *nc* 1 a framework with wires or bars, used for birds or animals. 2 a similar framework for workers in a mine.

cage² /keɪdʒ/ *vt* **cage sb/sth (in/up)** to keep a person, animal etc (as if) in a cage: *Long wet winter evenings make me feel caged in.*

ca·goule /kə'gu:l/ *nc* a thin (plastic) jacket with a hood, worn on walking holidays. ⇨ anorak.

ca·jole /kə'dʒəʊl/ *vt* to use flattery or deceit to persuade, get information etc from, (a person).

cake¹ /keɪk/ *n* 1 *nc, nu* a sweet mixture of flour, eggs, butter etc baked in an oven: *a birthday cake; a slice of cake.* **a piece of cake** (*sl*) very easy and pleasant work. 2 *nc* a shaped mixture of other kinds of food: *fish cakes.* 3 *nc* a shaped piece of other material or substances: *a cake of soap.*

cake² /keɪk/ *vt* **cake sth (with sth)** to cover clothes, shoes, the body etc (with mud etc): *Her face is caked with chocolate.*

cal. *abbr* calorie(s).

ca·lami·tous /kə'læmɪtəs/ *adj* (*formal*) disastrous: *a calamitous error of judgement.*

ca·lam·ity /kə'læmətɪ/ *nc* (*pl* **-ies**) (*formal*) a big and serious misfortune or disaster (e.g. an earthquake or flood).

cal·cium /'kælsɪəm/ *nu* soft white metal (symbol Ca), the chemical basis of many compounds essential to life, occurring in bones and teeth and also marble and chalk.

cal·cu·late /'kælkjʊleɪt/ *vt,vi* 1 to find out (something) by working with numbers: *calculate the cost of a journey.* 2 to consider etc and be confident (that something will happen etc): *I calculate that they'll arrive at 6 o'clock.* 3 (*passive*) designed to: *This TV ad is calculated to attract children.*

cal·cu·lated /'kælkjʊleɪtɪd/ *adj* (usually *attrib*) 1 deliberately planned: *a calculated lie.* 2 done after considering all the possibilities of failure: *a calculated risk.*

cal·cu·lat·ing /'kælkjʊleɪtɪŋ/ *adj* (*derog*) (of a person) using deceit or trickery to her or his advantage.

cal·cu·la·tion /ˌkælkjʊ'leɪʃn/ *nc, nu* the act, result etc of calculating: *I'm out in my calculations* (= have made a mistake).

cal·cu·la·tor /'kælkjʊleɪtə(r)/ *nc* a small machine that calculates automatically: *an electronic/a pocket calculator.*

cal·cu·lus /'kælkjʊləs/ *nu* the branch of mathematics that deals with variable quantities.

cal·en·dar /'kælɪndə(r)/ *nc* a list of the days, weeks, months of a particular year.

ˌcalendar 'month *nc* (**a**) any of the 12 named divisions in a year. (**b**) a period from a numbered day in one month to the same number in the next, e.g. 2 January to 2 February. Compare lunar month.

calf¹ /kɑːf/ *nc* (*pl* **calves** /kɑːvz/) the young of the cow and of the elephant, seal, whale and some other animals.

calf² /kɑːf/ *nc* (*pl* **calves** /kɑːvz/) the fleshy part of the back of the human leg, between the knee and the ankle.

cali·brate /'kælɪbreɪt/ *vt* to mark the scale of (a thermometer, gauge or other measuring instrument).

cali·bra·tion /ˌkælɪ'breɪʃn/ *nc,nu.*

cal·ibre (*US* = **cali·ber**) /'kælɪbə(r)/ *n* 1 *nc* (*tech*) the inside diameter of a pipe etc. 2 *nu* quality of mind or character: *a man of considerable calibre* (= importance).

cali·pers /'kælɪpəz/ *n pl* (*US*) = callipers.

call¹ /kɔːl/ *nc* 1 (something said using) a loud voice: *a call for help.* **a close call** (*informal*) an escape from a danger or disaster by only a small amount. **be within call** be able to hear or be heard. 2 a use of a telephone: *a local/long-distance call.* ⇨ callbox. **give sb a call** (*informal*) to telephone her or him. 3 (a use of a telephone, buzzer etc to send) a message, order, signal etc: *an early morning call* (i.e. to get out of bed); *calls for Dr White throughout the clinic.* **on call** (of doctors, firemen etc) ready to go on duty immediately if necessary. 4 (usually with negatives or in questions) something demanding a response or reply because of the situation: *Is there much call for fountain pens nowadays? There's no call for concern/no call to be rude.* Ⓝ 'Need' is also possible and is more usual. **the call of duty** something a person feels it is her or his responsibility to do. **a call of nature** (*informal*) a feeling that one needs to go to the toilet. 5 a short visit: *a doctor's calls. May I pay a call on you/pay you a call* (= visit you) *later today?* 6 the typical cry or sound of a bird or other animal. 7 (*card-games*) (a player's turn to make) a bid¹(2).

'call·box *nc* a small public kiosk for making telephone calls.

call² /kɔːl/ *v* 1 *vi,vt* to speak, say (something), in a loud voice: *'Is anyone at home?' she called. He called to his brother to help him/for help. I'll call the names once so listen carefully. The referee called a fault and McEnroe disagreed. She called and called but no-one came.* ⇨ call out. 2 *vi,vt* to telephone (a person): *I'll call you later. I called earlier, but there was no answer.* ⇨ call sb back. 2 *vt* to send a message, order etc to (a person) by speaking loudly, using an electronic signal etc: *Please call a doctor. I've been calling you on the bleep but you didn't answer. Can you call the children to dinner? Please call me* (= wake me) *at 7 tomorrow morning. She'll call you a taxi/call a taxi for you.* Ⓝ For uses with nouns such as *attention, bluff, election, halt, meeting, mind, strike* etc, ⇨ the noun entries. 4 *vt* to describe or name (a person, thing etc): *They called her Diana. Are you calling me a liar? Some say it's bravery but I call it stupidity. Her friends called her foolish for being so generous.* ⇨ call sb after sb. **call sb names** ⇨ name¹(1). 5 *vi* to visit a person, place etc for a short time: *I only called to give you this invitation. The postman called early this morning. Our salesperson will call on you/at your office.* ⇨ call by. 6 *vi,vi* (of a bird and other animals) to make its typical cry or sound. 7 *vi,vt* (*card-games*) to make a bid¹(2): *call two hearts.*

call (sb) about sb/sth to visit or telephone (a

person) to explain, ask about, a person or thing etc: *I'm calling about your advertisement in the newspaper.*

call sb/sth after sb/sth to give the same name to a person, animal, house etc: *Let's call the cat after Aunt Maud.*

call sb away (usually *passive*) to send a message for a doctor, police officer etc to go to an accident, emergency etc: *The nurse isn't here—he's been called away to another patient.*

call sb back ⇨ back²(4).

call by (*informal*) to visit a home, office etc for a short time: *We called by to thank you.*

call for sb/sth to visit a home, office etc to collect a person, tickets etc: *She'll call for you at 8 o'clock/for the tickets at reception. Has the van called for those parcels?* **call for sth** to demand, need, something: *The situation calls for maximum effort from everyone. Courage is called for if we are to succeed.*

call in (to do sth) to visit a home, office etc for a short time (to take or leave something etc). **call sth in** to order a book, product etc to be returned: *The manufacturer called in all new cars to check the brakes.* **call in at a place** to stop at a place (on the way to somewhere else): *We called in at your house on the way home but you were out.* **call in on sb** to visit a person for a short time.

call sth off (a) to give an order to stop or abandon something: *The wedding/picnic/meeting/ match/search has been called off.* (b) to order a dog etc to stop attacking.

call on sb (of a doctor, salesperson, candidate etc) to visit a person for business or official reasons: *He'll call on you at 10 o'clock.* **call on sb to do sth** to ask, invite a person to speak, help, give a lecture, be a chairperson etc: *I was called on to chair/address the meeting.*

call (sth) out to say something in a very loud voice: *'Hallo!' he called out, as loud as possible. They're calling out the names of the winners.* **call sb out** (a) to order the army, police etc to go somewhere (to deal with a crisis etc): *Extra police were called out to cope with the football crowd.* (b) to order workers to strike: *The union has called the car workers out.*

call round (at a place) to visit a home etc for a short time: *I'll call round this evening to see how you are. I called round at your mother's (house) last night.*

call sb up (a) to telephone a person, business etc. (b) (*mil*) to order a person to join the armed forces. Hence **'call-up** *nc*. **call sth up** (a) to cause a person to remember an event, childhood etc: *The smells called up memories of my mother's cooking.* (b) (*computers*) to order a computer to produce information: *Please call up the details of all our clients in the London area.*

call upon sb to do sth (*formal*) = call on sb to do sth.

cal·ler /'kɔːlə(r)/ *nc* a person who telephones or makes a short visit to a home etc.

cal·ligra·phy /kə'lɪgrəfɪ/ *nu* (*tech*) (the art of) beautiful handwriting.

cal·ling /'kɔːlɪŋ/ *nc* (a strong desire to work in) an occupation, profession or trade.

cal·li·pers /'kælɪpəz/ *n pl* **1** (*tech*) an instrument

used for measuring the diameter of round objects or the inside measurement of tubes etc. **2** the metal supports attached to the legs of a disabled person to enable her or him to walk.

cal·lous /'kæləs/ *adj* **1** (of the skin) made hard (by rough work etc). **2** (*fig; derog*) hardhearted, unsympathetic.

call-up /'kɔːl ʌp/ *nc* ⇨ call sb up(b).

cal·lus /'kæləs/ *nc* (*pl* **—es**) an area of thick, hardened skin.

calm¹ /kɑːm/ *adj* (**—er**, **—est**) **1** (of the weather) quiet; not windy. **2** (of the sea) without large waves. **3** (*fig*) not excited, untroubled: *keep calm.*

calm·ly *adv*

calm·ness *nu*

calm² /kɑːm/ *nc,nu* a time when everything is quiet and peaceful.

calm³ /kɑːm/ *vi,vt* **calm (sb) (down)** (to cause a person) to become calm(3).

cal·orie /'kælərɪ/ *nc* (abbr cal.) a unit of heat (from energy supplied by food): *An ounce of sugar supplies about 100 calories.* ⇨ joule.

cal·or·if·ic /,kælə'rɪfɪk/ *adj* (*attrib*) (*tech*) producing heat: *the calorific value of food* (= the quantity of heat produced by a given quantity). ⇨ joule.

ca·lyx /'keɪlɪks/ *nc* (*pl* **—es** or **calyces** /'keɪ-lɪsiːz/) (*biol*) a ring of leaves (called *sepals*) forming the outer support of the petals of an unopened flower-bud.

cam·ber /'kæmbə(r)/ *nc,nu* a slight rise in the middle of a surface (e.g. of a road).

came /keɪm/ *pt* of come.

cam·el /'kæml/ *nc* a kind of long-necked animal, with either one or two humps on its back, used in desert countries.

cam·era /'kæmrə/ *nc* **1** (also *attrib*) an apparatus used for taking photographs or for broadcasting TV programmes etc: *a pocket camera; a camera case/lens.* **2 in camera** privately: *The court heard the evidence in camera* (i.e. with no public present).

cam·ou·flage /'kæməflɑːʒ/ *vt, nu* (to give something) a colour, pattern, shape etc that makes it difficult to identify: *The camouflage of some insects is extraordinary.*

camp¹ /kæmp/ *nc* **1** a place where tourists, soldiers, explorers etc live in tents or huts. **break/ strike camp** to take down and pack up tents and other equipment. **2** a group of people with the same ideas (esp on politics or religion): *We're in the same camp* (= are in agreement).

camp² /kæmp/ *v* **1** *vi* to make, live in, a camp: *Where shall we camp tonight?* **go camping** to spend a holiday in tents: *The boys have decided to go camping next summer.* **2** *vt* **camp it up** (*informal*) to overact in a silly way.

camp·er *nc* a person who camps, esp on holiday.

cam·paign¹ /kæm'peɪn/ *nc* **1** a group of military operations with a shared purpose, usually in one area. **2** a series of planned activities to gain a particular result: *an advertising campaign; a political campaign.*

cam·paign² /kæm'peɪn/ *vi* to take part in, go on, a campaign: *campaigning for the Labour Party.*

cam·paign·er *nc* a person who campaigns.

cam·pus /'kæmpəs/ *nc* (*pl* **—es**) the grounds of a

school, college or university.

can¹ /kæn/ *nc* **1** a metal container used for liquids etc: *an oilcan.* **2** (formerly *US* but now also *GB*) (the contents of) a small airtight metal container (for food etc): *a can of beer.* ⇨ cannery, tin(2).

can² /kən *strong form:* kæn/ *auxiliary verb* Ⓝ 'Can' is a *modal auxiliary verb* used with another verb to express ability, possibility or permission. 'Can' has no infinitive or imperative forms and no participles. 'Can' is always followed by an infinitive without 'to'. Compare may, might, must, ought, should, will, would. (*Pres t* (*all persons*): **can**, *negative:* **cannot** /'kænɒt/, **can't** /kɑːnt/; *pt* (*all persons*): **could** /kəd *strong form:* kʊd/, *negative:* **could not, couldn't** /'kʊdnt/) **1** to have the ability to: *I can touch my toes. Can you do it without bending your knees? She couldn't even move the box. I can't imagine what he looks like. He could hear footsteps and he was afraid. She can only read with her glasses.* Ⓝ 'Be able to' is also possible but is not usual. 'Be able to' is used about future ability, as in *I'll be able to reach it if I stand on a chair,* and when referring to a particular ability shown on one occasion, as in *He wasn't able to mend the TV. Were you able to find carrots in the market?* **2** to know how to: *She can speak Russian. You can't operate a computer without training. He could read when he was three.* Ⓝ 'Be able to' is used for the future, as in *By the end of this year he'll be able to repair his own bike.* **3** (used to show possibility): *How many can I buy for £5? I can't afford it. Where can my glasses be? Can they be in the kitchen? It couldn't have been a nicer evening. Surely that can't be true? What can you mean?* ⇨ could(3). **4** to be allowed to: *You can watch TV for another half-hour. She said I could take some cake.* Ⓝ 'May' is also possible but is formal or is used when contrasting permission with ability, as in *Yes, you may borrow my pen if you can find it.* **5** to have the right (by law) to: *Men and women can vote at 18. You can't drive until you are 17.* **6** (used to make a request): *Can I have another potato? Can he borrow your pen?* Ⓝ 'Could' is preferred when one is being very polite or is uncertain or a little afraid, as in *Could I speak to you for a moment, please?* 'May' is also possible but is very formal. **7** (used to express surprise): *What can you mean—behaving like that!* **8** (used in conversation) (**a**) (joined to the end of a statement to form a question): *You can drive, can't you?* Ⓝ The short addition is always negative (e.g. *can't*) if the statement is positive (e.g. *can*) and always positive if the statement is negative. Statements with *neither, no, nobody, nothing* etc are considered to be negative and the short addition is always positive, as in *Nothing can be proved, can it?* (**b**) (used to make a short question): '*Boris can run very fast.*'—'*Can he?*' Ⓝ If the statement is positive, the short question is positive. If the statement is negative, the short question is negative. (**c**) (used to make a short answer): '*Can I borrow £5?*'—'*No, you can't.*' '*Can you meet me later?*'—'*Yes, I can.*' Ⓝ 'Can' is also used to give permission in a short answer after a question using could, as in '*Could I have 50p for some ice-cream?*'—'*Yes, you can.*' Be careful because *can, could* etc is used in (a), (b) and (c) only when *can, could* etc is used in the main statement. ⇨ be¹(4).

ca·nal /kə'næl/ *nc* **1** (C- in names) a long channel cut through land for boats or ships (e.g. *the Suez*

Canal) or to carry water to fields for irrigation. **2** a tube or pipe (or system of these) in a plant or animal, for food, air etc: *the alimentary canal.*

ca·nary /kə'neəri/ *n* (*pl* **-ies**) **1** *nc* a kind of small, yellow-feathered songbird. **2** *nu* (also *attrib*) its light yellow colour.

can·cel /'kænsl/ *vt,vi* (**-ll-**, *US* **-l-**) **1** to cross out, draw a line through, (words or figures) or make a mark on (e.g. postage stamps to prevent reuse). **2** to say that (something already arranged or decided) will not be done, will not take place etc: *The sports meeting was cancelled.* **3** *cancel* (*each other*) *out* (of similar conditions etc) to balance and so make them equal in importance, strength etc: *Their lower price plus delivery charges and our higher but inclusive price cancel (each other) out.*

can·cel·la·tion /ˌkænsə'leɪʃn/ *nc,nu*

can·cer /'kænsə(r)/ *nc,nu* (a kind of) diseased growth in the body, often causing death: *lung cancer.*

can·cer·ous /'kænsərəs/ *adj*

Can·cer /'kænsə(r)/ *n* **1** (*Tropic of Cancer*) the parallel of latitude 23½°N. ⇨ Capricorn. **2** the Crab, fourth sign of the zodiac.

can·did /'kændɪd/ *adj* (of a way of expressing an unpleasant opinion) honest and exact: *I'll be absolutely candid with you: I think you acted foolishly.* ⇨ candour.

can·did·ly *adv*

can·di·date /'kændɪdət/ *nc* **1** a person who wishes, or who is put forward by others, to take an office or position (e.g. for election to Parliament): *The Labour candidate was elected.* **2** a person taking an examination.

candle /'kændl/ *nc* a length of wax with a string (*wick*) through it, used for giving light.

'candle·stick *nc* a holder for a candle.

can·dour (*US* = **can·dor**) /'kændə(r)/ *nu* (*formal*) the quality of expressing an unpleasant opinion honestly. ⇨ candid.

cane /keɪn/ *nc* **1** a long, hollow, jointed stem of tall reeds and grass-like plants (e.g. bamboo). **2** *nu* (also *attrib*) this material: *a chair with a cane seat.*

ca·nine /'keɪnaɪn/ *adj* of, like, dogs.

can·is·ter /'kænɪstə(r)/ *nc* **1** a small box (usually metal) with a lid, used for holding tea etc. **2** a cylinder which when thrown or fired from a gun, bursts and scatters its contents: *a tear-gas canister.*

can·ker /'kæŋkə(r)/ *n* **1** *nu* a disease that destroys the wood of trees. **2** *nu* a disease that causes ulcers. **3** *nc* (*fig*) an evil influence or tendency that causes decay.

can·ker·ous /'kæŋkərəs/ *adj*

can·na·bis /'kænəbɪs/ *nu* a drug smoked or chewed to cause high spirits.

can·nery /'kænəri/ *nc* (*pl* **-ies**) a factory where food is put into cans.

can·ni·bal /'kænəbl/ *nc* a person or other animal that eats its own kind.

can·ni·bal·ism /-ɪzəm/ *nu*

can·ni·bal·is·tic /ˌkænɪbə'lɪstɪk/ *adj*

can·non /'kænən/ *nc* (*pl* often **—**) a large, heavy gun, esp the old kind that fired a solid ball of metal (a *cannon-ball*). Ⓝ 'Gun' and 'shell' are the words used for modern weapons.

can·not /'kænət/ ⇨ can².

ca·noe /kə'nu:/ *vi, nc* (to travel in) a long light-weight boat moved by one or more paddles.
ca·noe·ist *nc* a person who uses a canoe.
can·on /'kænən/ *nc* a church law.
ca·noni·cal /kə'nɒnɪkl/ *adj* of, according to, church law: *canonical books.*
can·on·ize (also **-ise**) /'kænənaɪz/ *vt* to make (a dead person) a saint.
can·opy /'kænəpɪ/ *nc* (*pl* **-ies**) a (usually cloth) covering over a bed, throne etc or held (on poles) over a person.
cant /kænt/ *nu* insincere talk.
can't /kɑ:nt/ = *cannot.* ⇨ **can².**
can·ta·loup (also **-loupe**) /'kæntəlu:p/ *nc* a kind of melon.
can·tank·er·ous /kæn'tæŋkərəs/ *adj* (*derog*) bad-tempered; quarrelsome.
can·teen /kæn'ti:n/ *nc* **1** a place (esp in factories, offices) where food and drink are sold and meals bought and eaten. **2** a box or chest of knives, forks, spoons. **3** a camper's eating and drinking utensils.
can·ter /'kæntə(r)/ *nc* (of a horse) a pace faster than a trot but slower than a gallop; period of riding at such a pace: *go for a canter.* □ *vt, vi* (to cause a horse) to move at a canter.
can·to /'kæntəʊ/ *nc* (*pl* **—s**) (*literature*) a main division of a long poem.
can·vas /'kænvəs/ *nc, nu* (*pl* **—es**) (a piece of) strong, coarse cloth used for tents, sails, bags etc and by artists for oil-paintings. *under canvas* in tents.
can·vass /'kænvəs/ *vt, vi* to go from person to person and ask for votes, orders for goods, subscriptions etc or to learn about people's opinions: *go canvassing (neighbours) (for support).* □ *nc, nu* (an instance of) canvassing: *a political canvass.*
can·yon /'kænjən/ *nc* (C- in names) a deep gorge (usually with a river): *the Grand Canyon.*
cap¹ /kæp/ *nc* **1** a head-covering worn by boys and men, without a brim but with a peak. ⇨ feather¹. **2** a special cap showing membership of a team, occupation etc. **3** a waterproof head-covering for swimming etc. **4** a cover (e.g. on a bottle, tube of toothpaste).
cap² /kæp/ *vt* (**-pp-**) **1** to put a cap(4) on (a bottle etc). **2** to do or say (something) more interesting than another person. *cap a joke/story* to tell a better one. *and to cap it all . . .* and the final, best etc reason, description etc is . . . **3** to award (a player) a cap(2) (as a member of a football team etc): *He's been capped 36 times for England.*
cap(s) /kæp(s)/ *abbr* capital(s): *write in caps.*
ca·pa·bil·ity /ˌkeɪpə'bɪlətɪ/ *n* (*pl* **-ies**) **1** *nu* power, fitness or capacity: *nuclear capability* (= power to use nuclear weapons). **2** (*pl*) a talent that can be developed: *The boy has great capabilities.*
ca·pable /'keɪpəbl/ *adj* **1** having mental or physical ability: *a very capable teacher.* **2** (*pred*) *capable of (doing) sth* (of a person, machine) having the power, ability or will to do something: *He's capable of any crime. The bike is capable of doing 40 miles per hour.* Compare incapable.
ca·pably *adv*
ca·pac·ity /ke'pæsətɪ/ *n* (*pl* **-ies**) **1** *nu* the quantity that can be contained, held, learned etc: *The hall has a seating capacity of 500.* **2** *nc* an official

position: *I am your friend but in my capacity as your manager I must ask you to resign.*
cape¹ /keɪp/ *nc* a sleeveless article of clothing, hanging from the shoulders.
cape² /keɪp/ *nc* (C- in names) a point of land going out into the sea: *the Cape of Good Hope.*
cap·il·lary /kə'pɪlərɪ/ *nc* (*pl* **-ies**) a small blood-vessel.
capi·tal /'kæpɪtl/ *nc* **1** (also *attrib*) a town or city where the government of a country, state or county is carried on: *Melbourne is the capital of Victoria. London, Paris and Rome are capital cities.* **2** (*pl*) a large separated style of writing letters: *Write your name in capitals* (e.g. JOHN). **3** *nu* the wealth, money or property that may be used to produce or start a business: *The company has a capital of £500 000.*
,capital 'gains tax *nu* (*GB*) a tax on the profit made after selling a business, property etc.
,capital 'letter *nc* e.g. A,B,C,D.
,capital 'punishment *nu* punishment by being killed.
capi·tal·ism /'kæpɪtəlɪzəm/ *nu* an economic and political system in which a country's trade and industry are controlled by the owners of capital(3). Compare socialism.
capi·tal·ist /'kæpɪtəlɪst/ *adj, nc* **1** (of) a person who supports capitalism. **2** (of) a person who controls much capital(3).
capi·tal·is·tic /ˌkæpɪtə'lɪstɪk/ *adj*
capi·tal·ize (also **-ise**) /'kæpɪtəlaɪz/ *vi* *capitalize (on sth)* (*fig*) to use a situation, mistake etc to one's advantage or profit: *You should not capitalize on her errors.*
ca·pitu·late /kə'pɪtjʊleɪt/ *vi* to surrender (on stated conditions).
ca·pitu·la·tion /kə,pɪtjʊ'leɪʃn/ *nu*
ca·price /kə'pri:s/ *nc* (a tendency towards) a sudden change of mind or behaviour that has no obvious cause.
ca·pri·cious /kə'prɪʃəs/ *adj*
Cap·ri·corn /'kæprɪkɔ:n/ *n* **1** (*Tropic of Capricorn*) the parallel of latitude 23½°S. ⇨ Cancer. **2** the Goat, tenth sign of the zodiac.
cap·si·cum /'kæpsɪkəm/ *nc* (*pl* **—s**) a kind of plant (*green* or *red pepper*) with large round seed-pods that are eaten as a vegetable.
cap·size /kæp'saɪz/ *vt, vi* (to cause a boat) to overturn in water.
cap·sule /'kæpsju:l/ *nc* **1** a seed-case of a plant. **2** a small soluble container for medicine. **3** a compartment in a spacecraft for the crew, which can be separated from the spacecraft.
Capt. *abbr* Captain.
cap·tain¹ /'kæptɪn/ *nc* (often C-) **1** a leader: *the captain of a football team.* **2** (*army*) an officer (below a major and above a lieutenant) who commands a company. **3** (*navy*) an officer below an admiral and above a commander.
cap·tain² /'kæptɪn/ *vt* to act as a captain of a team, ship etc.
cap·tion /'kæpʃn/ *nc* a set of words put with a diagram, photograph etc.
cap·ti·vate /'kæptɪveɪt/ *vt* to attract (a person): *He was captivated by Helen.*
cap·ti·vat·ing *adj*
cap·tive /'kæptɪv/ *adj, nc* (kept as) a prisoner.
,captive 'audience *nc* a person, group, that

cannot go easily and so avoid being persuaded.

,captive 'market *nc* a market for goods where there is much need, no competition etc.

cap·tiv·ity /kæp'tɪvətɪ/ *nu* the state of being held captive: *Some birds will not sing in captivity.*

cap·tor /'kæptə(r)/ *nc* a person who takes another prisoner.

cap·ture¹ /'kæptʃə(r)/ *nu* the act of capturing: *the capture of a thief.*

cap·ture² /'kæptʃə(r)/ *vt* **1** to make (a person, animal etc) a prisoner. **2** to get (something) as a prize by force, trickery, skill etc. **3** (*computers*) to put (information) into a computer. **4** to be successful in describing etc (a particular scene, person): *capturing the beauty of the early morning in music.*

car /kɑ:(r)/ *nc* **1** a vehicle designed for private use, for (usually four) passengers: *go by car.* **2** a coach of a train: *the dining-car.* **3** the part of a lift etc used by passengers.

'car-ferry *nc* a ferry used for taking cars (e.g. across the English Channel).

'car hire *nu* the renting of a car(1) for a period.

'car-park *nc* a place for parking cars(1).

'car·port *nc* an open-sided shelter for a car(1).

'car·sick *adj* feeling unwell and wanting to be sick while travelling in a car. Hence 'carsickness *nu*.

cara·mel /'kærəmel/ *n* **1** *nu* (also *attrib*) burnt sugar as used for colouring and flavouring: *caramel sauce.* **2** *nc* a small, shaped piece of boiled sugar.

cara·pace /'kærəpeɪs/ *nc* the shell on the back of a tortoise etc.

car·at /'kærət/ *nc* **1** a unit of measurement of weight (= 0·20 g) for precious stones. **2** a unit of measurement of the purity of gold, pure gold being 24 carat.

cara·van /'kærəvæn/ *nc* **1** a group of people making a journey together (across desert country). **2** a covered cart or wagon used for living in, e.g. by gipsies. **3** a modern structure on two wheels, used as a place to live by people on holiday and pulled behind a vehicle. ⇨ also trailer(2).

carbo·hy·drate /,kɑ:bəʊ'haɪdreɪt/ *nc,nu* (also *attrib*) a kind of organic compound, esp a sugar or starch.

car·bon /'kɑ:bən/ *n* **1** *nu* a non-metallic element (symbol C) that occurs in all living matter, in its pure form as diamonds and graphite and in an impure form as coal and charcoal. **2** *nc,nu* (also *carbon-paper*) (a piece of) thin paper coated with coloured matter, used between sheets of writing paper for making copies. **3** *nc* a copy made by the use of a carbon(2).

,carbon di'oxide *nu* a gas (symbol CO_2) present in the air, necessary to plant life and produced when animals breathe out.

,carbon mon'oxide *nu* a poisonous gas (symbol CO), as produced by the engine of a vehicle.

car·buncle /'kɑ:bʌŋkl/ *nc* (esp) a red (usually painful) inflamed swelling under the skin.

car·bu·ret·tor (also -retor) /,kɑ:bjʊ'retə(r)/ *nc* the part of an engine, e.g. in a car, in which petrol and air are mixed to make an explosive mixture to provide power.

car·cass (also car·case) /'kɑ:kəs/ *nc* a dead body of an animal (esp one prepared for cutting up as meat).

card /kɑ:d/ *nc* **1** a folded piece of stiff paper with a picture, as used for various purposes: *a Christmas/New Year/birthday card* (i.e. sent with greetings at Christmas etc). ⇨ also postcard. **2** (often *playing-card*) one of the 52 cards used for various games (whist, bridge, poker etc) and for telling fortunes. **on the cards** likely or possible; *Rain is on the cards.* **put one's cards on the table** to make one's plans, intentions etc known. **3** a small oblong-shaped piece of printed plastic, as used by bank customers to have an account at a shop etc: *a bank card; a credit card.* **4** a piece of stiff paper with information, used with others to produce a catalogue, file etc.

'card-game *nc* a game using playing-cards.

'card·holder *nc* a person owning a card(3).

,card 'index *nc* an index, catalogue, on cards(4).

card·board /'kɑ:dbɔ:d/ *nu* the thick, stiff kind of paper used for making boxes etc.

car·di·ac /'kɑ:dɪæk/ *adj* (*attrib*) of, concerning, the heart: *cardiac muscle/surgery; a cardiac arrest* (= heart failure).

car·di·gan /'kɑ:dɪgən/ *nc* a knitted woollen jacket that (usually) buttons up the front.

car·di·nal¹ /'kɑ:dɪnl/ *adj* (usually *attrib*) most important: *the cardinal virtues.*

,cardinal 'number *nc* any number expressing amount, e.g. 2, 5, 17 (contrasted with *second*, *fifth* etc). Compare ordinal number.

,cardinal 'points *n pl* the main points of the compass (N, S, E and W).

car·di·nal² /'kɑ:dɪnl/ *nc* (C- in names) a very high official of the Roman Catholic Church with the authority to elect Popes.

care¹ /keə(r)/ *n* **1** *nu* serious attention or effort: *You should take more care over your work.* **take care of sb/sth** (*informal*) to look after, deal with, be responsible for a person, duty etc. ⇨ careful(2). **2** *nu* protection; charge; responsibility: *The child was left in its sister's care.* **care of sb/sth** (*abbr* c/o) (used when sending a letter, parcel etc to a person at another person's address). **3** *nu* sorrow, anxiety caused by doubt or fear: *Care has made him look ten years older.* **4** *nc* (usually *pl*) a cause of sorrow and anxiety: *He was poor and troubled by the cares of a large family.*

care² /keə(r)/ *vi* **1** to feel concern or anxiety: *She never cares what people think. He failed in the examination but I don't think he cares very much. He doesn't seem to care about it/me. I couldn't care less* (= I am not at all interested). **not care a damn/a hoot/two hoots** to feel no concern or anxiety at all. **be past caring** to have no concern, energy, feeling, any longer. **2** (used before an infinitive with 'to' in the negative or in questions) to like; be willing: *Would you care to go for a walk?* **3 care for sb/sth** (a) to like a person: *I don't care for him at all.* (b) to like (to have) something: *Would you care for a drink?* (c) to enjoy something: *Do you care for modern music?* (d) to look after; provide food etc for a person, family: *Who will care for the children if their mother dies?*

ca·reer¹ /kə'rɪə(r)/ *nc* **1** a way of making a living; profession: *All careers are open to women.* **2** the development and progress of a person's life, political party etc: *the career of the Liberal Party* *since 1980.*

ca·reer² /kə'rɪə(r)/ *vi* **career (about)** to move wildly and fast.

care·free /'keəfriː/ *adj* (happy because) free from anxiety.

care·ful /'keəfəl/ *adj* **1** (of a person) thinking of, paying attention to, what one does, says etc: *Be careful not to break the eggs. Be more careful with your work.* **2** done with, showing, care: *a careful piece of work.* Opp careless.
care·ful·ly /-fəlɪ/ *adv*
care·ful·ness *nu*

care·less /'keəlɪs/ *adj* **1** (*derog*) (of a person) not taking care; thoughtless: *A careless driver is a danger to the public.* **2** (*derog*) done or made without care: *a careless mistake.* **3** (*pred*) **careless of sth** (*formal*) not concerned about: *He is careless of his reputation.* Opp careful.
care·less·ly *adv*
care·less·ness *nu*

ca·ress /kə'res/ *vt,nc* (to give a person) a loving or affectionate touch.

care·taker /'keəteɪkə(r)/ *nc* a person in charge of a building's cleaning, repairs etc: *a school caretaker.*

'caretaker government *nc* one in control for a short time until an election.

car·go /'kaːgəʊ/ *nc,nu* (*pl* **—es**) the goods carried in a ship, plane etc.

cari·ca·ture¹ /'kærɪkətjʊə(r)/ *n* **1** *nc* a picture, description, imitation, of a person's voice, behaviour etc stressing certain features in order to amuse or ridicule. **2** *nu* the art of doing this.

cari·ca·ture² /'kærɪkətjʊə(r)/ *vt* to make, give, a caricature of (a person's voice etc).

car·ies /'keərɪz/ *nu* (*tech*) the decay (of bones or teeth): *dental caries.*

car·nage /'kaːnɪdʒ/ *nu* the killing of many people.

car·nal /'kaːnl/ *adj* (*formal*) of sex or the body: *carnal desires.*

car·na·tion /kaː'neɪʃn/ *nc* a kind of garden plant with sweet-smelling white, pink or red flowers.

car·ni·val /'kaːnɪvl/ *nc,nu* (an instance of) public entertainment and feasting, usually with music and processions of people in fancy dress.

car·ni·vore /'kaːnɪvɔː(r)/ *nc* (*science*) an animal that eats meat. Compare herbivore, insectivore, omnivore.
car·niv·or·ous /kaː'nɪvərəs/ *adj* meat-eating.

car·ol /'kærəl/ *nc* a Christmas hymn.

carp /kaːp/ *vi* to make unnecessary complaints about small matters: *She's always carping (at her husband.*

car·pal /'kaːpl/ *adj, nc* (*anat*) (of) a bone in the wrist.

car·pen·ter /'kaːpɪntə(r)/ *nc* a person who makes or repairs wooden parts of buildings etc.
car·pen·try *nu* the work of a carpenter.

car·pet¹ /'kaːpɪt/ *nc* **1** a thick covering for floors or stairs, often with a pattern. **2** something like a carpet: *a carpet of moss.*

car·pet² /'kaːpɪt/ *vt* to cover (as if) with a carpet: *to carpet the stairs; a field carpeted with snow.*

car·riage /'kærɪdʒ/ *n* **1** *nc* a car or coach for passengers on a railway train. **2** *nc* a large four-wheeled vehicle pulled by a horse or horses, used for carrying people. **3** *nu* the manner of holding

the head or the body (when walking etc): *She has a graceful carriage.* **4** *nu* (*commerce*) (the cost of) carrying goods from place to place. **5** *nc* the wheeled support on which a heavy object may move or be moved: *a gun-carriage.* **6** *nc* a moving part of a machine, changing the position of other parts (e.g. the roller of a typewriter).

'car·riage·way *nc* the part of a road used by vehicles. ⇨ dual carriageway.

car·rier /'kærɪə(r)/ *nc* **1** (*commerce*) a person or business carrying goods or people for payment. **2** a support for luggage etc fixed to a bicycle etc. **3** a person, animal etc carrying a disease without suffering from it. **4** a vehicle, ship etc used for the transport of troops, aircraft etc: *an aircraft-carrier.*

,carrier 'bag *nc* a strong paper or plastic bag, used for carrying away purchases from shops.

'carrier pigeon *nc* a pigeon able to find its way home from a distant place.

car·rion /'kærɪən/ *nu* dead and decaying flesh.

car·rot /'kærət/ *nc,nu* (also *attrib*) (a plant with) an orange root, used as a vegetable: *carrot soup.*

car·ry /'kærɪ/ *v* (*pt,pp* **-ied**) **1** *vt* to support the weight of (a person, thing) and go from one place to another: *Carry these boxes to the car, please. He carried his daughter on his shoulder. This bus can carry 40 passengers. Some seeds are carried by the wind. She's carrying (= is pregnant with) her fourth child.* **2** *vt* to support (the weight of something): *The walls will not carry (the weight of) the ceiling.* **3** *vt* to keep (something) in one's mind: *How can you carry all those names/numbers/facts in your head? I'll carry your memory with me to the end.* **4** *vt* to (be able to) accept or have control of or responsibility for (something): *Since his illness, she's been carrying the business single handed. You'll carry the blame for any failures.* **5** *vt* to hold (oneself, part of the body) in a particular manner: *She carries herself like a champion. He carried his head high.* **6** *vt,vi* (of air, water etc) to be a substance in which something moves or exists: *Copper carries electricity well. Sound is carried in water. The disease was carried by the wind.* **7** *vt* (of pipes, wire etc) to allow (a substance) to move through to another place: *The sound is carried in underwater telephone cables. The aorta carries blood from the heart.* **8** *vt* (usually *passive*) to be positioned: *These pipes are carried under the road.* **9** *vt* (of a shop etc) to keep (something) in stock: *They carry 30 flavours of ice-cream.* **10** *vt* (of newspapers etc) to print (something): *The magazines carried pictures of their wedding.* **11** *vt* (of a crime) to have (something) as a result: *Rape must carry the severest penalty.* **12** *vt* (of investments, business agreements etc) to have (an amount to be paid etc) as agreed: *The loan will carry 25% interest.* **13** *vi,vt* (to cause sound, a ball, bullet etc) to move through the air: *My voice doesn't carry far. The ball was carried by the wind.* **14** *vt* to be successful in winning support from (a person, group): *Antony carried the crowd by appealing to their greed. The motion was carried by a large majority.* **15** *vt* (*maths*) to take (a number) to the next column when adding or multiplying: *9 and 17 are 26; write 6 and carry 2.*

be carried along by sb/sth (of a competitor,

team) to be encouraged, helped, (by supporters, committed interest): *The home team was carried along by the crowd. The research was carried along by the university's enthusiasm.*

be/get carried away to be filled with emotion, enthusiasm so that one loses self-control: *Don't get too carried away with your success—you may lose the next match. She was carried away by thoughts of his return.*

carry sb back to cause a person to remember: *The music carried me back to when I was a teenager.*

carry sth forward (*bookkeeping*) (abbr c/f) to write the total from the previous page on the top of the next one: *carry forward a profit of £120.*

carry sb/sth off to take a person, animal etc as a prisoner, for food etc: *The fox carried off the rabbit..The gunman carried off the children as hostages.* **carry sth off** to win an award, prize etc: *The Chinese team carried off the most medals.*

carry it off (*informal*) to manage a difficult situation successfully: *She came in covered in mud but was able to carry it off well in front of the other guests.*

carry on (**a**) to continue: *Please carry on (playing) while I answer the phone. Somehow plant life carries on in the coldest climates.* (**b**) to talk or quarrel loudly: *My dad carried on about the broken window all afternoon.* **carry sth on** to have, continue, a conversation etc: *carry on a discussion with the bank manager.* **carry on (with sb)** (*informal*) to have a love affair (with a person): *She's carrying on with a sailor.*

carry sth out (**a**) to perform an experiment, test etc: *carry out a medical check on all imported animals.* (**b**) to act and complete an obligation, threat, instructions etc: *Carry out her instructions carefully. He carried his threat out and resigned.*

carry sth over (**a**) to keep something for discussion, action etc until a later time: *The two last items on the agenda have been carried over to the next meeting.* (**b**) (*bookkeeping*) to keep a debt, transaction etc to be dealt with later: *This small debt can be carried over until next month's account.*

carry sb through sth to help a person to survive a difficult situation: *His trust in the doctors carried him through the crisis.* **carry sth through** to complete a plan, promise, threat etc: *Do we have enough money to carry the scheme through?*

carry sb/sth with one (**a**) to have a person or thing in one's mind: *We'll carry images of those starving children with us for a long time.* (**b**) to keep supporters etc with one: *The speaker seemed to carry the whole crowd with him.*

car·ry·cot /'kærɪ kɒt/ *nc* a portable cot for a baby.

cart[1] /kɑːt/ *nc* a kind of two-wheeled vehicle pulled by a horse. Compare waggon. **put the cart before the horse** to do things in the wrong order.

cart[2] /kɑːt/ *vt* **1** to carry (something) in a cart: *carting away the rubbish.* **2** (*informal*) to carry (something) in the hands etc: *Have we got to cart these parcels around for the rest of the day?*

'cart-horse *nc* a kind of strong horse used for heavy work.

'cart-load *nc* as much as a cart holds.

carte blanche /ˌkɑːt 'blɑːnʃ/ *nu* (*Fr*) full authority or freedom (to use one's own judgement etc): *be given carte blanche to do it.*

car·ti·lage /'kɑːtɪlɪdʒ/ *nc,nu* (a piece of) tough, white tissue attached to one of the joints in an animal.

car·tog·ra·pher /kɑːˈtɒɡrəfə(r)/ *nc* a person who makes maps and charts.

car·to·graph·ic /ˌkɑːtəˈɡræfɪk/ *adj* of cartography.

car·tog·ra·phy /kɑːˈtɒɡrəfɪ/ *nu* the science of drawing maps and charts.

car·ton /'kɑːtn/ *nc* a cardboard box used for holding goods: *a carton of cigarettes/tinned food.*

car·toon /kɑːˈtuːn/ *nc* **1** a drawing dealing with contemporary (esp political) events in an amusing way. **2** an animated film: *a Walt Disney cartoon.*

car·toon·ist *nc* a person who draws cartoons(1).

car·tridge /'kɑːtrɪdʒ/ *nc* **1** the detachable head of the device holding the *stylus*, which picks up sound on a record-player. **2** a (large) cassette, e.g. for a typewriter ribbon. **3** a case containing explosive (for blasting) or the explosive with a bullet etc (for firing from a rifle or shotgun).

carve /kɑːv/ *v* **1** *vt* to form (something) by cutting away material from a piece of wood or stone: *carve a statue out of wood; a boy carved from marble.* **carve out sth** to achieve something with effort: *carve out a career for oneself.* **2** *vt* to write (something) by cutting into a surface: *carve one's initials on a tree.* **3** *vt,vi* to cut up (cooked meat) into pieces or slices: *carving a leg of lamb. Would you carve, please.*

carv·ing *nc* something carved in wood etc: *a wood-carving.*

cas·cade[1] /kæˈskeɪd/ *nc* **1** a long, wide waterfall. **2** a similar length (of lace, cloth etc).

cas·cade[2] /kæˈskeɪd/ *vi* to fall (as if) in a cascade(1).

case[1] /keɪs/ *nc* **1** an example, instance, of the occurrence of something: *It's an obvious case of inexperience/of being too inexperienced. In some cases we charge for delivery but in most cases delivery is free. In nine cases out of ten children prefer chocolate ice-cream.* **a case in point** a particularly useful example. **(just) in case** (*conj*) as an action done in advance because of the possibility of something: *I'm taking my coat in case it rains. The sun's shining but take your umbrella just in case.* **in case of** (*prep*) (used in instructions to refer to something (dangerous) that can possibly happen) if there is: *Ring the bell in case of fire.* **in any case** (*adv*) whatever happens or might happen: *It's too late now, in any case.* **in that case** (*adv*) if that happens, has happened or will happen: *'She's gone to live in Berlin.'—'In that case, I'll use her room.'* **2** a particular situation or state of affairs: *If that's the case, you'd better take the job.* **3** (an instance of) a person suffering from a disease, injury etc: *five cases of flu among the staff.* **4** (*legal*) an issue (to be) decided in a law court: *When will my case come before the court?* **make out a case (against/for sth)** (*fig*) to give arguments (against/in favour of something): *It's not easy to make out a case for her promotion.* **5** a matter to be discussed: *the particular case being considered* *by the committee.* **6** (*gram*) (the change in) the form of a noun or pronoun showing how it relates to other words in a sentence: *The first-person pronoun has three cases: 'I', 'me' and 'my'.* ⇨ genitive, possessive case.

'**case-book** *nc* a record kept, e.g. by a doctor, of cases(3) dealt with.

,**case 'history** *nc* a record of the past history of a person's health, social state etc.

'**case-law** *nu* law based on decisions made by judges.

'**case-load** *nc* a list of cases(3) to be dealt with in a particular period: *Dr Jones has a heavy* (= large) *case-load tomorrow.*

'**case-study** *nc* a record of information, reports etc about a person (with social problems).

'**case-work** *nu* the work of helping a person or family with social problems.

case² /keɪs/ *nc* **1** a box, tin etc used as a container: *a cigarette case.* ⇨ also bookcase, pillowcase, suitcase etc. **2** as much as a case(1) holds. **3** (*printing*): *upper case* (= capital letters); *lower case* (= small letters).

case³ /keɪs/ *vt* to enclose (something) in a case²(1).

cash¹ /kæʃ/ *nu* **1** money in coin or notes: *I have no cash with me; may I pay by cheque?* ⇨ hard cash. **cash on delivery** (abbr **COD**) payment when the goods are delivered. **2** money in any form: *be short of cash* (= without money).

,**cash and 'carry** *nc* a large shop that sells goods (esp food) cheaply to other shops, restaurants etc.

'**cash card** *nc* a card(3) used to get money from a machine outside a bank.

'**cash crop** *nc* a foodcrop (e.g. coffee, maize) to be sold for cash. Compare subsistence crop.

'**cash desk** *nc* a desk or counter (in a shop etc) where payments (by cash or cheque) are made.

'**cash flow** *nc,nu* (*finance*) the movement of cash in a business.

'**cash price** *nc* the price if payment is immediate.

cash² /kæʃ/ *vt* to get or give cash for (a cheque etc): *I must cash this postal order before I go shopping. Will you cash me this cheque/cash this cheque for me?*

cash in (on sth) to take advantage of a situation: *Shopkeepers often cash in on a shortage of something by putting the price up.*

ca·shew /'kæʃuː/ *nc* (also *attrib*) (a tropical tree with) a small kidney-shaped nut: *a cashew-nut.*

cash·ier /kæ'ʃɪə(r)/ *nc* a person who receives and pays out money in a bank, store, restaurant etc.

cash·mere /kæʃ'mɪə(r)/ *nu* (also *attrib*) the fine soft wool of Kashmir goats of India: *a cashmere sweater.*

cas·ing /'keɪsɪŋ/ *nc,nu* (a kind of) covering; protective wrapping: *copper wire with a rubber casing.*

ca·si·no /kə'siːnəʊ/ *nc* (*pl* —**s**) a room or building for music, dancing and gambling.

cask /kɑːsk/ *nc* **1** a barrel for liquids. **2** as much as a cask holds.

cas·ket /'kɑːskɪt/ *nc* **1** a small box used to hold letters, jewels etc. **2** (*US*) a coffin.

cas·sa·va /kə'sɑːvə/ *nc,nu* (also *attrib*) (a kind of tropical plant with) a starchy root eaten as food.

cas·ser·ole /'kæsərəʊl/ *nc* **1** a heat-proof dish with a lid in which food is cooked. **2** the food so cooked: *a casserole of lamb.* □ *vt* to cook (food) in a casserole.

cas·sette /kə'set/ *nc* a sealed container for magnetic tape or for photographic film (*US* = *cartridge*).

cas'sette player *nc* a machine for playing music on cassettes.

cas'sette recorder *nc* a machine for playing and recording music, computer programs etc on cassettes.

cas·sock /'kæsək/ *nc* a long, close-fitting article of clothing, worn by priests.

cast¹ /kɑːst/ *nc* **1** a set of actors in a play. **2** an act of throwing a net or fishing line. **3** something made by casting(4) or by pressing soft material into a mould: *His leg was in a plaster cast.* **4** a mould for a cast(3).

cast² /kɑːst/ *v* (*pt,pp* **cast**) **1** *vt,vi* to throw (something); allow (it) to fall or drop: *The fisherman cast his net into the water.* ⇨ doubt¹; **vote¹**(1). **2** *vt* to send (an expression etc) in a particular direction: *casting a glance at her.* **3** *vt* to give (an actor) a part in a play: *He was cast for the part of Hamlet.* **4** *vt* to pour (liquid metal etc) into a mould (to make something): *a figure cast in bronze; gates made of cast iron.* ⇨ cast-iron.

cast sb/sth aside to abandon, throw away, a person, thing as useless, unwanted.

be cast down (*formal*) to be very unhappy. ⇨ downcast.

cast off (a) to remove ropes etc holding a boat etc. **(b)** to tie up the last row of stitches when knitting. **cast sth off** to remove clothing. ⇨ cast-off.

cast on to make the first row of stitches when knitting.

cast sb out to force a person to go away: *He was cast out from society because of his behaviour.*

cast round for sth to search quickly for a weapon, excuse, alibi etc.

cas·ta·nets /ˌkæstə'nets/ *n pl* (also *a pair of castanets*) instruments of wood etc used in pairs on the fingers to make rattling sounds as a rhythm for dancing.

cast·away /'kɑːstəweɪ/ *nc* a shipwrecked person in a strange country or on an island.

caste /kɑːst/ *nc* an exclusive social class, esp a Hindu one.

cas·ti·gate /'kæstɪgeɪt/ *vt* (*formal*) to punish (a person) severely with blows or by criticizing.
cas·ti·ga·tion /ˌkæstɪ'geɪʃn/ *nc,nu*

cast-iron /ˌkɑːst 'aɪən/ *adj* (*attrib*) (esp) very strong or convincing: *a cast-iron determination/ excuse.* ⇨ also cast²(4).

castle¹ /'kɑːsl/ *nc* **1** a large, strong building fortified against attack, esp as in olden times. **2** a chess piece (also called *rook*).

castle² /'kɑːsl/ *vt,vi* (*chess*) to move (the king) sideways two squares and place the castle on the square the king moved across.

cast-off /'kɑːst ɒf/ *nc* a piece of unwanted clothing.

cas·tor sug·ar /'kɑːstə ʃʊgə(r)/ *nu* a kind of white, finely powdered sugar.

cas·trate /kæ'streɪt/ *vt* to remove the sex organs of (a male animal).

cas·tra·tion /kæ'streɪʃn/ *nc,nu*

cas·ual /'kæʒʊəl/ *adj* **1** (*attrib*) happening by chance: *a casual meeting*. **2** informal: *casual clothes*. **3** (*derog*) not thorough or serious: *casual behaviour/work*. **4** (*attrib*) irregular; not permanent: *casual labourers*.

cas·ual·ly *adv*

casu·al·ty /'kæʒʊəltɪ/ *nc* (*pl* **-ies**) **1** a person killed or seriously injured in war or an accident: *The enemy suffered heavy casualties*. **2** a person or thing that suffers because of something else.

'**casualty ward/department** *nc* the part of a hospital to which injured people are taken.

cat /kæt/ *nc* **1** a kind of small, fur-covered animal that is often kept as a pet. **let the cat out of the bag** (*informal*) to tell a secret. **2** (*tech*) any animal of the group that includes cats, tigers, lions, panthers and leopards.

'**cat burglar** *nc* a burglar who enters a building by climbing up the outside.

'**cat·call** *vi,nc* (to make) a loud whistle expressing disapproval (e.g. at a political meeting).

cat's eye *nc* (P) a reflecting spot in the road at night.

'**cat·nap** *nc* a short sleep (in a chair etc not in bed).

'**cat·suit** *nc* a woman's tight-fitting one-piece clothing for the whole body.

cat. *abbr* catalogue.

cata·clysm /'kætəklɪzəm/ *nc* (*formal*) a sudden and violent change (e.g. an earthquake, a political or social revolution).

cata·clys·mic /ˌkætə'klɪzmɪk/ *adj*

cata·combs /'kætəkuːmz/ *n pl* a series of underground galleries for the burial of the dead (as in ancient Rome).

cata·logue (*US* also **cata·log**) /'kætəlɒg/ *vt,nc* (to make) a list of names, places, goods etc in a special order: *a library catalogue*.

cata·ma·ran /ˌkætəmə'ræn/ *nc* a kind of boat with twin hulls.

cata·pult¹ /'kætəpʌlt/ *nc* a Y-shaped stick with a piece of elastic, used for throwing stones.

cata·pult² /'kætəpʌlt/ *vt* to shoot (something) (as if) from a catapult: *be catapulted to stardom* (= achieve fame quickly).

cata·ract /'kætərækt/ *nc* **1** a large waterfall or fast, narrow part of a river. **2** a growth over the eyeball, that gradually reduces sight.

ca·tarrh /kə'tɑː(r)/ *nu* inflammation, esp in the nose and throat, causing flow of liquid as when one has a cold.

ca·tas·trophe /kə'tæstrəfɪ/ *nc* **1** a sudden event causing great suffering and destruction (e.g. a flood). **2** (*literature*) the final, most serious part of tragedy (usually the death of the hero or heroine).

cata·stroph·ic /ˌkætə'strɒfɪk/ *adj*

catch¹ /kætʃ/ *nc* **1** an act of catching (esp a ball): *That was a difficult catch*. **2** something caught or worth catching: *a fine catch of fish*. **3** something intended to trick or deceive: *There's a catch in her offer somewhere*. **4** a device used for fastening or securing a lock, door etc.

catch² /kætʃ/ *v* (*pt,pp* **caught** /kɔːt/) (N) Not used in the continuous tenses, e.g. *'is/was —ing'* in 3,4,6. **1** *vt* to stop (something moving) (e.g. by getting hold of it with the hands, by holding out

something into which it may come): *I threw the ball to him and he caught it*. ⇨ breath(2). **2** *vt* to get hold of (a person, thing etc): *catch a thief. How many fish did you catch?* **catch sb's eye** ⇨ eye¹(1). **catch sight/a glimpse of sb/sth** to see a person, thing, for a short time. **3** *vt* to discover suddenly (a person) doing something (wrong): *I caught the boys stealing apples from my garden*. **4** *vt,vi* (to cause something) to become fixed or prevented from moving; to cause (something) to be trapped: *I caught my fingers in the door. My dress caught on a nail*. **5** *vt* to arrive in time for and get on (a vehicle): *catch a bus/train to Venice*. **6** *vt* to understand (the meaning of something); hear (a sound): *I don't quite catch your meaning. I didn't catch the end of the sentence*. **7** *vt* to become infected with (a disease etc): *catch a disease/a cold*. ⇨ death(2). **8** *vt* to grasp (something): *He caught my arm as I passed*. ⇨ also fire¹(1).

catch on (**a**) (*informal*) to become popular: *Her records never really caught on* (*with the public*). (**b**) to understand: *He winked as he spoke but I didn't catch on*.

catch sb out (**a**) to discover a person doing something wrong, making a (deliberate) mistake etc. (**b**) (*cricket*) to defeat a batsman by catching a ball he or she has hit.

catch sb up; catch up with sb to reach the same place, position etc as a person: *You go ahead and I'll catch you up later*. **catch up** (*on sth*) (**a**) to get oneself up to date with news etc: *catch up on the latest developments*. (**b**) (*informal*) to work hard to do uncompleted, necessary etc work: *catch up on one's correspondence*. **be caught up in sth** to be very occupied, involved, in work etc: *caught up in one's studies*.

catch·ing /'kætʃɪŋ/ *adj* (usually *pred*) (*informal*) (esp of diseases) tending to spread from one person to another: *Yawning is catching*.

catch·phrase /'kætʃfreɪz/ *nc* (*lang*) a phrase used often and by many people (usually for a short period).

catch·word /'kætʃwɜːd/ *nc* (*lang*) (**a**) a word that is popular in informal speech (usually for a short period). (**b**) a word (e.g. in this dictionary) at the top of the page, used as a reference.

catchy /'kætʃɪ/ *adj* (**-ier, -iest**) (of a tune etc) easily remembered.

cat·echism /'kætɪkɪzəm/ *nc* a number of questions and answers for religious education.

cat·egori·cal /ˌkætɪ'gɒrɪkl/ *adj* (of a statement) unconditional and without doubt: *the categorical truth*.

cat·egori·cal·ly /-klɪ/ *adv*

cat·egor·ize (also **-ise**) /'kætɪgəraɪz/ *vt* to place (people, objects, ideas etc) in a category.

cat·egory /'kætɪgərɪ/ *nc* (*pl* **-ies**) a division in a system, order or type of group.

ca·ter /'keɪtə(r)/ *vi* **1** **cater for sth** to provide food for an event: *We cater for weddings and parties*. **2** **cater for/to sth** to make sure one takes into account people's favourite occupations etc: *TV programmes try to cater for all interests*.

ca·ter·er *nc* a person, business, that provides meals etc for offices etc or special occasions.

cat·er·pil·lar /'kætəpɪlə(r)/ *nc* a creature like a short worm with many legs (a *larva*) that will become a butterfly or moth.

ca·thar·sis /kəˈθɑːsɪs/ nu (literature) the effect in a tragedy of such qualities as fear and pity on the audience's emotions, especially feelings of relief and elation.

ca·thar·tic /kəˈθɑːtɪk/ adj 1 (literature) of, producing, catharsis. 2 (med) (of a drug etc) causing the bowels to empty.

ca·the·dral /kəˈθiːdrəl/ nc the main church in a diocese.

cath·ode /ˈkæθəʊd/ nc (tech) a negative electrode in a battery etc. Compare anode.

,cath·ode 'ray tube nc the part in a television set in which streams of electrons give out light to produce the picture.

cath·ol·ic /ˈkæθəlɪk/ adj general; including many or most things: a man with catholic interests.

Cath·ol·ic /ˈkæθlɪk/ adj, nc (a member) of the Roman Catholic Church.

Ca·tholi·cism /kəˈθɒlɪsɪzəm/ nu the teaching, beliefs etc of the Roman Catholic Church.

cat·kin /ˈkætkɪn/ nc a length of flowers hanging down from twigs of such trees as willows and birches.

cat·tery /ˈkætərɪ/ nc (pl -ies) a business with a place where cats can be left for a short time.

cattle /ˈkætl/ n pl farm animals, esp bulls and cows: twenty head of cattle. The cattle are grazing.

cat·ty /ˈkætɪ/ adj (-ier, -iest) (derog) (of a person, statement etc) sly and spiteful.

caught /kɔːt/ pt,pp of catch².

caul·dron /ˈkɔːldrən/ nc a large, deep pot in which things are boiled.

cauli·flower /ˈkɒlɪflaʊə(r)/ nc,nu (also attrib) (a kind of vegetable with) a large, white flowerhead: cauliflower cheese.

cau·sal /ˈkɔːzl/ adj of, expressing, cause(1).

cause¹ /kɔːz/ n 1 nc,nu something that produces an effect, that makes something happen: The cause of the fire was carelessness. 2 nu reason: You have no cause for complaint/no cause to complain. 3 nc a purpose for which efforts are made: fight in the cause of justice. **a lost cause** one that is sure to be unsuccessful.

cause² /kɔːz/ vt to be the cause of (something): What caused his death?

cause·way /ˈkɔːzweɪ/ nc a raised road or footpath, esp across wet land.

caus·tic /ˈkɔːstɪk/ adj 1 (attrib) able to burn or destroy by chemical action: caustic soda. 2 (fig; derog) sarcastic: caustic remarks.

caus·ti·cal·ly /-klɪ/ adv

cau·tion¹ /ˈkɔːʃn/ n 1 nu the act of paying attention (to avoid danger or making mistakes): When crossing a busy street we must use caution. 2 nc an official warning: The judge gave the prisoner a caution and set him free.

cau·tion² /ˈkɔːʃn/ vt to give an official warning to (a person): He cautioned me for being late.

cau·tion·ary /ˈkɔːʃənrɪ/ adj (no comp) giving advice or warning: cautionary tales.

cau·tious /ˈkɔːʃəs/ adj having or showing caution(1).

cau·tious·ly adv

cav·al·cade /ˌkævlˈkeɪd/ nc a procession of people on horseback or in carriages or vehicles. Compare motorcade.

cav·al·ry /ˈkævəlrɪ/ nc or pl (the —) soldiers who

fight on horseback.

cave¹ /keɪv/ nc a hollow place in the side of a cliff or hill or under the ground.

'cave·man nc a person living in a cave (very long ago).

cave² /keɪv/ vi,vt **cave in** to fall in, give way to pressure: The roof of the tunnel caved in.

cav·ern /ˈkævən/ nc (literary) a cave.

cavi·ar (also **cavi·are**) /ˈkævɪɑː(r)/ nu pickled eggs (roe) of the sturgeon or certain other large fish.

cav·ity /ˈkævətɪ/ nc (pl -ies) a small hole: a cavity in a tooth.

ca·vort /kəˈvɔːt/ vi **cavort (about)** (informal) to dance or jump about with excitement.

caw /kɔː/ vi,nc (to make) the call, cry of a raven, rook or crow.

cay·enne /keɪˈen/ nu (also cayenne pepper) a kind of very hot red pepper.

cc abbr 1 cubic centimetre(s). 2 centuries.

CD /ˌsiːˈdiː/ abbr 1 (Fr: Corps Diplomatique) Diplomatic Service. 2 Civil Defence. 3 compact disc.

Cdr abbr Commander.

cease /siːs/ vt,vi (formal) to stop (the usual word): Cease fire! (= Stop shooting!)

cease·less adj never ending.

cease·less·ly adv

ce·dar /ˈsiːdə(r)/ nc,nu (also attrib) (the wood of) a kind of evergreen tree with hard, red, sweet-smelling wood.

cede /siːd/ vt **cede sth to sb/sth** (formal) to give up rights, land etc to another person or country.

ce·dil·la /sɪˈdɪlə/ nc mark put under the c (ç) in the spelling of some French and Portuguese words (as in façade) to show that the sound is /s/.

ceil·ing /ˈsiːlɪŋ/ nc 1 the upper or overhead surface of a room. 2 the highest (practicable) level (to be) reached by an aircraft: a plane with a ceiling of 20 000 ft. 3 a maximum height, limit or level: price ceilings; wage ceilings.

cel·ebrate /ˈselɪbreɪt/ vt,vi to do something to show that (a day or an event) is important or an occasion for rejoicing: celebrating Christmas/ one's birthday.

cel·ebrated adj famous: a celebrated painter.

cel·ebra·tion /ˌselɪˈbreɪʃn/ nc,nu

ce·leb·ri·ty /sɪˈlebrətɪ/ nc (pl -ies) a popular and famous person.

cel·ery /ˈselərɪ/ nu (also attrib) a garden plant of which the white stems are eaten raw as salad or cooked as a vegetable: celery soup.

ce·les·tial /sɪˈlestɪəl/ adj (no comp) of the sky; of heaven: celestial bodies, e.g. the sun and the stars. Compare terrestrial(2).

celi·ba·cy /ˈselɪbəsɪ/ nu the state of living unmarried or not having sexual intercourse, esp as a religious obligation.

celi·bate /ˈselɪbət/ adj, nc (of) a person committed to celibacy.

cell /sel/ nc 1 a small room for one person (esp in a prison or a monastery). 2 (science) an extremely small unit of living matter: blood cells ⇨ cellular. 3 one of many shaped compartments in a larger structure, in a honeycomb. 4 (electricity) a unit of an apparatus (e.g. a battery) for producing electric current by chemical action.

cel·lar /'selə(r)/ nc **1** an underground room for storing coal, wine etc. **2** a (person's) store of wine.

cel·list /'tʃelɪst/ nc a person who plays a cello.

cello /'tʃeləʊ/ nc (pl —s) (also attrib) (also (formal) violoncello) a large stringed musical instrument with a deep sound, held between the knees when being played: a cello player.

cel·lo·phane /'seləfeɪn/ nu (P) a kind of thin, shiny transparent material, used to wrap things and to make sticky tape.

cel·lu·lar /'seljʊlə(r)/ adj (science) consisting of cells(2): cellular tissue.

cel·lu·lose /'seljʊleʊs/ nu the substance in the walls of plant cells(2), used to make plastics etc.

Cel·sius /'selsɪəs/ adj (science) = centigrade.

ce·ment¹ /sɪ'ment/ nu **1** a grey powder (made by burning lime and clay) which, after being wetted, becomes hard like stone and is used for building etc. ⇨ concrete². **2** any similar soft substance that sets firm, used for filling holes (e.g. in the teeth) or for joining things.

ce·ment² /sɪ'ment/ vt **1** to put (something) on or in, join (things), with cement. **2** (fig) to strengthen (a partnership, agreement etc): cement a friendship.

ce'ment-mixer nc (a vehicle with) a revolving drum in which cement is mixed.

cem·etery /'semɪtrɪ/ nc (pl -ies) an area of land (not a churchyard) used for burials.

cen·sor /'sensə(r)/ nc (esp) an official with authority to examine books, magazines, plays, films etc and to remove anything regarded as immoral or in other ways undesirable. □ vt to (act as a censor and) remove immoral or undesirable parts.

cen·sor·ship nu

cen·sure¹ /'senʃə(r)/ nu (formal) the act, expression, of unfavourable criticism.

cen·sure² /'senʃə(r)/ vt (formal) to criticize (a person) unfavourably: censuring her for being lazy.

cen·sus /'sensəs/ nc (pl —es) an official counting of the population, traffic etc.

cent /sent/ nc a 100th part of a dollar and some other metric units of currency; metal coin of this value. **per cent** (abbr %) in, by or for every 100. **one hundred per cent** completely: I agree one hundred per cent.

cen·ten·ar·ian /ˌsentɪ'neərɪən/ nc a person who is (more than) 100 years old.

cen·ten·ary /ˌsen'tiːnərɪ/ adj, nc (pl -ies) **1** (of) a period of 100 years. **2** (of) a 100th anniversary.

cen·ten·ni·al /sen'tenɪəl/ adj, nc (esp US) = centenary.

cen·ter /'sentə(r)/ nc, vt, vi (US) = centre.

cen·ti·grade /'sentɪgreɪd/ adj (symbol C) in or of the temperature scale that has 100 degrees between the freezing-point and the boiling-point of water: Water boils at 100° centigrade (100°C). Compare Fahrenheit.

cen·ti·metre (US = -meter) /'sentɪmiːtə(r)/ nc the 100th part of a metre.

cen·ti·pede /'sentɪpiːd/ nc a small, long, crawling creature with many legs.

cen·tral /'sentrəl/ adj **1** of, at, from or near the centre: The shops are central (= in the centre of the town). **2** (no comp) most important: the central idea of an argument. That fact is central to his explanation.

central 'heating nu a system of heating a building from a central source using radiators.

central 'nervous system nc (anat) the system of nerves controlling the activity of any animal life.

central 'processing unit nc (abbr CPU) (computers) the part of a computer system that analyzes the information according to instructions given.

cen·tral·ly adv: We live centrally.

cen·tral·ize (also -ise) /'sentrəlaɪz/ vt (esp) to put, bring, (something, esp government) under central control.

cen·tral·iz·ation (also -is·ation) /ˌsentrəlaɪ-'zeɪʃn/ nu

centre¹ (US = cen·ter) /'sentə(r)/ nc **1** a middle part or point: the centre of Frankfurt. **centre of gravity** the point in an object about which the weight is evenly balanced in any position. **2** a place of great activity, of special interest etc: a health centre; a shopping centre. **3** a person or thing that attracts interest, attention etc: She loves to be the centre of attraction. **4** a middle or moderate position (in politics): The Alliance tries to appeal to the centre.

centre² (US = cen·ter) /'sentə(r)/ vt, vi **1** to place (something) in, pass to, come to, be at, the centre: The defender centred the ball. **2** **centre (sth) on sth** (to cause one's thoughts etc) to be concentrated on something: Our thoughts centred on one idea.

cen·trifu·gal /sen'trɪfjʊgl/ adj (attrib; tech) moving, tending to move, away from the centre or axis.

cen,trifugal 'force nu (tech) the force which causes a body spinning round a centre to tend to move outwards.

cen·tury /'sentʃərɪ/ nc (pl -ies) **1** a period of 100 years. **2** one of the periods of 100 years before or since the birth of Jesus Christ: during the 20th century (= AD 1901–2000). **3** (cricket) 100 runs made by a batsman in one innings.

ce·ram·ic /sɪ'ræmɪk/ adj of the art of making and decorating pottery.

cer·am·ics /sɪ'ræmɪks/ n **1** n sing the art of making and decorating pottery. **2** n pl articles made of porcelain, clay etc.

cer·eal /'sɪərɪəl/ nc (also attrib) **1** any kind of grain used for food: cereal crops. **2** food prepared from cereals: breakfast cereals.

cer·ebral /'serɪbrəl/ adj (tech) of the brain: He had a cerebral haemorrhage.

cer·emo·ni·al /ˌserɪ'məʊnɪəl/ adj as used for ceremonies: ceremonial dress.

cer·emo·ni·al·ly adv

cer·emo·ny /'serɪmənɪ/ nc (pl -ies) **1** nc an act with special clothes, actions etc, such as a wedding, funeral, the opening of a new public building etc. **2** nu behaviour required by social customs during such special occasions: There's too much ceremony on official occasions. (**not**) **stand on ceremony** to pay (no) great attention to accepted rules of behaviour.

cert /sɜːt/ nc (sl) something considered certain to happen or that certainly has happened: It's a cert that he'll win. **a dead cert** an absolute certainty.

cert. abbr certificate.

cer·tain /'sɜ:tn/ *adj* **1** of which there is no possible doubt: *It is certain that two and two make four.* **2** having no doubt; confident: *I'm certain (that) he saw me.* (N) *'Sure'* is also possible. Opp uncertain. **for certain** without doubt: *I cannot say for certain* (= with complete confidence) *when he will arrive.* **make certain (of sth/ that . . .)** to inquire (about something) in order to be sure: *I think there's a train at 8.20 but you ought to make certain. I'll go and make certain of our seats.* **3** (used as a *det* or *pron*) **(a)** not named, stated or described (although it is possible to do so): *I'd come only on certain conditions. A certain person I met yesterday asked after you. Certain of them were already late.* **(b)** some but not much: *There was a certain coldness in her attitude towards me.*

cer·tain·ly *adv* **(a)** without doubt: *He will certainly die if you don't get a doctor.* **(b)** (used as an answer to questions) yes: *'Will you pass me the towel, please?'—'Certainly.'*

cer·tain·ty /'sɜ:tntɪ/ *n* (*pl* **-ies**) **1** *nc* something that is certain: *Prices have gone up—that's a certainty.* **2** *nu* the state of being certain: *We can have no certainty of success.*

cer·ti·fi·able /ˌsɜ:tɪ'faɪəbl/ *adj* that can be certified.

cer·tifi·cate /sə'tɪfɪkət/ *nc* an official written or printed statement that may be used as proof or evidence: *a birth/marriage certificate.*

cer·ti·fy /'sɜ:tɪfaɪ/ *vt* (*pt,pp* **-ied**) (*formal*) **1** to declare (usually by showing a certificate) that (something is true, correct): *I certify (that) this is a true copy of the will.* **2** to state (as an official) that something is correct etc: *Can you certify that she was not at the party?*

cer·vi·cal /sɜ:'vaɪkl/ *adj* (*med*) (esp) of the cervix: *a cervical smear* (= a test for cancer of the cervix).

cer·vix /'sɜ:vɪks/ *nc* (*anat*) the narrow opening of the womb.

ces·sa·tion /se'seɪʃn/ *nc,nu* (*formal*) the act of stopping: *the cessation of hostilities.*

cess·pit /'sespɪt/ (also **cess·pool** /'sespu:l/) *nc* a (usually covered) hole, pit or underground tank into which drains (esp for sewage) empty.

c/f *abbr* (*bookkeeping*) carried forward.

c.f. *abbr* (*commerce*) cost and freight.

c.f.i. *abbr* (*commerce*) cost, freight and insurance.

ch. *abbr* chapter.

c.h. *abbr* central heating.

chafe /tʃeɪf/ *v* **1** *vt,vi* (to cause skin) to become rough or sore by rubbing: *Her skin chafes easily.* **2** *vi* (*formal*) to feel irritation or impatience: *chafing at the delay/inefficiency; chafe under restraints.*

chaff¹ /tʃɑ:f/ *nu* the outer covering (*husks*) of grain, removed before the grain is used.

chaff² /tʃɑ:f/ *vt, nu* (to use) good-humoured teasing or joking (to (a person)).

chaf·finch /'tʃæfɪntʃ/ *nc* a kind of small European songbird.

chain¹ /tʃeɪn/ *nc* **1** a flexible line of connected metal rings or links, used for connecting, fastening, holding etc. **in chains** tied up as a prisoner. **pull the chain** to pull a chain or press a handle in order to cause water to flow and clean a lava-

tory bowl. **2** a number of connected things, events etc: *a chain of events/ideas/mountains.*

'chain-gang *nc* a group of prisoners in chains while at work outside their prison.

,chain re'action *nc* a change (chemical or *fig*) causing effects that themselves cause similar changes.

'chain-smoker *nc* a person who smokes cigarettes one after the other.

'chain-stitch *nc,nu* a style of sewing in which each stitch makes a loop through which the next stitch is taken.

'chain-store *nc* one of many shops owned and controlled by the same business company.

chain² /tʃeɪn/ *vt* **chain sb/sth (up)** to fasten a person, animal, using a chain(1).

chair¹ /tʃeə(r)/ *nc* **1** a separate movable seat with a back, for one person: *an armchair.* **take a chair** to sit down: *Please take a chair.* **2** the position of a person who controls a meeting. **be in/ take the chair** to act as a chairperson. **3** the position of a professor: *the chair of Philosophy.*

chair² /tʃeə(r)/ *vt* **1** to be in control of (a discussion etc) as a chairperson: *chair a meeting.* **2** to carry (a person who has won a contest): *The captain was chaired by the fans.*

'chair·man *nc* (*pl* **-men**) a man controlling a meeting.

'chair·person *nc* (*pl* **-persons**) a man or woman controlling a meeting.

'chair·woman *nc* (*pl* **-women**) a woman controlling a meeting.

cha·let /'ʃæleɪ/ *nc* **1** a wooden mountain hut with a tall, steep roof. **2** a cottage built in the same style. **3** a small house in a holiday camp etc.

chal·ice /'tʃælɪs/ *nc* a goblet, esp one used for the Eucharist.

chalk¹ /tʃɔ:k/ *n* **1** *nu* a kind of soft, white substance (a kind of limestone). **2** *nc,nu* this material or a similar material, white or coloured, made into sticks for writing and drawing.

chalk² /tʃɔ:k/ *vt* **1** to mark, write etc (something) using chalk(2). **2** **chalk sth up** (*fig*) to be successful in achieving something: *chalk up a victory.*

chal·lenge¹ /'tʃælɪndʒ/ *nc* **1** an invitation or call to play a game, run a race, have a fight etc to see who is better, stronger etc. **2** a request to prove the truth, existence etc of something. **3** a project, undertaking etc that is difficult but interesting: *Sailing round the world is a great challenge.*

chal·lenge² /'tʃælɪndʒ/ *vt* **1** to give a challenge(1,2) to (a person, team etc): *challenging her to a game of chess.* **2** to be a challenge(3) to (a person, her or his ability etc): *challenging his strength and endurance.*

chal·lenger *nc* a person who challenges(1).

cham·ber /'tʃeɪmbə(r)/ *n* **1** (*old use*) a room, esp a bedroom. **2** an enclosed space in the body of an animal or plant, and in some kinds of machinery: *the chambers of the heart.* **3** (often *C-*) (a hall used by) a group of legislators (often known as the *Upper Chamber* (e.g. the House of Lords) and the *Lower Chamber* (e.g. the House of Commons)). **4** (*pl*) a judge's room for hearing cases that need not be taken into court. **5** (*pl*) the offices of barristers etc esp in the Inns of Court. **6** (often *C-*) a group of people organized for purposes of trade: *a Chamber of Commerce.*

'**chamber·maid** *nc* a maid who keeps bedrooms in order in hotels.

'**chamber music** *nu* music for a small number of players (e.g. a string quartet).

'**chamber-pot** *nc* a vessel for urine.

cha·mele·on /kə'mi:liən/ *nc* **1** a small lizard with a long tongue whose colour changes according to its background. **2** (*fig*; often *derog*) a person who changes her or his voice, manner, opinions etc to suit the situation.

champ[1] /tʃæmp/ *nc* (*informal*) = champion(1).

champ[2] /tʃæmp/ *v* **1** *vt,vi* (of horses) to bite (food, the bit) noisily. **2** *vi* (*fig*) to show strong or angry emotion: *champ with impatience/rage.*

cham·pagne /ʃæm'peɪn/ *nc,nu* (a particular kind of) white sparkling French wine.

cham·pion[1] /'tʃæmpɪən/ *nc* **1** a person, team, animal etc taking the first place in a competition: *a boxing/tennis champion.* **2** a person who fights, argues or speaks in support of (another or of a cause): *a champion of free speech/of women's rights.*

cham·pion[2] /'tʃæmpɪən/ *vt* to support strongly (an idea, cause, person etc): *champion the release of political prisoners.*

cham·pion·ship /'tʃæmpɪənʃɪp/ *nc* a competition to find the best athlete, player, team etc: *the Australian tennis championship.*

chance[1] /tʃɑːns/ *adj* (*attrib*) happening unexpectedly: *a chance meeting.*

chance[2] /tʃɑːns/ *n* **1** *nu* the occurrence of events without an obvious cause, planning or warning: *Winning or losing in card-games depends on chance. He leaves nothing to chance* (= He tries to plan for every possible situation). *What part did chance* (= good luck) *play in his success?* **by chance** unexpectedly and not planned: *We met by chance.* **2** *nc,nu* a possibility of being either successful or not: *She has no/not much/a good chance of winning. The chances are that you'll lose.* **an even chance (of sth); a fifty-fifty chance (of sth)** an equal possibility of success or failure: *He has an even chance of winning.* **on the (off) chance (of doing sth)** in the hope of being able to (do something): *He went on the off chance of seeing her.* **(the) chances are (that)** . . . it is more likely (that) . . . **stand a (fair/good) chance (of sth)** to have a fair/ good possibility (of success). **take a chance (on sth)** to act knowing that one can be unlucky or unsuccessful: *I'm willing to take a chance on that new rope if you are.* ⇨ also ghost(2). **3** *nc* an opportunity: *a chance to prove his ability.* **the chance of a lifetime** ⇨ lifetime.

chance[3] /tʃɑːns/ *v* **1** *vi* (used before an infinitive with 'to') to happen, occur, without an obvious cause or without planning or warning: *I chanced to be there.* **2** *vt* **chance it** (*informal*) to act with the possibility of being unsuccessful: *I'm not sure I trust her but I'm prepared to chance it.* Ⓝ '*Risk*' is also possible.

chan·cel /'tʃɑːnsl/ *nc* the eastern part of a church round the altar, used by the priest(s) and choir.

chan·cel·lor /'tʃɑːnsələ(r)/ *nc* (C- in names) **1** a state or law official: *the Chancellor of the Exchequer.* **2** (of some universities) an honorary head or president (the duties being performed by the Vice-Chancellor). **3** (in some countries, e.g. West Germany) the chief minister of state.

chan·cy /'tʃɑːnsɪ/ *adj* (**-ier**, **-iest**) (*informal*) having a strong possibility of being unsuccessful: *It's chancy to travel in this bad weather.*

chan·de·lier /ˌʃændə'lɪə(r)/ *nc* a support for several lights hanging from a ceiling.

change[1] /tʃeɪndʒ/ *n* **1** *nc,nu* (an example, instance, of) a changed or different condition: *a change in the weather; a change for the better; a change of government/policy; a major change in the economy; be in favour of/be against change.* **for a change** in order to have variety or a difference in a routine: *Why don't you phone me for a change?* **the change of life** (*informal*) = menopause. **make a change** to produce a difference in conditions, routine etc: *Let's go camping this weekend—it'll make a nice change from working.* **2** *nc* something used in place of another or others: *Take a clean change of clothes with you. Did you give me your change of address?* **have a change of heart** to have a serious alteration of one's opinions, attitudes (esp to be kinder, forgiving etc). **a change of scene** new surroundings, environment (e.g. as when on holiday). **3** *nu* money in small(er) units; money that is the difference between the price or cost and the sum offered in payment: *Can you give me change for a pound?*

change[2] /tʃeɪndʒ/ *v* **1** *vi,vt* to take off (clothes) and put on other clothes: *My T-shirt's dirty so I'll change (it). She's gone home to change. He's changing the baby.* ⇨ change into/out of sth. **2** *vt* to take off (bedclothes) and put on other bedclothes: *change the sheets on this bed.* **change the bed** to put on different bedclothes. **3** *vt* to leave (a place, team, vehicle etc) and go to another: *change addresses; change sides; change trains at Victoria Station.* ⇨ also hand[1](1); place[1](1). **4** *vt* to give up (something) and get, have, use etc another: *She's changed her job. We've changed to a new brand of coffee. I didn't like the record so I changed it for this cassette.* ⇨ also tune[1](1). **5** *vt* to give (money) and get other money in return: *Can you change this twenty pound note?* (= Can you give me coins or smaller notes for it?) *I need to change more dollars into francs.* ⇨ change sth back (into sth). **6** *vt,vi* (to cause a person, thing, to become different: *His wife's death has changed him. This caterpillar will soon change out of all recognition. Will she ever change or will she always be selfish? Change gear when you turn the corner. The leaves change colour in autumn.* ⇨ also mind[1](3), subject[2](2).

change back (into sth) to become a previous form, shape: *It cannot change back into a kitten. She changed back into a witch.* **change back (into sth)** to put on clothes worn earlier: *You can change back into your jeans.* **change sth back (into sth)** to give back money and get the previous type in return: *change pounds back into dollars; change this note back into coins.*

change down (when driving) to use a lower gear: *change down to second gear.*

change (sb/sth) from sb/sth (into/to sb/ sth) (to cause a person, thing) to be altered: *It changed from a caterpillar into a butterfly. Her illness changed her from an active teenager to a sad young woman.*

change into sth (a) ⇨ above. **(b)** to change(1) into other clothes etc: *change into trainers.* **(c)** to change money into a different kind: *change dollars into pounds; change £10 into silver coins.*

change out of sth to take off clothes and put on others: *Wait for me while I change out of these wet clothes.*

change over (of two people) to change places, jobs etc with each other. **change over (from sth) (to sth)** to change(4) (from one thing or kind) (to another): *change over from butter to margarine. I've changed over to coffee for breakfast. They've changed over to robots in the factory.* Hence **'change-over** *nc* an act, instance, of changing over.

change round (of two people) to change places with each other.

change up (when driving) to use a higher gear: *change up to fourth gear.*

change·able /'tʃeɪndʒəbl/ *adj* likely to become different: *changeable weather.*

change-over /'tʃeɪndʒ əʊvə/ *nc* ⇨ change over (from sth) (to sth).

chan·nel¹ /'tʃænl/ *nc* **1** (C- in names) a stretch of water joining two seas: *the English Channel* (between France and England). **2** a passage along which a liquid may flow. **3** (*fig*) any way by which news, ideas etc may travel: *He has secret channels of information.* **through the usual channels** by the usual means of communication. **4** a band of radio or TV frequencies: *Britain has four TV channels.*

chan·nel² /'tʃænl/ *vt* (**-ll-**, *US* also **-l-**) **1** to form a channel(1,2) in (something): *The river channelled its way through the rock.* **2** to guide, send, (something) through a channel(3): *channelling information through to headquarters.*

chant /tʃɑːnt/ *vi,vt, nc* (to produce) prayer, words etc in a singing voice.

cha·os /'keɪɒs/ *nu* the complete absence of order or shape: *The room was in complete chaos when the burglars left.*

cha·ot·ic /keɪ'ɒtɪk/ *adj* in a state of chaos.
cha·oti·cal·ly /-klɪ/ *adv*

chap¹ /tʃæp/ *nc* (*dated informal*) a man or boy.

chap² /tʃæp/ *vt,vi* (**-pp-**) (to cause the skin) to become sore, rough, cracked: *My skin soon chaps in cold weather.* □ *nc* a sore crack in the skin.

chap. *abbr* chapter.

chap·el /'tʃæpl/ *nc* **1** a place used for Christian worship, e.g. in a hospital, prison etc. **2** a small place within a Christian church, used for private prayer. **3** a trade union group in a factory etc.

chap·er·on¹ /'ʃæpərəʊn/ *nc* an elderly person (usually a woman) in charge of a girl or young unmarried woman.

chap·er·on² /'ʃæpərəʊn/ *vt* to act as a chaperon.

chap·lain /'tʃæplɪn/ *nc* a priest or clergyman in the armed forces, a hospital etc.

chap·ter /'tʃæptə(r)/ *nc* **1** a main (usually numbered) division of a book. **chapter and verse** the exact origin of a quotation or exact details giving proof, identity etc: *provide chapter and verse about the source of the information.* **2** a particular historical period: *the most brilliant chapter in our history.*

char¹ /tʃɑː(r)/ *nu* (*GB sl*) tea: *a cup of char.*
char² /tʃɑː(r)/ *nc* = charwoman.

char³ /tʃɑː(r)/ *vi* (**-rr-**) to do the cleaning of offices, houses etc with payment by the hour or the day.

'char·woman *nc* a woman who earns money by charring.

char⁴ /tʃɑː(r)/ *vt* (**-rr-**) to cause the surface of (something) to become black by burning: *charred wood.*

char·ac·ter /'kærɪktə(r)/ *n* **1** *nu* the mental or moral qualities that make one person etc different from others: *a woman of fine/strong/good character; the character of the French.* **in/out of character** like/not like a person's known or expected behaviour or qualities. **2** *nu* moral strength; reputation: *a man of character.* **3** *nc* (*literature*) a person in the story of a book, drama etc: *a leading/main character; a minor character in the novel.* **4** *nu* all those qualities that make a thing, place etc what it is and different from others: *the character of the desert areas of N Africa.* **5** *nc* a letter, sign etc used in a system of writing or printing: *Greek/Chinese characters.* **6** *nc* (*computers*) any letter, number etc that is part of the computer code.

'character study (*literature*) a description of the physical, mental, emotional etc qualities and features identified in a character(3). ⇨ characterization.

char·ac·ter·less *adj* (*derog*) dull and ordinary: *a characterless design.*

char·ac·ter·is·tic¹ /,kærɪktə'rɪstɪk/ *adj* forming part of, showing, the typical qualities or features: *a characteristic laugh/smell. It's so characteristic of him.*

char·ac·ter·is·ti·cal·ly /-klɪ/ *adv*

char·ac·ter·is·tic² /,kærɪktə'rɪstɪk/ *nc* a typical feature or quality: *One of the tortoise's characteristics is to hibernate.*

char·ac·ter·iz·ation (also **-is·ation**) /,kærɪktəraɪ'zeɪʃn/ *nc,nu* (*literature*) an author's (ability to provide a) description of a character(3) through her or his actions, words, personality and other typical features so that the reader, viewer etc can identify her or him clearly.

char·ac·ter·ize (also **-ise**) /'kærɪktəraɪz/ *vt* (*often passive*) **1** to show or mark (something) in a special way: *Your work is characterized by great attention to detail.* **2** to describe the character(1) of (a person): *He was characterized as cruel and jealous.*

cha·rade /ʃə'rɑːd/ *nc* **1** a game in which a word is guessed after each syllable of it has been suggested by acting a little play. **2** any dishonest or mocking act: *His trial was a charade.*

char·coal /'tʃɑːkəʊl/ *nu* a black substance made by burning wood slowly in an oven with little air, used as fuel, for drawing etc.

charge¹ /tʃɑːdʒ/ *n* **1** *nc* a price (to be) paid for goods or services: *a charge of 10% for services; a service charge in a restaurant.* **2** *nc* a statement, written or spoken, that a person has done wrong, esp something illegal: *a charge of robbery with violence.* **bring a charge against sb** (or **prefer charges (against sb)** (*legal*)) to accuse a person of a crime. **3** *nu* care, control, responsibility for (a person, thing): *He has charge of the office keys.* **in charge (of sth)** in control (of something), responsible for something: *be in* charge of the sales department. *Who's in charge?* **take charge** *(of sth)* to become responsible (for something): *Ms Jones will take charge (of the equipment) while I'm on holiday.* **4** *nc* a sudden and strong attack (e.g. by a soldier, football player etc). **5** *nc* (*electricity*) **(a)** one of two forms of electrical force: *a negative/positive charge.* **(b)** a quantity of electricity measured by the amount and length of time it flows. ⇨ **coulomb.** **(c)** the total quantity of electricity stored (in a battery etc). **6** *nc* a quantity of explosive etc in a gun etc. **7** *nc* a formal instruction: *a judge's charge to a jury to ignore prejudice.*

charge² /tʃɑːdʒ/ *v* **1** *vt,vi* **charge (sb/sth) (for sth)** to ask (an amount) as a price: *charge him £10 for it; charge £25 a night; How much do you charge?* Ⓝ Compare *'cost',* as in *How much does it cost? It costs £10.* **2** *vt* **charge sb to do sth/with sth** (usually *passive; formal*) to give a person an order as a duty or task: *be charged to make certain that the children are safe; be charged with responsibility for the department.* **3** *vt* **charge sb (with sth)** (usually *passive*) (*legal*) to make a charge(2) against a person: *charge a man with murder.* **4** *vi* **charge (at/towards sb/sth)** to make a charge(4): *charging at the enemy; charge towards the goal. Charge!* **5** *vt,vi* (*electricity*) (to cause a battery etc) to take in electricity. **be on charge** (of a battery) to be in the process of charging(5). **6** *vt* to put a charge(6) in (a gun etc). **7** *vt* (*bookkeeping*) to state or record (the cost of something) as being owed: *charge postage; charge the goods to my account.*

charge·able /'tʃɑːdʒəbl/ *adj* **1** that can be charged(7): *Costs of repairs are chargeable to the owner.* **2** that can result in a charge(2): *Theft is a chargeable offence.*

chargé d'affaires /ˌʃɑːʒeɪ dæˈfeə(r)/ *nc* (*pl* **chargés d'affaires,** pronunciation unchanged) an official who takes the place of an ambassador who is absent.

charger /'tʃɑːdʒə(r)/ *nc* an apparatus for charging(5) a battery.

char·iot /'tʃærɪət/ *nc* a horse-drawn vehicle with two wheels, used in ancient times in fighting and racing.

char·io·teer /ˌtʃærɪəˈtɪə(r)/ *nc* a driver of a chariot.

cha·ris·ma /kəˈrɪzmə/ *nu* the natural ability to create enthusiasm and liking for oneself.

char·is·matic /ˌkærɪzˈmætɪk/ *adj*: *a charismatic personality.*

chari·table /'tʃærɪtəbl/ *adj* **1** showing kindness and understanding: *A charitable person would forgive him.* Opp **uncharitable.** **2** of a charity(2): *a charitable trust.*

chari·tably /-əblɪ/ *adv*

char·ity /'tʃærɪtɪ/ *n* (*pl* **-ies**) **1** *nu* (kindness in providing) money, food etc given to the poor. **2** *nc* a society or organization for helping the poor: *Oxfam is a well-known charity.* **3** *nu* the willingness to judge other persons with kindness and understanding.

char·la·tan /'ʃɑːlətən/ *nc* (*derog*) a person who claims to have more skill, knowledge or ability than he or she really has.

charm¹ /ʃɑːm/ *n* **1** *nc,nu* (an example of) the power to please or give pleasure: *Her charm made*

her very popular. **2** *nc* something believed to have magic power, good or bad: *a good-luck charm.*

charm² /tʃɑːm/ *vt* (*formal*) **1** to give pleasure to (a person): *We were charmed with the scenery.* **2** to influence (something) (as if) by magic: *She charmed the pain from his brow.*

charm·ing *adj* pleasing; delightful: *a charming child/face.*

chart¹ /tʃɑːt/ *nc* **1** a map used by sailors, showing the coasts, depth of the sea, position of rocks, lighthouses etc. **2** a sheet of paper with information in the form of curves, diagrams etc: *a weather chart.*

chart² /tʃɑːt/ *vt* to make, show, (something) on a chart(1,2).

char·ter¹ /'tʃɑːtə(r)/ *nc* a written statement of rights, permission, esp from a ruler or government (e.g. to a town, city or university).

'charter flight *nc* a flight in a plane hired for a special purpose, e.g. to take people on holiday. Compare **scheduled flight.**

char·ter² /'tʃɑːtə(r)/ *vt* to hire (a plane).

char·tered ac·count·ant /ˌtʃɑːtəd əˈkaʊntənt/ *nc* (*GB*) a qualified and registered accountant.

char·woman /'tʃɑːwʊmən/ *nc* ⇨ **char³.**

chary /'tʃeərɪ/ *adj* (**-ier, -iest**) cautious: *I'm chary of catching cold.*

char·ily /'tʃeərəlɪ/ *adv*

chase¹ /tʃeɪs/ *nc* an instance of chasing(1) a person or animal: *a long chase after the thief.*

chase² /tʃeɪs/ *v* **1** *vt,vi* **chase (after) sb/sth** to run after a person, animal, leaf etc in order to catch, overtake her, him or it: *Dogs like chasing rabbits.* **2** *vt* **chase sb/sth (away)** to run towards a person, animal, and shout etc to try to make her, him or it go away: *chasing the big dog away from the garden.* **3** *vi* (*informal*) to hurry; run: *The children chased out of the room.*

chasm /'kæzəm/ *nc* **1** a deep opening or crack in the ground. **2** (*fig*) a wide difference (of feeling or interests, between people, nations etc).

chas·sis /'ʃæsɪ/ *nc* (*pl* unchanged) the framework of a vehicle on which the body is fastened or built.

chaste /tʃeɪst/ *adj* (usually of young women) morally good and sexually pure. ⇨ **chastity.**

chas·ten /'tʃeɪsn/ *vt* (usually *passive*) (*formal*) to cause (a person) to be more sympathetic and understanding: *She was chastened by the experience of unemployment.*

chas·tise /tʃæˈstaɪz/ *vt* (*formal*) to blame, criticize, punish etc (a person) severely.

chas·tise·ment *nu*

chas·ti·ty /'tʃæstɪtɪ/ *nu* the state of being chaste.

chat¹ /tʃæt/ *nc* a friendly, informal talk: *I had a long chat with him.*

chat² /tʃæt/ *v* (**-tt-**) **1** *vi* to have a chat: *They were chatting (away) in the corner.* **2** *vt* **chat sb up** (*informal*) to talk to a person in order to win friendship: *chat up a girl at a party.*

'chat show *nc* (*informal*) a TV programme where celebrities are interviewed.

chat·ty *adj* (**-ier, -iest**) fond of chatting.

châ·teau /'ʃætəʊ/ *nc* (*pl* **—x/** -təʊz/) a castle or large country house in France.

chat·tel /'tʃætl/ *nc* (often *pl*) (*legal*) an article of personal movable property (e.g. a chair, a car).

chat·ter¹ /'tʃætə(r)/ *nu* **1** (the sound of) people talking quickly and informally together. **2** the similar sound of birds, machinery, teeth when cold etc.

chat·ter² /'tʃætə(r)/ *vi* **1** (of a person, people) to talk quickly or foolishly (and too much). **2** (of the cries of monkeys and some birds, of a person's teeth striking together from cold or fear) to make short, quick, sharp sounds.

'**chat·ter·box** *nc* (usually *derog*) a person who chatters(1).

chauf·feur /'ʃəʊfə(r)/ *nc* a man paid to drive a private car.

chau·vin·ism /'ʃəʊvɪnɪzəm/ *nu* too much support or enthusiasm for sexual superiority, a particular opinion etc.

'**chau·vin·ist** *nc* a person with such enthusiasm (esp for sexual superiority): *a male chauvinist.*

chau·vin·is·tic /ˌʃəʊvɪn'ɪstɪk/ *adj*

cheap¹ /tʃiːp/ *adj* (**—er, —est**) **1** costing little money: *cheap clothes/food; travel by the cheapest route.* Opp dear(3). **2** (*derog*) of poor quality: *cheap and nasty toys.* **3** (*derog*) (of behaviour etc) reducing a person's reputation because insincere, shameful etc: *cheap emotions/jokes. He played a cheap trick on her.*

cheap·ly *adv*: *behave cheaply.*

cheap·ness *nu*

cheap² /tʃiːp/ *adv* costing little money: *I got this dress cheap.*

cheap·en /'tʃiːpən/ *vt* **1** to cause (oneself, a person) to become cheap(2): *Don't cheapen yourself.* **2** to lower the price or quality of (goods).

cheat¹ /tʃiːt/ *nc* **1** (*derog*) a dishonest person (esp when playing games). **2** a dishonest or deceiving action.

cheat² /tʃiːt/ *v* **1** *vi* **cheat (at sth)** to act in a dishonest or deceitful way (e.g. when playing games): *cheat at cards; cheat in an exam.* **2** *vt* **cheat sb out of sth** to take something from a person dishonestly or deceitfully: *cheat him out of his inheritance.*

check¹ /tʃek/ *n* **1** *nc* **check (on sth)** an examination in order to learn whether something is correct: *a check on the labels for the parcels/on the equipment provided. The computer ran a check on the addresses of the major customers.* **a spot check** a quick one that is not planned. **2** *nc* **check (on sb/sth)** a person, thing, that prevents, controls, restrains another person, thing: *Wind acts as a check on speed.* **in check** under control: *It's often difficult to keep teenagers in check.* **3** *nc* (esp *US*) a receipt for articles (e.g. a bag, coat etc) left for a while in a shop, restaurant etc. **4** *nu* (*chess*) (a call stating) the position when one is directly threatening one's opponent's king. **5** *nu* (cloth with) a pattern of crossed lines of different colours. **6** *nc* (*US*) = cheque. **7** *nc* (*US*) a bill²(1) in a restaurant.

'**check·list** *nc* a list (of names, parts etc) to be identified when making a check(1).

'**check·point** *nc* a place (esp at a frontier) where officials, make a check(1) on vehicles, travellers' documents etc.

check² /tʃek/ *v* **1** *vt, vi* to examine (something) in order to learn whether it is correct: *check the bill; check the time.* ⇨ check on sb/sth. **2** *vt* to cause (an emotion, feeling etc) to stop: *He couldn't*

check his anger. ⇨ unchecked. **3** *vt, vi* (*chess*) to call, make, a check(4).

check in (at sth) to arrive and register at a hotel, airport. Hence '**check-in** *nc* a place at an airport etc where one checks in for a flight.

check sb/sth off to mark a person, item etc as correct, present, dealt with etc using a list: *check off their names.* ⇨ checklist.

check on sb/sth to examine, confirm, something, a person's health etc: *check on the score; check on the baby; check on a candidate.*

check out (of sth) to pay the bill, return keys etc and leave (a hotel). (*informal*) = check on sb/sth. ⇨ also check-out.

check sb/sth over (*informal*) = check on sb/sth.

check through sth to check(1) a list or series (to find errors, identify one item, person etc).

check up (on sb/sth) = check on sb/sth. ⇨ also check-up.

check-in /'tʃek ɪn/ *nc* ⇨ check in (at sth).

check·mate /'tʃekmeɪt/ *vt* (*chess*) to make a move that prevents the opponent's king from being moved away from a direct attack (and so win the game).

check-out /'tʃek aʊt/ *nc* a place in a supermarket where goods are paid for and wrapped.

check-up /'tʃek ʌp/ *nc* (esp) a medical examination.

Ched·dar /'tʃedə(r)/ *nu* (also *attrib*) a kind of hard cheese, very common in Britain: *Cheddar cheese*.

cheek¹ /tʃiːk/ *n* **1** *nc* either side of the face below the eye. **2** *nu* rudeness, esp when speaking to a parent, teacher, person in authority etc.

'**cheek·bone** *nc* the bone below the eye.

cheek·ily /-əlɪ/ *adv*

cheeky *adj* (**-ier, -iest**) (*derog*) rude, impolite.

cheek² /tʃiːk/ *vt* to speak rudely and without respect, esp to (a parent, teacher etc).

cheep /tʃiːp/ *vi, nc* (to make) a weak, high sound (as young birds do).

cheer¹ /tʃɪə(r)/ *n* **1** *nc* a shout of joy or encouragement: *give a loud cheer.* **2** *nu* the state of hope and gladness: *words of cheer* (i.e. of encouragement).

cheer² /tʃɪə(r)/ *v* **1** *vt, vi* to give (a person, team etc) shouts of joy, approval: *They cheered (her) loudly.* **2** *vt* **cheer sb/sth on** to give (a person, team etc) shouts of encouragement: *The crowd cheered him on as he ran the last 100 metres.* **3** *vi* **cheer up** to become happier: *She cheered up when he promised to telephone her.* **4** *vt* **cheer sb (up)** to cause a person to become happier, hopeful etc: *Your visit cheered us all (up).*

cheer·ing¹ /'tʃɪərɪŋ/ *adj* (*attrib*) causing a person to feel happier, encouraged etc: *cheering news.*

cheer·ing² /'tʃɪərɪŋ/ *nu* the sound of a cheer(1): *The cheering was heard a mile away.*

cheer·ful /'tʃɪəfəl/ *adj* **1** causing or suggesting happiness: *a cheerful room/smile.* **2** happy and contented: *cheerful workers/children.* Compare cheerless.

cheer·ful·ly /-fəlɪ/ *adv*

cheer·ful·ness *nu*

cheer·io /ˌtʃɪərɪ'əʊ/ *int* (*informal*) (used when parting) = goodbye.

cheer·less /'tʃɪəlɪs/ *adj* gloomy, miserable: *a wet*

and cheerless day. Compare cheerful.

cheery /'tʃɪərɪ/ *adj* (**-ier, -iest**) lively and happy: *a cheery smile/greeting.*

cheer·ily /-əlɪ/ *adv*

cheese /tʃiːz/ *n* **1** *nu* a kind of solid food made from milk curds. **2** *nc* a particular kind or shaped and wrapped portion of this.

'cheese·cake *nc,nu* (a kind of) food of cooked cheese and eggs between a biscuit base and fruit.

'cheese·cloth *nu* a kind of thin cotton cloth as put round some kinds of cheese or used to make shirts etc.

'cheese-paring *adj, nu* (*derog*) (showing) meanness with money.

cheesed off /ˌtʃiːzd 'ɒf/ *adj* (*pred*) (*sl*) bored (and feeling angry): *I'm cheesed off with this work.*

chee·tah /'tʃiːtə/ *nc* a kind of leopard.

chef /ʃef/ *nc* (*pl* —**s**) a chief cook in a hotel, restaurant etc.

chef-d'oeuvre /ˌʃeɪ 'dɜːvrə/ *nc* (*pl* **chefs-d'oeuvre** pronunciation unchanged) (*Fr*) a (person's) masterpiece.

chem·ical /'kemɪkl/ *adj* of, made by, chemistry: *chemical warfare* (e.g using poison gas etc). □ *nc* (often *pl*) a substance used in, or obtained using, chemistry.

chem·ical·ly /-klɪ/ *adv*

chem·ist /'kemɪst/ *nc* **1** an expert in chemistry. **2** a person, business, selling medical goods, toilet articles etc.

chem·is·try /'kemɪstrɪ/ *nu* the scientific study of how substances (*elements*) are made up, how they combine, how they act under different conditions.

cheque /tʃek/ *nc* a written order to a bank to pay money: *a cheque for £10. Can I pay by cheque?*

cross a cheque to draw lines across it so that it can only be paid into a bank account. (*US = check*)

'cheque-book *nc* a number of blank cheques fastened together.

'cheque card *nc* an identification for paying by cheque, cashing cheques etc.

cher·ish /'tʃerɪʃ/ *vt* (*formal*) **1** to care for (a person, animal, thing) lovingly: *cherishing her puppy.* **2** to keep alive (hope, ambition, memories etc): *For years she cherished the hope that her husband might still be alive.*

cher·ry¹ /'tʃerɪ/ *nc* (*pl* **-ies**) (also *attrib*) (a kind of tree with) a soft, small, round fruit that is red, yellow or black when ripe and with a hard seed in the middle: *cherry pie.*

cher·ry² /'tʃerɪ/ *adj, nu* bright red (colour).

cher·ub /'tʃerəb/ *nc* **1** (*pl* —**s**) (*art*) a small beautiful child with wings. **2** (*pl* **-ubim** /-bɪm/) one of the second highest order of angels.

chess /tʃes/ *nu* a board game for two players with sixteen pieces each (*chess men*), on a board with sixty-four squares (a *chess board*).

chest /tʃest/ *nc* **1** a large, strong (usually wooden) box with a lid, used for storing things. **2** the upper front part of the body, enclosed by the ribs, containing the heart and lungs. **get sth off one's chest** (*sl*) to say something that one is anxious to say.

,chest of 'drawers *nc* a piece of furniture with drawers for clothes.

chest·nut /'tʃesnʌt/ *n* (also *attrib*) **1** *nc,nu* (a kind of, wood of) a tree with smooth, bright reddish-brown nuts (some being edible): *a chestnut tree.* **2** *nu* the colour of the nut: *chestnut hair.*

chew¹ /tʃuː/ *nc* an act of chewing.

chew² /tʃuː/ *v* **1** *vt,vi* to move (food etc) about between the teeth in order to crush it: *Chew your food well before you swallow it.* **2** *vt* **chew sth over** (*informal*) to think about it carefully.

'chew·ing gum *nu* a sticky substance sweetened and flavoured for chewing.

chic /ʃiːk/ *adj* fashionable: *chic clothes; a chic woman.*

chick /tʃɪk/ *nc* a young bird, esp a young chicken.

chick·en¹ /'tʃɪkɪn/ *n* **1** *nc* a young bird, esp a hen. **(don't) count your chickens before they are hatched** (*saying*) (don't) be too hopeful of your chances of success etc. **2** *nu* (also *attrib*) its flesh as food: *chicken soup.* **3** *nc* (*sl; derog*) a scared, unwilling person.

'chicken-feed *nu* (*informal*) a small amount of money.

,chicken-'hearted *adj* (*derog*) not having courage.

'chicken-pox *nu* a disease producing red spots on the skin.

chick·en² /'tʃɪkɪn/ *vi* **chicken out (of sth)** (*informal*) to withdraw from, fail to do, an activity because of fear.

chic·ory /'tʃɪkərɪ/ *nu* (also *attrib*) **1** a kind of plant with long white leaves, used as a vegetable and for salad. **2** the root roasted and made into a powder (to be) used with coffee.

chide /tʃaɪd/ *vt,vi* (*pt* **chided** or **chid** /tʃɪd/, *pp* **chided** or **chidden** /'tʃɪdn/) (*formal*) to scold (a person); complain.

chief¹ /tʃiːf/ *adj* (no *comp*) **1** most important: *That's the chief thing to remember.* **2** (C- in names) highest in rank: *the Chief of Police.*

chief² /tʃiːf/ *nc* **1** a leader or ruler: *the chief of the group.* **2** a head of a department; highest official. **-in-chief** highest in rank: *the Commander-in-Chief.*

chief·ly /'tʃiːflɪ/ *adv* **1** above all: *Chiefly, I need someone to help in the shop on Saturdays.* **2** mostly: *Our products are chiefly sold outside Europe.* **3** mainly: *The failure was chiefly your responsibility.*

child /tʃaɪld/ *nc* (*pl* **children** /'tʃɪldrən/) **1** a young human being. **2** a son or daughter.

'child allowance *nc,nu* (*GB*) a payment by the government to parents of children under 16 or 18.

'child·birth *nu* the process of giving birth to a child.

'child·hood *nu* the state, period, of being a child.

'child·ish *adj* (*derog*) (of an adult) (behaving) like a child: *childish behaviour.*

'child·like *adj* innocent and loving as a child.

'child-minder *nc* a person who looks after a child (while the parents are working).

'child's play *nu* something very easily done.

'child-proof *adj* made so that a child cannot open, use, it: *child-proof caps on medicine bottles.*

chill¹ /tʃɪl/ *n* **1** *n sing* an unpleasant feeling of coldness: *There's quite a chill in the air this morning.* **2** *n sing* (*fig*) (something that causes) a depressed feeling: *The bad news cast a chill over the gathering.* **3** *nc* an illness caused by cold and damp with shivering of the body: *catch a chill.*

chil·ly *adj* (**-ier, -iest**) (**a**) a little cold: *feel chilly; a chilly morning.* (**b**) (*fig;* usually *attrib*) unfriendly: *a chilly welcome.*

chill² /tʃɪl/ *vt,vi* (to cause a person) to become cold or cool: *He was chilled to the bone/marrow* (= very cold).

chil·li /'tʃɪlɪ/ *nc,nu* (also *attrib*) the dried pod of a kind of red pepper, used to give a hot flavour: *chilli powder; chilli sauce.*

chime¹ /tʃaɪm/ *nc* (a series of notes sounded by) a tuned set of bells: *a chime of bells.*

chime² /tʃaɪm/ **1** *vt,vi* (to cause bells) to ring: *The bells are chiming.* **2** *vi* **chime in** to break in on the talk of others: *'I disagree' he chimed in.*

chim·ney /'tʃɪmnɪ/ *nc* (*pl* **—s**) **1** a structure in a roof etc through which smoke from a fire is carried away. **2** a narrow opening by which a rock face may be climbed.

'chimney-pot *nc* a pipe fitted to the top of a chimney(1).

'chimney-stack *nc* a group of chimneys.

'chimney-sweep(er) *nc* a man who sweeps soot from chimneys.

chimp /tʃɪmp/ *nc* (*informal*) = chimpanzee.

chim·pan·zee /ˌtʃɪmpæn'ziː/ *nc* a kind of African ape, smaller than a gorilla.

chin /tʃɪn/ *nc* the part of the face below the mouth. *a double chin* a fat chin with two folds. *keep one's chin up* to remain hopeful and happy.

'chin-strap *nc* the narrow band worn under the chin to keep a hat or helmet on.

china /'tʃaɪnə/ *nu* **1** baked and glazed fine white clay. **2** cups, saucers, plates etc made from this.

chink¹ /tʃɪŋk/ *nc* a narrow opening or crack.

chink² /tʃɪŋk/ *vt,vi, nc* (to make or cause) a sound of coins, glasses etc striking together.

chip¹ /tʃɪp/ *nc* **1** a small piece cut or broken off (from wood, stone, china, glass etc). *have a chip on one's shoulder* to feel miserable, quarrel etc because of feeling badly treated. **2** a long piece of potato: *fish and chips.* **3** a place (in china) from which a chip has come. **4** a flat plastic counter used as money (in gambling). **5** (*informal*) a very small electronic circuit: *a silicon chip.*

chip² /tʃɪp/ *v* (**-pp-**) **1** *vt,vi* (to cause china etc) to lose a small piece: *All the plates have chipped edges.* **2** *vt* to make (potatoes) into chips(2). **3** *vi* **chip in** (*informal*) (**a**) to interrupt. (**b**) to contribute money (to a fund).

chi·rop·odist /kɪ'rɒpədɪst/ *nc* an expert in the treatment of the feet.

chi·rop·ody /kɪ'rɒpədɪ/ *nu* the work of a chiropodist.

chirp /tʃɜːp/ *vi, nc* (to make) the short, sharp sound(s) of small birds or insects.

chirpy /'tʃɜːpɪ/ *adj* (**-ier, -iest**) (of a person) happy and cheerful.

chir·rup /'tʃɪrəp/ *vt, nc* (to make) a series of chirps.

chis·el /'tʃɪzl/ *nc* a kind of steel tool, used for shaping wood, stone or metal. □ *vt* (**-ll-**) **chisel** *(away) (at) sth* to cut or shape something using a chisel.

chit /tʃɪt/ *nc* (*informal*) a note of money owed.

chit-chat /'tʃɪt tʃæt/ *nu* informal conversation.

chiv·al·ry /'ʃɪvlrɪ/ *nu* good manners, esp qualities such as honour, courtesy, (towards women).

chiv·al·rous /'ʃɪvlrəs/ *adj*

chive /tʃaɪv/ *nc* (often *pl*) a kind of herb like a small leek, used to flavour food.

chiv·vy /'tʃɪvɪ/ *vt* (*pt,pp* **-ied**) *chivvy sb (along)* (*informal*) to encourage a person to be cheerful, finish a task etc by making frequent requests etc.

chlor·ine /'klɔːriːn/ *nu* a chemical substance (symbol Cl) used as a disinfectant etc.

chloro·form /'klɒrəfɔːm/ *nu* the thin, colourless liquid (formula $CHCl_3$) formerly given to make a person unconscious during a surgical operation.

chloro·phyll (*US:* **-phyl**) /'klɒrəfɪl/ *nu* (*biol*) the green colouring matter in leaves.

choc-ice /'tʃɒk aɪs/ *nc* a brick of ice-cream covered in chocolate.

chock-a-block /ˌtʃɒk ə 'blɒk/ *adv* (*informal*) very full; crowded: *The street was chock-a-block with people/cars.*

choc·olate /'tʃɒklət/ *n* (also *attrib*) **1** *nc,nu* a sweet substance (a bar, drink, powder) made from the crushed seeds of the cacao tree: *a bar of chocolate; a box of chocolates; chocolate cake.* **2** *nu* its dark brown colour.

choice¹ /tʃɔɪs/ *adj* (*attrib*) (**—r, —st**) (of fruit etc) of the best quality: *choice grapes; the choicest peaches.*

choice² /tʃɔɪs/ *n* **1** *nc* an act of choosing: *take your choice.* **2** *nu* the right or possibility of choosing: *I have no choice but to go.* **3** *nc* a variety from which to choose: *This shop has a large choice of bags.* **4** *nc* a person or thing chosen: *This is my choice.*

choir /kwaɪə(r)/ *nc* **1** a group of people trained to sing together. **2** the part of a church building for a choir.

choke¹ /tʃəʊk/ *nc* the valve in a petrol engine, used to control the intake of air.

choke² /tʃəʊk/ *v* **1** *vi* to be unable to breathe because of something in the windpipe: *choke over one's food.* **2** *vt* to stop the breathing of (a person, animal) by pressing the throat or by blocking the windpipe: *The chain was choking the dog.* **3** *vi* (*fig*) to be unable to breath because of strong emotion, tears etc: *be choked by/with anger.* **4** *vt* (often *passive*) to fill (something) partly or completely so that air, water etc cannot pass (easily): *a drain choked with leaves.*

choke sth back to keep tears, anger etc from appearing.

choke sth up to block a pipe etc (with dirt etc). *be choked up about sth* (*informal*) (of a person) to be very angry, upset.

choker /'tʃəʊkə(r)/ *nc* a kind of close-fitting necklace.

chol·era /'kɒlərə/ *nu* a kind of infectious and often fatal disease, common in hot countries.

choles·ter·ol /kə'lestrəl/ *nu* a substance found in animals and in food made from animal products (often associated with heart disease).

choose /tʃuːz/ *v* (*pt* **chose** /tʃəʊz/, *pp* **chosen** /'tʃəʊzn/) **1** *vt,vi* to pick out (a person, thing) from a large number; show what or which one wants by taking (something): *She took a long time to choose a new dress. You can choose one from*

the set. There's nothing/not much/little to choose between them (= They are equally good/bad etc).
⇨ also **beggar. 2** *vt* to decide (to do something): *He chose to stay at home.*

choosy /'tʃuːzɪ/ *adj* (**-ier, -iest**) (*informal; often derog*) (of a person) careful when choosing (and so difficult to please).

chop¹ /tʃɒp/ *nc* **1** a quick blow (as if) with a chopper. **2** a thick slice of meat with the bone in it.

chop² /tʃɒp/ *v* (**-pp-**) **1** *vt,vi* to cut (wood, food) into pieces using a chopper or knife: *chop wood; chop carrots into small pieces.* **2** *vt* **chop sth down** to use a chopper to cut a tree etc: *I'm going to chop that tree down.* **3** *vt* **chop sb/ sth up** (**a**) to cut meat, vegetables into small pieces. (**b**) (*informal*) to kill a person violently with an axe etc.

chop³ /tʃɒp/ *vi* (**-pp-**) **chop and change** to change one's decision, opinion etc often: *He's always chopping and changing.*

chop·per¹ /'tʃɒpə(r)/ *nc* a kind of heavy tool with a sharp edge for chopping meat, wood etc.

chop·per² /'tʃɒpə(r)/ *nc* (*informal*) a helicopter.

chop·py /'tʃɒpɪ/ *adj* (**-ier, -iest**) (of the sea) moving in short, irregular waves.

chop·sticks /'tʃɒpstɪks/ *n pl* (also *a pair of chopsticks*) sticks as used by Chinese and Japanese people for eating with.

chor·al /'kɔːrəl/ *adj* of, for, sung by or together with, a choir: *a choral society.*

chord /kɔːd/ *nc* **1** (*maths*) a straight line that joins two points on the circumference of a circle or the ends of an arc. **2** (*music*) a combination of two or more musical notes sounded together in harmony.

chore /tʃɔː(r)/ *nc* **1** a small task or piece of work, esp an ordinary everyday task in the home. **2** a small unpleasant duty.

chor·eogra·phy /ˌkɒrɪ'ɒɡrəfɪ/ *nu* the art of designing ballet and other dance for the stage.

chor·eogra·pher *nc* a person who designs ballet and other dancing.

chor·us¹ /'kɔːrəs/ *nc* (*pl* **—es**) **1** (music for) a group of singers. **2** (part of) a song for all to sing (after verses): *Mr White sang the verses and everybody joined in the chorus.* **3** a group of birds singing: *the dawn chorus.* **4** (*literature*) a group of actors, singers etc who comment on the action as part of a drama. **5** something said or cried by many people together: *a chorus of approval.*

chor·us² /'kɔːrəs/ *vt,vi* to sing, say, as a group.

chose /tʃəʊz/ *pt* of **choose**.

chosen /'tʃəʊzn/ *pp* of **choose**.

Christ /kraɪst/ *n* the title given to Jesus, the founder of Christianity.

christ·en /'krɪsn/ *vt* **1** to receive (a child) into the Christian church and give a name at the baptism. **2** to give a name to (a new ship when it is launched).

christen·ing *nc* a ceremony of baptism or naming a child.

Christen·dom /'krɪsndəm/ *n* (*dated*) all Christian people and Christian countries.

Chris·tian¹ /'krɪstʃən/ *adj* **1** of Jesus and his teaching. **2** of the religion, beliefs, churches etc based on this teaching.

Chris·tian² /'krɪstʃən/ *nc* a person believing in the religion of Christ.

'Christian name *nc* a name given at baptism.

Chris·ti·an·ity /ˌkrɪstɪ'ænətɪ/ *nu* the Christian religion.

Christ·mas /'krɪsməs/ *n* (also *Christmas Day*) the yearly celebration of the birth of Jesus Christ, 25 December.

'Christmas box *nc* a Christmas present, esp to a dustman, postman etc.

'Christmas card *nc* an illustrated card sent as a greeting to friends etc at Christmas.

ˌChristmas 'cracker *nc* a roll of brightly coloured paper which explodes harmlessly when the ends are pulled.

'Christmas present *nc* a present given at Christmas to a friend, relative etc.

'Christmas tree *nc* a small decorated evergreen tree set up at Christmas.

chro·mium /'krəʊmɪəm/ *nu* (*science*) an element (symbol Cr) used for covering taps etc and in stainless steel.

chro·mo·some /'krəʊməsəʊm/ *nc* (*science*) one of the tiny threads in every nucleus in animal and plant cells, carrying genes.

chron·ic /'krɒnɪk/ *adj* (of a disease or physical condition) continuing for a long time: *chronic rheumatism; a chronic illness.* Compare **acute²**.

chroni·cal·ly /-klɪ/ *adv*

chron·icle /'krɒnɪkl/ *vt, nc* (to make) a record of (events) in the order of their happening.

chrono·logi·cal /ˌkrɒnə'lɒdʒɪkl/ *adj* (arranged) in order of time: *Shakespeare's plays in chronological order* (= in the order in which they were written).

chrono·logi·cal·ly /-klɪ/ *adv*

chron·ol·ogy /krə'nɒlədʒɪ/ *nc* (*pl* **-ies**) an arrangement or list of events with dates.

chron·ometer /krə'nɒmɪtə(r)/ *nc* a kind of watch that keeps very accurate time.

chrysa·lis /'krɪsəlɪs/ *nc* (*pl* **—es**) **1** the form taken by an insect (e.g. a butterfly) between the time when it creeps or crawls (as a *larva*) and the time when it flies. **2** the sheath that covers it during this time.

chry·san·the·mum /krɪ'sænθəməm/ *nc* (*pl* **—s**) (the flower of) a kind of garden plant with large, colourful flowers in autumn.

chub·by /'tʃʌbɪ/ *adj* (**-ier, -iest**) fat and round: *chubby cheeks.*

chuck¹ /tʃʌk/ *nc* **1** a part of a lathe which grips the work to be operated on. **2** a part which grips the bit on a drill.

chuck² /tʃʌk/ *vt* (*informal*) **1** **chuck sb/sth (away/off/out)** to throw a person out of a place, something away etc: *chuck (away) rubbish; chuck a drunken man out of a pub* **2** **chuck sth in/up** to abandon, give up, a job etc: *chuck up one's job.*

chuckle /'tʃʌkl/ *vi, nc* (to make) a low, quiet laugh with closed mouth (showing satisfaction or amusement): *He was chuckling (away) to himself.*

chuf·fed /tʃʌft/ *adj* (usually *pred*) (*informal*) very pleased and proud.

chug /tʃʌɡ/ *vi, nc* (**-gg-**) (to make) the short explosive sound of an oil-engine or small petrol-engine running slowly: *The boat chugged along.*

chum /tʃʌm/ *nc* (*dated*) a close friend (esp used by boys).

chum·my *adj* (**-ier, -iest**) (*dated*) friendly.

chump /tʃʌmp/ *nc* **1** (also *attrib*) a thick piece of meat: *a chump chop*. **2** (*dated sl; derog*) a slightly foolish person.

chunk /tʃʌŋk/ *nc* a thick, solid piece or lump cut off a loaf, meat, pineapple etc.

chun·ky *adj* (**-ier, -iest**) short and thick.

church /tʃɜ:tʃ/ *n* **1** *nc* a building for public Christian worship. **2** *nu* a service in such a building: *What time does church begin?* **3** (the C-) an organization, profession, within the Christian religion: *the Church of England*. **enter the Church** to become a minister of religion.

'church-goer *nc* a person who goes to church regularly.

'church·yard *nc* a burial ground round a church. Compare cemetery.

churn¹ /tʃɜ:n/ *nc* **1** a tub in which cream is shaken or beaten to make butter. **2** a very large can in which milk is carried from the farm.

churn² /tʃɜ:n/ *v* **1** *vt* to make (butter) in a churn. **2** *vt* **churn sth (up)** to cause water etc to move about violently: *The ship's propellers churned up the waves.* **3** *vi* to be disturbed: *The accident made my stomach churn.* **4** *vt* **churn sth out** (*informal*) to produce writing, paintings etc quickly and without caring about quality, originality etc.

chute /ʃu:t/ *nc* **1** a long, narrow, steep slope down which things may slide: *an escape chute.* **2** a smooth, rapid fall of water over a slope.

chut·ney /'tʃʌtnɪ/ *nu* a hot-tasting mixture of fruit, peppers etc, eaten with curry, cold meat etc.

c.h.w. *abbr* constant hot water.

CIA /ˌsi: aɪ 'eɪ/ *abbr* (the —) (*US*) the Central Intelligence Agency.

cic·ada /sɪ'kɑ:də/ *nc* (*pl* **—s**) an insect with transparent wings, the male making a high noise.

CID /ˌsi: aɪ 'di:/ *abbr* (the—) (*GB*) Criminal Investigation Department.

ci·der /'saɪdə(r)/ *nc,nu* (a portion of) a drink made from fermented apple juice.

ci·gar /sɪ'gɑ:(r)/ *nc* a tight roll of tobacco leaves for smoking.

cig·ar·ette /ˌsɪgə'ret/ *nc* pieces of tobacco in a roll of thin paper for smoking.

ˌciga'rette-case *nc* a small flat case for carrying cigarettes.

ˌciga'rette-holder *nc* a tube in which a cigarette may be put for smoking.

ˌciga'rette-lighter *nc* a device for producing a small flame to light a cigarette.

C-in-C *abbr* Commander-in-Chief.

cinch /sɪntʃ/ *n sing* (*sl*) something that is certain, easy or sure: *It's a cinch!*

cin·der /'sɪndə(r)/ *nc* a small piece of coal, wood etc partly burned, no longer flaming and not yet ash.

cine-camera /'sɪnɪ kæmrə/ *nc* a kind of camera able to take moving pictures.

cine-projector /'sɪnɪ prədʒektə(r)/ *nc* a machine for showing films on a screen.

cin·ema /'sɪnəmə/ *n* **1** *nc* a place where films are shown (*US = movie house*). **2** *nu* (the—) films as an art form or industry (*US = the movies*).

cin·na·mon /'sɪnəmən/ *nu* (also *attrib*) a yellowish-brown spice from the inner bark of an E Indian tree, used in cooking: *cinnamon cakes.*

ci·pher /'saɪfə(r)/ *nc* **1** (a method of, key to) secret writing: *a message in cipher*. ⇨ decipher. **2** (*fig; derog*) a person or thing of no importance. **3**

(*tech*) the symbol 0, representing nought or zero.

cir·ca /'sɜ:kə/ *prep* (*Latin*) (abbr = c. or ca.) (used with dates) about: *born circa 150 BC*.

circle¹ /'sɜ:kl/ *nc* **1** (**a**) a space enclosed by a curved line, every point on which is the same distance from the centre. (**b**) the line enclosing this space. **2** a shape (of people, things) like a circle(1): *a circle of trees; standing in a circle.* Ⓝ *'Ring'* is also possible. **3** a group of seats in curved rows, between the highest part and the ground floor of a theatre or hall. **4** a group of people having the same or similar interests: *He has a large circle of friends.*

circle² /'sɜ:kl/ *vt,vi* to move, go round, draw, (something), in a circle: *The plane was circling (over) the city.*

cir·cuit /'sɜ:kɪt/ *nc* **1** a journey round a circle or closed route: *The circuit of the race track is three kilometres.* **2** (*electricity*) a closed path for an electrical current. ⇨ short-circuit.

cir·cu·itous /sɜ:'kju:ɪtəs/ *adj* (*formal*) going a long way round: *a circuitous route.*

cir·cu·lar¹ /'sɜ:kjʊlə(r)/ *adj* round or curved in shape; moving round: *a circular tour/trip* (= ending at the starting-point without visiting a place more than once).

cir·cu·lar² /'sɜ:kjʊlə(r)/ *nc* a printed advertisement, announcement etc of which many copies are made and distributed.

cir·cu·lar·ize (also **-ise**) /-aɪz/ *vt* to send circulars to (many people, homes etc).

cir·cu·late /'sɜ:kjʊleɪt/ *vt,vi* (to cause oneself, something etc) to go round a closed path; move from place to place freely: *Blood circulates through the body. Let's circulate among the other guests. I'll circulate this book among you.*

cir·cu·la·tion /ˌsɜ:kjʊ'leɪʃn/ *n* **1** *nu* the movement of the blood from and to the heart: *He has good/bad circulation.* **2** *nu* the state of being circulated: *When were British decimal coins put into circulation?* **3** *nc* a total quantity of copies of a newspaper or other periodical sold to the public.

cir·cum·cise /'sɜ:kəmsaɪz/ *vt* to remove the skin at the end of the sex organ of (a man).

cir·cum·ci·sion /ˌsɜ:kəm'sɪʒn/ *nc,nu*

cir·cum·fer·ence /sə'kʌmfərəns/ *nc* **1** a line that marks out a circle or other curved figure. **2** a distance round something: *The circumference of the earth is almost 25 000 miles or about 42 000 km.*

cir·cum·flex /'sɜ:kəmfleks/ *nc* a mark (ˆ) placed over a vowel to show how it is to be sounded (as in French *rôle*).

cir·cum·navi·gate /ˌsɜ:kəm'nævɪgeɪt/ *vt* to sail round (the world).

cir·cum·navi·ga·tion /ˌsɜ:kəmˌnævɪ'geɪʃn/ *nc,nu*

cir·cum·stance /'sɜ:kəmstəns/ *nc* **1** (usually *pl*) conditions, facts etc connected with an event or person: *Don't judge the crime until you know the circumstances.* **in/under the circumstances** such being the state of affairs. **under no circumstances** never. **2** a fact or detail: *He has plenty of money, which is a fortunate circumstance.* **3** (*pl*) (*dated*) financial condition: *His circumstances are poor.*

cir·cum·stan·tial /ˌsɜ:kəm'stænʃl/ *adj* (of evidence) based on details that suggest something strongly but do not provide direct proof.

cir·cum·vent /ˌsɜːkəmˈvent/ vt to find a way to get round (a law, rule etc).

cir·cum·ven·tion /ˌsɜːkəmˈvenʃn/ nu

cir·cus /ˈsɜːkəs/ nc (pl **—es**) **1** a (round or oval) place with seats on all sides, used for a show of performing animals, acrobats etc. **2** the people and animals giving such a show. **3** (C- in names) an open space where a number of streets meet: *Piccadilly Circus in London.*

cis·tern /ˈsɪstən/ nc a water tank, e.g. for a lavatory.

cite /saɪt/ vt **1** to give or mention (something) as an example (esp by quoting from a book to support an argument etc). **2** (*legal*) to call (a person) to appear in a law court: *be cited in divorce proceedings.*

ci·ta·tion /saɪˈteɪʃn/ nc (esp) a statement of an example of a brave or courageous act: *a citation for bravery in action.*

citi·zen /ˈsɪtɪzn/ nc **1** a person who lives in a town, not in the country: *the citizens of Paris.* **2** a person who has full rights in a State, either by birth or by gaining such rights: *immigrants who have become citizens of the United States.*

'citizen's band nc (abbr CB) a radio frequency for use by private citizens.

'citizen·ship nu the rights and duties of a citizen.

cit·ric /ˈsɪtrɪk/ adj **citric acid** acid from such fruits as lemons and limes. ⇨ citrous.

cit·ron /ˈsɪtrən/ nc (also *attrib*) (a tree with) a pale yellow fruit like a lemon but with a thicker skin.

cit·rous /ˈsɪtrəs/ adj of the citrus fruits.

cit·rus /ˈsɪtrəs/ nc (pl **—es**) (also *attrib*) (a fruit of) a tree including the lemon, lime, citron, orange and grapefruit: *citrus fruit.*

city /ˈsɪtɪ/ nc (pl **-ies**) **1** (also *attrib*) (C- in names) a large and important town: *Oxford City; the City Council.* **2** the people living in a city: *How did the city vote?* **3** (the C-) the oldest part of London, now the commercial and financial centre.

civ·ic /ˈsɪvɪk/ adj (usually *attrib*) of the official life and affairs of a town or a citizen: *civic pride; a civic centre* (where the official buildings, e.g. the town hall etc are grouped together).

civ·ics /ˈsɪvɪks/ n sing the study of city government, the rights and duties of citizens etc.

civ·il /ˈsɪvl/ adj **1** (*attrib*) (*no comp*) of human society or of individuals living together: *We all have civil rights and civil duties.* **2** politely helpful: *Can't you be more civil?* Opp uncivil.

civil de'fence nu the protection of civilians and property during a war.

civil diso'bedience nu a refusal to obey laws (as a non-violent protest against government policy).

civil engi'neering nu the design and building of roads, bridges, railways etc.

civil 'law nu the law dealing with private rights of citizens, not with crime.

civil 'marriage nc one without religious ceremony but recognized by law.

civil 'rights n pl the rights of a citizen to political, racial, legal and social freedom or equality.

civil 'servant nc a worker in the Civil Service.

Civil 'Service n (the —) all the government departments except the Navy, Army and Air

Force.

ci·vil·ly adv (*formal*) politely: *speak civilly to her.*

ci·vil·ian /sɪˈvɪlɪən/ adj, nc (of) a person who is not a member of the armed forces: *In modern wars civilians as well as soldiers are killed.*

ci·vil·ity /sɪˈvɪlətɪ/ nu (*formal*) politeness.

civi·liz·a·tion (also **-is·ation**) /ˌsɪvɪlaɪˈzeɪʃn/ n **1** nu the act, state, of civilizing or being civilized: *The civilization of mankind has taken thousands of years.* **2** nc a system or stage of social development: *the civilizations of ancient Egypt.* **3** nu people in society generally: *acts that horrify civilization.*

civi·lize (also **-ise**) /ˈsɪvɪlaɪz/ vt to bring (people) out of a lower social, cultural or economic state.

cl abbr **1** class. **2** centilitre(s).

clack /klæk/ vi, nc (to make) a short, sharp sound of flat objects struck together.

claim¹ /kleɪm/ n **1** nc an act of claiming something: *His claim to own the house is invalid.* **2** nc **claim (for sth)** a sum of money demanded, e.g. under an insurance agreement: *make/put in a claim (for a refund).* ⇨ no-claims bonus. **3** nu **claim (on sb/sth)** the right to ask for something from a person: *You have no claim on my sympathies.* **4** nc **claim (to sth)** something rightly claimed (e.g. land, a reputation etc): *Her only claim to fame is this one poem.* **lay claim to sth** to demand something as a right: *He laid claim to his father's land.*

claim² /kleɪm/ vt **1** to demand recognition of the fact that one is, owns or has a right to (something): *He claimed to be the owner of/claimed that he owned the land.* **claim damages** ⇨ damage¹(2). **2** to say that (something) is a fact: *He claimed to be the best basketball player in the school.* **3** to need, deserve, (a person's attention, time etc): *There are several matters that claim my attention.*

claim·ant /ˈkleɪmənt/ nc (*legal*) a person who makes a claim(2).

clair·voy·ance /kleəˈvɔɪəns/ nu the abnormal power of seeing in the mind what will happen or what exists beyond the normal range of the senses.

clair·voy·ant /kleəˈvɔɪənt/ nc a person with clairvoyance.

clam /klæm/ nc a kind of large shellfish, with a shell in two halves, used for food.

clam·ber /ˈklæmbə(r)/ vi to climb with difficulty using the hands and feet: *clamber up/over a wall.*

clam·my /ˈklæmɪ/ adj (**-ier**, **-iest**) damp and sticky to touch: *hot, clammy hands.*

clam·our (*US* = **clam·or**) /ˈklæmə(r)/ vi, nc, nu (to make) a loud confused noise or shout, esp of people complaining angrily or making a demand: *The foolish people were clamouring for war.*

clamp¹ /klæmp/ nc an apparatus used for holding things together tightly by means of a screw.

clamp² /klæmp/ v **1** vt to put a clamp on (something). **2** vi **clamp down (on sb/sth)** (*informal*) to put pressure on or against a person in order to stop something: *They clamped down on drug pushers.* Hence **'clamp-down** nc.

clan /klæn/ nc (*Scot*) a large family group.

clan·des·tine /klænˈdestɪn/ adj done secretly; kept secret: *a clandestine marriage.*

clang /klæŋ/ *vt,vi, nc* (to (cause something to) make) a loud ringing sound: *The clang of the fire bell alarmed the village.*

clang·er /'klæŋə(r)/ *nc* **drop a clanger** (*informal*) to make an indiscreet remark.

clank /klæŋk/ *vi,vt, nc* (to make) a ringing sound (not so loud as a clang): *prisoners clanking their chains.*

clan·nish /'klænɪʃ/ *adj* showing family closeness, esp by supporting one another against other people.

clap[1] /klæp/ *nc* **1** the sound, action, of bringing the open hands together. **2** a loud noise (of thunder).

clap[2] /klæp/ *v* (**-pp-**) **1** *vt,vi* to show one's approval (of a person) by striking the palms of the hands together; do this as a signal (e.g. to summon a waiter etc): *When the violinist finished, the audience clapped (her) for five minutes.* **2** *vt* to hit (a person) lightly with the open hand in a friendly way: *I clapped him on the back.* **clap eyes on sb** ⇨ eye[1](1). **3** *vt* to put (a person) (into prison) quickly or energetically: *He was clapped in prison.*

clapped out *adj* **1** (*derog*) (of an engine etc) old and broken. **2** (of a person) very tired.

clap·ping /'klæpɪŋ/ *nu* (the sound of) applause.

clar·et /'klærət/ *nu* (also *attrib*) **1** (a kind of) red wine from Bordeaux. **2** its dark red colour.

clar·ify /'klærɪfaɪ/ *vt,vi* (*pt,pp* **-ied**) **1** (to cause a statement etc) to become clear or intelligible. ⇨ clarity(2). **2** (*tech*) to make (a liquid) free from impurities.

clari·fi·ca·tion /,klærɪfɪ'keɪʃn/ *nu*

clari·net /,klærɪ'net/ *nc* a kind of wooden musical instrument, with finger-holes and keys.

clari·net·tist *nc* a person who plays the clarinet.

clar·ity /'klærətɪ/ *nu* **1** the state of being easy to see through. **2** the state of being easy to understand, hear etc: *clarity of thought.* ⇨ clarify(1).

clash[1] /klæʃ/ *nc* **1** a sound of clashing(1). **2** an instance of clashing(4): *a clash of colours/opinions.*

clash[2] /klæʃ/ *v* **1** *vi,vt* (to cause things) to make a loud, confused noise (as when metal objects strike together): *The cymbals clashed.* **2** *vi* to come suddenly together in conflict: *The two armies clashed outside the town.* **3** *vi* **clash (with sth)** (of an event) to interfere (with another) because it is (to be) at the same time on the same date: *It's a pity the two concerts clash because I want to go to both.* **4** *vi* **clash (with sb/sth)** to be in disagreement (with a person, thing): *I clashed with him/We clashed at the last meeting of the Council. The (colours of the) curtains clash with (the colours of) the carpet. They clash.*

clasp[1] /klɑːsp/ *nc* **1** a metal device used to fasten together two things or two parts of one thing (e.g. the ends of a necklace). **2** a firm hold (with the fingers or arms).

clasp[2] /klɑːsp/ *v* **1** *vt,vi* to hold (a person, thing) tightly or closely: *They were clasped in each other's arms. He stood with his hands clasped behind him.* **2** *vt* to fasten (something) with a clasp(1): *She clasped the watch on his wrist.*

class[1] /klɑːs/ *n* **1** *nu* (also *attrib*) the system of ranks in society: *It will be difficult to abolish class.*

Is the economy based on the class struggle? **2** *nc* the people in one of these ranks: *Should society be divided into upper, middle and lower classes?* **3** *nc* a group of people taught together; their course of teaching. **4** *nc* a grade or merit after examination: *take a first-/second-class degree.* **5** *nc* a group having qualities of the same kind: *As an actor she is not in the same class as Sarah* (= is not as good as Sarah). **6** *nu* (*informal*) good style (of manners, behaviour): *There's not much class about her. He has class.* **7** *nc* (*US*) a group of pupils or students who enter school or college in the same year and leave together: *the class of 1986.*

'class-mate *nc* a friend in the same class(3).

'class-room *nc* a room where a class(3) is taught.

class·less *adj* without distinctions of class(1): *Is a classless society possible?*

class[2] /klɑːs/ *vt* **class sb (as sth)** to describe a person as being the type, quality mentioned: *Would you class him as a fool/as unintelligent?*.

clas·sic[1] /'klæsɪk/ *adj* **1** of the highest quality; having a recognized high value or position: *It's the classic cure.* **2** of (the standard of) ancient Greek and Latin literature, art and culture. **3** famous because of a long history: *The Derby* (horse-race) *is a classic event.* **4** (of fashion) traditional: *a classic suit.*

clas·sic[2] /'klæsɪk/ *nc* **1** a writer, artist, book etc of the highest class: *John Milton is a classic. 'Robinson Crusoe' is a classic.* **2** an ancient Greek or Latin writer. **3** (the —s) (literature of) the ancient languages of Greece and Rome. **4** (*pl*) a university course in the classics(3): *He read classics at Oxford.* **5** a classic(3) event.

clas·si·cal /'klæsɪkl/ *adj* **1** in, of, the best (esp ancient Greek and Roman) art and literature: *a classical education.* **2** recognized for a very long time as being of a high intellectual standard: *classical literature/authors/artists.*

,classical 'music *nu* the traditional form (from the 18th century) of symphonies, sonatas, concertos etc.

class·si·cal·ly /-klɪ/ *adv*

clas·si·cist /'klæsɪsɪst/ *nc* **1** a follower of classic style. **2** a classical scholar: *Milton was a classicist.*

clas·si·fi·ca·tion /,klæsɪfɪ'keɪʃn/ *n* **1** *nu* the process of classifying or being classified. **2** *nc* a group into which something is put.

clas·si·fy 'klæsɪfaɪ/ *vt* (*pt,pp* **-ied**) to arrange (items) in categories or groups: *In a library, books are usually classified by subjects.*

clas·si·fied *adj* (**a**) arranged in categories or groups: *classified advertisements.* (**b**) officially secret: *classified information.* Opp unclassified.

clat·ter /'klætə(r)/ *vi, nc,nu* (to make) the continuous repeated noise (as of metal things falling or knocking together): *the clatter of cutlery. Pots and pans were clattering in the kitchen.*

clause /klɔːz/ *nc* **1** (*gram*) a part of a sentence with its own subject and predicate, esp one doing the work of a noun, adjective or adverb. ⇨ adjectival/adverbial/conditional/main clause. **2** (*legal*) a complete paragraph in an agreement, legal document etc.

claus·tro·pho·bia /,klɔːstrə'fəʊbɪə/ *nu* the abnormal fear of being in confined places (e.g. a lift).

clav·icle /ˈklævɪkl/ nc (anat) the collar-bone.

claw¹ /klɔ:/ nc **1** one of the pointed nails on the feet of some animals and birds; a foot with such nails. **2** (pl) the pincers of a shellfish (e.g. a lobster). **3** an instrument or device like a claw (e.g. a steel hook on a machine for lifting things).

claw² /klɔ:/ vt,vi to get hold of (soil, clothes etc), pull, scratch (as if) with claws.

clay /kleɪ/ nu (also attrib) **1** stiff, sticky earth that becomes hard when baked: clay soil. **2** a similar material used to make bricks, pots, earthenware etc: clay pots.

clean¹ /kli:n/ adj (—er, —est) **1** free from dirt: clean hands. Wash it clean. Opp dirty¹(1). **2** (attrib) not yet used: Give me a clean sheet of paper. **3** moral; free from evil: a clean joke. He has a clean record (= is not known to have done wrong). **4** even; regular; with a smooth edge or surface: A sharp knife makes a clean cut. **5** (attrib) not having dirty habits: a clean pet.
,clean-'cut adj clearly outlined: the clean-cut lines of the car's design.
,clean-'shaven adj with hair of the face shaved off.

clean² /kli:n/ adv completely; entirely: I clean forgot about it. **come clean** to make a full confession.

clean³ /kli:n/ n sing an act of cleaning something: give it a good clean.

clean⁴ /kli:n/ vt,vi (to cause a person, thing etc) to become clean(1): I must have this suit cleaned ⇨ dry-clean.
clean sth down to clean something by brushing or wiping it: clean down the walls.
clean sb out of sth (informal) to win, take, all of a person's money, stock etc: They've cleaned me out of bread.
clean sth out to clean the inside of something: clean out the saucepan. It's time you cleaned out your bedroom.
clean up (a) to make an area clean or tidy: You should always clean up after a picnic (= collect litter, empty bottles etc). (b) (informal) to win or take all the money. Hence 'clean-up nc (a) the process of cleaning up(a). (b) a large profit. **clean (oneself) up** to wash, change one's clothes etc: clean oneself up after a football match. **clean sth up** (informal) to get rid of criminal and immoral elements etc in a place: The mayor has decided to clean up the city.

clean·er /ˈkli:nə(r)/ nc **1** a person who cleans offices, roads etc. **2** a tool, machine, business, substance etc for cleaning: a vacuum cleaner; a household cleaner for floors and walls.

clean·ly¹ /ˈklenlɪ/ adj (-ier, -iest) (formal) having clean personal habits.
clean·li·ness nu.

clean·ly² /ˈkli:nlɪ/ adv exactly, sharply; neatly: He cut the cake cleanly.

cleanse /klenz/ vt **1** to make (something) thoroughly clean: cleansing a cut/graze. **2** (formal) to make (something) pure: cleanse the heart of/from sin.

clean-up /ˈkli:n ʌp/ nc ⇨ clean up.

clear¹ /klɪə(r)/ (—er, —est) **1** (attrib) easy to see through: clear glass; the clear water of a mountain lake. ⇨ clarity(1). **2** (attrib) without clouds: a clear sky/light. **3** without obstacles: Is the road clear? **4** (of sounds etc) easily heard; distinct: the clear note of a bell. ⇨ clarity(2). **5** (of the skin) without spots etc. **6** free from doubt or difficulty: It was clear (to everyone) that the war would not end quickly. Opp unclear. **make oneself/one's meaning/it clear** to make oneself understood. ⇨ clarity(2). **7** certain: I am not clear as to what you expect me to do. Opp unclear. **8** (pred) free: I wish I were clear of debt. **9** (attrib) complete: for three clear days. **10** (attrib) after all payments etc: a clear profit of £5.
,clear-'headed adj able to think well (because not tired, drunk or drugged).
,clear-'sighted adj able to see well.
'clear·way nc (GB) a section of a main road on which vehicles must not stop or park.

clear² /klɪə(r)/ adv **1** easily heard, seen, understood etc: speak loud and clear. **2** completely: The prisoner got clear away. **3** without touching; at or to a distance: Stand clear (of the gates)! He jumped ten centimetres clear of the bar. ⇨ also steer²(2).
clear·ness nu the state of being clear: clearness of vision.

clear³ /klɪə(r)/ nu **in the clear** (informal) free from suspicion, danger etc.

clear⁴ /klɪə(r)/ v **1** vi to become free of clouds, traffic or other obstacles: The sky/road cleared. **2** vt to remove, get rid of, (what is unwanted or unwelcome): clear the snow off the streets; clear the streets of snow; clear oneself (of a charge) (= prove one's innocence). This will clear your headache. **clear the air** ⇨ air¹(1). **clear the table** ⇨ table¹(1). **clear one's throat** ⇨ throat(2). **3** vt to get past or over (something) without touching it: Our car only just cleared the gatepost. **4** vt to make (an amount) as a gain or profit: clear £50. **5** vt to get (a ship or its cargo) free by doing what is necessary (e.g. signing papers, paying dues) on entering or leaving a port: clear goods through customs.
clear away (of clouds etc) to be no longer present. **clear sth away** to take away things no longer needed: clear away the plates.
clear off (usually imperative) to go away: This is my garden, so clear off! **clear sth off** to complete payment of money owed: clear off a debt.
clear off sth to leave a place quickly: Clear off my land!
clear out (of a place) (informal) to go away; leave: The police are after you, you'd better clear out! **clear sth out** to remove unwanted things from something: clear out a cupboard. Hence 'clear-out nc.
clear up to become clear: The weather/The sky is clearing up. **clear sth up** (a) to put things, a place etc in order; make it tidy: Who's going to clear up the mess? (b) to solve a mystery etc: clear up a misunderstanding.

clear·ance /ˈklɪərəns/ n **1** nc the act of clearing up, removing unwanted things, making something tidy. **2** nc,nu (a) free space, esp for moving past: There is not much/not enough clearance for large lorries passing under this bridge. Compare clearing.

clear-cut /ˌklɪə ˈkʌt/ adj (esp) easily understood and certain: a clear-cut decision.

clear·ing /ˈklɪərɪŋ/ nc an open space from which

trees have been cleared in a forest.

'clearing bank *nc* (*GB*) a major bank able to use the clearing-house.

'clearing-house *nc* the office at which banks exchange cheques etc and settle accounts, the balance being paid in cash.

clear·ly /'klɪəlɪ/ *adv* **1** so as to be (easily) understood: *speak/see clearly*. **2** without doubt: *Clearly, we must review our plans.* '*Was he mistaken?'—'Clearly'*.

clear·out /'klɪər aʊt/ *nc* ⇨ clear sth out.

cleav·age /'kliːvɪdʒ/ *n* **1** *nc,nu* (the direction of) a split or division. **2** *nc* (*informal*) the division between a woman's breasts.

cleave /kliːv/ *vt* (*pt* **clove** /kləʊv/, **cleft** /kleft/ or **cleaved** /kliːvd/, *pp* **cleft** or **cloven** /'kləʊvn/) (*dated*) to cut (something) into two (with a blow from a heavy axe etc): *cleave a block of wood in two.* Ⓝ '*Split'* is the usual word. **be in a cleft stick** ⇨ stick¹(1).

clef /klef/ *nc* (*music*) the symbol placed at the beginning of a stave to show the pitch of the notes.

cleft /kleft/ *pt* of cleave.

,cleft 'sentence *nc* (*gram*) a sentence using *it* or *what* to emphasize the subject or object, as in '*It wasn't you who telephoned, surely?' 'What I said was that I don't mind.'*

clem·en·cy /'klemənsɪ/ *nu* (*formal*) **1** mercy. **2** mildness (of temper or weather).

clem·ent /'klemənt/ *adj* (*formal*) **1** showing mercy. **2** (of the weather, a person's temper) mild.

clench /klentʃ/ *vt* to press or clasp (something) firmly together: *clench one's teeth; a clenched fist.*

cler·gy /'klɜːdʒɪ/ *nu* (the —) the priests or ministers of the Christian Church.

'clergy·man *nc* a member of the clergy.

cler·ic /'klerɪk/ *nc* (*dated*) = clergyman.

cleri·cal /'klerɪkl/ *adj* **1** (*attrib*) of the clergy: *clerical dress; a clerical collar.* **2** of, for, made by, a clerk or clerks(1): *a clerical error* (= one made when typing or writing).

clerk /klɑːk/ *nc* **1** a person employed in an office etc to keep records and accounts, copy letters etc: *a bank clerk.* **2** (often C-) an officer in charge of official records etc: *the Clerk to the Court.*

clev·er /'klevə(r)/ *adj* (**—er**, **—est**) **1** quick at learning and understanding things: *She's so/very clever. He's clever at arithmetic.* **2** (of things done) showing ability and skill: *a clever speech/book/ idea.* **3** thinking quickly; cunning: *clever at finding excuses.*

clev·er·ly *adv*

clev·er·ness *nu*

cli·ché /'kliːʃeɪ/ *nc* an expression that is or has been used too much (and now has no meaning or usefulness) e.g. '*Tomorrow is another day'*.

click¹ /klɪk/ *vt,vi, nc* (to make) a short, light sound (like that of a key turning in a lock): *The door clicked shut.*

click² /klɪk/ *vi* (*informal*) to be understood; understand: *His jokes didn't click with the audience. Suddenly I clicked.*

click³ /klɪk/ *vi* (*informal*) (of two people) to become friends easily.

cli·ent /'klaɪənt/ *nc* **1** a person who gets help or advice from any professional person: *a successful*

lawyer with hundreds of clients. **2** a customer (in a hairdresser's, beauty salon etc).

cli·en·tele /ˌkliːənˈtel/ *nu* customers: *His clientele is usually rich.*

cliff /klɪf/ *nc* a steep face of rock, esp at the edge of the sea.

'cliff-hanger *nc* an episode in a story or contest with an uncertain end, leaving the reader or spectator feeling excited, curious etc.

cli·mac·tic /klaɪˈmæktɪk/ *adj* forming a climax.

cli·mate /'klaɪmɪt/ *n* **1** *nc,nu* the weather conditions of a place or area over a (long) period: *A drier climate would be good for her health.* Compare weather. **2** *nu* (*fig*) a current condition: *the economic/political climate.*

cli·mat·ic /klaɪˈmætɪk/ *adj* (*attrib*) of, concerning, climate: *a climatic chart/region.*

cli·mati·cal·ly /-klɪ/ *adv*

cli·max /'klaɪmæks/ *nc* (*pl* **—es**) **1** the most interesting, intense, violent, energetic etc part (of an event, game, speech, storm etc). **2** (*literature*) the highest point of interest in a drama or story (often the turning-point of the plot) such as the discovery of the truth, the action that directly causes the tragedy etc. ⇨ climactic.

climb¹ /klaɪm/ *nc* an instance of climbing: *a climb up a mountain.*

climb² /klaɪm/ *v* **1** *vt,vi* to go or get down, over, up etc (a tree, wall, rope, stairs, mountain etc). **2** *vi* (of aircraft) to go higher. **3** *vi* to rise by effort in social rank, position etc. **4** *vi* **climb down** (*fig*) to admit that one has been mistaken, unreasonable etc. Hence **'climb-down** *nc.* **5** *vi* (of plants) grow upwards.

climb·er *nc* (**a**) a person who climbs mountains etc. (**b**) a climbing plant.

climb-down /'klaɪm daʊn/ *nc* ⇨ climb²(4).

clinch¹ /klɪntʃ/ *nc* an instance of clinching(2).

clinch² /klɪntʃ/ *v* **1** *vt* to settle (a bargain, an argument) completely: *clinch a deal. That clinches the argument.* **2** *vi* to put one or both arms round a person's body: *The boxers/lovers clinched.*

cling /klɪŋ/ *vi* (*pt,pp* **clung** /klʌŋ/) (often **cling to sth**) **1** to hold tightly: *They clung together when the time came to part.* **2** to keep something firmly in one's head: *They clung to a hope of being rescued. He clung to his ambition to become an actor.* **3** to keep close (to something): *He clung to the walls to avoid being seen.*

cling-film /'klɪŋ fɪlm/ *nu* (also **cling-wrap** /'klɪŋ ræp/-) a very thin plastic material used to cover or wrap food to keep it fresh: *Wrap the sandwiches in cling-film.*

clin·ic /'klɪnɪk/ *nc* **1** (a part of) a hospital or small institution where medical advice and treatment are given. **2** the teaching given to medical students in a clinic(1). **3** a medical department for the purpose mentioned: *an ante-natal clinic.*

clini·cal /'klɪnɪkl/ *adj*

,clinical 'death *nu* a condition when major areas of the brain are no longer in operation but some bodily functions can continue (only with machinery).

,clinical ther'mometer *nc* one used to find the body temperature.

clink /klɪŋk/ *vt,vi, nc* (to make) the sound of small bits of metal, glass etc knocking together:

the clink of keys/glasses.

clip[1] /klɪp/ *nc* a small metal etc device used for keeping papers etc together.

clip[2] /klɪp/ *nc* **1** an instance of clipping[4](1): *give her fringe a clip.* **2** (*informal*) a quick hit or slap: *a clip on the jaw/round the face.*

clip[3] /klɪp/ *vt* (**-pp-**) *clip sth (together)* to use a clip[1] to fasten papers etc.

clip[4] /klɪp/ *vt* (**-pp-**) **1** to cut (bushes, hair etc) with scissors or shears: *clip a hedge.* ⇨ clippers. **2** (*informal*) to give (a person) a quick hit or slap: *The man clipped him on the chin.*

clip·ping *nc* (esp) an article, picture etc cut from a newspaper etc.

clip·pers /'klɪpəz/ *n pl* (also *a pair of clippers*) an instrument used for clipping[4](1): *hair-clippers; hedge-clippers.*

clique /kli:k/ *nc* (often *derog*) a group of people with the same interests (who often discourage others from joining them).

cliqu·ish /'kli:kɪʃ/ *adj*

cloak[1] /kləʊk/ *nc* **1** a loose outer article of clothing without sleeves. **2** (*fig*) something used to hide or keep secret an activity: *under the cloak of darkness.*

'cloak·room *nc* a place where coats etc may be left (e.g. in a school, theatre).

cloak[2] /kləʊk/ *vt* (often *pp*) to hide (thoughts, intentions etc): *cloaked in secrecy/mystery.*

clock[1] /klɒk/ *nc* an instrument (not carried or worn like a watch) for measuring and showing the time. *round the clock* all day and all night.

'clock-face *nc* the front of a clock showing figures marking the hours etc.

'clock-tower *nc* a tall structure (forming part of a building, e.g. a church) with a clock high up on an outside wall.

'clock·wise *adv* in the same direction as the movements of the hands of a clock. Opp anti-clockwise.

'clock·work *adj* operated by wheels and springs like a clock: *a clockwork toy.* *like clockwork* as planned and without trouble: *The meeting went like clockwork.*

clock[2] /klɒk/ *vt* to do something (e.g. run a race, carry out a task) and measure the time taken: *He clocked 9·6 seconds for the 100 metres race.*

clock in/on to record the time of arrival at work: *We clocked in/on at 7 a.m.*

clock off/out to record the time of departure from work: *We clocked off/out at 4 p.m.*

clock up sth to record a distance travelled during a journey: *We clocked up 7000 km during the trip.*

clod /klɒd/ *nc* a lump (of earth or soil).

clog[1] /klɒg/ *nc* a shoe with a wooden sole or carved out of a block of wood.

clog[2] /klɒg/ *v* (**-gg-**) **1** *vt,vi* (often *passive*) (to cause something) to become blocked with dirt, grease etc so that movement, flow of liquid etc is difficult or prevented: *The vacuum cleaner is clogged (up) with dirt.* **2** *vt* (*fig*) to cause (one's mind) not to think clearly: *Don't clog your memory with useless facts.*

clois·ter /'klɔɪstə(r)/ *nc* a covered walk, usually on the sides of an open courtyard, with a wall on the outer side and columns or arches on the inner side.

clois·ter·ed /'klɔɪstəd/ *adj* (*formal*) away from active social life or influences: *be cloistered in the country.*

close[1] /kləʊs/ *adj* (**—r, —st**) **1** (*pred*) *close (to sb/sth)* at a short distance: *The house isn't very close (to my school). It's closer to the railway station.* ⓝ 'Near' is also possible but 'close' suggests a shorter distance away. Compare: *The house is close to the beach and It is near (to) the coast. close at hand* ⇨ hand[1](1). *at close quarters* ⇨ quarter[1](8). **2** (*attrib*) directly connected by birth: *a close relative* (e.g. a sister, first cousin). ⓝ 'Near' is also possible. Compare distant(2). **3** loved and trusted: *She's my closest friend. We're very close* (i.e. love and trust each other). **4** (in contests, games etc) each side having nearly the same (result): *a close contest/election/result.* ⇨ also call[1](1), second[5](1), shave[1], thing(4). **5** (of the atmosphere, weather) uncomfortably hot, damp, stale etc: *a close atmosphere/room.* **6** (*attrib*) thorough and concentrated: *On closer examination I found the faulty connection. I made a close study of the text. Pay close attention to what she says.* ⇨ also watch[1](2). **7** (usually *attrib*) not very different from the original, base, model etc: *a close translation; a close resemblance.* **8** (*pred*) not talking about one's private affairs; secretive: *She's so close about her boyfriends. He was close about his duties in the Royal Navy.*

,close-'fitting *adj* (of clothing) fitting the body tightly: *close-fitting trousers.*

close·ly *adv: Examine it closely. It was a closely fought contest* (⇨ close[1](4)). *That's a closely guarded secret* (⇨ close[1](8)).

close·ness *nu*

close[2] /kləʊs/ *adv* very near (in position): *sit close against the wall; following close behind; come closer together; live close to the river.* *close by* very near: *They live close by.* *close on* . . . very nearly . . . : *We have close on 50 members.* *close to* not far away: *Close to, the painting looks like thousands of small dots.* *be close to sth* (a) to be almost (a particular time): *It's close to midnight.* (b) to be about to do (something): *be close to death* (= dying).

,close-'set *adj* positioned close together: *close-set eyes.*

'close-up *nc* (a) a photograph taken near to an object etc and showing it in large scale. (b) a close view (using a microscope or telescope).

close[3] /kləʊs/ *nc* (C- in names) **1** a square surrounded by buildings as part of a cathedral, college etc. **2** an area of housing with short streets used only by residents.

close[4] /kləʊz/ *nu* the end (of a period of time): *at the close of (the) day; towards the close of the century.* *draw to a close* to come to an end: *The evening was drawing to a close.*

close[5] /kləʊz/ *v* **1** *vt,vi* (to cause something) to be put in a position of being covered or blocked, of having the edges together etc: *This box/The lid doesn't close properly. Please close the door. I closed the curtains/my eyes.* ⇨ also eye[1](1). ⓝ 'Shut' is also possible, as in *Please shut the window* but 'close' is preferred in situations using the form *be . . . ing* (the continuous tense), as in *The park gates are closing* and for situations using slow movement, as in *The electrically operated doors in the supermar-*

ket close automatically. 'Shut' is used to show anger or to be rude, as in *Shut that door! Oh, shut your face!* **2** *vt,vi* (to cause a business, place etc) to stop giving a service: *The shops are closing. This road is closed to traffic during repairs.* **3** *vt,vi* (to cause a meeting, performance etc) to come to an end: *close a discussion/meeting. The concert closed with an encore by Paul McCartney.* **4** *vt* to complete (an agreement etc) successfully: *close a deal for the supply of raw materials.*

close down (**a**) (of a business, factory etc) to stop production, trading etc completely: *During the 1970's in Europe many businesses closed down.* (**b**) (of a radio or TV station) to stop broadcasting: *BBC television is now closing down until tomorrow.* Hence **'close-down** *nc.*

close in (*formal*) (of day) to become shorter: *It's autumn and the days are closing in.* **close in (on sb/sth)** (**a**) to come near(er) a person, army etc and attack: *The enemy is closing in on us.* (**b**) to cover a person, place etc on all sides in an unpleasant way: *Darkness closed in. Winter closed in on the explorers.*

close up (of a flower) to close(1) the petals slowly (e.g. at night). **close (sth) up** to close(2) (a shop, office etc) (e.g. for the night): *You can go—I'll close up (the shop) tonight.* ⇨ *close-up* at close².

close-down /'kləʊz daʊn/ *nc* ⇨ close down.

closed /kləʊzd/ *adj* **1** having been closed(1): *a closed door.* **2** (*attrib*) for some people only: *a closed meeting* (e.g. for members only).

,closed 'book *n sing* (*informal*) (**a**) something that is impossible to understand: *Modern physics is a closed book to me.* (**b**) an issue that has been decided and cannot now be reconsidered.

,closed 'circuit *nc* (*electricity*) one that is complete and allows voltage to flow.

,closed-circuit television *nu* a TV system using telephone lines or cables.

,closed 'couplet *nc* (*literature*) two lines of rhyming verse containing a complete statement.

,closed 'shop *nc* a business, industry etc where employment is given to union members only.

clos·et /'klɒzɪt/ *nc* (now chiefly *US*) a small room for storing things.

close-up /'kləʊs ʌp/ *nc* ⇨ close².

clos·ing /'kləʊzɪŋ/ *adj* (*attrib*) **1** last: *his closing remarks.* **2** marking the end: *When's closing time?* Compare opening¹.

clo·sure /'kləʊʒə(r)/ *nc,nu* an act of closing (esp closing down a business etc): *pit closures.*

clot¹ /klɒt/ *nc* **1** a semi-solid lump formed from liquid, esp blood. **2** (*sl; derog*) a fool.

clot² /klɒt/ *vt,vi* (**-tt-**) (to cause blood, food etc) to form into clots: *clotted cream.*

cloth /klɒθ/ *n* **1** *nu* material made by weaving cotton, wool etc: *three metres of cloth.* **2** *nc* a piece of this material for a special purpose: *a dish-cloth.*

clothe /kləʊð/ *vt* to put on, supply, clothes for (a person): *He has to work hard in order to clothe his family.*

clothes /kləʊðz/ *n pl* (also *attrib*) coverings for a person's body: *baby-clothes; a clothes-brush.* ⇨ also bedclothes. **in plain clothes** (esp of the police) in ordinary clothes, not in uniform.

'clothes-line *nc* = washing-line.

'clothes-peg *nc* one used for fastening clothes to a washing-line.

cloth·ing /'kləʊðɪŋ/ *nu* (also *attrib*) clothes: *articles of clothing; a clothing allowance.*

cloud¹ /klaʊd/ *n* **1** *nc,nu* (a mass of) white or grey water vapour floating in the sky: *The top of the mountain was hidden under cloud.* **every cloud has a silver lining** (*saying*) there is always a little comfort, happiness etc possible however sad, disappointing etc the present situation is. **2** *nc* a similar mass of smoke etc in the air: *a cloud of insects.* **3** *nc* a similar mass as in a liquid or a transparent object: *a cloud on a photograph.* **4** *nc* something that causes unhappiness or fear: *the clouds of war.* **under a cloud** under suspicion, in disgrace: *He failed the exam and left school under a cloud.*

'cloud·burst *nc* a sudden rainfall.

cloudy *adj* (**-ier, -iest**) (**a**) covered with clouds: *a cloudy sky.* (**b**) (esp of liquids) not clear.

cloud² /klaʊd/ *vt,vi* **cloud sth (with sth); cloud over** (to cause something) to become unclear (as if) with cloud: *The sky clouded over. Her eyes were clouded with tears.*

clout /klaʊt/ *vt* (*sl*) to hit (a person).

clove¹ /kləʊv/ *pt* of cleave.

clove² /kləʊv/ *nc* a dried, unopened flower-bud of a kind of tropical tree used as a spice.

clove³ /kləʊv/ *nc* a small, separate section of some bulbs: *a clove of garlic.*

cloven /'kləʊvn/ *pp* of cleave.

clo·ver /'kləʊvə(r)/ *nu* a kind of low-growing plant with (usually) three leaves on each stalk. **be in clover** to be very happy.

'clover-leaf *nc* (esp) an intersection of motorways with flyovers etc in the form of a leaf of clover.

clown¹ /klaʊn/ *nc* **1** a person (esp in a circus or pantomime) who makes a living by dressing up and doing foolish or funny things. **2** a person who acts like a clown.

clown² /klaʊn/ *vi* **clown (about/around)** to behave like a clown: *Stop all this clowning!*

cloy /klɔɪ/ *vt,vi* (to cause something) to become unpleasant because of the sweet, rich taste or too much pleasure: *That chocolate cloys the palate.*

club¹ /klʌb/ *nc* **1** (a room or building used by) a society, group etc who come together as members for a particular purpose: *a bridge club; a football supporters' club.* ⇨ night-club. **2** (any of 13 playing-cards with a black symbol like three leaves joined together: *the ace of clubs.* Compare diamond(3), heart(4), spade(2). ⇨ suit¹(3). **3** (*golf*) a curved metal implement used to hit the ball. **4** a stick with a thick end used as a weapon.

club² /klʌb/ *v* (**-bb-**) **1** *vi* **club together** to act together as a group: *Let's club together and buy a present for Sheila.* **2** *vt* to hit (a person) with a heavy object: *He'd been clubbed to death.*

cluck /klʌk/ *vi, nc* (to make) the sound made by a hen, e.g. when calling her chickens.

clue /kluː/ *nc* a fact, idea etc that suggests a possible answer to a problem: *The spots provided a clue to her illness.* **not have a clue** (*informal*) to be completely ignorant, unable to explain etc.

clued /kluːd/ *adj* (*pred*) **be clued up (about/ on sth)** (*informal*) to have much knowledge (about something).

clue·less /'klu:lıs/ *adj* (*informal; derog*) (of a person) ignorant and stupid.

clump¹ /klʌmp/ *nc* a group (of trees, shrubs or plants): *growing in clumps.*

clump² /klʌmp/ *vi* **clump about** to walk heavily and noisily.

clum·sy /'klʌmzı/ *adj* (**-ier, -iest**) (*derog*) **1** careless, awkward in movement or construction: *The clumsy workman put his elbow through the window and broke it.* **2** (*attrib*) done without thought or care: *a clumsy remark.*

clum·si·ly /-əlı/ *adv*

clum·si·ness *nu*

clung /klʌŋ/ *pt,pp* of cling.

clunk /klʌŋk/ *vi, nc* (to make) the sound of heavy metals striking together.

clus·ter¹ /'klʌstə(r)/ *nc* **1** a group of things of the same kind growing closely together: *a cluster of flowers.* **2** a group of people, animals, objects etc close together: *a cluster of islands; consonant clusters* (in phonetics, e.g. *str* in *strong*).

clus·ter² /'klʌstə(r)/ *vi* **cluster (a)round/ together** to be in, form, a cluster(1).

clutch¹ /klʌtʃ/ *nc* **1** an instance of clutching. **2** (*pl*) (*fig*) control: *be in her mother's clutches.* **3** a device (in a car) used when operating the gears: *Let the clutch in/out smoothly when changing gear.* **4** a set of eggs put under a hen to hatch together. **5** the chicks produced from a clutch(4).

clutch² /klʌtʃ/ *v* **1** *vt* to take hold of, grip, (something) (as if) with the hands: *She clutched the rope we threw to her.* **2** *vi* **clutch at sth** to try to take hold of something: *She clutched at the rope but missed it.* **clutch at a straw** to make use of a small opportunity to survive, avoid failure etc.

clut·ter¹ /'klʌtə(r)/ *n sing* **in a clutter** in a mess: *Her files are in a clutter.*

clut·ter² /'klʌtə(r)/ *vt* **clutter sth (up)** to make something untidy or confused: *a desk cluttered up with papers.*

cm *abbr* centimetre(s).

Cmdr *abbr* Commander.

co. *abbr* **1** (Co.) (*commerce*) Company: *Smith & Co.* **2** (*informal* /kəʊ/) and the other people in the group: *I've asked Bob and co. to come.*

c/o *abbr* care of: *Miss B Jones, c/o Mrs V Jones.*

CO *abbr* Commanding Officer.

coach¹ /kəʊtʃ/ *nc* **1** (also *attrib*) a long-distance, single-decked bus: *travel by coach; a coach-tour of Europe.* **2** a railway carriage, often divided into compartments. (*US = car*). **3** a four-wheeled carriage pulled by four or more horses, used to carry passengers and mail before railways were built.

coach² /kəʊtʃ/ *nc* **1** a teacher who gives (private) lessons to prepare students for a public examination. ⇨ tutor(1). **2** a person who trains athletes and players: *a football/tennis coach.*

coach³ /kəʊtʃ/ *vt* to teach or train (a person).

co·agu·late /kəʊ'ægjʊleıt/ *vi* (*tech*) (of liquids) to change to a thick and solid state, as blood does in air.

co·agu·la·tion /kəʊ,ægjʊ'leıʃn/ *nu*

coal /kəʊl/ *n* (also *attrib*) **1** *nu* a kind of black mineral that burns and supplies heat: *a coal fire.* **2** *nc* a piece of this material.

'coal-face *nc* the part of a coal-seam from which coal is being cut.

'coal gas *nu* the mixture of gases made from coal, used for lighting and heating.

'coal·mine *nc* a mine from which coal is dug.

'coal-seam *nc* an underground layer of coal.

'coal tar *nu* a thick, black, sticky substance produced when coal-gas is made.

co·alesce /,kəʊə'les/ *vi* (*formal*) to come together, unite, into one group, substance etc: *Is the new group of students coalescing well?*

co·ales·cence /,kəʊə'lesns/ *nu*

co·ali·tion /,kəʊə'lıʃn/ *n* **1** *nu* the act of uniting. **2** *nc* (also *attrib*) a union of political parties for a special purpose: *a coalition government; form a coalition* (e.g. during a political crisis).

coarse /kɔ:s/ *adj* (**—r, —st**) **1** (of a substance) not fine; rough: *coarse sand/sugar; coarse cloth; a coarse skin/complexion.* **2** (*derog*) (of behaviour, language etc) not delicate or polite.

coarse·ly *adv*

coarse·ness *nu*

coars·en /'kɔ:sn/ *vt,vi* (to cause something) to become coarse.

coast¹ /kəʊst/ *nc* (the land near) a seashore: *We live near/on the coast. There are many islands off the coast.* **the coast is clear** there is no-one watching.

'coast·guard *nc* an officer on police duty on the coast (to prevent or detect smuggling, report passing ships etc).

'coast·line *nc* an edge of land, esp when referring to its type: *a rugged/rocky coastline.*

coast² /kəʊst/ *vi* **1** to ride a bicycle without pedalling (e.g. down a hill). **2 coast along** (*fig*) to make adequate progress (e.g. in a course of studies) without making much effort.

coast·al /'kəʊstl/ *adj* (*attrib*) of, near, the coast: *coastal waters/fishing.*

coat¹ /kəʊt/ *nc* **1** an outer article of clothing with sleeves, buttoned in the front. **2** a covering like a coat, e.g. an animal's hair or wool. **3** a layer of paint or other substance put on a surface: *The woodwork has had its final coat of paint.*

'coat-hanger *nc* a device on which clothes are hung in wardrobes etc.

,coat of 'arms *nc* a design used by a town, university, a noble family etc, e.g. on a shield.

coat² /kəʊt/ *vt* **coat sth (in/with sth)** to cover something (with a layer of something): *furniture coated with dust/red paint.*

coat·ing /'kəʊtıŋ/ *nc* a thin layer or covering: *A coating of oil stops metal rusting.*

coax /kəʊks/ *vt* **1** to persuade (a person or thing) to do something by using kindness, encouragement etc: *coax a child to take its medicine; coax a fire to burn.* **2** to get (something) by coaxing: *coax a smile from the baby.*

cob /kɒb/ *nc* **1** (also *corn-cob*) the inner part of an ear of maize on which the grain grows: *corn on the cob.* **2** (also *cob-nut*) a large kind of hazel-nut.

cob·bled /'kɒbld/ *adj* (of roads) made using small round stones.

cob·bler /'kɒblə(r)/ *nc* (*dated*) = shoe-repairer.

co·bra /'kəʊbrə/ *nc* a kind of poisonous snake of Asia and Africa.

cob·web /'kɒbweb/ *nc* a fine network of threads made by a spider.

co·caine /kəʊ'keın/ *nu* (also *attrib*) a kind of drug used as a local anaesthetic and also by drug addicts: *cocaine users*.

coc·cyx /'kɒksɪks/ *nc* (*anat*) the last bone at the bottom of the spine.

cochi·neal /ˌkɒtʃɪ'ni:l/ *nu* a bright red colouring-matter used in cooking.

coch·lea /'kɒklɪə/ *nc* (*anat*) the spiral-shaped part of the inner ear.

cock¹ /kɒk/ *nc* **1** an adult male chicken. Compare **hen**(1). **2** (in compounds) a male of other kinds of bird: *a peacock; a cock-robin*.
'**cock-crow** *nu* (*literary*) early dawn.

cock² /kɒk/ *nc* **1** a tap and spout for controlling the flow of a liquid or a gas, e.g. from a pipe. **2** a lever in a gun; position of this lever when it is raised and ready to be released by the trigger. **go off at half cock** (*fig*) (of an event, etc) to be organized, happen, without success because not well prepared.

cock³ /kɒk/ *vt* **1** to turn (the ears) upwards (showing attention, inquiry etc): *The horse cocked its ears*. **2** to raise the cock²(2) of (a gun) ready for firing. **3** *cock sth up* (*sl*) to make a mess of something: *They completely cocked up the arrangements for our holiday*. Hence '**cock-up** *nc*.

cocka·too /ˌkɒkə'tu:/ *nc* a kind of crested parrot, usually from Australia.

cock·erel /'kɒkrəl/ *nc* a young cock¹(1).

cock-eyed /'kɒk aɪd/ *adj* (*sl*) crooked; turned or twisted to one side.

cockle /'kɒkl/ *nc* a kind of edible shellfish.

cock·ney /'kɒknɪ/ *nc* (also *attrib*) a (working-class) person from London: *a cockney accent; cockney humour; cockney slang*.

cock·pit /'kɒkpɪt/ *nc* a compartment in a small plane for the pilot.

cock·roach /'kɒkrəʊtʃ/ *nc* a kind of large, dark-brown insect that comes out at night in kitchens and places where food is kept.

cocks·comb /'kɒkskəʊm/ *nc* the red flap of skin, like a comb, on a cock's head.

cock·sure /ˌkɒk'ʃʊə(r)/ *adj* = cocky.

cock·tail /'kɒkteɪl/ *nc* **1** a mixed alcoholic drink, esp one taken before a meal. **2** a mixture of fruit, fruit juices, small quantities of shellfish etc served as an appetizer: *prawn cocktail*.
'**cocktail party** *nc* a party held early in the evening where cocktails are served.

cock-up /'kɒk ʌp/ *nc* ⇨ cock³(3).

cocky /'kɒkɪ/ *adj* (**-ier, -iest**) (*informal; derog*) too confident or sure of one's ability etc: *Don't be so cocky!*

co·coa /'kəʊkəʊ/ *nc* the powder of crushed cacao seeds, as used with milk to make a hot drink.

coco·nut /'kəʊkənʌt/ *nc,nu* (also *attrib*) a large hard seed (of the *coconut-palm*) filled with milky juice and with a solid white lining: *coconut biscuits*.

co·coon /kə'ku:n/ *nc* a silky covering made by a caterpillar to protect itself while it is a chrysalis, esp that of the silkworm.

cod /kɒd/ *n* (*pl* —) **1** *nc* (also *codfish*) a kind of large sea-fish. **2** *nu* (also *attrib*) its flesh as food: *a cod pie*.

COD /ˌsi: əʊ 'di:/ *abbr* (*commerce*) cash on delivery.

coddle /'kɒdl/ *vt* **1** to treat (a person) with great care and tenderness: *coddling a child because it is*

in poor health. **2** to cook (eggs) in water just below boiling-point.

code¹ /kəʊd/ *nc* **1** a set of laws or rules: *a code of practice for a doctor*. **2** a system of rules and principles that has been accepted by society: *a high moral code*. **3** a set of numbers used for telephoning: *What is the code for London?* **4** a system of signs, writing etc used to write (secret) messages: *the Morse code*. **break/crack a code** to discover how to interpret a code(4). **5** (*computers*) a system of signs used to give instructions in a program. ⇨ binary code.

code² /kəʊd/ *vt* **1** to put (a message etc) into, send (it) in, a code(4). **2** (*computers*) to provide coded(5) instructions for (a computer, piece of information).

co·deine /'kəʊdi:n/ *nu* a kind of drug from opium, used to reduce strong pain.

codi·fy /'kəʊdɪfaɪ/ *vt* (*pt,pp* **-ied**) to put (laws etc) into a code(1).

co·ed /kəʊ'ed/ *nc* (*informal*) (a student at) a co-educational school.

co·edu·ca·tion /ˌkəʊedjʊ'keɪʃn/ *nu* education of boys and girls together.
co·edu·ca·tion·al /-ʃənl/ *adj: a coeducational school*.

co·ef·fi·cient /ˌkəʊɪ'fɪʃnt/ *nc* (*maths*) **1** the total value of everything except one variable: *The coefficient of x in $2xy^2$ is $2y^2$*. **2** a number in an algebraic expression: *The coefficient of 4ab is 4*.

co·erce /kəʊ'ɜːs/ *vt* **coerce sb (into doing sth)** to force a person to be obedient, do something etc.
co·er·cion /kəʊ'ɜːʃən/ *nu*
co·er·cive /kəʊ'ɜːsɪv/ *adj* of, using, coercion: *coercive methods/measures*.

co·exist /ˌkəʊɪg'zɪst/ *vi* (esp of two or more opposing political systems, countries) to exist (peacefully) at the same time.
co·exist·ence /-təns/ *nu*

C of E /ˌsi: əv 'i:/ *abbr* Church of England.

cof·fee /'kɒfɪ/ *n* **1** *nc* (also *attrib*) a kind of shrub with berries containing seeds (called *beans*) used for making a dark, bitter drink: *a coffee cup*. **2** *nc,nu* the drink.
'**coffee bar** *nc* a small café serving drinks and light refreshments.
'**coffee-pot** *nc* a pot for making or serving coffee.
'**coffee-table** *nc* a low table used (in a lounge etc) for magazines, ashtrays etc.
'**coffee-table book** *nc* an illustrated book for occasional light reading.

cof·fer /'kɒfə(r)/ *nc* (esp) a large, strong box for holding money or valuables.

cof·fin /'kɒfɪn/ *nc* a box for a dead person.

cog /kɒg/ *nc* one of a series of teeth on the rim of a wheel which transfers motion by locking into the teeth of a similar wheel.

co·gen·cy /'kəʊdʒənsɪ/ *nu* (*formal*) the force or strength (of arguments).

co·gent /'kəʊdʒənt/ *adj* (*formal*) (of arguments) strong and convincing.

cogi·tate /'kɒdʒɪteɪt/ *vi* **cogitate (on/upon sth)** (*formal*) to meditate (the usual word).

cog·nac /'kɒnjæk/ *nu* French brandy.

cog·nate¹ /'kɒgneɪt/ *adj* (*formal*) **1** (*pred*) **cognate with sth** having the same source or origin as something: *Dutch is cognate with German.* **2** related: *Physics and astronomy are cognate sciences.*

cog·nate² /ˈkɒgneɪt/ *nc* **1** (*lang*) a word with the same origin as another. *'House' in English and 'Haus' in German are cognates.* **2** (*gram*) an object of a verb that gives information about the verb and not the subject of a sentence, such as 'fishing' in 'He's gone *fishing'.*

co·hab·it /kəʊˈhæbɪt/ *vi* (of an unmarried couple) to live together as husband and wife.

co·hab·ita·tion /kəʊˌhæbɪˈteɪʃn/ *nu*

co·here /kəʊˈhɪə(r)/ *vi* **1** (*formal*) to stick together; be or remain united: *The wooden top and sides cohered well.* **2** (of an argument etc) to be consistent and reasonable. **3** (*literature*) (of writing) to be composed or arranged (e.g. in order of sentences, by use of paragraphs etc) so that the writer's intentions, the plot etc are easily understood.

co·her·ence /-rəns/ *nu*

co·her·ent /-rənt/ *adj* clear; reasonable: *coherent speech/arguments.* Opp incoherent.

co·her·ent·ly *adv*

C.O.I. *abbr* (*GB*) Central Office of Information.

coil¹ /kɔɪl/ *vt,vi* **coil (sth) (up)** (to cause something) to wind or twist into a continuous circular or spiral shape; curl round and round: *The snake coiled (itself) (up) round the branch.*

coil² /kɔɪl/ *nc* **1** (a single turn of) something coiled: *the thick coils of a python.* **2** (*electricity*) a length of wire wound in a spiral to produce electric current in another one or to produce a magnetic field. **3** (*informal*) a contraceptive device in the shape of a coil, used in the womb.

coin¹ /kɔɪn/ *nc,nu* (a piece of) metal money: *a small heap of coins.*

coin² /kɔɪn/ *vt* **1** to make (metal) into coins. **be coining money** to be earning money quickly or easily. **2** to invent (a new word etc): *to coin a phrase.*

ˈcoin·box *nc* (esp in a public telephone) the part of a machine where coins are placed.

coin·age /ˈkɔɪnɪdʒ/ *n* **1** *nu* the act of making coins. **2** *nc,nu* a system of coins in use: *decimal coinage.* **3** *nc,nu* (the inventing of) a new word or phrase.

co·in·cide /ˌkəʊɪnˈsaɪd/ *vi* **coincide (with sth)** **1** (of events) to happen at the same time; occupy the same period of time: *His free time never coincided with hers.* **2** (of ideas, interests etc) to be in harmony or agreement: *His hobbies coincide with those of his wife.*

co·inci·dence /kəʊˈɪnsɪdəns/ *nc,nu* (an example of) the condition when events happen at the same time as if this had been arranged: *By a curious coincidence we went on holiday during the same week.*

co·inci·den·tal /kəʊˌɪnsɪˈdentl/ *adj*

coke /kəʊk/ *nu* the substance that remains when gas has been taken out of coal, used as a fuel.

col /kɒl/ *nc* a low depression or pass in a mountain range.

Col. *abbr* Colonel.

col·an·der (also but rarely **cul·len·der**) /ˈkʌləndə(r)/ *nc* a pot with many small holes, used to drain off water from vegetables etc when cooking.

cold¹ /kəʊld/ *adj* (**—er, —est**) **1** having a low temperature, esp when compared with the human body: *cold weather; a cold wind; feel cold.* Opp hot(1). **have cold feet** ⇨ foot¹(1). **throw cold water on sth** ⇨ water¹(1). **(kill sb) in cold blood; make one's blood run cold** ⇨ blood(1). **2** (*fig*) unfriendly: *a cold greeting/welcome.* **3** (of colours) suggesting cold, e.g. grey and blue.

ˌcold-ˈblooded *adj* (**a**) (*no comp*) (of an animal) having a body temperature that changes according to the temperature of its surroundings (e.g. fish, reptiles). Compare warm-blooded. (**b**) (*fig*) (of a person, actions) without showing emotion: *cold-blooded murder.*

ˈcold cream *nu* an ointment used for cleansing and softening the skin.

ˌcold-ˈhearted *adj* (*derog*) unkind and unsympathetic. Opp warm-hearted.

ˌcold ˈmeat *nu* meat that has been cooked and is eaten cold.

ˌcold ˈsnap *nc* a short period of cold weather.

ˌcold ˈshoulder *n sing* **give sb the cold shoulder** to ignore her or him rudely. □ *vt* to ignore (a person) rudely.

ˈcold sore *nc* a sore on the lips caused by a virus.

ˌcold ˈstorage *nu* (**a**) a refrigerator: *put meat into cold storage.* (**b**) (*fig*) a temporary state of not being used, considered etc: *put plans/idea into cold storage.*

ˌcold ˈsweat *n sing* perspiration because of fear: *come out in a cold sweat.*

ˌcold ˈwar *nc* a struggle for superiority using propaganda, economic measures etc without actual fighting.

cold·ness *nu*

cold² /kəʊld/ *n* **1** *nu* (usually the —) the absence of heat; a low temperature (esp in the atmosphere): *He was shivering with cold. He hates the cold of winter. Don't stay outside in the cold— come indoors by the fire.* **(be left) out in the cold** (*fig*) (of a person) (to be) ignored or neglected. **2** *nc* an illness which causes a wet nose, sore throat, headache etc: *have/catch a cold.*

cole·slaw /ˈkəʊlslɔː/ *nu* a salad made of raw cabbage and carrot in mayonnaise.

Coll. *abbr* College.

col·lab·or·ate /kəˈlæbəreɪt/ *vi* **1** **collaborate (with sb) (on sth)** to work in partnership: *I'm collaborating with her on writing a biography.* **2** **collaborate (with sb)** to help an enemy of one's country, people involved in opposing authority etc, by giving information, advice etc.

col·lab·or·ation /kəˌlæbəˈreɪʃn/ *nu* the act of collaborating: *working in collaboration with others.*

col·lab·or·ator /kəˈlæbəreɪtə(r)/ *nc* (often *derog*) a person who collaborates (esp 2).

col·lage /ˈkɒlɑːʒ/ *nc* a picture made from an artistic combination of bits of paper, cloth, photographs etc.

col·lapse¹ /kəˈlæps/ *nc,nu* (an instance of) collapsing: *a collapse of the wall caused by the crash; a mental collapse; the collapse of discussions at the United Nations.*

col·lapse² /kəˈlæps/ *v* **1** *vt,vi* (to cause something) to fall down or break into pieces suddenly: *The roof collapsed under the weight of the snow.* **2**

vi to lose physical strength, courage, mental powers etc: *If you work too hard you may collapse.* **3** *vi* (of a plan etc) to fail or stop suddenly: *Our plans will collapse unless we get more help.* **4** *vi,vt* (to cause equipment etc) to fold into a small shape: *Does this table collapse?*

col·laps·ible /-əbl/ *adj* that can be collapsed(4): *a collapsible chair.*

col·lar¹ /'kɒlə(r)/ *nc* **1** the part of clothing that fits round the neck, esp the turned-over neckband of a shirt, dress etc. **hot under the collar** very angry or embarrassed. ⇨ blue-collar, white-collar. **2** a band of leather etc put round the neck of a dog, horse or other animal. **3** a piece of meat from the neck of an animal, eaten as food: *a collar of lamb.*

col·lar² /'kɒlə(r)/ *vt* **1** to take hold of (a person) (roughly) by the collar: *The policeman collared the thief.* **2** (*informal*) to stop (a person): *She collared me in the street and asked me my name.*

'col·lar·bone *nc* a bone joining the shoulder and the breastbone.

col·late /kə'leɪt/ *vt* **1** to examine and make a careful comparison between (manuscripts, books etc): *collate a new edition with an earlier edition.* **2** to put (pages) in correct (numerical) order (e.g. after photocopying, printing etc).

col·lat·er·al¹ /kə'lætərəl/ *adj* (*legal*) secondary or subordinate but from the same source: *collateral evidence.*

col·lat·er·al² /kə'lætərəl/ *nu* (*finance*) property or other valuables used as security for a loan: *use one's house as collateral when buying a business.*

col·league /'kɒliːg/ *nc* a person working with another or others: *When he left the company his colleagues bought him a present.*

col·lect¹ /'kɒlekt/ *nc* a short Christian prayer to be said on certain days.

col·lect² /kə'lekt/ *vt,vi* **1** to bring or gather (people, things) together: *Please collect all the empty bottles and put them over here. Several people collected round the injured motorcyclist.* **2** *vt* to obtain (books, stamps etc), e.g. as a hobby: *I collect foreign stamps.* **3** *vt* to go and bring back (a person, thing): *collect a child from school.* **4** *vt* to gather together, gain control of, (one's thoughts, energies, oneself): *Before you speak, you should collect your thoughts and ideas.*

col·lect·ed /kə'lektɪd/ *adj* (*informal*) (of a person) controlled and not afraid, angry, excited etc: *You must be cool, calm and collected during the interview.*

col·lec·tion /kə'lekʃn/ *n* **1** *nc,nu* (an instance of) collecting things: *How many collections of letters are there every day?* **2** *nc* a group of objects that have been collected (and that belong together): *a fine collection of paintings.* **3** *nc* a mass of material or objects that have come together: *a collection of dust/rubbish.* **4** *nc* an amount of money collected (at a meeting).

col·lec·tive /kə'lektɪv/ *adj* of a group (of people, nations etc) as a whole: *collective leadership* (= control or government by a group rather than an individual).

col,lective 'bargaining *nu* organized negotiations between an employer and a trade union to decide wages, conditions.

col,lective 'noun (*gram*) a noun that is singular

in form but stands for many individuals, such as *cattle, crowd, audience: In 'to catch fish' fish is a collective noun.*

col·lec·tor /kə'lektə(r)/ *nc* **1** a person who is employed to obtain something: *a tax-collector; a ticket-collector.* **2** a person who collects(2) things: *a stamp collector.*

col·lege /'kɒlɪdʒ/ *nc* **1** a place for higher or professional education; (a group of teachers and students forming) part of a university: *go to college; be at college.* **2** (often C-) a group of people with common aims, responsibilities etc: *the Royal College of Surgeons; the College of Cardinals* (who elect and advise the Pope).

col·lide /kə'laɪd/ *vi* **1** to come together violently by accident: *As the bus came round the corner it collided with a van. The ships collided in the fog.* **2** to be in a state of strong opposition: *If the aims of two countries collide there may be war.*

col·lier /'kɒlɪə(r)/ *nc* **1** a coalminer. **2** a ship that carries coal as cargo.

col·liery /'kɒljərɪ/ *nc* (*pl* **-ies**) a coalmine (and its buildings etc).

col·li·sion /kə'lɪʒn/ *nc,nu* (an instance of) colliding: *a railway collision.*

col·lo·cate /'kɒləkeɪt/ *vi* (*lang*) (of words) to combine in a way characteristic of language: *'Weak' collocates with 'tea'* (i.e. *weak tea* is good English) *but 'feeble' does not* (i.e. *feeble tea* is not good English).

col·lo·ca·tion /ˌkɒlə'keɪʃn/ *nc,nu* (*lang*) (an example of) collocating: *'Strong tea' and 'heavy drinker' are English collocations.*

col·lo·ca·tion·al /-ʃənl/ *adj*

col·lo·qui·al /kə'ləʊkwɪəl/ *adj* (*lang*) (of words, phrases, style) belonging to, suitable for, ordinary conversation and not formal or literary.

col·lo·qui·al·ly /-əlɪ/ *adv*

col·lo·qui·al·ism /-ɪzəm/ *nc* (*lang*) a colloquial word or phrase.

col·lo·quy /'kɒləkwɪ/ *nc* (*literature*) a book, essay etc written as a dialogue.

col·lu·sion /kə'luːʒn/ *nu* a secret agreement or understanding for a deceitful or fraudulent purpose: *act in collusion with a thief; be in collusion.*

co·lon¹ /'kəʊlən/ *nc* the lower and larger part of the large intestine.

co·lon² /'kəʊlən/ *nc* the punctuation mark (:). Ⓝ It is used in formal written style (a) to introduce a list, esp after expressions such as 'as follows'; (b) between numbers showing time or references, as in *9:0; Chap 4:1–6;* (c) between parts of a title or heading, as in *Shakespeare: A Personal View.*

co·lonel /'kɜːnl/ *nc* an army officer above a major (and in US commanding a regiment).

co·lo·ni·al¹ /kə'ləʊnɪəl/ *adj* (no *comp*) **1** of a colony or colonies(1). **2** (esp *US*) in the style of architecture in the British colonies in N America before and during the American Revolution.

co·lo·ni·al² /kə'ləʊnɪəl/ *nc* a person living in a colony(1), esp who helped to start or organize it.

co·lo·ni·al·ism /-ɪzəm/ *nu* (the belief in) the political system of having colonies(1).

co·lo·ni·al·ist *adj* of, like colonialism. □ *nc* a supporter of, believer in, colonialism.

col·on·ist /'kɒlənɪst/ *nc* a person who helped to start or organize a colony.

col·on·ize (also **-ise**) /'kɒlənaɪz/ *vt* to establish a colony in (a place): *The ancient Greeks colonized many parts of the Mediterranean.*

col·on·iz·a·tion (also **-is·ation**) /ˌkɒlənaɪ'zeɪʃn/ *nu*

col·on·nade /ˌkɒlə'neɪd/ *nc* a row of columns(1).

col·ony /'kɒlənɪ/ *nc* (*pl* **-ies**) **1** a country politically controlled by another country, often extensively settled with people from that country. **2** a group of people with the same trade, profession or occupation who live together: *a colony of artists.* **3** a number of animals or plants living or growing together: *a colony of ants.*

co·los·sal /kə'lɒsl/ *adj* very large.

col·our¹ (*US* = **col·or**) /'kʌlə(r)/ *n* **1** *nu* (also *attrib*) the varied visual sensation produced by rays of light (and different from looking at black and white only): *a colour TV/film/photograph; take a photograph in colour. There's so much colour in the garden in summer.* **2** *nc* one of the many different visual sensations produced by colour(1): *What colour are your eyes? Red, blue and yellow are primary colours, and the rest are mixtures of these. What are the colours of the rainbow?* **3** *nu* the (healthy) appearance of the face: *She has very little colour* (= looks pale). **off colour** (*informal*) ill: *be/feel/look off colour.* **4** *nu* (also *attrib*) the appearance of the skin according to racial origin: *Colour is the least important human characteristic. We must end colour prejudice.* **5** *nu* (*formal*) (details giving) evidence of truth: *The marks on his back gave colour to his claim of being beaten.* **6** *nu* general quality (of living conditions): *the colour of city life.* ⇨ local colour. **7** *nu* (*literature*) the particular feelings, qualities etc in the descriptions, characterization, style etc of a piece of writing. **8** *nu* (*music*) the particular quality of sound (in a composition, made by an instrument etc). **9** (*pl*) **one's (true) colours** one's personal and typical characteristics; what one is really like: *During the quarrel she was seen in/showed her true colours.* **10** (*pl*) the badge, uniform etc worn by a member of a society: *university/football colours.* **11** (*pl*) the particular flag (of a ship, regiment): *salute the colours.* **with flying colours** very successfully: *She passed her exams with flying colours.*

'colour-blind *adj* unable to distinguish between or to see certain colours.

'colour scheme *nc* a scheme for using colours in a design (e.g. decorating a room).

col·our·ful /-fʊl/ *adj* (**a**) full of colour(1): *a colourful garden.* (**b**) exciting and varied: *the colourful life of London.*

col·our·less *adj* (**a**) without colour(1): *a colourless scene.* (**b**) (*derog*) ordinary and dull: *a colourless existence; colourless writing.*

col·our² (*US* = **col·or**) /'kʌlə(r)/ *v* **1** *vt,vi* to give colour(1) to (something); produce colour(1): *She coloured her nails bright red. The children coloured in the flowers* (*in the picture*). *I love to watch the leaves as they colour during autumn.* **2** *vi* **colour (up)** to become red in the face (because of shame, nervousness etc): *She colours* (*up*) *whenever Peter speaks to her.* **3** *vt* to misrepresent facts in (a report) deliberately: *News is often highly coloured.* **4** *vt* to influence (an opinion) wrongly: *Her views are coloured by her experiences as a sailor's wife.*

col·our·ed /'kʌləd/ *adj* **1** having colour(1,2): *a coloured carpet; a cream-coloured wallpaper.* **2** (*derog*) (of a report) containing a great deal of deliberate misrepresentation: *a coloured account of what happened.*

col·our·ing /'kʌlərɪŋ/ *nu* **1** any substance used to produce colour(1). **2** (*art*) the style, process, of using colour(1). **3** (*derog*) (the form of) misrepresentation in a false or biased report.

colt /kəʊlt/ *nc* a young male horse up to the age of 4 or 5. Compare filly.

col·umn /'kɒləm/ *nc* **1** a tall, upright structure, usually of stone, supporting or decorating part of a building or standing alone as a monument. **2** something shaped like or suggesting a column: *a column of smoke; the spinal column* (= the backbone). **3** a vertical division of a printed page, (e.g. of this page or of a newspaper). **4** a series of numbers arranged under one another: *add up a long column of figures.* **5** (*mil*) a line of soldiers, ships etc, one behind the other.

Com. *abbr* **1** Communist. **2** Committee.

co·ma /'kəʊmə/ *nc* **in a coma** in an unnatural deep sleep because of injury or illness.

comb¹ /kəʊm/ *nc* **1** a flat object with a row of teeth, used for making the hair tidy. **2** a part of a machine with the look or use of a comb, esp for tidying and straightening wool etc. ⇨ also honeycomb, cockscomb.

comb² /kəʊm/ *vt* **1** **comb sth (out)** to use a comb on something (in order to remove something): *comb one's hair; combing out tangles/knots.* **2** **comb sb/sth out** (*fig*) to remove unwanted things, people from a group: *comb out a government department.* **3** **comb (through) sth** to search something thoroughly: *comb through the dog's fur for fleas; police combing (through) the fields/combing the town/countryside for the murderer.*

com·bat¹ /'kɒmbæt/ *nc,nu* (*mil*) (an act, example, of) fighting: *armed combat.*

com·bat² /'kɒmbæt/ *v* **1** *vt* to fight (soldiers etc): *combat the enemy.* **2** *vt,vi* to struggle (against something): *a ship combating with the wind and waves; take aspirin to combat a headache.*

com·bat·ant /'kɒmbətənt/ *nc* (*mil*) a person who fights as a soldier: *Both combatants and non-combatants will be killed in a nuclear attack.*

com·bi·na·tion /ˌkɒmbɪ'neɪʃn/ *n* **1** *nu* an act of joining or putting things together; the state of being joined: *Look at it in combination with other colours.* **2** *nc* a number of people, things, that are joined: *The college is supported by a combination of income from the government and fees from students.* **3** *nc* a formula or code for a lock etc: *How did the thieves learn the combination?*

com·bine /kəm'baɪn/ *vt,vi* (to cause things) to join together: *We can't always combine work with pleasure. Hydrogen and oxygen combine. Hydrogen combines with oxygen to form water.*

com·bine har·ves·ter /ˌkɒmbaɪn 'hɑːvɪstə(r)/ *nc* a kind of machine that reaps and threshes grain.

com·bust·ible /kəm'bʌstəbl/ *adj* (*tech*) able to catch fire and burn easily.

com·bus·tion /kəm'bʌstʃən/ *nu* (*tech*) the process of burning.

come /kʌm/ *v* (*pt* **came** /keɪm/, *pp* **come**) **1** *vi* to move towards, nearer to, (the speaker, a place): *They came to a river. Come here! Come and join us! Come over here and look at this. The children came running* (= ran) *to meet us. Why not come walking with us tomorrow? I'm coming! Are you coming? He refuses to come within ten miles of the city. We've come three miles and I'm exhausted already.* ⇨ also way²(4). **2** *vi* to arrive (where the speaker is, was or will be): *At what time/When will you come? Has he come? She's coming at 6 o'clock on Friday. I'll come when I've finished. She's coming to the party with John. He's come for the keys. She'll come later to fetch her bike. The sooner you can come the better. Come now or you'll miss the start of the race. The postman's come. Can you come for dinner?* **3** *vi* **come to sth** to reach, amount to, a mentioned quantity, level, condition, position etc: *The bill came to £30. The total amount travelled came to 8000 km. Her shorts come to her knees. The water came* (*up*) *to my waist.* Ⓝ For the use of 'come' with nouns such as *age, agreement, bit, blow, boil, decision, end, fashion, flower, nothing* etc, ⇨ the noun entries. **4** *vi* to occur; exist: *The sales analysis comes every three months. These shirts come in all sizes/four colours. What comes after the soup? May comes between April and June. I came first/second/last in the race. What comes next?* (= after this/that?). *He's as good as they come* (= as good as anyone). *Her success came as a surprise to us all.* **come again?** (*informal*) What did you say? **easy come, easy go** (*saying*) something easily achieved or obtained can as easily be lost. **5** *vt* **come to** + *verb*(a) to arrive at a state when one understands, knows etc: *He came to realize his stupidity. Now that I come to think of it, he wasn't there. How did you come to believe that?* (**b**) **come to pass** (*dated*) to happen: *It came to pass that* . . . **6** *vi* (used with adjectives, often with *un-*) to become: *The rope came loose. My shoelace came untied. The stitches are coming undone. My coat has come unbuttoned.* ⇨ get(4). **come clean** ⇨ clean². **come true** ⇨ true¹(1). **7** *vi* to become visible, obvious: *Daylight/Night came.* ⇨ also light⁴(5), notice¹(3), sight¹(3), view¹(1). **8** *vi* **come the** . . . (**with sb**) to become someone unpleasant (when talking etc to a person): *Don't come the bully with me!* **9** . . . **to come** (*adj* (*pred*)) in the future: *In years to come you'll remember this conversation. It will be painful for some time to come. Do you believe in the life to come?* ⇨ coming¹.

come aboard to go onto a plane or ship (and join the speaker).

come about (esp of a disaster, failure etc) to happen: *How did the accident come about?*

come across (of a voice, speech, style of writing etc) to be heard or understood: *Do the meanings/his feelings come across?* **come across sb/sth** (*no passive*) to find or meet, a person, thing, by chance: *He came across her at the railway station. I came across this old photograph in the cupboard.*

come after sb/sth (**a**) to be the next in order: *Your name comes after mine.* (**b**) to follow and try to catch a person, animal: *The police came after us with dogs.*

come along (**a**) (*imperative*) be quick! try

harder!: *Come along, we'll be late! Come along, someone knows the answer.* (**b**) to make progress: *The vegetables in the garden are coming along well.* (**c**) to occur: *When the right opportunity comes along I'll change my job.* **come along (to sth)** (esp used in invitations) to move from one place to another: *Do come along (to our party tomorrow) if you can.* **come along (with sb)** (esp used in commands etc) to accompany a person: *Come along with me—I want to ask you something.*

come apart to fall to pieces: *The vase came apart in my hands.*

come around = come round.

come at sb to attack a person: *He came at me with a knife.* **come at sth** (*formal*) to arrive at the truth, reasons etc: *We came at the real causes by accident.*

come away (*imperative*) (used to ask a person to leave a quarrel, fight etc). **come away (from sth)** to become separated (from something): *If the meat is well cooked, it will come away from the bone easily.*

come back (**a**) to return: *Please come back soon.* (**b**) to become fashionable, popular, again: *Are pointed shoes coming back? Jazz is coming back.* Hence **'come-back** *nc* (esp in) **make a come-back** to become popular again. **come back at sb** to give a reply to a person: *He came back at me with some useful advice.* **come back to sb** to be remembered by a person: *Their names are all coming back to me now.* Compare bring sth back(b).

come before sb/sth (**a**) to be earlier in order than a person, thing: *'Again' comes before 'against' in the dictionary.* (**b**) to be higher in rank, greater in importance, than a person, thing. *Should spending on education come before spending on defence?* (**c**) to be presented to an official or an official meeting, for consideration, judgement etc: *The issue came before the European Parliament last month.*

come between sb (and sb/sth) (**a**) to interfere with the private affairs of a person: *Never come between a man and his wife.* (**b**) to prevent a person from having, doing, something: *He never lets anything come between him and his daily jog.*

come by to pass: *A huge juggernaut came by.* **come by sth** (**a**) to obtain something by effort: *Jobs are not easy to come by these days.* (**b**) to get something (by chance etc): *How did you come by that scar?*

come down (**a**) (of rain, snow etc) to fall. (**b**) (of a structure, picture etc) to collapse, fall: *The ceiling has come down.* (**c**) (of aircraft) to fall to the ground: *The capsule came down in the sea.* (**d**) (of prices, costs) to become less. **come down (from sth)** to leave (a university) after graduating. **come down in the world** to become poorer, less important etc. Hence **'come-down** *nc* (*informal*) a loss of social position: *He's had to sell his large house—what a come-down!* **come down in favour of/on the side of sb/sth** to decide to support a person, plan etc: *He came down on the side of the government.* **come down on sb** to criticize a person strongly: *Why do you come down on your children so severely?* **come down to sb** to be passed on to a person:

stories that have come down to us from ancient times. **come down to sth** (a) to mean (eventually), be reduced to, something: So, it came down to a vague offer of a part-time job. Your choices come down to two—sell the car or lose the house. **come down to earth** ⇨ earth¹(2). **come down with sth** to become ill with a particular disease etc: The baby's come down with flu.

come forward (a) to present oneself (and offer one's services): Will anyone come forward as a candidate? (b) (of an issue, motion) to be presented for discussion: The housing document will come forward (for debate) at our next meeting.

come from sth (a) to have a country etc as a birthplace: She comes from Chile. (b) to have a substance as an origin: Coke comes from coal. (c) to have a family etc as ancestors: She comes from a rich family. (d) to be the result of something: Does football violence come from youth unemployment?

come in (a) (esp in polite requests) to enter (a room): Come in and close the door. (b) to become fashionable: Beards are coming in again. (c) to become available: Cheap fruit is coming in. (d) to have a part, role, in some activity: I see the new arrangement but where do I come in? (e) to get money etc as income: There's not much money coming in at present. (f) (of news) to be received: The report has just come in of an aircrash. (g) (radio; imperative) please speak to me: Come in, Flight BC319. (h) to gain power: When did Mrs Thatcher come in? (i) (of the tide) to move towards the coast. **come in handy/useful** to be useful (at some time or other): Don't throw paper bags away—they may come in handy. **come in for sth** to be the subject of the response mentioned: He came in for a lot of criticism. **come in on sth** to take part in an activity: If you want to come in on the new business you must offer some money. **come in with sb** to join a person as a partner, e.g. in a business.

come into sth (a) to enter a place: Come into a concert hall. (b) to inherit money etc: Come into a share of the company. (N) For uses of 'come into' with nouns such as being, contact, effect, existence, fashion, focus, force, line, power, season, sight etc ⇨ the noun entries.

come of sth (a) = come from(c). (b) to happen as a result of something: Can any good come of arguing with the manager? What good can come of it? ⇨ also age¹(1), become(3).

come off (a) to take place: Did your visit to China come off? (b) (of plans, efforts, experiments etc) to be successful: It was a good effort but the play didn't quite come off. **come off (sth)** (a) to become separated (from something): A button has come off (my coat). (b) to fall (from something): I came off (my motorbike) as I turned the corner. (c) to be removed (from something): Import duty will come off certain items. **come off it!** (imperative; informal) stop trying to deceive me (esp by talking nonsense).

come on (a) = come along. (b) to follow: You go to the party and I'll come on later. (c) (used as a challenge): Come on—I'll race you home. (d) (of lights, TV and other electrical equipment) to begin to work: All the lights suddenly came on. (e)

(of pain, illness etc) to begin to be felt: I can feel a cold coming on. (f) (of seasons) to begin to be noticeable: Winter is definitely coming on. (g) (of an actor) to appear on the stage. (h) (of a film, TV or radio programme) to be shown: The news came on at 7 o'clock (i) (of a woman) to begin menstruating. **come on in** (imperative; informal) come inside (and join me/us in my home, office, the swimming pool etc).

come out (a) to appear, be noticeable: The sun/stars/blossom came out. (b) to appear in the shops: When did his first novel come out? (c) (of workers) to strike: The drivers came out (on strike/in sympathy/in support of the miners). (d) (of a prisoner) to be released (from gaol): He came out (of gaol) last Saturday. (e) (of a secret etc) to become known: If the truth ever comes out, I'll be sacked. (f) to be reproduced (well/badly etc) in a photograph: You've come out well in this one. (g) (of stains etc) to be removed: The oil on your trousers won't come out. (h) (of colour etc) to disappear: Will the red come out if I wash it? (i) (of a person's character) to be noticeable: His arrogance comes out in conversation. (j) (of a candidate) to achieve a position mentioned (in an exam etc): She came out first/top/last/bottom. **come out even** to achieve the same score, profit etc. (k) (of exam results) to be announced: When will the results come out? **come out against sth** to indicate one's opposition to something: Will the Liberals come out against nuclear weapons? **come out at sth** (of totals, averages etc) to amount to a mentioned figure: The cost comes out at £30.50. **come out (for/to (do) sth)** to leave home (for an outing etc/to join an activity etc): Can you come out for a walk/to the theatre/to play? **come out of sth** to leave a place: When did he come out of prison/school/the bath? **come out in sth** to be (partly) covered in spots etc: I've come out in a rash. **come out on top** (informal) to prove one's superiority, abilities etc: After years of struggle she finally came out on top. **come out with sth** to say something (after an effort): He came out with a stupid lie.

come over to visit: Come over this weekend. **come over sb** (of a feeling, attack of dizziness etc) to affect a person: A sudden feeling of coldness came over me. You've behaved so badly—I don't know what's come over you today. **come over (to sth)** (a) to come to a country etc from a distance: When did you come over to England? (b) to join a person, group etc after changing one's opinion: Will he ever come over to our side?

come round (a) to visit: Come round at the weekend. (b) (of seasons) to occur again: Spring will soon come round. (c) to regain consciousness: He came round and found himself in hospital. (d) to use a route round: The city was busy so we came round by the bypass. **come round (to sth)** to agree (with another person's opinion): She'll soon come round (to our idea) if you offer her promotion.

come through to be delivered (by telephone, telex etc): Your posting has come through—it's Tokyo! A message is coming through on the telefax machine. **come through sth** to recover from a serious illness etc; survive a war etc. Compare pull through.

come to to regain consciousness: *He came to in the hospital.* **come to sth** (of totals etc) to amount to a figure: *Your bill comes to £150.* (N) For uses of *'come to'* with nouns such as *blow, boil, climax, conclusion, end, grip, point, rescue, term* etc ⇨ the *noun* entries.

come under sth (a) to be in a category: *What heading in the account does this cost come under?* Compare put sth under sth. (b) to be controlled by something: *He came under her notice/ influence/control.*

come up (a) (as a request, command etc) come upstairs: *Come up to my office.* (b) to swim, rise, to the surface of water: *Do frogs come up for air?* (c) (of an opportunity, vacancy etc) to occur: *I'll call you if a vacancy comes up.* (d) (of the time, date etc of an event) to be near: *The interview/ Her wedding is coming up.* (e) (of a problem, a person's name) to occur; be mentioned: *The issue is certain to come up at the next meeting. Her name comes up at every staff meeting.* Compare bring sth up(a). (f) (of a lawsuit etc) to be dealt with (in a law court): *Will my driving offence ever come up?* (g) (*informal*) (of food) to be returned to the mouth from the stomach: *His milk keeps on coming up.* Compare bring sth up(b). (h) (of a plant etc) to appear above the ground: *The peas haven't come up yet.* (i) (of a ticket, number, in a competition etc) to win: *I'll buy a yacht if my number comes up.* (j) (of the sun, moon) to appear over the horizon. **come up against sth** to be faced with a problem, difficulty etc: *After finding the address they came up against the problem of how to get there.* **come up for sth** to be considered as a candidate etc for a position etc: *You're coming up for election to the board of directors on Friday.* **come up for sale** to become available for sale (esp at an auction). **come up to sb** to approach a person. **come up to sth** (a) to reach the level mentioned: *The boots came up to her knees.* (b) to reach an acceptable standard: *Your work has not come up to expectation/the required level.* (c) to be near to the time, date etc of an event: *It's coming up to the exams/your birthday.* **be coming up to sth** to be near to an age, date etc: *He's coming up to 16. It's coming up to 4 o'clock. They're coming up to their final exams.* **come up with sth** to produce an excuse, cure etc: *come up with an answer.*

come upon sb/sth (*formal*) (a) (of a disaster etc) to attack a person, group etc suddenly: *Fear came upon us.* (b) to find, meet, a person, thing etc by chance: *We came upon a bargain at the market. He came upon her at the station.*

come within sth to become near enough to be heard, seen: *come within sight/range/earshot.*

come-back /'kʌm bæk/ *nc* ⇨ come back.

com·edi·an /kə'miːdɪən/ *nc* **1** an actor who plays comic parts in plays etc. **2** a person who behaves in a comic way and who cannot be taken seriously.

com·edi·enne /kə,miːdɪ'en/ *nc* a woman comedian.

come-down /'kʌm daʊn/ *nc* ⇨ come down.

com·edy /'kɒmədɪ/ *nc,nu* (*pl* **-ies**) **1** (*literature*) (an example of) a form of drama dealing with everyday life in a humorous way and with a happy ending. (N) *'Comedy'* has more plot, stronger charac-

ters and more developed dialogue than *'farce'* or other forms of humorous drama. Compare tragedy. **2** (an instance of) an amusing incident in real life.

,comedy of 'humours *nc,nu* (a) comedy relying on humorous characters, often with one exaggerated characteristic for each major figure in the drama.

,comedy of 'manners *nc,nu* (a) comedy relying on a humorous portrayal of the manners and conventions of so-called sophisticated society, with a witty dialogue and amusing handling of intrigue.

,comedy of ,situ'ation *nc,nu* (a) comedy relying on a clever and amusing plot and ridiculous situations such as mistaken identity, unexpected meetings and silly mistakes.

come·ly /'kʌmlɪ/ *adj* (**-ier, -iest**) (*literary*) (of a person) pleasant to look at.

com·et /'kɒmɪt/ *nc* a heavenly body (looking like a star with a bright centre and a less bright tail) that moves round the sun.

come-up·pance /,kʌm 'ʌpens/ *nu* **get one's come-uppance** (*informal*) to receive the punishment one deserves.

com·fort¹ /'kʌmfət/ *n* **1** *nu* the state of being free from suffering, anxiety, difficulties, pain etc: *living in great comfort.* **2** *nu* help or kindness to a person who is suffering: *a few words of comfort.* **3** *nc* a person or thing that brings relief or help: *Your letters/You have been a great comfort to me.*

com·fort² /'kʌmfət/ *vt* (*formal*) to give comfort(2) to (a person): *We try to comfort those who are in trouble.*

com·fort·able /'kʌmftəbl/ *adj* **1** pleasant to be in or on: *a comfortable chair/bed.* **2** having or providing comfort(1): *a comfortable life/income.* **3** at ease; free from (too much) pain, anxiety etc: *to be/feel comfortable.* Opp uncomfortable.

com·fort·ably /-əblɪ/ *adv*

com·ic¹ /'kɒmɪk/ *adj* **1** causing people to laugh: *a comic face/phrase.* **2** (*attrib*) of comedy: *a comic scene/actor.*

,comic 'opera *nc,nu* (a) light opera using comedy and with spectacular scenes and sung dialogue.

,comic re'lief *nu* the use of a humorous scene or episode in a serious drama to provide rest from tension or sadness, or to contrast with the rest of the play.

'comic strip *nc* a series of drawings telling an amusing story.

com·ic² /'kɒmɪk/ *nc* **1** a magazine with comic strips. **2** a professional comedian(2).

comi·cal /'kɒmɪkl/ *adj* amusing; odd: *a comical old hat.*

com·ing¹ /'kʌmɪŋ/ *adj* (*attrib*) that is to come or will come: *in the coming years.*

com·ing² /'kʌmɪŋ/ *n* (the —) the first sign: *the coming of spring.*

,comings and 'goings *n pl* arrivals and departures.

com·ma /'kɒmə/ *nc* the punctuation mark (,). (N) It is used (a) between several clauses, phrases, words in a sentence but not between the last two, as in *I looked in the window, saw a man and ran. It's a big, hairy spider;* (b) between parts of a date, address etc, as in *3 May, 1988; 8 High St, Oxford;* (c) after an introductory remark or phrase, as in *After adding the* sugar, stir well. Sorry, I didn't see you. Oh, what a mess! (**d**) either side of an explanatory phrase or other interruption, as in *The man, hoping to encourage me, offered me a cigarette. My brother, however, won a prize. You, I'm sure, would love the play. Mrs Brown, the owner, will see you now. The children, tired but happy, went to bed.* (**e**) either side of part of reported speech that refers to the speaker, as in '*I want it,' she said, 'and I'll get it!'* (**f**) to emphasize a contrast, as in *I said 'Nice day', not 'Go away'.* (**g**) before a short addition used to make questions, as in *You do like it, don't you?*

com·mand¹ /kə'mɑːnd/ n **1** nc an order: *His commands were quickly obeyed.* **2** nu **be in command of sth** to have authority, power, to control a group of soldiers, staff etc: *General Johnson is in command of the army.* **have/take command (of sth)** to have/take authority (over an army etc): *When the major was killed, the senior captain took command (of the company).* **3** nc (often C-) (*mil*) a part of an army, air force etc under separate command: *Bomber Command.* **4** nu or sing **command of sth** ability, skill: *He has a good command of the English language.* **5** nc (*computers*) an instruction expressed in computer language. **6** nc (*gram*) a form of a sentence giving an order.

com·mand² /kə'mɑːnd/ v Ⓝ Not used in the continuous tenses, e.g. '*is/was -ing*' in 3,4. **1** vt,vi to order (a person) (usually with the right to be obeyed): *Do as I command (you). The officer commanded his men to fire.* **2** vt to have authority over, be in control of, (a person, group): *The captain of a ship commands all the officers and men.* **3** vt to deserve and get (something): *Great personalities command our respect.* **4** vt (of a place) to be in a position that overlooks and may control (a place): *The fort commands the road to the valley.*

com·man·dant /'kɒməndænt/ nc (*mil*) an officer in command of a military establishment.

com·man·deer /ˌkɒmən'dɪə(r)/ vt (*mil*) to seize (provisions etc) for military use under martial law.

com·man·der /kə'mɑːndə(r)/ nc (*mil*) an officer in charge of a military operation.

com,mander-in-'chief nc the chief officer in a military operation.

com·mand·ing /kə'mɑːndɪŋ/ adj (*attrib*) **1** (*mil*) in charge: *a commanding officer.* **2** showing authority; deserving respect: *speak in a commanding voice.* **3** (*mil*) (of a military position) giving control, authority. **4** (in a contest) unable to be defeated or threatened: *have a commanding lead in a race.*

com·mand·ment /kə'mɑːndmənt/ nc (*esp*) one of the ten laws given by God to Moses.

com·man·do /kə'mɑːndəʊ/ nc (*pl* **—s** or **—es**) (*mil*) (one of) a group of soldiers specially trained for carrying out raids and making assaults.

com·mem·or·ate /kə'meməreit/ vt to keep or honour the memory of (a person, event); (of a thing) be in memory of (a person, event): *A monument was built to commemorate the victory.*

com·mem·or·ation /kəˌmemə'reiʃn/ n **1** nu an act of commemorating a person, thing: *It was built in commemoration of the victory.* **2** nc (a part of) a service in memory of a person or event.

com·mem·or·ative /kə'memrətɪv/ adj (usually attrib) serving to commemorate: *commemorative stamps/medals.*

com·mence /kə'mens/ vt (*formal*) to begin (the more usual word). Ⓝ For a comparison of *commence, begin* and *start,* ⇒ the note at begin(1).

com·mence·ment nu

com·mend /kə'mend/ vt (*formal*) to speak favourably of (a person, an achievement etc): *His work was highly commended.*

com·mend·able /-əbl/ adj worthy of praise.

com·men·sur·ate /kə'menʃərət/ adj **commensurate with sth** (*formal*) corresponding in amount, worth etc to something: *Was the pay you received commensurate with the work you did?*

com·ment¹ /'kɒment/ nc,nu (an) opinion, explanation or criticism in speech or writing about an event, book, state of affairs etc: *Have you any comments to make on my story?*

com·ment² /'kɒment/ vi **1** to make a remark: *He didn't comment (about my mistake).* **2** **comment on sth** to give comments: *comment on an essay.*

com·men·tary /'kɒməntri/ nc (*pl* **-ies**) **commentary (on sth) 1** a series of comments (on an event): *a commentary on a football match; a football commentary.* **2** a collection of written comments (e.g. on a book): *a Bible commentary.*

com·men·tate /'kɒmənteit/ vi **commentate (on sth)** to give a commentary(1).

com·men·ta·tor /'kɒmənteitə(r)/ nc a person who gives a radio or TV commentary(1).

com·merce /'kɒmɜːs/ nu the buying, selling and distribution of goods (esp between countries).

com·mer·cial¹ /kə'mɜːʃl/ adj of, concerning, commerce: *commercial banks.*

com,mercial 'traveller nc (not now used) a travelling salesman.

com·mer·cial·ly /-əlɪ/ adv

com·mer·cial² /kə'mɜːʃl/ nc an advertisement in a TV or radio programme.

com,mercial 'radio/'television nu the kind financed by charges made for commercials.

com·miser·ate /kə'mizəreit/ vi **commiserate (with sb)** to feel, say that one feels, pity for a person: *commiserate with a friend on his misfortunes.*

com·miser·ation /kəˌmizə'reiʃn/ nc,nu (an expression of) pity or sympathy.

com·mis·sion¹ /kə'miʃn/ n **1** nc,nu (an instance of) giving authority, permission, or a task, duty, to a person: *He has won a commission to design the new sports centre. The commission to write a new play for the National Theatre has not been decided.* **2** nu payment for the quantity of goods sold (by a salesman): *She gets 10% commission on sales.* **3** nc (often C-) a group of people given the duty to make an inquiry and produce a report: *A Royal Commission has been set up to consider drug addiction.* **4** nc (*mil*) an official document appointing an officer in the armed forces. **5** nu **out of commission** (of a machine, ship etc) not in a good working condition; not in use.

com·mis·sion² /kə'miʃn/ vt **1** to give a commission(1) to (a person): *be commissioned to photograph the Princess of Wales.* **2** (*mil*) to give a commission(4) to (a person): *be commissioned as* *a captain in the Royal Navy.*

com·mis·sion·aire /kə,mɪʃə'neə(r)/ *nc* a uniformed porter at the entrance to a hotel, large shop etc.

com·mis·sion·er /kə'mɪʃənə(r)/ *nc* 1 a member of a commission(3). 2 (C-) a government representative of high rank (in a Commonwealth country): *the British High Commissioner in Accra.*

com·mit /kə'mɪt/ *vt* (-tt-) 1 to perform (a crime etc): *commit murder/suicide/an offence.* 2 to hand over (a person) officially for guarding or treatment: *commit a man to prison; commit a patient to a mental hospital.* 3 *commit oneself (to do sth)* to promise to do, make oneself responsible for doing, something: *He has committed himself to support his brother's children.* 4 *commit sth to memory* to learn and remember it.

com·mit·ted *adj* (of a person) determined to be responsible for, to support, to do etc: *a committed campaigner for peace. How committed are you?* ⇨ uncommitted.

com·mit·ment *nc* (esp) something to which one is committed(3): *If you have a mortgage, a large family and a car on hire purchase you have a lot of commitments.*

com·mit·tee /kə'mɪtɪ/ *nc* or *n pl* (also *attrib*) a group of people appointed (usually by a larger group) to carry out special duties: *to attend a committee meeting; to be on/sit on/chair the committee. The committee is/are still discussing the problem.*

com·mod·ity /kə'mɒdətɪ/ *nc* (*pl* -ies) (*commerce*) an article of trade.

com·mo·dore /'kɒmədɔː(r)/ *nc* (*mil*) a naval officer having rank above a captain and below a rear-admiral.

com·mon¹ /'kɒmən/ *adj* (**—er**, **—est**) 1 belonging to, used by, coming from, done by, affecting, all or nearly all members of a group or society: *His wife is German but they have English as a common language.* 2 happening or found often and in many places: *Are snakes common in this country? Is this word in common use?* Opp uncommon. 3 (of a person) not of noble birth. ⇨ commoner. 4 (*derog*) (of people, their behaviour, possessions) of inferior quality or taste: *speak with a common accent.* 5 (*maths*) belonging to two or more quantities: *a common factor/multiple.*

,**common 'ground** *nu* (*fig*) the situation of sharing similar attitudes in an argument dispute etc: *be on common ground.*

,**common 'knowledge** *nu* something that is generally known: *It is common knowledge that you are dating Mary.*

,**common 'law** *nu* (*common-law* when *attrib*) (in England) unwritten law from customs and earlier legal decisions: *A common-law husband/ wife is one who is considered to be married because of many years of cohabitation.*

,**Common 'Market** *n* (the —) (officially *the European Community*) an economic, social and political union of most western European countries.

,**common 'noun** *nc* (*gram*) one referring to any person, thing, place etc that is not a name, such as

boy, road, box, plan.

'**common-room** *nc* a lounge for teachers or for students in a college, school etc.

,**common 'sense** *nu* practical good sense got from experience of life, not by study.

com·mon² /'kɒmən/ *nc* 1 an area of unfenced grassland for all to use: *Let's go for a walk on the village common.* 2 *in common* shared by all or both: *What interests do they have in common? in common with sb* the same as, another person or others: *In common with most students, she found the first term difficult.*

com·mon·er /'kɒmənə(r)/ *nc* a person who is not of noble birth. ⇨ common¹(3).

com·mon·ly /'kɒmənlɪ/ *adj* 1 usually: *That commonly happens.* 2 (*derog*) in a common(4) way: *be commonly dressed.*

com·mon·place /'kɒmənpleɪs/ *adj* ordinary or usual: *Chinese restaurants are commonplace here.*

Com·mons /'kɒmənz/ *n pl* (the —; usually *the House of Commons*) the assembly of the British Parliament elected by the people.

com·mon·wealth /'kɒmənwelθ/ *nc* 1 (the C-) the free association of independent states that were formerly colonies and dominions of GB. 2 a group of states (e.g. in Australia) associating politically.

com·mo·tion /kə'məʊʃn/ *nc,nu* (an instance of) noisy confusion or excitement: *You're making a great commotion about nothing.*

com·mu·nal /'kɒmjunl/ *adj* 1 of or for a community: *communal facilities.* 2 for shared use: *communal land/kitchens.*

com·mune¹ /'kɒmjuːn/ *nc* a group of people living together and sharing property and responsibilities.

com·mune² /kə'mjuːn/ *vi* *commune (with sb/sth)* (*formal*) to feel, be, in close spiritual touch with a person or thing: *communing with nature.*

com·muni·cable /kə'mjuːnɪkəbl/ *adj* (of ideas, illness etc) that can be communicated or passed on: *a communicable disease.*

com·muni·cant /kə'mjuːnɪkənt/ *nc* a person who (regularly) receives Holy Communion.

com·muni·cate /kə'mjuːnɪkeɪt/ *v* 1 *vt* to exchange, pass on, (news, information, feelings etc): *My parents are not communicating their views/feelings to each other.* 2 *vi communicate (with sb)* to share or exchange news etc (with a person): *We can communicate with people in most parts of the world by telephone.*

com·muni·ca·tion /kə,mjuːnɪ'keɪʃn/ *n* 1 *nu* the act of communicating: *Among the deaf and dumb communication is by means of sign language.* 2 *nc* something that is communicated (e.g. information): *This communication is confidential.* 3 *nc,nu* a means of communicating (roads, railways, telephone, radio and TV): *All communication with the north has been stopped because of snow.*

com·muni·cat·ive /kə'mjuːnɪkətɪv/ *adj* (of a person) ready and willing to talk and give information. Opp uncommunicative.

com·mu·nion /kə'mjuːnɪən/ *nu* 1 *communion (with sb/sth)* closeness in feeling, thought, (with a person, nature etc). 2 (C-; also *Holy Communion*) (in the Christian Church) the celebration of the Eucharist.

com·mu·ni·qué /kəˈmjuːnɪkeɪ/ *nc* an official announcement, e.g. as issued to the press.

com·mu·nism /ˈkɒmjʊnɪzəm/ *nu* (also C-) (a belief in) a social system in which the State owns and controls the means of wealth and production.

com·mu·nist /-ɪst/ *adj* (also C-) of, like, communism. □ *nc* a supporter of, believer in, communism.

com·mun·ity /kəˈmjuːnətɪ/ *nc* (*pl* **-ies**) **1** (the —) the people living in one place, district or country, considered as a whole: *work for the good of the community*. **2** a group of people having the same religion, race, occupation etc or with common interests: *a community of monks; the Greek community in London*.

com·mute /kəˈmjuːt/ *v* **1** *vi* to travel regularly, e.g. by train, between one's work and one's home: *I commute by bus*. **2** *vt* to exchange (one thing, esp one kind of payment) for another: *commute a weekly pension for a single payment*. **3** *vt* to reduce the severity of (a punishment) (to a less severe one): *commute a death sentence (to one of life imprisonment)*.

com·mu·ter *nc* a person who commutes(1).

com'muter belt *nc* an area outside a town or city where commuters live.

comp. *abbr* (*gram*) comparative.

com·pact¹ /kəmˈpækt/ *adj* closely packed together; neatly fitted.

,compact 'disc *nc* (abbr CD) a type of small disc (for reproducing sound) using technology that allows a lot of music, singing etc to be available with a very high standard of sound quality.

,compact 'disc player *nc* an electrical appliance for reproducing sound from a compact disc.

com·pact·ly *adv*

com·pact·ness *nu*

com·pact² /ˈkɒmpækt/ *nc* an official agreement; contract.

com·pact³ /ˈkɒmpækt/ *nc* a small, flat container for face-powder: *a powder compact*.

com·pan·ion /kəmˈpænɪən/ *nc* **1** a person who goes with, or is often or always with, another: *I enjoyed my companions on the trip*. **2** (also *attrib*) one of two things that go together; something that matches another or is one of a pair: *the companion volume*. **3** a woman paid to keep another person company. **4** (often C-) a handbook or reference book: *the Gardener's Companion*.

com·pan·ion·ship *nu* the fact of, warm feeling from, having companions.

com·pany /ˈkʌmpənɪ/ *n* (*pl* **-ies**) **1** *nu* the state of being together with another or others: *I shall be glad of your company* (= to have you with me) *on the journey. He came in company with* (= together with) *a group of boys*. **part company (with sb)** to separate (from a person) (and go in a different direction). **part company with sth** to give something one likes or values to another person: *He refused to part company with his favourite toy*. **2** *nu* visitors, guests etc: *We're expecting company next week*. **3** *nu* the warm feeling from having a companion: *She's good company*. **4** *nc* (C- in names; abbr Co) a group of people united for business or commerce: *a publishing company; a theatrical company*. **5** *nc* (mil)

a subdivision of an infantry battalion, commanded by a captain or major.

com·par·able /ˈkɒmprəbl/ *adj* (*formal*) that can be compared: *His achievements are comparable with the best/to yours*. Opp incomparable.

com·para·tive¹ /kəmˈpærətɪv/ *adj* **1** having to do with comparison or comparing: *comparative religion*. **2** measured or judged by comparing: *living in comparative comfort*. **3** (*gram*) a form of an adjective or adverb expressing a higher or stronger degree (usually made by adding *-er* or using *more*), such as *happier, longer, more likely*: *'Worse' is the comparative form of 'bad'*. Compare positive(9), superlative(2).

com·para·tive·ly *adv*

com·para·tive² /kəmˈpærətɪv/ *nc* (*gram*) a comparative(3) form: *'Better' is the comparative of 'good'*. Ⓝ Marked *comp* in this dictionary.

com·pare /kəmˈpeə(r)/ *vt* **compare sb/sth (to/with sb/sth)** **1** to examine, judge, to what extent (people or things) are similar or not similar: *compare two translations. Compared to/with yours my garden is untidy*.) **2** to point out the likeness or relation between (people, ideas, things etc): *Poets have compared death to sleep. As a dramatist Shakespeare cannot be compared* (= has no equal).

com·pari·son /kəmˈpærɪsn/ *n* **1** *nu* **by/in comparison (with sb/sth)** when compared (with): *The tallest buildings in London are small in comparison with those of New York. This is better by comparison if you ignore the bad spelling*. **2** *nc* an instance, act, of comparing: *She made a comparison between the eye and a camera*. **3** *nu* the ability to be compared favourably with: *There's no comparison between cotton and nylon. That's a good dictionary, but it won't/can't stand comparison with this one*. **4** *nu* (*gram*) the comparative and superlative form (of adjectives and adverbs), e.g. *better, best*.

com·part·ment /kəmˈpɑːtmənt/ *nc* one of several separate divisions of a structure. e.g. of a railway carriage or coach: *The first-class compartments are in front*.

com·pass /ˈkʌmpəs/ *nc* (*pl* **-es**) **1** an instrument with a needle that points to the magnetic north: *the points of the compass* (N, NE, E, SE, S, etc). **2** (*pl*) (also *a pair of compasses*) a V-shaped instrument with two arms joined by a hinge, used for drawing circles, measuring distances on a map or chart etc. **3** an extent; range: *The song was outside the compass of her voice*.

com·pas·sion /kəmˈpæʃn/ *nu* a feeling for the sufferings or difficulties of others, causing a wish to help: *She was filled with compassion for the refugees*.

com·pas·sion·ate /kəmˈpæʃənət/ *adj* showing or feeling compassion: *a compassionate headteacher. She was granted compassionate leave* (i.e. allowed to go home because of personal problems).

com·pat·ible /kəmˈpætəbl/ *adj* (often *pred*) (of people, ideas, machinery, principles etc) able to exist together: *driving a car at a speed compatible with safety*. Opp incompatible.

com·pati·bil·ity /kəmˌpætəˈbɪlətɪ/ *nu*

com·pat·ibly /-əblɪ/ *adv*

com·pa·tri·ot /kəmˈpætrɪət/ *nc* a person born

in, or a citizen of, the same country as another.

com·pel /kəm'pel/ vt (-ll-) to force (a person or thing) to do something: *His conscience compelled him to confess.*

com·pen·sate /'kɒmpənseɪt/ vt,vi **compensate (sb) (for sth)** to make a suitable payment, give something, to make up (for loss, injury etc): *Nothing can compensate (a person) for the loss of her or his health.*

com·pen·sa·tion /,kɒmpən'seɪʃn/ nc,nu (something given for) compensating: *He received £50 000 in compensation/by way of compensation/as compensation for the loss of his right hand.*

com·pen·sa·tory /kəm'pensətərɪ/ adj (formal) compensating.

com·père /'kɒmpeə(r)/ vt, nc (Fr) (to be) the presenter of a stage, TV or radio entertainment who introduces the performers, speakers etc.

com·pete /kəm'pi:t/ vi to take part (in a race, contest, examination etc): *We are competing against/with other countries for the contract. I'm competing for a prize.*

com·pet·ence /'kɒmpɪtəns/ nu **1** the state of being competent: *I doubt his competence in handling money/to handle money efficiently.* **2** (legal; formal) (of a court, committee etc) legal responsibility and ability: *This is an affair that is within/beyond the competence of the court.*

com·pet·ent /'kɒmpɪtənt/ adj **1** (of a person) having the necessary ability, power, authority, skill, knowledge etc: *Is she competent in her work/competent as a teacher/competent to teach French?* Opp incompetent. **2** (of qualities) sufficient; adequate: *Has she a competent knowledge of French?*

com·pet·ent·ly adv

com·pe·ti·tion /,kɒmpə'tɪʃn/ n **1** nu the act of competing: *Competition encourages trade.* **in competition with sb/sth** competing with a player, team, business company etc: *At the Olympic Games our teams were in competition with the best swimmers in the world.* **2** nc a contest of skill, strength, knowledge etc: *chess competitions.*

com·peti·tive /kəm'petɪtɪv/ adj **1** enjoying, engaged in, competition: *My son is not competitive.* **2** able to compete successfully: *We offer competitive prices* (= prices that are as low as those of other firms). Opp uncompetitive. **3** (of an activity) involving competition: *competitive sports.*

com·peti·tor /kəm'petɪtə(r)/ nc a person, firm, product etc that competes.

com·pi·la·tion /,kɒmpɪ'leɪʃn/ nc,nu (a result of) compiling.

com·pile /kəm'paɪl/ vt to collect (information) and arrange in (a book, list, report etc): *compiling a dictionary.*

com·piler nc a person who compiles information.

com·pla·cence /kəm'pleɪsəns/ nu (often derog) a feeling of personal satisfaction (but without caring about others).

com·pla·cen·cy /-sənsɪ/ nu

com·pla·cent /kəm'pleɪsənt/ adj (derog) pleased with oneself or one's ability (and not caring about others): *with a complacent smile/air.*

com·pla·cent·ly adv

com·plain /kəm'pleɪn/ vi to say that one is not

satisfied, that something is wrong, that one is suffering: *We have nothing to complain about/of.*

com·plain·ant /kəm'pleɪnənt/ nc (legal) a person who makes a formal complaint in a law court.

com·plaint /kəm'pleɪnt/ n **1** nc,nu (an instance, example, of) complaining: *Do you have good cause for complaint? Some children are full of complaints about their food.* **2** nc an illness; disease: *a heart/liver complaint.*

com·plais·ance /kəm'pleɪzəns/ nu (formal) the readiness, willingness, to please.

com·plais·ant /-zənt/ adj

com·ple·ment¹ /'kɒmplɪmənt/ nc **1** that which makes something complete; the full number or quality needed: *Do we have a full complement of staff?* **2** (gram) a word or group of words used after a verb to complete its meaning, such as a *direct object* (e.g. 'I've read *that book*.'), a *subjective complement* (e.g. 'That is *the book* I read.') and an *objective complement* (e.g. 'I find grammar *easy*.').

com·ple·ment² /'kɒmplɪmənt/ vt to be the complement(1) to (something).

com·ple·ment·ary /,kɒmplɪ'mentrɪ/ adj **1** serving to complete a set etc: *complementary volumes.* **2** (maths) making a right angle: *An angle of 60° needs a complementary angle of 30°.* ⇨ supplementary(2).

com·plete¹ /kəm'pli:t/ adj **1** having all its parts; whole: *a complete edition of Shakespeare's plays.* **2** finished: *When will the work be complete?* Opp incomplete. **3** thorough; in every way: *It was a complete surprise to me.*

com·plete·ly adv wholly; in every way: *The operation was completely successful.*

com·plete·ness nu

com·plete² /kəm'pli:t/ vt to finish doing or adding something and make (a whole): *I need one more volume to complete my set of Dickens.*

com·ple·tion /kəm'pli:ʃn/ nu the act of completing; state of being complete: *You may occupy the house on completion of contract.*

com·plex¹ /'kɒmpleks/ adj made up of many connected parts (and often difficult to understand or explain): *a complex argument/proposal/situation.*

,complex 'sentence nc (gram) a sentence with one independent clause and one or more dependent clauses, as in 'If my dad telephones, ask him to ring me again when he gets home from work'.

com·plex·ity /kəm'pleksətɪ/ nc,nu

com·plex² /'kɒmpleks/ nc **1** a group or number of different but related parts. **2** a mental state of strong concern or fear: *an inferiority complex.*

com·plex·ion /kəm'plekʃn/ nc **1** a natural colour, appearance etc of the skin, esp of the face: *a good/dark/fair complexion.* **2** (formal) the general character or aspect (of conduct, affairs etc): *This victory changed the complexion of the war.*

com·pli·ance /kəm'plaɪəns/ nu the state, act, of doing what is asked or ordered: *in compliance with your wishes.*

com·pli·ant /kəm'plaɪənt/ adj (formal) ready and willing to agree to a request etc and act.

com·pli·cate /'kɒmplɪkeɪt/ vt to make (something) difficult to do or understand: *This complicates matters.*

com·pli·ca·ted adj (a) having many (sometimes confusing) parts: *a complicated machine/business deal/personality*. (b) difficult to understand: *a complicated explanation. This problem is too complicated*.

com·pli·ca·tion /ˌkɒmplɪˈkeɪʃn/ nc something that adds new difficulties (e.g. of a person who is ill): *Here are further complications to worry us. She'll survive if no further complications set in*.

com·plic·ity /kəmˈplɪsətɪ/ nu the act of taking part with another person (in doing wrong): *complicity in a crime*.

com·pli·ment¹ /ˈkɒmplɪmənt/ nc 1 an expression of admiration, approval etc, either in words or by action: *Copying my design is a great compliment*. 2 (pl) greetings: *My compliments to your wife*.

com·pli·ment² /ˈkɒmplɪment/ vt to express admiration etc for (a person): *I complimented him on his skill*.

com·pli·men·tary /ˌkɒmplɪˈmentrɪ/ adj 1 (usually attrib) expressing admiration, praise etc: *complimentary words*. Opp uncomplimentary. 2 given free: *a complimentary ticket*.

com·ply /kəmˈplaɪ/ vi (pt,pp **-ied**) *comply (to/ with sth)* to act in agreement (with a request, command, wish etc): *He refused to comply (to my order/with her wishes)*. ⇨ compliant.

com·po·nent¹ /kəmˈpəʊnənt/ adj (attrib) helping to form (a complete thing): *component parts*.

com·po·nent² /kəmˈpəʊnənt/ nc a part of a larger or more complex object (esp a machine): *the components of a camera*.

com·port /kəmˈpɔːt/ v (formal) 1 v reflex to behave (in the way mentioned): *comport oneself with dignity*. 2 vi *comport (with sth)* to suit, be in harmony (with something): *His conduct did not comport with his high position*.

com·pose /kəmˈpəʊz/ vt 1 (often passive) (of parts) to make up (a whole): *Our party was composed of teachers, pupils and their parents*. 2 to put together (words, musical notes etc) in literary, musical etc form: *compose a poem/song/ speech/tune*. 3 to bring (feelings etc) under control: *compose one's thoughts/feelings*. ⇨ composure.

com·posed adj having, with, feelings etc under control.

com·posed·ly adv

com·po·ser /kəmˈpəʊzə(r)/ nc (esp) a person who composes music.

com·pos·ite /ˈkɒmpəzɪt/ adj made up of different parts or materials: *a composite illustration* (i.e. made by using several drawings etc).

com·po·si·tion /ˌkɒmpəˈzɪʃn/ n 1 nu the act or art of composing, e.g. a piece of writing or music. 2 nc that which is composed, e.g. a piece of music or writing, an arrangement of objects to be painted or photographed. 3 nu the parts of which something is made up: *Scientists studied the composition of the soil*.

com·pos men·tis /ˌkɒmpəs ˈmentɪs/ adj (pred; Latin) sane: *He's not quite compos mentis*.

com·post /ˈkɒmpɒst/ nu a prepared mixture, esp of rotted food, leaves, manure etc for use as a fertiliser.

com·po·sure /kəmˈpəʊʒə(r)/ nu the condition of feeling calm and controlled: *behave with com-posure*.

com·pound¹ /ˈkɒmpaʊnd/ adj (attrib) having many parts: *a compound substance/word*.

ˌcompound ˈfracture nc a breaking of a bone with an open wound in the skin.

ˌcompound ˈinterest nu interest on capital and on earlier accumulated interest.

ˌcompound ˈnoun nc (gram) = compound²(2).

ˌcompound ˈsentence nc (gram) a sentence with two or more independent clauses, such as 'Mary drinks coffee but I prefer tea'.

com·pound² /ˈkɒmpaʊnd/ nc 1 something made up of two or more combined parts: *Common salt is a compound of sodium and chlorine*. 2 (gram) a word made up of two or more parts, themselves usually words, e.g. *safety-pin*.

com·pound³ /ˈkɒmpaʊnd/ nc (a group of buildings inside) an enclosed area.

com·pound⁴ /kəmˈpaʊnd/ vt (formal) 1 to mix substances together to make (something): *compound a medicine; an ointment compounded of/ from oil and herbs*. 2 to add to, increase the seriousness of, (an offence or injury): *Your lies compound the offence*.

com·pre·hend /ˌkɒmprɪˈhend/ vt (formal) to understand (something) fully.

com·pre·hen·sible /ˌkɒmprɪˈhensəbl/ adj that can be understood fully: *a book that is comprehensible only to specialists*. Opp incomprehensible.

com·pre·hen·si·bil·ity /ˌkɒmprɪˌhensəˈbɪlətɪ/ nu

com·pre·hen·sion /ˌkɒmprɪˈhenʃn/ n 1 nu the mind's power of understanding: *The problem is above/beyond my comprehension*. 2 nc,nu a written exercise aimed at improving or testing one's understanding.

com·pre·hen·sive /ˌkɒmprɪˈhensɪv/ adj including many details: *a comprehensive description*.

ˌcompreˌhensive (motor) inˈsurance nu the kind that covers all possibilities of accidents and claims.

ˌcompreˈhensive school nc one that provides all kinds of secondary education.

com·pre·hen·sive·ly adv

com·press¹ /ˈkɒmpres/ nc a pad or cloth pressed on part of the body (to stop bleeding, reduce fever etc): *a cold/hot compress*.

com·press² /kəmˈpres/ vt 1 to press, get, (a substance or material) into a small(er) space: *compressed air*. 2 (formal) to put (ideas etc) into fewer words.

com·pres·sion /kəmˈpreʃn/ nu

com·prise /kəmˈpraɪz/ vt to be composed of (things, ideas etc); have (things etc) as parts or members: *The committee comprises people of widely different views*.

com·pro·mise¹ /ˈkɒmprəmaɪz/ nc,nu (an instance of) the settlement of a dispute by each side giving up something it has asked for; settlement reached in this way: *A compromise was reached at last*.

com·pro·mise² /ˈkɒmprəmaɪz/ v 1 vi to settle a dispute etc by making a compromise: *I agree to compromise*. 2 v reflex, vt to bring (oneself) under suspicion by unwise action etc: *You will compromise yourself/your reputation if you stay in that hotel*. 3 vt (formal) to risk (the safety of people, a business etc): *The passengers' safety was compromised by his careless driving.*

com·pul·sion /kəm'pʌlʃn/ *n* **1** *nc* a strong and uncontrollable desire: *Smoking cigarettes is a compulsion.* **2** *nu* the state of being forced to do something (often without wanting to). **under compulsion (to do sth)** (*formal*) forced (to): *I feel under compulsion to explain.*

com·pul·sive /kəm'pʌlsɪv/ *adj* caused by a compulsion(1): *a compulsive eater/liar.*

com·pul·sive·ly *adv*

com·pul·sory /kəm'pʌlsərɪ/ *adj* (no *comp*) that must be done: *Is English a compulsory subject in your school?* Compare optional.

com·pul·sor·ily /kəm'pʌlsərəlɪ/ *adv*

com·punc·tion /kəm'pʌŋkʃn/ *nu* (usually used in negative sentences) a feeling of regret for one's action: *She kept me waiting without the slightest compunction.*

com·pu·ter /kəm'pjuːtə(r)/ *nc* an electronic device which stores information (*data*), analyses it and produces further information as required.

com,puter-'aided/-as'sisted *adj* using a computer: *computer-aided accounting.*

com,puter 'disk *nc* a small flat disc used to store computerized information.

com,puter 'program *nc* a coded system used to put in, analyse and take out information.

com·pu·ter·ize (also **-ise**) /-raɪz/ *vt* (**a**) to store (information) using a computer. (**b**) supply (a business etc) with a computer (system).

com·rade /'kɒmreɪd/ *nc* **1** a trusted and loyal companion. **comrades in arms** fellow soldiers. **2** a fellow member of a trade union, a left-wing political party etc.

com·rade·ship /'kɒmreɪdʃɪp/ *nu*

Con. *abbr* Conservative.

con·cave /'kɒnkeɪv/ *adj* (of an outline or surface) curved inwards like the inner surface of a bowl. Compare convex.

con·ceal /kən'siːl/ *vt* **conceal sth (from sb)** to hide something; keep information secret: *He tried to conceal the truth from me.*

con·ceal·ment *nu*

con·cede /kən'siːd/ *vt* **1** to admit (something) as true: *conceding a point in an argument.* **2** to agree to give (something, esp when defeated): *We won't concede any territory.* ⇨ concession(1).

con·ceit /kən'siːt/ *nu* too high opinion of, too much pride in, oneself or one's abilities: *He's full of conceit.*

con·ceit·ed *adj* (*derog*) having conceit.

con·ceit·ed·ly *adv*

con·ceiv·able /kən'siːvəbl/ *adj* that can be thought of or believed: *Her bad behaviour is hardly conceivable (to me).* Opp inconceivable.

con·ceiv·ably /-əblɪ/ *adv*

con·ceive /kən'siːv/ *v* Ⓝ Not used in the continuous tenses, e.g. *'is/was -ing'.* **1** *vi* **conceive of sth** (*formal*) to form an idea, plan etc in the mind: *It's impossible/difficult to conceive of a person hating a child.* **2** *vt,vi* (of a woman) to become pregnant with (a child). ⇨ conception.

con·cen·trate /'kɒnsəntreɪt/ *v* **1** *vi* **concentrate (on sth)** to keep one's attention on something: *You'll solve the problem if you concentrate (on it).* **2** *vt* to bring (people, things) together in one place: *to concentrate soldiers in a town.* **3** *vt*

(*science*) to increase the strength of (a liquid) by reducing the amount of water etc in it (e.g. by boiling it).

con·cen·trated *adj* (**a**) very strong: *concentrated hate; a concentrated effort.* (**b**) (of a liquid) increased in strength through reduction of the amount of water etc in it (e.g. by being boiled): *concentrated orange juice.*

con·cen·tra·tion /ˌkɒnsən'treɪʃn/ *n* **1** *nu* attention: *a book that needs concentration. I must have your concentration if you hope to understand.* **2** *nc* an act, example, of concentrating(2): *concentrations of enemy troops.*

,concen'tration camp *nc* a place where political prisoners are kept.

con·cen·tric /kən'sentrɪk/ *adj* (*maths*) (of circles) having the same centre.

con·cept /'kɒnsept/ *nc* a creative idea: *the concept of evolution.*

con·cep·tion /kən'sepʃn/ *n* **1** *nc* an idea, plan etc that is formed in the mind: *Do you have any conception of our difficulties?* **2** *nc,nu* the act, result, of becoming pregnant. ⇨ conceive, contraception.

con·cern¹ /kən'sɜːn/ *n* **1** *nc* something in which one is interested or which is important: *It's no concern of mine. It's of no concern to me. It's an issue of deep/major concern to me.* **2** *nc* a business or undertaking: *The shop has now become a profitable concern.* **a going concern** an active and successful business. **3** *nu* anxiety: *There is some/no/much cause for concern.*

con·cern² /kən'sɜːn/ *vt* **1** to affect, be of importance to, (a person): *Does this concern me? As far as I'm concerned* (= I consider that) *he's wrong.* Ⓝ Not used in the continuous tenses, e.g. *'is/was -ing'.* **2** to be busy with, interest oneself in, (a subject, problem etc): *I'm concerned with child psychology.* **3** (usu *pp*) **concerned (about/for sb/sth)** feeling worried or unhappy: *I'm concerned about the weather/for his old uncle/for his future.*

con·cern·ed /kən'sɜːnd/ *adj* **1** (usu *attrib*) very worried: *a concerned look.* **2** (used after the noun) involved; interested: *Would the students concerned wait behind, please.*

con·cern·ing /kən'sɜːnɪŋ/ *prep* with reference to: *I'm telephoning concerning a bill you have not paid.* Compare about²(1).

con·cert /'kɒnsət/ *n* **1** *nc* a musical entertainment given to an audience by players or singers. **2** *nu* **in concert** (of voices, sounds) together; at the same time: *They shouted in concert.*

con·cert·ed /kən'sɜːtɪd/ *adj* (*attrib*) **1** (planned as a group and) done together: *a concerted attempt.* **2** (of effort) great: *make a concerted effort.*

con·cer·tina /ˌkɒnsə'tiːnə/ *nc* (*pl* —s) a musical wind instrument held in the hands and played by pressing keys at each end.

con·cer·to /kən'tʃeətəʊ/ *nc* (*pl* —s) a musical composition for one or more solo instruments supported by an orchestra: *a piano concerto.*

con·ces·sion /kən'seʃn/ *n* **1** *nc,nu* (a result of) agreeing to do or give something (esp after discussion, an argument etc): *As a concession to public opinion the Government reduced the tax on petrol.* ⇨ concede. **2** *nc* (esp) a right given by owner(s) of land or by a government to do something (e.g. take minerals from land): *American oil concessions in the Middle East.*

con·cili·ate /kən'sɪlɪeɪt/ *vt* (*formal*) to win the support, goodwill or friendly feelings of (a person, country etc); calm the anger of (a person, government) etc: *After the robbery the old woman could not be conciliated.*

con·cili·ation /kən,sɪlɪ'eɪʃn/ *nu*

con·cili·atory /kən'sɪlɪətrɪ/ *adj* (*formal*) intended or likely to conciliate: *a conciliatory act.*

con·cise /kən'saɪs/ *adj* (of speech, a style of writing, a person etc) giving much information in few words.

con·cise·ly *adv*

con·cise·ness *nu*

con·clude /kən'kluːd/ *v* **1** *vt,vi* (to cause a speech, discussion etc) to come to an end: *He concluded by thanking us.* **2** *vt* to arrange, bring about, (an agreement etc): *to conclude a treaty with the French.* **3** *vt* **conclude (from sth) that . . .** to arrive at a belief or opinion: *The jury concluded (from the evidence) that I was not guilty.* Ⓝ Not used in the continuous tenses, e.g. *'is/was -ing'.*

con·clu·sion /kən'kluːʒn/ *nc* **1** the last part: *at the conclusion of his speech.* **in conclusion** lastly: *I'd like to say in conclusion that I am glad I came.* **2** an arrangement; settlement: *the conclusion of a peace treaty.* **3** a judgement: *the conclusion is that John must have broken it.* **a foregone conclusion** something already decided (before a discussion, contest etc). **come to the conclusion that . . .** to decide that: *I've come to the conclusion that she is innocent.* **jump to conclusions** to make a judgement too quickly: *Don't jump to conclusions.* **reach a conclusion** to finally decide about something.

con·clus·ive /kən'kluːsɪv/ *adj* (of facts, evidence etc) convincing; removing all doubt: *conclusive evidence/proof.* Opp inconclusive.

con·clus·ive·ly *adv*

con·coct /kən'kɒkt/ *vt* **1** to prepare (something) by mixing things together: *to concoct a new kind of soup.* **2** to invent (a story, an excuse etc).

con·coc·tion /kən'kɒkʃn/ *nc* a mixture.

con·cord /'kɒŋkɔːd/ *n* **1** *nc,nu* (*formal*) (an instance of) agreement or harmony (between people or things): *live in concord (with them).* **2** *nu* (*gram*) the agreement of a verb with its subject, as in *'I do', 'She does'.*

con·cord·ance /kən'kɔːdəns/ *n* **1** *nu* (*formal*) agreement. **2** *nc* an arrangement in ABC order of the important words used by an author or in a book: *a Shakespeare concordance.*

con·course /'kɒŋkɔːs/ *nc* a place (in a building or enclosed by buildings) where people come together.

con·crete¹ /'kɒŋkriːt/ *adj* **1** (*tech*) existing in material form; that can be touched, felt etc: *A lamp is concrete but light is abstract.* **2** definite; positive: *concrete proposals/evidence/proof.*

con·crete² /'kɒŋkriːt/ *nu* a kind of building material made by mixing cement with sand, gravel etc.

'concrete-mixer *nc* a machine that makes concrete.

‚concrete 'noun *nc* (*gram*) one referring to anything we can experience directly, such as *ball,*

the sea, fog, a kiss. Compare abstract noun.

con·cur /kən'kɜː(r)/ *vi* (**-rr-**) (*formal*) to agree (with a person, an opinion): *I concur with the speaker in condemning what has been done.*

con·cur·rence /kən'kʌrəns/ *nu* (*formal*) agreement.

con·cur·rent /kən'kʌrənt/ *adj* happening together: *concurrent events.*

con·cur·rent·ly *adv*

con·cuss /kən'kʌs/ *vt* to injure the brain of (a person) by concussion.

con·cus·sion /kən'kʌʃn/ *nc,nu* (an) injury or violent shaking or shock (to the brain) as caused by a blow, knock or fall.

con·demn /kən'dem/ *vt* **1** to say that (a person) is, or has done, wrong or that (something) is wrong or unfit for use: *We all condemn cruelty to children.* **2** (*legal*) to give judgement against (a person): *He condemned the murderer to life imprisonment.* **3** to force (a person) to do something unwelcome or painful: *an unhappy housewife condemned to spend hours at the kitchen sink.*

con·dem·na·tion /,kɒndəm'neɪʃn/ *nu*

con·den·sa·tion /,kɒnden'seɪʃn/ *nu* (the process of) drops of liquid forming when vapour condenses: *A cloud is the result of the condensation of vapour. We have wet walls due to condensation.*

con·dense /kən'dens/ *v* **1** *vt,vi* (to cause a liquid, gas etc) to increase in density or strength, to become thicker: *condensed milk.* **2** *vt* to put (a speech, writing) into fewer words: *a condensed report.*

con·de·scend /,kɒndɪ'send/ *vi* to (agree to) do something that one's rank, abilities etc do not require one to do: *The Duke has graciously condescended to open the new playing field.*

con·de·scend·ing *adj* (*derog*) behaving graciously in order to show one's feeling of superiority: *Don't be so condescending!*

con·di·ments /'kɒndɪmənts/ *n pl* (*formal*) salt and pepper (to be) used at the table.

con·di·tion¹ /kən'dɪʃn/ *n* **1** *nc* something on which another thing depends: *A condition of my accepting the job is that I work on Saturdays.* **on condition that** (*conj*) only if; provided that: *You can go on condition that you come home early.* **2** *nu* the present state of a person, thing; quality, character of a person, thing: *The condition of my health prevents me from working. He's in no condition to travel* (= is not well or strong enough). *I refuse to work under these conditions.*

con·di·tion² /kən'dɪʃn/ *vt* (*formal*) **1** (usually *passive*) to determine, control, (something): *My holidays are conditioned by my income.* **2** to persuade (a person): *We'll never condition the workers to accept a wage freeze.*

con·di·tion·ed /kən'dɪʃnd/ *adj* **1** in a desired mental state through persuasion, force etc: *She was conditioned to feeling inferior.* **2** in the state mentioned: *air-conditioned.*

con·di·tion·al /kən'dɪʃənl/ *adj* **conditional (on sth)** depending (on certain things): *Your place at the university is conditional on you passing the exam.*

con‚ditional 'clause *nc* (*gram*) one beginning with 'if' or 'unless', such as *'If it's warm tomorrow shall we go for a walk?'*

con,ditional 'verb *nc* (*gram*) a verb form using *would*, as in 'He *would come* if you asked him' or *should*, as in 'I *should write* if I were you'.
con·di·tion·al·ly /-əlɪ/ *adv*

con·dol·ences /kən'dəʊlənsɪz/ *n pl* (*formal*) (expressions of) sympathy: *Please accept my condolences*.

con·dom /'kɒndɒm/ *nc* an elastic covering (to be) worn over the penis during sexual intercourse, used to prevent conception or passing on sexually transmitted diseases.

con·done /kən'dəʊn/ *vt* to ignore or forgive (an offence): *condone a child's bad behaviour*.

con·duc·ive /kən'djuːsɪv/ *adj* (*pred*) **conducive to sth** (*formal*) helping to produce an effect: *Good health is conducive to happiness*.

con·duct¹ /'kɒndʌkt/ *nu* **1** behaviour (the usual word): *good/bad conduct*. **2** the manner of directing or managing affairs: *People were not satisfied with the conduct of the war*.

con·duct² /kən'dʌkt/ *v* **1** *vt* to lead or guide (a person): *He conducted the visitors round the museum*. **2** *vt* to control, direct, manage, (a group, discussion etc): *to conduct a meeting/ negotiations*. **3** *vt,vi* to direct (an orchestra) during a performance. **4** *v reflex* (*formal*) to behave: *He conducts himself well*. **5** *vt* (*science*) to allow (heat, electricity) to pass along or through: *Copper conducts electricity well*.

con·duc·tion /kən'dʌkʃn/ *nu* the process of conducting(5).

con·duc·tor /kən'dʌktə(r)/ *nc* **1** a person who conducts(3). **2** a person who collects fares on a bus etc. **3** (*science*) a material that conducts(5). ⇨ insulator.

con·duc·tress /kən'dʌktrɪs/ *nc* a woman conductor(2).

cone /kəʊn/ *nc* **1** an object which narrows to a point from a round, flat base. ⇨ conic. **2** something of this shape whether solid or hollow: *an ice-cream cone*. **3** a fruit of certain evergreen trees (fir, pine, cedar). ⇨ conifer.

con·fec·tion·ery /kən'fekʃənrɪ/ *nu* (*commerce*) sweets, chocolates etc.

con·fed·er·acy /kən'fedərəsɪ/ *nc* (*pl* **-ies**) a formal union of states etc.

con·fed·er·ate /kən'fedərət/ *nc* **1** a state or political party joined with another or others. **2** an accomplice (in a plot, crime etc).

con·fed·er·ation /kən,fedə'reɪʃn/ *nc,nu* (the act of forming) a political union of states.

con·fer /kən'fɜː(r)/ *v* (**-rr-**) **1** *vt* **confer sth (on sb)** to give, grant, a degree, title, favour: *The University conferred an honorary degree on the President*. **2** *vi* **confer (with sb)** (*formal*) to consult or discuss (with a person): *confer with one's lawyer*.
con·fer·ment *nc,nu*

con·fer·ence /'kɒnfərəns/ *nc,nu* (a meeting for) discussion: *The Director is in conference/is holding a conference*.

con·fess /kən'fes/ *vt,vi* **1** **confess (to sth/ that . . .)** to say or admit (that one has done wrong): *He confessed that he had stolen the money*. *I confess to having a great fear of spiders*. **2** (*R C Church*) to make known one's sins to a priest: *confess one's sins*.

con·fes·sion /kən'feʃn/ *n* **1** *nc,nu* (an instance of) confessing: *The accused man made a full confession*. **2** *nc* a declaration (of religious beliefs etc): *a confession of faith*.

con·fes·sion·al /kən'feʃənl/ *nc* a private place in a church for confession(2).

con·fes·sor /kən'fesə(r)/ *nc* a priest who has authority to hear confessions.

con·fet·ti /kən'fetɪ/ *nu* small bits of coloured paper (to be) thrown at weddings.

con·fi·dant /,kɒnfɪ'dænt/ *nc* a person who is trusted with personal secrets.

con·fide /kən'faɪd/ *vt* to tell (personal troubles etc) secretly: *He confided his troubles to a friend*. **confide in sb** to tell personal secrets to a person one trusts: *confiding in my mother*.

con·fi·dence /'kɒnfɪdəns/ *n* **1** *nu* the act of confiding. **in (strict) confidence** expecting something to be kept secret. **2** *nc* a secret or piece of private information which is confided to a person. **3** *nu* belief in oneself, one's abilities or in others or in what is said, reported etc: *to have/lose confidence in oneself/her. He answered all the questions with confidence*. **vote of confidence** ⇨ vote¹.
'confidence trick *nc* a theft achieved by persuading a person to trust one.

con·fi·dent /'kɒnfɪdənt/ *adj* **confident (of sth/that . . .)** feeling or showing confidence(3): *He feels fairly confident of passing/that he will pass the examination*.
con·fi·dent·ly *adv*

con·fi·den·ti·al /,kɒnfɪ'denʃl/ *adj* (that is to be kept) secret: *confidential information*.
con·fi·den·ti·al·ly /-ʃəlɪ/ *adv*

con·fine /kən'faɪn/ *vt* **1** **confine oneself/sb/ sth to sth** to keep (oneself, a person, speech etc) within limits: *Please confine your remarks to the subject we are debating*. **2** to keep (a person, animal etc) shut up: *Is it cruel to confine a bird in a cage?*
con·fined *adj* (of space) limited; restricted.

con·fine·ment /kən'faɪnmənt/ *n* **1** *nu* the state of being shut up or imprisoned: *He was placed in confinement*. **2** *nc,nu* (an instance of) giving birth to a child.

con·fines /'kɒnfaɪnz/ *n pl* (the —) (*formal*) limits; boundaries: *beyond the confines of knowledge/this valley*.

con·firm /kən'fɜːm/ *vt* **1** to state, show, the truth of (opinions, feelings etc): *The report of an earthquake in Greece has now been confirmed*. **2** to state definite agreement to (a date for an event, an appointment, a contract etc): *I'm writing to confirm our arrangement to meet next Tuesday*. **3** to admit (a person) to full membership of the Christian Church.
con·firm·ed *adj* (*attrib*) (esp) unlikely to change or be changed: *a confirmed bachelor*.

con·fir·ma·tion /,kɒnfə'meɪʃn/ *nc,nu* **confirmation (of sth/that)** the act of confirming or being confirmed (all senses): *We are waiting for confirmation of the news*.

con·fis·cate /'kɒnfɪskeɪt/ *vt* to take possession of (private property) without payment (as punishment or to enforce authority): *Smuggled goods will be confiscated by Customs*.
con·fis·ca·tion /,kɒnfɪ'skeɪʃn/ *nc,nu*

con·flict¹ /'kɒnflɪkt/ *n* **1** *nc* a fight, struggle, quarrel etc: *a bitter conflict between employers and workers*. **2** *nc,nu* (of opinions, desires etc) opposition; disagreement: *conflict between duty and desire*. **3** *nu* (*literature*) the struggle between opposing forces in a plot, within the personality etc of a character or between two or more characters (which gives interest and excitement to the work).

con·flict² /kən'flɪkt/ *vi* **conflict (with sth)** to be in opposition or disagreement: *His account of the war conflicts with mine. They conflict (with each other).*

con·flict·ing *adj* (usually *attrib*): *conflicting evidence/reports*.

con·form /kən'fɔːm/ *vi* **conform (to/with sth)** to agree with, behave in the same way as, (generally accepted rules, standards etc): *You should conform to the rules/with the wishes of others*.

con·form·ity /kən'fɔːmətɪ/ *nu* **conformity (to/with sth)** agreement with, behaviour etc based on, (what is usual, accepted etc): *Unemployed teenagers can ignore conformity in the way they dress*.

con·found /kən'faʊnd/ *vt* (*formal*) to fill (a person) with confusion: *His behaviour amazed and confounded her*.

con·front /kən'frʌnt/ *vt* **confront sb/sth (with sth)** to bring (a person), come, face to face (with danger, unpleasant facts etc): *When confronted with the evidence he confessed at once. A soldier has to confront danger*.

con·fron·ta·tion /ˌkɒnfrən'teɪʃn/ *nc,nu* (an act, instance, of) determined opposition, esp when face to face: *the noisy confrontation between the police and the demonstrators*.

con·fuse /kən'fjuːz/ *vt* **1** to make (a person) feel uncertain, puzzled etc: *They asked so many questions that they confused me*. ⇨ confound. **2** to mistake (one thing for another): *Don't confuse a cheap racing bike with this one*. **3** to make (a situation etc) disorganized, mixed up: *Adding more detail will only confuse things*.

con·fus·ed·ly *adv* in a confused manner.

con·fu·sion /kən'fjuːʒn/ *nu* the state of being mixed up, disordered: *His unexpected arrival threw everything into confusion. There has been some confusion; it was Mr Smythe who came, not Mr Smith*. **be covered with confusion** to be very embarrassed. ⇨ confound.

con·geal /kən'dʒiːl/ *vt,vi* (to cause blood etc) to become stiff or solid.

con·gen·ial /kən'dʒiːnɪəl/ *adj* **1** (of a person) pleasant and having the same or a similar nature, interests etc: *congenial flatmates*. **2** (of the weather, a job etc) pleasant and enjoyable: *a congenial climate; congenial work*. Opp uncongenial.

con·gen·ial·ly /-ɪəlɪ/ *adv*

con·geni·tal /kən'dʒenɪtl/ *adj* (of diseases etc) present at or before birth.

con·ges·ted /kən'dʒestɪd/ *adj* **1** overcrowed: *streets congested with traffic*. **2** (*med*) (of parts of the body, e.g. the nose, lungs) having an abnormal amount of mucus, blood etc.

con·ges·tion /kən'dʒestʃən/ *nu* the state of being congested: *congestion of the lungs/of traffic in town*.

con·glom·er·ate /kən'glɒmərət/ *nc* (also *attrib*) **1** a number of things or parts together in a mass or ball (e.g. rock). **2** (*fig*) a large and complex business organization: *conglomerate businesses*.

con·glom·er·ation /kən,glɒmə'reɪʃn/ *nc,nu*

con·gratu·late /kən'grætjʊleɪt/ *v* **1** *vt* to tell (a person) that one is pleased about something good that has happened etc: *congratulate him on his marriage*. **2** *v reflex* (*literary*) to consider (oneself) fortunate: *I congratulated myself on my escape/on having escaped unhurt*.

con·gratu·la·tions /kən,grætjʊ'leɪʃnz/ *n pl* (used to express pleasure at another person's success): *Congratulations on passing the exam! Please give my heartiest congratulations to her*.

con·gratu·la·tory /kən,grætjʊ'leɪtərɪ/ *adj* (*attrib*) that congratulates: *a congratulatory telegram*.

con·gre·gate /'kɒŋgrɪgeɪt/ *vi* to come together: *People were congregating round the speaker*.

con·gre·ga·tion /ˌkɒŋgrɪ'geɪʃn/ *nc* a group of people (esp taking part in religious worship).

con·gress /'kɒŋgres/ *nc* **1** (C-) **(a)** the law-making body of the US and some other republics in America; **(b)** a political party in India. **2** a meeting, series of meetings, of representatives of (professions etc) for discussion: *a medical congress*.

'Con·gress·man/woman *nc* a member of Congress(1a).

con·gres·sion·al /kən'greʃənl/ *adj*

con·gru·ent /'kɒŋgrʊənt/ *adj* (*maths*) having the same size and shape: *congruent triangles*.

con·ic /'kɒnɪk/ *adj* (*tech*) of a cone(1): *conic sections*.

coni·cal /'kɒnɪkl/ *adj* cone-shaped.

coni·fer /'kɒnɪfə(r)/ *nc* a tree of the kind (e.g. *pine, fir*) that bears cones(3).

co·nif·er·ous /kə'nɪfərəs/ *adj*

conj *abbr* (*gram*) conjunction.

con·jec·ture /kən'dʒektʃə(r)/ *vi, nc* (*formal*) (to make) a conclusion, opinion, based on incomplete evidence: *The result was just as I conjectured. I was right in my conjectures*.

con·jec·tur·al /kən'dʒektʃərəl/ *adj*

con·ju·gal /'kɒndʒʊgl/ *adj* (*formal*) of marriage and married life; of husband and wife: *conjugal happiness/fidelity*.

con·ju·gate /'kɒndʒʊgeɪt/ *v* (*gram*) **1** *vt* to give the forms of (a verb) for number, tense etc. **2** *vi* (of a verb) to have these forms.

con·ju·ga·tion /ˌkɒndʒʊ'geɪʃn/ *n* **(a)** *nc,nu* (the process of giving) verb forms: *Appendix 2 of this dictionary lists the conjugations of irregular verbs*. **(b)** *nc* a group of verbs conjugated in the same way.

con·junc·tion /kən'dʒʌŋkʃn/ *n* **1** *nc* (*gram*) a word used to join other words, clauses etc, such as *and, but, because*. Ⓝ Marked *conj* in this dictionary. ⇨ coordinating/subordinating conjunction. **2** *nu* (*formal*) the process, state, of being joined: *the conjunction of skill and imagination in planning a garden*. **in conjunction with sb/sth** together with others: *to work in conjunction with other research students*.

con·junc·tive /kən'dʒʌŋktɪv/ *adj* (*gram*) concerning conjunctions(1).

con,junctive 'adverb *nc* (*gram*) one that joins two independent clauses, such as *when* in 'It was 6 o'clock *when* the telephone rang'.

con·jure /ˈkʌndʒə(r)/ *vt,vi* **1** to do clever tricks which appear magical: *conjuring a rabbit out of a hat.* **2** *vt* **conjure sth up** (a) to cause something to appear as if from nothing, or as an image in the mind: *conjuring up visions of the past.* (b) to cause a spirit etc to appear by calling and encouraging: *conjure up the spirits of the dead.*

con·jur·er (also **-or**) *nc* a person who performs conjuring(1) tricks.

con·nect /kəˈnekt/ *v* **1** *vt,vi* (to cause things) to become united as one (physical) thing: *The towns are connected by a railway. Have they connected up the electricity yet? The terminal is connected up to the main computer.* Ⓝ *'Join'* is also possible but is more informal. **2** *vt* to link (a person) by telephone: *Wait please, I'm trying to connect you.* **3** *vt* **connect sb/sth (with sth)** (a) to associate a person (with a business, a club, as a member or supporter etc): *He's been connected with this firm/club/college for many years.* (b) to think of something as being related (to another): *I connect high mountains and waterfalls with Austria.*

con·nec·tion /kəˈnekʃn/ *n* **1** *nc,nu* (an act of) connecting(1,2): *a telephone/an electrical connection.* **2** *nc* a (logical, imaginary) association (of ideas, themes etc): *What is the connection between these two poems? It's easy to make a connection between his new camera and the stolen money.* **3** *nc* a relationship between a word and its meaning, context, origin etc: *Does 'catacombs' have any connection with clean cats?* **4** **in connection with** (*prep*) concerning: *I'm writing in connection with your overdraft.* **5** (*pl*) (*informal*) a number of clients, rich or socially high relatives, influential friends etc: *He has excellent business connections. Her family provided useful connections. What connections do you have in the city?* **6** *nc* a train, bus etc that will leave a station soon after another has arrived: *If this bus is late, I'll miss my connection.*

con·nect·ive /kəˈnektɪv/ *adj* (*formal*) serving to join: *connective layers.*

con·nive /kəˈnaɪv/ *vi* **connive at sth** to encourage something that is wrong: *connive at an escape from prison.*

con·niv·ance /-əns/ *nu*

con·nois·seur /ˌkɒnəˈsɜː(r)/ *nc* a person with good judgement on matters in which knowledge or artistic taste is needed: *a connoisseur of wine.*

con·note /kəˈnəʊt/ *vt* (*formal*) (of a word) to suggest (something) in addition to its basic meaning: *The word 'Tropics' means a geographical area; it also connotes heat.*

con·no·ta·tion /ˌkɒnəˈteɪʃn/ *nc* something that is suggested: *Be careful not to use slang words which have obscene connotations.*

con·quer /ˈkɒŋkə(r)/ *vt* **1** to defeat (and take possession of) (a country, army etc) by force: *conquer a country.* **2** to climb (a mountain): *conquer Everest.* **3** (*fig*) to overcome (an illness, bad habit, difficulty etc).

con·quer·or /-rə(r)/ *nc* a person who conquers(1,2) something.

con·quest /ˈkɒŋkwest/ *n* **1** *nc,nu* the act of conquering: *the conquest of Annapurna/a serious illness.* **2** *nc* something achieved by conquering: *His conquests will live on after his death.*

Cons. *abbr* Conservative.

con·science /ˈkɒnʃəns/ *nc,nu* the consciousness within oneself of the choice one ought to make between right and wrong: *have a clear/guilty conscience.* **have no conscience (about sth)** to be as ready to do wrong as right. **(have sth/sb) on one's conscience** (to feel) troubled about something one has done or failed to do, or about a person one has harmed.

con·scien·tious /ˌkɒnʃɪˈenʃəs/ *adj* **1** (of a person) guided by one's sense of duty. **2** (of an action) done carefully and honestly: *conscientious work.*

consci,entious ob'jector *nc* a person who objects to serving in the armed forces because he or she believes it is morally wrong to fight and kill.

con·scien·tious·ly *adv*

con·scien·tious·ness *nu*

con·scious /ˈkɒnʃəs/ *adj* **1** able to think, feel, see etc. Opp unconscious. **2** knowing things because one is using the bodily senses and mental powers: *They were conscious of being/that they were being watched.*

con·scious·ly *adv*

con·scious·ness /ˈkɒnʃəsnɪs/ *nu* the state of being conscious: *He hit the ground and lost consciousness. He didn't recover/regain consciousness until two hours after the accident.*

con·script¹ /ˈkɒnskrɪpt/ *nc* a person who is conscripted.

con·script² /kənˈskrɪpt/ *vt* **conscript sb (into sth)** to force a person by law to serve in the armed forces: *be conscripted into the army.* ⇨ draft²(2).

con·scrip·tion /kənˈskrɪpʃn/ *nu*

con·se·crate /ˈkɒnsɪkreɪt/ *vt* to set (something) apart as sacred or for a religious purpose: *to consecrate a church.*

con·se·cra·tion /ˌkɒnsɪˈkreɪʃn/ *nc,nu*

con·secu·tive /kənˈsekjʊtɪv/ *adj* coming one after the other in regular order: *I found a parking space on five consecutive days.*

con·secu·tive·ly *adv*

con·sen·sus /kənˈsensəs/ *nc,nu* (*pl* **—es**) (a) general agreement: *a consensus of opinion.*

con·sent¹ /kənˈsent/ *nu* agreement: *He was chosen leader by general consent.* ⇨ age of consent.

con·sent² /kənˈsent/ *vi* **consent (to sth)** to give one's agreement or permission: *Anne's father would not consent to her marrying her boyfriend.*

con·se·quence /ˈkɒnsɪkwəns/ *n* **1** *nc* something that follows or is caused as the result or effect: *If you behave so foolishly you must be ready to take the consequences.* **2** *nu* importance: *It's of no consequence to me.*

con·se·quent·ly /ˈkɒnsɪkwəntlɪ/ *adv* therefore: *I crashed the car and consequently I must pay for the repairs.*

con·ser·va·tion /ˌkɒnsəˈveɪʃn/ *nu* preservation (esp the prevention of loss, waste etc by controlling use): *the conservation of forests. Energy conservation is a problem throughout the world.*

con·ser·va·tism /kənˈsɜːvətɪzəm/ *nu* (the belief in) a political and social system which maintains an established state of affairs without great or sudden change.

con·ser·va·tive¹ /kənˈsɜːvətɪv/ *adj* **1** in favour

of established ways, customs etc and opposed to great or sudden change: *Old people are usually more conservative than young people.* **2** careful not to be wrong: *a conservative estimate of one's future income.*
con·serva·tive·ly *adv*

con·ser·va·tive² /kən'sɜːvətɪv/ *nc* **1** a conservative(1) person. **2** (C-) a member, supporter, of the Conservative Party.

Con'servative Party *n* (the —) (*GB*) one of the main political parties, with conservative(1), right-wing views.

con·serva·tory /kən'sɜːvətrɪ/ *nc* (*pl* **-ies**) **1** (a part of) a building with glass walls and roof, used for growing plants. **2** a school for music or dramatic art.

con·serve /kən'sɜːv/ *vt* to keep (something) from change, loss or destruction: *conserve one's strength/energies/health.*

con·sid·er /kən'sɪdə(r)/ *vt* **1** to think about (a person, thing): *Please consider my suggestion. We are considering going to Canada. The jury considered their verdict. We are considering you for the job.* **2** to take into account, make allowances for, (a person, possible result etc): *We must consider the feelings of other people.* **all things considered** taking everything into account: *We hoped to win the competition, but all things considered we did well to reach the final.* **3** to have the opinion mentioned: *They considered themselves lucky to be alive. Do you consider it wise to interfere?*

con·sid·er·able /kən'sɪdrəbl/ *adj* large in amount, importance etc: *bought at considerable expense; with considerable influence.* Opp inconsiderable.

con·sid·er·ate /kən'sɪdərət/ *adj* thoughtful (of the needs of others): *It was considerate of you to bring me flowers.* Opp inconsiderate.
con·sid·er·ate·ly *adv*

con·sid·er·ation /kən,sɪdə'reɪʃn/ *n* **1** *nu* the act of giving attention to, thinking about, something: *Please give the matter your careful consideration.* **take sth into consideration** (esp) to make allowances for it: *When marking the examination, I took Tom's long illness into consideration.* **under (active) consideration** being discussed, thought about, now: *Your request for an assistant is under consideration.* **2** *nu* thoughtful attention to the wishes, feelings etc of others: *in consideration of/out of consideration for his youth.* **3** *nc* something which must be thought about; fact, thing etc thought of as a reason: *Time is an important consideration in this case.*

con·sid·er·ing /kən'sɪdərɪŋ/ *prep* taking into account; having regard to: *She's very active considering her age.*

con·sign /kən'saɪn/ *vt* **1** (*commerce*) to send (goods etc) for delivery: *The goods have been consigned by rail.* **2** (*formal*) to hand over, give up, (a person): *consign the girl to her uncle's care.*
con·sign·ment *nc,nu*

con·sist /kən'sɪst/ *vi* (*no passive*) Ⓝ Not used in the continuous tenses, e.g. *'is/was -ing'.* **1 consist of sb/sth** to be made up of people, things: *The committee consists of ten members.* **2 consist in sth** (*formal*) to have something as the main or only element: *The happiness of a country consists*

in the freedom of its citizens.

con·sist·en·cy /kən'sɪstənsɪ/ *n* (*pl* **-ies**) **1** *nu* the state of always being the same in standard, form, behaviour etc: *His work shows no consistency.* Opp inconsistency. **2** *nc,nu* the degree of thickness, firmness or solidity (esp of a liquid or something mixed with a liquid): *Mix flour and milk to the right consistency.*

con·sist·ent /kən'sɪstənt/ *adj* **1** (of a person, behaviour, principles etc) having a regular pattern: *The ideas in his various speeches are not consistent.* Opp inconsistent. **2 consistent (with sth)** in agreement (with): *What you say now is not consistent with what you said last week.*
con·sist·ent·ly *adv* often and regularly: *You have consistently refused to listen to my advice.*

con·so·la·tion /,kɒnsə'leɪʃn/ *n* **1** *nu* the act of giving comfort or sympathy: *a few words of/a letter of consolation.* **2** *nc* a person, object, situation etc that consoles: *Your friendship has been a great consolation to me.*
,conso'lation prize *nc* one given to a competitor who has just missed the main prize(s).

con·so·la·tory /kən'sɒlətrɪ/ *adj* (*formal*) intended to give comfort: *a consolatory letter.*

con·sole¹ /'kɒnsəʊl/ *nc* a flat panel for the controls of electronic or mechanical equipment.

con·sole² /kən'səʊl/ *vt* to give comfort or sympathy to (a person): *console him in his disappointment; consoling oneself with the thought that it might have been worse.*

con·soli·date /kən'sɒlɪdeɪt/ *vt,vi* **1** (to cause things) to become (more) solid or strong: *consolidate one's position/influence.* **2** (to cause things) to unite or combine into one: *consolidate debts/business companies. The different States have been consolidated into one federation.*
con·soli·da·tion /kən,sɒlɪ'deɪʃn/ *nc,nu*

con·som·mé /kən'sɒmeɪ/ *nu* (*Fr*) a kind of clear meat soup.

con·son·ance /'kɒnsənəns/ *nu* **1** harmony of spoken or musical sounds. Compare dissonance. **2** the similarity of sound between one word and another because they have the same final consonant (as in *best* and *mist*). ⇨ assonance.

con·son·ant /'kɒnsənənt/ *nc* (*lang*) (a letter or phonetic symbol representing) a speech sound produced by a complete or partial stoppage of the breath. Compare vowel.

con·sort¹ /'kɒnsɔːt/ *nc* a husband or wife of a ruler: *the prince consort* (= the reigning queen's husband).

con·sort² /kən'sɔːt/ *vi* **consort with sb** to spend time in the company of (usually bad) people: *consort with criminals.*

con·sort·ium /kən'sɔːtɪəm/ *nc* (*pl* **—s**) an association (of businesses, banks etc).

con·spicu·ous /kən'spɪkjʊəs/ *adj* easily seen; attracting attention: *Traffic signs should be conspicuous.* **make oneself conspicuous** to attract attention by unusual behaviour, clothes etc: *He made himself conspicuous at the party by wearing silver boots.* Opp inconspicuous.
con·spicu·ous·ly *adv*

con·spir·acy /kən'spɪrəsɪ/ *n* (*pl* **-ies**) **1** *nu* the act of conspiring. **2** *nc* a plan made by conspiring: *a conspiracy to overthrow the Government.*

con·spira·tor /kən'spɪrətə(r)/ *nc* a person who

conspires.

con·spire /kən'spaɪə(r)/ vi **1** to make secret plans (with others) (to do wrong): *conspiring with a friend to steal/against the teacher*. **2** (of events) to join to cause an effect: *Bad sales figures each month conspired to bring about his ruin*.

con·stable /'kʌnstəbl/ nc a policeman (now the usual word).

con·stabu·lary /kən'stæbjʊlərɪ/ nc (pl **-ies**) (*dated*) a police force.

con·stan·cy /'kɒnstənsɪ/ nu (*formal*) the quality of being firm, faithful, unchanging: *constancy of purpose*.

con·stant /'kɒnstənt/ adj **1** going on all the time: *constant complaints*. **2** (*formal*) faithful; unchanging: *a constant friend*.
con·stant·ly adv

con·stel·la·tion /ˌkɒnstə'leɪʃn/ nc a named group of fixed stars (e.g. *the Great Bear*).

con·ster·na·tion /ˌkɒnstə'neɪʃn/ nu surprise and fear: *News of the hijacking filled him with consternation*.

con·sti·pated /'kɒnstɪpeɪtɪd/ adj having bowels that are emptied infrequently or only with difficulty.

con·sti·pa·tion /ˌkɒnstɪ'peɪʃn/ nu difficult or infrequent emptying of the bowels.

con·stitu·en·cy /kən'stɪtjʊənsɪ/ nc (pl **-ies**) (a group of voters living in) a town or district that sends a representative to Parliament: *a Liberal/marginal/safe constituency*.

con·stitu·ent¹ /kən'stɪtjʊənt/ adj (attrib) (*formal*) **1** having the power or right to make or alter a political constitution: *a constituent assembly*. **2** helping to form a whole: *a constituent part*.

con·stitu·ent² /kən'stɪtjʊənt/ nc **1** a member of a constituency. **2** (*formal*) a part that helps to form a whole: *the constituents of happiness*.

con·sti·tute /'kɒnstɪtjuːt/ vt **1** to establish, give legal authority to, (a committee etc). **2** to make up (a whole); amount to: *Twelve months constitute a year*.

con·sti·tu·tion /ˌkɒnstɪ'tjuːʃn/ nc **1** a system (laws and principles) according to which a state is governed: *Great Britain has an unwritten constitution*. **2** the general physical structure and condition of a person's body: *Only people with strong constitutions should climb in the Himalayas*. **3** the general structure of a thing: *the constitution of a new committee*.

con·sti·tu·tion·al /ˌkɒnstɪtju:ʃənl/ adj **1** of a constitution(1): *constitutional government/reform*. ⇨ unconstitutional. **2** of a person's constitution(2): *a constitutional weakness*.

con·strain /kən'streɪn/ vt (usually *passive; formal*) to use force or strong persuasion on (a person): *I feel constrained to write and ask for your forgiveness*.

con·straint /kən'streɪnt/ n **1** nc something that forces one not to do something: *social/financial constraints*. **2** nu the control of one's (true) feelings or desires: *show constraint when punishing a child*. **act under constraint** to be, feel, forced to do something.

con·strict /kən'strɪkt/ vt **1** to make (e.g. a blood vessel) tight or smaller. **2** (*fig*) to make action difficult for (a person): *He feels constricted in a shirt and tie*.

con·stric·tion /kən'strɪkʃn/ nc,nu

con·struct /kən'strʌkt/ vt **1** to put together materials, parts, to make (a building or similar structure): *construct a factory/bridge*. **2** (*fig*) to use words, ideas etc to produce (something): *construct a sentence/theory*.

con·struc·tor /-tə(r)/ nc a person, business, that builds things: *building constructors*.

con·struc·tion /kən'strʌkʃn/ n **1** nu the act, process, manner, of constructing. **under construction** being built: *The new railway is still under construction*. **2** nc a structure; building: *a wooden construction*. **3** nc an interpretation of words, statements, acts etc: *Please do not put a wrong construction on his action*. **4** nc (*gram*) an example of the arrangement and relationship of words in a sentence: *This dictionary gives examples to illustrate constructions*.

con·struc·tion·al /-ʃənl/ adj of, requiring, construction: *constructional toys*.

con·struc·tive /kən'strʌktɪv/ adj (*esp*) helping to improve: *constructive criticism/proposals*. Compare destructive.
con·struc·tive·ly adv

con·strue /kən'struː/ vt (*formal*) **1** to interpret the meaning of (words, statements, acts etc): *His remarks were wrongly construed*. **2** (*gram*) to analyse the construction(4) of (a sentence).

con·sul /'kɒnsl/ nc a state official sent to help and protect her or his fellow citizens in a foreign country.

con·su·lar /'kɒnsjʊlə(r)/ adj

consu·late /'kɒnsjʊlət/ nc a consul's position or place of work.

con·sult /kən'sʌlt/ vt **1** to go to (a person, a book etc) for information, advice, opinion etc: *to consult a doctor/a map/the dictionary*. **2 consult with sb** to discuss something with a person: *Have you consulted with the other members of the team?*

con·sult·ing-room nc one in which a doctor examines patients.

con·sul·tant /kən'sʌltənt/ nc a person who gives expert advice (e.g. in medicine, business): *a consultant surgeon; a firm of business consultants*.

con·sul·ta·tion /ˌkɒnsəl'teɪʃn/ n **1** nu (*esp in consultation with sb*) the act, process, of consulting: *We'll decide in consultation with the director*. **2** nc a meeting for sharing opinions, getting advice: *The doctors had a consultation to decide whether to operate*.

con·sult·ative /kən'sʌltətɪv/ adj (usually *attrib*) for the purpose of sharing opinions, getting advice: *a consultative committee; a consultative document*.

con·sume /kən'sjuːm/ vt (*formal*) **1** to eat or drink (something). **2** to use up, get to the end of, (something): *consume a lot of petrol; consume all one's energies*. **3** to destroy (a building, person) (by fire): *be consumed in the flames*. **4** to waste (time, an opportunity): *consuming too much time*.

con·su·mer /kən'sjuːmə(r)/ nc (also *attrib*) a person who buys (manufactured) goods in shops etc: *consumer goods*. Compare producer(1).

con·sum·ing /kən'sjuːmɪŋ/ adj (usually *attrib*) dominating: *a consuming ambition*.

con·sum·mate /'kɒnsəmeɪt/ vt **1** to make (a

marriage) complete by sexual intercourse. **2** (*formal*) to make (a condition) perfect: *Her happiness was consummated when her father took her to Paris*.

con·sum·ma·tion /ˌkɒnsə'meɪʃn/ *nc,nu*

con·sump·tion /kən'sʌmpʃn/ *nu* **1** the process of consuming food, energy, materials etc or the quantity consumed: *Beer consumption did not go down when the tax was raised*. **2** (*informal*) tuberculosis of the lung.

cont. *abbr* continue(d).

con·tact¹ /ˈkɒntækt/ *n* **1** *nu* the process, state, of touching, exchanging information, coming together: *We are in contact with the boy's parents. A steel cable came into contact with an electric power line*. **make contact (with sb)** to meet or telephone a person (esp after searching etc): *I finally made contact with him in Amsterdam*. **2** *nc* a business, social etc associate: *He made many business contacts while he was in Canada*. **3** *nc* (*electricity*) (a device used for making) a connection (for electric current). **4** *nc* a person recently exposed to a contagious disease.

'contact lens *nc* one of thin glass or plastic made to fit over the eyeball to improve vision.

con·tact² /ˈkɒntækt/ *vt* to reach (a person) using a telephone, sending a message, visiting etc: *Where can I contact Mr Green?*

con·ta·gi·ous /kən'teɪdʒəs/ *adj* **1** (of a disease) spreading by contact: *Scarlet fever is contagious*. Compare infectious(1). **2** (of a person) in such a condition that he may spread disease. **3** (*fig*) spreading easily by example: *contagious laughter/enthusiasm*.

con·ta·gi·ous·ly *adv*

con·tain /kən'teɪn/ *vt* **1** to have or hold (things) within itself: *The atlas contains forty maps*. **2** to be capable of holding (people, things): *How much does this bottle contain? The stadium can contain 100 000 supporters*. **3** to keep (emotions, children, enemy forces etc) under control: *Can't you contain yourself/your enthusiasm?*

con·tain·er /kən'teɪnə(r)/ *nc* **1** a bottle, box, carton etc designed to hold something. **2** (also *attrib*) a very large metal box used to transport goods by road, rail, sea or air: *a container ship*.

con·tain·er·ize (also **-ise**) *vt* to put (goods) into containers(2).

con·tami·nate /kən'tæmɪneɪt/ *vt* to make (something) dirty, impure or diseased (by touching or adding something impure): *Flies contaminate food*.

con·tami·na·tion /kən,tæmɪ'neɪʃn/ *nc,nu*

contd *abbr* continued.

con·tem·plate /ˈkɒntempleɪt/ *vt* **1** to look at, think about, (oneself, ideas etc): *She stood contemplating herself in the mirror/her recent success*. **2** to think about (something) as an intention or possibility: *She was contemplating a visit to London*.

con·tem·pla·tion /ˌkɒntem'pleɪʃn/ *nu*

con·tem·pla·tive /ˈkɒntemplətɪv/ *adj* (*formal*) thoughtful: *be in a contemplative mood*.

con·tem·por·aneous /kən,tempə'reɪnɪəs/ *adj* (*formal*) originating, existing, happening, during the same period of time: *contemporaneous events*.

con·tem·por·ary¹ /kən'temprərɪ/ *adj* **1** belonging to the same time: *Dickens was contem-*

porary with Thackeray. **2** of the present time: *contemporary artists*. **3** in the most modern style: *contemporary music*.

con·tem·por·ary² /kən'temprərɪ/ *nc* (*pl* **-ies**) a person of the same age, belonging to the same period etc as another: *Jack and I were contemporaries at college*.

con·tempt /kən'tempt/ *nu* **1** the mental attitude of despising: *We feel contempt for cheats*. **hold sb in contempt** to despise a person: *A man who is cruel to his children should be held in contempt*. **2 be in contempt of sth** to show disregard or disrespect for something: *be in contempt of all rules and regulations*. **(be in) contempt of court** (to show) disobedience to a judge, legal procedures.

con·tempt·ible /kən'temptəbl/ *adj* (*derog*) deserving or causing contempt.

con·temp·tu·ous /kən'temptʃʊəs/ *adj* (*formal*) showing contempt: *a contemptuous expression; be contemptuous of public opinion*.

con·tend /kən'tend/ *v* **1** *vi* to struggle, compete: *contending with difficulties/for a prize*. **2** *vt* **contend that ...** (*formal*) to argue, insist (that something is true, happened etc). ⇒ contention(2).

con·tend·er *nc* a competitor for a title in a sports contest.

con·tent¹ /kən'tent/ *adj* (*pred*) **1** **content (with sth)** satisfied (with what one has): *Are you content with your present salary?* **2** **content (to do sth)** willing or ready (to do something): *I am content to remain where I am now*.

con·tent·ed *adj* showing or feeling satisfaction, happiness: *contended workers; with a contented look/smile*. Opp discontented.

con·tent·ed·ly *adv*

con·tent·ment *nu* the state of feeling content(1).

con·tent² /kən'tent/ *nu* the condition of being satisfied: *He looked with content at his new car*. Opp discontent. **to one's heart's content** ⇒ heart(2).

con·tent³ /ˈkɒntent/ *nu* or *sing* the information, story of a book, speech etc as opposed to its style: *the content of a report. The programme was entertaining but had little content*.

con·tent⁴ /kən'tent/ *vt* (usually *reflex*) (*formal*) to satisfy (oneself, a person): *You must content yourself with second place*.

con·tents /ˈkɒntents/ *n pl* **1** things contained in something: *the contents of a room/book/packet*. **2** the amount which a container, pocket etc can hold: *the contents of this bottle*.

con·ten·tion /kən'tenʃn/ *n* (*formal*) **1** *nu* the act of quarrelling or arguing: *This is not a time for contention*. **2** *nc* an opinion as given during a discussion: *My contention is that you took the bike*. ⇒ contend(2).

con·ten·tious /kən'tenʃəs/ *adj* likely to cause argument: *a contentious clause in a treaty*.

con·test¹ /ˈkɒntest/ *nc* a struggle, fight or competition: *a keen contest for the prize; a contest of skill*.

con·test·ant /kən'testənt/ *nc* a person who competes, fights etc.

con·test² /kən'test/ *vt* **1** to compete in, try to win, (something): *contest an election; contest a* *place on the Committee.* **2** to argue about the truth, value etc of (something): *contest a statement/point.*

con·text /'kɒntekst/ *nc,nu* **1** the words etc used before and after another word, phrase etc helping to fix or illustrate the meaning: *Can't you guess the meaning of the word from its context?* **2** the circumstances in which an event occurs: *We must consider the theft in the context of her child's illness.*

con·tex·tual /kən'tekstjʊəl/ *adj*

con·ti·nent /'kɒntɪnənt/ *nc* **1** one of the main land masses: *the continents of Europe, Asia, Africa etc.* **2** (the C-) the mainland of Europe.

con·ti·nen·tal /,kɒntɪ'nentl/ *adj* **1** belonging to, typical of, a continent: *a continental climate.* **2** of the mainland of Europe: *continental countries.*

,conti,nental 'breakfast *nc,nu* breakfast that includes coffee (or tea), bread rolls, jam etc.

,conti,nental 'quilt *nc* = duvet.

con·tin·gen·cy /kən'tɪndʒənsɪ/ *nc* (*pl* **-ies**) (also *attrib*) an uncertain event (esp one causing problems): *be prepared for all contingencies; make contingency plans.*

con·tin·gent¹ /kən'tɪndʒənt/ *adj* (*pred*) **contingent on sth** (*formal*) dependent on something that may or may not happen.

con·tin·gent² /kən'tɪndʒənt/ *nc* a group of soldiers, ships etc forming part of a larger group.

con·tin·ual /kən'tɪnjʊəl/ *adj* happening very often or with only short breaks: *Aren't you tired of his continual interruptions?* Compare continuous.

con·tin·ual·ly /-jʊəlɪ/ *adv*

con·tinu·ation /kən,tɪnjʊ'eɪʃn/ *n* **1** *nu* the act of continuing. **2** *nc* a part etc by which something is continued or extended: *The next issue will contain an exciting continuation of the story.*

con·tin·ue /kən'tɪnjuː/ *vi,vt* **1** to go on (being, doing, something): *The desert continued as far as the eye could reach. I hope this wet weather will not continue. How long will you continue working?* **2** to start (something) again after stopping: *The story will be continued in next month's issue. Let's continue (our discussions) tomorrow.*

con·ti·nu·ity /,kɒntɪ'njuːətɪ/ *nu* **1** the state of being continuous: *There is no continuity of subject in a dictionary.* **2** (in films, TV) an arrangement of parts of a story: *Films are often made out of continuity* (i.e. out of order of the events). **3** the comments, announcements etc made between radio or TV programmes.

con·tinu·ous /kən'tɪnjʊəs/ *adj* going on without stopping: *a continuous struggle for human rights.* Compare continual.

con,tinuous 'play *nu* the ability of a machine that plays recorded tapes to play the next side of the tape (or the second tape) without stopping.

con'tinuous tense *nc* (*gram*) ⇨ future/past/perfect continuous tense.

con·tin·uous·ly *adv*

con·tort /kən'tɔːt/ *vt* (often *passive*) to force or twist (the face) out of the usual shape or appearance: *Her face was contorted with pain.*

con·tor·tion /kən'tɔːʃn/ *nc,nu*

con·tour /'kɒntʊə(r)/ *nc* an outline (of a coast etc).

'contour (line) *nc* a line (on a map) joining points at the same height above sea-level.

contra·band /'kɒntrəbænd/ *nu* (trade in) goods brought into or taken out of a country illegally.

contra·cep·tion /,kɒntrə'sepʃn/ *nu* the practice, method, of preventing or planning conception(2).

contra·cep·tive /,kɒntrə'septɪv/ *adj, nc* (of) a device or drug used to prevent conception(2): *contraceptive pills/devices.*

con·tract¹ /'kɒntrækt/ *nc,nu* a formal agreement (between people, groups, states): *enter into/ make a contract* (*with a person*) (*for the purchase of a house*); *work to be done by private contract; a breach of contract.* Ⓝ In the last two examples, *'a/ an'* is not used.

con·trac·tor /-tə(r)/ *nc* a person, business, that makes a contract to do something: *building contractors.*

con·trac·tual /kən'træktʃʊəl/ *adj*

con·tract² /kən'trækt/ *v* **1** *vt,vi* to agree to (something) in writing: *to contract an alliance with another country.* **contract out** (**of sth**) to reject, abandon, an agreement. **2** *vt* to catch (an illness): *contract measles.*

con·tract³ /kən'trækt/ *vt,vi* (to cause something) to become smaller, tighter or shorter: *Metals contract in very cold conditions. 'I will' can be contracted to 'I'll'. You must contract muscles to move your arm.* Opp expand(1).

con·trac·tion /kən'trækʃn/ *n* **1** *nu* the act of contracting or being contracted: *the contraction of a muscle.* **2** *nc* (*lang*) the shortened form of a word, such as *can't* for *cannot.*

con·tra·dict /,kɒntrə'dɪkt/ *vt* **1** to deny the truth of (something said or written, a person who has given a decision etc): *to contradict a statement. Don't contradict me.* **2** (of facts, statements etc) to be opposite to (another): *The reports contradict each other.*

con·tra·dic·tion /,kɒntrə'dɪkʃn/ *nc,nu* (an instance of) contradicting.

con·tra·dic·tory /,kɒntrə'dɪktərɪ/ *adj* contradicting(2): *contradictory statements/reports.*

con·tral·to /kən'træltəʊ/ *nc* (*pl* **-s**) (a woman with) the lowest female voice.

con·trap·tion /kən'træpʃn/ *nc* (*informal*) a strange-looking apparatus or machine.

con·trary¹ /'kɒntrərɪ/ *adj* (*pred*) **contrary to sth** opposite to something: *What you have done is contrary to the doctor's orders. You have acted contrary to the rules.*

con·trary² /kən'treərɪ/ *adj* (*informal; derog*) (of a person, behaviour) obstinate, unreasonable: *a contrary personality.*

con·trar·ily /kən'treərɪlɪ/ *adv*

con·trary³ /'kɒntrərɪ/ *nc* (*pl* **-ies**) (usually *sing*; the —) the opposite: *The contrary of 'wet' is 'dry'.* **on the contrary** (used to deny or contradict what has been said, written): *'You've nothing to do now, I think'—'On the contrary, I have a lot of work to do'.* **to the contrary** (*formal*) saying the opposite: *I will come on Monday unless you write to me to the contrary.*

con·trast¹ /'kɒntrɑːst/ *n* **1** *nu* the act of contrasting people, things: *Contrast may make something appear more beautiful than it is when seen alone.* **2** *nc,nu* (something showing) a difference clearly seen when unlike things are put together: *The contrast between the two brothers is remarkable.*

In contrast (to you), I shall agree to the proposal. Harry's marks were poor but Tom's were excellent by contrast.

con·trast² /kən'trɑːst/ v **1** vt to compare (two or more people, things, ideas etc) so that differences are made clear: *She contrasted the features of a comedy with those of a tragedy.* **2** vi to show a difference when compared: *His poor abilities contrast badly with his brother's talent.*

con·tra·vene /ˌkɒntrə'viːn/ vt (formal) to act in opposition to (a law, a custom).

con·tra·ven·tion /ˌkɒntrə'venʃn/ nc,nu (an act of) contravening a law etc: *in contravention of the rules.*

con·trib·ute /kən'trɪbjuːt/ vt,vi **1** to join with others in giving (help, money ideas, suggestions etc): *contribute money to/towards a charity/new information on a scientific problem.* **2** to help to cause (something): *Drink contributed to his ruin.* **3** to write (an article etc) and send (it) in (to a magazine etc): *Mary Green has contributed (poems) to the magazine for several years.*

con·tribu·tor /-tə(r)/ nc a person who contributes.

con·tri·bu·tion /ˌkɒntrɪ'bjuːʃn/ n something contributed: *contributions to the relief fund.*

con·tribu·tory /kən'trɪbjutrɪ/ adj (attrib) **1** helping to cause something: *contributory negligence* (e.g. that helped to cause an accident). **2** to which contributions need to be made: *a contributory pension scheme.* Opp non-contributory.

con·trite /'kɒntraɪt/ adj (formal) filled with, showing, deep sorrow for having done wrong.

con·tri·tion /kən'trɪʃn/ nu

con·triv·ance /kən'traɪvəns/ n **1** nc a clumsy, strange, apparatus. **2** nu (formal) the capacity to invent things: *Some things are beyond human contrivance.*

con·trive /kən'traɪv/ vt to manage to do, cause, (something), esp by planning in advance: *to contrive a means of escape from prison.*

con·trived /kən'traɪvd/ adj (no comp; derog) deliberately forced; insincere: *a contrived smile.*

con·trol¹ /kən'trəʊl/ n **1** nu the power or authority to direct, order or restrain: *Some children are beyond parental control. The owners must have/keep control of their dogs. A good teacher has control over the class.* **be in control (of sth)** (a) to be in command, in charge, (of a group, situation etc). (b) (of a political party) to have the majority of elected places (in national or local government): *The Independents are in control (of Liverpool).* **be/get out of control** to be in/get into a state where authority etc is lost: *The children are/have got out of control.* **bring/get/keep sb/sth under control** to obtain or keep one's power or authority over a person, animal, situation etc. **lose control (of sth)** (a) to be unable to manage or restrain something: *lose control of one's temper.* (b) (of a political party) to fail to keep the majority of elected representatives (in national or local government): *The socialists lost control (of London).* **take control (of sth)** (a) to take authority (over something): *We must find someone to take control of the situation.* (b) (of a political party) to win the majority of elected places (in national or local government): *Labour has taken control of Birmingham.* **2** nu management: *control of traffic; traffic control.* **3** nc (the means of) regulating, restraining, keeping something in order: *government controls on trade and industry.* ⇨ birth-control. **4** (usually pl) the means by which a machine etc is operated or regulated: *the controls of an aircraft.*

con·trol² /kən'trəʊl/ vt (-ll-) **1** to have control of (something, children etc): *to control expenditure/one's temper/a plane.* **2** to regulate (prices etc).

con'trol tower nc the building in an airport where flights are controlled.

con·trol·lable /-əbl/ adj able to be controlled (1): *Is her temper/her son controllable?* Opp uncontrollable.

con·tro·ver·sial /ˌkɒntrə'vɜːʃl/ adj likely to cause controversy: *a controversial speech/decision.* Opp uncontroversial.

con·tro·ver·sial·ly /-ʃəlɪ/ adv

con·tro·ver·sy /kən'trɒvəsɪ/ also 'kɒntrəvɜːsɪ/ nc,nu (pl **-ies**) (a) strong argument, esp over social, moral or political matters: *be involved in (a) controversy with a neighbour; a decision that has caused much controversy.*

con·un·drum /kə'nʌndrəm/ nc a kind of riddle using a play on words, e.g. 'When is a door not a door?'—'When it's ajar.'

con·va·lesce /ˌkɒnvə'les/ vi to get one's health and strength back after an illness: *She is convalescing by the sea.*

con·va·les·cence /ˌkɒnvə'lesns/ nu the gradual recovery of health and strength.

con·va·les·cent /ˌkɒnvə'lesnt/ nc (also attrib) a person who is recovering from illness: *a convalescent home.*

con·vec·tion /kən'vekʃn/ nu (tech) the conveying of heat from one part of a liquid or gas to another by the movement of heated substances.

con·vene /kən'viːn/ vt,vi (to call people) to come together (for a meeting etc).

con·vener nc a person who convenes a meeting.

con·veni·ence /kən'viːnɪəns/ n **1** nu the quality of being convenient or suitable: *I keep my reference books near my desk for convenience. Please come at your earliest convenience.* ⇨ inconvenience. **2** nc an appliance, arrangement etc that is useful, helpful etc: *The house has all modern conveniences* (e.g. central heating).

con·veni·ent /kən'viːnɪənt/ adj **1** suitable; that avoids trouble or difficulty: *Will it be convenient for you to start work tomorrow? This is a convenient method of payment.* **2** easy to get to: *The car is parked in a convenient place.* Opp inconvenient.

con·veni·ent·ly adv

con·vent /'kɒnvənt/ nc a building in which women (nuns) lead a religious life away from others. Compare monastery. **enter a convent** to become a nun.

con·ven·tion /kən'venʃn/ n **1** nc (often C-) a conference of members of a business, club, political party etc: *the Democratic Party Convention.* **2** nc (often C-) an agreement between States, rulers etc (less formal than a treaty): *The Geneva Convention deals with the treatment of prisoners of war.* **3** nc,nu a usual practice or custom based on general consent: *Wearing a tie to work is a convention. It is silly to be a slave to convention.* **4** nc (in the arts) a device, style, arrangement etc that has become a generally accepted form of technique, e.g. using soliloquy in drama, classical ballet gestures, exaggerating size to help perspective in art etc.

con·ven·tion·al /kən'venʃənl/ adj **1** based on convention(3) (and so sometimes appearing insincere): *conventional greetings*. **2** following convention(4): *a conventional design for a carpet*.

con,ventional 'weapon nc one that does not use atomic power.

con·ven·tion·al·ly /-əlɪ/ adv

con·verge /kən'vɜ:dʒ/ vi *converge (on sb/ sth)* (of lines, people, moving objects, opinions) to come towards each other and meet at a point: *The roads converge here. The demonstrators converged on the government offices.*

con·ver·gence /-dʒəns/ nu

con·ver·gent /-dʒənt/ adj

con·ver·sant /kən'vɜ:sənt/ adj (pred) *conversant with sth* (formal) having a good knowledge of: *conversant with all the rules.*

con·ver·sa·tion /ˌkɒnvə'seɪʃn/ n **1** nu *in conversation with sb* talking with: *I saw him in conversation with a friend.* **2** nc an informal talk: *I've had several conversations with him.*

con·ver·sa·tion·al /-ʃənl/ adj (of words etc) used in, characteristic of, informal talk or informal letters.

con·verse¹ /'kɒnvɜ:s/ nc (the —) (also attrib) an idea, statement that is opposite (to another): *The converse (idea) is equally possible.*

con·verse·ly adv

con·verse² /kən'vɜ:s/ vi (formal) to talk.

con·ver·sion /kən'vɜ:ʃn/ n **1** nu the process, act, of converting: *the conversion of cream into butter/of children to Christianity/from dollars to pounds.* **2** nc an instance of this: *building conversions* (e.g. of large houses into flats).

con·vert¹ /'kɒnvɜ:t/ nc a person converted, esp to a religion or a political view: *a convert to socialism.*

con·vert² /kən'vɜ:t/ vt **1** *convert sth (from sth) (to/into sth)* to change (from one form, use etc) (into another): *to convert pounds into francs.* **2** *convert sb (to sth)* to cause a person to change her or his beliefs etc: *to convert a man to Christianity.* **3** (rugby) to score more points after scoring (a try) by kicking a goal.

con·vert·ed adj

con·vert·ible /kən'vɜ:təbl/ adj that can be converted: *Convertible currency can be exchanged by banks for other currencies.*

con·vex /'kɒnveks/ adj (of an outline or surface) curved outwards like the outside of a ball: *a convex lens.* Compare concave.

con·vey /kən'veɪ/ vt **1** *convey sth (from sth) (to sth)* to take, carry, (something): *Pipes convey hot water from this boiler to every part of the building.* **2** *convey sth (to sb)* to make known ideas, views, feelings etc (to another person): *This picture will convey to you some idea of the beauty of the scenery.*

con'veyor-belt nc (in a factory) a band or chain moving over wheels, used for carrying packages etc.

con·vict¹ /'kɒnvɪkt/ nc a person convicted of crime and being punished.

con·vict² /kən'vɪkt/ vt (of a jury or a judge) to declare in a law court that (a person) is guilty: *He was convicted of murder.*

con·vic·tion /kən'vɪkʃn/ n **1** nc,nu (an instance of) convicting a person for a crime: *He has had six previous convictions.* **2** nc,nu (a) firm and confident belief: *He spoke with such conviction.* **(not) carry much conviction** (to fail) to be convincing.

con·vince /kən'vɪns/ vt *convince sb (of sth/ that . . .)* to make a person feel certain, cause a person to realize: *I am convinced of his honesty/ that he is honest. We couldn't convince him of his mistake. I'm willing to be convinced* (= prepared to listen to your arguments).

con·vinc·ing adj able to convince: *a convincing argument.* Opp unconvincing.

con·vinc·ing·ly adv

con·viv·i·al /kən'vɪvɪəl/ adj friendly, pleasant; pleasing: *a convivial smile/person/climate.*

con·vol·uted /'kɒnvəlu:tɪd/ adj **1** coiled; twisted: *a convoluted horn.* **2** (fig) difficult to understand: *convoluted explanations/arguments.*

con·vol·ution /ˌkɒnvə'lu:ʃn/ nc,nu

con·voy /'kɒnvɔɪ/ nc a group of ships, vehicles etc travelling together for safety: *The convoy was attacked by submarines. We were part of a police convoy.*

con·vulse /kən'vʌls/ vt to cause (a person) to make violent movements or disturbances: *He was convulsed with laughter.*

con·vul·sion /kən'vʌlʃn/ nc **1** (usually pl) a very strong involuntary movement of (parts of) the body: *The child's convulsions filled us with fear.* **2** (pl) (informal) strong fits of laughter: *The story was so funny that we were all in convulsions.*

con·vuls·ive /kən'vʌlsɪv/ adj

coo /ku:/ vi, nc (to make) a soft, murmuring sound (as if) of doves.

cook¹ /kʊk/ nc a person who cooks food in a house, small hotel, school etc. Compare chef.

cook² /kʊk/ v **1** vi,vt to prepare (food) by heating (e.g. boiling, baking, roasting, frying). **2** vi to be cooked in the way mentioned: *These apples cook well.* **3** vt *cook sth up* to invent a story, excuse etc. **4** vt (informal) to make false statements in (an account): *cook the books/the accounts.*

cook·er /'kʊkə(r)/ nc **1** an apparatus used for cooking food: *an electric/gas cooker.* **2** a kind of fruit etc (esp apples) grown for cooking.

cook·ery /'kʊkərɪ/ nu (also attrib) the science or art of preparing, cooking and serving food: *cookery classes.*

'cookery book nc a book with recipes.

cookie /'kʊkɪ/ nc (US) a biscuit.

cook·ing /'kʊkɪŋ/ nu the practice of cooking: *Modern cooking is more a science than an art.*

cool¹ /ku:l/ adj (—er, —est) **1** between warm and cold: *cool autumn weather. The coffee's not cool enough to drink.* **2** calm; unexcited: *as cool as a cucumber* (= very calm). *Keep cool! He was always cool in the face of danger.* **play it cool** (informal) to deal calmly with a difficult situation. **3** (of behaviour) not showing interest or enthusiasm: *They gave the prime minister a cool reception.* Compare warm¹.

cool·ly adv

cool·ness nu

cool² /ku:l/ nu (the —) cool air: *in the cool of the*

evening. *Stay in the cool.*

cool³ /ku:l/ *v* **1** *vt,vi* (to cause something) to become cool: *The rain has cooled the air. Has the food cooled yet?* **2** *vi* **cool down/off** (*fig*) to become calm, less excited or enthusiastic: *I told him to cool down.*

cool·ant /'ku:lənt/ *nc* (*tech*) a substance (usually a liquid) used to cool a mechanical system.

coop¹ /ku:p/ *nc* a cage for hens with small chickens: *a hen coop.*

coop² /ku:p/ *vt* **coop sb/sth up 1** to put hens etc in a coop. **2** (*fig*) to keep a person in a place: *How long are we going to be cooped up in here?*

co-op /'kəʊ ɒp/ *nc* (the —) (*informal*) = cooperative (shop): *I buy my food at the co-op.*

co·op·er·ate, co-op- /kəʊ'ɒpəreɪt/ *vi* **cooperate (with sb (in doing sth))** to work or act together in order to bring about a result: *cooperate with friends in starting a social club.*

co·op·er·ator, co-op- /-tə(r)/ *nc* a person who cooperates.

co·op·er·ation, co-op- /kəʊ,ɒpə'reɪʃn/ *nu* the willingness shown by, an act of, working or acting together for a common purpose: *The workers, in cooperation with management, have increased output by 10%.*

co·op·er·ative¹, co-op- /kəʊ'ɒprətɪv/ *adj* **1** willing to cooperate: *be cooperative and help to organize the chairs for the meeting.* Opp uncooperative. **2** organized, done, by a cooperative: *cooperative milk production/farming.*

co·op·er·ative², co-op- /kəʊ'ɒprətɪv/ *nc* (also *attrib*) (a shop run by) people owning, producing and selling things as a group and sharing the profits: *agricultural cooperatives. This shop is owned by a cooperative society.*

co-opt /kəʊ 'ɒpt/ *vt* **co-opt sb (onto sth)** (of a committee) to add a person as a member by the votes of those who are already members: *co-opt a new member onto the committee.*

coord written *abbr* (*gram*) coordinating conjunction (as used in this dictionary).

co·or·di·nate¹ /kəʊ'ɔ:dɪnət/ *adj* of, concerning, coordination.

co·,ordinate 'clause *nc* (*gram*) one of several clauses in a sentence that have equal value, as in *'You're very dirty* and *you need a bath.'*

co·or·di·nate² /kəʊ'ɔ:dɪnət/ *nc* (usu *pl*; *geog, maths*) one of a set of numbers used to find an exact position (on a map, graph etc).

co·or·di·nate³ /kəʊ'ɔ:dɪneɪt/ *vt* to make (activity) happen, fit, together in harmony (with others): *coordinate the movements of the arms and legs when swimming.*

co,ordinating con'junction *nc* (*gram*) one used to join coordinate clauses, such as *but* in *'I like it but I haven't any money.'* (N) Marked *coord* in this dictionary. ⇨ subordinating conjunction.

co·or·di·na·tion /kəʊ,ɔ:dɪ'neɪʃn/ *nu* **1** the balanced position and related movement of muscles: *An athlete must have good coordination.* **2** the balanced relationship between parts.

coot /ku:t/ *nc* a kind of small, dark waterbird.

cop /kɒp/ *nc* (*sl*) a police officer.

co-part·ner /,kəʊ 'pɑ:tnə(r)/ *nc* a person who has a share in the profits of a business etc in addition to her or his salary or wages.

co-part·ner·ship /-ʃɪp/ *nc,nu*

cope /kəʊp/ *vi* **cope (with sb/sth)** to manage (a difficult person, situation etc) successfully: *coping with difficulties.*

cop·ing /'kəʊpɪŋ/ *nc* a line of stonework or bricks on top of a wall.

copi·ous /'kəʊpɪəs/ *adj* (*attrib; formal*) plentiful; having a large amount: *a copious supply/meal.*

copi·ous·ly *adv*

cop·per¹ /'kɒpə(r)/ *n* **1** *nu* (also *attrib*) a common reddish-brown metal (symbol Cu): *copper wire/cable/alloy.* **2** *nc* a coin made of copper (alloy). **3** *nu* (also *adj*) reddish-brown colour.

'copper beech *nc* a kind of beech tree with copper-coloured leaves.

,copper-'bottomed *adj* (*fig*) safe in every way: *copper-bottomed guarantees.*

cop·per² /'kɒpə(r)/ *nc* (*sl*) a police officer.

copse /kɒps/ *nc* a small area of shrubs and small trees.

cop·ula /'kɒpjʊlə/ *nc* (*pl* **—s**) (*gram*) the verb *be* when used to join a subject to its complement, as in 'The baby *is* a boy', 'It's Thursday today'.

copu·late /'kɒpjʊleɪt/ *vi* (*formal*) to have sexual intercourse.

copu·la·tion /,kɒpjʊ'leɪʃn/ *nc,nu*

copy¹ /'kɒpɪ/ *nc* (*pl* **-ies**) **1** something made like another; reproduction of an original: *Make three carbon copies of the letter.* **2** one example (of a book, newspaper etc) of which many have been made: *If you can't buy a copy (of the book), perhaps you can borrow one from the library.*

'copy-cat *nc* (*informal; derog*) a person who copies another person's actions, ideas etc.

copy² /'kɒpɪ/ *vt,vi* (*pt,pp* **-ied**) **1** to make a copy of (something): *copy notes.* ⇨ photocopy. **2** to (try to) do the same as (a person, form of behaviour etc): *You should copy his good example.*

copy sth down to write down something which is spoken or which is written somewhere else: *copy down names/an address.*

copy sth in to write information in the empty spaces of a document using information from somewhere else: *copy in the names of the winners.*

copy sth out (of sth) to write exactly what is written somewhere else: *copy out a poem; copy it out of a book.*

copy·right /'kɒpɪraɪt/ *vt, nu* (symbol ©) (to protect a work, author, with) the sole legal right to print, publish, sell, broadcast, perform, film or record the work or any part of it.

cor·al /'kɒrəl/ *nu* (also *attrib*) **1** the hard red, pink or white substance built on the seabed by the shells and bones of sea animals. **2** red or pink colour.

,coral 'island *nc* one formed by the growth of coral.

'coral reef *nc* a reef of coral.

cord /kɔ:d/ *n* **1** *nc,nu* (a length of) twisted strands, thicker than string, thinner than rope. **2** *nc,nu* (a length of) wires inside a plastic or rubber casing for an electric current. **3** *nc* a long part of the body like a cord(1): *the spinal cord; the vocal cords.*

cord·less *adj* without a cord(2): *a cordless telephone.*

cor·di·al /'kɔ:dɪəl/ *adj* friendly and sincere (in feeling, behaviour): *a cordial smile.*

cor·di·al·ly /-ɪəlɪ/ *adv*

cor·don[1] /'kɔ:dn/ *nc* a line, rope, ring of officials etc used as a barrier: *a police cordon*.

cor·don[2] /'kɔ:dn/ *vt* **cordon sth off** to keep people, a building etc separate using a cordon: *cordon off a road*.

cords /kɔ:dz/ *n pl* (*informal*) trousers made of corduroy: *wearing cords; dressed in cords*.

cor·du·roy /'kɔ:dərʌɪ/ *nu* (also *attrib*) thick, cotton cloth with raised lines on it: *corduroy trousers*.

core[1] /kɔ:(r)/ *nc* **1** a (usually hard) centre (with seeds) of such fruits as the apple and pear. **2** the central or most important part (of something): *the core of a nuclear reactor*. **to the core** thoroughly: *He's English to the core* (= is completely English in manner, speech, dress etc). **rotten to the core** (*fig; derog*) (of a person) thoroughly bad.

core[2] /kɔ:(r)/ *vt* to take out the core(1) of (fruit): *coring an apple*.

cork[1] /kɔ:k/ *n* **1** *nu* (also *attrib*) the light, brown, tough outer bark of a kind of tree (called the *cork-oak*): *floors made of cork; cork floors*. **2** *nc* a round piece of this material used as a stopper for a bottle.

'cork·screw *nc* an implement used for pulling corks out of bottles.

cork[2] /kɔ:k/ *vt* **cork sth (up)** to block the top of a bottle with a cork(2).

corn[1] /kɔ:n/ *n* **1** *nu* (the seed of) any of various grain plants, e.g. wheat, oats, rye, maize: *a field of corn; a corn field*. ⇨ **sweet corn**. **2** *nc* a single grain (of wheat, pepper etc).

'corn-cob *nc* the part of an ear of maize on which the grains grow.

'corn·flour (*US* **'corn·starch**) *nu* a fine flour made from maize, rice etc and used in cooking.

corn[2] /kɔ:n/ *nc* a small area of hardened skin on the foot, esp on a toe, often with a painful centre and root. **tread on sb's corns** (*fig*) to hurt her or his feelings.

cor·nea /'kɔ:nɪə/ *nc* (*pl* **—s**) (*anat*) the transparent covering for the front of the eye.

cor·ner[1] /'kɔ:nə(r)/ *nc* **1** (also *attrib*) the place, position, where two lines, sides, edges or surfaces meet: *the corner of this page; the dog on/at the corner; sitting in the corner of the room; the house just round the corner; the corner shop*. **in a (tight) corner** (*fig*) in a (very) difficult situation. **(a)round the corner** (*fig*) very near; happening soon: *Success is just round the corner*. **cut corners** (a) (of the driver of a vehicle) to go across, not round, corners of a road when travelling fast. **(b)** (*fig*) to ignore details, regulations etc to get work done quickly: *We've had to cut a few corners to get your visa ready in time*. **drive sb into a corner** (*fig*) to put a person in a difficult situation (e.g. in an argument) so that escape is almost impossible. **turn the corner** (*fig*) to pass a critical point in an illness, a period of (economic) difficulty etc. **2** (usually *pl*) a region: *to the four corners of the earth*. **3** (in football) a kick from the corner of the field, allowed when the ball has been kicked by an opponent over her or his own goal-line.

cor·ner[2] /'kɔ:nə(r)/ *v* **1** *vt* to force (a person) into a difficult position: *The escaped prisoner was cornered at last*. **2** *vi* (of a vehicle, its driver) to turn a

corner (on a road etc): *My new car corners well*. **3 corner the market** ⇨ market[1](3).

'corner-stone /'kɔ:nəstəun/ *nc* **1** a stone forming a corner of a foundation for a building. **2** (*fig*) the main reason, cause: *Charm was the corner-stone of his success*.

cor·net /'kɔ:nɪt/ *nc* **1** a small musical instrument of brass, like a trumpet. **2** a piece of biscuit etc twisted into the shape of a cone and used to hold ice-cream etc.

cor·nice /'kɔ:nɪs/ *nc* **1** a projecting part at the top of a column(1). **2** an ornamental moulding at the top of the walls of a room.

cor·ny /'kɔ:nɪ/ *adj* (**-ier, -iest**) (*sl; derog*) dull because often repeated: *corny jokes*.

co·rol·lary /kə'rɒlərɪ/ *nc* (*pl* **-ies**) a statement that must be true because an earlier and related statement is true.

cor·on·ary /'kɒrənrɪ/ *adj* arteries supplying blood to the heart: *coronary thrombosis* (= the formation of a clot in a coronary artery).

cor·on·ation /ˌkɒrə'neɪʃn/ *nc* a ceremony of crowning a king, queen or other sovereign ruler.

cor·on·er /'kɒrənə(r)/ *nc* an official who investigates the cause of any death thought to be from violent or unnatural causes: *a coroner's inquest* (i.e. such an inquiry).

cor·on·et /'kɒrənet/ *nc* a small crown.

Corp. *abbr* Corporation.

cor·por·al[1] /'kɔ:pərəl/ *adj* of the human body. **,corporal 'punishment** *nu* physical punishment, e.g. whipping, beating.

cor·por·al[2] /'kɔ:pərəl/ *nc* (*mil*) the lowest non-commissioned officer (below a sergeant) in the army.

cor·por·ate /'kɔ:pərət/ *adj* (*attrib*) **1** of, belonging to, a corporation(2): *corporate property*. **2** of, shared by, members of a group: *corporate responsibility/action*.

cor·por·ation /ˌkɔ:pə'reɪʃn/ *nc* or *n pl* (C- in names) **1** a group of people elected to govern a town: *the municipal corporation*. **2** a group of people authorized to act as one business organization: *The Post Office is a public corporation*.

cor·por·eal /kɔ:'pɔ:rɪəl/ *adj* (*formal*) of or for the body. Compare **spiritual**.

corps /kɔ:(r)/ *nc* (*pl* **corps** /kɔ:z/) (*mil*) **1** (C- in names) one of the technical branches of an army: *the Royal Army Medical Corps*. **2** a military force made up of two or more divisions.

,corps de 'ballet *nc* (*Fr*) a company of dancers in a ballet.

,Corps ,Diploma'tique *nc* (the —; *abbr* CD) (*Fr*) all the ambassadors, ministers and attachés of governments represented in another country.

corpse /kɔ:ps/ *nc* a dead human body.

cor·pu·lent /'kɔ:pjʊlənt/ *adj* (*formal*) (of a person) fat and heavy.

cor·pus /'kɔ:pəs/ *nc* (*pl* **corpora** /'kɔ:pərə/) a collection, esp of writings on a specified subject or of material for study.

cor·puscle /'kɔ:pʌsl/ *nc* (*anat*) one of the red or white cells in the blood.

cor·ral /kə'rɑ:l/ *nc* (esp in US) an enclosure for horses and cattle.

cor·rect[1] /kə'rekt/ *adj* **1** true; right: *the correct time*. **2** (of conduct, manners, dress etc) proper; agreeing with good taste or convention: *the cor-*

rect dress for a ceremony. Opp incorrect.

cor·rect·ly *adv*

cor·rect² /kə'rekt/ *vt* **1** to indicate the mistakes in (something): *Please correct my pronunciation.* **2** to (punish and) help to improve (a person): *correct a child for disobedience.*

cor·rec·tion /kə'rekʃn/ *n* **1** *nu* the act, process, of correcting something: *the correction of schoolchildren's work.* **2** *nc* something right that is written etc in order to show what is wrong: *a written exercise with corrections in red ink.*

cor·rect·ive /kə'rektɪv/ *nc, adj* (something) meant to correct(2): *corrective training* (e.g. for young offenders).

cor·re·late /'kɒrəleɪt/ *v* (*formal*) **1** *vi* to complement each other; have a relationship: *Do these two ideas correlate?* **2** *vt* **correlate sth (to/with sth)** to establish, show, a relationship between (things, ideas etc): *Research workers found it hard to correlate the two sets of figures/to correlate one set with the other.*

cor·re·la·tion /ˌkɒrə'leɪʃn/ *nc,nu.*

cor·re·spond /ˌkɒrɪ'spɒnd/ *vi* **1** **correspond (with sth)** to be the same; be in agreement (with something); to conform, be consistent, (with something): *His exam results do not correspond with his ability.* **2** **correspond (to sth)** to be equal (to something); be similar in position etc (to): *The American Congress corresponds to the British Parliament.* **3** **correspond (with sb)** to exchange letters: *We've been corresponding (with each other) for years.*

cor·re·spond·ing *adj* (*attrib*) similar; same: *Imports for July this year are 10% up on the corresponding period last year.*

cor·re·spond·ing·ly *adv*

cor·re·spon·dence /ˌkɒrɪ'spɒndəns/ *n* **1** *nu* writing letters; letters: *I have been in correspondence with him about the problem. Don't read my private correspondence.* **2** *nc,nu* (*formal*) agreement; similarity: *There is not much correspondence between their ideals and ours.*

cor·re·spon·dent /ˌkɒrɪ'spɒndənt/ *nc* **1** a person with whom one exchanges letters: *He's a good/bad correspondent.* **2** a person regularly contributing local news or special articles to a newspaper: *a war correspondent.*

cor·ri·dor /'kɒrɪdɔː(r)/ *nc* a long narrow passage from which doors open into rooms. **the corridors of power** the highest levels of government, the Civil Service, a political party etc.

cor·rob·or·ate /kə'rɒbəreɪt/ *vt* to give support or certainty to (a statement, belief, theory etc).

cor·rob·or·at·ive /kə'rɒbərətɪv/ *adj* (*formal*) tending to corroborate: *corroborative evidence.*

cor·rode /kə'rəʊd/ *vt,vi* (to cause a material) to wear away slowly by chemical action or disease.

cor·ro·sion /kə'rəʊʒn/ *nu* the process of corroding or being corroded.

cor·ros·ive /kə'rəʊsɪv/ *adj, nc* (of) a substance that corrodes: *Acids are corrosive.*

cor·ru·gated /'kɒrʊɡeɪtɪd/ *adj* (usu *attrib*) (of materials) in folds, wrinkles or furrows: *corrugated cardboard/iron.*

cor·ru·ga·tion /ˌkɒrʊ'ɡeɪʃn/ *nc,nu*

cor·rupt¹ /kə'rʌpt/ *adj* (*derog*) **1** (of a person, action) immoral; dishonest: *corrupt practices* (= offering and accepting bribes). **2** (of languages, texts etc) containing errors or alterations: *a corrupt form of English.*

cor·rupt·ly *adv*

cor·rupt² /kə'rʌpt/ *vt,vi* (to cause a person) to become corrupt: *young people whose attitudes have been corrupted by unemployment and boredom.*

cor·rupt·ible /-əbl/ *adj* who or that can be corrupted: *corruptible government officials.* Opp incorruptible(2).

cor·rup·tion /kə'rʌpʃn/ *nu*

cor·set /'kɔːsɪt/ *nc* a close-fitting type of underwear shaping the waist and hips.

cor·tège /kɔː'teɪʒ/ *nc* (*Fr*) a procession, e.g. at the funeral of a king or president.

cor·tex /'kɔːteks/ *nc* (*pl* **cortices** /'kɔːtɪsiːs/) (*anat*) the outer layer of grey matter of the brain.

cor·ti·sone /'kɔːtɪzəʊn/ *nu* (*med*) a kind of powerful drug used to treat rheumatism, allergies, cancers etc.

cos¹ /kɒs/ *nc* (also *attrib*) a kind of long-leaved lettuce: *a cos lettuce.*

cos² *abbr* (*maths*) cosine.

'cos /kəz/ *conj* (*GB informal*) = because.

cosh /kɒʃ/ *vt, nc* (*GB sl*) (to hit (a person) with) a length of metal, rubber etc.

co·sine /'kəʊsaɪn/ *nc* (*abbr* **cos**) (*maths*) **1** (of a triangle) the ratio of the length of the adjacent side to the hypotenuse. **2** (in a circle with a pair of axes meeting at the centre) a line from a point where a sine(2) meets an arc perpendicular to a radius that is at right angles to the one at the other end of the sine(2).

cos·met·ic /kɒz'metɪk/ *adj, nc* (of) a preparation, substance, that makes the skin or hair beautiful: *Face-cream, lipstick and eyeshadow are cosmetics.*

cos·mic /'kɒzmɪk/ *adj* of the whole universe: *cosmic rays* (i.e. from outer space).

cos·mo·naut /'kɒzmənɔːt/ *nc* = astronaut (the usual word).

cos·mo·poli·tan¹ /ˌkɒzmə'pɒlɪtən/ *adj* **1** of or from all, or many different parts of, the world: *London is a cosmopolitan city* (= has people from many parts of the world). **2** free from national prejudices because of wide experience of the world: *a statesman with a cosmopolitan outlook.*

cos·mo·poli·tan² /ˌkɒzmə'pɒlɪtən/ *nc* a cosmopolitan(2) person.

cos·mos /'kɒzmɒs/ *n* (the —) the universe.

cost¹ /kɒst/ *n* **1** *nc,nu* the amount of money (to be) paid for something: *the cost of repairs/of renting a flat/of learning to drive; without regard to cost* (= without considering how much money would be needed). Ⓝ *'Cost'* is used when referring to an amount to be paid (e.g. for building, repairs, paying fees etc) which involves paying people for labour, materials, rent, meals etc. *'Price'* is used when referring to payment to be paid when buying individual things as in shops. *'Cost'* is also used for general expenses such as running a car, living expenses etc. **the cost of living** the general expenses of rent, food, clothes etc. **2** *nu* or *sing* something done, needed or given to obtain something: *The battle was won at a great cost in human lives.* **at all costs** however severe the cost(2) may be. **to one's cost** according to one's own experience of pain, loss or disadvantage: *Wasps' stings are pain-*

my cost. **3** (*pl*) (*legal*) the expenses of having an action settled in a law court: *He was asked to pay a £50 fine and £15 costs.*

cost² /kɒst/ *v* (*pt, pp* —) (*no passive*) Ⓝ Not used in the continuous tenses, e.g. '*is/was -ing*'. **1** *vt, vi* to be obtainable at the price of, require the payment of, (an amount of money mentioned): *The house cost him £80 000.* **2** *vt* to result in the loss of (something): *Careless driving may cost you your life.*

cost³ /kɒst/ *vt* (*pt, pp* costed) *cost sth* ((*out*) *at sth*) to estimate the price to be charged for (an article, work etc) based on the expense of producing it: *I've costed the repairs out at £50.*

co-star /ˌkəʊ ˈstɑː(r)/ *nc, vi, vt* (-**rr**-) (an actor agreeing) to be a film star having equal status with another or others: *The film co-starred John Wayne and Clint Eastwood.*

cost·ly /ˈkɒstlɪ/ *adj* (-**ier, -iest**) **1** costing much money: *a costly new outfit.* Ⓝ '*Expensive*' is much more usual. **2** (*fig*) involving much loss or sacrifice: *a costly mistake.*

cos·tume /ˈkɒstʃuːm/ *n* **1** *nu* a style of dress: *actors wearing historical costume.* **2** *nc* a woman's jacket and skirt of the same material. ⇨ also swimming costume.

co·sy¹ (*US* = **co·zy**) /ˈkəʊzɪ/ *adj* (-**ier, -iest**) warm and comfortable: *a cosy little room.*
co·si·ly /-əlɪ/ *adv*
co·si·ness *nu*

co·sy² /ˈkəʊzɪ/ *nc* (*pl* -**ies**) a covering for a teapot or an egg in an egg-cup: *a tea-cosy; an egg-cosy.*

cot /kɒt/ *nc* **1** a bed for a young child (with sides to prevent the child from falling out). **2** (*US*) a camp-bed.

cot·tage /ˈkɒtɪdʒ/ *nc* a small house, esp in the country.
ˌcottage 'cheese *nu* a kind of white cheese in lumps.
ˌcottage 'industry *nc* a kind of paid work that can be carried on at home, e.g. pottery.
ˌcottage 'pie *nu* = shepherd's pie.

cot·ton¹ /ˈkɒtn/ *nu* (also *attrib*) **1** the soft, white fibrous substance (round the seeds of the *cotton plant*), used for making thread, cloth etc: *cotton yarn/cloth.* **2** thread spun from cotton: *sewing with a needle and cotton.*
ˌcotton 'wool *nu* absorbent cotton as used for cleaning wounds etc.

cot·ton² /ˈkɒtn/ *vi* **cotton on(to sb/sth)** (*informal*) to understand (a person, action etc) after some difficulty or when it is being kept secret etc: *Suddenly I cottoned on* (*to why she left the party early*).

couch¹ /kaʊtʃ/ *nc* **1** a long seat like a bed, used for sitting on or lying on during the day: *a studio couch.* **2** (*literary*) a bed.

couch² /kaʊtʃ/ *vi* (of an animal) to lie flat and ready to jump.

couch³ /kaʊtʃ/ *vt* (*formal*) (usually *passive*) to put (a thought etc) in the way mentioned: *The reply was couched in insolent terms.*

cou·gar /ˈkuːgə(r)/ *nc* a kind of large wild cat (also called a *puma*).

cough¹ /kɒf/ *nc* **1** an act, sound, of coughing: *He gave me a warning cough.* **2** an illness that causes a person to cough often: *to have a bad cough.*

cough² /kɒf/ *v* **1** *vi* to send out air from the lungs

violently and noisily (because of a cold etc). **2** *vt* **cough sth up** to get something out of the throat by coughing. **3** *vt, vi* **cough (sth) up** to say or produce (something) reluctantly.

could /kəd *strong form:* kʊd/ *auxiliary verb* Ⓝ '*Could*' is a *modal auxiliary verb* used with another verb to express possibility or permission. '*Could*' has no infinitive or imperative forms and no participles. '*Could*' is always followed by an infinitive without '*to*'. Compare can, may, might. (*Negative:* **could not, couldn't** /ˈkʊdnt/) **1** *pt* form of can². **2** (conditional form of can²): *He could be a first class student if he tried. If you held the table, I could stand on it.* **3** (**a**) (used to show possibility): *She could arrive at any time. He couldn't have done it. Could he run the school well? This letter could contain the photographs. You could be right. They look so alike, they could be sisters.* (**b**) (used to suggest the possibility is not likely): *Steve could break the world record but I doubt it. The sun could shine although the forecast is bad.* (**c**) (used of a possibility that (fortunately) did not happen): *You were lucky—that ball could have broken the window.* (**d**) (used when criticizing a person for not doing something): *You could have warned me about her snoring/that she snores!* ⇨ can²(3). **4** (used to make a request, especially when being very polite or when uncertain or a little afraid): *Could you help me with this heavy suitcase, please. I wonder if I could speak to you for a moment—if you're not too busy. Could I make a suggestion, though I realize I'm only an observer?* ⇨ the *note* at can²(6). **5** (used in conversation) (**a**) (joined to the end of a statement to form a question): *He couldn't make me a coffee, could he?* Ⓝ The short addition is always negative (i.e. *couldn't*) if the statement is positive (i.e. *could*) and always positive if the statement is negative. Statements with *neither, no, nobody, nothing* etc are considered to be negative and the short addition is positive, as in *No-one could see, could they?* (**b**) (used to make a short question): '*We could be there by 5 o'clock*'—'*Could you really?*' Ⓝ If the statement is positive, the short question is positive. If the statement is negative, the short question is negative. Statements with *neither, no, nobody, nothing* etc are considered to be negative. (**c**) (used to make a short answer): '*Could you be there by four?*'—'*Yes I could.*' Ⓝ '*Could*' is not used in a short answer to give permission. Use '*can*', as in '*Could I borrow your car?*'—'*Yes, you can*'/'*No, you can't*'. Be careful, because '*could*' is only used in (a), (b) and (c) when *could* is used in the main statement, but ⇨ the start of this note. Compare can²(7).

couldn't /ˈkʊdnt/ = could not. ⇨ can², could.

cou·lomb /ˈkuːlɒm/ *nc* (symbol C) (*science*) a unit of measurement for the amount of electricity transported in one second by a current of one ampere.

coun·cil /ˈkaʊnsl/ *nc* or *n pl* (often C-; also *attrib*) a group of people appointed, elected or chosen to give advice, make rules, carry out plans, manage affairs etc, esp of government: *a city/county council; a council meeting.*
ˈcouncil-chamber *nc* the room where a council meets.
ˈcouncil estate *nc* (*GB*) a housing estate built by a city or county council.

'**council house** *nc* a house on a council estate.

coun·cil·lor (*US* also **coun·cil·or**) /'kaʊn-sələ(r)/ *nc* a member of a council.

coun·sel /'kaʊnsl/ *n* **1** *nu* (*formal*) advice; opinions, suggestions. **2** *nc* (*pl* —) (*legal*) a barrister or group of barristers giving advice in a law case.

coun·sel /'kaʊnsl/ *vt* (**-ll-**; *US* also **-l-**) (*formal*) to give advice to (a person): *counsel students*.

coun·sel·ling /'kaʊnsəlɪŋ/ *nu* advice on personal matters given by a trained person such as a social worker.

coun·sel·lor (*US* also **coun·sel·or**) /'kaʊnsələ(r)/ *nc* (*formal*) an adviser, esp on personal matters.

count¹ /kaʊnt/ *nc* a title of European nobility (but not in GB) equal to an earl.

count² /kaʊnt/ *nc* **1** an act of counting; number got by counting: *Four counts were necessary before we were certain of the total.* **keep/lose count (of sth)** to continue/fail to continue to know the correct total. **2** (*legal*) one of a number of things of which a person has been accused: *He was found guilty on all counts.*

count³ /kaʊnt/ *v* **1** *vt,vi* to say, name, (the numerals in order): *count from 1 to 10. He can't count yet.* ⇨ **count up to sth. 2** *vt* to say, name, (numerals, things, people etc) to find the total in a collection: *Don't forget to count your change. Please count the passengers as they get on the bus.* **3** *vt* to include (people, things): *Fifty people are coming, not counting the children.* **4** *vt* to consider (oneself, a person, thing) to be in the state mentioned: *You can count yourself lucky that you weren't badly injured.* **5** *vi* to be important: *It's the thought that counts, not how much it cost you. My wishes don't seem to count.*

count (sth) against sb (of age, origins, failure etc) to be considered, consider (something), as a disadvantage: *She is an immigrant but that shouldn't count against her. Don't count his age against him.*

count (sb/sth) among sb/sth to be considered, consider (a person, thing) as: *Athens counts among one of the world's greatest cities. I count her among my best students.* Ⓝ Not used in the continuous tenses, e.g. *'is/was -ing'.*

count down to say numerals in reverse order (e.g. when sending a spacecraft into the sky). Hence '**count-down** *nc.*

count for sth to be of (some, no, little etc) importance: *Your previous experience ought to count for something. Surely all that hard work won't count for nothing!*

count sb in to include a person: *If you are going to Venice, count me in.*

count on sb to rely on a person (to help, give support etc): *We're counting on you to provide transport.*

count sb out to decide not to include a person: *If it's raining in Venice when you all go, count me out.* **count sth out** to count(2) money etc slowly: *The old woman counted out the money for the milk.*

count to sth = count up to sth.

count sth up to find the total of something: *This computer program can count up all the items left on the shelves and produce orders for new stock.* **count up to sth** to count(1,2) as far as a number: *I can count up to 1000 in Spanish.*

count·able /'kaʊntəbl/ *adj* that can be counted. ⇨ **countless.**

,**countable 'noun** *nc* (*gram*) one that may be used with *a*, *an* or *many* and with numerals and the plural form, as in '*a bird*', 'I need a lot of *pins*'. Ⓝ Marked *nc* in this dictionary. Compare uncountable noun.

count-down /'kaʊnt daʊn/ *nc* ⇨ count down.

coun·ten·ance /'kaʊntɪnəns/ *nc* (*formal*) a face, including its appearance and expression: *a woman with a fierce countenance.*

coun·ter¹ /'kaʊntə(r)/ *adj,adv* **counter to sth** (*formal*) opposite to something: *to act counter to a person's wishes.*

coun·ter² /'kaʊntə(r)/ *nc* a table or flat surface where goods are shown, customers served, in a shop, bank etc. **under the counter** (*fig*) (bought, sold, arranged) dishonestly.

coun·ter³ /'kaʊntə(r)/ *nc* **1** a small (round) flat piece of plastic etc used in games etc. **2** (in compounds) a device (in a machine etc) for keeping count: *a speed-counter.*

coun·ter⁴ /'kaʊntə(r)/ *vt,vi* **counter (sth (with sth))** to oppose (something); meet (an attack) (with a return attack): *They countered our proposal with one of their own.*

coun·ter·act /ˌkaʊntər'rækt/ *vt* to act against and make another (action, force) less strong: *This will counteract (the effects of) a poison.*

coun·ter-at·tack /'kaʊntər ətæk/ *vi, nc* (to make) an attack in reply to an attack by the enemy.

coun·ter·bal·ance /'kaʊntəbæləns/ *vt, nc* (to act as) a weight, force, equal to (another) and balancing it.

coun·ter·espion·age /ˌkaʊntər 'espɪənɑːʒ/ *nu* spying directed against the enemy's spying.

coun·ter·feit /'kaʊntəfɪt/ *vt, nc, adj* (to make) (something) made or done in imitation of another thing in order to deceive: *counterfeit money.*

coun·ter·foil /'kaʊntəfɔɪl/ *nc* a section of a cheque, receipt etc kept by the sender as a record.

coun·ter-in·fla·tion·ary /ˌkaʊntər ɪn'fleɪʃnrɪ/ *adj* intended to reduce inflation(b): *counter-inflationary economic policies.*

coun·ter-in·tel·li·gence /ˌkaʊntər ɪn'telɪdʒəns/ *nu* = counter-espionage.

coun·ter·mand /ˌkaʊntə'mɑːnd/ *vt* to cancel (a command) already given (e.g. by giving another).

coun·ter·meas·ure /'kaʊntəmeʒə(r)/ *nc* an action intended to reduce, remove, be a punishment for, another: *a countermeasure against vandalism.*

coun·ter-of·fer /'kaʊntərɒfə(r)/ *nc* an offer (of a price) made in reply to an earlier offer.

coun·ter·part /'kaʊntəpɑːt/ *nc* a person or thing exactly like, or closely corresponding to, another: *Sally is my counterpart in our rival company.*

coun·ter-rev·ol·ution /ˌkaʊntə ˌrevə'luːʃn/ *nc* a political movement directed against a revolution.

,**counter-,revo'lutionary** *adj, nc* (*pl* **-ies**) (a person) supporting, helping, a counter-revolution.

coun·ter·sign /'kaʊntəsaɪn/ *vt* to add another

signature to (a document) to give it authority.

count·ess /'kaontis/ *nc* **1** a wife or widow of a count or earl. **2** a woman who holds the rank of a count or an earl.

count·less /'kaontlis/ *adj* that cannot be counted (because there are too many): *countless mistakes*.

coun·try /'kʌntrɪ/ *n* (*pl* **-ies**) **1** *nc* a land occupied by a nation: *European countries*. **2** *nc* the land of a person's birth or citizenship: *to return to one's own country*. **3** (the —) all the people of a country(1): *Does the country want war?* **4** (the —; *also attrib*) the areas of land used for farming etc (and not a town or suburb): *to live in the country; country life; country roads*. **5** *nu* an area of land (with reference to its physical or geographical features): *We passed through miles of densely wooded country*.

coun·try·man /'kʌntrɪmən/ *nc* (*pl* **-men**) **1** a man living in the country(4). **2** a man of one's own country(2): *my fellow countrymen*.

coun·try·side /'kʌntrɪsaɪd/ *nu* the country(4,5): *The English countryside looks its best in May and June*.

coun·try·woman /'kʌntrɪwomən/ *nc* (*pl* **-women** /-wimɪn/) **1** a woman living in the country(4). **2** a woman of one's own country(2): *my own countrywomen*.

coun·ty /'kaontɪ/ *nc* (*pl* **-ies**) (C- in names) a division of Great Britain, the largest unit of local government: *the county of Kent; the Home Counties* (= those round London).

,county 'council *nc* a body of officials elected to administer a county.

coup /ku:/ *nc* (*pl* **—s** /ku:z/) (*Fr*) **1** a clever and sudden action to obtain a desired result: *He pulled off a great coup when he won the contract*. **2** = coup d'état.

coup d'état /,ku: deɪ'tɑ:/ *nc* (*Fr*) a violent or unconstitutional change in government.

couple¹ /'kʌpl/ *nc* **1** two people, things seen together or associated: *Here is a couple of pounds towards the expenses. I'll send a couple of men to help you. I'll ring you in a couple of days*. Compare pair¹. **2** two people in a relationship, activity etc: *married couples; dancing couples. They make a handsome couple*.

couple² /'kʌpl/ *v* **1** *vt* to fasten, connect, (two things) together: *We couple the name of Oxford with great learning*. **2** *vi* (of animals) to unite sexually.

coup·let /'kʌplɪt/ *nc* (*literature*) two successive lines of rhyming verse. ⇨ closed couplet.

cou·pon /'ku:pɒn/ *nc* **1** a ticket, part of a document, paper etc, giving the holder the right to receive or do something, e.g. given with a purchase to be exchanged for goods. **2** an application form in a newspaper etc for buying by post, obtaining information etc: *Fill in the coupon below and send it to us*.

cour·age /'kʌrɪdʒ/ *nu* the quality that makes a person able to control fear in the face of danger, pain etc. **have the courage of one's convictions** to be determined enough to do something that one believes is right or necessary. **pluck up courage; pluck up the courage to do sth; screw up one's courage** to ignore one's fears and become brave enough (to do something).

cou·ra·geous /kə'reɪdʒəs/ *adj* brave; fearless: *It was courageous of him to chase the gunman*.
cou·ra·geous·ly *adv*

cour·gette /kʊə'ʒet/ *nc* (also *attrib*) a kind of small green marrow(3) eaten as a vegetable: *courgette soup.* (*US* = zucchini).

cour·ier /'kʊrɪə(r)/ *nc* **1** a person who is paid to attend to details of travel (e.g. buying tickets, arranging for hotels etc) and (sometimes) accompanying travellers. **2** a messenger carrying news or important government papers.

course¹ /kɔ:s/ *n* **1** *nu* a forward movement in space or time: *a river in its course to the sea; the course of events.* **in due course** after the usual amount of time: *Sow the seeds now and in due course you will have the flowers.* **in the course of** (*prep*) during: *in the course of the evening/the conversation.* **2** *nc* a direction taken by something; line along which something moves: *a map that shows the courses of the chief rivers. The ship is on/off (her right) course. The course of the argument suddenly changed.* **run/take its course** to complete its stages of development: *The disease must run its course.* **as a matter of course** as an expected or natural result, way of acting etc: *I always take her flowers as a matter of course.* **3 of course** naturally; certainly: *'Do you study hard?'—'Of course (I do)!'* **4** *nc* one of the several parts of a meal, e.g. soup, fish, dessert: *a five-course dinner; the main course.* **5** *nc* a ground for certain games, sport: *a golf-course; a race-course.* **6** *nc* a series (of talks, treatments etc): *a course of lectures; a course of treatment.*

course² /kɔ:s/ *vi* (of a liquid) to move quickly: *The blood coursed through his veins.*

court¹ /kɔ:t/ *n* **1** *nc* (also *attrib*) a place where legal cases are heard and judged; the judges, magistrates and other officers who administer justice: *a court of law/a law court; a court-room. The prisoner was brought to court for trial. Silence in court!* **go to court** to take legal action. **settle out of court** to agree (the money to be paid as) a result and end a legal action. **take sb to court** to start a legal action against her or him. **2** *nc* a space marked out for certain games: *a tennis-court.* **3** (the C-) (the residence of a) king, queen, emperor, family and officials, councillors etc: *The Court went into mourning when the Queen's uncle died.* ⇨ courtier.

'court-card *nc* a playing-card with a king, queen or jack on it.

'court·yard *nc* an unroofed space with walls or buildings round it.

court² /kɔ:t/ *vt* **1** (*dated*) to try to win the affections of (a person) with a view to marriage: *He had been courting Jane for six months.* **2** (*formal*) to try to win or obtain (something): *to court a person's approval/support.* **3** to act in such a way that one may experience (something unpleasant): *That would be courting disaster.*

cour·teous /'kɜ:tɪəs/ *adj* having, showing, good manners; polite and kind (to a person). Opp discourteous.
cour·teous·ly *adv*

cour·tesy /'kɜ:tɪsɪ/ *n* (*pl* **-ies**) *nc,nu* (an instance of) courteous behaviour. Opp discourtesy. **by courtesy of sb/sth** as a favour or by permission of a person, business etc: *The photo-*

graphs were made available by courtesy of British Rail.

court·ier /'kɔːtɪə(r)/ nc (in earlier times) a person in attendance at the Court of a sovereign: the King and his courtiers.

court-mar·tial /ˌkɔːt 'mɑːʃl/ vt (-ll-), nc (pl courts-martial) (mil) (to try a person in) a military court; such a trial.

court·ship /'kɔːtʃɪp/ nc,nu (dated) (a period of) courting(1) a person: a brief courtship.

cous·in /'kʌzn/ nc (a) (also first cousin) the child of one's uncle or aunt. (b) (also second cousin) the child of one's parents' first cousin.

cove /kəʊv/ nc a small bay[1].

cov·en·ant /'kʌvənənt/ nc 1 (legal) a formal agreement that is legally binding. 2 a formal undertaking to make regular payments to a charity etc.

cov·er[1] /'kʌvə(r)/ n 1 nc something that covers another thing: Some chairs are fitted with loose covers. 2 nc a binding of a book, magazine etc: The book needs a new cover. **from cover to cover** (of a book etc) from beginning to end: I read the magazine from cover to cover. 3 nc a wrapper or envelope. **under separate cover** in a separate parcel or envelope: We are sending the photo under separate cover. ⇨ covering[1]. 4 nu shelter or protection: There was nowhere where we could find cover. **take cover** to find protection from (bad weather, enemy guns etc). **under cover of sth** with the protection of something: under cover of darkness. 5 nu insurance against loss, damage etc: Does your policy provide adequate cover against fire? 6 nc (informal) an activity, way of behaving etc used to hide a secret or illegal activity: They use the café as a cover for gambling.

cov·er[2] /'kʌvə(r)/ vt 1 to put something over or in front of (something else): We covered the seats with red cloth. Cover your eyes from the sun. It's best to cover your head in this heat. Please cover your clothes while you cook. 2 to extend over the surface of (something): Snow covered the ground. 3 to occupy, extend over, (a region): What areas do you cover as a salesperson? 4 to hide (an emotion): He laughed to cover his embarrassment. ⇨ cover sth up. 5 (of money, assets) to be enough for (a debt, loan etc): You don't have enough assets to cover your debts. 6 (usually pp) to insure (oneself, something etc) against loss, damage etc: Is my bike also covered in the policy? 7 to travel (the distance mentioned): We were able to cover 400km each day. ⇨ ground[1](1). 8 (of a book, lecture, research etc) to deal with (a subject, topics etc): a book covering African history; an exhibition that covered every aspect of arts and crafts. 9 (of a reporter, photographer or a magazine, broadcast etc) to report on (an event), deal with (a subject) etc: cover a war/a general election/a music concert/the famine in Africa. 10 to keep a gun etc aimed at (a person) e.g. so that he or she cannot escape: Keep him covered while I call the police.

be covered against sth to be insured against something harmful: Is your car covered against fire and theft?

cover for sb (a) to take the place of a person for a short time: Will you cover for me while I'm away on Friday? (b) = cover up for sb.

be covered in sth = be covered with sth.

cover sb/sth over (a) to protect a person, thing, with clothing, a blanket etc. (b) to hide a person, thing, by using cloth, branches, paint etc.

cover sb/sth up = cover sb/sth over. **cover sth up** to (try to) hide a mistake, emotion, crime etc. Hence **'cover-up** nc (an attempt at) the hiding of a mistake, immoral or illegal action etc: President Nixon was made responsible for the Watergate cover-up. **cover up for sb** to try to prevent a person's actions, bad behaviour etc from becoming known: He covered up for his wife by saying she had stayed with him.

cover oneself with sth to bring the reputation mentioned on oneself: cover oneself with glory/dishonour/disgrace. **be covered with sth** (a) (of trees etc) to have, display, a large amount of leaves etc: trees covered with blossom/fruit. (b) (of an animal etc) to have something as a coat: animals covered with fur. (c) to have something on the surface: walls covered with pretty wallpaper; doors covered with red paint; a wall covered with grape vines; a floor covered with wool carpet; furniture covered with dust; a face covered with mud. ⇨ also confusion, shame(1).

cov·er·age /'kʌvərɪdʒ/ nu 1 the type, amount, of risk in an insurance policy. 2 the (time, quantity etc of) reporting of an event by TV, radio, newspapers etc: coverage of the Olympic Games by the BBC. 3 the area reached by a TV station, sales campaign etc.

cov·er·ing[1] /'kʌvərɪŋ/ adj (attrib): a covering letter (= one sent with a document or with goods etc).

cov·er·ing[2] /'kʌvərɪŋ/ nc something that covers: a thin covering of snow.

cover-up /'kʌvʌp/ nc ⇨ cover sth up.

cov·ert[1] /'kʌvət/ adj (attrib; formal) (of glances, threats etc) hidden; disguised.

cov·ert·ly adv

cov·ert[2] /'kʌvət/ nc an area of thick bushes etc in which animals hide.

cov·et /'kʌvɪt/ vt to desire eagerly (esp something belonging to another person).

cov·et·ous /'kʌvɪtəs/ adj **covetous (of sth)** (formal) wanting things eagerly (esp something belonging to another person).

cov·et·ous·ly adv

cow /kaʊ/ nc 1 a fully grown female of any animal of the ox family, esp the domestic kind kept by farmers for producing milk. 2 a female elephant, rhinoceros, whale etc. Compare bull.

'cow·boy nc a man who looks after cattle in the western parts of the US.

'cow·hand, 'cow·herd nc a person who looks after grazing cattle.

'cow·man nc a man responsible for milking cows.

'cow·shed nc a building for cows.

cow·ard /'kaʊəd/ nc (derog) a person unable to control fear, e.g. who runs away from responsibility, dangerous situations etc.

cow·ard·ly adj

cow·ard·ice /'kaʊədɪs/ nu the feeling, way of behaviour, of a coward.

cow·er /'kaʊə(r)/ vi to shrink back because of cold, misery, fear, shame: The dog cowered under *the table when its master raised the whip.*

cowl /kaʊl/ *nc* a long, loose gown (as worn by monks) with a hood.

cox /kɒks/ *vt,vi, nc* (*informal*) (to act as) a person who guides rowers in a rowing-boat during races.

coy /kɔɪ/ *adj* (**—er, —est**) (esp of a woman) (pretending to be) shy, modest.
coy·ly *adv*

coy·ote /'kɔɪəʊt/ *nc* a prairie wolf of western N America.

Cpl *abbr* Corporal.

cps. *abbr* **1** characters per second (e.g. in a computer printer). ⇨ wpm. **2** cycles per second. ⇨ hertz.

CPU /ˌsiː piː 'juː/ *abbr* (*computers*) central processing unit.

cr *abbr* (*bookkeeping*) credit; creditor.

crab /kræb/ *n* **1** *nc* a sea animal with a wide shell and five pairs of legs. **2** *nu* (also *attrib*) its flesh as food: *crab paste.*

crack¹ /kræk/ *nc* **1** a line or division where something is broken but not into separate parts: *a cup with bad cracks in it.* **(at) the crack of dawn** (at) the beginning of the day. **2** a sudden, sharp noise: *the crack of thunder/of a whip.* **3** a sharp blow which can be heard: *give/get a crack on the head.* **4 have a crack at sth** (*informal*) to try to do something that is difficult. **5** a witty joke: *make cracks about/at her clothes.* **6** (*sl*) a form of cocaine used by drug addicts.

crack² /kræk/ *v* **1** *vt,vi* (to cause something) to have a crack(1): *crack an egg; crack open a peanut; glass cracking easily.* **2** *vt,vi* (to cause something) to make the noise of a crack(2): *crack one's fingers/a whip.* **3** *vt* to hit (something) with a sharp blow: *crack an egg; crack one's head on the post.* **4** *vt* **crack a code,** ⇨ code¹(4). **crack a joke,** ⇨ joke¹. **get cracking** (*informal*) (esp *imperative*) to get on with (a task).
crack down (on sb/sth) (*informal*) to use one's full authority to prevent or stop something bad: *crack down on drug pushers/violence.*
crack up (a) (of a person) to suddenly lose self-control and mentally collapse. **(b)** (of a person) to become physically ill (because of worry, age, too much work etc). **(c)** (*informal*) (of a person) to suddenly laugh uncontrollably.

crack·er /'krækə(r)/ *nc* **1** a thin, dry biscuit (as eaten with cheese). **2** a firework that makes cracking noises when set off. ⇨ also Christmas cracker, nutcrackers.

crack·ers /'krækəz/ *adj* (*sl; derog*) mad; crazy.

crackle /'krækl/ *vi, nc* (to make) the series of small cracking sounds as when one treads on dry twigs or when dry sticks burn: *A cheerful wood fire was crackling near the tents.*

crack·ling /'kræklɪŋ/ *n* **1** *nc,nu* the sound of a crackle. **2** *nu* the crisp skin of roast pork.

crack·pot /'krækpɒt/ *adj* (*attrib*), *nc* (*derog*) (of) a person with strange or mad ideas.

cradle¹ /'kreɪdl/ *nc* **1** a small bed, sometimes with a curved bottom, for a newborn baby. **from the cradle to the grave** from birth to death. **2** (*fig*) a place where something is born or begins: *Greece, the cradle of Western culture.* **3** the part of a telephone apparatus on which the receiver rests.

cradle² /'kreɪdl/ *vt* to place, hold, (a baby, young animal etc) (as if) in a cradle: *cradling a baby in one's arms.*

craft¹ /krɑːft/ *nc* **1** an occupation in which skill in using the hands is needed; such a skill: *the potter's craft; needlecraft; woodcraft; handicraft.* **2** (*pl —*) boat(s), ship(s): *The harbour was full of all kinds of craft.* ⇨ also aircraft, spacecraft.

craft² /krɑːft/ *nu* cunning; trickery; skill in deceiving: *Be careful when you do business with him—he's full of craft.* ⇨ crafty.

crafts·man /'krɑːftsmən/ *nc* (*pl* **-men**) a skilled workman who practises a craft(1).

crafts·woman /'krɑːftswʊmən/ *nc* (*pl* **-women**) a woman craftsman.

crafty /'krɑːftɪ/ *adj* (**-ier, -iest**) (often *derog*) showing skill in trickery or deceit.
craft·ily /-əlɪ/ *adv*
crafti·ness *nu*

crag /kræg/ *nc* a high, sharp mass of rock.
crag·gy *adj* (**-ier, -iest**) having many crags.

cram /kræm/ *vt* (**-mm-**) **1** to make (a space) too full; put, push, very much or too much of (something) (into something): *to cram food into one's mouth/cram one's mouth with food.* **2** to fill (a person's head) with facts (for an examination): *to cram pupils.*
cram·full /-'fʊl/ *adj, adv* as full as cramming(1) can make it.

cramp¹ /kræmp/ *nu* a sudden and painful tightening of the muscles, usually caused by cold or overwork, making movement difficult: *The swimmer was seized with/had cramp in the cold water.*

cramp² /kræmp/ *nc* a tool with a moveable part which can be screwed to a table etc to hold things.

cramp³ /kræmp/ *vt* **1** to keep (something) in a narrow space; reduce or prevent the movement, growth, of (something): *All these difficulties cramped his progress. We are/feel cramped for space here.* **2** to fasten (something) with a cramp².

cran·ber·ry /'krænbrɪ/ *nc* (*pl* **-ies**) (also *attrib*) a kind of small, red berry, used for making jelly and sauce: *turkey with cranberry sauce.*

crane¹ /kreɪn/ *nc* **1** a kind of large waterbird with long legs and neck. **2** a machine with a long arm that can be swung round, used for lifting and moving heavy weights.

crane² /kreɪn/ *vt,vi* to stretch (the neck): *to crane forward; to crane one's neck in order to see.*

crane-fly /'kreɪn flaɪ/ *nc* (*pl* **-ies**) a kind of fly with very long legs.

cran·ial /'kreɪnɪəl/ *adj* (*anat*) of the skull.

cran·ium /'kreɪnɪəm/ *nc* (*anat*) the bony part of the head enclosing the brain.

crank¹ /kræŋk/ *nc* an apparatus with an L-shaped arm and handle, used for making something turn. □ *vt* to move (a piece of machinery) by turning a crank: *to crank (up) an engine.*

crank² /kræŋk/ *nc* (*informal; derog*) a person with peculiar ideas or with skill that has not been proved: *Don't go to that doctor—he's a crank!*

cran·ny /'krænɪ/ *nc* (*pl* **-ies**) a small crack or opening, e.g. in a wall: *nooks and crannies.*

crap /kræp/ *nu* (*sl; derog*) nonsense: *Don't talk crap!*

crash¹ /kræʃ/ *adj* (*attrib*) using fast (and often severe) methods to be successful: *a crash diet; a crash course in typing.*

crash² /kræʃ/ nc 1 (the noise made by) a violent fall, blow or breaking: *The tree fell with a great crash. He was killed in a plane crash.* 2 a sudden collapse (e.g. in trade, finance): *The great crash on Wall Street in 1929 ruined international trade.*

crash³ /kræʃ/ 1 vt,vi (to cause something) to fall or strike suddenly, violently and noisily (esp in an accident): *I've crashed the car. The bus crashed into a tree. The aircraft crashed.* 2 vi (of a business company, computer program, government etc) to fail suddenly; come to ruin: *His great financial scheme crashed.* 3 vi **crash through sth** to move or break through something with great force: *elephants crashing through the jungle.*

'crash barrier nc a barrier used to keep vehicles etc apart (e.g. along a motorway).

'crash-helmet nc a hard helmet worn, e.g. by a motorcyclist, to protect the head in a crash.

'crash-land vi,vt (to cause a plane etc) to land wholly or partly out of control. Hence **crash-'landing** nc,nu.

crass /kræs/ adj (of ignorance, stupidity etc) very great.

crate /kreɪt/ vt, nc (to put (goods) in) a large framework of light boards or basketwork for transporting.

cra·ter /'kreɪtə(r)/ nc 1 a round hole at the top of a volcano. 2 a similar hole in the ground.

cra·vat /krə'væt/ nc a wide piece of cloth loosely folded and worn round the neck by men.

crave /kreɪv/ vt,vi **crave (for) sth** to have, state, a strong desire for something: *to crave (for) forgiveness; craving (for) a drink.*

crav·ing /'kreɪvɪŋ/ nc a very strong or uncontrollable desire: *He has a craving for whisky.*

crawl¹ /krɔːl/ nc 1 a very slow crawling movement: *Traffic in Oxford Street was reduced to a crawl during the rush hours.* 2 (the —) a swimming style, bringing the arms over the head while on one's stomach.

crawl² /krɔːl/ vi 1 to move slowly by pulling the body along close to the ground: *There were insects/babies/snakes crawling across the room.* 2 to move very slowly: *Our train crawled over the damaged bridge.* 3 **crawl with sth** to be full of, covered with, things that crawl: *The ground was crawling with ants.* Ⓝ Usually in the continuous tenses, e.g. *'is/was -ing'.* 4 (of the flesh) to feel as if covered with crawling things: *She says that the sight of snakes makes her flesh crawl.* 5 **crawl to sb** (*informal*) to behave too well in order to gain a person's affections, attention etc: *Don't crawl to the manager.*

cray·fish /'kreɪfɪʃ/ nc,nu (also *attrib*) a kind of freshwater shellfish like a lobster.

cray·on /'kreɪɒn/ vt,vi, nc (also *attrib*) (to use) a stick or pencil of coloured chalk or wax.

craze /kreɪz/ nc an enthusiastic interest that may last for a short time: *the modern craze for rock music.* ⇨ rage¹(3).

crazed /kreɪzd/ adj (*attrib*) wildly excited or mad: *a crazed look/expression.*

crazy /'kreɪzɪ/ adj (-ier, -iest) 1 (*pred*) wildly excited or enthusiastic: *I'm crazy about you, darling.* **like crazy** with much enthusiasm, energy: *We ran like crazy when we saw the police.* 2 (*derog*) mad; foolish: *a crazy suggestion. You were crazy to lend that man your money.*

craz·ily /-əlɪ/ adv

crazi·ness nu

creak /kriːk/ vi, nc (to make) a sound like an unoiled hinge of a door.

creaky adj (-ier, -iest).

cream¹ /kriːm/ nu 1 the fatty or oily part of milk which rises to the surface and can be made into butter. 2 a kind of food containing or resembling cream: *ice-cream.* 3 a substance like cream in appearance or consistency: *furniture cream; face-cream.* 4 (the —) the best part (of something): *be among the cream of the university students.* 5 (also *adj*) a yellowish-white colour: *cream paint.*

,cream 'cheese nu a kind of smooth white cheese.

,cream 'tea nc an afternoon meal with scones, jam and cream.

creamy adj (-ier, -iest) smooth and rich like cream; containing cream: *creamy butter.*

cream² /kriːm/ vt 1 to take the cream(1) from (milk etc). 2 to mix (e.g. butter and sugar, potatoes) to a soft, smooth mass. 3 **cream sb/sth off** (*fig*) to take the best of a group of people, objects: *cream off the more intelligent children.*

crease /kriːs/ vi,vt, nc (to make) a line on cloth, paper etc made by crushing, folding or pressing: *I've creased my shirt. This material creases easily. He likes a crease in his trousers.*

cre·ate /krɪ'eɪt/ vt 1 to make (something new or original): *God created the world. Dickens created many wonderful characters in his novels.* 2 to produce (an effect): *His behaviour is creating a bad impression. They created such a noise!.* 3 to give a person (a rank): *He was created a life peer.*

cre·ation /krɪ'eɪʃn/ n 1 nu the act of creating: *the creation of great works of art.* 2 nu the universe and all things. 3 nc a production of the human intelligence, esp one in which imagination has a part: *the creations of poets, artists, designers, composers and dramatists.*

cre·ative /krɪ'eɪtɪv/ adj able to produce new, exciting, stimulating etc ideas or things: *a creative writer; useful and creative work.*

cre·ative·ly adv

cre·ativ·ity /,kriːeɪ'tɪvətɪ/ nu creative ability.

cre·ator /krɪ'eɪtə(r)/ nc a person who creates something.

crea·ture /'kriːtʃə(r)/ nc 1 a living animal, esp a small one. 2 (*dated*) a living person: *poor creatures in refugee camps.*

crèche /'kreɪʃ/ nc a place where babies are looked after while their parents go to work, church etc.

cre·dence /'kriːdəns/ nu **attach/give credence to sth** (*formal*) to believe gossip, what is claimed etc.

cre·den·tials /krɪ'denʃlz/ n pl the letters or papers showing that a person is what he or she claims to be: *His credentials were so satisfactory that he was given the post of manager.*

cred·ible /'kredəbl/ adj that can be believed: *credible witnesses/reports.* Compare incredible(1).

cred·ibly /-əblɪ/ adv.

credi·bil·ity /,kredɪ'bɪlətɪ/ nu

cred·it¹ /'kredɪt/ n 1 nu the belief, reputation, that a person, business etc can pay debts: *have/be in good credit with the shops/bank.* 2 nu the practice of allowing a person to pay later: *No credit is given in this shop*. **on credit** paying (often in instalments) after the date of buying: *a car bought on credit*. **3** *nc,nu* the time allowed to pay a debt: *We were given 12 months' credit*. **4** *nc* (also *attrib*) the money owned by a person, business etc in a bank etc: *You have a credit/a credit balance of £1200*. **be in credit** to have money in the bank. **5** *nc* the money a bank etc has agreed that a person business etc can borrow: *a credit of £50 000*. **6** *nc* (*bookkeeping; abbr* cr) a record on the right-hand side of an account showing money received: *Must this item be entered as a credit or a debit?* **7** *nu* the quality of honour, trust, good reputation etc in a person or her or his actions: *This work does you credit. She has great credit as a nurse. He's wiser than I gave him credit for. He does almost no work but gets most of the credit. She deserves to take the credit for such a beautiful garden*. **8** *nc* a person who has approval, a good reputation, trust etc: *She's a credit to her family*. **9** *nc* (an award for) a high standard in an exam etc: *pass with credit*. Compare distinction(4). **10** *nc* (esp *US*) a section of an educational course completed satisfactorily. **11** (*pl*) the names (in a film, book, programme etc) of those who worked on the production.

'credit account *nc* an account with a shop etc with an agreement to pay at a later date.

'credit card *nc* (**a**) one issued by a business firm allowing the holder to obtain goods on credit(2). (**b**) one issued by a bank allowing the holder to have money from its branches or use cheques to buy goods up to a written amount.

'credit limit *nc* the amount of credit(5) allowed.

'credit side *nc* (**a**) (*bookkeeping*) the right-hand side of an account(9) showing payments received. (**b**) (*fig*) favourable comments about a person: *He is easily annoyed and can also be boring, but on the credit side he is generous*.

'credit squeeze *nc* a government policy of making it difficult to borrow money (as part of an economic policy).

'credit titles *n pl* = credits(11).

'credit-worthy *adj* (**-ier, -iest**) (accepted as being) safe to offer credit(2) to.

cred·it² /'kredɪt/ *vt* **1 credit sb/sth (with sth)** to believe that a person or thing has something or is able to do something: *Until now I've always credited you with more sense. The relics are credited with miraculous powers*. **2** (*bookkeeping*) to enter (an amount) on the credit side of an account of (a person): *credit a customer with £10; credit £10 to a customer/to her account*.

cred·it·able /'kredɪtəbl/ *adj* worthy of respect or praise: *a creditable attempt*.

cred·it·ably /-əblɪ/ *adv*

credi·tor /'kredɪtə(r)/ *nc* a person to whom one owes money: *He ran away from his creditors*. Compare debtor.

cre·du·lity /krɪ'dʒuːlətɪ/ *nu* (*formal*) too great a readiness to believe things.

credu·lous /'kredjʊləs/ *adj* (*formal*) too ready to believe things: *There are credulous people who accept all the promises of the politicians*. Compare incredulous.

credu·lous·ly *adv*

creed /kriːd/ *nc* (a system of) religious beliefs or opinions.

creek /kriːk/ *nc* **1** (*GB*) a narrow inlet of water on the coast or in a river-bank. **2** (*US*) a small river.

creep /kriːp/ *vi* (*pt,pp* **crept** /krept/) **1** to move along with the body close to the ground or floor: *The cat crept silently towards the bird*. **2** to move carefully, quietly or secretly: *The thief crept along the corridor*. **3** (of a plant) to grow along the ground, over the surface of a wall etc: *Ivy had crept over the walls*. **4** (of the flesh) to have the feeling that things are creeping over it (as a result of fear, horror etc): *The sight of the rats running about made her flesh creep*. ⇨ creeps.

creep in to begin to appear: *Lots of mistakes are creeping in*.

creep on (of age, time etc) to move ahead gradually: *I can feel old age creeping on. Time is creeping on—we must go*.

creep over sb to affect a person gradually: *A sudden fear crept over her*.

creep up behind/on sb to approach a person quietly or secretly.

creep·er /'kriːpə(r)/ *nc* **1** an insect, bird etc that creeps. **2** a plant that grows along the ground or over rocks, walls etc.

creeps /kriːps/ *n pl* **give sb the creeps** to make a person feel afraid. ⇨ creep(4).

creepy /'kriːpɪ/ *adj* (**-ier, -iest**) feeling or causing fear: *The ghost story made us all creepy/gave us a creepy feeling*.

cre·mate /krɪ'meɪt/ *vt* to burn (a dead person) to ashes: *He wants to be cremated, not buried*.

cre·ma·tion /krɪ'meɪʃn/ *nc*

cre·ma·tor·ium /ˌkreməˈtɔːrɪəm/ *nc* (*pl* —s) a furnace, building etc for cremations.

crêpe /kreɪp/ *nc* (also *attrib*) the name for kinds of wrinkled cloth or paper.

ˌcrêpe 'paper *nu* thin paper with a wavy or wrinkled surface.

ˌcrêpe 'rubber *nu* raw rubber with a wrinkled surface, used for the soles of shoes etc.

crept /krept/ *pt,pp* of creep.

Cres. *abbr* Crescent.

cres·cen·do /krɪ'ʃendəʊ/ *nc* (*pl* —s) **1** music to be played, a noise made, with increasing loudness. **2** (*fig*) any progress towards a climax.

cres·cent /'kresnt/ *nc* (C- in names) (something shaped like) the curve of the moon in the first quarter (esp a row of houses).

cress /kres/ *nu* (also *attrib*) a kind of plant with hot-tasting leaves, used in salads: *mustard and cress; watercress; cress sandwiches*.

crest /krest/ *nc* **1** a tall growth of feathers on a bird's head. **2** a decoration like a crest, on the top of a helmet. **3** a special design (e.g. on notepaper): *the family crest*. **4** the top of a slope or hill. **5** white top of a large wave. **on the crest of a wave** (*fig*) (of a person) very happy because of good luck or success.

crest·fal·len /'krestfɔːlən/ *adj* very sad and disappointed.

cre·tin /'kretɪn/ *nc* (*informal; derog*) a very stupid person.

cre·vasse /krɪ'væs/ *nc* a deep, open crack, esp in ice on a glacier.

crev·ice /'krevɪs/ *nc* a narrow opening or crack (in a rock etc).

crew[1] /kruː/ *nc* **1** all the people working a boat, ship or plane; all these except the officers: *passengers and crew; officers and crew.* **2** a group of people working together.

crew[2] /kruː/ *vi* to act as crew(1) on a boat etc: *Will you crew for me in tomorrow's race?*

crib[1] /krɪb/ *nc* **1** a wooden framework from which animals can pull out food. **2** a small bed for a new-born baby.

crib[2] /krɪb/ *vi* (-bb-), *nc* (to make) something copied dishonestly from the work of another.

crick·et[1] /'krɪkɪt/ *nc* a small, brown jumping insect which makes a shrill noise by rubbing its front wings together.

crick·et[2] /'krɪkɪt/ *nu* (also *attrib*) an outdoor game played on a field by two teams of eleven players each, with bats, a ball and wickets.

'cricket match *nc* a game of cricket.

crick·eter *nc* a person who plays cricket.

cried /kraɪd/ *pt,pp* of cry[2].

cries /kraɪz/ **1** *pres t* of cry[2]. **2** *pl* of cry[1].

crime /kraɪm/ *n* **1** *nc* an offence for which there is punishment by law: *to commit a crime.* **2** *nu* illegal actions: *It is the business of the police to prevent and detect crime and of the law courts to punish crime.* **3** *nc* (*fig*) a foolish or wrong act, not an offence against the law: *It would be a crime to send the boy out on such a cold, wet night.*

'crime wave *nc* a period when many crimes(1) are committed.

crimi·nal[1] /'krɪmɪnl/ *adj* **1** of a crime(1): *a criminal act.* **2** (*fig*) extremely, esp morally, bad: *a criminal lack of sympathy for the poor.*

crimi·nal·ly /-nəlɪ/ *adv*

crimi·nal[2] /'krɪmɪnl/ *nc* a person who commits a crime or crimes.

crimi·nol·ogy /ˌkrɪmɪ'nɒlədʒɪ/ *nu* the scientific study of crime.

crim·son /'krɪmzn/ *adj, nu* deep red (colour).

cringe /krɪndʒ/ *vi* **1** to move (the body) back or down in fear: *The dog cringed at the sight of the whip.* **2** to behave in a way that shows lack of self-respect; be too humble: *cringing to/before a policeman.*

crinkle /'krɪŋkl/ *vi,vt, nc* (to make, get) a small, narrow wrinkle (in material such as foil or paper).

cripple[1] /'krɪpl/ *nc* a person unable to walk or move properly because of injury or weakness in the spine or legs. (N) Not now used in GB. Use *'disabled/handicapped person'*.

cripple[2] /'krɪpl/ *vt* **1** to injure and make (a person) a cripple: *crippled soldiers.* **2** (*fig; often passive*) to damage (something) severely: *The business was crippled by lack of money/government support.*

crip·pling /'krɪplɪŋ/ *adj* **1** causing severe weakness: *a crippling disease.* **2** (*fig*) causing great harm: *a crippling rate of tax.*

cri·sis /'kraɪsɪs/ *nc* (*pl* crises /-siːz/) **1** a turning-point in an illness, life, history. **2** a time of serious difficulty, danger: *a financial crisis.*

crisp[1] /krɪsp/ *adj* (—er, —est) **1** (esp of food) hard, dry and easily broken: *crisp toast/biscuits.* **2** (of the air, the weather) frosty, cold: *the crisp air of an autumn morning.* **3** (of style, manners) quick, precise and decided; showing no doubts or hesitation: *a man with a crisp manner of speaking.*

crisp·ly *adv*

crisp·ness *nu*

crisp[2] /krɪsp/ *nc* a thin slice of potato, fried and dried (usually sold in packets) (*US* = chip).

criss-cross /'krɪskrɒs/ *vi,vt, nc* (also *attrib*) (to make) a pattern of crossed lines: *a criss-cross pattern/design.*

cri·teri·on /kraɪ'tɪərɪən/ *nc* (*pl* **-ria** /-rɪə/ or **—s**) a standard for judging something: *Success in making money is not always a good criterion of real success in life.*

crit·ic /'krɪtɪk/ *nc* **1** a person who gives judgements, esp about literature, art, music etc: *music/drama/literary critics.* **2** a person who finds fault, points out mistakes etc: *I am my own most severe critic.*

criti·cal /'krɪtɪkl/ *adj* **1** of or at a crisis: *We are at a critical time in our history. The patient's condition is critical* (= He or she is dangerously ill). **2** (*attrib*) of the work of a critic: *critical opinions on art and literature.* **3** (*attrib*) finding faults: *critical remarks.*

criti·cal·ly /-klɪ/ *adv* dangerously: *critically ill.*

criti·cism /'krɪtɪsɪzəm/ *n* **1** *nu* the art of making judgements about art, literature etc. **2** *nc* a judgement or opinion on literature, art etc. **3** *nc,nu* (an example of) the act of finding faults.

criti·cize (also **-ise**) /'krɪtɪsaɪz/ *vt,vi* **1** to give a judgement of the quality of (something): *criticize a painting.* **2** to find fault with (a person, work, behaviour): *Stop criticizing (me)!*

cri·tique /krɪ'tiːk/ *nc* an essay or review criticizing an author's work.

croak /krəʊk/ *vi, nc* (to make) a deep, hoarse sound (as made by frogs).

cro·chet[1] /'krəʊʃeɪ/ *nu* (also *attrib*) (cloth made by) crocheting: *a crochet stitch.*

cro·chet[2] /'krəʊʃeɪ/ *vt,vi* (-t-) to make (cloth) with a thread looped over others with the help of a small hooked needle (called *a crochet-hook*).

crock·ery /'krɒkərɪ/ *nu* plates, cups, dishes etc.

croco·dile /'krɒkədaɪl/ *nc* **1** (also *attrib*) a kind of large river reptile with a long body and mouth: *a crocodile belt.* **2** (*informal*) a group (e.g. of children) walking in procession, two by two.

'crocodile tears *n pl* insincere sorrow.

crook[1] /krʊk/ *nc* **1** a stick with a rounded hook at one end, as used by a shepherd. **2** a bend or curve, e.g. in a river. **3** (*informal*) a person who makes a living by dishonest or criminal means.

crook[2] /krʊk/ *vt* to bend (something) into the shape of a crook: *to crook one's finger/arm.*

crook·ed /'krʊkɪd/ *adj* **1** twisted; bent: *a crooked little man. You've got your hat on crooked.* **2** (*informal; derog*) (of a person, actions) dishonest: *a crooked salesman.*

crook·ed·ly *adv*

croon /kruːn/ *vt,vi* to sing softly and gently: *croon a lullaby.*

crop[1] /krɒp/ *nc* **1** a yearly (or season's) produce of grain, fruit etc: *the potato crop.* ⇨ cash crop. **2** (*pl*) agricultural plants in the fields: *to get the crops in.* **3** a quantity (of anything) appearing or produced together: *The Prime Minister's statement produced a crop of questions.*

crop[2] /krɒp/ *v* (-pp-) **1** *vt* (of animals) to bite off the tops of (grass, plants etc): *The sheep had cropped the grass short.* **2** *vt* to cut short (a person's hair). **3** *vi* to bear a crop: *The beans cropped* *well this year.* **4** *vi* **crop up/out** (of rock, minerals) to show above the earth's surface. **5** *vi* **crop up** to appear, happen, (esp unexpectedly): *All sorts of difficulties cropped up.*

cro·quet /'krəʊkeɪ/ *nu* an outdoor game played on short grass with wooden balls which are knocked with wooden mallets through hoops.

cross¹ /krɒs/ *adj* **1** angry; easily or quickly showing anger: *Don't be cross with the child for being late.* **2** (*attrib*) (of winds) moving across: *Strong cross-winds made it difficult for the yachts to leave harbour.*

cross² /krɒs/ *nc* **1** a mark made by drawing one line across another, e.g. ×, +: *The place is marked on the map with a cross.* **2** a post with another piece of wood across it like T or X. **3** (C- in names) a similar design as a decoration for personal courage or bravery: *the Victoria Cross.* **4** (**cut sth**) **on the cross** diagonally: *This skirt material was cut on the cross.* **5** a result of animals or plants from two different sorts or breeds: *A mule is a cross between a horse and an ass.*

cross³ /krɒs/ *v* **1** *vt* to go across, move from one side to the other side of, (something): *cross a road/river/bridge/the sea/the Sahara.* ⇨ **cross over.** ⇨ *also* **mind¹**(2). **2** *vt* to draw a line or lines across or near (writing): *Please cross the names of the winners.* **cross a cheque** ⇨ **cheque.** ⇨ **cross sth off/out/through. 3** *vt* to put, position, (something) across or over another: *cross one's legs.* ⇨ **finger¹. 4** *v reflex* to make the sign of a cross on one's face and chest as a Christian act. **cross my heart** ⇨ **heart**(2). **5** *vt,vi* to (meet and) pass (each other): *Our paths didn't cross once during the trip. Our letters have probably crossed in the post.* **6** *vi* (of telephone lines) to interfere with each other: *The lines are crossed and I can hear another conversation.* **7** *vt* to mix (one breed) with another: *crossing sheep to make stronger animals.* ⇨ **cross sth with sth, crossbred. 8** *vt* to oppose, obstruct, (plans, wishes etc): *He was angry to have his plans crossed.*

cross sth off to remove names, items etc from a list by drawing a line across.

cross sth out to draw a line across writing to show it is not wanted: *My name was crossed out!*

cross over (to sth) (**a**) to go across (to): *They crossed over (to the other side of the river).* (**b**) to change one's opinion and support the opposing political party, another club, candidate, group etc: *She's crossed over to the Liberal Party.*

cross sth through = cross sth out.

cross sth with sth to mix one breed with another breed: *cross British cattle with an Australian breed.*

cross·bar /'krɒsbɑː(r)/ *nc* a bar going across, e.g. joining the two posts of a goal in football etc or the front and back parts of a bicycle.

cross·bred /'krɒsbred/ *adj* produced by crossing(7) breeds: *crossbred sheep.*

cross·breed /'krɒsbriːd/ *nc* an animal, plant etc produced by crossing breeds.

cross-check /ˌkrɒs 'tʃek/ *vt,vi, nc* (to use) a method to test if (a calculation, process etc) is accurate by doing it a different way: *We cross-checked the results twice. We'd better do a cross-check on these figures.*

cross-coun·try /ˌkrɒs'kʌntrɪ/ *adj,adv* across

the country or fields, not along roads: *a cross-country race; run cross-country.*

cross-exam·ine /ˌkrɒs ɪg'zæmɪn/ *vt* to question (a person) closely, esp to test answers given to someone else, as in a law court.

cross-e,xami'nation *nc,nu*

cross-eyed /'krɒsaɪd/ *adj* with one or both eyeballs turned towards the nose.

cross-fer·ti·lize (also **-ise**) /ˌkrɒs 'fɜːtəlaɪz/ *vt* to carry pollen from one plant to another (plant). **cross-fer·ti·li·za·tion** (also **-li·sa·tion**) /ˌkrɒs ˌfɜːtəlaɪ'zeɪʃn/ *nu*

cross-fire /'krɒsfaɪə(r)/ *nu* the firing of guns from two or more points so that the lines of fire cross.

cross·ing /'krɒsɪŋ/ *nc* **1** the act of going across, esp by sea: *We had a rough crossing from England to France.* **2** a place where two roads, two railways, or a road and a railway cross. **3** a place on a street etc where pedestrians can cross. ⇨ **level crossing.**

cross-leg·ged /ˌkrɒs'legd/ *adv* (of a person sitting) with one leg placed across the other.

cross pur·poses /ˌkrɒs 'pɜːpəsɪz/ *n pl* **be at cross purposes** (of two people or groups) to misunderstand one another, have different and conflicting intentions.

cross-question /ˌkrɒs 'kwestʃən/ *vt* = cross-examine.

cross-ref·er·ence /ˌkrɒs 'refərəns/ *nc* a reference from one part of a book etc to another part.

cross·roads /'krɒsrəʊdz/ *n sing* **1** a place where two or more roads meet: *We came to a crossroads.* **2** (*fig*) a point when a decision is necessary between two or more alternatives: *be at a crossroads.*

cross-sec·tion /ˌkrɒs 'sekʃn/ *nc* **1** (a drawing of) a piece or slice made by cutting across, e.g. a tree trunk. **2** (*fig*) a typical or representative sample (of the whole): *a cross-section of the voters.*

cross-wind /'krɒs wɪnd/ *nc* ⇨ cross¹(2).

cross·word /'krɒswɜːd/ *nc* (also *crossword puzzle*) a puzzle in which words must be written (from numbered clues) vertically and horizontally into spaces on a pattern.

crotch /krɒtʃ/ *nc* the place where a pair of trousers or a person's legs meet at the top.

crotch·et /'krɒtʃɪt/ *nc* (*music*) a black-headed note with a stem (♩), half of a minim (*US = quarter note*).

crotch·ety /ˌkrɒtʃətɪ/ *adj* (*derog*) (of an old person) bad-tempered.

crouch /kraʊtʃ/ *vi* **crouch (down)** to lower the body with the limbs together (in fear or to hide, or ready to jump). □ *nc* a crouching position.

crow¹ /krəʊ/ *nc* a kind of large, black bird with a loud, rough call. **as the crow flies** in a straight line: *It's six miles away as the crow flies.*

'crow's feet *n pl* little lines on the skin near a person's eyes.

crow² /krəʊ/ *vi* **1** (of a cock) to make a loud, rough call. **2** (of a person) to make known a triumph in order to cause envy: *to crow over passing the exam with distinction.* □ *nc* a cry of a cock.

crow·bar /'krəʊbɑː(r)/ *nc* a straight, iron bar, often with a forked end, used as a lever for moving heavy objects.

crowd¹ /kraʊd/ nc **1** a large number of people together but without order or organization: *He pushed his way through the crowd.* **2** (*formal*) a particular group of people associated in some way: *I can't afford to go about with that crowd.* ⇨ clique. **3** a large number (of things, usually without order): *a desk covered with a crowd of books and papers.*

crowd² /kraʊd/ v vi to come together in a large group: *Now, don't all crowd together!* **2** vt to cause (a vehicle etc) to fill up: *The tourists crowded the buses.* **3** vt to fill (a place) in large numbers: *Students crowded the streets.*

crowd (sb) in to move (people) into a place in a crowd: *We could crowd a few more supporters in.*
crowd in (on sb) (of bad memories, unwanted people, large buildings etc) to become too obvious, come too close (and cause discomfort).
crowd into sth to go into a place in a crowd: *The fans crowded into the airport.*
crowd onto sth to get onto a bus, train etc in a crowd.
crowd out of sth to go out of a place in a crowd: *The workers crowded out of the station.*
crowd sb out (of sth) to cause a person to be kept out because of too many people: *The older members had come early and crowded out the young people.*
crowd round (sb/sth) to form a large group round a person, thing: *People crowded round to look at the injured.*

crowd·ed /ˈkraʊdɪd/ adj having large numbers of people: *crowded cities/trains.* ⇨ overcrowded.

crown¹ /kraʊn/ nc **1** an ornamental ring of gold, jewels etc worn on the head by a sovereign ruler. **2** the top of the head or of a hat. **3** a circle of flowers or leaves worn on the head, esp as a sign of victory. **4** the visible part of a tooth. **5** (*fig*) a point of perfection, completion: *the crown of one's success.*
'**crown prince** nc one next in succession to the throne.
'**crown princess** nc one next in succession to the throne.

crown² /kraʊn/ vt **1** to put a crown on (a king or queen) *the crowned heads* (= kings and queens) *of Europe.* **2** to reward (an attempt etc) (with a good result): *efforts that were crowned with success.* **3** to have (something) at the top of a hill etc: *The hill is crowned with a wood.* **4** to put a happy finishing touch to (an event): *to open a bottle of wine to crown a feast.* **to crown it all** to complete good or bad fortune: *It rained, we had no umbrellas, and, to crown it all, we missed the last bus and had to walk home.* **5** to put an artificial cover on (a broken tooth).

crown·ing adj (attrib; no comp) completing; making perfect: *Her crowning glory is her hair.*

cru·cial /ˈkruːʃl/ adj decisive; critical: *the crucial test/question; at the crucial moment.*
cru·cial·ly /-ʃəlɪ/ adv

cru·cible /ˈkruːsəbl/ nc a pot in which metals are melted, e.g. in a chemistry laboratory.

cru·ci·fix /ˈkruːsɪfɪks/ nc a model of a cross with the figure of Jesus on it.

cru·ci·fix·ion /ˌkruːsɪˈfɪkʃn/ nc,nu (an instance of) the act of putting a person to death, being put to death, on a cross(2): *the Crucifixion* (= that of Jesus).

cru·ci·fy /ˈkruːsɪfaɪ/ vt (pt,pp **-ied**) to kill (a person) by nailing or tying her or him to a cross(2).

crude /kruːd/ adj (**—r, —st**) **1** (of materials) in a natural state; not refined or manufactured: *crude oil* (= petroleum). **2** (*derog*) not having grace, taste or refinement: *crude manners.* **3** (*derog*) not made or finished properly; badly worked out: *crude schemes/methods/ideas.*
crude·ly adv

crud·ity /ˈkruːdətɪ/ nc,nu (an example of) the state or quality of being crude.

cruel /ˈkruːəl/ adj (**—er, —est**) **1** (of a person) taking pleasure in causing pain to, watching the suffering of, others: *a man who is cruel to animals.* **2** (of acts, objects) causing pain or suffering: *a cruel blow/punishment/disease/war.*
cruel·ly adv

cruel·ty /ˈkruːəltɪ/ nc,nu (pl **-ies**) (an act of) readiness to cause pain or suffering to others: *Cruelty to children is unforgiveable.*

cruise¹ /kruːz/ nc a journey by sea for pleasure: *to go on/go for a cruise.*

cruise² /kruːz/ vi **1** to sail about, either for pleasure, or, in war, looking for enemy ships. **2** (of cars, planes) to travel at the most economical speed: *The plane has a cruising speed of 500 miles an hour.*

cruiser /ˈkruːzə(r)/ nc **1** a fast warship. **2** (also *cabin cruiser*) a kind of motorboat for cruises.

crumb /krʌm/ nc **1** a very small piece (of bread, cake etc): *biscuit crumbs.* **2** (*fig*) a small amount: *a few crumbs of comfort.*

crumble /ˈkrʌmbl/ v **1** vt,vi (to cause something) to break, rub or fall into very small pieces: *Crumble the biscuit before adding the milk.* **2** vi (*fig*) to be destroyed; decay: *hopes that crumbled to dust* (= came to nothing). **3** vi (of a person) to lose self-confidence or determination.

crum·bly /ˈkrʌmblɪ/ adj (**-ier, -iest**) easily crumbled.

crum·my /ˈkrʌmɪ/ adj (**-ier, -iest**) (*informal; derog*) inferior in quality: *a crummy TV programme/pen.*

crum·pet /ˈkrʌmpɪt/ nc a kind of flat, round, unsweetened cake, to be toasted.

crumple /ˈkrʌmpl/ vt,vi **crumple (sth) (up)** (to cause something) to become full of folds or creases: *Some kinds of material crumple more easily than others. She crumpled (up) the sheet of paper.*

crunch¹ /krʌntʃ/ nc **1** an act, noise, of crunching. **2 come to the crunch** (*informal*) to reach a critical moment when a difficult decision must be made.

crunch² /krʌntʃ/ vt,vi **1** to crush (food) noisily with the teeth when eating: *People who crunch nuts in the cinema can be very annoying.* **2** (to cause something) to be crushed noisily under one's feet, under wheels etc: *The frozen snow crunched under the wheels of our car.*

crunchy /ˈkrʌntʃɪ/ adj (**-ier, -iest**) (of something hard) breaking with a definite cracking sound, esp when being eaten: *crunchy biscuits.*

cru·sade¹ /kruːˈseɪd/ nc **1** (*history*) one of the military expeditions by Christians during the Middle Ages to recover the Holy Land from the Muslims. **2** a struggle or movement in support of something believed to be good or against something believed to be bad: *a crusade against racial hatred.*

cru·sade² /kru:'seɪd/ *vi* to take part in a crusade: *crusading for peace.*

cru·sader *nc* a person taking part in a crusade.

crush¹ /krʌʃ/ *nc* 1 a crowd of people pressed together: *There was a crush at the gate into the stadium.* 2 **have a crush on sb** (*sl*) (to imagine oneself to) be in love with a person.

crush² /krʌʃ/ *v* 1 *vt* to press (something) so that there is breaking or injury: *The car was crushed in the accident. Wine is made by crushing grapes.* 2 *vt,vi* (to cause something) to become full of creases or irregular folds: *Her dresses were badly crushed when she took them out of the suitcase.* 3 *vt* to defeat (a person) completely: *He was not satisfied until he had crushed his enemies.* 4 *vt,vi* to press or push (people, things) in: *They all tried to crush into the front seats.*

crush·ing /'krʌʃɪŋ/ *adj* (*attrib*) 1 overwhelming: *a crushing defeat.* 2 in a manner intended to cause great embarrassment, disappointment, sadness etc: *a crushing reply/remark.*

crust¹ /krʌst/ *nc,nu* 1 (a piece of) the hard surface of bread or of a pie or tart. 2 a hard surface: *a thin crust of ice/frozen snow; the earth's crust.*

crust² /krʌst/ *vi* **crust (over)** to form into a crust: *The snow crusted over* (= froze hard on top) *during the night.*

crus·ta·cean /krʌ'steɪʃn/ *adj, nc* (*science*) (of) any member of the group of animals having a hard shell: *Crabs, lobsters, shrimps and prawns are crustaceans.*

crusty /'krʌstɪ/ *adj* (**-ier, -iest**) 1 having a crust; hard like a crust: *crusty bread.* 2 (*fig; derog*) (of a person, behaviour) bad-tempered.

crutch /krʌtʃ/ *nc* 1 a stick used as a support under the arm to help a disabled person to walk: *a pair of crutches.* 2 (*fig*) any moral support: *He uses his older sister as a crutch.* 3 = crotch.

crux /krʌks/ *nc* (*pl* **—es**) (the —) the part (of a problem) that is the most difficult to solve: *The crux of the matter is that you lied.*

cry¹ /kraɪ/ *nc* (*pl* **cries**) 1 a loud sound or statement (of fear, pain, grief, excitement etc): *a cry for help; the cry of an animal in pain; angry cries from the mob. 'Equal opportunities for women' was their cry.* **a far/long cry from sth** very different from something: *Being a junior clerk is a far cry from being one of the Directors.* 2 a fit of weeping: *have a good cry.*

'cry-baby *nc* (*pl* **-ies**) (*derog*) a young person who cries often or easily without good or apparent cause.

cry² /kraɪ/ *v* (*pt,pp* **cried**) 1 *vi* (of a person, animal) to make sounds that express feelings (e.g. pain, fear): *A baby can cry as soon as it is born. He cried with pain when the doctor pulled the splinter out.* 2 *vi* (of a person) to produce tears (with or without sounds): *The boy was crying because he had lost his money.* **cry oneself to sleep** to cry until one falls asleep. 3 *vt,vi* to call (something) out loudly in words: *'Help! Help!' he cried.*

cry for sth to cry(2) in order to get food, attention etc: *If you do that again I'll give you something to cry for. Paul often cries for nothing* (= for

no reason).

cry off (*informal*) (of a person) to withdraw from an earlier promise, arrangement: *Two people cried off so we didn't have a full team.*

cry out to call out loudly (in pain or fear): *I cried out to her to stop.* **cry one's heart out** ⇨ heart(2). **cry out (for sth)** to show an obvious need (for something): *The farm is crying out for development/to be developed.* ⇨ crying.

cry over sth to cry(2) because of something: *crying over a lost ball. It isn't worth crying over.*

cry·ing /'kraɪɪŋ/ *adj* (*attrib; no comp*) demanding attention: *a crying shame/evil/need.*

crypt /krɪpt/ *nc* an underground room of a church.

cryp·tic /'krɪptɪk/ *adj* with a hidden meaning or a meaning not easily understood: *a cryptic remark; a cryptic clue in a crossword puzzle.*

cryp·ti·cal·ly /-klɪ/ *adv*

crys·tal /'krɪstl/ *n* 1 *nu* a kind of transparent mineral like glass. 2 *nc* a piece of this as an ornament: *a necklace of crystals.* 3 *nc* a definite and regular shape taken naturally by the molecules of certain substances: *sugar and salt crystals; snow and ice crystals.* 4 *nu* glass of the best quality made into bowls, vases etc: *The dining-table shone with silver and crystal.*

crys·tal·lize (also **-ise**) /'krɪstəlaɪz/ *v* 1 *vt,vi* (to cause something) to form into crystals(3). 2 *vt* (often as a *pp*) to cover (fruit etc) with sugar-crystals: *crystallized ginger.* 3 *vt,vi* (*fig*) (to cause ideas, plans etc) to become clear and definite: *His vague ideas crystallized into a definite plan.*

crys·tal·li·za·tion (also **-sa·tion**) /ˌkrɪstəlaɪ'zeɪʃn/ *nu*

CSE /ˌsiː es 'iː/ *abbr* (*GB*) Certificate of Secondary Education.

cu *abbr* cubic.

cub /kʌb/ *nc* a young lion, bear, fox, tiger.

cubby-hole /'kʌbɪ həʊl/ *nc* a small, enclosed space.

cube¹ /kju:b/ *nc* 1 a solid body having six equal square sides: *cubes of sugar.* 2 (*maths*) the result of multiplying a number by itself twice: *The cube of 5* (5^3) *is* $5 \times 5 \times 5$ (= 125).

,cube 'root *nc* (*maths*) a number which when multiplied by itself twice gives a certain number: *The cube root of 27* ($\sqrt[3]{27}$) *is 3.*

cube² /kju:b/ *vt* 1 to cut (food etc) into cubes(1). 2 (*maths*) to find the cube(2) of (a number).

cu·bic /'kju:bɪk/ *adj* (abbr **cu**) (having the shape) of a cube: *one cubic metre* (= the measured volume of a cube whose edges are one metre long).

cu·bicle /'kju:bɪkl/ *nc* a small division of a larger room walled or curtained to make a separate compartment, e.g. for (un)dressing at a swimming-pool.

cub·ism /'kju:bɪzəm/ *nu* a style in art in which objects are represented so that they appear to be mostly of geometrical shapes.

cub·ist /'kju:bɪst/ *nc* an artist who practises cubism.

cuck·oo /'kʊku:/ *nc* a kind of European bird whose call is like its name.

cu·cum·ber /'kju:kʌmbə(r)/ *nc,nu* (a creeping plant with) a long, green-skinned vegetable, eaten in salads or made into pickle.

cud /kʌd/ *nu* the food which cattle bring back from the first stomach and chew again. **chew the cud** (*fig*) to think about a problem etc deeply.

cuddle¹ /'kʌdl/ *nc* an act of cuddling.

cuddle² /'kʌdl/ *v* **1** *vt* to hold (a person, thing) close and lovingly in one's arms: *She cuddled her doll.* **2** *vi* **cuddle up (to sb/sth)** to lie close and comfortably: *The children cuddled up (together) under the blankets.*

cud·dly /'kʌdlɪ/ *adj* suitable for cuddling: *a nice cuddly doll.*

cud·gel /'kʌdʒəl/ *vt* (**-ll-**, *US* also **-l-**), *nc* (to hit (a person) with) a short, thick stick or club.

cue¹ /kjuː/ *vt*, *nc* (to give) a signal (e.g. in a drama) which shows when a person is to do or say something. **take one's cue from sb** to observe what he or she does and do the same.

cue² /kjuː/ *nc* a long, tapering stick, used for hitting the ball in snooker etc.

cuff¹ /kʌf/ *nc* the end of a sleeve of a shirt, blouse or coat (at the wrist). **off the cuff** (*informal*) without preparation or planning: *speak off the cuff.*

'cuff-link *nc* a link used to fasten a cuff.

cuff² /kʌf/ *vt*, *nc* (*informal*) (to give a person) a light blow with the open hand.

cul-de-sac /'kʌl də sæk/ *nc* a street with an opening at one end only.

cu·li·nary /'kʌlɪnərɪ/ *adj* (*attrib*) (*formal*) for, of, cooking or a kitchen: *culinary plants* (e.g. herbs).

cull /kʌl/ *vt* **1** (*formal*) to select (things) (from a group): *extracts culled from the best authors.* **2** to take and kill (animals in a crowded place).

cul·len·der /'kʌləndə(r)/ *nc* = colander.

cul·mi·nate /'kʌlmɪneɪt/ *vi* **culminate in sth** (of efforts, hopes, careers etc) to reach the highest or most serious point: *misfortunes that culminated in bankruptcy.*

cul·mi·na·tion /ˌkʌlmɪ'neɪʃn/ *nu*

culp·able /'kʌlpəbl/ *adj* (*legal*) (of a person, behaviour, crime) deserving punishment: *hold a person culpable.*

cul·prit /'kʌlprɪt/ *nc* a person who has done wrong: *'My pens have gone—who is the culprit?'*

cult /kʌlt/ *nc* **1** a system of religious worship. **2** a devotion to a person, practice etc: *the cult of science fiction films.* **3** (a group of people devoted to) a popular fashion or craze: *join the cult of wearing large rings.*

cul·ti·vate /'kʌltɪveɪt/ *vt* **1** to prepare (land) by ploughing etc; help (crops) to grow (e.g. by breaking up the soil around them). **2** to give care, thought, time etc in order to develop (something): *to cultivate the mind/a person's friendship.*

cul·ti·vated /'kʌltɪveɪtɪd/ *adj* (of a person) cultured(1) (the more usual word).

cul·ti·va·tion /ˌkʌltɪ'veɪʃn/ *nu* the act of cultivating or being cultivated: *the cultivation of the soil; land that is under cultivation.*

cul·tur·al /'kʌltʃərəl/ *adj* having to do with culture: *cultural studies* (e.g. art, literature). **a cultural desert** (*derog*) a place where there are very few cultural activities.

cul·ture /'kʌltʃə(r)/ *n* **1** *nu* the expression of intellectual development (of arts, science etc) in society: *Universities should be centres of culture.* **2** *nc,nu* a particular form of intellectual develop-

ment: *We still owe much to Greek culture.* **3** *nu* the state of high development of the mind by experience and training: *the culture of an academic/literary mind.* **4** *nu* the rearing of animals, plants, bees etc: *He has five acres devoted to bulb culture.* **5** *nc* a growth of bacteria (for medical or scientific study): *a culture of cholera germs.*

cul·tured /'kʌltʃəd/ *adj* **1** (of a person) well-educated and with many cultural interests. Opp uncultured. **2** (of tastes, interests etc) highly developed.

cum·ber·some /'kʌmbəsəm/ *adj* (*derog*) heavy and awkward to carry: *a cumbersome parcel.*

cumu·lat·ive /'kjuːmjʊlətɪv/ *adj* increasing in amount by one addition after another: *cumulative interest on a savings account.*

cumu·lus /'kjuːmjʊləs/ *nc* (*pl* **-li** /-lɪ/) (*tech*) a kind of cloud made up of rounded masses on a flat base.

cun·ning /'kʌnɪŋ/ *adj*, *nu* (*derog*) (showing) ability to deceive easily: *a cunning old fox; a cunning trick. The boy showed a great deal of cunning in getting what he wanted.*

cun·ning·ly *adv*

cup¹ /kʌp/ *nc* **1** a small container with a handle, used with a saucer for tea, coffee etc: *a teacup.* **not my cup of tea** (*informal*) not what I like; not what suits me. **2** as much as a cup can hold: *I drank a cup of coffee.* **3** a silver or gold vessel given as a prize in competitions: *I hope Arsenal will win the cup!* **4** something shaped like a cup: *the cup of a flower; an egg-cup; the cups of a bra.*

'cup final *nc* a football match to decide the winner of a competition between many teams.

'cup-tie *nc* a football match to eliminate teams competing for a cup(3).

cup·ful /'kʌpfʊl/ *nc* (*pl* **—s**) as much as a cup can hold.

cup² /kʌp/ *vt* (**-pp-**) **1** to put (one's hands etc) into the shape of a cup: *to cup one's hands.* **2** to put one's hands round or over (something): *with her chin cupped in her hand.*

cup·board /'kʌbəd/ *nc* a piece of furniture with shelves and doors in front.

cur /kɜː(r)/ *nc* **1** a bad-tempered, low-bred dog. **2** (*fig*; *derog*) a cowardly or badly-behaved man.

cur·able /'kjʊərəbl/ *adj* that can be cured. Opp incurable.

cur·acy /'kjʊərəsɪ/ *nc* (*pl* **-ies**) the office and work of a curate.

cur·ate /'kjʊərət/ *nc* a clergyman who helps a parish priest (rector or vicar).

cura·tive /'kjʊərətɪv/ *adj* helping to, able to, cure disease or ill health: *the curative value of sunshine and sea air.*

cu·ra·tor /kjʊ'reɪtə(r)/ *nc* an official in charge of a museum or art gallery.

curb¹ /kɜːb/ *nc* **1** a chain or leather strap passing under a horse's jaw, used to control it. **2** (*fig*) something that holds one back or controls something: *put/keep a curb on one's anger/passions.* **3** (*esp US*) = kerb.

curb² /kɜːb/ *vt* to keep (feelings, emotions etc) under control: *to curb one's impatience/passion.*

curd /kɜːd/ *nc,nu* (often *pl*) the thick, soft substance formed when milk turns sour, used to make cheese·

curdle /'kɜːdl/ *vi,vt* **1** (to cause milk etc) to form into curds: *The lemon has curdled the cream.* **2** (*attrib*) (*fig*) to cause (blood) to seem thick and slow (because of great fear): *What a blood-curdling yell!*

cure¹ /kjʊə(r)/ *nc* **1** an instance of being made healthy again: *The doctor cannot guarantee a cure.* **2** a substance, treatment, which cures(1): *Is there a cure for cancer yet?* ⇨ curative. **3** (*fig*) a way of getting rid of something harmful or bad: *We must find a cure for poverty in Africa.*

cure² /kjʊə(r)/ *vt* **1** to cause (a person) to be healthy again after (a disease, ill health): *to cure (a man of) a disease.* **2** to cause (a person) to stop (bad behaviour): *to cure (a child of) bad habits.* **3** to get rid of (something harmful or bad) in (a place): *cure (a country of) inflation.* **4** to treat (meat, fish, skin, tobacco etc) in order to keep it in good condition by salting, smoking, drying etc: *well-cured leather.*

cur·few /'kɜːfjuː/ *nc* (*modern use*) a period (under martial law) when people must stay indoors: *be under a curfew; to lift/end the curfew.*

cur·io /'kjʊərɪəʊ/ *nc* (*pl* —s) an unusual or interesting object.

curi·os·ity /ˌkjʊərɪ'ɒsətɪ/ *n* (*pl* -ies) **1** *nu* being curious(1,2): *I'm dying of/burning with curiosity* (= very curious) *to know what happened.* **2** *nc* a strange or rare object or person.

curi·ous /'kjʊərɪəs/ *adj* **1** wanting very much (to learn, know): *I'm curious to know what he said.* **2** (*derog*) having or showing too much interest in the affairs of others: *curious neighbours.* **3** strange; unusual: *What a curious mistake! Isn't he a curious-looking little man!*
curi·ous·ly *adv*

curl¹ /kɜːl/ *n* **1** *nc* a mass of hair twisted into a coil or spiral: *curls (of hair) falling over a girl's shoulders.* **2** *nc* (*fig*) anything of a similar shape: *a curl of smoke rising from a cigarette.* **3** *nu* the state of being curly: *How do you keep your hair in curl?*

curl² /kɜːl/ *vt,vi* **1** (to cause hair etc) to grow, be, in curls: *Does her hair curl naturally?* **2 curl (sth) up** to form the shape of a curl: *curl up on the sofa; curling up her toes.* **3 curl (sth) round (sth)** (to cause something) to grow, twist round (a pole, tree etc).

cur·lew /'kɜːljuː/ *nc* a kind of waterbird with a long, narrow bill which curves down.

cur·ly /'kɜːlɪ/ *adj* (-ier, -iest) having, arranged, in curls: *curly hair; a curly-headed girl.*

cur·rant /'kʌrənt/ *nc* (also *attrib*) **1** a small, sweet, dried seedless grape used in cakes, puddings etc: *a currant bun.* **2** (a bush with) a small black, red or white juicy fruit growing in bunches: *a blackcurrant bush.*

cur·ren·cy /'kʌrənsɪ/ *n* (*pl* -ies) **1** *nc,nu* (a kind of) money that is in use in a country: *foreign currencies; a decimal currency.* **a hard currency** one that can be exchanged for another one. **2** *nu* the state of being in general use: *The belief soon gained currency among the population.*

cur·rent¹ /'kʌrənt/ *adj* **1** in common or general use now: *current opinions/beliefs; words that are no longer current.* **2** (*attrib*) now passing; of the present time: *the current year; a news broadcast showing current events.*

'current account *nc* (with a bank) one from which money may be taken without previous notice.

,current af'fairs *n pl* (the kinds, importance etc of) contemporary events, institutions etc.

,current 'assets *n pl* (*business*) assets easily changed into cash.

cur·rent·ly *adv* at the present time: *It is currently reported that she is in Spain.*

cur·rent² /'kʌrənt/ *nc* **1** a moving mass (of air, gas): *A cold current of air came in when the door was opened.* **2** a fast movement of water through slow or still water: *Although he was a strong swimmer he was swept away by the current and was drowned.* **3** a flow of electricity through something or along a wire or cable. **4** (*fig*) a course or movement (of events, opinions, thoughts etc): *to influence the current of thought.*

cur·ricu·lum /kə'rɪkjʊləm/ *nc* (*pl* —s or -la /-lə/) a course of study in a school, college etc.

cur,riculum 'vitae /'viːtaɪ/ *nc* (*Latin*) a brief written account of one's past history (e.g. education, employment), used when applying for a job etc.

cur·ry¹ /'kʌrɪ/ *vt, nc,nu* (*pl* -ies) (also *attrib*) to prepare) (a dish of) meat, fish, eggs etc cooked with hot-tasting spices: *Madras curries; curry powder.*

cur·ry² /'kʌrɪ/ *vt* (*pt,pp* -ied) **curry favour (with sb)** to try to win approval by using flattery etc.

curse¹ /kɜːs/ *nc* **1** a word, phrase or sentence calling for punishment, injury or destruction. **2** a cause of misfortune or ruin: *Gambling is often a curse.* **3** a word or words used in language expressing anger or hatred. **4** (the —) (*informal*) menstruation.

curse² /kɜːs/ *vt,vi* **1** to use a curse(1) against a person. **2** to use angry language against a person, thing: *to curse and swear; cursing at a stupid mistake.* **3 be cursed with sth** to suffer misfortune, trouble etc because of something bad: *to be cursed with a violent temper.*

cur·sor /'kɜːsə(r)/ *nc* (*computers*) a small area of light used on a screen to identify a place in the text.

cur·sory /'kɜːsərɪ/ *adj* (of work, reading etc) done without attention to details: *a cursory glance/inspection.*
cur·sor·ily /'kɜːsərəlɪ/ *adv*

curt /kɜːt/ *adj* (*derog*) (of a speaker, voice, person's manner etc) quick, impolite and bad-tempered: *I gave him a curt reply.*
curt·ly *adv*
curt·ness *nu*

cur·tail /kɜː'teɪl/ *vt* (*formal*) to make (something) shorter than was first planned: *curtail a speech/one's holidays.*
cur·tail·ment *nc,nu*

cur·tain¹ /'kɜːtn/ *nc* **1** a piece of cloth etc hung up at a window. **draw the curtains** to pull them together or apart. **2** a sheet of heavy material to lower in front of the stage in a theatre. **3** (*fig*) a cover or protection: *A curtain of mist hid the view.* **4** (*pl*) (*informal*) an end to a career etc: *If I'm late once more it will be curtains for me.*

cur·tain² /'kɜːtn/ *vt* to cover (windows etc) with curtains: *Is there enough material to curtain all the windows?* **2 curtain sth off** to separate or divide an area using curtains: *to curtain off part of a room.*

curt·sy (also **curt·sey**) /'kɜːtsɪ/ *vi, nc* (*pl* **-ies, —s**) (of a woman or girl) (to make) a formal sign of respect (by bending one or both knees) (e.g. to a queen).

cur·va·ture /'kɜːvətʃə(r)/ *nu* (*formal*) the state of being curved: *the curvature of the earth's surface.*

curve¹ /kɜːv/ *nc* a line of which no part is straight, e.g. part of the edge of a circle: *a curve in the road.*

curve² /kɜːv/ *vt,vi* (to cause something) to have the form of a curve: *The river curves round the hill.*

cush·ion¹ /'kuʃn/ *nc* **1** a bag of cloth filled with feathers, foam rubber etc, used to lie, sit or rest on. **2** something soft and like a cushion in shape or function: *a pincushion; a cushion of air.*

cush·ion² /'kuʃn/ *vt* **1** to supply (a room, chair etc) with cushions. **2** to protect (something) from shock with cushions: *cushioned seats.* **3** (*fig*) to protect (something) from harmful changes: *Our savings cushioned us against rising costs.*

cushy /'kuʃɪ/ *adj* (**-ier, -iest**) (*informal*) (of a job etc) not needing much effort: *get a cushy job in the Civil Service.*

cus·tard /'kʌstəd/ *nc,nu* (also *attrib*) a mixture of milk and flavoured cornflour eaten with fruit, pastry etc: *custard tarts.*

cus·tod·ian /kʌ'stəudɪən/ *nc* (*formal*) a person who has custody of something (e.g. a building, collection) or a child.

cus·tody /'kʌstədɪ/ *nu* **1** (the duty of) caring for, guarding, people or things: *Parents have the custody of children while they are young. You should leave your jewellery in safe custody* (e.g. with your bank). **2** (**be**) **in custody** (to be) in prison (e.g. awaiting trial).

cus·tom /'kʌstəm/ *n* **1** *nu* the usual and generally accepted behaviour among most people: *Don't be a slave to custom* (= Do not do things only because most people do them and have always done them). **2** *nc* a particular way of behaving which, because it has been long established, is accepted by most individuals and social groups: *Social customs vary in different countries.* Ⓝ 'Habit' is used to refer to an activity that is done regularly and which is difficult to give up, as in *Smoking is a dangerous habit.* **3** *nu* regular support given to a shop etc: *We should very much like to have your custom.* **4** (*pl*) taxes due to the government on goods imported into a country. **5** *pl;* (the) Customs) the government department that collects customs(4): *How long will it take us to get through (the) Customs?*

cus·tom·ary /'kʌstəmərɪ/ *adj* in agreement with, according to, custom(1): *the customary vote of thanks to the chairman.*

cus·tom·er /'kʌstəmə(r)/ *nc* **1** a person who buys things (regularly) from a shop etc: *Mr Jones has lost some of his best customers.* **2** (*informal*) a person (who is difficult or strange): *She's a queer/awkward/tough customer.*

cut¹ /kʌt/ *nc* **1** an act, result, of cutting; opening made by a knife or other sharp-edged tool etc: *a deep cut in the leg.* **2** a reduction (in size, amount etc): *a cut in prices/expenditure; a 1% cut in inter-*

est rates. **3** a part that is cut out: *There were several cuts in the film.* **4** a way across (from one place to another) that shortens the distance: *Let's take a short cut.* **5** (of food) a piece cut off a larger piece: *a nice cut of beef.* ⇨ **cutlet.** **6** a way of shaping clothes, hair etc by cutting. **7** a break in an electricity supply: *a power cut.* **8** a remark that hurts a person's feelings: *That remark was a cut at me.* **9** a refusal to recognize a person. ⇨ cut²(11). **10** (TV, films) a quick change from one scene to another. **11 be a cut above sb** (*informal*) to be better than another person: *She's a cut above the other girls in the office.*

cut² /kʌt/ *vt* (*pt,pp* **cut**) **1** *vt,vi* to make an opening, incision, wound etc in (something) using a knife, scissors or other implement: *Let's cut the cake now. He cut himself while shaving. I cut my leg on a broken bottle. She's very badly cut.* ⇨ also ground²(1), ice¹(1), open¹(1), way. **2** *vt* to remove or divide (something) by using a knife, scissors etc: *cut cloth/flowers.* ⇨ **cut sth away/off/out.** ⇨ also loose¹(1), short²(2). **3** *vt* to shorten (hair etc) by using scissors etc: *cut hair; cut a hedge.* **4** *vt* to make (a shape etc) by cutting(1): *I've cut a hole in the cloth.* **5** *vi* (of a knife, scissors etc) to be sharp and able to cut: *This knife cuts well.* **6** *vi* (of food, cloth etc) to be able to be cut: *This steak doesn't cut easily.* **7** *vt* to reduce (a size, time, quantity, price etc): *cutting wages/prices/unemployment/ the membership; cut 10 seconds off the world record.* ⇨ cut down on sth, cut-price. ⇨ also fine²(2), loss(3). **8** *vt* to make (a way) by cutting: *cut a path through a forest.* **9** *vt* **cut corners** ⇨ corner¹(1). **10** *vt* (*informal*) to stay away from (a lesson etc): *Let's cut the biology class/lecture.* **11** *vt* (*informal*) to refuse to recognize (a person) in a public place. **cut sb dead** to ignore her or him deliberately (esp when angry with her or him): *After our quarrel she cut me dead at the supermarket.* **12** *vt* to shorten (a text, programme, film etc) by removing part: *cut a speech because the audience is bored; cut a play by half an hour.* **13** *vt* (of a performer) to make (a recording): *cut a disc/ new album/record.* **14** *vt,vi* (*card-games*) to divide a pile of playing-cards: *Cut the cards. It's your turn to cut.* **15** (*pp*) **cut and dried** (of a decision, opinion etc) already decided and impossible to change.

cut across (sth) (a) to take a shorter way by going across: *cut across a field. It's a long way round—let's cut across.* **(b)** to be opposite to (usual arrangements, expectations etc): *Opinion on overseas aid cut clean across usual political loyalties.*

cut sth away to remove an infected area, dead or unwanted plant etc: *The infection in the wound has been cut away. They cut away all the larger branches.*

cut sth back to cut(3) (plants etc) close to the ground. **cut back (on) sth** to reduce staffing, loans, production etc: *We need not cut back on staffing. We must cut back our investments in America.* Hence **'cut-back** *nc.*

cut sb down (a) to kill or injure a person with a weapon. **(b)** to make a person seriously ill: *He was cut down in his prime.* **(c)** to persuade a person to accept a lower price: *We were able to cut her down to £10 for the bike.* **cut sth down (a)** to cause something to fall by using an axe etc: *cut down trees.* (**b**) to reduce a quantity, length etc: *cut down a dress. I must cut down the amount of wine I drink. I won't have a cigarette—I'm trying to cut down.* **cut down on sth** to reduce one's (excessive) smoking, drinking, food, spending etc: *cutting down on smoking/drinking beer/buying records.* **cut sb down (to sth)** to persuade a person to accept less (money): *We cut her down to £10 for the vase.* **cut sb down to size** ⇨ size¹(1).

cut in (**a**) to interrupt a conversation. (**b**) (of a driver of a vehicle, a cyclist etc) to move dangerously close to another vehicle when overtaking. **cut sb in** (*informal*) to include a person in an activity that will provide a share of the profits: *If you want my help you'll have to cut me in.* **cut sth in/into sth** to divide something in half, two etc or into equal parts etc: *cut the cake in two/into quarters.*

cut sb off (**a**) to stop a telephone link: *Operator, we've been cut off.* (**b**) to stop a person while speaking: *He cut me off just when I was about to explain.* (**c**) to prevent a person from moving by surrounding her or him: *She was cut off by the flood/snow/police road-blocks.* **cut sth off** (**a**) to remove something by cutting: *cut off a rose from the bush.* (**b**) to stop the supply of something: *cut off the electricity/gas/funds.*

cut out (**a**) (of electricity) to stop suddenly: *The electricity has cut out.* (**b**) (of a machine, engine) to stop working suddenly: *The engine has cut out. The air-conditioning cuts out when the temperature is normal.* Hence **'cut-out** *nc.* **cut sb out** (**a**) (*informal*) to defeat a rival, competitor: *He bought Jane a gold watch and that cut me out.* (**b**) to decide not to include a person in an activity: *If you're not taking safety precautions you can cut me out.* **cut sth out** (**a**) to remove an article in a magazine, a photograph in a newspaper etc by cutting. (**b**) to produce something by cutting the shape etc wanted: *cut out a dress; cut out new designs for machinery.* Hence **'cut-out** *nc.* (**c**) to make something by cutting(8): *cut out a path through the orchard.* (**d**) to stop using something or doing something such as swearing, smoking, drinking alcohol etc: *cut out cigarettes/beer/fats.* (**e**) to remove particular words, references etc from writing: *cut out all mention of sex.* **cut it/ that out** (*imperative; informal*) stop doing that. (**not**) **be cut out for sth** to (lack or) have the necessary ability, interest etc: *He's not cut out for this work.* **cut through sth** (**a**) to make a path through a forest, ice, jungle etc. (**b**) (*fig*) to be able to overcome difficulties, esp too many rules, etc: *cut through all the unnecessary regulations.*

cut to sb/sth (in TV, films) to change quickly to another actor, scene etc: *cut to a beach scene/to James Bond in prison.*

cut sb up (*sl*) to injure a person by cutting with a razor, knife etc. **cut sth up** to cut, chop, vegetables, meat, wood etc into pieces. **be cut up (about sb/sth)** (of a person) to be extremely sad (because of a person, event etc): *He was so cut up about her death.* **cut up rough** (*informal*) (of a person) to behave violently: *He'll cut up rough if you refuse.*

cut-back /'kʌt bæk/ *nc* ⇨ cut back (on) sth.

cute /kjuːt/ *adj* (**—r, —st**) **1** (*informal*) (of a girl or woman) pretty and charming. **2** (of any person) quick-thinking: *You're cute but I'm cleverer.*
cute·ly *adv*
cute·ness *nu*

cu·ticle /'kjuːtɪkl/ *nc* a layer of hardened skin at the base of a finger-nail or toe-nail.

cut·lery /'kʌtlərɪ/ *nu* knives, forks, spoons etc.

cut·let /'kʌtlɪt/ *nc* a slice of meat or fish.

cut-out /'kʌtaʊt/ *nc* **1** ⇨ cut out. **2** an article etc cut out of a newspaper etc. **3** (*electricity*) a device that disconnects a circuit.

cut-price /'kʌt praɪs/ *adj* (usu *attrib*) sold below the price of other manufacturers, organizers, or below cost: *cut-price holiday tours/groceries.*

cut·ter /'kʌtə(r)/ *nc* **1** a tool for cutting: *wire-cutters.* **2** a small boat for use between ship and shore.

cut·throat /'kʌtθrəʊt/ *adj, nc* (of, like) a murderer: *cutthroat competition* (= organized to ruin the weaker competitors).

cut·ting¹ /'kʌtɪŋ/ *adj* (usu *attrib*) **1** strong, cold and painful: *a cutting wind.* **2** (*derog*) unkind and sarcastic: *a cutting remark.*

cut·ting² /'kʌtɪŋ/ *nc* **1** a deep route along the ground for a road, railway, canal etc. **2** a piece cut from a newspaper etc: *press cuttings.* **3** a short piece of the stem of a plant, to be used for growing a new plant: *chrysanthemum cuttings.*

c.v. /ˌsiː 'viː/ *abbr* = curriculum vitae.

cwt *written abbr* hundredweight.

cy·an·ide /'saɪənaɪd/ *nu* a kind of poisonous compound substance: *potassium cyanide; sodium cyanide.*

cy·ber·net·ics /ˌsaɪbə'netɪks/ *nu* (*tech*) the scientific study of electronic and mechanical instruments (esp compared to natural or biological systems).

cycle¹ /'saɪkl/ *nc* **1** a series of events taking place in a regularly repeated order: *the cycle of the seasons.* **2** a complete set or series: *a song cycle.* **3** a bicycle or motorbike.

cycle² /'saɪkl/ *vi* to ride on a bicycle. Ⓝ *'Cycle'* is the usual verb form, not *'bicycle'.*

cyc·list /'saɪklɪst/ *nc* a person who cycles.

cyc·lic /'sɪklɪk/ (also **cyc·li·cal** /-kl/) *adj* repeated at regular intervals.

cyc·lone /'saɪkləʊn/ *nc* a violent, tropical windstorm.

cyc·lon·ic /saɪ'klɒnɪk/ *adj*

cyg·net /'sɪgnɪt/ *nc* a young swan.

cyl·in·der /'sɪlɪndə(r)/ *nc* **1** a solid or hollow body shaped like a pole or log. **2** (*tech*) the part of an engine where steam etc works a piston: *a six-cylinder engine/car.*

cy·lin·dri·cal /sɪ'lɪndrɪkl/ *adj* shaped like a cylinder(1).

cym·bal /'sɪmbl/ *nc* one of a pair of round brass plates (to be) struck together to make clanging musical sounds.

cyn·ic /'sɪnɪk/ *nc* (*derog*) a person who sees little or no good in anything and who has no belief in human progress (esp showing this by being sarcastic).

cyni·cism /'sɪnɪsɪzəm/ *nc,nu*

cyni·cal /'sɪnɪkl/ *adj* (*derog*) of, like, a cynic: *a cynical smile/remark.*

cyni·cal·ly /-klɪ/ *adv*

cy·pher /'saɪfə(r)/ *nc* = cipher.

cy·press /'saɪprəs/ *nc* (also *attrib*) a kind of ever-green tree with dark leaves and hard wood: *cypress forests*.

cyst /sɪst/ *nc* a hollow growth in the body containing liquid matter.

cys·ti·tis /'sɪstaɪtɪs/ *nu* inflammation of the bladder and the tubes where urine passes.

cy·tol·ogy /ˌsaɪ'tɒlədʒɪ/ *nu* (*science*) the scientific study of the structure and function of plant and animal cells.

czar /zɑː(r)/ *nc* = tsar.

czar·ina /zɑː'riːnə/ *nc* = tsarina.

Dd

D, d /diː/ (*pl* **D's, d's** /diːz/) **1** the fourth letter of the English alphabet. **2** the Roman numeral for 500. **3** (3-D) three dimensional (i.e. having or showing length, height and depth).

d. *abbr* **1** date. **2** day. **3** degree. **4** departs. **5** died.

'd used for *had* or *would* (esp after *I, we, you, he, she, they, who* as in *I'd, we'd, you'd* etc).

dab¹ /dæb/ *nc* **1** a small quantity (of paint etc) dabbed on something. **2** a light tap or small touch putting something on a surface without rubbing.

dab² /dæb/ *vt,vi* (**-bb-**) to touch, put (something) on (something), lightly and gently: *dab one's eyes with a handkerchief*.

dabble /'dæbl/ *v* **1** *vt* to splash (the hands, feet etc) about in water. **2** *vi* **dabble (at/in sth)** to be interested (in an activity, subject for study etc) as a hobby, not professionally: *dabbling in politics*.

dachs·hund /'dækshʊnd/ *nc* a kind of small dog with short legs.

dad /dæd/ *nc* (*informal*) = father.

dad·dy /'dædɪ/ *nc* (*pl* **-ies**) (a child's word for) father. ⇨ also sugar daddy.

,daddy-'long-legs *nc* a kind of long-legged flying insect (also called a *crane-fly*).

daf·fo·dil /'dæfədɪl/ *nc* a garden plant with a yellow flower and long narrow leaves, growing from a bulb.

daft /dɑːft/ *adj* (**—er, —est**) (*informal; derog*) silly; foolish: *a daft idea/person*.

dag·ger /'dægə(r)/ *nc* a short, pointed, two-edged knife, used as a weapon.

dai·ly¹ /'deɪlɪ/ *adj, adv* (happening, done, appearing) every day (or every weekday): *daily newspapers. Thousands of people cross this bridge daily.*

dai·ly² /'deɪlɪ/ *nc* (*pl* **-ies**) **1** a newspaper published every day or every weekday. **2** (*informal*) a woman who is paid to go to a person's home and do housework every day.

dain·ty /'deɪntɪ/ *adj* (**-ier, -iest**) (*dated*) **1** (of a girl or woman) pretty, neat and delicate in appearance and tastes: *a dainty little girl*. **2** (of a thing) pretty and easily damaged or broken: *dainty cups and saucers*.

dain·ti·ly /-təlɪ/ *adv*

dain·ti·ness *nu*

dairy /'deərɪ/ *nc* (*pl* **-ies**) **1** a (part of a) shop where milk, butter, eggs etc are sold. **2** (a part of)

a building where milk and milk products are prepared.

'dairy cattle *nu* cows raised to produce milk, not meat.

'dairy·maid *nc* a woman who works in a dairy(2).

dais /'deɪs/ *nc* (*pl* **—es** /-ɪz/) a raised platform in a large room for a speaker.

dai·sy /'deɪzɪ/ *nc* (*pl* **-ies**) a kind of small white flower with a yellow centre. **be pushing up the daisies** (*informal*) to be dead and buried.

dale /deɪl/ *nc* (esp in N England and in poetry) = valley.

dal·ly /'dælɪ/ *vi* (*pt,pp* **-ied**) **1** *dally with sth* to think slowly about something: *dally with an idea or proposal*. **2** to do something lazily: *Don't dally over your work*.

dam¹ /dæm/ *nc* a mother of some kinds of four-footed animals, e.g. horses. ⇨ sire.

dam² /dæm/ *nc* a barrier built to keep back water and raise its level (e.g. to form a reservoir).

dam³ /dæm/ *vt* (**-mm-**) **dam sth (up) 1** to make a dam across (a narrow valley etc); to hold (water etc) back by means of a dam: *dam (up) a river*. **2** (*fig*) to control, hold back, (feelings): *to dam up one's anger*.

dam·age¹ /'dæmɪdʒ/ *n* **1** *nu* harm or break that causes loss of value: *The insurance company will pay for the damage to my car*. Compare injury. **2** (*pl*) (esp) **claim damages** (*legal*) money claimed from or paid by a person who has caused loss or injury: *He claimed £5000 damages from his employers for the loss of his right arm*.

dam·age² /'dæmɪdʒ/ *vt* to cause damage(1) to (something): *furniture damaged by fire*.

dame /deɪm/ *nc* **1** (D-) (title of) a woman who has been awarded the highest grade of the Order of the British Empire: *Dame Agatha Christie*. Compare lady(6). **2** (*US sl*) a woman.

damn¹ /dæm/ *n sing* (*sl*) **not care/give a damn** to not care at all: *I don't give a damn what you think of me*.

damn² /dæm/ *vt* **1** (of God) to condemn (a person) to everlasting punishment. **2** (of a person) to say that (something or a person) is worthless, bad etc: *The book was damned by the critics*. **3** (used to express anger, annoyance, impatience etc): *I'll be damned if I go! Oh damn! Damn you!*

dam·na·tion /dæm'neɪʃn/ *nu* the state of being damned(1): *to suffer eternal damnation*.

damn·ed /dæmd/ *adj* (*attrib; informal*) (used to emphasize annoyance etc): *You damned fool!*

damp¹ /dæmp/ *adj* (**—er, —est**) a little wet: *damp clothes*. ⇨ dank.

damp·ish *adj* a little damp.

damp² /dæmp/ *nu* the state of being damp; damp air; moisture on the surface of, or existing throughout, something: *The damp rising from the ground caused the walls to stain badly*.

damp·ness *nu*

damp³ /dæmp/ *vt* **1** to make (something) damp: *damp clothes before ironing them*. **2** (also **damp·en**) to make (a person, feelings, interest etc) sad or less strong: *Nothing could damp his spirits*. **3** **damp sth down** to make a fire etc burn more slowly.

damp·en /'dæmpən/ *vt* = damp³(2).

damp·er /'dæmpə(r)/ *nc* **1** a movable metal plate

that regulates the flow of air, e.g. into a stove. **2** a person, thing, that discourages: *His complaints were a damper on the evening.*

dam·sel /'dæmzl/ *nc* (*old use*) a young unmarried woman.

dam·son /'dæmzn/ *n* **1** *nc* (also *attrib*) (a kind of tree producing) a small dark-purple plum: *damson jam.* **2** *nu* (also *adj*) a dark-purple colour.

dance¹ /dɑːns/ *nc* **1** (also *attrib*) (a series of) movements and steps in time with music: *May I have the next dance? What sort of dance music do you play?* **2** a social meeting for dancing: *Can I take you to the dance on Friday?.*

dance² /dɑːns/ *v* **1** *vi* to move in rhythmical steps, usually with music, either alone, with a partner or in a group: *They went on dancing until after midnight. I can't dance to this music.* **2** *vt* to perform (a named kind or set of such movements): *dancing a waltz/Swan Lake.* **3** *vi* to move in a lively way up and down etc: *The leaves were dancing in the wind.* **4** *vt* to cause (a person) to dance(3): *to dance a baby on one's knee.*

dan·cer *nc* a person who dances.

dan·cing *nu* (also *attrib*) the activity of people who dance: *a dancing-teacher; a dancing-partner; ballet-dancing.*

dan·de·lion /'dændɪlaɪən/ *nc* a kind of small wild plant with bright yellow flowers.

dan·druff /'dændrʌf/ *nu* dead skin in small pieces among the hair of the scalp.

dan·ger /'deɪndʒə(r)/ *n* **1** *nu* the possibility of suffering injury or loss of life: *Is there any danger of fire?* **in danger (of sth)** likely to experience injury, death: *His life was in danger. He was in danger of losing his life.* **out of danger** no longer seriously ill: *He has been very ill but the doctors say that he is now out of danger.* **2** *nc* a person, thing, that may cause danger: *That man is a danger to society.*

'danger money *nu* an extra fee paid for a dangerous task or job.

dan·ger·ous /'deɪndʒərəs/ *adj* likely to cause danger: *a dangerous bridge/journey/illness. The river is dangerous to bathe in.*

dan·ger·ous·ly *adv*: *dangerously ill; live dangerously.*

dangle /'dæŋgl/ *vt,vi* (to cause a child, object etc) to hang or swing loosely: *a bunch of keys dangling at the end of a chain.*

dank /dæŋk/ *adj* (**—er, —est**) damp in an unpleasant or unhealthy way: *a dank cave.*

dap·pled /'dæpld/ *adj* (of a horse or shaded area) marked with patches of different (shades of) colour.

dare¹ /deə(r)/ *n* (only in) **do sth for a dare** to do it because one has been dared³(1).

dare² /deə(r)/ *auxiliary verb* Ⓝ *'Dare'* is used as a modal auxiliary verb to express courage. *'Dare'* has no infinitive or imperative forms and no participles. *'Dare'* is always followed by an infinitive without *'to'*. For the use of *dare* as an ordinary verb, ⇨ dare³, esp dare³(2). *Present tense* (all persons) **dare**; *negative* **dare not** or **daren't** /deənt/; *dared not.* **1** to have the courage to (do something): *She daren't go out alone. Dare she try it again? We dared not even whisper.* Ⓝ *'Dare'* is not used except in negatives or in questions. Use *'not be afraid to'* for affirmative forms, as in *She's not afraid to go out*

alone/to try it again.* **2** (in conversation) **(a)** (joined to the end of a statement to form a question): *He daren't lie to me, dare he?* Ⓝ The statement is negative but the short addition is positive. **(b)** (used to make a short question): *'They daren't open the letter.'—'Daren't they?'* Ⓝ The statement is negative and the short question is also negative.

dare³ /deə(r)/ *v* **1** *vt* to challenge (a person) to do something (usually dangerous) suggesting he or she does not have the courage or ability: *He has dared me to swim across the channel. I dare you to ask her for a dance. She dares me to eat it.* ⇨ dare¹. **2** *vi* to have enough courage or impudence to do something: *He wouldn't dare (to) speak to me like that. Nobody dared (to) speak. And now she dares (to) accuse me of theft! You wouldn't dare!* Ⓝ Used with or without *'to'*. **3** *vi* (used to warn a person not to do something when one is angry): *Don't you dare (do that again)!* **4** *vt* (used to show anger with a person for doing something wrong): *How dare he/you/they (do that)!*

dare-dev·il /'deə devl/ *nc* a person who is very daring.

dare·n't /deənt/ = *dare not.* ⇨ dare²,³.

dar·ing¹ /'deərɪŋ/ *adj* bold and courageous or adventurous: *She's so daring! What a daring thing to do!*

dar·ing·ly *adv*

dar·ing² /'deərɪŋ/ *nu* bold and adventurous courage: *to show daring.*

dark¹ /dɑːk/ *adj* (**—er, —est**) **1** having no or very little light: *a dark night. It's getting too dark to take photographs.* Compare light¹(1). **2** (of a colour) not reflecting much light; nearer black than white: *dark blue/green/brown; dark-brown eyes.* Compare light¹(2). **3** (of the skin) not fair; a *dark complexion.* Compare light¹(3). **4** (*fig*) mysterious: *a dark personal history.* **keep it dark** (esp *imperative*) to keep a secret. **a dark horse** ⇨ horse(1). **5** hopeless; sad: *Don't look on the dark side of things.* Compare bright(4).

'Dark Ages *n pl* (the —) (in European history) period from the 6th to the 12th centuries.

,dark 'glasses *n pl* (*informal*) = sunglasses.

dark·ly *adv*

dark·ness *nu* the state of being dark: *The room was in complete darkness.*

dark² /dɑːk/ *nu* **1** the absence of light: *All the lights went out and we were left in the dark.* **after/before dark** after/before the sun goes down. **2** (the —) (*fig*) ignorance: *We were completely in the dark about his movements.*

darken /'dɑːkən/ *vt,vi* (cause sth to) become dark: *The sky darkened in the east.*

dar·ling /'dɑːlɪŋ/ *nc* a person who is loved very much.

darn /dɑːn/ *vi,vt* to mend (a hole in) (something) by sewing over it: *My socks need darning again.* □ *nc* a place mended by darning.

'darning-needle *nc* a large sewing needle, used for darning.

dart¹ /dɑːt/ *nc* **1** a quick, sudden, forward movement: *The child made a sudden dart across the road.* **2** a small, sharp-pointed object to be thrown at a target (marked with numbers for scoring) in the game called *darts.*

dart² /dɑːt/ *vi* to move forward suddenly and quickly: *The deer darted away when it saw us. She* *darted into the shop/across the road.*

dash¹ /dæʃ/ n 1 nc a sudden quick rush: *to make a dash for shelter/freedom.* **2** nc a small amount of something added or mixed: *water with a dash of whisky in it; red with a dash of blue.* **3** nc the punctuation mark (—). (N) It is used in informal style (a) to show hesitation, as in *She's—she's—er—dying;* (b) to emphasize, as in *It's over—over and done with;* (c) either side of a long interruption, as in *Mr Smith—I think you all know him well—has been appointed Director.* **4** nc a (sound of) liquid striking something or being thrown or struck: *the dash of the waves on the rocks.*

dash² /dæʃ/ v 1 vi to run quickly: *dash away/off/out; dash across the road.* **dash off a letter** to write one quickly. **2** vi,vt (to cause something) to move, hit (something), violently: *waves dashing (a boat) against/over the rocks.* ⇨ hope¹(1).

dash·board /ˈdæʃbɔːd/ nc a long piece below the windscreen inside a vehicle, with the speedometer, controls etc.

da·ta /ˈdeɪtə/ nu **1** information; facts: *I can't decide until sufficient data is available.* **2** (computers) information prepared for or stored by a computer: *The data is ready for processing.*

'database nc (computers) an organized store of computer data.

,data-'processing nu (computers) computer operations on data to obtain (more) information, solutions to problems etc.

date¹ /deɪt/ nc a kind of small brown fruit (of the *date-palm*).

date² /deɪt/ nc **1** a statement of the time, day, month, year (one or all three of these) when something happened or is to happen: *date of birth: 20 April 1984. What's today's date? What's the date today? Tell me the date of the discovery of America.* **2** a particular period of time: *Many ruins of Roman date* (= of the time of ancient Rome) *are to be seen in the south of France.* **(be/go) out of date** (written *out-of-date* when *attrib*) (to be/become) no longer used, old-fashioned: *out-of-date ideas.* **to date** so far; until now: *I've had five replies to date.* **(be/bring sb/ sth) up to date** (written *up-to-date* when *attrib*) **(a)** in line with, according to, what is now known, used etc: *up-to-date ideas/methods.* **(b)** up to the present time: *to bring a catalogue up to date.* **3** (informal) a social meeting arranged for a certain time and place: *I have a date with her next week.* **4** (informal) a boyfriend or girlfriend with whom dates(3) are arranged. ⇨ blind date.

date³ /deɪt/ v **1** vt to have, put, a date(1) on (something): *Don't forget to date your letters.* **2** vt to give a date(2) to (an old object): *to date old coins.* **3** vi **date back to/from (a particular period)** to have existed since: *The castle dates from the 14th century.* **4** vi to show signs of going out of date: *Isn't this textbook beginning to date?* **5** vt to make a date(3) with (a person).

dated adj no longer used; old-fashioned: *dated clothes/expressions/ideas.*

date-line /ˈdeɪt laɪn/ n (the —) (also usually *the international date-line*) an imaginary line from the North to the South Pole on or near meridian 180°, east and west of which the date differs.

daub /dɔːb/ vt to cover (a surface) thickly and roughly with (paint, clay, plaster etc): *to daub a*

wall with paint. My shirt was daubed with mud.

daugh·ter /ˈdɔːtə(r)/ nc a person's female child.

daughter-in-law /ˈdɔːtr ɪn lɔː/ (pl **—s-in-law**) the wife of one's son.

daunt·ing /ˈdɔːntɪŋ/ adj causing discouragement because difficult: *a daunting path up the mountain.*

dawdle /ˈdɔːdl/ vi to be slow and lazy: *You should stop dawdling and do something useful!*

dawn¹ /dɔːn/ nc **1** the first light of day: *We must start at dawn.* Compare dusk. **from dawn to dusk** all day long. **2** (fig) the beginning: *the dawn of civilization.*

dawn² /dɔːn/ vi **1** (of the day) to begin to become light: *The day was just dawning.* **2** vi **dawn (on sb)** (fig) to become clear (in a person's mind): *The truth began to dawn on him.*

,dawn 'chorus n sing (the —) (informal) the singing of many different birds very early each day.

day /deɪ/ n **1** nu the time between the sun or light appearing and disappearing: *I work during the day.* **day and night; night and day** through the period of day and night: *We travelled day and night/night and day without stopping.* **all day (long/through)** during the whole day: *I've been working all day.* **make sb's day** to make a person very pleased, happy: *Your kind letter has made my day.* **by day** during the day: *We travelled by day and camped every night.* **pass the time of day (with sb)** to have an informal conversation. **2** nc a period of twenty-four hours (from midnight): *There are seven days in a week. I'll come the day after tomorrow* (i.e. after two days). *She'll telephone in a day's time* (i.e. tomorrow). **any day (now)** very soon: *You should get a letter any day (now).* **day after day; day in, day out** for many days together: *It rained day in, day out.* **day by day** every or each day: *The situation is improving day by day.* **one day** (esp in stories) on a day (past or future). **one of these days** on an unknown day (soon): *One of these days you'll be sorry you did that.* **the other day** a few days ago: *I saw her the other day.* **some day** some time in the future: *Some day I'll find her again.* **that'll be the day** (used to express complete doubt that something will be done, happen etc). **3** nc the hours of the day given to work: *I've done a good day's work.* **call it a day** (informal) to stop working: *Let's call it a day.* **4** nc (often pl) time; period: *in the days of the Greek philosophers; in my parents' day.* **see better days** to experience times when one is richer, more successful etc: *Let's hope we'll soon see better days.* **the present day** (written *present-day* when *attrib*) the time we are now living in: *up to the present day; present-day* (= modern) *writers.* **(in) these days; in this day and age** at the present time. **in those days** during that period in the past; then: *People were happier in those days.*

'day-break nu dawn.

'day-dream vi, nc (to have) a period of imagining pleasant events, possibilities etc.

'day-light nu ⇨ separate entry.

'day-long adj, adv (lasting) for the whole day.

,day-re'turn nc (also *attrib*) a ticket to travel to a place and back on the same day.

'day shift *nc* (people working for) a period during the day, e.g. in a factory.

'day·time *nu* (also *attrib*) day(1): *in the daytime; daytime hours*.

'day-to-day *adj* (*attrib*) (for) each day: *day-to-day expenses/duties/problems*.

day·light /'deɪlaɪt/ *nu* **1** the light of day: *Can we reach our destination in daylight?* (= before it gets dark?) *in broad daylight* during the day when easily seen (and so surprising): *They robbed the bank in broad daylight! daylight robbery* (*informal*) an obvious instance of charging too much money. **2** dawn: *We must leave before daylight*.

daze¹ /deɪz/ *n sing in a daze* unable to think clearly; confused.

daze² /deɪz/ *vt* to make (a person) unable to think clearly: *He was dazed after the crash/was in a dazed state*.

dazzle /'dæzl/ *vt* to make (a person, animal) unable to see clearly or act normally because of too much light, brilliance, splendour etc: *dazzled by bright lights*.

db *written abbr* decibel(s).

DC /ˌdiː'siː/ *abbr* (*electricity*) direct current.

DDT /ˌdiː diː 'tiː/ *abbr* (**d**ichloro**d**iphenyl**t**richloroethane) a kind of powerful but dangerous insecticide.

dea·con /'diːkən/ *nc* an official in some Christian churches.

dea·con·ess /'diːkənɪs/ *nc* a woman deacon.

dead¹ /ded/ *adj* **1** (of people, animals, plants) no longer living: *dead flowers/leaves/flies/fish. drop dead* to die suddenly. **2** (*attrib*) complete: *come to a dead stop; experience a dead silence.* ⇨ **dead²** below. **3** no longer used, discussed, considered etc: *a dead language/custom/issue*. **4** (of a part of the body) no longer able to feel anything: *dead hands/toes* (e.g. because cold). **5** (of machinery, an apparatus etc) no longer working, able to be used etc: *a dead match/engine/battery. The telephone is dead/has gone dead*. **6** (*fig*) (of colours, sound, atmosphere etc) dull. **7** (*attrib*) exact: *The point must be at the dead centre*.

dead 'end *n sing* (*dead-end* when *attrib*) a situation, place, where more progress is impossible: *come to a dead end; a dead-end job*.

dead 'heat *nc* a race in which competitors finish at exactly the same time.

'dead·line *nc* a date fixed for completing a task.

dead 'loss *n sing* a complete failure.

dead 'weight *nc* (*fig; derog*) a useless, difficult etc member of a group.

dead 'wood *nu* (*fig; informal; derog*) useless people: *We must cut out the dead wood in the factory*.

dead² /ded/ *adv* (used to make an *adj* or *adv* stronger in meaning) completely; thoroughly; exactly: *be dead certain/drunk/easy/right/tired; dead ahead; be dead against doing it; be dead on time; stop dead* (= suddenly and quickly) *at the traffic lights*.

dead³ /ded/ *n* **1** *n pl* (the —) dead people. **2** *in the dead of sth* during the most silent and still part of a period: *in the dead of night/winter*.

dead·en /'dedn/ *vt* to cause (feelings, sound etc) to lose strength, brightness: *take drugs to deaden the pain; thick walls that deaden the noise*.

dead·lock /'dedlɒk/ *nc, nu* a total failure to reach agreement or to settle a quarrel: *reach (a complete) deadlock*.

dead·ly /'dedlɪ/ *adj* (**-ier, -iest**) **1** causing, likely to cause, death: *deadly weapons/poison*. **2** filled with extreme hate: *deadly enemies*.

dead·pan /'dedpæn/ *adj* (*attrib*) (of a face) showing no emotion: *a deadpan expression*.

deaf¹ /def/ *adj* (**—er, —est**) **1** unable to hear at all; unable to hear well: *to become/go deaf; a deaf child*. **2** *deaf to sth* (*pred; fig*) unwilling to listen: *deaf to all advice. fall on deaf ears* ⇨ ear¹(1). *turn a deaf ear (to sb/sth)* ⇨ ear¹(1).

'deaf-aid *nc* (*old use*) = hearing-aid.

deaf 'mute *nc* (*old use*) a person who is deaf and dumb.

deaf·ness *nu*

deaf² /def/ *n pl* (the —) deaf people.

deaf·en /'defn/ *vt* to make so much noise that it is difficult or impossible for (a person) to hear: *We were almost deafened by the uproar. There were deafening cheers when the speaker finished*.

deal¹ /diːl/ *n sing* **1** *a good/great deal (of sth)* a large or considerable quantity (of something): *He has had to spend a good deal of money on medicines. I have spent a great deal of trouble over this work*. **2** *a great deal* often; very much: *They see each other a great deal*.

deal² /diːl/ *nc* **1** a (business) agreement: *a business deal. make a deal (with sb)* to agree a business matter (with a person). *It's a deal* (*informal*) I agree/accept. *a raw/rough deal* unfair, bad, treatment. *a square deal* a fair and honest one. **2** (in card-games) a distribution of cards to players.

deal³ /diːl/ *v* (*pt,pp* dealt /delt/) **1** *vt, vi* (in card-games) to give out (cards) to the players: *Who dealt (the cards)?* **2** *vt* to give (a person) (a blow): *deal him a blow on the chin*.

deal sb in to include a person in a game by giving her or him cards. *deal in sth* to do business by buying and selling something: *deal in second-hand cars*.

deal sth out (a) to give out playing-cards. **(b)** to give justice, punishment etc (to a person).

deal with sb (a) to organize and give a punishment to a person. **(b)** to do business with a person, business: *We've been dealing with them/their company for years. deal with sth (a)* to settle, attend to, correspondence, a complaint, a problem etc. *deal with unemployment/an epidemic/ yesterday's post.* **(b)** (of a book, lecture etc) to have a topic etc as its subject: *It deals with Asian culture*.

deal·er /'diːlə(r)/ *nc* **1** a person who deals out playing-cards. **2** a person, business, that buys and sells something: *a car dealer*.

deal·ing /'diːlɪŋ/ *n* **1** *nu* behaviour towards others: *He is well known for fair dealing*. **2** (*pl*) business methods and relations: *I've always found him honest in his dealings with me*.

dealt /delt/ *pt,pp* of deal³.

dean /diːn/ *nc* (D- in names) **1** a Christian clergyman responsible for a number of parishes: *a rural dean*. **2** (in some universities) **(a)** a person with authority to maintain discipline. **(b)** a head of a department of studies.

dear¹ /dɪə(r)/ *adj* (**—er, —est**) **1** (*attrib*) loved;

lovable: *What a dear little child!* **2** (D-) (used at the beginning of letters): *Dear Madam/Sir; Dear Mr Green.* **3** high in price; (of a shop) asking high prices: *Everything is getting dearer.* **4** (*pred*) **dear (to sb)** precious (to a person); greatly valued (by a person): *He lost everything that was dear to him.* **dear·ness** *nu*

dear² /dɪə(r)/ *adv* at a high cost: *If you want to make money, you must buy cheap and sell dear.*

dear³ /dɪə(r)/ *nc* **1** a lovable person: *Isn't she a dear?* **2** (*informal*) (used to speak kindly to a person): *Yes, dear. Drink your milk up, dear.*

dear⁴ /dɪə(r)/ *int* (used to express surprise, impatience, wonder, dismay etc): *Oh dear! Dear me!*

dear·ly /dɪəlɪ/ *adv* **1** very much: *He would dearly love to see his mother again. He loves his mother dearly.* **2** at great cost: *Victory was dearly bought* (e.g. hundreds of soldiers were killed).

dearth /dɜ:θ/ *nc* (*formal*) a shortage (the usual word): *a dearth of food.*

deary (also **dearie**) /ˈdɪərɪ/ *nc* (*pl* **-ies**) (*informal*) (used by an elderly woman to a younger person, or a mother to her child) = **dear³**(2).

death /deθ/ *n* **1** *nc,nu* (the act, way, of) dying; end of life: *There have been several deaths from drowning here this summer. Two children were burnt to death in the fire.* **be at death's door** to be dying. **be sick to death of sb/sth** to be very fed up with a person, complaints etc. **bore sb to death** to bore a person extremely. **2** *nc,nu* (an act of) killing or being killed: *The murderer was sentenced to death.* **be the death of sb** to cause a person's death: *That motorbike will be the death of him.* **catch one's death of cold** to get a very serious cold. **put sb to death** to kill her or him (as a punishment). **3** *nu* the state of being dead: *find peace in death.* **a fate worse than death** ⇨ fate(2).

'death·bed *nc: She's on her deathbed* (= is dying).

'death certificate *nc* an official document giving cause of death.

'death duties *n pl* taxes (to be) paid on a person's property after death.

'death penalty *nc* (usu the —) an execution as a punishment for a crime.

'death-trap *nc* (*fig*) a very dangerous place, condition etc.

death·ly /ˈdeθlɪ/ *adj, adv* like death: *a deathly stillness; look deathly pale.*

de·bar /dɪˈbɑ:(r)/ *vt* (-rr-) **debar sb (from sth)** to prevent a person by a regulation (from doing or having something): *debar prisoners from voting at elections.*

de·base /dɪˈbeɪs/ *vt* to make (a person, currency etc) lower in value, poorer in quality etc: *The insults debased her reputation.*

de·base·ment *nu*

de·bat·able /dɪˈbeɪtəbl/ *adj* that can be argued about because uncertain: *It's debatable whether she will agree to it.*

de·bate¹ /dɪˈbeɪt/ *nc,nu* **1** a formal discussion, e.g. at a public meeting, by a committee: *After a long debate the bill was passed by the House of Commons.* **2** a contest between two or more speakers who give different opinions about the same issue.

de·bate² /dɪˈbeɪt/ *vt,vi* **1** to take part in a debate: *debating (about/on) secondary education.* **2** to think about and discuss (something) in order to decide: *We were debating whether to go to the mountains or to the seaside.*

de·bauch·ed /dɪˈbɔ:tʃt/ *adj* (*formal; derog*) immoral: *a debauched student.*

de·bauch·ery /dɪˈbɔ:tʃərɪ/ *nu* (*formal*) an immoral style of living: *a life of debauchery.*

de·bili·tat·ing /dɪˈbɪlɪteɪtɪŋ/ *adj* making (a person, her or his health) weak: *a debilitating climate.*

de·bil·ity /dɪˈbɪlətɪ/ *nu* weakness (of health): *After her long illness she is suffering from general debility.*

deb·it¹ /ˈdebɪt/ *nc* (*bookkeeping*) **1** an entry (in an account) of a sum owing. **2** the left-hand side of an account, on which such entries are made. Compare credit.

deb·it² /ˈdebɪt/ *vt* **debit sb/sth (with sth)** to put an amount on the debit side of (a person's) (account): *debit her/his account (with £5).*

de·bris /ˈdeɪbrɪ/ *nu* scattered broken pieces: *We searched for the box among the debris after the explosion.*

debt /det/ *nc,nu* **1** a payment which must be, but has not yet been, paid to a person: *If I pay all my debts I shall have no money left.* **a bad debt** one that is not, cannot be, paid. **be in debt/out of debt** to be owing/no longer owing money. **run (oneself/sb) into debt** (to cause oneself, a person) to start (suddenly) to owe money: *All that equipment will run you into debt.* **2** (*fig*) a condition of needing to do something in return for a kindness, good deed etc: *I owe him a debt of gratitude/am in debt to him for all he has done for me.*

debt·or /-tə(r)/ *nc* a person who owes money to another person. Compare creditor.

de·bug /ˌdi:ˈbʌg/ *vt* (-gg-) **1** (*computers*) to remove faults, problems from (a computer or a computer program). **2** to remove electronic listening devices from (a room).

de·bunk /dɪˈbʌŋk/ *vt* (*informal*) to show that (something generally believed) is not true (esp with sarcasm): *The newspaper report debunked the idea that all politicians are honest.*

dé·but /ˈdeɪbju:/ *nc* (of an actor, musician etc) a first appearance on a public stage: *to make one's début.*

Dec *written abbr* December.

dec·ade /ˈdekeɪd/ *nc* a period of ten years: *the first decade of the 20th century* (=1900–1909).

deca·dence /ˈdekədəns/ *nu* the fall to a lower standard (in morals, art, literature etc).

deca·dent /ˈdekədənt/ *adj* (*derog*) showing decadence: *decadent teenagers; decadent humour; decadent architecture.*

de·caf·fein·ated /ˌdi:ˈkæfɪneɪtɪd/ *adj* (no *comp*) with the caffein removed from the contents: *decaffeinated coffee.*

de·cant /dɪˈkænt/ *vt* to pour (wine etc) from a bottle into another vessel.

de·cant·er *nc* a vessel for wine.

de·capi·tate /dɪˈkæpɪteɪt/ *vt* to kill (a person) by cutting off her or his head.

de·capi·ta·tion /dɪˌkæpɪˈteɪʃn/ *nc,nu*

deca·syl·lab·ic /ˌdekəsɪˈlæbɪk/ *adj* (of a line of verse) having ten syllables.

de·cath·lon /dɪˈkæθlɒn/ nc a modern athletic contest in which each competitor takes part in ten events (involving running, jumping, hurdles, shot put, discus, pole vault and javelin).

de·cay¹ /dɪˈkeɪ/ n **be in/fall into decay** to be, begin to be, decaying (esp 2).

de·cay² /dɪˈkeɪ/ vi,vt **1** (to cause food) to go bad: *decaying vegetables*. **2** (to cause teeth, a building, beauty, a standard of performance etc) to become lower in health, quality, strength, ability etc.

de·ceased /dɪˈsiːst/ nc (pl —) (the —) (legal) the person who has recently died.

de·ceit /dɪˈsiːt/ n **1** nu the act of causing a person to accept as true or genuine something that is false: *She is incapable of deceit*. **2** nc a lie; dishonest trick.

de·ceit·ful /dɪˈsiːtfəl/ adj **1** (derog) often deceiving: *a deceitful child*. **2** intended to deceive: *deceitful words*.
    de·ceit·ful·ly /-fəli/ adv
    de·ceit·ful·ness nu

de·ceive /dɪˈsiːv/ vt to cause (a person) to believe something that is false: *You can't pass the examination without working hard, so don't deceive yourself*.
    de·ceiv·er nc a person who deceives.

De·cem·ber /dɪˈsembə(r)/ n (also attrib) (abbr Dec) the twelfth month of the year, with 31 days: *enjoy the December sunshine. Christmas Day is 25 December*. Ⓝ '25 December' is spoken as 'December the twenty-fifth' or 'the twenty-fifth of December'.

de·cen·cy /ˈdiːsnsɪ/ nu (the quality of) being decent: *I hope he'll have the decency to apologize*. ⇨ indecency.

de·cent /ˈdiːsnt/ adj **1** right and suitable: *decent clothes*. **2** not likely to shock or embarrass others: *decent language and behaviour*. Ⓝ This is the only sense for which *indecent* is the opposite.
    de·cent·ly adv in a decent(1,2) manner: *decently dressed; behave decently*.

de·cen·tra·lize (also **-ise**) /ˌdiːˈsentrəlaɪz/ vt to give greater powers for self-government etc to (regions, branches etc away from the centre).
    de·cen·tra·liz·ation (also **-is·ation**) /ˌdiːˌsentrəlaɪˈzeɪʃn/ nu

de·cep·tion /dɪˈsepʃn/ n **1** nu the act of deceiving or being deceived: *to practise deception on the public*. **2** nc an action intended to deceive: *His false smile is an obvious deception*.

de·cep·tive /dɪˈseptɪv/ adj deceiving: *a deceptive smile/appearance*.
    de·cep·tive·ly adv

deci·bel /ˈdesɪbel/ nc (abbr db) (science) a unit for measuring the loudness of sounds.

de·cide /dɪˈsaɪd/ v **1** vt to settle (a question or a doubt); give a judgement about (something): *It's difficult to decide between the two. The committee decided for/in favour of/against the plan*. **2** vi to think about something and come to a conclusion; make up one's mind: *The boy decided not to become/decided that he would not become a sailor. She decided to buy it. We decided against going/decided not to go for a holiday in Wales*. **3** vt (to cause a person) to decide(2): *What decided you to give up your job?*

de·cid·ed /dɪˈsaɪdɪd/ adj **1** (attrib) clear; definite: *There is a decided difference between them*. **2** (of a person) determined: *He's quite decided about it*. ⇨ undecided.
    de·cid·ed·ly adv definitely; undoubtedly: *This is decidedly better*.

de·cidu·ous /dɪˈsɪdjʊəs/ adj (of trees) losing their leaves annually (esp in autumn). Compare coniferous.

deci·mal /ˈdesɪml/ adj (attrib) of tens or one-tenths: *a decimal system* (for money etc).
    ,decimal 'fraction nc (maths) a number such as 15·61. Compare vulgar fraction.
    ,decimal 'point nc (maths) the point in, e.g., 15·61.

deci·mal·ize (also **-ise**) /-aɪz/ vt to change (money, measurement) to a decimal system: *decimalized currency*.
    deci·mal·iz·ation (also **-is·ation**) /ˌdesɪmələˈzeɪʃn/ nu

deci·mate /ˈdesɪmeɪt/ vt to kill or destroy a large number of (people, plants etc): *a population decimated by an earthquake*.

de·ci·pher /dɪˈsaɪfə(r)/ vt to find the meaning of (something written in code, bad handwriting etc).
    de·ci·pher·able /-əbl/ adj that can be deciphered. Opp indecipherable.

de·ci·sion /dɪˈsɪʒn/ n **1** nc,nu (a result of) deciding: *Have they reached/come to/arrived at/taken/made a decision yet?* **2** nu the ability to decide and act accordingly: *A person who is not capable of decision cannot hold a position of responsibility*. ⇨ indecision.

de·cis·ive /dɪˈsaɪsɪv/ adj **1** having a definite result: *a decisive victory* (= deciding which side wins the war). **2** showing decision(2): *He gave a decisive answer*. Opp indecisive.
    de·cis·ive·ly adv

deck¹ /dek/ nc **1** any of the floors of a ship in or above the hull: *Shall we go up on deck?* **2** any similar surface, e.g. in a bus: *Let's sit on the top deck of the bus*. **3** the flat part for the disc and arm on a record-player or for the tape in a tape-recorder: *a stereo cassette deck; a tape deck*. **4** a pack (of playing-cards).
    'deck-chair nc a collapsible wooden chair with a cloth seat, used out of doors, e.g. on the beach.

deck² /dek/ vt **deck sth (out) (in/with sth)** to decorate something: *streets decked with flags*.

de·claim /dɪˈkleɪm/ vt,vi **declaim (against) sb/sth** (formal) to speak with strong feeling and attack a person, plan etc.

dec·lar·ation /ˌdekləˈreɪʃn/ nc something that is declared: *a declaration of imported goods to Customs officials; a declaration of war*.

de·clare /dɪˈkleə(r)/ v **1** vt to make (something) known to everyone formally: *to declare the results of an election. I declare this meeting closed*. **declare war (on/against** a country, or (fig) a **disease, poverty** etc) to announce that a state of war exists. **2** **declare (that . . .)** to say (something) in order to show that one has no doubt: *The accused man declared that he was not guilty/declared himself innocent*. **3** vi **declare against/for sth** to say that one is not/is in favour of a proposal etc. **4** vt to make a statement (to Customs) of (imported goods) or (to a Tax Inspector) of (one's income): *Have you anything to declare?*

de·clen·sion /dɪˈklenʃn/ nu (gram) the process

of changing the endings of nouns, pronouns, and adjectives according to their use in a sentence.

de·cline¹ /dɪ'klaɪn/ *nc* a period of gradual and continued loss of importance, strength: *the economic decline of Europe; a decline in prices/health.*

de·cline² /dɪ'klaɪn/ *v* **1** *vt,vi* to say 'No'; refuse (something offered): *to decline an invitation to (go to) a party.* **2** *vi* to continue to become smaller, weaker, lower: *a declining birthrate; declining sales.* **3** *vi* (*formal*) (of the sun) to go down. **4** *vt* (*gram*) to give the endings etc of (a noun, pronoun or adjective) according to its use in a sentence.

de·clutch /ˌdiː'klʌtʃ/ *vi* to disconnect the clutch (of a vehicle) in order to change gear.

de·code /ˌdiː'kəʊd/ *vt* to find the true meaning of (something produced in code).

de·com·pose /ˌdiːkəm'pəʊz/ *vt,vi* (to cause a dead body etc) to become bad: *decomposed meat.*

de·com·po·si·tion /ˌdiːˌkɒmpə'zɪʃn/ *nu*

de·con·gest·ant /ˌdiːkɒn'dʒestənt/ *nc* (*med*) a substance that reduces (esp nasal) congestion.

dé·cor /'deɪkɔː(r)/ *n sing* the decorations, furniture etc, e.g. of a room or the stage of a theatre.

dec·or·ate /'dekəreɪt/ *v* **1** *vt* **decorate sth (with sth)** to make a place, food etc (more) beautiful (by placing ornaments on or in it): *decorating a street with flags/a birthday cake.* **2** *vt,vi* to paint etc the outside or inside of (a building). **3** *vt* to give (a person) a symbol (e.g. a medal) of distinction: *be decorated for bravery during a fire.*

dec·ora·tion /ˌdekə'reɪʃn/ *n* **1** *nu* the act of decorating. **2** *nc* something used for decorating: *cake decorations.* **3** *nc* a medal etc given and worn as an honour or award.

dec·or·ative /'dekrətɪv/ *adj* suitable for decorating(1): *Wild flowers can be very decorative.*

dec·or·ator /'dekəreɪtə(r)/ *nc* a person who decorates(2): *interior decorators.*

de·coy /'diːkɔɪ/ *nc* **1** a (real or imitation) bird used to attract others so that they can be caught. **2** (*fig*) a person, suggestion, object etc used to tempt a person into a position of danger.

de·crease¹ /'diːkriːs/ *nc,nu* (the result, amount of) decreasing: *a decrease in exports/applications/profits.* Opp increase.

de·crease² /dɪ'kriːs/ *vt,vi* (to cause something) to become shorter, smaller, less: *The population of the village has decreased from 1000 to 500.* Opp increase.

de·cree¹ /dɪ'kriː/ *nc* an order given by a ruler or authority and having the force of a law: *issue a decree; rule by decree.*

de·cree 'absolute *nc* an order for an immediate divorce.

de·cree 'nisi /dɪˌkriː 'naɪsaɪ/ *nc* an order for a divorce unless cause to prevent it is shown within a fixed period.

de·cree² /dɪ'kriː/ *vt* **decree (that) sth** to order (something) by a decree: *It has been decreed that all children will be examined.*

de·crep·it /dɪ'krepɪt/ *adj* made weak by old age or hard use: *a decrepit horse.*

de·cry /dɪ'kraɪ/ *vt* (*pt,pp* **-ied**) (*formal*) to speak against (something) esp with sarcasm: *He decried her efforts to win.*

dedi·cate /'dedɪkeɪt/ *vt* **1** to give (one's time,

energy etc) (to a special cause or purpose): *He dedicated his life to the service of his country.* **2** **dedicate sth to sb** to state that a book, performance etc is in honour of or in gratitude to a particular person.

dedi·ca·tion /ˌdedɪ'keɪʃn/ *nc,nu*

de·duce /dɪ'djuːs/ *vt* (*formal*) to arrive at (knowledge, a theory etc) by reasoning: *If you see a doctor leaving a house, you deduce that someone in the house is ill.*

de·duc·ible /-əbl/ *adj*

de·duct /dɪ'dʌkt/ *vt* to take away (an amount or part) (from a bill, wage etc): *deduct tax/rent.*

de·duc·tion /dɪ'dʌkʃn/ *nc,nu* **1** (an amount, result, of) deducting: *deductions from pay for insurance and pension.* **2** *nc,nu* (a conclusion reached by) reasoning from general laws to a particular case. ⇨ deduce.

deed /diːd/ *nc* **1** something done: *Deeds are better than promises.* **2** (*legal*) a signed agreement, esp about ownership or rights.

deem /diːm/ *vt* (*formal*) to consider, judge (it/ something) to be (the kind of condition mentioned): *She deemed it unnecessary to explain.* Ⓝ Not used in the continuous tenses, e.g. *is/was -ing.*

deep¹ /diːp/ *adj* (**—er, —est**) **1** going a long way down from the top: *a deep well/the deep end of a swimming-pool; a river 4 metres deep.* Opp shallow. ⇨ depth. **2** going a long way from the surface or edge: *a deep wound/drawer/shelf; deep in the woods.* **3** (*fig*) serious and sincere: *a deep thinker; deep feelings/sympathy.* **4** to a great extent: *deep in debt; in a deep sleep* (= from which one is not easily awakened). **5** (of a sound) low: *in a deep voice.* Opp high¹(6). **6** (of a colour) strong: *a deep red.* Opp pale¹(2). **7** **deep in sth (a)** ⇨ 4 above. **(b)** having all one's attention centred on something: *deep in thought/study/a book.*

deep·ly *adv* extremely: *He is deeply interested in the subject.*

deep·ness *nu*

deep² /diːp/ *adv* far down or in: *We had to dig deep to find water.*

deep-'freeze *vt* to freeze (food) at a very low temperature to keep it fresh for long periods: *deep-frozen fish.*

deep-'freeze/-'freezer *nc* a special type of refrigerator (or a special part of an ordinary refrigerator) used for deep-freezing.

deep-'fry *vt* (*pt,pp* **-ied**) to fry (food) in oil deep enough to cover it. Hence **deep-'fried** *adj.*

deep-'rooted *adj* not easily removed: *He has a deep-rooted dislike of hard work.*

deep-'sea *adj* (*attrib*) of, from, very low down in the sea: *deep-sea diving/fish.*

deep-'seated *adj* fixed firmly: *The causes of the trouble are deep-seated.*

deep³ /diːp/ *n* (the —) (*poetry*) the sea.

deep·en /'diːpən/ *v* **1** *vt,vi* (to cause a hole etc) to become deep(er). **2** *vi* (of a bad situation) to get worse: *the deepening crisis.*

deer /dɪə(r)/ *nc* (*pl* **—**) a kind of graceful, quick-running animal, the male of which usually has branched horns.

'deer·skin *nc,nu* (a) leather made of a deer's skin.

de·face /dɪ'feɪs/ *vt* to spoil the appearance of (something) by marking or damaging the surface.

de·face·ment *nc,nu*

de·fame /dɪ'feɪm/ *vt* (*formal*) to attack the good reputation of (a person).

defa·ma·tion /ˌdefə'meɪʃn/ *nu*

de·fama·tory /dɪ'fæmətrɪ/ *adj:* defamatory remarks.

de·fault¹ /dɪ'fɔːlt/ *nu* the act of defaulting: *to win a case/a game by default* (e.g. because the other person, team, player etc does not appear).

de·fault² /dɪ'fɔːlt/ *vi* **default (on sth)** (*legal*) to fail to perform a duty, to appear (e.g. in a law court) or to pay a debt.

de·fault·er *nc* a person who defaults.

de·feat¹ /dɪ'fiːt/ *nc,nu* (an instance of) defeating or being defeated.

de·feat² /dɪ'fiːt/ *vt* **1** to win a victory over (a player, team, rival): *to defeat another school at football*. **2** to cause (a purpose, hope etc) to fail: *Our hopes were defeated*.

de·feat·ed *adj:* *a defeated army.* Opp undefeated.

de·feat·ism *nu* the mental condition in which one expects to be defeated.

de·feat·ist *adj, nc* (of) a person who considers it impossible to win, be successful etc.

de·fe·cate /'defɪkeɪt/ *vi* (*formal*) to empty the bowels.

de·fect¹ /'diːfekt/ *nc* a fault; something that is not complete or perfect: *defects in a system of education*.

de·fect² /dɪ'fekt/ *vi* to desert one's country, a political party etc: *the journalist who defected to the East* (e.g. by asking for political asylum).

de·fec·tor /-tə(r)/ *nc* a person who defects: *defectors from the Republican Party.*

de·fec·tion /dɪ'fekʃn/ *nc,nu* (an instance of) defecting, e.g. to another political party (or its leader), to another religion etc: *defections from the Labour Party.*

de·fec·tive /dɪ'fektɪv/ *adj* **1** imperfect: *defective in workmanship; defective machinery*. **2** (*gram*) describing a verb without certain usual forms (e.g. *must* which has no past tense).

de·fence (*US* = **de·fense**) /dɪ'fens/ *n* **1** *nu* the act of defending from attack: *money used for national defence*. **2** *nc* something used for defending or protecting: *build high walls along the coast as a defence against floods during storms*. **3** *nc,nu* (*legal*) the arguments used to contest an accusation; the lawyers acting for an accused person: *The accused man made no defence. Counsel for the defence put in a plea for mercy.*

de·fence·less *adj* unable to defend oneself or itself.

de·fend /dɪ'fend/ *vt* **1** to guard, protect, (a person, thing): *to defend one's friend/country against enemies; defend a goal during a football match*. **2** to speak or write in support of (a person, idea, decision etc): *defend a decision/friend/claim; defend a lawsuit*.

de·fend·ant /dɪ'fendənt/ *nc* (*legal*) a person against whom a legal action is brought. Compare plaintiff.

de·fend·er /dɪ'fendə(r)/ *nc* **1** a person who defends an idea, decision etc. **2** (in sport) a player who guards the goal area against attacks from the other side.

de·fens·ible /dɪ'fensəbl/ *adj* (*formal*) able to be

defended(2). Opp indefensible.

de·fen·sive¹ /dɪ'fensɪv/ *adj* (*attrib*) used for, intended for, defending: *defensive weapons/measures*.

de·fen·sive² *n* **be on the defensive** to be careful about expressing one's ideas, doing things, because of criticism.

de·fens·ive·ly *adv*

de·fer¹ /dɪ'fɜː(r)/ *vt* (**-rr-**) to put off (an action, decision etc) until a later date or time: *I'll defer my departure for a week.*

de·fer·ment *nc,nu*

de·fer² /dɪ'fɜː(r)/ *vi* (**-rr-**) **defer to sb/sth** (*formal*) to agree with a person, opinion etc (often to show respect): *defer to his experience/to one's grandparents.*

de·fer·ence /'defərəns/ *nu* (*formal*) the act of giving way to the wishes, accepting the opinion or judgement, of another or others: *show deference to a judge*. **in deference to sth** because of respect for it: *in deference to her age*.

de·fer·en·tial /ˌdefə'renʃl/ *adj* (*formal*) showing respect: *a deferential bow*.

de·fi·ance /dɪ'faɪəns/ *nu* an obvious refusal to obey. **in defiance of sb/sth** refusing to obey a person, order etc: *to act in defiance of orders.*

de·fi·ant /dɪ'faɪənt/ *adj* (often *derog*) showing no fear about refusing to obey; openly disobedient. ⇨ defy.

defi·ant·ly *adv*

de·fi·cien·cy /dɪ'fɪʃnsɪ/ *nc,nu* (*pl* **-ies**) (an instance of) the state of being short of, less than, what is correct or needed: *suffering from a deficiency of food; a vitamin deficiency.*

de·fi·ci·ent /dɪ'fɪʃnt/ *adj* **deficient (in sth)** not having enough (of something): *deficient in courage.*

de·fi·cit /'defɪsɪt/ *nc* an amount by which something, esp a sum of money, is too small. Opp surplus.

de·file /dɪ'faɪl/ *vt* (*formal*) to make (a region, water; a person's thoughts etc) dirty or impure: *factories that defile rivers; horror films that defile the minds of teenagers.*

de·fine /dɪ'faɪn/ *vt* **1** to state precisely the meaning of (e.g. words). **2** to state, show, (something) clearly: *The powers of a judge are defined by law.*

de·fin·able /-əbl/ *adj* that can be defined. Opp indefinable.

defi·nite /'defɪnət/ *adj* clear; not doubtful or uncertain: *I want a definite answer—'Yes' or 'No'.* Opp indefinite.

definite 'article *nc* (*gram*) the word '*the*'.

defi·nite·ly *adv* **(a)** without doubt: *definitely the best*. **(b)** (*informal*) (used in answer to a question) yes, certainly.

defi·ni·tion /ˌdefɪ'nɪʃn/ *n* **1** *nc* a statement that defines a word, rule etc: *To give a definition of a word is more difficult than you think*. **2** *nu* (*formal*) clearness of outline or sound: *a recording that does not have true definition.*

de·fini·tive /dɪ'fɪnətɪv/ *adj* considered final and without the need for change or addition: *a definitive offer/answer.*

de·flate /dɪ'fleɪt/ *v* **1** *vt* to make (a tyre, balloon etc) smaller by letting out air or gas. **2** *vt* (*fig*) to lessen the conceit of (a person): *deflate a pompous politician*. **3** *vt,vi* (*economics*) to take action to reduce (the amount of money in circulation) in order to lower or keep steady the prices of saleable goods.

de·fla·tion /dɪ'fleɪʃn/ *nu* a decrease in economic activity by reducing the money supply. Compare reflation.

de·fla·tion·ary /-ərɪ/ *adj* (*economics*) designed or tending to produce deflation: *necessary deflationary measures by the Chancellor.*

de·flect /dɪ'flekt/ *vt,vi* (to cause something) to turn aside or move in a different direction: *The ball was deflected off a defender into the goal.*

de·flec·tion /dɪ'flekʃn/ *nc,nu*

de·form /dɪ'fɔ:m/ *vt* to spoil the form or appearance of (something, a person's body).

de·form·ed *adj* (of the body or a part of it) badly shaped: *The boy has a deformed foot and cannot play games.*

de·form·ity /dɪ'fɔ:mətɪ/ *nc* (*pl* **-ies**) a deformed part (esp of the body).

de·fraud /dɪ'frɔ:d/ *vt* to trick (a person) out of what is rightly hers or his.

de·freeze /,di:'fri:z/ *vt* to allow (food) to become unfrozen.

de·frost /,di:'frɒst/ *vt* **1** to remove, get rid of, ice or frost (e.g. in a refrigerator or on the windscreen of a vehicle). **2** to allow (food) to become unfrozen.

de·froze /,di:'frəʊz/ *pt* of defreeze.

de·frozen /,di:'frəʊzn/ *pp* of defreeze.

deft /deft/ *adj* (**—er, —est**) quick and clever (esp with the fingers).

deft·ly *adv*

deft·ness *nu*

de·funct /dɪ'fʌŋkt/ *adj* (of a law, method etc) no longer used.

de·fuse /,di:'fju:z/ *vt* **1** to make (e.g. an unexploded bomb) useless. **2** (*fig*) to prevent (a dangerous crisis): *defusing anger among the crowd.*

de·fy /dɪ'faɪ/ *vt* (*pt, pp* **-ied**) **1** to refuse to obey or show respect to (a person, government etc): *to defy one's parents.* ⇨ defiant. **2** to offer difficulties that cannot be solved by (something): *The problem defied solution* (= could not be solved).

deg. *abbr* degree.

de·gen·er·ate¹ /dɪ'dʒenərət/ *adj* (*derog*) having lost qualities (physical, moral or mental) that are considered normal and desirable: *degenerate teenagers with too much money.*

de·gen·er·ate² /dɪ'dʒenərət/ *nc* (*derog*) a degenerate person.

de·gen·er·ate³ /dɪ'dʒenəreɪt/ *vi* to pass from a state of goodness to a lower state by losing qualities which are considered normal and desirable: *Young people of today are not degenerating.*

de·grade /dɪ'greɪd/ *vt* to cause (a person) to be less moral or less deserving of respect: *degrading oneself by cheating.*

degra·da·tion /,degrə'deɪʃn/ *nu*

de·grad·ing /dɪ'greɪdɪŋ/ *adj* causing a person to be considered less moral or less deserving of respect: *degrading behaviour/clothes.*

de·gree /dɪ'gri:/ *nc* **1** a unit of measurement (of a circle) for angles: *An angle of ninety degrees (90°) is called a right angle. One degree of latitude equals about 115km.* **2** a unit of measurement for temperature: *Water freezes at 32 degrees Fahren-*

heit *(32°F) or zero degrees Celsius (0°C).* **3** an academic grade given by a university to a person who has passed an examination: *studying for/take a degree; the degree of Master of Arts.* **4** a step or stage in a scale or process: *first/second/third degree burns. The girls show various degrees of skill in their use of carpentry tools. He was not in the slightest degree* (= not at all) *interested.* **by degrees** gradually: *Their friendship grew by degrees into love.* **5** a position in society: *persons of high degree.* **6** (*music*) an interval from one note to another. **7** (*gram*) one of the three forms of comparison of an adjective or adverb. ⇨ comparative(3), positive(9), superlative(2).

de·hy·drate /,di:haɪ'dreɪt/ *v* (usually used as a *pp*) **1** *vt* to remove water or moisture from (food etc): *dehydrated vegetables.* **2** *vi* to lose water from one's body during hot weather, esp when one has nothing to drink.

de·hy·dra·tion /,di:haɪ'dreɪʃn/ *nu* (esp) the weak physical condition caused by lack of water in one's body: *suffer from dehydration.*

de-ice /,di: 'aɪs/ *vt* to remove ice, e.g. from (a windscreen etc).

de·ify /'di:ɪfaɪ/ *vt* (*pt, pp* **-ied**) to worship (a person) as a god.

de·ity /'deɪɪtɪ/ *nc* (*pl* **-ies**) a god or goddess: *Roman deities* (e.g. Neptune).

de·ject·ed /dɪ'dʒektɪd/ *adj* sad or gloomy: *Why is she looking so dejected.*

de·lay¹ /dɪ'leɪ/ *nc,nu* (an instance of) delaying or being delayed: *We must leave without delay. The race began after a delay of two hours.*

de·lay² /dɪ'leɪ/ *vt,vi* **1** to cause (a person, vehicle etc) to be slow or late: *The train was delayed (for) two hours.* **2** to put off (an action, decision etc) until later: *Why have you delayed opening the new school?*

de·lec·table /dɪ'lektəbl/ *adj* (*formal*) delicious; pleasant: *a delectable meal.*

del·ega·cy /'delɪgəsɪ/ *nc* (*pl* **-ies**) **1** an act, process, of delegating. **2** a group of delegates.

del·egate¹ /'delɪgət/ *nc* a person given a responsibility (esp a representative sent to a meeting).

del·egate² /'delɪgeɪt/ *vt* **1** to appoint and send (a person) as a representative to a meeting: *delegating her to attend the conference.* **2** to give (rights, duties) (to a person) for a period: *delegate rights to a deputy.*

del·ega·tion /,delɪ'geɪʃn/ *n* (**a**) *nu* the act of delegating or being delegated. (**b**) *nc* a group or team of delegates.

de·lete /dɪ'li:t/ *vt* to take out (something written or printed): *Several words had been deleted by the teacher.*

de·le·tion /dɪ'li:ʃn/ *nc,nu*

de·lib·er·ate¹ /dɪ'lɪbərət/ *adj* **1** intentional and not by chance: *a deliberate lie/insult.* **2** (*formal*) slow and cautious (in action, speech etc): *He entered the room with deliberate steps.*

de·lib·er·ate·ly *adv*: *deliberately rude.*

de·lib·er·ate² /dɪ'lɪbəreɪt/ *vt,vi* (*formal*) to think about, talk about, (something) carefully: *I've been deliberating whether to buy a new car.*

de·lib·er·ation /dɪ,lɪbə'reɪʃn/ *nc,nu* careful consideration and discussion: *After (a) long deliberation, they decided to accept the offer.*

deli·ca·cy /'delɪkəsɪ/ *n* (*pl* **-ies**) **1** *nu* the quality of being delicate (all senses): *The political situation is one of great delicacy* (= requires very careful handling). **2** *nc* a delicate(2) kind of food: *all the delicacies of the season.*

deli·cate /ˈdelɪkət/ *adj* **1** soft; tender: *the delicate skin of a baby.* **2** fine: *jewellery of delicate workmanship.* **3** (of food, its flavour) pleasing to the taste and not strongly flavoured: *Some kinds of fish have a more delicate flavour than others.* **4** easily damaged; becoming ill easily: *delicate china/plants; a delicate-looking child.* **5** needing careful treatment or handling: *a delicate surgical operation.* **6** (of colours) soft; not strong: *a delicate shade of pink.* **7** (of the senses, of instruments) able to appreciate or show very small changes or differences: *the delicate instruments needed by medical scientists.*
deli·cate·ly *adv*

deli·ca·tes·sen /ˌdelɪkəˈtesn/ *nc* a shop selling prepared foods (e.g. cooked meat, smoked fish, pickles).

de·li·cious /dɪˈlɪʃəs/ *adj* giving delight to the senses of taste and smell: *a delicious cake.*
de·li·cious·ly *adv*

de·light¹ /dɪˈlaɪt/ *n* **1** *nu* great pleasure: *To his great delight he passed the examination.* **take delight in (doing) sth** to find pleasure in (doing) it: *The cruel boy took great delight in pulling the cat's tail.* ⇨ **delight²(3). 2** *nc* a cause, source, of great pleasure: *Dancing is her chief delight.*

de·light·ful /-fəl/ *adj* giving pleasure: *a delightful holiday/painting/meal/performance.*
de·light·ful·ly /-fəlɪ/ *adv*

de·light² /dɪˈlaɪt/ *v* **1** *vt* to give great pleasure to (a person); please (a person) greatly: *Her singing delighted everyone.* **2** *vt* (*passive*) **be delighted** to be greatly pleased: *I was delighted to hear the news of your success/delighted at the news/ delighted that you were successful.* **3** *vi* **delight in (doing) sth** to take or find great pleasure in (doing) it: *He delights in teasing his young sister.*

de·lin·quen·cy /dɪˈlɪŋkwənsɪ/ *nc,nu* (*pl* **-ies**) (an instance of) behaving badly: *the serious problem of juvenile delinquency.*

de·lin·quent /dɪˈlɪŋkwənt/ *nc, adj* (*derog*) (a person) doing wrong, behaving badly.

de·liri·ous /dɪˈlɪrɪəs/ *adj* **1** suffering from delirium. **2** (*fig*) wildly excited: *We were delirious with joy.*
de·liri·ous·ly *adv: deliriously happy.*

de·lir·ium /dɪˈlɪrɪəm/ *nu* **1** a violent mental disturbance, often accompanied by uncontrolled movement and talk, esp during feverish illness. **2** (*fig*) wild excitement.

de·liv·er /dɪˈlɪvə(r)/ *vt* **1** to take (letters, parcels, goods etc) to houses, to the person(s) to whom they are addressed, to the buyer(s): *Did you deliver my message?* **2** to give (a speech): *to deliver a sermon/a course of lectures.* **3** (of a doctor, midwife etc) to help a woman in the birth of (a baby). **4** **deliver sb/sth (over/up)** to give, hand over, a person, thing: *to deliver up stolen goods/a prisoner; to deliver over the keys to the new house.* **5** **deliver sb from sth** (*formal*) to rescue, save, set free, a person: *I hope your conscience will deliver you from temptation.*
de·liv·er·ance /dɪˈlɪvərəns/ *nu*

de·liv·ery /dɪˈlɪvərɪ/ *n* (*pl* **-ies**) **1** *nu* the act of delivering letters, goods etc: *We guarantee prompt delivery.* **2** *nc* a particular act of delivering; the articles taken: *How many postal deliveries are there in your town every day?* **3** *nu* a style of speaking in lectures etc: *His delivery was good but his delivery was poor.*

dell /del/ *nc* a small valley, usually with trees.

del·ta /ˈdeltə/ *nc* (*pl* **-s**) **1** the Greek letter D (Δ). **2** land in this shape at the place where some rivers meet the sea and separate to make two or more branches: *the Nile delta.*
'delta wing *nc* (also *attrib*) an aircraft wing of this shape (Δ).

de·lude /dɪˈluːd/ *vt* to deceive or mislead (a person) (on purpose): *deluding oneself with false hopes. I deluded him/myself into believing that it was possible.*

del·uge¹ /ˈdeljuːdʒ/ *nc* **1** a large amount of water; violent rainfall. **2** (*fig*) anything coming in a large rush: *a deluge of words/questions/protests.*

del·uge² /ˈdeljuːdʒ/ *vt* to produce a large amount of (something) in a great rush: *He was deluged with questions.*

de·lu·sion /dɪˈluːʒn/ *n* **1** *nu* the act, state, of deluding or being deluded. **2** *nc* a false opinion or belief, esp one that may be a symptom of madness: *to be under a/the delusion that everyone is an enemy; to suffer from delusions.*
de·lus·ive /dɪˈluːsɪv/ *adj*
de·lus·ive·ly *adv*

de luxe /dɪˈlʌks/ *adj* (*attrib*) (*Fr*) of very high quality, standard of comfort etc: *a de luxe edition of a book; a de luxe meal/hotel.*

delve /delv/ *vi* **delve (among/into sth)** to search; investigate: *delving into his past/among her photos.*

dema·gogue /ˈdeməgɒg/ *nc* a political leader who tries to gain support by speeches appealing to the feelings instead of to reason.

de·mand¹ /dɪˈmaːnd/ *n* **1** *nc* an act of demanding(1); something that is demanded(1): *The workers' demands* (e.g. for higher pay) *were refused by the employers.* **on demand** when asked for: *a cheque payable on demand.* **make demands (on sth)** to use up (supplies): *Children make great demands on one's income/time.* **2** *nu* (or **a(n)** + *adj* + **demand**) the desire to buy, get etc: *There is a great demand for typists but a poor demand/not much demand for clerks.* **in demand** popular: *Our goods are in great demand.*

de·mand² /dɪˈmaːnd/ *vt* **1** to ask for (something) as if ordering or as if one has a right to: *I demand an apology from her.* **2** (*formal*) to need or require (something): *This sort of work demands great patience.*

de·mar·cate /ˈdiːmaːkeɪt/ *vt* to fix, mark, the limits of (e.g. a frontier).
de·mar·ca·tion /ˌdiːmaːˈkeɪʃn/ *nu*

de·mean /dɪˈmiːn/ *vt* (usually *reflex*) (*formal*) to lower (oneself, also a person) in dignity, reputation.
de·mean·ing *adj: demeaning behaviour.*

de·mean·our (*US* = **-or**) /dɪˈmiːnə(r)/ *nu* (*formal*) a way of behaving: *I don't like his pompous demeanour.*

de·ment·ed /dɪˈmentɪd/ *adj* mad: *be demented*

with grief.

deme·rara /ˌdeməˈreərə/ nu (also *demerara sugar*) a kind of light brown sugar.

de·mili·tar·ized (also **-ised**) /ˌdiːˈmɪlɪtəraɪzd/ adj (of a country or part of it) required by treaty or agreement to have no military forces or equipment in it: *a demilitarized zone.*

de·mise /dɪˈmaɪz/ nu (*legal*) death.

de·mist /ˌdiːˈmɪst/ vt to remove the mist from (e.g. a windscreen).

demo /ˈdeməʊ/ abbr (*informal*) = demonstration(2).

de·mo·bil·ize (also **-ise**) /dɪˈməʊbəlaɪz/ vt (*mil*) to release (a soldier) from military service.
   de·mo·bil·iz·ation (also **-is·ation**) /dɪˌməʊbəlaɪˈzeɪʃn/ nu

democ·ra·cy /dɪˈmɒkrəsɪ/ nc,nu (*pl*-ies) (a country with a) government in which adult citizens freely elect their political representatives to manage public affairs.

demo·crat /ˈdeməkræt/ nc **1** a person who favours or supports democracy. **2** (D-) (*US*) a member of the Democratic Party.

demo·crat·ic /ˌdeməˈkrætɪk/ adj **1** of, like, supporting, democracy(1): *a democratic form of government.* **2** supporting, based on, equal opportunities and rights for all: *take a democratic decision; a democratic head of department.* Opp undemocratic.
   Demo·cratic Party n (the —) (*US*) one of the two main political parties. ⇨ Republican.
   demo·crati·cal·ly /-klɪ/ adv

de·mol·ish /dɪˈmɒlɪʃ/ vt **1** to pull down (e.g. old buildings). **2** (*fig*) to destroy (e.g. an argument).
   demo·li·tion /ˌdeməˈlɪʃn/ nc,nu

de·mon /ˈdiːmən/ nc **1** (in stories) an evil, wicked or cruel supernatural being or spirit. **2** (*informal; derog*) a naughty and energetic child: *You little demon!*

de·mon·strable /dɪˈmɒnstrəbl/ adj (*formal*) that can be logically proved.
   de·mon·strably /-əblɪ/ adv

dem·on·strate /ˈdemənstreɪt/ v **1** vt to show (something) clearly by giving facts, examples etc: *How would you demonstrate that the world is round?* **2** vi **demonstrate (about/against/ for sth)** to take part in a demonstration(2): *The workers marched through the streets to demonstrate against the rising cost of living.*

dem·on·stra·tion /ˌdemənˈstreɪʃn/ nc,nu **1** an act of showing clearly the facts, how something works etc: *a demonstration of a new car.* **2** a public display of feeling or opinion, e.g. by marching, by a group, e.g. of workers, students: *a demonstration against nuclear weapons/for jobs.*

de·mon·stra·tive /dɪˈmɒnstrətɪv/ adj (of a person) (capable of) showing feelings: *Some children are more demonstrative than others.* Opp undemonstrative.

de,monstrative 'adjective nc (*gram*) one used to show or explain who or which (i.e. *this, that, these, those*), as in '*This* record is better than *that* one'.

de,monstrative 'pronoun nc (*gram*) one used to show or explain who or which (i.e. *this, that, these, those*), as in '*These* are better than *those*'.
   de·mon·stra·tive·ly adv

dem·on·stra·tor /ˈdemənstreɪtə(r)/ nc **1** a person who demonstrates(2): *There were thousands of demonstrators in Trafalgar Square.* **2** a person who teaches or explains by demonstrating(1).

de·moral·ize (also **-ise**) /dɪˈmɒrəlaɪz/ vt to weaken the courage, confidence, self-discipline etc of (e.g. an army).

de·mote /ˌdiːˈməʊt/ vt to reduce (a person) to a lower rank or grade.
   de·mo·tion /ˌdiːˈməʊʃn/ nu

de·mure /dɪˈmjʊə(r)/ adj (*formal*) (esp of a woman) quiet and serious: *a demure dancer.*
   de·mure·ly adv

den /den/ nc **1** an animal's hidden lying-place. **2** (*fig*) a secret place: *a den of thieves.* **3** (*informal*) a room in which a person studies.

de·nation·al·ize (also **-ise**) /ˌdiːˈnæʃənəlaɪz/ vt to transfer (a nationalized industry etc) to private ownership again. ⇨ privatize.
   de·nation·al·iz·ation (also **-is·ation**) /ˌdiːˌnæʃənəlaɪˈzeɪʃn/ nu

de·ni·able /dɪˈnaɪəbl/ adj that can be denied. Opp undeniable.

de·ni·al /dɪˈnaɪəl/ n **1** nc,nu (an instance of) denying; refusing a request: *the denial of justice/ of a request for help.* **2** nc a statement that something is not true: *She made repeated denials of being involved in the robbery.*

den·im /ˈdenɪm/ n **1** nu (usually pale blue) strong cotton cloth (used for jeans, overalls etc). **2** (*pl; informal*) jeans made from denim.

de·nomi·na·tion /dɪˌnɒmɪˈneɪʃn/ nc **1** a religious group or sect: *The Protestant denominations include the Methodists, Presbyterians and Baptists.* **2** a unit (in weight, length, numbers, money etc): *The US coin of the lowest denomination is the cent.*

de·nomi·na·tion·al /-ʃənl/ adj of religious groups: *inter-denominational meetings* (= of several groups together).

de·nomi·na·tor /dɪˈnɒmɪneɪtə(r)/ nc (*maths*) a number or quantity below the line in a fraction, e.g. 4 in $\frac{3}{4}$.

de·note /dɪˈnəʊt/ vt (*formal*) **1** to be the sign, name or symbol of (something): *In algebra 'x' usually denotes an unknown quantity.* **2** to indicate (something): *His silence denoted his objection to the policy.*

de·noue·ment /deɪˈnuːmɒn/ nc (*Fr*) (*literature*) the final solution, explanation, result etc of a plot in a story or play.

de·nounce /dɪˈnaʊns/ vt to speak publicly against (a person): *denouncing her as a spy.* ⇨ denunciation.

dense /dens/ adj (—r, —st) **1** (of liquids, vapour) not easily seen through: *a dense fog; dense smoke.* **2** (of people and things) crowded together in great numbers: *a dense crowd/forest.* **3** (*fig; derog*) (of a person) stupid.
   dense·ly adv: *a densely populated country.*
   dense·ness nu

den·si·ty /ˈdensətɪ/ n (*pl*-ies) **1** nu the quality of being dense: *the density of a forest/the population.* **2** nc,nu (*physics*) the relation of mass to volume.

dent[1] /dent/ nc **1** a hollow place in a hard surface as made by a blow or by pressure. **2** (*fig*) (*informal*) a bad effect: *a dent in one's income/pride.*

dent[2] /dent/ vt,vi (to cause something) to get a dent: *a car badly dented in a collision.*

den·tal /'dentl/ adj (attrib) of or for the teeth: a dental surgeon.

,dental 'floss nu threads of silk, etc used to clean between teeth.

,dental 'surgeon nc (formal) a dentist.

den·tist /'dentist/ nc a person whose work is filling, cleaning and taking out teeth, and fitting artificial teeth.

den·tist·ry nu the work of a dentist.

den·tures /'dentʃəz/ n pl artificial teeth.

de·nude /dɪ'njuːd/ vt to make (land etc) bare; remove a covering from (something): fields denuded by erosion.

de·nun·ci·ation /dɪ,nʌnsɪ'eɪʃn/ nc,nu (an act of) denouncing: the denunciation of a traitor.

de·ny /dɪ'naɪ/ vt (pt,pp **-ied**) **1** to say that (something) is not true: The accused man denied the charge. It cannot be denied that/There is no denying the fact that she's clever. **2** (legal) to refuse (responsibility for something): He denied liability for the accident. **3** to refuse to give something asked for or needed by (a person): He denies himself/his wife nothing. ⇨ deniable, denial.

de·odor·ant /,diː'əʊdərənt/ nc a substance that disguises or absorbs (esp body) smells.

dep. abbr departs.

de·part /dɪ'pɑːt/ vi **depart (from sth) 1** to go away (from a place); leave: The train departs (from Euston) at 3.30 p.m. **2** (formal) to behave in a way that differs from something: depart from routine/the truth.

de·part·ed n (the —) **(a)** n sing a person who has recently died. **(b)** n pl all those who have died: pray for the souls of the departed.

de·part·ment /dɪ'pɑːtmənt/ nc (often D-) (abbr Dept) one of several divisions of a government, business, shop, university etc: the Education Department/Department of Education.

de'partment store nc a large shop where many kinds of goods are sold in different departments.

de·part·ment·al /,diːpɑːt'mentl/ adj of a department (contrasted with the whole): departmental duties/administration.

de·par·ture /dɪ'pɑːtʃə(r)/ nc,nu (formal) **1** (an instance of) departing; going away: There are notices showing arrivals and departures of trains over there. **2** (an act of) changing in method etc: a departure from old custom; a new departure in medical science.

de·pend /dɪ'pend/ vi **depend (on sb/sth) 1** to need; rely (on the support etc of a person, thing) in order to exist, to be true or to succeed: Children depend on their parents for food and clothing. (N) Not often used in the continuous tenses, e.g. is/was -ing. **That/It (all) depends** (used to show that one is not sure about something): 'Will you come?'—'That depends—will Sue be there?' **2** to trust (a person); be certain about (something): You can always depend on John to be there when he is needed.

de·pend·able /-əbl/ adj

de·pend·ant (also, esp US, **-ent**) /dɪ'pendənt/ nc a person who depends on another or others for a home, food etc. Compare dependent¹.

de·pend·ence /dɪ'pendəns/ nu **dependence (on sb/sth) 1** the state of being supported by others: Why don't you find a job and stop this dependence on your parents? **2** confident trust:

He's not a man you can put much dependence on. **3** the uncontrollable state of needing something: a dependence on drugs.

de·pend·en·cy /dɪ'pendənsɪ/ nc,nu (pl **-ies**)

de·pend·ent¹ /dɪ'pendənt/ adj **dependent (on sth) 1** relying (on a person etc) for support: I'm dependent on my parents. **2** decided according to (facts, a person's decision etc): Promotion is dependent on your record of success. Compare independent.

de,pendent 'clause nc (gram) = subordinate clause.

dep·end·ent² /dɪ'pendənt/ nc (esp US) = dependant.

de·pict /dɪ'pɪkt/ vt **1** to describe (a person, thing) in the form of a picture: Many Mediterranean scenes are depicted in these photographs. **2** (formal) to describe (something): the exciting holiday depicted in her letters.

de·pic·tion /dɪ'pɪkʃn/ nu

de·plete /dɪ'pliːt/ vt to use up, empty, (supplies etc) until little or none remains: depleting a lake of fish; depleted supplies.

de·ple·tion /dɪ'pliːʃn/ nu

de·plore /dɪ'plɔː(r)/ vt to express great disapproval of, show one is very sorry about, (something): deploring violence.

de·plor·able /dɪ'plɔːrəbl/ adj (derog) that is, or should be, deplored: deplorable behaviour.

de·plor·ably /-əblɪ/ adv

de·ploy /dɪ'plɔɪ/ vt (mil) to cause (soldiers, military equipment) to get into position, go into battle etc.

de·popu·late /,diː'pɒpjʊleɪt/ vt to reduce the number of people living in (a place): a country depopulated by famine.

de·popu·la·tion /,diː,pɒpjʊ'leɪʃn/ nu

de·port /dɪ'pɔːt/ vt to send away (an unwanted person) from a country: The spy was imprisoned for two years and then deported.

de·port·ation /,diːpɔː'teɪʃn/ nc,nu

de·port·ment /dɪ'pɔːtmənt/ nu (esp) the position of the body when standing and walking.

de·pose /dɪ'pəʊz/ vt to remove (a ruler) from a position of authority.

de·pos·it¹ /dɪ'pɒzɪt/ nc **1** an amount of money that is deposited(2,3): The shopkeeper promised to keep the goods for me if I left/paid/made a deposit. **2** a substance that is deposited(1): A thick deposit of mud covered the fields. **3** a layer of metal, coal or other minerals underground: Valuable deposits of tin have been found in Bolivia.

de'posit account nc money in a bank that cannot normally be taken out without notice and on which interest is payable.

de·pos·it² /dɪ'pɒzɪt/ vt **1** to put (something) down (in or on a place): Some insects deposit their eggs in the ground. When the Nile floods, it deposits a layer of mud on the land. **2** to put (money, something of value) (in a place or store) for safe keeping: to deposit money in a bank/ papers with one's lawyer. **3** to make payment (of part of some money) that is or will be owed: We had to deposit 10% of the price of the house.

de·posi·tor /dɪ'pɒzɪtə(r)/ nc a person who deposits(2,3), eg money in a bank.

de·pot /'depəʊ/ nc **1** a storehouse or warehouse.

2 (*US*) a railway or bus station.

de·praved /dɪ'preɪvd/ *adj* (*derog*) morally bad; corrupt: *depraved people who sell drugs.*

de·prav·ity /dɪ'prævətɪ/ *nc,nu* (*pl* **-ies**)

de·pre·ci·ate /dɪ'priː.ʃɪeɪt/ *vi* to become lower in value: *Shares in this company have depreciated over the past few years.* Opp appreciate(3).

   de·preci·ation /dɪ,priː.ʃɪ'eɪʃn/ *nu*

de·press /dɪ'pres/ *vt* **1** to cause (a person) to be very sad: *The newspapers are full of depressing news such as of war, crime, disasters.* **2** to cause (something) to be less active: *When business is depressed there is an increase in unemployment.* **3** (*formal*) to press, push or pull (something) down: *to depress a lever/the keys of a piano.*

   de,pressed 'area *nc* a part of a country where industry is reduced (causing poverty and unemployment).

de·pres·sion /dɪ'preʃn/ *n* **1** *nu* the state of being depressed(1): *He committed suicide during a fit of depression.* **2** *nc* a hollow place in the surface of something, esp the ground: *It rained heavily and every depression in the road was soon filled with water.* **3** *nc* a period or time when business is depressed(2). **4** *nc* (*tech*) a lowering of, area of, atmospheric pressure; the system of winds round it: *a depression over Iceland.*

depri·va·tion /,deprɪ'veɪʃn/ *n* **1** *nu* the state of being deprived: *deprivation of one's rights as a citizen.* **2** *nc* something of which one is deprived: *social deprivations in poor countries.*

de·prive /dɪ'praɪv/ *vt* **deprive sb/sth (of sth)** to take something away from a person, country etc; prevent a person, building, place etc from having, using or enjoying something: *trees that deprive a house of light.*

   de·prived *adj* (of a person) without (enough) food, money etc: *deprived children.*

Dept *written abbr* Department.

depth /depθ/ *n* **1** *nc,nu* the state of being deep; distance from the top down, from the front to the back, from the surface inwards: *Water was found at a depth of 10 metres. The snow is one metre in depth.* **be/go out of one's depth** (**a**) to be/go in water too deep to stand in: *If you can't swim, don't go out of your depth.* (**b**) (*fig*) to become involved in something too difficult to understand, do: *When people start talking about computers I'm out of my depth.* **2** *nc* a deep level (of thought, feeling etc): *She showed a depth of feeling that surprised us.* **3** (*pl;* the —**s**) the deepest or most central parts: *in the depths of winter; in the depths of despair.*

depu·ta·tion /,depjʊ'teɪʃn/ *nc* a group of people with the right to act or speak for others.

depu·tize (also **-ise**) /'depjʊtaɪz/ *vi* **deputize (for sb)** to act as deputy: *Can you deputize for me?*

depu·ty /'depjʊtɪ/ *nc* (*pl* **-ies**) a person who is (to be) given another person's authority etc: *I must find someone to act as a deputy for me during my absence.*

de·rail /dɪ'reɪl/ *vt* to cause (a train etc) to run off the rails: *The engine was derailed.*

   de·rail·ment *nc,nu*

de·range /dɪ'reɪndʒ/ *vt* (*usu passive*) to make (a person) mad (because of worry, grief etc): *She was deranged by his death.*

der·el·ict /'derəlɪkt/ *adj* abandoned and left to fall into ruin: *a derelict house.*

de·ride /dɪ'raɪd/ *vt* (*formal*) to laugh at (a person, behaviour etc) and show contempt: *They derided his efforts as childish.*

de·ri·sion /dɪ'rɪʒn/ *nc,nu* (an instance of) laughing at a person, treating an effort etc as valueless.

de·ris·ive /dɪ'raɪsɪv/ (also **de·ris·ory** /dɪ'raɪsərɪ/) *adj* showing or deserving derision: *a derisive offer* (e.g. £50 for a bike that is worth £100).

deri·va·tion /,derɪ'veɪʃn/ *n* **1** *nu* an origin: *a word of Latin derivation.* **2** *nc* a statement of how a word was formed and how it has changed: *to study the derivations of words.*

de·riva·tive /dɪ'rɪvətɪv/ *adj, nc* (something, esp a word) derived from another: *The word 'assertion' is a derivative of 'assert'.*

de·rive /dɪ'raɪv/ *vt* **derive sth from sth 1** (*formal*) to get a feeling etc because of something: *deriving great pleasure from her latest novel.* **2** to have something as a source or origin: *Thousands of English words are derived from/derive from Latin.*

der·ma·ti·tis /,dɜːmə'taɪtɪs/ *nu* a diseased condition of the skin with redness and pain.

der·ma·tol·ogist /,dɜːmə'tɒlədʒɪst/ *nc* an expert in skin diseases.

der·ma·tol·ogy /,dɜːmə'tɒlədʒɪ/ *nu* the medical study of the skin and its diseases.

de·roga·tory /dɪ'rɒgətrɪ/ *adj* (of speech, words etc) showing bad behaviour, a bad quality etc or one's low opinion; damaging a good reputation: *derogatory statements about her character.*

der·rick /'derɪk/ *nc* **1** a large crane used for moving or lifting heavy weights, esp on a ship. **2** a framework over an oil well to hold the drill.

DES /,diː iː 'es/ *abbr* (the —) (*GB*) the Department of Education and Science.

de·scend /dɪ'send/ *vi,vt* **1** (*formal*) to come or go down (something): *descend a mountain. On turning the corner, we saw that the path descended steeply.* **2** (of property, qualities, rights) to pass (from parent to child) by inheritance.

   be descended from sb/sth to have as earlier members of one's family or species: *All animals are descended from simple organisms.*

   descend on sb/sth (**a**) to attack a person, army, place etc suddenly: *The enemy descended on the soldiers' camp.* (**b**) (*informal*) to arrive suddenly in a group: *All our friends descended on us during the summer.*

   descend to sth to act in the vulgar or mean way mentioned: *She would never descend to cheating/lying/being rude.*

   descend upon sb/sth (*formal*) = descend on sb/sth.

de·scend·ant /dɪ'sendənt/ *nc* a person or animal that is descended from another one (that is mentioned): *a descendant of William Shakespeare; an old woman with all her descendants.*

de·scent /dɪ'sent/ *n* **1** *nc,nu* (an act of) coming or going down: *The descent of the mountain took two hours.* **2** *nu* ancestry: *of French descent.* **3** *nc* **descent on sb/sth** a sudden attack on a person, army, place etc: *The Danes made many descents on the English during the 10th Century.*

de·scribe /dɪ'skraɪb/ *vt* **1** to say what (a person or thing) is like: *Words cannot describe the beauty of the scene.* **2 describe sb/sth as sb/sth** to say that a person, thing has the qualities mentioned: *He describes himself as a doctor.* **3** (*tech*) to mark out, draw, (esp a geometrical figure): *describing a circle with a pair of compasses.*

de·scrip·tion /dɪˈskrɪpʃn/ *n* **1** *nc,nu* (an act of) describing(1,2): *Her beauty is beyond description* (= is too great to be expressed in words). *Can you give me a description of the thief?* **2** *nc* (*informal*) a kind or type: *The harbour was crowded with boats of every description.*

de·scrip·tive /dɪˈskrɪptɪv/ *adj* containing description(1): *descriptive writing.*

des·ecrate /ˈdesɪkreɪt/ *vt* to use (a sacred thing or place) in an unworthy or wicked way.

des·ecra·tion /ˌdesɪˈkreɪʃn/ *nu*

des·ert[1] /ˈdezət/ *nc,nu* (also *attrib;* D- in names) (a large area of) land that is without water and trees, often sand-covered: *the Sahara Desert; the desert areas of southern Africa.*

ˌdesert ˈisland *nc* an island without people.

de·sert[2] /dɪˈzɜːt/ *v* **1** *vt* to go away from (a place): *deserted farms.* **2** *vt* to leave (one's job, family etc) without arranging help or support: *He deserted his wife and children.* **3** *vt* (*fig*) (of strong feeling, courage etc) to suddenly be absent: *His courage deserted him.* **4** *vt,vi* to leave (esp service in the armed forces) without authority or permission: *The soldiers have deserted.*

de·sert·er *nc* a person who deserts(4).

de·ser·tion /dɪˈzɜːʃn/ *nc,nu*

de·serts /dɪˈzɜːts/ *n pl* that which a person deserves: *to be rewarded/punished according to one's deserts.*

de·serve /dɪˈzɜːv/ *vt* to be worthy of (something) (because of actions, conduct, qualities): *He deserves a medal.* Ⓝ Not used in the continuous tenses, e.g *is/was -ing.*

de·serv·ed·ly /dɪˈzɜːvɪdlɪ/ *adv* according to what is deserved; rightly: *to be deservedly punished.* Opp undeservedly.

de·serv·ing /dɪˈzɜːvɪŋ/ *adj* (*attrib*) having merit; suitably good: *to give money to a deserving cause.*

des·ic·ca·ted /ˈdesɪkeɪtɪd/ *adj* dried out: *desiccated coconut.*

de·sign[1] /dɪˈzaɪn/ *n* **1** *nc* a drawing or outline from which something may be made: *designs for a dress/garden.* **2** *nu* the art of making such drawings etc: *a school of design.* **3** *nu* the general arrangement or plan (of a picture, building, machine etc): *The building is poor in design.* **4** *nc* a pattern as ornament: *a vase with a design of flowers on it.* **5** *nc,nu* an intention; plan: *Was it by accident or by design that he arrived too late to help?* **have designs on sb/sth** to intend (selfishly or evilly) to get possession of a person, thing: *That man has designs on your money/your life/that girl.*

de·sign[2] /dɪˈzaɪn/ *v* **1** *vt,vi* to prepare a plan, sketch etc of (something to be made): *design a dress/garden. He designs for a large firm of carpet manufacturers.* **2** *vt* (usu *passive*) to intend, plan, (something): *This room was designed for the children.*

des·ig·nate[1] /ˈdezɪɡnɪt/ *adj* (placed after the noun) appointed to a position (but not yet installed): *the bishop designate.*

des·ig·nate[2] /ˈdezɪɡneɪt/ *vt* (*formal*) **1** to mark or point out (something) clearly: *to designate the*

boundaries. **2** **designate sb as sb** to appoint a person to a position: *He designated Mary Smith as his successor.*

des·ig·na·tion /ˌdezɪɡˈneɪʃn/ *nc,nu*

de·sign·er /dɪˈzaɪnə(r)/ *nc* a person who designs something, e.g. machinery, clothes, books.

de·sir·able /dɪˈzaɪərəbl/ *adj* wished for; worth having: *a desirable house.* Opp undesirable.

de·sire[1] /dɪˈzaɪə(r)/ *n* **1** *nc,nu* (an instance of) strong longing (for something): *He has no/not much desire for wealth.* **2** *nc* something that is wished for: *Her main desire is to go to university.*

de·sire[2] /dɪˈzaɪə(r)/ *vt* (*formal*) to want (something) strongly: *I hope you achieve all you desire.* Ⓝ Not used in the continuous tenses, e.g. *is/was -ing.*

de·sir·ous /dɪˈzaɪərəs/ *adj* **desirous of sth** (*formal*) wanting something seriously: *desirous of peace.*

de·sist /dɪˈzɪst/ *vi* **desist (from doing sth)** (*formal*) to stop: *I must ask you to desist from taking photographs.*

desk /desk/ *nc* a table with a flat or sloping top and drawers at which to read, write or do business, e.g. in an office.

deso·late[1] /ˈdesələt/ *adj* **1** (of a place) in a ruined, neglected state: *a desolate, wind-swept area.* **2** (*formal*) (of a person) lonely and sad: *a desolate child.*

deso·la·tion /ˌdesəˈleɪʃn/ *nu*

deso·late[2] /ˈdesəleɪt/ *vt* to make (an area) desolate(1).

des·pair[1] /dɪˈspeə(r)/ *nu* the state of having lost all hope: *He gave up in despair. He was filled with despair when he read the examination questions.*

des·pair[2] /dɪˈspeə(r)/ *vi* **despair (of sb/sth)** to lose all hope (of a person, thing): *to despair of success/of ever succeeding/of one's son.*

des·patch /dɪˈspætʃ/ *n,vt* = dispatch.

des·per·ate /ˈdespərət/ *adj* **1** (of a person) filled with despair and ready to do anything regardless of danger: *I stole the food because I was desperate. He's desperate for work. They are all desperate criminals.* **2** extremely serious: *The economic state of the country is desperate.*

des·per·ate·ly *adv*

des·per·ation /ˌdespəˈreɪʃn/ *nu* **in desperation** in a state of being desperate(1): *They fought in desperation to get free.*

des·pic·able /dɪˈspɪkəbl/ *adj* (*derog*) deserving to be despised: *despicable behaviour/crimes/ criminals.*

des·pic·ably /-əblɪ/ *adv*

des·pise /dɪˈspaɪz/ *vt* to feel contempt for (a person); consider (a person) to be worthless: *Strikebreakers are despised by their workmates.*

des·pite /dɪˈspaɪt/ *prep* regardless of: *Despite what she says, I think she'll agree.* Ⓝ 'In spite of' is also possible and is less formal.

de·spon·den·cy /dɪˈspɒndənsɪ/ *nu* (*formal*) a state of feeling no hope: *to fall into despondency.*

de·spon·dent /dɪˈspɒndənt/ *adj* having or showing loss of hope: *Don't become too despondent.*

de·spon·dent·ly *adv*

des·pot /ˈdespɒt/ *nc* (*derog*) a ruler with unlimited powers, esp one who uses these powers wrongly or cruelly.

des·pot·ic /dɪˈspɒtɪk/ *adj* (*derog*) of or like a despot.

des·sert /dɪˈzɜːt/ *nc* a course of fruit etc at the end of a meal.

des·'sert·spoon *nc* a medium-sized spoon.

des·'sert·spoon·ful /-fʊl/ *nc* as much as a dessertspoon can hold.

de·sta·bil·ize (also **-ise**) /ˌdiːˈsteɪbəlaɪz/ *vt* (esp *fig*) to cause (something) to become unstable: *They tried to destabilize the government.* Compare **stabilize**.

des·ti·na·tion /ˌdestɪˈneɪʃn/ *nc* a place to which a person, thing, is going or being sent.

des·tine /ˈdestɪn/ *vt* (usually *passive*) to decide (something) in advance (esp by fate): *They were destined never to meet again.*

des·ti·ny /ˈdestɪnɪ/ *n* (*pl* **-ies**) **1** *nu* the invisible power believed to control future events: *tricks played on human beings by destiny.* **2** *nc* something that happens to a person thought of as determined in advance by fate: *It was his destiny to become famous.*

des·ti·tute /ˈdestɪtjuːt/ *adj* without food, clothes and other things necessary for life: *destitute children.*

des·ti·tu·tion /ˌdestɪˈtjuːʃn/ *nu*

de·stroy /dɪˈstrɔɪ/ *vt* to break (something) to pieces; make (something) useless; put an end to (hopes, a career etc): *Don't destroy that box—it may be useful. All his plans/hopes were destroyed.*

de·stroy·er /dɪˈstrɔɪə(r)/ *nc* (*mil*) a small, fast warship used for protecting larger ships.

de·struc·tion /dɪˈstrʌkʃn/ *nu* the act of destroying or being destroyed: *the destruction of a town by an earthquake.*

de·struc·tive /dɪˈstrʌktɪv/ *adj* (*derog*) **1** causing destruction: *destructive weapons.* **2** fond of, in the habit of, destroying: *Are all small children destructive?*

de·tach /dɪˈtætʃ/ *vt* to unfasten and take (something) apart: *to detach a label from a parcel.*

de·tach·able /-əbl/ *adj* that can be separated: *a detachable lining in a coat.*

de·tach·ed /dɪˈtætʃt/ *adj* **1** (of the mind) not influenced by personal opinion or by others: *to take a detached view of an event.* **2** (of a house) not joined to another building on either side. ⇨ **semi-detached**.

de·tach·ment /dɪˈtætʃmənt/ *n* **1** *nu* the act of detaching or being detached. **2** *nu* the state of not being influenced by personal opinions: *consider the proposal with detachment.* **3** *nc* (*mil*) a group of soldiers, ships etc separated from a larger group (for a special duty).

de·tail /ˈdiːteɪl/ *nc,nu* a small, particular fact or item: *Please give me all the details. The composition of the picture is good but there is too much detail.*

de·tail·ed *adj* containing many details: *a detailed report/description.*

de·tain /dɪˈteɪn/ *vt* to prevent (a person) from leaving, travelling etc: *He told his wife that he had been detained in the office. The police have detained two suspects.*

de·tain·ee /ˌdiːteɪˈniː/ *nc* a person who is detained (esp by the police etc as a suspect).

de·tect /dɪˈtekt/ *vt* to find out (the existence or presence of something): *The dentist could detect no sign of decay in her teeth.* (N) Not used in the con-

tinuous tenses, e.g. *is/was -ing.*

de·tect·able /-əbl/ *adj* that can be detected.

de·tec·tion /dɪˈtekʃn/ *nu*: *He tried to escape detection by disguising himself as an old man.*

de·tec·tive /dɪˈtektɪv/ *nc* a police officer whose job is to investigate a crime.

de'tective story/novel *nc* one in which the main interest is crime and the process of solving it.

de·ten·tion /dɪˈtenʃn/ *nu* the act, state, of detaining or being detained, e.g. keeping a pupil in school after ordinary hours as a punishment.

de'tention centre *nc* (*GB*) an institution where young offenders are kept for a short period.

de·ter /dɪˈtɜː(r)/ *vt* (**-rr-**) **deter sb (from (doing) sth)** to discourage or prevent a person: *Failure did not deter him from trying the exam again.* ⇨ **deterrent**.

de·ter·gent /dɪˈtɜːdʒənt/ *nc,nu* a washing powder or liquid that removes dirt, esp used to wash clothes etc.

de·teri·or·ate /dɪˈtɪərɪəreɪt/ *vi* to become of less value or worse (in quality): *Health quickly deteriorates in a cold, damp house.*

de·teri·ora·tion /dɪˌtɪərɪəˈreɪʃn/ *nu*

de·ter·mi·na·tion /dɪˌtɜːmɪˈneɪʃn/ *nu* **1** a seriousness in wanting to do something successfully: *a determination to improve one's English.* **2** (*formal*) the act of deciding: *the determination of the amount of metal in ore.*

de·ter·mine /dɪˈtɜːmɪn/ *vt* **1** (*formal*) to decide or fix (something): *to determine a date for a meeting.* **2** to find out (something) precisely: *to determine the speed of light.* **3** (to cause a person) to make (a decision): *His future has not yet been determined but he may study medicine.*

de·ter·mined *adj* (of a person, action) showing a serious wish to do something successfully: *a determined student/expression. He's determined to win.*

de·ter·min·er /dɪˈtɜːmɪnə(r)/ *nc* (*gram*) a word (e.g. *a/an, all, my, her, the, this, those, all, both* and numbers) used before a noun or noun phrase to show what or who it refers to. (N) Determiners cannot usually be used together. When they can, the first is called a *'predeterminer'*, such as *'half'* in *'half an hour'* or *'both'* in *'both his legs'.* Marked *'det'* in this dictionary.

de·ter·rent /dɪˈterənt/ *nc* something tending to or intended to discourage or prevent something: *Do you believe that the hydrogen bomb is a deterrent?* (i.e. that it will discourage countries from making war?).

de·test /dɪˈtest/ *vt* to hate (a person, thing) strongly: *I detest smoking.* (N) Not used in the continuous tenses, e.g. *is/was -ing.*

de·test·able /-əbl/ *adj* hated very much.

de·throne /dɪˈθrəʊn/ *vt* to remove (a king or queen) from power.

de·throne·ment *nu*

det·on·ate /ˈdetəneɪt/ *vt,vi* (to cause a bomb etc) to explode with a loud noise: *detonating bombs.*

det·on·ation /ˌdetəˈneɪʃn/ *nc,nu*

det·on·ator /ˈdetəneɪtə(r)/ *nc* a part of a bomb or shell that causes it to explode.

de·tour /ˈdiːtʊə(r)/ *nc* a way round, e.g. a way used when the usual road is blocked: *to make a* *detour.*

de·tract /dɪ'trækt/ *vi* **detract (from sth)** to take away (from the credit, value etc of something).

det·ri·ment /'detrɪmənt/ *nu* (*formal*) damage; harm: *I know nothing to his detriment* (= nothing to harm his good reputation).

det·ri·men·tal /detrɪ'mentl/ *adj* (*formal*) harmful: *activities that are detrimental to our interests.*

det·ri·men·tal·ly /-təlɪ/ *adv*

deuce /djuːs/ *nc* **1** the two on playing-cards or dice. **2** (*tennis*) the score of 40 each after which either side must gain two successive points to win the set.

de·value /ˌdiː'væljuː/ *vt,vi* (to cause the value of a currency) to become less (esp in exchange for other currencies): *to devalue the dollar/pound.*

de·valu·ation /ˌdiːvæljʊ'eɪʃn/ *nc*

dev·as·tate /'devəsteɪt/ *vt* (often *passive*) to ruin (a place) completely: *towns devastated by fire/ floods/war.*

dev·as·ta·tion /ˌdevə'steɪʃn/ *nu*

de·vel·op /dɪ'veləp/ *v* **1** *vt,vi* **develop (sth) (from/into sb/sth)** (to cause oneself, a plant, egg, business etc) to grow larger, fuller or more mature: *Plants develop from seeds. We must develop the natural resources of our country. Amsterdam developed into one of the greatest ports in the world.* **2** *vt,vi* (to cause something not at first active or noticeable) to come into a state in which it is active or visible: *He developed a cough. The bad weather is developing into a storm.* **3** *vt* to treat (an exposed film or plate) with chemicals so that the photographed image can be seen. **4** *vt* to use (an area of land) for the building of houses, shops, factories etc and so increase its value.

de·vel·oper *nc* (**a**) a person, business, authority, that develops land etc: *a property developer.* (**b**) a chemical substance used to develop film.

de·vel·op·ment /dɪ'veləpmənt/ *n* **1** *nu* the act of developing or being developed (all senses): *He is engaged in the development of his business. The development of photographic films requires a dark-room.* **2** *nc* a new stage or event in a process: *The latest developments in medical research.*

de·vi·ate /'diːvieɪt/ *vi* **deviate (from sth)** (*formal*) to turn, move away, leave (what is usual, customary, right etc): *deviating from the truth/a rule/ one's usual practice.*

de·vi·ation /ˌdiːvi'eɪʃn/ *nc,nu*

de·vice /dɪ'vaɪs/ *nc* **1** something carefully designed and made for a particular purpose such as an instrument or small piece of technical equipment: *a useful device for banging nails into walls.* **2** a careful scheme; trick: *Leave a light on in the house as a device to make a thief think people are inside.*

dev·il /'devl/ *nc* **1** (the D-) the spirit of evil. **2** (*derog*) a cruel or mischievous person. **3** (*dated*) unfortunate person: *Oh, you poor devil!* ⇨ also dare-devil.

devil·ment /'devlmənt/ (also **dev·il·ry** /'devəlrɪ/) *nu* mischief.

de·vi·ous /'diːviəs/ *adj* **1** going round and not taking the direct way: *a devious route avoiding busy streets.* **2** (*derog; formal*) cunning, deceitful: *devious people/methods.*

de·vi·ous·ly *adv*

de·vi·ous·ness *nu*

de·vise /dɪ'vaɪz/ *vt* to think out, invent, (a plan etc): *devising a scheme for making money.*

de·void /dɪ'vɔɪd/ *adj* (*pred*) **devoid of sth** without, empty of, something: *devoid of shame/sense.*

de·vol·ution /ˌdiːvə'luːʃn/ *nu* the giving, delegating or decentralizing (of power or authority).

de·volve /dɪ'vɒlv/ *vi* **devolve on sb** (*formal*) (of work, duties) to be transferred or passed to a person: *When the President is ill, his duties devolve on the Vice-President.*

de·vote /dɪ'vəʊt/ *vt* **devote sth/oneself to sth** to give up one's time, energy etc to something: *to devote one's life to sport. He devoted himself to charitable work for refugees.*

de·vot·ed *adj* very loving or loyal: *a devoted friend.*

devo·tee /ˌdevə'tiː/ *nc* **devotee (of sth)** a person who is very interested in something: *a devotee of sport/music.*

de·vo·tion /dɪ'vəʊʃn/ *nu* **1** **devotion (for sb/ sth)** deep, strong love: *the devotion of a mother for her children.* **2** **devotion (to sth)** the act of devoting or being devoted: *devotion to duty.*

de·vour /dɪ'vaʊə(r)/ *vt* **1** to eat (food, a meal) hungrily or greedily: *The hungry boy devoured his dinner.* **2** (*fig*) to use up, destroy etc (something) completely: *The fire devoured twenty acres of forest.*

de·vout /dɪ'vaʊt/ *adj* **1** paying serious attention to religious duties: *a devout Catholic.* **2** (*attrib*) (of feelings, wishes etc) serious; sincere: *a devout supporter; devout wishes for your success.*

de·vout·ly *adv*

de·vout·ness *nu*

dew /djuː/ *nu* tiny drops of moisture produced on cool surfaces from water vapour in the air: *The grass was wet with dew.*

'dew·drop *nc* a small drop of dew.

dewy *adj* (**-ier, -iest**) wet with dew.

dex·ter·ity /ˌdek'sterətɪ/ *nu* (*formal*) skill in doing things using one's hands.

dex·ter·ous (also **dex·trous**) /'dekstrəs/ *adj* (*formal*) clever, skilful, with one's hands.

dex·ter·ous·ly *adv*

dia·betes /ˌdaɪə'biːtɪz/ *nu* a disease of the pancreas in which sugar and starchy foods cannot be properly absorbed.

dia·bet·ic /ˌdaɪə'betɪk/ *adj, nc* (a person) suffering from diabetes.

dia·bol·ic /ˌdaɪə'bɒlɪk/ (also **dia·boli·cal** /-kl/) *adj* (*fig; derog*) very cruel, bad or wicked.

dia·boli·cal·ly /-klɪ/ *adv*

diag. *abbr* diagram.

di·ag·nose /'daɪəgnəʊz/ *vt* to determine the nature of (a disease) from symptoms: *The doctor diagnosed the illness as measles.*

di·ag·no·sis /ˌdaɪəg'nəʊsɪs/ *n* (*pl* **-noses** /-'nəʊsiːz/) **1** *nu* the act of diagnosing a disease. **2** *nc* (a statement of) the result of diagnosing.

di·ag·nos·tic /ˌdaɪəg'nɒstɪk/ *adj*

di·ag·on·al /daɪ'ægənl/ *nc, adj* (*maths*) (a line) going across (a straight-sided figure, e.g. an oblong) from corner to corner; slanting: *a diagonal path/pattern.*

di·ag·on·al·ly /-əlɪ/ *adv*

dia·gram /'daɪəgræm/ *nc* a drawing, design or plan used to explain or illustrate something.

dia·gram·mat·ic /ˌdaɪəgrə'mætɪk/ adj
dia·gram·mati·cal·ly /-klɪ/ adv

di·al¹ /'daɪəl/ nc **1** the face (of a clock or watch). **2** the marked face of an instrument that is for measuring. **3** the marked part of a radio etc with names or numbers, used for tuning into broadcasting stations. **4** the part of a telephone, with numbers and/or letters, used to make a connection.

di·al² /'daɪəl/ vt,vi (-ll-) to use a telephone dial to call (a number): *I dialled 01-230 1212.*

'dialling tone nc the sound in a telephone showing that the caller can dial a number.

dia·lect /'daɪəlekt/ nc,nu a form of a language (grammar, vocabulary, pronunciation) used in a part of a country or by a class of people: *the Yorkshire dialect.*

dia·lec·tal /ˌdaɪə'lektl/ adj

dia·logue (US also **dia·log**) /'daɪəlog/ n **1** nu (writing in the form of) a conversation or talk: *Plays are written in dialogue.* **2** nc an exchange of views; official talk: *a dialogue between the Prime Minister and the President.*

di·aly·sis /daɪ'æləsɪs/ nu (med) the artificial process of removing waste products from the blood, e.g. when the kidneys are not working.

diam. abbr diameter.

di·am·eter /daɪ'æmɪtə(r)/ nc (a measurement of) a straight line drawn from side to side through the centre of a circle: *the diameter of a tree-trunk.*

dia·met·ri·cal·ly /ˌdaɪə'metrɪklɪ/ adv completely; entirely: *diametrically opposed views.*

dia·mond /'daɪəmənd/ nc (also attrib) **1** a brilliant precious stone, the hardest substance known: *a ring with a diamond in it; a diamond ring/necklace.* **2** (maths) a figure with four equal sides whose angles are not right angles. **3** (any of 13 playing-cards with) this figure in red: *the ten of diamonds.* Compare club¹(2), heart(4), spade(2). ⇨ suit¹(3).

,diamond 'jubilee nc a 60th anniversary, esp of the start of a king's or queen's reign.

,diamond 'wedding nc the 60th anniversary of a wedding.

dia·phragm /'daɪəfræm/ nc **1** (anat) the muscle between the chest and the abdomen. **2** any vibrating disc or plate in an instrument, e.g. a telephone, that produces sound-waves.

di·ar·rhoea (also **-rrhea**) /ˌdaɪə'rɪə/ nu (illness with) too frequent emptying of the bowels.

di·ary /'daɪərɪ/ nc (pl **-ies**) (a book used for) a daily record of events, appointments etc: *keep a diary.*

dia·tribe /'daɪətraɪb/ nc a strong verbal attack: *a diatribe against the unions.*

dice¹ /daɪs/ (also (now rare) **die**) nc (pl **—**) a small cube marked with spots to indicate numbers, used in games.

dice² /daɪs/ vt to cut (food) into cubes: *dicing carrots.*

di·cey /'daɪsɪ/ adj (informal) uncertain; risky: *The weather/situation is dicey.*

di·chot·omy /daɪ'kɒtəmɪ/ nc (pl **-ies**) (formal) a division into two (usually opposite) groups or mutually exclusive pairs: *the dichotomy between fact and fiction/of truth and falsehood.*

dic·tate /dɪk'teɪt/ v **1** vt,vi to say, read, aloud (words to be written down by another or others):

dictating a letter to a secretary. **2** vt to state (something) with the force of authority: *to dictate terms to a defeated enemy.* **3** vi (derog) to give orders in an unfriendly way: *I won't be dictated to.*

dic·ta·tion /dɪk'teɪʃn/ n **1** nu the act of dictating or being dictated to: *The pupils wrote at their teacher's dictation.* **2** nc a piece of writing that is (to be) dictated.

dic·ta·tor /ˌdɪk'teɪtə(r)/ nc (derog) a ruler who has absolute authority, esp one who has obtained such power by force.

dic·ta·tor·ial /ˌdɪktə'tɔːrɪəl/ adj (derog) **(a)** of or like a dictator: *dictatorial government.* **(b)** too fond of giving orders: *his dictatorial manner.*

dic·ta·tori·al·ly /-əlɪ/ adv

dic·ta·tor·ship nc,nu (a country with) government by a dictator.

dic·tion /'dɪkʃn/ nu a person's style or way of speaking.

dic·tion·ary /'dɪkʃənrɪ/ nc (pl **-ies**) a book explaining the words of a language arranged in alphabetical order. Compare thesaurus.

did /dɪd/ pt of do²,³.

di·dac·tic /dɪ'dæktɪk/ adj (formal) intended to teach: *didactic poetry.*

diddle /'dɪdl/ vt **diddle sb (out of sth)** (informal) to cheat a person: *I was diddled (out of my fee).*

didn't /'dɪdnt/ = did not. ⇨ do².

die¹ /daɪ/ nc (pl **—s**) (tech) a block of hard metal with a design in it, used for shaping coins, medals etc.

die² /daɪ/ vi (pt,pp **died**, pres p **dying**) **1** to come to the end of life: *Flowers soon die if they are left without water.* **2** (fig) to be lost; pass from human knowledge: *His fame will never die.*

die away to lose strength, become faint or weak until gone: *The breeze/noise died away.*

die back (of stems of plants) to die as far as the root.

die down **(a)** (of a fire) to burn with less heat. **(b)** (of excitement etc) to become less strong. **(c)** (of noise etc) to become less loud.

be dying for sth to have a very strong wish for something: *We're dying for a drink.*

die from sth to have something as a cause of death: *die from cancer.*

die of sth **(a)** = die from sth: *die of pneumonia.* **(b)** (fig) (informal) to be in an extreme state of something: *dying of boredom/curiosity.*

die off to die one by one: *The leaves of this plant are dying off.*

die out to become extinct; come to a complete end: *Many old customs are gradually dying out.*

die·sel /'diːzl/ nu (also attrib) a type of heavy fuel used in specially designed engines (diesel engines) in buses, trains, lorries etc.

di·et¹ /'daɪət/ nc **1** the sort of food usually eaten (by a person, community etc): *a balanced diet of vegetables.* **2** the sort of food (to be) eaten by a person in order to lose (or gain) weight: *The doctor put her on a diet.*

di·et² /'daɪət/ vi to eat sorts of food in order to lose weight: *Is he still dieting?*

dif·fer /'dɪfə(r)/ vi **differ (from sb/sth) 1** to be unlike: *They look like each other but differ widely in their interests. How does French differ from English?* **2** to disagree; have another opinion: *I'm* *sorry to differ from you about that.* **agree to differ** to give up the attempt to convince each other.

dif·fer·ence /'dɪfrəns/ *nc,nu* **1** (an example of) the state of being unlike: *the difference between summer and winter.* **2** an amount, degree, manner, in which things are unlike: *The difference between 7 and 18 is 11. I can't see much difference between/in them.* ⇨ similarity(2). **split the difference** (when deciding a price, cost etc) to agree by accepting a middle figure. **tell the difference** (usually *negative*) to identify, notice, what is different between two or more people or things: *They look so alike that I can't tell the difference between them.* **3** **make a/some/no/not much etc difference** to be of some/no etc importance: *It won't make much difference whether you go today or tomorrow.* **4** (usually *pl*) a small disagreement: *Let's settle/sink our differences and be friends again.*

dif·fer·ent /'dɪfrənt/ *adj* **1** **different (from sb/ sth)** not the same (as a person, thing): *She wears a different dress every time I see her. Life today is different from life long ago.* Ⓝ *'Different to' is now often heard.* US speakers say *'different than'.* ⇨ similar. **2** (*attrib*) separate: *I called three different times but he was out.* Compare same¹(1).

dif·fer·ent·ly *adv*

dif·fer·en·tial /ˌdɪfəˈrenʃl/ *nc* a difference (expressed in a percentage) between things, e.g. wages of skilled and unskilled workers in the same industry.

dif·fer·en·ti·ate /ˌdɪfəˈrenʃɪeɪt/ *vt,vi* **differentiate (between sb/sth); (sth from sth)** to treat (something) as different; show things to be different: *to differentiate varieties of plants; differentiating one variety from another. It's wrong to differentiate between pupils according to their family background.*

dif·fi·cult /'dɪfɪkəlt/ *adj* **1** requiring much effort, strength, skill or ability: *a difficult problem/ language. The sound is difficult to pronounce. It is a difficult sound to pronounce.* Opp easy(1). **2** (*derog*) (of a person) not willing to agree, not easily pleased: *He's a difficult man to get on with.* Opp easy(6).

dif·fi·cul·ty /'dɪfɪkəltɪ/ *n* (*pl* **-ies**) **1** *nu* the state or quality of being difficult: *Do you have any difficulty in understanding English?* **2** *nc* something hard to do or understand: *have a difficulty with the car in cold weather.* **in difficulty/difficulties** suffering difficulties: *to be in financial difficulties.*

dif·fi·dence /'dɪfɪdəns/ *nu* (*formal*) the state of not having confidence in oneself.

dif·fi·dent /'dɪfɪdənt/ *adj* (usually *pred*) not having, not showing, much belief in one's own abilities: *to be diffident about one's ability to do it.*

dif·fi·dent·ly *adv*

dif·fuse¹ /dɪ'fju:s/ *adj* (*formal*) **1** (*derog*) using too many words: *a diffuse writer/style.* **2** spread out; scattered: *diffuse light.*

dif·fuse·ly *adv*

dif·fuse·ness *nu*

dif·fuse² /dɪ'fju:z/ *vt,vi* (*formal*) (to cause something) to spread out in every direction: *diffusing knowledge/light/heat.*

dif·fu·sion /dɪ'fju:ʒn/ *nu*

dig¹ /dɪg/ *nc* **1** a small push or thrust: *Give her a dig in the ribs.* **a dig at sb** a critical remark

against a person: *That was a dig at me.* **2** a site being excavated by archaeologists.

dig² /dɪg/ *v* (*pt,pp* **dug** /dʌg/; **-gg-**) **1** *vt,vi* to use a tool, a machine, claws etc to break up and move (soil etc); make (a way) through, into etc by doing this; make (a hole etc) by digging: *It is difficult to dig the ground when it is frozen hard. They are digging a tunnel through the hill.* **2** *vt* (*sl*) to enjoy (something); understand (a person, what is being said etc): *I don't dig modern jazz.*

dig sth in (a) to put something into the ground by digging: *dig in manure.* (b) to push something in: *He dug in his fork.* **dig in one's heels** ⇨ heel¹(1).

dig into sth (*informal*) to begin to eat food, a meal. **dig sth into sth** to push, thrust, poke something into something: *to dig a fork into a potato.*

dig sb/sth out (of sth) (a) to get a person, thing, out by digging: *He was buried by the avalanche and had to be dug out.* (b) (*informal*) to get facts by searching: *to dig information out of books and reports.*

dig sth up (a) to break up land, soil etc by digging: *to dig up land for a new garden.* (b) to remove plants etc from the ground by digging: *We dug the tree up by the roots.* (c) to discover what has been buried or hidden by digging: *An old Greek statue was dug up here last month.* (d) (*fig*) to discover information by searching: *The newspapers love to dig up scandals.*

di·gest¹ /'daɪdʒest/ *nc* a short, condensed account: *a digest of the week's news.*

di·gest² /daɪ'dʒest/ *v* **1** *vt,vi* (to cause food) to be changed in the stomach and bowels into a form that can be used in the body: *Some foods digest/ are digested more easily than others.* **2** *vt* to take (information) into the mind, esp in an organized order: *Have you digested everything that is important in the book?*

di·gest·ible /-əbl/ *adj* that can be digested. Opp indigestible.

di·ges·tion /daɪ'dʒestʃn/ *nu* the process of digesting; a person's ability to digest food. ⇨ indigestion.

di·ges·tive /daɪ'dʒestɪv/ *adj* of digestion (of food).

di'gestive system *nc* (the —) the alimentary canal.

di·git /'dɪdʒɪt/ *nc* **1** any one of the ten Arabic numerals 0 to 9: *The number 57 306 contains five digits.* **2** a finger or toe.

digi·tal /'dɪdʒɪtl/ *adj* of, using, digits: *a digital watch* (i.e. with numbers only).

ˌdigital com'puter *nc* one using combinations of characters in a special form (language) that are represented by the digits 0 and 1. ⇨ analog computer.

digi·tize (also **-ise**) /'dɪdʒɪtaɪz/ *vt* (*computers*) to translate (information) into a form (called a *language*) that can be processed by a digital computer.

dig·ni·fied /'dɪgnɪfaɪd/ *adj* having or showing dignity: *a dignified apology.*

dig·ni·tary /ˌdɪgnɪtrɪ/ *nc* (*pl* **-ies**) a person holding a high office, e.g. in government.

dig·ni·ty /'dɪgnətɪ/ *n* (*pl* **-ies**) **1** *nu* the quality that earns or deserves respect: *A man's dignity*

depends on his character, not his wealth. **2** nc a
calm and serious manner or style: *He's afraid of
losing his dignity* (i.e. of being made to look foolish) *and won't speak a foreign language.*

di·gress /daɪ'gres/ vi **digress (from sth)** (formal) (esp in speaking or writing) to move away
(from the main subject).
  di·gres·sion /daɪ'greʃn/ nc

digs /dɪgz/ n pl (*GB informal*) lodgings.

dike (also **dyke**) /daɪk/ nc **1** a ditch (used for
carrying away water from land). **2** a long wall of
earth etc (used to keep back water and prevent
flooding).

dil·api·dated /dɪ'læpɪdeɪtɪd/ adj falling to
pieces; in a state of disrepair: *a dilapidated old
house.*
  dil·api·da·tion /dɪ,læpɪ'deɪʃn/ nu

di·late /daɪ'leɪt/ vt,vi (to cause something) to
become wider, larger, further open: *The pupils of
your eyes dilate when you enter a dark room.*
  di·la·tion /,daɪ'leɪʃn/ nu

dila·tory /'dɪlətrɪ/ adj (*derog*) slow in doing
things.

di·lem·ma /dɪ'lemə/ nc (pl **—s**) a situation in
which one has to choose between two things, two
courses of action etc.

dili·gence /'dɪlɪdʒəns/ nu steady effort; showing
of care and effort.

dili·gent /'dɪlɪdʒənt/ adj hard-working; showing
care and effort: *diligent workers.*
  dili·gent·ly adv

di·lute /daɪ'luːt/ vt to make (a liquid or colour)
weaker or thinner (by adding water or other
liquid): *diluting orange squash with water.*

dim¹ /dɪm/ adj (**—mer, —mest**) **1** not bright;
not (to be) seen clearly: *the dim outline of buildings on a dark night.* **2** (*fig*) not clear: *dim memor-
ies/recollections of my childhood.* **3** (of the eyes,
eyesight) not able to see clearly: *His eyesight is
getting dimmer.* **take a dim view of sb/sth** ⇨
view¹(4). **4** (*informal*) unintelligent.
  dim·ly adv in a dim manner: *a dimly lit room.*
  dim·ness nu

dim² /dɪm/ vt,vi (**-mm-**) (to cause something) to
become dim: *eyes dimmed by tears.*

dim. abbr dimensions.

dime /daɪm/ nc a coin of US and Canada worth
ten cents.

di·men·sion /dɪ'menʃn/ n **1** nc a measurement
of any sort (esp length, height and width): *What
are the dimensions of the room?* ⇨ also fourth
dimension. **2** (*pl*) extent: *the dimensions of the
problem.*
  di·men·sion·al /-ʃənl/ suffix: *two-/three-
dimensional* (= having two, three, dimensions).

dim·in·ish /dɪ'mɪnɪʃ/ vt,vi (to cause supplies) to
become less: *diminishing food supplies.*

dim·inu·tive¹ /dɪ'mɪnjutɪv/ adj **1** unusually
small. **2** (*gram*) (of a suffix) indicating smallness,
e.g. *-let* in *booklet.*

dim·inu·tive² /dɪ'mɪnjutɪv/ nc a word formed by
the use of a diminutive suffix, e.g. *booklet* (= a
small book).

dimple /'dɪmpl/ nc a small natural hollow in the
chin or cheek, e.g. when a person smiles.

din /dɪn/ nu or sing a loud, confused noise: *The
children were making so much din/such a din that
I couldn't study.*

DIN /dɪn/ abbr (*photography*) (used to indicate
film speed, using a method developed in West
Germany). ⇨ ASA.

dine /daɪn/ vi to eat dinner: *dining off roast beef.*
  dine out to eat outside one's home (e.g. at the
house of friends or at a restaurant).
  'dining-room nc a room (in a house, hotel) in
which meals are eaten.
  'dining-table nc a table used for eating.

di·ner /'daɪnə(r)/ nc **1** a person who dines. **2** (*US*)
a small restaurant.

ding-dong /,dɪŋ 'dɒŋ/ nc, adv (with) a sound of
bells.

din·ghy /'dɪŋgɪ/ nc (pl **-ies**) **1** a kind of small
open boat. **2** an inflatable rubber boat.

din·gy /'dɪndʒɪ/ adj (**-ier, -iest**) (*derog*) dirty-
looking; not fresh or pleasant: *a dingy room.*
  ding·ily /-əlɪ/ adv: *dingily lit/dressed.*
  dingi·ness nu

din·ing /'daɪnɪŋ/ ⇨ dine.

din·ner /'dɪnə(r)/ nc (also *attrib*) the main meal of
the day, whether eaten at midday or in the evening: *It's time for dinner/dinner-time. He ate too
much dinner. Shall we ask him to dinner? Shall we
give a dinner/a dinner-party for her? The dinner
was too small.* Ⓝ *'A'* and *'the'* are rarely used.
  'dinner-jacket nc a jacket worn by men in the
evening for formal occasions.
  'dinner-service/-set nc a set of plates, dishes
etc for dinner.

dino·saur /'daɪnəsɔː(r)/ nc one of many kinds of
large extinct reptile.

di·ocesan /daɪ'ɒsɪsn/ adj of a diocese.

dio·cese /'daɪəsɪs/ nc (pl **—s** /-sɪsɪz/) a bishop's
district of responsibility.

dip¹ /dɪp/ nc **1** an act of dipping. **2** (*informal*) a
quick bathe or swim: *to have/take/go for a dip.* **3** a
downward slope: *a dip in the road.*

dip² /dɪp/ v (**-pp-**) **1** vt to put, lower, (something)
into a liquid: *to dip one's pen into the ink.* **2** **dip
into sth** (*fig*): *to dip into a book* (= take a hurried look). **3** vi to go below a surface or level: *The
sun dipped below the horizon.* **4** vt to lower (a
beam of light etc): *to dip the headlights of a car.*

dip. abbr diploma.

Dip. Ed. /,dɪp 'ed/ abbr Diploma in Education.

diph·theria /dɪf'θɪərɪə/ nu a serious disease of
the throat causing difficulty in breathing.

diph·thong /'dɪfθɒŋ/ nc (*lang*) a union of two
vowel sounds or vowel letters, e.g. /aɪ/ as in *pipe*
/paɪp/.

di·plo·ma /dɪ'pləʊmə/ nc (pl **—s**) a written
paper showing one has completed or passed an
examination in a course of study: *a diploma in
architecture; an education diploma.*

di·plo·ma·cy /dɪ'pləʊməsɪ/ nu **1** the (skill of)
management of a country's affairs by ambassadors and ministers living overseas. **2** (the skill of)
dealing with people so that business is done
smoothly.

dip·lo·mat /'dɪpləmæt/ nc a person employed in
diplomacy for her or his country (e.g. an
ambassador).

dip·lo·mat·ic /,dɪplə'mætɪk/ adj **1** (*attrib*) of
diplomacy(1): *the diplomatic service.* **2** tactful;
showing diplomacy(2): *a diplomatic answer; to be
diplomatic in dealing with people.* Opp undiplo-
matic.

diplomatic im'munity *nu* official immunity from paying taxes, being arrested etc because one is a diplomat.

dip·lo·mati·cal·ly /-klɪ/ *adv*

Dir. *abbr* Director.

dire /daɪə(r)/ *adj* **1** dreadful; terrible: *dire news.* **2** extreme: *to be in dire need of help.*

di·rect¹ /dɪ'rekt/ *adj* (no *comp*) **1** (going) straight; not curved or crooked; not turned aside: *in a direct line.* **2** with nothing or no-one in between; in an unbroken line: *as a direct result of this decision. He's a direct descendant of the Duke of Kent.* **3** exact: *the direct opposite.* **4** straightforward; going straight to the point: *He has a direct way of speaking/doing things.* (N) *'Direct'* is usually pronounced /'daɪrekt/ in the following compounds.

direct 'action *nu* the use of strikes etc by workers to get their demands.

direct 'current *nc,nu* (an) electric current flowing in one direction.

direct 'evidence *nu* (esp) evidence from a witness.

direct 'object *nc* (*gram*) the noun or clause in a sentence to which the action of the verb is related, such as 'the money' in 'He took *the money*'.

direct 'speech *nu* (*gram*) the speaker's actual words. Compare indirect speech.

direct 'tax/tax'ation *nu* tax on actual earnings, not on articles bought etc.

di·rect·ness *nu*

di·rect² /dɪ'rekt/ *vt* **1** to tell, show, (a person) how to do something, how to get somewhere: *Can you direct me to the post office?* **2** to speak or write to (a person): *My remarks were not directed to all of you.* **3** to manage; control, (a business, performance etc): *Who is directing the traffic/the play?* ⇨ director. **4** to send (a letter, query etc) (to a person, office): *Please direct all complaints to the manager.* **5** to order (people): *The officer directed his men to advance slowly.* ⇨ directive.

di·rec·tion /dɪ'rekʃn/ *n* **1** *nc* a course taken by a moving person or thing; point towards which a person or thing looks or faces: *Tom went off in one direction and Harry in another (direction).* **have a good/poor sense of direction** to be able/unable to determine well one's position when there are no known or visible landmarks. **2** *nc* (often *pl*) a piece of information or instructions about what to do, where to go, how to do something etc: *Directions about putting the parts together are printed on the card.* **3** *nu* management; control; guidance: *He did the work under my direction.*

di·rec·tive /dɪ'rektɪv/ *nc* an order giving general or detailed instructions: *a directive to staff to arrive on time.*

di·rect·ly¹ /dɪ'rektlɪ/ *adv* **1** in a direct manner; exactly: *He was looking directly at us.* **2** (*formal*) at once: *I'll be there directly.*

di·rect·ly² /dɪ'rektlɪ/ *conj* (*informal*) as soon as: *I reported it directly I knew I'd made a mistake.*

di·rec·tor /dɪ'rektə(r)/ *nc* **1** a person who manages or controls (esp one of a group called *the Board of Directors*) the affairs of a business company. **2** a person who supervises and instructs actors and actresses, the lighting, camera crew etc in plays and films.

di·rec·tory /dɪ'rektərɪ/ *nc* (*pl* **-ies**) **1** (a book

with) a list of people, businesses etc in a district. **2** (also *telephone directory*) a list of people, businesses etc with their telephone numbers and addresses in alphabetical order.

dirge /dɜːdʒ/ *nc* a song sung at a burial or for a dead person.

dirt /dɜːt/ *nu* **1** unclean matter (e.g. dust, mud), esp when it is where it is not wanted (e.g. on the skin, clothes, in buildings): *His clothes were covered with dirt.* **2** (also *attrib*) loose earth or soil: *a dirt road.* **treat sb like dirt** to treat a person as if he or she is worthless.

dirt 'cheap *adj* (*pred*) very cheap; almost valueless.

dirty¹ /'dɜːtɪ/ *adj* (**-ier, -iest**) **1** not clean: *dirty hands/clothes.* **2** causing one to be or become dirty: *dirty jobs.* **3** obscene: *write dirty words on lavatory walls.* **4** (*informal*) mean, dishonourable: *play a dirty trick on her; get/give him a dirty look* (= one expressing strong disapproval or disgust). **do the dirty on sb** (*informal*) to deceive her or him.

dirt·ily /-əlɪ/ *adv*

dirty² /'dɜːtɪ/ *vt* (*pt,pp* **-ied**) to cause (something) to become dirty: *Don't dirty your new dress.*

dis·abil·ity /ˌdɪsə'bɪlətɪ/ *n* (*pl* **-ies**) **1** *nu* the state of being disabled. **2** *nc* something that disables a person: *a hearing disability.*

dis·able /dɪs'eɪbl/ *vt* to make (a person) unable to do something, esp take away the power of using the limbs, or of seeing or hearing: *He was disabled in a car crash.*

dis·abled *adj* physically or mentally handicapped. □ *n pl* (the —) people with physical or mental handicaps.

dis·ad·van·tage /ˌdɪsəd'vɑːntɪdʒ/ *nc* an unfavourable condition; something that makes progress, success etc difficult: *It is a disadvantage to be small when you're standing in a crowd at a football match. If you don't study now you'll be at a great disadvantage later on.*

dis·ad·van·tage·ous /ˌdɪsˌædvən'teɪdʒəs/ *adj* (*formal*) causing a disadvantage (to a person): *Bad health is disadvantageous to an athlete.*

dis·af·fec·tion /ˌdɪsə'fekʃn/ *nu* (*formal*) political discontent; disloyalty.

dis·agree /ˌdɪsə'griː/ *vi* **1** *disagree (with sb/ sth)* to have different opinions; not agree: *I disagree. I'm sorry to disagree with you/with what you say.* **2** *disagree with sb* (of food, climate) to have a bad effect on a person: *The climate/That fish disagrees with me.*

dis·agree·able /-əbl/ *adj* (*derog*) unpleasant: *disagreeable weather; a disagreeable old man.*

dis·agree·ably /-əblɪ/ *adv*

dis·agree·ment /ˌdɪsə'griːmənt/ *n* **1** *nu* **in disagreement (with sb/sth)** the act of disagreement; the absence of agreement: *to be in disagreement with him/the plan.* **2** *nc* a difference of opinion; small quarrel: *disagreements between husbands and wives.*

dis·al·low /ˌdɪsə'laʊ/ *vt* (*formal*) to refuse officially to allow or accept (something) as correct: *The judge disallowed the claim.*

dis·ap·pear /ˌdɪsə'pɪə(r)/ *vi* to go out of sight; be seen no more: *Let's hope our difficulties will soon disappear. The sun disappeared behind the clouds.*

dis·ap·pear·ance /-rəns/ *nc,nu*

dis·ap·point /ˌdɪsə'pɔɪnt/ vt to fail to do or be equal to what is hoped for by (a person): *The book disappointed me. Don't disappoint your parents.*

dis·ap·point·ed adj sad at not getting what was hoped for or wanted: *We were disappointed when we heard that you could not come.*

dis·ap·point·ing adj causing a person to be disappointed: *Our holiday was disappointing.*

dis·ap·point·ment /ˌdɪsə'pɔɪntmənt/ n 1 nu the state of being disappointed: *To her great disappointment it rained on the day of the picnic.* 2 nc a person, something, that disappoints: *He had suffered many disappointments in love.*

dis·ap·prov·al /ˌdɪsə'pruːvl/ nu the state of disapproving: *He shook his head in disapproval (= to show that he disapproved).*

dis·ap·prove /ˌdɪsə'pruːv/ vi *disapprove (of sb/sth)* to have, express, an unfavourable opinion: *She wants to become an actress but her parents disapprove (of the idea).*

dis·ap·prov·ing·ly adv in a way that shows disapproval: *When Mary lit a cigar her father looked at her disapprovingly.*

dis·arm /dɪs'ɑːm/ v 1 vt to take away weapons and other means of attack from (a person): *Five hundred rebels were captured and disarmed.* 2 vi (of a nation) to reduce the size of, give up the use of, armed forces. 3 vt (fig) to make it difficult for (a person) to express anger, suspicion, doubt: *I felt angry but her smiles disarmed me.*

dis·arma·ment /dɪs'ɑːməmənt/ nu the act, policy, of disarming or being disarmed(2): *working for nuclear disarmament.*

dis·arm·ing adj making it difficult for another person to express anger, suspicion, doubt etc: *a disarming look/smile.*

dis·ar·ray /ˌdɪsə'reɪ/ vt, nu (to cause (people, things) to be in) a state of disorder: *The troops were in disarray.*

dis·as·so·ci·ate /ˌdɪsə'səʊʃɪeɪt/ vt = dissociate.

dis·as·ter /dɪ'zɑːstə(r)/ nc,nu (a) large or sudden misfortune (e.g. a flood or fire, an earthquake, a serious defeat in war, the loss of a large sum of money).

dis·as·trous /dɪ'zɑːstrəs/ adj causing disaster: *disastrous floods.*

dis·as·trous·ly adv

dis·band /dɪs'bænd/ vt,vi (to cause an organized group) to break up: *The society (was) disbanded.*

dis·be·lief /ˌdɪsbɪ'liːf/ nu the state of not believing: *We watched the chaos in total disbelief.*

dis·be·lieve /ˌdɪsbɪ'liːv/ vt to refuse to believe (something): *Why do you disbelieve her account of what happened?* Ⓝ *'Disbelieve'* is very rare and never used as an opposite for believe(1). Always use *'not believe'.*

disc /dɪsk/ nc 1 a record²(5). ⇨ also compact disc. 2 a thin, flat, round object: *a parking disc.* 2 a layer of strong flexible material between the small bones in the back. *a slipped disc* one that is not in the correct position. 3 (computers) = disk.

'disc jockey nc (abbr DJ) a person who introduces records and tapes (esp) of light and popular music on radio or TV.

dis·card /dɪ'skɑːd/ vt (formal) to throw away, give up, (something useless or unwanted): *to discard old clothes.*

dis·cern /dɪ'sɜːn/ vt (formal) to see (something) clearly (with the eyes or with the mind): *It is often difficult to discern the truth in newspapers.* Ⓝ Not used in the continuous tenses, e.g. *is/was -ing.*

dis·cern·ing adj able to, wanting to, see and understand well: *a discerning mind.*

dis·cern·ible /-əbl/ adj that can be discerned.

dis·charge¹ /dɪs'tʃɑːdʒ/ nc an act, result, of discharging or being discharged (all senses).

dis·charge² /dɪs'tʃɑːdʒ/ v 1 vt,vi to give or send out (liquid, gas, electric current etc): *Where do the sewers discharge their contents? Lightning is caused by clouds discharging electricity.* 2 vt *discharge sb (from sth)* to allow a person to leave: *discharge a patient from hospital . The accused man was found not guilty and was discharged.* 3 vt to take (cargo) off a ship. 4 vt (formal) to pay (a debt) in full. 5 vt (formal) to perform (a duty).

dis·ciple /dɪ'saɪpl/ nc a follower of any leader of religious thought, art, learning etc (esp one of the twelve personal followers of Jesus Christ).

dis·ci·pli·nar·ian /ˌdɪsɪplɪ'neərɪən/ nc a person able to maintain discipline(2): *My teacher is a good/strict/poor disciplinarian.*

dis·ci·plin·ary /ˌdɪsɪ'plɪnərɪ/ adj of, for, discipline: *to take disciplinary action.*

dis·ci·pline¹ /'dɪsɪplɪn/ nu 1 the training of the mind and character to produce self-control, obedience etc: *school discipline; military discipline.* 2 the result of such training: *The students showed perfect discipline during the ceremony.*

dis·ci·pline² /'dɪsɪplɪn/ vt 1 to apply discipline(1) to (a person); train, control (a person, group): *disciplining crowds at sports meetings.* 2 to punish: *We discipline students who never work.*

dis·ci·plined adj having, showing, discipline: *A disciplined student always produces written work on time.* Opp undisciplined.

dis·claim /dɪs'kleɪm/ vt to say that one does not own or have a connection with (a person, thing, action etc): *disclaim responsibility for the accident; disclaim all knowledge of the incident.*

dis·close /dɪs'kləʊz/ vt 1 to make (something) known: *disclosing a secret.* 2 to allow (something) to be seen by uncovering it: *He opened the box and disclosed a tiny jewel.*

dis·clos·ure /dɪs'kləʊʒə(r)/ nc,nu (an act, result, of) disclosing or being disclosed.

dis·co /'dɪskəʊ/ nc (informal for discotheque) a place where people dance to records of popular music.

dis·col·our (US = **-col·or**) /dɪs'kʌlə(r)/ vt,vi (to cause something) to change colour: *walls discoloured by damp; paper that discolours in strong sunlight.*

dis·col·our·ation (US = **-col·or-**) /dɪsˌkʌlə'reɪʃn/ nc,nu

dis·com·fort /dɪs'kʌmfət/ n (formal) 1 nu the absence of comfort. 2 nc something that causes this: *the discomfort of a toothache.*

dis·con·cert /ˌdɪskən'sɜːt/ vt (formal) to upset the calmness or confidence of (a person): *The Manager was disconcerted to discover that he had forgotten to bring his diary.*

dis·con·nect /ˌdɪskə'nekt/ vt to take (two things) apart: *Disconnect the TV set (e.g. by pulling out the plug) before you open the back of it.*

dis·con·nect·ed /ˌdɪskə'nektɪd/ adj (derog) (of speech, thought or writing) having the ideas etc badly ordered.

dis·con·so·late /dɪ'skɒnsələt/ adj (formal) very unhappy and without hope because of the loss of a person or thing.
  dis·con·so·late·ly adv

dis·con·tent /ˌdɪskən'tent/ nc,nu (formal) (a cause of) dissatisfaction.

dis·con·tent·ed /ˌdɪskən'tentɪd/ adj not satisfied: I'm discontented with my job.
  dis·con·tent·ed·ly adv

dis·con·tinue /ˌdɪskən'tɪnjuː/ vt (formal) to put an end to, stop (something): I'll discontinue the payments until the repairs are done.

dis·con·tinu·ous /ˌdɪskən'tɪnjʊəs/ adj not continuous.

dis·cord /'dɪskɔːd/ n 1 nu (formal) disagreement; quarrelling: What has brought discord into the family? 2 nc,nu (music) (an example of) the state of not having harmony between notes etc sounded together.

dis·cord·ant /dɪ'skɔːdənt/ adj (formal) (a) not in agreement: discordant opinions. (b) (of sounds) not harmonious: the discordant noises of car horns.

dis·co·theque /'dɪskətek/ nc ⇨ disco.

dis·count¹ /'dɪskaʊnt/ nc an amount of money which may be taken off the full price, e.g. for quick payment.

dis·count² /dɪ'skaʊnt/ vt (esp) to refuse complete belief in (news, a story etc): You should discount a great deal of what appears in the newspapers.

dis·cour·age /dɪ'skʌrɪdʒ/ vt 1 (to try) to take away the courage or confidence of (a person): Don't let one failure discourage you—try again. 2 **discourage sb/sth (from (doing) sth)** (to try) to stop something or stop a person from doing something: How can we discourage children from taking drugs? The wet weather is discouraging people from going to the meeting. We must discourage smoking in cinemas.
  dis·cour·age·ment nc,nu

dis·course¹ /'dɪskɔːs/ nc,nu (formal) (a) speech, talk.
  'discourse marker nc (lang) a word or phrase used to show a relation between one part of a speech and another, such as 'however', 'all the same', 'to put it another way'.

dis·course² /dɪ'skɔːs/ vi (formal) to give a serious or formal talk.

dis·cour·teous /dɪ'skɜːtɪəs/ adj (formal; derog) impolite (the usual word): It was discourteous of you to arrive late.
  dis·cour·teous·ly adv
  dis·cour·tesy /dɪ'skɜːtəsɪ/ nc,nu

dis·cov·er /dɪ'skʌvə(r)/ vt to find out (something) (by accident); get knowledge of (something existing but not yet known): Columbus discovered America. She's discovered a way of making chocolate. The dog discovered a bone in the garden.

dis·cov·er·er nc a person who has made a discovery.

dis·cov·ery /dɪ'skʌvərɪ/ n (pl -ies) 1 nu the act of discovering or being discovered: a voyage of discovery; the discovery of new chemical elements.

2 nc something that is discovered: She made important scientific discoveries.

dis·cred·it¹ /dɪs'kredɪt/ n 1 nu the loss of credit or good reputation: If you continue to behave in this way you will bring discredit on yourself. 2 n sing **a discredit to sb/sth** a person, something, causing such loss: You are a discredit to the school.

dis·cred·it·able /-əbl/ adj (formal; derog) bringing discredit: discreditable behaviour.

dis·creet /dɪ'skriːt/ adj careful, tactful, in what one says or does: I decided to maintain a discreet silence. Opp indiscreet.
  dis·creet·ly adv

dis·crep·an·cy /dɪ'skrepənsɪ/ nc,nu (pl -ies) (of statements and accounts) (a) difference; absence of agreement: There was considerable discrepancy/There were numerous discrepancies between the two accounts of the quarrel.

dis·cre·tion /dɪ'skreʃn/ nu 1 the state of being discreet: You must show more discretion in choosing your friends. Opp indiscretion(1). 2 the freedom to act according to one's own judgement of what seems right or best: Use your discretion.
  dis·cre·tion·ary /-ərɪ/ adj having discretion(2): discretionary powers.

dis·crimi·nate /dɪ'skrɪmɪneɪt/ vi 1 **discriminate (between sth and sth)** to express, show, see, a difference (between): discriminating between good and bad books. 2 **discriminate against/in favour of sb/sth** to treat a person, thing, idea etc as different or worse/better: The law should not discriminate against anyone because of their race.

dis·crimi·nat·ing adj (a) (formal) able to see or make small differences: a discriminating taste in literature. (b) treating (groups of people, societies etc) as worse or better: discriminating policies/laws. ⇨ indiscriminate.

dis·crimi·na·tion /dɪsˌkrɪmɪ'neɪʃn/ nu (a) the ability to discriminate(1): Some people do not show much discrimination in their choice of TV programmes. (b) a policy, state etc of discriminating(b): Is there racial discrimination in your country?

dis·crim·i·na·tory /dɪˌskrɪmɪ'neɪtərɪ/ adj

dis·cur·sive /dɪ'skɜːsɪv/ adj (formal; derog) (of a way of speaking or writing) wandering from one point or subject to another.
  dis·cur·sive·ly adv

dis·cus /'dɪskəs/ nc (pl —es) a heavy, round object of wood, stone or metal (to be) thrown in athletic contests.

dis·cuss /dɪ'skʌs/ vt to examine and argue about (a subject): discussing (with my friends) what to do/how to do it/where to go.

dis·cus·sion /dɪ'skʌʃn/ n 1 nu the state of discussing or being discussed: We agreed after much discussion. **under discussion** being discussed: The proposal is still under discussion. 2 nc a talk in order to discuss: After several long discussions we agreed.

dis·dain¹ /dɪs'deɪn/ nu (formal) contempt; scorn: a note of disdain in his voice.

dis·dain² /dɪs'deɪn/ vt (formal) to look on (something) with contempt; be too proud (to do or accept something): He disdained my offer of help.
  dis·dain·ful /-fəl/ adj showing contempt: disdainful looks.

dis·dain·ful·ly /-fəlɪ/ adv

dis·ease /dɪ'ziːz/ nc,nu (a particular) disorder of body or mind or of plants: *Measles, flu and malaria are all diseases. Dirt and poverty cause disease. Plants are attacked by many diseases.*

dis·eased /dɪ'ziːzd/ adj suffering from, injured by, disease: *diseased plants.*

dis·em·bark /ˌdɪsɪm'bɑːk/ vt,vi (to cause passengers) to leave a ship and go on shore. ⇨ embark.

dis·em·bar·ka·tion /ˌdɪsembɑː'keɪʃn/ nc,nu

dis·en·chant·ed /ˌdɪsɪn'tʃɑːntɪd/ adj (formal) not pleased or satisfied (with something); disillusioned: *He is disenchanted with his job.*

dis·en·chant·ment nc,nu

dis·en·fran·chise /ˌdɪsɪn'fræntʃaɪz/ vt = disfranchise.

dis·en·gage /ˌdɪsɪn'geɪdʒ/ vt to cause (one machine part) to become detached: *disengaging the gears of a car.* Compare engage.

dis·en·tangle /ˌdɪsɪn'tæŋgl/ vt **1** to cause (something) to become free from complications or confusion: *disentangling truth from fiction.* **2** to cause (something) to become clear of tangles: *I can't disentangle this wool.*

dis·fa·vour (US = **-fa·vor**) /ˌdɪs'feɪvə(r)/ nu (formal) the state of being out of favour; disapproval: *to be in disfavour; speak about her with disfavour.*

dis·fig·ure /dɪs'fɪgə(r)/ vt (usu passive) to spoil the appearance or shape of (a person, thing): *beautiful scenery disfigured by ugly houses; a face disfigured by a broken nose/an ugly scar.*

dis·fig·ure·ment nc,nu

dis·fran·chise /dɪs'fræntʃaɪz/ (also **disenfranchise**) vt to take away the right of (a person) to send a representative to parliament or the right to vote for a parliamentary representative. ⇨ enfranchise.

dis·gorge /dɪs'gɔːdʒ/ vt to throw (food) up or out (as if) from the throat.

dis·grace¹ /dɪs'greɪs/ n **1** nu the loss of respect, favour, good reputation: *A man who commits a crime and is sent to prison brings disgrace on himself and his family.* **2 be in disgrace** to have lost people's respect and liking: *He told a lie and is in disgrace.* **3** n sing something, a state of affairs, person etc that is a cause of shame or discredit: *These slums are a disgrace to the city authorities.*

dis·grace·ful /-fəl/ adj (derog) bringing or causing disgrace: *disgraceful behaviour.*

dis·grace·ful·ly /-fəlɪ/ adv: *to behave disgracefully.*

disgrace² /dɪs'greɪs/ vt **1** to be a disgrace to (a person, school, family): *disgracing the family name.* **2** to cause (an official etc) to lose people's respect or favour: *be disgraced by the newspapers.*

dis·gruntled /dɪs'grʌntld/ adj annoyed; angry; in a bad mood.

dis·guise¹ /dɪs'gaɪz/ n **1** nu **in disguise** with a deliberately strange or unusual appearance in order to hide one's identity: *He went among the enemy in disguise.* ⇨ also blessing(2). **2** nc,nu (a particular) dress, action, manner etc used for disguising: *He had tried all sorts of disguises.*

dis·guise² /dɪs'gaɪz/ vt **1** to use a strange or unusual appearance in order to deceive or to hide the identity of (a person, thing): *He disguised his*

looks but he could not disguise his voice. **2** to hide (something): *disguising his sorrow beneath a cheerful appearance.*

dis·gust¹ /dɪs'gʌst/ nu a very strong feeling of dislike (e.g. caused by a bad smell or taste, a horrible sight, very bad behaviour): *He turned away in disgust. She was disgusted at what she saw.*

dis·gust² /dɪs'gʌst/ vt (often passive) to cause disgust in (a person): *We were disgusted at/by/with her language.*

dis·gust·ing adj (derog): *disgusting smells.*

dis·gust·ing·ly adv

dish¹ /dɪʃ/ nc **1** a container with a wide flat bottom, used to serve food: *a meat-dish.* **2** n pl (the —es) the plates, bowls, cups and saucers etc used for a meal: *It's your turn to wash up the dishes.* **3** a meal: *His favourite dish is steak and kidney pie.*

'dish·cloth nc a cloth for washing dishes(2) etc.

'dish·washer nc an electric machine used for washing dishes(2), cutlery etc.

'dish·ful /-fʊl/ nc as much as a dish(1) can hold.

dish² /dɪʃ/ v **1** vt,vi **dish up (sth)** to put food into dishes: *dish up the dinner.* **2** vt **dish sth up** (fig) to prepare and produce (facts, arguments etc): *to dish up the usual arguments in a new form.* **3 dish sth out** (a) to give food to several people from a dish. (b) to give out a written programme, report etc to people (e.g. at a meeting).

dis·heart·en /dɪs'hɑːtn/ vt (usually passive) to cause (a person) to lose courage or confidence: *Don't be disheartened by what he says.*

dis·heart·en·ing /dɪs'hɑːtnɪŋ/ adj: *disheartening news.*

di·shev·elled (US = **-el·ed**) /dɪ'ʃevld/ adj (of the hair or clothes) untidy.

dis·hon·est /dɪs'ɒnɪst/ adj (derog) not honest: *dishonest methods/traders.*

dis·hon·est·ly adv

dis·honesty /dɪs'ɒnɪstɪ/ nu

dis·hon·our¹ (US = **-hon·or**) /dɪs'ɒnə(r)/ n **1** nu disgrace or shame; loss, absence, of honour and self-respect: *to bring dishonour on one's family.* **2** nc a person, activity etc that brings dishonour: *He was a dishonour to his family.*

dis·hon·our² (US = **-hon·or**) /dɪs'ɒnə(r)/ vt **1** to cause (one's family, employers, college etc) shame. **2** (of a bank): *dishonour a cheque* (= to refuse to pay the money on it because the bank's customer has not enough credit).

dis·hon·our·able /dɪs'ɒnrəbl/ adj (derog) without honour; shameful: *dishonourable acts.*

dis·hon·our·ably /dɪs'ɒnrəblɪ/ adv

dis·il·lu·sion /ˌdɪsɪ'luːʒn/ vt (often passive) to set (a person) free from mistaken beliefs: *They had thought that the holiday would be restful but they were soon disillusioned.*

dis·il·lu·sion·ed adj having a poor opinion of people, the future etc: *I became disillusioned after I was made redundant from work.*

dis·il·lu·sion·ment nu

dis·in·cli·na·tion /ˌdɪsˌɪnklɪ'neɪʃn/ nc,nu (formal) (an example of) unwillingness: *Some teachers have a strong disinclination for work.*

dis·in·clined /ˌdɪsɪn'klaɪnd/ adj (pred; formal) reluctant or unwilling: *He was disinclined to help me.*

dis·in·fect /ˌdɪsɪn'fekt/ vt to make (something) free from infection caused by bacteria: *The house* *was disinfected after Tom had had scarlet fever.*

dis·in·fec·tant /ˌdɪsɪnˈfektənt/ *nc,nu* a chemical substance used to disinfect.

dis·in·her·it /ˌdɪsɪnˈherɪt/ *vt* (often *passive*) to take away the right to inherit from (a person).

dis·in·heri·tance /ˌdɪsɪnˈherɪtəns/ *nc,nu*

dis·in·te·grate /dɪsˈɪntɪgreɪt/ *vt,vi* (to cause something) to break up into small pieces: *mud walls disintegrating in the rain; rocks disintegrated by frost and rain.*

dis·in·te·gra·tion /dɪsˌɪntɪˈgreɪʃn/ *nu*

dis·in·ter /ˌdɪsɪnˈtɜ:(r)/ *vt* (**-rr-**) to dig up (a body) from the ground (e.g. from a grave).

dis·in·ter·ment *nc,nu*

dis·in·ter·est·ed /dɪsˈɪntrɪstɪd/ *adj* not influenced by personal feelings or interests: *His action was not altogether disinterested.* Compare uninterested.

dis·in·ter·est·ed·ly *adv*

dis·joint·ed /dɪsˈdʒɔɪntɪd/ *adj* (of speech and writing) not having a good order or plan.

dis·joint·ed·ly *adv*

dis·joint·ed·ness *nu*

dis·junc·tive /dɪsˈdʒʌŋktɪv/ *adj* (*gram*) expressing contrast.

dis,junctive con'junction *nc* (*gram*) one expressing opposition or contrast, such as '*either . . . or*' and '*but*' in '*small but strong*'.

disk /dɪsk/ *nc* **1** (*computers*) a flat, round device used for storing information. **2** (an unusual variant spelling for) disc. ⇨ floppy disk.

'disk memory *nc* (*computers*) a system for storing information using disks(1).

dis·like¹ /dɪsˈlaɪk/ *nc* a feeling of not liking: *to have a dislike of/for cats.* **likes and dislikes** ⇨ likes. **take a dislike to sb** to begin not liking a person: *I took an instant dislike to her.*

dis·like² /dɪsˈlaɪk/ *vt* to not like (a person, thing): *disliking work/getting up early/being disturbed.* ⓝ Not used in continuous tenses, e.g. *is/was -ing.*

dis·lo·cate /ˈdɪsləkeɪt/ *vt* **1** to put (a bone in the body) out of position: *He fell from his horse and dislocated his shoulder.* **2** (often *passive*) to put traffic, machinery, business etc out of order: *Traffic was badly dislocated by the heavy fall of snow.*

dis·lo·ca·tion /ˌdɪsləˈkeɪʃn/ *nc,nu*

dis·lodge /dɪsˈlɒdʒ/ *vt* to cause (something, a person) to move from a (usual) place: *dislodging a stone from a building/the enemy from their positions.*

dis·lodge·ment *nc,nu*

dis·loy·al /dɪsˈlɔɪəl/ *adj* **disloyal (to sb/sth)** (*derog*) not loyal (to a person, one's country etc).

dis·loy·al·ly *adv*

dis·loy·al·ty *nc,nu*

dis·mal /ˈdɪzməl/ *adj* sad, gloomy; miserable: *dismal weather; in a dismal voice.*

dis·mal·ly /-əlɪ/ *adv*

dis·mantle /dɪsˈmæntl/ *vt* **1** to take (a machine etc) to pieces: *dismantling a car engine.* **2** to take away parts, furnishings etc from (something): *dismantling a large cupboard/an office.*

dis·may¹ /dɪsˈmeɪ/ *nu* the feeling of strong fear and discouragement: *The news that the enemy were near filled us with dismay.*

dis·may² /dɪsˈmeɪ/ *vt* to fill (a person) with dismay: *We were dismayed at/by/with the news.*

dis·mem·ber /dɪsˈmembə(r)/ *vt* to tear or cut

the limbs from (a person): *He was dismembered by the lion.*

dis·miss /dɪsˈmɪs/ *vt* **1** **dismiss sb (from sth)** to send a person away permanently (from employment): *She was dismissed (from her job) for being lazy and dishonest.* **2** to allow (a person) to go: *The teacher dismissed his class when the bell rang.* **3** to stop thinking or talking about (something): *to dismiss all thoughts of revenge.* **4** (*cricket*) (of the team that is fielding) to cause a batsman, team, to be out quickly: *The fast bowler dismissed Smith for ten runs.*

dis·mis·sal /-sl/ *nc,nu*

dis·mount /ˌdɪsˈmaunt/ *vt* to get down (from a horse, bike etc).

dis·obedi·ence /ˌdɪsəˈbi:dɪəns/ *nu* the failure or refusal to obey: *acts of disobedience; disobedience to orders.*

dis·obedi·ent /ˌdɪsəˈbi:dɪənt/ *adj* (*derog*) not obedient: *disobedient children.*

dis·obedi·ent·ly *adv*

dis·obey /ˌdɪsəˈbeɪ/ *vt* to refuse to obey (a person, order): *He's disobeyed me/my orders.*

dis·or·der /dɪsˈɔ:də(r)/ *n* **1** *nu* **in disorder** showing absence of order; confusion: *The burglars left the room in great disorder.* **2** *nc,nu* an absence of order, angry outburst of rioting, caused by political troubles etc: *Troops were called out to deal with the disorders in the cities.* **3** *nc,nu* (a kind of) disturbance of the normal working of the body or mind: *suffering from mental disorder.*

dis·or·der·ed *adj* without order: *a disordered mind.*

dis·order·ly /dɪsˈɔ:dəlɪ/ *adj* (*derog*) **1** (*formal*) very untidy: *a disorderly room/desk.* **2** causing a disturbance: *disorderly crowds/behaviour.*

dis·or·gan·ize (also **-ise**) /ˌdɪsˈɔ:gənaɪz/ *vt* (often *passive*) to cause (an organized system) to be in disorder: *The train service was disorganized by fog.*

dis·or·gan·iz·ation (also **-is·ation**) /ˌdɪsˌɔ:gənaɪˈzeɪʃn/ *nu*

dis·ori·en·tate /dɪsˈɔ:rɪənteɪt/ (also, esp *US*, **dis·ori·ent** /dɪsˈɔ:rɪənt/) *vt* (usually *passive*) to confuse (a person) so that he or she does not know a place, the time, date etc.

dis·own /dɪsˈəʊn/ *vt* to say that one does not know, that one has not or no longer wishes to have, any connection with (a person or thing): *The boy was so cruel that his father disowned him.*

dis·par·ag·ing /dɪˈspærədʒɪŋ/ *adj* suggesting that a person or thing is of little value or importance: *disparaging remarks.*

dis·par·ag·ing·ly *adv*

dis·par·age·ment *nu*

dis·par·ate /ˈdɪspərət/ *adj* (*formal*) that cannot be compared in quality, amount etc.

dis·par·ity /dɪˈspærətɪ/ *nc,nu* **disparity (between sth)** (an instance of) a difference in quality, size etc (between): *a disparity between our salaries.*

dis·pas·sion·ate /dɪˈspæʃənət/ *adj* (of a person) not favouring a particular side, opinion etc (in a quarrel).

dis·pas·sion·ate·ly *adv*

dis·patch¹ (also **des·patch**) /dɪˈspætʃ/ *n* **1** *nu* (*formal*) the process of dispatching or being dispatched (all senses): *Please hurry up the dispatch of these telegrams.* **2** *nc* a government, military or newspaper report: *London newspapers receive dispatches from all parts of the world.* **3** *nu* (*formal*) speed: *to act with dispatch.*

dis·patch² (also **des·patch**) /dɪ'spætʃ/ *vt* **1** to send (a person, post etc) off to a destination, on a journey: *to dispatch letters/a messenger.* **2** (*formal*) to finish, get through, (business etc).

dis·pel /dɪ'spel/ *vt* (**-ll-**) to cause (something) to go away or be removed: *The wind soon dispelled the fog. How can we dispel their doubts and fears?*

dis·pens·able /dɪ'spensəbl/ *adj* not necessary. Opp indispensable.

dis·pens·ary /dɪ'spensərɪ/ *nc* (*pl* **-ies**) a place where medicines are given out, e.g. in a hospital.

dis·pen·sa·tion /ˌdɪspen'seɪʃn/ *n* (*formal*) **1** *nu* the act of distributing: *the dispensation of justice/medicine/food.* **2** *nc,nu* (an instance of) permission to do something that is usually forbidden, or not to do something that is usually required (esp connected with religion): *be granted (a) dispensation from fasting during a journey.*

dis·pense /dɪ'spens/ *vt* **1** (*formal*) to give, distribute (something): *dispensing charity/justice.* **2** to prepare and give out (medicines): *to dispense a prescription.* **3** *dispense with sb/sth* (a) to do without a person, thing: *He is not yet well enough to dispense with the doctor's services.* (b) to make something unnecessary: *The new design dispenses with gears.*

dis·pen·ser *nc* (a) a professional person who dispenses medicines. (b) a container from which something can be obtained without removing a cover or lid: *a dispenser for liquid soap.*

di,spensing 'chemist *nc* one qualified to prepare and give out medicines.

dis·perse /dɪ'spɜːs/ *vt,vi* (to cause people, things) to go in different directions: *The police dispersed the crowd. The crowd was dispersing when the police arrived.*

dis·per·sal /dɪ'spɜːsl/ *nu*

dis·pir·it·ed /dɪ'spɪrɪtɪd/ *adj* discouraged; without confidence.

dis·place /dɪ'spleɪs/ *vt* **1** to put (a bone) out of the right or usual position: *displace a bone.* **2** to take the place of (a person): *Tom has displaced Harry in Mary's affections.*

di,splaced 'person *nc* one who must leave her or his country because of war etc.

dis·place·ment /dɪ'spleɪsmənt/ *nu*

dis·play¹ /dɪ'spleɪ/ *nc,nu* the act, result, of showing something: *a fashion display; a display of bad temper.*

dis·play² /dɪ'spleɪ/ *vt* **1** to organize (things) in attractive positions so that there is no difficulty in seeing them: *Department stores display their goods in the windows.* **2** to allow (something) to be seen; show signs of having (something): *to display one's ignorance. She displayed no sign of emotion.*

dis·please /dɪs'pliːz/ *vt* (often *passive; formal*) to annoy or offend (a person); make (a person) angry: *be displeased with her (for doing that); be displeased at her behaviour.*

dis·pleas·ure /dɪs'pleʒə(r)/ *nu* (*formal*) the state of feeling annoyed, angry or offended: *He deserves his father's displeasure.*

dis·pos·able /dɪ'spəʊzəbl/ *adj* made so that it can be used and then easily destroyed: *disposable plates/nappies.*

dis·pos·al /dɪ'spəʊzl/ *nu* **1** *disposal (of sth)* the act of disposing: *the disposal of rubbish; a bomb disposal squad* (= a group of men who try to make unexploded bombs harmless and remove them). **2** *at one's disposal* (*formal*) able to be used as one wishes: *My desk/report is at your disposal.*

dis·pose /dɪ'spəʊz/ *vt,vi dispose of sth* to get rid of something: *to dispose of rubbish.*

dis·posed /dɪ'spəʊzd/ *adj* (*pred*) *disposed to do sth* willing or ready to do it: *I'm not disposed/don't feel disposed to help my lazy sister.*

dis·po·si·tion /ˌdɪspə'zɪʃn/ *nc* (*formal*) **1** an arrangement (the more usual word): *the disposition of furniture in a room.* **2** a person's natural qualities of mind and character: *a man with a cheerful disposition.*

dis·pos·sess /ˌdɪspə'zes/ *vt dispossess sb (of sth)* to take away (property, esp land) from a person: *The nobles were dispossessed of their property after the Revolution.*

dis·pro·por·tion·ate /ˌdɪsprə'pɔːʃənət/ *adj* (*formal*) not equal; too large or small etc: *to give a disproportionate amount of one's time to watching TV.*

dis·pro·por·tion·ate·ly *adv*

dis·prove /dɪs'pruːv/ *vt* to prove (something) to be wrong or false: *disprove a theory.*

dis·put·able /dɪ'spjuːtəbl/ *adj* that can be disputed. Opp indisputable.

dis·pute¹ /dɪ'spjuːt/ *n* **1** *nu in dispute* being argued about: *The matter in dispute is the ownership of a house.* **2** *nc* a quarrel; argument: *a dispute about/over a wage increase.*

dis·pute² /dɪ'spjuːt/ *v* **1** *vt,vi dispute (about/over) (sth)* to argue; quarrel: *disputing (about) the cause of the accident.* **2** *vt* to discuss, question, the truth or validity of (something): *to dispute a statement/claim/decision.* ⇨ disputable.

dis·qual·ify /dɪs'kwɒlɪfaɪ/ *vt* (*pt,pp* **-ied**) *disqualify sb (from (doing) sth)* to state a person as unsuitable or unable: *Because he was a professional, he was disqualified from taking part in the Olympic Games.*

dis·quali·fi·ca·tion /dɪsˌkwɒlɪfɪ'keɪʃn/ *nc,nu*

dis·quiet /dɪs'kwaɪət/ *nu* (*formal*) anxiety (the more usual word): *The President's speech caused considerable disquiet in some European capitals.*

dis·quiet·ing *adj* (*formal*) causing anxiety: *disquieting news.*

dis·re·gard¹ /ˌdɪsrɪ'gɑːd/ *nu disregard (for sb/sth)* the absence of respect, interest etc (for): *show disregard for one's teacher/her feelings.*

dis·re·gard² /ˌdɪsrɪ'gɑːd/ *vt* (*formal*) to show no respect or interest for (a person, wish); ignore (the more usual word): *disregard a warning/your parents' wishes.*

dis·re·pair /ˌdɪsrɪ'peə(r)/ *nu in disrepair* (*formal*) in the state of needing repair: *The building was in bad disrepair.*

dis·repu·table /dɪs'repjʊtəbl/ *adj* (*derog*) having or producing a bad reputation; not respectable: *disreputable behaviour; a disreputable appearance.*

dis·re·pute /ˌdɪsrɪ'pjuːt/ *nu* the state of being

disreputable. **fall into disrepute** to lose a good reputation.

dis·re·spect /ˌdɪsrɪ'spekt/ *nu* the expression of one's low opinion of, lack of respect for, (a person): *He meant no disrespect by that remark.* ⇨ respect(1).

dis·re·spect·ful /-fəl/ *adj* (*derog*) showing disrespect.

dis·re·spect·ful·ly /-fəlɪ/ *adv*: *She spoke disrespectfully of/about him.*

dis·rupt /ˌdɪs'rʌpt/ *vt* to cause (a discussion, speech, flow of something etc) to be stopped or be in a state of disorder: *disrupt a meeting by shouting. Traffic was disrupted by the snow.*

dis·rup·tion /dɪs'rʌpʃn/ *nc,nu* (an instance of) disrupting or being disrupted: *serious disruptions in the factory by union members.*

dis·rup·tive /dɪs'rʌptɪv/ *adj* (*derog*) causing disorder: *disruptive people at the meeting.*

dis·sat·is·fac·tion /dɪˌsætɪs'fækʃn/ *nu* the state of being dissatisfied: *He expressed great dissatisfaction with my work.* Compare satisfaction.

dis·sat·is·fied /dɪ'sætɪsfaɪd/ *adj* **dissatisfied (with sb/sth)** not feeling happy or pleased (with): *dissatisfied with one's salary/job.* ⇨ satisfy. Compare unsatisfied.

dis·sect /dɪ'sekt/ *vt* (*science*) to cut up (parts of a body, plant etc) in order to study its structure.

dis·sec·tion /dɪ'sekʃn/ *nc,nu*

dis·semi·nate /dɪ'semɪneɪt/ *vt* (*formal*) to distribute or spread widely (ideas etc): *disseminating new political ideas.*

dis·semi·na·tion /dɪˌsemɪ'neɪʃn/ *nu*

dis·sen·sion /dɪ'senʃn/ *nc,nu* **dissension among/between sb/sth** (*formal*) (an instance of) angry quarrelling or disagreement: *dissension(s) between rival groups in politics.*

dis·sent¹ /dɪ'sent/ *nu* (*formal*) (the expression of) disagreement: *to express strong dissent.*

dis·sent² /dɪ'sent/ *vi* **dissent (from sth)** (*formal*) to express a different opinion (from something said or written): *I strongly dissent from what the last speaker has said.*

dis·ser·ta·tion /ˌdɪsə'teɪʃn/ *nc* a long written account (e.g. as prepared for a higher university degree): *a dissertation on/concerning modern poetry.*

dis·ser·vice /dɪs'sɜːvɪs/ *nu* or *sing* harmful or unhelpful action: *You are doing her a great disservice spreading such unfair rumours.*

dis·si·dent /'dɪsɪdənt/ *nc* (also *attrib*) a person who actively disagrees: *political dissidents; dissident students.*

dis·simi·lar /dɪ'sɪmɪlə(r)/ *adj* not the same; not like; not similar: *people with dissimilar tastes.*

dis·simi·lar·ity /dɪˌsɪmɪ'lærətɪ/ *nc,nu*

dis·si·pate /'dɪsɪpeɪt/ *v* **1** *vt,vi* (to cause fears, a bad smell, smoke etc) to go away gradually: *to dissipate fear/doubt/ignorance.* **2** *vt* to waste (time, leisure, money etc) foolishly: *Don't dissipate your efforts.*

dis·si·pated *adj* (*formal; derog*) behaving in a foolish and often harmful way: *to lead a dissipated life.*

dis·si·pa·tion /ˌdɪsɪ'peɪʃn/ *nu*

dis·so·ci·ate /dɪ'səʊʃɪeɪt/ *vt* **dissociate oneself/sb (from sb/sth)** to refuse to associate oneself/a person with, support, a person, idea

etc: *I wish to dissociate myself from what has just been said.*

dis·so·cia·tion /dɪˌsəʊʃɪ'eɪʃn/ *nu*

dis·so·lute /'dɪsəljuːt/ *adj* (*formal; derog*) (of a person, behaviour) immoral, evil: *to lead a dissolute life.*

dis·so·lute·ly *adv*

dis·so·lu·tion /ˌdɪsə'luːʃn/ *nc,nu* the breaking up or ending (of a marriage, partnership, formal meeting etc).

dis·solve /dɪ'zɒlv/ *v* **1** *vt* (of a liquid) to soak into a solid so that the solid itself becomes liquid: *Water dissolves salt.* **2** *vi* **dissolve in sth** (of a solid) to become liquid as the result of being taken into a liquid: *Salt dissolves in water.* **3** *vt* to cause (a solid) to dissolve: *He dissolved the salt in water.* **4** *vt,vi* (to cause something) to come to an end: *to dissolve a business partnership/a marriage/Parliament.*

dis·son·ance /'dɪsənəns/ *n* **1** *nu* (*formal*) very strong disagreement. **2** *nc* (*music*) a combination of notes that is discordant.

dis·son·ant /'dɪsənənt/ *adj* (*attrib*) (*formal*) **1** not agreeing. **2** harsh in (musical) tone.

dis·suade /dɪ'sweɪd/ *vt* **dissuade sb (from (doing) sth)** to advise a person against (doing something): *I tried to dissuade her from marrying him.* Compare persuade(2).

dis·sua·sion /dɪ'sweɪʒn/ *nu*

dis·tance /'dɪstəns/ *nc,nu* the amount, measure, of space or time between two points etc: *In the USA distance is measured in miles, not in kilometres. What is the distance from here to Cairo? It's hard to remember things over such a distance of time.* **at a/some distance (from sth)** a long way away (from): *The house is at a distance from the road.* **in the distance** far away: *A ship could be seen in the distance.* **be within striking distance** to be near enough to reach easily: *There's a good restaurant within striking distance of the hotel.* ⇨ also long-distance.

dis·tant /'dɪstənt/ *adj* **1** far away in space or time: *We had a distant view of Mount Everest.* Compare close-up. **2** (*attrib*) far off in family relationship: *She's a distant cousin of mine.* Compare close¹(2). **3** (of degree of similarity) not easily seen: *There is a distant resemblance between the cousins.* Compare close¹(7). **4** not friendly: *She's very distant with strangers.*

dis·tant·ly *adv* in a distant manner: *He is distantly related to me.*

dis·taste /dɪs'teɪst/ *nu* (*formal*) dislike: *I think of his rude behaviour with distaste.*

dis·taste·ful /-fəl/ *adj* (*formal*) disagreeable; unpleasant: *It is distasteful to me to have to say this but you have not told the truth.* Compare tasteful.

dis·taste·ful·ly /-fəlɪ/ *adv*

dis·tend /dɪ'stend/ *vt,vi* (to cause something) to swell out (by pressure from within): *a distended stomach.*

dis·til (*US* = **-till**) /dɪ'stɪl/ *vt* (**-ll-**) **1** (*science*) to change (a liquid) to gas by heating, and then cool the gas and collect drops of liquid: *Salt water can be distilled and made into drinking water.* **2** to make (whisky etc) by distilling.

dis·til·la·tion /ˌdɪstɪ'leɪʃn/ *nc,nu*

dis·til·ler /dɪ'stɪlə(r)/ *nc* a person, business, that distils (esp whisky).

dis·til·lery *nc* (*pl* **-ies**) a factory where alcoholic drinks such as gin or whisky are made.

dis·tinct /dɪ'stɪŋkt/ *adj* **1** easily heard, seen, understood; clearly marked: *a distinct smell of cigarette smoke. There is a distinct improvement in her typing.* Opp indistinct. **2** *distinct (from sth)* different in kind; separate: *Keep this design distinct (from that one).*

dis·tinct·ly *adv* clearly: *I remember her distinctly. He distinctly remembers telling you not to do it.*

dis·tinc·tion /dɪ'stɪŋkʃn/ *n* **1** *nc,nu* (an instance of) being distinct(2): *The President shook hands with everyone, without distinction of rank.* **draw/ make a distinction between sth (and sth)** to identify, state, a clear difference between: *It is difficult to make exact distinctions between all the meanings of a word.* **2** *nc* that which makes one thing different from another: *The distinction between poetry and prose is obvious.* **3** *nu* the quality of being superior, excellent: *pass an exam with distinction; a writer/novel of distinction.* **4** *nc* a mark or award of honour: *academic distinctions.*

dis·tinc·tive /dɪ'stɪŋktɪv/ *adj* marking (a person, thing) as clearly different: *Football teams wear distinctive clothes.*

dis·tinc·tive·ly *adv*

dis·tin·guish /dɪ'stɪŋgwɪʃ/ *v* **1** *vt,vi* **distinguish (between) sb/sth; distinguish sb/sth from (among) sb/sth** to identify, state, a difference between people, things (by looking, listening, thinking etc): *The twins were so alike that it was impossible to distinguish one from the other. A person with good eyesight can distinguish distant objects.* **2** *vt* to be a particular mark that makes (people, things) different: *Speech distinguishes man from the animals.* **3** *v reflex* to act, behave, so as to bring credit to (oneself): *to distinguish oneself in an examination.*

dis·tin·guish·able /-əbl/ *adj* **distinguishable (from sb/sth)** that can be distinguished(1): *Tom is hardly distinguishable from his twin brother.* Opp indistinguishable.

dis·tin·guish·ed /dɪ'stɪŋgwɪʃt/ *adj* well known as being of superior or excellent quality: *He is distinguished for his good knowledge of economics/ distinguished as an economist.* Opp undistinguished.

dis·tort /dɪ'stɔːt/ *vt* **1** (often *passive*) to pull, twist, (something) out of the usual shape: *Her face was distorted by pain.* **2** to give a false account of (something): *Newspaper accounts of international affairs are sometimes distorted.*

dis·tor·tion /dɪ'stɔːʃn/ *nc,nu*

dis·tract /dɪ'strækt/ *vt* **distract sb (from sth)** to take away (a person's) attention, concentration etc: *The noise in the street distracted me from my reading.*

dis·trac·tion /dɪ'strækʃn/ *n* **1** *nc,nu* (a person, thing) that distracts a person: *Noise is a distraction when you are trying to study.* **2** *nc* (*formal*) something that holds the attention and gives pleasure: *He complained that there were not enough distractions in the village.* **3** **to distraction** to a point of being very confused or emotional: *You'll drive me to distraction with your silly questions. He loves her to distraction.*

dis·traught /dɪ'strɔːt/ *adj* (*formal*) extremely troubled or upset: *be distraught with grief.*

dis·tress¹ /dɪ'stres/ *nu* **1** (a cause of) great pain, discomfort or sorrow: *He caused great distress to his parents.* **2** **in distress** in a state of serious danger or difficulty: *a ship in distress.*

dis·tress² /dɪ'stres/ *vt* to cause distress to (a person): *What are you looking so distressed about?*

dis·tress·ing *adj* causing distress: *distressing experiences.*

dis·trib·ute /dɪ'strɪbjuːt/ *vt* **distribute sth (among/to sb/sth)** to give, send out, (things) (to many people, houses etc): *distributing leaflets to people in the street.*

dis·tri·bu·tion /ˌdɪstrɪ'bjuːʃn/ *nc,nu* (an instance of) distributing or being distributed: *Is the distribution of wealth fair in your country?*

dis·tribu·tive /dɪ'strɪbjutɪv/ *adj* (**a**) of distribution: *the distributive trades* (e.g. keeping a shop). (**b**) (*gram*) concerning each individual or member of a class: *'Each', 'every', 'either' and 'neither' are distributive pronouns.*

dis·tribu·tive·ly *adv*

dis·tri·bu·tor /dɪ'strɪbjutə(r)/ *nc* **1** a person who distributes things. **2** (*tech*) a part of a car engine that sends electricity to the sparking plugs.

dis·trict /'dɪstrɪkt/ *nc* **1** a part of a country: *a mountainous district; the Lake District* (in England). **2** a part of a town or country marked out for a special purpose: *the London postal districts.*

ˌdistrict 'nurse *nc* a nurse who visits people at home, not in hospitals.

dis·trust¹ /dɪs'trʌst/ *nu* doubt or suspicion; absence of trust or confidence: *The child looked at the stranger in/with distrust.*

dis·trust² /dɪs'trʌst/ *vt* to have no trust in (a person, idea etc); be doubtful about (a person, idea etc): *He distrusted his own father.*

dis·trust·ful /-fəl/ *adj* (*formal*) suspicious (of a person, thing) (the usual word).

dis·turb /dɪ'stɜːb/ *vt* **1** to break the quiet, calm, peace, of (a person): *She opened the door quietly so as not to disturb the baby. He was disturbed to hear of your illness/by the news of your illness.* **2** to put (things) out of the right or usual order: *Who has disturbed the papers on my desk?*

dis·turb·ance /dɪ'stɜːbəns/ *nc,nu* (an instance of) disturbing or being disturbed: *Were there any political disturbances in the country last year?*

dis·uni·ty /dɪs'juːnətɪ/ *nu* (*formal*) absence of unity.

dis·use /dɪs'juːs/ *nu* the state of no longer being used: *be rusty from disuse; a machine that has fallen into disuse* (= is no longer used).

dis·used /dɪs'juːzd/ *adj* no longer used: *a disused railway line.*

ditch¹ /dɪtʃ/ *nc* a deep, long channel dug in or between fields, at the sides of a road etc, used to hold or carry off water.

ditch² /dɪtʃ/ *vt* (*informal*) to abandon, leave, (a person, stolen goods etc) suddenly: *He's ditched his girlfriend.*

dith·er /'dɪðə(r)/ *vi* **dither (about/over sth)** (*informal*) to hesitate about what to do; be unable to decide.

dit·to /'dɪtəu/ *nc* (*pl* **—s**) the same (used in lists to avoid writing words again): *One hat at £2.25; ditto at £4.50.*

dit·ty /'dɪtɪ/ *nc* (*pl* **-ies**) a short, simple song.

di·van /dɪ'væn/ nc a long seat or bed without a back.

dive¹ /daɪv/ nc 1 an act of diving into water: *the graceful dive of a duck.* 2 (*informal*) a place with a bad reputation, used for drinking, gambling etc.

dive² /daɪv/ vi 1 to go head first into water: *He dived from the bridge and rescued the drowning child.* 2 to move (e.g. the hand) quickly and suddenly downwards (into something): *He dived into his pocket and pulled out a handful of coins.* 3 (of a submarine) to go under water. 4 (of aircraft) to go quickly to a lower level: *The plane was diving steeply.*

diver nc a person who dives, esp one who goes under water in a diving-suit.

div·ing nu the act, sport, of going head first into water.

'diving-board nc a long platform from which to dive(1).

'diving-suit nc a kind of suit with heavy boots and a helmet, worn when going deep under the sea.

di·verge /daɪ'vɜ:dʒ/ vi **diverge (from sth)** (of lines, opinions, roads etc) to get farther apart (from a point or from each other) as they progress: *diverging from the path/truth.*

di·ver·gence /daɪ'vɜ:dʒəns/ nu

di·ver·gent /-dʒənt/ adj

di·verse /daɪ'vɜ:s/ adj of different kinds: *The wildlife in Africa is extremely diverse.*

di·verse·ly adv

di·ver·si·fy /ˌdaɪ'vɜ:sɪfaɪ/ vt,vi (pt,pp **-ied**) (*formal*) (to cause something) to become (more) varied: *diversify one's career to gain more experience.*

di·ver·si·fi·ca·tion /daɪˌvɜ:sɪfɪ'keɪʃn/ nu

di·ver·sion /daɪ'vɜ:ʃn/ n 1 nc,nu (an instance of) giving something a different direction: *the diversion of a stream to water the fields; traffic diversions because of road repairs.* 2 nc an activity which gives pleasure: *Chess and tennis are his favourite diversions.* 3 nc a method used to turn the attention away from something that one does not wish to be noticed: *to create/make a diversion.*

di·ver·sion·ary /daɪ'vɜ:ʃnərɪ/ adj

di·ver·si·ty /daɪ'vɜ:sətɪ/ nu or sing (*formal*) the state of being diverse; variety: *a wide diversity of subjects to study.*

di·vert /daɪ'vɜ:t/ vt 1 **divert sth (from sth)** to turn something in another direction: *divert a river from its course.* 2 **divert sb (from sth)** to take a person's attention away (from something): *divert her from her problems.*

di·vest /daɪ'vest/ vt **divest sb of sth** (*formal*) to take (something) away from (a person): *divest an official of power and authority.*

di·vide /dɪ'vaɪd/ v 1 vt,vi **divide (sth among/ between sb)** to separate or be separated: *We divided the money equally. They divided the cash among/between themselves. The road divides at this point.* 2 vt,vi **divide (sth) (by/into sth)** to find out how often (one number) is contained in another: *If you divide 6 into 30/ divide 30 by 6, the answer is 5.* 3 vt **divide sb (from sb)** to separate a person (from others): *dividing the boys from the girls.* 4 vi to separate in order to vote: *After a long debate, the House (= Parliament) divided.*

divi·dend /'dɪvɪdənd/ nc a (monthly, annual etc) payment of a share of profit: *The company paid a dividend of 10 pence per share.*

di·vid·ers /dɪ'vaɪdəz/ n pl (also *a pair of dividers*) (*maths*) an instrument used for measuring or marking distances, angles etc.

di·vine¹ /dɪ'vaɪn/ adj 1 (often D-; *no comp*) of, from, God: *Divine worship.* 2 (*informal*) excellent; very beautiful: *divine weather. She looks divine in that new dress.*

di·vine·ly adv

di·vine² /dɪ'vaɪn/ vt (*formal*) to discover, learn, about (future events, hidden things etc) without usual or obvious methods, as if by magic: *divining what the future has in store.*

div·ing /'daɪvɪŋ/ nu ⇨ dive².

di·vin·ity /dɪ'vɪnətɪ/ n 1 nu the quality of being divine¹(1): *the divinity of Christ.* 2 nu the study of theology: *a student of divinity.*

di·vis·ible /dɪ'vɪzəbl/ adj **divisible (by sth)** that can be divided: *8 is divisible by 2.*

di·vi·sion /dɪ'vɪʒn/ n 1 nu the process of dividing or being divided: *the division of time into months, weeks and days; a simple problem in division* (e.g. 50 ÷ 5). 2 nc an act, result, of dividing; one of the parts into which something is divided: *Is that a fair division of the money? He plays in the second division of the Football League.* 3 nu the process of dividing(2): *the division of 30 by 6.* 4 nc **division (between sth and sth)** something that separates things: *A hedge forms the division between his land and mine.* 5 nc (*mil*) a unit of two or more brigades.

di·vorce¹ /dɪ'vɔ:s/ nc,nu (also *attrib*) (an instance of) the legal ending of a marriage so that the man and woman are free to marry again: *sue for a divorce; to take/start divorce proceedings; to get a divorce (from Peter).*

di·vorce² /dɪ'vɔ:s/ vt 1 to end a marriage by law: *Did Mr Hill divorce his wife or did she divorce him?* 2 (*fig*) (*formal*) to separate things: *Can you divorce economics from politics?*

di·vor·cee /dɪˌvɔ:'si:/ nc a divorced person.

di·vulge /daɪ'vʌldʒ/ vt to make known (a secret): *divulging new plans to a competitor.*

DIY abbr do it yourself. ⇨ do³(1).

diz·zy /'dɪzɪ/ adj (**-ier, -iest**) 1 (of a person) feeling as if everything is turning round, as if unable to balance; mentally confused. 2 (of a place, condition) causing such a feeling: *a dizzy height.*

diz·zi·ly /-əlɪ/ adv

diz·zi·ness nu

DJ /ˌdi:'dʒeɪ/ abbr 1 disc jockey. 2 dinner jacket.

DNA /ˌdi: en 'eɪ/ abbr (**d**eoxyribo**n**ucleic **a**cid) the main chemical substance of all organisms.

do¹ /du:/ nc (pl **do's** or **dos** /du:z/) 1 (*informal*) a party or similar entertainment: *The Browns are having a big do to celebrate their anniversary.* 2 **do's and don'ts** (*informal*) regulations: *Are there too many do's and don'ts in your home?*

do² /də strong form: du:/ auxiliary verb Ⓝ *'Do'* as an auxiliary verb is used with the infinitive form of another verb without 'to', mainly to form negatives, questions and for emphasis.

1 do + verb without *'to'* replaces the present simple tense (e.g. *play*) or the past simple tense (e.g. *played*) (**a**) (used with *not* to form the negative): *I do not play tennis. He does not/doesn't want it. I didn't know. Don't worry about it. You don't have to come.* Ⓝ *'Do'* is not used with *never, no-one,*

do	Present participle **doing** /'du:ıŋ/; past participle **done** /dʌn/	

Positive statements	**Negative statements**	**Questions***
Present tense forms:		
I **do**	I do not, I **don't** /dəunt/	do I? don't I?
you **do**	you do not, you **don't**	do you? don't you?
he/she/it **does** /dəz, dʌz/	he/she/it does not, he/she/it **doesn't** /'dʌznt/	does he/she/it? doesn't he/she/it?
we **do**	we do not, we **don't**	do we? don't we?
you **do**	you do not, you **don't**	do you? don't you?
they **do**	they do not, they **don't**	do they? don't they?
Past tense forms (all persons):		
did /dɪd/	did not, **didn't** /'dɪdnt/	did I/he/you etc? didn't she/we/they etc?

The other tenses of 'do' are formed in the same way as those of other verbs, as in *will do the work, is doing her best, was doing that, has done well.*

* The negative question forms *do I not? did she not?* etc are also correct but are more formal.

nothing etc in negative sentences. **(b)** (used to form questions): *Do you play tennis? Does he want it? Didn't he go? Did her have to say that?* Ⓝ *'Do'* is not used in questions with *who, which* etc as the subject, as in *Who said that? Which came first?* ⇨ also 3(a) below. ⇨ have¹(2). **2** (use in affirmative sentences) **(a)** (to show emphasis): *I really do love you. She does play the piano. He did need you. Do be quiet!* **(b)** (to make a polite request): *Do please telephone me. Do have some more wine.* Ⓝ For *'do'* as an auxiliary verb used with *'do'* as an ordinary verb, as in *Do do your homework, please* or *Don't do that,* ⇨ do³(1a). **(c)** (used to replace another verb used earlier in a sentence): *I said I love you and I do. He promised to come and he did. Do you or don't you?* (e.g. like it?) *She doesn't want it but I do. He enjoys swimming and so do I.* ⇨ (d) below. **'do so** (used when referring to activity, esp when explaining how, why, when etc): *He asked me not to tell you but I did so because it was important. She promised to return the money and she did so as soon as she was paid.* **(d)** (used in comparisons): *She plays the guitar better than you do. He worked much harder than you did.* Ⓝ *'Do', 'did'* etc can be omitted, as in *She plays better than you.* **3** (used in conversation) **(a)** (joined to the end of a statement to form a question): *We leave on Saturday, don't we? She didn't say that, did she?* Ⓝ The short addition is always negative (e.g. *don't*) if the statement is positive (e.g. *leave*) and positive (e.g. *did*) if the statement is negative (e.g. *didn't say*). Statements with *neither, no, nobody, nothing* etc are considered to be negative and the short addition is always positive, as in *Nothing happened, did it?* **(b)** (used to make a short question): *'She won the race.'—'Did she?' 'They didn't go.'—'Didn't they?'* Ⓝ If the statement is positive the short question is also positive and if the statement is negative the short question is also negative. **(c)** (used to give a short answer showing approval, permission, responsibility etc): *'Do you like modern jazz?'—'No, I don't.'/'Yes, I do.' 'Shall I ask her to come?'—'Yes, please do.'/'Yes do.'/'Do.' 'I'll call the police.'—'No, please don't.'/'No, don't.'/'Don't.'*

'Who broke the window?'—'I did.' 'Which goes faster?'—'This one does.' Ⓝ The auxiliary verb *'do'* is only used in (a), (b) and (c) when there is no other auxiliary verb (e.g. *be, can, have*) in the main statement. Compare: be¹, have¹.

do³ /du:/ *v* **1** *vt* **(a)** to carry out, take part in, (an action or activity): *Who's doing the cooking tonight? He said he'd do it and he did. I have so much work to do. I've nothing to do and I'm bored. Can you do a handstand? I tried but I can't do it. You must do your duty. He would have done it if you'd asked. What are you doing in my office?* (i.e. *Why are you in my office?*) *She's doing her knitting. He does a little gardening each evening. How would you like your steak done* (= cooked)? *I like it well done* (= cooked completely). *What did you do after that? Does he do any exercise? What do you do for a living? Do the washing-up, Sam. Don't do that!* Ⓝ The last five examples show the use of *'do'* as an auxiliary verb (i.e. *. . . did you . . . , Does he . . . , do you . . . , Do do . . . , Don't do . . .*) with *'do'* as an ordinary verb. ⇨ overdo(2). ⇨ also *do so* at do²(2) above. **do it yourself** (abbr DIY) to carry out house repairs, decorate, make things out of wood etc, oneself (and not pay a professional worker). **(b)** to produce (something) as a result of activity: *do six copies/a translation/a Chinese meal.* Ⓝ *'Make'* is also possible and is used when referring to a particular production, construction or creation from parts, as in *make a model plane/a new dress/a contract,* or a result of an amount of work, thought etc, as in *'make arrangements/a mistake/money/a noise'.* *'Make'* is used much more often than *'do'.* ⇨ make²(1,2). **2** *vt* to solve, find the answer to, (something): *do a difficult calculation/a crossword/a puzzle.* **3** *vt* to study, learn, work at, (a subject): *I'm doing business studies/Spanish/education at college. Didn't she do science at school?* Ⓝ Compare *'do the cooking'* (= prepare a meal) and *'do cooking at college'* (= learn how to prepare a meal). **4** *vt* to arrange, tidy, fix, clean etc (something): *do one's hair/the flowers; do the garden; do one's teeth; do the house from top to bottom* (= clean it thoroughly). **5** *vt, vi* to behave; perform, act; cause (something as a result): *You can't do as you please. I'll do everything I can to help. You'll do more harm than good. She could do better. What will you do if she refuses? I can only do my best. He won't do himself any good by arguing.* **do or die** (*informal*) to have the choice of responding to a challenge or losing all hope, opportunity etc. **6** *vt* to travel, complete, (a distance): *They did the trip by air/in six hours. How many miles a day did you do?* **7** *vi* (*informal*) to happen: *What's doing at the club tonight?* **Nothing doing!** (*sl*) I refuse (to agree, accept, do it etc). **8** *vi* to be enough; be satisfactory: *£5 will do as a deposit. Will these shoes do for walking? They'll have to do. Will this do (until I find another one)?* Ⓝ Often used in the future tense. **make sth do; make do with sth** ⇨ make²(8). **9** *vi* to make progress; improve: *She's doing well/badly at school/at tennis/in her studies. He's done better than expected after such a long illness. How are you doing in your job?* **How do you do?** (used as a polite form of address when being introduced to a person). Ⓝ The reply is identical.

do sth about sb/sth to deal with a problem, difficult person etc: *What can be done about high unemployment? You must do something about your hair.*

do as sth to be a substitute for something: *This bottle will have to do as a vase.* ⇨ also 8 above.

do away with sth (*informal*) to abolish, get rid of, (something): *Do you think written exams should be done away with?*

be hard done by to be treated very unfairly: *She complained that she was hard done by.* **do well by sb** (*informal*) to be treated kindly and generously by a person: *The children did well by their grandfather.*

do sb/sth down (*informal*) to try to make a person, thing, seem unimportant, inferior etc: *She's always doing her husband down. Why do your country down by criticizing it so much?* ⇨ run sb/sth down.

do for sb (a) to be enough, be satisfactory, for a person: *A salary of £80 a week will do for him.* Ⓝ '*For him*' can be omitted, as in 8 above. (b) (*informal*) to carry out housework for a person: *She's been doing for me since my wife died.* **do for sth** (a) = do as sth: *That old box will do for a table.* (b) to manage to get something: *What shall we do for fuel during the winter?* **be done for** to be ruined, destroyed, dying etc: *If we can't borrow the money we're done for. The nurse could do nothing—he was done for.* **do well for oneself** to become successful, rich etc.

do sb in (*sl*) to kill a person: *Who did her in?* **done in** (*informal*) exhausted: *be/feel done in.*

do sth out to make a room, cupboard etc clean and tidy. **do sb out of sth** (*informal*) to use tricks etc to prevent a person from having something: *He tried to do me out of a job.*

do sb over (*sl*) to hit and hurt a person very badly. **do sth over** (*informal*) to redecorate a room etc: *The hall has been done over.*

do something to sb (*informal*) to cause a person to feel excitement, attraction etc: *You do something to me that mystifies me.*

do (sth) up (a) to fasten clothes, a bag etc using buttons, a zip etc: *Do up your coat.* (b) to be fas-

tened (in a place, way etc mentioned): *The dress does up at the back. How does it do up?* (c) to make something into a parcel, package etc: *The vase was done up in brown paper/with string.* (d) to decorate, modernize etc a room, building: *We're having the kitchen done up.*

do with sb/sth to deal, cope, with a person, thing: *What can I do with such a naughty child? I didn't know what to do with myself. I can't do with him and his bad temper. What can be done with unemployed teenagers?* **do with sth** (used in questions) to place, hide, use etc something: *What have I done with my glasses? What did he do with the money?* **can/could do with sth** to need, want, something: *He could do with a bath!* **have to do with sb/sth** (a) to be caused by (a person, thing); be connected with: *It had nothing/something/a little to do with the weather.* (b) to be associated with (a person, activity): *I warned you to have nothing to do with her.*

do without (sb/sth) to manage, work, exist etc without a person, thing: *I can't do without you. You'll have to do without a car for today. It's not ready yet so you'll have to do without.* ⇨ go without (sth). **can/could do without sb/sth** to be better without a person, thing: *I can certainly do without your interference.*

do. *abbr* ditto.

d.o. *abbr* (*commerce*) delivery order.

do·cile /'dəʊsaɪl/ *adj* (also *derog*) quiet; easily trained or controlled: *a docile child/horse.*

do·cil·ity /dəʊ'sɪlətɪ/ *nu*

dock¹ /dɒk/ *nc* a place in a criminal court for the prisoner: *to be in the dock.*

dock² /dɒk/ *n* **1** a place in a harbour, river etc where ships are (un)loaded or repaired. **2** (*pl*) (the —s) a group of docks with the sheds, offices etc round them.

dock·er *nc* a dockyard labourer.

'dock·yard *nc* a place with docks and facilities for building and repairing ships.

dock³ /dɒk/ *vi,vt* **1** (to cause a ship) to come or go into a dock. **2** (to cause a spacecraft) to join with another in space.

dock⁴ /dɒk/ *vt* (*esp*) to make (wages, supplies) less: *to dock a workman's wages; to have one's salary docked.*

dock·et /'dɒkɪt/ *nc* (*commerce*) **1** a list of goods delivered, jobs done etc. **2** a label on a package listing the contents, giving information about use etc.

doc·tor¹ /'dɒktə(r)/ *nc* (often D-) **1** a person who has been trained in medical science. ⇨ physician, surgeon. **2** a person who has received the highest university degree: *a Doctor of Laws/Philosophy.*

doc·tor² /'dɒktə(r)/ *vt* **1** (*informal*) to give medical treatment to (an illness): *doctor a cold.* **2** to use dishonest means to change (results, accounts, evidence etc) to one's advantage. **3** to make (esp food, drink) harmful by adding drugs etc.

doc·tor·ate /'dɒktərɪt/ *nc* a doctor's(2) degree. ⇨ D.Phil., Ph.D.

doc·tri·naire /ˌdɒktrɪ'neə(r)/ *adj* (*derog*) theoretical (and not thinking about practical problems): *doctrinaire politicians.*

doc·tri·nal /ˌdɒk'traɪnl/ *adj* of doctrine(s).

doc·trine /'dɒktrɪn/ *nc,nu* (a system of) principles of teaching, beliefs of a church, political party etc: *There is a doctrine that the Pope is infallible.*

docu·ment¹ /'dɒkjʊmənt/ *nc* a written account providing proof, evidence etc.

docu·ment² /'dɒkjʊment/ *vt* (often *passive*) to prove (something) by, supply (something) with, written evidence: *a well-documented report.*

docu·men·ta·tion /ˌdɒkjʊmen'teɪʃn/ *nu*

docu·men·tary¹ /ˌdɒkjʊ'mentrɪ/ *adj* (*attrib*) of, with, documents: *documentary proof/evidence.*

docu·men·tary² /ˌdɒkjʊ'mentrɪ/ *nc* (*pl* **-ies**) (also *documentary film*) a film providing facts about social topics, the natural world, science etc.

dod·der /'dɒdə(r)/ *vi* (*informal*) to walk, move, in a shaky way, e.g. because of old age: *doddering along.*

dod·der·er *nc* a person who dodders.

doddle /'dɒdl/ *n sing* (*informal*) something done very easily: *The interview was a doddle.*

dodge¹ /dɒdʒ/ *nc* **1** a quick movement to avoid something. **2** (*informal*) a deception: *He's up to* (= knows) *all the dodges.*

dodge² /dɒdʒ/ *v* **1** *vt,vi* to move quickly to one side, change position, in order to avoid something: *dodging traffic. I dodged behind a tree so that he could not see me.* **2** *vt* to avoid (difficulties, duties etc) by dishonesty or trickery: *He's dodging his turn to wash the dishes.*

dodg·er *nc* a cunning person.

dodgy /'dɒdʒɪ/ *adj* (**-ier, -iest**) (*informal*) **1** risky; not safe: *a dodgy piece of equipment.* **2** (*derog*) using clever and dishonest methods: *dodgy business methods.*

doe /dəʊ/ *nc* a female deer, rabbit or hare.

DOE /ˌdiː əʊ 'iː/ *abbr* (the —) (*GB*) the Department of the Environment.

do·er /'duːə(r)/ *nc* (*informal*) a person who does things (contrasted with a person who only talks about it etc): *He's a doer not a talker.*

does /dʌz/, **doesn't** /'dʌznt/ ⇨ do²,³.

dog¹ /dɒg/ *nc* **1** a common domestic animal of which there are many breeds. **go to the dogs** (of a person) to be ruined because of one's own foolishness. **lead a dog's life** to be troubled, unhappy, all the time. **lead sb a dog's life** to cause a person to be troubled, unhappy. **let sleeping dogs lie** to avoid or stop doing something (e.g. quarrelling) that causes trouble. **not stand (even) a dog's chance** to have no chance at all (of beating a stronger enemy, surviving a disaster etc). ⇨ also top dog, underdog. **2** a male of this animal and of the wolf and the fox. Compare bitch.

'dog-collar *nc* (*informal*) a clerical collar.

'dog-eared *adj* (of a book) having the corners of the pages turned down with use.

'dog-house *n sing* **be in the doghouse** (*sl*) to be in disgrace.

dog·gy /'dɒgɪ/ *nc* (*pl* **-ies**) (a child's word for) a dog.

dog² /dɒg/ *vt* (**-gg-**) **1** to keep close behind (a person, vehicle, one is following): *dog a suspected thief.* **2** **dogged by sth** (*fig*) often affected by something bad: *be dogged by misfortune/illness.*

dog·ged /'dɒgɪd/ *adj* determined and stubborn when trying to solve or complete something.

dog·ger·el /'dɒgərəl/ *nu* (*formal*) **1** nonsense. **2** (*literature*) a poor attempt at poetry (often done

to amuse).

dog·ma /'dɒgmə/ *nc,nu* (*pl* **—s**) a belief, system of beliefs (esp by the Church) to be accepted as true without question.

dog·mat·ic /dɒg'mætɪk/ *adj* **1** put forward as dogmas: *dogmatic theology.* **2** (*derog*) (of a person, statement) expressing opinions in an arrogant way.

dog·mati·cal·ly /-klɪ/ *adv*

dog·ma·tism /'dɒgmətɪzəm/ *nu* (the quality of) being dogmatic.

do-good·er /ˌduː 'gʊdə(r)/ *nc* (*informal*) a person who often works for charity etc.

dogs·body /'dɒgzbɒdɪ/ *nc* (*pl* **-ies**) a person who is made to do a lot of inferior work.

do·ing /'duːɪŋ/ *nu* activity; work: *Is this mess your doing? It will take a lot of doing to persuade her to stay.*

do·ings /'duːɪŋz/ *n pl* (*informal*) activities: *Tell me about all your doings in London.*

dol·drums /'dɒldrəmz/ *n pl* **be in the doldrums** (*fig*) to be sad, depressed.

Dolby /'dɒlbɪ/ *n* (*P*) (also *attrib*) a system that reduces hiss when tapes are played on a taperecorder.

dole¹ /dəʊl/ *nc* **be/go on the dole** (*informal*) to receive/begin to receive weekly payment from the State as an unemployed person.

dole² /dəʊl/ *vt* **dole sth (out)** to distribute food, money etc in small amounts (e.g. to poor people).

dole·ful /'dəʊlfəl/ *adj* sad, depressed.

dole·ful·ly /-fəlɪ/ *adv*

doll¹ /dɒl/ *nc* a model of a baby or person for a child to play with.

doll² /dɒl/ *v reflex* **doll oneself up** (of a woman) (*informal*) to dress up attractively: *She was all dolled up for the party.*

dol·lar /'dɒlə(r)/ *nc* a unit of money (symbol $) in the US, Canada, Australia etc.

dol·lop /'dɒləp/ *nc* (*informal*) a shapeless quantity (of food etc): *a dollop of ice-cream.*

dol·ly /'dɒlɪ/ *nc* (*pl* **-ies**) (a child's word for) a doll.

dol·phin /'dɒlfɪn/ *nc* a kind of sea animal smaller than a whale, with a long nose.

dolt /dəʊlt/ *nc* (*derog*) a stupid person.

do·main /də'meɪn/ *nc* (*formal*) **1** the lands under the rule of a government, ruler etc. **2** (*fig*) an area or topic of knowledge, activity or responsibility: *It's in the domain of biological research.*

dome /dəʊm/ *nc* a round roof with a circular base; something shaped like a dome: *the rounded dome of a hill.*

domed *adj* like a dome in shape: *a domed forehead.*

do·mes·tic¹ /də'mestɪk/ *adj* **1** related to the home, family, house: *domestic costs/duties/life/ help.* **2** of one's own country: *This newspaper provides more foreign news than domestic news.* **3** (of animals etc) kept by, living with, people: *Cows, dogs and cats are domestic animals.* ⇨ wild¹(1).

do·mestic ap'pliance *nc* any electrical or gas household equipment such as a washing-machine, cooker etc.

do·mestic 'bliss *nu* a very happy life at home.

do·mestic 'drama *nc,nu* (*literature*) drama using everyday life as themes for the plot.

do·mes·tic² /də'mestɪk/ *nc* a person who is

employed to do housework.

do·mes·ti·cat·ed /dəˈmestɪkeɪtɪd/ adj **1** able to do, interested in, housework: *I'm not at all domesticated.* Opp undomesticated. **2** (of animals) being kept on a farm or used as a pet.

do·mes·tic·ity /ˌdəʊmeˈstɪsətɪ/ nu (the enjoyment of) home or family life.

domi·cile /ˈdɒmɪsaɪl/ nc (*legal*) a place where a person lives permanently.

domi·nance /ˈdɒmɪnəns/ nu **dominance (of/over sb)** the state of being dominant.

domi·nant /ˈdɒmɪnənt/ adj **1** having strong control or authority; dominating: *a dominant personality.* **2** most important or influential: *the dominant partner in a business.* **3** overlooking others: *a dominant position above the town.* **4** (*science*) (of a gene) showing the strong characteristics which are passed to later generations, e.g. brown eyes and brown hair. Compare recessive.

domi·nant·ly adv

domi·nate /ˈdɒmɪneɪt/ vt,vi **1** to have strong control, authority or influence: *Mary dominated the conversation. Muhammed Ali dominated boxing for many years.* **2** (of part of a place) to overlook other parts: *The whole valley is dominated by this mountain.*

domi·na·tion /ˌdɒmɪˈneɪʃn/ nu

domi·neer /ˌdɒmɪˈnɪə(r)/ vi **domineer (over sb)** (*formal*) to act, speak, in a dominating manner: *Big boys sometimes domineer over their sisters.*

domi·neer·ing adj (*derog*): *He's a very domineering man.*

do·min·ion /dəˈmɪnɪən/ n **1** nu **dominion (over sb/sth)** authority to rule; control (over). **2** nc (often pl) the territory of a sovereign government. **3** nc (D-) one of the self-governing territories of the British Commonwealth: *the Dominion of Canada.*

dom·ino /ˈdɒmɪnəʊ/ nc (pl —es or —s) **1** a small, flat, oblong piece of wood or bone, marked with spots. **2** (pl) (used with a *sing v*) a game played with 28 of these.

do·nate /dəʊˈneɪt/ vt to give (esp money) (to a charity etc): *donating money/clothes to Oxfam.*

do·na·tion /dəʊˈneɪʃn/ nc,nu (an act of) donating something; something donated: *donations to the refugee fund.*

done¹ /dʌn/ adj **be not done** to be socially wrong: *It's not done to drink from a saucer.* **the done thing** accepted social behaviour.

done² /dʌn/ pp of do²,³. ⇨ also done in at do sb in.

don·key /ˈdɒŋkɪ/ nc (pl —s) an animal like a small horse but with long ears, used to carry loads. **(for) donkey's years** (*informal*) (for) a very long time: *I've lived here for donkey's years. It's donkey's years since we met.*

'donkey-work nu work needing great (physical) effort.

do·nor /ˈdəʊnə(r)/ nc **1** a person who donates something. **2** a person who gives part of his own body for medical use: *a kidney/blood donor.*

don't /dəʊnt/ = do not. **1** v ⇨ do². **2** do's and don'ts ⇨ do¹(2).

doodle /ˈduːdl/ vi,nc (*informal*) (to make) a meaningless scrawl or scribble.

doom¹ /duːm/ nu death; something evil that is to come: *to send a man to his doom.*

doom² /duːm/ vt (usually *passive*) to cause (something) to be destroyed, ruined etc: *The project is doomed to failure.*

Dooms·day /ˈduːmzdeɪ/ n the day of Judgement. **(from now) until Doomsday** for ever.

door /dɔː(r)/ nc **1** a movable flat object that closes the entrance to a room, cupboard etc: *The door opened/was opened and a man came out.* ⇨ back door, front door. **answer the door** to go and open the door to a house etc when a visitor arrives. **lay sth at sb's door** to say that he or she is responsible for something bad. **next door** ⇨ next¹(1). ⇨ outdoor, outdoors. **be at death's door** to be dying. **2** (*fig*) a means of obtaining or approaching something: *a door to success.* **by the back door** by using dishonest methods.

'door·bell nc a bell outside a building used to call a person who is inside.

'door·keeper nc a person on duty at the door of a building.

'door·man nc uniformed attendant at the entrance to a hotel etc.

'door·mat nc a mat by a door on which shoes can be wiped.

'door·step nc a step in front of a door.

'door-to-door adj (*attrib*) visiting homes (e.g. to sell something): *a door-to-door salesman.*

'door·way nc an opening into which a door fits: *standing in the doorway.*

dope¹ /dəʊp/ nu **1** (*informal*) any strong or harmful drug (e.g. opium). **2** (*sl; derog*) a stupid person. **3** (the —) (*sl*) the facts: *Give me all the dope.*

dope² /dəʊp/ vt to give dope(1) to (a person, animal): *Doping horses is illegal.*

do·pey (also **do·py**) /ˈdəʊpɪ/ adj (**dopier, dopiest**) (*sl*) **1** (as if) drugged. **2** (*dated; derog*) stupid.

dor·mant /ˈdɔːmənt/ adj in a state of inactivity but awaiting development or activity: *a dormant volcano. This project must remain dormant until we have enough staff.*

dor·mi·tory /ˈdɔːmɪtrɪ/ nc (pl -ies) a room for sleeping with several beds, e.g. in a school or institution.

dor·mouse /ˈdɔːmaʊs/ nc (pl **dormice** /ˈdɔːmaɪs/) a kind of small animal like a mouse, that sleeps during winter.

dor·sal /ˈdɔːsl/ adj (*tech*) of, on, near, the back(1): *the dorsal fin of a shark.*

dos·age /ˈdəʊsɪdʒ/ nc,nu (an act, quantity of) the giving of medicines in doses.

dose¹ /dəʊs/ nc **1** a quantity (of medicine) to be taken at one time: *The bottle contains six doses.* **2** (*informal; fig*) something given or taken: *Give her a dose of her own medicine* (= behave as badly as she does).

dose² /dəʊs/ vt to give dose(s) to (a person, animal): *dosing oneself with aspirin.*

doss /dɒs/ vi (*GB sl*) **doss down** to make a (cheap) temporary bed and go to sleep.

'doss-house nc a very cheap place to sleep.

dos·sier /ˈdɒsɪeɪ/ nc a set of papers giving information about a person or event, esp a personal record: *We've kept a dossier on her.*

dot¹ /dɒt/ nc **1** a small round mark (as over the letters i and j). **on the dot** (*informal*) at the exact time mentioned: *Be back by six o'clock on the dot.* **2** something like a dot in appearance: *We watched the ship until it was a mere dot on the horizon.*

,dot 'matrix *nc* (*computers*) the formation of a character or symbol by using dots.

dot² /dɒt/ *vt* (-tt-) to mark (something) with, make, cover, (something) with, dots. **a dotted line** e.g. for a signature: *Sign on the dotted line.* **dotted about** scattered here and there: *houses dotted about in the valley.*

do·tage /'dəʊtɪdʒ/ *nu* mental weakness caused by old age: *He's in his dotage* (= is becoming unable to remember etc).

dote /dəʊt/ *vi* **dote (on sb/sth)** to show (too) much fondness (for): *She dotes on her grandson.* do·ting *adj* (*attrib*) very loving: *a doting father.*

dot·ty /'dɒtɪ/ *adj* (-ier, -iest) (*informal*) **1** mad; eccentric. **2 be dotty about sb** to be in love with a person: *I'm dotty about her.*

double¹ /'dʌbl/ *adj* **1** twice as much, big, good etc: *He ate a double portion of meat. His income is double what it was two years ago.* **2** (*attrib*) having two like things or parts: *double doors.* **3** (*attrib*) made for two people or things: *a double bed; a double room* (e.g. for two guests in a hotel). **4** (*attrib*) combining two uses, qualities etc: *furniture that serves a double purpose* (e.g. as a seat and as a bed); *a word with a double meaning.*

,double 'agent *nc* a spy who supplies information to both sides.

,double-'barrelled *adj* (**a**) (of a gun) having two barrels. (**b**) (of a surname) hyphened.

,double-'bass *nc* the largest and lowest-pitched stringed musical instrument.

,double-'breasted *adj* (of a coat, jacket) made to cross over at the front with two rows of buttons.

,double-'check *vt,vi* to check²(1) (something) twice in order to be certain.

,double 'chin *nc* a chin with loose flesh underneath.

,double-'cross *vt* (*informal*) to cheat or betray (two people, groups, by pretending to support both).

,double-'dealing *adj, nc* (using) deceit (in business).

,double-'decker *nc* (**a**) a bus with an upper level. (**b**) a sandwich with two layers of filling.

,double 'Dutch *adj, nu* (*informal*) (speech) unable to be understood.

,double-'edged *adj* (*fig*) (of a compliment, remark etc) having two possible interpretations, one good and the other bad.

,double en'tendre *nc* ⇨ separate entry.

,double 'figures *n pl* numbers from 10 to 99 inclusive.

,double 'glazing *nu* two pieces of glass in a window (to reduce heat loss, sound).

,double-'jointed *adj* having joints (e.g. in the fingers) that bend in unusual ways.

,double 'negative *nc* (*lang*) the use of two negatives in a sentence etc when only one is correct, e.g. *I wouldn't tell nobody.* Ⓝ *'Neither', 'no', 'nobody', 'none' etc are considered to be negative and the use of 'not' is incorrect.*

,double-'quick *adj, adv* very quick(ly): *in double-quick time.*

'double-talk *nu* a kind of talk that really means the opposite of, or something quite different from, what it seems to mean.

double² /'dʌbl/ *adv* **1** twice (as much): *Many things now cost double what they did a year ago.* **2** in twos, in pairs or couples: *folded double.* **see double** to see two things when there is only one.

double³ /'dʌbl/ *nc* **1** a number, quantity, size etc that is two times as large: *Ten is the double of five.* **2** a person, thing, that looks (almost) exactly like another: *She's her mother's double.* **3 at the double** (**a**) (*mil*) at a slow run (about twice as fast as ordinary walking): *The troops advanced at the double.* (**b**) (*fig*) immediately: *Come here at the double!* **4** a quantity of alcoholic drink that is two times the usual one.

double⁴ /'dʌbl/ *v* **1** *vt,vi* (to cause something) to become twice as large: *doubling one's income.* **2** *vt* **double sth (over)** to bend, fold, something to make two layers: *If you are cold, double the blanket* (*over*).

double as/for sb/sth to be a substitute for a person, thing: *The actor is doubling as a soldier/ for another actor who is ill.*

double sth back to turn, fold, it back to make two layers: *double back the blankets.* **double back (on sb/sth)** to turn back quickly (to escape etc): *The prisoner doubled back on his tracks.*

double up (*informal*) (**a**) to bend over (in pain). (**b**) to begin to laugh a lot. **double sth up** to bend, fold, something in the middle: *He doubled up his legs to avoid the shark.*

double en·tendre /,du:blə ɑ:n'tɑ:ndrə/ *nc* (*Fr*) a word or phrase with two possible uses (often with one rude meaning and meant to amuse).

doubles /'dʌblz/ *n pl* (also *attrib*) (*tennis* etc) a game between two pairs: *mixed doubles* (= with men and women); *my doubles partner.*

doub·let /'dʌblɪt/ *nc* a type of close-fitting jacket worn by men (about 1400/1600).

doub·ly /'dʌblɪ/ *adv* (used before an *adj*) twice the extent or amount: *be doubly careful/sure.*

doubt¹ /daʊt/ *nc,nu* **(no/some etc) doubt (about sth/that sth)** (a feeling of) uncertainty: *There's some doubt about his health. He has no doubt that you'll succeed. There's no doubt about it.* ⇨ also benefit¹(1). **in doubt** uncertain: *The game is in doubt because of the rain. When in doubt about a word, use a dictionary.* **no doubt** (**a**) (used as a reply meaning 'I agree' but suggesting a little uncertainty): *'He's very intelligent.'— 'No doubt, but he's lazy.'* (**b**) very probably: *No doubt he wanted to win and he did.* **without doubt** certainly: *Without doubt she's telling the truth.* **cast doubt on sth** to express unwillingness to believe something; cause one to be uncertain about the truth, value of something.

doubt² /daʊt/ *vt* to feel uncertain about (something): *I doubt whether she'll agree/if he's telling the truth. She doesn't doubt that you tried your best.* Ⓝ Not used in continuous tenses, e.g. *is/was -ing. 'Doubt if/whether . . . ' is only possible in positive sentences. 'Doubt that . . . ' is usually only used in negative sentences.*

doubt·ful /'daʊtfəl/ *adj* **doubtful (about sth/ that sth)** feeling, causing, doubt: *I'm/feel doubtful (about) what I ought to do. The future/weather* *looks very doubtful.*

doubt·ful·ly /-fəlɪ/ *adv*

doubt·less /ˈdaʊtlɪs/ *adv* **1** without doubt: *Doubtless the bank will keep it safe.* **2** (*informal*) very probably: *Doubtless I'll be ill during the exams.*

dough /dəʊ/ *nu* **1** a mixture of flour, water etc, used to make bread, pastry etc. **2** (*sl*) money.

'dough·nut *nc* a piece of sweetened dough cooked in deep fat.

doughy *adj* of, like, dough.

dour /dʊə(r)/ *adj* (of a person's character, expression) gloomy, serious and unfriendly: *dour looks.*

dour·ly *adv*

douse (also **dowse**) /daʊs/ *vt* to put (something burning) into water; throw water over (a fire): *dousing a fire.*

dove /dʌv/ *nc* **1** a kind of pigeon (esp as a symbol of peace). **2** (*fig*) a person who favours promoting peace. Opp hawk[1](2).

dow·dy /ˈdaʊdɪ/ *adj* (**-ier, -iest**) **1** (of clothes etc) dull or unfashionable. **2** (of a person) dressed in such clothes.

dow·di·ly /-əlɪ/ *adv*: *dowdily dressed.*

dow·di·ness *nu*

dow·el /ˈdaʊəl/ *nc* a pin or peg used to keep two pieces of wood etc together.

down[1] /daʊn/ *adj* **1** (*pred*) sad; depressed; ill: *be/feel down.* **2 a down payment** ⇨ payment(2).

down[2] /daʊn/ *adverbial particle* Ⓝ For uses of *'down'* with verbs such as *bring, come, get, go, hold, keep, let, put, run, take, wind* etc, ⇨ the *verb* entries. **1** from a high(er) level to a low(er) one: *climb/go/jump down. We looked down and saw the ocean below us. The rain poured down. Get down from that tree! The sun is going down.* Opp up[2](1). Compare down[4](1). **2** from an upright position to a horizontal one: *The baby fell down. If you're tired, go and lie down. The telephone lines are down because of the storm. He was knocked down by a bus. She is/has gone down with* (= *is ill in bed because of*) *flu.* **3** (of a part of a person or thing) to a low(er) position: *She bent/sat down. Fold/Glue down the flap.* **4** in, to, a low(er) place: *deep down in the sea; down below the ground. The covers/blinds are down. Has Ben come down? Is Ben down* (= *downstairs*) *yet?* Compare up[2](2). **down below** under the ocean or sea. **5** to a small(er) volume, size, grade, standard etc: *The temperature is down. Who let the balloon/tyre down? The soup has boiled down to half the original quantity. Prices/Stocks are down. Trade is down. We are £100 down on last week's earnings/10% down on last month's sales. We are down to our last few pounds. Everyone must accept responsibility, from the management down.* Opp up[2](3). **down and out** (*adj*) unemployed and very poor. Hence **,down-and-'out** *nc* a very poor person. **down at heel** ⇨ heel[1](1) **be down on one's luck** ⇨ luck. **6** from a more active, loud etc level to a lower one: *calm/cool/die down. Turn that music/radio down!* Opp up[2](4). **7** in writing: *Note/Take/Write down her address and telephone number. Copy down these instructions. Our next meeting is down for June 1st. Put me down/my name down as a candidate.* **8** from north to south; from the town to the country; from a (more important) place to another: *travel down from Scotland; live down in Cornwall; work down south; down in the country; down on the farm; walk down to the post office; come down from university.* Opp up[2](6). **down under** (*informal*) in, to, Australia or New Zealand. **9** from an earlier time or period: *the history of Africa down to 1966; traditions that have been handed/passed down from our ancestors.* **10 down with sth** (*informal imperative*) I do not like, want etc: *Down with grammar!*

down[3] /daʊn/ *nu* the soft feathers of young birds, used to make pillows and cushions.

down[4] /daʊn/ *prep* **1** at, to, a low(er) level: *She ran down the hill. He looked down the microscope. Our camp is situated down the river.* Opp up[3](1). Compare down[2](1). **2** along: *I live down the road. The boat travels up and down the coast. Let's cut the cake down the middle.* Compare up[3](2).

down[5] /daʊn/ *vt* **1** to bring, throw, knock etc down: *He downed his attacker with one punch.* **down tools** (*informal*) to begin a strike by stopping one's work. **2** (*sl*) to swallow quickly: *She downed her coffee and ran for the bus.*

down-and-out /ˌdaʊn ənd ˈaʊt/ *nc* ⇨ down[2](5).

down·cast /ˈdaʊnkɑːst/ *adj* **1** (of a person) sad; depressed. **2** (of eyes) looking downwards (esp with sadness, shame etc).

down·fall /ˈdaʊnfɔːl/ *nc* **1** a heavy fall (of rain etc). **2** (*fig*) a fall from fortune or power; personal ruin: *His downfall was caused by gambling and drink.*

down·grade /ˌdaʊnˈɡreɪd/ *vt* (usually *passive*) to reduce (a person, thing) to a lower grade or rank. ⇨ upgrade.

down-heart·ed /ˌdaʊn ˈhɑːtɪd/ *adj* sad; depressed.

down·hill /ˌdaʊnˈhɪl/ *adv* in a downward direction: *walk downhill.* **go downhill** (*fig*) to go from bad to worse in health, behaviour, luck etc.

down·pour /ˈdaʊnpɔː(r)/ *nc* a heavy fall of rain.

down·right /ˈdaʊnraɪt/ *adj* (*attrib*) (of bad behaviour, actions etc) thorough: *It's a downright lie.* □ *adv* thoroughly: *He was downright rude.*

downs /daʊnz/ *n pl* (the D-) an area of low hills, esp the chalk hills of S England: *walking on the North/South Downs.*

Down's syn·drome /ˈdaʊnz sɪndrəʊm/ *nu* an abnormal condition in which a person is born mentally handicapped and with a flat, wide face.

down·stairs /ˌdaʊnˈsteəz/ *adv* **1** to, at, on, of, a lower floor; down the stairs: *Our neighbours downstairs* (= *on the lower floor*) *are very noisy. Your brother is waiting downstairs.* **2** /ˈdaʊnsteəz/ (used as an *adj* (*attrib*)): *the downstairs rooms.*

down-to-earth /ˌdaʊn tə ˈɜːθ/ *adj* (of a person) practical and realistic.

down·trod·den /ˈdaʊntrɒdn/ *adj* (of a person) (kept) poor and treated badly.

down·ward /ˈdaʊnwəd/ *adj* leading, going, pointing etc to what is lower: *a downward slope; prices with a downward tendency.*

down·wards /ˈdaʊnwədz/ *adv* towards what is lower: *She was too afraid to look downwards. He laid the picture face downwards on the table* (= with the picture facing the table). Ⓝ *'Down'* is more usual.

dow·ry /'daʊərɪ/ nc (pl **-ies**) an amount of, money, property, given by a bride's family to her husband.

dowse /daʊs/ vt = douse.

doz. abbr dozen.

doze¹ /dəʊz/ nc a short, light sleep.

doze² /dəʊz/ vi to sleep lightly; be half asleep: He was dozing during the lecture. **doze off** to fall asleep (e.g. in a chair).

doz·en /'dʌzn/ det, n (pl unchanged) twelve: Eggs were 50p a dozen. I want three dozen of these/a dozen eggs. **dozens of sth** a large number of things, occasions etc: I've been there dozens of times. **one's daily dozen** (informal) a short set of physical exercises each day: doing one's daily dozen to keep fit.

do·zy /'dəʊzɪ/ adj (**-ier, -iest**) 1 sleepy. 2 (fig) stupid.

D Phil /,di: 'fɪl/ abbr Doctor of Philosophy (an academic degree).

Dr abbr Doctor: Dr Lee.

drab /dræb/ adj (fig; derog) dull; uninteresting: drab colours; a drab existence.

　drab·ly adv

　drab·ness nu

draft¹ /drɑːft/ nc 1 (also attrib) an outline (usually in the form of rough notes or drawing) of something to be done: a draft for a speech; a draft design. 2 (also bankdraft) a written order for payment of money from one bank to another: a draft for £500 on London (e.g. one written by a Paris bank on its London branch). 3 (mil) a group of soldiers selected to do something. 4 (US) = draught.

draft² (US = draught) /drɑːft/ vt 1 to make a draft(1) of (something): draft a speech. 2 to order (a person) to join the armed forces.

drafts·man /'drɑːftsmən/ nc (US) = draughtsman.

drafty /'drɑːftɪ/ adj (US) = draughty.

drag¹ /dræg/ n 1 nc,nu the act, result, of dragging(1). 2 nc (informal; derog) a person, thing, that is boring, dull and annoying: She's/washing up is such a drag. ⇨ drag²(3). 3 nu (in) drag (sl) (with) a woman's clothes worn by a man: 'As You Like It' performed in drag (= with the women's parts acted by men dressed as women). 4 nc (sl) a puff (at a cigarette or cigar).

drag² /dræg/ v (**-gg-**) 1 vt to pull (something) along (esp with effort and difficulty): to drag a heavy box along the floor. 2 vt,vi (to cause, allow, a person, thing, oneself) to move slowly and with effort: Her scarf dragged through the mud. He could scarcely drag himself along. **drag one's feet** ⇨ foot¹(1). 3 vi (of time, work, an entertainment) to go on slowly in a dull manner: Time seemed to drag. 4 vt to use nets, tools etc to search the bottom of (a river, lake etc): They dragged the river for the missing child.

　drag sb down (informal) to cause a person to feel depressed, ill etc: Cold weather really drags me down.

　drag sb in/into sth to force a person to become involved: I was dragged into helping at the meeting. **drag sth in; into sth** to bring an unconnected subject into a conversation: Why do you drag politics into every discussion?

　drag sb off (informal) to take a person who does not want to go: She drags her husband off to all her concerts.

　drag on to continue for what seems a long and boring time: Their quarrels have dragged on for years.

　drag sth out to cause a meeting, decision etc to continue longer than necessary.

　drag sb/sth through the mud (fig) to say, do, something to harm the reputation of a person, her or his family name.

　drag sth up (informal) to cause an unpleasant, embarrassing event to be remembered: Must you drag up that old story of her affair again?

drag·on /'drægən/ nc 1 (in stories) an animal like a reptile but with wings and claws, able to breathe out fire. 2 (derog) an older, very strict woman.

drag·on-fly /'drægənflaɪ/ nc (pl **-flies**) a kind of insect with a long body and two pairs of long wings.

drain¹ /dreɪn/ nc 1 a pipe, channel etc used for carrying away water, sewage and other unwanted liquids; (pl) system of such pipes etc: There's a bad smell because of the drains. **go down the drain** (informal) to be wasted: When she changed her job, all that experience went down the drain. 2 (fig) something that continually uses up force, time, energy, wealth etc: Defence costs have been a great drain on the country's resources. ⇨ brain drain.

　'drain-pipe nc a pipe used in a system of drains.

drain² /dreɪn/ v 1 vi **drain away/off** (of liquid) to run or flow away: The water will soon drain away/off. 2 vt,vi (to cause land, crockery) to dry as water flows away: Land must be well drained for some crops. Leave the dishes to drain. 3 vt **drain sb/sth (of sth)** (fig) to cause a person, region to lose (strength, wealth etc) gradually: The country was drained of its wealth by the famine.

　'drain·ing-board nc a part at the side of a sink on which dishes etc are placed to drain.

drain·age /'dreɪnɪdʒ/ nu (a system for) draining or being drained.

drake /dreɪk/ nc a male duck.

dram /dræm/ nc 1 a unit of measurement of weight: 16 drams equals 1 ounce. 2 (Scot) a small drink of alcoholic spirits.

dra·ma /'drɑːmə/ n 1 nc (literature) a play for the theatre, radio or TV. 2 nu (also attrib) the writing, presentation and performance of plays: a student of drama; a drama student; be interested in drama. 2 nc,nu a series of exciting events: a holiday filled with drama. 3 nc an exaggerated (emotional) response to a problem: Don't make a drama out of such a small crisis.

dra·mat·ic /drə'mætɪk/ adj 1 (no comp) of drama(1): dramatic performances/criticism. 2 sudden and large or exciting: dramatic changes in the international situation. 3 (of a person, speech, behaviour) showing feelings, character, in a lively or exaggerated way.

　dra·mati·cal·ly /-klɪ/ adv

dra·mat·ics nu (a) dramatic works or performances: Are you interested in amateur dramatics? (b) (informal; usually derog) hysterical, excited behaviour.

dra·ma·tis per·so·nae /,drɑːmətɪs pə'səʊnaɪ/ n pl (Latin) (literature) a list of characters in a drama, e.g. listed in the text or in a theatre programme.

dra·ma·tist /'dræmətɪst/ *nc* (*literature*) a writer of plays. (N) *'Playwright'* is also possible.

dra·ma·tize (also **-ise**) /'dræmətaɪz/ *vt* **1** to put (a story, novel etc) into the form of a drama. **2** (*informal; derog*) to respond to (a problem) in an exaggerated way, esp to cause excitement.

dra·ma·tiz·ation (also **-is·ation**) /ˌdræmətaɪ-'zeɪʃn/ *nc,nu*

drank /dræŋk/ *pt* of drink².

drape /dreɪp/ *vt* **1** *drape sth over/round sth* to hang curtains, cloth, clothing etc over or round something: *draping his coat over a chair/round her shoulders.* **2** *drape sth in/with sth* to cover, decorate something using something: *walls draped with flags.*

dra·per /'dreɪpə(r)/ *nc* (*GB; dated*) a shopkeeper who sells cloth, linen, clothing etc.

dra·pery *nu* (also *attrib*) materials used for making clothes, curtains etc: *the drapery department of a large store.*

dras·tic /'dræstɪk/ *adj* (of actions, methods, medicines) having a very strong and serious effect: *use drastic measures to cure inflation/an illness.*

dras·ti·cal·ly /-klɪ/ *adv*

draught¹ (*US* = **draft**) /drɑːft/ *n* **1** *nc* (a current of) flowing air in a room, chimney or other enclosed place: *You'll catch cold if you sit in a draught.* **2** *nu* (also *attrib*) the drawing of liquid from a container (e.g. a barrel): *draught beer.* **3** *nc* (an amount drunk during) one continuous act of swallowing: *a draught of water.* **4** (*pl*) a board game for two players using twenty-four round pieces (called *draughts(men)*) (*US* = *checkers*). **5** *n sing* a depth of water needed to float a ship: *a ship with a draught of two metres.*

draughty (*US* = **drafty**) /'drɑːftɪ/ *adj* (**-ier**, **-iest**) with draughts(1) blowing through: *a draughty room.*

draw¹ /drɔː/ *nc* **1** the act of drawing(3,9): *the draw for the fourth round of the tennis tournament. The game ended in a draw* (= neither side won). **2** a person, event etc that attracts a large crowd: *He is always a great draw at political meetings.*

draw² /drɔː/ *v* (*pt* **drew** /druː/, *pp* **drawn** /drɔːn/) **1** *vt,vi* to make (pictures, plans etc) using a pen, pencil etc: *draw a picture/diagram/straight line/circle; drawing a line with chalk/with a stick.* **draw the line (at sth)** ⇨ line¹(4). **draw sth to scale** ⇨ scale²(5). ⇨ also draw sb/sth in. **2** *vt* to cause (something heavy) to move by pulling: *The horses drew the logs along the path.* **draw the curtains** ⇨ curtain¹(1). **3** *vt* to take (something) out by pulling: *draw a cork (from a bottle); draw a knife from a pocket; draw the winning ticket.* Dentists sometimes have to draw teeth. *She drew a card from the pack.* **draw a chicken** etc to take out the insides before cooking it. **4** *vi* to move, come etc (in the direction, to the position, mentioned): *The children drew near* (*to the ice-cream seller*). *The two runners drew level 100 metres from the finish. The train drew slowly into the station.* ⇨ draw away, back etc. **5** *vt* to attract (an audience, a reaction etc): *The pop singer always draws large crowds. Will that advertisement draw many new customers? Her loud crying drew a lot of attention.* **6** *vt* to cause (a person) to express feelings, opinion, information etc: *We tried to persuade her to tell us what she knew/to explain but she would not be drawn.* ⇨ draw sb out. **7** *vt* to obtain (something) (from a source): *draw money (from the bank)/water (from a well)/beer from a barrel. He drew inspiration from her encouragement.* **8** *vt* to compose, form, (an idea of the kind mentioned): *draw an analogy between my leg and a matchstick; draw a distinction between being tired and being lazy; draw the conclusion that all dogs are dangerous. The characters in Hardy's novels are well drawn.* **9** *vi* to make an equal score; end a contest without winning or losing: *The teams drew 1–1/one all.* **10** *vt* (*finance*) to write out (a cheque etc). **11** *vt* to take in (air etc): *draw a deep breath.* **12** *vi* (of a chimney etc) to allow air to move through: *This fire/pipe doesn't draw well.*

draw ahead (of sb/sth) to move in front (of).

draw apart (**a**) to move away: *The two groups of supporters drew apart as the police approached.* (**b**) (of a couple) to become emotionally separate.

draw sb aside to take a person where one can talk privately. **draw sth aside** to pull something to one side: *She drew the blankets/curtains aside.*

draw away (from sb/sth) (**a**) to go ahead (of): *Steve soon drew away (from the other runners).* (**b**) to move back or away (from): *The crowd drew away (from the horrible scene).*

draw back (from sb/sth) (**a**)= draw away (from sb/sth)(b). (**b**) (fig) to show one does not want, agree, to something: *draw back from actual fighting.* ⇨ drawback.

draw sth down to lower it: *draw down the blinds.*

draw sth from sb/sth to get comfort, inspiration etc from a person, activity etc: *draw inspiration from her/from nature.*

draw in (**a**) (of days) to become shorter. (**b**) (of a particular day) to come to an end. (**c**) (of a train) to enter a station. **draw sb/sth in** to fill a person, thing in as part of a diagram, drawing etc. **draw in one's breath** to breathe in deeply.

draw into sth (of a train) to enter a station etc.

draw sb off to attract a person away from a scene, place, situation: *A few soldiers drew off the fighters and the rest of us crossed the bridge.* **draw sth off** to remove liquid from something: *draw off the fatty liquid from the soup.*

draw on (of a season, day etc) to come near: *Winter is drawing on and we must mend the window.* **draw sth on** (not often used) to put on (clothing): *draw on a sock.* **draw on sth** to take, use, something as a source: *draw on her experience; draw on his savings; draw on one's imagination.*

draw out (of days) to become longer. **draw sb out** to make a person less reserved, quiet etc: *A good teacher should be able to draw the students out.* **draw sth out** to cause a discussion etc to take a long time: *draw out an argument.* ⇨ long-drawn-out. **draw sth out (of sb/sth)** to produce something (from); to remove something (from): *draw a gun (out of a desk drawer); draw a piece of wood out of my hand; draw money out of* *a bank; draw a confession out of him.*

be drawn to/towards sb/sth to be attracted to a person, thing (as if by magic or a magnetic force): *be drawn to her by her beauty.* **draw to a close** ⇨ close⁴.

draw up (of a bus, car etc) to come near and stop: *A car drew up and we got in.* **draw sth up** (a) to bring something near: *Do draw up a chair and sit down.* (b) to prepare a report, a list, a set of rules etc. **draw oneself up** to sit or stand upright (esp in a determined way): *She drew herself up, looked him in the eye and then slapped him.*

draw·back /ˈdrɔːbæk/ *nc* something which lessens one's satisfaction or makes progress or success less easy: *His age is a drawback.*

draw·bridge /ˈdrɔːbrɪdʒ/ *nc* a bridge that can be pulled up by chains (e.g. one across a river to allow boats to pass).

draw·er /drɔː(r)/ *nc* **1** a box-like container that slides in and out of a piece of furniture etc. ⇨ chest of drawers. **2** (usually /ˈdrɔːə(r)/) a person who draws pictures etc. **3** (usually /ˈdrɔːə(r)/) a person who cashes a cheque at a bank.

draw·ers /ˈdrɔːz/ *n pl* (*dated*) underpants with long legs.

draw·ing /ˈdrɔːɪŋ/ *n* **1** *nu* the art of representing objects, scenes etc by lines, pictures etc. **2** *nc* a diagram, picture, plan etc.

'drawing-pin *nc* a flat-headed, short pin used for fastening paper to a board etc.

draw·ing-room /ˈdrɔːɪŋ rʊm/ *nc* (*formal*) a lounge or living-room.

drawl /drɔːl/ *vi* to speak so that the sounds of the vowels are longer than usual: *The speaker drawled on.* □ *n sing* a slow way of speaking.

drawn /drɔːn/ **1** *pp* of draw². **2** *adj* (of a face etc) looking very tired, worried, full of pain etc. ⇨ also long-drawn-out.

dread¹ /dred/ *nu* or *sing* (a) great fear and anxiety: *to live in constant dread of poverty. Cats have a dread of water.*

dread² /dred/ *vt* to fear (something) greatly: *dread having to visit the dentist.*

dread·ed *adj* greatly feared.

dread·ful /-fəl/ *adj* (a) causing great trouble; terrible: *a dreadful disaster.* (b) (*informal*) very unpleasant: *What dreadful weather!*

dread·ful·ly /-fəlɪ/ *adv* (esp) (*informal*) extremely: *I'm dreadfully sorry!*

dream¹ /driːm/ *nc* **1** something which one seems to see or experience during sleep: *have a dream (about a waterfall).* Compare nightmare. **2** a state of mind in which things going on around one seem unreal: *She lives in a dream.* **3** a mental image of the future: *have dreams of wealth and happiness.* **4** a beautiful or pleasing person, thing, experience etc: *She looked a perfect dream.* **go like a dream** (of a car etc) to perform well.

dream·less *adj*

'dream·like *adj*

dream² /driːm/ *vi, vt* (*pt, pp* **dreamed** or **dreamt** /drempt/) **1** *dream (about/of sb/sth/ that sth)* to have dreams; see or experience (a person, thing) in a dream: *The explorer often dreamt of/about home/that he was home. I wouldn't dream of it/of doing such a thing* (= The idea would never occur to me). **2** *vt* **dream sth**

away to pass (time) in a dream(2): *dreaming away one's time/the hours.* **3 dream sth up** (*informal*) to think of an extraordinary excuse, plan etc.

dream·er *nc* (a) a person who dreams. (b) a person with impractical ideas etc.

dreamy /ˈdriːmɪ/ *adj* (**-ier, -iest**) **1** (of a person) with thoughts far away from her or his surroundings or work. **2** (of things, experiences) vague; unreal: *a dreamy recollection of what happened.*

dream·ily /-əlɪ/ *adv*

dreary /ˈdrɪərɪ/ *adj* (**-ier, -iest**) (*derog*) dull; uninteresting; gloomy: *dreary work/weather.*

drear·ily /-əlɪ/ *adv*

dredge /dredʒ/ *vt, vi* **dredge (sth) (for sth); (sth up)** to clear, clean, find, (something) by removing mud etc: *dredging (up) mud; dredge a channel/harbour.*

dredg·er *nc* (a ship with) a machine for digging, sucking etc underwater.

dregs /dregz/ *n pl* **1** bits of worthless matter which sink to the bottom of liquid in a glass, bottle, barrel etc. **2** (the —) (*fig*) the worst or useless section: *the dregs of society/humanity.*

drench /drentʃ/ *vt* to cause (a person) to be wet all over or all through: *be drenched with rain; drenched to the skin* (= made extremely wet).

dress¹ /dres/ *n* (also *attrib*) **1** *nc* an article of clothing with a top part and skirt, worn by a woman or girl: *dress material.* **2** *nu* clothing in general (for both men and women): *He doesn't care much about dress.* ⇨ also evening dress.

'dress circle *nc* the lowest balcony in a theatre.

'dress coat *nc* a black coat with long tails worn by men in an orchestra, for formal evenings etc.

'dress·maker *nc* a person who makes dresses.

'dress rehearsal *nc* a final rehearsal of a play in which actors wear their costumes.

dress² /dres/ *v* **1** *vt, vi* to put clothes on (a person, doll): *I'm busy dressing. He's too young/ill to dress himself. Mary was dressing her doll.* **2** *vt, vi* to put clothes on (a person) in the way mentioned: *Do you have to dress well in your job? She's badly dressed for a bank clerk.* ⇨ dress for sth, dress up. **3** *vt* to provide money for clothes for (a person): *It costs a lot to dress children these days.* **4** *vt* to clean and cover (a wound etc). ⇨ dressing(2). **5** *vt* to add a sauce to (food): *dress a salad.* ⇨ salad-dressing. **6** *vt* to prepare (a chicken, fish etc) for cooking. **7** *vt* to arrange articles for display in (a place) or on (a model): *dress a shop window.* ⇨ window-dresser.

dress sb down (*informal*) to criticize, blame, a person with angry words. Hence **,dressing- 'down** *nc.*

dress for sth to put on (more) formal clothes for an occasion: *dress for an interview/a wedding; dress for work.*

be dressed in sth (a) to be wearing something mentioned: *be dressed in national costume/in blue.* (b) (of food) to be covered with a sauce etc: *fish/salad dressed in a lemon sauce.*

dress up to put on formal or smart clothes: *We're visiting my parents on Sunday so dress up.*

dress up (as sb) to put on special or unusual clothes (for amusement or for a play): *They were dressed up as pirates.* **dress sth up** to make a piece of writing etc more impressive by using

special language, adding (too much) detail etc:
*There's no need to dress up your report with all
these long words.*

dress·er¹ /'dresə(r)/ *nc* a person who helps
actors and actresses to dress for the stage.

dress·er² /'dresə(r)/ *nc* a piece of kitchen furniture with shelves for dishes and cupboards below.

dress·ing /'dresɪŋ/ *n* **1** *nc,nu* (the process of
using) a sauce for food: *a salad-dressing; a French
dressing of oil and vinegar.* ⇨ dress²(5). **2** *nc,nu*
(the process of using) something to dress(4) a
wound, e.g. an ointment, a bandage etc. **3** *nu*
dressing (up) the act, process, of putting on
clothes.

'dressing-gown *nc* a kind of loose gown worn
over pyjamas etc.

'dressing-table *nc* a piece of bedroom furniture with drawers and a large mirror on the top.

drew /dru:/ *pt* of draw².

dribble /'drɪbl/ *vi,vt* **1** to cause a liquid to flow
drop by drop or slowly (esp from the side of the
mouth): *Babies often dribble on their bibs. She's
dribbling her soup.* **2** (*football*) to take (the ball)
forward by using many short kicks.

dried /draɪd/ *pt,pp* of dry².

dri·er /'draɪə(r)/ *adj* ⇨ dry¹. □ *nc* = dryer.

drift¹ /drɪft/ *n* **1** *nc,nu* (something caused by) a
drifting movement: *the drift of the tide; the drift of
young people towards the cities. Big drifts of
snow/snow drifts made driving slow and difficult.*
2 *nu* the general meaning: *Did you get/catch the
drift of the argument?* **3** *nu* the direction, manner,
in which events etc tend to move: *The general drift
of affairs was towards war.*

drift² /drɪft/ *vi* **1** to be carried along (as if) by a
current or wind: *The boat drifted out to sea.* **2** (*fig*)
(of a person, group) to move, change etc without
aim, purpose or self-control: *Is the country drifting towards bankruptcy? She drifts from one job to
another. We seem to have drifted apart in recent
years. The crowd drifted away.*

drift·er *nc* (**a**) a kind of fishing boat. (**b**) a person
who drifts(2).

drill¹ /drɪl/ *nc* a tool that turns quickly, used for
making holes in hard substances: *a dentist's drill.*

drill² /drɪl/ *n* **1** *nu* (*mil*) training in the handling of
weapons, marching etc: *The soldiers were at drill
in the barracks.* **2** *nc,nu* (a) thorough training by
practical experience, usually with much repetition: *drills in the English vowel sounds.* **3** *nc,nu*
(a) routine to be followed in an emergency: *fire-
drill; a lifeboat drill.*

drill³ /drɪl/ *nc* **1** a long channel where seeds are
(to be) sown. **2** a machine used for making these
and sowing seeds in them.

drill⁴ /drɪl/ *vt,vi* **1** to use a drill¹; to make (something) using a drill¹: *drilling a hole.* **2** to train (soldiers, students etc) using drill²(1). **3** to provide
practice for an emergency using drills²(3).

dri·ly /'draɪlɪ/ *adv* ⇨ dry¹.

drink¹ /drɪŋk/ *nc,nu* **1** (any) liquid for drinking:
*We have bottled drinks such as lemonade, beer
and orange juice.* **2** (a portion or kind of) alcoholic liquor: *He's too fond of drink.*

drink² /drɪŋk/ *vt,vi* (*pt* **drank** /dræŋk/, *pp*
drunk /drʌŋk/) **1** *vt,vi* **drink (sth) (up/down)**
to take (liquid) into the mouth and swallow: *to
drink a pint of milk. Drink (up) your coffee.*

*Drink (down) that medicine. You must drink in
hot weather.* **2** *vt* **drink sth (up)** (of plants, the
soil etc) to take in (liquid): *The thirsty plants
drank (up) the water I gave them.* **3** *vi* to take in
alcoholic drink, esp too much. **drink like a fish**
to drink(3) a great deal or often. **drink sb under
the table** to be able to drink(3) more than
another person. **4** *vi* **drink to sb/sth** to wish
good to a person while raising one's glass: *to drink
to him/his health/his success.*

drink·able /-əbl/ *adj* suitable, fit, for drinking:
Is this water drinkable? Opp undrinkable.

drink·er *nc* (esp) a person who drinks(3) too
often or too much: *He's a heavy drinker.*

drip¹ /drɪp/ *nc* **1** an act, sound or amount of liquid
falling in drops: *drips of rain/paint.* **2** (*informal;
derog*) a dull, weak person.

drip² /drɪp/ *vi,vt* (**-pp-**) (to cause liquid) to fall in
drops: *The tap was dripping. His hand was drip-
ping (with) blood. You're dripping paint all over
the floor.* **be dripping wet** to be very wet.

,drip-'dry *adj* (*attrib*) (of clothes etc) made of
cloth allowing them to drip until they are dry (so
that they do not need to be ironed): *drip-dry
shirts.* □ *vt,vi* (*pt,pp* **-ied**) to dry (clothes) in this
way.

drip·ping /'drɪpɪŋ/ *nu* (esp) fat etc from roasted
meat.

drive¹ /draɪv/ *n* **1** *nc* a journey in a car: *to go for a
drive. The station is an hour's drive away.* Ⓝ *'Ride'*
is used of buses, trains etc. **2** *nc* (also *driveway*) a
private road to a house or from a road to a garage.
3 *nc* a strong stroke or hit (of a ball e.g. in cricket,
golf): *a drive to the boundary.* **4** *nu* energy;
capacity to get things done: *The new headteacher
has no drive.* **5** *nc* a human need or motivation:
the sex-drive. **6** *nc* an organized effort or campaign: *an export drive.* **7** *nu* (*mechanics*) the
apparatus for keeping a vehicle moving: *My car
has four-wheel drive.*

drive² /draɪv/ *v* (*pt* **drove** /drəʊv/, *pp* **driven**
/'drɪvn/) **1** *vt,vi* to operate, direct the course of (a
car etc): *driving a taxi. Shall we drive home or
walk?* Ⓝ Compare ride home in a bus, taxi etc. **2** *vt*
to take, carry, (a person) in a car etc: *He drove me
to the station.* **3** *vt* to make (animals) move in a
particular direction: *to drive cattle to market.* **4** *vt*
(of steam, electricity or other kind of power) to
provide the power to operate (an engine,
machine): *The machinery is driven by steam.* **5** *vt*
(of wind, water) to send, throw, (something) in
the direction mentioned: *The gale drove the ship
onto the rocks. The wind was driving the rain
against the window-panes.* **6** *vt* to hit (something):
With one blow he drove the nail into the plank. **7** *vt*
to cause, force, (a person) to be (in the state mentioned): *Failure drove him to despair/to drink.
You're driving me mad.* ⇨ drive sb to (do) sth. **8** *vt*
to cause (oneself, a person) to work very hard: *He
drives himself/his staff very hard.*

be driving at sth to mean when saying something: *What are you driving at?* ⇨ get at.

drive away to drive a car etc away from somewhere.

drive back to return by driving a car. **drive sb/
sth back** to force a person, crowd etc to go back:
The police drove the fans back.

drive in to enter a park etc by driving a car etc.

Hence '**drive-in** *nc* a place (cinema, café, bank etc) where one can be served in one's car. *drive sth in* to force a nail to go in by hitting it.

drive sb into a corner ⇨ corner¹(1).

drive off = drive away.

drive out (of a place) to leave (a park etc) by driving a car etc.

drive sb to (do) sth to force, encourage, a person to do something or be in a certain state: *drive her to drink/to despair.*

drive up (to sb/sth) to approach by driving a car etc.

drive-in /'draɪv ɪn/ *nc* ⇨ drive in.

driv·el /'drɪvl/ *vt* (**-ll-**, *US:* **-l-**) *nu* (to talk) nonsense: *What's he drivelling (on) about?*

driv·en /'drɪvn/ *pp* of drive².

dri·ver /'draɪvə(r)/ *nc* a person who drives vehicles: *a taxi-driver; a bus-driver.* ⇨ chauffeur.

drive·way /'draɪvweɪ/ *nc* ⇨ drive¹(2).

dri·ving¹ /'draɪvɪŋ/ *adj* (*attrib*) (of rain, snow etc) being blown hard while falling.

dri·ving² /'draɪvɪŋ/ *nu* (also *attrib*) the activity of operating a vehicle: *driving lessons. I enjoy driving.*

'**driving licence** *nc* an official proof of being qualified to drive(1).

drizzle /'drɪzl/ *vi, nu* (to) rain (in many small fine drops): *It was drizzling all day.*

drom·edary /'drɒmədərɪ/ *nc* (*pl* **-ies**) a kind of camel with one hump.

drone¹ /drəʊn/ *n* **1** *nc* a male bee. **2** *nu* a low humming sound (as if) made by bees: *the drone of distant motorway traffic.*

drone² /drəʊn/ *vi* **1** to make a drone(2). **2** *drone (on)/(about sb/sth)* to talk in a slow, boring way: *droning on and on about his problems.*

drool /druːl/ *vi* **drool (about/over sb/sth)** to be very excited, enthusiastic.

droop /druːp/ *vi* to bend, hang, downwards (because of tiredness or weakness): *The flowers were drooping because they needed water. His spirits drooped* (= He became sad). □ *nc* a round, bending position.

drop¹ /drɒp/ *n* **1** *nc* a very small amount (of liquid): *raindrops.* **2** (*pl*) liquid medicine taken in drops: *ear/eye/nose drops.* **3** a very small amount: *There isn't a drop of milk left.* **a drop in the ocean** a very small or unimportant amount, event etc. **4** something like a drop in shape or appearance: *fruit drops* (= a kind of round sweet). **5** a movement from a higher to a lower level, esp the distance of a fall: *a sudden drop in the temperature; a drop in the price of meat; a drop of 100 metres.* **at the drop of a hat** at once and willingly.

'**drop-kick** *nc* (*rugby*) one in which the ball is dropped and kicked as it rises.

drop² /drɒp/ *v* **1** *vt, vi* (to cause liquid) to fall in drops: *Tears dropped (from her eyes). The car is dropping oil on the road.* **2** *vt* to allow (something) to fall, with or without wanting to: *He dropped his boots on the floor. They dropped the supplies by parachute. I'm sorry but I've dropped a plate.* ⇨ anchor, brick¹(1), clanger, stitch¹(2). **3** *vi* (of a person) to fall to the ground: *dropping with fatigue; drop to one's knees.* **drop dead** (a) to fall dead. (b) (*imperative; informal*) (used as a very rude way of saying) I refuse, go away etc. **4**

vi (of levels, amounts, prices etc) to become less: *The temperature is dropping. Prices have dropped.* ⇨ rise²(1). **5** *vt, vi* (to allow something) to become weaker, quieter etc: *The wind has dropped. Please drop your voice.* ⇨ rise²(6). **6** *vt* to stop a vehicle and allow (a person) to get out: *Kindly drop me at the station.* **7** *vt* to stop doing, seeing, discussing, meeting etc (something): *drop a subject at college/a hobby; drop a bad habit/a topic of discussion; drop all one's friends.* **8** *vt* to fail to select (a person): *I've been dropped (from the team) by the captain.* **9** *vt* (*informal*) to say (something) quickly or briefly: *drop a hint; drop a remark about him.* **10** *vt* (*informal*) to write and post (something short) quickly: *drop her a postcard/a note/a few lines.*

drop away to (gradually) become less: *Resistance is dropping away.*

drop back to go back to a position with others in front: *He's dropped back to third position.*

drop behind (a) = drop back. (b) to be left behind: *Europe has dropped behind Japan in car manufacturing.* ⇨ fall behind.

drop by/in (*informal*) to pay a short visit: *I'll drop by later. Do drop in if you are passing.* **drop in on sb** (*informal*) to visit a person: *He dropped in on us just as we were eating dinner.*

drop into a place (*informal*) to visit a place: *We've dropped into New York for a short holiday.*

drop off (a) to fall asleep, e.g. in a chair. (b) = drop away: *Orders are dropping off.* **drop sb off (at sth)** to stop a vehicle and allow a person to get out: *Can you drop me off at the post office?* ⇨ 6 above.

drop out (of sth) (a) to stop taking part, competing etc: *Three competitors have dropped out (of the race). She's dropped out of the team.* (b) (*informal*) to stop studying, accepting social behaviour etc: *drop out of school/society.* Hence '**drop-out** *nc* a person who does this.

drop-out /'drɒp aʊt/ *nc* ⇨ drop out (of sth).

drop·pings /'drɒpɪŋz/ *n pl* solid waste matter from animals.

drought /draʊt/ *nc, nu* (a) continuous (period of) dry weather causing suffering because of lack of food and water.

drove¹ /drəʊv/ *pt* of drive².

drove² /drəʊv/ *nc* **1** a large number of sheep or cattle being moved together. **2** (*fig*) a crowd of people moving together: *droves of sightseers; visitors arriving in droves.*

drov·er *nc* a man who moves cattle, sheep etc.

drown /draʊn/ *v* **1** *vi, vt* (to cause a person, animal) to die under water because unable to breathe: *Help! I'm drowning! He drowned the kittens.* **2** *vt* (usually *passive*) to cover (something) with water: *a boat drowned by the waves.* **3** *vt* **drown sth in sth** to make something wet with something: *a face drowned in tears.* **4** *vt* **drown sb/sth out** to prevent a person, voice etc from being heard: *The crowd drowned out the speaker. Her voice was drowned out by the shouting.*

drow·sy /'draʊzɪ/ *adj* (**-ier, -iest**) feeling sleepy; making a person feel sleepy.

drow·si·ly /-əlɪ/ *adv*

drow·si·ness *nu*

drudge /drʌdʒ/ *nc* a person who must work hard and long at unpleasant or uninteresting tasks. □ *vi* to work as a drudge does.

drudg·ery *nu* unpleasant or uninteresting work.

drug¹ /drʌg/ *nc* **1** a substance used as a medicine. **2** (also *attrib*) a substance (often habit-forming) used for pleasure or to remove pain and anxiety: *Heroin is a dangerous drug. He's a drug addict. How can we cure drug addiction?*

drug² /drʌg/ *vt* (**-gg-**) **1** to add harmful drugs to (food and drink): *His wine had been drugged.* **2** to give drugs to (a person), esp in order to make her or him unconscious: *They drugged the caretaker and then robbed the bank.*

drum¹ /drʌm/ *nc* **1** a kind of musical instrument usually made of a hollow round frame with skin stretched over it, played by beating it. **2** the sound (as if) of a drum. **3** a container, part of a machine etc shaped like a drum: *an oil drum.* ⇨ also eardrum.

'drum·stick *nc* (**a**) a stick used for beating a drum. (**b**) a lower part of the leg of a cooked chicken, turkey etc.

drum² /drʌm/ *v* (**-mm-**) **1** *vi* to play a drum by beating it with the hand or a stick. **2** *vt* to hit (one's fingers etc) (on something) with many small movements: *He was drumming his fingers on the table.*

drum sth into sb (*informal*) to cause a person to remember something by using repetition: *drum the spelling into their heads.*

drum on sth to tap, beat etc something with many short movements: *drumming on the table with her fingers.*

drum sth up (*informal*) to encourage, increase support, help etc by lots of asking, persuading: *drumming up votes; drum up support for an idea.*

drum·mer /'drʌmə(r)/ *nc* a person who plays a drum.

drunk¹ /drʌŋk/ **1** *pp* of drink². **2** *adj* (**a**) **be/get drunk** to be/become affected by drinking alcoholic liquor: *He was dead/blind* (= completely) *drunk. It's easy to get drunk on brandy.* (**b**) (*fig*) **drunk with sth** very excited, affected etc because of something: *He was drunk with joy/power/success.*

drunk² /drʌŋk/ (also **drunk·ard** /'drʌŋkəd/) *nc* a person who often gets drunk.

drunk·en /'drʌŋkən/ *adj* (*attrib*) **1** in the habit of drinking; often drunk: *a drunken man.* **2** caused by drinking: *a drunken fight.*

drunk·en·ly *adv*

dry¹ /draɪ/ *adj* (**drier, driest**) **1** not wet; having no moisture: *Is this wood dry enough to burn?* **(as) dry as a bone** ⇨ bone¹. ⇨ bone-dry. **high and dry** ⇨ high¹(3). **2** (**a**) not rainy: *dry weather.* (**b**) having a small rainfall: *a dry climate.* **3** not supplying water: *a dry well.* **4** (*attrib*) (of drink) not sweet, not fruity in flavour: *dry wines.* **5** (*pred; informal*) thirsty; causing thirst: *to feel dry.* **6** (*attrib*) without butter etc: *dry bread/toast.* **7** (*derog*) uninteresting; dull: *a dry lecture.* **8** (of humour, wit) quiet and appearing serious but very amusing.

,dry (cell) 'battery *nc* a battery with paste inside, not liquid.

,dry-'clean *vt* to clean (clothes etc) by using chemicals instead of water.

,dry-'cleaner's *nc* a shop that dry-cleans clothes etc.

,dry-'cleaning *nu*

dri·ly /'draɪlɪ/ *adv*

dry·ness *nu*

dry² /draɪ/ *vt,vi* (*pt,pp* **dried**) **1** (to cause something) to become dry: *Dry your hands on this towel. The clothes are drying on the line.* **2** (usually as a *pp*) to preserve (food) by extracting moisture: *dried fruit/milk.* **cut and dried** ⇨ cut²(15).

dry (sb) out (*informal*) (to cause a person, oneself) to become free of the need to take alcoholic drinks or drugs(2): *She's gone to a clinic to dry out/to be dried out.* **dry (sth) out** (to cause something) to become free of water: *dry out a building after a storm.*

dry up (**a**) to make dishes etc dry by using a cloth: *dry up after dinner.* (**b**) (of a river, well etc) to lose its water. (**c**) (*fig*) (of savings, excuses, ideas etc) to come to an end. (**d**) (*fig*) (of a person) to become unable to speak (because of fear, nervousness etc): *The actor dried up in the second act.*

dry·er (also **drier**) /'draɪə(r)/ *nc* **1** a machine, apparatus, that dries: *a hair-dryer; a spin-dryer.* **2** something on or in which clothes etc are put to dry: *a clothes-dryer.*

DT(s) /,di: 'ti:z/ *abbr* (**delirium tremens**) (*informal*) a serious physical disorder causing shaking because of drinking too much alcohol.

du·al /'dju:əl/ *adj* (*attrib*) of two; double; divided in two: *dual ownership.*

,dual 'carriageway *nc* a road divided down the centre (by a barrier, grass) with two lanes in each direction.

dub /dʌb/ *vt* (**-bb-**) **1** to make (a person) a knight. **2** to give (a person) a pet name: *They dubbed him 'Shorty' because he was so tall.* **3** to replace, add to, the soundtrack of (a film or tape) esp using a different language.

du·bi·ous /'dju:bɪəs/ *adj* **1** **dubious (about sb/sth)** (of a person) feeling doubt: *I feel dubious about his honesty.* **2** (of a person) causing doubt (because probably not very good or reliable): *He's a dubious character.* **3** (of things, actions etc) of which the value, truth etc is doubtful: *a dubious compliment.*

duch·ess /'dʌtʃɪs/ *nc* **1** a wife or widow of a duke. **2** a woman whose rank is equal to that of a duke.

duck¹ /dʌk/ *nc* (*pl* **—s**, but often unchanged when collective) **1** (also *attrib*) a common waterbird, often eaten as food: *duck soup.* ⇨ drake. **(take to sth) like a duck to water** to do, learn, it naturally and without fear, hesitation or difficulty. **like water off a duck's back** without producing any effect: *Her criticism was like water off a duck's back.* ⇨ also lame duck. **2** (*cricket*) a batsman's score of 0: *be out for a duck.*

duck² /dʌk/ *nc* **1** a quick downward or sideways movement of the head or body. **2** a quick dip below water (when bathing in the sea etc).

duck³ /dʌk/ *vt,vi* **1** to move, bend, (the head or body) down quickly (to avoid being seen or hit): *duck one's head. I ducked under the wire.* **2** to go, push (a person), quickly under water for a short time: *The big boy ducked all the small boys in the swimming-pool.* **3** **duck out of sth** (*informal*) to avoid a responsibility, a task etc: *duck out of the washing up.*

duck·bill·ed platy·pus /ˌdʌk bɪld 'plætɪpəs/ *nc* a small Australian egg-laying water mammal with webbed feet and a beak like a duck.

duck·ling /'dʌklɪŋ/ *nc* a young duck.

duct /dʌkt/ *nc* **1** (*biol*) a thin tube through which liquid in the body flows. **2** a tube, outlet, for air (e.g. in a plane): *The air duct above your seat can be adjusted.*

dud /dʌd/ *nc, adj* (*sl*) (a person, thing) of no value or use: *This cheque/diamond is a dud.*

due¹ /dju:/ *adj* **1** (*pred*) owing; to be paid: *When is the rent due? The wages due (to) him will be paid tomorrow.* **2** (*attrib; formal*) right; proper: *after due consideration.* **3** (*pred*) (because of arrangements, planning etc) expected: *The train is due (in) at 1.30.* **4 be due to** (*prep*) be caused by: *The accident was due to careless driving.* Compare because of, owing to.

due² /dju:/ *adv* (of the points of the compass) exactly: *due east/north.*

due³ /dju:/ *n* **1** *n sing* something that must be given to a person because it is right or owing: *This money is her due.* **give sb her/his due** to accept recognition of her/his good character etc: *To give Sue her due she did try to warn you.* **2** (*pl*) sums of money to be paid, e.g. for membership of a club.

du·el¹ /'dju:əl/ *nc* **1** (in history) a fight (usually with swords or pistols) between two people, esp to decide a point of honour. **2** any two-sided contest: *a duel of wits.*

du·el² /'dju:əl/ *vi* (*-ll-* US also **-l-**) to fight a duel.
duel·list (*US* = **duel·ist**) *nc* a person who fights a duel.

du·et /dju:'et/ *nc* a piece of music for two voices or two players.

dug /dʌg/ *pt,pp* of dig².

duke /dju:k/ *nc* a nobleman of high rank (next below a prince).

dul·cet /'dʌlsɪt/ *adj* (*formal*) (of sounds) sweet; pleasant.

dull¹ /dʌl/ *adj* (**—er**, **—est**) **1** not clear or bright: *a dull colour/sound/mirror/day/sky. The weather was dull.* **2** slow to understand: *dull pupils; a dull mind.* **3** (*derog*) not exciting or interesting: *a dull book/speech/sermon/play.* **as dull as ditch-water** (of a person, book etc) very boring. **4** not sharp: *a dull knife.* **5** (of pain) not felt distinctly: *a dull ache.* **6** (of trade) not active.
dull·ness *nu*

dull² /dʌl/ *vt,vi* to cause an edge, the mind, pain etc) to become dull: *dulling the edge of a razor; drugs that dull pain.*

du·ly /'dju:lɪ/ *adv* as expected; at the right time: *The letter duly arrived the next day.*

dumb /dʌm/ *adj* (**—er**, **—est**) **1** unable to speak: *He's deaf and dumb.* **2** temporarily silent: *The class remained dumb when the teacher asked a difficult question.* **strike sb dumb** (usually *passive*) to make a person unable to talk because of surprise, fear etc: *He was struck dumb with horror.* **3** (*informal; derog*) stupid: *a dumb idea/person.*
dumb·ly *adv*
dumb·ness *nu*

dumbbell /'dʌmbel/ *nc* a short bar with a metal ball at each end, used for exercising.

dumb·found (*US* also **dum·found**) /dʌm-'faʊnd/ *vt* (often *passive*) to astonish (a person).

dum·my /'dʌmɪ/ *nc* (*pl* **-ies**) an object made to look like and serve the purpose of the real person or thing: *a tailor's dummy* (i.e. for fitting clothes); *a baby's dummy* (i.e. sucked like the nipple of a mother's breast).
dummy 'run *nc* a trial attempt, performance etc.

dump¹ /dʌmp/ *nc* **1** a place where rubbish etc may be unloaded and left. **2** (*mil*) (a place with) a temporary store of military supplies: *an ammunition dump.* **3** (*sl; derog*) a poor, dirty or ugly place: *I'd hate to live in a dump like this.*

dump² /dʌmp/ *vt* **1** to put or throw (something) down carelessly: *Where can I dump this rubbish?* **2** to put (something) down with a heavy, loud movement: *They dumped the coal outside the shed instead of putting it inside.* **3** (*commerce*) to sell abroad at low prices (goods which are unwanted in the home market).

dump·ling /'dʌmplɪŋ/ *nc* **1** a small round piece of dough steamed or boiled with meat and vegetables. **2** a baked pudding made of dough with fruit inside it: *apple dumplings.*

dumps /dʌmps/ *n pl* **be (down) in the dumps** (*informal*) to be very depressed.

dum·py /'dʌmpɪ/ *adj* (**-ier**, **-iest**) (of a person) short and fat.

dunce /dʌns/ *nc* (*derog*) a slow, stupid learner.

dune /dju:n/ *nc* a low area of loose, dry sand near the coast.

dung /dʌŋ/ *nu* solid waste matter dropped by animals (esp cattle).

dun·ga·rees /ˌdʌŋgə'ri:z/ *n pl* (also *a pair of dungarees*) strong cotton trousers with a front flap attached by straps over the shoulders.

dun·geon /'dʌndʒən/ *nc* a dark underground cell used (in history) as a prison.

duo·de·nal /ˌdju:ə'di:nl/ *adj* of the duodenum: *a duodenal ulcer.*

duo·de·num /ˌdju:ə'di:nəm/ *nc* (*pl* **—s**) (*anat*) the first part of the small intestine immediately below the stomach.

duo·logue /'dju:əlɒg/ *nc* a conversation between two people.

dupe /dju:p/ *vt* to cheat; make a fool of (a person). □ *nc* a person who is duped.

du·pli·cate¹ /'dju:plɪkət/ *adj* (no *comp*) exactly like: *duplicate keys.* □ *nc* something that is exactly like another. **in duplicate** (of documents etc) with a copy: *typed in duplicate.*

du·pli·cate² /'dju:plɪkeɪt/ *vt* to make a copy of (a letter etc).
du·pli·ca·tion /ˌdju:plɪ'keɪʃn/ *nc,nu*
du·plic·ity /dju:'plɪsətɪ/ *nu* (*formal*) deliberate deception.

dur·able /'djʊərəbl/ *adj* likely to last for a long time: *a durable pair of shoes.*
dura·bil·ity /ˌdjʊərə'bɪlətɪ/ *nu*

dur·ation /djʊ'reɪʃn/ *nu* the time during which something lasts or exists: *for the duration of the war. Their friendship was of short duration.*

dur·ess (also **-esse**) /djʊ'res/ *nu* **under duress** using threats, imprisonment or violence (to compel a person to do something): *a confession signed under duress.*

dur·ing /'djʊərɪŋ/ *prep* **1** throughout (a length, period, of time): *The sun gives us light during the day.* Ⓝ *'During'* refers to when something happens, as in *sunny during the afternoon* and *'for'* refers to how long something occurs, as in *sleeping for two hours*. *'In'* can be used for *'during'*, as in *sunny in the afternoon*, but is preferred as an alternative for 2 below. *'During'* is used when referring to an activity, as in *'during the exam'*. **2** at some point in (a length, period, of time): *He called to see me during my absence*. (N) *'For'* is not possible. *'In'* can be used and is preferred when referring to an exact point of time, as in *He died in the middle of the night*.

dusk /dʌsk/ *nu* the time just before it is dark. Compare dawn¹.

dusky /'dʌskı/ *adj* (**-ier, -iest**) a little dark: *a dusky corridor; a dusky blue*.

dust¹ /dʌst/ *nu* dry powder from soil, waste etc on the surface of objects, blown about by the wind etc: *The dust was blowing in the streets*. **bite the dust** (*sl*) to be killed.

'**dust·bin** *nc* a container for household rubbish (*US = trashcan*).

'**dust bowl** *nc* an area that has no vegetation because of drought, poor farming etc.

'**dust-cart** *nc* a vehicle into which dustbins are emptied.

'**dust-jacket/-wrapper** *nc* a loose paper cover for a book.

'**dust·man** *nc* a man employed to empty dustbins and take away refuse.

'**dust·pan** *nc* a pan into which household dust is swept.

dust² /dʌst/ *vt* **1** to remove dust from (furniture etc) by wiping, brushing etc: *dusting a room/ table*. **2** to sprinkle (something) (with powder): *dusting a cake with sugar*.

dust·er *nc* a cloth used for removing dust from furniture etc.

'**dust-up** *nc* (*informal*) a fight; noisy argument.

dusty /'dʌstı/ *adj* (**-ier, -iest**) covered with, full of, like, dust.

Dutch /dʌtʃ/ *adj* **go Dutch (with sb)** to share expenses. ⇨ also double Dutch.

,**Dutch 'auction** *nc* a sale at which the price is reduced by the auctioneer until a buyer is found.

,**Dutch 'courage** *nu* (*informal*) courage obtained by drinking alcoholic drinks.

du·ti·able /'dju:tıəbl/ *adj* on which customs duties(2) must be paid: *dutiable goods*.

du·ti·ful /'dju:tıfəl/ *adj* showing respect and obedience: *a dutiful son*.

duti·ful·ly /-fəlı/ *adv*

du·ty /'dju:tı/ *n* (*pl* **-ies**) **1** *nc,nu* something a person must do because of morality, law, conscience etc: *Do not forget your duty to your parents. His sense of duty is strong*. **2** *nc,nu* **duty (on sth)** the payment demanded by the government for certain goods exported or imported (*customs duties*), or manufactured in the country (*excise duties*), or when property etc is transferred to a new owner by sale (*stamp duties*) or death (*estate duty*). **3** **on/ off duty** doing/not doing one's regular work (as a nurse, doctor, soldier etc): *She goes on duty at 8 and comes off duty at 6*.

,**duty-'bound** *adj* (*pred*) having to do something as one's moral duty.

,**duty-'free** *adj* (of goods) allowed to enter without the payment of customs duties(2).

du·vet /'dju:veı/ *nc* a bed quilt (filled with feathers or an artificial substitute) used in place of

blankets.

dwarf¹ /dwɔ:f/ *nc* (*pl* **—s**) **1** (also *attrib*) a person, animal or plant much below the usual size: *a dwarf rose*. **2** (in stories) a small being with magic powers.

dwarf² /dwɔ:f/ *vt* to cause (something) to appear small by contrast or distance: *The big liner dwarfed their little boat*.

dwell /dwel/ *vt* (*pt,pp* **dwelt** /dwelt/) **1** **dwell in a place** (*formal*) to have as one's home; live in (which is more usual). **2** **dwell on sth** to think, speak or write at length about a topic, subject: *She dwells too much on her past*.

dwel·ler *nc* (used in compounds) inhabitant: *city dwellers*.

dwel·ling *nc* (*formal*) a place of residence (a house, flat etc).

dwindle /'dwındl/ *vi* **dwindle (away)** to become gradually less or smaller.

dye¹ /daı/ *nc,nu* **1** a substance used for dyeing cloth. **2** a colour produced by dyeing.

dye² /daı/ *vt,vi* (*3rd pers sing, pres t* **dyes**, *pt,pp* **dyed**, *pres p* **dyeing**) to produce, take on, a colour, usually by dipping (something) in a liquid: *dyeing a white dress blue; have her hair dyed. This material does not dye well*.

,**dyed-in-the-'wool** *adj* (*attrib*) (*fig*) (of a person) having the strong opinions mentioned and not willing to change them: *a dyed-in-the-wool Tory*.

dy·ing /'daııŋ/ ⇨ die².

dyke /daık/ *nc* = dike.

dy·nam·ic /daı'næmık/ *adj* **1** (*science*) of physical power and forces producing motion. Compare static. **2** (of a person) having great energy, force of character etc.

dy,namic 'verb *nc* (*gram*) one expressing action (not conditions or states), such as *run, think, go*. Compare stative verb.

dy·nami·cal·ly /-klı/ *adv*

dy·nam·ics /daı'næmıks/ *nu* a branch of physics dealing with matter in motion.

dy·na·mite /'daınəmaıt/ *vt, nu* (to use) a powerful explosive (for mining and quarrying).

dy·na·mo /'daınəməυ/ *nc* (*pl* **—s**) a machine used for changing steam-power, water-power etc into electrical energy.

dyn·ast·ic /dı'næstık/ *adj* of a dynasty.

dyn·as·ty /'dınəstı/ *nc* (*pl* **-ies**) a succession of rulers belonging to one family: *the Tudor dynasty* (in England).

dys·en·tery /'dısəntrı/ *nu* a painful disease of the bowels which produces mucus and blood.

dys·lexia /dıs'leksıə/ *nu* serious difficulty in reading.

dys·lex·ic *adj*

dys·pep·sia /dıs'pepsıə/ *nu* (*formal*) indigestion (the usual word).

dys·pep·tic /dıs'peptık/ *adj*

Ee

E, e /i:/ (*pl* **E's, e's** /i:z/) the fifth letter of the English alphabet.

E *written abbr* east.

ea. *written abbr* (*commerce*) each.

each¹ /iːtʃ/ *adj* or *det* (of two or more people, things etc) the separate individuals or parts in a group: *Each one is a different colour. There are houses on each side of the road. Each team has a place to practise. There is one biscuit for each child. Each one of you is to blame.* Ⓝ '*Each*' is used with a singular noun and verb, as in *Each idea is a good one.* Compare all¹(2), both¹. '*Each*' and '*every*' can have the same meaning, as in *each/every day of the week*, but '*each*' is preferred when referring particularly to the separate individuals or parts, as in *Each member of the expedition has a different job to do.* '*Every*' is preferred when making a general statement or when referring to a group as a whole, as in *Every child has the right to be educated.* '*Every*' cannot be used to refer to only two. Use '*each*' or '*both*'. **each and every** (*informal*) all the individuals, things etc in a group without exception: *Each and every one of you will clear up this mess.*

each² /iːtʃ/ *adv* (of two or more people, things etc) for, of, every one: *They cost £10 each. You can take one cake each.*

each³ /iːtʃ/ *pron* (of two or more) the whole group, number etc; not only the one: *Each is an excellent example. Jane and Anne each bought a new coat. You will each receive an invitation. Each of you has a chance of winning. I sent a postcard to each of my friends.* Ⓝ '*Each*' is used with a singular verb. '*Each*' cannot be used in front of another determiner (e.g. *a, some, what, many*). '*Each of*' can be used in front of possessive pronouns (e.g. *my, your*), personal pronouns (e.g. *you, us*) and the, these, those etc, as in *Each of us has to sign. Each of the men received a bonus.* Compare all, both. **each other** (used when a fact, action etc relates to both people, things etc): *We promised each other that we'd stay together. The two boys hit each other on the nose. They smiled at each other.* Ⓝ '*One another*' is also possible, as in *We promised one another that we'd stay together*, but '*each other*' is preferred when referring to two, as in *They kissed each other*, and '*one another*' is preferred when referring to more than two, as in *The whole team was proud of one another.*

eag·er /ˈiːgə(r)/ *adj* **eager (for sth/to do sth)** full of, showing, strong desire or willingness: *eager for success/to succeed.*

  eag·er·ly *adv*

  eag·er·ness *nu*

eagle /ˈiːgl/ *nc* a kind of large strong bird of prey.

  eag·let /-lɪt/ *nc* a young eagle.

ear¹ /ɪə(r)/ *nc* **1** the part of the body on each side of the head used for hearing. **be all ears** to be listening eagerly: *Do tell me what happened—I'm all ears!* **be up to one's ears in sth** to be extremely concerned, busy etc with something: *be up to her ears in debt/work.* **be wet behind the ears** (of a person) to be very immature or weak in character. **box sb's ears** to hit a person (often used as a threat or warning): *I'll box your ears!* **close/shut one's ears to sth** to refuse to listen to criticism etc. **fall on deaf ears** to be ignored, not noticed: *My advice fell on deaf ears.* **go in one ear and out the other** to have no effect on the listener. **have the ear of sb/sb's ear** to be able to offer one's opinion and be trusted etc: *have the ear of the Managing Director.* **have an ear to the ground** to be well informed. **have a word in sb's ear** to talk to a person privately: *Can I have a word in your ear?* **make a pig's ear of sth** (*informal*) to carry out an activity very badly; produce a bad result. **prick up one's ears** to listen carefully when suddenly hearing an interesting conversation etc by accident. **be thrown out on one's ear** to be suddenly (and physically) removed (from a house, pub etc). **turn a deaf ear (to sb/sth)** to refuse to listen, respond etc: *The richer nations seemed to turn a deaf ear to our problems.* **2** *nu* or *sing* the sense of hearing. **by ear** using one's sense of hearing (and remembering): *I can play the tune by ear but I can't read music.* **have an ear/a good ear (for sth)** to be able to identify etc (a piece of music, a particular foreign accent etc). **play sth by ear** to play (music) without written notes. **play it by ear** to act according to the changing situation etc and not plan in advance.

  'ear·ache *nu* or *sing* (a) pain in the inner ear.

  'ear·drum *nc* the thin skin (in the inner ear) which vibrates when sound-waves strike it.

  'ear·lobe *nc* the flap at the bottom of the outer ear.

  'ear·ring *nc* an ornament worn on the earlobe.

  'ear·shot *nu* the distance within which a sound can be heard: *within/out of earshot.*

  'ear·splitting *adj* very loud and unpleasant.

ear² /ɪə(r)/ *nc* the top seed-bearing part (of corn, wheat, barley etc).

earl /ɜːl/ *nc* (a title of) a British nobleman of high rank. Compare countess.

  'earl·dom /-dəm/ *nc* the rank or lands of an earl.

ear·ly¹ /ˈɜːlɪ/ *adj* (**-ier, -iest**) **1** (*pred*) (arriving, starting etc) before the usual or agreed time or before others: *I'm early. The train is early. It's early in the morning and the birds are singing. He's 15 minutes early. The postman's earlier than usual.* **2** (*attrib*) near to the beginning, during the first part, of the day, season, period of time etc: *in the early part of the century; during the early morning; catch an early train.* **3 at the earliest** and not before (the usual or agreed time): *I can't leave work until six at the earliest.* Compare late¹.

ear·ly² /ˈɜːlɪ/ *adv* (**-ier, -iest**) **1** before the usual or agreed time or before others: *arrive/finish/ wake up/go to bed early. You've come 10 minutes too early.* **2 early (on) in** a period of time near to the beginning, during the first part, of: *He got married early (on) in life. Early in the year the trees have no leaves.* **earlier (on)** at an earlier time: *Your brother telephoned earlier (on) but you were out.* **3** long ago; not before: *I met her as early as 1975/no earlier than 1975.* Compare late².

  'early bird *nc* (*informal*) a person who gets up very early in the morning or who arrives before others.

  ,early 'man *nu* a prehistoric human being.

  ,early-'warning *adj* (*attrib*) (of radar) giving a warning of the approach of enemy aircraft, missiles etc: *an early-warning system.*

ear·mark /ˈɪəmɑːk/ *vt* to make a note of, put to one side, (money etc) for a particular use.

earn /ɜːn/ *vt* **1** to receive (money) in return for work or in payment for a loan: *earn £20 000 a* *year*. **2** to obtain (something) as a reward for one's qualities (good or bad) or one's actions: *His success earned him respect and admiration. Your refusal will only earn you more hostility. I had a well-earned rest.*

earn·ings *n pl* money earned.

ear·nest[1] /'ɜːnɪst/ *adj* serious and determined: *an earnest student.*

earn·est·ly *adv*

ear·nest[2] /'ɜːnɪst/ *n* **in earnest** in a determined and serious way: *She spoke in earnest about her problems.*

earth[1] /ɜːθ/ *n* **1** *n* (often E-) the planet on which we live: *The Earth goes round the sun. Who do you think was the greatest person on earth?* ⇨ **3** below. ⇨ axis. **2** *nu* the land surface of the world (contrasted with the sky). **the salt of the earth** ⇨ salt[2](1). ⇨ also heaven(1). **bring sb/come down/come back to earth** (*fig*) (to cause a person) to return to being realistic. **cost the earth** to be very expensive. **promise sb the earth** to make extravagant promises. **run sb/sth to earth** to find a person or thing after a long search. **3** ... **on earth** (*informal*) (used to emphasize anger, surprise etc in a question): *How on earth did you do it? Where on earth have you been? What on earth did she say?* **4** *nu* soil: *to cover the roots of a plant with earth.* **5** *nc, nu* (*electricity*) (a means of) electrical contact with the ground as the completion of a circuit.

earth[2] /ɜːθ/ *vt* **1** **earth sth up** to cover a plant, roots etc with earth: *to earth up the roots of a newly-planted shrub.* **2** (*electricity*) to connect (an apparatus etc) with the earth(5).

'earth·worm *nc* a common kind of worm that lives in the soil.

earthy *adj* (**-ier, -iest**) (**a**) of or like soil: *an earthy smell.* (**b**) (*fig*) coarse, unrefined: *earthy humour.*

earth·en·ware /'ɜːθənweə(r)/ *nu* (also *attrib*) pots etc made of baked clay: *an earthenware casserole.*

earth·ly /'ɜːθlɪ/ *adj* (*no comp*) **1** (*attrib*) of this world, not of heaven: *earthly pleasures/possessions.* **2** **not an/no earthly sth** (*informal*) no possibility of success etc: *You haven't an earthly (chance)* (= no chance at all). *There's no earthly use (in) crying* (i.e. it is pointless).

earth·quake /'ɜːθkweɪk/ *nc* a series of sudden, violent movements of the earth's surface.

ear·wig /'ɪəwɪg/ *nc* a kind of small insect with pincers at the back.

ease[1] /iːz/ *nu* **1** freedom from work, discomfort, trouble, difficulty, anxiety: *a life of ease.* **be/feel ill at ease** to be/feel uncomfortable, worried or embarrassed. **put sb at ease** to allow a person to feel relaxed, untroubled. **stand at ease** (*mil*) (as a command) to stand with the legs apart and the hands behind the back. **2** **with ease** (*formal*) without difficulty: *He passed the test with ease.*

ease[2] /iːz/ *v* **1** *vt, vi* to give relief to (the body or mind) from pain, discomfort, anxiety: *easing his anxiety; easing the pain; the ache is easing.* **2** *vt* (to cause a person, thing) to move slowly and carefully (in a small space): *I eased myself/the rope up through the hole.* **3** *vi* **ease (off)** to become less tense or troublesome: *The situation has eased*

(off). **4** *vi* **ease up** to reduce speed, effort etc: *Ease up* (e.g. in a car) *or there'll be an accident. Ease up* (= Don't work so hard) *or you'll be ill.* **5** *vt* to make (clothes etc) looser: *ease the shoulders of a jacket.*

eas·el /'iːzl/ *nc* a frame used to support a blackboard or a picture.

eas·ily /'iːzəlɪ/ *adv* **1** without difficulty: *I did it easily.* **2** without doubt: *easily the best TV programme.*

east[1] /iːst/ *adj* (*attrib*) from, in, towards, the east: *an east wind; living on the east side of the city.* ⇨ eastern.

east[2] /iːst/ *adv* towards the east: *to travel/face east.* **east of a place** farther east than.

east[3] /iːst/ *n* **1** (the —) the direction, point, where the sun rises. **2** (often the E-) that part of a country, the world etc in this direction: *the east of France; beautiful silk from the East* (= from Asia). ⇨ Far/Middle East.

Eas·ter /'iːstə(r)/ *n* (also *attrib*) the anniversary of the death and return to life of Christ: *the Easter holidays.*

east·er·ly /'iːstəlɪ/ *adj, adv* in an eastern direction or position.

east·ern /'iːstən/ *adj* of, from, in, the east part of a country, continent, the world etc: *eastern religions; eastern Europe.*

,Eastern 'Church *n* (the —) the Greek or Russian Orthodox Church.

,eastern 'bloc *nc* (the —) the group of eastern European countries under Russian control or influence.

,Eastern 'Hemisphere *n* (the —) Europe, Asia, Africa and Australasia.

east·ern·most /-məʊst/ *adj* farthest east.

east·ward /'iːstwəd/ *adj* towards the east: *in an eastward direction.*

east·wards *adv*: *to travel eastwards.*

easy[1] /'iːzɪ/ *adj* (**-ier, -iest**) **1** not difficult: *easy writing to read; an easy puzzle; an easy language to learn; as easy as ABC/anything* (= very easy). Opp hard[1](1). **2** not needing much (physical) effort: *an easy way up the mountain; easy to reach; easy to lift.* Opp difficult(1). **3** free from anxiety, problems, pain etc: *feel easy about going out at night. A student's life isn't always easy.* Compare hard[1](3), uneasy. **4** not fast or extreme: *an easy pace/speed.* **5** quickly persuaded or influenced: *an easy victim.* **6** (*informal*) willing to agree, let others decide etc: *I don't mind where we go—I'm easy. She's very easy to get on with.* Compare difficult(2).

'easy chair *nc* a comfortable armchair.

,easy-'going *adj* (of a person) tolerant, fair. ⇨ easy[1](6).

easy[2] /'iːzɪ/ *adv* **take it/things easy** (**a**) to stay calm, not get angry. (**b**) to avoid working too hard. ⇨ also come(4). **2** (*informal*) **go easy (on sb)** to punish a person more lightly than he or she deserves. **go easy (on sth)** to be careful, not use too much (of something): *Go easy on the milk—that's all we have.* **3** **be easier said than done** to be easier to talk about or promise than to do.

eat /iːt/ *v* (*pt* **ate** /et/, *pp* **eaten** /'iːtn/) **1** *vi* to have a meal: *There's no time to eat. Where shall we eat tonight?* **2** *vt* to take (food) into the mouth and swallow it: *You must eat a good breakfast. I* *don't eat spinach.* **eat one's head off; eat like a horse** (*informal*) to eat a great amount of food. **eat one's hat** ⇨ hat. **eat one's heart out** ⇨ heart(2). **eat one's words** ⇨ word(2). **3** *vt* to damage, destroy, (something) as if by eating: *Acids eat into metals. It ate a hole in the exhaust-pipe.*

eat sth away; eat away at sth (of chemicals, weather etc) to destroy, wear away a substance or material.

eat from sth ⇨ eat out of sth.

eat in to eat a meal at home, in college etc.

eat into sth (a) (of acid etc) to damage metals. **(b)** to use up savings, supplies etc, esp unwillingly: *The fees have eaten into my bank account badly.*

eat out to eat a meal in a restaurant, not at home. **eat out of sth** to use a dish, plate etc as a container when eating. **eat out of sb's hands** ⇨ hand¹(1).

eat (sth) up to finish a meal, food: *Eat your carrots up.* **be eaten up with sth** to be extremely affected by, filled with, hatred, envy etc.

eat·able /'iːtəbl/ *adj* edible (the usual word).

eaten /'iːtn/ *pp* of eat.

eat·er /'iːtə(r)/ *nc* **1** a person who eats: *He's a big eater* (= eats large quantities). **2** An apple etc suitable for eating uncooked.

eats /iːts/ *n pl* (*sl*) food: *There were plenty of eats but not enough drinks at her party.*

eau de Cologne /ˌəʊ də kəˈləʊn/ *nu* (*Fr*) a kind of perfumed toilet water.

eaves /iːvz/ *n pl* the overhanging edges of a roof.

eaves·drop /'iːvzdrɒp/ *vi* (**-pp-**) to listen secretly to a private conversation.

'eaves·drop·per *nc* a person who eavesdrops.

ebb¹ /eb/ *n sing* **1** the flowing out of the tide; *the ebb and flow of the sea/the tide.* **2** (*fig*) a low mood or state: *be at a low ebb.*

ebb² /eb/ *vi* **1** (of the tide) to flow back from the land to the sea. **2** (*fig*) to grow less; become weak or faint: *His fortune's beginning to ebb.*

ˌebb-'tide *n sing* = ebb(1).

eb·ony /'ebənɪ/ *adj, nu* (of) a kind of hard, black wood.

ebul·li·ence /ɪˈbʌlɪəns/ *nu* (*formal*) great excitement, enthusiasm.

ebul·li·ent /ɪˈbʌlɪənt/ *adj* (*formal*) very excited, enthusiastic: *an ebullient personality.*

EC /ˌiːˈsiː/ *abbr* European Community.

ec·cen·tric¹ /ɪkˈsentrɪk/ *adj* **1** (of a person, behaviour) odd; not normal (and often amusing). **2** (*maths*) (of circles) not having the same centre; (of an orbit) not circular.

ec·cen·tric·ity /ˌeksenˈtrɪsətɪ/ *nc,nu* (*pl* **-ies**)

ec·cen·tric² /ɪkˈsentrɪk/ *nc* an eccentric person.

ec·cle·si·as·tic /ɪˌkliːzɪˈæstɪk/ *nc* (*formal*) a clergyman.

ec·cle·si·as·ti·cal /-kl/ *adj* of the Christian Church; of clergymen.

ec·cle·si·as·ti·cal·ly /-klɪ/ *adv*

echo¹ /'ekəʊ/ *nc,nu* (*pl* **—es**) (a) sound reflected or sent back.

echo² /'ekəʊ/ *v* **1** *vt,vi* (to cause sound) to be sent back as an echo: *The valley echoed as he sang. The hills were echoing with sounds of their singing. The shot echoed through the woods.* **2** *vt* to repeat (the words, actions, etc) of another: *They were*

echoing every word of their leader.

éclair /ɪˈkleə(r)/ *nc* a pastry iced on top and filled with cream: *chocolate éclairs.*

eclipse¹ /ɪˈklɪps/ *nc* **1** a total or partial disappearance of the light of the sun (when the moon is between it and the earth), or of the moon (when the earth's shadow falls on it). **2** (*fig*) a loss of fame, power, etc: *After suffering an eclipse, he is famous again.*

eclipse² /ɪˈklɪps/ *vt* (*fig*) to make (a person or thing) appear dull, worse etc by comparison: *She was so beautiful that she eclipsed every other woman in the room.*

eco·logi·cal /ˌiːkəˈlɒdʒɪkl/ *adj* of ecology.

eco·logi·cal·ly /-klɪ/ *adv*

ecol·ogy /iːˈkɒlədʒɪ/ *nu* the scientific study of the habits of living things, esp their relation to their environment.

econ·om·ic /ˌiːkəˈnɒmɪk/ *adj* **1** producing a profit: *We sell our goods at an economic price.* **2** (*informal*) cheap: *It's an economic rent.* **3** of economics: *the government's economic policy.* **4** connected with commerce, systems of production etc: *economic resources.*

econ·omi·cal /ˌiːkəˈnɒmɪkl/ *adj* careful in using money, time, supplies etc: *an economical system for heating water.* Opp uneconomical.

econ·omi·cal·ly /-klɪ/ *adv*

econ·om·ics /ˌiːkəˈnɒmɪks/ *nu* the scientific study of the production, sale, distribution and use of goods and wealth.

econ·om·ist /ɪˈkɒnəmɪst/ *nc* **1** an expert in, student of, economics or political economy(2). **2** a person who is economical.

econ·om·ize (also **-ise**) /ɪˈkɒnəmaɪz/ *vi* **economize (on sth) (by doing sth)** to save (money, supplies etc); use or spend less than before: *She is economizing on bus fares by walking more.*

econ·omy /ɪˈkɒnəmɪ/ *n* (*pl* **-ies**) **1** *nc,nu* (an instance of) the avoidance of waste of money, supplies, strength or anything else of value: *By various little economies she managed to save enough money for a holiday.* **2** *nc,nu* (a system of) control and management of the money, goods and other resources of a community, society or household.

e'conomy class *nu, adv* the cheapest class of travel: *travel economy class.*

ec·stat·ic /ɪkˈstætɪk/ *adj* of, concerning, causing, feeling, ecstasy.

ec·stati·cal·ly /-klɪ/ *adv*

ec·sta·sy /'ekstəsɪ/ *nc,nu* (*pl* **-ies**) (a feeling of) great joy or pleasure; being very pleased: *be in an ecstasy of delight; to be in/go into ecstasies (over something).*

ecu·meni·cal /ˌiːkjuːˈmenɪkl/ *adj* of or representing (the uniting of) the whole Christian world.

ec·zema /'eksɪmə/ *nu* a kind of itching skin disease.

ed. *abbr* edited; edition; editor.

ed·dy /'edɪ/ *vi* (*pt,pp* **-ied**), *nc* (*pl* **-ies**) (of wind, smoke, fog, mist, dust, water) (to move in) a circular or spiral movement: *Eddies of mist rose from the valleys.*

edge¹ /edʒ/ *nc* **1** the sharp, cutting part of a knife, sword or other tool or weapon: *a knife with* *a blunt/sharp edge.* **2 be on edge** to be excited or worried because unsure. **have the edge on/over sb** (*informal*) to have an advantage over her or him. **set sb's/one's teeth on edge** ⇨ tooth(1). **3** (usually the —) (a line marking) the outer limit or boundary of a (flat) surface: *the edge of a table; a cottage on the edge of a forest/a lake. He fell off the edge of the cliff.* Compare end¹(1). **push sb over the edge** (*fig*) to make a person very angry, mad etc.

edge² /edʒ/ *v* **1** *vt* **edge sth (with sth)** to supply something (with something as a border): *edging a garden with plants; a road edged with grass.* **2** *vt,vi* (to cause a person) to move slowly forward or along: *edging one's way through a crowd/along a ledge.*

edge·ways (also **edge·wise**) /'edʒweɪz, -waɪz/ *adv* with the edge outwards or forwards. **not get a word in edgeways** (*informal*) to be unable to say anything because a very talkative person is speaking.

edg·ing /'edʒɪŋ/ *nc* a narrow border: *an edging of lace on a dress.*

edgy /'edʒɪ/ *adj* (**-ier, -iest**) (*informal*) nervous.

ed·ible /'edəbl/ *adj* fit to be eaten. Opp inedible.

edict /'iːdɪkt/ *nc* an official order.

edi·fice /'edɪfɪs/ *nc* (*formal*) a building (esp a large or grand one).

ed·it /'edɪt/ *vt* **1** to do the work of planning and directing the publication of a newspaper, magazine, book etc. **2** to prepare a film, tape etc by putting parts together.

edi·tion /ɪ'dɪʃn/ *nc* **1** a form in which a book, magazine etc is published: *a paperback edition.* **2** a number of copies (of a book, newspaper etc): *the first/a revised edition (of a dictionary).* ⇨ impression(3).

edi·tor /'edɪtə(r)/ *nc* a person who edits (part of) a newspaper, book or film or a TV or radio programme: *the sports/financial editor.*

edi·tor·ial¹ /ˌedɪ'tɔːrɪəl/ *adj* of the work of an editor.

edi·tor·ial² /ˌedɪ'tɔːrɪəl/ *nc* a special article in a newspaper etc written by the senior editor.

EDP /ˌiː diː 'piː/ *abbr* (*computers*) electronic data processing.

edu·cate /'edjʊkeɪt/ *vt* to give intellectual and moral training to (a person): *You should educate your children to behave well. They were well/badly educated.* **an educated guess** one based on experience, not facts.

edu·ca·tion /ˌedjʊ'keɪʃn/ *nc,nu* (an organized system of) intellectual and moral training and instruction: *Education must be a priority in every society. I had a good/poor education.*
edu·ca·tion·al /-ʃənl/ *adj* of, connected with, education: *educational books/toys.*

EEC /ˌiː iː 'siː/ *abbr* (the —) the European Economic Community. ⇨ the Common Market.

eel /iːl/ *nc* a kind of long fish like a snake.

eerie (also **eery**) /'ɪərɪ/ *adj* (**-ier, -iest**) causing a feeling of mystery and fear: *an eerie shriek.*
eer·ily /-əlɪ/ *adv*
eeri·ness *nu*

ef·face /ɪ'feɪs/ *vt* (*formal*) to remove (something) by rubbing or wiping: *effacing an inscription.* ⇨ also self-effacing.
ef·face·ment *nu*

ef·fect¹ /ɪ'fekt/ *n* **1** *nc,nu* a condition caused by something: *The children were suffering from the effects of the hot weather. Did the medicine have any effect/a good or bad effect?* **of little/no effect** not doing what was intended or hoped for: *The warning had no effect/was of little effect.* **in effect** (a) in fact, really: *Although he is the assistant, he is in effect the person who controls the business.* (b) in operation: *The rule/law is still in effect.* **be brought/come into effect** to be/come into force or operation: *When was that law brought into effect?* **take effect** (a) to produce the result intended or required: *When will the drug take effect?* (b) to come into force; to become active: *The new law will take effect from midnight.* **2** *nc* an impression produced on the mind of a spectator, hearer, reader etc: *sound effects.* **do sth for effect** to do it to impress or influence people to one's advantage: *Everything he says and does is done for effect.* **3** *nu* **to that/this effect** with the same meaning: *That is what he said, or words to that effect.* **4** (*pl*) possessions: *The hotel manager seized her personal effects because she could not pay her bill.*

ef·fect² /ɪ'fekt/ *vt* (*formal*) to cause (something) to happen as a result: *I hope this new drug will effect a cure.* Compare affect(1).

ef·fec·tive /ɪ'fektɪv/ *adj* **1** able to bring about the result intended: *effective measures to reduce unemployment.* Opp ineffective. **2** making a strong impression: *an effective scheme of decoration. That design isn't as effective.* **3** (*attrib; no comp*) actual or existing: *the effective strength of the army.* **4** (*pred*) (of a rule, law) in force: *When will the new parking law be effective?*
ef·fec·tive·ly *adv*

ef·fec·tu·al /ɪ'fektʃʊəl/ *adj* (*formal*) (not used of a person) bringing about the result required: *an effectual punishment.* Opp ineffectual. Ⓝ *'Effective'* is more usual.

ef·femi·nate /ɪ'femɪnət/ *adj* (of a man, his behaviour, clothes) like, of, a woman.

ef·fer·vesce /ˌefə'ves/ *vi* (*tech*) **1** (of a liquid) to produce bubbles of gas. **2** (of gas) to come out in bubbles.
ef·fer·ves·cence /-sns/ *nu*
ef·fer·ves·cent /-snt/ *adj*

ef·fete /ɪ'fiːt/ *adj* (*formal; derog*) weak, without energy; incapable (because too subtle, sensitive, refined): *an effete man.*

ef·fi·cien·cy /ɪ'fɪʃnsɪ/ *nu* the state, quality, of being efficient. Opp inefficiency.

ef·fi·cient /ɪ'fɪʃnt/ *adj* **1** (of a person) organized and able to perform duties well: *an efficient secretary/staff of teachers.* **2** producing a desired or satisfactory result: *efficient machines/businesses; efficient methods of teaching.* Opp inefficient.
ef·fic·ient·ly *adv*

ef·fi·gy /'efɪdʒɪ/ *nc* (*pl* **-ies**) a representation of a person (in wood, stone etc).

ef·flu·ent /'eflʊənt/ *nc,nu* (*tech*) waste liquid matter, sewage etc coming from a factory, town etc.

ef·fort /'efət/ *nc,nu* (an attempt at) trying hard; use of strength and energy (to do something): *Please make an effort to arrive early. I will make every effort (= do all I can) to help you. You made absolutely no effort to help us. That was a good* *effort. It needed a great deal of effort.*

ef·fort·less *adj* needing no effort: *done with effortless skill.*

ef·front·ery /ɪˈfrʌntərɪ/ *nc,nu* (*pl* **-ies**) (*formal*) (an instance of) rude behaviour without showing any fear, shame etc: *How can you have the effrontery to ask for another loan?*

ef·fu·sion /ɪˈfjuːʒn/ *nc,nu* (*formal*) (a result of) the sending or pouring out (of liquid, e.g. blood).

ef·fu·sive /ɪˈfjuːsɪv/ *adj* (*formal*) (of greetings, thanks etc) expressed with (too) much feeling: *effusive but insincere thanks.*

ef·fu·sive·ly *adv*

EFL /ˌiː ef ˈel/ *abbr* English as a foreign language.

e.g. /ˌiː ˈdʒiː/ *abbr* (*Latin: exempli gratia*) for example.

egali·tar·ian /ɪˌgælɪˈteərɪən/ *nc, adj* (a person) supporting equal rights, benefits and opportunities for all people. Compare élite, élitist.

egg[1] /eg/ *n* **1** *nc* an oval object with a shell, as produced by a bird: *Birds, reptiles and insects come from eggs.* **2** *nc,nu* (a chicken's, duck's etc) egg eaten as food: *Will you have your egg boiled or fried? You've got some egg on your chin.* **put all one's eggs in one basket** to risk everything in one attempt, venture etc. **teach one's grandmother to suck eggs** to give advice to a person who has much more experience than oneself. **3** *nc* (*science*) a very small cell produced by a female animal that joins a male cell to form a new life.

'egg·cup *nc* a small cup for a boiled egg.

'egg·head *nc* (*fig*) an intellectual person.

'egg·plant *nc,nu* (esp *US*) = aubergine.

'egg·shell *nc* the shell of an egg.

'egg·timer *nc* a device used for timing the boiling of an egg.

'egg·whisk *nc* a utensil for beating eggs.

egg[2] /eg/ *vt* **egg sb on** to urge a person to do something, usually bad.

ego /ˈiːgəʊ/ *nc* (*pl* **-s**) **1** the way a person thinks or feels about herself or himself: *The critic's praise boosted her ego.* **2** (*informal*) conceit.

'ego-trip *nc* (*informal*) a selfish activity for personal interest.

ego·cen·tric /ˌiːgəʊˈsentrɪk/ *adj* interested mainly in oneself.

ego·ism /ˈiːgəʊɪzəm/ *nu* **1** the theory that our actions are always caused by the desire to benefit ourselves. **2** the state of mind in which one is always thinking of oneself.

ego·ist /-ɪst/ *nc* a person who believes in egoism.

ego·ist·ic /ˌiːgəʊˈɪstɪk/ (also **ego·isti·cal** /-kl/) *adj* of egoism or an egoist.

ego·tism /ˈiːgətɪzəm/ *nu* the practice of talking too often or too much about oneself.

ego·tist /-tɪst/ *nc* (*derog*) a very selfish person.

ego·tis·tic /ˌiːgəʊˈtɪstɪk/ *adj* (*derog*) of egotism or an egotist.

eh /eɪ/ *int* (used to express surprise or doubt, or to invite agreement): *You believe me now, eh?*

eider·down /ˈaɪdədaʊn/ *nc* (*dated*) a quilted bed-covering filled with soft feathers. ⇨ duvet.

eight /eɪt/ *adj or det, nc* (of) 8.

eight·een /ˌeɪˈtiːn/ *adj or det, nc* (of) 18.

eighteenth /-ˈtiːnθ/ *adj or det, nc* (abbr 18th) (of) one of 18 parts or the next after 17.

eighth /eɪtθ/ *adj or det, nc* (abbr 8th) (of) one of

8 parts or the next after 7.

eight·ieth /ˈeɪtɪəθ/ *adj or det, nc* (abbr 80th) (of) one of 80 parts or the next after 79.

eighty /ˈeɪtɪ/ *adj, nc* (of) 80: *Eighty-two people came.* **in the eighties** (**a**) (of temperature, speed etc) between 80 and 89. (**b**) between '80 and '89 in a century.

ei·ther[1] /ˈaɪðə(r)/ *adj or det* (of two people, things etc) **1** the one or the other: *You can use either room—I don't mind which. They can study either language but not both. Take either half. Either one will do. I don't mind either way* (=which of the two alternatives you choose). Compare neither[1]. **2** the one and also the other: *There is a bus-stop on either side of the road. There are shops on either side of the street. The car was damaged at either end.* Ⓝ 'Either' is followed by a singular noun. 'Both' is also possible but is followed by a plural noun, as in *damaged at both ends.* 'Neither' means 'not the one and not the other'. Compare both[1].

ei·ther[2] /ˈaɪðə(r)/ *pron* (of two people, things etc) **1** the one or the other: *Either will be OK. I'll accept either/either of them. Either of your parents can sign the form. Either of the two days is convenient. Are/Is either of your parents at home? I don't think either of my bicycle wheels are/is damaged.* Ⓝ 'Either' cannot be used in front of another determiner (e.g. *a, some, the*). 'Either of' can be used in front of possessive pronouns (e.g. *my, your*), personal pronouns (e.g. *you, us*) and *the, these, those* etc, as in *Either of them can sign.* Compare: all, both, each. 'Either of' is usually used with a singular verb but is often used with a plural verb in informal questions and negative statements, as in *Are/Is either of your hands injured?* **2** (used as an adverb in negative statements): *I don't like the red one and I don't like the orange one either.* 'He doesn't like carrots'—'I don't either.' 'She can't swim'—'I can't either'. Ⓝ 'Too' and 'also' are used in positive statements, as in *I like it too, I also like it.* 'Also' is possible in negative statements but 'either' is more usual. Compare neither[2](2). **3** (used as a *conj*) **either . . . or . . .** (used to introduce the first of two (or more) possibilities): *We can come either this weekend or next. Either do your homework or go to bed. You can choose either red, green or yellow. Either the world is ending or the lights have fused.* Ⓝ 'Either' can be used in front of another determiner (e.g. *a, the, your, this* etc) when combined with 'or' in this way. Compare neither . . . nor . . .

ejacu·late /ɪˈdʒækjʊleɪt/ *vt,vi* (*science*) to send out (semen) from the penis.

ejacu·la·tion /ɪˌdʒækjʊˈleɪʃn/ *nc,nu*

eject /ɪˈdʒekt/ *v* **eject (sb/sth) (from sth)** **1** *vt,vi* (often *passive*) to force (a person) to leave (a place): *They were ejected from the meeting by the police.* **2** *vt,vi* (*tech*) to send out (liquid etc): *Lava was ejected from the volcano.* **3** *vi* to make an emergency exit, e.g. with a parachute.

ejec·tion /ɪˈdʒekʃn/ *nc,nu*

eke /iːk/ *vt* **eke sth out** to make a small supply of something enough to live on, enough for one's needs etc: *eking out one's grant by walking to college.*

elab·or·ate[1] /ɪˈlæbərət/ *adj* having much detail: *elaborate designs; elaborate plans.*

elab·or·ate² /ɪ'læbəreɪt/ *vi* **elaborate (on sth)** (*formal*) to explain, describe, something in detail: *Please elaborate (on your proposals) a little.*

elab·or·ation /ɪ,læbə'reɪʃn/ *nc,nu*

elapse /ɪ'læps/ *vi* (*formal*) (of time) to pass.

elas·tic¹ /ɪ'læstɪk/ *adj* **1** able to go back to the normal or previous size or shape after being pulled or pressed: *Rubber is elastic.* **2** (*fig*) able to be changed, adapted: *elastic rules/plans.*

elas·tic² /ɪ'læstɪk/ *nu* material made elastic by weaving rubber into it: *a piece of elastic.*

e,lastic 'band *nc* a circular strip of rubber, used to keep papers etc together.

elas·tic·ity /,elæ'stɪsəti/ *nu*

elat·ed /ɪ'leɪtɪd/ *adj* (usually *pred*) extremely happy, pleased, proud etc: *He was elated at the news/elated by his success/elated to find that he had won.*

ela·tion /ɪ'leɪʃn/ *nu*

el·bow¹ /'elbəʊ/ *nc* **1** (the outer part of) the joint in the middle of the arm. **at one's elbow** near by: *I always keep my dictionary at my elbow.* **2** the middle part of a long sleeve. **3** a sharp corner or joint (e.g. in a pipe) shaped like an elbow.

'elbow-grease *nu* (*informal*) hard work.

'elbow-room *nu* enough space to move freely.

el·bow² /'elbəʊ/ *vt* to push, force, (one's way through, forward etc): *elbow one's way through a crowd.*

el·der¹ /'eldə(r)/ *adj* (*attrib*) **1** (no *comp*) (referring to two brothers, sisters, daughters, sons etc) having lived longer: *My elder brother is an engineer.* **2** (*superl* **eldest**) (of several people in the same family) having lived longer: *Her two younger sons are at university and her eldest son works in a bank. My elder sister is a teacher and my other sisters are at school.* Ⓝ *'Elder' is only used of people. 'Older' is used of people and things, as in an older man/building, and is now used more often than 'elder' especially when referring to one of three or more people.*

,elder 'statesman *nc* a politician with a lot of experience whose advice is valued.

el·der² /'eldə(r)/ *n* **1** *n sing* the older of two people: *Who is the elder of the two? He's my elder by several years.* ⇨ eldest(2). Ⓝ *'Older' is not possible.* **2** (*pl*) people who have lived a long time: *Should we always follow the advice of our elders?*

el·der³ /'eldə(r)/ *nc* a kind of small tree with white flowers and red or black berries.

el·der·ly /'eldəli/ *adj* (of a person) old.

el·dest /'eldɪst/ **1** *adj* (*attrib*) ⇨ elder¹(2). **2** *n sing* the older of two or more people: *Who's the eldest?* ⇨ elder²(1).

elect¹ /ɪ'lekt/ *adj* (used after a noun) chosen but not yet in office: *the president elect.*

elect² /ɪ'lekt/ *vt* **1** to choose (an official) by voting: *to elect a president.* **2 elect to do sth** (*formal*) to decide to do something: *He had elected to become a lawyer.*

elec·tion /ɪ'lekʃn/ *nc,nu* (an instance of) the choosing of representatives for a committee, government etc by voting: *call/hold an election.* ⇨ by-election, general election, local election.

elec·tion·eer·ing /ɪ,lekʃə'nɪərɪŋ/ *nu* working in elections, e.g. by canvassing, making speeches.

elec·tive /ɪ'lektɪv/ *adj* (*attrib*) (*formal*) **1** having the power to elect: *an elective assembly.* **2**
decided or filled by election: *The presidency is an elective office.*

elec·tor /ɪ'lektə(r)/ *nc* a person having the right to vote in an election.

elec·tor·al /ɪ'lektərəl/ *adj* of an election.

electoral register *nc* a list of voters.

elec·tor·ate /ɪ'lektərət/ *nc* all the people who can vote in an election.

elec·tric /ɪ'lektrɪk/ *adj* **1** (usually *attrib*) (of machinery, systems, objects etc) of, worked by, capable of producing, electricity: *an electric current/torch/iron/shock; an electric guitar* (= one with an amplifier for the sound). Compare electrical. **2** (*fig*) causing a strong emotional effect: *The effect of the speech was electric.*

elec·tri·cal /ɪ'lektrɪkl/ *adj* (usually *attrib*) concerned with, related to, electricity: *an electrical fault; an electrical appliance; electrical engineering.*

elec·tri·cal·ly /-klɪ/ *adv*

elec·tri·cian /ɪ,lek'trɪʃn/ *nc* a person who sets up, repairs etc electrical apparatuses.

elec·tri·city /ɪ,lek'trɪsəti/ *nu* the power, energy, from the movement of electrons and protons, as obtained from an electric generator, battery etc and used to provide heat, light, work motors etc.

elec·tri·fy /ɪ'lektrɪfaɪ/ *vt* (*pt,pp* **-ied**) **1** to provide, equip, (a machine, system etc) with electricity: *electrify the railways.* **2** (*fig*) to excite, shock, (a person) suddenly: *to electrify an audience by making an unexpected announcement.*

elec·tri·fi·ca·tion /ɪ,lektrɪfɪ'keɪʃn/ *nu*

elec·tro·cute /ɪ'lektrəkjuːt/ *vt* to kill (a person, animal) by using electricity.

elec·tro·cu·tion /ɪ,lektrə'kjuːʃn/ *nc,nu*

elec·trode /ɪ'lektrəʊd/ *nc* (*electricity*) one of two solid points by which an electric current enters or leaves a battery etc. ⇨ anode, cathode.

elec·tron /ɪ'lektrɒn/ *nc* (*science*) a very small particle of matter, smaller than an atom, having a negative electric charge. ⇨ neutron, proton.

elec·tron·ic /ɪ,lek'trɒnɪk/ *adj* of electronics: *electronic music* (i.e. produced by using electric currents to change the sounds from a musical instrument or tape).

electronic data processing (abbr **EDP**) (*computers*) using computers to store, analyse etc information.

elec·tron·ics /ɪ,lek'trɒnɪks/ *nu* the scientific study, technology, industry, concerned with apparatuses such as radio, TV, tape-recorders, calculators, computers etc.

el·egance /'elɪgəns/ *nu* elegant quality or style.

el·egant /'elɪgənt/ *adj* showing, having, done with, good taste in design, style, movement, behaviour etc: *looking elegant in a long dress; elegant manners.* Opp inelegant.

el·egant·ly *adv*

el·egy /'elədʒi/ *nc* (*pl* **-ies**) (*literature*) a poem or song of sorrow, esp for the dead.

el·ement /'elɪmənt/ *nc* **1** (*science*) a substance which has not so far been split up into a simpler form by ordinary chemical methods: *Water is a compound containing the elements hydrogen and oxygen.* **2 in/out of one's element** in/not in suitable, comfortable, preferred etc surroundings: *He's in his element when they start talking about economics.* **3** (*pl;* the —s) the forces of nature, bad weather etc: *We spent a night on the mountain exposed to the elements* (= to winds, storms etc). **4** (*pl*) the beginnings or outlines (of a subject of study): *the elements of geometry*. **5** a necessary or characteristic feature: *Justice is an important element in good government*. **6** a suggestion, indication, trace, (of something): *There's an element of truth in his statement*. ⇨ atom(2). **7** the part of an electrical appliance (e.g. a kettle, boiler etc) that produces heat.

ele·men·tary /ˌelɪˈmentrɪ/ *adj* of, at or in the beginning stage(s); not difficult: *an elementary course; elementary arithmetic*. Compare advanced(2).

el·eph·ant /ˈelɪfənt/ *nc* a very large four-footed animal, with curved tusks and a long trunk. ⇨ also white elephant.

el·ev·ate /ˈelɪveɪt/ *vt* (*formal*) **1** to promote (a person, job) to a higher or more important position: *elevated to the Board of Directors*. **2** (*fig*) to make (the mind, morals) higher and better: *an elevating book/speech*.

el·ev·ation /ˌelɪˈveɪʃn/ *n* **1** *nc,nu* (*formal*) (an instance of) elevating or being elevated: *elevation to the House of Lords*. **2** *nc* (*tech*) a height (esp above sea-level): *an elevation of 2000 metres*. **3** *nc* (*tech*) a plan (drawn to scale) of one side of a building. Compare plan¹(1).

el·ev·ator /ˈelɪveɪtə(r)/ *nc* (*US*) = lift¹(2).

elev·en /ɪˈlevn/ *adj or det, nc* **1** (of) the number 11. **2** a team of eleven players for football, hockey or cricket.

elev·enth /ɪˈlevnθ/ *adj or det, nc* (abbr 11th) (of) one of 11 parts or the next after 10. **at the eleventh hour** at the latest possible time.

elf /elf/ *nc* (*pl* **elves** /elvz/) (in stories) a small fairy; mischievous little creature.
 elf·ish /ˈelfɪʃ/ *adj*

eli·cit /ɪˈlɪsɪt/ *vt* (*formal*) to cause (information) to become known: *eliciting the truth/the facts*.

eli·gible /ˈelɪdʒəbl/ *adj* **1** **eligible (for sth/as sb/to do sth)** fit, suitable, to be chosen; having the right qualifications: *eligible for promotion/as a member/to be a member*. Opp ineligible. **2** (*informal*) who would be a satisfactory choice as a husband or wife: *an eligible young man*.
 el·igi·bil·ity /ˌelɪdʒəˈbɪlətɪ/ *nu*

elim·in·ate /ɪˈlɪmɪneɪt/ *vt* **eliminate sth (from sth)** to remove (something); get rid of (something) because unnecessary or unwanted: *eliminating suspects from a list by interviewing them*.
 elim·in·ation /ɪˌlɪmɪˈneɪʃn/ *nu*

eli·sion /ɪˈlɪʒən/ *nu* (*lang*) the omission of a sound at the beginning or end of a word (esp in poetry), e.g. *'Tis* (= It is) *my delight . . . ; give 'em* (= them) *to me; that is the truth on't* (= on it)*; Were't* (= Were it) *not for you . . .* Compare syncope.

élite /eɪˈliːt/ *nc* a group in society considered (esp by itself) to be superior because of power, privileges etc: *the diplomatic élite*. Compare egalitarian.

élit·ist /ɪˈliːtɪst/ *adj* (*derog*) favouring, encouraging, the existence of an élite.

elix·ir /ɪˈlɪksə(r)/ *nc* a medicine which medieval scientists thought keeps a person alive for ever.

elk /elk/ *nc* one of the largest kinds of deer (*US* = *moose*).

el·lipse /ɪˈlɪps/ *nc* a regular oval.

el·lip·ti·cal /-kl/ *adj* shaped like an ellipse: *an elliptical orbit*.

el·lip·sis /ɪˈlɪpsɪs/ *nu* (*lang*) the omission of one or more words in a sentence, as in *a table and chair* (for *. . . a chair*)*; I promised to phone and I did* (for *. . . I did phone*)*; five coffees, please* (for *. . . cups of* coffee)*; he ran and fell over* (for *. . . he fell over*).

elm /elm/ *nc,nu* (the wood of) a kind of tree with wide leaves that grows to a great size.

elo·cu·tion /ˌeləˈkjuːʃn/ *nu* the art, style, of speaking well, esp in public.

elon·gat·ed /ˈiːlɒŋgeɪtɪd/ *adj* (*formal*) (made) long and thin: *an elongated leaf*.

elope /ɪˈləʊp/ *vi* (of lovers) to run away from home to get married.
 elope·ment *nc,nu*

elo·quence /ˈeləkwəns/ *nu* (*formal*) the skilful use of language to express oneself or persuade others.
 elo·quent /-ənt/ *adj*
 elo·quent·ly *adv*

else /els/ *adv* **1** in addition: *Did you go anywhere else? What else would you like?* **2** different: *Let's go somewhere else. How else could you do it? He's wearing someone else's coat. No-one/Nobody else will pay*. **3** apart from that: *How else could she have known? There's not much else I can add. Little else is known about the disease. Who else wants coffee (apart from me)? Nothing else, thanks*. **all else** ⇨ all³(1). **or else** (*conj*) (**a**) if not; otherwise: *Give it to me or else I'll tell your dad*. Ⓝ *'Else' can be omitted.* (**b**) (used to make a threat) or something painful, horrible etc will happen: *You'd better give it to me or else!*

else·where /elsˈweə(r)/ *adv* somewhere different: *If the restaurant is full we can go elsewhere*.

ELT /ˌiː el ˈtiː/ *abbr* English language teaching.

elu·ci·date /ɪˈluːsɪdeɪt/ *vt* (*formal*) to make clear, explain, (a problem, difficulty).
 elu·ci·da·tion /ɪˌluːsɪˈdeɪʃn/ *nc,nu*

elude /ɪˈluːd/ *vt* (*formal*) to escape (capture) by (a person) (esp by deceiving): *elude one's enemies*.

elu·sive /ɪˈluːsɪv/ *adj* **1** difficult to find, capture etc: *an elusive criminal*. **2** not easy to remember: *an elusive word/name*.

elves /elvz/ *pl* of elf.

'em /əm/ *pron* (*informal*) = them.

em·aci·at·ed /ɪˈmeɪsieɪtɪd/ *adj* (of a person) very thin because of illness, poverty etc.

ema·nate /ˈemə·neɪt/ *vi* **emanate (from sth)** (*formal*) to come, flow, proceed, (from a source or origin): *The rumour emanated from your department*.
 ema·na·tion /ˌeməˈneɪʃn/ *nc,nu*

eman·ci·pate /ɪˈmænsɪpeɪt/ *vt* to set (a person) free (esp politically).
 eman·ci·pated /-peɪtɪd/ *adj* (esp) free from social restrictions or conventions: *an emancipated woman*.
 eman·ci·pa·tion /ɪˌmænsɪˈpeɪʃn/ *nu*

em·balm /ɪmˈbɑːm/ *vt* to preserve (a dead body) by using oils, chemicals etc.
 em·balm·er *nc* a person who embalms bodies.

em·bank·ment /ɪmˈbæŋkmənt/ *nc* a wall of earth, stone etc built to hold back water, to support a road or railway.

em·bar·go /ɪm'bɑːgəʊ/ nc (pl **—es**) an order that forbids trade, movement of ships etc: lift/ raise/remove an embargo.

em·bark /ɪm'bɑːk/ v **1** vt,vi to go, put or take (passengers etc) on board a ship: The soldiers embarked for Malta. The ship embarked passengers and cargo. **2 embark on sth** (formal) to start an activity: embark on a new career.

em·bar·ka·tion /ˌembɑː'keɪʃn/ nc,nu

em·bar·rass /ɪm'bærəs/ vt to make (a person) feel uncomfortable, ashamed etc: His smile embarrassed her.

em·bar·rass·ing adj: embarrassing questions.

em·bar·rass·ing·ly adv

em·bar·rass·ment nc,nu

em·bas·sy /'embəsɪ/ nc (pl **-ies**) (also attrib) (E- in names) (the building of) an ambassador and her or his staff: the French Embassy in London; embassy officials.

em·bed /ɪm'bed/ vt (-dd-) **embed sth in sth** (usually passive) **1** to fix (something) firmly (in a surrounding substance): stones embedded in rock. **2** (fig) to keep (something) firmly (in one's mind etc): facts embedded in one's memory.

em·bel·lish /ɪm'belɪʃ/ vt **embellish sth (with sth)** to add details to (something) to make it more attractive, exciting etc: embellish a story with amusing details. ⇨ embroider(2).

em·bel·lish·ment nc,nu

em·ber /'embə(r)/ nc (usually pl) a small piece of burning wood or coal in a dying fire.

em·bezzle /ɪm'bezl/ vt,vi to use (money etc placed in one's care) illegally for one's own benefit: embezzle the committee's funds; be arrested for embezzling.

em·bezzle·ment nc,nu

em·bit·ter /ɪm'bɪtə(r)/ vt (usually passive) to cause (a person) to feel hate, envy, anger: She became embittered by repeated failures.

em·bit·ter·ment nu

em·blem /'embləm/ nc a device that represents something: The dove is an emblem of peace.

em·blem·at·ic /ˌemblə'mætɪk/ adj

em·body /ɪm'bɒdɪ/ vt (pt,pp **-ied**) (formal) Ⓝ Not often used in the continuous tenses, e.g. is/was -ing. **1** to express (ideas, feelings etc) (in writing, speech): embody one's ideas in a speech. **2** to include (something): The latest cameras embody many new features.

em·bodi·ment /ɪm'bɒdɪmənt/ nc **the embodiment of sth** (formal) an excellent example of a (good) quality: She is the embodiment of kindness.

em·boss /ɪm'bɒs/ vt **emboss sth (with sth)** to make (a pattern, writing etc) that stands out on the surface of (something): a silver vase embossed with a design of flowers.

em·brace¹ /ɪm'breɪs/ nc an act of embracing(1): a loving embrace.

em·brace² /ɪm'breɪs/ v **1** vt,vi to take (a person) in one's arms, as a sign of affection: She was embracing her son. They embraced. **2** vt (formal) to accept and make use of (something good): embrace an offer/opportunity. **3** vt (formal) (of things) to include (something): embrace many colours in a single design. Ⓝ Not often used in the continuous tenses, e.g. is/was -ing.

em·bro·ca·tion /ˌembrə'keɪʃn/ nu an oily medi-cine used for rubbing on a bruise etc.

em·broid·er /ɪm'brɔɪdə(r)/ vt,vi **1** to sew (cloth) with a design: a dress embroidered with flowers; a design embroidered in gold thread. **2** (fig) to add untrue details to (a story) for a better effect.

em·broid·ery nu the act, art, result, of embroidering.

em·bryo /'embrɪəʊ/ nc (pl **-s**) **1** (science) the young of an animal in the early stage of its devel-opment before birth (or before coming out of its egg). **2** (fig) something in its very early stage of development. **in embryo** (of a plan etc) at a very early stage.

em·bry·on·ic /ˌembrɪ'ɒnɪk/ adj

emend /ɪ'mend/ vt to remove errors from, make small improvements to, (writing, a speech): emend a piece of writing. Compare amend.

em·er·ald /'emərəld/ nc,nu, adj (the colour of) a bright green precious stone.

emerge /ɪ'mɜːdʒ/ vi **1 emerge (from/out of sth)** to appear, come, (from): The moon was emerging from behind the clouds. **2** (of facts, ideas) to become known: No new ideas emerged during the talks.

emerg·ence /-dʒəns/ nu

emerg·ent /-dʒənt/ adj

emerg·en·cy /ɪ'mɜːdʒənsɪ/ nc (pl **-ies**) (also attrib) **(in) an emergency** (in the event of) a serious and dangerous happening or situation needing quick action: This door is to be used only in an emergency. Use the emergency exit.

emi·grant /'emɪgrənt/ nc a person who emi-grates: emigrants from Italy to Canada. Compare immigrant.

emi·grate /'emɪgreɪt/ vi to go away from one's own country to live in another. Compare immi-grate.

emi·gra·tion /ˌemɪ'greɪʃn/ nc,nu

émi·gré /'emɪgreɪ/ nc (Fr) a person who has left her or his own country, usually for political reasons.

emi·nence /'emɪnəns/ nu the state of being famous or distinguished: achieve eminence as a scientist.

emi·nent /'emɪnənt/ adj (formal) (of a person) distinguished and famous: eminent as a sculptor; an eminent lawyer.

emi·nent·ly adv

emir /e'mɪə(r)/ nc a Muslim ruler.

emir·ate /e'mɪəreɪt/ nc the rank, lands etc of an emir: the great emirates of Northern Nigeria.

emis·sion /ɪ'mɪʃn/ n (formal) **1** nc,nu a sending out or giving off (of something): an emission of light/heat. **2** nc something (heat, radiation etc) that is sent out or given off.

emit /ɪ'mɪt/ vt (-tt-) (formal) to give or send out (something): A volcano emits smoke and ashes.

emo·tion /ɪ'məʊʃn/ n **1** nc a strong feeling of any kind: Love, hate, fear and envy are emotions. **2** nu an excited state of the mind; strength of feeling: He thought of his dead child with deep emotion.

emo·tion·al /-ʃnl/ adj **(a)** of, concerning, excit-ing emotions(1): an emotional appeal/response. **(b)** having strong or easily excited feelings: an emotional woman/husband.

emo·tion·al·ly /-əlɪ/ adv

emo·tion·less adj without (showing) emo-tion(1): She remained emotionless throughout her *trial.*

emot·ive /ɪˈməʊtɪv/ *adj* causing a strong emotional response: *emotive language.*

em·pale /ɪmˈpeɪl/ *vt* = impale.

em·pa·thy /ˈempəθɪ/ *nu* **empathy (with sb)** (the power of) sharing the feelings, mood of another person (and so understanding her or him).

em·per·or /ˈempərə(r)/ *nc* a ruler of an empire. Compare empress.

em·pha·sis /ˈemfəsɪs/ *nc,nu* (*pl* **-phases** /-siːz/) **1** the addition of a particular word or words, the spoken force used etc to make the significance clear or to show importance when speaking or writing. Ⓝ Changes in stress, the use of capital letters in writing, the use of words such as 'so' and 'such' and the repetition of words such as 'very, very' are all ways of showing emphasis in English. **2** *emphasis (on sth)* (the placing of) special value or importance (on): *Some dictionaries lay/ put special emphasis on grammar.*

em·pha·size (also **-ise**) /ˈemfəsaɪz/ *vt* **empha-size (that) sth** to give emphasis to (something): *He emphasized the importance of careful driving/ that we must drive carefully.*

em·phat·ic /ɪmˈfætɪk/ *adj* having, expressed with, emphasis; strong and firm: *an emphatic opinion/person.*

em,phatic 'pronoun *nc* (*gram*) one used to emphasize a noun or (more usually) a pronoun, as in 'I'll come *myself*', 'The chair *itself* is worth nothing.' Ⓝ Also called *intensive pronoun.*

em·phati·cal·ly /-klɪ/ *adv*

em·pire /ˈempaɪə(r)/ *nc* (E- in names) a group of countries under a single supreme authority: *the Roman Empire.* ⇨ emperor, empress.

em·piri·cal /ɪmˈpɪrɪkl/ *adj* (*formal*) relying on observation and experiment, not on theory: *empirical evidence.*

em·piri·cal·ly /-klɪ/ *adv*

em·piri·cism /ɪmˈpɪrɪsɪzəm/ *nu* the use of empirical evidence to decide the truth of something.

em·piri·cist /-sɪst/ *adj* of, concerning, empiri-cism. □ *nc* a supporter of empiricism.

em·ploy /ɪmˈplɔɪ/ *vt* **1 employ sb (as sb)** to give work to (a person) for payment: *He is employed as a clerk in a bank.* ⇨ unemployed. **2** (*formal*) to make use of (something): *How do you employ your spare time?*

em·ploy·ee /ˌemplɔɪˈiː/ *nc* a person who is employed: *an employee of the hospital.*

em·ploy·er *nc* a person who employs others.

em·ploy·ment /ɪmˈplɔɪmənt/ *nu* **1** the state of employing or being employed. Compare unem-ployment. **2** a person's regular work or occupa-tion: *be in/out of employment.*

em'ployment agency a business that helps people to find jobs.

em·por·ium /ɪmˈpɔːrɪəm/ *nc* (*pl* **—s**) a large (food) shop.

em·pow·er /ɪmˈpaʊə(r)/ *vt* (often *passive*) to give (a person) power or authority (to act).

em·press /ˈemprɪs/ *nc* **1** woman governing an empire. Compare emperor. **2** the wife, widow, of an emperor.

emp·ty¹ /ˈemptɪ/ *adj* (**-ier, -iest**) **1** having nothing inside: *an empty box; a cupboard empty*

of food. Compare full¹(1). **2** (*fig*) (of speech, writ-ing) having no meaning or purpose; not meant to be carried out: *empty words; an empty apology; empty promises; a letter empty of all feeling.*

empty-'handed *adj* (*pred*) bringing, carrying, nothing: *arrive empty-handed.*

empty-'headed *adj* (*derog*) not having com-mon sense; stupid.

emp·ti·ness /ˈemptɪnəs/ *nu*

emp·ty² /ˈemptɪ/ *vt,vi* (*pt,pp* **-ied**) (to cause a container etc) to become empty; remove (what is inside): *empty one's glass* (= drink everything in it); *empty (out) a drawer; empty one's pockets onto the table. The lesson finished and the room emptied. Please empty the rubbish into the dust-bin.* Opp fill²(1).

emu /ˈiːmjuː/ *nc* a kind of large flightless Austra-lian bird that runs fast.

emu·late /ˈemjʊleɪt/ *vt* (*formal*) to try to do as well as or better than (a person).

emu·la·tion /ˌemjʊˈleɪʃn/ *nu*

emul·sion /ɪˈmʌlʃn/ *nc,nu* (also *attrib*) (any kind of) creamy liquid containing oil or fat: *emulsion paint.*

en·able /ɪˈneɪbl/ *vt* to make (a person) able to do something by giving authority or means: *The new road is enabling us to arrive ten minutes earlier. Are children enabled to have a bank account?*

en·act /ɪˈnækt/ *vt* **1** to make (a law). **2** (*formal*) to perform (a part) on the stage: *enact the part of Romeo.* Ⓝ 'Act' or 'perform' is much more usual.

en·act·ment *nc,nu*

en·am·el¹ /ɪˌnæml/ *nu* **1** (also *attrib*) a hard, shiny substance used for protecting or decorating metal, porcelain etc: *enamel paint.* **2** the hard outer covering of teeth.

en·am·el² /ɪˈnæml/ *vt* (**-ll-,** *US* also **-l-**) to cover, decorate, (something) with enamel(1).

en bloc /ˌɑːn ˈblɒk/ *adv* (*Fr*) all together; as a body: *They voted en bloc to send aid.*

en·case /ɪnˈkeɪs/ *vt* (*formal*) to surround or cover (something) completely: *a diamond encased in gold.* Ⓝ Not used in the continuous tenses, e.g. *is/ was -ing.*

en·chant /ɪnˈtʃɑːnt/ *vt* **enchant sb (with sth)** (often *passive*) (*formal*) to charm or delight (a person): *She was enchanted by/with the flowers you sent her.*

en·chant·ed *adj* (in stories) affected by magic: *an enchanted garden.*

en·chant·ing *adj* (*formal*) charming.

en·chant·ment *nc,nu*

en·circle /ɪnˈsɜːkl/ *vt* **encircle sth (by/with sth)** (often *passive*) to surround something: *a lake encircled by/with trees.*

en·circle·ment *nc,nu*

encl. *abbr* (*commerce*) enclosed.

en·clave /ˈenkleɪv/ *nc* a part of a country wholly within the boundaries of another.

en·close (also **in·close**) /ɪnˈkləʊz/ *vt* **enclose sth (with sth)** (often *passive*) **1** to put a wall, fence etc round (something); shut (something) in on all sides: *enclose a garden with a wall.* **2** to put (something) inside an envelope, parcel etc: *A cheque for £5 is enclosed.*

en·clos·ure /ɪnˈkləʊʒə(r)/ *n* **1** *nc,nu* (an instance of) enclosing(1): *the enclosure of land.* **2** *nc* a fenced area: *an enclosure for horses.* **3** *nc* (usually *commerce*) something put inside a letter or parcel.

en·code /ɪnˈkəʊd/ *vt* to change (writing) into a code.

en·com·pass /ɪnˈkʌmpəs/ *vt* (*formal*) **1** to surround (something). **2** to include, consist of, (something): *The course will encompass poetry, drama and novels*.

en·core /ˈɒŋkɔː(r)/ *int* Repeat! Again! □ *nc* a repetition of a performance. *The singer gave three encores*.

en·coun·ter¹ /ɪnˈkaʊntə(r)/ *nc* a sudden or unexpected (esp unpleasant) meeting: *an encounter with the bank manager*.

en·coun·ter² /ɪnˈkaʊntə(r)/ *vt* (*formal*) **1** to find oneself faced by (danger, difficulties etc). **2** to meet (a friend etc) unexpectedly.

en·cour·age /ɪnˈkʌrɪdʒ/ *vt* **1** *encourage sb (in sth/to do sth)* to give hope, courage or confidence to (a person): *encouraging her to work harder; encourage a boy in his studies*. **2** to give support, money etc to (a business, team etc). **3** to show enthusiasm, give support etc to increase (cooperation, commitment etc).
en·cour·age·ment *nc,nu*

en·croach /ɪnˈkrəʊtʃ/ *vi* *encroach (on sth)* (*formal*) to go beyond, use more than, what is right or natural: *encroach on his rights/time/land*.
en·croach·ment *nc,nu*

en·crust /ɪnˈkrʌst/ *vt* *encrust sth with sth* (often *passive*) to cover (something) (with jewels etc): *a gold vase encrusted with precious stones*.

en·cum·ber /ɪnˈkʌmbə(r)/ *vt* *encumber sb/ sth with sth* (usually *passive*) (*formal*) to be a burden or difficulty to (a person, business, place etc) (and make action, movement difficult): *be encumbered with a large family; a room encumbered with old and useless furniture*.

en·cum·brance /ɪnˈkʌmbrəns/ *nc* *encumbrance (to sb)* (*formal*) a person, thing, that is a burden: *A lazy daughter can be an encumbrance to her parents*.

en·cy·clo·pae·dia (also **-pe·dia**) /ɪnˌsaɪkləˈpiːdɪə/ *nc* (*pl* —s) a book or set of books giving information about every branch of knowledge or about one subject: *a scientific encyclopaedia; an encyclopaedia of world history*.
en·cy·clo·pae·dic (also **-pe·dic**) /ɪnˌsaɪkləˈpiːdɪk/ *adj*

end¹ /end/ *nc* **1** the last part (of something); the place where (something) stops: *at the end of the street/the queue/the bed/the table. The front end has a point and the back end is flat. One end is broken. Both ends are pointed.* Compare edge¹(3), side²(1,2). *end on* (of two things) so that their ends touch: *The cars crashed end on.* Compare on end at 2 below. *end to end* (of many things) in a line and with their ends touching: *We arranged the tables end to end across the room. on (its) end* with one end on the ground, at the bottom, and the other high in the air: *Can you stand your pen on its end?* ⇨ hair(1). *the end of the road* (*fig*) the point after which survival is impossible. *get (hold of) the wrong end of the stick* to have the wrong idea, opinion, of something. *go off the deep end* to become suddenly very angry. *make (both) ends meet* to live using the money one has or earns, not bor-

row. **2** *the end (of sth)* the finish, conclusion (of a period of time, an activity etc): *at the end of the day/the week/the month/the year/the century; at the end of the morning/the afternoon; towards the end of June/winter; from the end of July to the beginning of September; at the end of the lesson/ race/conversation. I'm nearly at the end of this book. She's reaching the end of her patience.* ⇨ tether. *in the end* finally (after a long time): *I tried to telephone her many times and in the end I sent a telegram. no end of sb/sth* (*informal*) very many, much: *We met no end of interesting people. on end* without stopping: *It rained for two hours/ for days on end. to the (bitter) end* without stopping and doing all that is/was possible (even until death): *They fought to the bitter end. without end* without stopping: *work for weeks without end; have trouble without end. be at an end* to be finished: *At last their quarrel is at an end. come to an end* to finish: *Summer/The day/The meeting was coming to an end. make an end of sth* to cause (something) to finish, stop: *Let's make an end of our quarrel. put an end to sth* to stop a condition, activity etc from happening: *put an end to bad behaviour/poverty.* **3** a small piece that is left: *a cigarette end. odds and ends* ⇨ odds. **4** death; destruction: *She's nearing her end. This flu could be the end of me. Modern technology means the end of typewriters as we have known them. come to a sticky end* to be painfully killed or badly defeated. **5** an aim; purpose: *With this end in view, he bought the poison. She'll do anything to achieve her end. be an end in itself* (of an activity) to be considered as the main purpose or aim: *Studying is often not an end in itself but a means to getting a job. be at a loose end* (*informal*) to have nothing important or interesting to do.

'end-game *nc* the final stage of a game, esp chess.

,end-'product *nc* the final product in a manufacturing process.

end² /end/ *vt,vi* (to cause something) to come to an end: *The road ends here. How does the film end? They ended their quarrel by shaking hands. end it all* (*informal*) to kill oneself. *a sth to end all sth* (*informal*) something that is the best example of those things: *This is a camera to end all cameras.*
end in sth (**a**) to have something at the end: *Words that end in '-y' change to '-ies' in the plural.* (**b**) to finish in the state mentioned: *Their marriage ended in divorce.* (**c**) to have the result mentioned: *The trial ended in a victory for human rights. If you quarrel it will end in tears.*
end up (as) sb/sth to be or become finally the kind of person, thing mentioned: *It ends up as dog meat. You'll end up unemployed if you don't study. She ended up as a teacher. end up in a place* to be finally in (prison etc). *end up doing/ with sth* to finish by doing, having, something: *end up with a song; end up with cheese and coffee; end up crying.*
end with sth = end up with sth.

en·dan·ger /ɪnˈdeɪndʒə(r)/ *vt* to cause danger to (an opportunity etc): *endanger one's chances of success.*

en·dan·ger·ed *adj* (*attrib*) in danger of being

destroyed: *The tiger is an endangered species.*

en·dear /ɪn'dɪə(r)/ *vt* **endear oneself/sb to sb** (*formal*) to make oneself, a person, loved: *endear oneself to everyone.*

en·dear·ing *adj* causing feelings of liking or love: *an endearing smile.*

en·dear·ment *nc,nu* (*formal*) an act, word, expression, of affection: *'Darling' is a term of endearment.*

en·deav·our¹ (*US* = **-vor**) /ɪn'devə(r)/ *nc* (*formal*) an effort (the usual word): *Please make every endeavour to be early.*

en·deav·our² (*US* = **-vor**) /ɪn'devə(r)/ *vi* **endeavour to do sth** (*formal*) to try: *Endeavour to please your employer.*

en·dem·ic /en'demɪk/ *adj* (of a disease) often found in a country or area, or among a particular group of people: *Cholera is endemic in many poor countries.* Compare epidemic.

end·ing /'endɪŋ/ *nc* the last part (of a word, story, film etc).

en·dive /'endɪv/ *nc,nu* a kind of curly-leaved chicory, used as salad.

end·less /'endlɪs/ *adj* having no end; never stopping: *a woman with endless patience.*

end·less·ly *adv*

en·dorse /ɪn'dɔːs/ *vt* **1** to write one's name on the back of (a cheque). **2** to write comments etc on (a document): *His driving licence has been endorsed with a driving offence.* **3** (*formal*) to approve, support (an opinion, decision etc).

en·dorse·ment *nc,nu*

en·dow /ɪn'dau/ *vt* **1** to give money etc to provide a regular income for (e.g. a college). **2** **be endowed with sth** (*formal*) to be born with personal qualities etc mentioned: *be endowed with artistic talents.*

en·dow·ment /ɪn'daumənt/ *nc,nu*

en·dur·ance /ɪn'djuərəns/ *nu* the ability to endure: *He showed remarkable powers of endurance.* **past/beyond endurance** (of pain, loneliness, criticism etc) impossible to endure.

en'durance test *nc* a test of how long a person can put up with suffering, working hard, loneliness etc.

en·dure /ɪn'djuə(r)/ *v* (*formal*) **1** *vt* to suffer a long period of (pain, hardship etc): *enduring pain/loneliness/cold weather bravely.* **2** *vi* to last; continue in existence: *fame that will endure for ever.*

en·dur·able /-əbl/ *adj* able to be endured. Opp unendurable.

en·dur·ing *adj* lasting: *an enduring peace.*

end·ways /'endweɪz/ (also **-wise**) /-waɪz/) *adv* with the end towards the spectator: *Viewed endways (on), it looks like a cube.*

ENE *written abbr* east-north-east.

en·emy /'enəmɪ/ *nc* (*pl* **-ies**) **1** a person who feels hatred and tries or wishes to harm or attack: *A bad-tempered teacher will make many enemies among the pupils. They have been enemies for years* (= each is an enemy of the other). **2** (the —) (used with a *sing* or *pl verb*; also *attrib*) the armed forces of a nation with which one's country is at war: *The enemy was/were forced to retreat. We saw enemy aircraft/ships.* **3** (*fig*) anything that harms or injures: *Laziness is his chief enemy.*

en·er·get·ic /ˌenə'dʒetɪk/ *adj* full of, done with,

energy(1).

en·er·geti·cal·ly /-klɪ/ *adv*

en·er·gy /'enədʒɪ/ *n* (*pl* **-ies**) **1** *nu* (of a person) the force, strength, capacity, to do things and get things done: *He had so much energy that he did the work of three men. She's full of energy.* **2** (*pl*) (of a person) the powers used for working: *apply/ devote all one's energies to a task.* **3** *nu* the capacity for, power used for, working machines etc: *electrical energy.*

en·er·vate /'enəveɪt/ *vt* (*formal*) to cause (a person) to lose physical or moral strength.

en·er·vat·ing *adj: an enervating climate.*

en·fold /ɪn'fəuld/ *vt* (*formal*) to hold (a person) (in one's arms).

en·force /ɪn'fɔːs/ *vt* **1** to force obedience to (something), force (something) to be done: *enforce discipline/silence.* **2** to make sure that (a law etc) is carried out: *enforcing the new parking regulations.*

en·force·able /-əbl/ *adj* able to be enforced.

en·force·ment *nu*

en·fran·chise /ɪn'fræntʃaɪz/ *vt* (*formal*) to give the right to (a person) to vote at parliamentary elections: *In Great Britain women were enfranchised in 1918.* Compare disfranchise.

eng. *abbr* engine; engineer.

Eng. *abbr* England; English.

en·gage /ɪn'geɪdʒ/ *v* **1** *vt* **engage sb (as sb)** to employ a person (as): *engage him as a guide.* **2** *vt* **engage in sth** to take part in an activity: *engage in politics.* **be engaged (in sth)** to be busy (doing something): *be engaged in writing a novel.* **3** *vt* (*formal*) to attract (attention, a feeling): *Nothing engages his attention for long.* **4** *vt* to begin fighting with (soldiers etc): *The general did not engage the enemy.* **5** *vt,vi* **engage (sth) (with sth)** (to cause parts of a machine) to fit (into something): *The teeth of one wheel engage with those of the other.* Compare disengage.

en·gaged *adj* (a) having agreed to marry each other: *We're engaged.* (b) (of a telephone line) in use: *All the phones are engaged. The engaged tone you can hear means that someone else is using the line.*

en·gag·ing *adj* (*formal*) pleasant and attractive: *an engaging smile.*

en·gag·ing·ly *adv*

en·gage·ment /ɪn'geɪdʒmənt/ *n* **1** *nc* an agreement to marry: *Their engagement was announced in the papers.* **2** *nc* an arrangement to go somewhere, meet a person or do something, at a fixed time: *I can't come because of another engagement.* **3** *nc,nu* the process, act, of engaging (of part of a machine etc): *engagement of first gear.*

en'gagement ring *nc* one given by a man to a woman when they agree to marry.

en·gen·der /ɪn'dʒendə(r)/ *vt* (*formal*) to be the cause of (something): *Crime is often engendered by poverty.*

en·gine /'endʒɪn/ *nc* any kind of machine that changes energy (from petrol, electricity etc) into motion: *a new engine for a car.*

en·gin·eer¹ /ˌendʒɪ'nɪə(r)/ *nc* **1** a person who designs machines, bridges, railways etc: *a civil/ electrical engineer.* **2** a person in control of an engine or engines: *the chief engineer of a ship.*

en·gin·eer² /ˌendʒɪ'nɪə(r)/ *vt* (*formal*) to arrange

or bring about (a situation, plan etc) using careful planning: *engineer a scheme to win the contract.*

en·gin·eer·ing *nu* the profession of an engineer.

Eng·lish[1] /'ɪŋglɪʃ/ *adj* **1** of England. **2** of, written in, spoken in, the English language.

Eng·lish·man *nc* a man born in England.

Eng·lish·woman *nc* a woman born in England.

Eng·lish[2] /'ɪŋglɪʃ/ *n* **1** the English language. **2** (the —) (used with a *pl verb*) English people.

en·grave /ɪn'greɪv/ *vt* **1 engrave sth (on sth) (with sth)** to cut or carve lines, words, designs etc (on a hard surface): *a name engraved on a tombstone; glass engraved with a name.* **2 be engraved on sth** (*fig*) to be deeply impressed on the memory or mind: *My first trip to Venice is engraved on my memory.*

en·graver *nc* a person who engraves designs etc on stone, glass, metal etc.

en·grav·ing *n* (a) *nu* the art of cutting or carving designs on glass, metal etc. (b) *nc* a copy of a picture, design etc printed from an engraved metal plate.

en·gross·ed /ɪn'grəʊst/ *adj* (*pred*) **engrossed (in sth)** extremely busy with and interested (in an activity, book etc): *He's engrossed in his work.*

en·gulf·ed /ɪn'gʌlft/ *adj* (*pred*) **engulfed (in sth)** completely surrounded (by something): *be engulfed in the waves/flames.*

en·hance /ɪn'hɑːns/ *vt* (*formal*) to add to (the value, attraction, reputation etc): *It was an achievement that enhanced her reputation as a physicist.*

enig·ma /ɪ'nɪgmə/ *nc* (*pl* **—s**) a question, person, thing, circumstance, that is puzzling: *Where they hid the money will remain an enigma.*

enig·mat·ic /ˌenɪg'mætɪk/ *adj*

enig·mati·cal·ly /-klɪ/ *adv*

en·joy /ɪn'dʒɔɪ/ *vt* **1** to get pleasure from (something, an activity etc): *enjoy one's dinner.* **2** to have (a condition etc) as an advantage or benefit: *enjoy good health.* **3 enjoy oneself** to experience pleasure; be happy.

en·joy·able /-əbl/ *adj* (of experiences) pleasant: *an enjoyable meal/evening.* Opp unenjoyable.

en·joy·ably /-əblɪ/ *adv*

en·joy·ment /ɪn'dʒɔɪmənt/ *nc,nu*

en·large /ɪn'lɑːdʒ/ *vt,vi* **1** (to cause something) to become larger: *enlarge a photograph/one's house.* **2 enlarge on sth** (*formal*) to say or write more about something: *I need not enlarge on the plans which are explained in this report.*

en·large·ment *nc,nu*

en·light·en /ɪn'laɪtn/ *vt* **enlighten sb (about/ on sb/sth)** to give more knowledge to a person (about something); free a person from ignorance, misunderstanding or false beliefs: *Can you enlighten me about/on what really happened?*

en·light·en·ed *adj* free from ignorance, prejudice, superstition etc: *enlightened attitudes towards young people.* Opp unenlightened.

en·lighten·ment *nc,nu*

en·list /ɪn'lɪst/ *v* **1** *vt,vi* **enlist (sb) (in sth) (as sb)** (to cause a person) to enter the armed forces: *enlist a recruit; enlist as a volunteer in the army.* **2** *vt* (*formal*) to get (the support of) a person, thing: *Can I enlist your help in a charitable cause?*

en·list·ment *nc,nu*

en·liv·en /ɪn'laɪvn/ *vt* to make (an event, painting etc) (more) lively: *How can we enliven the party?*

en·mi·ty /'enmətɪ/ *nu* (*formal*) hatred.

enor·mi·ty /ɪ'nɔːmətɪ/ *n* (*pl* **-ies**) (*formal*) **1** *nc,nu* (an act of) great wickedness: *Does he realize the enormity of his offence?* **2** *nu* the very large size (of a difficulty): *the enormity of the problem of curing cancer.*

enor·mous /ɪ'nɔːməs/ *adj* very large; very much: *an enormous sum of money/room. Your gift has given me enormous pleasure.*

enor·mous·ly *adv* to a great extent: *The town has changed enormously. I'm enormously grateful.*

enough[1] /ɪ'nʌf/ *adv* **1** to the right or necessary degree, extent etc: *This meat isn't cooked enough. Are you warm enough? This work isn't good enough. You're old enough to know better. Are these boxes big enough for those books?* **2** only adequately (often suggesting something could be better etc): *She sings well enough but her dancing is poor.* (Ⓝ) Not used with negative verbs. **3** (used to make the meaning of an adverb stronger): *Strangely/Surprisingly enough, she resigned* (= It was very strange/surprising). **fair enough** ⇨ fair[2]. **sure enough** ⇨ sure[2](3).

enough[2] /ɪ'nʌf/ *det* or *adj* (*attrib*) as many or as much as is necessary: *Is there enough time for another coffee? Do you have enough money for the fare? Have we got enough big boxes for all those books?* (Ⓝ) *'Enough'* is sometimes used after a noun, as in *food enough for everyone*, but this style is very formal. ⇨ also the use of *'enough of'* below.

enough[3] /ɪ'nʌf/ *pron* **enough (of sth)** a quantity, number etc that is as many or as much as is necessary: *That's enough for one day's work. £10 isn't enough. Will that be enough to get you into a university? You've eaten enough of those biscuits for one day. I've had enough of your nonsense. That's enough!* (e.g. used to tell children to stop making a noise).

en·quire /ɪn'kwaɪə(r)/ *vt,vi* = inquire.

en·quiry /ɪn'kwaɪərɪ/ *nc* = inquiry.

en·raged /ɪn'reɪdʒd/ *adj* (*pred*) **enraged (at/by sb/sth)** very angry (because of a bad person, quality etc): *enraged at/by his stupidity.*

en·rap·tured /ɪn'ræptʃəd/ *adj* (*pred*) (*formal*) filled with great delight or joy: *They were enraptured by her singing.*

en·rich /ɪn'rɪtʃ/ *vt* **enrich sth (with sth)** (*formal*) to improve something in quality, flavour etc (using something): *enrich the mind (with knowledge); soil enriched with manure.*

en·rich·ment *nc,nu*

en·rol (also **en·roll**) /ɪn'rəʊl/ *vt,vi* **enrol (sb) (as sb) (in sth)** (to cause a person) to become a member of (a society or institute): *to enrol in evening classes; to enrol (a person) as a member of a society/club.*

en·rol·ment *nc,nu*: *a school with an enrolment of 800 pupils.*

en route /ˌɑːn 'ruːt/ *adv* (*Fr*) on the way: *We stopped at Paris en route from Rome to London.*

en·semble /ɑːn'sɑːmbl/ *nc* (*Fr*) **1** a set of things (e.g. clothing, furnishings etc) considered as a whole. **2** (*music*) a group of musicians who play together regularly (smaller than an orchestra).

en·sign /'ensaɪn/ *nc* (*mil*) **1** a naval flag or ban-ner. **2** a naval officer of lowest rank.

en·sue /ɪn'sjuː/ vi to happen later (as a result): *If the project fails, what will ensue? They quarrelled and in the ensuing fight the telephone was broken.*

en suite /ˌɑːn 'swiːt/ adv (*Fr*) forming part of a set: *a bedroom with a bathroom en suite.*

en·sure (*US* = **in·sure**) /ɪn'ʃʊə(r)/ vt **ensure sth/that . . .** to make sure (that) something will happen: *I can't ensure that he will be there in time.*

ENT /ˌiː en 'tiː/ abbr (*med*) Ear, Nose and Throat (Department in a hospital).

en·tail /ɪn'teɪl/ vt (*formal*) to make (an event) necessary: *That will entail an early start.*

en·tangle /ɪn'tæŋgl/ vt to catch (something) in an obstacle: *My skirt was entangled among/in the thorns.*

en·tangle·ment nc,nu: *emotional entanglements* (= difficulties).

en·tente /ɑːn'tɑːnt/ nc (a group of States with) a friendly understanding.

en,tente ,cordi'ale /ˌkɔːdɪ'ɑːl/ nc a friendly agreement between two governments.

en·ter /'entə(r)/ v **1** vt,vi (*formal*) to come or go into something: *The train entered a tunnel. She entered as I was leaving.* **2** vt to become a member of (a college, monastery, profession etc): *enter university.*

enter (sb) for sth (to give the name of a person) to become officially a competitor in a game, exam etc: *enter oneself for an exam; enter (her) for a TV quiz.*

enter sth in sth to make a record of something by writing in a book etc: *enter a payment in a cash book.*

enter into sth (a) to mention something: *Don't enter into unnecessary detail.* **(b)** to be a (necessary) part of something: *Forgiveness doesn't enter into it when the offence is so major.* **enter into sth (with sb)** to begin a conversation, negotiations, a business partnership etc (with a person).

enter on sth (*formal*) to make a start on an activity: *enter on a new career.*

enter sth up (in sth) to make a record of something by writing in a book etc: *The nurse entered up the drugs used by the patient (in the files).*

enter upon sth (*formal*) = enter on sth.

en·ter·prise /'entəpraɪz/ n **1** nc a plan, esp one that needs courage or boldness or that is difficult. **2** nu the courage needed for such a plan: *He is a man of great enterprise.* **3** nu a method of organizing commercial projects: *Do you prefer private enterprise to the nationalization of major industries?*

en·ter·pris·ing adj having, showing, enterprise(2). Opp unenterprising.

en·ter·tain /ˌentə'teɪn/ v **1** vt,vi to receive (a person) as a guest; give food and drink to (a person): *The Smiths entertain a great deal/do a great deal of entertaining* **2** vt,vi to amuse and interest (a person): *We were all entertained by his jokes.* **3** vt (*formal*) to have (something) in the mind: *entertain ideas/doubts.* Ⓝ Not used in the continuous tenses, e.g. is/was -ing.

en·ter·tain·er nc a person who entertains(2) for a living, e.g. a singer, comedian.

en·ter·tain·ing adj pleasing; amusing: *an entertaining speaker/film.* Opp unentertaining.

en·ter·tain·ment /ˌentə'teɪnmənt/ n **1** nu the

process of entertaining or being entertained(1,2): *Does the city provide enough entertainment for children? He fell into the water, much to the entertainment of the onlookers.* **2** nc a performance (at a theatre, cinema etc).

en·thral (also, esp *US*, **en·thrall**) /ɪn'θrɔːl/ vt (**-ll-**) (often *passive*) to take the whole attention of (a person); please (a person, audience etc) greatly: *be enthralled by an exciting story.*

en·throne /ɪn'θrəʊn/ vt to place (a king, queen or bishop) on a throne.

en·throne·ment nc,nu

en·thuse /ɪn'θjuːz/ vi **enthuse (about/over sb/sth)** (*formal*) to show great enthusiasm (for a person, thing): *enthusing over the new teacher/ carpets.*

en·thusi·asm /ɪn'θjuːzɪæzəm/ nu **enthusiasm (about/for sb/sth)** a strong feeling of admiration or interest: *feel no enthusiasm about/for the new play; an outburst of enthusiasm.*

en·thusi·ast (for sth) /ɪn'θjuːzɪæst/ nc **enthusiast (for sth)** a person with a strong interest (in sports, games etc): *a cricket enthusiast; an enthusiast for golf.*

en·thusi·as·tic /ɪnˌθjuːzɪ'æstɪk/ adj: *an enthusiastic teacher.* Opp unenthusiastic.

en·thusi·as·ti·cal·ly /-klɪ/ adv

en·tice /ɪn'taɪs/ vt to tempt or persuade (a person): *enticing her into doing something/to do something wrong; entice him away from the firm by offering him a large salary.*

en·tice·ment nc,nu

en·tire /ɪn'taɪə(r)/ adj (*attrib*) complete: *I spent the entire holiday lying on the beach.*

en·tire·ly adv completely: *entirely different. I disagree entirely.* ⇨ absolutely.

en·tire·ty /ɪn'taɪərətɪ/ nu **in its entirety** (*formal*) as a whole: *We must examine the question in its entirety.*

en·title /ɪn'taɪtl/ vt **1** to give (something) a title: *a book entitled 'Adam Bede'.* **2** **entitle sb (to sth)** (of conditions, circumstances, qualities etc) to give a person a right (to (do) something): *If you fail three times, you are not entitled to try again.*

en·title·ment nu

en·ti·ty /'entətɪ/ n (pl **-ies**) nc something that has an independent existence: *Are the trade unions one political entity?*

en·to·mo·logi·cal /ˌentəmə'lɒdʒɪkl/ adj of entomology.

en·to·mol·ogist /ˌentə'mɒlədʒɪst/ nc a student of, expert in, entomology.

ento·mol·ogy /ˌentə'mɒlədʒɪ/ nu the scientific study of insects.

en·tour·age /ˌɒntʊ'rɑːʒ/ nc people accompanying and attending an important or high-ranking person: *the emir and his entourage.*

en·trails /'entreɪlz/ n pl the bowels; intestines (esp of an animal).

en·trance¹ /'entrəns/ n **1** nc an opening, gate, door etc by which people enter: *The entrance to the cave had been blocked up. The crowd gathered round the main entrance.* **2** nc,nu (an act of) coming or going in: *Actors must learn their entrances and exits.* **3** nu the right of entering: *I was refused entrance.* Ⓝ '*Entry*' is also possible. **4** nu (also *attrib*) the act of joining, the right to join, a college, course of study, race etc: *university entrance* *examinations.* ⇨ entrant, entry(4).

en·trance² /ɪn'trɑːns/ *vt* to fill (a person) with wonder, delight etc as in a dream: *I was entranced by the music. She stood entranced at the sight.*

en·trant /'entrənt/ *nc* entrant *(for sth)* a person who enters (for a university place, competition, race etc).

en·treat /ɪn'triːt/ *vt* (*formal*) to ask (a person) earnestly: *I entreat you to show mercy.*

en·treaty /ɪn'triːtɪ/ *nc,nu* (*pl* -ies)

en·trée /'ɑːntreɪ/ *nc* a dish served between the fish and the meat course.

entre·pre·neur /ˌɑːntrəprə'nɜː(r)/ *nc* a person who starts and manages her or his own business.

en·trust /ɪn'trʌst/ *vt* to trust (a person) to complete or look after something: *Can I entrust the task to you/entrust you with the money?*

en·try /'entrɪ/ *n* (*pl* -ies) **1** *nc* entry *(into a place)* an act of coming or going in: *Thieves had forced an entry into the building.* **2** *nu* the right of entering: *to be refused entry.* (N) *'Entrance'* is also possible. *'No Entry' is a sign refusing permission or the right to enter.* **3** *nc* an item in, section of, a list; item noted in an account book: *dictionary entries; make an entry in the accounts.* **4** *nc* (a list, number, of) people etc entering for a competition etc: *a large entry for the examination/race.*

enu·mer·ate /ɪ'njuːməreɪt/ *vt* (*formal*) to count, go through, (a list); name (items etc) one by one.

enu·mer·ation /ɪˌnjuːmə'reɪʃn/ *nc,nu*

enun·ci·ate /ɪ'nʌnsɪeɪt/ *vt,vi* (*formal*) to say, pronounce, (words): *He was enunciating (his words) clearly.*

enun·ci·ation /ɪˌnʌnsɪ'eɪʃn/ *nu*

en·vel·op /en'veləp/ *vt* envelop *sb/sth (in sth)* (usually *passive*) to surround (a person, thing) completely: *hills enveloped in mist.*

en·velop·ment *nu*

en·vel·ope /'envələup/ *nc* a paper covering for a letter etc.

en·vi·able /'envɪəbl/ *adj* **1** causing envy: *an enviable career.* **2** who or that is to be envied: *an enviable colleague.* Opp unenviable.

en·vi·ous /'envɪəs/ *adj* envious *(of sb/sth)* full of, feeling, expressing, envy: *envious of her/her success; envious looks.* Compare jealous(2).

en·vi·ous·ly *adv*

en·vi·ron·ment /ɪn'vaɪərənmənt/ *nc* a kind of surroundings and conditions in which people, animals or plants live: *a healthy/hostile environment.*

en·vi·ron·ment·al /ɪnˌvaɪərən'mentl/ *adj*

en·vi·ron·ment·al·ist *nc* a person specializing in or interested in maintaining good environmental conditions.

en·vir·ons /ɪn'vaɪərənz/ *n pl* the districts surrounding a town etc: *Berlin and its environs.* (N) *'Suburbs' is now more usual.*

en·vis·age /ɪn'vɪzɪdʒ/ *vt* to have an idea of (something) as a future possibility: *He had not envisaged seeing her/that he would see her again.*

en·voy /'envɔɪ/ *nc* **1** a government messenger, esp one sent abroad on a special mission. **2** a diplomatic officer next in rank below an ambassador.

en·vy¹ /'envɪ/ *nu* **1** envy *(at sth/towards sb)* the feeling of annoyance or anger mixed with admiration when one wishes to have the same ability, achievement, luck etc as another person: *He was filled with envy at my success.* ⇨

green¹(2). Compare jealousy. **2** *the envy of sb* the object that causes such feeling in a person: *His splendid new car was the envy of all his friends.*

en·vy² /'envɪ/ *vt* (*pt,pp* -ied) envy *(sb) (sth)* to feel envy towards (a person, thing): *I envy you. I envy (you) your good fortune.*

en·zyme /'enzaɪm/ *nc* (*science*) an organic chemical substance formed in plants and animals, able to cause chemical changes without being changed itself.

ep·aul·ette /'epəlet/ *nc* a strip of cloth on the shoulder of a military uniform showing rank etc.

ephem·er·al /ɪ'femərəl/ *adj* (*formal*) living, lasting, for a very short time: *ephemeral popularity.*

ep·ic /'epɪk/ *adj, nc* **1** (*literature*) (of) a long poem telling the story of the deeds of one or more great heroes, usually over a long period of time: *Milton's 'Paradise Lost' is an epic.* **2** (of) a film made using large crowds and many locations. **3** (*informal*) impressive; very large: *an epic journey; a new concert hall/peace march/a diplomatic row of epic proportions.*

epi·centre /'episentə(r)/ *nc* (*science*) the area immediately above the origin of an earthquake.

Epi·cur·ean /ˌepɪ'kjuərɪən/ *adj* (*literature*) involving the pursuit of pleasure as a basic theme (after the Greek philosopher *Epicurus* /ˌepɪ'kjuərəs/).

epi·dem·ic /ˌepɪ'demɪk/ *adj, nc* (of) a disease attacking many people in one area for a time: *a flu epidemic.* Compare endemic.

epi·der·mis /ˌepɪ'dɜːmɪs/ *nu* (*anat*) the outer layer of the skin.

epi·gram /'epɪgræm/ *nc* (*literature*) a short saying expressing an idea in a clever and amusing way, e.g. 'To know you is to love you'.

epi·gram·mat·ic /ˌepɪgrə'mætɪk/ *adj*

epi·graph /'epɪgrɑːf/ *nc* **1** an inscription on a coin, statue etc. **2** (*literature*) a short quotation at the beginning of a book or chapter.

epi·lep·sy /'epɪlepsɪ/ *nu* a disease causing a person to fall unconscious with violent involuntary movements.

epi·lep·tic /ˌepɪ'leptɪk/ *adj, nc* (of) a person suffering from epilepsy: *an epileptic fit.*

epi·logue (*US* = **-log**) /'epɪlɒg/ *nc* (*literature*) the last part of a literary work, esp spoken by an actor at the end of a play.

epi·sode /'epɪsəud/ *nc* **1** an incident that is one continuous action (and, in a story etc, one of many used to create the plot): *an interesting episode during the debate.* **2** one of several separate parts in a radio, TV or other serial: *You can see the next episode on Monday.*

epi·sod·ic /ˌepɪ'sɒdɪk/ *adj*

epistle /ɪ'pɪsl/ *nc* (also E-) a letter in the New Testament, written by an apostle.

epi·taph /'epɪtɑːf/ *nc* an inscription (describing a dead person), usually on a tombstone.

epi·thet /'epɪθet/ *nc* (*lang*) an adjective or phrase used to describe the character of a person or thing, as in 'Alfred the *Great*'.

epit·ome /ɪ'pɪtəmɪ/ *nc* **1** *the epitome of sth* the typical example, personification, of a quality, characteristic: *She's the epitome of the successful modern woman.* **2** (*literature*) a short summary of a book etc.

epit·om·ize (also **-ise**) /ɪ'pɪtəmaɪz/ *vt* to be the

epitome of (something): *She epitomizes success.*

ep·och /'iːpɒk/ *nc* (a beginning of) a period of time in history, life etc marked by special events or characteristics: *The discovery of the structure of the DNA marked a new epoch in biology.*

epo·nym /'epənɪm/ *nc* (*lang*) a person who gives her or his name to a place or institution, such as *Leningrad* from *Lenin.*

equal¹ /'iːkwəl/ *adj* **1** (*no comp*) being the same in size, amount, number, degree, value etc: *equal pay for equal work; equal opportunity; divide it into two equal parts; two boys of equal height.* **2** *equal to sth* having enough strength, courage, ability etc for something: *She was equal to the occasion.*

'equal(s) sign *nc* the sign (=), as used in maths. ⇨ equation.

equal·ly /'iːkwəlɪ/ *adv* in an equal manner; in equal shares: *equally clever. Divide it equally.*

equal² /'iːkwəl/ *nc* a person or thing equal to another: *Is he your equal in strength?*

equal³ /'iːkwəl/ *vt* (**-ll-**, *US* also **-l-**) Ⓝ Not used in the continuous tenses, e.g. *is/was -ing.* **1** to be the same as (another one): *Does your salary equal his? He equals me in training but not in experience.* **2** to do something that is as good as (another one): *Coe equalled the world record.* **equal out** to be or become level or the same: *I owe you for the ticket but I paid for the meal—I think our debts equal out.*

equal·ity /ɪ'kwɒlətɪ/ *nu* the state of being equal: *social/racial/sexual equality.*

equal·ize (also **-ise**) /'iːkwəlaɪz/ *vi* (*sport*) to make a score equal: *Liverpool were losing by one goal to nil but equalized in the last minute.*

equal·iz·er (also **-is·er**) *nc* the goal scored when equalizing.

equa·nim·ity /ˌekwə'nɪmətɪ/ *nu* (*formal*) calmness of mind or temper: *bear misfortune with equanimity.*

equate /ɪ'kweɪt/ *vt* *equate sth to/with sth* to consider, treat, one thing as being the same as another: *I equate happiness with health.*

equa·tion /ɪ'kweɪʒn/ *n* **1** *nc* (*maths*) a statement of equality between two expressions by using the sign (=), as in $2x + 5 = 11$. **2** *nu* the act of equating two or more things: *The equation of wealth and happiness is a mistake.*

equa·tor /ɪ'kweɪtə(r)/ *n* (often the E-) (the region near) an imaginary line around the Earth, or drawn on maps, at an equal distance from the north and south poles.

equa·tor·ial /ˌekwə'tɔːrɪəl/ *adj* of, near, the equator: *equatorial Africa.*

eques·tri·an /ɪ'kwestrɪən/ *adj* of, concerning, horse-riding: *equestrian skill.*

equi·dis·tant /ˌiːkwɪ'dɪstənt/ *adj* *equidistant (from sth)* separated by equal distance(s).

equi·lat·eral /ˌiːkwɪ'lætərəl/ *adj* (*maths*) (of a triangle) having all sides equal.

equi·lib·ri·um /ˌiːkwɪ'lɪbrɪəm/ *nu* (*formal*) the state of being balanced (esp mentally or emotionally): *maintain/lose one's equilibrium.*

equine /'ekwaɪn/ *adj* (*formal*) of, like, horses.

equi·nox /'iːkwɪnɒks/ *n* (the —) the time of the year when day and night are of equal length: *the spring equinox* (= 20 March); *the autumnal equinox* (= 22 or 23 September). ⇨ solstice.

equip /ɪ'kwɪp/ *vt* (**-pp-**) *equip sb/sth (for/with sth)* to supply a person, oneself, a ship etc (with what is needed for a purpose): *equip a ship for a voyage/climbers with boots and ropes.*

equip·ment *nu* (**a**) the act of equipping or being equipped: *The equipment of his laboratory took time and money.* (**b**) things needed for a particular purpose: *radar equipment.*

equi·table /'ekwɪtəbl/ *adj* (*formal*) fair; just: *an equitable settlement after a disagreement.*

equi·tably /-əblɪ/ *adv*

equi·ty /'ekwətɪ/ *n* **1** *nu* (*formal*) the quality of fairness; right judgement: *the equity of lawyers.* **2** (*pl*) (**-ies**) (*finance*) ordinary stocks and shares not paying fixed interest.

equiv·al·ent¹ /ɪ'kwɪvələnt/ *adj* *equivalent (to sth)* equal in value, amount, meaning: *What is $5 equivalent to in French francs?*

equiv·al·ent² /ɪ'kwɪvələnt/ *nc* something that is equivalent: *Is there a French word that is the exact equivalent of the English word 'home'?*

equivo·cal /ɪ'kwɪvəkl/ *adj* (*formal*) **1** (of a word) having a double or doubtful meaning. **2** (of actions, behaviour etc) open to doubt: *an equivocal reply.* Opp unequivocal.

era /'ɪərə/ *nc* (*pl* **—s**) a period in history starting from a particular development or event: *the Elizabethan era; the Christian era.*

eradi·cate /ɪ'rædɪkeɪt/ *vt* to destroy or put an end to (something bad): *eradicating crime/typhoid fever.*

eradi·ca·tion /ɪˌrædɪ'keɪʃn/ *nu*

erase /ɪ'reɪz/ *vt* to rub or scrape out (something): *erasing pencil marks.*

eraser *nc* something used to erase writing etc.

erect¹ /ɪ'rekt/ *adj* upright: *stand erect.*

erect·ly *adv*

erect·ness *nu*

erect² /ɪ'rekt/ *vt* **1** (*formal*) to build (something): *erect a statue (to a leader).* **2** to fix, set, upright: *erect a tent/a mast.*

erec·tion /ɪ'rekʃn/ *n* (**a**) *n sing* the process of erecting: *the erection of a statue/mast.* (**b**) *nc* a hardening of the penis.

erg /ɜːg/ *nc* (*science*) a unit of measurement of energy, work, in the metric system.

er·go·nom·ics /ˌɜːgə'nɒmɪks/ *n sing* the scientific study of the relationship between workers and their environment.

er·mine /'ɜːmɪn/ *nc,nu* (the white winter fur of) a small animal from Europe and Asia (called a *stoat*).

erode /ɪ'rəʊd/ *vt* *erode sth (away)* (of acids, rain etc) to wear away, eat into, something: *Metals are eroded by acids.*

ero·sion /ɪ'rəʊʒn/ *nu* the act of eroding or being eroded: *soil erosion by wind and rain.*

ero·sive /ɪ'rəʊsɪv/ *adj*

erot·ic /ɪ'rɒtɪk/ *adj* (of pictures, films etc) showing, encouraging, sexual love or desire.

err /ɜː(r)/ *vi* to make mistakes; do or be wrong: *It is better to err on the side of mercy* (= to be too merciful than too severe).

er·rand /'erənd/ *nc* a short journey to take or get something, e.g. to buy goods from a shop: *to go on/run errands for him.*

er·rat·ic /ɪ'rætɪk/ *adj* (*derog*) **1** (of a person, behaviour) likely to do unusual or unexpected things. **2** uncertain or irregular in movement, standard etc: *an erratic athlete.*

er·rati·cal·ly /-klɪ/ *adv*

er·ra·tum /ɪˈrɑːtəm/ *nc* (*pl* **-ta** /-tə/) a mistake in writing or printing.

er·ro·neous /ɪˈrəʊnɪəs/ *adj* (*formal*) (of an opinion etc) incorrect; mistaken.

er·ro·neous·ly *adv*

er·ror /ˈerə(r)/ *n* **1** *nc* a mistake: *spelling errors; an error of judgement.* **2** *nu* the state of being wrong in belief or behaviour. **in error** by mistake: *I took it in error.* **trial and error** ⇨ trial(1).

eru·dite /ˈeruːdaɪt/ *adj* (*formal*) having, showing, great learning.

eru·dite·ly *adv*

erupt /ɪˈrʌpt/ *vi* **1** (of a volcano) to burst or break out (suddenly) (with smoke and a very hot semi-liquid substance called *lava*). **2** to break out suddenly or violently: *erupt with anger/cheering/in a painful rash.*

erup·tion /ɪˈrʌpʃn/ *nc,nu*

es·ca·late /ˈeskəleɪt/ *v* **1** *vi* (of prices, levels of unemployment, numbers of people opposing something etc) to increase quickly. **2** *vt* to make (violence, war etc) increase quickly.

es·ca·la·tion /ˌeskəˈleɪʃn/ *nu*

es·ca·la·tor /ˈeskəleɪtə(r)/ *nc* a moving stairway carrying people up or down between floors or different levels.

es·ca·pade /ˈeskəpeɪd/ *nc* a daring, mischievous or adventurous act, often one causing gossip or trouble.

escape¹ /ɪˈskeɪp/ *n* **1** *nc,nu* **escape (from/out of sth) (to a place)** (an act of) escaping; fact of having escaped: *There have been very few successful escapes from/out of this prison. There was a large escape to Switzerland.* **a narrow escape** a lucky success after almost failing. **2** *nc* (something that provides) temporary freedom from a dull routine: *She watches videos of murder stories as an escape from boredom.*

es·cap·ism /-ɪzəm/ *nu* the avoidance of unpleasant or dull routine by activities such as reading love stories, watching adventure films etc.

es·cap·ist *adj, nc* (of) an activity, thing, person providing escapism: *escapist literature.*

es·cape² /ɪˈskeɪp/ *v* **1** *vi* **escape (from/out of sth) (to a place)** to get out; find a way out: *Two of the prisoners have escaped. Gas is escaping from this hole. Many refugees escaped to Botswana.* **2** *vt* to avoid (something); keep free or safe from (something): *You were lucky to escape punishment/to escape being punished.* **3** *vt* to be forgotten or unnoticed by (a person): *His name escapes me for the moment.*

es'cape road *nc* (e.g. at the bottom of a steep hill) a road for a vehicle that goes out of control.

es·carp·ment /ɪˈskɑːpmənt/ *nc* (*tech*) a steep slope on a hill, mountain or cliff.

es·chew /ɪˈstʃuː/ *vt* (*formal*) to avoid (something): *eschew wine/evil.*

es·cort¹ /ˈeskɔːt/ *nc* **1** one or more people going with another or others to protect them or as an honour: *an escort of soldiers.* **under (sb's) escort** with (a person) as an escort: *under police escort.* **2** one or more ships, planes etc giving protection: *an escort of ten destroyers.*

es·cort² /ɪˈskɔːt/ *vt* (*formal*) to go with (a person) as an escort: *Who will escort this young lady home?*

ESE *written abbr* east-south-east.

ESL /ˌiː es ˈel/ *abbr* English as a second language.

ESN /ˌiː es ˈen/ *abbr* educationally subnormal.

esopha·gus /iːˈsɒfəgəs/ *nc* = oesophagus.

eso·ter·ic /ˌesəˈterɪk/ *adj* (*formal*) understood by, intended for, only a small number of people.

esp *abbr* especially.

ESP /ˌiː es ˈpiː/ *abbr* **1** extrasensory perception. **2** English for special/specific purposes.

es·pec·ial·ly /ɪˈspeʃlɪ/ *adv* to an unusual or exceptional degree; in particular: *She likes the country, especially in spring.* Ⓝ *'Specially'* is also possible but is preferred when referring to something that is extraordinary or has a particular purpose, as in *specially difficult; specially designed. 'Especially'* is always considered to be more formal and is most often used before a prepositional phrase, as in *especially on Sundays/in August.*

es·pi·on·age /ˈespɪənɑːʒ/ *nu* the practice of spying or using spies.

es·pouse /ɪˈspaʊz/ *vt* (*formal*) to give one's support to (a cause, theory etc): *espousing liberalism.*

Esq. *abbr* Esquire.

Es·quire /ɪˈskwaɪə(r)/ *nc* (*old use*) a title (written Esq.) used in the address of a letter after a man's family name (instead of *Mr* before it).

es·say¹ /ˈeseɪ/ *nc* a piece of writing (on any one subject).

es·say·ist *nc* a writer of literary essays.

es·say² /eˈseɪ/ *vt,vi* (*formal*) to attempt (the usual word): *essay a task.*

es·sence /ˈesns/ *n* **1** *nu* **essence (of sth)** the nature or most important quality (of something): *Caution is the essence of that man's character.* **in essence** really: *What she was trying to say, in essence, was that she wants to leave.* **2** *nc,nu* the most valuable, important, part of a substance in concentrated form: *meat essences.*

es·sen·tial¹ /ɪˈsenʃl/ *adj* **1** **essential (for/to sth)** necessary; most important: *A sense of humour is essential. Maths is essential for a career in computers. Is wealth essential to happiness?* **2** (*attrib*) basic: *Being reserved is said to be an essential part of the English character.*

es·sen·tial² /ɪˈsenʃl/ *nc* a basic part, feature etc: *the essentials of English grammar.*

es·sen·tial·ly /ɪˈsenʃəlɪ/ *adv* in reality; actually: *We are an essentially peace-loving people.*

est. *abbr* **1** established. **2** (*commerce*) estimate(d).

es·tab·lish /ɪˈstæblɪʃ/ *vt* **1** to start and organize (something): *establish a new state/government/business.* **2** to settle, place, (a person or oneself) (in a position, place etc): *She's now established herself as a respected lawyer. We are now comfortably established in our new house.* **3** to cause people to accept (a belief, claim, custom etc): *He succeeded in establishing a good reputation for himself as a doctor.* **4** to find out (something): *establish the truth.*

es·tab·lish·ment /ɪˈstæblɪʃmənt/ *n* **1** *nu* the process of establishing or being established: *the establishment of a new state.* **2** *nc* something that is established, e.g. a business firm. **3** (the E-) (*GB*) those people in positions of power, authority and influence.

es·tate /ɪ'steɪt/ *n* **1** *nc* a piece of property in the form of land, esp in the country: *He owns large estates in Scotland.* ⇨ council/housing/industrial/ real estate. **2** *nu* (*legal*) a person's whole property.

e'state agent *nc* a person, business, that buys and sells buildings and land for others.

e'state car *nc* a kind of car with door(s) at the back for easy loading of luggage etc.

es·teem¹ /ɪ'stiːm/ *nu* (*formal*) great respect. **hold sb in high esteem** to have a very high opinion of her or him.

es·teem² /ɪ'stiːm/ *vt* (*formal*) to have a high opinion of (a person): *No-one can esteem your father more than I do.* Ⓝ Not used in the continuous tenses, e.g. *is/was -ing.*

es·thet·ic /iːs'θetɪk/ *adj* = aesthetic.

es·ti·mate¹ /'estɪmət/ *nc* an approximate calculation (of size, cost etc): *I hope the builders don't exceed their estimate. I don't know enough about him to form a true estimate of his abilities.*

es·ti·mate² /'estɪmeɪt/ *vt,vi* to form a judgement about (something); calculate (the cost, value, size etc of something): *They estimated the cost at £8000. We estimate that it will take a month to do it.* Ⓝ Not used in the continuous tenses, e.g. *is/was -ing.*

es·ti·ma·tion /ˌestɪ'meɪʃn/ *nu* judgement; opinion: *in/by my estimation; in the estimation of most people.*

es·trange /ɪ'streɪndʒ/ *vt* **estrange sb (from sb)** (*formal*) to cause a person no longer to have friends etc: *foolish behaviour that estranged (him from) all his friends.*

es·trange·ment *nc,nu*

es·tu·ary /'estʃʊərɪ/ *nc* (*pl* **-ies**) (E- in names) a (usually long) mouth of a river into which the tide flows: *The Thames Estuary.*

e.t.a. /ˌiː tiː 'eɪ/ *abbr* estimated time of arrival (e.g. of a plane). ⇨ e.t.d.

et al. *abbr* (*Latin: et alia*) and others.

etc *abbr* (*Latin: et cetera*) and other things; and so on.

et cet·era /ɪt 'setrə/ (*Latin*) (always written etc) and other things; and so on.

etch /etʃ/ *vt,vi* to use a needle and acid to make (a picture) on a metal plate from which copies may be printed.

etch·er *nc* a person who etches.

etch·ing *n* (**a**) *nu* the art of the etcher. (**b**) *nc* an etched picture.

e.t.d. *abbr* estimated time of departure (e.g. of a plane). ⇨ e.t.a.

eter·nal /ɪ'tɜːnl/ *adj* **1** without beginning or end; lasting for ever: *The Christian religion promises eternal life.* **the eternal triangle** ⇨ triangle(2). **2** (*informal*) too frequent: *Stop this eternal chatter.*

eter·nal·ly /-əlɪ/ *adv*

eter·ni·ty /ɪ'tɜːnətɪ/ *n* (*pl* **-ies**) **1** *nu* time without end. **2** *n sing* a period of time that seems endless: *It seemed an eternity before news of his safety reached her.*

eth·ic /'eθɪk/ *n sing* a system of moral principles, rules of behaviour: *Is thinking only of oneself a good ethic for living?*

ethi·cal /-kl/ *adj* (esp) morally good: *All doctors*

must be ethical when treating patients. Opp unethical.

ethi·cal·ly /-klɪ/ *adv: behave ethically.*

eth·ics *n* (**a**) *nu* the science of morals: *Ethics is a branch of philosophy.* (**b**) *n pl* moral principles or behaviour: *The ethics of his decision are doubtful.*

eth·nic /'eθnɪk/, **eth·ni·cal** /-kl/ *adj* of, concerning, (the customs etc of) the nations, races etc of mankind: *ethnic minorities.*

eth·ni·cal·ly /-ɪklɪ/ *adv*

eth·no·logi·cal /ˌeθnə'lɒdʒɪkl/ *adj* of ethnology.

eth·nol·ogist /eθ'nɒlədʒɪst/ *nc* a student of, expert in, ethnology.

eth·nol·ogy /eθ'nɒlədʒɪ/ *nc* the scientific study of the races of mankind, their relations to one another etc.

eti·quette /'etɪket/ *nu* the rules for formal behaviour among people or a profession: *medical/legal etiquette.*

ety·mol·ogi·cal /ˌetɪmə'lɒdʒɪkl/ *adj* of etymology.

ety·mol·ogist /ˌetɪ'mɒlədʒɪst/ *nc* a student of, expert in, etymology.

ety·mol·ogy /ˌetɪ'mɒlədʒɪ/ *n* (*pl* **-ies**) **1** *nu* the scientific study of the origin and history of words. **2** *nc* an account of the history of a word.

EU /ˌiː'juː/ *abbr* (the —) the European Union (formerly EEC).

eu·ca·lyp·tus /ˌjuːkə'lɪptəs/ *nc,nu* (also *attrib*) (*pl* **—es**) (oil from) a kind of tall evergreen tree (including the Australian gum tree).

Eu·char·ist /'juːkərɪst/ *n* (the —) the Christian ceremony in which bread and wine are consecrated and taken.

eu·lo·gize (also **-ise**) /'juːlədʒaɪz/ *vt* (*formal*) to praise (a person, thing) highly in speech or writing.

eu·lo·gy /'juːlədʒɪ/ *nc,nu* (*pl* **-ies**) (a speech or writing full of) high praise.

eu·phem·ism /'juːfəmɪzəm/ *nc,nu* (an instance of) the use of less exact but less harsh words or phrases in place of words required by truth or accuracy: *'Pass away' is a euphemism for 'die'.*

eu·phem·is·tic /ˌjuːfə'mɪstɪk/ *adj*

eu·phem·is·ti·cal·ly /-klɪ/ *adv*

eu·phor·ia /juː'fɔːrɪə/ *nu* the state of feeling pleasantly excited and happy.

eu·phor·ic /juː'fɒrɪk/ *adj*

Eu·sta·chian tube /juːˌsteɪʃn 'tjuːb/ *nc* (*anat*) the tube connecting the middle ear with the pharynx.

eu·tha·na·sia /ˌjuːθə'neɪzɪə/ *nu* the painless killing of people suffering from incurable painful diseases.

evacu·ate /ɪ'vækjʊeɪt/ *vt* **1** to go away from (a place), esp because of a crisis: *evacuate a town.* **2** to remove (people) from a place or district because of danger: *The population was evacuated during the flood.*

evacu·ation /ɪˌvækjʊ'eɪʃn/ *nc,nu*

evacu·ee /ɪˌvækjuː'iː/ *nc* a person who is evacuated(2).

evade /ɪ'veɪd/ *vt* **1** to stay out of the way of (a bad person or thing): *evade a blow/one's enemies/an attack.* **2** to find a way of not doing (something unpleasant): *evade (paying) income tax.* **3** to avoid answering (a question) fully or honestly:

evading a question.

evalu·ate /ɪ'væljʊeɪt/ vt (formal) to find out, decide, the amount or value of (something).

evalu·ation /ɪˌvæljʊ'eɪʃn/ nc,nu

evan·geli·cal /ˌiːvæn'dʒelɪkl/ adj (Christianity) **1** of, according to, the teachings of the Gospel: *evangelical preaching*. **2** of those Protestants who stress the importance of personal faith and making amends for the death of Jesus Christ.

evan·gel·ist /ɪ'vændʒəlɪst/ nc (Christianity) **1** one of the writers of the Gospels. **2** a preacher, esp one who travels and holds religious meetings.

evap·or·ate /ɪ'væpəreɪt/ vt,vi **1** (to cause something) to change into vapour: *Heat evaporates water*. **2** (fig) (to cause a feeling) to disappear: *His hopes evaporated*.

evap·or·ation /ɪˌvæpə'reɪʃn/ nu

evas·ion /ɪ'veɪʒn/ n **1** nu the process of avoiding something: *evasion of responsibility*. **2** nc an act, statement, excuse etc used to avoid something: *His answers to my questions were all evasions*.

evas·ive /ɪ'veɪsɪv/ adj avoiding, trying to avoid, something: *an evasive answer*. **take evasive action** to do something in order to avoid disaster etc.

evas·ive·ly adv

evas·ive·ness nu

eve /iːv/ nc (E- in names) a day or evening before a religious festival or any date or event: *Christmas Eve* (= 24 December); *New Year's Eve* (= 31 December).

eve abbr evening.

even¹ /'iːvn/ adj **1** level: *Floors must be perfectly even*. Opp uneven(2). **2** regular; steady; of unchanging quality: *His even breathing showed that he had got over his excitement. The quality of her work is not very even*. Opp uneven(1). **3** (of amounts, distances, values) equal: *Our scores are now even*. **be/get even with sb** to have one's revenge on a person. **break even** ⇨ break²(8). ⇨ also come out(j). **4** (of a number) that can be divided by two: *The pages on the left side of a book have even numbers*. Opp odd(1).

even-'tempered adj not easily made angry.

even·ly adv

even·ness nu

even² /'iːvn/ adv **1** (used to show a comparison between what is stated and what might have happened, been done etc): *He never even opened the letter* (i.e. so he certainly did not read it). *It was cold there even in summer* (i.e. so you can imagine how cold it was in winter). *Even a child can understand the book* (i.e. so adults certainly can). Ⓝ Be careful because the position of 'even' in a sentence affects the meaning. Compare: *We didn't even see Jane at the party* (so we cannot be blamed for not speaking to her), *We didn't see even Jane at the party* (we had expected to see other people including Jane) and *We didn't see Jane even at the party* (we had expected to see her, particularly at the party). 'Even' relates to the word or phrase immediately after it. **2** (used to make comparisons stronger): *You know even less about it than I do. You seem even busier than usual today*. Ⓝ 'Even' can be omitted.

even as just at the time when: *Even as I gave the warning, the car skidded*.

even if (conj) (used to emphasize what follows): *I wouldn't do it even if you paid me!*

even now/then in spite of these or those circumstances etc: *Even now he won't believe me. Even then he would not admit his mistake*.

even so though that is the case; however: *It has many words missing—even so, it is quite a useful reference book*.

even though (conj) although: *She won't leave the TV set even though the family is waiting for dinner*.

even³ /'iːvn/ vt,vi **1 even (sth) out** (to cause something) to become equal, level: *The path needs to be evened out. The costs will soon even out. Whatever advantages he started with, things will even out eventually*. **2 even (sth) up** (to cause debts, amounts) to become balanced or settled: *I'll even up with you* (i.e. pay what I owe) *later*.

even·ing /'iːvnɪŋ/ nc (also attrib) the part of the day between afternoon and nightfall: *two evenings ago; this/tomorrow/yesterday evening; during/in the evening; on Sunday evening; an evening meal/paper*.

'evening dress nu clothes worn for formal occasions in the evening.

event /ɪ'vent/ nc **1** something (usually important) that happens or has happened: *the chief events of 1986. That was quite an event!* (what happened was unusual, memorable etc). **2** one of the races, competitions etc in a sports programme: *Which events have you entered for?* **3** a result; outcome: *People are wiser after the event*. **at all events** (adv) whatever might happen: *At all events I ought to arrive before dark*. **in any event** (adv) whatever happens: *I'll try to be there, but in any event I'll let you know nearer the time*. **in either event** (adv) whichever of the two possibilities happens. **in that event** if that happens: *In that event, I'll refuse to pay*. **in the event** in actual fact; actually: *He promised, but in the event he didn't arrive*. **in the event of sth** if something happens: *In the event of a fire, dial 999*.

event·ful /-fəl/ adj full of interesting, exciting etc events: *He had an eventful life*.

event·ual /ɪ'ventʃʊəl/ adj coming at last as a result: *his foolish behaviour and eventual failure*.

event·ual·ly /-tʃʊəlɪ/ adv in the end; after a long time: *After several attempts he eventually swam across*.

event·ual·ity /ɪˌventʃʊ'ælətɪ/ nc (pl -ies) an event(1,3) that is possible: *be prepared for any eventuality*.

ev·er /'evə(r)/ adv **1** at any (single) time: *Nothing ever happens in this village. Do you ever travel by train? If you ever do that again, I'll tell your father. If ever I find it, I'll telephone you*. Ⓝ 'Ever' is usually used in negative sentences, questions and sentences with if. ⇨ if(1). For a comparison of 'ever' and 'always', ⇨ the note at always(3). **hardly ever** almost never: *She hardly ever telephones me*. **2** at any time up to the present: *Have you ever been to Cairo? Did he ever reply to your letter? She hasn't ever owned a car*. Ⓝ 'Has never' is also possible for 'hasn't ever' and is more usual. 'Ever' is not used in answer to questions. Use 'Yes, I have', 'No, he didn't' etc. **3** (used to make comparisons stronger) at any time: *It's raining harder than ever. Her singing is better than ever. He's as kind as ever. This is the best work you've ever done*. **4** all the time; always:

They lived happily ever after. **for ever (and ever)** always: *I'll love you for ever.* Ⓝ *'Forever' is now used instead of for ever, especially meaning 'a very long time', as in This work will take forever to complete.* ⇨ evermore. **ever since** all the time (from that point) up to now: *He went to live in Germany in 1980 and has been there ever since. Ever since I heard you were here, I've been hoping to meet you.* **Yours ever** (formula used for ending an informal letter, e.g. to a friend). **5** (used in combinations) continuously: *ever-present; everfaithful/hopeful.* **6 ever so** (informal) very: *I'm ever so busy!* **7** (used to emphasize surprise, doubt etc): *How ever/Where ever did you lose it? What ever do you mean? Who ever can that be?* Ⓝ *'Ever' can be omitted without changing the meaning. Be careful because however, wherever, whatever, whoever etc have different meanings from how ever, where ever etc.*

ever·green /ˈevəgriːn/ *nc* (also *attrib*) **1** (a tree, shrub) having green leaves throughout the year. Compare deciduous. **2** (*fig*) always fresh, enjoyable: *evergreen songs/poetry.*

ever·last·ing /ˌevəˈlɑːstɪŋ/ *adj* **1** going on for ever: *everlasting fame/glory.* **2** (*informal; derog*) repeated too often: *I'm tired of him and his everlasting complaints.*

ever·more /ˌevəˈmɔː(r)/ *adv* (often **for evermore**) for ever. Compare nevermore.

every /ˈevrɪ/ *adj or det* **1** each one (of a group) with no exception: *I've read every book she's written/every one of her books. Every single one of my answers was wrong. Every word he said is true. I try to do my exercises every day.* Ⓝ *'Every' is used with a singular noun and verb. Compare:* all¹(1), both¹. For a comparison of 'every' and 'each', ⇨ the note at each¹. **every time (a)** on every occasion: *Our football team wins every time.* **(b)** on each occasion: *Every time I ask her out she refuses.* Ⓝ *'Whenever' is also possible, as in Whenever I telephone he's not there.* **each and every** ⇨ each¹. **2** all possible; complete: *He has every faith in you. I've every reason to believe her.* Ⓝ *'Every' is used with a singular noun. 'Every' cannot be used in negative sentences. Use 'no', as in He has no faith in you, or 'not any', as in He hasn't any faith in you.* **every bit as good etc as** ⇨ bit²(1). **in every way** ⇨ way²(5). **3** (used before a noun phrase to show repetition or intervals in time or space): *every two hours; every ten miles; every two steps; every other/second day; every few days/weeks; every third Monday; every few metres.* **every now and again/then** ⇨ now¹(1). **every so often** ⇨ often.

every·body /ˈevrɪbɒdɪ/ (also **every·one** /ˈevrɪwʌn/) *pron* every person: *In a small village everybody knows everybody else.* Ⓝ *'Everybody/everyone' is used with a singular verb. Compare* anybody, nobody, somebody.

every·day /ˌevrɪˈdeɪ/ *adj* (*attrib*) happening, used, daily; common and familiar: *an everyday occurrence; in his everyday clothes.*

every·thing /ˈevrɪθɪŋ/ *pron* **1** all things; each thing: *Tell me everything about it. Everything I have is in this suitcase.* Ⓝ *'Everything' is used with a singular verb.* **2** something of the greatest importance: *Money means everything to him.* Compare anything, nothing, something.

every·where /ˈevrɪweə(r)/ *adv* in, to, every place: *I've looked everywhere for it. Everywhere she went people cheered.* Compare anywhere, nowhere, somewhere.

evict /ɪˈvɪkt/ *vt* **evict sb (from sth)** to send a tenant away (from a house or land) by authority of the law: *They were evicted (from the house) for not paying the rent.*

evic·tion /ɪˈvɪkʃn/ *nc,nu*

evi·dence /ˈevɪdəns/ *n* **1** *nu* anything that gives a reason for believing, that makes clear or proves, something: *There wasn't enough evidence to prove him guilty. Is there any evidence that she was there? There was no evidence of damage. The scientist must produce evidence to support her or his theories.* **2 (be) in evidence** (to be) able to be clearly seen: *He was very much in evidence at the party.*

evi·dent /ˈevɪdənt/ *adj* plain and clear to the eyes or mind: *It must be evident to all of you that we need more customers.*

evi·dent·ly *adv*

evil¹ /ˈiːvl/ *adj* **1** very wicked, bad: *evil men/thoughts.* **2** likely to cause trouble: *an evil tongue.*

evil·ly *adv* in an evil way: *He eyed her evilly.*

evil² /ˈiːvl/ *n* **1** *nu* great wickedness; doing morally wrong: *the spirit of evil.* **2** *nc* a very bad thing; disaster: *War, famine and flood are terrible evils.* **be/choose the lesser of two evils** to be/accept the less harmful of two bad choices.

,evil-'mind·ed *adj* (*derog*) having evil thoughts and desires.

evince /ɪˈvɪns/ *vt* (*formal*) to show that one has (a feeling, quality etc): *a child who evinces great intelligence.*

evoca·tive /ɪˈvɒkətɪv/ *adj* that produces (good or bad) memories, feelings: *evocative words.*

evoke /ɪˈvəʊk/ *vt* (*formal*) to produce (an effect) in the mind: *evoke admiration/surprise/memories of the past.*

evol·ution /ˌiːvəˈluːʃn/ *nu* the (scientific) process of developing from an earlier or simpler state: *the evolution of a plant from a seed. The evolution of modern society.*

evolve /ɪˈvɒlv/ *vi,vt* **evolve (sth) (from/out of sth)** (to cause an idea, kind of animal or plant etc) to develop naturally and (usually) gradually: *The American constitution was planned; the British constitution evolved. All animals have evolved from tiny sea creatures.*

ewe /juː/ *nc* a female sheep. Compare ram¹.

ex·acer·bate /ɪɡˈzæsəbeɪt/ *vt* (*formal*) to make (pain, disease, a problem etc) worse.

ex·acer·ba·tion /ɪɡˌzæsəˈbeɪʃn/ *nu*

ex·act¹ /ɪɡˈzækt/ *adj* (*no comp*) **1** correct in every detail; free from error: *Give me his exact words. What is the exact size of the room?* Compare approximate¹. **2** capable of being correct in every detail: *exact sciences; an exact memory.*

ex·act·ly *adv* **(a)** completely: *Your answer is exactly right.* **(b)** (used to emphasize what is being said) just; precisely: *That's exactly what I expected.* **(c)** (used as an answer or confirmation) You are right: *'And he then went home?'—'Exactly.'*

ex·act² /ɪɡˈzækt/ *vt* **exact sth (from sb)** (*formal*) **1** to demand and get payment of something (from a person): *exact taxes (from people).* **2** to insist on (something): *exact obedience*.

ex·act·ing /ɪɡˈzæktɪŋ/ *adj* needing a lot of (mental or physical) effort: *This is an exacting piece of work*.

ex·ag·ger·ate /ɪɡˈzædʒəreɪt/ *vt,vi* to make (something) seem larger, better, worse etc than it really is: *You are exaggerating (the difficulties). If you always exaggerate, people will no longer believe you.*

ex·ag·ger·ation /ɪɡˌzædʒəˈreɪʃn/ *nc,nu*

ex·alt·ed /ɪɡˈzɔːltɪd/ *adj* of high rank or importance: *an exalted job in industry*.

ex·am /ɪɡˈzæm/ *nc* (*informal*) = examination(2).

ex·am·in·ation /ɪɡˌzæmɪˈneɪʃn/ *n* **1** *nu* the act of examining or being examined: *On examination, it was found that the signature was not genuine.* **be under examination** to be being questioned, studied carefully: *The prisoner/account is still under examination.* **2** *nc* a (usually written) test of knowledge or ability: *I failed/passed all my examinations last year. He took/sat five examinations last week. When will you do the last examination?* Ⓝ '*Exam*' is now much more usual. **3** *nc* a detailed inquiry into or inspection of something: *an examination of business accounts; a medical examination.* **4** *nc* (*legal*) a questioning by a lawyer in a law court: *an examination of a witness*.

ex·am·ine /ɪɡˈzæmɪn/ *vt* **1** to look at (a person, thing) carefully in order to learn something: *examine a car before buying it; have one's teeth/eyes examined.* **2** (*formal*) to put questions to (a person) in order to test knowledge or get information: *examine pupils in grammar.* **3** (*legal*) to question (a person): *examine a witness in a law court*.

ex·am·in·er *nc* a person who examines students etc.

ex·ample /ɪɡˈzɑːmpl/ *nc* **1** a fact, thing etc used to represent a group of similar ones: *This dictionary has many examples of how words are used in sentences. This is a good example of Shakespeare's sense of humour. Can you give me an example of a bird that cannot fly?* **for example** (abbr e.g.) using this or these as typical: *Many great men came from poor families—Lincoln and Edison, for example.* **2** a person, thing, behaviour etc to be copied or imitated because good: *You should follow her example.* **set an example/a good example (to sb)** to be, offer, a good standard (esp of behaviour) for others to copy. **3** something used as a warning: *Let her unhappiness be an example to you.* **make an example of sb** to punish a person severely as a warning to others.

ex·as·per·ate /ɪɡˈzɑːspəreɪt/ *vt* (usually *passive*) to produce anger, annoyance etc in: *be exasperated at/by his stupidity*.

ex·as·per·at·ing *adj* very annoying: *It is exasperating to miss a train by a minute*.

ex·as·per·ation /ɪɡˌzɑːspəˈreɪʃn/ *nu* the state of being annoyed: '*Stop that noise!*' *he cried out in exasperation*.

ex·ca·vate /ˈekskəveɪt/ *vt* to make, uncover, (something) by digging: *excavating for coal; excavate a hole/a buried city/an ancient ruin*.

ex·ca·va·tion /ˌekskəˈveɪʃn/ *nc,nu*

ex·ca·va·tor *nc* a person or machine that excavates something.

ex·ceed /ɪkˈsiːd/ *vt* **1** to be greater than (some-

thing): *Their success exceeded all expectations.* **2** to go beyond (what is allowed, necessary or advisable): *exceed the speed limit*.

exceed·ing·ly *adv* extremely; to an unusual degree: *an exceedingly difficult problem; be exceedingly grateful*.

ex·cel /ɪkˈsel/ *v* (**-ll-**) **1** *vi* excel (**in sth; at sth; as sb**) to be very good: *He excels in courage/at football/as a writer.* **2** *vt* **excel sb (at a sport)** to be, do, better than: *She excels all of us (at tennis)*.

ex·cel·lence /ˈeksələns/ *nu* the quality of being excellent: *a prize for excellence in French*.

Ex·cel·len·cy /ˈeksələnsɪ/ *nc* (*pl* **-ies**) a title of ambassadors, governors and their wives, and some other officers and Church officials.

ex·cel·lent /ˈeksələnt/ *adj* (*no comp*) very good; of the highest quality: *an excellent result/student*.

ex·cel·lent·ly *adv*

ex·cept¹ /ɪkˈsept/ *prep* **1** except (**for**) not including; but not: *I could do nothing except wait. He gets up early every day except Sunday. Nobody was late except (for) me. Your essay is good except for the spelling.* Ⓝ ⇨ the note at besides²(2). **2** except that apart from the fact that: *She knew nothing except that he was likely to be late*.

ex·cept² /ɪkˈsept/ *vt* to agree not to include (a person, thing) (which is more usual): *I will except the younger children but no-one else*.

ex·cept·ing *prep* (usually with *not*) leaving out; excluding: *I want to see the whole staff, not excepting* (i.e. including) *the heads of departments*.

ex·cep·tion /ɪkˈsepʃn/ *n* **1** *nc* a person or thing that is not included: *I enjoyed all his novels with the exception of his last.* **make an exception** to agree not to include a person or thing: *I'll make an exception in your case.* **make no exception(s)** to accept no reason to exclude a person, thing: *You must each pay for the damage—I can make no exceptions.* **without exception** with no exceptions. **2** *nc* something that does not follow the rule: *exceptions to a rule of grammar.* **the exception proves the rule** (*saying*) the theory is true for most cases so it is useful. **3** *nu* objection. **take exception (to sb/sth)** to object to, protest about, a person, action etc: *He took great exception to me/what I said*.

ex·cep·tion·al /ɪkˈsepʃənl/ *adj* (of something good or pleasant) unusual: *weather that is exceptional for June; exceptional value for money.* Opp unexceptional.

ex·cep·tion·al·ly *adv* unusually: *She's an exceptionally clever girl*.

ex·cerpt /ˈeksɜːpt/ *nc* a part taken (from a book etc).

ex·cess¹ /ˈekses/ *adj* (*attrib*) (*no comp*) **1** more than is usual, allowed etc: *excess luggage.* **2** additional: *pay an excess fare*.

ex·cess² /ɪkˈses/ **1** *nu* the fact, state, of being more than (what is needed, right, usual etc): *Excess* (i.e. too much) *food is a major cause of heart disease.* **in excess of** an amount more than: *a debt in excess of £1000.* **2** *nu* or *sing* (**an**) **excess of sth** (an) amount that is more than what is needed, right etc: *an excess of enthusiasm.* **3** *nu* **to excess** to an amount or degree beyond usual limits: *drink to excess. She is generous to excess.* **4** (*pl*) personal acts which go beyond the limits of good behaviour, morality or humanity:

The excesses (= acts of cruelty etc) committed by the soldiers when they occupied the city will never be forgotten.

ex·cess·ive /ɪk'sesɪv/ *adj* too large or too much: *excessive charges.*

ex·cess·ive·ly *adv*

ex·change¹ /ɪks't ʃeɪndʒ/ *n* **1** *nc,nu* (an instance, act, of) exchanging things: *an exchange of information.* **in exchange (for sb/sth)** in place of another: *He is giving her French lessons in exchange for English lessons.* **2** *nu* the giving and receiving of money from one country for that of another. ⇨ also stock exchange.

ex'change rate *nc* (also *rate of exchange*) the proportion in which money from one country can be exchanged for money from another: *'What's the exchange rate for dollars?'—'$1.80 to the pound'.*

ex·change² /ɪks't ʃeɪndʒ/ *vt* **exchange sth (for sth) (with sb)** to give and receive (one thing) in place of another: *exchange glances/greetings. I exchanged my dollars for pounds. Mary exchanged seats with Anne.*

ex·change·able /-əbl/ *adj*

ex·cheq·uer /ɪks't ʃekə(r)/ *nc* (the E-) (*GB*) the government department in charge of public money: *Chancellor of the Exchequer (= the head of this department).*

ex·cise /'eksaɪz/ *nu* (*finance*) a government tax on certain goods manufactured, sold or used within a country: *the excise on beer/tobacco; excise duties.*

ex·cise² /ɪk'saɪz/ *vt* **1** (*med*) to remove (a part of the body) by cutting. **2** (*formal*) to remove (something unwanted, e.g. parts of a piece of writing).

ex·ci·sion /ɪk'sɪʒn/ *nc,nu*

ex·cit·able /ɪk'saɪtəbl/ *adj* easily excited.

ex·cite /ɪk'saɪt/ *vt* **1** to cause strong feelings (of great pleasure, anger etc) in (a person): *Everybody was excited by the news of the victory. It's nothing to get excited about. Extremists were exciting the people to rebellion/to rebel.* **2** to cause (a feeling, action): *excite admiration/envy/affection; excite a riot.*

ex·cite·ment /ɪk'saɪtmənt/ *n* **1** *nu* the state of being excited: *news that caused great excitement.* **2** *nc* an exciting event etc: *He kept calm amid all these excitements.*

ex·cit·ing *adj* causing strong feelings of pleasure, interest etc: *exciting news; an exciting story.* Opp unexciting.

excl. *abbr* **1** excluding. **2** exclusive.

ex·claim /ɪk'skleɪm/ *v* **1** *vt* to say with strong feelings (the words quoted): *'What!' he exclaimed, 'Are you leaving without me?'* **2** *vi* to cry out suddenly because of pain, surprise, anger etc.

ex·cla·ma·tion /,eksklə'meɪʃn/ *nc* a word, phrase etc used to express surprise, strong feeling etc, e.g. *'Help!' 'How terrible!' 'Isn't she beautiful!' 'What a lovely dress!'*

,excla'mation mark *nc* (*lang*) the punctuation mark (!). Ⓝ It is used after expressions that show strong feelings of surprise, anger, fear, delight etc, as in *How nice! Don't you dare! What a surprise! How terrible! Go away!*

ex·clama·tory /ɪk'sklæmətərɪ/ *adj* (*attrib*) of using, containing, an exclamation: *an exclama-*

tory remark/sentence.

ex·clude /ɪk'sklu:d/ *vt* **1** *exclude sb/sth (from sth)* (**a**) to prevent (a person) (from getting in somewhere): *exclude him from membership.* Opp include. (**b**) to leave (something) out as not relevant: *We can exclude the possibility that the money won't arrive.* **2** to put (something) out of one's mind: *exclude all possibility of doubt.*

ex·clu·sion /ɪk'sklu:ʒn/ *nu* the act, state, of excluding other things or being excluded: *He watches TV to the exclusion of everything else.*

ex·clus·ive¹ /ɪk'sklu:sɪv/ *adj* **1** not willing to admit members or mix with others considered to be inferior in social position, education etc: *an exclusive society. He belongs to the most exclusive clubs.* **2** (*attrib*) for only the person(s) concerned: *have exclusive rights/an exclusive agency for the sale of Ford cars in a town; an exclusive interview* (e.g. given to only one newspaper). **3** *exclusive of sb/sth* not including (which is much more usual): *The ship had a crew of 57, exclusive of officers.* **4** (*formal*) only: *Teaching has not been his exclusive employment.*

ex·clus·ive·ly *adv*

ex·clus·ive² /ɪk'sklu:sɪv/ *nc* an article, report etc published by only one newspaper.

ex·cre·ment /'ekskrəmənt/ *nu* (*formal*) solid waste matter from the body.

ex·cre·ta /ɪk'skri:tə/ *n pl* (*formal*) waste matter (excrement, urine, also sweat) expelled from the body.

ex·crete /ɪk'skri:t/ *vt* (*science*) (of an animal or plant) to discharge (waste matter, sweat etc) from the body.

ex·cre·tion /ɪk'skri:ʃn/ *nc,nu*

ex·cru·ci·at·ing /ɪk'skru:ʃɪeɪtɪŋ/ *adj* (of pain, suffering, bodily or mental) extreme: *an excruciating toothache.*

ex·cru·ci·at·ing·ly *adv*

ex·cur·sion /ɪk'skɜ:ʃn/ *nc* a short journey, esp one made by a number of people together for pleasure: *go on an excursion to the mountains.*

ex·cus·able /ɪk'skju:zəbl/ *adj* (of bad behaviour, an error etc) that can be excused(1): *an excusable mistake.* Opp inexcusable.

ex·cuse¹ /ɪk'skju:s/ *nc* **excuse (for sth)** a reason given (true or invented) to explain or defend one's behaviour or actions: *He's always making excuses for being late. Those who are absent without (good) excuse will be punished.* Compare reason¹(1).

ex·cuse² /ɪk'skju:z/ *vt* **1** *excuse sb (for doing sth); excuse sth* to forgive (a person) for doing something wrong: *Please excuse me for being late/excuse my late arrival.* **2** *excuse sb (from sth)* to set a person free (from a duty etc): *He was excused (from) attendance at the lecture.* **3** to be a reason for (something): *His lack of experience does not excuse his bad behaviour.* **4** *excuse me* (used as an apology when one interrupts, asks, disagrees etc): *Excuse me, but is this seat vacant? Excuse me, but you're wrong.*

exec. *abbr* executive.

ex·ecute /'eksɪkju:t/ *vt* **1** *execute sb (for sth)* to kill a person (for a major crime): *He was executed for murdering his wife.* **2** (*formal*) to make (a speech), play (a piece of music) etc: *The speech/sonata was badly executed.* **3** (*formal*) to

ex·ecu·tion /ˌeksɪˈkjuːʃn/ n 1 nc,nu (an act of) punishment by being killed. ⇨ stay¹(2). 2 nu (formal) skill in making a speech, performing music etc: a pianist with marvellous execution. 3 nu (formal) the carrying out or performance of a piece of work etc: His execution of the plan was unsatisfactory.

ex·ecu·tion·er nc an official who executes criminals.

ex·ecu·tive¹ /ɪɡˈzekjʊtɪv/ adj (attrib) 1 having to do with managing or carrying out orders: executive duties. 2 having authority to make decisions, laws, decrees etc: the executive branch of the government.

ex·ecu·tive² /ɪɡˈzekjʊtɪv/ nc 1 (the E-) the executive branch of a government. 2 (in the Civil Service) a person who carries out what has been planned or decided. 3 a person, group, in a business with administrative or managerial powers.

ex·ecu·tor /ɪɡˈzekjʊtə(r)/ nc (legal) a person who is appointed to carry out the terms of a will.

ex·ecu·trix /ɪɡˈzekjʊtrɪks/ nc (legal) a woman executor.

ex·emp·lary /ɪɡˈzemplərɪ/ adj (formal) serving as an example or a warning: exemplary conduct/punishment.

ex·emp·li·fy /ɪɡˈzemplɪfaɪ/ vt (pt,pp -ied) (formal) to be an example of (esp ability).

ex·empt¹ /ɪɡˈzempt/ adj (pred) **exempt (from sth)** free (from a duty, payment etc): exempt from tax/military service.

ex·empt² /ɪɡˈzempt/ vt **exempt sb (from doing sth)** to free a person (from a duty, payment etc): be exempted from paying an entrance fee.

ex·emp·tion /ɪɡˈzempʃn/ nc,nu

ex·er·cise¹ /ˈeksəsaɪz/ n 1 nu the use of one's physical powers to make one healthier: Walking, running, rowing and cycling are all healthy forms of exercise. 2 nc an activity designed for bodily, mental or spiritual training: vocal/gymnastic exercises. 3 nc a set of questions etc as part of learning: grammar exercises. 4 nc a piece of work for practice: exercises for the piano. 5 nu (formal) the use of a mental power: The exercise of patience will be essential. 6 nc (mil) a series of movements for training troops, crews of warships etc: military exercises.

ex·er·cise² /ˈeksəsaɪz/ v 1 vt,vi (to cause a person) to use physical powers to become healthier: We get fat and lazy if we don't exercise enough. 2 vt to use (a power or right): exercise patience/one's right to vote. 3 vt (formal) to worry (a person, the mind etc): It is an economic problem that is exercising our minds.

ex·ert /ɪɡˈzɜːt/ vt 1 to bring (something powerful) into use: exert all one's energy/influence; exert pressure on someone to do something. 2 **exert oneself** to make an effort: Does she ever exert herself (to help you)?

exer·tion /ɪɡˈzɜːʃn/ nc,nu

ex·hale /eksˈheɪl/ vt,vi to breathe out (air, smoke etc). Opp inhale.

ex·ha·la·tion /ˌekshəˈleɪʃn/ nc,nu

ex·haust¹ /ɪɡˈzɔːst/ nc,nu (a pipe in an engine or machine for) gas, steam, vapour etc that is no longer wanted.

ex·haust-pipe nc an exhaust in a vehicle.

ex·haust² /ɪɡˈzɔːst/ vt 1 to use up (strength, energy etc) completely: exhaust one's patience; exhaust oneself by hard work; feeling exhausted. 2 to use all the supply of (something): exhaust one's supplies. 3 to say, find out, all there is to say about (something): We've exhausted that subject.

ex·haust·ing adj very tiring: exhausting work. Compare exhaustive.

ex·haus·tion /ɪɡˈzɔːstʃən/ nu

ex·haus·tive /ɪɡˈzɔːstɪv/ adj thorough; complete: an exhaustive inquiry.

ex·hi·bit¹ /ɪɡˈzɪbɪt/ nc 1 an object or collection of objects shown publicly, e.g. in a museum: Do not touch the exhibits. 2 (legal) a document, object etc produced in a law court as evidence.

ex·hi·bit² /ɪɡˈzɪbɪt/ vt 1 to show (something) publicly (for sale, in a competition etc): exhibit paintings. 2 (formal) to give clear evidence of (a condition, quality): exhibit symptoms of a disease. The girls exhibited great courage during the climb.

ex·hi·bi·tor nc a person, business, that exhibits(1) something.

ex·hi·bi·tion /ˌeksɪˈbɪʃn/ n 1 nc a collection of things shown publicly (e.g. of works of art, of commercial or industrial goods for sale etc): an exhibition of Chinese books. **on exhibition** being exhibited(1). 2 n sing (formal) an act of showing: an exhibition of bad manners; an opportunity for the exhibition of one's knowledge.

ex·hi·bi·tion·ism /ˌeksɪˈbɪʃənɪzəm/ nu extravagant behaviour designed to attract attention to oneself.

ex·hi·bi·tion·ist /-ɪst/ adj of, concerning, exhibitionism. □ nc (derog) a person who uses extravagant behaviour to attract attention.

ex·hil·ar·ate /ɪɡˈzɪləreɪt/ vt (usually passive) 1 to make (a person) very excited and happy: feel exhilarated. 2 to make (a person) feel healthier, more active: be/feel exhilarated by a long walk.

ex·hil·ar·at·ing adj: exhilarating news/walks.

ex·hil·ar·ation /ɪɡˌzɪləˈreɪʃn/ nu

ex·hort /ɪɡˈzɔːt/ vt (formal) to urge (a person) (to do something): exhort her to do good.

ex·hor·ta·tion /ˌeksɔːˈteɪʃn/ nc,nu

ex·hume /eksˈhjuːm/ vt to take out (a dead body) from the earth (for examination).

ex·hum·ation /ˌekshjuːˈmeɪʃn/ nc,nu

ex·ile¹ /ˈeɡzaɪl/ n 1 nu or sing an act of being sent away from one's country, esp as a punishment: be/live in exile; go/be sent into exile; return after an exile of ten years. 2 nc a person who is sent away from her or his country.

ex·ile² /ˈeɡzaɪl/ vt to send (a person) into exile.

ex·ist /ɪɡˈzɪst/ vi 1 to be real, actual: The idea exists only in the minds of poets. Does life exist on Mars? 2 to continue living: We cannot exist without food and water.

ex·ist·ence /-əns/ n (a) nu the state of being: Do you believe in the existence of ghosts? **in existence** still alive, present, here: This is the oldest skull in existence. (b) n sing a way of living: lead a happy existence.

ex·ist·ent /-ənt/ adj living; being real; present, here. Compare non-existent.

ex·it¹ /ˈeksɪt/ nc 1 a way out, e.g. from a theatre or cinema. 2 a departure of an actor from the stage: *make one's exit* (= leave a place).

ex·it² /'eksɪt/ *vi,vt* (esp used as a stage direction) to go out: *Exit Macbeth.*

ex·on·er·ate /ɪg'zɒnəreɪt/ *vt* **exonerate sb (from sth)** (*formal*) to free, release, a person (from blame etc): *exonerate him from responsibility.*

ex·on·er·ation /ɪg,zɒnə'reɪʃn/ *nu*

ex·or·bi·tant /ɪg'zɔːbɪtənt/ *adj* (of a price, charge or demand) much too high or great.

ex·hor·bi·tant·ly *adv*

ex·or·cize (also **-ise**) /'eksɔːsaɪz/ *vt* to drive out (e.g. an evil spirit) (from a person, place) by using prayers or magic.

ex·or·cism /-sɪzəm/ *nc,nu*

ex·or·cist /-sɪst/ *nc* a person who exorcizes.

ex·ot·ic /ɪg'zɒtɪk/ *adj* **1** (of plants, fashions, words, ideas) introduced from another country: *exotic food.* **2** attractive or pleasing because colourful, unusual etc: *exotic birds/plants.*

ex·pand /ɪk'spænd/ *v* **1** *vt,vi* (to cause something) to become larger: *Metals expand when they are heated. Our foreign trade has expanded during recent years. He expanded his short story into a novel.* Opp contract³(1). **2** *vi* **expand on sth** to give more details about a story, theory etc.

ex·panse /ɪk'spæns/ *nc* **expanse (of sth)** a wide and open area: *the broad expanse of the sea; the blue expanse of the sky.*

ex·pan·sion /ɪk'spænʃn/ *n* **1** *nu* the process of expanding or being expanded(1): *the expansion of gases when heated.* **2** *nc* an enlargement: *The novel was an expansion of his short story.*

ex·pan·sive /ɪk'spænsɪv/ *adj* (*formal*) **1** (of a person) friendly; talkative. **2** extravagant: *an expansive way of living.*

ex·pat·ri·ate /eks'pætrɪət/ *nc* a person living outside her or his own country: *American expatriates in Paris.*

ex·pect /ɪk'spekt/ *vt* **1** to believe, think, that (a person) will come: *Is the head teacher expecting you? You were expected yesterday.* **2** to believe, think, that (something) will happen: *'Will he be late?'—'I expect so.' I expect (that) she'll phone tonight. Rain is expected.* **3** **be expecting (a baby/boy/girl)** to be pregnant. **4** **expect sth (of sb)** to hope, consider, that a person will behave in a certain way, reach a certain standard: *Some parents expect too much of their children. All I expect of them is a little kindness. Is that too much to expect?* **5** **expect sb/sth to do sth** to consider that a person must do something, that something must happen: *I expect you to return the money to me by Friday. I expect this liquid to turn brown within one hour.*

ex·pect·an·cy /-ənsɪ/ *nu* the state of expecting something to happen: *with a look/an air of expectancy; a life expectancy* (= expected length of life) *of 70 years.*

ex·pect·ant /-ənt/ *adj* (*attrib*) **(a)** expecting something to happen: *an expectant look/ audience.* **(b)** (*med*) expecting a baby: *an expectant mother.*

ex·pec·ta·tion /,ekspek'teɪʃn/ *n* (*formal*) **1** *nu* **in expectation of sth** expecting something to happen: *He ate a light lunch in expectation of a good dinner.* **2** (often *pl*) something that is expected: *Will she live up to her father's expec-*

tations? **3** (*pl*) future prospects, esp something to be inherited: *a young man with great expectations.* **4** (*pl*) **beyond all expectations** much more than what is/was considered possible: *The salary they offered was beyond all expectations.*

ex·pedi·ence /ɪk'spiːdɪəns/ *nu* = expediency.

ex·pedi·en·cy /ɪk'spiːdɪənsɪ/ *nu* (*formal*) **1** self-interest: *act out of expediency and give no thought to others.* **2** the state, process, of being expedient.

ex·pedi·ent /ɪk'spiːdɪənt/ *adj* (of an act, action) likely to be useful or helpful for a purpose (but not necessarily desired): *Governments often do things which are expedient, not because they want to.*

ex·pedi·ent·ly *adv*

ex·pe·dite /'ekspɪdaɪt/ *vt* (*formal*) to help, speed up, the progress of (a plan, business etc).

ex·pedi·tion /,ekspɪ'dɪʃn/ *nc* (the people, equipment etc making) a journey or voyage for a special purpose: *a scientific expedition; go on an expedition to the Antarctic.*

ex·pedi·tion·ary /-ʃənrɪ/ *adj* (*attrib*) of, making up, an (esp military) expedition: *an expeditionary force.*

ex·pedi·tious /,ekspɪ'dɪʃəs/ *adj* (*formal*) acting quickly and efficiently.

ex·pel /ɪk'spel/ *vt* (**-ll-**) **1** **expel sb (from sth)** to send a person away, e.g. for doing wrong: *expel a boy from school.* ⇨ expulsion. **2** **expel sth (from sth)** (*formal*) to force something out: *expel air from the lungs.*

ex·pend /ɪk'spend/ *vt* **expend sth (on sth/in doing sth)** (*formal*) to use up money, time etc: *expend time and care in making the curtains.*

ex·pend·able /-əbl/ *adj* (esp) that may be used or sacrificed to achieve a purpose: *The general considered that these soldiers were expendable.*

ex·pen·di·ture /ɪk'spendɪtʃə(r)/ *n* (*formal*) **1** *nu* the act of spending or using (money): *the expenditure of money on new equipment.* **2** *nc* an amount of money spent or used: *an expenditure of £500 on new furniture.*

ex·pense /ɪk'spens/ *n* **1** *nu* the spending (of money etc): *I want the best you can supply, regardless of expense.* **at the expense of sth** at the cost of something: *He became a great scholar, but it was at the expense of his health.* **spare no expense** to do what is necessary and ignore the cost: *I want you to spare no expense.* **no expense spared** without economizing at all. **2** (usually *pl*) money used or needed: *travelling expenses. Illness, holidays and other expenses reduced his bank balance to almost nothing.*

ex'pense account *nc* (a list of) money (to be) spent (on fares, hotels etc) e.g. when doing one's job.

ex·pen·sive /ɪk'spensɪv/ *adj* costing a great deal of money, people, effort etc: *an expensive dress; too expensive for me to buy; an expensive war* (i.e. with many killed). Opp inexpensive.

ex·pens·ive·ly *adv*

ex·peri·ence¹ /ɪk'spɪərɪəns/ *n* **1** *nu* (the process of gaining) knowledge or skill by doing and seeing things: *Has he had much experience in work of this sort?* **by/from experience** using one's experience: *We all learn by/from experience.* **2** *nc* an event, activity, which has provided experience(1): *She wrote about her experiences in Africa.* **3** *nc* an event that affects one in some way: *an unpleasant/ unusual/agreeable experience.*

ex·peri·enced *adj* having knowledge or skill as the result of experience: *an experienced nurse/ teacher.* Opp inexperienced.

ex·peri·ence² /ɪkˈspɪərɪəns/ *vt* to get experience(1) of (something): *experience pleasure/pain/ difficulty.*

ex·peri·ment¹ /ɪkˈsperɪmənt/ *n* **1** *nc* a test or trial carried out carefully in order to study what happens and gain new knowledge: *perform/carry out an experiment in chemistry.* **2** *nu* the process of experimenting: *learn by experiment.*

ex·peri·men·ta·tion /ɪkˌsperɪmenˈteɪʃn/ *nu* (*formal*) the act of experimenting.

ex·peri·ment² /ɪkˈsperɪmənt/ *vi* **experiment (on sb/sth; with sth)** to make an experiment: *experiment on children/frozen specimens; experiment with new methods.*

ex·peri·men·tal /ɪkˌsperɪˈmentl/ *adj* of, used for, experiments: *experimental methods; an experimental farm.*

ex·pert¹ /ˈekspɜːt/ *adj* **expert (at/in sth)** highly trained or skilled: *expert advice; She's expert in teaching handicapped children/at making model boats.*

ex·pert·ly *adv*

ex·pert² /ˈekspɜːt/ *nc* **expert (at/in sth)** a person with special knowledge, skill or training: *an agricultural expert; an expert in economics; an expert at dealing with problems.*

ex·pert·ise /ˌekspɜːˈtiːz/ *nc,nu* (a particular) expert knowledge and skill.

ex·pire /ɪkˈspaɪə(r)/ *vi* **1** (of something lasting for a period of time) to come to an end: *When does your driving licence expire?* Ⓝ *'Run out'* is more usual. **2** (*literary*) to die.

ex·piry /ɪkˈspaɪərɪ/ *nu* **expiry (of sth)** (*formal*) the ending (of something lasting for a period of time): *the expiry of a driving licence.*

ex·plain /ɪkˈspleɪn/ *v* **1** *vt* to give the meaning of (something): *A dictionary tries to explain (the meanings of) words.* **2** *vi,vt* **explain sth (to sb); explain (to sb) that . . .** to make (something) clear by giving reasons, details etc: *He explained that he had been delayed by the weather.* **3** *vt* to provide reasons for (something): *Can you explain his behaviour? That explains his long absence.*

ex·pla·na·tion /ˌekspləˈneɪʃn/ *n* **1** *nu* the process of explaining: *The plan needs explanation to make it clear.* **2** *nc* a statement, fact etc that explains: *His illness is one explanation of his lack of energy.*

ex·plana·tory /ɪkˈsplænətrɪ/ *adj* (*attrib*) (of writing, speech) used to explain: *an explanatory letter.*

ex·ple·tive /ɪkˈspliːtɪv/ *nc* (*lang*) an exclamation showing anger, surprise etc, e.g. *'My goodness!' 'Damn!'*

ex·plic·able /ɪkˈsplɪkəbl/ *adj* that can be explained. Opp inexplicable.

ex·pli·cit /ɪkˈplɪsɪt/ *adj* (of a statement, regulations etc) clearly and fully expressed: *He was quite explicit about it.*

ex·pli·cit·ly *adv*

ex·pli·cit·ness *nu*

ex·plode /ɪkˈspləʊd/ *vt,vi* **1** (to cause something) to burst with a loud noise: *explode a bomb/a charge of gunpowder. The bomb exploded.* **2** (*fig*)

(of a person) to show violent emotion: *He exploded with rage.* **3** (*fig*) to prove completely that (an idea, theory etc) is false: *explode a superstition; an exploded idea.*

ex·ploit¹ /ˈeksplɔɪt/ *nc* a bold or adventurous act.

ex·ploit² /ɪkˈsplɔɪt/ *vt* **1** to use, work or develop (natural resources): *exploiting our natural minerals.* **2** to use (people, another person's ideas etc) selfishly or for profit: *exploit children.*

ex·ploi·ta·tion /ˌeksplɔɪˈteɪʃn/ *nu*

ex·plore /ɪkˈsplɔː(r)/ *vt* **1** to travel into or through (a country etc) for the purpose of learning about it: *explore the Arctic regions; go exploring in the Andes.* **2** to examine thoroughly (problems etc) in order to test, learn: *exploring every possibility of a solution.*

ex·plorer *nc* a person who explores(1).

ex·plo·ra·tion /ˌekspləˈreɪʃn/ *nc,nu* (an instance of) exploring: *the exploration of the ocean depths.*

ex·plora·tory /ɪkˈsplɔːrətrɪ/ *adj* done in order to examine and learn about something: *an exploratory surgical operation.*

ex·plo·sion /ɪkˈspləʊʒn/ *nc* **1** (a loud noise caused by) a sudden and violent bursting: *a bomb explosion. The explosion was heard a mile away.* **2** (*fig*) (a loud noise of) an outburst or outbreak (of anger, laughter etc). **3** a large and sudden increase: *the population explosion.*

ex·plos·ive /ɪkˈspləʊsɪv/ *nc, adj* (a substance) that can explode: *a shell filled with high explosive; an explosive charge.* **an explosive issue** a subject for discussion etc that will produce strong feelings, emotions.

ex·plos·ive·ly *adv*

expo /ˈekspəʊ/ *abbr* exposition(2).

ex·po·nent /ɪkˈspəʊnənt/ *nc* **exponent (of sth)** a person, thing, that explains or supports, or is an example (of): *Huxley was an exponent of Darwin's theory of evolution.*

ex·port¹ /ˈekspɔːt/ *n* **1** *nu* (also *attrib*) (the business of) exporting: *a ban on the export of gold; the export trade; export duties.* **2** *nc* something exported: *Last year exports exceeded imports in value.* Compare import¹(1).

ex·port² /ɪkˈspɔːt/ *vt* to send (goods) to another country: *export cotton goods.* Compare import²(1).

ex·port·er *nc* a person, business, that exports goods.

ex·port·able /-əbl/ *adj*

ex·por·ta·tion /ˌekspɔːˈteɪʃn/ *nu*

ex·pose /ɪkˈspəʊz/ *vt* **1** to leave (a person, thing) uncovered or unprotected: *expose one's body to the sunlight; expose workers to unnecessary risks.* **2** to make (a bad person, thing) known: *expose a plot/liar.* **3** (*photography*) to allow light to reach (film etc).

ex·po·sé /ɪkˈspəʊzeɪ/ *nc* an instance or example of making a crime or scandal known to the public: *an exposé in a newspaper.*

ex·po·si·tion /ˌekspəˈzɪʃn/ *n* **1** *nc,nu* (*formal*) (an instance of) explaining or describing a theory, plan etc. **2** *nc* (*abbr* expo) /ˈekspəʊ/ (*commerce*) an exhibition of goods etc: *an industrial exposition.*

ex·po·sure /ɪkˈspəʊʒə(r)/ *n* **1** *nu* the process, state, of exposing or being exposed (all senses):

The climbers lost their way on the mountain and died of exposure. The exposure of the plot against the President probably saved his life. **2** *nc* an instance of exposing or being exposed (all senses): *How many exposures have you taken?* (= How many pictures have you taken on the film?)

ex·pound /ɪk'spaʊnd/ *vt* (*formal*) to explain, make clear, (a theory) by giving details: *expound a theory.*

ex·press[1] /ɪk'spres/ *adj* (*attrib*) **1** clearly and openly stated, not suggested or implied: *It was his express wish that you should remarry.* **2** going, sent, quickly: *an express train; express mail.*

ex·press[2] /ɪk'spres/ *adv* by express delivery: *a letter sent express.*

ex·press[3] /ɪk'spres/ *n* **1** *nc* an express train: *the 8am express to Edinburgh.* **2** *nu* a service of the post office, railways, road services for sending goods quickly: *send goods (by) express.*

ex·press[4] /ɪk'spres/ *vt* **1** to make known, show, (something) by using words, looks, actions: *I find it difficult to express my meaning. Her eyes expressed the love she felt.* **2** **express sth (from/ out of sth)** (*formal*) to press or squeeze juices or oil (from fruit etc): *juice expressed from grapes.*

ex·pres·sion /ɪk'spreʃn/ *n* **1** *nc,nu* (an instance of) the process of expressing(1): *Please accept these flowers as an expression of my thanks. Is there freedom of expression* (= freedom to say or write what you think or believe) *in your country?* **find expression in sth** (*formal*) to be expressed by using something: *Her feelings at last found expression in tears.* **2** *nc* a word or phrase: *'Shut up'* (= Stop talking) *is not a polite expression.* **3** *nc,nu* an outward sign (on the face, in the voice etc) of an emotion: *He had an angry expression in his eyes.* **4** *nc* (*maths*) a set of symbols representing a quantity, e.g. $3xy^2$.

ex·pres·sion·less *adj* without any expression(3): *an expressionless face/voice.*

ex·press·ive /ɪk'spresɪv/ *adj* showing feelings, personality etc: *an expressive smile.*

ex·press·ive·ly *adv*

ex·press·ly /ɪk'spreslɪ/ *adv* plainly; definitely: *You were expressly forbidden to touch my papers.*

ex·pro·pri·ate /eks'prəʊprɪeɪt/ *vt* (*formal*) to take away (property owned by another person).

ex·pro·pri·ation /ˌeksˌprəʊprɪ'eɪʃn/ *nu*

ex·pul·sion /ɪk'spʌlʃn/ *nc,nu* (an instance of) expelling or being expelled: *the expulsion of a student from college.*

ex·pur·gate /'ekspɜːgeɪt/ *vt* (*literature*) to take out from (a book etc) what are considered to be (improper or objectionable parts): *an expurgated edition of a novel.*

ex·pur·ga·tion /ˌekspɜː'geɪʃn/ *nu*

ex·quis·ite /ek'skwɪzɪt/ *adj* of a very high quality: *exquisite workmanship.*

ex·quis·ite·ly *adv*

ex·tem·pore /ek'stempərɪ/ *adv, adj* (*formal*) (spoken or done) without previous thought or preparation: *speak extempore.*

ex·tend /ɪk'stend/ *v* **1** *vt* to make (something) longer (in space or time): *extend a railway; extend a visit.* **2** *vt* to lay or stretch out (the body, a limb or limbs) at full length: *extend one's hand to her.* **3** *vt* (*formal*) to give, offer, (an invitation, greeting etc): *extend an invitation/a warm welcome to him.*

4 *vi* **extend for a length** (of space, land etc) to continue or stretch for the length mentioned: *a road that extends for miles and miles.* **5** *vt* to cause (something) to reach or stretch: *extend a cable between two posts.*

ex·ten·sion /ɪk'stenʃn/ *n* **1** *nu* the act of extending or being extended: *the extension of useful knowledge.* **2** *nc* an additional part: *an extension of one's summer holidays; build an extension to a hospital; a telephone extension* (= an internal number, e.g. in a business); *get an extension of time* (e.g. for paying a debt).

ex·ten·sive /ɪk'stensɪv/ *adj* large in area, amount, degree etc: *extensive buildings/repairs/ enquiries.*

ex·ten·sive·ly *adv*

ex·tent /ɪk'stent/ *nu* **1** **extent (of sth)** the length, area, range etc (of something): *I was amazed at the extent of his knowledge.* **2** **to a certain/to some extent** to the mentioned degree: *I agree with you to a certain extent but I'm not totally convinced.*

ex·tenu·at·ing /ɪk'stenjʊeɪtɪŋ/ *adj* (*attrib*) making (bad behaviour) seem less serious (by providing an excuse): *There are extenuating circumstances in this case.*

ex·ter·ior[1] /ek'stɪərɪə(r)/ *adj* situated on or coming from outside: *the exterior wall of a building.* Opp interior[1].

ex,terior 'angle *nc* (*maths*) an angle contained between one extended line of a triangle etc and the adjacent line. Compare interior angle.

ex·ter·ior[2] /ek'stɪərɪə(r)/ *nc* the outside; outward appearance: *paint the exterior of the building; a good man with a friendly exterior.* Compare interior[2].

ex·ter·mi·nate /ɪk'stɜːmɪneɪt/ *vt* to destroy completely (a disease, a race etc).

ex·ter·mi·na·tion /ɪkˌstɜːmɪ'neɪʃn/ *nc,nu*

ex·ter·nal /ek'stɜːnl/ *adj* **1** on, of or for the outside: *This skin cream is for external use only. I took my degree as an external student* (i.e. I was not a full member of the university). **2** not concerning one's own people or country; foreign: *external trade.* Compare internal.

ex·ter·nal·ly *adv*

ex·tinct /ɪk'stɪŋkt/ *adj* **1** no longer burning or active: *an extinct fire/volcano.* **2** no longer in existence: *an extinct species; become extinct.*

ex·tinc·tion /ɪk'stɪŋkʃn/ *nu* the state of being, becoming, extinct: *a race threatened with extinction.*

ex·tin·guish /ɪk'stɪŋgwɪʃ/ *vt* to put out (a light, fire).

ex·tin·guish·er *nc* an apparatus used for putting out a fire.

ex·tol /ɪk'stəʊl/ *vt* (**-ll-**) (*formal*) to praise (a person, quality) highly: *extolling her virtues; extol him as a hero.*

ex·tort /ɪk'stɔːt/ *vt* to obtain (money) by using violence, threats etc: *extort money from him.*

ex·tor·tion /ɪk'stɔːʃn/ *nc,nu*

ex·tor·tion·ate /ɪk'stɔːʃənət/ *adj* (of demands, prices) much too high.

ex·tra[1] /'ekstrə/ *adj* additional; beyond what is usual, expected or arranged: *extra pay for extra work.*

ex·tra[2] /'ekstrə/ *adv* **1** more than usually: *extra* *fine quality.* **2** in addition: *price £1.30, postage and packing extra.*

ex·tra³ /'ekstrə/ *nc* **1** an additional thing; something for which an extra charge is made: *The bike costs £80—the pump and saddle-bag are extras.* **2** (in a film, on TV etc) a person employed for a small acting part, e.g. in a crowd scene.

ex·tract¹ /'ekstrækt/ *nu* **1** something that has been extracted(3): *beef extract.* **2** *nc* a passage extracted(4): *extracts from a long poem.*

ex·tract² /ɪk'strækt/ *vt* **extract sth (from sb/ sth)** **1** to take or get something out (usually with effort): *have a tooth extracted; extract a bullet from a wound.* **2** (*fig*) to obtain (something) by force: *extract money/information from a person.* **3** to obtain (juices etc) by pressing, boiling etc: *extract oil from olives.* **4** to select and copy out (words, examples, passages etc) (from a book).

ex·trac·tion /ɪk'strækʃn/ *nc,nu* (**a**) the act of extracting or being extracted(1): *the extraction of a tooth.* (**b**) the origin (of a family): *Is he of French extraction?*

ex·tra·cur·ricu·lar /ˌekstrəkə'rɪkjʊlə(r)/ *adj* outside the regular course of academic work or studies: *extracurricular activities such as sport and drama.*

ex·tra·dite /'ekstrədaɪt/ *vt* **extradite sb (from/to a place)** to send a person (from the country where he or she is living) to the police in a country where he or she is said to have committed a crime.

ex·tra·di·tion /ˌekstrə'dɪʃn/ *nu*

ex·trane·ous /ɪk'streɪnɪəs/ *adj* (*formal*) not belonging (to what is being dealt with); coming from outside: *extraneous information; extraneous interference.*

ex·tra·ordi·nary /ɪk,strɔ:dnrɪ/ *adj* **1** beyond what is usual or ordinary; remarkable: *a person of extraordinary ability; extraordinary weather.* **2** very strange: *an extraordinary remark.*

ex·tra·ordi·nar·ily /ɪk'strɔ:dnrəlɪ/ *adv*: *extraordinarily beautiful.*

ex·trapo·late /ɪk'stræpəleɪt/ *vt* (*formal*) to estimate (something not known) (from known data, information).

ex·trapo·la·tion /ɪk,stræpə'leɪʃn/ *nc,nu*

ex·tra·ter·res·tri·al /ˌekstrətə'restrɪəl/ *adj* from outer space: *extraterrestrial beings.*

ex·trava·gance /ɪk'strævəgəns/ *n* **1** *nu* the act, condition, of being extravagant: *His extravagance explains why he is always in debt.* **2** *nc* something that is extremely expensive: *His new car was an extravagance he could not afford.*

ex·trava·gant /ɪk'strævəgənt/ *adj* **1** (in the habit of) wasting money etc: *an extravagant man; extravagant tastes and habits.* **2** (*derog*) (of ideas, speech, behaviour) going beyond what is reasonable; not properly controlled: *extravagant praise/ behaviour.*

ex·trava·gant·ly *adv*

ex·treme¹ /ɪk'stri:m/ *adj* **1** (*attrib*) at the outer end; farthest possible: *the extreme edge of town.* **2** (*attrib*) (of age etc) at the end: *extreme old age.* **3** of the highest degree, intensity etc: *extreme patience/heat.* **4** very severe: *take extreme measures against terrorism.* **5** (of a person, opinions) going beyond the normal (usually political) limits: *the extreme left/right. She has more*

extreme views than her mother. Compare moderate¹(2).

ex·treme·ly *adv*

ex·treme² /ɪk'stri:m/ *nc* **1** (of behaviour, weather etc) the highest degree: *go from one extreme to the other* (= change from one extreme(3) state, position etc to another). **in the extreme** (used to emphasize a quality, state etc): *annoying in the extreme* (= very annoying). **2** (*pl*) qualities etc as widely different as possible: *the extremes of heat and cold. Love and hate are extremes.* **go/be driven to extremes** to do more than is usually considered right or desirable.

ex·trem·ist /-ɪst/ *adj, nc* (of) a person who holds extreme views (esp in politics).

ex·trem·ity /ɪk'stremətɪ/ *nc* (*pl* **-ies**) (*formal*) **1** extreme point, end or limit: *bad behaviour that reached serious extremities.* **2** *n sing* the highest degree (esp of misery, suffering).

ex·tri·cate /'ekstrɪkeɪt/ *vt* **extricate sb (from sth)** (*formal*) to set (a person, oneself) free (from being held, from an unwanted responsibility etc): *extricating oneself from a difficulty.*

ex·tro·vert /'ekstrəvɜ:t/ *nc* **1** a person more interested in what goes on around her or him than in personal thoughts and feelings. **2** (*informal*) a person who is cheerful and lively and enjoys being with others. Compare introvert.

ex·uber·ance /ɪg'zju:bərəns/ *nu* the state or quality of being exuberant(1): *The speaker's exuberance won over an apathetic audience.*

ex·uber·ant /ɪg'zju:bərənt/ *adj* **1** full of energy, excitement; lively: *an exuberant boy/personality.* **2** (*formal*) growing vigorously: *plants with exuberant foliage.*

ex·uber·ant·ly *adv*

ex·ude /ɪg'zju:d/ *v* (*formal*) **1** *vt,vi* (to cause liquid) to come out slowly: *Sweat exudes through the pores.* **2** *vt* (*fig*) (of a person) to express (a feeling etc) strongly: *He exudes happiness.*

ex·ult /ɪg'zʌlt/ *vi* **exult at/in/over sth** (*formal*) to be very pleased because of (success): *exult at/in a success; exult over a defeated rival.*

ex·ult·ant /-ənt/ *adj* (*formal*) triumphant.

ex·ul·ta·tion /ˌegzʌl'teɪʃn/ *nu*

eye¹ /aɪ/ *nc* **1** one of two parts of the body used for seeing: *She has blue eyes. I've got something in my eye that hurts. Close your eyes and go to sleep.* **an eye for an eye** punishment as severe as the injury suffered. **before one's very eyes** (of a surprising, harmful etc action, done) in one's presence (with no attempt to hide it). **in the eyes of the law** according to the law: *You're still a child in the eyes of the law.* **in the public eye** often seen, discussed etc generally. **through the eyes of sb** from the point of view of a person: *imagine life through the eyes of a child.* **with an eye to sth** hoping for something; with reference to something: *done with an eye to promotion.* **with one eye on sth** giving part of one's attention to something: *with one eye on the clock.* **with one's eyes open/shut** aware/not aware of the difficulties, problems etc: *I warned her not to buy the house but she went into the whole affair with her eyes shut.* **with the naked eye** without using a microscope etc: *Seen with the naked eye, the surface looks flat.* **be all eyes** to be watching eagerly. **be more in it**

than meets the eye to have more serious considerations, problems etc than is immediately obvious. *be a sight for sore eyes* ⇨ sight¹(4). *cast one's eyes over sth* to examine a document etc quickly, not in detail. *catch sb's eye* to obtain a person's attention by signalling. *clap eyes on sb* (*informal*) to meet a person by chance: *I hadn't clapped eyes on her for years.* *close/shut one's eyes to sth* to refuse to notice and respond to bad action, difficulties etc. *cry one's eyes out* (*informal*) to cry very much. *have an eye for sth* to be a good judge of something: *have an eye for a good bargain.* *have eyes for sb* to be attracted to a person: *I only have eyes for you.* *have eyes in the back of one's head* (*informal*) to (seem to) be able to know everything that is happening. *have one's eye on sth* to have seen and want to own something: *I've had my eye on that picture for a long time.* *hit sb in the eye* to be very obvious: *The poverty in the refugee camp/Her beauty hits you in the eye.* *keep your etc eyes off (sth)* (usually *imperative*) (*informal*) to have no hope of getting something: *Keep your eyes off (the food)—that's for me!* *keep an eye on sb/sth* to watch, look after a person, thing: *Please keep an eye on the baby/kettle while I answer the telephone.* *keep an eye open/out (for sb/sth)* (*informal*) to be ready to observe, notice (particular information about) a person, thing: *I need one more piece to make a set so keep an eye out for it while you're shopping.* *lay/set eyes on sb/sth* to see, meet, a person, thing by chance: *If I ever set eyes on another similar dress, I'll buy it.* *(can't) look sb in the eye* to (be unable to) look at a person without feeling embarrassed or ashamed. *make eyes at sb* (*informal*) to show that one is attracted to a person. *open sb's eyes to sth* to cause a person to realize the truth, esp about an enemy, difficulty etc. *run an eye over sth* to examine a document etc quickly, not in detail. *see eye to eye (with sb) (about sth)* to have the same opinion, agree: *We've never seen eye to eye about buying the boat.* *shut one's eyes to* ⇨ close one's eyes to sth. *(can't) take one's eyes off sb/sth* (*informal*) to (be unable to) look away from, ignore, a person, thing, because so beautiful, attractive. *turn a blind eye to sth* to ignore opposition, the rules, a plea etc deliberately. **2** something similar to an eye(1) in shape, size etc: *the eye of a needle* (= the hole for the thread); *an eye of a potato* (= a place where a root grows). ⇨ also private eye.

'**eye·ball** *nc* the eye within the lids and socket.

'**eye·brow** *nc* the hair above the eye. *raise one's eyebrows* to express surprise, doubt etc.

'**eye-catching** *adj* attractive.

'**eye·lash** *nc* a hair or row of hairs on the edge of the eyelid.

'**eye·lid** *nc* the upper or lower skin covering the eye when blinking. *not bat an eyelid* to show no sign of feeling surprise, fear etc.

'**eye-liner** *nc,nu* cosmetic colouring used round the eye.

'**eye-opener** *nc* a circumstance, event etc (often surprising) that makes one realize something: *Finding him kissing my best friend was a real eye-opener for me.*

'**eye-shadow** *nu* cosmetic colouring used on the upper eyelid.

'**eye·sight** *nu* the power, ability, to see: *to have good/poor eyesight.*

'**eye·sore** *nc* something unpleasant to look at: *That new building is an eyesore.*

'**eye-strain** *nu* a tired condition of the eyes.

'**eye·witness** *nc* (also *attrib*) a person who can give evidence of what he or she has seen: *an eye-witness account of a crime.*

eye² /aɪ/ *vt* **1** to observe, watch, (a person, event etc) carefully: *He eyed me with suspicion. They were eyeing us jealously.* **2** (*informal*) to look at (a woman) and show (sexual) attraction.

eye·let /'aɪlɪt/ *nc* a small hole in cloth etc used for putting a rope etc through.

Ff

F, f /ef/ (*pl* **F's, f's** /efs/) the sixth letter of the English alphabet.

F *symbol* Fahrenheit.

f *written abbr* female; feminine.

FA /ˌef ˈeɪ/ *abbr* (the —) the Football Association.

fab /fæb/ *adj* (*informal*) = fabulous(1).

fable /'feɪbl/ *n* **1** *nc* a short story that teaches a moral, esp one with animals in it. **2** *nc,nu* (a) myth; legend. ⇨ fabulous(2).

fabled /'feɪbld/ *adj* well-known in legends.

fab·ric /'fæbrɪk/ *nc,nu* **1** (a kind of) cloth: *woollen/silk fabrics.* **2** (*fig*) the (method of) structure (of society, of a committee etc).

fab·ri·cate /'fæbrɪkeɪt/ *vt* (*formal*) to make up (something false): *fabricating excuses/a lie.*

fab·ri·ca·tion /ˌfæbrɪ'keɪʃn/ *nc,nu.*

fabu·lous /'fæbjʊləs/ *adj* **1** (*informal*) (abbr fab) (of a performance, performer, new design etc) wonderful; excellent: *a fabulous production of 'Othello'.* **2** existing in a story, myth or legend: *fabulous beasts in children's literature.* ⇨ fable(2).

fabu·lous·ly *adv* extremely: *fabulously rich.*

fa·çade (also **fa·cade**) /fə'sɑːd/ *nc* **1** the front (of a building). **2** (*fig*) a false appearance: *a façade of indifference.*

face¹ /feɪs/ *nc* **1** the front part of the head (from the forehead to the chin): *a round, spotty face; a pretty/ugly face.* ⇨ facial. *face to face (with sb/sth)* physically opposite with the face towards the other: *standing face to face. They met face to face on television. Suddenly I came face to face with an angry dog.* *full face* with all the face visible (e.g. in a photograph). *to sb's face* directly, not in a letter or through another person: *I disapprove and I'll tell her so to her face. until one is blue in the face* for as long as one has strength (suggesting that success, a result etc is impossible): *You can argue until you are blue in the face but I'll never agree. fall flat on one's face* to fall forward onto the ground with the face downwards: *He fell flat on his face in the mud. go blue/red in the face* to become angry or cold/ embarrassed or ashamed. *have a red face* to be embarrassed, ashamed etc. *laugh in sb's face* to show one's lack of respect, dislike etc openly.

look sb in the face to look at a person without showing fear, embarrassment, shame etc. **put one's face on** (*informal*) to put on make-up. **show one's face** to allow oneself to be seen: *Don't you dare show your face in here again!* **stare sb in the face (a)** to look defiantly at a person. **(b)** (of a disaster, truth, explanation etc) to be very obvious or clear: *Defeat stared her in the face.* **throw sth in sb's face** to be deliberately unkind by reminding a person about something embarrassing, insulting etc: *Everyone knew his mother had been to prison, but his wife continued to throw it in his face.* **2** a look; expression: *a kind/sad face.* **a long face** a miserable expression. **keep a straight face** to hide one's amusement by not smiling or laughing: *When I saw her hat I could hardly keep a straight face.* **lose face** to lose one's reputation (and feel ashamed): *He pretended his parents were rich in order not to lose face.* **make/pull a face/faces (at sb)** to make an amusing, ugly etc expression. **put on a bold/brave face** to make oneself appear courageous (although one is afraid). **save (one's) face** to avoid losing one's reputation, being made to feel ashamed: *To save face she never invited her friends to her poor home.* Hence **'face-saving** *adj*. **3** the main side or front (of a building, object etc): *a clock face; the face of a mountain; a cliff face. Put the cards face down on the table.* **4** a surface: *the two faces of a coin/all six faces of a cube; the face of the earth.* **at (its/their) face value** according to its apparent value, meaning etc (suggesting that this may not be the real value, meaning etc): *At face value the two statements seem to contradict each other.* **5** (outward) appearance: *the unacceptable face of capitalism.* **on the face of it** judging by first appearances: *On the face of it, his excuse seems reasonable.* **change the face of sth** to make it very different: *Computers have changed the face of industry.* **fly in the face of sth** to oppose something that is usual, reasonable: *Wearing colourful clothes in tennis tournaments is flying in the face of tradition.*

'face-ache *nc* (*fig; derog*) an annoying person.

'face-cloth *nc* a small square towel used for washing the face and hands.

'face-cream *nu* a kind of cream for cleaning and softening the face.

face·less *adj* (*fig*) unknown to the public: *the faceless leaders of commerce and industry.*

'face-lift *nc* **(a)** a form of surgery to make the face look younger. **(b)** (*fig*) an improvement to the appearance (of a building etc).

'face-powder *nu* cosmetic powder for the face.

'face-saving *adj* ⇨ face¹(2).

face² /feɪs/ *v* **1** *vt,vi* to have, turn the face(1,3) in the direction or position mentioned: *Turn round and face me. Don't face the camera towards the sun. All the gardens face away from the motorway. My bedroom faces onto the street. The soldiers faced left as the President passed.* **2** *vt* to be opposite: *face the park; facing page 219.* **3** *vt* to meet (with confidence): *face the enemy; face the problem.* **face facts** ⇨ fact(2). **Let's face it.** Let's accept it as true: *Let's face it—you're a bad swimmer.* **face the music** ⇨ music(1). **face sth out** to act with courage etc (and ignore criticism etc): *He was ashamed to meet his friends after being released from prison but decided to go home and face it out.* **face up to sth** to accept and cope with something unpleasant: *She had to face up to the fact that she was no longer young.* **4** *vt* (of a difficulty etc) to present itself to a person: *recognize the problems facing us.* **5** *vt* to cover a flat surface with a layer of a different material: *a wall faced with concrete.* ⇨ facing.

fac·et /'fæsɪt/ *nc* **1** one of the many sides of a cut stone or jewel. **2** (*fig*) a point of view, part, e.g. of a problem.

fa·cetious /fə'siːʃəs/ *adj* (trying to be) amusing (esp about something serious): *a facetious remark about an important problem; a facetious young man.*

fa·cetious·ly *adv*

fa·cial /'feɪʃl/ *adj* (*attrib*) of or for the face: *facial cream; a facial massage.*

fa·cile /'fæsaɪl/ *adj* (*formal; derog*) **1** too easily done or obtained: *a facile victory.* **2** (of speech or writing) done easily but without real meaning or quality: *a facile remark/comment.*

fa·cili·tate /fə'sɪlɪteɪt/ *vt* (*formal*) (of machines, equipment) to lessen the difficulty of (an activity, process): *Modern inventions have facilitated housework.*

fa·cil·ity /fə'sɪlətɪ/ *n* (*pl* **-ies**) **1** *nc,nu* (an) ability, esp one that makes learning or doing things easy: *This electronic typewriter has the facility to draw graphs.* **2** *nc* (usually *pl*) a service, piece of equipment etc that makes it possible or easy to do things: *sports facilities such as swimming pools.*

fac·ing /'feɪsɪŋ/ *nc* a covering of a different material: *a facing of concrete.* ⇨ face²(5).

fac·sim·ile /fæk'sɪməlɪ/ *nc* an exact copy or reproduction of writing, a picture etc.

fact /fækt/ *n* **1** *nc* something that has happened or been done: *I need all the facts before I can decide who was responsible.* **2** *nc* something known to be true or able to be proved: *Is it a fact that God exists? Gravity is a scientific fact. I'm never going there again and that's a fact!* **the facts of life** (*informal*) how babies are conceived and born. **face facts** to accept something (unpleasant) as true: *Let's face facts, I'll never be a millionaire.* **3** *nc* a piece of information: *learn all the facts needed to pass the exam.* **facts and figures** full and exact information. **4** *nu* the truth; reality: *It's important to distinguish between fact and fiction.* Opp fiction(1). **as a matter of fact; in (actual) fact; in point of fact** (used to emphasize one's belief that something is true or certain): *I think I saw him—in fact I'm certain.* **the fact of the matter is . . .** the truth is . . .

'fact-finding *adj* (*attrib*) designed to discover what is true: *a fact-finding tour/committee.*

fac·tion /'fækʃn/ *n* **1** *nc* a group of people in a larger group (e.g. a political party) with different views, often ones that suit their own interests. **2** *nu* quarrelling among such groups.

fac·tor /'fæktə(r)/ *nc* **1** a fact, circumstance etc causing or influencing a result: *a major factor in making a decision; an unknown factor* (= something unknown that could influence a result). **2** (*maths*) a whole number (except 1) by which a larger number can be divided exactly: *2, 3, 4 and 6* *are factors of 12.*

fac·tory /'fæktərɪ/ *nc* (*pl* **-ies**) (also *attrib*) a building or buildings where goods are made (esp by machinery): *factory workers.*

fac·tu·al /'fæktʃʊəl/ *adj* concerned with, using, fact: *a factual report.* Compare fictional.

fac·ul·ty /'fækəltɪ/ *nc* (*pl* **-ies**) **1** a natural ability to do things: *one's mental faculties. I'll need all my faculties to understand this.* **2** (also F-) (in a university) (members of) a particular department or group of related departments: *the Faculty of Science; the Law Faculty.*

fad /fæd/ *nc* (*informal*) a brief fashion, interest: *Pointed shoes were/Her love was only a passing fad.*

fade /feɪd/ *v* **1** *vt,vi* (to cause something) to lose colour, freshness or strength: *The strong sunlight had faded the curtains. Flowers soon fade when cut.* **2** *vi* **fade (away)** to go slowly out of view, hearing or the memory: *Daylight faded away. His hopes faded.* **3** *vi* **fade away** (of a person) to die slowly. **4** *vt,vi* **fade (sth) (in/out)** (in filming, broadcasting) (to cause sound/a picture) to decrease or increase in strength: *fading a conversation out/in.*

fae·ces (*US*= **fe·ces**) /'fiːsiːz/ *n pl* (*formal*) solid waste matter from the body.

fag /fæg/ *n* **1** *n sing* a tiring job: *What a fag! It's too much of a fag.* **2** *nc* (*sl*) a cigarette.

fag·ged /fægd/ *adj* (*pred*) (*informal*) very tired.

fag·got (*US* also **fag·ot**) /'fægət/ *nc* **1** a bundle of sticks or twigs tied together for burning as fuel. **2** a kind of meatball.

Fahr·en·heit /'færənhaɪt/ *adj* (symbol F) in or of a temperature scale with freezing-point at 32° (32°F) and boiling-point at 212° (212°F). Compare Centigrade.

fail¹ /feɪl/ *n* (only in) **without fail** for certain, no matter what difficulties etc there may be: *I'll come at two o'clock without fail.*

fail² /feɪl/ *v* **1** *vt,vi* to be unsuccessful: *fail (in) an examination; fail to pass an examination. All our plans/attempts failed.* Opp succeed(1). ⇨ failure. **2** *vt* (of examiners) to decide that (a candidate) has been unsuccessful. **3** *vt,vi* to not provide enough, the expected result: *The crops failed because of drought. Words fail me.* **4** *vi* (of health, eyesight etc) to become weak: *His eyesight is failing.* **5** *vt* **fail to do sth** to not do or remember it: *They failed to arrive on time. He never fails to write* (= always writes) *to his mother every week.*

fail-safe /'feɪl seɪf/ *adj* (of machinery) able to be in a safe state if it stops working.

fail·ing¹ /'feɪlɪŋ/ *nc* a weakness or fault (of character): *We all have our little failings.*

fail·ing² /'feɪlɪŋ/ *prep* in the absence of: *failing this* (= if this does not happen)*; failing an answer* (= if no answer is received)*.*

fail·ure /'feɪljə(r)/ *n* **1** *nc,nu* (an instance of) being unsuccessful: *Success came after many failures. All his efforts ended in failure.* **2** *nc* a person who is unsuccessful: *I was a failure as a singer.* **3** *nc,nu* (an instance of) the state of failing(3): *heart failure. Failure of crops often results in famine.* **4** *nc,nu* (an example of) an occasion of not doing something: *His failure to help us was disappointing.* **5** a breakdown (of machinery, power etc): *an engine failure.*

faint¹ /feɪnt/ *adj* (**—er, —est**) **1** (of things known by the senses) weak; not clear: *The sounds of the music grew fainter in the distance. There was a faint smell of burning. I saw a faint light.* **2** (of things in the mind) weak; vague: *There is a faint hope that she may be cured. I haven't the faintest idea what you mean.* **3** (of the body's movements and functions) weak: *His breathing became faint.* **4** (of a person) about to lose consciousness: *She looks/feels faint.*

faint-'hearted *adj* having no courage. Compare stout-hearted.

faint·ly *adv*

faint² /feɪnt/ *nc* an act of losing consciousness: *fall down in a faint.*

faint³ /feɪnt/ *vi* to lose consciousness: *He fainted from the heat. She was fainting with hunger.*

fair¹ /feə(r)/ *adj* (**—er, —est**) **1** acting in a just and honest way; in accordance with justice or the rules (of a game etc): *Everyone must have a fair share. To be fair, she did apologize.* Opp unfair. **fair's fair** (*informal*) (used to show that one believes one has the right to something as repayment). **fair play** just and honest action: *I'm here to see fair play during the inquiry.* **2** average; quite good: *a fair chance of success.* **3** (of the weather) good; dry and fine: *hoping for fair weather.* **4** (of the skin, hair) light in colour: *fair-haired; a fair skin.*

fair-'minded *adj* acting justly.

fair 'play *nu* (*fig*) equally just treatment for all.

fair·ish /'feərɪʃ/ *adj* of average size, weight or quality.

fair·ness *nu* (esp) **in all fairness** to be fair(1): *In all fairness, she did warn you.*

fair² /feə(r)/ *adv* in a fair(1) manner. **play fair** to act justly. **fair enough** (*informal*) (used to show agreement, that a person has been reasonable, made a reasonable suggestion etc): *Fair enough, you deserve a holiday.* **fair and square** in a just and honest way: *They beat us fair and square*

fair³ /feə(r)/ *nc* **1** a market (esp for cattle, sneep, farm products etc). **2** a group of large machines, games etc used for public entertainment, travelling from place to place. **3** a large exhibition of commercial goods: *a world fair.*

'fair-ground *nc* an open space used for fairs(2).

fair·ly /'feəlɪ/ *adv* **1** justly; honestly: *treat him fairly.* **2** to a considerable extent; more than a little: *This is a fairly easy exam. I know Jim fairly well.*

fairy /'feərɪ/ *nc* (*pl* **-ies**) a small imaginary being with supernatural powers, able to help or harm human beings.

'fairy-land *nc* the home of fairies.

'fairy-story/-tale *nc* (**a**) a tale about fairies. (**b**) an untrue excuse, story, esp told by a child.

fait ac·com·pli /ˌfeɪt əkɒmˈpliː/ *nc* (*Fr*) something that has happened or been done and cannot be changed.

faith /feɪθ/ *n* **1** *nu* trust; unquestioning confidence: *I haven't much faith in this medicine.* **2** *nc,nu* (a system of) strong belief in divine truth: *the Christian, Jewish and Muslim faiths.* **3** *nu* loyalty; sincerity. **in bad/good faith** with/without the intention of deceiving: *She acted in good faith.*

'faith-healing *nu* (the belief in) the healing (of

disease etc) by using prayer etc.

faith·ful /'feɪθfəl/ adj **1** **faithful (to sb/sth)** loyal and true: *a faithful friend; be faithful to one's promise.* Opp unfaithful. **2** (attrib) true to the facts: *a faithful copy/description/account.*

faith·ful·ly /-fəlɪ/ adv in a faithful way: *I promise faithfully to come.* **Yours faithfully** (a formula used to end a formal letter).

faith·less /'feɪθlɪs/ adj (derog) disloyal.

faith·less·ly adv

fake¹ /feɪk/ adj not genuine: *fake furs.*

fake² /feɪk/ nc **1** a work of art etc that looks genuine but is not. **2** a person who tries to deceive by claiming falsely to be or have something.

fake³ /feɪk/ vt to make (e.g. a work of art) in order to deceive: *faking an oil-painting.*

fal·con /'fɔ:lkən/ nc a kind of small bird of prey trained to hunt and kill other small animals.

fall¹ /fɔ:l/ nc (⇨ also falls) **1** an act of falling: *a fall from a horse.* **break sb's/sth's fall** to reduce the force of a fall, e.g. by putting out one's hand, holding a branch etc. **2** **fall (in sth)** a decrease (in value, amount etc): *a sharp fall in prices/temperature.* Opp rise¹(2). **3** a reverse in progress: *a fall in social position.* Opp rise¹(3). **4** something that falls: *a heavy/light fall of rain/snow.* **5** an amount, distance, by which something falls or comes down: *The fall of the river is six metres.* **6** (the —) (US) autumn: *in the fall of 1970.*

fall² /fɔ:l/ vi (pt fell /fel/, pp —en /'fɔ:lən/) **1** to come, go, down to a lower level: *The climber lost her grip and fell. The apples begin to fall in August. The car had fallen 10 metres down the hillside. The rain was falling hard.* Compare rise²(1). **2** to be suddenly no longer standing: *He tripped over and fell. She has fallen and broken her leg. Did you hurt yourself when you fell?* **fall flat** (a) to be completely horizontal after falling: *She fell flat on her face.* (b) (of jokes, an attempt to persuade etc) to have no effect: *Even his best jokes fell flat.* **3** to use (a part of) the face to look sad, disappointed, ashamed etc: *His face fell when he read the report. Her eyes fell to the ground.* **4** to go down and break: *It fell in two/in pieces.* ⇨ fall apart. **5** to become less in quantity, size, degree etc: *The temperature fell sharply. Prices are falling. Standards seem to be falling.* **fall short (of sth)** ⇨ short²(2). **6** (of hair etc) to hang down: *Soft curls fell on her shoulders.* **7** (of a person) to be killed by an enemy: *My father fell during the war.* **8** (of a town etc) to be captured by an enemy: *The city fell quickly to the invading troops.* **9** (of a government) to be defeated, become unable to continue working. **10** to become (the condition mentioned): *She's fallen ill. He fell asleep/silent.* **11** to occur: *Night fell. Pay day falls late this month.* ⇨ fall on sth.

fall about (laughing/with laughter) (informal) to laugh a great deal.

fall apart (a) (of a structure, arrangement etc) to break into pieces: *The cup fell apart in my hands. Their marriage has fallen apart.* (b) (of a person) to lose self-control (because of personal or mental problems).

fall away (a) (of land etc) to slope away from a point. (b) (of a level of production, demand etc) to become less. (c) (of support, confidence etc) to disappear.

fall back to move to a position farther back or behind: *He fell back to defend the goal.* **fall back on sb/sth** to turn to, use, a person, thing for support when in difficulties: *We have enough money to fall back on if the cost increases. If this plan fails, is there another we can fall back on?*

fall behind (sb/sth) (of a competitor) to fail to keep level with another: *The runner fell behind the others. Our company is in danger of falling behind our competitors/overseas competition.* **fall behind (with sth)** to fail to pay, produce, something by the agreed, required, time: *He's fallen behind with his payments.*

fall below sth (of a level, standard etc) to fail to reach the agreed, required, level: *Production has fallen below expectations.*

fall down (a) to be suddenly no longer standing: *She fell down in the street.* (b) (of a structure) to collapse: *The tent/tree fell down in the storm.*

fall for sb/sth (informal) to be very attracted to a person, thing: *She falls for every man she sees. He falls for any ideas suggested by his boss.* **fall for sth** to believe it: *Tell him your car wouldn't start—I'm sure he'll fall for it. Do you expect me to fall for that old excuse?*

fall from sth to lose a powerful position: *He fell from power when the government changed.*

fall in (of part of a structure) to collapse: *The roof has fallen in.* **fall in love (with sb/sth)** ⇨ love¹(1). **fall in with sb/sth** to show one's support for a person, thing: *She realized her company would not win the contract and fell in with its rivals. He fell in with my plans.*

fall into sth (a) to go down into something: *fall into the water.* (b) (of a report etc) to be divided into parts etc: *My lecture falls into four main parts.* (c) (to begin to) have something: *fall into the habit of being late/bad habits; fall into conversation with a neighbour.* (d) to become the strong, serious state mentioned: *fall into a deep sleep/a coma; fall into decay/a decline.* **fall into line (with sb/sth)** ⇨ line¹(10). **fall into place** ⇨ place¹(1).

fall off (a) (of part of a structure) to break and go down: *The handle/My button has fallen off.* (b) (of a quantity) to become less: *Sales/Profits/ Attendances have fallen off recently.* (c) (of standards) to become worse: *The quality of their goods has definitely fallen off.*

fall on sb/sth (a) to attack a person, place etc: *The army fell on the town.* (b) (of a cost, expense, responsibility) to be borne by a person etc: *It fell on me to pay the fees.* **fall on sth** to occur on the day mentioned: *My birthday falls on a Friday this year.* **fall on one's feet** ⇨ foot¹(1).

fall out (of sth) to go down from an enclosed place to a lower level: *fall out of bed/the window.* **fall out (with sb)** (informal) to quarrel (with): *I've fallen out with my friend over the money. My girlfriend and I have fallen out.* **fall out of love (with sb)** ⇨ love¹(1).

fall outside sth (of a problem, question etc) to not be part of one's responsibility, area of interest or ability etc: *That problem falls outside the agreed terms of this inquiry.* ⇨ fall within sth.

fall over (a) (of a person) to be suddenly no longer standing. (b) (of an object) to become horizontal suddenly: *The lamp fell over.* **fall**

over backwards to do sth (*informal*) to take great care, try very hard: *She fell over backwards to show that he was forgiven.*

fall through (*informal*) (of a plan, agreement etc) to fail.

fall to to begin to eat or fight (with great energy): *The children fell to with a great appetite.*

fall to bits ⇨ bit².

fall under sth (**a**) (of an item or part in a report etc) to be placed in the position or category mentioned: *That item falls under 'correspondence' in the agenda.* (**b**) (of a person) to be strongly influenced, attracted, by something: *fall under their influence/control/spell.*

fall upon sb/sth (*formal*) = fall on sb/sth.

fall within sth (of a problem, question etc) to be part of one's responsibility, area of interest or ability: *The decision about prices falls within my section's control.* ⇨ fall outside sth.

fal·la·cious /fəˈleɪʃəs/ *adj* (*no comp*) (*formal*) (of an argument etc) wrong because based on error.

fal·la·cy /ˈfæləsɪ/ *n* (*pl* **-ies**) **1** *nc* a false or mistaken belief. **2** *nu* false reasoning or argument: *a statement based on fallacy.*

fal·len /ˈfɔːlən/ **1** *pp* of fall². **2** *n pl* (the —) people who have died (in a war).

fal·lible /ˈfæləbəl/ *adj* (of a person) liable to make errors. Opp infallible.

fal·li·bil·ity /ˌfæləˈbɪlətɪ/ *nu*

fal·ling /ˈfɔːlɪŋ/ *adj* (*attrib*) **falling action** (*literature*) the part of a story or drama (after the climax) when the leading character suffers (before the final catastrophe or resolution). Compare rising action.

Fal·lo·pian tube /fəˌləʊpɪən ˈtjuːb/ *nc* (*anat*) either of two tubes connecting the ovaries to the uterus.

fall-out¹ /ˈfɔːl aʊt/ *adj* (*attrib*) **1** containing, concerning fall-out: *a fall-out shelter.* **2** referring to people who leave a course of study, membership of a society etc: *a fall-out rate among science students.* ⇨ drop out.

fall-out² /ˈfɔːl aʊt/ *nu* radioactive dust in the atmosphere after a nuclear explosion etc: *dangerous levels of fall-out near a nuclear power station.*

fal·low /ˈfæləʊ/ *adj, nu* (land) ploughed but not sown or planted: *allow land to lie fallow.*

falls /fɔːlz/ *n pl* (F- in names) a place where a river falls down a steep slope: *Boyoma Falls. The falls stop boats from using the river.*

false /fɔːls/ *adj* **1** not true; incorrect: *a false statement; a false arrest.* **make a false start** (*athletics*) to start before the signal has been given. **2** not loyal or faithful: *be false to a friend; give a false impression.* Opp true¹(2). **3** not genuine; artificial: *false teeth.* **a false alarm** ⇨ alarm¹(1).

false·ly *adv*

false·hood /ˈfɔːlshʊd/ *nc* (*formal*) a lie (the usual word): *How can you utter such falsehoods?*

fal·si·fy /ˈfɔːlsɪfaɪ/ *vt* (*pt,pp* **-ied**) to make (something) false: *falsify records/accounts.*

falsi·fi·ca·tion /ˌfɔːlsɪfɪˈkeɪʃn/ *nc,nu*

fal·ter /ˈfɔːltə(r)/ *vi* **1** to move, walk or act in an uncertain or hesitating manner, from either weakness or fear. **2** (of a person) to speak in a hesitating way or with a broken voice: *He faltered as he asked for mercy.*

fal·ter·ing·ly *adv*

fame /feɪm/ *nu* (the condition of) being known or talked about by all; what people say (esp good) about a person: *His fame as a poet did not come until after his death.*

fam·ed *adj* (*pred*) famous: *famed for their courage.*

fam·il·iar /fəˈmɪlɪə(r)/ *adj* **1** **familiar (to sb)** well known to a person: *facts that are familiar to everybody.* Opp unfamiliar. **2** **familiar with sth** having a good knowledge of something: *I am not very familiar with European history.* Opp unfamiliar. **3** common; usual; often seen or heard: *the familiar voices of one's friends.* Opp unfamiliar. **4** close and friendly: *Are you on familiar terms with Mr Green? He got much too familiar with my wife.*

fam·il·iar·ly *adv*

fam·ili·ar·ity /fəˌmɪlɪˈærətɪ/ *n* (*pl* **-ies**) *nu* **1** **familiarity (with sth)** the state of being familiar: *His familiarity with the languages used in Nigeria surprised me.* **2** the state of being (too) friendly: *You should not treat her with such familiarity.* ⇨ familiar(4).

fam·ili·ar·ize (also **-ise**) /fəˈmɪlɪəraɪz/ *vt* **1** **familiarize oneself/sb (with sth)** to make oneself, a person, know (something) well: *familiarize oneself with the rules.* **2** to make (something) well known: *Television has familiarized the word 'newscast'.*

fam·ily /ˈfæmlɪ/ *n* (*pl* **-ies**) **1** *nc* (also *attrib*) parents and children: *How many families live in that house? I enjoy family life.* (N) *'Family'* is used with a sing verb when it is a collective noun, as in *Almost every family in the village grows vegetables,* and it is used with a pl verb when *it* means 'members of my family', as in *My family are early risers.* **2** *nc,nu* a set of children: *He has a large family.* **3** *nc* all those people with the same ancestors: *families that have been in the US for two hundred years.* **run in one's/the family** to be a characteristic of one's ancestors: *Red hair runs in our family.* **4** *nc* a group of living things (plants, animals etc) or of languages, with common characteristics and a common source: *animals of the cat family* (e.g. lions and tigers).

family 'doctor *nc* a general practitioner.

'family ,name *nc* = surname.

,family 'planning *nu* (the use of birth control for) planning the number of children in a family.

,family 'tree *nc* a plan of the way members of a family(3) are related.

fam·ine /ˈfæmɪn/ *n* **1** *nu* (an almost) complete lack of food in a region: *Parts of India have often suffered from famine.* **2** *nc* a particular occasion when there is such a condition: *a rice famine.*

fam·ish·ed /ˈfæmɪʃt/ *adj* very hungry.

fa·mous /ˈfeɪməs/ *adj* known widely; having fame: *a famous scientist.* Compare infamous.

fa·mous·ly /ˈfeɪməslɪ/ *adv* (*informal*) very well: *The two children are getting on famously.*

fan¹ /fæn/ *nc* **1** a machine or instrument used for making a current of air (e.g. to cool a room). **2** something that is or can be spread out flat, e.g. the tail of a peacock.

'fan belt *nc* a rubber belt used to turn the cooling-fan of an engine.

'fan heater *nc* a heater that blows hot air.

fan² /fæn/ v (**-nn-**) **1** vt to send a current of air onto (a person, thing): *fan oneself. The breeze fanned our faces.* **2** vi **fan out** to spread out: *The police fanned out across the fields.*

fan³ /fæn/ nc (*informal*) a very keen supporter: *football fans.*

'fan mail nu letters from fans, e.g. to a pop star.

fa·nat·ic /fə'nætɪk/ adj, nc (of) a person with excessive enthusiasm: *a health fanatic.*

fa·nati·cal /-kl/ adj

fa·nati·cal·ly /-klɪ/ adv

fan·ci·ful /'fænsɪfəl/ adj (*formal*) **1** (of a person) led by imagination instead of reason and experience: *a fanciful writer.* **2** unreal and strange: *fanciful drawings.*

fan·ci·ful·ly /-fəlɪ/ adv

fan·cy¹ /'fænsɪ/ adj **1** (*attrib*) (esp of small things) brightly coloured; made to please the eye: *fancy cakes.* **2** not plain or ordinary: *fancy dress* (= unusual costume as worn at parties).

fan·cy² /'fænsɪ/ n (*pl* **-ies**) **1** nu the ability to create images in the mind. Ⓝ *'Imagination'* means the activity as well as the ability and is used much more often than *'fancy'.* **2** nc a vague opinion or idea: *I have a fancy that she will be late.* **3** nc **fancy for sth** a desire for something: *I have a fancy for some wine with my dinner.* **4** nc **take a fancy to sb** to become fond of a person: *The children have taken quite a fancy to you.*

,fancy-'free adj (*pred*) not taking one's life, other people, seriously.

fan·cy³ /'fænsɪ/ vt (*pt,pp* **-ied**) **1 fancy oneself/sb as sb** to picture oneself, a person, in the mind as another: *Can you fancy me as a mother?* Ⓝ *'Imagine'* is also possible and is more usual. **2 fancy oneself (as sb)** to have a too high opinion of oneself (and imagine oneself to be a special person): *He fancies himself as an orator.* **3** (used to express surprise): *Fancy her saying such unkind things about you! Fancy that!* **4** to have a desire for something: *What do you fancy to eat/for dinner?* Ⓝ *'Imagine'* is not possible.

fan·fare /'fænfeə(r)/ nc a series of notes played loudly on trumpets or bugles.

fang /fæŋ/ nc a long, sharp tooth, e.g. of a snake.

fan·tas·tic /fæn'tæstɪk/ adj **1** wild and strange: *fantastic dreams/shapes/fashions.* **2** (of ideas, plans) impossible to carry out: *fantastic proposals.* **3** (*informal*) marvellous; wonderful: *She's a really fantastic girl!*

fan·tas·ti·cal·ly /-klɪ/ adv

fan·ta·sy /'fæntəsɪ/ n (*pl* **-ies**) **1** nu (also *attrib*) wild or extravagant creative thought or mental pictures: *She seems to live in a world of fantasy/a fantasy world.* Ⓝ *'Imagination'* does not include any idea of 'wild' or 'extravagant'. **2** nc a wild or strange product of the imagination.

FAO /,ef eɪ 'əʊ/ abbr Food and Agriculture Organization (of the United Nations).

far¹ /fɑ:r/ adj (*attrib*) (*comp* **farther** /'fɑ:ðə(r)/ or **further** /'fɜ:ðə(r)/, *superl* **farthest** /'fɑ:ðɪst/ or **furthest** /'fɜ:ðɪst/) **1** more distant: *on the far side of the river; at the far end of the room; in the far north. The farther north one travels, the colder it gets.* Ⓝ The comparative and superlative forms are not usually used except for examples such as the last one above. *'Farther'* and *'farthest'* are more usual than *'further'* or *'furthest'* when referring to distance.

Compare **near¹.** **2** (*no comp*) (*literary*) distant: *travel to a far country; pottery from far places.* Ⓝ *'Faraway'* is now more usual.

'far·away adj (*no comp*) (**a**) distant: *a faraway place.* (**b**) (of an expression) vague as if thinking of other things: *a faraway look in her eyes.*

,Far 'East n (the —) the countries of eastern Asia (e.g. China, Japan).

,far-'fetched adj (of an idea, excuse etc) difficult to believe, agree with, because almost certainly impossible.

,far-'flung adj widely distributed: *far-flung influence.*

,far 'gone adj very ill, mad, drunk etc.

'far-off adj distant: *far-off days.*

,far-'reaching adj having a wide influence, range, effect etc: *far-reaching decisions/plans.*

,far-'sighted adj (**a**) able to see distant objects more clearly than near ones. (**b**) (*fig*) having good judgement of future possibilities etc. Compare short-sighted, long-sighted.

far² /fɑ:r/ adv (*comp* **farther** /'fɑ:ðə(r)/ or **further** /'fɜ:ðə(r)/, *superl* **farthest** /'fɑ:ðɪst/ or **furthest** /'fɜ:ðɪst/) **1** (of space) at, from, to, a distance: *They couldn't travel very far yesterday. How far is it (from here)? It isn't far. How far did you get? Would you travel as far in such an old car?* Ⓝ *'Far'* is usually used in negative statements and questions. For affirmative statements use *'a long way',* as in *It's a long way from here. We've travelled a long way.* *'Farther'* and *'farthest'* are more usual than *'further'* or *'furthest'* when referring to distance. Compare **near².** **far and near/wide** everywhere: over a wide area: *search/travel far and wide.* **go far** (**a**) to be (almost) enough: *£1 doesn't go far these days.* (**b**) (of a person) to make good progress in life: *That boy will go far.* **go too far** (of a person) to go beyond the limits of acceptable behaviour. **2** (by) very much: *far better/richer. She's far too intelligent for me. It fell far short of expectations.* **far and away** by a very large amount: *far and away the best.* **3** (used with other *advs* or *preps*) a long length in space or time: *They sailed far away. I could see a light far off on the horizon. We were left far out at sea. He reads far into the night.* **as far as** (**a**) up to (a point, place, mentioned): *as far as the post office.* (**b**) up to the same point as: *We went as far as the others.* (**c**) (suggesting a limit) to the extent that: *As far as I know he'll be in London next week.* **far from** + *adj* (**a**) not at all: *Your work is far from satisfactory.* (**b**) more the opposite than the same as: *It's far from easy. Far from enjoying the music, I hated it.* **by far** by a large amount: *That's by far the best/the best by far.* **so far** up to this point, moment: *So far the work has been easy. I'm with you so far* (= I can understand). **so far as** = as far as (**c**). **so far, so good** up to now everything is progressing well.

farce /fɑ:s/ n **1** nc,nu (*literature*) (the style of) a play using exaggerated and ridiculous situations to make people laugh. **2** nc an important or serious event treated lightly or wrongly: *The trial was a farce.*

far·ci·cal /'fɑ:sɪkl/ adj

far·ci·cal·ly /-klɪ/ adv

fare¹ /feə(r)/ nc **1** a cost of a journey by bus, ship, taxi etc. **2** a paying passenger: *The taxi-driver had* *only six fares all day.*

fare² /feə(r)/ *nu* (*dated*) food.

fare³ /feə(r)/ *vi* (*formal*) to get on (e.g. badly, well): *How did you fare at the interview? We fared better than we'd hoped.*

fare·well /ˌfeə'wel/ *int* (*literary*) goodbye. □ *nc* (also *attrib*) an act of saying goodbye: *make one's farewells; a farewell speech.*

farm¹ /fɑːm/ *nc* **1** (also *attrib*) an area of land and its buildings, used for growing crops, raising animals etc: *working on the farm; farm animals.* **2** a farmer's house.

'farm·yard *nc* a space surrounded by farm buildings.

farm² /fɑːm/ *v* **1** *vi,vt* to use (land) for growing crops, raising animals, etc. *He farms 200 acres.* **2** *vt* **farm sth out** to send work etc out to be done by others.

farm·er /'fɑːmə(r)/ *nc* a person who owns or manages a farm.

far·ther¹ /'fɑːðə(r)/ *adj* (*comp* of far) at, to, a greater distance: *on the farther shore.*

far·ther² /'fɑːðə(r)/ *adv* (*comp* of far) at, to, a greater distance: *We can't go any farther without a rest. They went farther into the forest.*

far·thest /'fɑːðɪst/ *adv, adj* (*superl* of far) at, to, the greatest distance: *Which town is farthest from the coast?*

far·thing /'fɑːðɪŋ/ *nc* a former GB coin worth one quarter of a penny(2).

fas·cia /'feɪʃə/ *nc* **1** = dashboard. **2** (*GB*) a flat piece of wood or stone on the outside of a building.

fas·ci·nate /'fæsɪneɪt/ *vt* (often *passive*) to charm or attract (a person) greatly: *The children were fascinated by the exhibition.*

fas·ci·nat·ing *adj* very attractive, interesting: *a fascinating smile/idea/girl.*

fas·ci·na·tion /ˌfæsɪ'neɪʃn/ *nc,nu*

Fas·cism /'fæʃɪzəm/ *nu* a political system with strong government control, strong nationalism and cruel opposition to socialists.

Fas·cist /'fæʃɪst/ *adj* of, like, Fascism, □ *nc* a supporter of, believer in, Fascism.

fash·ion¹ /'fæʃn/ *n* **1** *nc,nu* (of clothes) the style considered the best during a period or at a place: *dressed in the latest fashion.* **in fashion** fashionable. **come into fashion** to become fashionable. **(go) out of fashion** (to become) no longer fashionable: *When did pointed shoes go out of fashion?* **2** *n sing* a way of doing something: *behave in a strange fashion.* **after a fashion** not particularly well: *He can speak Italian after a fashion.*

fash·ion² /'fæʃn/ *vt* (*formal*) to design, make, shape, (an object): *fashion a bowl out of clay.*

fash·ion·able /'fæʃənəbl/ *adj* **1** following the latest fashion(1): *a fashionable dress/woman.* **2** used, visited, by many people: *a fashionable summer resort.* Opp unfashionable. ⇨ also old-fashioned.

fash·ion·ably /-əblɪ/ *adv*

fast¹ /fɑːst/ *adj* (**—er, —est**) **1** (capable of) acting, moving etc, taking a short time: *a fast train/worker; the fast lane of the motorway* (= one allowing vehicles to move very quickly). Opp slow¹(1). Compare quick¹(1). **2** (of a clock etc) showing a time later than the accurate time: *My*

watch is fast. It's fast by five minutes/five minutes fast. Opp slow¹(2). **3** (of a person) eager and active (but not always sincere): *a fast talker.* **pull a fast one (on sb)** ⇨ one³(1). **4** (*sport*) (of a surface) helping quick speed: *a fast track/wicket.* Opp slow¹(7). **5** firmly fixed: *Check the ropes and make sure the boat is fast.* **6** (of a colour, dye) fixed, not easily removed. ⇨ fastness. **7** (*no comp*) reliable and loyal: *a fast friend.*

fast² /fɑːst/ *adv* **1** quickly: *learn/run fast. Don't speak so fast.* Opp slowly. **2** firmly: *tied fast to the pole; stuck fast in the mud; fast asleep.*

fast³ /fɑːst/ *nc* a period of not eating food.

fast⁴ /fɑːst/ *vi* to go without food or without certain kinds of food, esp as a religious duty.

fas·ten /'fɑːsn/ **1** *vt, vi* to join, fix, (things) firmly: *How can I fasten these together? Fasten them with these screws. This dress fastens down the back* (= has buttons etc at the back). Opp unfasten. **2** *vt, vi* to lock (something): *Are all the windows fastened?* **3** *vt* **fasten (sth) on sb/sth** (*formal*) **(a)** to direct (one's looks, thoughts, attention etc) on (a person): *He fastened his eyes on me.* **(b)** to take (an idea) eagerly: *He fastened on the idea of using a rope.*

fas·ten·er /'fɑːsnə(r)/ *nc* something that fastens things together: *a paper fastener; a zip-fastener.*

fas·tid·i·ous /fə'stɪdɪəs/ *adj* (*derog*) (of a person) difficult to please; quick fo find fault: *He is fastidious about his food.*

fa·stid·i·ous·ly *adv*

fast·ness /'fɑːstnɪs/ *nu* the quality of being fast¹(6): *We guarantee the fastness of these dyes.*

fat¹ /fæt/ *adj* (**—ter, —test**) **1** having much weight: *a fat man; as fat as a pig* (= very fat). ⇨ fatten. Opp thin¹(3). **2** (of meat) having much fat(1). ⇨ fatty. **3** (*informal*) large; well-filled: *a fat salary; a fat wallet.* **4** (*informal*) (used for ironic emphasis): *A fat lot of good he'll be!* (= He will be no use at all!)

fat·tish *adj* a little fat¹(1,3).

fat·ness *nu*

fat² /fæt/ *nc,nu* **1** (a kind of) white substance found under animals' skins. **chew the fat** (*informal*) to chat. **2** an oily substance found in seeds etc, used for cooking: *Fried potatoes are cooked in deep fat.* **live off the fat of the land** to live in luxury.

fa·tal /'feɪtl/ *adj* **1** causing, ending in, death: *a fatal accident/disease.* Opp non-fatal. **2** (*fig*) causing disaster: *a fatal decision/mistake.*

fa·tal·ly /'feɪtəlɪ/ *adv*: *be fatally injured/wounded.*

fa·tal·ism /'feɪtəlɪzəm/ *nu* the belief that events are decided by fate(1) and cannot be influenced.

fa·tal·ist /-lɪst/ *nc* a believer in fatalism.

fa·tal·is·tic /ˌfeɪtə'lɪstɪk/ *adj* believing that all that happens is inevitable (and usually bad): *a fatalistic attitude.*

fa·tal·ity /fə'tælətɪ/ *n* (*pl* **-ies**) *nc* (*formal*) a death by accident, in war etc.

fate /feɪt/ *n* **1** *nu* (often F-) the power considered to control all events in a way that cannot be influenced: *He had hoped to live to 80 but fate decided otherwise.* **2** *nc* the future (esp death) as decided by fate: *They abandoned the men to their fate.* **a fate worse than death** something bad to be greatly feared.

fate·ful /'feɪtfəl/ adj (attrib) important and decisive: on this fateful day.

fate·ful·ly /-fəlɪ/ adv

fa·ther¹ /'fɑːðə(r)/ nc 1 a male parent: You have been like a father to me. 2 (often F-) a title used of a man who is a first great example: The Father of English poetry was Chaucer. 3 (F- in names) a priest. 4 (F-) a title used in personifications: Father Christmas; Father Time.

'father figure nc an older man who gives advice or who helps.

'father·hood /-hʊd/ nu the state of being a father.

'father-in-law /'fɑːðər ɪn lɔː/ nc (pl fathers-in-law) the father of one's wife or husband.

'father·land /-lænd/ nc one's native country. Ⓝ 'Mother country' is more usual.

father·less adj without a living or known father.

father·ly adj of, like, a father: fatherly love.

fa·ther² /'fɑːðə(r)/ vt 1 to be the originator of (an idea, plan etc). 2 to be the father of (a child).

fath·om¹ /'fæðəm/ nc a unit of measurement (6 feet or 1·8 metres) of the depth of water: The ship sank in six fathoms.

fath·om² /'fæðəm/ vt (formal) to understand (something) fully: I cannot fathom his meaning.

fa·tigue¹ /fə'tiːg/ n 1 nu the condition of being very tired: After a long walk up the mountain he was dropping with fatigue. 2 nu (tech) weakness (in metals) caused by a lot of use: metal fatigue in engines.

fa·tigue² /fə'tiːg/ vt to make (a person) tired: fatiguing work.

fat·ten /'fætn/ vt **fatten sb/sth (up)** (to cause a person, animal) to become fat: fatten cattle.

fat·ty /'fætɪ/ adj (-ier, -iest) like, having much, fat(1): fatty bacon.

fatu·ous /'fætjʊəs/ adj (formal; derog) foolish (and showing self-importance): a fatuous smile/young man/reply.

fatu·ous·ly adv

fau·cet /'fɔːsɪt/ nc (US) = tap¹.

fault¹ /fɔːlt/ n 1 nc something that makes a person, thing etc imperfect: She loves me in spite of all my faults. There is a fault in the electrical connections. **at fault** in the wrong: You were at fault, so you should apologize. **find fault with sb/sth** to complain about a person, thing: I have no fault to find with your work. 2 n sing responsibility for being wrong: It's your (own) fault. 3 nc a place where there is a long break in an organized group of layers of rock etc.

'fault-finding adj (derog) (of a person) often complaining.

fault² /fɔːlt/ vt to find fault with (a person, person's work etc): No-one could fault his performance. Ⓝ 'Fault' is used with cannot, can't etc or with nobody, no-one etc and in questions. Use 'find fault with' for affirmative statements.

fault·less adj

fault·less·ly adv

faulty adj (-ier, -iest) (esp of a machine or engine) having a fault or faults.

fauna /'fɔːnə/ nu (science) all the animals of an area or a period of history: the fauna of E Africa.

faux pas /ˌfəʊ 'pɑː/ nc (pl unchanged) (Fr) an accidental mistake in behaviour or speech that offends other people: It was an unfortunate faux pas when she asked Jane how her husband was without knowing he had died.

fa·vour¹ (US = **fa·vor**) /'feɪvə(r)/ n 1 nc a kind act. **ask a favour of sb; ask sb a favour** to ask a person to do something kind for one's benefit: Could I ask you a favour—may I borrow your car? **do sb a favour** to do something kind: Would you do me a favour and lend me your pen? **grant sb a favour** (formal) = do sb a favour. **owe sb a favour** to need to do something kind for a person who has been kind to one: You owe me several favours so I expect you to help me. 2 nu approval; support: look with favour on her ideas. **be in favour of sb/sth** to approve of a person, thing: Are you in favour of John/appointing John? **be in/out of favour (with sb)** to have/ not have a person's support or approval. 3 nu an unfair advantage given to a person: He got the job more by favour than ability. 4 nu **in sb's favour** to a person's advantage: The wind/rate of exchange is in our favour. Please write the cheque in favour of my wife. (= write my wife's name on it).

fa·vour² (US = **fa·vor**) /'feɪvə(r)/ vt 1 to approve of, support, (something): He favours an increase in nursery education. 2 to give an unfair advantage to (a person, group etc): A teacher should not favour any pupils.

fa·vour·able (US = **-vor-**) /'feɪvrəbl/ adj giving or showing approval: She got a favourable report on/about her work. Opp unfavourable.

fa·vour·ably /-əblɪ/ adv in a favourable manner: speak favourably of a plan.

fa·vour·ite¹ (US = **-vor-**) /'feɪvrɪt/ adj (attrib; no comp) approved of, liked, more than any other: My favourite meal is hamburgers and chips.

fa·vour·ite² (US = **-vor-**) /'feɪvrɪt/ nc 1 a person or thing preferred above all others: She's/It's my favourite/one of my favourites. 2 a person given unfair advantage: A manager shouldn't have favourites. 3 (the —) (racing) the horse etc generally expected to win: The favourite came in third.

fa·vour·it·ism (US = **-vor-**) /-ɪzəm/ nu (the practice of) having favourites(2).

fawn¹ /fɔːn/ n 1 nc a young deer. 2 nu (also adj) light yellowish-brown (colour).

fawn² /fɔːn/ vi **fawn on sb** to try to win a person's favour(2) by pretending to like or approve of her or him.

FBI /ˌef biː 'aɪ/ abbr (the —) (US) the Federal Bureau of Investigation.

fear¹ /fɪə(r)/ n 1 nc,nu the unpleasant feeling caused by the nearness or possibility of danger or evil: My worst fear is that the plane will crash. They stood there shaking with fear. **for fear of sth** because of worry about something: She asked us not to be noisy for fear of waking the baby. 2 nu possibility: There's not much fear of my losing the money. **No fear!** ⇨ no¹(3).

fear·ful /-fəl/ adj (formal; dated) **(a)** terrible: a fearful railway accident. **(b)** (informal) annoying; very large: What a fearful mess! **(c) fearful of sth** afraid of something (which is much more usual): fearful of waking the baby.

fear·ful·ly /-fəlɪ/ adv (old use) very: I'm fearfully sorry.

feel

fear·less *adj* without fear: *a fearless racing driver*.
fear·less·ly *adv*
fear·less·ness *nu*
fear² /fɪə(r)/ *v* (*formal*) **1** *vt* to be afraid of (something) (which is more usual): *fear death*. **2** *vi* **fear for sb/sth** to feel anxiety about a person, thing: *We feared for his life/safety*. **fear the worst** ⇨ worst³.
feas·ible /'fiːzəbl/ *adj* **1** that can be done: *Finishing the work by Friday is feasible*. **2** (*informal*) that can be believed: *His story sounds feasible*.
feasi·bil·ity /ˌfiːzə'bɪlətɪ/ *nu* (also *attrib*): *a feasibility study*.
feast¹ /fiːst/ *nc* **1** a religious anniversary or festival, e.g. Christmas. **2** a splendid meal.
feast² /fiːst/ *v* **1** *vt,vi* to take part in, give (a person), a feast: *feast one's friends; feast (on good wine and food) all evening*. **2** *vt* **feast sth on sth** (*formal*) to get pleasure from something by using: *feast one's eyes on beautiful scenes*.
feat /fiːt/ *nc* something difficult that is well done, esp showing skill, strength or daring: *brilliant feats of engineering*.
feath·er¹ /'feðə(r)/ *nc* one of the light coverings that grow from a bird's skin. **birds of a feather** ⇨ bird(1). **a feather in one's cap** something one can be proud of.
'feather·weight *nc* (also *attrib*) a boxer weighing between 118 and 126 lb (53·5 and 57 kg).
feath·ery *adj* light and soft like feathers: *feathery snow*.
feath·er² /'feðə(r)/ *vt* **feather one's own nest** to give oneself comforts, esp wealth (often dishonestly). ⇨ also tar².
fea·ture¹ /'fiːtʃə(r)/ *nc* **1** one of the named parts of the face: *Her eyes are her best feature. He has handsome features*. **2** a characteristic or noticeable part: *geographical features*. **3** an important article in a newspaper. **4** a full-length film with a story.
fea·ture² /'fiːtʃə(r)/ *vt* **1** to have as a feature(2): *The area features many kinds of trees*. **2** to be about or include (in a film, TV programme, music programme, book etc): *The play features Julie Legrand as the star. The concert features the songs of Cole Porter*.
fea·ture·less *adj* (*derog*) uninteresting because without features(2): *a featureless view*.
Feb *abbr* February.
Feb·ru·ary /'februərɪ/ *n* (*abbr* Feb) the second month of the year, with 28 days (29 in a *leap year*): *He was born on 18 February*. Ⓝ *'18 February'* is spoken as *'February the eighteenth'* or *'the eighteenth of February'*.
feces /'fiːsiːz/ *n pl* = faeces.
fed /fed/ *pt,pp* of feed². **be fed up (with sb/sth)** ⇨ feed²(1).
fed·er·al /'fedrəl/ *adj* of, based on, federation: *In the USA, foreign policy is decided by the federal (i.e. central) government, and federal laws are made by Congress*.
ˌFederal ˌBureau of Inˌvestiˈgation *n* (the —) (*abbr* FBI) the US department which is responsible for investigating violations of federal law and safeguarding national security.
fed·er·al·ism /-ɪzəm/ *nu* a political policy favouring federation (1).

fed·er·al·ist *adj* of, like, federalism. □ *nc* a believer in, supporter of, federalism.
fed·er·ate /'fedəreɪt/ *vt,vi* (to cause states, organizations, societies) to unite into a federation.
fed·er·ation /ˌfedə'reɪʃn/ *n* **1** *nc,nu* (an act of) forming a political union of several states for control of foreign affairs, defence etc by the central (Federal) government but keeping regional (State) government for other things such as education. **2** *nc* an example of such a political union, e.g. the USA. **3** *nc* a similar union of societies, trade unions etc.
fee /fiː/ *nc* **1** a charge or payment for professional advice or services, e.g. from doctors, lawyers etc. **2** the cost of an examination, membership etc.
feeble /'fiːbl/ *adj* (**-r, -st**) without energy or force: *a feeble old man; a feeble cry/argument/joke*.
feebly /'fiːblɪ/ *adv*
feed¹ /fiːd/ *n* **1** *nc* (mainly of animals and babies) a meal: *We stopped to let the horses have a feed*. **2** *nu* food for animals: *There isn't enough feed left for the hens*.
'feed·back *nu* (*informal*) information etc (about a product) given by the user to the supplier, maker etc: *interesting feedback via the market research department*. ⇨ feed²(4).
feed² /fiːd/ *v* (*pt,pp* fed /fed/) **1** *vt* to give food to (a person, animal): *Have the cats been fed yet?* **be fed up (with sb/sth)** (*informal*) to feel angry or annoyed (because of a person, thing): *I'm fed up with your grumbling*. **2** *vi* (chiefly of animals) to eat: *The cows were feeding in the meadows*. **feed off sth** (**a**) to take food from something: *feed off a large plate*. (**b**) to use something as a supplier: *She often feeds off other people's ideas*. **feed on sth** to use something as food: *Cattle feed chiefly on grass*. **3** *vt* to supply (material, parts etc) to (a machine etc): *This moving belt feeds the machine with cotton thread*. **4** *vt* (*computers*) **feed sth into sth** to put information into a computer. **feed sth back** to send information etc back e.g. from the sales staff to the manufacturer. ⇨ feedback.
'feeding-bottle *nc* a bottle from which a baby is given milk.
feed·er /'fiːdə(r)/ *nc* **1** a person or animal that feeds (in the way mentioned): *a poor feeder*. **2** a feeding-bottle or bib for a baby.
feel¹ /fiːl/ *n sing* **1** the sensation characteristic of something when touching or being touched: *You can tell it's wool by the feel*. **get the feel of sth** to learn how an organization, machine etc works by experience: *get the feel of a new car*. **2** an act of feeling; being touched: *Let me have a feel*.
feel² /fiːl/ *v* (*pt,pp* felt /felt/) **1** *vt,vi* to (try to) learn about (something) by touching, holding in the hands etc: *I could feel a spider on my arm. Does the water feel warm? Feel this and tell me what it is. Feel her forehead and tell me if she's ill*. **feel one's way** ⇨ way²(1). **2** *vi* to search with the hands, feet, a stick etc: *He felt in his pocket (for a penny)*. ⇨ feel (about) for sth. **3** *vt,vi* to be aware of, know, one's emotional or physical state: *feel afraid/happy; feel the cold. I'm feeling cold/hungry/ill/fit/tired/much better. Can you feel any pain? He felt concern for the sick children. I*

feel sorry for you. He could feel his heart beating.
feel free (to do sth) ⇨ free². **feel like sth** to
have a desire for something: *I don't feel like eating
a big meal.* **not feel oneself** to feel unhealthy
or not content: *I'm not feeling myself today.* **4** vt
feel (that) . . . to consider something to be
true: *I feel (that) it was wrong to say that.* Ⓝ Not
used in the continuous tenses, e.g. *is/was -ing.* **5** vt
(of an object etc) to have (a quality mentioned)
when touched: *These sheets feel soft. These shoes
feel tight.*
feel as if/as though to have, give, the
emotional or physical sensation that: *I felt as if my
head would break. I feel as though I've known you
for years. It feels as if it has been wet.*
feel for sb to have sympathy for an unhappy
person, the poor etc: *It isn't easy to bring up four
children—I feel for you.* **feel (about) for sth** to
search for something using the hands, feet, a stick
etc: *The climber felt (about) for a place to hold on
to the rock.*
feel in one's bones (that . . .) ⇨ bone¹.
feel sb/sth out (*informal*) to (try to) learn
about a person's opinion or the general opinion
by using careful questions etc: *I must know what
she thinks about my idea so take her for a coffee
and try to feel her out.* **feel out of it** (*informal*)
to have the impression that one is not welcome or
very involved: *I feel out of it when I go to parties
because I'm so shy.*
feel up to sth (*informal*) to know one is able or
healthy enough to do something: *Don't get out of
bed if you're not feeling up to it.*
feel·er /'fi:lə(r)/ *nc* **1** (usually *pl*) a long and narrow part of an animal used for testing things by
touch, e.g. a whisker, an antenna(1). **2** (*pl*) (*fig*)
questions, suggestions etc used to test the
opinions of others: *put out feelers.*
feel·ing /'fi:lɪŋ/ *n* **1** *nu* the power and capacity to
feel: *He had lost all feeling in his legs.* **2** *nc* **feeling (of sth)** a physical or mental awareness: *a
feeling of hunger/gratitude/joy.* **3** *nc* an idea or
belief not based completely on reason: *a feeling of
danger. I have a feeling that she's lying.* **4** (*pl*) the
emotional side of a person's nature (contrasted
with the intellect): *Have I hurt your feelings?* (=
made you sad?) **have mixed feelings (about
sb/sth)** to be unable to decide one's opinion
(about a person, thing). **spare sb's feelings** to
avoid making a person unhappy or sad. **5** *nu* sympathy; understanding: *He doesn't show much feeling for the sufferings of others. She plays the piano
with feeling.* **6** *nc,nu* (a) general opinion: *The feeling of the meeting was against the idea. Feelings
over the election ran high.*
feet /fi:t/ *n pl* of foot¹. ⇨ foot¹(1) for phrases
using *feet,* e.g. *fall on one's feet.*
feint /feɪnt/ *nc* (*formal*) a pretence (the more
usual word).
fe·line /'fi:laɪn/ *adj* of, like, a cat: *walk with feline
grace.*
fell¹ /fel/ *pt* of fall².
fell² /fel/ *nc* an area of high land (esp in N England): *the Derbyshire Fells.*
fell³ /fel/ *vt* to cut down (a tree) or knock down (a
person) by hitting: *He felled his enemy with a
single blow.*
fel·low¹ /'feləʊ/ *adj* (*attrib*) of the same kind,

class etc: *fellow citizens/students/travellers.*
fellow-'feeling *nu* sympathy (the usual word).
fel·low² /'feləʊ/ *nc* **1** (*dated informal*) a man or
boy: *He's a pleasant fellow.* **2** (*dated;* usually *pl*) a
friend: *schoolfellows.* **3** (F-) a member of a
learned society: *Fellow of the British Academy.*
4 a member of the governing body of some
university colleges.
fel·low·ship /'feləʊʃɪp/ *n* **1** *nu* (*dated*) friendly
relationship: *enjoy fellowship with people.* **2** *nc*
(the people in) a group or society. **3** *nc* a position
of a college fellow(4): *be awarded a fellowship.*
fel·on /'felən/ *nc* (*legal*) a person guilty of a
serious crime.
fel·oni·ous /fɪ'ləʊnɪəs/ *adj* (*formal* or *legal*)
criminal (the usual word).
fel·ony /'felənɪ/ *nc,nu* (*pl* **-ies**) (*legal*) a serious
crime, e.g. murder, armed robbery, arson.
felt¹ /felt/ *pt,pp* of feel².
felt² /felt/ *nu* (also *attrib*) a kind of cloth made
from pressed wool, hair or fur: *felt hats/slippers.*
felt-tip(ped) '(pen) *nc* a kind of ink pen with a
pointed top of felt.
fem *abbr* female; feminine.
fe·male¹ /'fi:meɪl/ *adj* **1** of the sex that can give
birth: *a female child/dog.* **2** (of plants) producing
fruit.
fe·male² /'fi:meɪl/ *nc* a female person or animal:
My cat's a female.
femi·nine /'femɪnɪn/ *adj* **1** of, like, suitable for,
women: *feminine curiosity* (said to be typical of
women). **2** (*gram*) of the forms of words used to
refer to females: *Some feminine nouns and pronouns are 'actress', 'lioness', 'she', 'her'.* Compare
masculine.
femi·nin·ity /,femɪ'nɪnətɪ/ *nu* the quality of
being feminine.
fem·in·ism /'femɪnɪzəm/ *nu* the principle that
women must have the same (social, financial,
legal etc) rights as men.
fem·in·ist /-ɪst/ *adj* of feminism. □ *nc* a supporter of feminism.
fe·mur /'fi:mə(r)/ *nc* (*anat*) the thigh-bone.
fen /fen/ *nc* an area of low, wet land.
fence¹ /fens/ *nc* **1** a barrier made of wood or
wire, used round a garden etc or to divide two
areas. **be/sit on the fence** to be unable to form
an opinion or make a decision (esp when waiting
to see what is best for oneself). **2** (*sl*) a person
who sells stolen goods.
fence² /fens/ *v* **1** vt **fence sth in/off/round** to
surround, divide, provide something with a
fence(1). **2** vi to take part in the sport of fenc-
ing(2). **3** vi (*fig*) to avoid giving a direct answer to
a question or person: *She was fencing, refusing to
admit where she had been.*
fenc·er *nc* a person who fences(2).
fenc·ing /'fensɪŋ/ *nu* **1** material used to make a
fence(1). **2** the sport of fighting with long, narrow
swords (called *foils*).
fend /fend/ *vt* **1** **fend sb/sth off** to defend oneself from an attacker, a hit etc: *fend off a blow.* **2**
fend for oneself to look after oneself: *When
his father died, Tom had to fend for himself.*
fen·der /'fendə(r)/ *nc* **1** a metal frame on the
floor in front of an open fireplace. **2** (*US*) a guard
over the wheel of a vehicle.
fer·ment¹ /'fɜ:ment/ *n* **be in a ferment** (*fig*) to

be in a state of (social or political or personal) excitement or trouble.

fer·ment² /fə'ment/ *vt,vi* **1** (to cause a substance) to change chemically through the action of organic bodies (esp *yeast*) that change glucose into alcohol, e.g. in beer, wine. **2** (*fig*) (to cause a situation) to become (more) excited: *The police sometimes ferment social unrest.*

fer·men·ta·tion /ˌfɜ:men'teɪʃn/ *nu*

fern /fɜ:n/ *nc,nu* a (kind of) feathery, green-leaved flowerless plant.

fer·ocious /fə'rəʊʃəs/ *adj* fierce, cruel, violent: *a ferocious temper/dog.*

fer·ocious·ly *adv*

fer·oc·ity /fə'rɒsəti/ *n* (*formal*) *nc,nu* (an act of) violent cruelty.

fer·ret¹ /'ferɪt/ *nc* a kind of small animal used for catching rabbits and rats.

fer·ret² /'ferɪt/ *vi,vt* **ferret (about) for sth;** **ferret sth out** to (try to) discover something by searching: *ferret out the truth; ferret about for a lost book.*

fer·ry¹ /'ferɪ/ *nc* (*pl* **-ies**) **1** a ferry-boat: *cross the river by ferry.* **2** (a place where there is) a boat etc that carries people and goods across a river etc.

fer·ry² /'ferɪ/ *vt* (*pt,pp* **-ied**) to take (a person, thing) across in a ferry: *ferry people across a river.*

'ferry-boat *nc* one used for ferrying.

fer·tile /'fɜ:taɪl/ *adj* **1** (of land, plants etc) producing strong plants: *fertile soil.* Opp infertile. **2** (of a person, mind etc) full of ideas, plans etc: *a fertile imagination.* **3** able to produce children, young, fruit: *fertile seeds/eggs.* Compare sterile(1,2).

fer·til·ity /fə'tɪləti/ *nu* the state of being fertile.

fer·til·ize (also **-ise**) /'fɜ:tɪlaɪz/ *vt* **1** to make (soil) fertile(1): *fertilizing the soil.* **2** to make (an egg, seed etc) able to produce a new animal, plant.

fer·ti·liz·er (also **-is·er**) *nc,nu* (a kind of) natural or chemical substance used for fertilizing.

fer·ti·li·za·tion (also **-li·sa·tion**) /ˌfɜ:tɪlaɪ'zeɪʃn/ *nu*

fer·vent /'fɜ:vənt/ *adj* (*formal; usually attrib*) showing strong feeling: *fervent love/hatred.*

fer·vent·ly *adv*

fer·vour (US = **-vor**) /'fɜ:və(r)/ *nu* an enthusiastic feeling.

fes·ter /'festə(r)/ *vi* **1** (of a cut or wound) to become filled with poisonous matter (*pus*): *If the cut gets dirty, it will probably fester.* **2** (*fig*) to act like poison in the mind: *The insult festered in his mind.*

fes·ti·val /'festɪvl/ *nc* **1** (a day or season for) a public celebration: *Christmas is a Christian festival.* ⇨ feast¹(1). **2** a series of performances (of music, ballet, drama etc) given during a period in a place: *a festival of music.*

fes·tive /'festɪv/ *adj* of a feast or festival; very enjoyable: *a festive season* (e.g. Christmas).

fes·tiv·ity /fe'stɪvəti/ *n* (*pl* **-ies**) **1** *nu* the act of rejoicing, being merry and gay. **2** (*pl*) joyful celebrations: *wedding festivities.*

fes·toon /fe'stu:n/ *vt* **festoon sb/sth with sth** (often *passive*) to decorate (the usual word): *a girl festooned with flowers.*

fe·tal /'fi:tl/ *adj* (*US*) = foetal.

fetch /fetʃ/ *v* **1** *vt* to go for (a person, thing) and

bring back: *Fetch a doctor at once. Shall I fetch your coat (for you)?* Compare send(1), bring(1), take²(2). **2** *vt* (of goods) to be sold for (a price): *My bike fetched £50. These old books won't fetch (you) much.* **3** *vi* **fetch up at/in** a place (*informal*) (**a**) (of a person) to arrive at (a place), esp after a period when no-one knows where he or she is: *He fetched up at the station in Tokyo.* (**b**) (of things) to be found in (a place) after being lost for a period: *The wheel fetched up in the shed.*

fête¹ /feɪt/ *nc* a public entertainment, usually to raise money: *the village fête.*

fête² /feɪt/ *vt* (*formal*) to honour (a person) with ceremonies etc: *The hero was fêted wherever he went.*

fet·id /'fetɪd/ *adj* (of liquid) stinking.

fet·ish /'fetɪʃ/ *nc* **1** an object worshipped by people because they believe a spirit lives in it. **2** anything to which too much respect or attention is given: *Some women have a fetish about/make a fetish of clothes.*

fe·tus /'fi:təs/ *nc* (*US*) = foetus.

fet·ter /'fetə(r)/ *nc* (usually *pl*) chains for a prisoner. □ *vt* to keep (a person) from making progress (as if) by using fetters.

feud /fju:d/ *nc* a serious quarrel between two people, families or groups over a long period of time. □ *vi* **feud (about/over sth)** to quarrel; fight: *feud with a cousin over a will.*

feu·dal /'fju:dl/ *adj* of the method of holding land (by giving services to the owner) as in Europe until four hundred years ago.

feu·dal·ism /-ɪzəm/ *nu* the feudal system.

fe·ver /'fi:və(r)/ *n* **1** *nc,nu* a condition of the human body with a temperature higher than usual, esp when a sign of illness: *He has a high fever.* **at fever pitch** in a very excited state: *The family was at fever pitch on the day before the wedding.* **2** *nu* one of many diseases in which there is a high fever: *yellow/rheumatic fever.*

fe·ver·ish *adj* having symptoms of, caused by, causing, fever: *feeling feverish; feverish shivers.*

fe·ver·ish·ly *adv*

few¹ /fju:/ *adj* or *det* (**—er, —est**) **1** **a few sb/ sth** not many; a small number of: *a few children/ cars/mistakes/carrots. Please wait a few moments. A few students took the bus and the rest went by train. Quite a few* (= Many) *apples were bad.* ⇨ few²(1). Ⓝ *'Few'* is used to refer to 'a small number of', as in *few animals/clocks. 'A little'* is used to refer to 'a small amount of', as in *a little bread/time/kindness.* ⇨ the note at less¹. **fewer . . . than . . .** not so many . . . as . . . : *Fewer students took the bus than the train.* Compare less¹, many¹. **2** (used without *a*) almost none: *Few people would agree.* **few and far between** almost none and not often: *Opportunities for studying medicine are few and far between.* **every few days/weeks** *etc* ⇨ every(3). Compare less¹, many¹; little¹, much¹.

few² /fju:/ *pron* **1** **a few (of sb/sth)** a small number (of): *I know a few (of them). A few bought cakes and the rest bought sandwiches.* **a good few/quite a few (of sb/sth)** many: *A good few (of them) were bad.* ⇨ few¹(1). **fewer than . . .** not so many as . . . : *Fewer than ten people applied for the job.* **no fewer than . . .** as many as: *No fewer than 100 people came to the* *meeting.* Compare less[4], more[3]; little[3], much[3]. **2** (used without *a*) almost none: *Few would agree with you and fewer still* (or *still fewer*) *would vote for you.* **3** (the —) the smaller number (of people in a group or society): *We must not ignore the wishes of the few.* **the fewer, the better** (used to suggest one is happy even if only a small number do something): *He doesn't mind if he has only five students—the fewer, the better because he can give more time to each.*

ff *abbr* and the following (pages).

fi·an·cé /fɪ'ɑːnseɪ/ *nc* a man to whom a woman is engaged to be married.

fi·an·cée /fɪ'ɑːnseɪ/ *nc* a woman to whom a man is engaged to be married.

fi·as·co /fɪ'æskəʊ/ *nc* (*pl* **—s**, *US* also **—es**) (of something organized) a complete failure: *The new play was a fiasco.*

fib /fɪb/ *vi* (**-bb-**), *nc* (*informal*) (to make an) untrue statement (esp about something unimportant): *Don't tell fibs!*

fib·ber *nc* a person who tells fibs.

fi·bre (*US* = **fi·ber**) /'faɪbə(r)/ *n* **1** *nc* one of the very thin threads of which many animals and vegetable growths are formed, e.g. cotton, wool, nerves, muscles. **2** *nu* a substance formed of a mass of plant fibres, used in various materials: *rope made of a coarse fibre.* **3** *nu* a coarse substance found in all plants which, when eaten in food, helps digestion, prevents constipation and reduces the absorption of fat and sugar: *Brown bread, beans, peas and dried fruit are high in fibre.* (= contain a lot of fibre). Ⓝ *'Roughage'* is the dated word. **4** *nu* (*fig*) character: *a person of strong moral fibre.*

'fibre·glass *nu* a material of glass fibres in resin, used as insulation.

fi·brous /'faɪbrəs/ *adj* like, made of, fibres.

fib·ula /'fɪbjʊlə/ *nc* (*pl* **—s**) (*anat*) the outer and smaller of the two bones from the knee to the ankle.

fickle /'fɪkl/ *adj* (*derog*) (of a person) often changing one's feelings about another person.

fic·tion /'fɪkʃn/ *n* **1** *nu* or *sing* something invented or imagined: *Her explanation was a total fiction. Was the story fact or fiction?.* Opp fact(4). **2** *nu* (*literature*) writing that uses imagination, such as stories, novels etc.

fic·tion·al /-ʃənl/ *adj* invented or imagined: *The characters in this film are fictional.* Compare factual.

fic·ti·tious /fɪk'tɪʃəs/ *adj* (*no comp*) untrue; not real: *The account he gave of his movements was fictitious.*

fiddle¹ /'fɪdl/ *nc* **1** a violin; any instrument of the violin family. **play second fiddle (to sb)** to take a less important part (than another). **2** an instance of being dishonest: *She's on the fiddle.* ⇨ fiddle²(3).

fiddle² /'fɪdl/ *v* **1** *vi* to play a tune, etc on the fiddle. **2** *vi* to move something in one's fingers without a reason or purpose: *He was fiddling* (*about*) *with a piece of string.* **3** *vt* (*sl*) to make deliberately inaccurate records of figures (in business accounts etc): *fiddle one's expenses.*

fid·dler *nc* (**a**) a person who plays a fiddle(1). (**b**) a person who fiddles(3).

fid·dling *adj* (*informal*) small and unimportant:

fiddling little jobs.

fi·del·ity /fɪ'delətɪ/ *nu* **1** **fidelity (to sb/sth)** (*formal*) loyalty, faithfulness: *fidelity to one's principles.* **2** accuracy; exactness: *copy a painting with great fidelity.* ⇨ also high-fidelity.

fidg·et¹ /'fɪdʒɪt/ *nc* a person who fidgets.

fidg·et² /'fɪdʒɪt/ *vi* **fidget (about) (with sth)** to move the body (or part of it) about restlessly: *The boy was fidgeting with his knife and fork.*

fidg·ety *adj* (of a person) often fidgeting.

field¹ /fiːld/ *nc* **1** an area of land, usually surrounded by hedges, fences etc, used for cattle or for growing crops: *working in the fields.* **2** (*sport*) an area of land marked for a game: *a cricket/football field.* **3** an area of land from which minerals etc are obtained: *a new oilfield; coalfields.* **4** an area of land where a battle or war is or was fought: *the field of battle/battlefield.* **5** an area or department of study or activity: *the field of politics/medical research. That is outside my field* (= is not something that I have studied). **6** (the —) the area where there is direct activity or contact in one's work or study: *I obtained the facts in the field, not from books.* **7** an area or space with the use mentioned: *a magnetic field; a wide field of vision.*

'field day *n sing* **have a field day** to have great fun, success etc.

'field event *nc* an athletic event such as jumping or throwing which does not take place on a track.

'field glasses *n pl* binoculars designed for outdoor use.

'field hockey *nu* = hockey(1).

,field 'marshal *nc* an army officer of highest rank.

'field study *nc* a planned study of direct observations, interviews etc.

'field work *nu* (**a**) research done in the field(6). (**b**) = field study.

field² /fiːld/ *vt,vi* **1** (in cricket and baseball) (to stand ready) to catch or stop (the ball): *He fields well.* **2** to put (a team) into the field: *The school is fielding a strong team in its next match.*

field·er *nc* (in cricket etc) a player who fields.

fiend /fiːnd/ *nc* **1** (*derog*) a very wicked or cruel person. **2** (*informal*) a person devoted to or addicted to something: *a fresh-air fiend.*

fiend·ish *adj* (*derog*) savage and cruel.

fiend·ish·ly *adv* (*dated*) very: *fiendishly clever.*

fierce /fɪəs/ *adj* (**-r, -st**) **1** violent; cruel; angry: *fierce dogs/winds; look fierce; have a fierce look.* **2** (of heat, emotion etc) very strong: *fierce hatred.*

fierce·ly *adv*

fierce·ness *nu*

fi·ery /'faɪərɪ/ *adj* (**-ier, -iest**) **1** looking like, hot as, fire: *a fiery sky.* **2** (*derog*) (of a person, actions etc) quickly or easily made angry: *a fiery temper/speech.*

fier·ily /-ɪlɪ/ *adv*

FIFA /'fiːfə/ *acronym* International Federation of Association Football.

fif·teen /ˌfɪf'tiːn/ *adj* or *det, nc* (of) 15.

fif·teenth /ˌfɪf'tiːnθ/ *adj* or *det, nc* (abbr 15th) (of) one of 15 parts or the next after 14.

fifth /fɪfθ/ *adj* or *det, nc* (abbr 5th) (of) one of 5 parts or the next after 4.

,fifth 'column *nc* an organized group of people sympathizing and working for the enemy inside a country at war.

fifth·ly *adv*

fif·ti·eth /'fɪftɪəθ/ *adj* or *det, nc* (abbr 50th) (of) one of 50 parts or the next after 49.

fif·ty /'fɪftɪ/ *adj* or *det, nc* (*pl* -ies) (of) 50: *Fifty-three* (53). ⇨ chance²(2). **in the fifties (a)** (of a temperature, speed etc) between 50 and 59. **(b)** between '50 and '59 in a century. **go fifty-fifty (with sb); do sth on a fifty-fifty basis** to have equal shares, responsibility etc.

fig /fɪg/ *nc* (a kind of tree with) a soft, sweet fruit full of small seeds. **not care/give a fig (for sb/sth)** to fail to care about or value a person, thing, at all.

'fig-leaf *nc* a representation of a fig-leaf used for hiding the male genital organs in drawings etc.

fig. *written abbr* **1** figure¹(3). **2** (*lang*) figurative.

fight¹ /faɪt/ *n* **1** *nc* an act of fighting(1): *a fight between two boys/among the players.* **pick a fight (with sb)** to try to begin one. **2** (*fig*) a struggle: *the fight against poverty/racism.* **put up a fight (against sth)** to try to oppose or not to take or use something: *put up a strong fight against having to pay.* **3** *nu* the desire, spirit or ability to oppose or resist: *When she heard that the others had accepted the money, it took all the fight out of her.*

fight·er *nc* a person or machine that fights(1): *a professional fighter; a jet fighter.*

fight² /faɪt/ *v* (*pt,pp* **fought** /fɔːt/) **1** *vi,vt* to use force or violence with the hands or weapons: *They fought a difficult battle. We were fighting with real swords in the play. European countries have often fought each other. Professional boxers fight for money.* **fight to the finish** to fight until there is a decision or end. **2** *vt,vi* to use effort, struggle, to achieve something: *fight to survive; fight for freedom/to win a larger share of the market/to get a place in the team/against an incurable disease.* **fight shy of sb/sth** to keep away from, avoid, a person, thing. **fight tooth and nail** ⇨ tooth(1). **3** *vi* to quarrel: *I could hear his parents fighting in the kitchen.*

fight back (a) to use force or violence to resist attack: *If they attack we must fight back.* **(b)** (*fig*) to use effort to return to a previous condition or position: *You must fight your way back to a management position. She was fighting back but her health got worse.*

fight sth down to (try to) control, stop, a feeling: *fight down a feeling of jealousy.*

fight sb off to force a person to go away or stop fighting(1). **fight sth off** to struggle to prevent an illness, cold, sad feeling.

fight it out to fight(1,2) until a contest etc is decided.

fight·ing /'faɪtɪŋ/ *nu* the activity of a fight: *street fighting.* □ *adj* (*attrib*) **fighting fit** very healthy.

fig·ment /'fɪgmənt/ *nc* something invented or imagined: *It was a figment of your imagination.*

fig·urat·ive /'fɪgjʊrətɪv/ *adj* (*lang*) (of words and language) used not in the true sense but in an imaginative way to produce a stronger effect, as in 'a *heated* (*fig*) argument', 'a *deep* thinker'. ⓃMarked (*fig*) in this dictionary.

fig·ura·tive·ly *adv*

fig·ure¹ /'fɪgə(r)/ *nc* (abbr fig) **1** a symbol for a number, esp 0 to 9: *Please write the numbers in*

figures not words. *a five-figure salary* (= one of £10 000 or more). ⇨ double figures. **2** an amount: *a huge figure.* **3** a diagram or illustration, e.g. in a book: *a plane/solid figure. See the figure on page 48.* **4** a person or animal in a picture or carved: *a wooden figure of a cat.* **5** the human form, esp a person's appearance because of her or his shape: *a woman with a slender/trim figure; a fine figure of a man.* **keep/lose one's figure** to remain slender/become fat. **6** a person: *a great academic/political/theatrical figure.* **a figure of fun** a person who other people laugh at and try to make feel foolish. ⇨ father figure, mother figure.

'figure-head *nc* (esp) a person in a high position but with no real power: *Queen Elizabeth II is a figure-head.*

,figure of 'speech *nc* (*pl* **figures of speech**) (*lang*) an example of words used not in the true sense but in an imaginative way to produce a stronger effect: *Metaphors, similes, irony and personification are kinds of figures of speech.*

fig·ure² /'fɪgə(r)/ *v* **1** *vt* to represent (something) in a diagram, drawing etc: *This illustration figures six different animals.* **2** *vi* to appear, be included: *She doesn't figure much in the first act of the play. His research figures in most reports on pollution from petrol.* **3** *vt* (*informal*) to estimate: *I figure that the job will take six months.*

figure in sth to be included in something: *The cost of materials figures in the first account.*

figure sth out (a) to calculate something: *figure out the cost.* **(b)** to learn, work out, something by thinking: *figuring out a way to make another window.* **figure sb out** (*informal*) to understand a person: *I can't figure her out.*

figure on sth (*informal*) to allow for, rely on, something when making plans: *I'm figuring on a large increase in sales/on our doubling sales.*

fila·ment /'fɪləmənt/ *nc* a thin thread, e.g. of metal in an electric light-bulb.

filch /fɪltʃ/ *vt* to steal (something of small value).

file¹ /faɪl/ *nc* a metal tool with a rough surface, used for cutting or smoothing hard substances.

file² /faɪl/ *nc* **1** any kind of holder, case etc used for keeping papers etc together. **2** a set of papers (to be) kept in a file(1). **3** (*computers*) information on one topic etc stored on a cassette or disk. **on file** in or on a file(1) or computer.

fil·ing *nu* the work of placing papers in files.

file³ /faɪl/ *nc* (often **in single file**) (in) a line of people or things one behind the other.

file⁴ /faɪl/ *vt,vi* to use a file¹ on something: *filing one's nails.*

file⁵ /faɪl/ *vt* **1 file sth (away)** to place papers etc in a file: *filing letters.* **2** to send in an official paper: *filing a complaint/application.*

file⁶ /faɪl/ *vi* **file (in/out; into/out of a place)** to walk, march, in a line: *filing into the classroom; filing past their leader.*

fil·ial /'fɪlɪəl/ *adj* (*formal*) of a son or daughter: *filial duty.*

fil·ings /'faɪlɪŋz/ *n pl* bits removed by filing⁴.

fill¹ /fɪl/ *nu* as much as is wanted: *eat/drink one's fill.* **have had one's fill of sb/sth** (*informal*) to have had as much as one can bear: *I've had my fill of you/your rudeness.*

fill·ing *nc* something used to fill something: *a filling in a tooth.*

fill² /fɪl/ v **1** vt,vi (to cause something) to become full: *fill a tank with petrol. Tears filled her eyes. I was filled with admiration.* Opp empty². **2** vt to have (a job) and do the necessary work; put a person in (a job): *The vacancy has already been filled.* **fill the bill** ⇨ bill²(2).

fill in (for sb) to be a substitute: *Can you fill in for me while I go to the doctor tomorrow?* **fill sb in** (informal) to give a person information, e.g. about a future plan, necessary facts for a meeting etc. **fill sth in (a)** to add detail, shading etc to a drawing. **(b)** to complete an application form, a certificate etc by adding the information required, usually personal: *fill in a form when applying for a driving licence; fill in one's tax return.*

fill out to become larger, rounder or fatter: *Her cheeks began to fill out.* **fill sth out** = fill sth in(b).

fill (sth) up (to cause something) to become full: *fill up a petrol tank/a bottle with milk. The cinema is filling up.*

fil·let /'fɪlɪt/ nc a slice of fish or meat without bones. □ vt to cut (fish etc) into fillets: *filleted plaice.*

fil·lip /'fɪlɪp/ nc (fig) an encouragement or stimulus: *an advertising campaign that gave a fresh fillip to sales.*

fil·ly /'fɪlɪ/ nc (pl **-ies**) a young female horse.

film¹ /fɪlm/ n **1** nc a thin coating or covering: *a film of dust/mist.* **2** nu thin flexible material: *plastic film for wrapping food.* ⇨ cling film. **3** nc,nu a length of a special material used to take photographs: *a roll of film.* **4** nc (also attrib) a series of photographs that is shown quickly on a screen so that the people, objects etc in them appear to be moving: *a film about wild animals/a murder; a television film; film critics; a film show.* (US = movie).

'film star nc a very popular cinema actor or actress.

film² /fɪlm/ v **1** vt to make a film(4) of (a person, subject etc): *film a play.* **2** vi **film over** to become covered with a film(1): *The glass filmed over.*

fil·ter¹ /'fɪltə(r)/ nc **1** an apparatus used for holding back solid substances in a liquid passed through it: *an oil filter in a car engine; a coffee filter.* **2** (photography) a coloured piece of glass used on a camera lens to hold back particular forms of light. **3** = filter tip.

'filter tip nc a cigarette end containing material that acts as a filter (for nicotine etc).

'filter-tipped adj: *filter-tipped cigarettes.*

fil·ter² /'fɪltə(r)/ vt,vi **1** (to cause something) to flow through a filter(1,2): *filtered coffee/light.* **2** (fig) (to cause people, traffic, news, ideas etc) to pass or flow: *new ideas filtering into people's minds.*

filth /fɪlθ/ nu **1** a dirty mess. **2** obscene language, pictures etc.

filthy adj (**-ier, -iest**) **1** very dirty: *a filthy floor.* **2** obscene: *a filthy joke.*

fin /fɪn/ nc **1** a wide, thin part attached to a fish, used in swimming. **2** something shaped like or used in the same way as a fin, e.g. on the back of a plane.

fi·nal¹ /'faɪnl/ adj **1** (attrib) coming at the end: *the final chapter of a book.* **2** putting an end to doubt or argument: *a final decision/judgement. My decision is final.*

fi·nal² /'faɪnl/ nc (often pl) the last of a series: *take one's finals* (last examinations); *the tennis finals* (i.e. at the end of a tournament). ⇨ cup final.

fi·nal·ist nc **(a)** a player who takes part in the last of a series of contests. **(b)** a student in her or his last year as an undergraduate.

fi·nal·ly /-nəlɪ/ adv Ⓝ The meaning of *'finally'* depends on its position in a sentence or clause. **(a)** lastly; in conclusion: *Finally, I would like to thank my parents.* Ⓝ Used at the beginning of a sentence or clause. **(b)** after a long time: *We finally managed to find a sofa we both liked.* Ⓝ Used before the verb. **(c)** once and for all: *When the true facts became known we settled the matter finally.* Ⓝ Used at the end of a sentence or clause.

fi·na·le /fɪ'nɑ:lɪ/ nc the last part of a public performance. **the grand finale** the final, splendid part of a (musical) performance.

fi·nal·ity /faɪ'nælətɪ/ nu (formal) the state or quality of being final: *speak with an air of finality* (= as if there is nothing more to be said or done).

fi·nal·ize (also **-ise**) /'faɪnəlaɪz/ vt to give a final form to (something): *finalize plans for a meeting.*

fi·nance¹ /'faɪnæns/ n **1** nu the management of (esp public) money: *an expert in finance.* **2** (often pl) money (esp of a government or a business company): *How much finance will you need for next year? Are the country's finances sound?*

fi·nance² /'faɪnæns/ vt to provide money for (an expedition, business, scheme etc).

fi·nan·cial /faɪ'nænʃl/ adj of finance: *be in financial difficulties* (= be without enough money); *the financial year* (= the annual period for which accounts are made up). ⇨ fiscal.

fi·nan·cial·ly /-ʃəlɪ/ adv

fin·an·ci·er /faɪ'nænsɪər(r)/ nc an expert in finance.

finch /fɪntʃ/ nc a kind of small bird, e.g. chaffinch, bullfinch.

find¹ /faɪnd/ nc a person or thing found by accident or after effort, esp something remarkable or impressive: *This guitarist/diamond is a magnificent find.*

find² /faɪnd/ vt (pt,pp **found** /faʊnd/) Ⓝ **1, 3** not used in the continuous tenses, e.g. *is/was -ing.* **1** to get back (a person, thing) after a search: *I can't find my glasses. She's found her son. Did you ever find the pen you lost?* **2** to discover (something) after searching, studying, experiment or effort: *They've found a cure/remedy for rheumatism. We couldn't find our way home in the dark. Have you found a solution/answer to that problem? Gold has been found in Australia. The tiger is found in India.* ⇨ fault(1), foot¹(1). **3** to discover by chance: *Ben's found a £10 note in the street. We found her dead on the floor in the kitchen.* **4** to become aware of (something) by experience: *I find it impossible to work late at night. Do you find that bed comfortable? You don't find many people willing to nurse old people. I find that students work much harder these days. He finds TV very boring. She finds him difficult to speak to.* **5** to provide (something): *Who will find the money for the expedition?* ⇨ all-found. **6** to succeed in having or getting (something): *How do you find time for all your interests? Can you find room for one* *more potato?* ⇨ bearing(4). **7** (*legal*) to decide and declare a judgement on (a person): *The jury found him guilty/not guilty.*

find against sb (*legal*) to find(7) a person guilty.

find for sb (*legal*) to find(7) a person not guilty.

find out to discover a person's wrong behaviour, an error etc: *You've broken the vase and if your mother finds out she'll be very angry.* **find sb out** (**a**) to discover a person is not at home. (**b**) to discover that a person has done something wrong: *Don't steal pens—if you're found out there'll be trouble.* **find sth out** to learn something by study or inquiry: *Find out the cost and let me know. Please find out when the next train leaves.*

find·er /'faɪndə(r)/ *nc* a person who finds (an object) by accident: *Lost, a gold ring—finder will be rewarded.*

find·ings /'faɪndɪŋz/ *n pl* things learnt or discovered by study or inquiry: *the findings of the committee reviewing discipline in schools.*

fine¹ /faɪn/ *adj* (**—r, —st**) **1** (of weather) bright; clear; not raining: *It rained all morning but turned fine later.* **2** (*pred*) in good health: *I'm feeling fine.* **3** (*attrib*) enjoyable; pleasing; splendid: *a fine view; have a fine time; fine clothes.* **4** delicate; carefully made and easily damaged: *fine silk.* **5** of very small particles: *Sand is finer than gravel.* **6** slender; sharp: *a pencil with a fine point.* **not to put too fine a point on it** ⇨ point¹(1). **7** (of metals) refined; pure: *fine gold.* **8** (able to be) seen or noticed only with difficulty or effort: *a fine distinction.*

fine 'art *nu* (also **the ˌfine 'arts**) the visual arts that appeal to the sense of beauty, esp painting and sculpture.

fine·ly *adv* (**a**) splendidly: *finely dressed.* (**b**) into small pieces: *carrots finely chopped.*

fine·ness *nu*

fine² /faɪn/ *adv* **1** (*informal*) very well: *That will suit me fine.* **2 cut it fine** to leave only the smallest amount of time: *Your bus leaves in ten minutes and you haven't dressed yet—that's cutting it fine!*

fine³ /faɪn/ *vt, nc* (to punish a person by asking for) a sum of money (to be) paid as a penalty for breaking a law or rule: *I was fined £20.*

fin·ery /'faɪnərɪ/ *nu* beautiful and elegant clothes or appearance: *the garden in its summer finery* (= with its flowers etc).

fi·nesse /fɪ'nes/ *nu* a delicate way of dealing with a situation: *show finesse in dealing with people.*

fin·ger¹ /'fɪŋgə(r)/ *nc* one of the end parts of the hand or a glove: *There are four fingers and a thumb on each hand.* **burn one's fingers** (often *passive*) to cause harm or trouble for oneself: *I got my fingers burnt the first time I lent him money.* **have a finger in every pie** to be involved (often too much) in all that is going on. **keep one's fingers crossed** (*fig*) to hope that nothing will prevent success. **not lift a finger (to help sb)** to do nothing to help when help is needed. **pull one's finger out** (*informal*) to begin to work harder; hurry up. **put one's finger on sth** to find the cause of a trouble. **(let sth) slip through sb's fingers** (*fig*) (to allow an opportunity etc) to be missed: *Don't let such an opportunity slip through your fingers.* **twist sb round one's little finger** (*informal*) to per-

suade a person without difficulty to do things one wants her or him to do.

'finger-nail *nc* a nail at the tip of a finger.

'finger·print *nc* a mark made by a finger when pressed on a surface, used for identifying criminals.

'finger·tip *nc* the top of a finger. **have sth at one's fingertips** to be thoroughly familiar with it; know it well.

fin·ger² /'fɪŋgə(r)/ *vt* to touch (something) with the fingers: *finger a piece of cloth.*

fin·ish¹ /'fɪnɪʃ/ *n sing* **1** *n* the last part (of an activity): *the finish of a race; a contest with an exciting finish.* Compare end¹(2). **fight to the finish** to fight, compete etc until there is a decision. **2** *nc* a condition or appearance after being polished, painted etc: *wood with a beautiful/smooth finish.*

fin·ish² /'fɪnɪʃ/ *v* **1** *vt* to bring (an activity etc) to an end: *Have you finished (reading) that book? Finish your dinner! I hope to finish the work by tonight.* **finishing touch** a last small detail done to complete the production of something: *add the finishing touches to a painting.* **2** *vi* to come to an end: *When will the TV programme finish?*

finish sb off (*sl*) to kill a person (after a fight etc). **finish sth off** to complete the production of something by completing the last small details: *finish off (making) a coat.*

finish up (by doing sth) to end an activity (by): *They finished up by having drinks in a night-club.* **finish up (in a place)** to be finally in prison etc.

finish with sb to stop having a relationship with a person: *Oh, I finished with him months ago!*

finish with sth (**a**) to eat something as a final course: *Let's finish with cheese and biscuits.* (**b**) to have no more need or use for something: *Have you finished with that dictionary yet?*

fi·nite /'faɪnaɪt/ *adj* **1** limited: *Human understanding is finite.* Compare infinite. **2** (*gram*) (of a form of a verb) agreeing with a subject in number and person: *'Am', 'is', 'are', 'was' and 'were' are the finite forms of the verb 'to be'.* Compare non-finite.

fiord /fjɔːd/ *nc* = fjord.

fir /fɜː(r)/ *nc, nu* (also *attrib*) (the wood of) a kind of tall tree growing in cold regions with leaves like needles.

'fir-cone *nc* a hard fruit of a fir.

fire¹ /faɪə(r)/ *n* **1** *nu* the condition of burning: *Fire is extremely dangerous.* **catch fire** to begin to burn: *Paper catches fire easily.* **play with fire** to be involved in something dangerous or likely to result in failure. **2** *nc, nu* (an instance of) destructive burning: *There's a fire in the factory. Is your house insured against fire?* **on fire** burning: *The building is on fire!* **set sth on fire** to cause (a building etc) to burn. **set fire to sth** to cause it to burn: *set fire to garden rubbish.* **3** *nc* an amount of burning fuel, used to heat, cook etc: *a warm fire in the sitting-room.* **light a fire** to cause a fire(3) to begin to burn. **4** *nc* an apparatus using gas, electricity, paraffin etc for heating a room etc: *an electric fire.* **5** *nu* the process of shooting (from a gun etc). **cease/open fire** to stop/begin shooting. **hang fire** (of events) to be slow in developing or be delayed. **under fire** (**a**) being

shot at. **(b)** (*fig*) (of a person) being criticized. **6**
nu passion; angry or excited feeling: *speak with
fire; with fire in her eyes*.

'**fire alarm** *nc* an apparatus (bell etc) used as a
warning of fire(2).

'**fire·arm** *nc* a rifle, gun, pistol or revolver.

'**fire brigade** *nc* (the —) the organized team of
people who put out fires(2).

'**fire drill** *nc* a practice of the routine to be followed when fire(2) breaks out.

'**fire-engine** *nc* (a vehicle with) a machine for
putting out a fire(2).

'**fire-escape** *nc* **(a)** an outside staircase for leaving a burning building. **(b)** an apparatus used to
save people from a burning building.

'**fire extinguisher** *nc* a portable cylinder with a
chemical substance etc inside, used for putting
out a small fire(2).

'**fire-fighter** *nc* a person who works in a fire brigade.

'**fire·man** *nc* a man who works in a fire brigade.

'**fire·place** *nc* a place for a fire(3) in a room.

'**fire·proof** *adj* **(a)** that does not burn. **(b)** that
does not break when heated.

'**fire·side** *nc* (the —; also *attrib*) the part of a
room round the fireplace: *sitting at/by the fireside;
a fireside chair*.

'**fire station** *nc* a building for a fire brigade.

'**fire·wood** *nu* wood used for lighting fires or as
fuel.

'**fire·work** *nc* a device containing gunpowder
and chemicals, used for making a colourful display at night.

fire² /faɪə(r)/ *v* **1** *vt,vi* to shoot (bullets) using a
gun etc: *firing a gun. 'Fire!' shouted the captain.
fire (away) (at sb/sth) **(a)** to shoot (at a person,
thing): *firing (away) at an armed criminal*. **(b)**
(*fig*) to ask questions, make critical remarks etc
loudly and quickly: *Don't fire so many questions
at me—I need time to think. I'm ready for your
questions now, so fire away*. **2** *vt* (*informal*) to dismiss (a person) from a job: *You're fired!* **3** *vt* to
produce a strong feeling or emotion in (a person):
His speech has fired me with enthusiasm. **4** *vt* to
heat (clay, metal etc) in order to change its form
or shape: *fire clay pots in a kiln*.

'**firing-line** *nc* the front line where soldiers fire at
the enemy **be in the firing-line** (*fig*) to be
exposed to direct attack, criticism etc.

'**firing-squad** *nc* a number of soldiers ordered
to carry out a military execution.

firm¹ /fɜːm/ *adj* (**—er, —est**) **1** fixed in position:
Is the shelf firm? **2** solid; hard; not yielding when
pressed: *firm flesh/muscles*. **3** not easily changed
or influenced; showing strength of character and
purpose: *a firm promise; be firm with children* (=
insist on obedience and discipline). **4** steady,
stable: *walk with firm steps; a firm chair; be firm
on one's feet*.

firm·ly *adv* in a firm manner: *Is it nailed firmly to
the door? She spoke firmly to the children*.

firm·ness *nu*

firm² /fɜːm/ *adv* firmly: *stand firm; hold firm to
one's beliefs*.

firm³ /fɜːm/ *nc* (two or more people carrying on)
a business.

fir·ma·ment /ˈfɜːməmənt/ *n* (the —) the sky,
heavens and all that is in them.

first¹ /fɜːst/ *adj* or *det* (abbr 1st) *the/my/its* etc
first + *noun* coming before all others in order or
time, importance etc: *January is the first month of
the year. The first prize is a car. My first child was a
boy. I'll do it at the first* (= earliest) *opportunity*.
Compare last¹(1), next¹(1). **at first hand** ⇨
hand¹(1). **at first sight** ⇨ sight¹(2). **first thing**
⇨ thing(4).

,**first 'aid** *nu* treatment given to a sick or injured
person before a doctor comes.

,**first 'class** *nu* (also *attrib*: ,'first-class) the best
standard: *first-class hotels; a first-class* (university) *degree. Is this first class* (e.g. in a train, plane
etc)? □ *adv* in the best accommodation in a train,
plane etc: *travel first-class*.

,**first 'cousin** *nc* the child of one's aunt or uncle.
⇨ second cousin.

'**first-degree** *adj* (*attrib*) of the most serious
kind: *first-degree burns/murder*.

,**first 'floor** *nc* (*GB*) the floor immediately above
the ground floor; (*US*) the ground floor.

,**first ,gene'ration** *adj* (*attrib*) being the first of
the family to come: *first generation immigrants*.

,**first-'hand** *adj, adv* (obtained) directly from the
source: *first-hand information; learn something
first-hand*. ⇨ hand¹(1).

,**first 'lady** *nc* (the —) the wife of a president.

'**first name** *nc* a given name, e.g. David, Mary.
⇨ surname.

,**first 'person** *nu* (*gram*) the pronouns *I, me, we,
us* (and the verb forms used with them), used to
show the person speaking. ⇨ second/third person.

,**first-'rate** *adj* excellent: *first-rate acting*. □ *adv*
(*informal*) very well: *getting on first-rate*.

'**first school** *nc* one in Britain for children aged
5 to 9 years.

first² /fɜːst/ *adv* **1** before any other or others: *I
saw her first. What will do you first? First, I'd like
to thank my wife*. Compare last²(1), next²(1).
first of all (used for emphasis): *First of all we
must rescue the children*. **first and foremost**
(used for emphasis) before anything else: *First
and foremost you must check that the electricity is
off*. **2** for the first time: *I first met her in Paris
twenty years ago. When did you first have an interest in music?* Compare last²(2), next²(2). **3** more
willingly: *I won't work with him—I'd resign first!*
Ⓝ 'Rather' is also possible, but the structure
changes, as in *I'd rather resign* (than work for him)!

first³ /fɜːst/ *pron* (abbr 1st) **1** (the —) the first
person, thing or people, things etc: *He was/We
were the first to leave. It's the first of April/April
the first/1st April. I'm the first to agree that he's
intelligent*. Compare last³, next³. **at first** at the
beginning: *At first she refused to help but I soon
persuaded her. She refused at first*. **from the
first** from the beginning: *I knew from the first that
he was lazy*. **from first to last** from the beginning to the end (of a period of activity or time):
*He was a kind and generous manager from first to
last*. **2** *nc* (in examinations) a best standard in a
university examination: *He got a first in biology*.
⇨ first class.

first-born /ˈfɜːst bɔːn/ *adj* (*attrib*), *nc* an eldest
(child): *my first-born son*.

first·ly /ˈfɜːstlɪ/ *adv* before (saying) any other
thing: *Firstly, I'd like to apologize for replying so

late. Compare lastly.

firth /fɜ:θ/ *nc* (esp in Scotland) a river estuary or sea inlet.

fis·cal /'fɪskl/ *adj* (*attrib*) concerning public money, esp taxes: *a fiscal policy; the fiscal year.*

fish¹ /fɪʃ/ *n* (*pl* — or **—es**) **1** *nc* an animal living in water and breathing through gills: *catch a fish/two fishes/a lot of fish.* **have other fish to fry** to have other important business to attend to. **feel like a fish out of water** to feel uncomfortable or uneasy because of strange surroundings. **2** *nu* fish as food: *fish and chips.*

'fish cake *nc* a shaped piece of minced fish.

fish 'finger *nc* a long piece of fish in bread-crumbs.

'fish-knife *nc* a knife designed for eating fish.

'fish·monger *nc* a person, business, that sells fish.

'fish·paste *nu* a paste of fish or shellfish (spread on bread etc).

'fish-slice *nc* an implement for serving fish at table.

fishy *adj* (**-ier, -iest**) (**a**) smelling or tasting like fish: *a fishy smell.* (**b**) (*informal*) causing a feeling of doubt: *a fishy story.*

fish² /fɪʃ/ *v* **1** *vi* **fish (for sth)** to try to catch (fish): *go fishing.* **2** *vi* **fish for sth** (*fig*) to try to get something by indirect methods: *fish for information/compliments.* **3** *vt* **fish sth out** (*informal*) to take or pull out something: *He fished out a coin from his pocket.*

fish·ing *nu* catching fish for a living or for pleasure.

'fish·ing-line *nc* a line with a hook attached, used for fishing.

'fish·ing-rod *nc* a rod to which a fishing-line is fastened.

fisher·man /'fɪʃəmən/ *nc* (*pl* **-men**) a man who earns a living by fishing. Compare angler.

fis·sion /'fɪʃn/ *nc,nu* (*science*) a splitting or division, e.g. of an atom: *nuclear fission.*

fis·sure /'fɪʃə(r)/ *nc* (*tech*) a narrow opening: *a fissure in a rock.*

fist /fɪst/ *nc* a hand when tightly closed (as in boxing): *He struck me with his fist.*

fit¹ /fɪt/ *adj* (**—ter, —test**) **1** **fit (for sth/to do sth)** suitable or suited; good enough: *The food was not fit to eat. That man is not fit for the job.* **think/see fit (to do sth)** to consider an action, decision, to be right: *Do as you think fit.* Opp unfit(1). **2** in good health; in a good bodily condition: *feel fit after a long walk; be fit for work.* **keep fit** (also *attrib*) (to do exercises) to remain in good health: *go to keep-fit classes.* Opp unfit(2). **3** (used as an *adv*) **fit to + verb** (*informal*) ready to: *He was laughing fit to burst.*

fit·ness *nu* (**a**) **fitness for sth** suitability (for a job, use). (**b**) the state of being physically fit.

fit² /fɪt/ *nc* **1** a sudden (usually short) attack of illness: *a fit of coughing.* **2** a sudden attack, e.g. with loss of consciousness and violent movements: *fall down in a fit.* **give sb a fit** (*informal*) to do something that greatly shocks a person. **have a fit** (*informal*) to be greatly surprised or angered: *She almost had a fit when she saw the bill.* **throw a fit** to be suddenly angry. **3** a sudden outburst lasting for a short time: *a fit of energy/enthusiasm/temper.* **by fits and starts**

often starting and then stopping again: *do the job by fits and starts.*

fit·ful /-fəl/ *adj* irregular and restless: *fitful sleep.*

fit·fully /-fəlɪ/ *adv: sleep fitfully.*

fit³ /fɪt/ *n sing* a way something (e.g. clothing) fits(1): *This coat/wooden shelf is a good fit.*

fit⁴ /fɪt/ *v* (**-tt-**) Ⓝ **1**, **4** not used in the continuous tenses, e.g. *is/was -ing.* **1** *vt,vi* to be the right measure, shape and size for (a person, place): *shoes that fit (her) badly/well.* **2** *vt* to put on (esp clothing) to see that it is the right size, shape etc: *have a new coat fitted.* **fit like a glove** to fit well. **3** *vt* to put (something) into place: *fit a new lock on a door.* **4** *vt* to make (a person, something) suitable or competent: *Can we make the punishment fit the crime?*

fit in (with sth) (of a person) to be, feel, comfortable and right among particular people: *I never visit my sister because I don't feel that I fit in (with her family).* **fit sb/sth in** to find time to do something, see or speak to a person etc: *I'll see if I can fit you in this afternoon.* **fit sth in** to cause something to be suitable (in time or position): *Why must I fit my holiday plans in with yours?*

fit sb/sth out (for sth) to supply a person or ship etc with what is needed: *fit out an expedition for a long journey.*

fit sb/sth up (with sth) to supply a person, building etc: *a hotel fitted up with modern comforts.*

fit·ment /'fɪtmənt/ *nc* a piece of fitted furniture or equipment: *kitchen fitments.*

fit·ted /'fɪtɪd/ *adj* (usually *attrib*) **1** supplied with fixed cupboards in particular places: *a fitted kitchen.* **2** cut to cover a floor completely: *fitted carpets.* Compare fixture(1).

fit·ter /'fɪtə(r)/ *nc* **1** a person who cuts out, fits and alters clothes. **2** a workman who fits and adjusts parts of an engine, machine etc.

fit·ting¹ /'fɪtɪŋ/ *adj* right; suitable: *a fitting moment to apologize.*

fit·ting² /'fɪtɪŋ/ *nc* **1** act of fitting: *go to the tailor's for a fitting.* **2** (*pl*) things permanently fixed in a building: *gas and electric light fittings.* Compare fixture(1).

five /faɪv/ *adj or det, nc* (of) 5. ⇨ fifth.

'five·fold *adj, adv* 5 times as many or as much.

five·pence /'faɪfpəns/ *n* the value of 5 pence.

,five-pence 'piece *nc* (*pl* **,five-pence 'pieces**) a GB coin worth 5 pence.

'five-star *adj* of the best or luxury class: *a five-star hotel.*

fiv·er /'faɪvə(r)/ *nc* (*informal*) a £5 note.

fix¹ /fɪks/ *nc* **1** **be in/get (oneself) into a fix** to be in/get into a dilemma, an awkward situation. **2** a position found, e.g. when sailing, by taking bearings, observing the stars etc. **3** (*sl*) an injection of a drug, e.g. heroin.

fix² /fɪks/ *vt* **1** to make (something) firm so that it cannot be moved: *fix shelves to a wall.* **2** to determine or decide (something): *fix the rent/a date for a meeting; a man with fixed* (= definite and decided) *ideas.* **3** (*informal*) to repair (something): *fix a watch/car; have one's teeth fixed.* **4** (*informal*) to put (hair, clothes) in order: *fix one's hair/dress.* **5** to treat (photographic films, colours used in dyeing etc) so that light does not affect them. **6** (*sl*) (**a**) to use bribery or deception, improper influence on (an official): *Can you fix a judge in Britain?* (**b**) to have revenge on (a person): *I'll fix him!*

fix sth on sb/sth to direct one's attention, eyes etc on a person, thing: *fix one's attention on what one is doing* or *on an attractive film star.* **fix sth on/onto sth** to attach a fastener, piece of equipment etc on something: *fix a lock on a window.*

fix sb up with sb/sth (*informal*) to arrange for a person to have a friend, job, car etc: *He fixed me up with a new car/a girlfriend for the party. You can stay here until you're fixed up.* **fix sth up** (**a**) to arrange a meeting, a tour etc. (**b**) (*informal*) to repair something.

fix sb with sth (*formal*) to get and keep a person's attention using an angry or frightening look: *He fixed her with a hostile look.*

fix·ed /fɪkst/ *adj* (*no comp*) **1** firmly attached or fastened: *fixed cupboards.* ⇨ fixture(1). **2** (*attrib*) always the same: *have a fixed expression; meet at a fixed time each week.* **3** (*informal*) (of a trial, appointment for a job) using unfair or wrong methods: *a fixed trial* (= with a judge or jury prepared to accept unfair influence); *a fixed appointment/interview* (= when it is known in advance who will be given the job).

,**fixed 'assets** *n pl* (*finance*) valuable parts of a business that are permanent such as buildings, machinery, goodwill.

,**fixed 'charge** *nc* (*finance*) one that is the same each time it is paid.

'**fixed cost** *nc* (*finance*) a cost that does not change according to the number of things being produced, such as rent, salaries etc. Compare variable cost.

,**fixed 'disk** *nc* (*computers*) one that cannot be changed, e.g. shortened.

,**fixed ex'pression/'phrase** *nc* (*lang*) one that is always the same and cannot be changed, such as *flesh and blood, make oneself at home, cut corners* etc.

fix·ation /fɪk'seɪʃn/ *nc* a very strong feeling or emotion: *She has a fixation about bathing daily.*

fixa·tive /'fɪksətɪv/ *nc* any kind of substance which keeps something (e.g. paint, a specimen) in position or fixes(5) colours, film etc.

fix·ture /'fɪkstʃə(r)/ *nc* **1** something fixed in place, esp (*pl*) built-in cupboards etc which are bought with a building: *We were charged for fixtures and fittings.* Compare fitted, fitting²(2). **2** (a day fixed or decided for) a sporting event: *football and racing fixtures.* **3** (*informal*) a person who appears unlikely to move from a place: *Professor Green seems to be a permanent fixture in the college.*

fizz /fɪz/ *vi, nc* (to make) a hissing sound (as when gas escapes from a liquid).

fizzy *adj* (**-ier, -iest**) (of a drink) containing bubbles: *fizzy lemonade.*

fizzle /'fɪzl/ *vi* **fizzle out** (of a protest, meeting, party etc) to come to a weak, unsatisfactory end.

fjord (*also* **fiord**) /fjɔːd/ *nc* a long, narrow inlet of the coast between high cliffs or mountains, esp in Norway.

fl *written abbr* fluid.

flab·by /'flæbɪ/ *adj* (**-ier, -iest**) (of the muscles, flesh) soft; not firm: *A man who never takes any exercise is likely to have flabby muscles.*

flab·bi·ness *nu*

flag¹ /flæg/ *nc* a colourful piece of cloth, attached by one edge to a rope, used as the distinctive symbol of a country or as a signal: *the national flag of France.*

'**flag-pole** *nc* a pole for a flag.

flag² /flæg/ *vt* (**-gg-**) **flag sb/sth down** to signal (a driver, vehicle) to stop by waving.

flag³ /flæg/ *vi* (**-gg-**) **1** (of a plant) to hang down, become limp. **2** (*fig*) to become tired or weak: *His strength/interest in his work was flagging.*

flag·on /'flægən/ *nc* a large, round bottle in which wine etc is sold.

fla·grant /'fleɪgrənt/ *adj* (*derog*) (of a crime etc) openly and obviously wicked: *flagrant offences; a flagrant breach of the rules.*

fla·grant·ly *adv*

flag·stone /'flægstəʊn/ *nc* a flat piece of stone for a floor, path or pavement.

flair /fleə(r)/ *nu* or *sing* **have a flair for sth** to have a natural ability to do something well, to select or recognize what is best etc: *have a flair for languages.*

flake¹ /fleɪk/ *nc* a small, light, leaf-like piece: *snow-flakes; soap-flakes.*

flake² /fleɪk/ *vi* **1** **flake (off)** to fall off in flakes. **2** **flake out** (*informal*) (of a person) to collapse with exhaustion.

flaky *adj* (**-ier, -iest**) made up of flakes: *flaky pastry.*

flam·boy·ance /flæm'bɔɪəns/ *nu* being flamboyant.

flam·boy·ant /flæm'bɔɪənt/ *adj* **1** brightly coloured and decorated. **2** (of a person, behaviour, writing style etc) very energetic, lively etc.

flam·boy·ant·ly *adv*

flame¹ /fleɪm/ *n* **1** *nc,nu* (a portion of) burning gas: *He put a match to the papers and they burst into flame(s).* **in flames** burning. **2** *nc* a strong feeling: *a flame of anger/enthusiasm.* **3** *nc* **an old flame** (*dated; informal*) a sweetheart: *She's an old flame of his.*

flame² /fleɪm/ *vi* **1** to burn with, send out, flames. **2** (*fig*) to be or become like flames in colour: *trees that flame in autumn.*

flam·ing *adj: flaming trees.*

fla·min·go /flə'mɪŋgəʊ/ *nc* (*pl* **—s** or **—es**) a kind of large waterbird with a long neck, long legs, and pink feathers.

flam·mable /'flæməbl/ *adj* likely to burst into flames and to burn quickly. Ⓝ '*Flammable*' and '*inflammable*' have the same meaning. The opposite is '*non-flammable*'.

flan /flæn/ *nc* a tart containing fruit etc that is not covered with pastry.

flank¹ /flæŋk/ *nc* **1** the side of a human being or animal between the last rib and the hip. **2** a side of a mountain. **3** a right or left side of an army: *attack the left flank.*

flank² /flæŋk/ *vt* to be situated or move along the side of (a person, thing): *a road flanked with tall trees. We flanked the enemy and crossed the frontier.*

flan·nel¹ /'flænl/ *n* **1** *nu* a kind of loosely woven woollen cloth. **2** *nc* a face-cloth.

flan·nel² /'flænl/ *vi, nc* (*informal*) (to give) an indirect or useless answer to avoid commitment.

flap¹ /flæp/ *nc* **1** (a sound of) a flapping blow or

movement. **2** a piece of material that hangs down or covers an opening: *the flap of a pocket/an envelope.* **3** a part of the wing of a plane that can be raised or lowered to alter its height or speed. **4** *be in/get into a flap* (*sl*) to be in/get into a state of anxious excitement or confusion.

flap² /flæp/ *v* (**-pp-**) **1** *vt,vi* (to cause something) to move up and down or from side to side: *The sails were flapping against the mast. The bird was flapping its wings.* **2** *vt* **flap sth away/off** to give something a light blow with something soft and flat: *flap the flies off/away.* **3** *vi* (*sl*) to become anxious and excited: *Stop flapping!*

flare¹ /fleə(r)/ *n* **1** *nu* a bright burning light: *the flare of the Olympic torch.* **2** *nc* a device that produces bright light, used as a signal.

flare² /fleə(r)/ *vt* **1** to burn with a bright flame: *flaring torches.* **2** **flare up** (**a**) to burst into bright flame. (**b**) (*fig*) (of violence, anger) to break out suddenly: *She flares up at the least thing. Rioting flared up again later.* Hence **'flare-up** *nc*.

flare³ /fleə(r)/ *vt,vi* (to cause trousers, a skirt etc) to spread gradually outwards.

flared *adj: a flared skirt.*

flash¹ /flæʃ/ *nc* **1** a sudden burst of flame or light: *a flash of lightning.* **2** (*fig*) a sudden idea, realization etc. *in a flash* instantly, at once: *I realized in a flash that she was the thief.* *a flash in the pan* an effort that is quickly over or soon ends in failure. ⇨ also newsflash.

'flash·back *nc* a part of a film etc that shows a scene earlier in time than the rest.

'flash·bulb *nc* a bulb used in photography giving a flash of light. ⇨ flashlight (b).

'flash·gun *nc* = flashlight(b).

'flash·light *nc* (**a**) a light used for signals, in lighthouses etc. (**b**) a device for producing a brilliant flash of light for taking a photograph. (**c**) a small electric torch.

flash² /flæʃ/ *v* **1** *vt* to send, give out, a sudden bright light: *Lightning flashed across the sky.* **2** *vi* to come suddenly (into view, into the mind): *The idea flashed into/through his mind.* **3** *vt* to send (something) instantly: *flash news across the world* (by radio or TV). **4** *vt* to show or reflect (a feeling) suddenly: *Her eyes flashed defiance.* **5** *vt* *flash sth at sb/sth* to show something briefly: *flash a light/a document at him.* **6** *vi* to move quickly: *The train flashed past us.*

flashy /'flæʃɪ/ *adj* (**-ier, -iest**) (usually *derog*) shining and attractive but often a little vulgar: *flashy clothes/jewellery/men.*

flask /flɑːsk/ *nc* **1** a narrow-necked bottle. **2** = vacuum flask.

flat¹ /flæt/ *adj* (**—ter, —test**) **1** smooth and level; even: *as flat as a pancake* (= very flat). *The top of a table is flat. We need flat ground for putting up the tent. Do the walls have a flat surface?* *flat against sth* with one surface completely touching another: *I stood flat against the wall.* **2** not deep or high: *a flat dish/cap. The omelette/cake is flat. Where are my flat shoes?* **3** dull; boring: *The conversation/scenery/party/food is rather flat.* **4** (of a battery) no longer producing electricity. **5** (of a tyre) no longer having air inside. **6** (of drinks) no longer fizzy. **7** (of trade) not active. **8** (of colours) not bright or shiny; dull. **9** without variety in amount or kind: *speak in a flat voice.* **10**

(*attrib; no comp*) without any limitations or restrictions: *a flat refusal/denial.* **flat broke** completely without money. ⇨ also spin¹(3). **11** (*attrib; no comp*) without changing: *a flat charge/rate.* Ⓝ *'Fixed'* is also possible. **12** (*music*) lower than the true or acceptable pitch: *a flat note.* Compare sharp¹(7).

'flat-fish *nc* a fish (*sole, plaice,* etc) having a flat body and swimming on one side.

,flat-'footed *adj* (**a**) having feet with flat soles. (**b**) (*informal; derog*) (of behaviour) clumsy.

,flat 'spin *nc* (**a**) an (uncontrollable) descent of a spinning plane. (**b**) (*informal*) a mental state of great confusion: *be in a flat spin.*

flat·ly *adv* absolutely: *He flatly refused to help.*

flat·ness *nu*

flat² /flæt/ *adv* **1** in, into a flat(1) position: *lie flat on the floor; hold your hand out flat.* **2** exactly: *run a mile in four minutes flat.* **3** (used for emphasis) completely; without limitations or restrictions: *He told me flat that he did not like my dress. I asked for a job and was turned down flat. I'm flat broke until Friday.* **4** in a flat(12) way: *sing flat.* **5** *flat out* (*informal*) using all one's energy and strength and not stopping: *work flat out to finish the job.*

flat³ /flæt/ *nc* **1** a set of rooms on one floor of a building, used as a home: *convert a large house into flats; a new block of flats.* **2** an area of level ground: *mud flats.* **3** a flat surface: *the flat of the hand.* **4** a flat(5) tyre. **5** (*music*) (a symbol for) a flat(12) note. Compare sharp³.

flat·ten /'flætn/ *vt,vi* (to cause a person, thing) to become flat: *flatten out a map on the table; a field of wheat flattened by storms; flatten oneself against a wall.*

flat·ter /'flætə(r)/ *vt* **1** to praise (a person) too much or insincerely (in order to please). **flatter oneself that . . .** to be pleased with one's opinion of a person etc . . . : *I flatter myself that I'm a good judge of people's characters.* **2** (of a picture, artist etc) to show (a person) as better looking than he or she is: *This photograph flatters you.*

flat·ter·er *nc* a person who flatters(1).

flat·tery *nc,nu* (*pl* **-ies**) (a piece of) (usually insincere) praise: *Don't be deceived by her flatteries.*

flaunt /flɔːnt/ *vt* to show off in order to attract attention to (oneself, one's possessions): *flaunt oneself/one's riches.*

flau·tist /'flɔːtɪst/ *nc* a person who plays a flute.

fla·vour¹ (*US* = **-vor**) /'fleɪvə(r)/ *n* **1** *nu* the sensation of taste and smell: *Some food has very little flavour.* **2** *nc* a particular taste: *various flavours of ice-cream.* **3** *nc* a special quality: *a newspaper story with a flavour of romance.*

fla·vour² (*US* = **-vor**) /'fleɪvə(r)/ *vt* to give a flavour to (food etc): *flavour a sauce with onions.*

fla·vour·ing (*US* = **-vor-**) *nc* something used to give flavour to food etc.

flaw /flɔː/ *nc* something that lessens the value, beauty or perfection of a thing: *flaws in a jewel/an argument/a person's character.*

flaw·less *adj* perfect.

flaw·less·ly *adv*

flax /flæks/ *nu* a plant with fibre in its stem (used to make *linen*) and oil in its seed (used to make *linseed oil*).

flax·en /'flæksən/ adj (of hair) pale yellow.

flea /fliː/ nc a kind of small wingless jumping insect that feeds on the blood of humans and animals.

'flea market nc an open-air market selling cheap and second-hand goods.

fleck[1] /flek/ nc **1** a small spot or patch: flecks of colour on a bird's breast. **2** a small particle (of dust etc).

fleck[2] /flek/ vt (usually passive) to mark (something) with flecks: a sky flecked with clouds.

fled /fled/ pt,pp of flee.

fledged /fledʒd/ adj (of birds) with fully-grown wing feathers.

,fully-'fledged adj (attrib; fig) trained and experienced: a fully-fledged engineer.

fledg(e)·ling nc **(a)** a young bird just able to fly. **(b)** (fig) a young, inexperienced person.

flee /fliː/ vi,vt (pt,pp fled /fled/) to run or hurry away (from a place): He killed his enemy and fled the country.

fleece[1] /fliːs/ nc,nu (a piece of) the woolly covering of a sheep or similar animal: a coat lined with fleece.

fleecy adj (-ier, -iest) like, with, fleece: fleecy snow; a fleecy-lined coat.

fleece[2] /fliːs/ vt (informal) to rob (a person) by using trickery: He was fleeced of his money.

fleet /fliːt/ nc **1** a number of warships under one commander; all the warships of a country. **2** a number of vehicles moving or working under one command or ownership: a fleet of buses/taxis.

fleet·ing /'fliːtɪŋ/ adj (usually attrib) lasting for a short time: a fleeting visit; fleeting happiness.

flesh /fleʃ/ nu **1** the soft part, esp muscle, between the skin and bones of animal bodies: Tigers are flesh-eating animals. **flesh and blood** human nature with its emotions, weaknesses etc: This cruelty is more than flesh and blood can stand. **one's own flesh and blood** one's close relatives. **2** the body (contrasted with the mind and soul): The spirit is willing but the flesh is weak. **in the flesh** in actual bodily form: You say he wasn't there, but I saw him in the flesh. **3** the soft, juicy part of fruits and vegetables.

flew /fluː/ pt of fly[3].

flex[1] /fleks/ nc,nu a (length of) flexible covered wire for electric current.

flex[2] /fleks/ vt to stretch (e.g. a muscle, leg).

flex·ible /'fleksəbl/ adj **1** easily bent without breaking. **2** (fig) (of plans etc) easily changed to suit new conditions. **3** (fig) (of people) easily adapting to new conditions or decisions; (of persons) adaptable. Opp inflexible.

flexi·bil·ity /,fleksə'bɪlətɪ/ nu

flexi·time /'fleksɪtaɪm/ nu (the system of) working for a total amount of time with the hours and days chosen by the worker.

flick[1] /flɪk/ nc **1** a quick, sudden movement: a flick of the switch; a flick of the wrist. **2** a quick, light stroke: the flick of a whip.

flick[2] /flɪk/ vt **1** to move (something) with a flick: The cat flicked its paw and caught the butterfly. He flicked the whip, and the lion sat down. **2** to hit (something) lightly and quickly: I flicked the coin and it spun into the air.

flick sth away/from/off to remove something with a flick(2): flick away a piece of dust.

flick sth on/off to switch a light, lamp etc on/off quickly.

flick sth out to send something forward or out with a quick, sudden movement: The snake flicked out its tongue.

flick through sth to turn the pages of a magazine, book etc and look at it quickly: flicking through a telephone directory.

flick·er[1] /'flɪkə(r)/ nc an irregular or unsteady movement or appearance: a flicker of light; a flicker of hope.

flick·er[2] /'flɪkə(r)/ vi **1** (of a light) to burn or shine irregularly and unsteadily: The candle flickered and then went out. **2** (fig) (of hopes etc) to appear briefly: A faint hope still flickered in her heart.

fli·er /'flaɪə(r)/ nc = flyer.

flight[1] /flaɪt/ n **1** nu the act of flying through the air: study the flight of birds. **in flight** while flying. **2** nc a journey made by air: a non-stop flight from Paris to New York. **3** nc an instance of going beyond the ordinary: a flight of the imagination/fancy. **4** nc (also a flight of stairs) a series of stairs between two landings: My bedroom is two flights up. **5** nu the movement (and path) through the air: the flight of an arrow. **6** nc a number of birds or things moving together through the air: a flight of swallows/arrows/bombers.

'flight deck nc **(a)** (in a plane) the compartment used by the pilot, navigator, engineer etc. **(b)** (on an aircraft-carrier) the deck for taking off from and landing on.

'flight lieutenant nc an officer with a commissioned rank in the Air Force.

'flight path nc a (planned) course of an aircraft or spacecraft.

'flight·less adj (of birds) unable to fly.

flight[2] /flaɪt/ nc,nu (an act, instance of) running away or fleeing (from danger etc): seek safety in flight. **take (to) flight** to run away.

flim·sy /'flɪmzɪ/ adj (-ier, -iest) **1** (of material) light and thin. **2** (of objects) easily destroyed. **3** (fig; derog) weak: a flimsy excuse/attempt.

flim·si·ly /-əlɪ/ adv

flim·si·ness /nu

flinch /flɪntʃ/ vi to move back (because of fear, pain): have a tooth pulled out without flinching.

fling[1] /flɪŋ/ nc **1** an act of throwing something quickly. **2** (in Scotland) a kind of lively dance: the Highland fling. **3 have a fling** (informal) to enjoy a period of fun and pleasure: have a fling after the exams.

fling[2] /flɪŋ/ vt (pt,pp flung /flʌŋ/) **1** to throw, move, (something) quickly and with force: fling a stone; fling the doors and windows open; be flung into prison. **2** to move (oneself, one's arms etc) violently, quickly or angrily: fling one's clothes on (= dress quickly and carelessly). **3 fling oneself into sth** to work at a task etc with enthusiasm: He flung himself into his new job.

flint /flɪnt/ n **1** nu a kind of hard stone. **2** nc a piece of hard metal as used in a cigarette-lighter to produce sparks.

flip[1] /flɪp/ nc a quick, light hit to make something move: the flip of a coin.

flip[2] /flɪp/ v (-pp-) **1** vt to make (something) move by a light hit: flip a coin (down) on the counter. **2** vt **flip through sth** = flick through sth. **3** vi (*informal*) to become very angry: *My dad saw the damage to his car and flipped.*

'flip side *nc* (*informal*) the less popular side (of a record).

flip·pan·cy /'flɪpənsɪ/ *nu* the state, act, of being flippant.

flip·pant /'flɪpənt/ *adj* (*derog*) not showing deserved respect: *a flippant answer/remark.*

flip·pant·ly *adv*

flip·per /'flɪpə(r)/ *nc* **1** a flat limb of certain sea animals (not fish) used in swimming: *Seals, turtles and penguins have flippers.* **2** a similar device, usually of rubber, worn on the feet to aid swimming.

flirt /flɜːt/ *vi* to try to attract a person; show affection without serious intentions: *She flirts with every man she meets.* □ *nc* a person who flirts.

flit¹ /flɪt/ *nc* **do a moonlight flit** to leave a rented home etc secretly and quickly at night to avoid debts.

flit² /flɪt/ *vi* (**-tt-**) **1** to fly or move lightly and quickly: *bees flitting from flower to flower.* **2** (*fig*) to pass quickly: *fancies that flit through one's mind.*

float¹ /fləʊt/ *nc* **1** a piece of cork or other light material as used on a fishing-line or to support the edge of a fishing-net. **2** a low platform on wheels, as used for showing things in a procession. **3** an amount of money used, e.g. by shopkeepers, to provide change at the start of business dealings.

float² /fləʊt/ *v* **1** *vt,vi* (to cause a person, thing) to stay on the surface of a liquid, or up in air, gas: *Wood floats on water. A balloon floated across the sky.* Compare sink²(1). **2** *vt* (*commerce*) to get (esp financial) support in order to start (something): *float a new company.* **3** *vt* (*finance*) to allow the foreign exchange value (of a currency) to change: *float the dollar.*

float·ing *adj* (*attrib*) free from attachment; not fixed or settled: *a floating population.* **floating voters** those not committed to any political party.

flock¹ /flɒk/ *nc* **1** a group of birds, sheep or goats. **2** a crowd of people: *Visitors came in flocks to see the new bridge.*

flock² /flɒk/ *vi* **flock around sb/together** to come or go together in great numbers: *The children flocked round their teacher.*

floe /fləʊ/ *nc* a sheet of floating ice.

flog /flɒg/ *vt* (**-gg-**) **1** to beat (a person, animal) severely with a rod or whip. **flog a dead horse** to waste one's efforts. **flog sth to death** to try to persuade people so much that they lose interest: *flog an idea/joke to death.* **2** (*sl*) to (try to) sell (something): *flog one's old car.*

flog·ging *nc,nu*

flood¹ /flʌd/ *nc* **1** a large great quantity of water in a place that is usually dry: *The rainstorms caused floods in the low-lying areas.* **2** (*fig*) a large amount or outburst: *floods of tears; a flood of anger/letters.*

'flood·gate *nc* (**a**) a gate opened and closed to control water. (**b**) (*fig*) a beginning of a large rush of people or activity: *The floodgates were opened as people hurried to apply for jobs in the new factory.*

'flood·light *nc* an artificial light producing a bright and broad beam.

'flood·lit *adj* lit by floodlights: *a floodlit sports stadium.*

flood² /flʌd/ *vt,vi* (to cause a place, business etc) to become covered or filled (as if) with a flood: *Thousands of people were flooded out* (= forced to leave their homes because of flooding). *We've been flooded with requests. Requests are flooding in for the free tickets.*

floor¹ /flɔː(r)/ *nc* **1** the lower surface of a room etc on which people, furniture etc stand: *the kitchen floor.* **wipe the floor with sb** to defeat a person completely and openly, e.g. in an argument. **2** a collection of rooms etc on the same level in a building: *I live on the ground floor/top floor.* **3** the bottom (of the sea, of a cave etc). **4** the part of an assembly hall, e.g. a parliament, where members sit. **take the floor** to speak in a debate.

'floor·board *nc* a wooden plank for a floor.

'floor·cloth *nc* a piece of cloth for washing floors.

'floor show *nc* a cabaret entertainment.

'floor-walk·er *nc* (= *shop-walker*) a person employed in a large shop or store to direct customers, find shoplifters etc.

floor·ing *nu* material used for making floors.

floor² /flɔː(r)/ *vt* **1** to put (a floor) in a building. **2** to knock (a person) down: *floor a man who was rude to one's wife.* **3** (of a problem, argument etc) to defeat (a person): *Tom was floored by two questions in the examination.*

flop¹ /flɒp/ *adv* with a flop(1): *fall flop into the water.*

flop² /flɒp/ *nc* **1** an act or sound of flopping. **2** (*informal*) (of a play, book, record etc) a failure to please the public: *The film was a flop.*

flop³ /flɒp/ *vi* (**-pp-**) **1** to move, fall, sit etc suddenly and clumsily: *fish flopping about in the water. He flopped down in a chair.* **2** (*informal*) (of a play, book, record etc) to be a flop(2).

flop·py /'flɒpɪ/ *adj* (**-ier, -iest**) **1** hanging down loosely: *a floppy hat.* **2** (*informal*) without strength: *feeling tired and floppy.*

,floppy 'disk *nc* (*computers*) a flexible disk used for storing information.

flora /'flɔːrə/ *nu* (*science*) all the plants of an area or a period of history: *the flora of Europe.*

flor·al /'flɔːrəl/ *adj* of flowers: *floral designs.*

flor·id /'flɒrɪd/ *adj* **1** (*derog*) (too) rich in ornament and colour: *a florid writing style.* **2** (of a person's face) naturally red: *a florid complexion.*

flor·ist /'flɒrɪst/ *nc* a person, business, that sells flowers.

flounce /flaʊns/ *vi* to move, go, with quick, impatient or troubled movements: *flouncing into/out of the room.*

floun·der /'flaʊndə(r)/ *vi* **1** to make wild and usually useless efforts (as when one is in deep water and unable to swim). **2** (*fig*) to hesitate, make mistakes: *He floundered during the interview and couldn't remember the facts.*

flour /'flaʊə(r)/ *nu* a fine powder made from grain, used for making bread, cakes, pastry etc. □ *vt* to cover or sprinkle (food) with flour.

flour·ish¹ /'flʌrɪʃ/ *nc* **1** an exaggerated wave. **2** an exaggerated curve or decoration when writing e.g. one's signature. **3** a loud, excited playing of a musical instrument: *a flourish of trumpets.*

flour·ish² /'flʌrɪʃ/ v **1** vi to develop in a healthy manner; be well and active: *His business is flourishing. I hope you are all flourishing.* **2** vt to wave about and show (something): *flourish a cheque for £1000.*

flout /flaʊt/ vt to ignore, refuse to carry out, (something) by acting without respect: *flout his wishes/authority.*

flow¹ /fləʊ/ n sing **1** a flowing movement: *the flow of the tide.* **2** a quantity that flows: *a good flow of water.*

flow² /fləʊ/ vi (pt,pp —ed) **1** to move along or over as a river does: *Rivers flow into the sea. The tears flowed from her eyes.* **2** (of hair, clothes etc) to hang down loosely: *flowing robes; hair flowing down her back.* **3** *flow from sth* to come from; be the result of: *Wealth flows from industry.* **4** *flow over sb* (of noise, trouble, anger) to happen without affecting a person: *The children's quarrels flowed over me—I ignored them.*

flow·er /'flaʊə(r)/ nc **1** a part of a plant that produces seeds. *in flower* with the flowers out. *come into flower* to produce flowers. **2** *the flower of sth* (fig) the finest part: *in the flower of one's youth.* □ vi to produce flowers: *flowering plants.*

'flower-bed nc a small area of land in which flowers are grown.

flower·less adj not having, not producing, flowers: *flowerless plants.*

'flower·pot nc a pot in which a plant can be grown.

flow·ery adj (-ier, -iest) **(a)** having many flowers: *flowery fields.* **(b)** (fig; derog) having an elaborate style: *flowery language.*

flown /fləʊn/ pp of fly³.

Flt Lt written abbr Flight Lieutenant.

flu /fluː/ nu (informal) = influenza.

fluc·tu·ate /'flʌktʃʊeɪt/ vi (of levels, prices etc) to move up and down: *fluctuating prices.*
fluc·tu·ation /ˌflʌktʃʊ'eɪʃn/ nc,nu

flue /fluː/ nc a pipe used for carrying heat or smoke away from a boiler etc.

flu·en·cy /'fluːənsɪ/ nu being fluent.

flu·ent /'fluːənt/ adj **1** (of a person) able to speak easily and without hesitating: *a fluent speaker in Spanish.* **2** (of speech, movement) coming regularly and easily: *speak fluent French; make fluent movements.*
flu·ent·ly adv

fluff¹ /flʌf/ n **1** nu soft, loose material from blankets, wool etc. **2** nc (informal) a small error when doing something.

fluff² /flʌf/ v **1** vt *fluff sth (out/up)* to shake, puff or spread something out: *fluff up a pillow. The bird fluffed (out) its feathers.* **2** vt,vi (informal) to make an error in games, in speaking (one's lines in a play) etc.

fluffy adj (-ier, -iest) of, like, covered with, fluff: *a fluffy blanket.*

flu·id¹ /'fluːɪd/ adj (no comp) **1** (science) able to flow (as gases and liquids do). **2** (fig) (of ideas, etc) not fixed; capable of being changed: *fluid opinions/plans.*

flu·id² /'fluːɪd/ nc,nu (science) a liquid.

ˌfluid 'ounce nc a liquid measurement, one twentieth of a pint or approximately ·028 litres.

flu·id·ity /fluː'ɪdətɪ/ nu (science) the quality of

being fluid.

fluke¹ /fluːk/ nc an instance of accidental good luck: *It was only by a fluke that I noticed her in the crowded train.*

fluke² /fluːk/ nc **1** a flat end of each arm of an anchor. **2** (a lobe of) a whale's tail.

flung /flʌŋ/ pt,pp of fling².

flunk /flʌŋk/ vt (informal) to fail (an examination).

flu·or·es·cence /flʊə'resns/ nu (science) the emission of radiation, esp bright light.

flu·or·es·cent /flʊə'resnt/ adj (of substances) sending out bright light: *fluorescent lamps/lighting.*

fluor·ide /'flʊəraɪd/ nu a kind of chemical substance (as added to water and toothpaste to strengthen tooth enamel).

flur·ry¹ /'flʌrɪ/ nc (pl -ies) **1** a short, sudden rush (of wind or fall of rain or snow). **2** (fig) a nervous hurry: *in a flurry of excitement.*

flur·ry² /'flʌrɪ/ vt to cause (a person) to be confused, in a nervous hurry etc.

flush¹ /flʌʃ/ adj (no comp) **flush (with sth) 1** even; level: *doors flush with the walls.* **2** having plenty; well supplied: *flush with money; feeling flush.*

flush² /flʌʃ/ n **1** nc a rush (of water): *the flush of water in the toilet.* **2** nc a rush of blood to the face; rush of emotion, excitement caused by this: *feel a flush.* ⇒ flush³(1). **3** nu *the (first) flush of sth* the first sign or part of something pleasant: *the first flush of spring; in the (first) flush of youth.*

flush³ /flʌʃ/ v **1** vi (of a person, face) to become red because of a rush of blood to the skin: *She flushed when he spoke to her.* **2** vt,vi (to cause something) to become clean by using a flush(1): *flushing the toilet.* **3** *flush sth (out)* to clean it with a rush of water: *flush out the drains.* **4** *flush sb out* (informal) to force a criminal etc out of a hiding place: *flush an escaped prisoner out of a building.*

flus·ter /'flʌstə(r)/ vt to make a person nervous or confused. □ nu a nervous state: *be/get in a fluster.*

flus·ter·ed adj (pred) nervous and confused.

flute /fluːt/ nc a kind of metal or wooden musical wind instrument with holes to be stopped by keys. ⇒ flautist.

flut·ter¹ /'flʌtə(r)/ n **1** n sing a fluttering movement: *a heart flutter; a flutter of the curtains.* **2** n sing a state of nervous excitement: *be get/in a flutter.* **3** nu an interference in sound reproduced from a disc or tape, caused by faulty recording or reproduction. **4** nc (informal) a small bet: *have a flutter on a race.*

flut·ter² /'flʌtə(r)/ v **1** vt,vi (of birds) to move (the wings) hurriedly or irregularly: *The wounded bird fluttered to the ground.* **2** vt,vi (to cause something) to move about in a quick, irregular way: *curtains fluttering in the breeze.* **3** vi (of the heart) to beat irregularly.

flu·vial /'fluːvɪəl/ adj (tech) of, found in, rivers.

flux /flʌks/ nu a continuous succession of changes: *be in a state of flux.*

fly¹ /flaɪ/ nc (pl flies) a kind of two-winged insect (esp the housefly).

'fly·weight nc (also attrib) a boxer weighing 112 lb (50·8 kg) or less.

fly² /flaɪ/ nc (pl **flies**) **1** (pl) the flap of cloth covering a zip-fastener or buttonholes down the front of a pair of trousers. **2** a flap of cloth at the entrance to a tent.

'**fly·sheet** nc an outer covering of a tent.

fly³ /flaɪ/ v (pt **flew** /fluː/, pp **flown** /fləʊn/) **1** vi to move through the air as a bird does, or in a plane: *birds flying in the air; fly from London to Paris.* ⇨ also pig(2). **2** vt,vi to direct or control the flight of (planes); transport (goods or passengers) in a plane: *Five thousand passengers were flown to Paris during Easter weekend. Does British Airways fly to Cairo?* **3** vt to move over (a sea or ocean) in the air: *fly the Atlantic in 3 hours.* **4** vi to go or move quickly; rush along; pass quickly: *He flew down the road. The door flew open.* **fly off the handle** ⇨ handle¹. **fly in the face of sth** ⇨ face¹(5). **fly into a rage/temper** ⇨ rage¹(1). **send sb flying** to strike a person so that he or she falls over. **5** vt to cause (a kite) to rise and stay high in the air; raise (a flag) so that it waves in the air. **6** vt to flee from (a place): *fly the country.*

fly·er /'flaɪə(r)/ nc **1** (also **fli·er**) an animal, vehicle etc moving very fast. **2** (informal) a successful professional person.

fly·ing /'flaɪɪŋ/ adj **1** that flies, flutters or waves. a *flying bird/kite/flag.* **with flying colours** ⇨ colour¹(11). **2** (attrib) long and high: *a flying jump/leap over a river.* **get off to a flying start** (of a project, a person in a competition etc) to begin well.

,flying '**doctor** nc a doctor visiting patients by plane, as in Australia.

,flying '**saucer** nc (informal) a round, flat spacecraft that some people think comes from another planet.

'**flying-squad** nc a section of a police force organized (with fast cars) to chase criminals.

,flying '**visit** nc (informal) a very short visit.

fly·over /'flaɪəʊvə(r)/ nc a road which crosses above another road (as on a motorway).

fly·past /'flaɪpɑːst/ nc a flight of planes in formation as part of a military display.

FM written abbr **1** (radio) frequency modulation. **2** Field Marshal.

FO written abbr **1** (GB) Foreign Office. **2** Field Officer; Flying Officer.

foal /fəʊl/ nc a young horse. □ vi to give birth to a foal.

foam /fəʊm/ nu a white mass of small air bubbles as formed in or on a liquid. □ vi to produce, send out, foam: *waves foaming along the beach; foaming beer; foaming at the mouth.*

,foam '**rubber** nu rubber with air bubbles inside, used in cushions and seats.

foamy adj (-ier, -iest) having foam: *foamy water.*

fob /fɒb/ vt (-bb-) **fob sb off (with sth)** to get a person to accept something of little or no value by deceit or trickery: *He fobbed me off with promises that he never intended to keep.*

f.o.b. written abbr (commerce) free on board.

fo·cal /'fəʊkl/ adj of or at a focus: *the focal length/ distance of a lens* (= from the surface of a lens to its focus); *the focal point of a discussion/exhibition.* ⇨ focus¹(3).

fo·cus¹ /'fəʊkəs/ nc (pl **—es** or **foci** /'fəʊsaɪ/) **1** a meeting-point of rays of light, heat etc. **2** a

point, distance, where the sharpest outline is given (to the eye, through a telescope, through a lens on a camera etc): *The image is out of/in focus.* **3** a point at which interests, tendencies etc meet: *The focus of attention was on the baby.*

fo·cus² /'fəʊkəs/ v (-s- or -ss-) **1** vt,vi (to cause something) to come together at a focus; adjust (an instrument etc) so that it is in focus: *focus the picture onto the screen; focus a camera/the lens of a microscope.* **2** vt **focus sth on sb/sth** to concentrate attention etc on a person, thing: *focussing her attention on her studies; focus one's mind/ efforts on a problem.*

fod·der /'fɒdə(r)/ nu dried food used for farm animals, horses etc.

foe /fəʊ/ nc (poetic) an enemy.

foe·tal (US= **fe·tal**) /'fiːtl/ adj of, like, a foetus: *the foetal position* (as in the womb).

foe·tus (US= **fe·tus**) /'fiːtəs/ nc (pl **—es**) (science) a fully developed embryo in the womb or in an egg.

fog¹ /fɒg/ n **1** nu vapour in the atmosphere at or near the earth's surface, thicker than mist and difficult to see through. **2** nc a period of fog: *London used to have bad fogs in winter.*

'**fog·bound** adj unable to move safely because of fog: *fogbound traffic.*

'**fog·horn** nc an instrument used for warning ships in fog.

'**fog·lamp** nc a headlamp (on a vehicle) providing a strong beam of light for use in foggy weather.

fog·gy adj (-ier, -iest) **(a)** not clear because of fog: *a foggy evening.* **(b)** (fig) obscure, confused: *have only a foggy idea.*

fog² /fɒg/ vt,vi (-gg-) to cover (as if) with fog: *My glasses have fogged over/up.*

foible /'fɔɪbl/ nc a slight peculiarity or defect of character, often one of which a person is wrongly proud.

foil¹ /fɔɪl/ n **1** nu very thin, flexible metal sheet: *aluminium foil* (e.g. wrapped round chocolate). **2** nc a person or thing that contrasts with, and sets off, the qualities of another: *A plain old woman acts as a foil to her beautiful daughter.*

foil² /fɔɪl/ nc a light sword with a button on the point, used for the sport of fencing.

foil³ /fɔɪl/ vt (often passive) to frustrate or prevent (a person) from carrying out plans: *He was foiled in his attempt to deceive the girl.*

foist /fɔɪst/ vt **foist sth on sb** to trick a person into accepting a useless article etc: *foist a broken bike off on a buyer.*

fold¹ /fəʊld/ nc a part (of a card, paper etc) that is folded(1).

fold² /fəʊld/ nc **1** an enclosure for sheep. **2** (fig) members of a Church. **return to the fold** to rejoin a group of believers.

fold³ /fəʊld/ v **1** vt to bend one part of a thing back on itself: *fold (up) a newspaper; fold back the sheets.* **fold one's arms** ⇨ arm¹(1). **2** vi to become, be able to be, folded: *folding doors.* **fold up** to collapse; come to an end: *The business finally folded up last week.* **3** vt **fold sth into sth** (in cooking) to mix one ingredient, e.g. beaten eggs, gently into another: *Mix thoroughly and then gently fold in the beaten whites of two eggs.*

fold·er nc a holder (made of cardboard etc) for

loose papers.

fo·li·age /'fəʊlɪdʒ/ *nu* (*formal*) the leaves of a tree or plant.

fo·lio /'fəʊlɪəʊ/ *nc* (*pl* —**s**) **1** a sheet of (typed) manuscript numbered on one side only. **2** a volume made of such sheets: *the first folio* (= first edition) *of Shakespeare's plays*.

folk /fəʊk/ *n pl* **1** people in general: *Some folk are never satisfied*. **2** (*pl*) (*informal*) relatives: *the old folks at home*.

'**folk-dance** *nc* (music for) a traditional popular dance.

'**folk·lore** *nu* (the study of) the traditional beliefs, tales etc of a community.

'**folk-music/-song** *nu,nc* popular music/a popular song handed down from the past.

foll *abbr* following.

fol·low /'fɒləʊ/ *v* **1** *vt,vi* to come, go, after or along in the same direction: *You go first and I'll follow (you). Follow this road for about two hundred metres until you see a garage. My dog follows me when I go shopping.* ⇨ footstep, nose¹(1). **2** *vt,vi* to come after in order (space or time): *Which town follows Oxford on the river Thames? Monday follows Sunday.* **as follows** as I am now going to state: *The sizes available are as follows: children 22, 24, 26 and adults 10, 14, 16.* **to follow** next: *We'll have soup and then roast lamb to follow.* **3** *vt* to do (something) as suggested or ordered; accept (something) as correct: *follow instructions/her advice/a map; follow Darwin/Darwin's theory of evolution.* **4** *vt* to show an interest in (something): *follow his career with interest; follow the latest fashion; follow Manchester United Football Club.* **5** *vt,vi* to understand (a person, thing): *I can't follow her/her lesson because she speaks too quickly. Can you follow (me)?* **6** *vi* **follow (from sth) (that . . .)** to be necessarily true: *It follows from what you say that he has the keys.*

follow on (*cricket*) to be forced to bat again immediately after an innings because of a low score. Hence ,**follow-'on** *nc*.

follow through (in tennis, golf) to complete a movement of hitting the ball by moving the racket or club after the hit. **follow sth through** to continue to do something until it is completed: *Don't stop now—follow your ideas through and build that new machine.*

follow sth up (**a**) to try to find out more about it: *I'd like you to follow up that clue/that rumour about hidden treasure.* (**b**) to develop or continue a successful period by doing something as good or better: *Last month's sales were very good but can we follow them up with better ones?* Hence '**follow-up** *nc*.

fol·low·er /'fɒləʊə(r)/ *nc* supporter; admirer: *the football team and their followers.*

fol·low·ing¹ /'fɒləʊɪŋ/ *adj* (*attrib*) **1** next: *We returned the following day.* **2** about to be named etc: *Would the following people kindly remain behind?* ⇨ following²(2).

fol·low·ing² /'fɒləʊɪŋ/ *n* **1** *n sing* a group of supporters: *a pop star with an enormous following.* **2** (the —) those about to be named etc: *Would the following kindly remain behind?* ⇨ following¹(2).

fol·low·ing³ /'fɒləʊɪŋ/ *prep* after: *There will be a discussion following the film.*

follow-on /,fɒləʊ 'ɒn/ *nc* ⇨ follow on.

follow-up /'fɒləʊ ʌp/ *nc* ⇨ follow sth up.

fol·ly /'fɒlɪ/ *n* (*pl* -**ies**) *nc,nu* (an act of) foolishness.

fo·ment /fəʊ'ment/ *vt* to cause or increase (disorder, discontent, ill-feeling etc): *foment trouble by gossiping.*

fo·men·ta·tion /,fəʊmen'teɪʃn/ *nc,nu*

fond /fɒnd/ *adj* **1 be fond of sb/sth** to like, be full of love for, a person, thing: *be fond of babies/music.* **2** (*attrib*) loving and kind: *fond embraces.*

fond·ly *adv* (**a**) lovingly: *look fondly at her.* (**b**) in a foolishly optimistic manner: *He fondly imagined that he could learn French in six weeks.*

fond·ness *nu*

fondle /'fɒndl/ *vt* to touch or stroke (an animal etc) lovingly: *fondling a kitten.*

font /fɒnt/ *nc* a stone basin for baptism.

food /fuːd/ *n* **1** *nu* something that can be eaten by people or animals, or used by plants, to keep them living and for growth: *cold/hot food; pet food; plant food.* **food for thought** (*fig*) something to think about: *His suggestion gave me food for thought.* **2** *nc* a particular kind of food.

'**food chain** *nc* (*science*) a series of plants, animals etc in a region in which each member feeds on the next.

'**food mixer** *nc* an electrical household apparatus used to mix food for cooking.

'**food poisoning** *nu* an unhealthy condition from eating bad or unclean food.

'**food·stuff** *nc* a (kind of) material used as food.

fool¹ /fuːl/ *adj* (*attrib*) (*derog; informal*) foolish: *a scheme devised by some fool politician.*

fool² /fuːl/ *nc* (*derog*) a person without much sense; silly person: *What fools we were not to see the joke! She was fool enough* (= enough of a fool) *to believe him.* **make a fool of sb** to cause a person to seem like a fool. **act/play the fool** to appear deliberately to be stupid or foolish. ⇨ also April fool.

,**fool's 'paradise** *n sing* a state of happiness that is not real.

fool³ /fuːl/ *v* **1** *vi* **fool (about/around) (with sb/sth)** to behave like a fool (with): *Don't fool about with that knife. He's been fooling around with my wife* (i.e. having an affair). *Stop fooling (about)!* **2** *vt* to deceive (a person): *You can't fool me!*

fool·ery /'fuːlərɪ/ *n* (*pl* -**ies**) **1** *nu* foolish behaviour. **2** *nc* a foolish act, idea or word.

fool·hardy /'fuːlhɑːdɪ/ *adj* (*formal*) taking, involving, unnecessary risks.

fool·ish /'fuːlɪʃ/ *adj* (*derog*) without reason, sense or good judgement; silly: *It would be foolish for us to quarrel.*

fool·ish·ly *adv*

fool·ish·ness *nu*

fool·proof /'fuːlpruːf/ *adj* (*no comp*) incapable of failure, involving no risk: *a foolproof scheme.*

foot¹ /fʊt/ *nc* (*pl* feet /fiːt/) **1** a part of the body at the bottom of the leg below the ankle: *an injured foot; have big/flat/smelly feet.* **by foot** walking: *get there/go by foot.* **on foot** (**a**) walking; running: *manage to get there on foot.* (**b**) in progress: *A plan is on foot to build a new stadium.* **my foot!** (used as an exclamation of disbelief) I don't believe it: *She tried to help, my foot!* **be on**

foot! **be on one's feet** to be standing up: *I've been on my feet all day and I'm tired. The man was on his feet immediately to reply to the accusation.* **be rushed off one's feet** to be extremely busy. **drag one's feet** to make slow progress deliberately: *Will management drag its feet over the issue of a shorter working week?* **fall on one's feet** to be lucky: *I don't think she'll have problems finding a job or a house—she always falls on her feet.* **find one's feet** to become settled (e.g. in a new place or job), get to know the best methods etc: *Forgive me for asking so many questions—I'm still finding my feet.* **get/have cold feet** to become/be afraid or hesitant. **have a/ one foot in the door** to have completed the first stage (e.g. obtained an interview) towards achieving something (e.g. getting a job). **have one foot in the grave** to be seriously ill. **have/ keep one's feet on the ground** to be practical and realistic. **land on one's feet** to be lucky (esp after a disappointment or difficult period). **put one's foot down** (a) (when driving) to increase the speed of a vehicle by accelerating. (b) to act firmly (e.g. when insisting, protesting etc). **put one's best foot forward** to try to behave, act, well in order to achieve something. **put one's foot in it** to do or say something wrong, annoying or upsetting accidentally. **put one's feet up** to rest with one's legs in a horizontal position. **(not) put a foot wrong** (not) to make a bad impression or error: *He never puts a foot wrong at work.* **set foot in a place** to enter a house, country: *Don't you ever set foot in my house again! If he sets foot in this country he'll be arrested.* **set sb/sth on her/his/its feet** to help a person, business, country etc to become financially strong or able (again). **stamp one's feet** to put one's feet down on the ground noisily and heavily to show anger, impatience or cold. **stand on one's own two feet** to be (financially) independent. **sweep sb off her/his feet** to make a person feel suddenly in love with one. **wait on sb hand and foot** ⇨ hand¹(1). **walk sb off her/his feet** to make a person very tired by walking with them for a long distance. **2** the lowest part: *the foot of a hill/ladder/page.* **3** the bottom end: *the foot of the bed/garden.* **4** (abbr ft) a unit of measurement of length (equal to 12 inches or 30·5cm): *Everest is about 29 000 feet high. The room is 10 foot/feet by 12 foot/feet (10 ft × 12 ft). George is 6 foot/feet tall.* ⓝ 'Foot' or 'feet' can be used with numbers when describing dimensions, volume or a person's height. **5** the part of a sock or boot that covers a foot(1). **6** (*literature*) a division of a line of verse forming the basic unit of rhythm, and marked, as in *'For men/may come/ and men/may go'.*

'foot·ball *nu* (also *attrib*) (also called *soccer*) a game played by two teams of eleven players who kick a round ball (a *football*) into goals at each end of the field (a *football pitch*): *a game of football; a football game/player.*

'football pools *n pl* (*GB*) a system of betting money on the results of football matches.

'foot·bridge *nc* a bridge for people and not vehicles.

'foot·fall *nc* a sound of a footstep.

'foot·hills *n pl* low hills near a mountain.

'foot·hold *nc* (a) a secure place for the foot, e.g. when climbing. (b) (*fig*) a secure position, e.g. in a business.

'foot·note *nc* a note at the bottom of a page.

'foot·path *nc* a path for people who are walking.

'foot·print *nc* a mark left on a soft surface by a foot.

'foot·sore *adj* having sore feet, esp because of walking.

'foot·step *nc* (a sound of) a step of a person walking. **follow in sb's footsteps** to do as he or she did.

'foot·wear *nu* (*commerce*) boots, shoes etc.

'foot·work *nu* the manner of using the feet, e.g. in boxing, dancing.

foot² /fut/ *vt* **1** *nc* **foot it** (*informal*) to walk: *We've missed the last bus so we'll have to foot it.* **2 foot the bill** to (agree to) pay it.

foot·ing /'futɪŋ/ *n* **1** *nc* a placing of the feet; surface for standing on: *He lost his footing and fell.* **2** *n sing* a (mentioned) relationship (with people): *be on a friendly footing with them; on a peace/war footing.*

for /fə(r) *strong form:* fɔ:(r)/ *prep* ⓝ For uses of *'for'* with verbs such as *do, go, make, run, stand, take* etc, ⇨ the *verb* entries. **1** towards; in order to get to: *We set out for home. They all made for the forest. Where do I catch the train for Paris?* **2** aimed towards: *This letter/phone-call/present is for you. The flowers were meant for you. Who are they for?* **3** (showing purpose or use): *a pen for drawing; a tool for making holes; meat for animals; ointment for spots; a shampoo for dry hair. What do you want/need it for? What's it for? This is for your birthday. Do you want an egg for breakfast? She's gone for a walk. He's just left for a holiday.* ⓝ 'For' cannot be used in front of a verb. 'For' is used before the -ing form to refer to what something is used for, as in *a knife for carving meat.* **4** in order to have: *look/search/wish/pray for happiness; work for a living; reach for a stick; wait for a bus; shout for help.* **5** in order to do something: *get ready/ train/prepare for an expedition/the Olympics/ an exam.* **6** during (time or space): *They were gone for two hours. We've been here for a week. We'll be here for the next few days. I've loved her for many years. We could see only sand for several miles. Let's stay here for always/for good/for ever.* ⓝ 'For' is used to refer to the amount of time, as in *'lived here for 3 years'* and *'since'* is used to refer to when a period of time began, as in *'lived here since 1984'.* **7** to the amount of: *I bought it for £5. You can have it for nothing. For every six vouchers you get a free mug. He wouldn't hurt you for all the world. It's getting on for 2 o'clock. He's getting on for 30.* **8** (showing meaning): *What's that road sign for? Can you tell me the Russian for 'window'?* **9** representing: *B is for ball. Yellow is for jealousy.* **10** as a representative of: *be the MP for Cambridge; play football for England.* **11** in favour of: *I'm for private education but against private medicine. They argued/voted for disarmament.* **all for** ⇨ all². **12** because of: *I did it for you/for this reason. She received a reward for courage. He was fined for speeding.* **13** with regard to: *have a liking/taste for hot curries; be anxious for news.* **14** (showing suitability): *He's the right man for the job. You're fit for nothing.*

Are they good enough for your mother? Spinach is good for you. **15** considering (that it is): *She's tall for her age. It's warm for June/for this time of year.* **16** as (if) being: *I mistook him for your father. Do you take me for a fool? I for one don't believe a word of it.* **for certain** ⇨ certain(2). **for sure** ⇨ sure²(1). **17** in spite of: *For all his money he's not willing to help.* **18** *adj* + **for sb/sth to** + *verb* (used to refer to the object, usually after an *adj*, showing importance, necessity, frequency, degree etc): *It's necessary for you to complete this form. Is it normal for boys of his age to have spots? This question is too difficult for me to answer.*

for. *written abbr* **1** foreign. **2** forest.

for·age /'fɒrɪdʒ/ *vi* **forage (for sth)** to search (for): *foraging about/around for a screwdriver; forage for food.*

for·ay /'fɒreɪ/ *nc* a sudden attack (esp to get food, animals etc): *make/go on a foray.* □ *vi* to make a foray.

for·bad /fəˈbæd/, **for·bade** /fəˈbeɪd/ *pt* of forbid.

for·bear¹, **fore·bear** /'fɔːbeə(r)/ *nc* (usually *pl*) (*formal*) an ancestor: *My forbears were Romanian.*

for·bear² /fɔːˈbeə(r)/ *vi* (*pt* **forbore** /fɔːˈbɔː(r)/, *pp* **forborne** /fɔːˈbɔːn/) **forbear (from sth/ to . . .)** (*formal*) to stop, prevent oneself (from doing something): *I cannot forbear from going into details/to do so.*

for·bear·ance /fɔːˈbeərəns/ *nu* patience; self-control: *show forbearance in dealing with people.*

for·bid /fəˈbɪd/ *vt* (*pt* **forbad** /fəˈbæd/ or **for·bade** /fəˈbeɪd/, *pp* **forbidden** /fəˈbɪdn/; **-dd-**) to order (a person) not to do something: *I forbid you to use that word.*

for·bid·ding /fəˈbɪdɪŋ/ *adj* (usually *attrib*) serious and unfriendly; threatening: *a forbidding appearance.*

for·bore /fɔːˈbɔː(r)/ *pt* of forbear².

for·borne /fɔːˈbɔːn/ *pp* of forbear².

force¹ /fɔːs/ *n* **1** *nu* (*physics*) the measurable influence that causes an object to move or move faster or that makes a material or object able to bear weight: *the force of gravity.* **2** *nu* natural power or energy: *the force of an explosion; a gale-force wind.* **3** *nu* natural power or strength of mind; controlling influence: *the force of argument/of circumstances/of a strong personality.* ⇨ forceful. **4** *nc* a person, thing, idea etc that causes large changes: *the forces of evil; the forces of nature* (e.g. storms, earthquakes). *The United Nations ought to be a powerful force in world affairs.* **5** *nu* physical strength: *use force to open a locked door when the key is lost.* **by force** using violence: *I'll never give you my jewels—you'll have to take them by force.* **6** *nc* (often F-) an organized group of people trained to keep order, defend etc: *the Police Force; the armed forces.* **7** *nu* power of authority: *the force of law.* **in force** (a) (of a law) active and valid. (b) in large numbers: *attack in force.* **come into force** (of a law) to become active and valid: *When does the new parking law come into force?* **8 join forces (with sb)** to unite (with a person) to share effort: *join forces with a friend to try to win a competition.*

force² /fɔːs/ *vt* **1** to use physical strength to do or get (something): *forcing her way through a* crowd; *force a confession from him; force a door* (*open*). **2** to use strong influence to achieve (something): *He forced his ideas on the other committee members. I'm forced to agree with your father.* **3** to produce (something) with effort and unwillingly: *force a smile.* **4** to use unnatural heat and light to cause (plants) to mature earlier than usual.

force·ful /'fɔːsfəl/ *adj* (of a person, character, argument etc) convincing, believable: *a forceful speaker/style of writing.*

force·ful·ly /-fəlɪ/ *adv*

for·ceps /'fɔːseps/ *nc* (*pl* —) (also *a pair of forceps*) an instrument used by dentists (when pulling out teeth) and by doctors for gripping things.

forc·ible /'fɔːsəbl/ *adj* **1** (esp *legal*) done by, involving the use of, physical force: *a forcible entry into a building.* **2** having a strong influence: *a forcible argument.*

forc·ibly /-əblɪ/ *adv*

ford /fɔːd/ *vt, nc* (to cross a river using) a shallow place where it is possible to walk or drive across.

fore¹ /fɔː(r)/ *adj* (*attrib*) (of things in pairs, front and back) at the front: *the forelegs of a horse.* Compare hind.

fore² /fɔː(r)/ *n sing* **come to the fore** to come into a position of importance, prominence.

fore·arm¹ /'fɔːrɑːm/ *nc* the part of the arm from the elbow to the wrist or fingertips.

fore·arm² /fɔːrˈɑːm/ *vt* (*formal*) to prepare (a person) for trouble, in advance: *To be forewarned is to be forearmed.*

fore·bear *nc* = forbear¹.

fore·bod·ing /fɔːˈbəʊdɪŋ/ *nu* (*formal*) a feeling that trouble is coming: *be filled with foreboding.*

fore·cast¹ /'fɔːkɑːst/ *nc* a statement about what is likely to happen, based on experience or scientific study: *weather forecasts.*

fore·cast² /'fɔːkɑːst/ *vt* (*pt, pp* — or **—ed**) to say (what is likely to happen).

fore·court /'fɔːkɔːt/ *nc* an enclosed space in front of a building.

fore·fathers /'fɔːfɑːðəz/ *n pl* = ancestors.

fore·fin·ger /'fɔːfɪŋɡə(r)/ *nc* the finger next to the thumb.

fore·front /'fɔːfrʌnt/ *n sing* (the—) the most forward part: *in the forefront of the battle.*

fore·going /fɔːˈɡəʊɪŋ/ *adj* (*attrib*) (of speech, writing) already mentioned.

fore·gone /'fɔːɡɒn/ *adj* **a foregone conclusion** an ending that can be seen or could have been seen from the start.

fore·ground /'fɔːɡraʊnd/ *nc* **1** the part of a view nearest to the observer. **2** (*fig*) the most noticeable position: *keep oneself in the foreground.*

fore·hand /'fɔːhænd/ *adj, adv* (of a stroke in tennis etc) (made) with the palm turned forward. □ *nc* such a stroke.

fore·head /'fɒrɪd/ *nc* the part of the face above the eyes.

for·eign /'fɒrən/ *adj* (*no comp*) **1** of, in, from, another country, not one's own: *foreign languages/countries.* **2 foreign to sb/sth** not natural to a person, personality: *Lying is foreign to his nature.* **3** (*attrib*) coming or introduced from outside: *a foreign body* (e.g. dirt) *in her eye.*

foreign af·fairs *n pl* a country's political and economic relations with other countries.

,foreign ex'change *nu* (an office for) the system of exchanging one country's currency for another.

for·eign·er *nc* a person born or living in a foreign country.

fore·leg /'fɔ:leg/ *nc* one of the front legs of a four-footed animal.

fore·man /'fɔ:mən/ *nc* (*pl* **-men** /-mən/) **1** a workman in authority over others. **2** a chief member and spokesman of a jury.

fore·most /'fɔ:məʊst/ *adj* (*attrib*) most notable: *the foremost painter of his period*. □ *adv* first in position. **first and foremost** ⇨ first²(1).

fore·name /'fɔ:neɪm/ *nc* (as used, e.g. on application forms) = first name.

for·en·sic /fə'rensɪk/ *adj* (*attrib; formal*) of, used in, courts of law: *forensic medicine* (= medical knowledge as needed in legal enquiries, such as murder).

fore·run·ner /'fɔ:rʌnə(r)/ *nc* **1** a sign of what is to follow: *swallows, the forerunners of summer*. **2** a person who prepares for the coming of another person or thing.

fore·see /fɔ:'si:/ *vt* (*pt* **foresaw** /fɔ:'sɔ:/, *pp* **foreseen** /fɔ:'si:n/) to know (something) in advance: *foresee trouble*. ⇨ unforeseen.

fore·see·able *adj* (*no comp*) which can be described, known, in advance: *the foreseeable future*. Opp unforeseeable.

fore·shad·ow /fɔ:'ʃædəʊ/ *vt* to be a sign or warning of (something bad): *In drama certain events foreshadow the catastrophe*.

fore·shore /'fɔ:ʃɔ:(r)/ *nc* a part of the shore between the sea and land that is cultivated, built on etc.

fore·short·en /fɔ:'ʃɔ:tn/ *vt* (*tech*) to draw (an object) with some lines shortened to make it look the same as in real life.

fore·sight /'fɔ:saɪt/ *nu* the ability to see future needs: *have/use foresight*.

fore·skin /'fɔ:skɪn/ *nc* the fold of skin covering the end of the penis.

for·est /'fɒrɪst/ *n* **1** *nc,nu* (also *attrib*) (a large area of) land covered with trees; the trees growing there: *forest fires*. **2** *nc* (*fig*) something like a forest: *a forest of masts in a harbour*.

for·est·er *nc* an officer in charge of a forest (protecting wild animals, watching for fires etc); a man who works in a forest.

for·est·ry *nu* (the science of) planting and caring for forests.

fore·stall /fɔ:'stɔ:l/ *vt* to do (something) first and so prevent (another person) from doing it.

fore·swear /fɔ:'sweə(r)/ *vt* = forswear.

fore·taste /'fɔ:teɪst/ *nc* **foretaste (of sth)** an (often short) experience (of enjoyment or suffering) in advance.

fore·tell /fɔ:'tel/ *vt* (*pt,pp* **foretold** /-'təʊld/) to say (what will happen): *foretell her future*.

fore·thought /'fɔ:θɔ:t/ *nu* careful thought or planning for the future: *have the forethought to warn the neighbours about a party*.

fore·told /fɔ:'təʊld/ *pt,pp* of foretell.

for·ev·er /fə'reʊə(r)/ *adv* (for) a very long time: *It will take forever to finish this job*. ⇨ ever(4).

fore·warn /fɔ:'wɔ:n/ *vt* to warn (a person) in advance.

fore·wom·an /'fɔ:wʊmən/ *nc* (*pl* **-women** /-wɪmɪn/) a woman in authority over other workers.

fore·word /'fɔ:wɜ:d/ *nc* an introduction to a book, often describing the author.

for·feit¹ /'fɔ:fɪt/ *nc* something (to be) forfeited: *His health was the forfeit he paid for overworking*.

for·feit² /'fɔ:fɪt/ *vt* to suffer the loss of (something) as a punishment or result of an action: *forfeit one's salary because of ill health*.

for·gave /fɔ:'geɪv/ *pt* of forgive.

forge¹ /fɔ:dʒ/ *nc* **1** a workshop where metals are heated and shaped, esp one used for making shoes for horses. **2** (a workshop with) a furnace for melting metal.

forge² /fɔ:dʒ/ *vt* **1** to shape (metal) by heating and hammering. **2** (*fig*) to form or make (something): *Their friendship was forged by poverty*. **3** to make a copy of (e.g. a signature, banknote, will) in order to deceive.

forg·er *nc* a person who forges(3).

forg·ery /'fɔ:dʒərɪ/ *n* (*pl* **-ies**) **(a)** *nu* the act of forging(3) a document, signature etc. **(b)** *nc* a forged document, signature etc.

forge³ /fɔ:dʒ/ *vi* **forge ahead** to make good progress; take the lead (in a race etc).

for·get /fə'get/ *vt,vi* (*pt* **forgot** /fə'gɒt/, *pp* **forgotten** /fə'gɒtn/; **-tt-**) **1** to fail to keep (something) in the memory: *I forget/I've forgotten her name. She seems to have forgotten that you were coming. I shall never forget your kindness to me. He forgot all about it*. **2** to fail (to do something): *Don't forget to post the letters*. **3** to put (something) out of the mind; stop thinking about (something): *Let's forget our quarrels. 'I still owe you £1'—'Oh, forget (about) it!'*

for·get·ful /-fəl/ *adj* (usually *pred*) in the habit of forgetting: *Old people are sometimes forgetful*.

for·get·ful·ly /-fəlɪ/ *adv*

for·get·ful·ness *nu*

forget-me-not /fə'get mi: nɒt/ *nc* a kind of small plant with blue flowers.

for·give /fə'gɪv/ *vt* (*pt* **forgave** /fə'geɪv/, *pp* **forgiven** /fə'gɪvn/) to say that one will not punish (a person) or be angry because of (a wrong action): *forgive him for being rude; forgive his rudeness*.

for·giv·ing *adj* ready, willing, to forgive: *a forgiving nature*. Opp unforgiving.

for·give·ness *nu* the act of forgiving or being forgiven: *ask for forgiveness*.

for·go /fɔ:'gəʊ/ *vt* (*pt* **forwent** /fɔ:'went/, *pp* **forgone** /fɔ:'gɒn/) (*formal*) to do without, give up, (something): *forgo pleasures in order to study hard*.

for·got /fə'gɒt/ *pt* of forget.

for·got·ten /fə'gɒtn/ *pp* of forget.

fork¹ /fɔ:k/ *nc* **1** an implement with two or more points (*prongs*), used for lifting food to the mouth etc. **2** a farm or gardening tool like a fork(1). **3** a place where a road, tree-trunk etc divides or branches; one such branch: *take the left fork*. **4** a part of a bicycle frame to which a wheel is fixed. ⇨ also tuning fork.

fork² /fɔ:k/ *v* **1** *vt,vi* to lift, move, carry, (something) with a fork: *fork the ground over* (= turn the soil over with a fork). **2** *vi* (of a road, river etc) to divide into branches. **3** *vi* (of a person) to turn (left or right): *We forked right at the church*. **4** **fork out sth** (*informal*) to hand over, pay, something (unwillingly): *I've got to fork out a lot of money for lessons this year.*

fork-lift 'truck *nc* a small, powerful machine on wheels with a platform, used for lifting, moving and lowering goods.

fork·ed *adj* divided into two or more parts: *the forked tongue of a snake.*

for·lorn /fə'lɔːn/ *adj* (*literary*) unhappy.

for·lorn·ly *adv*

form¹ /fɔːm/ *n* **1** *nu* shape; outward appearance: *have the same form but different colours; a vase in the form of a swan.* **take form** to begin to have an identifiable shape: *The statue began to take form.* **2** *nc* a general shape of a person or animal: *A dark form could be seen in the distance.* **3** *nc* a particular kind or variety: *Ice, snow and steam are forms of water. Walking is an easy form of exercise. Which form of government do you prefer?* Compare kind²(1). **4** *nc* a particular way of behaving, speaking etc (esp as accepted by most people as right): *accepted forms of behaviour.* **form of address** a way of referring to a person, as on an envelope, e.g. *Miss, Ms, Dr, Sir.* **5** *nu* physical and mental condition (of an athlete, racehorse etc): *show good form.* **off/on form** not fit and badly prepared/fit and well prepared. **6** *nu* **be in/on (good etc) form** to be happy and sociable: *Jack was in great form at the party.* **7** *nc* a printed paper with spaces (to be) filled in giving details: *an application form; fill in/out a form for a driving licence.* **8** *nc* a class of schoolchildren: *be in the sixth form.* (US = *grade*). **9** *nc,nu* (*gram*) a way of spelling or changing a word in a particular structure: *What is the plural form of 'sheep'? Which of these verbs have irregular forms in the past tense? These words are different in form but identical in meaning.* **10** *nc* a long bench without a back, as used in a gymnasium.

form·less *adj* without shape.

form² /fɔːm/ *v* **1** *vt,vi* to make a shape; give a shape to (something): *form a statue out of stone. A green line began to form in the sky.* **2** *vt* to organize (something) (from parts): *They formed (themselves into) a committee. She tried to form a government but the Liberals refused to join her.* **3** *vt* to be (part of) (something): *This record forms part of a collection of his own songs.* **4** *vt* to develop, build up, (ideas, plans, relationships etc): *form a close friendship with a neighbour's son; form bad habits; form ideas/an opinion.* **5** *vt* (*gram*) to make a form(9) of (a word): *How do we form the singular of 'bacteria'? We form the past tense with '-ed'.*

for·mal /'fɔːml/ *adj* **1** (of words, ways of speaking or writing) used in situations when one must be particularly polite, impersonal, well-educated, traditional etc to give a good impression: *formal ways of writing a business letter; make a formal speech at a conference. 'Commence' is more formal than 'begin'.* Opp informal(1). **2** (of clothes, activities, behaviour etc) according to what is accepted by conventional society: *wear formal dress to a cocktail party. They had a formal wedding.* Opp informal(2). **3** (*attrib*) regular or geometric in design: *a formal garden/pattern.*

for·mal·ly /-məlɪ/ *adv*

for·mal·ity /fɔː'mælətɪ/ *n* (*pl* **-ies**) **1** *nc* an action required by custom or rules: *legal formalities.* **a**

mere formality something one is required or expected to do, but which has little meaning or importance. **2** *nu* attention to conventional rules and tradition: *Is there too much formality in British society?*

for·ma·tion /fɔː'meɪʃn/ *n* **1** *nu* the act, process, of forming or shaping: *the formation of character/of ideas in the mind.* **2** *nc* something that is formed: *Clouds are formations of condensed water vapour.* **3** *nc* a (style of) structure or arrangement: *rock formations.*

for·ma·tive /'fɔːmətɪv/ *adj* (*formal*) influencing the development of: *the formative years of a child's life.*

for·mer¹ /'fɔːmə(r)/ *adj* (*attrib; no comp*) of an earlier period: *in former times; my former students.* Compare latter¹.

for·mer² /'fɔːmə(r)/ *pron* the first (mentioned) of two people or things: *They have blue cars and dark green ones, and I prefer the former.* Compare latter².

for·mer·ly *adv* in earlier times.

for·mi·da·ble /'fɔːmɪdəbl/ *adj* (*formal*) **1** causing fear or anxiety: *a man with a formidable appearance.* **2** difficult to deal with or overcome: *formidable obstacles/opposition/enemies/debts.*

for·mi·da·bly /-əblɪ/ *adv*

for·mu·la /'fɔːmjulə/ *nc* (*pl* **—s**, or (*science*) **—e** /-liː/) **1** a group of words used regularly (e.g. *'How d'you do?', 'Excuse me', 'Yours sincerely'*) or used in legal documents etc. **2** (*science*) a statement of a rule, fact etc, esp one in letters, signs or numbers: *The chemical formula for water is H_2O.* **3** a set of directions for making something: *The formula for making this famous drink is a secret.* **4** a method of achieving something: *a formula for success.*

for·mu·late /'fɔːmjuleɪt/ *vt* (*formal*) to express, organize, (ideas etc) clearly and exactly: *formulate one's thoughts/a doctrine.*

for·mu·la·tion /ˌfɔːmju'leɪʃn/ *nc,nu*

for·ni·cate /'fɔːnɪkeɪt/ *vi* **fornicate (with sb)** to have sexual intercourse with a person who one is not married to.

for·ni·ca·tion /ˌfɔːnɪ'keɪʃn/ *nu*

for·sake /fə'seɪk/ *vt* (*pt* **forsook** /fə'suk/, *pp* **forsaken** /fə'seɪkn/) (*formal*) to abandon (a person, good behaviour etc): *forsake one's wife and children.*

for·swear /fɔː'sweə(r)/ *vt* (*pt* **forswore** /fɔː'swɔː(r)/, *pp* **forsworn** /fɔː'swɔːn/) (*formal*) to give up doing or using (something bad): *forswear bad habits.*

fort /fɔːt/ *nc* a building for military defence. **hold the fort** to take over responsibility (e.g. in an office) during a person's absence.

forte /'fɔːteɪ/ *n sing* something a person does particularly well: *Singing is not my forte.*

forth /fɔːθ/ *adv* (*formal*) **1** out (which is more usual): *set forth* (= begin a journey). **2** onwards; forwards: *from this day forth.* **and so forth** ⇨ so²(5). **back and forth** ⇨ back²(1). **3** **hold forth** ⇨ hold³.

forth·com·ing /ˌfɔːθ'kʌmɪŋ/ *adj* **1** (*attrib; no comp*) about to appear: *forthcoming books.* **2** (*pred; no comp*) available, ready when needed: *The money/help we hoped for was not forthcoming.* **3** (*pred; informal*) ready to be helpful, give information etc: *The girl at the reception desk was not very forthcoming.*

forth·right /ˈfɔːθraɪt/ *adj* clear and determined; straightforward: *Be forthright when you explain why you deserve promotion.*

forth·with /fɔːθˈwɪθ/ *adv* (*formal*) at once; without losing time: *He came forthwith.*

for·ti·eth /ˈfɔːtɪəθ/ *adj or det, nc* (abbr 40th) (of) one of 40 parts or the next after 39.

for·ti·fy /ˈfɔːtɪfaɪ/ *vt* (*pt,pp* **-ied**) **1** to strengthen (a place) against attack (with walls, weapons etc). **2** to support or strengthen (oneself, one's courage etc): *Fortify oneself against the cold.*
for·ti·fi·ca·tion /ˌfɔːtɪfɪˈkeɪʃn/ *nc,nu*

for·ti·tude /ˈfɔːtɪtjuːd/ *nu* (*formal*) calm courage, self-control, in the face of pain, danger or difficulty: *show fortitude in distress.*

fort·night /ˈfɔːtnaɪt/ *nc* a period of two weeks: *They've gone on holiday for a fortnight. They'll return in a fortnight's time. Have the money by Sunday fortnight* (= two weeks after Sunday).
fort·night·ly *adj, adv* happening regularly every fortnight.

fort·ress /ˈfɔːtrɪs/ *nc* a fortified building or town.

for·tu·itous /fɔːˈtjuːɪtəs/ *adj* (*formal*) happening by happy chance: *a fortuitous meeting.*
for·tu·itous·ly *adv*

for·tu·nate /ˈfɔːtʃənət/ *adj* (*formal*) having, bringing, brought by, good fortune; lucky (which is more usual): *You were very fortunate to escape being injured.* Opp unfortunate.

for·tu·nate·ly *adv* luckily: *I thought I'd lost her watch but fortunately I found it in my room. Fortunately for everyone, the principal has changed his mind.* Opp unfortunately.

for·tune /ˈfɔːtʃuːn/ *n* **1** *nc,nu* (an example of) chance, luck (good or bad) influencing a person's life: *have fortune on one's side. It was her good fortune to marry a rich man. Fortune was always against him.* ⇨ misfortune. **tell sb's fortune** to say, after looking at a person's hand, looking at playing-cards etc, what good or bad luck a person will have. **2** *nc* a large sum of money: *earn a fortune by selling shoes; spend a fortune in the supermarket.* **come into a fortune** to inherit one. **make a fortune** to earn or acquire one in business. **seek one's fortune** to try to earn or acquire one: *He's gone to Australia to seek his fortune.*

ˈfortune teller *nc* a person who claims to be able to tell a person's fortune.

for·ty /ˈfɔːtɪ/ *adj or det, nc* (of) 40: *forty-six* (46). **in the forties** (a) (of temperature, speed etc) between 40 and 49. (b) between '40 and '49 in a century.
ˌforty ˈwinks *n pl* a short sleep.

fo·rum /ˈfɔːrəm/ *nc* (*pl* **—s**) **1** (in ancient Rome) a public place for meetings. **2** any place or means for public discussion: *TV is an accepted forum for the discussion of public affairs.*

for·ward¹ /ˈfɔːwəd/ *adj* **1** towards the front or future: *a movement forward; forward planning* (i.e. for future needs etc). **2** making, having made, more than normal or expected progress (intellectually, economically, culturally, physically etc): *a forward child. His vegetables are further forward than mine.* **3** (*derog*) (too) eager or impatient: *a forward young girl.*

ˈ**forward-looking** *adj* using or encouraging progressive ideas.

for·ward² /ˈfɔːwəd/ *adv* Ⓝ For uses with verbs such as *bring, come, look, put* etc, ⇨ the *verb* entries. **1** towards the front (so as to make progress): *go/ rush forward.* **2** towards the future: *from this day forward.* ⇨ forwards.

for·ward³ /ˈfɔːwəd/ *nc* (*sport*) a player who attacks the opponent's goal (now often called a *striker*) in football, rugby, hockey etc.

for·ward⁴ /ˈfɔːwəd/ *vt* **1** to send (a letter, parcel, information etc) to: *We have forwarded you our new catalogue. Please forward my letters to my new address.* **2** (*formal*) to help the progress of (something): *training that will forward his plans/ career.*

for·wards /ˈfɔːwədz/ *adv* **1** = forward² (which is now more usual). **2 backwards and forwards** ⇨ backwards(3).

fos·sil /ˈfɒsl/ *nc* (a part or mark of) a prehistoric animal or plant once buried in earth, now hardened like rock.
fos·sil·ize (also **-ise**) /ˈfɒsəlaɪz/ *vt,vi* (to cause something) to become a fossil.

fos·ter /ˈfɒstə(r)/ *vt* **1** (*formal*) to help the growth and development of (something): *foster good relations/evil thoughts.* **2** to take (a child) into one's home and care for her or him without being a legal guardian. Compare adopt(1).
ˈ**foster-child/-parent** *nc* ⇨ 2 above.

fought /fɔːt/ *pt,pp* of fight².

foul¹ /faʊl/ *adj* (**—er**, **—est**) **1** causing disgust; having a bad smell or taste: *a foul taste; foul-smelling drains.* **2** (*attrib; informal*) very bad and strong: *a foul temper.* **3** (of language) obscene. **4** (of weather) stormy; rough.
ˌfoul ˈplay *nu* (a) (*sport*) an action that is against the rules. (b) a violent crime, esp murder: *Is foul play suspected?*
foul·ly /ˈfaʊllɪ/ *adv*

foul² /faʊl/ *nc* (*sport*) an action that is against the rules: *commit a foul.*

foul³ /faʊl/ *vt,vi* **1** (to cause something) to become very dirty, smell bad etc: *Cars foul the air in our cities.* **2** (*sport*) to commit a foul² against (a player). **3 foul sth up** (*informal*) to spoil it, make it unpleasant: *We were working well together until you joined us and fouled things up. His drinking fouled up the marriage.*

found¹ /faʊnd/ *pt,pp* of find².

found² /faʊnd/ *vt* **1** to establish (a society etc): *The Methodist Church was founded by John Wesley.* **2** to get (something) started by providing money: *found a new school.* **3 found sth on sth** to base an idea etc on something: *arguments founded on fact.*

foun·da·tion /faʊnˈdeɪʃn/ *n* **1** *nu* the act of establishing (a university, church etc). **2** *nc* (F- in names) a fund of money for charity, research etc: *the Ford Foundation.* **3** *nc* (often *pl*) a strong base of a building, on which it is built: *the foundation(s) of a block of flats.* **4** *nc,nu* a thing on which an idea, belief etc is based: *the foundations of religious beliefs.* **be without foundation** be completely untrue: *a story that is without foundation.*

foun'dation-stone *nc* a stone laid to celebrate the start of constructing a building.

found·er¹ /'faʊndə(r)/ nc a person who establishes a school etc.

,founder 'member nc one who joins a society etc at the beginning: *a founder member of the Social Democratic Party.*

foun·der² /'faʊndə(r)/ vi 1 (of a ship) to fill with water and sink. 2 (fig) to fail: *Our ideas foundered because of lack of money.*

foun·dry /'faʊndrɪ/ nc (pl -ies) a place where metal or glass is melted and shaped into objects.

foun·tain /'faʊntɪn/ nc 1 an apparatus producing a rush of water into the air. 2 (fig) a source or origin: *the fountain of my happiness.*

'fountain-pen nc a kind of pen with a supply of liquid ink inside the holder.

four /fɔː(r)/ adj or det, nc (of) 4: *a child of four* (= 4 years old); *an income in four figures* (= of £1000 or more). **on all fours** on the hands and knees.

'four·fold adj, adv 4 times as many or as much.

'four-ply adj (of wool etc) having 4 strands or thicknesses.

four·teen /,fɔː'tiːn/ adj or det, nc (of) 14.

four·teenth /,fɔː'tiːnθ/ adj or det, nc (abbr 14th) (of) one of 14 parts or the next after 13.

fourth /fɔːθ/ adj or det, nc (abbr 4th) (of) one of 4 parts or the next after 3.

the ,fourth di'mension n time.

'fourth·ly adv in the fourth place.

fowl /faʊl/ 1 nc (old use) any bird: *the fowls of the air.* 2 nc a domestic cock or hen: *keep fowls.* 3 nu flesh of fowls(2) as food.

fox¹ /fɒks/ nc (female = **vixen** /'vɪksn/) a wild animal of the dog family, with red fur and a bushy tail.

'fox·hound nc a kind of dog bred and trained to hunt foxes.

fox² /fɒks/ vt 1 to deceive (a person): *fox one's enemies.* 2 (often passive) to puzzle, be too difficult for, (a person): *The detective was completely foxed and had no idea how the murderer had escaped.*

foy·er /'fɔɪeɪ/ nc a large hall, e.g. an entrance hall in a hotel, cinema etc.

frac·tion /'frækʃn/ nc 1 a small part or bit: *The insurance company paid only a fraction of the cost.* 2 (maths) a number that is not a whole number (e.g. ⅓, 0·76). ⇨ decimal/vulgar fraction.

frac·tion·al /-ʃənl/ adj

frac·tious /'frækʃəs/ adj (formal; derog) (of a person) irritable; bad-tempered.

frac·ture¹ /'fræktʃə(r)/ nc,nu (an instance of) breaking or being broken, e.g. of a bone: *compound/simple fractures* (= with/without skin wounds).

frac·ture² /'fræktʃə(r)/ vt,vi (to cause esp a bone) to break: *fracture one's leg.*

frag·ile /'frædʒaɪl/ adj easily injured, broken or destroyed: *fragile china/health/happiness.*

fra·gil·ity /frə'dʒɪlətɪ/ nu

frag·ment¹ /'frægmənt/ nc 1 a part broken off: *fragments of a broken vase.* 2 a separate or incomplete part: *fragments of their conversation.*

frag·ment² /fræg'ment/ vi to break into pieces.

frag·men·tary /'frægməntrɪ/ adj made up of fragments(2): *a fragmentary report of an event.*

fra·grance /'freɪgrəns/ nc,nu (an example of) a pleasant, sweet smell.

fra·grant /'freɪgrənt/ adj smelling pleasant and sweet: *fragrant flowers.*

frail /freɪl/ adj (—er, —est) weak; fragile: *a frail child/chair.*

frail·ty /'freɪltɪ/ n (pl -ies) (formal) 1 nu the quality of being frail: *the frailty of human life.* 2 nc (literary) a moral fault: *He loved her in spite of her little frailties.*

frame¹ /freɪm/ nc 1 a border in which a picture, photograph, window or door is enclosed or set. 2 a structure that holds the lenses of a pair of spectacles. 3 the main structure used in the process of building a ship, building, plane etc. 4 (the shape of) a human or animal body: *a girl of slender frame.* 5 a structure of wood and glass for protecting plants from the cold: *a cold/heated frame.*

frame of mind a (mentioned) condition of mind: *be/feel in a cheerful frame of mind.*

'frame·work nc the part of a structure that gives shape and support: *a bridge with a steel framework.*

frame² /freɪm/ vt 1 to put a frame(1) round (something): *have a painting framed.* 2 to put (a plan etc) together: *frame a plan/theory/sentence.* 3 (sl) to make (an innocent person) appear guilty of something: *The accused man said he had been framed.*

'frame-up nc (sl) a scheme to make an innocent person appear guilty.

fran·chise /'fræntʃaɪz/ nc 1 (usually the —) full rights of citizenship given by a country or town, esp the right to vote at elections. 2 a special right given by public authorities to a person or company: *win a franchise for a bus service.*

frank¹ /fræŋk/ adj (—er, —est) showing clearly the thoughts and feelings: *a frank look; make a frank confession of one's guilt.* I'll be quite (= completely) *frank with you* (about my opinion).

frank·ly adv speaking honestly: *Frankly, I don't believe you.*

frank·ness nu

frank² /fræŋk/ vt to stamp (letters, parcels) to show the charge for sending.

frank·fur·ter /'fræŋkfɜːtə(r)/ nc a kind of smoked sausage.

fran·tic /'fræntɪk/ adj 1 **frantic (with sth)** extremely worried, anxious; full of pain: *frantic with worry; frantic cries for help.* 2 very busy, excited: *work at a frantic pace.*

fran·ti·cal·ly /-klɪ/ adv

fra·ter·nal /frə'tɜːnl/ adj (formal) brotherly: *fraternal love.*

fra·ter·nal·ly /-nəlɪ/ adv

fra·ter·ni·ty /frə'tɜːnətɪ/ n (pl -ies) 1 nc a society of men who treat each other as equals and who have the same common interests etc. 2 nc (US) a society of students, with branches in various colleges, usually with names made up of Greek letters. 3 nu (formal) brotherly affection.

frat·er·nize (also **-ise**) /'frætənaɪz/ vi **fraternize (with sb)** to become friendly (with).

frat·er·ni·za·tion (also **-ni·sa·tion**) /,frætə-naɪ'zeɪʃn/ nu

fraud /frɔːd/ n 1 nc,nu (legal) (an act of) criminal dishonesty: *get money by fraud.* 2 nc a person who pretends to be qualified, to have authority or to want to be kind, but who is or does not.

fraudu·lent /'frɔːdjʊlənt/ adj dishonest (the usual word): *fraudulent behaviour.*

fraudu·lent·ly *adv*

fraught /frɔːt/ *adj* **1 fraught with sth** involving, threatening, unpleasant consequences: *an expedition fraught with danger.* **2** (of a person) very worried: *looking fraught.*

fray¹ /freɪ/ *nc* (usually the —) a fight; contest.

fray² /freɪ/ *vt,vi* **1** (to cause cloth, rope etc) to become worn by rubbing so that there are loose threads: *Will this cloth fray?* **2** (*fig*) to cause exhaustion, wear out (a person's mental strength): *fray one's nerves; a frayed temper.*

freak¹ /friːk/ *adj* (*attrib; no comp*) unusual and unexpected: *a freak storm.*

freak² /friːk/ *nc* **1** a very unusual idea, act or happening: *By some freak* (*of nature*) *the drought was followed by floods.* **2** a person, animal or plant that is abnormal in form or behaviour: *That blue rose is a freak.* **3** (*informal*) a fanatic: *a football freak.*

freak·ish /-ɪʃ/ *adj* abnormal: *freakish behaviour.*

freak³ /friːk/ *vi* **freak (out)** (*informal*) to become extremely angry, excited, worried etc.

freckle /ˈfrekl/ *nc* a small light-brown spot on the human skin. □ *vi* to become covered with freckles: *Some people freckle more easily than others.*

free¹ /friː/ *adj* (—r, —est) **1** (of a person) not in the power of another person; not in prison; not controlled or restricted by rules and regulations: *as free as a bird/the air* (= completely free). *All people should be born free. You are free to go or stay—it is your decision. A free market allows equal competition for selling goods.* **free and easy** (of a person, behaviour) informal and tolerant: *a free and easy manner.* **give sb/have a free hand** to give a person/have permission to act without asking other people's advice, without the usual controls or restrictions. **2** (of a nation, its citizens and institutions) not controlled by a foreign government or a cruel and undemocratic government: *a free country; struggle to be free.* **3** (*no comp*) without payment: *have two free tickets for the show; entrance/admission free; admission is free of charge; win a free trip to Kenya. The best things in life* (e.g. health, sunshine) *are free.* **for free** (*informal*) without paying: *You can have my old TV for free.* **4** (*no comp*) (of a person) not doing anything; not occupied or committed: *Are you free next Saturday evening? The Manager will be free to see you at 3 o'clock. I'm not free to marry you—I've promised David.* **5** (*no comp*) not being used: *Is this seat free? The bathroom is free now. It's impossible to find a free telephone in the station.* **6** (*pred*) **free from sth** without, released from, something: *free from blame/error/ pain.* **7** without any obstruction: *a free flow of water; a free route to the sea.* **8** (*attrib*) not exact: *a free translation.* **9** (*pred*) **free with sth** generous and ready with help etc: *free with her advice/ money.*

free-for-all *nc* a disorganized quarrel in which everyone tries to give an opinion.

free·hand *adj* (of drawings) done by hand, no instrument being used: *a free-hand sketch.*

free·hold *nu* (*legal*) (the holding of) land in absolute ownership. Compare leasehold.

free·holder *nc* a person who owns freehold property.

free·lance /-lɑːns/ *adj, nc* (of) an independent journalist, writer etc.

free 'speech *nu* the right to speak in public without interference from the authorities.

free-standing *adj* (of furniture) not attached to anything.

free·style *nu* (*swimming*) (a race using) a style where the competitors choose their own stroke, usually the crawl.

free 'trade *nu* trade without customs duties to restrict imports.

free 'verse *nu* a style of poetry without a regular metre and rhyme.

free 'will *nu* an individual's personal power of guiding and choosing her or his actions: *I came of my own free will.*

free·ly *adv* in a free manner; readily.

free² /friː/ *adv* in a free way: *give the tickets away free.* **break free (from sb/sth)** to escape (from): *You must try to break free from that man's influence. The dog has broken free* (*from its lead*). **come free** to become unattached: *The boat came free and floated out to sea.* **feel free (to do sth)** (used as an informal way of inviting a person to ask for or do something): *Please feel free to ask my advice/borrow my bike whenever you want to.* **go free** to be released from prison, suspicion etc. **make free with sb** to be too familiar with, e.g. a person's wife. **set sb free** to release a person from prison, suspicion, an obligation etc.

free³ /friː/ *vt* (*pt,pp* **freed**) **free sb/sth (from sth)** **1** to give economic, political, personal etc liberty to a person: *free a prisoner; free the people* (*from tyranny*). **2** to release a person, animal, thing (from): *free a man from debt/pain/an obligation; free an animal* (*from a trap*); *free a skirt from a nail.*

free·dom /ˈfriːdəm/ *n* **1** *nu* the condition of being free(1,2): *freedom of thought/speech.* **2** *nc* a particular kind of freedom(1): *various political and economic freedoms.* **3** *nu* **freedom from sth** release from something unpleasant: *freedom from pain/debt.*

freedom fighter *nc* a person fighting for political freedom.

freeze¹ /friːz/ *nc* **1** a period of extremely cold weather: *A sudden freeze killed the roses.* **2** a fixing (of prices, wages etc) by a government: *a wage freeze.*

freeze² /friːz/ *v* (*pt* **froze** /frəʊz/, *pp* **frozen** /ˈfrəʊzn/) **1** *vt,vi* (to cause a substance) to become solid, esp as ice, because of extreme cold: *When water freezes it becomes ice. Are frozen vegetables as tasty as fresh ones?* ⇨ deep-freeze. **2** *vi* (of weather, temperature) to be extremely cold (so that water becomes ice): *It was freezing last night. This house is freezing—close the windows.* **3** *vi* to feel extremely cold: *I'm freezing—give me a jumper.* **freeze to death** to die because of extreme cold: *You'll freeze to death in that cotton dress.* **4** *vt,vi* (to cause a person, animal, liquid) to become still, stop moving, e.g. because of fear: *I was frozen to the spot when I heard the scream. The sound made my blood freeze.* **5** *vt* to fix (prices, wages etc) at a certain level: *Wages have been frozen for six months.*

freeze sb out (*informal*) (**a**) to prevent a rival

business or trader from competing by offering lower prices, refusing to cooperate etc. (**b**) to prevent a person from becoming a member by being unfriendly, uncooperative etc.

freeze over (of a lake, harbour etc) to become covered with ice.

freeze up (of an engine, pipe etc) to become filled with ice and not work.

freeze-dry /'fri:z draɪ/ *vt* (*pt,pp* **-ied**) to preserve (food) by rapid freezing and drying it in a vacuum.

freez·er /'fri:zə(r)/ *nc* an electrical apparatus, like a refrigerator, in which food is kept frozen.

freez·ing /'fri:zɪŋ/ *adj* extremely (cold): *freezing temperatures. I'm freezing (cold)*.

'freezing-point *nc* the temperature at which a liquid (esp water) freezes.

freight /freɪt/ *nu* (*commerce*) **1** (money charged for) the carrying of goods from place to place by water. **2** the goods carried. □ *vt* to send or carry (goods).

freight·er *nc* a ship, plane, that carries cargo.

fren·et·ic /frə'netɪk/ *adj* = frantic.

fren·zy /'frenzɪ/ *n sing* **in/into a frenzy (of sth)** violent excitement: *in a frenzy of despair; worked himself up into a frenzy*.

fren·zied *adj* wildly excited.

fre·quen·cy /'fri:kwənsɪ/ *n* (*pl* **-ies**) **frequency (of sth)** **1** *nu* frequent occurrence: *the frequency of earthquakes in Italy*. **2** *nc* a rate of occurrence; number of repetitions (in a given time): *a frequency of 25 per second*. **3** *nc* (*radio*) a particular frequency(2) for a radio signal.

fre·quent[1] /'fri:kwənt/ *adj* often happening: *Hurricanes are frequent here in autumn. He's a frequent visitor*.

fre·quent·ly *adv*

fre·quent[2] /frɪ'kwent/ *vt* to go often to, be often in or at, (a place): *Frogs frequent wet places*.

fresh /freʃ/ *adj* (**—er, —est**) **1** newly made, produced, gathered, grown, arrived etc: *fresh meat/ milk; fresh fruit* (= not cooked, tinned etc); *fresh supplies; fresh paint* (= still wet); *fresh water* (i.e. as in rivers, not salty as in the sea). **2** (*no comp*) new or different: *Is there any fresh news? I'll make a fresh pot of coffee/put fresh sheets on the bed.* **make a fresh start** to begin again. **3** (of the air, wind, weather) cool; refreshing: *go out for some fresh air*. **4** bright and clean: *fresh colours; a fresh face*. **5** (*informal; derog*) too friendly and lacking respect (towards a woman): *be/get fresh with a girl*. **6 be fresh out of sth** (*informal*) (**a**) to have just finished a supply of something: *I'm fresh out of sugar*. (**b**) to have just left school, university.

fresh·ly *adv* (only with a *pp*) recently: *freshly picked fruit*.

fresh·ness *nu*

fresh·en /'freʃn/ *vt,vi* **1** (to cause air, a room, clothes etc) to become fresh(1). **2 freshen (oneself) up** to make oneself feel fresh(4) by washing.

fret[1] /fret/ *nc* one of the metal ridges across the neck of a guitar, banjo etc.

fret[2] /fret/ *vi,vt* (**-tt-**) (to cause a person) to be worried or bad-tempered: *What are you fretting about/for? Stop fretting!*

fret·ful /-fəl/ *adj* crying because uncomfortable and unhappy: *a fretful baby*.

fret·ful·ly /-fəlɪ/ *adv*

fret[3] /fret/ *vt* (**-tt-**) to decorate (wood) with patterns by cutting or sawing.

'fret·saw *nc* a very narrow saw used for cutting designs.

'fret·work *nu* wood cut with patterns by using a fretsaw.

Fri *written abbr* Friday.

fri·ar /'fraɪə(r)/ *nc* a man who is a member of certain Christian groups, esp one who lives in poverty.

fric·tion /'frɪkʃn/ *n* **1** *nu* the rubbing of one thing against another. **2** *nc,nu* (an instance of) a difference of opinion leading to argument and quarrelling: *political friction between two countries*.

Fri·day /'fraɪdɪ/ *nc* (abbr **Fri**) the sixth day of the week: *Let's go out on Friday/next Friday evening. On Fridays* (= Every Friday) *I get paid*. ⇨ **Good Friday**.

fridge /frɪdʒ/ *nc* (*informal*) = refrigerator.

fridge-'freezer *nc* an electrical apparatus with a freezer and a fridge in one unit.

fried /fraɪd/ *pt,pp* of fry.

friend /frend/ *nc* **1** a person, not a relation, who one knows and likes well: *She's my best* (= favourite) *friend. He has been a good friend to me.* **be/make friends (with sb)** to be/become a friend of a person. ⇨ also befriend. **2** a helpful thing or quality: *Among gossips, silence can be your best friend.* **3** a helper or sympathizer: *a good friend of the poor.* ⇨ also Quaker.

friend·ly /'frendlɪ/ *adj* (**-ier, -iest**) **1 friendly (to/towards/with sb)** acting or ready to act as a friend: *be friendly to/towards her; be on friendly terms with her*. **2** (*attrib*) kind: *a friendly greeting/ smile*. **3** (*attrib*) helping: *a friendly breeze*. **4** done without strong feelings: *a friendly argument*. Opp unfriendly.

friend·li·ness *nu*

friend·ship /'frendʃɪp/ *nc,nu* (an instance, period, of) the feeling or relationship that exists between friends: *I enjoy my friendship with her. We have enjoyed a friendship of twenty years.*

frieze /fri:z/ *nc* an ornamental band or strip along (usually the top of) a wall.

frig·ate /'frɪɡət/ *nc* a kind of fast warship.

fright /fraɪt/ *nc,nu* (an instance of) great and sudden fear: *I nearly died of fright.*

fright·en /'fraɪtn/ *vt* to fill (a person, animal) with fright: *Did the noise frighten you?* **frighten sb/sth away** to cause a person, animal to go way because of fear.

fright·en·ed *adj* afraid: *be frightened of him/the storm/frightened at the idea of something happening/that she'll come/of failure.*

fright·en·ing *adj* causing fright: *a frightening experience.*

fright·ful /'fraɪtfəl/ *adj* **1** causing fear; dreadful: *a frightful accident.* **2** (*dated informal*) very unpleasant: *frightful weather.*

fright·ful·ly /-fəlɪ/ *adv* (*dated informal*) very: *I'm frightfully sorry!*

fri·gid /'frɪdʒɪd/ *adj* **1** cold: *a frigid climate.* **2** unfriendly: *a frigid manner.* **3** having no sexual desire.

fri·gid·ly *adv*

fri·gid·ity /frɪ'dʒɪdətɪ/ *nu*

frill /frɪl/ *nc* **1** a pleated border on a dress etc. **2**

(*pl*) (*fig; derog*) unnecessary adornments to speech or writing.

frilly *adj: a frilly dress.*

fringe¹ /frɪndʒ/ *nc* **1** a border of loose threads, e.g. on a rug. **2** an edge (of a crowd, forest etc): *on the fringe(s) of the desert.* **3** a part of the hair cut short and allowed to hang over the forehead.

,fringe 'benefit *nc* (*informal*) a car etc given by an employer as well as a salary.

fringe² /frɪndʒ/ *vt* to put a border on, be a border to, (something): *fringing a skirt with a frill; countries fringing the Sahara desert.*

frisk /frɪsk/ *v* **1** *vi* to jump and run about playfully. **2** *vt* to pass the hands over (a person) to search for concealed weapons.

frisky *adj* (**-ier, -iest**) lively.

frit·ter¹ /'frɪtə(r)/ *nc* a piece of fried batter with sliced fruit or meat in it: *banana fritters.*

frit·ter² /'frɪtə(r)/ *vt* **fritter sth away** to waste money, time etc on useless aims: *fritter away one's time/energy/money.*

friv·ol·ity /frɪ'vɒlətɪ/ *n* (*pl* **-ies**) **1** *nu* frivolous behaviour or character. **2** *nc* a frivolous act or statement.

friv·ol·ous /'frɪvələs/ *adj* **1** not serious or important: *frivolous remarks/behaviour.* **2** (*derog*) (of a person) not serious; enjoying pleasure (too much).

friv·ol·ous·ly *adv*

frizz /frɪz/ *vt,vi* (to cause hair) to form into masses of small curls.

friz·zy *adj* (**-ier, -iest**) (of hair) frizzed.

frizzle /'frɪzl/ *vt,vi* to cook (food), be cooked, in oil which spits: *bacon frizzling in the pan.*

fro /frəʊ/ *adv* (only in) **to and fro** ⇨ to¹(2).

frock /frɒk/ *nc* (*dated*) a woman's or girl's dress (now the usual word).

frog /frɒg/ *nc* a small, cold-blooded, jumping animal living in water and on land.

'frog·man *nc* a person skilled in swimming under water with the aid of flippers on the feet and breathing apparatus.

frol·ic /'frɒlɪk/ *vi* (*pt,pp* **—ked**) to play about in a gay, lively way. □ *nc* an instance of enjoying oneself in a gay, lively way.

from /frəm *strong form*: frɒm/ *prep* Ⓝ For uses of *from* with verbs such as *come, make, take* etc ⇨ the *verb* entries. **1** starting at (a place, position, amount etc): *from the beginning; start from £10; shout from the window; jump from a wall; slip from one's fingers; set out from London; travel from Rome to Venice; from person to person.* **2** starting at (a time, date, period): *from 2 o'clock; the end of May; from my childhood; from 1985 to 1988.* Compare *during, since.* **from now on** starting now and in future: *From now on I'll always believe you.* **from time to time** ⇨ time¹(4). **3** (showing distance): *ten miles from the coast; five kilometres from here.* **4** (showing limit, difference etc of quantity): *From 10 to 15 people were injured. 12 from 26 is 14.* **5** (showing origin, source etc): *a letter from my brother; quotations from Shakespeare; drawn from life; make wine from grapes; clothes from Marks and Spencer; steal from a shop; bought from a supermarket; released from prison; a family from India.* **6** as a result of; because of: *die from starvation; suffer from measles.* **7** (showing difference or change):

know an Englishman from an American; change from a caterpillar into a butterfly. Things are going from bad to worse. **8** (used in many adverbial and prepositional phrases of time and place): *from above/below/behind/afar/abroad/among the best.*

frond /frɒnd/ *nc* a part of a fern or palm-tree that is like a leaf.

front¹ /frʌnt/ *n* **1** **the front of sb/sth** (also *attrib*) the side nearer or towards one more often seen; most important side: *the front of a building; sitting in the front of the class; the front page of a newspaper* (= page 1). **in front** (*adv*) at, to, the front position: *Please go in front.* **in front of sb/ sth** (*prep*) at, to, the front position of something: *There are some trees in front of the house.* **2** *nc* (the —) (*mil*) the part where the fighting is taking place: *go/be sent to the front.* **3** *nc* a road etc bordering the part of a town facing the sea: *have a walk along the front.* **4** *nc* **put on a bold front** to face a situation with (apparent) courage. **5** *nc* a boundary between masses of cold and warm air: *a cold/warm front.*

,front 'door *nc* the main door of a building.

,front 'runner *nc* a leading contestant.

front² /frʌnt/ *v* **1** *vt,vi* **front (onto) sth** to be positioned opposite something: *I prefer a hotel room that fronts (onto) the sea.* **2** *vi* **front for sb** (*informal*) to act in a way that hides a person doing something illegal.

front·age /'frʌntɪdʒ/ *nc* an extent of a piece of land or a building along its front: *a building site with a road frontage of 500 metres.*

fron·tal /'frʌntl/ *adj* (*attrib*) of, on, to, the front: *a frontal attack; a full frontal painting of a person* (= of the whole body).

fron·tier /'frʌntɪə(r)/ *nc* **1** a part of a country bordering on another country; (land on each side of) a boundary. **2** (*fig*) an extreme limit: *the frontiers of knowledge.*

frost¹ /frɒst/ *n* **1** *nc,nu* (a period of) a weather condition with temperature below the freezing point of water: *ten degrees of frost.* **2** *nu* a white frozen coating of vapour on the ground, roofs, plants etc: *windows covered with frost.*

frost² /frɒst/ *v* **1** *vi* **frost (over)** to become covered with frost(2): *The windscreen of my car frosted over during the night.* **2** *vt* (usually *passive*) to give a roughened surface to (glass) so that it is not transparent: *frosted glass.* **3** *vt* to cover (a cake etc) with sugar.

'frost·bite *nu* an injury to skin tissue because of freezing weather, snow etc.

'frost-bitten *adj* having, suffering from, frostbite.

frosty /'frɒstɪ/ *adj* (**-ier, -iest**) **1** cold with frost: *frosty weather.* **2** (*fig; derog*) unfriendly: *a frosty welcome.*

froth /frɒθ/ *nu* a mass of small bubbles; foam: *a glass of beer with a lot of froth on it.* □ *vi* to have, produce, froth: *A mad dog may froth at the mouth.*

frothy *adj* (**-ier, -iest**) of, like, covered with, froth: *frothy beer.*

frown¹ /fraʊn/ *nc* a frowning expression: *a deep frown on the judge's face.*

frown² /fraʊn/ *v* **1** *vi* to draw the eyebrows together causing lines on the forehead (to express disapproval, puzzlement, deep thought etc). **2** *vt*

frown on sth to disapprove of an activity: *Gambling is frowned on here*.

froze /frəʊz/ *pt* of freeze².

frozen /'frəʊzn/ *pp* of freeze².

fru·gal /'fru:gl/ *adj* (*formal*) careful, economical (esp of food, cost): *a frugal meal*.

fru·gal·ity /fru:'gælətɪ/ *nc,nu*

fru·gal·ly /-gəlɪ/ *adv*

fruit¹ /fru:t/ *n* **1** *nc,nu* (*pl* unchanged) a part of a plant or tree that contains the seeds and is used as food, e.g. apples, bananas: *Do you eat much fruit?* **2** *nc* a part of any plant in which the seed is formed. **3** (*pl*) any plant or vegetable used for food: *the fruits of the earth*. **4** (*fig*) (often *pl*) profit, result or reward (of labour, study etc): *the fruits of industry*. **bear fruit** (*fig*) to show a good result: *When do you expect these improvements to begin to bear fruit?*

'fruit fly *nc* (*pl* **-ies**) a kind of a small fly that feeds on fermenting fruit.

,fruit 'salad *nu* a dish of various kinds of fruit cut up and mixed.

fruit·er·er *nc* a person, business, that sells fruit.

fruit·ful /-fəl/ *adj* (*fig*) producing good results: *a fruitful career*.

fruit·less *adj* (*fig*) without results or success: *fruitless efforts*.

fruit·less·ly *adv*

fruity *adj* (**-ier, -iest**) (**a**) of or like fruit. (**b**) (*informal; derog*) full of indecent humour: *a fruity novel*. (**c**) (*informal*) rich; mellow: *a fruity voice*.

fruit² /fru:t/ *vi* (of trees, bushes) to produce fruit.

fru·ition /fru:'ɪʃn/ *nu* (esp) **come to fruition** to achieve what was wanted or hoped for: *research ideas/business plans that come to fruition*.

frump /frʌmp/ *nc* (*informal; derog*) an unattractive woman.

frus·trate /frʌ'streɪt/ *vt* (*formal*) **1** (often *passive*) to prevent (a person) from doing something: *be frustrated by the bad weather*. **2** to prevent (plans) from being carried out.

frus·tra·tion /frʌ'streɪʃn/ *nc,nu*

fry /fraɪ/ *vt,vi* (3rd person sing, pres t **fries**, *pt,pp* **fried**) **1** to cook, be cooked, in boiling fat: *She's frying chicken.* ⇨ also fish¹(1). **2** (*fig; informal*) (of a person) to feel hot, become burned, in the sun.

'fry·ing-pan *nc* a shallow pan used for frying.

ft written *abbr* foot; feet.

fudge /fʌdʒ/ *nu* a kind of soft sweet made with milk, sugar and butter.

fu·el¹ /'fju:əl/ *nu* (*pl* = kinds of fuel) any substance used for producing heat or energy, e.g. coal, oil.

fu·el² /'fju:əl/ *v* (**-ll-**, *US* also **-l-**) **1** *vt* to supply (an aircraft etc) with fuel. **2** *vi* **fuel (up)** to take in fuel: *The plane is already fuelling up again*. **3** *vt* to cause (an argument etc) to begin or grow stronger.

fugi·tive /'fju:dʒətɪv/ *adj, nc* (of) a person running away from the police, danger etc: *a fugitive from justice*.

ful·crum /'fʌlkrəm/ *nc* (*pl* **—s**) (*tech*) a point on which a lever turns.

ful·fil (*US* also **ful·fill**) /fʊl'fɪl/ *vt* (**-ll-**) to carry out (a task, duty, promise etc): *fulfil one's duties/ an obligation/his hopes*.

ful·filled *adj* (of a person) satisfied with her or his job, life etc. Opp unfulfilled.

ful·fil·ment *nu*

full /fʊl/ *adj* (**—er, —est**) **1** completely filled; having or holding a lot (of): *The room was full of people. I have three full boxes left. The reservoir is full to the brim.* Compare empty¹(1). **full up** (*informal*) (**a**) (of a container) completely filled. (**b**) (of a person) having eaten enough. **2** **full of oneself** showing complete confidence and too much interest in one's ability, good qualities etc. **be full of sth** to be completely occupied with talking about something: *She was full of the news*. **3** reaching the usual or expected extent, limit, length etc: *wait a full hour; did it in full daylight*. **in full** without leaving out anything: *Write your name in full* (i.e. 'Ivor Brain', not 'I. Brain'). **to the full** to the greatest extent: *enjoyed myself to the full*. **at full speed** ⇨ speed¹(2). **4** (usually *attrib*) complete: *Write your full name and address. Give me full details of what happened. A fuller account will be sent later. There's a full moon tonight*. **5** (*attrib*) pleasantly rounded: *a full face/figure*. **6** (of clothes) wide and using a lot of material: *a full skirt; full sleeves*.

'full-back *nc* a player (*defender*) placed near the goal area (in football etc).

,full 'board *nu* hotel accommodation with all meals included.

,full-'length *adj* (**a**) (of a portrait) showing the whole figure. (**b**) of standard or usual length: *a full-length novel/play*.

,full 'point *nc* (*US*) = full stop.

,full-'scale *adj* (**a**) (of drawings, plans etc) of the same size, area etc as the object itself. (**b**) (*attrib*) using every available means: *a full-scale enquiry*.

,full 'stop *nc* (*lang*) the punctuation mark (.). Ⓝ It is used (**a**) at the end of a sentence, (**b**) after abbreviations, as in *e.g., No., approx., temp.* ⇨ the note at abbreviation.

',full-'time *adj, adv* occupying all normal working hours: *a full-time worker; working full-time*.

full·ness *nu*

ful·ly /'fʊlɪ/ *adv* **1** completely: *fully satisfied; fully automatic*. **2** at least: *The journey will take fully two hours.* ⇨ also fledged.

,fully-'grown *adj* mature.

fumble /'fʌmbl/ *v* **1** *vi* to feel about uncertainly with the hands; use the hands awkwardly: *fumbling about in one's pockets for a key*. **2** *vt,vi* to handle or deal with (something) nervously or incompetently: *fumbled a ball* (e.g. in sport); *fumbled (over) her speech*.

fume¹ /fju:m/ *nc* (often *pl*) a strong-smelling smoke, gas or vapour: *petrol fumes*.

fume² /fju:m/ *vi* **1** to give off fumes. **2** (*fig*) to show one's strong feeling of anger or irritation: *fuming at her incompetence*.

fu·mi·gate /'fju:mɪgeɪt/ *vt* to disinfect (a place) using chemical fumes: *fumigating a room*.

fu·mi·ga·tion /,fju:mɪ'geɪʃn/ *nu*

fun /fʌn/ *nu* **1** amusement; playfulness: *What fun the children had!* **make fun of sb; poke fun at sb** (to cause people) to laugh at (a person): *We made fun of dad in his smart suit*. **for/in fun** as a joke, for amusement; not seriously: *He did it for fun*. **2** a person, activity etc that causes laughter or pleasure: *Paul is great fun. Sailing is good fun*.

'**fun·fair** nc a public outdoor entertainment with various amusing activities.

'**fun run** nc (informal) a long road race on foot for pleasure more than competition.

func·tion[1] /ˈfʌŋkʃn/ nc **1** a special activity or purpose of a person or thing: the functions of a judge/of education; grammatical functions. A calculator has many functions (= can carry out many activities). **2** a public or formal ceremony or event: the numerous functions that a professor must attend.

func·tion[2] /ˈfʌŋkʃn/ vi to work, be active: The telephone was not functioning.

func·tion·al /ˈfʌŋkʃənl/ adj having, designed to have, practical use.

fund[1] /fʌnd/ nc **1** (often pl) a sum of money available for a purpose: a relief fund (e.g. to help in a disaster). **2** a large supply: a fund of jokes.

fund[2] /fʌnd/ vt to provide money for (an activity, organization): The research is funded by the University.

fun·da·men·tal[1] /ˌfʌndəˈmentl/ adj of great importance; basic: fundamental changes in education.

fun·da·men·tal·ly /-təlɪ/ adv

fun·da·men·tal[2] /ˌfʌndəˈmentl/ nc (usually pl) a basic or most important rule or principle; essential part: the fundamentals of mathematics.

fu·ner·al /ˈfjuːnərəl/ nc a (religious ceremony of) burial or cremation of a dead person.

'**funeral march** nc a piece of sad and solemn music.

fu·ner·eal /fjuːˈnɪərɪəl/ adj **1** suitable for a funeral: funereal dress. **2** (fig) sad and gloomy: a funereal look.

fun·gi·cide /ˈfʌŋgɪsaɪd/ nc,nu (an example of) a substance that destroys fungi.

fun·goid /ˈfʌŋgɔɪd/ adj (tech) of, like, fungi.

fun·gous /ˈfʌŋgəs/ adj of, like, caused by, fungi.

fun·gus /ˈfʌŋgəs/ nc,nu (pl -gi /-gaɪ/) a plant without leaves, flowers or green colouring (e.g. a mushroom), growing on other plants or on decaying matter (e.g. old wood).

fun·nel[1] /ˈfʌnl/ nc **1** a tube wide at the top and narrow at the bottom, used for pouring liquids or powders through small openings. **2** a tall outlet for smoke on a ship, railway engine etc.

fun·nel[2] /ˈfʌnl/ vt,vi (-ll-, US -l-) (to cause things) to move (as if) through a funnel.

fun·ni·ly /ˈfʌnəlɪ/ adv in an odd or an amusing way: speak funnily. **funnily enough** it is strange to say but: Funnily enough I believe her.

fun·ny /ˈfʌnɪ/ adj (-ier, -iest) **1** causing fun or laughter: funny stories. **2** strange; queer; causing surprise: A funny thing happened to me this morning. That's funny—I thought I left my keys here on the table. I feel funny (= sick). There's something funny about him/the affair (perhaps not quite honest or straightforward).

'**funny-bone** nc (informal) a part of the elbow over which a very sensitive nerve passes.

fur[1] /fɜː(r)/ n **1** nu the soft, thick hair covering certain animals, e.g. cats, rabbits. **2** nc (also attrib) an animal skin with the fur on it, esp when made into clothes: a fur coat. **3** nu the coating on a person's tongue when ill, on the inside of a kettle, boiler etc.

fur[2] /fɜː(r)/ vt,vi (-rr-) (to cause something) to become covered with fur(3): a furred tongue/kettle.

fur·ry /ˈfɜːrɪ/ adj (-ier, -iest) of, like, covered with, fur.

furi·ous /ˈfjʊərɪəs/ adj **1** (of a person) extremely angry: I'm furious with you. **2** very strong: a furious struggle/storm/quarrel.

furi·ous·ly adv

furl /fɜːl/ vt,vi (to cause sails, flags, umbrellas etc) to roll up: furl the sails of a yacht.

fur·long /ˈfɔːlɒŋ/ nc (abbr **fur.**) (esp horse-racing) a unit of measurement of length (equal to one eighth of a mile or 201·168 metres).

furn. written abbr furnished.

fur·nace /ˈfɜːnɪs/ nc an enclosed apparatus with a fire, used for heating metals, making glass etc in a factory.

fur·nish /ˈfɜːnɪʃ/ vt **1** to put furniture in (a building etc): furnish a room/an office. **2 furnish sth (with sth)** to supply: furnish a library (with books).

fur·nish·ings n pl furniture and equipment.

fur·ni·ture /ˈfɜːnɪtʃə(r)/ nu all the movable things such as chairs, beds, desks etc in a house, office etc.

fu·rore (US = **fu·ror**) /fjʊˈrɔːrɪ/ n sing a strong, excited public protest: The new play at the National Theatre created a furore.

fur·rier /ˈfʌrɪə(r)/ nc a person, business, that prepares or deals in furs.

fur·row[1] /ˈfʌrəʊ/ nc **1** a long cut in the ground made by a plough: newly turned furrows. **2** a long wrinkle on the forehead.

fur·row[2] /ˈfʌrəʊ/ vt to make furrows in (something): a forehead furrowed by old age/anxiety.

fur·ry /ˈfɜːrɪ/ adj ⇨ fur.

fur·ther[1] /ˈfɜːðə(r)/ adj **1** more; additional: We need further information. Ⓝ 'Farther' is not possible. **2** more distant: on the further side of the field. Ⓝ 'Farther' is more usual. ⇨ far[1].

further education nu (also attrib) any education after leaving school: a college of further education.

fur·ther[2] /ˈfɜːðə(r)/ adv **1** at, to, a greater distance: It's not safe to go any further. Ⓝ 'Farther' is more usual. **2** more: We needn't worry any further. Ⓝ 'Farther' is not possible. **3** in addition; moreover: He said he'd lost the key and further that it couldn't be found. Ⓝ 'Farther' is not possible. ⇨ far[2].

fur·ther[3] /ˈfɜːðə(r)/ vt to help the progress of (something): further the cause of peace.

fur·ther·ance /ˈfɜːðərəns/ nu **the furtherance of sth** (formal) the progress, development, of something: the furtherance of his career.

fur·ther·more /ˌfɜːðəˈmɔː(r)/ adv in addition; moreover: I love her, and furthermore I intend to marry her. ⇨ further[2](3).

fur·thest /ˈfɜːðɪst/ adj, adv (superl of far) at, to, the greatest distance: Let's see who can swim furthest/get to the furthest shore. Ⓝ 'Farthest' is more usual.

fur·tive /ˈfɜːtɪv/ adj done secretly so as not to attract attention: a furtive glance; furtive behaviour.

fur·tive·ly adv

fu·ry /ˈfjʊərɪ/ n (pl -ies) **1** nu a state of extreme anger: She was filled with fury. **2** nc a wild expression of anger: *He flew into a fury*.

fuse¹ /fju:z/ *nc* **1** (*electricity*) (a device with) a thin wire which melts and breaks the circuit when the electric current is too strong. **2** a tube, cord etc for carrying a spark to explode powder etc, e.g. in a firework, bomb.

fuse² /fju:z/ *vt,vi* **1** (*electricity*) (to cause an electric circuit) to break because a fuse(1) has melted. **2** (to cause wire etc) to join as the result of melting: *fuse two pieces of plastic together*.

fu·sel·age /'fju:zɪlɑ:ʒ/ *nc* the body of a plane (to which the engine(s), wings and tail are fitted).

fu·sion /'fju:ʒn/ *nc,nu* (a process of) mixing or uniting different things into one: *the fusion of copper and tin; a fusion of races/political parties*.

fuss¹ /fʌs/ *nu* or *sing* **1** unnecessary nervous excitement, esp about unimportant things: *Don't make so much fuss/such a fuss. What's all the/this fuss about?* **2** too much or unnecessary anxiety, concern. **make a fuss (of sb)** to give (a person) too much attention: *Don't make so much fuss of the children.*

fus·si·ness *nu*

fus·sy *adj* (**-ier, -iest**) (*derog*) (**a**) too concerned with unimportant details: *be too fussy about one's clothes.* (**b**) (of dress, writing style etc) too elaborate.

fuss² /fʌs/ *vi* **fuss (about/over sth)** to get into, be in, a fuss: *Stop fussing (about)! Don't fuss over the children so much.*

fu·tile /'fju:taɪl/ *adj* (of an action) of no use; having no effect: *a futile attempt.*

fu·til·ity /fju:'tɪlətɪ/ *nc,nu*

fu·ture¹ /'fju:tʃə(r)/ *adj* (*attrib*) **1** coming after the present: *his future wife* (= the woman he will marry). **2** of or in the future: *the future life* (= life after death).

fu·ture² /'fju:tʃə(r)/ *nc* a time, event, coming after the present: *I hope you have a happy future before you.* **in future** from this time onwards: *Try to live a better life in future.*

,future con'tinuous (tense) (the —) *nc* (*gram*) the verb form (*shall be/will be* and a *present participle*) used to describe an action or state that will be happening or continuing during the time mentioned or understood, as in 'He'*ll be coming* home tomorrow.' '*Will* she *be staying* long?'

,future 'perfect (tense) *nc* (the —) (*gram*) the verb form (*shall have/will have* and a *past participle*) used to describe an action or state that will be completed or have happened at a particular time, as in 'They'*ll have gone* before then.' '*Will* it *have finished* by midnight?'

,future ,perfect con'tinuous (tense) *nc* (the —) (*gram*) the verb form (*shall have been/will have been* and a *present participle*) used to describe an action or state, esp intended or expected, that will continue for a period mentioned or understood and be completed at a time further in the future, as in 'They'*ll have been travelling* for a month on Friday.'

,future pro'gressive (tense) *nc* = future continuous tense.

,future 'tense *nc* (the —) (also called the **future simple tense**) (*gram*) the verb form (*shall/will* and the *verb* without *to*) used to describe opinion, expectation etc about a future action or state, as in 'I *shall go* soon.' '*Will* they *come* soon?' (N) The future simple tense is used with adverbs describing 'how often', e.g. *never, rarely, sometimes, often, frequently, usually, always*. Avoid using a continuous tense with these adverbs.

fuzz /fʌz/ *nu* **1** a soft substance, e.g. from wool. **2** very curly hair. **3** *the fuzz* (*dated sl*) the police.

fuz·zy /'fʌzɪ/ (**-ier, -iest**) **1** not clear (in shape or outline): *a fuzzy photograph*. **2** very curly: *fuzzy hair; a fuzzy beard*. **3** (of a person) dizzy: *feeling fuzzy*.

fwd *written abbr* (*commerce*) forward.

Gg

G, g /dʒi:/ (*pl* **G's, g's** /dʒi:z/) the seventh letter of the English alphabet.

g *written abbr* gramme(s).

gabble¹ /'gæbl/ *nu* a way of talking fast that is difficult to understand.

gabble² /'gæbl/ *vt,vi* to speak, say, sing, things quickly so that it is difficult to be understood: *The little girl gabbled her prayers and jumped into bed. Listen to those children gabbling away.*

gad /gæd/ *vi* (**-dd-**) **gad about** (*informal*) to go from place to place for excitement or pleasure.

'gad·about *nc* a person who does this.

gadg·et /'gædʒɪt/ *nc* (*informal*) a small mechanical apparatus for a particular practical use: *a new gadget for opening tin cans.*

gaffe /gæf/ *nc* a tactless act or remark.

gag¹ /gæg/ *nc* **1** something put in or over a person's mouth to prevent her or him from speaking or crying out. **2** a joke, funny story, esp as part of a comedian's act.

gag² /gæg/ *vt* (**-gg-**) **1** to put a gag(1) into or over (a person's mouth). **2** (*fig*) to use regulations, political power etc to prevent (a person) from speaking freely.

ga·ga /'gɑ:gɑ:/ *adj* (*sl*) senile.

gage /geɪdʒ/ *nc* = gauge.

gaggle /'gægl/ *nc* a flock (= group) (of geese).

gai·ety /'geɪətɪ/ *n* (*pl* **-ies**) **1** *nu* the state of being cheerful; bright appearance: *flags and scarves that added to the gaiety of the Cup Final scene.* **2** (*pl*) joyful festive occasions: *the gaieties of the Caribbean carnival.* ⇨ gay.

gai·ly /'geɪlɪ/ *adv* in a cheerful way. ⇨ gay.

gain¹ /geɪn/ *n* **1** *nu* (the process of) getting possessions or wealth. **2** *nc* an increase in amount or power: *a gain in weight/health.*

gain·ful /-fəl/ *adj* (*formal*) providing money: *gainful occupations.*

gain·ful·ly /-fəlɪ/ *adv* in order to earn money: *gainfully employed.*

gain² /geɪn/ *v* **1** *vt* to obtain (something wanted or needed): *gain experience; gain an advantage over a competitor.* **gain access (to sb/sth)** ⇨ access¹(1). **gain time** ⇨ time¹(2). **gain the upper hand** ⇨ upper. **2** *vt,vi* to increase in an amount (of wealth, weight, speed etc): *The baby gained five pounds (in weight). The clock gains three minutes a day.* **gain ground** ⇨ ground¹(1). **3** *vt* **gain on sb/sth** (**a**) to get closer to a person, thing: *gain on the other runners in a race*. **(b)** to go faster than, get farther in advance of, (a person, car etc): *gain on the police*. **4** *vt* (*formal*) to reach, arrive at, (a desired place, esp with effort): *The swimmer gained the shore*.

gait /geɪt/ *nc* a manner of walking or running: *with an awkward gait*.

gal /gæl/ *n* (*dated informal*) = girl.

gal *written abbr* gallon(s).

ga·la /'gɑːlə/ *nc* **1** (also *attrib*) a festive occasion: *a gala performance* (e.g. at a theatre, with special actors, singers etc). **2** (also *swimming gala*) a swimming competition between teams.

ga·lac·tic /gəˈlæktɪk/ *adj* of the Galaxy.

gal·axy /'gæləksɪ/ *nc* (*pl* **-ies**) **1** any of the huge groups of stars in outer space. **2** (the G-) the one that includes our solar system (visible as a band of stars known as *the Milky Way*). **3** (*fig*) a group of people: *a galaxy of beautiful women*.

gale /geɪl/ *nc* **1** a strong wind, often with rain: *The ship lost her masts in the gale*. **2** a noisy outburst: *gales of laughter*.

gall[1] /gɔːl/ *nu* **1** = bile. **2** (*fig*) a bitter feeling. **3** (*informal*) impudence: *Of all the gall!*

'gall-bladder *nc* (*anat*) the part, attached to the liver, containing and discharging bile.

gall[2] /gɔːl/ *vt* (*fig*) to hurt (a person)'s feelings: *It was galling to have to ask for a loan*.

gall[3] *written abbr* gallon(s).

gal·lant /'gælənt/ *adj* **1** brave (now the usual word): *gallant deeds*. **2** (*literary*) (also /gəˈlænt/) showing special respect and courtesy to women: *He was very gallant at the ball*.

gal·lant·ly *adv*

gal·lant·ry *nu*

gal·lery /'gælərɪ/ *nc* (*pl* **-ies**) **1** a room or building for the display of works of art. **2** (the —) (people in) the highest and cheapest seats in a theatre. **3** a covered walk or corridor, partly open at one side. **4** a horizontal underground passage in a mine. ⇨ shaft(4).

gal·li·vant /ˌgælɪˈvænt/ *vi* **gallivant (about)** to go from place to place for excitement or pleasure.

gal·lon /'gælən/ *nc* (abbr gal(l)) a measure for liquids equal to 8 pints (4·5 litres).

gal·lop[1] /'gæləp/ *nc* (of a horse etc) the fastest pace, with all four feet off the ground at each stride; period of riding at such a pace: *He rode away at a gallop/at full gallop/went for a gallop*.

gal·lop[2] /'gæləp/ *v* **1** *vt,vi* (to cause a horse) to go at a gallop: *They galloped across the fields*. **2** *vi* **gallop through sth** to do and complete something quickly: *gallop through one's work/lecture/meal*.

gal·lows /'gæləʊz/ *n sing* a wooden framework on which to kill a criminal by hanging.

ga·lore /gəˈlɔː(r)/ *adj* (used after a noun) in plenty: *a meal with beer galore*.

ga·loshes /gəˈlɒʃɪz/ *n pl* (also *a pair of galoshes*) rubber overshoes (to be) worn in wet weather.

gam·bit /'gæmbɪt/ *nc* **1** a kind of opening move in chess. **2** (*fig*) any first move: *His opening gambit in the debate was a direct attack on Government policy*.

gamble[1] /'gæmbl/ *nc* (an attempt or activity with) a risk of loss or a chance of profit. **take a gamble (on sth)** to do it knowing it is risky.

gamble[2] /'gæmbl/ *v* **1** *vi* to play games to try to win money: *He lost his money gambling at cards*. **2** *vt* **gamble sth away** to lose money etc by gambling: *He has gambled away half his fortune*. **3** *vi* **gamble (on sth)** to take risks with the chance of making a profit, achieving something: *gambling on the success of a new product/on parking illegally without being caught*.

gam·bler *nc* a person who gambles(1).

gamb·ling *nu* playing games for money.

gam·bol /'gæmbl/ *vi* (**-ll-**, *US* also **-l-**), *nc* (to make) a quick, playful, jumping or skipping movement, e.g. of lambs, children.

game[1] /geɪm/ *adj* **game (for sth)** **1** brave; ready to go on fighting: *a game soldier*. **2** (*pred*) ready and willing: *Are you game for a 10-mile walk?*

game[2] /geɪm/ *n* **1** *nc* a form of play, sport, esp with rules, e.g. tennis, football, cards: *play games; have/enjoy a game of chess/table tennis*. **be off one's game** to be not playing well. **play the game (a)** to obey the rules. **(b)** (*fig*) to behave fairly. **2** *nc* a set of equipment needed for a game, e.g. a board, dice and counters. **3** (*pl*) athletic contests: *the Olympic/Commonwealth Games*. **4** *nc* a single round in some contests, e.g. tennis: *win four games in the first set; game, set and match*. **5** *nc* a scheme, plan, esp a trick: *I wish I knew what his game is*. **give the game away** to tell a secret plan etc. **play games (a)** (of children) to be naughty. **(b)** (of adults) to act without sincerity. **6** *nu* (the flesh of) animals and birds hunted for sport and food: *try to photograph big game* (e.g. elephants, lions, tigers).

'game·keeper *nc* a man employed to breed and protect birds as game(6).

gam·ma /'gæmə/ *nc* the third letter (γ) of the Greek alphabet.

'gamma ray *nc* (*science*) a ray of very short wavelength from radioactive substances.

gam·mon /'gæmən/ *nu* a kind of smoked ham.

gam·ut /'gæmət/ *nc* (the —) the complete extent or scope of anything: *the whole gamut of feeling* (e.g. from great joy to great despair or misery).

gan·der /'gændə(r)/ *nc* a male goose.

gang[1] /gæŋ/ *nc* **1** a number of workmen or prisoners working together. **2** a group of criminals. ⇨ gangster. **3** (children's use) a group of friends: *Can I join your gang?*

gang[2] /gæŋ/ *vi* **1** **gang together** to act as a group: *gang together to steal a car*. **2** **gang up against/on sb** to act as a group to oppose a person: *They've ganged up against her because she refused to share her chocolate*.

gan·gling /'gæŋglɪŋ/ *adj* (*derog*) (of a person) tall, thin and awkward.

gang·plank /'gæŋplæŋk/ *nc* a movable bridge as placed between a ship and the land.

gan·grene /'gæŋgriːn/ *nu* the decay of a part of the body because the supply of blood to it has been stopped.

gan·gren·ous /'gæŋgrɪnəs/ *adj*

gang·ster /'gæŋstə(r)/ *nc* a member of a gang of armed criminals.

gang·way /'gæŋweɪ/ *nc* **1** an opening in a ship's side; movable bridge from this to the land. **2** a passage between rows of seats, e.g. in a theatre.

gan·try /'gæntrɪ/ *nc* (*pl* **-ies**) a structure of steel bars, used to support a crane etc.

gaol¹ (*US* = **jail**) /dʒeɪl/ *n* **1** *nc* a prison. **2** *nu* confinement in prison: *be sentenced to (three years in) gaol.*

  gaol·er (*US* = **jail·er**, **jail·or**) /'dʒeɪlə(r)/ *nc* a person in charge of a prison or the prisoners.

gaol² (*US* = **jail**) /dʒeɪl/ *vt* to put (a person) in prison.

gap /gæp/ *nc* **1** a break or opening in a wall, hedge etc: *The sheep got out of the field through a gap in the hedge.* **2** an empty space; wide separation (of ideas etc): *a gap in a conversation; fill in gaps in an application form; a serious gap between the government and the unions.* ⇨ also generation gap. **3** a gorge or pass between mountains.

gape¹ /geɪp/ *nc* an act of staring with the mouth open.

gape² /geɪp/ *vi* to stare with the mouth open, esp when surprised: *country visitors gaping at the neon lights.*

gap·ing /'geɪpɪŋ/ *adj* (*attrib*) very wide: *a gaping hole.*

gar·age¹ /'gæraːʒ/ *nc* **1** a building in which to keep a car or cars. **2** a roadside petrol and service station.

gar·age² /'gæraːʒ/ *vt* to put (a vehicle) in a garage.

gar·bage /'gaːbɪdʒ/ *nu* **1** waste food (to be) thrown out, fed to pigs etc. **2** (*US*) rubbish, refuse (of any kind). **3** (*computers*) useless or wrongly programmed data.

  'garbage can *nc* (*US*) = dustbin.

garble /'gaːbl/ *vt* (usually *passive*) to make an incomplete or unfair selection from statements, facts etc, esp in order to give false ideas: *a garbled report of a speech.*

gar·den¹ /'gaːdn/ *n* **1** *nc,nu* (also *attrib*) (a piece of) ground used for growing flowers, fruit, vegetables etc: *a rose garden; have lunch in the garden; garden plants.* ⇨ market garden. **2** (usually *pl*) (abbr **Gdns**) a public park: *zoological gardens.*

  'garden centre *nc* a business selling garden plants, tools and other equipment.

  ,garden 'suburb *nc* a housing area with large gardens.

gar·den² /'gaːdn/ *vi* to work in a garden: *He's been gardening all day.*

  gard·en·er *nc* a person who works in a garden.

  gar·den·ing *nu* (also *attrib*) the act, process, of working in gardens: *be fond of gardening; gardening tools.*

gargle¹ /'gaːgl/ *nc* **1** a liquid used for gargling. **2** an act of gargling.

gargle² /'gaːgl/ *vi* to wash the throat with liquid kept in motion by breathing air out through it.

gar·goyle /'gaːgɔɪl/ *nc* a stone or metal spout, usually in the form of a strange-looking human or animal head, used to carry off rainwater from the roof of a building.

gar·ish /'geərɪʃ/ *adj* (*derog*) unpleasantly coloured; over-decorated: *garish clothes.*

  gar·ish·ly *adv*

gar·land¹ /'gaːlənd/ *nc* a circle of flowers or leaves used as an ornament or decoration or as a prize for victory etc.

gar·land² /'gaːlənd/ *vt* **garland sb/sth (with sth)** (usually *passive*) to decorate a person, statue etc with a garland.

gar·lic /'gaːlɪk/ *nu* a plant like an onion with a

strong taste and smell, used in cooking.

gar·ment /'gaːmənt/ *nc* (*commerce*) an article of clothing (which is more usual).

gar·net /'gaːnɪt/ *nc* a kind of semi-precious gem of deep transparent red.

gar·nish /'gaːnɪʃ/ *nc* something used to decorate food. □ *vt* to use garnishes on (food): *fish garnished with slices of lemon.*

gar·ret /'gærət/ *nc* a small room on the top floor of a house, esp in the roof.

gar·ri·son¹ /'gærɪsn/ *nc* a group of soldiers stationed in a town or fort.

gar·ri·son² /'gærɪsn/ **1** to supply (a town) etc with a garrison. **2** to place (soldiers etc) in a garrison.

gar·ru·lous /'gærələs/ *adj* (*formal; derog*) talking too much about unimportant things.

  gar·ru·li·ty /gə'ruːlətɪ/ *nu*

gar·ter /'gaːtə(r)/ *nc* an (elastic) band worn round the leg to keep a sock or stocking in place.

gas¹ /gæs/ *n* **1** *nc,nu* (*pl* —**es**) any substance like air (used chiefly of those that are not liquid or solid at ordinary temperatures): *Air is a mixture of gases.* ⇨ gaseous, gassy. **2** *nu* one of the gases or mixtures of gases used for lighting and heating: *We use natural gas for cooking.* **3** *nu* (*US*) = petrol. **4** *nc* (*informal*) an activity, object etc that is very exciting: *His new Ferrari is a gas!*

  'gas cooker *nc* an apparatus (with gas rings and an oven) for cooking by gas.

  'gas meter *nc* one for registering the amount of gas used, e.g. in a building.

  'gas oven *nc* an oven in a gas cooker.

  'gas ring *nc* a metal ring with small holes providing gas for boiling, frying etc.

  'gas stove *nc* (*dated*) = gas cooker.

  'gas station *nc* (*US*) = petrol station.

  'gas·works *nc* a place where coal gas is manufactured.

gas² /gæs/ *v* (**-ss-**) **1** *vt* to poison or (try to) kill (a person, animal) with gas. **2** *vi* (*informal; derog*) to talk for a long time without saying anything that is useful or interesting.

gas·eous /'gæsɪəs/ *adj* (*science*) of or like gas: *a gaseous mixture.*

gash /gæʃ/ *vt, nc* (to make) a long deep cut or wound (in).

gas·ket /'gæskɪt/ *nc* a strip of soft, flat material used to prevent steam, oil etc from escaping (e.g. in an engine).

gaso·line (also **-lene**) /'gæsəliːn/ *nu* (*US*) = petrol.

gas·ometer /gæ'sɒmɪtə(r)/ *nc* a large round tank in which gas is stored or measured.

gasp¹ /gaːsp/ *nc* a sudden quick breath because of surprise, pain etc: *give a gasp of amazement.*

gasp² /gaːsp/ *v* **1** *vi* **gasp (for sth)** to struggle (for breath). **2** *vi* **gasp (with sth)** to take sudden quick breaths (because of pain, surprise etc): *gasping with rage/surprise.* **3** *vt* **gasp sth out** to say something in a breathless way: *He gasped out a few words.*

gas·sy /'gæsɪ/ *adj* (**-ier**, **-iest**) of, like, full of, gas: *a gassy drink.*

gas·tric /'gæstrɪk/ *adj* (*attrib; science*) of the stomach: *a gastric ulcer; gastric juices.*

gas·tron·omy /gæ'strɒnəmɪ/ *nu* (*formal*) the art and science of choosing, preparing and eating good food.

gas·tron·om·ic /ˌgæstrə'nɒmɪk/ *adj*

gate /geɪt/ *nc* **1** an opening in a hedge, fence, wall etc able to be closed by a barrier. **2** a kind of barrier, usually of long pieces of wood or metal, used to close such an opening: *a garden gate.* **3** a barrier used to control the passage of water, e.g. into or out of a dam. **4** a number of spectators in a stadium etc: *the largest gate this season.* **5** (in an airport) an exit from the departure area to the plane.

'**gate·crash** *vt* to join (a private party or other event) without invitation or payment. Hence '**gate·crash·er** *nc* a person doing this.

'**gate-post** *nc* a post on which a gate is hung or against which it is closed. *between you (and) me and the gatepost* in strict confidence.

'**gate·way** *nc* (**a**) an opening that can be closed by a gate. (**b**) (*fig*) a means of access: *a gateway to fame/knowledge.*

gâ·teau /'gætəʊ/ *nc* (*pl* —**x** /-təʊz/) (*Fr*) a rich fancy cake.

gath·er /'gæðə(r)/ *v* **1** *vt,vi* **gather round (sb/sth)** to get, come or bring together: *A crowd soon gathered round him/the car.* **2** *vt* **gather sth (together/up)** to collect, form, things, people into a group: *gather one's papers and books together; gather up dead leaves; a skirt gathered at the waist.* **3** *vt* to obtain, increase, (something) gradually: *gather information/speed.* **4** *vt* **gather (from sb/sth) (that . . .)** to understand: *What did you gather from his statement?*

gath·er·ing *nc* a meeting.

gauche /gəʊʃ/ *adj* (*derog*) (of a person) socially shy and clumsy.

gaudy /'gɔːdɪ/ *adj* (**-ier, -iest**) (*derog*) too bright and showy: *cheap and gaudy jewels.*

gaud·ily /-əlɪ/ *adv*

gauge¹ (*US* also **gage**) /geɪdʒ/ *nc* **1** (an instrument used for measuring) the thickness of wire, sheets of metal, rubber on a tyre etc. **2** the distance between rails for a train (or between opposite wheels of a train). **3** an instrument used for measuring rainfall, strength of wind etc. **4** a standard measure or means of comparison: *take a gauge of her attitude towards having a pet.*

gauge² (*US* also **gage**) /geɪdʒ/ *vt* **1** to measure (something) using a gauge(1): *gauging the diameter of wire/the strength of the wind.* **2** (*fig*) to make an estimate, form a judgement, of (something): *gauge a person's character.*

gaunt /gɔːnt/ *adj* (of a person) thin because of hunger, ill-health or suffering.

gaunt·ness *nu*

gaunt·let /'gɔːntlɪt/ *nc* **1** a glove with metal plates, formerly worn by soldiers. *pick up/take up/throw down the gauntlet* to accept/give a challenge to a fight. **2** a kind of strong glove used for fencing etc.

gauze /gɔːz/ *nu* **1** a kind of thin, net material used on wounds and injuries. **2** a similar material of wire used for screening windows against insects etc.

gave /geɪv/ *pt* of give².

gaw·ky /'gɔːkɪ/ *adj* (**-ier, -iest**) (*derog*) (of a person) shy and clumsy.

gawp /gɔːp/ *vi* **gawp (at sb/sth)** to stare (at a person, scene) in a foolish way: *What are they all gawping at?*

gay /geɪ/ *adj* (—**er**, —**est**) **1** light-hearted; cheerful; happy and full of fun: *gay voices/looks/ laughter.* ⇨ gaiety, gaily. **2** suggesting happiness and joy: *gay colours.* **3** (*informal*) homosexual.

gay·ness *nu*

gaze¹ /geɪz/ *n sing* a long, steady look: *with a bewildered gaze.*

gaze² /geɪz/ *vi* **gaze (at/out of/out to sth)** to look long and steadily: *gazing (out) at the view/ out of the window/out to sea.*

ga·zelle /gə'zel/ *nc* a kind of small, graceful antelope.

ga·zette /gə'zet/ *nc* a government periodical with legal notices, news of appointments, promotions etc of officers and officials.

ga·zet·teer /ˌgæzə'tɪə(r)/ *nc* an index of geographical names, e.g. in an atlas.

GB *written abbr* Great Britain.

GCSE /ˌdʒi: si: es 'i:/ *abbr* General Certificate of Secondary Education (given to children in England and Wales who pass examinations at secondary school).

Gdns *written abbr* Gardens.

gds *written abbr* (*commerce*) goods.

gear¹ /gɪə(r)/ *n* **1** *nc* a set of toothed wheels working together in a machine, e.g. to connect the engine of a vehicle with the road wheels: *change gear.* **2** *nc* a mechanism, arrangement, of wheels, levers etc used for a particular purpose: *the landing-gear of an aircraft.* **3** *nu* equipment for an activity: *fishing gear.* **4** *nu* (*modern informal*) clothes: *wearing the latest gear.*

'**gear box** *nc* a case enclosing the gears in a machine or engine.

'**gear-lever/-shift/-stick** *nc* a device used for engaging or disengaging gears.

gear² /gɪə(r)/ *vt* **gear sth to sth** to adjust one thing to the working of another: *The country's economics must be geared to social needs.*

geese /giːs/ *n pl* of goose.

geisha /'geɪʃə/ *nc* a Japanese girl or woman trained to entertain men by singing and dancing at parties etc.

gela·tine /ˌdʒelə'tiːn/ (also **gela·tin** /'dʒelətɪn/) *nu* a clear, tasteless substance, made by boiling bones etc, used to make food set like a jelly.

gel·ati·nous /dʒɪ'lætɪnəs/ *adj*

gel·ig·nite /'dʒelɪgnaɪt/ *nu* a kind of powerful explosive made from nitric acid and glycerine.

gem /dʒem/ *nc* **1** a precious stone or jewel, esp cut or polished. **2** (*fig*) something valued, e.g. because of great beauty: *the gem of the collection.*

Gem·ini /'dʒemɪnaɪ/ *n* the third sign of the zodiac.

Gen. *written abbr* General.

gen·der /'dʒendə(r)/ *nc* (*gram*) a grouping of nouns and pronouns into classes (masculine, feminine and neuter).

gene /dʒiːn/ *nc* (*science*) one of the biological factors controlling heredity. ⇨ genetic.

ge·nea·logi·cal /ˌdʒiːnɪə'lɒdʒɪkl/ *adj* of genealogy.

ˌ**genea,logical 'tree** *nc* a diagram of the earlier members of a family, the origins of an animal, plant etc.

ge·nea·logi·cal·ly /-klɪ/ *adv*

ge·ne·al·ogy /ˌdʒiːnɪ'ælədʒɪ/ *n* (*pl* **-ies**) **1** *nu* (*science*) the scientific study of the development of plants and animals from earlier forms. **2** *nc* (a diagram illustrating) the development of a plant or animal from earlier forms, of a family from ancestors etc.

gen·era /ˈdʒenərə/ *n pl* of genus.

gen·er·al¹ /ˈdʒenrəl/ *adj* **1** (*attrib*) of, affecting, all or nearly all; not special, local or particular: *a matter of general interest* (= one in which all or most people are likely to be interested); *a general meeting* (= one to which all members (of a society etc) are invited); *a good general education* (= in all the chief subjects); *a word that is in general use* (= used by all people). **on general release** ⇨ **release¹**(1). **as a general rule; in general** in most cases; usually: *I don't eat red meat as a general rule. In general, people disagreed with us.* **2** (*attrib*) not in detail; not definite: *a general outline of a scheme; have a general idea of what a book is about.* **3** (used after an official title) chief: *postmaster-general; inspector-general.*

,general ,anaes'thetic *nc* one affecting the whole body, causing sleep. Compare local anaesthetic.

,general e'lection *nc* one to elect parliamentary representatives from the whole country. Compare by-election, local election.

,General 'Headquarters *n pl* (abbr GHQ) the central or chief offices of the armed forces.

,general 'hospital *nc* one providing treatment for a wide variety of illnesses and injuries.

,general 'knowledge *nu* knowledge of a wide variety of subjects.

,general prac'titioner *nc* (abbr GP) a doctor who is not a specialist or consultant and who treats patients in her or his surgery or in their homes.

,general 'strike *nc* one of all trade unionists.

gen·er·al² /ˈdʒenrel/ *nc* (abbr Gen) an army officer with the highest rank below Field Marshal.

gen·er·al·ity /ˌdʒenəˈrælətɪ/ *n* (*pl* **-ies**) **1** *nc* a vague or indefinite statement, remark etc: *I wish you would not form opinions from generalities.* **2** *nu* (*formal*) the quality of being general: *a rule of great generality* (= one with few exceptions).

gen·er·al·iz·ation (also **-is·ation**) /ˌdʒenrəlaɪˈzeɪʃn/ *nc,nu* (an act of making) a statement or decision that is based on too little detail or too few examples.

gen·er·al·ize (also **-ise**) /ˈdʒenrəlaɪz/ *v* **1** *vi* **generalize (about sth)** to make a general statement: *generalizing about teenagers.* **2** *vi* **generalize (from sth)** to form an opinion or principle using a small amount of information: *generalize from one bad experience and say all boys are naughty.* **3** *vt* to cause (something) to be used by everyone: *generalize a new invention.*

gen·er·al·ly /ˈdʒenrəlɪ/ *adv* **1** usually: *I generally get up at six o'clock.* **2** for the most part: *The new plan was generally welcomed* (= was welcomed by most people). **3** in a general sense, without paying attention to details: *I like babies, generally speaking/speaking generally.*

gen·er·ate /ˈdʒenəreɪt/ *vt* to cause (power, a feeling etc) to exist or occur: *generate heat/electricity; hatred generated by racial differences.*

gen·er·ation /ˌdʒenəˈreɪʃn/ *n* **1** *nu* the act, process, of causing power, feelings etc to exist: *the generation of electricity by water-power.* **2** *nc* a

single stage in family descent: *three generations* (i.e. children, parents and grandparents). **3** *nc* an average period (regarded as 30 years) in which children grow up, marry, and have children: *a generation ago.* **4** *nc* people born about the same time: *the young generation.*

,gene'ration gap *nc* the failure or inability of the younger and older generations to understand one another.

gen·er·ator /ˈdʒenəreɪtə(r)/ *nc* an apparatus that produces electricity, gas etc.

gen·er·ic /dʒɪˈnerɪk/ *adj* **1** (*attrib; science*) of a genus: *a generic name.* **2** common to a whole group or class: *'Food' is a generic term for things we eat.*

gen·eri·cal·ly /-klɪ/ *adv*

gen·er·os·ity /ˌdʒenəˈrɒsətɪ/ *n* (*pl* **-ies**) **1** *nu* the quality of being generous: *show generosity in dealing with a defeated enemy.* **2** *nc* a generous act.

gen·er·ous /ˈdʒenərəs/ *adj* **1** giving, ready to give, freely: *He is generous with his money/generous in giving help.* **2** (*attrib*) large: *a generous helping of meat and vegetables.*

gen·er·ous·ly *adv*

gen·esis /ˈdʒenəsɪs/ *n* **1** *nc* (*pl* **-eses** /-siːz/) (*literary*) the beginning; starting-point: *the genesis of civilization.* **2** *n* (G-) the first book of the Old Testament.

gen·et·ic /dʒɪˈnetɪk/ *adj* of genes or genetics.

gen·et·ics *n sing* the scientific study (branch of biology) of heredity, the ways in which characteristics are passed on from parents to offspring.

gen·eti·cist /dʒɪˈnetɪsɪst/ *nc* an expert in genetics.

ge·ni·al /ˈdʒiːnɪəl/ *adj* (*formal*) **1** kindly, sympathetic; sociable: *a genial old man; genial smiles.* **2** favourable to growth: *a genial climate.* ⇨ congenial.

ge·ni·al·ity /ˌdʒiːnɪˈælətɪ/ *nc,nu*

ge·ni·al·ly *adv*

ge·nie /ˈdʒiːnɪ/ *nc* (*pl* **—s** or **genii** /ˈdʒiːnɪaɪ/) (in Arabic stories) a spirit with strange powers.

geni·tal /ˈdʒenɪtl/ *adj* (*attrib*) of the reproductive organs of animals. ⇨ congenital.

gen·itals *n pl* the external sex organs.

geni·tive /ˈdʒenɪtɪv/ *nc* (also *attrib; esp genitive case*) (*gram*) a form of noun etc showing source or possession, as in *'Australia's* trees', *'Bob's* hotel', *'children's* clothes', *'boys'* games'.

gen·ius /ˈdʒiːnɪəs/ *n* (*pl* **—es**) **1** *nu* great and exceptional intelligence or artistic ability: *men of genius.* **2** *nc* a person having this ability: *Einstein was a mathematical genius.* **3** *n sing* **a genius for sth** a natural ability: *have a genius for languages/acting/making friends.* **4** *n sing* (the —) special character, spirit or principles of a language, a period of time, a person, place or institution etc: *the genius of the Renaissance period in Italy.*

geno·cide /ˈdʒenəsaɪd/ *nu* the extermination of a race or community by mass murder or by imposing conditions that make survival impossible.

genre /ˈʒɑːnrə/ *nc* **1** (*literature*) a type or category of literary work such as comedy, tragedy, novel, drama etc. **2** a type or category of any artistic work, esp painting.

gent /dʒent/ *abbr* (*informal*) gentleman.

gents *n sing* (the—) a public toilet for men and

boys.

gen·tile /'dʒentaıl/ adj, nc (of) a person not of the Jewish race.

gentle /'dʒentl/ adj (**—r, —st**) **1** kind, friendly; not rough or violent: *a gentle person/heart/look/ voice/call/touch; a gentle breeze.* **2** gradual: *a gentle slope.* ⇨ gently.

gentle·ness *nu*

gentle·man /'dʒentlmən/ nc (pl **-men** /-mən/) **1** a man who shows consideration for the feelings of others, who is honourable and well-bred: *a fine old gentleman; a true gentleman.* **2** (*formal*) any unknown man: *A gentleman has called to see you.* **3** (*pl*) (a polite form of address to male members of an audience): *Gentlemen! Ladies and Gentlemen!*

gentle·man·ly *adj*

gen·tly /'dʒentlı/ adv in a gentle manner: *Hold it gently* (= carefully). *The road slopes gently* (= gradually) *to the sea.*

gen·try /'dʒentrı/ nu (the —) (*dated*) the people of good social position next below the nobility.

genu·flect /'dʒenjuflekt/ vi (*formal*) to bend the knees briefly with one foot in front of the other, esp in a church.

genu·flec·tion /ˌdʒenjuˈflekʃn/ nc

genu·ine /'dʒenjuın/ adj (*no comp*) **1** true; really what it is said to be: *a genuine picture by Picasso.* **2** (of a person) sincere: *Were you being genuine when you said you love me?*

genu·ine·ly *adv*

ge·nus /'dʒiːnəs/ nc (pl **genera** /'dʒenərə/) (*science*) a division of animals or plants within a family.

ge·ogra·pher /dʒıˈɒɡrəfə(r)/ nc a student of, expert in, geography.

geo·graphi·cal /ˌdʒıəˈɡræfıkl/ adj of geography.

geo·graphi·cal·ly /-klı/ adv

ge·ogra·phy /dʒıˈɒɡrəfı/ nu **1** the scientific study of the earth's surface, physical features, divisions, climate, products, population etc. **2** the arrangement, location etc of the features of an area: *the geography of a house/region.*

geo·logi·cal /ˌdʒıəˈlɒdʒıkl/ adj of geology.

geo·logi·cal·ly /-klı/ adv

ge·ol·ogist /dʒıˈɒlədʒıst/ nc a student of, expert in, geology.

ge·ol·ogy /dʒıˈɒlədʒı/ nu **1** the scientific study of the earth's history as shown by its rocks etc. **2** the rock structure of a specific region.

geo·met·ric /ˌdʒıəˈmetrık/ adj (*maths*) of geometry; or like the lines, figures etc used: *geometric patterns.*

geo·metric pro·gression nc (*maths*) a series of numbers in which each is multiplied by a constant number to give the next, such as 3, 6, 12, 24 etc. Compare arithmetic progression.

geo·metric 'series nc (*maths*) a geometric progression written as a sum, such as $3+6+12+24$ etc.

geo·met·ri·cal·ly /-klı/ adv

ge·ometry /dʒıˈɒmətrı/ nu the scientific study of the properties and relations of lines, angles, surfaces and solids.

ger·ani·um /dʒəˈreınıəm/ nc (pl **—s**) a kind of plant with red, pink or white flowers.

geri·at·rics /ˌdʒerıˈætrıks/ nu the medical care

of old people.

geri·at·ric adj of, for, old people: *a geriatric hospital.*

germ /dʒɜːm/ nc **1** a very small organism (in the air, food etc) that can cause disease. **2** (*science*) a portion of a living organism capable of becoming a new organism. **3** (*fig*) the beginning or starting-point (of an idea etc).

germ 'warfare nu the use of bacteria as a weapon in war.

Ger·man measles /ˌdʒɜːmən ˈmiːzlz/ nu a mild disease, like measles in appearance, that can cause severely deformed babies if suffered by a woman during the first three months of pregnancy. Ⓝ The official name is *'rubella'*.

ger·mi·nate /'dʒɜːmıneıt/ vt,vi (to cause seeds) to start growing.

ger·mi·na·tion /ˌdʒɜːmıˈneıʃn/ nu

ger·und /'dʒerənd/ nc (also *verbal noun*) (*gram*) the *-ing* form of a verb when used as a noun, as in 'fond of *swimming*'.

gerund 'phrase nc (*gram*) a phrase containing a gerund that is used as a noun, as in '*Climbing in winter* can be dangerous'.

ges·ta·tion /dʒeˈsteıʃn/ nu (*science*) the process, period, of a baby, young animal, being carried in the womb between conception and birth.

ges·ticu·late /dʒıˈstıkjuleıt/ vi (*formal*) to use movements of the hands, arms or head to express oneself while speaking.

ges·ticu·la·tion /dʒıˌstıkjuˈleıʃn/ nc,nu

ges·ture¹ /'dʒestʃə(r)/ nc **1** nc a movement of the hand or head to show feeling etc: *a gesture of refusal.* **2** nc something done to show friendship etc: *give money as a gesture of support.* **3** nu the use of expressive movements: *an actor who is a master of the art of gesture.*

ges·ture² /'dʒestʃə(r)/ vi to make a gesture(1).

get /get/ v (pt,pp **got** /gɒt/; **-tt-**) Ⓝ 'Get' is used very often, and some people consider it is used too often. As alternatives, use the verbs given in the explanations. **1** vt to receive, obtain, (something): *He got first prize/a reward/an A in the exam. What did you get for your birthday? She gets a letter from him every week. How much will you get if you sell your record-player? If you can't see the colour you like, we can get it for you. I can't get the BBC World Service on my radio. If you multiply 13 by 4 you get 52. He got 6 months/a fine of £100* (i.e. as a punishment) *for dangerous driving.* Ⓝ For uses of *get* with nouns such as *better, boot, control, credit, sack, time, way, word, worst* etc, ⇨ the noun entries. **2** vt to bring or fetch (a person) (something, a person): *Please get me a pen/get my slippers for me. Can I get you anything? Get a doctor, quickly!* **3** vt to prepare (food): *get dinner for the family; get me a cup of coffee.* **4** vt,vi (used with *adjs*) (to cause a person, thing) to become (the mentioned state): *get cold/dressed/drunk/ wet; get a box open; get the children ready for school; get a cooker clean; get hungry after 2 o'clock; get too old for dancing. How did your bike get stolen?* Compare come(6) and go²(17). Ⓝ 'Get' is usually used to refer to a condition or state achieved after (deliberate) activity, as in *get married, get one's shoes dirty.* 'Come' is used to refer to a condition or state that is not deliberate, as in *come undone.* 'Go' is usually used to refer to a condition or state that becomes 'worse', as in *go blind/deaf/mad, go bad/stale*, or to a change in colour, as in *go pale, go blue with cold.* **get better; get better at sth** ⇨ better². **get well** ⇨ well¹(1). **5** *vt, vi* (often used with a present participle, e.g. *moving*) (to cause a person, thing) to begin doing something: *Can you get that old car going* (i.e. repair it)? *I can't get this clock to work. Let's get going* (= start). *Get going/ moving!* (i.e. as an order). **get cracking** ⇨ crack²(4). **6** *vt, vi* (used with many *adverbial particles* and *prepositions*) (to cause a person, thing) to move in the direction mentioned, esp with difficulty or effort; succeed in doing it: *get a screw in/a nail out/a lid off; get over a wall/through a barrier/ up a mountain.* (N) When difficulty or effort is not involved, *put, take, go* etc are used. For other uses of 'get' with adverbial particles and prepositions, ⇨ below. **7** *vt* **get sb to** + *verb* to cause, persuade, a person to do something: *get her to come; get him to stop arguing; get them to agree to the proposal. How can I get her to understand?* **8** *vi* **get to** + *verb* to reach a mentioned state: *get to know the neighbours; get to like the new house.* **9** *vi* (often **get to a place**) to arrive (at): *get to London on Thursday; get to work early; get to the top (of a mountain). What time will the bus get here? I'll get home at 6 o'clock.* **(never/not) get anywhere; get somewhere/nowhere** (to fail (ever)) to succeed or make progress; be successful/unsuccessful trying to achieve something: *You'll never get anywhere/You'll get nowhere if you are rude.* **10** *vt* to go to and enter (a vehicle etc): *get a bus/ coach/train/plane to Amsterdam.* **11** *vt* to become infected with (an illness): *get a cold; get flu; get the measles.* **12** *vt* **get sb (for sth)** (*informal*) (used as a threat) to have one's revenge on a person: *I'll get you (for reporting me)!* **13** *vt* (*informal*) to understand or hear (something): *I didn't get her name. Did you get what he was saying? I don't get it* (= don't understand). *I never get her jokes.* **14** *vt* (*informal*) to confuse, worry, (a person): *What she sees in him gets me. That's got you!* **15** *vt* (*informal*) to make (a person) angry or annoyed: *Loud pop music at night really gets me!* ⇨ get to sb. **16** *vt* (*informal*) to deal with (a telephone call, a visitor at the door etc): *'The phone's ringing/ There's someone at the door'—'I'll get it.'* **17 have got sth** ⇨ have²(1). **have got to** + *verb* ⇨ have¹(2).

get about (a) (of a person) to move, walk, go to places etc (esp after being ill or after obtaining a vehicle): *It's difficult to get about with a broken leg/without a car.* **(b)** (of news etc) to become known: *News of their divorce soon got about.* **get about on sth** to go to places using something: *get about on two walking sticks/on the bus.*

get across (sth) to succeed in crossing (something), esp with difficulty or effort. **get sth across (to sb)** to cause something to be understood: *I spoke slowly but my meaning didn't get across.*

get ahead (of sb) (a) to go forward and pass (a person): *get ahead of other people in the race.* **(b)** to make more progress (than a person): *get ahead of other students in the class.*

get along to make progress: *How are you getting along at your new school? How is your English getting along?* **get along (with sb)** to enjoy

being with, working with, a person: *My brother and his boss don't get along. We get along with each other very well.* **get along (with sth) (a)** to make progress (with one's studies, a new book, an activity): *I'm getting along well with my English/the decorating.* **(b)** to be able to use and enjoy using (a new tool etc): *I'm getting along well with my new cooker.* **get along without sb/sth** to manage to live or work without a person or thing: *I can't get along without you/your help/a screwdriver.*

get around = get about. **get around sb** = get round sb. **get around to sth/to doing sth** to reach the point of doing something, esp after delaying: *I ought to get around to mending the door this weekend. I'll soon get around to it.*

get at sb (*informal*) to criticize a person often: *The manager's always getting at me.* **get at sth (a)** to gain access to something: *I've put my money in the bank/the chocolate on a high shelf so that you can't get at it.* ⇨ get-at-able. **(b)** to discover or learn the truth, cause. **(c)** to suggest something: *What are you getting at?* **(d)** to begin working on a task: *Let's get at the garden.*

get away to go on holiday. **get away (from a place)** to manage to leave, escape: *I hope to get away from the library by 8 o'clock.* ⇨ getaway. **get sb/sth away (from a place)** to use effort to remove a person or thing: *get children away from a burning building.* **get sth away from sb/sth** to use effort to remove something from a person or animal: *get a bone away from a dog.* **get away from it all** (*informal*) to go somewhere far from work, worries etc. **get away with sth (a)** to steal and escape with something: *rob a bank and get away with £50 000.* **(b)** to receive a surprisingly light punishment: *I was lucky—I got away with a small fine.* **get away with it** (*informal*) to avoid being caught, suffering or being punished after doing wrong: *He cheated in the exam and thought he could get away with it.* ⇨ also murder.

get back (a) to return (to one's starting-point): *It's almost 11 o'clock—I must be getting back.* **(b)** to go back to a sensible distance (e.g. as a spectator): *The police asked the crowd to get back.* **(c)** to return to a position of authority or power: *The Democrats hope to get back at the next election.* **get sth back (a)** to have possession of something after losing, lending, it: *Don't lend her your records—you'll never get them back.* **(b)** to put something in its original or correct place, esp with difficulty or effort: *I took out the batteries but I can't get them back.* **get sb/sth back (to sb)** to return a person or thing: *I'll try to get the children back before dark.* **get one's own back (on sb)** ⇨ own². **get back to sb** (*informal*; usually future tense) to contact a person again (esp by telephone) (e.g. after obtaining information). **get back to sth** to return to (a place of) work: *get back to work/my studies/college.*

get behind (with sth) (a) to make too little progress: *get behind with one's work.* **(b)** to be late in making payments (e.g. of rent).

get by (a) to manage, earn enough to live etc: *She never works but somehow she gets by.* **(b)** to be sufficiently happy: *I'll get by as long as I have you.* **(c)** to be accepted: *Although it was a formal dinner, he thought he could get by in a brown* *jacket.* **get by (sth)** to pass (an obstacle). **get by on sth** to manage using a small income, a pension, a grant, a few supplies of food etc: *How do people get by on £50 a week?*

get down (a) to descend: *The cat's up the tree and can't get down.* (b) (of children) to leave the dining-table after a meal. **get sb down** (*no passive*) to cause a person to feel very sad: *Bad weather gets me down.* **get sth down** (a) to swallow something, esp with difficulty: *get medicine down.* (b) to write down a message, address, important details etc: *get a car number down after an accident.* **get down to (doing) sth** to begin an important or necessary task: *get down to work/revising for an exam.* ⇨ also business(3).

get in (a) to enter a room, building etc with difficulty or effort: *I've lost my key and I can't get in.* (b) (of a train, plane etc) to arrive: *What time does her coach get in? The bus gets in at 2 o'clock.* (c) to be elected: *Will the Liberals get in?* (d) to be accepted as a member of a university, team etc. **get sb in** (a) to cause a person to become a member of a university, club, team, committee, parliament etc. (b) to obtain the advice or services of: *get in an electrician.* **get sth in** to collect rent, fruit, crops, washing from the garden etc. **get in first** (*informal*) to make sure one is first to do something and so obtain an advantage. **not get a word in (edgeways)** ⇨ word¹(2). **get in on sth** (*informal*) to make sure one joins an activity: *get in on a free trip to Italy.*

get into sth (*no passive*) (a) to put on clothes: *get into something comfortable.* (b) to enter a room, car etc, esp with difficulty. (c) (of a train etc) to arrive at a station, town etc: *When does the bus get into Stockholm?* (d) to become a member of the Civil Service, the Air Force, a club, team etc. (e) to be elected to Parliament, a constituency etc. (f) to make a way into a place: *Some dust has got into my eye.* (g) (*informal*) to cause oneself to be in difficulty: *get into a mess/a muddle; get into debt/trouble.* (h) to begin to be in an angry state: *get into a temper/a rage.* (i) to become interested in a book, TV programme etc: *I can't get into this book.*

get off (a) to leave a bus, train: *I get off at the next station.* (b) to avoid being (found guilty and) punished: *She apologized to the judge and got off.* (c) to manage to avoid a severe punishment: *get off with only a warning.* (d) to suffer only small injuries (e.g. after an accident): *get off lightly/with only a bruise/without serious injury.* **get sb off** to help a person to avoid being found guilty in a law court. **get off sth** (a) to leave a (bus, train etc). (b) to take oneself off (a bike, motorbike, horse etc). (c) to stop standing, walking, driving etc on (a surface): *Get off the grass!* Ⓝ For uses of 'get off' with nouns such as *back, chest, ground, sleep* etc, ⇨ the *noun* entries. **get sth off** (a) to remove something with difficulty or effort: *get paint off a window.* (b) to organize the sending of a letter, telegram, message etc. **get off with sb** (*informal*) to begin an affair or close friendship with a person.

get on (a) to enter a bus, train. (b) to (begin to) do one's duties, work etc: *I must get on—it's 10 o'clock.* (c) to make progress in one's career, studies, life: *How are you getting on? He's getting*

on badly/well. (d) (of time) to become late: *It's getting on and I ought to go home.* (e) to become old: *This cooker/Our head teacher is getting on.*

get on (a) to enter (a bus, train etc). (b) to place oneself on (a bike, motorbike, horse etc). **get sth on** (a) to put on clothes etc, esp quickly or with difficulty: *I can't get these shoes on.* (b) to manage to put something in position: *Can you get this lid on?* Ⓝ For uses of 'get on' with nouns such as *grip, hand, move, nerve, skate* etc, ⇨ the *noun* entries. **be getting on for sth** (a) to be nearly the time mentioned: *It's getting on for 10 o'clock.* (b) to be nearly the age mentioned: *He's getting on for 60.* **get on (with sb)** = get along (with sb): *The new manager isn't easy to get on with.* **get on (with sth)** = get along (with sth): *I can't get on with this new pen.* **get on with sth** to (begin to) do one's work, duties etc: *Get on with your work!* **get on without sb/sth** = get along without sb/sth.

get onto sb/sth (about sb/sth) to contact a person, business, department etc, esp by telephone: *I'll get on to the sales manager/department about that problem.* **get onto sth** to progress from (one part of) an activity to another: *We can now get onto more difficult grammar.*

get out (a) to leave a bus, train: *I always get out here.* (b) (of news) to become known: *If it ever gets out that I came, we'll be in serious trouble.* **get sth out** to remove something, esp with difficulty or effort: *get a nail out.* **get out (of a place)** (a) to leave a room, building etc with difficulty or effort: *The door is locked and we can't get out (of the hall).* (b) to manage to escape from a cage, prison etc. (c) to leave a hospital, prison etc: *I'll telephone as soon as I get out (of hospital/here).* **get out of sth** (a) to take off (wet, dirty) clothes. (b) to leave a building, piece of furniture etc: *get out of bed; get out of town/the house for a few days.* (c) to manage to avoid an activity: *get out of (doing) the washing up.* **get sb out (of a place)** to help a person to leave (e.g. a burning building). **get sth out of sb** to use force to make a person provide information, admit doing something etc.

get over sb/sth (*informal*) to recover after a person's death, the loss of a person's love etc: *He never got over Jane/losing Jane.* **get over sth** (a) to manage to go over to the other side of a wall, gate etc. (b) to recover after an illness, shock, death etc. (c) (usually negative) to believe or understand a person, thing fully: *I can't get over her rudeness.* (d) to manage to control a feeling etc: *get over her shyness.* **get sth over to sb** to cause something to be understood by a person: *The doctor could not get the seriousness of her illness over to the patient.* **get sth over (and done) with** (*informal*) to do something necessary but unpleasant: *I hate going to the dentist but I must get it over (and done) with.*

get round to complete one full journey round a track, circuit, course etc: *He got round in 50 seconds.* **get round sb** (*informal*) to persuade a person to agree, to approve or to give or do something: *I'll try to get round my mother to lend me the money.* **get round sth** (a) to manage to pass round an obstacle. (b) to manage to avoid a law or regulation without acting illegally (but often acting dishonourably): *A clever accountant can get round certain tax laws.* **get round to sth/to doing sth** = get around to sth/to doing sth.

get through to manage to make contact, esp by telephone: *I rang several times but I couldn't get through.* **get through (sth) (a)** to manage to pass through (a barrier). **(b)** to eat, drink, spend etc (an amount mentioned): *get through £20 a day/50 cigarettes a day.* **(c)** to pass (an examination). **(d)** to manage to read, deal with, (correspondence, a report, a book etc). **get through to sb** (*informal*) to cause oneself to be understood; persuade a person to accept one's advice: *The tearful mother couldn't get through to her teenage son.* **get through (to sth)** (*sport*) to manage to progress as far as the final, the last round etc in a competition: *We've got through to the semifinals.* **get through with sb** (*informal*) to attack a person physically or verbally (e.g. in angry revenge): *When I get through with you, you'll wish you'd never said it.*

get to a place to arrive at: *get to the station; get to an interesting part of the story; get to the end.* **get to doing sth** (*informal*) to begin to: *I got to thinking about my father.* Ⓝ For uses of 'get to' with nouns such as *bottom, grip, point, top, work* etc, ⇨ the noun entries.

get together to meet, e.g. for a discussion or social reason: *Let's get together and talk about it.* Hence **'get-together** *nc* an informal meeting, e.g. of friends. **get sth together** to collect papers, equipment, a team etc. **get it together** (*informal*; often negative) to be able to organize one's personal affairs, an outing etc: *I can't get it together at the moment. We're trying to get it together to visit China.*

get under sth to manage to pass under a barrier. Ⓝ For uses of 'get under' with nouns such as *control, skin, way,* ⇨ the noun entries.

get up (a) to get out of bed. **(b)** to stand. **(c)** (of wind) to increase in strength: *The wind is getting up.* **get up sth** to manage to go up a hill, stairs etc. **get sb/oneself up (a)** to cause a person/oneself to get out of bed. **(b)** to dress, put make-up on etc a person: *She was got up as an old woman.* Hence **'get-up** *nc* an unusual way of dressing. **get sth up** (*informal*) to organize a party, a protest, an exhibition etc. **get up to sth (a)** to reach a certain level, standard or position: *get up to 1 metre/grade 2/page 16.* **(b)** to be active doing something wrong or bad: *What's he getting up to now? She gets up to a lot of mischief.*

get with it (*informal*; usually *imperative*) to become modern in life style, attitudes etc.

get within sth to reach a point where one can be seen or heard, where one has almost succeeded: *get within sight of him; get within the possibility of victory.*

get-at-able /get 'æt əbl/ *adj* (*informal*) able to be reached, used, visited etc: *The house is not easily get-at-able.*

get·away /'getəweɪ/ *n* **make one's getaway** escape from prison.

get-together /'get təgeðə(r)/ *nc* ⇨ get together.

get-up /'get ʌp/ *nc* ⇨ get sb/oneself up (b).

gey·ser /'gi:zə(r)/ *nc* **1** an underground spring[1](3) sending out hot water or steam. **2** an

apparatus used for heating water, e.g. by gas, in a bathroom etc.

ghast·ly /'gɑ:stlɪ/ *adj* (**-ier, -iest**) **1** (often *pred*) pale and ill: *looking ghastly.* **2** causing horror or fear: *a ghastly accident.* **3** (*informal*) very bad or unpleasant: *a ghastly dinner.*

gher·kin /'gɜ:kɪn/ *nc* a kind of small, green cucumber, usually pickled in vinegar.

ghet·to /'getəʊ/ *nc* (*pl* **—s**) a section of a town lived in by underprivileged classes or people who are discriminated against, e.g. because of race or religion.

ghost /gəʊst/ *nc* **1** (a spirit of) a dead person appearing to a person still living: *He looked as if he had seen a ghost* (= looked very frightened). **give up the ghost** to die. **2** something shadowy or without substance. **not have the ghost of a chance** to have no chance at all: *They don't have a ghost of a chance of winning.*

'ghost town *nc* a town now abandoned, e.g. in an area where coal was once mined.

'ghost writer *nc* a person who writes a book etc for someone else.

ghost·ly *adj* of, like, suggesting, a ghost.

gi·ant /'dʒaɪənt/ *nc* **1** (in stories) a very big, tall man. **2** (also *attrib*) a man, animal or plant much larger than normal: *giant strength; a giant cabbage; a giant-size bottle.* **3** (*fig*) a person of extraordinary ability or genius: *a literary giant.*

gib·ber·ish /'dʒɪbərɪʃ/ *nu* unintelligible talk; nonsense.

gib·bon /'gɪbən/ *nc* a kind of long-armed ape.

gib·bous /'dʒɪbəs/ *adj* (*attrib*) (of the moon) having the bright part greater than a semicircle and less than a circle.

gibe¹ (also **jibe**) /dʒaɪb/ *nc* a comment used to make fun of a person.

gibe² (also **jibe**) /dʒaɪb/ *vi* **gibe at sth** to make fun of something: *gibing at a boy's mistakes.*

gib·lets /'dʒɪblɪts/ *n pl* the heart, liver, gizzard etc of a goose, hen etc taken out before the bird is cooked.

gid·dy /'gɪdɪ/ *adj* (**-ier, -iest**) causing, having, the feeling that everything is turning round so that one cannot stand steady.

gid·di·ly *adv*

gid·di·ness *nu*

gift /gɪft/ *n* **1** *nc* something given freely (and to please): *gifts to charities.* ⇨ birthday/Christmas present. **2** *n sing* **have a gift for sth** to have a natural ability or talent: *have a gift for art/languages.*

'gift voucher *nc* a document to be exchanged for gifts.

gift·ed /'gɪftɪd/ *adj* talented: *a gifted writer/daughter.*

gig /gɪg/ *nc* (*informal*) a booking for musicians to perform (esp jazz).

gi·gan·tic /dʒaɪˈgæntɪk/ *adj* very large.

giggle¹ /'gɪgl/ *nc* a silly, nervous laugh.

giggle² /'gɪgl/ *vi* to laugh in a nervous and silly way.

gild /gɪld/ *vt* (*pt,pp* **—ed** or **gilt** /gɪlt/) to cover (something) with gold leaf or gold-coloured paint: *gild a picture frame.*

gill¹ /gɪl/ *nc* (usually *pl*) a part of a fish with which it breathes.

gill² /dʒɪl/ *nc* a liquid measure, one-quarter of a

pint (0·14 litres).

gilt /gɪlt/ **1** *pt,pp* of gild. **2** *nu* (also *attrib*) gold leaf or gold-coloured paint used for gilding.

gim·let /'gɪmlɪt/ *nc* a small tool used for making holes in wood etc.

gim·mick /'gɪmɪk/ *nc* any trick, phrase, article of clothing etc used esp by actors, advertisers, to attract attention, customers etc.

gin /dʒɪn/ *nc,nu* (a portion of) a kind of colourless alcoholic drink: *Two gins, please.*

gin·ger¹ /'dʒɪndʒə(r)/ *nu* (also *attrib*) **1** (a plant with) a hot-tasting root used in cooking and for making a kind of wine: *ginger biscuits.* **2** a light reddish-yellow colour: *ginger hair.*

ˌginger 'ale/'beer *nu* a kind of non-alcoholic drink flavoured with ginger.

gin·ger² /'dʒɪndʒə(r)/ *vt* **ginger sb/sth up** to make a person or thing more lively, tasty etc: *ginger up the supporters/a soup.*

gin·ger·ly /'dʒɪndʒəlɪ/ *adv* with great care to avoid causing anger or harm, making a noise etc.

gip·sy (also **gyp·sy**) /'dʒɪpsɪ/ *nc* (*pl* **-ies**) a member of a group of people travelling around Europe and living in caravans.

gi·raffe /dʒɪ'rɑːf/ *nc* a kind of African animal with very long legs and neck.

gir·der /'ɡɜːdə(r)/ *nc* an iron or steel beam used to support a floor, bridge etc.

girdle /'ɡɜːdl/ *nc* = corset.

girl /ɡɜːl/ *nc* **1** a female child up to the age of 17 or 18. **2** a daughter: *I have a boy and two girls.*

'girl·friend *nc* **1** a boy's or man's special female friend. **2** a female friend.

'girl·hood *nu* the time when one is or was a girl.

girl·ish /'ɡɜːlɪʃ/ *adj* **1** (esp of a man's hair, clothes, behaviour) like a woman. **2** (of an older girl or woman) childish.

gi·ro /'dʒaɪrəʊ/ *n* (also *attrib*) (the —; also G-) (*GB*) a banking system of paying of accounts or debts directly from one account to another: *the Post Office Giro; a giro cheque.*

girth /ɡɜːθ/ *nc* a measurement round anything like a pole in shape: *a tree 10 metres in girth.*

gist /dʒɪst/ *n* **the gist (of sth)** the main points: *Tell me the gist of what he said.*

give¹ /ɡɪv/ *nu* **1** the quality of being able to move or stretch a little: *These ropes/leather gloves/rubber mats have a lot of give in them.* ⇨ give²(12). **2** **give and take** (willingness by both sides in a discussion or argument to agree to) an exchange of concessions: *There must be give and take if the talks are to succeed.* Compare **give or take** at give²(4).

give² /ɡɪv/ *v* (*pt* **gave** /ɡeɪv/, *pp* **given** /'ɡɪvn/) **1** *vt* to present (something) to another person without being paid or receiving anything in exchange: *What did he give you for your birthday? I gave her a clean towel this morning. Give me the sugar, please. Can you give me another word for 'lovely'? Please give that knife to me. He has given all his money to charity. You've given me such happiness.* **2** *vt* to present (something) to another person in exchange for, in payment for or as compensation for something else: *I'll give you £10 for that bike. What will you give me for this watch? We were given £100 by the insurance company after the accident. I'd give a lot to know where she is.* **give as good as one gets** to act, speak etc

as severely as another person has acted, spoken etc against oneself. **3** *vt* to present and allow (a person) to carry, hold etc (something): *Give me that heavy suitcase. Give that box to me—I'll carry it.* **4** *vt* to allow (a period of time): *We gave ourselves half an hour for the journey. The bank has given me a month to pay the debt.* **give or take** (*informal*) a little more or a little less than: *She'll be here by 3 o'clock, give or take a few minutes.* Compare *give and take* at give²(2). **5** *vt* to provide, offer, (something): *He gave me his arm as we crossed the road. It gave me the opportunity/chance to visit my grandmother. Who gave you permission to come in here? You gave me good advice.* Ⓝ For uses with nouns such as *break, chance, go-ahead* etc, ⇨ the noun entries. **6** *vt* to act in some way to produce an effect: *give a smile/shout/wave; gave her a fright/scare; gave him a slap.* Ⓝ 'Give' can be used with many nouns to produce the same meaning as the verb alone, as in *give a cry* (= cry); *give her a surprise* (= surprise her). For uses of 'give' with nouns such as *boot, call, hand, lift, ring, sack* etc, ⇨ the noun entries. **7** *vt* to organize and have (an activity): *give a party/lecture.* **8** *vt* to produce (an effect) for (a person): *The sun gives us warmth and light. I hope the car will not give you any trouble. The computer analysis gives the following sales figures.* **9** *vt* to be the cause or origin of (an injury, illness): *The fall gave me a big bruise. You've given me your cold.* **10** *vt* to dedicate (one's time, energy, life etc): *He gave his life to fighting poverty.* **11** *vt* **Give me . . .** I prefer . . . : *Give me the simple life!* **12** *vi* (of materials such as wood, rubber, vinyl etc) to be able to stretch, bend etc because of weight or pressure: *The branch gave but didn't break.* **give way (to sb/sth)** ⇨ way²(1). ⇨ also give¹(1). **13 What gives?** (*informal*) What is happening?

give sb away (**a**) to tell something secret so that a person's action, hiding-place etc is known. (**b**) to hand over a woman to be married (as part of a wedding ceremony): *Her father gave her away.*

give sth away (**a**) to present something to another person free of charge: *give away free samples.* (**b**) to tell a secret. (**c**) to present prizes, certificates etc, esp at a ceremony: *The chairperson gave the prizes away.* ⇨ giveaway. **give the game away** ⇨ game²(5).

give sb back sth; give sth back (to sb) (**a**) to return something to the owner: *That's my ball—give it back (to me).* (**b**) to allow, make it possible for, a person to have eyesight, freedom etc again: *The surgeon gave her back the use of her fingers. Give them back their right to vote.*

give sth for sb/sth to organize, produce an event etc in honour of a person, organization etc: *give a farewell party for a colleague.* **give sth (to sb) for sth** ⇨ 2 above.

give in (*informal*) to admit defeat: *I give in—I don't know the answer.* **give in to sb/sth** to allow (a person, policy, situation etc) to have authority, power, be victorious etc: *give in to one's boss; give in to her experience; give in to blackmail/pressure from one's parents.* **give sth in** to hand over (equipment, a piece of writing etc) to a person with authority: *give in an exam paper; give in the tools after borrowing them.*

give sth off to produce smoke, a smell etc.

give out (of supplies, energy, patience etc) to become used up: *His strength finally gave out and he fell off the edge.* **give sth out** (a) to present something to each individual: *give out exam papers/leaflets.* (b) to make news, a decision, results etc known: *give out news of the exam results.*

give over (*informal;* usually *imperative*) to stop saying, thinking, doing, that.

give oneself to sb (*informal*) (of a woman) to have sexual intercourse with a person. (N) For the use of *'give . . . to'* with nouns such as *birth, place, rise, way* etc, ⇨ the noun entries.

give up = give in. **give oneself up** to stop avoiding capture: *I'm going to give myself up to the police. He gave himself up.* **give sb up** (a) to abandon a claim on, authority over, a person: *If you divorce me you must give up the children.* (b) (*informal*) to stop a relationship with a person: *He's not my boyfriend—I've given him up.* (c) to consider that a person will not arrive, will not recover etc: *The doctors have given her up. We'd given you up and gone home.* **give sth up** (a) to stop eating, drinking, smoking etc: *You must give up gambling/cigarettes/alcohol.* (b) to stop having a belief, interest etc: *give up believing in God; give up socialism.* (c) to hand over, sell etc something, e.g. because of poverty: *give up a beautiful house.* (d) to stop (attempts at) doing, achieving something: *give up thoughts of finding her/the search for him/trying to understand.* (e) to stop having and enjoying something: *give up a well-paid job; give up an exciting life to marry her.*

give·away /'gɪvəweɪ/ *n sing* something that (often by mistake) causes something secret to be known: *She tried to disguise herself but her height is a giveaway.*

giv·en /'gɪvn/ 1 *pp* of give². 2 (*adj; attrib*) (a) already agreed: *They are to meet at a given time and place.* (b) (*maths*) already known or decided: *a given quantity.* 3 (*adj*) with this fact, belief, as a condition: *Given good health, the work should take another month.* 4 (*adj; pred*) **be given to doing sth** to have something as a habit, addiction etc: *She's given to telling lies.*

'given name *nc* (also *first name*) a name chosen at birth. Compare family name, surname.

giv·er /'gɪvə(r)/ *nc* a person who gives (help, a present etc).

giz·zard /'gɪzəd/ *nc* a bird's second stomach, used for grinding food.

glacé /'glæseɪ/ *adj* (*attrib*) (of fruits) iced, sugared: *glacé cherries.*

gla·cial /'gleɪsɪəl/ *adj* (*tech*) of, caused by, ice.

gla·cier /'glæsɪə(r)/ *nc* a mass of ice, formed by snow on mountains, moving slowly along a valley.

glad /glæd/ *adj* (**—der, —dest**) 1 (usually *pred*) pleased: *be/look/feel glad about something. I'm glad to see you. I'll be glad to finish this job.* ⇨ gladly. 2 (*attrib*) causing or bringing happiness: *Have you heard the glad news?*

glad·den /'glædn/ *vt* to make (a person) glad or happy.

glad·ness *nu*

glade /gleɪd/ *nc* (*literary*) a clear, open space in a forest.

glad·ly /'glædlɪ/ *adv* (often used to reply politely to a request) willingly and happily: *'Will you lend me the money?'—'Gladly.' I'd gladly lend it to you but I haven't got it.*

glam·our (*US* also **glam·or**) /'glæmə(r)/ *nu* the state of being attractive and exciting (although often not for important reasons): *the glamour of city life; the glamour of beautiful film stars.*

glam·our·ize (also **-ise**) (*US* also **-or-**) /-aɪz/ *vt* to make (a person or thing) appear very attractive and exciting: *newspapers that glamourize the lives of pop stars.*

glam·our·ous (*US* also **-or-**) /-əs/ *adj* attractive and exciting: *glamorous film stars.*

glance¹ /glɑːns/ *nc* 1 a quick look: *take a glance at the newspaper headlines.* **at a glance** immediately: *I knew at a glance that it was impossible.* 2 a quick turning of the eyes: *loving glances.*

glance² /glɑːns/ *vi* 1 to take a quick look: *glancing at the clock; glance over/through a letter; glance round a room.* 2 **glance off sth** to hit something and bounce off: *The bullet glanced off his helmet.* 3 (of bright objects, light) to produce a flash of light: *Their helmets glanced in the sunlight.*

gland /glænd/ *nc* (*anat*) an organ that separates substances from the blood that are to be used by or expelled from the body: *sweat glands.*

glan·du·lar /'glændjʊlə(r)/ *adj* of a gland: *glandular fever.*

glare¹ /gleə(r)/ *n* 1 *nu* **the glare of sth** (a) a strong, unpleasant light: *the glare of the sun on the water.* (b) a strong, unpleasant effect: *in the full glare of publicity.* 2 *nc* an angry stare: *looking at her with a glare.*

glare² /gleə(r)/ *vi* 1 to shine in a dazzling or unpleasant way: *The tropical sun glared down on us all the day.* 2 **glare (at sb/sth)** to stare strongly and angrily: *They stood glaring at each other.*

glar·ing *adj* (a) extremely bright: *a car with glaring headlights; glaring colours.* (b) angry: *glaring eyes.* (c) huge, obvious: *a glaring mistake; glaring injustice.*

glass /glɑːs/ *n* 1 *nu* a kind of hard substance (as used in windows): *made of glass.* 2 *nc* a drinking container or its contents: *drink a glass (of milk).* ⇨ also magnifying-glass.

'glass·house *nc* a building with glass sides and roof, used for growing plants.

'glass·ware *nu* articles made of glass.

glass·ful /-fʊl/ *nc* as much as a drinking glass can hold: *a glassful of orange juice.*

glassy *adj* (**-ier, -iest**) (a) like glass in appearance; *glassy ice on the windows.* (b) expressionless, fixed: *a glassy stare.*

glass·es /'glɑːsɪz/ *n pl* (also *a pair of glasses*) two pieces of special glass in a frame, used by some people to see better. ⇨ sunglasses.

glaze¹ /gleɪz/ *nc,nu* (a substance producing) a thin shiny layer, as used on pots.

glaze² /gleɪz/ *v* 1 *vt* to fit glass into (a window etc): *glaze a window.* 2 *vt* to cover (pots etc) with glaze¹: *glaze pottery.* 3 *vi* **glaze (over)** (of the eyes) to become expressionless: *His eyes glazed over.*

glaz·ier /'gleɪzɪə(r)/ *nc* a worker who fits glass into windows etc.

gleam¹ /gliːm/ *nc* 1 a beam or ray of soft light: *the gleams of the morning sun.* 2 (*fig*) a brief show of some quality or emotion: *an occasional gleam of intelligence; a gleam of hope.*

gleam² /gli:m/ *vi* to send out gleams: *reflector studs gleaming in the road.*

glean /gli:n/ *vt* (*fig*) to collect (news, facts in small quantities).

glean·ings *n pl* small items of knowledge from various sources.

glee /gli:/ *nu* the feeling of joy caused by success or triumph: *shout with glee.*

glee·ful /-fəl/ *adj* feeling very happy.

glen /glen/ *nc* a narrow valley, esp in Scotland.

glib /glɪb/ *adj* (**—ber, —best**) (*derog*) (of a person, what is said or how it is said) eager and fluent but not sincere: *a glib talker; glib excuses.*

glib·ly *adv*

glide¹ /glaɪd/ *nc* a steady, gentle movement, e.g. by a plane or a skater.

glide² /glaɪd/ *vi* **1** to move in a steady, gentle and quiet way: *gliding across/over/through the water.* **2** to travel in a glider.

glid·er *nc* an aircraft without an engine.

glid·ing *nu* the sport of flying gliders.

glim·mer¹ /'glɪmə(r)/ *nc* **1** a weak, irregular light: *a glimmer of light through the curtains.* **2** (*fig*) a small, irregular sign: *a glimmer of hope.*

glim·mer² /'glɪmə(r)/ *vi* to send out a weak, irregular light: *lights glimmering in the distance.*

glimpse¹ /glɪmps/ *nc* a quick, incomplete view: *get/catch a glimpse of a bird in a tree.*

glimpse² /glɪmps/ *vt* to obtain a glimpse of (a person, thing).

glint /glɪnt/ *nc, vi* = gleam.

glis·ten /'glɪsn/ *vi* (esp of wet or polished surfaces) to shine brightly; sparkle: *eyes glistening with tears; snow glistening in the sunlight; diamonds that glisten.*

glit·ter /'glɪtə(r)/ *vi, nu* (to produce) a bright, irregular light: *stars that glitter.*

glit·ter·ing *adj*: *glittering jewels.*

gloat /gləʊt/ *vi* **gloat (over sth)** to look (at something) with selfish delight: *gloat over one's wealth.*

gloat·ing·ly *adv*

glo·bal /'gləʊbl/ *adj* (*attrib*) **1** of the whole world: *global war.* **2** of the whole of a group of facts, possibilities etc: *a global view of the economic potential.*

globe /gləʊb/ *nc* **1** an object shaped like a ball, used as a model of the earth. **2** (the —) the Earth: *people from all over the globe.* **3** any round glass bowl, esp a lampshade or a fishbowl.

globu·lar /'glɒbjʊlə(r)/ *adj* (*tech*) **1** shaped like a globe. **2** in the form of globules.

glob·ule /'glɒbjuːl/ *nc* (*tech*) a tiny drop.

gloom /gluːm/ *n* **1** *nu* (the —) semi-darkness. **2** *nc* a feeling of sadness and hopelessness: *The news cast a gloom over the village.*

gloomy /'gluːmɪ/ *adj* (**-ier, -iest**) **1** dark, unlit: *a gloomy room.* **2** giving very little happiness, hope: *feeling gloomy about the future; gloomy news.*

gloom·ily /-əlɪ/ *adv*

glor·ify /'glɔːrɪfaɪ/ *vt* (*pt, pp* **-ied**) **1** to praise (God). **2** to give honour and glory to (a hero). **3** (to try) to make (a person or thing) seem more beautiful, splendid etc than it is: *His cottage is a glorified barn.*

glori·fi·ca·tion /,glɔːrɪfɪ'keɪʃn/ *nu*

glori·ous /'glɔːrɪəs/ *adj* **1** splendid; magnificent: *a glorious sunset/view.* **2** great; honourable: *a glorious victory.* **3** (*informal*) very enjoyable: *have a glorious time; glorious weather.* **4** (*ironic*) dreadful: *What a glorious mess!*

glori·ous·ly *adv*

glory¹ /'glɔːrɪ/ *nu, nc* (*pl* **-ies**) **1** *nu* great fame and honour won by great achievements. **2** *nu* praise offered to God: *Glory to God in the highest!.* **3** *nu* the quality of being beautiful or magnificent: *the glory of a sunset.* **4** *nc* a reason for pride; something deserving respect and honour: *the glories of ancient Rome.*

glory² /'glɔːrɪ/ *vi* (*pt, pp* **-ied**) **glory in sth** to feel great happiness and pride because of a success: *glory in her success.*

gloss¹ /glɒs/ *n* **1** *nu* a smooth, bright, shining surface: *the gloss of silk.* **2** *n sing* (*fig*) a deceptive appearance: *a gloss of respectability.*

'gloss paint *nu* a kind of paint which produces a glossy surface. ⇔ matt.

glossy *adj* (**-ier, -iest**) (**a**) smooth and shiny: *a glossy surface.* (**b**) bright and colourful: *a glossy magazine.*

gloss² /glɒs/ *nc* (*tech*) an explanation (in a footnote etc) of a word in the text.

gloss³ /glɒs/ *vt* **1** to give something a glossy surface. **2** **gloss over sth** (**a**) to avoid explaining it fully: *gloss over a scientific detail.* (**b**) to avoid admitting or discussing something unpleasant: *gloss over her faults.*

gloss·ary /'glɒsərɪ/ *nc* (*pl* **-ies**) a list in a book with explanations of special vocabulary.

glove /glʌv/ *nc* a cover made for the hand. **fit like a glove** (*fig*) (of clothes) to fit perfectly. **be hand in glove (with sb)** ⇔ hand¹(1).

glow¹ /gləʊ/ *n sing* **1** a soft light from something hot without flames: *the glow of coal in a fire.* **2** any similar soft light: *the glow of the sky at sunset.* **3** a sign of warmth or happiness in the face, e.g. after exercise, because of good news etc: *a glow of enthusiasm/health/pride.*

glow² /gləʊ/ *vi* **1** to send out brightness or warmth without flame: *glowing logs/coal/charcoal.* **2** (*fig*) **glow (with sth)** to look, feel, warm (because of happiness, after exercise etc): *glowing with enthusiasm/health/pride.* **3** to show (strong or warm colours): *trees glowing with autumn tints.*

'glow-worm *nc* an insect of which the wingless female gives out a green light at its tail.

glow·ing *adj* (**a**) showing brightness or warmth: *a glowing fire.* (**b**) (*attrib*) (*fig*) showing enthusiasm and excitement: *give a glowing account of what happened.*

glow·ing·ly *adv*

glow·er /'glaʊə(r)/ *vi* **glower (at sb)** to look (at a person) in an angry or threatening way: *glower at her.*

glow·er·ing·ly *adv*

glu·cose /'gluːkəʊs/ *nu* natural sugar found in fruit.

glue¹ /gluː/ *nu* a kind of liquid substance used for sticking things.

glue² /gluː/ *vt* (*pres p* **gluing**; *pt, pp* **glued**) **1** to join (things) together using glue: *glue two pieces of wood together; gluing a piece of paper on to* something. **2** (*fig*) (often *passive*) to fix, direct, (one's eyes, attention etc): *His eyes were/His ear was glued to the keyhole. Why must you always be glued to the TV?* (= Why do you always watch it?).

glum /glʌm/ *adj* (**—mer, —mest**) sad and without hope.

> **glum·ly** *adv*

glut¹ /glʌt/ *nc* a supply in excess of demand: *a glut of pears in the market.*

glut² /glʌt/ *vt* (**-tt-**) **1** to supply too much to (a market): *glut the market (with fruit).* **2** to have too much for (an appetite): *glut one's appetite.*

glut·ton /'glʌtn/ *nc* **1** (*derog*) a person who eats too much: *You've eaten the whole pie, you glutton!* **2** a person who is willing and ready to do something: *He's a glutton for work.*

> **glut·ton·ous** /'glʌtənəs/ *adj* (*derog*) very greedy.
>
> **glut·ton·ous·ly** *adv*
>
> **glut·tony** /-tənɪ/ *nu* the habit or practice of eating too much.

gly·cer·ine (*US* = **-in**) /'glɪsərɪn/ *nu* a kind of sweet, colourless liquid, used in medical and toilet preparations and in explosives.

gm *written abbr* gramme(s).

gnarled /nɑːld/ *adj* twisted: *a gnarled old oak tree; gnarled fingers.*

gnash /næʃ/ *vt* to rub (one's teeth) together noisily because of anger or worry.

gnat /næt/ *nc* a kind of small two-winged fly that bites.

gnaw /nɔː/ *vt,vi* **gnaw (away at/at) sth 1** to bite steadily at (something): *The dog was gnawing (at) a bone.* **2** (*fig*) to affect (a person's mind, nerves etc) steadily: *Worry/Fear gnawed away at her thoughts.*

> **gnaw·ing** *adj* (*attrib*) continuous and painful: *a gnawing anxiety/pain/hunger.*

gnome /nəʊm/ *nc* a (statue of) a small bearded man with (in stories) magic powers.

GNP /ˌdʒiː en 'piː/ *abbr* Gross National Product (the total value of the goods produced and the services provided in a country in one year).

go¹ /gəʊ/ *nc* (*pl* **goes** /gəʊz/) (*informal*) **1** an opportunity to do, try, something, esp in one's correct order among others: *It's my go to use the computer. It's your go after me.* **at one go** using one attempt: *Can you blow out all the candles/ knock down all the blocks at one go?* **have a go (at sth)** to try (to achieve something): *He had several goes at the world record but never succeeded.* **make a go of sth** to try to make a success of one's career, a business, one's marriage etc. **2 from the word go** from the beginning: *I knew from the word go that she'd be successful.* **3** the quality of being active and energetic. **be full of go; have plenty of/a lot of go** to be full of energy and enthusiasm. **be on the go** to be busy doing one's work: *She's been on the go all day.* **4 be all the go** to be very popular: *Alloy bicycle parts are all the go.* ⇨ also **no-go area.**

go² /gəʊ/ *v* (*pres t 3rd person* **goes** /gəʊz/; *pres p* **going**; *pt* **went** /went/, *pp* **gone** /gɒn/) **1** *vi* to move from one place to another: *He went to the corner of the street. Don't go near the edge! Go over there and sit down. Where would you like to go this evening? I'm going home. Let's go for a*

walk. *They've gone on holiday. He's gone on a journey/trip to China. She's gone shopping* (i.e. gone to do her shopping). *Would you like to go camping/cycling/swimming with us?* Compare **come(1)**. ⇨ also **downhill, place¹(2). 2** *vi,vt* to travel: *go by bus/coach/plane/train; go on a bicycle/motorbike/horse; go miles trying to find petrol.* **3** *vi* **go to a place** (of a person) to visit a place for the purpose indicated by the place: *He's gone to hospital/the doctor's/the cinema/the seaside. I go to school/college/university* (i.e. I'm a student). *She's gone to work* (i.e. to her place of work). **4** *vi* to leave a place: *We must go at 9 o'clock. Let's go, this party is boring. Please don't go. He went as soon as he saw her.* **5** *vt* **go and** + **verb without 'to'** to move towards a person, place, in order to do something: *I'll go and see if it's ready. Please go and get/bring/make me a cup of coffee.* **has/have gone and** + *pp* (*informal*) (used to show surprise, anger etc): *She's gone and broken my calculator!* **6** *vi* (used as an imperative to show that one refuses, disagrees, is angry with a person etc): *Go to hell/to blazes! Go and jump in the lake!* **7** *vi* to make progress at a speed, to a distance, mentioned: *go at 40 mph; go fast/slow; go for miles; go a long way.* **go far; go too far** ⇨ **far²(1). go to great lengths/trouble to do sth** to use a lot of effort to achieve something: *He went to great trouble to make her happy.* **go a long way (towards sth)** ⇨ **way²(1). go slow** ⇨ **slow². 8** *vi* to reach, extend, as far as (a limit): *This road goes all the way to Tokyo.* **9** *vi* (usually *imperative*) (in competitions) to begin: *Go! Ready, steady, go!* **10** *vi* **. . . to go** (of a period of time) to pass; left: *There's an hour to go before the bell rings. We have 2 days to go and then it's our anniversary.* **11** *vi* to have as a usual or correct place: *The books go here/on this shelf/in the cupboard/over there. Where does this plate go? Where would you like this piano to go?* **12** *vi* (used when asking about or reporting on progress): *How are the exams going? My work is going well/badly. The interview went better than I expected.* **be going strong** ⇨ **strong². 13** *vi* (of a machine) to be able to work: *My radio/clock doesn't go/isn't going. Can you make this old car go again?* **14** *vi* (of a machine etc) (used when a person is reporting on its performance): *My bike is going well at the moment. His car goes like a dream* (i.e. works well). **15** *vi* to become weak; fade; disappear: *My eyesight/hearing is going. At last the loud noises went. My headache's gone.* **16** *vi* to be given, sold, lost, stolen, dismissed etc (according to the situation): *That cheap chair I saw in the window has gone. My watch has gone! That wardrobe will have to go. She'll have to go—she's too lazy.* **let go; let sb/sth go; let oneself go** ⇨ **let³(1). 17** *vi* (used with *adjs*) (**a**) to change to a mentioned (worse) state: *go blind/ lame/mad; go bad/sour/stale/flat.* (**b**) to change to a mentioned (worse) condition: *The batteries went dead. The clock's gone wrong. You'll go broke very quickly if you drink so much.* (**c**) to change to a mentioned colour or shade: *go pale; go white with fear; go brown in the oven.* ⇨ **get(4).** (**d**) to change to a mentioned belief or attitude: *The country's gone socialist. He goes serious when I mention her.* (**e**) to become, stay in, a mentioned state: *go hungry. She went free/unpunished. It went undiscovered for years.* **18** *vi,vt* to act (in a way mentioned): *Go carefully with that glass vase!* **go it alone**, to act without help. ⇨ also Dutch, easy²(2), half³(1), share¹(1). **19** *vi* to have a pleasing relationship: *These curtains won't go with the carpet. The wallpaper and the curtains don't go.* ⇨ go together. **20** *vi* to have the wording or tune mentioned: *How does that poem/song/melody go? It goes like this* . . . **21** *vt* to make (the sound mentioned): *A clock goes 'tick tock'. The balloon went 'pop'.* **22** *vi* **be going to** + *verb* (used to show what is intended, planned, probable, inevitable etc in the future): *I'm going to buy another one next Saturday. I'm going to tell you a story. It's going to rain. She's going to be twenty next month.* **be going to be** + *pp* (used as a form of the passive to show that something is/was intended, planned etc): *It was going to be sung on television but the singer was ill. It is going to be sung tomorrow.*

go about (a) to walk, travel, move, from place to place (used with a description of how, what one is doing etc): *go about in green boots/telling lies about her.* **(b)** (of a rumour etc) to be told by one person to another and then another: *There's a story going about that we have quarrelled.* **go about sth (a)** to be, keep, busy with an activity: *go about her usual duties.* **(b)** to make a start at something: *You're not going about it/that problem/the job in the right way.* **go about (with sb)** = go around (with sb).

go abroad to go to another country for a holiday or to live.

go across (to sth) (a) to move across (a street, bridge, river etc). **(b)** to change one's opinion and support, join, another group: *go across to the Democrats.*

go after sb/sth (a) to follow and try to catch a person, animal etc: *go after a thief/a dog.* **(b)** to try to get a person, job etc for oneself: *go after a job in Kuwait; go after a brilliant salesman who works for a competitor.* **(c)** to be after a person, thing, in a list, order of events etc: *Mrs White will go after you in the order of speakers.* Compare come after sb/sth.

go against sb to have an unsatisfactory result for a person: *The election/legal decision went against her.* **go against sth** to be opposed to, contrary to, something: *The use of animals in medical research goes against my principles.* ⇨ also grain(6).

go ahead (a) (often *imperative* to show approval or agreement) to do what one wants to do: *He went ahead and started his own business. If you think the bike is worth the money, go ahead and buy it.* **(b)** to make progress: *After the storm the building of the bridge went ahead quickly.* ⇨ go-ahead. **go ahead (of sb) (a)** = get ahead (of sb). **(b)** to continue a journey in front of others: *Some of us went ahead to find a place to camp.*

go along to proceed with an activity: *You'll find the job easier as you go along.* **go along with sb (a)** to accompany a person to a place: *I'll go along with you as far as the bus stop.* **(b)** to agree with a person: *I can't go along with you on that issue.*

go around = go round (b). **go around (with sb)** to keep company with a person as a boyfriend

or girlfriend: *Ben's been going around with the same girl for months.*

go astray (a) (of a personal possession, a pet etc) to be lost (with the belief that it will be found quickly): *My pen's gone astray.* **(b)** (of a young person) to behave immorally or illegally: *It is so easy for teenagers to go astray during periods of high unemployment.*

go at sb to attack, argue with, a person strongly: *The two leaders went at each other during the television debate.* **go at sth** to make great efforts to do something: *Once she decides to decorate a room she goes at the work/goes at it with such determination.*

go away (a) to leave a place, a house, a town etc, esp permanently: **(b)** (*imperative*) leave me (e.g. because I am tired of your interference, complaints etc).

go back (a) to return (to a place): *When do the students go back (to college)? Go back and tell her you're sorry.* **(b)** (of clocks etc) to be set to an earlier time: *When do the clocks go back in England?* **(c)** to have as its origin, date from: *Her love of literature goes back to her school days.* **go back on one's word** ⇨ word¹(3).

go before to live (and die) before: *Think of all the prime ministers who went before.* **go before sb** to appear before a person: *go before a judge/an interviewing committee.*

go behind to go to the back of a queue etc. ⇨ also back³(1).

go below (on a ship) to go to the lower (underwater) levels.

go-between ⇨ separate entry below.

go beyond sth to do more than what is allowed, necessary etc: *You've gone beyond your instructions.* ⇨ also joke¹.

go by (a) (of a period of time) to pass: *As the months went by she became more and more ill.* **(b)** (of traffic, a procession etc) to pass in front of a person, view etc: *The parade went by and the children clapped.* **(c)** (of an opportunity etc) to pass without being used. **go by sth** to be guided or directed by something: *Don't go by my watch—it's unreliable. Don't go by outward appearances—he may be a keen worker.* ⇨ also name¹(1).

go down (a) (of the sun, moon) to disappear below the horizon. **(b)** (of a ship etc) to disappear below the surface of the sea. **(c)** (of food, drink) to be eaten or swallowed: *That cup of coffee went down well!* **(d)** (of prices, costs etc) to be reduced in amount: *Meat has gone down this week.* **(e)** (of liquid, temperature, supplies etc) to be reduced. **(f)** (of wind etc) to become calm. **(g)** (of a student) to leave a university, e.g. at the end of term or end of a course. **go down (in sth)** to be written and recorded in something: *Your comments go down in the files. He'll go down in history as a man of peace.* **go down to sth (a)** to reach as far as something: *skirts that go down to the ankle.* **(b)** to travel to the sea, coast. **(c)** (of a book etc) to contain information up to a date mentioned: *a history book that goes down to 1966.*

go down with sb to be accepted, liked, by a person: *The new manager didn't go down well with the staff.* **go down with sth** to become ill with measles, flu etc.

go for sb (a) to attack a person physically or verbally: *The dog went for the postman. The newspapers went for the corrupt minister.* **(b)** to go to a place to bring back a professional person: *go for a doctor.* **(c)** to be true for a person: *What she says goes for me too.* **go for sb/sth** to be attracted to a person or thing: *go for tall handsome men/silk blouses/brightly coloured artwork.* **go for an amount of money** to be sold for: *It went for £100/a fair price/more than I expected.* **go for it** (*informal*) to try to achieve something.

go in (a) to enter (part of) a building. **(b)** (of the sun, moon) to disappear behind a cloud. **(c)** to be understood and remembered: *I've tried to teach him the rules of chess, but they just don't go in.* **go in (sth)** to be able to be put in something: *The key won't go in (the lock). My clothes will all go in this small bag.* ⇨ also **ear**[1](1). **go in for sth (a)** to enter as a candidate for an exam, contest, competition. **(b)** to choose something as one's career: *go in for medicine.* **(c)** to have something as an interest or hobby: *go in for aerobics.*

go into sth (a) to enter a building. **(b)** to be admitted to a place: *go into hospital.* **(c)** to make violent contact with something: *go into the back of another car.* **(d)** to become a member of an organization etc: *go into the army. When did Portugal go into the Common Market?* **(e)** to adopt something as a career: *go into politics/the family business.* **(f)** to examine, consider, something: *go into details/the facts.* **(g)** to begin to have a mentioned mental state: *go into fits of laughter/a mental decline/a coma/hysterics.* **(h)** (*maths*) to be able to divide another number: *10 into 8 won't/ doesn't go. 10 into 20 goes 2. 10 goes into 20 twice.* ⇨ also **abeyance.**

go off (a) (of food etc) to become unsuitable for eating: *The meat/milk has gone off.* **(b)** (of an event) to proceed (successfully, badly etc): *The meeting/play/interview/football match went off well.* **(c)** (of an alarm, bell) to make a sound: *My alarm clock didn't go off this morning.* **(d)** (of a source of power) to become unavailable: *The electricity has gone off again.* **(e)** (of a person) to leave a place, room etc: *go off on holiday; go off in a temper.* **(f)** (in a play) to leave the stage. **(g)** (of a person) to fall asleep. **go off sb/sth** to lose one's interest in or liking for a person, food etc: *go off beer/one's boyfriend.* ⇨ also **head**[1](2). **go off with sb/sth** to go away with a person, thing: *He's gone off with David's wife/with my coat in his car/to Oslo with Paul.*

go on (a) (of a light etc) to be lit: *The lamp won't go on. The street lights will go on at 6.30.* **(b)** to happen: *What's going on (in here)?* **(c)** to continue a journey: *We decided to go on although the weather was bad.* **(d)** to continue a journey ahead of other people: *You go on and try to catch the earlier train.* **(e)** (of time) to pass: *As the days went on she became worried.* **(f)** to behave, esp in an annoying, wrong, excited etc way: *If you go on like this you'll be dismissed.* **(g)** (of a state of affairs) to continue: *How long can the situation go on (before the firm collapses)?* **(h)** (in a play) to enter the stage. **(i)** (*informal*) (used as an exclamation) I don't believe you! I dare you to do it! (according to the situation). **go on sth (a)** to travel on something, esp for pleasure: *go on a supersonic plane/an elephant.* **(b)** to leave a place

for the purpose of something: *go on holiday/business/a trip.* **(c)** to be guided by something: *What evidence do we have to go on? I was going on her report/the computer analysis.* **(d)** to be spent on something: *All her money goes on the children.* **(e)** to begin to get help from something: *go on social security.* **go on (about sb/sth)** to talk or write (too) much (about a person, difficulties etc): *Please don't go on about your problems. She goes on and on about her husband.* **go on (at sb)** to criticize or complain (too much): *She goes on at her teenage son far too much!* **be going on for sth** = be getting on for sth (which is more usual). **go on (to sth/to do sth)** to do or say something next: *Let's go straight on to the next question. He went on to explain the cost.* **go on (with sth/ doing sth)** to continue: *Go on with your work until I return. These supplies are enough to be going on with* (i.e. for the present time).

go out (a) to leave a building, room etc: *He's not here—he went out at five o'clock. She's gone out dancing/to the cinema. Out you go!* **(b)** to attend parties, dinners etc: *She still goes out even at the age of 85! Out you go!* **(c)** (of a light, fire) to stop shining or burning: *All the lights went out. The fire's gone out.* **(d)** to stop being fashionable: *Have pointed shoes gone out?* **(e)** to become unconscious, esp in a certain way: *She went out within a minute* ⇨ **light**[4](1). **(f)** (of a year, month etc) to end: *As 1985 went out we remembered the series of air disasters.* **(g)** (of the sea, tide) to flow back from the land. **go out and about** to leave one's home etc and visit friends, shops etc, esp after being ill. **go out for sth** to leave one's home, work etc in order to enjoy or obtain something: *go out for some fresh air/a picnic/some bread.* **go out of sth (a)** to leave, using (e.g. a door) as a means of exit: *go out of the front gates.* **(b)** to disappear from, become reduced in: *The anger went out of his voice.* Ⓝ For uses of 'go out of' with nouns such as **business, fashion, mind, service, way** etc, ⇨ the noun entries. **go all out for sth/to do sth** to make every effort to achieve something: *go all out to win the prize.* **go out to sb** (of sympathy etc) to be offered, given over, to a person: *Our hearts went out to the victims of the earthquake.* **go out (to a place)** to travel to (a distant) place): *go out to Australia to live.* **go out together** to be involved together in a close personal relationship: *Sarah and Tom are going out together.* **go out with sb** to be involved with a person in a close personal relationship: *How long have you been going out with Mark?*

go over (of a speech, proposal, performance) to be received (by an audience): *The speech went over well at the conference.* **go over sth (a)** to examine, check, accounts, details in a report, arrangements etc. **(b)** to examine a car, house etc before deciding to buy. **(c)** to study and revise notes, a textbook, the text of a play etc. **(d)** to clean: *go over the furniture with a duster.* **(e)** to search luggage, clothes for illegal goods. ⇨ **going-over. go over (to a place)** to move across a street, river, stretch of sea etc; to the other side, an island etc. **go over to sth (a)** to change one's political opinion, beliefs, and join another group. **(b)** to give up one practice, interest etc and take on another: *go over to a vegetarian diet.*

go overseas to go to another continent to work, study or have a holiday.

go round (a) (of the world, a spinning top, one's head when feeling dizzy) to (seem to) move in circles. (b) to move from place to place or from person to person: *go round telling lies.* (c) = go about (b). **go round (sth)** (a) to move (from one place to another) using a route that is longer and not the quickest or usual one: *The city is so busy that I suggest we go round (it). The road was damaged and we had to go the long way round.* (b) to visit and look at the structure, contents, of a new house, a school, an art gallery, museum, factory etc. (c) to be enough (for everyone): *Is there enough food to go round? There are not sufficient blankets to go round all the refugees.* (d) (of a doctor, manager etc) to visit a ward, place of work etc and check on patients, workers etc: *go round the casualty department/the factory.* ⇨ also **bend¹**. **go round (to sb/sth)** to visit a person, place, near one's home: *go round to my mother/my mother's house.* **go round (with sb)** = go around (with sb).

go through (a) (of a business deal) to be agreed and finalized. (b) (of a piece of legislation) to be agreed and passed by a parliament etc. **go through (sth)** (a) to move from one side to the other (of a town, farm etc). (b) to pass from one side to the other, esp with difficulty: *This piano won't go through (the door).* (c) to hit and enter something by breaking: *The stone went through (the window).* (d) (of a pipe, electricity supply etc) to pass from one side to the other (of a wall etc). (e) to use up supplies: *go through a whole packet of biscuits in five minutes.* (f) to examine pockets, papers, files, drawers etc searching for something. (g) to discuss and examine something in detail: *Let's go through your account of what happened again.* (h) to take part in an official ceremony, experience etc: *She asked him to go through a religious and civil wedding. They went through a painful divorce.* (i) to practise the speeches and movements of a play: *Let's go through Act I again.* (j) to suffer anxiety, pain, a difficult period etc: *If only you knew what I must go through with all her complaints.* **go through with sth** to take part in an activity, esp unwillingly or against advice: *On the day before the wedding Pat wrote to say she couldn't go through with it.*

go to sb to be given or awarded to, pass into, a person's possession: *First prize went to John. In the will the house went to my sister.* **go to sb (for sth)** to visit a person in order to receive lessons, treatment, advice, money etc. **go to a place** ⇨ go²(3). Ⓝ For the use of 'go to' with nouns such as *hell, head, piece, sea, wall, waste* etc, ⇨ the noun entries.

go together (of colours, types of food, patterns etc) to be good, attractive or suitable to see, eat etc together: *Do red and green go together?* **go together (to a place)** to visit a cinema, party etc together: *Let's go to the disco together.*

go towards sth to be a contribution towards the cost of something.

go under (a) (of a person who cannot swim etc) to go below the surface of the sea. (b) (of a business, organization, businessman) to fail because there is no money left.

go up (a) (of prices, costs, temperature) to increase. (b) (of a level of water etc) to get higher. (c) (of the curtain in front of the stage in a theatre) to be raised. (d) (of buildings) to be built: *A new office block has gone up opposite the post office.* (e) to be destroyed by explosion or fire: *The whole city went up (in flames).* **go up sth** to climb up something: *a ladder, a mountain etc.* ⇨ wall¹(1). **go up to sb** to approach a person (to speak to her or him). **go up to sth** (a) to reach as high as something: *The water went up to my knees.* (b) (of a student) to begin studying at a university: *go up to university/Oxford/Sussex University.* (c) (formal) to visit an important city: *go up to London to shop.*

go with sb (a) to accompany a person (on a journey): *I went with my parents to Italy.* (b) to have a close personal relationship with a person: *Who does Eric go with at the moment?* **go with sth** (a) to be part of, be included with, something: *The belt goes with the trousers. The curtains go with the house.* (b) (of a colour, food, pattern etc) to be attractive, suited etc when combined with something: *Does gravy go with steak?*

go without (sth) (of a person) to not have (and suffer the absence of) something: *go without a meal/holiday. We have no money so you'll have to go without.* **go without saying** ⇨ saying²(1).

goad /gəʊd/ *vt* **goad sb on/into doing sth** to encourage, urge a person, esp to do wrong: *goad him on; goad him into stealing.*

go-ahead¹ /ˈgəʊ əhed/ *adj* (usually *attrib*) (of a person) showing spirit, enthusiasm and ambition.

go-ahead² /ˈgəʊ əhed/ *nc* (esp) **give sb/get the go-ahead** to give a person/get permission to begin an activity such as starting a business, building a house etc.

goal /gəʊl/ *nc* **1** (in games such as football) the posts between which (the *goal-mouth*) the ball is to be sent in order to score; point(s) made by doing this: *score/kick a goal; win by three goals to one.* **2** (*fig*) an aim of one's efforts or ambition: *His goal in life is to be happy.*

ˈgoal·keeper *nc* the player whose duty is to keep the ball out of the goal.

goat /gəʊt/ *nc* a kind of small, horned animal: *A she-goat* (or *nanny-goat*) *is kept for its milk. A male goat is called a he-goat* (or *billy-goat*). ⇨ kid¹(1).

ˈgoat·skin *nu* the skin of a goat, used to make rugs, containers for water etc.

gobble /ˈgɒbl/ *vt,vi* **gobble (sth (up))** to eat (food) quickly, noisily and greedily: *gobble an ice-cream.*

go-between /ˈgəʊ bɪtwiːn/ *nc* a person who makes arrangements for two people who do not meet at first: *In some countries, marriages are arranged by go-betweens.*

gob·let /ˈgɒblɪt/ *nc* a drinking-vessel with a stem, a base and no handles.

gob·lin /ˈgɒblɪn/ *nc* a mischievous demon.

god /gɒd/ *nc* **1** a being regarded or worshipped as having power over nature and control over human affairs: *Greek gods.* **2** (G-) the creator and ruler of the universe, according to Christians, Jews and Muslims. **Thank God!** (an expression used to show relief). **God willing** if possible. ⇨

also act[1](1).

'god·child/daughter/son *nc* a person for whom a godparent acts as sponsor at baptism.

'god·father/mother/parent *nc* a person who agrees, when a child is baptized, to take an active interest in its welfare (and see that he or she remains a Christian).

'god-forsaken *adj* (*attrib; derog*) (of places) unpleasant; poor.

'god·send *nc* something (unexpected and) welcome because it is needed.

god·dess /'gɒdɪs/ *nc* a female god, esp in Greek and Latin mythology: *Venus, the goddess of love.*

god·like /'gɒdlaɪk/ *adj* like God or a god in some way.

god·ly /'gɒdlɪ/ *adj* (**-ier, -iest**) religious.
 god·li·ness *nu*

goes /gəʊz/ **1** *pres t 3rd person* of go[2]. **2** *n pl* of go[1].

goggle /'gɒgl/ *vi* **goggle at sb/sth** to look with eyes wide open, e.g. in surprise or amazement: *goggling at her in surprise.*

goggles /'gɒglz/ *n pl* (also *a pair of goggles*) large glasses with special rims to protect the eyes from the wind, dust etc (as worn by motorcyclists).

go·ing[1] /'gəʊɪŋ/ *adj* (*attrib*) **a going concern** an active, profitable business. **the going rate** the current price, value.

go·ing[2] /'gəʊɪŋ/ *nu* **1** the act of leaving: *Your going is sure to upset her.* ⇒ also comings and goings. **2** a method or speed of travelling or working: *50 miles per hour is good going for this old car.* **keep going** ⇒ keep[2](2). **3** the condition of the ground, road etc when travelling: *The going was hard/soft (for the horses) on the mountain road.* **heavy going** ⇒ heavy. ⇒ also ongoing.

go·ing[3] /'gəʊɪŋ/ *pres p* of go[2]. ⇒ go[2](22).

going-over /ˌgəʊɪŋ 'əʊvə(r)/ *nc* (*pl* **goings-over**) (*informal*) **1** a (thorough) examination: *I gave the bike she was buying a thorough going-over.* **2** a beating of a person: *He gave the man a good going-over and then ran away.*

gold /gəʊld/ *nu* **1** (also *attrib*) a precious yellow metal used for making coins, ornaments, jewellery etc: *£500 in gold* (= in gold coins); *a gold watch/bracelet.* **2** (also *attrib*) the yellow colour of the metal. **3** (*fig*) highly respected or valued qualities: *a heart of gold.*

'gold·field *nc* an area in which gold is found.

'gold·fish *nc* a gold-coloured fish kept in bowls or ponds.

ˌgold 'medal *nc* the prize for first place in a sporting contest.

'gold-mine *nc* (**a**) a place where gold is mined. (**b**) (*fig*) any source of wealth.

gold·en /'gəʊldən/ *adj* **1** of or like gold in value or colour: *golden hair.* **2** (*attrib*) excellent: *a golden opportunity.*

ˌgolden 'handshake *nc* a sum of money given to a high-ranking member of a company when he or she retires (in recognition of good work).

ˌgolden 'jubilee *nc* a 50th anniversary, esp of the start of a king's or queen's reign.

ˌgolden 'rule *nc* (the —) any important rule of conduct.

ˌgolden 'wedding *nc* the 50th anniversary of a wedding.

golf /gɒlf/ *nu* a game during which players hit small, hard balls (with *golf-clubs*) into holes on land (called a *golf-course* or *golf-links*). □ *vi* to play golf.

golf·er *nc* a person who plays golf.

gon·do·la /'gɒndələ/ *nc* (*pl* **—s**) a long, flat-bottomed boat with high peaks at each end, used on canals in Venice.

gon·do·lier /ˌgɒndə'lɪə(r)/ *nc* a man who rows a gondola.

gone /gɒn/ *pp* of go[2].

gong /gɒŋ/ *nc* a metal disc that gives an echoing note when struck with a stick.

gon·or·rhea (also **-rhoea**) /ˌgɒnə'rɪə/ *nu* a kind of sexually transmitted disease.

good[1] /gʊd/ *adj* (**better** /'betə(r)/, **best** /best/) **1** having the correct or desired qualities: *That is a good* (= sharp) *knife but this one is better. This soil is good. She comes from a good* (i.e. respectable) *family. My eyesight isn't good. This is a good opportunity to prove your sincerity. Is he in good health? This work isn't good enough—do it again.* Compare poor[1](3). **2** efficient; competent: *a good teacher/driver. She's a good cook.* **be good at sth** to be able to do it well: *He's very good at mathematics/football. She's better at engineering than chemistry. Are you good at sewing on buttons?* **be in good hands** ⇒ hand[1](1). **3** reliable: *good brakes; a good watch; a good investment; good debts* (i.e. that will be paid). *This pen is no good. My car is good for another year.* **4** (of food) suitable for eating: *Fish doesn't stay good in hot weather.* **5** healthy; having a good effect: *Milk is very good for you. Exercise is good for the heart. Too much sun isn't good.* **6** pleasing; pleasant: *good news/weather; a good idea; good to be alive/home; has a good smell/feel/taste; have a good figure; feel good* (i.e. feel healthy and happy); *look good* (i.e. look attractive) *in a suit.* **be a good thing** ⇒ thing(3). **have a good time** ⇒ time[1](2). **put in/say a good word for sb** ⇒ word[1](2). **7** (*attrib; no comp*) kind; willing: *It was good of you to help them. Will you be good enough/be so good as to pass me my coat? My father has always been good to me.* **so far, so good** ⇒ far[2](3). **8** (of a person, esp a child, an animal) behaving well: *as good as gold* (= very well behaved). *Be a good boy while I make coffee. Sit down, Rover, there's a good dog!* **9** (of behaviour) morally excellent: *live a good life; do a good deed.* **10** genuine; valid: *offer a good excuse/ reason for being late.* **11** (*attrib; no comp*) thorough: *have a good rest; have a good look for the key.* ⇒ also account[1](2), mind[1](4). **12** (*no comp*) much in number or quantity: *a good deal of* (= much) *trouble/the responsibility/money; a good many* (= a large number of) *people; a good few* (= many) *visitors; live a good* (= long) *distance from the sea; have a good* (= large) *supply of food; will go a good way towards the cost.* Compare poor[1](4). **in good time** at a time when there is no risk of being late or too late: *Be there in good time if you hope to find a parking place.* **all in good time** without hurrying (because it is not necessary): *I'll mend the window all in good time.* **13** (*attrib; no comp*) not less than: *We waited a good hour. They work a good ten miles from home.* **14** **as good as** + *pt* practically (did something): *He as good as said I was a liar.* **15** (used in forms of greeting and saying farewell): *Good morning/afternoon/evening. Good night. Goodbye.* **16** (used in exclamations of surprise, shock etc): *Good gracious/heavens!* **17** (used as an exclamation of approval, thanks, wishing etc): *'I've finished doing that.'—'Good!' Good old Mike—he's agreed to do it! Good luck!*

'**good-for-nothing** *adj, nc* (*derog*) (of) a worthless person.

,**Good 'Friday** *n* (*Christianity*) the Friday before Easter; the day when Jesus died.

,**good 'humour** *nu* a cheerful, happy state of mind. Hence ,**good-'humoured** *adj*

,**good-'looking** *adj* beautiful; handsome.

,**good-'natured** *adj* kind, ready and willing to help others.

good² /gud/ *nu* **1** that which is beneficial, has the desired qualities, is morally right, is profitable etc: *Was his advice any good? This tout isn't any/ much good. It's no good (at all). It's no good (my) talking to her. There's some good in everyone. What good was it/does it do you? What's the good of lying? What good can come out of violence?* **for good (and all)** permanently: *He's left the country for good* (i.e. he will not return). *I'm leaving you for good and all!* **for one's/sb's own good** for one's/a person's personal benefit: *You must be home by midnight—it's for your own good.* **for the good of sb/sth** in order to benefit a person, country, community etc: *He did it for the good of his family/the school.* **be up to no good** to be doing something illegal or morally wrong. **do good (to sb)** to show kindness, concern, by doing something beneficial (to): *do good to one's neighbours/relatives.* **do sb good** (of an activity) to be beneficial to a person: *Eat more fruit—it will do you good. A holiday would do her a lot of good.* **make good** to become successful: *He went to live in Canada where he hoped to make good as a chef.* **make (sth) good** to repair (something), repay (a loss): *make good the wall round the new pipes. She hoped to make good her mistake by apologizing.* **2** morally excellent people: *Good and bad alike respected the new police chief. Only the good die young!*

good·bye /,gud'baɪ/ *int* (an expression used when leaving).

good·ies /'gudɪz/ *n pl* (*informal*) kinds of food, items etc that give pleasure, are unexpected etc: *What goodies did you buy?*

good·ish /'gudɪʃ/ *adj* (*attrib; no comp*) quite large, extensive etc: *It's a goodish walk from here.*

good·ness /'gudnɪs/ *nu* **1** the quality of being good: *goodness of heart.* **have the goodness to do sth** (*formal*) to be kind enough to do it: *Have the goodness to come this way, please.* **2** that part that is beneficial: *meat with all the goodness boiled out.* **3** (used as an exclamation of surprise, relief etc): *Goodness gracious! Goodness me! Thank goodness!*

goods /gudz/ *n pl* **1** movable property, esp thing to be sold or things (furniture, clothes, bedding etc) belonging to a person: *sell leather goods.* **deliver the goods** (*fig*) to do what one has promised. **goods and chattels** personal possessions. **2** (also *attrib*) large articles (to be) carried by trains or lorries: *a goods train; a heavy*

goods vehicle.

good·will /,gud'wɪl/ *nu* **1** a kind and friendly feeling: *a policy of goodwill in international relations.* **2** a beneficial, respected relationship of a business with its customers: *A large part of the price of the shop is for goodwill.*

goofy /'guːfɪ/ *adj* (**-ier, -iest**) (*sl; derog*) having long top teeth that stick out.

goose /guːs/ *n* (*pl* **geese** /giːs/) **1** *nc* a kind of waterbird larger than a duck. **2** *nu* its flesh as food.

'**goose-flesh/-pimples** *nu* a condition of the skin having raised spots, caused by cold or fear.

goose·berry /'guzbrɪ/ *nc* (*pl* **-ies**) (also *attrib*) (a kind of bush with) a green, hairy berry: *gooseberry jam.* **play gooseberry** to be present with two people who prefer to be alone.

gore /gɔː(r)/ *vt* (usually *passive*) to pierce, wound, (a person) with the horns or tusks: *be gored to death by a bull.* ⇨ **gory.**

gorge¹ /gɔːdʒ/ *nc* a deep, narrow opening, usually with a stream, between hills or mountains.

gorge² /gɔːdʒ/ *vt, vi, v reflex* to eat (food) greedily: *gorge (on) rich food; gorging oneself with meat.*

gorg·eous /'gɔːdʒəs/ *adj* **1** richly coloured; magnificent: *a gorgeous sunset.* **2** (*informal*) giving pleasure and satisfaction: *gorgeous weather; a gorgeous dress.*

gorg·eous·ly *adv*

gor·il·la /gə'rɪlə/ *nc* (*pl* **-s**) a kind of darkhaired tree-climbing African ape.

gorse /gɔːs/ *nu* a kind of evergreen shrub with sharp thorns and yellow flowers.

gory /'gɔːrɪ/ *adj* (**-ier, -iest**) involving blood and death: *a gory tale.*

gos·ling /'gozlɪŋ/ *nc* a young goose.

gos·pel /'gospl/ *n* **1** (the G-) (one of four books recording) the life and teachings of Jesus Christ. **2** *nu* (also *attrib*) something that may be believed with confidence: *the gospel truth.*

gos·sa·mer /'gosəmə(r)/ *nu* **1** the fine silky substance of webs made by small spiders. **2** (also *attrib*) a kind of soft, delicate cloth: *a gossamer veil.*

gos·sip¹ /'gosɪp/ *n* **1** *nu* talk (often critical) about the affairs of other people: *Don't believe all the gossip you hear.* **2** *nu* (also *attrib*) informal writing about people and social events, as in newspapers: *the gossip column* (of a newspaper); *a gossip writer.* **3** *nc* an instance of gossip(1): *have a good gossip with a neighbour over the garden fence.* **4** *nc* a person who is fond of gossip(1): *She's an old gossip.*

gos·sip² /'gosɪp/ *vi* to talk or write gossip.

got /got/ **1** *pt,pp* of get. **2** **has/have got** ⇨ have².

got·ten /'gotn/ *pp* (in US) of get.

gouge¹ /gaudʒ/ *nc* a tool with a sharp semicircular edge, used for cutting grooves in wood.

gouge² /gaudʒ/ *vt* **gouge sth (out)** to cut, shape or force something out (as if) with a gouge: *gouge out a person's eye with one's thumb.*

gou·lash /'guːlæʃ/ *nc,nu* (a dish of) stew of steak and vegetables, seasoned with paprika.

gourd /guəd/ *nc* (a large, hard-skinned fruit of) a kind of climbing or trailing plant.

gour·mand /ˈɡʊəmənd/ nc a lover of food.

gour·met /ˈɡʊəmeɪ/ nc a person who enjoys and is expert in the choice of good food, wines etc.

gout /ɡaʊt/ nu a disease causing painful swellings in joints, esp toes, knees and fingers.

gov·ern /ˈɡʌvn/ v **1** vt,vi to rule (a country, city etc). **2** vt to control (an emotion etc): *govern one's temper*. **3** vt (often *passive*) to determine, influence, (a decision, person etc): *be governed by the size of the hole/the opinions of others*.

gov·ern·ing adj (attrib) having the power or right to govern: *the governing body of a school/college*.

gov·ern·ess /ˈɡʌvənɪs/ nc a woman who lives with a family and teaches the children at home.

gov·ern·ment /ˈɡʌvnmənt/ n (abbr govt) **1** nu the power to govern: *What the country needs is strong government*. **2** nu the method or system of governing: *We prefer democratic government*. **3** nc (often G-) the group of people governing a State: *The Prime Minister has formed a Government. The Government was criticized by the Opposition.*

gov·ern·men·tal /ˌɡʌvn'mentl/ adj

gov·ern·or /ˈɡʌvnə(r)/ nc (G- in names) **1** a person who governs a province or (in US) a State: *the Governor of New York State*. **2** a member of the governing body of an institution (e.g. a prison, school, college, hospital).

,governor-'general nc (in the Commonwealth) a representative of the British king or queen having no special powers: *the Governor-General of Canada*.

govt *written abbr* government.

gown /ɡaʊn/ nc **1** a woman's long dress, esp one for an occasion mentioned: *a dressing-gown/night-gown; an evening gown*. **2** a loose (usually black) robe worn by members of a university, judges etc.

GP /ˌdʒiː 'piː/ abbr General Practitioner.

Gp Capt *written abbr* Group Captain.

GPO /ˌdʒiː piː 'əʊ/ abbr General Post Office (the old official title for the postal service in GB).

grab¹ /ɡræb/ nc a sudden attempt to take something roughly, selfishly or eagerly: *make a grab at something*. **be up for grabs** (*informal*) to be available for anyone to take, buy etc: *The house is up for grabs*. **make a grab at sth** to try to take it.

grab² /ɡræb/ vt,vi (**-bb-**) **grab (at) (sth)** to (try to) take (something) roughly, selfishly or eagerly: *The dog grabbed the bone and ran off with it. He grabbed at the opportunity of going abroad.*

grace¹ /ɡreɪs/ n **1** nu the quality of being pleasing and attractive, esp in structure, movement: *She danced with grace/with a grace that surprised us.* **2** (usually *pl*) pleasing manner or behaviour. **airs and graces** ⇨ air¹(3). **3** nu goodwill; willingness. **do sth with a good/bad grace** to do it willingly/reluctantly. **give sb a week's etc grace** to allow a person an extra week etc before he or she has to do something. ⇨ also saving¹. **4** nc,nu a short prayer of thanks before or after a meal: *say (a) grace*. **5** nu (*formal*) (the result of) God's mercy and favour towards mankind. **be in a state of grace** to be influenced by the strength and inspiring power of God; have received the Sacraments. **fall from grace** to fall to a lower

moral state. **6** nc (G-) (used as a title when speaking of or to an archbishop, duke or duchess): *His/Her/Your Grace*.

grace² /ɡreɪs/ vt to add honour, dignity, to (an event): *The occasion was graced by the presence of the Queen*.

grace·ful /-fəl/ adj having or showing grace(1): *a graceful dancer*.

grace·ful·ly /-fəlɪ/ adv

gra·cious /ˈɡreɪʃəs/ adj **1** pleasant; kind; polite: *a gracious wave/smile*. **2** (of God) merciful. **3** (used in exclamations to express surprise): *Good gracious! Goodness gracious!*

gra·cious·ly adv

gra·cious·ness nu

gra·da·tion /ɡrəˈdeɪʃn/ nc (*formal*) a step, stage or degree in development: *gradations of width/colour/difficulty*.

grade¹ /ɡreɪd/ nc **1** a step, stage or degree in rank, quality, value etc: *The rank of major is one grade higher than that of captain. This pupil has a high grade of intelligence*. **2** a mark (e.g. 80%) or rating (e.g. 'Excellent' or 'Fair') given to a student for work done. **make the grade** (*informal*) to reach a good standard; do as well as is required.

grade² /ɡreɪd/ vt **1** to put (things, people etc) in order in grades(1): *graded by size/intelligence*. **2** to make land (esp for roads) more level by reducing the slope.

gradi·ent /ˈɡreɪdɪənt/ nc an amount, degree, of the slope of land etc.

grad·ual /ˈɡrædjʊəl/ adj taking place, changing, slowly or a little at a time: *a gradual improvement/increase/decline*.

grad·ual·ly /-djʊlɪ/ adv

grad·uate¹ /ˈɡrædjʊət/ nc **1** (also *attrib*) (*GB*) a person who holds a university degree: *London graduates; a graduate student; post-graduate studies*. **2** (*US*) a person who has completed a course at an educational institution: *high-school graduates*.

grad·uate² /ˈɡrædjʊeɪt/ v **1** vi **graduate (from a college or university) (in a subject)** to complete an academic course successfully: *graduate from the London School of Economics. I graduated in philosophy*. **2** vt to mark (something) with degrees for measuring: *a ruler graduated with centimetres*.

gradu·ation /ˌɡrædjʊˈeɪʃn/ n (**a**) nu the act of graduating or being graduated. (**b**) nc a ceremony at which university degrees are conferred.

graf·fi·ti /ɡrəˈfiːtɪ/ n pl (*It*) drawings, words etc painted or written on a hard surface, esp a wall.

graft¹ /ɡrɑːft/ nc **1** a shoot from a branch or twig of a living tree, fixed in another tree to form a new growth. **2** (in surgery) a piece of skin, bone etc from a living person or animal, transplanted on another body or another part of the same body.

graft² /ɡrɑːft/ nc,nu (*derog*) (an instance of) getting business advantages, profit-making etc by taking wrong advantage of connections in politics etc.

graft³ /ɡrɑːft/ vt **graft sth (on/onto sth)** to put a graft¹(1,2) on something: *graft new skin (on a nose/onto a wound)*.

grain /ɡreɪn/ n **1** nu the small, hard seed of food plants such as wheat and rice: *a cargo of grain*. **2**

nc a single seed of such a plant: *eat up every grain of rice.* **3** *nc* a tiny, hard bit: *grains of sand/sugar.* **4** *nc* (*fig*) a small amount: *a boy without a grain of intelligence.* **5** *nu* the natural arrangement or pattern of lines in wood etc as seen on a surface that has been sawn or cut: *woods of fine/coarse grain.* **be/go against the grain** (*fig*) to be undesirable, unpleasant.

gram·mar /ˈgræmə(r)/ *nu* (the scientific study of) rules for the combination of words into sentences (called *syntax*), and the forms of words (called *morphology*).

'grammar school *nc* (*GB*) a kind of secondary school for children wishing to go to college or university. Compare comprehensive.

gram·mar·ian /grəˈmeərɪən/ *nc* an expert in grammar.

gram·mati·cal /grəˈmætɪkl/ *adj* of, conforming to, the rules of grammar: *a grammatical error.* Opp ungrammatical.

gram·mati·cal·ly /-klɪ/ *adv*

gram (also **gramme**) /græm/ (*abbr* g or gm) *nc* a metric unit of weight (the weight of one cubic centimetre of water at maximum density).

gramo·phone /ˈgræməfəʊn/ *nc* (*dated* but still used in the expression *gramophone record*) = record-player.

gran·ary /ˈgrænərɪ/ *nc* (*pl* **-ies**) a storehouse for grain.

grand /grænd/ *adj* (**—er, —est**) **1** (*attrib*) magnificent; splendid: *living in grand style.* **2** (*derog*) self-important and proud: *He puts on a very grand manner/air.* **3** (*informal*) very fine or enjoyable: *We had a grand time. The weather's grand!* **4** (*attrib*) full; complete: *the grand total* (i.e. including everything).

,grand fi'nale *nc* ⇨ finale.

,grand-'master *nc* (*chess*) a player of high standard.

,grand pi'ano *nc* a large piano with horizontal strings.

Grand Prix /ˌgrɒn 'priː/ *nc* (*motor-racing*) one of several international races.

'grand·stand *nc* a covered place in a stadium with seats for spectators.

,grand 'tour *nc* a tour of the major cultural centres and sights of a region or country.

grand·ly *adv*

grand- *prefix* (showing one generation back).

'grand·aunt/·uncle *nc* (*US*) an aunt/uncle of one's father or mother.

'grand·child/·daughter/·son *nc* a daughter/son of one's daughter or son.

'grand·father/·mother *nc* the father/mother of one's father or mother.

'grand·father clock *nc* a clock in a tall wooden case.

'grand·nephew/·niece *nc* (*US*) a son/daughter of one's nephew or niece.

gran·dad (also **grand-dad**) /ˈgrændæd/ *nc* (*informal*) = grandfather.

gran·deur /ˈgrændʒə(r)/ *nu* (*formal*) greatness; magnificence: *the grandeur of the Swiss Alps; a man with delusions of grandeur.*

gran·di·ose /ˈgrændɪəʊs/ *adj* (*formal*) planned on an impressive scale (often foolishly): *grandiose ideas.*

grand·ma /ˈgrænmɑː/ *nc* (*informal*) = grandmother.

grand·pa /ˈgrænpɑː/ *nc* (*informal*) = grandfather.

grange /greɪndʒ/ *nc* a country house with farm buildings attached.

gran·ite /ˈgrænɪt/ *nu* a kind of hard, grey stone, used for building.

gran·ny (also **gran·nie**) /ˈgrænɪ/ *nc* (*pl* **-ies**) (*informal*) = grandmother.

grant¹ /grɑːnt/ *nc* something granted, esp money from a government: *grants towards the cost of a university education.*

grant² /grɑːnt/ *vt* **1** (*formal*) to give or allow (what is asked for): *grant a favour/request.* **2** to agree (that something is true): *He's a nice person, I'll grant you that.* Ⓝ Not used in continuous tenses, e.g. *is/was -ing.* **take sth for granted** to accept it as true or as certain without discussion.

granu·lar /ˈgrænjʊlə(r)/ *adj* of, like, grains.

granu·lat·ed /ˈgrænjʊleɪtɪd/ *adj* in the form of grains: *granulated sugar.*

gran·ule /ˈgrænjuːl/ *nc* a tiny, hard bit.

grape /greɪp/ *nc* a green or purple berry growing in clusters on vines, as used for making wine: *a bunch of grapes.* **sour grapes** criticism about something that one cannot get but would like to have: *She said that she wouldn't want to go to such a party even if she were invited—but that was just sour grapes.*

'grape-vine *nc* (**a**) a kind of vine on which grapes grow. (**b**) (*fig*) a means by which news gets about, e.g. in an office, school or a group of friends: *I heard on the grape-vine that Jill is to be promoted.*

grape·fruit /ˈgreɪpfruːt/ *nc* (*pl* **—** or **—s**) a (usually yellow) fruit like a large orange but with a sour taste.

graph /grɑːf/ *nc* a diagram consisting of a line or lines showing the variation of two related quantities, e.g. the temperature at each hour.

'graph paper *nu* paper printed with small squares of equal size.

graph·ic /ˈgræfɪk/ *adj* **1** (*attrib*) of visual symbols (e.g. lettering, diagrams, drawings): *a graphic artist.* **2** (of descriptions) giving a clear and easily understood image: *a graphic account of the battle.*

graphi·cal·ly /-klɪ/ *adv* (**a**) using graphs, writing or diagrams. (**b**) in a way that is clear and easily understood: *describe the quarrel graphically.*

,graphic 'equalizer *nc* a part of a system for playing records and tapes that allows different frequencies within the total sound to be adjusted to suit the listener and that shows how each is set.

graph·ics /ˈgræfɪks/ *nu* the art, process, of producing diagrams, drawings, graphs etc: *Computer graphics are an important aid to business management.*

grapple /ˈgræpl/ *vi* **grapple (with sb/sth) 1** to hold and struggle with: *grapple with a thief.* **2** (*fig*) to try to deal with (a problem etc): *grappling with staff problems.*

grasp¹ /grɑːsp/ *nc* (usually *sing*) **1** a firm hold or grip: *a strong grasp.* **2** (*fig*) a strong hold, understanding, attraction etc: *in the grasp of a cruel parent; have a thorough grasp of the problem; a problem within/beyond my grasp* (= that I can/cannot understand).

grasp² /grɑːsp/ *vt* **1** to seize (a person, thing)

firmly with the hand(s) or arm(s): *grasp his hand/
a rope.* **2** to understand: *grasp an argument/her
meaning.* **3 *grasp (at) sth*** to accept a chance etc
eagerly: *grasp (at) an opportunity.*

grasp·ing *adj* (*derog*) greedy (for money etc):
He's so grasping.

grass /grɑːs/ *n* **1** *nu* (an area covered with) any
common, wild, low-growing, green plant: *sitting
on the grass.* **2** *nc* (*science*) any species of this kind
of plant (including cereals, reeds and bamboos).

'grass·land *nu* an area of land covered with
grass where there are few trees. Compare lawn.

,grass 'roots *n pl* (also *attrib*) ordinary people,
especially in relation to politics: *a grass-roots
rebellion.*

,grass 'widow *nc* a wife whose husband is temporarily not living with her, e.g. because of work.

gras·sy *adj* (**-ier, -iest**) covered with grass.

grass·hopper /'grɑːshɒpə(r)/ *nc* a kind of
jumping insect which makes a shrill, chirping
noise.

grate¹ /greɪt/ *nc* (a metal frame for holding coal
etc in) a fireplace.

grate² /greɪt/ *n sing* a harsh noise made by scraping (esp metals): *the grate of a door on its hinges.*

grate³ /greɪt/ *v* **1** *vt* to rub (esp food) into small
pieces: *grate cheese.* **2** *vi* **grate (on sth)** to make
a harsh noise by rubbing: *The gate grates on its
hinges.* **3** *vi* **grate (on sb)** (*fig*) to have an irritating effect (on a person): *His bad manners grated
on everyone.*

grater *nc* a utensil with a rough surface, used for
grating food etc: *a cheese grater.*

grate·ful /'greɪtfəl/ *adj* (usually *pred*) feeling or
showing thanks: *We are grateful to you for your
help.* ⇨ gratitude.

grate·ful·ly /-fəlɪ/ *adv*

grat·ify /'grætɪfaɪ/ *vt* (*pt,pp* **-ied**) (*formal*) **1** to
give pleasure or satisfaction to (a person): *I'm
gratified to know that you have been successful.* **2**
to give what is desired to satisfy (interest etc):
gratify a child's curiosity. Ⓝ *'Satisfy'* is more usual.

grat·ify·ing *adj* (*formal*) pleasing: *It is very grat-
ifying to know that you like this dictionary.*

grati·fi·ca·tion /,grætɪfɪ'keɪʃn/ *nc,nu*

grat·ing /'greɪtɪŋ/ *nc* a framework of wooden or
metal bars placed across an opening such as a window, used to keep out burglars or to allow air to
flow through.

grati·tude /'grætɪtjuːd/ *nu* the state of being
grateful: *We showed our gratitude by buying him a
present.*

gra·tu·itous /grə'tjuːɪtəs/ *adj* **1** given, obtained
or done without payment: *gratuitous service/
information/help/advice.* **2** done or given without
good reason: *gratuitous violence in some films.*

gra·tu·itous·ly *adv*

gra·tu·ity /grə'tjuːətɪ/ *nc* (*pl* **-ies**) **1** a gift (of
money in addition to pay or a pension) to a retir-
ing employee for her or his services. **2** (*formal*) a
gift of money to a porter, waiter etc.

grave¹ /greɪv/ *adj* (**—r, —st**) serious; very sad
and disappointing: *grave news.* ⇨ gravity(2).

grave·ly *adv: gravely ill.*

grave² /greɪv/ *nc* (a place with) a hole dug in the
ground for a dead body. **have one foot in the
grave** ⇨ foot¹(1).

'grave·stone *nc* a stone over a grave, with the

name etc of the person buried there.

'grave·yard *nc* a cemetery.

grave³ /grɑːv/ *nc* (also *grave accent*) the mark (`)
placed over a vowel to indicate how it is to be
sounded (as in French *mère*).

grav·el /'grævl/ *nu* a mixture of small stones with
coarse sand, used for roads and paths. □ *vt* (**-ll-,**
US also **-l-**) to cover (a path etc) with gravel.

gravi·tate /'grævɪteɪt/ *vi* **gravitate towards a
place** to move towards or be attracted to: *gravitate towards the cities.*

grav·ity /'grævətɪ/ *nu* **1** the force of attraction
between any two objects, esp that force which
attracts objects towards the centre of the earth:
Gravity makes things fall to the ground. **2** the
quality of being serious, dangerous etc: *the gravity of the international situation.*

gra·vy /'greɪvɪ/ *nu* (a sauce made using) the juice
which comes from meat while it is cooking.

'gravy-boat *nc* a jug in which gravy is served at
table.

gray /greɪ/ *adj, nu* (*US*) = grey.

graze¹ /greɪz/ *nc* a place where the skin has been
scraped or rubbed.

graze² /greɪz/ *vt* **1** to touch or scrape (something)
lightly in passing: *My handlebars grazed the corner as I rode round it.* **2** to scrape, rub, (the skin):
The boy grazed his knees when he fell.

graze³ /greɪz/ **1** *vi* (of cattle, sheep etc) to eat
growing grass: *cattle grazing in the fields.* **2** *vt* to
put (cattle etc) in fields to graze.

grease¹ /griːs/ *nu* **1** animal fat, esp when semi-
liquid. **2** any similar semi-liquid substance as used
in engines, cosmetics etc.

grease² /griːs/ *vt* to put or rub grease(2) in or on
(esp parts of a machine).

'grease-gun *nc* a device used for forcing
grease(2) into the parts of an engine, machine etc.

'grease-paint *nu* make-up used by actors.

'grease-proof *adj* not letting grease pass
through: *greaseproof paper.*

greasy /'griːsɪ/ *adj* (**-ier, -iest**) covered with
grease: *greasy fingers; a greasy road.*

great /greɪt/ *adj* (**—er, —est**) **1** well above average (in amount, size, extent): *a great amount of
work; a great number of supporters; a great quantity of vegetables; a great deal of talking; buildings
of great size.* Compare small¹(1). Ⓝ For a comparison of *great*, *big* and *large*, ⇨ big(1). **2** (used with
uncountable nouns) a lot of: *great generosity/
hunger/distress/joy; take great care of her.* **3** of
much more than average importance: *a great
friend of mine; a great occasion/event; a great
nation; a great moment in history.* Ⓝ For a comparison of *great* and *big*, ⇨ big(3). **4** having, showing,
special ability: *a great painter/musician/states-
man; a great work of art.* Ⓝ *'Big'* is not possible. **5**
(*informal*) splendid: *We had a great time in Paris.*
6 (*informal*) (used to show irritation, dislike etc,
according to the situation): *You great fool! Take
your great big head out of my light!* Compare little,
small.

,Great 'Britain *n* (*abbr* GB) England, Wales and
Scotland excluding Northern Ireland.

great·ly *adv* much; by much: *greatly amused.*

great·ness *nu*

great- *prefix* (showing one more generation back
than *grand-*): *my great-aunt/uncle/niece/nephew.*

ˌgreat-ˈgrandfather / ˌgreat-ˈgrand-mother nc one's mother's or father's grandfather/grandmother.

ˌgreat-great-ˈgrandfather / ˌgreat-great-ˈgrandmother nc one's grandmother's or grandfather's grandfather/grandmother.

greed /griːd/ nu the strong desire for more food, money etc, esp more than is right or reasonable.

greedy /ˈgriːdɪ/ adj (-ier, -iest) (derog) filled with greed: I'm not hungry, just greedy. He's greedy for success/honours.
greed·ily /-əlɪ/ adv
greedi·ness nu

green¹ /griːn/ adj (—er, —est) 1 of the colour of growing grass. **give sb/get the green light** to give/get permission to begin an activity. 2 (of the complexion) pale; looking ill: green with envy (= very jealous). 3 (of fruit etc) not ripe: green tomatoes/bananas. 4 (pred; informal) inexperienced; untrained: He's still green at his job. 5 (pred; informal) easily deceived: I'm not so green as to believe that.

ˌgreen ˈbelt nc a wide area of land round a town, where building is controlled so that there can be fields, woods etc.

ˌgreen ˈcard nc a document proving car insurance for overseas travel.

ˌgreen ˈfingers n pl (informal) skill in gardening.

ˈgreen·fly nc a kind of small insect (in science, called an aphid).

ˈgreen·gage /-geɪdʒ/ nc a kind of plum with greenish-yellow skin and flesh.

ˈgreen·grocer nc a shopkeeper selling vegetables and fruit.

ˈgreen·house nc a glass building used for growing plants.

ˌgreen ˈtea nu a kind of tea made from steam-dried leaves.

green² /griːn/ n 1 nc,nu the colour green: a girl dressed in green; a picture in greens and blues. 2 nc an area of land with growing grass that is (a) used by people in a community: the village green; (b) used for games such as golf.

green·ery /ˈgriːnərɪ/ nu green leaves and plants: the greenery of the woods in spring.

green·ish /ˈgriːnɪʃ/ adj a little green in colour (esp used in compounds): greenish-yellow.

greens /griːnz/ n pl kinds of leafy vegetables, boiled as food.

greet /griːt/ vt 1 to welcome (a person) on meeting: greet a friend by saying 'Good morning!'; greet someone with a smile. 2 (formal) (of sights and sounds) to meet the eyes and ears of (a person): the view that greeted us at the hill top; be greeted by a loud cheer.

greet·ing nc the first words or act used when meeting a person or writing to a person: 'Good morning' and 'Dear Sir' are greetings.

greg·ari·ous /grɪˈgeərɪəs/ adj 1 living in groups or societies: People are naturally gregarious. 2 liking the company of others: a gregarious child.

gre·nade /grɪˈneɪd/ nc a kind of small bomb (to be) thrown by hand.

grew /gruː/ pt of grow.

grey¹ (US = **gray**) /greɪ/ adj (—er, —est) nu (of) the colour between black and white, coloured like ashes: His hair has turned grey.

grey·ish /ˈgreɪɪʃ/ adj a little grey.

grey² (US = **gray**) /greɪ/ vi (of hair, the sky etc) to become grey in colour.

grey·hound /ˈgreɪhaʊnd/ nc a kind of thin, long-legged dog, able to run fast and used in racing.

grid /grɪd/ nc 1 a system of overhead cables carried on pylons, for distributing electric current over a large area. 2 a net-work of squares on maps, numbered for reference. 3 a set of bars over a hole in a road (a cattle-grid) or over a drain.

griddle /ˈgrɪdl/ nc a circular iron plate, used for cooking cakes.

grief /griːf/ n 1 nu deep or great sorrow: die of grief. ⇨ grieve. 2 nc something causing grief: His failure was a lasting grief to his parents. 3 nu **bring sb/come to grief** (to cause a person) to experience misfortune, injury or ruin.

griev·ance /ˈgriːvəns/ nc **grievance (against sb/sth)** a real or imagined cause for complaint or protest: A strike seemed to be the only way of expressing their grievances (e.g. against the government).

grieve /griːv/ vi **grieve (for sb; over sb/sth)** to suffer grief (because of a person, thing): grieve for the dead/over his death.

griev·ous /ˈgriːvəs/ adj (attrib; formal) severe: grievous pain; grievous bodily harm (as when a person injures another in a robbery etc).
griev·ous·ly adv

grill¹ /grɪl/ nc 1 a place in a cooker where food is cooked below the heat; the food cooked. 2 a set of bars for cooking food over a fire.

grill² /grɪl/ v 1 vt,vi to cook (food) under or over a grill(1,2). 2 vi (fig) to expose oneself to great heat: lie grilling in the hot sun. 3 vt (e.g. of the police) to question (a person) severely and without stopping: They grilled him for hours but he refused to give any names.

grille /grɪl/ nc a series of metal bars in an opening such as a window, as used in banks.

grim /grɪm/ adj (—mer, —mest) serious and severe; determined: a grim struggle; a grim smile/expression. **hold on like grim death** to hold on very firmly.
grim·ly adv
grim·ness nu

gri·mace /grɪˈmeɪs/ vi, nc (to make) a twisted expression of pain, disgust etc: He grimaced as the needle went in.

grime /graɪm/ nu (a coating of) dirt on the surface of something or on the body: a face covered with grime and sweat.

grimy /ˈgraɪmɪ/ adj (-ier, -iest) covered with grime.

grin¹ /grɪn/ nc an act, instance, of grinning.

grin² /grɪn/ vi (-nn-) to smile broadly so as to show the teeth, expressing amusement, satisfaction etc: grinning at the camera; grinning with delight; grin from ear to ear. **grin and bear it** to bear pain, disappointment etc without complaining.

grind¹ /graɪnd/ n 1 nc an act of grinding(1,2). 2 n sing (informal; derog) a long, boring task: Is learning English a grind?

grind² /graɪnd/ vt (pt,pp **ground** /graʊnd/) 1 to crush (a substance) to grains or powder: grind coffee beans; grind corn into flour. 2 to polish, shape or sharpen (something) by rubbing it on or

with a rough, hard surface: *grind a lens/knife.* ⇨
axe[1]. **3** to rub (something) harshly, esp with a circular motion: *grind one's teeth (together); grind
one's heel into the ground; grind dirt into the carpet.* **4 grind to a halt** ⇨ halt[1](2).
    grind away (at sth) *(informal)* to work with
great effort (at a task etc).
    grind sb down to make a person poor,
depressed, troubled (by using cruel or unfair
treatment). **grind sth down** to crush corn etc
into powder.
    grind on to make slow progress: *The war ground
on.*
grind·er /'graɪndə(r)/ *nc* an apparatus for grinding: *a coffee-grinder.*
grip[1] /grɪp/ *n* **1** *n sing* an act, manner or power of
gripping: *let go one's grip of a rope; have a good
grip* (fig = understanding) *of a problem; have a
good grip on an audience* (= hold their attention
and interest). **be at/come to/get to grips
with sth** to be attacking/begin to attack: *get to
grips with a problem.* **2** *nc* (dated) a small bag for
travelling: *a leather grip.*
grip[2] /grɪp/ *v* (**-pp-**) **1** *vt,vi* to take and keep a firm
hold of (a person, thing): *The frightened child
gripped its mother's hand. The brakes failed to
grip and the car ran into a wall.* **2** *vt* to hold the
attention of (a person): *The speaker gripped the
attention of his audience.*
grip·ping *adj* holding one's attention or interest:
The film is a gripping story of love and hate.
gris·ly /'grɪzlɪ/ *adj* causing horror or terror: *The
dead animal was a grisly sight.*
gristle /'grɪsl/ *nu* tough, elastic tissue in animal
bodies, esp in meat.
grit[1] /grɪt/ *nu* **1** tiny, hard bits of stone, sand etc:
spread grit on icy roads. **2** the quality of courage
and determination: *have plenty of grit.*
grit·ty *adj* (**-ier, -iest**) like, covered with,
grit(1).
grit[2] /grɪt/ *vt* (**-tt-**) **1** to spread grit on (a path etc):
grit the road when it snows. **2 grit one's teeth**
to keep the jaws tight together to show effort,
determination.
grizzle /'grɪzl/ *vi* (informal) (esp of children) to
cry irritably.
groan[1] /grəʊn/ *nc* a groaning sound.
groan[2] /grəʊn/ *vi* **1** to make a deep sound forced
out by pain, despair or distress: *The wounded
men lay there groaning. The teacher groaned with
dismay.* **2** (of things) to make a noise like that of
groaning: *The ship groaned during the storm.*
gro·cer /'grəʊsə(r)/ *nc* a shopkeeper who sells
food in packets, tins and bottles, and household
requirements such as polish, soap powders etc.
gro·cer·ies *n pl* items (to be) bought in a supermarket etc.
gro·cery *adj* (attrib): *a grocery store.*
grog·gy /'grɒgɪ/ *adj* (**-ier, -iest**) likely to collapse or fall: *You look rather groggy.*
groin /grɔɪn/ *nc* (anat) the front part of the body
below the stomach near the top of the legs.
groom[1] /gruːm/ *nc* **1** a person in charge of
horses. **2** = bridegroom.
groom[2] /gruːm/ *vt* **1** to feed, brush and in other
ways look after horses. **2** (of animals) to clean the
fur and skin: *a female ape grooming her mate.* **3**
(used in the *pp*) (of a person): *well/badly*

groomed (= looking/not looking clean and
smart). **4** (informal) to prepare (a person) for
success etc: *be groomed for stardom.*
groove /gruːv/ *nc* **1** a long, hollow area in the
surface of a hard material, esp one made for
something that slides along it, e.g. a sliding door
or window. **2** a spiral cut on a gramophone record
(in which the needle moves). **3** (fig) a way of living that has become a habit: *be in a groove.*
grope /grəʊp/ *vi,vt* to feel about, search for
(something), as one does in the dark: *He was
groping (about) for the door handle.*
gross[1] /grəʊs/ *adj* **1** (attrib) (of something
wrong) very obvious: *gross injustice/negligence.* **2**
(of a person) extremely fat. **3** (attrib; commerce,
finance) the total, whole: *his gross income.*
    'gross profit *nc* (finance) the profit after the
cost of materials etc has been taken off the
receipts from sales. Compare net profit.
gross·ly *adv*
gross[2] /grəʊs/ *nc* (pl —) (commerce) twelve
dozen; 144.
gross[3] /grəʊs/ *vt* to make or earn (a total
amount): *His last film grossed five million pounds.*
gro·tesque /grəʊ'tesk/ *adj* strange, ugly and
unnatural: *a grotesque appearance.*
gro·tesque·ly *adv*
grot·to /'grɒtəʊ/ *n* (pl **—es** or **—s**) a cave, esp an
attractive (artificial) one.
grot·ty /'grɒtɪ/ *adj* (**-ier, -iest**) (sl; derog) dirty;
unpleasant; bad: *a grotty idea/person/hotel.*
grouch /graʊtʃ/ *vi, nc* (informal) (to show) a fit
of bad temper.
ground[1] /graʊnd/ *n* **1** *nu* (or the —) (a part of)
the solid surface of the earth: *lie flat on/fall to/sit
on the ground. The house is on stony ground.*
above ground alive. **below ground/under
the ground** dead and buried. Compare under-
ground(1). **down to the ground** completely:
*The new arrangements suit me down to the
ground.* **on the ground** present: *I hope the staff
on the ground can deal with the problem.* **thin on
the ground** difficult to find or obtain: *Good
workers are thin on the ground.* **break fresh/
new ground** to begin work in a new area of
study. **cover the ground** to deal adequately
with a topic (e.g. in a book or lecture). **cover
much/some/the same etc ground** (of a
report or inquiry) to deal with a lot of/some/the
same information, questions etc. **gain ground**
(of a new idea etc) to become increasingly
accepted. **gain ground (on sb)** to get closer (to
a person one is trying to catch). **get off the
ground** (of a scheme etc) to make a successful
beginning. **give ground (to sb)** to fail to keep
one's advantage (over a person). **hold one's
ground** to maintain one's position (e.g. in an
argument, competition etc). **have/keep one's
feet on the ground** ⇨ foot[1](1). **lose ground
(to sb)** = give ground (to sb). **meet sb on
her/his own ground** to meet in the place
where a person lives, works etc. **run sb/sth to
ground** to find a person or thing after a long
search. **stand one's ground** to refuse to give
in (e.g. in an argument). **2** *nu* soil: *bury a bone
in the ground.* **3** *nc* an area of land used for a
purpose: *a football ground; a playground; a
parade ground.* **4** (pl) land, gardens round a

large house or buildings: *walk round the grounds of the hospital/university.* **5** (*pl*) small pieces of solid matter: *coffee grounds.* ⇨ grind²(1). **6** (*pl*) **grounds (for sth)** reasons for believing, acting etc in a certain way: *On what grounds?* (= For what reason) *do you suspect him? What are the grounds for divorce/for calling her a liar? I hope you have good grounds* (i.e. satisfactory reasons) *for calling the fire brigade.* ⇨ groundless.

'**ground control** *nu* the control of a plane (e.g. in an airport) from the ground.

,**ground 'floor** *nc* the floor of a building level with the ground.

'**ground·nut** *nc* = peanut.

'**ground rule** *nc* a basic principle.

'**ground·sheet** *nc* a waterproof sheet spread on the ground, e.g. in a tent.

'**ground speed** *nc* a plane's speed in relation to the ground.

'**ground·work** *nu* (*fig*) the preparation or first stages of a piece of work.

ground² /graʊnd/ *v* **1** *vi* (of a ship) to touch the sea bottom. **2** *vt* to order, force, (a plane) to stay on the ground: *All aircraft at London Airport were grounded by fog yesterday.*

ground³ /graʊnd/ *pt,pp* of grind².

ground·ing /'graʊndɪŋ/ *n sing* a thorough teaching of the basic details of a subject: *a good grounding in grammar.*

ground·less /'graʊndlɪs/ *adj* without good reason: *groundless fears.* ⇨ ground¹(6).

group¹ /gruːp/ *nc* a number of people or things gathered or placed together, or naturally associated: *a group of islands/trees/houses/girls/languages.*

'**group captain** *nc* (abbr Gp Capt) an officer above a squadron leader in the British air force.

,**group 'practice** *nc* a medical practice with several doctors sharing responsibilities.

,**group 'therapy** *nu* treatment for people with similar mental or emotional disorders who share their problems in discussions.

group² /gruːp/ *vt,vi* (to cause people, things) to form into a group or groups: *We were grouped according to age and ability. They were grouped round the painting. All the papers were grouped together in the files.*

grouse¹ /graʊs/ *nc* (*pl* unchanged) (a kind of) bird with feathered feet, shot for food.

grouse² /graʊs/ *vi, nc* (*informal*) (to make) a complaint.

grove /grəʊv/ *nc* a small group of trees.

grov·el /'grɒvl/ *vi* (-ll-, *US* also -l-) to behave in a way that shows one has no self-respect: *You can stop grovelling because I won't change my mind about sacking you.*

grov·el·ler *nc* (*derog*) a person who grovels.

grow /grəʊ/ *v* (*pt* **grew** /gruː/, *pp* **grown** /grəʊn/) **1** *vi* to increase in size, height, length etc; develop: *Rice grows in warm climates. Buy a larger bike because you're growing fast at the moment. How tall you've grown!* **2** *vt* to cause or allow (plants; one's hair, beard, nails etc) to develop and increase in size: *grow vegetables/flowers; grow a beard/one's fringe.* **3** *vi* to become gradually: *grow old/dark/rich/sad.* **grow to** + *verb* to reach the stage when one does something: *He grew to like his new boss. I've grown to enjoy*

modern jazz.

grow away from sb to stop loving, feeling friendly towards, a person gradually: *After going to university I seem to have grown away from my school friends.*

grow (sth) from sth (**a**) (to cause something) to develop using something as a source: *grow flowers from seed.* (**b**) to have something as its origin: *My interest in words grew from my studies at university.*

grow in sth to increase in size, quality: *grow in size/strength/importance/wisdom.*

grow into sb/sth to become a particular kind after a period of time: *grow into a beautiful woman/attractive dog/magnificent tree.* **grow into sth** to increase in size until one fits clothing: *grow into a school shirt.*

grow on sb (**a**) to become gradually more deeply rooted: *a habit that grows on you.* (**b**) to gradually become more attractive, pleasing: *I didn't like her music/painting/clothes at first, but they certainly grow on you.*

grow out of sth (**a**) to gradually become too big for clothing: *grow out of a school sweater.* ⇨ outgrow. (**b**) to abandon behaviour, habits etc as one gets older: *grow out of one's need for a father's advice/one's childish behaviour.* (**c**) to have something as its origin or cause: *The idea for a new sports centre grew out of the report on local amenities.*

grow (sth) over sth (to cause something) to cover something: *Weeds grew over the flower beds. I'm growing a rose over the fence.*

grow up (**a**) to develop into an adult: *I want to be a pilot when I grow up.* ⇨ grown-up. (**b**) to behave, think, like an adult: *When will you grow up?* (**c**) to develop: *A close friendship has grown up between them.* **grow up into sb** = grow into sb.

grow upon sb (*formal*) = grow on sb.

grow·er /'grəʊə(r)/ *nc* **1** a person who grows things: *a fruit-grower; rose-growers.* **2** a plant etc that grows in the way mentioned: *a fast grower.*

growl /graʊl/ *vi, nc* (of a person, animal) (to make) a low, threatening sound: *The dog/old man growled at me.*

grown /grəʊn/ **1** *pp* of grow. **2** *adj* (*attrib*): *a grown man/woman* (= a physically or mentally mature person).

grown-up /'grəʊn ʌp/ *nc* an adult.

growth /grəʊθ/ *n* **1** *nu* the process of growing or developing: *the rapid growth of our economy.* **2** *nc* an amount of something that grows or has grown: *three days' growth of beard.* **3** *nc* a diseased formation in the body, e.g. a cancer.

grub¹ /grʌb/ *n* **1** *nc* a first stage (*larva*) of an insect. **2** *nu* (*sl*) food.

grub² /grʌb/ *vi* (-bb-) to turn over the soil, esp in order to get something: *grubbing about among the bushes for food.*

grub·by /'grʌbɪ/ *adj* (-ier, -iest) dirty; unwashed: *a boy with grubby fingers.*

grudge¹ /grʌdʒ/ *nc* a feeling of dislike, envy with a little anger. **bear sb a grudge; have a grudge against sb** to feel a grudge towards a person.

grudge² /grʌdʒ/ *vt* to be unwilling to give or accept (something): *I don't grudge him his suc-*

grudg·ingly adv: to agree grudgingly.

gruel /'gru:əl/ nu liquid food of oatmeal etc boiled in water.

gruel·ling (US **gruel·ing**) /'gru:əlɪŋ/ adj exhausting: a gruelling race.

grue·some /'gru:səm/ adj causing horror and disgust: gruesome details of the murder.

grue·some·ly adv

gruff /grʌf/ adj (of a person, voice, behaviour) rough and abrupt.

gruff·ly adv

grumble[1] /'grʌmbl/ nc a complaint or protest: That girl's full of grumbles.

grumble[2] /'grʌmbl/ v 1 vi,vt **grumble (about sth/at sb)** to complain or protest in a bad-tempered way: He's always grumbling (about something). He grumbled a reply. 2 vi to make a low, rumbling sound: thunder grumbling in the distance.

grum·bler nc (derog) a person who grumbles.

grumpy /'grʌmpi/ adj (**-ier, -iest**) (informal; derog) a little bad-tempered.

grump·ily adv

grumpi·ness nu

grunt[1] /grʌnt/ nc a deep, rough sound.

grunt[2] /grʌnt/ v 1 vi (of animals, esp pigs) to make a deep, rough sound. 2 vt,vi (of a person) to make a similar sound expressing disagreement, boredom, irritation etc: grunt one's approval.

gt written abbr great.

gtd (commerce) written abbr guaranteed.

guar·an·tee[1] /ˌgærən'ti:/ nc 1 a formal promise or agreement that certain conditions agreed (e.g. when one buys something) will be fulfilled: a watch with a year's guarantee. 2 a formal promise given by one person to another that he or she will be responsible for payment of a debt. 3 something offered as security for the fulfilling of conditions in a guarantee(1,2): What guarantee can you offer? 4 (informal) something that seems to make an occurrence likely: Blue skies are not always a guarantee of warm weather.

guar·an·tee[2] /ˌgærən'ti:/ vt 1 to give a guarantee for (something): guarantee a camera for a year; guarantee a man's debts; guarantee to pay a man's debts. We can't guarantee our workers regular employment. 2 (informal) to promise (something) (without legal obligation): I guarantee you'll like it!

guar·an·tor /ˌgærən'tɔ:(r)/ nc a person who gives a guarantee(2).

guar·an·ty /ˌgærən'ti:/ nc (pl **-ies**) (legal) a guarantee(1,2,3).

guard[1] /gɑ:d/ n 1 nu a state of readiness or watchfulness against attack, danger or surprise: The soldier is on guard/was ordered to keep guard. 2 nu (esp **on guard**) a position of readiness to defend oneself, e.g. in fencing, boxing. 3 nc a soldier or group of soldiers keeping guard. 4 nc (GB) an official in charge of a train. 5 (pl; often the G-s) (in GB and some other countries) troops used to protect the sovereign: the Royal Horse Guards. 6 nc (also called warder) an official in charge of prisoners in a prison. 7 nc an apparatus designed to protect: a fire-guard (in front of a fireplace); a mudguard (over the wheel of a bicycle).

guard[2] /gɑ:d/ vt 1 to protect (a person, thing) from danger: guard a camp; guard a bank against thieves. 2 to watch over (a person) to prevent escape: guard prisoners. 3 **guard against sth** to use care and caution to prevent something: guard against disease/infection.

guard·ed adj (of statements etc) cautious: a guarded answer.

guard·ian /'gɑ:dɪən/ nc 1 a person who is legally responsible for the care of a child and her or his property. 2 a person, institution etc that protects: The police are guardians of law and order.

guardian 'angel nc a spirit which protects a person or place.

guard·ian·ship /-ʃɪp/ nu the position of a guardian(1).

gua·va /'gwɑ:və/ nc (pl **-s**) (also attrib) (a tropical tree with) a fruit with pink flesh and many seeds.

guer·ril·la (also **guer·i·lla**) /gə'rɪlə/ nc (pl **-s**) a person engaged in a guerrilla war.

guer,rilla 'war nc,nu fighting by small groups of civilians, usually for a political cause.

guess[1] /ges/ nc 1 **guess (at sth)** an attempt at guessing: have/make/take a guess at the answer. **an educated guess** one based on experience. 2 an opinion, idea, formed by guessing: My guess is that she's over fifty. **be anyone's guess** to be difficult to guess correctly.

guess[2] /ges/ vt,vi to form an opinion, give an answer, make a statement about (something) that is not based on very careful thought, calculation or definite knowledge: Can you guess my weight/what my weight is/how much I weigh? Guess how much I weigh. He guessed my age.

'guess·work nu (a result of) guessing: use guesswork.

guest /gest/ nc 1 a person staying at or paying a visit to another's house or being entertained at a meal: We're having guests to dinner. 2 a person who is invited out, e.g. to a concert, without having to pay: You're my guest for tonight. 3 a person paying to stay in a hotel.

'guest·house nc a private house offering rooms to paying guests.

guf·faw /gʌ'fɔ:/ vi, nc (to give) a noisy laugh.

guid·ance /'gaɪdəns/ nu advice or help on educational, personal, career etc matters.

guide[1] /gaɪd/ nc 1 a person who shows others the way, esp a person employed to point out interesting sights on a journey or visit. 2 something that directs or influences (conduct, etc): Instinct is not always a good guide. 3 a book used by travellers, tourists etc with information about a place: a guide to the British Museum. 4 a book of practical information: a guide to growing roses. 5 (G-) a member of an organization for girls similar to the Scouts.

guide[2] /gaɪd/ vt 1 (of a person) to act as a guide(1) to (a person): guide a visitor to the station; guiding visitors round a museum. 2 (of a person) to lead or show the way for (a vehicle, animal etc passing through a difficult place). 3 to advise or influence (a person): be guided by common sense.

,guided 'missile nc a weapon in a rocket which is directed while in flight by electronic devices.

'guide·line nc a point or principle used to decide how to act, to set standards etc.

guild /gɪld/ nc (G- in names) a society(2): *the Women's Guild.*

guile /gaɪl/ nu (formal) clever deceit: *full of guile.*
guile·less adj

guil·lo·tine¹ /'gɪləti:n/ nc 1 a machine used for beheading criminals with a heavy blade sliding in grooves dropped from a height. 2 a machine used for trimming sheets of paper etc.

guil·lo·tine² /'gɪləti:n/ vt to use a guillotine on (a criminal, paper etc).

guilt /gɪlt/ nu 1 a feeling of shame caused by having done wrong. 2 the fact of having done wrong: *The guilt of the accused man was not proved.* 3 responsibility for doing wrong: *The guilt lies with irresponsible builders.*

guilt·ily /-əlɪ/ adv
guilt·less adj innocent (the more usual word).
guil·ty adj (-ier, -iest) (a) having done wrong: *plead guilty to a crime; be guilty of a crime.* (b) showing or feeling guilt: *have a guilty conscience.*

guinea-pig /'gɪnɪ pɪg/ nc 1 a short-eared animal like a big rat, often used in experiments. 2 (fig) a person allowing herself or himself to be used in medical or other experiments.

gui·tar /gɪ'tɑ:(r)/ nc a stringed musical instrument, played by pulling the strings with the fingers or a piece of plastic etc.

gui·tar·ist nc a person who plays a guitar.

gulf /gʌlf/ nc 1 (G- in names) a part of the sea almost surrounded by land: *the Gulf of Mexico.* 2 **a gulf (between . . .)** (fig) a large difference (between opinions etc).

gull¹ /gʌl/ nc a kind of large, long-winged seabird.

gull² /gʌl/ vt to cheat, deceive, (a person): *gull a fool out of his money.*

gull·ible /-əbl/ adj (derog) easily deceived.
gulli·bil·ity /ˌgʌlə'bɪlətɪ/ nu

gul·let /'gʌlɪt/ nc (anat) the food passage from the mouth to the stomach.

gul·ly /'gʌlɪ/ nc (pl -ies) a narrow channel cut or formed by rainwater, e.g. on a hillside, or for carrying water away from a building.

gulp¹ /gʌlp/ nc 1 an act of gulping. 2 an amount gulped: *a gulp of beer.*

gulp² /gʌlp/ v 1 vt **gulp sth (down)** to swallow food or drink quickly or greedily: *gulp down a cup of tea.* 2 vi make a swallowing movement (e.g. because of fear, surprise).

gum¹ /gʌm/ nc (usually pl) the area of firm, pink flesh round the teeth.
gum·boil /'gʌmbɔɪl/ nc a boil or abscess on the gums.

gum² /gʌm/ n 1 nu a sticky substance obtained from some trees, used for sticking things together. 2 nu a gum that has been specially prepared for chewing: *chewing-gum.* 3 nc a kind of sweet like hard jelly.

gum³ /gʌm/ vt (-mm-) 1 to stick (things) together with gum; spread gum on the surface of: *gum two things together.* 2 **gum sth up** (informal) to ruin an activity: *gum up the works.*

gump·tion /'gʌmpʃn/ nu (informal) common sense and initiative.

gun¹ /gʌn/ nc any kind of weapon that sends shells or bullets from a metal tube: *a machine-gun.* **jump the gun** to act too soon. **stick to one's guns** to maintain one's position against attack or argument.

'gun·boat nc a small warship carrying heavy guns.

'gun-carriage nc a wheeled support for a big gun, or the part on which a gun slides when it recoils.

'gun·man nc a man who uses a gun to rob or shoot people.

'gun·point nu **at gunpoint** under the threat of being shot.

'gun·powder nu an explosive powder used in guns, fireworks etc.

'gun·shot nu the range of a gun: *be out of/within gunshot.*

gun² /gʌn/ v 1 vt **gun sb down** to shoot a person with a gun. 2 vi **be gunning for sb** to be trying to harm a person, destroy her or his reputation etc.

gun·ner /'gʌnə(r)/ nc (in the army) a soldier using big guns.

gur·gle /'gɜ:gl/ vi, nc (to make) a bubbling sound as of water flowing from a narrow-necked bottle: *gurgles of delight. The baby was gurgling happily.*

gu·ru /'guru:/ nc a Hindu or Sikh spiritual teacher.

gush¹ /gʌʃ/ nc a sudden rush or flow (of liquid, anger, enthusiasm etc).

gush² /gʌʃ/ vi 1 to burst, flow out, suddenly: *oil gushing from a new well; blood gushing from a wound.* 2 to talk with exaggerated enthusiasm: *girls who gush over handsome popstars.*
gush·ing adj: *gushing compliments.* ⇨ 2 above.

gus·set /'gʌsɪt/ nc a (usually triangular or diamond-shaped) piece of cloth inserted in clothing to add strength or size.

gust /gʌst/ nc a sudden rush (of air): *a gust of wind.*
gusty adj (-ier, -iest) windy.

gut¹ /gʌt/ nc 1 (pl) the lower intestines. **hate sb's guts** (sl) to hate a person very much. 2 (pl) (informal) courage and determination: *a man with plenty of guts.* 3 nu a kind of strong cord used for fishing lines, the strings of violins etc. 4 (pl) (informal) the important parts of something: *the guts of a car.*

gut² /gʌt/ vt (-tt-) 1 to take the guts(1) out of (a fish etc). 2 (often passive) to destroy the inside of or the contents of (something): *a building gutted by fire.*

gut·ter /'gʌtə(r)/ nc 1 a long semicircular pipe fixed under the edge of a roof to carry away rainwater. 2 a long deep channel at the side of a road for rainwater.

gut·tur·al /'gʌtərəl/ adj (tech) (of a sound) produced in the throat.

guy¹ /gaɪ/ nc a rope or chain used to keep something steady or secured, e.g. to hold a tent in place.

guy² /gaɪ/ nc (sl) a man.

guzzle /'gʌzl/ vi,vt (informal; derog) to eat or drink (something) greedily: *guzzling beer.*

gym /dʒɪm/ nc (informal) = gymnasium, gymnastics.

'gym-shoes n pl (also *a pair of gym-shoes*) rubber-soled canvas shoes used for sport or casual wear (now called *trainers*).

gym·kha·na /dʒɪm'kɑ:nə/ nc (pl —s) a public display of sports competitions with horses.

gym·na·si·um /dʒɪm'neɪzɪəm/ nc (pl —s) a

room or hall with equipment for gymnastics and sports.

gym·nast /'dʒɪmnæst/ *nc* a person who does gymnastics.

gym·nas·tic /dʒɪm'næstɪk/ *adj* of, for, bodily training.

gym·nas·tics *n pl* (forms of) exercises for physical training, using special equipment.

gy·nae·col·ogy (*US* = **gyne-**) /ˌgaɪnɪ'kɒlədʒɪ/ *nu* the scientific study of the diseases of women and pregnancies.

gy·nae·co·logi·cal (*US* = **gy·ne-**) /ˌgaɪnɪkə'lɒdʒɪkl/ *adj*

gy·nae·colo·gist (*US* = **gy·ne-**) /-dʒɪst/ *nc* an expert in gynaecology.

gyp·sy /'dʒɪpsɪ/ *nc* = gipsy.

gy·rate /ˌdʒaɪ'reɪt/ *vi* to move round in circles or spirals.

gy·ra·tion /ˌdʒaɪ'reɪʃn/ *nc,nu*

gy·ro·scope /'dʒaɪrəskəʊp/ *nc* (*tech*) a heavy wheel which, when spinning fast, keeps steady the object in which it is fixed.

Hh

H, h /eɪtʃ/ (*pl* **H's, h's** /'eɪtʃɪz/) the eighth letter of the English alphabet. **drop one's h's** to leave out the sound /h/, e.g. by saying '*ot* for *hot*.

H /eɪtʃ/ *symbol* (used on) a pencil with a hard lead which produces a thin line (also 2H, 3H etc on pencils with harder lead). Compare B, HB.

ha /hɑː/ *int* **1** (used to express surprise, joy, triumph, suspicion etc). **2** (when repeated as *Ha! Ha! Ha!*, used to represent laughter).

hab·er·dash·er /'hæbədæʃə(r)/ *nc* a shopkeeper who sells cloth, pins, cotton etc.

hab·er·dash·ery *nu* a shop, part of a large store, selling cloth, cottons, pins etc.

hab·it /'hæbɪt/ *n* **1** *nc* a person's usual or normal practice, esp one that cannot easily be given up: *try to give up the habit of smoking*. **out of habit** because it is a habit: *I bite my nails out of habit*. **break the habit** to give one up: *I want to stop smoking but I can't break the habit*. **fall/get into bad habits** to begin to have them. **get out of a habit** to give it up. **kick the habit** (*informal*) to succeed in giving one up (esp using drugs). Compare custom(2). **2** *nu* a form of usual behaviour that one no longer thinks about: *Are we all creatures of habit?* (= Do we do things because of habit and not because we have decided to?) **3** *nc* a style of clothing worn by monks and nuns.

hab·it·able /'hæbɪtəbl/ *adj* (esp of a building) fit to be lived in: *The old house is no longer habitable*. Opp uninhabitable. Compare inhabitable.

habi·tat /'hæbɪtæt/ *nc* (esp *science*) the usual natural place and conditions in which an animal or plant lives. ⇨ inhabit.

habi·ta·tion /ˌhæbɪ'teɪʃn/ *nu* the act of living inside: *houses that were not fit for habitation*.

ha·bit·ual /hə'bɪtjʊəl/ *adj* (*attrib*; *no comp*) **1** regular, usual: *He took his habitual seat in the train*. **2** having a habit mentioned: *a habitual liar*.

ha·bit·ual·ly /-tjʊlɪ/ *adv* as a habit: *be habitually*

late for school.

hack¹ /hæk/ *nc* **1** an old horse. **2** a person paid to do hard and uninteresting work as a writer.

hack² /hæk/ *vt,vi* to cut (something, a person) roughly or clumsily; chop: *He hacked (away) at the branch until it fell to the ground. The man had been hacked to death/hacked down*.

'hack·saw *nc* a saw with a thin replaceable blade in a frame, used for cutting through metal.

hackles /'hæklz/ *n pl* long feathers on the neck of a domestic cock. **make sb's hackles rise** to cause a person to feel and show anger.

hack·ney·ed /'hæknɪd/ *adj* (of sayings) repeated too often to have any meaning.

had /həd *strong form;* hæd/ *pt,pp* of have¹,².

had·dock /'hædək/ *nc* (*pl* —) a kind of seafish much used for food.

hadn't /'hædnt/ = *had not*. ⇨ have¹,².

hae·mo·glo·bin (also **he-**) /ˌhiːmə'gləʊbɪn/ *nu* (*science*) the colouring matter of the red corpuscles in the blood.

hae·mo·phil·ia (also **he-**) /ˌhiːmə'fɪlɪə/ *nu* (*med*) a (usually hereditary) disease in which blood, e.g. in wounds, does not thicken.

hae·mo·phil·iac (also **he-**) /-'fɪlɪæk/ *nc* (*med*) a person suffering from haemophilia.

haem·or·rhage (also **hem-**) /'hemərɪdʒ/ *nc,nu* (*med*) (an instance of) bleeding from bloodvessels.

haem·or·rhoids (also **hem-**) /'hemərɔɪds/ *n pl* (also called *piles*) (*med*) swollen (and bleeding) veins at or near the anus.

hag /hæg/ *nc* (*derog*) an ugly woman, esp one who does evil.

hag·gard /'hægəd/ *adj* (of a person, face) looking tired and lined, esp from worry: *a haggard woman/expression*.

hag·gis /'hægɪs/ *nc,nu* a kind of Scottish food using parts of a sheep, mixed with oatmeal and cooked in a sheep's stomach.

haggle /'hægl/ *vi* **haggle (over/about sth)** to argue: *haggling with the Manager over/about one's salary*.

hai·ku /'haɪkuː/ *nc* (*literature*) a Japanese verse form using 17 syllables in 3 lines.

hail¹ /heɪl/ *n* **1** *nu* frozen raindrops falling from the sky. **2** *n sing* something coming in great numbers and force: *a hail of blows*.

'hail·stone *nc* a small piece of hail.

'hail·storm *nc* a storm with hail.

hail² /heɪl/ *vi* (of hail) to fall: *It is hailing*.

hail³ /heɪl/ *v* **1** *vt* to call out to (a person, vehicle etc) in order to attract attention: *Let's hail a taxi, shall we?* **2** *vt* **hail sb/sth as sb/sth** to express one's belief and delight that a person or thing is: *They hailed him as a hero/hailed it as the best on the market.* **3** *vi* **hail from a place** to come from it: *He/The ship hails from the Caribbean.*

hair /heə(r)/ *n* **1** *nu* all the growths, like threads, on the human head and on the skin of animals: *brush one's hair; have one's hair cut*. **keep your hair on** (*sl*; *imperative*) don't lose your temper. **let one's hair down** (*fig*) to relax after a period of being formal. **make sb's hair stand on end** to fill a person with fright or horror. **set sb's hair** to arrange it in a particular style. **2** *nc* a single thread of hair: *find a hair in the soup*. **split hairs** to state or pretend to see differences of meaning, difficulties etc, so small that they are unimportant. **not turn a hair** to give no sign of being afraid or troubled.

hair's breadth *n sing* a very small distance: *escape by a hair's breadth.*

'hair·brush *nc* a brush for the hair.

'hair·cut *nc* an act or style of cutting the hair.

'hair-do *nc* (*informal*) an act or style of arranging a woman's hair.

'hair·dress·er *nc* a person who styles hair.

'hair-line *nc* (a) the edge of the hair above the forehead. (b) (used *attrib*) the width of a hair: *a hair-line fracture.*

'hair·pin *nc* a bent pin, used for keeping the hair in place.

,hairpin 'bend *nc* a sharp bend on a road.

'hair-raising *adj* terrifying.

'hair-style *nc* a way in which hair is cut, curled etc.

hair·less *adj* bald.

hairy *adj* (**-ier, -iest**) of, like, covered with, hair: *a hairy chest.*

hale /heɪl/ *adj* (only in) **hale and hearty** strong and healthy.

half¹ /hɑːf/ *adj* or *det* to the extent of ½: *a flag that is half green and half white; be half Greek and half Russian* (i.e. have a Greek and a Russian as parents); *have a half share in a business; work an extra half day to finish the job; half a pound/kilo/ metre; half an hour; half an orange; half the week/ day; half the country; half your time; half her pay; half their family.* (N) *'Half' can be used before another determiner such as a/an, the, etc and is then called a predeterminer, as in 'half a mile'; 'half the population'.* ⇨ halve.

half² /hɑːf/ *adv* to the extent of ½; partly: *This meat is only half cooked. She's half mad. I half wish I could join you.* **half (past) one, two** *etc* 30 minutes after one/two o'clock etc: *It's half past three already and I still have a lot to do. Be there by half two* (= 2.30). **not half** (*informal*) (a) not very: *He's not half careful enough when he drives.* (b) very (much): *I'm not half worried about her! 'Do you like ice-cream?'—'Not half!'* **not half bad** ⇨ bad¹(2). **not half so bad, ill** etc (**as expected** *etc*) not as bad, ill etc as thought or feared. (N) *'Half' can be combined with many adjectives or past participles meaning 'partly . . .', as with blind, crazy, dressed, forgotten, grown, inclined, open, remembered, starved, understood.* ⇨ halve.

,half a 'dozen, a ,half-'dozen *n sing* six.

'half-back *nc* (in football, hockey etc) (the position of) a player (defender) between the forwards and the backs.

,half-'baked *adj* (*informal; derog*) foolish: crude and inexperienced: *a half-baked idea/man.*

,half 'board *nu* hotel accommodation with breakfast and dinner included.

'half-brother/-sister *nc* a brother/sister by one parent only.

,half-'hearted *adj* (*derog*) done with, showing, little interest or enthusiasm: *a half-hearted attempt.* Hence **,half-'heartedly** *adv* Compare whole-hearted.

,half-'holiday *nc* a day of which half is free from work or duty.

,half-'hour *nc* (esp) **on the half-hour** at a point exactly 30 minutes after an hour marked on a clock or watch.

,half-'hourly *adj, adv* (done, occurring) every half hour.

,half-'measures *n pl* very little contribution, effort, (making an activity, policy etc fail).

half-penny /'heɪpənɪ/ *nc* a former British coin worth half a penny.

,half-'price *adv, adj* at half the usual price.

,half-'starved *adj* very hungry.

,half 'term *nu* (also *attrib*) a short holiday in the middle of a term: *a half-term holiday.*

,half-'time *nu* (a) work and pay for half the usual time: *The workers are on half-time this month.* (b) the interval between the two halves of a game of football etc: *The score at half-time was 2–2.*

'half-truth *nc* a statement that is (deliberately) only partly true.

,half-'way *adj, adv* (a) at or to an equal distance from two places: *Manchester is halfway between London and Glasgow.* (b) using only a little effort or enthusiasm: *In an emergency halfway measures are usually unsatisfactory.* **meet sb halfway** to settle a disagreement by agreeing to give up some of one's own conditions, opinion etc.

,half-'yearly *adj, adv* (done, occurring) every half year.

half³ /hɑːf/ *pron, nc* (*pl* **halves** /hɑːvz/) **1** ½; one of two equal parts: *Half of 6 is 3. Two halves make a whole. The film lasted an hour and a half. I'd like a kilo and a half of potatoes. Half of them are bad. I'll take half.* **by half** to a large degree: *He's too proud by half* (= much too proud). **in half** (a) into two separate parts: *He cut the apple in half.* (b) so as to make two joined parts: *Fold the letter in half and put it into the envelope.* **go halves (with sb) (on/in sth)** to share (the cost; work; food etc) equally. **the half of it** (*informal*) the most important part: *You haven't heard the half of it.* ⇨ halve. **2** something, e.g. a ticket, drink, that is half the standard price, quantity: *Two halves* (i.e. children's fares) *to Victoria Station, please. A half* (of lager), *please.* **3** one of two equal periods of a game such as a football match: *He scored one goal in the first half and two goals in the second half.*

hall /hɔːl/ *nc* **1** a (usually) long space into which the main entrance or front door of a building opens: *Leave your coat in the hall.* **2** (a building with) a large room for meetings, concerts, public business etc. **3** (in universities) a large room for meals. **4** a building for university students to live in: *a hall of residence.* **5** (in England) a large country house, usually on a large estate.

'hall·mark *nc* (a) a mark stamped on gold or silver articles as a guarantee of quality. (b) (*fig*) any indication of good quality.

hal·le·lu·jah /ˌhælɪ'luːjə/ *int, nc* (an expression of) praise to God.

hal·lo /hə'ləʊ/ *int, nc* a cry used to attract attention; greeting.

hal·low·ed /'hæləʊd/ *adj* holy: *hallowed ground.*

Hal·low·e·en /ˌhæləʊ'iːn/ *n* 31 October, when children dress up and play practical jokes on neighbours.

hal·lu·ci·na·tion /həˌluːsɪ'neɪʃn/ *nc,nu* (an instance of) seeming to see something not actually present: *Some drugs cause hallucinations.*

hal·luci·na·tory /hə'lu:sɪnətərɪ/ *adj*

ha·lo /'heɪleʊ/ *nc* (*pl* **—es** or **—s**) **1** a circle of light round the sun or moon. **2** (in paintings) a ring round or above the heads of Christ or sacred figures.

halt¹ /hɔ:lt/ *nc* **1** *call a halt (to sth)* to order (something unpleasant) to stop: *It's time to call a halt to vandalism.* **2** a stop or pause: *The train came to a halt.* *grind to a halt* (a) (of a machine, engine) to stop slowly and noisily. (b) (of activity, work etc) to stop slowly (e.g. because of low supplies, a strike etc).

halt² /hɔ:lt/ *v* **1** *vi* to stop marching. **2** *vt* to cause (a person, thing) to stop; end: *be halted by a fallen tree; halt a protest by blocking the road.*

hal·ter /'hɔ:ltə(r)/ *nc* a rope or leather strap put round a horse's head (for leading or fastening the horse).

halt·ing /'hɔ:ltɪŋ/ *adj* (*attrib*) hesitating; uncertain: *a halting voice.*

halt·ing·ly *adv*

halve /ha:v/ *vt* **1** to divide (something) into two equal parts: *halve an apple.* **2** to lessen (something) by one half: *The supersonic plane has halved the time needed for crossing the Atlantic.*

halves /ha:vz/ *n pl* of half³.

ham¹ /hæm/ *n* **1** *nu* (also *attrib*) the upper part of a pig's leg, salted and dried or smoked as meat: *a ham sandwich.* **2** *nc* (*derog*) a bad actor or performer. **3** *nc* an amateur who sends and receives radio messages: *a radio ham.*

ham-'handed/-'fisted *adj* (*derog*) clumsy when doing practical things.

ham² /hæm/ *vt,vi* (**-mm-**) (esp *ham it up*) (*informal*) to overact on the stage.

ham·bur·ger /'hæmbɜ:gə(r)/ *nc* **1** a portion of minced or chopped meat made into a round flat cake and fried. **2** a bread roll filled with this.

ham·let /'hæmlɪt/ *nc* a small village.

ham·mer¹ /'hæmə(r)/ *nc* **1** a tool with a heavy metal head, used for hitting nails etc. *be/go at it hammer and tongs* to fight, argue etc with great energy and noise. **2** an athletic competition in which a heavy metal ball fixed to a long wire is thrown as far as possible. **3** (in a piano etc) a part like a hammer that strikes the strings. **4** a wooden mallet used by an auctioneer. *be/come under the hammer* to be sold by auction. **5** (*anat*) a bone in the ear.

ham·mer² /'hæmə(r)/ *v* **1** *vt,vi* *hammer at sth; hammer sth in/out* to strike or beat something (as if) with a hammer: *hammer in a nail/hammer a nail in; hammer at the door* (= hit it with a stick or one's fists)*; hammer at the keys* (= play the piano loudly, without feeling)*; hammer out a tune on the piano.* **2** *vi* *hammer away at sth* to work hard at a task etc: *hammer away at a problem/a solution.* **3** *vt* *hammer sth into sb* to force a person to understand, believe, something: *hammer an idea into his head.* **4** *vt* (*informal*) to defeat (a person) heavily in a game.

ham·mock /'hæmək/ *nc* a hanging bed made of canvas or a network of ropes.

ham·per¹ /'hæmpə(r)/ *nc* a basket etc with a lid, used for carrying food: *a picnic hamper.*

ham·per² /'hæmpə(r)/ *vt* to prevent (a person) from moving or working easily: *be hampered by heavy boots.*

ham·ster /'hæmstə(r)/ *nc* an animal like a large rat, kept as a pet.

ham·string¹ /'hæmstrɪŋ/ *nc* (also *attrib*) (*anat*) the tendon at the back of the knee: *a hamstring injury.*

ham·string² /'hæmstrɪŋ/ *vt* (*pt,pp* **-strung** /-strʌŋ/) (*fig*) to destroy the power or efficiency of (a person, army etc).

hand¹ /hænd/ *n* **1** *nc* the end part of the arm after the wrist: *my left/right hand; have soft/hard/ rough hands; a cut on the back of his hand; holding a small kitten in the palm of her hand; because my hands are full* (i.e. I am carrying many things)*; hit a ball with the open hand.* *Hands off!* (*imperative*) Don't touch/interfere! *Hands up!* (*imperative*) Raise your hands! *a firm hand* determined, strong control: *Some teenagers need a firm hand.* *a heavy hand* unkind or cruel form of authority: *rule with a heavy hand.* *(close/ near) at hand* very near (in space or time): *live near at hand; victory being* (*close*) *at hand.* *at first, second etc hand* from the original source/from a person who was told before you: *hear the news at first hand; learn about the decision at second hand.* *by hand* (a) using the hands, not machinery: *knitted by hand; hand-knitted.* (b) not (sent) through the post but (brought) by a person: *deliver a letter by hand.* *from hand to hand* from one person to another: *information passing from hand to hand.* *in hand* (a) receiving attention, being dealt with: *busy with the business/job/ work in hand.* (b) available: *have money in hand to buy a textbook.* *hand in hand* (a) holding another person's hand: *walk hand in hand.* (b) in cooperation (with): *work hand in hand with the factory across the road.* ⇨ go hand in hand below. *in the hands of sb* owned by or kept by: *evidence in the hands of the committee.* *off one's hands* no longer one's responsibility: *I'll be glad when my sons are off my hands.* *on hand* present, near by: *We have a computer on hand to analyse the results.* *on one's hands* being one's responsibility: *I have too many pupils on my hands.* *on the one hand . . . and on the other (hand) . . .* (used when describing two different or contrasting conditions, possibilities etc). *out of hand* out of control: *He's got out of hand.* *hand over fist* to an excessive degree: *spend money hand over fist.* *to hand* near and ready: *have oxygen to hand in the ambulance.* *be in good hands* to be well cared for, esp medically. *be out of one's hands* to be something one cannot influence or control: *I'm sorry I can't help you—the decision is now out of my hands.* *be good with one's hands* to be able to do practical things well. *be hand in glove with sb* to be very involved with a person, esp to commit a crime. *clap hands* to bring one's two open hands together to make a noise. *eat out of sb's hands* to be willing to obey immediately: *have her eating out of your hands.* *change hands* (of property) to be sold, given, to another person. *fall into the wrong hands* (of information, evidence, important documents etc) to become known, owned etc by a person who may do harm. *force sb's hand* to force a person to agree or do something unwillingly. *gain/get/have the upper hand* ⇨ upper. *give sb a hand (with* *sth)* to help a person. *give sb a big hand* to show one's pleasure (e.g. after a speech or performance) by clapping loudly. *give sb/have a free hand* ⇨ free[1](1). *go hand in hand* to be very closely linked: *War and misery go hand in hand.* *have/take a hand in sth* to be involved: *have a hand in the preparations.* *have one's hands full* to be very busy. *have sth (well) in hand* to be dealing with a problem, task etc well. *have time on one's hands* ⇨ time[1](2). *hold hands* (of two people) to hold each other's hand. *join hands* (of several people) to join together by holding each other's hands. *keep one's hand in* to practise enough to keep one's skill. *keep one's hands off sth* (esp *imperative*) to stop or avoid touching something: *Keep your hands off my bicycle!* *lay one's hands on sb/sth* (a) to get possession of something: *He keeps everything he can lay his hands on.* (b) (usually *negative*) to find something: *I can't lay my hands on the calculator.* (c) to treat a person roughly or violently: *Don't you dare lay your hands on my son.* *lend sb a hand (with sth)* to help a person. *live from hand to mouth* to be forced to use all one's money to live and not save any. *play into sb's hands* to do something that benefits another person who planned this result. *seize sth with both hands* to use much effort to take advantage of an opportunity: *seize an opportunity with both hands.* *shake hands (with sb)* to hold a person's hand and move it up and down as a form of greeting. *show one's hand* to let other people know one's opinion, ability or plans. *take a hand (in sth)* to become involved in helping to do something. *take sb/sth in hand* to discipline a person; control or deal with a situation. *take the law into one's own hands* ⇨ law(3). *try one's hand at sth* to attempt a task to see if one can do it: *try your hand at wallpapering.* *turn one's hand to sth* (to be able) to do a task: *He can turn his hand to most household repairs.* *wait on sb hand and foot* to do anything that a person asks. *wash one's hands of sb/sth* to refuse to continue to be responsible for, involved with, interested in etc a person or thing: *After she refused to help me, I washed my hands of her.* *win hands down* to win easily and convincingly. **2** *nc* a person who works on a ship, in a factory etc: *The factory has taken on 50 extra hands this month.* *be an old hand at doing sth* to be very experienced: *He's an old hand at this sort of work.* **3** *nc* a pointer or similar indicator on the face of a clock or watch: *the minute/hour hand of a watch.* **4** *n sing* handwriting: *She has/writes a good hand.* **5** *nc* (*card-games*) a set of playing-cards held by a player: *a good/poor hand.*

'**hand·bag** *nc* a woman's bag for her money, keys etc.

'**hand·ball** *nu* a game played by hitting a ball with the hand against a wall or between two goals.

'**hand·brake** *nc* a brake operated by hand in a vehicle, used when it is not moving.

'**hand·clap** *nc* an act of clapping.

'**hand·cuff** *vt, nc* (to put on) one of a pair of metal rings joined by a chain, fastened round a prisoner's wrists.

hand·ful /-fʊl/ *n* (a) *nc* as much or as many as can be held in one hand. (b) *nc* a small number: *Only a handful of people came.* (c) *n sing (informal)* a person or animal that is difficult to control: *That young boy of hers is quite a handful.*

'**hand luggage** *nu* a small bag containing personal things for use during a journey, e.g. in a plane.

,**hand·'made** *adj* made by hand, not a machine: *handmade furniture.*

,**hand·'picked** *adj* carefully selected.

'**hand·rail** *nc* a railing along the side of a staircase, etc.

,**hand·'sewn** *adj* sewn by hand, not a machine.

'**hand·shake** *nc* a greeting given by shaking hands with a person.

'**hand·stand** *nc* an acrobatic feat of supporting oneself in an upright position on the hands: *do a handstand.*

'**hand·writing** *nu* (a person's style of) writing by hand.

hand² /hænd/ *vt* **1** to give or pass (a person, thing) (to a person): *Please hand me that book/ hand that book to me.* **2** to lead or help (a person) by using one's hands: *Hand the boy across to the policeman.*

hand sth back to sb to give a document, essay, exam paper etc to the owner: *The policeman handed my passport back to me/handed me back my passport.*

hand sth down (to sb) (a) to pass clothes, a bike etc to a younger or smaller child in the family. (b) (usually *passive*) to pass customs, traditions to a later generation: *traditions handed down from the past.* (c) (*legal*) to give a sentence to a criminal: *hand down a heavy fine.*

hand sth in to give an exam, equipment, uniform etc to an official (because completed or no longer wanted or needed).

hand sth on (to sb) to give, pass, knowledge, responsibility, objects etc to a person: *hand a magazine on to a friend; hand one's skill on to one's daughter.*

hand sth out (a) to give notes, equipment etc to each member of a group. (b) to offer free food, blankets etc to poor people, flood victims etc. Hence '**hand-out** *nc* something (a leaflet, equipment, food, clothes etc) handed out.

hand sb over (to sb) to deliver a person (to the authorities): *hand him over to the police.* *hand sth over (to sb)* (a) to give a weapon, money etc (to a person): *hand over a knife; hand over the rent to the landlord.*

hand it to sb (*informal*) to give a person credit or praise: *She's very clever—you've got to hand it to her.*

han·di·cap¹ /'hændɪkæp/ *nc* **1** (a competition, race, in which there is) a disadvantage imposed on a competitor to make the chances of success more equal for all. **2** anything likely to lessen one's chance of success: *Poor eyesight is a handicap to a student.*

han·di·cap² /'hændɪkæp/ *vt* (**-pp-**) to give or be a handicap to (a person): *handicapped children* (= suffering from a physical or mental disability).

handi·craft /'hændɪkrɑːft/ *nc, nu* (a kind of) art or craft needing skill with the hands, e.g. needlework, pottery.

handi·work /'hændɪwɜːk/ *nc, nu* (an example of)

work done by hand.

hand·ker·chief /'hæŋkətʃɪf/ *nc* **1** a square piece of cotton etc, used for blowing the nose. **2** a similar square worn round the neck.

handle¹ /'hændl/ *nc* a part of a tool, cup, bucket, door, drawer etc by which it may be held in the hand. **fly off the handle** (*informal*) to become very angry and lose self-control.

'handle·bars *n pl* a bar with a handle at each end, for steering a bicycle etc.

handle² /'hændl/ *vt* **1** to touch, hold, (something) with the hands: *I can't handle spiders.* **2** to manage, deal with, (a person, thing): *Can you handle the situation?* **3** to behave in the way mentioned towards a person: *The speaker was roughly handled by the crowd.* **4** to buy and sell (goods): *This shop does not handle imported goods.*

hand·out /'hændaʊt/ *nc* ⇨ hand sth out.

hand·some /'hænsəm/ *adj* **1** (of men) good-looking: *He's so handsome.* Compare pretty(1). **2** (of gifts, behaviour) generous: *He said some very handsome things about you. She made a handsome gift to the school.*

handy /'hændɪ/ *adj* (**-ier, -iest**) **1** (of a person) clever with the hands: *handy at repairing things.* **2** (of things) convenient to have and use: *A good toolbox is a handy thing to have in the house.* **come in handy** to be useful at some time or other: *Don't throw that plastic bag away—it may come in handy.* **3** (of things, places) not far away; available for use: *Always keep a first-aid kit handy.*

'handy·man/·woman *nc* a person who is clever at doing odd jobs of various kinds.

hand·ily /-əlɪ/ *adv*

hang¹ /hæŋ/ *n sing* **1** the way in which a thing hangs: *the hang of a coat/skirt.* **2** **get/have the hang of sth** (a) to see how something works or is managed: *I've been trying to get the hang of this new word processor.* (b) to see the meaning or significance of what is said or written: *I don't quite get the hang of your argument.*

hang² /hæŋ/ *vt,vi* (*pt,pp* **hung** /hʌŋ/ or, for 2 below, **—ed**) **1** to support (something), be supported, from above so that the lower end is free: *hang a lamp from the ceiling. Hang your coat on that hook.* **2** (*pt,pp* **—ed**) to kill (a person) by hanging her or him with a rope round the neck: *He was hanged for murder.*

hang about/around (sth) (*informal*) to stand doing nothing definite: *boys hanging about (on) street corners.*

hang back (from doing sth) to show unwillingness to act or advance: *She refused to hang back from giving her opinion.*

hang behind to stay in a place after others have left.

hang on (a) to hold tight: *He hung on until the rope broke.* (b) to keep on trying: *It's hard work, but if you hang on long enough you'll succeed.* (c) (*informal*) to wait (esp when telephoning). **hang onto sth** (*informal*) to keep a receipt, ticket etc in one's possession.

hang out (in a place) (*informal*) to live in; be in (a place) often: *The boys often hang out in the quarry.* **hang sth out** (a) to hang wet clothes etc from a line to dry. (b) to display a flag etc: *hang out flags.*

hang over sb (of failure, a threat of being dismissed, a possible defeat etc) to seem likely to happen. **hang sth over sth** to put a tablecloth, flag etc over a surface so that it covers it and falls over the side. ⇨ also hangover.

hang together (a) (of people) to support one another: *If we all hang together, our plan will succeed.* (b) to fit well together: *Their excuses don't hang together* (= are not consistent).

hang up to replace the receiver at the end of a telephone conversation. **hang up on sb** to end a telephone conversation quickly and suddenly by replacing the receiver, e.g. when angry. **be hung up (about sb/sth)** (*informal*) to feel worried and dissatisfied: *Everything seems to have gone wrong—I feel really hung up about things.* Hence **'hang-up** *nc* this feeling.

han·gar /'hæŋə(r)/ *nc* a building used for planes or helicopters.

hang·er /'hæŋə(r)/ *nc* an apparatus used for hanging something: *a coat-hanger.*

,hanger-'on *nc* (*pl* **hangers-on**) a person who forces her or his company on another or others in the hope of profit or advantage.

hang·ing /'hæŋɪŋ/ *nc* **1** a death by being hanged(2): *There were three hangings here last month.* **2** a decorated cloth etc (to be) hung on a wall.

,hanging 'participle *nc* (*gram*) one that does not contain a subject, as in '*Considering the weather,* the day was a success.'

hang·man /'hæŋmæn/ *nc* (*pl* **-men**) a man who hangs criminals.

hang·over /'hæŋəʊvə(r)/ *nc* **1** an unpleasant feeling after a period of drinking alcohol. **2** a continued effect, result, way of working, regulation etc from an early time. *This rule is a hangover from the past.*

hang-up /'hæŋʌp/ *nc* ⇨ be hung up (about sb/sth) at hang².

hank /hæŋk/ *nc* a twist (of wool, silk etc).

han·ker /'hæŋkə(r)/ *vi* **hanker after/for sb/sth** to have a strong desire for a person, thing: *hanker for sympathy/after wealth.*

'han·ker·ing *nc*: *have a hankering after/for fame.*

hanky (also **hankie**) /'hæŋkɪ/ *nc* (*pl* **-ies**) (*informal*) = handkerchief.

hap·haz·ard /hæp'hæzəd/ *adj,adv* happening without having been planned; depending on chance: *haphazard arrangements.*

hap·pen /'hæpn/ *vi* **1** (of an event) to take place (usually by chance): *How did it happen?* **2** **happen to sb/sth** to be a person's experience; to be done to something: *If anything happens to him* (= If he has an accident), *let me know. What happened to your new shoes?* **3** **happen to** + *verb* to do, be, have, by chance and not planned: *I happened to be out when he called.*

hap·pen·ing *nc* (often *pl*) an event: *There have been strange happenings here lately.*

hap·py /'hæpɪ/ *adj* (**-ier, -iest**) **1** feeling or expressing pleasure, contentment, satisfaction etc: *a happy face/child. Their marriage has been a happy one.* Opp unhappy. **Happy birthday; Many happy returns (of the day)** (used as a friendly greeting to wish a person well on her or his birthday). **Happy new year** (used as a friendly greeting to wish a person well for a new year). **2** (use in polite formulas) pleased: *We shall be happy to accept your kind invitation*. **3** (*attrib; formal*) (of language, behaviour, suggestions etc) suitable for the situation: *a happy thought/idea*.

,happy-go-'lucky *adj* (*dated*) not worrying about the future.

hap·pily /-əlɪ/ *adv*

hap·pi·ness *nu*

har·angue /həˈræŋ/ *vt* to attack (a person) with a long, loud speech.

har·ass /ˈhærəs/ *vt* to trouble, annoy, (a person) often: *be harassed by the cares of a large family*.

har·ass·ment *nu*

har·bour¹ (*US* = **-bor**) /ˈhɑːbə(r)/ *nc* **1** a place of shelter for ships. **2** (*fig*) any place of safety or shelter: *Her home is a harbour for criminals*.

har·bour² (*US* = **-bor**) /ˈhɑːbə(r)/ *vt* **1** to give shelter to (a person) in order to hide her or him: *harbour an escaped criminal*. **2** to hold (unkind thoughts) in the mind: *harbour thoughts of revenge*.

hard¹ /hɑːd/ *adj* (**—er, —est**) **1** solid and firm; not easy to bend, dent, cut etc: *as hard as iron/ rock* (= very firm and solid); *a hard metal/wood; a hard chair/bed*. Opp soft(1). **2** difficult (to do, explain, understand): *a hard exam question. She found it hard to make up her mind. He's hard to please/a hard man to please. It's hard to believe that she came*. Opp easy(1). **be hard of hearing** to be (partly) deaf. **3** (of conditions) causing unhappiness, pain, suffering; difficult to bear: *lead a hard life; give him a hard time*. **do/learn sth the hard way** to achieve/learn it by suffering, experiencing pain, using great effort etc. *hit sb hard* (*fig*) to cause a person to suffer: *The economic recession hit me hard*. Compare easy(3). **4** (of a person, personality etc) unsympathetic and serious: *as hard as nails* (= very severe); *a hard father; a hard tone; use hard words; have a hard heart*. ⇨ hard-hearted. **take a hard line** ⇨ line¹(10). Opp soft(6). ⇨ also bargain¹(1). **5** needing, using, much effort: *hard work; a hard worker. She tried her hardest to finish on time*. Compare soft(9). **6** (of weather) severe: *a hard winter; a hard frost*. **7** (of water) not soft(8). **8** (of drugs) very harmful. Compare soft(10).

'hard·back *nc* a book bound in a hard, stiff cover. Compare paperback.

'hard·board *nu* material like a thin sheet of wood, used to make doors, walls etc.

,hard-'boiled *adj* (of eggs) boiled so that the yolk is hard. Compare soft-boiled.

,hard 'cash *nu* coins and notes, not a cheque or a promise to pay.

,hard 'copy *nu* (*computers*) information that is printed on paper or shown on a display unit.

,hard 'core *nc* the members of a group with the strongest beliefs, who work most etc.

'hard court *nc* a tennis court with a hard surface, not of grass.

,hard 'currency *nu* one that is easily exchanged for another currency and so more likely to keep its value. Compare soft currency.

,hard 'drug *nc* ⇨ hard¹(8).

,hard 'facts *n pl* ones that cannot be ignored even if they are unpleasant.

,hard-'headed *adj* practical; not influenced by feelings: *a hard-headed businesswoman*.

,hard-'hearted *adj* (*derog*) unsympathetic; unkind. Opp soft-hearted.

,hard 'labour *nu* hard physical work (done by criminals as a punishment).

,hard 'liquor *nu* a kind with a high alcoholic content, such as whisky, gin, brandy.

,hard 'luck *nu* = bad luck.

,hard-'pressed *adj* in difficulties (because of competition, lack of time etc): *be hard pressed to complete the work by Friday*.

,hard 'shoulder *nc* a hard surface at the side of a motorway, to be used in an emergency.

'hard·ware *nu* (**a**) metal goods for domestic use, e.g. pots and pans. (**b**) (*computers*) mechanical equipment in a computer system e.g. the central processing unit, visual display unit etc. Compare software.

,hard-'wearing *adj* (of cloth) tough and lasting a long time.

'hard·wood *nu* heavy wood, e.g. oak, teak. Compare softwood.

,hard-'working *adj* working with much effort.

hard² /hɑːd/ *adv* (**—er, —est**) **1** with great energy, effort, force: *try hard to succeed; play hard and work hard*. **be hard at it** to be working hard. **be hard put to do sth** to find it very difficult to do: *I'd be hard put to explain why I don't like him*. **2** seriously and with determination: *think hard about a problem*. **3** so as to be solid: *paint left to go hard*. **4** **hard on sb/sth** close to a person, thing: *follow hard on his heels*. **5** **be hard up** to be needing money. Ⓝ Be careful, because *'hardly'* has completely different meanings and uses from *'hard'*.

hard·en /ˈhɑːdn/ *vt,vi* **1** (to cause something) to become solid: *Has the paint hardened?* **2** (to cause a person) to become confident and determined: *people who are hardened by poverty and bad experiences; a hardened criminal* (= one who refuses to stop doing wrong).

hard·ly /ˈhɑːdlɪ/ *adv* **1** only just; not quite; scarcely: *I hardly know her. I'm so tired I can hardly walk*. **2** (used to suggest that something is improbable, unlikely or unreasonable): *You can hardly expect me to lend you money again. I need hardly say* (= It is almost unnecessary for me to say) *that I am innocent*. **3** almost no, not, never: *He hardly ever goes to bed before midnight. There's hardly any coal left. Hardly anybody* (= Very few people) *came to the meeting*.

hard·ship /ˈhɑːdʃɪp/ *nc,nu* (an instance of) serious suffering; difficult conditions: *the hardships of war*.

hardy /ˈhɑːdɪ/ *adj* (**-ier, -iest**) **1** strong; able to put up with suffering: *A few hardy people broke the ice on the lake and had a swim*. **2** (of plants) able to survive very cold ground: *hardy annuals*.

hardi·ness *nu*

hare¹ /heə(r)/ *nc* an animal, similar to a rabbit but with long ears, able to run fast. **as mad as a March hare** ⇨ mad(1).

'hare-brained *adj* (*derog*) silly and impractical: *a hare-brained scheme*.

,hare·lip *nc* a person's upper lip divided (from birth) like that of a hare.

hare² /heə(r)/ *vi* **hare (off)** to run fast.

har·em /ˈheərəm, ˈhɑːriːm/ nc **1** the women's part of a Muslim household. **2** the women living in it.

hark /hɑːk/ vi **1 hark at sb** (informal) to listen to a person: *Just hark at him!* **2 hark back (to sth)** to refer to something done or said earlier.

har·le·quin /ˈhɑːləkwɪn/ nc a clown as in Italian comedy or English pantomime.

har·lot /ˈhɑːlət/ nc (old use; derog) a prostitute.

harm[1] /hɑːm/ nu damage; injury: *It will do you no harm. He meant no harm.* **out of harm's way** safe.

harm[2] /hɑːm/ vt to cause harm to (a person).

harm·ful /-fəl/ adj **harmful (to sb/sth)** causing harm (to): *It's harmful to humans.*

harm·less adj **harmless (to sb/sth)** not able to do harm (to): *harmless snakes; harmless to birds.*

harm·less·ly adv

har·mon·ica /hɑːˈmɒnɪkə/ nc (pl **—s**) = mouth organ.

har·moni·ous /hɑːˈməʊnɪəs/ adj **1** pleasingly or satisfactorily arranged: *a harmonious group of buildings.* **2** in agreement; friendly: *harmonious neighbours.*

har·moni·ous·ly adv

har·mon·ize (also **-ise**) /ˈhɑːmənaɪz/ vt,vi **1** (to cause the style, colour etc of something) to be pleasant to see with something else. **2** (music) to add notes (to a melody) to make harmonies.

har·mo·ny /ˈhɑːməni/ n (pl **-ies**) **1** nu a state of agreement (of feeling, interests, opinions etc): *racial harmony.* **2** nc,nu (an instance or example of) a pleasing combination of related things: *the harmony of colour in nature; colours in harmony when put together.* **3** nc,nu (music) (an instance of) a pleasing combination of notes sounded together to make chords.

har·ness[1] /ˈhɑːnɪs/ n **1** nu or sing all the leatherwork and metalwork by which a horse is controlled. **2** nc an arrangement of straps etc for fastening something to the body, e.g. a parachute.

har·ness[2] /ˈhɑːnɪs/ vt **1** to put a harness on (a horse). **2** to use (a river, waterfall etc) to produce electricity etc.

harp[1] /hɑːp/ nc a kind of upright musical instrument with vertical strings played with the fingers.

harp·ist /-ɪst/ nc a person who plays the harp.

harp[2] /hɑːp/ vi **harp on (about sth)** to talk repeatedly or too much (about something): *She is always harping on about her problems.*

har·poon /hɑːˈpuːn/ vt, nc (to use) a spear on a rope, thrown by hand or fired from a gun, for catching (large sea animals).

harp·si·chord /ˈhɑːpsɪkɔːd/ nc a kind of musical instrument like a piano, popular from the 16th to the 18th centuries.

har·row /ˈhærəʊ/ vt, nc (to use) a heavy frame with metal teeth or discs for breaking up (ground) after ploughing.

har·row·ing /ˈhærəʊɪŋ/ adj causing distress: *a harrowing experience in a hijacked plane.*

har·ry /ˈhærɪ/ vt (pt,pp **-ied**) **1** to attack (a country etc) frequently: *harry the English coast.* **2** to annoy or worry (a person): *money-lenders harrying their debtors.*

harsh /hɑːʃ/ adj (**—er**, **—est**) **1** rough and unpleasant: *a harsh voice.* **2** cruel, severe: *a harsh judge/punishment.*

harsh·ly adv

harsh·ness nu

har·vest[1] /ˈhɑːvɪst/ nc **1** (the season for) the cutting and gathering in of grain and other food crops; quantity obtained. **2** (fig) the result of an action or behaviour: *reap the harvest of one's hard work.*

harvest 'festival nc a service of thanksgiving in Christian churches after the harvest has been gathered.

har·ves·ter nc **(a)** a person who harvests. **(b)** a machine for cutting and gathering grain, esp the kind that also binds the grain into sheaves or (**combine harvester**) threshes the grain.

har·vest[2] /ˈhɑːvɪst/ vt to cut, gather, dig up, (a crop): *harvest rice.*

has /həz strong form: hæz/ ⇨ **have**[1].

hash /hæʃ/ n **1** nu (a meal of) cooked chopped meat. **2 make a hash of sth** (fig) to do something very badly; make a mess of it.

hash·ish /ˈhæʃiːʃ/ (also **hash**) nu = cannabis.

hasn't /ˈhæznt/ = has not. ⇨ **have**[1].

hasp /hæsp/ nc a metal fastening of a padlock, used with a staple.

hassle /ˈhæsl/ nu (informal) trouble; irritation: *Having to fill in this long application form is a real hassle.* □ vt to irritate or annoy (a person) by continually asking her or him to do something.

has·sock /ˈhæsək/ nc (in a church) a cushion used for kneeling on.

haste /heɪst/ nu (formal) quickness of movement or activity: *Why all this haste?* **more haste, less speed** (saying) too much haste when doing something can cause delays.

has·ten /ˈheɪsn/ v **1** vi **hasten (to do sth)** to move or act with speed: *hasten to tell him the good news.* **2** vt,vi (to cause something) to be done, to happen, quickly or earlier: *Artificial heating hastens the growth of plants.*

hasty /ˈheɪstɪ/ adj (**-ier**, **-iest**) said, made or done (too) quickly: *hasty decisions/preparations.*

hast·ily /-əlɪ/ adv

hasti·ness nu

hat /hæt/ nc a firm, shaped covering for the head, worn out of doors. ⇨ **old hat**. **at the drop of a hat** ⇨ **drop**[1](5). **eat one's hat** to admit that one was wrong. **keep sth under one's hat** to tell something to no-one. **take one's hat off to sb** (fig) to express admiration for a person's achievements. **talk through one's hat** (informal; derog) to talk foolishly.

hat·ter nc a person, business, that makes or sells hats.

hatch[1] /hætʃ/ nc **1** (the movable covering over) an opening in a ceiling or floor, esp (**hatchway**) one in a ship's deck through which cargo is lowered and raised. **2** an opening in a wall between two rooms, esp a kitchen and a dining room, through which dishes etc are passed.

hatch·back nc (also attrib) a car with a flap at the back used for loading or unloading.

hatch[2] /hætʃ/ v **1** vt,vi (to cause a bird, snake etc) to break out (of an egg): *hatch chickens.* ⇨ also **chicken**[1](1). **2** vt to think out and produce (a plan etc).

hatch·et /ˈhætʃɪt/ nc a short-handle axe. **bury**

---

have

Present participle **having** /'hævɪŋ/; past participle **had** /hæd/

Positive statements	Negative statements	Questions*
Present tense forms:		
I **have**, I've /aɪv/	I have not, I've not, I **haven't** /'hævnt/	have I? haven't I?
you **have**, you've / juːv/	you have not, you've not, you **haven't**	have you? haven't you?
he/she/it **has** /həz, hæz/, he's/she's/it's† /hiːz, ʃiːz, ɪts/	he/she/it has not, he's/she's/it's not, he/she/it **hasn't** /'hæznt/	has he/she/it? hasn't he/she/it?
we **have**, we've /wiːv/	we have not, we've not, we **haven't**	have we? haven't we?
you **have**, you've /juːv/	you have not, you've not, you **haven't**	have you? haven't you?
they **have**, they've /ðeɪv/	they have not, they've not, they **haven't**	have they? haven't they?
Past tense forms:		
I **had** /həd, hæd/, I'd /aɪd/	I had not, I'd not, I **hadn't** /'hædnt/	had I? hadn't I?
you **had**, you'd /juːd/	you had not, you'd not, you **hadn't**	had you? hadn't you?
he/she/it **had**, he'd/she'd/it'd /hiːd, ʃiːd, 'ɪtəd/	he/she/it had not, he'd/she'd/it'd not, he/she/it **hadn't**	had he/she/it? hadn't he/she/it?
we **had**, we'd /wiːd/	we had not, we'd not, we **hadn't**	had we? hadn't we?
you **had**, you'd /juːd/	you had not, you'd not, you **hadn't**	had you? hadn't you?
they **had**, they'd /ðeɪd/	they had not, they'd not, they **hadn't**	had they? hadn't they?

The other tenses of *'have'* are formed in the same way as those of other verbs, as in *will have come, is having lunch, was having a bath.*

* The negative question forms *have I not? had she not?* etc are also correct but are more formal.

† Be careful, because *he's, she's, it's* can mean either *he has, she has, it has* or *he is, she is, it is.*

---

the hatchet (*fig*) to end a quarrel or fight.

hatch·way /'hætʃweɪ/ *nc* ⇨ hatch¹(1).

hate¹ /heɪt/ *nu* extreme dislike.

hate² /heɪt/ *vt* **1** to have an extreme dislike of (a person, thing): *My cat hates dogs.* **2** (used as a polite way of saying something embarrassing): *I hate to trouble you but you're sitting on my hat.*

hate·ful /'heɪtfəl/ *adj* extremely unpleasant: *The bloodshed was hateful.*
hate·ful·ly /-fəlɪ/ *adv*

ha·tred /'heɪtrɪd/ *nu* a feeling of hate: *look with hatred.*

hat·ter /'hætə(r)/ *nc* ⇨ hat.

haughty /'hɔːtɪ/ *adj* (-**ier**, -**iest**) (*derog*) having or showing a high opinion of oneself: *treating staff with haughty contempt.*
haught·ily /-əlɪ/ *adv*
haugh·ti·ness *nu*

haul¹ /hɔːl/ *nc* **1** the act of hauling. **2** a distance along which something is hauled. **3** an amount gained, esp of fish in a net or stolen goods in a robbery.

haul² /hɔːl/ *vi, vt* **1** to pull (a heavy weight) along the ground with much effort: *haul logs.* **2** to pull up (a net) from the sea with much effort.

haul·age /'hɔːlɪdʒ/ *nu* (*commerce*) (the cost of) the transport of goods.

haul·ier /'hɔːlɪə(r)/ *nc* a person or business that contracts to carry goods by road.

haunch /hɔːntʃ/ *nc* (often *pl*) the part of the body between the waist and the thighs: *a dog sitting on its haunches.*

haunt¹ /hɔːnt/ *nc* a place often visited (by the (kinds of) people mentioned): *a haunt for/of criminals; one of my favourite haunts.*

haunt² /hɔːnt/ *vt* **1** to visit (a place) often: *haunt the pubs.* **2** (of ghosts and spirits) to appear often in (a place): *The murdered nun haunts the forest.* **3** (usually *passive*) to return to (the mind) repeatedly: *be constantly haunted by fear of discovery.*

haunt·ing /'hɔːntɪŋ/ *adj* (*attrib*) that stays in one's mind, thoughts: *a haunting smile/sound.*

have¹ /həv/ *strong form:* hæv/ *auxiliary verb* Ⓝ
'Have' is used with the past participle of another verb to form tenses, and with the infinitive form of another verb to express obligation.

1 (used with the past participle of another verb (e.g. *moved, done*) to form): (**a**) the present perfect tense: *They have finished. He's not eaten his dinner.* (**b**) the past perfect tense: *You had finished. Hadn't they played that tune before?* (**c**) the future perfect tense: *I'll have studied for two hours.* (**d**) the perfect conditional tense: *I would have told you tomorrow.* **2** '**have to** + verb (used to express obligation): *She has to leave. We had to pay. I lost it so I'll have to buy a new one. You'll have to wait if we arrive late. He didn't want to pay but he had to. 'Go to bed!'—'Do I have to?'*

(N) 'Have to' or 'had to' etc always expresses obligation and has no other meaning. 'Must' is also possible for 'have/has to', but 'had to' is always used for the past form because 'must' has no past form. When 'have to' is used at the end of a statement or in a question when the verb has already been mentioned, the verb need not be repeated, as in the last two examples above. **have got to** + verb (*informal*) (used to emphasize obligation): *I've got to pay. She hasn't got to go.* (N) It is also possible to say: *Do I have to pay? She doesn't have to go.* 'Have to' is preferred when the obligation is general or usual, as in *Do I have to apply for a visa?* Compare *have got to* in have²(1). **3 have sb/sth** + *-ing* (a) to cause something to be done or happen: *He'll have the television working again soon.* (b) to cause a person to do something (as a result of one's activity): *If you play your radio on the beach, you'll have everyone complaining.* **4 have sb/sth** + *past participle* (used to report another person's action that is a result of one's request): *We've had the children taught to swim. I'm having my car repaired.* (N) 'Do' is used to form questions, as in *Did you have the children . . . ?* and to form the negative, as in *I didn't have my car repaired.* Be careful because the order of the words changes the meaning. Compare *I had my car repaired* (= Somebody repaired it for me) and *I had repaired my car* (= I had repaired it myself). **5 I will not have sb/sth** + *verb* I will not allow a person (to do something): *I won't have you speak to your father like that!* **6 sb/sth had better** + *verb* (used to express an opinion, decision, warning etc) it would be better for a person or thing to: *You'd better apologize. I'd better leave now. That car had better be ready by tonight. She'd better not try to persuade me.* **7** (used in conversation) (a) (joined to the end of a statement to form a question): *I haven't got to go, have I? She has seen the film, hasn't she?* (N) The short addition is always negative (e.g. *hasn't*) if the verb in the statement is positive (e.g. *has seen*) and it is positive (e.g. *have*) if the verb in the statement is negative (e.g. *haven't got to go*). Statements with *neither, no, nobody, nothing* etc are considered to be negative and the short addition is always positive, as in *Nothing has happened, has it?* (b) (used to make a short question): *'It hasn't appeared.'—'Hasn't it?' 'He's apologized.'—'Has he?'* (N) If the statement is positive, the short question is also positive. If the statement is negative, the short question is also negative. Statements with *neither, no, nobody* etc are considered to be negative. (c) (used to give a short answer): *'Have you paid?'—'Yes, I have.' 'Had you been there before?'—'No, I hadn't.'* (N) The auxiliary verb 'have' is used in (a), (b) and (c) only when 'have' is used in the main statement. Compare: be¹, do².

have² /həv *strong form:* hæv/ *vt* **1** to possess, own (something); have (something) in the mind; suffer from (an illness): *I've blue eyes/a dog and a cat. He had the feeling/idea that you didn't believe him. She has flu.* **have got sth** (*informal*) (used esp in the present perfect tense): *I've blue eyes. She's got flu. How many children has he got? We haven't got any milk.* (N) Not used in continuous tenses, e.g. *is/was -ing: 'Do'* is also possible for questions, as in *Does she have blue eyes?*, but *Has he got blue eyes?* is less formal. 'Do' is preferred when the state or condition is general or usual, as in *Do you have free university education in your country? 'Do'* is also possible for negatives, as in *I don't have any money*, but *I haven't got any money* is less formal. 'Got' can be omitted but is now very usual in conversation. Compare *have got to* in have¹(2). **2** (used to refer to action where the meaning is the same as the activity mentioned): *have a swim/walk/bath/drink; have a look/try/go; have doubts.* (N) The verb form of the noun has the same meaning, e.g. *to have a wash* is the same as *'to wash'.* For special uses of 'have' with nouns such as *affair, baby, crack, time* etc, ⇨ the noun entries. **3** to take (a meal): *have lunch/breakfast. What are we having for dinner?* **4** to organize and give (a party, meeting etc); entertain (a person): *We're having a party on Friday. Let's have the neighbours to dinner.* **5** to experience (something): *We didn't have any difficulty. I'm having a marvellous holiday. We've had a disappointment.* **let sb have it** (*informal*) to attack a person physically or verbally. **6 be had** to be tricked or deceived: *I thought the story was true but I've been had.*

have sth against sb to feel angry with, oppose, a person: *have a grudge against a teacher. What have you got against me?* (= Why do you dislike me, feel angry etc?).

have sb around = have sb round.

have sth back to receive a possession again after lending or losing it: *I promise that you will have it back by tonight. I must have my radio back tomorrow.* **have one's own back** ⇨ back²(4).

have an ear, eye etc for sth ⇨ ear, eye, gift, time etc.

have sb in to organize for builders, decorators etc to come into one's home: *We've had the painters in for the past week.* ⇨ also hand, mind, say.

have sth of sth ⇨ control, courage etc.

have sb on (*informal*) to deceive a person: *He said he had won £500 but he was having me on.*

have sth on (a) to be wearing clothes: *have a hat on.* (b) to have an arrangement, commitment etc: *I haven't anything on this afternoon* (= I'm free).

have nothing/something etc on sb to have no cause/cause to believe a person has done something wrong. ⇨ also brain, eye, mind etc.

have sth out to arrange for a tooth etc to be taken out. **have sth out (with sb)** to discuss an issue fully, esp angrily: *We were determined to have it out with the landlord.*

have sb over = have sb round.

have sb round to entertain a person in one's home: *have him round for/to dinner.*

have sb up for (doing) sth (usually *passive*) (*informal*) to cause a person to appear in court: *He was had up for drunken driving.*

have sth with sb ⇨ affair(2), word¹(2) etc.

ha·ven /'heɪvn/ *nc* a place of safety or rest.

haven't /'hævnt/ = have not. ⇨ have¹.

hav·er·sack /'hævəsæk/ *nc* (*dated*) = backpack or rucksack (the usual words).

hav·oc /'hævək/ *nu* widespread damage; destruction: *The floods caused terrible havoc.*

hawk¹ /hɔːk/ *nc* **1** a kind of strong, swift, bird of prey. **2** (*fig*) a person who favours war or the use of military force. Opp dove(2).

hawk² /hɔːk/ *vt* **1** to go from house to house,

street to street, selling (goods). **2** (*fig*) to spread (information) about: *hawk news about.*

hawk·er *nc* a person who hawks(1).

haw·thorn /'hɔ:θɔ:n/ *nc* a kind of thorny shrub or tree with white, red or pink blossom and small red berries.

hay /heɪ/ *nu* grass cut and dried for use as animal food. **make hay (while the sun shines)** (*saying*) to use your opportunities while you have them.

'**hay fever** *nu* a condition with sneezing, a wet nose and sore eyes, caused by pollen in the air.

'**hay-fork** *nc* a long-handled two-pronged fork, used for turning and lifting hay.

'**hay-rick/·stack** *nc* a large pile of hay firmly packed for storing. ⇨ needle¹(1).

'**hay·wire** *adj* (*pred*) (*informal*) out of order; excited or distracted. **go haywire (a)** (of a person) to become very upset. **(b)** (of something, e.g. a plan) to become very disorganized.

haz·ard¹ /'hæzəd/ *nc* a danger: *health hazards* (e.g. smoking cigarettes).

haz·ard² /'hæzəd/ *vt* **1** to expose (a person etc) to danger: *Rock-climbers sometimes hazard their lives.* **2** (*formal*) to offer (a guess that is probably wrong).

haz·ard·ous /-əs/ *adj* dangerous: *a hazardous climb.*

haze /heɪz/ *nu* thin cloudy smoke or mist.

ha·zel /'heɪzl/ *n* **1** *nc* a kind of tree with small, round edible nuts. **2** *nu* (also *attrib*) the colour of the shell of the nut, reddish-brown: *hazel eyes.*

hazy /'heɪzɪ/ *adj* (**-ier, iest**) **1** misty: *a hazy sky.* **2** (*fig*) vague; uncertain: *be hazy about what to do next.*

haz·ily /-əlɪ/ *adv*

hazi·ness *nu*

HB /ˌeɪtʃ 'bi:/ *symbol* (used on) a pencil with a lead which produces a fairly dark line. Compare B, H.

HCF /ˌeɪtʃ si: 'ef/ *abbr* (*maths*) highest common factor. ⇨ factor(2).

he /hi:/ *pron* **1** (used as the subject of a verb) a male person or animal mentioned: *'Where's your brother?'—'Oh, he's in Paris.'* Compare him. **2** (often used as a *prefix*) male: *a he-goat. Is it a he or a she?*

head¹ /hed/ *nc* **1** the part of the body above the neck which contains the face and the brain: *lower/ raise one's head; have a head of curly hair.* **from head to foot/toe** over the whole length of one's body: *covered in mud from head to toe.* **off the top of one's head** without thinking or learning in advance: *speak off the top of one's head.* **on sb's/one's own head be it** (*saying*) the choice or responsibility is a person's/one's own and he/ she/one must suffer the results (often used as a warning): *If you want to lend her £50, on your own head be it.* **over sb's head (a)** without a more obvious candidate being considered: *She was promoted over my son's head.* **(b)** too difficult for a person to understand: *His speech went over my head.* **head over heels (a)** with one's body turning in a circle: *fall head over heels.* **(b)** completely: *be head over heels in love.* **be above sb's head** to be too difficult for a person to understand. **be off one's head** (*informal*) to be mad. **bite sb's head off** to speak angrily to a person because one is annoyed with her or him.

eat one's head off to eat a large quantity of food. **hold one's head high/up** to appear brave and not ashamed (e.g. because poor, having failed after sincerely trying). **keep one's head** to remain calm during a crisis. **keep one's head above water** to be able to manage, esp financially, during a difficult period. **laugh one's head off** to laugh with much energy. **lose one's head** to fail to stay calm during a crisis. **stand head and shoulders above sb** to be much more intelligent, moral etc than another person. **talk above/over sb's head** to use a style of educated speech about a serious subject so that another person cannot understand. **talk one's head off** to talk for a long time. **turn sb's head** to make a person conceited: *His Olympic medal turned his head.* ⇨ also big-head. **2** the mind, intellect, brain: *I need a clear head while I'm working.* **be wrong/not right in the head** to be behaving strangely; be a little mad. **be soft/weak in the head** to be not very intelligent. **clear one's head (a)** to reduce the effects of a cold: *take an aspirin to clear one's head.* **(b)** to empty one's mind (of unnecessary thoughts). **get sth into one's head** to understand and appreciate (the full effect that may or will result): *Please get it into your head that I am not rich.* **get sth out of one's head** to stop thinking that something is true. **give sb her/his etc head** to allow a person to act, think, freely. **go off one's head** (*informal*) to become mad. **go to sb's head (a)** (of alcoholic drink) to cause a person to become affected and behave stupidly. **(b)** (of success, praise etc) to cause a person to become too proud etc. **have a good head for sth** to be very capable when working at something: *have a good head for business/figures.* **have a good head on one's shoulders** to be intelligent; have good practical sense. **have a level head** to be able to judge issues well, think in an organized way etc. Hence ˌlevel-'headed *adj*. **have one's head screwed on (the right way)** (*informal*) to act sensibly. **have a thick head** to be unable to think clearly (e.g. because of tiredness). **put our/your/their heads together** to discuss together in order to solve a problem, to decide etc. **put sth into sb's head** to cause a person to think about a topic: *He wouldn't have believed his friend was a liar if you hadn't put it into his head.* **put sth out of one's head** to refuse to continue thinking about it. **3** a part at the top or end of an object: *the head of a pin/nail/hammer.* **4** the top or most important end: *at the head of a page/the stairs; the head of the bed* (i.e. where the head rests); *the head of a river* (i.e. near its source); *the head of a procession* (i.e. the front part). **5** (also *attrib*) the person with most responsibility in an organization, institution, government, department etc: *the head of a business/school/sales department; heads of government; the head waiter; head teachers; head office.* **6** *n sing* for each person: *We can supply a meal at £2 a head.* **7** the side of a coin with the head of a ruler on it. Compare tail¹(3). **be unable to make head or tail of sth** (esp of writing) to be completely unable to understand it. **8** the top of a swelling on the skin, esp when infected. **come to a head** (*fig*) to reach a critical stage when action is essential: *The problems at the new factory have come to a head.* **9** the layer of white bubbles on the surface of beer etc. **10** (H- in names) a long piece of coast pointing into the sea: *sail past Beachy Head.*

'**head·ache** *nc,nu* (**a**) a pain in the head. *a splitting headache* a severe one. (**b**) (*fig*) (*informal*) a troublesome problem: *Higher prices will cause headaches for the Government.*

'**head-dress** *nc* an ornamental covering for the head, e.g. as part of a national costume.

'**head·land** /-lənd/ *nc* a long piece of coast pointing into the sea.

'**head·light** *nc* a large light on the front of a vehicle.

'**head·line** *nc* a newspaper heading.

,**head·'master**/-'**mistress** *nc* a male/female head teacher.

'**head·phones** *n pl* an electrical apparatus with two parts fitting over each ear, used to listen to radio messages, records etc.

,**head·'quarters** *nc* or *pl* (abbr HQ) a main or central office of an army, the police, a business etc.

'**head·rest** *nc* something (e.g. on a car seat) that supports the head.

'**head·room** *nu* space (e.g. under a bridge) allowing tall vehicles, people etc to pass.

'**head·set** *nc* = headphones.

,**head 'teacher** *nc* the teacher who manages a school and its staff.

'**head wind** *nc* one that blows directly into one's face or against the course of a ship.

'**head·word** *nc* the first word of a dictionary entry.

head² /hed/ *v* **1** *vt* to be at the front or top of (something): *head a procession. Smith's name headed the list.* **2** *vt,vi* to strike, touch, (a ball etc) with the head (e.g. in football). **3** *vi* **head for sth** (**a**) to move towards a place: *be heading (for) home.* (**b**) (*fig*) to be tending towards a bad condition: *be heading for disaster.* **head** + *a place or direction* to go towards: *Let's head home/south.* **4** *vt* **head sth/sb off** to get in front of a person, animal, in order to turn her/him/it back or aside: *head off a flock of sheep.*

head·er /'hedə(r)/ *nc* **1** a fall, dive or jump with the head first: *take a header into a swimming pool.* **2** an act of heading²(2) a ball: *score a goal with a header.*

head·ing /'hediŋ/ *nc* a word or words printed at the top of a chapter or newspaper article to show the subject of what follows.

head·long /'hedloŋ/ *adj, adv* **1** with the head first: *a headlong fall; fall headlong.* **2** thoughtless(ly) and hurried(ly): *rush headlong into a decision.*

head-on /'hed ɒn/ *adj, adv* (/,hed 'ɒn/ when *adv*) (of collisions) with the front parts (of vehicles) hitting each other: *a head-on collision; collide head-on.*

head·strong /'hedstrɒŋ/ *adj* (*derog*) difficult to control; refusing advice.

head·way /'hedwei/ *nu* **make headway** to make progress: *Are the negotiations making headway?*

heady /'hedi/ *adj* (**-ier, -iest**) **1** (of alcoholic drink) having a quick effect on the senses. **2** (*fig*)

(e.g. of sudden success) having an exciting effect.

heal /hi:l/ *vt,vi* **1** (to cause a wound) to become healthy and sound: *The wound soon healed up/over.* **2** (*fig*) (to cause a quarrel etc) to end.

heal·er *nc* a person or thing that heals: *Time is a great healer.*

health /helθ/ *nu* **1** the condition of the body or the mind: *be in good/poor health.* **2** the state of being well and free from illness: *Health is more important than wealth.* ⇨ picture¹(5). **3** (*fig*) a (mentioned) state: *the economic health of Europe.*

'**health food** *nc,nu* (a kind of) natural food without chemicals that helps to produce good health.

'**health resort** *nc* a place or institution providing conditions (climate, diet, treatment) to produce good health.

'**health store** *nc* a shop selling health food.

healthy /'helθi/ *adj* (**-ier, -iest**) **1** having good health; well, strong and able to resist disease: *The children look very healthy.* **2** likely to produce good health: *a healthy climate.* **3** (usually *attrib*) showing good health: *a healthy appetite.* Opp unhealthy.

health·ily /-əli/ *adv*

heap¹ /hi:p/ *nc* **1** a number (of things), mass (of material), piled up: *a heap of sand.* **2** (*pl*) (*informal*) a large quantity: *We have heaps of books/time.*

heap² /hi:p/ *vt* **1** to put (things) in a heap: *heap (up) stones.* **2** to fill (something) with a heap: *heap a plate with food; a heaped spoonful* (= an amount that fills a spoon and rises above the edges).

hear /hiə(r)/ *v* (*pt,pp* **heard** /hɜːd/) **1** *vt,vi* to become aware of (sound) with the ears: *I can hear someone laughing. I heard a noise. Be quiet—I can't hear. Listen carefully and you'll hear the sea/rain.* Ⓝ Not used in continuous tenses, e.g. *is/was -ing.* Compare listen(1). **2** *vt* to be told, receive (information etc): *Have you heard the news? I've heard that taxes are going up.* ⇨ hear about sb/sth. **3** *vt* to pay attention to (something): *You'd better hear what they have to say.* Ⓝ 'Listen to' is also possible. **4** (*legal*) (of a judge) to listen to arguments in a law court. **5** *Hear! Hear!* (used to express approval at a meeting).

hear about sb/sth to be told about a person, thing: *Have you heard about John's success/their marriage?*

hear from sb to receive a letter, postcard etc from a person.

hear of sb/sth to receive information about a person, thing: *I heard of your promotion last night. I've never heard of it/her/blue leaves.* *I will not hear/I refuse to hear of it* (used to refuse a person's kind offer of help politely when one is in difficulty). *sb will hear more of sth* a (named) person will be criticized, blamed, punished etc again later.

hear sb out to listen to a person until he or she has finished saying something: *Don't judge me until you've heard me out.*

hear·ing /'hiəriŋ/ *n* **1** *nu* (also *attrib*) the ability to hear: *Her hearing is poor.* She has hearing difficulties. *be hard of hearing* ⇨ hard¹(2). **2** *nu* the distance within which one can hear: *in the* *hearing of strangers.* **within/out of hearing** near enough/not near enough to hear or be heard. **3** *nc* an opportunity to defend oneself. **(get) a fair hearing** an opportunity to have one's evidence, opinion etc heard fairly. **4** *nc* (*legal*) a trial of a case at law.

'**hearing-aid** *nc* an electronic device used to improve hearing.

hear·say /'hɪəseɪ/ *nu* what one has heard another person or other people say but does not know to be true: *I don't believe it: it's only hearsay.*

hearse /hɜːs/ *nc* a vehicle used for carrying a coffin at a funeral.

heart /hɑːt/ *nc* **1** the part inside the body which sends blood round: *have a strong/weak heart. I can feel your heart beating.* **2** this part of the body considered as the centre of emotions and feelings: *a man with a kind heart.* **after one's own heart** with a character that one prefers or likes: *He's a man after my own heart.* **at heart** in fact; really: *Although she shouts, she's a good mother at heart.* **by heart** so that one can say, sing or play it from memory: *learn/know the words/tune by heart.* **from the bottom of one's heart** very sincerely; genuinely: *I wish you success from the bottom of my heart.* **in one's heart (of hearts)** as one must admit to oneself as being true: *You know in your heart of hearts that I am innocent.* **to one's heart's content** for as long as, as much as, one wishes: *You can beg to your heart's content but I will not let you have it.* **with all one's heart** completely and willingly: *I love you with all my heart.* **heart to heart** openly and sincerely: *speak heart to heart about a problem.* **heart and soul** completely: *I'm yours heart and soul* (i.e. I love you). **sb's heart is/was not in it** a person is/was not really willing (or determined to succeed): *He tried but gave up as his heart wasn't in it.* **sb's heart is/was in the right place** a person has/had good intentions. **be sick at heart** to be extremely disappointed and sad. **bare one's heart (to sb)** to confess, tell, one's most personal thoughts or feelings. **break sb's heart** to make a person extremely sad. **cross my heart (and hope to die)** (used to show that a promise, reason, piece of evidence etc is sincere). **cry/sob one's heart out** to cry very much. **do sb's heart good** (of pleasant news, esp about a person's kindness) to make one feel happy, positive about human nature: *It did my heart good to see young people giving so much to the famine victims.* **eat one's heart out** to suffer very much and without showing one's sadness. **find it in one's heart to do sth** to be persuaded or decide to do it because of one's kindness and generosity: *Can you find it in your heart to forgive him?* **give one's heart to sb** to allow oneself to fall in love with a person. **have a heart** to be kind to a person. **have a change of heart** ⇨ change¹(2). **have a heart of gold/stone** to be extremely kind/unkind. **have one's heart in one's mouth** to be very afraid. **have one's heart in the right place** to be sympathetic. **have one's heart set on sth** to want it very much. **not have the heart to do sth** to be unable to do something unkind. **lose heart** to become discouraged. **lose one's heart to sb** to fall in love with a person. **set**

one's heart on (having/doing) sth to be very anxious to. have/do it. **sick at heart** extremely sad or disappointed. **take heart (from sth)** to feel encouraged because of (another person's experience, another good result etc). **take sth to heart** to feel the effects of unkind gossip, a poor exam result, a person's refusal etc very strongly. **3** the central part: *the heart of a cabbage/lettuce; the heart of a forest.* **the heart of the matter** the most important considerations in an argument, set of facts etc. **4** a heart-shaped design, esp (any of 13 playing-cards with) a red one: *the four of hearts.* Compare club¹(2), diamond(3), spade(2). ⇨ suit¹(3).

'**heart·ache** *nu* deep sorrow.

'**heart attack** *nc* a sudden dangerous condition of the heart, which stops working regularly, often causing death.

'**heart·beat** *nc* one movement of the heart.

'**heart-break** *nu* deep sorrow.

'**heart-break·ing** *adj* causing deep sorrow.

'**heart-broken** *adj* extremely sad.

'**heart·burn** *nu* a burning sensation in the lower part of the chest, caused by indigestion.

'**heart·felt** *adj* sincere: *heartfelt emotion/thanks.*

heart·less *adj* (*derog*) unkind; without pity.

heart·less·ly *adv*

'**heart-throb** *n* **1** *nu* the beating of a heart. **2** *nc* a man who many women find attractive.

heart·en·ing /'hɑːtnɪŋ/ *adj* giving courage: *heartening news.* Opp disheartening.

hearth /hɑːθ/ *nc* the area in front of a fireplace.

heart·ily /'hɑːtəlɪ/ *adv* **1** with force, courage or appetite: *eat heartily.* **2** very: *I'm heartily sick of this wet weather.*

hearty /'hɑːtɪ/ *adj* (-ier, -iest) **1** (usually *attrib*) (of feelings) strong; sincere: *give a person a hearty welcome.* **2** in good health. **hale and hearty** ⇨ hale. **3** (*attrib*) (of meals, appetites etc) big: *a hearty meal; a hearty laugh.*

heat¹ /hiːt/ *n* **1** *nu* or *sing* (an amount of) the burning sensation caused by a high temperature: *the heat of the sun's rays; cooked on a low heat.* ⇨ hot. **2** *nu* (*fig*) a strong feeling, esp of excitement or anger: *in the heat of the debate/argument.* ⇨ heated. **3** *nc* a stage in a competition to select those who will take part in (further competitions leading to) the finals: *He won his heat but not the final.* **4** *nu* **be on heat** (of female mammals) to be in a condition when conception is possible.

'**heat-stroke** *nu* a sudden illness caused by very hot weather.

'**heat·wave** *nc* a period of unusually hot weather.

heat² /hiːt/ *vt,vi* **heat (sth) (up)** (to cause something) to become hot: *heat (up) some water.*

heat·ed /'hiːtɪd/ *adj* showing excited or angry feelings: *a heated discussion/argument/debate.*

heat·ed·ly *adv* in an excited manner.

heat·er /'hiːtə(r)/ *nc* an apparatus for supplying warmth to a room or for heating water etc: *a water-heater* (which heats water); *an oil-heater* (which burns oil).

heath /hiːθ/ *nc* an area of wild land covered with small shrubs.

hea·then /'hiːðn/ *adj, nc* (*pl* — when used with *the*) (*old use*) (of) a person who does not belong to one of the main world religions.

heath·er /'heðə(r)/ *nu* a low shrub with small purple, pink or white flowers.

heave /hi:v/ *v* (*pt,pp* **—ed** or **hove** /həʊv/) **1** *vt,vi* to raise, lift up (something heavy): *heave the anchor.* **2** *vt* to produce (a sigh etc) by breathing heavily: *heave a sigh/groan.* **3** *vt* (*informal*) to lift (something heavy) and throw it: *heave a brick through a window.* **4** *vt* **heave (at)** *sth* to pull (at a rope etc). **5** *vi* (of the chest, a ship) to rise and fall regularly.

heav·en /'hevn/ *nc* **1** (also H-) the home of God and the saints: *die and go to heaven.* **move heaven and earth (to do sth)** to do everything possible (to help etc). **2** (used as an exclamation): *Good heavens! Thank heaven!* **3** (*fig*) a place, state, of supreme happiness: *Being with you is heaven!* **4** (often *pl*) the sky.

,heaven-'sent *adj* unexpected and fortunate: *a heaven-sent opportunity.*

heav·en·ward(s) /-wəd(z)/ *adj,adv.*

heav·en·ly /'hevnlɪ/ *adj* **1** of, from, like, heaven: *a heavenly angel/vision.* **2** (*informal*) very pleasing: *What a heavenly dress!*

,heavenly 'body *nc* the sun, moon, a planet etc.

heavy /'hevɪ/ *adj* (**-ier, -iest**) **1** having (a lot of) weight; difficult to lift, carry or move: *a heavy piano. It's too heavy for me to lift.* **2** of more than usual size, amount etc: *heavy rain; a heavy meal; a heavy smoker.* **3** not gentle; delicate: *cook with a heavy hand.* **4** (of work) needing a lot of energy or effort. **5** (of writing, films, music etc) serious; difficult and so dull: *a heavy opera; use a heavy writing style.* **6** (of punishment, taxes etc) difficult to bear: *be given a heavy sentence; a heavy tax on tobacco.* **7** (of sleep) not easily disturbed; (of a person asleep) difficult to wake. Compare deep¹(4), light²(7). **8** (of food) difficult to digest. **9** (of beer, wine etc) very strong. **10** (*informal*) (of criticism, disapproval, anger etc) very strong. **11** (of soil) difficult to dig and break up. **12** **heavy with sth** (of a person) inactive, sleepy, because of too much sleep, wine etc.

,heavy-'duty *adj* (*attrib*) made to survive rough use, bad weather etc: *heavy-duty shoes.*

,heavy 'going *adj* (*pred*) (of literature, work etc) difficult and boring.

,heavy-'handed *adj* (*derog*) clumsy.

,heavy-'hearted *adj* very sad. Compare light-hearted.

,heavy 'industry *nu* a mining or manufacturing industry using large machinery, e.g. the manufacture of cars. Compare light industry.

,heavy-'laden *adj* (a) carrying a heavy load. (b) (*fig*) very sad or worried.

'heavy·weight *nc* **1** (also *attrib*) a boxer weighing 175 lb (79·3 kg) or more. **2** (*fig*) an important person.

heav·ily /'hevəlɪ/ *adv: drink/sleep/breathe heavily* (i.e. to an unusual extent, degree etc). Compare lightly.

heavi·ness *nu*

heck /hek/ *n* (*sl*) (used in exclamations) hell: *Oh! What the heck!*

heckle /'hekl/ *vt,vi* to interrupt (a person) at a meeting by asking questions: *heckling the Socialist candidate.*

heck·ler /'heklə(r)/ *nc* a person who heckles.

hec·tare /'hekteə(r)/ *nc* a unit of metric measure of area, = 10 000 sq metres or 2·471 acres.

hec·tic /'hektɪk/ *adj* full of excitement and without rest: *lead a hectic life.*

he'd /hi:d/ = *he had; he would.*

hedge¹ /hedʒ/ *nc* **1** a row of bushes, shrubs or tall plants etc forming a boundary for a field, garden etc. **2** (*fig*) a means of defence against possible loss: *buy gold/diamonds as a hedge against inflation.*

hedge² /hedʒ/ *v* **1** *vt,* to put a hedge round (a garden etc): *hedge a field.* **2** *vi* to avoid giving a direct answer to a question: *Answer 'yes' or 'no'—don't hedge!* **3** *vt* **hedge one's bets** (*informal*) to do something to protect oneself from the effects of possible failure: *We hedged our bets and made some blue coats in case the red ones did not sell well.*

'hedge-row *nc* a row of bushes forming a hedge, esp along a road or path.

hedge·hog /'hedʒhɒg/ *nc* a kind of small insect-eating animal with spines covering its back.

he·don·ism /'hi:dənɪzəm/ *nu* the belief that pleasure is the most important thing in life.

he·don·ist /-ɪst/ *nc* a believer in hedonism.

he·don·is·tic /,hi:də'nɪstɪk/ *adj*

heed¹ /hi:d/ *nu* **pay heed to sth; take heed of sth** to give attention to advice, a warning etc: *She paid no heed to my advice.*

heed² /hi:d/ *vt* to pay attention to (advice etc): *heed advice/a warning.*

heed·ful /-fəl/ *adj* (*formal*): *heedful of advice.*

heed·less *adj: heedless of danger.*

hee·haw /'hi:hɔ:/ *nc* the sound made by an ass.

heel¹ /hi:l/ *nc* **1** the back part of the human foot. **at/on sb's/sth's heels** close behind: *Famine often follows on the heels of war.* **hot on sb's heels** following close behind. **down at heel** (of a person) untidy and poor. **head over heels** ⇨ head¹(1). **come to heel** (a) (of a dog) come, walk, close behind a person. (b) (*fig*) (of a person) to accept discipline and control. **dig in one's heels** to refuse to be persuaded or to go. **take to one's heels** to run away. **turn on one's heel** to turn sharply round. **2** the part of a sock etc covering the heel. **3** the part of a shoe under the heel to support it. **4** (*sl; derog*) an insincere person.

heel² /hi:l/ *vt* to put a heel(3) on (a shoe etc).

hef·ty /'heftɪ/ *adj* (**-ier, -iest**) (*informal*) big, strong: *a hefty increase/farm worker.*

heif·er /'hefə(r)/ *nc* a young cow.

height /haɪt/ *nc* (abbr ht) **1** a measurement from bottom to top: *What's your height?* (= How tall are you?) **2** the distance to the top of something, esp from sea-level or the ground: *the height of a mountain; flying at a height of 2000 metres.* **3** (often *pl*) a high place: *mountain heights; I don't like/have a poor head for heights.* **4** **the height of sth** the period of most activity, interest etc: *at the height of his ambition/popularity; be the height of fashion; during the height of the storm.* **at its height** at the point of most activity: *The famine claimed 100 lives each day at its height.*

height·en /'haɪtn/ *vt,vi* **1** (to cause something) to become high(er): *heighten a wall.* **2** (to cause) to become greater in degree: *heighten a person's anger.*

hei·nous /'heɪnəs/ *adj* (*attrib*) (of a crime) extremely bad.

hei·nous·ly adv

heir /eə(r)/ nc a person with the legal right to receive a title, property etc when the owner dies: *He is heir to a large fortune.*

heir·ess /'eərɪs/ nc a female heir.

heir·loom /'eəlu:m/ nc something valuable handed down in a family for several generations.

held /held/ pt,pp of hold³.

heli·cop·ter /'helɪkɒptə(r)/ nc a kind of aircraft with horizontal revolving blades (called *rotors*) on the top.

heli·port /'helɪpɔːt/ nc an airport for helicopters.

he·li·um /'hiːlɪəm/ nu a kind of colourless gas (symbol He) that is lighter than air and does not burn, used in balloons.

he·lix /'hiːlɪks/ nc (maths) a curved line in the shape of a spiral, as on a snail's shell.

hell /hel/ nc 1 (in some religions) a place of punishment after death. 2 a place, condition, of great suffering or misery: *suffer hell on earth.* 3 (informal) (used in exclamations to express anger, or to intensify a meaning): *What the hell do you want? He ran like hell* (= very fast). *I like him a hell of a lot* (= very much). **for the hell of it** for no serious reason.

he'll /hiːl/ = he will; he shall.

hel·lo /he'ləʊ/ int = hallo.

helm /helm/ nc a handle (also called *tiller*) or wheel, used for guiding a boat or ship. **at the helm (of sth)** (fig) in control (of a business etc).

hel·met /'helmɪt/ nc a hard covering for the head as worn by motorcyclists, soldiers, police etc.

help¹ /help/ n 1 nu the act of helping: *Thank you for your kind help.* 2 n sing a person or thing that helps: *Your advice was a great help.* 3 nu a cure: *There's no help for it.* 4 nc a woman paid to do the housework. ⇨ also home help.

help·ful /-fəl/ adj (a) giving help: *a helpful suggestion.* (b) willing to help: *helpful children.*

help·ful·ly /-fəlɪ/ adv

help·ing nc (esp) a portion of food served at a meal: *three helpings of pie.*

help·less adj (a) not receiving help. (b) dependent on others: *a helpless invalid.*

help·less·ly adv

help² /help/ v 1 vt,vi to do (part of) something to reduce a person's work or make it easier: *Could you please help me to lift these boxes? Can I help (you)? She often helps with the cooking. We helped the old man out of the car.* Ⓝ 'Assist' is also possible but much more formal. 2 vt **can/cannot/can't help** + **-ing/it/oneself** to avoid, prevent: *I can't help wondering where she is. She began to cry—she couldn't help herself/it. He avoids extra work if he can help it.* **it can't be helped** a situation, result etc is unavoidable or cannot be prevented. 3 vt to take (esp food, drink) for oneself: *Help yourself (to the fruit).* 4 vt,vi to make (a condition etc) better: *All the wishing in the world won't help (you) if you don't work. Apologizing might help.*

help sth along to cause a process, experiment, situation etc to progress.

help sb off/on with sth to help a person to take off/put on clothing.

help out to give a person help (during a crisis, a busy period etc): *My daughter helps (me) out on Saturdays.*

help sb to sth ⇨ 3 above.

help·er /'helpə(r)/ nc a person who helps.

hel·ter-skel·ter /ˌheltə 'skeltə(r)/ adv (done) in a hurry and without organization. □ nc a tall spiral slide¹(2) in a fairground etc.

hem¹ /hem/ nc a border or edge of cloth, esp one on an article of clothing when turned and sewn down.

hem² /hem/ vt (-mm-) 1 to make a hem on (clothing etc). 2 **hem sb/sth in** to surround a person, thing: *be hemmed in by the crowds.*

'hem·line nc (esp) the lower edge of a skirt or dress.

hemi·sphere /'hemɪsfɪə(r)/ nc 1 (maths) a half of a sphere. 2 a half of the Earth. ⇨ Eastern/Northern/Southern/Western hemisphere.

he·mo·glo·bin /ˌhiːmə'gləʊbɪn/ nu = haemoglobin.

he·mo·phil·ia /ˌhiːmə'fɪlɪə/ nu = haemophilia.

hem·or·rhage /'hemərɪdʒ/ nc,nu = haemorrhage.

hem·or·rhoids /'hemərɔɪdz/ n pl = haemorrhoids.

hemp /hemp/ nu 1 a kind of plant from which coarse fibres are obtained, used for making rope and cloth. 2 = marijuana.

hem-stitch /'hemstɪtʃ/ vt, nc (to sew the hem of a dress etc with) a decorative stitch made by pulling out some of the threads and tying the cross-threads in groups.

hen /hen/ nc 1 a female of the common domestic fowl. Compare cock¹(1). 2 a female of the bird mentioned: *guinea-hen; peahen.*

'hen-party nc (pl **-ies**) (informal) a party for women only. Compare stag-party.

'hen-pecked adj (informal; derog) (of a man) controlled and criticized by his wife.

hence /hens/ adv (formal) 1 from here; from now: *a week hence* (i.e. in a week's time). 2 for this reason: *I don't like her. Hence, I won't visit her.*

hence'forth, **hence'forward** adv from now on; in future.

hench·man /'hentʃmən/ nc (pl **-men**) a faithful supporter, esp one who obeys without question the orders of a leader.

hen·na /'henə/ nu (a kind of bush producing) a reddish-brown dye for colouring the hair etc.

hen·na·ed /'henəd/ adj dyed with henna.

hepa·ti·tis /ˌhepə'taɪtɪs/ nu (med) inflammation of the liver.

hep·ta·gon /'heptəgən/ nc (maths) a flat figure with 7 (esp equal) sides.

hep·tag·on·al /hep'tægənl/ adj

her¹ /hə(r) strong form: hɜː(r)/ possessive adj or det of, belonging to, a female person or animal (and sometimes a ship, country etc considered to be female): *That's her pen, not his. He's hijacked the plane and her crew.* Compare hers, his¹.

her² /hə(r) strong form: hɜː(r)/ pron (used as the object form of *she*) a female person or animal (and sometimes a ship, country etc considered to be female): *I love her. Give her the book. Give it to her. We sailed round the island in her.*

her·ald¹ /'herəld/ nc 1 a person (formerly) making public announcements for, and carrying messages from, a ruler. 2 a person or thing telling the coming of a person or thing: *In England the cuckoo is a herald of spring.*

her·al·dic /he'rældɪk/ *adj* of heraldry.

¹her·ald·ry *nu* the study of coats of arms and the descent and history of old families.

her·ald² /'herəld/ *vt* (*formal*) to announce the approach of (spring etc).

herb /hɜːb/ *nc* any small plant whose leaves or seeds, because of their scent or flavour, are used in medicine or for flavouring food, such as *sage, mint.*

herb·al /-əl/ *adj* using (esp) medicinal herbs: *herbal remedies.*

herb·al·ist /-əlɪst/ *nc* a person, business, that sells herbs or herbal remedies.

her·ba·ceous /hɜː'beɪʃəs/ *adj* (*science*) (of plants) having stems that are not woody: *a herbaceous border* (= a flowerbed with herbaceous plants).

her·bi·vore /'hɜːbɪvɔː(r)/ *nc* (*science*) an animal that eats plants. Compare carnivore, insectivore, omnivore.

her·biv·or·ous /hɜː'bɪvərəs/ *adj* plant-eating.

her·cu·lean /ˌhɜːkjʊ'liːən/ *adj* having, needing, great strength: *a herculean task.*

herd¹ /hɜːd/ *nc* **1** a number of animals, esp cattle, feeding or going about together: *a herd of cattle/ deer/elephants.* **2** (used mainly in compounds) keeper of a herd: *a cowherd.*

herd² /hɜːd/ *v* **1** *vt, vi* (to cause people) to gather (as if) into a herd: *We were herded together like cattle.* **2** *vt* to look after (cattle).

herds·man *nc* a person who looks after a herd.

here /hɪə(r)/ *adv* **1** in, at, to, towards, this place: *Come here. I live near here. Ben's not here. Here comes the bus. Here it comes. She is staying a mile from here.* **here you are/it is** this is what you want/are looking for. Compare there²(1). **2** at this point (in a series of events, during a process etc): *Here the speaker paused to have a drink. Here is where I disagree.* Compare there²(2). **here goes!** (used when beginning a new or daring activity): *I've never swum that far but here goes!* **3** (used to call attention or for emphasis) in this place, list etc: *My friend here was also at the wedding.* **4 here and now** in this place and immediately: *I'm warning you here and now that this is your last chance.* **here and there** in, to, various places: *She travelled here and there distributing food. He bought things here and there and soon spent all his money.* **here, there and everywhere** in, to, many different places: *I've looked/been here, there and everywhere, but I can't find it.* **be neither here nor there** to be unimportant, irrelevant: *He may deny it, but it's neither here nor there.* **5 here's to sb/sth** (used when drinking to a person's success, health, a scheme's success etc): *Here's to the bride and groom!*

ˌhere·a'bouts *adv* near here.

ˌhere·'after *adv, nu* (in) the future; the life after death.

ˌhere·'in *adv* (*legal*) in this (document).

ˌhere·'with *adv* (abbr h/w) (*commerce*) with this: *Herewith the report you asked for.*

her·ed·itary /hɪ'redɪtrɪ/ *adj* passed on from parent to child, from one generation to following generations: *hereditary rulers/diseases.*

her·ed·ity /hɪ'redətɪ/ *nu* the tendency to pass characteristics on to children etc.

her·esy /'herəsɪ/ *nc, nu* (*pl* **-ies**) (the holding of) a belief contrary to what is generally accepted in religion: *be guilty of heresy.*

her·etic /'herətɪk/ *nc* **1** a person guilty of, supporting, heresy. **2** a person who holds an unorthodox opinion.

her·eti·cal /hɪ'retɪkl/ *adj*

heri·tage /'herɪtɪdʒ/ *nc* that which has been or may be inherited: *our political heritage.*

her·met·ic /hɜː'metɪk/ *adj* (*science*) completely airtight.

her·meti·cal·ly *adv: hermetically sealed.*

her·mit /'hɜːmɪt/ *nc* a person living in isolation from others.

her·mit·age /-ɪdʒ/ *nc* a place where a hermit lives.

he·ro /'hɪərəʊ/ *nc* (*pl* **-es**) **1** a boy or man respected for bravery. **2** (*literature*) a main male character in a poem, story, play etc.

hero·ism /'herəʊɪzəm/ *nu* great courage.

her·oic /hɪ'rəʊɪk/ *adj* **1** having, needing, great courage: *heroic deeds/tasks.* **2** (*literature*) (of poetry) dealing with heroes: *heroic verse.*

he·roi·cal·ly /-klɪ/ *adv*

her·oics /hɪ'rəʊɪks/ *n pl* exaggerated expressions of anxiety, sorrow etc.

her·oin /'herəʊɪn/ *nu* a kind of narcotic drug prepared from morphine.

her·oine /'herəʊɪn/ *nc* a female hero.

her·on /'herən/ *nc* a kind of long-legged waterbird living in marshy places.

her·pes /'hɜːpiːz/ *nu* (*med*) a disease of the skin with blisters, esp on the lips, caused by a virus.

her·ring /'herɪŋ/ *nc* (*pl* **—**) a kind of seafish valued as food. ⇨ also red herring.

'her·ring·bone *adj, nu* a pattern for stitching (like the spine and bones of a herring).

hers /hɜːz/ *possessive pron* of, belonging to, her: *Is Jane his friend or hers? He's a friend of hers.* Compare her¹, his².

her·self /hə'self *strong form:* hɜː-/ *pron* **1** (used as the *reflexive* form of *her*): *She hurt herself. Jane ought to be ashamed of herself.* **(all) by herself** ⇨ by²(1). **2** (used for emphasis): *She told me the news herself.* **3** her usual self: *She's not herself/ doesn't look/seem herself today.*

hertz /hɜːts/ *nc* (*pl* **—**) (symbol Hz) a unit of frequency equal to one cycle per second. ⇨ megahertz.

he's /hiːz/ = he is, he has.

hesi·tant /'hezɪtənt/ *adj* tending to hesitate.

hesi·tant·ly *adv*

hesi·tance /-əns/, **hesi·tan·cy** /-ənsɪ/ *nu*

hesi·tate /'hezɪteɪt/ *vi* to show signs of uncertainty or unwillingness in speech or action: *He's still hesitating about joining.*

hesi·tat·ing·ly *adv*

hesi·ta·tion /ˌhezɪ'teɪʃn/ *n* **1** *nu* the state of hesitating. **2** *nc* an instance of this: *His doubts and hesitations were tedious.*

hes·sian /'hesɪən/ *nu* a kind of strong, coarse cloth made of jute.

het·ero·dox /'hetərədɒks/ *adj* (*formal*) not normal, accepted or established: *heterodox ideas.*

het·ero·gen·eous /ˌhetərə'dʒiːnɪəs/ *adj* (*formal*) (formed of parts) of different kinds: *the het-*

erogeneous population of the USA. Opp homogeneous.

het·ero·sex·ual /ˌhetərəˈseksjʊəl/ *adj* attracted to the opposite sex.

het-up /ˌhetˈʌp/ *adj* (*informal*) worried.

hew /hjuː/ *vt,vi* (*pt* —**ed**, *pp* —**ed** or —**n** /hjuːn/) to cut down (a tree etc), e.g. with an axe: *hew down a branch*.

hexa·gon /ˈheksəgən/ *nc* (*maths*) a flat figure with 6 (esp equal) sides.

hex·ag·on·al /hekˈsægənl/ *adj*

hex·ameter /hekˈsæmɪtə(r)/ *nc* (*literature*) a line of verse with six units of rhythm (called *metrical feet*).

hey /heɪ/ *int* (used to call attention, to express surprise etc): *Hey! What are you boys doing?*

hey·day /ˈheɪdeɪ/ *n sing* the time of greatest prosperity or power: *in the heyday of the railways*.

HGV /ˌeɪtʃ dʒiː ˈviː/ *abbr* heavy goods vehicle (a large vehicle used for transporting goods).

hi /haɪ/ *int* (esp *US*) = hallo.

hi·atus /haɪˈeɪtəs/ *nc* (*pl* —**es**) a gap in a series making it incomplete.

hi·ber·nate /ˈhaɪbəneɪt/ *vi* (of some animals) to pass the whole of the winter in a state like sleep.

hi·ber·na·tion /ˌhaɪbəˈneɪʃn/ *nu*

hic·cup (also **hic·cough**) /ˈhɪkʌp/ *vi, nc* (to have) a sudden stopping of the breath with a sound like a cough.

hid /hɪd/ *pt* of hide[3].

hid·den /ˈhɪdn/ *pp* of hide[3].

hide[1] /haɪd/ *nc* a hidden place where wild animals, birds etc may be observed, e.g. by photographers.

hide[2] /haɪd/ *nc,nu* (an) animal's skin.

hide[3] /haɪd/ *v* (*pt* **hid** /hɪd/, *pp* **hidden** /ˈhɪdn/) 1 *vt* to put or keep (a person, thing) in a place to prevent her, him, it from being seen, found or known: *Where shall I hide the money? Quick, hide yourself! The sun was hidden by the clouds. His words had a hidden meaning.* 2 *vi* to be or become hidden: *Where is he hiding?*

hid·eous /ˈhɪdɪəs/ *adj* filling the mind with horror: *a hideous crime/noise/face.*

hid·eous·ly *adv*

hid·ing[1] /ˈhaɪdɪŋ/ *nc* a beating: *give him a good hiding.*

hid·ing[2] /ˈhaɪdɪŋ/ *nu* **be in/go into hiding** to be hidden/hide oneself. **come out of hiding** to show oneself.

'hiding-place *nc* a place where a person or thing is or could be hidden.

hi·er·archy /ˈhaɪərɑːkɪ/ *nc* (*pl* -**ies**) an organization with grades of authority from lowest to highest.

hi·ero·glyph·ics /ˌhaɪərəˈglɪfɪks/ *n pl* a system of writing using a picture to represent a word or sound.

hi·ero·glyph·ic *adj*

hi-fi /ˌhaɪ ˈfaɪ/ *adj, nc* (*informal*) (of) electrical equipment reproducing recorded sound (using *high fidelity*).

high[1] /haɪ/ *adj* (—**er**, —**est**) 1 going, reaching, far up: *a high wall; a high mountain.* Ⓝ *'Tall'* is used for people and narrow objects, as in *a tall man/ tree/tower.* Opp low[1](1). ⇨ height. 2 above the usual or normal amount, level or intensity: *a high cost/temperature/speed/mark. The waves were*

high during the storm at sea. Opp low[1](2). **have a high opinion of sb** ⇨ opinion(1). 3 (situated) far above the ground: *a high shelf; flying high in the sky; the highest climber.* Opp low[1](3). **high and dry** (*fig*) without help or support: *They left me high and dry without any money.* 4 showing a lot of activity; happening often: *a high rate of success; a high mileage/voltage.* Opp low[1](4). 5 (*pred*) measuring (the distance mentioned) from the bottom to the top: *How high is Mount Everest? It's nearly 9000 metres high. The water was almost waist-high.* Ⓝ *'Tall'* is always used of people, as in *How tall are you? I'm 1·8 metres tall,* and can be used of narrow objects, as in *The tree is 50 metres tall.* Compare low[1](5). 6 (of sound) at, near, the top of the scale: *sing in a high voice.* Compare deep[1](5), low[1](6). 7 (of sound) loud: *That radio is on too high.* Opp low[1](7). 8 (*attrib*) of an important or superior social position or rank: *a high official; high society.* **high and mighty** (*informal; derog*) arrogant. 9 (*informal*) (of a person) under the influence of alcoholic drink or drugs. 10 noble; virtuous: *have high aims/ideals.* Compare low[1](10). 11 far advanced: *high summer; high noon.* **be high time** (*sb* + *past tense*) ⇨ time[1](4). 12 (of food) smelling or tasting a little bad: *high meat/fish.* 13 highly developed: *A mammal is a high form of life.* Opp low[1](11).

'high-born *adj* of noble birth.

'high·brow *adj, nc* (sometimes *derog*) (of) a person with intellectual tastes and interests. Compare lowbrow.

'high chair *nc* one with tall legs for a young child.

,high-'class *adj* of first-class quality.

,high 'comedy *nu* (*literature*) drama or novels with cultured, well-spoken characters. Compare low comedy.

,High Com'missioner *nc* the representative of one Commonwealth country in another, equivalent to an ambassador.

'High Court *nc* the supreme court of justice.

,high 'drama *nu* (*literature*) the kind that is serious in style and subject.

,higher ,edu'cation *nu* education at college, university, a polytechnic etc.

,high-fi'delity *nu* (abbr hi-fi) the method of producing sound giving faithful reproduction by the use of a wide range of sound waves.

,high fi'nance *nu* complex and important financial affairs.

,high-'flyer/-'flier *nc* an ambitious person.

,high-'flown *adj* (*derog*) pompous.

,high 'frequency *nc* (abbr hf) any radio frequency of between 3 and 30 megacycles per second.

'high-grade *adj* of superior quality: *high-grade petrol.* Opp low-grade.

,high-'handed *adj* (*derog*) using power or authority without consideration for the feelings of another person.

'high jump *nu* (the —) an athletic contest for jumping over an adjustable horizontal bar. ⇨ long jump.

'high·land *n* (**a**) *nc* a mountainous region. (**b**) (*pl*) any mountainous parts of a country.

'high-level *adj* (of conferences etc) involving people in important positions.

,**high-level** '**language** (*computers*) a system for coding near to ordinary language, e.g. BASIC, that can be learnt and used easily. Compare low-level language.

'**high life** *nu* (**a**) a fashionable and luxurious style of living. (**b**) (in W Africa) a popular kind of music and dance.

'**high·light** *vt* to give emphasis to (the more important details, facts).

'**highlights** *n pl* (**a**) luminous areas on a photograph, picture, in a person's hair etc which show reflected light. (**b**) (*fig; also sing*) most obvious or important parts: *the highlights of the week's events.*

,**High** '**Mass** *nc* (*RC Church*) one with a choir and much ceremony.

,**high-**'**minded** *adj* very serious about morals, ideals or principles.

,**high-**'**powered** *adj* (**a**) having, using, great power: *a high-powered engine.* (**b**) (of optical instruments) giving great magnification. (**c**) (of a person) important; energetic.

,**high** '**priest** *nc* a chief priest.

'**high-rise** *adj* (*attrib*) (of tall buildings) with many storeys or levels: *high-rise flats.*

'**high·road** *nc* a main road.

'**High School** *nc* a secondary school.

'**high season** *nu* (the —) (also *attrib*) the most popular period, e.g. at a hotel, when booking a plane, for a holiday: *travel in the high season.* Compare low season.

,**high so**'**ciety** *nu* the upper classes.

,**high-**'**spirited** *adj* bold; lively.

'**high spot** *nc* an outstanding feature, memory, event etc.

'**high street** *nc* (esp in proper names) the main street of a town.

,**high** '**tea** *nu* (*GB*) an early evening meal (or late tea) in homes where dinner is not eaten in the evening.

,**high** '**treason** *nu* treason against the State or a sovereign.

'**high·way** *nc* a main public road.

,**highway** '**code** *nc* (usually the —) (a book of) the rules for driving on public roads.

high² /haɪ/ *adv* at, in or to a high degree: *climb high.* **hold one's head high** ⇨ head¹(1). **high and low** everywhere: *hunt/look/search high and low for it.* **run high** (of feelings) to be very excited.

high³ /haɪ/ *nc* a high level: *Costs are at an all-time high.*

high·ly /'haɪlɪ/ *adv* in or to a large degree: *a highly-paid official; a highly amusing film.* **highly strung** very nervous; easily excited. **think highly of sb** to have a good opinion of a person.

high·ness /'haɪnɪs/ *n* **1** *nu* the state or quality of being high. **2** *nc* (H-) a title used of and to a royal person: *His/Her/Your Royal Highness.*

hi·jack /'haɪdʒæk/ *vt* **1** (to threaten) to use force against those in control of (a plane etc) in order to achieve certain aims or to reach a desired destination. **2** to stop (a vehicle) by force and steal the goods it is carrying.

hi·jack·er *nc* a person who hijacks a plane etc.

hike /haɪk/ *vi, nc* (*informal*) (to go for) a long walk in the country. ⇨ hitch-hike.

hiker *nc* a person who hikes.

hil·ari·ous /hɪ'leərɪəs/ *adj* very funny.

hil·ari·ous·ly *adv*

hil·ar·ity /hɪ'lærɪtɪ/ *nu* loud laughter.

hill /hɪl/ *nc* **1** an area of high land, lower than a mountain. **be over the hill** (of a person) to be no longer as good, active etc as he or she was. **2** the slope, e.g. on a road: *drive up a steep hill.* **3** a heap of earth: *a hill of sand; anthills.*

'**hill·side** *nc* a side of a hill.

'**hill·top** *nc* the top of a hill.

hilly *adj* (**-ier, -iest**) having many hills.

hill·ock /'hɪlək/ *nc* a small hill(1).

hilt /hɪlt/ *nc* the handle of a sword or dagger. **(up) to the hilt** (*fig*) completely: *His guilt was proved to the hilt.*

him /hɪm/ *pron* (used as the object form of *he*) a male person or animal: *I love him. Give him the money. Give it to him. I have a lot of respect for him.* Compare her.

him·self /hɪm'self/ *pron* **1** (used as the *reflexive* form of *him*): *He hurt himself. John ought to be ashamed of himself.* **(all) by himself** ⇨ by²(1). **2** (used for emphasis): *He told me the news himself.* **3** his usual self: *He's not himself/doesn't look/ seem himself today.*

hind /haɪnd/ *adj* (*attrib*) (of things in pairs, front and back) at the back: *the hind legs of a horse.* Compare fore¹.

'**hind·most** *adj* farthest behind or back.

'**hind·quarters** *n pl* the back part of a carcass of lamb, beef etc.

hin·der /'hɪndə(r)/ *vt* to make (progress) difficult; get in the way of (a person): *Don't hinder me in my work.*

hin·drance /'hɪndrəns/ *nc* a person or thing that hinders: *You are more of a hindrance than a help.*

hind·sight /'haɪndsaɪt/ *nu* the ability to understand why something happened or how it could have been prevented after the event has occurred.

Hin·di /'hɪndɪ/ *adj, n* (of) an official language of N India, also used by some Indians living in other countries.

Hin·du /'hɪnduː/ *adj, nc,nu* (of) (a person who believes in) Hinduism.

Hin·du·ism /'hɪnduːɪzm/ *nu* a religion from India with a strong philosophy, a belief that a person is born again after death and with a series of social ranks that cannot be changed.

hinge¹ /hɪndʒ/ *nc* **1** a joint on which a lid, door or gate turns or swings. **2** (*fig*) the central principle on which something depends.

hinge² /hɪndʒ/ *vt* **1** to support, attach (something) with a hinge or hinges. **2 hinge on sth** (*fig*) to depend on something: *Success hinges on the weather.*

hint¹ /hɪnt/ *nc* a small or indirect indication or suggestion. **take a hint** (*informal*) to realize (and do) what is suggested: *I know how to take a hint.*

hint² /hɪnt/ *v* **1** *vt,vi* **hint (that . . .)** to suggest; give a hint: *I hinted that he ought to work harder.* **2** *vi* **hint at sth** to refer indirectly to something: *He hinted at my bad pronunciation.*

hin·ter·land /'hɪntəlænd/ *nc* the areas of land away from the coast, esp when undeveloped.

hip¹ /hɪp/ *nc* the part on either side of the body

above the leg: *He stood there with his hands on his hips.*

'hip-flask *nc* a small flask (for brandy etc).

hip² /hɪp/ *nc* a fruit (red when ripe) of the wild rose.

hip³ /hɪp/ *int Hip, hip, hurrah!* (an expression of satisfaction or approval by a group).

hip·po /'hɪpəʊ/ *nc* (*pl* **—s**) (*informal*) = hippopotamus.

hip·po·pota·mus /ˌhɪpə'pɒtəməs/ *nc* (*pl* **—es** or **-mi** /-maɪ/) a kind of large, African river animal with a thick skin.

hip·py (also **hip·pie**) /'hɪpɪ/ *nc* (*pl* **-ies**) a person who rejects usual social values, e.g. by wearing casual and colourful clothes and living in groups.

hip·ster /'hɪpstə(r)/ *adj* (*attrib*) (of clothes) held at the hips (not at the waist): *hipster trousers.*

hire¹ /haɪə(r)/ *nu* (money paid for) the act of hiring: *Bicycles for hire, £3 a week.*

ˌhire-'purchase *nu* (abbr HP) an agreement to pay for something by instalments, having the use of it after the first payment: *I've bought this on HP.*

hire² /haɪə(r)/ *vt* **1** to obtain the use of (something) in return for payment: *hire a car.* **2** to employ (a person) for a period: *hire a gardener for the summer.* **3** *hire sth out (to sb)* to allow equipment etc to be used for a period in return for a payment: *They hire out sailing boats on the lake.*

his¹ /hɪz/ *possessive adj* or *det* of, belonging to, a male person or animal: *That's his book, not yours.* Compare **her¹**.

his² /hɪz/ *possessive pron* of, belonging to, him: *Is Jane her sister or his? She's a friend of his.* Compare **hers**.

hiss¹ /hɪs/ *nc* a hissing sound: *The speaker ignored the hisses.*

hiss² /hɪs/ *v* **1** *vi* to make the sound /s/ or the noise heard when water falls on a very hot surface. **2** *vt,vi* **hiss (at) sb/sth** to show disapproval by making this sound: *hiss (at) an actor.*

his·tor·ian /hɪ'stɔːrɪən/ *nc* a writer, student, of, expert in, history.

his·tor·ic /hɪ'stɒrɪk/ *adj* notable or memorable in history; associated with past times: *a historic event.*

hiˌstoric ˌpresent 'tense *nc* (*gram*) the simple present tense used to describe events in the past to make the description more lively, as in *I'm standing there when a man comes along and takes out a knife.*

his·tori·cal /hɪ'stɒrɪkl/ *adj* **1** belonging to history (as contrasted with legend and fiction): *a historical event.* **2** having to do with history: *historical studies.*

hiˌstorical 'novel *nc* a novel using characters and situations from history.

his·tori·cal·ly /-klɪ/ *adv*

his·tory /'hɪstərɪ/ *n* (*pl* **-ies**) **1** *nu* (the study of) the branch of knowledge dealing with past events of a country, a continent or the world. **make history** to do something which will be recorded in history. **2** *nc* a description of past events: *a new history of Europe.* ⇨ ancient/modern/natural history; medieval. **3** *nc* a set of events connected with a person or thing: *a house with a strange history; a person's medical history.*

his·tri·on·ic /ˌhɪstrɪ'ɒnɪk/ *adj* (of expressions of

feelings) insincere.

his·tri·on·ics *n pl* exaggerated expressions of feelings to create an effect.

hi-tech (also **high-tech**) /ˌhaɪ 'tek/ *adj* (*attrib*) (*informal*) using the latest technology: *hi-tech medical equipment.*

hit¹ /hɪt/ *nc* **1** a blow (that reaches a target); violent contact that causes damage: *a hit with one's fist/a stick; five hits and three misses; a direct hit on the front of the car.* **2** (*informal*) (of a performance, actor, new model, record etc) a success (because liked by the audience, buyers etc): *Their new record/The play/The latest model is a hit. She has been a hit on Broadway for six months.* **make a hit (with sb)** (*informal*) to cause a person to like you or be impressed with you.

hit² /hɪt/ *vt* (*pt,pp* **—**; **-tt-**) **1** to give a blow to (a person or thing): *hit a nail; hit a man accidentally. The lorry hit the back of my car.* ⇨ roof¹(1). **2** to use a bat, racket etc to send (a ball) to a target, a distance etc: *hit a ball into the crowd; hit a winning shot.* **3** to reach (a place): *hit the right path; hit town.* ⇨ sack². **4** to reach (a state, level etc): *Prices hit a new low.* **5** to affect (a person): *Her redundancy has hit her family hard* (i.e. they are suffering a great deal).

hit back (at sb/sth) to respond strongly or violently to a physical or verbal attack: *The government hit back at its critics by publishing a report on the economy.*

hit it off (together) (with sb) (*informal*) to enjoy a strong friendly relationship.

hit on sth to find a good idea etc by chance or unexpectedly: *hit on an idea/a solution.*

hit out (against/at sb/sth) to make a strong verbal or written attack (against a political leader or policy, immorality, a belief or principle etc).

hitch¹ /hɪtʃ/ *nc* **1** *a hitch (up)* a short pull or push (up). **2** a kind of noose or knot. **3** a temporary difficulty: *a technical hitch.* **go off without a hitch** to be done without difficulty. **4** (*informal*) an act of hitch-hiking.

hitch² /hɪtʃ/ *v* **1** *vt* **hitch sth up** to pull something up with a quick movement: *hitch up one's trousers.* **2** *vt* **hitch sth on/to sth** to fasten something on or to a hook etc: *hitch a horse to a fence.* **3** *vi* (*informal*) = hitch-hike.

hitch-hike /'hɪtʃhaɪk/ *vi* to get a free ride by asking for one (from the driver of a car, lorry etc).

hitch-hiker *nc* a person who hitch-hikes.

hith·er /'hɪðə(r)/ *adv* (*old use*) here.

hith·er·to /ˌhɪðə(r) 'tuː/ *adv* until now; until then: *We'd never been there hitherto.*

HIV /ˌeɪtʃ aɪ 'viː/ *abbr* Human Immunodeficiency Virus (the virus that is present in a person who may suffer from AIDS).

hive¹ /haɪv/ *nc* **1** a box for bees to live in; the bees living in the box. **2** (*fig*) a place full of busy people: *What a hive of industry!*

hive² /haɪv/ *vt* **hive (sth) off (from sth)** (*fig*) (to cause people, things) to become a separate (and perhaps independent) part or group.

h'm /həm/ *int* (used to call a person's attention to or express doubt or disapproval).

HMS /ˌeɪtʃ em 'es/ *abbr* Her/His Majesty's Ship (used before the names of British warships, naval colleges etc): *HMS Victory.*

HMSO /ˌeɪtʃ em es 'əʊ/ *abbr* Her/His Majesty's

Stationery Office (on government stationery).

ho /həʊ/ *int* (used to express surprise, disbelief etc).

hoard¹ /hɔːd/ *nc* a carefully saved and guarded store or collection of money, coins, food or other treasured or valuable objects.

hoard² /hɔːd/ *vt,vi* to save and store (money, valuable things): *hoard (up) gold.*

hoard·er *nc* a person who hoards.

hoar·frost /'hɔːfrɒst/ *nu* white frost on grass, leaves etc.

hoarse /hɔːs/ *adj* (**—r, —st**) sounding rough and harsh: *He shouted himself hoarse.*

hoarse·ly *adv*

hoarse·ness *nu*

hoax /həʊks/ *vt, nc* (to deceive a person using) a trick intended to make a person believe something that is not true and act unnecessarily.

hoax·er *nc* a person who uses hoaxes.

hobble /'hɒbl/ *vi* to walk with difficulty as when injured: *hobbling along the road.*

hob·by /'hɒbɪ/ *nc* (*pl* **-ies**) an activity done for pleasure during one's free time.

hob·by·horse /'hɒbɪhɔːs/ *nc* **1** a wooden horse on rockers as a child's toy. **2** a long stick with a horse's head. **3** a favourite idea or topic: *Now he's started on his hobbyhorse.*

hob·nob /'hɒbnɒb/ *vi* (**-bb-**) **hobnob (with sb)** to be friendly towards, chat with, a person in a higher position: *Paul was happily hobnobbing with the directors.*

hock¹ /hɒk/ *nc* the middle joint of an animal's back leg.

hock² /hɒk/ *nu* a kind of German white wine.

hock·ey /'hɒkɪ/ *nu* **1** '**field hockey** a game played on a field by two teams of eleven players, with sticks and a ball. **2** '**ice hockey** a game played on ice by two teams of six players wearing skates, with sticks and a rubber disc (called a *puck*).

'**hockey stick** *nc* a long curved or angled stick used to hit the ball or puck.

hoe /həʊ/ *nc* a garden implement used for loosening soil etc. □ *vt, vi* (*pt,pp* **—d**) to work with a hoe: *hoeing (up) weeds.*

hog¹ /hɒg/ *nc* **1** a castrated male pig reared for meat. **2** (*fig; derog*) a greedy, selfish person. **3 go the whole hog** to do something thoroughly.

hog² /hɒg/ *vt* (**-gg-**) to take or keep (something) greedily and selfishly.

Hog·ma·nay /'hɒgmənɛɪ/ *n* (in Scotland) New Year's Eve (and its festivities).

hoist¹ /hɔɪst/ *nc* **1** an apparatus used for hoisting. **2** (*informal*) a push up: *give him a hoist* (e.g. when he is climbing a wall).

hoist² /hɔɪst/ *vt* to lift (something) with an apparatus of ropes and pulleys: *hoist a flag/sail; hoist crates aboard.*

hoi·ty-toi·ty /ˌhɔɪtɪ 'tɔɪtɪ/ *adj* (*informal; derog*) snobbish and arrogant.

hold¹ /həʊld/ *n* **1** *nc,nu* the act, manner, power of holding: *Can you grab/get/take hold of the wheel? Keep hold of my hand.* **get hold of sb/sth** (esp) to find a useful person, thing: *You should get hold of a good lawyer.* **have a hold over sb** to know something about a person that gives one power or influence to get one's own way. **2** *nc* something that a person can hold: *The rock face provides few*

holds for climbers. ⇨ **foothold**. **3** (in boxing and wrestling) (a kind of) grip: *all-in wrestling with no holds barred.*

hold² /həʊld/ *nc* the part of a ship below deck where cargo is stored.

hold³ /həʊld/ *v* (*pt,pp* **held** /held/) **1** *vt,vi* to have or keep (a person, thing) in one's hands or arms and also any other part of the body such as the teeth or with a tool: *She held my hand. Hold the handle/rail/rope. He held the knife in his teeth. Hold the nut with this spanner while I turn the screw. John held his newborn son in his arms. Can you hold these tickets/this vase for me* (i.e. keep it for me) *until tomorrow?* **hold the line** ⇨ line¹(3). **2** *vt* to control (something) (in the position or state mentioned): *Hold your head up. Please hold your temper.* **hold everything/it** (*informal*) to stop an activity. **there's no holding sb/some people** it is impossible to control or stop a person/people. ⇨ also breath(2), head¹(1), horse¹(1), tongue(1). **3** *vt,vi* to support the weight of (a person, thing): *Will the ropes hold me? He held her head above the water.* **4** *vt* to be the owner of (something): *hold the world record; hold shares in a business.* **5** *vt* to have (a job etc): *hold a job in industry; hold office in local government.* **6** *vt* to have the space for (people, things): *The theatre can hold 60 000 people. The bowl holds two litres. Will this suitcase hold all your clothes?* Ⓝ Not used in continuous tenses, e.g. *is/was -ing.* ⇨ also holdall, water¹(1). **7** *vt* (*computers*) to keep (information) stored: *hold data on floppy disks.* **8** *vt* to believe (something): *He holds strange ideas about education. Does he hold himself responsible for the children? What does the future hold for us?* (= What do you believe will happen to us?) **9** *vt* to control the effects of (alcohol): *hold one's liquor.* **10** *vt* (of a vehicle) to keep a good contact with (the road): *hold the road.* **11** *vt* to defend (something) during an attack: *hold a bridge.* **hold at bay** ⇨ bay⁴. **hold the fort** ⇨ fort. **hold one's ground** ⇨ ground¹(1). **hold one's own** ⇨ own². **12** *vt* to keep the interest or attention of (a person, group): *hold an audience/the viewers/people's attention.* **13** *vt* to organize and have (a meeting etc): *hold an election/debate/inquiry.* **14** *vi* (of weather) to remain unchanged. **15** *vi* (of a theory, scheme etc) to remain true, possible, valid etc. Ⓝ Not used in continuous tenses, e.g. *is/was -ing.*

hold sth against sb to allow previous bad behaviour, a criminal record, a failure etc to affect one's judgement about a person.

hold back to hesitate because of fear or unwillingness: *She held back and allowed the others to go first.* **hold sb back** to prevent a person from making progress: *Her poor education/working-class accent/modern hairstyle seemed to be holding her back.* **hold sb/sth back** to use a barrier, officials such as the police etc to prevent water, plants etc or a person, crowd etc from moving forward. **hold sth back** to prevent or delay something becoming known or allowed: *hold back information; hold back a salary increase/a decision.*

hold sb down (**a**) to hold a person in a physically low position. (**b**) to prevent a person from making progress. **(c)** (of a dictator or tyrant) to keep a population, group under control and without freedom to object. **hold sth down (a)** to keep an object fixed to a lower object: *hold the wood down with nails.* **(b)** to prevent food from being brought up from the stomach. **(c)** to keep an amount at a low level: *hold prices/numbers down.* **hold a job down** ⇨ job(2).

hold forth to speak loudly and seriously (as if) to an audience.

hold sth in (a) to keep one's stomach tight and flat. **(b)** to control emotions: *hold in one's feeling of anger/frustration.* **hold sb in high esteem/ regard** to feel a great deal of respect for a person.

hold off (of bad weather or an enemy's attack) to be delayed, not occur: *The storm seems to be holding off.* **hold sb/sth off** to prevent a person, group, bad influence, social difficulties etc from having an effect: *hold off an attack/the fans/ the reporters; hold off inflation/an outbreak of flu.*

hold on (a) to remain in a dangerous position and continue to survive, avoid defeat etc: *Can you hold on while I go for help?* **(b)** (*informal*) to wait (esp on the telephone): *Hold on while I call my mother.* **hold sth on** to keep an object fixed in a position: *Ordinary glue won't hold the handle on.*

hold onto sb/sth (a) to keep one's grip on a person, thing, and not let go: *hold onto one's hat/ my hand/me.* **(b)** to refuse to give up the possession or ownership of something: *You should hold onto those savings certificates for a while.*

hold out (a) (of supplies) to remain available: *How long will our food hold out?* **(b)** to continue to resist an attack: *How long can the miners hold out against the government?* **hold out for sth** to refuse to give up until one has achieved something: *hold out for higher wages.* **hold out on sb** (*informal*) to refuse to share information with a person; oppose a person's wishes.

hold sth over to decide not to deal with a proposal, decision etc until the next meeting.

hold sb to sth to make a person keep to a promise, agreement, price etc. **hold to sth** to remain committed to something: *hold to one's beliefs.*

hold together (a) (of a machine etc) to remain joined: *Her old car is only just holding together.* **(b)** (of a group) to remain united: *Will the Labour Party hold together until the next general election?* **hold sb/sth together** to keep people, a country etc united: *Is he a leader who can hold the different groups together?*

hold sb up (a) to delay a person's progress: *I was held up by the bad weather.* **(b)** to stop and rob a person: *They were held up by bandits who took their money.* Hence **'hold-up** *nc.* **(c)** to offer a person as an example: *hold them up as model students.* **hold sth up (a)** to carry something high: *hold up an umbrella.* **(b)** to delay work, a vehicle etc: *Fog held up the traffic.* **(c)** to stop and rob a passenger vehicle: *hold up a train.* Hence **'hold-up** *nc.*

(not) hold with sth (used in either the negative or a question) to approve of something: *Do you hold with nudity on the stage?*

hold·all /'həʊld ɔːl/ *nc* a bag used for clothes etc when travelling.

hold·er /'həʊldə(r)/ *nc* **1** a person who possesses or owns something: *a passport holder; the holder of the contract.* **2** something that contains something mentioned: *a cigarette-holder.*

hold·up /'həʊld ʌp/ *nc* **1** a delay: *a traffic hold-up.* **2** an instance of stopping and stealing from a person, vehicle etc. ⇨ hold sb up, hold sth up.

hole¹ /həʊl/ *nc* **1** an opening or empty place in a solid thing: *a hole in a tooth; roads full of holes.* **make a hole in sth** (*fig*) to use a large amount of something: *The hospital bills made a large hole in his savings.* **pick holes in sb/sth** to find fault with a person, plan etc. **a square peg in a round hole** ⇨ peg¹(1). **2** (*informal*) an awkward situation: *I'm in rather a hole.* **3** a small animal's home: *a mouse's hole.* **4** (*fig*) a small, dark, wretched place: *What a wretched little hole he lives in!* **5** (*golf*) a hollow into which the ball must be hit; point scored by a player who does this with the fewest strokes: *win the first hole.*

hole² /həʊl/ *vt* **1** to make a hole in or through (something): *hole a ship.* **2** (*golf*) to get (a ball) into a hole(5).

holi·day /'hɒlədɪ/ *nc* **1** (often *pl*) a period of rest from work: *take a month's holiday in summer.* **on holiday** having a holiday. ⇨ vacation. **2** a day of rest from work: *Sunday is a holiday in Christian countries.* ⇨ bank holiday.

'holiday-maker *nc* a person on holiday.

holi·ness /'həʊlɪnɪs/ *n* **1** *nu* being holy or sacred. **2** (H-) a title used to the Pope: *Your Holiness.*

hol·low¹ /'hɒləʊ/ *adj* **1** not solid; with a hole or empty space inside: *a hollow tree.* **2** (of sounds) as if coming from something hollow: *a hollow groan.* **3** (*fig*) unreal; false; insincere: *a hollow laugh/ promise; a hollow victory* (= one without real value). **4** sunken: *hollow cheeks.*

hol·low² /'hɒləʊ/ *nc* a large, shallow hole: *a hollow in the ground.*

hol·low³ /'hɒləʊ/ *vt* **hollow sth out** **1** to make something by taking out the centre: *hollow out a boat from a tree trunk.* **2** (usually *passive*) to make an empty or deep space in something: *rocks hollowed out by a river.*

hol·ly /'hɒlɪ/ *nu* a kind of evergreen shrub with shiny, spiny leaves and red berries.

holo·caust /'hɒləkɔːst/ *nc* a large-scale destruction, esp of human lives: *a nuclear holocaust.*

holo·gram /'hɒləgræm/ *nc* a special kind of photograph which produces a three-dimensional image in some kinds of light.

holo·graph /'hɒləgrɑːf/ *nc* (*literature*) a book handwritten by the author.

hol·ster /'həʊlstə(r)/ *nc* a leather case for a gun.

ho·ly /'həʊlɪ/ *adj* (**-ier, -iest**) **1** (often H-) of God or religion: *the Holy Bible.* **2** devoted to religion: *live a holy life.*

hom·age /'hɒmɪdʒ/ *nu* **do/pay homage (to sb)** (*formal*) to express one's respect (for a person): *Many came to do the dead man homage.*

home¹ /həʊm/ *adj* (*attrib*) **1** made or done in one's own house: *home cooking.* ⇨ home-grown, home-made. **2** of one's own country: *home industries.* **3** (*sport*) played at a stadium etc in the town where the team is situated: *a home game.* Compare away¹(3).

home² /həʊm/ *adv* **1** at, in or to one's home or country: *Is he home yet? You should be going* *home.* **2** so as to be in the right place: *drive a nail home* (= hit it so that it is completely in). *bring sth/come home to sb* (to cause a person) to realize (an unpleasant truth). *drive a point/an argument home* to cause its full force to be understood.

home³ /həʊm/ *nc* **1** the place where one lives, esp with one's family: *He left home at the age of 16.* **at home** (a) in the house: *Is your mother at home? I've left my books at home.* **(b)** as if in one's own house; at ease: *The boy did not feel at home in such a splendid house. Please make yourself at home* (= relax here). *be nothing/something to write home about* (*informal*) to be (not) particularly interesting. **2** an institution or place (for the care of children, old or sick people etc): *a nursing home.* **3** a place where an animal, plant etc lives or exists naturally: *Africa is the home of the giraffe. The West Indies is the home of exciting cricket.*

'home·coming *nc* an instance of arriving home after a long time away.

,home com'puter *nc* a small personal computer for family use.

,home eco'nomics *nu* the study of child care, food, budgets etc in a home(1).

,home-'grown *adj* (of food, etc) produced in the country (not imported).

,home 'help *nc* a woman doing domestic work, e.g. for an elderly or sick person.

'home·land *nc* the country from which one's ancestors came.

,home-'made *adj* made at home (not bought from shops).

'Home Office *n* (the —) the government department controlling local government, immigration, police, prisons etc in England and Wales.

'home·sick *adj* sad because away from home. Hence **home·sick·ness** *nu*

,home 'town *nc* the town where a person lives or was born.

,home 'truth *nc* an unpleasant and obvious fact.

'home·work *nu* work which a pupil does at home. *do one's homework* (*fig*) to prepare for a meeting or discussion.

home·less *adj* having no home.

home·like *adj* like a home: *a hotel with a home-like atmosphere.*

home·ward /-wəd/ *adj* going towards home.

home·wards /-wədz/ *adv* towards home.

home·ly /'həʊmlɪ/ *adj* (**-ier, -iest**) **1** simple and plain: *a homely meal.* **2** like a home: *a homely atmosphere.*

home·li·ness *nu*

ho·meo·path *nc* = homoeopath.

homi·cide /'hɒmɪsaɪd/ *nu* the killing of a human being.

homi·cid·al /,hɒmɪ'saɪdl/ *adj* of homicide: *homicidal tendencies.*

hom·ing /'həʊmɪŋ/ *adj* (*attrib*) **1** (of pigeons) having the ability to fly home (from a long distance). **2** (of torpedoes, missiles) fitted with electronic devices that enable them to reach a target.

ho·moeo·path (*US* = **-meo-**) /'həʊmɪəpæθ/ *nc* a person who practises homoeopathy.

ho·moeo·pathy (*US* = **-meo-**) /,həʊmɪ'ɒpəθɪ/ *nu* the treatment of disease by very small doses of drugs that, if given in large quantities, would pro-

duce symptoms like those of the disease.

ho·mo·gene·ous /,həʊmə'dʒiːnɪəs/ *adj* (formed of parts) of the same kind. Opp heterogeneous.

hom·ogen·ize (also **-ise**) /hə'mɒdʒənaɪz/ *vt* (usually *passive*) (esp) to make (milk) more uniform in consistency by breaking down and blending the particles of fat.

homo·graph /'hɒməgrɑːf/ *nc* (*lang*) a word spelt like another but with a different meaning. e.g. lead¹ and lead².

homo·nym /'hɒmənɪm/ *nc* (*lang*) a homograph or homophone.

homo·phone /'hɒməfəʊn/ *nc* (*lang*) a word pronounced like another but different in meaning, spelling or origin, e.g. *sum* and *some*.

homo·sex·ual /,həʊmə'seksjʊəl/ *adj, nc* (of) a person sexually attracted to people of her or his own sex.

homo·sex·ual·ity /,həʊmə,seksjʊ'ælətɪ/ *nu*

Hon *written abbr* Honorary(1), Honourable(2).

Hons *written abbr* Honours(5).

hon·est /'ɒnɪst/ *adj* **1** (of a person) not telling lies; not cheating or stealing: *an honest man; honest in business*: *to be honest* speaking truthfully: *To be honest, I don't like her.* **2** (usually *attrib*) (of an action, appearance etc) showing, resulting from, an honest person: *an honest face; an honest opinion; an honest attempt; an honest piece of work.* Opp dishonest.

hon·est·ly *adv* (a) in an honest manner: *behave honestly.* **(b)** (speaking) truthfully: *Honestly, that's all the money I have.*

hon·esty *nu* the quality of being honest.

hon·ey /'hʌnɪ/ *nu* a sweet, sticky yellowish substance made by bees.

'hon·ey-bee *nc* an ordinary kind of bee that lives in hives.

hon·ey·comb /'hʌnɪkəʊm/ *nc,nu* (a container with) a wax structure of six-sided cells made by bees for honey and eggs.

hon·ey·moon /'hʌnɪmuːn/ *nc* **1** a holiday taken by a newly married couple. **2** (*fig*) a quiet, pleasant period at the start of an undertaking, etc □ *vi* to go on a honeymoon(1): *They will honeymoon in Paris.*

honk /hɒŋk/ *vi, nc* (to make) the sound of a car horn.

hon·or·ary /'ɒnərərɪ/ *adj* **1** (H- in names; abbr Hon) (of a position) unpaid: *the honorary secretary.* **2** (of a degree, rank) given as an honour: *an honorary degree/doctorate; an honorary vice-president.*

hon·our¹ (*US* = **hon·or**) /'ɒnə(r)/ *n* **1** *nu* (a sign of) great respect; high public regard: *win honour in war.* Opp dishonour¹(1). *in honour of sb/ sth* as a symbol of respect and appreciation for a person, thing: *statues in honour of those killed in battle.* **2** *nu* a reputation for good behaviour, loyalty, truthfulness etc: *Her honour was discredited in the newspapers.* *on one's word of honour* with a guarantee to fulfil an obligation, keep a promise etc. **3** *n sing* a person or thing bringing credit: *He is an honour to his school/ family.* Opp dishonour¹(2). **4** (*pl*) marks of respect, distinction etc: *birthday honours* (in GB a list of titles given to individuals by the State as a reward for social or professional services). **5** (*pl*

H-s, abbr Hons) (in universities) (a place in) the top level of marks in degree examinations. **6** *nc* (H-) (a title of respect to a judge): *Your/Her/His Honour*. **7** *n sing* (used in formal polite situations): *I have the honour to inform you that . . .*

hon·our² (US = **hon·or**) /'ɒnə(r)/ *vt* **1** to show respect to (a person, thing): *I feel highly honoured by the kind things you say about me*. **2** to keep (an agreement to pay) (and pay when due): *honour a bill/cheque*. Opp dishonour².

hon·our·able (US = **hon·or·**) /'ɒnrəbl/ *adj* **1** possessing or showing honour(1,2): *honourable conduct*. Opp dishonourable. **2** (abbr Hon) a title given to judges and some other officials, to the children of peers below the rank of Marquis, and (during debates) to members of the House of Commons: *my Honourable friend the member for Chester*.

hon·our·ably /-əblɪ/ *adv*

hood /hʊd/ *nc* **1** a covering for the head and neck, fastened to a coat etc so that it can hang down at the back when not in use. **2** anything like a hood in shape or use, e.g. a folding roof over a pram or sports car.

hood·lum /'hu:dləm/ *nc* (*sl; derog*) a dangerous criminal.

hood·wink /'hʊdwɪŋk/ *vt* to deceive or trick (a person).

hoof /hu:f/ *nc* (*pl* **—s** or **hooves** /hu:vz/) the hard, horny part of the foot of a horse, bull, cow or deer.

hook¹ /hʊk/ *nc* **1** a curved piece of metal or other material, used for catching hold or for hanging something on: *a fish-hook; a clothes-hook*. **get/ be let off the hook** to get out of/be let off a difficult situation or punishment. **2** a curved tool used for cutting (grain etc) or for chopping (branches etc): *a reaping-hook*. **3** (*boxing*) a short blow with the arm bent: *a left hook*.

'hook-nosed *adj* having a curved, pointed nose.

'hook·worm *nu* (a disease caused by) a worm which gets into people and animals through their skin.

hook² /hʊk/ *v* **1** *vt* to catch (a fish, person etc) (as if) with a hook(1): *hook a fish; hook a husband* **2** *vt,vi* (to cause something) to become attached, be held, with a hook(1): *a dress that hooks/is hooked at/down the back; hook a chain over a knob on the wall*. **3** *vt* to make (something) into the shape of a hook: *hook one's finger*. **4** *vt* **hook sb/sth up (with sb/sth)** (*broadcasting*) to connect a person or a radio or television station with another.

hook·ed /hʊkt/ *adj* **1** shaped like a hook(1): *a hooked nose*. **2** (*pred; informal*) **be hooked on sb** to be very attracted to a person. **be hooked on sth** (a) to be completely dependent on a drug, cigarettes etc: *be hooked on heroin*. (b) to enjoy something very much: *My aunt is hooked on holidays in Austria/on ice-cream*.

hoo·li·gan /'hu:lɪgən/ *nc* (*derog*) a person shouting, fighting or being rude in the streets or other public places.

hoo·li·gan·ism /-ɪzəm/ *nu*

hoop /hu:p/ *nc* **1** a circular band of wood or metal as put around a barrel etc. **2** a large ring with paper stretched over it through which circus riders and animals jump.

hoo·rah /hʊ'rɑ:/ = hurrah.

hoo·ray /hʊ'reɪ/ = hurrah.

hoot¹ /hu:t/ *nc* **1** the sound made by an owl. **2** the sound made by a car horn, foghorn etc. **3** *not care a hoot/two hoots* (*informal*) to refuse to care at all.

hoot² /hu:t/ *v* **1** *vt,vi* (to cause a car's horn) to make a hoot. **2** *vi* (of an owl) to make its characteristic sound: *an owl hooting in the garden*. **3** *vt* to show disapproval of (a person) by making a loud noise: *hoot an actor; hoot a speaker down*.

hoot·er *nc* (a) a device in a car that sounds to give a warning. (b) a signal with a similar sound used to announce when work will start and stop.

hooves /hu:vz/ *pl* of hoof.

hop¹ /hɒp/ *nc* a kind of tall climbing plant used to make beer.

hop² /hɒp/ *nc* **1** the action of hopping. **2** a short jump. **hop, step and jump** = triple jump. **3** one stage in a long-distance flight: *fly from Berlin to Tokyo in three hops*.

hop³ /hɒp/ *vi* (**-pp-**) **1** (of a person) to jump on one foot. **be hopping mad** ⇨ mad(3). **2** (of birds, frogs, grasshoppers etc) to jump with both or all feet together: *Sparrows were hopping about on the lawn*. **3** **hop over to a place** to make a quick journey, esp in a plane: *hop over to France*.

hope¹ /həʊp/ *n* **1** *nc,nu* a feeling of desire, trust, confidence: *There is not much hope that they are alive*. **beyond/past hope** with no possibility of success, recovery etc. **build one's hopes on sb/sth** = pin one's hopes on sb/sth. **build (up) one's hopes** to increase one's confidence of success. **dash sb's hopes** to destroy a person's confidence of success. **not have a hope (of sth)** to have no chance to succeed in doing something: *She hasn't a hope of seeing him again*. **hold out some/no/little/not much hope (of sth)** to give some etc encouragement or expectation: *The doctors could hold out no hope of his recovery*. **pin one's hopes on sb/sth** to rely completely on a person, a decision etc for success. **raise sb's hopes** to encourage a person to feel confident of success or better luck: *Don't raise his hopes too much*. **2** *nc* a person, thing, circumstance etc on which hope is based: *You are my last hope—if you can't help, I'm ruined*.

hope² /həʊp/ *v* **1** *vt* **hope that . . . /to** + *verb* to expect and desire something that is possible: *I hope that you can come/to see you tomorrow*. **2** *vi* **hope for sth** to want something very much: *hope for good weather. We've had no news from him but we're still hoping*. Compare wish for sth.

hope·ful /'həʊpfəl/ *adj* **1** having hope: *be/feel hopeful about the future*. **2** giving hope; promising: *The future does not seem very hopeful*.

hope·ful·ly /-fəlɪ/ *adv* **1** in a hopeful(1) way: *He struggled on hopefully*. **2** (used to express hope that something mentioned will happen): *Hopefully she'll be here soon*. Ⓝ This use is very common but is considered incorrect by some speakers.

hope·less /'həʊplɪs/ *adj* **1** feeling, giving, promising, no hope of recovery, improvement etc: *The doctors now say she is a hopeless case*. **2** (*attrib*) complete and unchangeable: *a hopeless fool*.

hope·less·ly *adv*
hope·less·ness *nu*

horde /hɔ:d/ *nc* a great number: *hordes of people/*

locusts.

hor·izon /hə'raɪzn/ *nc* **1** the line at which the earth or sea seems to meet the sky: *The sun sank below the horizon.* **2** *(fig)* the limit of one's knowledge, experience, thinking etc.

hori·zon·tal /ˌhɒrɪ'zɒntl/ *adj* parallel to the horizon; flat or level. Compare vertical. □ *nc* a horizontal line, bar etc.

hori·zon·tal·ly /-əlɪ/ *adv*

hor·mone /'hɔːməʊn/ *nc* (*science*) a kind of substance that passes into the blood and encourages physical development etc.

horn¹ /hɔːn/ *n* **1** *nc* one of the hard, pointed, usually curved parts on the heads of cattle, deer and some other animals. ⇨ bull¹(1). **2** *nu* (also *attrib*) the substance that a horn(1) is made of: *a horn spoon.* **3** *nc* one of several kinds of musical instrument with a coiled metal tube: *a French horn.* **4** *nc* an apparatus that gives a sound as a warning: *to blow a car horn; to sound a fog-horn.*

horn² /hɔːn/ *vi* **horn in (on sth)** to take part in a conversation etc without being invited.

hor·net /'hɔːnɪt/ *nc* a kind of large insect of the wasp family.

horny /'hɔːnɪ/ *adj* (**-ier, -iest**) (of skin, hands etc) hard and rough.

hor·oscope /'hɒrəskəʊp/ *nc* a statement about a person's future based on the position of the stars and planets.

hor·ren·dous /hə'rendəs/ *adj* (*informal*) extremely unpleasant.

hor·rible /'hɒrəbl/ *adj* **1** causing extreme disgust, fear etc: *horrible cruelty/crimes.* **2** (*informal*) unpleasant: *horrible weather.*

hor·ribly /-əblɪ/ *adv*

hor·rid /'hɒrɪd/ *adj* (*informal*) unpleasant: *horrid weather. Don't be horrid to her.*

hor·rid·ly *adv*

hor·rif·ic /hə'rɪfɪk/ *adj* (*informal*) horrifying.

hor·ri·fy /'hɒrɪfaɪ/ *vt* (*pt,pp* **-ied**) to fill (a person) with horror; shock: *We were horrified at/by the news/what we saw.*

hor·ror /'hɒrə(r)/ *nc,nu* (something that causes) a feeling of extreme fear, disgust or dislike: *To her horror she saw her husband knocked down by a bus. We have all read about the horrors of modern warfare.*

'horror story/film *nc* one that is intended to frighten people.

'horror-struck/-stricken *adj* (of a person) very frightened.

hors d'œuvres /ˌɔː'dɜːvrə/ *n pl* (*Fr*) food served at the beginning of a meal.

horse¹ /hɔːs/ *n* **1** *nc* a four-legged animal with solid hooves, used to carry loads, for riding etc. ⇨ colt, filly, foal, mare, stallion. **a dark horse** (*fig*) a person with greater ability than is apparent. **back the wrong horse** to support the loser in a contest. **be/get on one's high horse** to insist on being treated with proper respect. **flog a dead horse** to waste one's efforts or energy doing something that cannot succeed. **hold one's horses** (usually *imperative*) to wait before acting (to think about one's actions or until another person is ready). **(straight) from the horse's mouth** (of tips, advice, information) (given) directly from a person. ⇨ also cart¹. **2** *nc* a framework, often with legs, on which something

is supported: *a clothes-horse* (i.e. on which clothes may be dried).

'horse·back *nu* (only in) **on horseback** on a horse.

'horse-fly *nc* (*pl* **-flies**) a kind of large insect which troubles horses and cattle.

'horse·play *nu* rough, noisy fun or play.

'horse·power *nu* (abbr hp) a unit for measuring the power of an engine etc (550 foot-pounds per second).

'horse·shoe *nc* a U-shaped metal shoe for a horse.

horse² /hɔːs/ *vi* **horse about/around** (*informal*) to behave noisily and roughly for fun.

hor·ti·cul·tur·al /ˌhɔːtɪ'kʌltʃərəl/ *adj* of horticulture: *a horticultural show.*

hor·ti·cul·ture /'hɔːtɪkʌltʃə(r)/ *nu* (the science of) growing flowers, fruit and vegetables.

hose¹ /həʊz/ *nc,nu* (a length of) rubber or plastic tubing used for directing water onto fires, gardens etc.

'hose·pipe *nc* a length of hose.

hose² /həʊz/ *vt* **1** to use a hose to provide water for (something): *hosing a garden.* **2 hose sth (down)** to clean a car etc using a hose.

ho·siery /'həʊzɪərɪ/ *nu* (*commerce*) underwear, socks etc.

hosp *written abbr* hospital.

hos·pice /'hɒspɪs/ *nc* a place where people who are dying are cared for.

hos·pit·able /hə'spɪtəbl/ *adj* giving, liking to give, hospitality; being kind: *a hospitable man.* Opp inhospitable.

hos·pit·ably /-əblɪ/ *adv*

hos·pi·tal /'hɒspɪtl/ *nc* a place where people are treated for illness or injuries.

hos·pi·tal·ity /ˌhɒspɪ'tælətɪ/ *nu* being friendly and generous towards guests, esp in one's own home. ⇨ hospitable.

host¹ /həʊst/ *nc* a great number: *He has hosts of friends.*

host² /həʊst/ *nc* **1** a person who entertains guests. **2** (*biology*) an animal or plant from which a parasite feeds.

hos·tage /'hɒstɪdʒ/ *nc* a person kept as a guarantee that demands will be met: *The hijackers kept one of the travellers as a hostage.*

hos·tel /'hɒstl/ *nc* a building in which board and lodging are provided for students, people working away from home etc. ⇨ youth hostel.

host·ess /'həʊstɪs/ *nc* a woman who entertains guests. ⇨ air hostess.

hos·tile /'hɒstaɪl/ *adj* being or appearing unfriendly: *a hostile crowd/look; looking hostile.*

hos·til·ity /hɒ'stɪlətɪ/ *n* (*pl* **-ies**) **1** *nu* an unfriendly feeling; hatred: *show feelings of hostility.* **2** (*pl*) (acts of) war.

hot¹ /hɒt/ *adj* (**—ter, —test**) **1** having great heat or a high temperature: *hot weather; feel hot.* Opp cold¹(1). **hot and bothered (about sth)** restless and irritated or worried. **not so hot** (*informal*) (of a person, performance, idea etc) not particularly good. **hot on the heels of sb** close behind a person (in space or time): *arrive hot on his heels.* **be hot on sb's trail** to be near to reaching and catching an escaped prisoner etc. **be in/get into hot water** to be in/get into trouble. **be too hot to handle** (*informal*) to be too

309

housing

dangerous to become involved with. **blow hot and cold** (of a person) to be in turns enthusiastic and then unenthusiastic. **make it hot for sb** to cause a situation to become dangerous or unpleasant. ⇨ also collar(1), piping¹. **2** producing a burning sensation to the taste: *Pepper is hot*. **3** (*attrib*) intense; violent: *a man with a hot temper*. **4** (*sl*) (of stolen goods) difficult to sell (because the police are trying to find them).

,hot 'air *nu* insincere talk, promises etc.

,hot-'air balloon *nc* a large bag filled with air and with a flame underneath, used to travel in the air.

'hot·bed *nc* (*fig*) a place favourable to the growth of something evil: *a hotbed of vice/crime*.

,hot-'blooded *adj* passionate.

'hot dog *nc* a sausage served with onions and mustard in a bread roll.

'hot·foot *adv* eagerly: *follow the enemy hotfoot.* □ *vt* to go quickly: *hotfoot it down to the library.*

'hot·head *nc* (*derog*) a person who acts without thinking.

,hot-'headed *adj* (*derog*) acting quickly without thinking.

'hot·house *nc* a heated glass building, used for growing plants.

'hot line *nc* a direct line of communication (e.g. a telephone) between heads of governments.

'hot·plate *nc* a flat surface on a cooker that can be heated.

,hot po'tato *nc* (*informal*) a difficult problem or situation.

'hot seat *n* (the —) a difficult or dangerous position: *be in the hot seat.*

,hot-'tempered *adj* (*derog*) easily angered.

,hot-'water bottle *nc* a container (often of rubber) to be filled with hot water for warmth in bed.

hot·ly *adv* (a) energetically: *a hotly contested match.* (b) closely: *hotly pursued by the police.*

hot² /hɒt/ *vi* (**-tt-**) (*informal*) to become more exciting or dangerous; intensify.

hotch·potch /'hɒtʃpɒtʃ/ *n sing* a mixture (of different things, ideas etc).

ho·tel /həʊ'tel/ *nc* a building where rooms and meals are provided for travellers.

ho·tel·ier /həʊ'telɪeɪ/ *nc* a person who owns or manages a hotel.

hound¹ /haʊnd/ *nc* a kind of dog used for hunting and racing: *a foxhound; a bloodhound; a greyhound.*

hound² /haʊnd/ *vt* (often *passive*) to trouble, worry, (a person): *be hounded by one's creditors.*

hour /aʊə(r)/ *nc* (abbr hr) **1** a twenty-fourth part of a day; 60 minutes: *walk for hours (and hours); work for an hour and a half/one and a half hours; a three hours' journey.* **at the eleventh hour** ⇨ eleventh. **2** a point or period of time: *We waited for hours but no-one came. They disturb me at all hours of the day and night* (= often). **3** (*pl*) fixed periods of time, esp for work: *Office hours are 9 am to 5 pm.*

'hour hand *nc* the small hand on a clock or watch, pointing to the hour.

hour·ly¹ /'aʊəlɪ/ *adj* **1** done or occurring every hour: *an hourly bus service.* **2** (*attrib*) continual: *live in hourly fear of discovery.*

hour·ly² /'aʊəlɪ/ *adv* **1** every hour; once every hour: *This medicine is to be taken hourly.* **2** at any

hour: *We're expecting news hourly.* **3** by the hour: *paid hourly/hourly rates of pay.*

house¹ /haʊs/ *nc* (*pl* **—s** /'haʊzɪz/) **1** a building for people to live in: *New houses are going up everywhere.* **get on like a house on fire** (of people) to become friendly quickly. **keep house (for sb)** to be responsible for cleaning a person's house, cooking, shopping etc. **keep open house** to give a party and provide food and drink for everyone who comes. **move house** to take one's belongings and move to another house. **put one's house in order** to organize and deal with one's personal affairs. **set up house (together)** to start living in a house (together). ⇨ also safe¹(4). **2** (usually with a prefix) a building made or used for the mentioned purpose: *a warehouse; a store-house.* **3** (H- in names) (a building used by) an official assembly: *the House of Commons/Lords; the Houses of Parliament.* **4** (H-) an important family line: *the House of Windsor* (= the British royal family). **5** the audience in a theatre: *a full house* (= with every seat occupied). **bring the house down** to win very great applause and approval.

'house-agent *nc* (*GB*) a person, business, that sells or lets houses.

'house arrest *nu* **be/put sb under house arrest** to be forbidden to leave one's house, have visitors etc.

'house·boat *nc* a boat used to live in.

'house·father *nc* a man in charge of children in an institution.

'house-fly *nc* (*pl* **-flies**) a very common flying insect seen in buildings, esp near food.

'house·hold *nc* all the people (family, lodgers etc) living in a house.

'house·holder *nc* a person leasing or owning and occupying a house.

'house·keeper *nc* a woman employed to look after a household.

'house·master *nc* a teacher in charge of a school boarding-house.

'house·mother *nc* a woman in charge of children in an institution.

,House of 'Commons *n* (the —) (*GB*) the group of representatives elected to Parliament by the people.

,House of 'Lords *n* (the —) (*GB*) the group of people in Parliament consisting of the peers, bishops etc.

'house-proud *adj* concerned about the care and appearance of one's home.

'house physician/surgeon *nc* one who lives in a hospital.

,Houses of 'Parliament *n* (the —) (the building used by) the House of Commons and the House of Lords.

'house-trained *adj* (of pets) trained to empty their body waste outside buildings.

'house·wife *nc* a woman who stays at home, brings up the family etc.

'house·work *nu* work done in a house, such as cleaning, sweeping etc.

house² /haʊz/ *vt* to provide a home, room or shelter for (a person, thing): *We can house you and your friends if the hotels are full.*

hous·ing /'haʊzɪŋ/ *n* **1** *nu* accommodation in houses etc: *More housing is needed for old people.*

2 *nc* a solid cover for a machine.

'housing estate *nc* an area of houses planned and built as a group.

hove /həʊv/ *pt,pp* of heave.

hov·el /'hɒvl/ *nc* a small, poor house or hut.

hov·er /'hɒvə(r)/ *vi* **1** (of a bird) to remain in the air in one place: *A hawk was hovering overhead.* **2** (*fig*) (of a person) to wait nearby. **3** (*fig*) to remain in or near a mentioned condition: *hovering between life and death.*

hov·er·craft /'hɒvəkrɑːft/ *nc* a vehicle that moves over land or water supported by air blown underneath it.

how /haʊ/ *adv* **1** in what way or manner; by what means: *Do you know how snails breathe? Tell me how to spell the word. How is it spelt? How do birds fly? How can you work with all this noise?* **2** to what extent: *How old are you? How many legs has an insect got? How often do you go to the dentist? How much* (= What amount of money) *must I pay?/does it cost? How he's changed!* (= He's changed a great deal). *How warm it is today! How nice of you to remember! Ask her how long we will have to wait.* **3** in what state of health (when referring to a person): *How's your mother?* Ⓝ 'How' always refers to health. When asking about a person's character, appearance etc use *What is . . . like?* as in *What's your new teacher like?* **How are you?** (used when greeting a friend, relative etc or any other person one knows). Ⓝ The reply is *'I'm fine, thanks' 'Very well' 'I'm feeling better'* etc according to the situation. **How do you do?** (used when greeting a stranger, esp in formal situations). Ⓝ The reply is *'How do you do?'*, because the question is not intended to be answered. **4** in what state or condition (when referring to anything, but not people): *How's your English? How do you like your steak cooked? How was the weather during your holiday?* **5** (used when asking for an opinion or making a suggestion): *How did you like the TV programme? How was the film/meeting? How about coming to the pub with me?* **And how!** (*informal*) (used to emphasize one's agreement) very much so: *'Would you like to come fishing?' 'And how!'* **How's that?** (*informal*) (used when pointing to something) what is your opinion of that? **How's that for sth?** (*informal*) (**a**) is this or that thing acceptable according to size, price etc? (**b**) (used to emphasize one's opinion of an act, quality etc): *How's that for stupidity?*

how·ev·er¹ /haʊ'evə(r)/ *adv* in whatever way: *He'll never succeed, however hard he tries. However much you cry, I won't change my mind.* Ⓝ 'However' is often used as an emphatic form of *how*(1) in questions, as in *However did you do it?*

how·ev·er² /haʊ'evə(r)/ *conj* (*coord*) although that is true: *She's clever; however, she's lazy/she's lazy, however.*

howl¹ /haʊl/ *nc* **1** the long, loud sound made by e.g. a wolf. **2** a long cry of a person in pain, or expressing scorn, amusement etc: *howls of laughter.* **3** a long noise of a strong wind.

howl² /haʊl/ *vi* to make such noises: *The wind howled through the trees. They howled with delight.*

howl·ing *adj* (*attrib*): *a howling gale.*

HP /ˌeɪtʃ 'piː/ *abbr* hire-purchase.

hp *written abbr* horsepower.

HQ /ˌeɪtʃ 'kjuː/ *abbr* headquarters.

hr(s) *written abbr* hour(s).

HRH *written abbr* Her/His Royal Highness.

ht *written abbr* height.

hub /hʌb/ *nc* **1** the central part of a wheel from which the spokes radiate. **2** (*fig*) the central point of activity or importance: *a hub of industry/commerce.*

'hub-cap *nc* a metal or plastic shield for a hub(1).

hub·by /'hʌbɪ/ *nc* (*pl* **-ies**) (*GB informal*) = husband.

huddle¹ /'hʌdl/ *nc* a number of people or things close together without any order.

huddle² /'hʌdl/ *v* **1** *vt,vi* (to cause animals, people) to crowd together: *sheep huddling together for warmth.* **2** *vi* **huddle (up)** to curl up: *Tom was cold, so he huddled up against his brother in bed. They huddled (up) together.*

hue¹ /hjuː/ *nc* a (shade of) colour: *the dark hue of the ocean.*

hue² /hjuː/ *nc* (only in) **hue and cry** a general cry of alarm as when a criminal is being chased or to express opposition: *raise a hue and cry against new tax proposals.*

huff /hʌf/ *n sing* **be in/get into a huff** to be/ become bad-tempered.

hug¹ /hʌg/ *nc* an act of hugging: *She gave her mother a big hug.*

hug² /hʌg/ *vt* (**-gg-**) **1** to put the arms round (a person etc) tightly, esp to show love: *The child was hugging her doll.* **2** to keep close to the edge of (something): *The ship hugged the shore. The car hugged the kerb.*

huge /hjuːdʒ/ *adj* very big or notable: *a huge stain/building/mistake/stomach/success.*

hulk /hʌlk/ *nc* **1** an old ship no longer in use. **2** (*fig; derog*) a big, clumsy person or object.

hulk·ing *adj* (*derog*) clumsy: *Get out of my way, you big hulking creature!*

hull¹ /hʌl/ *nc* the body or frame of a ship.

hull² /hʌl/ *nc* the outer covering of some cereal plants and seeds, esp the pods of peas and beans. □ *vt* to remove the hulls of (plants).

hul·la·ba·loo /ˌhʌləbəˈluː/ *nc* (*dated*) an uproar; disturbance: *What's all this hullabaloo about?*

hul·lo /həˈləʊ/ *int* = hallo.

hum¹ /hʌm/ *nc* a humming noise: *the hum of bees/ of distant traffic/of voices.*

hum² /hʌm/ *v* (**-mm-**) **1** *vi* to make a continuous sound like that made by bees. **2** *vt,vi* to sing (a song etc) with closed lips: *She was humming (a tune) to herself.* **3** *vi* **hum (with sth)** to be active: *a factory humming with noise.*

hu·man¹ /'hjuːmən/ *adj* **1** of people (contrasted with animals or God): *human nature.* **2** having, showing, good moral qualities: *His cruelty shows that he is less than human.* Opp inhuman.

ˌhuman 'being *nc* a person.

ˌhuman 'nature *nu* behaviour etc expected from people.

ˌhuman 'race *nu* (the —) all people.

ˌhuman 'rights *n pl* the freedom of thought and expression, personal liberty, means to live etc justly claimed by all human beings.

hu·man·ly *adv* (*esp*) by human means; without divine help: *The doctors have done all that is humanly possible.*

hu·man² /'hjuːmən/ *nc* a person.

hu·mane /hju:'meɪn/ adj being kind and caring about the feelings of another: *a man of humane character*. Opp inhumane.
　hu·mane·ly adv

hu·mani·tar·ian /hju:ˌmænɪ'teərɪən/ adj, nc (of, holding the views of) a person who works for the welfare of all human beings by reducing suffering, reforming laws about punishment etc.

hu·man·ity /hju:'mænətɪ/ nu **1** all people: *crimes against humanity*. **2** the quality of being humane: *treat people and animals with humanity*. Compare inhumanity.
　humanities n pl (the —) the branches of learning concerned with art, languages, literature, history, philosophy.

hu·man·ize (also **-ise**) /'hju:mənaɪz/ vt to make (a person) human(2) or humane.

humble¹ /'hʌmbl/ adj (**—r, —st**) **1** showing that one is inferior, less able etc: *He is very humble towards his superiors*. **2** (of a person) low in rank or position; unimportant. **3** (of things) poor in appearance: *a humble home*. ⇨ humility.
　humb·ly adv in a humble way: *ask humbly for forgiveness*.

humble² /'hʌmbl/ vt to make (oneself, a person) lower in importance, confidence, position etc: *humble one's enemies*.

hum·bug /'hʌmbʌg/ n **1** nc,nu (*dated*) (an instance of) dishonest and deceiving behaviour or talk. **2** nc (*GB*) a hard-boiled sweet flavoured with peppermint.

hum·drum /'hʌmdrʌm/ adj dull because too ordinary: *live a humdrum life*.

hu·mer·us /'hju:mərəs/ nc (*anat*) the bone in the upper arm.

hu·mid /'hju:mɪd/ adj (esp of air, climate) damp.
　hu·mid·ity /hju:'mɪdətɪ/ nu (the degree of) moisture (in the air).

hu·mili·ate /hju:'mɪlɪeɪt/ vt to cause (a person) to feel ashamed; lower the dignity or self-respect of (a person): *humiliate one's family*.
　hu·mili·at·ing adj: *a humiliating defeat*.
　hu·mili·ation /hju:ˌmɪlɪ'eɪʃn/ nc,nu

hu·mil·ity /hju:'mɪlətɪ/ nu a humble condition or state of mind.

hu·mor·ist /'hju:mərɪst/ nc a humorous talker or writer.

hu·mor·ous /'hju:mərəs/ adj having or showing a sense of humour; funny: *a humorous remark*.
　hu·mor·ously adv

hu·mour¹ (*US* = **hu·mor**) /'hju:mə(r)/ n **1** nu (the capacity to cause or feel) amusement: *have a good sense of humour*. **2** nu (*formal*) a person's state of mind (esp at a particular time): *not in the humour for work*.

hu·mour² (*US* = **hu·mor**) /'hju:mə(r)/ vt to keep (a person) happy by agreeing, giving things etc: *Is it always wise to humour a child?*

hump¹ /hʌmp/ nc a round lump, e.g. on a camel's back or (as a deformity) on a person's back. ⇨ hunchback.

hump² /hʌmp/ vt **hump sth (up)** to make something into the shape of a hump: *The cat humped (up) her back when she saw the dog*.

hu·mus /'hju:məs/ nu earth formed by the decay of dead leaves, plants etc.

hunch¹ /hʌntʃ/ n sing **have a hunch that** . . . (*sl*) to have a vague feeling, idea, that . . . .

hunch² /hʌntʃ/ vt **hunch sth (up)** to make something into the shape of an arch: *with his shoulders hunched up*.

'hunch·back nc (a person with) a back with a hump. Hence **'hunch·backed** adj

hun·dred /'hʌndrəd/ n or det, nc (of) 100: *two hundred and three* (= 205); *three thousand, two hundred and six* (= 3206). Ⓝ The plural of *'hundred'* is hundred in spoken numbers.
　hundreds (of sth) very many: *hundreds of people*.
　'hundred·fold adj, adv a hundred times as many or as much.
　hun·dred·th /'hʌndrədθ/ adj or det, nc (abbr 100th) (of) the next after 99 or one of 100 equal parts.
　'hundred·weight nc (often written cwt) (*GB*) a twentieth of one ton (= 50·8kg).

hung /hʌŋ/ pt,pp of hang².

hun·ger¹ /'hʌŋgə(r)/ n **1** nu the desire for food: *die of hunger*. **2** n sing (*fig*) any strong desire: *a hunger for excitement*.
　'hunger-strike nc,nu a refusal to take food as a protest: *go on (a) hunger-strike*.

hun·ger² /'hʌŋgə(r)/ vi **hunger after/for sb/sth** to have a strong desire for: *hunger for news*.

hun·gry /'hʌŋgrɪ/ adj (**-ier, -iest**) **1** feeling, showing signs of hunger. **go hungry** to be, remain, without food. **2** (*attrib*) causing hunger: *hungry work*. **3** (*pred*) **hungry for sth** wanting or needing something very much: *hungry for news. The refugee child was hungry for affection*.
　hun·gri·ly /'hʌŋgrəlɪ/ adv

hunk /hʌŋk/ nc a thick piece cut off something: *a hunk of bread*.

hunt¹ /hʌnt/ n **1** n sing an act of hunting; search: *find something after a long hunt*. **2** nc a group of people who regularly hunt foxes with horses and dogs.
　hunt·er nc a person who hunts animals.
　hunt·ing nu the act of chasing wild animals, esp foxes: *He's fond of hunting*.

hunt² /hʌnt/ v **1** vt,vi to go after (wild animals): *hunt deer*. **2** vi to search: *hunt after/for food*. **hunt high and low** ⇨ high².
　hunt sb down to search for and find a person, animal: *hunt down a criminal*.
　hunt for sb/sth ⇨ 2 above.
　hunt sb/sth out to find a person, thing, by searching.

hurdle¹ /'hɜ:dl/ nc **1** a light frame to be jumped over (in a *hurdle-race*). **2** (*fig*) any difficulty to be overcome: *meet hurdles during the discussions*.

hurdle² /'hɜ:dl/ vi to take part in a race over hurdles(1).
　hur·dler nc a person who hurdles.

hurl /hɜ:l/ vt to throw (a person, thing) with force: *hurl a man to the ground; hurl a brick through a window*. □ nc a violent throw.

hur·rah /hʊ'rɑ:/ int (also **hoorah, hooray, hurray**) (used to express joy, approval etc).

hur·ri·cane /'hʌrɪkən/ nc an extremely strong wind with a storm.
　'hurricane lamp/lantern nc a lamp with the light protected from the wind.

hur·ry¹ /'hʌrɪ/ nu an act of doing something (too) quickly; a wish to do something very quickly: *Why all this hurry?* **in a hurry (a)** acting, anxious to act, quickly: *He was in a hurry to leave.* **(b)** *(informal)* soon and willingly: *I shan't ask that rude man to dinner again in a hurry.* **(c)** *(informal)* easily: *You won't find a better one than that in a hurry.*

hur·ry² /ˈhʌrɪ/ *vt,vi (pt,pp* **-ied)** (to cause a person) to move or do something (too) quickly: *It's no use hurrying her/trying to make her hurry.* ***Hurry up!*** Be quick! **hurry *sb/sth* up** to make a person do something (more) quickly; get a job done (more) quickly.

hur·ried *adj* done in a hurry: *a hurried meal.* Compare unhurried.

hurt¹ /hɜːt/ *nu* or **sing** a harm; an injury: *I intended no hurt to his feelings.*

hurt² /hɜːt/ *v (pt,pp* **—) 1** *vt* to cause injury or pain to (a person, animal etc): *He hurt himself when he fell.* **2** *vt* to make (a person) feel mental pain: *He was very hurt by their criticisms.* **3** *vt,vi* (to cause a part of the body) to feel pain: *My toe hurts. These boots hurt my feet. Stop it—you're hurting me!* **4** *vt,vi* (usually *negative*) to affect (a person) badly: *An extra hour's work won't hurt them* (i.e. it will do some good).

hurt·ful /-fəl/ *adj* causing mental pain; unkind: *a hurtful remark.*

hurtle /ˈhɜːtl/ *vi* to fall or be flung violently: *During the gale the tiles came hurtling down.*

hus·band /ˈhʌzbənd/ *nc* a man who a woman is married to. Compare wife.

hus·band·ry /ˈhʌzbəndrɪ/ *nu (formal)* farming: *animal husbandry.*

hush /hʌʃ/ *vt,vi* (to cause a person) to become silent or quiet: *Hush!* (= Be silent!) **hush *sth* up** to prevent it from becoming public knowledge: *She tried to hush up the fact that her husband was in prison.*

husk /hʌsk/ *nc* the dry outer covering of a seed, esp grain: *rice in the husk.*

husky¹ /ˈhʌskɪ/ *nc (pl* **-ies)** a kind of dog with thick hair living in cold climates.

husky² /ˈhʌskɪ/ *adj* **(-ier, -iest)** (of a person, voice) with a dry and almost whispering sound: *a husky voice/cough.*

husk·ily /-əlɪ/ *adv*

hustle¹ /ˈhʌsl/ *nu* (esp **hustle and bustle**) quick and energetic activity in a crowded and busy place.

hustle² /ˈhʌsl/ *v* **1** *vt* to push or move (a person) roughly: *The police hustled the thief into their van.* **2** *vt* to make (a person) act (too) quickly: *I don't want to hustle you into a decision.* **3** *vi* (esp *US*) *(informal)* to sell or obtain something by energetic (esp deceitful) activity.

hus·tler *nc* a person who hustles(2,3).

hut /hʌt/ *nc* a small, roughly made house or shelter.

hutch /hʌtʃ/ *nc* a box or cage, esp one used for rabbits.

hy·aena /haɪˈiːnə/ *nc* = hyena.

hy·brid /ˈhaɪbrɪd/ *adj, nc* (of) an animal or plant produced from two different kinds.

ˌhybrid comˈputer *nc* one combining features of digital and analog computers.

hy·drant /ˈhaɪdrənt/ *nc* a pipe for water (esp in a street) with a place where a hose can be attached.

hy·drau·lic /haɪˈdrɔːlɪk/ *adj* of, worked by, water or liquid moving through pipes: *hydraulic brakes.*

hy·drau·lics *nu* the science of using liquids to carry power.

hy·dro·chlor·ic acid /ˌhaɪdrəˌklɒrɪk ˈæsɪd/ *nu* an acid (symbol HCl) containing hydrogen and chlorine, used widely in industrial processes.

hy·dro·elec·tric /ˌhaɪdrəʊɪˈlektrɪk/ *adj* of electricity produced by water-power.

hy·dro·gen /ˈhaɪdrədʒən/ *nu* a gas (symbol H) without colour, taste or smell, that combines with oxygen to form water.

ˈhydrogen bomb *nc* (abbr H-bomb) a bomb with a force much greater than an atomic bomb.

hy·dro·pon·ics /ˌhaɪdrəˈpɒnɪks/ *nu* (the method of) growing plants in water without soil.

hy·dro·pho·bia /ˌhaɪdrəˈfəʊbɪə/ *nu* (an illness marked by) a great fear of water.

hy·ena (also **hy·aena**) /haɪˈiːnə/ *nc* a kind of wild animal, like a wolf, with a laughing cry.

hy·giene /ˈhaɪdʒiːn/ *nu* the science of, rules for, clean and healthy living.

hy·gien·ic /haɪˈdʒiːnɪk/ *adj* of hygiene; free from disease germs: *These are not very hygienic conditions.* Opp unhygienic.

hy·gieni·cal·ly /-klɪ/ *adv*

hymn /hɪm/ *nc* a song of praise to God, as used in a religious service.

hym·nal /ˈhɪmnəl/ *nc* a book of hymns.

hy·per·ac·tive /ˌhaɪpəˈræktɪv/ *adj* abnormally active: *a hyperactive child.*

hy·per·bola /haɪˈpɜːbələ/ *nc (pl* **—s** or **-lae** /-liː/) *(maths)* a curve of two equal parts formed by cutting through both bases of a double cone.

hy·per·bole /haɪˈpɜːbəlɪ/ *nc,nu (lang)* (an instance of) using exaggerated statement(s) made for effect and not to be taken literally as in *'waves as high as Everest'.*

hy·per·bol·ic /ˌhaɪpəˈbɒlɪk/ *adj (maths)* of a hyberbola.

hy·per·criti·cal /ˌhaɪpəˈkrɪtɪkl/ *adj (derog)* too critical, esp of small faults.

hy·per·mar·ket /ˈhaɪpəmɑːkɪt/ *nc* a very large supermarket selling many varieties of goods.

hy·per·sen·si·tive /ˌhaɪpəˈsensɪtɪv/ *adj (informal)* too easily upset or offended.

hy·phen /ˈhaɪfn/ *nc (lang)* the mark (-) used to join two words together, as in *Anglo-French*, between syllables, as in *co-op*, or to divide a word at the end of a written or printed line, as in *hyphen*.

hy·phen·ate /-eɪt/ *vt* to join ((parts of) words) with a hyphen.

hyp·no·sis /hɪpˈnəʊsɪs/ *nc (pl* **-ses** /-siːz/) (an artificially produced) state like deep sleep in which a person's acts may be controlled by another person.

hyp·not·ic /hɪpˈnɒtɪk/ *adj* of hypnosis: *in a hypnotic state.*

hyp·not·ism /ˈhɪpnətɪzəm/ *nu* (the use, effect of) hypnosis.

hyp·not·ist /-ɪst/ *nc* a person able to produce hypnosis.

hyp·not·ize (also **-ise**) /-aɪz/ *vt* to produce hypnosis in (a person).

hy·po·chon·dria /ˌhaɪpəˈkɒndrɪə/ *nu* a mental depression due to unnecessary anxiety about one's health.

hy·po·chon·dri·ac /-drɪæk/ adj of, affected by, hypochondria. □ nc a person suffering from hypochondria.

hy·poc·ri·sy /hɪˈpɒkrəsɪ/ nc,nu (pl **-ies**) (an example, instance, of) falsely making oneself appear to be virtuous or good.

hyp·ocrite /ˈhɪpəkrɪt/ nc a person who pretends to be virtuous or good.

hy·po·crit·i·cal /ˌhɪpəˈkrɪtɪkl/ adj of hypocrisy or a hypocrite: a hypocritical remark.

hy·po·crit·i·cal·ly /-klɪ/ adv

hy·po·der·mic /ˌhaɪpəˈdɜːmɪk/ adj (of drugs etc) injected beneath the skin: a hypodermic injection; a hypodermic syringe.

hy·pot·en·use /haɪˈpɒtənjuːz/ nc (maths) the side of a right-angled triangle opposite the right angle.

hy·po·ther·mia /ˌhaɪpəˈθɜːmɪə/ nu an abnormally low body temperature, as suffered by old people in cold weather.

hy·poth·e·sis /haɪˈpɒθəsɪs/ nc (pl **-ses** /-siːz/) an idea, suggestion, put forward as a starting-point for reasoning or an explanation.

hy·poth·esize (also **-ise**) /haɪˈpɒθəsaɪz/ vt,vi to produce (an idea etc) as a hypothesis: hypothesize about the economic future for Europe.

hy·po·thet·i·cal /ˌhaɪpəˈθetɪkl/ adj of, based on, a hypothesis (and not proved).

hys·ter·ec·to·my /ˌhɪstəˈrektəmɪ/ nc (pl **-ies**) (med) the removal of the womb by surgery.

hys·teria /hɪˈstɪərɪə/ nu 1 a disturbance of the nervous system, with outbursts of uncontrollable emotion. 2 uncontrolled excitement, e.g. in a crowd round a pop star.

hys·ter·i·cal /hɪˈsterɪkl/ adj caused by, suffering from, hysteria: hysterical laughter.

hys·ter·i·cal·ly /-klɪ/ adv

hys·ter·ics /hɪˈsterɪks/ n pl attack(s) of hysteria: be in/go into hysterics.

Hz symbol hertz.

Ii

I¹, i /aɪ/ (pl **I's, i's** /aɪz/) 1 the ninth letter of the English alphabet. 2 the Roman numeral 1.

I² /aɪ/ personal pron (used by a speaker or writer to refer to herself or himself): I can swim. You and I must do it. ⇔ the note at me.

IATA /aɪˈɑːtə/ acronym International Air Transport Association (an official international body governing standards of safety, financial security etc).

IBA /ˌaɪ biː ˈeɪ/ abbr (the —) (GB) the Independent Broadcasting Authority.

ICA /ˌaɪ siː ˈeɪ/ abbr (the —) (GB) the Institute of Contemporary Arts.

ice¹ /aɪs/ n 1 nu frozen water: Is the ice thick enough for skating? **break the ice** (fig) to do or say something to reduce tension or any uncomfortable feeling in a group of people. **cut no/not much ice (with sb)** to have no/very little effect on a person. 2 nc,nu (a piece of) flavoured ice or ice-cream: water-ice; two strawberry ices.

'Ice Age n (the —) the time when much of the Northern hemisphere was covered with glaciers.

'ice·berg nc a mass of ice moving in the sea.

'ice-bound adj (of harbours etc) blocked by ice in the sea.

'ice-box nc a box in which ice is used to keep food cool.

ice-'cream nc,nu (a portion of) cream flavoured and frozen.

'ice hockey nu ⇔ hockey.

'ice-lolly nc a piece of flavoured ice on a stick.

'ice-rink nc an indoor skating-rink with a floor of artificial ice.

'ice-skate nc a thin metal blade on a boot for skating on ice. □ vi to skate on ice. Hence **'ice-skating** nu.

ice² /aɪs/ vt 1 (often passive) to make (something) very cold: iced water. 2 vi **ice over/up** to become covered with ice: The pond is icing over. 3 vt to cover (a cake) with icing. ⇔ icing(1).

icicle /ˈaɪsɪkl/ nc a long piece of ice made by the freezing of dripping water.

ic·ing /ˈaɪsɪŋ/ nu 1 a mixture of sugar, white of egg etc used for covering cake(s). 2 the formation of ice, e.g. on the wings of an aircraft.

icon /ˈaɪkɒn/ nc a painting etc of a sacred person, used in the Christian churches of Greece and Eastern Europe.

icy /ˈaɪsɪ/ adj (**-ier, -iest**) 1 very cold, like ice: icy winds. 2 covered with ice: icy roads. 3 (fig) unfriendly: an icy welcome.

ic·ily /ˈaɪsəlɪ/ adv

ID /ˌaɪ ˈdiː/ abbr (informal) identification (documents): Have you got your ID?

I'd /aɪd/ = I had; I would.

idea /aɪˈdɪə/ nc 1 a picture in the mind; result of thinking and learning: have a good idea of life fifty years ago. You have no idea (of) how anxious we have been. 2 an opinion: You shouldn't force your ideas on other people. 3 a plan; intention as a result of thinking: He's full of new ideas; That's a good idea. **get ideas** (esp used with don't as a warning) to be determined (to escape, do something wrong etc): This dog will bite so don't get any ideas (about leaving the house). **have an idea (that . . .)** to have a vague belief, feeling that something is probable: I have an idea that she will be late.

ideal¹ /aɪˈdɪəl/ adj satisfying one's idea of what is perfect: ideal weather for a holiday; an ideal boyfriend.

ideal² /aɪˈdɪəl/ nc 1 an idea, example, looked on as perfect: Her ideal of a holiday is to walk in the mountains. 2 (pl) personal high standards of behaviour etc: His ideals prevent him from accepting second-rate solutions.

ideal·ism /aɪˈdɪəlɪzəm/ nu 1 (in art and literature) the showing of life and behaviour in a perfect form. 2 behaviour based on the belief that the highest standards can be achieved. Compare realism.

ideal·ist /-ɪst/ nc a person who believes in (often impractical) ideals(2). Compare realist.

ideal·is·tic /aɪˌdɪəˈlɪstɪk/ adj 1 showing idealism(1): an idealistic description of life on a farm. 2 believing in, based on, the idea that perfect standards are possible (and so often impractical): an idealistic person/belief.

ideal·is·ti·cal·ly /-klɪ/ *adv*

ideal·ize (also **-ise**) /aɪˈdɪəlaɪz/ *vt* to consider, describe (a state) as perfect.

ideal·iz·ation (also **-is·ation**) /aɪˌdɪəlaɪˈzeɪʃn/ *nu*

ideal·ly /aɪˈdɪəlɪ/ *adv* if what one desires most were possible; if conditions were perfect: *Ideally, I'd like to travel abroad but I haven't got the money.*

iden·ti·cal /aɪˈdentɪkl/ *adj* (*no comp*) **1** the same: *This is the identical knife with which the murder was committed.* **2** exactly alike: *Our views of what should be done are identical.*

i,**dentical 'twins** *n pl* twins from the same fertilized ovum.

iden·ti·cal·ly /-klɪ/ *adv*

iden·ti·fi·ca·tion /aɪˌdentɪfɪˈkeɪʃn/ *n* **1** *nu* the act of identifying a person, thing. **2** *nc* a proof of who a person is, e.g. a passport.

iden·ti·fy /aɪˈdentɪfaɪ/ *vt* (*pt,pp* **-ied**) **1** to show, prove, who or what (a person or thing) is: *Could you identify your umbrella among a hundred others?* **2** **identify sb/sth with sb/sth** to consider, treat a person or thing as being identical with another. **identify oneself with sb/sth** to be associated with: *He refused to identify himself with the new political party.*

i,**dentifying ,relative 'clause** *nc* (*gram*) one that explains which person, thing, is being referred to, as in 'There's the man *I was telling you about*'. Compare non-identifying relative clause.

iden·ti·ty /aɪˈdentətɪ/ *n* (*pl* **-ies**) **1** *nu* the state of being the same. **2** *nc,nu* facts that describe who a person is, what something is: *He was arrested because of mistaken identity.*

ideol·ogy /ˌaɪdɪˈɒlədʒɪ/ *nc* (*pl* **-ies**) a way of thinking, of ideas, characteristic of a person, group etc, esp as forming the basis of an economic or political system.

ideo·logi·cal /ˌaɪdɪəˈlɒdʒɪkl/ *adj*

ideo·logi·cal·ly /-klɪ/ *adv*

ideol·ogist /ˌaɪdɪˈɒlədʒɪst/ *nc* a person who believes in and acts according to an ideology.

idi·ocy /ˈɪdɪəsɪ/ *nc,nu* (*pl* **-ies**) (an act of) being stupid. ⇨ idiot(1).

idio·lect /ˈɪdɪəʊlekt/ *nc* (*lang*) the vocabulary, expressions etc used by one particular person: *Is the word 'corny' part of your idiolect?* Compare dialect.

id·iom /ˈɪdɪəm/ *nc* **1** (*lang*) a group of words with a meaning that is not obvious through knowledge of the individual words but must be learnt as a whole, e.g. *give up, in order to, be all ears.* **2** a particular way a person, group of people or country uses a language: *the idiom of modern American English.*

idio·mat·ic /ˌɪdɪəˈmætɪk/ *adj*

idi·om·at·ic·al·ly /ˌɪdɪəˈmætɪklɪ/ *adv*

idio·syn·cra·sy /ˌɪdɪəˈsɪŋkrəsɪ/ *nc* (*pl* **-ies**) a way of thinking or behaving that is peculiar to a person: *My mother has many idiosyncrasies such as talking to her vegetables to encourage them to grow.*

idio·syn·cra·tic /ˌɪdɪəsɪŋˈkrætɪk/ *adj*

id·iot /ˈɪdɪət/ *nc* **1** (*informal*; usually *derog*)) a fool: *'I've left my umbrella in the train. What an idiot I am!'* **2** (not now used) a person suffering

severe mental handicap.

idi·ot·ic /ˌɪdɪˈɒtɪk/ *adj* very foolish.

idi·oti·cal·ly /-klɪ/ *adv*

idle¹ /ˈaɪdl/ *adj* (**—r, —st**) **1** doing no work; not active or in use: *When people cannot find employment they are idle* (*though not necessarily lazy*). **2** (*attrib*) (of time) not spent in doing something: *We spent many idle hours during the holidays.* **3** (of a person) lazy (the more usual word for this sense): *an idle girl.* **4** (*attrib*) worthless: *Don't listen to idle gossip.*

idle² /ˈaɪdl/ *v* **1** *vt* to spend (time) in a lazy manner: *idling away your time. Don't idle.* **2** *vi* (also *tick over*) (of a car engine) to be switched on but not active or moving.

idler *nc* a person who is idle.

idly /ˈaɪdlɪ/ *adv*

idol /ˈaɪdl/ *nc* **1** an image in wood, stone etc of a god, esp used as an object of worship. **2** a person or thing greatly loved or admired: *He was an only child and the idol of his parents.*

idol·atry /aɪˈdɒlətrɪ/ *n* (*pl* **-ies**) *nc,nu* (an instance of) the worship of idols.

idol·ize (also **-ise**) /ˈaɪdəlaɪz/ *vt* to love or admire (a person, thing) too much.

idol·iz·ation (also **-is·ation**) /ˌaɪdəlaɪˈzeɪʃn/ *nu*

idyll /ˈɪdɪl/ *nc* **1** (*literature*) a short description, usually a poem, of simple country life, esp described as extremely pleasant. **2** a scene or event showing this.

idyl·lic /ɪˈdɪlɪk/ *adj* simple and extremely pleasant: *idyllic weather/life.*

i.e. /ˌaɪ ˈiː/ *abbr* (used after a word or phrase which is going to be explained) that is; which means: *the Arts, i.e. the theatre, music, literature etc.*

if /ɪf/ *conj* (*subord*) Ⓝ 'If' is mainly used to express the conditional form in English. Be careful: most mistakes are made because the wrong tense is used in the *if*-clause or the main clause. The main structures are therefore given before the explanations and examples. **1** on condition that: supposing that: **(a)** *if*-clause in present tense + *main clause* in future tense (used to express a condition or event that is possible or likely): *If you ask, he'll help you. You'll fail the exam if you don't work. If I have the time, I'll visit her. If I have some money left, I'll buy that record. She'll become ill if she doesn't eat more. If I become rich, I'll buy you a car.* Ⓝ 'If' used with a negative, as in 'if you do not go', has the same meaning as 'unless' with an affirmative, as in 'unless you go'. **(b)** *if*-clause in past tense + *main clause* in past tense (used to express a condition or event that is a likely or necessary explanation or result): *If she said that, she was really angry. He must have been very hungry if he stole the bread.* **(c)** *if*-clause in present tense + *main clause* in present or future tense (used to express a condition or event that always happens as a result): *If you mix yellow and blue paint you (will) get green paint. If there is high unemployment there is/will be increased social unrest.* **(d)** *if*-clause in present or past tense + main clause with *can/may* (used to express permission using the condition mentioned): *If you pay/have paid for a ticket, you can go in.* **(e)** *if*-clause in present or past tense + *main clause* with *must/ought to/should* (used to give advice or an order using the condition mentioned): *If your job is boring, you ought to look for a more interesting one.* Ⓝ If-clause + imperative is also possible when giving advice, as in *If you're tired, go to bed.* **(f)** *if-clause* in past tense + *main clause* with *would* (used to suggest a condition or event that is imagined): *If I were a millionaire, I'd buy you a large house.* Ⓝ Compare this with the last example in (a) above. ⇨ if ever. **(g)** *if-clause* in past perfect tense + *main clause* with *would have* (used to express a condition or event that was possible but did not happen): *If you had asked me* (but you did not) *I would have allowed you to go.* ⇨ if only. **as if** ⇨ as². **if any** supposing that there is/are any: *All the profits, if any, will be used to buy a new machine.* **if anything** (used to express an opinion) supposing any opinion can be given (which is unlikely) this is it: *If anything, it was a pleasant film to watch but it wasn't very good.* **if at all** supposing an action, event etc happens although it is very unlikely: *I'll be there by 6 o'clock, if at all.* Ⓝ For 'if at all sth', as in *if at all possible*, ⇨ (not) at all at: all³(4). **if ever** supposing that there is an occasion when something happened or happens although it is unlikely: *We must have met in Mexico, if ever.* Ⓝ For 'if ever sb/sth + verb', as in *If ever you leave me . . .* , ⇨ ever(1). **if need be** supposing the action etc is necessary, useful etc: *I could be in Rome by Friday, if need be.* **if not** supposing that the action, event, situation etc mentioned has not happened: *Did you lock the door? If not, do it now.* **if only** (used to express a strong desire or hope that was not fulfilled, esp in exclamations): *If only you had come to see me months ago!* (i.e. but you did not!) **if so** supposing an action, event etc mentioned has happened: *Have you finished your work? If so, you can watch television.* **if then** and it is unlikely that something would happen, be allowed, be done etc even on the condition mentioned: *I'd only allow you to use the car in an emergency, if then.* **if I were you** + main clause with *would* (used to give advice): *If I were you I would put the money in the bank.* **if it was/were not for sb/ sth** the person, state, event etc is the only reason that stops an action, event etc happening: *If it was/were not for my family/education, I'd be a rich man by now.* **if sb/sth will/would do sth (a)** (used to make a polite or formal request): *She'd be delighted if you would agree to visit her. If you'll be so kind as to sign this for me . . .* **(b)** (used with *like* or a similar verb as a polite form of permission): *If you'd like to write to me, please do.* **(c)** (used to express willingness): *If Mary would apologize, I would forgive her.* **(d)** (used to express unwillingness to stop or change): *If you will continue to make a noise, I'll report you.* **if and when** (or **when and if**) (used as an emphatic form of *if*) on that/this condition and occasion: *I'll telephone you if and when I can.* **What if . . . ?** (used as an emphatic form of *if*) supposing that: *What if I offered to pay? Would you agree to come?* **2** (used to introduce an indirect question, to suggest doubt or to express choice): *I wondered if you'd like to come for a drive. He doesn't know if there are any left. She can't remember if she's read that book or not.* Ⓝ 'Whether' is also possible, esp to express choice, as in *She can't decide whether to go or stay,* or in a sentence with 'if'

already included, such as *He asked whether, if John hated the area so much, he would sell the house.* 'Whether' can be used in front of an infinitive, as in *I don't know whether to go or not,* but 'if' cannot. Compare *I don't know whether/if I want to go or not.* **3** although: *The hotel, if a little more expensive, was good value.* **even if** ⇨ even²(2). **4** (used in polite requests, apologies etc): *Do you mind if I sit here? Forgive me if I said something rude.*

'if-clause *nc* (usually written: *if*-clause) (*gram*) a clause beginning with *if*, esp used to express the conditional form in English, as in '*If you try, you will succeed.*' ⇨ if(1).

ig·loo /'ɪgluː/ *nc* (*pl* **—s**) a house made of blocks of hard snow.

ig·neous /'ɪgnɪəs/ *adj* (*science*) (of rocks) formed by action from volcanoes.

ig·nite /ɪg'naɪt/ *vt,vi* (*science*) to set (something) on fire.

ig·ni·tion /ɪg'nɪʃn/ *n* **1** *nu* (*science*) the state of igniting or being ignited. **2** *nc* (in a car) an electrical mechanism used to make the petrol in an engine explode.

ig·nom·ini·ous /ˌɪgnə'mɪnɪəs/ *adj* (*formal*) causing public disgrace, shame: *an ignominious defeat.*

ig·nom·ini·ous·ly *adv*

ig·nom·iny /'ɪgnəmɪnɪ/ *nu* public disgrace or shame.

ig·nor·ance /'ɪgnərəns/ *nu* **ignorance (of sth)** the state of being ignorant: *We are in complete ignorance of his plans.*

ig·nor·ant /'ɪgnərənt/ *adj* **1** (of a person) knowing little or nothing: *I am still ignorant/was kept ignorant of his plans.* **2** resulting from lack of knowledge: *ignorant behaviour.*

ig·nor·ant·ly *adv*

ig·nore /ɪg'nɔː(r)/ *vt* to take no notice of (a person, thing): *ignoring rude remarks.*

I'll /aɪl/ = *I will; I shall.*

ill¹ /ɪl/ *adj* **1** (*pred*) in poor health: *He's very ill. Unwashed fruit can make you seriously ill. She's been ill with measles. Does society care about those who are mentally ill?* Compare well¹(1). **be taken/fall ill** to become ill. **2** (*attrib*) bad: *She suffers from ill health. The ill effects of the weather are obvious. He's noted for his ill manners.* Compare good¹(1). Ⓝ 'Worse' can be used as a comparative form of '*ill*', as in *He was very ill yesterday but today he's worse.*

ill² /ɪl/ *adv* (*no comp*) (often used as a prefix) badly: *It ill becomes a boy of your intelligence to do that. He's an ill-bred boy. Don't ill-treat your staff.* **be/feel ill at ease** to be/feel embarrassed and uncomfortable: *I always feel ill at ease in a suit.*

ill·ad'vised *adj* not sensible or wise: *an ill-advised remark.*

ill·'bred *adj* (*derog*) badly brought up.

ill·con'sidered *adj* unwise because not thought about carefully: *an ill-considered scheme.*

ill·dis'posed (towards sb/sth) *adj* (*pred*) unfriendly, unfavourable, (towards a person, plan etc).

ill·'fated *adj* unlucky; sure to fail.

ill 'feeling *nc* a feeling of being angry, jealous etc: *I hope there are no ill feelings between us.*

ill·'gotten *adj* (*attrib*) obtained dishonestly: *ill-*

gotten gains.

ill-'judged *adj* not sensible or wise.

ill-'mannered *adj* rude. Opp well-mannered.

ill-'timed *adj* done at a wrong or unsuitable time: *Your criticism was ill-timed—she's very ill*.

ill-'treat *vt* to treat (a person, property) badly or cruelly.

ill-'treatment *nu* bad or cruel treatment.

ill-'use *vt* (*formal*) = ill-treat.

ill 'will *nu* an unkind feeling.

ill³ /ɪl/ *n* **1** *nu* harm; evil: *do ill; wish her ill*. **2** *nc* (usually *pl*) an unfortunate experience; trouble: *the various ills of life*. Compare illness.

il·le·gal /ɪ'li:gl/ *adj* (*no comp*) not legal; forbidden by law: *It is illegal to drive before you are 17 in Britain*. Compare illicit, unlawful.

il·legal·ity /ˌɪlɪ'gælətɪ/ *nc,nu*

il·le·gal·ly /ɪ'li:gəlɪ/ *adv*

il·leg·ible /ɪ'ledʒəbl/ *adj* difficult or impossible to read: *illegible writing*. Opp legible.

il·leg·ibil·ity /ɪ,ledʒə'bɪlətɪ/ *nu*

il·leg·ibly /-əblɪ/ *adv*

il·legit·imate /ˌɪlɪ'dʒɪtɪmət/ *adj* (*no comp*) **1** born of parents who were not married to each other: *an illegitimate child*. **2** not according to law or public opinion of correct or moral behaviour: *an illegitimate excuse for causing a riot*. Compare legitimate.

il·legit·imate·ly *adv*

il·lib·er·al /ɪ'lɪbərəl/ *adj* (*formal*) intolerant.

il·lib·er·al·ly /-rəlɪ/ *adv*

il·li·cit /ɪ'lɪsɪt/ *adj* (*no comp;* usually *attrib*) **1** done against a law (esp one concerning conditions for an activity to be carried out): *illicit gambling; the illicit use of drugs*. **2** not permitted (though not illegal): *illicit smoking of cigarettes in school*. Compare illegal; Opp licit.

il·lic·it·ly *adv*

il·lit·er·ate¹ /ɪ'lɪtərət/ *adj* (*no comp*) unable to read or write. Compare literate(1).

il·lit·er·acy /-rəsɪ/ *nu*

il·lit·er·ate² /ɪ'lɪtərət/ *nc* **1** an illiterate person. **2** (*derog*) a person who (is unwilling and) has not learned facts by reading.

ill·ness /'ɪlnɪs/ *n* **1** *nu* the state of being ill: *There has been no/not much/a great deal of illness this winter*. **2** *nc* a specific reason for, occasion of, being ill: *She had one illness after another*.

il·logi·cal /ɪ'lɒdʒɪkl/ *adj* without, contrary to, logic.

il·logi·cal·ity /ɪ,lɒdʒɪ'kælətɪ/ *nc,nu*

il·logi·cal·ly /-klɪ/ *adv*

il·lumi·nate /ɪ'lu:mɪneɪt/ *vt* (*formal*) **1** to make (something) clear; help to explain (an idea, fact): *This dictionary provides examples to illuminate the definitions*. **2** to give light to (something): *a street illuminated by street lamps*. **3** to decorate (a place) with bright lights.

il·lumi·nat·ing *adj* (usually *pred*) (esp) explaining something clearly and in an interesting way: *I found his lectures illuminating*.

il·lumi·na·tion /ɪ,lu:mɪ'neɪʃn/ *nc,nu*

il·lu·sion /ɪ'lu:ʒn/ *nc* (the seeing of) something that does not really exist; a false or impossible idea: *Seeing water in a desert is often an optical illusion*. **be under the illusion that . . .** to believe that: *I was under the illusion that you owned your house*. **be under/have no illusion**

about sb/sth to have no false or wrong idea: *She was under no illusion about him*. Compare delusion.

il·lu·sive /ɪ'lu:sɪv/ *adj* (*no comp*) = illusory (esp when used about mental images): *an illusive picture of an imagined ideal design*.

il·lu·sive·ly *adv*

il·lu·sory /ɪ'lu:zərɪ/ *adj* (*no comp*) based on a false or impossible idea: *For many young people, ambitions to become rich are illusory*.

il·lus·trate /'ɪləstreɪt/ *vt* **1** to add pictures, diagrams, photographs etc to (something): *illustrating a book with colour drawings*. **2** to explain (something) by using examples etc: *The uses of words in this dictionary are illustrated with example sentences. Let me illustrate what I mean by telling you a story*.

il·lus·tra·tor /-tə(r)/ *nc* a person who draws pictures for books etc.

il·lus·tra·tion /ˌɪlə'streɪʃn/ *n* **1** *nu* the process, state of illustrating or being illustrated: *Illustration is often more useful than definition for giving the meanings of words*. **2** *nc* a picture, diagram, example etc used in a book etc.

il·lus·tra·tive /'ɪləstrətɪv/ *adj* (*no comp*) **illustrative (of sth)** (*formal*) used to explain the meaning (of something).

il·lus·tri·ous /ɪ'lʌstrɪəs/ *adj* (*formal*) celebrated as being a fine example; famous: *an illustrious writer*.

il·lus·tri·ous·ly *adv*

I'm /aɪm/ = *I am*. ⇨ be¹.

im·age /'ɪmɪdʒ/ *nc* **1** a likeness or copy of a god or person, esp made in wood, stone etc: *an image of Buddha*. **2** a mental picture: *have an image of what the house will look like*. **3** an exact likeness seen in a mirror or through the lens of a camera. **the spitting image (of sb)** an exact likeness: *She's the spitting image of her mother*. **4** a general opinion (of a government, business, person, organization): *How can we improve our (public) image?* **5** (*literature*) a descriptive representation (esp of a feeling or emotion) so that it can be imagined by the reader.

image·ry /'ɪmɪdʒrɪ/ *nu* (*literature*) the use of figurative language to produce an imaginative or emotional response or to make descriptions stronger, as in 'Your face is like a book in which people can read many strange things.'

im·agin·able /ɪ'mædʒɪnəbl/ *adj* (*no comp*) that can be imagined: *We had every imaginable difficulty/every difficulty imaginable to get here in time*. Opp unimaginable.

im·agin·ary /ɪ'mædʒɪnrɪ/ *adj* (*no comp*) existing only in the mind and not real: *imaginary problems/voices*.

im·agin·ation /ɪ,mædʒɪ'neɪʃn/ *n* **1** *nc,nu* (the ability to create) mental pictures of a person, situation etc that has not been experienced or is not present: *He hasn't much imagination. Her writing shows a strong imagination*. Compare fantasy(1). **2** *nc* the mind (when thinking creatively): *Use your imagination and try to explain how it happened*.

im·agin·ative /ɪ'mædʒɪnətɪv/ *adj* of, having, using, imagination: *an imaginative child/idea*. Opp unimaginative.

im·ag·ine /ɪ'mædʒɪn/ *vt* **1** to form a picture or

idea of (something) in the mind: *Can you imagine life without electricity? Can you imagine* **2** to think of (something) as probable: *Don't imagine that I'll lend you money each time you ask!* Ⓝ Not used in continuous tenses, e.g. *is/was -ing.* Compare fancy³.

im·bal·ance /ˌɪmˈbæləns/ *nc* an absence of balance between two quantities or totals: *We must control the increasing imbalance between rich and poor countries.*

im·be·cile /ˈɪmbəsiːl/ *adj (attrib)* foolish: *imbecile behaviour.* □ *nc* **1** a foolish person. **2** (not now used) a person with very low intelligence.
im·be·cil·ity /ˌɪmbəˈsɪləti/ *nc,nu*

im·bue /ɪmˈbjuː/ *vt (pt,pp* —**d)** *imbue sb with sth (formal)* to fill, inspire a person with a mentioned feeling etc: *be imbued with patriotism/ hatred.*

IMF /ˌaɪ em ˈef/ *abbr* International Monetary Fund (an international organization to encourage trade by ensuring that the major currencies are stable and lending money to countries with temporary need).

imi·tate /ˈɪmɪteɪt/ *vt* (try to) copy the behaviour, appearance, sound, actions etc of (a person, animal, thing): *Don't imitate her bad behaviour or you'll get into trouble. The wood was painted to imitate stone. Some birds can imitate human speech. The author has tried to imitate Tolstoy's style.*
imi·ta·tor /-tə(r)/ *nc* a person, animal, that imitates.

imi·ta·tion¹ /ˌɪmɪˈteɪʃn/ *adj (attrib)* not real: *imitation leather/diamonds.*

imi·ta·tion² /ˌɪmɪˈteɪʃn/ *n* **1** *nu* the act of imitating: *Imitation is the sincerest form of flattery.* **2** *nc* something made or done like something else: *This painting isn't a real Picasso—it's an imitation.*

imi·tat·ive /ˈɪmɪtətɪv/ *adj* *imitative (of sb/ sth) (formal)* trying to be like another.

im·macu·late /ɪˈmækjʊlət/ *adj (no comp)* completely clean; without faults: *immaculate clothes; looking immaculate; immaculate behaviour.*
im·macu·late·ly *adv: immaculately dressed.*

im·ma·teri·al /ˌɪməˈtɪərɪəl/ *adj (pred)* *immaterial to sb/sth* of no importance to a person, thing: *It is immaterial to me whether you go or stay.* Compare material¹(3).

im·ma·ture /ˌɪməˈtjʊə(r)/ *adj* not yet fully developed: *an immature girl; He's very bright, but his behaviour is rather immature.* Opp mature.
im·ma·tur·ity /ˌɪməˈtjʊərəti/ *nu*

im·meas·ur·able /ɪˈmeʒərəbl/ *adj* that cannot be calculated: *You've given me immeasurable happiness.* Compare measurable.

im·medi·ate /ɪˈmiːdɪət/ *adj* **1** occurring, done, at once: *take immediate action. His response was immediate.* **2** *(attrib)* without anything coming between: *my immediate neighbours; to my immediate left.*
im·medi·ate·ly *adv* **(a)** at once; without delay: *Come here immediately.* **(b)** directly or closely: *She's immediately behind the man in the red shirt.* □ *conj* as soon as: *You can go immediately he comes.*

im·mem·or·ial /ˌɪməˈmɔːrɪəl/ *adj (pred)* (esp) *from/since time immemorial* for a very long time: *That house has been there since time immemorial.*

im·mense /ɪˈmens/ *adj* **1** very large: *an immense airport/building.* **2** very great: *immense pleasure/ difficulties.*
im·mense·ly *adv* **(a)** to a very large degree: *immensely popular.* **(b)** *(informal)* very much: *They enjoyed themselves immensely.*
im·men·si·ty /ɪˈmensəti/ *nc,nu*

im·merse /ɪˈmɜːs/ *vt* **1** to put (a person, thing) under the surface of water or other liquid: *immerse one's head in the water.* **2** *immerse oneself etc in sth* to give all one's thoughts or attention to something: *She was immersed in her book/work.*
im·mer·sion /ɪˈmɜːʃn/ *nc,nu*
im'mersion heater *nc* an electric apparatus fixed in a tank of water to heat water.

im·mi·grant /ˈɪmɪɡrənt/ *nc* a person who immigrates: *Italian immigrants into Australia.* Compare emigrant.

im·mi·grate /ˈɪmɪɡreɪt/ *vi* to come to another country to live. Compare emigrate.
im·mi·gra·tion /ˌɪmɪˈɡreɪʃn/ *nc,nu*

im·mi·nence /ˈɪmɪnəns/ *nu (formal)* the state of being imminent.

im·mi·nent /ˈɪmɪnənt/ *adj* likely to come or happen very soon: *A storm is imminent.*
im·mi·nent·ly *adv*

im·mo·bile /ɪˈməʊbaɪl/ *adj* **1** not able to move or be moved: *My injury made me immobile for several weeks.* **2** *(no comp)* not moving: *an immobile object.*
im·mo·bil·ity /ˌɪməˈbɪləti/ *nu* the state of being immobile.
im·mo·bi·lize (also **-ise**) /ɪˈməʊbəlaɪz/ *vt* to make (a person, thing) immobile(1).
im·mo·bil·iz·ation (also **-is·ation**) /ˌɪməʊbəlaɪˈzeɪʃn/ *nu*

im·mod·er·ate /ɪˈmɒdərət/ *adj (formal)* too much: *immoderate eating and drinking.* Compare moderate¹(1).
im·mod·er·ate·ly *adv*

im·mod·est /ɪˈmɒdɪst/ *adj (derog)* not modest: *immodest behaviour.*
im·mod·est·ly *adv*

im·mor·al /ɪˈmɒrəl/ *adj (derog)* not moral; wicked and evil: *immoral conduct; an immoral act/person.*
im·mor·al·ity /ˌɪməˈræləti/ *nc,nu*
im·mor·al·ly *adv*

im·mor·tal /ɪˈmɔːtl/ *adj* **1** living for ever: *Humans are not immortal.* Compare mortal¹(1). **2** never forgotten: *immortal fame.*
im·mor·tal·ity /ˌɪmɔːˈtæləti/ *nu* endless life or fame.
im·mor·tal·ize (also **-ise**) /ɪˈmɔːtəlaɪz/ *vt* to give endless fame to (a person etc) (esp in literature): *Classical Greek writings have immortalized their gods.*

im·mov·able /ɪˈmuːvəbl/ *adj* **1** *(no comp)* that cannot be moved: *immovable property* (e.g. buildings, land). **2** not able, refusing, to be affected or changed: *The chairperson remained immovable on the cost of membership.*
im·mov·ably /-əblɪ/ *adv*

im·mune /ɪˈmjuːn/ *adj* **1** *immune (from sth)* protected (from disease, danger, punishment etc). **2** *immune (to sth)* not able to be affected (by); protected (against): *immune to her tears;*

immune to infection.

im·mun·ity /ɪˈmjuːnəti/ *nu* **immunity (from sth)** the condition of being free from disease, punishment: *Immunity from disease; diplomatic immunity.*

im·mu·nize (also **-ise**) /ˈɪmjʊnaɪz/ *vt* **immunize sb (against sth)** to make a person immune (to a disease).

im·mu·niz·ation (also **-is·ation**) /ˌɪmjʊnaɪˈzeɪʃn/ *nc,nu*

imp /ɪmp/ *nc* **1** (in stories) a little, wicked elf. **2** (*informal*) a mischievous child.

im·pact /ˈɪmpækt/ *n* **1** *nc,nu* (the force produced by) one object striking against another: *The cars hit each other with a great impact.* **on impact** at the moment of hitting together: *The two glasses broke on impact.* **3** *nc* a strong influence or effect: *the impact of his speech on the audience.*

im·pair /ɪmˈpeə(r)/ *vt* (*formal*) to weaken, spoil, (something): *impair one's health by overwork.*

im·pair·ment *nu*

im·pale /ɪmˈpeɪl/ *vt* **impale sb (on sth)** to stab a person (with a spear etc).

im·part /ɪmˈpɑːt/ *vt* (*formal*) to give, pass on, (a secret, news etc).

im·par·tial /ɪmˈpɑːʃl/ *adj* not favouring one more than another: *an impartial decision.* Compare partial(2).

im·par·tial·ity /ˌɪmˌpɑːʃɪˈælətɪ/ *nu*

im·par·tial·ly /-ʃəlɪ/ *adv*: *act impartially.*

im·pas·sable /ɪmˈpɑːsəbl/ *adj* (of roads etc) impossible to travel through or on. Compare passable(1).

im·passe /ˈæmpɑːs/ *nc* a position from which no progress is possible: *The talks reached an impasse.*

im·pas·sion·ed /ɪmˈpæʃnd/ *adj* full of, showing, deep feeling: *an impassioned speech/appeal.*

im·pas·sive /ɪmˈpæsɪv/ *adj* (*formal*) (of a person) showing no sign of feeling: *an impassive audience.*

im·pas·sive·ly *adv*

im·pa·tience /ɪmˈpeɪʃns/ *nu* the absence of patience: *He was beginning to show his impatience at the long delay.*

im·pa·tient /ɪmˈpeɪʃnt/ *adj* **1** (*pred*) **impatient for sth** very eager for something to happen: *The dog is impatient for its bone.* **2** **impatient (to do sth)** not able to wait quietly and with self-control: *The children were impatient to start.* **3** (*pred*) **impatient (with sb)** showing intolerance: *be impatient with a stranger who asks advice.* Compare patient[1].

im·pa·tient·ly *adv*

im·peach /ɪmˈpiːtʃ/ *vt* (*legal*) to accuse (a person) of a serious crime, e.g. against a profession or the State: *impeach a judge for taking bribes.*

im·peach·ment *nc,nu*

im·pec·cable /ɪmˈpekəbl/ *adj* (*no comp; formal*) faultless: *an impeccable character/record.*

im·pe·cuni·ous /ˌɪmpɪˈkjuːnɪəs/ *adj* (*formal*) having little or no money.

im·pede /ɪmˈpiːd/ *vt* to get in the way of (a person, activity etc): *What is impeding an early start?*

im·pedi·ment /ɪmˈpedɪmənt/ *nc* **1** a physical defect, esp in speech, e.g. a stammer. **2** something that hinders: *The lack of a degree will be an impediment to her career.*

im·pel /ɪmˈpel/ *vt* (**-ll-**) **impel sb (to do sth)** (often *passive; formal*) to force, urge, (a person): *He said he had been impelled to crime by poverty.*

im·pend·ing /ɪmˈpendɪŋ/ *adj* (usually *attrib*) that is about to happen: *her impending arrival.*

im·pen·etrable /ɪmˈpenɪtrəbl/ *adj* that cannot be penetrated: *impenetrable forests.*

im·peni·tent /ɪmˈpenɪtənt/ *adj* (*formal*) not sorry for having done wrong.

im·pera·tive[1] /ɪmˈperətɪv/ *adj* **1** (*no comp*) urgent; essential: *Is it imperative they should have/for them to have two cars?* **2** not to be disobeyed: *The colonel's orders were imperative.* **3** (*gram*) of the form of a verb used to express an order or command: *'Listen!' and 'Go away!' are in the imperative (mood).*

im·pera·tive·ly *adv*

im·pera·tive[2] /ɪmˈperətɪv/ *nc* (*gram*) an imperative(3) form of a verb.

im·per·cep·tible /ˌɪmpəˈseptəbl/ *adj* that cannot be seen; very slight or gradual: *The mistakes in the cloth are imperceptible. He's making imperceptible progress.* Opp perceptible.

im·per·cep·tibly /-əblɪ/ *adv*

im·per·fect /ɪmˈpɜːfɪkt/ *adj* **1** having faults: *imperfect glass.* **2** not complete: *an imperfect knowledge of English.* **3** (*gram*) of the imperfect tense.

im,perfect 'tense *nc* (*gram*) = past continuous (or progressive) tense.

im·per·fect·ly *adv*

im·per·fec·tion /ˌɪmpəˈfekʃn/ *n* **1** *nu* the state of being imperfect. **2** *nc* (*formal*) a fault (the usual word): *little imperfections in her character.*

im·per·ial /ɪmˈpɪərɪəl/ *adj* **1** of an empire or its ruler(s): *imperial trade.* **2** (*formal*) magnificent: *with imperial splendour.* **3** (of weights and measures) used by law in the United Kingdom: *an imperial pint/gallon.*

im·per·ial·ly /-ɪəlɪ/ *adv*

im·per·ial·ism /ɪmˈpɪərɪəlɪzəm/ *nu* (the belief in) a political system of gaining economic or political influence and control over other countries.

im·per·ial·ist /-ɪst/ *adj* of, like, imperialism: *an imperialist policy.* □ *nc* a supporter of, believer in, imperialism.

im·per·ial·is·tic /ɪmˌpɪərɪəˈlɪstɪk/ *adj*

im·per·il /ɪmˈperəl/ *vt* (**-ll-**, *US* also **-l-**) to put (a person, life, success etc) in danger.

im·peri·ous /ɪmˈpɪərɪəs/ *adj* (*formal; derog*) showing too much pride in oneself, esp that one is superior to others: *imperious gestures/looks.*

im·per·son·al /ˌɪmˈpɜːsənl/ *adj* **1** not influenced by personal feeling: *an impersonal decision.* **2** not referring to any particular person: *an impersonal discussion.* **3** (*gram*) of a verb form used after 'it' to make general statements such as 'It *is raining.*'

im·per·son·al·ly /-əlɪ/ *adv*

im·per·son·ate /ɪmˈpɜːsəneɪt/ *vt* to pretend to be (another person) by using the same behaviour etc: *She impersonated her teacher by altering her voice.*

im·per·son·ation /ɪmˌpɜːsəˈneɪʃn/ *nc,nu*

im·per·ti·nent /ɪmˈpɜːtənənt/ *adj* (*derog*) not showing proper respect; rude: *impertinent remarks.* Ⓝ *'Impertinent'* is not the opposite of *'pertinent'.*

im·per·ti·nent·ly *adv*: *behave impertinently.*

im·per·ti·nence /-əns/ *nc,nu*

im·per·turb·able /ˌɪmpəˈtɜːbəbl/ *adj (formal)* not easily troubled or excited.

im·per·vi·ous /ɪmˈpɜːvɪəs/ *adj* **impervious (to sth) 1** (of materials) not allowing water etc to pass through. **2** *(fig)* (of a person) not moved or influenced (by something): *impervious to criticism.*

im·petu·ous /ɪmˈpetjuəs/ *adj (derog)* done, acting, quickly and without enough thought or care: *impetuous remarks.*
　im·petu·ous·ly *adv*
　im·petu·os·ity /ɪmˌpetʃuˈɒsətɪ/ *nc,nu*

im·pe·tus /ˈɪmpɪtəs/ *n (pl —es)* **1** *nu (science)* the force with which a body moves. **2** *nc,nu (fig)* the strong encouraging feeling that makes a person do something: *He felt the impetus to fight back.* **3** *nc* an encouraging reason for activity: *The treaty will give an impetus to trade between the two countries.*

im·pinge /ɪmˈpɪndʒ/ *vi* **impinge on sth** *(formal)* to use something, e.g. time, too much or irresponsibly: *impinging on a person's time.*
　im·pinge·ment *nu*

im·pi·ous /ˈɪmpɪəs/ *adj (formal; derog)* wicked (the more usual word). Compare pious.
　im·pi·ous·ly *adv*

imp·ish /ˈɪmpɪʃ/ *adj* of, like, an imp.
　imp·ish·ly *adv*

im·plac·able /ɪmˈplækəbl/ *adj (formal)* that cannot be calmed or satisfied: *an implacable jealousy; an implacable enemy.*

im·plant /ɪmˈplɑːnt/ *vt* **implant sth (in/into sb/sth) 1** to fix or put ideas, feelings etc in a person's mind: *implant a respect for authority in school children.* **2** *(med)* to put a piece of body tissue, a machine etc in the body for medical reasons. Compare transplant²(2).

im·plaus·ible /ɪmˈplɔːzəbl/ *adj* not plausible.

im·ple·ment¹ /ˈɪmplɪmənt/ *nc* a tool or instrument used for doing work: *farm implements.*

im·ple·ment² /ˈɪmplɪment/ *vt* to carry out (an undertaking, agreement, promise etc): *implement a scheme.*
　im·ple·men·ta·tion /ˌɪmplɪmenˈteɪʃn/ *nu*

im·pli·cate /ˈɪmplɪkeɪt/ *vt* **implicate sb (in sth)** to show that a person is or was involved (in doing something wrong).

im·pli·ca·tion /ˌɪmplɪˈkeɪʃn/ *n* **1** *nu* the state of being involved: *Was his implication in the robbery serious?* **2** *nc* something that is implied: *What are the implications of this statement?*

im·pli·cit /ɪmˈplɪsɪt/ *adj (formal)* **1** **implicit (in sth)** implied though not openly expressed: *an implicit threat; a warning implicit in a statement.* **2** *(attrib; no comp)* done without questioning: *implicit belief.*
　im·pli·cit·ly *adv*

im·plore /ɪmˈplɔː(r)/ *vt* **implore sb (for sth; to do sth)** to ask a person earnestly (for or to do something): *imploring a judge for mercy.*
　im·plor·ing·ly *adv*

im·ply /ɪmˈplaɪ/ *vt (pt,pp -ied)* **imply (that) sth** to suggest (that) something is true without saying it: *Are you implying that I am not telling the truth?* ⇨ implication(2). Compare infer.

im·po·lite /ˌɪmpəˈlaɪt/ *adj* not polite.
　im·po·lite·ly *adv*

im·poli·tic /ɪmˈpɒlətɪk/ *adj (formal)* not judged well; not wise.

im·pon·der·able /ɪmˈpɒndrəbl/ *adj (fig)* of which the effect cannot at that point be judged as important or not, or cannot be estimated: *One imponderable fact in forecasting the profits for next year is the weather.* □ *nc* (often *pl*) an effect, result etc that is impossible to assess.

im·port¹ /ˈɪmpɔːt/ **1** *nc* (often *pl*) goods imported: *food imports.* Compare export¹(1). **2** *nu (formal)* meaning: *What is the import of his statement?* **3** *nu (formal)* importance: *questions of great international import.*

im·port² /ɪmˈpɔːt/ *vt* **1** to bring in (goods) from a foreign country: *import coffee from Brazil into Europe.* Compare export². **2** *(informal)* to bring in (a person, idea etc) in order to help: *We've imported the manager from our northern office to advise us.* **3** *(formal)* to mean (something): *What does this import?*
　im·por·ta·tion /ˌɪmpɔːˈteɪʃn/ *nc,nu* (an instance of) the act of importing goods.
　im·port·er *nc* a person, business that imports goods.

im·port·ance /ɪmˈpɔːtəns/ *nu* **1** the state of being important: *The matter is of great/no/not much/little importance to us.* **2** a high social or professional position: *a writer of (no) importance.*

im·port·ant /ɪmˈpɔːtənt/ *adj* **1** of great influence or value: *important decisions/books/discoveries/writers.* **2** (of a person) having a high social or professional position: *an important figure in the financial world.* **3** **important (to sb)** of value, concern, relevance (to a person): *Your future career is important to me.* Opp unimportant.
　im·port·ant·ly *adv*

im·por·tu·nate /ɪmˈpɔːtjʊnət/ *adj (formal)* (of a person) making repeated and annoying requests: *an importunate beggar.*

im·por·tune /ɪmˈpɔːtjuːn/ *vt (formal)* to beg (a person) urgently and repeatedly: *importuning a person for more money.*
　im·por·tun·ity /ˌɪmpɔːˈtjuːnətɪ/ *nc,nu*

im·pose /ɪmˈpəʊz/ *v* **impose (sb/sth) (on sb/sth) 1** *vt* to make (a tax, duty, regulation etc) officially necessary: *New duties were imposed on wines and spirits.* **2** *vt* to force (something, oneself, one's company) on others. **3** *vi* to ask a person to do, give etc something (esp causing a person more work, costs, worry etc): *Stop imposing on his kindness.*

im·pos·ing /ɪmˈpəʊzɪŋ/ *adj (formal)* making a strong impression because of size, character, appearance: *an imposing old lady.*
　im·pos·ing·ly *adv*

im·po·si·tion /ˌɪmpəˈzɪʃn/ *n* **imposition (on sb/sth) 1** *nu* the act of imposing(1): *the imposition of new taxes on the farmers.* **2** *nc (formal)* something imposed, e.g. a tax, burden, fine.

im·pos·sible¹ /ɪmˈpɒsəbl/ *adj* **1** not possible: *It is impossible to cure him.* **2** that cannot be put up with: *It's an impossible situation!*
　im·pos·si·bil·ity /ɪmˌpɒsəˈbɪlətɪ/ *nc,nu*
　im·pos·sibly /-əblɪ/ *adv*

im·pos·sible² /ɪmˈpɒsəbl/ *n sing* (the —) that which is not possible: *Don't ask me to do the impossible.*

im·pos·tor /ɪmˈpɒstə(r)/ *nc* a person pretending to be somebody else (esp in order to do something bad).

im·po·tence /'ɪmpətəns/ *nu* the state of being impotent.

im·po·tent /'ɪmpətənt/ *adj* (*no comp*) **1** (*formal*) not having enough strength, influence etc (to do something or prevent, act, change etc something): *On the question of persuading the manager to change his mind I am impotent.* **2** (of a man) incapable of sexual intercourse.

im·po·tent·ly *adv*

im·pound /ɪm'paʊnd/ *vt* to take possession of (something) by law or by authority: *The videotapes were impounded by customs officials.*

im·pov·er·ish /ɪm'pɒvərɪʃ/ *vt* (often *passive*; *formal*) to cause (a person) to become poor: *He was impoverished by university fees.*

im·prac·ti·cable /ɪm'præktɪkəbl/ *adj* that cannot be put into practice or used: *an impracticable scheme.* Opp practicable.

im·prac·ti·cably /-əblɪ/ *adv*

im·prac·ti·cal /ɪm'præktɪkl/ *adj* **1** not sensible because not doing well or achieving that which is intended: *He's full of impractical ideas like using one room as a library, classroom, gymnasium, theatre and sports hall!* **2** (*derog*) (of a person) not able to do things (such as household repairs etc) well: *an impractical husband.* Compare practical, unpractical.

im·pre·cise /ˌɪmprɪ'saɪs/ *adj* not precise: *imprecise measurements.*

im·preg·nable /ɪm'pregnəbl/ *adj* (*formal*) that cannot be overcome or taken by force: *impregnable defences.*

im·preg·nate /'ɪmpregneɪt/ *vt* **impregnate sth (with sth)** to cause a material or substance to be filled with another): *impregnating soap with perfume.*

im·pre·sario /ˌɪmprɪ'sɑːrɪəʊ/ *nc* (*pl* **—s**) a manager of a theatre or opera company.

im·press /ɪm'pres/ *vt* **1** (often *passive*) to have a strong favourable effect on (a person): *He was not impressed by/with the boy's behaviour. Your work has impressed the examiners. You may think because you work late that I think you work hard but I am not impressed.* **2** **impress sth on sb** to emphasize the importance, danger, necessity etc of something on a person: *We cannot impress on you too seriously the dangers of smoking cigarettes.* **3** to produce (a mark etc) by pressing one thing on another: *impress a design on writing-paper.*

im·pres·sion /ɪm'preʃn/ *nc* **1** an effect produced by a person or thing on a person's mind: *It's my impression that he won't come. Don't go by first impressions—later you may find that your boss is kind. My parents' love for each other has made a lasting impression on me.* **be under/get the impression that . . .** to have/get an idea that: *I get the impression that you don't like modern art.* **make a good impression (on sb)** to cause a person to have a favourable opinion about oneself. **2** a mark produced by pressing something on something: *We could see the impression of her feet in the sand.* **3** a single production of something, esp of a quantity of books: *A first impression of a novel is usually about 5000 copies.* ⇨ edition.

im·pres·sion·ism /-ɪzəm/ *nu* (sometimes I-) the method of painting or writing so as to give the general effect without elaborate detail.

im·pres·sion·ist /-ɪst/ *adj, nc* (sometimes I-) (of) a person who paints or writes using this method.

im·pres·sion·is·tic /ɪm,preʃn'ɪstɪk/ *adj* (a) (sometimes I-) of, characteristic of, impressionism. (b) producing only a general effect.

im·pres·sion·able /ɪm'preʃənəbl/ *adj* easily influenced: *He is at an impressionable age* (usually considered to be 14–18 years).

im·pres·sive /ɪm'presɪv/ *adj* having a strong effect on the mind and feelings: *an impressive ceremony.* Opp unimpressive.

im·pres·sive·ly *adv*

im·print¹ /'ɪmprɪnt/ *nc* **1** a mark produced by pressing or printing: *an imprint of a design on paper.* **2** (*formal*) an effect produced as a sign of something: *an imprint of suffering on her face.*

im·print² /ɪm'prɪnt/ *vt* **1** **imprint sth on sth** (*formal*) to establish something firmly in a person's mind: *imprint ideas on a young mind.* **2** to produce (a mark) by pressing or printing: *imprint a book title.*

im·pris·on /ɪm'prɪzn/ *vt* to put or keep (a person) in a prison.

im·prison·ment *nu*

im·prob·able /ɪm'prɒbəbl/ *adj* not likely to be true or to happen: *an improbable story/result.* Compare probable.

im·prob·abil·ity /ɪm,prɒbə'bɪlətɪ/ *nc,nu*

im·prob·ably /-əblɪ/ *adv*

im·promp·tu /ɪm'prɒmptjuː/ *adj, adv* without preparation: *an impromptu speech.*

im·prop·er /ɪm'prɒpə(r)/ *adj* **1** not paying attention to the conventions of society: *Laughing is improper at a funeral.* Compare proper(2). **2** incorrect: *an improper diagnosis of disease.* **3** indecent: *improper stories/language; make an improper suggestion.*

im·proper·ly *adv*

im·pro·pri·ety /ˌɪmprə'praɪətɪ/ *n* (*pl* **-ies**) (*formal*) **1** *nu* the state of being indecent. **2** *nc* an indecent or offensive act. Compare propriety.

im·prove /ɪm'pruːv/ *vt,vi* **1** (to cause a person, condition) to become better: *His health is improving.* **2** **improve on sb/sth** to manage to obtain a better standard, quality etc than a person, thing: *improve on a world record/last month's profits.*

im·prove·ment *n* (a) *nu* the act, state, of improving or being improved: *There is need for improvement in your handwriting.* (b) *nc* a better condition; something which adds to beauty, usefulness, value etc: *an improvement in the weather. We are making improvements to the house.*

im·pro·vi·dent /ɪm'prɒvɪdənt/ *adj* (*formal*) wasteful and not caring about future needs. Opp provident.

im·pro·vise /'ɪmprəvaɪz/ *vt,vi* **1** to compose music, words etc during the performance: *If an actor forgets his words, he has to improvise* (them). **2** to provide, make or do (something) quickly, using whatever happens to be available: *an improvised meal.*

im·pro·vis·ation /ˌɪmprəvaɪ'zeɪʃn/ *nc,nu*

im·prud·ent /ɪm'pruːdənt/ *adj* unwise or thoughtless (in one's behaviour): *an imprudent act/remark.* Opp prudent.

im·prud·ence /-əns/ *nc,nu*

im·pru·dent·ly *adv*

im·pu·dence /'ɪmpjudəns/ *nu* the state of being impudent: *I will not listen to your impudence!*

im·pu·dent /'ɪmpjudənt/ *adj* (*derog*) very rude, disrespectful: *What an impudent boy he is!*

im·pu·dent·ly *adv*

im·pulse /'ɪmpʌls/ *n* **1** *nc* a sudden desire to act without thought about the consequences: *feel an irresistible impulse to jump out of a window.* **2** *nu* the state of mind in which such desires occur: *a man who acts on impulse.* **3** *nc* a short increase in strength, force: *an electrical impulse.* **4** *nc* a particular encouragement: *They need to give a fresh impulse to state education.*

im·pul·sive /ɪm'pʌlsɪv/ *adj* (of a person, behaviour) acting on, resulting from an impulse(1): *a girl with an impulsive nature.*

im·pul·sive·ly *adv*

im·pul·sive·ness *nu*

im·pun·ity /ɪm'pju:nətɪ/ *nu* (*esp*) **(do sth) with impunity** without caring about the risk of injury or punishment.

im·pure /ɪm'pjʊə(r)/ *adj* (*formal*) **1** immoral: *impure motives.* Opp pure(2). **2** combined with something else: *an impure medicine.* Opp pure(1).

im·pur·ity /-ətɪ/ *nc,nu*

im·pu·ta·tion /ˌɪmpju'teɪʃn/ *nc,nu* (*formal*) (an instance of) suggesting (a fault, bad quality etc): *imputations of carelessness in his official letter.*

im·pute /ɪm'pju:t/ *vt* **impute sth to sb/sth** (*formal*) to consider that an act, quality or result is a person's responsibility or fault: *He was innocent of the crime imputed to him.*

in(s) *written abbr* inch(es).

in¹ /ɪn/ *adj* **1** (*pred*) **(a)** at home, present at work etc: *She'll be in later this evening.* **(b)** fashionable: *Long skirts are in.* **(c)** in power or in office: *The Liberals are in.* **(d)** available: *The library book you wanted is in.* **(e)** (of a player, team) playing, esp batting: *England is still in but with only two wickets left.* **(f)** (of the tide) high; nearest to the coast. Compare out¹(1). **2** (*attrib*) used for receiving things from another place: *an in tray/file.* Compare out¹(2). **3** (*attrib*) (esp **the in sth**) most fashionable: *Black seems to be the in colour this year.*

in² /ɪn/ *adverbial particle* Ⓝ For uses with verbs such as *call, cave, check, close, come, cut, do, get, give, join, lie, live, lock, run, settle, swear, take, turn* etc, ⇨ the *verb* entries. **1** at or to a place or position near or inside: *walk in; bring the dog in. When does the train get in? Everyone has gone in.* Opp out²(1). **2** at home, work etc: *Let's eat in tonight. We stayed in all day.* Compare inside²(2). Opp out²(2). Ⓝ *'Into'* is not possible as an alternative to *'in'* as an adverbial particle, but be careful because *'in to'* (two words with *'to'* as part of the infinitive form of a verb), as in *call in to see my parents,* is possible. **in between** ⇨ between¹(1). **be in for sth (a)** to have agreed to take part in a competition: *I'm in for the marathon/the tennis tournament.* **(b)** to be likely to experience usually something unpleasant: *We're in for a difficult period/a storm.* **be in on sth** (*informal*) to be involved, have a share, in a plan etc: *I'd like to be in on your new scheme.* **be (well) in with sb** (*informal*) to be (very) friendly with, thought of (very) highly by, a person. **have it in for sb** (*informal*) to be ready and wanting to harm, punish etc a person when there is an opportunity (esp because of jealousy etc).

in³ /ɪn/ *prep* Ⓝ For uses in phrases such as *in the clear, in control (of), in conclusion, in exchange for, in order (that/to)* etc, ⇨ the entry for the noun, as at *case, character, clear, coma, conclusion, contact, defence, effect, memory, order* etc. **1** within a place: *in Europe/England/London; in the country/the car/the crowd/the street/the sky/the sea; in a box/bottle; in bed/prison/hospital; in school; in the library/the newspapers.* Ⓝ *'In'* is used for large or important places (e.g. a country and city) and for structures, objects, situations etc that have, or seem to have, length, depth and height (e.g. buildings, vehicles, containers, books, a group of people). *'At'* is only possible when referring to a place (esp a building) when being physically inside is not absolutely necessary, as in *at the station/library.* Note also that *'at school'* can mean 'being a pupil', as in *My son's still at school,* as well as referring to where a person is at a particular time. However, *'at work'* always refers to where a person is, as in *She'll be at work until 6 o'clock* and *'in work'* means 'employed' as in *She hasn't been in work for months.* ⇨ the *note* at at(1). **2** (used of physical surroundings, conditions etc): *in the dark/the rain; in public/private; in secret; in chaos/good order; in poor health; in a dream/a hurry/a panic.* **3** (used of arrangement, shape etc): *in a circle/line; in alphabetical order; in large/small quantities; in packets of twenty.* **4** (used of numbers, quantities etc, e.g. when compared to another number or quantity): *There are 31 days in May. He pays 25p in the pound as tax. One in ten children could go to university.* **in all** ⇨ all³(4). **5** (used of occupation or activity): *in the army/the Civil Service; in teaching/social work. So much time is lost in silly quarrels.* **6** (used of a direction of motion or action): *He put his hand in his pocket. She broke/cut it in two.* Ⓝ *'Into'* is also possible and is much more usual, as in *get into a car; fall into the water; put a coin into the box.* Because *'in'* cannot be used with as many verbs as *into,* if you are not sure about using *'in',* use *'into'.* ⇨ also the *note* at in²(2): *'I invited her in'* is correct but *'into'* is not possible here because *'into'* cannot replace *'in'* as an adverbial particle. However, *'into'* as a preposition, as in *I invited her into the house,* is correct. **7** (used of a period of time) during the period of: *in 1988; in the summer; in the day time/night; in her holidays/lessons.* **8** (used of a period of time) inside a period of: *I'll be back in a few hours. He'll be ready in a moment.* **9** (used of age, temperature, speed etc) inside (the range mentioned): *a man in his forties; a temperature in the eighties.* **10** (used of a way of saying, writing, doing or producing something): *speaking in English; writing in ink/code; painting in oils; built in brick; paid for in cash.* **11** (used of colour, style etc of clothing): *dressed in white; arrived in uniform; appeared in his best suit.* **12 in as far as; in so far as** (*conj*) because; to the extent (of something's importance or relevance) that: *He is Russian in so far as he was born in Russia. . . . in it* between two possibilities, quantities etc: *There's nothing/very little in it.* (= There is no/almost no difference). **in itself** considered separately from a particular situation or condition: *Playing cards in itself is fun but playing cards for money can be harmful.* **-in·law; in·laws** ⇨ separate entries. **in that** = in as/so far as: *Gambling can be harmful in that it may make a family very poor.*

in⁴ /ɪn/ *n* (only in) **the ins and (the) outs** the different details or parts; the full details: *I know all the ins and outs of their problem.*

in·abil·ity /ˌɪnəˈbɪlətɪ/ *nu* the lack of power or means: *an inability to pay one's debts.*

in·ac·ces·sible /ˌɪnækˈsesəbl/ *adj* (*formal*) not accessible.
in·ac·ces·si·bil·ity /ˌɪnækˌsesəˈbɪlətɪ/ *nu*

in·ac·cur·acy /ɪˈnækjʊrəsɪ/ *nc,nu* (*pl* **-ies**) (an instance of) being inaccurate.
in·ac·cur·ate /ɪˈnækjʊrət/ *adj* not accurate.
in·ac·cur·ate·ly *adv*

in·ac·tive /ɪnˈæktɪv/ *adj* not active.
in·ac·tiv·ity /ˌɪnækˈtɪvətɪ/ *nu*

in·ad·equate /ɪnˈædɪkwət/ *adj* **1 inadequate (for sb/sth)** not adequate; not enough. **2** (of a person) not able, skilled or strong enough: *feeling inadequate.*
in·ad·equate·ly *adv*

in·ad·mis·sible /ˌɪnədˈmɪsəbl/ *adj* (*legal*) that cannot be admitted or allowed: *inadmissible evidence.*

in·ad·ver·tent /ˌɪnədˈvɜːtənt/ *adj* (*formal*) not intentional: *an inadvertent lie.*
in·ad·ver·tent·ly *adv*

in·ad·vis·able /ˌɪnədˈvaɪzəbl/ *adj* not advisable.

in·al·ien·able /ɪnˈeɪlɪənəbl/ *adj* (*formal*) (of legal or other rights etc) that cannot be taken away: *Voting is my inalienable right.*

in·ane /ɪˈneɪn/ *adj* silly: *an inane remark.*
in·ane·ly *adv*
in·an·ity /ɪˈnænətɪ/ *nc,nu* (*pl* **-ies**)

in·ani·mate /ɪnˈænɪmət/ *adj* **1** lifeless: *Rocks and stones are inanimate.* Opp animate. **2** (*formal*) without interest; dull: *inanimate conversation.*

in·ap·pli·cable /ɪnˈæplɪkəbl/ *adj* **inapplicable (to sb/sth)** not applicable (to).

in·ap·pre·ci·able /ˌɪnəˈpriːʃəbl/ *adj* too small or slight to be noticed: *an inappreciable difference.*

in·ap·proach·able /ˌɪnəˈprəʊtʃəbl/ *adj* not approachable: *an inapproachable bank manager.*

in·ap·pro·pri·ate /ˌɪnəˈprəʊprɪət/ *adj* **inappropriate (to sb/sth)** not appropriate or suitable.

in·apt /ɪnˈæpt/ *adj* (esp) not apt or relevant: *inapt remarks.*
in·ap·ti·tude /ɪnˈæptɪtjuːd/ *nu* the state of being inapt.

in·ar·ticu·late /ˌɪnɑːˈtɪkjʊlət/ *adj* **1** (of speech) not clear or distinct. **2** (of a person) not speaking distinctly, clearly or fluently. **3** (*science*) not jointed: *an inarticulate body* (e.g. a jellyfish).

in·ar·tis·tic /ˌɪnɑːˈtɪstɪk/ *adj* not artistic.

in·as·much as /ˌɪnəzˈmʌtʃ əz/ *conj* (*subord*) because of the fact that: *You are also to blame inasmuch as you knew the car had poor brakes.*

in·at·ten·tion /ˌɪnəˈtenʃn/ *nu* **inattention (to sth)** the state of not having, failure to pay, attention: *inattention to detail.*

in·at·ten·tive /ˌɪnəˈtentɪv/ *adj* not attentive.

in·aud·ible /ɪnˈɔːdəbl/ *adj* that cannot be heard.

Opp audible.
in·audi·bil·ity /ɪnˌɔːdəˈbɪlətɪ/ *nu*

in·aug·ural /ɪˈnɔːgjʊrəl/ *adj* done when inaugurating a person or thing: *an inaugural lecture.*

in·aug·ur·ate /ɪˈnɔːgjʊreɪt/ *vt* **1** to introduce (a new official, professor etc) at a special ceremony: *inaugurate a president.* **2** to open (an exhibition, a new public building etc) with ceremony. **3** (*formal*) to be the beginning of (something): *The invention of the silicon chip inaugurated a new era in data processing.*
in·aug·ur·ation /ɪˌnɔːgjʊˈreɪʃn/ *nc,nu*

in·aus·pi·cious /ˌɪnɔːˈspɪʃəs/ *adj* (*formal*) not favourable or promising; unlucky. Opp auspicious.
in·aus·pi·cious·ly *adv*

in·born /ˌɪnˈbɔːn/ *adj* (/ˈɪnbɔːn/ when *attrib*) (*no comp*) (of a quality) possessed (by a person or animal) at birth: *a talent which is inborn; an inborn talent.*

in·bred /ˌɪnˈbred/ *adj* (/ˈɪnbred/ when *attrib*) **1** inborn: *courtesy which is inbred; inbred courtesy.* **2** bred for several generations from ancestors closely related.

in·breed·ing /ˌɪnˈbriːdɪŋ/ *nu* the state, result of, breeding from closely related ancestors etc.

Inc *written abbr* Incorporated.

in·cal·cu·lable /ɪnˈkælkjʊləbl/ *adj* too great to be calculated: *This has done incalculable harm to our reputation.*

in·can·des·cent /ˌɪnkænˈdesnt/ *adj* giving out, able to give out, light when heated.

in·can·ta·tion /ˌɪnkænˈteɪʃn/ *nc,nu* (the use of) words used in magic.

in·ca·pable /ɪnˈkeɪpəbl/ *adj* **incapable (of (doing) sth)** not capable: *incapable of telling a lie.*
in·capa·bil·ity /ɪnˌkeɪpəˈbɪlətɪ/ *nu*

in·ca·paci·tate /ˌɪnkəˈpæsɪteɪt/ *vt* **incapacitate sb (for sth)** (*formal*) to make a person unfit (for work etc).

in·ca·pac·ity /ˌɪnkəˈpæsətɪ/ *nu* **incapacity (for sth; to do sth)** the state of not having enough ability, strength etc.

in·car·cer·ate /ɪnˈkɑːsəreɪt/ *vt* (*formal*) (usually *passive*) to imprison (a person).
in·car·cer·ation /ɪnˌkɑːsəˈreɪʃn/ *nu*

in·car·nate /ɪnˈkɑːnət/ *adj* in human form: *That prison officer is a devil incarnate.*

In·car·na·tion /ˌɪnkɑːˈneɪʃn/ *n* (the —) the taking of bodily form by Jesus.

in·cen·di·ary /ɪnˈsendɪərɪ/ *adj* (*attrib*), *nc* (*pl* **-ies**) **1** (of) a person setting fire to property unlawfully and with an evil purpose. **2** (of) a person, thing, tending to stir up violence: *an incendiary speech.* **3** (of) a bomb causing fire.

in·cense¹ /ˈɪnsens/ *nu* (the smoke of) a substance giving a sweet smell when burning.

in·cense² /ɪnˈsens/ *vt* (usually *passive* **incensed at/by sb/sth**) to make (a person) angry: *incensed by his conduct/at her remarks.*

in·cen·tive /ɪnˈsentɪv/ *nc,nu* (also *attrib*) that which incites or encourages a person: *He hasn't much incentive to work hard. They have agreed an incentive scheme* (e.g. more pay for more productivity).

in·cep·tion /ɪnˈsepʃn/ *nc* (*formal*) the start: *the inception of a disease.*

in·ces·sant /ɪn'sesnt/ adj continual; often repeated: *a week of incessant rain.*
in·ces·sant·ly adv

in·cest /'ɪnsest/ nu an act of sexual intercourse between close relations, e.g. a brother and sister.
in·ces·tu·ous /ɪn'sestjʊəs/ adj

inch[1] /ɪntʃ/ nc **1** (abbr **in**) a unit of measurement of length, = 1/12 foot or 25·4mm. **2** (fig) a small distance: *I refuse to move an inch.*

inch[2] /ɪntʃ/ vt,vi (to cause a person) to move along, back etc gradually: *We inched along a ledge on the cliff.*

in·ci·dence /'ɪnsɪdəns/ n sing the frequency, extent etc with which something occurs or affects things: *the incidence of a disease.*

in·ci·dent[1] /'ɪnsɪdənt/ adj **incident to sth** (formal) forming a natural or expected part of something: *the risks incident to the life of a racing driver.*

in·ci·dent[2] /'ɪnsɪdənt/ nc **1** an event, esp one that causes trouble in public or a small act of disagreement or a quarrel that may have serious results: *incidents of social unrest; a diplomatic incident with international consequences.* **2** a separate piece of action in a novel, play or poem.

in·ci·den·tal /ˌɪnsɪ'dentl/ adj **1** accompanying but not forming a necessary part: *incidental music to a film.* **2** small and comparatively unimportant: *incidental expenses.*
in·ci·den·tal·ly /-əlɪ/ adv (used to mention news, information etc suddenly remembered): *Incidentally, did you know that Mary had got married?*

in·cin·er·ate /ɪn'sɪnəreɪt/ vt to burn (rubbish) completely.
in·cin·er·ation /ɪnˌsɪnə'reɪʃn/ nu
in·cin·er·ator /-tə(r)/ nc an apparatus used for burning rubbish etc.

in·cipi·ent /ɪn'sɪpɪənt/ adj at an early stage: *incipient decay of the teeth.*

in·cise /ɪn'saɪz/ vt (formal; med) to make a cut in (a surface).
in·ci·sion /ɪn'sɪʒn/ n **(a)** nu the act of cutting (into something). **(b)** nc a cut, e.g. in surgery.
in·cis·ive /ɪn'saɪsɪv/ adj (of a person's mind, remarks) clear, apt and effective: *incisive criticism.*
in·cis·ive·ly adv: *speak incisively.*
in·cis·or /ɪn'saɪzə(r)/ nc (science) (in human beings) any one of the front cutting teeth with sharp edges.

in·cite /ɪn'saɪt/ vt to encourage, cause (an effect): *insults inciting violence.*
in·cite·ment nc,nu

incl written abbr including; inclusive.

in·clem·ent /ɪn'klemənt/ adj (formal) (of weather or climate) cold and stormy.
in·clem·en·cy /-ənsɪ/ nu

in·cli·na·tion /ˌɪnklɪ'neɪʃn/ n **1** nc,nu **inclination (for/to sth; to do sth)** a liking or tendency: *He showed an inclination for studying sciences/no inclination to leave.* **2** nc a slope or slant: *the steep inclination of the roof.*

in·cline[1] /'ɪnklaɪn/ nc a slope or degree of slope: *a mountain with a sharp incline.*

in·cline[2] /ɪn'klaɪn/ vt,vi **1** (to cause something) to lean, slope or slant. **2** to bend (the head, body, oneself) forward or downward: *incline the head in*

prayer. **3** (usually *passive* **be inclined to do sth**) to have a desire or tendency to do something: *He's inclined to be lazy.*

in·clude /ɪn'kluːd/ vt to consider, put in, (a person, thing) as part of the whole: *There were ten competitors, including six from America. I don't include her among my best friends. Have you included the cost of petrol?* Opp exclude.
in·clu·sion /ɪn'kluːʒn/ nu

in·clus·ive /ɪn'kluːsɪv/ adj **1** having as part of the whole: *from 1 May to 3 June inclusive* (= 1 May and 3 June being included). **2** containing everything: *an inclusive price.* ⇨ all-inclusive. **inclusive of sth** (of costs etc) including something: *a price inclusive of tax.*
in·clus·ive·ly adv

in·cog·ni·to /ˌɪnkɒg'niːtəʊ/ adj, adv (pred) disguised; with one's name, character etc concealed: *travel incognito.*

in·co·her·ent /ˌɪnkəʊ'hɪərənt/ adj not coherent[2].
in·co·her·ent·ly adv
in·co·her·ence /-əns/ nu

in·come /'ɪnkʌm/ nc money received during a given period (as salary, receipts from trade, interest from investments etc): *live within/beyond one's income* (= spend less/more than one receives).
'income tax nc a tax on wages or salary.

in·com·ing /'ɪnkʌmɪŋ/ adj (attrib) coming in: *the incoming tide/tenant.* Opp outgoing(1).

in·com·mu·ni·ca·do /ˌɪnkəˌmjuːnɪ'kɑːdəʊ/ adj, adv (pred) not allowed to contact other people, e.g. when under house arrest: *He's incommunicado.*

in·com·par·able /ɪn'kɒmprəbl/ adj without equal: *incomparable beauty.* Opp comparable.

in·com·pat·ible /ˌɪnkəm'pætəbl/ adj **incompatible (with sb/sth)** not able or suitable to exist together: *Smoking is incompatible with good health.* Opp compatible.
in·com·pati·bil·ity /ˌɪnkəmˌpætə'bɪlətɪ/ nu

in·com·pe·tent /ɪn'kɒmpɪtənt/ adj without ability or talent: *an incompetent teacher.* Opp competent(1).
in·com·pe·tent·ly adv
in·com·pe·tence /-əns/ (also **in·com·pe·ten·cy** /-ənsɪ/) nu being incompetent.

in·com·plete /ˌɪnkəm'pliːt/ adj not complete.
in·com·plete·ly adv

in·com·pre·hen·sible /ɪnˌkɒmprɪ'hensəbl/ adj **incomprehensible (to sb)** that cannot be understood. Opp comprehensible.
in·com·pre·hen·si·bil·ity /ɪnˌkɒmprɪˌhensɪ'bɪlətɪ/ nu

in·com·pre·hen·sion /ɪnˌkɒmprɪ'henʃn/ nu the failure to understand.

in·con·ceiv·able /ˌɪnkən'siːvəbl/ adj that cannot be imagined: *Thought of escape was inconceivable in such a place.* Opp conceivable.

in·con·clus·ive /ˌɪnkən'kluːsɪv/ adj (of evidence, arguments, discussions) not decisive or convincing. Opp conclusive.
in·con·clus·ive·ly adv

in·con·gru·ous /ɪn'kɒŋgrʊəs/ adj not in harmony or agreement; out of place: *A modern building looks incongruous in an old village.*
in·con·gru·ous·ly adv
in·con·gru·ity /ˌɪnkɒŋ'gruːətɪ/ nc,nu

in·con·se·quen·tial /ˌɪnˌkɒnsɪ'kwenʃl/ *adj* (*formal*) unimportant: *inconsequential criticism*.

in·con·sid·er·able /ˌɪnkən'sɪdrəbl/ *adj* of small size, value, importance etc. Opp considerable.

in·con·sid·er·ate /ˌɪnkən'sɪdərət/ *adj* (*derog*) (of a person, actions) thoughtless: *inconsiderate children/remarks*. Opp considerate.

in·con·sid·er·ate·ly *adv*

in·con·sist·en·cy /ˌɪnkən'sɪstənsɪ/ *nc,nu* (an instance of) the state of being inconsistent.

in·con·sist·ent /ˌɪnkən'sɪstənt/ *adj* **inconsistent (with sth)** not consistent; contradictory; having parts that do not agree: *Their accounts of what happened were inconsistent*. Opp consistent.

in·con·sist·ent·ly *adv*

in·con·sol·able /ˌɪnkən'səʊləbl/ *adj* that cannot be consoled: *inconsolable grief*.

in·con·sol·ably *adv*

in·con·spicu·ous /ˌɪnkən'spɪkjʊəs/ *adj* not striking or obvious: *dressed in inconspicuous colours*. Opp conspicuous.

in·con·spicu·ous·ly *adv*

in·con·stant /ɪn'kɒnstənt/ *adj* (*formal*) (of a person) having feelings, intentions etc that often change: *an inconstant lover*.

in·con·stan·cy /-ənsɪ/ *nc,nu*

in·con·test·able /ˌɪnkən'testəbl/ *adj* that cannot be disputed: *an incontestable right to vote*.

in·con·ti·nent /ɪn'kɒntɪnənt/ *adj* unable to control excretion, e.g. because ill.

in·con·tro·vert·ible /ˌɪnˌkɒntrə'vɜːtəbl/ *adj* (*no comp*) that cannot be disputed: *incontrovertible evidence*.

in·con·ven·ience /ˌɪnkən'viːnɪəns/ *nc,nu* (a cause or instance of) discomfort or trouble: *I suffered great inconvenience*. □ *vt* to cause inconvenience to (a person).

in·con·ven·ient /ˌɪnkən'viːnɪənt/ *adj* causing discomfort, trouble or annoyance. Opp convenient.

in·con·ven·ient·ly *adv*

in·cor·por·ate /ɪn'kɔːpəreɪt/ *vt* to cause (things) to become united in one group: *The library and market were incorporated into the design for the new shopping centre*.

in·cor·por·ated *adj* (abbr in company names Inc) (*legal*) organized as a business company, esp a corporation(2).

in·cor·por·ation /ɪnˌkɔːpə'reɪʃn/ *nu*

in·cor·rect /ˌɪnkə'rekt/ *adj* not correct.

in·cor·rect·ly *adv*

in·cor·ri·gible /ɪn'kɒrɪdʒəbl/ *adj* (of a person, bad behaviour) that cannot be corrected: *an incorrigible liar*.

in·cor·rupt·ible /ˌɪnkə'rʌptəbl/ *adj* **1** that cannot decay or be destroyed. **2** (of a person) who cannot be corrupted, esp by being bribed.

in·crease¹ /'ɪnkriːs/ *nc,nu* (an amount as the result of) increasing. **on the increase** becoming larger, more frequent, more serious etc: *Poverty is on the increase in many countries*. Opp decrease¹.

in·crease² /ɪn'kriːs/ *vt,vi* (to cause something) to become greater in size, number, degree etc: *Our difficulties/opportunities are increasing*. Opp decrease².

in·creas·ing·ly /ɪn'kriːsɪŋlɪ/ *adv* more and more: *increasingly sad/ill/dangerous*.

in·cred·ible /ɪn'kredəbl/ *adj* **1** (almost) impossible to believe (because shocking): *incredible news*. Compare credible. **2** (*informal*) very surprising: *an incredible victory for the English football team*.

in·cred·ibly /-əblɪ/ *adv*

in·cred·ib·il·ity /ɪnˌkredə'bɪlətɪ/ *nu*

in·cred·ul·ity /ˌɪnkrɪ'djuːlətɪ/ *nu* (*formal*) the state of not believing something.

in·credu·lous /ɪn'kredʒʊləs/ *adj* not believing; showing doubt: *incredulous looks*. Compare credulous.

in·credu·lous·ly *adv*

in·cre·ment /'ɪnkrɪmənt/ *nc* an (amount of) increase: *Salary £10 000 per annum, with yearly increments of £500*.

in·crimi·nate /ɪn'krɪmɪneɪt/ *vt* to say, be a sign, that (a person) is guilty of doing wrong: *incriminating a neighbour's son*.

in·crimi·na·ting *adj*: *incriminating evidence*.

in·cu·bate /'ɪnkjʊbeɪt/ *vt,vi* to hatch (eggs) by sitting on them or by using artificial warmth.

in·cu·ba·tion /ˌɪnkjʊ'beɪʃn/ *nu*

in·cu·ba·tor /-tə(r)/ *nc* (**a**) an apparatus used for hatching eggs by artificial warmth. (**b**) (*med*) an apparatus used for rearing small, weak babies.

in·cum·bent¹ /ɪn'kʌmbənt/ *adj* **be incumbent on sb** (*formal*) to be a person's duty: *It is incumbent on you to warn him not to smoke*.

in·cum·bent² /ɪn'kʌmbənt/ *nc* a person holding a position or appointment, esp in the church.

in·cur /ɪn'kɜː(r)/ *vt* (-**rr**-) to bring (something bad or unpleasant) on oneself: *incurring debts/hatred/great expense*.

in·cur·able /ɪn'kjʊərəbl/ *adj* that cannot be cured: *incurable diseases/habits*. Opp curable.

in·cur·ably /-əblɪ/ *adv*: *incurably ill*.

in·cur·sion /ɪn'kɜːʃn/ *nc* a sudden attack or invasion: *incursions into enemy territory; incursions on my leisure time*.

in·debt·ed /ɪn'detɪd/ *adj* (*pred*) **indebted to sb** very grateful to a person: *I am indebted to you for your help*.

in·de·cent /ɪn'diːsnt/ *adj* (*derog*) (of behaviour, talk etc) obscene or offensive: *indecent language; an indecent photograph*. Compare decent(2).

in·de·cent·ly *adv*

in·de·cen·cy /-nsɪ/ *nc,nu* (*pl* -**ies**)

in·de·ci·pher·able /ˌɪndɪ'saɪfrəbl/ *adj* that cannot be read or understood: *indecipherable handwriting*. Opp decipherable.

in·de·ci·sion /ˌɪndɪ'sɪʒn/ *nu* the state of being unable to decide. Compare decision(2).

in·de·cis·ive /ˌɪndɪ'saɪsɪv/ *adj* (*derog*) not decisive.

in·de·cis·ive·ly *adv*

in·deed /ɪn'diːd/ *adv* **1** (used to make one's statement, agreement etc stronger): *They are, indeed, great actresses*. '*Are you pleased at your son's success?*'—'*Yes, indeed*'. **2** (used to make a statement of thanks stronger): *Thank you very much indeed*. **3** (used as a comment to show interest, surprise etc): '*He spoke to me about you.*'—'*Oh, indeed!*' '*She thinks she got the job.*'—'*Does she indeed!*'

in·de·fens·ible /ˌɪndɪ'fensəbl/ *adj* that cannot be defended, justified or excused: *indefensible violence*. Opp defensible.

in·de·fin·able /ˌɪndɪˈfaɪnəbl/ *adj* (*formal*) that cannot be defined or put in words: *indefinable beauty*.

in·defi·nite /ɪnˈdefɪnɪt/ *adj* **1** not clear; vague: *'Maybe' is an indefinite answer.* **2** having no precise limit: *We must wait for an indefinite period of time.* Opp definite.

in,definite 'article *nc* (the —) (*gram*) the word *a* or *an* (now called *determiner*).

in,definite 'pronoun *nc* (*gram*) one that does not refer to a particular person or thing, e.g. *somebody*, *anyone*.

in·defi·nite·ly *adv*

in·del·ible /ɪnˈdelɪbl/ *adj* that cannot be rubbed out or removed: *indelible ink*.

in·del·ibly /-əbl/ *adv*

in·deli·cate /ɪnˈdelɪkət/ *adj* (*formal; derog*) (of a person, speech, behaviour etc) indecent or rude: *indelicate remarks*.

in·deli·ca·cy /-kəsɪ/ *nc,nu* (*pl* **-ies**)

in·dem·ni·fy /ɪnˈdemnɪfaɪ/ *vt* (*pt,pp* **-ied**) **indemnify sb (against/for sth)** (*legal, commerce*) to (promise to) pay a person for loss, damage; costs etc: *indemnify a person against harm/loss. I will indemnify you for any expenses.*

in·dem·ni·ty /ɪnˈdemnətɪ/ *nc,nu* (*pl* **-ies**) (an instance of, payment given for) security against damage or loss, or as compensation.

in·dent /ɪnˈdent/ *vt* **1** to break into the edge or surface of (something): *The sea has indented the hills at the coast.* **2** to start (a line of print or writing) farther from the margin than the others.

in·den·ta·tion /ˌɪndenˈteɪʃn/ *nc,nu*

in·de·pen·dence /ˌɪndɪˈpendəns/ *nu* the state of being independent: *Many countries are struggling to achieve economic independence.*

in·de·pen·dent¹ /ˌɪndɪˈpendənt/ *adj* **1** not dependent on or controlled by (another person or thing): *Campers are independent of hotels.* **2** acting freely; showing free thought: *an independent witness/inquiry/report.* **3** not governed or controlled by another country: *When did Namibia become independent?*

in·de·pen·dent·ly *adv*

in·de·pen·dent² /ˌɪndɪˈpendənt/ *nc* an elected officer or candidate etc who does not belong to a political party.

in·de·scrib·able /ˌɪndɪˈskraɪbəbl/ *adj* that cannot be described: *indescribable horror*.

in·de·struct·ible /ˌɪndɪˈstrʌktəbl/ *adj* that cannot be destroyed: *indestructible concrete buildings*.

in·de·ter·mi·nate /ˌɪndɪˈtɜːmɪnət/ *adj* not fixed; indefinite: *an indeterminate period of time.*

in·dex /ˈɪndeks/ *nc* (*pl* **—es** or, in science, **indices** /ˈɪndɪsiːz/) **1** something that points to or indicates; pointer (on an instrument) showing measurements: *Increasing unemployment was an index of the country's poverty.* **2** an alphabetical list of names, subjects etc at the end of a book or on cards (*a card index*) in a library etc.

'index finger *nc* the finger next to the thumb, used for pointing.

,index-'linked *adj* (of wages, savings) increasing according to the cost of living.

in·di·cate /ˈɪndɪkeɪt/ *v* **1** *vt* to point to (a person, thing): *He indicated the chair he wanted me to sit in.* **2** *vt* **indicate (that) sth** to make (some-

thing) known; be a sign of (something): *He indicated that the interview was over. The sudden rise in temperature indicated pneumonia.* **3** *vt,vi* (when driving) to signal that one is about to turn (left, right).

in·di·ca·tion /ˌɪndɪˈkeɪʃn/ *nc,nu*

in·dica·tive¹ /ɪnˈdɪkətɪv/ *adj* **1** (*pred*) **indicative of sth/that** . . . suggesting: *Is a high forehead indicative of intelligence?* **2** (*gram*) of the verb form used to state a fact or ask questions of fact: *'He can swim' and 'Is she coming?' are in the indicative mood.*

in·dica·tive² /ɪnˈdɪkətɪv/ *nc* (*gram*) an indicative(2) form of a verb.

in·di·ca·tor /ˈɪndɪkeɪtə(r)/ *nc* a person, apparatus, pointer etc that points out or gives information: *The indicator shows that the lift is on the first floor.*

in·di·ces /ˈɪndɪsiːz/ *n pl* of index.

in·dict /ɪnˈdaɪt/ *vt* (*legal*) to accuse (a person) of a crime: *He was indicted on a charge of murder/for murder.*

in·dict·able /-əbl/ *adj*

in·dict·ment *nc,nu*

in·dif·fer·ence /ɪnˈdɪfrəns/ *nu* the absence of interest, opinion or feeling: *We noticed his indifference towards the needs of other people.*

in·dif·fer·ent /ɪnˈdɪfrənt/ *adj* **1** **indifferent (to sb)** having no interest or opinion; neither for nor against: *It is indifferent to me whether you go or stay.* **2** (*attrib*) not of good quality or ability: *an indifferent footballer.*

in·dif·fer·ent·ly *adv*

in·dig·en·ous /ɪnˈdɪdʒɪnəs/ *adj* **indigenous (to a place)** (*formal*) having its origins in: *Kangaroos are indigenous to Australia.*

in·di·gest·ible /ˌɪndɪˈdʒestəbl/ *adj* difficult or impossible to digest. Opp digestible.

in·di·ges·tion /ˌɪndɪˈdʒestʃən/ *nu* (pain caused by) difficulty in digesting food: *suffer an attack of indigestion.*

in·dig·nant /ɪnˈdɪgnənt/ *adj* angry, esp because of injustice or undeserved blame etc.

in·dig·nant·ly *adv*

in·dig·na·tion /ˌɪndɪgˈneɪʃn/ *nu* anger caused by feelings of injustice etc.

in·dig·ni·ty /ɪnˈdɪgnətɪ/ *nc,nu* (*pl* **-ies**) (*formal*) (an instance, example of) rude treatment causing a person to feel shame or loss of respect: *forced to suffer all sorts of indignities.*

in·di·go /ˈɪndɪgəʊ/ *nu* a deep blue (dye).

in·di·rect /ˌɪndɪˈrekt/ *adj* not straight or direct: *an indirect answer to a question; an indirect tax* (= one not paid direct to a tax-collector but included in the price of goods). Compare direct¹(1,2,4).

,indirect 'object *nc* (*gram*) one referring to the person etc affected by the verb, e.g. *him* in '*Give him the money*'.

,indirect 'question *nc* (*gram*) one given in indirect speech, as in '*He asked if he could come*' (for *He asked 'Can I come?'*).

,indirect 'speech *nu* (*gram*) (also called *reported speech*) a way of expressing what a person said, as in '*He said he would come*' (for *He said 'I will come'*). Compare direct speech.

in·dir·ect·ly *adv*

in·dis·cern·ible /ˌɪndɪˈsɜːnəbl/ *adj* that cannot be seen; unnoticeable. Opp discernible.

in·dis·ci·pline /ɪn'dɪsɪplɪn/ *nu* the absence of discipline.

in·dis·creet /ˌɪndɪ'skriːt/ *adj* not discreet.
in·dis·creet·ly *adv*

in·dis·cre·tion /ˌɪndɪ'skreʃn/ *n* 1 *nu* the state of being indiscreet; indiscreet behaviour. Opp discretion(1). 2 *nc* an indiscreet remark or act.

in·dis·crimi·nate /ˌɪndɪ'skrɪmɪnət/ *adj* acting, given, without care: *indiscriminate praise; indiscriminate bombing.* ⇨ discriminating.
in·dis·crimi·nate·ly *adv*

in·dis·pens·able /ˌɪndɪ'spensəbl/ *adj* essential: *Air, food and water are indispensable to life.* Opp dispensable.

in·dis·posed /ˌɪndɪ'spəʊzd/ *adj* (*pred*) (*formal*) unwell.

in·dis·put·able /ˌɪndɪ'spjuːtəbl/ *adj* that cannot be disputed or questioned: *indisputable evidence.*

in·dis·tinct /ˌɪndɪ'stɪŋkt/ *adj* not distinct: *indistinct sounds/memories.*
in·dis·tinct·ly *adv*

in·dis·tin·guish·able /ˌɪndɪ'stɪŋgwɪʃəbl/ *adj* (usually *pred*) that cannot be distinguished between: *He is indistinguishable from his brother.*

in·di·vid·ual[1] /ˌɪndɪ'vɪdjʊəl/ *adj* 1 for one person or thing: *individual attention.* Compare general[1](1). 2 characteristic of a single person, animal, plant or thing: *an individual style of speaking.*

in·di·vid·ual[2] /ˌɪndɪ'vɪdjʊəl/ *nc* any one human being (esp contrasted with society): *the basic rights of the individual.*
in·di·vid·ual·ly *adv* separately; one by one: *be interviewed individually.*

in·di·vidu·al·ity /ˌɪndɪˌvɪdjʊ'ælətɪ/ *nc,nu* (*pl* **-ies**) all the characteristics that belong to an individual and that distinguish her or him from others.

in·di·vis·ible /ˌɪndɪ'vɪzəbl/ *adj* that cannot be divided. Opp divisible.

in·doc·tri·nate /ɪn'dɒktrɪneɪt/ *vt* to fill the mind of (a person) (with ideas or beliefs).
in·doc·tri·na·tion /ɪnˌdɒktrɪ'neɪʃn/ *nu*

in·do·lence /'ɪndələns/ *nu* (*formal*) laziness (the usual word).
in·do·lent /'ɪndələnt/ *adj* (*formal*) lazy.
in·do·lent·ly *adv*

in·domi·table /ɪn'dɒmɪtəbl/ *adj* (*formal*) that cannot be defeated or controlled: *indomitable courage.*

in·door /'ɪndɔː(r)/ *adj* (*attrib*) belonging, carried on, situated, inside a building: *indoor games.* Compare outdoor.

in·doors /ˌɪn'dɔːz/ *adv* in or into a building: *go/ stay indoors; kept indoors all week by bad weather.* Compare outdoors.

in·duce /ɪn'djuːs/ *vt* (often *passive*) 1 to persuade or influence (a person): *What induced you to do such a thing?* 2 to cause, bring about, (something): *illness induced by overwork.*

in·duce·ment *nc,nu* (an) incentive (the more usual word): *He hasn't much inducement to study English.*

in·duc·tion /ɪn'dʌkʃn/ *nu* 1 the act of introducing knowledge or experience, e.g. to a person beginning a new job. 2 a method of reasoning which obtains general laws from particular facts or examples; production of facts to prove a general statement. Compare deduction(2).
in'duction course *nc* one designed to introduce and provide general background knowledge.

in·duc·tive /ɪn'dʌktɪv/ *adj* (of reasoning) based on induction(2).

in·dulge /ɪn'dʌldʒ/ *v* 1 *vt* to give way to and satisfy (a person's desires etc): *indulge a sick child.* 2 *vi* **indulge in sth** to allow oneself the pleasure of something: *He occasionally indulges in the luxury of a good cigar.*

in·dul·gence /ɪn'dʌldʒəns/ *n* (*formal*) 1 *nu* the state, act of having or doing what one wants: *Constant indulgence in gambling brought about his ruin.* 2 *nc* something in which a person indulges: *Wine and cigarettes are her only indulgences.*

in·dul·gent /ɪn'dʌldʒənt/ *adj* inclined to indulge(1) a person: *indulgent parents.*
in·dul·gent·ly *adv*

in·dus·tri·al /ɪn'dʌstrɪəl/ *adj* 1 of industry: *industrial methods; industrial output.* 2 (of a country etc) having many industries: *an industrial nation; an industrial economy.* ⇨ industrious.

in,dustrial 'action *nu* any action (e.g. a strike, go-slow) by workers in industry: *take industrial action in support of higher wages.*

in,dustrial e'state *nc* an area of land planned and used for factories.

in,dustrial relations *n sing* or *pl* (the management of) relations between workers and managers in industry.

in,dustrial ,revo'lution *n* (the —) the social changes brought about by mechanical inventions in the 18th and early 19th centuries.

in·dus·trial·ist /-ɪst/ *nc* (esp) an owner of a large industry.

in·dus·tri·al·ize (also **-ise**) /ɪn'dʌstrɪəlaɪz/ *vt,vi* (to cause a country etc) to develop industries as an important or main part of the economy: *All countries see the need to industrialize.*

in·dus·tri·ous /ɪn'dʌstrɪəs/ *adj* willing to work long and hard. ⇨ industrial.

in·dus·try /'ɪndəstrɪ/ *n* (*pl* **-ies**) 1 *nc,nu* (a particular kind of) work in factories, mines etc to manufacture, obtain, things (contrasted with distribution and commerce): *the manufacturing industries.* ⇨ heavy/light industry, industrial. 2 *nu* (the quality of) working long and hard: *The manager was admired for his industry.* ⇨ industrious.

in·ebri·ated /ɪ'niːbrɪeɪtɪd/ *adj* (*formal*) drunk (the usual word).

in·ed·ible /ɪn'edəbl/ *adj* (of a kind) not suitable to be eaten: *inedible berries.* Opp edible.

in·ef·fec·tive /ˌɪnɪ'fektɪv/ *adj* not producing the effect(s) desired. Opp effective.
in·ef·fec·tive·ly *adv*
in·ef·fec·tive·ness *nu*

in·ef·fec·tual /ˌɪnɪ'fektʃʊəl/ *adj* (*formal; derog*) without confidence and unable to get things done: *an ineffectual teacher/leader.* Opp effectual.

in·ef·fi·cien·cy /ˌɪnɪ'fɪʃənsɪ/ *nu* the state or quality of being inefficient. Opp efficiency.

in·ef·fi·cient /ˌɪnɪ'fɪʃənt/ *adj* 1 (*derog*) (of a person) wasting time, energy etc in their work or duties: *an inefficient management/administration.* 2 (of machines, processes etc) not producing adequate results. Opp efficient.

in·ef·fi·cient·ly *adv*

in·el·egant /ɪnˈelɪgənt/ *adj* not elegant.

in·el·egant·ly *adv*

in·eli·gible /ɪnˈelɪdʒəbl/ *adj* **ineligible (for sth)** not eligible: *ineligible for the position.*

in·eli·gi·bil·ity /ˌɪnˌelɪdʒəˈbɪlətɪ/ *nu*

in·ept /ɪˈnept/ *adj* unsuitable; said or done at the wrong time: *inept remarks.*

in·ept·ly *adv*

in·ep·ti·tude /ɪˈneptɪtjuːd/ *nc,nu*

in·e·qual·ity /ˌɪnɪˈkwɒlətɪ/ *n* (*pl* **-ies**) *nc,nu* (an instance, example, of) the absence of equality in size, degree, rank, wealth: *Great inequalities in wealth cause social unrest.*

in·equi·table /ɪnˈekwɪtəbl/ *adj* (*formal*) unjust; unfair: *an inequitable division of the profits.*

in·ert /ɪˈnɜːt/ *adj* **1** (*science*) without power to move or act: *inert matter.* **2** (*chemistry*) without active chemical properties: *inert gases.* **3** (of a person) without the will or strength to move or think.

in·er·tia /ɪˈnɜːʃə/ *nu* **1** the state of being inert(3). **2** (*science*) the property of matter by which it remains in a state of rest or, if it is in motion, continues in the same direction and in a straight line unless it is acted on by an external force.

in·es·cap·able /ˌɪnɪˈskeɪpəbl/ *adj* that cannot be avoided: *I've come to the inescapable conclusion that he is a thief.*

in·es·ti·mable /ɪnˈestɪməbl/ *adj* (*formal*) too great, precious etc to be estimated.

in·evi·table /ɪnˈevɪtəbl/ *adj* **1** that cannot be avoided; that is sure to happen: *Death is inevitable.* **2** (*informal*) so frequently seen, heard etc that it is familiar and expected: *a Japanese tourist with his inevitable camera.*

in·evi·ta·bil·ity /ɪnˌevɪtəˈbɪlətɪ/ *nu*

in·ex·act /ˌɪnɪgˈzækt/ *adj* not exact.

in·ex·acti·tude /ˌɪnɪgˈzæktɪtjuːd/ *nc,nu*

in·ex·cus·able /ˌɪnɪkˈskjuːzəbl/ *adj* that cannot be excused: *inexcusable behaviour/delays.*

in·ex·haust·ible /ˌɪnɪgˈzɔːstəbl/ *adj* that cannot be exhausted: *My patience is not inexhaustible.*

in·ex·ped·ient /ˌɪnɪkˈspiːdɪənt/ *adj* not expedient.

in·ex·ped·ien·cy /-ənsɪ/ *nu*

in·ex·pen·sive /ˌɪnɪkˈspensɪv/ *adj* not expensive.

in·ex·pen·sive·ly *adv*

in·ex·pe·ri·ence /ˌɪnɪkˈspɪərɪəns/ *nu* the absence of experience.

in·ex·pe·ri·enced *adj* not experienced.

in·ex·plic·able /ˌɪnɪkˈsplɪkəbl/ *adj* that cannot be explained. Opp explicable.

in·ex·press·ible /ˌɪnɪkˈspresəbl/ *adj* that cannot be put into words: *inexpressible sorrow/anguish.*

in·ex·tri·cable /ɪnˈekstrɪkəbl/ *adj* that cannot be solved or escaped from: *inextricable confusion.*

in·fal·lible /ɪnˈfæləbl/ *adj* **1** incapable of making mistakes or doing wrong: *None of us is infallible.* **2** never failing: *infallible cures.* Opp fallible.

in·fal·li·bil·ity /ɪnˌfæləˈbɪlətɪ/ *nu*

in·fa·mous /ˈɪnfəməs/ *adj* wicked; shameful; disgraceful: *infamous behaviour, an infamous plot/traitor.* Compare famous.

in·fa·my /ˈɪnfəmɪ/ *nc,nu* (*pl* **-ies**) (an instance of) being infamous.

in·fan·cy /ˈɪnfənsɪ/ *nu* **1** the state of being,

period when one is, an infant. **2** *in its infancy* at an early stage of development or growth: *when space travel was still in its infancy.*

in·fant /ˈɪnfənt/ *nc* a child during the first few years of his life.

'infant school *nc* (a part of) a primary school for children under 7.

in·fan·ti·cide /ɪnˈfæntɪsaɪd/ *nu* the crime of killing an infant.

in·fan·tile /ˈɪnfəntaɪl/ *adj* (*derog*) very childish: *infantile behaviour.*

ˌinfantile paˈralysis *nu* (formerly used for) poliomyelitis.

in·fan·try /ˈɪnfəntrɪ/ *nc* or *pl* (also *attrib*) the soldiers who fight on foot: *an infantry regiment.*

in·fatu·at·ed /ɪnˈfætʃʊeɪtɪd/ *adj* (*pred*) **be infatuated with/by sb** to be filled with a wild and inexperienced feeling of love for a person: *He's infatuated with that girl.*

in·fatu·ation /ɪnˌfætʃʊˈeɪʃn/ *nc,nu*

in·fect /ɪnˈfekt/ *vt* **1** to cause (a person, part of the body, place etc) to have a disease: *The dirt has infected the wound. I think the water is infected with germs.* **2** (*fig*) to influence the feelings, ideas etc of (a person): *Mary's high spirits infected the whole class.*

in·fec·tion /ɪnˈfekʃn/ *n* **1** *nu* the process of infecting or being infected, esp the communication of disease through the air or water. **2** *nc* an infectious disease.

in·fec·tious /ɪnˈfekʃəs/ *adj* **1** (of disease) that can be spread by means of bacteria carried in the air or in water. Compare contagious(1). **2** (*fig*) quickly influencing others; likely to spread to others: *infectious humour. Yawning is infectious.*

in·fer /ɪnˈfɜː(r)/ *vt* (**-rr-**) **infer (from sb/sth) (that . . .)** to reach an opinion (from facts or reasoning): *Am I to infer from your remarks that you think I am a liar?* Compare imply.

in·fer·ence /ˈɪnfərəns/ *n* **1** *nu* the process of inferring. **by inference** as the result of making a judgement: *He never goes to the lessons and by inference I assume he thinks they are not useful.* **2** *nc* something that is inferred.

in·fer·ior¹ /ɪnˈfɪərɪə(r)/ *adj* **inferior (to sb/sth)** **1** worse than the average in quality: *inferior intelligence; ability/skill that is inferior to hers.* Opp superior¹(1). **2** of lower position or rank: *Your position is inferior to mine.* Opp superior¹(3). **3** (showing one feels) less able or important than others: *feeling inferior.* Compare superior¹(4).

in·fer·ior² /ɪnˈfɪərɪə(r)/ *nc* (often *derog*) a person (considered to be) of lower rank, importance, ability etc. Compare superior²(1).

in·fer·ior·ity /ɪnˌfɪərɪˈɒrətɪ/ *nu* the state of being inferior.

inˌferiˈority complex *nc* the feeling of being inferior, often producing behaviour such as boasting and aggression.

in·fer·nal /ɪnˈfɜːnl/ *adj* **1** of hell: *the infernal regions.* **2** (*informal*) very bad or unpleasant: *Stop that infernal noise!*

in·fer·no /ɪnˈfɜːnəʊ/ *nc* (*pl* **-s**) **1** hell. **2** (*informal*) a scene of horror, e.g. a blazing building in which people are trapped.

in·fer·tile /ɪnˈfɜːtaɪl/ *adj* not fertile.

in·fer·til·ity /ˌɪnfəˈtɪlətɪ/ *nu*

in·fest /ɪnˈfest/ *vt* (often *passive*) (of rats, insects, robbers etc) to be present in large numbers in (a building etc): *warehouses infested with rats.*

in·fi·del·i·ty /ˌɪnfɪˈdelətɪ/ *nc,nu* (*pl* **-ies**) (an act of) disloyalty or being unfaithful, esp to a wife or husband.

infight·ing /ˈɪnfaɪtɪŋ/ *nu* (*informal*) harmful competition between colleagues or rivals (esp in commerce and industry).

in·fil·trate /ˈɪnfɪltreɪt/ *v* **1** *vt,vi* to join (a group), enter (an area), in order to do harm, find information, influence changes etc. **2** *vt* (of ideas) to pass into (people's minds).
in·fil·tra·tion /ˌɪnfɪlˈtreɪʃn/ *nu*

in·fi·nite /ˈɪnfɪnət/ *adj* (*no comp*) endless; without limits; that cannot be measured, calculated, or imagined: *infinite space. Such ideas may do infinite harm.* Compare finite(1).
in·fi·nite·ly *adv* to an infinite degree: *Atoms and molecules are infinitely small.*

in·fini·tesi·mal /ˌɪnˌfɪnɪˈtesɪml/ *adj* (usually *pred*) extremely small.

in·fini·tive /ɪnˈfɪnətɪv/ *adj, nc* (*gram*) (of) the form of a verb used with or without *to*, e.g. 'let him *go*', 'allow him *to go*'. ⇨ finite², non-finite.
in,finitive 'particle *nc* (*gram*) *to* used with the infinitive, as in 'It's wrong *to steal*'.
in,finitive 'phrase *nc* (*gram*) a phrase containing an infinitive used as a subject or object of a sentence, as in '*To kick the dog* was very cruel of you'.

in·fin·ity /ɪnˈfɪnətɪ/ *nu* **1** (*maths*) an endless quantity (symbol ∞). **2** infinite space, time: *stretching to infinity.*

in·firm /ɪnˈfɜːm/ *adj* (*literary*) physically or mentally weak (esp through age): *walk with infirm steps.*
in·firm·ity /ɪnˈfɜːmətɪ/ *nc,nu* (*pl* **-ies**)

in·firm·ary /ɪnˈfɜːmərɪ/ *nc* (*pl* **-ies**) **1** a hospital (the usual word). **2** (in an institution etc) a room used for people who are ill or injured.

in·flame /ɪnˈfleɪm/ *vt,vi* **inflame (sb/sth) (with sth) 1** (to cause a person or thing) to become red, swollen and sore: *inflamed eyes.* **2** (*fig*) (to cause a person or thing) to become very excited: *inflamed with passion.*

in·flam·mable /ɪnˈflæməbl/ *adj* easily set on fire. ⇨ the *note* at flammable.

in·flam·ma·tion /ˌɪnfləˈmeɪʃn/ *nc,nu* (an example, instance of) an inflamed condition (esp of some part of the body): *inflammation of the eyes.*

in·flam·ma·tory /ɪnˈflæmətrɪ/ *adj* **1** of, producing, inflammation(1). **2** (*fig*) likely to produce anger, acts of violence etc: *inflammatory speeches.*

in·fla·table /ɪnˈfleɪtəbl/ *adj* that can be inflated: *an inflatable rubber dinghy.*

in·flate /ɪnˈfleɪt/ *vt* **1** to fill (a tyre, balloon etc) with air or gas. **2** (*fig*) (usually *passive*) to cause (a person) to become (too) proud: *inflated with pride.* **3** (*finance*) to take action to increase the amount of money in circulation in (an economic system) so that prices rise. Compare deflate.

in·fla·tion /ɪnˈfleɪʃn/ *nu* (a) the act, state, of being inflated. (b) (*finance*) (a rise in prices brought about by) the expansion of the supply of money, credit etc.

in·fla·tion·ary /ɪnˈfleɪʃənrɪ/ *adj* of, caused by, inflation(b): *inflationary policies.*

in·flect /ɪnˈflekt/ *vt* **1** (*gram*) to change the ending or form of (a word) to show its relationship to other words in a sentence. **2** to adapt, regulate (the voice). **3** (*tech*) (of a line etc) to bend inwards; curve.

in·flec·tion /ɪnˈflekʃn/ *n* **1** *nu* inflecting. **2** *nc* (*gram*) an inflected form of a word. **3** *nu* the rise and fall of the voice in speaking.

in·flex·ible /ɪnˈfleksəbl/ *adj* **1** that cannot be bent. **2** (*fig*) refusing to change or be influenced: *an inflexible will.* Opp flexible.
in·flex·ibly /-əblɪ/ *adv*
in·flexi·bil·ity /ɪnˌfleksɪˈbɪlətɪ/ *nu*

in·flict /ɪnˈflɪkt/ *vt* **inflict sb/sth on sb** to force a person or something unpleasant or unwanted on a person: *inflict a cruel leader on the community. I'm sorry to have to inflict my company on you.*
in·flic·tion /ɪnˈflɪkʃn/ *nc,nu*

in·flight /ˈɪnflaɪt/ *adj* (*attrib*) during a journey in a plane: *in-flight entertainment.*

in·flow /ˈɪnfləʊ/ *nc,nu* something (a liquid, gas etc) that flows in.

in·flu·ence¹ /ˈɪnfluəns/ *n* **1** *nu* (the use of) the power to affect a person's character, beliefs or actions or to get a result e.g. because of a strong personality, wealth etc: *Can you use your influence to get me a job? Does she have any influence with the authorities? Under her influence I improved enormously. He enjoys a powerful influence over the banks.* **2** *nc* a person, fact etc that exercises such power: *She's an influence for good in the town.* **3** *nu* **influence (on sth)** (*science*) the action of natural forces: *the influence of climate (on vegetation).*

in·flu·ence² /ˈɪnfluəns/ *vt* to have an effect on (a person, mind etc): *What was influencing him when he decided not to support the recommendation? Don't be influenced by what she says.*

in·flu·en·tial /ˌɪnfluˈenʃl/ *adj* having power to affect people or situations: *an influential politician/committee.*
in·flu·en·tial·ly /-ʃəlɪ/ *adv*

in·flu·en·za /ˌɪnfluˈenzə/ *nu* (usual short form **flu**) an infectious disease with fever, aches and a bad cold.

in·flux /ˈɪnflʌks/ *n* (*pl* **—es**) *nc* a constant flowing in of large numbers or quantities: *an influx of wealth/foreign cars/ visitors.*

info /ˈɪnfəʊ/ *abbr* (*informal*) information.

in·form /ɪnˈfɔːm/ *vt* **1 inform sb (about/of sth; that . . .)** to give information to a person: *Keep me informed of fresh developments. He's a well-informed man.* **2 inform against/on sb (to sb)** to give evidence against a person (to the police).
in·form·ant /-ənt/ *nc* a person who gives information.
in·form·er *nc* a person who informs(2) on a person.

in·for·mal /ɪnˈfɔːml/ *adj* **1** (of words, ways of speaking or writing) used in situations when one can be friendly and relaxed: *informal conversation/letters.* Opp formal(1). **2** (of clothes, activities, behaviour etc) not needing to follow social conventions: *informal clothes such as jeans; an informal visit.* Opp formal(2).
in·for·mal·ity /ˌɪnfɔːˈmælətɪ/ *nc,nu*

in·for·mal·ly /-əli/ adv

in·for·ma·tion /ˌɪnfə'meɪʃn/ nu news, facts or knowledge given: *That's a useful piece/bit of information.*

in·for·ma·tive /ɪn'fɔ:mətɪv/ adj giving useful information: *informative books; an informative talk.*

in·for·ma·tive·ly adv

in·fra-red /ˌɪnfrə 'red/ adj, nu (*science*) (of) the form of light (between visible colours and radio waves) producing heat.

in·fra·struc·ture /'ɪnfrəstrʌktʃə(r)/ nc the structure or system of organization for a business, government, school, society or other group.

in·fre·quent /ɪn'fri:kwənt/ adj not frequent; rare.

in·fre·quent·ly adv

in·fre·quen·cy /ɪn'fri:kwənsɪ/ nu

in·fringe /ɪn'frɪndʒ/ vt **1** to break (a rule etc). **2** *infringe on sth* to go beyond (what is right or natural): *Be careful not to infringe on the rights of other people.*

in·fringe·ment nc,nu

in·furi·ate /ɪn'fjʊərɪeɪt/ vt to cause (a person) to feel strong anger.

in·furi·at·ing adj: *infuriating delays.*

in·fuse /ɪn'fju:z/ v (*formal*) **1** vt to fill a person with (a quality, energy etc): *infusing courage into athletes; infusing students with new ideas.* **2** vt,vi (to cause something) to soak in (hot) water etc, e.g. to produce a tasty drink: *infuse herbs.*

in·fu·sion /ɪn'fju:ʒn/ nu

-ing form /'ɪŋ fɔ:m/ nc (*gram; informal*) = gerund.

in·geni·ous /ɪn'dʒi:nɪəs/ adj **1** (of a person) very clever and skilful (at making or inventing things). **2** (of things, excuses etc) skilfully done: *an ingenious method.*

in·geni·ous·ly adv

in·ge·nu·ity /ˌɪndʒɪ'nju:ətɪ/ nu cleverness and skill (used to produce something).

in·genu·ous /ɪn'dʒenjʊəs/ adj (*formal*) (of a person, remark) straightforward, trusting and innocent (often because of inexperience): *An ingenuous friend will believe anything you say.*

in·got /'ɪŋgət/ nc a (usually brick-shaped) lump of metal (esp gold or silver).

in·grain·ed /ˌɪn'greɪnd/ adj **1** (of habits, tendencies etc) deeply fixed: *ingrained prejudices.* **2** going deep: *ingrained dirt.*

in·gra·ti·ate /ɪn'greɪʃɪeɪt/ vt *ingratiate one·self with sb* (*formal*) to make oneself liked, esp in order to gain an advantage: *ingratiating herself with her manager.*

in·gra·ti·at·ing adj (*derog*): *an ingratiating smile.*

in·grati·at·ing·ly adv

in·grati·tude /ɪn'grætɪtju:d/ nu the absence of gratitude.

in·gredi·ent /ɪn'gri:dɪənt/ nc one of the parts of a mixture: *the ingredients of a cake.*

in·hab·it /ɪn'hæbɪt/ vt to live in (a place). ⇨ habitat.

in·hab·it·able /-əbl/ adj that can be lived in: *inhabitable forests.* Compare habitable. ⇨ also uninhabitable.

in·habit·ant /-ənt/ nc a person or animal living in a place.

in·hale /ɪn'heɪl/ vt,vi to breathe (something) in: *inhaling air/smoke/gas.* Opp exhale.

in·haler nc (*med*) a device used to make breathing easier.

in·her·ent /ɪn'hɪərənt/ adj *inherent (in sb/ sth)* existing as a natural and permanent part or quality of: *He has an inherent love of beauty. It's inherent in his behaviour.*

in·her·it /ɪn'herɪt/ v **1** vt,vi to receive (property, a title etc) as an heir: *inherited wealth. The eldest son will inherit (the title).* **2** vt to receive (qualities etc) from ancestors: *She inherited her mother's good looks.* Ⓝ Not used in continuous tenses, e.g. *is/was -ing.*

in·her·it·ance /-əns/ n (**a**) nu the process of inheriting something: *receive money by inheritance.* (**b**) nc something inherited(1).

in·hib·it /ɪn'hɪbɪt/ vt *inhibit sb (from doing sth)* to prevent or stop a person (from doing it): *The evidence about cancer inhibits me from smoking. Her wild temper inhibits us.*

in·hib·it·ed adj (of a person, personality) unwilling to express feelings or act independently.

in·hib·it·ing adj (of an action, behaviour) stopping or preventing a person from doing something: *an inhibiting look.*

in·hi·bi·tion /ˌɪnhɪ'bɪʃn/ nc,nu (an instance of) feeling unable or unwilling to act.

in·hibi·tory /ɪn'hɪbɪtrɪ/ adj causing inhibition: *an inhibitory remark.*

in·hos·pit·able /ˌɪnhɒ'spɪtəbl/ adj (*derog*) not hospitable.

in·hu·man /ˌɪn'hju:mən/ adj (*derog*) cruel; without moral feeling: *inhuman treatment.* Opp human¹(2).

in·hu·man·ity /ˌɪnhju:'mænətɪ/ nc,nu (an instance of) the absence of pity; cruelty: *man's inhumanity to man.* Compare humanity(2).

in·hu·mane /ˌɪnhju:'meɪn/ adj not humane.

in·hu·mane·ly adv

in·iqui·tous /ɪ'nɪkwɪtəs/ adj (*formal*) very wicked or unjust: *iniquitous laws.*

in·iqui·ty /ɪ'nɪkwətɪ/ nc,nu (pl **-ies**)

in·iti·al¹ /ɪ'nɪʃl/ adj of, at, the beginning: *the initial letter of a word.*

in·iti·al·ly /-ʃəlɪ/ adv at the beginning.

in·iti·al² /ɪ'nɪʃl/ nc a first letter of a word, esp of a person's names, e.g. *GBS* for *George Bernard Shaw.*

in·iti·al³ /ɪ'nɪʃl/ vt (-ll-, US also -l-) to mark, sign, (something) with one's initials.

in·iti·ate /ɪ'nɪʃɪeɪt/ vt **1** to cause (a scheme etc) to start working: *initiate a plan.* **2** to admit (a person) to membership of a group etc. **3** to give (a person) elementary instruction in a subject, e.g. someone who wants to become a priest.

in·iti·ation /ɪˌnɪʃɪ'eɪʃn/ nu

in·iti·at·ive /ɪ'nɪʃətɪv/ n **1** nu the first or introductory step or move. *act/do sth on one's own initiative* to decide and act without an order, request or suggestion from others. *have/ take the initiative* (to be in the position) to make the first move. **2** nu the ability to see what needs to be done and the will to do it: *A statesman must show initiative.*

in·ject /ɪn'dʒekt/ vt *inject sth into sb/sb with sth* **1** to force (a liquid, drug etc) into (a person,

thing) (as if) with a syringe: *inject a drug into the bloodstream; inject a patient with antibiotic.* **2** (*fig; informal*) to put (something) in: *Her appointment may inject some new life into the committee.*
in·jec·tion /ɪn'dʒekʃn/ *nc,nu*

in·ju·di·cious /ˌɪndʒʊ'dɪʃəs/ *adj* (*formal*) not having or showing good sense; not well-judged: *injudicious remarks.* Opp judicious.

in·junc·tion /ɪn'dʒʌŋkʃn/ *nc* (*legal*) an official order, esp from a law court, demanding that something shall or shall not be done.

in·jure /'ɪndʒə(r)/ *vt* to harm, damage, (a person, part of the body): *The old man fell and injured his back.*

in·jured *adj* (**a**) harmed; damaged: *an injured back.* (**b**) (*fig*) badly affected; showing a feeling of being harmed: *injured pride; an injured look.* □ *n* (the —) (used with a *pl verb*) the people who are hurt: *The injured are in hospital.*

in·juri·ous /ɪn'dʒʊərɪəs/ *adj* (*pred*) *injurious to sb/sth* (*formal*) causing, likely to cause, injury: *habits that are injurious to health.*

in·jury /'ɪndʒərɪ/ *n* (*pl* **-ies**) **1** *nu* harm; damage: *be insured against injury in the home.* **2** *nc* a hurt or damage to the body, caused by an accident: *a back injury.* Compare wound¹(1). **3** *nc* (*fig*) an act that damages (a reputation, career etc): *an injury to his reputation.*

in·jus·tice /ˌɪn'dʒʌstɪs/ *nc,nu* (an instance of) the absence of justice.

ink¹ /ɪŋk/ *nu* (any kind of) coloured liquid used for writing and printing.

ink² /ɪŋk/ *vt* to mark (something) with ink: *ink one's fingers.* **ink sth in** to draw (e.g. along lines), fill in (spaces), with ink: *ink in a drawing.*

ink·ling /'ɪŋklɪŋ/ *nc* **inkling** (*of sth; that* . . .) a vague idea: *have/get an inkling (of the truth).*

in·laid /ɪn'leɪd/ **1** *pt,pp* of inlay. **2** *adj* (/'ɪnleɪd/ when *attrib*) **inlaid (with sth)** having a different material in the surface: *a desk inlaid with leather.* ⇨ inlay.

in·land¹ /'ɪnlənd/ *adj* (*attrib*) **1** situated in the interior of a country, far from the sea or border: *inland towns.* **2** carried on, obtained, within the limits of a country: *inland trade.*
ˌInland 'Revenue *n* (the —) the government department that collects taxes.

in·land² /ɪn'lænd/ *adv* towards the centre of a country: *travel inland.*

-in-law *suffix* because of one's marriage: *my father-/sister-in-law.*

in-laws /'ɪnlɔːz/ *n pl* (*informal*) relatives by marriage.

in·lay /'ɪnleɪ/ *nc,nu* (an instance, result, of) using materials to inlay something. □ *vt* /ɪn'leɪ/ (*pt,pp* inlaid /ɪn'leɪd/) **inlay sth (with sth)** to put a different material in the surface of another: *inlay wood with metal strips.*

in·let /'ɪnlet/ *nc* **1** a long area of water extending into the land from a larger body of water or between islands. **2** an apparatus, place, for letting in water, gas etc. Opp outlet. **3** something inserted, e.g. a piece of material inserted into clothing.

in·mate /'ɪnmeɪt/ *nc* (*informal*) a person living in a prison or other institution.

in mem·ori·am /ˌɪn mə'mɔːrɪəm/ (*Latin*) (used in epitaphs etc) in memory of; as a memorial to.

in·most /'ɪnməʊst/ *adj* = innermost.

inn /ɪn/ *nc* a small hotel or public house.
'inn·keeper *nc* a person who runs an inn.

in·nards /'ɪnədz/ *n pl* (*informal*) **1** the stomach and bowels. **2** any inner parts: *the innards of a car engine.*

in·nate /ɪ'neɪt/ *adj* (usually *attrib*) (of a quality etc) possessed from birth and part of one's character: *her innate courtesy.*
in·nate·ly *adv*

in·ner /'ɪnə(r)/ *adj* (*attrib*) inside; of the inside: *an inner room.* Compare outer(1).
'inner tube *nc* a rubber tube inside a tyre.

in·ner·most /'ɪnəməʊst/ *adj* **1** (situated) farthest inside: *the innermost part of the library.* **2** (*fig*) most private or secret: *her innermost thoughts/wishes.*

in·nings /'ɪnɪŋz/ *n pl* **1** (*cricket*) the period during which a player or team is batting. **2** (*fig*) the period of power, e.g. of a political party, or of opportunity to show one's ability: *The old man said he had had a good innings.*

in·no·cence /'ɪnəsns/ *nu* the quality or state of being innocent.

in·no·cent /'ɪnəsnt/ *adj* **1** **innocent (of sth)** (*legal*) not guilty: *innocent of the crime.* **2** harmless: *innocent activities.* **3** knowing nothing of evil or wrong: *as innocent as a new-born babe.* **4** foolishly trusting: *Don't be so innocent as to believe everything he says.*
in·no·cent·ly *adv*

in·nocu·ous /ɪ'nɒkjʊəs/ *adj* (*formal*) (of behaviour, something said) causing no harm; not wanting to harm.

in·no·va·tion /ˌɪnə'veɪʃn/ *nc,nu* (an instance of) inventing, using, new ideas, methods: *technological innovations in industry.*

in·no·va·tor /'ɪnəveɪtə(r)/ *nc* a person who invents or uses new methods.

in·nu·en·do /ˌɪnjʊ'endəʊ/ *nc* (*pl* **-es**) an unfavourable suggestion about a person's character.

in·nu·mer·able /ɪ'njuːmrəbl/ *adj* too many to be counted: *innumerable mistakes.*

in·ocu·late /ɪ'nɒkjʊleɪt/ *vt* to inject a substance (a *serum* or *vaccine*) into (a person or animal) to produce a mild form of a disease in order to be a protection against it: *inoculating against cholera.*
in·ocu·la·tion /ɪˌnɒkjʊ'leɪʃn/ *nc,nu*

in·of·fen·sive /ˌɪnə'fensɪv/ *adj* not causing offence: *an inoffensive remark/person.*

in·op·er·able /ɪ'nɒprəbl/ *adj* **1** (*med*) not able to be treated by an operation. Opp operable. **2** (of a system, innovation) not able to be used.

in·op·er·at·ive /ɪn'ɒprətɪv/ *adj* (of laws, rules etc) having no effect; useless. Opp operative.

in·op·por·tune /ˌɪn'ɒpətjuːn/ *adj* (*formal*) not suitable or favourable: *at an inopportune time/remark.* Opp opportune.
in·op·por·tune·ly *adv*

in·or·di·nate /ɪ'nɔːdɪnət/ *adj* (*formal*) more than is usually asked for: *inordinate tax demands.*
in·or·di·nate·ly *adv*

in·or·gan·ic /ˌɪnɔː'gænɪk/ *adj* (*science*) not having an organized physical structure, esp as plants and animals have: *Rocks and metals are inorganic substances.* Compare organic.
in·or·gani·cal·ly /-klɪ/ *adv*

in-pa·tient /'ɪn peɪʃnt/ *nc* a patient living in a

hospital. Compare out-patient.

in·put[1] /'ınpʊt/ *nc* **1** something (a substance, idea, piece of information etc) provided during a process: *What was her input in the project?* **2** a place where something (power, information etc) enters a system: *The input for the electricity is on the wall.* **3** (*computers*) information (to be) put into a computer. Compare output.

in·put[2] /'ınpʊt/ *vt* (*computers*) to provide (information) and put it into a computer.

in·quest /'ınkwest/ *nc* an official inquiry to learn facts, esp concerning a death which may not be the result of natural causes.

in·quire (also **en-**) /ın'kwaıə(r)/ *vt* to ask in order to be told (something): *inquire what he wants/ where to stay.*

inquire (about sb/sth) to ask for information: *inquire about her/his health/the times of the trains.*

inquire after sb to ask about a person's health, happiness, news etc.

inquire into sth to make a careful study in order to get information: *inquire into the causes of social unrest.*

inquire sth of sb; inquire sb (to do sth) (*formal*) to ask a person to provide information, to do something: *inquire of her to write a report.*

in·quir·er (also **en-**) /ın'kwaıərə(r)/ *nc* a person who inquires.

in·quir·ing (also **en-**) /ın'kwaıərıŋ/ *adj* (*attrib*) in the habit of asking for information: *an inquiring mind.*

in·quir·ing·ly (also **en-**) *adv*

in·quiry (also **en-**) /ın'kwaıərı/ *n* (*pl* **-ies**) **1** *nu* the process of asking. **on inquiry** having asked: *On inquiry I discovered he was dead.* **2** *nc* **inquiry (into sth)** an investigation: *hold an official inquiry into the incident.*

in·qui·si·tion /ˌınkwı'zıʃn/ *nc* (esp) a formal investigation that ignores the legal and human rights of the people involved.

in·quisi·tive /ın'kwızətıv/ *adj* (*derog*) liking, showing a fondness for, having, (too much) interest in other people's affairs.

in·quisi·tive·ly *adv*

in·quor·ate /ın'kwɔːrət/ *adj* (*no comp*) without a majority of members (a *quorum*) present. Opp quorate.

in·road /'ınrəʊd/ *nc* **1** a sudden attack (into a country etc), esp to steal supplies. **2** (*pl*) **make inroads (into/on sth)** (*fig*) to use something up, obtain success in something etc gradually: *making inroads into one's savings/into finding a cure for cancer.*

in·rush /'ınrʌʃ/ *nc* a sudden movement, flow: *an inrush of water.*

in·sane /ın'seın/ *adj* **1** mentally ill. **2** (*informal*) foolish; with little or no purpose: *insane greed.* Compare sane.

in·sane·ly *adv*: *insanely jealous.*

in·san·ity /ın'sænətı/ *nu* madness.

in·sani·tary /ın'sænıtrı/ *adj* not sanitary: *insanitary conditions.*

in·sa·tiable /ın'seıʃəbl/ *adj* (*formal*) that cannot be satisfied: *insatiable appetites.*

in·sa·tiably /-ʃəblı/ *adv*

in·scribe /ın'skraıb/ *vt* (*formal*) to mark, write, (words, one's name etc in or on something).

in·scrip·tion /ın'skrıpʃn/ *nc* (esp) words on a stone, coin or medal.

in·scru·table /ın'skruːtəbl/ *adj* (*formal*) that cannot be understood or known: *the inscrutable ways of fate.*

in·sect /'ınsekt/ *nc* any of a kind of small animal, such as an ant, fly, beetle, having six legs and no backbone and a body divided into three parts.

in·sec·ti·cide /ın'sektısaıd/ *nc,nu* a substance used for killing insects.

in·sec·ti·vore /ın'sektıvɔː(r)/ *nc* (*science*) an animal that eats insects. Compare carnivore, herbivore, omnivore.

in·sec·tiv·or·ous /ˌınsek'tıvərəs/ *adj* insecteating.

in·se·cure /ˌınsı'kjʊə(r)/ *adj* **1** not safe; not providing good support; not to be relied on: *an insecure job.* Opp secure[1](2). **2** (of a person) feeling unsafe; without protection; without confidence. Opp secure[1](1).

in·se·cure·ly *adv*

in·se·cur·ity /ˌınsı'kjʊərətı/ *nu: suffer from feelings of insecurity.*

in·sen·sible /ın'sensəbl/ *adj* (*formal*) **1** unconscious as the result of injury, illness etc. **2 insensible (of sth)** unaware (of): *insensible of danger.*

in·sen·sibly /-əblı/ *adv*

in·sen·si·tive /ın'sensətıv/ *adj* not sensitive (to touch, light, to the feelings of other people).

in·sen·si·tive·ly *adv*

in·sen·si·tiv·ity /ˌınˌsensə'tıvətı/ *nu*

in·sep·ar·able /ın'seprəbl/ *adj* not able to be separated: *inseparable friends.*

in·sert /ın'sɜːt/ *vt* to put, fit, place, (something) (in, into, between etc): *insert a key in a lock.*

in·ser·tion /ın'sɜːʃn/ *nc,nu*

in·shore /'ınʃɔː(r)/ *adj* (*attrib*), *adv* close to the shore: *an inshore current; inshore fisheries.* Compare offshore(2).

in·side[1] /'ınsaıd/ *adj* (*attrib*) **1** situated in the interior area of: *an inside door; the inside pages of a newspaper.* Opp outside[1](1). **2** situated along the inner edge of: *the inside lane of a running track* (= nearest to the central area); *the inside lane of a motorway* (= nearest to the side of the road). Opp outside[1](2). **3** (*informal*) provided by, using, a person working for an organization: *inside information; an inside job* (= a robbery using an employee).

in·side[2] /'ınsaıd/ *adv* **1** in, into, towards, the interior area: *There's nothing inside. Have a look inside and see if it's empty.* Opp outside[2](1). **2** indoors: *He's inside. Go inside.* Opp outside[2](2). Compare in[2](2). **3** (*informal*) in prison: *How long has he been inside?* **4 inside of sth** in less than a mentioned time, distance: *inside of a week.* Opp outside[2](3).

in·side[3] /'ınsaıd/ *nc* (the —) **1** the interior area, enclosed space, of a container, building, vehicle, group, mass etc: *the inside of a box/house/car/forest.* **2** the inner side or surface: *the inside of a wall.* **inside 'out** (a) with the inner side on the outside: *He put his socks on inside out.* (b) thoroughly: *He knows the subject inside out.* **3** the inner part or edge of something, e.g. of a road, racing track, curve: *Never overtake on the inside.* ⇨ outside[3](1,2).

inside[4] /ın'saıd/ *prep* **1** in, into, towards, the interior area: *Don't bring that big, dirty dog inside* *this house!* ⇨ outside⁴(1). **2** in less than: *He can run a mile well inside 4 minutes. It will be ready inside an hour.* Ⓝ *'Within' is also possible.*

,inside **'left/'right** *nc* (in football etc) a player in the forward (attacking) line immediately to the left/right of the centre-forward.

in·**sider** *nc* (also *attrib*) a member of an organization etc who can obtain facts and information and so has advantages over others: *insider dealing in stocks and shares.* ⇨ outsider(1).

in·**sidi·ous** /ɪnˈsɪdɪəs/ *adj* doing harm secretly or unseen: *an insidious disease.*

in·**sidi·ous·ly** *adv*

in·**sight** /ˈɪnsaɪt/ *nc,nu* **insight (into sb/sth)** (an instance of) the power of understanding something: *On holiday, she had a good insight into what life would be like as his wife.*

in·**sig·nia** /ɪnˈsɪgnɪə/ *n pl* symbols of authority or position such as a badge, medal, crown, esp as part of a uniform.

in·**sig·nifi·cant** /ˌɪnsɪgˈnɪfɪkənt/ *adj* having little or no value, use, meaning or importance: *insignificant faults/costs.* Compare significant.

in·**sig·nifi·cant·ly** *adv*

in·**sig·nifi·cance** /-əns/ *nu*

in·**sin·cere** /ˌɪnsɪnˈsɪə(r)/ *adj* not sincere.

in·**sin·cere·ly** *adv*

in·**sin·cer·ity** /ˌɪnsɪnˈserətɪ/ *nu*

in·**sinu·ate** /ɪnˈsɪnjʊeɪt/ *vt* **1 insinuate oneself into sth** to make oneself accepted slowly and using dishonest means: *insinuating oneself into a person's favour.* **2 insinuate (to sb) that . . .** to suggest unpleasantly and indirectly: *insinuating (to her) that he is a liar.*

in·**sinu·ation** /ɪnˌsɪnjʊˈeɪʃn/ *nc,nu*

in·**sip·id** /ɪnˈsɪpɪd/ *adj* (*derog*) **1** without taste or flavour: *insipid food.* **2** (*fig*) without interest, spirit: *an insipid personality.*

in·**sip·id·ly** *adv*

in·**sist** /ɪnˈsɪst/ *vi,vt* **insist (on sth; that . . .)**) **1** to urge (something) strongly against opposition or disbelief: *insist on one's innocence/that one is innocent.* **2** to give (an order) that will not be changed: *I insisted that he should come with us/ insisted on his coming with us.*

in·**sist·ent** /-ənt/ *adj* (*formal*) **1** insisting: *be insistent about her innocence.* **2** (of actions) needing to be carried out: *insistent requests for more staff.*

in·**sist·ence** /-əns/ *nu*

in·**so·far as** /ˌɪnsəʊˈfɑː rəz/ *conj* = in so far as. ⇨ in³(12).

in·**so·lent** /ˈɪnsələnt/ *adj* (*derog*) insulting; rude: *insolent behaviour/boys.*

in·**so·lent·ly** *adv*

in·**so·lence** /-əns/ *nu*

in·**sol·uble** /ɪnˈsɒljʊbl/ *adj* **1** (of substances) that cannot be dissolved: *Sand is insoluble in water.* Opp soluble. **2** (of problems etc) that cannot be solved or explained. Opp solvable.

in·**sol·vent** /ɪnˈsɒlvənt/ *nc,* *adj* (of a person, business) unable to pay debts. Opp solvent¹(1).

in·**sol·ven·cy** /-ənsɪ/ *nu*

in·**som·nia** /ɪnˈsɒmnɪə/ *nu* the condition of being unable to sleep.

in·**som·ni·ac** /ɪnˈsɒmnɪæk/ *nc* a person suffering from insomnia.

in·**spect** /ɪnˈspekt/ *vt* **1** to examine (details) care-

fully. **2** to visit (a school, office etc) to see if the organization is running well and work is done properly.

in·**spec·tion** /ɪnˈspekʃn/ *nc,nu*

in·**spec·tor** /ɪnˈspektə(r)/ *nc* **1** an official who inspects, e.g. schools, factories. **2** an official who examines (manufactured articles, tickets etc): *a ticket inspector on a train.* **3** (*GB*) a police officer who is below a superintendent and above a sergeant.

in·**spec·tor·ate** /ɪnˈspektərət/ *nc* a group of inspectors(1).

in·**spi·ra·tion** /ˌɪnspəˈreɪʃn/ *n* **1** *nu* influence(s) producing creative activity in literature, music, art etc: *inspiration from nature.* **2** *nc* a person or thing that inspires: *His wife was a constant inspiration to him.* **3** *nc* (*informal*) a sudden good idea: *His idea to add a yellow flower to the design was an inspiration.*

in·**spire** /ɪnˈspaɪə(r)/ *vt* to put (encouraging, creative thoughts, feelings or aims etc) into (a person): *inspiring confidence in her. What inspired him to give such a brilliant performance?*

in·**spir·ed** *adj* filled with, showing inspiration: *inspired poets/artists.*

Inst written *abbr* Institute.

in·**sta·bil·ity** /ˌɪnstəˈbɪlətɪ/ *nu* the absence of stability (of character). Opp stability.

in·**stall** (*US* also in·**stal**) /ɪnˈstɔːl/ *vt* **1** to place (a person) in a new position of authority with the usual ceremony: *install a bishop.* **2** to place, fix, (apparatus) in position for use: *install central heating.* **3** to settle (oneself, family etc) in a place: *be installed in a new home.*

in·**stal·la·tion** /ˌɪnstəˈleɪʃn/ *nc,nu*

in·**stal·ment** (*US* also in·**stall·ment**) /ɪnˈstɔːlmənt/ *nc* **1** any one of the parts in which something is presented over a period of time: *a story that will appear on TV in instalments.* **2** any one of the parts of a payment spread over a period of time: *pay by monthly instalments.*

in·**stance** /ˈɪnstəns/ *nc* an example; fact or occasion etc supporting a general truth: *This is only one instance out of many.* **for instance** for example: *There are lots of things to do—for instance there's a cinema.* **in the first instance** (used to introduce a series of requests, facts etc) first; to begin with: *In the first instance I refused but then I realized I had to go.*

in·**stant¹** /ˈɪnstənt/ *adj* **1** coming or happening at once: *an instant success; instant relief.* **2** urgent: *be in instant need of help.* **3** (*attrib*) (of food, drink) that can be prepared quickly and easily: *instant coffee.*

in·**stant·ly** *adv* at once.

in·**stant²** /ˈɪnstənt/ *nc* **1** an exact point of time: *Come here this instant!* (= Come here immediately!) *I sent you the news the instant (that)* (= as soon as) *I heard it.* **2** a moment: *Help arrived not an instant too soon.*

in·**stan·ta·neous** /ˌɪnstənˈteɪnɪəs/ *adj* happening, done, extremely quickly (as a result of something): *Death was instantaneous. My instantaneous reaction was to lock the door.*

in·**stan·ta·neous·ly** *adv*

in·**stead** /ɪnˈsted/ *adv* as an alternative or substitute: *If Harry won't go with you, take me instead.* **instead of** (*prep*) in place of; as an alternative to or substitute for: *I will go instead of you. Use oil instead of butter.*

in·step /'ɪnstep/ *nc* the upper surface of the foot between the toes and the ankle; part of a shoe etc covering this.

in·sti·gate /'ɪnstɪgeɪt/ *vt* to cause (something) to happen by using strong and continual encouragement: *instigate a strike.*

in·sti·ga·tion /ˌɪnstɪ'geɪʃn/ *nu* (esp) **at the instigation of sb** encouraged by a person, group to do it, start.

in·sti·ga·tor /-tə(r)/ *nc* a person who instigates something.

in·stil (*US* = **in·still**) /ɪn'stɪl/ *vt* (**-ll-**) **instil sth into sb; sb with sth** to introduce ideas etc using continual effort: *instil discipline into school-children.*

in·stil·la·tion /ˌɪnstɪ'leɪʃn/ *nu*

in·stinct /'ɪnstɪŋkt/ *nc,nu* (an instance of) the natural tendency to behave in a certain way without reasoning or training: *Birds learn to fly by instinct. She has an instinct for always saying the right thing.*

in·stinc·tive /ɪn'stɪŋktɪv/ *adj* based on instinct, not from training or teaching: *an instinctive feeling that something was wrong.*

in·stinc·tive·ly *adv*

in·sti·tute¹ /'ɪnstɪtjuːt/ *nc* **1** (abbr **Inst**) a society or organization for a special (usually a social or educational) purpose. **2** the building(s) of an institute.

in·sti·tute² /'ɪnstɪtjuːt/ *vt* (*formal*) **1** to set up and start (rules etc) officially: *instituting new parking regulations.* **2** **institute sth (against sb/sth)** to start legal action (against an offender): *institute legal proceedings (against a dangerous driver).*

in·sti·tu·tion /ˌɪnstɪ'tjuːʃn/ *n* **1** *nu* the act, process, of instituting or being instituted: *the institution of rules.* **2** *nc* (a building of) an organization with a social purpose, e.g. an orphanage. **3** *nc* an established custom or practice: *the institution of marriage.* **4** *nc* (*informal*) a person who has been a member of an organization or community for a long time: *He's an institution in our office/village.*

in·sti·tu·tion·al /-ʃənl/ *adj*: *institutional food.*

in·struct /ɪn'strʌkt/ *vt* **1** **instruct sb (to do sth)** to give orders or directions to a person: *instruct him to start early.* **2** (*formal*) to give information to (a person): *I have been instructed by my bank that the money has arrived.* **3** **instruct sb (in sth)** (*formal*) to teach a person (esp a skill): *instruct a boy in mechanics.*

in·struc·tor /-tə(r)/ *nc* a person who teaches a skill: *a driving instructor.*

in·struc·tion /ɪn'strʌkʃn/ *n* **1** *nu* **instruction (in sth)** the act, process, of instructing or being instructed: *instruction in mechanics.* **2** *nc* (usually *pl*) direction; order: *give instructions to arrive early.*

in·struc·tion·al /-ʃənl/ *adj* educational (the usual word): *instructional films.*

in·struc·tive /ɪn'strʌktɪv/ *adj* giving or containing information: *instructive leaflets.*

in·stru·ment /'ɪnstrʊmənt/ *nc* **1** an apparatus designed to be used to perform an action, esp for delicate or scientific work: *optical instruments* (e.g. a microscope). **2** an object designed for pro-

ducing musical sounds (e.g. piano, violin, flute or drum): *musical instruments.* ⇨ string/wind instrument. **3** a person used by another for her or his own purposes: *be made the instrument of another's crime.*

in·stru·men·tal /ˌɪnstrʊ'mentl/ *adj* **1** **instrumental (in doing sth)** causing, responsible (for something): *be instrumental in finding work for a friend.* **2** of or for musical instruments: *instrumental music.*

in·stru·men·tal·ist /-təlɪst/ *nc* a person who plays a musical instrument.

in·sub·or·di·nate /ˌɪnsə'bɔːdɪnət/ *adj* (*formal; derog*) disobedient.

in·sub·or·di·na·tion /ˌɪnsəˌbɔːdɪ'neɪʃn/ *nc,nu*

in·sub·stan·tial /ˌɪnsəb'stænʃl/ *adj* (*formal*) **1** not solidly built. Compare substantial(1). **2** not enough: *an insubstantial supply/meal.* Compare substantial(2). **3** without enough evidence: *insubstantial proof.*

in·suf·fer·able /ɪn'sʌfrəbl/ *adj* unbearable: *insufferable insolence.*

in·suf·fi·cient /ˌɪnsə'fɪʃənt/ *adj* not sufficient: *insufficient evidence.*

in·suf·fi·cien·cy /-ʃənsɪ/ *nu*

in·suf·fi·cient·ly *adv*

in·su·lar /'ɪnsjʊlə(r)/ *adj* **1** having, showing, limited thought or experience: *insular habits and prejudices.* **2** (*tech*) of, concerning, an island.

in·su·lar·ity /ˌɪnsjʊ'lærəti/ *nu*

in·su·late /'ɪnsjʊleɪt/ *vt* **1** **insulate sth (against sth)** (esp *science*) to cover or separate something with material that stops heat, electricity etc from passing through: *insulate pipes against freezing.* ⇨ conduct²(5). **2** **insulate sb (from sth)** to keep a person separate (from bad, unpleasant experiences): *insulating children from harmful television programmes.*

'insulating tape *nu* a kind of plastic tape used to stop electricity from passing through.

in·su·la·tion /ˌɪnsjʊ'leɪʃn *US:* -sə'l-/ *nu*

in·su·la·tor /'ɪnsjʊleɪtə(r)/ *nc* (*science*) a material that insulates(1) something.

in·sult¹ /'ɪnsʌlt/ *nc* **insult (to sth)** a remark, act, that insults: *crowds yelling rude insults at the speaker. Your excuses are an insult (to my intelligence).*

in·sult² /ɪn'sʌlt/ *vt* to speak or act in a way that hurts or is intended to hurt (a person, a person's feelings or pride).

in·sult·ing *adj*: *insulting behaviour.*

in·sup·er·able /ɪn'sjuːprəbl/ *adj* (*formal*) = insurmountable.

in·sup·port·able /ˌɪnsə'pɔːtəbl/ *adj* (*formal*) intolerable: *insupportable rudeness.*

in·sur·ance /ɪn'ʃʊərəns/ *n* **1** *nc,nu* (an agreement by a business company or the State to provide) money because of ill health, death, loss of property etc paid in return for regular payments in advance: *take out medical/life insurance. When her husband died, she received £50 000 insurance.* **2** *nc* **insurance (against sth)** any measure taken as protection against loss, failure etc: *put an extra lock on the door as an insurance against burglary. Why not apply for a course at the college as an insurance against not getting into university?*

in·sure /ɪn'ʃʊə(r)/ *vt,vi* **insure (sb/sth) (against sth)** to make an agreement with a business that promises to pay money in case of accident, damage, loss, death etc: *insure one's house against fire. A car accident can cost you a lot if you're not insured.*

insured *nc* (the —) a person to whom payment will be made.

insurer *nc* (the —) a person or business promising to make payment in case of loss etc.

in·sur·gent /ɪnˈsɜːdʒənt/ *adj, nc* (of, like) a person wanting to take (political) power by force.

in·sur·mount·able /ˌɪnsəˈmaʊntəbl/ *adj* (of difficulties etc) too large or serious to oppose, deal with, successfully. Opp surmountable.

in·sur·rec·tion /ˌɪnsəˈrekʃn/ *nc,nu* (an instance of) the act of people using force against the government.

int. *written abbr* **1** interior; internal. **2** international.

in·tact /ɪnˈtækt/ *adj* (*pred*) complete and untouched or undamaged: *The radio is still intact even though I dropped it.*

in·take /ˈɪnteɪk/ *nc* **1** a quantity, number etc entering or taken in (during a given period): *an annual intake of 200 students.* **2** a place for letting in water, gas etc. Compare outlet.

in·tan·gible /ˌɪnˈtændʒəbl/ *adj* (*formal*) that cannot be known by means of the senses or fully understood, but can be sensed by the feelings: *an intangible idea of someone hiding upstairs.* Compare tangible(1).

in·tan·gi·bil·ity /ˌɪnˌtændʒəˈbɪlətɪ/ *nu*

in·te·ger /ˈɪntɪdʒə(r)/ *nc* (*maths*) a whole number.

in·te·gral /ˈɪntɪɡrəl/ *adj* (*attrib*) **1** necessary for completeness: *The arms and legs are integral parts of a human being.* **2** (*maths*) (made up) of integers.

in·te·gral·ly /-əlɪ/ *adv*

in·te·grate /ˈɪntɪɡreɪt/ *vt,vi* **integrate (sb/sth) (with sb/sth; into sth) 1** to join (parts) into a whole; complete (something) by adding parts: *integrating the old school with the new one (into a comprehensive school).* **2** (to cause people) to be together as one group: *integrate children from different backgrounds (into one community).*

integrated 'circuit *nc* (*computers*) an electronic circuit with many parts formed on a tiny silicon chip often only a few millimetres square.

in·te·gra·tion /ˌɪntɪˈɡreɪʃn/ *nu*

in·teg·ri·ty /ɪnˈteɡrətɪ/ *nu* the quality of being honest, moral: *commercial integrity.*

in·tel·lect /ˈɪntəlekt/ *nu* the power to reason (contrasted with emotions and instinct): *Intellect distinguishes man from other animals.*

in·tel·lec·tual /ˌɪntəˈlektʃʊəl/ *adj* (*attrib*) using, having or showing (pleasure in) the power of thought to reason and produce explanations or ideas: *intellectual people/interests.* Compare intelligent. □ *nc* an intellectual person.

in·tel·lec·tual·ly /-tʃʊəlɪ/ *adv*

in·tel·li·gence /ɪnˈtelɪdʒəns/ *nu* **1** the power to learn, understand and know: *A man of little/ some/great/no intelligence. Playing with matches is dangerous—use your intelligence!* **2** information, esp with reference to important events: *have secret intelligence of the enemy's plans.*

in'telligence test *nc* a method used to find a person's standard of intelligence(1).

in·tel·li·gent /ɪnˈtelɪdʒənt/ *adj* having, showing intelligence(1): *intelligent students/suggestions. It was intelligent of you to think of that possibility.*

in·tel·li·gent·ly *adv*

in·tel·li·gible /ɪnˈtelɪdʒəbl/ *adj* **intelligible (to sb)** that can be easily understood. Opp unintelligible.

in·tel·li·gibly /-əblɪ/ *adv*

in·tel·li·gi·bil·ity /ɪnˌtelɪdʒəˈbɪlətɪ/ *nu*

in·tend /ɪnˈtend/ *vt* to have (something) in mind as a purpose or plan: *What do you intend to do/ intend doing today?*

in·tense /ɪnˈtens/ *adj* **1** (of qualities) high in degree or strength: *intense heat.* **2** (of a person, feelings etc) strong and serious: *an intense hatred.*

in·tense·ly *adv*

in·ten·si·fi·er /ɪnˈtensɪfaɪə(r)/ *nc* (*gram*) an adjective or adverb that makes the meaning stronger, such as *very, awfully, extremely.*

in·ten·si·fy /ɪnˈtensɪfaɪ/ *vt,vi* (*pt,pp* **-ied**) (to cause something) to become stronger or more determined: *intensify one's efforts.*

in,tensifying 'adjective/'adverb *nc* = intensifier.

in·ten·si·ty /ɪnˈtensətɪ/ *nu* the state, quality, of being intense; strength (of feeling etc).

in·ten·sive /ɪnˈtensɪv/ *adj* **1** deep and thorough: *make an intensive study of a subject.* **2** (*gram*) of a word giving force and emphasis: *In 'a terribly hot day', 'terribly' is used as an intensive word.*

in,tensive 'care *nu* (a place used to give) specially thorough care to acutely ill patients.

in,tensive 'pronoun *nc* (*gram*) = emphatic pronoun.

in·ten·sive·ly *adv*

in·tent¹ /ɪnˈtent/ *adj* **1** (of looks) eager; earnest. **2 intent (on sth; doing sth)** (of a person) having, showing, serious and constant desire or attention: *He was intent on his work.*

in·tent·ly *adv*

intent² /ɪnˈtent/ *nu* purpose; intention: *shoot with intent to kill.* **to all intents (and purposes)** very nearly; in the essential details: *She was not the actual manager but did the same job to all intents and purposes.*

in·ten·tion /ɪnˈtenʃn/ *nc,nu* (an instance, example, of) an aim, determination to do something: *He hasn't the least intention of marrying yet.* ⇔ also best³(3), well-intentioned.

in·ten·tion·al /ɪnˈtenʃənl/ *adj* done on purpose: *If I hurt your feelings, it wasn't intentional.* Opp unintentional.

in·ten·tion·al·ly /-ʃənəlɪ/ *adv* on purpose.

in·ter /ɪnˈtɜː(r)/ *vt* (**-rr-**) (*formal*) to bury (a person). ⇔ interment.

in·ter·act /ˌɪntərˈækt/ *vi* **interact (with sb/ sth)** to have an effect on one another, another person or thing.

in·ter·ac·tion /-ˈækʃn/ *nc,nu*

in·ter·ac·tive /-ˈæktɪv/ *adj*

in·ter·cede /ˌɪntəˈsiːd/ *vi* **intercede (with sb)** (*formal*) to plead (with a person) to end a quarrel or to obtain a favour: *intercede with the father for/ on behalf of the daughter.*

in·ter·ces·sion /ˌɪntəˈseʃn/ *nc,nu*

in·ter·cept /ˌɪntəˈsept/ *vt* to stop and (usually) get hold of (a person or thing) between the starting-point and destination: *intercept a letter/a mes-*

senger.

in·ter·cep·tion /ˌɪntə'sepʃn/ *nu*

in·ter·cep·tor /-tə(r)/ *nc* a person who intercepts.

in·ter·change¹ /'ɪntətʃeɪndʒ/ *n* **1** *nc* a place where roads join a motorway etc. **2** *nc,nu* (an instance of) the exchange of ideas, methods etc.

in·ter·change² /ˌɪntə'tʃeɪndʒ/ *vt,vi* **interchange (sb/sth with sb/sth)** (to cause a person, group, things) to change places (with another).

in·ter·change·able /-əbl/ *adj* that can be interchanged: *True synonyms are interchangeable*.

in·ter·col·legi·ate /ˌɪntəkə'liːdʒɪət/ *adj* (usually *attrib*) of, carried on between, colleges: *intercollegiate games/debates*.

in·ter·con·ti·nen·tal /ˌɪntəˌkɒntɪ'nentl/ *adj* (usually *attrib*) of, carried on between, continents: *intercontinental travel*.

in·ter·course /'ɪntəkɔːs/ *nu* **1** the exchanges of trade, ideas etc between people, businesses, nations etc. **2** = sexual intercourse.

in·ter·de·pen·dent /ˌɪntədɪ'pendənt/ *adj* needing, depending on, each other: *interdependent nations in southern Africa*.

in·ter·de·pen·dence /-əns/ *nu*

in·ter·est¹ /'ɪntrəst/ *n* **1** *nc,nu* **interest (in sb/ sth)** (an instance of) wanting to know or learn (more) about a person or thing: *He feels/has/ takes no/not much/a great interest in politics*. **lose interest (in sb/sth)** to stop being interested (in). **2** *nu* **interest (to sb)** the quality that causes concern or curiosity: *It's of considerable/ not much/no/great interest (to me)*. **3** *nc* something which a person wants to and does spend time on: *His two great interests in life are music and painting*. **4** *nc* (often *pl*) advantage; profit; benefit: *You will soon learn something to your interest*. **be in one's interest (to do sth)** to be to one's benefit: *It is in your interest(s) to work hard*. **in the interest(s) of sb/sth** for the benefit of: *in the interests of truth*. **5** *nu* the money charged or paid for borrowing: *a poor rate of interest*. **6** *nc* a legal right to share in a business etc, esp in its profits: *have an interest in a clothing factory*. **7** (often *pl*) a group of people engaged in the same trade etc: *business/insurance/banking interests*.

'interest rate *nc* the amount of payment (usually a percentage) charged for a loan.

in·ter·est² /'ɪntrəst/ *vt* **interest sb (in sb/sth)** to cause a person to have, show, an interest(1): *Are you interested in wild birds? Can I interest you in this new soap?* (= Would you like to buy some?)

in·ter·est·ed *adj* (usually *attrib*) (a) having, showing interest(1): *an interested look*. (b) having an interest(6): *an interested party in an argument*. Compare disinterested, uninterested.

in·ter·est·ing *adj* holding the attention; causing interest(1): *an interesting conversation*.

in·ter·face /'ɪntəfeɪs/ *nc* **1** an edge, point of contact, shared between two things. **2** (*computers*) an apparatus used to join two different computer parts.

in·ter·fere /ˌɪntə'fɪə(r)/ *vi* **1** **interfere (in sth)** to break in on another person's affairs without right or invitation: *Please stop interfering in my*

business. **2** **interfere (with sth)** to touch and move parts about: *Do not interfere with this machine*. **3** **interfere (with sth)** (of events, circumstances etc) to be an obstacle; hinder or prevent something: *Do you ever allow pleasure to interfere (with duty)?* **4** **interfere with sb** to attack (esp) a child sexually. **5** (*radio*) to produce a noise that prevents sound being heard.

in·ter·fer·ence /ˌɪntə'fɪərəns/ *nu* (a) the process of interfering. (b) (*radio*) the noise that results from interfering(5).

in·ter·im¹ /'ɪntərɪm/ *adj* (*attrib*) **1** temporary (while more information is prepared, more supplies are obtained etc): *an interim payment/ report; interim measures to prevent flooding*. **2** of the time between: *The interim period was one of increasing poverty*.

in·ter·im² /'ɪntərɪm/ *n* **in the interim** during the period of time in between: *We'll arrive at 6 and the film starts at 8, so we could have a meal in the interim*.

in·ter·ior¹ /ɪn'tɪərɪə(r)/ *adj* of, situated in, suitable for, the inner area: *an interior room/wall. The interior regions of Central America have many beautiful birds. Interior paint cannot be used on the outside of a building.* Opp exterior¹.

in,terior 'angle *nc* one on the inside of two lines or a shape. Compare exterior angle.

in,terior 'decorator *nc* a person who paints and wallpapers rooms and staircases, etc.

in·ter·ior² /ɪn'tɪərɪə(r)/ *nc* (usually the —) **1** the inner area or parts of a region: *the Australian interior; the interior of the desert*. **2** the inside of a room, building etc, esp with reference to its design etc: *Let's use white paint throughout the interior*. Compare exterior².

in·ter·ject /ˌɪntə'dʒekt/ *vt,vi* (*formal*) to make (a remark etc) suddenly between statements made by another.

in·ter·jec·tion /ˌɪntə'dʒekʃn/ *nc* (*gram*) a word or phrase used as an exclamation, such as *Oh! Ugh! Ouch! Phew! Good Gracious!* Ⓝ Marked *int* in this dictionary.

in·ter·lace /ˌɪntə'leɪs/ *vt,vi* to join (things), be joined, (as if) by weaving or lacing together: *interlacing branches*.

in·ter·link /ˌɪntə'lɪŋk/ *vt,vi* (to cause systems, e.g. for travel) to link together.

in·ter·lock /ˌɪntə'lɒk/ *vt,vi* (to cause machine parts etc) to lock or join together.

in·ter·lo·per /'ɪntələʊpə(r)/ *nc* (*derog*) a person who, for profit or personal advantage, involves herself or himself without any right.

in·ter·lude /'ɪntəluːd/ *nc* **1** an interval between two activities or two periods of time of different character: *interludes of bright weather*. **2** a piece of music played during such an interval between parts of a concert, play etc.

in·ter·mar·ry /ˌɪntə'mærɪ/ *vi* (*pt,pp* **-ied**) (of people from different countries etc) to marry each other.

in·ter·mar·riage /ˌɪntə'mærɪdʒ/ *nu*

in·ter·medi·ary /ˌɪntə'miːdɪərɪ/ *adj, nc* (*pl* **-ies**) (of) a person acting as a link between (groups), esp to get agreement.

in·ter·medi·ate /ˌɪntə'miːdɪət/ *adj* situated or coming between in time, space, degree etc: *at an intermediate stage/standard*.

in·ter·medi·ate·ly *adv*

in·ter·ment /ɪn'tɜ:mənt/ *nc,nu* (*formal*) burial.

in·ter·mi·nable /ɪn'tɜ:mɪnəbl/ *adj* boring because (too) long: *an interminable debate*. Compare terminable.

in·ter·mi·nably /-əblɪ/ *adv*

in·ter·mit·tent /ˌɪntə'mɪtənt/ *adj* pausing or stopping at intervals: *intermittent fever*.

in·ter·mit·tent·ly *adv*

in·tern /ɪn'tɜ:n/ *vt* to force (people, esp aliens during a war) to live in certain areas or in a special building, camp etc.

in·tern·ment *nu*

in·ter·nal /ɪn'tɜ:nl/ *adj* 1 of, in, the inside: *suffer internal injuries*. 2 of, concerning, a country and its people; not foreign: *internal trade*. Compare external.

in·ter·nal·ly *adv*

in·ter·na·tion·al[1] /ˌɪntə'næʃənl/ *adj* of, concerning, carried on between, nations: *international relations/trade/talks*.

international date-line *nc* = date-line.

in·ter·na·tion·al·ist *nc* (of) a person, policy, in favour of cooperation between nations.

in·ter·na·tion·al·ly /-əlɪ/ *adv*: *internationally famous*.

in·ter·na·tion·al·ize (also **-ise**) /-aɪz/ *vt* to make (something) international, esp by putting it under international control: *Should the Suez Canal be internationalized?*

in·ter·na·tion·al[2] /ˌɪntə'næʃənl/ *nc* (a player in) a sports competition between different countries: *a football international*.

in·ter·ne·cine /ˌɪntə'ni:saɪn/ *adj* causing destruction to both sides: *internecine war*.

in·ter·play /'ɪntəpleɪ/ *nu* the effect of two things on each other: *the interplay of colours*.

in·ter·pose /ˌɪntə'pəʊz/ *vt,vi* (*formal*) 1 to make (a comment), put forward (an objection etc) as an interference: *Will they interpose (their veto) yet again?* 2 to use one's power, influence, advice etc during a dispute: *interpose (between two people) in a quarrel*.

in·ter·pret /ɪn'tɜ:prɪt/ *v* 1 *vt* to show, explain, the meaning of (something) (either in words or by artistic performance): *interpret a difficult passage in a book/the role of Hamlet*. 2 *vt* **interpret sth as sth** to consider something to mean something: *We interpreted his silence as a refusal*. 3 *vi* to act as an interpreter.

in·ter·pre·ta·tion /ɪnˌtɜ:prɪ'teɪʃn/ *nc,nu*

in·ter·preter *nc* a professional person who gives an immediate translation of words spoken in another language.

in·ter·ra·cial /ˌɪntə'reɪʃl/ *adj* between, involving, different races: *interracial harmony*.

in·ter·ro·gate /ɪn'terəgeɪt/ *vt* to question (a person) thoroughly or formally: *interrogating a prisoner*.

in·ter·ro·ga·tion /ɪnˌterə'geɪʃn/ *nc,nu*

in·ter·ro·ga·tor /-tə(r)/ *nc* a person who interrogates a person.

in·ter·roga·tive /ˌɪntə'rɒgətɪv/ *nc* (*gram*) a word or structure used to form a question.

inter,rogative 'adverb/'pronoun *nc* (*gram*) an adverb (e.g. *how, when, why*) or a pronoun (e.g. *what, which, who*) used to form questions.

in·ter·rupt /ˌɪntə'rʌpt/ *vt,vi* 1 to break the conti-

nuity of (something): *The war interrupted trade between the two countries*. 2 to (speak and so) break in on (a person speaking, doing something etc): *Don't interrupt (me) while I'm busy*.

in·ter·rup·tion /ˌɪntə'rʌpʃn/ *nc,nu*

in·ter·sect /ˌɪntə'sekt/ *vt,vi* 1 to divide (something) by cutting, passing or lying across. 2 (of lines) to cross each other.

in·ter·sec·tion /ˌɪntə'sekʃn/ *nc,nu*

in·ter·sperse /ˌɪntə'spɜ:s/ *vt* to place (something) between or among others: *music interspersed with dancing/between the speeches*.

in·ter·twine /ˌɪntə'twaɪn/ *vt,vi* to twist (things) together: *branches intertwined with vines*.

in·ter·val /'ɪntəvl/ *nc* 1 a period of time between acts of a play, parts of a concert etc: *Let's meet in the interval*. 2 a space before an event or activity: *After a short interval the speaker began again/the two men agreed*. 3 a space between two objects or points: *arranged at intervals of twenty metres*.

in·ter·vene /ˌɪntə'vi:n/ *vi* 1 (of events, circumstances) to happen between others in time: *I shall leave on Sunday if nothing intervenes*. 2 **intervene (between/in sth)** (of a person) to interfere (so as to try to stop something): *intervene in a dispute; intervene between people who are quarrelling*. 3 (of time) to come or be between: *during the years that intervened*.

in·ter·ven·tion /ˌɪntə'venʃn/ *nc,nu*

in·ter·view[1] /'ɪntəvju:/ *nc* 1 a meeting for discussion between employers and an applicant for a job. 2 a meeting of a reporter etc) with a person whose views are requested: *He refused to give any newspaper interviews*.

in·ter·view[2] /'ɪntəvju:/ *vt* to have an interview with (a person): *I was interviewed for the manager's job. She interviews many famous pop stars*.

in·ter·weave /ˌɪntə'wi:v/ *vt* (*pt* **-wove** /-'wəʊv/, *pp* **-woven** /-'wəʊvn/) to weave together (one with another).

in·tes·tate /ɪn'testeɪt/ *adj* (*pred; legal*) having not made a will before death occurs: *die intestate*.

in·tes·tine /ɪn'testɪn/ *nc* (usually *pl*) (*science*) the lower part of the food canal from below the stomach to the anus: *the small/large intestine*.

in·tes·ti·nal /ɪn'testɪnl/ *adj*

in·ti·ma·cy /'ɪntɪməsɪ/ *nu* (*formal*) **intimacy (with sb/sth)** the state of being intimate.

in·ti·mate[1] /'ɪntɪmət/ *adj* 1 close and familiar: *intimate friends*. 2 **be intimate (with sb)** to have sexual intercourse. 3 most private and personal: *the intimate details of one's life*. 4 resulting from close study or great familiarity: *an intimate knowledge of Greek*.

in·ti·mate·ly *adv*

in·ti·mate[2] /'ɪntɪmət/ *nc* (*formal*) a close friend.

in·ti·mate[3] /'ɪntɪmeɪt/ *vt* (*formal*) to make (one's opinion etc) known: *intimate one's approval*.

in·ti·ma·tion /ˌɪntɪ'meɪʃn/ *nc,nu*

in·timi·date /ɪn'tɪmɪdeɪt/ *vt* to make (a person) afraid in order to force her or him to do something: *intimidating a witness to make him change his evidence*.

in·timi·da·tion /ɪnˌtɪmɪ'deɪʃn/ *nu*

in·to /'ɪntə *strong form* 'ɪntu:/ *prep* (N) For uses with verbs such as come, get, go, inquire, look, run, settle, turn etc, ⇨ the verb entries. For the difference between *into* and *in to* (two words), ⇨ the *note* at in²(2). **1** (used of direction of motion or action) so as to be (towards the) inside: *She came into the house/put her hand into her pocket/got into her car/broke it into several pieces/fell into the water/ peeped into the room.* ⇨ in³(6). Ⓝ '*Into*' is most often used as the prepositional alternative to '*in*', as in *She went in/went into the library; The plane got in at six o'clock/got into the airport at six o'clock; They looked in and saw nothing/looked into the box and . . .* Compare onto. **2** (used of a change in arrangement, shape, condition etc): *get into a line/a circle/a mess; turn into a frog; burst into tears.* **3** so as to hit: *crash/drive into a wall.* **4** (*maths*) (used when dividing): *6 into 13 won't go* (i.e. there is 1 remaining). ⇨ also be into sth.

in·tol·er·able /ɪnˈtɒlərəbl/ *adj* that cannot be tolerated because too strong, painful etc: *intolerable heat/insolence.* Compare tolerable.

in·tol·er·ant /ɪnˈtɒlərənt/ *adj* not tolerant.
 in·tol·er·ant·ly *adv*
 in·tol·er·ance /-əns/ *nu*

in·ton·ation /ɪntəˈneɪʃn/ *nu* (*tech*) the rise and fall of the pitch of the voice in speaking.

in·toxi·cate /ɪnˈtɒksɪkeɪt/ *vt* (*formal*) **1** to cause (a person) to lose self-control as the result of taking alcoholic drink. **2** (*fig*) (usually *passive*) to excite (a person) greatly: *be intoxicated with joy.*
 in·toxi·ca·tion /ɪnˌtɒksɪˈkeɪʃn/ *nu*

in·tran·si·gent /ɪnˈtrænsɪdʒənt/ *adj* (*formal*) refusing to change one's opinion, esp about an important issue.

in·tran·si·tive /ɪnˈtrænsɪtɪv/ *adj* (*gram*) of an intransitive verb.
 in,transitive 'verb *nc* (*gram*) a verb used without a direct object, as in 'I *agree*'; 'they *quarrel*'; 'smoke *rises.*' Ⓝ Marked *vi* in this dictionary. Compare transitive verb.
 in·tran·si·tive·ly *adv*

in·tra·uter·ine /ˌɪntrəˈjuːtəraɪn/ *adj* (*tech*) (of a contraceptive device) placed in the uterus. ⇨ IUD.

in·tra·venous /ˌɪntrəˈviːnəs/ *adj* (*med*) into a vein or veins: *intravenous injections.*

in·trep·id /ɪnˈtrepɪd/ *adj* (*formal*) brave and fearless: *intrepid explorers.*
 in·trep·id·ly *adv*

in·tri·ca·cy /ˈɪntrɪkəsɪ/ *nc,nu* (*pl* **-ies**) (an example, instance, of) being intricate.

in·tri·cate /ˈɪntrɪkət/ *adj* **1** complicated: *an intricate pattern/arrangement.* **2** (of machinery etc) built with many parts and difficult to understand: *an intricate piece of machinery.*
 in·tri·cate·ly *adv*

in·trigue¹ /ˈɪntriːg/ *nc,nu* (an instance of) plotting secretly: *be involved in intrigue.*

in·trigue² /ɪnˈtriːg/ *v* **1** *vi* to make and carry out secret plans or plots: *intriguing with Smith against Robinson.* **2** *vt* to bring out the interest or curiosity of (a person): *The news intrigued all of us.*
 in·trigu·ing *adj* causing curiosity and interest: *an intriguing story.*
 in·trigu·ingly *adv*

in·trin·sic /ɪnˈtrɪnsɪk/ *adj* (of value, quality) belonging to, existing within, what is essential and natural (not caused or produced from outside): *a man's intrinsic worth.*
 in·trin·si·cal·ly /-klɪ/ *adv*

intro /ˈɪntrəʊ/ *abbr* (*informal*) introduction.

in·tro·duce /ˌɪntrəˈdjuːs/ *vt* **1** **introduce sb**

(**to sb**) to make a person known to another, usually by giving her or his name: *May I introduce John/my mother* (*to you*). *Allow me to introduce myself—I'm the new head teacher and my name is Miss Phitt.* **2** **introduce sth** (**into sth**) to bring something into use or operation for the first time: *introduce new ideas into a business.* **3** **introduce sth** (**to sb**) to give a person an experience of something (e.g. food, an idea, plan) for the first time: *introduce a man to British cooking.* **4** to bring (something) into an organization: *introduce a new computer system.* **5** **introduce sth** (**with sth**) to start a book, speech, report etc (with background information, an outline etc): *introduce a report with an account of past failures; introduce a television programme.*

in·tro·duc·tion /ˌɪntrəˈdʌkʃn/ *n* **1** *nu* the process of introducing or being introduced: *My next speaker needs no introduction. The introduction of a new system of accounting seems to have failed.* **2** *nc* an occasion of introducing people to one another. **3** *nc* an opening part of a letter, speech etc; explanatory article at or before the beginning of a book.

in·tro·duc·tory /ˌɪntrəˈdʌktərɪ/ *adj* that introduces(5): *introductory remarks; an introductory chapter.*

in·tro·spec·tion /ˌɪntrəˈspekʃn/ *nu* (*formal*) (the act of) examining one's own feelings and thoughts for a long time: *be lost in introspection.*
 in·tro·spec·tive /-tɪv/ *adj*

in·tro·vert /ˈɪntrəvɜːt/ *nc* **1** a person who is interested in her or his own thoughts and feelings than in things outside. **2** (*informal*) a quiet, antisocial person. Compare extrovert.
 in·tro·vert·ed *adj*

in·trude /ɪnˈtruːd/ *vt,vi* (to cause oneself, something) to enter when not invited or wanted: *I hope I'm not intruding.*
 in·truder *nc* (*derog*) a person or thing that intrudes, e.g. a burglar.

in·tru·sion /ɪnˈtruːʒn/ *nc,nu* **intrusion** (**on sb/ sth**) (an instance of) intruding: *Your questions are an intrusion on my privacy.*
 in·tru·sive /ɪnˈtruːsɪv/ *adj*
 in,trusive 'r' *nc* (*tech*) an 'r' with no grammatical or spelling justification, e.g. the r-sound often heard after *law* in '*law and order*'. /ˌlɔːr ən ˈɔːdə/.

in·tu·ition /ˌɪntjuːˈɪʃn/ *n* **1** *nu* (the power of) the immediate understanding of something without conscious reasoning or study: *My intuition tells me he's a liar. We had an intuition that you'd refuse.* **2** *nc* a piece of knowledge gained by this power.
 in·tu·itive /ɪnˈtjuːɪtɪv/ *adj*
 in·tu·itive·ly *adv*

in·un·date /ˈɪnʌndeɪt/ *vt* **inundate sb/sth** (**with sth**) (usually *passive*) to send a person, office etc large quantities as if flooding: *be inundated with requests for help.*
 in·un·da·tion /ˌɪnʌnˈdeɪʃn/ *nc,nu*

in·vade /ɪnˈveɪd/ *v* **1** *vt,vi* to enter (a country) with armed forces in order to attack. **2** *vt,vi* (*fig*) to crowd into (a place): *a city invaded by tourists.* **3** *vt* to interfere with (a person's rights etc): *invade her private life.* ⇨ invasion.
 in·vad·er *nc* a person who invades.

in·va·lid¹ /ɪnˈvælɪd/ *adj* not valid. ⇨ invalidate.

in·va·lid² /'ɪnvəlɪd/ adj **1** weak or disabled because of illness or injury: *invalid soldiers*. **2** (*attrib*) suitable for invalid persons: *an invalid chair/diet*.

in·va·lid³ /'ɪnvəliːd/ nc an invalid(2) person.

in·va·li·date /ɪn'vælɪdeɪt/ vt to make (a written agreement, guarantee etc) not valid.
  in·va·li·da·tion /ɪn,vælɪ'deɪʃn/ nc,nu

in·valu·able /ɪn'væljubl/ adj of a value too high to be measured: *Her services are invaluable to me*. Compare valuable.

in·vari·able /ɪn'veərɪəbl/ adj unchangeable; constant: *an invariable temperature*. Opp variable.
  in·vari·ably /-əblɪ/ adv usually; almost always: *She's invariably right*.

in·va·sion /ɪn'veɪʒn/ nc,nu (an instance of) invading or being invaded: *an invasion of privacy*.

in·vec·tive /ɪn'vektɪv/ nu (*formal*) angry, abusive language: *speeches filled with invective*.

in·vent /ɪn'vent/ vt **1** to make or design (something not existing before): *When was television invented?* Compare create(1), discover. **2** to make up, think of, (something) for the first time: *invent an excuse*. ⇨ inventive.
  in·ven·tor /-tə(r)/ nc a person who invents(1) something.

in·ven·tion /ɪn'venʃn/ n **1** nu the act, process, of inventing: *the invention of the telephone*. **2** nc something invented: *the many inventions of Edison*.

in·ven·tive /ɪn'ventɪv/ adj able to invent(2) easily; imaginative: *an inventive mind*.

in·ven·tory /'ɪnvəntrɪ/ nc (*pl* **-ies**) a detailed list, e.g. of household goods, furniture, stocks etc.

in·verse /ɪn'vɜːs/ adj (of) a reversed position or order: *The inverse of 'tops' is 'spot'*.
  in·verse·ly adv

in·ver·sion /ɪn'vɜːʃn/ n **1** nc,nu (an instance of) inverting or being inverted. **2** nc,nu (*gram*) a structure in which the verb is placed before its subject, as in 'Never *have I* seen such a mess!'

in·vert /ɪn'vɜːt/ vt to put (something) upside down or in the opposite position or order.
  in,verted 'commas nc (*lang*) = quotation marks.
  in,verted 'snobbery nu too much pride in being, or wanting to be, from a low social class.

in·vert·ebrate /ɪn'vɜːtɪbrət/ adj, nc (of) an animal without a backbone or spinal column, e.g. insects, worms. Compare vertebrate.

in·vest /ɪn'vest/ v **1** vt,vi **invest (money) (in sth)** to put (money) into a business etc: *invest £1000 in a business*. **2** vi **invest in sth** (*informal*) to buy something: *invest in a new hat*. **3** vt **invest sb (with sth)** (*formal*) (usually *passive*) to give a person (authority); decorate a person (with honours, medals): *be invested with the power to award degrees*.
  in·ves·tor /-tə(r)/ nc a person who puts money into a business etc.

in·ves·ti·gate /ɪn'vestɪgeɪt/ vt to examine, study, (something) carefully: *investigating a crime/the market for sales of a product*.
  in·ves·ti·ga·tion /ɪn,vestɪ'geɪʃn/ nc,nu
  in·ves·ti·ga·tor /-tə(r)/ nc an official who investigates accounts, legal matters etc.

in·ves·ti·ture /ɪn'vestɪtʃə(r)/ nc an official cer-

emony of investing a person with a rank, power etc.

in·vest·ment /ɪn'vestmənt/ n **1** nu the act of investing money: *careful investment of capital*. **2** nc a sum of money that is invested: *an investment of £1000*. **3** nc a business etc in which money is invested: *profitable investments*. **4** nc = investiture.

in·vet·er·ate /ɪn'vetərət/ adj (*attrib; formal*) (esp of habits, feelings) long-established: *She's an inveterate liar*.

in·vidi·ous /ɪn'vɪdɪəs/ adj (*attrib; formal*) likely to cause anger, envy, jealousy, (because of real or apparent injustice).
  in·vidi·ous·ly adv

in·vigi·late /ɪn'vɪdʒɪleɪt/ vi to watch over students during examinations.
  in·vigi·la·tion /ɪn,vɪdʒɪ'leɪʃn/ nu
  in·vigi·la·tor /-tə(r)/ nc a person who invigilates.

in·vig·or·ate /ɪn'vɪgəreɪt/ vt to give strength, energy or courage to (a person): *Your speech invigorated all of us*.
  in·vig·or·at·ing adj: *an invigorating climate*.

in·vin·cible /ɪn'vɪnsəbl/ adj too strong to be overcome or defeated: *an invincible will*.
  in·vin·cibly /-əblɪ/ adv

in·vis·ible /ɪn'vɪzəbl/ adj that cannot be seen: *stars that are invisible to the naked eye*. Opp visible.
  in,visible 'earnings n pl (*finance*) income from services (such as insurance) and not trade in goods. Compare visible earnings.
  in·visi·bil·ity /ɪn,vɪzə'bɪlətɪ/ nu
  in·vis·ibly /-əblɪ/ adv

in·vi·ta·tion /,ɪnvɪ'teɪʃn/ n **1** nu the act of inviting or being invited: *admission by invitation only*. **2** nc **invitation (from sb)(to sth)** a request to come or go somewhere, or do something: *send out invitations to a party*.

in·vite /ɪn'vaɪt/ vt **1** **invite sb (to sth/to do sth)** to ask (a person to do something, come somewhere etc): *invite a friend to one's house. We have all been invited*. **2** to encourage (something bad): *Don't leave the windows open—it's inviting theft*.
  in·vit·ing adj tempting; attractive: *an inviting smell of hot coffee*. Opp uninviting.

in·voice /'ɪnvɔɪs/ vt, nc (to prepare) a list of goods sold with the price(s) charged.

in·voke /ɪn'vəʊk/ vt **1** to call on (God, the power of the law etc) for help or protection. **2** to request (something) earnestly: *invoking revenge on one's enemies*. **3** to summon up (ghosts etc) (by magic): *invoke evil spirits*.

in·vol·un·tary /ɪn'vɒləntrɪ/ adj **1** done without a desire, thought or intention: *an involuntary response to fear*. **2** (of muscle, physical action) moving without conscious control: *involuntary muscles in the heart*. Compare voluntary(3).
  in·vol·un·tar·ily /ɪn'vɒləntrəlɪ/ adv

in·volve /ɪn'vɒlv/ vt **1** to have, include, (something) as necessary: *The training involves learning how to use a computer. What is involved if I agree to come? It involves a long journey by bus*. Ⓝ Not used in the continuous tenses, e.g. *is/was -ing*. **2** **involve sb/sth (in sth)** to cause a person, thing to take part (in trouble, a difficult situation etc):

Don't involve me in your quarrels. They are deeply involved in debt. **3** to have (something) as a necessary result: *The new design will involve a lot of extra work.*

in·volved *adj* (a) **involved (with sb)** joined in a serious (esp sexual) relationship. (b) complicated in form etc: *an involved sentence/style.*

in·volve·ment *nc,nu*

in·vul·ner·able /ɪn'vʌlnrəbl/ *adj* that cannot be wounded, hurt or attacked. Opp vulnerable.

in·ward /'ɪnwəd/ *adj* **1** situated on the inside; inner: *one's inward* (i.e. mental or spiritual) *nature.* **2** towards the inside: *an inward curve.* Opp outward.

in·ward·ly *adv* in mind or spirit: *suffer inwardly.* Compare outwardly.

in·wards /'ɪnwədz/ (also **in·ward**) *adv* towards the inside or middle: *point inwards.* Opp outwards.

iod·ine /'aɪədiːn/ *nu* a chemical substance widely used as an antiseptic, in photography etc.

ion /'aɪən/ *nc* (*electricity*) an electrically charged particle formed by losing or gaining electrons.

ion·ize (also **-ise**) /'aɪənaɪz/ *vt* to convert (a material) into ions.

iono·sphere /aɪ'ɒnəsfɪə(r)/ *n* (the —) (also known as the *Heaviside Layer*) a region of the earth's atmosphere, which reflects radio waves and causes them to follow the earth's shape.

iota /aɪ'əʊtə/ *nc* (*pl* **—s**) (usually **not an/one iota of sth**) an extremely small part: *not an iota of truth in the story.*

IOU /ˌaɪ əʊ 'juː/ *abbr* I owe you (a signed note stating that a person owes a certain amount of money).

IPA /ˌaɪ piː 'eɪ/ *abbr* International Phonetic Alphabet (as used in this dictionary).

IQ /ˌaɪ 'kjuː/ *abbr* Intelligence Quotient (a measure for comparing intelligence).

irate /aɪ'reɪt/ *adj* (*formal*) angry; causing anger: *an irate author/letter.*

ire /aɪə(r)/ *nu* (*poetic*) anger.

iri·des·cent /ˌɪrɪ'desnt/ *adj* (*tech*) showing colours like those of the rainbow.

iri·des·cence /ˌɪrɪ'desns/ *nu*

iris /'aɪərɪs/ *nc* **1** (*anat*) the coloured part round the pupil of the eye. **2** a kind of plant with a blue, yellow or white flower of three long petals and with long narrow leaves.

irk /ɜːk/ *vt* to annoy (a person).

irk·some /-səm/ *adj* annoying.

iron¹ /'aɪən/ *n* **1** *nu* the commonest metal (symbol Fe), used in manufacturing and building, and also forming an essential part of blood. **2** *nc* a flat-bottomed implement heated and used for smoothing clothes etc. **strike while the iron is hot** to act while conditions are in one's favour. **3** (*pl*) chains used for the ankles and wrists of a prisoner: *put him in irons.*

'Iron Age *n* (the —) the period in history when people used tools and weapons made of iron.

iron 'curtain *n* (the —) (also i- C-) the European frontier(s) that used to divide the former USSR and her allies from other countries.

iron 'lung *nc* (*med*) an apparatus fitted over the whole body, except the head, to provide artificial respiration.

'iron·mon·ger *nc* a dealer in metal and household goods.

'iron·mon·gery *nu* metal goods sold by an ironmonger (now usually called *hardware*).

iron 'rations *n pl* a store of food for use in an emergency as for troops or explorers.

iron² /'aɪən/ *vt,vi* to smooth (cloth, clothes etc) using an iron²: *She's been ironing all afternoon.* **iron sth out** (a) to remove something by ironing: *iron out wrinkles.* (b) (*fig*) to remove difficulties etc: *iron out misunderstandings.*

'iron·ing-board *nc* a long padded table, used to iron clothes etc.

iron·ic /aɪ'rɒnɪk/ (also **ironi·cal** /-kl/) *adj* of, using, expressing, irony: *an ironic smile.*

ironi·cal·ly /-klɪ/ *adv*

irony /'aɪərənɪ/ *n* (*pl* **ies**) **1** *nu* the act of expressing one's true opinion or intention by saying the opposite of one's thoughts in order to make one's remarks forceful, esp by praising and not blaming. **2** *nc* an event, situation etc which is itself desirable, but which, because of the circumstances, is of little or no value: *Inheriting a large fortune and dying a month later might be called one of life's ironies.*

ir·ra·tion·al /ɪ'ræʃənl/ *adj* **1** without the power to reason: *an irrational animal.* **2** absurd; not reasonable: *irrational fears/behaviour.* Opp rational.

ir,rational 'number *nc* (*maths*) any number that cannot be written using numbers, such as $\sqrt{17}$.

ir·ra·tion·al·ly *adv*

ir·rec·on·cil·able /ˌɪˌrekən'saɪləbl/ *adj* (of a person, opinions, plans etc) that cannot reach an agreement: *irreconcilable differences.* Opp reconcilable.

ir·re·cover·able /ˌɪrɪ'kʌvərəbl/ *adj* that cannot be recovered: *irrecoverable losses.*

ir·re·fut·able /ˌɪrɪ'fjuːtəbl/ *adj* that cannot be denied or proved false: *an irrefutable argument; irrefutable evidence.* Opp refutable.

ir·regu·lar /ɪ'regjʊlə(r)/ *adj* **1** contrary to rules, to what is normal and established: *an irregular request.* **2** not at the usual or equal intervals: *an irregular pulse; an irregular pattern.* **3** uneven; not regular in shape, arrangement, etc: *a coast with an irregular outline.* **4** (*gram*) (of words) not having the usual endings or forms: *'Child' has an irregular plural. 'Go' is an irregular verb.*

ir,regular 'verb *nc* (*gram*) a verb that does not have the usual forms for persons, tenses etc, such as *go, make, take.*

ir·regu·lar·ly *adv*

ir·regu·lar·ity /ˌɪˌregjʊ'lærətɪ/ *nc,nu*

ir·rel·evant /ɪ'reləvənt/ *adj* not to the point; having no relation or connection: *irrelevant remarks.* Compare relevant.

ir·re·li·gious /ˌɪrɪ'lɪdʒəs/ *adj* opposed to, showing no interest in, religion: *irreligious acts/people.*

ir·rep·ar·able /ɪ'reprəbl/ *adj* (of a loss, damage etc) that cannot be put right or restored. Opp reparable.

ir·re·place·able /ˌɪrɪ'pleɪsəbl/ *adj* too good, rare, special etc to be able to be replaced if lost, broken etc.

ir·re·proach·able /ˌɪrɪ'prəʊtʃəbl/ *adj* (*formal*) free from blame or fault: *irreproachable conduct/ politicians.*

ir·re·sist·ible /ˌɪrɪˈzɪstəbl/ adj too strong, convincing, delightful etc to be resisted: irresistible temptations.

ir·re·spec·tive /ˌɪrɪˈspektɪv/ adj **irrespective of** (prep) paying no attention to; regardless of (which is more usual): irrespective of the cost/danger. Compare respective.

ir·re·spon·sible /ˌɪrɪˈspɒnsəbl/ adj (esp) (doing things, done) without a proper sense of responsibility: irresponsible behaviour/people. Opp responsible(3).
  ir·re·spon·si·bil·ity /ˌɪrɪˌspɒnsəˈbɪlətɪ/ nu

ir·re·triev·able /ˌɪrɪˈtriːvəbl/ adj that cannot be retrieved or remedied: an irretrievable loss.

ir·rev·er·ence /ɪˈrevərəns/ nu the state of being irreverent.

ir·rev·er·ent /ɪˈrevərənt/ adj feeling or showing no respect for sacred things. Opp reverent.
  ir·rev·er·ent·ly adv

ir·re·vers·ible /ˌɪrɪˈvɜːsəbl/ adj that cannot be reversed or revoked: an irreversible decision. Compare reversible(a).

ir·revo·cable /ɪˈrevəkəbl/ adj final and unalterable: an irrevocable legal decision.

ir·ri·gate /ˈɪrɪɡeɪt/ vt to supply (land, crops) with water (by using rivers, pipes etc): irrigate desert areas to make them fertile.
  ir·ri·ga·tion /ˌɪrɪˈɡeɪʃn/ nu

ir·ri·table /ˈɪrɪtəbl/ adj easily annoyed or made angry.
  ir·ri·tably /-əblɪ/ adv
  ir·ri·ta·bil·ity /ˌɪrɪtəˈbɪlətɪ/ nu

ir·ri·tant /ˈɪrɪtənt/ adj, nc (of) an irritating substance.

ir·ri·tate /ˈɪrɪteɪt/ vt **1** to cause small but frequent feelings of anger or annoyance: I was irritated at/by the delays; irritated with her silly jokes; irritated to discover that it wasn't ready. **2** to cause discomfort to (part of the body): The smoke irritated her eyes.
  ir·ri·tat·ing adj: irritating delays; an irritating voice.
  ir·ri·ta·tion /ˌɪrɪˈteɪʃn/ nc, nu

is ⇨ be¹.

Is written abbr island.

Is·lam /ˈɪzlɑːm/ n the faith, religion, proclaimed by the Prophet Muhammad; all Muslims; all the Muslim world.
  Is·lam·ic /ɪzˈlæmɪk/ adj

is·land /ˈaɪlənd/ nc **1** a piece of land surrounded by water. **2** something like an island because it is detached, separate or isolated. ⇨ traffic island.
  is·land·er nc a person born, living, on an island.

isle /aɪl/ nc an island (not much used except in names): the British Isles.

is·let /ˈaɪlɪt/ nc (tech) a small island.

isn't /ˈɪznt/ = is not. ⇨ be¹.

iso·bar /ˈaɪsəʊbɑː(r)/ nc (tech) a line on a map joining places with the same atmospheric pressure at a particular time.

iso·late /ˈaɪsəleɪt/ vt to put or keep (a person, thing) apart from others: isolating the infected children.
  iso·lat·ed adj far from others: an isolated house/incident.
  iso·la·tion /ˌaɪsəˈleɪʃn/ nu (a) the state of isolating or being isolated: A country's policy of isolation means deliberately not being involved in

international political or economic affairs. (b) **in isolation** without an interest in other opinions, facts, people etc: live in isolation; act in isolation from the rest of the committee.

isos·celes /aɪˈsɒsɪliːz/ adj (maths) (of a triangle) having two sides equal.

iso·therm /ˈaɪsəʊθɜːm/ nc (tech) a line on a map joining places having the same average temperature.

iso·tope /ˈaɪsəʊtəʊp/ nc (science) a form of a chemical element having a nuclear mass different from other forms of the same element: radioactive isotopes.

is·sue¹ /ˈɪʃuː/ n **1** nu the act of sending, flowing, giving, out something: an issue of blood/free booklets. **2** nc a set of things (stamps, books, coins etc) produced and sent out for sale: the latest issue of a magazine. **3** nc an important question that needs discussion and a decision: political/social issues. **at issue** (a) disagreeing: They have been at issue for years. (b) needing discussion: The point at issue here is . . . **force the issue** to make a decision about something essential: His refusal to lend the money without her agreement should force the issue. **take issue (with sb)** (formal) to discuss a disagreement (with a person): I'd like to take issue with you on that point. **4** nc a result; consequence: await the issue of the enquiry. **5** nu (legal) children: die without issue. **6** nc (legal) a question to be settled in court.

is·sue² /ˈɪʃuː/ n **1** vt, vi **issue (from/out of sth)** to come, go, flow, out: blood issuing from a wound. **2** vt **issue sth (to sb)/sb with sth** to distribute (something) for use: issue travel tickets to the passengers; issue passengers with tickets. **3** vt to publish (books etc). **4** vt to put (stamps, banknotes etc) into circulation.

isth·mus /ˈɪsməs/ n (pl —es) (tech) a long, narrow piece of land joining two larger areas of land: the Isthmus of Panama.

it /ɪt/ pron (3rd person sing as subject or object) (pl: subject **they** /ðeɪ/, object **them** /ðəm/; possessive **its** /ɪts/ (pl **their** /ðeə(r)/); reflexive **itself** /ɪtˈself/) ⓝ For the difference between 'it's' and 'its', ⇨ its. For uses of 'it' in phrases such as be for it, come off it, hit it off, live it up, run for it, sleep on it etc, ⇨ the verb entries. **1** (used of a lifeless thing, or of an animal or a baby when the sex is unknown or unimportant) the thing mentioned: It has a wooden top. It's green and hairy. It was here on the table this morning. We can mend it. I've stopped writing the exam because I can't do it. What's it for? 'Where's the cat?'—'It's in the garden.' She's had the baby, and it's a girl. **2** (used to identify a person, thing etc): 'Who is it?'—'It's the postman.' 'What was that noise?'—'It was the wind.' ⓝ 'There is . . . ' is also used for identity, as in There is someone at the door. Is there anyone at home? **3** (used as the subject of a sentence with the verb be, esp describing weather, time etc): It is hot. It's raining/snowing. It was six o'clock. It's Monday 16 August. It's late/early. Is it far? It's a month since I saw her. It was my first visit for 10 years. ⓝ 'There is + noun', as in There is snow can be used for 'It is + adj', as in It is snowing, but not for dates or time, i.e. not for It is Monday/8 o'clock. **4** (used to emphasize part of a sentence): It was John I gave the book to, not Harry. It was Mary who said that.

It was in China that we first met. **5 (a)** (used as a grammatical subject to begin a sentence, referring to the real subject which follows): *It's nice to see you* (= To see you is nice). *Is it difficult to learn Russian? It doesn't matter if you come later. It's cold swimming in winter.* Ⓝ *'It'* used in this way is called the 'preparatory subject'. **(b)** (used as a grammatical object referring to the real object which is an infinitive or a clause beginning *that*): *We found it easy to get to the station.* (= To get to the station was easy for us). *She considers it important that I sit the exam.* Ⓝ *'It'* used in this way is called the 'preparatory object'. An adjective always follows *'it'* in these constructions. **6** (used as a grammatical subject for impersonal verbs such as *appear, look, seem* etc): *It looks as if we'll lose the game. It sounds as if she'll forgive you. It seems that you have won the prize.* **7** (exactly) what is needed or wanted: *That's (not) it. I've got it* (= I've remembered or understood)—*the policeman carried out the murder.* **8** (*informal*) the end: *Well, that's it—there's nothing left. I drove into a tree and that was almost it. This is it this time because we have no chance to pay off the loan.*

ital *written abbr* italics.

ital·ic /ɪˈtælɪk/ *adj* (of printed letters) sloping: *This is italic type.* □ *n (pl)* italic letters.

itch¹ /ɪtʃ/ *n* **1** *n sing* a feeling of irritation on the skin, causing a desire to scratch: *have/feel an itch.* **2** *nc* (*fig*) a restless desire or longing: *I've always had an itch to travel.*

itch² /ɪtʃ/ *vi* **1** to have an itch(1): *scratch where it itches.* **2** *itch for/to do sth* to have a strong desire to do it: *itching to go on holiday.*

itchy *adj* (**-ier, -iest**)

it'd /ˈɪtəd/ = *it had; it would.*

item /ˈaɪtəm/ *nc* **1** a single article or unit in a list etc: *items of clothing; the first item on the programme.* **2** a piece (of news): *interesting news items/items of news.*

item·ize (also **-ise**) /-aɪz/ *vt* to give, write, every detail or unit of (something): *an itemized account.*

itin·er·ant /aɪˈtɪnərənt/ *adj* (*attrib; formal*) travelling from place to place: *itinerant circus performers.*

itin·er·ary /aɪˈtɪnərəri/ *nc* (*pl* **-ies**) a plan for, details of, a journey.

it'll /ˈɪtl/ = *it will.*

it's /ɪts/ = *it is; it has.*

its /ɪts/ *det, pron* (*possessive* form of *it*) of, belonging to, it(1): *Look at that bird—it has broken its wing/its wing is broken.* Ⓝ Be careful because *'its'* is not the same as *'it's'.* *'It's'* is a short way of speaking and writing *'it is'* or *'it has'.* Although an apostrophe is used with words to show possession, as in *the bird's wing,* the apostrophe is not used in *its.*

it·self /ɪtˈself/ *pron* (*pl* **themselves** /ðəmˈselvz/) **1** (used as the *reflexive* form of *it*): *My dog has hurt itself. The community ought to be ashamed of itself.* **(all) by itself** ⇨ **by²**(1). **2** (used for emphasis): *The ring itself isn't valuable but I like it.* **in itself** considered separately from related facts, qualities, effects etc: *Power in itself need not be harmful but it so often leads to abuse. If you treat money as an end in itself it will only bring you unhappiness.* **3** its usual self: *The cat isn't itself/doesn't seem itself today.*

ITV /ˌaɪ tiː ˈviː/ *abbr* Independent Television (i.e.

not State-financed).

IUD /ˌaɪ juː ˈdiː/ *abbr* intrauterine device. ⇨ coil²(3).

I've /aɪv/ = *I have.*

ivory /ˈaɪvəri/ *adj, nu* **1** (of) the white substance forming the tusks of elephants. **2** (of) its colour.

ivy /ˈaɪvi/ *nu* a kind of climbing, evergreen plant with dark, shiny leaves.

Jj

J, j /dʒeɪ/ (*pl* **J's, j's** /dʒeɪz/) the tenth letter of the English alphabet.

J *symbol* (*science*) joule(s).

jab¹ /dʒæb/ *nc* **1** a sudden push (with something long and narrow): *a jab with a finger/umbrella.* **2** (*informal*) an injection: *tetanus jabs.*

jab² /dʒæb/ *vt, vi* (**-bb-**) to push (something) (with something long and narrow): *He jabbed at the lid with a knife. She jabbed her elbow into my side. Don't jab my eye out with your umbrella!*

jab·ber /ˈdʒæbə(r)/ *vt, vi* to talk excitedly or in a confused manner: *The frightened boy jabbered an excuse. Listen to those children jabbering away!* □ *nu* an instance of talking like this: *the jabber of monkeys.*

jack¹ /dʒæk/ *nc* **1** an apparatus used for raising a car off the ground so that a wheel may be changed. **2** a playing-card between 10 and the Queen in value: *the jack of clubs.*

Jack 'Frost *n* frost considered as a person.

Jack of 'all trades *nc* a person who has many skills.

jack² /dʒæk/ *vt* **jack sth (up)** to lift a vehicle with a jack(1): *I jacked (up) the car and changed the wheel.*

jack·al /ˈdʒækl/ *nc* a kind of wild animal like a dog.

jack·ass /ˈdʒækæs/ *nc* **1** a male ass. **2** (*dated; derog*) a foolish person.

jack·daw /ˈdʒækdɔː/ *nc* a bird of the crow family (noted for flying off with small bright objects).

jack·et /ˈdʒækɪt/ *nc* **1** a short coat with sleeves. **2** an outer covering round a tank, pipe etc. **3** a skin (of a potato): *potatoes baked in their jackets.* **4** (also *dust-jacket*) a paper cover for a book.

ˌjacket po'tato *nc* a potato baked in its skin.

jack-knife¹ /ˈdʒæk naɪf/ *nc* (*pl* **-knives**) a large pocket-knife with a folding blade.

jack-knife² /ˈdʒæk naɪf/ *vi* (esp of an articulated vehicle) to bend where the driver's area is joined to the carrier, e.g. when out of control.

jack·pot /ˈdʒækpɒt/ *nc* large prize in various games, increasing in value until won.

jade /dʒeɪd/ *adj, nu* **1** (of) a kind of hard green stone, carved into ornaments etc. **2** (of) its colour, bright green.

jad·ed /ˈdʒeɪdɪd/ *adj* worn out; tired and overworked: *She looks jaded.*

jag·ged /ˈdʒægɪd/ *adj* having rough, uneven edges: *jagged rocks.*

jag·uar /ˈdʒægjʊə(r)/ *nc* a large spotted animal of the cat family, found in Central and South America.

jail /dʒeɪl/ *nc, vt* = gaol.

jam¹ /dʒæm/ *nu* fruit boiled with sugar until it is thick, eaten esp on bread.

'**jam·jar** *nc* a glass jar for jam.

'**jam·pot** *nc* a pot for jam.

jam² /dʒæm/ *nc* **1** a number of people or things crowded together so that movement is difficult or impossible: *a traffic jam; a jam of shoppers at Christmas.* **2** a condition of a machine when parts cannot move because of a fault: *a jam in the engine.* **3** *be in/get into a jam* (*informal*) to be in/get into difficulty; be in a difficult situation: *I'm in a bit of a jam—my handbag has been stolen.*

jam³ /dʒæm/ *v* (**-mm-**) **1** *vt jam sb/sth into sth* to push people, things into a vehicle, container etc: *jam clothes into a suitcase; jam passengers into a bus.* **2** *vt, vi* (to cause parts of a machine, apparatus etc) to be unable to move because of a fault. *The handle has jammed and I can't open the door. This tool had jammed.* **3** *vt* (of people, things) to block (something) so that movement is difficult or impossible: *Children jammed the entrance to the funfair. Cars were jamming the roads near the city area. Hundreds of callers were jamming the telephone lines to the airport after the plane crash.* **4** *vt jam on sth* to push suddenly and forcefully to make (car brakes) go on: *When I saw the child crossing the road I jammed on my brakes.* **5** *vt* to prevent (a radio programme) from being heard by using a noise to interfere: *The enemy's radio was jammed during the war.*

jam·boree /ˌdʒæmbəˈriː/ *nc* **1** a merry meeting. **2** a large gathering of Scouts.

jam-pack·ed /ˌdʒæm ˈpækt/ *adj jam-packed (with sb/sth)* (*informal*) filled (with): *a book jam-packed with useful information; a school jam-packed with intelligent children.*

Jan *written abbr* January.

jangle /ˈdʒæŋgl/ *vt, vi* (to cause something) to make an unpleasant metallic noise. □ *nu* this noise.

Jan·uary /ˈdʒænjʊərɪ/ *n* (abbr **Jan**) the first month of the year, with 31 days: *I was born on 3 January.* Ⓝ '*3 January'* is spoken as *'January the third'* or *'the third of January'.

jar¹ /dʒɑː(r)/ *nc* an unpleasant (usually a harsh) sound or vibration: *We felt a jar when the train started to move.*

jar² /dʒɑː(r)/ *nc* (the contents of) a container made of glass, stone etc with a wide mouth: *a jar of jam; a jamjar.*

jar·ful /-fʊl/ *nc* as much as a jar can hold.

jar³ /dʒɑː(r)/ *v* (**-rr-**) **1** *vt, vi jar (on sb/sth)* (to cause something) to make an unpleasant sound; have an unpleasant effect (on one's feelings): *The way he laughs jars on my nerves.* **2** *vi jar (with sth)* to disagree, not be suitable (with): *The two patterns jar. His opinions jar with mine.*

jar·ring *adj*

jar·gon /ˈdʒɑːgən/ *nu* a style of a language full of technical or special words: *scientific jargon.*

jaun·dice /ˈdʒɔːndɪs/ *nu* **1** a disease marked by yellowness of the skin and the whites of the eyes. **2** (*fig*) a state of mind in which one is jealous, spiteful, envious and suspicious.

jaun·diced /ˈdʒɔːndɪst/ *adj* **1** suffering from jaundice(1). **2** having, showing, bad judgement because of prejudice or suspicion(2): *have a jaun-*diced opinion of her.

jaunt /dʒɔːnt/ *vi, nc* (to make) a short journey for pleasure.

jaun·ty /ˈdʒɔːntɪ/ *adj* (**-ier, -iest**) feeling, showing, self-confidence and self-satisfaction: *feeling jaunty.*

jaunt·ily /-əlɪ/ *adv*

jav·elin /ˈdʒævlɪn/ *nc* (also *attrib*) a light spear used for throwing (in sport): *a javelin thrower.*

jaw¹ /dʒɔː/ *nc* **1** either of the bone structures (*lower* and *upper jaw*) containing the teeth. **2** (*pl*) the parts of a tool, machine, etc between which things are gripped or crushed. **3** (*fig*) something like jaws(1): *the jaws of death.*

jaw² /dʒɔː/ *vi jaw (away)* (*informal*) to talk boringly for a long time.

jay /dʒeɪ/ *nc* a kind of noisy European bird with brightly coloured feathers.

'**jay-walker** *nc* a person who walks across a street at an unauthorized place.

jazz¹ /dʒæz/ *nu* popular music first played by Black groups in the southern USA in the early 20th century, characterized by improvisation and strong rhythms (called *traditional jazz*); similar music played by large bands for dancing; a later variation much influenced by the *blues* to produce an unhurried emotive style (called *modern jazz*).

'**jazz-band** *nc* a group of musicians playing jazz.

jazzy *adj* (**-ier, -iest**) (*informal*) (**a**) of or like jazz. (**b**) showy: *a jazzy sports car.*

jazz² /dʒæz/ *v* **1** *vi* to play, arrange, music in the style of jazz. **2** *vt jazz sth up* to make something more lively, bright etc: *jazz up a party; jazz up a room with brightly coloured cushions.*

JC *written abbr* Jesus Christ.

JCR /ˌdʒeɪ siː ˈɑːr/ *abbr* Junior Common Room (a place where students can relax in a university college). ⇨ SCR.

jeal·ous /ˈdʒeləs/ *adj* **1** feeling, showing, a wish to be unkind because one does not trust a partner or believes one is being cheated: *a jealous husband.* **2** *jealous of sb/sth* feeling, showing, unhappiness and a wish to be unkind because of another person's success, better luck, wealth etc: *jealous of their riches/her promotion/ his ability.* Compare envious. **3** *jealous of sth* (*formal*) determined to protect one's own rights, position, power etc: *We're jealous of our political freedom.*

jeal·ous·ly *adv*

jeal·ousy *n* (*pl* **-ies**) *nc, nu* (an instance, example, of) feeling jealous(1,2): *a child's jealousy of his schoolfriends.* Compare envy¹(1).

jeans /dʒiːnz/ *n pl* trousers (usually made of blue denim) worn informally.

jeep /dʒiːp/ *nc* a small vehicle designed for use over rough ground.

jeer /dʒɪə(r)/ *vi, vt jeer (at sb/sth)* to make fun of, laugh rudely (at): *a jeering crowd.* □ *nc* a jeering remark.

jeer·ing·ly *adv*

Je·ho·vah /dʒɪˈhəʊvə/ *n* the name of God used in the Old Testament.

jell (also **gel**) /dʒel/ *vi* **1** (*informal*) to take shape: *My ideas are beginning to jell.* **2** to set into a jelly.

jel·ly /ˈdʒelɪ/ (*pl* **-ies**) *nc, nu* **1** (a portion of) semi-solid food flavoured with fruit and often eaten with ice-cream. **2** any semi-solid substance.

'**jelly·fish** *nc* (*pl* unchanged) a kind of sea creature like jelly, with long tentacles.

jeop·ard·ize (also **-ise**) /'dʒepədaɪz/ *vt* to put (a person, chance etc) in a dangerous position: *jeopardize one's future by failing the exams.*

jeop·ardy /'dʒepədɪ/ *nu* **in jeopardy** in danger of losing, being injured or killed, failing etc: *His place in the football team is in jeopardy. His behaviour has put him in jeopardy of being dismissed.*

jerk¹ /dʒɜːk/ *nc* **1** a sudden push, pull, start, stop, twist, lift or throw: *The train stopped with a jerk.* **2** a sudden involuntary twitch of a muscle. **3** (*pl;* usually *physical jerks*) (*informal*) physical exercises.

jer·ky *adj* (**-ier, -iest**) with jerks: *a jerky ride in an old bus.*

jerk² /dʒɜːk/ *v* **1** *vi* to move with a jerk: *The car jerked to a halt at the corner.* **2** *vt* to pull, push, twist etc suddenly: *He jerked off the lid with a knife.*

jer·kin /'dʒɜːkɪn/ *nc* a short, sleeveless jacket (as worn by men in olden times).

jer·sey /'dʒɜːzɪ/ *n* (*pl* **—s**) **1** *nu* (also *jersey-wool*) a kind of soft knitted fabric used for clothes. **2** *nc* a jumper knitted with jersey-wool. **3** *nc* (J-) a cow of the breed that originally came from Jersey, one of the *Channel Islands* (near the French coast).

jest /dʒest/ *nc* a joke. **in jest** as a joke. □ *vi* to make jokes: *He's not a man to jest with.*

jes·ter /'dʒestə(r)/ *nc* a person who jests, esp (in olden times) a man paid to make jokes to amuse the court or nobles.

jet¹ /dʒet/ *adj, nu* (made of) a kind of hard, black, highly polished mineral.

jet 'black *adj* deep, glossy black.

jet² /dʒet/ *nc* **1** a fast, strong stream (of gas, liquid, steam or flame) forced out of a small opening: *a jet of water.* **2** a narrow opening from which a jet(1) comes out: *a gas jet.* **3** = jet plane.

jet 'engine *nc* one that is used to propel an aircraft by sending out gases in jets(1) at the back.

jet 'plane/'aircraft *nc* one operated by jet engines.

jet pro'pulsion *nu* a method of producing movement using jets(1) of air or water.

'jet set *n pl* (the —) the wealthy people who often travel in jet planes.

jet³ /dʒet/ *v* (**-tt-**) **1** *vt,vi* (to cause water etc) to come out as a jet(1). **2** *vi* **jet (about/around)** (*informal*) to travel in a jet plane.

jet·sam /'dʒetsəm/ *nu* goods thrown overboard from a ship at sea to lighten it, e.g. in a storm.

jet·ti·son /'dʒetɪsn/ *vt* to abandon, throw away, (what is unwanted).

jet·ty /'dʒetɪ/ *nc* (*pl* **-ies**) a long structure built on the edge of water, e.g. as a landing-place for ships and boats.

Jew /dʒuː/ *n* a person whose family comes from the ancient land of Israel and who now has religious and cultural links with other Jews throughout the world. ⇨ **Judaism.**

Jew·ish *adj*

jew·el /'dʒuːəl/ *nc* **1** a precious stone, such as a diamond, emerald or ruby. **2** (*pl*) ornaments of jewels(1) in gold, silver etc, worn on clothes etc. **3** (*fig*) a highly valued person or thing: *His wife is a jewel.*

jew·el·ler (*US* = **jew·el·er**) /'dʒuːələ(r)/ *nc* a

person who buys and sells jewels.

jew·el·lery, jew·el·ry *nu* jewels(2).

jib¹ /dʒɪb/ *nc* **1** a sail in front of the mast on a sailing boat. **2** a long arm of a crane.

jib² /dʒɪb/ *vi* (**-bb-**) **1** (of a horse, etc) to stop suddenly; refuse to go forwards. **2** **jib at sth** (*fig*) to show unwillingness to do it: *He jibbed at working overtime.*

jibe /dʒaɪb/ *vi* = gibe.

jif·fy /'dʒɪfɪ/ *nc* (*pl* **-ies**) (*informal*) a moment: *I won't be a jiffy.* **in a jiffy** soon: *I'll be with you in a jiffy.*

jig¹ /dʒɪg/ *nc* **1** (music for) a kind of quick, lively dance. **2** an apparatus that holds a piece of work and guides the tools that are used on it.

jig² /dʒɪg/ *v* (**-gg-**) **1** *vi* to dance a jig. **2** *vt,vi* (to cause a person, thing) to move up and down with short, quick movements: *jigging up and down in excitement.*

jig·saw /'dʒɪgsɔː/ *nc* (also *jigsaw puzzle*) a picture, map etc on cardboard or wood and cut in shaped pieces which are to be fitted together again.

ji·had /dʒɪ'hɑːd/ *nc* a religious war by Muslims against unbelievers.

jilt /dʒɪlt/ *vt* to give up, send away, (a person) after giving her or him encouragement or a promise to marry: *When he lost his job, she jilted him.*

jingle¹ /'dʒɪŋgl/ *nc* **1** a metallic ringing sound (as of coins, keys or small bells). **2** a short and simple phrase or poem, esp with a simple tune, that is easily remembered: *advertising jingles.*

jingle² /'dʒɪŋgl/ *vt,vi* (to cause things) to make a light, ringing sound: *He was jingling his keys.*

jinks /dʒɪŋks/ *n* (only in) **'high jinks** (*informal*) noisy merrymaking; uncontrolled fun.

jinx /dʒɪŋks/ *nc* (*sl*) a person, thing, that brings bad luck.

jit·ters /'dʒɪtəz/ *n pl* (the —) (*sl*) extreme nervousness: *give her/have/get the jitters.*

jit·tery /'dʒɪtərɪ/ *adj* nervous; frightened.

jive /dʒaɪv/ *nc* (1950's) a style of popular music with a strong beat; dancing to this. □ *vi* to dance to this music.

Jnr *written abbr* (also **Jr, Jun.**) junior.

job /dʒɒb/ *nc* **1** a piece of work: *Have you got any jobs for me to do?* **odd jobs** bits of work not connected with one another. **an odd-job man** one who makes a living by doing any work he is asked to do. **make a good/fine/poor etc job of sth** to do it well/badly. **2** (*informal*) employment; position: *He has lost his job.* **be out of a job** to be unemployed. **hold a job down** to keep one's job by doing it satisfactorily: *That man never seems to hold a job down for long.* **3** **a good job** a fortunate state of affairs: *He lost his seat in Parliament, and a good job, too!* **make the best of a bad job** ⇨ best³(3). **4** **be/have a (hard) job doing/to do sth** to be/have (great) difficulty. **5** **a job lot** a collection of various articles, bought together. **6** (*informal*) **just the job** exactly what is wanted: *This tool is just the job.* **7** **do a job** (*sl*) to do something dishonest, e.g. steal.

jock·ey¹ /'dʒɒkɪ/ *nc* (*pl* **—s**) a professional rider in horse-races. ⇨ also disc jockey.

jock·ey² /'dʒɒkɪ/ *vt,vi* **1** **jockey for sth** to try to get an advantage by pushing, cheating etc: *jockeying for position on the committee.* **2**

jockey sb out of sth to force a person to lose a position, esp by cheating: *He jockeyed Green out of his job.*

jo·cose /dʒə'kəʊs/ *adj* (*formal*) humorous.

jocu·lar /'dʒɒkjʊlə(r)/ *adj* (*formal*) funny.
jocu·lar·ly *adv*
jocu·lar·ity /ˌdʒɒkjʊ'lærətɪ/ *nc,nu*

joc·und /'dʒɒkənd/ *adj* (*formal*) merry; cheerful.
joc·und·ity /dʒəʊ'kʌndətɪ/ *nc,nu*

jodh·purs /'dʒɒdpəz/ *n pl* (also *a pair of jodh-purs*) breeches for horse-riding, close-fitting from the knee to the ankle.

jog¹ /dʒɒg/ *nc* **1** a slight push, shake etc: *a jog with an elbow.* **2** an act, instance, of jogging(3): *go for a jog.*

jog² /dʒɒg/ *v* (**-gg-**) **1** *vt,vi* to give a slight push or shake to (something): *jog up and down on a horse. He jogged my elbow.* **jog sb's memory** to (try to) make a person remember something. **2** *vi* **jog along/on** to make slow, patient progress: *We jogged along the bad roads.* **3** *vi* (of a person) to run slowly (esp for exercise). **4** *vi* (of a horse) to trot.

joie de vivre /ˌʒwɑː də 'viːvrə/ *nu* (*Fr*) carefree enjoyment of life.

join¹ /dʒɔɪn/ *nc* a place where two or more things have been joined together: *Can you see the join in this cloth?*

join² /dʒɔɪn/ *v* **1** *vt,vi* to unite; connect (two points, things) with a line, rope, bridge etc: *join one thing to another; join two things together.* **join hands** (of several people) to hold each other's hands. **join forces (with sb/sth)** to unite in action; work together. **2** *vi* to come together: *Parallel lines never join.* **3** *vt,vi* to become a member of (something): *join the army.* **4** *vt* to meet, associate with, (a person) as a friend, to do something together etc: *I'll join you in a few minutes.* **join in (sth)** to take part in (a meeting, singing, an activity etc): *Who invited you to join in? I'd like you to join in the last line of the song. I don't want to join in with the other people at the hotel.* **join sth on/sth onto sth** to attach or fix something (smaller) to another thing: *joining a handle onto a cup with glue.* **join together** (of several people) to act as a group to do something: *Let's all join together and shout for help.* **join (sth) together** to glue, sew, stick etc parts of something to make a complete object: *How does this model boat join together?* **join up** (*mil*) to become a member of the armed forces. **join up (with sb/sth)** to meet and unite (with a person or another part of a system): *Where do the roads join up? We hope to join up with the other tourists at the station.*

join·er /'dʒɔɪnə(r)/ *nc* a skilled worker who makes the inside woodwork of buildings etc.
join·ery *nu* the work of a joiner.

joint¹ /dʒɔɪnt/ *adj* (*attrib*) held or done by, belonging to, two or more people together: *joint responsibility.*
ˌjoint 'bank account, ˌjoint account *nc* a bank account in the name of more than one person, e.g. a husband and wife.
ˌjoint-'stock company *nc* a group of people who carry on a business with money contributed by all.
joint·ly *adv*

joint² /dʒɔɪnt/ *nc* **1** a place, line or surface at which two or more things are joined (esp bones): *a knee/elbow joint; have aching joints.* **put sb's nose out of joint** ⇨ nose¹(1). **2** a piece (esp from a shoulder, leg) of meat. **3** (*sl*) a place for gambling, drinking or drug-taking. **4** (*sl*) a cigarette containing a drug.

joint³ /dʒɔɪnt/ *vt* **1** to provide (an object) with a joint(1): *a jointed doll.* **2** to divide (meat) into joints(2).

joist /dʒɔɪst/ *nc* **1** one of the pieces of wood (from wall to wall) to which floors are fastened. **2** a steel bar supporting a floor or ceiling.

joke¹ /dʒəʊk/ *nc* something said or done to cause amusement. **be no joke** to be serious: *Your bad behaviour is no joke.* **beyond a joke** no longer fun, a game: *This game is going beyond a joke—someone will get hurt if you continue.* **cap a joke** to tell a better one. **carry a joke too far** to carry out a practical joke until it is no longer amusing. **crack a joke** to tell one. **play a joke on sb** to make a person the victim of a joke. **see the joke** to understand a joke; understand why something is funny: *I don't see the joke.* **take a joke** (usually *negative*) to accept a joke, trick on oneself: *She can't take a joke—she gets very angry if you tease her.* ⇨ practical joke.

joke² /dʒəʊk/ *vi* to make jokes: *I was only joking when I said that.* **joking apart** being serious: *Joking apart, I can't live with that ugly furniture any longer.*
jok·ing·ly *adv* in a joking manner.

jo·ker /'dʒəʊkə(r)/ *nc* **1** a person who is fond of making jokes. **2** an extra playing-card with the highest value, used in some games.

jol·ly¹ /'dʒɒlɪ/ *adj* (**-ier, -iest**) (*dated*) joyful; gay; merry.

jol·ly² /'dʒɒlɪ/ *adv* (*dated*) very: *Take jolly good care of it!*

jol·ly³ /'dʒɒlɪ/ *vt* (*pt,pp* **-ied**) **jolly sb along** to keep a person in a good humour (esp in order to win her or his cooperation).

jolt¹ /dʒəʊlt/ *nc* a sudden rough shake.

jolt² /dʒəʊlt/ *v* **1** *vt,vi* (to cause a person, thing) to shake roughly: *The bus jolted along. I was almost jolted onto the floor.* **2** *vt* **jolt sb out of sth** to cause a person suddenly to wake up, to stop thinking or believing something: *The noise of the telephone jolted her out of her sleep. What do I have to say to jolt you out of your ridiculous belief that you do not have to work hard?*

jostle /'dʒɒsl/ *vt,vi* to push (a person) roughly: *We were jostled by the crowd.*

jot¹ /dʒɒt/ *nc* a small amount: *not a jot of truth in it* (= no truth at all).

jot² /dʒɒt/ *vt* (**-tt-**) **jot sth down** to make a quick written note of it: *jot down my name and address.*
ˈjot·ter *nc* a notebook for rough notes.
ˈjot·tings *n pl* notes jotted down.

joule /dʒuːl/ *nc* (symbol J) (*science*) the unit of measurement for energy or work. ⇨ calorie.

jour·nal /'dʒɜːnl/ *nc* **1** a weekly or monthly magazine on a specialist subject: *the Economic Journal.* **2** a daily record of news, events, business accounts etc.

jour·nal·ese /ˌdʒɜːnə'liːz/ *nu* the style of a language used by some journalists.

jour·nal·ism /'dʒɜːnəlɪzəm/ *nu* the work of writing for, editing or publishing newspapers, magazines and journals.

jour·nal·ist /'dʒɜːnəlɪst/ nc a professional person who works in journalism.

jour·nal·is·tic /ˌdʒɜːnə'lɪstɪk/ adj of (the language of) journalism.

jour·ney[1] /'dʒɜːnɪ/ nc (pl —s) (the distance travelled by) going to a place, esp a distant place: go on a journey round the world.

jour·ney[2] /'dʒɜːnɪ/ vi **journey to a place** (formal) to travel (the usual word).

jov·ial /'dʒəʊvɪəl/ adj (formal) full of fun and good humour; merry: be in a jovial mood.
jov·ial·ly /-ɪəlɪ/ adv
jov·ial·ity /ˌdʒəʊvɪ'ælətɪ/ nc,nu

jowl /dʒaʊl/ nc the jaws; lower part of the face: a man with a heavy jowl.

joy /dʒɔɪ/ n **1** nu great pleasure or happiness: I wish you joy. **2** nc something that gives joy: the joys and sorrows of life.

'joy-ride nc (sl) a ride in a (stolen) car, at a fast speed for fun and thrills.

'joy-stick nc (sl) a control lever on a plane, computer etc.

joy·ful /-fəl/ adj (usually attrib) filled with, showing, causing, joy: joyful news/children.
joy·ful·ly /-fəlɪ/ adj
joy·ful·ness nu

joy·less adj without joy; gloomy; sad.

joy·ous /'dʒɔɪəs/ adj (attrib) full of joy: a joyous occasion.
joy·ous·ly adv

JP /ˌdʒeɪ 'piː/ abbr Justice of the Peace.

Jr written abbr (also **Jnr, Jun.**) junior.

ju·bi·lant /'dʒuːbɪlənt/ adj feeling, showing, great joy (esp at success): be jubilant after having won the race.
ju·bi·lant·ly adv

ju·bi·la·tion /ˌdʒuːbɪ'leɪʃn/ nc,nu (an instance of) happiness due to an important triumph.

ju·bi·lee /'dʒuːbɪliː/ nc a celebration of a special anniversary of some event, esp the start of a king's or queen's reign. ⇨ diamond/golden/silver jubilee.

Ju·da·ism /'dʒuːdeɪɪzəm/ n the religion and culture of Jews.

judge[1] /dʒʌdʒ/ nc **1** a public official with authority to hear and decide cases in a law court. **2** a person who decides in a contest, competition, dispute etc. **3** a person able to give opinions on merits and values: a good judge of horses.

judge[2] /dʒʌdʒ/ vt,vi (pres p **judging**) **1** to act as a judge(1). **2** to give a decision (in a competition etc): Who is going to judge the long-jump competition? **3** to estimate; consider; form an opinion about (something): Judging from what you say, he ought to succeed.

judge·ment (US and GB legal **judgment**) /'dʒʌdʒmənt/ n **1** nu the state of judging or being judged: sit in judgement on a case (i.e. in a law court); pass judgement on a prisoner (= give a decision after trial). **2** nc a decision of a judge or court: The judgement was in his favour. **3** nu the process of judging(3): an error of judgement. **4** nu the ability to decide, choose etc: He showed excellent judgement in choosing a secretary. **5** nc,nu (an) opinion: in the judgement of most people.

'Judgement Day; the ,Day of 'Judgement

n the day when God will judge everyone.

ju·di·cial /dʒuː'dɪʃl/ adj **1** (attrib) of, by, a court of justice or a judge: the judicial system. **2** (usually attrib) having, showing, the qualities of a judge(1): a judicial mind. Compare judicious.
ju·di·cial·ly /-ʃəlɪ/ adv

ju·dici·ary /dʒuː'dɪʃərɪ/ nc (pl **-ies**) (the —) the judges(1) of a State as a group.

ju·di·cious /dʒuː'dɪʃəs/ adj (formal) showing or having good sense; wise (the usual word). Opp injudicious. Compare judicial(2).
ju·di·cious·ly adv

ju·do /'dʒuːdəʊ/ nu a kind of wrestling and self-defence in which an opponent's own weight and strength are used against her or him.

jug /dʒʌg/ nc **1** a deep container for liquids, with a handle and lip: a milk jug. **2** its contents: a jug of milk.

jug·ful /-fʊl/ nc as much as a jug can hold.

jug·ger·naut /'dʒʌgənɔːt/ nc (informal) a huge long-distance transport vehicle.

juggle /'dʒʌgl/ vi,vt **1** to do tricks, perform (with balls, plates etc thrown into the air) to amuse people. **2** to arrange (facts, figures etc) to deceive people: juggling with the profits.

jug·gler nc a person who juggles(1).

jugu·lar /'dʒʌgjʊlə(r)/ adj (anat) of the neck or throat: jugular veins.

juice /dʒuːs/ nc,nu **1** the fluid part of fruits, vegetables and meat: a glass of orange juice. **2** fluid in parts of the body, e.g. the stomach: gastric juices. **3** (informal) electricity, petrol or other source of power.

juicy /'dʒuːsɪ/ adj (**-ier, -iest**) **1** containing much juice: juicy oranges. **2** (informal) interesting (esp because full of exciting details of a person's bad behaviour): juicy gossip.
juici·ness nu

juke-box /'dʒuːk bɒks/ nc a coin-operated record-player in pubs, cafés etc.

Jul written abbr July.

July /dʒuː'laɪ/ n (also attrib) (abbr Jul) the seventh month of the year, with 31 days: a fine July day. This year I shall be going on holiday on 2 July. ⓝ '2 July' is spoken as 'July the second' or 'the second of July'.

jumble /'dʒʌmbl/ vt,vi (to cause objects) to be mixed in a confused way: toys jumbled up together in the cupboard. □ nc a confused mixture.

'jumble sale nc a sale of a mixed collection of old or second-hand articles, usually for charity.

jum·bo /'dʒʌmbəʊ/ adj (attrib) unusually large: a jumbo jet.

jump[1] /dʒʌmp/ nc **1** an act of jumping. **2** a sudden movement caused by fear. **3** **jump (in sth)** a sudden rise (in amount, price, value etc): a jump in car exports.

jum·py adj (**-ier, -iest**) (informal) excited and nervous.

jump[2] /dʒʌmp/ v **1** vi to push oneself by using the strength in one's legs and feet until one is clear of the ground: We jumped up and down to keep warm. They were jumping for joy. **jump at sth** to be very willing to accept an offer, idea, opportunity etc: He jumped at the chance to earn an extra £50. **2** vt (to cause an animal) to jump(1) high or far enough to pass something: jump (over) a wall; jump across a river; jump through a hoop;

jump *a horse over a fence.* **3** *vt,vi* to move quickly out of or into (a place) (as if) by jumping(1): *jump off a wall; jump into a swimming-pool; jump out of a burning building; jump into/out of bed.* **4** *vi* to make a sudden movement because of surprise and fear: *That bang made me jump!* **5** *vt* to attack (a person) suddenly: *The thieves jumped me as I turned the corner.* **6** *vt* (*informal*) to drive quickly across (a set of traffic lights when they are red): *It is very dangerous to jump the lights.* **7** *vi,vt* to move quickly from (one part of a text) to another without reading: *She jumped a chapter/jumped to the bottom of the page because the story was boring.* **8** *vi* to change suddenly (from one to another): *The discussion jumped from one subject to another.* **9** *vi* (of prices, levels, quantities etc) to increase suddenly: *Our costs have jumped since last year. The temperature has jumped into the eighties.* (N) For uses of *'jump'* in phrases such as *jump bail, jump to conclusions, jump the gun, jump the queue* etc ⇨ the entry for the *noun,* e.g. *bail¹,* conclusion(3) etc.

jump·er /'dʒʌmpə(r)/ *nc* **1** an article of loose-fitting knitted clothing pulled on over the head and coming down to the hips. **2** a person, animal or insect, that jumps.

Jun *written abbr* **1** (Jun.; also **Jnr, Jr**) junior. **2** June.

junc·tion /'dʒʌŋkʃn/ *n* **1** *nc,nu* (an instance of) joining or being joined. **2** *nc* a place where roads, railway lines or sections of an electrical circuit meet. ⇨ T-junction.

junc·ture /'dʒʌŋktʃə(r)/ *nc* (*formal*) a state of affairs, esp in the phrase: *at this juncture* at this time.

June /dʒuːn/ *n* (also *attrib*) (abbr Jun) the sixth month of the year, with 30 days: *the hot June sun. We met on 20 June.* (N) *'20 June'* is spoken as *'June the twentieth'* or *'the twentieth of June'.*

jungle /'dʒʌŋgl/ *nc,nu* (land covered with) a thick forest with tall trees and lots of bushes and plants. *the law of the jungle* (*fig*) ruthless competition or exploitation.

jun·gly /'dʒʌŋglɪ/ *adj*

jun·ior /'dʒuːnɪə(r)/ *nc, adj* **1** (a person) younger than another: *He is my junior by two years. Tom Brown, Junior* (abbr Jun., Jnr, Jr; used of a son having the same names as his father). **2** (*attrib*) (a person) lower in rank than another: *a junior officer.* Compare senior.

junk¹ /dʒʌŋk/ *nu* (also *attrib*) (of) old, useless things; *a junk shop.*

'junk food *nu* food that is quick to prepare or ready to eat and that is unhealthy because it contains too much fat, sugar etc and chemicals to give it artificial colour and taste: *My son likes junk food such as crisps, sweets and fizzy drinks.*

junk² /dʒʌŋk/ *nc* a kind of flat-bottomed Chinese sailing ship.

junkie, junky /'dʒʌŋkɪ/ *nc* (*pl* -**ies**) (*sl*) a drug (esp heroin) addict.

jun·ta /'dʒʌntə/ *nc* (*pl* —**s**) a group of army officers who have seized power by force.

Jupi·ter /'dʒuːpɪtə(r)/ *n* **1** (in ancient Rome) the ruler of gods and men. **2** the largest planet of the solar system.

ju·ris·dic·tion /,dʒʊərɪs'dɪkʃn/ *nu* the right to administer justice; legal authority: *This matter does not come/fall within our jurisdiction* (= We have no authority to deal with it).

ju·ris·pru·dence /,dʒʊərɪs'pruːdəns/ *nu* the science and philosophy of law.

ju·rist /'dʒʊərɪst/ *nc* an expert in law.

ju·ror /'dʒʊərə(r)/ *nc* a member of a jury.

ju·ry /'dʒʊərɪ/ *nc* (*pl* -**ies**) **1** a group of people (in US and GB twelve) who swear to give a true decision (*a verdict*) on issues of fact in a law court: *The jury found the prisoner not guilty.* **2** a group of people chosen to decide in a competition.

'jury-box *nc* the place where a jury sits in a law court.

just¹ /dʒʌst/ *adj* **1** fair; in accordance with what is right: *a just man; be just to a person.* **2** (*attrib*) deserved; fair: *get/receive one's just rewards.* **3** reasonable: *just suspicions.* Opp unjust.

just·ly *adv*

just² /dʒʌst *strong form* dʒʌst/ *adv* **1** (of a completed activity) a short time ago: *I've just had dinner. We've just been talking about you. Haven't they just shown that film on TV?* **just now** (a) at this moment: *I'm busy just now but I'll meet you later.* (b) a short time ago: *Tom came in just now.* **2** exactly: *It's just two o'clock. That's just what I wanted.* **just as** exactly when: *He arrived just as I was leaving.* **just as** + *adj/adv* + **as** . . . exactly as + *adj/adv* + as . . . : *Leave everything just as* (*tidy as*) *you found it.* **just as . . . so . . .** in the same way as . . . so . . . : *Just as you dislike Mr Green so I dislike his wife.* **be just as well** ⇨ well²(2). **just so** exactly in this or that way: *He likes his letters to be typed just so.* **3** only: *He's just an ordinary man. It's just a mile from here. Would you walk five miles just to see a bird? I'm sorry—I just meant that you need a new car. We had just enough time* (or *We just had enough time*) *for a coffee before the bus came.* (**just**) **in case** ⇨ case¹(1). **4** (esp *only just*) barely; almost not: *We (only) just caught the train because we were late arriving at the station. I only just passed the exam. I passed the test but only just.* **just about** almost: *We're just about finished. 'Are you ready?'—'Just about!'* **5** (used to request attention or ask for a person to wait): *Just a moment, haven't we met before? Just a minute, please.* **6** (used when making a polite, easy request): *If you'd just sign at the bottom of the form, I'll bring your key.* **7** (used to make an order stronger or to emphasize one's anger, surprise etc): *Just stay here until I get back. Just listen to his nonsense—he's mad.* **8** (*informal*) absolutely: *The concert was just perfect.*

jus·tice /'dʒʌstɪs/ *n* **1** *nu* the quality of being right and fair: *treat all men with justice.* Compare injustice. **do sb justice; do justice to sb** to treat, judge, a person fairly. **do sth justice; do justice to sth** to show something to the best advantage: *This photograph does not do justice to her hair.* **2** *nu* the law and its administration: *a court of justice.* **bring sb to justice** to arrest and try a person in a law court. **3** *nc* a judge of the Supreme Courts: *the Lord Chief Justice.*

,Justice of the 'Peace *nc* (abbr JP) a magistrate.

jus·ti·fy /'dʒʌstɪfaɪ/ *vt* (*pt,pp* -**ied**) **1** to show that (a person, statement, act etc) is right, reasonable or proper: *You can hardly justify such conduct.* **2**

to be a good reason for: *Your wish to go for a walk cannot justify leaving the baby alone in the house.*

jus·ti·fi·able /ˌdʒʌstɪˈfaɪəbl/ *adj* that can be justified. Opp unjustifiable.

jus·ti·fi·ably /-əblɪ/ *adv*

jus·ti·fi·ca·tion /ˌdʒʌstɪʃɪˈkeɪʃn/ *nu* **justification (for sth)** proof, reasons, (for behaviour, an action).

jus·ti·fied *adj* able to be shown as right or reasonable: *Is his anger/refusal justified?* Opp unjustified.

jut /dʒʌt/ *vi* (**-tt-**) **jut out** to stand out from the edge: *The balcony juts out over the garden.*

jute /dʒuːt/ *nu* fibre from certain plants, used for making rope etc.

ju·ven·ile /ˈdʒuːvənaɪl/ *adj, nc* (of, suitable for) a young person: *a juvenile court; juvenile (= childish) behaviour.*

ˌjuvenile deˈlinquency *nu* law-breaking by young people.

ˌjuvenile deˈlinquent *nc* a young offender.

jux·ta·pose /ˌdʒʌkstəˈpəʊz/ *vt* (*formal*) to place (things) side by side: *The photographs were juxtaposed with the text in the book of poems.*

jux·ta·po·si·tion /ˌdʒʌkstəpəˈzɪʃn/ *nu*

Kk

K, k /keɪ/ (*pl* **K's, k's** /keɪz/) the 11th letter of the English alphabet.

k *symbol* kilo(s).

K *symbol* **1** (*science*) kelvin(s). **2** (*computers*) (also spoken) kilobyte (a unit of measurement of the amount of information a computer can store): *My computer is 64K.* **3** 1000: *He earns about 30K* (i.e. £30 000).

ka·leido·scope /kəˈlaɪdəskəʊp/ *nc* **1** a tube containing mirrors and small, loose pieces of coloured glass, turned to produce changing patterns. **2** (*fig*) a frequently changing pattern of bright scenes: *a kaleidoscope of colour in the landscape.*

ka·leido·scop·ic /kəˌlaɪdəˈskɒpɪk/ *adj*

kan·ga·roo /ˌkæŋgəˈruː/ *nc* an Australian animal that jumps along on its large back legs and which carries its young in a pocket of skin on its stomach.

kao·lin /ˈkeɪəlɪn/ *nu* fine white clay used in making porcelain etc.

ka·pok /ˈkeɪpɒk/ *nu* a soft material like cotton, used for filling cushions etc.

kar·at /ˈkærət/ = carat.

ka·rate /kəˈrɑːtɪ/ *nu* a Japanese method of fighting using blows made with the sides of the hands, foot, head or elbow.

KC /ˌkeɪ ˈsiː/ *abbr* King's Counsel (a barrister appointed by the Lord Chancellor when there is a King.) ⇨ QC.

ke·bab /kəˈbæb/ *nc* a dish of small pieces of meat, seasoned and roasted on metal rods or wooden sticks.

keel¹ /kiːl/ *nc* a wooden or steel structure on which the framework of a ship is built. **on an even keel** in a calm, steady state.

keel² /kiːl/ *v* **1** *vt, vi* to turn (a ship) over on one side for repair etc. **2** *vi* **keel over** (of a person) to collapse: *He keeled over and died.*

keen /kiːn/ *adj* (**—er, —est**) **1** (of interest, the feelings) strong; deep: *He has a keen interest in his work.* **2** (of a person, character etc) eager; anxious to do things: *a keen sportsman; as keen as mustard* (= very keen). **keen on sb/sth** (*informal*) enthusiastic about a person, thing: *keen on going abroad.* **3** (usually *attrib*) (of the mind, senses) active; sensitive: *keen eyesight.* **4** (usually *attrib*) (of points and edges) sharp: *a knife with a keen edge.* **5** (*fig*) sharp: *a keen* (= strong, cold) *wind.*

keen·ly *adv*

keen·ness *nu*

keep¹ /kiːp/ *n* **1** *nu* (the cost of) food and rent: *She doesn't earn enough money to pay for her keep. How does he earn his keep?* ⇨ upkeep. **2** **for keeps** (*informal*) for always: *This gold medal is yours for keeps.* **3** *nc* a large tower in a castle etc.

keep² /kiːp/ *v* (*pt,pp* **kept** /kept/) Ⓝ For uses of 'keep' in phrases with nouns such as *arm, balance, ball, control, count, eye, face, finger, head, mind, place, promise, secret, watch* etc, ⇨ the noun entries. **1** *vt* to continue to have (something); have (something) in one's possession and not give it back: *You can keep those shoes if you want to. Here's £5 to pay for the postage and you can keep any money left over. Waiter, here's £10—keep the change* (i.e. you can have any money left over). *May I keep the book (for) another week as I haven't finished it? Please keep the key for me while I am away.* **2** *vt, vi* (to cause a person) to remain in a particular condition or state; continue to do something: *This game will keep the children quiet/happy. Please keep quiet! Keep smiling! The cold weather kept us indoors. You must not keep your mother waiting. I hope you're all keeping well. Why does she keep (on) laughing at me?* ⇨ keep at/on/out of etc. **keep fit** ⇨ fit¹(2). **keep going** to continue to and not stop; not give up (an activity): *This is exhausting work but I manage to keep going.* **3** *vi* to continue in a particular direction or position: *Keep straight on until you come to a gate. Traffic in Britain keeps (to the) left.* **4** *vt* to carry out, fulfil, (a commitment): *keep a promise/an appointment.* Compare break²(9). **5** *vt* to celebrate (an anniversary): *keep Christmas/New Year.* **6** *vt* to provide what is needed for, maintain, (a person etc): *Does he earn enough to keep his family?* **7** *vt* to own or manage (something) as a way of earning money: *keep a shop; keep chickens.* **8** *vt* to have (something) in stock: *'Do you have any batteries?'—'I'm sorry but we don't keep them.'* **9** *vt* to make a regular record in (something) or of (something): *keep a diary; keep an account of the expenses.* ⇨ book-keeper. **10** *vi* (of food) to remain in good condition: *Milk does not keep in hot weather.* **11** *vt* to cause (a person) to be delayed or stopped: *I was kept at the office until very late finishing the report.*

keep abreast (of sb/sth) ⇨ abreast.

keep ahead (of sb/sth) ⇨ ahead.

keep at sth to continue to work hard at something: *The only way to finish the job is to keep at it.*

keep sb at sth to continue to encourage, force,

a person to do something: *My mother kept me at it until the exams were over.* ⇨ also arm¹(1), bay⁴.

keep (sb/sth) away (from sb/sth) (to cause a person, thing) to avoid or not come near: *Keep (the children) away from the edge! The fire is dangerous—keep away.*

keep (sb/sth) back (from sb/sth) **(a)** (to cause a person, thing) to remain at the back or not come near: *The police tried to keep the crowd back from the injured man. Please keep back, we need more space.* **(b)** to decide or agree not to tell a person, committee etc (news, information etc): *She can keep nothing back from her friends.* **(c)** to keep(1) something, not give it: *The boss keeps back £5 a month towards my uniform.*

keep down to remain in a low position (e.g. to avoid danger). **keep sb down** to continue to have (often unfair) control of a person to prevent her or his progress: *The government cannot keep the people down for much longer. You can't keep a good person down!* (i.e. You cannot prevent a person with ability and determination from succeeding). **keep sth down (a)** to stop an increase in prices etc: *keep down costs.* **(b)** to stop lifting up or not lift up a part of the body: *Keep your heads down!* **(c)** to control one's feelings: *He couldn't keep his anger down.* **(d)** to continue to have food in the stomach and not bring it up: *I feel ill, doctor, and I can't keep any food down.* **(e)** to prevent unwanted plants from growing: *keep the weeds down.*

keep sb/sth from doing sth to prevent a person, group, animal, machine etc from carrying out an activity: *The ice kept the car from working. What kept you from joining us?* **keep sth from sb** to not let a person know something: *We kept the seriousness of her illness from my mother for as long as possible.* ⇨ keep (sb/sth) back (from sb/sth)(b).

keep in to stay in (which is more usual). **keep sb in** to make a person remain inside as a punishment: *The children were kept in after school.*

keep sb in sth (a) to provide a person with a supply of something: *My money only keeps me in food and essential clothes.* **(b)** to maintain a person in a mentioned condition: *Her father's money has kept her in luxury for many years.* **keep sth in (a)** to hold one's stomach etc in. **(b)** to control one's feelings: *How did she manage to keep her anger in when he was so rude?* **keep in with sb** (*informal*) to remain friendly with a person, esp to benefit oneself: *If you want that job as supervisor, you'd better keep in with the boss.* Ⓝ For the use of 'keep in' with nouns such as *check*, *dark*, *line*, *mind*, *order*, *sight*, *step*, *touch* etc, ⇨ the noun entries.

keep off (a) (often *imperative*) do not touch, walk here etc: *The sign says 'Keep off!'.* **(b)** (of bad weather) to not happen: *I hope the rain keeps off.* **keep off sth (a)** to avoid touching, walking on it: *Keep off the grass!* **(b)** to avoid eating or drinking unhealthy etc food: *My doctor has warned me to keep off sugar.* **(c)** to avoid mentioning a particular subject: *I hope you'll keep off politics during dinner.* **keep sb/sth off (sb)** to cause a person, animal etc to stay away from (a person): *Keep him/your hands/that dog off (me)!*

keep on to continue moving: *Keep on until you get to a bridge.* **keep on (doing sth)** to continue

an activity: *She kept on (painting/trying/running) although she was in pain.* **keep sb on** to continue to employ a person: *I was kept on after the others to finish the last piece of work.*

keep sth on to continue to wear clothes: *Keep your coat on—it's cold outside.* **keep on about sb/sth** to talk about a person, situation, event etc without stopping: *He keeps on about his bank manager/his bad leg every time I see him.* **keep on at sb** to continue to worry, ask lots of questions, make demands etc: *I keep on at my son to tidy his bedroom but he often forgets to do it.* Ⓝ For uses of 'keep on' with nouns such as *eye*, *feet*, *hair*, *mind*, *tab* etc, ⇨ the noun entries.

keep out (usually *imperative*) do not come inside. **keep sb/sth out** to cause a person, animal, smell etc not to come inside: *We can't keep the old man/the insects/the smoke out.* **keep (sb/sth) out of sth (a)** to avoid (or cause a person, animal, thing etc to avoid) possible danger or a dangerous place: *Keep out of the sun. I hope they keep my name out of the newspapers. I warned you to keep out of trouble.* **(b)** to agree not to (or order a person, animal etc not to) come inside: *Keep her/your dirty boots/that cat out of my kitchen!*

keep to sth (a) to stay in a mentioned place, position in a road etc: *Keep to the path until you reach the river. Keep to the right on the stairs.* **(b)** to follow regulations, an agreed plan etc: *Keep closely to the rules if you want to pass your driving test. Here's a schedule for doing the work which I hope we can all keep to.* **(c)** to stay in a house, one's bed. **(d)** to continue with a subject being discussed: *I asked the speaker to keep to the subject/point.* **keep (sb) to sth** to (make a person) do what has been agreed: *He always keeps to his promises. You promised to help and I shall keep you to it.* **keep sth to oneself (a)** to agree or decide not to tell information, knowledge etc: *I'll tell you about my sister but I hope you'll keep this news to yourself.* **(b)** to refuse to share information: *Ben had the book and knew how to do the task but he kept the method to himself and so the rest of us failed.* **keep oneself to oneself** to avoid meeting people.

keep together (often *imperative*) to remain close together, do something at the same time: *We must keep together while climbing the mountain. The leader asked the musicians to keep together while playing the tune.* **keep sth together** to refuse to let a collection, set of papers etc become separated: *The sales records are kept together in my office.*

keep sb under (a) to make a person remain under the water. **(b)** to make a person remain unconscious (e.g. during a surgical operation). **(c)** = keep sb down. ⇨ also control¹, observation(1).

keep up (a) to move, work, progress etc at the same speed as another person. **(b)** (of weather) to continue without changing: *If this rain keeps up the garden will be ruined.* **keep sb up** to prevent a person from going to bed: *The noise/visitors/pain kept her up all night.* **keep sth up (a)** to prevent an object etc from falling, getting low: *Keep your chin up! I need a pin to keep my skirt up.* **(b)** to cause an amount, price etc to remain at a high level: *The high cost of materials keeps up prices. I* *hope sales will be kept up to the usual quantity.* (**c**) to continue an attack etc at a high level of activity: *The enemy kept up continuous gunfire.* (**d**) to continue to produce payment etc when asked: *keep up the rent/payments.* (**e**) to continue to practise, be involved in something: *keep up a friendship/a correspondence/the tradition of eating with the family on Fridays.* (**f**) to prevent courage, energy etc from becoming weaker: *I tried to keep my courage up with thoughts of you. Drink this—it will keep your strength up.* **keep it up** to continue an activity without slowing down: *He works far too hard; he'll never keep it up. You're behaving much better and if you keep it up you can go out on Saturday.* **keep up (with sb)** (**a**) to work, walk, dance etc with the same energy (as another person). (**b**) to have the same (high) standard of living (as neighbours, relatives etc). (**c**) to remain in contact (with old friends, people living abroad etc) by letter or visits: *I have no time to keep up with all my school friends.* **keep up with sth** (**a**) to remain informed about the latest news, opinion etc: *She likes to keep up with the latest fashions.* (**b**) to progress, rise, at the same speed as something else: *Are wages keeping up with inflation?*

keep·er /'ki:pə(r)/ *nc* **1** a guard, e.g. a person who looks after animals in a zoo. **2** (used in compounds) a person who looks after what is mentioned: *park-keeper; goalkeeper; shopkeeper; housekeeper.*

keep·ing /'ki:pɪŋ/ *nu* **1** care: *the keeping of bees.* **in safe keeping** being kept carefully. **2 be in/ out of keeping (with sth)** to be in/out of agreement: *His actions are not in keeping with his promises.*

keep·sake /'ki:pseɪk/ *nc* something kept in memory of the giver.

keg /keg/ *nc* a small barrel.

kelvin /'kelvɪn/ *nc* (symbol K) (*science*) a unit of measurement for temperature on the Absolute scale in which 0K (0 degrees kelvin) = −273·15°C.

ken·nel¹ /'kenl/ *nc* **1** a hut used to shelter a dog. **2** (*pl*) a place where dogs are looked after.

ken·nel² /'kenl/ *vt* (**-ll-**, *US* also **-l-**) to put, keep, (a dog) in a kennel.

kept /kept/ *pt,pp* of keep².

kerb (also **curb**) /kɜ:b/ *nc* a stone forming the edge of a path or pavement.

ker·nel /'kɜ:nl/ *nc* **1** the softer, inner part (of a nut or fruit-stone). **2** an inside part of a seed, e.g. a grain of wheat. **3** (*fig*) the central or important part (of a subject, problem etc).

kero·sene /'kerəsi:n/ *nu* paraffin.

kes·trel /'kestrəl/ *nc* a kind of small hawk.

ketch·up /'ketʃəp/ *nu* a red sauce made from tomato juice.

kettle /'ketl/ *nc* a pot with a lid, spout and a handle, used for boiling water.

kettle·drum /'ketldrʌm/ *nc* a large metal drum like half a ball.

key¹ /ki:/ *adj* (*attrib; no comp*) very important; essential; giving control or power: *a key worker; a key industry; a key position; the key speaker at the debate.*

key² /ki:/ *nc* **1** a shaped metal instrument for moving a lock. ⇨ also lock²(1). **2 key (to sth)**

(*fig*) something that provides an answer (to a problem or mystery). **3** a written set of answers to exercises or problems. **4** a part (lever or button) of a typewriter, piano, flute etc pressed down by a finger. **5** a winged fruit of some trees, e.g. the ash and elm. **6** (*music*) a scale of notes definitely related to each other and based on a particular note (called the *key-note*): *the key of C major.*

'key·board *nc* a row of keys(4) (on a piano, typewriter etc).

'key·hole *nc* a hole (in a door etc) for a key.

'key·note *nc* (**a**) a note on which a key(6) is based. (**b**) (*fig*) the most important idea: *The key-note of the Minister's speech was the need for higher productivity.*

'key·ring *nc* a ring for keeping keys together.

key³ /ki:/ *vt* **key sb/sth up** (usually *pp*) (*fig*) to excite, raise the standard of, (a person, activity etc): *The crowd was keyed up for the football match.*

key·stone /'ki:stəʊn/ *nc* **1** a stone at the top of an arch locking the others into position. **2** (*fig*) the central principle on which an argument, idea etc depends.

kg *symbol* kilogram(s).

KGB /,keɪ dʒi: 'bi:/ *abbr* (the —) the secret police of the USSR.

kha·ki /'kɑ:kɪ/ *nu, adj* (cloth, military uniform, of) a dull yellowish-brown.

kHz *symbol* kilohertz.

kick¹ /kɪk/ *nc* **1** an act of kicking: *The bruise was caused by a kick.* **2** (*informal*) a strong feeling of pleasure or excitement: *He gets a big kick out of motor-racing.*

kick² /kɪk/ *v* **1** *vi,vt* to hit, move, make, (something) with the foot: *kick a ball; kick a hole in the door; kick a goal.* ⇨ also bucket¹(1), habit(1). **2** *vi* (of a gun) to move suddenly when fired: *This old rifle kicks badly.*

kick against sth to protest about, try to resist rules, authority, fate etc: *It's useless to kick against one's destiny.*

kick sth around (*informal*) to discuss an idea, plan etc informally.

kick sth in to break open, damage, a door, teeth etc by kicking.

kick off (**a**) to start a game. Hence **'kick-off** *nc*. (**b**) to start a speech, discussion: *He kicked off with a description of the building.*

kick sb out (of a place) (*informal*) to force a person to leave a room, society, political party etc.

kick up sth (*informal*) to cause, produce, a fuss etc: *kick up a row/fuss.*

kick·back /'kɪk bæk/ *nc* (*informal*) a payment to a person who has helped one to make money.

kick-off /'kɪk ɒf/ *nc* ⇨ kick off(a).

kick-starter /,kɪk 'stɑ:tə(r)/ *nc* a lever on a motorbike etc used to start the engine by being pushed with the foot.

kid¹ /kɪd/ *n* **1** *nc* a young goat. **2** *nu* (also *attrib*) leather made from skin of this: *wearing kid gloves.* **handle sb with kid gloves** (*fig*) to deal with a person gently. **3** *nc* (*sl*) a child.

kid·dy *nc* (*pl* **-ies**) (*sl*) a child.

kid² /kɪd/ *vt,vi* (**-dd-**) (*sl*) to deceive (a person): *You're kidding (me)!*

kid·nap /'kɪdnæp/ *vt* (**-pp-**, *US* **-p-**) to steal (a child) (esp in order to demand payment for her or his return).

kid·nap·per *nc* a person who kidnaps a child.

kid·ney /'kɪdnɪ/ *nc* (*pl* **—s**) **1** one of two organs in the abdomen that separate urine from the blood. **2** (also *attrib*) a kidney of sheep, cattle etc as food: *kidney soup*.

'**kidney bean** *nc* a reddish-brown kidney-shaped bean.

'**kidney machine** *nc* (*med; informal*) an apparatus that does the work of diseased kidneys(1).

kill¹ /kɪl/ *n sing* an act of killing a wild animal.

kill² /kɪl/ *v* **1** *vt,vi* to cause the death of (a person, animal, plant): *kill animals for food*. Ⓝ '*Murder*' is used when a person's death is planned and caused by another person. Compare *She was murdered by her husband* and *He was killed in a car accident*. **kill sth off** to cause something's destruction: *The frost has killed off the roses/insects*. ⇨ also bird(1), kindness, time¹(2). **2** *vt* to make (something) ineffective by poor contrast: *That floral carpet kills the effect of your curtains*. **3** *vt* (*fig*) to cause the failure or defeat of (something): *kill a proposal*.

kill·er *nc* a person, animal etc that kills.

kill·ing *n sing* (esp) **make a killing** to make a lot of money in business.

'**kill·joy** *nc* (*derog*) a person who destroys other people's pleasure or enjoyment.

kiln /'kɪln/ *nc* a furnace or oven used for baking or drying (esp pots, bricks).

ki·lo /'kiːləʊ/ *nc* (*pl* **—s**) kilogram.

kilo·byte /'kɪləbaɪt/ *nc* (symbol K) (*computers*) 1000 bytes: *My computer has a 48K memory*.

kilo·gram (also **kilo·gramme**) /'kɪləgræm/ *nc* (symbol kg) 1000 grammes.

kilo·joule /'kɪlədʒuːl/ *nc* (symbol kJ) 1000 joules (= about 4·25 calories).

kilo·hertz /'kɪləhɜːts/ *nc* (symbol kHz) 1000 hertz.

kilo·litre /'kɪləliːtə(r)/ *nc* (symbol kl) 1000 litres.

kilo·metre (*US* = **-me·ter**) /'kɪləmiːtə(r)/ *also* kɪ'lɒmɪtə(r)/ *nc* (symbol km) 1000 metres.

kilo·watt /'kɪləwɒt/ *nc* (symbol kW) 1000 watts.

kilt /kɪlt/ *nc* a pleated skirt, worn as part of male dress in Scotland; similar skirt worn by women and children.

ki·mo·no /kɪ'məʊnəʊ/ *nc* (*pl* **—s**) a wide-sleeved, long gown as worn by Japanese women.

kin /kɪn/ *n* (used collectively) family; relations. *next of kin* nearest relation(s): *my next of kin*.

kind¹ /kaɪnd/ *adj* (**—er, —est**) having, showing, thoughtfulness, willingness or sympathy for others: *be kind to animals. It was kind of you to help us.* Opp unkind.

,**kind-'hearted** *adj* being kind; showing kindness.

kind·ly *adv* (**a**) in a kind manner: *treat her/speak kindly*. Opp unkindly. (**b**) (used to make a polite request): *Will you kindly tell me the time?* (**c**) **not take kindly to sth** to accept it unwillingly or with difficulty: *He doesn't take kindly to being cheated.*

kind·ness *n* (**a**) *nu* kind nature; being kind: *do something out of kindness.* **kill sb with kindness** to make an angry or unpleasant person become (more) pleasant by being kind to her or him. (**b**) *nc* a kind act: *He has done me many kindnesses.* Opp unkindness.

kind² /kaɪnd/ *nc* **1** a particular group, class, variety with the same characteristics or features: *What kind of tree is this? These birds are the same kind. Many kinds of animals have horns.* Ⓝ '*Sort*' and '*type*' are also possible, but '*sort*' is not often used in a scientific context and '*type*' is the most formal or scientific in usage. Compare: *There are all sorts of games to play. We have many kinds of tools in the shop. A prawn is a type of shellfish.* **a kind of sth** (used to express uncertainty) a vague idea of: *I had a kind of suspicion that he was a liar.* **of a kind** (**a**) of the same kind: *Those brothers are two of a kind.* (**b**) almost not deserving the name: *They gave us coffee of a kind.* ⇨ also nothing². **2** **in kind** (**a**) in essential character: *Their bad behaviour differs in degree but not in kind.* (**b**) (of payment) in goods but not in money. (**c**) in the same way: *repay abuse in kind.* **4 kind of** (*adv*) (*informal*) a little: *kind of jealous/miserable/tired. He spoke kind of confidentially.* Compare sort¹(1).

kin·der·gar·ten /'kɪndəgɑːtn/ *nc* a school for children below five years old.

kindle /'kɪndl/ *v* **1** *vt,vi* (to cause something) to catch fire or burst into flames or flaming colour: *The sparks kindled the dry wood.* **2** *vt* to encourage (strong feeling, interest etc): *kindling the interest of an audience.*

kind·ly¹ /'kaɪndlɪ/ *adj* (**-ier, -iest**) friendly; sympathetic: *give kindly advice.*

kind·ly² /'kaɪndlɪ/ *adv* ⇨ kind¹.

kin·dred /'kɪndrɪd/ *adj* (*attrib*) **1** related; having a common origin: *kindred languages.* **2 a kindred spirit** a person with the same interests, ideas, personality etc as oneself.

ki·net·ic /kaɪ'netɪk/ *adj* (*science*) of, relating to, produced by, motion.

ki,netic 'energy *nu* (*science*) the energy of a moving body (measured in *joules*).

ki·net·ics *nu* the science of the relations between the motions of bodies and the forces acting on them.

king /kɪŋ/ *nc* **1** a male ruler of a country. **2** (*chess*) the most important piece. **3** the most prominent member of a group, category etc: *the king of beasts* (= the lion); *the king of the forest* (= the oak). **4** a playing-card between the queen and ace in value: *the king of spades.*

'**king·pin** *nc* (**a**) a vertical bolt used as a pivot. (**b**) (*fig*) an indispensable or essential person or thing.

,**king 'prawn** *nc* a kind of large prawn.

'**king-size** *adj* extra large: *king-size cigarettes.*

king·dom /'kɪŋdəm/ *nc* **1** a country ruled by a king or a queen: *the United Kingdom.* **2** any one of the three divisions of the natural world: *the animal, vegetable and mineral kingdoms.*

king·fish·er /'kɪŋfɪʃə(r)/ *nc* a kind of small brightly-coloured bird that feeds on fish.

kink /kɪŋk/ *nc* **1** a twist (in a length of wire, pipe, cord etc) such as may cause a break or obstruction. **2** (*fig*) something abnormal in a person's way of thinking.

kinky *adj* (**-ier, -iest**) (*informal; derog*) abnormal (esp referring to sexual behaviour): *a kinky sense of humour.*

kin·ship /'kɪnʃɪp/ *nu* a relationship by blood.

ki·osk /'kiːɒsk/ *nc* **1** a small open-fronted structure used for the sale of newspapers, sweets, cigarettes etc. **2** a small place for a public telephone.

kip /kɪp/ *n* (*GB sl*) sleep: *have a kip*. □ *vi* (**-pp-**) to sleep. ***kip down*** to go to bed: *It's time to kip down*.

kip·per /ˈkɪpə(r)/ *nc* a salted herring, dried or smoked.

kirk /kɜːk/ *nc* (*Scot*) a church.

kiss¹ /kɪs/ *nc* an act of kissing. ***blow sb a kiss*** to kiss one's hand and then blow it towards a person. **,kiss of 'death** *n sing* (the —) (*fig*) (*informal*) an action etc with disastrous consequences. **,kiss of 'life** *n sing* (the —) the act of breathing air into the mouth, e.g. of a person rescued from drowning.

kiss² /kɪs/ *vt,vi* to touch (a person) with the lips to show affection, love or as a greeting: *kiss the children goodnight*.

kit¹ /kɪt/ *n* **1** *nu* all the equipment (esp clothing) of a soldier, sportsman or traveller: *packing one's kit for an expedition*. **2** *nc* the tools etc needed by a worker: *a plumber's kit*.

kit² /kɪt/ *vt* (**-tt-**) ***kit oneself/sb out (with sth)*** to obtain, provide sb with, (a) kit. **'kit·bag** *nc* a long bag in which kit(1) is carried by a soldier, sailor etc.

kit·chen /ˈkɪtʃɪn/ *nc* a room in which meals are cooked or prepared. **'kitchen unit** *nc* a piece of furniture designed for kitchen equipment, e.g. a sink and a storage cabinet.

kit·chen·ette /ˌkɪtʃɪˈnet/ *nc* a small room or space used as a kitchen (esp in a small flat).

kite /kaɪt/ *nc* **1** a framework covered with paper or cloth, made to fly in the wind at the end of a long string or wire. **2** a bird of prey of the hawk family.

kith /kɪθ/ *n* (only in) ***kith and kin*** friends and relations.

kit·ten /ˈkɪtn/ *nc* a young cat.

kit·ty¹ /ˈkɪtɪ/ *nc* (*pl* **-ies**) a playful name for a kitten.

kit·ty² /ˈkɪtɪ/ *nc* (*pl* **-ies**) **1** (in some games) the money to be played for. **2** (*informal*) any collected money, e.g. savings.

ki·wi /ˈkiːwiː/ *nc* a New Zealand bird with undeveloped wings.

kl *symbol* kilolitre(s).

kJ *symbol* kilojoule(s).

klep·to·ma·nia /ˌkleptəˈmeɪnɪə/ *nu* an uncontrollable wish to steal. **klep·to·ma·ni·ac** /-nɪæk/ *nc* person with kleptomania.

km *symbol* kilometre(s).

knack /næk/ *n sing* ***the knack (of sth)*** the ability (usually after practice) enabling one to do something skilfully: *It's quite easy to drive once you have/get the knack (of it)*.

knack·er·ed /ˈnækəd/ *adj* (*pred; sl*) very tired: *I'm knackered*.

knap·sack /ˈnæpsæk/ *nc* = backpack.

knave /neɪv/ *nc* **1** (*old use*) a dishonest man. **2** = jack(2).

knead /niːd/ *vt* **1** to make (flour and water) into a firm paste (*dough*) by working with the hands: *knead bread*. **2** to mix (water and clay) to make pots. **3** to move (muscles) by pushing and rubbing

to take away pain etc.

knee /niː/ *nc* **1** the joint in the middle of the leg. ***be on/go (down) on one's knees*** to be kneeling/kneel down. ***bring sb to her/his knees*** to force her or him to give in. **2** a part of an article of clothing covering the knees: *the knees of a pair of trousers*.

'knee-breeches /ˈbrɪtʃɪz/ *n pl* breeches reaching (below) the knees.

'knee·cap *nc* the flat bone at the front of the knee.

,knee-'deep *adj, adv* so deep as to reach the knees: *The water was knee-deep*. ***knee-deep in debt*** owing a lot of money.

kneel /niːl/ *vi* (*pt,pp* **knelt** /nelt/) ***kneel (down)*** to be or go down on one's knees: *They knelt in silent prayer. Can you kneel down while I do your hair?*

knell /nel/ *n sing* the sound of a bell, esp for a death or at a funeral.

knelt /nelt/ *pt,pp* of kneel.

knew /njuː/ *pt* of know².

knick·ers /ˈnɪkəz/ *n pl* = panties.

knick-knack /ˈnɪk næk/ *nc* a small ornament, piece of jewellery etc.

knife¹ /naɪf/ *nc* (*pl* **knives** /naɪvz/) a sharp blade with a handle, used as a cutting instrument or as a weapon: *a table knife; a pocket knife*. ***get one's knife into sb*** to have the wish to harm a person. **'knife-edge** *nc* the cutting edge of a knife. ***on a knife-edge*** (of an important outcome, result etc) extremely uncertain.

knife² /naɪf/ *vt* (*pres p* **knifing**; *pt,pp* **—d**) to injure (a person) with a knife.

knight¹ /naɪt/ *nc* **1** (in history) a soldier honoured for his courage. **2** a man who has been given an honorary title (below a lord) as a reward for services to the State or to a political party. Ⓝ The title *'Sir'* is used before the first name, as *Sir James Hill*. Compare lady(5). **3** (*chess*) a piece with a horse's head.

knight² /naɪt/ *vt* to make (a person) a knight(2). **'knight·hood** *nc,nu* such an act or honour.

knit /nɪt/ *vt,vi* (*pt,pp* **—ted** or **—**; **-tt-**) **1** to make (an article of clothing etc) by looping wool etc on long needles: *She often knits while reading. I'm knitting a jumper for my son*. **2** to unite (people) firmly or closely: *The two families are knit together by common interests. They are a close-knit family*. **3** ***knit one's brows*** to frown.

knit·ter *nc* a person who knits.

knit·ting *nu* (**a**) the act of a person who knits. (**b**) something being knitted. **'knit·ting-machine** *nc* a machine that knits. **'knit·ting-needle** *nc* a long rod used to knit. **'knit·wear** /-weə(r)/ *nu* (*commerce*) knitted clothes.

knives /naɪvz/ *pl* of knife.

knob /nɒb/ *nc* **1** a round handle of a door, drawer etc. **2** a round control of a radio, television etc.

knob·bly /ˈnɒblɪ/ *adj* (**-ier, -iest**) having round lumps: *knobbly knees*.

knock¹ /nɒk/ *nc* **1** (the short, sharp sound of) a blow: *He got a nasty knock on the head when he fell. I heard a knock at the door*. **2** (*sl*) an unlucky experience (esp a financial loss): *He's taken a bad knock*.

knock² /nɒk/ *v* **1** *vt,vi* to hit (something); strike;

cause (something) to be (in a mentioned state), make (something), by hitting: *Someone is knocking at the door. He knocked the bottom out of the box. He knocked* (= accidentally hit) *his head on/against the wall. Let's knock a hole in the wall.* ⇨ shape[1](1). **2** *vt* (*sl*) to surprise, shock, (a person): *I was knocked flat by her news.* **3** *vt* (*informal*) to give a poor opinion of (a person, thing): *Why must you always knock British products?*

knock sb about to hit a person repeatedly. **knock about with sb** (*informal*) to be often in company with a person.

knock at sth to hit a door etc using one's closed hand or a knocker.

knock sb back (*informal*) (of costs for buying something) to cost a person (a sum of money): *The wedding knocked me back about £200.*

knock sth back (*informal*) to drink quickly a portion of medicine, whisky etc: *knock back a pint of beer.*

knock sb down to cause a person to fall to the ground by hitting: *He was knocked down by a bus.*

knock sth down (**a**) to destroy something by hitting: *These old houses are to be knocked down.* (**b**) to take something to pieces: *The machines will be knocked down before being packed for shipment.* (**c**) to lower a price: *He knocked down the price by ten per cent.*

knock sth in/sth into sth to strike something so that it goes in: *knock in a nail; knock a nail into the wood.* ⇨ sense[1](4).

knock off (work) to stop work. **knock sb off** (*sl*) to murder a person: *knock off a police officer.* **knock sth off (sth)** (**a**) to take off an amount: *I'll knock 50p off the price.* (**b**) (*informal*) to produce something quickly: *knock off a letter to the bank.* (**c**) (*sl*) to steal from a place: *knock off a bank.* **knock it off** (*imperative*) to stop making a noise, asking questions etc.

knock sb out (**a**) to make a person unconscious by hitting her or him. (**b**) (of a drug) to cause a person to go to sleep. (**c**) (*fig*; usually *passive*) to shock a person: *She was knocked out by the news.*

knock sb/sth out (of sth) (**a**) to remove an object by hitting. (**b**) to defeat a person, team and so cause her, him or them to leave a competition.

knock sth together to make furniture etc roughly or quickly: *The bookshelves had obviously been knocked together.*

knock sb up (*GB informal*) to wake a person by knocking at the door etc. **knock sth up** (**a**) to arrange, put together, something quickly: *knock up a meal.* (**b**) to score runs at cricket.

knock-down /'nɒkdaʊn/ *adj* (*attrib*) (of prices) the lowest at which goods are to be sold.

knock·er /'nɒkə(r)/ *nc* a hinged device on a door, used for knocking(1).

knock-kneed /ˌnɒk'niːd/ *adj* having legs curved so that the knees touch when walking.

knock-out /'nɒkaʊt/ *nc* **1** (abbr KO) a blow that knocks a boxer out. **2** (*informal*) an impressive or attractive (person, thing): *Isn't she a knock out!* **3** (*sl*) (also *attrib*) a drug that causes sleep: *knock out pills.*

knoll /nəʊl/ *nc* a small hill.

knot[1] /nɒt/ *nc* **1** parts of one or more pieces of string, rope etc twisted together to make a fasten-

ing: *tie/make a knot.* **2** a hard lump in wood where a branch once grew. **3** a group (of people or things): *People were standing about in knots, anxiously waiting for news.* **4** a measure of speed for ships (= one nautical mile per hour).

'knot-hole *nc* a hole (in a board) from which a knot(2) has come out.

knot·ty *adj* (**-ier, -iest**) full of knots(1,2). **a knotty problem** one that is difficult to solve.

knot[2] /nɒt/ *vt* (**-tt-**) to make a knot in (string etc); join (string etc) using a knot: *knot two ropes together.*

know[1] /nəʊ/ *n* (only in) **be in the know** (*informal*) to have information about a person, plan etc that is not available to everyone.

know[2] /nəʊ/ *v* (*pt* **knew** /njuː/, *pp* **known** /nəʊn/) Ⓝ Not used in continuous tenses, e.g. *is/was -ing.* **1** *vt,vi* to feel certain about, understand, (a fact, method, information, way, result etc): *Every child knows* (*that*) *two and two make four. You should know that by now. Do you know the way to my house? I don't know how to get there. Did you know that peanuts grow under the ground? Does she know enough to pass the test? I don't want to know what happened to you yesterday. Do you know how to play chess? 'You've got a parking-ticket.'—'I know.' I already know* (*that*). Ⓝ *'Know'* is not possible immediately before an infinitive. Use *'know how to',* as in *He knows how to cook/how to mend his car.* **for all I know** from my own (limited) information: *For all I know, he could have gone away by now.* **I know what . . .** I have a suggestion to make: *I know what, let's go out for dinner.* **let me know** (*imperative*) tell me: *Let me know when Peter gets back.* **know one's (own) mind** ⇨ mind[1](3). **there's no knowing sth** it is impossible to know it: *There's no knowing when we shall meet again.* **you know** (used to make a pause in conversation): *You know, I'm not sure that I want it.* **you know sth/what . . .** (*informal*) I'm going to tell you something: *You know something/what, I think you're beautiful.* **you never know** you cannot be certain: *You never know, she may change her mind.* **2** *vt* to be acquainted with (a person): *I've known her for a long time. Do you know Mr Hill? They've known each other since 1980.* ⇨ well-known. **be known as sb** to be considered to be: *She's known as a great actress.* **3** *vt* to have experienced (something): *She's known good times and bad times.* **4** *vt* to be able to recognize (a good example of a person, thing): *He knows a good painting when he sees one.* **know the ropes** ⇨ rope[1](2). **know a thing or two** ⇨ thing(3).

know about sb/sth to have information about a person, an event etc: *I knew about her wedding last week.*

know sth backwards ⇨ backwards(2).

know better (than to do sth) ⇨ better[2](1).

know sb by name/sight to know a person's name/what a person looks like (and nothing more).

(not) know sb/sth from sb/sth to be able/unable to tell the difference between two people or things: *My doctor doesn't know one patient from another.*

know of sb/sth to have knowledge of a person,

lace

thing: *I know of a cheap café near here. I know of a dentist in town but I've never been to see her.* **not that I know of** not according to my knowledge or information.

know sb through and through (*informal*) to understand a person's character thoroughly: *After a long holiday together, we knew each other through and through.*

be known to sb (of a criminal, poor family, patient etc) to be on the records of an authority: *He's known to the police/the social services.* **sb has been known to (do sth)** it is generally known that, recorded that, a person has done something bad before: *She's never been known to hit her children.*

know-all /'nəʊ ɔ:l/ *nc* (*derog*) a person who claims to know everything about a subject etc.

know-how /'nəʊ haʊ/ *nu* practical ability through experience: *He hasn't got the know-how.*

know·ing /'nəʊɪŋ/ *adj* (*attrib*) having, showing that one knows something: *knowing looks.*

know·ing·ly *adv* (**a**) intentionally: *I didn't hurt her knowingly.* (**b**) in a knowing way: *look knowingly at somebody.*

knowl·edge /'nɒlɪdʒ/ *nu* **1** understanding: *A baby has no knowledge of good and evil.* **2** information or familiarity gained by experience: *My knowledge of French is poor. It has come to my knowledge* (= I have been informed) *that you have been spreading gossip about me.* **to the best of my knowledge** ⇨ best³(3).

knowl·edge·able /-əbl/ *adj* (of a person) having much knowledge(2).

known /nəʊn/ *pp* of know².

KO /ˌkeɪ 'əʊ/ *abbr* knock-out.

kph /ˌkeɪ pi: 'eɪtʃ/ *abbr* kilometres per hour (to measure speed). ⇨ mph.

knuckle¹ /'nʌkl/ *nc* **1** a bone at a finger-joint. **2** (in animals) a knee-joint; the part joining a leg to a foot, eaten as food.

knuckle² /'nʌkl/ *vi* **1** *knuckle down to sth* to do work with great effort and energy. **2** *knuckle under* to obey, give in to, a person's pressure: *He is unwilling to knuckle under and study.*

ko·ala /kəʊ'ɑ:lə/ *nc* an Australian tree-climbing mammal, like a small bear.

Ko·ran /kə'rɑ:n/ *n* (the —) the holy book of the Muslim religion.

Ko·ran·ic /kə'rænɪk/ *adj*

ko·sher /'kəʊʃə(r)/ *adj* of, concerning, food that religious Jews eat.

kow·tow /ˌkaʊ'taʊ/ *vi* to obey a person (too) humbly.

Kt *written abbr* Knight(2).

kung fu /ˌkʊŋ 'fu:/ *nu* a kind of Chinese fighting, like karate.

kW *symbol* kilowatt(s).

Ll

L, l /el/ (*pl* **L's, l's** /elz/) **1** the 12th letter of the English alphabet. **2** the Roman numeral 50.

l. *symbol* litre(s). □ *written abbr* **1** line (in a book). **2** left (side or turn).

L *symbol* **1** large size (clothing). **2** (on a car) learner driver. □ *written abbr* **1** (esp on a map) lake. **2** length.

'L-plate *nc* a sign put on the front and back of a car to show that a learner is driving.

lab /læb/ *nc* (*informal*) = laboratory.

Lab. *written abbr* The Labour Party.

la·bel¹ /'leɪbl/ *nc* **1** a piece of paper or other material used for describing what something is, where it is to go etc: *put labels on one's luggage.* **2** a short word or phrase describing a person or thing: *be given the label of thief.*

la·bel² /'leɪbl/ *vt* (**-ll-**, *US* **-l-**) **1** to put a label on (a parcel, clothes, a suitcase etc): *properly labelled luggage.* **2** to give a label(2) to (a person): *labelled as untrustworthy.*

la·bi·al /'leɪbɪəl/ *adj* (*tech*) of, made with, the lips: *labial sounds* (e.g. m, p, b).

la·bor /'leɪbə(r)/ *n* (*US*) = labour.

lab·ora·tory /lə'bɒrətrɪ/ *nc* (*pl* **-ies**) a room, building, used for scientific experiments, research etc. ⇨ language laboratory.

la·bori·ous /lə'bɔ:rɪəs/ *adj* needing, showing, great effort: *a laborious task; a laborious style of writing.*

la·bori·ous·ly *adv*

la·bour¹ (*US* = **la·bor**) /'leɪbə(r)/ *n* **1** *nc,nu* (a piece of) work needing physical or mental effort: *manual labour.* **a labour of love** a task gladly undertaken (e.g. one for a person one loves). **2** *nu* workers as a class (contrasted with the owners of capital etc): *skilled and unskilled labour.* **3** *nu* the process of childbirth. **in labour** giving birth.

la·bour² (*US* = **la·bor**) /'leɪbə(r)/ *v* **1** *vi* to work; try hard: *labour in the cause of peace.* **2** *vi* to move, breathe, slowly and with difficulty: *The old man laboured up the hillside.* **3** *vi* **labour under sth** to be the victim of, suffer because of, difficulties: *labour under the disadvantage of being poor.* **4** *vt* to speak about, stress, (something) at great length: *There's no need to labour the point.*

labour-in'tensive *adj* (of work in a factory, industry etc) needing many workers: *Building is a labour-intensive industry.*

'Labour Party *n* (the —) (*GB*) the political party representing socialist opinion.

labour re'lations *n pl* relations(3) between labour(2) and employers.

'labour-saving *adj* reducing the amount of physical work needed: *labour-saving kitchen utensils.*

la·bour·ed (*US* = **la·bor·ed**) /'leɪbəd/ *adj* **1** slow and troublesome: *laboured breathing.* **2** not easy or natural; showing too much effort: *a laboured style of writing.*

la·bour·er (*US* = **la·bor·er**) /'leɪbərə(r)/ *nc* a person who does heavy unskilled work: *farm labourers.*

lab·yr·inth /'læbərɪnθ/ *nc* **1** a set of winding paths, roads etc that is difficult to get through. **2** (*fig*) any similar confused state.

lab·yr·in·thine /ˌlæbə'rɪnθaɪn/ *adj*

lace¹ /leɪs/ *n* **1** *nu* a kind of delicate material with the threads making patterns: *a lace collar.* **2** *nc* a string or cord put through small holes in shoes etc to fasten edges together: *shoelaces.*

lace² /leɪs/ *vt* **1** *lace sth (up)* to fasten or tighten clothes, shoes etc with laces(2): *lacing (up) one's* *shoes*. **2 lace sth (with sth)** to flavour or strengthen a drink (with an alcoholic spirit): *milk laced with rum*.

lac·er·ate /'læsəreɪt/ *vt* (*formal*) to cut or tear (the flesh).
lac·er·ation /ˌlæsə'reɪʃn/ *nc,nu*

lack¹ /læk/ *nc,nu* an absence of or need for (something): *a lack of money*.

lack² /læk/ *vt* to be without, not have, have less than enough of, (something): *He lacks courage*.
be lacking (in sth) to be in short supply, not be available: *Money was lacking/We were lacking in money to complete the building*.

lacka·daisi·cal /ˌlækə'deɪzɪkl/ *adj* (*derog*) (appearing) tired, unenthusiastic.
lacka·daisi·cal·ly /-klɪ/ *adv*

lack·ey /'lækɪ/ *nc* (*pl* **—s**) (*derog*) a person who does jobs for an important person as if he or she is a servant: *I refuse to become your lackey!*

la·con·ic /lə'kɒnɪk/ *adj* (*formal*) using, expressed in, few words: *a laconic person/reply*.
la·coni·cal·ly /-klɪ/ *adv*

lac·quer¹ /'lækə(r)/ *nc,nu* **1** (any kind of) varnish used to give a hard, bright surface to metal (esp brass). **2** a kind of colourless paint used for wood. **3** a substance put on hair to keep it shiny and in position: *hair lacquer*.

lac·quer² /'lækə(r)/ *vt* to use lacquer on (metal, woodwork, hair etc).

la·crosse /lə'krɒs/ *nu* an outdoor game played with a ball which is caught in, carried in and thrown from a racket (called a *crosse*).

lac·tic /'læktɪk/ *adj* (*science*) of milk.

lacy /'leɪsɪ/ *adj* (**-ier, -iest**) of or like lace(1).

lad /læd/ *nc* (*informal*) a boy; young man.

lad·der¹ /'lædə(r)/ *nc* **1** two lengths of wood, metal or rope, with crosspieces (called *rungs*), used to climb up and down. **2** a fault which looks like a ladder in a sock or in tights. **3** (*fig*) a means of progressing: *the ladder of success*.

lad·der² /'lædə(r)/ *vi,vt* (to cause a stocking etc) to develop ladders(2): *Have you any tights that won't ladder?*
'ladder-proof *adj* impossible, difficult, to ladder.

lad·die /'lædɪ/ *nc* = lad

la·den /'leɪdn/ *adj* **laden (with sth)** carrying a large number (of something): *trees laden with apples*.

la·dies /'leɪdɪz/ *pl* of lady.

la-di-da /ˌlɑː dɪ 'dɑː/ *adj* (*pred; informal*) behaving with too much self-importance (esp by speaking with a false, aristocratic accent).

lad·ing /'leɪdɪŋ/ *nu* (esp) **bill of lading** (details of) a ship's cargo.

ladle /'leɪdl/ *nc* a large, deep spoon used for serving liquids: *a soup ladle*. □ *vt* **ladle sth (out)** to serve food with a ladle: *ladle (out) soup*.

la·dy /'leɪdɪ/ *nc* (*pl* **-dies**) **1** a woman belonging to the upper classes. ⇨ gentleman(1). **2** a woman who has good manners: *act like a lady*. **3** a woman (now the more usual word): *ladies' fashions*. **4** (*pl*) (used to address women in a formal speech): *'Ladies and Gentlemen, . . . '* **5** (L-) (title in GB used of and to a woman who is a noble, or to wives and daughters of some nobles). Compare dame(1).

Ladies' *nc* (the **—**; also *attrib*) a public toilet for

women and girls.

'lady-killer *nc* (*derog*) a man with a reputation for attracting women.

'lady·like *adj* behaving like a lady(2).

lady·bird /'leɪdɪbɜːd/ *nc* a kind of small red beetle with black spots.

lag¹ /læg/ *nc* (*sl; derog*) a person convicted of a crime: *an old lag* (= one who has often been in prison).

lag² /læg/ *vi* (**-gg-**) **lag (behind)** to go too slowly; not keep up with others.

lag³ /læg/ *vt* (**-gg-**) **lag sth (round); lag sth with sth** to wrap (pipes etc) with material to prevent heat from escaping.
lag·ging *nu* material used for this.

la·ger /'lɑːgə(r)/ *nc,nu* (a glass, can or bottle of) a kind of light beer.

la·goon /lə'guːn/ *nc* a lake separated from the sea by a sandbank or coral reef.

laid /leɪd/ *pt,pp* of lay².

lain /leɪn/ *pp* of lie⁴.

lair /leə(r)/ *nc* a home, sleeping-place, of a wild animal.

laird /leəd/ *nc* (*Scot*) a landowner.

la·ity /'leɪətɪ/ *nu* (the **—**) all people who are not members of the clergy. ⇨ lay¹(1).

lake /leɪk/ *nc* a large area of water enclosed by land.

'Lake District *nc* (the **—**) the area of NW England with many lakes.

'Lake Poet *nc* a poet who lived in the Lake District, e.g. Coleridge, Wordsworth.

la·ma /'lɑːmə/ *nc* (*pl* **—s**) a Buddhist priest in Tibet or Mongolia.

lama·sery /'lɑːməsərɪ US: -serɪ/ *nc* (*pl* **-ies**) a monastery of lamas.

lamb¹ /læm/ *n* **1** *nc* a young sheep. **2** *nu* (also *attrib*) its flesh as food: *roast lamb; lamb stew*. **3** *nc* an innocent, mild person. **like a lamb** without resistance or protest.

'lamb·skin *nc,nu* (leather from) the skin of a lamb with the wool on it.

lamb² /læm/ *vi* to give birth to lambs: *the lambing season*.

lame¹ /leɪm/ *adj* (**—r, —st**) **1** not able to walk normally because of an injury or defect. **2** (of an excuse, argument etc) weak and unsatisfactory.
,lame 'duck *nc* (*informal*) (**a**) (*derog*) a disabled or weak person. (**b**) a business or commercial organization in financial difficulties.
lame·ly *adv*
lame·ness *nu*

lame² /leɪm/ *vt* to make (a person) lame.

lamé /'lɑːmeɪ/ *nu* a kind of cloth made of metal threads.

la·ment¹ /lə'ment/ *n* **1** an expression of grief. **2** a song or poem expressing grief: *a funeral lament*.

la·ment² /lə'ment/ *vt,vi* **lament (over) (sb/sth)** to feel, express, great sorrow or regret: *lament (over) the death of a friend*.

lam·en·table /'læməntəbl/ *adj* (*formal*) poor, unsatisfactory, distressing: *a lamentable performance*.
lam·en·tably /-əblɪ/ *adv*
lam·en·ta·tion /ˌlæmən'teɪʃn/ *nc,nu*

lami·nat·ed /'læmɪneɪtɪd/ *adj* (of material) made by sticking several thin layers together: *laminated wood*.

lamp /læmp/ nc an apparatus for giving light (using oil, electricity, gas etc).

'**lamp·light** nu light from a lamp: *reading by lamplight*.

'**lamp-post** nc a tall post for a street light.

'**lamp·shade** nc a covering placed round or over a lamp.

lam·poon /læm'puːn/ nc (*literature*) a piece of writing attacking and ridiculing a person. □ vt to write a lampoon about (a person).

lance[1] /laːns/ nc a long weapon with a pointed steel head.

lance[2] /laːns/ vt (*med*) to cut (the skin, an infected area) with a kind of small sharp knife.

lance-corporal /ˌlaːns 'kɔːprəl/ nc (*GB*) a non-commissioned officer in the army, at lowest rank.

lan·cet /'laːnsɪt/ nc (*med*) a pointed, two-edged knife as used by surgeons.

land[1] /lænd/ n 1 nu the solid part of the earth's surface (contrasted with *sea*): *travel over land and sea*. **by land** (travelling) by train, car etc, not by plane, ship etc. Compare ground(1). *the land of the living* this present existence. *the lie of the land* ⇨ lie[1]. *see/find out how the land lies* (*fig*) to learn how things are; learn the general state of affairs. 3 nu (sometimes pl) property in the form of land: *Do you own much land here?* 4 nc a country (the usual word) and its people: *my native land*.

'**land-agent** nc a person employed to look after, buy, or sell land(3).

'**land·holder** nc an owner or tenant of land(3).

'**land·lady** nc (**a**) a woman who lets others live in her property for money. (**b**) a woman owner, manager of a pub, lodging-house etc.

'**land·lock·ed** adj (of a country) with no frontier at the sea.

'**land·lord** nc (**a**) a man who lets others live in his property for money. (**b**) an owner, manager, of a pub, lodging-house etc.

'**land·mark** nc (**a**) an object that marks the boundary of a piece of land. (**b**) an object etc easily seen by travellers and helpful to them. (**c**) (*fig*) an event, discovery, change etc that is an important stage or turning-point: *landmarks in the course of social history*.

'**land-mine** nc an explosive put in the ground and exploded by vehicles, footsteps etc.

'**land·owner** nc an owner of land(3).

'**land·slide** nc (**a**) a fall of earth, rock etc from the side of a hill etc. (**b**) (also *attrib*) a sudden change in political opinion resulting in a very large majority of votes for one side in an election: *a Democratic landslide; a landslide victory*.

land[2] /lænd/ v 1 vt,vi (to cause a plane etc) to come down from the air to stop on the ground or the sea: *The airliner landed safely. The pilot landed the plane safely. The cat fell out of the tree but landed on its feet. land on one's feet* ⇨ foot[1](1). 2 vt to get (a fish) onto land. 3 vt (of a ship etc) to put (cargo, passengers) onto land. 4 vt *land a job* (*informal*) to get a job: *land a job on a ship*.

land (sb) in sth (*informal*) to get (a person) into trouble, difficulties: *What a mess you've landed us all in!*

land up (*informal*) to reach a point or position (after a journey, series of events etc): *We landed up teaching in China. land (up) in a place* to come eventually to be in a place: *He landed in prison/in Berlin*.

land sb with sb/sth (often *passive*) to make a person accept a responsibility, task etc: *I've been landed with the job of cleaning the floors/with her youngest baby*.

land·ed adj (*attrib*) (**a**) consisting of land: *landed property*. (**b**) owning land: *the landed classes*.

land·ing /'lændɪŋ/ nc 1 the act of a plane etc coming, or bringing a plane etc, down to land: *The pilot made an emergency landing*. 2 a place where people and goods may be landed from a ship etc. 3 an area at the top of a set of stairs.

'**landing-gear** nu equipment with wheels etc for landing an aircraft.

'**landing-stage** nc = landing(2).

land·scape /'lændskeɪp/ n 1 nc (a picture of) inland scenery. 2 nu the branch of art dealing with this.

,**landscape 'gardening/'architecture** nu the planning of parks, gardens etc.

lane /leɪn/ nc 1 a narrow country road. 2 (L- in names) a narrow street: *Drury Lane*. 3 a marked division of a road to guide motorists; line of vehicles within such a division: *keep to the inside/outside lane*. 4 a marked division to guide competitors in a race (e.g. on a running track or in a swimming pool).

lang. *written abbr* language.

lan·guage /'læŋgwɪdʒ/ n 1 nu the system of human communication of knowledge, ideas, feelings etc using sounds and words. *bad language* swearing. *strong language* swearing or using abusive words. 2 nc a particular form of this: *foreign languages*. 3 nu the words, phrases etc used by a particular profession or class: *medical/legal language; computer language*. 4 nc a system of signs used as language: *sign language* (i.e. as used by the deaf). 5 nc (*fig*) an expression of feelings etc: *the language of flowers*.

'**language laboratory** nc a room where languages are taught using tape-recorders etc.

lan·guid /'læŋgwɪd/ adj (*formal*) (of a person) having no energy.

lan·guid·ly adv

lan·guish /'læŋgwɪʃ/ vi (*formal*) 1 *languish (in a place)* to lose, be without, energy, health or happiness (during one's time in a place): *languish in prison*. 2 *languish (for sth)* to be unhappy because of a desire (for something): *languish for love and sympathy*.

lan·guor /'læŋgə(r)/ nu (*formal*) the (cause of) loss of energy, health and happiness.

lan·guor·ous /-əs/ adj

lank /læŋk/ adj (usually *derog*) (of hair) straight and limp.

lanky /'læŋkɪ/ adj (**-ier, -iest**) (of a person) tall and thin: *a lanky girl*.

lano·lin /'lænəlɪn/ nu the fat from sheep's wool, used in ointments for the skin.

lan·tern /'læntən/ nc a container for a light from a flame, used to protect it from the wind.

lap[1] /læp/ nc one complete journey round a track or race-course. □ vt (**-pp-**) to overtake (another competitor) who is a lap behind.

lap[2] /læp/ nc the front part of a person from the waist to the knees, when sitting: *The mother had* the baby on her lap. Ⓝ *'Lap'* is not used in the *pl* when referring to one person. **the lap of luxury** a fortunate or wealthy state or condition.

lap³ /læp/ *nc* **1** an act of lapping. **2** a sound of lapping: *the lap of the waves against the side of the boat.*

lap⁴ /læp/ *v* (**-pp-**) **1** *vt,vi* **lap (sth) (up)** to drink by taking up (liquid) with the tongue as a cat does. **2** *vt* **lap sth up** (*fig*) (of a person) to take praise etc quickly or eagerly: *lap up compliments.* **3** *vi* (of water) to move with a sound like the lapping up of liquid: *waves lapping on the shore.*

la·pel /lə'pel/ *nc* a front part of a coat or jacket that is folded back and forms part of the collar.

lapse¹ /læps/ *nc* **1** a small error in speech, behaviour, memory etc. **2** a gradual passing (of time): *a long lapse of time.* **3** (*legal*) an ending of a right etc because of failure to use it or renew it.

lapse² /læps/ *vi* **1** to make a lapse¹(1). **2 lapse (into sth)** to change from good ways (into bad ways): *lapsing into bad habits.* **3** (of time) to pass: *Several hours lapsed before he woke up.* **4** (*legal*) (of rights etc) to be lost because not used or renewed.

lar·ceny /'lɑːsənɪ/ *n* (*pl* **-ies**) *nc,nu* (*legal*) (an instance of) stealing.

lard /lɑːd/ *nu* the fat of pigs used in cooking. □ *vt* to put lard on (food etc). **lard sth with sth** (often *derog*) to fill a speech, report etc with too much of something: *a speech larded with boring quotations.*

lar·der /'lɑːdə(r)/ *nc* a room or cupboard used for storing meat etc.

large¹ /lɑːdʒ/ *adj* (**—r, —st**) **1** above average (in amount, size, extent): *a large house/hole/meal/family/town. She takes a large size in dresses. This furniture is too large for the space. His debts are large. There has been a large increase in unemployment.* Ⓝ For a comparison of *large, big* and *great,* ⇨ the *note* at big¹(1). **as large as life** obvious when seen (esp when not expected): *He said he was ill but I saw him at the disco as large as life.* **larger than life** (**a**) (of a picture, model etc) more than the actual size. (**b**) (of an event, person etc) exaggerated in order to impress: *accounts of the battle/expedition/her qualities that were larger than life.* **2** (*fig; formal*) very generous, sympathetic: *He has a large heart.*

‚large in'testine *nc* (the **—**) (*anat*) the lower part of the *alimentary canal* (near the *anus*).

'large-scale *adj* (*attrib*) (**a**) extensive: *large-scale operations.* (**b**) made or drawn to a large scale: *a large-scale map.* Opp small-scale.

larg·ish /-ɪʃ/ *adj* rather large.

large·ly *adv* to a great extent; mainly: *His success was largely due to luck.*

large² /lɑːdʒ/ *adv* **by and large** ⇨ by¹(5).

large³ /lɑːdʒ/ *n* (only in) **at large** (**a**) (of a criminal or wild animal) free: *The escaped prisoner is still at large.* (**b**) in general; as a whole: *Did the people at large approve of the government's decision?* (**c**) in full detail; at length (which is more usual): *talk/write at large about the discovery.*

lark¹ /lɑːk/ *nc* (any of many kinds of) small brown songbird: *the skylark.*

lark² /lɑːk/ *nc* (*informal*) a bit of fun: *He did it for a lark. What a lark!* (= How amusing!).

lark³ /lɑːk/ *vi* **lark (about/around)** to be foolish and waste time: *Stop larking about and get on with your work.*

lar·va /'lɑːvə/ *nc* (*pl* **larvae** /'lɑːviː/) (*science*) an insect in the first stage of its development after coming out of the egg.

lar·val /'lɑːvl/ *adj*

lar·yn·gi·tis /ˌlærɪn'dʒaɪtɪs/ *nu* (*med*) inflammation of the larynx.

lar·ynx /'lærɪŋks/ *nc* (*anat*) the upper part of the windpipe where the vocal cords are.

las·civ·ious /lə'sɪvɪəs/ *adj* (*formal; derog*) feeling, causing, showing, lust.

las·civ·ious·ly *adv*

la·ser /'leɪzə(r)/ *nc* (also *attrib*) an apparatus used for generating, amplifying and concentrating light waves into a powerful beam, used to cut metal and jewels, to aim weapons etc: *a laser beam; a laser tool.*

lash¹ /læʃ/ *nc* **1** (a blow using) the flexible part of a whip: *given twenty lashes.* **2** = eyelash.

lash² /læʃ/ *v* **1** *vt,vi* to strike (a person, thing) violently (as if) with a whip: *The rain was lashing (against) the windows. The tiger lashed its tail angrily. He lashed the horse across the back with his whip.* **2** *vi* **lash out (against/at sb/sth)** to attack (a person, policy etc) violently with blows or words: *He lashed out against the government.* **3** *vt* **lash sth (down) (to sth)** to fasten something tightly with rope etc.

lash·ing /'læʃɪŋ/ *n* **1** *nc* a cord or rope used for tying or fastening. **2** *nc* an instance of whipping or beating. **3** (*pl*) **lashings of sth** (*informal*) plenty of something: *lashings of cream.*

lass /læs/ *nc* (*informal*) a girl; young woman.

las·sie /'læsɪ/ *nc* = lass.

las·so /læ'suː/ *nc* (*pl* **—s** or **—es**) a looped rope with a knot, used for catching horses and cattle. □ *vt* to catch (animals) with a lasso: *lassoing horses.*

last¹ /lɑːst/ *adj* or *det* **1** (**the, my,** etc) **last** + noun coming after all others in order or time: *December is the last month of the year. Will the last person to come in please close the door. That is my last* (= final) *word on the subject.* Compare first¹, next¹(1). **have the last laugh** ⇨ laugh¹. **be on one's/its last legs** ⇨ leg¹(1). **have the last word** ⇨ word¹(2). ⇨ also resort¹(2). **2** (**a**) **the last day, year** etc the period (day, year etc) immediately before now (or the period mentioned or known): *You've been absent for the last hour. She's been in New York for the last two months. The last month was a sad one.* (**b**) **last week, year** etc during the period immediately before this: *I telephoned you last night/Sunday. I was ill last weekend but I feel better now. Last year we went to Italy. On Tuesday last* (= Last Tuesday) *I lost my bag. Is the rent for this month* (i.e. now) *or last month?* Compare next¹(2). **3** only remaining: *I wouldn't marry you if you were the last person on earth! This opportunity will be your last.* **4 the last thing in sth** the latest, most modern, example of something: *This cordless telephone is the last thing in electronic equipment for the home.* ⇨ word¹(1).

last² /lɑːst/ *adv* after all others: *I was chosen last. What did you do last? I'm to speak last at the meeting.* Compare first²(1), next²(1). **last of all** (used for emphasis) finally: *Last of all you must* *not forget to switch off the lights.* **last but not least** (used for emphasis) after all others in order but not in importance: *And last but not least I'd like to thank you all for coming.* ⇨ lastly. **2** on the occasion immediately before (this, that): *She was still married when I last saw her* (or *saw her last*). *When did you last see your father?* Compare first²(2), next²(2).

last³ /lɑːst/ *pron* (the —) the last person, thing or people, things etc: *He was/They were the last to arrive. These are the last of our apples. I'd be the last to harm you.* Compare first³(1), next³. **at last** after a long time or delay: *At last she agreed to come. He came at last.* **at long last** after a very long time: *At long last we were able to finish the work.* **from first to last** ⇨ first³(1). **(the) last but one** the one immediately before the last: *She was (the) last but one to arrive.* **see the last of sb/sth** to have finished being with a person, dealing with a job etc that is unpleasant, boring: *I'll be glad to see the last of this job.* **to the last** until the final moment possible; until death: *fight to the last.*

last⁴ /lɑːst/ *vt,vi* **1** **last ((for) sth)** to continue (for a period of time): *How long will this good weather last? Her speeches often last (for) hours.* **2** **last ((for) sth)** to remain fresh, not change, (for the length of time mentioned): *The meat ought to last (for) one more day. How long can he last without water?* **3** **last (sb) ((for) sth)** to satisfy the needs of (a person) (for a length of time mentioned): *Your shoes will have to last (you) until I get paid/(for) another month.*

last·ing /ˈlɑːstɪŋ/ *adj* (*attrib*) continuing for a long time: *a lasting peace.* ⇨ everlasting.

last·ly /ˈlɑːstlɪ/ *adv* (used at the end of a list) finally: *Lastly, I'd like to thank my father.* Ⓝ *'Last of all'* is also possible. Compare firstly.

lat. *written abbr* latitude.

latch¹ /lætʃ/ *nc* a fastening for a door or gate, with a bar falling into a catch and being lifted by a small lever.

latch² /lætʃ/ *v* **1** *vt,vi* to fasten (a door etc) with a latch. **2** *vt* **latch onto sb/sth** (*informal*) **(a)** to hold onto a person, thing and not let go. **(b)** to understand a person, thing: *latch onto what he meant.* **3** *vi* **latch on** (*informal*) to understand.

late¹ /leɪt/ *adj* (**—r, —st**) **1** (*pred*) (arriving, starting etc) after the usual or agreed time or after others: *You're late. Dinner will be late. It's late* (or *It's late in the day*) *and I'm tired. She's an hour late. The train is later than usual.* **2** (*attrib; no comp*) near to the end, during the last part, of the day, season, period of time etc: *have a late lunch; during the late afternoon; catch a late bus home.* **3** **at the latest** and not after (the usual or agreed time): *Be here by Monday at the latest.* Compare early¹(3). **4** (*attrib*) most modern or recent: *the latest fashions; the late news programme.* **5** (*attrib; no comp*) who is now dead: *her late husband.* **6** (*attrib; no comp*) who no longer has that position: *the late prime minister.*

late² /leɪt/ *adv* (**—r, —st**) **1** after the usual or agreed time or after others: *arrive/start/get up late. The buses are running late. The doctor came 5 minutes too late.* **sooner or later** ⇨ soon(2). **2** **late (on) in** a period of time near to the end, during the last part, of: *She became a writer late*

on in life. Later in the year this tree has flowers. **later (on)** at a later time: *You go to the disco and I'll join you later* (on). **3** recently; not after: *I saw him as late as yesterday/no later than 9 o'clock this morning.* Compare early².

late·comer /ˈleɪtkʌmə(r)/ *nc* a person who is late(1).

lat·ish /ˈleɪtɪʃ/ *adj, adv* (*no comp*) rather late: *have a latish breakfast; come latish to the meeting.*

late·ly /ˈleɪtlɪ/ *adv* during recent times; recently: *Have you been to the cinema lately? It is only lately that she has been well enough to go out.*

la·tent /ˈleɪtənt/ *adj* (*no comp*) present but not yet active, developed or visible: *latent energy/ability.*

lat·er·al /ˈlætərəl/ *adj* (*attrib*) of, at, from, to, the side(s): *a lateral branch.*

ˌlateral ˈthinking *nu* a way of solving a problem by simple, unusual or illogical methods (e.g. as a child may).

la·tex /ˈleɪteks/ *nu* the kind of thick white liquid produced by a rubber tree.

lathe /leɪð/ *nc* a machine used for holding and turning pieces of wood or metal while they are being shaped etc.

la·ther /ˈlɑːðə(r)/ *nu* the soft mass of white froth from soap and water. □ *vt,vi* (to cause soap etc) to form a lather on (something): *lather one's chin before shaving.*

lati·tude /ˈlætɪtjuːd/ *n* **1** *nc* (*tech*) the distance north or south of the equator measured in degrees. **2** *nu* freedom of action or opinion: *She was given too much latitude as a child.*

lati·tudi·nal /ˌlætɪˈtjuːdɪnl/ *adj*

la·trine /ləˈtriːn/ *nc* (in camps etc) a ditch (to be) used as a toilet.

lat·ter¹ /ˈlætə(r)/ *adj* (*attrib; no comp*) of a later period: *the latter half of the year.* Compare former¹.

lat·ter² /ˈlætə(r)/ *pron* (the —) the second (mentioned) of two people or things: *I can study history or geography and I prefer the latter.* Compare former².

lat·ter·ly *adv* recently.

lat·tice /ˈlætɪs/ *nc* (also *attrib*) a framework of crossed wooden or metal strips, used as a fence etc: *a lattice window.*

laud·able /ˈlɔːdəbl/ *adj* (*formal*) deserving praise: *a laudable effort to complete the work on time.*

laud·ably /-əblɪ/ *adv*

laugh¹ /lɑːf/ *nc* an act, sound, of laughing: *We had such a good laugh watching the children playing in the mud.* **have the last laugh** to be successful, defeat a person etc after earlier failure. **raise a laugh** to do something to cause laughter. ⇨ also belly-laugh.

laugh² /lɑːf/ *v* **1** *vi* to make sounds and expressions to show amusement: *His jokes made me laugh. I was laughing so much I almost cried.* ⇨ laugh at/over sb/sth. **be laughing** (*informal*) to be successful, have enough money etc: *Now that she's won the competition she's laughing.* **laugh like a drain** to laugh long and loudly. **2** *vt,vi* to make the sounds of laughing to show one's feelings (of disrespect, hate, arrogance etc): *She laughed her contempt. How he laughed when she tried to apologize.* **3** *v reflex* to cause oneself to be (a condition mentioned) by laughing: *She laughed herself sick/silly.*

laugh at sb/sth (a) to laugh(1) because of an amusing person, joke etc. (b) to make fun of a person, thing: *It is cruel to laugh at a poor old man/at his clothes.* (c) to pay no serious attention to, show no respect for, (danger): *She laughed at the warning about bad weather.*

laugh sth away to laugh in order to hide pain, fear, tears etc.

laugh in sb's face ⇨ face¹(1).

laugh sth off (*informal*) to try to hide one's mistake, responsibility etc by not being serious: *You were in charge when the accident happened so it's useless to try to laugh it off.* **laugh one's head off** ⇨ head¹(1).

laugh over sb/sth to laugh(1,2) because of a person, situation etc: *laugh over his failure.*

laugh up one's sleeve ⇨ sleeve(1).

laugh·able /ˈlɑːfəbl/ *adj* amusing; ridiculous: *a laughable mistake/attempt.*

laugh·ably /-əblɪ/ *adv*

laugh·ing /ˈlɑːfɪŋ/ *adj* (*attrib*) showing amusement: *laughing faces.* **no laughing matter** ⇨ matter¹(4). □ *nu* laughter.

laugh·ter /ˈlɑːftə(r)/ *nu* the act, sound, of laughing: *I was aching with laughter at the end of the play.*

launch¹ /lɔːntʃ/ *nc* a kind of boat with an engine (used on rivers and lakes and in harbours).

launch² /lɔːntʃ/ *nc* an act of launching a ship or spacecraft.

launch³ /lɔːntʃ/ *v* **1** *vt,vi* to put (a ship, esp a new one) in the sea for the first time: *launch a new passenger liner.* **2** *vt* to send (something) high into the air: *launch a missile/spacecraft.* **3** *vt* to begin (an attack). **4** *vt* (*fig*) to get (a business, scheme etc) started: *launch a new business.* **5** *vi* **launch (out) into sth** to make or start (on an activity): *launch into a new career.*

'launching pad *nc* a base or platform from which spacecraft etc are launched.

'launching site *nc* a place for launching-pads.

laun·der /ˈlɔːndə(r)/ *vt* (*formal; commerce*) to wash and iron (clothes): *Send these sheets to be laundered.*

laun·der·ette /ˌlɔːndəˈret/ *nc* a place with coin-operated automatic washing-machines and dryers.

laun·dry /ˈlɔːndrɪ/ *n* (*pl* **-ies**) **1** *nc* a place where clothes, sheets etc are sent to be washed. **2** *nu* clothes (to be) washed and ironed: *Has the laundry come back yet?*

laur·el /ˈlɒrəl/ *nc* an evergreen shrub with smooth, shiny leaves (used by ancient Romans and Greeks as an emblem of victory, success and distinction). **look to one's laurels** to be on the look out for possible successes among rivals. **rest on one's laurels** to be content with present achievements.

lav /læv/ *nc* (*informal*) = lavatory.

la·va /ˈlɑːvə/ *nu* hot semi-liquid material flowing from a volcano: *a stream of lava.*

lava·tory /ˈlævətrɪ/ *nc* (*pl* **-ies**) **1** a toilet. **2** a room for washing the hands and face in.

lav·en·der /ˈlævɪndə(r)/ *adj, nu* (of the (smell, colour of) a kind of plant with tall stems having small pale purple flowers.

lav·ish¹ /ˈlævɪʃ/ *adj* **1** (of a person) giving or producing freely, liberally or generously: *be lavish in giving money to charity.* **2** (*attrib*) given in great amounts: *receive lavish praise.*

lav·ish·ly *adv*

lav·ish² /ˈlævɪʃ/ *vt* **lavish sth (on sb)** to give care, praise, attention etc generously to (a person): *lavish care on an only child.*

law /lɔː/ *n* **1** *nc* a rule made by authority for the proper regulation of a community or society or for behaviour: *traffic laws.* ⇨ by-law. **2** (the —) the whole body of laws as a group: *If a man breaks the law he can be punished.* ⇨ -in-law, in-laws. **lay down the law** to speak in a forceful, demanding way: *She's been laying down the law all week-end about which flowers to plant.* **3** *nu* (also *attrib*) the legal profession; legal system: *study law; law students; commercial/international law.* **law and order** the state of respect for, the keeping of, laws: *Law and order must be maintained.* **take the law into one's own hands** to try to get justice without legal help or by ignoring the law(2). **4** (the —) (*informal*) the police. **5** *nc* a rule of action or procedure in sport, art or life: *the laws of tennis; a mathematical law; the laws of perspective; the laws of good behaviour.* **be a law unto oneself** to ignore general rules and conventions. **6** *nc* (also *law of nature* or *natural law*) a statement of what always happens in the natural world: *Newton's law; the law of supply and demand.*

'law-abiding *adj* obeying the law(2).

'law-breaker *nc* a person who disobeys the law(2).

'law court *nc* a court of justice.

'law-suit *nc* a case in a law court.

law·ful /-fəl/ *adj* (*no comp*) allowed by law: *We must ask whether it is lawful to build a fence here.* Opp unlawful. ⇨ also legal; licit.

law·ful·ly /-fəlɪ/ *adv*

law·less *adj* not according to, not conforming to, the law: *a lawless society.*

law·less·ness *nu*

lawn /lɔːn/ *nc* an area of grass cut short and smooth.

'lawn-mower *nc* a machine used for cutting grass.

lawn 'tennis *nu* tennis played on a grass court.

law·yer /ˈlɔːjə(r)/ *nc* a person who practises law, esp an attorney or solicitor.

lax /læks/ *adj* (*formal*) **1** not taking care. **2** **lax (in sth)** not strict or severe: *lax in morals.*

lax·ity /ˈlæksətɪ/ *nc,nu*

laxa·tive /ˈlæksətɪv/ *nc, adj* (a medicine, drug) causing the bowels to empty.

lay¹ /leɪ/ *adj* (*attrib*) **1** of, for, done by, people who are not members of the clergy: *a lay preacher.* ⇨ laity. **2** non-professional (esp referring to law or medicine): *lay opinion.*

'lay·man *nc* (a) a lay(1) person. (b) a person without professional knowledge: *technical explanations for the layman.*

lay² /leɪ/ *v* (*pt,pp* laid /leɪd/) Ⓝ For uses of 'lay' with nouns such as *blame, charge, claim, door, finger, hand, rest, seige* etc, ⇨ the noun entries. Be careful because 'to lay' may be mistaken for the past tense of the verb 'to lie' (which is also 'lay', as in *I lay down on the bed*). 'To lay' always has a direct object as in *lay your coat over a chair; lay an egg; lay a table* but *'to lie'* never has a direct object. Compare: *We were laying a carpet on the floor* and *We were lying on the grass looking at the stars.* **1** *vt* to put (something) on, over etc something: *He laid his coat over my shoulders. Please do not lay bicycles against this wall. Lay those books on the table.* **2** *vt* to put (something) in a particular place or position: *lay a carpet; lay a trap.* **3** *vt* to put (something) in a particular arrangement or order: *lay a table (for breakfast); lay a fire.* **4** *vt* to cause (a person or thing) to be in the condition mentioned: *The horse laid its ears back.* **be laid low** ⇨ low[1](9). **lay oneself open to sth** to make oneself able to be hurt by criticism, abuse etc. **laid waste** ⇨ waste[1](1). **5** *vt* to cause (dust, dirt etc) to settle: *use water to lay the dust.* **6** *vt* to offer, put down, (money) as a bet: *I'll lay you £5 that he'll win.* **7** *vt,vi* (of birds, fish, insects etc) to produce (an egg or eggs). **8** *vt* (usually *passive*) to place, set (a story, event etc) (in a place): *The scene is laid in Rome.*

lay sth aside (a) to keep money etc for future use: *lay aside a certain amount each week.* (b) to put something down (which is more usual): *He laid his book aside and looked at me.*

lay sth before sb/sth (*formal*) to present a plan, proposal etc to an official, committee etc.

lay sth by = lay sth aside(a). ⇨ also lay-by.

lay sb down to place a person in a flat position (on or in a place): *I was laying the baby down in her cot.* (N) Compare the use of *'to lie'* as in *The baby was lying in her cot.* **lay sth down** (a) to put an object down: *He laid the box down on the step to rest.* Compare lie down. (b) to advise or order a regulation, method etc: *Follow the instructions laid down in the manual.* (c) to put wine etc in a special place to improve. ⇨ also arms(1), law(1), life(4).

lay sth in to provide a supply, stock etc for oneself: *lay in wood for the fire/food for the winter.*

lay into sb (*informal*) to attack a person (physically or verbally): *My parents will lay into me because I'm late.*

lay off (*imperative*) stop (doing something unpleasant or annoying). **lay sb off** to take a person's job away (usually for a short time): *The factory laid off twenty men last week.* Hence **'lay-off** *nc.* **lay off sb/sth** to stop annoying a person, causing trouble to a person, her or his property etc: *He warned us to lay off his son/dog/chickens/apples.* **lay off sth** (*informal*) to stop doing, eating something unpleasant or harmful: *lay off shouting/smoking/cigarettes/alcohol.*

lay sth on (a) to organize an exhibition, party, food etc: *A reception has been laid on for the visitor.* (b) to provide gas, electricity or a driver, guard: *A car has been laid on for you.* (c) (*informal*) to make one's feelings, problems etc seem bigger: *Isn't saying she has no money while wearing gold and diamond rings laying it on a bit thick?* ⇨ also eye[1](1), hand[1](1), stress[1](2).

lay sb out (*informal*) to hit a person unconscious. **lay sth out** (a) to spread out clothes, equipment, tools etc ready for use. (b) to plan, arrange, something (in the way mentioned): *well laid-out streets; lay out photographs in an album.* (c) (*informal*) to spend money: *lay out a lot of*

money on the dinner party. ⇨ outlay.

lay sb up (of an injury, illness) to make a person inactive, keep a person in bed: *A bad cold laid me up for the weekend.* **lay sth up** (a) (usually *passive*) to put a vehicle, boat etc out of use: *My car has been laid up for a week with a broken starter.* (b) to make certain because of one's behaviour that one will experience trouble: *The government is laying up serious economic difficulties for itself by cutting taxes.*

lay[3] /leɪ/ *pt* of lie[4].

lay·about /'leɪəbaʊt/ *nc* (*GB informal; derog*) a person who avoids work.

lay-by /'leɪbaɪ/ *nc* (*GB*) an area at the side of a road used for vehicles to park.

lay·er /'leɪə(r)/ *nc* **1** a thickness of material (esp one of several) over a surface or forming one division: *a layer of dust; a layer of cake; a layer of clay.* **2** (of hens): *good/bad layers* (= laying eggs in large/small numbers). ⇨ also bricklayer.

lay·ette /leɪ'et/ *nc* an outfit for a newborn baby.

lay·man /'leɪmən/ *nc* ⇨ lay[1].

lay-off /'leɪ ɒf/ *nc* ⇨ lay sb off.

laze /leɪz/ *vi,vt* **laze (about/around); laze sth away** to be lazy: *lazing away the afternoon; lazing about in the sun.*

la·zy /'leɪzɪ/ *adj* (**-ier, -iest**) **1** (*derog*) unwilling to work; doing little work: *a lazy girl.* **2** suitable for, causing, inactivity: *a lazy afternoon.* Compare idle.

'lazy-bones *nc* (*informal*) a lazy person.

lazi·ly *adv*

lazi·ness *nu*

lb. *written abbr* pound(s) (weight).

l.b.w. /ˌel biː 'dʌbljuː/ *abbr* (*cricket*) leg before wicket (a way of defeating a batsman).

l.c. *written abbr* (*commerce*) letter of credit.

LCD /ˌel siː 'diː/ *abbr* (*maths*) least/lowest common denominator. ⇨ denominator. **2** liquid crystal display (a kind of flat surface on which information can be shown, used esp in digital watches, calculators etc).

LCM /ˌel siː 'em/ *abbr* (*maths*) least/lowest common multiple (the smallest number that is exactly divisible by each member of a set of numbers): *12 is the LCM of 2, 3 and 4.* ⇨ multiple[2].

Ld *written abbr* Lord(4).

LEA /ˌel iː 'eɪ/ *abbr* Local Education Authority (responsible for education in a particular area).

lead[1] /led/ *n* **1** *nu* a kind of soft, heavy, easily melted, grey metal (symbol Pb), used for pipes etc. ⇨ leaden(1). **2** *nc, nu* (a stick of) grey substance (called *graphite*) as used in a pencil.

,lead 'poisoning *nu* a diseased condition caused by taking lead(1) into the body.

lead[2] /liːd/ *n* **1** *n sing* an action of guiding or giving an example; direction given by going in front: *follow the manager's lead; give the competitors a lead by explaining the first problem.* **2** (the —) the first place or position: *be in/have/gain the lead in a race.* **take the lead** to take first place (in a race, competition, set of statistics): *Our business has taken the lead in paper production.* **3** *n sing* a distance by which a person, business, political party etc leads: *an actual lead of two metres.* **4** *nc* a cord, strap or chain used for leading a dog. **5** *nc* a principal part in a play; actor or actress who plays such a part. **6** *nc* a wire etc for an electric current.

7 *nc* a piece of useful information (to be used to solve a problem): *The police have no leads on the crime yet.*

lead³ /li:d/ *v* (*pt,pp* **led** /led/) **1** *vt,vi* to bring, take, (a person, animal) by going in front: *lead a group of children across the road. She led and the children followed her.* **lead the way** ⇨ way²(1). **2** *vt,vi* to direct the movement of (a person, animal) by using one's hands, a rope etc: *lead a blind person/horse through the field.* **lead sb astray** ⇨ astray. **3** *vt,vi* to act as a leader, chief of (something): *lead an expedition/orchestra/army; lead the Liberal Party.* **4** *vi* to have the first place in a race, competition, set of statistics): *Which horse/political party/business is leading?* **5** *vi* **lead** (*to a place*) to be a direction, road etc (to): *Where does this road lead (to)?* **6** *vt* to influence (a person) (to do something): *What led you to think I would agree?* **7** *vt* to experience (a kind of life etc mentioned): *lead a hard life/a miserable existence/an unhappy childhood.* ⇨ dog¹(1).

lead off (with sth) to start a talk, discussion (with a particular subject): *We led off with a discussion of last month's sales.*

lead on (*imperative*) to go in front and lead(1).

lead sb on (*informal*) to try to persuade a person to believe, agree etc by using false information or promises: *Do television advertisements lead us on?*

lead to sth (a) ⇨ 5 above. (b) to have something as a result: *Your bad behaviour will lead to trouble. Such a policy could lead to war.*

lead up to sth to be a preparation for something in increasing stages: *discussions leading up to a final agreement; events leading up to the war. You've spoken for a long time—what are you leading up to?*

lead with sth = lead off (with sth).

lead·en /'ledn/ *adj* (*formal*) **1** having the grey colour of lead¹(1): *leaden clouds.* **2** dull and sad: *a leaden heart.*

lead·er /'li:də(r)/ *nc* **1** a person who leads: *the leader of an army/an expedition/the Labour Party; a political leader.* **2** a business, design, country etc that has first place in a competition, set of statistics etc): *Japan is a market leader in car production.* **3** a chief lawyer in a lawsuit: *the leader for the defence.* **4** (*GB*) a leading article (in a newspaper).

lead·er·less *adj*

lead·er·ship *nu* (a) the position of a leader. (b) the power, qualities, of a leader.

lead·ing /'li:dɪŋ/ *adj* (*attrib*) chief; most important: *the leading men of the day.*

,**leading 'article** *nc* (in a newspaper) one giving editorial opinions on events, policies etc.

,**leading 'lady** *nc* the most important actress in a play etc.

,**leading 'light** *nc* (*informal*) an important and influential person.

,**leading 'question** *nc* one formed and used to suggest the answer that is hoped for.

leaf¹ /li:f/ *n* (*pl* **leaves** /li:vz/) **1** *nc* one of the parts (usually green and flat) growing from the side of a stem or branch or direct from the root of a tree, bush, plant etc. **be in leaf** to have leaves: *The trees will soon be in leaf.* **2** *nc* one sheet of paper forming two pages of a book. **turn over a**

new leaf (*fig*) to make a new and better start. **3** *nc* a hinged flap of a table (used to make it larger). **4** *nu* a very thin sheet of metal, esp of gold or silver: *gold leaf.*

leafy *adj* (**-ier, -iest**) covered with, having, made by, leaves: *a leafy shade.*

leaf² /li:f/ *vi* **leaf through sth** to look through a book, magazine etc quickly.

leaf·let /'li:flɪt/ *nc* a printed sheet (sometimes folded) with announcements etc, esp one for free distribution.

league /li:g/ *nc* **1** (an agreement made between) people, groups or nations working for their common benefit. **in league with sb/sth** (a) having made an agreement with a person, organization. (b) connected with a person, group (usually in order to do illegal or immoral things). **2** a group of sports clubs or teams playing matches among themselves: *the football league.*

leak¹ /li:k/ *nc* **1** a small hole, crack etc through which a liquid, gas etc may get in or out: *a leak in the roof.* **spring a leak** to produce a leak suddenly: *The boat has sprung a leak.* **2** the liquid, gas etc that gets out or in: *I can smell a petrol leak.* **3** (*fig*) an instance of leaking(2): *a leak of secret information.*

leak² /li:k/ *vt,vi* **1** (to allow a liquid, gas) to pass out or in through a hole, crack etc: *The rain is leaking in.* **2** **leak sth (to sb/sth); leak out** (to cause news, secrets etc) to become known by chance or deliberately: *Who leaked the news to the press? How did the news leak out?*

¹**leak·age** /-ɪdʒ/ *nc,nu*

lean¹ /li:n/ *adj* (**—er, —est**) **1** (of people and animals) having less than the usual amount of fat. **2** (of meat) containing little or no fat. **3** poor: *a lean harvest.*

lean·ness *nu*

lean² /li:n/ *nu* meat with little or no fat.

lean³ /li:n/ *vt,vi* (*pt,pp* **—ed** or **—t** /lent/) **1** (to cause oneself, an object) to rest against or be supported by something: *lean a ladder against a wall; lean on one's elbows.* **2** (to cause oneself etc) to bend from an upright position: *lean over a wall; lean out of a window; lean one's head back; lean forward in one's chair.*

lean on sb/sth (for sth) (a) (*informal*) to depend on a person, evidence etc (for support, advice etc): *I know I can always lean on my teacher for advice.* (b) (*sl*) to use threats or violence to force a person to do or get something: *Some small criminals lean on weak people for money or information.*

lean over (sb) to bend one's body near to or look over the top (of a person): *She leant over and whispered in my ear. Don't lean over me while I'm reading.* **lean over backwards (to do sth)** to make a great effort (to understand, cooperate etc): *I've leant over backwards to help you, but you make no effort yourself.*

lean towards sth to have, show, a tendency to support, approve of, be interested in etc something: *She leans towards socialism.* ⇨ leaning.

lean·ing /'li:nɪŋ/ *nc* **leaning (towards sth)** a tendency: *a leaning towards a career in industry.* ⇨ lean towards sth.

leap¹ /li:p/ *nc* **1** a sudden upward movement off the ground by a person: *a leap over a wall/across a*

leap /li:p/ or —t /lept/) **1** *vi* to make
a sudden upward movement off the ground: *leap
with delight.* (N) *'Jump'* is also possible and is more
usual, but *'leap'* can suggest a more energetic movement. **2** *vt* **leap (over) sth** to jump across or over
something: *leap a wall/river.* **3** *vi* **leap over** to
move across quickly and with enthusiasm: *He
leapt over to shake her hand.* **4** *vi* **leap at sth** to
be very willing to accept an offer, opportunity,
idea etc: *leap at the chance to earn a lot of money.*

leap year /li:p jɪə(r)/ *nc* a year in which February
has 29 days (every fourth year).

learn /lɜ:n/ *v* (*pt,pp* **—ed** or **—t** /lɜ:nt/) **1** *vt,vi* to
gain knowledge of, become skilled in, (a subject
being studied, a particular activity): *learn a
foreign language; learn (how) to swim; learn to be
a typist. I knew nothing about life in Spain but I'm
learning (fast).* Compare teach(1). **2** *vt* to put
(something) into one's memory: *learn one's part
in a play.* **learn sth by heart** ⇨ heart(2). **3** *vt,vi*
to be told or hear (information): *How did you
learn about the meeting? We haven't yet learnt if
they arrived safely.*

learn·ed /lɜ:nɪd/ *adj* (usually *attrib*), having,
showing, a great deal of knowledge: *learned
teachers/books/societies.*

learn·ed·ly *adv*

learn·er *nc* a person who is learning.

learn·ing *nu* (knowledge gained by) study.

lease¹ /li:s/ *nc* a written agreement by which the
owner of land or a building (*the lessor*) agrees to
let another (*the lessee*) have the use of it for a certain time for a fixed money payment (*rent*). **a
new lease of life** a chance of living longer, of
being happier etc.

lease·hold *adj, nu* (of) land (to be) held on
lease. Compare freehold.

'lease·hold·er *nc* a person who has a lease.

lease² /li:s/ *vt* **1** to have (a building, land) under a
lease: *I've leased this flat for a year.* **2** **lease sth
(to sb)** to give a building, land (to a person)
under a lease: *He leased this flat to me.*

leash /li:ʃ/ *nc* a length of leather, chain etc used
for leading or controlling a dog.

least¹ /li:st/ *adj* or *det* (the — . . .) the smallest
amount of: *the least worry/trouble/money.* ⇨
least³. (N) *'Least'* is the superlative form of *'a little',*
as in *He has a little food, I have less food and he has
the least food.* *'The least'* is used to refer to *'the smallest amount of,'* as in *the least pain/luck/bread. 'The
fewest'* is used to refer to *'the smallest number of',* as
in *the fewest places/people/possibilities.* **at least**
(a) not less (than): *The car will cost at least £6000
(or £6000 at least).* **(b)** if nothing else: *He didn't
win but at least he tried.* **last but not least** ⇨
last²(1). Compare most¹, less¹.

least² /li:st/ *adv* to the smallest extent: *This is the
least useful. He is least likely to help.* **least of all**
(used to express a strong opinion or feeling) particularly not: *None of you should complain,
Charles least of all.* Compare most², less².

least³ /li:st/ *pron* (**the**) **least (of sth)** the smallest amount (of): *He has a little money, she has less
and I have (the) least. That's the least of my worries.* **not in the least** not at all: *It doesn't matter
in the least.* **to say the least** expressing the
smallest possible dislike, disapproval etc: *Her
voice isn't very good to say the least.* Compare
most³, less⁴.

'least·wise (also **'least·ways**) *adv* if nothing
else: *Leastwise he did try.* ⇨ at least(b).

leath·er /'leðə(r)/ *nu* the material from animal
skins, used for making shoes, bags etc.

leath·ery *adj* **(a)** hard and tough: *leathery meat.*
(b) like leather: *a leathery look/texture.*

leave¹ /li:v/ *n* **1** **nu leave (to do sth)** permission (the usual word): *be given leave to speak.*
by your leave with your permission. **2** *nc,nu*
(often **leave of absence**) permission to be,
stay, away from work, duty: *five days' sick leave;
be granted a month's leave of absence.* **on leave**
away from work, duty etc with official permission: *go home on leave for the weekend.* **put
in for leave** to ask officially for leave(2). **3** *nu*
take one's leave (*formal*) to say goodbye.
take leave of sb/sth to say goodbye to a person, place etc. **take leave of one's senses**
(usually asked as a question to show surprise at a
person's foolish actions) to go mad: *Have you
taken leave of your senses?* (= Are you mad?)

leave² /li:v/ *v* (*pt,pp* **left** /left/) **1** *vt,vi* to go away
from (a person, place etc): *Would you please
leave the room. What time did they leave? They left
at 8 o'clock. I'm leaving you because you argue too
much.* **2** *vt,vi* to go away from (a place) permanently: *When did you leave school? I'm leaving
(London/hospital) on Tuesday.* **3** *vt,vi* to stop
being a member of (a club, society etc): *If they
increase the fees, I'll leave (the club).* **4** *vt,vi* to
stop working for, studying at, (a university, business etc): *I'm leaving my job in July. He left London University in 1980.* **5** *vt* to cause (a person,
thing) to remain somewhere (often by mistake): *I
left my bag in the shop. Don't leave her waiting
outside. The postman has left a parcel for you. Is
there any tea left in the pot?* **6** *vt* to cause (a person, thing) to be, remain, in a particular state:
*Who left the window open? All our expenses have
left us very poor.* **leave go of sb/sth; leave
hold of sb/sth** to stop holding a person or thing.
7 *vt* to hand over (work, responsibility etc) to a
person: *I'll leave the problem/the rest of the work/
it to you. He left his son to look after the house.* **8**
vt to give, have, (money, children) when one dies:
*He left me £500. Mr Jones leaves a wife and two
children.* **9** *vt* to go beyond (a place) in the direction mentioned: *Leave the garage on your right
and go up the hill.* **10** *vt* (*maths*) to have (an
amount) afterwards: *Three from ten leaves seven.*

leave sth about *a place* to allow (clothes, toys,
papers etc) to be out of their correct place: *leave
newspapers about the house.*

leave sb/sth alone to agree or refuse to touch,
spoil, interfere with etc a person, thing: *Leave*

that cake alone!

leave it at that to do, say, nothing more.

leave sb/sth behind to cause a person, thing, to remain somewhere: *Don't leave your diary behind. We're leaving the children behind while we visit the caves. I left my purse behind by mistake.*

leave sth down to allow a switch etc to remain in the 'down' position.

leave for a place to travel to it: *We leave for home/London tomorrow.* **leave sb/sth for sb/sth** to abandon a person, job etc and follow, take, a new person, career etc: *He left Jane for Mary. He's leaving teaching for a job in industry.*

leave sb for dead to go away from a person believing he or she is dead.

leave sth in (sth) to allow something to remain inside: *Leave the clothes in the water overnight. I suggest you leave that information in your report.*

leave off (a) *(informal; imperative)* stop doing that. **(b)** *(of rain etc)* to stop: *Will this wind ever leave off?* **leave sth off (a)** to allow a switch, television etc to remain in the 'off' position. **(b)** to decide not to wear or put on clothes: *It's hot so I'm leaving my jacket off.* **leave off sth** to stop work, arguing, fighting etc: *Does she ever leave off talking about her children?*

leave sth on (a) to allow a switch, television etc to remain in the 'on' position: *Leave the water heater on because I'll have a bath later.* **(b)** to continue to wear clothes: *You can leave your coats on if you feel cold.* **(c)** to allow a light, fire etc to continue to burn: *Leave the oven on because I'm making a cake. Who has left the lights on?*

leave sb out to decide not to include a person in one's arrangements. **leave sb/sth out (of sth)** to fail to include or mention a person, thing: *He's left out the details in his drawing. We left your name out of the list. Leave me out of your arguments.* **be left out in the cold** ⇨ cold²(1).

leave sth over *(usually passive: be left over)* **(a)** to leave as an amount remaining: *All the food that was left over was thrown away. When I have bought your present I'll have no money left over.* ⇨ leftovers. **(b)** to keep a task, topic for discussion etc until a later date: *Discussion on the new design will be left over until next week.*

leave sth to sb (a) to give money, property to a person after one's death: *I'm leaving my money to my children.* **(b)** to allow a person to have responsibility for arrangements, organization etc: *You can leave all the details/the agenda/things/it to me.* ⇨ chance²(1).

leave sth up (a) to allow a switch etc to remain in the 'up' position. **(b)** to allow a poster, flag, display etc to remain high and visible. **leave sth up to sb** to allow an important decision etc to be a person's responsibility or choice: *I'm not sure which is better so I'll leave it up to you to choose.*

leaves /li:vz/ *pl of* leaf¹.

lech·er·ous /'letʃərəs/ *adj (derog)* having, showing, strong sexual desires.

lech·er /'letʃə(r)/ *nc (derog)* a lecherous man.

lech·ery /'letʃəri/ *nu*

lec·tern /'lektɜ:n/ *nc* a tall, sloping desk, used for reading aloud.

lec·ture¹ /'lektʃə(r)/ *nc* **lecture (about/on sth)** a talk for the purpose of teaching: *a course of*

philosophy lectures. **give sb a lecture** to tell a person off or state one's disapproval.

lec·ture² /'lektʃə(r)/ *vt,vi* **1 lecture (about/on sb/sth) (to sb/sth)** to give a lecture: *lecturing on English grammar to a group of students.* **2 lecture (at) sb** to tell a person off or state one's disapproval: *Stop lecturing (at) me!*

lec·turer *nc* a person who gives lectures at a college or university.

lec·ture·ship *nc* a position as a lecturer.

led /led/ *pt,pp* of lead³.

ledge /ledʒ/ *nc* a narrow shelf coming out from a wall, cliff, rock or other upright surface: *a window ledge.*

ledg·er /'ledʒə(r)/ *nc* a book in which a business firm's accounts are kept.

leech /li:tʃ/ *nc* **1** a small blood-sucking worm living in wet places. **2** *(fig; derog)* a person who takes money from others.

leek /li:k/ *nc* a vegetable like an onion with a long, white bulb.

leer /lɪə(r)/ *nc* an unpleasant look that suggests immoral thoughts. □ *vi* **leer (at sb)** to look with a leer: *leering at his neighbour's wife.*

lee·way /'li:weɪ/ *nu* a small amount of time etc given to make success possible: *He was given leeway to pay his debts.*

left¹ /left/ *adj* **1** *(attrib)* of the side of the body etc towards the west when the front is towards the north: *In Britain people drive on the left side of the road. He writes with his left hand.* **2** *(attrib)* worn on a left hand or foot: *a left shoe.* **3** *(often L-)* *(politics)* having radical views, expressing radical opinions: *a left newspaper; a party that is left of centre. Which group is more Left?* Compare right¹(3).

left² /left/ *adv* on, in, to, the left side: *Look left!* **left, right and centre** *(also right, left and centre)* everywhere: *We searched left, right and centre.*

left³ /left/ *nu* **1** the left side, direction, position, part etc: *Keep to the left.* **be on the left** be on the left side: *Our house is on the left when you face the river.* **2** *(usually the L-)* the political group, party etc having radical views: *vote for the Left.* Compare right⁵(2).

left⁴ /left/ *pt,pp* of leave².

left-hand /'left hænd/ *adj (attrib)* on the left side: *a left-hand turning.*

left-hand·ed /,left 'hændɪd/ *adj* **1** using the left hand to write, throw etc. **2** *(attrib)* designed to be used in the left hand: *left-handed scissors.* **3** *a left-handed compliment* one that deliberately causes doubt about its sincerity.

left·ist /'leftɪst/ *adj* supporting, expressing, radical political views.

left·overs /'leftəʊvəz/ *n pl* unused parts (esp of food or cloth).

left·wards /'leftwədz/ *adv* towards the left(1): *sloping leftwards.*

left wing /,left 'wɪŋ/ *adj, nc,nu (left-wing when attrib)* **1** *(often (the) L-)* *(of)* the political group, party etc having (more) radical views: *the left wing of the Labour Party. It's a left-wing group.* **2** *(of)* *(the position of)* a player on the left edge of a football or other sports field. ⇨ right wing.

leg¹ /leg/ *nc* **1** one of the parts on which an animal stands, walks etc: *She has long legs. How many* *legs does a spider have?* **be on one's/its last legs** to be very weak and likely to collapse, die etc. **give sb a leg up** (a) to help a person to climb up a tree, wall etc. (b) *(fig)* to help a person to make progress in a career, in business etc. **not have a leg to stand on** to have no evidence, reason etc for one's opinion, behaviour etc. **pull sb's leg** to make a person do, say, something a little foolish for fun, e.g. saying there is a spider on her or his back when it is not there. **stretch one's legs** to walk around for exercise, e.g. because of sitting for a long time. **2** the part of clothes that covers a leg: *a trouser leg.* **3** one of the parts that support a table, chair etc. **4** one section of a journey: *complete the first leg of a round-the-world flight.* **5** one of a series of games in a competition.

leg² /leg/ *vt* (**-gg-**) (only in) **leg it** *(informal)* to run fast.

leg·acy /'legəsɪ/ *nc* (*pl* **-ies**) **1** money etc (to be) given to a person at the wish of another person who has died. **2** *(fig)* something handed down from ancestors or predecessors: *a legacy of firm government.*

le·gal /'liːgl/ *adj* allowed by law; connected with law: *It's legal to park here at this time of the day. She's a member of the legal profession.* Opp illegal. Compare licit, lawful. **take legal action (against sb/sth)** ⇨ action(5).
 ,**legal 'tender** *nu (finance)* currency that must by law be accepted from a person paying a debt.
 le·gal·ly /'liːgəlɪ/ *adv*

le·gal·ity /liːˈgælətɪ/ *nc,nu* the state or quality of being legal: *the legality of an act.*

le·gal·ize (also **-ise**) /'liːgəlaɪz/ *vt* to make (something) legal: *legalize the sale of alcoholic drinks.*

le·ga·tion /lɪˈgeɪʃn/ *nc* (the offices of) a group of officials representing their government in a foreign country.

legend /'ledʒənd/ *n* **1** *nc* an old story handed down from the past, esp one of doubtful truth: *the Greek legends.* **2** *nu* the literature of such stories: *heroes who are famous in legend.* **3** *nc* explanatory words on a map, picture etc.
 legend·ary /'ledʒəndrɪ/ *adj* famous; known only in legends: *legendary heroes.*

leg·gings /'legɪŋz/ *n pl* an outer covering (for small children) for the whole of the leg: *a pair of leggings.*

leg·gy /'legɪ/ *adj* (**-ier, -iest**) (esp of young children and animals) having long legs.

leg·ible /'ledʒəbl/ *adj* (of handwriting, print) that can be read easily. Opp illegible.
 leg·ibly /-əblɪ/ *adv*
 legi·bil·ity /ˌledʒəˈbɪlətɪ/ *nu*

le·gion /'liːdʒən/ *nc* **1** a large group of soldiers. **3** any great amount or number: *legions of supporters.*

leg·is·late /'ledʒɪsleɪt/ *vi* to make laws: *legislate against gambling.*
 leg·is·la·tion /ˌledʒɪsˈleɪʃn/ *nu*

leg·is·lat·ive /'ledʒɪslətɪv/ *adj (attrib)* of, having the duty or purpose of, making laws: *legislative reforms/assemblies.*

leg·is·la·tor /'ledʒɪsleɪtə(r)/ *nc* a member of a legislative assembly.

leg·is·la·ture /'ledʒɪsleɪtʃə(r)/ *nc* an assembly

which makes laws, e.g. Parliament in GB.

le·git·ima·cy /lɪˈdʒɪtɪməsɪ/ *nu* the state of being legitimate.

le·git·imate /lɪˈdʒɪtɪmət/ *adj (no comp)* **1** born of parents who are married to each other. **2** according to law or public opinion of correct or moral behaviour: *a legitimate reason for being away from work.* Compare illegitimate.
 le·git·imate·ly *adv*

le·gu·mi·nous /lɪˈgjuːmɪnəs/ *adj (science)* of, like, the botanical family that includes peas and beans (and other seeds in pods).

lei·sure /'leʒə(r)/ *nu* time free from work. **at one's leisure** when one is free and without hurrying: *Please fill in the form at your leisure and post it to me.*
 lei·sure·ly *adj, adv* without hurrying: *leisurely movements; work leisurely.*

lem·on /'lemən/ *n* **1** *nc* (a tree with) a pale yellow fruit with acid juice, used for drinks and flavouring. **2** *nu* the colour of this fruit.
 ,**lemon 'curd** *nu* a kind of jam made from lemons boiled with sugar.
 ,**lemon 'squash** *nu* a drink of lemon-juice and water.
 'lemon-squeezer *nc* a utensil for pressing juice out of a lemon.

lem·on·ade /ˌleməˈneɪd/ *nc,nu* (a glass etc of) a drink made from lemons, sugar and water.

le·mur /'liːmə(r)/ *nc* an animal similar to a monkey but with a face like a fox.

lend /lend/ *vt* (*pt,pp* **lent** /lent/) **1** to give (a person) the use of (something) on the understanding that it or its equivalent will be returned: *I will lend you £100/my bike. I've lent my pen to him. Can you lend me £1 until tomorrow?.* Compare borrow(1). **lend sb a hand (with sth)** ⇨ hand¹(1). **2** *(formal)* to add (something) (to an idea, event etc): *facts that lend probability to a theory.*
 lend·er *nc* a person who lends something.

length /leŋθ/ *nc* **1** a measurement from end to end (space or time): *a river 300 miles in length; run the whole length of the way; the length of time needed for the work.* **at length** (a) after a long time; at last (which is more usual): *We arrived at length close to the water's edge.* (b) for a long time: *speak at (great) length.* (c) in detail; thoroughly: *treat a subject at length.* **2** a measurement of a particular thing from end to end: *The horse won by a length* (= by its own length). **3** **go to any/great/ some lengths (to do sth)** to do whatever is necessary (to get what one wants or needs). **4** a piece of material etc long enough for a purpose: *a dress length; a length of tubing/pipe.*
 length·en /'leŋθən/ *vt,vi* (to cause something) to become longer: *lengthen a skirt. The days are lengthening.*
 'length·ways (also **'length·wise**) *adv, adj* in the direction from end to end: *cut it lengthwise.*
 lengthy *adj* (**-ier, -iest**) (of speech, writing) long: *a lengthy essay.*

le·ni·ent /'liːnɪənt/ *adj* **lenient (towards sb)** not severe (esp in punishing people): *be lenient towards juvenile offenders.*
 le·ni·ence /-əns/, **le·ni·en·cy** /-ənsɪ/ *nu* the state of being lenient.
 le·ni·ent·ly *adv*

lens /lenz/ *nc* (*pl* **—es**) **1** a piece of glass (or substance like glass) with one or both sides curved, used in spectacles, cameras, telescopes, microscopes and other optical instruments. **2** (*anat*) the transparent part of the eye through which light is refracted.

lent /lent/ *pt,pp* of lend.

Lent /lent/ *n* the forty days before Easter when Christians go without food, special privileges etc.

len·til /'lentɪl/ *nc* (also *attrib*) (a kind of bean plant with) a seed eaten as food: *lentil soup*.

Leo /'li:əʊ/ *n* the Lion, the fifth sign of the zodiac.

leop·ard /'lepəd/ *nc* a large animal of the cat family with a yellow coat and dark spots.

leo·tard /'li:ətɑ:d/ *nc* an article of clothing fitting close to the body from the shoulders to the top of the legs, worn by (women) dancers, acrobats, people doing exercises etc.

lep·er /'lepə(r)/ *nc* a person suffering from leprosy.

lep·ro·sy /'leprəsɪ/ *nu* a kind of skin disease that causes loss of feeling which can lead to the loss of fingers, toes etc.

lep·rous /'leprəs/ *adj* of, having, leprosy.

les·bian /'lezbɪən/ *adj, nc* (of) a homosexual woman: *a lesbian relationship*.

le·sion /'li:ʒn/ *nc* (*med*) a wound; cut.

less[1] /les/ *adj* or *det* not so much; a smaller amount of: *less speed/trouble/patience; less butter/paint/paper.* ⇨ **less**[4]. Ⓝ '*Less*' is the comparative form of '*a little*', as in *She has a little money, I have less money and he has the least money.* '*Less*' is used to refer to '*a smaller amount of*', as in *less furniture/happiness/time.* '*Fewer*' is used to mean '*a smaller number of*' as in *fewer apples/ideas/places/people.* **less . . . than . . .** not so much . . . as . . . : *He has had less opportunity than you.* Compare **few**[1](1), **more**[1], **least**[1], **little**[1](1). ⇨ also **lesser**[1].

less[2] /les/ *adv* not so much; to a smaller extent: *I slept less last night. We see each other much less now.* **less . . . (than sb/sth)** not so . . . (as): *Tom is less clever (than me). Norway is less hot than Spain.* **even/still less** (used to express a strong opinion or feeling): *I hate hamburgers but I like white bread even/still less.* **less and less** to an extent that gets smaller: *It's less and less easy.* ⇨ **more and more.** **less so (than)** not as much (as): '*Was the book interesting?*'—'*Yes, but less so than I expected.*' **much/still less** (used with a negative to express a strong opinion or feeling): *I don't want to go out tonight, much less go to a boring meeting.* Compare **more**[2], **least**[2].

less[3] /les/ *prep* without (an amount mentioned): *I'm paid £100 a week less £40 for my room and food.*

less[4] /les/ *pron* **less (of sth)** an amount that is not so much; a smaller amount (of): *I have a little food, he has less and she has the least. I've seen less of her than you.* Use *less of the butter.* **less than . . .** not so much as . . . : *You have less than anyone else.* **no less than . . .** as much as . . . : *He won no less than £50.* **none the less** ⇨ **none**(1). **the less . . ., the less . . .** (used to express a relationship between two ideas etc): *The less you learn, the less you'll know.* Compare **least**[3](2), **more**[3].

les·see /le'si:/ *nc* ⇨ lease.

less·en /'lesn/ *vt,vi* (to cause something) to

become less in size, importance, effect etc: *to lessen the impact/effect.*

less·er[1] /'lesə(r)/ *adj* (*attrib*) not so great as the other: *choose the lesser evil; a lesser-known poet.* **to a lesser extent** smaller in range, importance, value etc.

less·er[2] /'lesə(r)/ *pron* **the lesser of . . .** the one that is smaller in size, amount, importance: *the lesser of two evils.*

les·son /'lesn/ *nc* **1** something to be learnt or taught; period of time given to learning or teaching: *English lessons.* **2** something serving as an example or a warning: *Let his unhappiness be a lesson to you all!* **teach sb a lesson** to be a bad experience that a person will not want to cause to be repeated: *Her poverty has taught her a lesson about lending money.* **3** a passage from the Bible read aloud during a church service.

les·sor /les'ɔ:(r)/ *nc* ⇨ lease.

lest /lest/ *conj* (*subord*) (*old use*) for fear that: *He ran away lest he should be seen. We were afraid lest he arrive too late.* Ⓝ Used with a subjunctive.

let[1] /let/ *nc* (in tennis, squash etc) a small error allowing a point to be played again.

let[2] /let/ *nc* (*informal*) an instance of letting(5).

let[3] /let/ *vt* (*pt,pp* —; *-tt-*; *let us* often shortened to **let's**) Ⓝ '*Let*' is usually followed by an infinitive without *to*. The passive is not possible in 1,2,3,4 below. Use '*be allowed to*'. **1** to allow (a person, thing) (to do something or to happen): *My mother won't let me come (write to you). Please let me come. Don't let her see me. Let me pay for it. You mustn't let the rope get too long. Why not let them all come? Who let the water escape?* **let alone** (*conj*) without considering; not to mention (something more difficult, expensive, important etc): *The walking will be difficult, let alone carrying our bags. We can't afford a holiday, let alone one in another country.* **let sb/sth alone/be** to agree not to touch, move, interfere with a person or thing: *Why don't you let her/the dog be?* **let sb/sth go** to allow a person, thing to be free: *We've let the spider go.* **let oneself go** to act in a way that shows one's true feelings or desires without embarrassment or fear. **let it go (at that)** to do, say, no more about it: *I disagree but we'll let it go at that.* **let sb know (sth)** to tell a person (information about a person, thing): *I'll let you know when the next meeting is. Don't forget to let me know if I can help you.* **let sth pass** to decide not to discuss, deal with, something: *You're late but I'll let it pass this time.* **let me see** (used to get a short pause while speaking) allow me to think for a moment: *Now, let me see—couldn't you try another shop?* **let things slide** to stop taking enough care, not organize things correctly. **let sth slip** (**a**) to allow something to fall out of one's hands etc. (**b**) to tell a secret accidentally. **live and let live** ⇨ live[2](2). **2** (used to express a suggestion, an order, or a threat or warning): *Let's go to the cinema tonight. Don't let's start yet. Let's see if you can do it. Let me find you here again and I'll call the police.* **let's face it** ⇨ face[2](3). **let go (of sb/sth)** (often *imperative*) to stop holding, preventing, a person, thing: *Let go of my arm. Don't let go!* **3** to allow (air, light, liquid etc) to enter, leave: *Open the curtains and let the sunshine in. Someone has let the air* *out of my tyres.* **4** (*maths, science*) to make, allow, (something) to have a particular value in order to explain, solve etc something: *Let x equal 15. If we let the middle quantity be the average, then* . . . **5** (the *passive* is possible) to give (a room, building etc) to be used in exchange for payment: *The offices have been let to a lawyer. Are you letting your house while you are away?* **to let** available for renting: *Is this flat to let, please?* ⇨ let².

let sb down (often *passive*) to disappoint (a person), be unreliable: *I thought you could be trusted but you've let me down. The shop let me down badly over the delivery dates.* Hence **let-down** *nc* a disappointment. **let sth down** to lower something: *let one's dress down a few centimetres*; *let a rope down a wall*; *let a window down for some fresh air*; *let one's hair down and brush it.* ⇨ also hair(1), side²(9).

let sb in (open a door and) allow a person to enter. **let sth in** (a) to allow something to enter: *My shoes let in water. The roof lets the rain in.* (b) to provide a possibility for something to enter: *The windows let in light and air. The water is let in through this pipe.* (c) to make clothes narrower: *let in a jacket.* **let oneself/sb/sth in for sth** to force oneself, a person, a business etc to take responsibility for loss, difficulty, hard work etc: *I didn't realize how much work I was letting myself in for when I agreed to do it.* **let sb in on sth** to allow a person to know about a plan, agreement etc: *Who let you in on our plans?*

let sb into sth to allow a person to know a secret: *She had been let into the secret.* **let sth into sth** to set, fix, something into an open place in a wall etc: *The book shelves can be let into that wall.*

let sb off (a) to allow, help, a person to leave a boat, bus, plane etc. (b) to allow a person not to be punished or to receive only a small punishment: *He was let off (with only a small fine) and not sent to prison.* (c) to allow a person not to do an unpleasant duty: *I'll let you off doing the washing-up tonight. I was going to make the fire but I've been let off.* **let sth off** (a) to explode a gun, fireworks etc. (b) to let(5) (part of) a building: *let a house off as flats.* (c) (*sl*) (*do not use!*) to produce wind from the anus: *let off a fart.* ⇨ also hook¹(1), steam¹(3).

let on (about sb/sth; that . . . **)** (*informal*) to tell secret information: *She never let on about her wealth. Don't let on that I've been here. I knew who did it but I didn't let on.*

let sb out to (open a door and) allow a person to leave (esp an institution, prison etc): *When were you let out of prison? We are let out every Saturday night.* **let sth out** (a) to provide a possibility for something to leave: *These holes let the bad smells out. Who let the water out of my bath?* (b) to make a cry, scream etc: *He let out a loud cry of pain.* (c) to tell information, news etc: *let out the news to the press.* (d) = hire sth out (to sb). (e) to make clothes wider or larger: *let out a dress at the waist.*

let sb through (a) to (take away a barrier and) allow a person to move on. (b) to allow a person to pass an exam: *I only got 40% so they wouldn't let me through.* **let sth through** to allow goods etc to pass a control point: *The customs let our cases through without opening them.*

let up (*informal*) to stop (making an effort); relax: *She doesn't let up all day. The wind hasn't let up all night.* Hence **'let-up** *nc: There's been no let-up in the rain.*

let-down /'let daʊn/ *nc* ⇨ let sb down.

le·thal /'liːθl/ *adj* causing, able to cause, death: *a lethal dose of poison.*

leth·ar·gy /'leθədʒɪ/ *nu* the state, feeling, of being tired, lacking interest.

le·thar·gic /lɪ'θɑːdʒɪk/ *adj*

let's /lets/ = *let us.* ⇨ let³(2).

let·ter /'letə(r)/ *nc* **1** a symbol or character representing a sound, of which words in writing are formed: *capital letters* (A, B, C etc) *and small letters* (a, b, c etc). *Do you have any letters* (e.g. BA) *after your name?* **2** a written message, request, sent by one person to another: *I have some letters to write.* **do sth to the letter** to pay strict attention to the actual wording, to every detail: *carry out an order to the letter.*

'letter-bomb *nc* an exploding device put in an envelope.

'letter box *nc* (a) a slot in a door for letters. (b) a box (in the street, at a post office) in which letters are posted.

'letter·head *nc* a printed name and address, e.g. of a business firm.

,letter of 'credit *nc* (*commerce*) authority from a bank allowing a person to take money up to a certain amount.

let·ter·ing /'letərɪŋ/ *nu* letters, words, esp with reference to their style and size: *the lettering on a book cover.*

let·tuce /'letɪs/ *nc,nu* a garden plant with crisp green leaves, used in salads.

let-up /'let ʌp/ *nc* ⇨ let up.

leu·ke·mia (also **-kae-**) /luː'kiːmɪə/ *nu* a serious disease of the blood causing anaemia.

lev·el¹ /'levl/ *adj* **1** having a horizontal surface: *level ground.* **2** (*pred*) **level (with sth)** equal in measurement, standard: *My shoulder is level with yours.* **3 do one's level best** ⇨ best³(3). **have a level head** ⇨ head¹(2).

,level 'crossing *nc* a place where a road and a railway cross on the same level.

,level-'headed *adj* reliable and balanced in one's behaviour.

,level 'pegging *nu* (*informal*) equality (between two people in a competition).

lev·el² /'levl/ *adv* so as to be level: *be/draw level with the other runners.*

lev·el³ /'levl/ *n* **1** *nc* a horizontal line or surface. **be on the level** (*fig*) to be honest and sincere: *Is he on the level?* **2** *nc* an instrument used to show whether a surface is level(1): *A spirit-level is used by builders.* **3** *nc* an instrument used to find out the height of land. **4** *nc,nu* a surface with reference to its height: *It is 1000m above sea level.* **5** *nc* a position, stage, in a set of values: *a sound-level.* **one's own level** the social, educational, professional etc standard that is one's own: *bring her down to/find one's own level in society.* ⇨ also top-level.

lev·el⁴ /'levl/ *v* (**-ll-**, *US:* **-l-**) **1** *vt,vi* (to cause something) to become level(1) or flat: *levelling the top of a cake.* **2** *vt* to make (two or more people, things) equal in position, standard. **3** *vt* to make (a building) collapse. **4** *vt* to aim (criticism, a stare) at a person.

level sth against sb to accuse a person of something: *level a charge of/an accusation of stealing against a neighbour*.

level sth at sb/sth to aim a gun, criticism etc at a person, thing.

level sth down to reduce amounts, prices, wages, standards etc of a few to the same level as the rest.

level off (a) (of prices, costs, amounts) to remain the same after rising: *Inflation seems to have levelled off at 10%*. **(b)** (of a plane) to become horizontal after climbing: *The plane levelled off at 15 000 feet*. **level sth off** to make a surface smooth and even: *level the wood off*.

level out = level off (a,b). **level sth out** to remove bumps, lumps etc and make something smooth and even: *level out the rough bits*.

level up (with sb) (*informal*) to pay or receive the money that is owed. **level sth up** to increase amounts, prices, wages, standards etc of a few to the same level as the rest.

level with sb (*informal*) to give a person one's honest opinion, all the information etc.

le·ver¹ /'li:və(r)/ *nc* **1** a bar or other tool used to lift something or to force something open. **2** a bar or handle of a machine used to make it work: *pull this lever*. **3** (*fig*) a means (in a discussion) by which force may be used: *using our oil as an economic lever in the negotiations*.

le·ver² /'li:və(r)/ *vt* to move (something) with a lever(1): *levering it into position*.

lev·er·et /'levərɪt/ *nc* a young hare.

levi·tate /'levɪteɪt/ *vt,vi* (to cause a person, thing) to rise and float in the air.

levi·ta·tion /ˌlevɪ'teɪʃn/ *nc,nu*

lev·ity /'levətɪ/ *nc,nu* (*pl* **-ies**) (*formal*) (an instance of) a lack of seriousness.

levy¹ /'levɪ/ *nc* (*pl* **-ies**) (an act, demand, amount of) money collected.

levy² /'levɪ/ *vt* (*pt,pp* **-ied**) **1** to collect (money) by authority or force: *levy a tax (on petrol); levy a fine*. **2** **levy war (on/against sb/sth)** to declare, make, war (on a person, country).

lewd /lu:d/ *adj* (*derog*) indecent; showing, having, lust: *a lewd look/joke/person*.

lewd·ly *adv*

lexi·cal /'leksɪkl/ *adj* (*tech*) of the vocabulary of a language.

lexi·cal·ly /-klɪ/ *adv*

lexi·con /'leksɪkn/ *nc* a dictionary (esp of Greek, Latin or Hebrew).

lex·is /'leksɪs/ *nu* (*tech*) vocabulary.

lia·bil·ity /ˌlaɪə'bɪlətɪ/ *n* (*pl* **-ies**) **1** *nu* **liability (to do sth)** the state of being liable: *liability to pay taxes*. **2** *nc* (often *pl*) an amount of debt that must be paid. **3** *nc* (*informal*) something that causes difficulties, uses a lot of money, is a problem etc: *His house is more of a liability than an asset*. Compare asset(1).

li·able /'laɪəbl/ *adj* **1** **liable (for sb/sth)** responsible according to law: *Is a man liable for his son's debts in your country?* **2** **be liable to sth** to be likely to have, suffer etc something: *be liable to a heavy fine; be liable to flu in winter*. **3** **be liable to do sth** to have a tendency to, be likely to do it: *We are all liable to make mistakes occasionally*.

li·aise /lɪ'eɪz/ *vi* **liaise (between/with sb)**

(about sb/sth) to work, act, together, inform each other etc: *liaising with the union about holiday arrangements*.

li·ai·son /lɪ'eɪzn/ *nc* **liaison (between/with sb)** **1** a working association between two or more people, committees etc. **2** (*dated*) a sexual relationship between unmarried people.

li·ar /'laɪə(r)/ *nc* (*derog*) a person who tells, or who has told, a lie.

lib /lɪb/ *n* (*informal*) liberation: *women's lib*.

Lib. *written abbr* the Liberal Party.

li·bel¹ /'laɪbl/ *nc,nu* (the publishing of) a written or printed statement that damages a person's reputation: *sue for libel*. Compare slander.

li·bel² /'laɪbl/ *vt* (**-ll-**, *US*: **-l-**) to publish a libel against (a person).

li·bel·lous (*US* = **li·bel·ous**) /'laɪbələs/ *adj* **1** containing a libel: *libellous reports*. **2** in the habit of using libels: *a libellous person/magazine*.

lib·er·al /'lɪbərəl/ *adj* **1** giving or given freely; generous: *a liberal supply of food and drink*. **2** having, showing, a mind free from prejudice. **3** (of education) directed mainly towards creating a tolerant mind with a wide knowledge, not specially to professional or technical needs. **4** (often L-) having moderate or progressive views, expressing moderate or progressive opinions.

liberal 'arts *n pl* (the —) (usually *the arts*) subjects such as fine arts, literature, languages, history etc.

'Liberal Party *n* (the —) (*GB*) a political party representing moderate or progressive views.

'liberal studies *nu* a course in a college for science or technical students to learn about the arts.

lib·er·al·ity /ˌlɪbə'rælətɪ/ *nu* (*formal*) generosity; freedom from prejudice.

lib·er·al·ly /'lɪbərəlɪ/ *adv* generously.

lib·er·ate /'lɪbəreɪt/ *vt* to set (a person, people) free: *liberate women; liberating a country from a military regime*.

lib·er·ation /ˌlɪbə'reɪʃn/ *nu*

lib·er·ator /-tə(r)/ *nc* a person who liberates.

lib·er·ty /'lɪbətɪ/ *n* (*pl* **-ies**) **1** *nu* the state of being free (from imprisonment, control, government by others etc); right or power to decide for oneself what to do, how to live etc: *They fought to defend their liberty*. **at liberty (a)** (of a person) free; not imprisoned. **(b)** having permission or the right (to do something): *You are now at liberty to leave any time*. **2** *nc* **take the liberty of doing sth** to decide and do it: *I took the liberty of borrowing your lawn-mower while you were away on holiday*. **take liberties with sb** to take advantage of a person's friendship, trust: *You must stop taking liberties with her*.

li·bi·do /lɪ'bi:dəʊ/ *nc* (*tech*) a natural sexual desire or interest.

Li·bra /'li:brə/ *n* the Scales or Balance, the seventh sign of the zodiac.

li·brar·ian /laɪ'breərɪən/ *nc* a person in charge of a library(1).

li·brary /'laɪbrərɪ/ *nc* (*pl* **-ies**) **1** (also *attrib*) (a room, building, for) a collection of books: *a public library; a reference library; a library book*. **2** (a room for) a collection of records, toys etc that may be borrowed.

lice /laɪs/ *n pl* of louse.

li·cence (*US* = **li·cense**) /'laɪsns/ *n* 1 *nc,nu* (a written statement giving) permission from a person in authority to do something: *a licence to drive a car/a driving licence.* **2** *nu* an excessive or wrong use of freedom: *The licence shown by the troops when they entered enemy territory disgusted everyone.* ⇨ also off-licence, poetic licence.

li·cense (also **li·cence**) /'laɪsns/ *vt* (usually *passive*) to give a licence to (a business etc): *shops licensed to sell tobacco.*

li·cen·see /ˌlaɪsn'siː/ *nc* a person holding a licence (esp to sell alcohol).

li·cen·tious /laɪ'senʃəs/ *adj* (*derog*) immoral about sexual matters: *licentious thoughts.*

li·cen·tious·ly *adv*

li·chee (also **li·chi**) /'laɪtʃiː/ *nc* ⇨ litchi.

lic·it /'lɪsɪt/ *adj* usually *attrib*) 1 done legally (esp concerning conditions for an activity to be carried out: *the licit use of drugs.* 2 permitted: *licit smoking in cinemas.* Opp illicit. Compare legal, lawful.

lick¹ /lɪk/ *nc* an act of licking(1). **a lick and a promise** a quick and not thorough clean: *give one's shoes a lick and a promise.*

lick² /lɪk/ *vt* **1** to move the tongue over or under (something): *The cat was licking its paws.* **lick one's lips** ⇨ lip(1). **lick sb/sth into shape** ⇨ shape¹(1). **2** (esp of waves, flames) to touch (something) lightly: *The flames licked the dry grass.* **3** (*informal*) to defeat (a competitor, illness, problem etc).

lid /lɪd/ *nc* **1** a movable cover for an opening, esp at the top of a container: *the teapot lid.* **2** = eyelid.

li·do /'liːdəʊ/ *nc* (*pl* **—s**) an open-air swimming pool.

lie¹ /laɪ/ *n sing* **the lie of the land** (a) the natural features of the land in an area. **(b)** (*fig*) the general state of affairs: *find out the lie of the land before deciding.*

lie² /laɪ/ *nc* (esp **tell a lie; tell (sb) lies**) a statement that one knows to be not true: *She often tells lies. That's a lie!* ⇨ pack¹(3), white lie.

lie³ /laɪ/ *vi* (*pres p* **lying**; *pt,pp* **lied**) **lie (to sb) (about sb/sth)** to make a statement that one knows to be not true: *He's lying to you. I lied about my expenses.*

lie⁴ /laɪ/ *vi* (*pres p* **lying**; *pt* **lay** /leɪ/, *pp* **lain** /leɪn/) Ⓝ Be careful because *'lay'* as the past tense of *'lie'* may be mistaken for the verb *'to lay'.* ⇨ the note at lay². **1** to be, put oneself, flat on a surface: *He lay on the grass looking at the stars. The baby was lying on its back/on her side. She's still lying in bed. Let's lie by the river and talk.* **lie awake** ⇨ awake¹. **lie low** ⇨ low². **2** (of people, things) to be in the position(s) mentioned: *The books/bodies were lying all over the floor. Thick dust lay on the furniture. The letter lay open near the chair. The mountains lie to the north of the city. The valley lay before us.* **3** to be, remain, in the condition mentioned: *machinery lying idle; money lying in the bank doing nothing.* **4** (of trouble, interest etc) to exist, be caused by: *The difficulty lies with the organizers. The trouble lies in the engine. He knows where his best interests lie* (i.e. where he can have the best advantage).

lie about (of a person) to be very lazy.

lie back (in sth) (of a person) to lean back (in a chair etc).

lie behind sb to be in a person's past: *Sad memories lay behind them. Behind lay months of illness.* **lie behind sth** to be the cause, explanation, of something: *What lay behind his refusal to help?*

lie down (a) (of a person, animal) to put oneself in a horizontal position. Compare lay sth down. (b) (of a person) to rest on a bed or sofa. Hence **'lie-down** *n sing* a rest on a bed etc: *have a lie-down.* **not take sth lying down** to refuse to accept something, agree too easily and without protest or trying to stop it: *I won't take your insults lying down.*

lie in to stay in bed after the usual time for getting up: *lying in on Sundays.* Hence **'lie-in** *nc.* ⇨ also ruin¹(3), store¹(2), wait¹(2).

lie with sb to be a person's responsibility: *The fault/decision lies with you.*

lie-down /'laɪ daʊn/ *nc* ⇨ lie down (b).

lie-in /'laɪ ɪn/ *nc* ⇨ lie in.

lieu /luː/ *n* (only in) **in lieu (of)** (*prep*) instead (of): *I get a room and food in lieu (of pay).*

lieu·ten·ant /lef'tenənt/ *nc* **1** an army officer below a captain; junior officer in the Navy. **2** (in compounds) an officer with the highest rank under: *lieutenant-colonel; lieutenant-commander.*

life /laɪf/ *n* (*pl* **lives** /laɪvz/ **1** *nu* the state, condition of existing (e.g. growing, moving, reproducing): *Only animals and plants have life. Metals, rocks and liquids do not have life. Do you believe in life after death?* ⇨ alive. **2** *nu* living things in general or as a group: *How did life on earth begin? Is there life on Mars? Pollution destroys life in rivers. Is there any sign of life in the sand?* ⇨ wildlife. **3** *nu* human existence: *a sad loss of life because of the earthquake.* Compare death(1). **the change of life** ⇨ change¹(1). **for dear life** with great energy or effort (as if to protect one's life: *run for dear life.* **the facts of life,** ⇨ fact(2). **the good life** the (real or imaginary) life of wealth, comfort and leisure. **the kiss of life** ⇨ kiss¹. **larger than life** exaggerated in order to appear more important: *His description of his father's achievements was larger than life.* **a matter of life and death** ⇨ matter¹(4). **a new lease of life** ⇨ lease¹. **(in) real life** (in) life as most people live it (not as described in novels, films and plays): *Nobody speaks like that in real life. The film is about real-life situations.* **such is life** (*saying*) that is what real life is like: *I didn't get the job I wanted but such is life.* **that's life** (*saying*) that is what can happen in real life: *I failed the exam but that's life.* **true to life** exactly as happens in real life. **a way of life** the usual way a person or group lives and works: *If you come to live in our country you must learn our way of life.* **bring sb to life** to cause a person to recover from a serious illness or recover consciousness. **come to life** to recover one's consciousness, energy, interest etc. **have seen life** to have had a lot of experience about the way people live. **4** *nc* the period between birth and death: *lead the life of a soldier/rich woman. He lived all his life in London.* **cannot for the life of one . . .** (used for emphasis) cannot at all: *I cannot for the life of me remember her name.* **a dog's life** a life without pleasure or comfort. **early (on) in life** (when) still young. **a hard life** a life that is full of problems and suffering.

late (on) in life (when) getting old. **not on your life** (*informal*) (used to express disagreement or a refusal) definitely not. **one's private life** the part of one's life not connected with work, duties, public affairs etc: *He should try to stop his career from interfering with his private life.* **cost sb her/his life** to be the cause of a person's death: *Smoking has cost too many people their lives.* **have the time of one's life** ⇨ time¹(2). **lay down one's life (for sb/sth)** to allow oneself to die (for one's country, a good cause, one's beliefs etc). **run for one's life** to escape, hurry, (as if) because one's life is in danger. **take sb's life** to murder a person. **take one's own life** to kill oneself. **5** *nc* a living person: *How many lives were lost/saved during the famine?* **6** *nc* the amount of time something is useful or active: *the life of a battery; the average life of a family car.* **7** *nc,nu* an active state or way of living in society: *I prefer life in the country to life in town* (or *town life*). *Is there much life in your village?* **full of life** lively and cheerful: *The children were full of life.* **the life and soul (of the party)** the person who is the most lively and amusing (in a group). **8** *nc* a biography: *a life of Mozart.* **9** *nu* imprisonment until one dies: *be given life for murder.*

'life·belt *nc* a ring or cork or other material worn to keep a person afloat in water.

'life-blood *nu* **(a)** blood necessary to life. **(b)** (*fig*) something that gives essential strength and energy.

'life·boat *nc* a boat built for saving people in danger at sea.

'life·buoy *nc* a large ring used to save a person in danger in water.

'life cycle *nc* (*science*) a progression through different stages of development: *the life cycle of a frog* (i.e. from the egg to the final stage).

'life ,force *nu* the vital energy thought of as working for the survival of the human race and the individual.

'life-giving *adj* (usually *attrib*) that strengthens or restores physical or spiritual life.

'life-guard *nc* a trained swimmer on duty at dangerous places where people swim.

'life history *nc* **(a)** the record of the life cycle of an organism. **(b)** the history of a person's life.

,life im'prisonment *nu* imprisonment until one dies.

'life-jacket *nc* one designed to keep a person afloat in water.

'life-like *adj* **(a)** resembling real life. **(b)** looking like the person represented: *a lifelike portrait.*

'life-line *nc* (*fig*) anything on which one's happiness, survival, depends.

'life-long *adj* (*attrib*) continuing (as if) for a lifetime: *a lifelong ambition.*

,life 'peer *nc* (*GB*) a member of the House of Lords whose title cannot be inherited.

'life science *nc* a scientific study of living things, e.g. biology, botany, zoology.

'life-size(d) *adj*, *adv* (of pictures, statues etc) having the same size, proportions etc as the person represented: *a life-size portrait.*

'life-span *nc* the period during which a person, animal, machine etc lives or is active.

'life-style *nc* the way of life of a person or group.

'life·time *nc* a duration of a person's life. **the chance/opportunity of a lifetime** a good opportunity that will probably never come again.

'life-less *adj* **(a)** dead: *a lifeless body.* **(b)** dull; not lively: *answer in a lifeless manner.*

'life-less·ly *adv*

'lif·er /'laɪfə(r)/ *nc* (*sl*) a person sentenced to life imprisonment.

lift¹ /lɪft/ *nc* **1** an act of lifting(1). **2** an electrical compartment in a building that moves up and down from one floor to another. **3** a free ride in a car etc: *Can you give me a lift to the station.* **thumb a lift** ⇨ finger¹. **4** (*informal*) a sudden feeling of increased energy, interest, excitement: *Her compliments/The music/The good news gave us a tremendous lift.*

lift² /lɪft/ *v* **1** *vt,vi* (to cause a person, thing) to rise up: *lift a heavy bag; lift a child out of a cot; lift one's head: This box is too heavy for me to lift.* **not lift a finger** ⇨ finger¹. **2** *vi* (of clouds, fog etc) to rise up: *The mist began to lift.* **3** *vt* to end (a restriction, ban etc): *lift a ban on demonstrating.* **4** *vt* to make (a voice etc) louder. **5** *vt* to cause (a person) to appear more important, necessary etc: *The victory lifted him above the other athletes.* **6** *vt* to make (a person, personality) more lively: *The news lifted her/his spirits.* **7** *vt* (*informal*) to steal (goods) from a shop, a person's pocket etc. ⇨ shoplifter.

lift sb/sth down (from a place) to take (a person, object) from a higher place to a lower one: *lift a book down from a shelf.*

lift off (of a spacecraft) to rise straight up (from the ground). Hence **'lift-off** *nc,nu.* **lift sth off (sth)** to use force to take a lid, glue etc off (a container, surface etc).

lift sb up = lift(1) or lift(6).

lift-off /'lɪft ɒf/ *nc* ⇨ lift off.

liga·ment /'lɪgəmənt/ *nc* (*tech*) a band of strong tissues that holds two or more bones together.

light¹ /laɪt/ *adj* (**—er**, **—est**) **1** with some or much light: *It's still light outside. It's beginning to get light.* Compare dark¹(1). **2** (of a colour) reflecting much light; nearer white than black: *light-blue/-green/-brown.* Compare dark¹(2), deep¹(6). **3** (of the skin) fair: *a light complexion.* Compare dark¹(3).

light² /laɪt/ *adj* (**—er**, **—est**) **1** having (very) little weight: *a light suitcase; as light as air/a feather* (= very light). **2** of very little size, amount etc: *a light fall of snow; a light breakfast; a light smoker.* **3** gentle: *a light touch on the shoulder.* **4** (of work) needing little energy or effort. **5** (of writing, plays, music) not serious; intended to amuse: *light opera; light music; light comedy.* **6** (of punishment, taxes etc) not difficult to bear: *get off with a light sentence; a light tax on clothes.* **7** (of sleep) easily disturbed; (of a person asleep) easily woken. Compare heavy(7), deep¹(4). **8** (of food) easy to digest. **9** (of beer, wine etc) not strong. **10** (*informal*) (of criticism, disapproval, anger etc) not strong. **11** (of soil) easy to dig and break up. **12** (*pred*) below the correct amount: *We're about £50 light on the day's takings.*

,light-'fingered *adj* (*derog*) enjoying, good at, stealing from a person's pockets.

,light-'footed *adj* moving with gentle, easy steps.

,light-'headed *adj* dizzy.

,light-'hearted *adj* cheerful; gay. Compare heavy-hearted.

,light-'heavyweight *nc* (also *attrib*) a boxer weighing between 160 and 175 lb (72·5 and 79·3 kg).

,light 'industry *nu* manufacturing industry that does not use large machinery and makes small articles such as clothes, toys etc. Compare heavy industry.

'light·weight *nc* (also *attrib*) (a) a boxer weighing between 126 and 135 lb (57 and 61 kg). (b) (*informal; derog*) a person of little influence or importance.

light·ness *nu*

light³ /laɪt/ *adv* with little luggage: *travel light.* **make light of sth** to treat a serious problem, issue etc as if it is not important.

light⁴ /laɪt/ *n* **1** *nu* that which makes things visible: *the light of the sun/a lamp/the fire; moonlight; sunlight.* **in a good/bad light** (a) so as to be seen well/badly: *The picture has been hung in a bad light.* (b) (*fig*) so as to make a good/bad impression: *Press reports always make him appear in a bad light.* **(go) out like a light** (to fall) asleep, faint etc quickly. **see the light** to realize the truth of something that one has been opposed to. **2** *nc* something that gives light such as a lamp, torch, candle: *traffic lights. Turn/Switch the lights on/off.* **3** *nc* (something used for producing) a spark or flame: *Can you give me a light, please?* **4** *nu* brightness or liveliness in a person's face (esp in the eyes) suggesting happiness or interest or excitement. **5** *nc,nu* (an example of) knowledge or information that helps understanding. **in the light of** because of: *In the light of your evidence, I'm willing to believe you.* **come/bring sth to light** to become/cause something to be visible or known: *Much new evidence has come to light/has been brought to light in recent years.* **shed/ throw (a new) light on sth** to make something clearer, provide new information. **6** *nc* a way in which something appears: *I've never viewed the matter in that light.* **7** *nc* a person (to be) regarded as a good example or model: *one of the leading lights of our age.*

'light-bulb *nc* an electric light enclosed in glass.

'light·house *nc* a tower or other tall structure containing a strong, flashing light for warning or guiding ships at sea.

'light-year *nc* the distance travelled by light in one year (about 6 million million miles) used to measure distances in space.

light⁵ /laɪt/ *v* (*pt,pp* lit /lɪt/ or **—ed**) **1** *vt,vi* (to cause something) to begin burning or to give out light: *light a cigarette/fire. The wood won't light.* **2** *vt* (often *passive*) to provide lights(2) to or for (something): *Our streets are lit by electricity.* **3** *vt* to cause (something) to become bright: *The room was lit by a single candle. The burning building lit up the whole district.* **4** *vt,vi* **light up (with sth)** to become bright (because of something): *Her face lit up with pleasure.*

light·en¹ /'laɪtn/ *v* **1** *vt* to make (something) (more) light or bright: *using white paint to lighten the room.* **2** *vi* to become (more) light or bright: *The eastern sky lightened.*

light·en² /'laɪtn/ *vt,vi* **1** (to cause something) to become less heavy; reduce the weight of (something): *lighten a ship's cargo.* **2** (*fig*) (to cause a person) to become more cheerful: *She/her face lightened when she heard the news.*

light·er /'laɪtə(r)/ *nc* **1** a device used for lighting cigarettes or cigars. **2** a person or apparatus that lights lamps, fires etc.

light·ly /'laɪtlɪ/ *adv* less than the usual extent, degree: *sleep/breathe lightly.* Compare heavily. **get off lightly** (*informal*) to avoid having to pay a lot, be punished severely etc.

light·ning /'laɪtnɪŋ/ *nu* a flash of bright light produced by natural electricity between clouds in the sky or clouds and the ground, often with thunder: *be struck/killed by lightning.* **like lightning; with lightning speed** very fast.

lights /laɪts/ *n pl* the lungs of sheep, pigs, cattle, used as food for pet animals.

lik·able (also like·able) /'laɪkəbl/ *adj* of a kind that is, or deserves to be, liked: *He's a very likable person.* Opp unlikable.

like¹ /laɪk/ *adj* (*attrib*) having the same or similar qualities: *I refuse to discuss this and like subjects.* ⇨ like³(2). Compare unlike. ⇨ also childlike, ladylike, lifelike.

like² /laɪk/ *conj* (*subord*) **1** in the same way as: *She can't cook like her mother does. The grass is turning brown like it did last year.* Compare like⁴(1). **2** (*informal; esp US*) as if (which is more usual): *I feel like I've been here before. You look like you need a drink.*

like³ /laɪk/ *n* **1 and the like** and similar people, things, qualities etc: *I enjoy acting, dancing and the like. I enjoy meeting old school friends and the like.* **2 the likes of sb/sth** people, things, similar to the one or ones mentioned: *She would never go to parties with the likes of you. Have you ever seen the likes of this garden?* ⇨ also likes below.

like⁴ /laɪk/ *prep* **1** similar to: *He can't cook like his mother. She's (not/a little/a lot/so) like her sister. It's hot like last Sunday. Your drawing is nothing like (= not at all like)/something like (= a little similar to) an elephant.* Compare like²(1). **2** characteristic of: *Isn't that just like a man? That's more like it!* (i.e. is nearer to the description, to what I expected etc). **3** such as: *There's a lot of work to do, like cleaning the kitchen and washing the floors.* **4** in that manner; in the same way as: *Don't talk to me like that! She was acting like an idiot.* ⇨ anything(1,5), clockwork, crazy, hell, mad(2), shot(1), wildfire. **5** (used in many expressions to emphasize the verb; 'like a sth' has a similar meaning to 'a lot' or 'well'): *drink like a fish; eat like a horse; fit like a glove; go like a bomb.* **5** (used as an *adv*) **feel like sth** ⇨ feel²(3). **look like** ⇨ look²(2).

like⁵ /laɪk/ *v* **1** *vt* to be fond of (a person, animal, thing): *I like you very much but I don't love you. I like cats but I don't like dogs. Do you like bright jewellery?* **2** *vt* to enjoy (an activity, food etc): *Do you like carrots? I like watching sport on TV. We like to walk in the summer. How did you like the play?* (i.e. What was your opinion of it?) **3** *vt,vi* to prefer (the kind mentioned): *I like people to be honest. Which do you like—baths or showers? How do you like your steak cooked?* **if you like** (used to express agreement, willingness or to make a suggestion) if you wish (it): *I'll go if you*

like. If you like, we could go to the cinema.
would like (often used to make a polite suggestion or question about a choice, something one wishes to have, do etc): *Would you like another coffee? She'd like some chocolate cake. I'd like to go to the cinema. Which one would you like? What would you like for your birthday? We wouldn't like to miss the chance of seeing you.* **4** vt **not like to (do sth)** to be unwilling to (do it): *I didn't like to disturb you.*

like·li·hood /'laɪklɪhʊd/ nu *or sing* **likelihood (of sth)** probability: *There is a strong likelihood of rain tomorrow.*

like·ly¹ /'laɪklɪ/ adj (-ier, -iest) **1** probable: *It is likely that he'll win. That's the likely result.* **2** that seems reasonable or suitable for a purpose: *What do you think is the likeliest/the most likely time to find him at home? That's a likely story/excuse!* (= I don't believe you). **2 be likely to + verb/ that . . .** to be expected (to . . .): *He is not likely to succeed. It's highly* (= very) *likely that he will succeed.*

like·ly² /'laɪklɪ/ adv **more than/most/very likely** probably: *More than likely, I shall be here again next month.* **as likely as not** probably: *He will succeed as likely as not.* **not likely** (informal) certainly not: *'Will you come to the pop concert?' 'Not likely!'*

lik·en /'laɪkn/ vt **liken sth to sth** to compare one thing to another: *liken the heart to a pump.*

like·ness /'laɪknɪs/ n **1** nu the condition of being like: *I can't see much likeness between the two boys.* **2** nc a detail, instance, of being like: *There's a family likeness in all of them.*

likes /laɪks/ n pl (only in) **likes and dislikes** things that one likes(3) and does not like(3): *It's impossible to satisfy everyone's likes and dislikes.*

like·wise /'laɪkwaɪz/ adv **1** in the same or a similar way: *Watch him and do likewise.* **2** (used as a *conj*) also; in addition: *You must take a raincoat, likewise you'll need strong boots.*

lik·ing /'laɪkɪŋ/ n **1** nu the state of being fond of a person, thing: *Liking is not the same as loving.* **2** n sing a feeling of fondness. **have a liking for sb/ sth** to like a person, thing. **be to one's liking** to be as one likes it; satisfactory: *Is everything to your liking?* **take a liking to sb** to begin to like a person.

li·lac /'laɪlək/ n **1** nc (a small tree with) sweet-smelling pale purple or white blossom. **2** nu (also adj) a pale purple colour.

li·lo /'laɪləʊ/ nc (pl **-s**) (P) an airbed.

lily /'lɪlɪ/ nc (pl **-ies**) (one of many kinds of) plant growing from a bulb often with white, long flowers: *water-lilies.*

'lily-livered adj (derog) cowardly.

,lily-'white adj pure white.

limb /lɪm/ nc **1** a leg, arm or wing. **2** a large branch (of a tree). **out on a limb** (informal) **(a)** alone because of unpopular opinions: *His refusal to agree left him out on a limb.* **(b)** in a difficult position and easy to attack: *Don't go out on a limb for such a silly cause.*

lim·ber /'lɪmbə(r)/ vi **limber up** to do exercises to make oneself fit for athletics or sport.

lim·bo /'lɪmbəʊ/ nu **in limbo** (informal) in a state between two extremes; not (to be) decided: *The idea is in limbo until the new manager is*

appointed.

lime¹ /laɪm/ nu a white substance, used in making cement or as a fertilizer.

lime² /laɪm/ nc (a tree with) a fruit like, but more acid than, a lemon.

'lime juice nu juice of this fruit used for flavouring and as a drink.

lime·light /'laɪmlaɪt/ n **be in/be fond of the limelight** to be enjoying/enjoy a lot of public attention.

lim·er·ick /'lɪmərɪk/ nc (literature) a humorous or nonsense poem of five lines.

lime·stone /'laɪmstəʊn/ nu a kind of rock containing lime¹, used for building and to make cement.

lim·it¹ /'lɪmɪt/ nc a line or point that may not or cannot be passed; greatest or smallest amount, extent etc of what is possible: *within a limit of five miles/a five-mile limit. We must set a limit to the expense of the trip. She has reached the limit of her patience.* ⇨ also age limit. **within limits** to a limited degree: *I'm willing to help you, within limits.*

lim·it² /'lɪmɪt/ vt to keep (something) within or up to a certain amount, size, extent etc: *We must limit our spending to what we can afford. I'm limited in ways to help you.*

lim·ited adj small in amount, size etc: *Accommodation is very limited.*

,limited ,lia'bility company nc (abbr Ltd placed after the name) a business whose members are liable for its debts only up to the amount they have provided.

lim·it·less adj without a limit: *limitless ambitions.*

limi·ta·tion /,lɪmɪ'teɪʃn/ n **1** nu the state of limiting or being limited. **2** nc a condition, fact or circumstance that limits: *He knows his limitations* (= knows the extent of his ability).

lim·ou·sine /'lɪməzi:n/ nc a large expensive car, esp with the front seats separated from the back seats by a glass window.

limp¹ /lɪmp/ adj not stiff or firm; without strength: *The flowers looked limp in the heat.*

limp·ly adv

limp·ness nu

limp² /lɪmp/ nc an uneven way of walking because of injury etc: *walk with a limp.*

limp³ /lɪmp/ vi **1** to walk unevenly as when one leg or foot is hurt: *The wounded footballer limped off the field.* **2** (fig) **limp back/home** (of a vehicle, boat etc) to manage to return with difficulty because of damage.

lim·pet /'lɪmpɪt/ nc a small shellfish that fastens itself tightly to rocks.

linch·pin /'lɪntʃpɪn/ nc **1** a bar passed through the end of an axle to keep the wheel in position. **2** (fig) a person who keeps a business, organization etc successful.

line¹ /laɪn/ nc **1** a thin long mark on a surface: *draw a straight line; a thin/thick line; sign on the dotted line; many lines in the rock; the lines on a map showing the height of the land; the lines on a tennis court; the pattern of lines on a television screen.* ⇨ linear(1). **2** a long piece of rope, string, wire etc: *a clothes/fishing/washing-line.* **3** a telephone wire; telephone or radio link: *A bird was sitting on the telephone line. I can't hear because* there is another voice on the line. The line is engaged (= Another person is speaking to the person you wish to contact). **get one's lines crossed** (fig) to misunderstand (each other) because of mistaken information. **hold the line** (often used as a request) to keep listening and not put the telephone down (e.g. while one fetches something). ⇨ also hot line. **4** a long deep mark on the skin: lines under her eyes. **5** an (imaginary) edge or boundary: kick the ball over the line; cross the line into Mexico; cross enemy lines; the dividing line between right and wrong. **draw the line (at sth)** to set limits by refusing to accept, allow, do, something: I don't mind your jokes but I draw the line at rudeness. It's difficult to know where to draw the line. **6** a row (of people or things): a line of children/players/trees. **all along the line** at every point: They'd made mistakes all along the line during the investigation. **be in line for sth** to be likely to get something: be in line for promotion. She's next in line for (= next to get) a free ticket. **stand in line** (esp US) to form a queue. **7** a row (of words, letters, symbols etc): a line of writing; lines of poetry; page 5 line 10; an actor learning her lines for a play. **drop sb a line** (informal) to write a person a short letter. **read between the lines** to find a fact, idea etc in a letter etc that is not actually written down: Reading between the lines, I don't think he'll come although he doesn't say so. **8** a railway track or system: a branch/main (railway) line. **the end of the line** (fig) the point after which more effort is useless. **9** a system of travelling, carrying goods, sending information etc: an airline; a shipping line; lines of communication. **10** a direction, course, of movement: You're in my line of vision. Don't stand in his line of fire (i.e. where he is pointing his gun). That won't solve the problem; why not try a different line of approach (= a different way or method)? **the line of least resistance** the easiest way of avoiding trouble or difficulty when dealing with a problem: choose/follow/take the line of least resistance when deciding who to dismiss. **be in line with sb** to agree with a person. **be on the right/wrong lines** to be likely/unlikely to succeed because using the right/wrong method. **be out of line with sb** to disagree with a person. **come/fall into line (with sb/sth)** to agree to accept a person's opinion, plan etc. **follow the party line** ⇨ party(4). **take a firm/hard/strong line** to deal with a problem, difficult person, criminal etc by using determined or harsh methods. **toe the line** to behave properly; obey orders. **11** an occupation, profession, business: He's in the grocery line. Teaching football isn't really in my line (i.e. I'm not qualified or interested). **12** a type of goods for sale: A department store sells many different lines. They stock a cheap line in jeans. **13** a design, shape, style, of clothes, buildings, vehicles etc: the soft lines in women's jackets; a new concert hall with strong lines produced by the brickwork; the sporty lines of the latest saloon cars. **14** a series of people living, having power or position etc after each other: a direct line of descent; a long line of doctors in our family; a line of monarchs since 1066. ⇨ lineal.

line² /laɪn/ v **1** vt to mark (something) with lines: a face that had been lined with worry. **2** vt,vi to place (people, things), be formed, in a row or rows: Children were lining the streets hoping to see the princess. The road was lined with trees. **3 line (sb/sth) up** (to cause people, things) to be, get, into a row: They were lining up at the bus-stop. ⇨ line-up.

line³ /laɪn/ vt **1** to attach an inside layer of material to (a bag, box, drawer etc or to clothing): a box lined with paper; fur-lined gloves. ⇨ lining. **2** to cover the surface of (something): a wall lined with books. **3** (fig) to fill (something): pockets lined with money.

lin·eage /ˈlɪnɪɪdʒ/ nu (formal) = ancestry.

lin·eal /ˈlɪnɪəl/ adj (formal) in the direct line of descent (from father to son etc): a lineal descendant/heir.
lin·eal·ly /-ɪəlɪ/ adv

lin·ear /ˈlɪnɪə(r)/ adj (attrib) **1** of or in lines: a linear design. **2** of length: linear measurement.

lin·en /ˈlɪnɪn/ nu **1** a kind of cloth made of flax. **2** articles made from this cloth, esp sheets, tablecloths etc. **wash one's dirty linen in public** to discuss family quarrels, unpleasant personal affairs etc in the presence of other people.

line-print·er /ˈlaɪn prɪntə(r)/ nc (computers) a machine that reproduces a line(7) of words etc at a time extremely quickly.

lin·er /ˈlaɪnə(r)/ nc **1** a passenger ship or plane: a jet airliner. **2** a cosmetic pencil used for drawing lines round the eyes: an eye-liner.

lines·man /ˈlaɪnzmən/ nc (pl -men) (also **lineswoman**) (sport) a person who helps the umpire or referee by saying whether the ball crosses a line(5).

line-up /ˈlaɪn ʌp/ nc **1** an arrangement of people, things, in a line(6). **2** a way in which people, countries are grouped politically or economically. **3** a formation of players ready for action (in a game such as football). **4** an arrangement of items (esp in a radio or TV programme): This evening's line-up includes an interview with the Chairman of British Rail.

ling. written abbr linguistics.

lin·ger /ˈlɪŋɡə(r)/ vi to be late or slow in going away or finishing; stay at or near a place: linger about/around the school gates; linger over a meal; a pain that lingered (on) for hours.
'ling·er·er nc a person who lingers.
ling·er·ing adj (attrib) lasting a long time: a lingering illness; a lingering look; a few lingering doubts.
ling·er·ing·ly adv

linge·rie /ˈlɒnʒərɪ/ nu (Fr) (commerce) women's underwear.

lin·go /ˈlɪŋɡəʊ/ nc (pl —es) (informal) a language that one does not know; way of talking, vocabulary, of a particular group of people: the strange lingo used by disc jockeys.

lin·gua fran·ca /ˌlɪŋɡwə ˈfræŋkə(r)/ nc a language adopted for local communication over an area in which several languages are spoken, e.g. Swahili in E Africa.

lin·guist /ˈlɪŋɡwɪst/ nc **1** a person skilled in foreign languages: She's a good linguist. **2** a person who makes a scientific study of language(s).

lin·guis·tic /lɪŋˈɡwɪstɪk/ adj of (the scientific study of) languages.

lin·guis·tic·al·ly /-klɪ/ adv

lin·guis·tics nu the scientific study of language, e.g. of its structure, relationship to other forms of communication etc.

lini·ment /'lɪnɪmənt/ nc,nu (a kind of) liquid for rubbing on stiff or aching parts of the body.

lin·ing /'laɪnɪŋ/ nc,nu (a layer of) material added to the inside of something: a fur lining.

link¹ /lɪŋk/ nc **1** one ring or loop of a chain. **the missing link** (fig) the piece of information, fact etc that provides a solution to a problem or explanation. **2** one of a pair of fasteners for the cuffs of a shirt: cuff-links. **3** a person, idea etc that unites or connects two others: the links between the past and the future.

link² /lɪŋk/ v **1** vt **link sth (together)** to cause things to be joined (as if) with a link(1): They linked arms. Use the string to link the papers together. What do you think links the various incidents? (i.e. What is the shared fact?) The towns are linked by a motorway. **2** vi **link up (with sb/ sth)** to (meet and) join (a person, office etc) either physically or by telephone: Where shall we link up?

links /lɪŋks/ n **1** n pl grassy land, esp near the sea. **2** nc a golf-course.

lin·seed oil /'lɪnsɪd ɔɪl/ nu a kind of oil, used in making ink, paint etc.

lint /lɪnt/ nu a soft cotton material, used for putting on wounds.

lin·tel /'lɪntl/ nc a horizontal piece of wood or stone forming the top of the frame of a door or window.

li·on /'laɪən/ nc a large, strong, animal of the cat family, found in Africa and S Asia, **the lion's share** the larger or largest part.

li·on·ess /-es/ nc a female lion.

li·on·ize (also **-ise**) /'laɪənaɪz/ vt to treat (a person) as a celebrity.

lip /lɪp/ nc **1** one or other of the fleshy edges of the mouth: the lower/upper lip. **bite one's lip** to hide one's feelings. **curl one's lip** to show anger or scorn. **give/pay lip-service to sth** to make insincere promises, express insincere regret. **keep a stiff upper lip** ⇨ upper. **lick/smack one's lips** (fig) to show (anticipation of) enjoyment. **2** an edge of a hollow container or opening: the lip of a bowl/crater.

'lip-reading nu a method (taught to deaf people) of understanding speech from lip movements. Hence **'lip-read** vt,vi.

'lip-service nu ⇨ lip(1).

'lip·stick nc (a stick of) cosmetic material for colouring the lips.

lique·fy /'lɪkwɪfaɪ/ vt,vi (pt,pp **-ied**) (to cause a substance) to become liquid. ⇨ liquidize.

li·queur /lɪ'kjʊə(r)/ nc,nu (also attrib) (a kind of) strong-flavoured alcoholic drink, e.g. brandy: a liqueur glass (= a small one for liqueurs).

liq·uid¹ /'lɪkwɪd/ adj (usually attrib) **1** (esp of solids) now in the form of a liquid: liquid food; liquid metals. **2** (of sounds) clear; pure: the liquid notes of a blackbird. **3** (finance) easily sold or changed into cash: liquid assets.

liq·uid² /'lɪkwɪd/ nc,nu (a kind of) substance like water or oil that flows freely and is neither a solid nor a gas.

liqui·date /'lɪkwɪdeɪt/ vt **1** to bring (esp an unsuccessful business company) to an end by dividing up its property to pay debts. **2** (informal) to get rid of, put an end to, kill, (a person): gangsters who liquidate their rivals.

liqui·da·tion /ˌlɪkwɪ'deɪʃn/ nu liquidating or being liquidated. **go into liquidation** (of a business) to become bankrupt.

liqui·da·tor /-tə(r)/ nc an official who liquidates(1) a business company.

li·quid·ity /lɪ'kwɪdətɪ/ nu **1** (finance) the ability to sell assets and pay debts. **2** (science) the state of being liquid(1).

liq·uid·ize (also **-ise**) /'lɪkwɪdaɪz/ vt to crush (e.g. fruit, vegetables) to a liquid.

liq·uid·izer (also **-iser**) nc an electrical device for liquidizing fruit etc.

liq·uor /'lɪkə(r)/ nu (a kind of) strong alcoholic drink.

liq·uor·ice (US = **lic·or·ice**) /'lɪkərɪs/ nu a black substance with a strong flavour, used in medicine and in sweets.

lisp¹ /lɪsp/ nc a lisping way of speaking: The child has a bad lisp.

lisp² /lɪsp/ vi,vt to fail to use the sounds /s/ and /z/ correctly (e.g. by saying /θɪk'θeɪ:n/ for sixteen): She lisps.

lis·som (also **lis·some**) /'lɪsəm/ adj (formal) quick and graceful in movement.

list¹ /lɪst/ nc a number of names (of people, things etc) written or printed: a shopping list. ▢ vt to make a list of (things); put (things) on a list.

'list price nc (commerce) a published or advertised price.

lis·ten /'lɪsn/ vi (usually **listen (to sb/sth)**) **1** (to pay attention in order to) hear: We listened but heard nothing. The boys were not listening to me. **listen in (to sth)** (a) to listen to a radio programme: Did you listen in to the Prime Minister yesterday evening? (b) to listen secretly (to a conversation). **2** to take (a person's) advice: Don't listen to him—he wants to get you into trouble. **listen to reason** ⇨ reason¹(3).

lis·ten·er nc a person who listens (esp to the radio). Compare viewer.

list·less /'lɪstlɪs/ adj too tired to show interest or do anything.

list·less·ly adv

lit /lɪt/ pt,pp of light⁵.

lit·any /'lɪtənɪ/ nc (pl **-ies**) a form of Christian prayer used in church services.

lit·chi /'laɪtʃiː/ nc (a tree producing) a round fruit with a thin reddish-brown shell and white juicy flesh.

li·ter /'liːtə(r)/ n (US) = litre.

lit·er·acy /'lɪtərəsɪ/ nu the ability to read and write.

lit·er·al /'lɪtərəl/ adj **1** corresponding exactly to the original: a literal translation. **2** taking words in their usual and obvious sense without exaggeration etc: the literal sense of a word.

lit·er·al·ly /'lɪtrəlɪ/ adv (a) exactly: carry out orders too literally. (b) (informal) without exaggeration: The children were literally starving.

lit·er·ary /'lɪtərərɪ/ adj (attrib) of literature or authors: a literary style (= as used in literature).

lit·er·ate /'lɪtərət/ adj **1** able to read and write: What percentage of the world's population is literate? Compare illiterate. **2** (formal) having read and learned much: *Ben's a remarkably literate young man.*

lit·era·ture /'lɪtərətʃə(r)/ *nu* **1** (the writing or the study of) books etc valued as works of art (i.e. novels, drama, essays, poetry, biography etc but not textbooks and journalism). **2** books dealing with a special subject: *travel literature.* **3** printed material giving information, e.g. brochures: *We shall be glad to send you some literature about our package holidays.*

lithe /laɪð/ *adj* (of a person etc) bending, twisting or turning easily: *lithe movements.*

liti·gant /'lɪtɪgənt/ *nc* (*legal*) a person engaged in a lawsuit.

liti·gate /'lɪtɪgeɪt/ *vi,vt* (*legal*) to make or oppose a claim at a law court.

liti·ga·tion /,lɪtɪ'geɪʃn/ *nu*

lit·mus /'lɪtməs/ *nu* (also *attrib*) (*science*) a blue colouring that is turned red by acid and can then be restored to blue by alkali: *litmus-paper.*

li·totes /'laɪtəʊtiːz/ *nc* (*pl* unchanged) (*literature*) an expression of a positive feeling or affirmative statement by using a negative one, as in '*I shall not be sorry when it's over*' (meaning 'I shall be very glad').

litre (*US* = **liter**) /'liːtə(r)/ *nc* a unit of measurement for liquid, = 1·75 pints.

lit·ter¹ /'lɪtə(r)/ *n* **1** *nu* unwanted pieces of paper, wrappings, bottles etc left lying about in a room or public place: *Pick up your litter after a picnic.* **2** *nc* all the young ones of an animal born at the same time: *a litter of puppies.*

'litter-basket/-bin *nc* a container for litter(1).

lit·ter² /'lɪtə(r)/ *vt* to make (something) untidy with litter(1): *litter a desk with papers; litter up one's room.*

little¹ /'lɪtl/ *adj* or *det* **1** *a little sth* a small amount of: *He has a little money. With a little effort you'll succeed. She speaks only a little Japanese. I'll walk a little way with you. I need a little more time. Can you wait a little while? She has a little food, I have less food and he has the least food.* Ⓝ '*Small*' is not possible. The comparative form of '*a little*' is '*less*' and the superlative form is '*least*'. ⇨ the notes at less¹ and least¹. ⇨ also few¹(1). **no little sth** a large amount of: *She gives no little care to her children.* **2** not much: *There's little chance of meeting her. You've done little work today. We have very little time left. But it would cost you so little money!* Ⓝ '*Small*' is not possible. The comparative form is '*less*' and the superlative form is '*least*'. '*Not much*' is more usual than '*little*', as in *There's not much hope of a cure, We haven't got much time left.* '*Little*' is more usual only when it is used with *so, too, very* etc, as in '*so little opportunity*', '*too little patience*', '*very little money*'. **3** (*attrib*) small in size: *my little finger/toe; a little fish in a big pond. He's a little man with a big heart. What a horrible little mind you have!* Ⓝ The comparative and superlative forms are '*littler*' and '*littlest*' but they are rarely used. '*Small*' is also possible but is used to refer to physical size only, as in *a small room/ box/town/space.* '*Little*' is preferred when expressing an emotional idea with the size, as in *He has a nasty little temper. I can afford only a little present.* Compare big(1). **4** (*attrib*) young: *Here's my little girl. I teach the little ones in the first class.* Ⓝ The comparative and superlative forms are '*littler*' and '*littlest*'

but they are rarely used. **5** (*no comp*) not important: *It's a little problem so don't worry.* Compare big, small¹(3). **6** (*informal*) younger: *my little brother/sister.* Compare big(2).

little² /'lɪtl/ *adv* **1** not much: *He's little known. She slept very little last night. I see him so little these days.* Ⓝ The comparative form is '*less*' and the superlative form is '*least*', as in '*sleep less*' and '*pay the least money*'. **little by little** gradually: *Little by little they moved towards the top. We saved the money little by little.* **little . . . than sb/sth** almost as much or the same as: *He left little more than an hour ago. She's little better than a thief.* **2** *verb* + *a little* to a small extent: *cry/laugh/smile a little.* **a little** + *adj* to a small degree or extent: *It's a little heavy/too big. Spain is a little hotter than France. I'm a little afraid.* Ⓝ The comparative form is '*less*' and the superlative is '*least*'. **not a little** + *adj* very: *not a little annoyed.* Compare less², least². **2** (used with verbs referring to mental activity) not at all: *He little thought/imagined/ guessed that she would agree. Little did she realize that he was a thief.*

little³ /'lɪtl/ *pron* **a little (of sth)** a small amount (of): *I know a little (of the music). Only a little of it was bad. She's eaten (a) very little (of her dinner). Let's keep a little for tomorrow. There's quite a little* (= much) *left over.* Compare less⁴, least³, few². **after/for a little** after/for a small amount of time or distance: *After a little, a car appeared. Let's wait for a little.* **little or nothing** almost nothing: *We could see little or nothing in the fog.*

lit·ur·gy /'lɪtədʒɪ/ *nc,nu* (*pl* **-ies**) (a form of) public worship in a Christian church.

li·tur·gi·cal /lɪ'tɜːdʒɪkl/ *adj*

liv·able (also **live·able**) /'lɪvəbl/ *adj* **1** (of a house, room, climate etc) fit to live in. **2** (of life) worth living. **livable with** (of a person) easy to live with.

live¹ /laɪv/ *adj* (*no comp*) **1** (*attrib*) having life; living: *live fish; live bacteria.* Compare alive(1), dead¹(1). **a real live sb/sth** an actual person or animal (not an actor or model): *We saw a real live elephant.* **2** charged with electricity: *a live (rail-way) line. Is this wire live?* **3** burning: *live coals.* **4** not yet used: *a live match.* **5** (*attrib*) actively being discussed, studied, thought about: *a live issue.* Compare alive(2). **6** (also used as an *adv*) (of a radio or TV programme etc) happening while it is being heard or seen, not recorded: *a live broad-cast/concert. We are reporting live from the festi-val.*

live² /lɪv/ *v* **1** *vi* to exist; be alive (the more usual words): *We can't live without oxygen. She lived in the last century.* Compare die²(1). **2** *vi* to continue to exist; remain alive: *She's very ill and the doctors don't think she will live much longer.* **3** *vi* to pass, spend, one's life (in the way mentioned): *live hap-pily/honestly.* **live and learn** to get knowledge from the experience of living: *I didn't think such hatred was possible but you live and learn!* **live and let live** (*saying*) to be tolerant and do not try to change the way others organize their lives. **live well** to enjoy a high standard of living. **4** *vt* to conduct oneself in life in (the way mentioned): *She lived an honest/clean/interesting life. He lived and died a bachelor.* **5** *vi* to have one's home: *liv-ing abroad/at home/in England/on a farm. Where* *are you living now? This isn't a nice place to live.* ⇨ **live at/in/on** a place. **6** *vi* to be able to buy the things needed for one's existence: *Does the job pay you enough to live?* **7** *vi* to have a pleasant and interesting life: *'I want to live,' she said 'not spend all day cleaning the house.'* **8** *vi* to continue to exist: *No ship could live in such a storm! His memory lives in our hearts.*

live above one's income to spend more money than one earns.

live apart (from sb) (of a married couple) to have separate homes.

live at a place to have one's home at (an address, place of work or study): *live at home/at the hospital/at the university. I live at 14 Church Road.*

live beyond one's income/means = live above one's income.

live by sth to live(3) a style of life according to a belief, philosophy: *living by one's faith.* **live by sth/doing sth** to live(6) using something: *living by one's writing/by writing.* **live by oneself** to live(3) alone.

live sth down to live(3) in such a way that one's failures, bad past etc are forgotten: *She can never live down her time spent in prison.*

live in to live(5) where one works. ⇨ **live out**.

live in a place to have one's home in a building, tent, a city, town etc; a country or continent; a forest, the countryside etc: *live in a flat/house; live in Bombay/a village; live in Italy/Africa; live in a wood.* **lived in** (*adj*) (of a house, room etc) having a comfortable and relaxing atmosphere: *Her new flat looks lived in already.*

live off sb to get money to live(6) from another person: *live off one's parents.* **live off sth** (**a**) to eat (only) food one has grown on a place: *live off the land/one's vegetable patch.* (**b**) to get money to live(6) from the government etc: *live off the state.*

live on (**a**) to continue to be alive: *Her husband died but she lived on for another ten years.* (**b**) to continue to live(5) (in a place): *The children have left but the old people still live on in the village.* (**c**) (of reputation) to continue to exist: *His fame will live on for years to come.* **live on a place** to have one's home on a boat; a farm; a housing estate or university campus etc: *live on a ship/yacht; live on a farm/on the land; live on a council estate; live on campus.* **live on sth** (**a**) to use something in order to live(3): *live on one's salary.* (**b**) to eat something as one's diet: *live on fruit and vegetables.* **live on air** ⇨ air¹(1). **live on one's own** to live(3) alone.

live out to live(5) away from one's place of work. ⇨ live in. **live out of sth** to have one's possessions in a bag etc because one has no fixed home: *live out of a suitcase/plastic bag.*

live sth over (again) (**a**) to experience it again, esp in the imagination: *She continued to live over her experiences as a hostage for many years.* (**b**) to live(3) a second time: *If I had my life to live over, I'd do the same again.*

live through sth to experience and survive a war, revolution, a difficult period, an unpleasant experience: *We've lived through the worst years.*

live to an age (*informal*) to live(2) until: *live to an old age/to the age of 90.* **live to do sth** to continue to exist until one does something: *You'll live*

to regret this. I'll live to see my children married.

live together (with sb) (**a**) to share the same house. (**b**) to live(3) as husband and wife although not married.

live under sth to experience while living(3) the rule of a political system, a particular kind of ruler etc: *live under socialism/a military ruler.*

live up to sth to reach a standard one wants while living or expected by others; act as (good or bad) as expected: *live up to one's high principles; live up to a reputation for being kind/stupid.* **live it up** (*informal*) to have fun and pleasure: *living it up in London.*

live upon sth (*formal*) = live on sth(b).

live with sb = live together (with sb). **live with sth** to accept and bear a sad fact, disability, failure etc: *You must learn to live with the fact that you are getting old.*

live·li·hood /'laɪvlɪhʊd/ *nc* a way in which one earns money: *earn/gain one's livelihood by teaching. Writing is my livelihood.*

live·long /ˌlɪvlɒŋ/ *adj* (only in) **the livelong day/night** all day/night.

live·ly /'laɪvlɪ/ *adj* (**-ier, -iest**) **1** full of life and spirit; gay and cheerful: *The patient seems a little livelier/a little more lively this morning.* **2** energetic; quick: *a lively imagination/tune.* **3** interesting and enthusiastic: *a lively description of a football game.*

live·li·ness *nu*

liven /'laɪvn/ *vt,vi* **liven (sb/sth) (up)** (to cause a person, situation) to become lively: *How can we liven things up?*

liv·er¹ /'lɪvə(r)/ *n* **1** *nc* (*anat*) the large, reddish-brown organ in the body which produces bile and cleans the blood. **2** *nu* an animal's liver as food.

liv·er² /'lɪvə(r)/ *nc* a person who lives in the way mentioned: *a clean/loose liver.*

liv·ery /'lɪvərɪ/ *nc* (*pl* **-ies**) **1** uniform worn by male staff in a very rich household. **2** (also *livery-stable*) a place where horses are fed and looked after for payment.

lives /laɪvz/ *pl* of life.

live·stock /'laɪvstɒk/ *nu* (esp) farm animals kept for use or profit.

liv·id /'lɪvɪd/ *adj* (usually *pred*) (of a person, expression) extremely angry: *be livid with her.*

liv·id·ly *adv*

liv·ing¹ /'lɪvɪŋ/ *adj* **1** alive, esp now: *living relatives.* **in/within living memory** ⇨ memory(1). **2** being used still: *a living language.* **3** (of a likeness) true to life: *He's the living image of* (= is exactly like) *his father.*

liv·ing² /'lɪvɪŋ/ *n pl* (the —) those people now alive: *He's still in the land of the living.*

liv·ing³ /'lɪvɪŋ/ *n* **1** *sing* a means of keeping alive; of earning what is needed for life. **make a/one's living** have as a means of earning money to live: *make a living as an artist/by painting/from one's paintings.* **2** *nu* a way of life: *fast/good living; enjoy a high standard of living.*

'living-room a room for general use such as watching TV, relaxing, entertaining.

liz·ard /'lɪzəd/ *nc* a kind of small, creeping, long-tailed, four-legged reptile.

ll. *written abbr* lines (used when referring to certain lines in a book): *See ll. 50–55.*

lla·ma /'lɑːmə/ *nc* a kind of S American animal

with a thick woolly coat.

lo /ləʊ/ *int* (*old use*) Look! See!

load¹ /ləʊd/ *nc* **1** an amount which is (to be) carried. **a load of** (*informal*) complete: *Her excuse is a load of nonsense.* **loads of** (*informal*) much or many: *loads of money/fun/times.* **2** (*fig*) an amount of care, responsibility etc: *a heavy/light work load. a heavy load on one's shoulders.* ⇨ also mind¹(2). **3** an amount of people which a vehicle can carry: *a bus-load of passengers.* **4** the work that an engine etc is required to do. **5** (*electricity*) an amount of electric current carried by a circuit.

load² /ləʊd/ *v* **1** *vt,vi* to put a load in or on (a person, vehicle, animal): *load sacks onto a lorry; a poor old woman loaded* (*down*) *with her shopping.* **load** (*sth*) **up** to fill (a vehicle) with goods etc: *Have you finished loading up* (*the van*) *yet?* **2** *vi* (of a bus, plane etc) to begin to take on passengers: *The plane to Rome is now loading.* **3** *vt* to put (information) into a computer. **4** *vt* to put (film) into (a camera); put (video-tape) into (a video machine). **5** *vt* to put (a cartridge or shell) into (a gun).

load·ed *adj* (*sl*) having a lot of money.

loaf¹ /ləʊf/ *nc* (*pl* **loaves** /ləʊvz/) **1** a shaped piece of bread: *a brown/white loaf* (*of bread*). **2** *nc,nu* (a quantity of) food shaped and cooked: (*a*) *meat loaf.* **3** (*sl*) **use one's loaf** to think intelligently.

loaf² /ləʊf/ *vi* **loaf** (*about*) to waste time by doing nothing: *Don't loaf about while there's so much work to be done.*

loaf·er *nc* (*derog*) a person who is lazy.

loam /ləʊm/ *nu* fertile soil.

loamy *adj* (**-ier, -iest**) of, like, loam.

loan¹ /ləʊn/ *nc* **1** something lent, esp a sum of money: *a bank loan.* **2** *nu* (esp **on loan**) the act of lending or being lent: *I have the book out on loan from the library.*

loan² /ləʊn/ *vt* **loan sth** (*to sb/sth*) to lend something, esp for a long time (to a person, organization etc): *These pictures are on permanent loan to the museum.*

loath (also **loth**) /ləʊθ/ *adj* **loath** (*to do sth*) unwilling; reluctant; *I'm loath to agree but it seems that I must.*

loathe /ləʊð/ *vt* **1** to feel disgust because of (something): *She loathed the smell of greasy food.* **2** (*informal*) to dislike (a person, thing): *He loathes travelling by air.*

loath·ing *nu* disgust (the usual word).

loath·some /-səm/ *adj* disgusting; extremely unpleasant: *a loathsome disease/smell.*

loaves /ləʊvz/ *pl* of loaf¹.

lob /lɒb/ *vi,vt* (**-bb-**) to send (a ball) in a high arc (as in tennis). □ *nc* a ball that is lobbed.

lob·by¹ /'lɒbɪ/ *nc* (*pl* **-ies**) **1** a large room inside the entrance to (a building): *the lobby of a hotel/ theatre.* **2** a group of people who try to influence others to support or oppose a social or political cause.

lob·by² /'lɒbɪ/ *v* (*pt,pp* **-ied**) **1** *vt,vi* **lobby** (*sb/ sth*) (*for/about sth*) to meet (officials) to try to gain support (for a social or political cause). **2** *vi* to act as (part of) a lobby(2).

lobe /ləʊb/ *nc* **1** (also *earlobe*) the flap at the bottom of the outer ear. **2** a division of the lungs or the brain.

lob·ster /'lɒbstə(r)/ *n* **1** *nc* a kind of shellfish with eight legs and two claws, bluish-black before and pink after being boiled. **2** *nu* (also *attrib*) its flesh as food: *lobster soup.*

lo·cal¹ /'ləʊkl/ *adj* **1** of, in, a place or district: *the local doctor/newspaper.* **2** affecting a part only, not the whole: *a local pain/injury/anaesthetic.*

,**local** ,anaes'thetic *nc,nu* one affecting only a part of the body. Compare general anaesthetic.

,**local au'thority** *nc* officers elected to administer local government.

,**local 'colour** *nu* (*literature*) details of the scenes and period described in a story, added to make the story more real.

,**local e'lection** *nc* one to decide representatives for local government. Compare general election.

,**local 'government** *nu* the administration of the affairs of a district (roads, education, refuse, parks etc) by representatives elected by the residents.

,**local 'time** *nu* time at a particular place in the world.

lo·cal·ly /-kəlɪ/ *adv*

lo·cal² /'ləʊkl/ *nc* **1** (usually *pl*) a person living in a particular district: *a shopping-centre for the locals.* **2** (*informal*) a pub near one's home: *Let's pop into the local for a pint.*

lo·cale /ləʊ'kɑːl/ *nc* a scene of an event, e.g. in a novel etc.

lo·cal·ity /ləʊ'kælətɪ/ *nc* (*pl* **-ies**) a district or place, esp in which an event occurs.

lo·cal·ize (also **-ise**) /'ləʊkəlaɪz/ *vt* to keep (something) inside a particular part or area: *There is little hope of localizing the disease.*

lo·cate /ləʊ'keɪt/ *vt* **1** to discover, show, the position of (something): *locate a town on a map.* Ⓝ Not used in continuous tenses, e.g. *is/was -ing.* **2** (often *passive*) to establish (something) in a place: *Where is the new factory to be located?*

lo·ca·tion /ləʊ'keɪʃn/ *n* **1** *nc* a position or place: *suitable locations for new factories.* **2** *nc,nu* a place, not a film studio, where (part of) a film is photographed. **on location** making a film in this way.

loch /lɒx/ *nc* (*Scot*) a lake.

lock¹ /lɒk/ *nc* a portion of hair that naturally hangs or clings together.

lock² /lɒk/ *nc* **1** a device used to fasten a door, lid etc that needs a key to work it. **under lock and key** locked inside something, esp a prison. **pick a lock** to use wire etc to open a lock without using a key. **2** a mechanism by which a gun is fired. **lock, stock and barrel** completely: *They sold everything, lock, stock and barrel.* **3** an enclosed section of a canal where the water level changes, used for raising or lowering boats. **4** the amount of turn of a steering wheel: *full lock* (= with the steering wheel turned as far as it will go).

'**lock·smith** *nc* a maker and mender of locks.

lock³ /lɒk/ *v* **1** *vt,vi* (to cause something) to become fastened using a lock: *The car door locks on the inside. Are all the doors locked? This window doesn't lock* (i.e. it has no lock or the lock is broken). Opp unlock. **2** *vt* to make (a building) safe from unwanted people by fastening all the ways of entering. **3** *vt,vi* (to cause something) to become unable to move: *The wheels of the car* have locked. *The muscle in my leg locked as I jumped for the ball.* **4** *vt* to join (arms etc) together: *They locked arms.*

lock sb away to put a person in prison. **lock sth away** to put something in a place, e.g. a box, cupboard, drawer, that is then locked.

lock sb in to prevent a person (deliberately or accidentally) from leaving a room etc by locking the door. **be locked in sth** to be very busy with an activity: *be locked in battle.*

lock on (to sth) (a) (of a missile etc) to find and follow a target automatically, e.g. using radar. (b) (*informal*) to become determined or decided about an idea or plan: *She's firmly locked on to the idea of becoming an engineer.*

lock sb out to prevent workers from entering a factory etc, e.g. during an argument between management or owners and the workers. Hence 'lock·out *nc* an act, situation, of this kind. **lock sb out (of a place)** to prevent a person (deliberately or accidentally) from entering a building etc by locking the door.

lock up to lock the doors of a house, business etc: *Let's lock up and go to bed. It's time to lock up and go home.* **lock sb up (in a place)** to put a person in a place, e.g. a prison (and lock the door). **lock sth up (a)** = lock sth away. **(b)** to make a building safe from unwanted people by fastening the doors and windows. **(c)** to put money into a business, saving system etc so that it cannot easily be changed back into cash: *All my savings are locked up in the building society.*

lock·er /'lɒkə(r)/ *nc* a cupboard, esp one for storing one's clothes, e.g. at a swimming-pool.

'**locker-room** *nc* (e.g. in a sports centre) a room with lockers.

lock·et /'lɒkɪt/ *nc* a metal (often gold or silver) case for a portrait, a lock of hair etc, worn round the neck on a chain.

lock-out /'lɒk aʊt/ *nc* ⇨ lock sb out.

loco·mo·tion /,ləʊkə'məʊʃn/ *nu* movement, ability to move, from place to place.

loco·mo·tive¹ /,ləʊkə'məʊtɪv/ *adj* (*science*) of, having, causing, locomotion.

lo·co·mo·tive² /,ləʊkə'məʊtɪv/ *nc* a railway engine.

lo·cust /'ləʊkəst/ *nc* a kind of African and Asian winged insect which flies in large groups and destroys crops and vegetables.

lodge¹ /lɒdʒ/ *nc* **1** a small house, esp one at the entrance to the grounds of a large house. **2** a small house for temporary use: *a skiing lodge.* **3** a local branch of a trade union.

lodge² /lɒdʒ/ *v* **1** *vt* to supply (a person) with a room or place to sleep in for a time: *The shipwrecked sailors were lodged in the local school.* **2** *vi* to live in as a paying guest: *Where are you lodging now?* **3** *vt,vi* **lodge (sth) in a place (a)** (to cause something) to enter and become fixed: *The bullet lodged in his jaw.* **(b)** to put (money etc) somewhere for safety: *lodge one's valuables in the bank.* **4** *vt* **lodge sth (with sb)** to make a statement etc to an official: *lodge a complaint with the police.*

lodger *nc* a person lodging(2) in a house: *taking in lodgers.*

lodg·ings /'lɒdʒɪŋz/ *n pl* a place (not in a hotel) rented to live in: *Where can we find lodgings for*

the night?

loft¹ /lɒft/ *nc* a room, place, under the roof of a building.

loft² /lɒft/ *vt* to hit (a ball) high into the air.

lofty /'lɒftɪ/ *adj* (usually *attrib*) **(-ier, -iest) 1** (of a mountain etc) looking large and impressive. **2** (of thoughts, aims, feelings etc) impressive because very noble or moral: *lofty sentiments.* **3** (too) proud: *speak in a lofty manner.*

loft·ily /-əlɪ/ *adv*

lofti·ness *nu*

log¹ /lɒg/ *nc* **1** a length of tree-trunk that has fallen or been cut down. **sleep like a log** to sleep very deeply and well. **2** a short piece of a branch etc for a fire. **3** (also *log-book*) an official record of the journey of a ship or plane.

,**log 'cabin** *nc* one made of logs.

log² /lɒg/ *vt* (**-gg-**) to enter (facts) in the log(3) of a ship or plane.

log³ /lɒg/ *nc* (*abbr*) logarithm.

lo·gan·ber·ry /'ləʊgənbərɪ/ *nc* (*pl* **-ies**) (a large red berry from) a plant that is a cross²(5) between a blackberry and a raspberry.

log·ar·ithm /'lɒgərɪðəm/ *nc* (*maths*) one of a series of numbers set out in tables which make it possible to work out problems in multiplication and division by adding and subtracting.

log·ger·heads /'lɒgəhedz/ *n* (only in) **at loggerheads (with sb)** disagreeing or quarrelling: *He's constantly at loggerheads with his wife.*

log·ic /'lɒdʒɪk/ *nu* **1** the scientific method of organized reasoning. **2** (a person's) ability to think and express thoughts systematically: *argue with logic.*

logi·cal /-kl/ *adj* **(a)** in accordance with the rules of logic: *a logical conclusion.* **(b)** able to reason well: *a logical mind.*

logi·cal·ly /-klɪ/ *adv*

loins /lɔɪnz/ *n pl* the lower part of the body on both sides between the waist and the hips.

loi·ter /'lɔɪtə(r)/ *vi* to go slowly and stop frequently; stand about: *loiter on one's way home.*

loi·ter·er *nc* a person who loiters.

loll /lɒl/ *v* **1** *vi* **loll (about/around)** to rest, sit or stand in a lazy way. **2** *vt,vi* **loll (sth) (out)** (to allow the tongue) to hang out: *The dog's tongue was lolling out.*

lol·li·pop /'lɒlɪpɒp/ *nc* **1** a large sweet of boiled sugar on a stick. **2** (also *lolly*) a piece of flavoured ice on a stick.

lol·ly /'lɒlɪ/ *n* (*pl* **-ies**) **1** *nc* (*informal*) a lollipop: *iced lollies.* **2** *nu* (*sl*) money.

lone /ləʊn/ *adj* (*attrib*) without other people: *a lone soldier.*

lone·ly /'ləʊnlɪ/ *adj* (**-ier, -iest**) **1** without other people: *a lonely traveller.* **2** unhappy because one has no friends, support etc: *feel lonely.* **3** (of places) not often visited; far from where (other) people live: *a lonely mountain village.*

lone·li·ness *nu* the state of being lonely(2).

lone·some /'ləʊnsəm/ *adj* **1** lonely(2). **2** (esp *US*) not often visited: *a lonesome valley.*

long¹ /lɒŋ/ *adj* (**—er** /'lɒŋgə(r)/, **—est** /'lɒŋgɪst/) **1** having much extent in space (length): *a long rope; a long dress; a long way down; a long journey in a bus; a long nose; long sleeves; an animal with long fur. How long is that table?* Opp short¹(1). **2** having, taking, much time: *a long* holiday; *a long friendship/business association; a long flight between London and Chicago; be ill for a long time.* Opp short¹(3). **3** (*pred*) (of particular measurement) along the whole length; from end to end: *a road 6 miles long; a dress 1·5 metres long; a car exactly 4 metres long.* **4** (*pred*) (of particular measurement) from beginning to end (of time): *a film that was 2 hours long; a week long holiday.* **5** (of shape) measuring much more in one direction (esp up and down) than another (e.g. across): *a long face/room.* **6** not likely to be successful: *a long bet/chance.* ⇨ short¹(6), shot¹(3). **7** (used in many phrases). **at long last** ⇨ last³. **in the long run** ⇨ run¹(8). **in the long term** ⇨ term¹(1). **be long in the tooth** ⇨ tooth(1). **a long way** ⇨ way²(1).

,**long-'distance** *adj* (*attrib*) covering a long distance: *a long-distance race/telephone call/lorry driver.*

'**long·hand** *nu* ordinary handwriting (contrasted with *shorthand* and *typing*).

'**long johns** *n pl* (*informal*) long underpants for men.

'**long jump** *n* (the —) an athletic contest for jumping along the ground. ⇨ high jump.

,**long-playing 'record** *nc* (abbr LP) one playing many tunes or songs, or one long piece of music.

'**long-range** *adj* (*attrib*) of long periods, distances: *a long-range weather forecast* (e.g. for one month ahead).

,**long-'sighted** *adj* (usually *pred*) able to see only things a great distance away clearly. Compare short-sighted, far-sighted.

'**long-term** *adj* (*attrib*) related to a long period of time: *long-term agreements.*

'**long wave** *nu* (*radio*) one of 1000 metres or more.

,**long-'winded** *adj* (*derog*) taking a long time and boring: *a long-winded lecture/lecturer.*

long² /lɒŋ/ *adv* **1** (for) a long time: *Have you been waiting long? No, not (for) long. How long have you been here? How much longer must we be here? I haven't worked long in this office. The work won't take long. Please stay (for) as long as you want to.* **as/so long as** (**a**) during the length of time that; while: *You'll never enter this house as/so long as I live.* (**b**) on condition that: *You can borrow my bike as/so long as you return it.* **so long!** ⇨ so²(1). **2** at a distant time (from the time shown or mentioned): *long ago/after/before/since; not long ago/after/before/since.* **3 a long/any/no/much longer** after this time (mentioned or shown): *Are you staying any/much longer? I've often gone a lot longer without a meal. He can't live much longer than a year. I'm no longer interested.*

,**long-drawn-'out** *adj* unnecessarily or inappropriately long: *a long-drawn-out visit from my mother-in-law.*

'**long-running** *adj* (*attrib*) (of a disagreement, difficulty; a film or show etc) continuing for a long time: *a long-running argument; a long-running play.*

'**long-standing** *adj* (*attrib*) (of an agreement or arrangement) existing for a long time.

'**long-suffering** *adj* patient and uncomplaining: *his long-suffering wife.*

long³ /lɒŋ/ *n* **before long** soon: *She'll be back before long.* **for long** (usually used in questions) for a long time: *Have you been living here for long?* **the long and the short of it** all that needs be said about it: *He stole the bike, and the long and the short of it is that he's now in prison.*

long⁴ /lɒŋ/ *vi* **long (for sb/sth) (to do sth)** to want, wish for, a person, thing very much: *She longed for him to say something. I'm longing to see you.*

long·ing·ly *adv*

long. *written abbr* longitude.

lon·gev·ity /lɒnˈdʒevətɪ/ *nu* (*formal*) long life: *food that promotes longevity.*

long·ing /ˈlɒŋɪŋ/ *nc,nu* a strong desire: *a longing to be home.*

longi·tude /ˈlɒndʒɪtjuːd/ *nc* (abbr long) a distance east or west (measured in degrees) from a particular point (called a *meridian*) on a map.

longi·tu·di·nal /ˌlɒndʒɪˈtjuːdɪnl/ *adj* (**a**) of longitude. (**b**) along the length: *longitudinal stripes.*

long·ways (also **-wise**) /ˈlɒŋweɪz, -waɪz/ *adv* = lengthways.

loo /luː/ *nc* (*GB informal*) = lavatory, toilet.

loo·fah /ˈluːfə/ *nc* a piece of the inside of a tropical plant with many fibres, used as a sponge¹(2) for washing.

look¹ /lʊk/ *nc* **1** an act of looking: *Let me have a look at your new car.* **take a look (at sb/sth)** (*informal*) to examine a person, animal, machine etc because of a problem. **2** an expression (on the face): *There were angry looks from the neighbours.* **3** an appearance: *The town has an Italian look.* **not like the look of sb/sth** to be worried about her/his/its appearance. **4** (*pl*) a person's beauty or appearance: *She's beginning to lose her looks.*

look² /lʊk/ *v* **1** *vi* to use one's ability to see in order to search, examine, be entertained etc: *We looked everywhere but we couldn't see it.* Ⓝ 'Look' is almost always used with an adverbial particle or preposition to show where or why one is looking, as in *look at a book/the flowers/television; look down/up; look across the road.* 'See' is used when referring to having the ability of sight, as in *I can't see in the dark/without my glasses,* or when a particular visual impression happens (either accidentally or deliberately), as in *Did you see* (i.e. notice) *the roses in her garden? Suddenly we saw a shadow in the next room.* **2** *vi,vt* (usually *imperative*) to pay attention by looking carefully (at a person, thing, or in a particular direction): *Look where you're going. Look what I've made! Look who's here!* **look before you leap** (*proverb*) don't decide or do something until you have thought carefully about it. **Look here!** (used either to demand attention or to make one's doubt, protest etc stronger). **Look sharp!** Hurry up! **3** *vi* **look + adj** to appear or seem to be: *He looks old/ill/well/sad/tired/happy. That looks interesting/boring/expensive.* **(not) look oneself** to appear (not) to be as healthy or happy as usual. **look one's age** to appear to be as old as one is: *You don't look your age in that dress.* **look one's best (in sth)** to appear one's most attractive: *She looks her best in bright colours.* **look as if . . .** (**a**) to have the appearance that indicates . . . : *You look as if you've seen a ghost!* (**b**) = look like sth(b): *It looks as if it will* *rain/will be a good day.* **look like sb** to have the same physical (esp facial) appearance as another person: *He looks like his sister.* **look like sth (a)** to have an appearance that reminds one of something else: *Your car looks like an old bus.* **(b)** to seem as if there will probably be rain, snow, fog etc: *It looks like rain/a good day.* **4** *vi* to face (a direction mentioned): *Our garden looks south.*

look about (a place) (for sb/sth) to observe, search (in a place) (for a person, thing): *Are you still looking about for a job? We looked about the town in the afternoon.*

look after sb to take care of a person: *A mother looks after her children.* **look after sth (a)** to take responsibility for the safety of something: *Please look after my watch while I go swimming.* **(b)** to take care of a person's affairs: *Who looks after her legal affairs/the marketing side of the business?* **(c)** to pay a bill: *I'll look after this restaurant bill.*

look ahead (to sth) (a) to think about and prepare (for future events or situations). **(b)** to think of oneself at a future date or time: *I'm looking ahead (several years) when I talk about computers being in every home.* **(c)** to expect something with pleasure: *I'm looking ahead to having a super holiday.* ⇨ look forward to sth.

look around/round (sth) to observe, examine what is nearby: *look around (a room/museum). If you want to see the effects of greed, look around you.*

look at sb (a) to observe a person closely: *Look at that man on the roof!* **(b)** (of a doctor etc) to examine a person for possible illness etc. **look at sth (a)** to observe something closely: *look at a fly's eye through a microscope; look at a wall to see if it is damaged.* **(b)** to consider a possibility, proposal etc: *Let's look at his idea that vegetables feel pain.* **not look at sth** to refuse to consider a suggestion, proposal etc: *They won't look at a price below £300.* **... to look at** (*informal*) when considering a person's, object's etc outward appearance: *He's/The car's not much to look at.* **to look at sb/sth** considering the outward appearance of a person, object etc: *To look at her/her house, you'd think she was rich.*

look away (from sb/sth) to turn one's eyes away: *She looked away (from the manager), ashamed and embarrassed.*

look back to turn and look(1) behind. **look back (on sth)** to consider an event, period in the past: *look back on one's childhood.* **look back to sth** to return one's thoughts to an earlier event or period: *When I look back to my schooldays, I remember you well.*

look down to lower one's eyes and look(1) towards the ground. **look down on sb** to consider oneself to be better than another person. **look down one's nose at sb/sth** ⇨ nose¹(1).

look for sb/sth to search for, try to find, a person, something one has lost, a job, a place to live, a way to sell something etc. **be looking for trouble** ⇨ trouble¹(1).

look forward to sth to think about something that will happen in the future with pleasure: *I'm looking forward to meeting you/hearing from you/going home. He's not looking forward to his exam results.*

look in (at a place/on sb) to make a short visit: *look in at the party; look in on my mother to see if she is well. The doctor will look in (to see you) this afternoon.* ⇨ look-in.

look into sth (a) to look(1) inside a box, room etc. **(b)** to look(1) at a mirror, water, a person's eyes etc and observe what one sees. **(c)** to inquire into, make a careful study of something: *look into a possibility of working in China. Your suggestion is certainly worth looking into.*

look on to be an observer or spectator: *Why don't you learn to play tennis instead of just looking on?* **look on sb/sth as sb/sth** to consider a person, thing to be the kind mentioned: *He was looked on as a first class athlete. Look on the whole affair as one of life's bad experiences.* **look on sb/sth with sth** to have the opinion mentioned of a person, situation, event, plan etc: *He seems to look on me with disapproval/suspicion.*

look out (usually *imperative*) to be careful; take care: *Look out, there's a child running across the road!* **look sb/sth out (for sb)** to search for a person, thing and produce her, him or it: *I'll run out some old records for you.* **look out (for sb/sth) (a)** to search or watch carefully for a person, thing: *The police are looking out for pickpockets in the crowd.* **(b)** (often *imperative*) to watch carefully in order to find: *Look out for thieves/dangerous corners. Please go to the bus-station and look out for my mother.* **look (out) onto sth** to provide a view of something: *The hotel room looks onto the beach.* ⇨ look-out.

look out (of sth) to look(1) through a window, door, hole etc. **look out on sth** = look (out) onto sth.

look over sth (a) to make a careful inspection of a house, factory; a piece of expensive china etc. **(b)** to examine carefully business accounts, a legal agreement etc. Compare overlook.

look round to turn one's head and look(1) behind. **look round (sth)** = look around (sth): *I looked round the room but I couldn't see him.*

look through (sth) to look(1) through a window, space; telescope, binoculars. **look through sth** to study or examine a set of papers, a legal agreement etc (but often not thoroughly): *I only have time to look through these accounts.* Compare look over sth.

look to sb/sth (for sth; to do sth) to rely on a person, organization: *Don't look to me for any help. They are looking to the government to provide the money.*

look towards sth to face towards: *The front of the building looks towards the sea/west/car park.*

look up (a) to raise one's eyes and look(1) towards the sky. **(b)** (of business, one's money, career; opportunities; the weather etc) to improve: *Business is/Things are looking up.* **look sb up** to find a person's home and visit her or him: *The next time I come to London I'll look you up.* **look sth up (in sth)** to search for an address, telephone number, piece of information (in a reference book etc): *If you don't know the word, look it up in a good dictionary.* **look sb up and down** to look(1) at a person with envy, contempt etc. **look up to sb** to show admiration or respect for a parent, teacher etc.

look upon sb/sth as/with sb/sth (*formal*) =

look on sb/sth as/with sb/sth.

look-in /'lʊk ɪn/ *n sing* **get/give sb a look-in** to get/give a person a chance to be involved, share a profit etc: *I'd like to study in Bristol but I don't think I'll get a look-in with all those qualified applicants.*

look-out /'lʊk aʊt/ *n* **1** *n sing* the state of watching carefully: *be on the look-out for bargains; keep a sharp (= deliberate, careful) look-out for her.* **2** *nc* (a person in) a place from which to watch carefully: *Who is the look-out for tonight?* **3 be sb's (own) look-out** (*informal*) to be a person's (own) concern or responsibility: *It's your own look-out whether you pass or fail the exam.*

loom[1] /luːm/ *nc* a machine used for weaving cloth.

loom[2] /luːm/ *vi* **1** to appear in a threatening way: *The dark outline of another ship loomed (up) through the fog.* **2** (*fig*) to seem very important or dangerous and fill the mind: *The threat of war loomed large in their minds.*

loony /'luːnɪ/ *nc, adj* (**-ier, -iest**) (*sl*) = lunatic.

loop[1] /luːp/ *nc* (the round shape produced by) string, ribbon etc crossing itself.

loop[2] /luːp/ *vi,vt* **1** to form or bend (string etc) into a loop. **2** to fasten (things) using a loop: *loop things together.*

loop·hole /'luːphəʊl/ *nc* (*fig*) a means of avoiding a commitment: *find a loophole in the law.*

loose[1] /luːs/ *adj* (**—r, -st**) **1** (*no comp*) not held, tied up, fastened, packed or contained in something: *That dog is too dangerous to be left loose.* **break/get loose** to escape from being held or locked in: *One of the tigers in the zoo has broken/got loose.* **cut sb/sth loose (a)** to cut rope etc that is holding a person, animal, flag etc. **(b)** (*fig*) to make oneself, a person free from obligations: *cut oneself loose from one's family.* **2** not tight[1](1): *a loose knot; loose-fitting clothes.* **3** not fully stretched: *a loose rope/string.* Opp tight[1](2). **4** moving more freely than is right or usual: *a loose tooth.* **come/work loose** (of a fastening, bolt etc) to become unfastened or insecure. **be at a loose end** ⇨ end[1](5). **5** (of talk, behaviour etc) not controlled: *a loose (= immoral) woman.* **6** not exact; (of translations) not close to the original: *a loose argument.* **7** not closely packed: *loose soil; cloth with a loose weave.* ⇨ tight[1](4). **8** careless, inaccurate: *loose passes* (e.g. in football).

‚loose ˈchange *nu* money in the form of coins.

ˈloose-leaf *adj* (*attrib*) (of a file, album etc) designed so that pages can be removed or added.

loose·ly *adv* in a loose manner.

loose[2] /luːs/ *n* **be on the loose** to be free from the control of the police: *There's a mad gunman on the loose.*

loos·en /'luːsn/ *vt,vi* (to cause something) to become loose or looser: *Loosen the screw. I must exercise and loosen up my muscles.* Opp tighten.

loot[1] /luːt/ *nu* goods stolen, e.g. by thieves.

loot[2] /luːt/ *vt* to steal goods from (shops, homes etc).

loot·er *nc* a person who loots.

lop /lɒp/ *vt* (**-pp-**) **lop sth (off)** to cut, chop branches etc from a tree.

lope /ləʊp/ *vi* to move along with long, easy steps or strides. □ *nc* a loping step or stride.

lop·sided /ˌlɒp 'saɪdɪd/ *adj* with one side lower than the other: *a lopsided hat.*

lord /lɔːd/ *nc* **1** (L- in names) a male peer. ⇨ House of Lords. **2** (L-) a male official: *the Lord Mayor.* **3** a man or animal with the highest power: *the lord of the manor; the lord of the jungle.* **4** (L-) Jesus Christ. **5** (used in exclamations, esp of surprise): *Good Lord!*

lord·ly /'lɔːdlɪ/ *adj* (**-ier, -iest**) **1** (*derog*) arrogant; feeling superior. **2** like, suitable for, a lord(1).

lore /lɔː(r)/ *nu* (*formal*) knowledge, esp from the past or possessed by a class of people: *folk lore.*

lor·ry /'lɒrɪ/ *nc* (*pl* **-ies**) a kind of strong vehicle, used for carrying goods (*US* = truck).

lose /luːz/ *v* (*pt,pp* **lost** /lɒst/) Ⓝ For the use of 'lose' with nouns such as balance, bearings, control, count, face, ground, head, interest, place, sight, temper, track etc, ⇨ the noun entries. **1** *vt* to have (something) no longer because of accident, theft, carelessness etc: *I've lost my handbag/the keys of the car. We lost our way in the dark.* **2** *vt* to stop having, possessing, (a person, thing): *lose one's job; lose a leg in a car accident; lose one's husband* (i.e. because he has died). **3** *vt* to not make use of (time, an opportunity): *She's lost her chance of becoming a pilot. There's not a moment to lose if we are to save him. We lost no time in arranging a loan* (i.e. did it immediately). **4** (*passive*) **be/get lost** to not know where one is: *They were lost for three days on the mountain.* **5** *vt* to be too late for (a passenger vehicle): *lose one's train/bus/plane.* Ⓝ 'Miss' is much more usual. **6** *vt,vi* to fail to win, gain or get (something); *lose a competition/football match/battle/lawsuit; lose an argument/bet; lose money on a business deal.* **7** *vt,vi* (of profit, weight, time etc) to decrease in amount: *I lost 10 kilos when I was ill. My watch loses two minutes a day.* Opp gain[2](2). **8** *vt* to cause (a person) to not see, hear or understand: *I'm sorry but I'm lost/ you've lost me—could you explain the directions again?* **9** *vt* (usually *passive*) to cause the death of (a person): *Two hundred lives were lost in the air disaster.*

lose by sth to suffer personally or financially because of something: *There's little to lose by trying. How much will you lose by selling the house now?*

lose sth in sb/sth (a) to have no longer any trust, confidence, interest etc in a leader, business, one's studies etc: *I've completely lost faith in your promises.* **lose oneself in sth** to become very interested or involved in a book, studies, game, TV programme etc. **be lost in sth** to be extremely occupied or filled with admiration, wonder, thought etc: *be lost in amazement.*

lose on sth to have an amount of money no longer as the result of a bet, business deal, currency exchange etc. **be lost on sb** (of a joke, wit, comment) to be unnoticed or not understood by a person.

lose out (on sth) to be unsuccessful; do less well than others: *Hurry or you'll lose out (on the bargains).* **lose out to sb/sth** to fail or make a loss because of a person, thing: *The small shops are losing out to the supermarkets.*

be/feel lost without sb/sth (*informal*) to be unable to live, win, work well, be happy etc unless one has a person, information, friendship, **map**

etc: *I'm lost without my watch/newspaper/diary/ wife/you.*

los·er /'luːzə(r)/ *nc* a person who loses or is defeated: *He's a good/bad loser* (= is cheerful/ bad-tempered when he loses). Opp winner.

loss /lɒs/ *n* **1** *nu* the act, fact or process of losing: *Loss of health is more serious than loss of money. The loss of the game was a big surprise.* **2** *n sing* a failure to keep, maintain or use something: *an enormous loss. There was a temporary loss of power.* **3** *nc* a person, thing, amount etc that is lost: *suffer heavy losses in war. Such a man is no great loss* (= We need not regret losing his services). **cut one's losses** to end a business that is losing money before the situation gets worse. ⇨ dead loss. **4 at a loss for sth/to do sth** uncertain (about what to do or say): *He was at a loss for words/to know what to say.*

lost /lɒst/ *pt,pp* of lose.

lot¹ /lɒt/ *nc* (*informal*) **1** (the —) the whole number or amount: *I bought the lot. The lot of them are bad. That's the lot* (= That's all or everything). *Take the (whole) lot.* **2 a lot (of)** a large amount or number (of): *What a lot of time you take to dress! We've not got a lot (of money). There are a lot (of visitors) here. I saw quite a lot of her* (= saw her often) *when I was in London last month.* **lots (and lots) (of)** (*informal*) a (very) large amount or number (of): *lots of milk/possibilities/time; have lots* (= many things) *to say/eat.* **3 a lot +** adj (used as an *adv*) very much: *He's feeling a lot better today.*

lot² /lɒt/ *nc* **1** an item, or number of items, (to be) sold at an auction sale: *Lot 46: six chairs.* **a job lot** ⇨ job(5). **2** a collection of objects of the same kind: *We have received a new lot of coats from Paris.* **3** (one of a set of objects used in) the making of a selection or decision by methods depending on chance: *They drew lots to decide who should begin.* **4** *nc* a decision or choice resulting from this: *The lot came to/fell on me.* **5 a bad lot** (*informal; derog*) an immoral, unkind etc person. **6** a plot of land: *a vacant lot.*

loth /ləʊθ/ *adj* = loath.

lo·tion /'ləʊʃn/ *nc,nu* (a kind of) liquid mixture for use on the skin: *lotions for insect bites.*

lot·tery /'lɒtəri/ *nc* (*pl* **-ies**) **1** an arrangement to give prizes to buyers of tickets with winning numbers. **2** (*fig*) something considered to be uncertain: *Is marriage a lottery?*

lo·tus /'ləʊtəs/ *nc* (*pl* **—es**) one of many kinds of pink or white water-lily.

loud¹ /laʊd/ *adj* (**—er**, **—est**) **1** producing, having, much sound: *loud voices/cries/laughs.* **2** (of a person's behaviour; of colours) unpleasant because too obvious or extreme.

loud·ly *adv* in a loud manner: *Someone knocked loudly at the door.*

loud·ness *nu*

loud'speaker *nc* (often shortened to *speaker*) a part of a radio etc that changes electric impulses into sound.

loud² /laʊd/ *adv* in a loud manner: *Don't talk so loud.* **out loud** in a loud voice: *shout/cry out loud.*

lounge¹ /laʊndʒ/ *nc* a comfortable sitting-room, esp in a club or hotel.

lounge² /laʊndʒ/ *vi* to sit, stand about, (leaning against something) in a lazy way: *lounging at street corners.*

lour (also **low·er**) /'laʊə(r)/ *vi* to frown; look bad-tempered.

louse /laʊs/ *nc* (*pl* **lice** /laɪs/) **1** a kind of small insect living on the bodies of people and animals. **2** (*sl; derog*) a bad person deserving criticism: *He's an absolute louse.*

lousy /'laʊzi/ *adj* (**-ier, -iest**) **1** filled with lice. **2** (*informal; derog*) very bad: *a lousy meal/cook/ film.* **3 lousy with money** (*sl*) having a great deal of money.

lout /laʊt/ *nc* (*derog*) a rough, ill-mannered man.

lout·ish /-ɪʃ/ *adj*: *loutish behaviour.*

lov·able /'lʌvəbl/ *adj* deserving, worthy of, love: *a lovable child; a child's lovable ways.*

love¹ /lʌv/ *n* **1** *nu* a very strong, pleasant feeling about a person; sexual feeling or desire: *whisper words of love. My love for you is deeper than the sea.* **be/fall in/out of love (with sb/sth)** to have/begin to have love/no love (for a person, thing). **make love (to sb)** to have sexual intercourse (with a person). **2** *nu* a strong, kind feeling: *a mother's love for her children.* **not to be had for love or money** impossible to get however hard one tries. **there is/was no love lost between them** they dislike/disliked each other. **a labour of love** ⇨ labour¹(1). **3** *nc,nu* a strong interest and pleasure: *a love of sport; a love of adventure.* **4** *nc* (a way of speaking to) a person who one loves: *Of course, my love.* **5** *nc* (*informal*) (a friendly way of addressing a person): *Are you all right, love?* **6** *nu* (in games, e.g. tennis) no score, nothing, nil: *love all* (= no score for either side).

'love affair *nc* a (sexual) relationship between people in love.

'love-letter *nc* a letter between lovers(1).

'love-lorn /-lɔːn/ *adj* (*dated*) = lovesick.

'love-sick *adj* suffering because of (unreturned) love.

'love-song *nc* a song about love.

'love-story *nc* (*pl* **-ies**) a novel or story of which the main theme is love.

love² /lʌv/ *vt* Ⓝ Not usually used in continuous tenses, e.g. *is/was -ing.* **1** to have a very strong affection and desire for (a person): *I'll never stop loving you.* **2** to have kind and warm feelings for (a person, thing): *love one's parents/one's country.* **3** to be very fond of, like very much, find pleasure in, (something): *love ice-cream/going to parties. 'Will you come with me?'—'I'd love to'.*

love·ly /'lʌvli/ *adj* (**-ier, -iest**) **1** beautiful; attractive; pleasant: *a lovely view; lovely hair.* **2** (*informal*) very pleasant: *We had a lovely holiday. What lovely weather! It's lovely and warm here by the fire.*

love·li·ness *nu*

lov·er /'lʌvə(r)/ *nc* **1** a person who is having a (sexual) relationship with another person. **2** a person who is fond of or devoted to (something): *a lover of music/horses/good wine.*

lov·ing /'lʌvɪŋ/ *adj* feeling or showing love: *a loving husband; loving parents.*

lov·ing·ly *adv* in a loving way.

low¹ /ləʊ/ *adj* (**—er**, **—est**) **1** not going, reaching, far up: *a low wall; a low hill.* Ⓝ 'Short' is used for people and narrow objects, as in *'a short man/*

pole'. Opp high¹(1). **2** below the usual or normal amount, level or intensity: *a low price/tempera-ture/speed/wage. The rivers were low during the summer months.* Opp high¹(2). **be/get/run low** (of supplies) to be/become small in amount: *The sugar is (getting/running) low.* ⇨ also opinion(1). **3** (situated) not far above the ground: *a low ceil-ing/shelf; flying low in the sky; the lowest climber.* Opp high¹(3). **4** showing not much activity; not happening often: *a low rate; a low mileage/volt-age.* Opp high¹(4) **5** (*pred*) measuring (the small distance mentioned) from the top to the bottom: *How low is that fence? It's a metre lower than that one.* Ⓝ It is much more usual to use *'high'*. ⇨ high¹(5). **6** (of sound) at, near, the bottom of the scale: *the low notes of a cello.* Compare high¹(6). **in a low key** ⇨ key(8). **7** (of sound) not loud: *speak in a low voice.* Opp high¹(7). **8** of an unim-portant or inferior social position or rank: *men of low birth; a low job.* **9** (of a person) weak; sad: *in a low state of health; be low/be in low spirits.* **be laid low** to be ill in bed. **10** immoral and unpleasant (behaviour): *a low way of behaving; low deceit; a low trick.* Compare high¹(10). **11** not highly developed: *Is a worm a low form of life?* Opp high¹(13).

,low-'born *adj* of low(8) birth.

'low·brow *nc, adj* (*derog*) (a person) showing little interest in intellectual things. Compare highbrow.

,low 'comedy *nu* (*literature*) (part of) a drama without a serious purpose or an intellectual or cul-tured appeal. Compare high comedy.

'low-grade *adj* of inferior quality: *low-grade petrol.* Opp high-grade.

'low·land *n* (a) *nc* a region without mountains. (b) (*pl*) flat parts of a country.

'low-level *adj* (of meetings etc) concerning people in less senior positions.

,low-level 'language *nc* (*computers*) a system for coding that is like the computer's machine code and is far from ordinary language. Compare high-level language.

,Low 'Mass *nc* one without a choir.

'low·ness *nu*

'low-rise *adj* (*attrib*) (of buildings) having only one or two storeys.

'low season *nu* (also *attrib*) the less popular period, e.g. at a hotel, when booking a plane, for a holiday: *low-season holidays.* Compare high season.

,low-'spirited *adj* depressed; sad.

low² /ləʊ/ *adv* (**—er, —est**) at, in or to a low po-sition: *aim/shoot low; buy low* (= at low prices) *and sell high.* **lie low** to hide or stay hidden (until the danger has passed). Opp unlucky. **high and low** ⇨ high².

low³ /ləʊ/ *nc* a low level or figure: *Several indus-trial shares reached new lows yesterday.*

low⁴ /ləʊ/ *nu* the sound made by cows. □ *vi* (of a cow) to make this sound.

low·er¹ /'ləʊə(r)/ *adj* (*attrib*) in or being the bot-tom part; situated below: *the lower lip; the lower arm.* Opp upper.

'lower case *nu* (in printing) small letters, not capitals, e.g. *a, b, c.*

,lower 'class(es) *nu* or *pl* (the —) (also *attrib*) the lower levels of society, e.g. the working class.

'Lower House *n* (the —) (in Parliament) the

House of Commons.

low·er² /'ləʊə(r)/ *v* **1** *vt, vi* to let or bring (some-thing) down: *lower the sails/a flag.* **2** *vt, vi* (to cause something) to become less (strong etc): *lower the rent of a house. He lowered his voice to a whisper.* **3** *vt* **lower oneself** to cause one's reputation to be harmed: *He would never lower himself by taking bribes.* **4** *vt* to weaken (one's health etc): *Poor diet lowers resistance to illness.*

low·er³ /'laʊə(r)/ *vi* = lour.

low·er·most /'ləʊəməʊst/ *adj* = lowest.

low·ly /'ləʊlɪ/ *adj* (**-ier, -iest**) humble; modest: *a lowly clerical job.*

low·li·ness *nu*

loy·al /'lɔɪəl/ *adj* **loyal (to sb/sth)** true and faithful (to): *loyal supporters; loyal to one's country.* Opp disloyal.

'loyal·ist /-ɪst/ *nc* a person who is loyal to a ruler and government.

loy·al·ly /'lɔɪəlɪ/ *adv*

loy·al·ty *n* (*pl* **-ies**) (a) *nu* being loyal; loyal behaviour: *loyalty to one's parents.* (b) (*pl*) feel-ings of being loyal: *family loyalties.*

loz·enge /'lɒzɪndʒ/ *nc* **1** (*maths*) a four-sided, diamond-shaped figure. **2** a flat sweet of this shape: *cough lozenges.*

LP /,el 'piː/ *abbr* a long-playing record.

L-plate /'el pleɪt/ *nc* ⇨ L, l.

LSD /,el es 'diː/ *abbr* lysergic acid diethylamide (a drug that causes hallucinations).

Lt. *written abbr* Lieutenant.

Ltd *written abbr* a limited liability company.

Lt. Gen. *written abbr* Lieutenant General.

lu·bri·cant /'luːbrɪkənt/ *nu* a substance that lubricates.

lu·bri·cate /'luːbrɪkeɪt/ *vt* to make (a machine) work or move easily, e.g. by adding oil or grease.

lu·bri·ca·tion /,luːbrɪ'keɪʃn/ *nu*

lu·cid /'luːsɪd/ *adj* (*formal*) **1** clear; easy to under-stand: *a lucid mind; a lucid explanation.* **2** men-tally sound; able to think and speak clearly.

lu·cid·ly *adv*

luck /lʌk/ *nu* **1** something that happens (good or bad) by chance: *have good/bad luck. As luck would have it, . . .* (= Fortunately . . . or Unfortunately . . . , according to context). **be down on one's luck** to have bad luck. **2** good fortune: *Wish me luck! Bad luck!* (used to express sympathy). *Good luck!* (used to encourage, express hopes of good fortune etc). *Hard luck!* = Bad luck!

lucky /'lʌkɪ/ *adj* (**-ier, -iest**) having, bringing, resulting from, good luck: *a lucky man/guess/escape. You are lucky to be alive after being in that accident.* Opp unlucky.

luck·ily /'lʌkɪlɪ/ *adv* fortunately: *Luckily for me the train was late so I caught it.*

lu·cra·tive /'luːkrətɪv/ *adj* profitable.

lu·di·crous /'luːdɪkrəs/ *adj* ridiculous.

lu·di·crous·ly *adv*

lug /lʌg/ *vt* (**-gg-**) to pull or drag (something) roughly and with much effort: *lugging two heavy suitcases up the stairs.*

lug·gage /'lʌgɪdʒ/ *nu* bags etc and their contents (to be) taken on a journey: *six pieces of luggage* (*US = baggage*).

'luggage-rack *nc* a shelf (above the seats) in a train, coach etc, used for luggage.

lu·gu·bri·ous /luː'guːbrɪəs/ adj (formal) dismal; mournful; unhappy.
lu·gu·bri·ous·ly adv

luke·warm /'luːkwɔːm/ adj **1** (of liquids etc) neither very warm nor cold. **2** (fig) not eager either in supporting or opposing something: give only lukewarm support to a cause.

lull[1] /lʌl/ nc a short period of quiet or calm: a lull in the storm/in the conversation.

lull[2] /lʌl/ vt to cause (a person) to become quiet or less active: lull a baby to sleep (e.g. by rocking it and singing to it).

lul·la·by /'lʌləbaɪ/ nc (pl -ies) a song for encouraging a baby to sleep.

lum·ba·go /lʌm'beɪgəʊ/ nu a muscular pain in the lumbar regions.

lum·bar /'lʌmbə(r)/ adj (attrib; science) of the lower part of the back: the lumbar region.

lum·ber[1] /'lʌmbə(r)/ nu **1** timber (the usual word). **2** (chiefly GB) useless or unwanted articles.
'lum·ber-room nc one used for storing lumber(2).

lum·ber[2] /'lʌmbə(r)/ vt **1** lumber sth (up) to fill a room etc with lumber(2): a room lumbered up with useless articles; (fig) a mind that is lumbered (up) with useless bits of information. **2** lumber sb (with sb/sth) (informal) to leave an unpleasant or unwanted person or thing with a person: be lumbered with one's in-laws for the weekend.

lum·ber[3] /'lʌmbə(r)/ vi to move in a heavy, clumsy, noisy way: The tanks lumbered along/by/past.

lum·ber·jack /'lʌmbədʒæk/ nc a person who cuts down trees and produces timber.

lu·mi·nous /'luːmɪnəs/ adj giving out light; visible in the dark: luminous paint.
lu·min·os·ity /ˌluːmɪ'nɒsətɪ/ nu

lump[1] /lʌmp/ nc **1** a solid mass, usually without a regular shape: a lump of coal/sugar. **a lump sum** ⇨ sum[1](1). **2** a swelling or bump: He has a bad lump on the forehead. **have a lump in one's throat** to have a feeling of pressure (as caused by strong emotion). **3** (informal; derog) a dull person.
lumpy adj (-ier, -iest) full of, covered with, lumps: lumpy soup.

lump[2] /lʌmp/ vt lump sth together (informal) to put things together: Can we lump all these items together under the heading 'Costs'?

lump[3] /lʌmp/ vt (only in) lump it (informal) to put up with something unpleasant or unwanted: If you don't like it you can lump it.

lu·na·cy /'luːnəsɪ/ nu madness.

lu·nar /'luːnə(r)/ adj of the moon.
,lunar 'module nc a section of a spacecraft that travels round the moon and can land on it.
,lunar 'month nc a period in which the moon makes one complete revolution(1), about 29 days. Compare calendar month.

lu·na·tic /'luːnətɪk/ nc a foolish person. □ adj mad; extremely foolish: a lunatic proposal/idea.
'lunatic asylum nc (not now used) a mental home or hospital.
,lunatic 'fringe n (the —) the minority group with extreme views or engaged in eccentric activities.

lunch /lʌntʃ/ nc a meal taken in the middle of the day: They were at lunch when I called. □ vi,vt to eat, provide (a person) with, lunch.

lunch·eon /'lʌntʃən/ nc (formal) = lunch.

lung /lʌŋ/ nc (science) either of the two organs in the chest of man and other animals, used for breathing.

lunge /lʌndʒ/ vi, nc (to make) a sudden forward movement (e.g. with a sword), or forward movement of the body (e.g. when aiming a blow): lunging out suddenly.

lurch[1] /lɜːtʃ/ n (only in) **leave sb in the lurch** to leave a person when he or she is in difficulties and needs help.

lurch[2] /lɜːtʃ/ nc a sudden change of weight to one side; sudden roll or pitch: The ship gave a lurch.

lurch[3] /lɜːtʃ/ vi to move along with unsteady steps: The drunken man lurched across the street.

lure[1] /lʊə(r)/ nc **1** something used to attract animals or fish. **2** (fig) something that attracts or invites: the lure of the sea; the lures used by a rich man/pretty woman.

lure[2] /lʊə(r)/ vt to attract, tempt, (a person): luring him away from his duty.

lu·rid /'lʊərɪd/ adj **1** (too) bright and strong: a lurid colour; a lurid sky/sunset. **2** (fig) shocking and unpleasant: lurid details of a railway accident.
lu·rid·ly adv
lu·rid·ness nu

lurk /lɜːk/ vi to be, keep, out of view, waiting or ready to attack: a man lurking in the shadows. Some suspicion still lurked in his mind.

lus·cious /'lʌʃəs/ adj having a sweet and pleasant taste and smell: luscious peaches/lips.

lush /lʌʃ/ adj (usually attrib) (esp of grass and plants) growing thickly and well: lush meadows.

lust[1] /lʌst/ nc,nu lust (for sth/sb) (an instance of) a great desire to possess something, esp strong sexual desire: a lust for gold/power; a lust for a woman; be filled with lust.

lust[2] /lʌst/ vi lust (after/for sb/sth) to feel lust (for): lust after/for wealth/power/a woman.
lust·ful /-fəl/ adj full of lust.
lust·ful·ly /-fəlɪ/ adv

lustre (US = **lus·ter**) /'lʌstə(r)/ nu brightness, esp of a smooth or polished surface: the lustre of pearls.
lus·trous /'lʌstrəs/ adj having lustre: lustrous pearls/eyes.

lusty /'lʌstɪ/ adj (-ier, -iest) healthy and strong: a lusty girl; lusty cheers.
lust·ily /-əlɪ/ adv

lute /luːt/ nc stringed musical instrument (14th to 17th centuries) associated with poets and poetry.
lut·an·ist (also **-ten-**) /'luːtənɪst/ nc a person who plays the lute.

lux. written abbr luxury.

lux·u·ri·ant /lʌg'ʒʊərɪənt/ adj (of grass and plants) growing thickly and well: the luxuriant vegetation of the tropics. Compare luxurious.
lux·u·ri·ant·ly adv

lux·u·ri·ous /lʌg'ʒʊərɪəs/ adj supplied with luxuries; very comfortable: a luxurious hotel. Compare luxuriant.
lux·u·ri·ous·ly adv

lux·ury /'lʌkʃərɪ/ n (pl -ies) **1** nu (also attrib) a state of rich, comfortable living (good food and drink, clothes, comfort, beautiful surroundings):

live in luxury; a life of luxury; a luxury hotel. **the lap of luxury** ⇨ lap². **2** *nc* something not essential but which gives enjoyment and pleasure, esp something expensive: *His salary is low and he gets few luxuries.*

LW *written abbr (radio)* long wave.

ly·chee /'laitʃi/ *nc* = litchi.

ly·ing /'laiɪŋ/ *pres p of* lie³, lie⁴.

lymph /limf/ *nu (science)* a colourless fluid in animals, like blood but with no colour.

  lym·phat·ic /lim'fætik/ *adj* of, carrying, lymph.

lynch /lintʃ/ *vt* to put (a person) to death (usually by hanging) without a lawful trial.

lynch·pin /'lintʃpin/ = linchpin.

lynx /liŋks/ *nc* a kind of short-tailed wild animal of the cat family, noted for its good eyesight.

lyre /laiə(r)/ *nc* a kind of harp with strings fixed in a U-shaped frame.

lyr·ic¹ /'lirik/ *adj* of a lyric(1).

lyr·ic² /'lirik/ *nc* **1** *(literature)* a type of poetry about emotions, love, death etc. **2** *(pl) (informal)* the words of a song.

lyri·cal /'lirikl/ *adj* **1** of, like, a lyric(1): *a lyrical drama.* **2** (of music, singing) having a pleasant, light quality. **3** (of a person) expressing strong approval or praise: *She was very lyrical about her daughter's performance.*

  lyri·cal·ly /-klɪ/ *adv*

Mm

M, m /em/ *(pl* **M's, m's** /emz/) **1** the 13th letter of the English alphabet. **2** the Roman numeral 1000.

m *written abbr* **1** male. **2** married. **3** month. □ *symbol* **1** metre(s). **2** mile(s). **3** million(s). **4** minute(s).

M *symbol* **1** Mach number. **2** medium size (clothes). **3** Motorway: *the M5 from Birmingham to Exeter.*

'm /m/ (only in *I'm*) = am.

MA /,em 'ei/ *abbr* Master of Arts.

ma /ma:/ *nc (informal)* mamma, mother.

mac /mæk/ *n (GB informal)* = mackintosh: *Put your macs on—it's raining.*

ma·cabre /mə'ka:brə/ *adj* horrible, causing fear (because suggesting death).

maca·roni /,mækə'rəuni/ *nu (It)* flour paste *(pasta)* made into hollow tubes, cooked by boiling: *macaroni cheese.*

mace /meis/ *nc* **1** (in history) a heavy club with a metal head covered with spikes. **2** a ceremonial rod carried by an official, e.g. a Mayor.

Mach /ma:k/ *n (abbr M)* (also *Mach number*) the ratio of the air speed of an aircraft to the speed of sound: *Mach two equals twice the speed of sound.*

ma·chete /mə'tʃeti/ *nc* a wide, heavy knife used in Latin America as a tool and weapon.

mach·ia·vel·li·an /,mækiə'veliən/ *adj* (also M-) *(derog)* using any means to get what one wants and not caring about morality etc.

machi·na·tion /,mækɪ'neiʃn/ *nc (formal)* an evil plot or scheme.

ma·chine¹ /mə'ʃi:n/ *nc* **1** an appliance or mechanical device with parts working together, often using electricity: *a sewing-machine.* **2** people organized to control a political group: *the party machine.*

ma'chine code *nc (computers)* the language understood directly by the computer: *A computer changes programs written in a computer language such as BASIC into a machine code that the computer can understand.*

ma'chine-gun *nc* one that fires continuously while the trigger is pressed.

ma,chine-'made *adj* made using a machine. Compare handmade.

ma,chine 'readable *adj (computers)* that can be understood by a computer: *machine readable data.*

ma'chine tool *nc* a tool worked by electricity, used for cutting or shaping metals and materials.

ma·chine² /mə'ʃi:n/ *vt* to make (something) using a machine(1).

ma·chin·ist /mə'ʃi:nist/ *nc* **(a)** a person who makes or repairs machine tools. **(b)** a person who works a machine, e.g. a sewing-machine.

ma·chin·ery /mə'ʃi:nəri/ *n (pl* **-ies)** **1** *nc,nu* the moving parts of a machine; machines collectively: *How much new machinery has been installed?* **2** *nu* a system of methods, organization, (e.g. of government): *the machinery of state.*

macho /'mætʃəu/ *adj* (of a man, behaviour etc) having, showing, strong interest in male strength, pride etc.

mack·erel /'mækrəl/ *nc (pl* **—)** a kind of grey sea-fish, eaten as food.

mack·in·tosh /'mækintoʃ/ *nc (GB) (dated)* a raincoat made of cloth treated with rubber.

mac·ro·bi·ot·ic /,mækrəubai'ɒtik/ *adj* believed to make one live longer: *macrobiotic food* (i.e. without chemicals added).

mac·ro·cosm /'mækrəukɒzəm/ *nc* **1** (the —) the world or universe. **2** any large and complex thing or system. ⇨ microcosm.

macro-zoom /'mækrəu zu:m/ *nc* a kind of lens for a camera able to magnify close up as well as cause distant objects to appear closer. ⇨ zoom lens.

mad /mæd/ *adj* (**—der, —dest**) **1** mentally ill. **as mad as a March hare/as a hatter** very mad. **drive/send sb mad** to cause a person to become mad. **2** *(informal)* very excited; filled with great enthusiasm: *mad about pop music.* **like mad** *(informal)* with much effort, enthusiasm etc: *run like mad.* **be/go mad** to be/ become wildly excited, angry, upset etc. **3 mad at/about sth; mad at/with sb** *(informal)* very angry: *They were mad at/about missing the train. Dad was mad at/with me for coming home late.* **be hopping mad** to be very angry.

'mad·man/-woman *nc* a person who is mad(1).

mad·ly *adv* **(a)** in a mad manner: *run about madly.* **(b)** *(informal)* extremely: *madly excited/in love.*

mad·ness *nu* **1** the state of being mad. **2** mad behaviour: *It's madness to meet in secret like this.*

mad·am /'mædəm/ *nc* **1** a respectful form of address to a woman (married or unmarried) e.g. by a shop assistant: *Can I help you, madam?* **2** (a form of address used in formal letters): *Dear Madam.* Compare sir. **3** *(informal)* a woman or girl who likes to give people orders: *She's a bit of a madam.*

mad·den /'mædn/ *vt* to make (a person) angry; annoy (a person): *Her slow walk maddened me.*
mad·den·ing *adj: maddening delays.*

made /meɪd/ *pt,pp* of make².

Ma·don·na /mə'dɒnə/ *n* **1** (the —) Mary, Mother of Jesus Christ. **2** *nc* a picture or statue of her.

mad·ri·gal /'mædrɪgl/ *nc* a song for several voices without musical accompaniment.

mael·strom /'meɪlstrɒm/ *nc* (*formal*) **1** a violent whirlpool. **2** (*fig*) a violent or destructive force or series of events: *the maelstrom of war.*

maes·tro /'maɪstrəʊ/ *nc* (*pl* **maestri** /'maɪstrɪ/) (*It*) a great musical composer, teacher or conductor.

mag /mæg/ *nc* (*informal*) = magazine(1): *the colour mags.*

maga·zine /ˌmægə'ziːn/ *nc* **1** (a weekly or monthly) paper book, with stories, pictures etc. **2** a store for arms, explosives etc. **3** a place for holding cartridges in a rifle or gun.

ma·gen·ta /mə'dʒentə/ *adj, nu* (of) a kind of dark red colour.

mag·got /'mægət/ *nc* a creature like a short worm (called a *larva* or *grub*) that is the young of a fly or other insect.
mag·goty *adj* having maggots: *maggoty cheese.*

ma·gic¹ /'mædʒɪk/ *adj* (*attrib*) done (as if) by magic; possessing, used in magic: *magic arts/ words; a magic touch.* ⇨ the *note* at magical.

ma·gic² /'mædʒɪk/ *nu* **1** the art of controlling events by the (pretended) use of supernatural forces, superstitious belief etc. **as if by/like magic** in a way that is impossible to explain. ⇨ black magic. **2** the art of producing mysterious results by using tricks: *use magic to produce a rabbit.* **3** (*fig*) any quality or effect produced as if by magic: *the magic of poetry.*

ma·gi·cal /-kl/ *adj* produced (as if) by magic. Ⓝ *'Magical'* is usually *attrib* but it can be *pred*, as in *The effect of the lighting was magical.* *'Magical'* is preferred to *'magic'* when describing a particularly beautiful or dramatic scene or event, as in *magical beauty; a magical effect.*
ma·gi·cal·ly /-kl/ *adv*

ma·gi·cian /mə'dʒɪʃn/ *nc* a person skilled in magic(2).

ma·gis·teri·al /ˌmædʒɪ'stɪərɪəl/ *adj* **1** of, conducted by, a magistrate. **2** (*formal*) having or showing authority: *a magisterial manner.*
ma·gis·teri·al·ly /-ɪəlɪ/ *adv*

ma·gis·trate /'mædʒɪstreɪt/ *nc* an officer acting as a judge in the lowest courts; Justice of the Peace.

magistrates' court *nc* a law court dealing with minor crimes and first hearings.

mag·nani·mous /mæg'nænɪməs/ *adj* (*formal*) having, showing, great generosity.
mag·na·nim·ity /ˌmægnə'nɪmətɪ/ *nu*
mag·nani·mous·ly *adv*

mag·nate /'mægneɪt/ *nc* a wealthy and powerful leader of business or industry.

mag·nesia /mæg'niːʃə/ *nu* a white substance (formula MgO), used in medicine and industry.

mag·nesium /mæg'niːzɪəm/ *nu* a silver-white metal (symbol Mg), used in the manufacture of

aluminium and flash bulbs.

mag·net /'mægnɪt/ *nc* **1** an object or substance that can attract iron etc, either naturally or by using an electric current. **2** (*fig*) a person or thing that attracts.

mag·net·ic /mæg'netɪk/ *adj* **1** of magnetism: *magnetic force.* **2** having the properties of a magnet(1): *Is copper magnetic?* **3** (*fig*) attracting attention: *a magnetic smile/personality.*

mag,netic 'field *nc* (*tech*) the area in which a magnetic force can be detected.

mag,netic 'needle *nc* a magnetized steel rod which indicates north and south.

mag,netic 'north *nc* (*tech*) the point indicated by a magnetic needle.

mag,netic 'pole *nc* (*tech*) the point near the North or South Pole to which the compass needle points.

mag,netic 'tape *nc* a kind of tape used to record sound and vision.

mag·neti·cal·ly /-klɪ/ *adv*

mag·net·ism /'mægnɪtɪzəm/ *nu* **1** (the science of) (the power of) magnets. **2** (*fig*) great personal charm and attraction.

mag·net·ize (also **-ise**) /'mægnɪtaɪz/ *vt* **1** to give magnetic properties to (an object or substance). **2** (*fig*) to attract (people) as a magnet attracts things.

mag·ni·fi·ca·tion /ˌmægnɪfɪ'keɪʃn/ *nu* (*esp*) the act, amount, power, of magnifying.

mag·nifi·cent /mæg'nɪfɪsnt/ *adj* superb; splendid: *a magnificent house; a magnificent ceremony.*
mag·nifi·cent·ly *adv*

mag·ni·fi·er /'mægnɪfaɪə(r)/ *nc* an instrument etc that magnifies.

mag·ni·fy /'mægnɪfaɪ/ *vt* (*pt,pp* **-ied**) **1** to make (a person or thing) appear larger (as with a lens or microscope). **2** to exaggerate (something): *magnify dangers.*

'magnifying glass *nc* a lens for making objects appear larger.

mag·ni·tude /'mægnɪtjuːd/ *nu* (*formal*) **1** size. **2** (degree of) importance: *a crime of great magnitude.*

mag·num opus /ˌmægnəm 'əʊpəs/ *nc* (*Latin*) a great literary work, esp a person's chief literary work.

mag·pie /'mægpaɪ/ *nc* **1** a noisy black-and-white bird which is attracted by, and often takes away, small, bright objects. **2** (*fig*) a person who steals small things.

ma·hog·any /mə'hɒgənɪ/ *nc,nu* (a tropical tree with) a hard dark-brown wood, used to make furniture.

maid /meɪd/ *nc* **1** (*literary*) a girl. **2** (*old use*) a young, unmarried woman. ⇨ old maid. **3** (*modern use*) a woman who does cleaning in a hotel etc: *Has the maid cleaned my room yet?*

,maid of 'honour *nc* (**a**) the senior bridesmaid at a wedding. (**b**) an unmarried woman attending a queen or princess.

maid·en¹ /'meɪdn/ *adj* (*attrib*) **1** first or earliest: *a ship's maiden voyage.* **2** (of an older woman) unmarried: *my maiden aunt.*

'maiden name *nc* a woman's family name before her marriage.

,maiden 'over *nc* (*cricket*) a set of six bowls (throws) of the ball (called an *over*) without the batsman scoring.

maiden 'speech *nc* a first speech, e.g. in Parliament as a new member.

maid·en² /'meɪdn/ *nc* **1** (*old use*) a young, unmarried woman. **2** = maiden over.

'maiden·like, maiden·ly *adj* gentle; modest; like a young woman.

mail¹ /meɪl/ *nu* armour of metal rings or plates: *a coat of mail; chain-mail.*

mail² /meɪl/ *n* **1** *nu* a system of collecting, carrying and delivering letters and parcels: *send a letter by airmail.* **2** *nu* (esp *US*; in GB *post* is more usual) letters, parcels etc sent or delivered by post; the letters etc sent, collected or delivered at one time: *Was there any mail this morning?*

'mail-bag *nc* a strong bag for mail(2).

,mail 'order *nc* an order for goods to be delivered by post.

mail³ /meɪl/ *vt* (esp *US*; in GB *post* is more usual) to send (letters etc) by post.

'mail·ing list *nc* a list of names of people to whom something, e.g. a catalogue, is regularly sent.

maim /meɪm/ *vt* to wound or injure (a person) so that some part of the body is useless: *He was seriously maimed in the war.*

main¹ /meɪn/ *adj* chief; most important: *the main thing to remember; the main street of a town; the main point of my argument; the main course of a meal.*

,main 'clause *nc* (*gram*) one that includes the main verb in a complex sentence, as in, 'If she asks you, *tell her that I'm visiting the doctor*'.

'main·frame *nc* (also *attrib*) (*computers*) a large computer.

,main 'verb *nc* (*gram*) the verb in the main clause of a sentence, as in 'I *explained* that children are often ill'.

main·ly *adv* chiefly; for the most part: *You are mainly to blame.*

main² /meɪn/ *n* **1** *nc* (usually *pl*) a principal pipe (bringing water or gas), principal wire (bringing electricity), into a building: *My new house is not yet connected to the mains.* **2** **in the main** in the majority of cases; on the whole: *In the main, people realize that smoking is dangerous.* **3** **with (all one's/sb's) might and main** ⇨ might¹. **4** (*poetry*) the sea.

main·land /'meɪnlænd/ *nc* (usually the —) the land area of a country or continent without its islands.

main·stay /'meɪnsteɪ/ *nc* a chief support: *She was the mainstay of the committee.*

main·stream /'meɪnstriːm/ *n* **1** *nc* the most important or chief kind, tendency etc: *the main-stream of literary criticism.* **2** *nu* (also *attrib*) (a style of jazz) between traditional and modern.

main·tain /meɪn'teɪn/ *vt* **1** to keep or continue (something) at a certain level: *to maintain friendly relations (with them); maintain current prices; maintain law and order; maintain a speed of 60 miles an hour.* **2** to provide food, clothes etc for (a person, family): *maintain a wife and eight children.* **3** to continue to claim (something) to be true: *maintain one's innocence/that one is innocent.* **4** to keep (a machine, building etc) in good repair or working order: *maintain the roads.*

main·tain·able /-əbl/ *adj*

main·ten·ance /'meɪntənəns/ *nu* **1** the act or state of maintaining or being maintained. **2** a means of providing what is needed to support life: *A divorced woman may claim maintenance* (= money) *for her children.*

mai·son·ette /ˌmeɪzə'net/ *nc* a home that uses two storeys in a building.

maize /meɪz/ *nu* (also called *mealie* in some areas) a kind of plant with large yellow grains on a long head (called a *cob*). ⇨ corn-cob.

Maj. *written abbr* Major².

ma·jes·tic /mə'dʒestɪk/ *adj* having, showing, majesty.

ma·jes·ti·cal·ly /-klɪ/ *adv*

maj·esty /'mædʒəstɪ/ *n* (*pl* **-ies**) **1** *nu* (conduct, speech, appearance, manner, causing) great respect and dignity. **2** *nc* (*His/Her/Your M—; Their/Your Majesties*) (a form of address used when speaking of or to a king or queen).

ma·jor¹ /'meɪdʒə(r)/ *adj* (*attrib*) greater or more important (than others): *major injuries; a major fault; a major actress/part in a play; major roads.* Compare minor¹.

ma·jor² /'meɪdʒə(r)/ *nc* (abbr Maj.) an army officer between a captain and a colonel.

,major-'general *nc* (abbr Maj.-Gen.) an army officer between a brigadier and a lieutenant-general.

ma·jor³ /'meɪdʒə(r)/ *vi* **major in sth** to specialize in (a certain subject, at college or university): *Brian majored in economics.*

ma·jor·ity /mə'dʒɒrətɪ/ *nc* (*pl* **-ies**) **1** **majority (of sth)** (used with a *sing* or *pl verb*) the largest number or part: *The majority were/was in favour of the proposal. The majority of people agree.* **be in the majority** (of a group) to have the largest number (e.g. of supporters). **2** the number by which votes for one side are more than those for the other side: *He was elected by a large majority/by a majority of 3749.* **3** (usually *sing*) the legal age of becoming an adult (e.g. 18 in GB): *He will reach his majority next month.* Compare minority.

ma,jority 'verdict *nc* one by the majority (of a jury etc).

make¹ /meɪk/ *n* **1** *nc* a particular (style of) product from a particular business company: *What make is your car? They sell all makes of washing-machines.* **2** **on the make** (*sl*) interested in and busy making a profit or gaining an advantage.

make² /meɪk/ *v* (*pt,pp* made /meɪd/) Ⓝ *'Make'* is used with many nouns where *'make'* + the noun has the same meaning as the verb form of the noun, as in *make a decision* (= decide), *make a promise* (= promise), *make a telephone call* (= telephone). For other examples, ⇨ the noun entries, such as: *allowance, application, arrangement, attempt, contact, effort, note, offer, success. 'Make'* is also used with many nouns in special senses, as in *make a bed* (= tidy the bedclothes), *make a fortune* (= become very rich). For other examples, ⇨ the noun entries, such as: *best, bid, bone, break, change, day, demand, difference, end, eye, face, fun, fuss, go, grade, history, love, man, mess, most, much, name, night, pass, peace, point, room, sense, war, way, weather.* **1** *vt* to produce, construct, shape, form, (something) (esp using parts or materials): *make bread; make a cup of coffee; make a fire; make a chair using some old* *wood; make a model house. It was made in Portugal. Who made this cake? How do you make ice-cream?* (N) For a comparison of *'do'* and *'make'*, ⇨ do³(1b). ⇨ make sth from/of/out of sth. **2** *vt* to be suitable to use for (something): *This coat will make a warm blanket.* **3** *vt* to cause (the effect or state mentioned): *make trouble/mischief/peace/war; make merry* (= enjoy oneself). **4** *vt,vi* (to cause a person) to be or become the state mentioned): *make her happy/well; make oneself understood.* ⇨ also certain, clear, sure, worth. **5** *vt* to cause (a person) to be the kind mentioned: *make friends/enemies (of one's neighbours); make an honest man of him.* **6** *vt* to cause (something) to occur by breaking etc: *make a hole in the sleeve.* **7** *vt* to form, prepare, (something): *make a rule/law; make an agreement/a contract/a deal.* **8** *vt* to force (a person) to do something: *make her apologize; make him write her name down. What made you do it? I was made to wait outside/to stand for six hours.* (N) In this sense *'make'* is always used with the infinitive form of the verb without *'to'*, as in *make her eat.* But *'to'* is used in the passive, as in *She was made to eat.* **make sth do; make do with sth** to manage by using something although it may not be enough or may not be satisfactory: *You'll have to make do with soup for supper/with coffee without milk.* ⇨ do³(8). **9** *vt* to cause (something) to happen: *make a car start; make her smile. You're making me shake. How do I make the wheels turn? What makes cakes rise?* (N) In this sense, *'make'* is used with the infinitive form of the verb without *'to'*. ⇨ also blood(1), hackles, hair(1). **10** *vt* to cause (something) to seem to be the kind mentioned: *These shoes make my feet look big.* **11** *vt* to appoint, elect, select, (a person) as the kind mentioned: *make her a judge; be made captain of the team. Let's make the main character in the story an old woman.* **12** *vt* (to cause a person) to turn out, prove, to be the kind mentioned: *He'll make a good lawyer/husband. What makes a successful businessman?* **13** *vt* to cause (something) to be the result: *make a habit of it; make an example of her; make a fool of oneself.* **14** *vt* to earn, gain, get, win, (money, a reputation etc): *make a profit/loss; make a living as an artist; make a name/reputation as a singer; make £200 a week.* **make it** (*informal*) to be successful in one's career or ambition. **have (got) it made** (*informal*) to be sure of being successful. **15** *vt* to find out (something) using numbers; estimate: *How much do you make the bill? I make the total cost £140. What do you make the time? What size do you make the carpet? I make the distance about 50 miles. That makes the fifth time that you've visited us.* **16** *vt* to amount to, equal (an amount etc): *A hundred pence makes a pound. 5 and 7 make 12.* **17** *vt* (*informal*) to travel (a distance): *make 15 miles in one day.* **18** *vt* to arrive at (a place): *Can we make London by midnight? We ought to make it back to the hotel by 7 o'clock. You'll never make it.* **19** *vt* to be in time for (a means of transport): *Let's try to make the early train.* **20** *vi* **make (as if/though) to** + *verb* to start an action with the intention mentioned: *He made to leave but stopped at the door. She made as if/though to kiss him.*

make after sb/sth to run and try to catch a person, animal etc: *make after a thief/dog.*
make as if/though to + *verb* ⇨ 20 above.
make at sb to attack a person: *He made at me with a knife.*
make away with sth = make off with sth.
make for a place to move, travel, towards: *make for home/the sea.* **make for sb** to move quickly towards a person (as if) to attack: *The dog made for me with his mouth open.* **make for sth** to help to make something possible: *Learning the language makes for a better knowledge of a country.*
make sth from sth to produce an article using materials: *a house made from old bricks; making a dress from a curtain.*
make sb/sth into sb/sth to cause a person, thing to change and become another: *You'll make her into a cruel parent. We can make this house into several flats.* **make sth into sth** to use material to produce something: *make a curtain into a dress.*
make of sb/sth to understand, interpret a person, writing etc (to the extent mentioned): *I could make nothing/very little of her handwriting. Tell me honestly what you make of* (i.e. what your opinion is of) *her son.* **make sth of sth** to produce an article using the material mentioned: *clothes made of nylon. What's it made of?* (N) Make + noun + of sb/sth is often used with special meaning, as in *make fun of him, make the most of a situation.* For uses of this kind, ⇨ the noun entries.
make off to leave quickly (esp to escape): *She made off down the road in my car!* **make off with sb/sth** to steal a person, thing and run away: *He made off with their daughter/the jewels.*
make sth on sth to gain a profit from a piece of business: *make £10 000 on the sale of the house.*
make out (*informal*) to be successful, progress, earn enough money: *How is he making out (as an engineer)?* (N) Used only in questions. To reply, use do well/badly/fine etc. **make out that . . .** to claim, maintain, (esp) something untrue: *Let's make out that we were here all day.* **can/can't make sb out** to be able/not able to understand a person's character: *I can't make her husband out.* **make sb/sth out** to manage to see a person, thing: *It's impossible to make her/the house out in this fog.* **make sb/sth out to be sb/sth** to claim, maintain, a person, thing is the kind mentioned: *Is she really as clever as she makes herself out to be? The doctors are making the new drug out to be a major discovery.* **make sth out** (a) to write and complete a cheque, an application form etc. (b) to manage to read or interpret bad handwriting, a poor photograph etc. ⇨ make sb/sth out. **can/can't make sth out** to understand/fail to understand a reason, cause etc: *I can't make out why they quarrelled.* **make sth out of sth** = make sth of sth. **make out with sb** (*informal*) to begin and develop a friendship with a person: *How is Bob making out with Emma?*
make sth over (to sb/sth) to transfer the ownership or control of something (to a person or organization): *His house has been made over to the government as a museum.*
make up to end a quarrel: *Let's kiss and make up.* **make (sb/sth) up** to put cosmetics on (oneself, an actor, a face, one's eyes etc): *I make*

(myself) up every morning. Do you make up your eyes? It takes an hour to make him up as Othello. Hence **'make-up** *nu.* **make sb/sth up** (a) to invent a story, excuse etc, esp an untrue one: *You made up the story about the accident—it wasn't true. Your rich girlfriend doesn't exist—you made her up. Stop making things up* (i.e. telling lies). (b) to compose a tune, poem etc: *He can make up tunes very quickly on his guitar.* (c) to form something from parts: *Our bodies are made up of millions of cells. How was the committee made up?* Hence **'make-up** *nc.* **make sth up** (a) to prepare a mixture such as medicine: *I asked the chemist to make up my cough medicine.* (b) to prepare food for a journey etc: *We made up hundreds of sandwiches for the children.* (c) to prepare a place to sleep: *She made up a bed on the sofa for me.* ⇨ also unmade-up. (d) to cause something needed to be complete: *We need £50 to make up the money they asked for.* (e) to use up a gap or difference in distance, time etc: *He had twenty metres to make up on the leader in the race. Work hard because there's a lot of time to make up.* (f) to add fuel to a fire etc. **make up one's mind** ⇨ mind¹(3). **make up for sth** to use as a suitable repayment or alternative for something: *Can interesting work make up for a low wage? He gave the money to make up for all the misery he had caused.* **make up for lost time** ⇨ time¹(2). **make sth up from sth** = make sth from sth. **make sth up (into sth)** to use material to produce clothes: *This cloth will make up into two dresses.* **make up to sb** *(informal)* to be pleasant to a person in order to try to get something: *Don't make up to the boss thinking she'll promote you.* **make it up to sb** to do something, give a person something, to repay responsibility for suffering: *I'm sorry that you can't go on holiday but I'll make it up to you.* **make it up (with sb)** to end a quarrel or disagreement (with a person): *Have Ben and Sue made it up yet? Has Fred made it up with Mary?*

make with sth *(sl)* to produce food, money, entertainment etc: *Make with the music—I want to dance!*

make-believe /'meɪk bɪliːv/ *nu* an act of pretending: *Don't be frightened; the play is all make-believe.*

maker /'meɪkə(r)/ *nc* **1** (often used in compounds) a person, business that produces a product: *My radio doesn't work so I sent it back to the maker. She's a good dressmaker.* **2** (M-) a title given to God: *our Maker and Defender.*

make-shift /'meɪkʃɪft/ *adj (attrib; no comp)* used for a time until something better is obtained: *a makeshift bed/home.*

make-up /'meɪkʌp/ *n* **1** *nu* cosmetics. ⇨ make (sb/sth) up. **2** *nc* the result or method of forming something. ⇨ make sb/sth up(c). **3** *n sing* (of a person) a character and personality: *a man with a strong make-up.*

mak-ing /'meɪkɪŋ/ *n* **1** (often used in compounds) the act of producing something: *dressmaking.* **2** **be the making of** to cause a person to develop well: *The two years he served in the Army were the making of him.* **3** **have the makings of sb** to have the necessary qualities for becoming the kind of person mentioned: *He has the makings of a great swimmer.*

mal·ad·just·ed /,mælə'dʒʌstɪd/ *adj* (of a person) unable to adapt properly to society.

mal·ady /'mælədɪ/ *nc* (*pl* **-ies**) *(formal)* a disease; illness.

mal·aise /mæ'leɪz/ *n sing (formal)* a feeling of discomfort but without clear signs of a particular illness.

mala·prop·ism /'mæləprɒpɪzəm/ *nc* an incorrect use of a word that is similar to another one, such as 'a city with many *aversions*' (for *diversions*).

ma·laria /mə'leərɪə/ *nu* a kind of disease with chills, sweating and fever, carried by a particular type of insect (*mosquito*).

　　ma·lar·ial /-ɪəl/ *adj*

male /meɪl/ *adj, nc* (of) the sex that does not give birth to children or young.

mal·for·ma·tion /,mælfɔː'meɪʃn/ *nc,nu* (the state of having) a badly formed or shaped part: *a malformation of the spine.*

mal·form·ed /,mæl'fɔːmd/ *adj* badly formed or shaped.

mal·ice /'mælɪs/ *nu* the desire to harm others. **bear sb malice** feel hatred for a person.

ma·li·cious /mə'lɪʃəs/ *adj* feeling, showing, caused by, malice: *malicious gossip.*

　　ma·li·cious·ly *adv*

ma·lig·nan·cy /mə'lɪgnənsɪ/ *nu* the state of being malignant.

ma·lig·nant /mə'lɪgnənt/ *adj* (of diseases) harmful to life: *malignant cancer.* Compare benign.

ma·lin·ger /mə'lɪŋgə(r)/ *vi* to pretend to be ill etc in order to escape duty or work.

　　ma·lin·ger·er *nc* a person who malingers.

mal·lard /'mælɑːd/ *nc* a kind of wild duck.

mal·le·able /'mælɪəbl/ *adj* **1** *(science)* (of metals) that can be hammered or pressed into new shapes. **2** *(fig)* (e.g. of a person's character) easily influenced; adaptable.

　　mal·lea·bil·ity /,mælɪə'bɪlətɪ/ *nu*

mal·let /'mælɪt/ *nc* a hammer with a wooden head.

mal·nu·tri·tion /,mælnjuː'trɪʃn/ *nu* the condition caused by not getting (enough of) (the right) food.

mal·prac·tice /,mæl'præktɪs/ *nc,nu (legal)* (an instance of) doing wrong; neglect of duty (esp by a professional person such as a doctor or lawyer).

malt /mɔːlt/ *nu* grain (usually *barley*), used to make beer etc.

mal·treat /mæl'triːt/ *vt (formal)* to treat (a person, animal) roughly or cruelly.

　　mal·treat·ment *nu*

ma·ma /mə'mɑː/ *nc (dated)* = mother.

mam·ba /'mæmbə/ *nc* (*pl* **-s**) a kind of black or green poisonous African tree snake.

mam·mal /'mæml/ *nc (science)* any of the class of animals of which the females feed their young with milk from the breast: *Cats, rabbits, cows, monkeys and whales are all mammals.*

　　mam·ma·li·an /mæ'meɪlɪən/ *adj*

mam·mary /'mæmərɪ/ *adj (science)* of, concerning, the female breast: *The mammary glands produce milk.*

mam·moth¹ /'mæməθ/ *adj (attrib)* very big: *a mammoth task.*

mam·moth² /'mæməθ/ *nc* a kind of hairy elephant that does not exist any more.

man¹ /mæn/ n (pl **men** /men/) **1** nc (often used in combinations) an adult male human being: *a post-man/clergyman*. *There's a man at the door*. **man and boy** from boyhood onwards: *He has worked for the firm, man and boy, for thirty years*. **the man in the street** a person regarded as representing the interests and opinions of ordinary people. **a man of the world** a person with wide experience of business and society. **2** (usually pl; dated) a human being; person: *All men must die*. **odd man out** ⇨ odd(3). **3** nu the human race: *Man is mortal*. **4** (usually pl) a male person under the authority of another: *officers and men*. **5** n sing a male person having the qualities (e.g. strength, confidence) associated with men: *Don't give up trying—be a man!* **make a man of sb** to show him how to be strong, confident etc. **6** nc a husband: *man and wife*. **7** nc a player's piece in chess etc. **8** nc (informal) a suitable person: *If you want a good teacher, here's your man!*
'**man·hood** nu (a) the state of being a man: *reach manhood*. (b) men in general.
'**man-hour** nc (pl **—s**) an amount of work done by one person in one hour.
,**man-'made** adj (a) made by humans and not machines. (b) produced from synthetic materials.
'**man·power** nu the number of people available for work etc: *a shortage of manpower in the coal-mines*.
'**man·slaughter** nu the act of killing a human being unlawfully but not deliberately.
,**man-to-'man** adj frank, not holding feelings or opinions back: *a man-to-man discussion*.

man² /mæn/ vt (**-nn-**) to supply (something) with men for service or defence: *man a ship; man the barricades*.

man·acle /'mænəkl/ vt to tie up (a person etc) using chains(1).

man·acles /'mænəklz/ n pl chains(1) used for tying a person up.

man·age /'mænɪdʒ/ v **1** vt to organize and control (something): *managing a business/one's family/a theatre*. **2** vt,vi to succeed in doing or dealing with (something) (esp using help, tools, money etc): *Can you manage the suitcases if I carry the parcels? We can't manage with these poor tools*. **3** vi **manage (on sth/without sb/sth)** to live, survive: *I can't manage without you/on only £50 a week*. **4** vt **can/can't manage sth** (informal) to be able/unable to eat something: *Can you manage another slice of cake?*
man·age·able /-əbl/ adj that can be dealt with or controlled. Opp unmanageable.

man·age·ment /'mænɪdʒmənt/ n **1** nu the practice of managing or being managed: *The shop is under new management*. **2** nu skilful treatment or handling: *It needed a good deal of management to persuade them to give me the job*. **3** nc,nu all the people managing an industry etc: *joint consultations between workers and (the) management*.

man·ager /'mænɪdʒə(r)/ nc a person who organizes and controls a business, a professional sportsperson etc: *the sales manager; the manager of a tennis player*.

man·ager·ess /,mænɪdʒə'res/ nc a woman who controls a business etc, esp a shop.

mana·ger·ial /,mænɪ'dʒɪərɪəl/ adj (usually attrib) of managers or management: *managerial skill*.

man·ag·ing /'mænɪdʒɪŋ/ adj (attrib) having (senior) control: *a managing director*.

man·date /'mændeɪt/ nc **1** the authority given to representatives by voters, members of a trade union etc: *the mandate given to us by the electors/workers*. **2** an official order from a superior person.

man·da·tory /'mændətrɪ/ adj (of a command or power) that must be obeyed.

man·dible /'mændəbl/ nc (science) **1** the lower jaw in mammals and fishes. **2** either part of a bird's beak. **3** (in insects) either half of the upper pair of jaws.

mane /meɪn/ nc the set of long hair on the neck of a horse or lion.

man·ga·nese /'mæŋɡəniːz/ nu a kind of hard, brittle, light-grey metal (symbol Mn), used in making steel, glass etc.

mange /meɪndʒ/ nu a skin disease of dogs and cats.
mangy /'meɪndʒɪ/ adj (**-ier, -iest**)

manger /'meɪndʒə(r)/ nc a long, open box for horses or cattle to feed from.

mangle¹ /'mæŋɡl/ nc a machine with rollers for pressing out water from clothes etc.

mangle² /'mæŋɡl/ vt to cut up, tear, damage, (a person, thing) badly: *be badly mangled in a car accident*.

man·go /'mæŋɡəʊ/ nc (pl **—es** or **—s**) (also attrib) (a tropical tree with) a large fruit with a large flat stone and yellow flesh when ripe: *mango chutney*.

man·grove /'mæŋɡrəʊv/ nc (also attrib) a tropical tree growing in or near water and sending down long roots from its branches: *mangrove swamps*.

man·handle /'mænhændl/ vt **1** to move (something) using physical strength: *manhandling heavy boxes*. **2** to hold or move (a person) roughly: *be manhandled by the police*.

ma·nia /'meɪnɪə/ n **1** nu a serious mental illness causing great excitement, violence. **2** **have a mania for sth** to have extreme enthusiasm, excitement for it: *have a mania for powerful motor bikes/hard work*.

ma·ni·ac /'meɪnɪæk/ nc **1** a mad person. **2** (fig) a person with extreme enthusiasm.
ma·ni·acal /mə'naɪəkl/ adj
ma·ni·acal·ly /-klɪ/ adv

mani·cure /'mænɪkjʊə(r)/ nu the care of the hands and finger-nails. □ vt to cut, clean and polish (the finger-nails).
'**mani·cur·ist** /-ɪst/ nc a person who manicures finger-nails as a profession.

mani·fest¹ /'mænɪfest/ adj clear and obvious: *a manifest truth*.

mani·fest² /'mænɪfest/ vt **1** to show (something) clearly: *manifest the truth of a statement*. **2** to give signs of (something): *She doesn't manifest much desire to marry him*. **3** (reflexive) to appear: *No disease manifested itself during the long voyage*.
mani·fest·ly adv
mani·fes·ta·tion /,mænɪfe'steɪʃn/ nc,nu
mani·fes·to /,mænɪ'festəʊ/ nc (pl **—es** or **—s**) a public declaration of principles, policy, intentions etc by a ruler, political party etc.

mani·fold /'mænɪfəʊld/ adj (formal) many (uses, reasons etc): manifold ways of using it.

man·ila (also **-il·la**) /məˈnɪlə/ nu (also manila paper) a kind of strong, brown paper.

ma·nipu·late /məˈnɪpjʊleɪt/ vt **1** (formal) to operate, handle, (machines, tools) with skill: manipulate machinery. **2** to control, (people, organizations, opinions etc) esp by using one's influence or unfair methods: A clever politician knows how to manipulate his supporters/public opinion.

ma·nipu·la·tion /mə,nɪpjʊˈleɪʃn/ nc,nu

man·kind /,mæn'kaɪnd/ nu **1** the human race. **2** /'mænkaɪnd/ the male sex; all men. ⇨ woman-kind.

man·like /'mænlaɪk/ adj having the qualities (good or bad) of a man: a manlike voice.

man·ly /'mænlɪ/ adj (**-ier**, **-iest**) having the qualities expected of a man: manly courage. Compare manlike, mannish.

man·li·ness nu

man·na /'mænə/ nu **1** (in the Bible) food provided by God. **2** (fig) something unexpected that gives hope, determination etc.

man·ned /mænd/ adj operated by a person and not a machine. Opp unmanned.

man·ne·quin /'mænɪkɪn/ nc a model(2) (the usual word).

man·ner /'mænə(r)/ n **1** nc a way in which something is done or happens: Do it in this manner. **2** n sing a person's way of behaving towards others: I don't like his manner. **3** (pl) social behaviour: good/bad manners. **4** nc a style in literature or art: a painting in the manner of Raphael. **5** nc a kind, sort: What manner of man is he? **not by any manner of means** absolutely not at all. **all manner of sb/sth** every kind of person, thing etc: He gave us all manner of excuses.

man·nered adj (used in compounds): ill-/well-mannered (= having bad/good manners(3)).

man·ner·ism /'mænərɪzəm/ nc a peculiar kind of behaviour, way of speaking etc, esp one that is a habit.

man·nish /'mænɪʃ/ adj **1** (of a woman) like a man. **2** more suitable for a man than for a woman: a mannish style of dress. Compare manlike, manly.

ma·noeu·vre¹ (US = **ma·neu·ver**) /məˈnuːvə(r)/ nc **1** (often pl) a (group of) planned movements (of a person driving or operating a machine, or of an army etc): learn the manoeuvres for the battle. **2** a clever movement or plan, made to deceive, to escape, or to win or do something: the desperate manoeuvres of some politicians.

ma·noeu·vre² (US = **ma·neu·ver**) /məˈnuːvə(r)/ vi,vt (to cause something) to perform manoeuvres: manoeuvring a car into a parking space.

ma·noeu·vrer (US = **ma·neu·ver·er**) nc a person who uses manoeuvres(2).

ma·noeu·vrable (US = **ma·neu·ver·able**) adj that can be manoeuvred. Opp unmanoeu-vrable.

ma·noeu·vra·bil·ity (US = **-neu·ver-**) /mə,nuːvrəˈbɪlətɪ/ nu

man·or /'mænə(r)/ nc an area of land with a large house (called the manor-house), owned by one family.

ma·nor·ial /məˈnɔːrɪəl/ adj of a manor.

man·sion /'mænʃn/ nc a large house.

man·tel·piece /'mæntlpiːs/ nc a shelf above a fireplace.

man·tis /'mæntɪs/ nc (science) a kind of long-legged insect: a praying mantis.

mantle /'mæntl/ nc **1** a loose, sleeveless cloak. **2** (fig; literary) covering: hills with a mantle of snow. **3** a metal cover fixed round the flame of a light from gas.

man·ual¹ /'mænjʊəl/ adj (usually attrib) of, done with, the hands: manual labour.

man·ual·ly /-jʊəlɪ/ adv

man·ual² /'mænjʊəl/ nc a book giving explanations of how to do something: a technical manual.

manu·fac·ture¹ /,mænjʊ'fæktʃə(r)/ nu the making or production (of goods and materials): the manufacture of toys/plastic.

manu·fac·ture² /,mænjʊ'fæktʃə(r)/ vt **1** to make, produce, (goods etc) using machinery: manufacturing industries; manufactured goods. **2** to invent (a story, an excuse etc): manufacturing lies.

manu·fac·turer nc a person, business, that manufactures things.

ma·nure /məˈnjʊə(r)/ nu waste from animals mixed with soil to make it produce better food. □ vt to put manure in (soil).

manu·script /'mænjʊskrɪpt/ nc (abbr MS, pl MSS) a book etc as first written out or typed.

many¹ /'menɪ/ adj or det (comp **more**, superl **most**) **1** a large number of: many chairs/visitors/ideas. How many cakes do you want? Give me as many books as possible. Many people think so. Ⓝ 'A lot of' is also possible in statements and is more informal. 'Many' refers to 'a large number of', as in many children. 'Much' is used to refer to 'a large amount of', as in much food/noise/sadness. Compare few¹. **2 many a** + sing noun a large number of + pl noun: Many a man (= many men) would like such an opportunity.

many² /'menɪ/ pron **many (of sb/sth)** a large number (of): I have some sweets but not many. Many of them are broken. Give me as many as you can. Do you need so many? (= such a large number?) Many (of us) agree. **a good many ((of the) sb/sth)** a particularly large amount (of): A good many (apples/of the apples) were bad. **as many again** the same number again: Ten were killed and as many again were injured. Compare few², much³.

map¹ /mæp/ nc a drawing on paper etc of the earth's surface or a part of it, showing hills, rivers, countries, vegetation, economic resources etc. **(put sth) on the map** (fig) (to cause it to be) considered important: John's success in athletics put his college on the map.

'map-reader nc a person who is able to get information from maps: He's a good/poor map-reader.

map² /mæp/ vt (**-pp-**) **1** to make a map of (an area); show (an area) on a map. **2 map sth out** (fig) to plan, arrange, an activity: map out one's visit.

maple /'meɪpl/ nc,nu a kind of tree grown for its wood and maple-sugar.

'maple-sugar/-syrup nu a kind of sugar/syrup obtained from one kind of maple.

mar /mɑː(r)/ vt (-rr-) (formal) to spoil (beauty, a feeling etc): Nothing marred their happiness.

Mar written abbr March.

mara·thon /'mærəθən/ nc **1** (also M-) a long-distance race on foot (about 26 miles (or 41·8 kilometres) at modern sports meetings). **2** (fig) (also attrib) a test of a person's endurance: a marathon performance.

ma·raud /mə'rɔːd/ vi to go about in search of things to steal or damage.

ma·raud·er nc a person or animal that marauds.

marble /'mɑːbl/ n **1** nc,nu (also attrib) (an example of) a kind of hard stone with patterns, used when polished for building and sculpture: a marble statue. **2** nc small ball of coloured glass used in games played by children.

March /mɑːtʃ/ n (also attrib) (abbr Mar) the third month of the year, with 31 days: cold March winds. I was born on 14 March. (N) '14 March' is spoken as 'March the fourteenth' or 'the fourteenth of March'.

march¹ /mɑːtʃ/ n **1** nc,nu (an instance of) marching; distance travelled: a march of ten miles. **2 on the march** marching. **3** n sing (fig) the progress: the march of events/time. **4** nc a piece of music for marching to: military marches. **5** nc a large public demonstration(2) by people walking: a march in support of human rights.

march² /mɑːtʃ/ v **1** vt,vi (to cause a person) to walk as soldiers do, with regular steps: The troops marched by/past/in/out/off/away. He was marched off to prison (= taken to prison). **2** vi to take part in a march(5). **3** vi (fig) to make progress: Time marches on.

march·er nc (a) a person who marches. (b) a person who walks in a march(5).

mar·chion·ess /ˌmɑːʃə'nes/ nc **1** a wife or widow of a marquis. **2** a woman who holds a position equal to that of a marquis.

mare /meə(r)/ nc a female horse, donkey.

mar·gar·ine /ˌmɑːdʒə'riːn/ nu a yellow food substance, used like butter, made from animal or vegetable fats.

marge /mɑːdʒ/ nu (informal) = margarine.

mar·gin /'mɑːdʒɪn/ nc **1** an empty space round writing or printing on a page. **2** an edge or border: the margin of a lake. **3** an amount (of time, money etc) above what is estimated as necessary. **4** an amount (of profit etc) remaining: good profit margins. **5** a condition near the limit, below or after which something is impossible: He escaped defeat by a narrow margin.

mar·gin·al /-nl/ adj **(a)** small and not important: a marginal error/difference/increase. **(b)** (of a result of an election, the office being contested) where a small number of votes will decide the winner. **(c)** (of written notes) put in a margin(1).

mar·gin·al·ly /-nəlɪ/ adv

mari·jua·na (also **-hua·na** /ˌmærɪ'wɑːnə/ nu (also called cannabis, hashish, pot) dried leaves and flowers of Indian hemp smoked in order to cause excited feelings.

ma·ri·na /mə'riːnə/ nc (pl —s) a harbour for pleasure boats (small yachts etc).

mari·nade /ˌmærɪ'neɪd/ nc,nu (a kind of) a mixture of wine, vinegar and spice; fish or meat soaked in this. □ vt (also **mari·nate** /'mærɪneɪt/) to soak (fish, meat) in (a) marinade.

ma·rine¹ /mə'riːn/ adj (attrib) **1** of, by, found in, produced by, the sea: marine fishing. **2** of ships, trade by sea, the navy etc: marine insurance.

ma·rine² /mə'riːn/ n **1** nu shipping in general. **2** nc a soldier serving on a warship.

mari·ner /'mærɪnə(r)/ nc (literary) a sailor.

mari·on·ette /ˌmærɪə'net/ nc a jointed puppet moved by strings.

mari·tal /'mærɪtl/ adj of marriage: marital bliss.

mari·time /'mærɪtaɪm/ adj (usually attrib) **1** connected with the sea or ships: maritime law. **2** situated or found near the sea: maritime countries.

mark¹ /mɑːk/ nc **1** a line, scratch, cut, stain etc that spoils the appearance of something: Who made all these dirty marks on my new book? **2** a noticeable spot on the body by which a person or animal may be recognized: a birthmark. **make one's mark** to become famous. **3** a sign or indication: the marks of old age/suffering. **4** a figure, design etc made as a sign or symbol: punctuation marks; trademarks. **5** a numerical or alphabetical symbol, e.g. A+, to show a level or standard in an examination or performance: He got the best marks of his year. **full marks** an excellent standard. **up to/below the mark** equal to/below the necessary standard. **6** a target: His shot was off the mark. **be/fall wide of the mark** to be very inaccurate: Your guess/calculation is wide of the mark. **7** (athletics) a line showing the starting-point of a race: On your marks, get set, go! (= words used by the starter). **8** (often M-) (used with numbers) a model or type: a Honda Civic Mark 3.

mark² /mɑːk/ v **1** vt,vi (to cause something) to have a mark(1): You've marked the table. This cloth is marked. It marks easily. **2** vt to give marks(5) to (a piece of work): mark examination papers. **3** vt to indicate (something) by putting a mark, e.g. a cross, on or against: mark an answer wrong. **4** vt to watch (a person, method) carefully: Mark carefully how it is done. **(You) mark my words** Note what I say and you will find that I am right. **5** vt to signal, be a sign of, (something): His death marked the end of the war. Ceremonies marked an anniversary. **6** vt to be a distinguishing feature of (a person, thing): What are the qualities that mark a great leader?

mark sth down to reduce the price of something for sale.

mark sth off to put marks on something to show edges, measurements etc.

mark sth out to put lines on something to show boundary lines etc: mark out a tennis-court.

mark sth up to increase the price of something for sale.

mark·ed /mɑːkt/ adj noticeable; obvious: There has been a marked difference/improvement. **a marked man** a person who is being watched or who is in danger.

mark·ed·ly /'mɑːkɪdlɪ/ adv

mark·er /'mɑːkə(r)/ nc **1** a person or tool that marks, esp a person who marks the score at games. **2** a person who marks examination papers. **3** something that marks or indicates something, e.g. a flag or post on a playing field.

mar·ket¹ /'mɑːkɪt/ nc **1** an open space or a building where people meet to buy and sell goods: She went to (the) market to buy food for the family. **2**

an occasion during which such a meeting takes place: *The next market is on Monday.* **3** a trade in a class of goods: *the coffee market.* **corner the market** to gain control of a particular trade by obtaining most of the particular goods. **4** the state of trade as shown by prices: *The market rose/fell/ was steady.* **play the market** to buy and sell to make profit. **5** a demand: *There's no/not much/ only a poor market for these goods.* **6** (*sing* only) buying and selling. **be in the market for sth** to have the desire to buy something. **be on/come on(to)/put sth on the market** to be offered/ offer something for sale: *This house will probably come on the market next month.* **7** an area, country, in which goods may be sold: *We must find new markets for our manufacturers.* ⇨ Common Market.

'market day *nc* the day when a market(2) is regularly held.

,market 'garden *nc* a place where vegetables are grown for selling. Hence **,market 'gardening** *nu*

'market-place *nc* an open place for a market(2).

,market 'price *nc* (often the —) a price for which something is usually sold.

,market re'search *nu* a study of why people buy or do not buy certain goods, of the effect of advertising etc.

'market town *nc* one where a market(2) (esp one for cattle and sheep) is held.

mar·ket² /'mɑːkɪt/ *vt* to prepare and offer (something) for sale.

mar·ket·able /-əbl/ *adj* that can be, fit to be, sold.

mar·ket·ing *nu* the theory and practice of (large-scale) selling.

mark·ing /'mɑːkɪŋ/ *nc* (esp) a pattern of colours of feathers, fur etc: *a tiger's marking(s).*

marks·man /'mɑːksmən/ *nc* (*pl* **-men** /-mən/) a person who can use a gun well: *a police marksman.*

mar·ma·lade /'mɑːməleɪd/ *nu* jam made from oranges (or lemons, grapefruit).

ma·roon¹ /mə'ruːn/ *adj, nu* (of) a brownish-red colour.

ma·roon² /mə'ruːn/ *vt* (usually *passive*) to put (a person) on an island or place where no-one lives: *be marooned on a deserted beach.*

mar·quee /mɑː'kiː/ *nc* a very large tent.

mar·quis (also **mar·quess**) /'mɑːkwɪs/ *n* (*GB*) a nobleman between an earl and a duke. ⇨ marchioness.

mar·riage /'mærɪdʒ/ *n* **1** *nc,nu* (an instance of) a legal union of a man and woman as husband and wife; the state of being married: *Do you believe in marriage?* (= Do you think people should marry?) *A marriage has been arranged between Jane and Tom.* **a broken marriage** one that has ended in separation or divorce. **2** *nc* a wedding (the usual word). ⇨ marital.

mar·riage·able /-əbl/ *adj* old enough, fit for, marriage: *a girl of marriageable age.*

mar·ried /'mærɪd/ *adj* united in marriage; of marriage: *married couples; married life; my married sister.* Opp unmarried. **get married** to marry(1): *Let's get married.*

mar·row /'mærəʊ/ *n* **1** *nu* the soft, fatty substance that fills the inside of bones. **be chilled/**

chill sb to the marrow (to cause a person) to be extremely cold. **2** *nc,nu* (*GB*) (also *vegetable marrow*) a vegetable like a large fat cucumber, cooked as food.

mar·ry /'mærɪ/ *v* (*pt,pp* **-ied**) **1** *vt,vi* to take (a person) as a husband or wife: *Bill has married Sue. They've married.* **2** *vt* (of a priest, a civil official) to join (two people) as husband and wife: *Which priest is going to marry them?* **3** *vt* to give (a son, daughter etc) to be married: *He married both his daughters to farmers.* **4** *vt* (*informal*) to obtain (money, property etc) by marrying a rich person: *marry money/wealth.*

Mars /mɑːz/ *n* **1** (in Roman myth) the god of war. **2** the planet fourth in order from the sun.

marsh /mɑːʃ/ *nc,nu* (an area of) low-lying, wet land.

marshy *adj* (**-ier, -iest**) of, like, a marsh.

mar·shal¹ /'mɑːʃl/ *nc* **1** an army or air force officer of highest rank. **2** an official responsible for important public events or ceremonies.

mar·shal² /'mɑːʃl/ *vt* (**-ll-**, *US* **-l-**) **1** to arrange (things) in proper order: *marshal facts/military forces.* **2** to organize or lead (people, vehicles) into the correct position or place.

mar·su·pial /mɑː'suːpɪəl/ *adj, nc* (*science*) (of) an animal with a flap or bag (*pouch*) on the mother's abdomen used to carry its young.

mar·tial /'mɑːʃl/ *adj* (*formal*) of, associated with, war: *martial music.*

,martial 'art *nc* (usually *pl*) a form of fighting in sports such as *karate, kung fu.*

,martial 'law *nu* government by army officers.

mar·tin /'mɑːtɪn/ *nc* (also *house-martin*) a bird of the swallow family that builds a nest on walls etc.

mar·tyr /'mɑːtə(r)/ *nc* a person who is put to death or caused to suffer greatly for the sake of a great cause, religious belief or principle: *the early Christian martyrs in Rome.*

mar·tyr·dom /-dəm/ *nu* a martyr's suffering or death.

mar·vel¹ /'mɑːvl/ *nc* **1** something causing great surprise, wonder, astonishment: *the marvels of modern science.* **work marvels** to produce a highly successful result: *The drug worked marvels and I felt better immediately.* **2** **a marvel of sth** a fine example: *She's a marvel of patience.*

mar·vel² /'mɑːvl/ *vi* (**-ll-**, *US* **-l-**) **marvel (at sb/ sth)** to be greatly surprised (at a person, event etc): *marvel at her patience.*

mar·vel·lous (*US* = **mar·vel·ous**) /'mɑːvələs/ *adj* astonishing; wonderful: *such a marvellous story/performance; marvellous scenery/weather.*

mar·vel·lous·ly (*US* = **mar·vel·ous·ly**) *adv*

Marx·ism /'mɑːksɪzəm/ *n* (the belief in) the main theory of Karl Marx (1818–83) that social and political changes are caused by a struggle between social classes and that socialism will eventually replace capitalism.

Marx·ist /'mɑːksɪst/ *adj* of, concerning, Marxism. □ *nc* a supporter of, believer in, Marxism.

mar·zi·pan /'mɑːzɪpæn/ *nu* a mixture of ground almonds, sugar etc, used on cakes.

masc. *written abbr* masculine.

mas·cara /mæ'skɑːrə/ *nu* a cosmetic for darkening the eyelashes.

mas·cot /'mæskət/ *nc* a person, animal or object thought to bring good luck.

mas·cu·line /'mæskjʊlɪn/ adj **1** of, like, suitable for, men: *a masculine style.* **2** (*gram*) of the form of words used to refer to males: *'He' and 'him' are masculine pronouns.* Compare feminine.

mas·cu·lin·ity /ˌmæskjʊ'lɪnətɪ/ nu the quality of being masculine.

mash¹ /mæʃ/ nu **1** grain etc cooked in water as food for animals. **2** (*informal*) mashed potatoes: *sausage and mash.*

mash² /mæʃ/ vt to beat or crush (food): *mashed potato.*

mask¹ /maːsk/ nc **1** a covering for (part of) the face. **2** a thin piece of cloth worn over the mouth and nose by doctors and nurses. **3** a face carved in wood.

mask² /maːsk/ vt **1** to cover (the face) with a mask(1,2). **2** (*fig*) to hide (a feeling): *mask one's hatred under an appearance of friendliness.*

maso·chism /'mæsəkɪzəm/ nu (sexual pleasure from) enjoying the feeling of (self-inflicted) pain or humiliation. Compare sadism.

maso·chist /-kɪst/ nc a person suffering from masochism.

maso·chis·tic /ˌmæsə'kɪstɪk/ adj

ma·son /'meɪsn/ nc a worker who builds or works with stone.

ma·son·ry /'meɪsnrɪ/ nu stone used in a building.

mas·quer·ade¹ /ˌmæskə'reɪd/ nc **1** a dance where people wear masks(1). **2** (*fig*) a false show or pretence.

mas·quer·ade² /ˌmæskə'rɑːd/ vi **masquerade as/under the name etc of sb** to pretend to be, have the same name as another person.

mass¹ /mæs/ adj (*attrib*) of, for, very many people: *a mass meeting.*

ˌmass 'media n pl (the —) (sometimes used with a *sing verb*) television, newspapers etc, with a large audience.

ˌmass 'noun nc (*gram*) = uncountable noun.

ˌmass pro'duction nu the manufacture of large numbers of identical articles. Hence **ˌmass pro·'duce** vt

mass² /mæs/ n **1** nc a lump, quantity of matter, without regular shape: *masses of dark clouds in the sky; a mass of colour in the garden.* **2** (*pl*; the masses) ordinary people or workers. **3** nu (*science*) a quantity of matter in an object. Compare size¹(1).

mass³ /mæs/ vt,vi (to cause people, things) to come together in large numbers: *Students are massing in the examination hall.*

Mass /mæs/ n the main religious service (in the Roman Catholic Church).

mass·acre¹ /'mæsəkə(r)/ nc a cruel killing of very many people.

mass·acre² /'mæsəkə(r)/ vt **1** to kill (very many people). **2** (*fig*) to defeat or destroy (a person, thing) completely: *massacring an opponent/a song.*

mass·age /'mæsɑːʒ/ nc,nu (an instance of) pressing and rubbing the body with the hands in order to lessen pain, stiffness etc. □ vt to give a massage to (a part of the body).

mass·eur /mæ'sɜː(r)/ nc a man who practises massage.

mass·euse /mæ'sɜːz/ nc a woman who practises massage.

mas·sive /'mæsɪv/ adj **1** large, heavy and solid: *a massive monument.* **2** (*fig*) large and complete: *a massive victory.*

mass·ive·ly adv

mast /maːst/ nc a tall pole for a flag, a ship's sails, a TV aerial etc.

mas·ter¹ /'maːstə(r)/ adj (*attrib*) having, showing, the best professional skill: *a master builder/carpenter.*

mas·ter² /'maːstə(r)/ nc **1** master (of sth) a person who has control (of something): *He is master of the situation* (= has it under control). **2** (title used with a boy's name) young Mr: *Master Charles Smith.* **3** (*dated*) a male owner of a dog, horse etc: *Who's its master?* **4** a male teacher (esp in a private school): *the mathematics master.* Compare mistress(3). **5** (also M-) a title of the head of a college: *the Master of Balliol.*

ˌMaster of 'Arts/'Science nc (abbr MA, MSc) a holder of a university degree above a first (*Bachelor*) degree.

'master-key nc one that will open many different locks.

'master·mind vt to plan, direct, (a scheme): *Who masterminded the bank robbery?*

'master·piece nc something made with very great skill; the best example: *Which book is her masterpiece?*

'master-stroke nc a very clever act (of policy etc): *To tell the thief that the stolen goods were poisonous was a master-stroke.*

mas·ter³ /'maːstə(r)/ vt (*formal*) **1** to gain skill in (a subject, language etc): *master Japanese.* **2** to gain control of (a strong feeling): *master one's anger/fear.*

mas·ter·ful /'maːstəfəl/ adj showing control, determination: *speak in a masterful manner.*

mas·ter·ful·ly /-fəlɪ/ adv

mas·ter·ly /'maːstəlɪ/ adj very skilful: *She finished with a few masterly strokes of the brush.*

mas·tery /'maːstərɪ/ nu **mastery (of sth/over sb)** complete control or knowledge: *his mastery of the violin.*

mas·ti·cate /'mæstɪkeɪt/ vt (*formal*) to chew (food).

mas·ti·ca·tion /ˌmæstɪ'keɪʃn/ nu

mas·tiff /'mæstɪf/ nc a kind of large, strong dog much used as a watchdog.

mas·tur·bate /'mæstəbeɪt/ vt,vi to produce sexual excitement by manual or other stimulation of the genital organs (of oneself, a person).

mas·tur·ba·tion /ˌmæstə'beɪʃn/ nu

mat¹ /mæt/ adj = matt.

mat² /mæt/ nc **1** a piece of material used to cover a part of the floor: *a door mat.* **2** a small piece of material placed under vases, ornaments or plates etc on a table: *a table mat.* **3** anything thickly tangled or twisted together: *a mat of weeds.*

mat³ /mæt/ vt,vi (-tt-) (to cause something) to become tangled or knotted: *matted hair.*

mata·dor /'mætədɔː(r)/ nc a man whose task is to kill the bull in a bull-fight.

match¹ /mætʃ/ nc a short piece of wood, waxed paper etc with a top that burns when rubbed on a rough surface.

'match·box nc a box for matches.

match² /mætʃ/ nc **1** a contest; game: *a football/tennis match.* **2** match (for sb) a person with the same strength, skill etc as another: *You are no match for him.* **3** a person or thing exactly like, corresponding to, or combining well with, another: *colours/materials that are a good match.* **4** (*informal*) a person considered from the point of view of marriage: *He's a good match.*

,match 'point *nc* the final point needed to win a match²(1).

match³ /mætʃ/ *v* **1** *vt,vi* to be equal to, be suitable for, (something) (because of colour, design etc): *The carpets should match the curtains.* Compare clash²(4). **2** *vt* **match sth (up)** to find a match(3) for something: *Can you match this particular design?* **3** *vt* to be equal to (another in quality, ability etc): *He/This car can't be matched for speed.*

match·less *adj* (*formal*) without an equal: *matchless beauty.*

match·et /'mætʃit/ *nc* = machete.

mate¹ /meit/ *n* **1** (*informal*) a man: *Where are you going, mate?* ⇨ also class-mate, playmate. **2** one of a pair of birds or animals: *the lioness and her mate.* **3** a ship's officer (not an engineer) below the rank of captain. **4** a worker who helps another: *a plumber's mate.*

mate² /meit/ *vt,vi* (to cause birds or animals) to unite for the purpose of producing young.

ma·teri·al¹ /mə'tiəriəl/ *adj* **1** (*tech*) made of, connected with, matter or substance: *the material world.* ⇨ spiritual¹. **2** (usually *attrib*) of the body; of physical needs: *material needs* (e.g. food and warmth). **3** (*legal*) important; essential: *material evidence.* **material to sth** (*formal*) very important, essential, to a situation. Compare immaterial.

ma'terial noun *nc* (*gram*) one naming a material, e.g. *stone, wood, wool.*

ma·teri·al·ly /-iəli/ *adv* (*formal*) to an important degree: *Nothing has improved materially..*

ma·teri·al² /mə'tiəriəl/ *n* **1** *nc,nu* thing out of which something is (to be) made or with which something is done: *raw materials* (= substance to be used in manufacture); *dress materials* (= cloth); *writing materials* (i.e. pen, ink, paper etc). **2** *nu* (*fig*) facts, information (to be) used in a book etc: *the material from which history is made.*

ma·teri·al·ism /mə'tiəriəlizəm/ *nu* **1** the belief that only material things exist. **2** (*derog*) the policy or practice of giving too much value to wealth, pleasure etc.

ma·teri·al·ist /-ist/ *adj, nc* (of) a believer in, supporter of, materialism(1, 2).

ma·teri·al·is·tic /mə,tiəriə'listik/ *adj* supporting materialism(2).

ma·teri·al·is·ti·cal·ly /-kli/ *adv*

ma·teri·al·ize (also **-ise**) /mə'tiəriəlaiz/ *vi* **1** to become visible or touchable. **2** to happen, become fact: *Our plans did not materialize.*

ma·ter·nal /mə'tɜːnl/ *adj* **1** of, like, a mother: *maternal care/instincts; feel maternal.* **2** (*attrib*) related through the mother: *my maternal grandfather.* Compare paternal.

ma·ter·nal·ly /-nəli/ *adv*

ma·tern·ity /mə'tɜːnəti/ *adj* (*attrib*), *nu* (of) being a mother: *a maternity ward/hospital* (= for women who (are about to) become mothers).

math·emat·ical /,mæθə'mætikl/ *adj* of mathematics.

math·emat·ical·ly /-kli/ *adv*

math·ema·ti·cian /,mæθəmə'tiʃn/ *nc* an expert in mathematics.

math·emat·ics /,mæθə'mætiks/ *nu* (also *attrib*) the science of size and numbers (of which arithmetic, algebra, geometry etc are parts): *a mathematics lesson.*

maths (*US* = **math**) /mæθs *US:* mæθ/ *abbr* mathematics.

mati·née /'mætinei/ *nc* an afternoon performance at a cinema or theatre.

ma·tri·arch /'meitriɑːk/ *nc* a woman head of a family or tribe. Compare patriarch(2).

ma·tri·ar·chal /,meitri'ɑːkl/ *adj*

ma·tri·archy /-ɑːki/ *nc* a kind of society in which women have authority.

ma·trices /'meitrisiːz/ *pl* of matrix.

mat·ri·cide /'mætrisaid/ *nc,nu* (*tech*) (an instance of) killing one's mother. ⇨ patricide.

mat·ri·mo·ny /'mætriməni/ *nu* the state of being married.

mat·ri·mo·ni·al /,mætri'məuniəl/ *adj*

ma·trix /'meitriks/ *n* (*pl* **matrices** /'meitrisiːz/ or **—es**) **1** a shaped mould into which hot metal or other material is poured to make something. **2** a substance in which a jewel, mineral etc is found in the ground. **3** (*maths*) an organized arrangement of numbers etc. **4** (*computers*) an arrangement of information in the form of a table(3).

ma·tron /'meitrən/ *nc* **1** a woman who manages the nursing staff of a hospital. **2** a woman in charge of domestic affairs in a school, old people's home etc.

ma·tron·ly *adj* (**a**) with calm, confident authority: *run the home in a matronly way.* (**b**) (as of an older woman) a little fat: *a matronly figure.*

matt (also **mat**; *US* = **matte**) /mæt/ *adj* (of surfaces) dull; not shiny or glossy: *paint that dries with a matt finish.* ⇨ gloss paint.

mat·ter¹ /'mætə(r)/ *n* **1** *nu* any substance that forms a physical thing (contrasted with *mind, spirit* etc): *organic/inorganic matter.* **2** *nc* the subject for one's thoughts or for a book, speech etc (contrasted with the form or style). **3** *nu* something printed or written: *buy some reading matter.* **4** *nc* something, e.g. a subject, concern, issue, affair, to which attention is given: *money matters.* **as a matter of course** ⇨ course¹(2). **as a matter of fact** ⇨ fact(4). **be no laughing matter** (of a difficulty etc) to be serious. **a matter of life and death** an extremely serious affair. **a matter of opinion** something about which people have different personal opinions. **for 'that matter** so far as that (i.e. the subject being mentioned) is concerned. **5** *nu* importance. **(make/be) no matter** (to be) of no importance: *It's no matter/makes no matter whether you arrive early or late.* **no matter how/who/ what/where** etc it is of no importance how etc. **6** *nu* **the matter (with sb/sth)** wrong (with a person, thing): *There's something the matter with her. What's the matter?* **7** **a matter of sth** about an amount mentioned: *a matter of 20 weeks/10 miles/£50; within a matter of hours.* **8** *nu* (*med*) yellow liquid in a wound.

,matter-of-'fact *adj* (of a person, manner) unimaginative; concerned with facts only.

mat·ter² /'mætə(r)/ *vi* to be important: *It doesn't*

matter (to me) whether you stay or leave. Ⓝ Not used in continuous tenses, e.g. *is/was -ing.*

mat·ting /'mætɪŋ/ *nu* rough material for floors and packing goods: *coconut-matting.*

mat·tock /'mætək/ *nc* a kind of tool with a long iron bar, used for breaking up hard ground etc.

mat·tress /'mætrɪs/ *nc* a flat pad of foam rubber, springs etc on which to sleep. ⇨ spring mattress.

ma·ture¹ /mə'tʃʊə(r)/ *adj* **1** fully grown or developed: *mature trees.* **2** (of people, behaviour) sensible (because of age and experience). **3** (of food etc) ready for use: *mature cheese/wine.* **4** (of a plan, scheme etc) ready. Opp immature.

ma·ture·ly *adv*

ma·tur·ity /mə'tʃʊərəti/ *nu* the state of being mature.

ma·ture² /mə'tʃʊə(r)/ *vt,vi* (to cause a person, behaviour, food etc) to become fully developed or ready for use: *His character matured during these years.*

maud·lin /'mɔːdlɪn/ *adj* (*formal*) very sad and full of self pity.

maul /mɔːl/ *vt* to hurt or injure (a person or animal) badly: *be mauled by a tiger.*

mau·so·leum /ˌmɔːsə'liːəm/ *nc* a large stone tomb.

mauve /məʊv/ *adj, nu* pale purple (colour).

max. *written abbr* maximum.

max·im /'mæksɪm/ *nc* a short statement offering practical advice based on experience about how to live etc, as in '*Look before you leap*'.

maxi·mize (also **-ise**) /'mæksɪmaɪz/ *vt* to make (a profit, opportunity etc) as large as possible: *maximizing educational opportunities.* Opp minimize.

maxi·mum¹ /'mæksɪməm/ *adj* (*attrib*) of the largest possible: *the maximum temperature/ number/speed.* Opp minimum.

maxi·mum² /'mæksɪməm/ *nc* (*pl* **—s**) the largest possible or recorded amount, degree etc: *a maximum of 40 passengers on the bus.* Opp minimum.

may /meɪ/ *auxiliary verb* Ⓝ '*May*' is a *modal auxiliary verb* used with another verb to express permission or possibility. '*May*' has no infinitive or imperative form and no participles. '*May*' is always followed by an infinitive without '*to*'. Compare can². (*Present* and *future* tenses (all persons): **may**; *negative* **may not**, **mayn't** /meɪnt/; after a verb in the *past tense*: **might** /maɪt/, *negative* **might not**, **mightn't** /'maɪtənt/; *might have* can be shortened to **might've** /'maɪtəv/; for special uses of might, ⇨ 2,3,5,6 below) **1** (**a**) to be allowed to; to have permission to: *You may go home when you've finished. She said I might take another one.* Ⓝ '*Can*' is also possible and is much more usual. ⇨ can²(4). '*May*' is not usually used to express a right by law to do something. Use '*can*', as in *You can vote at 18.* '*May*' is sometimes used to express a right in a particular situation, as in *You may use a dictionary in the examination.* For structures in the past perfect and passive use '*allow to*', as in *She allowed him to take her home, He wasn't allowed to visit her again.* (**b**) (used to make a formal request): *May I look at the picture again? She asked if she might look at it again.* Ⓝ '*Can*' is much more usual. ⇨ can²(6). **2** (used to express possibility): *He may/might have missed the train. Ask Mary—she may/might know. That may or may not*

be true. *If you shout they may/might hear you. She knew that she might be forced to agree. Why tell Mary?—She might tell everyone else! If you'd asked earlier we might've been able to help.* Ⓝ The examples show when to use '*may*' and '*might*'. Both are possible except after a verb in the past tense when '*might*' must be used, as in *I said I might be there.* '*Might*' is usually preferred when needing to express more doubt about a possibility. '*May/might*' are not usually used to introduce a question. Use *Do you think . . . ?* Finally, '*may/might*' is particularly useful when expressing uncertainty with an *if*-clause. Compare: *If I have the money I may/might help you* (possible but not certain) and *If I have the money I will help you* (certain). **may/might well** + *verb* (used to express probability): *Ask him—he may well* (= I am fairly certain that he will) *help you.* **3** **may/ might (just) as well** + *verb* (used to suggest that there is good reason to do something): *I may/ might as well leave tomorrow. We might just as well* (= It seems equally reasonable to) *stay where we are.* **4** (used to express a wish or hope): *May you both be very happy!* Ⓝ '*Might*' is not possible. **5** (used to express annoyance about something done or not done etc): *You might have* (= I think you ought to have and so I am annoyed) *warned me about that dog.* Ⓝ '*May*' is not possible. **6** (used in conversation) (**a**) (joined to the end of a statement to form a question): *I may have it, may I not/mayn't I? He might have come, mightn't he?* Ⓝ The short addition is always negative (e.g. *may I not?*) if the statement is positive (e.g. *I may/might*) and always positive if the statement is negative. Statements with *nobody, nothing* etc are considered to be negative. (**b**) (used to make a short answer): '*May I come in now?*'—'*No, you may not*'/'*Yes, you may.*' ⇨ can²(8).

May /meɪ/ *n* (also *attrib*) the fifth month of the year, with 31 days: *He came on 6 May.* Ⓝ '*6 May*' is spoken as '*May the sixth*' or '*the sixth of May*'.

'May Day *n* **1** May, celebrated (**a**) as a spring festival; (**b**) in some countries as a holiday in honour of the working class.

may·be /'meɪbɪ/ *adv* possibly: *Maybe it will be warmer tomorrow. Maybe I will come and maybe I won't.* Ⓝ '*Perhaps*' is also possible and is more usual in Britain except when expressing indecision as in the last example above.

mayn't /meɪnt/ = *may not.* ⇨ may.

may·on·naise /ˌmeɪə'neɪz/ *nu* a thick yellow mixture of eggs, oil etc, used on salads.

may·or /meə(r)/ *nc* a head of a city or town council.

may·or·ess /'meərɪs/ *nc* **1** a woman mayor. **2** the wife of a mayor.

maze /meɪz/ *nc* **1** a set of lines, paths etc, arranged to make it difficult to find the centre. **2** any similarly difficult route or confused state: *a maze of narrow roads; a maze of disorganized facts.*

MBE /ˌem biː 'iː/ *abbr* Member of the Order of the British Empire (an honorary award for service to the community, achievement in sport etc).

mcp /ˌem siː 'piː/ *abbr* male chauvinist pig (a derogatory name for a man who treats women as less important or intelligent than men).

MD /ˌem 'diː/ *abbr* Doctor of Medicine.

me /miː/ *personal pron* (used as the object form of

l): *He loves me. Give me the pen. Give it to me. She made the coat for me. 'Who's there?'—'It's me.'* Ⓝ *'It is I'* is a formal alternative for *'It is me'.*

mead·ow /'medəʊ/ *nc* (a field of) grassland for cows or sheep.

meagre (*US* = **mea·ger**) /'miːgə(r)/ *adj* not enough: *a meagre meal/amount.*

meagre·ly (*US* = **mea·ger·ly**) *adv*

meagre·ness (*US* = **mea·ger·ness**) *nu*

meal[1] /miːl/ *nc* **1** an occasion of eating: *three meals a day.* **a square meal** one that is big enough. **make a meal of sth** (*fig*) to do a task as if it is much more difficult than it is. **2** a selection of food eaten at one time: *I hope you enjoy your meal.*

'meal·time *nc* the usual time for eating a meal.

meal[2] /miːl/ *nu* grain made into a rough powder: *oatmeal.*

mealie /'miːlɪ/ *nu* ⇨ maize.

mealy /'miːlɪ/ *adj* (**-ier, -iest**) of, like, containing, meal[2].

,mealy-'mouthed *adj* (*derog*) (of a person) tending to avoid giving straightforward, honest explanations, answers etc.

mean[1] /miːn/ *adj* (**—er, —est**) **1** (*derog*) not generous; selfish: *Her husband is so mean about money/with his money.* **2** (*derog*) (of a person, behaviour, action etc) cruel, unkind: *Don't be so mean to your little brother. That was a mean trick! It was mean of you to take all the oranges.* **3** poor in appearance: *a mean house in a mean street.* **4** (*pred; informal*) ashamed: *I feel rather mean for not helping more.* **5** (*attrib*) of low rank or birth: *We offer justice even to the meanest citizens.* **6** (usually *attrib*) poor in quality: *This should be clear even to the meanest intelligence.*

mean·ly *adv*

mean·ness *nu*

mean[2] /miːn/ *adj* (*attrib; no comp*) occupying the middle position between two extremes: *the mean annual temperature in Malta.*

mean[3] /miːn/ *nc* **1** a condition, quality, course of action etc that is halfway between two extremes. **2** (*maths*) a term halfway between the first and the last of a series: *The mean of 2, 3 and 10 is 6.* Compare average[2](1).

mean[4] /miːn/ *vt* (*pt,pp* **meant** /ment/) Ⓝ Not used in continuous tenses, e.g. *is/was -ing* except (rarely) in 4. **1** (of words, sentences etc) to have (something) as an explanation: *A dictionary tries to tell you what words mean.* **2** (of signs, symbols etc) to represent (something): *What does that road sign mean?* **3** to be a sign of, be likely to result in, (something): *These new orders will mean working overtime.* **4** to have (something) as a purpose; intend (to do something): *What do you mean by saying that? Do you mean* (= Are you referring to) *Miss Ann Smith or Miss Angela Smith? It is a building meant for offices. Is this figure meant to be a 1 or a 7? I'm sorry if I hurt your feelings—I didn't mean to. I've been meaning to ask him but I keep on forgetting.* **mean business** ⇨ business(3). **5 be meant to** + *verb* must; be expected to: *You're meant to attend every lesson. He's not meant to clean the windows.* **6 mean sth to sb** to be of importance or value to a person: *Your friendship means a great deal to me. £20 means a lot/nothing to her.* **7 'mean**

well to have good intentions (though perhaps not the will or ability to carry them out): *His plans never work but he means well.*

mean·ing[1] /'miːnɪŋ/ *adj* (used in compounds) full of strong (e.g. good) intentions: *He's a well-meaning person.*

mean·ing[2] /'miːnɪŋ/ *n* **1** *nc* what is understood by a word, phrase etc: *What is the meaning of 'perhaps'?* **2** *nc* what is understood by a sign, symbol etc. **3** *nc* what is intended: *What is the meaning of promising to help and not helping?* Ⓝ As a question *'meaning'* is often used to show anger. **4** *nu* value: *My life has no meaning without you.*

mean·ing·ful /-fəl/ *adj* having importance or a purpose: *a meaningful look.*

mean·ing·ful·ly /-fəlɪ/ *adv*

mean·ing·less *adj* without importance or a purpose: *meaningless violence.*

me·ander /mɪ'ændə(r)/ *vi* **1** (of a river, road etc) to follow a bending and turning course. **2** (*fig*) to speak or move in a disorganized way.

means /miːnz/ *n pl* **1 means (of sth)** (often used as a *sing*, as in the examples) a method, process, by which a result may be obtained: *There is/are no means of learning what is happening. Does the end always justify the means?* (= If the aim or purpose is good, may any methods, even if bad, be used?) **by means of sth** with the help of: *Thoughts are expressed by means of words.* **by 'all means** certainly: *'Can I stay?'—'By all means.'* **by 'no means** not at all: *You're by no means prepared for the exam.* **2** money; wealth; resources: *a man of means* (= a rich man). **live beyond/within one's means** to spend more/less than one's income.

meant /ment/ *pt,pp* of mean[4].

mean·time /'miːntaɪm/ *adv, n sing* **(in the) meantime** (during the) interval between two events: *Let's have a drink in the meantime. Meantime let's listen to some music.*

mean·while /ˌmiːn'waɪl/ *adv* during the time between (e.g. while waiting): *Meanwhile let's discuss tomorrow's walk.*

measles /'miːzlz/ *nu* (used with a *sing* verb) an infectious disease, with fever and small red spots that cover the whole body.

meas·ly /'miːzlɪ/ *adj* (**-ier, -iest**) (*informal; derog*) of little value; of poor quality; of small size or amount: *What a measly helping of ice-cream!*

meas·ure[1] /'meʒə(r)/ *n* **1** *nc,nu* the size, quantity, degree, mass etc as found by a standard or unit: *a small measure of salt; give her a measure of freedom.* **beyond measure** very big: *Her joy was beyond measure.* **made to measure** (of articles of clothing) specially made for a person after taking measurements. **2** *nc* a standard or system used in stating size, quantity or degree: *metric measure.* **3** *nc* an instrument or device used to find size, quantity etc. **4** *nc* an action used to obtain a particular result: *They took strong measures against dangerous drivers.* **5 for good measure** **(a)** in addition: *add another egg for good measure.* **(b)** as an extra action to avoid possible failure etc: *put on an extra layer of glue for good measure.*

meas·ure[2] /'meʒə(r)/ *vt* **1** to find the size, mass, amount, etc of (a person, thing): *measure an area of ground/the strength of an electric current/ the* *size of the floor.* **2** to be (the length etc mentioned): *This room measures 10 metres across.* **3 measure sth out** to take or mark a measured quantity of something: *measure out a dose of medicine.*

meas·ur·able *adj* that is noticeable: *a measurable difference.* Compare immeasurable.

meas·ured *adj* (*formal*) (of language) carefully chosen: *measured words.*

measure·ment *n* (**a**) *nu* the process, system, of measuring: *the metric system of measurement.* (**b**) (*pl*) a result of measuring(1): *the measurements of a room.*

meat /miːt/ *nu* **1** the flesh of animals used as food. (N) *'Meat'* usually refers to cattle, sheep etc (*red meat*) but is also used for chickens, ducks etc (*white meat*) and sometimes the flesh of fish. **2** (*fig*) useful or suitable contents: *There's not much meat in his argument.*

'meat·ball *nc* a small ball of minced meat.

meaty /'miːtɪ/ *adj* (**-ier, -iest**) (*fig*) full of facts, interest: *a meaty story.*

mech. *written abbr* mechanic; mechanical.

mech·an·ic /mɪ'kænɪk/ *nc* a skilled workman, esp one who repairs or adjusts machinery: *a motor mechanic.*

mech·an·ical /mɪ'kænɪkl/ *adj* **1** of, connected with, produced by, machines: *mechanical engineering.* **2** (of a person, action) done like machines (as if) without thought: *mechanical movements.*

mech·an·ical·ly /-klɪ/ *adv*

mech·an·ics /mɪ'kænɪks/ *n* **1** (usually used with a *sing verb*) the science of motion and force; science of machinery: *Mechanics is taught by Mr Hill.* **2** (*pl*) (the method of) organizing and producing something: *the mechanics of writing plays.*

mech·an·ism /'mekənɪzəm/ *nc* **1** the structure or arrangement of parts that work together (as the parts of a machine do): *the mechanism of a clock.* **2** the way in which something works or is constructed: *the mechanism of the heart/of government.*

mech·an·ize (also **-ise**) /'mekənaɪz/ *vt* to use machines to carry out (a task) (and not people): *mechanized farming.*

mech·an·iz·ation (also **-is·ation**) /ˌmekənaɪ-'zeɪʃn/ *nu*

med·al /'medl/ *nc* a flat piece of metal given as an award for a brave act, a sports achievement etc: *win a gold/silver/bronze medal.*

med·al·list (*US* = **med·alist**) /'medəlɪst/ *nc* a person who has been awarded a medal, e.g. for achievement in sport: *a gold medallist.*

me·dal·lion /mɪ'dælɪən/ *nc* a large medal used as decoration.

meddle /'medl/ *vi* **meddle (in sth; with sb/ sth)** to become involved without being asked to do so; interfere: *Don't meddle in my affairs. Who's been meddling with my papers?*

med·dler *nc* a person who meddles.

'meddle·some /-səm/ *adj* (*derog*) (of a person) in the habit of meddling.

me·dia /'miːdɪə/ *n pl* (the —) (sometimes used with a *sing verb*) television, radio, newspapers, magazines etc as used to give information to everyone. ⇨ mass media.

medi·aeval /ˌmedɪ'iːvl/ = medieval.

me·di·ate /'miːdɪeɪt/ *v* **1** *vi* **mediate (be-**

tween sb and sb; in sth) to act to obtain agreement: *mediating between the workers and management; mediate in a dispute.* **2** *vt* (*formal*) to produce (something) as a result by doing this: *mediating a wage settlement.*

me·dia·tion /ˌmiːdɪ'eɪʃn/ *nu*

me·dia·tor /-tə(r)/ *nc* a person who mediates.

medi·cal¹ /'medɪkl/ *adj* (*attrib*) **1** of, concerning, the treatment of disease: *a medical practitioner* (= a doctor); *a medical school.* **2** of the use of medicine (contrasted with *surgery*): *The hospital has a medical ward and a surgical ward.*

medi·cal·ly /-klɪ/ *adv*

medi·cal² /'medɪkl/ *nc* an examination of the body to check health.

medi·cated /'medɪkeɪtɪd/ *adj* (*no comp*) filled with a medicinal substance: *medicated soap.*

medi·ca·tion /ˌmedɪ'keɪʃn/ *nc,nu* (any kind of) medicine or ointment.

med·ici·nal /mɪ'dɪsɪnl/ *adj* able to heal or cure: *medicinal preparations; for medicinal use.*

medi·cine /'medsɪn/ *n* **1** *nu* the science of the prevention and cure of disease. **2** *nc,nu* (any kind of) substance used to treat disease, esp a pill or liquid that is drunk: *a medicine box; medicine for headaches.* **3** *nu* (*fig*) deserved punishment: *He took his medicine well.*

medi·eval (also **medi·aeval**) /ˌmedɪ'iːvl/ *adj* of the period in Europe between 1100 and 1500: *medieval history.*

me·di·ocre /ˌmiːdɪ'əʊkə(r)/ *adj* (*derog*) not very good: *a mediocre performance.*

me·di·oc·rity /ˌmiːdɪ'ɒkrətɪ/ *nc,nu*

medi·tate /'medɪteɪt/ *vi* **meditate (about/on sth)** to (fix one's attention on something and) think seriously and deeply (about it): *meditating about/on world peace.*

medi·ta·tion /ˌmedɪ'teɪʃn/ *nc,nu* the process, result, of meditating: *deep in meditation.*

me·di·um¹ /'miːdɪəm/ *adj* (usually *attrib*) of middle size, quality etc: *be of medium weight/ height; a medium-sized business company.*

'medium wave *nc,nu* (*radio*) a radio wave between 100 and 1000 metres in length.

me·di·um² /'miːdɪəm/ *nc* (*pl* **—s** or **media** /'miːdɪə/ for 1,2) **1** that by which something is expressed: *Commercial television is a medium for advertising.* ⇨ media. **2** a substance, surrounding, in which something exists or moves: *Air is the medium of sound.* **3** a person who claims to be able to speak to dead people. **4** (*sing* only) a middle degree, quality, size etc: *the medium between being hot and being cold.*

med·ley /'medlɪ/ *nc* (*pl* **—s**) a mixture of pieces of musical, people, ideas, styles etc: *a musical medley; the 400 metres medley* (= a swimming race where each swimmer uses a different style).

meek /miːk/ *adj* (**—er, —est**) gentle and patient: *as meek as a lamb* (= very meek).

meek·ly *adv*

meek·ness *nu*

meet¹ /miːt/ *nc* a gathering of people, esp on horses to go after a fox.

meet² /miːt/ *v* (*pt,pp* **met** /met/) **1** *vt,vi* (of people) to come together from different places by arrangement or by accident: *We met in the street. Let's meet for lunch. I'll meet you at 6 o'clock by the post office. The society meets every Tuesday* *evening. We met (each other) at a party and have been friends ever since.* **meet up (with sb)** to come together, esp after separating: *We all met up at midnight. They met up with the others later in the afternoon.* **2** *vt,vi* (of roads, rivers, areas of land, colours, lines etc) to come into contact: *The two paths meet at the bottom of the hill. There's a row of trees where the field meets the river. Mark on the diagram where the two lines meet.* **make (both) ends meet** ⇨ end¹(1). **3** *vt* to be present at the arrival of (a traveller, bus etc): *meet the train from Madrid. I'll meet you off the 8 o'clock bus.* **4** *vt,vi* to be introduced to (and get to know) (a person): *I know Mrs Hill by sight but we've never met. Come and meet my mother. I'm very pleased to meet you.* **5** *vt,vi* to oppose (a person, team) in a sports event: *They met in the semifinals.* **6** *vi* **meet with sth** to experience something bad: *meet with an accident.* **7** *vt* to do something to satisfy (a demand etc): *meet his wishes/ the required standard/all the expenses.* **meet sb halfway** (*fig*) to give up certain demands in order to reach agreement.

meet·ing /'miːtɪŋ/ *nc* **1** a coming together of a number of people at a certain time and place, esp for discussion: *political meetings.* **call a meeting** to say one will be held and organize it. **2** any coming together for a purpose: *a race meeting; a sports meeting.*

'meeting-place *nc* a place fixed for a meeting.

mega·cycle /'megəsaɪkl/ *nc* the old name for megahertz.

mega·hertz ('megəhɜːts) *nc* (*pl* —) (symbol MHz) (*science*) a unit of frequency equal to one million hertz or cycles (of changes of current) per second.

mega·lo·ma·nia /ˌmegələ'meɪnɪə/ *nu* a mental illness in which a person has exaggerated ideas of her or his importance, power, wealth etc.

mega·lo·ma·ni·ac /-nɪæk/ *nc* a person suffering from megalomania.

mega·phone /'megəfəʊn/ *nc* a device used for making a voice louder.

mega·ton /'megətʌn/ *nc* a measurement of explosive force equal to one million tons of TNT.

mel·an·chol·ic /ˌmelən'kɒlɪk/ *adj*, (*formal*) (of a person) suffering from melancholy.

mel·an·choly /'melənkəlɪ/ *adj, nu* (*formal*) sad(ness), esp often or for long periods.

mel·low¹ /'meləʊ/ *adj* (—er, —est) **1** soft and sweet in taste: *mellow wine.* **2** soft, pure, rich in colour or sound: *mellow tones; a mellow orange.*

mel·low·ness *nu*

mel·low² /'meləʊ/ *vt,vi* (to cause a taste, feeling ·etc) to become less strong: *The sound/taste has mellowed. His apology helped to mellow her/her anger.*

mel·od·ic /mɪ'lɒdɪk/ *adj* of, having, melody; melodious: *melodic poetry.*

mel·odi·ous /mɪ'ləʊdɪəs/ *adj* (*formal*) sounding tuneful: *melodious music.*

mel·odi·ous·ly *adv*

melo·drama /'melədrɑːmə/ *n* **1** *nc* (*literature*) a play, film etc with a romantic plot that appeals strongly to one's emotions in an exaggerated or sensational way. **2** *nc,nu* feeling, behaviour etc that is exaggerated in the same way: *She turns every small difficulty into (a) melodrama.*

melo·dram·at·ic /ˌmelədrə'mætɪk/ *adj*

melo·dram·ati·cal·ly /-klɪ/ *adv*

mel·ody /'melədɪ/ *nc* (*pl* **-ies**) **1** a simple song or tune: *old Irish melodies.* **2** a tuneful section or theme in music: *The melody is next taken up by the flutes.*

mel·on /'melən/ *nc* (any kind of) a large round fruit with a soft, sweet flesh and many seeds (called *pips*).

melt /melt/ *vt,vi* **1** (to cause ice etc) to become liquid through heating: *Snow melts when the sun shines.* **2** *vi* (of soft food) to dissolve, be softened, easily: *This cake melts in the mouth.* **3** *vt,vi* (to cause a person etc) to become (more) sympathetic: *She/Her heart melted with pity.*

melt away to become less; disappear (as if) by melting: *The snow soon melted away when the sun came up. Her fears melted away.*

melt sth down to reduce metal objects such as jewelry to ordinary metal by heating.

melt into sth to fade slowly and become something: *One colour melted into another.*

mem·ber /'membə(r)/ *nc* **1** a person belonging to a group, society etc: *Every member of her family came to her wedding. I've become a member of the swimming club.* **2** (*old use*) a part of a human or animal body.

,Member of 'Parliament *nc* (*abbr* MP) an elected representative in the House of Commons.

'mem·ber·ship *n* (**a**) *nu* the state of being a member (of a society etc): *agree to her membership of the society.* (**b**) *nc* a number of members: *The club has a membership of 80.*

mem·brane /'membreɪn/ *nc* (*science*) a soft, thin layer of (skin) tissue or covering.

mem·bra·nous /'membrənəs/ *adj*

mem·en·to /mɪ'mentəʊ/ *nc* (*pl* **—s** or **—es**) something that reminds one of a person or event: *We bought a picture as a memento of our visit.*

memo /'meməʊ/ *nc* (*pl* **—s**) (abbr for) memorandum.

mem·oirs /'memwɑːz/ *n pl* a person's written account of her or his own life or experiences: *my memoirs as a disc jockey.*

mem·or·able /'memrəbl/ *adj* deserving to be remembered because special: *a memorable occasion.*

mem·or·ably /-əblɪ/ *adv*

mem·or·an·dum /ˌmemə'rændəm/ *nc* (*pl* **-da** /-də/ or **—s**) (abbr memo) an informal business communication.

mem·or·ial /mɪ'mɔːrɪəl/ *nc* **1** something built to remind people of an event, person etc: *a war memorial.* **2** something that reminds people of a person, event etc: *a song written as a memorial to his work for the poor.* ⇨ also immemorial.

mem·or·ize (also **-ise**) /'meməraɪz/ *vt* to learn and remember (something) deliberately: *memorizing a speech.*

mem·ory /'memrɪ/ *n* (*pl* **-ies**) **1** *nc,nu* (an) ability to keep facts in the conscious mind and to recall them at will: *have a poor/good memory for names.* **from memory** using what one has remembered: *play a tune from memory.* **in memory of sb** so that a person will be remembered: *We planted a tree in memory of our friend who died in a car accident.* **to the best of my memory** as far as I can remember: *To the best of* *my memory he was wearing a blue jacket.* **in/ within living memory** during the period that people alive now can remember: *the worst disaster in living memory.* **commit sth to memory** to learn and remember it. **refresh one's/sb's memory** to help oneself/a person to remember. **2** *nc* something remembered: *memories of childhood.* **3** *nc* (*computers*) the part of a computer in which information is stored.

men /men/ *n pl* of **man¹**.

men·ace¹ /'menəs/ *nc* **menace (to sb/sth)** a danger; threat: *a menace to world peace. That woman is a menace* (= is a nuisance).

men·ace² /'menəs/ *vt* (often *passive*) (*formal*) to be a threat to (something): *countries menaced by/ with war.*

men·ac·ing *adj* looking able to harm: *menacing weapons/looks/clouds.*

men·ac·ing·ly *adv*

men·ag·erie /mɪ'nædʒərɪ/ *nc* a collection of wild animals in captivity.

mend¹ /mend/ *nc* a damaged or torn part that has been mended: *The mends were almost invisible.* **on the mend** (of a person) improving in health.

mend² /mend/ *v* **1** *vt* to remake, repair, (something broken, worn out or torn); restore (something) to good condition or working order: *mend shoes/a broken window.* **mend one's ways** ⇨ **way²(3)**. **2** *vi* to become healthy again: *Her leg is mending nicely.*

'mend·ing *nu* (**a**) things to be repaired: *Your sock is with the other mending.* (**b**) an act of mending(1): *the mending of a sock.*

men·da·cious /men'deɪʃəs/ *adj* (*formal*) untruthful: *mendacious newspaper reports.*

men·dac·ity /men'dæsətɪ/ *nu* (*formal*) untruthfulness; a tendency to be untruthful.

me·ni·al /'miːnɪəl/ *adj* not important or interesting: *menial tasks such as washing pots and pans.*

me·ni·al·ly /-ɪəlɪ/ *adv*

men·in·gi·tis /ˌmenɪn'dʒaɪtɪs/ *nu* a serious illness with inflammation of the brain or spinal cord.

meno·pause /'menəpɔːz/ *nu* a gradual stopping of a woman's monthly bleeding after about 45 years of age.

men·ses /'mensiːz/ *n pl* (*science*) a woman's monthly bleeding.

men·stru·al /'menstrʊəl/ *adj* of the menses: *menstrual bleeding.*

men·stru·ate /'menstrʊeɪt/ *vi* (*formal*) (of a woman) to bleed (from the *uterus*) every month.

men·stru·ation /ˌmenstrʊ'eɪʃn/ *nu*

men·tal /'mentl/ *adj* (*attrib*) **1** of, in, the mind: *a mental illness.* **2** (for people) suffering from an illness of the mind: *a mental patient/hospital.*

ˌmental a'rithmetic *nu* done in the mind without using written figures or a calculator.

ˌmental 'health *nu* the general condition of the mind.

'mental home/hospital *nc* one for mental patients.

ˌmental 'illness *nc, nu* (an) illness of the mind.

men·tal·ly /'mentəlɪ/ *adv*

ˌmentally 'ill *n pl* (the —) people with mental illness.

men·tal·ity /men'tælətɪ/ *n* (*pl* -**ies**) **1** *nu* the general intellectual character; degree of intellec-

tual power: *persons of average mentality.* **2** *nc* an attitude of mind: *a war mentality.*

men·thol /'menθɒl/ *nu* a solid white substance obtained from oil of peppermint, used medically and as a flavouring.

men·tho·lated /'menθəleɪtɪd/ *adj*

men·tion¹ /'menʃn/ *nc,nu* (an act of) mentioning or naming something: *He made no mention of your request.*

men·tion² /'menʃn/ *vt* to speak or write something about (a person, thing): *I'll mention it to him. I mentioned that you'd like to see her. Did I hear my name mentioned?* **Don't mention it** (used to show that thanks, an apology etc are welcome but unnecessary). **not to mention . . .** (*conj*) and also: *He has a huge house, not to mention his three cars.* ⇨ above-mentioned.

men·tor /'mentɔː(r)/ *nc* a wise and trusted adviser and helper.

menu /'menjuː/ *nc* **1** a list of meals that are available in a restaurant: *Is fish on the menu?* **2** (*computers*) a list of choices in a program to help the user find the information or facility required.

mer·can·tile /'mɜːkəntaɪl/ *adj* of trade, commerce and merchants.

ˌmercantile ma'rine *nc* a country's ships and seamen used in trade and commerce.

mer·cen·ary¹ /'mɜːsənrɪ/ *adj* (*derog*) working only for money or power: *mercenary politicians; act from mercenary motives.*

mer·cen·ary² /'mɜːsənrɪ/ *nc* (*pl* -**ies**) a soldier paid to serve in a foreign army.

mer·chan·dise /'mɜːtʃəndaɪz/ *nu* (*commerce*) goods bought and sold. □ *vt* to buy and sell (goods).

mer·chant /'mɜːtʃənt/ *nc* a person, business that buys and sells goods: *a wine merchant.*

ˌmerchant 'bank *nc* a bank that accepts foreign bills and lends money to businesses.

mer·ci·ful /'mɜːsɪful/ *adj* having, showing, mercy: *a merciful captain.*

mer·ci·ful·ly /-flɪ/ *adv*

mer·ci·less /'mɜːsɪlɪs/ *adj* (*derog*) having, showing or feeling no mercy: *merciless terrorists.*

mer·ci·less·ly *adv*

mer·cur·ial /mɜː'kjʊərɪəl/ *adj* (*formal*) (of a person) often changing (in opinion, temper etc).

mer·cury /'mɜːkjʊrɪ/ *nu* a heavy, silver metal (symbol Hg) usually liquid, as used in thermometers and barometers.

Mer·cury /'mɜːkjʊrɪ/ *n* the planet nearest the sun.

mer·cy /'mɜːsɪ/ *n* (*pl* -**ies**) **1** *nu* (the show of) willingness to forgive, not cause suffering, not punish severely: *We were given no mercy. He threw himself on my mercy* (= begged me not to punish him). **at the mercy of sb/sth** in the power of a person, thing: *The ship was at the mercy of the waves.* **2** *nc* a piece of good fortune; something to be thankful for: *It's a mercy that you were not killed. We must be thankful for small mercies.*

mere /mɪə(r)/ *adj* (*no comp*, but *the merest* can be used for emphasis) not more than: *She's a mere child. It's a mere/the merest trifle* (= nothing at all important, nothing of any value). ⇨ formality.

mere·ly *adv* only; simply: *I merely asked his name. I said it merely as a joke.*

merge /mɜːdʒ/ v **1** vt,vi **merge (with sth) (into sth)** (to cause business companies) to become one unit: *The small banks merged/were merged into one large organization.* **2** vi **merge into sth (a)** to fade or change gradually into something: *Twilight was merging into darkness.* **(b)** to become part of something else: *The thief soon merged into the crowds of shoppers.*

merger nc a merging(1) of business companies.

mer·id·ian /məˈrɪdɪən/ nc (either half of) an imaginary line round the earth, passing through the north and south poles, as used on maps.

me·ringue /məˈræŋ/ nc,nu (a cake of) whites of egg mixed with sugar and baked.

mer·it[1] /ˈmerɪt/ n **1** nu the quality or fact of deserving approval or praise: *a certificate of merit.* **2** nc a fact, action etc that deserves reward (or, less often, punishment): *We must decide the case on its merits* (i.e. according to the facts without being influenced by personal feelings).

mer·it[2] /ˈmerɪt/ vt to deserve, be worthy of, (something): *merit reward.*

meri·toc·ra·cy /ˌmerɪˈtɒkrəsɪ/ nc (pl **-ies**) (a system of government or control by) people with the best practical or intellectual ability.

meri·tori·ous /ˌmerɪˈtɔːrɪəs/ adj (formal) deserving praise or reward: *a prize for meritorious conduct.*

mer·maid /ˈmɜːmeɪd/ nc (in stories) a woman with a fish's tail in place of legs.

mer·ry /ˈmerɪ/ adj (-ier, -iest) **1** happy; cheerful; bright and gay: *a merry laugh. I wish you a merry Christmas.* **2** (informal) having had a little too much alcoholic drink.

'merry-go-round nc a revolving machine with horses etc on which children ride at funfairs.

mer·ri·ly /ˈmerəlɪ/ adv

mer·ri·ment /ˈmerɪmənt/ nu

mesh[1] /meʃ/ n **1** nu (a piece of) material with holes between the threads: *wire mesh.* **2** (pl) a network of threads: *the meshes of a spider's web.*

mesh[2] /meʃ/ vi **mesh (with sth)** (of wheels, organized parts; opinions) to connect, be connected: *Do the gears in the car mesh easily?* ⇨ synchromesh.

mess[1] /mes/ nc a place for soldiers to have their meals.

mess[2] /mes/ nc (used with a, an, but rarely pl) **1** a state of confusion, dirt or disorder: *The workmen cleaned up the mess before they left. The accounts are (in) a mess.* **make a mess of sth (a)** to do a task badly: *make a mess of one's exams.* **(b)** to cause something to be spoiled: *You've made a mess of my holiday.* **2** (informal) an untidy, dirty person: *My son looks a mess.*

messy adj (-ier, -iest) dirty; in a state of disorder: *a messy job; look messy.*

mess[3] /mes/ vt to make (clothes, hair etc) dirty: *mess one's new dress; mess her hair.*

mess about/around to pass one's time without any plan, purpose etc: *messing about in London for a few days.* **mess about/around (with sth)** to work (with tools, materials etc) in a thoughtless or careless way: *Don't mess about with fire.* **mess sb about/around** to interfere with the arrangements or plans of a person; to treat a person roughly.

mess sth up (a) to make clothes, a piece of

work etc untidy or dirty. **(b)** to do a task, exam etc badly: *mess up a painting.*

mess with sb (informal) to become involved with the police, a senior official etc in a way that annoys or that will get one into trouble. **mess with sth** to use something carelessly: *Don't mess with dangerous drugs.*

mess·age /ˈmesɪdʒ/ nc **1** a piece of news or a request sent to a person: *Will you take this message to my brother?* **2** the reason, central idea, (for an action, in a piece of writing etc): *What is the message in the story? How can I get my message across?*

mess·en·ger /ˈmesɪndʒə(r)/ nc a person carrying a message(1).

Mess·iah /məˈsaɪə/ n (the —) (in Christianity) Jesus Christ.

Messrs /ˈmesəz/ abbr (commerce) pl of Mr, esp in the names of companies: *a letter from Messrs Brighter Paints.*

met /met/ pt,pp of meet[2].

me·tab·ol·ism /mɪˈtæbəlɪzəm/ nu the chemical processes in living things producing energy, growth etc.

meta·bol·ic /ˌmetəˈbɒlɪk/ adj

meta·car·pal /ˌmetəˈkɑːpl/ adj, nc (anat) (of) a bone in the hand.

met·al /ˈmetl/ nc,nu any mineral substance such as tin, iron, gold and copper that can be used to make things. *Is it made of wood or metal?*

me·tal·lic /mɪˈtælɪk/ adj of, like, metal: *metallic sounds.*

met·al·lur·gy /ˈmetələːdʒɪ/ nu the scientific study of obtaining and using metals.

meta·mor·pho·sis /ˌmetəˈmɔːfəsɪs/ nc (pl **-pho·ses** /-siːz/) a complete change of form, e.g. by natural growth or development: *the metamorphosis in the life of an insect* (i.e. from the egg to the adult).

meta·phor /ˈmetəfə(r)/ nc,nu (lang) (an example of) the use of words (figure of speech) to express an idea by comparing one thing with another (without using 'like' or 'as'), to show a similarity, as in *She was a feather* (i.e. weighed very little) *in his arms.* Compare simile.

meta·phori·cal /ˌmetəˈfɒrɪkl/ adj

meta·phori·cal·ly /-klɪ/ adv

meta·phys·ic·al /ˌmetəˈfɪzɪkl/ adj **1** based on thought and reasoning: *metaphysical philosophy.* **2** (literature) (of poetry) intellectual and psychological, usually about themes such as love, religion and death.

meta·phys·ics /ˌmetəˈfɪzɪks/ nu the scientific study of existence and thought.

meta·tar·sal /ˌmetəˈtɑːsl/ adj, nc (anat) (of) a bone in the foot.

mete /miːt/ vt **mete sth out** (formal) to give punishment etc out (in portions): *Justice was meted out to them.*

me·teor /ˈmiːtɪə(r)/ nc a small body coming from outer space into the earth's atmosphere and becoming bright (as a *shooting star*) as it is burnt up.

me·teor·ic /ˌmiːtɪˈɒrɪk/ adj **1** of, like, of meteors. **2** (fig) fast and astonishing: *a meteoric rise to fame.*

me·teor·ite /ˈmiːtɪəraɪt/ nc a meteor that has landed on the earth.

me·teoro·logi·cal /ˌmiːtɪərəˈlɒdʒɪkl/ *adj* of meteorology.

me·teor·ol·ogist /ˌmiːtɪəˈrɒlədʒɪst/ *nc* an expert in meteorology.

me·teor·ol·ogy /ˌmiːtɪəˈrɒlədʒɪ/ *nu* the scientific study of the weather.

me·ter¹ /ˈmiːtə(r)/ *nc* an apparatus which measures the amount of whatever passes through it, the distance travelled, fare payable etc: *an electricity meter; a parking-meter.*

me·ter² /ˈmiːtə(r)/ *n* (*US*) = metre.

meth·od /ˈmeθəd/ *n* **1** *nc* a way of doing something: *modern methods of teaching arithmetic.* **2** *nc,nu* an organized system of doing or arranging something: *computer methods.*

meth·odi·cal /mɪˈθɒdɪkl/ *adj* **1** using order or method: *methodical work.* **2** using careful and organized methods: *a methodical worker.*
meth·odi·cal·ly /-klɪ/ *adv*

Meth·od·ism /ˈmeθədɪzəm/ *n* (belief in) the Christian faith and practices started by John Wesley (1703–91).

Meth·od·ist /-ɪst/ *adj, nc* (of) a believer in, supporter of, Methodism.

meth·od·ol·ogy /ˌmeθəˈdɒlədʒɪ/ *nu* the system of methods used, e.g. in academic study.

meths /meθs/ *nu* = methylated spirits.

meth·yl·ated spirits /ˌmeθɪleɪtɪd ˈspɪrɪts/ *nu* (informal *meths*) a form of alcohol as a violet liquid, used for lighting and heating.

me·ticu·lous /mɪˈtɪkjʊləs/ *adj* giving, showing, great care and attention to detail.
me·ticu·lous·ly *adv*

metre¹ (*US* = **me·ter**) /ˈmiːtə(r)/ *nc* a unit of measurement of length in the metric system.

metre² (*US* = **me·ter**) /ˈmiːtə(r)/ *nc,nu* (*literature*) rhythm in poetry formed by a pattern of stressed and unstressed syllables.

met·ric /ˈmetrɪk/ *adj* of metre¹.
metric 'mile *nc* (*athletics*) a race of 1500 metres.
'metric system *n* (the —) the decimal measuring system based on the metre as the unit of length, the kilogram as the unit of mass and the litre as the unit of capacity.
metri·ca·tion /ˌmetrɪˈkeɪʃn/ *nu* conversion to the metric system.
metric 'ton *nc* = tonne.

met·ro·nome /ˈmetrənəʊm/ *nc* (*music*) an instrument used to give the speed for playing music.

me·trop·olis /məˈtrɒpəlɪs/ *nc* (*pl* **—es**) a chief city of a country; capital city (which is more usual).

met·ro·poli·tan¹ /ˌmetrəˈpɒlɪtən/ *adj* of a capital city: *the metropolitan police.*

met·ro·poli·tan² /ˌmetrəˈpɒlɪtən/ *nc* a person who lives in a large city (often suggesting that he or she is therefore experienced in the energy and variety of city life).

mettle /ˈmetl/ *nu* (*formal*) courage: *a man of mettle.* **be on one's mettle; put sb on her/his mettle** to be/put her or him in a position that tests courage and will-power.

mew /mjuː/ *nc, vi* = miaow.

mez·za·nine /ˈmetsəniːn/ *adj, nc* (of) a floor between the ground floor and first floor.

mg *symbol* milligram(s).

MHz *symbol* megahertz.

MI5 /ˌem aɪ ˈfaɪv/ *abbr* Military Intelligence, Department 5 (GB; responsible for counter-espionage).

MI6 /ˌem aɪ ˈsɪks/ *abbr* Military Intelligence, Department 6 (GB; responsible for espionage).

mi·aow /miːˈaʊ/ *nc* the sound made by a cat. □ *vi* to make this sound.

mice /maɪs/ *n pl* of mouse.

mi·cro /ˈmaɪkrəʊ/ *nc* a microcomputer.

mi·crobe /ˈmaɪkrəʊb/ *nc* any very small creature, esp one causing disease.

mi·cro·chip /ˈmaɪkrəʊtʃɪp/ *nc* a very small electronic chip¹(5).

mi·cro·cir·cuit /ˈmaɪkrəʊsɜːkɪt/ *nc* a very small electronic circuit as used in a microchip.

mi·cro·com·pu·ter /ˈmaɪkrəʊkəmpjuːtə(r)/ *nc* any kind of computerized system using very small parts.

mi·cro·cosm /ˈmaɪkrəkɒzəm/ *nc* something considered as representing on a small scale a larger or complex system. ⇨ macrocosm.

mi·cro·dot /ˈmaɪkrəʊdɒt/ *nc* a photograph that is no bigger than the head of a pin.

mi·cro·elec·tron·ics /ˌmaɪkrəʊ ˌɪlekˈtrɒnɪks/ *n* (used with a *sing verb*) electronic equipment of a very small size.

mi·cro·fiche /ˈmaɪkrəʊfiːʃ/ *nc* a piece of microfilm.

mi·cro·film /ˈmaɪkrəʊfɪlm/ *nc,nu* (a section of) very small photographic film.

mi·crom·eter /maɪˈkrɒmɪtə(r)/ *nc* an instrument for measuring very small objects.

mi·cron /ˈmaɪkrɒn/ *nc* (*science*) a unit of length (symbol μ) equal to one millionth of a metre.

mi·cro·phone /ˈmaɪkrəfəʊn/ *nc* an instrument for increasing the volume of sound, as in telephones, radio etc.

mi·cro·pro·ces·sor /ˌmaɪkrəʊˈprəʊsesə(r)/ *nc* (*computers*) a type of small computer that can be programmed to do different things.

mi·cro·scope /ˈmaɪkrəskəʊp/ *nc* an instrument for making very small objects appear larger.

mi·cro·scop·ic /ˌmaɪkrəˈskɒpɪk/ *adj* very small.
mi·cro·scopi·cal·ly /-klɪ/ *adv*

mi·cro·wave /ˈmaɪkrəʊweɪv/ *nc* a very short wave (as used in radio and radar).

microwave (oven) *nc* a type of oven using microwaves to cook or heat food very quickly.

mid /mɪd/ *adj* (*no comp*) in the middle of; middle: *from mid June to mid August; in mid winter.*

mid·day¹ /ˈmɪddeɪ/ *adj* (*attrib*) at 12 o'clock in the day: *the midday meal.* Compare midnight.

mid·day² /ˌmɪdˈdeɪ/ *nu* 12 o'clock in the day. Compare midnight.

middle¹ /ˈmɪdl/ *adj* (*attrib*) at the centre: *the middle house in the row.*

middle² /ˈmɪdl/ *n* **1** (the —) the point, position or part which is at an equal distance from two or more points etc or between the beginning and the end: *the middle of a room. They were in the middle of dinner* (= were having dinner) *when I called.* **2** *nc* (*informal*) the waist: *holding her round her/the middle.*

middle 'age *nu* the period between youth and old age. Hence **middle-'aged** *adj: He's middle-aged/a middle-aged man.*

Middle 'Ages *n* (the —) the period in European

history from about AD 1100 to 1400 (or, in a wider sense, AD 600—1500). ⇨ medieval.

middle 'class n (the —) the class of society between the lower and upper classes (e.g. businessmen, professional workers). Hence **middle-'class** adj: middle-class voters.

Middle 'East n (the —) the countries from Egypt to Iran.

'middle·man nc any trader who buys goods from a producer and sells them.

middle 'name nc the second of two given names, e.g. Bernard in George Bernard Shaw.

'middle·weight nc (also attrib) a boxer weighing between 154 and 160 lb (70 and 72·5 kg).

mid·dling /'mɪdlɪŋ/ adj (informal) of average size, quality, grade etc: a town of middling size.

midge /mɪdʒ/ nc a small, winged insect .

midg·et¹ /'mɪdʒɪt/ adj (attrib) very small: a midget camera.

midg·et² /'mɪdʒɪt/ nc (do not use) an extremely short person.

mid·night¹ /'mɪdnaɪt/ adj (attrib) at 12 o'clock in the night: a midnight swim. Compare midday.

mid·night² /'mɪdnaɪt/ nc 12 o'clock in the night: at/before/after midnight. Compare midday.

mid·riff /'mɪdrɪf/ nc the part of the front of the body above the waist.

midst /mɪdst/ n (literary; old use) the middle part: in the midst of the battle.

mid·sum·mer /'mɪdsʌmə(r)/ nu (also attrib) the middle of summer: midsummer day.

midsummer 'day n 24 June.

mid·way /ˌmɪd'weɪ/ adj, adv in the middle (of a length, distance, speed etc). **midway between** halfway between.

mid·week /'mɪdwiːk/ adj (attrib), n (in) the middle of the week: a midweek visit.

mid·wife /'mɪdwaɪf/ nc (pl midwives /-waɪvz/) a professional woman who helps a woman during childbirth.

mid·wifery /'mɪdwɪfərɪ/ nu the profession and work of a midwife.

mid·winter /'mɪdwɪntə(r)/ nu (also attrib) the middle of the winter: a midwinter evening.

might¹ /maɪt/ nu great effort, power; strength: work with all one's might. **with (all one's) might and main** making every possible effort.

might² /maɪt/ auxiliary verb Ⓝ 'Might' is a modal auxiliary verb used with another verb to express permission or possibility. 'Might' has no infinitive or imperative form and no participles. 'Might' is always followed by an infinitive without 'to'. ⇨ may (esp 2,3,5,6).

mightn't /'maɪtənt/ = might not. ⇨ may.

might've /'maɪtəv/ = might have. ⇨ may.

mighty¹ /'maɪtɪ/ adj (-ier, -iest) 1 having great power: a mighty nation. 2 (literary) large: the mighty ocean. 3 **high and mighty** ⇨ high¹(8).

might·ily /-əlɪ/ adv

mighty² /'maɪtɪ/ adv (informal) very: think oneself mighty clever.

mi·graine /'miːgreɪn/ nc a very strong headache.

mi·grant /'maɪgrənt/ nc a person who, bird which, migrates. ⇨ emigrant, immigrant.

mi·grate /maɪ'greɪt/ vi **migrate (from/to a place)** 1 (of birds and fish) to go to another part of the world regularly each year. 2 (of people) to move regularly from one place to another (to live

there). ⇨ emigrate, immigrate.

mi·gra·tion /maɪ'greɪʃn/ nc,nu

mi·gra·tory /'maɪgrətrɪ/ adj having the habit of migrating: migratory birds.

mike /maɪk/ nc (informal) = microphone.

mild /maɪld/ adj (—er, —est) 1 gentle; not severe: mild weather; a mild answer/punishment/ temper. 2 (of food, drink etc) not sharp or strong in taste or flavour: mild cheese/cigars.

mild·ly adv in a gentle manner.

mild·ness nu

mil·dew¹ /'mɪldjuː/ nu a disease causing a white cover on plants, leather, food etc in warm and damp conditions.

mil·dew² /'mɪldjuː/ vt,vi (to cause plants, leather, food etc) to become covered with mildew.

mile /maɪl/ nc 1 a unit of measurement of distance equal to 1760 yards or 1609 metres: He ran the mile in under 4 minutes. My car can do 40 miles to the gallon. ⇨ metric/nautical mile. **a mile off** a long way away and clearly and obviously: see/ hear/recognize her a mile off. **run a mile** to be careful to avoid a person, thing: run a mile from trouble/debt/the police. **stand/stick out a mile** to be very obvious: The mistake/mark/reason stands out a mile! 2 (pl) (informal) any long distance: walk for miles (and miles). There's no-one within miles of him as a tennis player (= no-one anywhere near as good as him.) 3 (pl) (informal) a great deal: She's feeling miles better today.

mile·om·eter ⇨ milometer.

'mile·stone nc (a) a stone at the side of a road showing places and distances. (b) (fig) an important stage or event in history, research etc.

mile·age /'maɪlɪdʒ/ n 1 nc the distance travelled, measured in miles: a used car with a low mileage. 2 nu a fixed allowance for travelling expenses.

mili·tan·cy /'mɪlɪtənsɪ/ nu the state of being militant.

mili·tant¹ /'mɪlɪtənt/ adj using, supporting the use of, force or violence: use militant action to obtain political freedom.

mili·tant² /'mɪlɪtənt/ nc a militant person.

mili·tary¹ /'mɪlɪtrɪ/ adj of or for soldiers, an army, war on land: military training.

mili·tary² /'mɪlɪtrɪ/ n (the—) soldiers; the army.

mili·tate /'mɪlɪteɪt/ vi **militate against sb/sth** (formal) to be a reason against the success or acceptance of a person, thing: Several factors combined to militate against the success of our plan.

mil·itia /mɪ'lɪʃə/ nc (usually the —) civilians trained as soldiers but not part of the regular army.

milk¹ /mɪlk/ nu 1 the white liquid produced by female mammals as food for their young, esp that of cows which is drunk by human beings and made into butter and cheese. **It's no use crying over spilt milk** There is no point in feeling sad about a loss or error for which there is no remedy. 2 a juice like milk of some plants and trees: coconut milk.

milk 'chocolate nu the light brown kind.

'milk shake nc a milk drink with ice-cream or flavouring mixed into it.

'milk-tooth nc one of the first (temporary) teeth in children and young animals.

milk² /mɪlk/ vt **1** to take milk from (a cow, ewe, goat etc). **2** (fig) to get money, information etc (by deceit or dishonesty) from (a person or institution).

milky /'mɪlkɪ/ adj (**-ier, -iest**) **1** of, like, milk: mixed with milk. **2** (of a liquid) cloudy, not clear. ˌMilky 'Way n (the —) ⇨ galaxy(2).

mill¹ /mɪl/ n **1** (a building (flour-mill) with) machinery or apparatus for grinding grain into flour. **go/put sb through the mill** (to cause a person) to undergo hard training or experience. ⇨ run-of-the-mill. **2** a building, factory, workshop, for an industry: a cotton/paper-mill. **3** a small machine for grinding: a coffee/pepper-mill. 'mill·stone nc (**a**) one of a pair of circular stones between which grain is ground. (**b**) (fig) a heavy burden: The mortgage has been (like) a millstone round my neck.

mill² /mɪl/ v **1** vt to put (seeds etc) through a machine for grinding; produce (flour etc) by doing this: mill grain/flour. ⇨ miller. **2** vi **mill about/around** (of cattle, crowds of people) to move about in a disorganized group.

mil·len·nium /mɪ'lenɪəm/ nc (pl **-nia** /-nɪə/ or **—s**) **1** a period of 1000 years. **2** (the —) (fig) a future time of great happiness and prosperity for everyone.

mil·le·pede (also **mil·li-**) /'mɪlɪpiːd/ nc a kind of small, long creature with many pairs of legs.

mil·ler /'mɪlə(r)/ nc an owner or tenant of a flour-mill.

mil·let /'mɪlɪt/ nu a cereal plant producing a large crop of small seeds; the seeds.

mil·li·bar /'mɪlɪbɑː(r)/ nc (science) a unit of atmospheric pressure.

mil·li·litre /'mɪlɪliːtə(r)/ nc (symbol ml) one thousandth part of a litre.

mil·li·metre /'mɪlɪmiːtə(r)/ nc (symbol mm) one thousandth part of a metre.

mil·lin·er /'mɪlɪnə(r)/ nc a person, business, that makes and sells women's hats, lace etc.

mil·lin·ery /-nrɪ/ nu (the business of making or selling) women's hats, lace etc.

mil·lion /'mɪlɪən/ adj or det, nc **1** (of) one thousand thousand (1 000 000): two million, five thousand, six hundred and forty (= 2 005 640). Ⓝ The plural of 'million' is million in spoken numbers. **millions (of sth)** a very large number: millions of insects. **make a million** to earn, gain, a great deal of money.

mil·lionth /'mɪlɪənθ/ adj or det, nc (abbr 1 000 000th) (of) the next after 999 999 or one of a million equal parts.

mil·lion·aire /ˌmɪlɪə'neə(r)/ nc a person who has a million pounds, dollars etc; a very rich person.

mil·li·pede /'mɪlɪpiːd/ = millepede.

mi·lom·eter (also **mileometer**) /maɪ'lɒmɪtə(r)/ nc a device (in a vehicle) recording the number of miles travelled.

mime¹ /maɪm/ n **1** nu the use of only actions and facial expressions to tell a story. **2** nc,nu (an example of) a kind of drama without words.

mime² /maɪm/ vt,vi to act (a character, event) using only actions and facial expressions.

mim·ic¹ /'mɪmɪk/ nc a person who is clever at imitating others, esp in order to make fun of their habits, appearance etc.

mim·ic² /'mɪmɪk/ vt (pt,pp **-cked**) **1** to make fun of (a person, behaviour etc) by imitating: He was mimicking his uncle's voice. **2** (of things) to look like (something) closely: wood painted to mimic marble.

mim·ic·ry nu

min. written abbr **1** minute. **2** minimum.

min·aret /ˌmɪnə'ret/ nc a tall, slender tower of a mosque, from which Muslims are called to prayer.

mince¹ /mɪns/ nu (GB) minced(1) meat.

mince² /mɪns/ v **1** vt to cut or grind (meat etc) into very small pieces. **2** vi to try to appear elegant when speaking or walking.

'mince·meat nu a mixture of raisins, sugar, orange peel, apples, suet etc, used in pies. **make mincemeat of sb/sth** (informal) completely defeat a person, an argument etc.

mind¹ /maɪnd/ nc **1** a memory: She has a tired mind that cannot remember dates. **out of sight, out of mind** ⇨ sight¹(2). **bear/keep sb/sth in mind; bring/call sb/sth/to mind** to remember her/him/it. **go out of/slip sb's mind** to be forgotten. **2** the part of a person's brain responsible for thoughts and feelings: No two minds think exactly alike. Such an idea never entered my mind. Her mind's full of silly thoughts. **in the mind's eye** in one's imagination. **of sound/ unsound mind** (legal) sane/not sane. **on one's mind** in one's thoughts, esp because a cause of worry, needing to be dealt with etc: My poor brother/That tax bill has been on my mind all day. What have you got on your mind? **mind over matter** the ability to control pain or other strong physical feelings or desires: To stop smoking is a question of mind over matter. **be all in the mind** to be imagined and not true or real. **be a load off one's mind** to cause a person to feel less worried. **(must) be out of one's (tiny) mind** (must) be mad. **blow one's mind** (informal) (of drugs, extraordinary sights, sounds etc) to cause great mental excitement. Hence 'mind-blowing** adj. **cross sb's mind** to come into a person's thoughts suddenly. **(not) enter sb's mind** (of an idea, thought etc) to (not) come into a person's mind: The possibility never entered my mind. **have sb/sth in mind (for sth)** to be considering choosing a person, tool, material etc to use (to do a task etc): Who do you have in mind for the job? **set sb's mind at rest** to make a person feel less worried. **3** an opinion: To my mind (= In my opinion) he's very intelligent. **be of the same mind** to have the same opinion. **be in two minds (about sb/sth)** to be undecided. **change one's mind (about sb/sth)** to change one's opinion. **give sb a piece of one's mind** ⇨ piece¹(2). **have a mind of one's own** to have an independent opinion. **have/keep an open mind** to be willing to change one's opinion or decision. **know one's (own) mind** to know what one prefers or wants. **make up one's mind** to decide: I've made up my mind to study law. Her mind's made up (= She has decided and is determined). **speak one's mind** to give one's opinion. **4** an intention: Nothing could be further from my mind. **have a good mind to do sth** to be very willing or ready to do something: I've a good mind to report you to the police. **have half a mind to do sth**

to be thinking about doing something but not yet decided: *I've half a mind to join the army.* **keep one's mind on sth** to continue to pay attention to it: *Keep your mind on your work.* **put one's mind to sth** to give one's attention to it: *You could finish the job in an hour if you put your mind to it.* **take one's/sb's mind off sb/sth** to stop oneself, a person thinking about a person, activity, event etc that is unpleasant. **turn one's mind to sth** to begin to think seriously about it. **5** an intelligent, capable, person: *one of the great minds of this century.*

mind² /maɪnd/ v **1** vt to take care or charge of (a person, thing): *Would you mind our house while we are away? Who is minding the baby? Please mind the shop while I am out.* **mind one's P's and Q's** ⇨ P. **mind one's own business** ⇨ business(3). **2** vt,vi to be careful (about something): *Mind that car! Mind how you carry that box. Mind your language in front of children.* **mind out** (usually *imperative*) to be careful: *Mind out or you'll fall into the water. Mind out— there's glass on the floor!* **Mind you** (used when giving more information, to emphasize a fact etc): *Mind you, he's not the only capable person in the office. I'm not so sure about her cooking, mind you.* **3** vt (*imperative*) to make certain: *Mind he returns the tools in good order. Mind you don't lose it.* **4** vt,vi to be offended or troubled (by an activity, condition etc): *He doesn't seem to mind cold weather. Do you mind (if I smoke)? I don't mind cigarettes but I do mind cigars.* Ⓝ Usually used in questions or negative sentences. **Would you/he etc mind . . . ?** (used as a polite way of making a request): *Would you mind opening the window?* **I/we etc would not mind sth** (used to suggest that a person would like something): *I wouldn't mind a glass of cold beer* (= I would like one). **5** vt,vi **Never mind** (. . .) do not worry; it is not important: *'I've lost your pen.'—'Never mind, I'll buy another one.' Never mind how much it costs, buy it.*

mind-blowing /maɪnd bləʊɪŋ/ adj ⇨ blow one's mind at mind¹(2).

mind·ful /maɪndfəl/ adj (*formal*) **mindful of sth** giving care and thought to something: *mindful of one's duties/the nation's welfare.*

mind·less /maɪndlɪs/ adj **1** **mindless of sth** giving no care or thought to something: *mindless of danger.* **2** not having or not requiring intelligence: *mindless layabouts; mindless jobs.* **3** not having a purpose; thoughtless: *mindless violence.* **mind·less·ly** adv

mine¹ /maɪn/ nc **1** a hole made in the ground from which coal etc is taken: *a coal-mine; a gold-mine.* **2** (*fig*) a rich source: *A good dictionary/My grandmother is a mine of information.* **3** an explosive using electricity, contact, a time fuse etc: *The lorry was destroyed by a land-mine.*

'mine-detector nc a device for finding mines(3).

'mine·field nc an area of land or sea where mines(3) have been laid.

mine² /maɪn/ *possessive pron* of, belonging to, me: *Is this book yours or mine? It's mine. He's a friend of mine.*

mine³ /maɪn/ v **1** vt,vi **mine (for)** (sth) to dig (for coal etc) from the ground; obtain (coal etc)

from mines: *mining gold; mining for tin.* **2** vt to lay a mine(3) in (a place); destroy (something) by using mines(3): *mine a bridge.*

miner /maɪnə(r)/ nc a man who works in a mine: *coal-miners.*

min·er·al¹ /mɪnərəl/ adj (usually *attrib*) of, containing, mixed with, minerals: *mineral ores.*

min·er·al² /mɪnərəl/ nc any natural substance (not vegetable or animal) got from the ground by mining.

'mineral kingdom n (the —) all mineral substances. ⇨ kingdom(2).

'mineral water nu (a) a kind of water that naturally contains a mineral substance, esp one said to have medicinal value. (b) (*GB*) a non-alcoholic flavoured drink containing soda-water.

min·er·al·ogy /ˌmɪnəˈrælədʒɪ/ nu the scientific study of minerals.

min·er·al·ogist /ˌmɪnəˈrælədʒɪst/ nc an expert in, student of, mineralogy.

mingle /mɪŋgl/ vt,vi to mix (things): *mingle with* (= go about among) *the crowds.*

min·gy /mɪndʒɪ/ adj (-ier, -iest) (*GB informal*) small; ungenerous: *a mingy amount.*

min·ia·ture¹ /mɪnɪtʃə(r)/ adj (*attrib*) much smaller than usual or normal: *a miniature railway.*

min·ia·ture² /mɪnɪtʃə(r)/ nc **1** a very small painting of a person. **2** a small-scale copy or model of any object. **in miniature** on a small scale.

min·im /mɪnɪm/ nc (*music*) a note with half the value of a semibreve.

mini·mal /mɪnɪml/ adj smallest in amount or degree: *On these cliffs vegetation is minimal.*

mini·mize (also **-ise**) /mɪnɪmaɪz/ vt to reduce (something) to the smallest amount or degree: *She tried to minimize her difficulties.* Opp maximize.

mini·mum¹ /mɪnɪməm/ adj (*attrib*) of the smallest possible: *the minimum fee/speed/height/temperature.* Opp maximum.

mini·mum² /mɪnɪməm/ nc (pl —s) the smallest possible or recorded amount, degree etc: *a minimum of 15 people in each group; reduce the price to a minimum.* Opp maximum.

min·ing /maɪnɪŋ/ nu the process of getting coal, gold etc from mines.

min·ion /mɪnɪən/ nc (*derog*) a worker who, in order to win favour, obeys orders too readily.

min·is·ter¹ /mɪnɪstə(r)/ nc **1** (also M-) a person at the head of a government department: *the Minister for Defence.* ⇨ prime minister. **2** a Christian clergyman in the Protestant church.

min·is·ter² /mɪnɪstə(r)/ vi **minister to sb/sth** (*formal*) to give help or service to a person, her or his needs: *minister to* (the needs of) *a sick man.*

min·is·ter·ial /ˌmɪnɪˈstɪərɪəl/ adj of a minister(1): *ministerial functions/duties.* **min·is·ter·ial·ly** /-rəlɪ/ adv

min·is·try /mɪnɪstrɪ/ n (pl -ies) **1** nc (also M-) a government department: *the Ministry of Defence.* **2** n (the —) ministers of religion as a profession. **enter the ministry** to become a minister(2).

mink /mɪŋk/ adj, nc,nu (made of) (the valuable brown fur skin of) a small animal like a stoat: *a mink coat.*

mi·nor¹ /maɪnə(r)/ adj smaller or less important (than others): *minor repairs; a minor injury; a* minor part in a play; a minor character in a story. Compare major[1].

mi·nor[2] /'maɪnə(r)/ nc (legal) a person not yet legally of age (under 18 in GB).

mi·nor·ity /maɪ'nɒrətɪ/ nc (pl **-ies**) **1** *minority (of sth)* (used with a sing or pl verb) the smaller number or part (of a group): *The minority were/ was against the idea. The minority of voters agreed.* **be in the minority** (of a group) to have the smaller number (e.g. of supporters). **2** the number by which votes for one side are less than those for the other side: *We were in a minority of three.* **3** (usually sing) the state of being below the legal age of becoming an adult (e.g. 18 in GB). Compare majority.

mint[1] /mɪnt/ nu (one of many kinds of) a plant whose leaves are used for flavouring food.

mint[2] /mɪnt/ nc **1** a place where coins are made. **make/earn a mint** to earn a lot of money. **2** *in mint condition* (of stamps, pictures, books etc) in excellent condition.

mint[3] /mɪnt/ vt to make (a coin): *mint coins of 50p.*

mi·nus[1] /'maɪnəs/ adj **1** (attrib) (of a number) less than 0: *minus ten degrees.* **2** (pred) below the standard mentioned: *He was given A— for his essay.* Compare plus[1].

minus sign nc the sign – used (**a**) in front of minus numbers, e.g. −5; −2x; −10°C; (**b**) to show that one number is to be taken away from the previous one, as in 5−2 = 3. Compare plus sign.

mi·nus[2] /'maɪnəs/ nc a minus sign or quantity. Compare plus[2].

mi·nus[3] /'maɪnəs/ prep **1** reduced by taking away (a number): *6 minus 4 is 2.* **2** (informal) without: *He returned from the expedition minus a toe.* Compare plus[3].

min·us·cule /'mɪnəskjuːl/ adj extremely small.

min·ute[1] /maɪ'njuːt/ adj (no comp, but the min-utest can be used for emphasis) **1** very small: *minute particles of dust.* **2** giving small details; careful and exact: *the minutest details.*
mi·nute·ly adv

min·ute[2] /'mɪnɪt/ nc **1** the sixtieth part of one hour: *It's seven minutes to six/ten minutes past two. We arrived ten minutes early.* **in a minute** soon: *I'll come in a minute.* **the minute (that . . .)** (conj) as soon as: *I'll give him your message the minute (that) he arrives.* **Just a minute** (used to stop a person, pause to think etc before asking a question): *Just a minute—haven't we met before?* ⇨ up-to-the-minute. **2** the sixtieth part of a degree (in an angle): *37° 30′* (= 37 degrees 30 minutes). **3** (often pl) a summary, record, of what is said and decided at a meeting, esp of a society or committee.

'minute-hand nc the long hand on a watch or clock pointing to the minute.

min·ute[3] /'mɪnɪt/ vt to make a record of (a decision, agreement etc).

mir·acle /'mɪrəkl/ nc a remarkable, surprising act or event (good or welcome) which does not follow the known laws of nature: *I'll try my best but I cannot perform miracles. It's a miracle that anyone survived the crash.*
mir·acu·lous /mɪ'rækjʊləs/ adj
mir·acu·lous·ly adv

mi·rage /'mɪrɑːʒ/ nc an effect, produced by hot air conditions, causing something (not existing) to become visible (or upside down), esp the appearance of water in the desert.

mire /'maɪə(r)/ nu soft, muddy ground.

mir·ror[1] /'mɪrə(r)/ nc **1** a piece of glass used to look in and see oneself. **2** any polished surface that produces similar images. **3** (fig) something that describes or gives an idea: *Shakespeare's plays are a mirror of the times he lived in.*

mir·ror[2] /'mɪrə(r)/ vt to produce images of (something) as if in a mirror: *The still water of the lake mirrored the hillside.*

mirth /mɜːθ/ nu (formal) the state of being merry, happy; happy laughter.

mis·ad·ven·ture /misəd'ventʃə(r)/ nc,nu (for-mal; legal) (an event caused by) bad luck or an accident. **death by misadventure** death caused by an accident.

mis·an·thrope /'mɪzənθrəʊp/ nc (formal) a person who hates people and avoids them.
mis·an·throp·ic /mɪzən'θrɒpɪk/ adj
mis·an·thropy /mɪ'zænθrəpɪ/ nu (formal) hatred of mankind.

mis·ap·pre·hen·sion /misæprɪ'henʃn/ nc,nu (formal) misunderstanding: *be under a/the misap-prehension* (= believe incorrectly) *that he refused.*

mis·ap·pro·pri·ate /misə'prəʊprɪeɪt/ vt (for-mal) to take (a person's money) and use it wrongly (esp for one's own advantage): *The treasurer misappropriated the society's funds.*

mis·be·have /mɪsbɪ'heɪv/ vi (esp of children) to behave badly or improperly.
mis·be·hav·iour (US = **-ior**) /mɪsbɪ'heɪvɪə(r)/ nu

misc. written abbr miscellaneous.

mis·cal·cu·late /mɪs'kælkjʊleɪt/ vt,vi to calcu-late (amounts etc) wrongly.
mis·cal·cu·la·tion /mɪs,kælkjʊ'leɪʃn/ nc,nu

mis·car·riage /'mɪskærɪdʒ/ nc,nu **1** (**a**) *mis-carriage of justice* (an instance of) a failure of a court to administer justice properly. **2** (an instance of) a failure to deliver to the correct des-tination: *miscarriage of goods.* **3** (an instance of) the producing of a baby long before the correct time of birth.

mis·car·ry /mɪs'kærɪ/ vi (pt,pp **-ied**) **1** (formal) (of plans etc) to fail. **2** (of letters etc) to fail to reach the destination. **3** (of a woman) to have a miscarriage(3).

mis·cast /mɪs'kɑːst/ vt (pt,pp —) (usually pas-sive) (of an actor) to be cast unsuitably: *She was badly miscast as Juliet.*

mis·cel·la·ne·ous /mɪsə'leɪnɪəs/ adj of various kinds; having various qualities and characteris-tics: *a miscellaneous collection of goods.*

mis·cel·la·ny /mɪ'selənɪ/ nc (pl **-ies**) (literature) a collection of writings on various subjects by various authors.

mis·chance /mɪs'tʃɑːns/ nc,nu (an instance of) bad luck: *lose by mischance.*

mis·chief /'mɪstʃɪf/ nu foolish, bad behaviour (as by children) that is not serious: *Boys often get up to mischief. You can go to the park but keep out of mischief.*

mis·chiev·ous /'mɪstʃɪvəs/ adj **1** filled with, engaged in, mischief: *mischievous looks/children.* **2** causing trouble: *a mischievous letter/rumour.*

mis·con·ceive /ˌmɪskən'siːv/ vt (usually *passive; formal*) to organize, decide etc (something) without understanding or thinking about the facts properly: *Her plans were misconceived.*

mis·con·cep·tion /ˌmɪskən'sepʃn/ nc,nu **be under a/the misconception (that . . .)** to be wrong in one's opinion, decision because of misunderstanding.

mis·con·duct /ˌmɪs'kɒndʌkt/ nu (*formal*) bad behaviour, esp immoral behaviour.

mis·con·struc·tion /ˌmɪskən'strʌkʃn/ nc,nu (*formal*) (an instance of) inaccurate or wrong understanding: *Her friendliness is open to misconstruction.*

mis·con·strue /ˌmɪskən'struː/ vt (*formal*) to get a wrong idea of (something): *You have misconstrued my words/meaning.*

mis·deed /ˌmɪs'diːd/ nc (*formal*) a wicked act; crime: *be punished for one's misdeeds.*

mis·de·mean·our (*US* = **-mean·or**) /ˌmɪsdɪ'miːnə(r)/ nc (*legal*) an offence which is less serious than murder, violence etc.

mis·di·rect /ˌmɪsdɪ'rekt/ vt to give the wrong directions to (a person, letter etc): *misdirect a letter* (= put the wrong address on it).

mis·do·ings /ˌmɪs'duːɪŋz/ n pl misdeeds.

mi·ser /'maɪzə(r)/ nc (*derog*) a person who loves wealth for its own sake and spends as little as possible.

mi·ser·ly adj

mis·er·able /'mɪzrəbl/ adj **1** very unhappy, sad: *feeling miserable; as miserable as sin* (= very miserable). **2** poor in quality: *a miserable attempt/meal; miserable weather.*

mis·er·ably /-əblɪ/ adv

mis·ery /'mɪzərɪ/ n (pl **-ies**) **1** nu the state of being very unhappy; great suffering (of mind or body): *suffer misery from toothache.* **2** (pl) great misfortunes; *the miseries of war.* **3** nc (*informal*; *derog*) a person who is always unhappy and complaining.

mis·fire /ˌmɪs'faɪə(r)/ vi **1** (of a gun) to fail to send a bullet. **2** *misfire (on sb)* (*informal*) (of a joke, plan etc) to fail to have the intended effect: *His joke misfired badly (on him).*

mis·fit /'mɪsfɪt/ nc a person who is unable to live or work happily with others.

mis·for·tune /ˌmɪs'fɔːtʃuːn/ nc,nu (*formal*) (an instance of) bad luck (which is more usual): *suffer misfortune. He bore his misfortunes bravely.* ⇨ fortune(1).

mis·giv·ing /ˌmɪs'gɪvɪŋ/ nc,nu (*formal*) (a feeling of) doubt, suspicion, distrust: *a heart full of misgiving(s).*

mis·gov·ern /ˌmɪs'gʌvən/ vt to govern (a country) badly.

mis·gov·ern·ment nu

mis·guid·ed /ˌmɪs'gaɪdɪd/ adj (of behaviour) foolish and wrong (because of bad judgement).

mis·han·dle /ˌmɪs'hændl/ vt to deal with (a situation, person etc) roughly, inefficiently or without ability.

mis·hap /'mɪshæp/ nc,nu (an instance of) bad luck; unlucky accident: *meet with a slight mishap; arrive without mishap.*

mis·in·form /ˌmɪsɪn'fɔːm/ vt (often *passive*) to give wrong information to (a person): *I was misinformed about the price.*

mis·in·ter·pret /ˌmɪsɪn'tɜːprɪt/ vt to give a wrong interpretation or meaning to (something): *He misinterpreted her silence as giving consent.*

mis·judge /ˌmɪs'dʒʌdʒ/ vt to judge (a person, measurement etc) wrongly; form a wrong opinion of (a person, thing): *He misjudged the distance and fell into the stream.*

mis·lay /ˌmɪs'leɪ/ vt (pt,pp **mislaid** /-'leɪd/) to put (something) where it cannot easily be found: *I've mislaid my passport.*

mis·lead /ˌmɪs'liːd/ vt (pt,pp **misled** /-'led/) to cause (a person) to have the wrong idea or opinion or, to act incorrectly: *This information is misleading.*

mis·man·age /ˌmɪs'mænɪdʒ/ vt to manage (a business, accounts etc) badly.

mis·man·age·ment nu

mis·no·mer /ˌmɪs'nəʊmə(r)/ nc a wrong use of a name or word: *It's a misnomer to call this place a first-class hotel.*

mis·ogyn·ist /mɪ'sɒdʒɪnɪst/ nc a person who hates women.

mis·place /ˌmɪs'pleɪs/ vt **1** = mislay (the usual word). **2** (usually *passive*) to have (strong, good feelings) for a person, business etc that are shown to be wrong: *misplaced confidence/trust.*

mis·pro·nounce /ˌmɪsprə'naʊns/ vt to pronounce (a word) wrongly.

mis·pro·nun·ci·ation /ˌmɪsprəˌnʌnsɪ'eɪʃn/ nc,nu

mis·quote /ˌmɪs'kwəʊt/ vt to quote (a person, book etc) wrongly.

mis·quo·ta·tion /ˌmɪskwəʊ'teɪʃn/ nc,nu

mis·read /ˌmɪs'riːd/ vt (pt,pp **misread** /-'red/) to read or interpret (information) wrongly: *misread one's instructions.*

mis·rep·re·sent /ˌmɪsˌreprɪ'zent/ vt to give a false account or description of (a person, opinion etc).

mis·rep·re·sen·ta·tion /ˌmɪsˌreprɪzen'teɪʃn/ nc,nu

mis·rule /ˌmɪs'ruːl/ nu bad government.

miss[1] /mɪs/ nc **1** (M-) (used in front of the name of an unmarried woman or girl who has no other title): *Miss Smith.* Compare Mrs, Ms, Mr. **2** (used by children to a female teacher, to a shop assistant etc): *Good morning, miss! Two cups of coffee, miss.* Compare mister(2).

miss[2] /mɪs/ nc a failure to hit, catch, reach, see etc; *ten hits and one miss.* *a near miss* (*fig*) a result of an action that is not quite successful. *give sth a miss* (*informal*) to decide not to do it, visit it etc.

miss[3] /mɪs/ v **1** vt,vi to fail to hit, catch, reach, see, understand etc (something): *I threw the ball at the post and missed (it). He missed the world record by half a second. I'm sorry I'm late—I missed the 8 o'clock train. The house is the big red one on the corner, you can't miss it* (= can't fail to see it). *You've missed* (= failed to understand) *the main point of my argument.* *miss the boat/bus* ⇨ boat. **2** vt to feel unhappy or sorry about the absence of (a person): *I miss you so much—please come home.* **3** vt to feel unhappy or sorry about the absence of (something): *He's so rich that he wouldn't miss £100. I miss being able to visit you every day.* **4** vt to realize, discover, that (a person or thing) is lost or not there: *When did you first* *miss your purse?* ⇨ **missing. 5** *vi* **miss out (on sth)** to lose a chance to benefit, gain something etc: *If you don't come to the disco, you'll miss out on all the fun.* **6** *vt* **miss sth out** to fail to include, add etc something: *She missed out several important details.*

miss·ing *adj* not to be found; not in the place where it ought to be: *a book with two pages missing; missing persons.*

mis·shap·en /ˌmɪsˈʃeɪpn/ *adj* (esp of a part of the body) badly formed: *a misshapen cake.*

mis·sile /ˈmɪsaɪl/ *nc* **1** a powerful weapon that is sent through the air towards a distant target: *nuclear missiles.* **2** any object, e.g. a stone, bottle, sent through the air as a violent act.

mis·sion /ˈmɪʃn/ *nc* **1** a group of people sent abroad to perform a special task: *a mission of nuns to teach in Africa; a trade mission to S America.* **2** the purpose, task, of such a group: *Your mission is to report on the condition of the land.* **one's mission in life** the work one feels is one's duty, esp religious duty. **3** a place where missionaries work or where charitable or medical work is carried on among poor people.

mis·sion·ary /ˈmɪʃənrɪ/ *nc* (*pl* **-ies**) a person sent abroad to teach about religion and help the local people.

mis·sive /ˈmɪsɪv/ *nc* (used humorously for) a long, serious letter.

mis·spell /ˌmɪsˈspel/ *vt* (*pt,pp* **—ed** or **misspelt** /-ˈspelt/) to spell (a word) wrongly.
mis·spell·ing *nc,nu*

mis·spent /ˌmɪsˈspent/ *adj* (of time, ability, opportunity) used wrongly or foolishly: *a misspent youth.*

mist¹ /mɪst/ *nc,nu* (occasion when there is, an area with) water vapour in the air, at or near the earth's surface, less thick than fog: *hills hidden/covered in mist; mist on the car window.*

mist² /mɪst/ *vi,vt* **mist over; mist (sth) up** (to cause something) to become covered with mist: *The mountain misted over. The car windows have misted up. The hot air misted up my glasses.*
misty *adj* (**-ier, -iest**) with mist: *misty weather.*

mis·take¹ /mɪˈsteɪk/ *nc* a wrong opinion, idea or act because of wrong information, lack of ability or skill etc: *spelling mistakes. We all make mistakes occasionally.* **by mistake** as the result of a mistake, carelessness etc: *I took your umbrella by mistake.*

mis·take² /mɪˈsteɪk/ *vt* (*pt* **mistook** /mɪˈstʊk/, *pp* **mistaken** /mɪˈsteɪkn/) **1** to be wrong, have a wrong idea, about (something): *I mistook her true motives. He mistook her suggestion as a promise.* **2 mistake sb/sth for sb/sth** (often *passive*) to identify a person, thing wrongly: *She is often mistaken for her twin sister.*
mis·tak·en *adj* wrong: *a case of mistaken identity; have mistaken ideas.* **be mistaken (about sth)** to be wrong: *If I'm not mistaken, there's the man we met on the train.*
mis·tak·en·ly *adv*

mis·ter /ˈmɪstə(r)/ *nc* **1** (always written Mr) (used in front of the name of a man who has no other title): *Mr Green.* **2** (used by children to a man): *Please, mister, can I have my ball back?* Compare miss(2).

mis·timed /ˌmɪsˈtaɪmd/ *adj* said or done at an unsuitable time: *a mistimed intervention.*

mistle·toe /ˈmɪsltəʊ/ *nu* an evergreen plant with white berries, used as a Christmas decoration.

mis·took /mɪˈstʊk/ *pt* of mistake².

mis·treat /ˌmɪsˈtriːt/ *vt* to behave badly towards (a person); use, handle, (a machine, object) badly.
mis·treat·ment /ˌmɪsˈtriːtmənt/ *nc,nu*

mis·tress /ˈmɪstrɪs/ *nc* **1** a woman having regular sexual intercourse with a man who is not married to her. **2** (*dated*) a woman owner of a dog, horse etc: *Who's its mistress?* Compare master²(3). **3** (*dated*) a woman teacher, esp in a private school: *the games mistress.* Compare master²(4). **4** (*formal*) a woman in control (of a situation, a large household etc): *Is she mistress in her own home?* Compare master²(1).

mis·tri·al /ˌmɪsˈtraɪl/ *nc* (*legal*) a trial which is made invalid because of some legal error.

mis·trust¹ /ˌmɪsˈtrʌst/ *n sing* the absence of trust or confidence: *a strong mistrust of anything new.*

mis·trust² /ˌmɪsˈtrʌst/ *vt* to feel no trust or confidence in (a person, thing): *mistrust the newspapers.*

misty /ˈmɪstɪ/ ⇨ mist².

mis·un·der·stand /ˌmɪsʌndəˈstænd/ *vt* (*pt,pp* **-stood** /-ˈstʊd/) **1** to fail to have the correct idea or meaning about (a person, something said, written etc): *misunderstand a message/instructions. Don't misunderstand me, I do like you.* **2** to fail to identify the true character of (a person): *She had always felt misunderstood.* Compare understand(1).

mis·un·der·stand·ing *nc,nu* a failure to understand correctly, esp when this causes anger, suspicion etc: *Misunderstandings between nations may lead to war.* Compare understanding²(1).

mis·use¹ /ˌmɪsˈjuːs/ *nc,nu* (an instance of) using power, an instrument, money etc wrongly: *a misuse of political power.*

mis·use² /ˌmɪsˈjuːz/ *vt* to use (something) for a bad or wrong purpose: *misusing information.*

mite /maɪt/ *nc* **1** a kind of very small creature that can carry disease. **2** a small, esp poor, child: *Poor little mite!* **3** a very small or modest contribution or offering: *offer a mite of comfort.*

miti·gate /ˈmɪtɪgeɪt/ *vt* (*formal*) to make (anger, punishment etc) less serious or severe.
mitigating 'circumstance *nc* one that may make a mistake, crime, seem less serious.
miti·ga·tion /ˌmɪtɪˈgeɪʃn/ *nu*

mitre (*US* = **mi·ter**) /ˈmaɪtə(r)/ *nc* a kind of tall hat worn by bishops.

mitt /mɪt/ *nc* **1** a mitten. **2** (*sl*) a hand; fist.

mit·ten /ˈmɪtn/ *nc* (also *a pair of mittens*) a kind of glove covering four fingers together and the thumb separately.

mix¹ /mɪks/ *nc* **1** a variety of substances put together for a purpose: *a cake mix.* **2** a group of different kinds (of people): *an odd mix of people at the wedding.*

mix² /mɪks/ *v* **1** *vt,vi* to put (a variety of substances) together to make a new substance: *mix flour and water to make paste; mix cement. Oil and water will not mix.* **2** *vt* to carry out (several different activities) at about the same time: *I don't like to mix business and/with pleasure.* **3** *vi* (of a person) to enjoy, get on well with, other people: *He* *doesn't mix (well) at parties.* **4** *vt* **mix sb/sth up (a)** to put people, things in the wrong order: *mix up the correspondence.* **(b)** to confuse people, things: *mix up my brother/her letter with yours.* **mixed up** *(adj (pred))* confused: *He feels very mixed up about life.* **5** **be/get mixed up (in sth)** to be/become involved (in): *Don't get mixed up in politics.*

mix·ed /mɪkst/ *adj* of different sorts: *a mixed school* (= for boys and girls). **have mixed feelings (about sth)** to be undecided.

,mixed 'blessing *nc* a result etc having both advantages and disadvantages.

,mixed 'doubles *nc* (in tennis etc) with two players, one man and one woman, on each side.

,mixed e'conomy *nc* (*economics*) a government policy with some state-owned industry and some private enterprise.

,mixed 'metaphor *nc* (*literature*) the use of two unrelated metaphors in one phrase or statement, as in *'pull one's weight in the oceans of time'.*

mix·er /'mɪksə(r)/ *nc* **1** a machine that mixes: *a cement/food mixer.* **2** (*informal*) a person who is at ease with others on social occasions: *a good social mixer.* ⇨ mix²(3).

mix·ture /'mɪkstʃə(r)/ *nc* **1** the activity of mixing or being mixed. **2** something made by mixing: *a cough mixture. Air is a mixture of gases.* **3** (*sing only*) a variety (of qualities, feelings etc) at the same time: *I heard the news with a mixture of relief and sadness.*

mix-up /'mɪks ʌp/ *nc* (a mistake caused by) a disorganized state, confused arrangement etc: *Due to a mix-up with the dates, we missed the meeting.*

Mk *written abbr* Mark. ⇨ mark¹(8).

mkt *written abbr* (*commerce*) market.

ml *symbol* **1** millilitre(s). **2** mile.

mm *symbol* millimetre(s).

Mme *written abbr* (*Fr*) Madame (Mrs).

MO /ˌem 'əʊ/ *abbr* **1** Medical Officer. **2** *written abbr* mail order (an order for goods by post from a catalogue). **3** *written abbr* money order.

moan¹ /məʊn/ *nc* **1** a long, low sound produced by pain, suffering etc: *the moans of the injured.* **2** a long, low sound made by the wind. **3** (*informal*) a long complaint or expression of self-pity, gloom etc: *the moans of ungrateful children.*

moan² /məʊn/ *vi* **1** to make a low sound produced by pain, suffering etc. **2** (of the wind) to make a similar low sound. **3** (*informal*) (of a person) to complain, express self-pity etc: *Stop moaning about losing your watch. She moaned on and on.*

moat /məʊt/ *nc* a long, deep ditch filled with water, used round a castle etc as a defence.

mob¹ /mɒb/ *nc* **1** a disorganized crowd, esp one that has gathered to make trouble or attack. **2** a gang of criminals.

mob² /mɒb/ *vt* (**-bb-**) (of people) to crowd round in great numbers, either to attack or to admire: *The pop singer was mobbed by teenagers.*

mo·bile¹ /'məʊbaɪl/ *adj* moving, able to be moved, easily and quickly from place to place: *be mobile once the car is repaired; a mobile exhibition/home.*

mo·bil·ity /məʊ'bɪlətɪ/ *nu* being mobile.

mo·bile² /'məʊbaɪl/ *nc* an ornamental structure with hanging parts that move in air.

mo·bi·lize (also **-ise**) /'məʊbɪlaɪz/ *vt,vi* (to cause people, help etc) to group together in order to carry out a particular task: *mobilize support for a new hotel.*

mo·bi·liz·ation (also **-is·ation**) /ˌməʊbɪlaɪ-'zeɪʃn/ *nu*

mock¹ /mɒk/ *adj* (*no comp*) not real or genuine: *a mock fight.*

mock² /mɒk/ *vt,vi* to make fun of (a person, way of speaking etc) (esp by copying in an unkind or disrespectful way): *The cruel boys mocked the blind man.*

mock·ery /'mɒkərɪ/ *n* (*pl* **-ies**) **1** *nu* the act of mocking. **2** *nc* a person or thing that is mocked. **3** *nc* a very bad example: *His trial was a mockery of justice.* **make a mockery of sb/sth** to cause a person, thing to appear valueless, foolish: *Your exam results make a mockery of your true ability.*

mod /mɒd/ *abbr* modern. ⇨ mod cons.

mo·dal¹ /'məʊdl/ *adj* (*gram*) related to the mood (e.g. showing possibility) of a verb.

modal auxiliary verb *nc* (*gram*) a verb that is used with another verb to express possibility, necessity, probability, certainty etc. *Can, could, may, might, must, ought, shall, should, will, would* are all *modal auxiliary verbs.* Ⓝ For details, ⇨ the entry for the particular verb. ⇨ auxiliary verb.

mo·dal² /'məʊdl/ *nc* (*gram*) (also *modal verb*) = modal auxiliary verb.

mod cons /ˌmɒd 'kɒnz/ *n pl* (*informal*) (used in advertisements for houses, hotels etc) *modern conveniences* (e.g. such as heating, hot water).

mode /məʊd/ *nc* a way of speaking, behaving, dressing etc: *in the modern mode.*

mod·el¹ /'mɒdl/ *adj* (*attrib*) **1** perfect as an example: *a model wife/kitchen.* **2** small-scale: *a model railway.*

mod·el² /'mɒdl/ *nc* **1** a small-scale reproduction or representation of something: *a model of an ocean liner.* **2** a person employed, statue used, to wear clothes, hats etc so that possible buyers may see them. **3** a person who poses for sculptors, painters or photographers. **4** a design or structure of which many copies or reproductions are (to be) made: *the latest models of Ford cars.* **5** an article of clothing, hat etc shown by models(2): *the latest Paris models.* **6** (*informal*) a person or thing exactly like another: *She's the perfect model of her mother.* **7** a person, thing, that is a perfect example: *He's a model of kindness.*

mod·el³ /'mɒdl/ *v* (**-ll-**, *US* **-l-**) **1** *vt* to shape (something) (using a soft substance): *model her head in clay.* **2** *vt,vi* to work as a model(2,3): *She earns a living by modelling (clothes/hats).* **3** **model oneself on/upon sb** to use a person as a good copy or example: *model oneself on one's father.*

mo·dem /'məʊdem/ *nc* (*computers*) a device for joining two computers using a telephone link.

mod·er·ate¹ /'mɒdərət/ *adj* **1** limited: *a moderate appetite.* Compare *immoderate.* **2** (of an opinion, a desire, feelings etc) in the middle; within reasonable limits: *a moderate political party; be moderate in one's demands.* Compare *extreme(5).*

mod·er·ate·ly *adv*

mod·er·ate² /'mɒdərət/ *nc* a person who holds moderate opinions, esp in politics.

mod·er·ate³ /'mɒdəreɪt/ vt,vi (to cause one's opinion etc) to become less violent or extreme: *moderate one's enthusiasm/demands*.

mod·er·ation /,mɒdə'reɪʃn/ nu the quality of being moderate. **in moderation** in a moderate manner or degree: *Will alcoholic drinks be harmful if taken in moderation?*

mod·ern /'mɒdən/ adj **1** of the present or recent times: *modern technical achievements*. **2** new and up-to-date: *modern methods and ideas*.

,**modern 'history** nu the period from AD 1500 to the present.

mod·ern·ize (also **-ise**) /'mɒdənaɪz/ vt to make (something) suitable for present-day needs; bring (a thing, system etc) up to date: *have one's kitchen modernized*.

modernized (also **-ised**) adj: *a modernized kitchen*.

mod·est /'mɒdɪst/ adj **1** having, showing, a low but honest opinion of one's own merits, abilities etc: *be modest about one's achievements*. **2** not large in size or amount: *a modest house. My needs are quite modest*. **3** taking care not to do or say anything indecent or improper: *modest in speech, dress and behaviour*. Compare immodest.

mod·est·ly adv

mod·esty /'mɒdɪstɪ/ nu

modi·fi·ca·tion /,mɒdɪfɪ'keɪʃn/ n **1** nu the process of making changes. **2** nc a change to something, esp one that makes it less extreme: *make modifications to the basic design*.

modi·fi·er /'mɒdɪfaɪə(r)/ nc (gram) a word that limits or explains the particular meaning or use of another word, as in *'white hair', 'walk fast', 'very fast', 'bad-tempered', 'air letter'*. Ⓝ Adjectives and adverbs are the usual modifiers.

mod·ify /'mɒdɪfaɪ/ vt (pt,pp **-ied**) **1** to make changes in (something); make (something) different: *The industrial revolution modified the whole structure of society*. **2** to make less severe, violent etc: *You'd better modify your language*. **3** (gram) to change the meaning or use of (a word), e.g. by making the sense less general: *In 'red shoes', 'red' modifies 'shoes'*. ⇨ modifier.

,**modifying 'adjective/'adverb** nc ⇨ modify(3).

modu·late /'mɒdjʊleɪt/ vt,vi to adjust, adapt, the level, pitch etc of (sound).

modu·la·tion /,mɒdjʊ'leɪʃn/ nc,nu

mod·ule /'mɒdjuːl/ nc **1** a standard uniform part used in the structure of a building. **2** (computers) a unit of electronic components. **3** an independent unit of a spacecraft: *a lunar module*.

modu·lar /'mɒdjʊlə(r)/ adj

mo·hair /'məʊheə(r)/ nu (cloth made from) the fine, silky hair of the Angora goat.

Mo·ham·med·an /mə'hæmɪdən/ adj, nc = Muhammadan.

moist /mɔɪst/ adj slightly wet: *eyes moist with tears*.

mois·ten /'mɔɪsn/ vt,vi (to cause something) to become moist: *moisten the lips*.

mois·ture /'mɔɪstʃə(r)/ nu steam or water vapour (on a surface).

mois·tur·ize (also **-ise**) /'mɔɪstʃəraɪz/ vt to add moisture to (the skin, air etc): *an expensive moisturizing cream for the face*.

mois·tur·izer (also **-iser**) nu a kind of cream

that moisturizes the skin.

mo·lar /'məʊlə(r)/ nc, adj (one) of the back teeth used for grinding food.

mo·las·ses /mə'læsɪz/ n pl (used with a sing verb) a thick, dark syrup obtained from raw sugar.

mole¹ /məʊl/ nc a small, dark spot on the human skin.

mole² /məʊl/ nc **1** a small, dark-grey fur-covered animal living in tunnels (or burrows). **2** (informal) an employee who gives information to another government, business etc.

'mole·hill nc a small pile of earth thrown up by a mole(1). **make a mountain out of a molehill** to treat an unimportant matter as very important.

mol·ecule /'mɒlɪkjuːl/ nc (science) the smallest unit (usually a group of atoms) into which a substance can be divided without a change in its chemical nature.

mol·ecu·lar /mə'lekjʊlə(r)/ adj

mo·lest /mə'lest/ vt to trouble or annoy (a person) intentionally, esp making sexual attacks.

mol·li·fy /'mɒlɪfaɪ/ vt (pt,pp **-ied**) (formal) to make (a person, feelings) calmer: *mollifying his anger*.

mol·lusc (US also **mol·lusk**) /'mɒləsk/ nc one of a class of animals with soft bodies and no backbone (and often hard shells): *Oysters, mussels, cuttlefish, snails and slugs are all molluscs*.

mol·ten /'məʊltən/ adj (attrib) (pp of melt) (of metals) melted: *molten steel*.

mo·ment /'məʊmənt/ nc a very brief period of time: *It was all over in a few moments. Just a moment, please*. ⇨ spur¹(2). **the moment (that)** . . . (conj) as soon as: *The moment I saw you I knew you were angry with me*.

mo·men·tary /'məʊməntrɪ/ adj lasting for, done in, a very brief period of time: *a momentary pause in order to think before replying*.

mo·men·tar·ily /'məʊməntrəlɪ/ adv

mo·men·tous /mə'mentəs/ adj extremely important or serious: *a momentous occasion*.

mo·men·tum /mə'mentəm/ nu **1** (science) the quantity of motion of a moving body: *Do falling objects gain momentum?* **2** (of events) the force or strength (as) gained by activity: *Opposition to the idea is gaining/losing momentum*.

Mon written abbr Monday.

mon·arch /'mɒnək/ nc a king, queen, emperor or empress.

mon·ar·chic /mə'nɑːkɪk/ adj

mon·ar·chist /'mɒnəkɪst/ nc a believer in, supporter of, monarchy.

mon·archy /'mɒnəkɪ/ n (pl **-ies**) (a) nu government by a monarch. (b) nc a state ruled by a monarch.

mon·as·tery /'mɒnəstrɪ/ nc (pl **-ies**) a building in which men (monks) lead a religious life away from others. Compare convent. **enter a monastery** to become a monk.

mon·as·tic /mə'næstɪk/ adj of monks or monasteries: *monastic vows* (i.e. of poverty, chastity and obedience).

Mon·day /'mʌndɪ/ nc (also attrib) the second day of the week: *They're coming next Monday/on Monday afternoon. On Mondays* (= Every Monday) *I have sandwiches*.

mon·et·ar·ist /'mʌnɪtərɪst/ adj, nc (of) a supporter of monetarism.

mon·et·ar·ism /'mʌnɪtərɪzəm/ *nu* (the belief in) an economic policy of regulating the money supply as the basic method of controlling a country's economy.

mon·et·ary /'mʌnɪtrɪ/ *adj* of money or coins: *The monetary unit in the USA is the dollar.*

mon·ey /'mʌnɪ/ *nu* coins and printed paper used when buying and selling: *How much money do you earn a month?* **be made of money** to be very rich. **make money** to earn it or obtain it by making a profit. **put money into sth** to give finance to a business etc. **put money on sth** to place a bet on a horse etc. **throw one's money about** to spend one's money without thought or care. ⇨ ᵣun¹(1).

'money-box *nc* a box used for saving money.

'money-lender *nc* a person whose business is to lend money at interest.

'money market *n* (the —) (*finance*) the bankers, financiers etc who decide the rates of interest on borrowed capital.

'money-order *nc* an order for money bought from a post office for payment at another post office to a named person.

'money-spinner *nc* (*informal*) an item for sale that makes a lot of money.

mon·gol /'mɒŋgl/ *nc* (not now used) a person suffering from *Down's Syndrome*.

mon·gol·ism /'mɒŋgəlɪzəm/ *nu* (not now used) Down's Syndrome.

mon·goose /'mɒŋguːs/ *nc* (*pl* —**s**) a small animal with a long tail, clever at destroying snakes.

mon·grel /'mʌŋgrəl/ *adj, nc* (of) a dog of mixed breed.

moni·tor¹ /'mɒnɪtə(r)/ *nc* **1** a senior pupil given duties in a school. **2** a person, apparatus, that listens to or watches foreign radio and television programmes. **3** (*computers*) a screen on which information can be shown. **4** (*computers*) a book that contains a list of the commands needed to operate the computer system.

moni·tor² /'mɒnɪtə(r)/ *vt* to listen to, check, note, record, (radio or TV programmes, the quality of things being produced, the progress of something etc).

monk /mʌŋk/ *nc* a man who, after taking religious vows, lives with other men in a monastery in the service of God. Compare nun.

mon·key¹ /'mʌŋkɪ/ *nc* (*pl* —**s**) **1** an animal of the group with long tails and hairy bodies that often look like humans. **2** a person, esp a child, who is fond of mischief: *You little monkey!*

'monkey-wrench *nc* a tool with a jaw that can be adjusted to various lengths.

mon·key² /'mʌŋkɪ/ *vi* **monkey about (with sth)** to play carelessly or foolishly (with something): *Stop monkeying about with those tools!*

mono·chrome /'mɒnəkrəum/ *adj* having, using, only one colour: *a monochrome TV set.*

mon·ocle /'mɒnəkl/ *nc* a framed lens for one eye.

mon·og·amist /mə'nɒgəmɪst/ *nc* a person who practises monogamy.

mon·og·amous /mə'nɒgəməs/ *adj* practising monogamy.

mon·og·amy /mə'nɒgəmɪ/ *nu* the practice of being married to one person. Compare bigamy,

polygamy.

mono·gram /'mɒnəgræm/ *nc* two or more letters (esp a person's initials) combined in one design (on notepaper etc).

mono·graph /'mɒnəgrɑːf/ *nc* a detailed (scientific) account, esp a published report on one particular subject.

mono·lin·gual /ˌmɒnəu'lɪŋgwəl/ *adj* using, concerning, one language: *a monolingual dictionary* ⇨ bilingual(2).

mono·lith /'mɒnəlɪθ/ *nc* a tall, upright block of stone (as a pillar or monument).

mono·lith·ic /ˌmɒnə'lɪθɪk/ *adj*

mono·logue /'mɒnəlɒg/ *nc* **1** (*literature*) a scene in a play in which only one person speaks. **2** any long talk by one person in a conversation.

mon·op·ol·ize (also **-ise**) /mə'nɒpəlaɪz/ *vt* to get or keep control of the whole of (something), so that others cannot share: *Don't let me monopolize the conversation.*

mon·op·oly /mə'nɒpəlɪ/ *nc* (*pl* **-ies**) **1** (a private business, State company etc with) the exclusive right to control the supply of a particular kind of goods or services: *The State Railways are a monopoly controlling all rail transport.* **2** any exclusive control by one person or group: *You don't have a monopoly over what TV programmes we shall watch tonight.*

mon·op·ol·ist /-lɪst/ *adj* of, like, a monopoly. □ *nc* (**a**) a supporter of, believer in, monopolies. (**b**) a person who has a monopoly.

mon·op·ol·is·tic /mə,nɒpə'lɪstɪk/ *adj*

mono·syl·lable /'mɒnəsɪləbl/ *nc* (*lang*) a word of one syllable.

mono·syl·lab·ic /ˌmɒnəsɪ'læbɪk/ *adj*

mon·ot·on·ous /mə'nɒtənəs/ *adj* (uninteresting because) unchanging, without variety: *a monotonous voice; monotonous work.*

mon·ot·on·ous·ly *adv*

mon·ot·ony /mə'nɒtənɪ/ *nu* the state of being monotonous.

mon·soon /mɒn'suːn/ *nc* **1** the seasonal wind blowing in the Indian Ocean from SW from April to October (*the wet monsoon*) and from NE during the other months (*the dry monsoon*). **2** the rainy season that comes with the wet monsoon.

mon·ster /'mɒnstə(r)/ *nc* **1** a person, animal or thing of extraordinary or strange size, shape etc. **2** (in stories) a strange, usually frightening, imaginary creature: *dragons are monsters.* **3** (*derog*) a person who is remarkable for some bad or evil quality: *a monster of cruelty.*

mon·stros·ity /mɒn'strɒsətɪ/ *nc* (*pl* **-ies**) a large and ugly object.

mon·strous /'mɒnstrəs/ *adj* **1** of a large size and strange shape. **2** causing horror and disgust: *monstrous crimes.* **3** (*informal*) absurd; scandalous: *It's monstrous that men should be paid more than women for the same job.*

mon·strous·ly *adv*

mon·tage /'mɒntaːʒ/ *nc,nu* (*Fr*) (an instance of) the process of using many designs, materials etc to make a picture.

month /mʌnθ/ *nc* a period of approximately one twelfth of a year: *A baby of three months; a three-month-old baby.* **not in a month of Sundays** (almost) never. ⇨ calendar/lunar month.

month·ly¹ /'mʌnθlɪ/ *adj, adv* **1** done, happening

etc once a month: *a monthly meeting; writing monthly*. **2** valid for one month: *a monthly ticket*.

month·ly² /'mʌnθlɪ/ *nc* (*pl* **-ies**) a magazine etc issued once a month.

monu·ment /'mɒnjʊmənt/ *nc* **1** a building, column, statue etc in memory of a person or event: *a monument to a great scientist*. **2** a very old and interesting building: *an ancient monument*.

monu·men·tal /ˌmɒnjʊ'mentl/ *adj* (*formal*) **1** of a monument: *a monumental inscription*. **2** (of books, studies etc) of lasting value. **3** (of qualities, tasks) very great: *monumental ignorance; a monumental achievement*.

moo /muː/ *nc* the sound made by a cow or ox. □ *vi* to make this sound.

'moo-cow *nc* (a child's word for) a cow.

mood¹ /muːd/ *nc* a state of mind or spirits: *not in the mood for music; in no mood for a holiday*.

moody *adj* (**-ier**, **-iest**) having moods that often change, esp being bad-tempered.

mood·ily /-əlɪ/ *adv*

mood² /muːd/ *nc* (*gram*) one of the groups of forms that a verb may take to show whether things are regarded as certain, possible, doubtful etc: *the indicative/imperative mood*.

moon¹ /muːn/ *nc* **1** (the —) the body which moves round the earth once in a month and shines at night. **2** (used with *a*, *an*) this body as it is seen each month: *Is it a new moon or a full moon?* **promise sb the moon** to make extravagant promises. **3** a similar body moving round other planets: *How many moons has the planet Jupiter?*

'moon·light *nu* the light of the moon.

'moon·lit *adj* having light from the moon.

'moon·stone *nc,nu* a kind of semi-precious stone.

moon² /muːn/ *vi* **moon about/around** to move around or look slowly and without energy or interest.

moor¹ /mɔː(r)/ *nc* (also *moorland*) (an area of) open, uncultivated land, esp if covered with heather.

moor² /mɔː(r)/ *vt,vi* to make (a boat, ship etc) secure (to land or buoys) by using ropes etc.

moor·ings /'mɔːrɪŋz/ *n pl* (**a**) the ropes, anchors etc by which a ship or boat is moored. (**b**) a place where a ship is moored.

moose /muːs/ *nc* (*pl* — or **-s** /-sɪz/) a sort of large deer found in the forests of N America and in northern Europe (where it is called an *elk*).

moot¹ /muːt/ *adj* (only in) **a moot point/question** one about which there is uncertainty.

moot² /muːt/ *vt* (usually *passive*) to raise or bring forward (a subject) for discussion: *This question has been mooted before*.

mop¹ /mɒp/ *nc* **1** a bundle of strings, cloth etc fastened to a long handle, used for cleaning floors etc; similar material on a short handle for cleaning dishes etc. **2** a mass of thick, untidy hair.

mop² /mɒp/ *vt* (**-pp-**) to clean, wipe, (a floor etc) (as if) with a mop: *mop the floor; mop one's brow*.

mope /məʊp/ *vi* **mope about/around** to go about feeling sad or in low spirits: *moping (about) in the house all day*.

mo·ped /'məʊped/ *nc* (*GB*) a bicycle fitted with a small petrol engine.

mo·raine /mɒ'reɪn/ *nu* earth, rock etc carried and deposited by a glacier.

mor·al¹ /'mɒrəl *US:* 'mɔːrəl/ *adj* **1** concerning (principles of) right and wrong: *moral standards/law*. **a moral victory** an outcome of a struggle in which the weaker side is comforted because it has shown that its cause is right or just. **give sb moral support** to say one thinks her or his cause is just but not give any actual help. **2** good and virtuous: *a moral life/man*. Compare **immoral**. **3** able to understand the difference between right and wrong: *At what age do we become moral beings?*

,moral phi'losophy *nu* the scientific study of right and wrong in human behaviour.

mor·al·ly /-rəlɪ/ *adv*

mor·al² /'mɒrəl/ *nc* **1** a point about right and wrong, justice etc that a story, event or experience teaches: *And the moral is that a young girl should not speak to strange men*. **2** (*pl*) standards of good behaviour: *a man without morals*.

mo·rale /mə'rɑːl/ *nu* the state or degree of determination to act, continue to try to believe in the ability to win: *Their morale was high/low after their good/poor results*.

mor·al·ist /'mɒrəlɪst/ *nc* a person who criticizes other people's morals(2).

mor·al·is·tic /ˌmɒrə'lɪstɪk/ *adj* criticizing other people's morals(2).

mor·al·ity /mə'rælətɪ/ *n* (*pl* **-ies**) **1** *nu* (the standards, principles, of) good behaviour: *standards of commercial morality*. Compare **immorality**. **2** *nc* a particular system of morals: *Different religions have different moralities*.

mor·al·ize (also **-ise**) /'mɒrəlaɪz/ *vi* **moralize about/on sth** to talk or write on the right and wrong of an action, behaviour etc: *moralize about/on war*.

mo·rass /mə'ræs/ *nc* **1** an area of low, wet land. **2** (*fig*) a difficult, complicated situation: *a morass of problems*.

mora·tor·ium /ˌmɒrə'tɔːrɪəm/ *nc* (*pl* **—s** or **-ria** /-rɪə/) **1** (*legal*) (a period of) legal authorization to delay payment of debts. **2** a temporary and agreed delay or stopping.

mor·bid /'mɔːbɪd/ *adj* having, showing, an interest in horrible, unhealthy or depressing things: *a morbid sense of humour*.

mor·bid·ly *adv*

more¹ /mɔː(r)/ *adj* or *det* **1** a larger amount of: *more money/pain/speed; more bread/information/success*. ⇨ **more³** below. Ⓝ *'More'* when referring to 'a larger amount of' is the comparative form of *'much'*, as in *She has much food, I have more food and he has the most food*. **no more** . . . not any: *There's no more food left*. **2** a larger number of: *more men/apples/houses/ideas*. Ⓝ *'More'* when referring to 'a larger number of' is the comparative form of *'many'*, as in *He has many friends, I have more friends and she has the most friends*. Compare **less¹**.

more² /mɔː(r)/ *adv* Ⓝ *'More'* is used to form the comparative of adjectives and adverbs, as in *more intelligent, more easily, more quickly than you*. ⇨ **most²**. **1** to a larger extent: *You need to sleep more. Eat less and exercise more. Is Greece more beautiful than France? I think Italy is much more beautiful. He likes Spain even more*. **any more** ⇨ **any²**(1). **once more** ⇨ **once¹**(1). **more and more** to an extent that gets larger: *Life is becom-*

ing more and more expensive. ⇨ less and less at less². **more or less** approximately: *The house is more or less a mile from here.* **more so (than . . .)** (used to refer to an idea, fact already mentioned): *'Was the course helpful?'—'Yes, more so than we expected.'* **2 (the) more** + noun . . . (used for emphasis): *The more fool you* (= You are foolish) *to believe her.* Compare less².

more³ /mɔː(r)/ *pron* **more (of sth)** a larger amount or number (of): *I need a lot of money, he needs more and she needs the most. We've got more of them than you. He eats more than her. Let's buy a few/a little/some/three more. I want no more of your rudeness!* ⇨ most³. **the more . . ., the more . . .** (used to express a relationship between two ideas etc): *The more you have, the more you want.* Compare less⁴.

more·over /mɔːrˈəʊvə(r)/ *adv* in addition (to this); besides: *You're too old and moreover you're now much too big.*

morgue /mɔːg/ *nc* a building in which bodies of unidentified dead people are kept. Compare mortuary.

mori·bund /ˈmɒrɪbʌnd/ *adj* about to come to an end: *moribund civilizations.*

morn /mɔːn/ *nc* (*poetic*) morning.

morn·ing¹ /ˈmɔːnɪŋ/ *adj* (*attrib*) of, during, the part of the day before 12 o'clock: *a morning walk; an early morning swim.*

morn·ing² /ˈmɔːnɪŋ/ *nc* the early part of the day between dawn and 12 o'clock: *in/during the morning; this morning; yesterday/tomorrow morning; every morning; on Sunday/Monday morning; a few mornings ago.* **good morning** ⇨ good¹(15).

mo·ron /ˈmɔːrɒn/ *nc* (*informal; derog*) a stupid person.

mo·ron·ic /məˈrɒnɪk/ *adj*

mo·rose /məˈrəʊs/ *adj* gloomy; bad-tempered.

mo·rose·ly *adv*

mor·pheme /ˈmɔːfiːm/ *nc* (*lang*) the smallest meaningful part into which a word can be divided: *'Run-s' contains two morphemes and 'un-man-ly' contains three.*

mor·phine /ˈmɔːfiːn/ (also **mor·phia** /ˈmɔːfɪə/) *nu* a drug made from opium, used for reducing severe pain.

mor·ris dance /ˈmɒrɪs dɑːns/ *nc* an old English folkdance for men.

mor·row /ˈmɒrəʊ/ *n* (*literary*) the day after today or after any day mentioned.

Morse /mɔːs/ *n* (also the *Morse code*) a system of communication using short and long symbols, sounds, light etc as letters of the alphabet and numbers.

mor·sel /ˈmɔːsl/ *nc* a tiny piece (of food): *not a morsel (of food) anywhere.*

mor·tal¹ /ˈmɔːtl/ *adj* **1** who or that cannot live for ever: *Man is mortal.* Compare immortal(1). **2** (*attrib*) causing death: *a mortal wound.*

,mortal 'combat *nu* a fight only ended by the death of one of the fighters.

,mortal 'enemy *nc* an enemy whose hatred will not end until death.

,mortal 'sin *nc* one causing loss of life after death.

mor·tal·ly /-təlɪ/ *adv* (a) so as to cause death: *mortally wounded.* (b) extremely: *I was mortally*

offended.

mor·tal² /ˈmɔːtl/ *nc* (*literary*) a person.

mor·tal·ity /mɔːˈtælətɪ/ *nu* **1** the state of being mortal. **2** (the rate of) deaths caused by a disaster, disease etc): *an epidemic with a heavy mortality; infant mortality.*

mor·tar¹ /ˈmɔːtə(r)/ *nu* a mixture of lime, sand and water used to hold bricks, stones etc together in building.

mor·tar² /ˈmɔːtə(r)/ *nc* **1** a bowl of hard material in which substances are crushed (using a *pestle*). **2** a large gun used for firing shells at high angles.

mort·gage¹ /ˈmɔːgɪdʒ/ *nc* **1** a written agreement about money lent to a person buying a house. **2** the amount of money lent. **3** an act of mortgaging.

mort·gage² /ˈmɔːgɪdʒ/ *vt* to give a building society etc the right to own (one's house) in return for money lent to buy it.

mor·tice /ˈmɔːtɪs/ *nc* = mortise.

mor·ti·fy /ˈmɔːtɪfaɪ/ *vt* (*pt,pp* **-ied**) (usually *passive*) to cause (a person) to feel ashamed, humiliated or hurt: *be mortified by the news of her failure.*

mor·tise (also **mor·tice**) /ˈmɔːtɪs/ *nc* (*tech*) a shaped hole cut in a piece of wood to receive the end of another piece (the *tenon*).

mor·tu·ary /ˈmɔːtʃʊərɪ/ *nc* (*pl* **-ies**) a place, e.g. part of a hospital, where dead bodies are kept until burial. Compare morgue.

mo·sa·ic /məʊˈzeɪk/ *adj, nc* (of) a work of art in which designs etc are made by fitting together coloured pieces of stone etc.

Mos·lem /ˈmɒzləm/ *adj, n* = Muslim.

mosque /mɒsk/ *nc* a building in which Muslims worship.

mos·qui·to /məˈskiːtəʊ/ *nc* (*pl* **-es**) a small, flying, blood-sucking insect, esp the sort that spreads malaria.

moss /mɒs/ *nu* sorts of small green or yellow plant growing in thick masses on wet surfaces.

mossy *adj* (**-ier, -iest**)

most¹ /məʊst/ *adj* or *det* **1 the most . . .** (a) the largest amount of: *the most happiness/food/pain.* ⇨ most³ below. Ⓝ 'Most' when referring to 'the largest amount of' is the superlative form of 'much', as in *She has much money, I have more money and he has the most money.* **for the most part** usually: *Japanese cameras are, for the most part, of excellent quality.* (b) the largest number of: *the most mistakes/records/pens.* Ⓝ 'Most' when referring to 'the largest number of' is the superlative form of 'many', as in *You play many games, I play more games and she plays the most games.* **2** (used without *the*) the majority of: *Most people think so. Most time is spent sleeping.* Compare least¹.

most² /məʊst/ *adv* Ⓝ 'Most' is used to form the superlative of adjectives and adverbs, as in *most difficult, most willingly.* ⇨ more². to the largest extent: *I need most sleep. Which is the most beautiful? This is a most useful book. He was most polite to me. Her voice pleased me most.* **most of all** (used to express a strong opinion or feeling) particularly: *All of you deserve a prize, but Jane most of all.* Compare least².

most³ /məʊst/ *pron* **most (of sth)** the largest amount or number (of): *I ate a lot of food, she ate more food and he ate the most. He was ill most of* the summer. *Who earns the most? Most of us agree.* ⇨ **more³**. **at the (very) most** not more than: *I can pay only £20 a week at the most.* **make the most of sth** to use an opportunity etc to one's best advantage: *We have only one day left in Berlin so let's make the most of it.* Compare least³.

most·ly /'məʊstlɪ/ *adv* **1** in the majority of instances: *We are mostly out on Sundays.* **2** mainly: *The medicine was mostly (made of) sugar and water.*

MOT /ˌem əʊ 'tiː/ *abbr* Ministry of Transport road test (an annual safety test on all cars more than 3 years old).

mo·tel /məʊ'tel/ *nc* a hotel for people travelling by car to stop overnight.

moth /mɒθ/ *nc* a kind of winged insect flying mainly at night.

'moth-eaten *adj* (of cloth) eaten or destroyed by moths.

moth·er¹ /'mʌðə(r)/ *nc* **1** a female parent: *You've been like a mother to me.* **2** the institution, quality or condition that is the cause or originator: *The House of Commons is sometimes called 'the mother of Parliaments'.* **3** (often M-) a woman in charge of a religious community.

'mother country *nc* the country where one was born.

'mother-figure *nc* a woman who gives one care, advice etc.

'mother·hood /-hʊd/ *nu* the state of being a mother.

mother-in-law /'mʌðər ɪn lɔː/ *nc* (*pl* **mothers-in-law**) the mother of one's wife or husband.

‚mother'tongue *nc*

mother·less *adj* without a living or known mother.

mother·ly *adj* of, like, a mother: *motherly love.*

moth·er² /'mʌðə(r)/ *vt* to take care of (a person) as a mother does.

mo·tif /məʊ'tiːf/ *nc* **1** a repeated theme in music. **2** a main (and often repeated) feature in a work of art.

mo·tion¹ /'məʊʃn/ *n* **1** *nu* (the manner of) moving. **in slow motion** (as if) with movements that are much slower than usual: *watch a bird fly in slow motion on TV.* **put/set sth in motion** to cause it to begin to work, happen. **2** *nc* a particular movement: *All her motions were graceful.* **go through the motions** (*informal*) to do something in a disinterested or insincere manner. **3** *nc* an idea, proposal to be discussed and voted on at a meeting: *The motion was adopted/carried/rejected/lost by a majority of six.*

mo·tion² /'məʊʃn/ *vt,vi* **motion (to) sb** to signal or direct a person by moving one's hand etc: *He motioned (to) me to enter.*

mo·tion·less *adj* not moving; still.

mo·ti·vate /'məʊtɪveɪt/ *vt* to be a reason or encouragement for (a person) to do something: *He felt motivated by his success to try for another prize.*

mo·tiv·ation /ˌməʊtɪ'veɪʃn/ *nc,nu*

mo·tive /'məʊtɪv/ *nc* a cause or reason for doing something: *do it from motives of kindness.*

mot·ley /'mɒtlɪ/ *adj* of various sorts, shapes etc: *a motley crowd.*

mo·tor¹ /'məʊtə(r)/ *adj* (*attrib*) of, concerning,

vehicles: *the motor industry.*

mo·tor² /'məʊtə(r)/ *nc* a machine which produces or uses power (esp electric power) to produce motion: *electric motors.*

'motor·bike, -bicycle *nc* a vehicle like a bicycle with a motor.

'motor·boat *nc* a boat with a motor.

'motor·cade *nc* a procession of motor vehicles.

'motor car *nc* (*car* is now more usual) an enclosed motor vehicle with space for passengers.

'motor·cycle *nc* = motorbike (which is more usual).

'motor scooter *nc* = scooter(1).

'motor vehicle *nc* any road vehicle such as a car, bus, motorbike etc.

'motor·way *nc* a wide road designed for fast traffic, going over or under other roads.

'mo·tor·ist /-ɪst/ *nc* a person who drives a car.

mo·tor³ /'məʊtə(r)/ *vi* (*dated*) to travel by car: *motoring from London to Cambridge.*

mot·tled /'mɒtld/ *adj* marked with spots or different colours without a pattern.

mot·to /'mɒtəʊ/ *nc* (*pl* **—es** or **—s**) a short sentence or phrase used as a guide or rule of behaviour, as used by a school, club etc or expressed as a personal rule of conduct, such as '*Every man for himself*'.

mould¹ (*US* = **mold**) /məʊld/ *nu* a soft, green growth appearing on damp surfaces, bread etc.

mouldy *adj* (-**ier**, -**iest**) **(a)** covered with, smelling of, mould: *mouldy cheese.* **(b)** (*fig; derog*) (of a person) mean and unhelpful.

mould² (*US* = **mold**) /məʊld/ *nc* **1** a hollow container into which a liquid substance is poured to set into a desired shape. **2** something formed in this way: *We're having a lemon mould for supper.*

mould³ (*US* = **mold**) /məʊld/ *vt* **1** to make (something) (as if) in a mould²(1): *mould a head out of/in clay.* **2** (*fig*) to guide or control the development of (something): *mould a person's character.*

moult (*US* = **molt**) /məʊlt/ *vt,vi* **1** (of birds) to lose (feathers) before a new growth. **2** (of dogs and cats) to lose (hair) in the same way.

mound /maʊnd/ *nc* a mass of piled-up earth: *a mound of soil.*

mount¹ /maʊnt/ *nc* (*abbr* Mt) a mountain: *Mt Everest.*

mount² /maʊnt/ *v* **1** *vt,vi* **mount sth, mount (up)** to get on (a horse etc): *He mounted (his horse) and rode away.* Compare dismount. **2** *vt,vi* to go up (a hill, ladder, stairs etc). **3** *vi* **mount (up)** to become larger in amount: *Our expenses are mounting (up).* **4** *vt* to fix (something) onto a surface: *mount photographs in an album.* **5** *vt* to organize and produce (a display): *mount an exhibition.*

moun·tain /'maʊntɪn/ *nc* **1** a mass of very high land going up to a peak: *Everest is the highest mountain in the world.* **2** (*fig*) a very large amount: *a mountain of debts/letters.*

moun·tain·eer /ˌmaʊntɪ'nɪə(r)/ *nc* a person who climbs mountains.

moun·tain·eer·ing *nu* the act of climbing mountains (as a sport).

moun·tain·ous /'maʊntɪnəs/ *adj* **(a)** having mountains: *mountainous country.* **(b)** (*fig*) huge: *mountainous waves.*

mourn /mɔ:n/ *vi,vt* **mourn (for/over) (sb/sth)** to feel, show, sorrow or regret: *mourn a dead child; mourn for a dead child; mourn over the child's death.*

mourn·er *nc* a person who mourns at a funeral.

mourn·ful /-fəl/ *adj* sad; expressing sorrow: *mournful music.*

mourn·ful·ly /-fəlɪ/ *adv*

mourn·ing /'mɔ:nɪŋ/ *nu* (the wearing of) black clothes as a sign of grief: *go into mourning for three weeks.*

mouse /maʊs/ *nc* (*pl* **mice** /maɪs/) **1** one of many kinds of small furry animals with a long tail, e.g. the *field-mouse* living in fields, the *house-mouse* living in buildings. **2** (*fig*) a shy, timid person. **3** (*computers*) a device held in the hand and used to select a particular computer operation without using the keyboard.

'**mouse·trap** *nc* a trap for catching mice.

mousse /mu:s/ *nc,nu* (a dish of) flavoured cream beaten and frozen: *chocolate mousse.*

mous·tache (*US* = **mus-**) /mə'stɑ:ʃ/ *nc* hair allowed to grow on the upper lip.

mousy /'maʊsɪ/ *adj* (**-ier, -iest**) **1** (esp of hair) having a dull brown colour. **2** (*derog*) (of a person) timid, shy.

mouth[1] /maʊθ/ *nc* (*pl* **—s** /maʊðz/) **1** the opening through which animals take in food. **by word of mouth** ⇨ word[1](1). **down in the mouth** sad, depressed. **make one's mouth water** to make one feel hungry or thirsty. **put words into sb's mouth; take the words out of sb's mouth** ⇨ word[1](2). **2** an opening or way out (of a bag, bottle, tunnel, cave, river etc).

mouth·ful /-fʊl/ *nc* (*pl* **—s**) as much as can be put into the mouth comfortably at one time: *have only a mouthful of food.*

'**mouth·organ** *nc* a small musical instrument, played by passing it along the lips and blowing.

'**mouth·piece** *nc* (**a**) the part of a musical instrument etc placed at or between the lips. (**b**) a person, newspaper etc that expresses the opinions of others: *Which newspaper is the mouthpiece of the Socialists?*

mouth[2] /maʊð/ *vt,vi* to move the lips as if speaking (words) but not make any sounds.

mov·able /'mu:vəbl/ *adj* **1** that can be moved. Compare portable. **2** varying in date: *Easter is a movable feast.*

move[1] /mu:v/ *nc* **1** an act of changing position: *a slight move of the head.* Ⓝ *'Movement' is more usual.* **2** an act of changing one's place: *a move to a different part of the beach.* **on the move** (*informal*) travelling or moving(4) from one place to another. **3** one of several actions as part of a plan, purpose: *What's our next move?* **get a move on** (*informal*; usually *imperative*) to hurry up. **make a move** to begin to act: *Unless we make a move soon, we'll miss the train.* **4** an act of changing one's home, business etc to a new address: *a move to a bigger house/to another job.* **5** a movement of a piece that is allowed in a board game: *the moves in chess.* **6** a player's turn to move a piece in a board game: *It's your move, I think.*

move[2] /mu:v/ *v* **1** *vt,vi* (to cause a person, thing) to change from one position to another: *moving one's leg. Don't move while I take the photograph.* **2** *vt,vi* (to cause a person, thing) to change pos-

ition: *We moved from the front of the theatre to the back. Move your chair nearer the fire.* **3** *vt,vi* (to cause a person, thing) to be in motion: *It was calm and not a leaf moved. Don't jump on the bus while it's moving.* **4** *vi,vt* **move (sb/sth) (to . . .)** to change the address of (one's home, business etc): *moving (the family) to a new house; move to another job.* **move house** to take all one's furniture etc to another home. ⇨ move (sb) in/out. **5** *vt,vi* (to cause a person) to do something: *Nothing seems to move her. If we don't move soon another business will win the order.* **6** *vt* to have an effect on (a person, feelings, emotions): *I was moved by her sad story. His sadness moved me to tears.* ⇨ moving. **7** *vt,vi* to change the position of (a piece) in a board game: *I can't move (either of my bishops).* **8** *vt* (*formal*) to put (an idea, motion etc) forward for discussion and decision at a meeting: *I move that the money be spent on books.* **9** *vi* to make progress: *This work is moving far too slowly.* **10** *vi* to pass one's time with people: *moving in the best society.*

move about to be sent, go, to many different places, e.g. because of one's job: *As an international lawyer, she moves about a great deal.*

move along (**a**) (often *imperative*) to go away: *The police asked the crowd to move along.* (**b**) to make progress: *How is the job moving along?*

move down (sth) (used as a request by an official) to move away from the entrance and farther into the bus, train etc: *Move down (the bus), please!*

move (sb) in (to help a person) to take possession of another home, office etc. **move in (on sb/sth)** to come closer (to a person, thing): *The camera moved in (on the two climbers).*

move into a place to take possession of another home, office etc.

move off (of a vehicle, a procession) to begin to move(3).

move on (**a**) to change to another job, home etc: *It's time to move on.* (**b**) to go forward: *Time is moving on.* **move sb on** (of an official, e.g. the police) to tell a person to go somewhere else.

move out (of an expedition, army etc) to begin a planned series of movements. **move (sb) out** (to help a person) to leave a home, office etc (to go to another one).

move over (often *imperative*) to move away in order to make space for another.

move towards sth (**a**) to move nearer to something. (**b**) to make progress towards an agreement etc: *The two leaders are moving towards a better understanding.*

move up (of prices, rates, stocks) to increase. **move up (sth)** = move down (sth). **move sb up** to promote an employee. **move up (in) sth** to make progress in one's work, in society etc: *He quickly moved up the ranks. She's moved up in the world since she married Charles.*

move·ment /'mu:vmənt/ *n* **1** *nc,nu* (an act of) changing position: *a slight movement of the head. Any movement could damage your knee.* ⇨ move[1](1). **2** *nc* a change of place or position, esp as part of a series: *movements in chess/ballet dancing.* **3** *nc* a moving part of a machine or a group of such parts: *the movement of a clock or a watch.* **4** *nc* a united action and effort of a group of people for a purpose: *the movement to abolish nuclear armaments.* **5** *nc* (*music*) a main division of a musical work: *the final movement of the Ninth Symphony.* **6** *nu* (*commerce*) activity (in a stock market etc): *There was not much movement in oil shares.*

mov·ed /muːvd/ *adj* (*pred*) (of a person) made to feel sympathy, sadness etc: *I was moved by her sad story.*

movie /'muːvɪ/ *nc* (*informal* or *US*) film[1](4). **the movies** the cinema (industry).

mov·ing /'muːvɪŋ/ *adj* causing an effect on a person's feelings or emotions: *a moving account of life in a refugee camp.* ⇨ **move**[2](6).

mow /məʊ/ *vt* (*pt* **—ed**, *pp* **—n** /məʊn/) **1** to cut (grass etc) (with a *lawn-mower*). **2 mow sb down** to destroy, kill, people in large numbers: *Our men were mown down by the enemy's guns.*

MP /ˌem 'piː/ *abbr* **1** Member of Parliament (in the House of Commons). **2** Military Police.

mpg /ˌem piː 'dʒiː/ *abbr* miles per gallon (of petrol).

mph /ˌem piː 'eɪtʃ/ *abbr* miles per hour (to measure speed). ⇨ **kph**.

Mr /'mɪstə(r)/ *abbr* mister.

Mrs /'mɪsɪz/ (used in front of the name of a married woman who has no other title).

Ms /məz/ (used in front of the name of a woman (married or unmarried) who has no other title).

MS *written abbr* manuscript.

MSc /ˌem es 'siː/ *abbr* Master of Science.

Mt *written abbr* Mount[1].

mth *written abbr* month.

much[1] /mʌtʃ/ *adj* or *det* a large amount of: *We haven't much time. Did you have much food left? How much money will it cost? Tell me how much money you need. There's too much pepper in this soup. He has so much money that he owns four cars. We did (just) as much (= the same amount of) work as you.* ⇨ **much**[3]. ⓝ *'Much'* is usually used only in negative statements and questions, unless the context is very formal, as in *Much happiness filled the house. 'A lot of', 'a great deal of', 'plenty of'* are much more usual. However, *'much'* is used in affirmative sentences when used with *how, too, so* and *as*, as in the examples above. Compare **few**[1], **less**[1], **many**[1].

much[2] /mʌtʃ/ *adv* **1** *much + comparative* to a larger, an even larger, extent or degree: *It's much longer. I'm much happier/sadder.* **much more *+ adj =* much + comparative:** *I'm much more excited/depressed.* **so much so that . . .** to such an (extreme) extent that: *He worked hard, so much so that he became ill.* **2** (used with verbal phrases) to a large extent or degree: *It doesn't matter much. He doesn't like cabbage much. It costs too much. I love you very much. 'Do you like it?'—'Not much.' 'Yes, very much.'* ⓝ *'Much'* is usually used only in negative statements but *'much'* can be used in affirmative statements with *too, very* etc as in the examples above. Compare **less**[2], **more**[2]. **much less . . .** (used to show that what has been mentioned is more significant etc than what follows): *I didn't see him, much less speak to him.* **much the same (as sb/sth)** about the same, similar (to a person, thing): *Her health is much the same (as yesterday).*

much[3] /mʌtʃ/ *pron* **much (of sth)** a large

amount (of): *I have some money but not much. Eat as much as you like. Much of what you say is true. Did she say much? How much did it cost? You've given me too much. I have so much that there's no room for it all. I earn (just) as much as you.* ⇨ **much**[1]. Compare **few**[2], **little**[3]. **as much** to that extent: *I thought as much* (= That is what I thought). **as much again** the same amount again: *A third of the town was destroyed and as much again was seriously damaged.* **a bit much** (*informal*) (of behaviour, an action) an amount, degree, that is unacceptably large: *I don't mind taking you, but it's a bit much to ask me to pay!* **much as** (*conj*) although: *Much as I like you, I won't marry you.* **not much of a sb/sth** not a good example of: *She's not much of a cook.* **so much for (that/sb/sth)** that is all that needs to be said, done etc about (that/her/him/it): *So much for the organizing; now, what about the cost?* **not make much of sth** to fail to understand it: *I didn't/couldn't make much of her lecture.* **not think much of sb/sth** to have a poor opinion of a person, thing. Compare **less**[4], **many**[2].

much·ness /'mʌtʃnɪs/ *n* (only in) **be much of a muchness** to be very similar.

muck[1] /mʌk/ *nu* **1** the solid waste matter of animals (to be) used as manure. **2** dirt; filth. **make a muck of sth** (*informal*) to do a task badly.

muck[2] /mʌk/ *v* **1** *vi* **muck about/around** (*informal*) to do useless or unnecessary activities: *He's mucking about when he should be working.* **2** *vi* **muck in** (*informal*) to do work with others; share duties and responsibilities. **3** *vt* **muck sth up** (**a**) to do a task badly. (**b**) to make clothes, paper, cloths etc dirty.

mu·cous /'mjuːkəs/ *adj* of, like, covered with, mucus.

,mucous 'membrane *nc* (the —) (*anat*) the skin that lines the nose, mouth and food canal.

mu·cus /'mjuːkəs/ *nu* a sticky, slimy substance (as) produced by the mucous membrane: *Snails and slugs leave a trail of mucus.*

mud /mʌd/ *nu* soft, wet earth: *Rain turns soil into mud.*

'mud·guard *nc* a curved cover over a wheel (of a bicycle etc)

muddle[1] /'mʌdl/ *n sing* a confused state: *Everything was in a muddle and I couldn't find what I wanted.*

muddle[2] /'mʌdl/ *v* **1** *vt* **muddle sb; muddle sth (up)** to put a (person, group of things) in a state of confusion or disorder: *muddling (up) the photos. I was muddled by all the different advice.* **2** *vi* **muddle along/on** to live, act with no clear purpose or plan: *He's still muddling along/on.* **3** *vi* **muddle through** to complete a task in spite of inefficiency, obstacles of one's own making etc.

mud·dy[1] /'mʌdɪ/ *adj* (**-ier, -iest**) full of, covered with, mud: *muddy roads/shoes.*

mud·dy[2] /'mʌdɪ/ *vt* (*pt,pp* **-ied**) to cover, stain, (something) with mud: *You've muddied the carpet.*

mues·li /'mjuːzlɪ/ *nu* a mixture of grain, fruit, nuts etc, eaten with milk.

mu·ez·zin /muːˈezɪn/ *nc* a man who calls people to prayer in a mosque.

muff /mʌf/ *nc* a covering, open at both ends, used

to keep the hands warm.

muffle /'mʌfəl/ vt (usually passive) **1** to wrap or cover (a person, thing) for warmth or protection: muffled (up) in a heavy overcoat. **2** to cover (a machine etc) to reduce the sound it makes. ⇨ muffler(2).

muf·fler /'mʌflə(r)/ nc **1** (dated) a cloth worn round the neck for warmth. **2** something used to reduce sound: the muffler in a car engine.

mug¹ /mʌg/ nc **1** a drinking vessel with a handle, for use without a saucer: a beer-mug. **2** as much as a mug holds: a mug of coffee. **3** (sl) a face: What an ugly mug you have! **4** (sl) a foolish person: You're a mug to believe him.

mug² /mʌg/ vt (-gg-) (sl) to attack (a person) violently and rob, e.g. in a dark street.

mug·ger nc a person who mugs.

mug·ging nc,nu such an attack.

mug³ /mʌg/ vt (-gg-) mug sth up (informal) to (try to) become familiar with information etc on which one is soon to be tested.

mug·gins /'mʌgɪnz/ nc (pl —es) (derog) a fool.

mug·gy /'mʌgɪ/ adj (-ier, -iest) (of the weather etc) unpleasantly damp and warm.

muggi·ness nu

Mu·ham·mad /mə'hæmɪd/ n the founder of Islam.

Mu·ham·mad·an /-ən/ adj, nc (of) a believer in Islam.

mul·ber·ry /'mʌlbərɪ/ nc (pl -ies) a tree with broad, dark-green leaves on which silkworms feed; its fruit (dark purple or white).

mule¹ /mju:l/ nc an animal that is the young of a horse and a donkey. ⇨ stubborn.

mule² /mju:l/ nc a slipper without a heel.

mull /mʌl/ vt mull sth over to think about something carefully.

mul·led /'mʌld/ adj (attrib) (of wine) heated with spices added.

mul·ti·far·ious /ˌmʌltɪ'feərɪəs/ adj (formal) many and various: his multifarious duties.

mul·ti·lat·er·al /ˌmʌltɪ'lætərəl/ adj involving two or more participants: multilateral nuclear disarmament (i.e. after agreement between two or more countries).

mul·ti·na·tion·al /ˌmʌltɪ'næʃnəl/ adj, nc (of) a very large business with offices in many countries.

mul·tiple¹ /'mʌltɪpl/ adj (no comp) having many parts or elements: a multiple-choice exercise (with several answers given, of which one is right).

mul·tiple² /'mʌltɪpl/ nc (maths) a quantity which contains another quantity an exact number of times: 28 is a multiple of 7. ⇨ LCM.

multi·pli·ca·tion /ˌmʌltɪplɪ'keɪʃn/ nc,nu (an example of) the process of multiplying or being multiplied: The symbol '×' stands for multiplication. 3 × 11 is an easy multiplication.

mul·ti·plic·ity /ˌmʌltɪ'plɪsətɪ/ nu (formal) a large variety or number: a multiplicity of duties.

mul·ti·ply /'mʌltɪplaɪ/ vt,vi (pt,pp -ied) **1** multiply (sth) (by sth) to increase (a number) by the number of times mentioned: 6 multiplied by 5 is 30 (i.e. 6 × 5 = 30). **2** to increase in number: The money multiplied until he was very rich.

mul·ti-storey /ˌmʌltɪ 'stɔ:rɪ/ adj (attrib) having many storeys: a multi-storey car park.

mul·ti·tude /'mʌltɪtju:d/ nc **1** a large number (esp of people gathered together). **2** (the —) the

ordinary people: policies which appeal to the multitude.

mul·ti·tud·in·ous /ˌmʌltɪ'tju:dɪnəs/ adj (formal) large in number.

multi-word verb /ˌmʌltɪ ˌwɜːd 'vɜːb/ nc (gram) a verb made up of several words, e.g. come about, go into something, keep a person on, make for a place, set up house. ⇨ phrasal verb, prepositional verb.

mum /mʌm/ nc (informal) mother.

mumble /'mʌmbl/ vi,vt mumble (away); mumble sth to say something unclearly: The old man was mumbling away to himself. She mumbled an excuse.

mum·bo-jum·bo /ˌmʌmbəʊ 'dʒʌmbəʊ/ nu meaningless language.

mum·mi·fy /'mʌmɪfaɪ/ vt (pt,pp -ied) to preserve (a dead body). ⇨ mummy².

mum·my¹ /'mʌmɪ/ nc (pl -ies) (informal) mother.

mum·my² /'mʌmɪ/ nc (pl -ies) a dead body preserved from decay by using certain chemicals etc.

mumps /mʌmps/ nu (the —) (used with a sing verb) a contagious disease with painful swellings in the neck.

munch /mʌntʃ/ vi,vt munch (away at) sth to chew (food) with a lot of movement of the jaw: munching (away at) a hard apple.

mun·dane /mʌn'deɪn/ adj dull and unexciting: mundane jobs in factories.

mung bean /'mʌŋ bi:n/ nc a plant from Asia with a small green bean, used to grow bean sprouts as food.

mu·ni·ci·pal /mju:'nɪsɪpl/ adj of a town or city: municipal buildings (e.g. the town hall, public library).

mu·ni·ci·pal·ly /-plɪ/ adv

mu·ni·ci·pal·ity /mju:ˌnɪsɪ'pælətɪ/ nc (pl -ies) **1** a town, city, district, with local self-government. **2** the governing body of such a town etc.

mu·ni·tions /mju:'nɪʃnz/ n pl military supplies, esp guns, shells, bombs etc.

mur·al /'mjʊərəl/ adj of, like, on, a wall: a mural painting. □ nc a painting on a wall.

mur·der¹ /'mɜːdə(r)/ n **1** nc,nu (an instance of) the unlawful killing of a person on purpose: commit murder; guilty of murder. **get away with murder** (informal) to do whatever one wishes and not be punished. **2** nu (fig; informal) a very unpleasant experience: Driving in London is murder.

mur·der² /'mɜːdə(r)/ vt **1** to kill (a person) unlawfully and on purpose. **2** (fig) to spoil (something) by not having skill or knowledge: murder a piece of music (= play it very badly).

mur·der·er nc a person guilty of murder.

mur·der·ess /-ɪs/ nc a woman murderer.

mur·der·ous /-əs/ adj concerning, suggesting, designed for, murder: a murderous-looking villain.

murky /'mɜːkɪ/ adj (-ier, -iest) dark; gloomy: a murky night/river.

murk·ily /-əlɪ/ adv

mur·mur¹ /'mɜːmə(r)/ nc **1** a low, continuous, indistinct sound: the murmur of bees in the garden; the murmur of distant traffic. **2** a quiet expression of feeling: They paid the higher taxes without a murmur (i.e. without complaining).

mur·mur² /'mɜ:mə(r)/ v 1 vi to make a murmur(1): a murmuring brook. 2 vt to say (something) in a quiet voice: murmur a prayer.

muscle¹ /'mʌsl/ n 1 nc,nu (a band or bundle of) elastic substance in the body that can be tightened or loosened to produce movement: Don't move a muscle! (= Stay perfectly still!) 2 nu (fig) power: The new information will add more muscle to our argument.

muscle² /'mʌsl/ vi muscle in (on sb/sth) (informal) to use force to gain a share or an advantage: muscling in on a business deal.

mus·cu·lar /'mʌskjʊlə(r)/ adj 1 (no comp) of the muscles: muscular rheumatism. 2 having strong muscles: a muscular man.

muse /mju:z/ vi muse (over/on sth) to think deeply or dreamily, ignoring what is happening around one: musing over memories of the past.

mu·seum /mju:'zɪəm/ nc a building in which objects concerning art, history, science etc are displayed.

mush /mʌʃ/ nu a soft, thick mass.

mushy adj (-ier, -iest) like mush: mushy peas.

mush·room¹ /'mʌʃrʊm/ nc 1 a fast-growing flowerless plant (called a fungus) of which some kinds can be eaten. 2 (fig) a sudden, rapid development: the mushroom of London suburbs.

mush·room² /'mʌʃrʊm/ vi to grow, spread, rapidly: English language schools are mushrooming in London.

mu·sic /'mju:zɪk/ nu 1 an art form of making pleasant combinations of sounds, esp using a specially designed instrument: pop music; classical music. face the music (informal) to be prepared to suffer the results of one's (bad) behaviour or activity. 2 the written or printed signs representing these sounds: sheet music.

'music centre nc a unit containing a radio, record-player and tape-recorder.

'music-stand nc a framework for holding sheets of printed music.

mu·si·cal¹ /'mju:zɪkl/ adj of, fond of, skilled in, music.

‚musical 'comedy nc a light, romantic play or film with songs and dancing.

‚musical 'instrument nc one designed for playing music, e.g. the piano, violin, flute.

mu·si·cal·ly /-klɪ/ adv

mu·si·cal² /'mju:zɪkl/ nc a film with music and singing.

mu·si·cian /mju:'zɪʃn/ nc a person skilled in playing or composing music.

musk /mʌsk/ nu a strong-smelling substance produced in glands by male deer, used in the manufacture of perfumes.

Mus·lim /'mʊzlɪm/ (also **Moslem**) adj, nc (of) a believer in Islam.

mus·lin /'mʌzlɪn/ nu a kind of very fine cotton cloth, used for dresses etc.

mus·sel /'mʌsl/ nc a kind of sea animal (a mollusc) with a black shell, eaten as food.

must¹ /mʌst/ n a must (informal) something that it is essential to see, do, hear etc: Tom Stoppard's new play is a must.

must² /məst strong form: mʌst/ auxiliary verb Ⓝ 'Must' is a modal auxiliary used with another verb to express obligation. 'Must' has no infinitive or imperative form and no participles. 'Must' is always

followed by an infinitive without 'to'. Compare have¹(2), need²(1), ought, should. (Present and future tenses (all persons) must, negative must not, mustn't /'mʌsnt/; must have can be shortened to must've /'mʌstəv/) 1 (used to express an obligation or an order): You must finish your work before you go. When it gets dark you must come home. Cars must not be parked near the corner. I broke the vase so I must buy a new one. I must try to remember to telephone tomorrow. Must I complete this application form? He told me that I mustn't tell anyone. Ⓝ 'Must not' expresses an order not to do something, as in Visitors must not feed the birds. 'Need not' or 'do not have to' are used to say that something is not necessary, as in You needn't pay until it arrives, He doesn't have to sign it. 'Must' cannot be used to talk about the past. Use 'had to', as in I had to buy a new one because I broke it. 'Shall/will have to' is used for future obligation, as in You'll have to pay if you break it. 2 (used to express strong advice): You must do something about your hair. Compare ought(2). 3 (used to express strong possibility or certainty): You must be tired after such a long walk. There must be some mistake because I wasn't there. You must be joking! The telephone's ringing—it must be your mother. He must've left the bag on the bus. 'I didn't do it'—'You must have.' Ⓝ 'Must' is only possible in affirmative sentences. Use 'can/can't' in questions and negative sentences, as in Who can that be? It can't be true. You can't be serious! 'Must have' is used to express certainty. Compare She must have (= I think it is certain that she) missed the train and She may/might have (= I think it is possible that she) missed the train. Compare may(2).

mus·tache nc = moustache.

mus·tard /'mʌstəd/ nu (a plant with yellow flowers and seeds that produce) a fine, yellow powder, made into hot sauce.

mus·ter /'mʌstə(r)/ vt,vi to collect or gather (people, support etc) together: Go and muster (up) all the men you can find.

mustn't /'mʌsnt/ = must not. ⇨ must².

must've /'mʌstəv/ = must have. ⇨ must².

musty /'mʌstɪ/ adj (-ier, -iest) smelling or tasting mouldy: a musty room/book.

musti·ness /'mʌstɪnɪs/ nu

mu·ta·tion /mju:'teɪʃn/ nc,nu (science) (an instance of) a change in the basic structure of a living or developing organism which can affect the shape, size etc.

mute¹ /mju:t/ adj 1 making no sound: staring at me in mute amazement. 2 (of a person) dumb. 3 (of a letter in a word) not sounded: The 'b' in 'dumb' is mute.

mute² /mju:t/ nc 1 a dumb person. 2 a piece of bone or metal used to soften the sound of a musical instrument.

mu·ti·late /'mju:tɪleɪt/ vt to damage (a person, thing) by breaking, tearing or cutting off a necessary part.

mu·ti·la·tion /ˌmju:tɪ'leɪʃn/ nc,nu

mu·ti·nous /'mju:tɪnəs/ adj guilty of mutiny; rebellious: mutinous sailors.

mu·tin·eer /ˌmju:tɪ'nɪə(r)/ nc a person guilty of mutiny.

mu·ti·ny /'mju:tɪnɪ/ nc,nu (pl -ies) (an instance of) a rebellion against lawful authority, esp on a ship. □ *vi* (*pt,pp* **-ied**) to take part in a mutiny.

mut·ter /ˈmʌtə(r)/ *vi,vt* **mutter (away); mutter sth** to say something in a low voice not meant to be heard: *He was muttering away to himself.* □ *nc* a muttered speech or sound.

mut·ton /ˈmʌtən/ *nu* the flesh of fully grown sheep, eaten as food.

mu·tu·al /ˈmjuːtʃʊəl/ *adj* (*no comp*) **1** (of love, friendship, respect, feelings, opinions etc) shared: *mutual suspicion/affection.* **2** each to the other(s): *mutual aid.* **3** common to two or more people: *our mutual friend Bob* (i.e. a friend of both of us).

mu·tu·al·ly /-tʃəlɪ/ *adv*

muzzle¹ /ˈmʌzl/ *nc* **1** the nose and mouth of an animal (e.g. a dog or fox). **2** a guard of straps or wires placed over this to prevent biting etc.

muzzle² /ˈmʌzl/ *vt* **1** to put a muzzle on (a dog etc). **2** (*fig*) to prevent (a person, newspaper etc) from expressing opinions freely.

muz·zy /ˈmʌzɪ/ *adj* (**-ier, -iest**) (of a person, thoughts) confused (e.g. because of alcohol).

MW *written abbr* (*radio*) medium wave.

my /maɪ/ *possessive adj* or *det* **1** of, belonging to, me: *Where's my hat? That's my pen, not yours.* ⇨ mine. **2** (used as a part of a form of address): *Yes, my dear. My dear Anne, . . .* **3** (used in exclamations): *My goodness!*

my·opia /maɪˈəʊpɪə/ *nu* an inability to see objects that are far away.

my·op·ic /maɪˈɒpɪk/ *adj*

myr·iad /ˈmɪrɪəd/ *nc* **myriad (of) sth** (*formal*) a very large number of things: *a myriad flowers.*

myrrh /mɜː(r)/ *nu* a sweet-smelling, bitter-tasting substance, used to make incense and perfumes.

myrtle /ˈmɜːtl/ *nc* a kind of evergreen shrub with shiny leaves and sweet-smelling white flowers.

my·self /maɪˈself/ *pron* **1** (used as the *reflexive* form of *my*): *I hurt myself. I must look after myself.* (**all**) **by myself** ⇨ by²(1). **2** (used for emphasis): *I will carry it myself.* **3** my usual self: *I'm not/don't feel myself today.*

mys·teri·ous /mɪˈstɪərɪəs/ *adj* full of, suggesting, mystery: *a mysterious visitor; a mysterious-looking parcel.*

mys·teri·ous·ly *adv*

mys·tery /ˈmɪstərɪ/ *n* (*pl* **-ies**) **1** *nc* something of which the cause or origin is impossible to explain or understand: *The murder is an unsolved mystery.* **2** *nu* the quality, state, of being mysterious: *Agatha Christie's books are filled with mystery.*

mys·tic /ˈmɪstɪk/ *nc* a believer in, practiser of, mysticism.

mys·ti·cal /ˈmɪstɪkl/ *adj* having, concerning, hidden meaning or spiritual power; causing feelings of awe and wonder: *mystical rites and ceremonies.*

mys·ti·cism /ˈmɪstɪsɪzəm/ *nu* the teaching and belief that a knowledge of God and of real truth can be obtained through prayer and meditation.

mys·ti·fy /ˈmɪstɪfaɪ/ *vt* (*pt,pp* **-ied**) to puzzle, bewilder, (a person).

mys·ti·fi·ca·tion /ˌmɪstɪfɪˈkeɪʃn/ *nc,nu*

mys·tique /mɪˈstiːk/ *nc* an atmosphere of mystery, power etc that surrounds a (kind of) person, profession, object etc: *the mystique of computers.*

myth /mɪθ/ *n* **1** *nc* a well-known story used long ago to explain natural events, the history of a society or race etc: *Greek myths.* **2** *nu* such stories collectively: *famous in myth and legend.* **3** *nc* a person, thing etc that is imaginary or invented: *That rich uncle of whom he boasts is only a myth.*

mythi·cal /ˈmɪθɪkl/ *adj* (*no comp*) (**a**) of, existing only in, myth: *mythical heroes.* (**b**) imaginary: *mythical wealth.*

myth·ol·ogy /mɪˈθɒlədʒɪ/ *nc,nu* (*pl* **-ies**) (a system, collection, of) myths: *Greek mythology.*

mytho·logi·cal /ˌmɪθəˈlɒdʒɪkl/ *adj*

Nn

N, n /en/ (*pl* **N's, n's** /enz/) **1** the 14th letter of the English alphabet. **2** (*maths*) an indefinite or unknown number or amount.

n *written abbr* (*gram*) noun.

N *written abbr* North.

nab /næb/ *vt* (**-bb-**) (usually *passive; informal*) to catch (a thief etc): *be nabbed by the police.*

na·dir /ˈneɪdɪə(r)/ *nc* (**the —**) (*fig; formal*) the lowest, weakest, point: *at the nadir of one's hopes.* Compare zenith.

nag¹ /næg/ *nc* (*informal*) an old horse.

nag² /næg/ *vt,vi* (**-gg-**) **nag ((at) sb) (about sth)** to find fault with a person often: *She nagged (at) him all day long.*

nag·ger *nc* (*derog*) a person who nags.

nail¹ /neɪl/ *nc* **1** the layer of hard substance over the outer tip of a finger (ˈfinger-nail) or toe (ˈtoe-nail). **2** a piece of metal, pointed at one end and with a flat head at the other, (to be) hammered into articles to hold them together etc. ⇨ hard¹(4). **hit the nail on the head** to guess, say, do etc the right thing.

nail² /neɪl/ *vt* **1** to fasten, join etc (something) using a nail(2): *nail a lid on a box; nail down a carpet; nail up a poster.* **nail sb down (to sth)** to make a person say clearly what he or she intends to do. **2** (*informal*) to get (a person)'s attention: *He nailed me in the corridor.*

nail-biting *adj* anxious; causing anxiety.

ˈnail-brush *nc* one for cleaning nails(1).

ˈnail-file *nc* a small, flat file for shaping nails(1).

ˈnail-scissors *n pl* small scissors for trimming nails(1).

ˈnail-varnish/-polish *nu* the kind for giving a shiny colour to nails(1).

naïve (also **naive**) /naɪˈiːv/ *adj* (because) young and inexperienced: *a naïve girl/remark.*

naïve·ly *adv*

naïve·ty (also **naïve·té**) /naɪˈiːvɪtɪ/ *nu* the state of being naïve.

na·ked /ˈneɪkɪd/ *adj* **1** without clothes on: *as naked as the day he was born.* **2** (*fig*) without the usual covering: *a naked light* (i.e. without a lamp-shade). **with the naked eye** without using a microscope, telescope or other aid. **3** without hiding or leaving out anything: *the naked facts; the naked truth.*

na·ked·ly *adv*

na·ked·ness *nu*

name¹ /neɪm/ *n* **1** *nc* the word(s) by which a person, animal, place, thing etc is known: *The teacher knows all the pupils by their first names.*

What is your family/maiden name? **answer to the name of sb** to have as one's name. **be/go by/under the name of** ... to be called ... **call sb names** to call a person insulting names such as 'liar', 'coward'. **give sb a bad name** to cause a person to be considered bad. **not have a penny to one's name** to be without money. **take sb's name in vain** to use a name disrespectfully. **2** *n sing* reputation; fame: *have a name for being honest.* **give sb/sth a bad name; get a bad name (for oneself)** to cause a person, business, school etc to have/get (for oneself) a bad reputation. **make a name for oneself** to become well-known. **3** *nc* a famous person: *the great names of history.*

'name-dropping *nu* the practice of mentioning the names of important people (as if they were friends) in order to impress people. Hence **'name-drop** *vi* (**-pp-**).

'name-sake *nc* a person, thing, with the same name as another.

name² /neɪm/ *vt* **1** to give a name to (a person thing): *They named the child John.* ⇨ family/first/given name. **name sb after sb** to give that person the same name as another person. **2** to say the name(s) of (things): *Can you name all the plants and trees in this garden?* **3** to choose or select and state (a person, date, place etc): *Mr Brown has been named as the new chairman. Name your price! Please name the day for our wedding.*

name·less /'neɪmlɪs/ *adj* **1** having an unknown name: *a nameless grave; a well-known person who shall be nameless* (= whose name I shall not mention). **2** too bad to be named: *nameless vices.*

name·ly /'neɪmlɪ/ *adv* that is to say: *Only one boy was absent, namely Harry.*

nan·ny /'nænɪ/ *nc* (*pl* **-ies**) a woman employed by a family to look after the babies and young children.

nan·ny-goat /'nænɪ gəʊt/ *nc* a female goat. Compare billy-goat.

nap¹ /næp/ *nc* a short sleep (esp during the day): *have/take a nap after lunch.*

nap² /næp/ *vi* (**-pp-**) to have a nap¹. **catch sb napping** to find a person not carrying out her or his duties.

na·palm /'neɪpɑːm/ *nu* a kind of jellied petroleum, used in making bombs.

nape /neɪp/ *nc* the back of the neck.

nap·kin /'næpkɪn/ *nc* (also **'table-napkin**) a piece of cloth used at meals for protecting clothing, for wiping the lips etc.

nap·py /'næpɪ/ *nc* (*pl* **-ies**) a towel folded round a baby's bottom and between its legs.

nar·cis·sus /nɑːˈsɪsəs/ *nc* (*pl* **—es** or **-cissi** /-ˈsɪsaɪ/) one of many kinds of bulb plant (*daffodil* etc) with white or yellow flowers in the spring.

nar·cot·ic /nɑːˈkɒtɪk/ *adj, nc* **1** (of) a drug which produces sleep or reduces pain and is dangerous if taken in large amounts: *Opium is a narcotic* (*drug*). **2** (of) a person addicted to narcotics.

nar·rate /nəˈreɪt/ *vt* (*formal*) to tell (a story); give an account of (something): *narrating one's adventures.*

nar·ra·tion /nəˈreɪʃn/ *nc,nu*

nar·ra·tor /-tə(r)/ *nc* a person who tells a story.

nar·ra·tive /'nærətɪv/ *adj, nc,nu* (*literature*) (of) (an example of) a style of writing giving a series of

events as a story, as used in novels and poetry.

nar·row¹ /'nærəʊ/ *adj* (**—er, —est**) **1** measuring a small amount across in comparison with length: *a narrow bridge.* Opp broad¹(1), wide¹(1). **2** small, limited: *a narrow circle of friends.* Opp wide¹(2). **3** by, with, a small amount: *a narrow escape from death; elected by a narrow majority.* **4** covering a small range: *What does the word mean in the narrowest sense?* Opp broad¹(3), wide¹(2). **5** (of the mind, ideas) not liberal or tolerant: *narrow political views.* Opp broad¹(6). ⇨ also straight³.

,narrow-'minded *adj* (*derog*) not willing to listen to or respect the opinions, ideas, of others. Opp broad-minded.

nar·row·ly *adv* only just: *She narrowly escaped drowning.*

nar·row·ness *nu*

nar·row² /'nærəʊ/ *vt,vi* (to cause something) to become narrow.

NASA /'næsə/ *acronym* National Aeronautics and Space Administration (the US government department for space exploration).

na·sal /'neɪzl/ *adj* of, for, in, the nose: *nasal sounds* (e.g. /m, n, ŋ/).

nas·ty /'nɑːstɪ/ *adj* (**-ier, -iest**) **1** disgusting, unpleasant: *medicine with a nasty smell and a nastier taste.* **2** immoral; threatening: *a man with a nasty mind; a nasty temper/look in his eye.* **a nasty piece of work** (*informal; derog*) an unpleasant person.

nas·ti·ly /-əlɪ/ *adv*

nas·ti·ness *nu*

na·tal /'neɪtl/ *adj* of, from, birth. ⇨ antenatal, postnatal.

na·tion /'neɪʃn/ *nc* a large community of people in a particular territory, having a society under one government. ⇨ State²(2).

'na·tion-wide *adj* concerning, happening, throughout a nation.

na·tion·al¹ /'næʃənl/ *adj* of, concerning, the (whole) nation; of a particular nation: *national dress.*

,national 'anthem *nc* the official song of a nation (e.g. 'God Save the Queen' in GB).

,national in'surance *nu* (*GB*) State contributions from earnings, used for health, pensions, unemployment pay etc.

,national 'park *nc* a public area of land for the use and enjoyment of the people.

,national 'service *nu* a period of compulsory service in the armed forces.

na·tion·al·ly /'næʃənəlɪ/ *adv*

na·tion·al² /'næʃənl/ *nc* a citizen of a nation.

na·tion·al·ism /'næʃnəlɪzəm/ *nu* **1** a strong feeling of loyalty to one's country. **2** (the belief in) a political attitude or system based on a feeling that (a) one's country should be politically independent; (b) one's country and way of life is superior.

na·tion·al·ist /'næʃnəlɪst/ *adj* of, based on, supporting, nationalism. □ *nc* a supporter of, believer in, nationalism.

na·tion·al·ity /ˌnæʃəˈnælətɪ/ *nc,nu* (*pl* **-ies**) the fact or state of being a member of a nation: *What is your nationality?*

na·tion·al·ize (also **-ise**) /'næʃnəlaɪz/ *vt* **1** (of a government) to transfer (an industry etc) from private to State ownership: *nationalize the rail-*

ways. ⇨ privatize. **2** to make (a person) a national: *nationalized Poles and Greeks in the USA.*

na·tion·al·iz·ation (also **-is·ation**) /ˌnæʃnəlaɪ-ˈzeɪʃn/ *nu*

na·tive[1] /ˈneɪtɪv/ *adj* **1** (*attrib*) of, connected with, the place of one's birth: *my native land; a native speaker of English.* **2 native to a place** (of plants, animals etc) having their origin in: *One of the animals native to India is the tiger.*

na·tive[2] /ˈneɪtɪv/ *nc* **1** a person born in a place, country etc: *a native of London/Britain/India/Kenya.* **2** an animal or plant natural to and having its origin in a certain area: *The kangaroo is a native of Australia.*

Na·tiv·ity /nəˈtɪvətɪ/ *n* (the —) the birth of Jesus Christ.

NATO /ˈneɪtəʊ/ *acronym* North Atlantic Treaty Organization (a military association between the US, Canada and several western European countries).

nat·ter /ˈnætə(r)/ *vi* (*informal*) to grumble, chatter, (esp to oneself): *What's she nattering (on) about now?*

natu·ral /ˈnætʃrəl/ *adj* **1** of, concerning, produced by, nature: *animals living in their natural* (= wild) *state; a country's natural resources* (= its minerals, forests etc). **2** (*attrib*) belonging to a person from birth, not because of surroundings or learning: *natural gifts/abilities.* **3** (of a person) born with the qualities or powers mentioned: *He's a natural orator* (= makes speeches easily). *Being kind is natural to her.* **4** ordinary; normal: *It is natural for a bird to fly. It's only natural that she would want her mother to be at her wedding.* **5** not exaggerated or self-conscious: *speak in a natural voice.*

ˌnatural ˈdeath *nc* one from age or disease, not as the result of an accident, murder etc.

ˌnatural ˈforces/pheˈnomena *n pl* the forces of nature, e.g. storms, thunder, lightning.

ˌnatural ˈgas *nu* gas for fuel found under the ground, not manufactured.

ˌnatural ˈhistory *nu* the scientific study of animals, plants, rocks etc.

ˌnatural ˈscience *nu* the scientific study of the natural world, e.g. biology, chemistry, geology.

ˌnatural seˈlection *nu* the theory that animals and plants survive or not in accordance with their ability to adapt themselves to their environment.

natu·ral·ism /ˈnætʃrəlɪzəm/ *nu* the accurate representation of nature in literature and art.

natu·ral·ist /ˈnætʃrəlɪst/ *nc* **1** a person who makes a special study of animals or plants. **2** a believer in, practiser of, naturalism.

natu·ral·is·tic /ˌnætʃrəlˈɪstɪk/ *adj* representing living things, objects etc as they really are: *a naturalistic painting/painter.* Compare abstract art.

natu·ral·ize (also **-ise**) /ˈnætʃrəlaɪz/ *vt* **1** to give (a person from another country) rights of citizenship: *naturalize immigrants into the US.* **2** to take (a word) from one language into another: *English sporting terms have been naturalized in many languages, e.g. 'football'.*

natu·ral·iz·ation (also **-is·ation**) /ˌnætʃrəlaɪ-ˈzeɪʃn/ *nu*

nat·ur·al·ly /ˈnætʃrəlɪ/ *adv* **1** because of the

ability from birth: *She's naturally musical.* **2** of course; as might be expected: *'Did you answer her letter?'—'Naturally!'* **3** without artificial help etc: *Her hair curls naturally.* **4** without exaggeration, pretence etc: *She speaks and behaves naturally.*

na·ture /ˈneɪtʃə(r)/ *n* **1** *nu* the whole universe and every created thing: *Is nature at its best in spring? Miracles are contrary to nature.* **2** *nc,nu* the qualities and characteristics, physical, mental and spiritual, which belong to a person or animal from birth: *It is in the nature of a dog to bark. It's not in his nature to be cruel.* ⇨ good-natured, human nature, second nature. **3 the nature of sth** (*science*) the essential qualities of something: *Chemists study the nature of gases.* **4** *n sing* sort; kind: *Things of this nature do not interest me.*

ˈnature cure *nc* a treatment of disease using natural remedies (e.g. sunlight, diet, exercise).

naught /nɔːt/ *n* nothing, esp in the phrases: **care naught for sb/sth** to have no interest in a person or thing; consider her, him or it worthless. **come to naught** (of a plan, idea) to fail.

naughty /ˈnɔːtɪ/ *adj* (**-ier**, **-iest**) (of children, behaviour etc) bad; wrong (but usually not seriously).

naught·ily /-əlɪ/ *adv*

naughti·ness *nu*

nausea /ˈnɔːzɪə/ *nu* a feeling of sickness or disgust: *be filled with nausea after eating octopus/at the sight of cruelty to animals.*

naus·eate /ˈnɔːzɪeɪt/ *vt* to cause (a person) to feel nausea.

naus·eat·ing /ˈnɔːzɪeɪtɪŋ/ *adj* causing nausea: *a nauseating smell.*

naus·eous /ˈnɔːzɪəs/ *adj* (*formal*) disgusting: *a nauseous joke.*

nauti·cal /ˈnɔːtɪkl/ *adj* of ships, sailors or navigation: *nautical experience.*

ˈnautical mile *nc* a measurement of distance, one 60th of a degree(1), 2025 yards (= 1852 metres). ⇨ knot[1](4).

na·val /ˈneɪvl/ *adj* (*attrib*) of a navy or warships: *naval officers/battles.*

nave /neɪv/ *nc* the central part of a church where the people sit.

na·vel /ˈneɪvl/ *nc* the small, round mark in the middle of the belly.

navi·gable /ˈnævɪɡəbl/ *adj* (of rivers, seas etc) suitable for ships: *The Rhine is navigable as far up as Switzerland.*

navi·gate /ˈnævɪɡeɪt/ *vt,vi* to plan or control the direction of (a ship or aircraft). **2** *vt* to sail over (a sea); sail up or down (a river).

navi·ga·tor /-tə(r)/ *nc* a person who navigates(1).

navi·ga·tion /ˌnævɪˈɡeɪʃn/ *nu* the act, science, of navigating.

na·vy /ˈneɪvɪ/ *nc* (*pl* **-ies**) **1** a country's warships. **2** the officers and men of a country's warships: *join the navy.*

ˌnavy ˈblue *adj, nu* dark blue (colour).

NB /ˌen ˈbiː/ *abbr* (Latin: *nota bene*) take special note; observe carefully.

nd *written abbr* (used only after 2) second: *2nd, 32nd* etc.

NE *written abbr* north-east.

nea·poli·tan /ˌnɪəˈpɒlɪtən/ *adj* with many flavours and colours: *neapolitan ice-cream.*

near¹ /nɪə(r)/ adj (**—er, —est**) **1** at a short distance from (in space or time): *the nearest parking place to here; on the near side of the river. Take the one near/nearest you. The beach is quite near. Summer is getting nearer all the time.* Ⓝ For a comparison of *near* and *close*, ⇨ the note at close¹(1). Compare far¹(1). **near at hand** ⇨ hand¹(1). **2** (attrib) directly connected by birth: *a near relation* (e.g. a brother, first cousin). Ⓝ '*Close*' is also possible. **3 near and dear** loved and trusted: *neighbours who are near and dear to us.* Compare close¹(3). **4 a near miss** ⇨ miss². **a near thing** ⇨ thing(4). **5** (attrib) on the side nearest to the edge of a road: *the near(side) lane of the motorway; the near front wheel.* Compare off¹(3).
,near-'sighted adj able to see near objects more clearly than far ones.
near·ly adv ⇨ separate entry.
near·ness nu

near² /nɪə(r)/ adv at a short distance: *I live (quite/very) near. Do you work anywhere near?* **as near as . . .** (suggesting a limit) to the extent that: *As near as I can guess, there were forty people present. They're the same height, or as near as makes no difference.* **nowhere near (as)** not at all (as): *She's nowhere near as clever.* **near by** very near: *There's a good hotel near by.* Compare nearby. **be near to sth** to be about to: *She was near to tears* (= almost crying). Ⓝ '*Close to*' is also possible. **near and far; far and near** everywhere: *search near and far.* Compare far²(1).

near³ /nɪə(r)/ prep at a short distance from (in space, time etc): *live near (to) the centre of town. Don't go (too) near the edge! It's nearer 6.30 than 6 o'clock.* **2** having a small difference only (in ability, similarity etc): *Who comes nearest her in beauty/intelligence?*

near⁴ /nɪə(r)/ vt (formal) to come, travel, near to (something): *He's nearing the end of his performance. The ship was nearing land.*

near·by /'nɪəbaɪ/ adj not far away: *a nearby restaurant.* Ⓝ '*Nearby*' is also often used as an adverb /,nɪə'baɪ/ as in *the family living nearby.*

near·ly /'nɪəlɪ/ adv not far from (in space, time etc): *We're nearly there. It's nearly one o'clock. I'm nearly finished/ready.* Ⓝ For a comparison of *nearly* and *almost*, ⇨ the note at *almost.* Compare hardly, scarcely. **not nearly . . .** not at all near (in amount etc): *I have £20 but that isn't nearly enough for my fare.*

near·side /'nɪəsaɪd/ adj (attrib) on the side nearest to the edge of a road: *the nearside door of a car.* Compare offside(1). ⇨ near¹(5).

neat /niːt/ adj (**—er, —est**) **1** (liking to have everything in good order, done carefully: *a neat worker; a neat desk; neat writing.* **2** cleverly said or done: *a neat reply/conjuring trick.* **3** (no comp) (of wines and spirits) without water etc added: *drink one's whisky neat.*
neat·ly adv
neat·ness nu

neath /niːθ/ prep (poetic) beneath.

nebu·la /'nebjʊlə/ nc (pl **nebulae** /-liː/) a group of very distant stars, mass of gas, seen in the night sky as a patch of light.
nebu·lar /-lə(r)/ adj of nebulae.
nebu·lous /'nebjʊləs/ adj (fig) without structure; vague: *a nebulous argument.*

nec·es·sar·ily /,nesə'serəlɪ/ adv as a necessary result: *Big men are not necessarily strong men.*

nec·ess·ary /'nesəsrɪ/ adj that must be; that cannot be avoided: *Sleep is necessary for/to good health. Is that really necessary? Is it necessary to play your records so loudly?* Opp unnecessary.

ne·ces·sit·ate /nɪ'sesɪteɪt/ vt (formal) to make (something) necessary: *The increase in population necessitates a greater food supply.*

ne·ces·sity /nɪ'sesətɪ/ n (pl **-ies**) **1** nu or sing the state, condition (e.g. a law of nature, a (serious) need, a social rule etc) that makes a certain result unavoidable: *He was driven by necessity to steal food for his starving children. Working twelve hours a day is a matter of necessity. Is there a necessity to play the music so loud? Is it a necessity that prices go up if wages go up? In times of necessity everyone must share what they have.* **2** nc (often pl) something that one cannot be, live etc without: *the necessities of life* (i.e. food, clothing and shelter).

neck¹ /nek/ n **1** nc the part of the body that connects the head and the shoulders: *wrap a scarf round one's neck.* **neck and neck** level in a race or struggle. **a pain in the neck** ⇨ pain(2). **break one's neck (to do sth)** (fig) to work extremely hard (to achieve something). ⇨ also breakneck. **risk one's neck** (informal) to do something dangerous. **stick one's neck out** (informal) to do or say something at the risk of severe criticism, pain etc. **talk through (the back of) one's neck** (informal) to talk, argue, foolishly. **2** nc the part of clothing going round the neck. **3** nu flesh of an animal's neck as used for food: *neck of lamb.* **4** nc something like a neck in shape or position: *the neck of a bottle; a narrow neck of land; the neck of a guitar.*
'neck·lace /-lɪs/ nc a string with beads etc worn round the neck as an ornament.
'neck·line nc (of fashions for women's clothes) a line or edge at or near the neck.
'neck·tie nc (the usual word) a tie¹(1).

neck² /nek/ vi (sl) to exchange kisses, caresses and hugs: *necking in the park.*

nec·tar /'nektə(r)/ nu **1** (science) the sweet liquid in flowers, collected by bees. **2** (fig) any delicious drink.

nec·tar·ine /'nektərɪn/ nc a kind of peach with thin, smooth skin and firm flesh.

née /neɪ/ adj (Fr) (put after the name of a married woman and before her father's family name): *Mrs J Smith, née Brown.*

need¹ /niːd/ n **1** nu or sing (**a) need (for sth/to do sth)** a condition, fact, of feeling that something necessary is absent: *There's a need for more engineers. There's no need (for you to start yet). There's a real need to improve our newspapers. Do you have any need for these boxes?* **if need be** if necessary: *If need be I'll ask Ben to help me.* **be in need of sb/sth** to lack something that is necessary: *be in need of a rest.* **2** (pl) things considered to be necessary: *My needs are few.* **3** nu (literary) misfortune; bad circumstances: *He helped me in my hour of need.*

need² /niːd/ auxiliary verb Ⓝ '*Need*' is a modal auxiliary verb used with another verb to express necessity or obligation. '*Need*' has no infinitive or imperative forms and no participles. '*Need*' is always followed by an infinitive without 'to'. Compare have¹(2), must²(1), ought, should. (*Present and future tense* (all persons): **need**, *negative* **need not, needn't** /'ni:dnt/; *Need* has no past tense.) **1 need** + *verb* (used to express a necessity or obligation): *You needn't eat the skin if you don't want to. He need not stay until the end. Need I explain everything twice? Need it have happened?* Ⓝ 'Need' is rarely used in affirmative sentences. Use 'need to + verb', as in need³(1) below. 'Need' is not often used in questions. Use 'must I/he?' For the difference between 'need not' and 'must not', ⇨ the note at must²(1). 'Need' cannot be used to talk about the past. Use 'had to', as in *Yesterday, he had to wait an hour*. 'Shall/will have to' is used for future obligation, as in *Tomorrow she'll have to work all day*. **need not have** + *pp*, was unnecessary: *You needn't have worried*. Ⓝ 'Did not need to + verb' and 'did not have to + verb' are more usual, as in *He didn't need to go, We didn't have to worry*. **2** (used in conversation) **(a)** (joined to the end of a statement to form a question): *'I needn't go, need I?'* Ⓝ The statement is always negative and the short addition is positive. **(b)** (used to make a short question): *'You needn't wait'—'Needn't I?'* Ⓝ The statement is always negative and the short question is also negative. **(c)** (used to give a short answer): *'Need I explain?'—'No, you needn't'*. Ⓝ Only a negative answer is possible. Use 'Yes, you must' for a positive answer.

need³ /ni:d/ *vt* Ⓝ 'Need' as a transitive verb has an infinitive form and participles and can be followed by an infinitive with 'to'. Compare need². **1 need to do sth** to have to do something as a necessity; must: *You need to work harder. I need to sleep. Do I need to fill in this application form? I agree that she needs to be told about the arrangements. You don't need to eat it. She didn't need to pay. Won't you need to take some food?* **2 need sb/ sth** to have a need for a person or thing: *This bath needs more hot water. We all need plenty of exercise. Do you need any help? I'm here if you need me. Will you be needing me this afternoon?* **3 need sth** to deserve something because of something done, said etc: *That boy needs a slap!*

need·ful /'ni:dfʊl/ *adj* (*formal*) necessary (the usual word): *do what is needful*.

needle¹ /'ni:dl/ *nc* **1** a thin, pointed piece of polished steel with a small hole at one end for thread, used in sewing. **look for a needle in a haystack** to search hopelessly. ⇨ also pins and needles. **2** a long, thin piece of metal used for knitting. **3** a pointer used as an indicator in a measuring instrument, compass etc. **4** anything like a needle(1) in shape: *pine-needles*. **5** a stylus used in playing records.

'needle·craft/·work *nu* sewing; embroidery.

needle² /'ni:dl/ *vt* (*informal*) to make (a person) annoyed or irritated.

need·less /'ni:dles/ *adj* (*attrib*) unnecessary: *needless work*. **needless to say, . . .** (used to introduce a statement giving more information) it is/seems unnecessary to add . . . : *Needless to say, I'm also very hungry*.

need·less·ly *adv*

needn't /'ni:dnt/ = *need not*. ⇨ need².

ne'er /neə(r)/ *adv* (*poetic*) never.

ne·ga·tion /nɪ'geɪʃn/ *nc,nu* (*formal*) (an act of) denying, refusing: *a negation of one's responsibilities*.

nega·tive¹ /'negətɪv/ *adj* **1** expressing 'no', 'not', a refusal: *give a negative answer. Negative statements and questions in English have 'not' with the verb*. Compare affirmative. **2** lacking commitment, enthusiasm: *negative criticism* (= that does not help by making useful suggestions). Opp positive¹(3). **3** (*maths*) (of a number or amount) less than zero. Opp positive¹(5). **4** (*electricity*) of, concerning, the sort based on electrons: *the negative plate in a battery*. Opp positive¹(6). **5** (*photography*) having the lights and shades of the actual scene reversed: *negative film*. Compare positive¹(7). **6** (*med*) showing that a disease is not present: *Your tests were negative*. Opp positive¹(8).

nega·tive·ly *adv*

nega·tive² /'negətɪv/ *nc* **1** a word, phrase etc meaning 'no': *'No', 'not', 'neither' and 'nowhere else' are negatives*. **2** (*maths*) a quantity that is less than zero (e.g. $-5x$). **3** a developed film etc on which lights and shades are reversed. ⇨ positive².

ne·glect¹ /nɪ'glekt/ *nu* the act, condition, of neglecting or being neglected: *neglect of duty. The garden was in a state of neglect*.

ne·glect² /nɪ'glekt/ *vt* **1** to pay no attention to (a person, thing); give no or not enough care to (a person, thing): *neglecting one's studies/children/ health*. **2 neglect to** + *verb* (*formal*) to omit or fail to: *He neglected to say 'Thank you'*.

ne·glect·ful /-ful/ *adj* **neglectful (of sth)** (*formal*) in the habit of neglecting (things): *neglectful of her appearance*.

nég·li·gé (also **négligée**) /'neglɪʒeɪ/ *nc* a loose, thin nightdress.

neg·li·gence /'neglɪdʒəns/ *nu* (*formal*) **1** carelessness; failure to take proper care or precautions: *The accident was due to negligence*. **2** a neglected condition or appearance.

neg·li·gent /'neglɪdʒənt/ *adj* **negligent (in/of sth)** (*formal*) taking too little care; guilty of neglect: *He was negligent in his work/of his duties*.

neg·li·gent·ly *adv*

neg·li·gible /'neglɪdʒəbl/ *adj* of little or no importance or size: *a negligible quantity/effect*.

ne·go·ti·able /nɪ'gəʊʃɪəbl/ *adj* **1** that can be negotiated(2): *Is the price/my salary negotiable?* **2** (*finance*) that can be changed into cash or used instead of cash: *negotiable securities*. **3** (of roads, rivers etc) that can be passed over or along. ⇨ non-negotiable.

ne·go·ti·ate /nɪ'gəʊʃɪeɪt/ *v* **1** *vi* to discuss in order to come to an agreement: *We've decided to negotiate with the employers about our wage claims*. **2** *vt* to arrange (something) by discussion: *negotiating a sale/a loan/a treaty/peace*. **3** *vt* to get past or over (something): *This is a difficult corner for any car to negotiate*.

ne·go·ti·ator /-tə(r)/ *nc* a person who negotiates an agreement etc.

ne·go·ti·ation /nɪˌgəʊʃɪ'eɪʃn/ *nc,nu* (an instance of) negotiating: *enter into/start/carry on negotiations with him. Price is a matter of negotiation*.

Ne·gress /'ni:grɪs/ *nc* (*tech* or *dated*) a Negro woman or girl.

Ne·gro /'ni:grəʊ/ *nc* (*pl* **—es**) (*tech* or *dated*) a person of, from, one of the black African races. (*Black* is the usual word.)

neigh /neɪ/ *vi,nc* (to make the) cry of a horse.

neigh·bour (*US* = **-bor**) /'neɪbə(r)/ *nc* **1** a person living in a house, street etc near another: *We're next-door neighbours* (i.e. Our houses are side by side). **2** a building, country etc that is near(est) another: *Britain's nearest neighbour is France.*

neigh·bour·ing *adj* (usually *attrib*) near or next to each other: *neighbouring countries/villages.*

neigh·bour·hood (*US* = **-bor-**) /'neɪbəhʊd/ *nc* **1** (people living in) a part of a town, city etc; the area near the place mentioned: *There's some beautiful scenery in our neighbourhood. He lives in the neighbourhood of London.* **2 in the neighbourhood of** near to: *He lost a sum in the neighbourhood of £500.*

neigh·bour·ly (*US* = **-bor-**) /'neɪbəlɪ/ *adj* friendly (the usual word): *That town wasn't very neighbourly!*

neigh·bour·li·ness (*US* = **-bor-**) *nu*

nei·ther¹ /'naɪðə(r)/ *adj* or *det* (of two people, things etc) not the one and not the other: *Neither leg was injured. Neither parent could come. Neither side scored a goal. In neither case can I agree. Neither one will do.* Ⓝ *'Neither' cannot be used with a negative verb because its meaning is negative. 'Neither' is followed by a singular noun.* Compare either¹(1), both¹.

nei·ther² /'naɪðə(r)/ *pron* (of two people, things etc) **1** not the one and not the other: *Neither of his parents was able to come. Are/Is neither of your feet feeling better? Neither will sign the form. Neither of the two options is acceptable. I think neither of my bicycle wheels are/is damaged.* Ⓝ *'Neither' cannot be used in front of another determiner (e.g. a, some, the). 'Neither of' can be used in front of possessive pronouns (e.g. my, your), personal pronouns (e.g. you, us) and the, these, those etc, as in Neither of us/them can sign.* Compare: all, both, each. *'Neither of' is usually used with a singular verb but is often used with a plural verb in informal questions and statements, as in the above examples.* **2** (used as an *adverb* in short answers): *'I don't like her.'—'Neither do I.' 'He can't sing.'—'Neither can I.'* Compare either²(2). **3 neither . . . nor . . .** (*conj*) (of two or more) not the one (or more) and not the other: *Neither you nor I knew what happened. We like neither the American design nor the European one. He bought neither dollars, pounds nor francs.* Ⓝ *'Neither' can be used in front of another determiner (e.g. a, the, you, this etc) when combined with nor in this way.* Compare either . . . or . . . **be neither here nor there** ⇨ here(4).

neo·co·lo·ni·al·ism /ˌniːəʊ kə'ləʊnɪəlɪzəm/ *nu* economic control by powerful countries over less developed countries.

neo·co·lo·ni·al·ist /-ɪst/ *adj* of, like, neo-colonialism. □ *nc* a supporter of, believer in, neo-colonialism.

ne·on /'niːɒn/ *nu* a kind of colourless gas (symbol Ne) occurring in small amounts in the atmosphere, used in lighting.

,neon 'light *nu* an orange-red light produced when an electric current passes through neon.

,neon 'sign *nc* an advertisement etc in which

neon light is used.

neph·ew /'nefjuː/ *nc* a son of one's brother or sister. Compare niece.

nep·ot·ism /'nepətɪzəm/ *nu* the giving of special favour to one's relatives, esp good jobs, because one is in a powerful position.

Nep·tune /'neptjuːn/ *n* **1** the Roman god of the sea. **2** one of the farthest planets of the solar system.

nerve /nɜːv/ *n* **1** *nc* a fibre or bundle of fibres carrying messages concerning feeling and movement between the brain and all parts of the body. ⇨ neural. **2** (*pl*) condition of being easily excited, worried, irritated: *He is suffering from nerves.* **a bundle of nerves** (*fig*) a very nervous person. **get on one's nerves** to annoy one: *That noise/ man gets on my nerves.* **3** *nu* the quality of being bold; courage: *A test pilot needs plenty of nerve.* **have a nerve** (*informal*) to be impudent: *He's got a nerve, going to work dressed like that!* **have the nerve to do sth** (a) to have the necessary courage etc. (b) (*informal*) to be impudent enough: *He had the nerve to suggest that I was cheating!* **lose one's nerve** to lose one's courage.

'nerve-cell *nc* (*anat*) a cell that sends messages in nerves(1).

'nerve-centre *nc* (a) a group of nerve-cells. (b) (*fig*) any centre of power or control.

'nerve-racking *adj* causing great fear and worry: *a nerve-racking wait for the exam results.*

ner·vous /'nɜːvəs/ *adj* **1** (*attrib*) of the nerves(1): *the nervous system.* **2** easily afraid, timid: *Are you nervous in the dark?* ⇨ wreck¹(3).

,nervous 'breakdown *nc* a mental illness with exhaustion and severe loss of confidence.

,nervous 'energy *nu* (*informal*) energy produced when in an excitable, sometimes uncontrolled, state.

'nervous system *nc* (the —) the nerves(1) and nerve-centres as a whole.

ner·vous·ly *adv*

ner·vous·ness *nu*

nest¹ /nest/ *nc* **1** a place made or chosen by a bird for its eggs. **2** a place in which certain insects etc keep their young: *a wasps' nest.* **3** a number of like things (esp boxes, tables) fitting one inside another. **4** (*fig*) a place (esp one for wrong or unpleasant activities): *a nest of crime/vice.*

'nest-egg *nc* (*fig*) a sum of money saved for future use.

nest² /nest/ *vi* to make and use a nest(1): *The swallows are nesting in the woodshed.*

nestle /'nesl/ *v* **1** *vi* to settle comfortably and warmly: *nestle (down) among the cushions.* **2** *vt,vi* to press oneself, (one's head etc) lovingly (to a person, animal): *The child was nestling (its head) closely against/nestled up to her mother.*

net¹ (also **nett**) /net/ *adj* (*no comp*) remaining when nothing more is to be taken away: *make £100 net; net profit* (= when expenses have been taken away); *net weight* (= without the weight of the container, packing etc). ⇨ net⁴.

net² /net/ *n* **1** *nc,nu* a kind of material with loose threads of cotton, wire etc. **2** *nc* an object made using this: *a hairnet; fishing-nets; tennis nets.*

net³ /net/ *vt* (**-tt-**) **1** to catch (fish, animals etc) with or in a net. **2** to cover (something) with a net or nets: *net strawberries*.

net⁴ /net/ *vt* (**-tt-**) to gain (an amount) as a profit: *He netted £500 from the deal*. ⇨ **net¹**.

net·ball /'netbɔːl/ *nu* a game for two teams of 7 women or girls who score goals by throwing a ball through a net on top of a post.

nett = **net¹**.

net·ting /'netɪŋ/ *nu* = net²(1).

nettle¹ /'netl/ *nc* a common wild plant that stings when touched.

'nettle-rash *nu* red patches on the skin (like those) caused by nettles.

nettle² /'netl/ *vt* to make (a person) angry; annoy: *She looked nettled by my remarks*.

net·work /'netwɜːk/ *nc* **1** a system of lines, wires etc that cross each other: *a railway network*. **2** a system of radio or television companies sharing programmes. **3** (*fig*) any system of linked parts: *a computer network*.

neu·ral /'njʊərəl/ *adj* of, concerning, the nerves(1): *a neural pain*.

neur·al·gia /njʊə'rældʒə/ *nu* a sharp pain along the path of a nerve.

neu·rol·ogist /njʊə'rɒlədʒɪst/ *nc* an expert in, student of, neurology.

neur·ol·ogy /njʊə'rɒlədʒi/ *nu* the branch of medical science that is concerned with nerves.

neur·osis /njʊə'rəʊsɪs/ *nc* (*pl* **-oses** /-siːz/) a mental illness with anxiety, excited behaviour, abnormal concern etc caused by disorders of the nervous system or by something in the subconscious mind.

neur·ot·ic /njʊə'rɒtɪk/ *adj, nc* **1** (of) a person suffering from a neurosis. **2** (*informal*) (of) a person who is often very anxious.

neu·ter¹ /'njuːtə(r)/ *adj* **1** (*gram*) (of gender) neither feminine nor masculine. **2** (of insects, e.g. worker ants) sexually undeveloped.

neu·ter² /'njuːtə(r)/ *nc* **1** (*gram*) a neuter noun or gender. **2** an animal after its sexual organs have been removed.

neu·ter³ /'njuːtə(r)/ *vt* = castrate.

neu·tral¹ /'njuːtrəl/ *adj* **1** supporting neither side in a disagreement or quarrel: *neutral nations*. **2** belonging to a country that supports no side in a war: *neutral territory/ships*. **3** (of gear mechanism) of the position in which no power is transmitted: *leave a car in neutral gear*. **4** having no definite characteristic, colour etc: *neutral tints*. **5** (*chemistry*) neither acid nor alkaline.

neu·tral·ity /njuː'trælətɪ/ *nu* the state of being neutral, esp in war.

neu·tral² /'njuːtrəl/ *n* **1** *nc* a neutral person, country etc. **2** *nu* a neutral position of the gears of a vehicle: *park in neutral*.

neu·tral·ize (also **-ise**) /'njuːtrəlaɪz/ *vt* to take away the effect or special quality of (something) by using something with an opposite effect or quality: *neutralize a poison*.

neu·tron /'njuːtrɒn/ *nc* (*science*) a particle carrying no electric charge and forming part of the nucleus of an atom. ⇨ electron, proton.

nev·er /'nevə(r)/ *adv* **1** not at any time: *She never writes letters. He has never been abroad. I can never find you when I need you. Have you never travelled by plane? Never eat meat that smells bad. Never in all my life have I heard such nonsense!* Compare always, ever. **2** not at any time up to the present: *Such courage has never been known before.* **3** (used for emphasis in place of *not*): *This food will never do!* **4** **never mind!** it is not important, do not worry etc: *'I've broken it.'—'Never mind!'*

never·more /ˌnevə'mɔː(r)/ *adv* never again. Compare evermore.

never·the·less /ˌnevəðə'les/ *adv* in spite of that: *There was no news; nevertheless, she went on hoping.*

new¹ /njuː/ *adj* (**—er, —est**) **1** not existing before; seen, heard of, introduced, for the first time; of recent origin, growth, manufacture etc: *a new invention/film/idea/baby; the newest* (= latest) *fashions*. **as good as new** in very good condition. **2** already in existence but only now seen, discovered etc: *learn new words in a foreign language*. **3** (*pred*) **new to sth** unfamiliar with, not yet accustomed to, it: *I am new to this town/job*. **4** (**the — noun**) modern: *the new style of management*. **5** beginning again: *start a new life after a divorce*.

'new·comer *nc* a person who has recently arrived in a place.

'new·fangled *adj* (*attrib*) (*informal*) recently in use or fashion (and often suggesting poor in quality): *newfangled ideas*.

,new 'moon *nc* the moon seen as a thin crescent after being invisible.

,New 'Testament *n* (the —) the second part of the Bible.

,New 'World *n* (the —) N and S America.

,new 'year *n* (the —) the coming year or one recently begun: *Happy New Year!*

,New Year's 'Day *n* 1 January.

,New Year's 'Eve *n* 31 December.

new·ness *nu*

new² /njuː/ *adv* (used in combinations) recently: *new-born; new-laid eggs*.

new·ly /'njuːlɪ/ *adv* **newly** + *pp* **1** recently: *a newly married couple*. **2** in a new or different way: *newly arranged furniture*.

'newly-wed *nc* (usually *pl*) a recently married person.

news /njuːz/ *nu* (also *attrib*) new or fresh information; report(s) of what has most recently happened: *Have you heard the news about the air disaster? The news is bad. Here are the news headlines. Here are some interesting pieces/bits of news. That's news to me* (= I did not know that). *That's no news to me* (= I already know that). **no news is good news** while there is no information we, you etc can still hope.

'news·agent *nc* a person, business that sells newspapers, magazines etc.

'newscaster *nc* = news-reader.

'news·flash *nc* a short piece of important news on television or radio.

'news·letter *nc* a letter or printed paper sent out to members of a society etc.

'news·paper *nc* a printed publication, usually issued daily, with news, advertisements etc.

'news·reader *nc* a person who reads the news aloud on the radio or TV.

'news·stand *nc* a stall in the street for the sale of newspapers etc.

'news·worthy *adj* sufficiently interesting for reporting, e.g. in a newspaper.

newt /nju:t/ nc a small animal like a lizard which spends most of its time in the water.

next¹ /nekst/ adj or det **1 the, my, its** etc **next** + **noun** coming immediately after another or others in order or time: *April is the next month of the year after March. Take the next turning on the right. The next person to arrive was my uncle. When's the next bus due? For my next experiment I need a volunteer. This next meal could be your last one.* Compare first¹, last¹(1). **next door** at, in, the house, office etc immediately to the side: *a party in the house/room next door.* Hence '**next-door** adj (attrib): *our next-door neighbours.* **2 (a) the next week, year** etc the week, year etc immediately after now (or the period mentioned or known): *I'll be out for the next hour. She'll be in Rome for the next six weeks. He was ill on Monday and the next day he died. The next month will be expensive.* **(b)** (used without *the*) during the period immediately after this, that: *I'll phone you next week/Monday. Let's go to Spain next summer. Next year I'm going to travel. On Friday next (= Next Friday) we can paint the doors. Is he coming this weekend or next weekend?* (i.e. during or for the weekend immediately after now or the one after it?) Compare last¹(2), this¹(3).

next² /nekst/ adv **1** immediately after (this, that): *What are you going to do next? You can go in next. Next, I'd like to thank my parents.* Compare first²(1), last²(1). **2** on the occasion immediately after (this, that): *When I next saw her, she was about to get married. When will you next be in London?* Compare first²(2), last²(2). **3 next to sb/sth** immediately at, to, the side of a person, thing: *sit next to the chairman/fire; lives in the street next to mine.* **next to nothing** ⇨ nothing².

next³ /nekst/ pron **the next** the next person, thing etc: *Who was the next to arrive? You take this bus and I'll wait for the next. She'll be the next to complain.* **or next** or the one after: *Are they coming this weekend or next?* Compare first³(1), last³. **(the) next but one** the one immediately after the next: *You're (the) next but one to see the doctor.* **next of kin** ⇨ kin.

next-door /'nekstdɔ:(r)/ adj (attrib) ⇨ next¹(1).

NHS /,en eɪtʃ 'es/ abbr (the —) the National Health Service (the GB state medical service).

nib /nɪb/ nc a pointed metal piece on the end of a pen.

nibble¹ /'nɪbl/ nc **nibble (at sth)** an act of nibbling: *a nibble at one's food.*

nibble² /'nɪbl/ vt,vi **1 nibble ((away) at) sth** to take very small bites of (something): *She only nibbled (at) her supper. We watched the monkeys nibbling away.* **2** (fig) to show (only) a little willingness to accept (an offer), agree (to a suggestion) etc: *The customer is nibbling at the idea of accepting our offer.*

nice /naɪs/ adj (**—r, —st**) **1** pleasant; kind; friendly: *a nice day/taste/dress/voice; medicine that is not very nice to take. It was nice of you to say so. She isn't a very nice person.* **nice and ...** pleasant because ... : *It's nice and warm by the fire.* **2** (formal) needing care and exactness; sensitive: *nice shades of meaning.* **3** (ironic) difficult; bad: *You've got us into a nice mess!*

nice·ly adv in a nice manner; well: *nicely dressed; speak nicely.* **be doing nicely** (informal) to be making good progress: *The patient is doing nicely.*

nice·ness nu

ni·ce·ty /'naɪsətɪ/ nc (pl **-ies**) (formal) a very small difference or distinction: *all the niceties of justice.*

niche /nɪtʃ/ nc **1** a hollow place in a wall, e.g. for a statue or ornament. **2** (fig) a suitable or satisfactory position: *He found the right niche for himself in the Civil Service.*

nick¹ /nɪk/ nc **1** a small V-shaped cut. **2 in the nick of time** only just in time: *He arrived in the nick of time.* **3** (sl) prison.

nick² /nɪk/ vt to make a nick(1) in (something).

nick·el /'nɪkl/ n **1** nu a hard, silver-white metal (symbol Ni), used in alloys. **2** nc (US) a coin worth 5 cents.

nick·nack /'nɪknæk/ nc = knick-knack.

nick·name¹ /'nɪkneɪm/ nc a name used instead of a real name (e.g. *Fatty* for a fat boy).

nick·name² /'nɪkneɪm/ vt to give a nickname to (a person): *They nicknamed him 'Spotty'.*

nic·otine /'nɪkəti:n/ nu a poisonous, oily substance in tobacco leaves.

niece /ni:s/ nc a daughter of one's brother or sister. Compare nephew.

niggle /'nɪgl/ v **1** vi **niggle (about/over sth)** to give too much time or attention (to something); complain about unimportant details: *niggling over the cost.* **2** vt to annoy (a person): *Her bad manners niggled me.*

nig·gling adj (attrib) small or unimportant but annoying: *a niggling pain.*

nigh /naɪ/ adv, prep (old use and poetic) near.

night /naɪt/ nc the time between sunset and sunrise: *in/during the night; on the night of 13 June.* **at night** during the night: *sleep well at night; 6 o'clock at night* (i.e. 6 pm). **by night** during the darkness of night: *travel by night.* **all night (long)** during the whole night. **night after night; every night; night in, night out** for many nights together. ⇨ nightly. **one of these nights** on an unknown night (soon): *One of these nights you'll dream about it.* **the other night** a few nights ago: *I dreamt about you the other night.* **make a night of it** to spend the night having fun, e.g. at a party. **spend the night with sb (a)** to stay at a person's home as a guest. **(b)** to sleep with a person.

'**night·cap** nc a drink (esp alcoholic) taken before going to bed.

'**nightclub** nc a club that is open until very late for dancing, entertainment etc.

'**night·dress** nc a dress worn by a woman or girl in bed.

'**night·fall** nu the beginning of night.

'**night·gown** nc = nightdress.

'**nightie, 'nighty** nc (informal) = nightdress.

'**night-life** nu entertainment, e.g. nightclubs, available in a town late at night: *the night-life of London.*

'**night-long** adj lasting the whole night.

'**night·mare** /-meə(r)/ nc **(a)** a frightening dream. **(b)** (a memory of) a horrible experience: *Travelling on those bad mountain roads was a nightmare.*

'**night-school** nc one giving lessons in the evening.

'night-time *nu* the time of darkness during a night.

,night-'watchman /-mən/ *nc* a man employed to guard a factory etc at night.

night-ly *adj, adv* (taking place, happening, existing) every night.

night-in-gale /'naɪtɪŋɡeɪl/ *nc* a small reddish-brown bird that sings sweetly at night.

nil /nɪl/ *n* (esp in sport) nothing: *The result of the football match was 3–0* (say *'three-nil'*). ⇨ the note at zero¹(1).

nimble /'nɪmbl/ *adj* (**—r, —st**) moving, doing things, quickly and easily: *nimble fingers; as nimble as a goat* (= very nimble).

nim-bly /'nɪmblɪ/ *adv*

nine /naɪn/ *adj or det, nc* (of) 9: *He's nine (years old).* ⇨ stitch(1).

nine-teen /ˌnaɪn'tiːn/ *adj or det, nc* (of) 19. *(talk) nineteen to the dozen* (to talk) continuously.

nine-teenth /ˌnaɪn'tiːnθ/ *adj or det, nc* (abbr *19th*) (of) one of 19 parts or the next after 18.

nine-ti-eth /'naɪntɪəθ/ *adj or det, nc* (abbr *90th*) (of) one of 90 parts or the next after 89.

nine-ty /'naɪntɪ/ *adj or det, nc* (*pl* **-ies**) (of) 90. *ninety-nine times out of a hundred* almost always. *in the nineties* (a) (of a person's age, temperature, etc) between 90 and 99. (b) between '90 and '99 in a century.

ninth /naɪnθ/ *adj or det, nc* (abbr *9th*) (of) one of 9 parts or the next after 8.

nin-ny /'nɪnɪ/ *nc* (*pl* **-ies**) (*dated*) fool.

nip¹ /nɪp/ *nc* **1** a small, sharp pinch or bite. *a (cold) nip in the air* a sharp feeling of cold air. ⇨ nippy. **2** a small (alcoholic) drink: *a nip of brandy.*

nip² /nɪp/ *v* (**-pp-**) **1** *vt,vi* to press (something) together hard (e.g. between finger and thumb): *He nipped his finger in the door.* **2** *vi* **nip in/out** (*informal*) to go in/out quickly or for a short time: *nip out to buy a newspaper.* **3** *vt* (of frost, wind etc) to stop the growth of (a plant). *nip sth in the bud* ⇨ bud.

nip-per /'nɪpə(r)/ *nc* (*sl*) a small child.

nipple /'nɪpl/ *nc* **1** the part of the breast through which a baby gets its mother's milk; similar part on the breast of a man. Ⓝ *'Teat'* is used for animals. **2** something like a nipple in shape: *greasing nipples in an engine.*

nip-py /'nɪpɪ/ *adj* (**-ier, -iest**) (*informal*) (of air etc) feeling cold.

nir-vana /nɪə'vɑːnə/ *nu* (*Buddhism*) the desired state after death in which the individual becomes part of the supreme spirit (God).

nit¹ /nɪt/ *nc* an egg of a louse etc (e.g. as found in the human hair).

nit² /nɪt/ *nc* (*sl*) a fool.

ni-trate /'naɪtreɪt/ *nc,nu* (*science*) a salt formed by the chemical reaction of nitric acid with an alkali, esp *potassium nitrate* and *sodium nitrate*, used as fertilizers.

ni-tric /'naɪtrɪk/ *adj* of, containing, nitrogen. *,nitric 'acid nu* a powerful acid (formula HNO_3) that eats into and destroys most substances.

ni-tro-gen /'naɪtrədʒən/ *nu* a gas (symbol N) without colour, taste or smell, forming about four-fifths of the earth's atmosphere.

ni-tro-glycer-ine /ˌnaɪtrəʊ'ɡlɪsəriːn/ *nu* a powerful explosive.

nit-wit /'nɪtwɪt/ *nc* (*sl*) a fool.

NNE *written abbr* north-north-east.

NNW *written abbr* north-north-west.

no¹ /nəʊ/ *adj or det* **1** not any; not a: *She has no money. No other person can do it. No two people think alike. No news is good news. He's no friend of mine. It's no joke! I've no time for such nonsense. We had no idea you were coming. No fewer than 60 people applied for the job.* Ⓝ *'No'* is used with an affirmative verb to express a negative in the same way that *'not + verb + any'* does. *I ate no chips* means the same as *I did not eat any chips.* Compare not. *be no good/use* to be useless: *It's no good worrying about her now. by no means* ⇨ means(1). *in no time (at all)* ⇨ time¹(2). *no doubt* ⇨ doubt¹. *no end of sth* ⇨ end¹(2). *no more* ⇨ more¹(2). **2** *No + -ing* (used to state that something is not allowed): *No Parking! No Smoking.* **3** *No + noun* (used to express a strong feeling against, a refusal etc): *No fear!* (= I certainly will not!) *No way!* (= Nothing will persuade me!)

,no-'claims bonus *nc* a reduction from an insurance fee because no claim has been made.

,no-'go area *nc* a part of a town etc which police etc cannot or will not enter.

'no-one *pron* = nobody(1). *no-one else* ⇨ else(2).

no² /nəʊ/ *adv* **no** + *comparative* not any; not at all: *He's feeling no better. I'm no wiser than I was yesterday. She no longer cares. He's no more ill than I am!* (i.e. He's not at all ill!) Compare none(2).

no³ /nəʊ/ *int* (used as a short addition or in short answers to express a negative, refusal etc): *'Is it Monday today?'—'No, it isn't.' 'Do you like peas?'—'No, I don't.' 'Can I come?'—'No, you can't.' 'Would you like some?'—'No, thanks.' 'Give it to me.'—'No!' 'Is it a big house?'—'No, it's a small one.'* Compare yes.

no⁴ /nəʊ/ *nc* (*pl* **noes**) **1** a person who votes 'no': *The noes won the vote.* **2** a negative answer, refusal etc. *never/not take no for an answer* to refuse to give up trying.

no(s), No(s) *written abbr* number(s): *page no 6.*

nobble /'nɒbl/ *vt* (*informal*) to get the attention of (a person): *nobbling a busy manager on his way to lunch.*

no-bil-ity /nəʊ'bɪlətɪ/ *nu* **1** the quality of being noble. **2** (the —) the nobles as a class: *a member of the nobility.*

noble¹ /'nəʊbl/ *adj* (**—r, —st**) **1** of high social rank or birth. **2** having or showing impressive character and qualities: *a noble leader; noble sentiments.*

noble² /'nəʊbl/ *nc* (also *nobleman*) a person born into the highest social class; peer (the usual word).

no-bly /'nəʊblɪ/ *adv* in a manner that deserves praise: *nobly said.*

no-body /'nəʊbədɪ/ *pron* (*pl* **-ies**) **1** (also **no-one**) *n* not anybody; no person: *We saw nobody we knew there. He said he would marry me or nobody. Nobody could find their luggage.* Compare anybody. *nobody else, no-one else* ⇨ else(2). **2** (used with *a*) an unimportant person:

Don't marry a nobody like James. Compare **somebody**.

noc·tur·nal /nɒkˈtɜːnəl/ *adj* active or happening in the night: *nocturnal birds.*

nod[1] /nɒd/ *nc* a quick movement downwards (of the head), esp to show agreement, approval etc.

nod[2] /nɒd/ *v* (**-dd-**) **1** *vt,vi* to make a nod to show (something): *She nodded her approval. He nodded (to me) as he passed.* **2** *vi* to let the head fall forward as if sleepy or falling asleep: *She sat nodding by the fire.* **nod off** (*informal*) to fall asleep.

nod·ule /ˈnɒdjuːl/ *nc* a small rounded lump, knob or swelling.

nod·ular /-lə(r)/ *adj*

No·el /nəʊˈel/ *n* = Christmas (which is more usual).

no·how /ˈnəʊhaʊ/ *adv* (*informal*) in no way; not at all: *Nohow am I willing to lend you the money.*

noise[1] /nɔɪz/ *nc,nu* any (usually unpleasant) sound, esp a loud one: *the noise of jet aircraft. Did you hear a noise outside? Don't make so much noise/such a loud noise!* Compare **sound**[4](1).

noise·less *adj* making little or no noise: *with noiseless footsteps.*

noise·less·ly *adv*

noise[2] /nɔɪz/ *vt* to make known (information): *It was noised everywhere that he had been arrested.*

noisy /ˈnɔɪzɪ/ *adj* (**-ier, -iest**) making, having or accompanied by a lot of noise: *noisy children/ games; a noisy classroom.*

nois·ily /-əlɪ/ *adv*

noisi·ness *nu*

no·mad /ˈnəʊmæd/ *nc* a member of a community that wanders from place to place with no fixed home.

no·mad·ic /nəʊˈmædɪk/ *adj* of nomads: *lead a nomadic way of life.*

nom de plume /ˌnɒm də ˈpluːm/ *nc* (*pl* **noms de plume**) (*Fr*) = pen-name.

no·men·cla·ture /nəʊˈmeŋklətʃə(r)/ *nc,nu* (*formal*) a system of naming: *botanical nomenclature.*

nomi·nal /ˈnɒmɪnl/ *adj* **1** existing etc in name only and not in fact: *the nominal ruler of the country.* **2** (of a price, cost etc) very small: *pay a nominal rent.* **3** (*gram*) of a noun or nouns.

nomi·nal·ly /-nəlɪ/ *adv*

nomi·nate /ˈnɒmɪneɪt/ *vt* to put (a person) forward for election to a position: *We are nominating a woman for the Presidency.*

nomi·na·tion /ˌnɒmɪˈneɪʃn/ *nc,nu* (an instance of) nominating: *How many nominations have there been so far?*

nomi·na·tive /ˈnɒmɪnətɪv/ *nc* (*gram*) (also *nominative form*) the form of a word when it is the subject in a sentence. Compare **accusative**.

,nominative 'case *nc* (*gram*) = subjective case.

,nominative 'pronoun *nc* (*gram*) the form of a pronoun when it is the subject in a sentence, as in '*I love you*' '*They want some*'. Compare **accusative pronoun**.

nomi·nee /ˌnɒmɪˈniː/ *nc* a person who is nominated for an office or appointment.

nona·gen·ar·ian /ˌnɒnədʒəˈneərɪən/ *adj, nc* (concerning) a person who is between 90 and 99 years old.

non-ag·gres·sion /ˌnɒn əˈgreʃn/ *adj* (*attrib*),

nu (of) a condition of being willing to agree or refusing to fight: *a non-aggression treaty.*

non-aligned /ˌnɒn əˈlaɪnd/ *adj* not a member of a powerful group of nations: *a non-aligned state.*

non-align·ment *nu*

non-ap·pear·ance /ˌnɒn əˈpɪərəns/ *n* (usually *sing*) a failure to arrive, come.

non·cha·lance /ˈnɒnʃələns/ *nu* (*formal*) the state of being nonchalant.

non·cha·lant /ˈnɒnʃələnt/ *adj* (*formal*) having or showing no interest or enthusiasm.

non·cha·lant·ly *adv*

non-com·mer·cial /ˌnɒn kəˈmɜːʃl/ *adj* **1** (*derog*) showing poor ability or interest in business. **2** not producing a profit.

non-com·mit·tal /ˌnɒn kəˈmɪtl/ *adj* not agreeing to or expressing a definite decision or opinion: *a non-committal answer.*

non-con·duc·tor /ˌnɒn kənˈdʌktə(r)/ *nc* (*electricity*) a substance that cannot carry electricity.

non-con·form·ist /ˌnɒnkənˈfɔːmɪst/ *adj, nc* (of) a person who does not agree with and act like most people.

non-con·form·ity /-ətɪ/ *nu*

non-con·tribu·tory /ˌnɒn kənˈtrɪbjʊtrɪ/ *adj* not contributory(2).

non-de·script /ˈnɒndɪskrɪpt/ *adj* (*derog*) (of a person, thing) having no definite or outstanding feature (and so not a good example): *a nondescript play/performance/singer.*

none /nʌn/ *pron* **1** (of uncountable nouns and more than two people, things): not any; not (even) one: *I needed some milk but there was none in the house. None of the food was fresh. Were none of them the right size? None of the visitors has/have returned. None is/are suitable.* Ⓝ '*None*' cannot be used in front of another determiner (e.g. *a, the, some*). '*None of*' can be used in front of possessive pronouns (e.g. *your, their*), personal pronouns (e.g. *us, you*) and *the, that, those* etc, as in *None of them came. None of this will do.* '*None of*' is usually used with a singular verb but it is often used with a plural verb in informal statements and questions. Compare **either**[2], **neither**[2]. *none at all* (used for emphasis): '*Is there any petrol left?*'–'*No, none at all.*' *none but . . .* (*formal*) only: *None but the brave would dare to say that.* **none other than . . .** (used for emphasis) no other person than: *The speaker was none other than the Prime Minister herself.* **bar none** ⇨ **bar**[3]. **second to none** ⇨ **second**[2]. **2** *none the* + *comparative* (used as an *adv*) not at all: *I hope you're none the worse for your accident. I'm still none the wiser.* Compare **no**[2](1).

non·en·ti·ty /nɒnˈentətɪ/ *nc* (*pl* **-ies**) (*derog*) a person without importance, particular ability, character etc.

none·the·less /ˌnʌnðəˈles/ *adv* = nevertheless (which is more usual).

non-event /ˌnɒn ɪˈvent/ *nc* an event that is not as good, effective etc as expected: *The meeting turned out to be a non-event.*

non-ex·ist·ent /ˌnɒn ɪgˈzɪstnt/ *adj* not present, real: *The difference is almost non-existent.* Compare **existent**.

non-fa·tal /ˌnɒn ˈfeɪtl/ *adj* not fatal: *a non-fatal illness.*

non-fiction /ˌnɒn ˈfɪkʃn/ *nu* (*literature*) writing

that deals with real people, events, facts etc (not novels etc).

non-finite /ˌnɒn 'faɪnaɪt/ *adj* (*gram*) (of a form of a verb) not able to be used with a subject: *'Be', 'being' and 'been' are the non-finite forms of the verb 'to be'.* Compare finite(2).

non-flam·mable /ˌnɒn 'flæməbl/ *adj* not able to burst into flames. ⇨ the note at flammable.

non-ident·ify·ing /ˌnɒn aɪ'dentɪfaɪɪŋ/ *adj* (esp used in) ˌnon-iˌdentifying ˌrelative 'clause *nc* (*gram*) one that does not explain who, what, is being referred to (because he/she/it is already known), as in 'I met John White yesterday, *who said he has been in Kenya for a year'.* Compare identifying relative clause.

non-in·ter·ven·tion /ˌnɒn ˌɪntə'venʃn/ *nu* the practice, principle, of keeping out of arguments or disputes, esp between nations.

non-mem·ber /'nɒn membə(r)/ *nc* a person who is not a member (of a society): *Members £3, non-members £5.*

non-met·al·lic /ˌnɒn mə'tælɪk/ *adj* not a metal.

non-ne·go·ti·able /ˌnɒn nɪ'gəʊʃɪəbl/ *adj* that is not negotiable (esp 1,2).

non-nu·clear /ˌnɒn 'njuːklɪə(r)/ *adj* not using nuclear energy; not having nuclear weapons: *non-nuclear missiles; a non-nuclear defence policy.*

non-pay·ment /ˌnɒn 'peɪmənt/ *nu* a failure to pay (rent, a debt).

non·plus·sed /nɒn'plʌst/ *adj* (*pred*) very surprised or puzzled: *be completely nonplussed.*

non-prof·it-mak·ing /ˌnɒn 'prɒfɪt meɪkɪŋ/ *adj* not producing a profit.

non-pro·lif·er·ation /ˌnɒn prəˌlɪfə'reɪʃn/ *adj* (*attrib*) limiting the manufacture, spread etc of something, esp dangerous weapons: *a non-proliferation treaty.*

non-resi·dent /ˌnɒn 'rezɪdənt/ *adj, nc* (concerning) a person who visits (a hotel) but is not staying there. Compare resident.

non-re·sis·tant /ˌnɒn rɪ'zɪstnt/ *adj* **non-resistant (to sth)** not able to oppose the effect of a disease, chemical etc.

non·sense /'nɒnsəns/ *nu* or *sing* something said, written etc that is foolish or does not make any sense; stupid behaviour: *Your plans are nonsense. Her mind is filled with nonsense. 'I've been here all day'—'Nonsense!' 'What nonsense!' 'I won't listen to such nonsense!' These figures make a nonsense of your budget.*

'nonsense verse *nc,nu* a kind of poem (e.g. a *limerick*) with an illogical (often humorous) theme or story.

non·sen·si·cal /ˌnɒn'sensɪkl/ *adj* not making any sense: *nonsensical remarks.*

non·se·qui·tur /ˌnɒn'sekwɪtə(r)/ *nc* (*Latin*) a statement or conclusion that does not (seem to) have any connection to what was said or written before.

non-slip /ˌnɒn 'slɪp/ *adj* (of material used for floors) preventing a person from slipping.

non-smoker /ˌnɒn 'sməʊkə(r)/ *nc* **1** a person who does not smoke. **2** a place, e.g. a compartment on a train, where smoking is not allowed.

non-start·er /ˌnɒn 'stɑːtə(r)/ *nc* (*informal; derog*) a person, plan, idea etc with no possibility of being successful.

non-stative /ˌnɒn 'steɪtɪv/ *adj* (*gram*) of a non-

stative verb.

non-ˌstative 'verb *nc* (*gram*) a verb describing an activity, event or action (and not a condition or state). Compare stative verb.

non-stick /ˌnɒn 'stɪk/ *adj* (of cooking utensils etc) made so that food will not stick to the surface.

non-stop /ˌnɒn 'stɒp/ *adj, adv* without stopping: *a non-stop flight to Mexico; talk non-stop about her.*

non-U /ˌnɒn 'juː/ *adj* (*informal*) not fashionable.

non-union /ˌnɒn 'juːnɪən/ *adj* (*attrib*) not belonging to a trade union: *non-union labour.*

non-verb·al /ˌnɒn 'vɜːbl/ *adj* written or signalled, not spoken: *non-verbal communication.* Opp verbal(2).

non-vio·lence /ˌnɒn 'vaɪələns/ *nu* a practice or policy of not using physical force, e.g. when showing one's opposition (but using peaceful methods).

noodle /'nuːdl/ *n* (usually *pl*) (also *attrib*) paste of water and flour (and eggs) prepared in long, narrow strips: *chicken noodle soup.*

nook /nʊk/ *nc* a (hidden) corner: *search every nook and cranny* (= search everywhere).

noon /nuːn/ *n* 12 o'clock in the middle of the day: *at/by/before noon.* ⇨ midday.

no-one /'nəʊ wʌn/ *pron* = nobody.

noose /nuːs/ *nc* a loop of rope that becomes tighter when the rope is pulled.

nope /nəʊp/ *int* (*informal*) no³.

nor /nɔː(r)/ *conj* **1** (used after *neither* or *not*) and not: *I have neither time nor money for pop festivals. She won't agree, nor me.* ⇨ neither²(3). **2** also not: *He can't do it; nor can I, nor can you, nor can anybody. 'She doesn't like it.'—'Nor do I.'*

norm /nɔːm/ *nc* **1** a standard of behaviour, appearance, speech etc expected or asked for: *the norms of society.* **2** an average standard of achievement (e.g. in an exam): *The norm for maths was 60%.*

nor·mal¹ /'nɔːml/ *adj* in agreement with what is usual, average or regular: *the normal temperature of the human body.*

nor·mal·ly /'nɔːməli/ *adv*

nor·mal² /'nɔːml/ *n sing* only in ***above/below normal*** above/below the average or usual level or standard.

north¹ /nɔːθ/ *adj* (*attrib*) from, in, towards, the north: *a north wind; the north side of the street.* ⇨ northern.

north² /nɔːθ/ *adv* towards the north: *to travel/ face north.* ***north of a place*** farther north than: *Brussels is north of Paris.*

north³ /nɔːθ/ *n* (abbr N) **1** (the —) the direction, point, to the left of a person facing towards the sunrise (i.e. towards the east). **2** that part of a country, the world etc in this direction: *live in the north of England; cold winds from the north.*

ˌNorth 'Pole *n* (the —) (the ice regions of) the point of the world that is farthest north.

ˌnorth-'east, ˌnorth-'west *n, adj, adv* (abbr NE, NW) (a point, direction, region) midway between north and east or north and west.

ˌnorth-'eastern /-'iːstən/ *adj* of, from, in, the north-east.

ˌnorth-north-'east, ˌnorth-north-'west *n, adj, adv* (abbr NNE, NNW) (a point, direction, region) midway between north and north-east or north-west.

,north-'western /-'westən/ *adj* of, from, in, the north-west.

north·er·ly /'nɔːðəlı/ *adj, adv* **1** (of winds) from the north. **2** (of direction) towards, in or to the north.

north·ern /'nɔːðən/ *adj* of, from, in, the north part of a country, continent, the world etc: *northern France; northern areas of Britain.*

,Northern 'Hemisphere *n* (the —) the countries north of the Equator.

north·ern·er *nc* a person born in or living in the north regions of a country.

north·ern·most /-məust/ *adj* farthest north.

north·ward /'nɔːθwəd/ *adj* towards the north: *in a northward direction.*

north·wards *adv*: *to travel northwards.*

nose¹ /nəuz/ *nc* **1** the part of the face above the mouth, through which breath passes and used to smell things: *hit a man on the nose.* **as plain as the nose on sb's face** obvious. **(right) under sb's (very) nose** (a) directly in front of a person. (b) obviously or openly and ignoring disapproval: *He stole it under my very nose!* **cut off one's nose to spite one's face** to do something to damage one's own interests in a fit of bad temper. **follow one's nose** (a) to go straight forward. (b) to be guided by one's feelings or instinct. **keep one's nose clean** (*fig*) to avoid trouble. **lead sb by the nose** to make a person do everything one wants her or him to do. **look down one's nose at sb/sth** to show that one considers oneself to be superior to a person/thing. **pay through the nose** to pay too much. **poke/stick one's nose in/into sb else's business** to ask questions etc without being asked to do so. **put sb's nose out of joint** to cause a person to become annoyed or offended. **rub sb's nose in it** (*informal*) to remind a person unkindly of her or his recent failure. **turn up one's nose (at sb/sth)** to show one's lack of interest in, liking for, a person, thing. **2** a sense of smell: *a dog with a good nose.* **3** (*fig*) a good sense for finding out: *a reporter with a nose for news/ scandal.* ⇨ nose²(3). **4** something like a nose in shape or position, e.g. the open end of a pipe or the front part of an aircraft.

'nose·bleed *nc* a bleeding from the nose.

'nose-cone *nc* the most forward section of a spacecraft that usually separates during flight.

'nose·dive *nc, vi* (of an aircraft) (to make) a quick descent with the nose(4) pointing down.

'nose·gay *nc* (*dated*) a bunch of cut flowers.

nose² /nəuz/ *v* **1** *vt,vi* to go forward carefully, push (one's way): *The ship nosed its way slowly through the ice.* **2** *vt* **nose sth out** to find something by using smell: *dogs nosing out bombs.* **3** *vi* **nose about (for)/into sth** to search (esp rudely): *nosing into other people's affairs; nosing about for information.*

nos·tal·gia /nɒ'stældʒə/ *nu* nostalgia (for sth) the liking of and longing (for something one has known in the past): *be full of nostalgia for one's childhood.*

nos·tal·gic /nɒ'stældʒɪk/ *adj* of, feeling, causing, nostalgia: *nostalgic memories.*

nos·tal·gi·cal·ly /-klı/ *adv*

nos·tril /'nɒstrıl/ *nc* either of the two external openings into the nose.

nosy (also **nosey**) /'nəuzı/ *adj* (**-ier, -iest**) (*derog*) too interested in other people's private affairs.

Nosy Parker /'nəuzı pɑːkə(r)/ *nc* (*sl; derog*) a nosy person.

not /nɒt/ *adv* Ⓝ *'Not'* is often shortened to **-n't** /-nt/ after *can, do, have, must, will* etc, as in *can't, doesn't, hasn't, mustn't, won't* etc. **1** (used to make (part of) a sentence, question etc negative): **(a)** *auxiliary verb + not* (the most usual way to form the negative in English): *It's not easy. I haven't got any. Isn't it here? Why not? They cannot believe it. You must not go. She didn't say anything. Aren't you coming? He's not ready. He's not yet finished. He's still not finished.* Ⓝ For the imperative form, use *'do not'*, as in *Don't go near the edge!* **(b)** (used in other positions in a sentence): *I have a white car, not a red one. He asked us not to be late. 'Do you watch TV?'—'Not much/Not a lot.' Not all birds can fly.* (= 'Some birds cannot fly' which is the more usual structure). **(c)** (used with *be afraid, hope, suppose, trust* etc meaning 'that it is not possible' 'one cannot' etc): *'Can you meet me later?'—'I'm afraid not'. 'Are we too late?'—'I hope not.'* Compare so²(5). **(d)** (used to express refusal, denial, surprise etc): *Certainly not! Surely not!* **not (all) that + adj** (used for emphasis) not very: *It's not all that easy.* **not at all** ⇨ all³(4). **not half** ⇨ half². **not half bad** ⇨ bad¹(2). **not half so bad, ill etc (as expected etc)** ⇨ half². **not only . . . but also . . .** (used to express a connection between two facts) both (the one) and (the other): *She not only looks beautiful but she dresses well.* **not quite** almost: *I'm not quite ready. 'Have you finished?'—'Not quite.'* **not so/ as + adj + as . . .** (used to compare two ideas, things, qualities etc with the first being less than the second): *It's not so/as big as yours. Japanese isn't as easy as English.* **not that . . .** (*conj*) although it is not suggested that . . . : *We may be a day late, not that it matters. Did you do it?—Not that I care, of course.* **not that + adj** ⇨ not (all) that . . . **2** (used for emphasis in some phrases): *not a few* many. *not without reason* with very good/many reasons. *not often* on only a few occasions.

notable /'nəutəbl/ *adj* deserving to be noticed; remarkable: *notable events/speakers.* Ⓝ Because of possible difficulties when reading, it is better not to divide *'notable'* when writing or printing it.

no·tably /-əblı/ *adv*

no·ta·tion /nəu'teɪʃn/ *nc,nu* (a system of) signs or symbols representing numbers, amounts, musical notes etc.

notch¹ /nɒtʃ/ *nc* **notch (in/on sth)** a V-shaped cut.

notch² /nɒtʃ/ *vt* **1** **notch sth (in sth)** to make something shaped like a notch (in something). **2** **notch up sth** (*informal*) to win a victory; gain something as a profit.

note¹ /nəut/ *n* **1** *nc* a short written reminder: *He spoke for an hour without notes. Make a note of his name.* **compare notes (with sb) (on sth)** to exchange views, ideas etc. **take note (of sb/ sth)** to pay attention (to a person, result, event etc). **2** *nc* a short letter: *a note of thanks.* **3** *nc* a

short comment or explanation: *a new edition of 'Hamlet' with notes at the back.* ⇨ footnote. **4** *nc* a piece of paper money: *a £5 note.* ⇨ banknote. **5** *nc* (*music*) a single sound of a certain pitch and duration: *play notes on the piano.* **strike a note for sth** to contribute openly towards a cause: *strike a note for freedom.* **strike the right note** (*fig*) to speak, act, in a way that gets approval or sympathy. **6** *nc* (*music*) a sign used to represent a sound in printed music. **7** *n sing* a quality or tone (esp of voice) showing feelings, attitude etc: *There was a note of pleasure in his speech.* **8** *nu* of **note** of distinction; importance: *a family of note.*
'**note·book** *nc* a pad(2) for writing notes.
'**note·paper** *nu* paper for writing letters.
note² /nəʊt/ *vt* **1** to notice (something); pay attention to: *Note how I did it.* **2 note sth (down)** to make a written note of it: *The police officer was noting down every word I said.*
noted /'nəʊtɪd/ *adj* **noted (as/for sth)** celebrated; well-known: *a town noted for its pottery/ as a health resort.*
note·worthy /'nəʊtwɜːðɪ/ *adj* deserving to be noted; remarkable: *noteworthy efforts.*
noth·ing¹ /'nʌθɪŋ/ *adv* **nothing like** ⇨ like⁴(1).
noth·ing² /'nʌθɪŋ/ *pron* not anything: *There's nothing wrong with it. He's had nothing to eat all day. Nothing ever pleases her. Is there nothing I can do? 'You've hurt your arm'—'It's nothing.'* (i.e. It is not serious, important etc.) ⇨ something(1). **for nothing (a)** free: *I got it for nothing.* **(b)** without a purpose, result, reward etc: *It's not for nothing that he worked so hard! Her hard work was all for nothing.* **next to nothing** almost no money: *I paid next to nothing for it.* **Nothing doing!** (*informal*) I refuse! **nothing of the kind/sort** not at all similar: *You've made a mistake—I said nothing of the kind.* **be nothing to sb** of no concern or interest to a person: *She's nothing to him.* **be nothing to it** to be very easy: *You can build a boat—there's nothing to it!* **come to nothing** to fail: *All her schemes came to nothing.* **have nothing on (a)** to be naked. **(b)** to have made no arrangement to do something: *I've nothing on next Monday—let's go dancing.* **have nothing to do with sb/sth (a)** to have no dealings, relationship etc with a person, activity etc: *I advise you to have nothing to do with her/it.* **(b)** to have no connection to, not be the business of, a person or thing: *This has nothing to do with you.* **have nothing to show for it** to have no evidence, reward etc for one's effort, success etc. **mean nothing to sb (a)** to be of no concern or interest to a person: *He means nothing to her.* **(b)** to have no meaning for a person: *Computer terms mean nothing to me.* **to say nothing of . . .** and also: *He has a big house, to say nothing of a farm near the coast.* **stick/stop at nothing** to be prepared to take any risk in order to get what one wants. **think nothing of sth** to consider an action as ordinary or unremarkable: *Barbara thinks nothing of walking 5 miles a day.* **want for nothing** to have everything one needs or desires.
noth·ing³ /'nʌθɪŋ/ *nc* (*informal*) a person or thing of no importance or value.
no·tice¹ /'nəʊtɪs/ *n* **1** *nc* a written statement

about something that will happen or that has happened: *put up a notice about the meeting.* **(do sth) at short notice** to do it with little warning, time for preparation etc. **2** *nu* attention. **bring sth/ come to sb's notice** (*formal*) to call a person's attention or have one's attention called to something: *It has come to my notice that some students are always late for their lessons.* **take no notice (of sb/sth)** to pay no attention (to a person, thing): *Take no notice of them/of what they're saying about you.*
no·tice·able /-əbl/ *adj* easily seen or noticed. Opp unnoticeable.
no·tice·ably /-əblɪ/ *adv*
no·tice² /'nəʊtɪs/ *vi,vt* **notice (sb/sth/that . . .)** to see or observe (a person, thing, that): *I didn't notice (you). I noticed that she'd gone.*
no·ti·fi·ca·tion /ˌnəʊtɪfɪ'keɪʃn/ *nc,nu* (an instance of) notifying a person.
no·ti·fy /'nəʊtɪfaɪ/ *vt* (*pt,pp* **-ied**) **notify sb (of sth/that . . .)** to tell a person, group etc officially (about something): *notify the police of a loss; notify the authorities that you will not be available.*
no·tion /'nəʊʃn/ *nc* (esp **have a, no, some etc notion of sth/that . . .**) an idea; opinion: *I have no notion of what he means.*
no·tion·al /-ʃənl/ *adj* existing only in thought or calculation: *a notional loss.*
no·tor·iety /ˌnəʊtə'raɪətɪ/ *nu* the state of being notorious.
no·tori·ous /nəʊ'tɔːrɪəs/ *adj* well-known (esp for something bad): *a notorious criminal.*
no·tori·ous·ly *adv*
not·with·stand·ing /ˌnɒtwɪð'stændɪŋ/ (*formal*) *adv* all the same; in spite of that: *They threatened to sack the workers but they refused to work, notwithstanding.* □ *prep* in spite of: *They refused to go back to work, notwithstanding the threats by the management.*
nou·gat /'nuːgɑː/ *nu* a kind of hard, white or pink sweet made of sugar, nuts etc.
nought /nɔːt/ *nc* the figure 0: *point nought one* (i.e. ·01). **come to nought** to fail: *Our plans came to nought.*
noun /naʊn/ *nc* (*gram*) a word (not a *pronoun*) which can function as the subject or object of a verb, or the object of a preposition. Ⓝ Marked *n* in this dictionary. ⇨ abstract/collective/common/ concrete/countable/mass/proper/uncountable noun.
,**noun 'clause** *nc* (*gram*) one that acts as the subject or object of a sentence, as in 'Are you going to translate *the letters she wrote?*'
,**noun 'phrase** *nc* (*gram*) one that acts as the subject or object of a sentence, as in '*The last train leaves at 8.*'
nour·ish /'nʌrɪʃ/ *vt* (*formal*) **1** (of particular kinds of food) to make or keep (a person) alive and well: *This hot soup will nourish her.* **2** to cause (soil etc) to become good for growing plants: *This fertilizer will nourish the soil.* **3** (*fig*) to allow (a particular feeling) to grow stronger: *She nourished thoughts of revenge.*
nour·ish·ing *adj* (of food) making or keeping a person healthy: *nourishing soup.*
nour·ish·ment *nu* (*formal*) food.

Nov *written abbr* November.

nov·el¹ /'nɒvl/ *adj* strange; new; of a kind not previously known: *novel ideas.*

nov·el² /'nɒvl/ *nc (literature)* a story in prose, long enough to fill one or more volumes, about either imaginary or historical people: *the novels of Dickens.*
'novel·ist /-ɪst/ *nc* a person who writes novels.

nov·el·ty /'nɒvltɪ/ *n (pl* **-ies) 1** *nu* the quality of being new or strange: *the novelty of his surroundings.* **2** *nc* a previously unknown or unfamiliar thing, idea etc: *Eating apples with salt is a novelty.* **3** *nc* a cheap toy, decoration or ornament.

No·vem·ber /nəʊ'vembə(r)/ *n* (also *attrib*) the eleventh month of the year, with 30 days: *a wet November day. Come on 5 November.* Ⓝ *'5 November'* is spoken as *'November the fifth'* or *'the fifth of November'.*

nov·ice /'nɒvɪs/ *nc* **1** a person who is still learning and who has no experience. **2** a person training to become a monk or a nun.

now¹ /naʊ/ *adv* **1** at the present time: *Where are you living now? I believed you earlier but now I'm not so sure. Yesterday it rained and now it's sunny again.* Compare then²(1). **as of now** *(informal)* from this moment: *As of now you're the new deputy.* **for now** temporarily: *These shoes will have to do for now.* **just now** ⇨ just²(1). **(every) now and again/then** occasionally: *We go to a pop concert now and then.* **(right) now** immediately: *Do it (right) now!* **until/till/up to now** until this moment: *I've been lucky until now.* **2** because of this/that: *You broke it and/so now you must pay for it.* **3 (a)** (used for emphasis to express a warning, anger, comfort etc): *Now stop quarrelling and listen to me. Do that again now, and you'll be in trouble. Now come on—wipe your tears and forget him.* **(b)** (used to introduce a new or important topic, activity etc): *Now, let us consider the chemical effects. I'll tell you the story now.* **now then** (used at the beginning of a sentence etc) **(a)** (with the same meaning as 3(a) above): *Now then, listen to me!* **(b)** (with the same meaning as 3(b) above): *Now then, mix all the dry ingredients.* **(c)** (as a mild warning): *Now then, don't make so much noise!*

now² /naʊ/ *conj* **now (that)** because of the fact that: *Now (that) you're married, you should buy a house.*

now³ /naʊ/ *pron* (of a period of time) this one: *Now is the best season to be in Devon.*

now·adays /'naʊədeɪz/ *adv* during these times; at the present time: *Nowadays children are much healthier.*

no·where /'nəʊweə(r)/ *adv* not anywhere: *The boy was nowhere to be found. He's nowhere about/around.* Compare anywhere. **nowhere near (as)** ⇨ near².

nox·ious /'nɒkʃəs/ *adj (formal)* harmful: *noxious gases.* ⇨ obnoxious.

nozzle /'nɒzl/ *nc* the shaped end of a hose etc through which liquid or air is directed.

nr *written abbr* near.

NSPCC /,en es ,pi: si: 'si:/ *abbr* (the —) *(GB)* the National Society for the Prevention of Cruelty to Children.

NT *written abbr* **1** New Testament (in the Bible). **2** National Trust (a GB organization that protects

historic buildings and beautiful parts of the country).

nu·ance /'nju:ɑns/ *nc (formal)* a small difference in meaning, opinion, colour etc.

nu·bile /'nju:baɪl/ *adj* (of a girl) old enough to marry.

nu·clear /'nju:klɪə(r)/ *adj* of a nucleus; using nuclear energy. ⇨ non-nuclear.
,nuclear 'bomb *nc* one using nuclear energy.
,nuclear dis'armament *nu* the agreement not to develop, stock or use nuclear weapons.
,nuclear 'energy *nu* energy for industry etc produced by nuclear fission or nuclear fusion.
,nuclear 'fission *nu* the dividing of an atom (to produce energy).
,nuclear 'fuel *nc,nu* a means of providing nuclear energy.
,nuclear 'fusion *nu* the uniting of two nuclei (to produce energy).
,nuclear 'physics *nu* the scientific study of the atomic nucleus and its behaviour.
,nuclear 'power *n* **(a)** *nu* power from nuclear energy. **(b)** *nc* a country having nuclear weapons.
'nuclear-powered *adj* using nuclear energy: *a nuclear-powered submarine.*
,nuclear re'actor *nc* a device that generates power by nuclear fission.
,nuclear 'warfare *nu* the use of nuclear bombs.

nu·clei /'nju:klaɪ/ *n pl* ⇨ nucleus.

nu·cle·ic acid /nju:,kleɪk 'æsɪd/ *nc* a chemical substance that is an essential part of all living cells.

nu·cleus /'nju:klɪəs/ *nc (pl* **nuclei** /-klaɪ/) **1** *(science)* the central part of an atom, consisting of protons and neutrons. **2** *(fig)* a central part, round which other parts are grouped or round which other things collect: *These lessons form the nucleus of the language course.*

nude /nju:d/ *adj* naked. ☐ *nc* a nude human figure (esp in art). **in the nude** naked: *swim in the nude.*

nu·dism *nu* (the belief in) living without clothes.
nu·dist /-ɪst/ *adj* concerning nudism. ☐ *nc* a believer in, person who practises, nudism.
'nudist camp/colony *nc* a place where nudists practise their beliefs.

nu·di·ty /-ətɪ/ *nu* nakedness.

nudge¹ /nʌdʒ/ *nc* a slight touch or push.

nudge² /nʌdʒ/ *vt* to touch or push (a person) slightly (with the elbow) in order to attract her or his attention.

nug·get /'nʌgɪt/ *nc* a lump of metal as found in the earth: *gold nuggets.*

nui·sance /'nju:sns/ *nc* a person, insect, thing, act etc that causes trouble or offence: *These flies are a nuisance.*

null /nʌl/ *adj* **null and void** *(legal)* not valid.

nul·li·fy /'nʌlɪfaɪ/ *vt (pt,pp* **-ied)** to make (something) null and void: *nullify a marriage.*
nul·li·fi·ca·tion /,nʌlɪfɪ'keɪʃn/ *nu*

numb¹ /nʌm/ *adj* **(—er, —est) numb (with sth)** without ability to feel or move (because of something): *numb with cold/shock.*

numb² /nʌm/ *vt* **numb sb (with sth)** (often *passive*) to make a person numb (because of something): *numbed with grief.*
numb·ness *nu*

number¹ /'nʌmbə(r)/ *nc* **1** a written sign or symbol for a quantity; particular quantity: *3, 13, 33 and 103 are numbers.* **2** a particular quantity or amount: *a large number of people. A number of books* (= several books) *are missing from the library.* **in number** as a total quantity: *They were fifteen in number.* **without number** too many to be counted. **3** (usually shortened to No, with *pl* Nos, before a figure): *Room No 145* (e.g. in a hotel). **4** one issue of a magazine: *the current number of 'Punch'.* ⇨ **back number.** **5** a dance, song etc for the stage. **6** *nu̇* (*gram*) the way of showing the difference between singular and plural, such as *child/children; tree/trees; box/ boxes.*

number² /'nʌmbə(r)/ *vt* **1** to give a number to (members of a group, list etc): *Let's number them from 1 to 10.* **2** to amount to, add up to, (an amount mentioned): *We numbered 20 in all.* **3** to include (a person, thing): *number her among one's friends.* **4** (*passive*) to be restricted in number: *His days are numbered* (= He has not long to live).

'**number-plate** *nc* a sign showing the official number of a vehicle.

nu·mer·al /'nju:mərəl/ *adj, nc* (a word, figure or sign) used for a number; (of) number: *Roman numerals.*

nu·mer·ate /'nju:mərət/ *adj* (of a person) having good basic ability in mathematics. Compare literate.

nu·mer·ator /'nju:mərettə(r)/ *nc* (*maths*) the number above the line in a fraction, e.g. 3 in ¾. Compare denominator.

nu·meri·cal /nju:'merɪkl/ *adj* of, used to show, numbers: *numerical symbols.*

nu·meri·cal·ly /-klɪ/ *adv* in quantity: *The enemy were numerically superior.*

nu·mer·ous /'nju:mərəs/ *adj* very large in number: *her numerous friends.*

nun /nʌn/ *nc* a woman who, after taking religious vows, lives with other women in a convent in the service of God. Compare monk.

nun·nery /'nʌnərɪ/ *nc* a convent.

nup·tials /'nʌpʃəlz/ *n pl* (*formal*) wedding.

nurse¹ /nɜ:s/ *nc* **1** a professional person who cares for people who are ill or injured (in a hospital etc). **2** a woman employed to look after babies and young children in a family.

nurse² /nɜ:s/ *vt* **1** to take care of (people who are ill, injured etc). **2** to hold (a baby, a young animal etc) carefully and lovingly. **3** to give special care to (something): *nursing young plants.* **4** to have (something) in mind, think about (something) a great deal: *He was nursing feelings of revenge.*

nurs·ery /'nɜ:sərɪ/ *nc* (*pl* **-ies**) **1** a room (in a house etc) for the special use of small children. **2** a place where young plants and trees are raised.

'**nurs·ery·man** /-mən/ *nc* a man who owns a nursery(2).

'**nursery rhyme** *nc* a traditional poem or song for young children.

'**nursery school** *nc* one for children of 3 to 5.

'**nursery slope** *nc* a skiing slope suitable for learners.

nurs·ing /'nɜ:sɪŋ/ *nu* the profession or duties (as) of a nurse(1): *Careful nursing will be needed.*

'**nursing home** *nc* a building, usually privately owned, for the sick or aged.

nur·ture /'nɜ:tʃə(r)/ *vt* (*formal*) to give care to the growth or development of (a person, plan, business): *a delicately-nurtured girl/tree.*

nut /nʌt/ *nc* **1** a fruit consisting of a hard shell round a part (kernel) that can be eaten. *a hard nut to crack* (*fig*) a difficult problem to solve. **2** a small piece of metal with a threaded hole for screwing on to a bolt. **3** (*sl*) the head of a person. *be off one's nut* (*sl*) to be insane. ⇨ **nuts.**

'**nut-crackers** *n pl* (also *a pair of nutcrackers*) a utensil for cracking nuts open.

'**nut·shell** *nc* the hard outside covering of a nut. *(put sth) in a nutshell* (*fig*) (to say, write, it) in the fewest possible words.

nut·meg /'nʌtmeg/ *nc,nu* (the powder from crushing) a sweet-smelling seed of an E Indian tree, used as a flavouring.

nu·tri·ent /'nju:trɪənt/ *adj, nc* (*science*) (of) any mineral substance needed as food by plants or animals.

nu·tri·ment /'nju:trɪmənt/ *nc,nu* (*formal*) nourishing food.

nu·tri·tion /nju:'trɪʃn/ *nu* (*formal*) **1** the process of supplying and receiving healthy food. **2** the scientific study of food values.

nu·tri·tious /nju:'trɪʃəs/ *adj* (*formal*) having high value as food.

nuts /nʌts/ *adj* (*sl*) crazy; mad: *be/go nuts.* *be nuts about/over sb/sth* (*sl*) to be very much in love with a person, object, idea etc.

nut·ty /'nʌtɪ/ *adj* (**-ier, -iest**) **1** tasting, looking, like nuts(1). **2** (*sl*) mad; crazy.

nuzzle /'nʌzl/ *vt,vi* **nuzzle** ((*up*) *against*) *sb/ sth* to press, rub or push the nose against a person, thing: *The horse nuzzled* (*up against*) *my shoulder.*

NW *written abbr* north-west.

ny·lon /'naɪlɒn/ *n* **1** *nu* a manmade material with many varieties, used for clothes, rope, utensils etc: *nylon blouses; a nylon hairbrush.* **2** (*pl*) (*dated*) nylon stockings.

nymph /nɪmf/ *nc* **1** (*literary*) a beautiful young woman. **2** (in Greek or Roman stories) a young spirit(2) living in woods etc.

Oo

O, o /əʊ/ (*pl* **O's, o's** /əʊz/) **1** the 15th letter of the English alphabet. **2** zero (esp when saying telephone numbers).

O, oh /əʊ/ *int* a cry of surprise, fear, pain, sudden pleasure etc.

oak /əʊk/ *nc,nu* (the wood of) a large tree with leaves that have lobed edges.

OAP /ˌəʊ eɪ 'pi:/ *abbr* (*dated*) Old Age Pensioner (now called *senior citizen*).

oar /ɔ:(r)/ *nc* a pole with a flat blade, used to move a boat through the water. *put/shove one's oar in* (*informal*) to interfere. *rest on one's oars* to relax one's efforts.

oa·sis /əʊ'eɪsɪs/ *nc* (*pl* **oases** /-si:z/) **1** a place with water in a desert. **2** (*fig*) an experience etc that is pleasant in the middle of what is dull, unpleasant etc.

oath /əʊθ/ *nc* (*pl —s* /əʊðz/) **1** a solemn promise to do something. **2** a solemn statement (e.g. in a law court) that something is true. *be on/under oath* (*legal*) to have sworn to tell the truth. **3** an immoral use of religious words.

oats /əʊts/ *n* **1** *n pl* grain from a cereal plant used as food (*oats* for horses, *oatmeal* for people). *sow one's wild oats* to lead a life of pleasure while young. **2** *nu* porridge.
'**oat·meal** *nu* crushed oats.

ob·du·ra·cy /'ɒbdjʊərəsɪ/ *nu* (*formal*) stubbornness.

ob·du·rate /'ɒbjʊərət/ *adj* (*formal*) stubborn.
ob·dur·ate·ly *adv*

OBE /ˌəʊ biː 'iː/ *abbr* (Order of the) Order of the British Empire (a GB award for helping the country, doing well at sport etc).

obedi·ence /ə'biːdɪəns/ *nu* being obedient; showing obedience: *act in obedience to orders*.

obedi·ent /ə'biːdɪənt/ *adj* doing, willing to do, what one is told to do; behaving well: *obedient children*. Opp disobedient.
obedi·ent·ly *adv*

ob·elisk /'ɒbəlɪsk/ *nc* a tall, pointed, four-sided stone pillar.

obese /əʊ'biːs/ *adj* (*formal*) (of a person) very fat.
obes·ity /əʊ'biːsətɪ/ *nu*

obey /ə'beɪ/ *vt, vi* to do what one is told to do by (a person); carry out (a command): *They refused to obey. I was only obeying orders.*

obitu·ary /ə'bɪtʃʊərɪ/ *nc* (*pl -ies*) (also *attrib*) a printed notice of a person's death, often with a short account of his life: *obituary notices* (e.g. in a newspaper).

ob·ject[1] /'ɒbdʒɪkt/ *nc* **1** something that can be seen or touched; a material thing: *Tell me the names of the objects in this room.* **2** *object of sth* a person, thing, to which action, feeling or thought is directed: *an object of pity/admiration.* **3** a purpose: *with no object in life; fail/succeed in one's object. be no object* (*informal*) to be no problem: *Money is no object.* **4** (*gram*) a noun, clause etc towards which the action of the verb is directed, or to which a preposition indicates some relation. ⇨ direct/indirect/preparatory/prepositional object.

ob·ject[2] /əb'dʒekt/ *vi object* (*to sb/sth*) to state that one is not in favour (of a person, thing); make a protest (against): *I object to all this noise/to being treated like a child. He stood up and objected in strong language.*
ob·jec·tor /-tə(r)/ *nc* a person who objects. ⇨ conscientious objector.

ob·jec·tion /əb'dʒekʃn/ *n* **1** *nc, nu* a statement or feeling of dislike, disapproval or opposition: *He has a strong objection to getting up early. take objection to sb/sth* to state one's disagreement with or disapproval of a person, thing: *He took objection to what I said.* **2** *nc* something that one objects to: *Do you have any objections?*

ob·jec·tion·able /-əbl/ *adj* (*formal; derog*) very unpleasant: *an objectionable smell; objectionable remarks.*

ob·jec·tive[1] /əb'dʒektɪv/ *adj* influenced by what exists or is real, what can be seen, touched etc and not by emotions: *an objective view of a situation.* Compare subjective.

ob'jective case *nc* (*gram*) the use of a word or phrase as the object(4) in a sentence. Compare subjective case.

ob'jective form *nc* (*gram*) the form of a word used as an object(4): *The objective form of 'I' is 'me'.* Compare subjective form.
ob·jec·tive·ly *adv* in an objective manner.

ob·jec·tive[2] /əb'dʒektɪv/ *nc* an aim, purpose: *Her objective was to finish by November.*

ob·jec·tiv·ity /ˌɒbdʒek'tɪvətɪ/ *nu* an objective or unprejudiced judgement.

ob·li·gate /'ɒblɪgeɪt/ *vt* (usually *passive*) to force or compel (a person) (to do something): *He felt obligated to help.*

ob·li·ga·tion /ˌɒblɪ'geɪʃn/ *nc* a promise, duty or condition that shows what action ought to be taken (e.g. the law, one's duty, a sense of what is right): *the obligations of conscience. We are under an/no obligation to help* (= have to/do not have to help).

ob·li·ga·tory /ə'blɪgətrɪ/ *adj* that is required by law; essential: *Is attendance at the meeting obligatory or optional?*

ob·lige /ə'blaɪdʒ/ *vt* **1** (often *passive*) to force, compel, (a person) to do something (by law, a necessity etc): *They were obliged to* (= had to) *sell their house in order to pay their debts.* Ⓝ Not used in continuous tenses, e.g. *is/was -ing.* **2** (*formal*) to do something for (a person) as a favour or in answer to a request: *Please oblige me by closing the door. I'm much obliged to you* (= I'm grateful for what you've done).

oblig·ing *adj* willing to help: *obliging neighbours.*
oblig·ing·ly *adv*

ob·lique /ə'bliːk/ *adj* sloping; slanting.
o'blique angle *nc* (*maths*) an angle that is not a right angle (i.e. more or less than 90°).
ob·lique·ly *adv*

ob·lit·er·ate /ə'blɪtəreɪt/ *vt* to remove all signs of (something); destroy (something).
ob·lit·er·ation /əˌblɪtə'reɪʃn/ *nu*

ob·liv·ion /ə'blɪvɪən/ *nu* the state of being completely forgotten or having forgotten.

ob·livi·ous /ə'blɪvɪəs/ *adj* (*pred*) *oblivious* (*of sth*) unaware, having no memory, (of something): *oblivious of one's surroundings/of what was happening.*

ob·long /'ɒblɒŋ/ *adj, nc* (*maths*) (of) a figure having four straight sides and angles at 90°, longer than it is wide.

ob·nox·ious /əb'nɒkʃəs/ *adj* (*formal; derog*) (of smell, behaviour etc) very unpleasant.
ob·nox·ious·ly *adv*

oboe /'əʊbəʊ/ *nc* a woodwind musical instrument with a mouthpiece that has a double reed.
'**obo·ist** /-ɪst/ *nc* a person who plays the oboe.

ob·scene /əb'siːn/ *adj* (of words, thoughts, pictures etc) morally disgusting, offensive (esp because describing sex indecently).
ob·scene·ly *adv*

ob·scen·ity /əb'senətɪ/ *n* (*pl -ies*) *nc, nu* (an instance of) being obscene, bad language etc.

ob·scure[1] /əb'skjʊə(r)/ *adj* **1** hidden; not clearly seen: *an obscure view/corner.* **2** not easily understood: *Is the meaning still obscure to you?* **3** not well known: *an obscure poet.*

ob·scure[2] /əb'skjʊə(r)/ *vt* **1** to hide (a person,

thing): *Clouds were obscuring the moon.* **2** to make (something) difficult to understand: *The long words obscured the meaning.*

ob·scure·ly *adv*

ob·scur·ity /əb'skjʊərətɪ/ *n* (*pl* -ies) (*formal*) **1** *nu* the state of being hidden or unknown: *be content to live in obscurity.* **2** *nc* something that is obscure: *a philosophical essay full of obscurities.*

ob·se·qui·ous /əb'si:kwɪəs/ *adj* (*formal*) too eager to obey or serve; showing too much respect (esp hoping for reward or advantage): *be obsequious to the manager.*

ob·sequi·ous·ly *adv*

ob·serv·able /əb'zɜ:vəbl/ *adj* that can be seen or noticed.

ob·serv·ance /əb'zɜ:vns/ *n* **1** *nu* the keeping or observing(2,3) of a law, custom, festival etc: *the observance of Independence Day.* **2** *nc* an act performed as part of a ceremony or as a sign of respect or worship.

ob·serv·ant /əb'zɜ:vnt/ *adj* **1** quick at noticing things: *an observant boy.* Opp unobservant. **2** (*pred*) **observant of sth** (*formal*) careful to observe(2) laws, customs etc: *observant of the rules.*

ob·serv·ant·ly *adv*

ob·ser·va·tion /ˌɒbzə'veɪʃn/ *n* **1** *nu* the act, state, of observing or being observed: *observation of the stars; be kept under medical observation.* **2** *nu* the power of noticing carefully: *a man with poor powers of observation.* **3** (usually *pl*) collected and recorded information: *observations on bird life in the Antarctic.* **4** *nc* a measuring of the altitude of the sun etc in order to find one's exact position.

ob·serv·atory /əb'zɜ:vətrɪ/ *nc* (*pl* -ies) a building from which the sky can be observed.

ob·serve /əb'zɜ:v/ *vt* **1** to see and notice, watch, (a person, act etc): *observing the behaviour of birds. The accused man was observed entering the bank.* **2** to pay attention to (rules etc). **3** to celebrate (the usual word) (festivals, birthdays etc): *Do they observe Christmas in that country?* **4** **observe (that) sth** (*formal*) to say something as one's opinion etc (that): *He observed that the house seemed to be too small.*

ob·server *nc* a person who observes: *an observer of nature. An observer at a conference cannot vote or speak.*

ob·sess /əb'ses/ *vt* (usually *passive*) (of a fear etc) to occupy the mind of (a person) continually: *obsessed by fear of unemployment/failure.*

ob·ses·sion /əb'seʃn/ *nc* something such as a fixed idea that occupies one's mind completely.

ob·sess·ive /əb'sesɪv/ *adj* of, like, an obsession: *an obsessive hobby.*

ob·so·les·cence /ˌɒbsə'lesns/ *nu* the state of being obsolescent.

ob·so·les·cent /ˌɒbsə'lesnt/ *adj* becoming out of date; passing out of use.

ob·sol·ete /'ɒbsəli:t/ *adj* no longer used; out-of-date: *obsolete ideas/methods/words.*

ob·stacle /'ɒbstəkl/ *nc* something that stops progress or makes it difficult: *obstacles to world peace.*

'obstacle race *nc* (**a**) a race in which obstacles have to be crossed. (**b**) (*fig*) an aim etc with many difficulties to be dealt with.

ob·ste·tri·cian /ˌɒbste'trɪʃn/ *nc* an expert in obstetrics.

ob·stet·rics /əb'stetrɪks/ *nu* the branch of medicine and surgery connected with childbirth.

ob·sti·na·cy /'ɒbstɪnəsɪ/ *nu* (*formal*) the state of being obstinate; stubbornness.

ob·sti·nate /'ɒbstɪnət/ *adj* not easily agreeing to an argument or being persuaded; stubborn: *as obstinate as a mule* (= very obstinate).

ob·sti·nate·ly *adv*

ob·struct /əb'strʌkt/ *vt* **1** to block up (a road, view etc): *Trees obstructed the view.* **2** to make (the progress etc of something) difficult: *They shouted to obstruct justice in the law court.*

ob·struc·tion /əb'strʌkʃn/ *n* (*formal*) **1** *nu* the act of obstructing or being obstructed: *a diplomatic policy of obstruction.* **2** *nc* something that blocks a way, prevents progress: *obstructions on the road.*

ob·struc·tive /əb'strʌktɪv/ *adj* **obstructive (to sth)** (*formal*) causing, likely or intended to cause, obstruction: *a policy obstructive to our plans.*

ob·tain /əb'teɪn/ *v* **1** *vt* (*formal*) to get (something) (the usual word): *Where can I obtain the book?* **2** *vi* (*formal; dated*) (of rules, customs) to be established or in use: *The custom still obtains in some districts.*

ob·tain·able /-əbl/ *adj* that can be obtained. Opp unobtainable.

ob·trude /əb'tru:d/ *vt,vi* (*formal*) to push (oneself, opinions etc) forward, esp when unwanted.

ob·trus·ive /əb'tru:sɪv/ *adj* (*formal*) very (often too) noticeable or obvious: *an obtrusive smell.* Opp unobtrusive.

ob·trus·ive·ly *adv*

ob·tuse /əb'tju:s/ *adj* (*formal*) **1** not trying to be gentle or polite: *an obtuse remark.* **2** (*derog*) (of a person) stupid.

ob'tuse angle *nc* (*maths*) one between 90° and 180°.

obtuse·ly *adv*

ob·tuse·ness *nu*

ob·vi·ate /'ɒbvɪeɪt/ *vt* (*formal*) to get rid of (needs, dangers, difficulties etc).

ob·vi·ous /'ɒbvɪəs/ *adj* **1** easily seen: *an obvious error.* **2** easily understood or known: *an obvious liar.*

ob·vi·ous·ly *adv*

oc·ca·sion[1] /ə'keɪʒn/ *n* **1** *nc* a time when a particular event takes place or should take place: *On this/that occasion he won. She loses on rare occasions. He has had few occasions to speak French.* **on occasion** now and then: *I do go to the opera on occasion.* **rise to the occasion** to show that one is capable of doing what needs to be done. **2** *nc,nu* a reason; cause: *I've had no occasion to visit him recently.*

oc·ca·sion[2] /ə'keɪʒn/ *vt* (*formal*) to cause (something): *The boy's behaviour occasioned his parents much anxiety.*

oc·ca·sion·al /ə'keɪʒənl/ *adj* (*attrib*) happening, coming, seen etc from time to time, but not regularly: *He pays me occasional visits.*

oc·ca·sion·al·ly *adv* now and then; sometimes: *Occasionally I listen to jazz.*

oc·cu·pan·cy /'ɒkjupənsɪ/ *nc,nu* (*pl* -ies) an act, fact, period, of occupying a house, land etc.

oc·cu·pant /'ɒkjʊpənt/ nc a person who occupies a house, office, room, seat etc.

oc·cu·pa·tion /ˌɒkjʊ'peɪʃn/ n 1 nu the act, time, of occupying: *the occupation of a house by a family*. 2 nc a profession, trade etc: *What is your occupation?* 3 nc an activity that uses up one's time, either permanently or as a hobby etc.

oc·cu·pa·tion·al /-ʃənl/ adj concerning, caused by, a person's job: *occupational risks/diseases*.

ˌoccuˌpational 'therapy nu the treatment of illness etc by organized mental or physical activity.

oc·cu·pier /'ɒkjʊpaɪə(r)/ nc a person living in a building; occupant.

oc·cu·py /'ɒkjʊpaɪ/ vt (pt,pp **-ied**) 1 to live in, be in, (a house, office, seat etc): *Is this seat occupied?* 2 to take by force and keep possession of (towns, countries etc): *occupy the enemy's capital.* 3 to take up, fill, (space, time, attention, the mind): *Many anxieties occupy my mind. He is occupied with playing chess.* ⇨ preoccupy. 4 to hold (a job): *She occupies an important position in industry.*

oc·cur /ə'kɜː(r)/ vi (-rr-) 1 to take place; happen: *When did the accident occur?* 2 **occur to sb** to come into a person's thoughts: *Did it ever occur to you that he was lazy?* 3 to exist; be found: *Sadly poverty occurs in every country.*

oc·cur·rence /ə'kʌrəns/ n 1 nc a happening; event: *a sad occurrence.* 2 nu the fact or process of occurring: *of frequent/rare occurrence.*

ocean /'əʊʃn/ nc 1 (the —) the great body of salt water that surrounds the land masses of the earth. 2 (O-) one of the main divisions of this: *the Atlantic/Pacific Ocean.* 3 **oceans of sth** (informal) a great number or quantity: *oceans of time.*

ocean·ic /ˌəʊʃɪ'ænɪk/ adj of, like, living in, the ocean: *oceanic life.*

ochre (US also **och·er**) /'əʊkə(r)/ nu (a kind of soil producing) a pale yellowish-brown colour.

o'clock /ə'klɒk/ adverbial particle (used after numbers to ask and tell the time) the hour mentioned: *He left at five o'clock. I'll be there between 5 and 6 o'clock. It is nearly one o'clock at night/in the morning. We'll be on the 10 o'clock train.*

Oct written abbr October.

oc·ta·gon /'ɒktəgən/ nc (maths) a flat figure with eight sides and angles.

oc·tag·on·al /ɒk'tægənl/ adj

oc·tane /'ɒkteɪn/ nc,nu a form of petrol of high quality.

oc·tave /'ɒktɪv/ nc 1 (music) an interval of eight notes between two notes so that the first has a pitch double the value of the other. 2 (poetry) the first eight lines of a sonnet; verse of eight lines.

oc·tet (also **oc·tette**) /ɒk'tet/ nc (a piece of music for) eight singers or players.

Oc·to·ber /ɒk'təʊbə(r)/ n (also attrib) the tenth month of the year, with 31 days: *a cold October morning. Her birthday's on 12 October.* Ⓝ *'12 October'* is spoken as *'October the twelfth'* or *'the twelfth of October'.*

oc·to·gen·arian /ˌɒktədʒɪ'neərɪən/ adj, nc (of) a person between 80 and 89 in age.

oc·to·pus /'ɒktəpəs/ nc (pl **—es**) a sea animal with a soft body and eight arms (tentacles) with suckers.

ocu·list /'ɒkjʊlɪst/ nc a medical specialist in diseases of the eye.

odd /ɒd/ adj (no comp except 6 below) 1 (of a number) not exactly divisible by two: *1, 3, 5 and 7 are odd numbers.* Opp even¹(4). 2 (attrib) of one of a pair when the other is missing: *an odd shoe/ glove.* 3 (attrib) of one or more of a set or series when not with the rest: *two odd volumes of an encyclopaedia.* **odd man out** (informal) a person who cannot fit into the society, community etc of which he or she is a member. 4 (used after numbers) with a little extra: *thirty-odd years* (= between 30 and 40); *twelve pounds odd* (= £12 and some pence extra). 5 (attrib) not regular, habitual or fixed: *make a living by doing odd jobs; knit at odd times/moments.* 6 (**—er, —est**) strange; peculiar: *He's an odd/odd-looking old man. How odd!*

odd·ly adv in a strange manner: *Oddly enough* (= Although it may seem strange), *he was quite right!*

odd·ity /'ɒdətɪ/ nc (pl **-ies**) a strange act, thing or person.

odd·ment /'ɒdmənt/ nc something left over; spare piece: *The chair was sold as an oddment at the end of the auction.* Compare odds and ends.

odds /ɒdz/ n pl 1 the chances in favour of or against something happening: *The odds are in our favour/against us.* (= We are likely/unlikely to succeed). 2 the difference in amount between the money betted and the money that will be paid if a bet is successful: *odds of ten to one.* 3 **be at odds (with sb) (over sth)** to be quarrelling or disagreeing.

ˌodds and 'ends n pl small articles, bits and pieces, of various sorts and usually of small value.

ode /əʊd/ nc (literature) a lyric poem expressing noble or enthusiastic feelings.

odi·ous /'əʊdɪəs/ adj (formal; derog) extremely unpleasant: *an odious remark/old man.*

odi·ous·ly adv

odour (US = **odor**) /'əʊdə(r)/ nc a pleasant or unpleasant smell.

odour·less (US = **odor-**) adj

od·ys·sey /'ɒdɪsɪ/ nc (pl **—s**) (literature) a long, adventurous journey or series of adventures.

oecu·meni·cal /ˌiːkjuː'menɪkl/ adj = ecumenical.

o'er /ɔː(r)/ adv, prep (poetic) = over.

oesoph·agus /iː'sɒfəgəs/ nc (pl **—es** or **-agi** /-gaɪ/) (anat) the passage from the throat to the stomach.

of /əv strong form ɒv/ prep Ⓝ For uses with verbs such as *come, make, speak, taste, think* etc, ⇨ the verb entries. 1 (showing association, relationship) belonging to; associated with: *a friend of mine/ his/yours; one of my/her/their friends; the leg of the table; the colour of this ink; the countries of Europe; the President of the USA; the members of the committee; the University of Oxford; the writer of the letter; the people of Asia; first/last/second of all; the opposite of what I meant; the last warm day of summer; the second month of the year; your letter of 4 July.* 2 containing; having: *a bottle of wine; a cup of tea; a volume of poetry; a photograph of a flower; a girl of 10; a smell of onions; a look of horror.* 3 (showing a quantity, measure, part): *a pint of milk; a gallon of petrol; a kilo of sugar; six of them; some of my friends; all/many of* *us; nothing of the kind; a lot of the time.* **4** made using; made by: *a dress of pure cotton; built of brick; a camera of Japanese manufacture; a heart of gold.* **5** (showing a connection due to authorship, origin, cause): *the plays of Shakespeare; the cause of the accident; with the help of my family; of African descent.* **6** (showing a connection such as activity or ability): *a student of English; a repairer of bicycles; a Doctor of Medicine; be fond of music/dancing.* **7** (a) concerning: *be found guilty of theft; a matter of life or death; a case of measles; the fear of being killed. Of what am I accused? What of* (= What about) *the risks?* (b) due to: *die of hunger; afraid of spiders; happy because of him.* **8** (showing time, distance) in relation to: *south of London; within 5 miles of the frontier; inside the first minute of the football match.* **9** (showing loss, removal, separation): *a loss of power/appetite; short of money; cured of an illness; free of tax; independent of help; get rid of an old chair; be deprived of love.* **10** (formal) during: *I watch TV of an evening.*

off¹ /ɒf/ *adj* **1** (*pred*) cancelled; delayed: *The meeting/strike is off.* Opp on¹(1). **on the off chance** ⇨ chance²(2). **2** (*pred*) so as to be working; available: *The switch/tap/TV is on. Is the gas/water/electricity on?* Opp on¹(2). **in the off position** (of a switch etc) so that the electricity, water, air etc cannot pass. **3** (*attrib*) of the side furthest from the edge of a road: *the offside lane of the motorway; the off front wheel.* ⇨ near¹(5). **4** (*attrib*) (of a period of time) (a) with less activity: *the off season.* (b) not as good as usual: *have an off day.*

off² /ɒf/ *adverbial particle* ⓝ For uses with verbs such as *be, come, get, kick, pull, ring, show, take* etc, ⇨ the verb entries. **1** so as to be no longer present or in a particular position: *Take your coat off. Why not take the day off? I must be off now. The town is 5 miles off. It's not far off.* Compare on²(1). **2** so as to be no longer available or working: *Turn the switch/TV/electricity/gas off.* Opp on²(2). **off and on** (also **on and off**) from time to time; now and again: *It rained off and on.* **3** so as to be no longer there: *I've paid off the loan.* **4** (of food) no longer fresh: *This meat/fish has gone off.* **a bit off** (informal) (a little) annoying: *It's a bit off, making me work during the weekend.* **5** so as to have a little or a lot of something, esp money: *better/worse off than you; badly/comfortably/well off.*

off³ /ɒf/ *prep* ⓝ For uses of with verbs such as *go, keep, knock, put* etc, ⇨ the verb entries. **1** away from; down from: *Keep off the grass! He fell off the ladder/bike. She broke a piece of the loaf. He jumped off the bus. Can you take a little off the price?* **off duty** ⇨ duty(3). **2** situated near: *an island off the coast; a village just off* (= close to) *the motorway.* **3** (of a road etc) extending from (a larger one): *a narrow lane off the main road.* **4** not taking, using, wanting: *be off cigarettes/smoking; be off one's food; go off people.* **5** (used in combination with a colour) almost: *off-white.* **off colour** ⇨ colour¹(3).

of·fal /ˈɒfl/ *nu* the internal parts of an animal (e.g. heart, liver, kidneys), used for food.

off-beat /ˌɒf ˈbiːt/ *adj* (informal) (modern and) unusual: *off-beat clothes.*

of·fence (*US* = **of·fense**) /əˈfens/ *n* **1** *nc* **offence (against sb/sth)** a crime, sin, breaking of a rule: *an offence against the law/good manners; be charged with a serious offence.* **2** *nu* the condition of being hurt in one's feelings: *No offence meant* (used to say 'I did not intend to hurt your feelings'). ⇨ offensive¹(1). **take offence (at sth)** to be offended (because of something): *He's quick to take offence.* **3** *nu* the act, condition, of attacking: *They say that the most effective defence is offence.* **4** *nc* something that annoys or causes anger: *That dirty house is an offence to the neighbourhood.*

of·fend /əˈfend/ *v* **1** *vt* to hurt the feelings of, upset, (a person): *I'm sorry if I've offended you/if you were offended by my remarks.* **2** *vi* **offend against sth** (formal) to do wrong: *offend against good manners/the law/tradition.* **3** *vt* to annoy or be unpleasant to (a person etc): *ugly buildings that offend the eye.*

of·fend·er *nc* a person who does wrong, esp by breaking the law.

of·fense /əˈfens/ *n* = offence.

of·fen·sive¹ /əˈfensɪv/ *adj* **1** very unpleasant; causing offence(2): *fish with an offensive smell; offensive language.* **2** used for, connected with, attacking: *offensive weapons/wars.* Compare defensive¹.

of·fen·sive·ly *adv*

of·fen·sive·ness *nu*

of·fen·sive² /əˈfensɪv/ *nc* an attack: *launch an offensive against the enemy.* **take the/mount an offensive** to begin to attack.

of·fer¹ /ˈɒfə(r)/ *nc* **1** a statement offering to do or give something: *an offer of help.* **2** an amount (of money etc) offered: *an offer of £200 for my car.* **be open to offers** to be willing to consider prices offered.

of·fer² /ˈɒfə(r)/ *v* **1** *vt,vi* to suggest, say, (what one is willing to pay, do, give or exchange): *I'll offer you £10 for your bike. Let's offer them coffee while they are waiting. They offered a £50 reward. I've been offered a job in Spain. He offered to help me. He offered me his help.* **2** *vt* (formal) to try to do (something): *offer no resistance to the enemy.* **3** *vt* **offer sth ((up) to God)** to give praise etc (to God): *offer prayers.*

of·fer·ing /ˈɒfərɪŋ/ *n* **1** *nu* the act of trying to offer(1): *the offering of bribes.* **2** *nc* something offered or presented, esp for a good cause: *peace offerings.*

off·hand¹ /ˌɒfˈhænd/ *adj* **1** without thought or preparation: *offhand remarks.* **2** (of behaviour, etc) careless; impolite: *act in an offhand way.*

off·hand² /ˌɒfˈhænd/ *adv* without thought or preparation: *I can't say offhand whether I agree.*

of·fice /ˈɒfɪs/ *nc* **1** (often *pl*) room(s) used as a place of business: *a lawyer's/business office. Our offices are on the top floor.* ⇨ booking-/box-office. **2** (O-) a government department: *the Foreign Office.* **3** the position, duties, (of a person with responsibility): *the office of chairperson.* **be in office** to have the right or power to govern: *Which party will be in office after the next general election?* **hold office** to have a public position of authority. **4** (*pl*) (formal) attentions, help: *through the good offices* (= kind help) *of a friend.*

'office-block *nc* a large building with business

offices.

'**office hours** *n pl* the period during the day when a business is active.

'**office-worker** *nc* an employee in an office(1).

of·fi·cer /'ɒfɪsə(r)/ *nc* **1** a person appointed to command others in the armed forces, the police force etc: *officers and men/crew*. **2** a person with a (public) position of authority, e.g. in the government: *executive/clerical officers; a customs officer*. Compare official². **3** the form of address to a police officer.

of·fi·cial¹ /ə'fɪʃl/ *adj* **1** of, concerning, a position of trust or authority: *official responsibilities/ records; in his official uniform*. **2** done by people with authority: *official statements. The news is not yet official*. Opp unofficial. **3** characteristic of, suitable for, people holding office: *written in official style*.

of·fi·cial² /ə'fɪʃl/ *nc* a person holding an office(3) (e.g. in government, an organization). Compare officer(2).

of·fi·cial·ly /-ʃəlɪ/ *adv* (**a**) according to what has been said or written to an official (but possibly not actually true): *Officially she's at the dentist, but actually she's gone shopping*. Opp unofficially. (**b**) with ceremony and formalities: *The new sports centre will be opened officially by the Queen*. (**c**) as an official: *Are you here at the meeting officially?* Opp unofficially.

of·fici·ate /ə'fɪʃɪeɪt/ *vi* (*formal*) to do the duties expected of an officer(2): *officiate as chairman; officiate at a marriage ceremony*.

of·fi·cious /ə'fɪʃəs/ *adj* (*formal; derog*) too eager or ready to use one's authority, rank etc.
of·fi·cious·ly *adv*

off·ing /'ɒfɪŋ/ *n* **be in the offing** (*fig*) to be possible: *Promotion is in the offing*.

off-licence /'ɒf laɪsns/ *nc* **1** a licence to sell beer and other alcoholic drinks for drinking off the premises. **2** a shop, part of a pub, where such drinks may be bought and taken away.

off-line /'ɒf laɪn/ *adj* (*attrib*) (*computers*) not directly connected to the central unit. Compare on-line.

off-load /ɒf 'ləʊd/ *vt* to unload (things): *off-load a cargo; off-load shares onto the market* (i.e. sell them).

off-peak /'ɒf piːk/ *adj* (usually *attrib*) concerning a service, period of time, with much less activity: *off-peak electricity; an off-peak holiday*.

off·print /'ɒfprɪnt/ *nc* a separate printing of an article from a longer book.

off-putting /ɒf 'pʊtɪŋ/ *adj* (*informal*) unpleasant ⇨ put sb off.

off·set /'ɒfset/ *vt* (**-tt-**) to balance, make up for, (something): *He has to offset his small salary with freelance work*.

off·shoot /'ɒfʃuːt/ *nc* **1** a stem or branch growing from a main stem. **2** (*fig*) a branch (of a family, theory etc).

off·shore /'ɒfʃɔː(r)/ *adj* **1** in a direction away from a shore or land: *offshore breezes*. Compare onshore. **2** at a short way out to sea: *offshore islands/fisheries*. Compare inshore.

off·side /ɒf'saɪd/ *adj* **1** (*attrib*) on the side furthest from the edge of the road: *the offside wheels of a car*. Compare nearside. ⇨ off¹(3). **2** (also *adv*) (in football, hockey etc) (of a player) nearer the other team's goal than any player in the other team in a way that is against the rules: *be offside; the offside rule*. Compare onside.

off·spring /'ɒfsprɪŋ/ *nc* (*pl* —) a child; children; young of animals: *He's the offspring of a scientist and a dancer*.

off-the-record /ɒf ðə 'rekɔːd/ *adj* (*no comp*) not meant to be recorded or reported as official(2): *an off-the-record remark*.

off-white /ɒf 'waɪt/ *adj* almost white.

oft /ɒft/ *adv* (*poetic*) = often: *many a time and oft* (= very often).

'**oft-times** *adv* (*archaic*) = often.

of·ten /'ɒfn/ *adv* Ⓝ '*More/Most often*' is much more usual than '*oftener/oftenest*'. many times on different occasions; in a large number of instances: *We often go there. How often do the buses run? We've been there quite often* (= several times). Ⓝ '*Often*' refers to *several* occasions. For something happening many times on *one* occasion, use *a lot of/many* etc times, keep on + *-ing*, as in *I laughed many times/I kept on laughing during the performance*. Compare seldom. **as often as not; more often than not** very frequently: *During foggy weather the trains are late more often than not*. **every so often** occasionally: *Every so often we go to the theatre*. **once too often** once more than is wise, acceptable etc: *You've let me down once too often and I shall not trust you again*.

ogle /'əʊgl/ *vi,vt* **ogle ((at) sb/sth)** to stare at (a person) (suggesting sexual attraction or longing): *ogling all the pretty girls*.

ogre /'əʊgə(r)/ *nc* (in stories) a cruel man-eating giant.

ogress /'əʊgrɪs/ *nc* a female ogre.

oh /əʊ/ *int* (used to express surprise, fear etc).

ohm /əʊm/ *nc* a unit of electrical resistance (symbol Ω).

OHMS *written abbr* On Her (or His) Majesty's Service (printed on envelopes in GB carrying government letters etc).

oho /əʊ'həʊ/ *int* (used to express surprise, success, make fun of a person etc).

oil¹ /ɔɪl/ *nc,nu* **1** (any of many kinds of) liquid which does not mix with water, obtained from animals (e.g. *cod-liver oil*), plants (e.g. *olive oil*), or found underground (*petroleum*). **burn the midnight oil** to stay up late at night to study etc. **strike oil** (**a**) to find petroleum in the ground. (**b**) (*fig*) to become very prosperous or successful. **2** (*pl*) oil colours for painting. **paint in oils** to paint with oil colours.

'**oil-can** *nc* a container with a long spout, used to carry oil for machinery.

'**oil colours** *n pl* paints made by mixing colouring matter in oil.

'**oil-field** *nc* an area where petroleum is found.

'**oil-fired** *adj* burning oil as fuel: *oil-fired central heating*.

'**oil-painting** (**a**) *nu* the art of painting in oils. (**b**) *nc* a picture painted in oil.

'**oil-rig** *nc* a structure for drilling (e.g. in the seabed) for oil.

'**oil-slick** *nc* a layer of oil on the sea.

'**oil-tanker** *nc* a ship for carrying oil.

'**oil well** *nc* a well producing oil.

oil² /ɔɪl/ *vt* to put oil into or on (esp machinery).

oily /'ɔɪlɪ/ adj (-ier, -iest) 1 of, like, oil: an oily liquid. 2 covered or soaked with oil: oily fingers.

oint·ment /'ɔɪntmənt/ nc,nu (sorts of) medicinal paste made from oil or fat and used on the skin (e.g. to heal injuries).

OK¹ (also **okay**) /,əʊ'keɪ/ adj (pred), adv (informal) in good order; all right: Everything's OK. Are you feeling OK?

OK² (also **okay**) /,əʊ'keɪ/ vt (informal) to give one's approval to (a plan, idea etc): Did she OK the project?

ok·ra /'ɒkrə/ nc,nu (a tropical plant with) pointed green seed pods, used as a vegetable.

old¹ /əʊld/ adj (—er, —est) 1 (used with a period of time, and with how) of age: He's forty years old/a forty-year-old/a 60-year-old grandfather. How old are you? He's old enough to know better. ⇨ also elder¹, eldest. 2 having lived a long time; no longer young or middle-aged: as old as the hills (= very old). He's far too old for the job. What will he do when he grows/is/gets old? Compare young¹(1). 3 having existed for a long time: old clothes; old customs/families/civilizations/times. Compare young¹(2), new¹(1), modern(2). 4 (attrib) familiar; known for a long time: an old friend of mine; an old story. 5 (attrib) former; previous: This was my old office but now I work downstairs. 6 (attrib) having much experience or practice: He's an old supporter of the club/member of the committee. 7 (attrib) (informal) (used in addressing persons): 'Good old John!' 'Hullo, old thing!' 8 (informal) (used for emphasis): Any old thing (= Anything whatever) will do.

old 'age nu the period of life from about 60 years.

old-age 'pensioner nc = senior citizen.

old country nc (usually the —) a person's country of origin.

old-'fashioned adj out-of-date.

old 'hand nc a person with long experience (at something): an old hand at negotiating.

old 'hat adj, nc (informal; derog) (a person or thing that is) boringly familiar.

old 'maid nc (derog) an older woman thought unlikely to marry.

old 'master nc a great painter or painting.

Old 'Nick n (informal) the devil.

Old 'Testament n (the—) the first part of the Bible.

old-time adj (attrib) belonging to former times: old-time dancing.

old-'timer nc a person having a long association with a place, job, group etc.

Old World n (the —) Europe, Asia and Africa.

old² /əʊld/ n 1 n pl (the —) old people. 2 of old in, from, the past: in days of old; the men of old.

old·en /'əʊldən/ adj (attrib) (literary) of a former age: in olden times/days.

old·ish /'əʊldɪʃ/ adj (no comp) a little old.

oli·garchy /'ɒlɪgɑːkɪ/ nc,nu (pl -ies) (a country with, system of) government by a small group of powerful people; such a group.

ol·ive /'ɒlɪv/ nc 1 (an evergreen tree common in S Europe with a) small fruit with a hard seed like a stone and a bitter taste, eaten or used to make an oil (olive oil) which is used for cooking, in salads etc. 2 a leaf, branch or wreath of olive branches as an emblem of peace.

Olym·pic /ə'lɪmpɪk/ adj (attrib) (as in the Olympic Games (informal) the Olympics) of the international athletic and sports competitions held in modern times every four years in a different country: an Olympic gold medal.

ome·ga /'əʊmɪgə/ nc 1 the last letter of the Greek alphabet (Ω). 2 (fig) the last of a series.

om·elette (also **om·elet**) /'ɒmlɪt/ nc a meal of eggs beaten together and fried.

omen /'əʊmen/ nc,nu (something, a happening, regarded as) a sign of something good or warning of evil fortune: an event of good/bad omen.

om·in·ous /'ɒmɪnəs/ adj (formal) threatening: an ominous silence.
om·in·ous·ly adv

omis·sion /ə'mɪʃn/ n 1 nu the act of omitting, leaving out, something. 2 nc something that is omitted: serious omissions in the report.

omit /ə'mɪt/ vt (-tt-) 1 to fail to include (a person, thing); decide and leave out (a person, thing): The bill has been omitted from the accounts. 2 omit to + verb; omit + -ing (formal) to fail (to do something): omit to say/omit saying who wrote it.

om·ni·bus¹ /'ɒmnɪbəs/ adj (attrib) with several works (by the same author) or several episodes from a serial: an omnibus edition.

om·ni·bus² /'ɒmnɪbəs/ nc (pl —es) (former name for) a bus.

om·ni·di·rec·tion·al /,ɒmnɪdaɪ'rekʃnl/ adj (tech) (of an aerial, microphone etc) able to receive signals from any direction.

om·nip·otence /ɒm'nɪpətəns/ nu (formal) infinite power: the omnipotence of God.

om·nip·otent /-ənt/ adj having infinite power.

om·ni·vore /'ɒmnɪvɔː(r)/ nc (science) an animal that eats many different kinds of food. Compare carnivore, herbivore, insectivore.

om·niv·or·ous /ɒm'nɪvərəs/ adj eating many different kinds of food.

on¹ /ɒn/ adj 1 (pred) not cancelled: The meeting/trip is on. Opp off¹(1). 2 (pred) not turned off: The switch/light/radio is on. Is the gas on? Opp off¹(2). **in the on position** (of a switch etc) so that the electricity, gas, air etc can pass. 3 = near¹(5) (which is more usual). Opp off¹(3).

on² /ɒn/ adverbial particle (Ⓝ) For uses with verbs such as be, come, get, go, hang, keep etc, ⇨ the verb entries. 1 so as to be in a particular position or present: Put your shoes on. Your hat isn't on straight. I'm staying on for another year. The station is a mile further on. Compare off²(1). (Ⓝ) For notes about 'on to', ⇨ onto. 2 so as to be available or working: Turn the lights/tap/radio/water on. Opp off²(2). **on and off** ⇨ off²(2). 3 (showing progress forward; continuous activity): We went on until we came to a café. You go and I'll follow on. Come on—let's run! **on and on** without stopping: We walked on and on until we reached the river. **and so on** ⇨ so²(6).

on³ /ɒn/ prep (Ⓝ) For uses with verbs such as act, keep, put, spend etc, ⇨ the verb entries. For the use of 'on' in phrases such as on purpose; on condition that; on edge, ⇨ the noun entries, as at air, card, condition, contrary, conscience, duty edge, fire etc. 1 supported by, attached to, in contact with: put the bottle on the table; the carpet on the floor; sit on the grass; write on the postcard; lean on a wall; on a bike; on (= inside) a bus/train. (Ⓝ) 'Upon' is also possible but is much more formal. ⇨ also onto. **2** in the position, direction, of: *on the left; on the edge/ side; on the coast/river.* **3** towards: *turn one's back on her.* **4** (referring to time) during; exactly at: *on Sundays/weekends/1 May; on that day; on this occasion; on my arrival.* Ⓝ For the differences between *on, at* and *in,* ⇨ at(2). **5** about; covering: *a programme on jazz; a book/lecture/talk on Shakespeare.* **6** according to; because of: *a story based on fact; acting on your advice; arrested on a charge of murder.* **7** a member of: *be on the committee/staff.* **8** occupied with, busy with: *on business/duty/holiday.* **9** using: *walk on tiptoe; a car running on petrol; crawl on one's hands and knees; work on batteries; live on £50 a week; survive on one meal a day.*

once¹ /wʌns/ *adv* **1** for one time, on one occasion only: *I've been there once. I've seen her more than once. We write once a month. He goes to see his parents once (in) every six months.* **once more** one more time: *I'll try once more.* **once or twice** a very small number of times: *I've met her once or twice.* **(every) once in a while** occasionally. **once and for all** for the last time (and never again): *I'm warning you once and for all— don't do that!* **2** during some indefinite time in the past: *He once lived in Munich. There once lived a king who had twelve beautiful daughters.* **3** even for one time: *He didn't once/He never once offered to help.* **(just) for once** on this one occasion, as an exception: *Why don't you pay for once?* **4 at once** (a) without delay; immediately: *I'm leaving for Rome at once. Come here at once!* (b) at the same time: *Don't all speak at once! I can't do two things at once.* **all at once** suddenly: *All at once the rope broke.*

once² /wʌns/ *conj* as soon as; when: *Once you understand this particular instruction, you will have no further difficulty.*

on·com·ing /ˈɒnkʌmɪŋ/ *adj* (*attrib*) advancing; approaching: *oncoming traffic.*

one¹ /wʌn/ *adj* or *det* **1** a single (person, thing etc); of 1: *one pen and two pencils; one thousand pounds; twenty-one students; one and a half hours; one kilo/metre; at one o'clock.* **one and only sth** the single example (with no other as good): *my one and only true friend.* **one or two sth** a few . . . : *be out for one or two hours.* **2** a (but no particular occasion): *One day (= Some time in the future) you'll be sorry. We met one morning* (i.e. during a morning) *last month.* **3** a particular example: *That's one way of doing it (but I know a better one). That's the one thing I need.* **for one thing** ⇨ thing(3). ⇨ also accord¹. **4** (*attrib*) the same: *They all went off in one direction.*

one² /wʌn/ *nc* **1** (number, portion, piece etc): *We can only afford one. One from twenty leaves nineteen. It's half past one.* **by/in ones and twos** a few at a time: *People left the meeting in ones and twos.* **in one** combined: *He's the treasurer and secretary in one.* **be one up on sb** to have an advantage over, be one stage ahead of, another person.

one³ /wʌn/ *pron* **1 one (of sth)** a single person, thing, (from a group): *One is big and the other is small. Can you lend me one? She's one of my friends. Is one of them yours? He's treated as one*

of the family. *If one of us fails, another must try. I, for one, do not approve. The one's rich and the other's poor. Students who get the highest marks are not always the ones with the highest intelligence. Would you like this table or that one? I'd like this large one. Which ones do you want?* Ⓝ 'One' cannot be used in front of a determiner (e.g. *a, the, her*). 'One of' can be used in front of *determiners,* as in *One of them laughed. One of us is responsible.* The plural form of 'one of' is 'some of', as in *Some of my books are missing,* except after 'if' when it is 'any of', as in *If any of my pens are missing I'll be angry.* The plural form of 'that/this one' can be 'those/these', as in *'Would you like these apples or those?'* except when there is an adjective in which case 'one' is necessary, as in *I'd like these small ones.* **one after another/the other** one person, thing, then another: *We walked across the bridge one after another.* **one another** (used when a fact, action etc relates to two or more people): *All the members congratulated one another. They enjoyed meeting one another's families.* Ⓝ For a comparison of 'one another' and 'each other', ⇨ the note at each³. **one by one** one person, thing, at a time: *We were allowed in one by one.* **one of these days** some time soon: *One of these days I'll telephone you.* **pull a fast one (on sb)** to deceive a person. **2** (*impersonal pron*) (*formal*) any person but no particular individual; anybody: *One cannot always be right. One doesn't like one's word doubted.* Compare (2), you(2). ⇨ oneself(2).

one-act play /ˌwʌn ækt ˈpleɪ/ *nc* (*literature*) a (modern) form of drama using one act only (similar to the short story in prose).

one-off /ˌwʌn ˈɒf/ *adj* (*attrib*), *n sing* (of) something done, made, once only: *a one-off chance.*

on·er·ous /ˈɒnərəs/ *adj* **onerous (to sb)** (*formal*) needing much effort: *onerous duties; a duty that was onerous to him.*

on·er·ous·ly *adv*

one·self /wʌnˈself/ *pron* **1** (used as the reflexive form of one³(2)): *wash/dress oneself. One must look after oneself.* **(all) by oneself** ⇨ by²(1). **2** (used for emphasis) *To be sure one must check the quality oneself.*

one-sided /ˌwʌn ˈsaɪdɪd/ *adj* (of an argument, judgement etc) favouring one side unfairly.

one-track /ˈwʌn træk/ *adj* (*attrib*) interest in one subject only (usually sex): *have a one-track mind.*

one-way /ˈwʌn weɪ/ *adj* (*attrib*) in which traffic can move in one direction only: *a one-way street.*

on·go·ing /ˈɒngəʊɪŋ/ *adj* continuing; in progress: *ongoing research.*

onion /ˈʌnɪən/ *nc* a vegetable plant which has a (usually) round white bulb with a strong smell and flavour, used in cooking.

on-line /ˈɒn laɪn/ *adj* (*attrib*) (*computers*) directly connected to the central system. Compare off-line.

on·look·er /ˈɒnlʊkə(r)/ *nc* a person who watches something happening without taking part.

on·ly¹ /ˈəʊnlɪ/ *adj* (*attrib*) **1 the only sb/sth** the one, single, example: *It's the only way to do it. She's the only person who knows.* **one and only sth** ⇨ one¹(1). **2 the only** + *pl noun* that are all the examples: *We were the only people to arrive on time.* **3 an only sb** without any brothers or sisters: *an only child/son.*

on·ly² /'əʊnlɪ/ *adv* **1** and no other; and nothing else or more: *I only saw Mary—I didn't speak to her. It'll only take a minute.* Ⓝ Be careful because the position of *'only'* in a sentence can change the meaning. Compare *Only he speaks Greek* (= He is the one person), *He only speaks Greek* (i.e. He cannot read or write Greek), *He speaks only Greek* (i.e. He cannot speak another language). **not only . . . but also . . .** ⇨ not(1). **only too** + *pp* very: *I'll be only too pleased to help.* **2** and no-one, nothing, else (more important, significant, interesting): *It was only a worm. It's only me—can I come in?* **3** (used with *if* to emphasize an idea etc that might have an effect on a situation): *If we'd only thought about it, we could have telephoned sooner.* **if only** ⇨ if(1). **only if** not at all unless: *I'll sign only if you promise to pay the full amount.* **4** not earlier than: *It was only this morning that the truth became known.*

on·ly³ /'əʊnlɪ/ *conj* **1** but it must be added that: *I like the book very much only it's too expensive.* **2** (*informal*) (used to introduce a condition or reason): *You can borrow my bike, only don't leave it in the rain. I would've been here sooner, only the bus was late.* Ⓝ *'But'* is considered to be more acceptable and is more usual.

o.n.o. /ˌəʊ en 'əʊ/ *abbr* or nearest offer (of stated prices), as in '*£5000 o.n.o*'.

ono·mato·poeia /ˌɒnəʊˌmætə'piːə/ *nu* (*lang*) the use of words (in poetry etc) so that the sense is suggested by the sounds, such as *hiss, crunch, ping*.

on·rush /'ɒnrʌʃ/ *nc* a strong movement or flow toward: *an onrush of water/of football supporters.*

on·set /'ɒnset/ *nc* the start (of something bad): *at the first onset of the disease.*

on·shore /'ɒnʃɔː(r)/ *adj* in a direction towards the shore or land. Compare offshore(1).

on·side /ˌɒn'saɪd/ *adj, adv* (in football, hockey etc) (of a player) in a legal or permitted position: *be onside.* Compare offside.

on·slaught /'ɒnslɔːt/ *nc* **onslaught (on sb/ sth)** a violent attack (on).

on·to /'ɒntə *strong form* 'ɒntuː/ *prep* to a position on: *get onto the bus. The room looks out onto the park.* Ⓝ *'Onto'* is most often used as a prepositional alternative to *on*, as in *get on/onto the train. 'Onto'* is often written as two separate words, especially at the end of a sentence, as in *There's nothing to hold on to.* Be careful because *'onto'* is not possible as an alternative to *on* (as an adverbial particle) with *to* (as part of the infinitive form of a verb), as in *stay on to wait for the others.* Compare into(1).

onus /'əʊnəs/ *n sing* responsibility for doing something: *The onus of proof rests with you.*

on·ward /'ɒnwəd/ *adj* (*attrib*) going, pointing etc toward: *an onward march.*

on·wards /'ɒnwədz/ *adv* towards the front: *move onwards.* Ⓝ *'On'* is more usual.

oodles /'uːdlz/ *n pl* **oodles of sth** (*sl*) large amounts of something: *oodles of money/love.*

ooze¹ /uːz/ *nu* soft liquid mud, esp on a river-bed, the bottom of a pond, lake etc.

ooze² /uːz/ *v* **1** *vi* **ooze (from sth)** (of moisture, thick liquids) to pass slowly through small openings: *Blood was still oozing from the wound.* **2** *vt* to produce (moisture): *He was oozing sweat.* **3** *vt* (*fig*) to produce (a quality) slowly: *ooze charm.* **4**

vi **ooze away** to go slowly away: *Their courage was oozing away.*

opac·ity /əʊ'pæsətɪ/ *nu* (*formal*) the quality of being opaque.

opal /'əʊpl/ *nc* a kind of semi-precious stone.

opaque /əʊ'peɪk/ *adj* (*tech*) not allowing light to pass through; that cannot be seen through.
   opaque·ly *adv*

op art /'ɒp ɑːt/ *nu* a form of modern abstract art using geometrical patterns which produce optical illusions of movement.

op. cit. /ˌɒp 'sɪt/ (*Latin*) in the same book as previously referred to.

OPEC /'əʊpek/ *acronym* Organization of Petroleum Exporting Countries (an international organization that controls the supply and price of petrol).

open¹ /'əʊpən/ *adj* **1** not closed; allowing (things, people) to go in, out, through: *an open gate; sleep with open windows; leave the back door open.* **2** (*attrib*) ready for business or for the admission of the public: *Are the shops open yet?* **3** not enclosed, fenced in, barred or blocked: *open country; the open sea.* **4** (*attrib*) not covered in or over: *an open boat; an open car.* **in the open air** ⇨ air¹(1). **5** spread out; unfolded: *The flowers were all open. The book lay open on the table.* **with open arms** ⇨ arm¹(1). **6** (usually *attrib*) not limited to any special people but for anyone to enter: *an open competition/championship.* **7** (usually *pred*) not settled or decided: *leave a matter open. The job is still open* (= No-one has yet been appointed.) ⇨ mind¹(3). **8** known to all: *an open quarrel/scandal.* **9** (usually *pred*) honest and not hiding one's opinion: *Let me be quite open with you.* **10** friendly and social: *The office is full of warm, open people.* **11** (*pred*) **open to sth** likely to experience bad criticism etc: *open to ridicule/attack.*

   ˌopen-and-'shut *adj* (of an issue needing a decision) easily decided: *an open-and-shut case.*

   'open-air *adj* taking place out of doors; not covered: *an open-air swimming-pool.*

   'open cheque *nc* one that is not crossed and may be cashed at the bank named.

   ˌopen-'ended *adj* with no time limit, restriction or selection in advance: *an open-ended debate.*

   ˌopen-'handed *adj* generous.

   ˌopen-'hearted *adj* kind and generous.

   ˌopen-heart 'surgery *nu* surgery on the heart during which the blood flow is kept going by machine.

   ˌopen 'market *nc* one with free competition for sellers and buyers.

   ˌopen-'minded *adj* without prejudice.

   ˌopen-'mouthed *adj* amazed; surprised.

   'open-plan *adj* (of an office etc) without walls between staff areas.

   ˌopen 'prison *nc* one with fewer restrictions.

   ˌopen 'sandwich *nc* one slice of bread etc with meat, cheese etc on top.

   ˌopen 'secret *nc* something meant to be secret but known to all.

   ˌOpen ˌUni'versity *n* (the —) the British university (founded in 1969) whose students live at home and are taught mainly by correspondence, textbooks and radio and TV programmes.

   ˌopen 'verdict *nc* a jury's agreement that a

crime was committed but not naming the criminal, not giving the cause of death etc.

open·ly *adv* honestly; frankly; publicly: *speak openly*. ⇨ open¹(9).

open·ness *nu* frankness.

open² /'əʊpən/ *n* (the—) the places outside buildings: *enjoy being in the open all day*. **come out into the open** (*fig*) (a) (of ideas, plans) to be made public. (b) (of a person) to make opinions, plans etc known.

open³ /'əʊpən/ *v* 1 *vt,vi* (to cause something) to become open(1) or unfastened: *open a box. The door opened and a man came in*. 2 *vt,vi* to spread (something) out; unfold: *open one's hand/a book/a newspaper/an envelope/a map. The flowers are opening*. 3 *vt* to declare, show, that (a business etc) may now start: *open a shop/an office; open Parliament*. 4 *vt* to start (something): *open a bank account; open a debate*. 5 *vt* to cut or make an opening in or a passage through (something): *open a new road through a forest*.

open onto sth (of a door, window etc) to allow a person to move or look out into a garden, road, field etc: *The door opens onto a large garden*.

open out (a) (of flowers etc) to open(2). (b) (of a part of the countryside) to widen: *The river opens out near the coast*. **open sth out** to spread out a map, newspaper etc.

open up (a) to open a door etc to allow officials to enter: *Open up!* (b) (*informal*) to talk frankly: *After a few drinks she began to open up about her part in the affair*. **open sth up** (a) to unfasten a lock; unwrap a parcel etc. (b) to begin the development of a business etc: *open up a new industry*.

open with sth (of a book, ceremony, speech etc) to begin with something: *The story opens with a murder*.

open·er /'əʊpənə(r)/ *nc* a device (or person) that opens: (used chiefly in compounds) *a tin-/bottle-opener*. ⇨ also eye-opener.

open·ing¹ /'əʊpnɪŋ/ *adj* (*attrib*) 1 first: *her opening remarks*. 2 marking the start: *opening times for pubs*. Compare closing.

open·ing² /'əʊpnɪŋ/ *nc* 1 **opening** (**in sth**) a way in or out: *an opening in a hedge*. 2 a beginning: *the opening of a book/speech*. 3 the process of becoming open: *the opening of a flower*. 4 a position (in a business, firm) which is vacant; opportunity: *an opening in the advertising section*. 5 a known system of early moves in a game such as chess. Compare end-game.

op·era /'ɒprə/ *n* (*pl* —**s**) 1 *nc* a dramatic composition with music, in which the words are sung. 2 *nu* (also *attrib*) works of this kind: *be fond of opera; the opera season*.

op·er·at·ic /,ɒpə'rætɪk/ *adj*

op·er·able /'ɒpərəbl/ *adj* (of a disease etc) that can be treated using surgery. Opp inoperable.

op·er·ate /'ɒpəreɪt/ *v* 1 *vt,vi* (to cause a machine etc) to work, be in action: *operate a machine. The lift was not operating properly. The company operates two factories*. 2 *vi* to try to treat an ill person by cutting open the body and removing or mending a diseased or injured part: *The doctors decided to operate at once*.

'operating-table *nc* the table on which the patient lies during an operation(1).

'operating-theatre *nc* a room in a hospital used for operations(1).

op·er·ation /,ɒpə'reɪʃn/ *n* 1 *nc* an act of operating(2): *have an operation to remove a lump in the breast*. 2 *nu* the way in which something works: *the operation of new business methods*. **in operation** working: *Is this rule in operation yet?* **come into operation** to begin to be used: *When will the new law come into operation?* 3 *nc* something (to be) done: *building/banking operations*. 4 (usually *pl*) (*mil*) movements of troops, ships, aircraft etc.

op·er·ation·al /-ʃənl/ *adj* (a) of, for, used in an operation: *operational methods*. (b) (*pred*) ready for use: *When will the new airliner be operational?*

op·er·at·ive /'ɒprətɪv/ *adj* (*pred*) (*formal*) 1 being used; having an effect: *This law became operative on 1 April* Opp inoperative. 2 able to be used: *The new lifts will be operative from Monday*.

op·er·ator /'ɒpəreɪtə(r)/ *nc* 1 a person who works a machine: *telephone operators*. 2 (*sl*) a confident, efficient person (in business, love affairs etc): *He's a smooth operator*.

oph·thal·mic /ɒf'θælmɪk/ *adj* (*science*) of, concerning, the eyes.

opin·ion /ə'pɪnjən/ *n* 1 *nc* a belief or judgement not based on complete knowledge: *political opinions. What's your opinion of the new President? In my opinion/In the opinion of most people, the scheme is unsound*. **be of the opinion that . . .** to feel, believe, that . . . **have a high/low opinion of sb** to consider a person to be/not to be intelligent, able, honest etc. 2 *nu* the beliefs, judgement, of a group: *Opinion is changing in favour of stronger penalties for armed robbery*. **a matter of opinion** ⇨ matter¹(4). **opinion poll**. 3 *nc* a professional judgement or piece of advice: *You ought to get a lawyer's opinion on the question*.

o'pinion poll *nc* (also *public opinion poll*) a survey of general opinion by questioning a section of the community.

opin·ion·ated /ə'pɪnjəneɪtɪd/ *adj* (*derog*) often expressing (too much) confidence in one's own opinion.

opi·um /'əʊpɪəm/ *nu* a drug prepared from poppy seeds, used to relieve pain and as a narcotic.

opp *written abbr* opposite.

op·po·nent /ə'pəʊnənt/ *nc* a person against whom one fights, struggles, plays games, contests an election or argues.

op·por·tune /'ɒpətjuːn/ *adj* (*formal*) suitable, favourable: *arrive at an opportune moment; an opportune remark*. Opp inopportune.

op·por·tune·ly *adv*

op·por·tun·ism /,ɒpə'tjuːnɪzəm/ *nu* (the belief in) taking advantage of a good opportunity (sometimes against the interest of others).

op·por·tun·ist /,ɒpə'tjuːnɪst/ *nc* (usually *derog*) a person who is (more) anxious to gain an advantage for herself or himself (than to consider whether it is fair).

op·por·tun·ity /,ɒpə'tjuːnətɪ/ *nc,nu* (*pl* -ies) a favourable time or chance: *to find an opportunity to speak to him; have no/little/not much opportunity for hearing good music. I'd live in Africa given* (= if I had) *the opportunity*. **a golden opportunity** an excellent one. **take the**

opportunity of doing/to do sth to make use of a favourable moment to act.

op·pose /ə'pəuz/ *vt* **1** to be, fight, against (a person, organization, plan, idea etc): *opposing the Government/a scheme.* **2 as opposed to** in contrast to; unlike: *I hate fish, as opposed to Mary who loves it.*

op·po·site¹ /'ɒpəzɪt/ *adj* **1 opposite (to) (sb/ sth)** facing; front to front or back to back: *the house opposite (to) mine; on the opposite side of the road; with a window exactly opposite the door.* **2** (*attrib*) other; different: *in the opposite direction.* **sb's opposite number** a person occupying the same or a similar position in another group, business etc. **the opposite sex** the other sex (i.e. men in contrast to women and women in contrast to men).

op·po·site² /'ɒpəzɪt/ *prep* in front of and facing: *stop opposite the house.*

op·po·site³ /'ɒpəzɪt/ *nc* a word, idea etc that is completely different: *Black and white are opposites. I think the opposite.*

op·po·si·tion /,ɒpə'zɪʃn/ *nu* **1** the state of being opposed(1): *a great deal of opposition to the design.* **in opposition** (esp in politics, of a political party) not having power, and opposing the government: *The Socialist Party was in opposition.* **2** (the O-) members of the political party or parties opposing the Government: *the leader of the Opposition.* **3** an act, state, of fighting (against a person, thing): *Our forces met with strong opposition.*

op·press /ə'pres/ *vt* **1** to rule (people) unjustly or cruelly. **2** (*fig*) (usually *passive*) to cause (a person) to feel troubled, uncomfortable: *be oppressed by being poor; feel oppressed with the heat.*

op·pres·sion /ə'preʃn/ *nu* (an instance of) the condition of being oppressed: *a feeling of oppression; victims of oppression; severe oppression.*

op·press·ive /ə'presɪv/ *adj* (a) unjust: *oppressive laws/rules.* (b) hard to bear: *oppresive heat/ taxes.*

op·press·ive·ly *adv*

op·pres·sor /-sə(r)/ *nc* (*derog*) a cruel or unjust person, ruler.

opt /ɒpt/ *vi* **1 opt for sb/sth** to decide in favour of a person, thing: *More students are opting for science courses nowadays.* **2 opt out (of sth)** to choose to take no part (in something): *young people who have opted out (of society).*

op·tic /'ɒptɪk/ *adj* (*attrib*) of the eye or the sense of sight: *the optic nerve.*

op·tics *nu* the scientific study of light and the laws of light.

op·ti·cal /'ɒptɪkl/ *adj* (*attrib*) concerning the sense of sight.

,**optical il'lusion** *nc* something which one believes to exist because one sees it but which is not present: *A mirage is an optical illusion.*

,**optical 'instrument** *nc* one used for looking through, e.g. *a microscope, telescope.*

op·ti·cal·ly /-klɪ/ *adv*

op·ti·cian /ɒp'tɪʃn/ *nc* a person, business, that makes or supplies spectacles.

op·ti·mal /'ɒptɪml/ *adj* = optimum.

op·ti·mism /'ɒptɪmɪzəm/ *nu* the attitude or belief that the best thing is most likely to happen, that good will defeat evil. Compare pessimism.

op·ti·mist /-mɪst/ *nc* a believer in optimism. Compare pessimist.

op·ti·mis·tic /,ɒptɪ'mɪstɪk/ *adj* believing that something (a result, the future) will be good: *an optimistic view of events.*

op·ti·mis·ti·cal·ly /-klɪ/ *adv*

op·ti·mum /'ɒptɪməm/ *adj* (*attrib*) best or most favourable: *the optimum temperature for making wine.*

op·tion /'ɒpʃn/ *n* **1** *nu* the right or power to choose: *I haven't much option in the matter.* **2** *nc* something that is or may be chosen: *None of the options is satisfactory.* **keep/leave one's options open** to avoid committing oneself. **3** *nc* (*commerce*) a right to buy or sell at a certain price within a certain period of time: *have an option on a piece of land.*

op·tion·al /'ɒpʃənl/ *adj* which may be chosen or not as one wishes: *optional subjects at school.* Compare compulsory.

or /ɔː(r)/ *conj coord* **1** (used to express two or more alternatives): *Is it green or blue? You can have soup, salad or sandwiches. Are you coming or not? I don't know whether to go or stay. She's not a teacher or a student. He's never at home or at work. Will you have that one or this? You'll have to come now or phone again later.* Ⓝ When there are several possibilities *'or'* is placed before the last one; as in *small, medium or large.* **either . . . or . . .** ⇨ either²(3). **or other** ⇨ other³(2). **or else** ⇨ else(3). **2** (used to show that two statements etc are equivalent): *It holds 5 litres or 1·1 gallons. It's worth £2 or $3.* **or rather** ⇨ rather(3). **or so** ⇨ so²(6).

or·acle /'ɒrəkl/ *nc* a wise person considered able to give reliable guidance.

oral¹ /'ɔːrəl/ *adj* (*attrib*) **1** spoken, not written: *an oral examination.* **2** (*anat*) of, by, for, the mouth: *oral medicine.* Compare aural.

oral·ly /'ɔːrəlɪ/ *adv*

oral² /'ɔːrəl/ *nc* (*informal*) an oral(1) examination.

or·ange¹ /'ɒrɪndʒ/ *adj, nu* reddish-yellow (colour).

or·ange² /'ɒrɪndʒ/ *nc* (also *attrib*) (a tree with) a round fruit with orange flesh and skin (also called *peel*): *orange juice.*

orange·ade /,ɒrɪndʒ'eɪd/ *nc,nu* (a glass of) drink made of orange juice.

orang-utan /ɔː,ræŋ uː'tæn/ (also **-outang** /-'tæŋ/) *nc* a large ape with long arms and red hair.

orate /ɔː'reɪt/ *vi* (*formal*) to speak in public.

ora·tion /ɔː'reɪʃn/ *nc* a formal speech made on a public occasion: *a funeral oration.*

ora·tor /'ɒrətə(r)/ *nc* a person who makes public speeches.

ora·tory /'ɒrətrɪ/ *nu* (the art or skill of) speaking in public.

ora·tori·cal /,ɒrə'tɒrɪkl/ *adj*

orb /ɔːb/ *nc* a ball covered in jewels, held by a king, queen etc as a symbol of power.

or·bit¹ /'ɔːbɪt/ *nc* a path followed by a heavenly body, e.g. a planet, or by a man-made object, e.g. a satellite, round another body: *the earth's orbit round the sun. How many satellites have been put in orbit round the earth?*

or·bit² /'ɔːbɪt/ vt,vi (to cause something) to move in an orbit: *The spacecraft orbits the earth every 10 hours.*

or·bi·tal¹ /'ɔːbɪtl/ adj of, concerning, an orbit.

or·bi·tal² /'ɔːbɪtl/ nc a circular motorway round a city: *the London Orbital.*

or·chard /'ɔːtʃəd/ nc a piece of ground (usually enclosed) with fruit trees.

or·ches·tra /'ɔːkɪstrə/ nc (pl —s) a group of people playing musical instruments (including stringed instruments) together: *He plays in a symphony orchestra.*

or·ches·tral /ɔː'kestrəl/ adj of, for, by, an orchestra: *orchestral instruments/performances.*

or·ches·trate /'ɔːkɪstreɪt/ vt to compose, arrange, score, (music) for an orchestra.
  or·ches·tra·tion /ˌɔːkɪ'streɪʃn/ nc,nu

or·chid /'ɔːkɪd/ nc a kind of plant of which the tropical kinds have flowers of brilliant colours and fantastic shapes.

or·dain /ɔː'deɪn/ vt **1** to make (a person) a priest or minister: *He was ordained priest.* **2** ordain *(that . . .)* (of God, law, authority) to give orders (that): *God has ordained that all men shall die.*

or·deal /ɔː'diːl/ nc any severe or painful test of character or endurance: *suffer terrible ordeals.*

or·der¹ /'ɔːdə(r)/ n **1** nu the careful way in which things are placed in relation to one another: *put names in alphabetical order.* **in order of sth** arranged according to something: *in order of size/ importance.* **be out of order** not in any particular arrangement. ⇨ order¹(2). ⇨ also reverse¹, disorder. **2** nu the condition in which everything is carefully arranged; working condition: *Is the house back in order after the party?* **in (good etc) running/working order** *The engine has been tuned and is now in perfect running order.* **(not) in order** (not) as it should be: *Is your passport in order?* (= Is it valid?) **out of order** (of a machine etc) not working correctly: *The lift/ phone is out of order.* ⇨ order¹(1). **3** nu (the condition that is the result of) good and firm government, obedience to law, rules, authority: *It is the business of the police to keep order.* **law and order** ⇨ law(3). **4** nu an organized system of living, working etc: *I can't think without order in my life. This office needs more order.* ⇨ disorder(1). **in order** acceptable; correct: *Is it in order to interrupt?* **5** nu **(on) a point of order** (on) a point (= question) of what is officially allowed. **in order to do sth** with the purpose of doing something: *I've cleaned the window in order (for you) to see clearly.* **in order that** (conj) so that: *We'll meet an hour later in order that he can be here in time.* **6** nc a command (esp one given with authority): *Soldiers must obey orders. Those were my parents' orders.* **by order of sb/sth** (formal) according to directions given by authority of an official; organization etc: *by order of the Governor.* **a tall order** (fig) a difficult or unreasonable request. **7** nc a request to supply goods; the goods (to be) supplied: *place an order for more blue dresses; an order worth £50.* **on order** requested but not yet supplied. **8** nc a written instruction (esp to a bank or post office) to pay money, or giving authority: *a postal order.* **9** nc a rank or class in society: *the order of knights/baronets.* **10** nc a

group of people belonging to or appointed to a special class (as an honour or reward): *the Order of Merit.* **11** nc (biology) one of the highest divisions in the grouping of animals, plants etc: *The rose and the bean families belong to the same order.* **12** nc kind; sort: *intellect of a high order.* **13** n pl **take holy orders** to become a priest. ⇨ ordination.

or·der² /'ɔːdə(r)/ vt **1** to give an order(6,7) to (a person): *The doctor ordered me to (stay in) bed. The judge ordered that the prisoner should be remanded. I've ordered lunch for 1.30.* **order sb about** to keep on telling a person to do things. **2** to arrange or organize (something): *order one's life according to strict rules.*

or·der·ing /'ɔːdərɪŋ/ nc,nu an arrangement: *the ordering of words in an index.*

or·der·ly¹ /'ɔːdəlɪ/ adj **1** well arranged; in good order; tidy: *an orderly room/desk.* Opp disorderly(1). **2** methodical: *a man with an orderly mind.* **3** well-behaved: *an orderly crowd.* Opp disorderly(2).
  or·der·li·ness nu

or·der·ly² /'ɔːdəlɪ/ nc (pl -ies) **1** an (army) officer's messenger. **2** an attendant in a hospital.

or·di·nal number /ˌɔːdɪnl 'nʌmbə(r)/ nc a number showing order or position in a series, such as *first, second, third.* Compare cardinal number.

or·di·nance /'ɔːdɪnəns/ nc (formal) an official order, rule: *the ordinances of the City Council.*

or·di·nary /'ɔːdɪnrɪ/ adj normal; usual; average: *an ordinary day's work; in ordinary dress.* **in the ordinary way** in the usual way. **out of the ordinary** not as expected or as usual. ⇨ also extraordinary.
  or·di·nar·ily /'ɔːdɪnrəlɪ/ adv in the usual or normal way: *behave quite ordinarily.*

or·di·na·tion /ˌɔːdɪ'neɪʃn/ nc,nu (an instance of) the ceremony of ordaining a priest or minister.

ore /ɔː(r)/ nc,nu (any kind of) rock, earth, mineral etc from which a metal can be obtained: *iron ore.*

or·gan¹ /'ɔːgən/ nc **1** any part of an animal body or plant with an essential purpose: *the organs of speech* (= the tongue, teeth, lips, etc); *the reproductive organs.* **2** the means of getting something done: *organs of public opinion* (= the press, radio, TV etc); *Parliament is the chief organ of government.*

or·gan² /'ɔːgən/ nc a musical instrument with a keyboard, from which sounds are produced by air forced through pipes.
  'or·gan·ist /-ɪst/ nc a person who plays the organ.

or·gan·ic /ɔː'gænɪk/ adj (science) **1** of an organ or organs of the body: *organic diseases.* **2** of, concerning, living plants and animals: *organic chemistry/life.* ⇨ inorganic. **3** (of food) produced without artificial fertilizers.
  or·gani·cal·ly /-klɪ/ adv

or·gan·ism /'ɔːgənɪzəm/ nc (science) a living plant or animal.

or·gan·iz·ation (also **-is·ation**) /ˌɔːgənaɪ-'zeɪʃn/ n **1** nu the act of organizing; condition of being organized: *busy with the organization of a new committee.* Compare disorganization. **2** nc an organized group of people (e.g. a business); organized system: *The human body has a very* *complex organization.*

or·gan·ize (also **-ise**) /'ɔːgənaɪz/ *vt* to arrange (people, things etc) (in a system or particular order): *organize a trade union/one's work/one-self/a holiday.* Compare disorganize.

or·gan·ized (also **-ised**) *adj* (a) having a system or order: *highly organized forms of life.* (b) (of a business etc) with official trade union representation.

or·gan·izer (also **-iser**) *nc* a person who organizes things: *a good/bad organizer.*

or·gasm /'ɔːgæzəm/ *nc* a point of feeling most sexual pleasure.

or·gy /'ɔːdʒɪ/ *nc* (*pl* **-ies**) **1** an occasion of wild merry-making. **2** a drunken or immoral act for amusement.

Ori·ent /'ɔːrɪənt/ *n* (the —) (*literary*) the countries of the Far East.

ori·ent /'ɔːrɪənt/ *vt* (*US*) = orientate.

Orien·tal /ˌɔːrɪˈentl/ *adj* of the Orient: *Oriental civilization/art/rugs.*

orien·tate /'ɔːrɪənteɪt/ (*US* = **ori·ent**) *v* **1** *v reflex* to cause oneself to become familiar with a situation, surroundings etc: *I need time to orientate myself in my new job/house.* **2** *vt* to place or determine exactly the position of (something) using a compass.

orien·ta·tion /ˌɔːrɪənˈteɪʃn/ *nu*

ori·fice /'ɒrɪfɪs/ *nc* (*tech*) an opening.

ori·gin /'ɒrɪdʒɪn/ *nc,nu* a place or reason from which something starts: *the origin of a quarrel; the origin(s) of civilization; words of Greek origin; of poor origins.*

orig·inal¹ /əˈrɪdʒɪnl/ *adj* **1** (*attrib; no comp*) first or earliest known: *the original inhabitants of the country.* **2** (*no comp*) newly created; not copied or imitated: *an original design.* **3** able to produce new ideas etc: *an original thinker/mind.*

orig·inal² /əˈrɪdʒɪnl/ *nc* an original(2) thing: *This is a copy—the original is in Madrid.* **in the original** in the language in which it was first written: *study Plato in the original.*

o,riginal 'sin *nu* a state of having sinned which Christians believe is passed down from Adam, the first man.

orig·in·al·ity /əˌrɪdʒɪˈnælətɪ/ *nu* the state or quality of being original(3): *work that shows no originality.*

orig·in·al·ly /-nəlɪ/ *adv* (a) in the beginning: *The school was originally quite small.* (b) producing new ideas; in a new way: *write originally.*

orig·inate /əˈrɪdʒɪneɪt/ *vi,vt* (to cause something) to begin: *The quarrel originated in Paris. It originated from Poland. He originated a new style of dancing.*

orig·in·ator /-tə(r)/ *nc* a person who originates something.

or·na·ment¹ /'ɔːnəmənt/ *nc* an object used to add beauty or to decorate: *a shelf crowded with ornaments.*

or·na·men·tal /ˌɔːnəˈmentl/ *adj* decorative.

or·na·ment² /'ɔːnəment/ *vt* (*formal*) to decorate (something) (the usual word): *ornament a dress with lace.*

or·nate /ɔːˈneɪt/ *adj* **1** richly decorated. **2** (*literature*) not simple in style or vocabulary.

or·nate·ly *adv*

or·ni·tho·logi·cal /ˌɔːnɪθəˈlɒdʒɪkl/ *adj* of or-

nithology.

or·ni·thol·ogist /ˌɔːnɪˈθɒlədʒɪst/ *nc* an expert in, student of, ornithology.

or·ni·thol·ogy /ˌɔːnɪˈθɒlədʒɪ/ *nu* the scientific study of birds.

or·phan¹ /'ɔːfn/ *nc* (also *attrib*) a child who has lost one or both parents by death: *an orphan child.*

or·phan·age /-ɪdʒ/ *nc* a place where orphans live.

or·phan² /'ɔːfn/ *vt* (usually *passive*) to cause (a child) to become an orphan: *be orphaned by war.*

or·tho·dox /'ɔːθədɒks/ *adj* (having opinions, beliefs etc which) generally accepted or approved: *orthodox behaviour.*

or·thogra·phy /ɔːˈθɒgrəfɪ/ *nu* (*formal*) (a system of) spelling.

or·tho·pae·dic (also **-pe·dic**) /ˌɔːθəˈpiːdɪk/ *adj* of the treatment of deformities and diseases of bones: *orthopaedic surgery.*

or·tho·pae·dics (also **-pe·dics**) *nu* the branch of surgery dealing with bone deformities and diseases.

OS /ˌəʊ 'es/ *abbr* Ordnance Survey (the GB government department that produces the official maps of the country).

os·cil·late /'ɒsɪleɪt/ *vi* **1** to swing backwards and forwards as the pendulum of a clock does. **2** (*fig*) to change between extremes of opinion etc.

os·cil·la·tion /ˌɒsɪˈleɪʃn/ *nc,nu*

os·mo·sis /ɒsˈməʊsɪs/ *nu* the gradual and unconscious adoption or acceptance of ideas, facts: *learn by osmosis.*

os·prey /'ɒspreɪ/ *nc* (*pl* **-s**) a kind of large hawk that eats fish.

os·si·fy /'ɒsɪfaɪ/ *vt,vi* (*pt,pp* **-ied**) (*formal*) **1** (to cause something) to become hard like bone; change into bone. **2** (*fig*) (to cause a person) to become rigid in one's opinions.

os·si·fi·ca·tion /ˌɒsɪfɪˈkeɪʃn/ *nu*

os·ten·sible /'ɒstensəbl/ *adj* (*attrib*) (*formal*) (of reasons etc) put forward in an attempt to hide the real reason.

os·ten·sibly /-əblɪ/ *adv* apparently (but not really).

os·ten·ta·tion /ˌɒstenˈteɪʃn/ *nu* an exaggerated display of wealth, skill etc to get admiration or envy.

os·ten·ta·tious /ˌɒstenˈteɪʃəs/ *adj*

os·ten·ta·tious·ly *adv*

os·tra·cize (also **-ise**) /'ɒstrəsaɪz/ *vt* to refuse to meet, talk to, (a person): *She was ostracized by all her neighbours after her imprisonment.*

os·trich /'ɒstrɪtʃ/ *nc* (*pl* **-es**) (also *attrib*) a fast-running bird, the largest in existence, unable to fly: *ostrich feathers.*

OT *written abbr* Old Testament (in the Bible).

oth·er¹ /'ʌðə(r)/ *adj* or *det* **1** of the second of two people, things etc: *It's on the other side of the street. The other wheel of my bike is broken. I liked my old bike but I find this other one uncomfortable. You use this chair and I'll use the other one.* Ⓝ 'Other' cannot be used after *a*, e.g. to refer to 'an additional one'. Use *'another'.* **the other day, night** etc one day/night recently: *I met your sister the other evening.* **every other sb/sth** each alternate person, thing: *Write on every other line. The doctor called every other day* (= on each second day). **on the other hand** ⇨ hand¹(1). **2** (used of more than two people, things etc) apart from oneself, that etc: *Learn from other people's mistakes. Any other man could have done the job. No other person behaves like you. Some other facts are necessary. What other advice can I give you?*

oth·er² /'ʌðə(r)/ *adv* **other than** different from; except: *I couldn't say anything other than 'sorry'.* Ⓝ Usually used with a negative verb.

oth·er³ /'ʌðə(r)/ *pron* **1** (the —) the second of two people, things etc: *You hold one of her hands and I'll hold the other. They look so alike I can't tell one from the other.* **one after the other** ⇨ one³(1). **2** (used of more than two) people, things, apart from that, those etc: *Those are yours and the others are mine. My parents and six others went to the meeting. Others will offer better prices but is the quality as good? Will you have any others next week? Some others are very similar. I love you and I want no other.* **each other** ⇨ each³. **none other than** ⇨ none(1). **or other** (used to suggest lack of certainty or particular decision): *Someone or other phoned you yesterday. I'll phone some time or other next week.*

other·wise¹ /'ʌðəwaɪz/ *adv* **1** in another or different way: *You evidently think otherwise.* **2** apart from that: *The rent is high, but otherwise the house is satisfactory.*

oth·er·wise² /'ʌðəwaɪz/ *conj* if not: *Do what you're told, otherwise you'll be punished.*

OTT /ˌəʊtiː'tiː/ *abbr* (*informal*) over the top. ⇨ over⁴(10). Ⓝ 'OTT' is often used as a verb to mean 'exaggerate' in informal conversation, as in *Don't OTT!*

ot·ter /'ɒtə(r)/ *nc* a furry, fish-eating animal with webbed feet and a flat tail.

OU /ˌəʊ'juː/ *abbr* (the —) the Open University.

ouch /aʊtʃ/ *int* (used to express sudden pain).

ought /ɔːt/ *auxiliary verb* Ⓝ 'Ought' is a *modal auxiliary verb* used with another verb to express duty or obligation, opinion or advice. 'Ought' has no infinitive or imperative form and no participles. 'Ought' is always followed by an infinitive with 'to'. Compare have¹(2), need²(1), must, should. (*Verb form* (all persons): **ought**, *negative* **ought not**, **oughtn't** /'ɔːtnt/) **ought to** + *verb* **1** (used to tell a person about a present or past duty or obligation): *We ought to report the accident. You didn't apologize and you ought to. Ought I to explain if I'm asked? People ought not to interfere. You ought to have done that sooner. Oughtn't he to pay this time?* Ⓝ 'Ought to' expressing an obligation is not often used in the negative. Use 'must not' or 'should not', as in *You must not/should not interfere.* 'Need not' or 'do not have to' are used to say that there is no duty or obligation, as in *You don't have to explain.* 'Ought to have + pp' or 'should have + pp' are used to talk about a past duty or obligation that was not carried out. 'Shall/will have to' is used to talk about future obligation. Compare should, must. **2** (used to express an opinion, give advice etc about the present or past): *You ought to see a doctor about that pain. There ought to be a law against smoking. This ought to be enough. She ought not to wear those shoes. He ought not to have to pay until he's 18. They really ought to work harder. We never ought to have stayed out so late.*

Compare must²(2), should(3). **3** (used to express probability): *Steve ought to win the race. A holiday in Spain ought to be fun. It ought to be hot in July. It oughtn't to rain very much. They ought to have arrived by now.* Compare must²(3), should.

oughtn't /'ɔːtnt/ = ought not. ⇨ ought.

ounce /aʊns/ *nc* (*abbr* oz) a unit of measurement of mass, one sixteenth of a pound or about 28 grams.

our /ɑː(r) *strong form*: aʊə(r)/ *possessive adj* or *det* of, belonging to, us: *We've done our share. It's our problem, not yours.*

ours /aʊəz/ *possessive pron* (the one or ones) belonging to us: *This house is ours. Ours is larger than theirs.*

our·selves /aʊə'selvz/ *pron* **1** (used as the reflexive form of *we* or *us*): *We helped ourselves to more food. It's no use worrying ourselves about that.* **(all) by ourselves** ⇨ by²(1). **2** (used for emphasis): *We've often made that mistake ourselves.* ⇨ between²(4).

oust /aʊst/ *vt* **oust sb (from sth)** to force a person to leave (a home, job etc): *He's been ousted from the committee.*

out¹ /aʊt/ *adj* **1** (*pred*) **(a)** not at home, present at work etc: *I'll be out until 3 o'clock.* **(b)** not fashionable: *Wide ties are out this year.* **(c)** not allowed: *Playing loud music is definitely out.* **(d)** not burning or being used: *The fire/light is out.* **(e)** not in power or in office: *The Conservatives will be out next year.* **(f)** on strike: *The miners are out.* **(g)** unconscious: *She was out for two days.* **(h)** not worth considering: *The idea is out because we can't afford it.* **(i)** visible: *The blossom/sun is out.* **(j)** known: *The secret is out.* **(k)** not available: *The book I wanted is out* (i.e. not in the library). **(l)** (of the tide) low; furthest from the coast. Compare in¹(1). **2** (*attrib*) used for sending things to another place: *an out tray/file.* Compare in¹(2). ⇨ out-and-out.

out² /aʊt/ *adverbial particle* Ⓝ For uses with verbs, such as *be, come, get, go, have, keep, let, make, mind, miss, set, watch* etc, ⇨ the *verb* entries. **1** in, to, a place or position away from or outside: *walk out; find one's way out; order him out; put the cat out; keep out while it's wet.* Opp in²(1). **2** away from home, work etc: *We don't go out much. Let's eat out tonight. He stayed out all night. They flew out to China.* Opp in²(2). **3** (used to express distance): *live out in the country; out at sea; few opportunities out there.* **4** so as to be removed or stopped: *turn out the light; scratch/paint out a sign; put out a cigarette.* **5** completely: *tired/worn out.* **6** in a loud voice: *cry/shout out.* **out loud** ⇨ loud². **straight out** ⇨ straight²(3). **7** (used to express error): *We're £10 out in the accounts.* **not far out/a long way out (in sth)** not a lot/very much in error: *Your estimate was not far out.* **8** (in games, sport) no longer playing because beaten. **9** (used after a *superlative*) in existence: *the best doctor out; the tallest building out.*

inside out ⇨ inside³(2).

out and about ⇨ about¹(6).

out for sth trying to achieve, obtain, something: *out for a good time/a big profit.*

out of ⇨ out⁴.

out to determined to: *be out to cause trouble.*

out³ /aʊt/ *n* (only in) **the ins and outs of sth** ⇨

in⁴.

out⁴ /aʊt/ *prep* **out of** Ⓝ For uses of *'out of'* in special phrases such as *out of date, out of doors, out of the way* etc, ⇨ the noun entries, as in *breath, character, date, depth, door, ordinary.* **1** at, to, a place outside: *out of reach/range/place/ danger.* **out of it** (a) unhappy because not invited or involved: *feel out of it.* (b) not involved: *I'm glad to be out of it.* **2** because of: *out of poverty/kindness/anger/a desperate need.* **3** using (something) as material: *built/made out of stone.* **4** no longer having (something) in order to use or sell: *out of breath/petrol/stock; out of one's mind; cheat her out of her money.* **5** from among: *9 out of 10 disagree.* **6** from: *drink out of a cup; take one out of the jar; a scene out of a play; good out of evil.*

out-and-out /ˌaʊt ən ˈaʊt/ *adj* (*attrib*) complete and thorough: *an out-and-out liar.*

out·back /ˈaʊtbæk/ *n* (the —) (esp in Australia) the areas far from the cities.

out·bid /ˌaʊtˈbɪd/ *vt* (**-dd-**) to offer more money than (another person).

out·break /ˈaʊtbreɪk/ *nc* a sudden and violent breaking out: *an outbreak of fever/hostilities.*

out·build·ing /ˈaʊtbɪldɪŋ/ *nc* a building, e.g. a shed, separate from the main building.

out·burst /ˈaʊtbɜːst/ *nc* a sudden and violent expression (of an emotion etc): *an outburst of laughter/anger.*

out·cast /ˈaʊtkɑːst/ *nc, adj* (a person) sent away from home or society.

out·class /ˌaʊtˈklɑːs/ *vt* to be, do, much better than (another person, team etc): *He was outclassed from the start of the race.*

out·come /ˈaʊtkʌm/ *nc* an effect or result (of an event or of circumstances).

out·crop /ˈaʊtkrɒp/ *nc* that part of a layer (of rock etc) which can be seen.

out·cry /ˈaʊtkraɪ/ *nc* (*pl* **-ies**) **outcry (against sb/sth)** a public protest.

out·dated /ˌaʊtˈdeɪtɪd/ *adj* = out-of-date.

out·dis·tance /ˌaʊtˈdɪstəns/ *vt* to travel faster than (another) and leave her, him or it behind.

out·do /ˌaʊtˈduː/ *vt* (*3rd pers sing, pres t* **-does** /-ˈdʌz/, *pt* **-did** /-ˈdɪd/, *pp* **-done** /-ˈdʌn/) to do more or better than (a person): *Not to be outdone, he tried again.*

out·door /ˈaʊtdɔː(r)/ *adj* (*attrib*) done, existing, used, outside a house or building: *leading an outdoor life; outdoor sports; an outdoor swimming pool.* Compare indoor.

out·doors /ˌaʊtˈdɔːz/ *adv* (also **out-of-doors**) in the open air; outside: *It's cold outdoors. Let's eat outdoors.* Compare indoors.

out·er /ˈaʊtə(r)/ *adj* (*attrib*) **1** of, on, the outside: *the outer walls of a house.* Compare inner. **2** farther from the middle or inside: *the outer layers.* **'outer·most** /-məʊst/ *adj* farthest from the inside or centre. ⇨ outlying.

ˌouter ˈspace *nu* the universe beyond the earth's atmosphere.

out·fit¹ /ˈaʊtfɪt/ *nc* a set of clothing, equipment, esp needed for a purpose: *a camping outfit.*

out·fit² /ˈaʊtfɪt/ *vt* (**-tt-**) to equip (a person, business etc).

out·fox /ˌaʊtˈfɒks/ *vt* to defeat (a person) by being more cunning.

out·go·ing /ˈaʊtɡəʊɪŋ/ *adj* **1** (*attrib*) going out; leaving: *the outgoing tenant/tide.* Opp incoming. **2** (*informal*) friendly and pleasant: *be outgoing; have an outgoing personality.*

out·go·ings /ˈaʊtɡəʊɪŋz/ *n pl* expenditure.

out·grow /ˌaʊtˈɡrəʊ/ *vt* (*pt* **-grew** /-ˈɡruː/, *pp* **-grown** /-ˈɡrəʊn/) **1** to grow too large or too tall for (something, e.g. one's clothes). **2** to grow faster or taller than (another person). **3** to leave behind, as one grows older (bad habits, childish interests, opinions etc).

out·growth /ˈaʊtɡrəʊθ/ *nc* something growing out of something else: *an outgrowth on a tree.*

out·house /ˈaʊthaʊs/ *nc* (*pl* **—s** /-haʊzɪz/) a small building near to the main building.

out·ing /ˈaʊtɪŋ/ *nc* a short holiday; pleasure trip: *go for an outing to the seaside.*

out·land·ish /ˌaʊtˈlændɪʃ/ *adj* looking or sounding very odd, strange (esp to shock): *outlandish dress/behaviour/ideas.*

out·land·ish·ly *adv*

out·last /ˌaʊtˈlɑːst/ *vt* to last or live longer than (another).

out·law¹ /ˈaʊtlɔː/ *nc* (in olden times) a person punished by being placed outside the protection of the law.

out·law² /ˈaʊtlɔː/ *vt* to make (something) illegal; ban (it) officially: *outlaw smoking in cinemas.*

out·lay /ˈaʊtleɪ/ *nc* **outlay (on/for sth)** an amount of money that is spent: *a large outlay on/ for scientific research.*

out·let /ˈaʊtlet/ *nc* **1** a way out (for water, steam etc): *an outlet for water.* Compare inlet(2), intake(2). **2** (*fig*) a means of or occasion (for showing one's feelings etc).

out·line¹ /ˈaʊtlaɪn/ *nc* **1** a line showing the shape: *an outline map of Great Britain; draw it in outline.* ⇨ broad¹(5). **2** a statement of the chief facts, points etc: *an outline for an essay/a lecture.*

out·line² /ˈaʊtlaɪn/ *vt* to draw, give, (something) in outline(2): *outlining ideas for the stage design/ for future activities.*

out·live /ˌaʊtˈlɪv/ *vt* **1** to live longer than (another person): *outlive one's wife.* **2** to live until (something) is forgotten: *outlive a disgrace.*

out·look /ˈaʊtlʊk/ *nc* **1** a view on which one looks out: *a pleasant outlook over the valley.* **2** what seems likely to happen: *a bright outlook for trade; further outlook, dry and sunny* (e.g. in a weather forecast): **3 outlook (on sth)** (a person's) way of looking at something: *have a narrow outlook on life.*

out·lying /ˈaʊtlaɪɪŋ/ *adj* (*attrib*) far from the centre: *outlying villages.*

out·match /ˌaʊtˈmætʃ/ *vt* (often *passive*) to be more than equal to (another person, team etc): *be outmatched in skill and endurance.*

out·mod·ed /ˌaʊtˈməʊdɪd/ *adj* out of fashion or no longer in use: *outmoded methods.*

out·num·ber /ˌaʊtˈnʌmbə(r)/ *vt* to be larger in number than (another).

out-of-date /ˌaʊt əv ˈdeɪt/ *adj* (usually *attrib*) no longer in fashion, in use or valid: *They are out-of-date statistics.* Ⓝ Hyphens are used when *out-of-date* is used with (and usually before) a noun. For *'be/ go out of date'*, ⇨ date²(2).

out-of-doors /ˌaʊt əv ˈdɔːz/ ⇨ outdoors.

out-of-the-way /ˌaʊt əv ðə ˈweɪ/ *adj* **1** far away;

secluded: *an out-of-the-way cottage.* **2** not generally known: *out-of-the-way items of knowledge.*

out-pa·tient /'aʊtpeɪʃnt/ *nc* a person visiting a hospital for treatment but not living there. Compare in-patient.

out·play /ˌaʊt'pleɪ/ *vt* to play better than (another person, team): *The English were outplayed by the Brazilians.*

out·post /'aʊtpəʊst/ *nc* a distant settlement: *an outpost of the Roman Empire.*

out·pour·ing /'aʊtpɔːrɪŋ/ *nc* (usually *pl*) a strong expression of feeling: *outpourings of sadness at her death.*

out·put /'aʊtpʊt/ *nc* **1** a quantity of goods etc produced: *the output of a goldmine/a factory.* **2** a quantity of work, energy etc produced: *Our output is too low.* **3** (*computers*) the information produced from a computer. Compare input.

out·rage¹ /'aʊtreɪdʒ/ *nc,nu* **outrage (against sb/sth)** (an act of) extreme violence, cruelty or indecency: *The use of torture is an outrage (against humanity).*

out·rage² /'aʊtreɪdʒ/ *vt* to offend, shock, (a person) greatly: *outrage public opinion; be outraged by his bad language.*

out·rage·ous /ˌaʊt'reɪdʒəs/ *adj* **1** shocking; offensive: *outrageous behaviour; an outrageous remark.* **2** (*informal*) far too large or extravagant: *an outrageous price/hairstyle.*

out·rage·ous·ly *adv*

out·ran /ˌaʊt'ræn/ *pt* of outrun.

out·rank /ˌaʊt'ræŋk/ *vt* to hold a higher rank or position than (another person).

out·right¹ /ˌaʊtraɪt/ *adj* (*attrib*) **1** thorough; complete: *an outright denial; outright wickedness; an outright liar.* **2** without doubt: *On the voting for secretary, Smith was the outright winner.*

out·right² /'aʊtraɪt/ *adv* **1** openly, with nothing held back: *tell a man outright what one thinks of his behaviour.* **2** completely; at one time: *buy a house outright* (i.e. not with a mortgage)*; be killed outright* (e.g. by a single blow).

out·ri·val /ˌaʊt'raɪvl/ *vt* (**-ll-**, *US* also **-l-**) to be or do better than (a rival).

out·run /ˌaʊt'rʌn/ *vt* (*pt* **-ran** /-'ræn/, *pp* **-run**; **-nn-**) to run faster than (a person, animal).

out·sell /ˌaʊt'sel/ *vt* (*pt,pp* **-sold** /-'səʊld/) to sell more, be sold in more, quantities than (others).

out·set /'aʊtset/ *n* **at/from the outset** at/from the beginning: *I warned you from the outset that I don't like spiders.*

out·shine /ˌaʊt'ʃaɪn/ *vt* (*pt,pp* **-shone** /-'ʃɒn/) **1** to shine more brightly than (any other). **2** (*fig*) to be more attractive, successful, than (others).

out·side¹ /'aʊtsaɪd/ *adj* (*attrib*) **1** situated in the exterior area of: *an outside wall; the outside pages of a newspaper.* Opp inside¹(1). **2** situated along the outer edge of: *the outside lane of a motorway* (= nearest to the central division). Opp inside¹(2). **3** not likely or probable: *an outside chance.* **4** largest possible: *an outside estimate.*

out·side² /aʊt'saɪd/ *adv* **1** in, into, towards, the exterior area: *It's cold outside. Have a look outside and see if it's raining.* Opp inside²(1). **2** out of doors: *They're playing outside. Go outside.* Opp inside²(2). **3** **outside of sth** in a time, distance etc more than the one mentioned: *outside of an hour.* Opp inside²(4).

out·side³ /aʊt'saɪd/ *nc* (the —) **1** the outer side or surface: *the outside of a house/cupboard/bus.* **2** the outer part or edge of something, e.g. of a road, bend etc: *Always overtake on the outside.* ⇨ inside³(2,3). **3** **at the (very) outside** at the most: *There were only 20 people present at the outside.*

out·side⁴ /aʊt'saɪd/ *prep* **1** in, into, towards, the exterior area: *Take that dirty animal outside this house.* ⇨ inside⁴(1). **2** not including; apart from: *Outside you and me, no-one knows what really happened.* **3** further than; beyond: *It's outside our present experience/knowledge.* ⇨ within(2).

out·sid·er /ˌaʊt'saɪdə(r)/ *nc* **1** a person who is not (considered to be) an accepted member of a group, society etc. ⇨ insider. **2** a contestant, applicant etc thought to have little chance of being successful.

out·size /'aʊtsaɪz/ *adj* (*attrib*) (esp of clothing) larger than the usual size.

out·skirts /'aʊtskɜːts/ *n pl* (the —) the outer areas (esp of a town): *on the outskirts of Paris.*

out·smart /ˌaʊt'smɑːt/ *vt* (*informal*) to be more clever, cunning, than (another person, animal).

out·sold /aʊt'səʊld/ *pt,pp* of outsell.

out·spo·ken /ˌaʊt'spəʊkən/ *adj* saying freely what one thinks: *outspoken comments; be very outspoken.*

out·spo·ken·ly *adv*

out·spread /ˌaʊt'spred/ *adj* spread or stretched out: *with outspread arms/arms outspread.*

out·stand·ing /ˌaʊt'stændɪŋ/ *adj* **1** (attracting attention because) better than others: *an outstanding performance/result.* **2** (of problems, work, payments etc) still to be attended to: *outstanding debts; work that is still outstanding; pay the amount outstanding.*

out·stand·ing·ly *adv* extremely: *outstandingly successful.*

out·stay /ˌaʊt'steɪ/ *vt* to stay at a party etc longer than (other people): *outstay the other guests.* **out·stay one's welcome** to stay too long.

out·stretch·ed /ˌaʊt'stretʃt/ *adj* stretched out: *lie outstretched on the grass; with outstretched arms.*

out·strip /ˌaʊt'strɪp/ *vt* (**-pp-**) to do better, go faster, than (another).

out·ward /'aʊtwəd/ *adj* **1** situated on the outside; outer: *her outward appearance.* **2** towards the outside: *an outward slope.* Opp inward.

out·ward·ly *adv* on the surface; in appearance: *Though frightened, she seemed outwardly calm.* Compare inwardly.

out·wards /'aʊtwədz/ (also **out·ward**) *adv* towards the outside or away from the centre: *bend outwards.* Opp inwards.

out·wear /ˌaʊt'weə(r)/ *vt* (*pt* **-wore** /-'wɔː(r)/, *pp* **-worn** /-'wɔːn/) to last longer than (others): *Leather shoes will outwear plastic ones.*

out·weigh /ˌaʊt'weɪ/ *vt* to be more in value or importance than (something): *Do the many disadvantages outweigh the advantages?*

out·wit /ˌaʊt'wɪt/ *vt* (**-tt-**) to defeat (a person) by being cleverer or more cunning.

out·wore /ˌaʊt'wɔː(r)/ *pt* of outwear.

out·worn /ˌaʊt'wɔːn/ **1** *pp* of outwear. **2** *adj* (*informal*) no longer used: *outworn ideas/methods.*

ova /'əʊvə/ n pl of ovum.

oval /'əʊvl/ nc, adj (a shape or outline that is) like an egg or ellipse.

ovary /'əʊvərɪ/ nc (pl **-ies**) (anat) **1** either of the two reproductive organs in which eggs are produced in female animals. ⇨ ovum. **2** a part for seeds in a plant.

ova·tion /əʊ'veɪʃn/ nc an enthusiastic expression (e.g. clapping, cheering) of welcome or approval: be given a standing ovation (i.e. by people standing up to clap).

ov·en /'ʌvn/ nc an enclosed space (in a cooker) heated for baking, roasting etc: Bread is baked in an oven. ⇨ microwave (oven).

'oven-ready adj (attrib) already prepared for cooking: oven-ready chickens.

'oven·ware /-weə(r)/ nu heat-proof dishes for use in an oven.

over¹ /'əʊvə(r)/ adj (pred) ended; finished: Is the concert over yet? The meeting/storm/war is over. **all over; over and done with** completely finished: As far as I am concerned the quarrel is over and done with.

over² /'əʊvə(r)/ adv Ⓝ For uses with verbs such as change, get, give, look, make, pull, run, stop, take, think, turn etc, ⇨ the verb entries. **1** down from a standing position: fall/slip over; knocked it over. **2** so that the other or a different side is shown: turn/roll over. **3** downwards: bend over; boil over. **4** so as to exchange places: change/swop over. **5** across a space: move over; go over there. **6** from one side to another: jump over. Ⓝ 'Across' is also possible. **7** so as to be covered: paint/cover it over. **8** more: of 16 years and over. Opp under¹(2). **9** remaining: Is there any left over? I'll have just £10 over when I've paid all my debts. 7 into 30 goes 4 times with 2 over. **10** (used in combinations) more than usual, wise etc: over-anxious; overeat. **11** (used to express repetition): be warned many/several times over. **(all) over again** (used for emphasis) another time: I had to repeat the course all over again. **over and over (again)** (used for emphasis) several times: You were told over and over again not to do that.

over³ /'əʊvə(r)/ nc (cricket) six balls (to be) bowled by each bowler in turn.

over⁴ /'əʊvə(r)/ prep **1** above and not touching: lean over the table; be seen high over the mountains. Compare above²(1). **2** covering a surface and touching: spread a handkerchief over his eyes; pull a hat over her face; the snow lying over the fields. **3** across (a space): living over the road. **4** from one side to the other of: escape over the border; look over the wall; jump over a hole. **5** down from: fall/climb over the edge. **6** in many parts of: travel over northern Europe. **all over a place** in every part of: travelled all over China. **over there** in the distance: I can see a house over there behind the trees. **7** (showing authority or power): rule over a great nation; has no command over her students. **8** concerning: have difficulty over finding a good hotel. **9** using; by means of: over the phone/radio. **10** more than: over 15 years old/60 people/10 metres. Compare under²(3). **over age** ⇨ age¹(1). **over and above** in addition to: You will be given a uniform and free meals over and above your salary. **over the top** (of behaviour etc) beyond what is acceptable; exaggerated. ⇨

OTT.

over·abun·dant /,əʊvər ə'bʌndənt/ adj too abundant.

over·act /,əʊvər'ækt/ vi to do something, perform, in an exaggerated way.

over·ac·tive /,əʊvər'æktɪv/ adj doing too many things; using too much energy.

over·all¹ /'əʊvər'ɔːl/ adj (attrib), adv **1** including everything: the overall measurements; be 10 acres overall. **2** on the whole: It's becoming warmer overall.

over·all² /'əʊvərɔːl/ nc an apron.

over·alls /'əʊvərɔːlz/ n pl (also a pair of overalls) loose fitting trousers with shoulder straps, as worn by workmen.

over·anx·ious /,əʊvər'æŋkʃəs/ adj too anxious.

over·arm /'əʊvərɑːm/ adv (cricket) with the arm moving over the shoulder: bowl overarm; an overarm bowler; overarm bowling.

over·awe /,əʊvər'ɔː/ vt to fill (a person) with complete respect, fear etc. ⇨ awe.

over·bal·ance /,əʊvə'bæləns/ vi to fall over: He overbalanced and fell in.

over·bear·ing /,əʊvə'beərɪŋ/ adj forcing others to do what one wants: an overbearing manner.

over·bear·ing·ly adv

over·board /'əʊvəbɔːd/ adv over the side of a ship or boat into the water: fall/jump overboard. **go overboard** (informal) to show too much enthusiasm, liking, for a person, idea etc.

over·bur·den /,əʊvə'bɜːdn/ vt **overburden sb (with sth)** to make a person carry, have, suffer etc too much: overburdened with grief.

over·came /,əʊvə'keɪm/ pt of overcome.

over·cast /,əʊvə'kɑːst/ adj (of the sky) darkened by clouds.

over·cau·tious /,əʊvə'kɔːʃəs/ adj too cautious.

over·charge /,əʊvə'tʃɑːdʒ/ vt, vi **1** to charge too high a price: We were overcharged for the eggs. Compare undercharge. **2** (electricity) to fill or load (something) too much: overcharge an electric circuit.

over·cloud·ed /,əʊvə'klaʊdɪd/ adj covered with clouds or shadows.

over·coat /'əʊvəkəʊt/ nc a long coat worn over other clothes in cold weather.

over·come /,əʊvə'kʌm/ vt (pt **-came** /-'keɪm/, pp **-come**) **1** to defeat, be too strong for, (a person, habit etc) overcome the enemy/a bad habit/ temptation. **2** (usually passive) to make (a person) weak, unhappy or ill: be overcome by emotion/tiredness/sadness/whisky/fumes.

over·con·fi·dent /,əʊvə 'kɒnfɪdənt/ adj too confident.

over·cook /,əʊvə'kʊk/ vt to cook (food) for too long.

over·criti·cal /,əʊvə 'krɪtɪkl/ adj too critical.

over·crowd·ed /,əʊvə'kraʊdɪd/ adj (of places, transport) having too many people: overcrowded beaches/trains.

over·crowd·ing nu

over·do /,əʊvə'duː/ vt (pt **-did** /-'dɪd/, pp **-done** /-'dʌn/) to do, say etc (something) in an exaggerated way, too strongly etc: He overdid his part in the play. **overdo it** (informal) (a) to work etc too hard: Don't overdo it and make yourself ill. (b) to go too far in order to achieve one's aim: He tried to show sympathy for us, but didn't he overdo it?

over·done /ˌəʊvə'dʌn/ **1** pp of overdo. **2** adj (of food) cooked for too long: overdone beef.

over·dose /'əʊvədəʊs/ nc an amount of a drug that is too much. □ vi to take an overdose.

over·draft /'əʊvədrɑːft/ nc an amount of money by which a bank account is overdrawn.

over·drama·tize (also -ise) /ˌəʊvə'dræmətaɪz/ vt to exaggerate (the report of a happening, one's feelings etc).

over·drawn /ˌəʊvə'drɔːn/ adj having used, taken out, more money than one has in a bank account: I'm/My account is overdrawn. I have an overdrawn account. ⇨ overdraft.

over·dress /ˌəʊvə'dres/ vi to dress too richly or too formally.

over·due /ˌəʊvə'djuː/ adj beyond the time fixed (for arrival, payment etc): The train is overdue (= is late). These bills are all overdue (= ought to have been paid). The baby is two weeks overdue (= is still not born two weeks after the expected date of birth).

over-eag·er /ˌəʊvər 'iːgə(r)/ adj too eager.

over·eat /ˌəʊvər'iːt/ vi to eat too much food.

over-emo·tion·al /ˌəʊvər ɪ'məʊʃnl/ adj too emotional.

over-em·pha·size (also -ise) /ˌəʊvər 'emfəsaɪz/ vt to give too much importance to (something): I cannot over-emphasize how disappointed I am.

over-en·thu·si·as·tic /ˌəʊvər 'enθjuːzɪæstɪk/ adj too enthusiastic.

over·estimate /ˌəʊvər'estɪmeɪt/ vt to make (one's estimates) too large.

over-ex·cit·ed /ˌəʊvər 'ɪksaɪtɪd/ adj far too excited.

over-ex·pos·ed /ˌəʊvər 'ɪkspəʊzd/ adj (photography) (of a film) exposed for too long.

over·flow¹ /ˌəʊvə'fləʊ/ nc an act, instance, amount, of overflowing.

over·flow² /ˌəʊvə'fləʊ/ v **1** vt,vi to flow over the edges or limits; spread beyond the ordinary or usual area: The river overflowed its banks. The crowds were so big that they overflowed into the street. **2** vi to be more than filled: a heart overflowing with love.

over·grown /ˌəʊvə'grəʊn/ adj **1** having grown too fast: an overgrown schoolboy. **2** covered with something that has grown over: a garden overgrown with weeds.

over·hang /ˌəʊvə'hæŋ/ vt,vi (pt,pp -hung /-'hʌŋ/) to hang, project, over (something) like a shelf: The cliffs overhang the stream. The ledge overhangs several feet.

over·haul¹ /'əʊvəhɔːl/ nc an examination to discover and repair faults.

over·haul² /ˌəʊvə'hɔːl/ vt **1** to examine (something) thoroughly in order to learn about its condition: have the engine of a car overhauled. **2** to overtake (a person, vehicle etc); catch up with (a person, vehicle etc): The fast cruiser soon overhauled the old cargo boat.

over·head /ˌəʊvə'hed/ adj, adv above one's head; in the sky: the people in the room overhead; the stars overhead; overhead wires/cables.

over·heads /'əʊvəhedz/ n pl expenses, from running a business (e.g. rent, salaries, light), not manufacturing costs.

over·hear /ˌeʊvə'hɪə(r)/ vt (pt,pp -heard /-'hɜːd/)

to hear (a person, conversation etc) without the knowledge of the speaker(s), deliberately or by chance.

over·hung /ˌəʊvə'hʌŋ/ pt,pp of overhang.

over-in·dulge /ˌəʊvər 'ɪndʌldʒ/ vi overindulge (in sth) (formal) to eat, drink, play etc too much.

over-in·dul·gence nu

over·joy·ed /ˌəʊvə'dʒɔɪd/ adj overjoyed (at sth) very pleased (about one's success etc).

over·kill /'əʊvəkɪl/ nu **1** an ability to use more nuclear bombs than would be necessary. **2** (informal) exaggerated behaviour: Sending her so many roses was overkill!

over·land adj /'əʊvəlænd/, adv /ˌəʊvə'lænd/ across the land (contrasted with the sea): take the overland route; travel overland.

over·lap¹ /'əʊvəlæp/ nc an amount by which things overlap.

over·lap² /ˌəʊvə'læp/ v (-pp-) **1** vt,vi to cover (something) in part by extending beyond one edge: tiles that overlap (one another). **2** vi (fig) to coincide, be the same, in part: His duties/authority and mine overlap.

over·leaf /ˌəʊvə'liːf/ adv on the other side of the page (of a book etc).

over·load /ˌəʊvə'ləʊd/ vt to put too great a load of electric current, weight on (something, a person).

over·look /ˌəʊvə'lʊk/ vt **1** to have a view of (something) from above: Our garden is overlooked from the neighbour's windows. **2** to fail to notice (something); pay no attention to (it): His services have been overlooked by his employers (i.e. They have not properly rewarded him). **3** to allow (a wrong act, mistake etc) to pass without punishment: overlook a fault.

over·man·ned /ˌəʊvə'mænd/ adj (pred) (of an industry) having too many workers. ⇨ overstaffed.

over·man·ning nu

over·much /ˌəʊvə 'mʌtʃ/ adj, adv too much (which is more usual): an author who is praised over-much.

over·night¹ /'əʊvənaɪt/ adj (attrib) for, during, the night: an overnight bag/journey.

over·night² /ˌəʊvə'naɪt/ adv **1** for, during, the night: stay overnight at a friend's house (= sleep there for the night). **2** (informal) very quickly: become successful overnight.

over·pay /ˌəʊvə'peɪ/ vt (pt,pp -paid /-'peɪd/) to pay (a person) too much: Has Jack been overpaid for his work?

over·popu·lated /ˌəʊvə 'pɒpjʊleɪtɪd/ adj having far too many people: over-populated cities.

over·popu·la·tion nc,nu

over·pow·er /ˌəʊvə'paʊə(r)/ vt to defeat (a person) because of greater strength or numbers: The criminals were easily overpowered by the police.

over·power·ing adj too strong or powerful: an overpowering smell; overpowering grief.

over·rate /ˌəʊvə'reɪt/ vt to put too high a value on (a person, thing): overrate her abilities.

over·rated adj: an overrated book.

over·reach /ˌəʊvə'riːtʃ/ vt reflex overreach oneself to fail, damage one's own interests, by being too ambitious.

over·ride /ˌəʊvə'raɪd/ vt (pt -rode /-'rəʊd/, pp

-ridden /-'rɪdn/) **1** to refuse to agree with or accept (an opinion, decision, wish, claim etc): *They overrode my wishes*. **2** to ignore (an instruction) because of special conditions.

over·ripe /ˌəʊvə'raɪp/ *adj* too ripe.

over·rule /ˌəʊvə'ruːl/ *vt* to decide against (a person, decision etc) (esp by using one's higher authority): *The judge overruled the previous decision*.

over·run /ˌəʊvə'rʌn/ *vt* (*pt* -ran /-'ræn/, *pp* -run) **1** to spread over and occupy (something): *a country overrun by enemy troops; a garden overrun with weeds*. **2** to go beyond (a time limit): *speakers who overrun the time allowed them*.

over·seas /ˌəʊvə'siːz/ *adj* (*attrib*), *adv* across the sea: *overseas students* (i.e. students from other countries); *go/live overseas*.

over·see /ˌəʊvə'siː/ *vt* (*pt* -saw /-'sɔː/, *pp* -seen /-'siːn/) to supervise, control, (work or workers).

over·sen·si·tive /ˌəʊvə'sensɪtɪv/ *adj* (*derog*) (of a person) far too sensitive.

over·shad·ow /ˌəʊvə'ʃædəʊ/ *vt* **1** (*fig*) to cause (a person, event etc) to seem less important or obvious: *She was overshadowed by her sister/her sister's success*. **2** to cause (something) to seem less pleasant, good: *Her happiness at her wedding was overshadowed by her mother's death*.

over·shoe /'əʊvəʃuː/ *nc* (also *a pair of overshoes*) a rubber shoe worn over an ordinary one in wet weather.

over·shoot /ˌəʊvə'ʃuːt/ *vt* (*pt,pp* -shot /-'ʃɒt/) to travel over or beyond (a mark or limit): *The aircraft overshot the runway*.

over·sight /'əʊvəsaɪt/ *nc,nu* (an instance of) the failure to notice: *Because of a very unfortunate oversight, your letter was left unanswered*.

over·sim·pli·fi·ca·tion /ˌəʊvə ˌsɪmplɪfɪ'keɪʃn/ *nc,nu* (an instance of) making a process, an explanation etc seem too easy.

over·sim·pli·fy /ˌəʊvə 'sɪmplɪfaɪ/ *vt* (*pt,pp* -ied) to make (a process, explanation etc) seem too easy.

over·sleep /ˌəʊvə'sliːp/ *vi* (*pt,pp* -slept /-'slept/) to sleep too long or after the time for waking: *He overslept and was late for work*.

over·spill[1] /'əʊvəspɪl/ *nu* **1** the amount of a liquid etc that has overflowed. **2** (*fig*) the people who cannot find places in a meeting, to live or work in a city etc: *build new towns for London's overspill*.

over·staf·fed /ˌəʊvə'stɑːft/ *adj* (*pred*) (of an office, business) having too many workers. ⇨ **overmanned**.

over·state /ˌəʊvə'steɪt/ *vt* **1** to express or state (something) too strongly: *She overstated her anger*. **2** to state more than is true about (something): *Don't overstate the injuries you suffered. You've overstated your case*.

over·state·ment *nc,nu*

over·step /ˌəʊvə'step/ *vt* (-pp-) to go beyond (a limit): *overstep one's authority*.

over·stock /ˌəʊvə'stɒk/ *vt* to supply, fill, (something) with too much stock: *overstock a shop*.

over·strung /ˌəʊvə'strʌŋ/ *adj* (*derog*) (of a person, personality) extremely nervous; easily excited; too sensitive.

over·sub·scrib·ed /ˌəʊvə səb'skraɪbd/ *adj* (*finance*) (of an issue of shares etc) with more applications than what is offered.

overt /'əʊvɜːt/ *adj* (*formal*) done or shown openly, publicly: *overt hostility*.

overt·ly *adv*

over·take /ˌəʊvə'teɪk/ *vt* (*pt* -took /-'tʊk/, *pp* -taken /-'teɪkən/) **1** to catch up with and pass (a person, vehicle etc): *overtake other cars on the road*. **2** (usually *passive*) (of storms, troubles etc) to happen suddenly, by surprise: *be overtaken by/ with fear/surprise*.

over·tax /ˌəʊvə'tæks/ *vt* **1** to tax (a person, business etc) too heavily. **2** to put too much strain on (something): *overtax one's strength/her patience*.

over·throw /ˌəʊvə'θrəʊ/ *vt* (*pt* -threw /-'θruː/, *pp* -thrown /-'θrəʊn/) to force (a government, ruler etc) to give up power: *overthrow the government*. □ *nc* /'əʊvəθrəʊ/ an act of overthrowing.

over·time /'əʊvətaɪm/ *nu*, *adv* (time spent at work) after the usual hours: *working overtime; be on overtime; get overtime pay*.

over·took /əʊvə'tʊk/ *pt* of overtake.

over·ture /'əʊvətʃʊə(r)/ *nc* **1** *overture (to sb)* (*formal*) an approach made (to a person) with the aim of starting discussions: *peace overtures; make overtures to strikers*. **2** (*music*) a composition played as an introduction, esp to an opera.

over·turn /ˌəʊvə'tɜːn/ *vt,vi* (to cause something) to turn over; upset: *He overturned the boat. The car overturned*.

over·weight /ˌəʊvə'weɪt/ *adj* more than the weight (i.e. mass) allowed or than is normal: *If your luggage is overweight, you'll have to pay extra*.

over·whelm /ˌəʊvə'welm/ *vt* **1** to defeat (a person, army etc) completely: *be overwhelmed by the enemy*. **2** to cause (a person) to feel confused or embarrassed: *overwhelmed by all the publicity/ cameras/crowds*.

over·work /ˌəʊvə'wɜːk/ *vt,vi* (to cause a person) to work too hard or too long: *overwork a horse. It's foolish to overwork*. □ *nu* an act of working too much or too long: *made ill through overwork*.

over·wrought /ˌəʊvə'rɔːt/ *adj* tired out by too much work or excitement.

ovi·duct /'əʊvɪdʌkt/ *nc* (*anat*) = Fallopian tube.

ovum /'əʊvəm/ *nc* (*pl* ova /'əʊvə/) (*science*) a cell in female animals, capable of developing into a new individual when fertilized (by male *sperm*).

owe /əʊ/ *vt* Ⓝ Not used in continuous tenses, e.g. is/ was -ing. **1** *owe sb money (for sth)* to be in debt to (a person) (for something): *He owes (his father) £50. Owing money is a bad thing*. **2** *owe sth to sb* to feel grateful to a person for something: *We owe a great deal to our parents*. **3** *owe sth to sth* to accept that something is due to something: *He owes his success more to good luck than to ability*.

ow·ing /'əʊɪŋ/ *adj* (*pred*) still to be paid: *large sums still owing*. *owing to* (*prep*) because of: *Owing to the rain, they could not come*. ⇨ the *note* at because of.

owl /aʊl/ *nc* a bird that flies at night and eats small birds and animals.

own[1] /əʊn/ *adj* or *det* Ⓝ 'Own' is always used after a possessive pronoun, e.g. *my, her*, for emphasis. **1** belonging to her, him, me etc: *I saw it with my own eyes. Do you own your own house? I'll cook my own supper*. *all of its own* that is unique: *This fruit has a flavour all of its own*. **2** done, produced by, her, him, them etc: *This is all my own work. She makes her own clothes.*

own² /əʊn/ *pron* Ⓝ *'Own'* is always used after a possessive pronoun, e.g. *my, her,* for emphasis. belonging to, produced by, her, him, me etc: *It's my own. She'd love a bedroom of her own.* **(all) on one's own (a)** without help: *I did it (all) on my own.* **(b)** alone: *live (all) on one's own; walking on her own.* Ⓝ *'(All) by myself, herself etc'* is also possible. **get/have one's own back (on sb)** to have one's revenge. **hold one's own** to manage to keep one's position (against competition).

own³ /əʊn/ *v* Ⓝ Not used in continuous tenses, e.g. *is/was -ing.* **1** *vt* to possess (something); have (something) as property: *This house is mine; I own it.* **2** *vt* **own (that) sth** *(formal)* to admit or agree (that): *I own that your claim is justified.* **3** *vi* **own up (to sth)** to confess (something) fully.

own·er /'əʊnə(r)/ *nc* a person who owns something: *Who's the owner of this house?*

own·er·ship /-ʃɪp/ *nu*

ox /ɒks/ *nc* (*pl* **ox·en** /'ɒksn/) (*esp*) a fully-grown castrated male of cattle.

OXFAM /'ɒksfæm/ *acronym* Oxford Committee for Famine Relief (a GB independent organization for overseas aid).

ox·ide /'ɒksaɪd/ *nc,nu* (*science*) any kind of chemical substance made of oxygen and another chemical element: *lead oxide.*

oxi·dize (also **-ise**) /'ɒksɪdaɪz/ *vt,vi* (*chemistry*) (to cause a chemical element) to combine with oxygen.

oxy·acety·lene /ˌɒksɪə'setɪliːn/ *adj, nu* (*tech*) (of) a mixture of oxygen and acetylene: *oxyacetylene welding.*

oxy·gen /'ɒksɪdʒən/ *nu* a chemical element (symbol O); gas without colour, taste or smell, present in the air and necessary to the existence of all forms of life.

'oxygen mask *nc* a mask placed over the nose and mouth to supply oxygen.

'oxygen tent *nc* an apparatus in a hospital that allows a patient to breathe air with a greater oxygen content.

oy·ster /'ɔɪstə(r)/ *nc* a kind of shellfish used as food, usually eaten uncooked.

oz *written abbr* ounce(s).

Pp

P, p /piː/ (*pl* **P's, p's** /piːz/) the 16th letter of the English alphabet. **mind one's P's and Q's** to be careful about what one says or does.

p /piː/ *symbol* **1** penny, pence. □ *written abbr* **2** page.

P *symbol* **1** (*chemistry*) phosphorus. **2** (*physics*) pressure; power. **3** (on road signs) parking area.

pa /paː/ *nc* (*informal*) = papa.

p.a. *written abbr* per annum.

pace¹ /peɪs/ *nc* **1** (the distance covered by) a single step when walking or running. **2** a rate of walking or running. **keep pace (with sb/sth)** to progress at the same rate (as a person, thing):

He finds it hard to keep pace with all the developments in nuclear physics. **set the pace** to decide the rate at which a person or group carries out an activity.

pace² /peɪs/ *v* **1** *vi,vt* to walk, trot etc with slow or regular steps (in an area): *pace up and down* (often suggesting restlessness, impatience); *be pacing the room.* **2 pace sth off/out** to measure something by counting paces: *pace off 30 metres; pace out a room.* **3** to set the pace(2) for (a rider or runner in a race).

'pace-maker *nc* **(a)** (also **'pace-setter**) a rider, runner etc who sets the pace for another in a race. **(b)** (*med*) an electronic device used to correct weak or irregular heartbeats.

paci·fi·ca·tion /ˌpæsɪfɪ'keɪʃn/ *nu* (*formal*) the act, policy, of pacifying.

paci·fism /'pæsɪfɪzəm/ *nu* (the belief in) the principle that war should and could be abolished.

paci·fist /'pæsɪfɪst/ *adj* concerning pacifism. □ *nc* a supporter of, believer in pacifism.

pac·ify /'pæsɪfaɪ/ *vt* (*pt,pp* **-ied**) to calm (a person, a person's anger, excitement etc).

pack¹ /pæk/ *nc* **1** a number of things tied or wrapped up together for carrying. **2** a number of wild animals that go about together: *Wolves hunt in packs.* **3** a number of bad things or people: *a pack of thieves/liars/lies.* **4** a complete set (usually 52) of playing-cards. **5** (*esp US*) = packet: *a pack of cigarettes.*

'pack-horse/-animal *nc* one used for carrying packs(1).

'pack-ice *nu* a large area of ice in the sea.

pack² /pæk/ *v* **1** *vt,vi* to put (things) into a box, bundle, bag etc: *pack clothes into a suitcase. Have you packed your things/your bag? You must begin packing at once. Her husband takes a packed lunch* (e.g. sandwiches etc in a container) *to work every day.* Compare unpack. **send sb packing** (*informal*) to send a person away (because one is angry, upset etc). **2** *vt* to crowd together into (a place or period of time): *a bus packed with school-children.* ⇨ **pack sb/sth into sth. 3** *vt* to wrap (objects) in material and put them in a container. ⇨ **pack sth in sth. 4** *vt* to prepare and put (meat, fruit etc) in tins for preservation. **5** *vt* to choose the members of (a committee etc) so that their decisions will be in one's favour.

pack sth away to put things into a container that is put in a safe place until needed.

pack sb in (a) to put many people into a bus, stadium, hotel etc. **(b)** (*informal*) to stop seeing a girlfriend or boyfriend. **pack sth in (a)** (*sl*) to stop a habit, bad behaviour etc: *pack in smoking.* **(b)** to manage to do many things in a short time: *She packed in a lot of sightseeing.* **pack it in** (*sl; esp imperative*) to stop doing it. **pack sth in sth** to pack(1) objects in material to protect them: *glass packed in newspaper.*

pack sb/sth into sth to put many people, things, activities into a vehicle, container, building, a period of time etc: *They packed the workers into the buses. They packed several visits into their short holiday.*

pack sb off (to a place) (*informal*) to send a person away: *be packed off to school.*

pack sth out to fill a building completely: *The meeting/room was packed out.*

pack up (a) to pack(1) one's belongings. (b) (*informal*) to stop doing something: *If you're not willing to work you'd better pack up. The engine packed up after a mile or two.* ***pack sth up*** to pack(1) one's belongings. ***pack it up*** = pack it in.

pack·age¹ /'pækɪdʒ/ *nc* a number of things packed together and wrapped.

,package 'holiday/'tour *nc* (*informal*) a holiday including travel, hotel, food etc arranged in advance and sold at a fixed price.

pack·age² /'pækɪdʒ/ *vt* to place (something) in, make (something) into, a package.

pack·er /'pækə(r)/ *nc* a person who packs(1,3,4).

pack·et /'pækɪt/ *nc* **1** a small parcel: *a packet containing the invitations.* **2** a carton: *a packet of 20 cigarettes.* **3** (*sl*) a large sum of money: *cost a packet.* ***make a packet*** (*informal*) to earn a lot of money; make a large profit.

pack·ing /'pækɪŋ/ *nu* **1** the process of packing goods: *I'm doing my packing* (= putting things in my suitcase). **2** material used in packing(3).

pact /pækt/ *nc* (often P-) an agreement: *the Peace Pact.*

pad¹ /pæd/ *nc* **1** (a mass of, container filled with) soft material used to prevent damage, give comfort or improve the shape of something: *a pad of cotton wool.* **2** a number of sheets of writing-paper fastened together along one edge: *a writing pad.* **3** = launching pad. **4** a guard for the leg or other parts of the body (in cricket and other games). **5** the soft part of a paw. **6** (*sl*) a room etc to stay in.

pad² /pæd/ *vt* (**-dd-**) **1** to put pads(1) in or on (something) to prevent injury, to give comfort or to fill out spaces etc. **2** *pad sth (out)* (*informal*) to make a book, essay, etc longer by using unnecessary material.

,padded 'cell *nc* one with padded walls (as used in a mental hospital).

pad·ding /'pædɪŋ/ *nu* material used for padding(1).

paddle¹ /'pædl/ *nc* **1** a short oar, wide at one or both ends, used to move a canoe through the water. **2** an act or period of moving a boat with a paddle.

paddle² /'pædl/ *vi* to use a paddle. ***paddle one's own canoe*** (*fig*) to depend on oneself alone.

paddle³ /'pædl/ *vi* to walk with bare feet in shallow water (as children do at the seaside).

'paddling pool *nc* a pool where children can paddle³.

pad·dock /'pædək/ *nc* **1** a small field used for exercising horses. **2** an enclosed area where horses are assembled before a race.

pad·dy /'pædɪ/ *nu* rice that is still growing.

'paddy-field *nc* a field where rice is grown.

pad·lock /'pædlɒk/ *vt, nc* (to fasten (a door, object) using) a lock with a hook that can be removed: *padlock a bike to a lamp-post.*

padre /'pɑːdreɪ/ *nc* a priest, esp in the army and navy.

pae·di·at·ri·cian (also **pedi-**) /,piːdɪə'trɪʃn/ *nc* a physician who specializes in paediatrics.

pae·di·at·rics (also **pedi-**) /,piːdɪ'ætrɪks/ the branch of medicine concerned with children and their illnesses.

pa·gan /'peɪgən/ *adj, nc* (not now used) (of) a person who is not a believer in any of the chief religions of the world.

page¹ /peɪdʒ/ *nc* **1** one side of a piece of paper in a book etc. **2** one piece of paper in a book etc: *Several pages have been torn out.*

page² /peɪdʒ/ *nc* **1** (also *page-boy*) a young male member of a hotel staff. **2** a boy attending a bride at a wedding.

page³ /peɪdʒ/ *vt* to call the name of (a person) in a hotel, hospital etc: *paging Dr Green.*

pag·eant /'pædʒənt/ *nc* **1** a public entertainment, esp one in which there is a procession of people in fine costumes.

pag·eant·ry /'pædʒəntrɪ/ *nu* a rich and splendid ceremony or display.

pa·goda /pə'gəʊdə/ *nc* (*pl* —s) a religious building, typically a sacred tower shaped like a pyramid (Hindu temple), or of several storeys (Buddhist tower).

paid /peɪd/ *pt,pp* of pay².

pail /peɪl/ *nc* a round vessel of metal or wood, used for carrying liquid: *a pail of milk.*

pail·ful /-fʊl/ *nc* as much as a pail can hold.

pain¹ /peɪn/ *n* **1** *nu* the feeling of physical suffering or hurt: *be in (great) pain; cry with pain; feel some/no/not much/a great deal of pain.* Compare ache¹. **2** *nc* a particular kind of this feeling: *a pain in the knee.* ***a pain in the neck*** (*sl; derog*) an annoying person. **3** *nu* mental suffering or anxiety.

'pain-killer *nc* a kind of medicine for stopping pain(1).

pain·ed *adj* showing sadness, stress: *She had a pained look.*

pain·ful /-fəl/ *adj* causing pain or mental suffering: *a painful bite. This duty is painful to me.*

pain·ful·ly /-fəlɪ/ *adv*

pain·less *adj* without, causing no, pain: *painless methods of killing animals.*

pain·less·ly *adv*

pain² /peɪn/ *vt* to cause (a person) to suffer.

pains /peɪnz/ *n pl* trouble; effort: *work hard and get very little for all one's pains.* ***go to/take (great) pains to do sth*** to make a great effort to do it.

pains·taking /'peɪnsteɪkɪŋ/ *adj* very careful; thorough: *a painstaking enquiry.*

paint¹ /peɪnt/ *n* **1** *nu* a solid colouring matter (to be) mixed with oil or other liquid and used to give colour to a surface: *give the doors two coats of paint.* **2** (*pl*) a collection of colouring materials.

'paint-box *nc* a box with paints(2).

'paint-brush *nc* one used for painting.

paint² /peɪnt/ *vt,vi* **1** to put paint on (a surface): *paint a door.* ***paint the town red*** ⇨ town(1). **2** to make a picture of (a person, thing) with paint: *paint flowers; paint in oils/in water-colours.* ***paint sth in*** to add something to a painting: *paint in the foreground.* **3** (*fig*) to describe (a person, etc) vividly in words: *paint a person's character.*

paint·er /'peɪntə(r)/ *nc* **1** an artist who paints pictures. **2** a worker who paints buildings etc.

paint·ing /'peɪntɪŋ/ *n* **1** *nu* the practice, art, of using paint. **2** *nu* the occupation of a painter. **3** *nc* a painted picture.

pair¹ /peə(r)/ *nc* **1** two things of the same kind (to be) used together: *a pair of shoes; four pairs of gloves. I'd like two pairs, please.* **2** a single article with two parts always joined: *a pair of trousers/ tights/scissors.* **3** two people closely associated, e.g. a married couple: *They make a happy pair.* **in pairs** in twos: *They came out of the gate in pairs.*

pair² /peə(r)/ *v* **1** *vi* (of animals) to form a pair in order to produce young. **2** *vt,vi* **pair (sb/sth) off/up** (to cause (people, things)) to form a pair: *I was paired off with a boring cousin at the wedding.*

pa·ja·mas /pə'dʒɑːməz/ *n pl* = pyjamas.

pal¹ /pæl/ *nc* (*informal*) a friend.

pal·ly /'pælɪ/ *adj* (**-ier, -iest**) (*informal*) friendly.

pal² /pæl/ *vi* (**-ll-**) **pal up (with sb)** (*informal*) to become friendly (with a person).

pal·ace /'pælɪs/ *nc* **1** the official residence of a king or queen, archbishop or bishop. **2** any large and splendid building. ⇨ palatial.

pal·at·able /'pælɪtəbl/ *adj* (*formal*) **1** agreeable to the taste: *a palatable meal.* **2** (*fig*) pleasing; acceptable: *a palatable idea.* Opp unpalatable.

pal·ate /'pælət/ *nc* **1** the top of the mouth. **2** the sense of taste: *have a good palate for wines.*

pa·la·tial /pə'leɪʃl/ *adj* of, like, a palace: *own a palatial residence.*

pale¹ /peɪl/ *adj* (**—r, —st**) **1** (of a person's face) having little colour: *He turned pale at the news.* **2** (of a colour) not strong: *pale blue.* Compare deep¹(6).

pale·ness *nu*

pale² /peɪl/ *vi* to become pale(1).

pal·ette /'pælɪt/ *nc* a board (with a hole for the thumb) on which an artist mixes colours.

'palette-knife *nc* a wide, flat knife, used by artists and in cookery.

pal·in·drome /'pælɪndrəʊm/ *nc* (*lang*) a piece of writing giving the same meaning backwards or forwards, as in 'Madam, I'm Adam'.

pall¹ /pɔːl/ *nc* **1** a heavy cloth spread over a coffin. **2** (*fig*) any dark, heavy covering: *a pall of smoke.*

'pall·bear·er *nc* a person who walks by the side of a coffin at a funeral.

pall² /pɔːl/ *vi* to become distasteful or boring because done, used etc for too long a time: *pleasures that pall after a time.*

pal·let /'pælɪt/ *nc* a portable platform for loads.

pal·lid /'pælɪd/ *adj* pale; looking ill.

pal·lid·ly *adv*

pal·lor /'pælə(r)/ *nu* paleness of the face.

pal·ly /'pælɪ/ *adj* ⇨ pal.

palm¹ /pɑːm/ *nc* the inner surface of the hand.

palm² /pɑːm/ *nc* one of many trees growing in warm climates, with no branches and a mass of large wide leaves at the top: *date-palms; coconut-palms.*

palm³ /pɑːm/ *vt* **palm sth off (on sb)** to use deceit to persuade a person to buy or take something.

pal·pable /'pælpəbl/ *adj* (*formal; no comp*) **1** that can be felt or touched: *a palpable hit.* **2** obvious: *a palpable error.*

pal·pably /-əblɪ/ *adv*

pal·pi·tate /'pælpɪteɪt/ *vi* (of the heart) to beat irregularly or fast.

pal·pi·ta·tion /ˌpælpɪ'teɪʃn/ *nc,nu* (an instance of) an irregular or fast beat of the heart.

pal·try /'pɔːltrɪ/ *adj* (**-ier, -iest**) (*derog*) worthless because small; of no importance: *a paltry salary/amount.*

pam·pas /'pæmpəs/ *n sing* (the —) the flat, treeless, areas in S America. Ⓝ Compare *'prairie'* in N America and *'savanna'* in central America and W Africa.

pam·per /'pæmpə(r)/ *vt* to be too kind and generous to (a person, animal): *a pampered child/ dog.*

pamph·let /'pæmflɪt/ *nc* a small paper-covered book, esp on a topic of public interest.

pamph·let·eer /ˌpæmflə'tɪə(r)/ *nc* a person who writes pamphlets.

pan¹ /pæn/ *nc* **1** a metal container with a handle, used for cooking. ⇨ saucepan. **2** a bowl of a lavatory. **3** a wide and shallow hollow in the ground: *a salt-pan.* **4** either of the dishes on a pair of scales.

pan² /pæn/ *v* (**-nn-**) **1** *vt,vi* to wash (soil, rock, etc) and look (for gold, jewels etc): *panning for gold.* **2** *vi* **pan out** (*fig*) to succeed; turn out: *How did things pan out?* **3** *vt* (*informal*) to criticize (a person, product) harshly: *His play was panned severely.*

pan³ /pæn/ *vi,vt* to make (a camera) follow a moving object.

pana·cea /ˌpænə'sɪə/ *nc* (*pl* **—s**) (*formal*) a remedy for all troubles, diseases etc.

pa·nache /pæ'næʃ/ *nu* (*formal*) (an air of) confidence: *He does everything with panache.*

pan·cake /'pænkeɪk/ *nc,nu* a mixture of flour, eggs and milk, fried on both sides.

pan·creas /'pæŋkrɪəs/ *nc* (*anat*) the gland near the stomach, producing a juice which helps digestion.

pan·cre·at·ic /ˌpæŋkrɪ'ætɪk/ *adj*

pan·da /'pændə/ *nc* (*pl* **—s**) (also **giant panda**) a mammal of Tibet and China, with black legs and a black and white body.

pan·de·mo·nium /ˌpændɪ'məʊnɪəm/ *nu* a state of wild and noisy disorder.

pan·der /'pændə(r)/ *vi* **pander to sb/sth** to give help or encouragement to a person or thing that is weak, bad or undesirable: *newpapers that pander to the public interest in crime; pander to low tastes.*

P & L *written abbr* (*commerce*) profit and loss (account).

p. & p. *written abbr* (*commerce*) (usually the cost of) postage and packing.

pane /peɪn/ *nc* (also **window-pane**) a piece of glass in (a division of) a window.

pan·el /'pænl/ *nc* **1** a separate part of the surface of a door, wall etc raised above or sunk below the surrounding area. **2** a large piece of material of a different kind or colour put in a dress. **3** a board or other surface for controls and instruments: *the instrument panel* (i.e. of an aircraft or vehicle)*; the control panel* (i.e. on a radio or TV set). **4** a list of names of doctors who (in GB) work for the National Health Service. **5** a group of speakers chosen to speak, answer questions, take part in a game etc before an audience: *a discussion panel.*

'panel game *nc* a question game on TV or radio between two or more groups.

pan·el·led *adj* having panels(1).

pan·el·ling *nu* a series of panels(1).

pang /pæŋ/ *nc* a sudden, sharp feeling (of pain, guilt etc).

pan·ic¹ /'pænɪk/ *nc,nu* (an instance of) uncontrolled, quickly spreading fear: *There is always* *danger of (a) panic when a building catches fire.*

pan·ic² /'pænɪk/ *vi* (**-ck-**) to be affected with panic: *Stop panicking!*

pan·icky /'pænɪkɪ/ *adj* (*informal*) easily affected by, in a state of , panic.

'panic-stricken *adj* terrified; filled with panic.

pan·nier /'pænɪə(r)/ *nc* **1** one of a pair of baskets placed across the back of a horse or donkey. **2** one of a pair of bags on either side of the back of a bike or motorbike.

pan·or·am·a /ˌpænə'rɑːmə/ *nc* (*pl* **—s**) a wide, uninterrupted view.

pan·or·am·ic /ˌpænə'ræmɪk/ *adj*

pan·sy /'pænzɪ/ *nc* (*pl* **-ies**) a kind of small garden flower with big, colourful petals.

pant¹ /pænt/ *nc* a short, quick breath (e.g. because tired).

pant² /pænt/ *v* **1** *vi* to take short, quick breaths: *The dog was panting after the run.* **2** *vt* to say (something) while panting: *He panted (out) his message.*

pan·tech·ni·con /pæn'teknɪkən/ *nc* (*GB*) a large closed van, used for moving furniture.

pan·the·ism /'pænθɪɪzəm/ *nu* (the belief in) the theory that God is in everything and that everything is God.

pan·the·ist /-ɪst/ *adj* concerning pantheism. □ *nc* a believer in pantheism.

pan·the·is·tic /ˌpænθɪ'ɪstɪk/ *adj*

pan·ther /'pænθə(r)/ *nc* a leopard, esp a black one.

pan·ties /'pæntɪz/ *n pl* (*informal*) (a woman's or girl's) close-fitting, short knickers.

pan·to /'pæntəʊ/ *nc* (*pl* **—s**) (*informal*) = panto-mime.

pan·to·mime /'pæntəmaɪm/ *nc,nu* (an example of) a kind of English drama based on a traditional story, with music, dancing and clowning.

pan·try /'pæntrɪ/ *nc* (*pl* **-ies**) **1** a room (in a large house, hotel etc) in which silver, glass etc are kept. **2** a large cupboard, small room, in which food is kept.

pants /pænts/ *n pl* **1** (esp *US*) trousers. **2** under-pants; knickers.

pa·pa /pə'pɑː/ *nc* (a child's word for) father.

pa·pa·cy /'peɪpəsɪ/ *nc* (*pl* **-ies**) the position, authority, of the Pope.

pa·pal /'peɪpl/ *adj*

pa·paw (also **paw·paw**) /pə'pɔː/ *nc* (a tropical tree like a palm with) a large fruit with yellow flesh and many black seeds.

pap·aya /pə'paɪə/ = papaw.

pa·per¹ /'peɪpə(r)/ *n* **1** *nu* (also *attrib*) a sub-stance in the form of sheets, used for writing, printing, drawing, wrapping, packing etc: *a sheet of paper; a paper bag.* **2** *nc* = newspaper: *the evening papers.* **3** (*pl*) documents showing who a person or thing is, what authority he or it has etc: *identification papers; a ship's papers.* **4** *nc* a set of examination questions on a given subject: *The biology paper was difficult.* **5** *nc* an essay, esp one to be read to a learned society: *a paper on cur-rency reform.*

'paper·back *nc* a book in paper covers. Com-pare hardback.

'paper-clip *nc* a device, usually of wire, used for holding sheets of paper together.

'paper-mill *nc* a factory where paper is made.

'paper'tape *nu* (*computers*) a thin strip of paper used to store information using coded holes.

'paper 'tiger *nc* (*derog*) a person, country etc that seems to be, but is not, powerful.

'paper·work *nu* written work (in an office etc, e.g. letters, notes, forms etc, contrasted with practical affairs dealing with people): *He's good at paperwork.*

pa·per² /'peɪpə(r)/ *vt* to put wallpaper on (a wall etc): *paper the dining-room.* **paper over sth** (*fig*) to hide faults etc using a weak disguise.

pap·rika /'pæprɪkə/ *nu* a sweet, red pepper used in cooking.

par /pɑː(r)/ *nu* **1** an average or normal amount, degree, value etc: *above/at/below par.* **on a par with** of the same (high) standard as: *intelligence on a par with Einstein's.* **under par** (*informal*) not as healthy, efficient etc as usual. **2** (*golf*) the number of strokes considered necessary for a player to complete a hole or course.

para. *written abbr* paragraph.

par·able /'pærəbl/ *nc* a simple story used to teach a moral lesson.

par·ab·ola /pə'ræbələ/ *nc* (*pl* **—s**) (*tech*) a flat curve formed by cutting a cone along a line parallel to its side.

para·bol·ic /ˌpærə'bɒlɪk/ *adj*

para·chute¹ /'pærəʃuːt/ *nc* an apparatus used for a jump from a plane or for dropping supplies etc.

para·chute² /'pærəʃuːt/ *vt,vi* (to cause a person, thing) to drop, descend, from a plane using a parachute.

para·chut·ist /-ɪst/ *nc* a person who jumps using a parachute. ⇨ paratroops.

par·ade¹ /pə'reɪd/ *n* **1** *nu* (esp **on parade**) an official gathering of soldiers etc, esp for a cer-emony. **2** *nc,nu* (an instance of) gathering for a viewing ceremony or procession: *a circus parade; a fashion parade.* **3** *nc* a wide area for walking along the seafront.

pa'rade-ground *nc* area on which parades(1) are held.

par·ade² /pə'reɪd/ *v* **1** *vt,vi* (to cause soldiers etc) to gather together for drilling, inspection etc. **2** *vi* to march in procession: *clowns parading in the cir-cus ring.* **3** *vt* to make a display of (people, ani-mals, things); try to attract attention to (something): *parading wild animals; parade one's wealth.*

para·dise /'pærədaɪs/ *n* **1** (P-) (in the Bible) the Garden of Eden, home of Adam and Eve. **2** (P-) Heaven. **3** *n sing* any place of perfect happiness. ⇨ fool's paradise. **4** *nu* the condition of perfect happiness: *Loving you is paradise.*

para·dox /'pærədɒks/ *nc* **1** statement that seems to say something opposite to common sense or the truth but that may be true, e.g. 'More haste, less speed', i.e. if you hurry too much, you may find you take longer. **2** a situation that seems to demonstrate opposite ideas, possibilities etc such as a doctor being a heavy smoker.

para·doxi·cal /ˌpærə'dɒksɪkl/ *adj*

para·doxi·cal·ly /-klɪ/ *adv*

par·af·fin /'pærəfɪn/ *nu* (*GB*) a kind of oil obtained from petroleum, coal etc used as a fuel (*US* = kerosene).

para·gon /'pærəgən/ *nc* (*formal*) a model (of

excellence); apparently perfect person or thing: *a paragon of virtue.*

par·a·graph /'pærəgrɑːf/ *nc* **1** a division (usually a group of several sentences dealing with one main idea) of a piece of writing, started on a new line. **2** a small item of news in a newspaper.

para·keet /'pærəkiːt/ *nc* a kind of small parrot.

par·al·lel[1] /'pærəlel/ *adj* (*no comp*) **1** (of lines) always at the same distance from one another: *in a parallel direction* (*with/to another*). **2** (*fig*) similar: *a parallel job in another company; a job that is parallel to mine.*

,**parallel bars** *n pl* gymnastic equipment using a pair of horizontal bars.

par·al·lel[2] /'pærəlel/ *nc* **1** a parallel line. **2** *in parallel* (*electricity*) (of the parts of a circuit) with the supply of current taken to each part independently. Compare in series(b). **3** a person, event etc that is similar: *a brilliant career without* (*a*) *parallel in modern times.* **4** *draw a parallel* (*between/with sb/sth*) to compare.

par·al·lel[3] /'pærəlel/ *vt* (**-l-** or (*GB*) **-ll-**) **1** to quote, produce or mention (a comparison). **2** to be the same as (another): *His experiences parallel mine in many instances.*

par·al·lelo·gram /,pærə'leləgræm/ *nc* (*maths*) a four-sided plane figure whose opposite sides are parallel.

para·lyse (*US* = **-lyze**) /'pærəlaɪz/ *vt* **1** to affect (a person, animal) with paralysis. **2** (*fig*) to make (a person, animal) helpless: *paralysed with fear.*

par·al·ysis /pə'rælɪsɪs/ *nu* **1** the loss of feeling or power to move in any or every part of the body. **2** (*fig*) a state of total powerlessness.

para·lyt·ic /,pærə'lɪtɪk/ *adj* (**a**) suffering from paralysis(1). (**b**) (*fig*) uncontrollable: *paralytic laughter.* (**c**) (*informal*) very drunk.

pa·ram·eter /pə'ræmɪtə(r)/ *nc* (*tech*) a variable factor in an analysis or experiment.

para·mili·tary /,pærə'mɪlɪtrɪ/ *adj* acting, dressing, organized etc like official military forces.

para·mount /'pærəmaʊnt/ *adj* (*attrib; formal*) **1** supreme, superior in power: *paramount chiefs.* **2** pre-eminent, superior: *of paramount importance.*

para·noia /,pærə'nɔɪə/ *nu* a mental illness marked by fixed delusions, e.g. of persecution.

para·noid /'pærənɔɪd/ *nc, adj* (a person) suffering from paranoia.

para·pet /'pærəpɪt/ *nc* a protective wall at the edge of a flat roof, side of a bridge etc.

para·pher·na·lia /,pærəfə'neɪlɪə/ *nu* numerous small possessions, tools, instruments etc: *a plumber with all his paraphernalia.*

para·phrase /'pærəfreɪz/ *vt, nc* (to produce) a version of a piece of writing or speech in other (fewer or simpler) words.

para·ple·gia /,pærə'pliːdʒə/ *nu* paralysis of the lower part of the body, including both legs, caused by injury to the spinal cord.

para·ple·gic /,pærə'pliːdʒɪk/ *nc, adj* (a person) suffering from paraplegia. Compare quadriplegic.

para·site /'pærəsaɪt/ *nc* **1** an animal or plant living on or in another and getting its food from it. **2** (*fig; derog*) a person supported by another and giving nothing in return.

para·sit·ic /,pærə'sɪtɪk/ *adj*

para·sol /'pærəsɒl/ *nc* an umbrella used to give

shade from the sun.

para·troops /'pærətruːps/ *n pl* soldiers trained for being dropped by parachute.

para·troop·er /'pærətruːpə(r)/ *nc* one of these soldiers.

par·boil /'pɑːbɔɪl/ *vt* to boil (food) a short time until partially cooked.

par·cel[1] /'pɑːsl/ *nc* something or things wrapped and tied up for carrying, sending by post etc. *be part and parcel of sth* ⇨ part[1](1).

par·cel[2] /'pɑːsl/ *vt* (**-ll-**, *US* also **-l-**) **1** *parcel sth* (*up*) to make things into a parcel. **2** *parcel sth out* to divide something into portions and distribute it: *parcelling out food.*

parched /pɑːtʃt/ *adj* **1** hot and dry: *the parched deserts of N Africa.* **2** (*pred*) (*fig*) extremely thirsty: *I'm parched!*

parch·ment /'pɑːtʃmənt/ *n* **1** *nc, nu* (a manuscript on) writing material prepared from the skin of a sheep or goat. **2** *nu* a kind of paper like parchment.

par·don[1] /'pɑːdn/ *n* **1** *nc, nu* (an instance of) forgiveness: *ask for pardon.* **2** *I beg your pardon* (used to show politeness, e.g. when disagreeing with a person, or when not hearing or understanding somebody). *Pardon?* (used as a polite way of saying that one did not hear, understand what a person has said): *'Take the first road to the left, then . . .'—'Pardon, could you repeat that?'* Ⓝ *'Sorry'* is more usual. **3** *nc* an act of freeing a person from legal punishment: *a general pardon* (= one for groups of offenders, not individuals).

par·don·able /-əbl/ *adj* that can be forgiven: *a pardonable offence.*

par·don[2] /'pɑːdn/ *vt* to forgive or excuse (a person): *pardon her for doing wrong.*

pare /peə(r)/ *vt* **1** to cut away the outer part, edge or skin of (something): *pare the claws of an animal.* **2** *pare sth* (*down*) (*fig*) to reduce something little by little: *pare down one's expenses.*

par·ent /'peərənt/ *nc* (also *attrib*) a father or mother: *parent meetings at schools.*

'**par·ent·age** /-ɪdʒ/ *nu* **1** the state of having particular people as parents: *Her parentage is uncertain.* **2** the origin of something.

par·en·tal /pə'rentl/ *adj* (*attrib*) of a parent: *showing parental care.*

'**parent·hood** *nu* the state of being a parent.

par·enth·esis /pə'renθəsɪs/ *nc* (*pl* **-eses** /-əsiːz/) **1** (*gram*) a sentence or phrase within another sentence, marked off by commas, dashes or brackets. **2** (usually *pl*) round brackets ( ) for this: *a comment in parentheses.* ⇨ square brackets.

par·en·thet·ic /,pærən'θetɪk/ (also **par·en·theti·cal** /-ɪkl/) *adj*

par·en·theti·cal·ly /-klɪ/ *adv*

par·ish /'pærɪʃ/ *nc* a division of a county with its own church and clergymen.

par·ish·ion·er /pə'rɪʃənə(r)/ *nc* a member of a parish.

par·ity /'pærətɪ/ *nu* (*formal*) the state of being equal: *The two currencies have now reached parity* (= are equal in value).

park[1] /pɑːk/ *nc* **1** a public garden in a town or city. **2** an area of grassland, trees etc round a large country house or mansion. ⇨ also car park, national park.

park² /pɑːk/ *vi,vt* to place or leave (a vehicle) in a car park etc: *Where can we park (the car)?*

par·ka /'pɑːkə/ *nc* = anorak.

park·ing /'pɑːkɪŋ/ *nu* (an area for) the parking of vehicles: *No parking.*

'parking-meter *nc* a coin-operated meter for parking a vehicle in a public place.

Par·kin·son's dis·ease /'pɑːkɪnsəns dɪziːz/ *nu* a very serious, progressive disease with shaking, muscular rigidity and general weakness.

par·lia·ment /'pɑːləmənt/ *nc* (also P-) a supreme law-making assembly (in GB the House of Commons and the House of Lords): *Members of Parliament.*

par·lia·men·tar·ian /ˌpɑːləmən'teərɪən/ *nc* a person skilled in the rules and procedures of parliament.

par·lia·men·tary /ˌpɑːlə'mentrɪ/ *adj*

par·lour (*US* = **-lor**) /'pɑːlə(r)/ *nc* **1** (*old use*) an ordinary sitting-room for the family in a private house (now called a *sitting-room* or *living-room*). **2** (esp *US*) a shop: *a beauty parlour; an ice-cream parlour.*

par·ochi·al /pə'rəʊkɪəl/ *adj* **1** of a parish. **2** (*fig; derog*) limited, narrow: *a parochial mind/attitude.*

par·ochi·al·ly /-kɪəlɪ/ *adv*

par·ody¹ /'pærədɪ/ *n* (*pl* **-ies**) **1** *nc,nu* (a piece of) writing intended to amuse by imitating the style of writing used by somebody else. **2** *nc* a poor example: *a parody of justice.*

par·ody² /'pærədɪ/ *vt* (*pt,pp* **-ied**) to make a parody of (something).

pa·role¹ /pə'rəʊl/ *nu* a prisoner's solemn promise that he or she will not repeat a crime. **on parole** freed after making such a promise. Compare on probation(2).

pa·role² /pə'rəʊl/ *vt* to free (a prisoner) on parole.

par·ox·ysm /'pærəksɪzəm/ *nc* a sudden attack (of pain, anger, laughter etc).

par·ri·cide /'pærɪsaɪd/ *nc,nu* (*tech*) (a person guilty of) the murder of one's parent.

par·rot /'pærət/ *nc* **1** any of many kinds of bird with a short, hooked bill and (often) brightly coloured feathers, of which some kinds can copy human speech. **2** (*derog*) a person who repeats what others say, often without understanding.

'parrot-fashion *adv* (*informal*) without thinking of the meaning or importance: *learn poetry parrot-fashion.*

par·ry /'pærɪ/ *vt* (*pt,pp* **-ied**) **1** to avoid (a blow). **2** (*fig*) to avoid answering (a question).

parse /pɑːz/ *vt* (*gram*) to describe (a word or sentence) grammatically.

par·si·moni·ous /ˌpɑːsɪ'məʊnɪəs/ *adj* (*formal; derog*) ungenerous; too careful with money.

pars·ley /'pɑːslɪ/ *nu* a kind of plant with small curly leaves, used as a herb.

pars·nip /'pɑːsnɪp/ *nc* a kind of long, white root, cooked as a vegetable.

par·son /'pɑːsn/ *nc* a parish priest.

,parson's 'nose *nc* (*informal*) the tail end of a cooked chicken, duck etc.

'par·son·age /-ɪdʒ/ *nc* a parson's house.

part¹ /pɑːt/ *nc* **1 part (of sth)** (often *sing* without *a, an*) some but not all (of a thing or a number of things); something less than the whole: *We spent (a) part of our holiday in France. Parts of the book are interesting. One part is painted red and the other is green. Which part is bigger?* ⇨ partly. **for the greater part of sth** for most of (a period of time). **for the most part** ⇨ most¹(1). **in part** to some extent or degree: *I agree in part but I'm very worried.* **be part and parcel of sth** to be an essential part of a plan, opinion, discussion etc. **2** (*pl*) region; district: *in these/those parts.* **3** any one of a number of equal divisions: *A minute is the sixtieth part of an hour.* **4** a person's share in some activity, duty or responsibility: *have an important part in a play/in a conference.* **play one's part** to be involved, do what is expected. **take part (in sth)** to have a share (in); be involved (in): *Are you going to take part in the discussion?* **5** a person's side in a dispute, discussion agreement, arrangement etc: *What's your part in the affair?* **for my part** as far as I am concerned: *For my part I am quite happy about the division of the money.* **take sb's part** to support a person: *He always takes his brother's part.* **6 take sth in good part** to show that one is not offended by it. **7** an issue of a work published in sections: *a new encyclopaedia to be issued in monthly parts.* **8** an essential piece or section of a machine etc: *Where can I get a part for my bike?* ⇨ spare part.

,part of 'speech *nc* (*gram*) one of the classes of words, e.g. *noun, verb, adjective.*

,part-'time *adj, adv* for only a part of the working day or week: *be employed part-time; part-time teaching.* Hence **,part-'timer** *nc*

part² /pɑːt/ *v* **1** *vi,vt* (to cause people or things) to separate or divide: *We tried to part the two fighters. Let's part as friends.* **part company (with sb/sth)** ⇨ company(1). **2** *vt* **part with sth** to give away something: *He hates to part with his money.* **3** *vt* to divide (one's hair) by combing it in opposite directions.

part·ing *n* **(a)** *nc* a line where the hair is parted(3). **(b)** *nc,nu* (an act of) leaving a person: *Parting was so painful.* **at the parting of the ways** at the point when one has to choose between courses of action.

par·take /pɑː'teɪk/ *vi* (*pt* **-took** /-'tʊk/, *pp* **-taken** /-'teɪkən/) **partake of sth** (*formal*) to share in something: *They partook of our simple meal.*

par·tial /'pɑːʃl/ *adj* **1** (*no comp*) forming only a part; not complete: *a partial success; a partial eclipse of the sun.* **2** (usually *pred*) showing too much favour to one person or side: *examiners who are partial towards students they like.* Compare impartial. **3** (*pred*) **partial (to sth)** having a liking for it: *partial to French wines* ⇨ partiality (b).

par·ti·al·ity /ˌpɑːʃɪ'ælətɪ/ *n* **(a)** *nu* the condition of being partial(2) in one's treatment of people etc. **(b)** *nc* (*formal*) a liking: *a partiality for chocolate cake.*

par·tial·ly /'pɑːʃəlɪ/ *adv* (esp) partly; not completely: *partially blocked/cooked/deaf/blind.*

par·tici·pant /pɑː'tɪsɪpənt/ *nc* **participant (in sth)** a person who takes part (in an activity).

par·tici·pate /pɑː'tɪsɪpeɪt/ *vi* **participate (in sth)** to have a share, be involved (in something): *participate in a plot.*

par·ti·ciple /'pɑːtɪsɪpl/ *nc* (*gram*) a form of a

verb (*present/past participle*) used to form tenses and as an adjective: '*Hurrying*' and '*hurried*' are the present and past participles of '*hurry*'. Ⓝ '*Past participle*' is marked *pp* in this dictionary. ⇨ hanging/past/present participle.

par·ti·cip·ial /ˌpɑːtɪˈsɪpɪəl/ *adj*
parti'cipial adjective/adverb *nc* (*gram*) a participle used as an adjective/adverb, as in 'Add the *finishing* touches', 'She lay *stretched out* on the beach'.

parti'cipial clause/phrase *nc* (*gram*) one with a participle, used to give more information about a noun, a verb or a whole sentence, e.g. '*Hoping for another chance*, she apologized.' 'He went home, *disappointed by the exam result.*'

par·ti·cle /ˈpɑːtɪkl/ *nc* **1** a very small bit: *particles of dust.* **2** (*gram*) any (usually short) word that is not a verb, subject or object but is a necessary part of a phrase, sentence or verb. ⇨ adverbial particle.

par·ticu·lar /pəˈtɪkjʊlə(r)/ *adj* **1** (*attrib; no comp*) relating to one as distinct from others: *in this particular case.* **2** (*attrib*) special; worth notice; outstanding: *for no particular reason. He took particular trouble to get it right.* **in particular** especially: *I remember the colour in particular.* **3** difficult to please or satisfy: *She's very particular about what she wears.*

par·ticu·lar·ly *adv* to an unusual extent: *He was particularly noticeable.*

par·ticu·lars /pəˈtɪkjʊləz/ *n pl* details: *We need full particulars of the people involved.* **go into particulars** to give full details.

part·ing /ˈpɑːtɪŋ/ ⇨ part².

par·ti·san¹ /ˌpɑːtɪˈzæn/ *adj* showing (too) much preference, devotion, to one side, cause, group etc.

par·ti·san² /ˌpɑːtɪˈzæn/ *nc* **1** a person committed to a political party, group or cause. **2** (*esp*) a member of an armed resistance movement in a country occupied by enemy forces.

par·ti·tion¹ /pɑːˈtɪʃn/ *n* **1** *nu* the division (e.g. of a country) into parts: *the partition of India in 1947.* **2** *nc* something that separates or divides, e.g. a thin wall between rooms.

par·ti·tion² /pɑːˈtɪʃn/ *vt* (usually **partition sth off**) to divide (an area) into sections, e.g. using a partition(2): *partition off a room.*

par·ti·tive /ˈpɑːtɪtɪv/ *nc, adj* (*gram*) (a word) showing part, an amount, of something: '*Some*' and '*any*' are partitives.

part·ly /ˈpɑːtlɪ/ *adv* to some extent: *I partly agree with you. It's partly green in daylight.*

part·ner¹ /ˈpɑːtnə(r)/ *nc* **1** a person who takes a part with another or others in some activity: *partners in crime; business partners.* ⇨ sleeping partner. **2** one of two persons dancing together or playing tennis, cards etc together. **3** a husband or wife.

part·ner² /ˈpɑːtnə(r)/ *vt* **1** to be a partner to (a person): *I'll partner you at tennis.* **2** to bring, put (people) together as partners: *You've been partnered with Kim.*

'part·ner·ship /-ʃɪp/ (a) *nu* the state of being a partner: *enter/go into partnership (with her).* (b) *nc* a business with two or more partners.

par·took /pɑːˈtʊk/ *pt* of partake.

par·tridge /ˈpɑːtrɪdʒ/ *nc,nu* (the meat of) a bird of the same family as the pheasant.

par·ty /ˈpɑːtɪ/ *n* (*pl* **-ies**) **1** *nc* a gathering of people for pleasure: *a dinner/birthday party.* **throw a party** to organize and have one. **2** *nc* a group of people travelling or working together, or on duty together: *a party of tourists.* **3** *nc* (also P-) a group of people united in policy and opinion, in support of a cause, esp in politics: *political parties; the Conservative Party.* **4** *nu* (also *attrib*) a kind of government based on political parties: *party politics. Our best men put public interest before party.* **follow the party line** to speak, vote, in agreement with the established policy of a political party. **5** *nc* a person taking part in a legal agreement or dispute. **6** *nc* **party to sth** a person taking part in and approving of or being aware of what is going on: *be party to a decision.*

'party line *nc* (a) a telephone line shared by two or more people. (b) the agreed policy of a political party.

pass¹ /pɑːs/ *n* **1** *nc* an act of passing. **2** *nc* (also *attrib*) a success in an examination, esp success in satisfying the examiners but without distinction: *get a pass in History; a pass degree.* **3** *nc* a paper, ticket etc giving permission or authority to travel, enter a building, etc: *No admittance without a pass.* **4** *nc* an act of kicking, throwing or hitting the ball to another player in the same team. **5** *nc* a narrow way over or through mountains; such a way viewed as the entrance to a country. **6** **make a pass (at sb)** (*sl*) to make a (possibly unwelcome) friendly or amorous approach.

'pass·key *nc* a key which opens a number of different locks.

'pass·mark *nc* the minimum mark needed to pass an examination.

'pass·word *nc* a secret word or phrase which enables a person to be recognized as a friend and not an enemy.

pass² /pɑːs/ *v* **1** *vt, vi* to move towards and beyond (a place, other people etc); leave (a person, vehicle etc) behind as one goes forward: *Please let me pass. The road was too narrow for cars to pass. The two ships passed each other during the night. Turn right after passing the post office. We passed (each other) on the stairs. I passed your aunt in the street.* **2** *vt, vi* to go through, across or between (something): *The ship passed the channel. No complaints passed her lips.* **3** *vt, vi* to give (something) from one person to another: *Please pass (me) the butter. The news passed from person to person.* **4** *vi* (of time) to go by: *Six months/Winter passed and still we had no news of them.* **come to pass** ⇨ come(5). **5** *vt* to spend (time): *How shall we pass the evening?* **pass the time** ⇨ time¹(2). **6** *vt* to say (something): *pass a remark.* **pass the time of day (with sb)** ⇨ time¹(2). **7** *vt, vi* (to cause a person, piece of policy etc) to be examined and accepted: *The examiners passed most of the candidates. The candidates passed (the examination). Parliament passed the Bill. The Bill passed and became law.* **8** *vt* to give (an opinion, judgement etc): *I can't pass an opinion on your work without seeing it.* ⇨ sentence¹(1). **9** *vi* to be accepted without criticism or blame: *His rude remarks passed without comment. I don't like it, but I'll let it pass.* **10** *vi* to end: *The pain will soon pass.* **11** *vt* (to cause something) to circulate: *He was imprisoned for passing forged banknotes.* **12** *vi* (*card-games*) to let one's turn go by without bidding or playing. **13** *vi* (in football, hockey, etc) to kick, throw, hit, (the ball) to a player of one's own side.

pass along (sth) (*esp imperative*) to move further into a bus, train etc.

pass as sb = pass for sb.

pass away to die: *He passed away peacefully/in his sleep.*

pass between sb to be exchanged by people: *Don't tell anyone about what has passed between us* (i.e. about what we have discussed).

pass by (sb/sth) to go past. ⇨ passer-by. **pass sb by** to fail to affect a person: *The importance of the result seemed to pass him by.* ⇨ also bypass.

pass down = pass along (sth). **pass sth down (to sb)** = hand sth down (to sb).

pass for sb/sth to be accepted as a person, thing: *Do I speak French well enough to pass for a Frenchman?*

pass off (of an event) to take place: *The meeting of the strikers passed off quietly.* **pass sb off as sb** to present a person falsely as another: *I passed her off as my wife.* **pass sth off** to turn public attention from something (to avoid embarrassment): *pass off an awkward situation.*

pass on (of a person) to die. **pass on (to sth)** to move on (to a new topic, activity, stage etc). **pass sth on (to sb)** to hand or give something to a person.

pass out (*informal*) = faint³. **pass out (of sth)** to leave (a military) college etc having passed one's examinations. **pass sth out** to give out exam papers, free offers, gifts etc.

pass over (of a storm, pain, bad experience) to come to an end. **pass sb over** to fail to consider a person for promotion etc: *They passed me over in favour of a younger man.* **pass sth over** to fail to notice or include something: *pass over an important mistake and hope it will not be noticed.*

pass sth round (a) to send a box of chocolates, food etc round a group and offer them. (**b**) to send a container round a group asking for contributions.

pass through (sth) to go through (a town etc) without stopping. **pass through sth (a)** to complete a course at a (military) college: *pass through college.* (**b**) to experience, suffer something: *pass through a difficult period after a divorce.*

pass to sb to go from one person's possession or control to another: *The land/money/power passed to his daughter.*

pass sth up (*informal*) to fail to or decide not to take advantage of an offer etc: *pass up an opportunity.* **pass sth up (to sb)** to give something to a person who is at a higher level.

pass·able /'pɑːsəbl/ *adj* **1** (*pred*) (of roads etc) that can be passed over or crossed: *Are the roads passable yet?* Compare impassable. **2** (usually *attrib*) that can be accepted as fairly good but not excellent: *a passable knowledge of German.*

pass·ably /-əblɪ/ *adv*

pas·sage /'pæsɪdʒ/ *n* **1** *nc* a (narrow) way through: *force a passage through a crowd.* **2** *nc* a long entrance hall in a building: *She has to keep her bicycle in the passage.* **3** *nc* a short extract from a speech or piece of writing. **4** *nc* a journey from one point to another by sea or air: *book one's passage to New York.* **work one's passage** to earn the cost of a passage(4) by working during the journey. **5** *nu* an act of going past, through or across: *right of passage.* **6** *nu* **the passage of time** the period while time passes or passed.

'pas·sage·way *nc* = passage(2).

pas·sen·ger /'pæsɪndʒə(r)/ *nc* **1** a person travelling by bus, taxi, tram, train, ship, plane etc. **2** a member of a team etc who does not work.

pass·er-by /,pɑːsə 'baɪ/ *nc* (*pl* passers-by) a person who walks past a person, place etc in the street.

pass·ing¹ /'pɑːsɪŋ/ *adj* (*attrib*) going by; not lasting: *the passing years.*

pass·ing² /'pɑːsɪŋ/ *nu* the act of going by: *the passing of the old year.*

pas·sion /'pæʃn/ *nc,nu* (a) strong, enthusiastic feeling esp of love, hate or anger.

pas·sion·less *adj*

pas·sion·ate /'pæʃənət/ *adj* filled with, showing, love or anger: *a passionate speech; a passionate man/nature; passionate language.*

pas·sion·ate·ly *adv*

pas·sive /'pæsɪv/ *adj* **1** showing no enthusiasm, interest etc: *In spite of my efforts the boy remained passive.* **2** not willing to fight when attacked or oppressed: *The poor people stayed passive.* **3** (*gram*) in the passive voice.

,passive re'sistance *nu* the expression of disapproval of or opposition to a cruel government or law, using non-violent methods.

'passive (voice) *n* (the —) (*gram*) the verb form (forms of be and a *past participle*) used when the object of the verb is more important than the subject; the verb describes what happens, happened or will happen to a person or thing, e.g. 'Cigarettes *are* not *sold* to children.' 'The car *was driven* by him.' '*Have* you *been told* about the meeting?' 'It's *going to be finished* by Friday.' ⇨ go²(22). Compare active (voice).

pass·ive·ly *adv*

pass·key /'pɑːskiː/ *nc* ⇨ pass¹.

Pass·over /'pɑːsəʊvə(r)/ *n* the Jewish religious festival in memory of the freeing of the Jews from slavery in Egypt.

pass·port /'pɑːspɔːt/ *nc* **1** an official identity document (to be) carried by a person travelling abroad. **2** (*fig*) something that enables one to win or obtain something: *Is flattery a passport to success with that teacher?*

pass·word /'pɑːswɜːd/ *nc* ⇨ pass¹.

past¹ /pɑːst/ *adj* **1** of, concerning, all the time before the present: *past generations; in times past.* **2** of a particular period of time before the present: *during the past week/few minutes.* **3** (before the present time and) no longer existing: *past success/failures/happiness.* **4** (*attrib*) of a person no longer alive or in power: *a past prime minister/chairperson.* **5** (*gram*) of verb tenses used to describe activity, state etc begun or completed before the present time. Ⓝ Be careful not to use *'passed'* for *'past'*. *'Passed'* is the past tense and past participle of *'to pass'*, as in *An hour passed/has passed.* *'Past'* is an adjective, as in *for the past hour*, or an adv/prep, as in *walk past; run past the school; be past caring.*

past con'tinuous tense *nc* (the —) (*gram*) the verb form (*was/were* and a *present participle*) used to describe an action or state that continued during a period of time in the past with the precise limits unknown or unimportant, as in '*I was living* in Berlin in 1980.' 'He *was getting* better', and also to report a person's earlier speech about a present state or activity, as in 'She said she *was staying* at home so she ought to be there.'

past 'participle *nc* (*gram*) a verb form used to form the past and future perfect tenses, to form the passive and sometimes used as an adjective, e.g. *passed, ended, loved, begun, driven, taken.* Ⓝ Irregular forms are marked *pp* in this dictionary.

past 'perfect tense *nc* (the —) (*gram*) the verb form (*had* and a *past participle*) used to describe an action or state that had already happened when mentioning the past or when the conversation took place, as in 'When I got back she *had eaten* all the ice-cream.' 'I'*d fallen asleep* during the film'. 'We warned him that he'*d* not *done* enough work.'

past ,perfect con'tinuous tense *nc* (the —) (*gram*) the verb form (*had been* and a *present participle*) used to describe longer actions or states which continued up to the point in the past mentioned, as in 'When I got back *she had been writing* a letter.' 'We'*d been considering* a move to Manchester until this happened.'

past pro'gressive tense *nc* = past continuous tense.

'past tense *nc* (the —) (also called the **past simple tense**) (*gram*) the verb form (*past tense* without an *auxiliary verb*) used to describe actions or events completed in the past (esp at a time mentioned), actions that occupied a period in the past, a person's past habits, and in *if*-clauses, as in 'I *went* home yesterday.' 'She *worked* in India from 1982–84.' 'We always *telephoned* each other'. 'If she *owned* a car, she'd sell her motorbike.' Ⓝ The negative is formed by using '*did not*' and the infinitive without '*to*', as in 'I *didn't go* home yesterday.' '*Didn't* she *work* in Japan?' Irregular past tense forms (e.g. *began, drove, took*) are marked *pt* in this dictionary. The past simple tense is used with adverbs describing 'how often', e.g. *never, rarely, sometimes, often, frequently, usually, always.* Avoid using a continuous tense with these adverbs.

past² /pɑːst/ *adv* **1** up to and beyond: *go/walk/run past.* **2** ago (which is more usual): *for at least a month past.*

past³ /pɑːst/ *n* **1** (the —) all the time before the present: *We cannot relive the past. In the past people lived in smaller groups. Let's forget the past and start again.* **2** a person's, country's, organization's etc history or experience: *We know nothing of his past.* **3** (*gram*) a past tense.

past⁴ /pɑːst/ *prep* **1** beyond in time: *It's past 6 o'clock/noon. She's past middle age.* **2** (used when telling the time) after the hour mentioned: *Its five (minutes) past nine. It starts at a quarter past two.* ⇨ to³(5). Ⓝ We never use '*past*' and '*o'clock*' in the same sentence. **3** beyond in space or position: *He walked past the house. The chemist is past the post office.* Ⓝ Be careful not to use '*passed*' for '*past*'. '*Passed*' is the past tense and past participle of '*to pass*', as in *We passed the garage.* **4** beyond the limits, power or range of: *The pain is past*

bearing. The old man is past work (e.g. too old). **be past caring** ⇨ care²(1). **be past it** (*informal*) to be no longer able to do things as when younger. **would not put it past sb (to do sth)** to consider a person capable of doing something bad, daring, unusual: *I wouldn't put it past her to take the chocolates.*

pas·ta /'pæstə/ *nu* (*It*) (food made using) a mixture of flour, eggs and water, e.g. *macaroni, spaghetti.*

paste¹ /peɪst/ *nu* **1** a soft mixture used for sticking things together, e.g. paper on walls. **2** a preparation of fish, meat etc made into a soft, moist mass: *fish paste.*

paste² /peɪst/ *vt* **paste sth (on/together/up)** to stick something using paste(1): *pasting up a poster; paste wallpaper to a wall.*

pas·tel /'pæstl/ *nc* **1** (a picture drawn with) coloured crayons. **2** (also *attrib*) a soft, light shade of colour: *pastel blue.*

pas·teur·ized (also **-ised**) /'pæstʃəraɪzd/ (of milk, cream) with bacteria that produce disease killed by heating.

pas·tiche /pæˈstiːʃ/ *nc* (*Fr*) (*literature, art*) a literary work or work of art using different styles or one in the style of another.

pas·tille /'pæstl/ *nc* a small flavoured tablet to be sucked, e.g. one containing medicine for the throat.

pas·time /'pɑːstaɪm/ *nc* anything done to pass time pleasantly: *Reading is his favourite pastime.*

pas·tor /'pɑːstə(r)/ *nc* a Christian minister(2), esp of a Nonconformist church.

pas·tor·al¹ /'pɑːstərəl/ *adj* **1** (*literature*) of, concerning, shepherds and country life: *pastoral poetry.* **2** (esp) of a bishop: *a pastoral letter.* **3** of (duties towards) the welfare of people: *pastoral care/ responsibilities.*

pas·tor·al² /'pɑːstərəl/ *nc* (*literature*) a pastoral poem.

pas·try /'peɪstrɪ/ *n* (*pl* **-ies**) **1** *nu* a mixture of flour, fat etc baked in an oven. **2** *nc* a kind of food made using this, e.g. a pie or tart.

pas·ture /'pɑːstʃə(r)/ *nc,nu* (an area of) grassland for cattle. ⇨ meadow.

pas·ty¹ /'peɪstɪ/ *adj* (**-ier, -iest**) white (and unhealthy): *a pasty complexion.*

pas·ty² /'pæstɪ/ *nc* (*pl* **-ies**) a pastry(2) containing meat, potatoes etc and baked without a dish: *a Cornish pasty.*

pat¹ /pæt/ *nc* **1** a tap with the open hand. **2** a small mass of something, e.g. butter, formed by patting. **3** a light sound made by hitting something with a flat object.

pat² /pæt/ *vt* (**-tt-**) to tap (a person, animal, thing) gently with the open hand or with something flat: *pat a dog.* **pat sb/oneself on the back** (*fig*) to show approval of, congratulate, a person, oneself.

patch¹ /pætʃ/ *nc* **1** a small piece of material put over a hole or a damaged or worn place: *a coat with patches on the elbows; a patch on the inner tube of a tyre.* **2** a piece of plaster put over a cut or wound. **3** a pad worn to protect an injured eye. **4** a small, irregular, differently coloured part of a surface: *a dog with a white patch on its neck.* **5** a small area: *a patch of ground; patches of fog.* **not a patch on** not nearly as good as. **a bad patch**

a period of bad luck, difficulty, unhappiness etc:
go through a bad patch.

patch² /pætʃ/ *vt* to put a patch(1) on (something).
patch sb/sth up to put a patch(1,2) on an
injured person, a cut, tear, injury etc. **patch up
a quarrel (with sb)** to agree and end it.

patchy *adj* (**-ier**, **-iest**) **1** made up of patches(5):
patchy fog. **2** uneven in quality: *patchy work*.

patch·work /'pætʃwɜːk/ *nu* (also *attrib*)
material made up of pieces of cloth of various
sizes, shapes and colours: *a patchwork quilt*.

pâté /'pæteɪ/ *nu* a cooked mixture of (esp) liver,
chicken and flavouring in a smooth paste.

pa·tel·la /pə'telə/ *nc* (*anat*) = kneecap.

pat·ent¹ /'peɪtənt/ *adj* **1** **be patent (to sb)**
(that . . .) to be evident, easily seen: *It was
patent to everyone that he disliked the idea*. **2**
(*attrib*) protected by a patent(1): *patent medicines*
(i.e. allowed to be made by one firm or person
only).

,**patent 'leather** *nu* a kind of leather with a
shiny surface.

pa·tent·ly *adv* clearly; obviously: *Patently, he
had been lying to us*.

pat·ent² /'peɪtənt/ *nc* **1** a government authority
giving exclusive right to make or sell a new invention. **2** something protected by a patent.

pat·ent³ /'peɪtənt/ *vt* to obtain a patent for (an
invention or process).

pa·ter·nal /pə'tɜːnəl/ *adj* **1** of, like, a father:
paternal care. **2** (*attrib*) related through the
father: *my paternal grandfather*. Compare maternal.

pa·ter·nal·ism /-ɪzəm/ *nu* (the practice of)
governing a country, controlling a business etc by
making decisions, policies etc considered to be
good but without giving the right to choose.

pa·ter·nal·ly /-nəlɪ/ *adv*

pa·ter·ni·ty /pə'tɜːnətɪ/ *nu* being a father; origin
on the father's side: *paternity unknown*.

path /pɑːθ/ *nc* (*pl* —**s** /pɑːðz/) **1** a way made
(across fields, through woods etc) by people walking: *Keep to the path or you may lose your way*. ⇨
footpath. **2** a line along which a person or thing
moves: *the flight path of a plane*.

'**path·way** *nc* = path(1).

pa·thet·ic /pə'θetɪk/ *adj* **1** sad; causing pity: *a
pathetic sight; pathetic ignorance*. ⇨ pathos. **2**
weak and useless: *a pathetic excuse/attempt*.

pa·theti·cal·ly /-klɪ/ *adv*

patho·logi·cal /ˌpæθə'lɒdʒɪkl/ *adj* **1** (*tech*) of
the nature of disease. **2** (*informal*) caused by an
uncontrolled desire: *a pathological liar*.

patho·logi·cal·ly /-klɪ/ *adv*

path·ol·ogist /pə'θɒlədʒɪst/ *nc* a student of,
expert in, pathology.

pa·thol·ogy /pə'θɒlədʒɪ/ *nu* the scientific study
of the causes, types etc of diseases.

pa·thos /'peɪθɒs/ *nu* (*literature*) the quality which
produces a feeling of pity, sympathy or tenderness. ⇨ pathetic(1).

pa·tience /'peɪʃns/ *nu* **1** (an ability for) suffering
trouble, inconvenience etc without complaining:
*She has no patience with people who are always
grumbling*. **2** the willingness to wait for results, to
deal with problems, calmly and slowly. Opp
impatience.

pa·tient¹ /'peɪʃnt/ *adj* having, showing,

patience: *a patient listener; be patient with a child*.
Compare impatient.

pa·tient·ly *adv*

pa·tient² /'peɪʃnt/ *nc* a person who has received
or is receiving medical treatment.

pat·io /'pætɪəʊ/ *nc* (*pl* —**s**) a paved area near a
house, used for eating outside etc.

pa·tis·serie /pə'tiːsərɪ/ *nc* (*Fr*) a shop specializing in pastry and cakes.

pa·tri·arch /'peɪtrɪɑːk/ *nc* **1** a respected old
man. **2** a male head of a family or tribe. Compare
matriarch. **3** a high-ranking bishop.

pa·tri·arch·al /ˌpeɪtrɪ'ɑːkl/ *adj*

pat·ri·cide /'pætrɪsaɪd/ *nc,nu* (*tech*) (an instance
of) killing one's father. ⇨ matricide.

pa·tri·ot /'pætrɪət/ *nc* a person who loves and is
ready to defend her or his country.

pa·tri·ot·ic /ˌpætrɪ'ɒtɪk/ *adj* having or showing
patriotism. Opp unpatriotic.

pa·tri·oti·cal·ly /-klɪ/ *adv*

pa·triot·ism /-ɪzəm/ *nu* the feelings and qualities of a patriot.

pa·trol¹ /pə'trəʊl/ *n* **1** *nu* (also *attrib*) (esp **on
patrol**) the act of patrolling: *soldiers on patrol; a
police patrol car* (e.g. on a motorway). **2** *nc* a person, group, ship or aircraft that is on patrol.

pa·trol² /pə'trəʊl/ *vt,vi* (**-ll-**) to go round (a place)
to see that all is well, to look out for people doing
wrong, in need of help etc.

pat·ron /'peɪtrən/ *nc* **1** a person who gives
encouragement, moral or financial support, to a
person, cause, the arts etc: *Modern artists have
difficulty in finding wealthy patrons*. **2** a regular
customer at a shop.

,**patron 'saint** *nc* a saint regarded as the special
protector (of a place, travellers etc).

pat·ron·age /'pætrənɪdʒ/ *nu* (*formal*) **1** the support given by a patron(1): *with/under the patronage of the Duke of Cornwall*. **2** the right to
appoint a person to a high position, office, to
grant privileges etc: *He's an influential man, with
a great deal of patronage in his hands*. **3** a customer's support (to a shopkeeper etc): *I took
away my patronage because of poor service and
high prices*. **4** the act of treating a person as if one
is more important or superior. ⇨ patronize(1).

pat·ron·ize (also **-ise**) /'pætrənaɪz/ *vt* **1** to treat
(a person) in a pleasant and helpful way but really
wanting to show one is more important or superior. **2** to act as patron(1) towards (a person): *pat-
ronize a young musician/the corner shop*.

pat·ron·iz·ing (also **-is·ing**) *adj* (*derog*) pretending to be friendly or helpful but really feeling
more important, better etc.

pat·ron·iz·ing·ly (also **-is·ing·ly**) *adv*

pat·ter¹ /'pætə(r)/ *nu* fast talk, e.g. of a person
trying to sell something.

pat·ter² /'pætə(r)/ *nu* the sound of quick, light
taps or footsteps: *the patter of rain on a roof; the
patter of tiny feet*. ⇨ pitter-patter.

pat·ter³ /'pætə(r)/ *vi* to make quick, light tapping
sounds.

pat·tern¹ /'pætən/ *nc* **1** a regular design repeated
on cloth, wallpaper, carpets etc. **2** the shape of
something used as a guide: *a dress pattern*. **3** a
way in which something happens, develops, is
arranged etc: *new patterns of family life. It follows
the usual pattern* (= the expected behaviour,

result, procedure etc).

pat·tern² /'pætən/ *vt* (*formal*) **1** *pattern oneself on sb* to use another person as a model for oneself: *He patterns himself on his father.* **2** to decorate (something) with a pattern(1).

pau·city /'pɔːsətɪ/ *nu* *paucity of sth* (*formal*) a very small amount or number of something: *There is a paucity of good restaurants here.*

paunch /pɔːntʃ/ *nc* a (large) belly: *He's getting quite a paunch.*

pau·per /'pɔːpə(r)/ *nc* a very poor person.

pause¹ /pɔːz/ *nc* a short interval or stop (while doing or saying something): *during a pause in the conversation.*

pause² /pɔːz/ *vi* to stop for a short time: *pause to look round.*

pave /peɪv/ *vt* to put flat stones, bricks etc on (a path etc): *a path paved with brick.* **pave the way for sth** ⇨ way(1).

pave·ment /'peɪvmənt/ *nc* an area at the side of a street for people to walk on (*US = sidewalk*).

pav·ing /'peɪvɪŋ/ *nu* (material for) a paved area: *brick/stone paving.*

pa·vil·ion /pə'vɪlɪən/ *nc* **1** a building on a sports ground for the use of players, spectators etc. **2** an ornamental building for concerts, dancing etc. **3** a large tent as used for an exhibition.

paw¹ /pɔː/ *nc* any animal's foot that has claws or nails.

paw² /pɔː/ *vt* **1** (of animals) to feel or scratch (something) with the paw(s). **2** (of a person) to touch (a person) with the hands, awkwardly, rudely or with improper familiarity: *No girl likes being pawed (about) by men.*

pawn¹ /pɔːn/ *nc* **1** (*chess*) the least valuable piece. **2** (*fig; derog*) a person made use of by others for their own advantage.

pawn² /pɔːn/ *vt* to deposit (clothing, jewellery etc) as security for money borrowed: *The medical student pawned his microscope to pay his rent.* □ *nu* (usually *in pawn*) the state of being pawned: *My watch is in pawn.*

'pawn·broker *nc* a person licensed to lend money at interest on pawned goods.

'pawn·shop *nc* a pawnbroker's place of business.

paw·paw /'pɔːpɔː/ *nc* = papaw.

pay¹ /peɪ/ *nu* the money paid for regular work or services: *get an increase in pay.* **be in the pay of sb** to be employed by a person (often with a suggestion of dishonour): *in the pay of the enemy.*

'pay·day *nc* the day on which wages, salaries etc are (to be) paid: *Friday is pay-day!*

'pay·load *nc* (**a**) that part of the load (of a ship, plane etc) for which payment is received, e.g. passengers and cargo, but not fuel. (**b**) a warhead of a missile.

'pay·off *nc* (*informal*) a (time of) full and final settlement of accounts or of revenge.

'pay·packet *nc* a packet containing pay.

'pay phone *nc* a coin-operated telephone.

'pay·roll/·sheet *nc* (**a**) a list of people to be paid and the amounts due to each. (**b**) the total amount of wages, salaries etc to be paid.

'pay·slip *nc* a piece of paper showing how pay has been calculated.

pay² /peɪ/ *v* (*pt,pp* **paid** /peɪd/) **1** *vt,vi* to give (a person) money for goods, services etc: *You must*

pay me what you owe. I'm paid by the hour/paid £8 an hour. How much will you pay for the work? I paid you the money last week. He paid £600 for that car. Let me pay.* **2** *vi* to be useful, give a person an advantage, reward etc: *Crime doesn't pay.* **3** *vt,vi* to settle (debts etc): *Have you paid all your taxes?* **put paid to sth** (*informal*) to stop something planned from happening: *The storm put paid to our plans to go for a walk.* **4** *vt* to give (attention, respect etc) to (a person etc): *Please pay more attention to your work. He seldom pays his wife any compliments.* **pay one's way** ⇨ way²(1). **pay through the nose** ⇨ nose¹(1).

pay a call/visit to make a short visit: *pay a visit to the dentist.*

pay sb back (for sth) (**a**) to return to a person money owed. (**b**) to have one's revenge (for something): *I've paid him back for the trick he played on me.* **pay sth back** to return money etc that has been borrowed.

pay for sth (**a**) to give money owed for something: *pay for the use of the room.* (**b**) to suffer pain or punishment for doing wrong, a mistake, failure etc: *He'll be made to pay for his stupidity.*

pay into sth to put money into a bank, savings etc account: *Please pay this sum into my/my wife's account.*

pay off (*informal*) to succeed: *The idea/gamble paid off and she gained £100.* **pay sb off** to give a person her or his wages and dismiss her or him. **pay sth off** to pay money owed in full: *pay off one's debts.*

pay sth out (**a**) to give money, e.g. in settlement of debts, expenses: *paying out (money) on rent.* (**b**) to allow rope etc to move freely through one's hands and get longer.

pay up (*informal*) to pay in full what is owing: *If you don't pay up, I'll take legal action.*

pay·able /'peɪəbl/ *adj* (*pred*) which must or may be paid: *The cheque/money is payable to my mother.*

PAYE /ˌpiː eɪ waɪ 'iː/ *abbr* Pay As You Earn (a method of paying income tax).

pay·ee /peɪ'iː/ *nc* a person to whom something is (to be) paid.

pay·er /'peɪə(r)/ *nc* person who pays or is to pay.

pay·ment /'peɪmənt/ *n* **1** *nu* the act of paying or being paid: *demand immediate payment; send a cheque in payment for services given.* **2** *nc* a sum of money (to be) paid: *ten monthly payments of £5.* **a down payment** a deposit. **3** *nc,nu* (*fig*) a reward or punishment: *You deserve payment for a good/bad job.*

p.c. *written abbr* postcard.

PC /piː 'siː/ *abbr* **1** Police Constable. **2** personal computer.

pd *written abbr* (*commerce*) paid.

PDSA /ˌpiː diː es 'eɪ/ *abbr* (the —) the People's Dispensary for Sick Animals (the charitable GB organization that takes care of animals that are sick or not cared for).

PE /ˌpiː 'iː/ *abbr* physical education (esp sports at school).

pea /piː/ *nc* (a round, green seed of) a plant with seeds inside a long green case, used as food.

ˌpea·'green *adj, nu* light-green (colour).

peace /piːs/ *nu* **1** (also *attrib*) the condition of being free from war: *be at peace with neighbour-*

ing countries; work for international peace; a peace march. **2** the condition of freedom from quarrelling or fighting among people. *a breach of the peace* ⇨ breach¹(1). *disturb the peace* to cause disorder in the community. *keep the peace* to obey the law. *make one's peace (with sb)* to settle a quarrel. ⇨ also Justice of the Peace. **3** rest; quiet; calm: *the peace of the countryside. in peace* peacefully: *live in peace with one's neighbours. peace and quiet* freedom from noisy interference: *I need peace and quiet while I read. peace of mind* a calm and contented mental state.

'**peace·maker** *nc* a person who restores friendly and cooperative relations.

'**peace-offering** *nc* something used or done to show that one is willing to end a quarrel.

peace·ful /'pi:sfəl/ *adj* **1** preferring or enjoying, peace(1,2): *peaceful nations/communities.* **2** calm; quiet: *a peaceful evening.*
peace·ful·ly /-fəlɪ/ *adv*
peace·ful·ness *nu*

peach /pi:tʃ/ *nc* **1** (a tree with) a round, juicy fruit with yellow or red skin and a large, rough seed. **2** (*sl*) a very attractive person or thing: *Isn't she/it a peach!*

pea·cock /'pi:kɒk/ *nc* a kind of large male bird noted for its long tail feathers.
,**peacock-'blue** *adj, nu* bright blue (colour).
pea·hen /'pi:hen/ *nc* the female of the peacock.

peak /pi:k/ *nc* **1** a (pointed) top of a mountain. **2** a front part of a hat, used to shade the eyes. **3** (also *attrib*) a highest point in a record of figures: *when traffic is at its peak; peak hours of traffic* (= times when the traffic is heaviest). ⇨ off-peak.
peak·ed *adj* having a peak: *a peaked cap.*

peal¹ /pi:l/ *nc* **1** a loud ringing of a bell or of a set of bells with different notes. **2** a loud echoing noise: *a peal of thunder; peals of laughter.*

peal² /pi:l/ *vi, vt* (to cause a bell) to ring or sound loudly: *The bells pealed.* Compare toll².

pea·nut /'pi:nʌt/ *n* **1** *nc* a kind of nut growing underground in pairs in a thin shell. **2** (*pl*) (*sl*) a small amount of money: *I earn peanuts.*
,**peanut 'butter** *nu* (also *attrib*) a paste of roasted ground peanuts: *peanut butter sauce.*

pear /peə(r)/ *nc* (also *attrib*) (a tree with) a sweet, juicy fruit, like an apple but narrower towards the stalk: *pear juice.*

pearl /pɜ:l/ *nc* **1** (also *attrib*) a silvery-white or bluish-white round deposit found inside the shells of some oysters, valued as a gem: *a necklace of pearls; a pearl necklace.* **2** something that looks like a pearl, e.g. a dew drop. **3** (*fig*) a very precious person or thing: *pearls of wisdom. She's a pearl among women.*

peas·ant /'peznt/ *nc* a person working on the land, either for wages or on a very small farm which he or she either rents or owns. Ⓝ *'Peasant'* is now used only of people in poor countries.
peas·ant·ry /'pezntrɪ/ *nu* (the —) the peasants of a country.

peat /pi:t/ *nu* partly decayed plant material, used as a fuel and fertilizer.
peaty *adj* of, like, smelling of, peat.

pebble /'pebl/ *nc* a small stone made smooth and round by water.
peb·bly /'pebəlɪ/ *adj* having pebbles: *a pebbly*

beach.

peck¹ /pek/ *nc* **1** a quick hit or tap with the beak. **2** (*informal*) a quick kiss: *a peck on the cheek.*

peck² /pek/ *v* **1** *vt, vi* **peck (at) (sth)** (to try) to get, make, hit, (something) with the beak: *hens pecking at the corn/each other; pecking a hole in the sack.* **2** *vi* **peck (at sth)** (*informal*) (of a person) to eat only small amounts (of food): *peck at one's food.* **3** *vt* (*informal*) to kiss (a person) quickly.

peck·ish /'pekɪʃ/ *adj* (*pred; informal*) a little hungry: *I'm feeling peckish.*

pec·toral /'pektərəl/ *adj* (*science*) of, for, the chest or breast: *a pectoral muscle/fin.*

pe·cu·li·ar /pɪ'kju:lɪə(r)/ *adj* **1** (*pred*) **peculiar to sb/sth** owned, used, adopted, practised, only by a particular person, country etc: *customs peculiar to these islands.* **2** strange; unusual; odd: *I can smell something peculiar in the bathroom.*
pe·cu·li·ar·ly *adv* in a strange or special way: *behaving peculiarly.*
pe·cu·li·ar·ity /pɪ,kju:lɪ'ærətɪ/ *n* (*pl* **-ies**) (*formal*) **1** *nu* the quality of being peculiar. **2** *nc* a characteristic: *What are an elephant's peculiarities?* **3** *nc* something odd or strange: *a peculiarity in her way of speaking.*

pe·cu·ni·ary /pɪ'kju:nɪərɪ/ *adj* (*formal*) of money: *pecuniary reward.*

peda·gog·ic /,pedə'gɒdʒɪk/ (also **peda·gogi·cal** /-ɪkl/) *adj* (*tech*) educational (which is more usual).

peda·gogue (*US* also **-gog**) /'pedəgɒg/ *nc* (usually *derog*) a dogmatic teacher.

ped·al¹ /'pedl/ *nc* a lever on a bicycle, sewing-machine etc worked by the foot or feet.

ped·al² /'pedl/ *vi, vt* (**-ll-**, *US* also **-l-**) to use, work (something) by using, a pedal or pedals: *pedalling (a bicycle) uphill.*

ped·ant /'pedənt/ *nc* (*derog*) a person who pays too much attention to unimportant rules, e.g. in language.
pe·dan·tic /pɪ'dæntɪk/ *adj*
pe·dan·ti·cal·ly /-klɪ/ *adv*
ped·ant·ry /'pedəntrɪ/ *nc, nu*

peddle /'pedl/ *vt* **1** to go from place to place trying to sell (things): *peddling drugs.* ⇨ pedlar. **2** (*fig*) to give (something) out in small quantities: *She loves to peddle gossip round the village.*

ped·es·tal /'pedɪstl/ *nc* a base of a pillar, statue etc. *put/set sb on a pedestal* to treat a person as very important or special.

pe·des·tri·an¹ /pɪ'destrɪən/ *adj* **1** connected with walking: *a pedestrian area for shopping.* **2** (*derog*) (of writing, a person's way of making speeches etc) uninteresting, unexciting, ordinary.

pe·des·tri·an² /pɪ'destrɪən/ *nc* a person walking in a street etc: *Too many pedestrians are killed in traffic accidents.*
pe,destrian 'crossing *nc* a place marked on a road where pedestrians may walk across.

pe·di·at·rics /,pi:dɪ'ætrɪks/ = paediatrics.

pedi·cure /'pedɪkjʊə(r)/ *nc* a treatment of the feet, toe-nails etc.

pedi·gree¹ /'pedɪgri:/ *adj* (*attrib*) holding a good pedigree: *pedigree cattle/dogs.*

pedi·gree² /'pedɪgri:/ *nc, nu* a line of ancestors: *a poor/fine pedigree.*

ped·lar /'pedlə(r)/ *nc* a person who goes from

house to house selling small articles.

pee /piː/ *nc, nu (sl)* (an act of passing) urine: *I need to have a pee.* □ *vi (sl)* to pass urine.

peek¹ /piːk/ *nc* a quick look: *have a peek at the answers before doing the exercises.*

peek² /piːk/ *vi* to take a quick look: *peek through a crack.*

peel¹ /piːl/ *nu* the skin of oranges, apples, bananas, potatoes etc.

peel² /piːl/ *v* **1** *vt* to take the skin off (fruit or vegetables): *peel a banana; peel potatoes.* **2** *vi* to come off in strips or flakes: *The wallpaper is peeling (off). After a day in the hot sun my skin began to peel/my face peeled.*

peel·er *nc* a device used for peeling fruit and vegetables: *a potato peeler.*

peep¹ /piːp/ *nc* a short, quick look, often secret or cautious: *have a peep at her through the keyhole.*

peep² /piːp/ *nc* a weak, high sound made by a mouse, whistle etc. □ *vi* to make this sound.

peep³ /piːp/ *vi* to take a peep: *neighbours peeping from behind the curtains.*

Peeping 'Tom *nc* a man who enjoys secretly watching a woman undress.

peer¹ /pɪə(r)/ *nc* **1** a person who is equal in age, rank etc: *It is best if she plays with her peers, not much older girls. It will not be very easy to find his intellectual peer.* **2** (in GB) a member of one of the nobility, e.g. a duke, marquis, earl, viscount or baron.

'peer group *nc* a group of people of the same age.

'peer of the 'realm *nc* a peer(2). ⇨ peerage.

peer·ess /'pɪərɪs/ *nc* **(a)** a woman peer(2). **(b)** a wife of a peer(2).

peer² /pɪə(r)/ *vi* to look closely as if unable to see well: *peer at the small writing; peer into dark corners; peering over his spectacles.*

peer·age /'pɪərɪdʒ/ *nc,nu* the whole group or ranks of peers(2).

peg¹ /peg/ *nc* **1** a wooden or metal pin or bolt, used to fasten parts of woodwork together. *a square peg in a round hole* (fig) a person unsuited to a particular kind of work. **2** a short piece of metal etc used to fasten things: *a clothes peg; a tent peg.* **(buy sth) off the peg** (informal) (to buy clothes) ready-made. **3** a wooden screw used for tightening or loosening the strings of a violin, guitar etc. **take sb down a peg (or two)** to make a person feel less important.

peg² /peg/ *vt* (**-gg-**) **1** to fasten (something) with pegs: *peg a tent (down).* **2** to mark (an area), e.g. by using pegs fixed in the ground. **3** (commerce) to keep (prices, wages etc) unchanged: *pegging prices for six months.*

peg away (at sth) (informal) to keep on working to complete (a target, piece of work, investigation etc) successfully.

peg sb down (fig) to force a person to keep to a decision, agreement, set of rules etc. **peg sth down** ⇨ peg²(1).

peg out (sl) to die. **peg sth out** to fix washing, clothes etc on a clothes-line using pegs.

pe·jor·at·ive /prɪˈdʒɒrətɪv/ *adj* (formal) having or giving an idea of a person, thing etc being unimportant, bad or valueless: *pejorative remarks.*

pe·jor·at·ive·ly *adv*

pe·kin·ese /ˌpiːkɪˈniːz/ *nc* a kind of small dog with long, silky hair.

peli·can /'pelɪkən/ *nc* a kind of large waterbird with a long bill that has a bag underneath for storing food.

pel·let /'pelɪt/ *nc* **1** a small ball of something soft, made by rolling it between the fingers: *a paper pellet.* **2** a type of small metal ball, used for a gun.

pel·met /'pelmɪt/ *nc* an ornamental strip above a window or door, used to hide a curtain rod.

pelt¹ /pelt/ *nc* an animal's skin with the fur or hair on it.

pelt² /pelt/ *n* **at full pelt** (running) as fast as possible.

pelt³ /pelt/ *v* **1** *vt* **pelt sb/sth (with sth)** to attack a person etc by throwing things at her, him or it: *pelt them with stones/snowballs/mud.* **2** *vi* **pelt (down) (with sth)** (of rain, etc) to fall heavily: *It was pelting (down) with rain. The rain was pelting down.*

pel·vic /'pelvɪk/ *adj* of the pelvis.

pel·vis /'pelvɪs/ *nc* (anat) the bony frame with the hip-bones and the lower part of the backbone, holding the kidneys, colon, bladder etc.

pen¹ /pen/ *nc* an instrument used for writing with ink. ⇨ ball-point (pen), felt-tip(ped) (pen), fountain pen. **put pen to paper** to begin to write.

pen-and-'ink *adj* (attrib) drawn using a pen and ink: *a pen-and-ink sketch.*

pen² /pen/ *nc* **1** a small enclosure for cattle, sheep, poultry etc. **2** = play-pen.

pen³ /pen/ *vt* (**-nn-**) (formal) to write (one's name, a letter etc).

pe·nal /'piːnl/ *adj* (usually attrib; legal) connected with punishment: *penal laws; a penal offence (= one for which there is legal punishment).*

penal 'servitude *nu* (formal) imprisonment with hard labour.

pe·nal·ize (also **-ise**) /'piːnəlaɪz/ *vt* **1** **penalize sb (for sth)** to punish a person, make a person suffer a disadvantage, (because of a wrong act, failure and often unfairly): *be penalized for not having the correct equipment.* **2** to give a penalty(4) to (a player, competitor etc).

pen·al·ty /'penltɪ/ *n* (pl **-ies**) **1** *nu* punishment for doing wrong, for failure to obey rules or to keep an agreement: *The penalty is two years' imprisonment.* **2** *nc* something given (imprisonment, a fine etc) as punishment: *the expense of several parking penalties.* **3** *nu* (fig) a disadvantage, suffering, caused by a person to herself or himself or others: *The penalty for not working will be failing the exams.* **4** *nc* (in sport) a disadvantage forced on a player or team for breaking a rule: *The referee awarded a penalty.*

'penalty area *nc* (football) the area in front of the goal where a free kick at goal is given.

'penalty kick *nc* (football) a free kick at goal.

'penalty spot *nc* (football) the mark in the penalty area where a penalty kick is taken.

pen·ance /'penəns/ *nu* (formal) punishment which one imposes on oneself to show one is sorry.

pence /pens/ *n pl* of penny.

pen·cil¹ /'pensl/ *nc* an instrument for drawing or writing, esp a wooden one containing lead or coloured wax.

pen·cil² /'pensl/ *vt* (**-ll-**, *US* also **-l-**) to write, draw, mark, (something) using a pencil: *pencilled sketches/eyebrows*. **pencil sth in** use a pencil to draw or write something: *pencil in a design*.

pen·dant /'pendənt/ *nc* an ornament attached to a necklace etc.

pend·ing¹ /'pendıŋ/ *adj* (*pred*) waiting to be decided or settled: *The lawsuit was still pending*.

pend·ing² /'pendıŋ/ *prep* until: *No money will be given pending his acceptance of the offer*.

pen·du·lous /'pendʒʊləs/ *adj* (*formal*) hanging down and swinging freely: *pendulous branches filled with fruit*.

pen·du·lum /'pendjʊləm/ *nc* (*pl* **-s**) a weight hung so that it swings freely, esp to regulate the movement of a clock.

pen·etrable /'penıtrəbl/ *adj* (*formal*) that can be penetrated. Opp **impenetrable**.

pen·etrate /'penıtreıt/ *v* **1** *vt* to make or force a way into or through (something): *The cat's sharp claws penetrated my skin. The smell penetrated the room*. **2** *vt* (fig) to go into or through (something): *Our eyes could not penetrate the darkness. A scream penetrated the silence*. **3** *vi, vt* (*informal*) to be understood; understand: *The real importance of her warning didn't penetrate at first. Did it penetrate that she was serious?*

pen·etrat·ing *adj* (**a**) (of a person, mind) able to see and understand quickly and well. (**b**) (of sound) loud and clear: *penetrating screams*.

pen·etrat·ing·ly *adv*

pen·etra·tion /,penı'treıʃn/ *nu* **1** the act of penetrating. **2** the ability to understand quickly and well.

pen-friend /'pen frend/ *nc* a person (esp in another country) who one has a friendship with by exchanging letters.

pen·guin /'peŋgwın/ *nc* a black and white seabird of the Antarctic with small wings like flippers used for swimming.

peni·cil·lin /,penı'sılın/ *nu* an antibiotic drug that kills bacteria.

pen·in·su·la /pə'nınsjʊlə/ *nc* (*pl* **-s**) a long piece of land, e.g. Italy, almost surrounded by water.

pen·in·su·lar /-lə(r)/ *adj*

pe·nis /'piːnıs/ *nc* the sex organ of a man or male animal.

peni·tence /'penıtəns/ *nu* (*formal*) sorrow and regret (for doing wrong, sin).

peni·tent /'penıtənt/ *adj* (*formal*) feeling or showing deep regret.

peni·tent·ly *adv*

peni·ten·tiary /,penı'tenʃərı/ *nc* (*pl* **-ies**) (esp US) a prison.

pen·knife /'pennaıf/ *nc* (*pl* **-knives** /-naıvz/) small knife with one or more folding blades.

pen-name /'pen neım/ *nc* a name used by an author instead of a real name.

pen·nant /'penənt/ *nc* a long, pointed flag, used on a ship for signalling etc.

pen·ni·less /'penılıs/ *adj* without any money: *I'm penniless until pay-day*.

pen·ny /'penı/ *nc* (*pl* **pence** /pens/ when combined with numbers, as in *sixpence, tenpence, eighteen pence*; *pl* **pennies** /'penız/ when used of individual coins: *Please give me ten pennies (for this tenpence piece)*. **1** (abbr p) a British coin worth one hundredth of a pound: *These are 80 pence/80p* /pi:/ *a packet*. **the penny (has) dropped** the meaning of a remark was/has been understood etc. (*cost*) *a pretty penny* (to cost) a lot of money. **spend a penny** (*informal*) to use a toilet. **2** (until 1971) a British coin worth one twelfth of a shilling.

'penny-pinching *adj* (*informal; derog*) unwilling to spend money.

pen·sion¹ /'penʃn/ *nc* a regular payment made to a person who is no longer working because he or she is old or ill: *a retirement/State/private pension*.

pen·sion·able /-əbl/ *adj* giving the right to a pension.

pen·sion·er *nc* a person receiving a pension.

pen·sion² /'penʃn/ *vt* **pension sb off** to dismiss a person or allow a person to retire with a pension.

pen·sive /'pensıv/ *adj* (*formal*) seriously thoughtful: *pensive looks; looking pensive*.

pen·sive·ly *adv*

pen·ta·gon /'pentəgən/ *nc* (*maths*) a plane figure with five sides and five angles.

pen·tath·lon /pen'tæθlən/ *nc* an athletic contest in which each competitor takes part in five events (running, horseback riding, swimming, fencing and shooting with a pistol).

pent·house /'penthaus/ *nc* an apartment or flat built on the roof of a tall building.

pent-in /,pent 'ın/ *adj* closely confined: *I feel pent-in on a crowded train*.

pent-up /'pent ʌp/ *adj* **1** = pent-in: *feeling pent-up*. **2** not expressed: *pent-up anger*.

pen·ul·ti·mate /pe'nʌltımət/ *nc, adj* (*attrib*) (a word, event, occasion etc which is) last but one. ⇨ ultimate.

pen·ury /'penjʊərı/ *nu* (*formal*) poverty.

people¹ /'piːpl/ *n* **1** *n pl* two or more persons: *How many people were there? Only two people went. The room was full of people. The people in the village like the new doctor*. Ⓝ ⇨ the note at person(1). **2** *npl* (the —) all the people forming a nation; esp those who are not nobles, not high in rank etc: *government of the people, by the people, for the people. He's the people's choice*. **3** *nc* a race, tribe, nation: *the peoples of Asia; a brave and intelligent people*.

people² /'piːpl/ *vt* **people a place (with sb)** to fill a place with human beings.

pep /pep/ *nu* (*sl*) strength; energy; spirit. □ *vt* (**-pp-**) **pep sb (up)** to give energy or life to a person: *This soup will pep you up*.

'pep pill *nc* a pill with a drug that makes a person feel energetic.

'pep talk *nc* a talk or speech intended to produce encouragement and enthusiasm: *giving the team a pep talk before the match*.

pep·per¹ /'pepə(r)/ *n* **1** *nc, nu* (a kind of plant producing) (a berry used to make) a hot-tasting powder for seasoning food. **2** *nc* (also called *capsicum*) (a plant with) a red or green seed-pod used as a vegetable: *stuffed peppers*.

pep·pery *adj* tasting of pepper.

'pep·per·corn *nc* the dried, black berry of the pepper(1) plant.

'pep·per·mill *nc* a small device used for grinding pepper by hand.

'pep·per·mint *n* (**a**) *nu* a kind of mint grown for its oil, used in medicine and confectionery. (**b**) *nc* a sweet with this flavour.

per /pɜː(r)/ *prep* for each: *per pound; 30 miles per gallon; charge £10 per person.* **as per** according to: *as per instructions.* **as per usual** (*informal*) as usual.

,**per 'annum** /ˈænəm/ *adv* for each year.

,**per 'capita** /ˈkæpɪtə/ *adj, adv* for each person.

,**per 'cent** (abbr %) *adv* for, in, each hundred: *40% income tax.* ⇨ percentage.

per·ceive /pəˈsiːv/ *vt* (*formal*) to become conscious of or aware of (something): *perceive that something is wrong.* (N) Not used in continuous tenses, e.g. *is/was -ing.*

per·cen·tage /pəˈsentɪdʒ/ *nc* a rate, amount or number as a share of one hundred parts: *What percentage of his income is paid in income tax?*

per·cep·tible /pəˈseptəbl/ *adj* (*formal*) that can be seen or noticed. Opp imperceptible.
  per·cep·tibly /-əblɪ/ *adv*

per·cep·tion /pəˈsepʃn/ *nu* the process, act, by which we become aware (through seeing, hearing etc). ⇨ perceive.

per·cep·tive /pəˈseptɪv/ *adj* showing that one has understood or noticed: *perceptive remarks. It was perceptive of you to notice that.*
  per·cep·tive·ly *adv*

perch¹ /pɜːtʃ/ *nc* **1** a bird's resting-place, e.g. a branch. **2** (*informal*) a high position occupied by a person: *a perch on a ladder.*

perch² /pɜːtʃ/ *v* **perch (on sth) 1** *vi* to settle: *The birds perched on the television aerial.* **2** *vt, vi* (to cause a person) to sit (on something tall): *perched on a ladder/stool; perch a child on a wall.* **3** *vt* (used chiefly in *pp*) (of buildings) to be situated high up: *a castle perched on a rock.*

per·co·late /ˈpɜːkəleɪt/ *v* (*formal*) **percolate (through (sth)) 1** *vi* (of liquid) to pass slowly (through gaps in material): *Has the water percolated through yet?* **2** *vi* (*fig*) to become known slowly: *Has the news percolated through?* **3** *vt* to make (coffee) by percolating(1).

per·co·la·tor /-tə(r)/ *nc* a pot in which hot water percolates through coffee.

per·cus·sion /pəˈkʌʃn/ *nu* **1** (*formal*) the striking together of two (usually hard) objects; sound or shock produced by this. **2** (the —) (also *attrib*) musical instruments played by percussion, e.g. drums, cymbals: *the percussion section; percussion instruments.*

per·cus·sion·ist /-ɪst/ *nc* a player of a percussion instrument.

per·emp·tory /pəˈremptərɪ/ *adj* (*formal*) **1** (of commands) not to be disobeyed or questioned. **2** (*derog*) (of a person, manner) insisting (too much) on obedience.
  per·emp·tor·ily /-trəlɪ/ *adv*

per·en·ni·al¹ /pəˈrenɪəl/ *adj* **1** continuing throughout the whole year. **2** lasting for a very long time: *a perennial complaint.* **3** (of plants) living for more than two years. Compare annual²(2).
  per·en·ni·al·ly /-nɪəlɪ/ *adv*

per·en·ni·al² /pəˈrenɪəl/ *nc* a perennial plant.

perf. *written abbr* perfect.

per·fect¹ /ˈpɜːfɪkt/ *adj* **1** with everything needed: *a perfect solution to a problem.* **2** without fault; excellent: *a perfect holiday/wife; perfect weather.* **3** exact; accurate: *a perfect circle/fit.* **4** (*attrib*)

complete: *a perfect stranger/fool; perfect nonsense.*

,**perfect con'ditional** *nc* (the —) (*gram*) the verb form using *should/would have* and a *past participle* as in 'We *should have helped* them'.

,**perfect in'finitive** *nc* (the —) (*gram*) the verb form using *to have* and a *past participle*, as in '*To have run* would have been wrong'.

'**perfect tense** *nc* (the —) (*gram*) the verb form (*have* and a *past participle*) about a period up to the present. ⇨ future perfect (continuous), past perfect (continuous), present perfect (continuous tense). ⇨ also imperfect tense.

per·fect² /pəˈfekt/ *vt* to make (a skill, ability etc) perfect: *I've been perfecting my French.*

per·fec·tion /pəˈfekʃn/ *nu* **1** the process, act, of making something perfect: *busy with the perfection of detail.* **2** a perfect quality or example: *It was the perfection of beauty.* **3** (usually **to perfection**) the best possible state or quality: *beef roasted/done to perfection.*

per·fec·tion·ist /-ɪst/ *nc* (*informal*) a person who is satisfied with nothing less than what he or she thinks is perfect.

per·fect·ly /ˈpɜːfɪktlɪ/ *adv* **1** completely; very: *I'm perfectly happy. It's perfectly possible.* **2** extremely well: *speak German perfectly.*

per·fidi·ous /pəˈfɪdɪəs/ *adj* (*formal; derog*) deceitful; faithless: *a perfidious lover.*
  per·fidi·ous·ly *adv*

per·for·ated /ˈpɜːfəreɪtɪd/ *adj* having a hole or holes in: *a perforated sheet of postage stamps.*

per·for·ation /ˌpɜːfəˈreɪʃn/ *nc,nu* (a) set of small holes.

per·form /pəˈfɔːm/ *v* **1** (*formal*) *vt* to carry out, do, (a piece of work, something one is ordered or has promised to do): *perform a task.* **2** *vt, vi* to act a part in (a play), play (music), sing etc before an audience: *perform 'Hamlet' well; perform at a charity concert.*

per·form·er *nc* a person who performs (esp 2).

per·form·ance /pəˈfɔːməns/ *n* **1** *nc* an act of performing(2): *The orchestra/musicians gave a fine performance. She gives/does two performances a day.* **2** *nu* (*formal*) an act of performing(1): *faithful in the performance of his duties.* **3** *nc* (*fig*) a bad-tempered act etc: *What a performance!* (= What bad behaviour!)

per·fume /ˈpɜːfjuːm/ *nc,nu* (a kind of prepared liquid with) a sweet smell, esp from an essence of flowers. □ *vt* /pəˈfjuːm/ to give a perfume to, put perfume on, (a person, thing).

per·func·tory /pəˈfʌŋktərɪ/ *adj* (*formal*) done as a duty or routine but without care, sincerity or interest: *a perfunctory apology.*
  per·func·tor·ily /-trɪlɪ/ *adv*

per·haps /pəˈhæps/ *adv* possibly; it may be or may have been: *Perhaps it will rain. There were three men, or perhaps four. 'Will you be there?'—'Perhaps.' 'I didn't mean to be rude.'—'Perhaps not, but I was upset.'*

per·il /ˈperɪl/ *n* **1** *nu* serious danger: *be in peril of one's life.* **do sth at one's peril** to do it with the probability of being in serious danger. **2** *nc* something that causes danger: *the perils of the ocean* (i.e. storms etc).

per·il·ous /ˈperɪləs/ *adj* very dangerous: *a perilous journey.*

peril·ous·ly *adv: perilously close to death.*

per·im·eter /pəˈrɪmɪtə(r)/ *nc* (the measurement of) the outer boundary of a closed figure or area.

peri·na·tal /ˌperɪˈneɪtl/ *adj* (*med*) of the time immediately before and after childbirth.

peri·od /ˈpɪərɪəd/ *nc* **1** a length or portion of time, e.g. hours, days, months and years: *periods of sunny weather; the period when the disease is contagious; twenty teaching periods a week.* **2** a portion of time in the life of a person, a nation, a stage of civilization etc: *a period spent working overseas; the period of the French Revolution.* **3** a flow of blood from a woman each month. **4** (*astron*) the time taken for a planet etc to make one revolution. **5** (esp *US*) a full stop.

peri·od·ic /ˌpɪərɪˈɒdɪk/ *adj* occurring or appearing at regular intervals: *periodic headaches.*

periodic 'table *nc* (*chem*) a chart of the elements(1) according to their atomic weights.

peri·od·ical·ly /-klɪ/ *adv* (**a**) at regular intervals: *a magazine issued periodically.* (**b**) occasionally: *go to the theatre periodically.*

peri·od·ical /ˌpɪərɪˈɒdɪkl/ *nc* a magazine or booklet produced regularly, e.g. monthly.

peri·pa·tet·ic /ˌperɪpəˈtetɪk/ *adj* going from place to place: *peripatetic teachers.*

pe·riph·er·al /pəˈrɪfərəl/ *adj* **1** of, on, forming, a periphery. **2** (*formal*) having only a little importance: *a peripheral meeting.*

pe·riph·ery /pəˈrɪfərɪ/ *nc* (*pl* **-ies**) an external boundary or surface: *on the periphery (of a group/ town).*

peri·scope /ˈperɪskəʊp/ *nc* (*tech*) an instrument, as used in submarines, with mirrors and lenses so that things above can be seen.

per·ish /ˈperɪʃ/ *v* **1** *vi* to be destroyed, die: *Hundreds of people perished in the earthquake.* **2** *vt, vi* (to cause food, a material etc) to lose natural qualities: *Fruit perishes quickly. Leather perishes in water. Oil will perish tyres.*

per·ish·able /-əbl/ *adj, nc* (of) any kind of food that goes bad quickly.

per·ish·ed *adj* (*pred*) extremely cold: *My feet are perished!*

per·ito·ni·tis /ˌperɪtəˈnaɪtɪs/ *nu* inflammation of the lining of the abdomen.

per·jure /ˈpɜːdʒə(r)/ *v reflex* to make a false statement knowingly after taking an oath to tell the truth.

per·jur·er /ˈpɜːdʒərə(r)/ *nc* a person who has perjured herself or himself.

per·jury /ˈpɜːdʒərɪ/ *nc, nu*

perk /pɜːk/ *v* **1** *vi* **perk up** (of a person) to become (more) lively and active. **2** *vt* **perk sb/ sth up** to cause a person, thing to appear, be, more lively: *The horse perked up its ears.*

perky *adj* (**-ier, -iest**) lively; showing interest.

perks /pɜːks/ *n pl* (*informal*) advantages, such as a car, money in the form of paid expenses etc, given in addition to salary: *an executive's salary with the usual perks.*

perm /pɜːm/ *nc* (*informal*) = permanent wave: *go to the hairdresser's for/have a perm.* □ *vt* to give a perm to (a person's) hair.

per·ma·nence /ˈpɜːmənəns/ *nu* the state of being permanent.

per·ma·nent /ˈpɜːmənənt/ *adj* not expected to change; going on for a long time; intended to last:

my permanent address. Compare temporary.

ˌpermanent 'secretary *nc* a senior civil servant.

ˌpermanent 'wave *nc* a process of putting artificial curls in the hair so that they last several months.

per·ma·nent·ly *adv*

per·me·ate /ˈpɜːmɪeɪt/ *vt, vi* to pass, flow or spread into every part of (something): *water permeating (through) the soil; new ideas that have permeated (through/among) society.*

per·me·ation /ˌpɜːmɪˈeɪʃn/ *nu*

per·mis·sible /pəˈmɪsəbl/ *adj* (*formal*) that is allowed: *More than one visitor is not permissible.*

per·mis·sibly /-əblɪ/ *adv*

per·mis·sion /pəˈmɪʃn/ *nu* the act of allowing something: *Has he given you permission to leave?*

per·mis·sive /pəˈmɪsɪv/ *adj* (usually *derog*) allowing (too) much personal freedom: *permissive parents.*

per,missive so'ciety *n* (the —) (in GB, 1967 onwards) term used for social changes, including greater sexual freedom, abolition of censorship in the theatre, use of slang words etc.

per·miss·ive·ness *nu*

per·mit[1] /ˈpɜːmɪt/ *nc* a written authority giving permission: *You won't get in without a permit.*

per·mit[2] /pəˈmɪt/ *v* (**-tt-**) **1** *vt* (*formal*) to allow (something, a person to do something): *Smoking is not permitted in this cinema.* **2** *vi* to make something possible: *We'll play football, weather permitting.* **3** *vt* **permit of sth** (*formal*) to allow something as at all possible: *The situation does not permit of any delay.*

per·mu·ta·tion /ˌpɜːmjʊˈteɪʃn/ *nc* (*maths*) a change in the order of a set of things arranged in a group; any one such arrangement: *The permutations of x, y and z are xyz, xzy, yxz, yzx, zxy, zyx.*

per·ni·cious /pəˈnɪʃəs/ *adj* (*formal*) extremely harmful, causing distress: *pernicious gossip.*

per·ni·cious·ly *adv*

per·nick·ety /pəˈnɪkətɪ/ *adj* (*derog*) too concerned with unimportant details.

per·ox·ide /pəˈrɒksaɪd/ *nu* (also *hydrogen peroxide*) a colourless liquid (formula H_2O_2), used as an antiseptic and as a bleach.

per·pen·dicu·lar[1] /ˌpɜːpənˈdɪkjʊlə(r)/ *adj* **1** *perpendicular (to sth)* (*maths*) at an angle of 90° (to another line or surface). **2** upright: *a perpendicular wall.* Compare horizontal, vertical.

per·pen·dicu·lar[2] /ˌpɜːpənˈdɪkjʊlə(r)/ *nc* a perpendicular line or direction.

per·pe·tra·te /ˈpɜːpɪtreɪt/ *vt* to commit (a serious crime, error): *Several violations of human rights are being perpetrated.*

per·pe·tra·tor /-tə(r)/ *nc* a person, government, that commits a crime etc.

per·pe·tra·tion /ˌpɜːpɪˈtreɪʃn/ *nu*

per·pet·ual /pəˈpetʃʊəl/ *adj* going on for a long time or without stopping: *have a perpetual fear of dying.*

per,petual 'motion *nu* (*science*) the motion of a machine, if it could be invented, which would go on for ever without a source of energy.

per·pet·ual·ly /-ʃʊəlɪ/ *adv*

per·petu·ate /pəˈpetʃʊeɪt/ *vt* (*formal*) to preserve (something) from being forgotten or from going out of use: *perpetuate his memory by erecting a statue of him.*

per·petu·ation /pə,petʃu'eɪʃn/ *nu*

per·petu·ity /,pɜːpɪ'tjuːətɪ/ *nu* (*formal*) the condition of being perpetual. **in perpetuity** (*formal*) for ever (which is more usual).

per·plex /pə'pleks/ *vt* to puzzle or confuse (a person): *perplex her with questions.*

per·plex·ed *adj* confused.

per·plex·ity /-ətɪ/ *nu* (*formal*) the state of being puzzled, confused: *He looked at us in perplexity.*

per·se·cute /'pɜːsɪkjuːt/ *vt* to treat (a person, group) cruelly because of beliefs or opinions.

per·se·cu·tion /,pɜːsɪ'kjuːʃn/ *nc,nu*

per·se·cu·tor /-tə(r)/ *nc* a person who persecutes a person.

per·se·ver·ance /,pɜːsɪ'vɪərəns/ *nu* the constant effort to achieve something.

per·se·vere /,pɜːsɪ'vɪə(r)/ *vi* to make an effort to continue with, do, (esp something difficult or tiring): *persevere at/with/in one's studies.*

per·se·ver·ing *adj*

per·sist /pə'sɪst/ *vi* **1** **persist (in sth)** to refuse, in spite of argument, opposition, failure etc to make any change (in what one is doing, one's beliefs etc): *She persists in thinking he is innocent.* **2** **persist (with sth)** to continue to work hard (at something): *persist with one's studies.* **3** to continue to exist: *The fog is likely to persist in most areas.*

per·sist·ence /-əns/ *nu*

per·sist·ent /pə'sɪstənt/ *adj* (**a**) continuing to do something (e.g. to believe, refuse, lie etc) in spite of warnings etc: *a persistent liar.* (**b**) continuing to exist or happen: *persistent denials/efforts/coughing.*

per·sist·ent·ly *adv*

per·son /'pɜːsn/ *nc* **1** a man or woman (the usual words): *Who is this person? There's a strange person outside looking at our car.* **in person** physically present: *He'll collect his certificate in person* (= will be there himself). Ⓝ *'Persons'* is the standard plural of person but is only used in formal situations, as in *Persons under 16 may not enter.* In usual contexts use *'people'*, as in *Six people came. How many people came? More people like it than disapprove.* **2** (*gram*) the method used to describe who a verb or pronoun refers to (the speaker, the individual being spoken to or a person being spoken about). ⇨ *first/second/third person.*

per·son·able /'pɜːsnəbl/ *adj* good-looking and pleasant.

per·son·age /'pɜːsnɪdʒ/ *nc* an important person.

per·son·al /'pɜːsənl/ *adj* **1** private; individual; of a particular person: *my personal affairs/needs/opinions; your personal rights.* **2** done, made, by a person (not a deputy etc): *The Prime Minister made a personal appearance at the meeting.* **3** done, made, for a particular person: *give him one's personal attention. He did me a personal favour.* **4** of or about a person in a critical or hostile way: *I object to such personal remarks.* **5** (*attrib*) of the body or self: *Personal cleanliness is important to health.*

,personal as'sistant *nc* one who helps an official, e.g. by making travel arrangements, organizing meetings etc.

'personal column *nc* a place (in a newspaper

etc) in which private messages or advertisements appear.

,personal com'puter *nc* one that is small and is used in the home.

,personal 'pronoun *nc* (*gram*) a form of a pronoun (subject or object) used instead of a noun when the person or thing is known or obvious, as in 'Ask *him* to come in.' '*We're* going out and *you* can't come with *us.' 'Tell them* to wait.' '*It's* a big one.' '*It's* hot/10 o'clock/Friday.'

,personal 'stereo *nc* an apparatus (a small cassette player or radio with small headphones) for individual listening.

per·son·al·ly /-əlɪ/ *adv* (**a**) in person, not through a representative: *He showed me round the exhibition personally.* (**b**) giving one's own opinion: *Personally, I have no objection to your joining us.*

per·son·al·ized (also **-ised**) /'pɜːsnəlaɪzd/ *adj* printed with one's address (*personalized stationery*) or sewn with one's initials (*personalized handkerchiefs*).

per·son·al·ity /,pɜːsə'nælətɪ/ *n* (*pl* **-ies**) **1** *nc,nu* the qualities that make up a person's character: *a man with little personality; a woman with a strong personality.* **2** *nc* (*modern use*) a person who is well-known in a particular context: *a TV personality.*

per·son·ify /pə'sɒnɪfaɪ/ *vt* (*pt,pp* **-ied**) **1** to regard or represent (something) as a person: *personify the sun and moon by using 'he' and 'she'.* **2** to be a good example of (a quality): *That man is greed personified.*

per·soni·fi·ca·tion /pə,sɒnɪfɪ'keɪʃn/ *n* (**a**) *nc,nu* (an instance of) personifying something. (**b**) (the —) the best example (of a quality): *He's the personification of every virtue.*

per·son·nel /,pɜːsə'nel/ *nu* or *pl* the people employed in a business or organization: *Five airline personnel died in the plane crash. The personnel is/are satisfied with the decision.*

person'nel manager/officer *nc* a person employed to deal with staff, their salaries, training etc.

per·spec·tive /pə'spektɪv/ *n* **1** *nc,nu* the art of drawing solid objects on a flat surface so as to show their relative height, width, depth, distance etc: *the trees are in/out of perspective.* **2** *nu* the relation between different aspects of a problem: *He sees things in their right perspective.* **3** *nc* (*literary; fig*) a view: *perspectives of Britain's history.*

per·spex /'pɜːspeks/ *nu* (*P*) a tough plastic material used as a substitute for glass.

per·spi·ca·cious /,pɜːspɪ'keɪʃəs/ *adj* (*formal*) quick to judge and understand.

per·spi·cac·ity /,pɜːspɪ'kæsətɪ/ *nu*

per·spire /pə'spaɪə(r)/ *vi* to sweat (which is less formal).

per·spir·ation /,pɜːspə'reɪʃn/ *nu*

per·suade /pə'sweɪd/ *vt* **1** to make (a person) feel certain about, believe something: *How can I persuade you of my sincerity/that I am sincere?* **2** to cause (a person) by discussion, reasoning etc (not) (to do something): *We persuaded him/He was persuaded to try again.* Compare dissuade.

per·suad·able /-əbl/ *adj*

per·sua·sion /pə'sweɪʒn/ *n* **1** *nu* the act of persuading or being persuaded: *the power of persua-*

sion. **2** *nc* (*formal*) a group of people with a particular belief: *various political persuasions.*

per·sua·sive /pə'sweɪsɪv/ *adj* able to influence or persuade: *She has a persuasive manner/voice.*
per·sua·sive·ly *adv*

pert /pɜ:t/ *adj* not showing proper respect: *a pert child/answer.*

per·tain /pə'teɪn/ *vi* **pertain to sth** (*formal*) to belong to something as a part: *the farm and the lands pertaining to it.*

per·ti·na·cious /ˌpɜ:tɪ'neɪʃəs/ *adj* (*formal*) determined; stubborn.
per·ti·na·cious·ly *adv*
per·ti·nac·ity /ˌpɜ:tɪ'næsətɪ/ *nu* (*formal*) determination.

per·ti·nent /'pɜ:tɪnənt/ *adj* (*formal*) referring directly; relevant: *a pertinent reply; information that is pertinent to the discussion.* Ⓝ *'Pertinent'* is not the opposite of *'impertinent'.*
per·ti·nent·ly *adv*

per·turb /pə'tɜ:b/ *vt* (*formal*) to make (a person) anxious or concerned.

pe·rus·al /pə'ru:zl/ *nc,nu* (*formal*) (an act of) reading something carefully.

pe·ruse /pə'ru:z/ *vt* (*formal*) to read (something) carefully: *He perused the contract.*

per·vade /pə'veɪd/ *vt* (*formal*) (of a smell, belief etc) to spread through every part of (something): *The ideas that pervade all these magazines may do great harm.*
per·va·sion /pə'veɪʒn/ *nu*

per·va·sive /pə'veɪsɪv/ *adj* (*formal*) tending to pervade: *pervasive influences.*

per·verse /pə'vɜ:s/ *adj* **1** (*derog*) (of a person) deliberately continuing to do wrong. **2** (of behaviour) unreasonable.
per·verse·ly *adv*
per·verse·ness *nu*

per·ver·sion /pə'vɜ:ʃn/ *n* **1** *nu* the act of perverting or being perverted. **2** *nc* a change from right to wrong, to something abnormal, unnatural etc: *a perversion of justice; sexual perversions.*

per·ver·sity /pə'vɜ:sətɪ/ *n* (*pl* **-ies**) *nc,nu* (an act of) being perverse.

per·vert¹ /'pɜ:vɜ:t/ *nc* (*derog*) a person whose (sexual) behaviour is abnormal.

per·vert² /pə'vɜ:t/ *vt* **1** to turn (something) to a wrong use: *pervert the course of justice.* **2** to cause (a person, mind) to turn away from right behaviour, belief etc: *pervert (the mind of) a child.*

pes·si·mism /'pesɪmɪzəm/ *nu* the attitude or belief that the worst thing is most likely to happen, that everything is basically evil. Compare optimism.

pes·si·mist /-ɪst/ *nc* a believer in pessimism. Compare optimist.
pes·si·mis·tic /ˌpesɪ'mɪstɪk/ *adj*
pes·si·mis·ti·cal·ly /-klɪ/ *adv*

pest /pest/ *nc* **1** a troublesome or destructive thing, animal etc: *garden pests* (e.g. mice, snails). **2** (*informal; derog*) a child who is a nuisance: *You little pest!*

pes·ter /'pestə(r)/ *vt* to annoy or trouble (a person): *be pestered with flies/by requests for help.*

pes·ti·cide /'pestɪsaɪd/ *nc,nu* a chemical substance used to destroy pests.

pes·ti·lence /'pestɪləns/ *nc,nu* (any kind of) fatal epidemic disease.

pestle /'pesl/ *nc* a stick with a thick end used to crush things in a mortar.

pet¹ /pet/ *adj* (*attrib*) **1** of, for pets(1): *pet food; a pet shop.* **2** favourite: *a pet theory; a pet aversion/hate* (= something one hates most).

pet² /pet/ *nc* **1** an animal kept as a companion, e.g. a cat or a dog. **2** a person treated as a favourite: *Mary is the teacher's pet.*

pet³ /pet/ *v* (**-tt-**) **1** *vt* to touch (a person, animal) lightly to show affection: *pet a dog.* **2** *vi* to kiss and caress: *sit petting in the park.*

pet name /ˌpet 'neɪm/ *nc* a name other than a real name used by friends and family: *Christopher's pet name is 'Kit'.*

pet·al /'petl/ *nc* one of the (usually colourful) divisions of a flower: *rose-petals.*

pe·ter /'pi:tə(r)/ *vi* **peter out** (of supplies, sound etc) to come gradually to an end.

pe·ti·tion¹ /pɪ'tɪʃn/ *nc* **1** an earnest request or appeal (esp a written document signed by a large number of people). **2** (*legal*) a formal application made to a court of law.

pe·ti·tion² /pɪ'tɪʃn/ *v* **1** *vt* to make an appeal to (a person, organization): *petition Parliament to stop unemployment.* **2** *vi* **petition for sth** (*legal*) to ask for something earnestly: *petition for a retrial.*

pe·ti·tion·er *nc* (*legal*) a person who petitions, esp in a divorce suit.

pet·ri·fy /'petrɪfaɪ/ *v* (*pt,pp* **-ied**) **1** *vt,vi* (to cause a substance) to change into stone. **2** *vt* (*fig*) to make (a person) extremely afraid: *I'm petrified of spiders.*

pet·rol /'petrəl/ *nu* refined petroleum, used as a fuel in vehicles, planes etc: *fill up with petrol* (US = *gasoline*).

'petrol station *nc* a place where vehicles can be filled with petrol.

pe·tro·leum /pɪ'trəʊlɪəm/ *nu* a mineral oil found underground, used as a fuel.

pet·ti·coat /'petɪkəʊt/ *nc* a woman's underskirt.

pet·ty /'petɪ/ *adj* (**-ier, -iest**) **1** small; unimportant: *petty regulations enforced by petty officials.* **2** on a small scale: *petty farmers/shopkeepers.* **3** having or showing no sympathy: *petty spite.*

petty 'cash *nu* (*business*) money for or from small payments.

petty 'larceny *nu* theft of articles of little value.

petty 'officer *nc* a naval officer below commissioned rank.

pet·ti·ly /'petəlɪ/ *adv*
pet·ti·ness *nu*

petu·lance /'petʃʊləns/ *nu* (*formal*) unreasonable and impatient behaviour.

petu·lant /'petjʊlənt/ *adj* (*formal; derog*) unreasonably impatient or irritable.
petu·lant·ly *adv*

pew /pju:/ *nc* a long bench in a church.

pew·ter /'pju:tə(r)/ *nu* (objects made of) a grey alloy of lead and tin.

PG /ˌpi: 'dʒi:/ *symbol* (*films*) (entry only with) parental guidance. □ *abbr* a paying guest (in a boarding house).

pH /ˌpi: 'eɪtʃ/ *nc* (*science*) a measure of the acid or alkaline content of a substance (by which pure water has a pH of 7, acid solutions have a pH less than 7 and alkaline solutions have a pH greater than 7).

phal·anx /'fælæŋks/ nc (pl —es or **phalanges** /fə'lændʒi:z/) **1** a group of people formed for a common purpose. **2** (anat) a bone in a finger or toe.

phal·lic /'fælɪk/ adj of a phallus: phallic symbols/ emblems.

phal·lus /'fæləs/ nc (pl —es or **phalli** /'fælaɪ/) an image of the penis, used as a symbol of fertility.

phan·tom /'fæntəm/ nc a ghost.

phar·ma·ceuti·cal /ˌfɑːməˈsjuːtɪkl/ adj (attrib) of, engaged in, medicines.

phar·ma·cist /'fɑːməsɪst/ nc a person skilled in preparing medicines. ⇨ chemist.

phar·ma·col·ogist /ˌfɑːməˈkɒlədʒɪst/ nc an expert in, student of, pharmacology.

phar·ma·col·ogy /ˌfɑːməˈkɒlədʒɪ/ nu the scientific study of medicines and drugs.

phar·ma·cy /'fɑːməsɪ/ n (pl **-ies**) **1** nu the preparation and dispensing of medicines and drugs. **2** nc (a part of) a shop where medical goods are sold (US = drugstore).

phar·yn·gi·tis /ˌfærɪnˈdʒaɪtɪs/ nu inflammation of the pharynx.

phar·ynx /'færɪŋks/ nc (anat) the space (with the muscles etc that enclose it) at the back of the mouth.

phase¹ /feɪz/ nc **1** a stage of development: the critical phase of an illness. **2** (of the moon) an amount of bright surface visible from the earth.

phase² /feɪz/ vt to plan, carry out, (something) by phases: a well-phased plan. **phase sth in/out** to introduce/withdraw something gradually.

PhD /ˌpiː eɪtʃ 'diː/ abbr Doctor of Philosophy.

pheas·ant /'feznt/ nc a kind of long-tailed game bird.

phe·nom·ena /fəˈnɒmɪnə/ n pl ⇨ phenomenon.

phe·nom·enal /fəˈnɒmɪnl/ adj extraordinary or unusual (often referring to a large degree or size): phenomenal power/ability; a profit that is phenomenal.

phe·nom·enal·ly /-nəlɪ/ adv

phe·nom·enon /fəˈnɒmɪnən/ nc (pl **-ena** /-ɪnə/) **1** something that is known to exist by the senses: the phenomena of nature. **2** an unusual or extraordinary person, thing, amount, event etc.

phew /fjuː/ int (used to express astonishment, disgust, tiredness etc according to context).

phial /'faɪəl/ nc (formal or old use) a small bottle, esp one for liquid medicine.

phil·an·throp·ic /ˌfɪlənˈθrɒpɪk/ adj kind and helpful.

phil·an·thropi·cal·ly /-klɪ/ adv

phil·an·thro·pist /fɪ'lænθrəpɪst/ nc a person who helps those who are poor or in trouble.

phil·an·thropy /fɪ'lænθrəpɪ/ nu love and sympathy for people.

phil·ately /fɪ'lætəlɪ/ nu the activity of collecting stamps.

philo·logi·cal /ˌfɪlə'lɒdʒɪkl/ adj of philology.

phil·ol·ogist /fɪ'lɒlədʒɪst/ nc a student of, expert in, philology.

phil·ol·ogy /fɪ'lɒlədʒɪ/ nu the scientific study of the development of language or a particular language. Compare linguistics.

phil·os·opher /fɪ'lɒsəfə(r)/ nc **1** a person studying or teaching philosophy. **2** (informal) a person who lets reason control her or his life.

philo·sophi·cal /ˌfɪlə'sɒfɪkl/ adj **1** of, devoted to, guided by, philosophy. **2** (informal) (of a person, behaviour) guided by reason and not feelings: take a philosophical view of failure.

philo·sophi·cal·ly /-klɪ/ adv

phil·os·ophize (also **-ise**) /fɪ'lɒsəfaɪz/ vi **philosophize (about sth)** to think, discuss something, like a philosopher.

phil·os·ophy /fɪ'lɒsəfɪ/ n (pl **-ies**) **1** nu the search for knowledge, esp the nature and meaning of existence. **2** nc a system of thought resulting from such a search for knowledge: a man with a practical philosophy. **3** nu a calm, quiet attitude towards life, even in the face of unhappiness, danger, difficulty etc.

phleb·itis /flɪ'baɪtɪs/ nu inflammation of a vein.

phlegm /flem/ nu the thick, semi-fluid substance produced by coughing.

phleg·mat·ic /fleg'mætɪk/ adj (formal) calm and unemotional (about trouble).

phleg·mati·cal·ly /-klɪ/ adv

pho·bia /'fəʊbɪə/ nc (pl —s) an unhealthy and strong fear or dislike.

phone¹ /fəʊn/ nc, vt,vi (informal) telephone. **phone in** to contact a person, TV or radio programme by telephone. Hence **'phone-in** nc **'phone booth/box** nc a telephone box.

'phone-in nc a radio or TV programme in which the public take part on the telephone.

phone² /fəʊn/ nc (linguistics) a single speech-sound (vowel or consonant).

pho·neme /'fəʊniːm/ nc (linguistics) one of the sounds of a language.

pho·nemic /fə'niːmɪk/ adj

pho·net·ic /fə'netɪk/ adj **1** concerned with the sounds of speech. **2** providing a symbol for each phoneme of language: a phonetic transcription of a word. **3** (of a language) having a system of spelling close to the sounds represented by the letters: Spanish spelling is phonetic.

pho·neti·cal·ly /-klɪ/ adv

pho·net·ics nu (a) the scientific study of speech sounds. (b) the system of sounds (with symbols to represent them) in a language.

pho·neti·cian /ˌfəʊnɪ'tɪʃn/ nc a student of, expert in, phonetics.

pho·ney, phony /'fəʊnɪ/ adj (**-ier, -iest**) (sl) not genuine or real. □ nc (sl) a phoney person: He's a complete phoney.

pho·nol·ogy /fə'nɒlədʒɪ/ nu (linguistics) the scientific study of the organization of speech sounds, esp in a particular language.

phoo·ey /'fuːɪ/ int (used to express disgust, disbelief etc).

phos·pho·res·cence /ˌfɒsfə'resns/ nu (science) the giving out of light without burning or heat that can be felt.

phos·pho·res·cent /-snt/ adj

phos·pho·rus /'fɒsfərəs/ nu (science) a yellow, non-metallic element (symbol P) which catches fire easily and gives out a faint light in the dark.

pho·to /'fəʊtəʊ/ nc (informal) = photograph.

pho·to·copy /'fəʊtəkɒpɪ/ nc, vt (pt,pp **-ied**) (to make) a copy of (a document etc) using a photographic method.

pho·to·cell /'fəʊtəʊsel/ nc (tech) a device which gives out an electric current when light falls on it, as used for alarms.

photo·finish /ˌfəʊtəʊ'fɪnɪʃ/ *nc* a finish of a race that is so close that a photograph is needed to decide the winner.

pho·to·fit /'fəʊtəʊfɪt/ *nc,nu* (an example of) a method of combining facial features to give the police etc an idea of what a person looks like.

pho·to·gen·ic /ˌfəʊtə'dʒenɪk/ *adj* (of a person) looking attractive in photographs.

photo·graph /'fəʊtəgrɑːf/ *nc* a picture made by means of a camera. □ *vt* to take a photograph of (a person, thing).

pho·tog·ra·pher /fə'tɒɡrəfə(r)/ *nc* a person (esp professional) who takes photographs.

pho·to·graph·ic /ˌfəʊtə'ɡræfɪk/ *adj* of, related to, used in, taking photographs.

photo·graphi·cal·ly /-klɪ/ *adv*

pho·tog·ra·phy /fə'tɒɡrəfɪ/ *nu* the art or process of taking photographs.

pho·ton /'fəʊtɒn/ *nc* (*science*) a unit of electro-magnetic energy.

photo·stat /'fəʊtəstæt/ *nc* = photocopy.

pho·to·syn·the·sis /ˌfəʊtəʊ'sɪnθəsɪs/ *nu* (*science*) (in plants) the combining of carbon dioxide and water using light energy in chlorophyll to produce organic compounds.

pho·to·syn·thet·ic /-sɪn'θetɪk/ *adj*

phrasal /'freɪzl/ *adj* of, concerning, a phrase.

ˌphrasal 'verb *nc* (*gram*) a verb with an *adverbial particle* which has a meaning not identifiable from the individual words. (N) A *'phrasal verb'* always consists of an intransitive verb + adverbial particle, e.g. *'come apart'*, *'find out'*, *'walk out'*, *'get up'*, or a transitive verb + adverbial particle where the object can be placed before or after the adverbial particle, e.g. *'make up a story/make a story up'*, *'pull down a building/pull a building down'*. These verbs are listed at the end of the entry for the *verb*. Compare prepositional verb, prepositional phrasal verb.

phrase¹ /freɪz/ *nc* **1** (*gram*) a group of words (without a finite verb) forming part of a sentence, e.g. *in the garden, in order to, first of all.* ⇨ gerund / infinitive / noun / participial / prepositional / verb phrase. **2** (*music*) a short, independent piece forming part of a longer passage.

phrase² /freɪz/ *vt* to express (something) in words: *a neatly phrased compliment.*

phras·eol·ogy /ˌfreɪzɪ'ɒlədʒɪ/ *nu* (*formal*) the manner of choosing and organizing words in writing, speech etc.

physi·cal /'fɪzɪkl/ *adj* **1** of material things that are known through the senses (contrasted with moral and spiritual things): *the physical world; a physical impossibility.* **2** of the body: *physical exercise.* **3** (*attrib*) of the natural features of the world: *physical geography/chemistry/science.*

physi·cal·ly /-klɪ/ *adv*

phy·si·cian /fɪ'zɪʃn/ *nc* a doctor of medicine and surgery.

phys·i·cist /'fɪzɪsɪst/ *nc* a student of, expert in, physics.

phys·ics /'fɪzɪks/ *nu* the scientific study of matter and energy (heat, light, force etc).

phys·io·logi·cal /ˌfɪzɪə'lɒdʒɪkl/ *adj* of physiology.

physi·ol·ogist /ˌfɪzɪ'ɒlədʒɪst/ *nc* an expert in, student of, physiology.

physi·ol·ogy /ˌfɪzɪ'ɒlədʒɪ/ *nu* the scientific study

of how living things work (e.g. grow, move, digest food etc).

phys·io·thera·pist /ˌfɪzɪəʊ'θerəpɪst/ *nc* a person trained to give physiotherapy.

phys·io·ther·apy /ˌfɪzɪəʊ'θerəpɪ/ *nu* the treatment of disease by means of exercise, massage, light, heat, electricity etc.

phy·sique /fɪ'ziːk/ *nu* the appearance and structure of the body: *a strong physique.*

pia·nist /'pɪənɪst/ *nc* a person who plays the piano.

pi·ano /pɪ'ænəʊ/ *nc* (*pl* **—s**) a large musical instrument played by using a long keyboard.

pic·ca·lil·li /ˌpɪkə'lɪlɪ/ *nu* a kind of yellow, hot-tasting pickle.

pic·colo /'pɪkələʊ/ *nc* (*pl* **—s**) a kind of small flute.

pick¹ /pɪk/ *nc* a selection. **the pick of the bunch** (*fig*) the best of all of them.

pick² /pɪk/ *nc* **1** (also *pickaxe*) a heavy tool with an iron head having two pointed ends, used for breaking up hard surfaces. **2** a small, sharp-pointed instrument: *a toothpick.*

pick³ /pɪk/ *vt* **1** to take up, remove, pull away, (something) with the fingers: *pick flowers/fruit.* **pick and choose** to choose (too) slowly and carefully. **pick sb's brains** ⇨ brain¹(3). **2** to make (a hole etc) by picking. **pick holes in sb/sth** ⇨ hole¹(1). **3** to remove, clean, empty etc (something) by picking: *pick one's teeth/nose.* **pick sb's pocket** ⇨ pocket²(1). ⇨ pickpocket. **pick a lock** ⇨ lock²(1). **have a bone to pick with sb** ⇨ bone¹. **4** to choose or select (a person, group etc): *pick a team; pick the winner.* **pick a fight/quarrel (with sb)** ⇨ quarrel¹(2).

pick at sth (a) (of a bird) to take up (grain, etc) in the bill. **(b)** (of a person) to eat (food etc) in small amounts: *She only picked at her food.*

pick sb off to shoot and kill a person deliberately.

pick on sb to choose a person again and again for punishment, criticism etc: *You're always picking on me.*

pick sb/sth out (a) to choose a person, thing from others. **(b)** to distinguish a person, thing from surrounding people, objects etc: *pick out a friend in a crowd.*

pick sth over to examine something carefully and make a selection: *pick over a basket of grapes.*

pick up to improve: *His health/The profit is picking up.* ⇨ pick-me-up. **pick sb up (a)** to take a person as a passenger: *pick up a hitch-hiker.* **(b)** to find and arrest a suspect: *I was picked up in the street and questioned by the police.* **(c)** (*informal*) to meet a person deliberately and become acquainted: *pick up a girl at a party.* ⇨ pick-up(3).

pick sth up (a) to take hold of something and lift it: *pick up one's hat/parcels.* **(b)** to gain or get something: *pick up a foreign language* (= learn it without taking lessons or studying); *pick up bits of information; pick up a bargain at a sale.* **(c)** succeed in seeing or hearing something (by means of apparatus): *Enemy planes were picked up by our searchlights/radar/radio.* **pick oneself up** to stand up after a fall: *She slipped and fell but quickly picked herself up again.*

pick·er /'pɪkə(r)/ *nc* a person or device that picks (fruit etc).

pick·et /'pɪkɪt/ *nc* a worker or group of workers at the gates of a factory etc during a strike, to try to persuade others not to go to work. □ *vt,vi* to be, place, a picket at (a place of work etc): *picket a factory.*

pickle¹ /'pɪkl/ *n* **1** *nu* salt water, vinegar etc used for keeping vegetables etc in good condition. **2** a mixture of vegetables kept in pickle: *onion pickle.* **3** *n sing* **be in a pickle** to be in a difficult or disorganized condition.

pickle² /'pɪkl/ *vt* to preserve (food) in pickle: *pickled onions.*

pickled *adj* (*sl*) very drunk.

pick-me-up /'pɪk mɪ ʌp/ *nc* a drink etc that gives new energy, cheerfulness.

pick·pocket /'pɪkpɒkɪt/ *nc* a person who steals from pockets. ⇨ pocket²(1). □ *vi* to steal something in this way.

pick-up /'pɪk ʌp/ *nc* (*pl* **—s**) **1** the part on the arm of a record-player that holds the needle. **2** (also *attrib*) a small van or truck, open and with low sides: *a pick-up truck.* **3** (*sl*) a person one meets deliberately, e.g. at a party.

pic·nic¹ /'pɪknɪk/ *nc* **1** a pleasure trip in which food is carried to be eaten outdoors. **2** (*informal*) something easy and enjoyable: *Life is no picnic.*

pic·nic² /'pɪknɪk/ *vi* (**-ck-**) to take part in a picnic: *picnicking in the woods.*

pic·tor·ial /pɪk'tɔ:rɪəl/ *adj* of, having, represented in, pictures: *a pictorial record of the wedding.*

pic·ture¹ /'pɪktʃə(r)/ *nc* **1** a painting, drawing, sketch, photograph etc, esp as a work of art. **2** a beautiful scene, object, person etc: *The apple tree is a picture in spring.* **3** a film (to be) shown at the cinema. **4** the image, scene etc on television or a similar screen. **5** a very good example (of something): *be the picture of health.* **6** (*fig*) an account or description that enables a person to imagine an event etc. **be/put sb in the picture** (to cause a person) to be aware of all the facts of a situation.

pic·ture² /'pɪktʃə(r)/ *vt* to imagine (something): *Picture me as a tennis star!*

pic·tur·esque /ˌpɪktʃə'resk/ *adj* (of a place or view) attractive and pleasant: *a picturesque village.*

piddle /'pɪdl/ *vi, nu* (*sl*) (to pass) urine.

pidg·in /'pɪdʒɪn/ *n* **1** any of several languages having elements of a local language and English, French or Dutch. **2** (*informal*) (only in) **be (not) one's pidgin** to be (not) one's job or concern.

pie /paɪ/ *nc,nu* (a shaped case of) meat or fruit covered with pastry and baked in a dish. **pie in the sky** a hope, idea etc that is hopeless, very uncertain, unrealistic.

piece¹ /pi:s/ *nc* **1** a part or bit of a solid substance or thing: *a piece of paper/string. Will you have another piece (= slice) of cake? The vase is in pieces. The teapot fell and was broken to pieces.* **in one piece** undamaged; not broken. **be a piece of cake** to be easy (to do). **come to pieces** to divide into its parts: *Does this machine come to pieces?* **fall to pieces** to break into pieces: *It just fell to pieces in my hands.* **go (all) to pieces** (*informal*) (of a person) to break up physically, mentally or morally. **pull sth to pieces** (*fig*) to criticize a theory, essay etc in detail. **take sth to pieces** to separate it into its parts. **2** a separate instance or example: *a piece of news/luck/advice/information/furniture.* **give sb a piece of one's mind** to criticize a person strongly. **a nasty piece of work** (*derog*) an unpleasant person. **3** a single composition (in art, music etc): *a fine piece of work/music/poetry.* **4** a single part of a set: *a dinner service of 50 pieces.* **5** one of the objects moved on a board in such games as chess. **6** a coin: *a tenpence piece.*

piece² /pi:s/ *vt* **piece sth together** to put parts etc of something together; make something by joining or adding pieces together: *piecing together cloth/information.*

piece·meal /'pi:smi:l/ *adj, adv* one (part) at a time: *work done piecemeal.*

pier /pɪə(r)/ *nc* **1** a structure of wood, iron etc built out into the sea as a landing-stage or for walking on for pleasure. **2** (*tech*) a pillar supporting a bridge etc.

pierce /pɪəs/ *vt* **1** (of a sharp-pointed instrument) to go into or through (something) (and make a hole): *The arrow pierced his shoulder.* **2** (*fig*) (of cold, pain, sounds etc) to force a way into or through (something): *Her screams pierced the air.*

pierc·ing *adj* (esp of cold, voices) sharp and unpleasant: *a piercing wind/scream.*

pierc·ing·ly *adv: a piercingly cold wind.*

pi·ety /'paɪətɪ/ *nc,nu* (*pl* **-ies**) (*formal*) an act showing) respect and love for God.

pig /pɪg/ *n* **1** *nc* a type of farm and wild animal, often pink and without fur, that does not chew grass. **pigs might fly** the impossible might happen. **2** *nu* a pig's flesh as meat. ⇨ bacon, ham¹(1), pork. **3** *nc* (*informal; derog*) a dirty, greedy or ill-mannered person. **make a pig of oneself** to eat or drink too much.

'pig-'headed *adj* (*sl; derog*) stubborn.

'pig·sty /-staɪ/ *nc* (*pl* **-ies**) (**a**) a small building for pigs. (**b**) (*informal; derog*) a dirty home.

'pig·tail *nc* a plait of hair hanging down the back of the neck.

pi·geon /'pɪdʒɪn/ *nc* one of many kinds of bird of the dove family. ⇨ also stool-pigeon.

'pigeon-breasted *adj* (of a human being) having a large, round chest.

'pigeon-hole *nc* one of a number of small open boxes for keeping papers in. □ *vt* to put (papers etc) in a pigeon-hole (esp in order to ignore or forget them): *The scheme was pigeon-holed.*

'pigeon-toed *adj* having the toes turned inwards.

pig·let /'pɪglɪt/ *nc* a young pig.

pig·ment /'pɪgmənt/ *n* **1** *nc,nu* (an example of) a colouring matter used for making dyes, paint etc. **2** *nu* the natural colour in the skin, hair etc.

pig·my /'pɪgmɪ/ *nc* = pygmy.

pil·chard /'pɪltʃəd/ *nc* a small sea-fish like a herring.

pile¹ /paɪl/ *nc* **1** a number of things lying one on another: *a pile of books.* **2** (*informal*) a large amount (of money). **make a pile** to earn, gain, a lot of money.

pile² /paɪl/ *nc* a heavy length of timber, steel, concrete etc in the ground, used as a support for a building, bridge etc.

pile³ /paɪl/ *nu* a soft, thick surface like hair as on velvet, carpets etc.

pile⁴ /paɪl/ *v vt* to put (things) on or in a pile(1):

piling dishes on a table; a field piled high with rub-bish. ⇨ pile on below.

pile in to enter in a large, disorganized group: *The door opened and the children piled in.*

pile into sb (*informal*) to attack a person violently.

pile into *a place* to enter a place in a large, disorganized group.

pile off *a vehicle* to leave a bus, train etc in a large, disorganized group.

pile sth on (sth) to put something on top (of something) to make a pile: *pile coal on the fire.*

pile it on (*informal*) to exaggerate, make one's suffering, difficulties etc seem more dramatic.

pile onto *a vehicle* to get on a bus, train etc in a large, disorganized group.

pile out (of a place) to leave (a place) in a large, disorganized group.

pile up (a) (of work, supplies etc) to increase in amount (e.g. because of a stoppage or delay). **(b)** (of vehicles) to crash into each other. Hence '**pile-up** *nc* a crash involving many vehicles.

piles /pailz/ *nu* (*informal*) = haemorrhoids.

pile-up /'pail ʌp/ *nc* ⇨ pile up(b) above.

pil·fer /'pilfə(r)/ *vt,vi* to steal (things) in small quantities: *pilfering coins.*

pil·fer·er *nc* a person who pilfers.

pil·grim /'pilgrim/ *nc* a person who travels to a sacred place as a religious act: *pilgrims to Mecca.*

'**pil·grim·age** /-idʒ/ *nc* a journey by a pilgrim.

pill /pil/ *nc* a small ball or tablet of medicine. **be on/go on/use the pill** to be taking/start to take contraceptive pills regularly.

pil·lar /'pilə(r)/ *nc* **1** an upright column of stone etc as a support or ornament. **2** **pillar of sth** (*fig*) a strong supporter of something: *a pillar of the Church.* **3** something in the shape of a pillar, e.g. a column of smoke.

'**pillar-box** *nc* (*GB*) a round, tall container in which letters are posted.

pil·lion /'piliən/ *nc* a seat for a passenger on a motorbike.

pil·low /'piləu/ *nc* a long cushion used for the head when lying in bed. □ *vt* (*formal*) to rest, support, (one's head) (as if) on a pillow.

'**pillow-case/-slip** *nc* a cover for a pillow.

pi·lot¹ /'pailət/ *adj* (*attrib*) **1** of a pilot(1): *a pilot error.* **2** first and experimental: *a pilot scheme.* **3** showing the way (through): *a pilot ship.*

pi·lot² /'pailət/ *nc* **1** a person trained to operate the controls of an aircraft. **2** a person able to direct ships in a port, harbour etc.

pilot³ /'pailət/ *vt* to be a pilot of (a plane, ship etc).

pimp /pimp/ *nc* a man who finds men for a prostitute. □ *vi* to be a pimp.

pimple /'pimpl/ *nc* a small sore spot on the skin.

pim·ply /'pimpli/ *adj* (*-ier, -iest*) having many pimples: *a pimply face.*

pin¹ /pin/ *nc* **1** a short, thin piece of metal with a sharp point and a round head, used for fastening together parts of a dress, papers etc. ⇨ safety-pin. **2** a similar piece of wood or metal for various purposes. ⇨ drawing-pin, hairpin, rolling-pin.

,**pins and** '**needles** *nu* a tingling sensation in a part of the body.

'**pin·cushion** *nc* a pad for pins(1).

pin² /pin/ *vt* (*-nn-*) **1** to fasten (something) with a

pin or pins: *pin papers together; pin up a notice* (e.g. using drawing-pins). **pin sth on sb** to make a person appear responsible or deserve blame. **pin one's hopes on sb/sth** to rely completely on a person, decision etc. **2** to make (a person, thing) unable to move: *He was pinned under the wrecked car. He pinned me against the wall.* **pin sb down** (*fig*) to get a person to decide, choose etc.

pina·fore /'pinəfɔ:(r)/ *nc* a loose article of clothing worn over a dress to keep it clean.

pin·cers /'pinsəz/ *n pl* (also *a pair of pincers*) **1** an instrument used for gripping things, pulling nails out of wood etc. **2** the pincer-shaped claws of certain shellfish.

pinch¹ /pintʃ/ *nc* **1** a painful squeeze using the fingers and thumb: *He gave her a spiteful pinch.* **2** (*fig*) an effect of stress: *feel the pinch of poverty.* **3** an amount which can be taken up with the thumb and finger: *a pinch of salt.* **at a pinch** if there is a need and if there is no other way: *We can get ten people round the table at a pinch.*

pinch² /pintʃ/ *v* **1** *vt,vi* to squeeze (skin) between the thumb and finger: *He pinched the boy's cheek.* **2** *vt,vi* to be too tight; hurt (a person) by being too tight: *These shoes pinch (me).* **3** *vt* (*informal*) to take (something) without permission: *Who's pinched my dictionary?* **4** *vt* (usually *passive*) (*sl*) (of the police) to arrest (a person): *be pinched for stealing.*

pine¹ /pain/ *n* (also *attrib*) **1** *nc* any kind of evergreen tree with needle-shaped leaves ('*pine-needles*) and cones ('*pine-cones*). **2** *nu* the wood of this tree: *pine tables.*

pine² /pain/ *vi* **1** **pine (away)** to waste away because of sorrow or illness: *pining from hunger.* **2** **pine for sth/to do sth** to have a strong desire for or to do something: *pining for home/to return home.*

pine·apple /'painæpl/ *nc,nu* (also *attrib*) (a tropical plant with spiny leaves above) a large, sweet, juicy fruit: *pineapple juice; tinned pineapple.*

ping /piŋ/ *vi, nc* (to make) a short, sharp, ringing sound as of a small bell being hit.

ping·pong /'piŋpoŋ/ *nc* = table tennis.

pin·ion /'piniən/ *vt* to prevent (a person, bird etc) from moving by holding down arms, wings etc.

pink /piŋk/ *adj, nu* (of) a pale colour between red and white: *rose-pink.* **in the pink** (*informal*) very well.

pin-money /'pin mʌni/ *nu* a small amount of cash: *earn pin-money by washing cars.*

pin·nacle /'pinəkl/ *nc* **1** a tall, pointed part of a roof. **2** a high, slender mountain peak. **3** **the pinnacle of sth** (*fig*) the highest point: *at the pinnacle of his profession.*

pin·ny /'pini/ *nc* (*pl -ies*) (*informal*) = pinafore.

pin·point /'pinpoint/ *vt* to (try to) find or describe the exact cause of (a disaster or failure or the exact position of something).

pin·prick /'pinprik/ *nc* a small mark (as if) from a pin(1).

pin-striped /'pin straipt/ *adj* (*attrib*) (of cloth, clothes) having thin lines going up and down: *a pin-striped suit.*

pint /paint/ *nc* (abbr pt) a unit of measurement for liquids and certain dry goods, equal to one-eighth of a gallon or about ·57 of a litre: *a pint of milk/*

beer.

pin-up /'pɪn ʌp/ *nc* a picture of an attractive person, esp a woman.

pion·eer¹ /ˌpaɪə'nɪə(r)/ *nc* **1** a person who goes into an unexplored or undeveloped country to settle or work there. **2** the first person to begin a new branch of study, method etc.

pion·eer² /ˌpaɪə'nɪə(r)/ *vt* to be a pioneer of (something): *pioneering the development of learners' dictionaries.*

pi·ous /'paɪəs/ *adj* having, showing, sincere devotion to religion. Compare impious.
   pi·ous·ly *adv*

pip¹ /pɪp/ *nc* a seed (esp) of a lemon, orange, apple or pear.

pip² /pɪp/ *nc* a short note of a time-signal on the telephone or radio.

pipe¹ /paɪp/ *nc* **1** a tube through which liquids or gases can flow: *water-pipes; gas-pipes; drainpipes.* **2** (often *pl*) a musical wind instrument like a pipe or pipes, played by blowing. ⇨ **bagpipes. 3** a tube with a bowl, used for smoking tobacco. **put that in your pipe and smoke it** (*informal;* usually *imperative*) to think about that and accept it whether you want to or not. **4** a long hollow part in the body: *the windpipe.*
   'pipe·ful /-ful/ *nc* as much as a pipe(3) can hold: *a pipeful of tobacco.*

pipe² /paɪp/ *v* **1** *vt* to carry, send (water etc) through pipe: *pipe water into a house.* **2** *vt,vi* to play (music) on a pipe. **pipe down** (*informal*) to be less noisy. **pipe up** to speak, sing, more loudly. **3** *vt* to welcome (passengers etc) on board with a pipe(2): *piping the captain on board.* **4** *vt* to add a strip of (cloth, icing etc) as a decoration to a dress, cake etc. ⇨ piping(2)

pipe·dream /'paɪpdriːm/ *nc* a plan, idea etc that cannot happen or be successful.

pipe·line /'paɪplaɪn/ *nc* a system of pipes(1) (usually underground) used for carrying water, oil, cables etc. **be in the pipeline** (of supplies, schemes etc) to be being completed, prepared etc; be coming.

pi·per /'paɪpə(r)/ *nc* a person who plays on a pipe or bagpipes.

pip·ette /pɪ'pet/ *nc* (*science*) a thin tube for small quantities of liquid, esp used in chemistry.

pip·ing¹ /'paɪpɪŋ/ *adv* **piping hot** very hot.

pip·ing² /'paɪpɪŋ/ *nu* **1** a length of pipe(1): *ten metres of lead piping.* **2** a narrow strip or cord used to decorate the edges of clothes; lines of icing sugar used to decorate cakes etc. **3** the act of playing on, sound produced from, a pipe(2).

pi·quan·cy /'piːkənsɪ/ *nu* (*formal*) the quality of being piquant.

pi·quant /'piːkənt/ *adj* (*formal*) pleasantly sharp or hot to the taste: *a piquant sauce.*

pique /piːk/ *vt* to hurt the pride, self-respect, of (a person). □ *nu* this feeling: *resign in a fit of pique.*

pi·ra·cy /'paɪərəsɪ/ *nc,nu* (*pl* **-ies**) **1** (an instance of) robbery on the high seas. **2** (an instance of) illegally reproducing books, a design etc.

pi·rate¹ /'paɪərət/ *nc* **1** a person who stops ships at sea and steals from them. **2** a person who copies something, e.g. a book, design etc, without permission.

pi·rate² /'paɪərət/ *vt* to take and copy (another person's book, idea, design etc). ⇨ plagiarize.

pir·ou·ette /ˌpɪru'et/ *nc* a ballet dancer's fast turn on the front end of the foot. □ *vi* to dance a pirouette.

Pis·ces /'paɪsiːz/ *n* the Fish, twelfth sign of the zodiac.

piss /pɪs/ *vi, nu* (*vulgar sl*) (to pass) urine.
   pissed *adj* (*vulgar sl*) very drunk.

pis·ta·chio /pɪ'staːtʃɪəu/ *nc* (*pl* **—s**) (a kind of tree with) a kind of green edible nut.

pis·til /'pɪstl/ *nc* (*science*) the seed-producing part of a flower.

pis·tol /'pɪstl/ *nc* a small gun.

pis·ton /'pɪstən/ *nc* (in an engine) a round, short piece of metal fitting closely inside a tube in which it moves to cause motion.

pit¹ /pɪt/ *nc* **1** a large hole in the earth, esp one from which material is dug out: *a coal-pit.* **2** a covered hole used as a trap for dangerous animals etc. **3** a hollow in an animal or plant body: *an armpit; the pit of the stomach.* **4** a hole in the floor (of a garage, workshop) from which the underside of a vehicle can be examined and repaired. **5** a place at which cars stop (at racecourses) for fuel, new tyres etc. **6** (the people in) the area on the ground floor of a theatre: *the orchestra pit.*

pit² /pɪt/ *vt* (**-tt-**) **pit oneself/sb against sb** to set, match, oneself, a person against another in a competition, struggle.

pit-a-pat /ˌpɪt ə 'pæt/ *adv* with the sound of light, quick taps: *Her heart/The rain went pit-a-pat.* ⇨ pitter-patter.

pitch¹ /pɪtʃ/ *nc* **1** (*sl*) a place where a person (esp a street trader) usually does business. **queer sb's pitch** (*sl*) to upset a person's plans. **2** an area for playing football etc. **3** (*cricket*) the part of the ground between the wickets. **4** (in music and speech) the degree of highness or lowness: *the pitch of a voice.* **5** an amount or extent: *The noise reached such a pitch that . . .* ⇨ fever(1). **6** an amount of slope (esp of a roof).

pitch² /pɪtʃ/ *nu* a black, semi-liquid substance, used to make roofs waterproof etc.
   ˌpitch-'black/'dark *adj* very black or dark.

pitch³ /pɪtʃ/ *v* **1** *vt* to set up, erect, (a tent, camp). **2** *vt,vi* to throw (a ball etc). **3** *vt* (*music*) to set a pitch(4): *This song is pitched too low for me.* **4** *vt,vi* (to cause a person, boat etc) to fall heavily forwards or outwards: *The boat overturned and the passengers were pitched out.* **5** *vi* (of a ship) to move up and down as the front rises and falls. ⇨ roll²(6). **6** *vi* **pitch in** to begin to work with energy. **pitch into sth** (**a**) to attack something violently. (**b**) to get busy with work etc: *We pitched into the work/the food.* **7** *vt,vi* (*cricket*) (to cause the ball) to strike the ground near or around the wicket. **8** *vt* to lift or move (hay etc) with a fork.
   'pitch·fork *nc* a long-handled fork for lifting hay etc.

pitch·er¹ /'pɪtʃə(r)/ *nc* a large jug.

pitch·er² /'pɪtʃə(r)/ *nc* (*baseball*) a player who throws the ball.

pit·eous /'pɪtɪəs/ *adj* (*formal*) arousing pity.
   pit·eous·ly *adv*

pit·fall /'pɪtfɔːl/ *nc* an unexpected danger or difficulty (esp one that is not easy to identify).

pith /pɪθ/ *nu* **1** the soft, white substance that fills the stems of some plants and trees. **2** the similar substance lining the peel of oranges etc. **3** (*fig*) an essential part (of something): *the pith of his argument/speech*.

pithy *adj* (**-ier, -iest**) (**a**) of, like, full of, pith. (**b**) relevant, strong and meaningful: *pithy remarks*.
 pith·ily /-əlɪ/ *adv*

piti·able /'pɪtɪəbl/ *adj* = pitiful(3).
 piti·ably /-əblɪ/ *adv*

piti·ful /'pɪtɪfəl/ *adj* **1** feeling, showing, pity: *a pitiful cry*. **2** causing pity: *a pitiful sight*. **3** (*derog*) (of effort) weak and deserving to be criticized: *a pitiful attempt*.
 piti·ful·ly /-fəlɪ/ *adv*

piti·less /'pɪtɪlɪs/ *adj* showing no pity: *a pitiless boss; pitiless revenge*.
 piti·less·ly *adv*

pit·tance /'pɪtəns/ *nc* a very small payment: *work all day for a pittance*.

pit·ted /'pɪtɪd/ *adj* having many small hollow marks: *a pitted skin*.

pit·ter-pat·ter /'pɪtə pætə(r)/ *nu, vi* (to make) a quick succession of light sounds: *the pitter-patter of rain*. ⇨ pit-a-pat.

pi·tu·itary /pɪ'tjuːɪtərɪ/ *nc* (*pl* **-ies**) (also *pituitary gland*) (*anat*) the small gland at the base of the brain, giving hormones that influence growth etc.

pity¹ /'pɪtɪ/ *n* (*pl* **-ies**) **1** *nu* a feeling of sorrow for the troubles, sufferings etc of another person: *be filled with/feel pity for her*. **have/take pity on sb** to help a person who is in trouble etc. **for pity's sake** (used when asking for urgent action, a decision etc): *For pity's sake leave her alone*. **out of pity (for sb)** because of a feeling of pity: *I did it out of pity for her seven children*. **2** *n sing* (an event which gives) a cause for regret or sorrow: *What a pity* (= How unfortunate) (*that*) *you can't come with us!*

pity² /'pɪtɪ/ *vt* (*pt,pp* **-ied**) to feel pity for (a person): *I pity you having to work such long hours*.

piv·ot¹ /'pɪvət/ *nc* **1** a central pin or point on which something turns. **2** (*fig*) something on which an argument or discussion depends.

piv·ot² /'pɪvət/ *vt,vi* (to cause a person, thing) to turn (as if) on a pivot.

pixie /'pɪksɪ/ *nc* (*pl* **-ies**) a small fairy.

piz·za /'piːtsə/ *nc,nu* (*It*) (food made by baking) a layer of dough covered with a mixture of cheese, tomatoes etc.

Pk *written abbr* Park(1).

pkt *written abbr* packet.

Pl *written abbr* Place.

pl *written abbr* plural (as used in this dictionary).

plac·ard /'plækɑːd/ *nc* a written or printed notice or announcement.

pla·cate /plə'keɪt/ *vt* (*formal*) to make (a person) feel less angry.

place¹ /pleɪs/ *nc* **1** a particular part of space (to be) occupied by a person or thing: *You'll find a place for the cups on that shelf. I can't be in two places at once*. **all over the place** in or into order: *The wind blew my papers all over the place*. **in/out of place** (**a**) in/not in the right or proper place: *I like to have everything in place*. (**b**) (*fig*) suitable/unsuitable: *His remarks were out of place*. **in place of sth** instead of (which is more usual): *We need friendship in place of hostility*. **change places (with sb)** to take a person's

seat, job etc and give her or him one's own. **fall into place** to form a recognizable pattern: *Don't worry if you don't understand—everything will soon fall into place*. **put sb in her/his place** to tell a person that he or she is not so important. **put oneself in sb else's place** to imagine that one is that person and has the same problems. **take the place of sb/sth** to be used, substituted, for a person, thing: *Plastics have taken the place of many materials*. **swop places (with sb)** to exchange seats, jobs etc. **take place** to happen. **2** a city, town, village etc: *travel to different places and see things* (i.e. travel as a tourist). **go places** (*informal*) to have increasing success. **3** a building or area of land used for a particular purpose: *a place of worship* (= a church, mosque etc); *a place of business*. **4** (*informal*) a house or other home: *He has a nice little place in the country. Come round to my place one evening*. **5** a particular area on a surface: *a sore place on my neck*. **6** a position in a book, group, race etc: *Will you keep my place while I buy a newspaper? I've lost my place on the committee. Whose horse got the first place?* **7** a seat for one person in a bus, theatre, restaurant etc: *We have no places left*. **8** (*sport*) a position in a team. **9** (*maths*) a position of a figure in a series: *calculated to two decimal places* (e.g. 6·57). **10** a stage in an argument etc: *In the first/second place, . . .* **11** a position at a school, university etc: *get a place at Cambridge*.

place² /pleɪs/ *vt* **1** to put (a person, thing etc) in a particular place: *They're placing the food on the table. Place them in the right order*. **2** to state that (a person, animal etc) has achieved a particular position (e.g. in a competition, race, set of standards etc): *be placed third; be placed among the best students*. **3** to invest (money): *place £500 in a building society*. **4** to put (an order for goods etc) with a business firm: *place an order for books with the bookshop*. **5** to show or state (a feeling of trust etc) (in a person): *place confidence in a leader*. **6** to recognize (a person etc) by connecting her or him with one's past experience: *I know that man's face, but I can't place him*.

place name /'pleɪs neɪm/ *nc* a name of a town, region, country etc: *This dictionary does not include place names*.

pla·cen·ta /plə'sentə/ *nc* (*pl* **—s**) (*science*) an organ in the womb during pregnancy, through which the baby is fed.

pla·cid /'plæsɪd/ *adj* calm; not easily annoyed: *a placid husband*.
 pla·cid·ly *adv*

pla·giar·ism /'pleɪdʒərɪzəm/ *nc,nu* (an instance of) plagiarizing.
 pla·giar·ist /-ɪst/ *nc* a person who plagiarizes.

pla·giar·ize (also **-ise**) /'pleɪdʒəraɪz/ *vt* to take and use somebody else's ideas, words etc as if they were one's own.

plague¹ /pleɪg/ *nc,nu* **1** a kind of fatal disease which spreads quickly. **2** (*fig*) a cause of serious trouble or disaster: *a plague of locusts/flies*.

plague² /pleɪg/ *vt* **plague sb (with sth)** to annoy a person (esp with repeated requests or questions).

plaice /pleɪs/ *nc* (*pl* **—**) (also *attrib*) a brown, European flat-fish with spots, eaten as food: *plaice fillets*.

plaid /plæd/ *nc,nu* (a long piece of) woollen cloth worn over the shoulders by Scottish Highlanders.

plain[1] /pleɪn/ *adj* (**—er, —est**) **1** easy to see, hear or understand: *plain English. The meaning is quite plain.* **2** simple; ordinary; without luxury or ornament: *plain cooking; a plain blue dress.* **plain and simple** clear, not complicated: *plain and simple instructions.* **in plain clothes** (esp of policemen) in ordinary clothes, not in uniform. **3** (of people, thoughts, actions etc) honest and open about one's opinion or feeling: *He was plain with me and said he did not like my idea.* **4** (of a person's appearance) not pretty or handsome. **5** (of flour) ordinary and needing the addition of baking-powder, yeast etc when used to make cakes, bread etc. Compare self-raising.

'plain chocolate *nu* the dark kind with a bitter taste.

‚plain 'sailing *nu* (*fig*) a course of action that is simple and free from difficulties: *After we found a guide, the trek was plain sailing.*

‚plain-'spoken *adj* speaking honestly and sincerely: *a plain-spoken doctor.*

plain·ly *adv*: *It was plainly visible.*

plain·ness *nu*

plain[2] /pleɪn/ *nc* a large area of level land: *the wide plains of Canada.*

plain[3] /pleɪn/ *nc* (*knitting*) a basic way of knitting into the back of each stitch. ⇨ purl.

plain·tiff /'pleɪntɪf/ *nc* (*legal*) a person who brings an action at law. Compare defendant.

plain·tive /'pleɪntɪv/ *adj* (*formal*) sounding sad: *a plaintive tune.*

plain·tive·ly *adv*

plait[1] /plæt/ *nc* something made by plaiting: *wearing her hair in a plait.*

plait[2] /plæt/ *vt* to twist (lengths of hair, string etc) under and over one another into one length.

plan[1] /plæn/ *nc* **1** an outline drawing (of or for a building) showing the relative size, positions etc of the parts, esp as if seen from above: *plans for a new school.* Compare elevation(2). **2** a diagram (of the parts of a machine). **3** a diagram showing how a garden, park, town or other area of land has been, or is to be, laid out. Ⓝ '*Map*' is used for a large area of land. **4** an arrangement for doing or using something, considered in advance: *make plans for the school holidays.* **go according to plan** to happen as planned.

plan[2] /plæn/ *vt* (**-nn-**) to make a plan of (something, an activity): *plan a house/a holiday/an expedition. We're planning to visit London this summer.* **plan ahead** to make plans(4) in advance.

plan·ner *nc* a person who makes plans (esp (3)): *a town planner.*

plane[1] /pleɪn/ *adj* (*maths*) having length and breadth only: *a plane figure* (e.g. a square). Compare solid[1](8).

plane[2] /pleɪn/ *nc* **1** a flat or level surface. **2** (*fig*) a standard or stage (of development etc): *on a higher social plane.* **3** = aeroplane.

plane[3] /pleɪn/ *nc* a tool used for removing the surface of wood by taking shavings from it. □ *vt,vi* to use a plane: *planing wood.*

plane[4] /pleɪn/ *nc* one of several kinds of tree (a *plane tree*) with spreading branches, broad leaves and thin bark.

plan·et /'plænɪt/ *nc* one of the large bodies (e.g. *Mars, Venus*) that move round the sun.

plan·et·ary /'plænɪtrɪ/ *adj*

plank /plæŋk/ *nc* **1** a long, flat piece of wood. **2** a basic principle in a political policy.

plank·ton /'plæŋktən/ *nu* the very small forms of life in the sea.

plant[1] /plɑ:nt/ *nc* **1** any living organism that is not an animal, esp the kind smaller than trees and shrubs: *garden plants; a flowerless plant.* **2** the apparatus, fixtures, machinery etc used in an industrial or manufacturing process: *heavy plant.* **3** a large factory: *an industrial plant.* **4** (*informal; derog*) a person who joins a group in order to get information against them.

plant[2] /plɑ:nt/ *v* **1** *vt,vi* to put plants, bushes, trees etc in (a garden etc): *plant a garden with rose-bushes.* **2** *vt* (*fig*) to cause (an idea) to form in the mind: *plant the idea of organizing a demonstration among the members.* **3** *vt* to place (something) in position: *He planted his feet firmly on the ground.* **4** *vt* to place (a blow etc) with deliberate aim: *plant a blow on his ear.* **5** *vt* (*informal*) to place (a person or object) secretly, esp in order to deceive, to cause an innocent person to seem guilty etc: *He planted the stolen pen in my room.*

plan·tain /'plæntɪn/ *nc* (a tropical plant with) a fruit similar to the banana.

plan·ta·tion /plæn'teɪʃn/ *nc* **1** an area of land planted with trees: *plantations of fir and pine.* **2** an area of land on which a cash crop is grown: *a sugar plantation.*

plant·er /'plɑ:ntə(r)/ *nc* a person who grows crops on a plantation: *tea-planters.*

plaque /plɑ:k/ *n* **1** *nc* a flat metal or stone plate fixed on a wall as a memorial. **2** *nu* the yellow substance that forms on the teeth and causes decay.

plas·ma /'plæzmə/ *nu* (*tech*) the clear liquid in which the blood cells are carried.

plas·ter[1] /'plɑ:stə(r)/ *n* **1** *nu* a mixture of lime, sand, water etc, used for coating walls and ceilings. **2** *nc,nu* (a small piece of) fabric used to cover a wound etc. **3** *nu* a white substance that dries quickly, used round broken bones etc: *My leg was in plaster for two weeks.*

plas·ter[2] /'plɑ:stə(r)/ *vt* **1** to cover (a wall etc) with plaster(1). **2** to put a plaster(2,3) on a wound, bone etc. **3** *plaster sth (with sth)* to cover something thickly: *hair plastered with oil.*

'plaster·board *nu* material made of plaster and cardboard, used for making inside walls and ceilings.

‚plaster of 'Paris *nu* = plaster[1](3).

plas·ter·ed *adj* (*informal*) drunk.

plas·tic[1] /'plæstɪk/ *adj* **1** (*tech*) (of materials) easily shaped or moulded: *Clay is a plastic substance.* **2** (of goods) made of plastic: *plastic raincoats.* **3** (*tech*) of the art of modelling: *the plastic arts.*

plas·tic[2] /'plæstɪk/ *nc,nu* (one of many kinds of) manmade material which can be shaped or moulded and which keeps its shape when hard: *a plastic cup/toy.* ⇨ polymer.

‚plastic 'surgery *nu* the restoration of (deformed or diseased) parts of the body (by grafting skin etc).

plas·tic·ity /plæ'stɪsətɪ/ *nu* (*tech*) the state or quality of being plastic(1).

plas·ti·cine /'plæstɪsiːn/ *nu* (*P*) a substance like soft clay, used for modelling.

plate¹ /pleɪt/ *n* **1** *nc* an almost flat dish from which food is served or eaten: *a dinner/soup/dessert plate; a plate of beef and vegetables*. **hand/ give sb sth on a plate** (*informal*) to give a person an opportunity, reward etc without that person making any effort. **2** *nu* (*collective*) gold or silver articles, e.g. spoons, dishes, bowls. **3** *nc* a flat, thin piece (of metal, glass etc). **4** *nc* a piece of plastic with one or more false teeth: *a dental plate*. **5** *nc* a piece of metal with a person's name etc on it: *a door plate*. **6** *nc* a flat piece of metal, plastic etc from which the pages of a book are printed.
plate·ful /-fʊl/ *nc* as much as a plate can hold.

plate² /pleɪt/ *vt* to cover (another metal) with gold, silver or tin: *silver-plated spoons*.

pla·teau /'plætəʊ/ *nc* (*pl* **—s** or **—x** /-təʊz/) a large area of level land high above sea-level.

plat·form /'plætfɔːm/ *nc* **1** a flat area built at a higher level than the railway line in a train station: *Which platform does your train leave from?* **2** a flat structure raised above floor-level for speakers etc. **3** a statement of a political party's policies.

plat·ing /'pleɪtɪŋ/ *nu* a thin coating of gold, silver etc. ⇨ **plate²**.

plati·num /'plætɪnəm/ *nu* a grey metal (symbol Pt), used for jewellery and in industry.

plati·tude /'plætɪtjuːd/ *nc* a remark or statement that is obviously true but is used too often and is not interesting, e.g. 'Life has its ups and downs'.
plati·tudi·nous /ˌplætɪ'tjuːdɪnəs/ *adj*

pla·ton·ic /plə'tɒnɪk/ *adj* without sexual love: *platonic love/friendship*.

pla·toon /plə'tuːn/ *nc* a small group of soldiers (a subdivision of a company).

plat·ter /'plætə(r)/ *nc* (*esp US*) a large, shallow dish used for serving food, esp meat and fish.

platy·pus /'plætɪpəs/ *nc* = duck-billed platypus.

plau·dit /'plɔːdɪt/ *nc* (*usually pl*) (*formal*) a clapping or other sign of approval: *We were pleased at the plaudits of the audience.*

plaus·ible /'plɔːzəbl/ *adj* seeming to be right or believable: *a plausible excuse/explanation*. Opp implausible.
plaus·ibly /-əblɪ/ *adv*

play¹ /pleɪ/ *n* **1** *nc* a story (to be) performed on a stage, on TV or radio. **put on a play** to organize and produce a play on stage. **2** *nu* any activity for amusement or recreation: *The children are at play* (= playing). **a play on words** = pun. **3** *nu* (the manner of) playing a game: *rough play in a football match*. **in/out of play** (of the ball in football, cricket etc) in/not in a position where the rules of the game allow it to be. **make a play for sb** (*informal*) to try to attract a person. **make a play for sth** to try to gain a business deal, an advantage etc. ⇨ **fair play**. **4** *n sing* a turn or move in sport or in a game: *It's your play*. **5** *nu* a light, quick, movement: *the play of sunlight on water*. **6** *nu* (space for) free and easy movement (esp looseness): *too much play on the rope; give free play to one's emotions*. **7** *nu* (*formal*) the effect or action: *the play of natural forces*. **8** **bring sth into/come into play** (to cause it) to begin to operate or be active: *His long experience as a lawyer came into play*.

'play-acting *nu* (*fig*) pretence.

'play·boy *nc* a rich, pleasure-loving man.

'play·goer *nc* a person who often goes to the theatre.

'play·group *nc* a school for children under five.

'play·ground *nc* an outside area of a school etc for children to play on.

'play·house *nc* a theatre.

'play·mate *nc* (of children) a friend one plays with.

'play·pen *nc* a portable enclosure for a baby to be left to play.

'play reading *nc,nu* a reading aloud of the text of a play by a group.

'play·school *nc* = playgroup.

'play·thing *nc* (a) a toy. (b) (*fig*) a person treated like a toy.

play² /pleɪ/ *v* Ⓝ For uses of '*play*' in special expressions such as *play with fire, play for time, play it safe, play the game* etc, ⇨ the noun or *adjectival* entries, as at *ball, cool, ear, fair, fire, fool, game, hand, hell, joke, market, safe, time, truant*. **1** *vi,vt* to do (something) to pass time pleasantly, as children do: *Let's go and play. She was playing with the kitten. They were playing (at being) spacemen.* **2** *vt,vi* to take part in (a sport or game): *play football for Liverpool; play cards/chess. France is playing (against) Wales. Are you playing on Saturday?* **3** *vt* to strike or hit (a ball etc) during a game in a particular way: *Martina played that stroke well.* **4** *vt* to choose and move (a card, piece etc) in a game: *play an ace/the yellow one/a pawn.* **5** *vt,vi* to act (a part in a play) in the theatre, on TV etc: *play Hamlet; play in 'Twelfth Night'.* **6** *vi* to be produced in a theatre, shown in a cinema etc: *A new Shaffer drama is playing in the National Theatre. What's playing (at the cinema)?* **7** *vt,vi* to produce music using (an instrument): *play the piano/the violin/the guitar. He plays well. What can you play?* **8** *vt* to perform (a musical work): *play one of Lennon's tunes on the piano.* ⇨ **ear¹**(1). **9** *vt* to operate (a record-player, tape-recorder, or a record, tape, disc): *I'll play my new LP/cassette. Don't play your radio so loud!* **10** *vi* (of a radio etc) to produce sound. **11** *vt* to do (something) and have a particular effect: *He's played a nasty trick (on me)* (= deceived me). **12** *vt* to direct (a hose etc) in order to send out (liquid): *The firemen played their hoses on the flames.* **13** *vt* to send out a continuous length of (something): *play the rope along the side of the boat.* **14** *vt,vi* to direct (light etc) on, across etc: *The sunlight played on the water. They played coloured lights across the disco floor.* **15** *vt* to pretend to be (a condition mentioned): *play dead/ stupid.*

play about (with sb/sth) to use, treat etc a person, thing in an irresponsible way: *Stop playing about (with my money/my wife)*.

play along (with sb) to agree (with a person), esp because it is to one's advantage.

play around (with sb/sth) = play about (with sb/sth).

play at sb/sth (a) to pretend to be a person, profession etc for fun: *play at soldiers/doctors*. (b) to do an activity casually, with little interest: *Try harder—you're only playing at studying!* (c) to do an activity, esp a foolish one: *What are they playing at!*

play sth back to operate a tape-recorder, video etc and produce what has been recorded. **play sth back (to sb)** to pass, throw, a ball back (to a player).

play sth down to try to treat a pain, illness, crisis, defeat etc as less important than it really is: *He tried to play down his part in the robbery.*

play for sth (a) to represent a team, country etc in a game or sport: *play for Scotland.* (b) to try to get. **play for time** ⇨ time¹(2).

play off (of teams, players etc with equal scores) to play a deciding match. Hence **'play-off** *nc*.

play sb off against sb to try to encourage opposition between people in order to gain an advantage.

play on to continue to play a game. **play on sth** to use fear, sympathy, kindness etc in order to gain an advantage: *He tried to play on her sympathy.* ⇨ also joke¹, trick¹(2).

play sth out (a) (*fig*) to continue doing something to the finish: *The argument between them is not yet played out.* (b) to send out rope etc in a continuous length. **be played out** to be exhausted, out-of-date, no longer of a good standard: *He's played out as a professional footballer. Isn't that theory played out?* (= no longer worth considering?)

play up (a) (of children) to be naughty: *The twins are playing up.* (b) (of a bad leg, sore back etc) to produce pain: *My knee is playing up again.*

play sth up to try to treat an illness, problem etc as more important than it really is. **play up to sb** to say nice things to, do things for, a boss etc in order to gain an advantage.

play upon sth (*formal*) = play on sth.

play with sb/sth to treat a person, feelings etc in an irresponsible and casual way: *Don't play with her affections.* **play with sth** (a) to amuse oneself by touching, handling an animal, thing: *play with the dog.* (b) to consider an idea etc but not seriously: *We're playing with the idea of walking in Nepal.*

play·er /'pleɪə(r)/ *nc* a person who plays a game: *a football/tennis player.*

play·ful /'pleɪfəl/ *adj* in a mood for play; not serious: *as playful as a kitten; in a playful manner.*
play·ful·ly /-fəlɪ/ *adv*

play·ing-card /'pleɪŋ kɑːd/ *nc* a card(2).

play·ing-field /'pleɪŋ fiːld/ *nc* a field for games such as football and cricket.

play·let /'pleɪlɪt/ *nc* a short play.

play-off /'pleɪ ɒf/ *nc* ⇨ play off.

play·wright /'pleɪraɪt/ *nc* a person who writes plays.

plaza /'plɑːzə/ *nc* (*pl* —s) an open square or market-place.

plc, PLC /ˌpiː el 'siː/ *abbr* (*commerce*) (used after the name of a business that is) a public limited company (owned by the shareholders).

plea /pliː/ *nc* **1** (*legal*) a statement made by or for a person charged in a law court. **2** *plea (for sth)* a request: *a plea for mercy.*

plead /pliːd/ *vt,vi* (*pt,pp* **—ed** or *US* **pled** /pled/) **1** *vt,vi* (*legal*) to admit or deny that one is guilty: *How do you plead? Did you plead not guilty?* **2** *vt* to offer (something) as an explanation or excuse: *The thief pleaded poverty.* **3** *vi* **plead (with sb)** to make a serious and solemn request (to a per-

son): *He pleaded with his son to be less trouble to his mother.* **4** *vt* (*formal*) to argue in favour of (something): *plead the cause of political freedom.*

pleas·ant /'pleznt/ *adj* **1** giving pleasure to the senses, to one's thoughts and feelings: *a pleasant afternoon/taste/meal/surprise.* **2** (of a person) friendly, polite; showing understanding: *be pleasant towards a colleague; be pleasant about a mistake.* Opp unpleasant.
pleas·ant·ly *adv*
pleas·ant·ness *nu*

pleas·ant·ry /'plezntrɪ/ *nc* (*pl* **-ies**) (*formal*) an informal and friendly remark.

please /pliːz/ Ⓝ Not used in continuous tenses, e.g. *is/was -ing.* **1** (used as a polite form of request): *Come in, please. Please come in. Two coffees, please. Please don't do that. 'Would you like one?'—'Yes, please.'* Ⓝ Compare: *No, thanks.* **2** *vi,vt* to give pleasure or satisfaction to (a person): *She's hard to please. It's difficult to please everybody. Are you pleased with your new clothes?* **please oneself** to do what one wants to. **3** *vi* **as sb pleases** as a person prefers, chooses, thinks is best: *I shall do as I please. Take as many as you please.*

pleas·ed /pliːzd/ *adj* **pleased (with sb/sth)** feeling or showing satisfaction: *with a pleased smile. He looked pleased with himself. I'm very pleased with what he has done.*

pleas·ing /'pliːzɪŋ/ *adj* (*formal*) **pleasing (to sb/sth)** **1** giving pleasure (to): *pleasing to me/the eye.* **2** attractive: *a pleasing design.*
pleas·ing·ly *adv*

pleas·ur·able /'pleʒərəbl/ *adj* (*formal*) enjoyable (the usual word).
pleas·ur·ably /-əblɪ/ *adv*

pleas·ure /'pleʒə(r)/ *n* **1** *nu* the feeling of enjoyment, of being happy or satisfied: *It gave me such pleasure to hear of your success. Some boys take great pleasure in teasing their little sisters.* **2** *nu* **for pleasure** for enjoyment (not work): *I'm going to Athens for pleasure, not on business.* **3** *nc* something that gives happiness: *the pleasures of friendship. My greatest/only pleasure in life is walking.*

'pleasure-boat/-craft *nc* one used for enjoyment only.

pleat /pliːt/ *nc* a fold made by doubling cloth on itself. □ *vt* to make pleats in (cloth etc): *a pleated skirt.*

ple·be·ian /plɪ'biːən/ *adj, nc* (*informal* **pleb** /pleb/) (*derog*) (of) a person who does not have intellectual interests, good taste etc.

plebi·scite /'plebɪsaɪt/ *nc* (a decision made by) the votes of all qualified citizens.

plec·trum /'plektrəm/ *nc* a small piece of metal, plastic etc, used for plucking the strings of some instruments, e.g. the guitar.

pledge¹ /pledʒ/ *n* **1** *nc* something left with a person to be kept until the giver has done whatever he/she has to do: *You can keep this record as a pledge until I bring the money.* **2** *nu* the state of being left on these conditions: *put/hold goods in pledge.* **3** *nc* (formal) something given as a sign of love, approval etc. **4** *nc,nu* a serious promise, agreement: *under pledge of secrecy.* **take/sign the pledge** to make a written promise not to take alcoholic drink.

pledge² /pledʒ/ *vt* **1** *pledge sth (to sb)* to

make a serious promise (to give) (something) freely: *pledge £100 to the disaster fund.* **2 pledge that . . .** to make a serious promise or agreement that: *pledging that the money will be returned quickly.* **3 pledge sb to sth** (usually *passive*) to obtain a serious promise from a person about something: *be pledged to secrecy.*

ple·na·ry /'pli:nərɪ/ *adj* (*formal*) **1** (of powers, authority) unlimited; absolute. **2** (of meetings) attended by all who have a right to attend: *The meeting will be a plenary session.*

pleni·po·ten·ti·ary /ˌplenɪpə'tenʃərɪ/ *adj, nc* (*pl* **-ies**) (*formal*) (of) a person having full power to act, make decisions etc as an official representative (of a government etc).

plen·teous /'plentɪəs/ *adj* (*literary*) plentiful.

plen·ti·ful /'plentɪfʊl/ *adj* (usually *pred*) available in large quantities or numbers: *Apples are plentiful at this time of the year.* Compare scarce.
  plen·ti·ful·ly /-fəlɪ/ *adv*

plen·ty /'plentɪ/ *nu* **plenty (of sb/sth)** as much as or more than is needed or desired; a large number or quantity: *There are plenty of eggs. She has plenty of friends. We must get to the station in plenty of time. Six will be plenty* (= are as many as I need).

ple·th·ora /'pleθərə/ *n sing* (*formal*) an amount that is too much or too many: *a plethora of unhelpful suggestions.*

pleur·isy /'plʊərɪsɪ/ *nu* inflammation of the lining of the chest and lungs.

pli·able /'plaɪəbl/ *adj* **1** easily bent, shaped or twisted: *pliable wire.* **2** (of the mind) easily influenced.
  pli·abil·ity /ˌplaɪə'bɪlətɪ/ *nu*

pli·ant /'plaɪənt/ *adj* = pliable.

pli·ers /'plaɪəz/ *n pl* (also *a pair of pliers*) a kind of tool with long, flat jaws, used for holding, bending or cutting wire etc.

plight /plaɪt/ *nc* a serious and difficult condition: *His affairs were in a terrible plight.*

plim·soll /'plɪmsəl/ *nc* (also *a pair of plimsolls*) (*dated*) a casual shoe of canvas with a rubber sole. Ⓝ 'Trainer' or 'tennis shoe' is now used.

plinth /plɪnθ/ *nc* a square base or block on which a pillar or statue stands.

plod /plɒd/ *vi* (**-dd-**) **1** to walk slowly with a heavy step. **2 plod (away) at sth** to continue working etc slowly and without resting: *plod away at a task.*
  plod·der *nc* (often *derog*) a slow but determined worker.
  plod·ding *adj*

plonk¹ /plɒŋk/ *nu* (*sl*) cheap wine.

plonk² /plɒŋk/ *nc* a dull sound of something heavy dropping: *the plonk of a shoe falling down the stairs.*

plonk³ /plɒŋk/ *vt* **plonk sth down (on sth)** to put something down heavily: *plonk the book down on the table.*

plop¹ /plɒp/ *nc* a sound (as if) of a small smooth object dropping into water without a splash.

plop² /plɒp/ *vi* (**-pp-**) to make, fall with, a plop.

plot¹ /plɒt/ *nc* **1** a piece of ground (usually small): *a building plot; a plot of vegetables.* **2** (a secret) plan (good or bad) (to do something): *a plot to overthrow the government.* **3** the planned series of events or incidents in a story or play (usually lead-

ing to a climax).

plot² /plɒt/ *v* (**-tt-**) **1** *vt,vi* to make a (secret) plan: *plotting to buy the house; plot against the government.* **2** *vt* to mark (the position or movement of something) on a diagram or map: *plot the course of a ship.* **3** *vt* to show on a graph etc (changes, movement, amounts, comparisons etc). **4** *vt* **plot sth out** to divide land etc into small areas.

plot·ter /'plɒtə(r)/ *nc* a person who plots²(1).

plough¹ (*US* = **plow**) /plaʊ/ *nc* **1** a farming implement used for breaking and turning soil. **2** any similar implement: *a snow plough.*

plough² (*US* = **plow**) /plaʊ/ *v* **1** *vt,vi* to break up (soil, land) with a plough: *plough a field.* **2** *vt* **plough sth back** (*fig*) to put back money into a business: *plough back the profits.* **3** *vi* **plough through sth** to force a way through something: *plough through the mud/a dull textbook.* **4** *vt* (*informal*) to fail (a person) in an examination.

ploy /plɔɪ/ *nc* (*informal*) something said or done to gain an advantage over a person: *crying as a ploy to gain sympathy.*

pluck¹ /plʌk/ *n* **1** *nu* courage; spirit: *a boy with plenty of pluck.* **2** *nc* a short, sharp pull: *a pluck at her sleeve.*

pluck² /plʌk/ *v* **1** *vt* to pull the feathers off (a chicken etc): *Has this goose been plucked?* **2** *vt* to pick (flowers, fruit etc). **3** *vt,vi* **pluck (at) sth** to take hold of and pull something: *He was plucking at his mother's skirt.* **4 pluck up courage** to overcome one's fears.

plucky /'plʌkɪ/ *adj* (**-ier, -iest**) brave.

plug¹ /plʌg/ *nc* **1** a piece of rubber etc used to stop up a hole, e.g. in a bath. **2** a device used for making a connection with a supply of electric current: *put the plug in the socket.* ⇨ also spark plug. **3** (*sl*) a piece of favourable publicity (e.g. in a radio or TV programme) for a commercial product. ⇨ 4 below.

plug² /plʌg/ *v* (**-gg-**) **1** *vt* to fill (a hole etc) using a plug(1): *plug a leak.* **2** *vt* **plug sth in** to make a connection for an electrical appliance using a plug(2): *plug in the TV set.* **3** *vi* **plug away at sth** (*informal*) to work hard at a task etc. **4** *vt* (*sl*) to advertise (something) repeatedly: *plug a new song* (e.g. on TV).

plum /plʌm/ *nc* (also *attrib*) (a kind of tree with) a round, smooth-skinned fruit: *plum jam.*

plum·age /'plu:mɪdʒ/ *nu* a bird's feathers: *brightly coloured plumage.*

plumb¹ /plʌm/ *adv* (*informal*) exactly: *plumb in the middle/centre.*

plumb² /plʌm/ *nc* a ball or piece of lead tied to the end of a rope (*a plumb-line*) used for finding the depth of water or testing whether a wall is vertical.

plumb³ /plʌm/ *vt* (*fig*) to find the essential or basic cause or reason of (something): *plumb the depths of a mystery.*

plumb·er /'plʌmə(r)/ *nc* a worker who fits and repairs water-pipes.

plumb·ing /'plʌmɪŋ/ *nu* **1** the work of a plumber. **2** the pipes, water tanks, cisterns etc in a building.

plume¹ /plu:m/ *nc* **1** a feather, esp a large one used as a decoration. **2** something suggesting a feather by its shape: *a plume of smoke.*

plume² /plu:m/ *vt* (of a bird) to clean and smooth

(feathers).

plum·met /'plʌmɪt/ vi (-tt-) to fall steeply: *Share prices have plummetted.*

plump¹ /plʌmp/ adj (—er, —est) (of an animal, a person, parts of the body) fat in a pleasant way: *a baby with plump cheeks.*

plump² /plʌmp/ vt **plump sth up** to cause something to become rounded: *plump up a pillow.*

plump³ /plʌmp/ v 1 vt,vi (to cause a person, thing) to fall or drop suddenly and heavily: *plump (oneself) down in a chair; plump down a heavy bag.* 2 vt **plump for sb** to vote for, choose a person, plan etc: *plump for the Liberal candidate.*

plun·der /'plʌndə(r)/ vt,vi to steal things from (a town etc), esp during war or civil disorder: *plunder (the citizens of) a conquered town.* □ nu the things taken.

plunge¹ /plʌndʒ/ nc 1 an act of plunging, e.g. from a diving-board into water. 2 **take the plunge** to do something decisive, e.g. marry, accept a new job offer.

plunge² /plʌndʒ/ v 1 vt,vi (to cause a person, thing) to go suddenly and with force (into something): *plunging one's hand into cold water; plunging into a swimming-pool.* 2 vi to go down steeply: *Prices plunged. Her dress has a plunging* (= very low) *neckline.*

plung·er /'plʌndʒə(r)/ nc an implement used for clearing a blocked pipe by suction.

plu·per·fect /ˌpluː'pɜːfɪkt/ n **the pluperfect tense** (gram) (dated) = past perfect tense.

plu·ral /'plʊərəl/ adj, nc (gram) (of) a form of a noun or pronoun used to refer to more than one, as in *children, men, cakes, these.* Ⓝ Marked pl in this dictionary.

ˌplural 'noun nc (gram) (a) a plural form of a noun. (b) a noun that is always used as a plural, as in 'My son has *brains.*' Ⓝ Marked n pl or (pl) in this dictionary. Compare singular/collective noun.

plus¹ /plʌs/ adj (often written +) 1 (attrib) (of a number) more than 0; more than the amount mentioned: *plus ten degrees.* 2 (pred) above the standard mentioned: *He was given B+ for his school work.* Compare minus¹.

'plus sign nc the sign + used (a) in front of a plus number or after a plus standard, e.g. +10°; B+. (b) to show that one number is to be added to the previous one, as in 5+2=7 (five plus two equals seven). Compare minus sign.

plus² /plʌs/ nc 1 a plus sign or quantity. Compare minus². 2 (informal) an additional advantage: *To see mountains with snow on them is a definite plus.*

plus³ /plʌs/ prep 1 with the addition of a number: *6 plus 4 is 10.* 2 with the (unexpected) addition of: *return from the climb plus an injury or two.* Compare minus³.

plush /plʌʃ/ (also **plushy** (-ier, -iest)) adj (informal) smart, expensive: *work in a plush(y) restaurant.*

Pluto /'pluːtəʊ/ n the planet farthest from the sun.

plu·to·cra·cy /pluː'tɒkrəsɪ/ nc,nu (pl -ies) (government by) a rich and powerful class.

plu·to·crat /'pluːtəkræt/ nc a person who is powerful because of wealth.

plu·to·crat·ic /ˌpluːtə'krætɪk/ adj

plu·to·ni·um /pluː'təʊnɪəm/ nu (an artificially produced) radioactive element (symbol Pu), used in nuclear power.

ply¹ /plaɪ/ nc 1 a layer of wood or thickness of cloth: *three-ply wood* (= with 3 layers glued together). 2 one strand in wool, rope etc: *four-ply wool.*

'ply·wood nu a kind of board made by gluing together thin layers of wood.

ply² /plaɪ/ v (pt,pp **plied**, pres p **plying**) 1 vi **ply between** one place and another (of ships, buses etc) to go regularly to and from: *ships that ply between Glasgow and New York.* 2 vt **ply sb with sth** to keep a person constantly supplied with food, questions etc.

pm /ˌpiː 'em/ abbr 1 (Latin: post meridiem) after noon: *2.30 pm.* 2 (written abbr) per month.

PM written abbr (often the—) the Prime Minister.

pneu·mat·ic /njuː'mætɪk/ adj 1 worked or driven by compressed air: *pneumatic drills.* 2 filled with compressed air: *pneumatic tyres.*

pneu·mati·cal·ly /-klɪ/ adv

pneu·mo·nia /njuː'məʊnɪə/ nu a serious illness with inflammation of one or both lungs.

PO written abbr 1 Post Office. 2 postal order.

poach¹ /pəʊtʃ/ vt 1 to cook (an egg) by cracking the shell and dropping the contents into boiling water. 2 to cook (fish) in water or milk that is boiling gently.

poach² /pəʊtʃ/ vt,vi 1 (to go on private land and) take (animals, fish etc) illegally. 2 (fig) to take (good workers or good ideas) from another business etc.

poach·er nc a person who poaches.

PO Box /pɪ 'əʊ bɒks/ abbr post office box (used with the number, as in *'PO Box 141, Oxford'*).

pock·et¹ /'pɒkɪt/ adj (attrib) of a size suitable for carrying in a pocket: *a pocket camera/dictionary.*

pock·et² /'pɒkɪt/ nc 1 a small bag forming part of an article of clothing, used for carrying things in. **be in/out of pocket** (a) to have money/have no money. (b) to have gained/lost money as a result of a business deal. **pick sb's pocket** to steal from a person's pocket. ⇨ pickpocket. 2 (informal) a small area: *a pocket of iron-ore; pockets of unemployment.*

'pocket-money nu a small amount of money given to children.

pocket·ful /-fʊl/ nc as much as a pocket(1) can hold.

pock·et³ /'pɒkɪt/ vt 1 to put (something) into one's pocket: *He pocketed the money.* 2 to keep (money) for oneself (dishonestly): *He pocketed half the profits.*

pod¹ /pɒd/ nc a long, green part of a plant, in which peas or beans grow.

pod² /pɒd/ vt (-dd-) to take (peas) out of pods.

POD written abbr (commerce) pay on delivery.

podgy /'pɒdʒɪ/ adj (-ier, -iest) (usually derog) (of a person, finger etc) short and fat.

po·em /'pəʊɪm/ nc a piece of creative writing in a rhythmic (and often rhyming) form, usually designed to express deep feelings and thoughts.

po·et /'pəʊɪt/ nc a writer of poems.

po·et·ic /pəʊ'etɪk/ (also **po·eti·cal** /-ɪkl/) adj of poets and poetry: *poetic genius.*

po,etic 'justice nu an accidental form of justice, with suitable rewards and punishments: *Arriving late and losing the opportunity of a free* *meal was poetic justice*.

po‚etic 'licence *nu* the freedom from using the normal rules of grammar etc (as in poetry).

po·eti·cal·ly /-klɪ/ *adv*

po·et·ry /'pəʊɪtrɪ/ *nu* **1** the art of a poet; poems in general. **2** a quality that produces feelings as produced by poems: *the poetry of motion* (e.g. in some kinds of dancing).

poig·nan·cy /'pɔɪnjənsɪ/ *nu* (*formal*) the state or quality of being poignant.

poign·ant /'pɔɪnjənt/ *adj* (*formal*) causing pity and sadness: *poignant memories*.

poign·ant·ly *adv*

point¹ /pɔɪnt/ *n* **1** *nc* a sharp end (of a pin, pencil etc). **not to put too fine a point on it** to express (an opinion etc) honestly and fully. **2** *nc* a marked place or position in space or time: *At which points in the journey did you stop to eat? There is a petrol station at the point where the two roads meet. Going to India was an important point in my life*. **at that/this point** at that/this place or moment. **if/when it comes to the point** if/when the moment for action or decision comes: *When it came to the point, he refused to help*. **a point of view** (*pl* —*s of view*) (**a**) a position from which something is viewed. (**b**) (*fig*) a way of considering a question: *Imagine the difficulties from my point of view*. **the point of no return** the stage in an activity, procedure etc after which stopping is not possible. **be at the point of death** to be dying. **be on the point of doing sth** to be about to do it. **3** *nc* a small dot (as if) made by the point of a pencil etc. ⇨ also decimal point, full point. **4** *nc* a mark on a scale; unit of measuring: *the points on the compass; the boiling-point of water*. **5** *nc* a score of one in some games, sports and competitions. **6** *nc* one item, detail, idea etc: *There are several points on which we've agreed to differ*. **a point of order** (*pl* —*s of order*) a question made during a meeting about the agreed rules or procedure. **stretch a point** to allow something important not to be used or taken into account (when deciding). **7** *nc* a main piece of information, idea or thought in an argument: *The point is that she knew all the time*. **be beside the point** to be of little or no importance (compared to the main evidence, topic etc): *Your private opinion is beside the point—look at the results of the computer analysis!* **a case in point** ⇨ case¹(1). **in point of fact** ⇨ fact(4). **to the point** relevant: *Her explanation was clear and to the point*. **come to/get to/reach the point** to give the essential, relevant fact. **get/ see/miss the point (of sth)** to understand/fail to understand: *She missed the point of the joke*. **make a point of doing sth** to do it because it is important or necessary. **take sb's point** (during a discussion) to understand the idea etc used in a person's argument. **8** *nu* reason, purpose: *There's no/not much point in protesting* (= It won't help). **9** *nc* a particular or noticeable characteristic: *What are her best points as a secretary?* **10** *nc* (*GB*) (also *power point*) an outlet for electric current. **11** *nc* a long piece of land with a narrow end.

point² /pɔɪnt/ *v* **1** *vt,vi* **point (sth) at sb/sth; point to sb/sth** to direct attention to (the position of) a person, thing by directing a finger or other object towards her, him, it: *He pointed to the door. She was pointing a gun at him*. **2** *vi* **point to sth** to show, be a sign of something: *All the evidence points to his guilt*. **3** *vt* **point sth out** to direct attention to something: *point out a mistake. I must point out that the price is too high*.

point-blank /ˌpɔɪnt 'blæŋk/ *adj* (*attrib*), *adv* **1** (of a shot) fired at very close range: *fired at point-blank range*. **2** (*fig*) (of something said) in a manner that leaves no room for doubt: *a point-blank refusal. I asked him point-blank whether he intended to help*.

point·ed /'pɔɪntɪd/ *adj* (*fig*) intended to be against a person or group although not said directly to her, him, them: *Jack was making pointed comments about his neighbour's garden*.

point·ed·ly *adv*

point·er /'pɔɪntə(r)/ *nc* **1** a stick etc used to point to things on a map etc. **2** an indicator on a dial or balance. **3** **pointer (to sth)** an indication (of something): *The rise in unemployment is a pointer to the failure of their economic policies*.

point·less /'pɔɪntlɪs/ *adj* (*fig*) with little or no sense, aim or purpose: *It seemed pointless to argue*.

point·less·ly *adv*: *argue pointlessly*.

poise¹ /pɔɪz/ *nu* **1** the way in which one carries oneself, holds one's head etc. **2** self-confidence and self-control.

poise² /pɔɪz/ *vt* to balance (oneself, something etc) in a particular place or manner (esp a difficult one): *be poised in mid-air; poising the ball on his nose*.

poi·son¹ /'pɔɪzn/ *nc,nu* a substance causing death or harm if absorbed by a living thing (animal or plant): *poison for killing weeds/mice*.

poi·son² /'pɔɪzn/ *vt* **1** to put poison on or in (food, plants, animals etc): *poison the rats*. **2** (*fig*) to put harmful ideas into (a person's mind) deliberately: *poison somebody's mind against another person*.

pois·on·er *nc* a person who murders another person by using poison.

pois·on·ous /'pɔɪzənəs/ *adj* **1** having poison; causing death or injury: *poisonous plants*. **2** deliberately causing harm to a person's feelings, reputation etc: *a man with a poisonous tongue*.

pois·on·ous·ly *adv*

poke¹ /pəʊk/ *nc* an act of poking.

poke² /pəʊk/ *v* **1** *vt,vi* to push (a person, thing) sharply using a stick, one's finger etc: *poke a man in the ribs; poke the fire*. ⇨ fun(1), nose¹(1). **2** *vt,vi* to put, move, (something) with a sharp push through an opening: *Don't let him poke his head out of the (train) window—it's dangerous!* **3** *vi* **poke about** to search: *Who's that poking about in the garden?* **4** *vt* to make (a hole) by poking.

po·ker¹ /'pəʊkə(r)/ *nc* a metal bar used for moving coal in a fire.

po·ker² /'pəʊkə(r)/ *nu* a card-game used for gambling.

po·ky /'pəʊkɪ/ *adj* (-**ier**, -**iest**) (*derog*) (of a place) too small: *a poky little room*.

po·lar /'pəʊlə(r)/ *adj* (*attrib*) of, near, the North or South Pole: *polar regions*.

ˌpolar 'bear *nc* the white kind living in the north polar regions.

po·lar·ity /pəʊ'lærətɪ/ *nu* (*formal*) the possession

of two contrasted or opposite qualities, principles or tendencies.

po·lar·ize (also **-ise**) /'pəʊləraɪz/ vt,vi (to cause something) to centre on two opposite, conflicting or contrasting positions: *Inflation has polarized opinion for the next election.*

po·lar·iz·ation (also **-is·ation**) /ˌpəʊləraɪ'zeɪʃn/ nu

Po·lar·oid /'pəʊlərɔɪd/ nu (P) the thin transparent film used in sun-glasses, etc to reduce sun glare.

pole¹ /pəʊl/ nc **1** (usually P-) either of the two ends of the earth's axis: *the North Pole; the South Pole.* **2** (tech) either of the two ends of a magnet or the terminal points of an electric battery: *the negative/positive pole.* **be poles apart** to have opposite opinions in an argument: *The employers and the trade union leaders are still poles apart.*

pole² /pəʊl/ nc a thin, long, rounded piece of wood or metal, e.g. as a handle for a broom etc. **up the pole** (sl) (a) in difficulty. (b) slightly mad.

'pole-vault nc,nu (an athletic contest) jumping with the help of a long pole over a high bar which can be raised or lowered.

pol·em·ic /pə'lemɪk/ adj (formal) involving argument or disagreement. □ nc (formal) an argument or disagreement (esp about a belief).

po·lice¹ /pə'liːs/ n pl (the —) an official group of men and women whose job is to protect people and property, catch criminals etc: *The police have not made any arrests.*

po'lice·man /-mən/ nc a male police officer.

po'lice force nc (often the —) the police of a country or region.

po'lice officer nc a member of the police force.

po'lice state nc a country controlled by political police.

po'lice station nc an office of a local police force: *I was taken to the police station.*

po'lice·woman nc a female police officer.

po·lice² /pə'liːs/ vt to keep order in (a place) by using the police or a similar official group: *The United Nations soldiers are policing the area.*

pol·icy¹ /'pɒləsɪ/ nc,nu (pl **-ies**) a plan of action, statement of aims and ideals, e.g. one made by a government, political party, business company etc: *What is their policy on education? Is honesty the best policy?* (= the best way to act?)

pol·icy² /'pɒləsɪ/ nc (also attrib) a written statement of the conditions of an insurance agreement: *an insurance policy; a policy-holder.*

po·lio /'pəʊlɪəʊ/ nu (informal) = poliomyelitis.

po·lio·mye·li·tis /ˌpəʊlɪəʊˌmaɪə'laɪtɪs/ nu an infectious disease often causing loss of control of the muscles.

pol·ish¹ /'pɒlɪʃ/ n **1** nc,nu a substance used for polishing a surface: *furniture/shoe polish.* **2** nc a shining surface produced by polishing: *shoes with a good polish.* **3** nu a quality of elegance, good manners etc (in behaviour, speech etc).

pol·ish² /'pɒlɪʃ/ v **1** vt,vi (to cause the surface of something) to become smooth and shiny by rubbing (esp with a special substance): *polish furniture/shoes.* **2** vt **polish sth (up)** to improve something as much as possible: *polish a speech; polish up one's English.* **3** vt **polish sth off** (informal) to finish a meal, task etc quickly: *pol-*

ish off one's breakfast/an essay.

pol·ish·ed /'pɒlɪʃt/ adj (usually attrib) done to a high standard: *a polished performance.*

Pol·it·buro /pə'lɪtbjʊərəʊ/ nc (pl **—s**) the chief executive committee of a Communist party.

pol·ite /pə'laɪt/ adj having, showing, good manners and consideration for other people: *a polite boy/remark; be polite.* Opp impolite.

pol·ite·ly adv

pol·ite·ness nu

poli·tic /'pɒlɪtɪk/ adj (formal) **1** (of a person) acting or judging wisely. **2** (of an action) well-judged: *a politic remark at the conference.*

pol·iti·cal /pə'lɪtɪkl/ adj **1** concerning the State, government or public affairs in general: *political parties/beliefs.* **2** because of politics: *political censorship.* **3** interested in politics.

po,litical a'sylum nu protection given to a person who has left a country for political reasons.

po,litical 'prisoner nc a person who is imprisoned because he or she disagrees with the (system of) government.

po,litical 'science nu the scientific study of government and politics.

po,litical 'surgery nc an occasion and place when people can talk with their Member of Parliament.

po·liti·cal·ly /-klɪ/ adv

poli·ti·cian /ˌpɒlɪ'tɪʃn/ nc **1** a person taking an active part in government, esp as an elected representative. **2** a person with a (good or bad) ability to express an opinion, persuade a person etc: *a clever/poor politician.*

poli·tics /'pɒlɪtɪks/ n **1** n sing or pl the science or business of government: *Is politics taught at the school?* **2** n pl opinions, views about government: *What are your politics?*

pol·ka /'pɒlkə/ nc (a piece of music for) a kind of lively dance.

poll¹ /pəʊl/ nc **1** the process of voting at an election: *a light/heavy poll* (= a small/large number of voters). **2** = opinion poll.

poll² /pəʊl/ vt to receive (a mentioned number of votes): *Mr Hill polled over 3000 votes.*

'poll·ing-booth/-station nc a place where voters go to vote.

'poll·ing-day nc a day of an election by voting.

pol·len /'pɒlən/ nu the fine powder (usually yellow) formed on flowers, which fertilizes other flowers when carried to them by the wind, insects etc.

'pollen count nc the amount of pollen in the atmosphere.

pol·lin·ate /'pɒlɪneɪt/ vt to fertilize (a plant) by using pollen.

pol·li·na·tion /ˌpɒlɪ'neɪʃn/ nu

poll·ster /'pəʊlstə(r)/ nc a person who conducts public opinion polls.

pol·lu·tant /pə'luːtənt/ nc,nu any substance that pollutes(1): *pollutants in petrol/from factory chimneys.*

pol·lute /pə'luːt/ vt **1** to make (air, rivers etc) dirty, impure: *rivers polluted with waste from factories.* **2** (fig) to make (a person's mind) immoral: *polluting young minds.*

pol·lu·tion /pə'luːʃn/ nu **1** the act of polluting. **2** (a mixture of) substances that pollute: *pollution in the cities/rivers.*

po·lo /'pəʊləʊ/ *nu* an outdoor game played on horseback with long wooden hammers. ⇨ water polo.

po·lo-neck /'pəʊləʊ nek/ *adj, nc* (having) a rolled collar: *polo-neck sweaters.*

poly·ester /ˌpɒlɪ'estə(r)/ *nu* a kind of manmade fabric, used for clothing.

po·lyga·mist /pə'lɪgəmɪst/ *nc* a man who practises polygamy.

po·lyga·mous /pə'lɪgəməs/ *adj* of, practising, polygamy.

po·lyga·my /pə'lɪgəmɪ/ *nu* (the custom of) having more than one wife at the same time. Compare bigamy, monogamy.

poly·gon /'pɒlɪgən/ *nc* (*maths*) a flat figure with five or more straight sides.

poly·mer /'pɒlɪmə(r)/ *nc,nu* (*tech*) a kind of light, strong and durable plastic used in machines, vehicles etc.

poly·sty·rene /ˌpɒlɪ'staɪriːn/ *nu* (*tech*) a kind of light plastic material used to make containers.

poly·tech·nic /ˌpɒlɪ'teknɪk/ *nc* (also *attrib*) (P- in names) an educational institution for students studying mainly scientific and technical subjects: *Manchester Polytechnic; polytechnic students.*

poly·thene /'pɒlɪθiːn/ *nu* (*tech*) a kind of plastic material used for waterproof packaging etc.

poly·un·satu·rat·ed /ˌpɒlɪʌn'sætʃʊreɪtɪd/ *adj* of, containing, a group of vegetable and animal fats with a structure that is easily absorbed in digestion: *polyunsaturated margarine.*

poly·ure·thane /ˌpɒlɪ'jʊərəθeɪn/ *nu* (*tech*) a kind of manmade material used to make plastic foam and to make a kind of hard, strong paint or varnish.

pom·egran·ate /'pɒmɪɡrænɪt/ *nc* (a tree with) a thick-skinned round fruit which, when ripe, has a centre full of pink seeds.

pomp /pɒmp/ *nu* a grand ceremony or display, esp at a public event.

pom·pos·ity /pɒm'pɒsətɪ/ *nc,nu* (*pl* -**ies**) (*formal*) (an instance of) being pompous.

pom·pous /'pɒmpəs/ *adj* full of, showing (too much) self-importance: *a pompous official.*

pon·cho /'pɒntʃəʊ/ *nc* (*pl* —**s**) a large piece of cloth with a hole in the middle for the head, worn as a cloak.

pond /pɒnd/ *nc* a small area of water, e.g. in a garden.

pon·der /'pɒndə(r)/ *vt,vi* **ponder (about/on/ over) (sth)** (*formal*) to think (about something): *He pondered (over) the incident.*

pon·der·ous /'pɒndərəs/ *adj* (*formal*) **1** slow and heavy: *ponderous movements* (e.g. of a fat man). **2** (of written style) serious and dull.
pon·der·ous·ly *adv*

pong /pɒŋ/ *nc* (*sl*) a bad smell. □ *vi* (*sl*) to smell badly.

pon·tiff /'pɒntɪf/ *nc* (also P-) the Pope.

pon·tifi·cal /pɒn'tɪfɪkl/ *adj* of, concerning, the Pope.

pon·tifi·cate /pɒn'tɪfɪkeɪt/ *vi* **pontificate (about/over sth)** (*formal*) to speak in an arrogant and pompous way.

pon·toon¹ /pɒn'tuːn/ *nc* **1** a flat-bottomed boat. **2** (also *attrib*) many of these supporting a roadway over a river: *a pontoon bridge.*

pon·toon² /pɒn'tuːn/ *nu* a kind of card-game

used for gambling.

po·ny /'pəʊnɪ/ *nc* (*pl* -**ies**) a kind of small horse.

'pony-trekking *nu* the making of a journey for pleasure on ponies.

poodle /'puːdl/ *nc* a kind of dog with thick curling hair.

pooh /puː/ *int* (used to indicate a bad smell).

pool¹ /puːl/ *nc* **1** a small area of water (smaller than a pond). **2** a quantity of liquid lying on a surface: *He was lying in a pool of blood.* **3** = swimming-pool.

pool² /puːl/ *nc* **1** a total amount of money used by gamblers. **2** (*pl*) = football pools: *win a fortune on the pools.* **3** an arrangement by business firms to share business and divide profits, to avoid competition and agree on prices. **4** a common fund, supply or service, provided by or shared among many: *a typing-pool.*

pool³ /puːl/ *vt* to put (money, resources etc) together for the use of all who contribute: *They pooled their savings and bought a car.*

poor¹ /pʊə(r)/ *adj* (—**er**, —**est**) **1** (having only a little or no money and) not able to get the basic necessities of life: *poor families; poor countries.* Compare rich¹(1). **2** having poor people: *poor areas of our cities.* **3** not having the correct or desired qualities: *poor soil/eyesight; in poor health; a poor piece of work/attempt.* Compare good¹(1). **4** small in quantity: *a poor supply of food; a poor salary; a poor number of voters.* Compare good¹(12). **5** (*pred*) **poor in sb/sth** containing a small quantity or supply: *a country poor in natural resources; a world poor in people concerned about the destruction of the rain forests.* Compare rich¹(3). **6** giving little or no interest, enjoyment: *a poor play/performance.* **7** not able to enjoy life, our environment fully: *Without television/a hobby/areas where birds are protected, we/life would be much poorer.* **8** (*attrib*) needing, deserving help or sympathy: *The poor little cat had no home. Poor Ben has lost his bike again.*

poor² /pʊə(r)/ *n pl* (the —) poor people. Compare rich².

poor·ly¹ /'pʊəlɪ/ *adj* (*pred*) (*informal*) unwell: *He's very poorly this morning.*

poor·ly² /'pʊəlɪ/ *adv* **1** badly: *poorly-lit streets.* **2** **poorly off** having very little money: *She's been poorly off since her husband died.* Opp richly(a).

poor·ness /'pʊənɪs/ *nu* the absence of some necessary quality or element: *the poorness of the soil.* Compare poverty.

pop¹ /pɒp/ *adj* (*informal*) = popular: *pop music/ pop singers/pop groups* (= singers and players whose records sell in large numbers and who are popular on radio, TV and in discos).
'pop concert *nc* one with pop music.
'pop festival *nc* a large outdoor gathering of people to hear pop singers and musicians.
'pop star *nc* a famous pop singer or musician.

pop² /pɒp/ *adv* with the sound of popping: *I heard it go/The balloon went pop.*

pop³ /pɒp/ *nc* **1** a short, sharp, explosive sound: *the pop of a cork.* **2** (*informal*) a kind of fruit drink with gas in it: *a bottle of pop.*

pop⁴ /pɒp/ *nc* (*informal*) = father¹(1).

pop⁵ /pɒp/ *vt,vi* (-**pp**-) (to cause something) to make a sharp, quick sound (as when a cork comes out of a bottle).

pop across (to a place) ⇨ pop over (to a place) below.

pop (sth) in (to cause something) to go or come in quickly (giving the idea of rapid or unexpected movement or activity): *He popped his head in at the door. The neighbours' children are always popping in and out* (= are very frequent visitors).
pop sth into sth to put it there quickly: *She popped the gin bottle into the cupboard as the vicar entered the room.*
pop off (*sl*) to die.
pop (sth) out (to cause something) to go or come out quickly: *I'm popping out for a few minutes to buy some milk.*
pop out of sth to come out of something suddenly: *His eyes almost popped out of his head when he saw that he had won.*
pop over (to a place) to make a quick, short visit (to): *She's popped over to the grocer's.*
pop up (of toast, pictures in a book) to spring up quickly. Hence **'pop-up** *adj* (*attrib*): *a pop-up toaster/book.*

pop. *written abbr* **1** popular. **2** population.
pop·corn /'pɒpkɔːn/ *nu* dried maize heated until it bursts open, eaten with honey, salt etc.
pope /pəup/ *n* (also P-) the head of the Roman Catholic Church.
pop·py /'pɒpɪ/ *nc* (*pl* **-ies**) a kind of plant, with large, esp red, flowers.
popu·lace /'pɒpjʊləs/ *nc* (usually the —) (*formal*) the general public.
popu·lar /'pɒpjʊlə(r)/ *adj* **1** liked, admired, enjoyed by many people: *popular music; a popular film; a teacher who is popular with the students.* Opp unpopular. **2** (*attrib*) suited to the tastes, needs, educational level etc of the general public: *popular entertainment on TV.* **3** (*attrib*) of, for, the general public: *popular opinion/government.*
,popular 'front *nc* (in politics) an organized grouping of political parties opposed to reaction and fascism.
popu·lar·ly *adv*
popu·lar·ity /,pɒpjʊ'lærətɪ/ *nu* the quality of being popular(1).
popu·lar·ize (also **-ise**) /'pɒpjʊləraɪz/ *vt* to make (a new idea, product) known and liked: *popularize a new book.*
popu·late /'pɒpjʊleɪt/ *vt* to supply (an area of land) with people: *the thickly populated parts of India.*
popu·la·tion /,pɒpjʊ'leɪʃn/ *nc* (a number of) people living in a place, country etc or a special section of them: *the population of London; the working-class population.*
por·ce·lain /'pɔːsəlɪn/ *nu* (articles, e.g. cups and plates, made of) a kind of fine china with a shiny coating (called *glaze*).
porch /pɔːtʃ/ *nc* a roofed doorway or entrance to a building.
por·cu·pine /'pɔːkjʊpaɪn/ *nc* a small animal (larger than a hedgehog) covered with spines that it sticks out if attacked.
pore¹ /pɔː(r)/ *nc* a tiny opening in the skin through which fluids (e.g. sweat) pass.
pore² /pɔː(r)/ *vi* **pore over sth** to examine, study, something in detail: *poring over a letter/book.*
pork /pɔːk/ *nu* (also *attrib*) the flesh of a pig used

as food: *a pork chop; roast pork.* ⇨ bacon, ham¹(1).

porn /pɔːn/ *nu* (*informal*) = pornography.
'porn shop *nc* a place where pornographic books etc are sold.
por·nogra·phy /pɔː'nɒgrəfɪ/ *nu* **1** the treatment of sexual subjects in an offensive and immoral way using writing, pictures etc. **2** such writing, pictures etc.
por·no·graph·ic /,pɔːnə'græfɪk/ *adj*
po·rous /'pɔːrəs/ *adj* allowing liquid to pass through: *Sand is porous.*
por·poise /'pɔːpəs/ *nc* a kind of sea animal like a small whale.
por·ridge /'pɒrɪdʒ/ *nu* a kind of soft food made by boiling oatmeal in water or milk: *a bowl/plate of porridge.*
port¹ /pɔːt/ *nc* **1** a harbour: *a naval port. We reached port.* **2** a town or city with a harbour, esp one where customs officers are stationed.
port² /pɔːt/ *nu* the left-hand side of a ship or plane as one faces forward. Compare starboard.
port³ /pɔːt/ *nu* a strong, sweet, dark-red wine of Portugal.
port·able /'pɔːtəbl/ *adj* that can be carried about: *portable radios/typewriters.* Compare movable(1).
por·tal /'pɔːtl/ *nc* an elaborate doorway of a large building.
por·tend /pɔː'tend/ *vt* (*formal*) to be a sign or warning of (a future event etc): *This portends war.*
por·tent /'pɔːtent/ *nc* (*formal*) an omen.
por·ten·tous /pɔː'tentəs/ *adj* (*formal*) (esp) threatening that something bad will happen.
por·ter /'pɔːtə(r)/ *nc* **1** a person whose work is to carry luggage etc at stations, airports, hotels etc. **2** a doorkeeper (at a hotel, public building etc). **3** a person carrying a load on his back or head (usually in country where there are no roads for vehicles).
port·fo·lio /pɔːt'fəʊlɪəʊ/ *nc* (*pl* **—s**) **1** a flat case used for keeping papers, documents, drawings etc. **2** the position and duties of a minister of state: *He is minister without portfolio* (= is not in charge of any particular department). **3** a list of securities and investments (stocks, shares etc) owned by a person, bank etc.
port·hole /'pɔːthəʊl/ *nc* a small (usually round) window on the side of a ship or plane.
port·ico /'pɔːtɪkəʊ/ *nc* (*pl* **—es** or **—s**) a roof on pillars, esp at the entrance of a building.
por·tion¹ /'pɔːʃn/ *nc* **1** a part, esp a share, (to be) given when something is distributed: *pay back a portion of the loan; be given a portion of the profits.* **2** a quantity (of any kind of food) as served in a restaurant: *a generous portion of roast duck.*
por·tion² /'pɔːʃn/ *vt* **portion sth out (among/ between sb)** to share something out (which is more usual).
port·ly /'pɔːtlɪ/ *adj* (*formal*) (of a person) round, fat.
por·trait /'pɔːtrɪt/ *nc* **1** a painted picture, drawing or photograph of a person or animal. **2** a vivid description in words.
'por·trait·ure /-tʃə(r)/ *nu* the art of making portraits.

por·tray /pɔː'treɪ/ vt (formal) **1** to show (a person, thing) in a picture, photograph etc: portray a forest scene. **2** to describe (something) vividly in words. **3** to act (a character) in a play.

por·tray·al /pɔː'treɪəl/ nc,nu

pose¹ /pəʊz/ nc **1** a position in, for, a painting, photograph etc: an unusual pose. **2** a dishonest way of behaving, intended to impress people: That rich man's socialism is a mere pose.

pose² /pəʊz/ v **1** vt to put (a person) in a position before making a portrait, taking a photograph etc: All the children are well posed. **2** vi **pose for sb/sth** to take up a position for a photograph, painter etc: Will you pose for me? **3** vt to suggest, offer, cause, (a problem, difficulty): The increase in student numbers poses many problems for the universities. **4** vi **pose as sb** to pretend to be the type of person mentioned: posing as an expert on old coins. **5** vi to behave in a dishonest and important way hoping to impress people: She's always posing.

posh /pɒʃ/ adj (informal; often derog) elegant and smart (and intended to impress people): a posh hotel; posh clothes; her posh friends.

po·si·tion¹ /pə'zɪʃn/ n **1** nc a place where a person, thing, place etc is or stands: a position on a map/graph. **in/out of position** in/not in the right place. **2** nc a way of sitting, standing etc: sit/ lie in a comfortable position. **3** nc a person's place or rank in relation to others in employment, in society etc: a pupil's position in class; a high/low position in society. **4** nc (formal) a job: apply for the position of assistant manager. **5** n sing a condition: I'm sorry but I am not in a position (= am unable) to help you. **6** nc an opinion: What's your position on this problem?

po·si·tion² /pə'zɪʃn/ vt to place, put, (a person, thing) in position(1): position a chair in the corner.

posi·tive¹ /'pɒzɪtɪv/ adj **1** definite; sure; leaving no room for doubt: We want a positive answer— yes or no. I gave you positive instructions. **2** (pred) (of a person) quite certain, esp about opinions: Are you positive (that) it was after midnight? **3** practical and constructive; that definitely helps: a positive suggestion; positive advice/help; positive criticism. Opp negative(2). **4** (attrib) (informal) complete: That man is a positive fool. **5** (maths) greater than zero: a positive amount/number. Opp negative¹(3). **6** (electricity) of the sort caused by a lack of electrons: a positive charge. Opp negative(4). **7** (photography) showing light and shadows as in nature. Compare negative(5). **8** (med) showing presence of a disease etc: The blood tests were positive. Opp negative(b). **9** (gram) (of adjectives and adverbs) of the form (e.g. green) that is not a comparative (e.g. greener) or superlative (e.g. greenest).

,positive 'thinking nu deliberately considering, deciding, acting, in a way that shows confidence in an idea, plan, solution.

posi·tive·ly adv **1** definitely: express positively one's willingness to pay. **2** (informal) without doubt: This is positively the last time that I will remind you.

posi·tive² /'pɒzɪtɪv/ nc **1** (gram) a positive adjective or adverb. **2** (maths) an amount more than 0. **3** a positive photograph or film. ⇨ negative².

poss /pɒs/ abbr (informal) possible: I'll be there,

if poss, by 9 o'clock.

pos·sess /pə'zes/ vt Ⓝ Not used in continuous tenses, e.g. is/was -ing. **1** (formal) to own (something): possess nothing; lose all that one possesses. **2** to influence (a person, mind): What possessed you to do that?

pos·ses·sor /-sə(r)/ nc (formal) an owner.

pos·ses·sion /pə'zeʃn/ n **1** nu ownership: How did it come into your possession? How did you get possession of it? The information in my possession is strictly confidential. Is she in full possession of her senses? (= Is she sane?) **2** nc (usually pl) property: lose all one's possessions in a fire.

pos·sess·ive /pə'zesɪv/ adj **1** of possession or ownership: She has a possessive nature (= is eager to own things or wants the whole of (a person's) love or attention). **2** (gram) (of a pronoun, adjective) showing possession.

pos,sessive 'adjective nc (gram) (one kind of possessive pronoun) used before a noun etc to show possession, e.g. my, your, her, their.

pos'sessive case nc (gram) (the —) the form of pronouns, nouns and adjectives used to show possession or association, e.g. Tom's, the boys', a boy's.

pos,sessive 'pronoun nc (gram) the form of a pronoun used to show possession, e.g. mine, yours, hers, theirs and also my, your, her, their.

pos·si·bil·ity /ˌpɒsə'bɪlətɪ/ n (pl **-ies**) **1** nu the state, degree, of being possible: Is there any/much possibility of your getting to London this week? Help is still within the bounds of possibility (= is possible). **2** nc something that is possible: I see great possibilities for this scheme.

pos·si·ble /'pɒsəbl/ adj **1** that can happen or be done, or may prove to be correct: Come as soon as possible. I'd like it back tomorrow if (at all) possible. Frost is possible, though not probable. Compare probable. Opp impossible(1). **2** that is reasonable or suitable: He is the only possible man for the position.

pos·sibly /-əblɪ/ adv **(a)** (used for emphasis): You can't possibly mean that. I will come as soon as I possibly can. **(b)** perhaps: 'Will the manager put your salary up?'—'Possibly.'

post¹ /pəʊst/ nc an upright length of wood or metal supporting or marking something: a lamp post; a gate post; the goal posts.

post² /pəʊst/ nc **1** a job: be given the post as manager. **2** a place where a soldier is (to be) on duty.

post³ /pəʊst/ n (the —) **1** the system of collecting, sorting and delivering letters, parcels etc (US = mail). **by post** using this system: sent by post. Compare by hand. **by return of post** in the next possible delivery or collection: Please reply by return of post. **2** one delivery or collection: the afternoon post. **3** the letters, parcels etc that are delivered: Has the post arrived?

'post·box nc an official container for letters and small parcels sent by post.

'post·card nc an oblong card (usually with a picture on one side) used for sending short messages.

'post·code nc a set of letters and numbers as part of an address, used to make the sorting and delivery easier.

'post·man nc a man employed to deliver letters etc (US = mailman).

'post·mark *nc* an official mark on letters showing the date and place of posting.

'post office *nc* a place where postal business is carried on.

'post office box *nc* (abbr **PO Box**) a numbered box in a post office where letters are kept for collection by an individual or company.

,post-'paid *adj, adv* with postage already paid.

'post·woman *nc* a woman employed to deliver letters etc.

post⁴ /pəust/ *vt* **1** to put (letters, parcels etc) in a post-box or take (them) to a post office: *Have you posted all the invitations?* **2 keep sb posted** to keep a person supplied with the latest information. **3** to send (a person) to a place to work, carry out a duty etc: *be posted to Brussels. Guards were posted at the gates.*

post⁵ /pəust/ *vt* **post sth (up)** to put up an announcement, list etc on a wall or board for people to read: *The names of the winners were posted (up) in the shop.*

post·age /'pəustɪdʒ/ *nu* the cost charged for carrying letters etc: *What is the postage for an air-letter?*

'postage stamp *nc* (*formal*) = **stamp¹**(1).

post·al /'pəustl/ *adj* (*attrib*) of, concerning, the post³(1): *postal rates; a postal vote* (= one sent by post).

'postal order *nc* a written form for money (to be) cashed at a post office.

post-date /,pəust'deɪt/ *vt* **1** to put on (a letter, cheque etc) a date later than the date of writing. **2** to give to (an event) a date later than its actual date.

post·er /'pəustə(r)/ *nc* a large, printed announcement or picture.

pos·ter·ior¹ /pɒ'stɪərɪə(r)/ *adj* near(er) the back.

pos·ter·ior² /pɒ'stɪərɪə(r)/ *nc* (*formal*) one's buttocks.

pos·ter·ity /pɒ'sterətɪ/ *nu* people who will live after us; future generations: *We should each plant a tree for posterity.*

post·gradu·ate /,pəust'grædʒuət/ *adj, nc* (of) a person studying for a degree after having received a first (*Bachelor*) degree.

post·haste /,pəust'heɪst/ *adv* (*formal*) very quickly; as quickly as possible.

post·hum·ous /'pɒstʃuməs/ *adj* coming or happening after death: *posthumous fame.*

post·hum·ous·ly *adv*

post me·rid·iem /,pəust mə'rɪdɪəm/ *adv* (abbr **pm** which is more usual) after midday. Compare **am²**.

post·modi·fi·er /,pəust'mɒdɪfaɪə(r)/ *nc* (*gram*) an *adjective* or *adverb* placed after the word it modifies, as in 'the person *injured* in the accident.'

post-mor·tem /,pəust 'mɔːtəm/ *nc* **1** a medical examination made after death: *A post-mortem showed that the man had been poisoned.* **2** (*informal*) a review of an event etc in the past: *There will have to be a post-mortem on the poor profits gained last month.*

post·natal /,pəust'neɪtl/ *adj* existing or occurring after birth: *postnatal depression.*

post·pone /pə'spəun/ *vt* to change (an agreed time to meet, decide etc) to a later time: *postpone a meeting.*

post·pone·ment *nc, nu*

post·posi·tive /,pəust'pɒzɪtɪv/ *adj* (*gram*) = predicative.

post·script /'pəuskrɪpt/ *nc* (abbr **PS**) writing added to a letter after the signature.

pos·tu·late /'pɒstjuleɪt/ *vt* (*formal*) to claim, suggest (something) as necessary, esp as a basis for reasoning: *postulate that the material will not break if heated.*

pos·ture¹ /'pɒstʃə(r)/ *nc* **1** a way of holding the body: *Good posture helps you to keep well.* **2** an attitude: *Will the Government alter its posture over aid to the railways?*

pos·ture² /'pɒstʃə(r)/ *vi* to pose so that one will be admired: *She was posturing before a mirror.*

po·sy /'pəuzɪ/ *nc* (*pl* **-ies**) a small bunch of cut flowers.

pot¹ /pɒt/ *n* **1** *nc* a round container for liquids or solids, or for cooking things in etc: *pots and pans; a teapot/coffee-pot/flower-pot.* **2** *nc* the contents of such a container: *a pot of tea.* **3** (used in phrases) **go (all) to pot** (*sl*) to be (completely) ruined or (mentally) destroyed: *His work/He has gone to pot.* **take pot luck** to take whatever is available (without choice). **the pot calling the kettle black** the accuser having the same fault as the accused. **4** *nc* (*informal*) a large amount: *make a pot/pots of money.* **5** *nu* (*sl*) marijuana.

,pot-'bellied *adj* (of a person) having a large, round belly.

'pot-hole *nc* **(a)** a hole in a road made by rain and traffic. **(b)** a deep hole, often underground, worn in rock by water.

'pot-holer *nc* a person who explores pot-holes in caves.

,pot 'luck *nu* ⇨ take pot luck at 3 above.

'pot plant *nc* one grown (indoors) in a pot.

pot² /pɒt/ *vt* (**-tt-**) **1** to put (meat, fish paste etc) in a glass jar to preserve it: *potted shrimps.* **2** to put (a plant) in a flower-pot. **3** (*informal*) to put (a baby) on a potty.

po·tass·ium /pə'tæsɪəm/ *nu* a soft, shining, white metallic element (symbol K).

po·ta·to /pə'teɪtəu/ *nc, nu* (*pl* **—es**) (also *attrib*) (a plant with) a rounded white lump (*tuber*) growing underground, eaten as a vegetable: *baked potatoes; potato soup. May I have some more potato?* ⇨ sweet potato.

po·ten·cy /'pəutənsɪ/ *nu* (*formal*) strength (esp of drugs).

po·tent /'pəutənt/ *adj* (*formal*) (esp of drugs or alcoholic drink) strong.

po·ten·tial¹ /pə'tenʃl/ *adj* (*attrib*) that will possibly happen or come into existence: *potential wealth; the potential sales of a new book.*

po·ten·ti·al·ly /-ʃəlɪ/ *adv*: *a potentially rich country.*

po·ten·tial² /pə'tenʃl/ *nu* what a person or thing is capable of achieving: *He/It hasn't much/shows little potential.*

po·ten·ti·al·ity /pə,tenʃɪ'ælətɪ/ *nu* = potential (the usual word).

po·tion /'pəuʃn/ *nc* (*formal*) a single amount (*dose*) of liquid medicine, poison etc.

pot·ted /'pɒtɪd/ *adj* (*attrib*) **1** (of food) preserved in a pot or jar: *potted shrimps.* **2** (of a book etc) shortened: *a potted version of a classical novel.*

pot·ter[1] /'pɒtə(r)/ *nc* a person who makes pots out of clay, stone etc.

pot·tery *n* (*pl* -ies) (a) *nu* clay or stone pots. (b) *nu* a potter's work. (c) *nc* a potter's workshop.

pot·ter[2] /'pɒtə(r)/ *vi* **potter (about)** to move about doing small jobs: *pottering (about) in the garden.*

pot·ty[1] /'pɒtɪ/ *adj* (-ier, -iest) (*informal*) **1** unimportant; insignificant: *potty little jobs.* **2** (of a person) mad. **3 potty about sb** in love with a person: *He's potty about his new girlfriend.*

pot·ty[2] /'pɒtɪ/ *nc* (*pl* -ies) a child's pot used as a toilet.

pouch /paʊtʃ/ *nc* **1** a small bag carried in the pocket or fastened to the belt. **2** a bag of skin on the front of some female animals, e.g. the kangaroo, in which she carries her young.

pouffe /puːf/ *nc* a large cushion, used as a seat.

poul·tice /'pəʊltɪs/ *nc* a heated mass of a soft substance, e.g. mud, put on the skin to relieve pain etc.

poul·try /'pəʊltrɪ/ *n* **1** *n pl* hens, ducks, geese etc: *The poultry are being fed.* **2** *nu* poultry(1) considered as food: *Poultry is cheap at the moment.*

pounce /paʊns/ *vi* **pounce (at/on sb/sth)** to make a sudden jump or attempt (to get a person, thing): *The hawk pounced on its prey. He pounced at the first chance of a holiday.*

pound[1] /paʊnd/ *nc* **1** a unit of measurement of mass, equal to 16 ounces or 0·45kg. **2** the British unit of money: *five pounds* (written £5); *a five-pound note.* **3** a unit of money in some other countries, e.g. Egypt.

pound[2] /paʊnd/ *nc* a place where homeless dogs and cats, and vehicles left in unauthorized places, are kept until claimed.

pound[3] /paʊnd/ *v* **1** *vt,vi* to hit or beat (something) heavily and repeatedly: *Someone was pounding (at) the door with his fist. She could feel her heart pounding as she finished the 100 metres race.* **2** *vt* to crush (something) to powder or so as to break to pieces: *pound crystals in a mortar; a ship being pounded to pieces on the rocks.*

pour /pɔː(r)/ *v* **1** *vt,vi* (to cause a liquid or a substance like a liquid) to flow in a continuous stream: *Pour yourself another cup of tea. I poured (out) six cups of coffee. The sweat was pouring off him.* **2** *vi* **pour in/out; pour into/out of a place** to flow in a continuous stream: *Tourists pour into London during the summer months. The crowds were pouring out of the football ground. Letters of complaint poured in.* **3** *vi* **pour (down)** (of rain) to come down heavily: *The rain poured down.* ⇨ downpour. **4** *vt* **pour sth out** to tell, describe, something in a long speech: *He poured out his story of the road crash.*

pout /paʊt/ *vi* to push out the lips (as a sign of not being pleased). □ *nc* this expression.

pov·er·ty /'pɒvətɪ/ *nu* the state of being poor: *live in poverty.*

'poverty-stricken *adj* extremely poor.

POW /,piː əʊ 'dʌbljuː/ *abbr* Prisoner of War.

pow·der[1] /'paʊdə(r)/ *nc,nu* (any kind of) substance that has been crushed, rubbed or worn to dust, for use on the skin (*face-powder, talcum powder*), for cleaning things (*soap powder*) or for cooking (*baking-powder*) etc.

,powder-'blue *adj, nu* pale blue (colour).

pow·der·ed *adj* made into powder: *powdered milk/eggs.*

pow·der[2] /'paʊdə(r)/ *vt* to put powder on (the skin): *She powdered her face.*

pow·er /'paʊə(r)/ *n* **1** *nu* (in living things) the ability to do or act: *It is not within/It is beyond/It is outside my power to help you. I will do everything in my power to help.* **2** *nc,nu* something a living thing can do: *I have the power to hurt you. She has lost her power of speech. He's a man of great intellectual powers.* Compare ability, skill. **3** *nu* strength; force: *the power of a blow.* **4** *nu* energy that can be used to do work: *electric power.* ⇨ horsepower. **5** *nu* authority; influence: *be in a position of power; the power of the law; the power of Congress.* **in power** (of a political party) having the right to govern. ⇨ also balance of power. **6** *nc* a right possessed by, or granted to, a person or group: *The President has exceeded his powers* (= has done more than he has authority to do). **7** *nc* a person or organization having great authority or influence: *Is the press a great power in your country?* **8** *nc* a nation having great authority and influence in international affairs: *a world power.* **9** *nc* (*maths*) the result obtained by multiplying a number or quantity by itself a certain number of times: *x to the power of 3 is written x^3.* **10** *nu* the capacity to magnify: *the power of a lens; a telescope of high power.* **11** *nu* (*informal*) a large amount: *This beer does me a power of good.*

'power-boat *nc* a kind of motorboat.

'power-house/-station *nc* a building where electric power is produced.

'power-point *nc* ⇨ point[1](10).

'power politics *nu* diplomacy backed by force.

pow·er·ed *adj* (usually in *compounds*) (a) having, able to produce, mechanical energy: *a high-powered car.* (b) (*fig*) having great energy: *a high-powered salesman.*

pow·er·ful /'paʊəfəl/ *adj* having or producing great power: *a powerful enemy; a powerful drug.*

pow·er·ful·ly /-fəlɪ/ *adv*

pow·er·less /'paʊəlɪs/ *adj* (of a person) without energy, authority or influence: *be powerless to resist.*

pow·er·less·ly *adv*

pp *written abbr* **1** pages. **2** past participle. **3** (used before a name when another person has signed) on behalf of: *Yours sincerely, James Cooper, pp Angela Bright.*

pr *written abbr* **1** pair. **2** price.

PR /,piː 'ɑː(r)/ *abbr* Public Relations.

prac·ti·cable /'præktɪkəbl/ *adj* (of ideas, suggestions) that can be done or used or put into practice: *ideas that are not practicable.* Opp impracticable. Ⓝ For a comparison of *practicable* and *practical*, ⇨ practical(1).

prac·ti·cably /-əblɪ/ *adv*

prac·ti·cal /'præktɪkl/ *adj* **1** concerned with the process of doing something and the results: *a suggestion/proposal with little practical value.* Ⓝ *'Practical'* and *'practicable'* often have the same usage but *'practical'* is preferred when referring to *'usefulness'* and *'practicable'* is preferred when referring to the *'ability to do something'*. *The idea of giving everyone a full medical examination each year has practical value but is it practicable?* *'Practicable'* cannot be used for 2 or 3 below. Compare theoretical.

2 (of a person, character etc) clever at doing and making things: *a practical husband/mind.* Opp unpractical. **3** useful: *Your invention is clever but not very practical.* Compare impractical.

,**practical 'joke** *nc* a trick in which a person is made to appear ridiculous.

prac·ti·cal·ly /'præktɪklɪ/ *adv* **1** in a practical manner: *Practically, your invention seems to be of no use.* **2** almost: *We've had practically no sunshine this month.*

prac·ti·cal·ity /,præktɪ'kælətɪ/ *nc,nu* (*pl* **-ies**) (a detail concerning) the condition of being practical: *Let's get down to practicalities* (i.e. to considering the things to be done and the methods).

prac·tice (*US* also **prac·tise**) /'præktɪs/ *n* **1** *nc* something done regularly: *the practice of closing shops on Sundays. He made a practice of cheating in examinations.* **2** *nc,nu* regular and frequent repetition or exercise to improve ability: *Piano-playing needs a lot of practice. It takes years of practice to become an expert.* **out of practice** not having given enough time recently to practice. **practice makes perfect** (*saying*) regular practice is needed in order to be able to do something well. **3** *nu* (the process of) doing something: *Her plan must be put into practice* (= must be carried out). **in practice** when actually done: *Her idea may never work in practice.* Compare in theory. **4** *nc,nu* the business of a doctor, lawyer or accountant: *She has her own practice in Oxford. He hopes to set up practice* (i.e. to start a business) *in New York.* ⇨ general practitioner.

prac·tise (*US* also **prac·tice**) /'præktɪs/ *v* **1** *vt,vi* to do (something) repeatedly or regularly in order to become skilful: *practise* (*the piano*) *two hours every day.* **2** *vt* to make a habit of doing (something): *practise getting up early.* **practise what one preaches** to do what one advises others to do. **3** *vt* to be employed in (a profession etc): *practise medicine/the law* (= work as a doctor/lawyer).

prac·tised (*US* also **-ticed**) *adj* (*attrib*) skilled; having had much practice.

prac·ti·tion·er /præk'tɪʃənə(r)/ *nc* a professional person, esp in medicine or law. ⇨ general practitioner.

prag·mat·ic /præg'mætɪk/ *adj* concerned with useful results, the possibility of actually being done (and not theory or principles).

prag·mati·cal·ly /-klɪ/ *adv*

prag·ma·tism /'prægmətɪzəm/ *nu* the belief that the truth or value of a theory depends on its practical use.

prag·ma·tist /-tɪst/ *nc* a believer in pragmatism.

prairie /'preərɪ/ *nc* the flat, treeless areas in N America. Ⓝ Compare *'pampas'* in S America and *'savanna'* in central America and W Africa.

praise¹ /preɪz/ *nu* **1** (an expression of) admiration or approval: *His heroism is worthy of great praise/is beyond praise* (= is impossible to praise too much). **2** honour and thanks (to God): *Praise be to God.*

'**praise·worthy** *adj* deserving praise.

praise² /preɪz/ *vt* **1** to say that one admires or approves of (a person, thing): *praise a woman for her courage/the meal as the best of its kind.* **sing sb's praises** to say complimentary things about a person. **2** to give honour and thanks to (God).

pram /præm/ *nc* (*GB*) a four-wheeled carriage, pushed by hand, for a baby.

prance¹ /prɑ:ns/ *nc* a prancing movement.

prance² /prɑ:ns/ *vi* **1** (of a horse) to lift the front legs and jump from the back legs. **2** (*fig*) to move in an arrogant manner. **3** (*fig*) dance or jump happily and gaily.

prank /præŋk/ *nc* a playful or mischievous trick: *play pranks on her.*

prattle /'prætl/ *vi* (*derog*) to talk in a simple, childish way. □ *nu* such talk.

prawn /prɔ:n/ *nc* (also *attrib*) a shellfish like a large shrimp, eaten as food: *prawn cocktail.*

pray /preɪ/ *vi* to speak, offer thanks, make a request etc (esp in one's thoughts) to God: *pray to God for help. They knelt down and prayed.*

pray·er /preə(r)/ *n* **1** *nu* the act of praying: *He knelt down in prayer.* **2** *nc* (often P-) a form of church worship: *Morning/Evening Prayer.* **3** *nc* a form of words used in praying: *His prayers were answered when she phoned him.*

'**prayer-book** *nc* one containing prayers for use in church services.

'**prayer-mat/-rug** *nc* a small rug used by Muslims to kneel on when they pray.

'**prayer-wheel** *nc* a revolving cylinder with prayers inside, used by the Buddhists of Tibet.

preach /pri:tʃ/ *v* **1** *vt,vi* to give a talk (in church) about religion or morals. **2** *vt,vi* **preach (sth) (to sb)** to give (moral advice) (to a person): *He was preaching to the students about being lazy.* ⇨ practise(2). **3** *vt* to advise, urge, that (something) is right or best: *preach forgiveness and sympathy.*

preach·er *nc* a person who preaches(1).

pre·am·ble /pri:'æmbl/ *nc* an introduction or preliminary statement (esp to a formal document).

pre·ar·range /,pri:ə'reɪndʒ/ *vt* to arrange (something) in advance.

pre·ar·range·ment *nc,nu*

pre·cari·ous /prɪ'keərɪəs/ *adj* (*formal*) uncertain; unsafe; depending on chance: *make a precarious living as an author.*

pre·cari·ous·ly *adv*

pre·cast /,pri:'kɑ:st/ *adj* (of concrete) in blocks ready for use in building.

pre·cau·tion /prɪ'kɔ:ʃn/ *nc,nu* (an instance of) care taken in advance to avoid a risk: *take an umbrella as a precaution.*

pre·cau·tion·ary /,prɪ'kɔ:ʃnərɪ/ *adj*

pre·cede /prɪ'si:d/ *vt,vi* to come or go before (another or others) in time, place or order: *The singer who is preceding the pop group in the programme is very good.*

pre·ced·ing *adj* existing or coming before: *the preceding event on the programme.*

pre·ced·ence /'presɪdəns/ *nu* (*formal*) (the right to) a position or attention before others: *We must deal with the problems in order of precedence* (= starting with the most important or urgent ones). **have/take precedence (over sb/sth)** to have the right to be considered first.

pre·ced·ent /'presɪdənt/ *nc* (*formal*) an earlier happening, decision etc used as an example or rule for what comes later: *set/create/establish a precedent.*

pre·cept /'pri:sept/ *nc* (*formal*) a rule or guide for behaviour: *moral precepts.*

pre·cinct /'pri:sɪŋkt/ *nc* **1** the space enclosed by

outer walls or boundaries, e.g. of a cathedral or university. **2** (*modern use*) an area (of a town) for a particular use: *a shopping precinct.*

pre·cious[1] /'preʃəs/ *adj* **1** of great value: *my precious possessions.* **2 precious to sb** greatly loved by a person: *Her children are very precious to her.*

,**precious 'metal/'stone** *nc,nu* one that is highly valued, e.g. *gold/silver; diamond/ruby.*

pre·cious[2] /'preʃəs/ *adv* **precious few/little** (*informal*) very few/little: *I have precious little money left. There were precious few visitors.*

preci·pice /'presɪpɪs/ *nc* a very steep side of a rock, cliff or mountain.

pre·cipi·tate[1] /prɪ'sɪpɪtət/ *adj* (*formal*) (doing things, done) without thought or care: *a precipitate judgment.*

pre·cipi·tate[2] /prɪ'sɪpɪteɪt/ *nc,nu* (*science*) solid matter separated from a liquid because of chemical action, e.g. one that forms at the bottom of a liquid.

pre·cipi·tate[3] /prɪ'sɪpɪteɪt/ *vt* **1** (*formal*) to cause (an event) to happen suddenly, quickly: *precipitate a crisis.* **2** (*science*) to separate (solid matter) from a solution, using chemical action.

pre·cipi·ta·tion /prɪ,sɪpɪ'teɪʃn/ *n* (*formal*) **1** *nc* the amount of fall of rain, snow etc: *the annual precipitation in Scotland.* **2** *nu* the state of being too hurried: *act with precipitation.* **3** *nc,nu* (*science*) an act of precipitating(2).

pre·cipi·tous /prɪ'sɪpɪtəs/ *adj* (*formal*) very steep: *a precipitous mountain road.*

pré·cis /'preɪsiː/ *nc* (*pl* **précis** /-siːz/) a shortened form of a speech or piece of writing, with the main ideas, points etc.

pre·cise /prɪ'saɪs/ *adj* **1** exact (in measurement, detail etc): *precise measurements; precise information; at the precise moment when she sat down.* **2** taking care to be exact: *a very precise man.* Opp imprecise.

pre·cise·ly *adv* (**a**) exactly: *at 2 o'clock precisely.* (**b**) (used to express agreement that something is true): *'And he thinks that I should apologize?'—'Precisely.'*

pre·ci·sion[1] /prɪ'sɪʒn/ *adj* (*attrib*) (of an instrument or process) giving exact measurements or results: *precision tools.*

pre·ci·sion[2] /prɪ'sɪʒn/ *nu* accuracy: *to draw a map with precision.*

pre·clude /prɪ'kluːd/ *vt* (*formal*) to prevent (something): *preclude all doubts.*

pre·clu·sion /prɪ'kluːʒn/ *nu*

pre·co·cious /prɪ'kəʊʃəs/ *adj* **1** (of a person) having developed intelligence earlier than is normal. **2** (of actions, behaviour etc) showing this.

pre·co·cious·ly *adv*

pre·con·ceived /,priːkən'siːvd/ *adj* (of ideas, opinions) formed in advance (without knowledge or experience): *visit a foreign country with preconceived ideas.*

pre·con·cep·tion /,priːkən'sepʃn/ *nc* a preconceived idea, opinion.

pre·cur·sor /,priː'kɜːsə(r)/ *nc* (*formal*) a person or thing coming before and as a sign of what is to follow.

pre·cur·sory /-sərɪ/ *adj* (*formal*).

pred·ator /'predətə(r)/ *nc* a predatory animal.

preda·tory /'predətərɪ/ *adj* (*formal*) (of animals)

attacking and killing others.

pre·de·ces·sor /'priːdɪsesə(r)/ *nc* **1** a person who held an office or position before another person: *I was Mr Green's predecessor on the Board.* **2** something considered, used etc before something else: *Is the new proposal any better than its predecessor?*

pre·des·ti·na·tion /priː,destɪ'neɪʃn/ *nu* the theory or belief that everything about life and the future has already been decided (by God, fate etc) and cannot be changed.

pre·des·tine /priː'destɪn/ *vt* (usually *passive*) (of God, fate etc) to decide (something) in advance: *It was as if she was predestined to succeed.*

pre·de·ter·mine /,priːdɪ'tɜːmɪn/ *vt* (*formal*) to decide (something) in advance: *Does social class predetermine a person's career?*

pre·de·ter·min·er /,priːdɪ'tɜːmɪnə(r)/ *nc* (*gram*) a determiner used before another determiner, as in '*half* the cost', '*both* the boxes', '*all* her money' '*those* few examples'. ⇨ determiner.

pre·dica·ment /prɪ'dɪkəmənt/ *nc* an unpleasant situation from which escape seems difficult: *be in an awkward predicament.*

predi·cate[1] /'predɪkət/ *nc* (*gram*) the part of a statement that says something about the subject as in 'Life *is short*'.

predi·cate[2] /'predɪkeɪt/ *vt* (*formal*) (usually *passive*) to make (something) necessary as a consequence: *These policies were predicated by Britain's decision to join the Common Market.*

predi·cat·ive /prɪ'dɪkətɪv/ *adj* (*gram*) (of an *adjective*) placed after the verb, as in 'She's *asleep*' and 'live *apart*'. Compare attributive. Ⓝ Marked (*pred*) in this dictionary.

pre·dict /prɪ'dɪkt/ *vt* **predict (that) sth** to say, tell, something in advance: *predict a good harvest/ that there will be an earthquake.*

pre·dict·able /-əbl/ *adj* that can be predicted: *predictable errors.* Opp unpredictable.

pre·dic·tion /prɪ'dɪkʃn/ *nc,nu* (an example of) the act of predicting.

pre·dis·pose /,priːdɪ'spəʊz/ *vt* **predispose oneself/sb to do sth** (*formal*) to influence oneself, a person to do something, respond etc in the way mentioned: *His early training predisposed him to travel widely.*

pre·domi·nance /prɪ'dɒmɪnəns/ *nu* (a state of) superiority in strength, numbers etc.

pre·domi·nant /prɪ'dɒmɪnənt/ *adj* (*formal*) having more power, numbers or influence than others: *Her predominant characteristic is her friendliness.*

pre·domi·nant·ly *adv* for the most part: *a predominantly energetic people.*

pre·domi·nate /prɪ'dɒmɪneɪt/ *vi* (*formal*) to be superior in numbers, strength, influence etc: *a forest in which oak trees predominate.*

pre·emi·nent /priː'emɪnənt/ *adj* (*formal*) best of all: *His ideas are pre-eminent.*

pre·emi·nent·ly *adv*

pre·empt /priː'empt/ *vt* (*formal*) to do (something) before others (and have more success or influence): *He pre-empted her attack by sending an explanation to the committee.*

pre·emp·tion /priː'empʃn/ *nu*

pre·emp·tive /-tɪv/ *adj* done before another has a chance to act: *a pre-emptive attack/bid.*

preen /pri:n/ vt (of a bird) to clean, tidy, (its feathers) with its beak.

pre·fab·ri·ca·ted /pri:'fæbrɪkeɪtɪd/ adj (of parts of a building) produced in a factory in advance (to be put together later): prefabricated walls.

pre·fab·ri·ca·tion /pri:ˌfæbrɪ'keɪʃn/ nu

pref·ace¹ /'prefɪs/ nc an author's explanatory remarks at the beginning of a book.

pref·ace² /'prefɪs/ vt **1** to provide (a book etc) with a preface. **2** to begin (a talk etc) with: He prefaced his remarks with some sharp knocks on the table.

prefa·tory /'prefətərɪ/ adj (formal) introductory: after a few prefatory remarks.

pre·fect /'pri:fekt/ nc **1** (in some English schools) one of a number of senior pupils given responsibility, e.g. for keeping order. **2** (in some countries) the title of the chief officer of a police department.

pre·fer /prɪ'fɜ:(r)/ vt (-rr-) **1** to like (something) better: Which would you prefer, tea or coffee? I prefer walking to cycling. Ⓝ Not used in continuous tenses, e.g. is/was -ing. **2** prefer charges (against sb) ⇨ charge¹(2).

pre·fer·able /'prefərəbl/ adj (pred) **preferable (to sb/sth)** better; superior: an idea that is preferable to his.

pre·fer·ably /-əblɪ/ adv

pref·er·ence /'prefərəns/ n **1** nc,nu (an example of) liking for, wanting, one thing rather than another or others: have a preference for modern jazz. I'll study this evening in preference to tomorrow. **2** nu the act of favouring one person, group, more than another: giving preference to families with many children.

pref·er·en·tial /ˌprefə'renʃl/ adj (formal) of, giving, receiving, preference(2): get preferential treatment.

pre·fix¹ /'pri:fɪks/ nc **1** (lang) a word or syllable, e.g. pre-, co-, placed in front of a word to add to or change its meaning. Compare suffix. **2** a word used before a person's name, e.g. Mr, Dr.

pre·fix² /pri:'fɪks/ vt to add a prefix to (a word, name etc).

preg·nan·cy /'pregnənsɪ/ nc,nu (pl -ies) (an instance of) the state of being pregnant.

preg·nant /'pregnənt/ adj **1** (of a woman or female animal) having a baby or young animal in a stage of development before birth. **2** pregnant (with sth) (fig; formal) full of (significance): words pregnant with meaning; a pregnant pause in a play.

pre·his·tor·ic /ˌpri:hɪ'stɒrɪk/ (also -tori·cal /-kl/) adj of the time before recorded history: prehistoric man.

pre·his·tory /pri:'hɪstərɪ/ nu

pre·judge /ˌpri:'dʒʌdʒ/ vt to make a decision, form an opinion, about (a person, cause, action etc) before hearing the evidence, making a proper inquiry etc.

pre·judge·ment nc,nu

preju·dice¹ /'predʒʊdɪs/ nc,nu (an instance of) unfair opinion formed without adequate knowledge or experience: racial prejudice.

preju·dice² /'predʒʊdɪs/ vt **1** to cause (a person) to have a prejudice(1): be prejudiced against women. **2** to harm, weaken, (a person's advan-

tage etc): He prejudiced his claim by asking too much.

preju·diced adj

preju·di·cial /ˌpredʒʊ'dɪʃl/ adj (pred) **prejudicial to sb/sth** (formal) causing harm.

prel·ate /'prelət/ nc a bishop or other churchman of equal or higher rank.

pre·limi·nary¹ /prɪ'lɪmɪnərɪ/ adj (attrib) coming first and preparing for what follows: a preliminary examination; after a few preliminary remarks.

pre·limi·nary² /prɪ'lɪmɪnərɪ/ nc (pl -ies) (usually pl) preliminary actions, remarks etc.

prel·ude /'prelju:d/ nc **1** an action, event etc that acts as an introduction (to something more important). **2** (music) an introductory movement (to a longer piece).

pre·mari·tal /ˌpri:'mærɪtl/ adj before marriage: premarital sex.

pre·ma·ture /'premətʃə(r)/ adj done, happening, doing something, before the right or usual time: premature birth.

pre·ma·ture·ly adv: agree prematurely.

pre·medi·tated /pri:'medɪteɪtɪd/ adj planned in advance: premeditated murder.

pre·medi·ta·tion /ˌpri:ˌmedɪ'teɪʃn/ nu

prem·ier¹ /'premɪə(r)/ adj (attrib) first in position, standard, importance etc: a premier cause/influence/actor.

prem·ier² /'premɪə(r)/ nc a head of the government in some countries.

pre·mière /'premɪə(r)/ nc the first performance of a play or (film première) first public showing of a cinema film.

prem·ise /'premɪs/ nc a statement on which an opinion, argument, reason etc is based.

prem·ises /'premɪsɪz/ n pl a building with its sheds, land etc: business premises. **off/on the premises** not in/in the building or property: No one is allowed on the premises after 6 o'clock.

pre·mi·um /'pri:mɪəm/ nc (pl -s) **1** an amount of money paid for an insurance policy. **2** an addition to ordinary charges, rent etc: He had to pay the agent a premium before he could rent the house.

pre·modi·fi·er /ˌpri:'mɒdɪfaɪə(r)/ nc (gram) an adjective or adverb placed before the word it modifies, as in 'the winning ticket'.

pre·mon·ition /ˌpremə'nɪʃn/ nc a feeling of uneasiness considered as a warning (of danger etc): have a strong premonition of failure.

pre·moni·tory /prɪ'mɒnɪtərɪ/ adj

pre·na·tal /pri:'neɪtl/ adj before birth.

pre·nomi·nal /ˌpri:'nɒmɪnl/ adj (gram) = attributive.

pre·oc·cu·pa·tion /ˌpri:ɒkjʊ'peɪʃn/ n **1** nu a state of mind in which something takes up all a person's thoughts. **2** nc the subject etc that takes up all a person's thoughts: His greatest preoccupation was saving money for a holiday in Europe.

pre·oc·cu·py /pri:'ɒkjʊpaɪ/ vt (pt,pp -ied) to fill all (a person's mind) so that attention is not given to other matters: preoccupied with thoughts of a holiday.

pre·or·dain /ˌpri:ɔ:'deɪn/ vt (of God, fate etc) to determine (something) in advance.

pre·pack·aged /pri:'pækɪdʒd/ (also **pre·pack·ed** /pri:'pækt/) adj (of food products) cut, wrapped, packed, before being supplied to shops.

pre·paid /ˌpriː'peɪd/ *adj* paid for in advance: *postage prepaid; a prepaid reply.*

prep·a·ra·tion /ˌprepə'reɪʃn/ *n* **1** *nu* the act, process, of preparing: *Preparation for exams is essential.* **in preparation** being prepared: *The book is in preparation.* **2** *nc* (often *pl*) something done to get ready: *make preparations for a journey; practise as a preparation for a race.* **3** *nc* a kind of medicine, food etc that is specially prepared: *chemical preparations.*

pre·para·tory /prɪ'pærətərɪ/ *adj* done as part of getting ready: *preparatory measures/training.*

pre,paratory 'object/'subject *nc* (*gram*) the word *it* used when the object/subject of a sentence is an infinitive or clause, as in 'Please make *it* known that I disapprove' (object), '*It* is raining' or '*It* is well known that dogs can swim' (subject).

pre·pare /prɪ'peə(r)/ *vi,vt* **prepare (sb/sth) (for sth)** to get or make (a person, thing) ready: *prepare a meal; prepare (students) for an examination; be prepared for anything to happen.*

pre·pared /prɪ'peəd/ *adj* **1** (*no comp*) that has been made ready in advance: *a prepared speech. We are now prepared* (= ready) *and can begin the journey immediately.* Opp unprepared. **2** (*pred*) **prepared to do sth** willing to do something: *I'm prepared to help you if you work hard.*

pre·pon·der·ance /prɪ'pɒndərəns/ *nu* **a preponderance of sth** (*formal*) a larger amount or number of it, them: *a preponderance of women/of green in the design.*

pre·pon·der·ant /prɪ'pɒndərənt/ *adj*

pre·pon·der·ant·ly *adv*

prep·osi·tion /ˌprepə'zɪʃn/ *nc* (*gram*) a word or group of words (e.g. *from, in, to*) often placed before a noun or pronoun to show place, direction, source, method etc, as in 'come *from* Holland', '*in* July', 'turn *to* the right'. (N) Marked prep in this dictionary. Compare adverb.

prep·osi·tion·al /-ʃənl/ *adj* of, containing, a preposition.

,prepo,sitional 'object *nc* (*gram*) an object(4) connected to the sentence by a preposition, as in 'I gave the money to *the treasurer.*'

,prepo,sitional 'phrasal verb *nc* (*gram*) a verb with an *adverbial particle* and a *preposition*, e.g. '*put up with* a small salary', '*come down to* one choice', '*sit in on* a meeting'.

,prepo,sitional 'phrase *nc* (*gram*) (**a**) a phrase acting as a preposition, e.g. *in front of; on top of.* (**b**) a preposition and the noun following it, e.g. *in the night; on the beach.*

,prepo'sitional verb *nc* (*gram*) a verb with a *preposition* which has a meaning not identifiable from the individual words. (N) A '*prepositional verb*' consists of a transitive verb + preposition where the preposition is always placed before the object, e.g. '*come from* England', '*set on* thieves', '*put pressure on* her'. These verbs are listed at the end of the entry for the *verb.* Compare phrasal verb.

pre·pos·sess·ing /ˌpriːpə'zesɪŋ/ *adj* (*formal*) attractive; making a good impression: *a prepossessing appearance.* Opp unprepossessing.

pre·pos·ter·ous /prɪ'pɒstərəs/ *adj* (*formal*) completely impossible or ridiculous.

pre·pos·ter·ous·ly *adv*

pre·requi·site /ˌpriː'rekwɪzɪt/ *nc, adj* (something) necessary as a condition for something

else: *Three passes at 'A' level are a prerequisite for university entrance.*

pre·roga·tive /prɪ'rɒgətɪv/ *nc* (*formal*) a special right or privilege, esp of a ruler.

Pres. *written abbr* President.

Pres·by·ter·ian /ˌprezbɪ'tɪərɪən/ *adj, nc* (a member) of a Protestant group governed by officials of equal rank.

pres·by·tery /'prezbɪtərɪ/ *nc* (*pl* **-ies**) **1** (in a church) the eastern part of the chancel beyond the choir. **2** the ruling body of the Presbyterian Church. **3** the home of a Roman Catholic priest.

pre·scribe /prɪ'skraɪb/ *vt* **1** to advise or order the use of (something): *prescribe a medicine/a textbook.* **2** (*formal*) to say with authority (what course of action is to be followed): *penalties prescribed by the law.*

pre·scrip·tion /prɪ'skrɪpʃn/ *n* **1** *nc* (also *attrib*) (a doctor's written order for) a medicine, ointment etc: *prescription charges.* **2** *nu* the act of prescribing.

pres·ence /'prezns/ *nu* **1** the state of being present: *in the presence of his friends.* **presence of mind** the ability to act or decide quickly when necessary. Compare absence(1). **2** a personal way of standing, moving etc: *a man of noble presence.*

pres·ent¹ /'preznt/ *adj* **1** (*pred*) in this/that place: *The Smiths were present at the ceremony.* Compare absent¹(1). **2** (*attrib*) being discussed or dealt with now: *the present topic* (= the one being talked about). **3** (*attrib*) existing now: *the present government.* ⇨ present-day.

,present con'tinuous tense *nc* (the —) (*gram*) the verb form (present tense of *to be* and a *present participle*) used to describe an action or state happening now and also to describe a plan or arrangement to happen soon, as in: 'The sun *is shining.*' '*I'm learning* English at school.' '*We're watching* TV tonight.' (N) The present continuous tense can also be used with *always* to describe an action or state that is often repeated, as in '*They are always watching* TV.' Compare present tense.

,present 'participle *nc* (*gram*) a verb form (usually ending in *-ing*) used to form the continuous tenses, as in 'She *is playing*', 'She was *playing*', 'She will be *playing*', and also in some adjectival or adverbial phrases, as in '*Playing* the piano is her favourite pastime'. ⇨ gerund.

,present 'perfect tense *nc* (the —) (also called the **perfect tense**) (*gram*) the verb form (*has/ have* and a *past participle*) used to refer to an action or state that happened in the past and can be repeated now, and also for an action beginning in the past and continuing now, as in 'Yes, I *have learned* how to do it', 'We *have found* many flowers in these fields.' 'They *have lived* in India for many years.' This tense is also used with *yet*, as in 'She *hasn't arrived* yet', and with *just*, as in 'She *has* just *arrived.*' (N) ⇨ the note at present perfect continuous tense.

,present ,perfect con'tinuous tense *nc* (the —) (*gram*) the verb form (*has/have been* and a *present participle*) used to describe an action or state that began in the past and is continuing now, as in 'She *has been cooking* all day.' '*Have you been waiting* long?' (N) With verbs such as *live, work, sleep, wait* both the present perfect tense (e.g. 'He *has* *worked* in America for a long time') and the present perfect continuous tense (e.g. He *has been working* in America for a long time') are possible.

,**present pro'gressive tense** *nc* = present continuous tense.

'**present tense** *nc* (the —) (also called the **present simple tense**) (*gram*) the verb form (*present tense* without an *auxiliary verb*) used to describe actions or events that happen all the time, to give information, instructions or advice, and to report plans for the future: 'Fish *swim*.' 'Do you *eat* meat?' 'Then you *turn* left.' 'The instructions *say* we must take a tent.' 'They *arrive* at 6 o'clock.' This tense is also used for certain verbs (*like, want, believe, seem, agree* etc) that cannot be used in the *present continuous*, as in 'I *love* you.' 'He *agrees*.' Ⓝ The *negative* is formed by using '*do/does not*' + the infinitive without '*to*', as in 'He *doesn't agree*'. The present simple tense is used with adverbs describing 'how often', e.g. *never, rarely, sometimes, often, frequently, usually, always*. Avoid using a continuous tense with these adverbs.

pres·ent² /'preznt/ *n* (the —) **1** the time now passing: *the past, the present, and the future*. **at present** at this time; now: *We don't need any more at present*. **2** (*gram*) = present tense.

pres·ent³ /'preznt/ *nc* something given to a person for pleasure: *birthday presents*.

pres·ent⁴ /prɪ'zent/ *vt* (*formal*) **1** to give (something), esp as part of a ceremony: *That clock was presented to me when I retired*. **2** to introduce (a person) to a more important person: *May I present my father (to you)? I was presented to the Queen*. **3** to organize and provide (a play etc) for the public: *The Playhouse will present 'Hamlet' next week. The BBC will present a new documentary on pollution*. **4** (*reflex*) to appear: *A new opportunity has presented itself*. **present oneself (for sth)** to attend officially: *Please present yourself for trial on Monday*. **5** to offer (something) for discussion: *present a report at the meeting*.

pre·sent·able /prɪ'zentəbl/ *adj* fit to appear, be shown, in public: *I've just washed my hair and I'm not presentable at the moment*.

pre·sent·ably /-əblɪ/ *adv*: *presentably dressed*.

pres·en·ta·tion /ˌprezn'teɪʃn/ *n* **1** *nc,nu* (an instance of) presenting(1) something: *The presentation of the medals will be at 3 o'clock*. **2** *nc* a method used to arrange or describe objects, ideas etc: *a lovely presentation of flowers; a successful presentation of the scheme*.

present-day /ˌpreznt 'deɪ/ *adj* (*attrib*) existing now: *present-day problems of unemployment*.

pre·sen·ti·ment /prɪ'zentɪmənt/ *nc* (*formal*) a vague feeling that something (esp unpleasant or undesirable) is about to happen.

pres·ent·ly /'prezntlɪ/ *adv* **1** (*formal*) soon: *I'll be with you presently*. **2** (esp *US*) at the present time: *The Secretary of State is presently in Africa*.

pres·er·va·tion /ˌprezə'veɪʃn/ *nu* **1** the act of preserving something: *the preservation of food/one's health/wild life*. **2** the condition of something that has been preserved: *paintings in a good state of preservation*.

pre·serv·ative /prɪ'zɜːvətɪv/ *nc, adj* (substance) used for preserving (e.g. food): *This ice-cream is free from artificial preservatives*.

pre·serve¹ /prɪ'zɜːv/ *n* (*formal*) **1** *nc* an activity or responsibility of a particular person or group: *Choosing the menu is my preserve*. **2** *nu* (often *pl*) jam (the usual word). **3** *nc* an area of land where animals or birds are kept for protection or for sport.

pre·serve² /prɪ'zɜːv/ *vt* (*formal*) **1** *preserve sb/sth (from sth)* to keep a person, animal etc safe (from harm or danger): *preserving old people from the loneliness of old age; preserve one's eyesight; preserve fish in the lake*. **2** to keep (food) from going bad by freezing, drying, bottling etc: *preserve fruit*. **3** to keep (a name, memory) known and discussed: *Few of his early poems are preserved*.

pre·side /prɪ'zaɪd/ *vi* **preside (at/over sth)** to control a meeting, group etc: *The Prime Minister presides at meetings of the Cabinet. The city council is presided over by the mayor*.

presi·den·cy /'prezɪdənsɪ/ *nc* (*pl* **-ies**) **1** (the —) the office and functions of president. **2** a period as a president: *during Lincoln's presidency*.

presi·dent /'prezɪdənt/ *nc* (also P-) **1** the elected head of government in the USA and some other republics. **2** a head of some government departments: *the President of the Board of Trade*. **3** a head of some business companies, colleges, societies etc.

presi·den·tial /ˌprezɪ'denʃl/ *adj* (*attrib*) of, for, concerning, a president: *the presidential election*.

press¹ /pres/ *n* **1** *nc* an act of pressing with an iron: *give something a light press*. **2** (the —) newspapers etc and) journalists: *The book was favourably reviewed by/in the press/had a good press. The freedom of the press* (= The right of newspapers to report events, express opinions etc freely) *is very important*. **3** *nc* a business for printing (and sometimes publishing) books or magazines. **4** *nu* (usually with *the*) pressure (the usual word): *the press of modern life*.

'**press conference** *nc* an occasion when journalists get information and ask questions about an important issue, or when a well-known person etc talks about policy, achievements etc.

'**press-cutting/-clipping** *nc* an article etc cut out from a newspaper or magazine.

'**press photographer** *nc* a photographer who works for a newspaper or magazine.

press² /pres/ *v* **1** *vt,vi* to push steadily against (something): *press against the barrier; press (down) the accelerator (of a car); press the button* (e.g. of an electric bell). **2** *vt* to use an iron to get (cloth) smooth or flat: *press a suit/skirt*. **3** *vt* to use force to get liquid out of (fruit): *press (the juice out of) oranges*. **4** *vt* to use a weight to make (flowers etc) flat. **5** *vt* to hold (a person, hand etc) tightly in order to express affection or sympathy: *He pressed her arm*. **6** **be pressing** (**a**) (of a decision, issue) to be urgently in need of attention. (**b**) (of time etc) to be becoming (too) short. ⇨ be pressed for sth below. **7** *vt* (*fig*) to obtain (support, agreement etc) using a determined, organized effort: *press one's point home in the debate*.

press ahead (with sth) to continue (an activity) using a determined effort: *press ahead with urgent reforms*.

press down on sb to be a heavy burden: *The*

new taxes pressed down on everyone.
press (sb) for sth to demand (from a person) action, a decision etc often and strongly: *press for a new enquiry.* **be pressed for sth** to have (almost) too little of something: *be pressed for time/money/space.*
press on (with sth) = press ahead (with sth).

press·ing /'presɪŋ/ *adj* urgent; requiring immediate attention: *pressing business.* ⇨ press²(6).

press-stud /'pres stʌd/ *nc* a device for fastening cloth on clothes etc by pressing a metal knob into a metal hole.

press-up /'pres ʌp/ *nc* a form of exercise by lying on the floor and raising one's body by pushing against the floor.

press·ure /'preʃə(r)/ *nc,nu* **1** the act of pressing; (amount of) force on or against something: *I hope that the tyre pressure is right. The pressure must not be too high/low.* ⇨ blood pressure. **2** a force or strain: *He pleaded pressure of work and resigned his place on the committee.* **under pressure** feeling forced (to act): *He's under strong pressure to agree. They resigned under pressure.* **put pressure on sb/sth (to do sth)** to use force or influence: *The reduced price of oil put pressure on the pound.*
'**pressure-cooker** *nc* an airtight saucepan used for cooking quickly with steam under pressure.
'**pressure group** *nc* an organized group that tries to use influence for the benefit of its members.

press·ur·ize (also **-ise**) /'preʃəraɪz/ *vt* **pressurize sb (into doing sth)** (*informal*) to use pressure(2) on a person: *She was pressurized into helping with the cooking.*

press·ur·ized (also **-ised**) /'preʃəraɪzd/ *adj* (of a plane etc) with its internal air-pressure controlled.

pres·tige /pre'stiːʒ/ *nu* the respect that results from the good reputation (of a person, nation etc) and power or influence coming from this: *Some universities/writers have more prestige than others.*

pres·tig·ious /pre'stɪdʒəs/ *adj* having or producing respect, influence etc.

pre·sum·ably /prɪ'zjuːməblɪ/ *adv* one can suppose that: *Presumably you would agree to giving him more responsibility.*

pre·sume /prɪ'zjuːm/ *vt,vi* (*formal*) to suppose (something) to be true: *In Britain an accused person is presumed (to be) innocent until proved guilty.*

pre·sump·tion /prɪ'zʌmpʃn/ *n* **1** *nc* something which seems likely although there is no proof: *on the presumption that he was drowned.* **2** *nu* (*formal*) arrogance (the usual word): *What presumption to say that he is better than me!*

pre·sump·tu·ous /prɪ'zʌmptʃʊəs/ *adj* (*formal; derog*) (of behaviour etc) too self-confident or arrogant.
pre·sump·tu·ous·ly *adv*

pre·sup·pose /ˌpriːsə'pəʊz/ *vt* (*formal*) to suppose, assume, (something) in advance: *Let's presuppose that the weather will be fine.* Ⓝ Not used in continuous tenses, e.g. *is/was -ing.*
pre·sup·po·si·tion /ˌpriːsʌpə'zɪʃn/ *nc,nu*

pre·tence (*US* also **pre·tense**) /prɪ'tens/ *nc,nu* a false claim or excuse made to deceive: *It's all*

pretence. It is only a pretence of friendship. **false pretences** (*legal*) acts intended to deceive: *get money by/on/under false pretences.*

pre·tend /prɪ'tend/ *vt,vi* to make oneself appear (to be (doing) something) either in play or to deceive others: *pretend to be asleep. They pretended that they didn't see us.*

pre·ten·sion /prɪ'tenʃn/ *n* (*formal*) **1** *nc* (often *pl*) (a statement of) a claim: *He makes no pretensions to expert knowledge of the subject.* **2** *nu* the quality of being pretentious: *Pretension is his worst fault.*

pre·ten·tious /prɪ'tenʃəs/ *adj* claiming (without justification) great ability, qualities or importance: *a pretentious student/speech; use pretentious language.* Opp unpretentious.
pre·ten·tious·ly *adv*

pret·er·ite /'pretərɪt/ *nc* (*gram*) (*dated*) = past tense.

pre·text /'priːtekst/ *nc* **pretext (for sth)** a reason that is not true (for an action etc): *find a pretext for refusing the invitation. He phoned on/under the pretext of asking about mother but he really wanted to speak to my sister.*

pret·ty¹ /'prɪtɪ/ *adj* (**-ier, -iest**) **1** pleasing and pleasant to look at: *a pretty girl/garden/picture/piece of music.* Compare handsome(1). **2** (*attrib*) (*informal*) large in amount or extent: *a pretty big fine for such a minor offence; a pretty mess.* **a pretty kettle of fish** a state of confusion. **(cost) a pretty penny** a large amount of money.
pret·tily /-əlɪ/ *adv: prettily dressed.*
pret·ti·ness *nu*

pret·ty² /'prɪtɪ/ *adv* to a certain extent: *The situation seems pretty hopeless. It's pretty cold outside.* **pretty much** very nearly: *The result of the ballot is pretty much what we expected.* **pretty nearly** almost: *The car is new, or pretty nearly so.* **pretty well** almost: *We've pretty well finished the work.* **sitting pretty** ⇨ sit(1).

pre·vail /prɪ'veɪl/ *vi* **1** to gain victory (over something): *Truth/Justice will prevail.* **2** to be generally seen, done etc: *the conditions now prevailing in Africa.* **3 prevail on sb (to do sth)** (*formal*) to persuade a person (to do something): *prevail on a friend to lend £10.*

pre·vail·ing *adj* (*no comp*) most frequent or usual: *the prevailing fashions.*

pre·va·lence /'prevələns/ *nu* **prevalence (of sth)** (*formal*) the state of being usual: *prevalence of bribery among officials.*

pre·va·lent /'prevələnt/ *adj* **prevalent (among/in a place/group)** (*formal*) common, seen or done everywhere (at the time in question): *Is malaria still prevalent (in that country)?*

pre·vari·cate /prɪ'værɪkeɪt/ *vi* (*formal*) to make untrue or partly untrue statements (to avoid telling the (whole) truth).
pre·vari·ca·tion /prɪˌværɪ'keɪʃn/ *nc,nu*

pre·vent /prɪ'vent/ *vt* **prevent (sb) (from doing) sth** to stop or keep (a person) from doing (something); stop (something) from happening: *Who can prevent us (from) getting married?*

pre·vent·able /-əbl/ *adj* that can be prevented.

pre·ven·tion /prɪ'venʃn/ *nu* the act of preventing: *Prevention is better than cure.*

preventive /prɪ'ventɪv/ *adj* serving or designed

to prevent.

pre,ventive 'medicine *nu* (scientific) research into ways of avoiding, or protecting people against, disease, illness.

pre·view /'pri:vju:/ *nc* a view of a film, play etc before it is shown to the general public. □ *vt* to give or see a preview of (a film).

pre·vi·ous /'pri:vɪəs/ *adj* (*no comp*) **1** (*attrib*) coming earlier in time or order: *on a previous occasion.* **2** *previous to* (*prep*) (*formal*) before: *Previous to that I worked in Africa.*

pre·vi·ous·ly *adv*

prey¹ /preɪ/ *n sing* an animal, bird etc hunted for food: *The eagle was eating its prey.* ⇨ **bird of prey.**

prey² /preɪ/ *vi* **prey (on sb/sth)** **1** to take, hunt, animals as prey: *hawks preying on small birds.* **2** to attack and steal from people, boats etc: *Our ships were preyed on by pirates.* **3** (of fears etc) to produce strong feelings of worry, fear (in a person, one's mind): *anxieties/losses that prey on my mind.*

price¹ /praɪs/ *n* **1** *nc* an amount of money for which something is (to be) sold or bought: *What price are you asking? It's a high/low price.* **2** *nu* value; worth: *a pearl of great price.* ⇨ **priceless.** **3** *nc* something that must be done, given or experienced to obtain or keep something: *I don't think giving up an hour or two is too high a price to pay for learning the piano.*

price² /praɪs/ *vt* to fix, ask about, the price of (something); mark (goods) with a price. *price oneself/one's goods out of the market* to fix prices so high that orders decrease or stop. ⇨ **asking price.**

'price control *nu* the control or fixing of prices by a government, manufacturers etc.

'price war *nc* (*informal*) a form of business competition using low prices to attract buyers.

price·less *adj* too valuable to be priced: *priceless paintings.*

pricey /'praɪsɪ/ *adj* (*informal*) expensive.

prick¹ /prɪk/ *nc* **1** a small mark or hole caused by the act of pricking: *pricks made by a needle.* **2** a short pain: *I can still feel the prick.*

prick² /prɪk/ *v* **1** *vt* to make a hole or a mark in (something) with a sharp point: *prick a balloon.* **2** *vt,vi* (to cause a person, animal) to feel pain from a sharp point or points: *prick one's finger with/on a needle.* **3** *vt* (*fig*) to cause an uneasy feeling in (a person, one's conscience): *His conscience pricked him.* **4** *prick up one's ears* ⇨ **ear¹(1).**

prickle¹ /'prɪkl/ *nc* a pointed growth on the leaf or stem of a plant, or on the skin of some animals.

prick·ly /'prɪklɪ/ *adj* (a) having prickles. (b) (*informal; derog*) easily irritated or annoyed.

prickle² /'prɪkl/ *vt,vi* (to cause a person) to have a pricking sensation.

pride¹ /praɪd/ *n* **1** *nu* a feeling of satisfaction because of what one has done, or because of a person, thing etc one is concerned with: *look with pride at one's garden. They took (a) great pride in their success.* ⇨ **proud.** **2** *nu* self-respect: *Don't say anything that may wound his pride.* **3** *nu* too high an opinion of oneself, one's position, possessions etc: *be puffed up with pride.* **4** *nc* a person, thing, that is valued: *a girl who is her mother's pride and joy.* **5** *nc* a group: (only) *a pride of lions/peacocks.*

pride² /praɪd/ *vt* **pride oneself on sth** to be pleased and satisfied about something: *He prides himself on his skill as a pianist.*

priest /pri:st/ *nc* **1** a clergyman of a Christian Church. Compare clergyman, minister(2). **2** (of non-Christian religions) a person trained to perform special acts of religion, medicine etc.

priest·ess /'pri:stɪs/ *nc* a woman priest(2).

'priest·hood /-hʊd/ *nc* (the —) priests(1) as a group.

prig /prɪg/ *nc* (*dated; derog*) a person showing too much self-satisfaction or pride.

prim /prɪm/ *adj* (**—mer, —mest**) **1** neat; formal: *a prim garden.* **2** (often *derog*) (of a person, manner, speech etc) showing dislike of anything rough, rude, improper: *a very prim and proper old lady.*

prim·ly *adv*

pri·ma /,pri:mə/ *adj* (*It*) first.

,prima ,balle·rina *nc* a leading woman performer in ballet.

,prima 'donna /'dɒnə/ *nc* (a) a leading woman singer in opera. (b) (*informal; derog*) a conceited and bad-tempered person.

pri·mae·val /praɪ'mi:vl/ *adj* = primeval.

pri·mar·ily /'praɪmrəlɪ/ *adv* mainly; above all: *I do paint pictures but primarily I'm a designer.*

pri·mary /'praɪmərɪ/ *adj* first in rank, importance, extent etc: *of primary importance.*

,primary 'colour *nc* red, blue or yellow, from which all other colours can be obtained by mixing two or more.

'primary school *nc* (*GB*) one for children aged 5 to 9 or 11.

'primary stress *nc* the strongest stress(2) used in a word. (N) Marked¹ in print.

pri·mate¹ /'praɪmeɪt/ *nc* an archbishop.

pri·mate² /'praɪmeɪt/ *nc* (*science*) one of the highest order of mammals (including men, apes, monkeys and lemurs).

prime¹ /praɪm/ *adj* (*attrib; no comp*) **1** main; most important: *his prime motive.* **2** excellent; first-rate: *prime (cuts of) beef.*

,prime 'minister *nc* (often the —; also P- M-) the head of a government.

,prime 'number *nc* (*maths*) one divisible only by itself and the number 1 (e.g. 7, 17, 41).

prime² /praɪm/ *nu* the state of highest perfection; the best part: *in the prime of life.*

prime³ /praɪm/ *vt* **1** to supply (a person) with facts, instructions etc: *The witness had been primed by a lawyer.* **2** to cover (a surface) with the first coat of paint, oil, varnish etc. **3** to get (a machine) ready by adding fuel etc: *prime a pump.*

primer /'praɪmə(r)/ *nu* a special kind of paint for priming(2).

pri·meval (also **-mae·val**) /praɪ'mi:vl/ *adj* of the earliest time in the world's history: *primeval forests.*

primi·tive /'prɪmɪtɪv/ *adj* **1** (*attrib*) of the earliest times; of an early stage of social development: *primitive man; primitive culture.* **2** simple; old-fashioned; having undergone little development: *primitive machines/methods.*

primi·tive·ly *adv*

pri·mor·di·al /praɪ'mɔːdɪəl/ *adj* existing at or from the beginning: *primordial forests.*

prim·rose /'prɪmrəʊz/ *n* **1** *nc* a common wild

plant with pale yellow flowers; the flower. **2** *nu* (also *adj*) its colour.

prince /prɪns/ *nc* (P- in names) **1** a ruler, esp of a small state. **2** a male member of a royal family, esp (in GB) a son or grandson of the king or queen.

prince·ly *adj* (**-ier, -iest**) **(a)** concerning a prince: *princely duties*. **(b)** (*formal*) splendid; generous: *a princely gift*.

prin·cess /prɪn'ses/ *nc* (P- in names) **1** a wife of a prince. **2** a daughter of a king or queen.

prin·ci·pal¹ /'prɪnsəpl/ *adj* (*no comp*) first in order of importance: *the principal rivers of Europe*.

prin·ci·pal² /'prɪnsəpl/ *nc* **1** (also P- in names) a title of some heads of colleges and of other organizations. **2** (*finance*) money lent, put into a business etc on which interest is payable.

prin·ci·pal·ly /-plɪ/ *adv* mostly; mainly: *I'm principally interested in designing cars*.

prin·ci·pal·ity /ˌprɪnsɪ'pælətɪ/ *nc* (*pl* **-ies**) a country ruled by a prince.

prin·ciple /'prɪnsəpl/ *nc* **1** a generally known truth or belief guiding an activity: *the (first) principles of geometry*. **2** a general standard or rule for behaviour: *moral principles*. **in principle** concerning the basic idea (but possibly not concerning the particular details): *I agree with you in principle but I need more information*. **on principle** because of personal beliefs about what is moral: *He refuses to fight on principle*. **3** a basic method of working of a machine etc: *These machines work on the same principle*.

print¹ /prɪnt/ *n* **1** *nc* a mark, pattern, on a surface of a shape, left by the pressure of something: *fingerprints; footprints*. **2** *nc* a picture, design etc made by printing on paper etc: *old Japanese prints*. **3** *nc* a photograph printed from a negative. **4** *nu* the words etc in printed form. **in/out of print** (of a book) (not) printed(2) and available.

print² /prɪnt/ *v* **1** *vt,vi* to produce (words, pictures etc) on paper. **2** *vt,vi* to make (books etc) in this way: *print 6000 copies of a novel*. **3** *vt,vi* to shape (one's letters), write (words) without joining the letters: *Please print your name and address*. **4** *vt* to make (a photograph) from a negative film. **5** *vt* to mark (cloth) with a coloured design. **6** *v reflex* (*fig*) to make an impression: *The accident printed itself on her memory*.

'printout *nc,nu* (*computers*) information from a computer in printed(1) form.

print·able /-əbl/ *adj* suitable to be printed: *Her angry words are not printable!* Opp unprintable.

print·er /'prɪntə(r)/ *nc* **1** (a worker in) a business that prints books, magazines, packets, posters etc. **2** (*computers*) a machine that produces printouts.

pri·or¹ /'praɪə(r)/ *adj* (*no comp*) earlier in time, order or importance: *have a prior claim (to the money)*. **prior to** (*prep*) before: *The house was sold prior to auction* (= before the day of the auction).

pri·or² /'praɪə(r)/ *nc* a head of a priory.

pri·or·ess /'praɪərɪs/ *nc* a woman prior.

pri·or·ity /praɪ'ɒrətɪ/ *n* (*pl* **-ies**) **1** *nu* **priority (for sth) (over sb)** the right to have or do something before others: *I have priority over you in my claim*. **2** *nc* a high place among competing claims:

Road building is a first/top priority.

pri·ory /'praɪərɪ/ *nc* (*pl* **-ies**) a place where nuns or monks live.

prise (also **prize, pry**) /praɪz/ *vt* to use force to get (a box, lid etc) open or off: *prising a lid off*.

prism /'prɪzəm/ *nc* **1** (*maths*) a solid figure with a flat base and sides that are triangles or parallelograms. **2** a solid of this form, made of glass, which breaks up white light into the colours of the rainbow.

pris·mat·ic /prɪz'mætɪk/ *adj* (*tech*) **1** like, having the shape of, a prism. **2** (of colours) brilliant and varied.

pris·on /'prɪzn/ *nc* **1** a building in which a person who commits a crime is kept locked up: *She was sent to prison for stealing*. (N) *'Gaol'* is also possible. **2** any place where a person is shut up against her or his will: *In wet, cold weather this house is a prison*. **3** *nu* the condition of being in such a place: *escape/be released from prison*.

pris·on·er *nc* **(a)** a person kept in prison for crime or until tried in a law court. **(b)** a person, animal, kept locked up but not because of a crime: *political prisoners*.

ˌprisoner of 'conscience *nc* a person kept in prison because of her or his religious, political etc beliefs.

priv·acy /'prɪvəsɪ/ *nu* the state of being away from (the noise of) other people: *I don't want my privacy disturbed*.

pri·vate¹ /'praɪvɪt/ *adj* **1** of, for the use of, concerning, one person or group, not people in general: *a private letter; a private conversation; my private address*. Compare public¹(1). **in private** with no other people involved, listening etc: *talk in private*. **2** secret; kept secret: *have private information about it*. **3** (*attrib*) having no official position; not holding any public office: *act in one's private capacity* (i.e. not as an official etc). **4** not organized or paid for by the government: *a private hospital; private education*. ⇨ privatize.

ˌprivate 'enterprise *nu* the owning and management of industry etc by private individuals, companies etc. Compare public ownership.

ˌprivate 'eye *nc* (*informal*) a detective.

ˌprivate 'parts *n pl* (also (*informal*) **privates**) external sex organs.

ˌprivate 'practice *nu* a doctor's business that is owned by her or him: *go into private practice*.

ˈprivate school *nc* one at which fees are paid by individuals. Compare State school.

private·ly *adv*

pri·vate² /'praɪvɪt/ *nc* (also P-) a soldier with the lowest rank in the army.

pri·va·tion /praɪ'veɪʃn/ *nc,nu* (*formal*) a lack of the necessities of life: *the privations of unemployment. It was a painful privation not being able to meet her*.

pri·vat·ize (also **-ise**) /'praɪvətaɪz/ *vt* (of a government) to transfer (an industry etc) from State to private ownership: *privatize British Airways*. ⇨ nationalize(1).

pri·vat·iz·ation (also **-is·ation**) /ˌpraɪvətaɪ-'zeɪʃn/ *nu*

priv·et /'prɪvɪt/ *nu* (also *attrib*) a common shrub used for garden hedges: *a privet hedge*.

privi·lege /'prɪvɪlɪdʒ/ *nc* **1** a right or advantage available only to a person, class or rank etc: *the* *privileges of a good education.* **2** a special experience or benefit giving pleasure: *It was a privilege to hear her sing.*

privi·leged *adj* (of a person) having privileges(1). Compare underprivileged.

prize¹ /praɪz/ *adj* (*attrib; no comp*) **1** of the best quality: *prize cattle.* **2** used as a prize: *prize money.*

prize² /praɪz/ *nc* something (to be) awarded to a person who succeeds in a competition etc: *win first prize.*

prize³ /praɪz/ *vt* to value (a person, thing) highly: *my most prized possessions.*

prize⁴ /praɪz/ *vt* = prise.

pro /preʊ/ *nc* (*pl* **-s**) **1** *abbr* (*informal*) a professional (player): *a tennis pro.* **2 the pros and cons** the arguments for and against (esp when deciding).

PRO /piː ɑːr 'əʊ/ *abbr* **1** Public Relations Officer. **2** Public Records Office.

prob·abil·ity /ˌprɒbəˈbɪlətɪ/ *n* (*pl* **-ies**) **1** *nu* the quality of being probable. **in all probability** most probably: *In all probability she'll be late.* **2** *nu* likelihood: *There is not much probability of his succeeding.* **3** *nc* a probable event or result: *What are the probabilities?*

prob·able /ˈprɒbəbl/ *adj* that is very likely to happen or to prove correct: *the probable result; a probable winner.* Compare possible(1). ⇨ improbable.

prob·ably /-əblɪ/ *adv* **(a)** very likely: *I'll probably telephone tomorrow.* **(b)** it is very likely: *'Will he pass the exam?'—'Probably'.*

pro·ba·tion /prəˈbeɪʃn/ *nu* (esp **on probation**) **1** the testing of a person's conduct, abilities, qualities etc before he or she is finally accepted for a job etc: *an officer on probation.* **2** a system by which an offender is allowed to go unpunished for a first offence if he or she does not break the law again: *be on/get three years' probation.*

pro'bation officer *nc* an official who watches over people on probation(2).

pro·ba·tion·al /-əl/ *adj*

pro·ba·tion·er *nc* a person on probation(2).

probe¹ /prəʊb/ *nc* **1** (*med*) a thin instrument used by doctors etc for learning about the depth and direction of a wound etc. **2** (*journalism*) a careful investigation. **3** an object used to investigate an unknown area: *a space probe to the moon.*

probe² /prəʊb/ *vt* **1** to examine (a person, part of the body) with a probe(1). **2** to investigate or examine (e.g. the causes of something) thoroughly.

prob·lem /ˈprɒbləm/ *nc* a question to be solved or decided, esp something difficult: *mathematical problems.*

prob·lem·at·ic /ˌprɒbləˈmætɪk/ *adj* (esp of a result or future) doubtful.

prob·lem·ati·cal·ly /-klɪ/ *adv*

pro·bos·cis /prəˈbɒsɪs/ *nc* (*pl* **—es**) (*science*) **1** an elephant's trunk. **2** a long part of the mouth of some insects.

pro·ce·dure /prəˈsiːdʒə(r)/ *nc,nu* a (usual and agreed) way or order of doing something: *the usual procedure at committee meetings.*

pro·ce·dur·al /prəˈsiːdʒərəl/ *adj*

pro·ceed /prəˈsiːd/ *vi* (*formal*) **1 proceed (from sth) (to sth)** to continue, go on: *Let us*

proceed (to the next item: on the agenda). **2 proceed (with sth)** to start and continue (an activity): *She proceeded with her cooking.*

pro·ceed·ing /prəˈsiːdɪŋ/ *n* **1** *nu* (a way of) doing something, behaving: *What is our best way of proceeding?* **2** (*pl*) happenings: *There have been suspicious proceedings in committee meetings.* **3** (*pl*) **proceedings (against sb/sth)** (*legal*) action in a law court: *start/take legal proceedings against a person.* **4** (*pl*) (often P-s) official records (of the activities of a society etc): *the Proceedings of the Archaeological Society.*

pro·ceeds /ˈprəʊsiːdz/ *n pl* money, profits, of an undertaking: *All the proceeds from the sale will go to the Red Cross.*

pro·cess¹ /ˈprəʊses/ *n* **1** *nc* (*science*) a connected series of actions, changes etc, esp if they are involuntary or unconscious: *the processes of digestion, reproduction and growth.* **2** *nc* a series of operations deliberately undertaken: *Unloading the cargo was a slow process.* **3** *nc* a method, esp one used in manufacture or industry: *the process of melting iron.* **4** *nu* **in process of sth** (of an activity) being done: *a building in process of construction.* **5** *nc* (*legal*) an action at law.

pro·cess² /ˈprəʊses/ *vt* to use a process(3) to produce (something): *process a film; processed cheese; process information in a computer.*

pro·cess³ /prəˈses/ *vi* (*formal*) to walk (as if) in procession: *They processed towards the statue.*

pro·ces·sion /prəˈseʃn/ *n* **1** *nc* a number of people, vehicles etc moving forward and following each other in an orderly way: *a funeral procession.* **2** *nu* the act of moving forward in this way: *walking in procession through the streets.*

pro·ces·sion·al /-ʃənl/ *adj* of, for, used in, processions: *processional music.*

pro·ces·sor /ˈprəʊsesə(r)/ *nc* a machine that is used to produce something: *a food processor* (i.e. a machine that mixes or changes food); *a word processor* (i.e. a machine that produces a typed text).

pro·claim /prəˈkleɪm/ *vt* (*formal*) to make (something) known publicly or officially; declare (the usual word): *proclaim war/peace; proclaim a man (to be) a traitor/that he is the winner.*

proc·la·ma·tion /ˌprɒkləˈmeɪʃn/ *n* (*formal*) **1** *nu* the act of proclaiming: *by public proclamation.* **2** *nc* something that is proclaimed: *issue/make a proclamation.*

pro·cras·ti·nate /prəˈkræstɪneɪt/ *vi* (*formal*) to avoid starting an activity without any reason: *He procrastinated until it was too late.*

pro·cras·ti·na·tion /prəˌkræstɪˈneɪʃn/ *nu*

pro·cre·ate /ˈprəʊkrɪeɪt/ *vt* (*formal*) to give birth to (children, young animals).

pro·cre·ation /ˌprəʊkrɪˈeɪʃn/ *nc,nu*

pro·cure /prəˈkjʊə(r)/ *vt* (*formal*) to obtain (something), esp with care or effort: *procure the release of a prisoner.*

prod¹ /prɒd/ *nc* a prodding action: *She gave him a prod with her umbrella.*

prod² /prɒd/ *vt,vi* (**-dd-**) **1 prod (at sb/sth) (with sth)** to push or poke (a person, thing) (with something pointed): *prodding (at) the bear through the bars of the cage.* **2** (*fig*) to urge (a person) to act: *I was always prodding her to see her doctor.*

prodi·gal /'prɒdɪgl/ adj (formal; derog) spending or using too much: *the prodigal son.*

pro·di·gious /prə'dɪdʒəs/ adj (formal) surprisingly large or good: *a prodigious sum of money.*

pro·di·gious·ly adv

prod·igy /'prɒdɪdʒɪ/ nc (pl **-ies**) a person who has unusual or remarkable abilities or who is a remarkable example of something.

pro·duce¹ /'prɒdjuːs/ nu something that is produced, esp by farming: *garden/farm/agricultural produce.* (N) For a comparison of produce and product, ⇨ the note at product(1).

pro·duce² /prə'djuːs/ vt **1** to show, put forward, (something) to be looked at or examined: *produce one's railway ticket when asked to do so.* **2** to grow; cause to exist: *We must produce more food and import less. Sweden has produced a number of good tennis players.* **3** to give birth to (young); lay (eggs). **4** to cause, bring about (something) as a result: *success produced by hard work and enthusiasm; an incident that produced a smile/a protest.* **5** to organize (a play, film) for the stage, TV etc.

pro·duc·er /prə'djuːsə(r)/ nc **1** a person or business that manufactures goods: *a producer of cheap manufactured items.* Compare consumer. **2** a person responsible for presenting a play in the theatre or for the production of a film or a radio or TV programme. Compare director(2).

prod·uct /'prɒdʌkt/ nc **1** something produced, esp in factories: *importing cheap products from Hong Kong.* (N) 'Product' is preferred when referring to manufactured items and 'produce' is preferred for fruit, vegetables etc. **2** a result; outcome: *The plan was the product of many hours of careful thought.* **3** (maths) a quantity obtained by multiplication. **4** (science) a substance obtained by chemical reaction.

pro·duc·tion /prə'dʌkʃn/ n **1** nu the process of producing: *the production of crops/manufactured goods.* ⇨ mass production. **2** nu a quantity produced: *a fall/increase in production.* **3** nc something produced: *his early productions as a writer.*

pro·duction line nc a series of workers and machines producing something in a factory.

pro·duc·tive /prə'dʌktɪv/ adj **1** able to produce (esp food) well: *productive land.* **2** producing things economically: *productive methods.* Opp unproductive.

pro·duc·tive·ly adv

pro·duc·tiv·ity /,prɒdʌk'tɪvətɪ/ nu (also attrib) the quality of being productive: *a productivity bonus for workers.*

produc'tivity agreement nc (as part of a wage settlement) one giving better pay and conditions for an increased output.

Prof /prɒf/ abbr **1** (informal) Professor. **2** (written abbr) (title of a) Professor.

pro·fane /prə'feɪn/ adj (formal) having or showing contempt for God and sacred things: *profane language.*

pro·fane·ly adv

pro·fan·ity /prə'fænətɪ/ nc,nu (pl **-ies**) (formal) (an instance of) profane speech or language.

pro·fess /prə'fes/ vt (formal) **1** to declare that one has (beliefs, likes, ignorance, interests etc): *He professed a great interest in my welfare.* (N) Not used in continuous tenses, e.g. is/was -ing. **2** to

claim (something): *I don't profess to be an expert on that subject.*

pro·fes·sion /prə'feʃn/ nc **1** an occupation, esp one needing advanced education and special training, e.g. the law, teaching, medicine. **2** (formal) a declaration (of belief, feeling etc): *professions of faith/loyalty.*

pro·fes·sion·al¹ /prə'feʃənl/ adj (no comp) **1** of a profession(1): *professional skill; professional people.* **2** doing or practising something for payment or to make a living: *professional football.* Compare amateur. **3** doing something in a way that shows care or concern: *My doctor has a good professional attitude.* Compare unprofessional.

pro·fes·sion·al·ly /-nəlɪ/ adv

pro·fes·sion·al² /prə'feʃənl/ nc **1** (abbr pro) a person who does something for payment that others do (without payment) for pleasure, e.g. athletics, musicians. **turn professional** to become a professional. **2** (informal) a person with good ability or attitude: *She's a true professional.*

pro·fes·sion·al·ism /-ɪzəm/ nc

prof·es·sor /prə'fesə(r)/ nc (abbr Prof) a university teacher at the highest level.

prof·es·sor·ial /,prɒfɪ'sɔːrɪəl/ adj

prof·es·sor·ship /-ʃɪp/ nc a professor's post.

prof·fer /'prɒfə(r)/ vt (formal) to offer (esp advice).

pro·fi·cien·cy /prə'fɪʃnsɪ/ nu the quality of being skilled: *a certificate of proficiency in English.*

pro·fi·cient /prə'fɪʃnt/ adj skilled: *proficient in using a calculator.*

pro·fi·cient·ly adv

pro·file¹ /'prəʊfaɪl/ nc **1** a side view, esp of the head. **keep a low profile** to stay away from being noticed or observed. **2** an edge or outline of something seen against a background. **3** a brief biography, as given in a magazine or on TV.

pro·file² /'prəʊfaɪl/ vt to draw, show, (a person, building etc) in profile.

prof·it¹ /'prɒfɪt/ n **1** nu an advantage obtained from something: *gain profit from one's studies.* **2** nc,nu the money gained in trade, business etc: *sell a bike at a good profit.*

'profit-margin nc a difference between the cost of purchase or production and the selling price.

'profit-sharing nu the sharing of profits between employers and employees.

profit·less adj

prof·it² /'prɒfɪt/ vi (formal) (of a person) to gain or be helped: *I have profited from your advice.*

prof·it·able /'prɒfɪtəbl/ adj **1** bringing profit: *profitable investments.* **2** (fig; formal) giving an advantage; useful: *a deal that was profitable to all of us.*

prof·it·ably /-əblɪ/ adv

profi·teer /,prɒfɪ'tɪə(r)/ vi to make large profits unfairly. □ nc (derog) a person who does this.

prof·li·gate /'prɒflɪgət/ adj (formal; derog) **1** (of a person, behaviour) shamelessly immoral. **2** (of the spending of money) very extravagant: *profligate of one's inheritance.* □ nc (derog) a profligate person.

pro·found /prə'faʊnd/ adj **1** (formal) deep (the usual word): *a profound sleep.* **2** showing, having, great knowledge: *a man of profound learn-*

ing.

pro·found·ly *adv* (*formal*) deeply; extremely: *profoundly grateful*.

pro·fun·dity /prə'fʌndətɪ/ *nu* (*formal*) thoroughness: *the profundity of his knowledge*.

pro·fuse /prə'fju:s/ *adj* (*formal*) **1** very plentiful: *profuse gratitude*. **2** (*pred*) extravagant: *He was profuse in his apologies*.

pro·fuse·ly *adv*

pro·fu·sion /prə'fju:ʒn/ *nu* (esp **in profusion**) (*formal*) a great supply: *flowers in profusion*.

prog·eny /'prɒdʒənɪ/ *n pl* (*formal*) children; the young of an animal.

prog·no·sis /prɒg'nəʊsɪs/ *nc* (*pl* **-noses** /-si:z/) (*med*) a forecast of the probable course of a disease or illness. Compare **diagnosis**.

pro·gram¹ /'prəʊgræm/ *nc* (*computers*) a coded collection of instructions (to be) put into a computer.

pro·gram² /'prəʊgræm/ *vt* (**-mm-**) **1** to produce (a set of instructions) for a computer. **2** to arrange (information) in a coded form for a computer.

pro·gram·mable /prəʊ'græməbl/ *adj* (*computers*) (of information) able to be programmed.

pro·gramme¹ (*US* **-gram**) /'prəʊgræm/ *nc* **1** a list of items, events etc for a concert, for radio or TV, a sports meeting etc. **2** a printed list of names of singers at a concert, actors in a play etc. **3** a plan of what is to be done: *What's the programme for tomorrow?* (= What are we/you going to do?) *Do you agree with their political programme?*

pro·gramme² /'prəʊgræm/ *vt* to plan or arrange (something) as a programme: *The oven has been programmed to go on at 6 o'clock*.

,programmed 'learning *nu* a system of learning using a series of graded self-test units.

pro·gram·mer /'prəʊgræmə(r)/ *nc* (*computers*) a person who produces programs for a computer.

pro·gress¹ /'prəʊgres/ *nu* forward movement; improvement: *making fast/slow progress*. **in progress** happening; being made, done: *The meeting is still in progress*. **make good progress** (a) to improve (in health etc). (b) to do a task etc well.

pro·gress² /prə'gres/ *vi* **1** to come nearer to completion: *The work is progressing steadily*. **2** to improve in quality, size, health etc: *She is progressing well in her studies*.

pro·gres·sion /prə'greʃn/ *nu* the action of moving forward or improving.

pro·gres·sive¹ /prə'gresɪv/ *adj* **1** making continuous forward movement. **2** increasing by regular amounts: *progressive taxation*. **3** (of a disease) getting worse. **4** supporting or favouring new ideas, reform, modernization: *a progressive political party*. **5** (*gram*) = continuous tense.

pro,gressive in'finitive *nc* (*gram*) a form of the infinitive with '*be*' and a *present participle*, as in 'You ought not *to be studying* so late'.

pro'gressive tense *nc* (*gram*) = continuous tense.

pro·gres·sive·ly *adv*

pro·gres·sive² /prə'gresɪv/ *nc* a person with progressive(4) ideas or beliefs. Compare **reactionary**.

pro·hib·it /prə'hɪbɪt/ *vt* to say that (something) must not be done, that (a person) must not do something: *You are prohibited from entering that*

room. Smoking is strictly prohibited in libraries.

pro·hib·ition /,prəʊɪ'bɪʃn/ *n* **1** *nu* the act of prohibiting. **2** *nc* a law or order that bans something: *a prohibition against smoking*.

pro·hibi·tive /prə'hɪbɪtɪv/ *adj* **1** intended to prohibit: *prohibitive laws to stop racialism*. **2** (*informal*) having the result of preventing something: *prohibitive prices* (i.e. too high for most people to be able to pay).

pro·ject¹ /'prɒdʒekt/ *nc* (a plan for) a scheme or undertaking: *a project to build a new airport*.

pro·ject² /prə'dʒekt/ *v* **1** *vt,vi* (to cause something) to stand out beyond the surface: *a balcony that projects over the street*. **2** *vt* to cause (light, a shadow, a picture from a film etc) to fall on a surface: *project a beam of light onto a wall*. **3** *vt* (*formal*) to throw, send, (something): *to project one's voice from the stage; to project missiles into space*. **4** *vt* to draw (a solid thing) on a flat surface using straight lines through every point of it from a centre to make a map, diagram etc. **5** *vt* (*formal; usually passive*) to put forward (a plan): *A better system is being projected*. **6** *vt* to say a person has (feelings, usually unpleasant ones such as guilt, inferiority) that one has oneself: *She always projects her own bad temper onto her colleagues*. **7** *vt* to make known the characteristics of (something): *Does the BBC World Service adequately project life in Great Britain?*

pro·jec·ted /prə'dʒektɪd/ *adj* planned but not yet carried out: *a projected holiday/visit*.

pro·jec·tile /prə'dʒektaɪl/ *nc* something (esp a weapon) (to be) sent forward, esp from a gun or launching pad.

pro·jec·tion /prə'dʒekʃn/ *n* **1** *nu* the act, process, of projecting (all senses). **2** *nc* something that projects(1): *a projection from a wall*. **3** *nc* a statement of what one thinks will happen based on known evidence: *sales projections for next year*. **4** *nu* the process of making maps etc by projecting(4): *map projection*.

pro·jec·tor /prə'dʒektə(r)/ *nc* an apparatus for projecting pictures from film onto a screen: *a cinema/slide projector*.

pro·let·ar·iat /,prəʊlɪ'teərɪət/ *nc* (*modern use*) the wage-earners in society contrasted with the owners of industry and capital (who are called the *bourgeoisie*).

pro·let·ar·ian /-ɪən/ *nc, adj* (a member) of the proletariat.

pro·lif·er·ate /prə'lɪfəreɪt/ *vi* (*formal*) to exist or increase in large numbers: *guerrillas proliferating in the hills*.

pro·lif·er·ation /prə,lɪfə'reɪʃn/ *nu*

pro·lif·ic /prə'lɪfɪk/ *adj* (*formal*) producing much or many: *a prolific author*.

pro·logue /'prəʊlɒg/ *nc* (*literature*) the introductory (part of a) poem or play.

pro·long /prə'lɒŋ/ *vt* to make (an activity) longer: *prolong a visit*.

pro·long·ed *adj* continuing for a long time: *a prolonged discussion*.

prom·en·ade /,prɒmə'nɑ:d/ *nc* (a place suitable for) a walk or ride along the waterfront at a seaside resort. □ *vi* to walk along a promenade.

promi·nence /'prɒmɪnəns/ *n* **1** *nu* the state of being prominent. **2** *nc* a higher or more obvious part or place: *a prominence in the middle of a* *plain.*

promi·nent /'prɒmɪnənt/ *adj* **1** standing out; easily seen: *prominent cheekbones; the most prominent feature in the landscape.* **2** well-known and respected: *prominent politicians; play a prominent part in public life.*

promi·nent·ly *adv*

prom·is·cu·ity /ˌprɒmɪ'skjuːətɪ/ *nu* the act, state, of being promiscuous.

pro·mis·cu·ous /prə'mɪskjʊəs/ *adj* having many sexual partners: *promiscuous teenagers.*

pro·mis·cu·ous·ly *adv*

prom·ise¹ /'prɒmɪs/ *n* **1** *nc* a written or spoken serious statement or agreement (not) to do, give etc: *make/give/keep/carry out/break a promise. It was a promise so I'm doing it.* **2** *nc,nu* (something that gives) hope of success or good results: *a writer who shows much promise* (= seems likely to succeed).

prom·ise² /'prɒmɪs/ *v* **1** *vi,vt* to make a promise(1) to (a person): *He promised to be here/that he would be here at 6 o'clock. 'Will you come?'—'I promise (that I'll be there).' You promised me.* **2** *vt* (*formal*) to give cause for expecting (something): *The clouds promise rain.*

prom·is·ing *adj* likely to succeed, having (the possibility of) good results etc: *make a promising start as a student; a promising actress. His work is promising.*

prom·on·tory /'prɒməntrɪ/ *nc* (*pl* -ies) a high point of land standing out from the coastline.

pro·mote /prə'məʊt/ *vt* **1** to give (a person) a higher position or rank: *He was promoted sergeant/to director/to the board.* **2** to help to organize and start (something): *try to promote good feelings (between them).* **3** to try to increase the sales of (a product), the popularity of (a performer) etc.

pro·mo·ter *nc* (esp) a person who actively encourages a business, the sale of a product, the success of a professional person etc.

pro·mo·tion /prə'məʊʃn/ *n* **1** *nu* the state of promoting or being promoted: *He has got/gained promotion.* **2** *nc* an instance of promoting or being promoted: *He resigned because promotions were few.* **3** *nc,nu* (an instance of) advertising (a product for sale).

prompt¹ /prɒmpt/ *adj* acting, done, sent, given, without delay: *a prompt reply; at 6 pm prompt.*

prompt·ly *adv*

prompt·ness *nu*

prompt² /prɒmpt/ *nc* **1** a person who prompts³(2). **2** an instance of prompting³(2).

prompt³ /prɒmpt/ *vt* **1** to be the reason causing (a person) to do something: *He was prompted by patriotism.* **2** to follow the text of a play and tell (an actor) what to say if he or she forgets.

prompt·er /'prɒmptə(r)/ *nc* = prompt²(1).

prom·ul·gate /'prɒməlgeɪt/ *vt* (*formal*) **1** to announce officially (a decree, a new law etc). **2** to make known (beliefs, knowledge).

prom·ul·ga·tion /ˌprɒməl'geɪʃn/ *nu*

pron *written abbr* pronoun.

prone /prəʊn/ *adj* **1** (stretched out, lying) face downwards: *in a prone position.* **2** (*pred*) **prone (to sth)** having a tendency (to): *prone to accidents. Some people seem to be accident-prone.*

prong /prɒŋ/ *nc* (something like) one of the long, pointed parts of a fork.

pro·noun /'prəʊnaʊn/ *nc* (*gram*) a word used in place of a noun or noun phrase, e.g. *he, it, hers, me, them.* Ⓝ Marked *pron* in this dictionary. ⇨ demonstrative / emphatic / indefinite / interrogative/nominative/personal/possessive/reflexive/ relative pronoun.

pro·nounce /prə'naʊns/ *v* **1** *vt,vi* to make the sound of (a word etc): *The 'b' in 'debt' is not pronounced.* **2** *vt* to declare or announce (something) formally, solemnly or officially: *Has judgement been pronounced yet?*

pro·nounced *adj* definite; easy to notice: *a man with a pronounced foreign accent.*

pro·nounce·ment *nc* a formal statement or declaration.

pro·nun·ci·ation /prəˌnʌnsɪ'eɪʃn/ *n* **1** *nu* the way in which a language is spoken: *the pronunciation of English.* **2** *nu* a person's way of speaking a language: *His pronunciation is improving.* **3** *nc* a way in which a word is pronounced: *Which of these pronunciations do you recommend?*

proof¹ /pruːf/ *adj* (*pred*) **proof (against sth)** able to resist; giving protection against: *proof against being deceived.* Ⓝ 'Proof' is most often used in combinations such as foolproof, sound-proof, waterproof.

proof² /pruːf/ *n* **1** *nc,nu* (an example of) evidence that is sufficient to show that something is a fact: *Is there any proof that the accused man was at the scene of the crime? He produced documents in proof of his claim.* **2** *nc* a trial copy of something printed etc for approval before other copies are printed. **3** *nu* the standard of strength of alcoholic liquors: *This rum is 30% proof.*

prop¹ /prɒp/ *nc* **1** a support used to keep something up: *a clothes-prop.* **2** (*fig*) a person who supports another person: *He is the prop of his parents in their old age.* **3** (often *pl*) (*theatre*) any of the furniture, movable objects etc used on a stage during a performance.

prop² /prɒp/ *vt* (-pp-) **1** **prop sth (open/up)** to support, keep, something in position: *Use this box to prop the door open/to prop up the ladder.* **2** **prop sb up** to give support to a person: *He can't always expect his colleagues to prop him up.*

propa·gan·da /ˌprɒpə'gændə/ *nu* (also *attrib*) (methods for) the spreading of (esp untrue) information, doctrines, ideas etc: *political propaganda; propaganda plays/films.*

propa·gate /'prɒpəgeɪt/ *v* (*formal*) **1** *vt* increase the number of (plants, animals, diseases): *Trees propagate themselves by seeds.* **2** *vt,vi* (of animals and plants) to reproduce. **3** *vt* to cause (something) to spread more widely: *propagate news/ knowledge.*

propa·ga·tion /ˌprɒpə'geɪʃn/ *nu*

pro·pel /prə'pel/ *vt* (-ll-) to force (something) to move forward: *a boat propelled by oars.*

pro·pel·lant (also -**lent**) /-ənt/ *adj, nc* (of) something used to produce forward motion, e.g. fuel that burns to fire a rocket etc.

pro·pel·ler *nc* two or more blades which turn to move a ship, helicopter, plane etc.

pro,pelling 'pencil *nc* a pencil with a lead that can be extended by turning the outer casing.

pro·pen·sity /prə'pensətɪ/ *nc* (*pl* -ies) **propensity for sth/to do sth** (*formal*) a natural tendency: *She has a propensity to exaggerate.*

prop·er /'prɒpə(r)/ *adj* **1** (*attrib; no comp*) suitable, correct, for the purpose, situation etc: *Are you doing it the proper way? Is this the proper tool for the job?* **2** paying attention to the conventions of society: *proper behaviour.* Compare improper(1). **3** (placed after the *noun*) strictly so called: *architecture proper.* **4** (*attrib*) (*informal*) great: *We're in a proper mess.*

‚proper 'fraction *nc* (*maths*) (e.g. ½, ¾) one in which the number above the line is smaller than that below the line.

‚proper 'name/'noun *nc* (*gram*) a word used for an individual person, town, object, place etc, e.g. *Mary, Prague, Mars.* Ⓝ *Proper names/nouns always begin with a capital letter.*

prop·er·ly /'prɒpəlɪ/ *adv* in a correct manner: *behave properly; properly dressed.* Opp improperly.

prop·er·ty /'prɒpətɪ/ *n* (*pl* **-ies**) **1** *nu* things owned; possessions: *Don't take my bike—it's not your property.* **2** *nc,nu* an area of land (and buildings): *He has a small property near the coast.* **3** *nc* a special quality that belongs to something: *the chemical properties of iron.* **4** *nc* (theatre) = prop¹(3).

proph·ecy /'prɒfɪsɪ/ *n* (*pl* **-ies**) **1** *nu* the power of telling what will happen in the future: *have the gift of prophecy.* **2** *nc* a statement that tells what will happen: *His prophecy came true.*

proph·esy /'prɒfɪsaɪ/ *vt,vi* (*pt,pp* **-ied**) to say what will happen: *prophesy war/that war will break out.*

proph·et /'prɒfɪt/ *nc* **1** a person who teaches religion and claims that his teaching comes to him directly from God: *the prophet Isaiah.* **2** a pioneer of a new theory, cause etc: *William Morris was one of the early prophets of socialism.* **3** (*informal*) a person who claims to tell what will happen in the future: *I'm not a good weather-prophet.*

prophet·ess /'prɒfɪtɪs/ *nc* a woman prophet.

pro·phet·ic /prə'fetɪk/ *adj* indicating correctly what will happen: *Her dreams were prophetic.*

pro·pheti·cal·ly /-klɪ/ *adv*

pro·pi·tious /prə'pɪʃəs/ *adj* (*formal*) favourable: *propitious weather.*

pro·pi·tious·ly *adv*

pro·por·tion /prə'pɔːʃn/ *n* **1** *nu* the relation of one thing to another in quantity, size etc; relation of a part to the whole: *The proportion of imports to exports is worrying the government.* **in proportion to sth** based on the amount etc of something: *payment in proportion to work done.* **get sth/be out of proportion (to sth)** to (cause it to) have a wrong relation in size, importance etc (to something): *When you're angry, you often get things out of proportion* (= have an exaggerated view of things). **2** *nc* a part; share: *You have not done your proportion of the work.* **3** (*pl*) the correct or pleasing relation of (the sizes of) the several parts: *a room of good proportions.* **4** (*pl*) size; measurements: *export trade of substantial proportions.* **5** *nu* (maths) the equality of relationship between two sets of numbers (e.g. 4 is to 8 as 6 is to 12).

pro·por·tion·al /prə'pɔːʃənl/ *adj* **proportional (to sth)** (*formal*) corresponding in degree or amount (to something): *payment proportional*

to the work done.

pro‚portional ‚represen'tation *nu* a system of voting so that parties have a number of representatives according to the size of their success in the election.

pro·por·tion·al·ly /-nəlɪ/ *adv*

pro·por·tion·ate /prə'pɔːʃənət/ *adj* (*formal*) = proportional. ⇨ disproportionate.

pro·por·tion·ate·ly *adv*

pro·po·sal /prə'pəʊzl/ *n* **1** *nc* a suggested plan or scheme: *a proposal for peace.* **2** *nc* an offer (esp of marriage): *She had five proposals in one week.*

pro·pose /prə'pəʊz/ *v* **1** *vt* to offer or put forward (an idea) for consideration, as a suggestion, plan or purpose: *I propose starting early/an early start/ that we should start early.* **2** *vt,vi* to offer (marriage) (to a person). **3** *vt* to suggest (a person) for an office: *I propose Mr Smith for chairman.*

pro·poser *nc* a person who proposes.

prop·osi·tion¹ /‚prɒpə'zɪʃn/ *nc* **1** a suggestion (with or without the answer or solution): *Tunnelling under the English Channel is a big proposition.* **2** (*informal*) an indecent request about sex made to a woman. **3** (*formal*) a statement of an idea that supports or denies something: *a proposition about evolution.*

prop·osi·tion² /‚prɒpə'zɪʃn/ *vt* (*sl*) to make a proposition(2) to (a woman).

pro·pound /prə'paʊnd/ *vt* (*formal*) to offer (an idea etc) for consideration: *propound a theory.* ⇨ proposition(3).

pro·pri·etary /prə'praɪətrɪ/ *adj* owned or controlled by a person, business: *a proprietary name* (e.g. 'Kodak' for cameras and film).

pro·pri·etor /prə'praɪətə(r)/ *nc* an owner, esp of a hotel, shop, land.

pro·pri·etress /prə'praɪətrɪs/ *nc* a woman proprietor.

pro·pri·ety /prə'praɪətɪ/ *n* (*pl* **-ies**) (*formal*) **1** *nu* the state of being correct in behaviour and morals: *act with propriety.* **2** (*pl*) details of correct social behaviour: *observe the proprieties.* Compare impropriety.

props /prɒps/ *n pl* (theatre) ⇨ prop¹(3).

pro·pul·sion /prə'pʌlʃn/ *nu* a propelling force: *jet propulsion.*

pro·sa·ic /prəʊ'zeɪɪk/ *adj* (*formal; derog*) dull; uninteresting; commonplace: *a prosaic description.*

pro·sa·ical·ly /-klɪ/ *adv*

pro·sceni·um /prə'siːnɪəm/ *nc* (*pl* **—s**) (theatre) the opening of a stage and the area between this and the front edge.

pro·scribe /prəʊ'skraɪb/ *vt* to denounce (a person, practice etc) as dangerous.

pro·scrip·tion /prəʊ'skrɪpʃn/ *nc,nu*

prose /prəʊz/ *nu* the form of language that is not in verse form.

pros·ecute /'prɒsɪkjuːt/ *vt,vi* (of a person, her or his legal representative) to accuse (a person) of a crime and try to prove it in a law court: *Trespassers will be prosecuted. She was prosecuted for theft.*

pros·ecu·tion /‚prɒsɪ'kjuːʃn/ *n* **1** *nc,nu* (an instance of) prosecuting or being prosecuted: *make oneself liable to prosecution; start a prosecution against him.* **2** *n sing* (legal) a person and the legal officials responsible for accusing another person of a crime and trying to prove it in a law court: *the case for the prosecution.* Compare defence(3).

pros·ecu·tor /'prɒsɪkjuːtə(r)/ *nc* a person (or legal representative) who prosecutes.

pros·pect¹ /'prɒspekt/ *n* **1** *nc,nu* (an example of) an expectation or hope: *I see no/little/not much prospect of his recovery. There are good prospects for me if I accept the job.* **2** *nc* a wide view over land or sea. **3** *nc* something that is likely: *We must face the prospect of higher bus fares.* **4** *nc* a person who is likely to be successful, to buy one's goods etc: *He's a good prospect for the gold medal.*

pros·pect² /prə'spekt/ *vi* **prospect (for sth)** to search (in the ground) (for minerals): *prospecting for gold.*

pros·pec·tive /prə'spektɪv/ *adj* (*attrib*) probable or possible: *a prospective buyer; the prospective Labour candidate.*

pros·pec·tor /'prɒspektə(r)/ *nc* a person who explores a region looking for gold or other valuable substances.

pro·spec·tus /prə'spektəs/ *nc* (*pl* **—es**) a leaflet or small book advertising something, e.g. an educational course.

pros·per /'prɒspə(r)/ *vi* to succeed (esp financially): *The business prospered.*

pros·per·ity /prɒ'sperətɪ/ *nu* the state of being financially successful: *a life of happiness and prosperity; live in prosperity.*

pros·per·ous /'prɒspərəs/ *adj* financially successful: *a prosperous family/business; prosperous years.*

pros·per·ous·ly *adv*

pros·ti·tute¹ /'prɒstɪtjuːt/ *nc* a person who offers herself or himself for sexual intercourse for payment.

pros·ti·tute² /'prɒstɪtjuːt/ *v* **1** *v reflex* (*old use*) to make a prostitute of (oneself). **2** *vt* (*formal*) to put (one's name etc) to a wrong or unworthy use: *prostitute one's reputation.*

pros·ti·tu·tion /ˌprɒstɪ'tjuːʃn/ *nu*

pros·trate¹ /'prɒstreɪt/ *adj* (usually *pred*) lying stretched out on the ground, usually face downward.

pros·trate² /prɒ'streɪt/ *vt* (*formal*) **1** to cause (oneself, something) to be prostrate: *The Buddhists prostrated themselves before the altar.* **2** (usually *pp*) to make (a person) helpless: *She is prostrated with grief.*

pro·tag·on·ist /prə'tægənɪst/ *nc* (*literature*) the main character in a drama or novel. Compare antagonist(2).

pro·tect /prə'tekt/ *vt* to keep (a person, thing) safe (from danger, enemies, attack): *well protected from the cold/against the weather/against infection.*

pro·tec·tion /prə'tekʃn/ *nu* **protection (against/from sb/sth)** **1** the state of protecting or being protected: *These plants need protection against the sun.* **2** *nc* a person or thing that protects: *wearing a heavy coat as a protection against the cold.*

pro·tec·tive /prə'tektɪv/ *adj* **1** (*attrib*) giving protection: *a protective covering.* **2** (usually *pred*) **protective (towards sb)** (of a person) with a wish to protect a person: *A mother will naturally feel protective (towards her children).*

pro·tec·tor /prə'tektə(r)/ *nc* **1** a person who protects. **2** something made or designed to give protection.

pro·tégé /'prɒtɪʒeɪ/ *nc* a person (esp with a talent) given guidance and help by a rich or influential person.

pro·tein /'prəʊtiːn/ *nc,nu* a kind of body-building substance, essential to good health, in such foods as milk, eggs, meat, fish.

pro tem /ˌprəʊ 'tem/ *abbr* (*Latin: pro tempore*) for the time being. ⇨ time¹(2).

pro·test¹ /'prəʊtest/ *nc,nu* a statement of disapproval or objection: *He paid without protest.* **do sth under protest** to do it but unwillingly.

'protest march *nc* a public demonstration expressing objection to a government policy etc.

pro·test² /prə'test/ *v* **1** *vi* to express one's strong disapproval or objection: *I protested about the dirty bath to the manager. He protested against being called a fool.* **2** *vi* to take part in a protest march or demonstration. **3** *vt* (*formal*) to state (something) firmly against opposition: *protest one's innocence.*

pro·test·er *nc* a person who protests.

pro·test·ing·ly *adv*

Prot·es·tant /'prɒtɪstənt/ *n, adj* (a member) of any of the Christian groups that has separated from the Roman Catholic Church.

prot·esta·tion /ˌprɒtɪ'steɪʃn/ *nc* (*formal*) a serious or formal declaration: *protestations of innocence.*

pro·to·col /'prəʊtəkɒl/ *nu* a code of behaviour as practised on diplomatic occasions: *Was the seating arranged according to protocol?*

pro·ton /'prəʊtɒn/ *nc* (*science*) a positively charged particle forming part of an atomic nucleus. ⇨ electron, neutron.

pro·to·type /'prəʊtətaɪp/ *nc* the first or original example from which others have been or will be copied or developed.

pro·to·zoa /ˌprəʊtə'zəʊə/ *n pl* (*science*) (a division of the animal kingdom consisting of) animals of the simplest type, formed of a single cell.

pro·tract·ed /prə'træktɪd/ *adj* (*formal*) taking a long time: *a protracted visit/argument.*

pro·trac·tor /prə'træktə(r)/ *nc* an instrument, usually a semicircle, marked 0° to 180°, used for measuring and drawing angles.

pro·trude /prə'truːd/ *vi* (*formal*) to stick out or project.

pro·trud·ing *adj* sticking out: *protruding teeth.*

pro·tru·sion /prə'truːʒn/ *nc,nu*

pro·tu·ber·ance /prə'tjuːbərəns/ *nc* (*formal*) a bulge or swelling.

proud /praʊd/ *adj* (**—er, —est**) **1** (used in a good sense) having or showing a proper pride or dignity: *proud of their success/of being so successful; as proud as a peacock* (= very proud). **2** (*derog*) having or showing a too high opinion of one's importance: *He was too proud to join our party.* **3** (*attrib*) of which one is or may be rightly proud: *It was a proud day for the school when its team won the championship.* ⇨ also houseproud.

proud·ly *adv*

Prov. *written abbr* Province.

prov·able /'pruːvəbl/ *adj* that can be proved.

prove /pruːv/ *v* **1** *vt* to supply proof of (something); show (something) beyond doubt to be true: *prove that he is guilty. Can you prove it (to me)?* ⇨ exception(2). **2** *vt* to establish the genuineness, quality or accuracy of (something): *prove a person's worth.* **3** *vt,vi* (to cause a person, thing) to be shown to be the state or quality mentioned: *Our wood supply proved (to be) insufficient.*

proven /'pru:vn/ *adj* **1** (usually *attrib*) tested and known to be true, successful: *proven ability/methods.* **2** (*pp* of prove(1)) (*legal*) shown to be true: *His guilt was easily proven.*

prov·erb /'prɒvɜ:b/ *nc* a popular short saying giving a general truth, usually advice or warning, e.g. *'It takes two to make a quarrel'.* Ⓝ An *'adage'* is a familiar statement based on the wisdom of experience; an *'aphorism'* expresses a general truth; an *'apothegm'* is a statement of more practical use; an *'axiom'* is a statement of a self-evident truth; a *'maxim'* is usually advice based on experience; a *'proverb'* is the same as an *'aphorism'* but is from an unknown author.

prov·erb·ial /prə'vɜ:bɪəl/ *adj* widely known and talked about: *His stupidity is proverbial.*

prov·erb·ial·ly /-əlɪ/ *adv*

pro·vide /prə'vaɪd/ *vt* **1** **provide sth (for sb)** to give, supply, what is needed or useful, esp in order to live: *providing the children with food; provide food and clothes for the family.* **2** **provide that . . .** (*formal*) to state that . . . : *The agreement provides that the tenant shall pay for repairs.*

pro·vid·ed /prə'vaɪdɪd/ *conj* **provided (that)** on condition (that): *I'll come provided (that) he stays away.*

provi·dence /'prɒvɪdəns/ *nc,nu* (also P-) (an example of) God's care for human beings.

provi·dent /'prɒvɪdənt/ *adj* (*formal*) (careful in) providing for future needs or events, esp in old age. Opp improvident.

provi·dent·ly *adv*

pro·vid·ing /prə'vaɪdɪŋ/ *conj* **providing (that)** = provided (that) (which is more usual).

prov·ince /'prɒvɪns/ *nc* **1** a large, administrative division of a country. **2** (the —s) the country outside the area of the capital: *The pop group is now touring the provinces.* **3** an area of learning or knowledge: *That is outside my province.*

prov·in·cial¹ /prə'vɪnʃl/ *adj* (*attrib*) **1** of a province(1): *provincial government.* **2** of, in, the provinces(2): *provincial roads.* **3** having, typical of, the speech, manners, views etc of a person living in the provinces: *a provincial accent.*

prov·in·cial·ly /-ʃəlɪ/ *adv*

prov·in·cial² /prə'vɪnʃl/ *nc* a person from the provinces(2).

pro·vi·sion /prə'vɪʒn/ *n* (*formal*) **1** *nu* the act of providing. **2** *nu* preparation (esp for future needs): *make provision for one's old age.* **3** *nc* an amount provided: *issue a provision of meat to the campers.* **4** (*pl*) food; food supplies: *have a good supply of provisions.*

pro·vi·sion·al /prə'vɪʒənl/ *adj* **1** for the present only and to be changed or replaced later: *a provisional government/chairman.* **2** (of an appointment or agreement) to be confirmed if certain conditions are met: *get a provisional place at university.*

pro·vi·sion·al·ly /-nəlɪ/ *adv*

pro·viso /prə'vaɪzəʊ/ *n* **with the proviso**

that . . . (*conj*) on condition that . . .

provo·ca·tion /ˌprɒvə'keɪʃn/ *n* **1** *nu* the act of provoking or being provoked: *She shouts at/on the slightest provocation.* **2** *nc* something that annoys: *It needs only a slight provocation to make him angry.*

pro·voca·tive /prə'vɒkətɪv/ *adj* causing, likely to cause, anger or (sexual) excitement.

pro·voke /prə'vəʊk/ *vt* **1** to cause (a person or animal) to become angry. **2** to cause (an angry feeling): *anger provoked by her lies.*

prow /praʊ/ *nc* the pointed front of a ship or boat.

prow·ess /'praʊɪs/ *nu* (*formal*) unusual skill or ability.

prowl¹ /praʊl/ *n* **be on the prowl** to be prowling.

prowl² /praʊl/ *vi* **prowl (about)** to go about quietly looking for a chance to get food (as wild animals do) or to steal etc.

prow·ler *nc* a person, animal, that prowls.

prox·im·ity /prɒk'sɪmətɪ/ *nu* (*formal*) nearness. **in (close) proximity to** (very) near to: *I live in close proximity to the school.*

proxy /'prɒksɪ/ *n* (*pl* **-ies**) **1** *nc,nu* (a document giving) authority to represent or act for another (esp in voting at an election): *vote by proxy.* **2** *nc* a person given a proxy.

prude /pru:d/ *nc* (*derog*) a person who is extremely moral (often exaggerated or affected) in behaviour or speech: *She's such a prude—she objects to bikinis.* ⇨ prudish.

pru·dery /'pru:dərɪ/ *nc,nu*

pru·dence /'pru:dns/ *nu* careful thought or planning in advance (esp about money).

pru·dent /'pru:dnt/ *adj* showing, having, careful thought or planning: *be prudent when spending money; a prudent shopper.* Opp imprudent.

pru·dent·ly *adv*

prud·ish /'pru:dɪʃ/ *adj* (*derog*) easily shocked; extremely (often too) moral. ⇨ prude.

prud·ish·ly *adv*

prune¹ /pru:n/ *nc* a kind of dried plum.

prune² /pru:n/ *vt* **1** to cut away parts of (trees, bushes etc) in order to control growth or shape: *pruning the rose-bushes.* **2** (*fig*) to take out unnecessary parts from (something): *prune a report of unnecessary detail; prune a business of unwanted staff.*

pry¹ /praɪ/ *vi* (*pt,pp* **pried** /praɪd/) **pry (into sth)** to inquire too curiously (into other people's affairs).

pry² /praɪ/ *vt* (*pt, pp* **pried**) = prise.

Ps *written abbr* Psalm.

PS /ˌpi:'es/ *abbr* postscript.

psalm /sɑ:m/ *nc* (often P-) a sacred song or hymn in the Bible.

pseu·do·nym /'sju:dənɪm/ *nc* a name used by an author instead of a real name.

pseud·ony·mous /sju:'dɒnɪməs/ *adj*

psy·che /'saɪkɪ/ *nc* the human mind, soul or spirit.

psy·che·del·ic /ˌsaɪkɪ'delɪk/ *adj* **1** (of drugs) causing very strong feelings of excitement, fear etc. **2** (of visual and sound effects) acting on the mind like psychedelic drugs: *psychedelic music.*

psy·chi·at·ric /ˌsaɪkɪ'ætrɪk/ *adj* (*attrib*) of psychiatry: *a psychiatric ward/clinic.*

psy·chia·trist /saɪ'kaɪətrɪst/ *nc* an expert in psychiatry.

psy·chia·try /saɪˈkaɪətrɪ/ nu the scientific study and treatment of mental illness.

psy·chic /ˈsaɪkɪk/ (also **psy·chi·cal** /ˈsaɪkɪkl/) adj **1** of the soul or mind. **2** of phenomena and conditions which appear to be outside physical or natural laws, e.g. telepathy.

psy·cho·an·al·yse (US = **-lyze**) /ˌsaɪkəʊˈænəlaɪz/ vt to treat (a person) using psychoanalysis.

psy·cho·an·aly·sis /ˌsaɪkəʊəˈnæləsɪs/ nu the method of treating some mental illness by looking at and discussing the effects of events in the patient's life as possible causes.

psy·cho·anal·yst /ˌsaɪkəʊˈænəlɪst/ nc a person who practises psychoanalysis.

psy·cho·an·a·lyt·ic (also **-ical**) /ˌsaɪkəʊˌænəˈlɪtɪk(l)/ adj relating to psychoanalysis.

psy·cho·logi·cal /ˌsaɪkəˈlɒdʒɪkl/ adj of psychology.

psycho·logical 'warfare nu an attempt to win a struggle by destroying the opponent's confidence.

psy·cho·logi·cal·ly /-klɪ/ adv

psy·chol·ogist /saɪˈkɒlədʒɪst/ nc a student of, expert in, psychology.

psy·chol·ogy /saɪˈkɒlədʒɪ/ nu the scientific study of the mind and its processes.

psy·cho·path /ˈsaɪkəʊpæθ/ nc a person suffering from severe emotional disorder, esp one who is aggressive and antisocial.

psy·cho·path·ic /ˌsaɪkəʊˈpæθɪk/ adj

psy·cho·sis /saɪˈkəʊsɪs/ nc (pl **-cho·ses** /-ˈkəʊsiːz/) a severe mental disorder in which a person loses contact with reality.

psy·cho·ther·apy /ˌsaɪkəʊˈθerəpɪ/ nu the treatment by psychological methods of mental, emotional and nervous disorders.

psy·cho·'thera·pist nc a doctor who practises psychotherapy.

pt written abbr **1** pint(s). **2** part. **3** payment. **4** point.

PT /ˌpiː ˈtiː/ abbr Physical Training.

PTA /ˌpiː tiː ˈeɪ/ abbr Parent-Teacher Association (a committee concerned with school matters).

PTO /ˌpiː tiː ˈəʊ/ abbr please turn over (at the bottom of a page).

Pty written abbr (commerce) (used in the title of a business that is) privately owned and controlled.

pub /pʌb/ nc a place (not a club, hotel etc) selling alcoholic drinks to be drunk on the premises.

pu·ber·ty /ˈpjuːbətɪ/ nu the stage at which a person becomes physically able to become a parent.

pu·bic /ˈpjuːbɪk/ adj of the lower front part of the abdomen: pubic hair.

pub·lic¹ /ˈpʌblɪk/ adj **1** (attrib) of, for, connected with or owned by people in general: a public library/park; public opinion; a public bus service. Compare private¹(1). **2** known to many people: It's public gossip that they're married. The news was made public yesterday. ⇨ also eye¹(1).

public 'house nc (formal) = pub.

public o'pinion poll nc ⇨ opinion poll.

public 'ownership nu ownership (of an industry or service) by the State. Compare private enterprise.

public re'lations n pl (esp) relations between a government department, business organization etc and ordinary people.

'public school nc (GB) a kind of private school for fee-paying pupils.

pub·lic·ly /-klɪ/ adv

pub·lic² /ˈpʌblɪk/ n **1** (the —) people in general: The public are not admitted. **in public** so that people can see and know: be seen together in public. **2** nc a particular section of the community: the reading public.

pub·li·ca·tion /ˌpʌblɪˈkeɪʃn/ n **1** nu the act of making something known to the public, by publishing something. **2** nc something published, e.g. a book or magazine.

pub·lic·ity /pʌbˈlɪsətɪ/ nu **1** the state of being known to, seen by, everyone: an actress who seeks/avoids publicity. **2** (also attrib) (the business of providing) information, advertising: a publicity campaign.

pub·li·cize (also **-ise**) /ˈpʌblɪsaɪz/ vt to bring (something) to the attention of the public: publicize a meeting.

pub·lish /ˈpʌblɪʃ/ v **1** vt,vi (to cause a book, magazine, article etc) to be printed and offered for sale. **2** vt to make (something) known to the public: publish the news.

pub·lish·er nc a person or business that publishes books.

puck /pʌk/ nc a hard rubber disc used like a ball in ice hockey.

puck·er /ˈpʌkə(r)/ vt,vi **pucker (sth) (up)** (to cause something) to come together into small folds or wrinkles: pucker up one's lips.

pud·ding /ˈpʊdɪŋ/ nc,nu **1** (a dish of) food, usually a soft, sweet mixture, eaten after a meat or fish course. **2** a kind of sausage: black pudding.

puddle /ˈpʌdl/ nc a small pool of rainwater.

pudgy /ˈpʌdʒɪ/ adj (**-ier, -iest**) (derog) short, thick and fat: pudgy fingers.

puer·ile /ˈpjʊəraɪl/ adj (derog) childish: puerile behaviour; ask puerile questions.

puff¹ /pʌf/ nc (the sound of) a short, quick sending (in and) out of breath, air etc: have a puff at a pipe.

'puff-adder nc a poisonous African snake which can inflate the upper part of its body.

puf·fy adj (**-ier, -iest**) swollen: a face that is puffy under the eyes.

puff² /pʌf/ v **1** vi to breathe quickly (as after running): He was puffing hard when he jumped onto the bus. **2** vi (of smoke, steam etc) to come out in puffs. **3** vi,vt to take a puff(1) at (a cigarette etc): He was puffing (away) (at) his cigar. **4** vt to send out (something) in puffs: He puffed smoke into my face. **5** vt **puff sth out** to cause something to swell with air: He puffed out his chest with pride.

puf·fin /ˈpʌfɪn/ nc a kind of North Atlantic seabird with a large bill.

pug /pʌg/ nc a kind of small dog with a flat nose.

pug·na·cious /pʌgˈneɪʃəs/ adj (formal; derog) fond of, in the habit of, fighting.

puke /pjuːk/ vi,nu (sl) (to be) sick(1).

pull¹ /pʊl/ n **1** nc an act or instance of pulling: give a pull at a rope. **2** nc a hard effort: It was a long pull (= a long, hard climb) to the top of the mountain. **3** nu or sing (informal) power or influence to get help or attention, e.g. with people in high positions: He has a strong pull/a great deal of pull with the Managing Director.

pull² /pʊl/ v Ⓝ For uses of 'pull' in special

expressions such as *pull a face, pull sb's leg, pull a fast one,* ⇨ the noun entries as at *chain, face, finger, leg, one, piece, sock, string, weight, wool.* **1** *vt,vi* to use force or effort on (a person or thing) so as to move (her, him, it) towards oneself or behind oneself and in the same direction: *He pulled me into the room. The child pulled the toy across the floor. Pull your chair nearer the fire. I tried to pull the door open. You must pull harder!* Compare push²(1). **2** *vt,vi* to take hold of (a person or thing) and use force to move her, him, it, away: *Stop pulling my hair. She pulled my sleeve. Pull (the string) to make the bell ring.* **3** *vt* to injure (a muscle etc) by stretching or tearing it. **4** *vt,vi* to drive (a vehicle) in the direction mentioned: *pull away from the kerb; pull out of an entrance; pull a van into the fast lane.* **5** *vt* (*informal*) to attract (an audience): *The pop group pulled a big crowd.* **6** *vt* to take out (a tooth, the inside parts of a chicken). **7** *vt* to produce (a weapon) from clothing: *pull a knife/gun on him.* **8** *vt,vi* to move (a boat) by using oars: *They pulled for the shore.*

pull sb/sth about to treat a person, furniture, clothing etc roughly.

pull ahead (of sb/sth) (of a driver, runner etc or business) to go in front of and beyond a competitor.

pull sth apart to use force to separate something into parts.

pull sth aside to move a curtain etc to one side.

pull back (of soldiers etc) to go back to a position further away.

pull sth down (a) to make a blind, hat, cover lower. (b) to destroy a building.

pull in (a) (of a vehicle) to be driven towards the side of a road. (b) (of a train) to arrive at a station: *The express train pulled in at 2 o'clock.* ***pull sb in*** (*informal*) (of the police) to take a suspected criminal to a police station. ***pull sth in*** (a) to tighten muscles in order to draw in one's stomach, toes etc. (b) (*informal*) to earn a good wage. (c) (*informal*) to attract a crowd or audience.

pull sth off (a) to remove clothing using force. (b) to remove (part of) something using force: *I pulled the handle off by mistake.* (c) (*informal*) to succeed at a business deal, an attempt to persuade a person etc: *We've pulled off the contract!*

pull on sth to draw smoke from a pipe, cigarette. ***pull sth on*** to put on clothing: *He pulled on his sweater.* ***pull sth on sb*** ⇨ 7 above.

pull out (of a place) (of a vehicle, train, soldiers, etc) to leave (a place). ***pull sth out*** to take out a tooth, pages from a magazine etc.

pull over (often an order from the police) (of a vehicle) to be driven to the side of the road and stop.

pull (sb) round (*informal*) to (help a person to) become conscious again: *Cold water will pull him round.*

pull (sb) through (a) to (help a person to) recover from a serious illness. (b) to (help a person to) avoid failing an exam, financial ruin etc.

pull together (of a group of people) to work together using all the abilities and effort. ***pull oneself together*** (*informal*) to take firm control of one's feelings and behave sensibly.

pull sb under (a) to cause a person to go under water. (b) (*informal*) to be (partly) responsible

for a person's failure (esp financially).

pull up (at a place) (of a vehicle) to stop (at): *pull up at the traffic lights.* ***pull sb up*** (*informal*) to express one's disapproval of a person's behaviour.

pul·let /'pʊlɪt/ *nc* a young hen.

pul·ley /'pʊlɪ/ *nc* (*pl* **—s**) an apparatus with a wheel and ropes or chains, used for lifting things.

pull·over /'pʊləʊvə(r)/ *nc* a knitted article of clothing (to be) pulled on over the head.

pul·mon·ary /'pʌlmənərɪ/ *adj* (*anat*) of, in, concerning, the lungs: *the pulmonary arteries.*

pulp¹ /pʌlp/ *nu* **1** the soft, fleshy part of fruit. **2** a soft mass of other material: *wood pulp.*

pulp² /pʌlp/ *vt* to cause (fruit, wood etc) to become pulp.

pul·pit /'pʊlpɪt/ *nc* a raised and enclosed structure in a church, used when preaching.

pul·sate /pʌl'seɪt/ *vi* to beat or throb; expand and contract rhythmically.

pul·sa·tion /pʌl'seɪʃn/ *nc,nu*

pulse¹ /pʌls/ *nc* (often *pl*) a seed of a pea, bean or lentil used as food.

pulse² /pʌls/ *nc* **1** the regular beat of the arteries, e.g. felt at the wrist, as the blood is pumped through them by the heart. **2** (*fig*) the activities or thrill of life or emotion: *the pulse of life in a big city.*

pulse³ /pʌls/ *vi* to beat; throb: *news that sent the blood pulsing through his veins.*

pul·ver·ize (also **-ise**) /'pʌlvəraɪz/ *v* **1** *vt,vi* (to cause something) to become powder or dust. **2** *vt* to defeat (a person, team etc) completely.

pu·ma /'pju:mə/ *nc* (*pl* **—s**). = cougar.

pum·ice /'pʌmɪs/ *nu* (also *pumice-stone*) a light, grey stone (from *lava*) used for cleaning and polishing.

pum·mel /'pʌml/ *vt* (**-ll-**, *US* also **-l-**) to beat (a person, thing) repeatedly with the fists.

pump¹ /pʌmp/ *nc* a machine for forcing liquid, gas or air into, out of or through something: *a petrol pump; a bicycle pump.*

pump² /pʌmp/ *v* **1** *vt,vi* to force (water, air etc) into, from, (something) using a pump: *pump petrol into a car; pump (up) a tyre.* **2** (*fig*) *vt* to explain, teach etc (something) using repetition etc: *pump facts into the heads of dull students.* **3** *vt* (*fig*) to get (information) using many questions: *pump information out of her.*

pump·kin /'pʌmpkɪn/ *nc,nu* (a trailing plant with) a large, round, orange-yellow fruit, used as a vegetable.

pun¹ /pʌn/ *nc* (also called *a play on words*) a humorous use of words which sound the same or of two meanings of the same word, e.g. 'The soldier laid down his *arms.*'

pun² /pʌn/ *vi* (**-nn-**) to make a pun.

punch¹ /pʌntʃ/ *n* **1** *nc* a blow made with a closed hand: *a punch on the nose.* **2** *nu* (*fig*) energy and effect: *a speech with plenty of punch.*

punch² /pʌntʃ/ *nc* a tool used for cutting holes or pressing designs into leather etc.

punch³ /pʌntʃ/ *nu* a drink of wine, spices etc.

punch⁴ /pʌntʃ/ *vt* to hit (a person) with a punch¹(1): *I punched him on the chin.*

punch⁵ /pʌntʃ/ *vt* to use a punch² to make (holes or designs) in something.

punc·tili·ous /pʌŋk'tɪlɪəs/ *adj* (*formal*) very

careful to carry out duties correctly, arrive on time etc.

punc·til·i·ous·ly *adv*

punc·tual /'pʌŋktʃʊəl/ *adj* coming, doing something, at the agreed or fixed time: *be punctual for the lecture/in the payment of one's rent.*

punc·tu·al·i·ty /ˌpʌŋktʃʊ'ælətɪ/ *nu*

punc·tu·al·ly /-ʊəlɪ/ *adv*

punc·tu·ate /'pʌŋktʃʊeɪt/ *vt* 1 to put (marks, e.g. . , ; : ? !) into a piece of writing. 2 (often *passive*) to interrupt (a speech etc) from time to time: *a speech punctuated with cheers.*

punc·tu·a·tion /ˌpʌŋktʃʊ'eɪʃn/ *nu* (also *attrib*) (the use of) the marks . , : ; ? ! in writing: *punctuation marks.*

punc·ture¹ /'pʌŋtʃə(r)/ *nc* a small hole, esp one made accidentally in a tyre.

punc·ture² /'pʌŋtʃə(r)/ *vt,vi* to make or get a puncture in (something): *Two of my tyres punctured while I was on that stony road.*

pun·dit /'pʌndɪt/ *nc* a person who knows a great deal about a subject.

pun·gent /'pʌndʒənt/ *adj* (*formal*) 1 (of smells, tastes) very strong, sharp: *a pungent sauce.* 2 (*fig*) (of remarks) very painful: *pungent criticism.*

pun·ish /'pʌnɪʃ/ *vt* 1 to cause (a person) to suffer for doing wrong: *punish a man with/by a fine.* 2 to treat (a person) roughly; hit (a person): *The champion punished his opponent severely.*

pun·ish·able /-əbl/ *adj* that can be punished (by law).

pun·ish·ment *n* **(a)** *nu* the act of punishing or being punished: *Does the punishment fit the crime?* **(b)** *nc* a particular penalty for doing wrong: *The punishment for murder is severe.*

pu·ni·tive /'pjuːnɪtɪv/ *adj* (*formal*) 1 (intended for) punishing: *punitive measures.* 2 very severe: *punitive fines.*

punk /pʌŋk/ *adj* (*attrib*) (GB in the 1970's) describing young people who deliberately shock society through their clothes, language, pop music etc.

punk 'rock *nu* (1970's) a style of fast, loud rock music using violent or antisocial themes.

pun·net /'pʌnɪt/ *nc* a small basket (for fruit): *strawberries, 60p a punnet.*

pu·ny /'pjuːnɪ/ *adj* (-ier, -iest) (*derog*) small and weak: *What a puny little man!*

pup /pʌp/ *nc* = puppy.

pu·pa /'pjuːpə/ *nc* (*pl* —s or —e /-piː/) (*science*) = chrysalis.

pu·pil¹ /'pjuːpl/ *nc* a child at school.

pu·pil² /'pjuːpl/ *nc* (*anat*) the round opening in the centre of the eye.

pup·pet /'pʌpɪt/ *nc* 1 (**string puppet**) a small figure of a person, animal etc with jointed limbs moved by wires or strings. 2 (**glove puppet**) a doll of which the body can be put on the hand like a glove, moved by the fingers. 3 (often *attrib*) a person or group whose acts are completely controlled by another: *a puppet government/State.*

pup·py /'pʌpɪ/ *nc* (*pl* -ies) a young dog.

pur·chase¹ /'pɜːtʃɪs/ *n* 1 *nu* the act of buying. 2 *nc* (*formal*) something bought (esp something large and expensive such as a house or car).

pur·chase² /'pɜːtʃɪs/ *vt* (*formal*) to buy (something, esp something large and expensive such as a house or car).

pur·chaser *nc* a buyer (the usual word).

pure /pjʊə(r)/ *adj* (—r, —st) 1 not mixed with any other substance etc: *pure air/gold.* Opp impure(2). 2 without evil or sin: *pure in body and mind.* Opp impure(1). 3 (of sounds) clear and distinct: *a pure note.* 4 (*attrib; no comp*) dealing with, studied for the sake of, theory only: *pure mathematics/science.* 5 (*attrib; no comp*) complete; thorough: *a pure waste of time.* **pure and simple** (*informal*) (used for emphasis) absolutely: *It's a matter of working even harder, pure and simple.*

pu·rée /'pjʊəreɪ/ *nu* a soft mixture of vegetables, fruit etc boiled and pressed through a sieve: *apple purée.*

pure·ly /'pjʊəlɪ/ *adv* entirely; completely; merely: *I met her purely by accident.*

pur·ga·tive /'pɜːgətɪv/ *nc, adj* (a substance) having the power to empty the bowels.

pur·ga·tory /'pɜːgətrɪ/ *nu* 1 (esp in Roman Catholic doctrine) a condition or place after death in which the soul has to be purified by suffering. 2 (*fig*) any place of suffering.

purge¹ /pɜːdʒ/ *nc* an act of removing unwanted people from (a society, political party).

purge² /pɜːdʒ/ *vt* 1 to make (oneself, a person) free (of sin): *be purged of/from sin; purging away one's sins.* 2 to clear (oneself or a person of a charge, of suspicion). 3 to remove unwanted people from (a political party, society etc).

pu·ri·fy /'pjʊərɪfaɪ/ *vt* (*pt,pp* **-ied**) to make (air, water etc) pure or clean: *purifying the air in a factory.*

pu·ri·fi·ca·tion /ˌpjʊərɪfɪ'keɪʃn/ *nu*

pu·rist /'pjʊərɪst/ *nc* (often *derog*) a person who pays (too) much attention to the correct use of words, grammar, style etc.

puri·tan /'pjʊərɪtn/ *adj, nc* (*derog*) (of) a person who is strict in morals and who considers many kinds of fun and pleasure as sinful: *Don't marry a puritan.*

puri·tani·cal /ˌpjʊərɪ'tænɪkl/ *adj*

puri·tani·cal·ly /ˌpjʊərɪ'tænɪklɪ/ *adv*

pu·ri·ty /'pjʊərətɪ/ *nu* the state or quality of being pure.

purl /pɜːl/ *nc* (*knitting*) a basic way of knitting into the front of each stitch. ⇨ plain³.

pur·loin /pɜː'lɔɪn/ *vt* (*formal*) to steal (something).

purple /'pɜːpl/ *adj, nu* (of) red and blue mixed together.

pur·port¹ /'pɜːpət/ *nu* (*formal*) the general meaning or intention of something said or written: *the purport of what he said.*

pur·port² /pə'pɔːt/ *vt* (*formal*) 1 to seem to mean (something): *The statement purports that he is guilty.* 2 to claim (something): *It's purported to be an original but it is really a fake.*

pur·pose /'pɜːpəs/ *n* 1 *nc* intention; reason: *This van is used for various purposes. What's the purpose of doing that?* **serve its/one's purpose** to be satisfactory for a particular use or need. 2 *nu* (*formal*) the power of forming plans and keeping to them: *weak of purpose.* 3 **on purpose** deliberately: *She sometimes smiles at him on purpose just to annoy me.*

purpose-'built *adj* made for a particular reason or use: *purpose-built offices.*

pur·pose·ful /-fəl/ *adj*
pur·pose·ful·ly /-fəlɪ/ *adv*
pur·pose·ly *adj* deliberately.

purr /pɜː(r)/ *vi, nc* **1** (of a cat) (to make) a low, continuous sound expressing pleasure. **2** (of a car engine) (to make) a similar vibrating sound.

purse¹ /pɜːs/ *nc* **1** a small bag for money. **2** (*US*) = handbag.

purse² /pɜːs/ *vt* to draw (the lips) together in tiny folds or wrinkles.

purs·er /'pɜːsə(r)/ *nc* an officer responsible for a ship's accounts and stores, the welfare of passengers etc.

pur·su·ance /pə'sjuːəns/ *n* **in pursuance of sth** (*formal*) during the carrying out or performance of one's duties etc.

pur·sue /pə'sjuː/ *vt* **1** to go after (a person, animal, car etc) in order to catch or kill: *They were pursuing a robber/a bear. Make sure that you are not being pursued.* **2** (*formal*) to continue with (something): *pursue one's study of English after leaving college.* **3** (*formal*) to have (something) as an aim or purpose: *pursue pleasure/a teaching career.*

pur·su·er *nc* a person who pursues(1).

pur·suit /pə'sjuːt/ *n* **1** *nu* the act of pursuing: *a dog in pursuit of rabbits.* **2** *nc* something to which one gives time (for work or pleasure): *scientific/ literary pursuits.*

pur·vey /pɜː'veɪ/ *vt* (*formal*) to supply (food, basic goods) from a shop or store.

pur·vey·or /-ə(r)/ *nc* (*commerce*) a supplier (the usual word).

pus /pʌs/ *nu* the thick, yellowish-white liquid formed in and coming out of an infected place in the body, e.g. a cut.

push¹ /pʊʃ/ *n* **1** *nc* an act of pushing: *Give the door a hard push.* **2** *nc* a great effort: *We must make a push to finish the job this week.* **3 get/ give sb/be given the push** (*sl*) (to cause a person) to be dismissed from employment. **4** *nu* the confidence to put oneself forward, attract attention etc: *He hasn't enough push to succeed as a salesman.*

push² /pʊʃ/ *v* **1** *vt,vi* to use force or effort on (a person or thing) so as to move (her, him, it) away from oneself or in front of oneself in the same direction: *The woman was pushing the baby's pram. Please push the table against the wall. I was pushed out of the bus. I pushed the door shut. Don't push!* Compare pull²(1). **2** *vt,vi* to put one's hand, shoulder etc on (a person or thing) and use pressure to move it away from one: *Someone pushed me in the back. Push the button and the bell will ring.* **3** *vt* to make (one's way) through a crowd by pushing: *We pushed our way up the stairs.* **4** *vt,vi* to encourage, urge, try to persuade (others) to do something: *He pushed me into applying for the job. They're pushing us for payment/for a decision. She's pushing for agreement on the new prices.* **5** *vt* to try to sell (something illegal): *push drugs.* ⇨ pusher. **6 be pushing fifty** etc (*informal*) be nearing the age mentioned.

push sb about (*informal*) to order a person to do things in an unfriendly way.

push ahead (with sth) (*informal*) to continue to carry out (work, a plan): *The snow has gone*

and we can push ahead (*with building*).

push along (*informal*) to leave a social gathering: *I must be pushing along now.*

push sb around = push sb about.

push by (sb) to pass a person and push her or him out of the way.

push for sth to make repeated, serious requests for something: *push hard for a new investigation.*

push oneself forward to force oneself on the attention of others in order to gain an advantage.

push off (usually *imperative*) to go away.

push on (**a**) to go forward in a determined way: *push on up the hill.* (**b**) to continue working in a steady way: *push on with the work.*

push sb/sth over to cause a person, thing to fall over by pushing. ⇨ also push-over.

push past (sb) = push by (sb).

push sth through to cause a committee, official body etc to agree to, accept etc a proposal by using determination: *push a budget through the finance committee.*

push sth up to force prices, wages, temperature etc to increase.

push-bike /'pʊʃbaɪk/ *nc* (*informal*) bicycle.

push-chair /'pʊʃ tʃeə(r)/ *nc* an apparatus like a chair on wheels, for a small child to sit in.

push·er /'pʊʃə(r)/ *nc* (*informal*) a person who pushes(5) drugs.

push-over /'pʊʃəʊvə(r)/ *nc* (*informal*) a person, team etc that is easily defeated.

puss /pʊs/ *nc* (*informal*) a cat.

pus·sy /'pʊsɪ/ *nc* (*pl* **-ies**) (also *pussy-cat*) (*informal*) a cat.

put /pʊt/ *v* (*pt,pp* —; *pres p* **putting**) Ⓝ For uses of *put* in special expressions, such as *put one's foot down, put one's back up, put the blame on sb,* ⇨ the noun entries, as at *act, action, back, blame, boot, death, ease, end, foot, mind, money, place, play, pressure, right, root, stop, test, word.* **1** *vt* to move (something) into a certain place or position: *He put the book on the table/his hands in his pockets. It's time to put the baby to bed. They've put men on the moon.* **2** *vt* to cause (something) to be in a particular state: *put all one's papers in order; put a picture straight.* **not know where to put oneself** (*informal*) to be very embarrassed. **3** *vt* to write or indicate (something): *put a cross by each name/a price on each box/one's signature to an agreement.* **4** *vt* to express or state (something): *How shall I put it?* (= say it?) *That can all be put in a few words. To put it bluntly, I don't like you.* **5** *vt* to offer (an idea etc) for consideration: *put an idea to the committee/a question to the vote.* **6** *vt* to give (money) as an investment or contribution: *put £1000 into the business.* **7 put paid to sth** ⇨ pay²(3). **stay put** ⇨ stay²(1).

put sth about to pass gossip, information etc from one person to another: *Don't believe what he puts about.*

put sth above sth to treat honour, reputation, survival etc as more important than anything else.

put sth across (to sb) to explain, tell, communicate, something successfully: *How can I put the idea across?* **put sth across sb** to trick a person into believing something.

put sth aside (**a**) to put something down and leave it: *put aside one's book.* (**b**) to save money, food etc for future use. (**c**) to ignore something:

Let's put aside the fact that he's been to prison.

put sth at sth to calculate, estimate, something to be the amount, age, price etc mentioned: *I'd put her weight at 60 kilos.*

put sb away *(informal)* to place a person in a mental hospital. **put sth away (a)** to place something in a box, drawer etc: *Put your clothes/ books away.* **(b)** = put sth aside(b). **(c)** *(informal)* to consume a large amount of alcoholic drinks, food: *put away several potatoes/whiskies.*

put sth back (a) to return something to its correct place. **(b)** to move the hands of a clock back to an earlier time. **(c)** to cause a delay to a schedule, finishing a task etc: *The strike put deliveries back by a month.*

put sth before sb/sth to present an idea, plan etc for consideration by a person, committee. **put sth before sth** = put sth above sth.

put sth behind one to refuse to allow a bad experience, failure etc to affect one in future: *The exam results were bad but he's put that behind him now.*

put sth by = put sth aside(b).

put sb down (a) (of a driver) to allow a person to get off a bus, train or out of a taxi, car. **(b)** to silence an opponent, critic, rebel etc. **(c)** to make a person appear inferior or foolish in public deliberately. **put sth down (a)** to set or place something on a surface: *Put down that knife!* **(b)** to kill a dangerous or seriously ill animal. **(c)** to write a name, thought, date etc (in a book, diary, list etc). **(d)** to press a pedal, lever etc down. **put sb down as sb (a)** to write a person down as another person: *She put herself down as Mrs Smith.* **(b)** to consider a person to be the kind of person mentioned: *I put him down as a good businessman.* **put sth down as sth** to write something in a record etc as (related to) something, often to deceive: *She put the petrol costs down as business expenses.* **put sb down for sth (a)** to enter oneself, a child etc for a school, course, university etc: *I've put myself down for Oxford University.* **(b)** to record that a person is willing to give an amount of money mentioned: *You can put me down for £5.* **put sth down to sth (a)** to enter an amount in a particular account: *put the petrol down to business expenses.* **(b)** to regard behaviour, failure, disease etc as caused by ignorance, conditions, age etc: *Can we put the delay down to poor management?*

put sb forward (for sth) to recommend oneself, a person (for a job, an award etc). **put sth forward (a)** to suggest or propose an idea, theory. **(b)** to move the hands of a clock forward to a later time.

put in (at a place) (of a boat etc) to stop at: *put in at Tunis.* **put sth in (a)** to include, write in, a detail, colour, punctuation mark etc: *I'll put in that bit about teaching in Ghana.* **(b)** to cause something to be inside: *He put his head in the window.* **(c)** to spend a period of time doing something: *put in an hour's work before breakfast.* **(d)** to present a claim to an official: *put in an hour's overtime.* **(e)** to fit something into its particular opening: *put a plug in a socket.* **(f)** to build or fit a heating system, machine, new part etc in a building: *put in central heating/a new bath.* **put (sb) in for sth** to enter oneself, a person for a compe-

tition, a job, an award etc: *Let's put her in for the 3000m race.*

put sb inside *(informal)* to put a person in prison.

put into a place = put in (at a place). **put sth into sth** to devote effort, time, thought etc to work, a plan, arrangement: *put a lot of effort into improving one's Spanish.*

put sb off (sth) (a) = put sb down(a): *They put the rude boys off the bus.* **(b)** to cause a person to lose interest or liking: *She taught me so badly that it put me off maths for life. The dirty kitchen put me off eating.* **(c)** (of appearance, behaviour etc) to cause a person not to like or respond to a person: *Don't be put off by his hair-style.* **(d)** (of noise etc) to disturb a person: *The sound of the machine is putting me off (my studies).* **(e)** to delay seeing a person: *We'll have to put them off until next week.* **put sth off** to delay doing something: *put off a decision.*

put sth on (a) to cause a light, apparatus to be working: *put a light/the TV on.* Ⓝ Opposite is *'put sth out'* or *'turn sth off'.* **(b)** to put clothes on oneself: *put on one's shirt/shoes.* Ⓝ Opposite is *'take sth off'.* **(c)** to add an amount to the cost, price etc: *The increase in petrol prices will put pounds on the cost of transport.* **(d)** to add more vehicles to a transport service: *put on extra buses.* **(e)** to increase speed, weight etc. **(f)** to pretend to be, feel, something: *Her shyness is put on* (i.e. is not genuine). **(g)** to display or have a particular manner, pose, way of speaking: *Her upper class voice is put on to impress you.* **put sth on sb** to put physical or mental pressure on a person. **put sth on sb/sth** to bet money on a competitor in a race, an event.

put sb on to sb to tell a person where another person is or what that person is doing (e.g. so that he or she can be arrested).

put sb out (a) (often *passive*) to spoil a person's arrangements or make them difficult: *He was put out by our late arrival.* **(b)** (usually *passive*) to upset, cause annoyance to a person: *She was very put out (by his rudeness).* **(c)** to make a person unconscious: *One moment in the smoke put her out for an hour.* **put sth out (a)** to cause a light, fire etc to stop working or burning: *put out the lights/fire/gas.* **(b)** to issue a statement, report, warning etc to the public: *put out an announcement.* **(c)** to broadcast something on TV or radio: *the news put out by the BBC.* **(d)** to cause a bone in a joint to be knocked out of position: *put one's knee/shoulder out.* **(e)** (of movement, temperature etc) to cause an instrument, number etc to be inaccurate: *Wrong calculations put out the measurements by several centimetres.* **put sb out (of a place)** to use force to remove a troublemaker (from a place).

put sth over (to sb) = put sth across (to sb). **put one/sth over on sb** *(informal)* = put sth across sb.

would not put it past sb (to do sth) *(informal)* to consider a person capable (of doing something bad, illegal etc): *I wouldn't put it past her to steal.*

put sb/sth through (to sb/sth) to connect a person, call by telephone. **put sb through sth** to make it possible for a person to do a course of study etc: *Who'll put him through university?* **put sb through it** (*informal*) to make a person suffer while doing a test, examination. **put sth through** to carry out a programme of work, a business deal etc.

put sth to sb; put it to sb that . . . to suggest to a person that: *I put it to you that you stole the money.* ⇨ also 5 above. **put sth to sth** to use something for the purpose of something: *put one's experience to good use.* **be hard put to do sth** ⇨ hard²(1).

put sth together to fit together parts to make a whole: *It's easier to take a machine apart than to put it together again.* ⇨ head¹(2), two.

put sth towards sth to give money etc as a contribution to a cost, fund etc.

put sth under sth to place an example, item etc in a category: *Put that cost under general expenses.*

put up (at a place) to stay (at a hotel etc): *Where shall we put up for the night?* **put sb up** to provide a person with food and a place to sleep: *We can easily put you up for the weekend.* **put sth up** (a) to raise, hold up something: *put up one's hand/a flag.* (b) to fasten something on a wall etc: *put up a notice.* (c) to increase a price, cost etc: *Will they put our wages up?* (d) to lend, give the money needed: *put up the money for a new factory.* (e) to build something from parts: *put up a statue/tent/fence.* (f) to offer some action in return: *put up a strong resistance/a good fight.* (g) to pretend to feel something in order to deceive: *put up a show of being pleasant/a confident front.* (h) to offer something (to be bought): *put a house up for sale.* **put sb up for sth** = put sb forward (for sth). **put sb up to sth** to encourage a person to do something wrong, behave badly etc: *Who put her up to it?* **put up with sb/sth** to tolerate, bear an unattractive person, a noise, bad manners etc: *You married her and you must put up with her. Do I have to put up with noisy neighbours?*

be/feel put upon (by sb) to be/feel deceived or tricked (by a person).

pu·ta·tive /'pjuːtətɪv/ *adj* (*attrib*) (*formal*) generally considered to be: *his putative father.*

pu·tre·fy /'pjuːtrɪfaɪ/ *vt,vi* (*pt,pp* -**ied**) (*formal*) (to cause meat etc) to decay (the usual word).

pu·tre·fac·tion /ˌpjuːtrɪ'fækʃn/ *nc,nu*

pu·trid /'pjuːtrɪd/ *adj* having become decayed and smelling bad: *putrid fish.*

putt /pʌt/ *vi,vt* (*golf*) to hit (a golf-ball) gently so that it rolls along the ground.

put·ty /'pʌtɪ/ *nu* a soft mixture of white powder and oil, used for fixing glass in window frames etc.

puzzle¹ /'pʌzl/ *nc* **1** a question or problem that is difficult to understand or answer: *Why she said that is a puzzle (to me).* **2** a game, toy etc designed to test a person's knowledge, skill or patience: *a jigsaw puzzle; a crossword puzzle.* **3** *n sing* a condition caused by something that is difficult to explain: *be in a puzzle.*

puzzle² /'pʌzl/ *vt* **1** to cause (a person) to be confused, worried, (about the solution to a problem): *This letter puzzles me.* **2** *vt* **puzzle sth out** to (try to) find the answer or solution to something by thinking hard. **3** *vi* **puzzle over sth** to think very much about something.

PVC /ˌpiːviː'siː/ *abbr* (*tech*) polyvinyl chloride (a plastic substance used in materials that need to bend e.g. a hosepipe).

pyg·my (also **pig·my**) /'pɪgmɪ/ *nc* (*pl* -**ies**) a very small animal etc.

py·ja·ma /pə'dʒɑːmə/ ⇨ *note* at pyjamas.

py·ja·mas (*US* = **pa·ja·mas**) /pə'dʒɑːməz/ *n pl* (also *a pair of pyjamas*) a loose-fitting jacket and trousers for sleeping in. Ⓝ *'Pyjamas'* is singular when used as an attrib adjective, as in *pyjama tops/ bottoms.*

py·lon /'paɪlən/ *nc* a tall, steel framework for electric cables.

pyra·mid /'pɪrəmɪd/ *nc* (*maths*) a solid figure with a triangular or square base and sloping sides meeting at a point.

pyre /paɪə(r)/ *nc* a large pile of wood used for burning a corpse.

py·thon /'paɪθn/ *nc* a kind of large snake that kills by twisting its body round an animal.

Qq

Q, q /kjuː/ (*pl* **Q's, q's** /kjuːz/) the 17th letter of the English alphabet. **mind one's P's and Q's** ⇨ P.

QC /ˌkjuː'siː/ *abbr* Queen's Counsel (a title given while a queen is ruling to) a barrister.

qr *written abbr* quarter(s).

qt *written abbr* quart(s).

qty *written abbr* quantity.

qu. *written abbr* question.

Qu *written abbr* Queen.

quack¹ /kwæk/ *vi, nc* (to make) the cry of a duck.

quack² /kwæk/ *nc* (also *attrib; derog*) a person dishonestly claiming to have medical knowledge and skill: *quack remedies.*

quad /kwɒd/ *nc* **1** = quadrangle. **2** (= quadruplet) one of four babies at one birth. Ⓝ Usually used in the plural, i.e. *'one of the quads'*, not *'a quad'*.

quad·rangle /'kwɒdræŋgl/ *nc* (abbr quad) a space in the form of a rectangle, (almost) surrounded by buildings.

quad·ran·gu·lar /kwɒ'dræŋgjʊlə(r)/ *adj*

quad·rant /'kwɒdrənt/ *nc* (*maths*) **1** a quarter of a circle or its circumference. **2** an instrument shaped like a quarter of a circle, for measuring angles in astronomy and navigation.

quad·ri·lat·er·al /ˌkwɒdrɪ'lætərəl/ *adj, nc* (*maths*) (of) a four-sided shape, esp a square or oblong.

quad·ri·ple·gic /ˌkwɒdrɪ'pliːdʒɪk/ *adj, nc* (a person) suffering paralysis of all four limbs, caused by injury to the spinal cord. Compare paraplegic.

quad·ru·ped /'kwɒdrʊped/ *nc* (*formal*) a four-footed animal.

quad·ruple¹ /kwɒ'druːpl/ *adj* made up of four parts, groups etc: *a quadruple champion; quadruple alliance.*

quad·ruple² /kwɒ'druːpl/ *nc* (*maths*) a number or amount four times as great as another: *20 is the quadruple of 5.*

quad·ruple³ /kwɒ'druːpl/ *vt,vi* to multiply (a

quad·ru·plet /'kwɒdrʊplɪt/ nc (formal) ⇒ quad(2).

quag·mire /'kwɒgmaɪə(r)/ nc an area of soft, wet land.

quail¹ /kweɪl/ nc a kind of small bird, similar to a partridge, valued as food.

quail² /kweɪl/ vi **quail (at sth)** to feel or show fear: *He quailed at the thought of meeting the President.*

quaint /kweɪnt/ adj (**—er**, **—est**) attractive or pleasing because unusual or old fashioned: *American visitors to England admire our quaint villages/customs.*
    quaint·ly adv

quake /kweɪk/ vi **1** (of the earth) to shake: *The ground quaked under his feet.* **2 quake (with sth)** (of a person) to tremble (because of something): *quaking with fear/cold.*

Quaker /'kweɪkə(r)/ nc a member of the Quakers or the Society of Friends, a Christian group that holds informal meetings and is opposed to violence.

quali·fi·ca·tion /ˌkwɒlɪfɪ'keɪʃn/ n **1** nc a diploma, degree etc that proves a person has trained for something. **2** nc,nu (formal) something which restricts, modifies or limits: *You can accept his statement without qualification/with certain qualifications.*

qual·ify /'kwɒlɪfaɪ/ vt (pt,pp **-ied**) **1** vt,vi (to cause a person) to become trained, educated and approved as having the required standard: *He's qualified/His training qualifies him as a teacher of English/for this post.* **2** vt,vi (to cause a person) to have the necessary experience, conditions, age etc: *He's the manager's son but that does not qualify him to criticize my work. Do you qualify for the vote/to vote?* **3** vt to limit (something); make (it) less general: *The statement 'Boys are lazy' needs to be qualified* (e.g. by saying 'Some boys' or 'Many boys'). **4** vt (gram) = modify(3).
    quali·fied /-faɪd/ adj (**a**) having the necessary qualifications: *a qualified doctor.* (**b**) (attrib) limited: *give a scheme one's qualified approval.* Opp unqualified.
    quali·fi·er /-faɪə(r)/ nc (gram) = modifier.

quali·ta·tive /'kwɒlɪtətɪv/ adj concerning, relating to, quality: *a qualitative analysis.* Compare quantitative.

qual·ity /'kwɒlətɪ/ n (pl **-ies**) **1** nc,nu (a high standard of) goodness or worth: *We aim at quality rather than quantity.* **2** nc something that is special in, or that distinguishes, a person or thing: *One quality of leadership is that one must be trusted.*

qualm /kwɑːm/ nc (often pl) **1** a feeling of doubt (esp about whether one is doing or has done right): *He felt no qualms about borrowing money from friends.* **2** a temporary feeling of sickness in the stomach: *qualms which spoilt his appetite.*

quan·dary /'kwɒndərɪ/ nc **be in a quandary (about sth)** to be in a state of doubt or confusion: *be in a quandary about what to do next.*

quan·go /'kwæŋgəʊ/ nc (pl **—s**) a government committee or organization with limited power.

quan·ti·fy /'kwɒntɪfaɪ/ vt (pt,pp **-ied**) **1** to measure (an amount): *My love cannot be quanti-*

fied. **2** (gram) to express the amount of (a word) (e.g. by using many, some, no, all etc.)
    quan·ti·fi·able /ˌkwɒntɪ'faɪəbl/ adj

quan·ti·tat·ive /'kwɒntɪtətɪv/ adj concerning, relating to, quantity: *a quantitative analysis.* Compare qualitative.

quan·ti·ty /'kwɒntətɪ/ n (pl **-ies**) **1** nu the property of things which can be measured, e.g. size, mass, number: *I prefer quality to quantity.* **2** nc an amount, total or number: *There's only a small quantity* (i.e. not much or not many) *left.* **3** (often pl) a large amount or number: *He buys things in large quantities.* **4 an unknown quantity** (**a**) (maths) a symbol (usually x) representing an unknown value in an equation. (**b**) (fig) a person or thing whose ability etc is not known: *The Union's candidate is an unknown quantity.*
    ,quantity sur'veyor nc an expert who estimates quantities and costs of materials needed in building.

quar·an·tine /'kwɒrəntiːn/ nc,nu (a period of) separation (of imported animals) from others until it is known that there is no danger of spreading disease: *be in/out of quarantine.* □ vt to put (an animal) in quarantine.

quar·rel¹ /'kwɒrəl/ nc **1** an angry argument; strong disagreement: *have a quarrel with him about the weather.* **2** a cause for being angry; reason for protest or complaint: *I have no quarrel with/against him.* **pick a quarrel (with sb)** to find an occasion or excuse for disagreement etc. ⇒ patch².

quar·rel² /'kwɒrəl/ vi (**-ll-**, US also **-l-**) **quarrel (with sb/sth) (about/over sth) 1** to have, take part in, a quarrel: *The thieves quarrelled with one another about how to divide the money.* **2** to disagree (with); complain about: *It's not the fact of examinations I'm quarrelling with; it's the way they're organized.*
    'quar·rel·some /-səm/ adj (derog) often causing arguments.

quar·ry¹ /'kwɒrɪ/ nc (pl **-ies**) (usually sing) a hunted animal, bird etc.

quar·ry² /'kwɒrɪ/ nc (pl **-ies**) a place (not underground) where stone etc is obtained. □ vt,vi (pt,pp **-ied**) to get (a mineral substance) from a quarry: *quarry stone.*

quart /kwɔːt/ nc (abbr qt) a unit of measurement of capacity equal to two pints (about 1·14 litres).

quar·ter¹ /'kwɔːtə(r)/ nc **1** a fourth part (¼); one of four equal or corresponding parts: *a quarter of a mile; a mile and a quarter; a quarter of an hour; an hour and a quarter; scored ten points in the first quarter of the game; the first quarter of this century; three-quarters of an hour ago.* **2** a point of time 15 minutes before or after any hour: *a quarter to two; a quarter past six.* **3** three months, esp as a period for which rent and other payments are made. **4** a district: *live in the rich quarter of the city; travel in every quarter of the globe.* **5** a person, group as a source of help etc: *As his father was penniless, he could expect no help from that quarter.* **6** a direction; a main point of the compass: *Letters arrived from the four quarters of the earth.* **7** a fourth part of a lunar month: *the moon at the first quarter/in its last quarter.* **8 at close quarters** close together; very near: *I took the photograph at close quarters.*

,**quarter-'final** *nc* (*sport*) one of four competitions or matches, the winners of which play in the semifinals.

quar·ter² /'kwɔːtə(r)/ *vt* **1** to divide (something) into quarters. **2** (*mil*) to place (soldiers) in lodgings: *quarter troops on the villagers*.

quar·ter·ly¹ /'kwɔːtəlɪ/ *adj*, *adv* (happening) once in each three months: *quarterly payments; to be paid quarterly*.

quar·ter·ly² /'kwɔːtəlɪ/ *nc* (*pl* **-ies**) a magazine etc published every three months.

quar·ters /'kwɒtəz/ *n pl* a place to stay (esp in the armed forces): *married quarters*.

quar·tet (also **quar·tette**) /kwɔː'tet/ *nc* (a piece of music for) four players or singers.

quartz /kwɔːts/ *nu* a kind of hard mineral substance as used in clocks and watches.

quash /kwɒʃ/ *vt* (esp *legal*) to end, reject (something) as not valid (by legal procedure): *quash a verdict*.

quat·er·cen·ten·ary /ˌkwɔːtəsen'tiːnərɪ/ *adj*, *nc* (*pl* **-ies**) (of) the 400th anniversary (of an event): *the quatercentenary celebrations in 1964 of Shakespeare's birth*.

qua·ver¹ /'kweɪvə(r)/ *nc* **1** a trembling sound. **2** (*music*) a note with half the value of a crotchet.

qua·ver² /'kweɪvə(r)/ *vi* (of the voice or a sound) to shake; tremble: *speak in a quavering voice*.

quay /kiː/ *nc* a flat area to which ships are tied up for loading and unloading.

queasy /'kwiːzɪ/ *adj* (**-ier**, **-iest**) **1** (of the stomach) easily upset. **2** (of a person) feeling sick.

queen /kwiːn/ *nc* **1** (often Q-) a female ruler of a country: *the Queen of England; Queen Elizabeth II*. (N) '*Queen Elizabeth II*' is spoken as '*Queen Elizabeth the Second*'. **2** (often Q-) a wife of a king. **3** a woman regarded as first of a group: *a beauty queen*. **4** (*chess*) the most powerful piece for attack or defence. **5** (*playing-cards*) a card with the picture of a queen: *the queen of spades/hearts*. **6** an egg-producing female of bees, ants etc.

,**queen 'mother** *nc* (often Q- M-) the mother of a reigning king or queen.

queer /kwɪə(r)/ *adj* (**—er**, **—est**) **1** strange; unusual: *a queer way of talking*. **2** causing doubt or suspicion: *queer noises in the attic*. **3** (*informal*) unwell; sick: *feel very queer; a queer feeling*.
queer·ly *adv*

quell /kwel/ *vt* to suppress, stop, (a rebellion, riot etc).

quench /kwentʃ/ *vt* **1** to put out (flames, fire). **2** to satisfy (thirst).

queru·lous /'kwerʊləs/ *adj* (*formal; derog*) full of complaints: *speak in a querulous tone*.

query¹ /'kwɪərɪ/ *nc* (*pl* **-ies**) **1** a question raising a doubt about the truth of something: *raise a query*. **2** a mark (e.g. ?) put against something as a sign of doubt.

query² /'kwɪərɪ/ *vt* **1** to express doubt about (something): *query a person's instructions*. **2** to put a mark (e.g. ?) against (something).

quest /kwest/ *nc* (*formal*) a search: *the quest for gold*.

ques·tion¹ /'kwestʃən/ *nc* **1** (*gram*) a form of a sentence which asks for information, an answer etc. *a leading question* one formed in a way that suggests the answer required. **2** something which needs to be decided; difficulty: *economic*

questions. *Success is only a question of time* (= will certainly come sooner or later). *The question is* (= What we want to know, What we must decide, is) *who shall we choose?* **in question** being talked about: *Where's the man in question?* **out of the question** impossible: *We can't go out in this weather; it's out of the question*. **pop the question** (*informal*) to ask a person to marry one. **3** *nu* (the putting forward of) doubt, objection: *There is no question about/some question as to his honesty*. **beyond (all) question; without question** certain(ly); without doubt: *His honesty is beyond all question. Without question, he's the best man for the job*.

'**question mark** *nc* (**a**) (*lang*) the mark (?) at the end of a written question. (**b**) (*fig*) an instance of doubt: *There's a question mark about/over her suitability for the job*.

'**question tag** *nc* (*lang*) a short expression added to a sentence to make a question, as in 'You will come, *won't you?*' 'He can't do it, *can he?*'

ques·tion² /'kwestʃən/ *vt* **1** to ask (a person) questions officially: *He was questioned about the robbery by the police*. **2** to express or feel doubt about (something): *question her honesty; question the value/importance of games at school*.
ques·tion·able /-əbl/ *adj* doubtful: *a questionable account of what happened*.
ques·tion·ably /-əblɪ/ *adv*

ques·tion·naire /ˌkwestʃə'neə(r)/ *nc* a list of questions to be answered by a group of people, esp to get facts or information.

queue¹ /kjuː/ *nc* **1** a line of people waiting for their turn (e.g. to enter a cinema, get on a bus): *form a/stand in a queue*. **jump the queue** (**a**) to go ahead of others in a queue. (**b**) (*fig*) to do or get something without waiting for one's turn. **2** a line of vehicles waiting to proceed: *A queue of cars was held up by the traffic lights*.

queue² /'kjuː/ *vi* **queue (up) (for sth/to do sth)** to get into, be in, a queue: *We are queuing up for tickets/to buy tickets*.

quib·ble¹ /'kwɪbl/ *nc* an attempt to avoid an honest answer by using a secondary or doubtful meaning of a word or phrase.

quib·ble² /'kwɪbl/ *vi* **quibble (about/over sth)** to argue about small points or differences: *quibbling about/over nothing of importance*.

quick¹ /kwɪk/ *adj* (**—er**, **—est**) **1** (of an activity, movement) done in a short time: *a quick reply; have a quick meal; a quick telephone call home; a quick run to the shops*. Compare **fast¹**(1), **slow¹**(1). **2** enthusiastic and intelligent: *a quick child/mind; quick at working out the cost*. Compare **slow¹**(4). **3** (*pred*) enthusiastic and ready: *She's quick to seize an opportunity/to criticize others*. **4** easily excited: *a quick temper*.

quick·ly *adv* taking a short time: *walk quickly across the road. Quickly, open the door.* ⇨ **quick²**.

quick² /kwɪk/ *adv* (**—er**, **—est**) (*informal*) quickly: *He hopes to get rich quick. Quick, pass me that knife. Come as quick as possible.* (N) '*Quick*' is not often used as an adverb except in combined forms such as *quick-moving, quick-setting, quick-thinking*, or as a comparative (*quicker*), as in *The buses are arriving quicker than usual*. Compare: **slow²**.

quick·en /'kwɪkən/ *vt,vi* (*formal*) **1** (to cause the speed of a person, thing) to become quick(er): *We quickened our pace. Our pace quickened.* **2** (to cause something) to become more lively or active: *His pulse quickened.*

quick·sand /'kwɪksænd/ *nc,nu* (an area of) loose, wet, deep sand which sucks down whatever tries to cross it.

quick-tem·per·ed /ˌkwɪk 'tempəd/ *adj* easily made angry.

quick-wit·ted /ˌkwɪk 'wɪtɪd/ *adj* understanding and acting quickly.

quid /kwɪd/ *nc* (*pl* —) (GB *sl*) = pound¹(2): *earning twenty quid* (= £20) *a week*. **quids in** (*sl*) making a large profit.

qui·et¹ /'kwaɪət/ *adj* (—er, —est) **1** with little or no sound: *a quiet classroom; as quiet as a mouse* (= very quiet). **2** free from excitement, trouble, anxiety: *live a quiet life in the country.* **3** gentle; not rough (in attitude etc): *a quiet personality.* **4** (of colours) not bright. **5** not open or expressed: *harbouring quiet resentment.* **keep sth quiet; keep quiet about sth** to keep it a secret.

qui·et² /'kwaɪət/ *nu* the state of being quiet (all senses): *live in peace and quiet.* **on the quiet** (or (*informal*) **on the q t** /ˌkju: 'ti:/) secretly: *have a whisky on the quiet.*

qui·et·en /'kwaɪətn/ *vt,vi* (to cause a person, thing) to become quiet: *quieten children/fears/ suspicions. The city quietened down after the political disturbances.*

quiff /kwɪf/ *nc* a lock of hair brushed up above the forehead.

quill /kwɪl/ *nc* **1** a large wing or tail feather. **2** a long spine of a porcupine.

quilt /kwɪlt/ *nc* (also *continental quilt*) a thick bed-covering of two layers of cloth padded with soft material that is kept in place by cross-lines of stitches. ⇨ duvet.

quilt·ing *nu* padded material for a quilt.

quin /kwɪn/ *nc* (= quintuplet) one of five babies at one birth. Ⓝ Usually used in the plural, i.e. *'one of the quins'*, not *'a quin'*.

quin·cen·ten·ary /ˌkwɪnsən'ti:nərɪ/ *adj, nc* (*pl* -ies) (of) the 500th anniversary (of an event).

quin·ine /kwɪ'ni:n/ *nu* a bitter medicine used for fevers such as malaria.

quin·tes·sence /kwɪn'tesns/ *nc* (*formal*) a perfect example: *the quintessence of virtue.*

quin·tet (also **quin·tette**) /kwɪn'tet/ *nc* (a piece of music for) five players or singers.

quin·tu·plet /'kwɪntju:plɪt/ *nc* (*formal*) ⇨ quin.

quip /kwɪp/ *vi* (-pp-), *nc* (to make) a clever, witty or sarcastic remark or saying.

quirk /kwɜ:k/ *nc* an odd act or behaviour.

quis·ling /'kwɪzlɪŋ/ *nc* (*derog*) a person who co-operates with the enemy.

quit¹ /kwɪt/ *adj* (*pred*) free, clear: *We are well quit of him.*

quit² /kwɪt/ *vt,vi* (*pt* quitted or quit; -tt-) **1** to go away from (something); leave: *I've quitted my job. We've had notice to quit* (= a warning that we must give up the house we rent). **2** (*informal*) to stop (doing something): *He quit work when the bell rang.*

quit·ter *nc* (*informal; derog*) a person who (often) does not finish what he or she has started.

quite /kwaɪt/ *det, adv* Ⓝ *'Quite'* is often used as a predeterminer as shown in the examples below. **1** completely; altogether: *I quite agree/understand. She was quite alone. Are you quite sure you want to? I'm not quite certain. It's quite a problem. It's quite the best I've seen. That's quite another* (= completely different) *story.* **2** to a certain extent; a little more (so) than not: *It's quite warm today. He's quite a good player but he needs to practise.* **quite a few/a lot** several: *There are quite a few left.* **3** really; truly: *She's quite a beauty.* **4** (used to show agreement, understanding etc): *'It's a difficult situation'—'Quite (so)!' 'I'm sorry, I'm afraid I'm late.'—'Oh, that's quite all right'.*

quits /kwɪts/ *adj* (*pred*) **be quits (with sb)** to be on even terms (by repaying a debt of money, punishment etc): *We're quits now.* **call it quits** to agree that things are even, that a dispute or quarrel is over.

quiv·er¹ /'kwɪvə(r)/ *nc* a container for arrows.

quiv·er² /'kwɪvə(r)/ *vi* to tremble slightly or vibrate: *a quivering leaf; quivering with fear.* □ *nc* a quivering sound or movement.

quix·ot·ic /kwɪk'sɒtɪk/ *adj* (*formal*) generous, unselfish, imaginative, in a way that disregards one's own welfare.

quiz¹ /kwɪz/ *nc* (*pl* quizzes) a general knowledge test or game.

quiz² /kwɪz/ *vt* (-zz-) to ask (a person) questions as a test of knowledge.

quiz·zi·cal /'kwɪzɪkl/ *adj* (*formal*) **1** causing amusement; teasing: *a quizzical smile.* **2** expressing disbelief, puzzlement: *a quizzical look.*

quiz·zi·cal·ly /-klɪ/ *adv*

quoit /kɔɪt/ *nc* a rubber ring etc to be thrown over a peg in a game (called *quoits*).

quor·ate /'kwɔ:reɪt/ *adj* having a quorum. Opp inquorate.

quo·rum /'kwɔ:rəm/ *nc* (*pl* —s) a number of people who must be present at a meeting before it can have authority: *have/form a quorum.*

quo·ta /'kwəʊtə/ *nc* (*pl* —s) a limited share, amount or number: *The quota of trainees for this year has already been filled.*

quo·ta·tion /kwəʊ'teɪʃn/ *n* **1** *nu* the act of quoting(1). **2** *nc* something quoted(1): *quotations from Shakespeare.* **3** *nc* an estimate of the cost of a piece of work: *Can you give me a quotation for building a garage?*

quo'tation marks *n pl* (*lang*) the marks ' ' or " " enclosing words spoken or quoted.

quote¹ /kwəʊt/ *nc* (*informal*) = quotation(2, 3).

quote² /kwəʊt/ *vt* **1 quote (from) sb/sth** to repeat, write (words used by another, from a book, an author etc): *quoting from the newspaper; quote the chairman.* **2** to give (an example etc) to support a statement: *Can you quote (me) a recent instance?* **3** to offer (a person) (a price): *This is the best price I can quote you.*

quo·tient /'kwəʊʃənt/ *nc* (*maths*) a number obtained by dividing one number by another.

q.v. /ˌkju: 'vi:/ *abbr* (*Latin: quod vide*) which may be referred to (used to suggest that a reader should refer to a book etc just mentioned).

QWERTY key·board /'kwɜ:tɪ ki:bɔ:d/ *nc* (*computers*) a computer keyboard with its keys arranged in the same order as a typewriter (i.e. the first six letters of the top row are QWERTY).

Rr

R, r /ɑː(r)/ (*pl* **R's, r's** /ɑːz/) the 18th letter of the English alphabet. **the three R's** reading, (w)riting and (a)rithmetic as the basis of a child's education.

r *written abbr* **1** radius (of a circle). **2** right.

R *written abbr* **1** Royal, as in *The RA*. **2** (*Latin*) Rex (King)/Regina (Queen), as in *Elizabeth R*.

® *symbol* Registered trade mark (used on products by the manufacturer).

RA /ˌɑːr 'eɪ/ *abbr* (the —) the Royal Academy of Arts.

rab·bi /'ræbaɪ/ *nc* (*pl* **—s**) a teacher and religious leader of the Jews.

rab·bini·cal /rə'bɪnɪkl/ *adj*

rab·bit /'ræbɪt/ *nc,nu* (also *attrib*) (the meat of) a small animal with long ears that lives in a hole in the ground: *rabbit stew*.

rabble /'ræbl/ *nc* a disorderly crowd; mob.

'rabble-rousing *adj, nu* (the act of) encouraging excitement in a disorderly crowd.

rab·id /'ræbɪd/ *adj* affected with rabies.

ra·bies /'reɪbiːz/ *nu* a fatal disease that can affect animals with a spine, passed on by biting.

RAC /ˌɑːr eɪ 'siː/ *abbr* Royal Automobile Club.

race¹ /reɪs/ *n* **1** *nc,nu* (also *attrib*) any of several subdivisions of mankind sharing certain physical characteristics, esp colour of skin, colour and type of hair, shape of eyes and nose: *people of the same race but of different culture. Can race relations be improved by legislation?* **2** *nc* a group of people having the same culture, history or language: *the German race*. ⇨ human race.

race² /reɪs/ *nc* a contest or competition in speed, e.g. to see who can finish a piece of work or get to a certain place first: *a horse-race; run a race.* **a race against time** an effort to finish something before the time allowed or available ends. ⇨ also rat race.

race³ /reɪs/ *v* **1** *vi,vt* to take part in a race² against (a person etc): *I'll race you home. We're racing against the other school next week.* **2** *vt,vi* (to cause a person, vehicle etc) to go very quickly: *We were racing along in our new car. They raced the injured passengers to the hospital.* **3** *vi* **race by** (of time, an activity) to pass quickly: *The afternoon/holiday raced by.* **4** *vt* to cause (an animal, vehicle etc) to take part in a race²: *She races horses.* **5** *vi* (*informal*) (of thoughts, one's mind) to work (too) quickly: *My mind was racing at the idea of visiting China.*

ra·cial /'reɪʃl/ *adj* concerning race¹(1): *racial conflict/minorities/discrimination/harmony.*

ra·cial·ly /-ʃəlɪ/ *adv*

ra·cial·ism /-ɪzəm/ *nu* = racism.

ra·cial·ist /-ɪst/ *nc* = racist.

rac·ily, raci·ness ⇨ racy.

rac·ing /'reɪsɪŋ/ *nu* the hobby, sport, profession of racing(4) horses, cars etc.

rac·ism /'reɪsɪzəm/ *nu* (a policy, way of behaving, based on) the belief that one's own race¹ is superior to others.

rac·ist /-ɪst/ *nc* a believer in, supporter of, racism.

rack¹ /ræk/ *nc* **1** a framework with bars, pegs etc, used for holding things, hanging things on etc: *a plate-rack; a tool-rack.* **2** a shelf over the seats of a train, bus etc for light luggage: *a luggage-rack.*

rack² /ræk/ *n* (only in) **go to rack and ruin** to fall into a ruined state.

rack³ /ræk/ *vt* **1** to place (something) in, on, a rack¹(1): *rack wine; have one's music system racked.* **2** (usually *passive*) (of a physical or mental pain) to hurt (a person) a lot: *be racked with pain.* **3** **rack one's brains (for sth)** to make great mental efforts (in order to find an answer, method etc).

rack·et¹ (also **rac·quet**) /'rækɪt/ *nc* a stringed bat used for hitting the ball in tennis, squash etc.

rack·et² /'rækɪt/ *n* **1** *n sing* a loud noise: *The young men in the pub kicked up such a racket.* **2** *nc* (*informal*) a dishonest way of getting money (by deceiving or threatening etc). **3** *nu* (a time of) great social activity: *I hate the racket of living in London.*

rack·et·eer /ˌrækɪ'tɪə(r)/ *nc* (*derog*) a person who is engaged in a racket(2).

rac·on·teur /ˌrækɒn'tɜː(r)/ *nc* (*formal*) a person who tells stories with skill and wit.

rac·quet *nc* = racket¹.

racy /'reɪsɪ/ *adj* (**-ier, -iest**) (of speech or writing) full of activity and (often) about sex: *a racy style/novel.*

rac·ily /-əlɪ/ *adv*

raci·ness *nu*

RADA /'rɑːdə/ *acronym* Royal Academy of Dramatic Art.

ra·dar /'reɪdɑː(r)/ *nu* (*tech*) (the use of) an apparatus that shows on a screen (by means of radio echoes) solid objects that come within its range (used by pilots etc).

ra·di·al /'reɪdɪəl/ *adj* **1** relating to a ray, rays or a radius. **2** (of spokes in a bicycle wheel etc) arranged like rays or radii.

,radial 'tyre *nc* one designed (by having the material inside the tyre wrapped in a direction radial to the hub of the wheel) to hold a road surface better.

ra·di·al·ly /-ɪəlɪ/ *adv*

ra·di·ance /'reɪdɪəns/ *nu* a radiant quality.

ra·di·ant /'reɪdɪənt/ *adj* (*formal*) **1** sending out rays of light; shining: *the radiant sun.* **2** (of a person, expression) showing great happiness or love: *a radiant face. You're looking radiant today.* **3** (*science*) sent out by radiation: *radiant heat/energy.*

ra·di·ant·ly *adv*

ra·di·ate /'reɪdɪeɪt/ *v* **1** *vt* to send out rays of (light or heat). **2** *vt* (*fig*) to send out (happiness etc): *a bride who radiates joy.* **3** *vi* **radiate (from sth)** to come out or spread out in many directions from something: *heating radiating from a fire; roads radiating from a roundabout.*

ra·di·ation /ˌreɪdɪ'eɪʃn/ *n* **1** *nu* the act of radiating(1). **2** *nc* something radiated: *radiations emitted by an X-ray apparatus.*

ra·di·ator /'reɪdɪeɪtə(r)/ *nc* **1** an apparatus producing heat in a room, usually from hot water supplied through pipes. **2** a device used for cooling the engine of a vehicle: *This car has a fan-*

cooled radiator.

rad·ical¹ /'rædɪkl/ *adj* **1** thorough and complete: *radical changes.* **2** (*politics*) favouring complete reform; of the extreme left in opinions and policies: *a radical group of members/set of policies.*
  radi·cal·ly /-klɪ/ *adv*

rad·ical² /'rædɪkl/ *nc* a person with radical(2) opinions.

ra·dii /'reɪdɪaɪ/ *n pl* ⇨ radius.

ra·dio /'reɪdɪəʊ/ *nc* (*pl* **—s**) **1** *nc* (also *attrib*) an apparatus for receiving sound broadcast programmes: *a transistor radio; radio listeners. Do you often listen to the radio?* **2** *nc* a similar apparatus for sending and receiving sound messages: *The police used their radio to ask for help.* **3** *nu* the sending or receiving of sound by using a radio: *send a message by radio.*
  radio-cas'sette (player) *nc* an apparatus with a radio and a cassette tape player.

ra·dio·active /,reɪdɪəʊ 'æktɪv/ *adj* (*science*) (of such metals as *uranium*) having atoms that break up and, in so doing, send out electrically charged particles that can be harmful: *radioactive dust from nuclear explosions.*
  ,ra·dio·ac'tiv·ity *nu*

ra·di·ogra·phy /,reɪdɪ'ɒɡrəfɪ/ *nu* the production or use of X-ray photographs.
  ,radi·'ogra·pher *nc* a person who is trained in radiography.

ra·dio-iso·tope /,reɪdɪəʊ 'aɪsətəʊp/ *nc* (*science*) a radioactive form of an element, used in medicine, industry etc.

ra·dio-tele·scope /,reɪdɪəʊ 'telɪskəʊp/ *nc* (*science*) an apparatus that uses radio waves to find stars etc in space.

ra·dio·ther·apist /,reɪdɪəʊ'θerəpɪst/ *nc* a person trained in radiotherapy.

ra·dio·ther·apy /,reɪdɪəʊ'θerəpɪ/ *nu* the use of radiation(2) to treat diseases.

rad·ish /'rædɪʃ/ *nc* a plant with a white or red root that tastes hot, used in salads.

ra·dius /'reɪdɪəs/ *nc* (*pl* **radii** /-dɪaɪ/) **1** (*maths*) (the length of) a straight line from the centre of a circle or sphere to any point on the edge or surface. **2** a circular area measured by its radius: *The police searched all the fields and woods within a radius of two miles.* **3** (*anat*) the outer of the two bones in the forearm.

RAF /,ɑːr eɪ 'ef/ *abbr* (the —) the Royal Air Force.

raf·fia /'ræfɪə/ *nu* the fibre from the leaf-stalks of a kind of palm-tree, used for making baskets, hats, mats etc.

raffle /'ræfl/ *nc* a sale of things using numbered tickets which are picked to choose the winners. □ *vt* to sell (something) in a raffle: *We're raffling (off) a television.*

raft /rɑːft/ *nc* a kind of boat made by tying logs together.

raf·ter /'rɑːftə(r)/ *nc* one of the sloping beams of a roof.

rag¹ /ræɡ/ *nc* **1** an odd bit of cloth: *a rag to polish the car with.* **2** (*derog*) a newspaper of low quality: *Why do you read that worthless rag?*

rag² /ræɡ/ *nc* an amusing procession of students, painted vehicles etc, usually to collect money for charity.

rag³ /ræɡ/ *vt* (**-gg-**) (*informal*) to make fun of (a person).

rage¹ /reɪdʒ/ *n* **1** *nc,nu* (an outburst of) extreme or violent anger: *shouting with rage.* **be in/fly into a rage** to be, become, very angry. **2** *nc,nu* (*fig*) (an outburst of) violent movement: *the rage of the sea during a storm.* **3** *nu* **be (all) the rage** (*informal*) to be something for which there is strong temporary enthusiasm: *Long hair on men is all the rage this summer.*

rage² /reɪdʒ/ *vi* **1** to be extremely angry: *He had been raging against me for not letting him have his own way.* **2** (of storms etc) to be violent: *The storm/battle raged all day.*

rag·ged /'ræɡɪd/ *adj* **1** (with clothes) badly torn or in rags: *a ragged coat/old man.* **2** having rough or irregular edges or outlines or surfaces: *a dog with a ragged coat of hair; a sleeve with ragged edges.* **3** (*derog*) (of work etc) not keeping to a good standard all the time: *a ragged performance.*
  rag·ged·ly *adv*

rag·lan /'ræɡlən/ *adj* (*attrib*) (of a knitted sweater) having a seam from the neck to under the arm: *a raglan sleeve.*

raid¹ /reɪd/ *nc* **1** a surprise attack made by troops, ship(s) or aircraft: *make a raid on the enemy's camp.* **2** a sudden visit by police to make arrests: *a raid on a casino.* **3** a sudden attack for the purpose of stealing money etc: *a raid on a bank by armed men; a bank raid.*

raid² /reɪd/ *vt* to carry out a raid on (something): *Boys have been raiding my orchard.*
  raid·er *nc* a person, ship, aircraft etc that makes a raid.

rail¹ /reɪl/ **1** *nc* (one of) a series of horizontal or sloping bars or rods as part of a fence etc: *metal rails round a monument. He was leaning over the (ship's) rails.* **2** *nc* a similar bar or rod used for things to hang on: *a towel-rail.* **3** *nc* a continuous line of such bars, laid on the ground for trains: **off the rails** (**a**) (of a train) off the track. (**b**) (*fig*) out of order, out of control. (**c**) (*informal*) mad. **4** *nu* trains as a means of transport *send goods by rail.*
  rail·ings *n pl* a fence made with rails.
  'rail-road *nc,nu* (*US*) = railway.
  'rail·way *n* (**a**) *nc* the track on which trains run: *build a new railway.* (**b**) *nu* (also *attrib*) a system of such tracks with the trains etc and the organization controlling the system: *work on/nationalize the railway; a railway station/bridge.*

rail² /reɪl/ *vt* **rail sth off/in** to put rails(1) round (something): *fields railed off from the road.*

rail³ /reɪl/ *vi* **rail (at sb) (about/for sth)** to criticize a person angrily.

rai·ment /'reɪmənt/ *nu* (*literary*) clothing.

rain¹ /reɪn/ *n* **1** *nu* the moisture of the atmosphere falling as separate drops: *It looks like rain* (= as if there will be a fall of rain). *Don't go out in the rain.* **(come) rain or shine** (**a**) whatever the weather is like: *We walk every morning, rain or shine.* (**b**) (*fig*) whether conditions are favourable or not: *He's always there, (come) rain or shine.* **(as) right as rain** ⇨ right²(4). **2** **a + adj + rain** a (type of) fall of rain: *There was a heavy/light rain last night.* **3** (*pl*; the —**s**) the season in tropical countries when there is heavy and continuous rain. **4** *n sing* a fall of something like rain: *a rain of arrows/bullets.*
  'rain·drop *nc* one drop of rain.

'rain·fall *nc,nu* an amount of rain falling within a given area in a given time.

'rain forest *nc,nu* hot wet forest in tropical areas, where rainfall is heavy and there is no dry season.

'rain·proof *adj* able to keep rain out.

'rain·water *nu* water that has fallen as rain and has been collected.

rain² /reɪn/ **1** *vi* to fall as rain: *It was raining.* **It never rains but it pours** (*proverb*) if one disaster happens, others will follow. **2** *vt,vi* (to cause something) to fall like rain: *Tears rained down her cheeks. The audience rained flowers on the actress.*

rain·bow /'reɪnbəʊ/ *nc* an arch containing the colours of the spectrum, formed in the sky.

rain·coat /'reɪnkəʊt/ *nc* a light, waterproof coat.

rainy /'reɪnɪ/ *adj* (**-ier, -iest**) (*attrib*) having much rain: *rainy weather; a rainy day/climate; the rainy season.* **put away/keep/save sth for a rainy day** to save money for a time when one may need it.

raise¹ /reɪz/ *nc* (*esp US*) an increase in wages or salary. Ⓝ *Rise* is more usual.

raise² /reɪz/ *vt* **1** to move, lift, (a part of the body, thing etc) from a low(er) to a high(er) level: *raising a flag; raise a man to his feet; raise the lid and look inside; raise a hand as if to wave.* ⇨ eyebrow. Compare lower². **2** to increase (something) in amount, extent etc: *raise prices/wages/the speed/ temperature.* ⇨ hope¹(1), voice¹(1). Compare lower². **3** to cause (something) to appear: *raise a cloud of dust; shoes that raise blisters on my feet; a long, hot walk that raised a good thirst.* ⇨ laugh¹, roof¹. **4** to bring (something) up for discussion or attention: *raise a new point/a question/a protest/ an objection.* **5** to produce and grow (crops); breed (animals), bring up (a family): *raise corn/ cattle/children.* ⇨ rear²(1). **6** to (manage to) get (something) together: *raise an army; raise a loan; raise money for a new swimming-pool.*

rai·sin /'reɪzn/ *nc* a kind of dried, sweet grape, used in cakes etc.

rake¹ /reɪk/ *nc* a long-handled tool with prongs, used for pulling together dead leaves, moving soil etc.

rake² /reɪk/ *nc* (*dated; derog*) an immoral man.

rake³ /reɪk/ *v* **1** *vt,vi* to make (land) smooth with a rake: *raking the garden path.* **2** *vt* to gather (things) together with a rake: *raking dead leaves together; raking up the leaves.*
rake about/around (for sth) to search (for something) among other things: *rake about in a drawer for a letter.*
rake sth in (*fig*) to earn, make, a lot of money: *The business is raking in the money/is raking it in.*
rake sth over to search untidily in a set of papers, a box etc.
rake through sth to search through a pile, set of things etc.
rake sth up (**a**) ⇨ 2 above. (**b**) to talk about a bad or sad experience that it is better not to mention: *raking up old quarrels/the past.*

rake-off /'reɪk ɒf/ *nc* (*informal*) a (usually dishonest) share of the profits: *Since I found you a buyer, I expect a rake-off.*

rak·ish /'reɪkɪʃ/ *adj* (usually *attrib*) **1** wild and daring: *a rakish appearance.* **2** on one side: *set one's hat at a rakish angle.*

rak·ish·ly *adv*

ral·ly¹ /'rælɪ/ *nc* (*pl* **-ies**) **1** a large public gathering for a political or social cause: *a political rally; a peace rally.* **2** a meeting of car drivers or motorcyclists for a competition etc. **3** (in tennis etc) an exchange of several strokes.

ral·ly² /'rælɪ/ *vt,vi* (*pt,pp* **-ied**) **1** (to cause people etc) to come together again, esp to make new efforts: *The troops rallied round their leader. The leader rallied his supporters. They rallied to the support of the Prime Minister.* **2** to recover health, strength: *rally one's strength/spirits; rally from an illness. The pound rallied after the large fall in its value yesterday.*

ram¹ /ræm/ *nc* a male sheep. Compare ewe.

ram² /ræm/ *nc* a heavy device for striking or pushing something with great force.

ram³ /ræm/ *vt* (**-mm-**) to strike and push (something) heavily: *ram a post into the ground.*

RAM /ræm/ *acronym* (*computers*) random access memory (also known as *read/write memory*) (the amount of memory that a user has available to store, examine, read or change computer information). ⇨ ROM.

Rama·dan /ˌræmə'dɑːn/ *n* the ninth month of the Muslim year, when Muslims fast between sunrise and sunset.

ramble¹ /'ræmbl/ *nc* a walk in the countryside for pleasure.

ramble² /'ræmbl/ *vi* **1** to walk for pleasure, esp with no special destination: *rambling over the hills.* **2 ramble (on) (about sth)** (*fig*) to wander in one's talk, not keeping to the subject: *ramble on about one's family.* ⇨ rambling(2). **3** (of a plant) to grow with long shoots that extend up or along: *rambling roses.*

ram·bler *nc* a person or plant that rambles.

ram·bling /'ræmblɪŋ/ *adj* **1** (esp of buildings, streets, towns) extending in various directions as if built without planning. **2** (*derog*) (of a speech etc) disorganized.

ramp /ræmp/ *nc* a slope from one level to another, used instead of stairs or steps.

ram·page /ræm'peɪdʒ/ *vi* to rush about in wild excitement or rage. □ *n* /'ræmpeɪdʒ/ **be/go on the rampage** to be/go rampaging.

ram·pa·geous /ræm'peɪdʒəs/ *adj* (*formal*) excited and noisy.

ram·pant /'ræmpənt/ *adj* (of diseases, social evils, physical activity etc) very active and beyond control: *Revenge was rampant in the village.*

ram·pant·ly *adv*

ram·part /'ræmpɑːt/ *nc* (often *pl*) a wide bank of earth built to defend a fort etc.

ram·shackle /'ræmʃækl/ *adj* (*attrib*) (*derog*) almost collapsing: *a ramshackle house/old bus.*

ran /ræn/ *pt* of run².

ranch /rɑːntʃ/ *nc* (in N America) a very large farm, esp one for animals.

ranch·er *nc* person who owns, manages or works on a ranch.

ran·cid /'rænsɪd/ *adj* having the smell or taste of stale fat or butter.

ran·cour (*US* = **-cor**) /'ræŋkə(r)/ *nu* (*formal*) the deep and long-lasting feeling that one has after being ignored, injured or insulted: *full of rancour* (*against him*).

ran·cor·ous /'ræŋkərəs/ *adj*

ran·dom¹ /'rændəm/ adj (attrib) done, made, taken, at random: *a random remark/selection/ sample.*

,random 'access memory nc (computers) ⇨ RAM.

ran·dom² /'rændəm/ nu **at random** without any particular reason: *choosing children at random to help.*

rang /ræŋ/ pt of ring⁴.

range¹ /reɪndʒ/ nc **1** a row, line or series (of hills, mountains): *a magnificent range of mountains; a mountain range.* **2** a distance at which one can see or hear, or to which sound will carry: *within/out of range.* **3** a distance between limits: *the range of a plane; a wide range of colours; the annual range of temperature; a long-range weather forecast.* **4** an area inside which a particular plant or animal may be found: *What is the range of the elephant in Africa?* **5** an area (of study, interest): *a wide range of interests; a subject that is outside my range.* **6** an area of ground with targets for shooting at: *a rifle-range.* **7** a distance to which a gun will shoot or to which a missile etc can be fired: *in/ within/out of/beyond range.* **8** a kind of stove for heating or cooking, using wood or coal.

range² /reɪndʒ/ v **1** vt,vi to be, put (people, things) or take one's place in an order, class or group; arrange (the usual word): *The general ranged his men along the river bank.* **2** vi to go, move, wander: *animals ranging through the forests/over the hills.* **3** vi **range over sth (a)** (fig) to cover an area. **(b)** (fig) to cover a set of topics: *researches that ranged over a wide field; a wide-ranging discussion.* **(c)** (of a gun, telescope etc) to cover an area. **4** vi **range between sth and sth/from sth to sth** to change, extend, vary between limits: *prices ranging from £7 to £10/ between £7 and £10.*

rang·er /'reɪndʒə(r)/ nc **1** (N America) a policeman on horseback. **2** a forest keeper.

rank¹ /ræŋk/ n **1** nc,nu (a position in) a category or class; grade in the armed forces: *promoted to the rank of captain; be in the ranks of the unemployed.* **the rank and file** ordinary people (not the upper class, the rich or famous). **2** (pl; the —s) ordinary soldiers, not officers. **3** nc a line of people or things: *Take the taxi at the head of the rank.*

rank² /ræŋk/ v **1** vt to put or arrange (a person, thing) in a position or grade mentioned: *Would you rank him among the world's great statesmen?* **2** vi to have a position: *A major ranks above a captain.* (Ⓝ) Not used in continuous tenses, e.g. *is/ was -ing.*

rankle /'ræŋkl/ vi to continue to be a painful or annoying memory: *The insult rankled (in his mind).*

ran·sack /'rænsæk/ vt to search (a place) untidily and thoroughly: *ransack a drawer for money/to find money.*

ran·som¹ /'rænsəm/ nc,nu (money paid for) the freeing of a person who has been kidnapped. **hold sb to ransom** to keep a person as a prisoner and ask for money.

ran·som² /'rænsəm/ vt to obtain the freedom of (a person), set (a person) free, in exchange for ransom: *ransom a kidnapped diplomat/politician.*

rant /rænt/ vi to use loud, boasting language: *rant-ing and raving on the stage.*

rap¹ /ræp/ nc **1** (a sound of) a light, quick blow: *I heard a rap on the door.* **2 take the rap (for sth)** (informal) to be punished etc (for a wrong) (esp when innocent).

rap² /ræp/ vt,vi (-pp-) to hit (something) quickly: *He rapped my hand with a stick. I rapped at/on the door.*

ra·pa·cious /rə'peɪʃəs/ adj (formal; derog) greedy (esp for money).
ra·pa·cious·ly adv

rape /reɪp/ vt, nc (to commit) the crime of forcing sexual intercourse on (a person).
ra·pist /'reɪpɪst/ nc a person who rapes a person.

rap·id /'ræpɪd/ adj moving, happening, very quickly: *a rapid heartbeat/recovery/decision.*
rap·id·ity /rə'pɪdəti/ nu
rap·id·ly adv

rap·ids /'ræpɪdz/ n pl a part of a river where a steep slope causes the water to flow fast.

ra·pier /'reɪpɪə(r)/ nc a light sword.

rap·port /ræ'pɔː(r)/ nu **rapport (with sb/sth)** a sympathetic understanding and agreement: *feel rapport with her/her difficulties.* Compare empathy.

rapt /ræpt/ adj so deep in thought, so carried away by feelings, that one is unaware of other things: *listening to the news with rapt attention; be rapt in a book.*

rap·ture /'ræptʃə(r)/ nu the state of being extremely pleased and happy: *gazing with rapture at the face of the girl he loved.* **go into raptures (over sb/sth)** to express extreme pleasure and enthusiasm: *She went into raptures over the dresses they showed her.*
rap·tur·ous /'ræptʃərəs/ adj (formal) showing great pleasure: *rapturous applause.*
rap·tur·ous·ly adv

rare¹ /reə(r)/ adj (—r, —st) not often seen, found, happening etc: *a rare bird/butterfly/ occasion/metal. It is very rare for her to arrive late.*
rare·ly adv not often: *rarely seen.*
rare·ness nu

rare² /reə(r)/ adj (of meat) cooked so that the redness and juices are kept: *a rare steak.*

rare·fied /'reərɪfaɪd/ adj (of air) thin, clear and clean: *rarified mountain air.*

rar·ing /'reərɪŋ/ adj (pred) **raring to do sth** (informal) full of eagerness: *They're raring to go.*

rar·ity /'reərəti/ n (pl **-ies**) **1** nu the condition of being rare. **2** nc something unusual (and so valuable): *The person who is always happy is a rarity.*

ras·cal /'rɑːskl/ nc **1** (derog) a dishonest person. **2** (playfully) a naughty child.

rash¹ /ræʃ/ adj (derog) done, doing things, too quickly, without enough thought of the possible result: *a rash act/statement/man.*
rash·ly adv
rash·ness nu

rash² /ræʃ/ nc **1** (an appearance, patch, of) tiny red spots on the skin: *a heat rash.* **2** (fig) a sudden spread: *a rash of new houses on a country road.*

rash·er /'ræʃə(r)/ nc a slice (of bacon).

rasp¹ /rɑːsp/ nc **1** a metal tool like a coarse file, used for scraping. **2** the rough, grating sound produced by this tool.

rasp² /rɑːsp/ v **1** vt,vi to use a rasp(1) on (something). **2** vt (fig) to have an irritating effect on (something): *rasping my nerves.* **3** *vt* to say (something) in a rough, serious voice: *rasp (out) orders/insults.*

rasp·ing·ly *adv*

rasp·berry /'rɑːzbərɪ/ *nc* (*pl* **-ies**) **1** (also *attrib*) (a bush with) a kind of small, soft, red berry: *raspberry jam.* **2** (*sl*) a noise made with the tongue between the lips or by wind passing out of the anus.

rat¹ /ræt/ *nc* **1** an animal like, but larger than, a mouse. **smell a rat** (*fig*) to suspect that something wrong is being done. **2** (*fig; derog*) a person who deserts a cause that he or she thinks is about to fail.

'rat race *nc* (the —) the endless and undignified competition for success in one's career etc.

rat² /ræt/ *vi* **rat (on sb)** (*informal*) to break a promise, tell a secret (about a person).

rate¹ /reɪt/ *nc* **1** the amount, value, speed etc obtained by comparing two or more numbers or amounts: *the birth/death rate; walk at the rate of 3 miles an hour.* **2** a speed: *travelling/increasing at a great rate.* **3** an amount, level of cost, pay etc: *What is the postage rate to Australia? What rates (of pay) are they offering?* **the going rate** the present price, wage etc: *What's the going rate for this job?* **4** **at this/that rate** if this/that is true, if this/that state of affairs continues: *We'll never finish the job at this rate.* **at any rate** in any case; at least: *At any rate, say you're sorry.* **5** (also *attrib*) (used with ordinal numbers) class or grade: *first rate* (= excellent); *second rate* (= fairly good); *third rate* (= poor); *a first-rate teacher.* **6** (usually *pl*) (*GB*) a tax on property (land and buildings) paid to local authorities for local purposes.

‚rate of ex'change *nc* = exchange rate.

'rate-payer *nc* a person paying rates(6).

rate² /reɪt/ *vt* **1** to judge or estimate the size, value or qualities of (a person, thing): *How do you rate her chances of succeeding? What do you rate his wealth at? He was rated as kind and hospitable.* **2** (*GB*) to value (property) for the purpose of assessing rates(4): *My property was rated at £400 a year.*

rate·able /'reɪtəbl/ *adj: the rateable value of a house* (= its value used to decide the rates(6) to be paid).

ra·ther /'rɑːðə(r)/ *adv* **1** to a fairly large extent or degree: *a rather surprising result/rather a surprising result; the rather attractive design; this rather bad weather; feeling rather better today; eaten rather too many cakes; rather exhausted; rather a pity/shame. I think they'll rather enjoy* (= will enjoy quite a lot) *fish for dinner.* Ⓝ *'Rather' cannot be used with a negative structure in this sense. When used with an adjective, 'rather' can be placed before or after 'a', as in 'rather a long way/a rather long way'. When used before 'a' it is called a predeterminer.* **2** **rather than** in preference to: *Let's travel in May rather than June. He agreed to pay rather than go to prison.* **would rather . . . (than . . .)** would more willingly, would prefer: *I'd rather fail the exam than cheat. I'd rather you came tomorrow (than today). Then we'd rather not come at all. What would you rather do? Thank you, but I'd rather not.* **3** **or rather** or more accurately: *He arrived late last night or rather in the early morning. She's a doctor, or rather a gynae-*

cologist. **4** /rɑː'ðɜː/ (*dated*) (used to express strong agreement to a suggestion etc): *'Would you like to come?'—'Rather!'*

rat·ify /'rætɪfaɪ/ *vt* (*pt,pp* **-ied**) (*formal*) to give one's formal approval to (an agreement) by signing etc.

rati·fi·ca·tion /ˌrætɪfɪ'keɪʃn/ *nu*

rat·ing /'reɪtɪŋ/ *nc* **1** a position in a grade, classification etc: *a business with a poor credit rating.* **2** the amount of popularity of a record, TV programme etc. **3** (*mil*) a sailor who is not an officer.

ra·tio /'reɪʃɪəʊ/ *nc* (*pl* **—s**) a relation between two amounts determined by the number of times one contains the other: *The ratios of 1 to 5 and 20 to 100 are the same.*

ra·tion¹ /'ræʃn/ *nc* a fixed quantity or share, esp of food, allowed to one person or group.

ra·tion² /'ræʃn/ *vt* **1** to limit (a person) to a fixed ration. **2** to limit (food, water etc): *We'll have to ration the water.*

ra·tion·al /'ræʃnl/ *adj* **1** (of a person) able to think and reason. **2** (of behaviour, a discussion, idea) sensible; reasonable: *rational behaviour; a rational argument.* Opp irrational.

ra·tion·al·ly /-nəlɪ/ *adv*

ra·tion·al·ity /ˌræʃə'nælətɪ/ *nu*

ra·tion·ale /ˌræʃə'nɑːl/ *nc* the basic reasons (for a belief, decision, course of action etc).

ra·tion·al·is·tic /ˌræʃnə'lɪstɪk/ *adj* using or accepting a reasonable argument.

ra·tion·al·ize (also **-ise**) /'ræʃnəlaɪz/ *vt* **1** to think and offer reasons for (something that seems unreasonable): *rationalize one's fears/behaviour.* **2** to reorganize (an industry etc) in order to reduce or end waste in time, labour, expense etc.

ration·al·iz·ation (also **-is·ation**) /ˌræʃnəlaɪ'zeɪʃn/ *nu*

rattle¹ /'rætl/ *n* **1** *nu* a rattling sound: *the rattle of a window in the wind.* **2** *nc* a baby's toy that produces a rattling sound.

rattle² /'rætl/ *v* **1** *vt,vi* (to cause something) to make a series of short, sharp sounds: *The windows were rattling in the wind.* **2** *vt* (often *passive*) (*informal*) to make (a person) nervous and frightened: *He was rattled by the accident.*

rattle away (at sth) to operate a machine that rattles(1): *rattling away at a typewriter.*

rattle sth off to say, repeat, something quickly and without thinking: *rattle off a poem.*

rattle on (about sth) to continue to talk quickly and without thinking: *He can rattle on for hours about stupid things.*

rattle through sth to complete work, a speech etc quickly and without serious attention.

rattle·snake /'rætlsneɪk/ *nc* a kind of poisonous American snake that makes a rattling noise with its tail.

rat·ty /'rætɪ/ *adj* (**-ier, -iest**) (*informal; derog*) bad-tempered; irritable.

rau·cous /'rɔːkəs/ *adj* (of sounds) rough and loud: *the raucous cries of the crows; raucous laughter.*

rau·cous·ly *adv*

rav·age¹ /'rævɪdʒ/ *nc* (usually *pl*) a destructive effect: *the ravages of time.*

rav·age² /'rævɪdʒ/ *vt* (often *passive*) to damage (something) badly: *forests ravaged by fire.*

rave¹ /reɪv/ *nc* **1** (often *attrib*) (*informal*) an instance of enthusiastic praise: *a rave review* (e.g. of a book). **2** (*sl*) a wild, exciting party etc.

'rave-up *nc* (*sl*) a rave(2).

rave² /reɪv/ *vi* **1** to talk wildly, violently, angrily: *The patient began to rave.* **2** (of the sea, wind etc) to rage. **3** *rave about/over sb/sth* to talk with (too) much enthusiasm: *She was raving about the food she had had in France.*

ra·ven /'reɪvn/ *nc* **1** a kind of large, black bird. **2** (also *attrib*) glossy, shining black: *raven-black hair.*

rav·en·ous /'rævənəs/ *adj* very hungry.
rav·en·ous·ly *adv*

ra·vine /rə'viːn/ *nc* a deep, narrow valley.

rav·ing /'reɪvɪŋ/ *adj* (*attrib*) talking wildly: *a raving lunatic.* □ *adv* to the point of talking wildly: *You're raving mad!*

ravi·oli /ˌrævɪ'əʊlɪ/ *nu* (*It*) flour paste (*pasta*) made in square pieces and filled with chopped meat etc.

rav·ish /'rævɪʃ/ *vt* **1** (often *passive*) to fill (a person) with delight: *ravished by the view.* **2** (*old use*) to rape (a person).

rav·ish·ing *adj* very beautiful: *You look ravishing in that dress.*

rav·ish·ing·ly *adv*

raw /rɔː/ *adj* **1** uncooked: *raw meat.* **2** (*attrib*) in the natural state, not manufactured or prepared for use: *raw m..terials* (e.g. coal, ores). **3** (*attrib*) (of a person) untrained; inexperienced: *raw recruits.* **4** (*attrib*) (of the weather) damp and cold: *a raw February morning.* **5** (of the skin) sore and painful. **6** *a raw deal* (*informal*) unfair or cruel treatment.

ray¹ /reɪ/ *nc* **1** a line, beam, of radiant light, heat, energy: *the rays of the sun; X-rays.* **2** (*fig*) a small sign: *a ray of hope.* **3** (*maths*) any one of a number of lines coming out from a centre.

ray² /reɪ/ *nc* (*pl* —s or —) a kind of large sea-fish, such as a *skate*, with a broad, flat body.

ray·on /'reɪɒn/ *nu* a kind of cloth that is made from artificial fibres but looks like silk.

raze /reɪz/ *vt* to destroy (towns, buildings) completely, esp by making them level with the ground: *a city razed* (*to the ground*) *by an earthquake.*

ra·zor /'reɪzə(r)/ *nc* an instrument with a sharp blade or cutters, used for shaving hair from the skin.

'razor-blade *nc* a piece of thin metal with a sharp edge, used for shaving hair from the skin.

RC /ˌɑːr 'siː/ *abbr* **1** Roman Catholic. **2** Red Cross.

rd *written abbr* (used only with 3) third: *23rd, 33rd* etc.

Rd *written abbr* Road.

RE /ˌɑːr 'iː/ *abbr* Religious Education.

reach¹ /riːtʃ/ *n* **1** *n sing* an act of stretching out an arm etc: *a reach for the ball.* **2** *nu* the extent to which a hand etc can be reached out: *This boxer has a long reach. I have my reference books within my reach/within easy reach.* **3** *nc* a length of a river between two bends.

reach² /riːtʃ/ *v* **1** *vt* to get, go, as far as (a place, person, amount etc): *reach London by midnight; reach the end of a chapter. When did the news reach you? Tell me when the temperature reaches 150°. Will the carpet reach as far as the door?* ⇨

agreement(1). **2** *vt,vi* to stretch out an arm or hand and touch (a person, thing): *Can you reach that book on the top shelf? I'd like to get it but I can't reach* (= it is too high). ⇨ reach down/for/ out (for) below. **3** *vt* to make contact with (a person) in order to give a message: *You can reach her on this telephone number.*

reach sth down to take an object from a higher level by stretching up: *Can you reach me down that pot, please?*

reach for sth to stretch out an arm or hand to (try to) touch and hold something: *She reached for a pen. He reached for the branch and fell.*

reach out (for sth) to try to hold something by stretching with effort: *He reached out (for my hand) but I was too far away.* **reach out to sb** (of a political group, a sympathetic person etc) to try to make contact with a poor or unhappy person, the unemployed etc.

reach to sth to stretch as far as something: *The rope will reach (from here) to that tree.*

re·act /rɪ'ækt/ *vi* **1** *react (against sb/sth) (to sth)* to behave differently, be changed, as a result: *The people will react against the government if prices continue to rise. Do children react to kind treatment by becoming more self-confident?* **2** *react on sb/sth* to have an effect on a person or thing: *Criticism can react badly on a writer.* **3** *react (on/with sth)* (*science*) (of one substance applied to another) to have an effect (on it): *How do acids react on metals?*

re·ac·tion /rɪ'ækʃn/ *n* **1** *nc* a response to earlier action or activity: *What was your reaction when you heard the news? There is bound to be a reaction to the poor sales figures.* **2** *nu* opposition to progress or change: *The forces of reaction made reform difficult.* **3** *nc,nu* (*science*) (an instance of) a change in one substance caused by another: *a chemical reaction.*

re·ac·tion·ary /rɪ'ækʃənərɪ/ *adj, nc* (*pl* **-ies**) (of) a person opposing social progress or reform. Compare progressive².

re·ac·tor /rɪ'æktə(r)/ *nc* = nuclear reactor.

read¹ /riːd/ *nc* (*informal*) a period of time spent reading: *Have a quick read of/through this letter.*

read² /riːd/ *v* (*pt,pp* read /red/) **1** *vt,vi* to look at and (be able to) understand (something written or printed): *I can't read your writing. I enjoy reading in bed. She reads maps well. He read an extract from his book. Can you read French/music?* **2** *vt,vi* *read (sth) (to sb)* to say (with one's voice or in one's mind) written words: *She was reading the letter aloud/to herself/to the children.* ⇨ read sth out. **3** *vt,vi* to get (information) by reading: *read the account in the newspaper; read that she won the race; read about the fire.* **4** *vt* to bring (oneself, a person) into the state mentioned by reading: *She read herself/the children to sleep.* **5** *vt* to study (a subject, esp at a university): *He's reading physics.* ⇨ read for sth. **6** *vt* to interpret, learn the significance of (something): *read a person's thoughts.* **7** *vt,vi* (of writing) to have the quality, meaning or sense mentioned: *The notice reads 'No visitors'. Her reports read well.* **8** *vt,vi* (of instruments, graphs etc) to show (something): *What does the thermometer read?*

read about sb/sth to get information about a person, event etc in a book, magazine etc.

read for sth to study for a degree, diploma etc.

read sth back to say aloud a message one has written (to check it).

read between the lines ⇨ line¹(6).

read sth into sth to find a meaning, idea etc in a person's writing or statement that is not intended.

read sth off to say aloud a written list, measurement etc.

read sth out (loud) to say aloud (to an audience) something of particular interest: *read out the names of the winners*.

read sth over to read a letter, statement etc completely (in order to check it).

read round sth to read books etc that will give general information about a subject.

read through sth ⇨ read sth over.

read sth up, read up on sth to read books etc to find out as much as one can about something.

read·able /'ri:dəbl/ *adj* that is easy or pleasant to read. Opp unreadable.

re·address /ˌri:ə'dres/ *vt* to change the address on (a letter etc).

read·er /'ri:də(r)/ *nc* **1** a person who reads, esp one who spends much time in reading: *a good/ poor reader*. **2** (*GB*) a senior lecturer. **3** a textbook with selections for reading by a person learning a language: *a German reader*. **4** a person who can interpret what is hidden or obscure, esp *a mind-/thought-reader*.

'reader·ship /-ʃɪp/ *nc* (**a**) (of a magazine etc) the number of people who read it: *a readership of 20 000*. (**b**) the position of a reader(2).

readi·ly /'redɪlɪ/ *adv* **1** without hesitation; willingly: *She readily agreed to work late*. **2** without difficulty: *The record is readily obtainable*.

readi·ness /'redɪnɪs/ *nu* **1** willingness: *readiness to accept the plan*. **2** *in readiness (for sb/sth)* (*formal*) ready (for): *have everything in readiness for an early start*.

read·ing /'ri:dɪŋ/ *n* **1** *nu* the act of a person who reads. ⇨ play reading. **2** *nu* books etc to be read: *Suitable reading for children*. **3** *nc* a way in which something is interpreted or understood: *My reading of the situation is . . .* **4** *nc* a figure of measurement etc as shown on a scale etc: *The readings on my thermometer last month were well above the average*.

'reading-lamp *nc* a shaded lamp used for reading.

'reading matter *nu* magazines, books etc for reading (e.g in a waiting-room).

'reading-room *nc* a room (in a library) for reading.

re·adjust /ˌri:ə'dʒʌst/ *vt,vi* **readjust (oneself/ sth) (to sth)** to get (oneself, a thing) into an earlier condition, position etc: *readjust to work after the weekend*.

re·adjust·ment *nc,nu*

read-only memory /ˌri:d 'əʊnlɪ memərɪ/ *nc* (*computers*) ⇨ ROM.

ready¹ /'redɪ/ *n* (only in) *at the ready* (**a**) (of a rifle) in the position for aiming and firing. (**b**) in the correct position, condition.

ready² /'redɪ/ *adj* (**-ier, -iest**) **1** *ready (for sth) (to do sth)* in the condition needed for use; prepared: *ready for work; ready to leave. We're all ready to go*. Opp unready. ⓝ Be careful not to con-

fuse *'all ready'* (i.e. prepared as a group) and *'already'*. *make ready (for sth)* (*formal*) to prepare: *We made ready for the journey. rough and ready* ⇨ rough¹(4). **2** *ready to* + *verb* willing to: *He's always ready to help*. **3** (*attrib*) quick and prepared: *a ready answer*. **4** (*pred*) able to be easily reached or obtained: *have a notebook ready; have your tickets ready*.

,ready-'cooked *adj* (of food) ready to eat.

,ready-'made *adj* ready to wear or use: *ready-made clothes*.

,ready 'money *nu* coins or notes to use for payment at the time when goods are bought (contrasted with *credit*).

re·admit /ˌri:əd'mɪt/ *vt* (**-tt-**) to allow (a person) back (into a society, theatre, room etc).

re·admit·tance /-təns/ *nu*

re·af·firm /ˌri:ə'fɜ:m/ *vt* to state (something) again: *reaffirm one's prices/loyalty*.

real /rɪəl/ *adj* existing in fact; not imagined or artificial: *Was it a real man you saw or a ghost? Things that happen in real life are sometimes stranger than in stories. Who is the real manager of the business? Tell me the real* (= true) *reason for your anger.* Compare genuine, unreal.

'real estate *nu* (*legal*) property in land and buildings (contrasted with *personal estate*).

re·align /ˌri:ə'laɪn/ *vi, v reflex* to join (oneself, itself etc) with others in agreement (with a person, nation, group) again: *Some countries have realigned (themselves) with those wanting an end to the war*.

re·align·ment /-mənt/ *nc,nu*

real·ism /'rɪəlɪzəm/ *nu* **1** (in art and literature) the showing of objects, life, facts etc in a true way. **2** behaviour based on an honest opinion of the facts and a commitment to act without the influence of emotions or feelings. Compare idealism.

real·ist /-ɪst/ *nc* a believer in, supporter of, realism. Compare idealist.

real·is·tic /ˌrɪə'lɪstɪk/ *adj* **1** showing realism(1): *a realistic painting*. **2** practical and based on actual facts, not theory: *a realistic price; a realistic political policy. Let's be realistic about your ability.* Compare idealistic.

real·is·ti·cal·ly /-klɪ/ *adv*

re·al·ity /rɪ'ælətɪ/ *n* (*pl* **-ies**) **1** *nu* the quality of being real: *the reality of a situation. in reality* in actual fact: *She says she's poor but in reality she has a lot of money*. **2** *nc* something seen or experienced: *the grim realities of war*. **3** *nu* (in art etc) a lifelike copy of the original: *The TV broadcast described what was happening with extraordinary reality*.

real·iz·ation (also **-is·ation**) /ˌrɪəlaɪ'zeɪʃn/ *nu* the realizing(2) (of a plan, one's ambitions or hopes).

real·ize (also **-ise**) /'rɪəlaɪz/ *vt* **1** *realize (that) sth* to be fully conscious of, understand, (something): *He realized that he was wrong. Do you realize what I'm saying? I hope you fully realize what you've done!* ⓝ Not used in continuous tenses, e.g. *is/was -ing*. **2** to change (a hope, plan etc) into a fact: *realize one's hopes/ambitions/ dreams*. **3** (*finance*) to exchange (property, business shares etc) for money: *Can these shares/ bonds be realized at short notice?* **4** to obtain (money etc) as a price or as a profit: *How much did you realize on the paintings you sent to the sale?*

real·ly /'rɪəlɪ/ *adv* **1** in fact; without doubt; truly: *What do you really think about it? He's really not sure. We're not really angry. I'm really sorry. I don't like it, really. Really,* (= Speaking honestly) *you shouldn't be here.* (N) *'Really' can be used in many positions but is most often used in front of the verb, as in He really can fly, except when used with 'be' when it usually comes after, as in I'm really sorry. When used with 'not' the position can change the meaning a little. Compare She's really not coming* (emphasizing 'not', i.e. there is no doubt) *and She's not really coming* (suggesting that she was pretending or lying). *really do/don't + verb* (used for emphasis): *I really do/don't like you.* **2** (used to express interest, surprise, protest etc): *'We're going to Mexico next month.'—'Oh, really?' Really! This noise is terrible!*

realm /relm/ *nc* **1** (also R-) (*poetic* or *legal*) a kingdom: *the defence of the Realm.* **2** (*fig*) a region: *the realms of the imagination.*

reams /riːmz/ *n pl* (*informal*) a great quantity (of writing): *She has written reams of verse.*

reap /riːp/ *v* **1** *vt,vi* to cut and collect a crop of (grain) from a field etc: *reap the corn.* **2** *vt* (*fig*) to gain (something): *reap the rewards/benefits.*

reap·er *nc* a person, machine, that reaps.

re·appear /ˌriːə'pɪə(r)/ *vi* to appear again (after disappearing).

re·appear·ance /-rəns/ *nc,nu*

re·apprais·al /ˌriːə'preɪzl/ *nc* a new examination and judgement: *a reappraisal of our business interests in Chicago.*

rear[1] /rɪə(r)/ *nc* **1** (also *attrib*) a back part: *the rear mirror/wheels of the car. The kitchen is in/to the rear of the house.* **2** the last part of any army, fleet etc: *attack the enemy in the rear.* **bring up the rear** to come/be last.

rear-'admiral *nc* (*mil*) a naval officer below a vice-admiral.

'rear·guard *n sing* or *pl* soldiers with the duty of guarding the rear of an army.

rearguard 'action *nc* a fight between an army in retreat and the enemy.

rear·most /'rɪəməʊst/ *adj* farthest back.

rear[2] /rɪə(r)/ *v* **1** *vt* to help (a child, farm animal) to grow and develop; bring up: *rear poultry/cattle; rear children.* ⇨ raise[2](5). **2** *vi* (esp of a horse) to rise on the back legs. **3** *vt* to lift up (the head etc): *The snake reared its head.*

re·arm /riːˈɑːm/ *vt,vi* to supply (an army etc) with weapons again or with new weapons.

re·arma·ment /riːˈɑːməmənt/ *nu*

re·ar·range /ˌriːəˈreɪndʒ/ *vt* to arrange (things etc) in a different way: *rearrange one's books/schedule.*

re·ar·range·ment /-mənt/ *nc,nu*

rea·son[1] /'riːzn/ *n* **1** *nc,nu* (a fact suggested or used as) a cause of or justification for something: *What is the reason for all this noise? Is there any reason why you are late? The reason why he's late is that/because there was a breakdown on the railway.* **by reason of** (*prep*) (*formal*) because of: *He was excused by reason of his age.* **with reason** correctly: *He complains with good reason that he has been punished unfairly.* Com-

pare cause[1](2), excuse[1]. **2** *nu* the power to think, understand, form opinions etc: *Only human beings have reason.* **lose one's reason** to go mad. **3** *nu* what is right or practicable; good sense. *(do anything) within reason* (to do anything) that is sensible or reasonable. **listen to reason** to pay attention to sensible advice etc. **see reason** to accept sensible advice etc. **without rhyme or reason** ⇨ rhyme[1](1). **it stands to reason (that) . . .** it is obvious to sensible people, most people will agree, (that).

rea·son[2] /'riːzn/ *v* **1** *vi* to use one's power to think and decide: *Mankind's ability to reason is unique.* **2** *vt* **reason that . . .** to say, using reasons, that: *He reasoned that we must start early and avoid the traffic.*

reason sb out of sth to use reasons to persuade a person not to do, feel etc something: *reason him out of his fears/doubt.*

reason with sb to use reasons when trying to persuade a person: *She reasoned with me for an hour but it was no use—I refused to go.*

rea·son·able /'riːznəbl/ *adj* **1** sensible: *a reasonable way to behave; be reasonable and accept the offer.* Opp unreasonable. **2** fair: *a reasonable price/offer; a reasonable excuse.* **3** of an acceptable standard or level: *reasonable weather.*

rea·son·ably /-əblɪ/ *adv*

rea·son·ing /'riːznɪŋ/ *nu* the process of arguing, persuading etc using sensible advice, facts etc: *use clear reasoning.*

re·as·sure /ˌriːəˈʃʊə(r)/ *vt* to remove the fears or doubts of (a person): *reassuring him about his health; be reassured by the doctor; feel reassured after listening to her.*

re·as·sur·ance /-rəns/ *nu*

re·as·sur·ing·ly *adv*

re·bate /'riːbeɪt/ *nc* an amount of money by which a payment may be reduced: *There is a rebate of £1.50 if the account is settled before 31 December.*

reb·el[1] /'rebl/ *nc* (also *attrib*) a person who takes up arms against, or refuses to accept, the established government, authority or control: *rebels fighting against the government; the rebel forces.*

re·bel[2] /rɪ'bel/ *vi* (-ll-) **rebel (against sb/sth) 1** to fight (against a government or authority). **2** to protest strongly (against): *The children rebelled against having three hours' homework each evening.*

re·bel·lion /rɪ'belɪən/ *n* **1** *nc,nu* (an instance of) fighting: *rise in rebellion (against the government); a rebellion against the dictator.* **2** *nu* (an instance of a) refusal to obey: *rebellion by teenagers against their parents.*

re·bel·li·ous /rɪ'belɪəs/ *adj* **1** taking part in a rebellion: *rebellious soldiers.* **2** not easily controlled: *a child with a rebellious temper.*

re·bel·li·ous·ly *adv*

re·birth /ˌriːˈbɜːθ/ *nc* (*formal*) **1** a change in moral attitude causing a person to lead a new kind of life. **2** a revival (the usual word): *the rebirth of learning.*

re·born /ˌriːˈbɔːn/ *adj* (*pred*) (*poetic*) having new energy and strength: *Her courage was reborn.*

re·bound /'riːbaʊnd/ *n* **on the rebound (a)** while bouncing back: *hit a ball on the rebound.* **(b)** (*fig*) while still reacting to depression or disappointment: *She quarrelled with Paul and then married Peter on the rebound.*

re·bound² /rɪ'baʊnd/ vi **1** to spring or bounce back after hitting something: *The ball rebounded from the wall.* **2 rebound on sb** to have an effect on oneself, a person as a result: *The nasty things you say could rebound on yourselves.*

re·buff /rɪ'bʌf/ nc an unkind refusal (of an offer of or request for help, friendship etc). □ vt to give a rebuff to (a person).

re·build /ˌriː'bɪld/ vt (pt,pp **-built** /-'bɪlt/) to build or put together (something) again: *a rebuilt engine; rebuild a business after failure.*

re·buke /rɪ'bjuːk/ vt (formal) to speak severely to (a person) for doing something wrong: *rebuking an employee for being rude.* □ nc an act of rebuking a person.

re·but·tal /rɪ'bʌtl/ nc an act of proving an accusation to be false, esp by giving alternative evidence.

re·cal·ci·trance /rɪ'kælsɪtrəns/ nu (formal) the state of being disobedient.

re·cal·ci·trant /rɪ'kælsɪtrənt/ adj (formal) refusing to obey (esp after being punished).

re·call¹ /rɪ'kɔːl/ n **1** nc,nu a request to return (esp to an ambassador): *a letter of recall.* **2** nu an ability to remember: *have instant recall.*

re·call² /rɪ'kɔːl/ vt **1** to ask (a person) to come back: *recall an ambassador (from his post/to her own country).* **2** to remember (something): *I don't recall his name/face/meeting him/where I met him.*

re·cant /rɪ'kænt/ vt,vi (formal) to give up (an opinion, a belief) publicly; admit (a statement) was false: *The torturers could not make him recant.*

re·cap /'riːkæp/ vt,vi (informal) recapitulate.

re·cap·itu·late /ˌriːkə'pɪtʃʊleɪt/ vt,vi to repeat the main points of (something that has been said, discussed, argued about etc).

re·cap·itu·la·tion /'riːkəˌpɪtʃʊ'leɪʃn/ nc,nu

re·cap·ture /riː'kæptʃə(r)/ vt **1** to capture (a person, animal etc) again. **2** to think about, imagine (something): *try to recapture the past.*

recd written abbr (commerce) received.

re·cede /rɪ'siːd/ vi to (seem to) go back (from an earlier position): *As the tide receded we were able to explore the beach.*

re·ced·ing adj (attrib) going or sloping back: *A receding hairline/chin.*

re·ceipt /rɪ'siːt/ n **1** nu an occasion of receiving or being received: *on receipt of the news.* **2** (pl) money received (in a business etc). **3** nc a written statement that money or goods has or have been received: *get a receipt for the goods; sign a receipt.*

re·ceive /rɪ'siːv/ v **1** vt to accept, take, get, (something offered, sent etc): *When did you receive the letter/news/telegram? He has received a good education.* **2** vi to take possession of stolen property: *Smith was caught receiving soon after his release from prison.* **3** vt,vi to accept (a person) as a member: *He was received into the Church.*

re·ceiv·er /rɪ'siːvə(r)/ nc **1** a person who receives, esp who knowingly receives stolen goods. **2** (the R-) the government official appointed to take charge of the property and affairs of a bankrupt. **3** a part of an apparatus for

receiving something, e.g. the part of a telephone that receives and produces sound.

re·cent /'riːsnt/ adj (often attrib) (having existed, been made, happened) a short time ago: *recent news; a more recent event; within recent memory.*

re·cent·ly adv not long ago: *I lived in London until recently.*

re·cep·tacle /rɪ'septəkl/ nc (formal) a container: *a receptacle for pens and pencils.*

re·cep·tion /rɪ'sepʃn/ n **1** nu (also attrib) an act of receiving or being received: *prepare rooms for the reception of guests; a reception centre for refugees.* **2** nc a formal social occasion at which guests are received: *There was a reception after the wedding ceremony.* **3** nc a welcome or greeting of a kind mentioned; demonstration of feeling: *The new book/minister had a favourable reception.* **4** nu the quality (of) receiving of radio or TV signals: *Is radio reception good in your district?*

re'ception desk nc (in a hotel etc) a counter where guests ask for rooms etc.

re·cep·tion·ist /-ʃənɪst/ nc a person employed in a hotel, or by a doctor or other professional person, to receive clients.

re·cep·tive /rɪ'septɪv/ adj **receptive (to sth)** quick or ready (to listen to, accept, suggestions, new ideas etc): *receptive to new ideas; a receptive mind.*

re·cep·tive·ly adv

re·cess /rɪ'ses/ n **1** nc,nu a period of time when work or business is stopped: *The court is now in recess.* **2** nc a part of a room where the wall is set back from the main part. **3** nc a deep, inner part: *the recesses of a cave; in the recesses of the mind.*

re·ces·sion /rɪ'seʃn/ nc,nu (an occasion of) the slowing down of business and industrial activity: *Did the recent recession in Europe cause a lot of unemployment?*

re·ces·sive /rɪ'sesɪv/ adj **1** (science) (of a gene) showing the weak characteristics which are passed on to later generations, e.g. blue eyes and blond hair. Compare dominant(4). **2** showing weak characteristics of personality.

re·charge /ˌriː'tʃɑːdʒ/ vt **1** to fill (a battery) with an electric charge again: *recharge a battery.* **2** (fig) to fill (oneself) with new energy and determination.

re·charge·able /-əbl/ adj

recipe /'resɪpɪ/ nc **1** a detailed explanation of how to prepare (food): *a recipe for a fruit cake.* **2** (fig) a piece of advice: *Have you a recipe for happiness?*

re·cipi·ent /rɪ'sɪpɪənt/ nc **recipient (of sth)** (formal) a person who receives something.

re·cip·ro·cal /rɪ'sɪprəkl/ adj **1** (usually attrib) given and received in return: *reciprocal affection/help.* **2** (gram) (of a pronoun) showing that action relates to both, as in 'We love *each other*', 'They gave *one another* a present'.

re·cip·ro·cal·ly /-klɪ/ adv

re·cip·ro·cate /rɪ'sɪprəkeɪt/ vt,vi (formal) to do or give (something) in return or as payment: *He reciprocated by wishing her a pleasant journey.*

re·cit·al /rɪ'saɪtl/ nc **1** a detailed account of a number of connected events etc: *We were bored by the long recital of his adventures.* **2** a musical performance by a soloist or small group, or of the works of one composer: *a piano recital.*

reci·ta·tion /ˌresɪ'teɪʃn/ *n* **1** *nu* the act of reciting(2): *a boring recitation of his grievances*. **2** *nc,nu* (an instance of) a public performance of prose or poetry learnt by heart: *a Dickens recitation*.

re·cite /rɪ'saɪt/ *v* **1** *vt,vi* to say (poems, speeches in a play) aloud from memory: *The little girl refused to recite at the party*. **2** *vt* to give a list of, tell one by one, (names, facts etc): *recite the names of all the capital cities of Europe*.

reck·less /'reklɪs/ *adj* (usually *derog*) not thinking or caring about the effects, consequences: *a reckless spender/driver*.

reck·less·ness *nu*

reck·on /'rekən/ *vt* **1** to calculate (something) (the usual word): *reckon the cost of a holiday*. **2** to consider, suppose, (something): *One fourth of the country is reckoned to be unproductive*. (Ⓝ) Not used in continuous tenses, e.g. *is/was -ing*. **3** (esp US) (*informal*) to assume (something): *I reckon we'll need £10*.

reckon sb among/as sth to consider a person to be (best, worst) in a group: *He reckons me among his best friends*.

reckon on sth to depend on something (which is more usual): *We're reckoning on your help*.

reckon with sb (a) to deal with a person: *If you hurt her, you'll have me to reckon with*. (b) (usually *passive*) to consider a person: *He's a man to be reckoned with* (= who cannot be ignored).

reckon up sth to find the total cost etc.

reckon upon sth (*formal*) = reckon on sth.

reck·on·ing /'rekənɪŋ/ *n* **1** *n sing* a payment for a debt, being wronged etc: *If you treat your parents badly, there will be a reckoning*. **the day of reckoning** the time when one must be punished for doing something. **2** *nu* an act of calculating: *We've spent £48 by my reckoning*.

re·claim /rɪ'kleɪm/ *vt* **1** to return (waste land etc) to a useful condition, a state of cultivation etc. **2** (*formal*) to reform (a person): *a reclaimed drunkard*. **3** to demand that (something) be given back: *reclaim tax*.

rec·la·ma·tion /ˌreklə'meɪʃn/ *nu*

re·cline /rɪ'klaɪn/ *v* (*formal*) **1** *vi* to place oneself, be, in a position of rest; lie back or down: *reclining against a wall/on a couch/in a chair*. **2** *vt* to lean (something) in the position mentioned: *She reclined her head on my shoulder*.

re·cluse /rɪ'kluːs/ *nc* a person who lives alone and avoids other people.

rec·og·ni·tion /ˌrekəg'nɪʃn/ *nu* the act of recognizing or being recognized: *He was given a cheque for £25 in recognition of his services*. *Official recognition of the new State is unlikely*. **change beyond/out of (all) recognition** to change completely: *The town has changed out of all recognition since I was there ten years ago*.

rec·og·nize (also **-ise**) /'rekəgnaɪz/ *vt* (Ⓝ) Not used in continuous tenses, e.g. *is/was -ing*. **1** to (be able to) identify again (a person, thing) that one has seen, heard etc before: *recognize a tune/an old friend*. **2** to be willing to accept (a person, thing) as real, legal etc: *recognize an important medical discovery*. **3** to be prepared to admit (something): *He recognized that he was not qualified for the post*.

rec·og·niz·able (also **-nis·able**) /-əbl/ *adj* that

can be identified. Opp unrecognizable.

rec·og·niz·ably (also **-nis·ably**) /-əblɪ/ *adv*

re·coil¹ /'riːkɔɪl/ *nc,nu* an act of recoiling.

re·coil² /rɪ'kɔɪl/ *vi* **1** *recoil (at/from sth)* to draw or jump back: *recoil from doing something cruel*. **2** (of a gun, spring) to go back quickly. **3** *recoil on sb* to have an effect on the person responsible: *Revenge may recoil on the person who takes it*.

rec·ol·lect /ˌrekə'lekt/ *vt* to succeed in remembering (something): *recollect childhood days*.

rec·ol·lec·tion /ˌrekə'lekʃn/ *n* (a) *nu* the time, act or power of remembering: *It has not happened within my recollection*. (b) *nc* a fact about a person or event that is remembered: *letters with many recollections of my father*.

rec·om·mend /ˌrekə'mend/ *vt* **1** to speak favourably of (a person, thing); say that one thinks (something) is good (for a purpose) or that (a person) is suitable (for a post etc): *I can recommend this soap. He has been recommended for first class honours. Can you recommend Miss Hill as a typist?* **2** to approve of (something) as wise or suitable: *Do you recommend raising the school-leaving age?* **3** (of a quality etc) to cause (a person) to be or appear pleasing, satisfactory: *Behaviour of that sort will not recommend you*.

rec·om·men·da·tion /ˌrekəmen'deɪʃn/ *n* (a) *nu* the act of recommending: *buy it on the recommendation of a friend*. (b) *nc* a suggestion that is favourable: *The jury brought in a verdict of guilty, with a recommendation to mercy*. (c) *nc* something that causes a person to be well thought of: *Good cooking is a recommendation in a husband or wife*.

rec·om·pense¹ /'rekəmpens/ *nc,nu* (*formal*) a payment; reward: *work hard without recompense. Here is £1 in recompense for your help*.

rec·om·pense² /'rekəmpens/ *vt* (*formal*) to reward (a person), esp repay (a person) (for a loss, injury etc): *recompense a person for being injured in a car crash*.

rec·on·cile /'rekənsaɪl/ *vt* **1** (often *passive*) to become friendly with (a person) after a quarrel: *He refused to be reconciled (with his brother)*. **2** *reconcile oneself/sb to sth* to cause oneself, a person to accept something: *You must reconcile yourself to a life of poverty*. **3** *reconcile sth with sth* to cause something to agree with something: *I can't reconcile what you say with the facts of the case*.

rec·on·cil·able /-əbl/ *adj* willing to be reconciled(1). Opp irreconcilable.

rec·on·cil·iation /ˌrekənsɪlɪ'eɪʃn/ *nc,nu*

re·con·di·tion·ed /ˌriːkən'dɪʃnd/ *adj* (of an engine, machine) repaired and put into a good condition again.

re·con·nais·sance /rɪ'kɒnɪsəns/ *nc,nu* an act of getting information about something: *make a reconnaissance of the planned campaign*.

re·con·noitre (US = **-ter**) /ˌrekə'nɔɪtə(r)/ *vt,vi* to go to or near (a place or area occupied by enemy forces) to learn about their position, strength etc: *reconnoitring the area*.

re·con·sid·er /ˌriːkən'sɪdə(r)/ *vt,vi* to think about (a decision etc) again and perhaps change one's opinion.

re·con·struct /ˌriːkən'strʌkt/ *vt* **1** to build

(something) again: *reconstruct an engine/a model*. **2** to (form) a complete description of (something of which one has only partial evidence): *The detective tried to reconstruct the crime*.

re·con·struc·tion /ˌriːkənˈstrʌkʃn/ *nc,nu*

re·cord¹ /ˈrekɔːd/ *adj (attrib)* **1** concerning a record²(5): *a record shop/cover*. **2** being the best yet: *a record harvest*. ⇨ record²(6).

rec·ord² /ˈrekɔːd/ *n* **1** *nc* a written statement of facts, events etc: *keep a record of school attendances/of road accidents*. **2** *nu* **on record** the state of being recorded or preserved in writing, esp as evidence: *I don't want to go on record/don't want you to put me on record as saying that I think the President a fool*. **off the record** (*informal*) unofficial: *What the President said was off the record*. **put the record straight** to give an accurate statement of the facts (to replace an inaccurate one). **3** *nc* the facts known about the past of a person or thing: *He has an honourable record of service/a good record. That airline has a bad safety record*. **4** *nc* something that provides evidence or information: *Our museums are full of records of past history*. **5** *nc* a disc on which sound has been registered: *gramophone records*. ⇨ recording. **6** *nc* a limit, score, point, mark etc (high or low), not reached before; (esp in sport) the best yet done: *Who holds the record for the 5000 metres?* **break/beat/smash the record** to do better than has been done before. Hence **'record-breaking** *adj*

'record-player *nc* an electrical apparatus for reproducing sound from discs.

re·cord³ /rɪˈkɔːd/ *vt* **1** to write (something) down; put (something) into a computer etc: *record the results*. **2** to put (sound or vision) on tape or disc: *The programme was recorded*. **3** (of an instrument) to show (a measurement) on a scale: *The thermometer recorded 40°C*.

ˌrecorded deˈlivery *nu* (*GB*) a post system for which a signature is required to confirm safe delivery.

re·cord·er /rɪˈkɔːdə(r)/ *nc* **1** an apparatus that records (sound or vision). ⇨ tape/video recorder. **2** a kind of wooden musical instrument like a flute.

re·cord·ing /rɪˈkɔːdɪŋ/ *nc* (esp for radio, TV, record-players etc) a programme, piece of music etc on a disc, tape, film etc: *a BBC recording*.

re·count /rɪˈkaʊnt/ *vt* (*formal*) to tell (a story etc): *He recounted the story of his adventures in Mexico*.

re·count /ˌriːˈkaʊnt/ *vt* to count (something) again: *re-count the votes*. □ *nc* /ˈriːˈkaʊnt/ another count: *One of the candidates demanded a re-count*.

re·coup /rɪˈkuːp/ *vt* to get (something) back after losing it: *recoup one's losses*.

re·course /rɪˈkɔːs/ *nu* (*formal*) **1** an act or method of seeking help: *I still have recourse to the moneylenders*. **2** a method used as a help: *Your only recourse is legal action against them*.

re·cover /rɪˈkʌvə(r)/ *v* **1** *vt* to get back (something lost etc); get back the use of (something): *recover what was lost; recover consciousness* (i.e. after fainting); *recover one's sight/hearing*. **2** *vi* **recover (from sth) (a)** to become well again:

He is slowly recovering (from his illness). **(b)** to get back to a former position of strength, wealth etc: *Has the country recovered from the effects of the war yet?*

re·cover·able /-əbl/ *adj* that can be recovered(1): *Is the deposit I've paid recoverable?*

re·cov·ery *nu* an act of recovering: *make a quick recovery after the operation. The pound made a slow recovery against the dollar*.

re-cover /ˌriːˈkʌvə(r)/ *vt* to supply a new cover for (something): *This chair needs to be re-covered*.

rec·re·ation /ˌrekrɪˈeɪʃn/ *nc,nu* (also *attrib*) (a form of) activity for enjoyment: *a recreation centre; walk in the mountains for recreation. Sports, games and hobbies are recreations*.

rec·re·ation·al /-ʃənl/ *adj*: *recreational facilities*.

re·crimi·na·tion /rɪˌkrɪmɪˈneɪʃn/ *nc,nu* an accusation made as a reply to one already made.

re·crimi·na·tory /rɪˈkrɪmɪnətərɪ/ *adj* (*formal*) accusing: *speak in a recriminatory tone*.

re·cruit¹ /rɪˈkruːt/ *nc* a new member of an army, a society, group etc: *gain a few recruits to one's political party*.

re·cruit² /rɪˈkruːt/ *vt,vi* to get (new members): *recruit new people onto the committee*.

re·cruit·ment *nc,nu*

rect written abbr (*commerce*) receipt.

rec·tal /ˈrektl/ *adj* (*anat*) of the rectum.

rec·tangle /ˈrektæŋgl/ *nc* (*maths*) a four-sided shape with four right angles.

rec·tangu·lar /rekˈtæŋgjʊlə(r)/ *adj*

rec·ti·fy /ˈrektɪfaɪ/ *vt* (*pt,pp* **-ied**) (*formal*) to put (an error etc) right: *mistakes that cannot be rectified*.

rec·ti·lin·ear /ˌrektɪˈlɪnɪə(r)/ *adj* (*maths*) in a straight line; characterized by straight lines.

rec·tor /ˈrektə(r)/ *nc* **1** (Church of England) a clergyman in charge of a parish. **2** a head of certain universities, colleges or religious institutions.

rec·tory /ˈrektərɪ/ *nc* (*pl* **-ies**) a rector's residence.

rec·tum /ˈrektəm/ *nc* (*pl* **—s**) (*anat*) the lower and final part of the large intestine.

re·cum·bent /rɪˈkʌmbənt/ *adj* (*formal*) (esp of a person) lying down: *a recumbent figure on a tomb*.

re·cu·per·ate /rɪˈkuːpəreɪt/ *vt,vi* (to cause a person, thing) to become strong again after illness, exhaustion or loss: *recuperate one's health; go to the seaside (in order) to recuperate; recuperate one's losses*.

re·cu·per·ation /rɪˌkuːpəˈreɪʃn/ *nu*

re·cu·per·at·ive /rɪˈkuːpərətɪv/ *adj* helping, relating to, recuperation.

re·cur /rɪˈkɜː(r)/ *vi* (**-rr-**) to happen again; be repeated: *a problem/pain which recurs frequently*.

re·cur·rence /rɪˈkʌrəns/ *nc,nu*

re·cur·rent /-ənt/ *adj*

re·cycle /ˌriːˈsaɪkl/ *vt* to treat (a substance already used) so that it can be used again: *recycle waste paper*.

red¹ /red/ *adj* (**—der, —dest**) **1** of the colour of fresh blood: *red cabbage/wine; be/go red with anger/embarrassment*. **paint the town red** ⇨ town(1). **2** (R-) (*informal*) Communist.

'red·brick *adj* (*attrib*) of, concerning, British

universities founded in the 19th century, esp as opposed to Oxford and Cambridge.

,red 'carpet *nc* one put out for the reception of an important visitor.

,Red 'Cross *n* (the —) (the emblem of) the international organization that looks after victims of war, famine, earthquakes etc.

,red 'flag *nc* (usually the —) a red flag used as (a) a symbol of danger. (b) a symbol of Communism or Socialism.

,red-'handed *adj* (*pred*) (of a person) committing a crime: *be caught red-handed.*

'red·head *nc* a person having red hair.

,red 'herring *nc* (esp) something doubtful or irrelevant mentioned to take attention away from the subject being discussed.

,red-'hot *adj* (a) extremely hot. (b) (*fig*) very recent: *red-hot news.*

,red-'letter day *nc* (*fig*) one that is memorable because something good happened.

'red meat *nu* beef and lamb. Compare white meat.

,red 'tape *nu* too much attention to (government) rules and regulations: *red tape in government offices.*

red² /red/ *n* 1 *nc,nu* a (shade of) red colour: *the reds and browns of the woods in autumn.* **see red** to lose control of oneself and become very angry. 2 *nu* red clothes: *dressed in red.* 3 *nc* (R-) (*informal*) a believer in, supporter of, Communism. 4 the side of business accounts showing money owed. **be in/get into/out of the red** to be in/ get into/out of debt.

red·den /'redn/ *vt,vi* (to cause a person) to blush.

red·dish /'redɪʃ/ *adj* a little red.

re·deem /rɪ'di:m/ *vt* to get (something) back by payment or by doing something: *redeem a mortgage; redeem one's honour.*

re·deem·able /-əbl/ *adj*

re,deeming 'feature *nc* a good quality in a person's character that makes up for faults.

re·demp·tion /rɪ'dempʃn/ *nu* (*formal*) the act of redeeming or being redeemed: *the redemption of a mortgage.* **beyond/past redemption** too evil or bad to be completely forgiven, trusted, improved etc: *She/Her work is past redemption.*

re·de·ploy /,ri:dɪ'plɔɪ/ *vt* to move (soldiers, workers etc) in order to use them more efficiently.

re·de·ploy·ment *nu*

re·do /,ri:'du:/ *vt* (*pt* -did /-'dɪd/, *pp* -done /-'dʌn/) to do (something) again: *We must have the house redone* (= redecorated).

redo·lent /'redələnt/ *adj* (*pred*) **redolent of sth** (*formal*) having a strong smell that reminds one of something: *sheets redolent of lavender.*

re·double /,ri:'dʌbl/ *vt* to cause (effort etc) to become greater or stronger.

re·dress¹ /rɪ'dres/ *nu* compensation for a wrong: *ask for redress for an injury at work.*

re·dress² /rɪ'dres/ *vt* (*formal*) to set (a wrong) right again: *How can you redress the damage you have caused?* **redress the balance** to make things equal again.

re·duce /rɪ'dju:s/ *v* 1 *vt,vi* to make (something), become, smaller in size, number, degree, price etc: *reducing speed/costs; reduce the size of a photograph; reduce (one's weight) from 60kg to*

55kg. 2 *vt* **reduce sb/sth to sth** to bring a person, thing to a certain condition, way of living etc: *reduce a girl to tears* (= make her cry); *reduce him to silence* (= cause him to stop talking). *They were reduced to begging or starving.*

re·duc·ible /-əbl/ *adj*

re·duc·tion /rɪ'dʌkʃn/ *nc,nu* (an instance, example, of) reducing or being reduced: *a reduction in/of numbers; great reductions in prices; price reductions; a photographic reduction.*

re·dun·dan·cy /rɪ'dʌndənsɪ/ *nc,nu* (*pl* -ies) (an instance of) being made redundant: *redundancy caused by increasing use of computers; more redundancies in the mines.*

re·dun·dant /rɪ'dʌndənt/ *adj* 1 (usually *pred*) no longer needed (esp a person being made unemployed): *When the factory closes down many workers will become redundant.* 2 no longer or not used or useful: *Now that we have a car, our motorbike is redundant. In 'the two twins' the word 'two' is redundant.*

reed /ri:d/ *n* 1 *nc,nu* a kind of tall, coarse grass growing in or near water. 2 *nc* (in some wind instruments, e.g. the oboe, clarinet) a strip cut from a reed that vibrates to produce sound.

reef /ri:f/ *nc* a line of rock etc just below or above the surface of the sea: *a coral reef.*

reek¹ /ri:k/ *nu* a strong, bad smell: *the reek of stale tobacco smoke.*

reek² /ri:k/ *vi* **reek (of sth)** to smell unpleasantly of something: *He reeks of whisky/garlic.*

reel¹ /ri:l/ *nc* a kind of (music for a) lively Scottish dance.

reel² /ri:l/ *nc* a long, round object on which cotton, thread, wire, photographic film, magnetic tape etc is wound.

reel³ /ri:l/ *vt* 1 to roll or wind (thread, a fishing-line etc) onto a reel, or with the help of a reel: *reel in the fish.* 2 **reel sth off** to tell, say or repeat something without pause or effort: *reel off a list of names.*

reel⁴ /ri:l/ *vi* 1 to be shaken (physically or mentally) by a blow, a shock etc: *His mind reeled when he heard the news.* 2 to walk or stand unsteadily, moving from side to side: *He reeled like a drunken man.* 3 to seem to move: *The street reeled before him as the bike hit him.*

re·en·try /,ri: 'entrɪ/ *nc* (*pl* -ies) an act of a person, thing re-entering a place (e.g. the return of a spacecraft into the earth's atmosphere).

re·ex·port /,ri: 'ekspɔ:t/ *vt* to export (materials imported), esp after using them to produce something.

ref. *written abbr* 1 refer (to). 2 reference.

re·fec·tory /rɪ'fektərɪ/ *nc* (*pl* -ies) a large dining-room (e.g. in a college).

re·fer /rɪ'fɜ:(r)/ *v* (**-rr-**) **refer (sb/sth) to sb/sth** 1 *vi* (of a speaker, what is said etc) to speak about (a person, thing); be relevant to: *When I said that some people are stupid I wasn't referring to you. Does that remark refer to me?* 2 *vi* to turn to, go to, (a person, thing) for information etc: *The speaker often referred to his notes.* 3 *vt* to send, hand over, (something) (to a person, thing) to be dealt with, decided etc: *The dispute was referred to the United Nations. I was referred to the Manager.*

ref·er·able (also ref·er·rable) /rɪ'fɜ:rəbl/ *adj*

(*pred*) **referable to sb/sth** (*formal*) caused by: *Lung cancer is referable to smoking cigarettes.*

ref·er·ee[1] /ˌrefəˈriː/ *nc* **1** a person who controls matches, judges games etc. Ⓝ '*Referee*' is used for *basketball, boxing, football, hockey, rugby, wrestling* and for *billiards* and *snooker*. Compare umpire[1]. **2** a person who examines and decides a dispute. **3** a person who writes a reference(2) for a person.

ref·er·ee[2] /ˌrefəˈriː/ *vt,vi* to act as a referee(1,2) in (a game, etc).

ref·er·ence /ˈrefrəns/ *n* **1** *nc,nu* (an instance of) mentioning something: *The book is full of references to places that I know well.* **in/with reference to sb/sth** concerning: *I'm writing in reference to your advertisement.* **terms of reference** ⇨ terms(1). **2** *nc* a statement about a person's character or abilities: *The clerk has excellent references from former employers.* ⇨ referee[1](3). **3** *nc* a note telling where certain information may be found: *a book with references to earlier examples.* ⇨ cross-reference. **4** *nu* an act of using (a book, list etc) to find information: *a telephone directory for easy reference.*

'reference book *nc* one that is not read through but consulted for information, e.g. a dictionary or encyclopaedia.

'reference library *nc* one containing reference books.

ref·er·en·dum /ˌrefəˈrendəm/ *nc* (*pl* —**s** or **-da** /-də/) the referring of a political question to a direct vote of all the people.

re·fill[1] /ˈriːfɪl/ *nc* (a container with) an amount used to refill.

re·fill[2] /ˌriːˈfɪl/ *vt* to fill (a pen, bowl, petrol tank etc) again.

re·fine /rɪˈfaɪn/ *vt* **1** to free (something) from other substances: *refine sugar/oil/ores.* **2** to make small improvements to (writing, a speech etc).

re·fined /rɪˈfaɪnd/ *adj* (of a person, speech, manners etc) showing education and cultured taste: *refined language/manners/speech/taste.*

re·fine·ment /rɪˈfaɪnmənt/ *n* (*formal*) **1** *nu* the state of being well-mannered, cultured etc. **2** *nc* a small improvement (to writing etc).

re·fin·ery /rɪˈfaɪnərɪ/ *nc* (*pl* **-ies**) a place, building etc where oil or sugar is refined: *a sugar refinery.*

re·fit /ˌriːˈfɪt/ *vt,vi* (**-tt-**) (to cause a ship etc) to be made ready for use again by renewing or repairing parts. □ *n* /ˈriːfɪt/ *nc* an act of refitting a ship etc.

re·fla·tion /riːˈfleɪʃn/ *nu* (*finance*) an increase in economic activity (to previous levels) by increasing the money supply. Compare deflation, inflation(b).

re·flect /rɪˈflekt/ *v* **1** *vt* (of a surface) to throw back (light, heat, sound); (of a mirror) send back an image of (something): *Look at the trees reflected in the lake.* **2** *vt* to show the nature of (something): *Her sad looks reflected the thoughts passing through her mind.* **3** *vt,vi* **reflect** (**sth**) **on sb** (**a**) (of actions, results) to bring credit or discredit on a person: *The results reflect the greatest credit on all concerned.* (**b**) to injure the good reputation of a person: *Your rude behaviour reflects on yourself and your family.* **4** *vi* **reflect on sth** (*formal*) to consider, think about, something: *I must reflect on what answer to give.*

re·flec·tion /rɪˈflekʃn/ *n* **1** *nu* the act of reflecting or being reflected: *the reflection of heat.* **2** *nc* something reflected, esp an image reflected in a mirror or in water. **3** *nu* thought (the usual word): *be lost in reflection.* **on reflection** after reconsidering the matter: *On reflection, I decided not to write the letter.* **4** *nc* something that causes a bad reputation: *This is a reflection on your honour.* **5** *nc* (*formal*) an expression of a thought in speech or writing: *reflections on the pleasures of being idle.*

re·flec·tor /rɪˈflektə(r)/ *nc* something that reflects heat, light or sound, e.g. a piece of glass for reflecting light on the back of a bicycle.

re·flex /ˈriːfleks/ □ *nc* a reflex action: *test one's reflexes.*

'reflex action *nc* a movement that is an involuntary response to a stimulation of the nerves, e.g. lifting the leg after a tap on the knee.

'reflex angle *nc* (*maths*) one that is bigger than 180°.

'reflex camera *nc* one in which, by using a mirror, the image to be photographed can be focused up to the moment of exposure.

re·flex·ive /rɪˈfleksɪv/ *adj, nc* (*gram*) (of) a word or verb form showing that the action of a sentence is on the person or thing doing it, as in *I washed* (*myself*).

re,flexive 'pronoun *nc* (*gram*) a pronoun that refers to the subject, e.g. *myself, themselves.*

re,flexive 'verb *nc* (*gram*) one showing that the subject and object are the same, as in: '*He cut himself*'.

re·form[1] /rɪˈfɔːm/ *nc,nu* (an act, instance, of) reforming: *demonstrate for social or political reform; a reform in teaching methods.*

re·form[2] /rɪˈfɔːm/ *vt,vi* to (cause a person, thing) to become better by removing or putting right what is bad or wrong: *reform one's character/the world; a criminal who is determined to reform.*

re·form·er *nc* a person trying to get or carrying out reforms.

re-form /ˌriːˈfɔːm/ *vt,vi* to organize (members, soldiers) into the previous order or a new order.

re-for·ma·tion /ˌriːfɔːˈmeɪʃn/ *nc,nu*

ref·or·ma·tion /ˌrefəˈmeɪʃn/ *n* **1** *nc,nu* (an example of) the act of reforming or being reformed. **2** (the R-) the 16th-century movement for religious reform resulting in the establishment of the Protestant Churches.

re·fract /rɪˈfrækt/ *vt* (*science*) to cause (a ray of light) to bend where it enters water, glass etc. **re·frac·tion** /rɪˈfrækʃn/ *nu*

re·frain[1] /rɪˈfreɪn/ *nc* a repeated part of a song.

re·frain[2] /rɪˈfreɪn/ *vi* **refrain from doing sth** (*formal*) to agree with and not do something: *Please refrain from smoking.*

re·fresh /rɪˈfreʃ/ *v* **1** *vt, v* **reflex** to give new strength to (oneself, one's energy etc): *refresh oneself with a warm bath.* **2** *vt* **refresh one's memory** to think again, remember (by referring to notes etc). **3** *v reflex* (*formal*) to eat or drink: *They stopped at a pub to refresh themselves.*

re·fresh·er /rɪˈfreʃə(r)/ *nc* (*informal*) a refreshing drink.

re·fresh·ing /rɪˈfreʃɪŋ/ *adj* **1** strengthening; giving rest and comfort: *a refreshing breeze/sleep.* **2** pleasing and interesting because rare or unexpected: *The news that the children were doing things to help the old man was refreshing.*

re·fresh·ment /rɪˈfreʃmənt/ *n* **1** *nu* the act of refreshing or being refreshed: *refreshment of mind and body.* **2** (*pl*) food and drink: *Refreshments will be served during the interval.*

re·frig·er·ate /rɪˈfrɪdʒəreɪt/ *vt* to make (food) cold to keep it in good condition.

re·frig·er·ation /rɪˌfrɪdʒəˈreɪʃn/ *nu*

re·frig·er·ator /rɪˈfrɪdʒəreɪtə(r)/ *nc* (common short form *fridge*) an apparatus in which food and drinks are kept cold. ⇨ freezer.

re·fu·el /ˌriːˈfjuːəl/ *vt,vi* (-**ll**-, *US* also -**l**-) to supply (a vehicle etc) with, take on, more fuel.

ref·uge /ˈrefjuːdʒ/ *nc,nu* (a place giving) shelter or protection from trouble, danger etc: *seek refuge from the floods.*

refu·gee /ˌrefjuˈdʒiː/ *nc* (also *attrib*) a person who has been forced to leave her or his home or country because of danger from floods, war, political persecution etc: *political refugees; refugee camps.*

re·fund¹ /ˈriːfʌnd/ *nc,nu* (a) repayment: *obtain a refund of £20.*

re·fund² /rɪˈfʌnd/ *vt* to pay back (money): *refund the cost of postage.*

re·fur·bish /ˌriːˈfɜːbɪʃ/ *vt* to make (a room, furniture etc) clean or bright again, (as if) new.

re·fus·al /rɪˈfjuːzl/ *nc,nu* (an instance of) an act of refusing: *We were surprised at his refusal to do what I asked.* **first refusal** the right to decide whether to accept or refuse something before it is offered to others: *If you ever decide to sell your car, please give me first refusal.*

ref·use¹ /ˈrefjuːs/ *nu* waste or worthless objects, materials etc (to be burnt etc).

'refuse-collector *nc* = dustman.

re·fuse² /rɪˈfjuːz/ *vt,vi* **1** to say 'no' to (a request or offer): *refuse permission. I refuse!* **2** to show unwillingness to accept, do, (something): *refusing a gift. She refused to help although it was her turn.*

re·fute /rɪˈfjuːt/ *vt* (*formal*) to prove (a person, statements, opinions etc) to be wrong or mistaken: *refute an argument/an opponent.* Compare deny.

re·fut·able /ˈrefjʊtəbl/ *adj* (*formal*) that can be proved wrong. Opp irrefutable.

refu·ta·tion /ˌrefjuˈteɪʃn/ *nc,nu*

re·gain /rɪˈgeɪn/ *vt* **1** to get back (something), get possession of (something) again: *regain consciousness; regain one's freedom.* **2** (*formal*) to get back to (a place or position): *regain one's footing* (i.e. recover one's balance).

re·gal /ˈriːgl/ *adj* of, for, fit for, a king or queen: *regal splendour/power.*

re·gal·ly /-gəlɪ/ *adv*

re·gale /rɪˈgeɪl/ *vt* (*formal*) to give pleasure or delight to (oneself, a person): *regaling themselves with stories of their childhood.*

re·ga·lia /rɪˈgeɪlɪə/ *n pl* or *nu* the objects and costume of important officials, power etc: *royal regalia.*

re·gard¹ /rɪˈgɑːd/ *n* **1** *nu* thought; concern; consideration: *He has very little regard for the feelings of others. More regard must be paid to safety on the roads.* **in/with regard to** (*prep*) with reference to: *I'm writing in regard to your advertisement.* **2** *nu* respect: *hold a person in high/low*

regard. **3** (*pl*) kind thoughts and wishes (e.g. at the end of a letter): *Please give my regards to your brother.*

re·gard² /rɪˈgɑːd/ *vt* **1** to consider (a person, thing) (to be the kind mentioned): *regard her as a heroine; regard torture as a crime. How is he regarded locally? He is regarded with disfavour/unfavourably.* **2** (*formal*) to look at (a person, thing): *He regarded her through the trees.* **3** *as* **regards** = regarding (which is more usual).

re·gard·ing /rɪˈgɑːdɪŋ/ *prep* concerning; with reference to: *Regarding your offer to help, please telephone us.*

re·gard·less /rɪˈgɑːdlɪs/ *adj* (*pred*) **regardless of sb/sth** paying no attention to a person or thing: *He came regardless of the expense.* □ *adv* paying no attention to dangers, difficulties, a warning etc: *He carried on regardless.*

regards /rɪˈgɑːdz/ *n pl* ⇨ regard¹(3).

re·gat·ta /rɪˈgætə/ *nc* (*pl* —**s**) a meeting for boat races (rowing-boats or yachts).

re·gen·cy /ˈriːdʒənsɪ/ *nc* (*pl* -**ies**) the (period of) rule by a regent.

re·gent /ˈriːdʒənt/ *nc* (also R-) a person appointed to perform the duties of a ruler who is too young, old, ill etc.

reg·gae /ˈregeɪ/ *nu* a kind of modern popular music from the Caribbean, with a strong rhythm.

regi·cide /ˈredʒɪsaɪd/ *nc,nu* (an instance of) killing a king.

re·gime (also **ré·gime**) /reɪˈʒiːm/ *nc* **1** a method or system of government or administration: *a military regime.* **2** a set of rules for diet, exercise etc for improving one's health and physical well-being.

regi·ment¹ /ˈredʒɪmənt/ *nc* **1** a large group of soldiers under a colonel. **2** *a regiment of sb* (*informal*) a large number of people: *a regiment of children.*

regi·men·tal /ˌredʒɪˈmentl/ *adj* of a regiment: *a regimental badge.*

regi·ment² /ˈredʒɪment/ *vt* to organize and discipline (a group): *regiment the members of the Union.*

re·gion /ˈriːdʒən/ *n* **1** *nc* a large area or division without definite boundaries: *the densely populated regions of Europe.* **2** (*pl*) areas away from the capital: *live in the regions.* **3** *n sing* range: *In what region will you price your house?* **in the region of** an amount about: *in the region of £10/60 kilos.*

re·gion·al /-nl/ *adj* of, for, a region: *regional government.*

re·gion·al·ly /-nəlɪ/ *adv*

reg·is·ter¹ /ˈredʒɪstə(r)/ *nc* **1** (a book containing) a record or list: *the register of voters.* **2** the range of the human voice or of a musical instrument: *the lower register of the clarinet.* **3** a style (of speech, writing): *a formal register.*

reg·is·ter² /ˈredʒɪstə(r)/ *v* **1** *vt* to write (something), cause (something) to be written, in a record: *register one's car.* **2** *vi* to put one's name in, have one's name put in, a record: *I am a foreigner here; must I register with the police? She was registered at the Grand Hotel.* **3** *vt* (of instruments) to show (an amount): *The thermometer registered only two degrees above freezing-point.* **4** *vt* to show (emotion etc): *Her face registered* *surprise.* **5** *vt* to send (a letter or parcel) by registered post.

,registered 'post *nu* (*GB*) a post system by which a paper is given showing proof of postage and payment made if the letter, parcel etc is lost.

reg·is·trar /ˌredʒɪˈstrɑː(r)/ *nc* a person whose duty is to keep records e.g. for a town council or a university.

reg·is·tra·tion /ˌredʒɪˈstreɪʃn/ *nc,nu* (a record of) an act of registering something: *registration of letters; registration of students for an examination/ an academic course.*

,regis'tration mark/number *nc* the numbers and letters on a vehicle, used to identify it.

reg·is·try /ˈredʒɪstrɪ/ *nc* (*pl* -**ies**) a place where registers are kept.

'registry office *nc* (also *attrib*) (esp) a place where a marriage is conducted without a religious ceremony: *They had a registry-office wedding.*

re·gress /rɪˈgres/ *vi* (*formal*) to return to an earlier or less developed form or state: *regress mentally/culturally.*

re·gres·sion /rɪˈgreʃn/ *nc,nu*

re·gres·sive *adj* causing to regress.

re·gret¹ /rɪˈgret/ *n* **1** *nu* the feeling of being sorry or unhappy at the loss of something; a disappointment or a sad event: *hear with regret that a friend is ill. Much to my regret I am unable to accept your kind invitation.* **2** (*pl*) feelings of regret: *I have no regrets about resigning my job.*

re·gret·ful /-fəl/ *adj* sad; sorry.

re·gret·ful·ly /-fəlɪ/ *adv* (*formal*) sadly; with regret: *Regretfully, I cannot afford the bike.*

re·gret² /rɪˈgret/ *vt* (-**tt**-) (*formal*) **1** to be or feel sorry about (something): *I deeply regret being so rude/that I was so rude. He regrets his rudeness.* **2** to be sorry for the loss of (something); wish to have again: *regret lost opportunities.*

re·gret·table /-əbl/ *adj* (*formal*) that one should feel sorry about: *regrettable failures.*

re·gret·tably /-əblɪ/ *adv*

re·group /ˌriːˈɡruːp/ *vt,vi* (to cause (people)) to form again into groups or into new groups.

regu·lar¹ /ˈreɡjʊlə(r)/ *adj* **1** evenly arranged; systematic: *regular teeth; a regular wallpaper design; driving at a regular speed.* **2** (*attrib*) coming, happening, done, again and again at equal intervals: *as regular as clockwork* (= very regular); *a regular customer; keep regular hours* (e.g. getting up and going to bed at the same times every day). *He has no regular work* (i.e. no permanent job). **3** (*attrib*) properly qualified or trained: *the regular army* (i.e. of professional soldiers). **4** (*pred*) in agreement with what is considered correct procedure or behaviour: *I doubt whether your method of bringing in cigarettes would be considered regular by the Customs officials!* **5** (*gram*) (of verbs, nouns etc) having normal inflections: *The verb 'go' is not regular/is not a regular verb.* ⇨ **irregular**(4). **6** (*attrib*) (*informal*) thorough; complete: *He's a regular nuisance.*

regu·lar·ly *adv* at regular(2) intervals or times.

regu·lar² /ˈreɡjʊlə(r)/ *nc* **1** (*mil*) a soldier of the regular army. **2** (*informal*) a frequent customer or client, e.g. at a shop.

regu·lar·ity /ˌreɡjʊˈlærətɪ/ *nu* (*formal*) the state of being systematic, on time etc: *The doctor will*

test the regularity of your hearbeat.

regu·lar·ize (also **-ise**) /ˈreɡjʊləraɪz/ *vt* (*formal*) to make (something) lawful or correct: *regularize the proceedings.*

regu·late /ˈreɡjʊleɪt/ *vt* **1** to control (something) using rules: *regulate one's expenditure; regulate the traffic.* **2** to adjust (an apparatus, mechanism) in order to get the desired result: *regulate the speed of a machine/clock.*

regu·la·tion /ˌreɡjʊˈleɪʃn/ *n* **1** *nc* an official rule or order: *safety regulations; traffic regulations.* **2** *nu* an act of regulating: *the regulation of a clock/of prices.*

re·gur·gi·tate /rɪˈɡɜːdʒɪteɪt/ *vt* to bring (swallowed food) up again to the mouth.

re·ha·bili·tate /ˌriːhəˈbɪlɪteɪt/ *vt* **1** to make (a criminal, a person who has been ill) able to live a normal life again. **2** to restore (e.g. old buildings) to a good condition.

re·ha·bili·ta·tion /ˌriːhəˌbɪlɪˈteɪʃn/ *nu*

re·hears·al /rɪˈhɜːsl/ *nc,nu* (an occasion of) rehearsing: *have a rehearsal; put a play into rehearsal.* ⇨ **dress rehearsal.**

re·hearse /rɪˈhɜːs/ *vt,vi* to practise (a play, music, a speech etc) before a public performance: *rehearsing (the parts in) a play.*

re·house /ˌriːˈhaʊz/ *vt* to provide (a person, family) with another house: *be rehoused after the fire.*

reign¹ /reɪn/ *nc* (a period of) a rule: *during the reign of King George.*

reign² /reɪn/ *vi* **1 reign (over sb/sth)** to rule as a king or queen: *The king reigned over the country for ten years.* **2** (*formal*) to exist: *Silence reigned everywhere.*

reign·ing *adj* (*attrib*) existing now: *the reigning tennis champion.*

re·im·burse /ˌriːɪmˈbɜːs/ *vt* to pay back (money) (to a person): *You will be reimbursed for your expenses.*

re·im·burse·ment *nc,nu*

rein /reɪn/ *nc* (usually *pl*) a long, narrow strap used for controlling a horse. **give free rein to sb/sth** to allow freedom to a person, thing: *give free rein to one's imagination.* **hold/take the reins** (*fig*) to have/take control: *hold the reins of government.* **keep a tight rein on sb/sth** to allow a person, country, business etc very little freedom.

re·in·car·nate /ˌriːɪnˈkɑːnɪt/ *adj* (usually *pred*) born again in a new body.

re·in·car·na·tion /ˌriːɪnkɑːˈneɪʃn/ *nc,nu* (an example of) returning to life after death, in a new body.

rein·deer /ˈreɪndɪə(r)/ *nc* (*pl* unchanged) a kind of large deer with branched horns (called *antlers*), living in cold regions.

re·in·force /ˌriːɪnˈfɔːs/ *vt* to make (something) stronger by adding or supplying more people or material: *reinforce an army/a fleet; reinforcing a bridge.*

,re·in·forced 'concrete *nu* concrete strengthened with steel bars or metal netting.

re·in·force·ment *n* **(a)** *nu* the act of reinforcing or being reinforced. **(b)** (*pl*) soldiers, ships etc sent to strengthen an army, navy etc.

re·in·state /ˌriːɪnˈsteɪt/ *vt* to put (a person) in her or his former position: *reinstate the chairman.*

re·in·state·ment *nc,nu*

re·is·sue /ˌriːˈɪʃuː/ *vt* to issue(2) (something) again: *reissue stamps/books.* □ *nc* something reissued.

re·iter·ate /riːˈɪtəreɪt/ *vt* to say (something) again several times: *reiterate a command.*

re·iter·ation /ˌriːˌɪtəˈreɪʃn/ *nc,nu*

re·ject¹ /ˈriːdʒekt/ *nc* something rejected.

re·ject² /rɪˈdʒekt/ *vt* **1** to put aside, send back, throw away, (something) as not good enough: *reject fruit that is overripe.* **2** to refuse to accept (a person, thing): *reject an offer of help/of marriage. The meter rejected the bent coin. I applied for the job but I was rejected.*

re·jec·tion /rɪˈdʒekʃn/ *nc,nu*

re·joice /rɪˈdʒɔɪs/ *vi* (*formal*) to feel or show great joy or happiness: *rejoicing over a victory; rejoice at her success.*

re·joic·ing *nu* (*formal*) happiness; joy.

re·join /riːˈdʒɔɪn/ *vt* **1** to join (a company of soldiers, crew, meeting etc) again: *rejoin one's regiment/ship.* **2** to join (two parts) (together) again: *I rejoined the two ends of the rope.*

re·join·der /rɪˈdʒɔɪndə(r)/ *nc* (*formal*) something that is said in reply.

re·ju·ven·ate /riːˈdʒuːvɪneɪt/ *vt* (often *passive*) to cause (a person) to feel young or active again: *be rejuvenated by a long swim.*

re·ju·ven·ation /rɪˌdʒuːvɪˈneɪʃn/ *nu*

re·kindle /riːˈkɪndl/ *vt,vi* **1** (to cause a fire etc) to burn again: *rekindle a fire.* **2** (*fig*) (to cause a feeling etc) to be active again: *Our hopes were rekindled.*

re·laid /ˌriːˈleɪd/ *pt,pp* of relay².

re·lapse¹ /ˈriːlæps/ *nc* a change back into bad health, behaviour etc: *The patient had a major relapse.*

re·lapse² /rɪˈlæps/ *vi* to change back again (into bad health, behaviour, silence etc).

re·late /rɪˈleɪt/ *v* **1** *vt* (*formal*) to tell (a story): *He related amusing stories about his employer.* **2** *vt* **relate sb/sth to/with sth** to connect a person, thing in thought or meaning: *It is difficult to relate these results with/to any known cause.* **3** *vi* **relate to sb/sth** to concern, be about, a person, thing: *She is a girl who notices nothing except what relates to herself.* **4** *vt* (*passive*) **be related (to sb)** to be connected by family (to): *She says she is related (by marriage) to the Queen.*

re·lated *adj* (*attrib*) of the same kind; connected: *physics and other related science subjects.* Opp unrelated. ⇨ also relate(4).

re·la·tion /rɪˈleɪʃn/ *n* **1** *nc* a member of the same family as another person: *All my relations are coming to the wedding.* (N) 'Relative' is also possible but is sometimes considered more formal. **2** *nu* connection: *The effort and expense needed for this project bore no relation/were out of all relation to the results.* **in/with relation to** (*prep*) concerning: *I am writing in/with relation to your complaint.* **3** (usually *pl*) dealings; affairs; what a person, group, country etc has to do with another: *have business relations with a firm in Stockholm; the friendly relations between my country and yours; diplomatic relations.* ⇨ public relations.

re·la·tion·ship /rɪˈleɪʃnʃɪp/ **1** *nu* connection; relation(2): *the relationship of electricity to magnetism/between heat and energy.* **2** *nc* a connection by family or marriage: *What is your relationship to her?* **3** *nc* the feelings, work, dealings, between one person or group and another: *the relationship between the football supporters and the police; a business relationship.* **4** *nc* an important friendship or love affair: *He said he could never have a lasting relationship with Susan.*

rela·tive¹ /ˈrelətɪv/ *adj* **1** (*attrib*) compared (to each other or others): *the relative advantage of gas and electricity for cooking. They are living in relative comfort.* **2** (*pred*) **relative to sb/sth** having a connection with: *the facts relative to this problem.* **3** having meaning, importance only when compared to another or others: *Our idea of being poor is only relative.*

,**relative 'adverb** *nc* (*gram*) one, e.g. *where* in 'the place *where* the accident occurred', connecting a relative clause.

,**relative 'clause** *nc* (*gram*) one giving more information about the rest of the sentence and joined by a relative adverb or pronoun (as shown in *italics* in the examples above and below).

,**relative 'pronoun** *nc* (*gram*) one, e.g. *who* in 'the man *who* came yesterday', connecting a relative clause.

rela·tive² /ˈrelətɪv/ *nc* a relation(1).

rela·tive·ly /ˈrelətɪvlɪ/ *adv* when compared: *The matter is relatively unimportant.*

re·lax /rɪˈlæks/ *vt,vi* **1** (to cause something) to become less tight, stiff or rigid: *relax one's grip/hold on something; relaxing the muscles.* **2** (to cause a person, part of the body) to become less tense, active etc: *His face relaxed in a smile. Let's stop working and relax for an hour.*

re·lax·ation /ˌriːlækˈseɪʃn/ *n* (**a**) *nu* the act of relaxing or being relaxed: *relaxation of the muscles.* (**b**) *nc,nu* (*formal*) (something done for) recreation: *Fishing is his favourite relaxation.*

re·lay¹ /ˈriːleɪ/ *nc* **1** a group of people working in turn with others: *working in relays.* **2** (*tech*) an apparatus that receives and sends out radio or TV signals, etc. **3** (short for) a relay race: *the 400 metres relay.*

'**relay race** *nc* one between two teams, each member of the team running one section of the total distance.

'**relay station** *nc* a place where radio programmes are broadcast after being received from another station.

re·lay² /rɪˈleɪ/ *vt* (*pt,pp* —**ed**) to send out (radio or TV signals etc).

re·lay³ /ˌriːˈleɪ/ *vt* (*pt,pp* -**laid** /-ˈleɪd/) to lay (a cable, carpet etc) again.

re·lease¹ /rɪˈliːs/ *n* **1** *nc,nu* (an instance of) releasing or being released: *an order for his release from prison; a press release* (i.e. of a news item to journalists); *the latest release* (e.g. of a record or film). **on general release** (of films) available for seeing at local cinemas. **2** *nc* a handle, lever etc that releases part of a machine: *the carriage release* (i.e. on a typewriter).

re·lease² /rɪˈliːs/ *vt* **1** **release sb (from a place)** to allow a person, thing to go free: *release a man from prison; release a bomb (from an aircraft).* **2** to let (one's hold or grip) go: *release one's grip; release (one's hold on) a girl's arm.* **3** to allow (news) to be known or published; allow (a film) to be shown; allow (goods) to be placed on sale: *recently released films/records.*

rel·egate /'relɪgeɪt/ *vt* to put (a player, team etc) into a lower position: *Will our team be relegated (to the second division)?*

rel·ega·tion /ˌrelɪ'geɪʃn/ *nu*

re·lent /rɪ'lent/ *vi* to become less severe or cruel (esp by agreeing to something after refusing): *At last mother relented and let us watch TV.*

re·lent·less *adj* without pity (and determined): *suffer relentless persecution.*

re·lent·less·ly *adv*

rel·evance /'reləvəns/ *nu* **relevance (to sb/ sth)** the state of being relevant: *What relevance does your theory have to the facts?*

rel·evant /'reləvənt/ *adj* **relevant (to sb/sth)** connected (with the topic, problem, person etc receiving attention): *have all the relevant documents: the papers relevant to the meeting.* Compare irrelevant.

rel·evant·ly *adv*

re·li·able /rɪ'laɪəbl/ *adj* that may be trusted or depended on: *reliable tools/assistants/information/witnesses.* Opp unreliable.

re·li·ably /-əblɪ/ *adv*

re·lia·bil·ity /rɪˌlaɪə'bɪlətɪ/ *nu*

re·li·ance /rɪ'laɪəns/ *nu* **reliance (on sb/sth)** (formal) dependence, trust: *Do you place much reliance on his information?*

re·li·ant /rɪ'laɪənt/ *adj* **reliant (on sb/sth)** having, showing, trust or dependence: *Don't become too reliant on her/her help.*

rel·ic /'relɪk/ *nc* **1** something that belonged to a saint, kept as an object of reverence. **2** something from the past that keeps memories alive: *a relic of early civilization.*

re·lief¹ /rɪ'li:f/ *n* **1** *nu* (sometimes used with *a, an* as in the example) a lessening, ending or removal of pain, distress, anxiety etc: *The doctor's treatment gave/brought some/not much relief. She sighed with relief. It was a great relief to find the children safe.* **2** *nu* (also *attrib*) help (e.g. food, money, clothes etc) given to those in need: *provide relief for refugees; a relief fund.* **3** *nu* something that makes a change from monotony or that relaxes tension: *Shakespeare introduced comic scenes into his tragedies by way of relief.* **4** *nc* (often *attrib*) a person, group replacing another on duty: *a relief driver.*

re·lief² /rɪ'li:f/ *nc,nu* (a design, painting, carving made using) a method in which a design stands out from a flat surface: *a profile of Mozart in relief.*

re'lief map *nc* one showing hills, valleys etc.

re·lieve /rɪ'li:v/ *vt* **1** to lessen or remove (pain or distress): *We were relieved to hear that you had arrived safely. The fund is for relieving suffering among the flood victims.* **2** to take on a period of duty, a job etc after (a person): *relieve the guard/ the watch/a sentry.* **3** (formal) to take a burden from (a person): *Let me relieve you of your suitcase.* **4** *vt* (formal) to dismiss (a person) from employment. **5** *v reflex* (old use) to go to the toilet.

re·lieved /rɪ'li:vd/ *adj* (pred) made less anxious or pained: *She was relieved to know the boys were safe.*

re·lig·ion /rɪ'lɪdʒən/ *n* **1** *nu* the belief in the exist-

ence of a supernatural ruling power, the creator and controller of the universe. **2** *nc* one of the various systems of faith and worship based on such belief: *the great religions of the world such as Buddhism, Christianity, Islam, Judaism.*

re·lig·ious /rɪ'lɪdʒəs/ *adj* **1** (attrib) of religion: *a religious leader.* **2** (of a person) devout; having faith. **3** (attrib; formal) (doing work, duties) very carefully: *a religious worker; do one's work with religious care.*

re·lig·ious·ly *adv*

re·line /ˌri:'laɪn/ *vt* to put a new lining in (e.g. a coat).

re·lin·quish /rɪ'lɪŋkwɪʃ/ *vt* (formal) to give up (something): *relinquish all hope/a habit/a belief; relinquish one's rights/shares to a partner.*

rel·ish¹ /'relɪʃ/ *n* **1** *nc,nu* (something used to give or which has) a special flavour or attractive quality: *Olives and sardines are relishes. Some pastimes lose their relish when one grows old.* **2** *nu* (formal) liking: *I have no further relish for camping now that I am 90.*

rel·ish² /'relɪʃ/ *vt* (often negative) to enjoy, get pleasure out of, (doing something): *She won't relish having to get up before 5am!*

re·live /ˌri:'lɪv/ *vt* to imagine, live through (an experience) again: *It's an experience I don't want to relive.*

re·lo·cate /ˌri:ləʊ'keɪt/ *vt* (usually *passive*) to cause (a business etc) to become established in a new place or area: *The factory is being relocated in Devon.*

re·lo·ca·tion /ˌri:ləʊ'keɪʃn/ *nu*

re·luc·tance /rɪ'lʌktəns/ *nu* the state of being reluctant.

re·luc·tant /rɪ'lʌktənt/ *adj* **reluctant (to do sth)** (slow to act because) unwilling: *He seemed reluctant to join us.*

re·luc·tant·ly *adv*

re·ly /rɪ'laɪ/ *vi* (pt,pp **-ied**) **rely on sb/sth 1** to depend on (a person, thing): *We rely on that bus to get to the shops.* **2** to trust (a person, thing) with confidence: *He can always be relied on for help.*

re·made /ˌri:'meɪd/ *pt,pp* of remake.

re·main /rɪ'meɪn/ *vi* Ⓝ Not usually used in continuous tenses, e.g. *is/was -ing.* **1** to be still present after a part has gone or has been away: *After the fire very little remained of my house.* **2** to continue in the same place or condition: *How many weeks will you remain (= stay) here? He remained silent.*

re·main·der /rɪ'meɪndə(r)/ *nc,nu* something that remains; the rest: *Twenty people came in and the remainder stayed outside.*

re·mains /rɪ'meɪnz/ *n pl* **1** the part that is left: *the remains of a meal; ancient remains of Rome.* **2** (formal) a dead body: *His remains are buried in the churchyard.*

re·make /ˌri:'meɪk/ *vt* (pt,pp **-made** /-'meɪd/) to make (a bed, film etc) again. □ *n* /'ri:meɪk/ *nc* something made again: *a remake of a film.*

re·mand¹ /rɪ'mɑ:nd/ *nu* **on remand** while waiting to be tried in a law court: *be in prison on remand.* ⇨ parole, probation.

re'mand centre *nc* a place where young offenders are kept while waiting to be tried in a law court.

re·mand² /rɪ'mɑ:nd/ *vt* to send (an accused person) back (from a law court) to prison, e.g. while waiting for a report: *be remanded for a week.*

re·mark¹ /rɪ'mɑːk/ *nc* a comment or opinion: *pass rude remarks about her; make a few remarks.*

re·mark² /rɪ'mɑːk/ *v* (*formal*) **1** *vt* **remark (that) sth** to say something (which is more usual): *He remarked that he would be absent the next day.* **2** *vi* **remark on sth** to say something by way of comment: *It would be rude to remark on her appearance.*

re·mark·able /-əbl/ *adj* deserving or attracting attention: *a remarkable event/boy.* Opp unremarkable.

re·mark·ably /-əblɪ/ *adv*

re·mar·ry /ˌriː'mærɪ/ *vi* (*pt,pp* **-ied**) to get married again.

re·me·di·al /rɪ'miːdɪəl/ *adj* providing, or intended to provide, a remedy: *remedial education/classes* (i.e. for less able children).

re·me·di·able /rɪ'miːdɪəbl/ *adj* that can be remedied.

rem·edy¹ /'remɪdɪ/ *nc,nu* (*pl* **-ies**) a cure (for a disease etc); method used for putting something right: *a good remedy for colds. Your only remedy is to see a lawyer.*

rem·edy² /'remɪdɪ/ *vt* (*pt,pp* **-ied**) (often *passive*) to put (something) right; provide a cure for (something bad, a defect): *Your faults of pronunciation can be remedied.*

re·mem·ber /rɪ'membə(r)/ *v* **1** *vt,vi* to bring (a person, thing) back to the mind, esp after forgetting for a while: *Can you remember where you were? I remembered* (= did not forget) *to post your letters.* **2** *vt* to have, keep, (a person, thing) in the mind: *I shall always remember her as a slim young girl.* **3** *vt* to make a present to (a person): *I hope you'll remember me in your will.* **4** *vt* to give or send (one's greetings) (to a person): *Please remember me to your brother.*

re·mem·brance /rɪ'membrəns/ *n* (*formal*) **1** *nu* memory (the usual word): *have no remembrance of something; a service in remembrance of those killed in the war.* **2** *nc* something given or kept in memory of a person or thing: *He sent us a small remembrance of his visit.*

re·mind /rɪ'maɪnd/ *vt* to cause (a person) to remember (to do something etc); cause (a person) to think (of something): *Please remind me to answer that letter. He reminds me of his brother. That reminds me . . .* (= What you have just said makes me remember . . .).

re·mind·er *nc* something that helps a person to remember something: *He hasn't paid the money yet—I must send him a reminder.*

remi·nisce /ˌremɪ'nɪs/ *vi* to talk or write about past events and experiences.

remi·nis·cences /ˌremɪ'nɪsənsɪz/ *n pl* remembered experiences (spoken or written): *reminiscences of my days in the Navy.*

remi·nis·cent /ˌremɪ'nɪsnt/ *adj* (*pred*) **reminiscent of sb/sth** reminding one of past people, experiences etc: *music that is reminiscent of Mozart.*

remi·nis·cent·ly *adv*

re·miss /rɪ'mɪs/ *adj* (*pred; formal*) careless; negligent: *That was very remiss of you.*

re·mis·sion /rɪ'mɪʃn/ *n* **1** *nc,nu* (an instance of) reducing a period of imprisonment: *a remission of six months for good behaviour.* **2** *nu* (*formal*) a

lessening or weakening (of pain, disease, efforts etc): *remission of a fever.*

re·mit /rɪ'mɪt/ *vt* (**-tt-**) **1** (*formal*) to send (money etc) by post: *Kindly remit £20 by cheque.* **2** (*legal*) to cancel (a payment, punishment): *The fine cannot be remitted.* **3** (*formal*) to take or send (a question to be decided) (to some authority): *The matter has been remitted to a higher tribunal.*

re·mit·tance /-təns/ *nu* the sending of money. □ *nc* an amount of money sent.

rem·nant /'remnənt/ *nc* **1** (usually *pl*) a small part that remains: *remnants of a meal; remnants of former power.* **2** (esp) a length of cloth offered cheaply after most has been sold.

re·mon·strate /'remənstreɪt/ *vi* **remonstrate (against sth)** (*formal*) to make a protest; argue in protest: *remonstrate against cruelty to children.*

re·morse /rɪ'mɔːs/ *nu* (*formal*) a strong feeling of regret for doing wrong: *feel/be filled with remorse for one's failure to help her; in a fit of remorse.*

re·morse·ful /-fəl/ *adj* feeling remorse.

re·morse·ful·ly /-fəlɪ/ *adv*

re·morse·less *adj* without mercy.

re·morse·less·ly *adv*

re·mote /rɪ'məʊt/ *adj* (**—r, —st**) **remote (from sb/sth)** **1** very far away in space or time: *in the remotest parts of Asia; live in a house remote from any town or village.* **2** widely separated: *a remote link between a lizard and a snake.* **3** (often used in the superlative) slight: *a remote possibility. I haven't the remotest idea of what you mean.*

re·mote con·trol *nu* the control of an apparatus (e.g. a plane) from a distance using radio signals.

re·mote·ly *adv* (**a**) distantly: *remotely related.* (**b**) slightly: *not even remotely possible.*

re·mote·ness *nu*

re·mov·al /rɪ'muːvl/ *nc,nu* (an instance of) the act of removing: *the removal of furniture.*

re·mov·al van *nc* a large, closed van used to take furniture etc to a new home.

re·move /rɪ'muːv/ *vt* **remove sb/sth (from sth)** **1** to take something away, off or out (from a place): *remove the cloth from the table; remove doubts/fears. What do you use for removing ink from clothes?* **2** to dismiss a person (which is more usual): *remove a Civil Servant.*

re·mov·able /-əbl/ *adj* that can be removed: *a removable stain.*

re·moved *adj* (**a**) (**far**) **removed from sth** (very) distant from something, a place: *an explanation far removed from the truth; a factory too removed from the motorway.* (**b**) (of cousins) different by one generation: *my first cousin once removed* (= my first cousin's child).

re·mover /rɪ'muːvə(r)/ *n* (used in compounds) something that removes(1): *a stain remover.*

re·mun·er·ate /rɪ'mjuːnəreɪt/ *vt* (*formal*) to pay or reward (a person) (for work or services).

re·mun·er·ation /rɪˌmjuːnə'reɪʃn/ *nc,nu*

re·mun·er·ative /rɪ'mjuːnərətɪv/ *adj* (*formal*) profitable (the usual word).

re·nais·sance /rɪ'neɪsns/ *n* **1** (the R-) (the period of) revival of art and literature in Europe in the 14th, 15th and 16th centuries: *Renaissance art.* **2** *nc* any similar revival.

re·nal /'riːnl/ *adj* (*anat*) of or in the (region of the) kidneys: *the renal artery.*

re·name /riː'neɪm/ *vt* to give (a person, thing) a

new name: *rename a boat.*

rend /rend/ *vt* (*pt,pp* **rent** /rent/) (*literary*) **1** **rend sth** *(apart/in two)* to divide something violently: *a country rent in two by civil war. Loud cries rent the air.* **2** **rend sb/sth away/off** to cause a person, thing to separate violently: *Children were rent away from their mothers' arms by the brutal soldiers.*

ren·der /ˈrendə(r)/ *vt* (*formal*) **1** to give (something): *render good for evil; render help to those in need; render a service to him/render him a service; a reward for services rendered.* **2** (*finance*) to present, send in, (an account for payment): *You will have to render an account of your expenditure.* **3** (often *passive*) to cause (a person, thing) to be (in the condition mentioned): *be rendered helpless by an accident.* **4** to give a performance of (something); express (something) in another language: *There are many English idioms that cannot be rendered into other languages.*

ren·der·ing /ˈrendərɪŋ/ *nc* a way of performing or translating something: *renderings of Chaucer.* ⇨ **4** above.

ren·dez·vous /ˈrɒndɪvuː/ *nc* (*pl —*) /-vuːz/ **1** (a place for) a meeting at an agreed time. **2** a place where people often meet: *This café is a rendezvous for writers and artists.* □ *vi* to meet at a rendezvous.

ren·di·tion /renˈdɪʃn/ *nc* (*formal*) = rendering.

ren·egade /ˈrenɪɡeɪd/ *nc* (*derog*) a person who changes her or his political or religious beliefs and joins a rival group.

re·new /rɪˈnjuː/ *vt* **1** to begin (something) again: *renew one's studies; renew an acquaintance with a former friend.* **2** to put new life and strength into (something): *begin again with renewed enthusiasm.* **3** to replace (something out of date) with another: *renew a lease/contract; renew one's subscription to a magazine.*

re·new·able /-əbl/ *adj* that can be renewed(3): *Is the ticket renewable?*

re·new·al /-əl/ *nc,nu*

re·nounce /rɪˈnaʊns/ *vt* **1** to declare formally that one will no longer have anything to do with (a person, belief etc): *renounce one's faith/one's family.* **2** (*formal*) to give up (a claim, right, possession): *renouncing one's claim to an inheritance.* ⇨ renunciation.

reno·vate /ˈrenəveɪt/ *vt* to restore (an old building, painting etc) to a good condition.

reno·va·tion /ˌrenəˈveɪʃn/ *nc,nu*

re·nown /rɪˈnaʊn/ *nu* (*formal*) fame (for good qualities): *win renown; a man of high renown.*

re·nown·ed *adj* (*formal*) famous: *He was renowned for his skill as a surgeon.*

rent¹ /rent/ *nc* **1** a torn place in cloth etc: *a rent in the balloon.* **2** (*fig*) a division or split (in a political party etc).

rent² /rent/ *nc,nu* (a) regular payment for the use of land, a building, offices, machinery etc: *You owe me three weeks' rent.*

ˌrent-ˈfree *adj, adv* (used) without rent to be paid: *live rent-free; live in a rent-free house.*

rent·al /ˈrentl/ *nc* an amount of rent paid or received.

rent³ /rent/ *vt* **1** **rent sth** *(from sb)* to use a building, land etc and pay rent: *rent a house from the council.* **2** **rent sth** *(out)* *(to sb)* to allow a building, land etc to be used in return for rent: *We've rented (out) our house while we're away.*

rent⁴ /rent/ *pt,pp* of rend.

re·nun·ci·ation /rɪˌnʌnsɪˈeɪʃn/ *nu* the act of renouncing(1,2).

re·open /ˌriːˈəʊpən/ *vt,vi* (to cause something) to open again after closing or being closed: *reopen a shop; reopen a discussion. School reopens on Monday.*

re·or·gan·ize (also **-ise**) /ˌriːˈɔːɡənaɪz/ *vt,vi* to change the organization of (something): *They've reorganized the furniture in their living-room.*

re·orien·tate /ˌriːˈɔːrɪənteɪt/ (also **re·orient** /riːˈɔːrɪənt/) *vt,vi* to orient(ate) again or in a new way.

rep /rep/ *nc* (*informal abbr* of) **1** repertory. **2** representative.

re·paid /ˌriːˈpeɪd/ *pt,pp* of repay.

re·pair¹ /rɪˈpeə(r)/ *n* **1** *nu* the act of repairing or being repaired: *This road is under repair* (= being repaired). **2** (usually *pl*) the work or process of repairing: *The shop will be closed during repairs.* **3** *nu* a condition (mentioned): *This machine is in a bad state of repair/in good repair.*

re·pair² /rɪˈpeə(r)/ *vt* **1** to restore (something worn or damaged) to good condition: *repair the roads/a watch.* **2** (*formal*) to put (a bad or wrong act or result) right again: *repair an error/harm done.*

re·pair·able /-əbl/ *adj* that can be repaired. Compare reparable.

re·pair·er *nc* a person who repairs things: *a shoe repairer.*

re·pair³ /rɪˈpeə(r)/ *vi* **repair to a place** (*formal*) to go (often in large numbers) to: *repair to the seaside for the summer.*

rep·ar·able /ˈrepərəbl/ *adj* (of damage, a loss etc) that can be put right or restored. Opp irreparable.

rep·ar·ation /ˌrepəˈreɪʃn/ *nu* **reparation (for sth)** (*formal*) compensation (for loss or damage).

rep·ar·tee /ˌrepɑːˈtiː/ *nu* (the making of) amusing remarks and answers.

re·past /rɪˈpɑːst/ *nc* (*formal*) a meal: *a luxurious repast in the banqueting hall.*

re·pat·ri·ate /riːˈpætrɪeɪt/ *vt* to send or bring (a person) back to her or his own country: *repatriate refugees after a war.*

re·pat·ri·ation /ˌriːpætrɪˈeɪʃn/ *nu*

re·pay /rɪˈpeɪ/ *vt* (*pt,pp* **-paid** /-ˈpeɪd/) **1** to pay back (money): *If you'll lend me 75p, I'll repay you next week.* **2** to give something to (a person) in return: *How can I repay Jim for his kindness?*

re·pay·able /-əbl/ *adj* that can or must be paid back.

re·pay·ment *nc,nu*

re·peal /rɪˈpiːl/ *vt* to end, cancel, (a law etc) officially. □ *nc,nu* (an instance of) repealing.

re·peat¹ /rɪˈpiːt/ *nc* (also *attrib*) another supply, performance etc: *a repeat of the basic pattern in the design. This is a repeat performance.*

re·peat² /rɪˈpiːt/ *vt* **1** *vt* to say or do (something) again: *repeat a word/mistake.* **2** *vt* to say (what somebody else has said or what one has learnt by heart): *You must not repeat what I've told you; it's very confidential.* **3** *vi* (of food) to continue to be tasted after being eaten: *Do you find that onions repeat?* **4** *vt* to supply (a further amount, order etc): *We regret that we cannot repeat this design.*

re·peat·ed·ly /adv/ again and again; often.

re·pel /rɪ'pel/ vt (-ll-) **1** to drive (a person, thing) back or away: *repel the enemy/temptation.* Opp attract(3). **2** to cause (a person) to feel dislike: *His long, rough beard repelled her.* Opp attract(1).

re·pel·lent¹ /rɪ'pelənt/ adj unattractive; uninviting: *repellent work/food/manners.* (N) Compare *'repulsive',* which has a much stronger meaning.

re·pel·lent² /rɪ'pelənt/ nc something that causes something else to go or stay away: *an insect repellent.*

re·pent /rɪ'pent/ vi,vt **repent (of) (sth)** (formal) to be sorry about having done, wish one had not done, (something bad): *Don't you repent (of) having wasted your money so foolishly?*
re·pent·ance /-əns/ nu
re·pent·ant /-ənt/ adj
re·pent·ant·ly adv

re·per·cus·sion /ˌriːpə'kʌʃn/ nc (usually pl) a strong result or effect (of an event etc): *The assassination of the President was followed by repercussions throughout the whole country.*

rep·er·toire /'repətwɑː(r)/ nc all the plays, songs, pieces etc which a company, actor, musician etc is prepared to perform: *She has a large repertoire of songs.*

rep·er·tory /'repətərɪ/ nc (pl -ies) = repertoire.
'repertory company/theatre nc (usual abbr **rep**) one in which the actors or plays are changed regularly.

rep·eti·tion /ˌrepɪ'tɪʃn/ nc,nu (an instance of) repeating or being repeated: *after numerous repetitions. Let there be no repetition of this* (i.e. Don't do it again).

re·peti·tive /rɪ'petətɪv/ (also **rep·eti·tious** /ˌrepɪ'tɪʃəs/) adj characterized by repeated action: *the repetitive work in many factories.*

re·phrase /ˌriː'freɪz/ vt to say, write, (something) again using different words: *rephrase a question.*

re·place /rɪ'pleɪs/ vt **1** to put (something) back in its place: *replacing a dictionary on the shelf; replace the receiver* (i.e. after telephoning). **2** to take the place of (a person, thing): *Can anything replace a mother's love and care?* **3** to supply, use, (a person, thing) as a substitute: *replace coal by/with oil.*

re·place·able /-əbl/ adj that can be replaced. Opp irreplaceable.

re·place·ment n **(a)** nu the act of replacing or being replaced. **(b)** nc a person or thing that replaces: *get a replacement while one is away on holiday.*

re·play /ˌriː'pleɪ/ vt to play (e.g. a record, football match) again. □ nc /'riːpleɪ/ a replaying of a record, a football match etc.

re·plen·ish /rɪ'plenɪʃ/ vt (formal) to fill (something) up again; get (a supply of something) again: *replenish the shelves/supplies.*

re·plete /rɪ'pliːt/ adj (pred) (formal) filled (with food): *replete with food; feeling replete.*

rep·li·ca /'replɪkə/ nc (pl —s) an exact copy (esp of a work of art).

re·ply¹ /rɪ'plaɪ/ nc an act of replying; what is replied; answer: *He made no reply.* **in reply** as an answer: *What was said in reply?*

re·ply² /rɪ'plaɪ/ vt,vi (pt,pp -ied) **reply (sth) (to sb/sth)** to give (something) as an answer (to a person, about something): *He failed to reply to (to*

my question). *'Certainly', he replied. He replied that he was very sorry.*

re·port¹ /rɪ'pɔːt/ n **1** nc an account of, statement about, something heard, seen, done etc: *newspaper reports; an annual report of a business company; a school report* (e.g. by teachers about a pupil). **2** nc,nu (a piece of) gossip; rumour: *Report has it that . . .* (= People are saying that . . .). **3** nc the sound of an explosion: *the loud report of a gun.*

re·port² /rɪ'pɔːt/ v **1** vt,vi to give information or an account of (something seen, heard, done etc): *The discovery of another moon near Saturn has been reported.* **2** vi,vt **report (on) sth** to give news or information concerning (something): *report on a meeting.* **3** vi,vt **report (on) sb** to make a complaint against (a person) (to authorities): *report an official for insolence. Please don't report on me/report me to the police.* **4** vi **report (to sb) (for sth)** to go somewhere and announce (to a person) that one has come, that one is ready (for work, duty etc): *report for duty at the office; report to the Manager.*

re,ported 'speech nu (gram) = indirect speech.

re·por·ter nc a person who supplies news to a newspaper, for radio or TV.

re·pose nu (formal) rest; sleep: *Her face is beautiful in repose.*

re·posi·tory /rɪ'pɒzɪtrɪ/ nc (pl -ies) (formal) a place where things are (to be) stored: *Desks are repositories for all sorts of useless papers.*

rep·re·hend /ˌreprɪ'hend/ vt (formal) to disapprove of (a person, behaviour etc) strongly: *reprehend his conduct.*

rep·re·hen·sible /ˌreprɪ'hensəbl/ adj (formal) (of bad behaviour etc) deserving to be strongly disapproved of.

rep·re·sent /ˌreprɪ'zent/ vt **1** to be a picture, sign, symbol or example of (a person, thing): *Phonetic symbols represent sounds. This painting represents a hunting scene.* **2** to act officially for (a person), e.g. as a lawyer, member of parliament, union leader etc: *He is representing the older workers in the dispute.*

rep·re·sen·ta·tion /ˌreprɪzen'teɪʃn/ n **1** nu (the act of) representing or being represented: *legal representation.* ⇨ proportional representation. **2** nc something that is represented(1): *This model is a representation of the space shuttle.* **3** nc (formal) (esp) a polite protest: *make representations to the Inspector of Taxes.*

rep·re·sen·ta·tive¹ /ˌreprɪ'zentətɪv/ adj **1** **representative (of sth)** being or containing an example or examples (of another or others): *being representative of their abilities and interests; a representative collection of her paintings.* **2** consisting of elected members: *representative government/institutions.* Opp unrepresentative.

rep·re·sen·ta·tive² /ˌreprɪ'zentətɪv/ nc a person elected or appointed to represent or act for others: *send a representative to a conference; a sales representative in a business; our representative* (= MP) *in the House of Commons.*

re·press /rɪ'pres/ vt (formal) **1** to prevent, control, (something) (often cruelly): *repress a revolt.* **2** to keep (a feeling, desire) private: *repressed emotions.*

re·pres·sion /rɪˈpreʃn/ *nu*

re·pres·sive /rɪˈpresɪv/ *adj* (of control by government, law) cruel and severe: *repressive laws; a repressive regime.*

re·prieve[1] /rɪˈpriːv/ *nc* (an order giving authority for) the delay or cancelling of punishment (esp by death): *grant a prisoner a reprieve.*

re·prieve[2] /rɪˈpriːv/ *vt* to delay or cancel punishment (esp by death) for (a person): *The prisoner was reprieved at the last minute.*

rep·ri·mand[1] /ˈreprɪmɑːnd/ *nc* an official expression of disapproval.

rep·ri·mand[2] /ˌreprɪˈmɑːnd/ *vt* to express strong disapproval to (a person) officially (because of a fault etc): *be reprimanded for being late.*

re·pris·al /rɪˈpraɪzl/ *n* 1 *nu* the act of doing harm to a person who has wronged or hurt one: *do something by way of reprisal.* 2 (*pl*) such acts, esp by one country on another during a war.

re·proach[1] /rɪˈprəʊtʃ/ *n* (*formal*) 1 *nu* the act, condition, of reproaching: *a term/look of reproach.* **above/beyond reproach** perfect, blameless: *She/Her behaviour is beyond reproach.* 2 *nc* an instance, word, phrase etc of reproach.

re·proach·ful /-fəl/ *adj: a reproachful look.*

re·proach·ful·ly /-fəlɪ/ *adv*

re·proach[2] /rɪˈprəʊtʃ/ *vt* (*formal*) to find fault with (a person) (usually with a feeling of disappointment or sadness): *reproach one's son for being late home.*

re·pro·duce /ˌriːprəˈdjuːs/ *v* 1 *vt* to cause (something) to be seen, heard etc again: *reproduce music from magnetic tape; reproduce copies of an original painting.* 2 *vi* (of animals, plants) to produce young or offspring: *bacteria that reproduce easily.*

re·pro·duc·tion /ˌriːprəˈdʌkʃn/ *n* 1 *nu* the act, process, of reproducing. 2 *nc* something reproduced, esp a work of art.

re·pro·duc·tive /ˌriːprəˈdʌktɪv/ *adj* for, relating to, reproducing (esp (2)): *the female reproductive organs.*

re·proof /rɪˈpruːf/ *n* (*formal*) 1 *nu* blame (the more usual word): *a glance of reproof; conduct deserving of reproof.* 2 *nc* an expression of blame or disapproval.

re·prove /rɪˈpruːv/ *vt* (*formal*) to express one's strong disapproval to (a person) of her or his behaviour: *The head teacher reproved the boys for misbehaving.*

re·prov·ing·ly *adv: speak reprovingly to them.*

rep·tile /ˈreptaɪl/ *nc* (*science*) a cold-blooded animal that lays eggs, e.g. a lizard, tortoise, crocodile, snake.

rep·til·ian /repˈtɪlɪən/ *adj* (*science*) of, like, a reptile.

re·pub·lic /rɪˈpʌblɪk/ *nc* (a country with) a system of government by elected representatives and with an elected head (the President).

re·pub·li·can /rɪˈpʌblɪkən/ *adj* of, relating to, supporting the principles of, a republic. □ *nc* a believer in, supporter of, government as a republic.

Re'publican Party *n* (the —) (*US*) one of the two main political parties. ⇨ **Democratic Party**.

re·pudi·ate /rɪˈpjuːdɪeɪt/ *vt* (*formal*) 1 to refuse to accept or acknowledge (something): *repudiate the authorship of an article.* 2 to refuse to pay (a debt).

re·pudi·ation /rɪˌpjuːdɪˈeɪʃn/ *nu*

re·pug·nance /rɪˈpʌɡnəns/ *nu* (*formal*) a strong dislike.

re·pug·nant /rɪˈpʌɡnənt/ *adj* (*formal*) causing a feeling of strong dislike: *I find his views/proposals repugnant.*

re·pulse /rɪˈpʌls/ *vt* (*formal*) 1 to drive back (the enemy); resist (an attack) successfully. 2 to refuse to accept (a person's help, friendly offers etc); discourage (a person) by being unfriendly.

re·pul·sion /rɪˈpʌlʃn/ *nu* 1 the strong feeling of disgust: *feel repulsion for him.* 2 (*science*) the tendency of bodies to repel each other. Opp attraction(3).

re·pul·sive /rɪˈpʌlsɪv/ *adj* 1 causing a strong feeling of disgust: *a repulsive sight.* 2 (*science*) showing repulsion(b): *repulsive forces.*

re·pul·sive·ly *adv*

repu·table /ˈrepjʊtəbl/ *adj* respected; having a good reputation: *reputable occupations.* Compare disreputable.

repu·tably /-əblɪ/ *adv*

repu·ta·tion /ˌrepjʊˈteɪʃn/ *nc,nu* 1 the general opinion about the character, qualities etc of a person or thing: *have a good/bad reputation as a doctor.* **live up to one's reputation** to act in the way that people expect (good or bad). 2 a good general opinion of a person: *make a reputation for oneself as a writer.*

re·pute /rɪˈpjuːt/ *nu* 1 a reputation (good or bad): *know a man by repute.* 2 a good reputation: *a doctor of repute.* Compare disrepute.

re·put·ed /rɪˈpjuːtɪd/ *adj* 1 (*pred*) **reputed (as/ to be sb)** generally considered or reported (to be): *He is reputed to be very wealthy. He is reputed as/to be the best surgeon in Paris.* 2 (*attrib*) generally considered to be (but with some doubt): *the reputed father of the child.*

re·put·ed·ly /-ədlɪ/ *adv*

re·quest[1] /rɪˈkwest/ *n* 1 *nu* the act of asking or being asked: *We came at your request/at the request of Mr Brown.* **on request** if requested: *Samples will be sent on request.* 2 *nc* an expression of desire for something: *repeated requests for help.* 3 *nc* something asked for: *All my requests were granted.*

re·quest[2] /rɪˈkwest/ *vt* (*formal*) to ask (for) (something): *Visitors are requested not to touch the paintings.*

re·qui·em /ˈrekwɪəm/ *nc* (a musical setting for) a special mass for the souls of the dead.

re·quire /rɪˈkwaɪə(r)/ *vt* (*formal*) 1 to need (the usual word): *We require extra help.* 2 to demand (something); insist on (something) as a right or by authority: *Students are required to take three papers in English literature. I have done all that is required by law.*

re·quire·ment *nc* (*formal*) something asked for: *We cannot meet all your requirements from our existing supplies.*

requi·site /ˈrekwɪzɪt/ *nc, adj* (*formal*) (something) that is necessary: *We supply every requisite for travel/all travelling requisites. Do you have the requisite number of tickets?*

requi·si·tion /ˌrekwɪˈzɪʃn/ *nc* a formal, written request: *a requisition for supplies/that the supplies should be sent.* □ *vt* to ask for (something) formally: *requisition a cheque for £100.*

re·scind /rɪ'sɪnd/ vt (*legal*) to cancel (a law, contract etc).

res·cue¹ /'reskju:/ nc,nu (an instance of) rescuing or being rescued: *a successful/daring rescue. John came to my rescue at the meeting.*

res·cue² /'reskju:/ vt **rescue sb/sth (from sb/ sth)** to save (a person, thing) (from danger, disaster, attack, being held prisoner etc): *rescuing a child (from drowning); rescue a business by lending money.*

res·cu·er nc a person who rescues a person, thing.

re·search¹ /rɪ'sɜ:tʃ/ nc,nu (a) detailed study or investigation to discover new facts, get additional information etc: *be engaged in research; much research work; carry out a research/researches into the causes of cancer. His researches have been successful.*

re·search² /rɪ'sɜ:tʃ/ vi **research (into sth)** to make a detailed study or investigation (of something): *She is researching into the causes of cancer.*

re·search·er nc a person engaged in research.

re·sem·blance /rɪ'zembləns/ nc,nu **resemblance (between sb/sth)** (a point of) likeness, similarity (between people, things): *There's very little resemblance between them.*

re·semble /rɪ'zembl/ vt to be like, similar to, (a person, thing): *She resembles her mother.* Ⓝ Not used in continuous tenses, e.g. *is/was -ing.*

re·sent /rɪ'zent/ vt to feel annoyed or angry about (something considered to be unfair): *resent criticism. He resents my being here.*

re·sent·ful /-fəl/ adj

re·sent·ful·ly /-fəlɪ/ adv

re·sent·ment nu the angry and disappointed feeling that one has when insulted, ignored etc: *bear/feel no resentment against anyone.*

res·er·va·tion /ˌrezə'veɪʃn/ n **1** nc,nu (a cause, feeling, of) doubt: *accept a plan without reservation* (= completely). **2** nc an arrangement to keep something for a person to use, e.g. a seat in a train, a room in a hotel: *My travel agents have made all the reservations for my journey.* **3** nc: *the central reservation of a motorway* (= the land dividing the two carriageways).

re·serve¹ /rɪ'zɜ:v/ n **1** nc something stored (for later use): *a reserve of food.* **2** nu **in reserve** kept and available if needed: *have/hold/keep a little money in reserve.* **3** nc a player who is officially allowed to replace another player during a game. **4** nc a place or area reserved for some special use or purpose: *a game reserve* (e.g. in Africa, for wild animals). **5** nu the quality of being slow to express feelings or opinions: *break through his reserve* (i.e. get him to talk and be sociable). ⇨ reserved(1). **6** nc,nu (*formal*) (an instance of) feeling doubt: *We accept your statement without reserve* (= believe it completely). **7** n sing or pl (*mil*) soldiers etc trained but not members of the army etc and kept for use if needed.

re·serve² /rɪ'zɜ:v/ vt **1** to store, keep, (something) for a later occasion: *Reserve your strength for the climb.* **2** to keep (a person, thing) for a special purpose: *We are reserving these seats for special guests. These players are reserved for the more difficult games.* **3** to arrange to keep (something) for a person to use: *reserve rooms at a*

hotel.

re·serv·ed /rɪ'zɜ:vd/ adj **1** (of a person, character) slow to express feelings or opinions: *He is too reserved to be popular.* **2** (of a seat in a train, room in a hotel etc) kept for a person's later use.

res·er·voir /'rezəvwɑ:(r)/ nc **1** a place or an artificial lake) where water is stored. **2** (*fig*) a supply (of facts, knowledge etc).

re·settle /ˌri:'setl/ vt,vi (to help a person) to settle in a new country: *resettle European refugees in Canada.*

re·settle·ment nc,nu

re·shuffle¹ /ˌri:'ʃʌfl/ nc a change of responsibilities, duties etc again: *a Cabinet reshuffle.*

re·shuffle² /ˌri:'ʃʌfl/ vt **1** to mix (playing-cards) again. **2** to shuffle(3) (responsibilities of committee members) again.

re·side /rɪ'zaɪd/ vi (*formal*) **1** to live (the more usual word): *residing abroad.* **2 reside in sb** (of power, rights etc) to be the property of the person mentioned: *The supreme authority resides in the President.*

resi·dence /'rezɪdəns/ n (*formal*) **1** nu the act of residing: *take up residence in a new house.* **in residence** living in the house etc officially provided. **2** nc a place (esp a large one) where a person lives: *this desirable family residence for sale.*

resi·dent /'rezɪdənt/ adj **resident (at/in a place)** having a home (in the place mentioned): *a resident student. Are you resident in Oxford?* □ nc a person who lives in a place, has a room in a hotel etc (not a visitor): *The restaurant is for residents only.* ⇨ non-resident.

resi·den·tial /ˌrezɪ'denʃl/ adj **1** (*attrib*) concerning where one lives: *residential qualifications for voters.* **2** having houses and flats (and not factories or offices): *residential parts of the town.* **3** making it necessary to live in the place where one works: *a residential job in a hospital.*

re·sid·ual /rɪ'zɪdjʊəl/ adj (*formal*) remaining: *residual income after tax.*

resi·due /'rezɪdju:/ nc the part that remains after some is taken or used.

re·sign /rɪ'zaɪn/ v **1** vt,vi **resign (from) (sth)** to give up (a job, claim etc): *resign one's post; resign from the committee.* **2** v *reflex* **resign oneself (to sth)** to be ready to put up with or accept (something) without complaining: *resign oneself to one's fate.*

re·sign·ed /rɪ'zaɪnd/ adj having or showing acceptance (of something unpleasant): *with a resigned look; be resigned to failure.*

re·sign·ed·ly /-ədlɪ/ adv

res·ig·na·tion /ˌrezɪg'neɪʃn/ n **1** nu (an act, process, of) resigning(1). **2** nc an instance of this; letter stating this: *offer/send in/hand in one's resignation (from the committee).* **3** nu (*formal*) the state of accepting something unpleasant: *accept failure with resignation.*

re·sil·ience /rɪ'zɪlɪəns/ nu **1** the quality of quickly recovering the original shape or condition after being pulled, pressed, crushed etc: *the resilience of rubber.* **2** (*fig*) the power of recovering quickly: *the resilience of the human spirit.*

re·sil·ient /-ənt/ adj

res·in /'rezɪn/ nc,nu **1** a kind of sticky substance, esp from fir and pine trees, used in making varnish, lacquer etc. **2** a similar manmade substance, widely used in industry.

re·sist /rɪˈzɪst/ v 1 vt,vi to use force against (a person, thing) in order to stop her, him or it: *resist the enemy/a plan/a disease/authority.* 2 vt to be undamaged or unaffected by (something): *a kind of glass that resists heat.* 3 vt,vi to try not to give in, not to take or use (something): *resist temptation. She can't resist chocolates. How can I resist?*

re·sis·tance /rɪˈzɪstəns/ n 1 nu **resistance (to sth)** (the act, power, of) resisting: *resistance to infection; resistance to her ideas.* 2 (the —) (also *attrib*) (in a country occupied by an enemy) a group of people organized to oppose the enemy: *a resistance movement'.* 3 nu (*science*) an opposing force: *An aircraft has to overcome the resistance of the air.* **line of least resistance** ⇨ line¹(10).

re·sis·tant /rɪˈzɪstənt/ adj **resistant (to sth)** able to be unaffected (by something): *insects that are resistant to chemicals.*

re·sis·tor /rɪˈzɪstə(r)/ nc (*electricity*) a device used to reduce the power in an electric circuit.

re·sole /ˌriːˈsəʊl/ vt put a new sole on (a shoe).

res·ol·ute /ˈrezəluːt/ adj (*formal*) very determined: *a resolute man.*

re·sol·ute·ly adv

res·ol·ution /ˌrezəˈluːʃn/ n 1 nc a formal expression of opinion by an official meeting: *pass/ carry/adopt/reject a resolution (for/against/in favour of closing the school).* 2 nc something one makes up one's mind to do: *a New Year('s) resolution to work harder.* 3 nu (*formal*) the quality of being determined: *show great resolution; a man with no resolution.* 4 nu (*formal*) the ending (of a doubt, problem etc) by supplying an answer. ⇨ resolve(2).

re·solve¹ /rɪˈzɒlv/ nc (*formal*) a serious decision: *my resolve to help her get her job back.*

re·solve² /rɪˈzɒlv/ v 1 vt,vi to decide (something), esp with determination: *He resolved that nothing should prevent him from succeeding. He resolved to succeed.* 2 vt to end (doubts, difficulties etc) by supplying an answer.

res·on·ance /ˈrezənəns/ nu the quality of being resonant.

res·on·ant /ˈrezənənt/ adj (of sound) low and vibrating: *a deep, resonant voice.*

res·on·ate /ˈrezəneɪt/ vt,vi (to cause something) to produce resonant sounds.

re·sort¹ /rɪˈzɔːt/ n 1 nc a place visited for pleasure or for health reasons: *a holiday/seaside resort; a health resort.* 2 nu **resort (to sth)** the act of using (a method mentioned) to do something or succeed: *Can you do it without resort to force?* **as a/in the last resort** when every other method has failed: *We can always sell the house as a last resort.*

re·sort² /rɪˈzɔːt/ vi **resort to sth** to make use of a method or means in order to achieve something, esp after failure: *resort to force/violence; resort to using one's savings.*

re·sound /rɪˈzaʊnd/ vi (of a voice, instrument, sound, place) to be heard clearly and continually: *The hall resounded with the fans' screaming.*

re·sound·ing /rɪˈzaʊndɪŋ/ adj (*attrib*) (esp) very great: *a resounding success/failure.*

re·sound·ing·ly adv

re·source /rɪˈsɔːs/ n 1 (*pl*) a supply of goods, raw materials etc that a person, country etc has or can use: *the natural resources of our country* (i.e. its mineral wealth etc). 2 nc something that helps in doing something, that can be turned to for support or consolation: *Leave him to his own resources* (= to amuse himself, find his own way of passing the time). 3 nu the ability to solve difficulties: *She showed resource in coping with her personal problems.*

re·source·ful /-fəl/ adj showing resource(3): *a resourceful mind.*

re·source·ful·ly /-fəlɪ/ adv

re·spect¹ /rɪˈspekt/ n 1 nu the feeling of honour, high opinion or regard (for a person or quality): *I have great respect for her as a writer. The Prime Minister is held in the greatest respect.* Compare disrespect. 2 nu consideration; attention: *show respect for older people.* **with respect to** (*prep*) (*formal*) concerning: *With respect to your refusal to pay, . . .* 3 nc a detail; particular aspect: *They resemble one another in some/a few respects.* 4 (*pl*) (*formal*) regards; polite greetings: *My father sends you his respects.*

re·spect² /rɪˈspekt/ vt 1 (often *passive*) to show respect(1) for (a person): *He is respected by everyone.* 2 to show consideration for (something): *We must respect his wishes.*

re·spec·ter nc (only in) **no respecter of sb/ sth** a person etc paying little or no attention to wealth, social rank etc: *A flea is no respecter of class. Death is no respecter of persons.*

re·spect·able /rɪˈspektəbl/ adj 1 showing, having, qualities or standards that are acceptable: *a respectable person; look respectable for an interview.* 2 of a fairly large size, quality, importance etc: *He earns a respectable income.*

re·spect·ably /-əblɪ/ adv in a respectable manner: *respectably dressed.*

re·spect·ful /rɪˈspektfəl/ adj (*formal*) showing respect(1): *They stood at a respectful distance from the President.* Compare disrespectful.

re·spect·ive /rɪˈspektɪv/ adj (*attrib*) of, for, belonging to, each one: *The men were given work according to their respective abilities.* Compare irrespective.

re·spect·ive·ly adv separately and in the order mentioned: *Rooms for men and women are on the first and second floors respectively.*

res·pir·ation /ˌrespəˈreɪʃn/ nu breathing (the usual word). ⇨ artificial respiration.

res·pir·ator /ˈrespəreɪtə(r)/ nc (*med*) an apparatus used to help people to breathe.

res·pir·at·ory /rɪˈspɪrətrɪ/ adj (*attrib*) connected with breathing: *respiratory diseases.*

re,spiratory 'tract nc (*anat*) the system of organs used for breathing.

re·spire /rɪˈspaɪə(r)/ vi (*formal*) to breathe (the usual word).

res·pite /ˈrespaɪt/ nc,nu **respite (from sth)** a period of relief or rest (from work, suffering, anything unpleasant): *work without (a) respite.*

re·splen·dent /rɪˈsplendənt/ adj (*formal*) looking rich and colourful: *a resplendent display.*

re·splen·dent·ly adv

re·spond /rɪˈspɒnd/ vi 1 **respond (to sth)** to reply (the usual word): *respond to a speech of welcome.* 2 to act in answer to, or because of, the action of another: *When Tom insulted the referee, he responded by ordering him off the field.* 3

respond to sth (esp concerning illness) to be affected by a form of treatment: *The illness/patient quickly responded to treatment.*

re·sponse /rɪ'spɒns/ *n* **1** *nc* an answer (the usual word): *My letter of inquiry brought no response.* **2** *nc,nu* (a) reaction: *My appeal to her pity met with no response.*

re·spon·si·bil·ity /rɪˌspɒnsə'bɪlətɪ/ *n* (*pl* **-ies**) **1** *nu* **responsibility (for sb/sth)** the state, quality, of being responsible: *I'll lend you my camera if you will take full responsibility for it.* **2** *nc* something for which a person is responsible; duty: *the many responsibilities of the Prime Minister.*

re·spon·sible /rɪ'spɒnsəbl/ *adj* **1** (*pred*) **responsible (for sb/sth)** (of a person) legally or morally having to carry out a duty, care (for a person, thing): *The pilot of an airliner is responsible for the safety of the passengers. Who is responsible for the education of our children?* **be responsible for sth** to be the cause or source of something: *Who's responsible for this mess in the kitchen?* **2** (*pred*) involving the obligation to make decisions for others and bear the blame for their mistakes: *I've made you responsible and you must decide what to do.* **3** (usually *attrib*) who can be relied on: *Give the task to a responsible man.* Opp irresponsible.

re·spon·sibly /-əblɪ/ *adv*

re·spon·sive /rɪ'spɒnsɪv/ *adj* (*pred*) **responsive (to sth)** (*formal*) reacting easily or quickly: *responsive to affection/treatment.*

re·spon·sive·ly *adv*

rest¹ /rest/ *n* **1** *nu* the condition of being free from activity, movement, disturbance: *Rest is necessary after hard work. Have a rest (from work) this afternoon. She had a good night's rest* (= sleep). **at rest** (a) not moving. (b) dead. **be laid to rest** to be buried. **come to rest** to stop moving: *The ball came to rest by the river.* **set sb's mind at rest** ⇨ mind¹(2). **2** *nc* an object etc on which something is supported: *an armrest/headrest.*

'rest-cure *nc* a course of treatment for people suffering from nervous disorders.

'rest-home *nc* a home for old people.

'rest-room *nc* public toilet.

rest² /rest/ *n* (always the —) **1** (used with a *sing verb*) something that is left; the remainder: *Take what you want and throw the rest away. Her hat was red, like the rest of her clothes.* **for the rest** . . . concerning other matters . . . **2** (used with a *pl verb*) the others: *John and I are going to play tennis—what are the rest of you going to do?*

rest³ /rest/ *v* **1** *vt,vi* (to allow a person) to be free from activity, movement, disturbance: *We rested (for) an hour after lunch. He will not rest* (= will have no peace of mind) *until he knows the truth.* *vt* to give rest or relief to (a person, animal, part of the body): *He stopped to rest his horse. These dark glasses rest my eyes.* **3** *vt,vi* **rest (sth) against/on sth** (to cause something) to be supported: *Rest the ladder against the wall. She rested her elbows/Her elbows were resting on the table.* **4** *vi* to be buried or left alone: *He rests in the churchyard. Let her rest in peace. She won't let matters rest.*

'resting-place *nc* (esp) a place of burial.

rest⁴ /rest/ *vi* (*formal*) **1** to continue to be in (the state mentioned): *You may rest assured that*

everything possible will be done. **2 rest with sb** to be a person's responsibility: *It rests with you to decide.* **3 rest on sb/sth** (*formal*) to depend on (a person, thing): *His fame rests on his plays more than on his novels.*

re·state /ˌriː'steɪt/ *vt* to state (something) again or in a different way: *restate one's conditions.*

re·state·ment *nc,nu*

res·taur·ant /'restrɒnt/ *nc* a place where meals can be bought and eaten.

rest·ful /'restfl/ *adj* still and quiet; giving (a feeling of) rest¹(1): *a restful scene/sleeper/night; colours that are restful to the eyes.* Compare restless.

res·ti·tu·tion /ˌrestɪ'tjuːʃn/ *nu* (*formal*) the act of restoring (of something stolen etc) to its owner: *restitution of property.*

res·tive /'restɪv/ *adj* (*formal*) (of a person, audience etc) unwilling or unable to be still and patient.

rest·less /'restlɪs/ *adj* never still or quiet: *a restless sleeper/night.* Compare restful.

rest·less·ly *adv*

rest·less·ness *nu*

re·stock /ˌriː'stɒk/ *vt* to put fresh supplies into or onto (something): *restock the shelves in a shop.*

res·to·ra·tion /ˌrestə'reɪʃn/ *nu* the act, process, of restoring or being restored: *restoration to health and strength; restoration of stolen property.* **Restoration 'comedy** *nu,nc* (an example of) a kind of humorous drama from England in the 17th century, using satire of social conventions and containing witty speeches.

re·stora·tive /rɪ'stɔːrətɪv/ *adj* (*formal*) (of food, medicine) tending to restore health and strength.

re·store /rɪ'stɔː(r)/ *vt* **1** to give (something stolen, borrowed, lost etc) back: *restoring stolen property/borrowed books.* **2** to bring (something) back into use: *restore old customs.* **3** to make (a person) well or normal again: *be restored to health; feel completely restored.* **4** to bring (something) back to a former condition: *Law and order have been restored.* **5** to rebuild (something) as before: *restore a ruined abbey.* **6** to place (a person) in a former position etc: *restore an employee to his old post/an officer to his command.*

re·storer *nc* a person, substance, that restores old paintings etc.

re·strain /rɪ'streɪn/ *vt* **restrain sb (from doing sth); restrain sth** to prevent (a person or thing) (from doing something): *restrain a child from (doing) mischief; restrain one's anger.*

re·strain·ed *adj* (esp) not showing one's feelings (esp of anger): *He was so restrained as he talked to the man who had damaged his car.* Opp unrestrained.

re·straint /rɪ'streɪnt/ *n* **1** *nu* the quality of being restrained: *show restraint when accusing her.* **2** *nc* (*formal*) something that restrains; controlling influence: *the restraints of poverty.*

re·strict /rɪ'strɪkt/ *vt* **restrict sb/sth (to sb/sth)** to keep (a person, thing) within limits: *Discussion at the meeting was restricted to the agenda. Driving is restricted to 30 miles an hour in built-up areas. My view was restricted by the low roof.*

re·stric·tion /rɪ'strɪkʃn/ *nc,nu* (an instance, example, of) restricting or being restricted: *restriction of expenditure; currency restrictions (e.g.*

on money that can be used for foreign travel).

re·strict·ive /rɪ'strɪktɪv/ adj (formal) tending to restrict: *My father's rules were too restrictive.*

re·strict·ive·ly adv

re·style /,ri:'staɪl/ vt 1 to give a new name to (a person, thing): *The chairman has been restyled 'the President'.* 2 to redesign (something): *They have restyled the seats for the new model of this car.*

re·sult¹ /rɪ'zʌlt/ nc 1 something produced because of an activity or cause; effect: *exam results. What was the result of your discussions? She failed as a result (of not working hard).* 2 nc an answer (to a mathematical problem etc).

re·sult² /rɪ'zʌlt/ vi (formal) 1 **result (from sth)** to happen (because of something): *Any damage resulting from negligence must be paid for by the borrower.* 2 **result in sth** to cause something: *Their quarrels resulted in war.*

re·sult·ant /-ənt/ adj (attrib) coming as a result: *the resultant effect.*

re·sume /rɪ'zjuːm/ v 1 vt,vi to begin (something) again after stopping for a time: *resume one's work/a story.* 2 vt to take or occupy (something) again: *resume one's seat.*

ré·sumé /'rezuːmeɪ/ nc a summary (the more usual word): *a résumé of a speech.*

re·sump·tion /rɪ'zʌmpʃn/ nc,nu (an instance of) an activity beginning again.

re·sur·face /,ri:'sɜːfɪs/ v 1 vt to put a new surface on (a road etc). 2 vi (of a submarine) to come to the surface again. 3 vi (fig) (of a person, idea etc) to reappear among people.

re·sur·gence /rɪ'sɜːdʒəns/ nu a return to a state of activity, life etc: *a resurgence of energy/pacifism.*

re·sur·gent /rɪ'sɜːdʒənt/ adj (attrib) (formal) coming back to activity, strength etc (after defeat etc): *resurgent hopes.*

res·ur·rect /,rezə'rekt/ vt to bring (something) back into use: *resurrect an old custom.*

res·ur·rec·tion /,rezə'rekʃn/ nu 1 (the R-) (in Christianity) the rising of Jesus from the tomb. 2 a revival after disuse, inactivity etc: *the resurrection of hope.*

re·sus·ci·tate /rɪ'sʌsɪteɪt/ vt to bring (a person) back to consciousness: *resuscitate a person who has been nearly drowned.*

re·sus·ci·ta·tion /rɪ,sʌsɪ'teɪʃn/ nu

re·tail¹ /'riːteɪl/ adj (attrib) concerning retail: *retail prices.*

re·tail² /'riːteɪl/ adv by retail: *buy them retail.*

re·tail³ /'riːteɪl/ nu (also attrib) the sale of goods to the general public: *a business involved in retail.* Compare wholesale(1).

re·tail⁴ /'riːteɪl/ v 1 vt to sell (goods) by retail. 2 vi **retail at a price** (commerce) (of goods) to be sold to the public at: *The pen retails at £1.*

re·tail·er nc a person, business, that sells goods by retail.

re·tain /rɪ'teɪn/ vt to continue to have, keep possession of, (something): *retain an interest in the business. She retains a clear memory of her schooldays.* ⇨ retention, retentive.

re·take /,ri:'teɪk/ vt (pt **-took** /-'tʊk/, pp **-taken** /-'teɪkən/) to capture, photograph, (something) again.

re·tali·ate /rɪ'tælɪeɪt/ vi to return the same sort of

bad treatment that one has received: *He retaliated by kicking the other boy on the ankle. If we increase our import duties on their goods, they may retaliate (against us).*

re·tali·ation /rɪ,tælɪ'eɪʃn/ nu

re·tard /rɪ'tɑːd/ vt to prevent or hinder (something): *retard progress/development.*

re·tard·ed adj (of a person) slow or behind in (emotional, intellectual, physical) development: *a mentally retarded child.*

retch /retʃ/ vi to make (involuntarily) the sound and physical movements of vomiting but without bringing up anything from the stomach.

retd written abbr retired.

re·tell /,ri:'tel/ vt (pt,pp **-told** /-'təʊld/) to tell (a story etc) again or in a different way or language: *old Greek tales retold for children.*

re·ten·tion /rɪ'tenʃn/ nu (formal) an act of retaining or being retained: *the retention of funds for emergency use.*

re·ten·tive /rɪ'tentɪv/ adj (formal) having the power to remember: *a retentive memory.*

re·think /,ri:'θɪŋk/ vt (pt,pp **-thought** /-'θɔːt/) to think about (something) again; reconsider: *They will have to rethink their policy towards China.*

reti·cence /'retɪsns/ nu the quality of being reticent.

reti·cent /'retɪsnt/ adj in the habit of saying little; not saying all that is known or felt: *She was reticent about what Tom had said.*

reti·cent·ly adv

ret·ina /'retɪnə/ nc (pl **—s** or **-nae** /-niː/) (anat) the part at the back of the eyeball that is sensitive to light.

reti·nue /'retɪnjuː/ nc a group (of staff, officers etc) travelling with a person of high rank.

re·tire /rɪ'taɪə(r)/ v 1 vi **retire (from/to a place)** to go away: *He retired to his cabin/from the world.* 2 vi (formal) to go (to bed): *My wife usually retires (to bed) at 10 o'clock.* 3 vt,vi (to cause a person) to give up work, a position etc: *He will retire on a pension at 65. We must retire the head clerk.*

re·tired adj (attrib) having retired(3): *a retired civil servant.*

re·tir·ing adj (attrib) (a) (of a person, way of life etc) avoiding meeting people or talking: *a girl of a retiring nature.* (b) about to retire: *the retiring chairman.*

re·tire·ment nu (a) (formal) the act of going away: *retirement from the world.* (b) the condition of being retired(3): *be/live in retirement.* **go into retirement** to retire(3).

re·told /,ri:'təʊld/ pt,pp of retell.

re·took /,ri:'tʊk/ pt of retake.

re·tort¹ /rɪ'tɔːt/ nc (formal) a quick reply (to an accusation).

re·tort² /rɪ'tɔːt/ vi (formal) to answer back quickly, cleverly or angrily (esp to an accusation): *'It's entirely your fault,' he retorted.*

re·touch /,ri:'tʌtʃ/ vt to improve (a photograph, painting etc) by adding a little paint with a brush etc.

re·trace /,ri:'treɪs/ vt 1 to go back over or along (something): *retrace one's steps.* 2 to go over (past actions etc) in the mind: *retracing her movements.*

re·tract /rɪ'trækt/ vt,vi 1 to take back or withdraw (a statement, offer, opinion etc): *Even when confronted with proof the accused man refused to retract his statement.* **2** to (be able to) draw (a claw, blade etc) in or back: *A cat can retract its claws.*

re·trac·tion /rɪ'trækʃn/ *n/ nc,nu*

re·treat¹ /rɪ'tri:t/ *n* **1** *nc,nu* (an instance of) retreating: *The army was in full retreat. We made our retreat.* **beat a hasty retreat** to go back very quickly. **2** *nc* a signal to go back: *sound the retreat* (e.g. on a bugle). **3** *nc,nu* (a place for) a period of quiet and rest: *a quiet country retreat.* **go into retreat** to go to a quiet place (esp for religious reasons).

re·treat² /rɪ'tri:t/ *vi* (esp of an army) to go back; withdraw: *force the enemy to retreat.*

re·trial /ˌri:'traɪəl/ *nc* an occasion of repeating a trial in a law court.

ret·ri·bu·tion /ˌretrɪ'bju:ʃn/ *nu* (*formal*) deserved punishment: *Retribution for immoral acts does not always come in this life.*

re·tri·bu·tive /rɪ'trɪbjʊtɪv/ *adj*

re·triev·able /rɪ'tri:vəbl/ *adj* that can be retrieved. Opp irretrievable.

re·triev·al /rɪ'tri:vl/ *nu* (*formal*) **1** an act of retrieving: *the retrieval of one's fortunes.* **2** the possibility of recovery: *beyond/past retrieval.*

re·trieve /rɪ'tri:v/ *vt* **retrieve sth (from sth)** (*formal*) to get possession of something again: *retrieve a lost umbrella; retrieving information from a computer.*

retro·ac·tive /ˌretrəʊ'æktɪv/ *adj* (of laws etc) applying to or from the past: *a retroactive decision.*

retro·ac·tive·ly *adv*

retro·grade /'retrəgreɪd/ *adj* likely to cause worse conditions: *a retrograde policy.*

retro·gress /ˌretrə'gres/ *vi* (*formal*) to go back (to a worse state).

retro·gres·sion /ˌretrə'greʃn/ *nu*

retro·gres·sive /ˌretrə'gresɪv/ *adj* returning, tending to (cause a) return, to a worse state.

retro·rocket /'retrəʊrɒkɪt/ *nc* a jet engine fired to slow down or alter the course of a missile, spacecraft etc.

retro·spect /'retrəspekt/ *nu* **in retrospect** looking back at past events etc.

retro·spec·tive /ˌretrə'spektɪv/ *adj* **1** looking back on past events etc: *a retrospective review.* **2** (of a law, payment etc) applying to the past: *retrospective legislation; a retrospective* (= payable from an earlier date) *wage increase.*

retro·spec·tive·ly *adv*

re·turn¹ /rɪ'tɜ:n/ *adj* (*attrib*) concerned with going or coming back: *a return ticket; the return journey.*

re·turn² /rɪ'tɜ:n/ *n* **1** *nc,nu* (an instance of) coming, going, giving, sending, putting, back: *the return of spring. What is the date of your return?* **by return** in the next post: *Please send a reply by return.* **in return (for sth)** in exchange (for something): *I'll give you it in return for your bike.* **Many happy returns (of the day)** (used as a greeting on a person's birthday). **on sb's return** when a person gets/got back: *On my return I discovered that Mary had telephoned.* **point of no return** ⇨ point¹(2). **2** *nc* an official report or statement: *make one's return of income to the tax*

office.

re·turn³ /rɪ'tɜ:n/ *v* **1** *vi* to come or go back: *return from Japan; return to Paris from London. I shall return to this point later in my lecture.* **2** *vi* to go back (to a former state): *He has returned to his old habits.* **3** *vt* to give, put, send, pay, carry, (something) back: *When will you return the book I lent you/the money? She returned the compliment* (= said something pleasant after a compliment had been paid to her). **4** *vt* (of a constituency) to elect (a person) as representative to Parliament. **5** *vt* to express (something) officially: *The jury returned a verdict of guilty.*

re·turn·able /-əbl/ *adj* that may be sent, given, back: *Is this bottle returnable?*

re·un·ion /ˌri:'ju:nɪən/ *n* **1** *nu* the act of reuniting or being reunited. **2** *nc* a meeting of old friends, former colleagues etc after separation: *a family reunion.*

re·unite /ˌri:ju:'naɪt/ *vt,vi* (to cause people) to come together again: *reunite friends after long years of separation; be reunited with one's family.*

rev¹ /rev/ *abbr* revolution (per minute) of a car engine, as in '*4000 revs*'.

rev² /rev/ *vt,vi* (*-vv-*) **rev (sth) (up)** (*informal*) to increase the speed of revolutions in (a car engine): *Don't rev (up) (the engine) so hard.*

re·val·ue /ˌri:'vælju:/ *vt* **1** to put another price on (something). **2** to increase the exchange value of (money): *revalue the currency.*

re·valu·ation /ˌri:ˌvælju:'eɪʃn/ *nc,nu*

re·vamp /ˌri:'væmp/ *vt* (*informal*) to improve the condition of (something): *revamp an old book with new illustrations.*

Rev(d) *written abbr* Reverend.

re·veal /rɪ'vi:l/ *vt* **1** to allow or cause (something) to be seen: *Bikinis reveal more than swimming costumes do.* **2** **reveal sth (to sb)** to make something known: *One day the truth about these events will be revealed. The doctor did not reveal to him his hopeless condition.*

re·veille /rɪ'vælɪ/ *n sing* (in the armed forces) music used as a signal to get up in the morning: *sound (the) reveille.*

rev·el¹ /'revl/ *nc* (usually *pl*) an occasion of revelling.

rev·el² /'revl/ *vi* (*-ll-*, *US* also *-l-*) **1** **revel in sth** to take great delight in something: *revel in one's success; people who revel in gossip.* **2** to have a happy, lively time: *They revelled until dawn.*

rev·el·ler (*US* = **rev·el·er**) /'revlə(r)/ *nc* a person who revels.

rev·el·ation /ˌrevə'leɪʃn/ *n* **1** *nu* the making known (of something secret or hidden). **2** *nc* something surprising that is revealed: *It was a revelation to John when Mary said she had married him for money.*

rev·el·ry /'revlrɪ/ *nu* or *pl* (*-ies*) a time of noisy, happy festivity and merrymaking: *when the revelry/revelries ended.*

re·venge¹ /rɪ'vendʒ/ *nu* deliberate harm to a person in return for harm done: *take revenge on her; have/get one's revenge (on him); do it out of/in revenge (for an insult).*

re·venge·ful /-fʊl/ *adj* feeling or showing a desire for revenge.

re·venge·ful·ly /-fəlɪ/ *adv*

re·venge² /rɪ'vendʒ/ *vt* **1** to do something to get

satisfaction for (harm to oneself or another): *revenge an injustice/insult*. **2** to get satisfaction by deliberately causing harm because of (oneself or another person) having suffered: *revenge a friend; be revenged on a persecutor*. Compare **avenge**.

rev·enue /'revənju:/ *nu* or *pl* income, esp the total annual income of the State. ⇨ Inland Revenue.

re·ver·ber·ate /rɪ'vɜːbəreɪt/ *vi* **1** (of sound) to be sent or thrown back again and again: *The roar of the train reverberated/was reverberated in the tunnel*. **2** (*fig*) to have a repeated effect: *The result of the strike reverberated through the whole community*.

re·ver·ber·ation /rɪˌvɜːbə'reɪʃn/ *nc,nu*

re·vere /rɪ'vɪə(r)/ *vt* (*formal*) to have deep respect for (a person): *I revered my grandfather*.

rev·er·ence /'revərəns/ *nu* the feeling of deep respect: *He was held in reverence by everyone*.

Rev·er·end /'revərənd/ *n* (abbr Rev(d)) (a title used of a clergyman, as in *'Rev John Smith'*, which is spoken as *'the Reverend John Smith'*).

Reverend 'Mother *nc* a Mother Superior of a convent.

rev·er·ent /'revərənt/ *adj* (*formal*) feeling or showing deep respect: *a reverent student*. Opp irreverent.

rev·er·ent·ly *adv*

rev·erie /'revərɪ/ *nc,nu* (*literary*) (an instance, occasion, of) a condition of being lost in dreamy, pleasant thoughts: *She sat by the river, lost in reverie*.

re·vers /rɪ'vɪə/ *nc* (*pl* —) the turned-back edge of a coat etc showing the reverse side, as on a lapel.

re·vers·al /rɪ'vɜːsl/ *nc,nu* (an instance of) reversing or being reversed: *a reversal of the normal procedure; a reversal of last year's marks*.

re·verse¹ /rɪ'vɜːs/ *adj* (*attrib*) opposite in position or order: *the reverse side of a coin*. **in reverse order** from the end to the start, or in the opposite order.

re·verse² /rɪ'vɜːs/ *n* **1** *nu* (the —) the opposite: *do the reverse of what one is expected to do*. **2** *nc* (the —) the back (of a coin, medal, disc etc): *The Queen's head is on this side; what is on the reverse?* **3** *nc,nu* (the position of) a part of a machine that causes backward movement: *Most cars have three forward gears and a reverse. Put the car into reverse*. **4** *nc* a change to bad fortune: *My finances have suffered a slight reverse*.

re·verse³ /rɪ'vɜːs/ *v* **1** *vt,vi* (to cause a vehicle etc) to go in the opposite direction: *reverse one's car into the garage*. **2** *vt* to change (the order or position of) (people, things): *Their positions are now reversed; Tom is poor and Ben is rich*. **3** *vt* to change (a decision, opinion) to the opposite: *reverse the decision of a lower court*. **4** *vt* to make (the charge for a telephone call) payable by the person who receives it: *reverse charges*.

re·vers·ible /-əbl/ *adj* (a) that can be changed: *a reversible decision*. Compare **irreversible**. (b) (of cloth etc) that can be reversed.

re·vert /rɪ'vɜːt/ *vi* **revert (to sb/sth)** **1** to return (to a former state, condition, topic etc): *The fields have reverted to moorland*. **2** (*legal*) (of property rights etc) to return at some named time or under certain conditions to the original owner).

re·view¹ /rɪ'vjuː/ *n* **1** *nc,nu* (an act, instance of)

reviewing: *a review of the year's sporting events*. **be/come under review** to be considered or examined. **2** *nc* an article that critically examines a new book, play etc: *write film reviews for a magazine*. **3** *nc* (*mil*) an inspection of military etc forces: *hold a review*.

re·view² /rɪ'vjuː/ *v* **1** *vt* to consider or examine (something) again: *review the situation/her medical condition in a month*. **2** *vt,vi* to write a review(2) about (a book, play etc): *His new novel has been favourably reviewed*. **3** *vt* (*mil*) to inspect (soldiers etc) formally.

re·view·er *nc* person who writes reviews(2).

re·vile /rɪ'vaɪl/ *vt* (*formal*) to use abusive language about (a person, thing): *revile one's persecutors*.

re·vise /rɪ'vaɪz/ *v* **1** *vt* to read (something) carefully, esp in order to correct and improve it: *revise one's estimates*. **2** *vt* to reconsider and change (something): *revise one's opinion*. **3** *vt,vi* to study (what one has learned) for an exam.

re·viser *nc* a person who revises.

re·vi·sion /rɪ'vɪʒn/ *n* (a) *nc,nu* (an instance of) revising or being revised: *Several revisions have been made to the plan*. (b) *nc* something that has been revised; corrected version: *This is a revision of an earlier edition*. (c) *nu* an act, occasion, of revising(3): *How much revision have you done?*

re·vi·tal·ize (also **-ise**) /riː'vaɪtəlaɪz/ *vt* to put new life, restore power or strength etc into (a person, plan etc).

re·vi·tal·iz·ation (also **-is·ation**) /ˌriːˌvaɪtəlaɪ'zeɪʃn/ *nu*

re·vi·val /rɪ'vaɪvl/ *n* **1** *nc,nu* (an instance of) reviving or being revived: *a revival of trade; a revival of former crafts; a revival of an old play*. **2** *nc* (also *attrib*) (a meeting intended to produce) an increase of interest in religion: *a religious revival; revival meetings*.

re·vi·val·ist /-ɪst/ *nc* a person who organizes or conducts revival meetings.

re·vive /rɪ'vaɪv/ *vt,vi* **1** (to cause a person, business etc) to come back to consciousness, health or a good state: *revive a person who has fainted; revive after nearly drowning*. **2** *vt* (to cause something) to come into use again: *customs which have never been revived; revive an old play*.

re·voke /rɪ'vəʊk/ *vt* (*formal*) to cancel, end, (a decree, consent, permission etc): *revoke a driving licence*.

re·volt¹ /rɪ'vəʊlt/ *nc,nu* = rebellion(1): *a state of revolt; rise up in revolt against the cruel rulers*.

re·volt² /rɪ'vəʊlt/ *v* **1** *vi* **revolt (against sb/sth)** to fight (against a government or authority): *The people revolted against their rulers*. **2** *vt* to fill (a person) with disgust or horror: *scenes that revolted all who saw them*.

re·volt·ing /rɪ'vəʊltɪŋ/ *adj* very bad and unpleasant: *a revolting taste/habit/smell*.

re·volt·ing·ly *adv* in a way that disgusts: *a revoltingly dirty child*.

rev·ol·ution /ˌrevə'luːʃn/ *n* **1** *nc* an act of revolving or going round: *the revolution of the earth round the sun*. **2** *nc* (abbr rev) a complete turn of a wheel etc: *65 revolutions a minute*. **3** *nc,nu* (sometimes R-) (an instance of) a complete change (in conditions, ways of doing things, esp in methods of government when caused by the overthrow of one system by force): *the Russian Revolution (of 1917)*; *revolutions in business practice because of computers*.

rev·ol·ution·ary¹ /ˌrevəˈluːʃənrɪ/ *adj* **1** (*attrib*) involved in, supporting, revolution(3): *a revolutionary policy/party/thinker*. **2** completely different: *a revolutionary idea*.

rev·ol·ution·ary² /ˌrevəˈluːʃənrɪ/ *nc* a supporter of (a) political revolution(3).

re·vol·ution·ize (also **-ise**) /ˌrevəˈluːʃənaɪz/ *vt* to make a complete change in (something); cause (something) to be entirely different: *The use of nuclear energy will revolutionize the lives of future generations*.

re·volve /rɪˈvɒlv/ *v* **1** *vi* **revolve around/round sb/sth** to go round in a circle: *The earth revolves round the sun. The life of the home revolves around the mother*. **2** *vt* (*formal*) to think about all sides of (a problem etc): *revolving a problem in one's mind*.

re·volv·er /rɪˈvɒlvə(r)/ *nc* a kind of gun with a revolving part that makes it possible to fire a number of bullets without reloading.

re·vue /rɪˈvjuː/ *nc* a theatrical entertainment with dances, songs and jokes.

re·vul·sion /rɪˈvʌlʃn/ *nu* (often used with *a, an*) (a) (sudden and complete change of feeling to) deep hatred or opposition: *be filled with revulsion; a revulsion against torture*.

re·ward¹ /rɪˈwɔːd/ *nc,nu* (something given) in return for work or services, the returning of lost or stolen property, the capture of a criminal etc: *offer a reward of £10 for information about a stolen necklace. What will you give me in reward for my help?*

re·ward² /rɪˈwɔːd/ *vt* to give a reward to (a person) (for something): *reward a man for his honesty*.

re·wire /ˌriːˈwaɪə(r)/ *vt* to provide (a building) with new wiring for electric current.

re·word /ˌriːˈwɜːd/ *vt* to express (something) again using different words: *If we reword the telegram we can save one-third of the cost*.

re·write /ˌriːˈraɪt/ *vt* (*pt* **-wrote** /-ˈrəʊt/, *pp* **-wrote** /-ˈrɪtn/) to write (something) again in a different style etc.

rhap·so·dy /ˈræpsədɪ/ *nc* (*pl* **-ies**) an enthusiastic expression of delight (in speech, poetry etc): *Everyone went into rhapsodies over Olivier's performance as Othello*.

rhet·oric /ˈretərɪk/ *nu* **1** (the art, theory, of) presenting facts and ideas in clear and convincing language. **2** (*derog*) exaggerated, insincere language: *the rhetoric of politicians*.

rhe·tori·cal /rɪˈtɒrɪkl/ *adj* (often *derog*) (too) concerned with the style of speaking and writing and not with the content.

rhe,torical 'question *nc* one asked for the sake of effect or to impress people, no answer being needed or expected.

rhe·tori·cal·ly /-klɪ/ *adv*

rheu·mat·ic /ruːˈmætɪk/ *adj* relating to, causing, caused by, suffering from, rheumatism. □ *nc* a person who suffers from rheumatism.

rheu·ma·tism /ˈruːmətɪzəm/ *nu* a painful disease with stiffness and inflammation of the muscles and joints.

rheu·ma·toid /ˈruːmətɔɪd/ *adj* of rheumatism:

rheumatoid arthritis.

rhi·no /ˈraɪnəʊ/ *nc* (*pl* **—s** or **—**) (*informal*) = rhinoceros.

rhi·noc·eros /raɪˈnɒsərəs/ *nc* (*pl* **—es** or **—**) a thick-skinned, heavy animal of Africa and Asia with one or two horns on its nose.

rhom·boid /ˈrɒmbɔɪd/ *adj* (*maths*) of the shape of a rhombus. □ *nc* a rhombus with only its opposite sides equal.

rhom·bus /ˈrɒmbəs/ *nc* (*pl* **—es**) (*maths*) a four-sided figure with equal sides, and angles which are not right angles (e.g. a diamond or lozenge shape).

rhu·barb /ˈruːbɑːb/ *nu* **1** (a garden plant with) thick, pink stalks which are cooked and eaten like fruit. **2** (*informal*) the noisy talk of many speakers.

rhyme¹ (*US* also **rime**) /raɪm/ *n* **1** *nu* the similarity of sound of two or more words at the ends of lines of verse, e.g. *say, play; measure, pleasure; puff, rough*. **without rhyme or reason** without meaning or sense. **2** *nc* a word which provides a rhyme: *Is there a rhyme for 'hiccups'?* **3** *nu* the use of rhyme: *The story should be written in rhyme*. **4** *nc* a short, simple verse using rhyme. ⇨ nursery rhyme.

rhyme² (*US* also **rime**) /raɪm/ *v* **1** *vt* to put (words) together to form a rhyme: *Can we rhyme 'hiccups' with 'pick-ups'?* **2** *vi* (of words or lines of verse) to be in rhyme: *'Ship' doesn't rhyme with 'sheep'*.

,rhyming 'slang *nc* a style of slang using words that rhyme to replace other words, e.g. *a terrible boat-race* (= *an ugly face*).

rhythm /ˈrɪðəm/ *nc,nu* (an instance, example, of) a regular succession of weak and strong stresses, accents, sounds or movements (in speech, music, movement etc).

rhyth·mic /ˈrɪðmɪk/ (also **rhyth·mi·cal** /ˈrɪðmɪkl/) *adj* having rhythm: *the rhythmic noise of a typewriter*.

RI /ˌɑːr ˈaɪ/ *abbr* Religious Instruction.

rib¹ /rɪb/ *nc* **1** any one of the 12 pairs of bones round the chest of a person or animal. **2** (a pattern of) a raised line in a piece of knitting.

rib² /rɪb/ *vt* (**-bb-**) **1** to knit (wool etc) in ribs(2) as round the bottom edge of a sweater. **2** (*esp US*) (*informal*) to make fun of (a person).

rib·bon /ˈrɪbən/ *n* **1** *nc,nu* (a length of) cotton or other material woven in a long, narrow strip or band, used for decoration, tying things etc: *She had a ribbon in her hair*. **2** *nc* a piece of ribbon of a special design, colour etc, worn to show membership of an order or as a military decoration (when medals are not worn). **3** *nc* a long, narrow strip of cloth: *His clothes were in ribbons* (= were badly torn).

,ribbon de'velopment *nu* (the building of) long lines of houses along main roads leading out of a town.

rice /raɪs/ *nu* (a plant with) white grain used as food.

rich¹ /rɪtʃ/ *adj* (**—er, —est**) **1** having a lot of money or property: *rich people*. Compare poor¹(1). ⇨ also strike²(6). **2** (of clothes, jewels, furniture etc) well designed and expensive. **3** (*pred*) **rich in sth** producing, having, a lot of it: *a country rich in minerals*. Compare poor¹(5). **4** (of food) containing a large proportion of fat, oil, butter, eggs etc: *a rich fruit cake.* **5** (of land, soil) able to produce strong plants. **6** (of colours, sounds etc) full; strong: *the rich colours of the national flags; his rich voice.*

rich·ly *adv* (**a**) expensively and attractively: *richly dressed.* Opp poorly². (**b**) thoroughly; fully: *He richly deserved the punishment he received.*

rich·ness *nu* the quality or state of being rich (esp 4,5,6).

rich² /rɪtʃ/ *n pl* (the —) rich people. Compare poor².

rich·es /'rɪtʃɪz/ *n pl* wealth; being rich: *go from rags to riches* (= from poverty to being rich).

rick /rɪk/ *nc* a pile of hay, straw, corn etc (in a field).

rick·ety /'rɪkɪtɪ/ *adj* likely to break and collapse: *rickety furniture.*

rick·shaw /'rɪkʃɔ:/ *nc* a two-wheeled vehicle for one or two passengers, pulled by a man.

rico·chet¹ /'rɪkəʃeɪ/ *nc,nu* (an instance of) the movement in another direction (of a stone, bullet etc) after hitting something.

rico·chet² /'rɪkəʃeɪ/ *vi* (**-t-**) (of a stone, bullet etc) to change direction after hitting something: *The bullet ricocheted off his helmet.*

rid /rɪd/ *vt* (*pt,pp* —; **-dd-**) **rid sb/sth of sb/sth** to make (a person, animal, place etc) free of: *rid oneself of debt/a country of malaria.* **be/get rid of sb/sth** to be/become free of a person, thing: *These stains are difficult to get rid of.*

rid·dance /'rɪdəns/ *nu* (usually **good riddance**) (used to express one's pleasure at being free of an unwanted person or thing.): *Good riddance to bad rubbish!* (said of an unwanted person who has left).

rid·den /'rɪdn/ *pp* of ride².

riddle¹ /'rɪdl/ *nc* a question, statement or description, intended to make a person think hard in order to know the answer or meaning: *Do you know the answer to this riddle?*

riddle² /'rɪdl/ *vt* **riddle sb/sth with sth** **1** to make many holes in a person, thing: *riddle a man with bullets.* **2** **riddled with sth** (*fig*) full of something: *writing riddled with mistakes.*

ride¹ /raɪd/ *nc* a journey on horseback, on a bicycle, bus etc: *Let's go for a bike ride. Have a ride on an elephant!* **take sb for a ride** (*informal*) to deceive or cheat a person.

ride² /raɪd/ *v* (*pt* **rode** /rəʊd/, *pp* **ridden** /'rɪdn/) **1** *vi,vt* to sit on a horse, bicycle, motorbike etc and cause it to go forward: *He jumped on his horse and rode off/away. He was riding fast. Have you ever ridden a motorbike?* **2** *vi* to go out regularly on horseback (as a pastime, for exercise etc): *I've given up riding.* **3** *vt* to float on (something): *a ship riding the waves.* **4** **let sth ride** (*informal*) to take no action over it: *I wanted to complain but I let it ride for a week or two.*

ride in sth to be carried in a passenger vehicle: *ride in a bus/taxi.*

ride on sth (**a**) to be supported by something: *a bird riding on the wind; a boy riding on his father's shoulders.* (**b**) (of money) to be bet on a horse-race: *I have £10 riding on the 2 o'clock race.*

ride sth out to survive bad weather, a difficult period etc. ⇨ storm¹(1).

ride up (of clothing) to move up the body: *My skirt rides up under this coat.*

rider /'raɪdə(r)/ *nc* **1** a person who rides a horse, bike, motorbike etc. **2** **rider to sth** an addition to a statement, agreement, verdict etc: *The jury added a rider to their verdict recommending mercy.*

ridge /rɪdʒ/ *nc* **1** a raised line where two sloping surfaces meet: *the ridge of a roof.* **2** a long mountain range. **3** a long stretch of high land between the tops of a line of hills.

ridi·cule¹ /'rɪdɪkju:l/ *nu* the act, state, of being made fun of; unkind joking: *She has become an object of ridicule.* **hold sb up to ridicule** (*formal*) to make fun of a person.

ridi·cule² /'rɪdɪkju:l/ *vt* to make fun of (a person, idea etc); cause (a person, idea etc) to appear foolish: *Why do you ridicule my proposal?*

rid·icu·lous /rɪ'dɪkjʊləs/ *adj* deserving to be laughed at; foolish: *You look ridiculous in that old hat. What a ridiculous idea/old man!*

rid·icu·lous·ly *adv*

rife /raɪf/ *adj* (*pred*) widespread; common: *Is superstition still rife in the country?*

rifle¹ /'raɪfl/ *nc* a kind of gun with a long barrel, (to be) fired from the shoulder.

rifle² /'raɪfl/ *vt* to search (something) thoroughly in order to steal: *The thief rifled every drawer in the room.*

rift /rɪft/ *nc* **1** **rift (in sth)** a split or crack: *a rift in the clouds.* **2** **rift (between sb)** (*fig*) a disagreement, quarrel: *a rift between friends.*

'rift-valley *nc* (*tech*) a steep-sided valley caused by sinking of the earth's surface.

rig¹ /rɪg/ *nc* **1** a way in which a ship's sails etc are arranged. **2** equipment for a special purpose. ⇨ oil rig.

rig² /rɪg/ *vt* (**-gg-**) **1** to supply (a ship) with ropes, sails etc. **2** **rig sb out** to provide a person with necessary clothes, equipment etc: *rig the children out for school.* ⇨ rig-out. **3** **rig sth up** to put something together quickly or with any materials that may be available: *They rigged up some scaffolding for the workmen.*

'rig-out *nc* (*informal*) a person's clothes: *What a queer rig-out!*

rig³ /rɪg/ *vt* (**-gg-**) to arrange, manage, (an event) dishonestly, esp for private profit or gain: *rig an election.*

rig·ging /'rɪgɪŋ/ *nu* the ropes, sails etc on a ship.

right¹ /raɪt/ *adj* **1** (*attrib*) of the side of the body etc that is towards the east when the front is toward the north: *In France people drive on the right side of the road. She holds her racket in her right hand. Take the right turning.* ⇨ right-hand, right-handed. **2** (*attrib*) worn on the right hand or foot: *a right glove.* **3** (often R-) (*politics*) having conservative views, expressing conservative opinions: *a policy that is right of centre.* Compare left¹(3).

right² /raɪt/ *adj* **1** (*pred*) (of behaviour etc) morally good, legal, just: *You were quite right to refuse. I try to do what's right. Is it right to hit children? It wouldn't be right if she got the job.* Opp wrong¹(1). **2** (of facts, reasons, time etc) correct, true: *Is this answer right? The answers are all right* (i.e. All the answers are correct). *Is your watch right? Is that the right time? Have you got the right* *fare? Which is the right side of this cloth? What she said isn't right.* Opp **wrong¹**(2). **all right** ⇨ **all²**(1). **get/keep on the right side of sb** ⇨ **side²**(6). **put sb right (about sb/sth)** to give a person the correct information. **put sth right** (a) to repair a machine, engine etc. (b) to correct an error: *I've offended you—what can I do or say to put it/things right?* (c) to make a clock or watch have the correct time. **3** most suitable: *The conditions are not right for sailing. The time isn't right for selling the house. She's the right person for the job.* Opp **wrong¹**(3). **4** in a satisfactory or healthy condition: *Everything seems to be right so let's begin. Are you all right?* Compare **wrong¹**(4). **(as) right as rain** (*informal*) healthy: *You'll be as right as rain after a holiday.* **put sb right** to make a person healthy again: *This medicine will soon put you right.* **5** (*maths*) (of an angle) measuring 90°.

right³ /raɪt/ *adv* on, in, to, the right side: *Turn right at the corner. Look right!* **right, left and centre** = left, right and centre. ⇨ **left²**.

right⁴ /raɪt/ *adv* **1** correctly: *if I remember right. Did he guess right? Can't you ever do anything right?* Opp **wrong²**. **get sth right** to do it correctly. **go right** (of a machine etc) to operate, work, correctly. **serve sb right** to be what a person deserves: *It serves you/her/them right!* **2** all the way: *We stayed right to the end. There's a fence right round the building. He turned right round. The prisoner got right away. The pear was rotten right through. The stain has gone right through the cloth.* **3** immediately: *I'll be right over* (= I'll come immediately). *She's right beside me.* **right away/now** immediately; without any delay: *I'm coming right away/now.* **4** exactly: *Put it right in the middle. The pain's right here.* **5** in a favourable way: *It all turned out right in the end.* **6** (used in many phrases to express agreement, approval etc): *Right! Right you are! Right oh! Right on!* ⇨ **all right** (**all²**(1)).

right⁵ /raɪt/ *nu* **1** the right side, direction, position, part etc: *Keep to the right.* **be on the right** to be on the right side: *The garage is on the right.* **2** (usually the R-) the political group, party etc having conservative views: *vote for the Right.* Compare **left³**(2).

right⁶ /raɪt/ *n* **1** *nu* what is morally good, legal, just: *He knows the difference between right and wrong.* **be in the right** to have behaved or acted correctly; deserve justice. Opp **wrong³**. **2** *nc,nu* (a claim concerning) what is legally, morally, traditionally etc accepted as true, justified: *What gives you the right to say that? I know my rights. You have no right to hit him. It's your right to have a pension.* ⇨ human rights. **by right (of sth); by rights** according to a legal or just claim: *He's British by right of birth. By rights you ought to pay the debt.* **in one's own right** due to one's personal qualifications: *She's a peer in her own right.* **right of way** (a) a right to go before other vehicles etc: *Cyclists have right of way here.* (b) a right (for people) to be on (an area of) private land: *Is there a right of way across these fields?*

right⁷ /raɪt/ *v* **1** *vt,vi* (to cause a boat etc) to come to the normal, usual etc position (esp upright): *The boat righted (itself) after the big wave had passed.* **2** *vt* to make (something) correct or true.

3 *vt* to make amends for (something): *to right a wrong.*

right·eous /ˈraɪtʃəs/ *adj* **1** (of a person) doing what is morally right; obeying the law. **2** (*attrib*) justifiable: *righteous anger.*
right·eous·ly *adv*
right·eous·ness *nu*

right·ful /ˈraɪtfəl/ *adj* (*attrib*) according to law and justice: *the rightful owner of the land.*
right·ful·ly /-fəlɪ/ *adv*

right-hand /raɪt hænd/ *adj* (*attrib*) on the right side: *a right-hand turning.* **one's right-hand man** one's most valued assistant.

right-handed /,raɪt ˈhændɪd/ *adj* **1** using the right hand to write, throw etc. **2** (*attrib*) designed to be used in the right hand: *right-handed scissors.*

right·ist /ˈraɪtɪst/ *adj* supporting, expressing, conservative political views.

right·ly /ˈraɪtlɪ/ *adv* morally; justly; for a good reason: *be rightly upset. She was sacked, and rightly so.* Compare wrongly.

right-minded /,raɪt ˈmaɪndɪd/ *adj* having opinions or principles that are fair, moral etc: *All right-minded people hate violence.*

right wing /raɪt ˈwɪŋ/ *adj, nc,nu* (*right-wing* when attrib) **1** (often (the) R-) (of) the political group, party etc having (more) conservative views: *the right wing of the Labour Party; very right-wing attitudes.* **2** (of) (the position of) a player on the right edge of a football or other sports field. ⇨ left wing.

ri·gid /ˈrɪdʒɪd/ *adj* **1** stiff; that cannot be bent: *a rigid support for a tent.* **2** (*formal*) firm; strict; not changing: *a rigid disciplinarian; practise rigid economy.*
ri·gid·ity /rɪˈdʒɪdətɪ/ *nu*
ri·gid·ly *adv*

rig·ma·role /ˈrɪgmərəʊl/ *nc* (*informal*) a long, disorganized account or description.

rigor mor·tis /,rɪgə ˈmɔːtɪs/ *n* (*Latin*) the stiffening of the muscles after death.

rig·or·ous /ˈrɪgərəs/ *adj* **1** careful and determined: *a rigorous search for drugs.* **2** harsh; severe: *a rigorous climate.*
rig·or·ous·ly *adv*

rig·our (*US* = **rig·or**) /ˈrɪgə(r)/ *n* (*formal*) **1** *nu* strict enforcement (of rules etc): *use the rigour of the law.* **2** (often *pl*) harsh; severe conditions: *the rigours of prison life.*

rile /raɪl/ *vt* (*informal*) to annoy or anger (a person): *It riled him that no-one believed him.*

rim /rɪm/ *nc* the outer edge of a wheel, cup, bowl etc.

rind /raɪnd/ *nu* the thick outside skin or covering (of some fruits, e.g. melons, or of bacon and cheese).

ring¹ /rɪŋ/ *nc* **1** a circular band of metal worn round a finger: *a wedding ring.* **2** a similar band for other parts of the body: *an ear-ring.* **3** a circular band of metal, wood etc for a purpose: *a key-ring.* **4** a circular shape. **run rings round sb** to argue, do things, better than he or she does. **5** a group of people (traders, politicians etc) working together for their own advantage: *a ring of trade union activists.* ⇨ ringleader. **6** an enclosed space for an activity: *a circus-/boxing-ring.*

'ring-finger *nc* the third finger of the left hand.

'ring·leader *nc* a person who leads others who

are doing something bad or wrong.

'ring road *nc* a road round a town to keep traffic out of the centre. ⇨ orbital.

ring² /rɪŋ/ *n* **1** *n sing* a clear musical sound (as if) of a bell. *a ring of truth (to sth)* a feeling of sincerity: *There was a ring of truth to his statement.* ⇨ ring true. **2** *nc* an act of ringing(2): *There was a ring at the door. I'll give you a ring* (= telephone you) *later.* **3** *n sing* a continuous sound: *the ring of happy voices; a ring in my ears.* ⇨ ring⁴(3,4).

ring³ /rɪŋ/ *vt* (*pt,pp* —ed) **1** to make, draw, a circle round (something): *Please ring the correct answer. The soldiers ringed the airport.* **2** to put a ring(3) on (something): *ring a bird's leg/a bull's nose.*

ring⁴ /rɪŋ/ *v* (*pt* **rang** /ræŋ/, *pp* **rung** /rʌŋ/) **1** *vi* (of a bell etc) to produce a clear, musical sound: *The* (*church*) *bells are ringing. I can hear the doorbell ringing. The alarm clock rang at 7 o'clock. Did the telephone ring? Who rang?* (= Who telephoned?). *ring true* to seem sincere: *Her excuse rings true.* **2** *vt* to cause (a bell etc) to sound, esp as a warning, signal, summons etc: *ring the doorbell. Did the cyclist ring his bell? Please ring* (= telephone) *a doctor. If you have any problems, ring the police. I'll ring you later.* ⇨ ring for sb/sth, ring (sb) up. *ring a bell* ⇨ bell. **3** *vi* (of the ears) to be filled with a long, high sound: *The noise of the bells made my ears ring. His last words are still ringing in my ears* (= I still think about them). **4** *vi* (of a place) to be filled with continuous sound: *The playground rang with happy shouts.*

ring (sb) back to telephone (a person) again: *She isn't here—please ring back later. I can't talk now—can I ring you back?*

ring for sb/sth to use a bell or telephone to call for a doctor, maid, waiter etc or a meal, taxi etc: *I'll ring for an ambulance.* ⇨ 2 above.

ring off to end a telephone call by putting down the receiver.

ring out to make a sudden, loud noise: *Then a scream/shot rang out.*

ring round to telephone one person or business after another (e.g. to find the best price.)

ring (sb) up to call (a person) on the telephone: *I'll ring (you) up after work. ring sth up* to record a sale etc on a cash-register.

ring (with sth) ⇨ 4 above.

ring·let /'rɪŋlɪt/ *nc* small curl of hair: *She arranged her hair in ringlets.*

ring·worm /'rɪŋwɜːm/ *nu* an infection of the skin producing circular markings.

rink /rɪŋk/ *nc* a specially prepared area of ice (for skating or hockey), or floor (for roller-skating).

rinse¹ /rɪns/ *nc* **1** an act of rinsing: *Give your hair a good rinse after you've used shampoo.* **2** a kind of solution used for colouring the hair: *a blue rinse.*

rinse² /rɪns/ *vt* **1** *rinse sth (out)* to wash something with clean water in order to remove unwanted substances etc: *rinsing soap out of the clothes; rinse the plates; rinse (out) the mouth.* **2** *rinse sth down* to help food down with a drink: *Rinse it down with a glass of beer.*

ri·ot¹ /'raɪət/ *n* **1** *nc,nu* (a) wild outburst of anger, disapproval, disorder etc: *Riots during the election were dealt with/put down by the police.* **run**

riot (a) to become noisy and wild. (b) (of plants) to be out of control by growing fast in wrong places. **2** *n sing* (*literary*) a great supply: *The flowerbeds in the park were a riot of colour.* **3** *n sing* (*informal*) a very amusing person or event: *The production of his play is a riot.*

ri·ot² /'raɪət/ *vi* to take part in a riot(1): *They were rioting all night after the elections.*

riot·er *nc* a person who riots.

ri·ot·ous /'raɪətəs/ *adj* noisy and wild: *a riotous crowd; riotous behaviour.*

riot·ous·ly *adv*

rip¹ /rɪp/ *nc* a long cut or tear.

rip² /rɪp/ *v* (**-pp-**) **1** *vt,vi* to pull, tear or cut (something) quickly and with force: *rip open a letter; rip off the cover; rip out* (= remove) *worn bricks and replace them; rip a pocket.* **2** *vi* (of material) to tear. **3** *vt rip sb/sth off* (*sl*) to rob a person; steal something: *rip off books from the library.*

'rip-off *nc* (a) (*sl*) an instance of robbing or stealing. (b) (*informal*) an instance of being tricked.

RIP /ˌɑːr aɪ 'piː/ *abbr* (may he/she/they) rest in peace.

ripe /raɪp/ *adj* (**—r, —st**) **1** (of fruit, grain etc) ready to be gathered and used: *ripe fruit; cherries not ripe enough to eat.* Opp unripe. **2** (of cheese) ready to be eaten. **3** (*attrib*) *ripe for sth* ready, fit, prepared for something: *land that is ripe for development* (e.g. for building houses or factories). **4** *when the time is ripe* at the most suitable moment.

ripe·ly *adv*

ripe·ness *nu*

rip·en /'raɪpən/ *vt,vi* (to cause fruit etc) to become ripe: *These apples are ripening beautifully.*

rip-off /'rɪp ɒf/ *nc* ⇨ rip².

ri·poste /rɪ'pɒst/ *nc* **1** (*fencing*) a quick push with a sword as a response. **2** (*formal*) a quick, angry reply in an argument.

ripple¹ /'rɪpl/ *nc* **1** (a sound of) a small movement on the surface of water, crops etc, e.g. made by a gentle wind. **2** a sound of quiet laughter or gossip in a crowd: *A long ripple of laughter passed through the audience.*

ripple² /'rɪpl/ *v* **1** *vt,vi* (to cause something) to move in ripples(1): *The wheat rippled in the breeze.* **2** *vi ripple (through sth)* to make the sound of a ripple: *the wind rippling through the trees.*

rise¹ /raɪz/ *nc* **1** a small hill; upward slope: *on the rise of a hill; a rise in the ground.* **2** *rise (in sth)* an increase (in value, temperature etc): *a rise in prices; have a rise in wages* (*US* = raise). Opp fall¹(2). **3** a progress (in development): *a rise in social position/in business influence; the rise and fall of the British Empire.* Opp fall¹(3). **4** (of a river, line of hills) a starting-point: *The river has its rise among the hills. give rise to sth* to be the cause of (usually) something unwanted or bad: *Such behaviour might give rise to misunderstandings.*

rise² /raɪz/ *vi* (*pt* **rose** /rəʊz/, *pp* —**n** /'rɪzn/) **1** to go, come, up or higher; reach a high(er) level or position: *The river has risen by a metre. Prices continue to rise. The temperature is rising. The water rose above the edge. The cake is rising in the oven. Smoke rose from the fire. His voice rose in* *anger/excitement. She has risen to the position of manager. New office blocks are rising in our town.* Compare drop²(4), fall²(1). **2** (of the sun, moon, stars) to appear above the horizon: *The sun rises in the East.* Opp set³(11). **3** to get up from a lying, sitting or kneeling position: *The wounded man fell and was too weak to rise. The horse rose on its back legs. The hair rose on her neck.* **4** (*formal*) to get out of bed: *He rises very early.* **5** to become visible above the surroundings: *A range of hills rose on our left. The mountain rose above the other hills.* **6** to become stronger: *The wind is rising* ⇨ drop²(5). **7** to come to the surface: *Bubbles rose from the bottom of the lake.* **8** to slope upwards: *The road rises at this point.* **9** to have as a starting-point: *Where does the Nile rise?* **10 rise (up) (against sb/sth)** to become active in opposing (a leader, government etc) by force. ⇨ uprising.

ris·ing /ˈraɪzɪŋ/ *adj* (*attrib*) **1** increasing in position, rank etc: *a rising politician/lawyer.* **2** developing; growing: *the rising generation* (i.e. teenagers).

'rising action *nu* (*literature*) the part of a story or drama when the plot is developed to produce interest and excitement that leads to the climax. Compare falling action.

risk¹ /rɪsk/ *n* **1** *nc,nu* (an instance of) a possibility or chance (of meeting danger, suffering loss, injury etc): *There's no/not much risk of injury if you obey the rules.* **at risk** threatened (by disease, failure, loss etc): *Is the Government's income policy seriously at risk?* **at one's own risk** accepting personal responsibility and agreeing to make no claims for loss, injury etc: *If you climb it, you do so at your own risk.* **at the risk of sth** with the possibility of loss etc: *He was determined to get there even at the risk of being killed.* **run a/the risk of sth; take risks** to put oneself in a position where there is risk: *She's too sensible to take risks when she's driving. He was ready to run the risk of being taken prisoner by the enemy.* **2** *nc* a person or thing that is insured; the amount insured: *He's a good/poor risk.*

risk² /rɪsk/ *vt* **1** to place (something) in danger: *risk one's health in the jungle.* **risk one's neck** ⇨ neck¹(1). **2** to take the chance of (something bad happening): *We mustn't risk getting caught in a storm.*

risky *adj* (**-ier, -iest**) likely to fail, cause injury etc: *a risky undertaking.*

ri·sot·to /rɪˈzɒtəʊ/ *nu* a dish of rice cooked with butter, cheese, onions etc.

ris·qué /ˈriːskeɪ/ *adj* (of a story, remark, situation in a drama etc) likely to be considered indecent.

ris·sole /ˈrɪsəʊl/ *nc* a small, fried ball of minced meat, fish etc.

rite /raɪt/ *nc* a ceremony (esp in religious services): *burial rites.*

rit·ual¹ /ˈrɪtʃʊəl/ *adj* (*formal*) done as (part of) a traditional ceremony: *ritual dancing/clothes.*

rit·ual² /ˈrɪtʃʊəl/ *n* **1** *nc,nu* (an example of) the forms connected with a traditional ceremony, religious service etc: *the ritual of the Catholic Church.* **2** *ħc* any procedure regularly followed as if it were a ritual: *He went through his usual ritual of cutting and lighting his cigar.*

ri·val¹ /ˈraɪvl/ *adj* (*attrib*) competing (with): *a*

rival business.

riv·al² /ˈraɪvl/ *nc* **rival (for sb/sth) (in sth)** a person who competes with another: *business rivals; a rival for her love/for the job; rivals in love/business.*

riv·al³ /ˈraɪvl/ *vt* (**-ll-,** *US* also **-l-**) to be as good as (another person, thing): *Can cricket rival football in excitement?*

ri·val·ry /ˈraɪvlrɪ/ *nc,nu* (*pl* **-ies**) (an instance of) being rivals: *the rivalries between the political parties.*

riv·er /ˈrɪvə(r)/ *nc* **1** (R- in names) a large, natural flow of water to the sea or to a lake, or joining another river: *the River Thames.* **sell sb down the river** (*fig*) to betray a person. **2** a similar flow of liquid: *a river of lava; rivers of blood* (as in war).

'river-basin *nc* (*tech*) an area drained by a river and its tributaries.

'river-bed *nc* the ground over which a river flows.

riv·et¹ /ˈrɪvɪt/ *nc* a metal pin for fixing metal plates (e.g. in a ship's sides), the end being hammered flat to prevent slipping.

riv·et² /ˈrɪvɪt/ *vt* **1 rivet sth (together)** to fasten something using rivets. **2** (usually *passive*) (*fig*) to fix or concentrate one's eyes, attention etc on: *His eyes were riveted on the scene.*

riv·et·ing /ˈrɪvɪtɪŋ/ *adj* of great interest: *Some television documentaries are riveting.*

rivi·era /ˌrɪvɪˈeərə/ *nc* (R- in names) a length of coast in a warm country that is popular for holidays: *the French/Italian Riviera.*

rivu·let /ˈrɪvjʊlɪt/ *nc* a small stream.

rm *written abbr* **1** room. **2** ream (of paper).

RM *written abbr* **1** Royal Marines. **2** Royal Mail.

RN *written abbr* Royal Navy.

RNA /ˌɑːr en ˈeɪ/ *abbr* (*ribonucleic acid*) a chemical substance present in living cells that helps produce proteins.

road /rəʊd/ *nc* **1** (R- in names; abbr Rd) a specially prepared way between places for the movement of vehicles and people: *travel by road. Is this the road to Brighton? Which road do you live in? Is this the main road? The Old Kent Road leads south. I live at 10 King's Rd, Swinton.* Ⓝ *'Road' can be used of the routes in the countryside as well as in towns and cities. 'Street' is used only in towns and cities.* **on the road** travelling. **2** one's way or route: *You're in the/my road* (= obstructing me). **3 the road to sth** the method of obtaining or achieving something: *the road to success. Is too much drinking the road to ruin?*

'road-block *nc* a barrier across a road to stop traffic (e.g. to catch a prisoner).

'road-hog *nc* (*derog*) a motorist who ignores the wishes of other drivers.

'road-map *nc* one showing routes between cities etc for vehicles.

,road 'safety *nu* safety from road accidents.

'road sense *nu* the ability to behave intelligently on roads: *Harry/Harry's dog has no road sense.*

'road·side *nc* the area along the side of a road.

'road·way *nc* (usually the —) the central part of a road, used by vehicles: *Dogs should be kept off the roadway.*

'road-works *n pl* an area where repairs are

being made to a road.

'road·worthy *adj* (of a vehicle, bike etc) fit for use on the roads.

roam /rəʊm/ *vi,vt* to walk or travel without any definite aim or destination over or through (a country etc): *roam about the world/from town to town; roaming the streets.*

roar¹ /rɔː(r)/ *nc* a loud, deep sound as of a lion, thunder etc: *the roars of a tiger; the roar of London's traffic; roars of laughter.*

roar² /rɔː(r)/ *v* 1 *vi* to make a loud, deep sound (as if) of a lion, thunder etc: *lions roaring in the distance. Several lorries roared past.* 2 *vt,vi* to say, sing, (something) loudly: *roar with laughter/pain; roar (out) an order.*

roar·ing *adj* (*attrib*) (esp) lively: *do a roaring trade.* □ *adv* (*informal*) extremely: *roaring drunk.*

roast¹ /rəʊst/ *adj* (*attrib*) (of meat) that has been roasted: *roast beef/lamb/chicken.*

roast² /rəʊst/ *nc,nu* (a piece of) roasted meat.

roast³ /rəʊst/ *vt,vi* 1 (to cause meat, potatoes etc) to be cooked in a hot oven or over a hot fire: *roast a joint. The meat was roasting in the oven.* Compare bake(1). 2 to heat (oneself) by sitting near a fire, sunbathing etc: *roast oneself by the fire; lie in the sun and roast.*

rob /rɒb/ *vt* (**-bb-**) 1 **rob sb/sth (of sth)** to take property from a person or place unlawfully (and often by force): *The bank was robbed last night. I was robbed of my watch.* Ⓝ Compare 'I had my watch stolen'. 2 to refuse to let (a person) have what is due: *He was robbed of an opportunity because he was ill.*

rob·ber *nc* a person who robs: *a bank robber.*

rob·bery /'rɒbərɪ/ *nc,nu* (*pl* **-ies**) (an instance of) robbing: *robbery with violence.* **daylight robbery** (*informal*) obviously charging prices that are too high.

robe /rəʊb/ *nc* 1 a long, loose dress: *a bathrobe.* 2 (*US*) = dressing-gown. 3 (often *pl*) a long, loose gown worn as a sign of rank or office: *magistrates'/judges in their black robes.*

robed *adj* (often **robed in sth**) wearing the kind of robe mentioned: *robed in black; professors robed in their academic gowns.*

rob·in /'rɒbɪn/ *nc* a kind of small, brownish bird with a red breast.

ro·bot /'rəʊbɒt/ *nc* a machine in a factory made to act like a person: *a car built by robots.*

ro·bot·ic /rəʊ'bɒtɪk/ *adj*

ro·bust /rəʊ'bʌst/ *adj* strong, active; fit, healthy: *a robust young man; a robust appetite.*

ro·bust·ly *adv*

rock¹ /rɒk/ *n* 1 *nu* the solid stony part of the earth: *a house built on rock.* 2 *nc,nu* (a) mass of rock standing out from the earth's surface or from the sea. **as firm/solid as a rock** (a) ⇨ solid¹(3). (b) (*fig*) (of a person) reliable; dependable. **on the rocks** (of a marriage) likely to end in divorce or separation. 3 *nc* a large stone: *rocks rolling down the side of a mountain.* 4 *nu* (*GB*) a length of hard, sticky sweet.

,rock-'bottom *nu* (also *attrib*) the lowest point: *His morale has reached rock-bottom; rock-bottom prices.*

'rock climbing *nu* the sport of climbing rocky mountainsides (with ropes etc).

'rock-crystal *nu* a natural transparent quartz.

rock·ery *nc* (*pl* **-ies**) an area of a garden with stones and small plants.

rock² /rɒk/ *nu* (also *attrib*) a kind of highly rhythmic popular music for dancing, using electric instruments: *rock music.*

'rock band/concert/festival *nc* one playing, of, rock.

rock³ /rɒk/ *vt,vi* (to cause a person, thing) to swing backwards and forwards, or from side to side: *rock a baby to sleep. The town was rocked by an earthquake.* **rock the boat** (*fig*) to do something that upsets the smooth progress of an undertaking etc.

rock·er *nc* (**a**) one of the curved pieces of wood on which a rocking-chair etc rests. (**b**) = rocking-chair. (**c**) **off one's rocker** (*sl*) crazy; mad.

'rock·ing-chair *nc* one fitted with rockers on which it rests.

'rock·ing-horse *nc* a toy horse with rockers for a child to ride on.

rock·et¹ /'rɒkɪt/ *nc* 1 a tube-shaped case filled with fast-burning material, which launches itself into the air (as a firework, a signal of distress, or as used to launch a spacecraft). 2 (*informal*) a severe scolding: *get/give him a rocket.*

rock·et² /'rɒkɪt/ *vi* (*informal*) to go up very fast: *Prices are rocketing!*

rock-'n-roll /,rɒk ən 'rəʊl/ *nu* (also *rock and roll*) = rock².

rocky /'rɒkɪ/ *adj* (**-ier, -iest**) 1 of rock, full of rocks; hard like rock: *a rocky road; rocky soil.* 2 (*informal*) unstable; insecure: *The table is rather rocky. His business is very rocky.*

rod /rɒd/ *nc* a thin, straight piece of wood or metal: *a fishing-rod.*

rode /rəʊd/ *pt* of ride².

ro·dent /'rəʊdənt/ *nc* an animal, e.g. a rat, rabbit, squirrel, which gnaws things with its strong teeth specially adapted for this purpose.

ro·deo /'rəʊdɪəʊ/ *nc* (*pl* **—s**) (in western US) a contest of skill in catching cattle with a rope, riding wild horses etc.

roe /rəʊ/ *nc,nu* a mass of eggs (*hard roe*) or male seed (*soft roe*) of a fish, eaten as food.

rogue /rəʊg/ *nc* a dishonest person.

role (also *rôle*) /rəʊl/ *nc* 1 an actor's part in a play: *play the role of Ophelia in 'Hamlet'.* 2 a person's task or duty in an undertaking: *What is your new role on the Committee?*

roll¹ /rəʊl/ *nc* 1 something made into the shape of a tube by being rolled: *a roll of carpet/photographic film; a man with rolls of fat on his neck.* 2 a small loaf of bread for one person: *a bread roll.* 3 a rolling(6) movement: *The slow, steady roll of the ship made us sick.* 4 an official list or record, esp of names. **call the roll** to read the names (to check who is present and who absent). Hence **'rollcall** *nc*. 5 a rolling sound: *the distant roll of thunder/drums.*

roll² /rəʊl/ *v* 1 *vt,vi* (to cause a person, thing) to move (along) by turning over and over: *The coin fell and rolled under the table. The brakes failed and the car rolled down the hill. They rolled the log down the hill. He rolled himself (up) in a blanket. The dog rolled over and over in the snow.* ⇨ ball¹(1). 2 *vt* to make (something) into the shape of a ball or tube: *roll a ball of string; roll the wool into a ball; roll a cigarette.* 3 *vt* to move (something) on wheels: *roll a piano into the corner.* **4** *vt* to cause (something) to become flat by rolling a heavy object on top: *roll pastry.* ⇨ roll sth out. **5** *vt,vi* (to cause cloud, smoke etc) to flow in a rolling movement: *fog rolling across the fields.* ⇨ roll away. **6** *vt,vi* (to cause a person, boat etc) to move from side to side: *The ship was rolling on the waves. The old man rolled down the street.* ⇨ pitch³(5). **7** *vi* to produce a long, deep sound: *The thunder rolled in the distance.* **roll one's r's** to say them with the tongue making quick taps against the roof of the mouth. **8** *vi* (*informal*) to begin and progress: *Let the good times roll!*

roll away (of cloud, smoke, fog etc) to reduce and disappear.

roll back (of waves, clouds etc) to move back gradually: *The waves rolled back and we saw the shell in the sand.* **roll sth back** to remove a carpet, cover etc by rolling it into a tube.

roll by (of time) to pass: *The years rolled by and we never met.*

roll down (one's cheeks) (of tears) to fall.

roll in to arrive in regular amounts: *Offers of help/Gifts of money were rolling in.* **be rolling in sth** (*informal*) **(a)** to have large amounts of money, jewels etc. **(b)** to be living in the rich state mentioned: *be rolling in luxury.*

roll on = roll by. **roll on sth** (*informal; imperative*) (of the hope or wish mentioned) to come soon: *Roll on pay day!* **roll sth on** to put something on by rolling(1): *roll one's tights on.*

roll sth out to make pastry etc flat by rolling(4).

roll over to move to face the other way by rolling or to turn over.

roll up (*informal*) to arrive (esp as a group): *My family always rolls up late.* **roll sth up** to make something into a ball or tube: *roll up a carpet. He rolled up his sleeves.*

roll-call /'rəʊlkɔːl/ *nc* ⇨ roll¹(4).

roll·er /'rəʊlə(r)/ *nc* **1** a tube-shaped object, usually part of a machine, used for pressing, smoothing, crushing etc. **2** a tube-shaped piece placed under an object to make movement easy, or round which something may be rolled easily: *The luggage in the airport is moved on rollers.* **3** a long, rolling wave.

'roller-skate *nc* a skate with wheels for use on a smooth surface: *a pair of roller-skates.*

roll·ing /'rəʊlɪŋ/ *adj* (*attrib*) having gentle slopes: *rolling hills/fields/land.*

roll·ing-pin /'rəʊlɪŋ pɪn/ *nc* a tube-shaped piece of wood etc for rolling pastry flat.

ROM /rɒm/ *acronym* (*computers*) read-only memory (the permanent memory that a computer uses to operate. The contents can be read but not changed or deleted). ⇨ RAM.

Ro·man /'rəʊmən/ *adj* of, concerning, ancient Rome: *the Roman Empire.* ◻ *nc* a person belonging to ancient Rome.

,Roman 'numeral *nc* I, IV, XL, M etc.

Ro·man Cath·olic /,rəʊmən 'kæθəlɪk/ *adj, nc* (a member) of the Christian group with the Pope in Rome as its leader.

ro·mance /rə'mæns/ *n* **1** *nc* a story or novel of love or adventure. **2** *nu* the class of literature consisting of love stories. **3** *nc* a strong friendship of people in love: *I still remember my teenage*

romances. **4** *nu* the qualities and experiences characteristic of love and adventure, esp when looked for in one's own life: *travel abroad in search of romance.*

ro·man·tic¹ /rə'mæntɪk/ *adj* **1** having, producing, feelings or ideas about love: *romantic music/ scenes; a romantic novel/woman/hero.* **2** having, producing, feelings or ideas about adventure and excitement: *a romantic journey.* **3** (of an account) imagined and untrue: *a romantic description of one's school days.* **4** (also R-) a movement (18th and 19th centuries) in art, literature and music concerning themes of love and beauty: *the romantic poets.*

ro·man·ti·cal·ly /-klɪ/ *adv*

ro·man·tic² /rə'mæntɪk/ *nc* **1** a person with strong feelings and ideas about love and happiness. **2** (a person favouring) a romantic(4) approach in art, literature or music.

ro·man·ti·cize (also **-ise**) /rə'mæntɪsaɪz/ *vt,vi* (to cause an event, account) to seem more romantic(2) than it was.

romp¹ /rɒmp/ *nc* an instance of romping(1): *have a romp in the fields.*

romp² /rɒmp/ *vi* **1** **romp (about)** (esp of children) to play about, esp running, jumping and being noisy. **2** to win or succeed quickly or without apparent effort: *John romped through his examinations.* **romp home** (of a horse, runner) to win a race easily.

roof¹ /ruːf/ *nc* (*pl* **—s**) **1** the top covering of a building, tent, bus, car etc: *How can you live under the same roof as her?* (= in the same building?) **hit/raise the roof** (*informal*) to become very angry and noisy. **2** (used for the top or high part): *the roof of the mouth; the roof of the world* (= a high mountain range).

roof² /ruːf/ *vt* **roof sth (with sth)** to put a roof on a building: *a shed roofed with wood.*

rook¹ /rʊk/ *nc* a kind of large black bird like a crow.

rook² /rʊk/ *nc* = castle¹(2).

rook³ /rʊk/ *vt* (*informal*) to get money from (a person) by cheating or by charging a ridiculously high price.

room /rʊm/ *n* **1** *nc* a part of a house or other building enclosed by walls and a ceiling. **2** *nu* a space that is or might be occupied, or that is enough for a purpose: *Is there room for me in the car? This table takes up too much room.* ⇨ roomy. **make room (for sb/sth)** to make enough space (for a person, thing): *Can you make room on that shelf for some more books?* **3** *nu* a need; opportunity: *There's room for improvement in your work. There's no room for doubt.*

'room-mate *nc* one of two or more people sharing a room or flat.

roomy /'ruːmɪ/ *adj* (**-ier, -iest**) having plenty of space: *a roomy cabin/cupboard.*

roost¹ /ruːst/ *nc* a branch, pole etc on which a bird, esp a hen, sleeps. **come home to roost** to affect the person responsible: *Her extravagance came home to roost a month later.* **rule the roost** to behave as, be the leader.

roost² /ruːst/ *vi* (of a bird) to settle down for the night to sleep.

roost·er /'ruːstə(r)/ *nc* a domestic cock.

root¹ /ruːt/ *nc* **1** the part of a plant, tree etc in the ground and which takes water and food from the soil: *pull up a plant by the roots*. **take root** (a) (e.g. of a plant) to send out roots. (b) (*fig*) to become established: *The new idea/method soon took root among the workers*. **root and branch** (*adv*) (*fig*) thoroughly; completely: *We must examine our business methods root and branch*. **2** the part of a hair, tooth, the tongue, a finger-nail etc that is like a root in position, function etc. **3** (*fig*) a basis: *He has no roots in society* (= is not settled, does not belong to any particular group or place). *Is money the root of all evil?* **get at/to the root of sth** to deal with a problem at its source. **pull up one's roots** (*fig*) to move from a home, job etc to start a new life elsewhere. **put down new roots** (*fig*) to settle in a new place. **strike at the root of sth** to attack, deal with, the origin of a problem, difficulty. **4** (*gram*) a form of a word on which other forms of that word are based: *'Walk' is the root of 'walks', 'walked', 'walking', and 'walker'*. **5** (*maths*) a quantity which, when multiplied by itself a certain number of times, produces another quantity: *4 is the square root of 16 and the cube root of 64*.

'**root crop** *nc* a plant with a root used as food.

'**root sign** *nc* (*maths*) the symbol $\sqrt{}$.

root·less *adj* (of a person) without an established place in society.

root² /ruːt/ *v* **1** *vt,vi* (to cause a plant) to send out roots and begin to grow: *Some cuttings root easily*. **2** *vi* **root about (for sth)** to search (for something) by turning things over: *rooting about among piles of papers for a missing document*. **3** *vt* **root sb/sth out** (a) to find a person, thing by searching: *I managed to root out a copy of the document*. (b) to get rid of a bad person, thing completely: *root out the troublemaker*.

root·ed /'ruːtɪd/ *adj* **1** (*pred*) **rooted to sth** fixed and unable to move: *He stood there rooted to the spot*. **2** firmly established: *a rooted objection to cold showers; deeply-rooted affection*.

rope¹ /rəʊp/ *n* **1** *nc,nu* a (length of) thick, strong cord or wire made by twisting fine cords or wires together. **give (plenty of) rope** (*fig*) to allow a person (much) freedom of action. **give sb enough rope to hang herself/himself** to leave her/him to cause her/his own ruin. **2** *n pl* (the —s) those round a boxing-ring or other place used for sport or games. **know/learn/show sb the ropes** know/learn etc the conditions, rules, procedure (of an action). **3** *nc* a number of things twisted, strung or threaded together: *a rope of onions*.

rope² /rəʊp/ *vt* **1** to fasten (a person, thing) using rope: *roping climbers together*. **2** **rope sb in** to persuade a person to help in some activity. **3** **rope sth off** to enclose an area with a rope: *Part of the field was roped off*.

'**rope-ladder** *nc* a ladder made of ropes.

ro·sary /'rəʊzərɪ/ *nc* (*pl* -ies) **1** a form of prayer used in the RC Church. **2** a string of beads used for counting these prayers.

rose¹ /rəʊz/ *n* **1** *nc* (a bush with prickles on its stems and producing) a colourful and usually sweet-smelling flower. **a bed of roses** a pleasant, easy condition of life. **be not all roses** to be not perfect; have some discomfort and disadvantages. **2** *nu* a pinkish-red colour. ⇨ **rosy. see**

things through rose-coloured/-tinted spectacles to be very optimistic.

'**rose-bed** *nc* a flowerbed of roses.

'**rose-bud** *nc* a bud of a rose.

,**rose-'red** *adj* red like a rose.

'**rose-water** *nu* perfume made from roses.

rose² /rəʊz/ *pt* of rise².

rose·mary /'rəʊzmərɪ/ *nu* an evergreen shrub with fragrant leaves used as a herb.

ro·sette /rəʊ'zet/ *nc* a small rose-shaped badge or ornament.

ros·ter /'rɒstə(r)/ *nc* = rota (which is more usual).

ros·trum /'rɒstrəm/ *nc* (*pl* —s or **-tra** /-trə/) a platform for public speaking.

ro·sy /'rəʊzɪ/ *adj* (**-ier, -iest**) **1** of the colour of red roses: *rosy cheeks*. **2** (*fig*) full of good possibilities: *rosy prospects; a rosy future*.

rot¹ /rɒt/ *nu* **1** the condition of being bad: *Rot has set in.* ⇨ dry rot. **2** (*sl*) nonsense: *Don't talk rot!* **3** (in sport, business etc) a succession of failures: *How can we stop the rot?*

rot² /rɒt/ *v* (**-tt-**) **1** *vt,vi* (to cause something) to decay: *Oil will rot your tyres. The wood was rotting away*. **2** *vi* (*fig*) (of a prisoner etc) to waste away: *She was left to rot in gaol*.

ro·ta /'rəʊtə/ *nc* (*pl* —s) (*GB*) **1** a list of people who are to do things in turn. **2** a list of the duties to be done in turn.

ro·tary /'rəʊtərɪ/ *adj* (of motion) moving in circles round a central point.

ro·tate /rəʊ'teɪt/ *vt,vi* **1** (to cause something) to move round a central point. **2** (to cause something) to take place in succession: *The office of Chairman rotates*.

ro·ta·tion /rəʊ'teɪʃn/ *n* **1** *nu* the act of rotating or being rotated: *the rotation of the earth*. **2** *nc* one complete turn: *five rotations an hour*. **3** *nc,nu* the regular coming round of things or events in succession: *the rotation of duties to be done; the rotation of crops* (i.e. varying the crops grown each year on the same land to avoid exhausting the soil). **in rotation** in turn; in regular succession.

ro·ta·tory /'rəʊtətərɪ/ *adj* relating to, causing, moving in, rotation: *rotatory movement*.

ro·tor /'rəʊtə(r)/ *nc* an assembly of horizontally rotating blades on a helicopter.

rot·ten /'rɒtn/ *adj* **1** having gone bad: *rotten eggs*. **2** (*sl*) very unpleasant, ill, bad etc: *What rotten luck! I'm feeling rotten* (= unwell). *How rotten of you to say that!*

ro·tund /rəʊ'tʌnd/ *adj* (*formal*) **1** (of a person, face) round and plump. **2** (of the voice) rich and deep.

rouge /ruːʒ/ *nu* a kind of fine, red powder or cream, used for colouring the cheeks.

rough¹ /rʌf/ *adj* (**—er, —est**) **1** (of surfaces) not level, smooth or polished: *a rough skin; rough to the touch*. Opp smooth¹(1). **2** not calm, with uncomfortable movements: *a rough ride by car*. Opp smooth¹(2). **3** not gentle; acting violently: *rough behaviour/children*. **a rough tongue** ⇨ tongue(1). **cut up rough** ⇨ cut up. **have a rough time** ⇨ time¹(2). **4** made or done without attention to detail, esp as a first attempt: *a rough sketch/translation; a rough draft* (e.g. of a letter). **rough and ready** only good enough for ordinary or general purposes, occasions etc: *rough and ready methods*. **5** (of sounds) harsh: *a rough voice*. **6** (*pred*) **rough (on sb)** (*informal*) unfair; bad luck: *It was rough (on her) to have to pay for everyone*.

rough·ly *adv* (**a**) in a rough(3) manner: *treat him roughly*. (**b**) approximately: *It cost roughly £5. It took three hours, roughly speaking*.

rough·ness *nu* the quality of being rough.

rough² /rʌf/ *adv* **1** in a rough(3) manner: *play rough*. **2 live rough** to live in the open (as a homeless person does). **sleep rough** (of a homeless person) to sleep in the open air etc.

rough³ /rʌf/ *n* **1** *nu* a rough state, ground or surface; unpleasant condition. **take the rough with the smooth** to accept what is unpleasant with what is pleasant. **2** *nu* **in rough** in a rough(4) way: *write it out in rough first*. **3** *nu* (the —) the part of a golf-course where the ground is uneven and the grass uncut. **4** *nc* a rough(3) person: *A gang of roughs knocked him down and took all his money*.

rough⁴ /rʌf/ *vt* **1** to make (something) untidy or uneven: *Don't rough (up) my hair*. **2 rough sb up** (*sl*) to hit a person: *He was roughed up by a group of boys*. **3 rough it** (*informal*) to live without the usual comforts of life: *Some students have to rough it*.

rough·age /'rʌfɪdʒ/ *nu* the coarse part of food e.g. the outer part of seeds, fruit etc. ⇨ fibre(3).

rough·en /'rʌfn/ *vt,vi* (to cause something) to become rough(1).

rough·ly /'rʌflɪ/ *adv* ⇨ rough¹.

rou·lette /ruːˈlet/ *nu* a gambling game in which a ball falls by chance into a numbered hole in a wheel.

round¹ /raʊnd/ *adj* **1** shaped like a circle or a ball: *a round plate/window/table*. **2** (*attrib*) done with, involving, a circular motion; going and returning: *round trip/tour/voyage*. **3** (*attrib*) complete: *a round dozen*. **in round figures/numbers** given to the nearest 10, 100, 1000 etc (and so not completely accurate).

round·ness *nu*

round² /raʊnd/ *adverbial particle* Ⓝ For uses of *'round'* with verbs such as **come, get, go, take** etc, ⇨ the *verb* entries. *'Round'* is less formal than *'around'* and is more usual in GB English than US English. **1** moving in a circle or curve to face the opposite way: *Turn your chair round and face me*. **the wrong way round** with the front at the back. **2** moving in a complete circle: *The wheels went round and round. The hour hand of a clock goes right round in twelve hours. Christmas will soon be round again*. **all (the) year round** during all the year. **3** (so as to be) in a circle: *A crowd soon gathered round*. **4** from one (place, point, person etc) to another: *Please hand these papers round. The news was soon passed round*. **5** by a longer way or route; not by the direct way: *The taxi-driver brought us a long way round*. **6 round about** (**a**) about: *It costs round about £10*. (**b**) in the neighbourhood: *in all the villages round about*. **7** measuring in a circle: *Her hips are a metre round*.

round³ /raʊnd/ *nc* **1** a (regular) set or series of events: *the doctor's round of visits; the postman's round* (i.e. to deliver letters). *The inspector makes his rounds of the factory every evening*. **2** (in games, contests etc) one stage: *a boxing-match of ten rounds; the sixth round of the football competition; have a round of cards; play a round of golf*. **3** a share, allowance, distributed or measured out: *pay for a round of drinks* (i.e. for every member of the group); *another round of wage claims*. **4 in the round** so as to be viewed from all sides: *theatre in the round* (= with the audience on (near) all sides of the stage). **5** a song for several people or groups, the second singing the first line while the first is singing the second line etc. **6** a slice (of bread): *a round of toast*.

round⁴ /raʊnd/ *prep* Ⓝ *'Round'* is less formal than *'around'* and is much more usual in GB English than US English. **1** (of movement) in a circle: *The earth moves round the sun. Drake sailed round the world*. **all/right round** all the way round: *We walked right round the lake/looked all around the room*. **2** (of movement) in a path changing direction: *walk/follow her round a corner. This road will take you round* (i.e. not through) *the town*. **be/go round the bend** ⇨ bend¹. **3** (of position) so as to be on all sides of: *They were sitting round the table. He had a scarf round his neck*. **4** in every direction: *He looked round the room. Can I show you round (the house)?*

round⁵ /raʊnd/ *v* **1** *vt,vi* (to cause something) to become round: *Can you round your hands to catch the ball? These stones have been rounded by the sea*. **2** *vt* to go, travel, round (something): *He rounded the bend/corner*.

round sth down to give a price, weight etc to the nearest whole number or 10, 100 etc by lowering it: *£10.18 rounded down to £10*.

round sth off (**a**) to make a corner, edge etc smooth. (**b**) to give something a satisfactory finish or end: *round off a speech with a toast; round off a meal with coffee; round off a career by becoming the managing director*.

round on sb to turn and become suddenly angry with a person: *His father rounded on him and asked why he was so late home*.

round sth out to provide a plan, painting, story etc with more detail.

round sb up to collect together a group of tourists, suspects, children etc. **round sth up** (**a**) to collect together animals, pieces of information, evidence etc. (**b**) to give a price, weight etc to the nearest whole number or 10, 100 etc by increasing it: *£147 rounded up to £150*.

round·about¹ /'raʊndəbaʊt/ *adj* (*attrib*) not using the shortest or most direct route: *I heard the news in a roundabout way. What a roundabout way of doing things!*

round·about² /'raʊndəbaʊt/ *nc* **1** a circular area where several roads meet causing traffic to go round instead of directly across. **2** = merry-go-round.

roun·ders /'raʊndəz/ *n pl* an outdoor game for two teams with a bat and ball, the players running through four points (called *bases*) arranged in a square.

rouse /raʊz/ *vt* (often *passive*) **1** (*formal*) to wake (a person) up: *I was roused by the ringing of a bell*. **2** to cause (a person) to be more active, interested etc: *be roused to anger by insults*.

rout¹ /raʊt/ *nc* a complete defeat and disorderly retreat: *The defeat became a rout.* □ *vt* to defeat (an army etc) completely: *rout the enemy.*

rout² /raʊt/ *vt* **rout sb out (of sth)** to get a person up and out (of a room etc): *We were routed out of our cabins before breakfast.*

route¹ /ru:t/ *nc* a way (to be) taken from one place to another: *The climbers had tried to find a new route to the top of the mountain.* **en route** /ˌɒn 'ru:t/ on the way: *They died en route (to the top).*

route² /ru:t/ *vt* to send (a person, ship etc) by a particular route: *We were routed through Dover.*

rou·tine¹ /ru:'ti:n/ *adj (attrib)* using a routine; usual: *a routine duty/method.*

rou·tine² /ru:'ti:n/ *nc,nu* the fixed and usual way of doing things: *use the standard routine.*

rove /rəʊv/ *vi (literary)* to wander (the more usual word): *roving over sea and land.*

rover *nc* a wanderer (the usual word).

row¹ /rəʊ/ *nc* a number of people or things in a line: *a row of books/houses/desks/cabbages; sitting in a row/in rows.*

row² /raʊ/ *n* **1** *nu* a noisy conversation, activity or disturbance: *How can I study with all this row going on outside my window?* **2** *nc* a noisy or violent quarrel: *have a row with the neighbours.* **3** *nc* an instance of being in trouble, told off etc: *get into a row for being late at the office.*

row³ /raʊ/ *vi* **row (with sb)** to quarrel noisily: *He's always rowing with his neighbours.*

row⁴ /rəʊ/ *vt,vi* **1** to move (a boat) by using oars. **2** to carry or take (a person) in a boat with oars: *Shall I row you up/down/across the river?* □ *nc* a journey in a boat moved by oars: *go for a row.*

row·er *nc* a person who rows a boat.

row·ing *nu* the sport, act of people who row.

'rowing-boat *nc* one moved by the use of oars.

'rowing-club *nc* one for people who row.

row·dy /'raʊdɪ/ *adj (-ier, -iest)* rough and noisy: *There were rowdy scenes at the elections.*

row·di·ly /-əlɪ/ *adv*

row·di·ness *nu*

roy·al /'rɔɪəl/ *adj (attrib;* R- in titles) of, suitable for, belonging to, a king or queen: *Her/His Royal Highness; the Royal Family; the Royal Navy/Air Force; a royal event.*

roy·al·ly /'rɔɪəlɪ/ *adv* in a splendid manner: *We were royally entertained.*

roy·al·ist /'rɔɪəlɪst/ *nc* a supporter of a king or queen, or of the idea of a monarchy.

roy·al·ty /'rɔɪəltɪ/ *n (pl -ies)* **1** *nu* royal people: *The play was performed in the presence of royalty.* **2** *nu* the position, power etc of a royal person. **3** *nc* a payment of money as a share of the profit, e.g. to a writer: *a royalty of 10%.*

rpm *written abbr* revolutions (of an engine) per minute.

RSPCA /ˌɑ:r es ˌpi: si: 'eɪ/ *abbr* (the —) the Royal Society for the Prevention of Cruelty to Animals.

RSVP /ˌɑ:r es vi: 'pi:/ *abbr (French: répondez s'il vous plaît)* please reply.

rt *written abbr* right.

Rt Hon *written abbr* Right Honourable (a title used by senior government ministers, some peers etc).

rub¹ /rʌb/ *nc* an act of rubbing: *Give the bruise a good rub with this cream.*

rub² /rʌb/ *v (-bb-)* **1** *vt,vi* to move (something) backwards and forwards on the surface of another: *He was rubbing his hands together. Rub this oil on your skin. Rub yourself dry on this towel. The dog rubbed itself/its head against my legs. I rubbed until my arm ached.* **2** *vi* to come into, be in, contact with something by sliding up and down: *What is the wheel rubbing on/against?* **rub against sth** ⇨ 2 above.

rub sth away to remove a mark, pain etc by rubbing it.

rub sb/sth down (a) to rub oneself, a person, animal thoroughly, e.g. with a towel, to make dry and clean: *He rubbed himself down after his bath.* **(b)** to make a surface smooth or level by rubbing: *Rub the walls down well before applying new paint.*

rub sth in/into sth (a) to force ointment etc into e.g. the skin, by rubbing: *Rub the ointment in well/well into the skin.* **(b)** to force a humiliating or unpleasant fact into a person's mind: *rub the fact that he's poor.* **rub it in** to remind a person repeatedly of a fault, failure etc: *I know I behaved foolishly but you needn't rub it in.* ⇨ also **nose¹**(1).

rub off to appear less bright, remarkable etc: *Their success has begun to rub off.* **rub sth off** to remove something (from a surface) by rubbing.

rub off on/onto sb *(informal)* to pass from one person to another by contact or close association: *Don't let the criticism of him rub off on you.*

rub sth out to remove a mark, writing etc by rubbing: *rub out a word/pencil marks/mistakes.*

rub sth up to polish something by rubbing: *rub up the silver spoons.* **rub sb up the wrong way** to irritate a person, make a person angry.

rub·ber /'rʌbə(r)/ *n* **1** *nu* a tough, elastic substance made from the milky liquid that flows from certain trees when the bark is cut, used for making tyres etc. **2** *nc* a piece of rubber material for rubbing out pencil marks etc (also called an *eraser).*

,rubber 'band *nc* a band made of rubber, used for keeping papers etc together.

rub·bing /'rʌbɪŋ/ *nc* an impression of something, e.g. a coin, by rubbing with wax etc on paper laid over it: *brass-rubbings.*

rub·bish¹ /'rʌbɪʃ/ *nu* **1** anything that is (to be) thrown away as worthless: *I put the rubbish in the dustbin (US = garbage).* **2** nonsense: *She talks rubbish. This book/What you said is rubbish.*

'rubbish bin *nc* a container for rubbish.

rub·bishy *adj (informal)* worthless: *rubbishy designs.*

rub·bish² /'rʌbɪʃ/ *vt (informal)* to (try to) make (written a report, idea etc) seem worthless by using (unfair or irrelevant) criticism: *The report on the city's housing problems was rubbished by the minister.*

rubble /'rʌbl/ *nu* bits of broken stone, rock or brickwork: *build roads with a foundation of rubble; a building reduced to rubble.*

ru·bella /ru:'belə/ *nu* = German measles.

ru·by /'ru:bɪ/ *nc (pl -ies)* a kind of red precious stone. □ *adj, nu* (of) a deep red (colour).

ruck /rʌk/ *nc* a irregular fold or crease (esp in cloth). □ *vi,vt* **ruck (sth) up** (to cause something) to be in rucks: *The sheets have rucked up.*

ruck·sack /'rʌksæk/ *nc* a bag carried on one's back, used by people on a walking holiday etc.

ruc·tions /'rʌkʃnz/ *n pl* angry words or protests: *There'll be ructions if you refuse.*

rud·der /'rʌdə(r)/ *nc* a flat piece of wood or metal at the back of a boat or plane, used for steering.

rud·dy /'rʌdɪ/ *adj* (**-ier, -iest**) (of the face) red and showing good health: *ruddy cheeks.*

rude /ru:d/ *adj* (**—r, —st**) **1** (of a person, speech, behaviour) not showing respect or good manners: *It's rude to interrupt/to point at people. Don't be rude to your teacher.* **2** (*attrib*) strong and unexpected: *get a rude shock.* **3** (*attrib*) indecent: *a rude joke.* **4** (*attrib; dated*) roughly made; simple: *the rude prehistoric implements.*

rude·ly *adv* in a rude manner.

rude·ness *nu*

ru·di·men·tary /,ru:dɪ'mentrɪ/ *adj* **1** including the first stage only: *a rudimentary knowledge of mechanics.* **2** undeveloped: *rudimentary wings.*

ru·di·ments /'ru:dɪmənts/ *n pl* **1** the first steps or stages (of an art or science): *learn the rudiments of chemistry/grammar.* **2** the earliest stage (of a development): *A new-born chick has only the rudiments of wings.*

rue /ru:/ *vt* (*old use* or *literary*) to think of (something) with sadness or regret: *You'll rue the day when you refused.*

rue·ful /'ru:fəl/ *adj* showing, feeling or expressing regret.

rue·ful·ly /'ru:fəlɪ/ *adv*

ruff /rʌf/ *nc* **1** a band of different feathers round a bird's neck, or of hair round an animal's neck. **2** a wide, stiff frill worn round the neck in Europe in the 16th century.

ruf·fi·an /'rʌfɪən/ *nc* a rude and violent young man.

ruffle /'rʌfl/ *v* **1** *vt,vi* (usually *passive*) (to cause a person) to become annoyed: *Ann is easily ruffled.* **2** *vt* **ruffle sth (up)** to disturb the smooth surface of something: *The bird ruffled (up) its feathers. The wind ruffled (up) my hair.*

rug /rʌg/ *nc* **1** a mat of thick material (smaller than a carpet). **2** a thick covering or blanket: *a travelling-rug.*

rug·by /'rʌgbɪ/ *nu* (also R-) a kind of football using an oval-shaped ball which may be handled: *Rugby League* (a form of rugby with thirteen players and allowing professionalism)*; Rugby Union* (with fifteen players and having amateur teams only).

rug·ged /'rʌgɪd/ *adj* **1** uneven and rocky: *a rugged coast.* **2** having wrinkles: *a rugged face.* **3** strong and determined: *a rugged personality/ expression.*

rug·ged·ly *adv*

rug·ged·ness *nu*

rug·ger /'rʌgə(r)/ *nu* (*informal*) = rugby.

ru·in¹ /'ru:ɪn/ *n* **1** *nu* a destroyed state: *brought to ruin by gambling and drink. The castle has fallen into ruin.* **go to rack and ruin** ⇨ rack². **2** *nu* a state of financial collapse: *Without any help from the bank, our business faces ruin.* **3** *nc* a building that has been destroyed. **in ruins** destroyed: *The house is in ruins. The town lay in ruins. Without you, my life is in ruins.* **4** *n sing* a cause of ruin(1): *Gambling was his ruin.*

ru·in² /'ru:ɪn/ *vt* **1** to destroy (something): *The*

storm has ruined the vegetables. **2** to cause (a person, business) to lose all money: *Expensive cars ruined her/the business.*

ru·in·ous /'ru:ɪnəs/ *adj* causing ruin: *ruinous expenditure.*

ruin·ous·ly *adv: ruinously expensive.*

rule¹ /ru:l/ *n* **1** *nc* an order, law or custom which guides or controls behaviour or action: *obey the rules of the game. It's against the rules to handle the ball in soccer. Is it possible to learn all the rules of English grammar?* **(by) rule of thumb** (using) a method based on experience or practice. **bend a rule/the rules** to interpret a rule loosely in order to do, allow, something that should not be allowed. **work to rule** to pay exaggerated attention (deliberately) to regulations and so slow down output: *Instead of coming out on strike, the men decided to work to rule.* **2** *nc* a habit: *He makes it a rule to do an hour's work in the garden every day.* **as a rule** usually; more often than not: *He's late as a rule.* **3** *nu* authority: *countries that were under French rule.*

rule² /ru:l/ *v* **1** *vt,vi* **rule (sb/sth); rule over sb/sth** to govern (people, a country etc); have authority (over): *King Charles I ruled (over England) for eleven years without a parliament.* **2** *vt* (usually *passive*) to have power or influence over (a person, thing): *Is it true that Mrs Jones rules her husband? Don't be ruled by your passions/by hatred.* **3** *vt* **rule (that) sth** to give something as a decision: *The chairman ruled the motion out of order/that the motion was out of order.* **rule sth out** to declare that something cannot be considered, is not possible: *That's a possibility that can't be ruled out* (= It is something we must consider). **4** *vt* to make (a line or lines) on paper: *ruled notepaper.* **rule sth off** to separate, end, something by drawing a line under it.

rul·er /'ru:lə(r)/ *nc* **1** a person who rules or governs. **2** a straight length of wood, plastic, metal etc used for drawing straight lines or for measuring length.

rul·ing¹ /'ru:lɪŋ/ *adj* (*attrib*) strongest: *his ruling passion.*

rul·ing² /'ru:lɪŋ/ *nc* (*esp*) a decision made by a person in authority, e.g. a judge.

rum /rʌm/ *nc,nu* (a portion of) a kind of alcoholic drink made from sugar-cane juice.

rumble¹ /'rʌmbl/ *nc* a deep, heavy, continuous sound: *the rumble of juggernauts through the village.*

rumble² /'rʌmbl/ *v* **1** *vi* to move with a deep, heavy, continuous sound: *thunder/gunfire rumbling in the distance.* **2** *vt* to say (something) in a deep voice: *rumble (out) a few comments.*

ru·mi·nant /'ru:mɪnənt/ *nc, adj* (*tech*) (an animal) that ruminates(2), e.g. a cow.

ru·mi·nate /'ru:mɪneɪt/ *vi* **1** (*formal*) to think seriously: *ruminate over/about/on recent events.* **2** (*tech*) (of some animals) to swallow food and then return it to the mouth later and chew it.

rum·mage /'rʌmɪdʒ/ *vi* to turn things over, move things about, while looking for something: *rummaging (about) in a desk drawer.*

ru·mour¹ (*US* = **ru·mor**) /'ru:mə(r)/ *n* **1** *nu* general talk, gossip: *Rumour has it that she will be promoted.* **2** *nc* a statement, report, story that is generally known (and possibly untrue): *There is a* *rumour that there will be a general election in the autumn.*

ru·mour² /'ru:mə(r)/ *vt* (usually *passive*) to say (something) as a rumour: *He is rumoured to have escaped to Dublin.*

rump /rʌmp/ *nc* an animal's buttocks.

,rump 'steak *nc,nu* beef cut from near the rump.

rumple /'rʌmpl/ *vt* to crease (something): *Don't sit on my lap or you'll rumple my dress.*

rum·pus /'rʌmpəs/ *n sing* (*informal*) a noisy quarrel or disturbance: *What's all this rumpus about?* **kick up/make a rumpus** to cause a noisy disturbance.

run¹ /rʌn/ *nc* **1** an act of running on foot: *go for a short run across the fields.* **at a run** running: *He started off at a run but soon tired and began to walk.* **on the run** (a) running away: *He's on the run from the police.* (b) continuously active and moving about: *I've been on the run all day.* **get/ give sb a (good) run for her/his money** to give a person strong competition: *We must give him a good run for his money.* **2** a short journey in a car, train etc: *Can we have a trial run in the new car? It's an hour's run by train from Oxford.* **3** a regular route taken by vehicles, ships etc: *The bus was taken off its usual run.* **4** a series of performances: *The play had a long run/a run of six months.* **5** a set of similar results, events etc: *a run of bad luck.* **6** a period of eager activity. *a run on a bank* a demand by many customers together for immediate repayment. **7** **get/give sb the run of sth** to get/give permission to use it: *I have the run of his library.* **8** the way in which things tend to happen: *The run of events is rather puzzling.* **in the long run** in the end: *It pays in the long run to buy goods of high quality.* **9** (in some games, e.g. cricket) a unit of scoring made by running over a marked length. **10** a long slope (for skiing). **11** the usual sort: *the common run of people; a hotel out of the common run* (i.e. different or better). **12** a place (for chickens etc): *a chicken-run.* **13** a long hole (in cloth) where a thread has broken: *a run in my tights.*

run² /rʌn/ *v* (*pt* **ran** /ræn/, *pp* —; **-nn-**) **1** *vi,vt* (of people, animals) to move with quick steps: *run fast; run upstairs; run three miles. We ran to help him. Don't run across the road!* **2** *vt,vi* (to cause an animal etc) to take part in (a race) on foot: *run the 100 metres; run in the 1500 metres. Are you running your horse in the next race?* ⇨ also-ran. **3** *vt,vi* (to cause something) to move quickly over, through, to the end of etc: *A shadow ran across the room. The car ran down the hill/into a tree. A shiver ran down his spine. I ran my eyes over the page. He ran his fingers through her hair. A thought ran through my mind. A pain ran up my arm. A whisper ran round the room.* **run its course** ⇨ course¹(2). **4** *vi* (of liquid, sand etc) to flow: *The river runs to the sea. Tears ran down her cheek. Who left the water running?* **5** *vi* (of a tap etc) to allow liquid to flow: *Who left the tap running? My nose is running.* **6** *vt* to cause (liquid) to flow and fill (something): *run a bath.* **7** *vt,vi* (to cause an engine etc) to work, operate: *Don't leave the engine running. He ran the programme on the new computer.* ⇨ run on sth. **8** *vi* (of transport) to travel as arranged: *The buses run every five*

minutes. Do the trains run on Sundays? **9** *vt* to transport (a person, goods): *I'll run you home in my car.* **10** *vt* to own, control, organize (a business etc): *What kind of business does she run? I can't afford to run a car. Who runs the house while you're away?* **11** *vi* (of a ship etc) to move quickly into the position mentioned: *The ship ran aground/onto the rocks.* **12** *vi* to become the condition mentioned: *Supplies are running low. I'm running short of money. The film is running late* (= is late finishing). **run high** ⇨ high². **run riot** ⇨ riot¹(1). **run wild** ⇨ wild². ⇨ also temperature. **13** *vi* to continue or extend (over the space mentioned): *shelves running round the room; lines running down the wall; a scar running across his cheek; a road running through the farm.* **14** *vi* to continue or extend (during the period mentioned): *The play ran for six months. The lease runs for a year/has a year to run.* **15** *vi,vt* to have (something) as a tendency or possibility: *Inflation is running high. You run the chance/risk of being killed.* **run in the family** ⇨ family(3). **16** *vi* (of colour, dye) to spread (into the water): *Will the colour/dress run if I wash it?* **17** *vi* (of cloth) to produce a long hole or series of holes because of a broken thread: *My tights have run.*

run across sb/sth to meet or discover a person, thing by chance: *I ran across her in Paris last week.*

run after sb to follow a person (in the hope of attracting her or him): *She runs after every man in the village.* **run after sb/sth** to run to try to catch a person, bus etc: *run after a ball/a thief/a bus.*

run against sb to compete with a person (in a race or in an election).

run aground ⇨ 11 above.

run along (esp *imperative*) (to a child) to go away.

run at sb (with sth) to attack a person (with a sword, long knife etc).

run away (from/to sth) to leave (an unpleasant place) quickly: *She ran away from home. He's run away to sea* (= become a sailor). **run away (from sb/sth)** to try to avoid a person, situation because one is afraid, shy etc: *Don't run away (from me/your responsibilities).* **run away with sb** (a) (of a vehicle) to go too fast to be controlled: *Don't let the car run away with you.* (b) (of feelings etc) to gain complete control: *Too often her temper runs away with her.* (c) to leave home with a person, usually to marry without permission or to live together: *John has run away with the boss's daughter.* **run away with sth** (a) to steal and run carrying something: *He ran away with the secret plans.* (b) to win a contest easily: *Martina ran away with the first set.* (c) to assume (wrongly) that something is true: *Don't run away with the idea that I'll lend you the money.*

run back to return running. **run sb back** (*informal*) to drive a person back to a place. ⇨ 9 above. **run sth back** to wind a film, tape etc again so that it is ready to use. **run over sth** to review events, information, a period of time etc.

run (an amount of time) behind (sth) (of a schedule, plan) to be late ending or starting (by the amount of time mentioned): *My appointments* *are running (twenty minutes) behind. I'm running ten minutes behind schedule.*

run down (a) (of a battery) to become weak and stop working. (b) (used as an *adj* (*pred*)) exhausted and weak: *She's very run down.* **run sb down** (a) to knock a person down while driving, cycling etc. (b) to say unkind things about a person: *My boss is always running me down.* (c) to find a person after a long search: *At last I ran her down in Madrid.* **run sth down** (a) to say unkind things about a business, job, design, plan etc. (b) to allow a factory etc to become less active, have fewer workers etc: *The coal industry is being run down.*

run for sth (a) ⇨ 14 above. (b) to compete for an elected office: *Are you willing to run for treasurer? Who's running for president?* **run for it** to run quickly in order to escape.

run sb in (*informal*) (of the police) to arrest and take a suspect to a police station. **run sth in** to prepare a car engine by driving a car slowly and carefully when it is new.

run into sb = run across sb. **run into sb/sth** to hit a person, thing, while driving, cycling etc. **run into sth** (a) to meet bad weather: *We ran into a storm.* (b) (of a salary, debt, amount) to reach the size mentioned: *His income runs into six figures.* (c) to reach the bad condition mentioned: *We've run into debt/difficulties/trouble/problems.*

run off to go quickly. **run sb off (sth)** to force a person to leave one's land, property etc. **run sth off** (a) to produce a number of copies of something by photocopying etc: *Can you run off 100 copies of this leaflet?* (b) to produce a piece of writing quickly: *run off an article for a magazine.* (c) to cause liquid to flow away: *run off the oil from the engine.* **run off with sb/sth** to (steal and) go away with a person, thing, quickly: *His daughter's run off with a married man/with the funds.*

run on (a) to talk without stopping. (b) (of time) to pass quickly. **run sth on** to join letters when writing, sentences instead of making paragraphs etc. **run on sth** (a) to use something as fuel: *This calculator runs on solar energy.* (b) to be concerned with something: *Our talk ran on problems in Africa.*

run out to come to an end: *Our stock/Time/The lease/Her patience is running out.* **run out (of sth)** to finish supplies (of something): *We're running out of milk/money/time.* **run out on sb** to desert, abandon, a person: *Poor Jane! Her husband has run out on her.*

run over to overflow: *The bath is running over.* **run sb over** = run sb down(a). **run over sth** (a) to read through notes, a speech etc quickly. (b) to practise a part in a play etc again. **run over to sb/sth** to make a quick visit to a person, home, shop etc.

run round to sb/sth = run over to sb/sth.

run through sth (a) (of a whisper, gossip) to pass quickly through a crowd, audience etc. (b) to read and check a list, report etc. (c) to examine details etc again: *I'll run through the main parts of my speech.* (d) to practise a piece of music, a part in a play etc again. (e) to spend a grant, allowance, fortune etc quickly and irresponsibly.

run to sth (a) to reach an amount or number mentioned: *The cost runs to £600.* (b) to be enough for something: *My salary won't run to a holiday in Mexico.* (c) to extend to something: *His novel runs to 800 pages.* ⇨ also **earth¹**(2), **ground¹**(1).

run sth up (a) to cause a flag etc to be raised. (b) to make (esp) clothing quickly: *run up a dress.* (c) to cause a debt to grow quickly: *She's run up a huge overdraft.* **run up against sth** to meet a difficulty, problem etc: *run up against a misunderstanding.* **run up to sth** to amount to a figure mentioned: *Costs are running up to £100 a day.*

rung¹ /rʌŋ/ *nc* **1** a short piece forming a step in a ladder. **2** (*fig*) a particular level in society, one's employment etc: *start on the lowest/reach the highest rung (of the ladder).*

rung² /rʌŋ/ *pp* of ring⁴.

run·ner /'rʌnə(r)/ *nc* **1** a person, animal etc that runs (a race): *How many runners were there in the Derby?* **2** a messenger. **3** a part on which something slides or moves along: *the runners of a sledge.*

,runner-'up *nc* a person or animal taking second place in a race.

run·ner bean /ˌrʌnə 'biːn/ *nc* (a climbing plant with) a kind of long, flat, green container of beans, eaten as food.

run·ning¹ /'rʌnɪŋ/ *adj* **1** (*attrib*) done, made, carried on, while or immediately after running: *a running kick/jump/fight.* **2** (*attrib*) (of water) flowing: *All bedrooms in this hotel have hot and cold running water.* **3** (usually *attrib*) (of sores etc) with liquid (*pus*) coming out.

,running 'commentary *nc* a commentary as the event occurs, e.g. of a football match.

'running costs *n pl* costs of production (not preparation, planning).

run·ning² /'rʌnɪŋ/ *adv* one after the other: *win three times running.*

run·ning³ /'rʌnɪŋ/ *nu* the act of a person or animal that runs, esp in racing. **in/out of the running** (of competitors) having some/no chance of winning. **make the running** (*literally* and *fig*) to set the pace. **take up the running** to take the lead.

run·ny /'rʌnɪ/ *adj* (**-ier, -iest**) (*informal*) **1** semi-liquid: *runny soup.* **2** tending to run(5): *a runny nose.*

run-of-the-mill /ˌrʌn əv ðə 'mɪl/ *adj* (*derog*) (too) ordinary; unexciting: *a run-of-the-mill job.*

run-up /'rʌn ʌp/ *nc* **run-up (to sth)** the period leading to an activity, election etc: *the run-up to the general election.*

run·way /'rʌnweɪ/ *nc* a prepared surface on which planes take off and land.

rup·ture¹ /'rʌptʃə(r)/ *nc,nu* (an instance of) something breaking or tearing: *a rupture of a muscle.*

rup·ture² /'rʌptʃə(r)/ *vt,vi* to break or tear (e.g. a blood-vessel).

ru·ral /'rʊərəl/ *adj* in, of, characteristic of, suitable for, the countryside: *rural scenery/life.* Compare urban.

ruse /ruːz/ *nc* a clever but deceitful way of doing something; trick.

rush¹ /rʌʃ/ *nc* a kind of marsh plant with a tall leafless stem, often dried and used for weaving into baskets etc.

rush² /rʌʃ/ n 1 nc,nu (an instance of) a quick movement. 2 nu hurried activity: *I don't like the rush of city life. Why all this rush?*

'rush-hour nc (the —) (also attrib) the period when crowds of people are travelling to or from work in a large town: *We were caught in the rush-hour traffic.*

rush³ /rʌʃ/ vt,vi 1 (to cause a person, thing) to go or come, do something, quickly: *The children rushed out of the school gates. They rushed more supplies to the hospital.* 2 vt to get through, over, into etc (something) by pressing eagerly or violently forward: *rush the gates of the football ground.* 3 vt to force (a person) into hasty action: *I must think things over, so don't rush me.* 4 vt (sl) to charge (a person) a very high price: *How much did you rush you for this?*

rush into sth to do something (too) quickly: *Don't rush into marriage.*

be rushed off one's feet ⇨ foot¹(1).

rush sth through to arrange for a decision, law etc to be agreed and confirmed quickly: *The new Bill was rushed through Parliament.*

rusk /rʌsk/ nc a piece of bread or biscuit baked hard and crisp.

rus·set /'rʌsɪt/ adj, nu reddish-brown (colour).

rust¹ /rʌst/ nu the reddish-brown coating formed on iron etc by the action of water and air.

rusti·ness nu

rusty adj ⇨ separate entry.

rust² /rʌst/ vt,vi (to cause something) to become covered with rust: *Water rusts iron.*

rus·tic¹ /'rʌstɪk/ adj (usually attrib) (literary) 1 characteristic of country people: *rustic simplicity.* 2 rough; unrefined: *rustic speech/manners.*

rus·tic² /'rʌstɪk/ nc (literary) a person living in the countryside, e.g. a farm worker.

rus·ti·cate /'rʌstɪkeɪt/ vt (GB) to send (a student) temporarily away from the university as a punishment.

rustle¹ /'rʌsl/ nu a gentle, light sound as of dry leaves blown by the wind: *the rustle of paper.*

rustle² /'rʌsl/ v 1 vt,vi (to cause something) to make a gentle, light sound (like dry leaves blown by the wind): *Did you hear something rustling in the hedge? I wish people wouldn't rustle their programmes in theatres.* 2 vt **rustle sth up** (informal) to get something together quickly: *rustle up some food for an unexpected guest.*

rusty /'rʌstɪ/ adj (-ier, -iest) 1 covered with rust(1): *rusty needles.* 2 (fig) (of knowledge etc) needing to be revised or practised: *My German is a little rusty.*

rut /rʌt/ nc 1 a deep line or track (as if) made by wheels in soft ground. 2 (fig) a way of doing something, behaving, living etc that has become (too) established. **be in/get into a rut** to be in/get into a fixed (and boring) way of living so that it becomes difficult to change.

ruth·less /'ruːθlɪs/ adj (of a person, behaviour, act) showing no pity, sympathy or mercy.

ruth·less·ly adv

rye /raɪ/ nu 1 (also attrib) (a kind of plant with) a grain used for making flour: *rye bread.* 2 a kind of whisky made from rye.

Ss

S, s /es/ (pl **S's, s's** /'esɪz/) the 19th letter of the English alphabet.

s symbol 1 second(s). 2 (former GB currency) shilling(s).

S written abbr South. □ symbol (commerce) small size (clothes).

Sab·bath /'sæbəθ/ n the day of rest, Saturday for Jews, Sunday for Christians: *to break/keep the Sabbath.*

sab·bati·cal /sə'bætɪkl/ adj, nc (of) a period of freedom from routine duties given to teachers, lecturers etc so that they can travel or study.

sable /'seɪbl/ nc,nu (the fur from) a kind of small animal with a bushy tail.

sab·otage¹ /'sæbətɑːʒ/ nu the deliberate damaging of machinery, materials etc to weaken an opponent's activity during an industrial or political dispute.

sab·otage² /'sæbətɑːʒ/ vt to carry out an act of sabotage on (machinery, a scheme etc).

sab·oteur /ˌsæbə'tɜː(r)/ nc a person who carries out sabotage.

sac /sæk/ nc a bag of skin (usually containing liquid) in an animal or plant.

sac·cha·rine (also **-rin**) /'sækərɪn/ nu (also attrib) a sweet substance often used instead of sugar: *saccharine tablets.*

sach·et /'sæʃeɪ/ nc 1 a small perfumed bag. 2 a small plastic bag (for shampoo etc).

sack¹ /sæk/ nc (an amount held by) a large bag of strong cloth or paper, used for storing and carrying heavy goods: *two sacks of potatoes.*

sack·ing nu strong cloth used to make sacks.

sack² /sæk/ nc (sl) a bed. **hit the sack** (sl) to go to bed.

sack³ /sæk/ n sing (the —) (informal) dismissal from employment: *He got the sack for stealing.* □ vt to dismiss (a person) from employment.

sack⁴ /sæk/ vt (of a victorious army) to steal from, destroy, (a captured city etc). □ nc the act of sacking a captured town etc: *The citizens lost everything they had during the sack of the town.*

sac·ra·ment /'sækrəmənt/ nc a solemn Christian religious ceremony (e.g. baptism, Communion).

sac·ra·men·tal /ˌsækrə'mentl/ adj

sa·cred /'seɪkrɪd/ adj 1 (attrib) connected with religion: *a sacred building.* 2 serious because of respect for a person: *a sacred duty. I believe his promise to be sacred.* ⇨ sacrilege.

sac·ri·fice¹ /'sækrɪfaɪs/ n 1 nc,nu (an instance of) (an) offering of something precious to a god: *the sacrifice of an ox; kill a sheep as a sacrifice.* 2 nc an example of giving up something of great value to oneself, e.g. so that another person will benefit: *Parents often make sacrifices (e.g. go without things) for their children.*

sac·ri·fice² /'sækrɪfaɪs/ 1 vt,vi to make a sacrifice(1) of (something): *sacrificing a lamb to the gods.* **2** *vt* to give up (something) as a sacrifice(2): *He sacrificed his life to save the drowning child.*

sac·ri·fi·cial /ˌsækrɪˈfɪʃl/ *adj* of, for or like a sacrifice.

sac·ri·lege /ˈsækrɪlɪdʒ/ *nc,nu* an act of treating with great lack of respect something that should be sacred: *It would be a sacrilege to steal from a church/to pull down the old theatre.*

sac·ri·le·gious /ˌsækrɪˈlɪdʒəs/ *adj*

sac·ro·sanct /ˈsækrəʊsæŋkt/ *adj* **1** (protected from all harm because) sacred or holy. **2** (*fig*) not to be treated with disrespect: *He regards his privacy as sacrosanct.*

sad /sæd/ *adj* (**—der, —dest**) **1** unhappy; causing unhappy feelings: *It was a sad day for Mary when her mother died. Why is he looking so sad?* **2** (*attrib*) bad: *a sad state/mess/condition/result.*
sad·ly *adv*
sad·ness *nu*

sad·den /ˈsædn/ *vt,vi* (to cause a person) to feel sad.

saddle¹ /ˈsædl/ *nc* **1** a seat for a rider on a horse, donkey or bicycle. ***in the saddle*** (**a**) on horseback. (**b**) (*fig*) in a position of control or power. **2** the long part of an animal's back eaten as meat: *a saddle of lamb.* **3** a line or ridge of high land rising at each end to a high point.

saddle² /ˈsædl/ *v* **1** *vt,vi* ***saddle sth; saddle up*** to put a saddle on (a horse). **2** (often *passive*) ***saddle sb with sth*** to give a person a heavy responsibility or burden: *be saddled with a wife and ten children.*
'saddle-bag *nc* (**a**) one of a pair over the back of a horse or donkey. (**b**) a bag at the back of a bicycle saddle.

sad·dler /ˈsædlə(r)/ *nc* a person, business, that makes leather goods for horses.

sa·dism /ˈseɪdɪzəm/ *nu* (sexual pleasure from) enjoying cruelty to other people. Compare masochism.

sa·dist /-ɪst/ *nc* a person practising sadism.
sa·dis·tic /səˈdɪstɪk/ *adj*

s.a.e. *written abbr* stamped addressed envelope.

sa·fari /səˈfɑːrɪ/ *nc,nu* **1** a hunting expedition, overland journey, esp in E and Central Africa (where *safari* can also mean any short trip away from home). **2** an organized tour (for people on holiday) to game reserves etc. ***on safari*** (esp) hunting or visiting wild animals.

safe¹ /seɪf/ *adj* (**—r, —st**) **1** (*pred*) ***safe (from sb/sth)*** free, protected, (from danger etc): *safe from attack/enemies.* **2** unhurt and undamaged: *a safe journey.* ***safe and sound*** unharmed: *return safe and sound from a dangerous expedition.* **3** not causing or likely to cause harm or danger: *Is driving at 120 kilometres an hour safe on this road? Are these toys safe for small children?* Opp unsafe. **4** (of a place etc) giving security: *as safe as houses* (= very safe). *Keep it in a safe place.* Opp unsafe. **5** that can be depended on: *a safe bet. Is this a safe seat for the Tories?* (= Is it certain that the Tory candidate will be elected?) **6** not likely to be difficult or risky: *They appointed a safe man as Headmaster. It's safe to say* (= probably true) *that most people like chips.* ***to be on the safe side*** ⇨ side²(8). ***better safe than sorry*** (*saying*) it is better to be very cautious than

to take risks.
safe·ly *adv*

safe² /seɪf/ *nc* **1** a strong box or compartment with a special lock, in which money and other valuables are kept. **2** a cool cupboard used to protect food from flies etc: *a meat-safe.*

safe·guard¹ /ˈseɪfɡɑːd/ *nc* a condition, act, that prevents harm or injury: *a safeguard against disease.*

safe·guard² /ˈseɪfɡɑːd/ *vt* to keep (a person, area etc) protected from harm: *safeguard the children against illness/injury.*

safe·keep·ing /ˌseɪfˈkiːpɪŋ/ *nu* the act, state, of being kept safe: *Leave your jewels in the bank for safekeeping.*

safe·ty /ˈseɪftɪ/ *nu* the state of being safe; freedom from danger: *The safety of the children is our first concern. We are doing this for your own safety. You are putting the safety of others at risk.* ⇨ road safety.
'safety-belt *nc* = seat-belt.
'safety curtain *nc* a fireproof screen that can be lowered between the stage and the audience of a theatre.
'safety match *nc* one that lights only when rubbed on the side of a matchbox.
'safety-net *nc* one used to catch an acrobat etc if he or she falls.
'safety-pin *nc* one with a guard for the point.
'safety razor *nc* one with a guard to prevent the blade from cutting the skin.

saf·fron /ˈsæfrən/ *adj,nu* (of) an orange substance from a plant, used as a dye and for flavouring food.

sag¹ /sæɡ/ *nc* an instance of sagging: *a sag in the seat of an old chair; a sag in sales.*

sag² /sæɡ/ *vi* (**-gg-**) **1** to sink or curve down under weight or pressure: *The roof is sagging.* **2** (*fig*) to become lower; drop: *Profits are sagging. Our spirits sagged as the weather got colder.*

saga /ˈsɑːɡə/ *nc* (*pl* **—s**) **1** a long story, e.g. a number of connected novels about a family, social group etc: *the Forsyte Saga.* **2** a long account (of troubles, bad experiences etc): *I had to listen to boring sagas about her holiday.*

sa·ga·cious /səˈɡeɪʃəs/ *adj* (*formal*) wise.
sa·ga·cious·ly *adv*

sa·gac·ity /səˈɡæsətɪ/ *nu* (*formal*) wisdom.

sage¹ /seɪdʒ/ *adj, nc* (of) a wise and experienced man.

sage² /seɪdʒ/ *nu* a plant with dull greyish-green leaves, used as a herb: *sage and onions.*
ˌsage-'green *adj, nu* (of) a light green colour.

Sag·it·ta·ri·us /ˌsædʒɪˈteərɪəs/ *n* the Archer, ninth sign of the zodiac.

sa·go /ˈseɪɡəʊ/ *nu* (also *attrib*) hard, white grains (to be) cooked in milk and sugar: *sago pudding.*

said /sed/ *pt,pp* of say².

sail¹ /seɪl/ *n* **1** *nc,nu* a sheet of cloth spread to catch the wind and move a boat or ship forward: *hoist/lower the sails.* ***under sail*** (moving) with sails spread. ***set sail (from/to/for a place)*** to begin a voyage. **2** *nc* a set of boards attached to the arm of a windmill to catch the wind. **3** *nc* (rarely *pl*) a voyage or trip on water for pleasure: *go for a sail. How many days' sail is it from Hull to Oslo?*

sail² /seɪl/ *v* **1** *vi,vt* (of a person) (to cause a ship etc) to travel across the sea, a lake etc: *We sailed (the boat) along/up the river.* **2** *vi* (of a ship etc) to travel in water: *The yachts sailed into the harbour. When does this ship sail?* **3** *vi,vt* to be able to control and direct (a sailing boat etc): *Do you sail? Can you sail a yacht?* **4** *vi* to move smoothly: *The clouds sailed across the sky.* **5** *vi* to achieve something easily: *She sailed into a new job/sailed through the interview.* ⇨ plain sailing.

sail·ing *nu* the sport, act, of controlling and directing a sailing-boat.

'sail·ing-boat *nc* any boat with sails.

sail·or /'seɪlə(r)/ *nc* a member of a ship's crew or a navy.

saint /seɪnt/ *GB usual form immediately before names:* sənt/ *nc* **1** (S- in names; abbr St) a person who lived a holy and worthwhile life and so (according to Christians) is among the blessed in Heaven. ⇨ patron saint. **2** an unselfish or patient person: *What a saint my wife is!*

St ,Agnes 'Eve *n* 20 January night.

St Bernard /'bɜːnəd/ *nc* a large, powerful breed of dog.

St 'Andrew's Day *n* 30 November (the patron saint of Scotland).

St 'David's Day *n* 1 March (the patron saint of Wales).

St 'George's Day *n* 23 April (the patron saint of England).

St 'Patrick's Day *n* 17 March (the patron saint of Ireland).

St 'Valentine's Day *n* 14 February. ⇨ Valentine.

saint·ly *adj* (also **'saint·like**) very holy or good: *The boy had a saintly expression on his face.*

sake /seɪk/ *n* **for the sake of sb/sth; for my, your** *etc* **sake** for the good or benefit of a person, thing; because of an interest in or desire for: *He argues for the sake of arguing* (i.e. only because he likes arguing). *Do it for my sake* (i.e. if only to please me). ⇨ also pity¹(1).

sa·la·cious /sə'leɪʃəs/ *adj* (*formal*) (of a speech, book, picture etc) obscene; indecent.

sa·la·cious·ly *adv*

sal·ad /'sæləd/ *n* **1** *nc,nu* (also *attrib*) (a cold dish of) (usually uncooked) vegetables such as lettuce, cucumber, tomatoes: *a green salad; cold beef and salad; salad cream.* ⇨ fruit salad. **2** *nu* lettuce or other green vegetables for eating raw.

'salad days *n pl* the period of inexperienced youth.

'salad-dressing *nu* a mixture of oil, vinegar etc used with salad.

sa·la·mi /sə'lɑːmɪ/ *nu* a kind of cooked sausage, salted and flavoured with garlic.

sal·ary /'sælərɪ/ *nc* (*pl* **-ies**) a (weekly, monthly) payment for employment based on a total amount for a year: *a salary of £12 000 a year.* Compare wage.

sal·ar·ied *adj* receiving a salary.

sale /seɪl/ *n* **1** *nu* an exchange of goods or property for money; act of selling: *The sale of his old home made him sad.* **for sale** intended to be sold: *Is the house for sale?* **on sale** (of goods in shops etc) offered for buying. **put sth up for sale** to offer it to be sold: *I've put my house up for sale.* **2** *nc* an instance of selling something: *Sales are up/down this month* (= more/fewer goods

have been sold). **3** *nc* the offering of goods at lower prices than usual: *visit the sales; the winter/ summer sales. I bought it in a sale.*

'sale-room *nc* a room where goods are sold by public auction.

'sales department *nc* the part of a business company that is concerned with selling.

'sales·man (*pl* **-men** /-mən/) *nc* a man selling goods to businesses or to customers in shops.

'sales·man·ship /-mənʃɪp/ *nu* the skill of selling goods.

'sales·person *nc* (*pl* **-persons**) a person selling goods to businesses or to customers in shops.

'sales talk *nu* talk (to a prospective customer) in order to sell something.

'sales·woman *nc* (*pl* **-women**) a woman selling goods to businesses or to customers in shops.

sa·li·ent /'seɪlɪənt/ *adj* (*attrib; formal*) most important or most significant; easily noticed: *the salient points of a speech.*

sa·line /'seɪlaɪn/ *adj* (*tech*) containing salt: *a saline solution.* □ *nu* a solution of salt and water.

sa·li·va /sə'laɪvə/ *nu* the natural liquid present in the mouth.

sa·li·vary /'sælɪvərɪ US: -verɪ/ *adj* of, producing, saliva: *the salivary glands.*

sali·vate /'sælɪveɪt/ *vi* to produce saliva (e.g. when thinking of food or something pleasurable).

sal·low /'sæləʊ/ *adj* (**—er, —est**) (of the skin) having an unhealthy yellow colour.

sal·ly¹ /'sælɪ/ *nc* (*pl* **-ies**) a sudden breaking out by soldiers who are surrounded by the enemy.

sal·ly² /'sælɪ/ *vi* **1** to make a sally. **2** *sally forth* (*dated*) to go out for a walk.

salm·on /'sæmən/ *nc,nu* (*pl* **—**) (also *attrib*) (the flesh of) a large fish with firm pink flesh, eaten as food: *smoked salmon sandwiches.*

,salmon·'pink *adj, nu* yellowish-pink (colour).

sal·on /'sælɒn/ *nc* **1** a meeting of fashionable, intelligent etc people at the house of a rich and famous lady (esp in Paris). **2** a business offering services connected with fashion etc: *a beauty salon.*

sa·loon /sə'luːn/ *nc* **1** a comfortable room for social use (e.g. drinking alcohol) in a pub, hotel, ship etc. **2** (*GB*) (also *saloon car*) a car for 4 or 5 passengers with a roof and windows.

sa'loon bar *nc* = saloon(1).

salt¹ /sɔːlt/ *adj* (*attrib*) containing, tasting of, salt: *salt-water.* Compare fresh(1).

salty *adj* (**-ier, -iest**)

salt² /sɔːlt/ *n* **1** *nu* the white powder used to flavour food: *table salt. Would you pass the salt, please?* **rub salt in the wound** (*fig*) to make a person feel more shame, suffering etc. **take sth with a pinch of salt** to feel a little doubt about whether a statement etc is true. **the salt of the earth** a person with very high or worthy qualities. **2** *nc* (*science*) any chemical compound made from a metal and an acid. **3** (*pl*) medicine used to empty the bowels: *take a dose of (Epsom) salts.* **4** *nu* (*fig*) something that gives flavour or appeal: *Adventure is the salt of life to some people.*

'salt-cellar *nc* a small container for salt, used during meals.

salt³ /sɔːlt/ *vt* to put salt in or on (food).

SALT /sɔːlt/ *acronym* Strategic Arms Limitation Talks (to reduce, especially, nuclear weapons in

Europe).

sa·lu·bri·ous /sə'lu:briəs/ adj (formal) (esp of climate) making people healthy: *the salubrious air of Switzerland.*

salu·tary /'sæljʊtrɪ/ adj (usually *attrib*) favouring mental or physical health: *salutary exercise/advice.*

salu·ta·tion /ˌsæljʊ'teɪʃn/ nc,nu (formal) (an act or expression of) greeting or goodwill (e.g. a bow or a kiss).

sa·lute¹ /sə'lu:t/ nc 1 an act to welcome a person or to show respect or honour, esp (e.g. in the armed forces) the raising of the hand to the forehead: *give a salute.* 2 any friendly greeting such as a wave.

sa·lute² /sə'lu:t/ v 1 vt,vi to give a salute (to a person): *The soldier saluted (his officer).* 2 vt to greet (a person) (e.g. by waving).

sal·vage¹ /'sælvɪdʒ/ nu (also *attrib*) 1 the saving of property from loss (in a fire or other disaster, e.g. a wrecked ship): *a salvage company.* 2 the property saved. 3 (the saving of) waste material that can be used again after being processed.

sal·vage² /'sælvɪdʒ/ vt to save (property) from loss, fire, wreck etc.

sal·va·tion /sæl'veɪʃn/ nu 1 the act of saving, the state of having been saved, from sin. 2 something that prevents loss, disaster etc: *Government loans have been the salvation of several small businesses.* **Sal·vation 'Army** n (the —) a Christian organization for the revival of religion and for helping the poor.

salve¹ /sælv/ nc,nu (a kind of) oily medicinal substance, used on wounds, sores or burns: *lipsalve.*

salve² /sælv/ vt to calm (one's conscience): *It is pointless trying to salve one's conscience by giving stolen money to charity.*

Sa·mari·tan /sə'mærɪtən/ n a member of a group (the *Samaritans*) giving help to people in despair.

same¹ /seɪm/ adj 1 **the same** + *noun* not different or changed: *He's the same age as me. We lived in the same house for 50 years. Is it the same address? Put it back in the same place (that you took it from). I've got the same pen as you.* **at the same time** ⇨ time¹(4). **the same thing** ⇨ thing(3). ⇨ also boat, breath(2). Compare different. 2 (used with *this, that, these, those*) already mentioned, referred to or thought of: *On Monday I wasn't at work and on that same day the factory caught fire.*

same² /seɪm/ adv **the same** in the same way: *Older people don't feel the same about pop music.*

same³ /seɪm/ pron **the same** the same person, thing etc: *I'd do exactly the same if I were you. He thinks all children are the same. Waitress—I'll have the same again, please.* (i.e. the same drink). **all the same** ⇨ all²(1). **And the same to you** (sl) I hope you experience the same (bad luck or experience). **much the same** ⇨ much²(2). **be all/just the same to sb** to make no difference to a person: *You can do it now or later; it's all the same to me.* **Same here!** The same (idea, feeling, effect etc) applies to me too: *'I'm very hungry'—'Same here!'*

same·ness nu the condition of being the same (and so being uninteresting).

samo·var /'sæməvɑ:(r)/ nc a container used in Russia for making tea.

sam·pan /'sæmpæn/ nc a kind of small, flat-bottomed boat, used in the Far East.

sample¹ /'sɑ:mpl/ nc one of a number, part of a whole, used to show what the rest is like.

sample² /'sɑ:mpl/ vt to take a sample of (something); test a part of (it): *sampling the quality of the wine.*

sana·tor·ium /ˌsænə'tɔ:rɪəm/ nc (*pl* —**s**) a place for the treatment of people who have been ill and need rest and care.

sanc·ti·fy /'sæŋktɪfaɪ/ vt (*pt,pp* -**ied**) to make (a building etc) holy: *sanctify a church.*

sanc·ti·moni·ous /ˌsæŋktɪ'məʊnɪəs/ adj (derog) making a show (often insincere) of being religious.

sanc·ti·moni·ous·ly adv

sanc·tion¹ /'sæŋkʃn/ n 1 nu the right or permission given by authority to do something: *You cannot translate a book without the sanction of the author.* 2 nc an action used against a person, country etc breaking a rule of acceptable moral behaviour, a law etc: *apply economic sanctions against a country.* 3 nc (formal) a reason for obeying a rule etc: *The best moral sanction is that of conscience.*

sanc·tion² /'sæŋkʃn/ vt to approve of, allow, (an action, method etc) officially: *Torture should never be sanctioned.*

sanc·ti·ty /'sæŋktətɪ/ nu holiness: *break the sanctity of an oath.*

sanc·tu·ary /'sæŋktʃʊərɪ/ n (*pl* -**ies**) 1 nc a holy or sacred place, esp in a church, temple or mosque. 2 nc a country offering safety from unfair or cruel treatment: *Britain has been a sanctuary of political refugees.* 3 nu (the right of offering) freedom from arrest: *to seek/be offered sanctuary.* 4 nc an area where it is illegal to harm or kill birds, animals etc: *a bird sanctuary.*

sand¹ /sænd/ n 1 nu (a mass of) finely crushed rock as seen on the beach, in deserts etc. 2 (often *pl*) an expanse of sand (on the seashore or a desert).

'sand·bag nc a bag filled with sand, used in groups as a defensive wall (against flooding etc).

'sand·bank nc a hill of sand in a river or the sea.

'sand·bar nc a long high bar of sand at the mouth of a river or harbour.

'sand·blast vt to send a fast flow of sand against (e.g. stonework) to clean it, or against (glass) to make a design on it.

'sand·dune nc a hill of sand (as in the desert).

'sand·fly nc a kind of small fly found on beaches.

'sand·paper nu a strong paper with sand glued to it, used for rubbing surfaces smooth. □ vt to make (something) smooth with sandpaper.

'sand·piper nc a kind of small bird living in wet, sandy places.

'sand·pit nc an enclosure with sand for children to play in.

'sand·stone nu (also *attrib*) a type of rock formed of sand: *sandstone walls.*

'sand·storm nc a storm in a sandy desert with clouds of sand raised by the wind.

sandy adj (-**ier**, -**iest**) (**a**) covered with, of, sand: *a sandy beach.* (**b**) (of hair etc) yellowish-red.

sand² /sænd/ vt 1 to cover (a surface) with sand.

2 *sand sth (down)* to make a surface smooth by using sandpaper: *She sanded down the wood.*

san·dal /'sændl/ *nc* (also *a pair of sandals*) a kind of shoe made of a sole with straps to hold it on the foot.

san·dal·wood /'sændlwʊd/ *nu* a yellowish-brown hard, sweet-smelling wood; its smell.

sand·wich¹ /'sænwɪdʒ/ *nc* two pieces of bread with cheese, meat etc between: *jam/chicken/cheese sandwiches.*

'sandwich course *nc* a course of study, e.g. at a polytechnic, between periods of practical work in industry.

sand·wich² /'sænwɪdʒ/ *vt* to put (one thing or person) between two others, esp when there is little space: *I was sandwiched between two fat men on the bus.*

sane /seɪn/ *adj* (**—r, —st**) **1** mentally healthy. Compare insane. **2** sensible: *a sane policy; sane judgement.* ⇨ sanity. Compare insane.
sane·ly *adv*

sang /sæŋ/ *pt* of sing¹.

san·guine /'sæŋgwɪn/ *adj* (*formal*) hopeful; optimistic: *a sanguine student; sanguine about her chances of success.*

sani·tary /'sænɪtrɪ/ *adj* **1** clean; free from any dirt that might cause disease: *sanitary conditions.* **2** of, concerned with, the protection of (public) health.

'sanitary towel *nc* (spoken abbr ST) an absorbent pad used during menstruation.

sani·ta·tion /ˌsænɪ'teɪʃn/ *nu* arrangements to protect public health.

san·ity /'sænətɪ/ *nu* **1** the state of being sane. Compare insanity. **2** quality of being sensible. ⇨ sane(2).

sank /sæŋk/ *pt* of sink².

San·ta Claus /'sæntə klɔ:z/ *n* the person who, small children are told, brings them toys by night at Christmas.

sap¹ /sæp/ *nu* **1** the liquid in a plant, carrying food to all parts. **2** (*fig*) (anything that provides) strength or energy.

sap² /sæp/ *vt* (**-pp-**) to destroy or weaken (a person's strength, energy, confidence etc): *The climate sapped his health. The criticism sapped his confidence.*

sap·ling /'sæplɪŋ/ *nc* a young tree.

sap·phire /'sæfaɪə(r)/ *n* (also *attrib*) **1** *nc* a bright blue precious stone. **2** *nu* a bright blue colour.

sar·casm /'sɑ:kæzəm/ *nu* words or expressions intended to mean the opposite, used to hurt a person's feelings as in *'I like the colour,' she said, knowing that the wrong paint had been used.*

sar·cas·tic /sɑ:'kæstɪk/ *adj* of, using, sarcasm: *make a sarcastic comment.*
sar·cas·ti·cal·ly /-klɪ/ *adv*

sar·copha·gus /sɑ:'kɒfəgəs/ *nc* (*pl* **-gi** /-gaɪ/ or **—es**) a stone coffin.

sar·dine /sɑ:'di:n/ *nc* (also *attrib*) a kind of small fish (usually preserved in oil): *a sardine sandwich.*
packed like sardines closely crowded together.

sar·don·ic /sɑ:'dɒnɪk/ *adj* scornful; cynical: *a sardonic smile.*
sar·doni·cal·ly /-klɪ/ *adv*

sa·ri /'sɑ:rɪ/ *nc* (*pl* **—s**) a length of cotton or silk cloth wrapped round the body, worn by Hindu women.

sa·rong /sə'rɒŋ/ *nc* a long strip of cotton or silk material worn round the middle of the body in Malaysia, Indonesia etc.

sash /sæʃ/ *nc* a long strip of cloth worn round the waist or over one shoulder, esp as part of a uniform.

,sash-'window *nc* one with a frame that slides up and down on ropes.

sat /sæt/ *pt,pp* of sit.

Sat *written abbr* Saturday.

Sa·tan /'seɪtn/ *n* the Devil.
Sa·tan·ic /sə'tænɪk/ *adj* of, like, the Devil.

satch·el /'sætʃl/ *nc* (*dated*) a school-bag (now the usual word).

sate /seɪt/ *vt* (*formal*) = satiate.

sat·el·lite /'sætəlaɪt/ *nc* **1** a small body moving round a planet. **2** an artificial object put in orbit round a planet etc: *a communications satellite* (i.e. for sending back to the earth telephone messages, radio and TV signals). **3** (*fig*) (often *attrib*) a person, state, depending on and taking the lead from another: *a satellite state.*

sati·able /'seɪʃəbl/ *adj* (*formal*) (esp of appetite) that can be fully satisfied. Opp insatiable.

sati·ate /'seɪʃɪeɪt/ *vt* (*formal*) (often *passive*) to satisfy (a person, appetite) fully or too much: *be satiated with food/pleasure.*

sat·in /'sætɪn/ *adj, nu* (of) a kind of silk material that is shiny on one side: *satin ribbons.*

sat·ire /'sætaɪə(r)/ *nc,nu* (*literature*) (a piece of) amusing writing intended to make a person or idea etc appear foolish or absurd.
sa·tiri·cal /sə'tɪrɪkl/ *adj*
sa·tiri·cal·ly /-klɪ/ *adv*

sat·ir·ist /'sætərɪst/ *nc* a person who writes or uses satire.

sat·ir·ize (also **-ise**) /'sætəraɪz/ *vt* to describe (a person, idea etc) using satire.

sat·is·fac·tion /ˌsætɪs'fækʃn/ *n* **1** *nu* the state of feeling pleased or contented: *have the satisfaction of being successful in life.* Compare dissatisfaction. **2** *nc* (rarely *pl*) something that satisfies: *It is a great satisfaction to know that he is well again.* **3** *nu* (an opportunity of getting) revenge or compensation for an injury or insult: *The angry man demanded satisfaction but the other refused it* (i.e. would not apologize or fight).

sat·is·fac·tory /ˌsætɪs'fæktrɪ/ *adj* good enough for a purpose: *a satisfactory answer. Will these shoes be satisfactory for a long walk?* Opp unsatisfactory. Ⓝ *'Satisfactory'* is used when referring to something being 'good enough' but not particularly good. *'Satisfying'* is used when referring to something being enough in amount and also giving pleasure. Compare *'a satisfactory meal'* and *'a satisfying meal'.*
sat·is·fac·tor·ily /-əlɪ/ *adv*

sat·is·fy /'sætɪsfaɪ/ *vt* (*pt,pp* **-ied**) Ⓝ Not used in continuous tenses, e.g. *is/was -ing,* except sometimes in 3 below. **1** to make (a person) pleased: *I'm not satisfied with this work. Nothing satisfies him; he's always complaining.* ⇨ dissatisfied. **2** to be enough for (one's needs); be equal to (what one hopes for or desires): *satisfy one's hunger.* ⇨ unsatisfied. **3** to make (a person) free from doubt: *He satisfied me that he would come.*

sat·is·fy·ing *adj* enough in amount and giving

pleasure: *satisfying work.* ⇨ the *note* at satisfactory.

satu·rate /'sætʃəreɪt/ *vt* **1** **saturate sb/sth (with sth)** to make a person, thing thoroughly wet; soak: *His hair was saturated with mud. We were caught in the rain and came home saturated.* **2** to fill (a market, need etc) completely: *The market for used cars is saturated.* **3** (*science*) to cause (one substance) to absorb the greatest possible amount of another: *a saturated solution of salt.*

satu·ra·tion /ˌsætʃə'reɪʃn/ *nu* the state of being saturated.

ˌsatu'ration point *nc* the stage beyond which no more can be absorbed.

Sat·ur·day /'sætədɪ/ *nc* (also *attrib*) (abbr Sat) the seventh and last day of the week: *Let's meet on Saturday/next Saturday afternoon. On Saturdays* (= Every Saturday) *I work in a shop.*

Sat·urn /'sætən/ *n* (*astron*) the large planet with many rings round it.

sat·yr /'sætə(r)/ *nc* (in Greek and Roman myth) a god of the woods, half man and half animal.

sauce /sɔːs/ *n* **1** *nc,nu* (a kind of) (semi-)liquid preparation served with food to give flavour: *spaghetti and tomato sauce.* **2** *nu* (*informal*) rude remarks (often more amusing than annoying): *What sauce!* (= How rude!)

sauc·ily *adv* rudely.

saucy *adj* (**-ier, -iest**) slightly rude.

sauce·pan /'sɔːspən/ *nc* a deep cooking pot with a lid and a handle.

sau·cer /'sɔːsə(r)/ *nc* a small curved dish on which a cup stands. ⇨ also flying saucer.

sau·er·kraut /'sauəkraut/ *nu* chopped, pickled cabbage.

sau·na /'saunə/ *nc* (*pl* **—s**) (a place for) a bath in very hot steam.

saun·ter /'sɔːntə(r)/ *vi* to walk in a slow way: *saunter along Oxford Street window-shopping.* □ *nc* a slow walk.

saus·age /'sɒsɪdʒ/ *nc,nu* (also *attrib*) (a section of) chopped up meat etc in a casing or tube of thin skin: *a sausage sandwich.*

'sausage-dog *nc* (*GB informal*) = dachshund.

'sausage-meat *nu* meat minced for making sausages.

ˌsausage 'roll *nc* a piece of sausage-meat baked in pastry.

sau·té /'səuteɪ/ *adj* (*attrib*) (*Fr*) (of food) quickly fried in a little fat: *sauté potatoes.* □ *vt* (*pt,pp* **—d** or **—ed; —ing**) to fry (food) in this way.

sav·age¹ /'sævɪdʒ/ *adj* **1** of, in, an uncivilized state: *savage traditions/people.* **2** fierce; cruel: *a savage dog/attack; savage criticism.*

sav·age·ly *adv*

sav·age·ry /'sævɪdʒrɪ/ *nu* the state of being savage; savage behaviour.

sav·age² /'sævɪdʒ/ *nc* a savage person.

sav·age³ /'sævɪdʒ/ *vt* to attack, bite etc (a person, animal): *a lion savaging a dog.*

sa·van·nah (also **-na**) /sə'vænə/ *nc* the treeless, flat areas in America and W Africa. Ⓝ Compare *'prairie'* in N America and *'pampas'* in central S America.

save¹ /seɪv/ *nc* the act of saving a goal (in football, hockey etc).

save² (also **sav·ing**) /seɪv/ *prep* (*dated*) except: *all save him.*

save³ /seɪv/ *v* **1** *vt* **save sb/sth (from sb/sth)** to make, keep, a person, thing safe (from loss, death, injury etc): *save her from drowning; save his life.* **save (one's) face** ⇨ face¹(2). **save one's skin** ⇨ skin¹(1). **2** *vt,vi* **save (sth) (up)** to keep (something) for future use: *save (up) for a holiday; save some of the meat for tomorrow. He is saving himself/saving his strength for the swim back.* **3** *vt* to free (a person) from the need of using (something): *That will save you 50 pence a week/a lot of trouble.* **4** *vt* to stop a player from scoring (a goal) in football, hockey etc. **5** *vt* (in the Christian religion) to set (a person) free from (eternal punishment for) sin: *Jesus Christ came into the world to save sinners.*

sav·ing¹ /'seɪvɪŋ/ *adj* (*attrib*) that makes up for (a loss, injury, fault etc). **saving grace** a good feature of a person's character, looks etc that makes up for the bad ones: *Being polite was the boy's saving grace.*

sav·ing² /'seɪvɪŋ/ *nc* a way of keeping an amount (of money, time etc): *a useful saving of time/£10.*

sav·ing³ /'seɪvɪŋ/ *prep* ⇨ save².

sav·ings /'seɪvɪŋz/ *n pl* money saved(2): *keep one's savings in a building society.*

'savings account *nc* (with a bank) one on which interest is paid.

'savings bank *nc* a bank which holds and gives interest on savings.

sav·iour (*US* = **-ior**) /'seɪvɪə(r)/ *nc* **1** a person or thing that saves a person from danger. **2** (The/Our S-) Jesus Christ.

sa·vour¹ (*US* = **-vor**) /'seɪvə(r)/ *nc,nu* (*formal*) **1** a taste or flavour (of something): *soup with a savour of garlic.* **2** (*fig*) a quality (of something): *His political views have a savour of Fascism.*

sa·vour² (*US* = **-vor**) /'seɪvə(r)/ *v* (*formal*) **1** *vt* to taste, smell (something): *savouring the wine.* **2** *vi* **savour of sth** to have the quality of something: *His speech savours of a humane approach.*

sa·voury¹ (*US* = **-vory**) /'seɪvərɪ/ *adj* having a salty or sharp (not a sweet) taste: *a savoury omelette.* Compare unsavoury.

sa·voury² (*US* = **-vory**) /'seɪvərɪ/ *nc* (*pl* **-ies**) a savoury dish, biscuit etc.

sa·voy /sə'vɔɪ/ *nc,nu* (a kind of) winter cabbage with wrinkled leaves.

saw¹ /sɔː/ *nc* one of many kinds of tool with a toothed edge, used for cutting wood, metal.

saw² /sɔː/ *v* (*pt* **—ed**, *pp* **—n** /sɔːn/) **1** *vt,vi* to cut (wood) with a saw: *saw wood; saw a log in two.* **saw sth off** to remove something using a saw: *saw a branch off a tree.* **saw sth up** to saw something into pieces. **2** *vi* to be capable of being sawn: *This wood saws easily.*

'saw·dust *nu* tiny bits of wood falling off when wood is sawn.

'saw·mill *nc* a factory where wood is sawn by machines.

saw³ /sɔː/ *pt* of see².

saxo·phone /'sæksəfəun/ *nc* (abbr sax) a curved, brass musical wind instrument with a reed in the mouthpiece and keys for the fingers.

sax·ophon·ist /sæk'sɒfənɪst/ *nc* a person who plays a saxophone.

say¹ /seɪ/ *n sing* **1** **have/say one's say (in sth)** to express one's opinion (during a discussion, about an affair): *Let him have his say.* **2** a right of sharing a discussion, decision etc: *She didn't have/ was not allowed much say in the choice of the carpets.*

say² /seɪ/ (*3rd person, pres t* **says** /sez/, *pt,pp* **said** /sed/) **1** *vt* to use one's ordinary voice (not singing etc) to produce (words, sentences): *Did you say anything? He said that his friend's name was Smith. Say what you want to be. 'I'm sorry,' he said.* **easier said than done** ⇨ easy²(3). **that is to say** (abbr i.e.) or to use other words: *He's 15, that is to say he's very young.* **to say nothing of** ⇨ nothing². **to say the least** ⇨ least³. **You can say that again!** (*informal*) (used for emphasis) I agree. **You don't say!** (*informal*) (used to express surprise when hearing news etc). **it goes etc without saying** it is etc too obvious or well known to need saying: *It goes without saying that he's the best person for the job.* **say no more** you need not add anything because I agree. **say so** (*imperative*) say what you think, feel: *If you think I have lied to you, say so.* **say the word; say a good word (for sb)** ⇨ word(2). Ⓝ *'Say'* is almost always followed by an object that is not a person, i.e. 'we say *something'.* *'Tell'* is usually followed by an object that is a person, i.e., 'we tell *someone'* or 'we tell *someone* something'. **2** *vt* to make known (information): *She spoke for an hour but didn't say much.* **3** *vt,vi* to express an opinion concerning (something): *There is no saying when peace will be achieved.* **and so say all of us** that is the opinion of us all. **They say/It is said (that)** . . . (used to introduce rumours) people generally believe that . . . : *They say/It's said that he's a thief.* **4** *vt* to estimate or suggest (something): *You could speak English in, let's say, six weeks.* **be hard to say** to be difficult to estimate: *When I'll return is hard to say.* **5** *vt* to suppose (something): *Say you do get the job, will you accept it?* **6** *vt* (of writing or a clock, dial etc) to state (something): *The notice says 'No Smoking'. My watch says 10 o'clock.*

say·ing /'seɪɪŋ/ *nc* a short, well-known phrase, remark etc: *'More haste, less speed', as the saying goes.*

s/c *written abbr* (of a flat etc) self-contained.

scab /skæb/ *nc* **1** a dry crust formed over a wound or sore. **2** (*informal*) a worker who refuses to join a strike or who takes a striker's job.

scab·by *adj* (**-ier, -iest**) having scabs(1).

scab·bard /'skæbəd/ *nc* a long container for the blade of a sword, knife etc.

sca·bies /'skeɪbɪːz/ *nu* a kind of skin disease causing itching.

scaf·fold /'skæfəʊld/ *nc* **1** a structure put up for workers round a building which is being built or repaired. **2** a platform on which criminals are executed: *go to the scaffold* (= be executed).

scaf·fold·ing /'skæfəldɪŋ/ *nu* (materials for) a scaffold(1).

scald¹ /skɔːld/ *nc* an injury to the skin from hot liquid or steam.

scald² /skɔːld/ *vt* **1** to burn (the skin) with hot liquid or steam: *I scalded my hand with hot fat.* **2** to clean (instruments etc) with boiling water or steam.

scale¹ /skeɪl/ *n* **1** *nc* one of the thin pieces of hard material that cover the skin of many fish etc:

scrape the scales off a herring. **2** *nc* a small piece like a scale, e.g. of skin that comes off the body. ⇨ scaly. **3** *nu* the chalky deposit inside kettles, water-pipes etc.

scale² /skeɪl/ *nc* **1** one of the two pans on a balance. **2** (*pl* or *a pair of scales*) a simple balance or instrument for weighing by comparing something with a known mass. **3** any machine used for weighing: *bathroom scales.*

scale³ /skeɪl/ *nc* **1** a series of marks at regular intervals, used for measuring (as on a thermometer): *It has one scale in Centigrade and another in Fahrenheit.* **2** a system of units used for measuring: *the decimal scale.* **3** an arrangement in steps or degrees: *a salary scale.* ⇨ sliding scale. **4** a proportion between the size of something and the map, diagram etc which represents it: *a map using a scale of ten kilometres to the centimetre.* **draw sth to scale** to draw a map etc using the same scale for all the parts. **5** a relative size, extent etc: *They are preparing to demonstrate on a large scale.* **6** (*music*) a series of tones arranged in order (esp a series of eight starting on a keynote): *practise scales on the piano.*

scale⁴ /skeɪl/ *vt* **1** to make a copy or representation of (something), according to a certain scale(4): *scale a map/building.* **2** **scale sth up/ down** to increase/decrease something (by a mentioned proportion or scale(4)): *All wages/ marks were scaled up by 10%.*

scale⁵ /skeɪl/ *vt* to remove scales¹(1) from (fish).

scale⁶ /skeɪl/ *vt* to climb up (a wall, mountainside etc).

scal·lop /'skɒləp/ *nc* a kind of shellfish with a hinged double shell, eaten as food.

scalp /skælp/ *nc* the skin and hair of the head, excluding the face.

scal·pel /'skælpəl/ *nc* a small, light knife as used by surgeons.

scaly /'skeɪlɪ/ *adj* (**-ier, -iest**) covered with, coming off in, scales¹(1,2): *scaly fish.*

scamp /skæmp/ *nc* (*dated; derog*) (used playfully of) a naughty child.

scam·per /'skæmpə(r)/ *vi* (of small animals, e.g. mice or rabbits when frightened, or of children and dogs at play) to run quickly. □ *nc* a short, quick run.

scam·pi /'skæmpɪ/ *nu* (a dish of) large cooked prawns.

scan¹ /skæn/ *nc* an act, instance of scanning, esp to examine a person for disease or to find information in a computer.

scan² /skæn/ *v* (**-nn-**) **1** *vt* to examine (something) closely: *The shipwrecked sailor scanned the horizon anxiously every morning.* **2** *vt* (*modern use*) to look at (something) quickly but not very thoroughly: *He scanned the newspaper while having his breakfast.* **3** *vi* (*literature*) (of verse) to have a regular rhythm: *This line does not/will not scan. The verses scan well.* ⇨ scansion. **4** *vt* (*computers*) to search through (stored information) to find a particular part. **5** *vt* to use special equipment to examine (a person) for internal disease. ⇨ scanner. **6** *vt* (*radar*) to pass electronic beams across (an area) in search of something.

scan·dal /'skændl/ *n* **1** *nc,nu* (action, behaviour etc that causes) general shock, anger, opposition: *The way they treat the poor is a scandal.* **2** *nu* careless or unkind talk which can damage a person's reputation: *Most of us enjoy a bit of scandal.*

'scandal·monger /-mʌŋgə(r)/ *nc* a person who gossips.

scan·dal·ize (also **-ise**) /-aɪz/ *vt* to offend the (moral) feelings of (a person): *scandalize the neighbours by sunbathing in the nude.*

scan·dal·ous /-əs/ *adj* **(a)** shocking: *scandalous language/costs.* **(b)** (*attrib*) (of reports, rumours) containing scandal.

scan·dal·ous·ly *adv* in a scandalous way.

scan·ner /'skænə(r)/ *nc* (*med*) an electronic device used to examine a person for internal disease.

scan·sion /'skænʃn/ *nu* (*literature*) the way (a particular) verse scans²(3).

scant /skænt/ *adj* (*attrib*) (having) hardly enough: *I paid scant attention to her advice.*

scant·ily /-əlɪ/ *adv* in a scanty manner: *scantily dressed.*

scan·ty *adj* (**-ier, -iest**) only just large enough: *a scanty bikini.* Compare ample.

scape·goat /'skeɪpgəʊt/ *nc* a person blamed or punished for the mistake(s) or fault(s) of another or others.

scap·ula /'skæpjʊlə/ *nc* (*pl* **—s**) (*anat*) = shoulder-blade.

scar¹ /skɑ:(r)/ *nc* **1** a mark on the skin caused by a cut or other injury. **2** (*fig*) a visible effect of suffering, bad planning etc: *Mining can leave a scar on the countryside.*

scar² /skɑ:(r)/ *vt* (**-rr-**) **1** to mark (something) with a scar: *a face scarred by smallpox.* **2** (*fig*) to mark (a place) with effects of industry, suffering etc: *Many cities have been scarred by war.*

scar·ab /'skærəb/ *nc* a kind of beetle, esp one regarded as sacred in ancient Eygpt.

scarce /skeəs/ *adj* (**—r, —st**) not available in sufficient quantity; difficult to find: *Jobs are scarce this month.* Compare plentiful. **make oneself scarce** (*informal*) to go away suddenly.

scar·city /'skeəsətɪ/ *nc,nu* (*pl* **-ies**) an instance, state of being scarce: *a scarcity of fruit.*

scarce·ly /'skeəslɪ/ *adv* only just (and possibly not): *There were scarcely a hundred people present. I scarcely know him.* Ⓝ Barely and hardly are also possible.

scare¹ /skeə(r)/ *nc* a feeling, state, of alarm or fear: *I got quite a scare when I read my medical report.*

scare² /skeə(r)/ *vt,vi* (to cause a person, animal) to become afraid: *The dogs scared the thief away. He was scared by the thunder. He scares easily/is easily scared. He feels scared at night. She's scared of the dark. The lights should scare them away/off.* **scare sb stiff** (*informal*) to make a person very afraid, nervous: *He's scared stiff of women.* **scare sb out of her/his wits** to make a person extremely frightened: *The sound of footsteps outside the door scared her out of her wits.*

'scare·crow *nc* a figure in old clothes, used in fields to scare birds away from crops.

'scare-monger /-mʌŋgə(r)/ *nc* a person who spreads alarming news.

scary /'skeərɪ/ *adj* (**-ier, -iest**) (*informal*) causing alarm or fear: *a scary film.*

scarf /skɑ:f/ *nc* (*pl* **scarves** /skɑ:vz/ or **—s**) a piece of cloth worn over the head or shoulders,

round the neck etc.

scar·let /'skɑ:lət/ *nu, adj* bright red (colour). **go scarlet** to blush deeply.

¸scarlet 'fever *nu* a kind of infectious disease with red marks on the skin.

scath·ing /'skeɪðɪŋ/ *adj* (of criticism etc) severe; harsh: *a scathing review of a new book.*

scath·ing·ly *adv*

scat·ter /'skætə(r)/ *v* **1** *vt,vi* (to cause people, animals, things) to go in different directions: *The police scattered the crowd. The crowd scattered.* **2** *vt* to throw (things) in various directions: *scatter seed.*

scat·ter·ed *adj* (*attrib*) not situated together: *a few scattered villages.*

scat·ter-brain /'skætə breɪn/ *nc* (*derog*) a person who cannot keep her or his thoughts on one subject for long.

'scatter-brained *adj*

scat·ty /'skætɪ/ *adj* (**-ier, -iest**) (*informal; derog*) behaving as if a little mad: *a scatty woman.* **drive sb scatty** to cause a person to become mad.

scav·enge /'skævɪndʒ/ *vt,vi* to look among rubbish for (food, useful things): *scavenging in dustbins.*

scav·en·ger /'skævɪndʒə(r)/ *nc* **1** an animal or bird that lives on decaying flesh. **2** a person who looks among rubbish for food, useful things.

scen·ario /sɪ'nɑ:rɪəʊ/ *nc* (*pl* **—s**) (*literature*) an outline of a play, opera, film etc with details of the characters, scenes etc.

scene /si:n/ *nc* **1** the place of an actual or imagined event: *the scene of a great battle. The scene of the novel is set in Scotland.* **2** (a description of) an event or experience: *There were distressing scenes when the earthquake occurred.* **3** (an event characterized by) a show of strong feelings of anger etc: *She made a scene/We had a scene when I arrived late.* **4** a view: *The boats in the harbour make a beautiful scene.* **change of scene** ⇨ change¹(2). **5** (*literature*) (abbr Sc) one of the parts, shorter than an act, into which some plays and operas are divided: *'Macbeth', Act 2, Sc 1.* **6** a place represented on the stage of a theatre: *The scenes are changed during the intervals.* **behind the scenes** **(a)** out of sight of the audience. **(b)** (*fig*) kept from public knowledge: *What happens behind the scenes in a hospital?* **set the scene** to describe in speech or writing the place and characters in a story, play etc or in an event being reported on TV or radio. **7** (*informal*) an area of activity: *the drug scene in our big cities.*

scen·ery /'si:nərɪ/ *nu* **1** the natural features of a district, e.g. mountains, valleys, forests: *mountain scenery; stop to admire the scenery.* **2** the painted areas, furniture etc used on the stage of a theatre.

sce·nic /'si:nɪk/ *adj* of (esp beautiful) scenery: *a scenic trip across the Alps.*

sceni·cal·ly /-klɪ/ *adv*

scent¹ /sent/ *n* **1** *nc,nu* (a particular) smell, esp of something pleasant: *a rose that has no scent; scents of fresh coffee.* **2** *nu* perfume: *a bottle of scent.* **3** *nc* (usually *sing*) a smell left by (the track of) an animal: *follow/lose/recover the scent.* **off/on the scent** (*fig*) not having/having the right clue. **put/throw sb off the scent** (*fig*) to give a person false information. **4** *nu* the sense of smell (in dogs): *hunt by scent.*

scent² /sent/ *vt* **1** to learn the presence of (an animal etc) by smell: *The dog scented a rat.* **2** to begin to suspect the presence, likelihood or existence of (something): *scent a crime; scent danger/ trouble.* **3** to put scent(2) on (something): *scent a handkerchief.*
scent·ed *adj* (*attrib*) having a perfume: *scented flowers.*

scep·ter /'septə(r)/ *n* ⇨ sceptre.

scep·tic (*US* = **skep·tik**) /'skeptɪk/ *nc* a person who doubts the truth of a particular claim, theory, belief etc.
scep·ti·cal (*US* = **skep-**) /-kl/ *adj* in the habit of not believing, of questioning the truth of, claims, statements etc.
scep·ti·cal·ly (*US* = **skep-**) /-klɪ/ *adv*
scep·ti·cism (*US* = **skep-**) /'skeptɪsɪzəm/ *nu* a doubting state of mind or attitude.

sceptre (*US* = **scep·ter**) /'septə(r)/ *nc* a decorated rod carried as symbol of power or authority by a ruler.

Sch *written abbr* school.

sched·ule¹ /'ʃedjuːl/ *nc* a list or statement of details, esp of times for doing things: *a production schedule* (e.g. in a factory). **a tight schedule** one that is difficult to keep to. **on/behind schedule** on/not on time: *The train arrived on schedule.*

sched·ule² /'ʃedjuːl/ *vt* (often *passive*) **1** *vt* to put (events, payments etc) in an order of times, dates: *schedule flights; schedule a debt. It is scheduled to arrive at 9.* **2** to put (something) in a list of arrangements: *The President is scheduled to make a speech tomorrow.*
'scheduled flight *nc* one made regularly according to a timetable. Compare charter flight.

scheme¹ /skiːm/ *nc* **1** an arrangement; ordered system: *a colour scheme* (e.g. for a room so that colours of walls, carpets, curtains etc match). **2** a plan or design (for work or activity): *a scheme for manufacturing paper from straw.* **3** a secret and dishonest plan: *a scheme to avoid paying taxes.*

scheme² /skiːm/ *vi* to make a (esp dishonest) scheme: *They schemed to defeat/for the overthrow of the government.*
schemer *nc* a person who schemes.
schem·ing /'skiːmɪŋ/ *adj* (*attrib; derog*) (of a person) making schemes(3).

schism /'sɪzəm *or* 'skɪzəm/ *nc,nu* (an instance of) a division of an organization (esp a Church) into two or more groups.

schizo·phre·nia /ˌskɪtsə'friːnɪə/ *nu* a kind of mental illness producing a loss of sense of what is true or real, and emotional difficulties, antisocial behaviour etc.
schizo·phren·ic /ˌskɪtsəʊ'frenɪk/ *adj, nc* (a person) suffering from schizophrenia.

schnor·kel /'ʃnɔːkl/ *n* = snorkel.

schol·ar /'skɒlə(r)/ *nc* (*dated*) a boy or girl at school. **2** a person who is awarded money or other help so that he or she can attend a university, college etc: *British Council scholars.* **3** a person with much knowledge (usually of a particular subject): *This book is written by Professor Key, the famous Greek scholar.*
schol·ar·ly *adj* having or showing much learn-

ing; fond of learning: *a scholarly translation/ young woman.*

schol·ar·ship /'skɒləʃɪp/ *n* **1** *nc* a payment to a student so that he or she can study: *win a scholarship to the university.* **2** *nu* (*formal*) knowledge obtained by study.

school¹ /skuːl/ *n* **1** *nc* an institution for educating children: *primary and secondary schools.* **2** *n sing* (not used with *the, a* or *an*) the process of being educated in a school: *Is he old enough for school/ to go to school? He left school when he was sixteen. School begins at 9am. There will be no school* (= no lessons) *tomorrow.* **3** (the —) all the (staff and) pupils in a school: *The whole school hopes that its football team will win.* **4** *nc* (often S-) a place for the study of a particular subject: *an art school; the Law/Medical School.* **5** a group of people who are followers or imitators of an artist, a philosopher etc: *the Dutch school of painting.*
school of thought a way of thinking: *There are several schools of thought about AIDS.*
'school-bag *nc* one for carrying school-books and equipment.
'school·boy *nc* a boy at school.
'school-days *n pl* the period of being at school: *look back on one's school-days with pleasure.*
'school·girl *nc* a girl at school.
school·ing *nu* education (the usual word): *He had very little schooling.*
'school·master/·mistress *nc* a teacher (esp in a private school).
'school·mate *nc* a boy or girl at the same school.
'school·teacher *nc* a person who teaches in a school.

school² /skuːl/ *nc* **school (of sth)** a large number (of fish) swimming together.

school³ /skuːl/ *vt* (*dated*) to give (a person) practical training or experience: *Children are schooled to be polite.*

schoo·ner /'skuːnə(r)/ *nc* **1** a kind of sailing-ship with two or more masts. **2** a tall drinking-glass for sherry.

schwa /ʃwɑː/ *nc* (*pl* —s) (*tech*) the symbol /ə/ as used in phonetics.

science /'saɪəns/ *nu* (often the —s; also *attrib*) academic subjects, areas of study, in which exact measurement, observation and calculation are used: *study science/the sciences/science subjects at school.* Compare arts, natural/political/physical/ social science. ⇨ also Bachelor/Master of Science.
science 'fiction *nu* stories about imagined scientific developments and discoveries.
scien·tist /'saɪəntɪst/ *nc* a student of, expert in, one of the natural or physical sciences.
scien·ti·fic /ˌsaɪən'tɪfɪk/ *adj* **1** (*attrib*) of, for, connected with, used in, science: *scientific methods; scientific instruments.* **2** using, showing, organized methods as used in science: *a scientific approach; be scientific in one's planning.* Opp unscientific.
scien·ti·fi·cal·ly /-klɪ/ *adv*

sci fi /ˌsaɪ faɪ/ *abbr* science fiction.

scimi·tar /'sɪmɪtə(r)/ *nc* a curved sword.

scin·til·late /'sɪntɪleɪt/ *vi* to sparkle.

scin·til·lat·ing *adj* interesting and attractive: *scintillating conversation.*

scis·sors /'sɪzəz/ *n pl* (also *a pair of scissors*) an instrument with two blades which cut as they come together: *Where are my scissors?*

scis·sor *adj* (*attrib*) using, like scissors: *a scissor cut; a scissor kick; a scissor-like movement.*

scoff¹ /skɒf/ *vi* **scoff (at sb/sth)** to say disrespectful things (about a person, belief etc).

scoff² /skɒf/ *vt* (*sl*) to eat (food) greedily: *Who's scoffed all the pastries?*

scold /skəʊld/ *vt,vi* to blame (a person) with angry words: *scold a child for being lazy. She's always scolding.*

scold·ing *nc* a complaint using angry words: *get/give her a scolding for being late.*

scol·lop /'skɒləp/ *nc* = scallop.

scone /skɒn/ *nc* a kind of cake of oatmeal or flour etc baked quickly.

scoop¹ /sku:p/ *nc* **1** a short-handled tool like a small shovel, used for taking up and moving grain, flour, sugar etc. **2** an amount a scoop holds: *a scoop of sugar.* **3** (*informal*) a piece of news obtained and published by one newspaper before its competitors. **4** (*commerce*) a large profit from sudden luck.

scoop² /sku:p/ *vt* **1** **scoop sth out/up** to lift something (as if) with a scoop: *scoop out the sand with one's hands.* **2** to make (a hole etc) (as if) with a scoop: *scoop out a hole in the sand.* **3** (*informal*) to get (news, a profit etc) as a scoop(3,4): *He scooped the market.*

scoot /sku:t/ *vi* (*informal*) to run away.

scoot·er /'sku:tə(r)/ *nc* **1** (also *motor-scooter*) a kind of motorbike with a small engine. **2** a child's toy, a vehicle with two wheels, a platform and a handle, one foot being used to move it by pushing against the ground.

scope /skəʊp/ *nu* **1** **scope (for sth)** an opportunity: *work that gives scope for one's abilities.* **2** a range of action or observation: *Economics is beyond the scope of a child's mind.*

scorch¹ /skɔːtʃ/ *nc* a brown mark on the surface of something (esp cloth), made by dry heat.

scorch² /skɔːtʃ/ *vt,vi* to burn or discolour the surface of (something) with dry heat: *You scorched my shirt when you ironed it. The long, hot summer scorched the grass. Some cloth scorches more easily than others.*

scorch·ing *adj, adv* extremely (hot): *scorching hot.*

score¹ /skɔː(r)/ *nc* **1** (a record of) points, goals, runs etc made by a player or team in sport: *The score in the tennis final was 6–4, 3–6, 7–5. The half-time score* (e.g. football) *was 2–1.* **keep the score** to keep a record of the score as it is made. **2** a reason; point: *His particular score is that you ignored him.* **on that score** as far as that point is concerned: *You need have no anxiety on that score.* **3** a copy of written music showing what each instrument is to play, each voice is to sing: *follow the score while listening to music.* **4** a cut, scratch or notch made on a surface: *scores on rock.* **5** (a set of) twenty: *a score of people; three score and ten* (= 70). **scores of times** very often: *I've been there scores of times.* **6** (*sl*) a remark or act by which a person gains an advantage in an argument etc: *a politician who is clever at making scores off opponents.* **7** **an old score** a past disagreement or offence: *I've an old score to*

settle with him.

'score-board/-book/-card *nc* one on which the score(1) is recorded.

score² /skɔː(r)/ *v* **1** *vi* to make or keep a record of scores(1): *Who's scoring?* **2** *vt,vi* to win (points etc) in a game or sport; make (a goal, run, try etc) towards winning a game: *score a goal; score a century* (= 100 runs at cricket). *He kicked the ball and scored.* **score an advantage (over sb)** ⇨ advantage(1). **score off sb** (*informal*) to gain an advantage by making a person appear foolish. **score sth up** to record a point, goal etc that is won. **3** *vt* to write (music), esp for an orchestra or group. **4** *vt* to mark (a surface) with scratches, cuts, lines etc: *Don't score the floor by pushing heavy furniture about.* **score sth out** to draw a line or lines through something: *Three words had been scored out.*

scorer *nc* (**a**) a person who keeps a record of points, goals, runs etc scored in a game. (**b**) a player who scores runs, goals etc.

scorn¹ /skɔːn/ *nu* **1** the feeling that a person or thing deserves no respect: *be filled with scorn for her; dismiss a suggestion with scorn.* **laugh sb/sth to scorn** to laugh in a manner showing that he/she/it is inferior, worthless. **2** a person who is scorned: *He was the scorn of the school.*

scorn·ful /-fəl/ *adj* showing or feeling scorn: *a scornful smile.*

scorn·ful·ly /-fəlɪ/ *adv*

scorn² /skɔːn/ *vt* to refuse to accept, believe, (something) because one has no respect or trust: *He scorned my advice.*

Scor·pio /'skɔːpɪəʊ/ *n* the Scorpion, eighth sign of the zodiac.

scor·pion /'skɔːpɪən/ *nc* a small creature of the spider group with a poisonous sting in its long, jointed tail.

Scot /skɒt/ *nc* a person from Scotland.

scot-free /ˌskɒt 'friː/ *adj* (*pred*) unharmed; unpunished: *He went/got off scot-free.*

Scotch /skɒtʃ/ *adj* of Scotland: *Scotch whisky.* □ *nc,nu* (a portion of) Scotch whisky.

ˌScotch 'egg *nc* a boiled egg fried in sausage-meat.

Scots /skɒts/ *adj* of, concerning, a person from Scotland: *a Scots accent.*

Scot·tish /'skɒtɪʃ/ *adj* of, from, Scotland: *Scottish music; a Scottish accent.*

scoun·drel /'skaʊndrəl/ *nc* (*derog*) a person who does wicked things.

scour¹ /'skaʊə(r)/ *vt* to make (a dirty surface) clean or bright by using a rough cloth or pad and soap etc: *scour the pots and pans; scour the rust off/away.*

scour·er *nc* a pad of stiff nylon or wire, used for cleaning pots and pans etc.

scour² /'skaʊə(r)/ *vt* to look everywhere in (a place) (for a person, thing): *The police scoured London for the thief.*

scourge /skɜːdʒ/ *nc* (*fig*) a cause of suffering to people: *After the earthquake came the scourge of disease.*

scout¹ /skaʊt/ *nc* **1** a person, ship or small, fast plane, sent out to get information about the enemy. **2** (S-) a member of an organization training boys in character, developing self-reliance, discipline and social awareness. **3** a person employed to look for talented sportsmen and women for a professional team: *a talent scout.*

scout² /skaʊt/ *vi* **scout about/around (for sb/sth)** to go about looking (for a person, thing): *scout around for a cheap restaurant.*

scowl /skaʊl/ *vi, nc* (to make) a bad-tempered expression: *The prisoner scowled at the judge.*

SCR /ˌes siː ˈɑːr/ *abbr* Senior Common Room (a place where staff can relax in a university, college). ⇨ JCR.

scrabble /ˈskræbl/ *vi* **scrabble about (for sth)** to move quickly to find or collect things: *a mouse scrabbling about for food.*

scrag·gy /ˈskrægɪ/ *adj* **(-ier, -iest)** thin and bony: *She has scraggy arms.*

scram /skræm/ *vi* **(-mm-)** (usually *imperative; sl*) to go away quickly.

scramble¹ /ˈskræmbl/ *nc* **1** a walk, motorbike competition etc, over or through obstacles, rough ground etc. **2** an eager and rough struggle: *There was a scramble for the best seats.*

scramble² /ˈskræmbl/ *v* **1** *vi* to climb (with difficulty) or crawl (over steep or rough ground): *scramble up the side of a cliff/over a rocky hillside.* **2** *vi* to do something quickly (and untidily): *She scrambled into her clothes and ran to the bus-stop.* **3** *vi* **scramble for sth** to struggle with others to get something: *The players were scrambling for possession of the ball.* **4** *vt* to cook (eggs) by beating them and then heating them in a saucepan with butter and milk. **5** *vt* to make (a message sent by telephone etc) unintelligible.

scrap¹ /skræp/ *n* **1** *nc* a small (usually unwanted) piece: *scrap of paper/broken glass.* **2** *nc* (*fig*) a small amount: *not a scrap of food left/of truth in her statement.* **3** *nu* (also *attrib*) waste or unwanted articles, esp those of value only for the material they are made of: *He offers good prices for scrap* (*metal*).

'**scrap-book** *nc* a book of blank pages on which to keep pictures, photographs, stories from magazines etc.

'**scrap-heap** *nc* a pile of waste or unwanted material or articles. **throw sb/sth on the scrap-heap** to reject her/him/it as no longer wanted or useful.

scrap² /skræp/ *nc* (*dated informal*) a fight or quarrel (between children).

scrap³ /skræp/ *vt* **(-pp-) 1** to throw (something) away as useless or worn-out: *You ought to scrap that old bicycle and buy a new one.* **2** to reject (a plan, idea etc): *This idea won't work, let's scrap it.*

scrap⁴ /skræp/ *vi* **(-pp-)** (*dated; informal*) (of children) to fight or quarrel.

scrape¹ /skreɪp/ *nc* **1** an act or sound of scraping: *the scrape of a fork across a plate.* **2** a place on the skin that is scraped: *a bad scrape on the elbow.* **3** (*informal*) an awkward situation because of foolish or thoughtless behaviour: *That boy is always getting into scrapes.*

scrape² /skreɪp/ *v* **1** *vt* to make (something) clean, smooth or level by pushing a hard edge of a tool, something rough etc along the surface: *scrape a piece of wood smooth.* **2** *vt* to remove (something) from a surface by scraping(1): *scraping paint off a door.* **3** *vt* to (try to) make (a hole etc) by scraping: *scrape (out) a hole.* **4** *vt, vi* to pass (something) while touching it slightly or

almost touching it: *branches scraping (against) the window.* **bow and scrape** ⇨ bow⁴(1). **5 scrape a living (by doing sth)** = scrape along/by.

scrape along/by to manage with effort to make enough money to live.

scrape through (sth) to manage with effort to gain enough marks to pass: *He scraped through (the exams).*

scrape sb/sth together to use care and effort to obtain enough people, things: *We were able to scrape together an audience/enough money for a short holiday.*

scraper /ˈskreɪpə(r)/ *nc* a tool used for scraping, e.g. paint from woodwork.

scrap·py /ˈskræpɪ/ *adj* **(-ier, -iest) 1** made up of bits: *a scrappy dinner.* **2** incomplete or disorganized: *a scrappy idea/report.*

scratch¹ /skrætʃ/ *adj* (*attrib*) using whatever or whoever is available at the time: *a scratch team/uniform.*

scratch² /skrætʃ/ *n* **1** *nc* a mark, cut, injury, wound, made by scratching(1): *It's only a scratch. He escaped without a scratch.* **2** *n sing* an act of scratching(2): *The dog enjoys having a good scratch.* **3** *n sing* (used without *the*, *a* or *an*) the starting line for a race. **start (sth) from scratch** (*fig*) to start (an activity) at the beginning without any experience etc. **be up to scratch** (*fig*) to be ready and able to do what is expected or required: *Will you be up to scratch for the examination?*

scratchy *adj* **(-ier, -iest) (a)** (of writing, drawings) done carelessly. **(b)** (of a pen or gramophone record) making a scratching noise.

scratch³ /skrætʃ/ *v* **1** *vt, vi* to make (marks) on or in a surface, damage (one's skin), with something pointed or sharp, e.g. a pointed object, fingernail: *This cat scratches. Who has scratched the paint? He scratched his hands badly on a rose-bush.* **scratch the surface** (*fig*) to deal with a subject without going deeply into it: *The teacher only scratched the surface of the subject.* **2** *vt, vi* to rub, scrape, (the skin) because of an unpleasant irritating feeling: *scratch an insect bite. Stop scratching (yourself).* **scratch one's head** to do so to show signs of being puzzled or confused. **3** *vt* to mark (something) on a surface using a pointed object: *scratch a name on a door.* **4** *vt* **scratch sth off/out** to remove paint, a message etc from a surface by scratching(1): *scratch out one's name.* **5** *vi* to make the sound of scratching(1): *This pen scratches.* **6** *vt* to remove (oneself, an animal etc) from a race or competition.

scrawl¹ /skrɔːl/ *nc, nu* (an example of) shapeless, untidy handwriting: *His signature was a scrawl.*

scrawl² /skrɔːl/ *vi, vt* to write or draw (something) quickly or carelessly: *He scrawled a few words on a postcard to his wife. Who has scrawled all over this wall?*

scrawny /ˈskrɔːnɪ/ *adj* **(-ier, -iest)** (*derog*) thin and bony: *scrawny arms.*

scream¹ /skriːm/ *nc* **1** a loud, high, cry or noise: *screams of pain/laughter.* **2** (*informal*) a person or thing that causes much laughter: *He/It was a perfect scream.*

scream² /skriːm/ *v* **1** *vi* (of people, birds, animals) to give a loud, high cry (as if) of fear or pain: *The baby has been screaming for an hour.* **2** *vt,vi* to shout (something) in a high voice: *She screamed (out) that there was a burglar under the bed.* **scream with laughter** to laugh noisily. **3** *vi* (of the wind, machines etc) to make a loud, high noise: *The wind screamed through the trees.*

scree /skri:/ *nu* a mass of small loose stones on a mountain.

screech¹ /skri:tʃ/ *nc* a screeching cry or noise: *the screech of tyres on wet roads.*

screech² /skri:tʃ/ *vi* to make a harsh, high sound: *monkeys screeching in the trees. The brakes screeched as the car stopped. The car screeched to a halt.*

screed /skri:d/ *nc* a long, dull letter or speech.

screen¹ /skri:n/ *nc* **1** an (often movable) upright framework (some made to fold), used to divide a room etc. **2** anything that is or can be used to give shelter or protection from observation, the weather etc: *a screen of trees; a smoke-screen.* **3** a surface on which films, photographs, TV pictures etc are shown. **4** a frame with fine wire netting to keep out insects: *a door-screen.*
'screen·ing *nu* **(a)** fine wire netting for a screen(4). **(b)** the process of screening(4 or 5).
'screen·play *nc* a script of a film.
'screen test *nc* a test of a person's suitability for acting in films or on TV.

screen² /skri:n/ *vt* **1** to shelter, protect, hide, (a person, thing) using a screen(1,2): *The trees screen our house/us from view.* **2** **screen sth (off)** to hide something (as if) using a screen(1): *screen off a road accident; grow a tree to screen off the shed.* **3** (*fig*) to protect (a person) from blame, discovery, punishment: *I'm not willing to screen you from blame.* **4** to look at (a person's) history, test (a person's) ability, health, loyalty etc to decide whether he or she is suitable for a job. **5** to show (a film etc) in a cinema or on TV.

screw¹ /skru:/ *nc* **1** a metal piece with a spiral groove round its length, (to be) twisted into wood, metal etc for fastening and holding things together. **2** something that is turned like a screw and is used for producing pressure, tightening etc. **put the screws on sb** (*informal*) to use pressure to force her or him to agree, join in etc. **3** an action of turning: *This isn't tight enough yet—give it another screw.* **4** = propeller. **5** (*sl*) a prison warder.
'screw·driver *nc* a tool used for turning screw(1).

screw² /skru:/ *v* **1** *vt* to fasten or tighten (something) with a screw: *screw a lock on a door; screw down the lid of a coffin.* **have one's head screwed on (the right way)** ⇨ head¹(2). **2** *vt,vi* to twist (something) round to make it tight, or loose: *screw a lid on/off a jar.* ⇨ unscrew. **3** *vt* **screw sth out of sb** (*informal*) to force money, information etc from a person: *screw more taxes out of people.* **4** *vt* **screw sth up (a)** to twist paper etc into a tight ball (e.g. to throw it away). **(b)** to make (a part of) the face tight, to show pain, disapproval etc: *screw up one's eyes/face.* **be (all) screwed up** (*informal*) to be very worried or uncertain. **screw up (one's/the) courage** ⇨ courage.

screwy /'skru:ɪ/ *adj* (**-ier, -iest**) (*informal; derog*) crazy.

scribble¹ /'skrɪbl/ *nc,nu* (an example of) careless handwriting or meaningless marks.

scribble² /'skrɪbl/ *vt,vi* **1** to write (something) quickly or carelessly. **2** to make (meaningless marks) on paper etc.

scribe /skraɪb/ *nc* a person who, before the invention of printing, made handwritten copies of books etc.

script /skrɪpt/ *n* **1** *nu* handwriting. **2** *nc* (short for) a manuscript or typescript.
'script-writer *nc* a person who writes scripts for radio, TV, films.

Scrip·tures /'skrɪptʃəz/ *n pl* (the —) the Bible.
scrip·tur·al /'skrɪptʃərəl/ *adj* based on the Bible.

scroll /skrəʊl/ *nc* **1** a roll of paper or parchment with writing on. **2** a design cut in stone like a scroll.

scrooge /skru:dʒ/ *nc* (*derog*) a person who loves wealth and spends as little as possible.

scro·tum /'skrəʊtəm/ *nc* (*pl* **—s**) (*anat*) the bag of skin enclosing the testicles.

scrounge /skraʊndʒ/ *vi,vt* **scrounge (sth) (off sb)** (*informal*) to get what one wants (esp money or food) by begging or persuasion and never working for it.
scrounger *nc* (*derog*) a person who scrounges.

scrub¹ /skrʌb/ *nu* (land covered with) small trees and bushes.

scrub² /skrʌb/ *nc* an act of scrubbing: *The floor needs a good scrub.*

scrub³ /skrʌb/ *v* (**-bb-**) **1** *vt,vi* to clean (something, one's body etc) by rubbing hard, esp with a stiff brush, soap and water: *scrub the floor.* **2** *vt* (*informal*) to cancel (something): *scrub an order.*
'scrub·bing-brush *nc* a kind of stiff brush, used for scrubbing floors etc.

scruff /skrʌf/ *n* (only in) **the scruff of the neck** the back of the neck when used for grasping: *He held the boy by the scruff of the neck.*

scruf·fy /'skrʌfɪ/ *adj* (**-ier, -iest**) (*informal; derog*) dirty and untidy: *scruffy children/clothes.*

scrum /skrʌm/ *nc* (*informal*) = scrummage.
,scrum·'half *nc* (*rugby*) the half-back who puts the ball into the scrum.

scrum·mage /'skrʌmɪdʒ/ *nc* (*rugby*) the play when the forwards of both sides pack together with their heads down while the ball is thrown into the middle of them.

scruple¹ /'skru:pl/ *nc,nu* (a feeling of doubt caused by) a troubled conscience: *Have you no scruples about borrowing things without permission?*

scruple² /'skru:pl/ *vi* to hesitate because of scruples: *He doesn't scruple to tell a lie if he thinks it useful.* Ⓝ Usually *negative*.

scru·pu·lous /'skru:pjʊləs/ *adj* **1** paying great attention to small details: *with scrupulous care.* **2** careful to do nothing morally wrong: *A solicitor must act with scrupulous honesty.* Opp unscrupulous.
scru·pu·lous·ly *adv*

scru·ti·nize (also **-ise**) /'skru:tɪnaɪz/ *vt* to make a detailed examination of (something).

scru·ti·ny /'skru:tɪnɪ/ *nu* a thorough and detailed examination: *careful scrutiny to detect any faults.*

scuff /skʌf/ *vt* to mark (shoes etc) by walking without lifting the feet from the ground properly.

scuffle /'skʌfl/ vi, nc (to take part in) a rough fight or struggle: *The police were scuffling with the burglars. There was a noisy scuffle.*

scull¹ /skʌl/ nc **1** one of a pair of oars used by a rower. **2** a kind of lightweight boat for one person.

scull² /skʌl/ vt, vi to row a scull(2).

scul·ler nc a person who sculls.

scul·lery /'skʌlərɪ/ nc (pl -ies) a room in a large house next to the kitchen, where dishes, pots etc are washed up.

sculpt /skʌlpt/ = sculpture².

sculp·tor /'skʌlptə(r)/ nc an artist who sculptures.

sculp·ture¹ /'skʌlptʃə(r)/ n **1** nu the art of making representations in stone, wood, metal etc by carving or modelling. **2** nc, nu (a piece of) such work.

sculp·ture² /'skʌlptʃə(r)/ vt, vi to carve or model (something) (using a material mentioned): *The horse has been sculptured in wood.*

scum /skʌm/ nu **1** a grey layer of dirty substances that forms on the surface of water, e.g. in a bath, a pond etc. **2** (fig; derog) the worst kind of people.

scup·per /'skʌpə(r)/ vt **1** to sink (a ship) deliberately. **2** (fig) (informal) to ruin (a scheme, business).

scurf /skɜːf/ nu small bits of dead skin on the scalp.

scurfy adj having, covered with, scurf.

scur·ri·lous /'skʌrɪləs/ adj using rude and strong words of abuse: *scurrilous attacks on the Prime Minister.*

scur·ry¹ /'skʌrɪ/ n sing an act or sound of scurrying: *the scurry of feet/mice.*

scur·ry² /'skʌrɪ/ vi (pt, pp -ied) to run with short, quick steps: *The rain sent everyone scurrying about/scurrying for shelter.*

scuttle¹ /'skʌtl/ vi = scurry.

scuttle² /'skʌtl/ vt to cut holes in (a ship) to sink it: *The captain scuttled his ship to avoid its being captured by the enemy.*

scythe¹ /saɪð/ nc a tool with a long curved blade on a long wooden pole with two short handles, used for cutting long grass, grain etc.

scythe² /saɪð/ vt to use a scythe to cut (grass etc).

SE written abbr south-east.

sea /siː/ n **1** (the —) the salt water that covers most of the earth's surface: *Ships sail on the sea. The sea covers nearly three-quarters of the world's surface.* **the high seas** areas of the sea away from land masses. **2** (used in names; often S-) a particular area of sea which is smaller than an ocean: *the Mediterranean Sea.* **3** (used in various phrases without the, a or an) **at sea** away from, out of sight of, the land: *He was buried at sea.* **all at sea** (fig) puzzled: *He was all at sea when he began his new job.* **by sea** in a ship: *travel by sea.* **go to sea** to become a sailor. **4** n sing **a sea of sth** a large amount or extent of things: *a sea of up-turned faces.*

,sea 'air nu the air at the seaside, considered to be good for health.

'sea anemone nc a popular name for a kind of sea-creature like a flower.

'sea-animal nc any animal living in the sea, e.g. fish, whales, crabs etc.

'sea·bed nc the floor of the sea.

'sea·bird nc any bird living close to the sea.

'sea-breeze nc a breeze blowing inland from the sea.

'sea·faring /-feərɪŋ/ adj (attrib) of, concerning, work or voyages in ships: *a seafaring man.*

'sea-fish nc, nu (a) fish living in the sea.

'sea·food nu edible fish or shellfish from the sea.

'sea·front nc (usually the —) the part of a town facing the sea.

'sea-going adj (of ships) built for crossing the sea, not for coastal voyages only.

,sea-'green adj, nu bluish-green (colour).

'sea·gull nc a common seabird with long wings.

'sea-horse nc a kind of small fish with a head like a horse.

'sea-level nc the level of sea halfway between high and low tide, used as the basis for measuring height of land and depth of sea: *100 metres above/below sea-level.*

'sea-lion nc a kind of large seal¹.

'sea mile nc = nautical mile.

'sea·plane nc a plane designed so that it can come down on and rise from water.

'sea·port nc a town with a harbour used by seagoing ships.

'sea·scape nc a picture of a scene at sea. ⇨ landscape.

'sea·shell nc a shell of any shellfish living in the sea.

'sea·shore nc the land nearest the sea.

'sea·sick adj (usually pred) (feeling) sick because of the movement of a ship.

'sea·side nu (the —; also attrib) a place, town etc by the sea, esp a holiday resort: *go to the seaside; a seaside town.*

,sea-'wall nc a wall built to stop the sea from approaching the land.

'sea·ward /-wəd/ adj towards the sea; in the direction of the sea.

'sea·wards /-wədz/ adv

'sea-water nu water from the sea.

'sea·weed nu any kind of plant growing in the sea, esp on the rocks washed by the sea.

'sea·worthy adj (of a ship) fit for a voyage.

seal¹ /siːl/ nc a large sea-animal with short fur and wide flippers.

'seal·skin nc, nu the skin of a seal.

seal² /siːl/ nc **1** a piece of wax, lead etc stamped with a design, attached to a document to show that it is genuine, or to a letter, packet, box, bottle, door etc to show that it has not been opened. **2** something used instead of a seal(1), e.g. a paper disc stuck to a document. **3** something used to make an opening airtight or watertight. **4** **seal of approval** (fig) an act, event etc regarded as guaranteeing or approving something: *This latest design has my seal of approval.*

seal³ /siːl/ vt **1** to put a seal(1) on (something): *seal a letter.* **2** to fasten or close (something) tightly: *seal an envelope; seal up a drawer.* **3** **seal sth in/off** to prevent entry to or exit from an area: *seal off an area of land.* **4** to make (something) certain: *an agreement sealed with a toast/kiss. His fate is sealed.*

seal·ed adj closed with glue or a seal: *a sealed envelope.* Opp unsealed.

'seal·ing-wax nu a kind of wax used to seal

string round parcels etc.

seam /siːm/ nc **1** a line where two edges of cloth are turned back and sewn together. **2** a line where two edges of material meet. **3** a layer of coal etc in the ground.

seam·stress /ˈsiːmstrɪs/ (also **semp·stress** /ˈsempstrɪs/) nc a woman who makes a living by sewing clothes etc.

se·ance /ˈseɪɑːns/ nc a meeting for communicating with the spirits of the dead through a medium(3).

sear /sɪə(r)/ vt to burn or scorch the surface of (cloth etc), esp with a heated iron.

sear·ing /ˈsɪərɪŋ/ adj (attrib) sudden and sharp: a searing pain.

search¹ /sɜːtʃ/ nc,nu **search (for sb/sth)** an act of searching: a search for a missing aircraft; go in search of a missing child.

search² /sɜːtʃ/ v **1** vt,vi **search (sb/sth) (for sb/sth)** to examine carefully (a person, a person's clothes, inside furniture, a place etc) (in order to find a person or thing): search the house for a letter; search through a cupboard; search a man/his pockets (for the stolen watch); search for a missing child. **Search me!** (informal) I don't know! **2** vt **search for sth** to carry out research in order to find a cure, cause of a fault etc: searching for a cancer cure. **3** vt **search sb/sth out** to find a person or thing by searching.

search·er nc a person who searches.

'search·light nc a powerful light with a beam that can be turned in any direction to search for escaped prisoners etc.

'search-party nc a group of people looking for a person or thing that is lost.

'search-warrant nc an official authority to enter and search a building.

sea·son¹ /ˈsiːzn/ nc **1** one of the four main divisions of the year, i.e. spring, summer, autumn, winter. **2** a period of the year according to the usual weather: the dry/rainy season. **3** a period suitable for something, or closely associated with it: the football season; the holiday/tourist season. **in/out of season** available/not available: Strawberries are out of season now.

'season-ticket nc one that gives the owner the right to travel between places any number of times for a mentioned period of time.

sea·son² /ˈsiːzn/ vt **1** to add salt, pepper etc to (food) to improve the taste. **2** to make (wood) suitable for use by leaving it to dry.

sea·son·ed adj (of wood) dry and ready to use.

sea·son·able /ˈsiːzənəbl/ adj **1** (of the weather) of the kind expected at the time of year. **2** (of help, advice, gifts etc) coming at the right time.

sea·son·al /ˈsiːzənl/ adj happening during a particular season; changing with the seasons: seasonal occupations (e.g. fruit-picking).

sea·son·al·ly /-əlɪ/ adv

sea·son·ing /ˈsiːznɪŋ/ nu something used to season(1) food, e.g. salt, pepper, spices.

seat¹ /siːt/ nc **1** something used or made for sitting on, e.g. a chair, box, bench: The back seat of the car is wide enough for three people. **take a seat** to sit down: Won't you take a seat? **take one's seat** to sit down in one's place, e.g. in a hall or theatre. **take a back seat** to stay in the background: I took a back seat during the dis-

cussions. **2** that part of a chair, stool, bench etc on which one sits (contrasted with the back, legs etc): a chair-seat. **3** the part of clothing on which one sits: He tore the seat of his pants. **4** a place as an official member: a seat on the committee. Mr Smith has a seat in the House of Commons (= is a member). **win a seat/lose one's seat** to win/ be defeated in an election. **5** a place where something is, or where something is carried on: In the USA, Washington is the seat of government. A university is a seat of learning. **6** a large house in the country: He has a country seat as well as a house in London.

'seat-belt nc a strap for fastening across a passenger in a car or plane.

seat² /siːt/ vt **1** to have enough seats for (the number of people mentioned): This theatre seats 500 people. **2** **seat oneself/sb** (formal) (to organize for a person) to sit down: She seated herself at the table. **be seated** (used as an invitation): Please/Kindly be seated, ladies and gentlemen.

sec. /sek/ abbr **1** (of time) second(s). **2** (position) second.

Sec. written abbr **1** Secondary (school). **2** Secretary.

seca·teurs /ˌsekəˈtɜːz/ n pl (also a pair of secateurs) short, strong scissors, used for cutting stems and small branches.

se·cede /sɪˈsiːd/ vi **secede (from sth)** (formal) (of a group) to leave (membership of a group, organization etc).

se·ces·sion /sɪˈseʃn/ nc,nu

se·clude /sɪˈkluːd/ vt (formal) to keep (a person, oneself) away from the company of others: seclude oneself from society; keep a wife secluded in the kitchen.

se·cluded adj (of a place) separate and quiet.

se·clu·sion /sɪˈkluːʒn/ n **1** nu the state of being secluded: live in seclusion. **2** n sing a secluded place: in the seclusion of one's own home.

sec·ond¹ /ˈsekənd/ adj or det (abbr 2nd) **1** **the/ my/this etc second** + noun next after the first in order, time, importance etc: February is the second month of the year. The second prize is a holiday. You won't have a second chance. Compare first¹. ⇨ second⁵. **at second hand** ⇨ hand¹(1). **on second thoughts** ⇨ thought¹(2). **second to none** (pred) the best of all: As a teacher he was second to none. **2** additional; extra: Did you bring a second pair of shoes? **3** another (similar example of): He acts like a second Napoleon!

,second-'best adj ('second-best when attrib) next after the best: my second-best suit. □ adv: I won't accept/put up with second-best. **come off second-best** to be defeated.

,second-'class adj ('second-class when attrib) of the standard next after the first: a second-class hotel; take a second-class (university) degree; second-class citizens (i.e. treated as inferior). □ adv in the next after the best accommodation in a train, plane etc: go second-class.

,second 'cousin nc the child of one's parent's first cousin. ⇨ first cousin.

'second-degree adj (attrib) of the kind next to the most serious: second-degree burns.

,second 'floor nc the floor above the first (GB

two floors up; *US* one floor up).

,second-,gene'ration *adj* (*attrib*) having parents who were the first people in a family to be something: *second-generation immigrants*.

,second-'hand *adj* (a) previously owned by someone else: *second-hand furniture/books*. (b) (also *adv*) (obtained) from others: *second-hand information; hear news second-hand*.

,second 'name *nc* = surname.

,second 'nature *nu* a tendency that has become a habit: *Kindness is second nature to him*.

,second 'person *nu* (*gram*) the pronoun *you* (and the verb form used with it), used to show the person being spoken to. ⇨ first/third person.

,second-'rate *adj* (*derog*) not of the best quality; inferior: *a man with second-rate ideas*.

,second 'sight *nu* the power to see future events.

,second 'string *adj, nc* (of) an alternative course of action after initial failure.

,second 'teeth *n pl* those which grow after a child's first teeth come out. ⇨ milk tooth.

,second 'wind *nu* renewed strength, energy.

sec·ond² /'sekənd/ *adv* in the next position after the first: *The German team came second. Second, I'd like to thank my mother. second of all* (used for emphasis) after the first (mentioned): *Second of all we must save the women*. ⇨ secondly.

sec·ond³ /'sekənd/ *nc* **1** the sixtieth part of a minute or a degree: *The winner's time was 1 minute and 5 seconds. 1° 6' 10" means one degree, six minutes, and ten seconds*. **2** a moment; short time: *I'll be ready in a second or two/in a few seconds*.

'second hand *nc* an extra hand in some watches and clocks recording seconds. ⇨ also second-hand at second¹.

sec·ond⁴ /'sekənd/ *nc* **1** (*pl*) goods below the best in quality: *There are many cheap seconds of china in the sale*. **2** a helper of a boxer or wrestler.

sec·ond⁵ /'sekənd/ *pron* (abbr 2nd) **1** (the —) the next after the first person, thing or people, things etc: *I was/We were the second to arrive. This is the first prize but what is the second? Today is 2 May* (or *the second of May or May the second*). *a close second* (a person, score, etc that is very near to the first): *Coe won the race but Jones was a close second*. **2** *nc* (in examinations) the next standard after the best: *She got a second in Chemistry*. ⇨ second-class.

sec·ond⁶ /'sekənd/ *vt* **1** to support (esp a boxer, wrestler). **2** to speak formally in support of (a motion in a debate etc): *Mr Smith proposed and Mr Green seconded a vote of thanks to the lecturer*. sec·ond·er *nc* a person who seconds(2) a motion.

se·cond⁷ /sɪ'kɒnd/ *vt* (often *passive*) to send (a member of staff) to work in another department, for another company etc for a while: *be seconded by the BBC to work for another radio station*. se·cond·ment *nu* (esp) *on secondment* seconded to work in another place.

sec·ond·ary /'sekəndrɪ/ *adj* **1** (*attrib*) coming after the first: *secondary education*. **2** less important or less strong: *secondary symptoms*.

'secondary school *nc* one for children over 11 years of age.

'secondary stress *nc,nu* (*lang*) a weaker stress

(marked /ˌ/ in this dictionary) as shown in 'pronunciation' /prəˌnʌnsɪ'eɪʃn/.

sec·ond·ar·ily /-dərɪlɪ/ *adv*

sec·ond·ly /'sekəndlɪ/ *adv* after the first (mentioned): *Secondly, we must check the water level*. ⇨ second of all at second².

se·cre·cy /'siːkrəsɪ/ *nu* (the habit of) keeping secrets; state of being kept secret: *I depend on your secrecy. swear sb to secrecy* to make a person promise to keep a secret.

se·cret¹ /'siːkrɪt/ *adj* **1** (that is to be) kept from the knowledge or view of others; of which others have no knowledge: *It was a secret marriage*. ⇨ secretive. *keep sth secret (from sb)* to refuse to tell it (to a person). **2** (of places) quiet and unknown. ⇨ top secret.

,secret 'agent *nc* a member of the secret service.

,secret po'lice *nu* (the —) the police acting in secret (against political opposition).

,Secret 'Service *nu* (the —) the government department concerned with spying.

se·cret·ly *adv*

se·cret² /'siːkrɪt/ *n* **1** *nc* something that is secret. *keep a secret* to refuse to tell anyone: *Can you keep a secret? (be) an open secret* (of something thought to be secret) to be (in fact) widely known. **2** *nc* an unknown cause, explanation, way of doing or getting something etc: *What is the secret of his success?* **3** *nu* *in secret* without anyone else knowing: *I was told about it in secret*.

sec·re·tar·ial /ˌsekrə'teərɪəl/ *adj* (*attrib*) of (the work of) secretaries: *secretarial duties/training/colleges*.

sec·re·tar·iat /ˌsekrə'teərɪət/ *nc* an official department with administrative duties, esp of an international organization.

sec·re·tary /'sekrətrɪ/ *nc* (*pl* -ies) **1** a person in an office who deals with correspondence, keeps records, makes arrangements and appointments etc. **2** an official who has charge of the correspondence, records, and other business affairs of a society, club or other organization. **3** (often S-) a government officer or minister of high rank.

,Secretary of 'State *nc* (*GB*) a minister in charge of a government department: *the Secretary of State for Industry*.

se·crete /sɪ'kriːt/ *vt* **1** (*science*) to produce (a liquid) by secretion(1). **2** *secrete sth (away)* to put, keep, something in a secret place.

se·cre·tion /sɪ'kriːʃn/ *n* **1** *nc,nu* (*science*) (a liquid substance from) the process by which certain liquid substances in a plant or animal body are produced, e.g. sweat, saliva. **2** *nc* (*formal*) an act of hiding things: *the secretion of stolen goods*.

se·cret·ive /'siːkrətɪv/ *adj* (having the habit of) hiding one's knowledge, feelings etc.

se·cre·tive·ly *adv*

sect /sekt/ *nc* a group of people united by (esp political or religious) beliefs or opinions.

sec·tar·ian /sek'teərɪən/ *adj* of a sect or sects: *sectarian politics* (= in which the advantage of a particular sect is considered more important than the whole group). ⇨ sectional(b).

sec·tion /'sekʃn/ *nc* **1** one of the parts into which something has or may be divided: *the sections of an orange*. **2** one of a number of parts which can be put together to make a structure: *glue the sec-*

tions of the model together. **3** a division of an organization: *the exports section.* **4** a part of a community or area of land: *the poorer sections; the industrial section of a town.* **5** (*tech*) a view of something (as if) cut from top to bottom and examined from the side.

sec·tion·al /-ʃənl/ *adj* (*attrib*) (**a**) made or supplied in sections(2): *a sectional fishing-rod.* (**b**) of one or more sections of a community etc: *sectional interests.*

sec·tion·al·ism /-ɪzəm/ *nu* concern about sectional interests and not the community as a whole.

sec·tor /'sektə(r)/ *nc* **1** (*maths*) a part of a circle lying between two straight lines drawn from the centre to the circumference. **2** one of the parts into which an area is divided or used for a purpose. **3** a branch (of industry etc): *the public and private sectors of industry.*

secu·lar /'sekjʊlə(r)/ *adj* not religious or spiritual: *secular music.*

se·cure¹ /sɪ'kjʊə(r)/ *adj* (rarely —r, —st) **1** free from anxiety: *feel secure about the future.* Opp insecure(2). **2** certain; guaranteed: *He has a secure position as a university lecturer.* Opp insecure(1). **3** fastened; fixed: *Are you sure the doors and windows are secure? Is that ladder secure?* **4 secure (against/from sth)** (*formal*) safe: *Are we secure from attack?*

se·cure² /sɪ'kjʊə(r)/ *vt* **1** (*formal*) to lock (something) (the usual word): *Secure all the doors and windows before leaving the house.* **2** to make (something) safe or firm: *By strengthening the embankments they secured the village against/ from floods.* **3** (*formal*) to succeed in getting (something which is difficult to get): *She has secured a good teaching job.*

se·cure·ly *adv*

se·cur·ity /sɪ'kjʊərətɪ/ *n* (*pl* -ies) **1** *nc,nu* (something that provides) safety, freedom from danger or anxiety: *the security of parental care.* ⇨ insecurity. **2** *nc,nu* something valuable, e.g. a life insurance policy, given as a guarantee for the repayment of a loan or the fulfilment of a promise etc: *lend money on security; offer a house as (a) security for a loan.*

se·date¹ /sɪ'deɪt/ *adj* (of a person, behaviour) calm; serious.

se·date·ly *adv*

se·date² /sɪ'deɪt/ *vt* to give (a person) a sedative.

se·da·tion /sɪ'deɪʃn/ *nu* medical treatment using sedatives. **be under sedation** to have taken sedatives.

seda·tive /'sedətɪv/ *adj, nc* (a medicine, drug) used to calm the nerves and reduce stress: *After taking a sedative she was able to get to sleep.*

sed·en·tary /'sedntrɪ/ *adj* (*formal;* usually *attrib*) **1** (of work) done sitting down (at a desk etc). **2** spending much of the time seated: *lead a sedentary life.*

sedi·ment /'sedɪmənt/ *nu* any substance (e.g. sand, dirt) that settles on the bottom of a liquid.

sedi·men·tary /ˌsedɪ'mentrɪ/ *adj* of, formed from, sediment: *sedimentary rock.*

se·di·tion /sɪ'dɪʃn/ *nu* words or actions intended to make people rebel against authority, disobey the government etc.

se·di·tious /sɪ'dɪʃəs/ *adj* containing, using,

sedition: *seditious speeches/writers.*

se·duce /sɪ'djuːs/ *vt* **1** to persuade (a person who is less experienced) to have sexual intercourse. **2** to persuade (a person) to do wrong: *be seduced by the offer of money into betraying one's country.* **3** to persuade (a person) to do or decide something good, pleasant etc: *be seduced by the warm sun to live in Florida.*

se·ducer *nc* a person who seduces, esp(1).

se·duc·tion /sɪ'dʌkʃn/ *n* **1** *nc,nu* (an instance of) seducing or being seduced. **2** *nc* something attractive that may lead a person to do or decide something (but often with no implication of doing wrong): *the seductions of country life.*

se·duc·tive /sɪ'dʌktɪv/ *adj* (**a**) likely to seduce(1): *a seductive dress.* (**b**) attractive: *a seductive offer.*

se·duc·tive·ly *adv*

sedu·lous /'sedjʊləs/ *adj* (*formal*) serious and determined: *He paid her sedulous attention.*

see¹ /siː/ *nc* the office, district, of a bishop.

see² /siː/ *v* (*pt* saw /sɔː/, *pp* seen /siːn/) Ⓝ Not used in continuous tenses, e.g. *is/was -ing* in 1, 5–9, 11 below. **1** *vi, vt* to have, use, the power of sight: *I can't see in this light. On a clear day we can see the island. What can you see? I can see a big dog. I saw her in the street. We saw that you were angry. Couldn't you see that I was worried? I looked everywhere but he was not to be seen* (= could not be found). Ⓝ 'See' in this sense is not used in continuous tenses, e.g. *is/was -ing.* Use 'can/could see', as in *He can/could see a bird,* or 'is/was looking at', as in *He is/was looking at a bird.* For a comparison of *see* and *look,* ⇨ the note at look²(1). **seeing is believing** (*saying*) one must see something before believing it exists or is happening. ⇨ also back³(1), last³, red(1), sights¹(4), star¹(1), thing(1). **2** *vt* to watch a film, TV programme etc: *I saw it on TV. What are you seeing tonight? Which film are you seeing/are you going to see?* Ⓝ The continuous tenses are possible but 'going to see' is more usual. **3** *vt* to meet or interview (a person): *The manager can/will see you for five minutes. I'm seeing her/going to see her this afternoon.* **See you (later)** (*informal*) (an expression used to say goodbye, the reply being (*Yes,*) *see you!*). **4** *vt* to visit (a professional person): *You should see a doctor about that cough. Fred is seeing* (= is visiting regularly) *a psychiatrist.* **5** *vt, vi* to learn (something) by reading it in the newspaper etc: *I see that the Prime Minister is in China.* **6** (*imperative*) to look at (something): *See page 60.* **7** *vt* to have knowledge or experience of (something): *He's seen a great deal in his short life. I never saw such rudeness!* **see better days** = day(4). **8** *vt, vi* to understand (a person, thing): *Do you see what I mean? I can't see why I should believe you. We're taking a tent, see, so we'll be OK. You see/ See, I told you so!* (i.e. *You understand now, ...*) Ⓝ 'See' in this sense is not used in continuous tenses, e.g. *is/was -ing.* Use 'can/could see'. **as far as I can see; as I see it** in my opinion. ⇨ also joke¹, point¹(7) light⁴(1), reason¹(3), sense¹(4), side²(8). **9** *vi* to think: *Let me see, who shall I choose?* **10** *vt* to make sure (that) (something): *See that all the doors are locked/the children have enough to eat.* **11** *vt* to allow (a person) to be in the condition mentioned: *No-one can see people* *in pain without wanting to help.*

see about sb/sth to deal with a person, thing: *He promised to see about my broken window.* **see sb about sth** to visit a person for advice about something: *I must see a builder about my roof.*

see sb across sth to help, guide, a person across a road etc.

see sb/oneself as sb to imagine a person, oneself, to be the person mentioned: *He sees himself as a hero.*

~~see sb back~~ to take a person back to a place, e.g. home.

see beyond sth to be able to understand future events or possibilities: *A business manager must see beyond one year's activities.*

see by sth to use something in order to be able to see: *I had a torch to see by.*

see for oneself to find out personally (in order to be convinced or satisfied): *If you don't believe me, go and see for yourself!*

see a lot/less/more etc of sb to meet, visit, a person less/more often etc: *We don't see much of you these days. Nothing was seen of her for weeks.*

see sb off (a) to go to a station, airport etc to say goodbye to a passenger: *Will you come (to the bus station) and see me off?* **(b)** to chase (a person) away.

see sb out (of a place) to go with a person to the exit (of a building): *My secretary will see you out.*

see over sth to visit and examine a building, exhibition etc: *We saw over a house we wanted to buy.*

see round sth = see over sth.

see through (sth) (to be able) to see from one side to the other: *see through a window.* Hence **'see-through** *adj: see-through material.* **see through sb/sth** to understand the true nature of a person or situation that seems pleasant etc but is not. **see sb through (sth)** to give a person help, support during a crisis, trouble etc. **see sth through** to continue with an activity until it is successfully or happily achieved.

see to sb/sth to take care of a person, task: *Can you see to the children? I'll see to the meal* (= cook it). **see to it** to deal with something: *'That's the doorbell!' — 'I'll see to it.'* **see to it (that . . .)** to make sure (that . . .): *See to it (that) you're home early.*

seed¹ /si:d/ *n* **1** *nc,nu* a small part of a plant or fruit from which another plant can grow; a quantity of seeds: *a packet of seed(s).* **run/go to seed (a)** to stop flowering as seed is produced. **(b)** *(fig)* to become careless of one's appearance and manners. **2** *nc* **seed (of sth)** a cause or origin (of something): *sow the seeds of unhappiness in her.* **3** *nu* = semen. **4** *nc (sport)* a seeded(4) player: *England's number 1 seed* (e.g. in a tennis championship).

'seed-bed *nc* an area of fine soil in which to sow seed.

seed·less *adj* having no seed: *seedless raisins.*

seed² /si:d/ *v* **1** *vi* (of a plant) to produce seed when full grown. **2** *vt* to sow (soil) with seed: *seed a field with wheat.* **3** *vt* to remove seeds from (fruit etc): *seed raisins.* **4** *vt (sport)* to separate (the best players or teams) from the rest when organizing competitions (in order to have good matches

later): *seeded tennis players.*

seed·ling /'si:dlɪŋ/ *nc* a young plant growing from a seed(1).

seedy /'si:dɪ/ *adj* (-ier, -iest) **1** *(informal; derog)* old, neglected etc: *a seedy hotel; a seedy-looking person.* **2** *(pred; informal)* unwell: *feel seedy.*

seed·ily /-əlɪ/ *adv*

seek /si:k/ *v* (*pt,pp* sought /sɔ:t/) **1** *vt,vi* to look for (a person, thing); try to find: *seek advice; seek out a relative in Australia; seek shelter from the rain; seek a cure for AIDS.* **seek one's fortune** ⇨ fortune(2). **2** *vt (formal)* to ask for (something): *I will seek my doctor's advice.* **(much) sought after** (of tickets, valuable paintings, a reliable doctor etc) wanted by many people.

seem /si:m/ *vi* Ⓝ Not used in continuous tenses, e.g. *is/was -ing.* to have or give the impression or appearance of being or doing; appear to be: *You seem tired. There seems to be no one here. What seems easy to some people seems difficult to others. He seems to think so. He seems to be the winner. That seems (to be) the best idea. The book seems (to be) quite interesting. It seems as if I was wrong. That seems like a good idea.* Ⓝ 'Seem' cannot be used with an adverb. 'Seem' must be used with 'to be' when it comes immediately before a noun, as in *She seems to be the manager.* 'To be' can be omitted if it comes before an adjective.

seem·ing /'si:mɪŋ/ *adj (attrib)* apparent but perhaps not real or genuine: *In spite of his seeming friendship he gave me no help.*

seem·ing·ly *adv* apparently (the more usual word). *Seemingly, she wanted to leave early.*

seem·ly /'si:mlɪ/ *adj* (-ier, -iest) (usually *pred*) (of behaviour) proper or correct (for the occasion or circumstances): *It isn't seemly to praise oneself.* Opp unseemly.

seen /si:n/ *pp* of see¹.

seep /si:p/ *vi* (of liquids) to flow slowly (into, out of, through etc): *water seeping through the roof.*

~~seep·age~~ /-ɪdʒ/ *nu*

seer /sɪə(r)/ *nc* a person claiming to see into the future.

see·saw¹ /'si:sɔ:/ *nc,nu* **1** (a game played on) a long plank with a person sitting on each end which can rise and fall alternately. **2** *(fig)* any up-and-down or to-and-fro: movement: *the seesaw of bank interest charges.*

see·saw² /'si:sɔ:/ *vi* **1** to play on a seesaw. **2** *(fig)* to move up and down or to and fro: *Prices seesawed.*

seethe /si:ð/ *vi* **seethe (with sth)** to be very angry or upset (because of a strong emotion): *seethe with anger; a country seething with discontent.*

seg·ment¹ /'segmənt/ *nc* **1** *(maths)* a part cut off or marked off by a line: *a segment of a circle.* **2** a section: *a segment of an orange.*

seg·ment² /seg'ment/ *vi,vt* (to cause something) to divide into segments.

seg·re·gate /'segrɪgeɪt/ *vt* to put (a person, thing) apart from the rest; separate: *segregate the boys from the girls.*

seg·re·ga·tion /ˌsegrɪ'geɪʃn/ *nu*

seis·mic /'saɪzmɪk/ *adj (tech)* of earthquakes.

seis·mo·graph /'saɪzməgrɑːf/ *nc (science)* an instrument which records the strength, duration and distance away of earthquakes.

seis·mol·ogist /saɪz'mɒlədʒɪst/ *nc* a scientist studying earthquakes.

seis·mol·ogy /saɪz'mɒlədʒɪ/ *nu* the scientific study of earthquakes.

seize /siːz/ *v* **1** *vt* to take hold of (a person, thing) suddenly and with force: *seize a thief by the collar.* **2** *vt* **seize (on)** *sth* to take and use (something): *seize (on) an idea/a chance/an opportunity.* **3** *vt* (*legal*) to take possession of (property etc): *seize her house for payment of a debt.* **4** *vi* **seize (up)** (of moving parts of machinery) to become unable to move, e.g. because of too much heat or not enough oil: *The engine has seized (up).*

seiz·ure /'siːʒə(r)/ *n* **1** *nc,nu* (an act of) seizing (esp 3): *seizure of drugs by Customs officers.* **2** *nc* a heart attack.

sel·dom /'seldəm/ *adv* not often; rarely: *She seldom goes out. She goes out very seldom.*

se·lect¹ /sɪ'lekt/ *adj* (*attrib*) **1** carefully chosen: *select fruit; select passages from 'Hamlet'.* **2** of or for a particular group, not for all: *a play to be shown to a select audience.* ⇨ selective.

se·lect² /sɪ'lekt/ *vt* to choose (a person, thing, as being the most suitable etc): *select a book/a present for a child. Who has been selected to speak at the meeting?*

se·lec·tion /sɪ'lekʃn/ *n* **1** *nu* the act of choosing. ⇨ natural selection. **2** *nc* a collection or group of (a) selected things or examples; (b) a number of things from which to choose: *That shop has a good selection of handbags.*

se·lec·tive /sɪ'lektɪv/ *adj* **1** (*pred*) choosing carefully: *be selective when buying fruit.* **2** characterized by choosing (e.g. choosing to affect some and not others): *selective taxes.*

se·lec·tive·ly *adv*

se·lec·tor /sɪ'lektə(r)/ *nc* a person, machine etc that selects, e.g., a member of a committee, team etc.

self /self/ *n* (*pl* **selves** /selvz/) *nc,nu* a person's nature, special qualities; one's own personality: *my former self* (= myself as I used to be). *I'm not my usual self today* (= I feel ill, tired etc).

,self-ab'sorbed *adj* thinking of one's own interests only, unaware of other people.

,self-as'sertion *nu* the putting forward of oneself or one's ideas in an effort to be noticed by everyone.

,self-as'surance *nu* confidence in one's abilities. Hence **,self-as'sured** *adj*

,self-'catering *adj* (of a holiday flat, camp etc) where a visitor provides her or his own food.

,self-'centred *adj* (*derog*) interested mainly in oneself and one's own affairs.

,self-con'fessed *adj* admitted by oneself: *a self-confessed thief.*

,self-'confidence *nu* belief in one's own abilities. Hence **,self-'confident** *adj*

,self-'conscious *adj* shy; embarrassed. Hence **,self-'consciousness** *nu*

,self-con'tained *adj* (a) (of a person) not dependent on others. (b) (of a flat) complete in itself (not sharing the kitchen, bathroom etc with other people).

,self-con'trol *nu* the control of one's own feelings, behaviour etc: *lose one's self-control.*

,self-de'fence *nu* the defence of one's own body, property, rights etc: *kill a person in self-defence* (i.e. while defending oneself against an attack).

,self-de'nial *nu* the act of going without things in order to help others.

,self-ef'facing *adj* (*formal*) keeping oneself in the background (and avoiding praise, attention).

,self-em'ployed *adj* working for oneself, as an owner of a business etc.

,self-e'steem *nu* the state of having a good (sometimes exaggerated) opinion of oneself.

,self-'evident *adj* clearly true and not needing further proof or evidence. Hence **,self-'evidently** *adv*

,self-ex'planatory *adj* able to be understood without (further) explanation.

,self-'government *nu* independent government by a country's own people.

,self-im'portant *adj* (*derog*) having too high an opinion of oneself: *a self-important official.* Hence **,self-im'portance** *nu*

,self-im'posed *adj* (of a duty, task etc or suffering) that one has forced on oneself: *self-imposed misery/exile.*

,self-in'dulgent *adj* (*derog*) wanting to do or have things that please oneself and not others. Hence **,self-in'dulgence** *nu*

,self-'interest *nu* one's own interests and personal advantage.

,self-'made *adj* having obtained wealth or power because of one's own efforts.

,self-'pity *nu* (exaggerated) pity for oneself.

,self-pos'sessed *adj* calm, confident: *a self-possessed young woman.*

,self-,preser'vation *nu* keeping oneself safe from harm or destruction: *the instinct of self-preservation.*

,self-'raising *adj* (of flour) not needing the addition of baking-powder etc for cakes etc to rise. Compare plain(5).

,self-re'liant *adj* having or showing confidence in one's own ability, judgement etc. Hence **,self-re'liance** *nu*

,self-re'spect *nu* the feeling that one is behaving and thinking in ways that will not cause one to be ashamed of oneself: *lose all self-respect.*

,self-re'specting *adj* (*attrib*) having self-respect: *No self-respecting man could agree to do such a thing.*

,self-re'straint *nu* = self-control.

,self-'righteous *adj* (*derog*) convinced of one's own goodness and that one is better than others.

,self-'rule *nu* = self-government.

,self-'sacrifice *nu* the giving up of one's own interests and wishes for the sake of other people. Hence **,self-'sacrificing** *adj*

'self-same *adj* (*attrib*) identical: *Tom and I reached Paris on the selfsame day.*

,self-satis'faction *nu* (often *derog*) (too) much satisfaction with one's achievement(s) or position.

,self-'service *adj, nu* (a) (of) a canteen, restaurant at which people collect their own food and carry it to tables. (b) (of) a shop at which customers collect what they want from counters or shelves (in wire baskets) and pay as they leave. (c) (of) a garage at which customers fill their cars with petrol.

,self-'styled *adj* (*attrib*; usually *derog*) using a

name, title etc which one has given oneself (and to which one has no right): *a self-styled expert on music.*

,self-suf'ficient *adj* needing no help from others: *The country is now self-sufficient in oil.*

,self-sup'porting *adj* **(a)** (of a person) earning enough money to keep oneself: *I have more money now that my children are self-supporting.* **(b)** (of a business etc) not needing financial help.

,self-'taught *adj* having educated oneself, not taught by others.

,self-'will *nu* the determination to do as one wishes and not be guided by others. Hence **,self-'willed** *adj*

self·ish /'selfɪʃ/ *adj* (*derog*) thinking mainly of oneself and one's own wishes: *act from selfish motives.* Opp unselfish.

self·ish·ly *adv*

self·ish·ness *nu*

sell /sel/ *v* (*pt,pp* **sold** /səʊld/) **1** *vi,vt* **sell sb sth; sell (sth (to sb))** to give (something) in exchange for money: *sell sweets; sell me your bike/sell your bike to me. I'll sell it to you. She won't sell (it).* ⇨ sell at/for sth. **sell sb short** ⇨ short²(2). ⇨ also sale. **2** *vi* to be bought: *Your home won't sell—it's too expensive.* **3** *vt* to cause (something) to be sold: *It's the low prices which sell our goods.* **4** *vt* to persuade (a person) to agree, accept (an idea etc): *He tried to sell (me) the idea of buying a new carpet.* ⇨ be sold on sth.

sell oneself (a) to present oneself in an attractive or convincing way (e.g. when applying for a job). **(b)** to do something dishonourable for money or reward. **5 be sold** (*informal*) to be cheated or deceived (by being sold poor quality goods or because a person had no intention to honour an agreement): *I've/You've been sold!* ⇨ be sold on sth below.

sell (sth) at sth to give (something) in exchange for a mentioned price: *These oranges sell at/We sell these oranges at 10p. I sold my car at a loss.*

sell (sth) for sth to give (something) in exchange for money: *I'll sell it to you for £5. It was sold for £100. What did you sell it for? 'I'm selling my bike'—'How much (are you selling it) for?'*

sell sth off to get rid of goods cheaply: *They're selling off the old stock of shirts.*

be sold on sth (*informal*) to agree completely with an idea, plan etc: *Are they sold on the idea of a holiday in Spain?*

sell out (of sth) to sell all one's supplies (of goods): *We've sold out (of tickets/smaller sizes).*

sell out to sb (*informal*) to agree (secretly) to work with the enemy and so be disloyal to one's side: *The union leaders were accused of selling out to the management.* Hence **'sell-out** *nc*

sell up to sell one's house, a business (e.g. because of debt, moving to another town etc).

sell·er /'selə(r)/ *nc* a person who sells something: *a bookseller.* ⇨ also bestseller.

sell-out /'selaʊt/ *nc* **1** an event (a football match, concert etc) for which all tickets have been sold. **2** (*informal*) a betrayal: *government policies which are a sell-out.* ⇨ also sell out to sb above.

sel·vage (also **sel·vedge**) /'selvɪdʒ/ *nc* the edge of cloth made so that threads do not come apart.

selves /selvz/ *pl* of self.

sem·an·tic /sɪ'mæntɪk/ *adj* (*lang*) relating to

meaning in language.

se·man·tics *n sing* (*lang*) the branch of linguistics concerned with studying the meanings of words, phrases etc.

sema·phore /'seməfɔː(r)/ *nu* the system (code) for sending signals, e.g. by using one's arms or flags held in the hands, with various positions for the letters of the alphabet.

sem·blance /'sembləns/ *nc* **semblance (of sth)** (*formal*) an (untrue) appearance: *put on a semblance of gaiety.*

se·men /'siːmən/ *nu* the fertilizing fluid produced by male animals.

semi- /semɪ/ *prefix* half of; partly; midway: *semi-literate.*

'semi·circle *nc* half a circle.

,semi·'circular *adj* having the shape of half a circle.

,semi·'colon *nc* the punctuation mark (;). Ⓝ It is used to separate parts of a sentence that are already divided by commas, as in *The box contains two pots, each with lids; four plates, all the same size; and four cups.* It is also used in formal style to separate main clauses, as in *Kind thoughts won't help; we need money. Thanks for the thought; however, we need money.*

,semi·con'ductor *nc* (*science*) a material that allows electricity to pass through (when heated) but not as easily or as much as a conductor. ⇨ insulator.

,semi·'conscious *adj* partly conscious.

,semi·de'tached *adj* (of house) joined to another on one side.

,semi·'final *nc* (*sport*) a match or round before the final (e.g. in a football competition). Hence **,semi·'finalist** *nc* a player, team, in the semi-finals.

,semi·'liquid *adj, nc* any kind of (very) thick liquid.

,semi·of'ficial *adj* (esp of announcements etc made to newspapers) with the condition that they must not be considered as coming from an official source.

,semi·'skilled *adj* having or needing some training but less than skilled: *semi-skilled labour.*

sem·in·ar /'semɪnɑː(r)/ *nc* a group studying a problem and meeting for discussion with a tutor or professor.

semo·li·na /,semə'liːnə/ *nu* (also *attrib*) hard grains from wheat, used for making pasta and in milk puddings etc: *semolina pudding.*

semp·stress /'sempstrɪs/ = seamstress.

Sen. *written abbr* **1** (also **Snr, Sr**) Senior. **2** Senator.

SEN /,es i: 'en/ *abbr* State Enrolled Nurse.

sen·ate /'senət/ *nc* **1** the senior part (house) of a two part legislative assembly in some countries, e.g. France, US. **2** the governing council of some universities.

sena·tor /-tə(r)/ *nc* a member of senate(1).

sena·tor·ial /,senə'tɔːrɪəl/ *adj*

send /send/ *v* (*pt,pp* **sent** / sent/) **1** *vt* to cause or order (a person, thing) to be carried to, go to a place without going oneself: *send a telegram/message to her; send her a letter. I'll send my son to fetch the parcel. The children were sent to bed.* Compare fetch(1), bring(1), take²(2). **2** *vt* to use force to cause (a person, thing) to move quickly:

The wind sent the vase crashing to the floor. **send sb flying** ⇨ fly²(4). **send sb packing** ⇨ pack²(1). **3** *vt* to cause (a person) to become the state mentioned: *The noise sent me crazy.* **4** *vt* (*informal*) (of music, modern designs etc) to cause (a person) to feel very pleased and excited: *Her singing sends me!*

send after sb to ask a person to go and tell another person something: *She's left her gloves but I'll send one of the children after her.*

send sb/sth ahead to cause a person, luggage etc to go before oneself or the main group.

send sb away to tell an employee that he or she is no longer wanted. **send away for sth** to order goods by post: *I've sent away to the travel agent for their new brochure.*

send sth back to return goods to a shop or to a supplier by post.

send sb down (a) to dismiss a student from a university. (b) (*informal*) (of a judge) to give an offender a prison sentence. **send sth down** to cause prices, temperatures etc to fall: *The president's bad health sent the stock market down.*

send (sb) for sb/sth to ask, order, a person to come, or for a person, thing, to be brought to oneself: *send (one's daughter) for a newspaper; send for a doctor/taxi; send for the manager.*

send sth in (a) to enter a solution, article, entry-form etc for a competition. (b) to send(1) an application form etc to an official: *send in one's passport.*

send sb off (a) to go to a station, airport etc and say goodbye to a person: *All the staff went to the airport to send her off.* Hence **'send-off** *nc*. (b) to order a player to leave a sports field because of a serious offence. **send sth off** to post a letter, parcel. **send off for sth** = send away for sth: *I've sent off for more information.*

send sth on (a) = send sth ahead. (b) to post letters to a person at a new address.

send sth out to produce, give out, something: *The sun sends out heat and light.* **send sb out (of a place)** to order a person to leave. **send (sb) out for sth** to order (a person) to go and fetch food, a newspaper etc.

send sb to a place to arrange for a person to attend a university, college etc. **send sb to sth** to cause a person to experience a state mentioned: *The music sent me to sleep. His bad judgement sent him to his death.*

send sb/sth up (*informal*) to cause a person, tradition, accent etc to appear ridiculous: *The comedian sent up the Prime Minister.* Hence **'send-up** *nc*. **send sth up** to cause prices, temperatures etc to increase: *The shock sent her blood pressure up.*

send·er /'sendə(r)/ *nc* person or thing that sends something: *Who was the sender of the telegram?*

send-off /'send ɒf/ ⇨ send sb off(a).

send-up /'send ʌp/ ⇨ send sb/sth up.

se·nile /'siːnaɪl/ *adj* suffering from physical or mental weakness because of old age; lacking intelligence because of old age: *senile decay.*

sen·il·ity /sɪ'nɪlətɪ/ *nu*

sen·ior /'siːnɪə(r)/ *adj* **1** older in years; higher in rank, authority etc: *Smith is the senior partner in* (= the head of) *the firm.* **2** (a person) older than another: *She is my senior by ten years. He is ten*

years senior to me. Tom Brown, Senior (abbr Sen., Snr, Sr; used of a father having the same names as his son). **3** (a person) higher in rank than another: *a senior officer.* Compare junior.

,senior 'citizen *nc* a person over the age of retirement.

sen·ior·ity /ˌsiːnɪ'ɒrətɪ/ *nu* the condition of being older, higher in rank, longer in a job etc: *Should promotion be through merit or seniority?*

sen·sa·tion /sen'seɪʃn/ *n* **1** *nc,nu* the ability to feel; feeling produced by the senses: *lose all sensation in one's legs; have a sensation of warmth/ dizziness/falling.* **2** *nc* (an instance of) a general excited state: *The news created a great sensation.*

sen·sa·tion·al /-ʃənl/ *adj* (a) causing a sensation(2): *a sensational murder.* (b) (of newspapers etc) presenting news in a manner designed to cause sensation(2): *a sensational writer/newspaper.*

sen·sa·tion·al·ism /-ɪzəm/ *nu* the act of deliberately causing sensation(2): *Try to avoid sensationalism in your writing.*

sen·sa·tion·al·ist /-ɪst/ *nc* a person who writes or speaks in an exaggerated way to shock or excite people.

sen·sa·tion·al·ly /-nəlɪ/ *adv*

sense¹ /sens/ *nc* **1** any of the five powers of the body by which a person is conscious of things (i.e. sight, hearing, smell, taste and touch): *have a keen sense of hearing.* ⇨ sensory. ⇨ also sixth sense. **2** *nu* the power of judging; good, practical, judgement: *Haven't you any sense? There's a lot of sense in what he says. There's no sense in* (= There's no good reason for) *doing that.* ⇨ common sense. **3** *nc* a meaning: *In what sense are you using the word?* **in a sense** using one possible meaning: *He's right in a sense but I still disapprove.* **make (good/much/no/little) sense** to seem to have (a lot of/no/little) meaning that can be understood: *It just doesn't make sense* (= seems to have no useful meaning). **4** (*pl*) the normal state of mind: *in one's (right) senses* (= sane); *out of one's senses* (= insane). **bring sb to her/ his senses** to cause her or him to stop behaving foolishly: *Perhaps a month in prison will bring you to your senses.* **come to one's senses** to stop behaving foolishly. **knock (some) sense into sb** (*informal*) to force a person to behave sensibly. **see sense** to realize one is behaving foolishly and stop. **take leave of one's senses** ⇨ leave¹(3). **5** *n sing* (used with *a, an* or a *possessive pronoun*) an appreciation or understanding of the value or worth of: *a sense of humour; my sense of duty.* ⇨ direction(1). **6** *nu* consciousness: *have no sense of shame.* **7** *nu* a general feeling or opinion among a number of people: *take the sense of a public meeting.* ⇨ consensus.

'sense-organ *nc* a part of the body, e.g. an ear, eye, used to experience a sense(1).

sense² /sens/ *vt* to become vaguely aware of (something): *He sensed that his proposals were unwelcome.*

sense·less /'senslɪs/ *adj* **1** foolish: *a senseless idea.* **2** (*pred*) unconscious: *fall senseless to the ground.*

sense·less·ly *adv*

sense·less·ness *nu*

sen·si·bil·ity /ˌsensə'bɪlətɪ/ *n* (*pl* **-ies**) **1** *nu* the power of delicate, artistic feeling: *the sensibility of an artist or poet.* **2** (*pl*) (*formal*) strong feelings of what is right, good etc: *Her sensibilities are quickly injured.*

sen·sible /'sensəbl/ *adj* having or showing good sense(2): *a sensible woman; wearing sensible clothes. That was sensible of you.*

sen·sibly /-əblɪ/ *adv* in a sensible way: *sensibly dressed for hot weather.*

sen·si·tive /'sensətɪv/ *adj* **1** *sensitive (to sth)* quickly or easily receiving impressions: *The eyes are sensitive to light. The government should be sensitive to public opinion.* **2** (of feelings) easily hurt or offended: *He is very sensitive about his big nose.* **3** (of a person) showing awareness of people's feelings: *A sensitive son does not want his parents to worry about him.* Opp insensitive. **4** (of instruments) able to record or reproduce small changes: *a sensitive microphone.*

sen·si·tiv·ity /ˌsensə'tɪvətɪ/ *nu*

sen·sory /'sensərɪ/ *adj* of the senses(1): *sensory nerves.*

sen·su·al /'senʃʊəl/ *adj* **1** (*formal*) of the senses and not the mind: *sensual experience.* **2** enjoying, of, physical pleasures such as eating and drinking and sex: *sensual enjoyment.*

sen·su·al·ity /ˌsenʃʊ'ælətɪ/ *nu*

sen·su·al·ly *adv*

sen·su·ous /'senʃʊəs/ *adj* (*formal*) giving feelings of pleasure: *sensuous music/paintings.*

sent /sent/ *pt,pp* of send.

sen·tence¹ /'sentəns/ *nc* **1** (a statement by a judge etc of) a punishment: *pass sentence (on him); be under sentence of death.* **2** (*gram*) a set of words used to form a statement, question, command etc (and, when written, beginning with a capital letter and ending with a full stop, question mark or exclamation mark). ⇨ cleft/complex/ compound/simple sentence. ⇨ also command¹(6), question¹(1), statement(5).

'sentence adverb *nc* (*gram*) an adverb that refers to the complete sentence, as in '*Surprisingly, she didn't mind at all*'.

sen·tence² /'sentəns/ *vt* *sentence sb (to sth)* to state that a person is to have a certain punishment: *sentence a thief to six months' imprisonment.*

sen·ti·ment /'sentɪmənt/ *n* **1** *nc,nu* (a) mental feeling of love, happiness, pity, sadness etc: *show no sentiment when dismissing the workers.* **2** *nu* (the tendency to be affected by) emotional feeling: *There's no place for sentiment in business.* **3** *nc* an opinion or judgement: *The ambassador explained the sentiments of his government.*

sen·ti·men·tal /ˌsentɪ'mentl/ *adj* **1** having to do with emotions (and not practical or sensible judgement): *have a sentimental attachment to one's birthplace. The bracelet had only sentimental value* (e.g. because it belonged to one's mother). **2** (usually *derog*) producing, expressing, (often too strong) feelings: *She's far too sentimental about her cats.*

sen·ti·men·tal·ity /ˌsentɪmen'tælətɪ/ *nu* the quality of being (too) sentimental.

sen·ti·men·tal·ly /-təlɪ/ *adv*

sen·try /'sentrɪ/ *nc* (*pl* **-ies**) a soldier keeping a watch or guard.

'sentry-box *nc* a hut for a sentry.

sep. *written abbr* separate.

Sep *written abbr* September.

sep·ar·able /'sepərəbl/ *adj* that can be separated. Opp inseparable.

sep·ar·ate¹ /'seprət/ *adj* **1** *separate (from sth)* divided, not joined: *Cut it into two separate parts. The toilet is separate from the bathroom.* **2** (*attrib*) different: *There are four separate reasons for going.*

sep·ar·ate² /'sepəreɪt/ *v* **1** *vt,vi* *separate (sb/ sth) (off) (from sb/sth)* (to cause a person, thing) to be or become divided, not joined (to a person, thing): *separate the boys from the girls. England is separated (off) from France by the Channel.* **2** *vi* (of a number of people or a married couple) to leave each other: *We talked until midnight and then separated. My parents have separated.* **3** *vt,vi* *separate (sth) out* (to cause things) to be clearly different: *separate out two possible causes.*

sep·ar·ates /'seprəts/ *n pl* clothes (e.g. blouses, skirts, jackets etc) that can be worn in different combinations.

sep·ar·ation /ˌsepə'reɪʃn/ *n* **1** *nu* (an act of) separating or being separated or separate: *Separation from his friends made him sad.* **2** *nc* an instance, period, of not being together: *a separation of five years.*

se·pia /'si:pɪə/ *adj, nu* dark brown (colour, ink or paint).

Sept *written abbr* September.

Sep·tem·ber /sep'tembə(r)/ *n* (also *attrib*) the ninth month of the year, with 30 days: *Helen and I were married on 1 September.* Ⓝ '*1 September*' is spoken as '*September the first*' or '*the first of September*'.

sep·tic /'septɪk/ *adj* causing, caused by, infection (with disease germs): *A dirty wound may become/ turn septic.* ⇨ antiseptic.

sep·ulchre (*US* = **-cher**) /'seplkə(r)/ *nc* a tomb, esp one of stone.

se·quel /'si:kwəl/ *nc* *sequel (to sth)* **1** that which follows or arises out of (an earlier event): *Famine has often been the sequel to war.* **2** a story, film etc continuing the plot etc (of an earlier one).

se·quence /'si:kwəns/ *nc* **1** a connected series of events, ideas etc: *a sequence of five burglaries in the area.* *in sequence* in order (not mixed up). **2** a part or period (during a play, piece of music etc): *a sequence during the performance when the lights went out.*

se·quin /'si:kwɪn/ *nc* a tiny shining disc (to be) sewn on cloth as an ornament.

ser·en·ade¹ /ˌserə'neɪd/ *nc* (a piece of) music (to be) sung or played outdoors at night.

ser·en·ade² /ˌserə'neɪd/ *vt* to sing or play a serenade to (a person): *serenading her by moonlight.*

ser·ene /sɪ'ri:n/ *adj* happy and calm: *a serene sky/ look/smile.*

ser·ene·ly *adv*

ser·en·ity /sɪ'renətɪ/ *nu*

serf /sɜːf/ *nc* (in history) a person who worked on the land and was sold with it like a slave.

serf·dom /-dəm/ *nu* (**a**) the economic and social system using serfs. (**b**) a serf's condition of life.

ser·geant /'sɑːdʒənt/ nc (abbr Sgt) **1** (mil) a non-commissioned army officer above a corporal. **2** a police officer below an inspector.

sergeant-'major nc (abbr Sgt-Maj.) (mil) a non-commissioned army officer.

se·ri·al¹ /'sɪərɪəl/ adj (attrib) of, in or forming a series: *the serial number of a banknote or cheque.*

se·ri·al² /'sɪərɪəl/ nc a story, TV play etc produced in parts.

se·ri·al·ize (also **-ise**) /'sɪərɪəlaɪz/ vt to publish or produce (a book, play etc) as a serial.

se·ries /'sɪəriːz/ nc (pl unchanged) a number of connected things, events etc coming one after another: *a series of stamps; a television series* (i.e. a number of programmes each complete in itself and linked by cast, theme etc). **in series (a)** in an orderly arrangement. **(b)** (electricity) (of the parts of a circuit) with the supply of current fed directly through each part.

se·ri·ous /'sɪərɪəs/ adj **1** thoughtful; not funny, silly or for pleasure: *a serious attempt/appearance/face; look serious. Stop laughing and be serious for a moment.* **2** important because of possible danger: *a serious illness/mistake. The international situation looks serious.* **3** committed; sincere: *a serious worker. Please be serious about your work.*

se·ri·ous·ly adv in a serious manner: *be seriously ill.*

se·ri·ous·ness nu the state of being serious: *the seriousness of unemployment.* **in all seriousness** very seriously: *I tell you this in all seriousness* (i.e. I am not joking, being insincere etc).

ser·mon /'sɜːmən/ nc a spoken or written speech given in a church.

ser·pent /'sɜːpənt/ nc **1** a snake (the more usual word). **2** (fig; derog) a sly, deceptive person.

ser·rat·ed /sɪ'reɪtɪd/ adj having notches on the edge like a saw: *a serrated edge on a knife.*

se·rum /'sɪərəm/ nc,nu (pl **—s**) (a dose of) fluid taken from the blood of an animal, that can fight disease, used for inoculations.

ser·vant /'sɜːvənt/ nc a person who works in a household for wages, food and lodging. Ⓝ *'Servant' is not now used. Use* (a member of) *staff.* ⇨ also civil servant.

serve¹ /sɜːv/ nc (sport) an act of serving(6). ⇨ ace(3).

serve² /sɜːv/ v **1** vt to attend to (customers) in a shop, restaurant etc: *There was no-one in the shop to serve me. Are you being served, Madam? Which waiter is serving you?* **2** vt to offer (food) to people: *Mint sauce is often served with lamb. What time is dinner served?* ⇨ serving. **3** vt,vi to carry out duties (for a person, one's country): *serving one's country* (e.g. in Parliament or in the armed forces). **4** vt,vi to be satisfactory (for a need or purpose): *This box will serve as/for a seat.* **serve its/one's purpose** ⇨ purpose(1). **5** vt to spend (a period of time) (in a position, in prison etc): *He served his time as manager for five years. He has served five years of his sentence.* **6** vt,vi (sport) to put (the ball) into play (in tennis etc) by hitting it to an opponent: *serve a ball; serve well/badly.*

serve as/for sth ⇨ 4 above.

serve on sth to be a member of a committee, a board of directors etc. **serve sth (on sb)** (legal)

to deliver a notice (to a person) to attend a law court.

serve under sb to be a member of an army, expedition etc under a leader: *One of my ancestors served under Nelson.*

serve sth up to offer food during a meal.

server /'sɜːvə(r)/ nc **1** a person who serves(2,6). **2** a tray for dishes of food.

ser·vice¹ /'sɜːvɪs/ n **1** nc,nu (an act of) help or assistance to another or others: *Do you need the services of a lawyer? His services to the country* (i.e. his public duties) *were enormous.* **be at sb's service** to be ready to help or assist a person. **be of service (to sb)** (formal) (used in questions) to be able to help: *Can I be of any service (to you)?* **on active service** fighting as a soldier etc in a war. **2** nc (often S—) an organized system of work etc for the needs of the public: *a bus/train/postal service; the Diplomatic Service.* ⇨ civil service. **3** nu the serving of customers in a shop, restaurant etc: *The food is good but the service is poor.* ⇨ self-service. **4** nc the checking and repair of machines, vehicles etc: *My car needs a service. Has this washing-machine had a service before?* **5** nc a particular form of worship (for an occasion): *the marriage service.* **6** nc a complete set of plates, dishes etc for a meal: *a dinner/tea service.* **7** nu (formal) employment with a family: *Miss White has been in our service for five years.* **8** nc (sport) an act of serving(6): *It's your service.*

'service charge nc an additional charge for service(3).

'service flat nc a flat in which domestic help (sometimes with meals) is provided.

'service industry nc an industry providing services, not making things.

'service-line nc (in tennis etc) the line near the centre of one half of the court over which the ball may not be served(6).

'service road nc a branch off a main road giving access to houses etc.

'service station nc a petrol station with facilities for servicing vehicles.

ser·vice·able /-əbl/ adj suitable for strong and hard use: *serviceable clothes for children.*

ser·vice² /'sɜːvɪs/ vt to check and repair (a machine, vehicle etc): *My car is being serviced.*

ser·vi·ette /ˌsɜːvɪ'et/ nc = napkin.

ser·vile /'sɜːvaɪl/ adj (formal; derog) (of a person, behaviour) being too obedient or too ready to help, esp to gain an advantage: *a servile assistant; servile to public opinion.*

ser·vil·ity /sə'vɪlɪtɪ/ nu

serv·ing /'sɜːvɪŋ/ nc an amount of food (to be) given to one person: *four servings of soup.*

ser·vi·tude /'sɜːvɪtjuːd/ nu (formal) the condition of being forced to work for others and having no freedom.

ses·ame /'sesəmɪ/ nc (also attrib) a plant with seeds used in various ways as food and producing an oil: *sesame seeds; sesame oil.*

ses·sion /'seʃn/ nc **1** (the time used by) a meeting of a formal body or organization: *the autumn session of Parliament; go into secret session.* **in session** (of an organization) active (not on holiday). **2** a university term. **3** a meeting for an activity: *a recording session* (e.g. of a radio programme).

set¹ /set/ *adj* **1** (usually *attrib*) decided and fixed: *work set hours/a set number of hours; set habits; a set book; a set speech; the pattern has been set.* **2** (usually *attrib*) (of opinions, habits etc) fixed and not to be changed. **be set in one's ways** ⇨ way²(4). **3** (*attrib*) fixed and unmoving: *a set smile/expression; a set purpose.* **4** (*attrib*) regular and usual: *set forms of prayer; set phrases* (= idioms). **5** (*pred*) **be set on (doing) sth** to be determined to do or have something: *I'm set on becoming a doctor/on that new car.* **6** (*pred*) **be (all) set to** + *verb* to be ready and prepared to do something: *We were set to start early.*

set² /set/ *nc* **1** a group of things that belong together: *a set of tools; a dinner/tea set; a cutlery set; a maths set* (= of instruments); *a new set of false teeth; a set of lectures.* **2** a group of people with similar work, interests etc: *the literary/golfing set; the smart set; the jet set.* **3** an apparatus for receiving sound or pictures: *a radio/TV set.* **4** an act, process, of arranging a person's hair: *a hair set; a shampoo and set.* **5** the scenery for (part of) a play, film, TV programme etc. **6** (*sport*) a group of games (in tennis etc). **7** (*maths*) a group of similar things. **8** *n sing* the position (of the body, clothes etc).

set³ /set/ *v* (*pt,pp* —; **-tt-**) (N) For the use of 'set' in special phrases such as 'set an example', 'set eyes on her', 'set the scene' etc, ⇨ the noun entries, as at clock, example, eye, fashion, fire, hair, heart, house, mind, music, pace, price, sail, scene, shop, store, table, watch. **1** *vt* to move, place, put, (something) in a place or position: *She set the food on the table. When did you last set pen to paper* (= write a letter)? ⇨ set sth down. **set sb/sth on her/his/its feet** ⇨ foot¹(1). **2** *vt* to cause (a person, animal, thing) to be in the condition mentioned: *Let's set the bird free. Someone has set the house alight/on fire! ***3** *vt* to cause (a person, machine etc) to begin doing something: *It's time we set the machine going. That set me thinking.* **4** *vt* to prepare, put into order, (something) for use: *set a trap; set a table; set a clock/watch.* **5** *vt* to decide and fix (a time, price etc): *set a price; set a date for the meeting; set a book for an examination.* ⇨ set¹(1). **6** *vt,vi* (to cause something) to form a fixed position or state: *Has the jelly/glue set? I'm having my hair set tomorrow. It was a gold ring with a diamond set in it. The doctor took half an hour to set my broken bone/arm.* **7** *vt* to gain and establish (the best speed, time, distance): *set a world record.* **8** *vt* to give (oneself, a person) a task or duty: *I set my son to chop wood. You've set yourself a difficult task.* **9** *vt* to describe (the surroundings for a story etc): *The scene is set in Africa.* **10** *vi* (of plants) to form and develop seeds or fruit. **11** *vi* (of the sun, moon etc) to go down below the horizon. Opp rise²(2). ⇨ sunset.

set about sb (*informal*) to attack a person. **set about (doing) sth** to begin a task with energy: *Then you must set about (the job of) finding the boat. I don't know how to set about it* (= how to begin).

set sb against sb to cause one person, group, to become an enemy of another. **set sth against sth** to consider one fact etc in relation to a related difficulty or issue: *You must set the cost of a new bike against the cost of repairing your old one.*

set sb/sth apart (from sb/sth) to show (that one considers) her/him/it to be special: *Her use of beautiful phrases sets her apart from other writers.*

set sth aside (**a**) to put a book, knitting etc to one side. (**b**) to postpone a plan, task etc: *Work on the new school will have to be set aside for another year.* (**c**) to decide to ignore something: *Let's set aside our personal feelings.* (**d**) (*legal*) to cancel a judgement, decision.

set sb back sth to cost a person an amount of money: *The wedding will set us back a few hundred pounds.* **set sth back** (**a**) to place a building away from the road etc: *The house was set back twenty metres.* (**b**) to interrupt the progress of something: *The bad weather set the building programme back. The scandal set the Tories back in the opinion polls.* Hence **'set-back** *nc*

set sth by sth to set(4) a watch, clock, using something: *set one's watch by the radio.*

set sb down to allow a passenger to leave a bus, taxi etc. **set sth down** (**a**) to write something on paper. (**b**) to put something heavy down: *I set my suitcase down on the step.*

set forth (*formal*) = set off. **set sth forth** (*formal*) = set sth out: *The pamphlet set forth their political views.*

set in to begin and seem likely to continue: *The bad weather seems to have set in.* **be set in sth** (*passive* only) to be established in a routine etc: *be set in one's ways.*

set off ⇨ set off (on sth). **set sb off (doing sth)** to cause a person to begin (laughing, crying etc). **set sth off** (**a**) to cause a firework, explosive etc to explode. (**b**) to cause a rumour, activity, to begin: *The threat of a strike set off increased sales of gold shares.* (**c**) to make something more attractive by comparison: *Her red hair sets off her green eyes.* **set sth off against sth** to balance a cost, loss, fault etc against an income, profit, good quality: *set off expenses against tax relief.* ⇨ offset. **set off (on sth)** to begin (a journey): *set off on a walk/trip; set off on holiday. They set off at dawn.*

set on sb to attack a person: *She was set on by muggers.*

set out ⇨ set out (on sth). **set sth out** to present goods, ideas etc in an organized way: *set plates out on the table; set out articles for sale; set out one's ideas in a letter; set out the rules in a new booklet.* **set out (on sth)** = set off (on sth). ⇨ outset.

set sb over sb to place one person in a senior position to another.

set to to begin to do something: *The men set to and repaired the car.*

set sb up (**a**) (*informal*) to make a person healthier etc: *A holiday will soon set you up.* (**b**) (*informal*) to put a person in a position of danger, ridicule etc: *The boys set up the teacher by putting a bag of flour on the door.* **set sth up** (**a**) to place a camera, telescope, flag etc in position. (**b**) to build a statue. (**c**) to establish a business, an office, a trade union etc. Hence **'set-up** *nc*. (**d**) to arrange a meeting, discussion. (**e**) (of a climate, habit, condition) to cause an infection, rash etc. **set oneself/sb up as sb/sth** (**a**) to establish oneself, a person, in business as a person, thing: *set oneself up as a taxi-driver.* (**b**) to consider oneself, a person, to be special in the way mentioned: *set one's husband up as perfect.* **set up house (together)** ⇨ house¹(1).

set upon sb (*formal*) = set on sb.

set-back /'set bæk/ *nc* ⇨ set sth back(b).

set square /'set skweə(r)/ *nc* (*maths*) a flat, triangular piece of wood, plastic etc used for drawing lines and angles.

set·tee /se'ti:/ *nc* = sofa.

set·ter /'setə(r)/ *nc* **1** a kind of long-haired dog, used for hunting birds and small animals. **2** (often used with another word) a person, thing, that sets (various meanings): *a modern setter of hair; a typesetter.*

set·ting /'setɪŋ/ *nc* **1** something in which something else is fixed or fastened: *the setting of a jewel.* **2** an area; surroundings: *a beautiful setting for a picnic.* **3** a position on an instrument such as 'high' or 'low'. **4** (also *attrib*) the act of (the sun, moon etc) going down: *the setting sun.*

settle /'setl/ *v* **1** *vt,vi* (to cause a person, animal) to be, rest, in a comfortable or new position: *The nurse settled her patients for the night. A bird settled on the telephone wire. Settle yourselves by the fire and I'll make coffee.* **2** *vi* to become established in a new place, job, way of life etc: *I don't feel settled yet. They've settled in London.* ⇨ settled(2) **3** *vt,vi* to make an agreement about (a dispute): *It's time you settled the argument. Nothing is settled* (= decided) *yet. The lawsuit was settled out of court* (e.g. the money to be paid was agreed between the lawyers, not decided by the court). *Do you think the lawyers will settle?* **4** *vt* to pay (a debt). ⇨ account¹(8). **5** *vi* to come down and cover an area: *Fog settled over the town. Will the snow settle (on the ground)?* **6** *vi* to sink in a liquid: *The sand settled on the bottom.* **7** *vi* (of weather) to become calm and pleasant. ⇨ settled(1).

settle back to sit comfortably in a chair etc: *We settled back to watch TV.*

settle down (a) (of noise, noisy people) to become quiet and calm. **(b)** (of a person) to become quiet and comfortable in bed: *Now settle down and go to sleep.* **(c)** to make oneself comfortable in a seat etc: *Settle down everyone!* **(d)** to begin a responsible, organized way of living: *It's time you married and settled down.* **settle sb down** to make a person such as a patient comfortable. **settle down in sth (a)** to make oneself comfortable in a seat. **(b)** to establish oneself in a job, school etc. **settle down to sth (a)** to become established in a new job, way of life etc: *settle down to married life.* **(b)** to give one's attention to work: *settle down to writing.*

settle for sth (a) to accept an amount of money mentioned as payment: *I wanted £600 for my old car but I had to settle for £400.* **(b)** to accept something less exciting, demanding etc: *I'm not prepared to settle for life as an ordinary housewife.*

settle in (of weather, good or bad) to become established: *This rain seems to be settling in.* ⇨ settled(1). **settle in a place** ⇨ 2 above.

settle (sb) in (to help a person) to move into a new house, start a new job etc: *Do come and visit us when we've settled in.*

settle (sb) into sth (to help a person) to move into, become a member of, a house, college etc:

The children are settling into their new school.

settle on sth (a) ⇨ 1, 5 above. **(b)** to decide to take, buy etc something: *Which coat have you settled on?* **settle sth on sb** to give money or property (e.g. in a will) to a person.

settle up (with sb) to pay (a person) what one owes: *Can I settle up with you next week?*

settle with sb to punish a person for harm one has suffered.

set·tled /'setld/ *adj* **1** (*attrib*) fixed; unchanging; permanent: *settled weather; a man of settled opinions.* **2** (of a person) feeling comfortable and established in a new home, place etc. **3** (of a bill) paid. Opp unsettled.

settle·ment /'setlmənt/ *n* **1** *nc,nu* (an instance of) making an agreement (about a dispute etc): *The strikers have reached a settlement with the employers.* **2** *nc,nu* (an instance of) payment (of a debt etc): *I enclose a cheque in settlement of your account.* **3** *nc* (a statement of) property given to a person: *a marriage settlement.* **4** *nc,nu* (the establishment of) a community, group of homes etc: *mountain settlements.*

set·tler /'setlə(r)/ *nc* a person who has made a home in a new place.

set-up /'set ʌp/ *nc* = set sth up (c).

sev·en /'sevn/ *adj* or *det, nc* (of) 7. ⇨ sin¹(1).

sev·en·teen /ˌsevn'ti:n/ *adj* or *det, nc* (of) 17.

sev·en·teenth /ˌsevn'ti:nθ/ *adj* or *det, nc* (abbr 17th) (of) one of 17 parts or the next after 16.

sev·en·ti·eth *adj* or *det, nc* (abbr 70th) (of) one of 70 parts or the next after 69.

sev·enth /'sevnθ/ *adj* or *det, nc* (abbr 7th) (of) one of 7 parts or the next after 6.

sev·en·ty /'sevntɪ/ *adj* or *det, nc* (of) 70. **in the seventies (a)** (of temperature, speed etc) between 70 and 79. **(b)** between '70 and '79 in a century.

sev·er /'sevə(r)/ *v* **1** *vt* (*formal*) to cut (the usual word): *sever a rope.* **2** *vt* (*fig*) to break (something) off: *sever one's connections with her.* **3** *vi* (*formal*) to break (the usual word): *The rope severed under the strain.*

sev·er·ance /'sevərəns/ *nu*: severance pay (= money paid to an employee, e.g. when a contract has ended).

sev·er·al¹ /'sevrəl/ *adj* (*attrib*) or *det* **1** some but not many (three or more): *You will need several more. I've read it several times.* **2** separate; individual: *They went their several ways.*

sev·er·al² /'sevrəl/ *pron* **several (of sb/sth)** some but not many (three or more): *Several of us refused. Several are to be sold and the rest will be kept here.*

se·vere /sɪ'vɪə(r)/ *adj* **1** serious and strict; not kind: *severe looks; be severe with one's children.* **2** (of the weather, attacks of disease etc) strong, extreme: *a severe storm; severe pain.* **3** making great demands on skill, ability, patience etc: *The pace was too severe to be kept up for long.*

sev·ere·ly *adv*

se·ver·ity /sɪ'verətɪ/ *nu* (*pl* **-ies**) (*formal*) the quality of being severe: *the severity* (= extreme cold) *of the winter in Canada.*

sew /səʊ/ *v* (*pt* **—ed**, *pp* **—n** /səʊn/) **1** *vt,vi* to join, make, (things) using a needle and thread: *She sat sewing by the fire. He was sewing a badge/ button on/onto a jacket.* **2** *vt* to make (clothing) by sewing(1): *sew a dress. Was your blouse sewn by hand or by machine?* ⇨ handsewn, sewing-machine. **3** *vt* **sew sth up (a)** to join the edges of something with stitches. **(b)** (*fig; informal*) to complete arrangements for something: *sew up a deal/contract.* **(c)** (used as a *pp*) having obtained control of something: *We've got the market for dictionaries sewn up.*

sew·age /'su:ɪdʒ/ *nu* water and waste matter from baths and toilets, carried off in pipes.

sew·er¹ /'səʊə(r)/ *nc* a person who sews.

sew·er² /'su:ə(r)/ *nc* an underground pipe etc used to carry off sewage.

sew·ing /'səʊɪŋ/ *nu* **1** the act of using a needle and thread: *I enjoy sewing.* **2** the material (for clothes etc) being sewn: *Where is my sewing?*

'sewing-machine *nc* a machine for sewing clothes, curtains etc.

sewn /səʊn/ *pp* of sew.

sex¹ /seks/ *adj* (*attrib*) **1** connected with being male or female: *sex appeal* (i.e. the ability to attract a person of the opposite sex). **2** connected with sexual activity: *sex organs; sex films.*

sex² /seks/ *n* **1** *nu* the condition of being male or female: *What is the cat's sex? Help them all, without distinction of race, age or sex.* **2** *nc* either males or females as a group: *the opposite sex.* **3** *nu* sexual activity or intercourse, and everything connected with it: *teenage sex; sex in films/on TV.*

sex·ism /'seksɪzəm/ *nu* the belief that one sex(2) is superior to the other.

sex·ist /'seksɪst/ *adj* concerning sexism: *sexist policies.* □ *nc* a believer in sexism (esp a man who considers women to be inferior).

sex·tant /'sekstənt/ *nc* (*tech*) an instrument used to find the position of a ship or aircraft.

sex·ual /'sekʃʊəl/ *adj* **1** of, concerning, sex(3): *sexual attraction.* **2** of, concerning, the sexes(2): *sexual reproduction.* ⇨ asexual.

,sexual 'intercourse *nu* the physical union of male and female people or animals that produces young.

sexu·al·ity /,sekʃʊˈælətɪ/ *nu* the state of being interested in sex(3): *a person with strong sexuality.*

sex·ual·ly *adv* of, concerning, sex(esp 3).

,sexually trans,mitted dis'ease *nc* (abbr STD) a disease (e.g. *AIDS, gonorrhea, syphilis*) that is transferred by sexual intercourse.

sexy /'seksɪ/ *adj* (**-ier, -iest**) attractive, exciting, sexually: *a sexy man/dress.*

sex·ily /-əlɪ/ *adv*: *sexily dressed.*

SF /,es 'ef/ *abbr* science fiction.

sgd *written abbr* signed.

Sgt *written abbr* Sergeant.

Sgt-Maj. *written abbr* Sergeant-Major.

shab·by /'ʃæbɪ/ *adj* (**-ier, -iest**) **1** in a bad state of repair; poorly dressed: *wearing a shabby hat. You look shabby in those old clothes.* **2** (*derog*) (of behaviour) unkind and unfair.

shab·bi·ly /'ʃæbəlɪ/ *adv*

shack /ʃæk/ *nc* a small, wooden hut or house.

shackle¹ /'ʃækl/ *nc* **1** one of a pair of iron rings joined by a chain, used for fastening a prisoner's wrists or ankles. **2** (*fig*) something that prevents freedom of action: *the shackles of convention.*

shackle² /'ʃækl/ *vt* **1** to put shackles on (a person). **2** (*fig*) to prevent (a person) from acting freely.

shade¹ /ʃeɪd/ *n* **1** *nu* darkness caused by cutting off direct light: *a temperature of 35°C in the shade. The trees give a pleasant shade.* Compare shadow(1). **put sb/sth in the shade** to cause a person, thing to appear small, unimportant etc by contrast: *You are so clever that my poor efforts are put in the shade.* **2** *nc* something that produces shade(1): *a lampshade.* **3** *nu* the darker part(s) in a picture, etc: *There is not enough light and shade in your drawing.* **4** *nc* a degree or depth of colour: *cloth in several shades of blue.* **5** *nc* a small difference: *a word with many shades of meaning.*

shade² /ʃeɪd/ *v* **1** *vt* to keep direct light from (a person, thing): *He shaded his eyes with his hands.* **2** *vt* to keep direct heat from (a person, thing): *She shaded the children from the fire.* **3** *vt* **shade sth (in)** to darken parts of a drawing etc to give the appearance of light and dark. **4** *vi* **shade off** to change gradually: *red shading off into pink.*

shad·ow¹ /'ʃædəʊ/ *n* **1** *nc* a dark shape on the ground, a wall etc because of shade(1): *Can you stand on your own shadow's head? The shadows become longer in the afternoon.* **2** *nc* a form that is not as real, typical etc as usual: *He's a shadow of his former self* (= is very thin and weak). **3** *nc* a dark area: *have shadows round the eyes.* **4** *n sing* a very small amount or degree: *without/beyond a shadow of doubt.*

shad·ow² /'ʃædəʊ/ *vt* **1** to form a shadow or shadows on (something). **2** to follow closely and watch the movements of (a person): *The suspect was shadowed by detectives.*

,Shadow 'Cabinet *nc* (the —) the members of the Opposition in Parliament who would form a Cabinet if they were in power.

,shadow 'spokesperson/-man/-woman *nc* an MP selected to speak for the Opposition on a particular issue.

shad·owy *adj*

shady /'ʃeɪdɪ/ *adj* (**-ier, -iest**) **1** giving shade from sunlight; situated in shade: *the shady side of the street.* **2** (*fig*) of doubtful honesty: *a shady deal.*

shaft /ʃɑːft/ *nc* **1** the long handle of an axe or other tool. **2** one of the pair of bars (wooden poles) between which a horse pulls a cart etc. **3** the long part of a pillar. **4** a long, narrow space, usually vertical, e.g. in a coalmine. **5** a long bar joining parts of a machine. **6** a ray (of light).

shag·gy /'ʃægɪ/ *adj* (**-ier, -iest**) **1** (of hair) rough, coarse and untidy. **2** covered with rough, coarse hair: *a shaggy dog; shaggy eyebrows.*

shake¹ /ʃeɪk/ *nc* an act of shaking: *a shake of the head* (e.g. to indicate 'no').

shake² /ʃeɪk/ *v* (*pt* **shook** /ʃʊk/, *pp* **shaken** /'ʃeɪkən/) **1** *vt,vi* (to cause something, oneself) to move from side to side, up and down etc: *shake a bottle to mix the contents; shake a rug; shake a man by the hand; shake hands* (i.e. each other's hand); *shake one's head* (e.g. to indicate 'no', doubt, disapproval etc); *shake one's fist at him* (e.g. to show anger etc). *He was shaking with laughter/cold.* **2** *vt* (often *passive*) to shock or trouble, (a person): *They were badly shaken by the news.* **3** *vi* (of a person's voice) to tremble; become weak: *Her voice shook with emotion.* ⇨ shaky(1).

shake down (*informal*) to become adjusted to a

new environment, new conditions etc: *The new teaching staff is shaking down nicely.*

shake sth from sth to get something from, out of, something by shaking: *shake apples from a tree.*

shake sb off to free oneself from a follower: *The thief ran fast and soon shook off the police.*

shake sth off to get rid of an illness, bad feeling etc quickly: *shake off a cold/a fit of depression.*

shake on it (*informal*) to shake hands and agree: *Let's shake on it.*

shake sth out (a) to remove dirt etc by spreading out and shaking something: *shake out a table-cloth.* (b) (*fig*) to remove lazy workers, bad methods etc from a business. Hence **'shake-out** *nc.* **shake sth out of sth** to get dirt etc out of something by shaking: *shake sand out of a shoe.*

shake sb up (a) to disturb or shock a person: *The bad news/old car shook me up badly.* (b) to cause a person to behave, work etc better: *Some of these managers need shaking up—they're asleep on the job.* Hence **'shake-up** *nc*: *We need a good shake-up in our office.* **shake sth up** (a) to mix something well by shaking: *shake up a bottle of medicine.* (b) to restore something to its shape by shaking it: *shake up a cushion.*

shak·ing /'ʃeɪkɪŋ/ *nc* an act of shaking a person or thing: *give a pillow a good shaking.*

shaky /'ʃeɪkɪ/ *adj* (-ier, -iest) **1** (of a person, movements etc) weak; unsteady: *shaky hands; speak in a shaky voice; feel very shaky.* **2** unsafe; unreliable: *a shaky table.* **3** (*fig*) weak: *My French is a little shaky.*

shak·ily /-əlɪ/ *adv*

shale /ʃeɪl/ *nu* a kind of soft rock that splits easily into layers.

shall /ʃəl *strong form:* ʃæl/ *auxiliary verb* Ⓝ 'Shall' is a (modal) auxiliary verb used with another verb to form the future tense, to ask questions and to express duty or obligation. 'Shall' has no infinitive or imperative form and no participles. 'Shall' is always followed by an infinitive without 'to'. Compare will², must², should. (*Present tense* (all persons) **shall**; *he shall, she shall* often shortened to **he'll** /hiːl/, **she'll** /ʃiːl/, *I shall* to **I'll** /aɪl/ and *we shall* to **we'll** /wiːl/; *negative* **shall not** or **shan't** /ʃɑːnt/; *pt* **should** /ʃəd *strong form* ʃʊd/, *negative* **should not** or **shouldn't** /'ʃʊdnt/) **1** (used with *I* and *we* as an auxiliary to form the future tense): *I shall come as soon as I can. We shall arrive early tomorrow morning. I'll go and buy some. We'll be late. I/We shan't be able to join you. We'll be seeing her tonight. I shall have been in this job four years next October.* Ⓝ 'Will' is now more usual than 'shall'. **2** (used with *I* and *we* to ask questions): *Shall I* (= Do you want me to) *close the door? Shall we* (= Do you think we shall) *see anyone we know? How shall we recognize you? Where shall we go? What shall I say?* Ⓝ 'Will I' cannot be used instead of 'shall I' as in the first example but 'will we' is becoming more usual for 'shall we' except when asking advice as in the last two examples. ⇨ should(1) for questions about past actions and reported speech. **3** **shall have to** + *verb* (used with *I* and *we* to express future obligation): *I shall have to tell your mother. If you break it, we shall have to pay.* Ⓝ 'Will have to' is now more usual. ⇨ the *note* at must²(1). **4** (used to

emphasize a duty, obligation or intention): *You shall wash up, whether you want to or not! He shall not marry you! It shall be done!* ⇨ should(2). **5** (used, esp in written notices, to state an order or rule). *Members shall have one vote each.* ⇨ should(7). Compare must²(1).

shal·lot /ʃə'lɒt/ *nc* a kind of small onion.

shal·low /'ʃæləʊ/ *adj* **1** of little depth: *shallow water.* **2** (*fig; derog*) not showing much intelligence or ability: *a shallow thinker/argument.*

sham¹ /ʃæm/ *n* **1** *nc* (*derog*) a person who shams; something intended to deceive: *His love was only a sham.* **2** *nu* pretence: *What he says is all sham.*

sham² /ʃæm/ *vi,vt* (-mm-) to pretend (to be in the condition mentioned): *He shammed anger/death. He's only shamming.*

shamble /'ʃæmbl/ *vi* to walk without lifting the feet properly: *The old man shambled up to me.* ☐ *nc* a shambling walk.

shambles /'ʃæmblz/ *n sing* a scene of untidiness or confusion: *His flat is a complete shambles.*

shame¹ /ʃeɪm/ *n* **1** *nu* the sad feeling with loss of self-respect, caused by wrong, dishonourable or foolish behaviour, failure etc (of oneself, one's family etc): *feel shame at having told a lie; hang one's head in shame. He has no shame/is without shame* (i.e. does not feel shame). ⇨ ashamed. **be covered with shame** to feel shame strongly. **bring shame on sb/oneself** to cause dishonour to a person, oneself. **put sb/sth to shame** to cause a person to feel shame, cause work to be considered bad, because the quality of her or his work is poor (esp by producing a much better quality). **2** *n sing* something unworthy; something that causes shame; a person or thing that is wrong: *It's a shame to take the money for doing such easy work. He's a shame to his family.* **3** *n sing* **What a shame!** That is bad luck, a pity etc.

,shame·'faced *adj* looking ashamed.

shame·ful /-fəl/ *adj* very bad; causing or bringing shame: *shameful conduct.*

shame·ful·ly /-fəlɪ/ *adv*

shame·less *adj* without any self-respect: *The shameless girl had no clothes on.*

shame² /ʃeɪm/ *vt* **1** to bring disgrace on (a person, group): *shame one's family.* **2** **shame sb into doing sth** to make a person (not) do something by causing her or him to feel ashamed: *shame a man into apologizing.*

sham·poo /ʃæm'puː/ *nc,nu* (a special liquid for) a washing of the hair: *baby shampoo; give her a shampoo and set.* ☐ *vt* to wash (the hair): *Have you shampooed your hair yet?*

sham·rock /'ʃæmrɒk/ *nc* a plant with (usually) three leaves on each stem.

shan·dy /'ʃændɪ/ *nc,nu* (*pl* -dies) (a glass etc of) a drink of beer and lemonade.

shan't /ʃɑːnt/ = shall not. ⇨ shall.

shan·ty /'ʃæntɪ/ *nc* (*pl* -ies) a poorly made hut or home.

'shanty town *nc* an area with shanties.

shape /ʃeɪp/ *n* **1** *nc,nu* the outer form, outline, of something: *There were clouds of different shapes. What's the shape of his nose? I saw a shape in the darkness.* **lick sb/sth into shape** to make a person, a business, school etc organized and able to carry out tasks well. **knock sth into/ out of shape** to put it into/out of the right shape. **take shape** to become definite in form or basic organization: *The new building/His plan is beginning to take shape.* **2** *nc* a sort: *I've had no help from him in any shape or form* (= none of any sort). **3** *nu* condition: *He is in good shape* (= is physically fit). *Her affairs are in a bad shape* (= are not well organized). **get into shape** (of a person) to get fit.

shape² /ʃeɪp/ *v* **1** *vt* to give a form to (something): *shape a pot on a wheel. It was shaped like a pear/pear-shaped.* **2** *vi* to give signs of future development: *Our plans are shaping well* (= showing promise of success).

SHAPE /ʃeɪp/ *acronym* Supreme Headquarters Allied Powers Europe (a major centre for senior military staff).

shape·less *adj* with no definite shape.

shape·ly /'ʃeɪplɪ/ *adj* (**-ier, -iest**) (esp of a person) having a pleasing shape: *She has a shapely pair of legs.*

share¹ /ʃeə(r)/ *nc* **1** a part that a person owns, does, gets or gives: *I've done my share (of the work). You must take your share of the blame. We shall all have a share in the profits.* **the lion's share** ⇨ lion. **go shares (with sb) (in sth)** to divide profits, costs etc (with others); become part owner (with others); pay (a part of an expense): *Let me go shares with you in the taxi fare.* **2** (*commerce*) one of the equal parts into which the capital of a business company is divided: *I own 100 oil shares.*

share² /ʃeə(r)/ *v* **1** *vt* **share sth (out) (among/ between sb/sth)** to give a share of something (to others); divide and distribute: *share (out) £100 among/between five men.* ⇨ share-out. **2** *vt,vi* **share (sth) (between/with sb)** to have, use etc (something) (with others): *There are not enough books so you'll have to share. Can I share your umbrella? I'll share the cost with you. Will you two share a bedroom between you?* **share and share alike** (*informal*) to have equal use of, an equal part of, what is available: *A happy family has learned to share and share alike.*

share·hold·er /'ʃeə həʊldə(r)/ *nc* a person who owns shares(2) in a business.

share-out /'ʃeər aʊt/ *nc* an act of sharing(1).

shark /ʃɑːk/ *nc* **1** a kind of seafish, often large and dangerous. **2** (*fig; derog*) a person who cheats to get money.

sharp¹ /ʃɑːp/ *adj* (**—er, —est**) **1** with a fine cutting edge and able to divide a solid easily: *a sharp knife.* Opp blunt(1). **2** with a fine point: *a sharp pin/needle.* Opp blunt(1). **3** well-defined; clear: *a sharp outline.* **4** (of curves, slopes, bends) changing direction quickly: *a sharp bend in the road.* **5** (of a rise or fall) by a sudden, large amount: *a sharp rise in prices.* **6** (of a sound) high and sudden: *a sharp cry of distress.* **7** (*music*) (*no comp*) higher than the true or acceptable pitch¹(4): *a sharp note.* Compare flat³(12). **8** quickly aware of things: *a sharp intelligence/sense of smell; as sharp as a needle* (= very quick to understand). **keep a sharp look-out (for sb/sth)** ⇨ look-out. **9** (of feelings, taste) producing a strong physical sensation: *a sharp pain; the sharp taste of a lemon.* **10** harsh; severe: *sharp words.* **have a sharp ton-**

gue ⇨ tongue(1). **11** intelligent and quick to take advantage: *a sharp mind/lawyer.*

sharp·ly *adv*

sharp·ness *nu*

sharp² /ʃɑːp/ *adv* (*pred*) **1** exactly the time mentioned: *Be here at 1 (o'clock) sharp.* **2** (of direction) immediately: *turn sharp left.*

sharp³ /ʃɑːp/ *nc* (*music*) (a symbol for) a sharp(7) note. Compare flat³(5).

sharp·en /'ʃɑːpən/ *vt,vi* (to cause something) to become sharp: *sharpen a pencil.*

sharp·en·er /'ʃɑːpənə(r)/ *nc* a device that sharpens something: *a pencil-sharpener.*

shat·ter /'ʃætə(r)/ *vt,vi* **1** (to cause something) to break suddenly into small pieces: *The explosion shattered every window in the building.* **2** (*fig; usually passive*) to destroy (dreams, hopes etc): *Our hopes were shattered.*

shave¹ /ʃeɪv/ *nc* an act of shaving(1). **a close/ narrow shave** a lucky, almost unsuccessful escape from injury, disaster etc.

shave² /ʃeɪv/ *v* **shave sth (off)** **1** *vt,vi* to cut (hair) off the chin etc with a razor: *He is shaving off his beard.* **2** *vt* to take off (a thin layer etc): *shave off a piece of wood.*

shaver *nc* an electrical apparatus used for shaving(1). ⇨ razor.

'shaving-brush *nc* a brush used for spreading lather over the face before shaving.

shav·ings *n pl* thin pieces of wood or metal which have been shaved(2) off.

shav·en /'ʃeɪvn/ *suffix* having shaved(1): *He is clean-shaven.*

shawl /ʃɔːl/ *nc* a large piece of cloth worn round the shoulders or head of a woman, or wrapped round a baby.

she /ʃiː/ *pron* **1** (used as the subject of a verb) a female person or animal already mentioned: *My sister says she is going for a walk.* Compare her. **2** (often used as a *prefix*) a female: *a she-goat. Is it a he or a she?*

sheaf /ʃiːf/ *nc* (*pl* **sheaves** /ʃiːvz/) **1** a group of cereal plants tied together. **2** a group (of arrows etc) tied together.

shear /ʃɪə(r)/ *vt* (*pt* **—ed**, *pp* **shorn** /ʃɔːn/ or **—ed**) **1** to cut the wool off (a sheep) with shears. **2** to remove all of a person's hair: *a shorn head.*

shears /ʃɪəz/ *n pl* (also *a pair of shears*) a large cutting instrument shaped like scissors, used to cut hedges etc.

sheath /ʃiːθ/ *nc* (*pl* **—s** /ʃiːðz/) **1** a cover for the blade of a knife etc: *Put the dagger back in its sheath.* **2** = condom.

'sheath-knife *nc* a knife with a blade that fits into a sheath.

sheathe /ʃiːð/ *vt* to put (a knife etc) into a sheath(1).

sheaves /ʃiːvz/ *n pl* of sheaf.

shed¹ /ʃed/ *nc* a small building, usually of wood, used for storing things: *a bicycle/coal-/wood-shed.*

shed² /ʃed/ *vt* (*pt,pp* **—; -dd-**) **1** to let (leaves etc) come off, fall: *Some trees shed their leaves in autumn.* **shed blood** ⇨ blood(1), bloodshed. **shed tears** ⇨ tear¹. **2** to take off (clothes); get rid of (covering): *People on the beach began to shed their clothes as it got hotter. Some insects shed their skins.* **3** to spread or send out (heat, light etc): *a fire that sheds warmth; a woman who sheds happiness.* **shed light on sth** ⇨ light⁴(5).

she'd /ʃiːd/ = *she had; she would.*

sheen /ʃiːn/ *nu* shiny brightness: *the sheen of silk.*

sheep /ʃiːp/ *nc* (*pl* —) a grass-eating animal kept for its flesh as food (*mutton*) and its wool. ⇨ ewe, lamb¹(1), ram¹.

'sheep-dog *nc* a dog trained to help a shepherd to look after sheep.

'sheep-fold *nc* an enclosure for sheep.

'sheep-skin *nc,nu* (also *attrib*) (a rug of) a sheep's skin with the wool on it: *a sheepskin coat.*

sheep-ish /'ʃiːpɪʃ/ *adj* **1** awkwardly self-conscious: *a sheepish smile.* **2** (feeling) foolish or embarrassed because of having done something wrong.

sheep-ish-ly *adv*

sheer /ʃɪə(r)/ *adj* **1** (*attrib*) complete; thorough; absolute: *sheer nonsense; a sheer waste of time; by sheer chance.* **2** (*attrib*) (of cloth etc) finely woven and almost transparent: *sheer nylon.* **3** (almost) without a slope: *a sheer drop of 50 metres.*

sheet /ʃiːt/ *nc* **1** a piece of cloth used in pairs for sleeping between: *put clean sheets on the bed.* **2** a flat, thin piece (of a material): *a sheet of glass/ notepaper.* **3** a wide expanse (of ice, snow, flame etc): *The rain came down in sheets* (= very heavily).

,sheet 'lightning *nu* the kind that comes in wide flashes of brightness.

'sheet music *nu* music published on sheets of paper, not in a book.

sheet-ing *nu* material used for making sheets(1).

sheik (also **sheikh**) /ʃeɪk/ *nc* **1** an Arab prince or chieftain. **2** a head of an Arab village etc.

sheik-dom (also **sheikh-**) /'ʃeɪkdəm/ *nc* an area ruled by a sheik.

shelf /ʃelf/ *nc* (*pl* **shelves** /ʃelvz/) **1** a flat piece of wood, metal etc fastened to a wall or in a cupboard etc, used to stand things on: *bookshelves; a shelf for food.* **on the shelf** (*informal*) (**a**) (of a person) considered too old to work. (**b**) (of a woman) unmarried and considered as being unlikely to marry. **2** a piece of rock on a mountain etc like a shelf (as used by rock-climbers).

'shelf-life *nc* (*commerce*) the time food etc will remain fresh in a shop etc.

shell¹ /ʃel/ *nc* **1** the hard outer covering of eggs, nuts, some seeds etc and of some animals (e.g. snails, crabs) or parts of them. **go/retire into/ come out of one's shell** to become/stop being shy, reserved, quiet. **2** = seashell. **3** the outside walls etc of a building, ship etc: *After the fire, only the shell of the house was left.* **4** a metal case filled with explosive, to be fired from a gun.

shell² /ʃel/ *v* **1** *vt* to take (a pea etc) out of a shell(1): *shelling peas.* **2** *vt* to fire shells(4) at (an army, place): *shell the enemy.* **3** *vt,vi* **shell (sth) out** (*informal*) to pay (money) out: *Must I shell out (the money) for the party?*

'shell-fish *nc,nu* any kind of sea-animal (*crab, lobster* etc) with a shell(1).

'shell-proof *adj* built so that a shell(4) cannot break it.

she'll /ʃiːl/ = *she will; she shall.*

shel-ter¹ /'ʃeltə(r)/ *n* **1** *nu* the condition of being kept safe: *take shelter from the storm.* **2** *nc* something that gives safety or protection: *a bus shelter*

(i.e. for people waiting for buses).

shel-ter² /'ʃeltə(r)/ *v* **1** *vt* **shelter sb/sth (from sb/sth)** to protect a person, thing: *trees that shelter a house from cold winds; shelter an escaped prisoner.* **2** *vi* **shelter (from sb/sth)** to take shelter: *shelter (from the rain) under the trees.*

shelve¹ /ʃelv/ *vt* (*fig*) to set aside (a plan, problem) until later: *We are shelving a decision until later.*

shelve² /ʃelv/ *vi* (of land) to slope (down or up) gently.

shelves /ʃelvz/ *pl* of shelf.

shep-herd¹ /'ʃepəd/ *nc* a person who takes care of sheep.

,shepherd's 'pie *nu* a baked meal of minced meat covered with mashed potato.

shep-herd² /'ʃepəd/ *vt* **1** to take care of (sheep). **2** to guide or direct (people): *The passengers were shepherded across the tarmac to the airliner.*

shep-herd-ess /'ʃepədɪs/ *nc* a woman shepherd.

sher-bet /'ʃɜːbət/ *nu* a flavoured powder that produces bubbles in the mouth.

sher-iff /'ʃerɪf/ *nc* (*US*) a chief law-enforcing officer of a county.

sher-ry /'ʃerɪ/ *nu* a kind of strong yellow or brown wine from Spain, Cyprus etc.

she's /ʃiːz/ = *she is; she has.*

shied /ʃaɪd/ *pt,pp* of shy².

shield¹ /ʃiːld/ *nc* **1** a piece of metal, leather etc carried to protect the body. **2** a small representation of a shield used as a badge or an award. **3** (*fig*) a person or thing that protects a person from danger, heat etc: *He used the woman as a shield as he walked away from the police. The motor has a metal shield to prevent accidents.*

shield² /ʃiːld/ *vt* **shield sb/sth (from sb/sth)** **1** to protect a person, thing, (from a harmful person, thing): *shield one's eyes with one's hand.* **2** to protect (a person) (from suffering etc): *shield a friend from criticism.*

shift¹ /ʃɪft/ *nc* **1** a change of place, direction or character: *a shift to a new place; a shift in public opinion; a shift in emphasis.* **2** a change of one thing for another: *a shift from cars to bicycles.* **3** a group of workers that starts work as another group finishes; period for which such a group works: *on (the) day/night shift.* **4** a mechanism for changing gears in a vehicle. **5** a woman's narrow dress without a waistline.

'shift-work *nu* work organized, done, in shifts(3).

shift² /ʃɪft/ *v* **1** *vt* to change the position or direction of (something): *shift luggage from one hand to the other. Don't try to shift the blame (on)to somebody else.* **2** *vt,vi* (*motoring*) to change (gears): *shift into second/third gear.* **3** *vi* **shift for oneself** to manage as best one can to make a living etc without help: *When our father died we had to shift for ourselves.*

shift-less /'ʃɪftləs/ *adj* (*derog*) lazy (the usual word).

shifty /'ʃɪftɪ/ *adj* (-**ier**, -**iest**) (*derog*) not to be trusted: *a shifty customer; shifty behaviour.*

shil-ling /'ʃɪlɪŋ/ *nc* **1** (until 1971) a British coin with the value of twelve old pennies. **2** a unit of currency in Kenya, Uganda etc.

shim·mer /'ʃɪmə(r)/ vi, nu (to shine with) a wavering soft light: *moonlight shimmering on the water.*

shin[1] /ʃɪn/ nc the front part of the leg below the knee.

'shin-bone nc the inner and thicker of the two bones below the knee.

shin[2] /ʃɪn/ vi (-nn-) **shin up sth** to climb up something (using arms and legs to grip): *shin up a tree.*

shine[1] /ʃaɪn/ n sing an act of polishing: *Give your shoes a good shine.*

shine[2] /ʃaɪn/ v (pt, pp **shone** /ʃɒn/, but ⇨ 3 below) **1** vi to give out bright light: *The moon is shining. His face shone with excitement.* **2** vi **shine (at/in sth)** (fig) to show particular ability or intelligence: *He didn't shine in the exams. I don't shine at tennis.* **3** vt (pt, pp **—d**) (informal) to polish (the more usual word): *shine shoes.*

shiny adj (-ier, -iest) (as if) polished; bright: *shiny shoes.*

shingle /'ʃɪŋgl/ nu an area of small, rounded pebbles on the seashore.

shin·gly /'ʃɪŋglɪ/ adj

shingles /'ʃɪŋglz/ n sing a skin disease with irritating spots (often round the waist).

ship[1] /ʃɪp/ nc **1** a large boat with an engine that can travel on the sea. **2** (informal) a spacecraft. **3** (US informal) a plane.

'ship·builder nc a person, business, that builds ships. Hence **'ship·building** nu

'ship's-chandler nc a trader who sells equipment for boats and ships.

'ship·load nc as much cargo, or as many passengers, as a ship can carry.

'ship·mate nc a person belonging to the same crew: *Harry and I were shipmates in 1972.*

'ship·owner nc a person who owns a ship or ships.

ship·ping nu all the ships of a country, port etc.

'ship·shape adj tidy; in good order.

'ship·wreck nc, nu (an instance of) the loss or destruction of a ship at sea. □ vt (usually passive) to destroy (a ship etc) by shipwreck.

'ship·wright nc a shipbuilder.

'ship·yard nc a place where ships are built.

ship[2] /ʃɪp/ vt, vi (-pp-) **1** to take, send, (goods) in a ship: *ship oil to Europe.* **2** **ship water** (of a boat etc) to be flooded with water.

ship·ment n (a) nu the act of shipping(1) goods. (b) nc an amount of goods shipped.

ship·per nc a person, business, that arranges for goods to be shipped.

'ship·ping-agent nc a shipowner's representative at a port.

shire /'ʃaɪə(r)/ nc = county (the usual word): *the best in the shire.* □ suffix /-ʃə(r)/ (used in the names of certain counties): *Hampshire; Yorkshire.*

shirk /ʃɜːk/ vt, vi to try to avoid (doing something, responsibility, duty etc): *He's shirking (his duty).*

shirk·er nc (derog) a person who avoids work.

shirt /ʃɜːt/ nc an article of clothing with a collar and sleeves worn by a man, e.g. under a jacket. ⇨ also T-shirt. **keep one's shirt on** (sl) to control one's temper. **in one's shirt-sleeves** not wearing a jacket.

shirty /'ʃɜːtɪ/ adj (-ier, -iest) (sl; derog) easily

annoyed; bad-tempered.

shit[1] /ʃɪt/ n (vulgar; do not use) **1** nu solid waste matter from the body. **2** nu nonsense: *Don't talk such shit.* **3** nu a worthless, unpleasant person: *You little shit!*

shit[2] /ʃɪt/ vi (pt, pp **—**, **-ed** or **shat** /ʃæt/; -tt-) (vulgar; do not use) to pass solid waste matter from the body.

shitty /'ʃɪtɪ/ adj (-ier, -iest) (vulgar; do not use) very bad, unpleasant: *shitty weather/people.*

shiv·er[1] /'ʃɪvə(r)/ nc an act of trembling: *The sight sent cold shivers down my spine.*

shiv·er[2] /'ʃɪvə(r)/ vi to tremble, esp from cold or fear: *shivering like a leaf.*

shoal[1] /ʃəʊl/ nc a shallow place in the sea, esp where there are sandbanks.

shoal[2] /ʃəʊl/ nc a large number (of fish) swimming together: *a shoal of herring.* □ vi to form shoals.

shock[1] /ʃɒk/ n **1** nc (the effect caused by) a violent blow or shaking (e.g. as caused by a fall, collision or explosion): *the shock of a fall.* **2** nc an experience of electricity passing through the body: *If you touch that live wire you'll get a shock.* **3** nc, nu (the condition caused by) a sudden and very strong feeling of surprise, fear, worry etc (caused by bad news, unusual clothes etc): *The news of her mother's death was a terrible shock to her. She died of shock in the car crash.*

'shock absorber nc a device in a vehicle etc which absorbs the vibrations etc.

'shock tactics n pl a way of acting using sudden force to get a particular result, e.g. slapping a person to stop her or him screaming.

'shock treatment/therapy nu the use of electric shocks to cure mental illness.

shock[2] /ʃɒk/ vt to cause (a person) to feel shock(3): *I was shocked at the news of her death.*

shock·er nc (informal; often derog) an unpleasant person who shocks people by behaving very badly.

shock·ing /'ʃɒkɪŋ/ adj **1** (derog) very bad or wrong: *shocking writing/behaviour.* **2** causing shock(3): *a shocking hairstyle; shocking news.* **3** (informal) severe: *a shocking headache.*

shock·ing·ly adv

shod /ʃɒd/ pt, pp of shoe[2]

shod·dy /'ʃɒdɪ/ adj (-ier, -iest) (informal; derog) of poor quality: *a shoddy piece of work.*

shoe[1] /ʃuː/ nc **1** an outer covering of leather etc for the foot, esp one which does not reach above the ankle: *a pair of shoes.* **2** = horseshoe. **3** the part of a brake that presses against the wheel (of a bicycle etc).

'shoe·horn nc a device with a curved blade for getting the heel easily into a shoe.

'shoe·lace nc a length of string etc for fastening a shoe.

'shoe·maker nc a person who makes shoes and boots.

'shoe·repairer nc a person who mends shoes and boots.

'shoe-string nc (US) = shoelace. **do sth on a shoe-string** to do it (e.g. start a business) with a very small amount of money.

shoe[2] /ʃuː/ vt (pt, pp **shod** /ʃɒd/) to fit (a horse, also a person) with shoes: *shoe a horse; be well shod for wet weather.*

shone /ʃɒn/ *pt,pp* of shine.

shoo /ʃuː/ *int* (used to tell children, pets, birds etc to go away). □ *vt* (*pt,pp* **—ed**) *shoo sb/sth away* to make this cry (and wave one's hand) to make a person, animal go away.

shook /ʃʊk/ *pt* of shake².

shoot¹ /ʃuːt/ *nc* **1** a new, young growth on a plant or bush. **2** a group of people shooting birds, animals.

shoot² /ʃuːt/ *v* (*pt,pp* **shot** /ʃɒt/) **1** *vt,vi* to move, come, go, send (something), suddenly or quickly (out, in, up etc): *Flames were shooting up from the burning house. The meteor shot across the sky. She shot an angry look at him/shot him an angry look. shoot up* (**a**) (of a plant, child) to grow tall quickly. (**b**) (of prices etc) to increase quickly. **2** *vi* (of a plant, bush) to send out new twigs or branches from a stem. **3** *vi* (of pain) to happen suddenly and go quickly: *The pain shot down/up his arm.* **4** *vt* (to cause a boat) to move quickly over, through etc something: *The canoe shot a bridge on the left side.* **5** *vt,vi* to aim and fire (a gun, an arrow): *They were shooting at a target.* **6** *vt* to wound or kill (a person, animal etc) by using a gun: *The soldier was shot* (= executed by shooting) *for desertion. The seven bombers were shot down in flames. He had his arm shot off.* **7** *vt* to photograph (a scene in a film). **8** *vt,vi* (*sport*) to (try to) score (a goal) (in football, hockey etc).

,**shooting 'star** *nc* a meteor seen as a moving star.

shop¹ /ʃɒp/ *nc* **1** a place, business, where goods are shown and sold: *a butcher's shop. set up shop* to start a business as a shopkeeper. *all over the shop* (*informal*) (**a**) in a great mess: *His clothes were all over the shop.* (**b**) in every direction: *We looked for him all over the shop.* **2** *nu* a person's profession etc and things connected with it. *talk shop* to talk about one's work, profession etc. **3** (also *attrib*) = workshop: *a machine shop; the men on the shop floor* (= the workers, not the management). ⇨ closed shop.

'**shop assistant** *nc* a person who serves in a shop.

'**shop-front** *nc* the front of a shop with its window display etc.

'**shop-keeper** *nc* an owner of a (small) shop.

'**shop-lifter** *nc* a person who steals things from shops. Hence '**shop-lifting** *nu*

,**shop 'steward** *nc* an official representative of a branch of a trade union elected by the workers.

,**shop-'window** *nc* a window used for the display of things on sale in a shop.

shop² /ʃɒp/ *v* (-pp-) **1** *vi* to go to shops to buy things: *Do you often shop here? I go shopping early in the morning.* Ⓝ '*To go shopping*' is more usual than '*to shop*'. *shop around* (*informal*) to visit many shops, markets etc to obtain the best value for one's money etc. **2** *vt shop (on) sb* (*informal*) to inform against a person, esp to the police: *shop (on) an accomplice.*

shop-per *nc* a person who is shopping.

shop-ping *nu* (also *attrib*) (an act of) going to the shops to buy things: *go shopping; do one's shopping; a shopping bag/basket.*

'**shopping centre** *nc* the part of a town where there are the main shops.

shore¹ /ʃɔː(r)/ *nc* the land at the edge of a sea or lake: *a house on the shore(s) of a lake.*

shore² /ʃɔː(r)/ *vt shore sth up* to give something support (using a long piece of thick wood etc).

shorn /ʃɔːn/ *pp* of shear.

short¹ /ʃɔːt/ *adj* (**—er, —est**) **1** having only a little extent in space (length): *a short stick; short hair; a short way down; a short journey by train; short sleeves; a dog with a short tail. How short is your bed?* Opp long¹(1). **2** (of a person, mountain etc) below the average or usual height: *a short man.* Opp tall¹(1). **3** having, taking, a little time: *a short interval; a short holiday; a short flight; a short friendship; be away for a short time.* Opp long¹(2). *short and sweet* brief and (therefore) pleasant: *His speech was short and sweet. short shrift* ⇨ shrift. **4** (*pred*) (of particular measurement) not long enough by (the amount mentioned): *The cloth is 10cm short. be short of sth* to have not enough of it: *I'm short of breath/ money/time. little/nothing short of sth* the same as something: *Our escape was nothing short of a miracle. be in short supply* ⇨ supply¹(1). **5** (of a person) saying something with few words (and perhaps impatiently): *give a short reply. Her answer was short and to the point. short for sth; be sth for short* to be something as an abbreviation: *Benjamin, called Ben for short. Ben is short for Benjamin.* **6** likely to be successful: *a short bet; short odds.* ⇨ long¹(6). **7** (used in many phrases) *(do sth) at short notice* ⇨ notice¹(1). *have a short temper* ⇨ temper¹. *in the short term* ⇨ term¹(1).

,**short 'change** *nu* less than the correct amount. □ *vt* to give (a person) less than the correct amount of money.

'**short cut** *nc* a way of getting somewhere, doing something, that is quicker than the usual way: *take a short cut across the fields.*

,**short-'distance** *adj* covering a short distance: *a short-distance race.*

'**short-hand** *nu* a system of writing using special symbols.

,**short-'handed** *adj* having not enough workers or helpers.

'**short list** *nc* a list of candidates (e.g. for a job) reduced to small number from which the final choice is to be made: *be on the short list.* Hence '**short-list** *vt* to add (a person) to a small group on a list.

,**short-'lived** *adj* lasting for a short time: *a short-lived success.*

'**short-range** *adj* (**a**) (of plans etc) of use for a limited period. (**b**) (of a weapon) able to go a short distance only: *short-range bombers.*

,**short-'sighted** *adj* (**a**) (usually *pred*) able to see only close objects clearly. (**b**) (*derog*) not thinking about the future: *a short-sighted decision to refuse help.* Compare far-sighted, long-sighted.

,**short-'tempered** *adj* (*derog*) easily made angry.

'**short-term** *adj* related to a short period of time: *short-term loans.*

'**short wave** *adj* (*radio*) using a wave of between 10 and 100 metres.

,**short-'winded** *adj* quickly breathless after physical activity.

short-ness *nu*

short² /ʃɔːt/ adv **short (of sth) 1** suddenly (and before something bad or dangerous): *stop short; stop short of the edge. He committed every crime short of* (= except) *murder.* **2** before the expected distance, time or amount. **cut sb/sth short** to cause an activity to stop before a person has finished speaking, a performance has ended etc: *The chairman had to cut short the discussion/his speech.* **fall short (of sth)** to be not enough; fail to satisfy (expectations etc): *Your exam results fell short of our hopes.* ⇨ also shortfall. **go short (of sth)** to be without: *I don't want you to go short of money/blankets.* **run short (of sth)** to become low in supplies etc: *run short of bread/ money.* **sell sb short (a)** to cheat a person by giving too little. **(b)** (*fig*) to fail to describe all of a person's abilities or qualities. **be taken short** (*informal*) to need suddenly to go to the toilet when there is not one near.

short³ /ʃɔːt/ nc **1** a small amount of a strong alcoholic drink without water, lemonade etc. **2** a short film. **3** = short-circuit. **4 in short** using a few words: *I was hungry, wet and cold—in short I was very annoyed!*

short⁴ /ʃɔːt/ nc, vi, vt = short circuit.

short·age /ˈʃɔːtɪdʒ/ nc, nu (an amount caused by) not having enough: *food shortages; a shortage of staff.*

short circuit /ˌʃɔːt ˈsɜːkɪt/ nc an electrical fault that stops a machine working. Hence ˌ**short-ˈcircuit** vi, vt to have such a fault; produce one in (something).

short·comings /ˈʃɔːt kʌmɪŋz/ n pl faults; failures to reach the necessary standard, to do one's duty: *I'm aware of his shortcomings.*

short·en /ˈʃɔːtn/ vt, vi (to cause something) to become shorter: *Can you shorten my dress? The days are beginning to shorten.*

short·fall /ˈʃɔːtfɔːl/ nc an amount by which a supply etc is not enough.

short·ly /ˈʃɔːtlɪ/ adv **1** soon; in a short time: *I'll be home shortly. He came shortly before 10 o'clock. She arrived shortly afterwards.* **2** briefly (and showing impatience): *answer shortly.* ⇨ short¹(5).

shorts /ʃɔːts/ n pl (also *a pair of shorts*) short trousers ending above the knees, as worn by children, by adults for games etc: *tennis shorts.*

shot¹ /ʃɒt/ n **1** nc (a sound of) the act of firing a gun etc: *hear shots in the distance.* **(do sth) like a shot** at once; without hesitation: *He took the job like a shot.* **2** nc (an attempt at) a throw, stroke, hit etc in certain games. **3** nc an attempt at doing something successfully. **a long shot** a wild guess: *It's a long shot but I think John must have stolen the bike.* **a shot in the dark** a guess. **have a shot (at sth)** to try to do it: *Have a shot at solving the problem. Let me have a shot at it.* **4** nc a photograph: *The exterior shots* (i.e. of a film) *were taken in Bermuda.* **5** nc a heavy iron ball thrown in an athletic competition (called the shot-put): *putting the shot.* **6** nu (also *lead shot*) a quantity of tiny balls of lead used in a sporting gun (instead of a bullet). **7** nc a person who shoots a gun etc (with reference to skill): *He's a first-class/ good/poor shot.* **8** nc (*informal*) an injection (of a drug).

ˈ**shot·gun** nc a gun using shot(6).

ˈ**shot-put** nc ⇨ 5 above.

shot² /ʃɒt/ pt, pp of shoot².

should /ʃəd strong form ʃʊd/ auxiliary verb Ⓝ 'Should' is a (modal) auxiliary verb used with another verb as the past tense form of *'shall'* when asking questions or in reported speech, and to express duty or obligation. 'Should' has no infinitive or imperative form and no participles. 'Should' is always used with an infinitive without 'to'. Compare would, ought, shall. (*Present tense* (all persons) **should**; *negative* **should not** or **shouldn't** /ˈʃʊdnt/; **should have** can be shortened to **should've** /ˈʃʊdəv/) **1** (used as the past tense form of *shall*) **(a)** (to ask questions about past actions): *Should I have closed the door? Where should we have gone? Who should I have asked?* **(b)** (used in reported speech or thought): *We said we should arrive early. Tom asked if he should post the letter. I thought I should try once more.* Ⓝ 'Should' often means the same as 'ought to' here. *We shall arrive early. Shall I post the letter? 'I shall try once more,' I thought* are the possible equivalents for these examples in direct speech. **2** (used to express duty or obligation): *We should all offer to help. I should go home but I don't want to. He shouldn't be so angry. Shouldn't you pay this time?* **should have** + pp **(a)** ⇨ 1(a) above. **(b)** (used to express a past duty or obligation that was not carried out): *She should have warned you* (but she did not). **(c)** (used to give an opinion about an event that is (not) likely to happen or have happened): *The train should have arrived by now* (but it has not). *He should have saved enough money by then* (it is possible). ⇨ the *note* at ought(1). **3** (used to express an opinion or to ask for or give advice): *She should be there by now. It should be much warmer in April. They suggest that you should try again. We shouldn't have to wait so long. I should think so* (= I believe that to be true, possible etc). *How should I dress? When should we come? Why should you think that? 'Lend me a pound'—'Why should I?'* **4** (used with *I* and *we* in formal uses to express the conditional): *If I were you, I shouldn't bother. If it hadn't rained, we should have walked.* Ⓝ 'Would' is now much more usual. **5** (used to express the conditional referring to a future possible event): *Should the bell ring* (= If the bell rings), *come and get me.* **6** (used after *that* to express one's feelings or thought): *It's strange that Anne should be so worried.* **7** (used to express a formal rule or order): *Men should wear jackets in the dining room.* Ⓝ 'Must' is more usual. ⇨ shall(5).

shoul·der¹ /ˈʃəʊldə(r)/ nc **1** that part of the body where an arm (or front leg of an animal) joins the neck: *He has one shoulder a little higher than the other.* **straight from the shoulder** honestly and fully: *I told him straight from the shoulder that he was not good enough.* **give sb the cold shoulder** to ignore a person deliberately. **have a chip on one's shoulder** ⇨ chip¹(1). **put one's shoulder to the wheel** to work very hard at a task. **stand head and shoulders above sb** ⇨ head¹(1). **2** (*pl*) the part of the back between the shoulders: *give a child a ride on one's shoulders.* **3** a part of a mountain etc like a shoulder in shape. ⇨ also hard shoulder.

ˈ**shoulder-blade** nc either of the flat bones

behind and below the neck.

'**shoulder-strap** nc the narrow strap on the shoulders of a military uniform or on a woman's underwear or a dress.

shoul·der² /'ʃəʊldə(r)/ vt **1** to take on, bear, (the responsibility, weight etc): *Don't shoulder the responsibility for his debts.* **2** to push (a person, thing) with the shoulder: *be shouldered to one side.*

shouldn't /'ʃʊdnt/ = should not.

should've /'ʃʊdəv/ = should have.

shout¹ /ʃaʊt/ nc a loud call or cry: *They greeted him with shouts of 'Long live the President!'*

shout² /ʃaʊt/ v **1** vi,vt **shout (sth) (out)** to speak, call, say (something), in a loud voice: *Don't shout at me! He shouted to attract attention. He shouted out (my name). He shouted to me/ shouted for me to come. 'Go back!' he shouted.* **2** vt **shout sb down** to shout to prevent a person from being heard: *The crowd shouted the speaker down.*

shout·ing nu shouts. **be all over bar the shouting** (of a struggle, fight etc) to be finished except for the praise, cheers, etc to follow.

shove¹ /ʃʌv/ nc (informal) a push: *Give it a shove!*

shove² /ʃʌv/ vt,vi (informal) to push (a person, furniture etc) (often carelessly): *shove a boat into the water. He shoved me in the back.*

shov·el¹ /'ʃʌvl/ nc **1** a tool like a spade, used for moving coal, soil. **2** a large device used for the same purpose, mechanically operated from a crane in a vehicle.

shov·el² /'ʃʌvl/ vt (**-ll-**, US **-l-**) to lift, move, (something) away, using a shovel: *shovel the snow away from the garden path.*

shovel·ful /-fʊl/ nc as much as a shovel can hold.

show¹ /ʃəʊ/ n **1** nc a collection of things for people to look at: *a flower/horse/cattle show.* **on show** exhibited. **2** nc a natural display: *Those trees make a fine show.* **3** nc a kind of public entertainment, e.g. a performance by several different artists in a theatre, on TV etc: *Have you seen any good shows lately?* **4** nc (informal) a way of behaving, working etc: *a show of anger; put up a good/poor show* (= do something well/badly). **steal the show** to attract all the attention: *He was the best speaker and he stole the show at the conference.* **5** nc (informal) an organization; business; *Who's running this show?* (= Who is in control?) **6** n sing an outward appearance: *He didn't offer even a show of resistance.* **7** nu something done to attract envy: *She does it for show. They're fond of show.*

'**show business** nu the business of entertaining the public.

'**show-case** nc a cupboard, case, with glass sides and (or) top, for displaying articles in a shop, museum etc.

'**show-down** nc (sl) a full and frank declaration of one's intentions, opinion etc.

'**show·girl** nc a woman who sings or dances in a musical show(3).

'**show-jumping** nu the sport of showing skill in riding horses over fences, barriers etc.

'**show·man** nc **(a)** an organizer of public entertainments. **(b)** a person who uses publicity etc to attract attention to himself: *Some politicians are great showmen and very little else.*

'**show-place** nc a place that tourists go to see: *castles and other show-places.*

show² /ʃəʊ/ v (pt **—ed**, pp **—n** /ʃəʊn/) **1** vt to cause, allow, (a person, thing) to be seen: *You must show your ticket to the inspector. This diagram shows how our sales have improved. What films are they showing this week?* **2** vt,vi (to allow something) to be noticeable or obvious: *Does my petticoat show? He's pleased and it shows. His anger showed in his letter. That little mark won't show. A dark suit shows the dirt. My shoes are showing signs of wear. She showed great courage.* **show one's face** ⇨ face¹(1). **show one's hand** ⇨ hand¹(1). ⇨ also nothing². **3** vt to prove (something): *This key shows (that) he's guilty. The book shows that she's a great writer. That shows how little you know. It all goes to show that you can do it when you try.* **4** vt to make (methods, reasons etc) clear; cause (a person) to understand something: *He showed me how to do it. Show them how you managed it.* **show sb the ropes** ⇨ rope¹(2). **show sb the way** ⇨ way²(1). **5** vt to guide (a person) round, out of, to etc a place: *Let me show you to your seat. We were shown into the waiting-room.* ⇨ show sb around/ in/out/round/up. **6** vt to act towards (a person) in the way mentioned: *He showed me great kindness.*

show sb around to take a person to visit a large area: *show her around the city/my farm.*

show sb in to take a person into an office, a doctor's room etc.

show sb into a place = show sb in.

show off to draw attention to one's wealth, ability, knowledge etc to impress people: *Stop showing off!* Hence '**show-off** nc (derog) a person who shows off. **show sb/sth off** to draw attention to a person, possession etc because one feels (too) proud: *She drove up and down showing off her new car.*

show sb out (of a place) to take a person out (of an office, large building etc): *My secretary will show you out (of the office).*

show sb over sth to take a visitor, possible buyer etc to look at a factory, new house etc.

show sb round = show sb around (but usually preferred for a smaller area such as a house or factory).

show through to be visible under a covering: *We painted the wall but the marks still show through.*

show up (a) to be easily visible: *The marks show up badly in this light.* **(b)** (informal) (of a person) to arrive or appear: *I waited for an hour but he never showed up.* **show sb up (a)** to take a visitor upstairs (to an office etc). **(b)** to make a person feel embarrassed and criticized: *Some children show up their parents by crying in shops.* **show sb up as sb** to prove a person to be the kind of person mentioned: *The letter showed her up to be a liar.*

show·er¹ /'ʃaʊə(r)/ nc **1** a brief fall of rain, snow etc: *April showers.* **2** (an act of washing by using) an apparatus that produces a fall of water. **3** (fig) a large number of things arriving together: *a shower of stones/insults.*

show·ery *adj* (of the weather) with frequent showers.

show·er² /'ʃauə(r)/ *v* **1** *vt,vi* **shower sb with sth; shower (down) on sb** to fall in a shower(1,2): *They showered the hero with honours. The snow showered down on us. Good wishes showered (down) on the bride.* **2** *vi* to have a shower(2): *I shower every morning.*

shown /ʃəʊn/ *pp* of show².

show-off /'ʃəʊ ɒf/ *nc* ⇨ show off.

showy /'ʃəʊɪ/ *adj* (**-ier, -iest**) (*derog*) attracting attention because (too) colourful, bright etc: *a showy dress.*

shrank /ʃræŋk/ *pt* of shrink.

shrap·nel /'ʃræpnəl/ *nu* the pieces of an exploded shell or bullet.

shred¹ /ʃred/ *nc* **1** a small strip or piece scraped, torn or broken off something. **2** (*fig*) a very small amount: *There is not a shred of truth in what she says. You do not have a shred of evidence against me.*

shred² /ʃred/ *vt* (**-dd-**) to tear (paper, cloth) into small pieces.

shrew /ʃruː/ *nc* **1** a small animal like a mouse that feeds on insects. **2** (*derog*) a bad-tempered woman.

shrewd /ʃruːd/ *adj* (**-ier, -est**) **1** having or showing, judgement and common sense: *shrewd businessmen; shrewd arguments.* **2** likely to be correct or effective: *make a shrewd guess.*

shrewd·ly *adv*

shrewd·ness *nu*

shriek /ʃriːk/ *vt,vi* to make, say (something) in, a loud screaming voice: *shriek out a warning; shriek with laughter.*

shrift /ʃrɪft/ *nu* **get/give sb short shrift** to get/give little attention to a person because he or she does not deserve it: *They gave us/We got short shrift.*

shrill /ʃrɪl/ *adj* (**-er, -est**) (of sounds, voices etc) very high and long: *a shrill voice/whistle.*

shrimp /ʃrɪmp/ *nc* a kind of small shellfish with many legs and a long tail, used for food.

shrine /ʃraɪn/ *nc* **1** a place of worship with special associations or memory. **2** a place associated with a deeply respected person.

shrink /ʃrɪŋk/ *v* (*pt* **shrank** /ʃræŋk/ or **shrunk** /ʃrʌŋk/, *pp* **shrunk**) **1** *vt,vi* (to cause cloth, clothes etc) to become smaller through wetting: *Will this soap shrink woollen clothes? That dress will shrink in the wash.* ⇨ shrunken. **2** *vt,vi* (*fig*) (to cause the amount of sales, profits, opportunities etc) to become less: *Our car sales to Africa have shrunk to almost none.* **3** *vi* **shrink (back) (from sth)** to move back, show unwillingness (to do something) because of fear, shame, dislike etc: *A shy man shrinks from meeting strangers.*

'shrink·age /-ɪdʒ/ *nu* the process, degree, of shrinking: *The shrinkage in our export trade is serious.*

‚shrink-'wrapped *adj* (of food, goods) in an airtight packet or covering.

shriv·el /'ʃrɪvl/ *vt,vi* (**-ll-**, *US* also **-l-**) (often **shrivel up**) (to cause something) to become dried or curled (through heat, frost, dryness or old age): *The heat shrivelled (up) the leaves.*

shroud¹ /ʃraʊd/ *nc* **1** a cloth (to be) wrapped round a dead body. **2** (*fig*) something which covers and hides something: *a shroud of mist.*

shroud² /ʃraʊd/ *vt* **1** to wrap (a dead body) in a shroud. **2** (*usually passive*) **shrouded in sth** covered, hidden, by something: *be shrouded in darkness/mist; a crime shrouded in mystery.*

shrub /ʃrʌb/ *nc* a small bush with a woody stem.

shrub·bery /'ʃrʌbərɪ/ *nc* (*pl* **-ies**) a place, e.g. part of a garden, planted with shrubs.

shrug¹ /ʃrʌg/ *nc* a shrugging movement: *with a shrug (of the shoulders); a shrug of despair.*

shrug² /ʃrʌg/ *v* (**-gg-**) **1** *vt,vi* to lift (the shoulders) slightly (to show indifference, doubt etc). **2** *vt* **shrug sth off** to treat a difficulty, criticism etc as not important.

shrunk /ʃrʌŋk/ *pt,pp* of shrink.

shrun·ken /'ʃrʌŋkən/ *adj* (*attrib*) smaller (esp through wetting or age, illness etc): *shrunken curtains; a shrunken face.*

shud·der¹ /'ʃʌdə(r)/ *nc* an act of shuddering.

shud·der² /'ʃʌdə(r)/ *vi* to shake uncontrollably because of fear or disgust: *shudder with cold/horror; shudder at the sight of blood. He shuddered to think of it.*

shuffle¹ /'ʃʌfl/ *nc* **1** a shuffling movement. **2** an act of changing positions: *give the cards a shuffle; a shuffle of the committee members.*

shuffle² /'ʃʌfl/ *v* **1** *vi* to walk without lifting the feet properly. **2** *vt* to move (playing-cards etc) one over the other to change their positions: *He shuffled the papers together and put them in a drawer.* **3** *vt* to give the members of (a committee) different responsibilities: *The Prime Minister has shuffled his Cabinet.* ⇨ reshuffle(2).

shun /ʃʌn/ *vt* (**-nn-**) to avoid (the usual word): *shun publicity/society.*

shunt /ʃʌnt/ *v* **1** *vt* to send (a train etc) from one track to another. **2** *vi* (of a train) to move to another track. **3** *vt* (*fig*) to send (a person etc) to a different (usually worse) position: *be shunted aside.*

shush /ʃʊʃ/ *int* (used to call for silence).

shut /ʃʌt/ *v* (*pt,pp* **—**; **-tt-**) *vt,vi* (to cause something) to be put in a position of being covered or blocked, or having the edges together: *Please shut the door.* Ⓝ For a comparison of *shut* and *close*, ⇨ the *note* at close⁵(1). ⇨ also ear¹(1), eye¹(1).

shut oneself/sb away (in a place) to keep (oneself, a person) in a quiet or safe/locked place: *I shut myself away (in the library) in order to finish the work.*

shut down (of a business, factory etc) to stop production, trading etc for a short time or permanently. **shut sth down** (of a manager, owner etc) to cause a factory etc to shut down. Hence **'shut-down** *nc* an act of shutting (a factory) down.

shut sb in (a) to lock a person in a room, building. (b) to surround a person completely: *We were shut in by high mountains.*

shut sb off to keep a person away, unable to enter: *We were shut off by the floods.* **shut sth off** to stop the supply of water, gas etc, e.g. by closing a tap.

shut sb out (of a place) to lock (a person) out.

shut sth out (of sth) (a) to prevent (something) from getting in: *use curtains to shut out the light.* (b) to stop (a thought etc) from entering one's mind.

shut up (usually *imperative*) to be quiet. **shut sb up** to make a person stop talking: *Can't you shut her up!* **shut sth up (a)** to shut doors and windows (e.g. for the night, before going on holiday etc). **shut sb/sth up (in sth)** to lock a person, possessions, an animal etc up (in a prison, box, cage etc).

shut-down /'ʃʌt daʊn/ ⇒ shut sth down.

shut·ter /'ʃʌtə(r)/ *nc* **1** a movable cover for a window, used to keep out light. **put up the shutters** (*fig*) to stop doing business (for the day or permanently). **2** (*photography*) the device that opens to admit light through the lens of a camera.

shuttle /'ʃʌtl/ *nc* **1** a transport vehicle (esp an aircraft or spacecraft) that makes regular journeys to and from a place. **2** (in a loom) an instrument with two pointed ends by which thread is carried between other threads. **3** (in a sewing-machine) a piece that carries the lower thread.

shuttle·cock /'ʃʌtlkɒk/ *nc* a piece of cork with feathers in it, used in playing badminton.

shy[1] /ʃaɪ/ *adj* (**—er**, **—est**) **1** (of a person) self-conscious and uncomfortable in the presence of others; (of behaviour etc) showing this: *He's not at all shy with women. She gave him a shy look/ smile.* **2** (of animals etc) easily frightened.

shy·ly *adv*

shy·ness *nu*

shy[2] /ʃaɪ/ *vi* (*pt,pp* **shied** /ʃaɪd/) **1** (of a horse) to move away suddenly in fear or alarm: *The horse was shying at the hedge.* **2** **shy away from sb/ sth** (*informal*) to avoid an unpleasant person, thing.

SI /ˌes 'aɪ/ *abbr* (*Fr: Système International (d'Unités)*) (*tech*) the international system of units of measurement: *SI units* (e.g. the metre, kilogram, ampere, kelvin).

sib·ling /'sɪblɪŋ/ *nc* (*formal*) a brother or sister (the usual words).

sick[1] /sɪk/ *adj* **1** (usually *pred*) likely to throw up food from the stomach: *The journey made me feel sick.* **be sick** to throw up food from the stomach. ⇒ carsick, seasick. **2** ill; not well: *We now have four sick animals. He's been sick for six weeks.* **fall sick** to become ill. (N) *'Ill' or 'unwell'* is more usual when referring to people. *'Sick' is more usual in US English.* **3** (*attrib*) connected with being ill: *one's sick-bed* (= one's bed while one is ill); *sick-pay* (= payment by the government to a worker who is ill). **4** **sick (and tired) of sth; sick to death of sth** (*pred; informal*) wanting to experience no more of and hating: *I'm sick of your lies. She's sick and tired of/sick to death of all his excuses.* **sick at heart** ⇒ heart(2). **5** **feel sick about/at sth** (*informal*) to feel very sorry and unhappy: *I feel sick about failing the exam.* ⇒ homesick. **make sb sick** (*sl*) to make a person very annoyed: *Your arrogance makes me sick!* **6** (*informal*) treating bad luck, sadness etc as funny: *sick jokes. Her humour is sick.*

'sick-bay *nc* a medical centre in a university, a ship etc.

'sick-leave *nu* time spent away from duty or work because of illness: *be/go on sick-leave.*

sick[2] /sɪk/ *n pl* (the —) sick people.

sick[3] /sɪk/ *vt* **sick sth up** (*informal*) to be sick(1).

sick·en /'sɪkn/ *v* **1** *vi* **sicken for sth** to be in the first stages of an illness: *The child is sickening for something.* **2** *vt,vi* (to cause a person) to feel disgust: *Torture is sickening. Her cruelty sickened me. They sickened at the sight of so much waste.*

sick·en·ing /'sɪkənɪŋ/ *adj* disgusting; extremely unpleasant: *sickening smells/news.*

sickle /'sɪkl/ *nc* a short-handled tool with a curved blade, used for cutting grass etc.

sick·ly /'sɪklɪ/ *adj* (**-ier, -iest**) **1** often ill: *a sickly child.* **2** weak: *a sickly smile; These plants are/ look sickly.* **3** (usually *attrib*) causing, or likely to cause, a feeling of sickness or disgust: *a sickly smell/taste.*

sick·ness /'sɪknɪs/ *n* **1** *nu* illness; ill health. **2** *nc,nu* (a particular) illness or disease: *suffering from sea-sickness.* **3** *nu* a tendency to vomit.

'sickness benefit *nu* a (State) payment to a person absent from work through illness.

side[1] /saɪd/ *adj* (*attrib*) **1** apart from the main or usual one: *the side effects of a drug; the side dishes at a meal.* **2** at, by, the side(4) of a building etc: *the side entrance; a side street.* ⇒ also the combined words after side[2], e.g. sideline; side-step.

side[2] /saɪd/ *nc* **1** one of the flat surfaces of something: *the six sides of a cube. Please carry the box this side up* (= with this side on the top). **2** a flat surface that is not the top or bottom: *A box has a top and bottom and four sides.* **3** one of the two surfaces of something flat, e.g. paper, cloth, a coin: *Write on one side only. Which is the right side of this cloth?* **4** an upright surface (of a building etc): *There's a window in the left side. There's snow on the side of the mountain.* **5** an edge: *the three sides of a triangle; a fence along the sides of the garden.* **6** one of (two) sections produced by a real or imagined central line: *the left/right/sunny side of the street; the east side of town; the profit and loss sides of an account; a pain in my left side.* **side by side** next to each other. **get/keep on the right side of sb** to do something to make sure that a person continues to like one. **split one's sides (laughing/with laughter)** (*informal*) to laugh a great deal. **7** an area next to the left or right side(6): *come and sit by my side. There's a path on the side of the house.* **on/from all sides/every side** everywhere; in all directions: *Praise came from all sides.* **put sth on/to one side** to put it down (and delay dealing with it). **8** a particular opinion, part etc considered in relation to others: *look on the bright side; study all sides of a question; a man with many sides to his character. There are two sides to every argument. She's a little on the weak/heavy side. Prices are on the high/low side.* **be on the safe side** to be careful, prepared for something that may happen: *Bring an umbrella to be on the safe side.* **see both sides of sth** to agree with, understand both (different) opinions in a discussion, argument etc. **9** (one group with) a particular position in an argument, discussion, politics etc: *Whose side are you on? There are faults on both sides. They tried to bring the two sides together.* **let the side down** to disappoint one's supporters. **take sides (with sb)** to support a person or group. ⇒ side[3]. **10** a team: *Our side is better than yours. Which side is winning?* **11** (*informal*) a TV station: *What's on the other side?* **12** a line of descent (either of one's parents): *an aunt on my mother's side*.

side³ /saɪd/ *vi* **side with sb** to support a person in an argument or quarrel: *I'm siding with you*.

side·board /'saɪdbɔ:d/ *nc* a low cupboard used in a sitting-room etc.

side·boards /'saɪdbɔ:dz/ *n pl* = side-whiskers.

side·line /'saɪdlaɪn/ *nc* **1** a type of goods sold in addition to the main goods. **2** an occupation which is not one's main work. **3** (*sport*) a line marking the long edges of a football pitch, tennis-court etc.

side·long /'saɪdlɒŋ/ *adj, adv* (directed) to or from one side: *a sidelong glance*.

side-road /saɪdrəʊd/ *nc* a small road branching off a main road.

side·step /'saɪdstep/ *vt,vi* (**-pp-**) **1** to avoid (a blow etc) by moving to one side. **2** (*fig*) to avoid answering (a question).

side-street /'saɪdstri:t/ *nc* a small street.

side-stroke /'saɪdstrəʊk/ *nu* a kind of stroke used in swimming in which one side of the body is above and the other below the water.

side·track /'saɪdtræk/ *vt* (often *passive*) to turn (a person's attention) from her or his main work or study.

side·ways /'saɪdweɪz/ (also **side·wards** /wədz/) *adj, adv* to, towards the side, with the side edge first: *look sideways at her; a sideways glance; walk/carry a chair sideways through a narrow opening*.

side-whiskers /'saɪd wɪskəz/ *n pl* (of men) hair on the sides of the face near the ears.

sidle /'saɪdl/ *vi* **sidle up (to sb)** to move up (to a person) in a shy or nervous way: *The little girl was sidling up to me*.

siege /si:dʒ/ *nc* an operation of armed forces who surround a town etc and prevent supplies from going in: *a siege of fifty days*.

si·en·na /si:'enə/ *nu* a kind of reddish-yellow earth used as a colouring matter.

si·es·ta /si:'estə/ *nc* a short rest or sleep in the afternoon.

sieve¹ /sɪv/ *nc* a utensil with wire network, used for separating small and large lumps etc. **have a head/memory like a sieve** (*informal*) to be incapable of remembering things.

sieve² /sɪv/ *vt* to put (flour etc) through a sieve: *sieving soil*.

sift /sɪft/ *v* **1** *vt,vi* to put (something), separate (something) by putting, through a sieve: *sift flour*. **2** *vt* **sift (through) sth** (*fig*) to examine something carefully: *sift the evidence*.

sigh¹ /saɪ/ *nc* an act, sound, of sighing: *with a sigh of relief*.

sigh² /saɪ/ *vi* **1** to take a deep breath that can be heard (showing sadness, tiredness, relief etc). **2** (of the wind) to make a sound like sighing. **3** to feel a longing (for): *sigh for the return of a lost friend*.

sight¹ /saɪt/ *n* **1** *nu* the power of seeing: *lose one's sight; have long/short/near sight; have good/poor sight*. Ⓝ 'Eyesight' is more usual. **know sb by sight** to be able to recognize a person: *I know him by sight but I don't know his name*. **2** *nu* the act of seeing or being seen: *Their first sight of land came after three days at sea*. **at first sight** when first seen or experienced: *He fell in love with her at*

first sight. *At first sight the climb seemed impossible*. **at the sight of sb/sth** when a person, action etc is seen: *They all laughed at the sight of the old man dancing*. **out of sight out of mind** quickly forgotten when not reminded by seeing (a person, task to be done etc). **catch sight of sb/sth** to see a person, thing suddenly; succeed in seeing a person, thing: *If ever I catch sight of him again, I'll ask for the money he owes me*. **lose sight of sb/sth** (a) to stop being able to see a person, thing. (b) (*fig*) to stop being aware of something: *lose sight of one's ambition*. **3** *nu* distance within which seeing is possible: *The train was still in/within sight/was not yet out of sight. Victory was not yet in sight* (= not yet thought of as probable). **come into/go out of sight** to come near enough/go too far away to be seen. **keep out of sight** to stay where one cannot be seen. **4** *nc* (often *pl*) something seen or worth seeing such as beautiful scenery, buildings etc: *tourist sights*. ⇨ sightseeing. **be a sight for sore eyes** to be a person, thing, one enjoys seeing. **see the sights** to visit well-known places, buildings etc as a tourist. **5** *n sing* (*derog*) (*informal*) a person, thing, that is unpleasant or unattractive to look at: *What a sight you are in that dress! She does look a sight!*

sight² /saɪt/ *vt* (*formal*) to get sight of (something), esp by coming near: *After many months at sea, Columbus sighted land*. Ⓝ Not used in continuous tenses, e.g. *is/was -ing*.

sight·see·ing /'saɪtsi:ɪŋ/ *nu* the act of visiting sights(4) as a tourist.

sight·seer *nc* a person who visits sights(4).

sight·ing /'saɪtɪŋ/ *nc* an occasion on which something is seen: *sightings of a new star/of land*.

sign¹ /saɪn/ *nc* **1** a mark, object, symbol etc used to represent something: *mathematical signs*, such as +, −, ×, ÷. **2** a word or words, design etc on a board or plate to give a warning, or to give directions: *traffic signs*. **3** something that gives evidence, points to the existence or probability of something: *the signs of suffering on his face. Are dark clouds a sign of rain?* **4** a movement of the hand, head etc used with or instead of words; signal: *wave as a sign of friendship*. **5** a symbol, name etc used to advertise a business: *shop signs*.

sign² /saɪn/ *vt,vi* **1** to write (one's name) on (a letter, application form etc): *sign a cheque; sign one's name. Who will sign first?* ⇨ signature. **2** to use a sign(4) to make something known: *He signed to me to stop. Is she signing at you?* Ⓝ 'Signal' is more usual.

sign sth away to give up rights, property etc by signing(1) a written agreement.

sign (oneself/sb) in to sign(1) (for oneself, a friend) as one enters a hotel, club etc.

sign off (a) to end a letter etc by signing(1) it. (b) to end a radio or TV programme by saying good-bye etc.

sign on (*informal*) to register officially as unemployed and available for work. **sign sb on** to take on a player, worker, by written agreement.

sign (oneself/sb) out to sign(1) (for oneself, a friend) when leaving a hotel, club etc.

sign sth over (*commerce*) to confirm a sale of goods in writing.

sign up to sign(1) a written agreement to become

employed, join the army, become a member etc.
sign sb up = sign sb on.

sig·nal¹ /'sɪgnəl/ *nc* **1** a movement, light, sound etc used to give a warning, an order or information: *traffic signals. Wave as a signal to cross the road.* **2** an event which is the immediate cause of another activity etc: *The arrival of the President was the signal for an outburst of cheering.* **3** a sound or picture sent by radio or TV: *an area with a poor/excellent TV signal.*

sig·nal² /'sɪgnəl/ *v* (**-ll-**; *US* **-l-**) **1** *vi* to make a signal(1): *signal to the waiter.* **2** *vt,vi* to make (something) known by using a signal(1): *signal (the waiter) for more bread; signal that you are about to turn left.* **3** *vt* to be a sign(3) of (an event, condition, effect etc): *The storm signalled the end of summer.*

sig·na·tory /'sɪgnətrɪ/ *nc* (*pl* **-ies**) a person, country etc that has signed a formal agreement: *the signatories to the Treaty.*

sig·na·ture /'sɪgnətʃə(r)/ *nc* a person's name signed by herself or himself: *Can I have your signature on these letters?*

'signature tune *nc* a short tune identifying a particular radio or TV programme.

sig·ni·fi·cance /sɪg'nɪfɪkəns/ *nu* a special meaning, importance: *a speech of great/little significance.* Opp insignificance.

sig·ni·fi·cant /sɪg'nɪfɪkənt/ *adj* having a special or important meaning: *a significant speech/event/improvement.* Compare insignificant.
sig·ni·fi·cant·ly *adv*

sig·ni·fy /'sɪgnɪfaɪ/ *vt* (*pt,pp* **-ied**) (*formal*) **1** to make known (one's views, intentions etc); be a sign of (something): *He signified his agreement/that he agreed by nodding. Does a high forehead signify intelligence?* **2** (*formal*) to be a sign(3) of (a degree of importance): *It signifies much/little.*

sign language /'saɪn læŋgwɪdʒ/ *nu* a system of talking by using hand signals, used by deaf people.

sign·post /'saɪnpəʊst/ *nc* a notice by the side of a road etc giving directions to places etc.

Sikh /siːk/ *n* a member of an Indian religious group believing in one God, founded in the 16th century.

si·lage /'saɪlɪdʒ/ *nu* dry grass etc used as cattle food.

si·lence¹ /'saɪləns/ *nu* **1** the absence of sound: *the silence of night.* **2** the condition of not speaking, answering (questions, spoken or written) or making comments etc: *Your silence on recent events surprises me. There was a short silence and then uproar broke out.* **an awkward silence** a period of quiet embarrassment. **in silence** without speaking or making a noise: *listen in silence to a speaker.*

si·lence² /'saɪləns/ *vt* **1** to force (a person, radio etc) to stop speaking, expressing opinions etc: *silence one's critics; silence the opposition by not allowing newspapers to report their views.* **2** to make (a gun etc) stop making a noise.
si·lencer *nc* a part that reduces the noise made by an engine, a gun etc.

si·lent /'saɪlənt/ *adj* **1** making no or little sound: *a silent night; with silent footsteps.* **2** saying little or nothing: *You'd better be silent about what happened. Her husband is the strong silent type.* **3**

written but not spoken: *The letter 'b' in doubt is silent.*
,silent 'film *nc* one without a sound track.
si·lent·ly *adv*

sil·hou·ette¹ /ˌsɪluː'et/ *nc* a picture in solid black showing only the outline; outline of a person or object seen from the side: *silhouettes of famous authors.* **in silhouette** produced as a silhouette.

sil·hou·ette² /ˌsɪluː'et/ *vt* (*passive*) to be shown as a silhouette: *It was silhouetted against the sky.*

sili·con /'sɪlɪkən/ *nu* a non-metallic element (symbol Si) found in sand, granite etc, used in electronics and alloys.
,silicon 'chip *nc* (*microelectronics*) a tiny electronic circuit contained in silicon crystal.

silk /sɪlk/ *nu* (also *attrib*) a fine, soft thread from the cocoons of certain insects, used to make cloth: *silk scarves.*
'silk·worm *nc* a kind of caterpillar that produces silk.

silk·en /'sɪlkən/ *adj* soft and smooth or shining: *a silken voice; silken hair.*

silky /'sɪlkɪ/ *adj* (**-ier, -iest**) soft, shiny and smooth like silk: *a silky feel/voice.'*

sill /sɪl/ *nc* a flat shelf at the base of a window: *a vase of flowers on the window-sill.*

sil·ly /'sɪlɪ/ *adj* (**-ier, -iest**) (*derog*) not sensible; foolish: *say silly things. How silly of you to do that! Don't be silly! Silly me—I forgot the key!*

silt¹ /sɪlt/ *nu* the sand, mud etc carried by moving water (and left at the mouth of a river etc).

silt² /sɪlt/ *vt,vi* **silt (sth) up** (to cause a river etc) to become blocked with, full of, silt: *The sand has silted up the mouth of the river.*

sil·ver¹ /'sɪlvə(r)/ *adj* **1** made of silver: *a silver ring.* **2** of the colour of silver: *use silver paint.* **Every cloud has a silver lining** ⇨ cloud¹(1).
sil·very *adj* like silver: *a silvery colour.*

sil·ver² /'sɪlvə(r)/ *nu* **1** a shining white metal (symbol Ag) used to make knives and forks, jewellery, coins etc. **2** things made of silver, e.g. dishes, candlesticks, trays: *have all one's silver taken by burglars.* **3** the colour of silver. **4** silver(2) coins: *£20 in notes and £5 in silver.*

,silver 'jubilee *nc* a 25th anniversary, esp the start of a king's or queen's reign.

,silver 'medal *nc* a medal of silver given as the second prize.

,silver 'paper *nu* thin, light foil made of tin or aluminium (as used for packing chocolates etc).

'silver·smith *nc* a person who makes silver articles.

,silver 'wedding *nc* the 25th anniversary of a wedding.

simi·lar /'sɪmɪlə(r)/ *adj* **similar (to sb/sth)** like; of the same sort: *My wife and I have similar tastes in music. Your guitar is similar to mine. They are similar.* Compare different(1).
simi·lar·ly *adv*

simi·lar·ity /ˌsɪmɪ'lærətɪ/ *n* (*pl* **-ies**) **1** *nu* the state of being similar. **2** *nc* a point or part in which there is likeness: *There are many similarities between the two men.* Compare difference(2).

sim·ile /'sɪmɪlɪ/ *nc,nu* (*lang*) (an example of) the use of words (*figure of speech*) to express an idea by comparing one thing with another, using 'like' or 'as' to show similarity, as in *He's as brave as a lion.* Compare metaphor.

sim·mer /'sɪmə(r)/ v **1** vt,vi (to cause food) to cook gently, almost at boiling-point: *Simmer the stew for an hour.* **2** vi **simmer with sth** (fig) to be filled with anger etc which is only just kept under control: *simmer with rage/annoyance.* **simmer down** (fig) to become calm (after being angry or excited).

sim·per /'sɪmpə(r)/ vi, nc (to give) a silly, self-conscious smile.

simple /'sɪmpl/ adj (—r, —st) **1** without much decoration; ordinary: *simple food; a simple style/design.* Ⓝ *'Plain'* is also possible. ⇨ simply(1). **2** easily done or understood: *written in simple English. The method is very simple. It was a simple task.* **3** inexperienced (and so easily deceived): *I'm not as simple as you think.* Compare easy¹(5). **4** (attrib) with nothing added: *a simple fact.* ⇨ simply(2). **plain and simple** ⇨ plain¹(2). **pure and simple** ⇨ pure(5). **5** (of a tool, machine etc) not having many parts. **6** (science) not highly developed: *simple forms of life.*

,simple 'fraction nc (maths) = vulgar fraction.

,simple-'minded adj (derog) showing very little intelligence.

'simple sentence nc (gram) one with one verb only, as in *I saw her yesterday.*

'simple tense nc (gram) one that is not continuous or perfect, as in 'I *eat* chips', 'I *ate* chips'. ⇨ future/past/present tense.

simple·ton /'sɪmpltən/ nc (dated; derog) a foolish person, esp one who is easily deceived.

sim·pli·ci·ty /sɪm'plɪsətɪ/ nu (formal) the state of being simple: *A small child often has a look of simplicity.* **be simplicity itself** (informal) (of a task) to be extremely easy to do.

sim·pli·fy /'sɪmplɪfaɪ/ vt (pt,pp -ied) to make (something) easy to do or understand: *a simplified reader/text.*

sim·pli·fi·ca·tion /ˌsɪmplɪfɪ'keɪʃn/ nc,nu

sim·ply /'sɪmplɪ/ adv **1** in a simple(1) way: *dress simply; simply dressed.* **2** nothing more than: *It's simply a matter of working hard.* **3** absolutely; without doubt: *You're looking simply lovely. His pronunciation is simply terrible.*

simu·late /'sɪmjʊleɪt/ vt (formal) to pretend to be, have or feel (something): *insects that simulate dead leaves.*

simu·la·tion /ˌsɪmjʊ'leɪʃn/ nu

sim·ul·ta·ne·ous /ˌsɪml'teɪnɪəs/ adj happening or done at the same time: *a simultaneous signing of an agreement.*

sim·ul·ta·neous·ly adv

sin¹ /sɪn/ n **1** nc,nu (an example of) breaking God's laws, behaviour that is against the principles of morality: *stealing is a sin; confess one's sins to a priest.* ⇨ original sin. **the seven deadly sins** pride, jealousy, lust, anger, greed, envy, laziness. **2** nc (informal) something considered to be not common sense: *It's a sin to stay indoors on such a fine day.*

sin·ful /-fəl/ adj wrong; wicked.

sin² /sɪn/ vi (-nn-) to commit sin; do wrong: *We are all capable of sinning.*

sin·ner /'sɪnə(r)/ nc a person who sins or has sinned.

sin³ written abbr (maths) sine.

since¹ /sɪns/ adv **1** (used to refer to when a period of time began) between then and now (or the time

mentioned): *He left home in 1980 and has not been seen since* (then/that time). *The house was burned down ten years ago but has since been rebuilt.* Ⓝ *'Since'* is always used with a perfect tense, i.e. not 'is/was being seen since' or 'was built since'. **ever since** ⇨ ever(4). **2** (dated) ago: *He wrote it many years since/long since.*

since² /sɪns/ conj (subord) **1** from a period of time onwards: *How long is it since you were in London? Where have you been since I last saw you? It's ages since we met! She has been sad (ever) since you went away.* **2** (used to state a reason for (not) doing something) because of the reason that: *Since we've no money, we can't buy it.* ⇨ the note at as²(3).

since³ /sɪns/ prep during the period of time after: *I haven't been to London since 1982. Since the car accident she won't drive. He's the greatest artist since Picasso.* ⇨ the note at for(6).

sin·cere /sɪn'sɪə(r)/ adj **1** (of feelings, behaviour etc) genuine: *It is my sincere belief that he is innocent.* **2** (of a person) not expressing feelings that are false: *a sincere friend.* Opp insincere.

sin·cere·ly adv in a sincere manner. **Yours sincerely** (used to end a letter to a friend or informally to end a business letter).

sin·cer·ity /sɪn'serətɪ/ nu the quality of being sincere. **in all sincerity** very sincerely and honestly.

sine /saɪn/ nc (abbr sin) (maths) **1** (of a triangle) the ratio of the length of the opposite side to the hypotenuse. **2** (in a circle with a pair of axes meeting at the centre) a line from one end of an arc on the circumference perpendicular to a radius from the other end.

sin·ew /'sɪnjuː/ nc a strong cord joining a muscle to a bone.

sin·ewy adj (of meat) not easy to eat.

sing¹ /sɪŋ/ v (pt sang /sæŋ/, pp sung /sʌŋ/) **1** vi,vt to produce (musical sounds or words) with the voice: *She sings well. He was singing a French song. He was singing to the guitar. She sang the baby to sleep.* ⇨ praise²(1). **2** vi to make a humming, buzzing or ringing sound: *The kettle was singing (away) on the cooker.*

sing·er nc a person who sings: *a pop singer.*

sing·ing nu (also attrib) (esp) the art of the singer: *teach singing; take singing lessons.*

sing² written abbr (gram) singular (as used in this dictionary).

singe /sɪndʒ/ vt to burn (hair, cloth etc) lightly: *Careful! You're singeing that dress!* □ nc a light burn (on cloth etc).

single¹ /'sɪŋgl/ adj **1** (attrib) one only: *offer not even a single excuse; a single ticket* (= for a journey to a place but not back). **in single file** ⇨ file³. **2** not married: *single men and women; remain single.* **3** (attrib) for the use of, used for, done by, one person: *a single bed; reserve* (at a hotel) *two single rooms and one double room.*

,single-'breasted adj (of a coat) having only one row of buttons down the front.

,single-'handed adj, adv done by one person without help from others.

,single-'minded adj having only one aim: *a single-minded student.*

sing·ly /'sɪŋglɪ/ adv one by one; by oneself.

single² /'sɪŋgl/ nc **1** (pl) (sport) a game with

one person on each side. **2** a gramophone record with one song etc on each side. **3** a single ticket: *two second-class singles to Leeds.*

single³ /'sɪŋgl/ *vt* **single sb/sth out** to choose a person, thing, from others (for special attention, etc): *He singled me out for criticism.*

sin·glet /'sɪŋglɪt/ *nc* (*GB*) a kind of sleeveless vest.

sing·song /'sɪŋsɒŋ/ *nc* an informal meeting of friends to sing songs together: *have a singsong round the piano.*

sin·gu·lar¹ /'sɪŋgjʊlə(r)/ *adj* **1** (*dated*): strange: *look singular in a dress.* **2** (*formal*) outstanding: *a man of singular courage and honesty.* **3** (*gram*) of a form of a noun, pronoun, used to refer to one person or thing: *The singular of 'children' is 'child'.*

,singular 'noun *nc* (*gram*) **(a)** a singular(3) form of a noun, e.g. *child*. **(b)** a noun that is always used as a singular, as in 'a *sense* of humour'. Ⓝ Marked *n sing* in this dictionary.

sin·gu·lar² /'sɪŋgjʊlə(r)/ *nc* (*gram*) (abbr *sing*) a form of a noun, pronoun used to refer to one person, thing etc: *What is the singular of 'parties'?*

sin·gu·lar·ly *adv* (*formal*) particularly: *singularly odd behaviour.*

sin·is·ter /'sɪnɪstə(r)/ *adj* suggesting evil or the likelihood of bad luck: *a sinister beginning; a sinister face; sinister looks.*

sink¹ /sɪŋk/ *nc* a basin in a kitchen used for washing up etc.

sink² /sɪŋk/ *v* (*pt* **sank** /sæŋk/ or **sunk** /sʌŋk/, *pp* **sunk**) **1** *vt,vi* (to cause a person, ship etc) to go down below the surface of water: *Wood does not sink in water. The ship sank to the bottom. We sank the boat with stones.* **sink one's differences** ⇨ difference(4). Compare float²(1). **2** *vi* (of the sun, moon) to go down (below the horizon etc): *The sun sank (below the fields).* ⇨ rise²(2). **3** *vi* (of an amount, number, level etc) to become less or lower: *Sales are sinking.* Ⓝ *'Fall'* is more usual. **4** *vi* to become weaker: *The injured child was sinking fast* (= dying). *His voice sank to a whisper.* ⇨ sunken. **5** *vi* to fall down: *She sank to the floor.* **6** *vi* to lose hope etc: *His heart sank at the idea of failure.* ⇨ sinking. **7** *vt* to produce (something), put (something) in, by digging the ground: *sink a well; sink a post into the ground.*

sink in to be fully understood: *She said nothing while the news of the accident gradually sank in.*

sink into sth (a) to fall into a deep sleep. **(b)** to become involved in a bad state or activity: *sink into crime/debt.* **(c)** to allow oneself to sink heavily in something: *sink into a chair.* **sink sth into sth (a)** (*informal*) to put money etc into a business opportunity. **(b)** to put a weapon, one's teeth etc into a body etc.

sink·ing /'sɪŋkɪŋ/ *adj* (*attrib*) sad, full of fear etc caused by worry or lack of hope: *a sinking feeling.*

sinu·ous /'sɪnjʊəs/ *adj* (*formal*) full of curves and twists: *the sinuous movement of a snake.*

si·nus /'saɪnəs/ *nc* (*pl* **—es**) one of several air-filled holes in the bones of the skull linked to the nose: *I have a cold and my sinuses are blocked.*

sip¹ /sɪp/ *nc* (an act of taking) a small amount of drink: *have a sip of hot coffee.*

sip² /sɪp/ *vt,vi* (**-pp-**) to drink a very small amount of (something): *sip (one's) coffee.*

si·phon¹ (also **sy·phon**) /'saɪfn/ *nc* **1** a bent or curved tube, pipe etc arranged so that liquid will flow up through it and then down. **2** a bottle from which soda-water can be forced out by the pressure of gas in it.

si·phon² (also **sy·phon**) /'saɪfn/ *vt* **siphon sth off/out** to draw liquid out or off (as if) through a siphon.

sir /sɜː(r)/ *n* (often S-) **1** (used by children to a male teacher, by a shop assistant to a man etc): *Please sir, can I have a pencil? Can I help you, sir?* **2** (used to begin a formal letter to a man): *Dear Sir.* Compare **madam**. **3** (used in front of the name of a knight or baronet): *Sir Winston Churchill.*

sire¹ /saɪə(r)/ *nc* the male parent of a horse. Compare dam¹.

sire² /saɪə(r)/ *vt* (esp of horses) to be the sire of another: *a Derby winner sired by Pegasus.*

si·ren /'saɪərən/ *nc* an apparatus used for producing a long loud noise (as a warning etc): *an ambulance with its sirens wailing; a ship's siren.*

sir·loin /'sɜːlɔɪn/ *nc,nu* (also *attrib*) (a piece of) the best part of meat from a cow's back: *sirloin steak.*

si·sal /'saɪzl/ *nc,nu* (a plant with long leaves which provide) strong fibre used for making rope.

sis·sy /'sɪsɪ/ *nc, adj* (*pl* **-ies**) (*derog*) (a boy or young man who is) girlish or without the qualities of courage and strength.

sis·ter /'sɪstə(r)/ *nc* **1** a daughter of the same parents as oneself or another person: *my/your/his sister.* ⇨ half-sister, stepsister. **2** *n sing* a woman who behaves like a sister: *She was a sister to him.* **3** a senior hospital nurse. **4** (also S-) a member of a religious society; nun: *Sisters of Mercy.* **5** a woman of the same trade union, socialist party etc as another.

sis·ter·hood /-hʊd/ *nu* **(a)** the feeling of a sister for a sister. **(b)** *nc* (members of) an organization of women with the same interests and aims, esp a religious or socialist organization.

sister-in-law /'sɪstər ɪn lɔː/ *nc* (*pl* **sisters-in-law**) **(a)** a sister of one's husband or wife; **(b)** the wife of one's brother.

sis·ter·ly *adj* of, like, a sister: *sisterly love.*

sit /sɪt/ *v* (*pt,pp* **sat** /sæt/; **-tt-**) **1** *vi* to be in, take, a position with one's body upright and one's bottom resting on the ground, a seat etc: *sit (down) on a chair/on the floor/in an armchair/at a table/ by the fire.* **be sitting pretty** (*informal*) to be in an advantageous or favourable position: *She isn't worried about the increase in bus fares—she cycles to work so she's sitting pretty.* **sit still** ⇨ still¹(1). **sit tight (a)** to remain firmly in one's seat (e.g. while on a motorbike or horse). **(b)** (*fig*) to remain patient and unwilling to act, change one's opinion, give in: *If you sit tight, you'll get the money back.* **2** *vt* to sit (a child etc) in a place: *He sat the baby on the floor.* **3** *vi* (of a bird etc) to rest (on a branch etc): *sit on the fence; a hen sitting on her eggs.* **4** *vt,vi* (to cause something) to be in a place: *sit books on a shelf; a town sitting on the edge of the forest.* **5** *vt* (*informal*) to take (an exam): *sit one's university exams.* ⇨ sit for sth. **6** *vi* (of a committee, council, law court, parliament etc) to meet and be active: *The House of Commons sat until 3 am.* ⇨ sitting²(1). **7** *vi* (of clothes) to fit (in the way mentioned): *This coat sits badly across the shoulders.* **8** *vi* to act as a baby-sitter: *sit for one's neighbours.*

sit about/around to be lazy and do nothing useful: *sitting about in pubs.*

sit back (a) to make oneself comfortable (in a chair etc). **(b)** to rest after a lot of activity: *You can sit back now and we'll finish the work.* **(c)** to refuse to (continue to) be involved: *How can you sit back and let them suffer?*

sit down (a) ⇨ sit(1). **(b)** to take a seat: *Please sit down, everyone.* **(c)** (of workers, students etc) to sit down in a factory, building etc and refuse to leave. Hence **'sit-down** *nc* **(a)** a short rest in a chair. **(b)** (also *attrib*) an act, instance of sitting down **(c)**: *a sit-down strike.*

sit for sb to be a model for an artist. ⇨ sitting²(3). **sit for sth** to take an exam: *sit for a university scholarship.*

sit in (of workers, students etc) to stay in a factory, building etc and refuse to leave (as a protest). Hence **'sit-in** *nc* such an act. **sit in on sth** to take part in a meeting etc as an observer only.

sit on sb (*fig; informal*) to prevent a person from interfering, being involved etc. **sit on sth (a)** to be a member of a committee, jury etc. **(b)** to do nothing about a report, criticism, inquiry etc: *They've been sitting on my application for months.* ⇨ also fence¹(1).

sit out to sit outside. **sit sth out (a)** to take no part in a dance etc. **(b)** to stay until the end of a (bad) performance etc.

sit through sth = sit sth out (b).

sit up (a) to move into a sitting position after lying flat. **(b)** to sit with one's back straight: *Sit up, children.* **(c)** to stay out of bed (until later than usual). **(make sb) sit up and take notice** (*informal*) (to cause a person) to become aware and interested.

si·tar /sɪ'tɑː(r)/ *nc* an Indian stringed musical instrument with a long neck.

sit-down /'sɪt daʊn/ *nu* ⇨ sit down.

site¹ /saɪt/ *nc* a place where something was, is, or is to be: *a site for a new school; a building site.*

site² /saɪt/ *vt* to position, place, (a building): *Where have they decided to site the new factory?*

sit-down /'sɪt daʊn/ *nc* ⇨ sit down.

sit-in /'sɪt ɪn/ *nc* ⇨ sit in.

sit·ter /'sɪtə(r)/ *nc* **1** a person who is sitting for a portrait. **2** = baby-sitter.

sit·ting¹ /'sɪtɪŋ/ *adj* (*attrib*) who now occupies (an official place, a house etc): *a sitting member/tenant.*

sit·ting² /'sɪtɪŋ/ *nc* **1** the time during which a meeting, law court, parliament etc sits(6): *a long sitting.* **2** the time during which one is engaged continuously in a particular occupation: *finish reading a book at one sitting.* **3** an act of posing for a portrait or photograph. **4** an occasion of many people sitting down (for a meal etc): *In this hotel 100 people can be served at one sitting.*

sit·ting duck /ˌsɪtɪŋ 'dʌk/ *nc* a person who is or will be easily defeated.

sit·ting-room /'sɪtɪŋ rʊm/ *nc* = living-room.

situ·ated /'sɪtjʊeɪtɪd/ *adj* (*pred*) (of a town, building etc) placed: *The village is situated in a valley/by the river.*

situ·ation /ˌsɪtjʊ'eɪʃn/ *nc* **1** a position (of a town,

building etc). **2** a condition, state of affairs esp at a certain time: *be in an embarrassing situation.* **3** (*formal*) a job; employment: *Situations vacant, Situations wanted* (used to introduce newspaper advertisements of employment offered and asked for).

six /sɪks/ *adj* or *det, nc* (of) 6. **be six of one and half a dozen of the other** to be very little difference between the one and the other. **be at sixes and sevens** to be in a confused state: *We were at sixes and sevens while the house was being decorated.*

six·teen /sɪk'stiːn/ *adj* or *det, nc* (of) 16.

six·teenth /siːk'stiːnθ/ *adj* or *det, nc* (abbr 16th) (of) one of 16 parts or the next after 15.

sixth /sɪksθ/ *adj* or *det, nc* (abbr 6th) (of) one of 6 parts or the next after 5.

,sixth 'sense *n sing* (*informal*) the power to be aware of things independently of the five senses.

sixth·ly *adv*

six·ti·eth /'sɪkstɪəθ/ *adj* or *det, nc* (abbr 60th) (of) one of 60 parts or the next after 59.

six·ty /'sɪkstɪ/ *adj* or *det, nc* (of) 60. **in the sixties (a)** (of temperature, speed etc) between 60 and 69. **(b)** between '60 and '69 in a century.

size¹ /saɪz/ *n* **1** *nu* the extent of largeness or smallness: *about the size of* (= about as large as) *a duck's egg. They're both of a size* (= are the same size). **be (about) the size of it** (of information) to be correct. **cut sb down to size** to make an arrogant person realize her or his true value, ability etc. **2** *nc* one of the degrees of size in which articles of clothing etc are made: *size five shoes; three sizes too big. I take size ten.*

size² /saɪz/ *vt* **1** to arrange (people, things) according to size. **2 size sb/sth up** (*informal*) to form a judgement or opinion of a person, thing.

size·able /-əble/ *adj* fairly large: *a sizeable difference.*

sizzle /'sɪzl/ *vi, nc* (*informal*) (to make) the hissing sound (as if) of something cooking in fat: *sausages sizzling in the pan.*

skate¹ /skeɪt/ *nc* (a sharp-edged steel blade to be fastened to) a boot for moving smoothly over ice: *a pair of skates.* **get your skates on** (*informal; imperative*) to hurry up. ⇨ roller-skate.

skate² /skeɪt/ *vi* **1** to move on skates. **2** (*fig*) **skate over/round a difficulty/problem** to treat it lightly and not thoroughly or seriously.

'skate·board *nc* a small board on wheels, used to stand on and ride as a sport.

skater *nc* a person who skates.

'skat·ing *nu* (the sport of) moving on skates.

'skat·ing-rink *nc* a specially prepared surface for skating.

ske·daddle /skɪ'dædl/ *vi* (*informal*) (esp of children) to run away.

skein /skeɪn/ *nc* a length of silk or wool or thread coiled loosely into a bundle.

skel·eton /'skelɪtn/ *nc* **1** the bony framework of an animal body. **a skeleton in the cupboard** something of which a person is ashamed and which he or she tries to keep secret. **2** an outline, plan etc to which details are to be added.

'skeleton key *nc* one that will open a number of different locks.

'skeleton staff/crew/service etc *nc* one reduced to the smallest number needed.

sketch¹ /sketʃ/ nc **1** a rough, quickly made drawing: *make a sketch of a harbour.* **2** a short account or description without details: *He gave me a sketch of his plans for the expedition.* **3** a short, humorous play or piece of writing.

sketch² /sketʃ/ v **1** vt to make a sketch of (a person, view, thing). **sketch sth out** to produce a rough plan of something without detail: *sketch out plans for a new road.* **2** vi to practise the art of making sketches: *I often go into the country to sketch.*

sketch·ing nu (the art of) making sketches(1).

sketchy adj (**-ier, -iest**) (**a**) done roughly and without detail or care: *a sketchy drawing.* (**b**) incomplete: *He has a sketchy knowledge of geography.*

skew·er /ˈskjuːə(r)/ nc a pointed piece of wood or metal, used for holding meat etc together while cooking. □ vt to fasten (meat, fish etc) with a skewer.

ski¹ /skiː/ nc (pl **—s**) (also *a pair of skis*) a long, narrow strip of wood, metal, plastic etc fixed to a special boot for moving over snow.

'ski-jump nc a steep slope before a sharp drop to let a skier leap through the air.

'ski-lift nc a machine with a cable used for taking skiers uphill in chairs or a cabin or by pulling them on their skis.

ski² /skiː/ vi (pt,pp **skied**, present participle **ski·ing**) to move over snow on skis: *go skiing.*

ski·er /ˈskiːə(r)/ nc a person who skies.

skid¹ /skɪd/ nc a movement, often sideways, of the wheels of a car etc on a slippery or icy road, or while turning a corner: *How would you get out of/correct a skid?*

skid² /skɪd/ vi (**-dd-**) (of a car etc) to move or slide sideways etc.

skies /skaɪz/ pl of sky.

skiff /skɪf/ nc a small, light, rowing boat.

skil·ful (*US* = **skill·ful**) /ˈskɪlfəl/ adj having or showing skill: *skilful driving.*

skil·ful·ly /-fəlɪ/ adv

skill /skɪl/ n **skill (in (doing) sth) 1** nu the ability (from training and practice) to do something well: *He shows no skill in painting.* **2** nc a particular kind of skill: *Reading is a basic skill.*

skill·ed adj using, having, needing skill: *skilled workmen/jobs; be skilled in the use of a tool.* Compare semi-skilled, unskilled.

skim /skɪm/ v (**-mm-**) **1** vt to remove (floating matter) from (the surface of a liquid): *skim milk; skim cream off the milk.* **2** vt,vi to move lightly over (a surface), not touching, or only lightly or occasionally touching (it): *The swallows were skimming (over) the water.* **3** vi,vt **skim (through) (sth)** to read something quickly, noting only the main points: *skim through a newspaper.*

skimp /skɪmp/ vi **skimp (on sth)** to buy, use, the minimum of what is needed: *They are so poor that they have to skimp (on their meals).*

skimpy /ˈskɪmpɪ/ adj (**-ier, -iest**) (*derog*) being (almost) too small: *a skimpy blouse/breakfast.*

skimp·ily adv

skin¹ /skɪn/ n **1** nu (the substance forming) the outer covering of the body of a person. **by the skin of one's teeth** only just: *We escaped by the skin of our teeth.* **be soaked to the skin** to

be very wet (because of heavy rain etc). **get under one's skin** (*fig*) (of a person) to cause irritation or anger. **have a thin/thick skin** (*fig*) to be easily hurt/not easily hurt by unkindness, bad criticism etc. Hence ˌthin-/ˌthick-'skinned adj. **save one's (own) skin** to avoid personal injury, suffering. **2** nc an animal's skin with or without the hair or fur: *rabbit skins.* **3** nc,nu the outer covering of a banana, peach, plum etc: *slip on a banana skin.* **4** nc,nu the thin layer that forms on some liquids, e.g. paint, milk.

ˌskin-'deep adj (of beauty, feelings etc) only on the surface and not lasting.

'skin-diving nu a sport in which a person swims under the water with goggles and a snorkel or aqualung to help breathing.

'skin·flint nc (*sl; derog*) = miser.

'skin-graft nc (in surgery) the removal of layers of skin from one part of the body to another part, e.g. to grow over a bad scar.

ˌskin-'tight adj (of clothing) fitting closely to the body: *skin-tight jeans.*

skin·ny adj (**-ier, -iest**) (*derog*) having (too) little flesh: *skinny legs; a skinny person.*

skin² /skɪn/ vt (**-nn-**) to take the skin(2) off (an animal etc): *skin a rabbit.*

skint /skɪnt/ adj (*pred*) (*sl*) very poor: *I'm skint.*

skip¹ /skɪp/ nc a large metal container for carrying away builders' refuse etc.

skip² /skɪp/ nc a skipping movement: *a hop, skip and jump.*

skip³ /skɪp/ v (**-pp-**) **1** vi to jump lightly and quickly: *The lambs were skipping about in the fields.* **2** vi to jump over a rope which is turned over the head and under the feet as one jumps. **3** vi to go from one place to another quickly: *skip over/across to Paris for the weekend. He skipped off* (= left) *without saying anything to any of us.* **4** vi to change from one subject to another when talking: *He skips from one excuse to another.* **5** vt to go from (one part of a book etc) to another without reading, paying attention etc: *We'll skip the next chapter.*

'skip·ping-rope nc a rope with handles, used for skipping(2).

skip·per¹ /ˈskɪpə(r)/ nc **1** a captain, esp of a small merchant ship or fishing-boat. **2** (*informal*) a captain of a team in games such as football and cricket.

skip·per² /ˈskɪpə(r)/ vt (*informal*) to act as captain of (a team etc): *skipper a team.*

skir·mish /ˈskɜːmɪʃ/ vi, nc (to take part in) a fight between small groups.

skirt¹ /skɜːt/ nc **1** a woman's article of clothing that hangs from the waist. **2** a part of a dress etc that hangs from the waist.

skirt² /skɜːt/ vt **1** to be on or pass along the edge of (something): *Our road skirted the forest.* ⇨ also outskirts. **2** (*fig*) to avoid (details): *skirt (round) a problem/question.*

'skirt·ing-board nc a long board fixed round the walls of a room close to the floor.

skit /skɪt/ nc (*literature*) a short piece of humorous writing making fun of a person, idea, style etc: *a skit on 'Macbeth'.*

skittles /ˈskɪtlz/ n sing (a game in which a ball is thrown to knock down) a number of bottle-shaped pieces of wood (each called a *skittle*).

skulk /skʌlk/ vi to hide, move secretly, because afraid, to avoid work or duty, or with an evil purpose: *skulking about in the corridors*.

skull /skʌl/ nc (anat) the bony framework of the head.

skunk /skʌŋk/ nc a kind of small N American animal able to send out a strong unpleasant smell when attacked.

sky /skaɪ/ nc (pl **skies** /skaɪz/) the space we look up to from the earth, where we see the sun, moon and stars: *The sky is clear. It's a clear, blue sky.* Ⓝ 'Sky' is usually used with 'the' but with 'a, an' when used after an adjective, as in 'a blue sky'. 'Skies' is only used in poetic or literary situations. ⇨ also pie.

sky·blue adj, nu (of) the bright blue colour of the sky on a cloudless day.

sky-'high adv so as to reach the sky: *When the bomb exploded, the bridge was blown sky-high*.

'sky·line nc the outline of hills, buildings etc seen against the sky: *the skyline of New York*.

sky·lark /'skaɪlɑːk/ nc a kind of small bird that sings as it flies up into the sky.

sky·rock·et /'skaɪrɒkɪt/ vi (informal) (of prices, costs etc) to increase quickly be a large amount.

sky·scraper /skaɪskreɪpə(r)/ nc a very tall building.

slab /slæb/ nc a thick flat piece: *paved with slabs of stone; a slab of chocolate*.

slack¹ /slæk/ adj (—er, —est) **1** (derog) giving little care or attention to one's work: *Don't get slack at your work*. **2** (pred) having not much work to be done or business being done: *Trade/ Business is slack this week*. **3** loose, not pulled tight: *a slack rope*.

slack·ly adv

slack·ness nu

slack² /slæk/ n sing (the —) the part of a rope etc that hangs loosely.

slack³ /slæk/ vi to be lazy: *Stop slacking!*

slack·en /'slækn/ vt,vi **1** (to cause something) to become slower, less active etc: *The ship's speed slackened*. **2** (to cause a rope etc) to become loose(r): *slacken the ropes/reins*.

slacks /slæks/ n pl (dated) trousers, not part of a suit, worn informally.

slag /slæg/ nu waste matter remaining when metal has been taken from rock.

slain /sleɪn/ pp of slay.

slake /sleɪk/ vt (formal) to satisfy (thirst).

sla·lom /'slɑːləm/ nc a ski-race along a zigzag course marked out by poles with flags.

slam¹ /slæm/ nc **1** a noise of something being slammed: *the slam of a car door*. **2** (in card-games) an act of winning (almost) all the tricks.

slam² /slæm/ v (-mm-) **1** vt,vi (to cause a lid, door etc) to shut violently and noisily: *slam the door (in his face). The door slammed (to)*. **2** vt to put, throw or knock (something) with force: *She slammed the box down on the table*. **3** vt **slam sth on** to move something quickly and violently: *She slammed on the brakes*. **4** vt (informal) to criticize (a person, organization) severely: *The newspapers slammed the child murderer*.

slan·der /'slɑːndə(r)/ nc,nu (an offence of making) a false statement that damages a person's reputation. □ vt to use slander against (a person). Compare libel.

slan·der·er nc a person who uses slander.

slan·der·ous /-əs/ adj using or containing slander.

slang /slæŋ/ nu words, phrases, meanings etc sometimes used in very informal conversation but not suitable for writing or for more formal occasions, e.g. *bloke* (= man); *grub* (= food), *sloshed* (= drunk). Ⓝ Marked *sl* in this dictionary.

slangy adj (-ier, -iest) using or containing slang.

slant¹ /slɑːnt/ nc **1** a line or direction going up or down at an angle. **2** (informal) a particular way of considering (an opinion, facts etc): *a new slant on the political situation*.

slant² /slɑːnt/ v **1** vt,vi (to cause something) to go up or down at an angle: *His handwriting slants from right to left*. **2** vt to present (information etc) using a particular (often prejudiced) point of view.

slap¹ /slæp/ adv directly: *The car ran slap into a wall*.

slap² /slæp/ nc a quick blow with the open hand or with something flat.

slap³ /slæp/ vt (-pp-) **1** to hit (a person, thing) with the open hand; smack: *She slapped his face/ slapped him on the face*. **2** to put (something) down with a slapping noise: *He slapped the book down on the table*. **3** vt **slap sb down** (informal) to stop a loud critic, protesting person etc from speaking etc.

slap·dash /'slæpdæʃ/ adj, adv (derog) careless(ly): *a slapdash worker*.

slap-hap·py /'slæphæpɪ/ adj (derog) (of a person) pleasant and cheerful but lazy.

slap·stick /'slæpstɪk/ nu comedy using practical jokes.

slap-up /'slæpʌp/ adj (attrib; sl) extremely good: *a slap-up dinner at a slap-up restaurant*.

slash¹ /slæʃ/ nc **1** an act of slashing(1). **2** a long cut.

slash² /slæʃ/ vt **1** to make a cut or cuts in (something) with long strokes: *His face had been slashed with a razor-blade*. **2** (informal) to cut (prices etc) by a large amount: *slash prices/taxes/salaries*. **3** to hit (a person, animal) with a whip.

slat /slæt/ nc a thin narrow piece of material used in rows in some blinds or doors.

slate¹ /sleɪt/ n **1** nu (also attrib) a kind of blue-grey stone that splits easily into thin, flat layers: *a slate quarry*. **2** nc a piece of these layers used for making roofs. **3** nc a piece of slate used for writing on. *a clean slate* no more cause for criticism, hate etc. *wipe the slate clean* to forgive all past offences.

slate² /sleɪt/ vt **1** to cover (a roof etc) with slates. **2** (informal) to criticize (a book, play etc) severely.

slaugh·ter¹ /'slɔːtə(r)/ nu **1** the killing of animals for food. **2** the cruel killing of many people or animals.

slaugh·ter² /'slɔːtə(r)/ vt **1** to kill (animals) for food. **2** to kill cruelly (many people or animals).

'slaughter-house nc a place where animals are killed for food.

slaugh·ter·er nc (a) a person who kills animals for food. (b) a person who kills many people.

slave¹ /sleɪv/ nc **1** a person who is the property of another person. **2** a person forced to work very hard for someone else: *You mustn't make slaves* *of your workers.* **3 slave to sth** a person completely under the control of a habit etc: *a slave to duty/passion/convention/drink.*

'slave-driver *nc* (*derog*) a person who makes others work very hard.

slav·ery /'sleɪvərɪ/ *nu* (**a**) the condition of being a slave: *sold into slavery.* (**b**) the custom of having slaves: *men who worked for the abolition of slavery.*

slave² /sleɪv/ *vi* to work hard: *Poor Jim! He's been slaving away* (e.g. cooking) *for three hours!*

slay /sleɪ/ *vt* (*pt* **slew** /sluː/, *pp* **slain** /sleɪn/) (*literary*) to murder (a person) or kill (a wild animal).

sleazy /'sliːzɪ/ *adj* (**-ier, -iest**) (*informal; derog*) (of a place) dirty, untidy: *a sleazy hotel.*

sled /sled/ *nc* = sledge.

sledge¹ /sledʒ/ *nc* a vehicle with long, narrow strips of wood or metal instead of wheels, used to travel on snow.

sledge² /sledʒ/ *vi* to travel by sledge: *go sledging.*

sledge-hammer /'sledʒ hæmə(r)/ *nc* a heavy hammer with a long handle, used for banging posts into the ground etc.

sleek /sliːk/ *adj* (**—er, —est**) (of hair, an animal's fur etc) soft, smooth and glossy.

sleep¹ /sliːp/ *n* **1** *nu* the condition of the body and mind at rest in which the eyes are closed and the muscles, nervous system etc are relaxed: *How many hours' sleep do you need?* ⇨ asleep. **cry oneself to sleep** to cry until one is asleep. **get (off) to sleep** to manage to fall asleep: *I couldn't get to sleep last night.* **go to sleep** to begin to sleep. **2** *n sing* a period of sleep: *have a short/good/restful sleep.*

sleep² /sliːp/ *v* (*pp,pt* **slept** /slept/) **1** *vi* to be or fall asleep: *We go to bed to sleep. She slept for eight hours.* **sleep like a top/log** to sleep very well. **2** *vt* to provide beds for (people): *This hotel sleeps 300 guests.*

sleep around (*informal*) to have sexual intercourse with many people.

sleep in (**a**) (of a nurse, hotel staff etc) to live or sleep where one works. (**b**) to stay in bed asleep until late.

sleep sth off (*informal*) to recover from a party, headache etc by sleeping: *sleep off a bad headache/a hangover.*

sleep on to continue to sleep: *Don't wake him up—let him sleep on for another hour.* **sleep on it/sth** to leave a decision, solution to a problem etc until the next day.

sleep through sth to fail to be woken up by a noise, the alarm-clock etc.

sleep together = sleep with sb.

sleep with sb to have sexual intercourse with a person during the night.

sleep·er /'sliːpə(r)/ *nc* **1** a person who sleeps: *a heavy/light sleeper.* **2** (a bed in) a sleeping-car on a train. **3** a heavy beam of wood (or similarly shaped piece of other material) under a railway track. **4** a plain gold band used as an earring.

sleep·ing /'sliːpɪŋ/ (used in compounds):

'sleeping-bag *nc* a warm, waterproof bag in which to sleep, e.g. in a tent.

'sleeping-car *nc* a railway coach with beds.

,sleeping 'partner *nc* a person who owns a share in a business but does not do any work in it.

'sleeping-pill *nc* one that contains a drug to encourage sleep.

sleep·less /'sliːplɪs/ *adj* (*attrib*) without sleep: *pass a sleepless night.*

sleepy /'sliːpɪ/ *adj* (**-ier, -iest**) **1** needing, ready for, sleep: *feel/look sleepy.* **2** (of places etc) quiet; inactive: *a sleepy little village.*

sleep·ily /-əlɪ/ *adv*

sleet /sliːt/ *nu* a falling snow mixed with rain. ⬚ *vi* (of sleet) to fall: *It was sleeting.*

sleeve /sliːv/ *nc* **1** a part of clothing that covers all or part of the arm: *shirt-sleeves.* **have sth up one's sleeve** to have an idea, plan etc that one keeps secret for future use. **laugh up one's sleeve** to be secretly amused. **2** a stiff envelope for a gramophone record.

sleeve·less *adj* without sleeves.

sleigh /sleɪ/ *nc* a sledge, esp one drawn by a horse: *go for a sleigh-ride/a ride in a sleigh.*

sleight /slaɪt/ *n* (usually in) **sleight of hand** great skill in using the hand(s) to perform tricks, deceive etc.

slen·der /'slendə(r)/ *adj* (**-er, -est**) **1** small in width or circumference compared with height or length: *slender fingers; a slender waist.* **2** only just enough: *have slender means; a slender chance of passing.*

slen·der·ness *nu*

slept /slept/ *pt,pp* of sleep².

slew /sluː/ *pt* of slay.

slice¹ /slaɪs/ *nc* **1** a thin, wide, flat piece cut off something, esp bread or meat. **2** a part, share: *Smith deserves a slice of the credit for our success.* **3** a utensil with a wide, flat blade, used for cutting, serving or lifting (e.g. cooked fish, fried eggs). **4** (*sport*) (in tennis etc) a stroke that causes the ball to go spinning off in a different direction.

slice² /slaɪs/ *vt* **1 slice sth (up)** to cut bread, meat etc into slices: *slicing (up) a loaf.* **2** (*sport*) to hit (a ball) with a slice(4).

slick /slɪk/ *adj* (**—er, —est**) (*informal;* often *derog*) **1** done efficiently and well (but perhaps with a little deceit): *a slick business deal.* **2** (of a person) doing things in a slick way: *a slick salesman.*

slid /slɪd/ *pt,pp* of slide².

slide¹ /slaɪd/ *nc* **1** an act of sliding(1): *have a slide on the ice.* **2** (an apparatus with) a smooth slope down which children or things can slide. **3** a fall down a slope: *a rock slide.* ⇨ landslide. **4** a picture, diagram etc on photographic film and in a frame (looked at through an apparatus that makes it bigger). **5** (*science*) a glass plate on which something is placed to be examined under a microscope.

'slide projector *nc* an apparatus used for viewing slides(4).

slide² /slaɪd/ *v* (*pt,pp* **slid** /slɪd/) **1** *vt,vi* (to cause a person, thing) to move smoothly over, slip along, a polished surface: *children sliding on the ice. The drawers of this desk slide in and out easily.* **let sth/things slide** to fail to take care of, organize, do, it/them. **2** *vi* **slide into sth** to act gradually in the way mentioned without being fully aware: *slide into dishonesty/bad habits.* **3** *vt,vi* (to cause a person, thing) to move quickly, esp to avoid being seen: *The thief slid behind the curtains. She slid a coin into his hand.*

,slid·ing 'door *nc* one that is pulled across an opening (instead of swinging on hinges).

,slid·ing 'scale *nc* a scale by which one thing, e.g. wages, goes up or down in relation to changes in something else, e.g. the cost of living.

slight¹ /slaɪt/ *adj* (**—er, —est**) **1** small and thin: *a slight figure.* **2** small and not serious or important: *a slight error; a slight headache; without the slightest difficulty* (= with no difficulty at all). *She takes offence at the slightest thing* (= is very easily offended).

slight·ly *adv* (**a**) small and thin: *a slightly built boy.* (**b**) to a small extent: *The patient is slightly better today. I know her slightly.*

slight² /slaɪt/ *nc* an instance of treating a person without respect or good manners: *suffer slights.*

slight³ /slaɪt/ *vt* to treat (a person) without proper respect or good manners: *She felt slighted because no-one spoke to her.*

slim¹ /slɪm/ *adj* (**—mer, —mest**) **1** (of a person, part of the body) not fat; attractively thin: *slim legs; a slim waist/girl.* **2** (*informal*) almost not enough: *slim hopes/chances of success.*

slim·ness *nu*

slim² /slɪm/ *vi* (**-mm-**) to eat less, take exercise etc in order to become slim(1).

slime /slaɪm/ *nu* **1** soft, sticky mud. **2** a sticky substance from snails etc: *a trail of slime.*

slimy /'slaɪmɪ/ *adj* (**-ier, -iest**) (**a**) of, like, covered with slime. (**b**) (*fig; derog*) unpleasantly flattering and deceitful: *That slimy boy gets everything he wants.*

sling¹ /slɪŋ/ *nc* **1** a length of rope, chain etc put round an object, e.g. a barrel, to support or lift it. **2** a piece of cloth tied round the neck, used to support an injured arm. **3** a strip of leather used to throw stones to a distance. **4** an act of throwing a stone etc.

sling² /slɪŋ/ *vt* (*pt,pp* **slung** /slʌŋ/) **1** to throw (a stone etc) with force: *naughty boys slinging stones at girls.* **2** to throw (something) carelessly: *sling one's coat down; sling a rope over the cliff; with his bag slung over his shoulder.* **3** **sling sb out** (*informal*) to force a person to leave a room, party etc.

'sling-back *adj* (*attrib*) (of shoes) with a strap at the back, not a heel: *sling-back shoes.*

slink /slɪŋk/ *vi* (*pt,pp* **slunk** /slʌŋk/) to go or move quietly and secretly in order to deceive: *slinking away/in/out/off/by.*

slip¹ /slɪp/ *nc* **1** an act of slipping. **give sb the slip** (*informal*) to escape, get away, from a person. **2** a small error caused by carelessness: *make a slip.* **a slip of the tongue/pen** an error in speaking/writing. **3** a women's loose sleeveless clothing worn under a dress. **4** a young, thin person: *a (mere) slip of a boy/girl.* **5** (also *slipway* or *the slips*) a sloping path down to the water for ships or boats. **6** a small piece of paper (e.g. given as a receipt etc): *a sales slip.*

slip² /slɪp/ *v* (**-pp-**) **1** *vi* to (almost) fall as the result of losing one's balance: *He slipped on the icy road and broke his leg.* **2** *vt,vi* to go, move or put (something) quietly or quickly, esp without attracting attention: *She slipped away/out/past without being seen. He slipped a pound coin into my pocket.* **3** *vi* to pass without being noticed: *As the months slipped by, he began to recover his*

health. **4** *vi* to get away, escape, fall, by being difficult to hold or by not being fastened: *The fish slipped out of my hand. The blanket slipped off the bed.* **let sth slip** (**a**) to allow work etc to be neglected. (**b**) to allow an opportunity etc to be lost: *Don't let the opportunity slip.* (**c**) to tell a secret accidentally. **slip through one's fingers** ⇨ **finger¹**. **slip one's mind** ⇨ **mind¹**(1). **5** *vt,vi* to put, pull on or push off, (clothing) with a quick, easy movement: *slip a coat on/off; slip into/out of a dress.* **6** *vi* to move smoothly and effortlessly; go with a gliding motion: *The ship slipped through the water.* **7** *vi* to fall in standard or quality: *Her work has slipped recently.* **slip up** (*informal*) to make a mistake, e.g. by forgetting an arranged time, date, for something. Hence **'slip-up** *nc* such a mistake.

slip·ped disc /ˌslɪpt 'dɪsk/ *nc* a painful condition caused by one of the small bones in the back being out of position.

slip·per /'slɪpə(r)/ *nc* (also *a pair of slippers*) a loose-fitting, soft shoe worn in the home.

slip·pery /'slɪpərɪ/ *adj* (**-ier, -iest**) **1** (of a surface) smooth, wet, polished etc so that it is difficult to stand or to move on, or hold: *slippery roads.* **2** (*fig*) needing care: *We're on slippery ground when dealing with this subject.* **3** (*fig; derog*) (of a person) not to be trusted: *He's as slippery as an eel* (= impossible to trust).

slip-road /'slɪprəʊd/ *nc* a road used to join or leave a motorway.

slip-up /'slɪp ʌp/ ⇨ **slip²**(7).

slip·way /'slɪpweɪ/ ⇨ **slip¹**(5).

slit¹ /slɪt/ *nc* a long, narrow cut, tear or opening.

slit² /slɪt/ *vt* (*pt,pp* **-tt-**) to make a slit in (something); open (it) by slitting: *slit a sack of flour; slit an envelope open.*

slith·er /'slɪðə(r)/ *vi* to slide or slip unsteadily: *slither down an ice-covered slope.*

sliv·er /'slɪvə(r)/ *nc* **1** a small, thin strip (of wood). **2** a thin piece (of something) cut off a large piece: *a sliver of cheese.*

slob·ber /'slɒbə(r)/ *vi* to let saliva run from the mouth (as a baby does).

slog¹ /slɒg/ *nc* (*informal*) **1** a wild hit at (a ball). **2** a long and boring job: *Is writing a dictionary a slog?*

slog² /slɒg/ *v* (**-gg-**) (*informal*) **1** *vt* to hit (a ball) hard and wildly. **2** *vi* to work long and hard: *slogging away at one's work.*

slog·ger *nc* a person who slogs(2).

slo·gan /'sləʊgən/ *nc* an easily remembered phrase used to advertise something or to make clear the aim(s) of a group, campaign etc: *political slogans.*

sloop /sluːp/ *nc* **1** a small sailing-ship. **2** (*modern use*) a small warship.

slop¹ /slɒp/ *n* **1** (*pl*) dirty waste water from the kitchen. **2** (*pl*) urine, excrement (in buckets, as in a prison cell). **3** *nu* semi-liquid food for pigs.

slop² /slɒp/ *v* (**-pp-**) **1** *vi* (of liquids) to spill over the edge: *The tea slopped (over) into the saucer.* **2** *vt* to cause (a liquid) to spill: *slop beer over the table.* **3** *vt* to make a mess with (a liquid): *slopping paint all over the floor.* **4** *vt,vi* **slop (sth) out** to empty (buckets) containing urine etc: *The prisoners had to slop out every morning.*

slope¹ /sləʊp/ *n* **1** *nc,nu* a slanting line, position or direction: *the slope of a roof; a hill with a slope of 1 in 5.* **2** *nc* an area of rising or falling ground: *mountain slopes; ski slopes.*

slope² /sləʊp/ *vi* **1** (of land) to have a slope: *Our garden slopes* (*down*) *to the river.* **2** **slope off** (*informal*) to go away (to avoid a person or escape doing something): *children sloping off after a meal to escape the washing-up.*

slop·py /'slɒpɪ/ *adj* (**-ier, -iest**) **1** (*informal; derog*) careless and untidy: *a sloppy workman/ piece of work.* **2** (*informal*) (of clothes) loose and fitting badly. **3** (*informal*) foolishly sentimental; weakly emotional: *sloppy talk about girlfriends and boyfriends.* **4** wet and dirty: *sloppy floors.*

slop·pi·ly /-əlɪ/ *adv* in a careless way: *eating sloppily; sloppily* (= carelessly) *dressed.*

slop·pi·ness *nu*

slosh /slɒʃ/ *v* **1** *vt* (*sl*) to hit (a person): *slosh him on the chin.* **2** *vi* **slosh about** to splash about in water or mud.

slosh·ed /'slɒʃt/ *adj* (*sl*) drunk.

slot¹ /slɒt/ *nc* **1** a narrow opening through which something is to be put, e.g. for a coin in a machine to buy a ticket, cigarettes, sweets. **2** a long groove or channel into which something fits or along which it slides. **3** (*informal*) a (right or suitable) place for something in a system, set of activities etc: *too many advertising slots on TV.*

slot² /slɒt/ *vt* (**-tt-**) **slot sb/sth in; slot sb/sth into sth** to put (a person, thing) into a slot(2,3): *slot 30 000 graduates a year into jobs.*

sloth /sləʊθ/ *n* **1** *nu* (*formal*) laziness. **2** *nc* a S American animal which lives in the branches of trees and moves very slowly.

sloth·ful /-fəl/ *adj*

slouch¹ /slaʊtʃ/ *nc* a lazy way of standing or walking.

slouch² /slaʊtʃ/ *vi* to stand, sit or move, in a lazy, tired way: *people who slouch about at street corners all day.*

slov·en·ly /'slʌvnlɪ/ *adj* (*derog*) untidy, dirty, careless: *a slovenly appearance/child.*

slow¹ /sləʊ/ *adj* (**—er, —est**) **1** (capable of) acting, moving etc taking a long time: *a slow train/ runner; a slow journey; the slow lane of the motorway* (= one where vehicles move slowly). Opp fast¹(1). Compare quick¹(1). **2** (*pred*) (of a clock) showing a time earlier than the accurate time: *My watch is slow. It's slow by half an hour/an hour slow.* Opp fast¹(2). **3** at less than the usual rate or speed: *They were slow to answer my letter.* **in slow motion** ⇨ motion¹(1). **4** (of a person) not able to understand or learn something quickly: *a slow child/learner.* Compare quick¹(2). **5** (*attrib*) having an effect only after a long time: *a slow poison; a slow-acting drug.* **6** (*pred*) not very interesting or lively: *The party was a little slow.* **7** (*sport*) (of a surface) not helping quick speed: *a slow track/wicket.* Opp fast¹(4).

slow·ly *adv* in a slow(1) manner. Opp fast²(1).

slow·ness *nu*

slow² /sləʊ/ *adv* (**—er, —est**) at a slow(1) speed; slowly (which is more usual): *Please drive slower.* **go slow** (**a**) to be less active: *Go slow until you feel really well again.* (**b**) (of workers) to work slowly as a protest. Hence **'go-slow** *nc* such a form of protest. (N) *'Slow'* is not often used as an adverb except in combined forms such as *slow-mov-*

ing, slow-going, or as a comparative (*slower*), as in *The queue is moving slower than usual.* Compare: quick².

slow³ /sləʊ/ *vt,vi* (to cause a person, vehicle etc) to move, work etc at a slower speed: *The weather slowed us a little.* **slow down** (**a**) (of a car etc) to lessen its speed. (**b**) (of a person) to be less active; not work so hard: *You should slow down if you want to avoid becoming ill.* **slow sb down** to cause a person to be less active, work less etc: *Her chatter slows me down. That injury has slowed her down a lot.* **slow up** = slow down(b).

slow·coach /'sləʊkəʊtʃ/ *nc* (*informal; derog*) a person who moves or works (too) slowly.

slow-worm /'sləʊ wɜːm/ *nc* a kind of small, legless European lizard.

sludge /slʌdʒ/ *nu* **1** thick mud. **2** thick, dirty oil or grease.

slug¹ /slʌg/ *nc* a kind of slow-moving creature, like a snail but without a shell.

slug² /slʌg/ *nc* (*informal*) a bullet.

slug³ /slʌg/ *vt* (**-gg-**) (*US informal*) **1** to shoot²(5) (a person). **2** to hit (a person) hard.

slug·gish /'slʌgɪʃ/ *adj* not very active; slow-moving: *a sluggish river. I'm feeling sluggish.*

slug·gish·ly *adv*

sluice¹ /sluːs/ *nc* **1** an apparatus for regulating the level of water by controlling the flow into or out of a canal, lake etc. **2** a channel for water.

sluice² /sluːs/ *vt* **sluice sth out** to wash out a bowl, shed etc using running water.

slum¹ /slʌm/ *nc* a street of dirty, crowded houses; such a house: *live in a slum.*

slum·my *adj* (*derog*) dirty and in bad condition like slums: *a slummy part of the town.*

slum² /slʌm/ *vi* (**-mm-**) **slum (off sb)** (*informal*) to live very cheaply: *They've been slumming off me for years.*

slum·ber /'slʌmbə(r)/ *vi, nc,nu* (*literary*) (to be in) a state of peaceful sleep.

slump¹ /slʌmp/ *nc* **1** a serious fall (in prices etc). **2** a period when business is bad.

slump² /slʌmp/ *vi* **1** (of a person) to sit down, fall, heavily: *Tired from his walk, he slumped into a chair.* **2** (of prices, trade, business activity) to decrease a lot or suddenly.

slung /slʌŋ/ *pt,pp* of sling².

slunk /slʌŋk/ *pt,pp* of slink.

slur¹ /slɜː(r)/ *nc* **1** a suggestion of having done wrong: *cast a slur on her reputation; keep one's reputation free from* (*all*) *slurs.* **2** an act of slurring sounds when speaking.

slur² /slɜː(r)/ *vi,vt* (**-rr-**) to say (words) so that they are difficult to understand, e.g. because ill.

slush /slʌʃ/ *nu* **1** melting, dirty snow. **2** (*fig*) foolish sentiment (as in love stories etc).

'slush fund *nc* an amount of money used for bribes.

slut /slʌt/ *nc* (*derog*) a dirty or immoral woman.

slut·tish /-ɪʃ/ *adj*

sly /slaɪ/ *adj* (**—er, —est**) deceitful; keeping or doing things secretly: *a sly look; a sly child.* **do sth on the sly** to do it secretly.

sly·ly *adv*

smack¹ /smæk/ *nc* (a sound of) a blow given with the open hand, of the lips parted suddenly or a whip: *with a smack of the lips* (suggesting enjoyment of food or drink).

smack² /smæk/ adv (*informal*) violently and suddenly: *It hit me smack in the eye.*

smack³ /smæk/ vt **1** to hit (a person) with the open hand: *If you say that again, I'll smack your face.* **2** to part (the lips) with a smacking sound to show pleasure (at food or drink etc).

smack·ing nc,nu (an instance of) hitting with the palm of the hand: *That child needs a good smacking.*

smack⁴ /smæk/ vi **smack of sth** to have a slight flavour or suggestion of something: *opinions that smack of heresy.*

small¹ /smɔːl/ adj (**—er, —est**) **1** below average (in amount, size, extent): *a small room/meal/group/lump/cut. He takes a small size in shoes. The hole is too small for the pipe. His debts are small. There has been a small increase in prices.* ⓃFor a comparison of *small* and *little*, ⇨ little¹, esp little¹(3). Compare big, great, large. **it's a small world** ⇨ world²(1). **2** (*attrib*) not doing things on a big scale: *small farmers/business people.* **in a small way** ⇨ way²(5). **3** unimportant: *a small mistake.* Opp big(3). **4** (*derog*) (of a person) ungenerous and unpleasant: *a small man with a small mind.* Hence **ˌsmall-ˈminded** adj. Compare big-hearted. **5** (*attrib*) only slight: *He has only a small chance of winning. She failed and small wonder!* (= it is not surprising!)

ˈsmall ads n pl short advertisements in a newspaper or magazine.

ˈsmall arms n pl weapons that are light enough to be carried in the hand.

ˌsmall ˈbeer adj (*pred*) (*informal*) less or not important in amount, kind etc: *Sales on Monday are small beer compared to Saturday.*

ˌsmall ˈchange nu coins of small value: *Can you give me small change for this note?*

ˈsmall fry n pl (*derog*) people of no importance.

ˈsmall·holder nc a person owning a smallholding.

ˈsmall·holding nc a piece of land under fifty acres in size.

ˈsmall hours n pl (the —) the three or four hours after midnight.

small letters n pl ones that are not capitals.

ˌsmall-ˈminded adj (*derog*) ⇨ small¹(4).

ˈsmall-scale adj (**a**) limited: *small-scale fighting/industry.* (**b**) made or drawn to a small scale: *small-scale maps.* Opp large-scale.

ˈsmall talk nu conversation about unimportant social matters.

small·ness nu

small² /smɔːl/ n **1 the small of sth** the narrow part (of something): *the small of the back.* **2** (the —) small people.

small·pox /ˈsmɔːlpɒks/ nu a kind of serious disease leaving permanent marks on the skin.

smalls /smɔːlz/ n pl small articles of clothing, esp socks, pants etc.

smart¹ /smɑːt/ adj (**—er, —est**) **1** neat and clean in appearance : *a smart dress/suit/car. You look very smart.* **2** (*attrib*) fashionable; part of high society: *a smart dresser; the smart set.* **3** intelligent: *a smart student.* **4** quick: *walk at a smart pace.* **Look smart!** Hurry up!

smart·ly adv

smart·ness nu

smart² /smɑːt/ vi **1** to become painful: *The smoke made my eyes smart.* **2** to feel angry, annoyed: *She was smarting with anger. He was smarting over the insult.*

smart·en /ˈsmɑːtn/ vt,vi **smarten (oneself/sb) up** (to cause oneself, a person) to become smart(1): *smarten oneself up to see visitors.*

smash¹ /smæʃ/ adv violently: *run smash into a wall.* Ⓝ 'Smack' is more usual.

smash² /smæʃ/ nc **1** an act, sound, of something breaking to pieces. **2** (*sport*) (in tennis etc) a hard stroke in which the ball is hit hard.

smash³ /smæʃ/ vt,vi **1** (to cause something) to break with force into small pieces: *smash a window. The firemen smashed in/down the doors.* **2** (to cause something) to go violently (into, against etc): *The car smashed into a wall. He smashed the car against a tree.* **3** vt to defeat (an army etc) thoroughly: *smash the enemy.* **smash a record** ⇨ record²(6). **4** (*sport*) (in tennis etc) to hit (a ball) downwards over the net with a hard stroke.

smash·er /ˈsmæʃə(r)/ nc (*informal*) a person or thing considered to be a fine example: *That girl's a smasher!*

smash·ing /ˈsmæʃɪŋ/ adj (*dated sl*) excellent.

smat·ter·ing /ˈsmætərɪŋ/ n sing **a smattering of sth** a little knowledge (of): *have a smattering of French.*

smear¹ /smɪə(r)/ nc **1** a mark made by smearing(1): *a smear of paint.* **2** (also *attrib*) (*med*) a test for disease etc using a sample of skin, fluid etc: *a smear test for cancer of the cervix.* **3** a deliberate (often untrue) remark made against a person, product, business etc.

smear² /smɪə(r)/ v **1** vt to mark (something) with something oily or sticky; spread (something oily etc) on (something): *smear one's hands with grease; hands smeared with blood; smear butter on the newspaper.* **2** vi (of paint, oil, ink etc) to spread over, onto a surface. **3** vt (*fig*) to use a smear(3) or smears against (a person, business etc).

smell¹ /smel/ n **1** nu the sense using the nose: *Smell is stronger in dogs than in people.* **2** nc something that is noticed by using the nose; quality that affects this sense: *What a nice/horrible/unusual smell!* **3** n sing (used without an *adj*) a bad or unpleasant quality that affects the nose: *What a smell!* **4** n sing an act of breathing in through the nose to get the smell(2) of something: *Have a smell of this egg and tell me whether it's good.*

smell² /smel/ v (*pt,pp* **smelt** /smelt/) Ⓝ Not used in continuous tenses, e.g. *is/was -ing,* in 1, 2, 4 and 5 below. **1** vt to become aware of (a person, thing) through the sense of smell: *Can you smell anything unusual? I could smell something burning.* Ⓝ 'Smell' is often used with 'can/could'. **2** vt (*fig*) to become aware of (something) by having a slight feeling: *smell danger/trouble.* **smell a rat** ⇨ rat¹(1). **3** vt to use one's sense of smell in order to learn (something): *Smell this and tell me what it is.* **smell sth out** to discover information (as if) by smelling. **4** vi to have the sense of smell: *Can fishes smell?* **5** vi (used without an *adj*) to have a bad or unpleasant smell: *He/His breath smells.* **6** vi (used with an *adj* or *adv*) to have a kind of smell mentioned: *The flowers smell sweet. Your breath smells of brandy.*

smelly /ˈsmelɪ/ adj (**-ier, -iest**) (*informal; derog*) having a bad smell: *smelly feet.*

smelt¹ /smelt/ *vt* to melt (ore) in order to separate (metal) from it.

smelt² /smelt/ *pp,pt* of smell².

smile¹ /smaɪl/ *nc* a pleased, happy, amused expression on the face, with (usually a parting of the lips and) loosening of the face muscles: *There was a pleasant/amused smile on her face.* **be all smiles** to look very happy and pleased. Compare grin, laugh.

smile² /smaɪl/ *v* **1** *vi* to produce a smile: *He never smiles. What are you smiling at?* **2** *vt* to express (something) by means of a smile: *Father smiled his approval.* **3** *vi* **smile on sb** (*formal*) (of good luck, success etc) to affect, act on, a person: *May fortune smile on you.*

smirk /smɜːk/ *vi, nc* (to give) a silly (often rude), self-satisfied smile.

smite /smaɪt/ *vt,vi* (*pt* **smote** /sməʊt/, *pp* **smitten** /'smɪtn/) (*old use*) to affect (a person, hearing etc) strongly: *The sound of an explosion smote our ears.* ⇨ smitten.

smith·er·eens /ˌsmɪðə'riːnz/ *n pl* **into/to smithereens** into very small pieces: *The cup broke into/to smithereens.*

smit·ten /'smɪtn/ **1** *pp* of smite. **2** *adj* (*pred*) **smitten (with sb/sth)** (a) extremely affected: *smitten with guilt/grief.* (b) (*informal*) very attracted (to a person), in love (with a person): *He's smitten (with that pretty woman).*

smock /smɒk/ *nc* a loose shirt (with smocking on it) like an overall.

smock·ing *nu* a kind of decorative sewing on clothing made by gathering the cloth tightly with stitched patterns.

smog /smɒg/ *nu* fog with smoke, exhaust fumes from vehicles etc.

smoke¹ /sməʊk/ *n* **1** *nu* a visible gas coming from a burning substance: *smoke pouring from factory chimneys; cigarette smoke.* **go up in smoke** (a) to be destroyed by fire: *The factory has gone up in smoke.* (b) (*fig*) to end leaving nothing permanent or worthwhile behind: *After the quarrel, his holiday plans went up in smoke.* **2** *nc* (*informal*) (an act of smoking) a cigarette etc: *stop working and have a smoke.*

'smoke-screen *nc* (a) (*mil*) smoke used to hide military operations. (b) (*fig*) an act, explanation etc designed to deceive people about one's real intentions etc.

smoke·less *adj* (*attrib*) (a) that burns without smoke: *smokeless fuel.* (b) where smoke is not allowed: *a smokeless zone.*

smoky *adj* (**-ier, -iest**) (a) full of smoke: *smoky chimneys/fires.* (b) (*attrib*) like smoke in smell, taste or appearance: *smoky bacon.*

smoke² /sməʊk/ *v* **1** *vi* to give out smoke or something thought to be like smoke: *a smoking chimney/volcano.* **2** *vt,vi* to breathe in smoke from (a cigarette etc): *smoke a pipe/cigar. Can I smoke in here?* **3** *vt* to dry and preserve (meat, fish) in smoke (from wood fires). **4** *vt* to stain, darken, (something) with smoke: *smoked glass.* **5** *vt* **smoke sb/sth out** to use smoke to force a person, insect or animal to come out: *smoke out snakes from a hole.*

smoked *adj* (*attrib*) (of food) treated by smoking(3): *smoked bacon.*

smoker *nc* a person who smokes(2): *a heavy/light smoker* (= a person who smokes often/not often).

smok·ing *nu* the habit, act, of smoking(2).

smol·der /'sməʊldə(r)/ = smoulder.

smooth¹ /smuːð/ *adj* (**—er, —est**) **1** (of surfaces) level or polished, like glass: *smooth paper/skin; smooth to the touch; a smooth sea.* Opp rough¹(1). **2** calm and free from uncomfortable movement: *a smooth journey.* Opp rough¹(2). **3** (of a liquid mixture) free from lumps: *mix to a smooth paste.* **4** (of sounds) not harsh: *a smooth voice.* **5** (of drink etc) pleasant and not sour: *a smooth wine.* **6** (*derog*) (of a person, behaviour) flattering and polite (often with a suggestion of insincerity): *smooth manners; a smooth talker.*

smooth·ly *adv* in a smooth manner: *Things are not going very smoothly* (= There are problems, obstacles, interruptions etc).

smooth·ness *nu*

smooth² /smuːð/ *v* **1** *vt* to make (something) smooth(1): *smooth a bedcover; smooth (away/out) the creases.* **2** *vt* **smooth sb over** to make a person calm (by making promises, paying part of a debt etc). **smooth sth over** to make a difficulty, problem etc less serious: *smooth over her anger.* **3** *vi* **smooth down** (of a rough sea, quarrel etc) to become calm.

smoth·er /'smʌðə(r)/ *vt* **1** to kill (a person, animal) by keeping air from the mouth. **2** to use a cover or covering to put out (a fire). **3** to cover (a person, thing): *smother a grave with flowers/a child with kisses/one's wife with kindness; be smothered with/in dust by passing cars.* **4** to control, hold back (something): *smother a yawn/one's anger.*

smoul·der (*US* = **smol-**) /'sməʊldə(r)/ *vi* **1** to burn slowly without flame. **2** (*fig*) (of angry feelings) to exist but be controlled and unseen: *smoulder with discontent/hatred.*

smudge¹ /smʌdʒ/ *nc* a dirty mark: *You've got a smudge on your cheek.*

smudge² /smʌdʒ/ *v* **1** *vt* to make a smudge on (something). **2** *vi* (of ink, paint etc) to become smeared: *Ink smudges easily.*

smug /smʌg/ *adj* (**—ger, —gest**) (*derog*) too pleased with oneself and one's abilities and without kindness for others etc: *a smug smile/young man.*

smug·ly *adv*

smuggle /'smʌgl/ *vt* **1** to get (goods) secretly and illegally to and from a place: *smuggling drugs into/out of a country; smuggle a dog across the border.* **2** to take (a person or thing) secretly (and against rules and regulations): *smuggle a letter/news into a prison.*

smug·gler *nc* a person who smuggles.

smut¹ /smʌt/ *n* **1** *nc* (a mark made by) a bit of soot, dirt etc. **2** *nu* (*derog*) indecent or obscene talk, words: *Don't talk smut.*

smut·ty *adj* (**-ier, -iest**) (a) dirty with smuts. (b) (*derog*) containing smut(2): *smutty stories.*

smut² /smʌt/ *vt* (**-tt-**) to mark (something) with smuts(1).

snack /snæk/ *nc* a light meal (of sandwiches etc).

'snack-bar/-counter *nc* a place where snacks may be bought and eaten.

snag /snæg/ *nc* (*informal*) a hidden, unknown or

unexpected difficulty: *There's a snag in this plan somewhere.*

snail /sneɪl/ *nc* a kind of small animal with a soft body, no limbs and a shell on its back. **at a snail's pace** very slowly.

snake¹ /sneɪk/ *nc* **1** any one of a group of long, legless reptiles, some of which are poisonous. **2** (*fig; derog*) an insincere, harmful person who pretends to be a friend.

snake² /sneɪk/ *vi* to move in twists and glides: *The road snakes through the mountains.*

snap¹ /snæp/ *adj* (*attrib*) (*informal*) done immediately: *a snap decision/election.*

snap² /snæp/ *nc* **1** an act, sound, of snapping: *The dog made a snap at the meat. The lid shut with a snap.* **2** = snapshot. **3** a kind of small biscuit: *ginger snaps.*

snap³ /snæp/ *v* (**-pp-**) **1** *vt,vi* (to cause something) to break with a short loud sound: *The rope snapped. He snapped his pencil.* **2** *vt* to close (a lid etc of a container) making this noise: *snap a box shut; snap down the lid.* **3** *vi* (of a person's confidence etc) to end suddenly: *His patience/nerves snapped.* **4** *vi* to (try to) catch something with the teeth: *The dog snapped.* ⇨ **snap at sb/sth.** **5** *vt,vi* (of a person) to speak, say (something), in a quick angry way: *'You can't have it', he snapped.* ⇨ **snap sth out.** **6** *vt* to take (a photograph).

snap at sb/sth (a) to snap(4) at something: *snap at a leg/bone.* **(b)** to snap(5) at a person. **(c)** to (try to) take, get, use, something quickly: *snap at a chance/offer/opportunity.*

snap sth out to say something in a quick, angry voice. **snap out of it** (usually *imperative*) (*informal*) to force oneself to end a bad temper, sad mood etc immediately.

snap sb/sth up (*informal*) to get possession of an excellent worker, a cheap article etc eagerly and quickly.

snap·shot /ˈsnæpʃɒt/ *nc* a photograph taken quickly with a simple camera.

snap·py /ˈsnæpɪ/ *adj* (*pred*) (*no comp; informal*): *Be snappy!/Make it snappy!* Hurry up!

snare¹ /sneə(r)/ *nc* **1** a trap for small animals and birds. **2** (*fig*) something dangerous or deceitful that tempts a person: *His promises are a snare and a delusion.*

snare² /sneə(r)/ *vt* to catch (an animal) in a snare: *snare a rabbit.*

snarl¹ /snɑːl/ *vi, nc* **1** (of an animal) (to make) a sound, act, of growling with the teeth showing. **2** (of a person) (to speak in) a low, angry voice.

snarl² /snɑːl/ *nc* **1** a confused state: *traffic snarls in our cities.* **2** a knot, tangle (in wool etc).

snarl³ /snɑːl/ *vt,vi* **snarl (sth) up** (to cause something) to become confused or complicated: *The traffic was snarled up. The accident snarled up the traffic.*

'snarl-up *nc* (*informal*) a confused group of vehicles that are unable to move.

snatch¹ /snætʃ/ *nc* **1** an act of snatching: *make a snatch at the letter.* **2** a short outburst or period: *overhear snatches of conversation; snatches of warm weather.*

snatch² /snætʃ/ *v* **1** *vt,vi* to put out the hand suddenly and (try to) take (something): *He snatched the letter from me/snatched but was not quick enough.* **2** *vt* to get (something) quickly or when a

chance occurs: *snatch an hour's sleep/meal; snatch a kiss.*

snatch·er *nc* (*derog*) a person who snatches(1).

sneak¹ /sniːk/ *nc* (*informal; derog*) a person who deceives in a cowardly way.

sneak² /sniːk/ *v* **1** *vi* to move quietly and secretly in order to deceive: *sneak across/in/out/away/ upstairs.* **2** *vt* to take, put, (something) secretly: *sneak a look; sneak a sandwich; sneak a key back.* **3** *vi* to behave like a sneak. **4** *vi* **sneak (on sb)** (*informal*) to give information (about a person) secretly to an official, parent etc.

sneak·er /ˈsniːkə(r)/ *nc* (also *a pair of sneakers*) (esp *US*) a canvas shoe with a rubber etc sole; tennis shoe.

sneak·ing /ˈsniːkɪŋ/ *adj* (*attrib*) **1** secret: *have a sneaking respect/sympathy for him.* **2** vague: *a sneaking feeling/suspicion.*

sneer¹ /snɪə(r)/ *nc* a sneering look, smile etc.

sneer² /snɪə(r)/ *vi* to show one's dislike by using a wrinkled nose and an insincere smile (and perhaps despising words): *sneer at politics.*

sneer·ing·ly *adv*

sneeze¹ /sniːz/ *nc* a sudden, uncontrollable outburst of air through the nose and mouth: *Coughs and sneezes spread diseases.*

sneeze² /sniːz/ *vi* to make a sneeze: *sneezing into a handkerchief.* **not to be sneezed at** (*informal*) worth having even though it is small: *A prize of £5 is not to be sneezed at.*

snick /snɪk/ *vt, nc* (to make) a small cut in something.

snick·er /ˈsnɪkə(r)/ *vi, nc* = snigger.

snide /snaɪd/ *adj* (usually *attrib; derog*) sneering; suggesting unpleasant thoughts: *snide remarks about their friendship.*

sniff¹ /snɪf/ *nc* an act or sound of sniffing: *One sniff of this stuff is enough to kill you.*

sniff² /snɪf/ *v* **1** *vi* to draw air in through the nose so that there is a sound: *sniffing and sneezing.* **2** *vt,vi* **sniff (at) (sb/sth)** to draw in through the nose and smell (a person, thing): *sniff the sea air; sniff (at) a rose. The dog was sniffing (at) me.*

snig·ger /ˈsnɪgə(r)/ *vi, nc* (to make) a short, unpleasant laugh (esp at something rude or to show lack of respect).

snip¹ /snɪp/ *nc* **1** a cut made by snipping; thing cut off (something large). ⇨ snippet(1). **2** (*informal*) a bargain: *Only 50p! It's a snip!*

snip² /snɪp/ *vt* (**-pp-**) to cut (something) with scissors in short, quick strokes: *snip off the ends of the string.*

snipe¹ /snaɪp/ *nc* (*pl* unchanged) a kind of bird with a long bill which lives in marshes.

snipe² /snaɪp/ *vi* **snipe (at sb/sth)** **1** to fire shots (at a person, thing) from a hiding-place. **2** (*fig*) to say unkind or critical things (about a person, thing).

sniper *nc* a person who snipes(1).

snip·pet /ˈsnɪpɪt/ *nc* **1** a small piece cut off: *a snippet of cloth to use as a sample.* **2** (*pl*) small amounts (of information, news etc): *catch only snippets of the conversation.*

snitch /snɪtʃ/ *v* (*sl*) **1** *vt* to steal (something of little or no value). **2** *vi* **snitch (on sb)** to report (about a person) to an official.

sniv·el /ˈsnɪvl/ *vi* (**-ll-**, *US* **-l-**) to complain, cry, in a miserable way: *a poor woman with six snivelling* *children.*

snob /snɒb/ nc (*derog*) a person who pays too much attention to social position or wealth, or who does not like people in lower social positions.
snob·bery /'snɒbərɪ/ nu the state, quality, of being snobbish. ⇨ inverted snobbery.
snob·bish /-ɪʃ/ adj of, like, a snob.
snob·bish·ly adv

snook·er /'snu:kə(r)/ nu an indoor game played by hitting 1 white ball, 15 red balls and 6 balls of other colours with a long stick (a *cue*).

snoop /snu:p/ vi **1** *snoop (into sth)* to enquire (into matters one is not concerned with). **2** *snoop around* to look around for information etc, esp to gain an advantage.

snooty /'snu:tɪ/ adj (-ier, -iest) (*informal*; *derog*) (behaving) like a snob.
snoot·ily /-əlɪ/ adv

snooze /snu:z/ vi, nc (*informal*) (to take) a short sleep (esp in the daytime): *have a snooze after lunch.*

snore /snɔ:(r)/ vi to breathe roughly and noisily while sleeping. □ nc a sound of snoring: *His snores woke me up.*
snorer nc a person who snores.

snor·kel (also **schnor·kel**) /'snɔ:kl, 'ʃn-/ nc a short, bent tube held in the mouth, used by a swimmer to take in air while under water.

snort¹ /snɔ:t/ nc an act, sound, of snorting: *give a snort of disapproval.*

snort² /snɔ:t/ v **1** vi to force air out through the nose (esp to show impatience, contempt etc): *snort with rage (at her/the idea).* **2** vt to express (something) by snorting: *snort (out) a reply.* '*Never!*' *he snorted.*

snot /snɒt/ nu (*vulgar*) the semi-liquid produced in the nose.
snot·ty adj (-ier, -iest) (a) full of snot. (b) (*derog*) full of snot.

snout /snaʊt/ nc a nose (and sometimes the mouth or jaws) of an animal (esp a pig).

snow¹ /snəʊ/ nu frozen water falling from the sky in soft, white pieces.
'**snow·ball** nc (a) a mass of snow pressed into a hard ball for throwing in play. (b) (*fig*) something that increases quickly in size as it progresses. □ vi to grow quickly in size, importance etc: *Opposition to the war snowballed.*
'**snow-blind** adj (temporarily) unable to see because the eyes are tired by the glare of the sun on snow.
'**snow-bound** adj unable to travel because of heavy falls of snow.
'**snow·drift** nc snow heaped up by the wind.
'**snow·fall** nc (esp) an amount of snow that falls.
'**snow·flake** nc a small piece of snow.
'**snow-plough** (*US* -**plow**) nc a wide tool on a vehicle, used for pushing snow from roads etc.
'**snow·storm** nc a heavy fall of snow, esp with strong wind.
,**snow-'white** adj as white as snow.

snow² /snəʊ/ vi (of snow) to fall: *It snowed all day. be snowed in/up* to be prevented by heavy snow from going out. *be snowed under (with sth)* to be busy, burdened, (with something): *She was snowed under with work/with invitations to parties.*

snowy adj (-ier, -iest) (a) covered with snow:

snowy roofs. (b) characterized by snow: *snowy weather*

Snr written abbr (also **Sen., Sr**) Senior.

snub¹ /snʌb/ nc an act, instance, of snubbing a person.

snub² /snʌb/ vt (-bb-) to ignore, treat rudely, (a person): *He snubbed me by ignoring me when I spoke to him.*

snub nose /'snʌb nəʊz/ nc a short, turned up nose: *The baby has a snub nose.*
'**snub-nosed** adj

snuff¹ /snʌf/ nu powdered tobacco to be taken up into the nose by sniffing: *take a pinch of snuff.*
'**snuff-box** nc a box for snuff.

snuff² /snʌf/ vt *snuff sth out* to put out the flame of a candle.

snuffle /'snʌfl/ vi to breathe noisily (as when the nose is partly blocked). □ nc an act, sound, of snuffling.

snug /snʌg/ adj (-gg-) **1** sheltered from wind and cold; warm and comfortable: *snug in bed.* **2** neat and tidy; rightly or conveniently placed or arranged: *a snug room.* **3** warm and comfortable: *a snug jacket.*
snug·ly adv

snuggle /'snʌgl/ vi **1** *snuggle down* to make oneself warm and comfortable: *She snuggled down in bed.* **2** *snuggle up* to lie close to a person for warmth, comfort or affection: *The child snuggled up to her mother.*

so¹ /səʊ/ adj (*pred*) (used with forms of the verb 'be', e.g. *is/was*) true; like that: *I must admit that it isn't/wasn't so.* ⇨ also so-so.

so² /səʊ/ adv **1** (used for emphasis) to such a large (or small) extent (that): *The room is so small/ untidy. He was so ill (that) we had to send for a doctor. We had so little time that we had to run fast. There were so many books (that) we had no space for them. I ate so much (food) that I felt sick.* Ⓝ For a comparison of '*so + adj*' and '*such a . . .*', ⇨ the note at such¹(2). *not so + adj + as . . . =* not as . . . as . . . (which is more usual): *It's not so big as I thought. so far; so far, so good* ⇨ far²(3). *So long!* (*informal*) Goodbye! *so long as* ⇨ long²(1). *so much for that/sb/sth* ⇨ much³. *so much so that* ⇨ much²(1). **2** (used to emphasize a feeling, opinion etc): *I'm so pleased! We're so glad you could come. I love you so (much).* **3** in this or that way: *It's warm and sunny and I hope it will remain so for a long time. As you treat me, so will I treat you. Please stand exactly so while I take the photograph. 'It was cold yesterday'—'So it was.'* (= That is true.) *So it was that* (= That is how) *I became a sailor. even so* ⇨ even². *just so* ⇨ just²(2). **4** (used with auxiliary verbs such as *can, do, will*) also: *and so do/can/ have/was/will I.* Ⓝ For the negative, use '*neither*' or '*nor*'. **5** (used with verbs such as *believe, expect, hope, think*) to refer to a fact, event, situation etc already mentioned): '*Is she pleased?*'—'*I think/ hope so.*' '*Am I too late?*'—'*I'm afraid so.*' '*He's got the job.*' '*So I believe/was told/heard.*' Compare not(1.c). **6** (used in special phrases): *and so on* (also *and so forth*, which is less usual) and other things of the same kind: *We need blankets, bandages, disinfectant and so on.* Ⓝ The abbreviation '*etc*' is often used, as in *blankets, bandages etc. I told you so* ⇨ tell(1). *do so* ⇨ do²(2). *if so* ⇨

if(1). *quite so* ⇨ quite(4). *less so (than)* ⇨ less². *more so (than)*, ⇨ more²(1). *or so* approximately: *We have 100 members or so. I live a mile or so from the station.* Ⓝ '*About*' is more usual, as in *We've about 100 members.* *say so* ⇨ say²(1). *so be it* (*formal*) (used to express one's reluctant agreement): *If you must go, (then) so be it.*

so³ /səʊ/ *conj* (*subord*) **1** that is why; with the result that: *The shop was closed so I couldn't buy any milk. She asked me to go so I went. No-one said anything so I thought the water was clean.* **2** (used to express purpose) *so (that)* with the purpose that; in order that: *I'll leave the light on so (that) you can see where the lock is. Speak slowly so (that) they can understand you. Please be quiet so (that) I can sleep. We have arranged things so (that) one of us is always on duty.* *so as to +* *verb* (*informal*) in order to (which is more usual): *I'll have everything ready so as not to keep you waiting.* **3** (used at the beginning of a sentence to express surprise, irony etc): *So that's where I put it! So you think you're special!* *So what?* (*informal*) I'm not interested, don't care etc.

soak¹ /səʊk/ *nc* an act of soaking: *Give the sheets a good soak.* *in soak* being soaked: *The sheets are in soak.*

soak² /səʊk/ *v* **1** *vt,vi* (to cause a person, thing) to become completely wet: *The rain has soaked my clothes. The child fell in the pond and was soaked (through). Soak the stains for one hoʊr before washing. The clothes are soaking in soapy water. I love to soak for a long time in the bath.* *be soaked to the skin* (*informal*) to be, become completely wet (by rain etc). ⇨ sodden. **2** *vt,vi* (of a liquid) to go into or through (a substance): *The blood soaked through (the bandage). The rain is soaking in.*

soak oneself in sth (**a**) to spend a long time in a bath. (**b**) to take in as much tradition, atmosphere etc as possible: *soak oneself in the atmosphere of Venice.* *soak sth in sth* ⇨ 1 above.

soak through (**a**) (*passive*) to be made completely wet: *Your shirt's soaked through!* ⇨ 1 above. (**b**) ⇨ 2 above.

soak sth up (**a**) to take in a liquid; remove liquid from a carpet etc by doing this: *Sand quickly soaks up water. Soak up the coffee with this paper.* (**b**) (*fig*) to take in knowledge, atmosphere etc: *Soak up all the information you can. We sat listening to the music and soaking up the atmosphere of Spain.*

so-and-so /'səʊ n səʊ/ *nc* (*informal; derog*) a rude or unpleasant person: *He's an old so-and-so!*

soap¹ /səʊp/ *nu* **1** a substance made of fat or oil etc, used for washing and cleaning: *a bar of soap; use plenty of soap and water.* **2** (*informal*) flattering praise or silly romantic talk (esp insincere).

'**soap-box** *nc* a wooden box used by a speaker to stand on (in a street, park etc).

'**soap-bubble** *nc* a ball of soapy water, full of air.

'**soap powder** *nu* a substance used to wash clothes.

'**soap opera** *nc* a TV or radio serial on domestic and romantic themes.

'**soap·suds** *n pl* bubbles of soap and water.

soapy *adj* (**-ier, -iest**) of, like, soap: *This bread* has a soapy taste.

soap² /səʊp/ *vt* **1** to apply soap(1) to (a person): *soap oneself down.* **2** (*informal*) to use flattery to try to please (a person). ⇨ soft soap(b).

soar /sɔː(r)/ *vi* **1** (of a bird, plane) to fly or go up high in the air. **2** (*fig*) to increase quickly: *Prices soared when war broke out.*

sob¹ /sɒb/ *nc* an act, sound, of sobbing.

sob² /sɒb/ *v* (**-bb-**) **1** *vi* to draw in the breath sharply and irregularly while crying: *She sobbed her heart out* (= cried a great deal). **2** *vt* to tell (something) while sobbing: *She sobbed (out) the story of her son's death in the car crash.*

'**sob-story** *nc* an account of something unpleasant that happens to oneself told to get sympathy.

so·ber¹ /'səʊbə(r)/ *adj* **1** serious and in control of oneself: *make a sober estimate of what is possible.* **2** not drunk: *Does he ever go to bed sober?* **3** (of colours, tastes etc) ordinary and dull.

so·ber·ly *adv* in a controlled, serious way.

so·ber² /'səʊbə(r)/ *vt,vi* **sober up; sober one-self/sb** (*up*) **1** *vt* to cause (oneself, a person) to become sober(1): *The bad news sobered all of us.* **2** *vt,vi* (to cause oneself, a person) to become sober(2): *Leave him to sober up.*

so·bri·ety /sə'braɪətɪ/ *nu* (*formal*) the condition of being sober(1).

Soc. *written abbr* Society.

so-called /'səʊ kɔːld/ *adj* having the description mentioned, but wrongly: *Your so-called friends won't help you.*

soc·cer /'sɒkə(r)/ *nu* = football.

so·ciable /'səʊʃəbl/ *adj* friendly; liking company. Opp unsociable. Compare antisocial.

so·ciably /-əblɪ/ *adv*

so·cia·bil·ity /ˌsəʊʃə'bɪlətɪ/ *nu*

so·cial¹ /'səʊʃl/ *adj* **1** living in groups, not separately: *social ants. Man is a social animal.* **2** (usually *attrib*) of society or communities; of relations between people and communities: *social class/customs/reforms/welfare.* **3** of or for one's free time with one's friends: *a busy social life; a social club.* **4** = sociable.

,**Social 'Democrat** *nc* (*politics*) a person who wishes society to change gradually to a system of democratic socialism.

,**social se'curity** *nu* government financial help for people who are unemployed, ill, disabled etc: *The family is on social security* (= receiving such help).

,**social 'science** *nc,nu* (the study of) history, economics, politics, psychology, sociology etc.

'**social worker** *nc* a professional person who works to improve the welfare of individuals.

so·cial·ly /-ʃəlɪ/ *adv*

so·cial² /'səʊʃl/ *nc* an informal gathering for eating, dancing etc, esp organized by a club.

so·cial·ism /'səʊʃəlɪzəm/ *nu* (the belief in) a political and social system in which everyone has the same rights and opportunities, with State ownership or control of the major means of wealth and production. Compare capitalism.

so·cial·ist /-ɪst/ *adj* of, like, socialism. □ *nc* a supporter of, believer in, socialism.

so·cial·ite /'səʊʃəlaɪt/ *nc* a person who is well known in fashionable society.

so·cial·ize (also **-ise**) /'səʊʃəlaɪz/ *vi* to be friendly in the company of other people.

so·ci·ety /səˈsaɪətɪ/ n (pl **-ies**) **1** nu the system in which people live together in organized communities. **2** nc (often S-) an organization of people with a particular interest or purpose: *the school debating society; a society for the care of animals; the Geographical Society.* **3** nc a particular social community: *modern industrial societies.* **4** nu companionship; friendly company: *spend an evening in the society of one's friends.* **5** nu people of fashion or distinction; the upper classes: *fashionable society. Who do you know in society?* ⇨ high society.

so·cio·logi·cal /ˌsəʊsɪəˈlɒdʒɪkl/ adj of sociology.

so·cio·logi·cal·ly /-klɪ/ adv

so·ci·ol·ogist /ˌsəʊsɪˈɒlədʒɪst/ nc a student of, expert in, sociology.

so·ci·ol·ogy /ˌsəʊsɪˈɒlədʒɪ/ nu the scientific study of the nature and growth of society and social behaviour.

sock¹ /sɒk/ nc **1** a woollen, cotton etc covering for the foot and ankle: *a pair of football socks.* **pull one's socks up** (fig) to improve, make a greater effort: *You won't pass the exam if you don't pull your socks up!* **2** a loose sole used inside a shoe.

sock² /sɒk/ nc (sl) a blow given with the fist: *Give him a sock on the jaw!*

sock³ /sɒk/ vt (sl) to hit (a person) with the fist: *Sock him on the jaw!*

sock·et /ˈsɒkɪt/ nc **1** a hollow into which something fits: *the eye-sockets; a socket for an electric light bulb.* **2** a device (e.g. in a wall) with a set of holes, used with a plug to make an electrical connection.

sod /sɒd/ nc,nu (a piece of) earth including the grass with its roots.

so·da /ˈsəʊdə/ nu a common chemical substance used to make soap, glass etc.

'soda-water nu water with gassy bubbles.

sod·den /ˈsɒdn/ adj soaked through: *clothes sodden with rain.*

so·di·um /ˈsəʊdɪəm/ nu (science) a silver-white metal (symbol Na) occurring naturally only in compounds.

so·fa /ˈsəʊfə/ nc a soft, covered seat with sides and a back, for two or more people.

soft /sɒft/ adj (**—er**, **—est**) **1** not solid or firm; easy to bend, dent etc: *soft mud/butter; a soft chair/bed.* Opp hard¹(1). **2** pleasant and smooth to touch: *soft fur.* Compare rough¹(1). **3** (of light, colours) restful to the eyes: *a soft green colour.* **4** (of sounds) quiet (and pleasant): *soft music/voices.* Compare loud(1). **5** (of a wind etc) gentle: *a soft breeze.* **6** (of a voice, personality etc) sympathetic; loving: *a soft tone of voice; have a soft heart.* Opp hard¹(4). ⇨ soft-hearted. **7** (informal; derog) (of a person) easily persuaded, influenced or deceived: *He's not as soft as he looks.* **be soft on sb** to be filled with (foolish) love for a person. **be soft in the head** ⇨ head¹(2). **8** (of water) free from mineral salts (and so gentle to touch): *as soft as rainwater.* Opp hard¹(7). **9** (of work etc) not needing much effort: *a soft job; a soft option* (= a chosen task that is easier). Compare hard¹(5). **10** (of drugs) not very harmful. Compare hard¹(8).

soft-'boiled adj (of eggs) boiled so that the yolk is liquid. Compare hard-boiled.

soft 'currency nc,nu one that cannot easily be changed for another currency or for gold and so is not likely to keep its value. Compare hard currency.

'soft drink nc (a) non-alcoholic fruit juice.

soft 'fruit nc,nu the small kind without a stone, e.g. strawberries, currants.

soft-'hearted adj sympathetic; kind. Opp hard-hearted.

soft 'pedal vi (fig) to make (a previous promise, statement etc) less definite.

soft soap (a) liquid soap. **(b)** (fig) flattery. □ **soft-'soap** vt to flatter (a person).

soft-'spoken adj having a gentle voice; saying pleasant, friendly things.

'soft·ware nu (computers) information and programs. Compare hardware(b).

soft·wood nc,nu easily sawn wood, e.g. pine. Compare hardwood.

soft·ly adv

soft·ness nu

sof·ten /ˈsɒfn/ v **1** vt,vi (to cause something) to become soft etc: *curtains that soften the light; a substance used to soften water.* **2** vt,vi (to cause a person) to become kind, sympathetic etc: *She softened/was softened when she heard his sad story.* **3** vt to make (something) easier to bear: *Her gentle manner softened the effect of the news.* **soften the blow** ⇨ blow¹(2).

soft·en·er nc a substance used to soften water.

sog·gy /ˈsɒgɪ/ adj (**-ier**, **-iest**) (esp of ground) heavy with water.

sog·gi·ness nu

soil¹ /sɔɪl/ nc,nu the upper layer of earth in which plants, trees etc grow: *good/poor/sandy soil; a man of the soil* (= one who works on the land (and likes to do so)).

soil² /sɔɪl/ v **1** vt to make (something) dirty: *He refused to soil his hands.* **2** vi to become soiled: *material that soils easily.*

sol·ace /ˈsɒlɪs/ nc,nu (formal) (something that gives) comfort or relief (when one is in trouble or pain): *The blind man found solace in music.*

so·lar /ˈsəʊlə(r)/ adj of the sun.

solar 'cell nc (science) a device that converts solar energy into electric energy.

solar 'energy nu (science) energy from the sun as used to make electricity.

solar 'panel nc (tech) an apparatus (in a roof etc) that attracts solar energy (as a method of heating, lighting).

solar-'powered adj (tech) using solar energy.

'solar system n (the —) the sun and the planets which revolve round it.

'solar year n (the —) the time taken by the earth to go round the sun, about 365 days, 5 hours, 48 minutes and 46 seconds.

sold /səʊld/ pt,pp of sell.

sol·der /ˈsɒldə(r)/ nu an easily melted alloy used, when melted, to join harder metals, wires etc. □ vt to join (things) with solder.

'soldering-iron nc a tool used to solder things together.

sol·dier¹ /ˈsəʊldʒə(r)/ nc a member of an army: *three soldiers, two sailors and one civilian.*

sol·dier² /ˈsəʊldʒə(r)/ vi **soldier on** to continue bravely with one's work etc in the face of difficulties.

sole¹ /səʊl/ adj (attrib) **1** one and only: the sole cause of the accident. **2** belonging to one person, company etc: We have the sole right of selling the article. ⇨ solely.

sole² /səʊl/ nc the lower surface of a human foot, or of a sock, shoe etc. □ vt to put a sole on (a shoe etc): send a pair of shoes to be soled and heeled.

sole³ /səʊl/ nc a kind of flat seafish with a delicate flavour.

sole·ly /'səʊllɪ/ adv only: You are solely (= Only you are) responsible. I did it solely because of you.

sol·emn /'sɒləm/ adj **1** serious and sincere: a solemn oath. **2** (attrib) done formally and with ceremony: a solemn occasion. **3** serious and not smiling: solemn faces; looking solemn.
    sol·emn·ly adv

sol·em·ni·ty /sə'lemnətɪ/ n (pl -ies) (formal) **1** nu the condition of being solemn. **2** nc,nu a formal and solemn(2) act.

sol·em·nize (also -ise) /'sɒləmnaɪz/ vt (formal) to perform (esp a wedding) with the usual formal ceremony.

sol·icit /sə'lɪsɪt/ v **1** vt,vi solicit (for) sth to ask (for) (something) seriously: Both the candidates solicited my vote. **2** vi to offer to have sexual intercourse for payment, esp in a public place.

sol·ici·tor /sə'lɪsɪtə(r)/ nc (GB) a lawyer who prepares legal documents, advises clients on legal matters and speaks for them in lower courts. Compare barrister.

sol·ici·tous /sə'lɪsɪtəs/ adj solicitous (of/for sb/sth; to do sth) (formal) anxious to help, showing concern (for a person, thing): solicitous to please; solicitous for her comfort.
    sol·ici·tous·ly adv

sol·ici·tude /sə'lɪsɪtjuːd/ nu solicitude (for sb/sth) (formal) concern or anxiety: my deep solicitude for your welfare.

sol·id¹ /'sɒlɪd/ adj **1** not in the form of a liquid or gas: When water freezes and becomes solid we call it ice. When can the baby eat solid food? **2** without holes or spaces: a solid ball. Opp hollow. **3** of strong material or construction; able to support weight etc: solid buildings/furniture; as solid as a rock (= very solid). **4** that can be depended on: solid arguments; a solid (= financially sound) business firm; a man of solid character. **5** (attrib) of the same substance throughout: made of solid gold. **6** unanimous; undivided: There was a solid vote in favour of the proposal. **7** continuous; without a break: wait for a solid hour; sleep ten solid hours/ten hours solid. **8** (maths) having length, breadth and thickness: a solid figure (e.g. a cube). Compare plane¹.
    'solid-state adj (attrib) (science) (of electronic equipment) using devices, esp transistors or integrated circuits, that make use of the electrical properties of solid substances: a solid-state amplifier.
    sol·id·ly adv
    sol·id·ity /sə'lɪdətɪ/ nu (formal) the quality of being solid: the solidity of a building/argument.

sol·id² /'sɒlɪd/ nc **1** a body or substance which is solid, not a liquid or a gas. **2** (maths) a solid(8) figure.

soli·dar·ity /ˌsɒlɪ'dærətɪ/ nu unity because of common aims, beliefs, interests or feelings:

national solidarity in the face of danger.

sol·id·ify /sə'lɪdɪfaɪ/ vt,vi (pt,pp -ied) (to cause a substance) to become solid, hard or firm.

sol·il·oquy /sə'lɪləkwɪ/ nc,nu (pl -ies) (literature) (in drama) (an instance of) speaking one's thoughts without a listener.

sol·il·oquize (also -ise) /sə'lɪləkwaɪz/ vi (formal) to speak one's thoughts.

soli·taire /ˌsɒlɪ'teə(r)/ nc (an ornament, e.g. an earring with) one jewel.

soli·tary /'sɒlɪtrɪ/ adj **1** (attrib) without companions: a solitary life; a solitary walk. **2** (preferring to be) alone: a solitary person. **3** (attrib) single: not a solitary one/instance. **4** seldom visited: a solitary valley.
    ˌsolitary con'finement nu punishment by which a person is kept alone in a prison cell.
    soli·tar·ily /'sɒlɪtrəlɪ/ adv

soli·tude /'sɒlɪtjuːd/ nu the state of being alone: live in solitude.

so·lo¹ /'səʊləʊ/ adj (attrib), adv alone; by one person: his first solo flight; fly solo; a solo performance.

so·lo² /'səʊləʊ/ nc (pl —s) **1** a piece of music (to be) performed by one person: a violin/piano solo. **2** any performance by one person.
    'solo·ist /-ɪst/ nc a person who gives a solo(1).

sol·stice /'sɒlstɪs/ nc either time (summer solstice, the longest day, about 21 June; winter solstice, the shortest day, about 21 December in the northern parts of the world) when the sun is farthest N or S of the equator. ⇨ equinox.

sol·uble /'sɒljʊbl/ adj that can be dissolved: soluble in water. Opp insoluble(1).
    solu·bil·ity /ˌsɒljʊ'bɪlətɪ/ nu

sol·ution /sə'luːʃn/ n **1** nc solution (to sth) an answer (to a question etc); way of dealing with a difficulty: Perhaps economy is the solution to your financial troubles. **2** nu the process of finding an answer or explanation: problems that defy solution (= that cannot be solved). **3** nu (science) the process of dissolving a solid or a gas in liquid: the solution of sugar in tea. **4** nc,nu (science) (a kind of) liquid that results from this process: a solution of salt in water; a salt solution.

solv·able /'sɒlvəbl/ adj (of a difficulty, problem) that can be solved or explained. Opp insoluble(2).

solve /sɒlv/ vt to find the answer to (a problem etc); explain (a difficulty): solving a crossword puzzle.

sol·vent¹ /'sɒlvənt/ adj **1** having money enough to meet one's debts. Opp insolvent. **2** (science) of, having, the power of dissolving or forming a solution: the solvent action of water.
    sol·ven·cy /'sɒlvənsɪ/ nu the state of being solvent(1).

sol·vent² /'sɒlvənt/ nc (science) a substance (usually a liquid) able to dissolve another substance: a grease solvent (e.g. petrol).

sombre (US = **som·ber**) /'sɒmbə(r)/ adj dark; gloomy: a sombre January day; sombre clothes/ colours.
    sombre·ly (US = **som·ber·ly**) adv

some¹ /səm strong form sʌm/ adj (attrib) or det **1** (of an amount or number etc that is more than two) a little, a few: I need some milk. There are some children outside. Won't you have some cake? If we had some money, we could buy it. I'd *like some more (coffee), please.* Ⓝ For the differences between *some* and *any*, ⇨ any¹(3). **2** (always /sʌm/) a certain amount or number (but not the rest or others): *Some people learn English grammar easily but others find it difficult. Some work is boring. That's some help towards understanding the problem.* **3** (always /sʌm/) a fairly large amount of (esp time, distance): *He's been ill for some weeks. It's some distance from the hotel. I'll be away for some time* (i.e. for a long time). **4** (used to refer to a person, place etc that is not known or named): *I read it in some book or other. He's living at some address* (= somewhere) *in London. Let's meet some day soon and have a meal together. Some day I'll find you. Why don't you ring me some time?* Ⓝ Be careful not to confuse *'some time'*, as in the examples in 3 and 4 above, and *'sometime'* (= at a particular point in time), as in *We bought it sometime in April.* **5** approximately: *It happened some 20 years ago. He lives some ten miles away.* Ⓝ *'About'* is more usual but *'some'* is preferred when suggesting that the amount, distance etc is large. ⇨ also *or so* at so²(6).

some² /səm *strong form* sʌm/ *pron* **some (of sb/ sth)** (more than two) a little (of); a few (of); part (of): *Can I have some? Some of the work is too difficult. Some of you look untidy. Would you like some? I agree with some of what you say. Greece has some of the best scenery in the world. Some* (= Some people) *think that the world is mad. If I find some, I'll tell you. I can answer some, but the others are too difficult.*

some·body /'sʌmbədɪ/ (*also* **some·one** /'sʌmwʌn/) *pron* **1** a person but not a particular or known one: *There's somebody at the door.* Ⓝ For the difference between *somebody/someone* and *anybody/anyone*, ⇨ anybody(1). **2** (often used with *a*) a person of some importance: *If you had studied harder at college you might have become somebody. He's a nobody here but he's a somebody in his own village.* Compare nobody(2).

some·how /'sʌmhaʊ/ *adv* **1** in some way (or other); by one means or another: *We must find money for the rent somehow (or other). We shall get there somehow.* **2** because of an unknown reason: *Somehow I don't trust that man.*

some·one /'sʌmwʌn/ *pron* = somebody.

some·place /'sʌmpleɪs/ *adv* (*US informal*) = somewhere: *I've left my bag someplace.*

som·er·sault /'sʌməsɔːlt/ *vi*, *nc* (to make) a leap or fall in which one turns over completely before landing on one's feet: *turn a somersault.*

some·thing /'sʌmθɪŋ/ *pron* **1** a thing, reason, event etc that is unknown: *There's something on the floor. I want something to eat. Is there something I can do for you? Something's happened to her! There's something* (= some truth, some point) *in what he says.* Ⓝ For the difference between *something* and *anything*, ⇨ anything(1). **2** **or something** (used to show lack of exact or known information): *I hear he has broken an arm or something* (i.e. or suffered a similar injury). **something or other** a cause, fault, statement etc but I don't know exactly what: *There's something or other wrong with this camera. She mentioned something or other about a book you have.* **something like** ⇨ like⁴(1).

some·time /'sʌmtaɪm/ *adv* at an unknown point in time: *I saw him sometime in May. It was sometime last summer. I will speak to him about it sometime.* Ⓝ ⇨ the *note* at some¹(4).

some·times /'sʌmtaɪmz/ *adv* occasionally; from time to time: *I sometimes have letters from him. I have sometimes had letters from him. 'Do you ever go to discos?'—'Sometimes.'*

some·way /'sʌmweɪ/ *adv* (*US informal*) = somehow.

some·what /'sʌmwɒt/ *adv* to some extent; in some degree; a little: *I was somewhat surprised/ disappointed.* Ⓝ Not used with a negative verb.

some·where /'sʌmweə(r)/ *adv* **1** in, to, a place but not a particular or known one: *It must be somewhere near here. Let's go somewhere and talk. He lost it somewhere between here and the station.* Ⓝ For the differences between *somewhere* and *anywhere*, ⇨ anywhere(1). **2** a place: *I need somewhere to keep my bike. Let's find somewhere quiet.* **get somewhere** ⇨ get(9).

son /sʌn/ *nc* **1** a person's male child. **2** (*literary*) a person associated with a particular activity: *sons of the soil* (= farmers' sons).

Son of 'God/'Man *n* (the—) Jesus Christ.

'son-in-law *nc* (*pl* **—s-in-law**) the husband of one's daughter.

so·na·ta /sə'nɑːtə/ *nc* (*pl* **—s**) a piece of music for one instrument (e.g. the piano) or two (e.g. a piano and violin).

song /sɒŋ/ *n* **1** *nc* a poem set to music and intended to be sung: *pop songs.* **2** *nu* the act of singing: *burst into song.* **3** *nc,nu* the musical sound of a bird: *bird song; the song of the birds.*

'song·bird *nc* a kind of bird (e.g. blackbird, thrush) noted for its attractive musical sound.

'song·book *nc* a collection of songs (with both words and music).

son·ic /'sɒnɪk/ *adj* (*tech*) relating to sound, sound-waves or the speed of sound. ⇨ supersonic, ultrasonic.

son·net /'sɒnɪt/ *nc* (*literature*) a kind of poem containing 14 lines each of 10 syllables, and with a formal pattern of rhymes.

son·ny /'sʌnɪ/ *n sing* (*informal*) (a form of address to) a young boy.

son·or·ous /'sɒnərəs/ *adj* (*formal*) **1** having a full, deep sound: *the sonorous note of a large bell.* **2** (of language, words etc) making a deep impression: *a sonorous style.*

son·or·ous·ly *adv*

soon /suːn/ *adv* (**—er, —est**) **1** not long after the present time or the time mentioned: *We shall soon be home. We shall be home. We shall be home quite soon now. He'll be here very soon. It will soon be five years since we came to live in London.* **soon after** a short time after: *He arrived soon after three.* Ⓝ The opposite of *'soon after'* is *'a little before'.* **2** early: *How soon can you be ready? Must you leave so soon? The sooner* (i.e. The earlier) *you begin, the sooner you'll finish.* **the sooner the better** it is better to begin or carry out (a task etc) as early as possible. **as soon as** (**a**) at the moment when: *He rang me as soon as he received the news.* (**b**) as quickly or early as: *Please reply as soon as possible. We didn't arrive as soon as we had hoped.* **no sooner . . . than . . .** at the moment when (something happened), (something else happened): *He had no sooner arrived/*

No sooner had he arrived than he was asked to go out again. **sooner or later** now or definitely later on: *You'll get it back sooner or later.* **sooner ... than ...** in preference to: *He would sooner resign/resign sooner than be involved in bribery.*

soot /sʊt/ *nu* a black powder in smoke or left after burning coal etc.

sooty *adj* (**-ier, -iest**) black with, like, soot.

sooth·sayer /'su:θseɪə(r)/ *nc* (*old use*) a fortune-teller.

soothe /su:ð/ *vt* **1** to make (a person, a person's feelings or emotions) quiet or calm: *soothe a crying baby; soothing an angry man.* **2** to make (pains, aches) less sharp or severe: *soothe a cut/burn.*

sooth·ing *adj* able to soothe: *soothing ointment; a soothing voice.*

sooth·ing·ly *adv*

sop¹ /sɒp/ *nc* something offered to please a person who is disappointed, upset etc: *She only gave me the present as a sop to my injured pride.*

sop² /sɒp/ *vt* **sop sth up** to take up liquid with a soft cloth etc: *sop up the water with this towel.*

sop·ping *adj, adv* thoroughly (wet): *sopping wet. It's sopping.*

soph·is·ti·cated /sə'fɪstɪkeɪtɪd/ *adj* **1** having lost natural simplicity through education or because of experience from high social living: *a sophisticated girl; with sophisticated tastes.* Opp unsophisticated. **2** having the latest design, methods etc (and sometimes suggesting it is complicated or needs a lot of effort): *a sophisticated language course* (e.g. with attractive books, tapes, videos etc).

soph·is·ti·ca·tion /sə,fɪstɪ'keɪʃn/ *nu*

sop·or·if·ic /,sɒpə'rɪfɪk/ *nc, adj* (a substance, drink etc) producing sleep.

sop·ping /'sɒpɪŋ/ *adj, adv* ⇨ sop².

sop·py /'sɒpɪ/ *adj* (**-ier, -iest**) (*dated informal; usually derog*) foolishly sentimental: *I'm soppy about his sister. It's a soppy love story.*

so·pra·no /sə'prɑːnəʊ/ *adj, nc* (*pl* **—s**) (of) (a person having) the highest singing voice of women and girls (and boys).

sor·cer·er /'sɔːsərə(r)/ *nc* a man who practises magic with the help of evil spirits.

sor·cer·ess /'sɔːsərɪs/ *nc* a woman sorcerer.

sor·cery /'sɔːsərɪ/ *nu* = witchcraft (the usual word).

sor·did /'sɔːdɪd/ *adj* (*derog*) **1** (of conditions) poor, dirty, uncomfortable: *a sordid slum; living in sordid poverty.* **2** (of a person's behaviour) extremely unpleasant and dishonourable.

sor·did·ly *adv*

sore¹ /sɔː(r)/ *adj* (**—r, —st**) **1** (of a part of the body) painful; hurting when touched or used: *a sore knee/throat.* **a sight for sore eyes** ⇨ sight¹(4). **2** (*poetic*) filled with sorrow; sad: *a sore heart.* **a sore point** a subject that hurts the feelings when talked about: *Now that he's unemployed, having holidays abroad is a sore point with him.* ⇨ sore²(2). **3** (*pred*) hurt in one's feelings: *I felt sore about not being invited to the party.* **4** (*pred*) (*informal*) sorry: *She feels sore about behaving so badly.*

sore² /sɔː(r)/ *nc* **1** a place on the body (where the skin or flesh is injured). **2** (*fig*) a painful subject or

memory: *Let's not recall old sores.*

sore·ly *adv* (**a**) (*formal*) severely: *be sorely missed.* (**b**) very much: *More financial help is sorely needed.*

sore·ness *nu*

sor·row¹ /'sɒrəʊ/ *nc,nu* (a cause of) sadness or regret: *express sorrow for having done wrong; feel sorrow at the news of her death; be filled with sorrow over the sight of hungry children; and to my great sorrow he never wrote to me again.*

sor·row·ful /-fəl/ *adj* causing, feeling, sorrow.

sor·row² /'sɒrəʊ/ *vi* **sorrow (at/for/over sb/ sth)** (*formal*) to feel very sad or sorry: *sorrowing over her child's death.*

sor·ry /'sɒrɪ/ *adj* (**-ier, -iest**) **1** (*pred*) (used as a form of apology saying one is) feeling unhappy and disappointed with oneself for something one did or did not do: *I'm sorry (that) I was rude. I lost your pen and I'm sorry. He's very sorry and wants to apologize. Aren't you at all sorry for what you did? Sorry about that letter—can you forgive me? She's really/truly sorry. I'm so sorry, I've not finished it yet. 'You've broken my bike!'—'Sorry!'* (i.e. I'm sorry). Ⓝ *'Sorry'* is the usual form of apology. Expressions using *'apologize'* or *'forgive'* are much more formal. **2** (*pred*) feeling sad or sympathetic: *We were sorry to hear of your father's death. I'm very sorry that you didn't get the job. I'm sorry for anyone who has to drive in this storm. I feel sorry for you with all the work you have to do.* ⇨ also safe¹(6). **3** (used as a polite refusal to a request or to say one does not believe something): *'Can you lend me a pound?'—'Sorry, but I can't.' I'm sorry, but I don't think he's telling the truth.* **4** (used as a polite way of saying that one did not hear): *'The number's 21864.'—'Sorry, could you repeat that please?'* Ⓝ *'Pardon'* is much more formal. ⇨ also excuse²(4). **5** (*attrib*) causing a feeling of pity or sympathy: *The old man's room was a sorry mess/sight/was in a sorry state.*

sort¹ /sɔːt/ *nc* **1** a particular group, class, variety etc with the same characteristics or features: *Pop music is the sort she likes most. What sort of food do you like to eat? Many sorts of toys can be dangerous. Are they the same sort as these? We don't approve of this sort of thing/these sorts of things/things of this sort.* Ⓝ For the differences between *sort, kind* and *type* ⇨ kind²(1). ⇨ also assorted. **a sort of sth** something very similar to something else: *It's a sort of machine but without an engine.* **sort of + adj** (*adv*) (*informal*) to some extent; a little: *It's sort of green and sticky.* Compare kind²(1). **of a sort** = of a kind(b). ⇨ also nothing². **out of sorts** (*informal*) unwell; miserable: *He's feeling out of sorts.* **2** (*informal*) a person: *She's a good sort/not a bad sort* (i.e. She has good qualities).

sort² /sɔːt/ *vt,vi* to arrange (people, things) in groups, classes etc with the same characteristics or features: *I'm sorting all my own clothes into piles. These stamps need sorting. This test will sort the men from the boys* (e.g. will prove who are strongest).

sort sb/sth into sth to put people, things into particular groups.

sort sb out (*informal*) to punish, deal with, a person who causes trouble: *Stop that noise or I'll soon sort you out!* **sort oneself out** (**a**) to organize oneself into a new routine: *I'll ring you as soon as I've sorted myself out.* **(b)** (of two or more people) to settle disagreements: *Let's leave John and Ann to sort themselves out.* **sort sb/sth out** to arrange or put people, things, in groups: *sorting out the applicants/post.* **sort sth out (a)** to put things in a drawer, desk, room etc in good order: *sort out a drawer/a pile of socks.* **(b)** to deal with a problem: *I'll leave you to sort that out.* **sort sb/sth out from sth** to separate one person, thing, from another: *sort out the better athletes from the rest; sort out the lies from the truth.*

sort over sth to examine things in a disorganized pile to find particular ones or to arrange them in groups.

sort through sth to look through a container, things, in order to find something: *I sorted through the cupboard/my clothes but I couldn't find my gloves.*

SOS /ˌes əʊ 'es/ *nc* a signal for help that is known and understood internationally and is used esp by ships and planes in trouble.

so-so /'səʊ səʊ/ *adj* (*pred*), *adv* (*informal*) not very good (but not bad either): *'How are you feeling?'—'So-so'.*

souf·flé /'suːfleɪ/ *nc* (*Fr*) a baked dish of beaten eggs, milk, cheese etc.

sought /sɔːt/ *pt,pp* of seek.

soul /səʊl/ *n* **1** *nc* the part of a human that is not the body and cannot be touched: *He eats hardly enough to keep body and soul together* (= to keep himself alive). *That man has no soul* (= is unfeeling, selfish). *heart and soul* ⇨ heart(2). **2** *nc* a person regarded as the ideal (of some virtue or quality): *He is the soul of honour/discretion.* ⇨ life(7). **3** *nc* a person: *There wasn't a soul to be seen. I won't tell a soul.* **4** *nu* an attractive quality of being sincere and thoughtful: *The speech/music/performance lacked soul.* **5** *nu* (*informal*) all those qualities that make one able to be in harmony with oneself and others (expressed through a particular style of pop music).

'soul brother/sister *nc* (*informal*) a fellow Black person in society.

'soul-destroying *adj* killing the will-power or spirit: *soul-destroying work.*

'soul music *nu* modern popular blues music with strong rhythm for dancing.

soul·ful /-fəl/ *adj* having, affecting, showing, deep feeling: *soulful eyes/music.*

soul·less *adj* (*derog*) **(a)** (of a person) without pity, sympathy or care for others. **(b)** (of work etc) without interest; dull.

sound¹ /saʊnd/ *adj* (**—er, —est**) **1** healthy; in good condition; not hurt, damaged or decayed: *as sound as a bell* (= very healthy); *sound fruit/teeth.* **safe and sound** ⇨ safe¹(2). **2** reliable; based on truth, logic, facts: *a sound argument/policy/building; sound advice.* **of sound mind** ⇨ mind¹(2). Opp unsound. **3** strong, secure, capable: *a sound company to deal with; a sound business partner.* **4** (*attrib*) deep; thorough: *be a sound sleeper; give him a sound beating.*

sound·ly *adv* deeply; thoroughly: *sleep soundly; be soundly beaten at tennis.*

sound·ness *nu*

sound² /saʊnd/ *adv* **sound asleep** sleeping deeply.

sound³ /saʊnd/ *nc* (S- in names) a narrow channel of water between two larger areas: *Long Island Sound* (between Long Island and Rhode Island near New York, USA).

sound⁴ /saʊnd/ *n* **1** *nc,nu* something that is or can be heard: *We heard the sound of voices/footsteps. Try not to make a sound.* Compare noise¹. **2** *n sing* an idea, mental impression, produced by something stated (or read): *I don't like the sound of his excuses.* ⇨ sound⁵(4).

'sound barrier *nc* a point at which a plane's speed equals that of sound-waves.

'sound effect *nc* a sound (recorded on tape, film etc) for use in radio and TV programmes etc.

'sound-proof *adj* that sound cannot pass through or into: *a soundproof room.*

'soundtrack *nc* the music etc used in a film.

sound⁵ /saʊnd/ *v* **1** *vt,vi* (to cause something) to produce (a) sound: *If there is a fire, sound the alarm* (e.g. by ringing a bell). *The trumpets sounded. Why didn't you sound your (car) horn?* **2** *vt* to produce (a warning etc) using sound: *The bell sounded a warning.* **3** *vi* to give the impression mentioned when heard: *That sounds too loud. How sweet the music sounds!* **4** *vi* (*fig*) to give the idea mentioned when heard; seem: *His excuse sounds genuine.* **sound like . . .** to seem to be: *That sounds like a good idea.*

sound off (about sth) (*informal*) **(a)** to speak loudly (about one's own abilities, possessions, influence etc): *Bill's always sounding off about his boat.* **(b)** to speak noisily (about a particular topic in a critical and unsympathetic way): *I wish she'd stop sounding off about modern teenagers.*

sound sb out (about sth) to try to get a person's opinion, feeling or intention (about an election, issue etc): *Have you sounded him out about that job in Spain?*

soup¹ /suːp/ *nu* liquid food made by cooking meat, vegetables etc in water: *chicken/pea/tomato soup.* **in the soup** (*informal*) in trouble: *The police stopped him because he was driving too fast and now he's really in the soup.*

soup² /suːp/ *vt* **soup sth up** (*sl*) to fit a vehicle or its engine with a special part (to increase its power and so its speed).

'souped-up *adj* (*attrib*): *a souped-up engine.*

sour /'saʊə(r)/ *adj* **1** having a sharp taste (like that of vinegar, a lemon or an unripe apple etc). Opp sweet(1). Compare bitter¹(1) **sour grapes** ⇨ grape. **2** having a taste of having gone bad: *sour milk. The milk has turned sour.* ⇨ fresh(1). **3** (*fig*) bad-tempered: *sour looks; be made sour by disappointments.*

sour² /'saʊə(r)/ *vt,vi* (to cause something) to become sour: *The hot weather has soured the milk. Their marriage has soured* (= become unpleasant).

sour·ly *adv*

sour·ness *nu*

source /sɔːs/ *nc* **source (of sth) 1** the starting-point (of a river): *the sources of the Nile. Where does the Rhine have its source?* **2** a place or person from which something comes or is got: *The news comes from a reliable source. Is that water the source of the infection?* **3** (*pl*) original documents etc for an academic study.

south¹ /saʊθ/ *adj* (*attrib*) from, in, towards, the

south: *a south wind; living on the south coast.* ⇨ southern.

south² /saʊθ/ *adv* towards the south: *to travel/ face south.* **south of** *a place* further south than.

south³ /saʊθ/ *n* **1** (the —) the direction, point, to the right of a person facing towards the sunrise (i.e. towards the east). **2** that part of a country, the world etc in this direction: *living in the south of Italy; warm winds from the south.*

,**South 'Pole** *n* (the —) (the ice regions of) the point of the world that is farthest south.

,**south-'east,** ,**south-'west** (abbr SE, SW) *n, adj, adv* (a point, direction, region) midway between south and east or south and west.

,**south-'eastern** /-'iːstn/ *adj* of, from, in, the southeast.

,**south-south-'east,** ,**south-south-'west** (abbr SSE, SSW) *n, adj, adv* (a point, direction, region) midway between south and south-east or south-west.

,**south-'western** /-'westn/ *adj* of, from, in, the south-west.

south·er·ly /'sʌðəlɪ/ *adj, adv* **1** (of winds) from the south. **2** towards, in or to the south.

south·ern /'sʌðən/ *adj* of, from, in the south part of a country, continent, the world etc: *southern Europe; the Southern States of the USA.*

,**Southern 'Hemisphere** *n* (the —) countries south of the Equator.

south·ern·er *nc* a person born or living in the south regions of the country.

'**south·ern·most** /-məʊst/ *adj* farthest south.

south·ward /'saʊθwəd/ *adj* towards the south: *in a southward direction.*

south·wards *adv*: *to travel southwards.*

sou·ve·nir /ˌsuːvə'nɪə(r)/ *nc* something taken, bought or received as a gift, and kept as a reminder of a person, place or event.

sov·er·eign¹ /'sɒvrɪn/ *adj* (*attrib*) (of power) highest; ruling a country: *a sovereign prince.*

sov·er·eign² /'sɒvrɪn/ *nc* a ruler, e.g. a king or queen.

sov·er·eign·ty *nu* sovereign power.

So·vi·et /'səʊvɪət/ *adj* of the USSR. □ *nc* (in the former USSR) an elected council at local, regional or national level forming part of the system of government.

sow¹ /saʊ/ *nc* a fully grown female pig.

sow² /səʊ/ *v* (*pt* —**ed**, *pp* —**n** /səʊn/ or —**ed**) **1** *vt,vi* to plant (seed) in the ground: *sow seeds; sow a plot of land with grass.* **2** *vt* (*fig*) to cause (something): *sow (the seeds of) hatred.*

sow·er *nc* a person who sows seeds, young plants.

soya /'sɔɪə/ *nu* (also *attrib*) (a plant grown as food and for) the oil obtained from its seeds (*soya beans*): *soy(a) sauce.*

sozzled /'sɒzld/ *adj* (*sl*) very drunk.

spa /spɑː/ *nc* (*pl* —**s**) (a place with) a spring of mineral water having medicinal properties.

space¹ /speɪs/ *n* **1** *nu* (also *attrib*) that in which all objects exist and move: *The universe exists in space. Travel through space to other planets interests many people today. Spacecraft/Space-capsules/Space-vehicles are used for travel beyond the earth's atmosphere.* **2** *nc,nu* a measurable interval or distance between two or more objects: *the spaces between printed words; separated by a*

space of ten metres. There isn't enough space in this office for two desks.* **3** *n sing* a period of time: *during a space of three years.*

space² /speɪs/ *vt* **space sb/sth out** to set people, things out with regular spaces between: *space out the posts three metres apart.*

'**space·craft/-vehicle** *etc nc,nu* ⇨ space¹(1).

spa·cious /'speɪʃəs/ *adj* having much space: *a spacious room.* Compare spatial.

spa·cious·ly *adv*

spade /speɪd/ *nc* **1** a tool with a flat blade having a sharp edge, used for digging. **2** (any of 13 playing-cards with) a black symbol like a wide leaf with a stem: *the five of spades.* Compare club¹(2), diamond(3), heart(4). ⇨ suit¹(3).

'**spade·work** *nu* (*fig*) the hard, basic, work: *He got all the credit for the research but I did all the spadework.*

spa·ghet·ti /spə'getɪ/ *nu* (*It*) flour paste (*pasta*) in narrow rods, cooked by boiling.

span¹ /spæn/ *nc* **1** the distance between the tips of a person's thumb and little finger when stretched out. **2** the distance or part between the supports of an arch or bridge: *The arch has a span of 60 metres.* **3** a length in time, from beginning to end: *for a short span of time.* ⇨ life-span.

span² /spæn/ *vt* (**-nn-**) **1** to extend across (something) (from side to side): *The Thames is spanned by many bridges.* **2** (of time) to extend from (one period or point to another): *His life spanned almost all of the 19th century.*

spangle /'spæŋgl/ *nc* a tiny disc of shining metal, esp one used for ornament on a dress etc.

span·iel /'spænɪəl/ *nc* a kind of dog with short legs and long ears.

spank /spæŋk/ *vt* to punish (a child) by slapping on the buttocks with the open hand.

spank·ing *nc,nu* (an instance of) slapping on the buttocks.

span·ner /'spænə(r)/ *nc* a kind of tool used for gripping and turning nuts on screws, bolts etc (*US = wrench*).

spar¹ /spɑː(r)/ *nc* a strong wooden or metal pole, used as a mast, boom etc.

spar² /spɑː(r)/ *vi* (**-rr-**) **1** to make the motions of attack and defence with the fists (as in boxing). **2** (*fig*) to quarrel or argue.

spare¹ /speə(r)/ *adj* **1** (*attrib*) kept for use when needed: *Is there a spare wheel in your car?* **2** additional to what is being or will be used: *I have very little/no spare time/time spare for walking. If there is any spare food/food spare, can we have it?* **3** (of a person) thin; lean: *a tall, spare man.*

,**spare 'part** *nc* a part to replace a broken or worn-out part of a machine, an engine etc.

,**spare-'rib** *nc* a rib (of pork) with most of the meat cut off.

spare² /speə(r)/ *nc* a spare part (for a machine or engine).

spare³ /speə(r)/ *vt* **1** (to agree) to avoid hurting, punishing, destroying, (a person, building etc): *spare a prisoner's life.* **spare sb's feelings** ⇨ feeling(4). **2** to be able to give (time, money, an object etc) to a person or for a purpose; manage without (a person, thing): *Can you spare an extra ticket for me? Can you spare me a few minutes (of your time)? We cannot spare any of our tools/ workers while we are so busy. We haven't enough* *to spare* (i.e. We need all of them/it). **no expense spared** ⇨ expense(1). **spare a thought for sb/sth** ⇨ thought¹(2). **3** to prevent (a person) from suffering because of (something): *Can't you spare us the more painful details?*

spar·ing /'speəriŋ/ *adj* (*pred*) **sparing (of sth)** economical, careful: *You should be more sparing of your money/time/energy.*

spar·ing·ly *adv*

spark¹ /spɑːk/ *nc* **1** a tiny piece of a burning substance in a fire, or produced by hard metal and stone banging together or by the breaking of an electric current: *sparks from the fire.* **2** (*fig*) a small sign or quantity: *He hasn't a spark of generosity in him.*

spark² /spɑːk/ *v* **1** *vi* to give out sparks. **2** *vt* **spark sth off** (*fig*) to be the immediate cause of something: *His statement sparked off a quarrel between them.*

'spark-plug (also **'sparking-plug**) *nc* a device used for making an electric spark in an engine.

sparkle¹ /'spɑːkl/ *nc* a bright spark(1).

sparkle² /'spɑːkl/ *vi* **1** to send out flashes of light: *Her diamonds sparkled in the bright light.* **2** (*fig*) to be shining (with happiness etc): *Her eyes sparkled (with excitement).* **3** (*fig*) (of a person) to show obvious ability, intelligence etc.

spar·row /'spærəʊ/ *nc* a kind of very common, small brownish-grey bird.

sparse /spɑːs/ *adj* not crowded: *a sparse population.*

sparsely *adv*: *a sparsely furnished room* (i.e. with only a few pieces of furniture).

spasm /'spæzəm/ *nc* a sudden and involuntary tightening of a muscle or muscles: *in a spasm of pain/excitement; a coughing spasm.*

spas·mod·ic /spæz'mɒdɪk/ *adj* **1** irregular: *spasmodic laughter/shouts.* **2** happening in, affected by, spasms: *spasmodic pain.*

spas·modi·cal·ly /-klɪ/ *adv*

spas·tic /'spæstɪk/ *nc, adj* (a person) physically disabled because of difficulty in controlling voluntary muscles.

spat /spæt/ *pt,pp* of spit³.

spate /speɪt/ *n sing* **spate (of sth)** a sudden rush (of business etc): *a spate of orders.*

spa·tial /'speɪʃl/ *adj* (*tech*) of, in relation to, space: *spatial considerations when planning a building.* Compare spacious.

spa·tial·ly /-ʃəlɪ/ *adv*

spat·ter /'spætə(r)/ *v* **1** *vt* to cause (liquid etc) to splash, scatter, in drops: *spatter grease on one's clothes/spatter one's clothes with grease.* **2** *vi* (of liquid) to fall or spread out in drops: *rain spattering down on the tent.*

spat·ula /'spætʃʊlə/ *nc* (*pl —*s) a utensil with a wide, flat blade, used for mixing or spreading various substances.

spawn¹ /spɔːn/ *nu* the eggs of fish and certain water animals, e.g. frogs.

spawn² /spɔːn/ *v* **1** *vi* to produce spawn. **2** (*fig*) *vt* to produce (something) in large numbers: *committees which spawn subcommittees.*

speak /spiːk/ *v* (*pt* **spoke** /spəʊk/, *pp* **spoken** /'spəʊkən/) **1** *vi* **speak (to sb) (about sth)** to use one's voice to say words: *Please speak more slowly. She speaks with a French accent. I was speaking to him about our holiday plans. Can I speak to you for a moment, please? Sally and Liz aren't speaking (to each other)* (i.e. because they have quarrelled). *If you're late again, I'll have to speak to* (= complain to) *the manager. If you'd like some, speak to* (= ask) *my father. I've a sore throat and I can hardly speak. I can't hear you; please speak louder* (e.g. on the telephone). *She speaks so softly I can't hear her.* Ⓝ *'Speak'* and *'talk'* have the same uses in many situations such as when referring to conversation, as in *She was speaking/talking about her new car. Can I speak/talk to you for a minute? 'Speak'* is considered to be more formal than *'talk'* and is preferred when referring to the quality of one's voice, as in *speak slowly/softly,* or when one has an important or formal reason for speaking, as in *You must speak to the children and tell them to behave, Have you spoken to your lawyer yet? 'Tell'* is only possible as an alternative to *'speak to a person'* meaning *'make a complaint'*, as in *If you don't stop that, I'll speak to/tell your parents.* **generally/roughly** etc **speaking** using words in a general/rough etc sense: *Strictly speaking, you ought to be wearing uniform. Our sales have improved, generally speaking.* **so to speak** if I can express it in this way: *She was, so to speak, a good wife but a poor mother.* **to speak of** of any importance or value worth mentioning: *He had no possessions to speak of/had achieved nothing to speak of.* **be on (good/bad) speaking terms (with sb)** ⇨ terms(3). ⇨ also speech, wellspoken. **2** *vt* to know and be able to speak (a language): *Do you speak English? He speaks six languages. I can't speak German. He speaks Greek with a Japanese accent.* Ⓝ For a comparison of talk (*a language*) and speak (*a language*), ⇨ the note at talk²(3). ⇨ speak in a language below. **3** *vi* to give a formal speech: *The chairperson spoke for almost an hour.* ⇨ speak on sth. **4** *vt* to express (an idea) (as if) in words: *speak the truth. Actions speak louder than words.* **speak volumes for sb/sth** ⇨ volume(1).

speak about sb/sth ⇨ 1 above.

speak against sb/sth to give a formal speech against a person, idea, proposal etc.

speak for sb/sth (**a**) to speak(3) in favour of a person, idea, proposal etc. (**b**) to express the wishes, opinion etc of another person or group.

speak for itself (*informal*) (of a report, result, achievement etc) to be obvious and so make any spoken words unnecessary: *The sales figures speak for themselves.* **speak for yourself** (*informal; imperative*) Do not make decisions for me: *'We're all having coffee.'—'Speak for yourself, I'm having orange juice.'*

speak in a language to give a formal speech using a particular language: *I spoke in Russian at the conference. We had to speak in Spanish during the debate.* Compare talk in a language.

speak on (and on) to give a long (and boring) speech: *She spoke on and on for hours.* **speak on sth** to give a formal speech on a subject, topic: *I'm speaking on public health.*

speak out (against sb/sth) to speak(3) with courage and determination (in opposition to an idea, proposal etc): *If you don't agree, why don't you speak out?*

speak to sb (**a**) to tell a person something in the

hope of getting something done: *I'll speak to the owner about that broken window.* (**b**) to complain to a person: *You must speak to the neighbours about the noise.* ⇨ also 1 above.

speak up (**a**) to speak in a loud(er) voice: *Speak up—I can't hear you.* (**b**) to express one's opinion, the truth etc: *Speak up and tell us what you think! He was too frightened to speak up.*

speak·er /'spiːkə(r)/ *nc* **1** a person who talks formally about a subject: *Do we have a speaker for next month's meeting?* **2** a person who makes speeches in the way mentioned: *He's a good/poor public speaker.* **3** = loudspeaker.

spear¹ /spɪə(r)/ *nc* a weapon with a metal point on a long pole.

spear² /spɪə(r)/ *vt* to injure, catch, make a hole in, (an animal) with a spear: *spear fish.*

'**spear·head** *vt, nc* (to be) the individual or group chosen to lead (an attack): *spearhead the campaign for human rights.*

spear·mint /'spɪəmɪnt/ *nu* a variety of mint used for flavouring, esp chewing-gum.

spe·cial /'speʃl/ *adj* **1** not usual or ordinary: *A wedding is a special occasion. She thinks she's special. Wear something special tonight—I'm taking you to a concert. What's so special* (= unusual) *about owning a computer? There's something really special about that singer. He did it for her as a special favour.* **2** for a particular person, thing or purpose: *It's a special tool for removing paint. She has a special uniform.*

,**special de'livery** *nu* a delivery of a letter, parcel etc by a messenger instead of by the usual postal services.

spe·cial·ly /-ʃəlɪ/ *adv* particularly: *I came here specially to see you. The exam was specially difficult.* Ⓝ For the difference between *specially* and *especially,* ⇨ especially.

spe·cial·ist /-ʃəlɪst/ *nc* **specialist (in sth)** an expert (in a profession, esp medicine): *an eye specialist; a specialist in tropical diseases.*

spe·ci·al·ity /ˌspeʃɪˈælətɪ/ *nc* (*pl* -ies) **1** an activity, area of study, to which a person gives particular attention: *Modern art is her speciality. Mending old cars is his speciality.* **2** a product for which a business or place is well known: *Cheap wine is their speciality. This food is an Italian speciality.*

spe·cial·ize (also -**ise**) /'speʃəlaɪz/ *vi* **specialize (in sth)** to study or train (in a particular area) in order to become an expert: *specialize in biochemistry.*

spe·cial·iz·ation (also -**is·ation**) /ˌspeʃəlaɪˈzeɪʃn/ *nc,nu*

spe·cies /'spiːʃiːz/ *nc* (*pl* unchanged) (*science*) a group of animals or plants having similar characteristics and able to reproduce with each other: *What species of insect/flower is this?*

spe·ci·fic /spəˈsɪfɪk/ *adj* **1** detailed and exact: *specific orders. I can't be more specific than that!* **2** (*attrib*) relating to one particular thing etc, not general: *The money is to be used for a specific purpose.*

spe·cifi·cal·ly /-klɪ/ *adv* in an exact and particular way: *You were specifically warned not to smoke.*

spe·cifi·ca·tion /ˌspesɪfɪˈkeɪʃn/ *n* **1** *nu* the act of specifying. **2** *nc* (usually *pl*) details, instructions

etc for the design and materials of something to be made or done: *specifications for* (*building*) *a garage.*

spe·ci·fy /'spesɪfaɪ/ *vt* (*pt,pp* -**ied**) to state (a particular one, type etc): *Please will you specify which colours to use.*

speci·men /'spesɪmɪn/ *nc* (also *attrib*) **1** one used as an example: *specimens of rocks and ores.* **2** a part taken to represent the whole: *specimen pages of books; supply the doctor with a specimen of one's blood.*

spe·cious /'spiːʃəs/ *adj* (*formal*) seeming to be right or true but not really so: *It is a specious argument that if he was not there he was not involved.* Compare spurious.

speck /spek/ *nc* **1** a very small spot or piece (of dirt etc): *specks of dust.* **2** (*fig*) a small visible spot: *The ship was a speck on the horizon.*

speck·ed *adj*

speckle /'spekl/ *nc* a small mark, esp one of many on feathers etc.

speckled *adj*

specs /speks/ *n pl* (*informal*) = spectacles: *Where are my specs?*

spec·tacle /'spektəkl/ *nc* **1** a grand and attractive public ceremony, show etc: *The annual carnival is always a great spectacle.* **2** a view, scene that is extraordinarily attractive etc: *The sunset on the mountains was a tremendous spectacle.* **3** (*informal; derog*) something that is worth making fun of: *You'll make a spectacle of yourself/look a spectacle in those yellow trousers!*

spec·tacles /'spektəklz/ *n pl* (also *a pair of spectacles*) (abbr *specs*) (*formal*) = glasses.

spec·tacu·lar /spek'tækjʊlə(r)/ *adj* extremely attractive, grand: *spectacular scenery.*

spec·tacu·lar·ly *adv*

spec·ta·tor /spek'teɪtə(r)/ *nc* a person looking at (a sport, game, show etc).

spectre (*US* = **spec·ter**) /'spektə(r)/ *nc* a ghost (the usual word).

spec·tral /'spektrəl/ *adj* (*tech*) of the spectrum: *spectral colours.*

spec·trum /'spektrəm/ *nc* (*pl* -**tra** /-trə/) **1** the band of colours as seen in a rainbow and usually described as red, orange, yellow, green, blue, indigo and violet. **2** (*fig*) a wide range or sequence: *the whole spectrum of political opinion.*

specu·late /'spekjʊleɪt/ *vi* **1** (*formal*) to think, consider, form opinions (without having complete knowledge): *speculate about/on the future of the human race.* **2** to buy and sell goods, shares etc with the hope of profit from changes in their market value: *speculate in oil shares.*

specu·la·tor /-tə(r)/ *nc* a person who speculates(2).

specu·la·tion /ˌspekjʊˈleɪʃn/ *nc,nu* **1** (an instance of) speculating(1): *Such an opinion is only speculation.* **2** (a business deal as a result of) speculating(2).

specu·lat·ive /'spekjʊlətɪv/ *adj* **1** (*formal*) concerned with speculating(1): *speculative philosophy.* **2** concerned with speculating(2): *speculative purchases of grain.*

specu·la·tive·ly *adv*

sped /sped/ *pt,pp* of speed².

speech /spiːtʃ/ *n* **1** *nu* the power, act, manner, of speaking: *A human is the only animal that has the* *power of speech*. **2** *nc* a formal set of spoken statements to a group: *make a speech on/about human rights*.

'**speech marks** *n pl* (*informal*) = quotation marks.

'**speech therapy** *nu* treatment for incorrect speech, e.g. for stuttering.

speech·less *adj* (**a**) (*pred*) unable to speak, esp because of deep feeling: *Anger left him speechless*. (**b**) (*attrib*) that causes a person to be unable to speak: *speechless rage*.

speed[1] /spiːd/ *n* **1** *nc* a rate of moving: *at a speed of thirty miles an hour*. **2** *nu* fast movement: *need more speed to arrive on time*. **at (full/top) speed** (as) fast (as possible): *travelling at full/top speed*. ⇨ also breakneck, haste.

speed[2] /spiːd/ *v* (*pt,pp* **sped** /sped/ but ⇨ **2** below) **1** *vi* to move along, go fast: *cars speeding past the school*. **2 speed sth up** (*pt,pp* —**ed**) to increase the rate of something: *They have speeded up production/the train service*.

'**speed·boat** *nc* a motorboat designed for high speeds.

speed·ing *nu* (of motorists) the act of travelling at an illegal speed: *be fined £10 for speeding*.

'**speed limit** *nc* the fastest speed allowed.

speedy /ˈspiːdɪ/ *adj* (**-ier, -iest**) quick; coming, done, without delay: *I wish you a speedy recovery* (*from illness*).

speed·om·eter /spɪˈdɒmɪtə(r)/ *nc* an instrument showing the speed of a vehicle.

spell[1] /spel/ *nc* **1** words considered to have magic power: *cast a spell over him; put a spell on him; be/fall under a spell*. **2** an attraction caused by a person, place, activity etc: *the spell of Mozart's music*.

'**spell·bound** /-baʊnd/ *adj* (usually *pred*) with the attention held as if by a spell: *The speaker held his audience spellbound*.

spell[2] /spel/ *nc* **1** a period of time: *a long spell of warm weather*. **2** a period of activity or duty, esp one at which two or more people take turns: *take a spell at the wheel* (i.e. drive for a period).

spell[3] /spel/ *v* (*pt,pp* **spelt** /spelt/ or —**ed**) **1** *vt,vi* to name or write the letters of (a word): *How do you spell your name? These children can't spell. Do I spell it with a 'g'?* **2** *vt* (of letters) to form (a word) when put together in a particular order: *C-A-T spells cat*. **3 spell sth out** (**a**) to make something clear and easy to understand. (**b**) to give details of something: *Our ideas have been spelt out in this booklet*. **4** *vt* to cause something as a result: *Does laziness always spell failure?*

spell·er *nc* a person who spells (in the way mentioned): *a good/poor speller*.

spell·ing *nu* the way a word is spelt: *Do you use English or American spelling?*

spelt /spelt/ *pt,pp* of spell[3].

spend /spend/ *vt* (*pt,pp* **spent** /spent/) **1** to pay out (money) for goods, services etc: *spend all one's money. We spent our savings on a holiday.* **spend a penny** ⇨ penny(1). **2** to use up (time, energy etc): *spend a lot of time cleaning the car. He spent his life working to help others. Let's spend the weekend in London.* ⇨ also night.

spend·er *nc* a person who spends money (in the way mentioned): *an extravagant/big spender*.

'**spend·thrift** *nc* (*derog*) a person who spends

money extravagantly.

sperm /spɜːm/ *nu* the fertilizing fluid of a male animal.

spew /spjuː/ *vt,vi* = vomit.

sphere /sfɪə(r)/ *nc* **1** (*tech*) any object or mass in the shape of a ball, such as a planet. **2** a person's range of interests, activities, surroundings etc: *gardening is outside the sphere of my activities*. **3** a range, extent: *a sphere of influence*.

spheri·cal /ˈsferɪkl/ *adj* (*tech*) shaped like a sphere.

sphe·roid /ˈsfɪərɔɪd/ *nc* (*tech*) a solid that is almost spherical.

spice[1] /spaɪs/ *n* **1** *nc,nu* a substance from a plant (such as *ginger, cinnamon*) used to flavour food. Compare herb. **2** *nu* (*fig*) excitement or interest: *a story without spice*.

spicy *adj* (**-ier, -iest**) (**a**) of, flavoured with, spice. (**b**) (*fig*) exciting or interesting (because a little immoral): *spicy gossip about a pop star's love life*.

spice[2] /spaɪs/ *vt* **spice sth (with sth)** **1** to add flavour to something (using something). **2** to add excitement or interest to something (using something).

spick /spɪk/ *adj* (only in) **spick and span** bright, clean and tidy: *His room is spick and span*.

spi·der /ˈspaɪdə(r)/ *nc* a kind of creature with eight legs that can make a net (*web*) to catch insects.

spied /spaɪd/ *pt,pp* of spy.

spike[1] /spaɪk/ *nc* a pointed piece of metal, e.g. on a fence or on running-shoes.

spike[2] /spaɪk/ *vt* **1** to put spikes on (shoes etc): *spiked running-shoes*. **2** to catch (an animal) using a spike: *spike fish*.

spiky *adj* (**-ier, -iest**) having sharp points: *spiky hair*.

spill /spɪl/ *vt,vi* (*pt,pp* **spilt** /spɪlt/ or —**ed**) (to cause liquid) to go over the side of the container: *Who has spilt the milk? My coffee has spilt.* **spill the beans** ⇨ bean(2).

spin[1] /spɪn/ *n* **1** *nc,nu* (an instance of) the movement, act, of going round and round: *I could see the spin on the ball*. **2** *nc* (*informal*) a short ride in a car, on a motorbike etc: *Let's go for a spin in my new car*. **3 in a flat spin** in a panic: *We were in a flat spin one hour before the start because we just weren't ready*.

spin[2] /spɪn/ *v* (*pt,pp* **spun** /spʌn/; **-nn-**) **1** *vt,vi* to make (thread) by making wool, cotton etc go round and round and become long and thin. **2** *vt,vi* (of spiders etc) to make (a net (*web*)) by spinning(1) thread from their bodies. **3** *vi* (e.g. of a car wheel) to turn round and round very quickly: *My head spun* (i.e. It seemed to be spinning) *and I felt dizzy*. **4** *vt* to cause (something) to go round and round: *spin a coin; spin clothes in a washing-machine*. ⇨ spin-drier. **5** *vi* (of a vehicle) to move forward and turn when not under control: *The crash sent the car spinning across the road*. **6** *vt* (*fig*) to tell (a, usually untrue, story): *spin a tale about having caught a huge fish*.

spin along (of a car etc) to go smoothly along.

spin-off ⇨ below.

spin sth out to make money, time, a story etc last as long as possible.

spin round to turn round very quickly: *I spun*

round and grabbed the rock.

spin·ach /'spɪnɪdʒ/ *nu* (a kind of plant with) dark green leaves, eaten as a vegetable.

spi·nal /'spaɪnl/ *adj* (*anat*) of the spine: *a spinal injury.*

,spinal 'column *nc* (the —) the backbone.

spindle /'spɪndl/ *nc* **1** a thin rod used for spinning(1). **2** a bar on which something turns (e.g. an *axle*).

spin·dly /'spɪndlɪ/ *adj* (**-ier, -iest**) (usually *derog*) long and thin; (too) tall and thin: *spindly legs.*

spin-dri·er (also **-dry·er**) /ˌspɪn 'draɪə(r)/ *nc* an electrical machine for spinning washed clothes, sheets etc to remove the water.

,spin-'dry *vt* (*pt,pp* **-dried**) to dry (clothes etc) in a spin-drier.

spine /spaɪn/ *nc* **1** = backbone. **2** a sharp, pointed part on some plants and animals. **3** the part of a book's cover, usually with the book's title on it, covering the edge where the pages are joined.

spine·less *adj* (**a**) (*science*) having no spine(1): *spineless creatures.* (**b**) (*fig; derog*) (of a person) without courage to make decisions.

spin·ney /'spɪnɪ/ *nc* (*pl* **—s**) a small wood with thick bushes etc.

spin-off /'spɪn ɒf/ *nc* an extra advantage, benefit or product from a larger activity or process: *One spin-off from the research was the discovery of a new method for testing metals.*

spin·ster /'spɪnstə(r)/ *nc* (usually official or legal use) an unmarried woman, esp an older woman. Compare bachelor.

spi·ral¹ /'spaɪərəl/ *nc, adj* (a curve) going round a central point and moving towards the centre or up: *A snail's shell is spiral.*

spi·ral² /'spaɪərəl/ *vi* (**-ll-**, US also **-l-**) **spiral (up)** to move in a spiral: *The smoke spiralled up.*

spire /spaɪə(r)/ *nc* a pointed structure above a tower (esp of a church).

spir·it¹ /'spɪrɪt/ *n* **1** *nc,nu* a person's soul, mind: *The spirit is willing but the flesh is weak* (= One is willing (in theory) to do it but actually unable to do it). **in spirit** in one's thoughts: *We're with you in spirit.* **2** *nc* an invisible being, e.g. a ghost, fairy, elf etc: *Do you believe in spirits?* **3** (*pl*) state of mind: *be in high/low spirits* (= very happy/ sad). **4** *nu* the quality of having courage, determination: *Put a little more spirit into your work. That young athlete shows such spirit.* ⇨ spirited. **5** *n sing* a mental or moral attitude: *It depends on the spirit in which you apologized. She didn't seem to enter into the spirit of things* (i.e. didn't seem to enjoy herself or want to take part). **6** *n sing* the real meaning or purpose of a law, rule etc: *obey the spirit of the law.* **7** *nc* (usually *pl*) a kind of strong alcoholic drink (e.g. *whisky, gin, brandy, rum*): *Do you drink spirits?*

spir·it² /'spɪrɪt/ *vt* **spirit sb/sth away** to take a person or thing quickly, secretly or mysteriously: *She has been spirited away to another department.*

spir·it·ed /'spɪrɪtɪd/ *adj* **1** showing courage, determination: *a spirited attack/woman/reply.* Opp spiritless. **2** (in combinations) having the kind of spirits(3) mentioned: *high-/low-spirited* (= happy/sad).

spir·it·less /'spɪrɪtlɪs/ *adj* (*derog*) not having or

showing spirit(4): *a spiritless performance.* Opp spirited.

spiri·tu·al¹ /'spɪrɪtʃʊəl/ *adj* of the soul, not of material things; of, from, God: *concerned about one's spiritual welfare.* Compare corporeal.

spiri·tu·al·ly /-tʃʊlɪ/ *adv*

spiri·tu·al² /'spɪrɪtʃʊəl/ *nc* a religious song as first sung by Black people in the US.

spiri·tu·al·ism /'spɪrɪtʃʊəlɪzəm/ *nu* the belief in the possibility of receiving messages from the dead. ⇨ medium²(3).

spiri·tu·al·ist /-ɪst/ *nc* a believer in, supporter of, person who practises, spiritualism.

spirt /spɜːt/ *vi, nc* = spurt.

spit¹ /spɪt/ *nc* **1** a long pointed metal rod used for roasting meat. **2** a long, narrow piece of land.

spit² /spɪt/ *n* **1** *nu* the liquid in the mouth. **2** *nc* an act of spitting.

spit³ /spɪt/ *v* (*pt,pp* **spat** /spæt/) **1** *vi* to send liquid out of the mouth: *He spat into a bowl/on the ground/in the man's face. Don't spit! The cat spat at me.* **2** *vi* (of hot oil, a fire etc) to send out very small parts with a soft sharp sound: *The food was spitting in the pan.* **3** *vi* (of rain) to fall in a few light drops. **4** *vt* **spit sth out** (**a**) to spit(1) and send out something from the mouth: *spit out a pip.* (**b**) to say something quickly and angrily: *He spat out a curse.* (**c**) to send something out violently: *The wound spat blood. The chips spat fat onto the floor.*

spite¹ /spaɪt/ *nu* **1** the desire to annoy or harm another person because one does not like her or him: *do something out of/from spite.* **2 in spite of** (*prep*) without worrying about; although (something happened, is true etc): *They went out in spite of the rain. In spite of all his efforts, he failed.*

spite·ful /-fəl/ *adj* (*derog*) using, showing, spite.

spite·fully /-fəlɪ/ *adv*

spite·ful·ness *nu*

spite² /spaɪt/ *vt* to annoy or harm (a person) because of spite: *They play their radio loudly in the garden just to spite us.*

spittle /'spɪtl/ *nu* the liquid in the mouth.

splash¹ /splæʃ/ *n* **1** *nc* a noise, mark etc made by splashing: *He jumped into the water with a splash. She added splashes of green paint to the wall.* **2** *n sing* (usually **make a splash**) (*fig*) (to get) sudden and obvious public attention: *Her new record made a big splash.*

splash² /splæʃ/ *v* **1** *vt,vi* to cause (a liquid) to be flung about in drops; make (a person, thing) wet: *Children love to splash about/to splash water over each other.* **2** *vi* (of a liquid) to be flung about and fall in drops: *rain splashing on the stones.* **3** *vt,vi* **splash out** (**money**) (**on sb/sth**) (*informal*) to spend (a mentioned amount of) money extravagantly: *I've splashed out (£20) on a new shirt.*

splat /splæt/ *adv* with sound of a flat, wet object hitting a surface: *The fish fell splat on the floor.*

splay /spleɪ/ *vt,vi* **splay (sth) (out)** (to cause something) to be or become wider at one end: *Her toes splay out.*

spleen /spliːn/ *nc* (*anat*) the organ near the stomach that causes changes in the blood.

splen·did /'splendɪd/ *adj* **1** very beautiful and attractive to look at: *a splendid sunset/house.* **2** (*informal*) excellent: *a splendid dinner/idea.*

splen·did·ly adv

splen·dour (US = **-dor**) /'splendə(r)/ nu (formal) the condition of being splendid: the splendour of the moonlight over the sea.

splice /splaɪs/ vt to join together (rope, film, recording tape etc). **get spliced** (informal) to get married.

splint /splɪnt/ nc a strip of wood etc used to keep a broken bone in the right position.

splin·ter /'splɪntə(r)/ nc a small piece of hard material (wood, glass etc) split, torn or broken off a larger piece: have a splinter in one's finger. □ vt,vi (to cause something) to break into splinters.

'splinter group/party nc (politics) a group of people who have left the main political party.

split¹ /splɪt/ adj (attrib) divided: a split match; a split personality.

,split in'finitive nc (gram) a structure (often considered incorrect) when an adverb, etc comes between to and the infinitive, as in 'to hardly eat anything'.

,split 'second nc a brief moment.

split² /splɪt/ nc **1** a break or tear in cloth, wood etc: Can you mend this split in my trousers? **2** a separation, division, into groups: a split in the Labour Party. **3** **do the splits** to sit on the floor with one's legs pointing in opposite directions.

split³ /splɪt/ v (pt,pp —) **1** vt,vi (to cause something) to break along the length or at natural division: Some wood splits easily. He can split a match in two. Her dress has split along the sleeve/down the middle. ⇨ split¹. **split hairs** ⇨ hair(2). **split one's sides (laughing/with laughter)** ⇨ side²(6). **2** vt,vi (to cause people, things, areas) to separate, divide into groups: The issue has split the country (into several groups). ⇨ also split (sb/sth) up. **3** vt to share (something): split the cost/workload. **split the difference** ⇨ difference(2). **4** vi (informal) (of two people either married or in a close relationship) to stop living together, meeting etc. ⇨ split up. **5** vi (sl) (of people) to separate and go in opposite directions; to leave a party etc: Let's split.

split away (of one part) to leave a larger part or group: Some members split away to form a new party.

split on sb (informal) to give information about a person that will cause her or him to get into trouble.

split up (informal) = 4 above: My parents have split up. **split (sb/sth) up** (to cause a group, amount etc) to divide into parts: The children split up into teams. We split the work up among various people.

splut·ter¹ /'splʌtə(r)/ nu the act, sound, of talking in a confused way (as if) while coughing or when excited.

splut·ter² /'splʌtə(r)/ vi,vt **splutter (sth) (out)** to say (words) quickly and in a confused way.

spoil /spɔɪl/ v (pt,pp —t /spɔɪlt/ or —ed) **1** vt to make (something) useless or unsatisfactory: fruit spoilt by insects; holidays spoilt by bad weather. **2** vt to harm (a child's personality) by too much kindness or lack of discipline: parents who spoil their children. **3** vt to pay much attention to the comfort and wishes of (a person): He likes having a wife who spoils him. **4** vi (of food etc) to become bad, unfit for use: Some kinds of food soon spoil.

spoils /spɔɪlz/ n pl **1** stolen goods: The thieves shared the spoils. **2** the advantages, benefits etc from having power: the spoils of high office.

spoil-sport /'spɔɪl spɔːt/ nc (derog) a person who does things that interfere with the enjoyment of other people.

spoke¹ /spəʊk/ nc any one of the bars or wire rods connecting the centre of a wheel with the outer edge.

spoke² /spəʊk/ pt of speak.

spoken /'spəʊkən/ pp of speak.

spokes·man /'spəʊksmən/ nc (pl **-men**) a male spokesperson.

spokes·person /'spəʊkspɜːsn/ nc (pl **—s**) a person speaking, or chosen, as the representative of a group.

spokes·woman /'spəʊkswʊmən/ nc (pl **-women**) a female spokesperson.

sponge¹ /spʌndʒ/ n **1** nc a simple sea-animal with a body full of holes and able to absorb water easily. **2** nc one of these or something similar, used for washing, cleaning etc. **3** nc,nu = sponge-cake.

'sponge-bag nc a small bag for soap, a toothbrush etc, used when travelling.

'sponge-cake nc,nu a kind of soft, plain cake.

sponge² /spʌndʒ/ v **1** vt to wash, wipe or clean (something) with a sponge(2): sponging a wound/a child's face. **2** vt to remove (dirt, marks etc) with a sponge(2). **3** vi (informal) to take money etc without any intention to repay it: He's always sponging. Hence **sponger** nc (derog) a person who does this. ⇨ sponge from/off/on sb.

sponge sb/sth down to use a sponge(2) to wipe an area, animal, a person who is ill etc.

sponge from/off sb (informal) to take money etc from a parent, friend etc without any intention to repay it.

sponge on sb (informal) to live at another person's expense without any intention to pay them: I'm tired of my family sponging on me.

sponge sth up to use a sponge(2) to remove a liquid that has been spilt.

sponger /'spʌndʒə(r)/ nc ⇨ sponge²(3).

spon·sor¹ /'spɒnsə(r)/ nc **1** a person, business etc paying for a sports event, a team, an exhibition etc in return for advertising a product or trade name. **2** a person who presents a proposal etc to an official meeting: a sponsor of a bill on free transport for old people.

spon·sor² /'spɒnsə(r)/ vt to act as a sponsor for (something): sponsor a football team; sponsor a motion to increase students' grants.

spon·ta·ne·ous /spɒn'teɪnɪəs/ adj done, happening, from feelings, not suggested or planned: He made a spontaneous offer of help.

spon·ta·ne·ity /ˌspɒntə'neɪətɪ/ nu

spon·ta·ne·ous·ly adv

spoof /spuːf/ vt, nc (informal) (to produce) an amusing and exaggerated or deceptive account: a spoof on life as a prime minister.

spook /spuːk/ nc a ghost (the usual word).

spooky adj (**-ier**, **-iest**) causing fear because suggesting ghosts: a spooky house.

spool /spuːl/ nc a round holder (for thread, wire, photographic film, magnetic tape etc).

spoon¹ /spuːn/ nc a utensil with a shallow bowl on a handle, used for stirring, serving and taking up food: *a dessert-/soup-/table-/tea-spoon*.

'spoon·ful /-fʊl/ *nc* as much as a spoon can hold.

spoon² /spuːn/ *vt* to take, lift, (something) using a spoon: *spoon one's soup*. **spoon sth out** to serve food with a spoon: *spoon out the peas*.

'spoon-feed *vt* (*pt,pp* **-fed** /-fed/) (**a**) to feed (a baby etc) from a spoon. (**b**) (*fig*) to give (a person) too much help or teaching: *Some teachers spoon-feed their pupils*.

spor·ad·ic /spəˈrædɪk/ *adj* happening occasionally: *sporadic pain; sporadic increases in profits*.

spor·adi·cal·ly /-klɪ/ *adv*

spore /spɔː(r)/ *nc* (*science*) a single cell by which a flowerless plant (e.g. moss, a fern) reproduces itself.

spor·ran /ˈspɒrən/ *nc* a small bag worn in front of a kilt.

sport¹ /spɔːt/ *n* **1** *nc,nu* (a kind of) activity, esp outdoors, done for amusement and exercise: *fond of sport; watch sport on TV. Football and tennis are among my favourite sports*. ⇨ game²(1). **2** *nc* (*informal*) a person who takes defeat well. **3** *nc* (*informal*) an unselfish, kind person: *Be a sport and help me with this suitcase*. ⇨ also spoil-sport.

sport² /spɔːt/ *vt* (*informal*) to have or wear (something) proudly: *sport a moustache/a new uniform*.

sport·ing /ˈspɔːtɪŋ/ *adj* **1** (*attrib*) connected with, interested in, sport: *a sporting man*. **2** showing fairness: *give her a sporting chance. To allow the younger children to have the front seats was very sporting of you*. Opp unsporting.

sport·ing·ly *adv*

sports /spɔːts/ *n pl* (also *attrib*) a meeting for taking part in a sport(1): *school sports; a sports field/ meeting/report*.

'sports car *nc* a car designed for driving fast.

'sports·man/·woman *nc* a person who takes part in a sport(1).

'sports·man·like *adj* being fair. ⇨ sporting(2). Opp unsportsmanlike.

'sportsmanship *nu* the quality of being fair and helpful.

,sports·wear *nu* (*commerce*) clothes used for playing sports.

spot¹ /spɒt/ *nc* **1** a small round mark on a surface: *a red scarf with white spots*. **knock spots off sb** (*informal*) to do an activity, task etc better than another person. **2** a dirty mark: *grease/mud/ink spots*. **3** a small infected area on the skin. ⇨ spotty. **4** a small drop (of liquid): *spots of rain*. **a spot of sth** (*informal*) a small amount of something: *I need a spot of milk in this coffee. I'm having a spot of bother* (= a little difficulty) *with this problem*. **5** a particular place: *the very* (= exact) *spot where he was killed; a popular spot for picnics*. **on the spot** (**a**) at the place where one is needed: *Within a few minutes an ambulance was on the spot*. (**b**) immediately: *The car hit the wall and the driver was killed on the spot*. **be in a bit of a/a tight spot** (*informal*) to be in a little difficulty: *Can I borrow your car—I'm in a bit of a spot*.

spot² /spɒt/ *vt* (**-tt-**) **1** to recognize or notice (a person, thing) suddenly: *spot a friend in a crowd; spot a mistake in the pattern*. **2** to mark (something) with spots.

spot·ted *adj* marked with spots(1) as a design: *a*

spotted handkerchief.

spot·less /ˈspɒtlɪs/ *adj* (*no comp*) **1** completely clean: *a spotless room/dress*. **2** without anything considered bad: *a spotless reputation/character*.

spot·less·ly *adv*: *spotlessly clean*.

spot check /ˈspɒt ˌtʃek/ *vt, nc* (to make) a quick test without warning: *a spot check on vehicles*.

spot·light¹ /ˈspɒtlaɪt/ *nc* (an electrical apparatus used for sending) a strong light directed onto a particular place or person, e.g. the stage of a theatre. **be in/hold the spotlight** (*fig*) to be, have, the centre of attention.

spot·light² /ˈspɒtlaɪt/ *vt* (*pt,pp* **-lit** /-lɪt/) to show the importance of (something) (as if) with a strong light: *spotlight difficulties in the scheme*.

spot·ty /ˈspɒtɪ/ *adj* (**-ier, -iest**) (of the skin) having spots(3): *a spotty face*.

spouse /spaʊz/ *nc* (*legal*) a husband or wife.

spout¹ /spaʊt/ *nc* **1** a pipe from which liquid pours, e.g. for tea from a teapot. **2** a stream of liquid coming out with great force. **3** **up the spout** (*dated sl*) (of a person) in difficulties.

spout² /spaʊt/ *vt,vi* **1** (to cause liquid) to come or be sent out with great force: *blood spouting from a wound*. **2** (*informal*) to speak (lots of words, verses etc) with energy and (too much) pride: *spouting political slogans*.

sprain /spreɪn/ *vt* to injure (a joint, esp the wrist or ankle) by twisting it violently so that there is pain and swelling: *sprain one's wrist*. □ *nc* an injury caused by spraining a joint.

sprang /spræŋ/ *pt* of spring³.

sprat /spræt/ *nc* a kind of small European sea-fish used as food.

sprawl¹ /sprɔːl/ *nc* **1** a sprawling(1) position. **2** a spread (of homes) on the edge of a town: *an urban sprawl*.

sprawl² /sprɔːl/ *vi* **sprawl (out)** **1** to sit or lie with the arms and legs loosely spread out: *sprawling on the sofa; lie sprawled out in the mud*. **2** (of plants etc) to spread out loosely and irregularly. **3** (*fig*) (of buildings) to spread over much space: *suburbs that sprawl out into the countryside*.

spray¹ /spreɪ/ *nc* **1** a small branch of a tree or plant with smaller stems, esp as an ornament. **2** an ornament in a similar shape: *a spray of diamonds*.

spray² /spreɪ/ *n* **1** *nc,nu* (an example of) liquid sent through the air in tiny drops (by the wind, or through an apparatus): *sea-spray; a spray of insecticide*. **2** *nc* an apparatus that sprays perfume etc.

spray³ /spreɪ/ *vt* to put (a liquid) on (something), using a spray(2) or making a spray(1): *spray fruit trees*.

spray·er *nc* (**a**) a person who sprays. (**b**) an apparatus used for spraying.

spread¹ /spred/ *n* **1** *nu* the process, act, of spreading(4): *the spread of disease/knowledge/ information*. **2** *nu* extent; range: *the spread of a bird's wings*. **3** *n sing* a range, space, (of space or time): *a spread of many months/miles between one and the other*. **4** *nc* a part of a page with writing and illustrations, esp over the whole area. **5** *n sing* (*informal*) a table with many good things to eat and drink on it: *What a superb spread!* **6** *nc,nu* (an example of) a kind of soft food (to be) spread(3) with a knife etc: *cheese spread*.

spread² /spred/ v (pt,pp —) **1** vt **spread sth (out)** to cause (something) to become wider, longer etc by unfolding or unrolling: *spread out a map; spread (out) one's arms. The bird spread its wings.* **2** vi **spread out** to separate and go off in different directions over an area: *The police spread out to search for the body in the woods.* **3** vt to cover (something) by spreading: *spread a table with a cloth.* **4** vt to put (a substance) on a surface and extend its area by flattening etc: *spread butter on bread/a slice of bread with butter.* **5** vt,vi to cause something to become more widely extended or distributed: *spread knowledge. Coughs and sneezes spread diseases. The water spread over the floor. The rumour quickly spread through the village. The fire spread from the factory to the houses next door.* **6** vi to extend in space: *desert spreading for hundreds of miles.* **7** vt **spread sth over sth** to cause something to cover a period of time: *a course of studies spread over three years; spread payments over twelve months.*

spread-'eagled adj (usually pred) in a lying position with arms and legs stretched out: *sunbathers spread-eagled on the grass.*

spree /spriː/ nc **1** a time of fun and pleasure: *a holiday/drinking spree; have a spree in town.* **2** an occasion of spending money for pleasure: *a spending/buying spree.*

sprig /sprɪg/ nc **sprig (of sth)** a small branch (of the plant mentioned): *a sprig of holly.*

spright·ly /'spraɪtlɪ/ adj (-ier, -iest) lively; active and cheerful.

spring¹ /sprɪŋ/ nc **1** a length of twisted, bent or coiled metal which returns to its shape or position after being pulled, pushed or pressed: *the spring of a watch.* **2** an act of springing or jumping up. **3** (a place where there is) water coming up from the ground: *a hot spring; a mineral spring.* **4** nu an ability to stretch and go back to the normal shape: *rubber bands that have lost their spring.*

spring 'balance nc (science) an instrument that measures weight by how much the object pulls a spring down.

spring·board nc one used to give a springing motion to a person jumping from it.

springy adj (-ier, -iest) (of movement) showing energy, satisfaction etc: *walk with a youthful springy step.*

spring² /sprɪŋ/ nc (often S-) (also attrib) the season between winter and summer when many plants and flowers begin to grow: *flowers that appear in (the) spring; spring flowers/weather.*
'spring·like adj: *springlike weather.*
'spring·time nu the period of spring.

spring³ /sprɪŋ/ v (pt **sprang** /spræŋ/, pp **sprung** /sprʌŋ/) **1** vi to move suddenly or with energy (down, up, out etc) from being still: *He sprang down from the wall/out of bed/to his feet/out from behind a bush/up from his seat. The branch sprang back and hit me in the face. Where have you sprung from?* (= appeared from suddenly?) **2** vt to cause (a device, part of a machine etc) to move by freeing a spring(1): *spring a bolt/lever.* **3** vt to cause (something) to happen suddenly: *He sprang a surprise on me.* **spring a leak** ⇨ leak¹(1). **4** vt (informal) to organize (a prisoner) to escape. **5** vi **spring up (a)** (of

plants) to appear suddenly and grow: *Weeds were springing up everywhere.* **(b)** (of buildings) to be suddenly and quickly built: *New offices sprang up in the town centre.* **(c)** to occur suddenly: *A doubt/suspicion/new idea sprang up in her mind.*

spring-clean /ˌsprɪŋ 'kliːn/ vi,vt to clean (a house, room) thoroughly. Hence ,spring-'cleaning nu

spring onion /ˌsprɪŋ 'ʌnjən/ nc,nu a kind of small, long onion, often used in salads.

sprinkle¹ /'sprɪŋkl/ nc an act of, small amount caused by, sprinkling: *a sprinkle of sugar.*

sprinkle² /'sprɪŋkl/ vt to direct, throw, a small amount of (liquid or powder) on (a surface): *sprinkling water on a dusty path; sprinkle the floor with sand.*

sprink·ler /'sprɪŋklə(r)/ nc an apparatus used for sprinkling water.

sprink·ling nc a small amount or number: *There was a sprinkling of young people in the audience.*

sprint¹ /sprɪnt/ nc **1** an act of sprinting. **2** a short race, e.g. 100 metres.

sprint² /sprɪnt/ vi to run a short distance at full speed: *He sprinted past his competitors just before reaching the tape.*

sprin·ter nc a person who sprints.

sprite /spraɪt/ nc a fairy; elf.

sprout¹ /spraʊt/ nc **1** a new part of a plant. **2** = brussels sprout.

sprout² /spraʊt/ v **1** vt,vi (to cause a plant, leaf etc) to grow: *The leaves are sprouting from the stem. The bush is sprouting new leaves.* **2** vi **sprout up (a)** (of plants) to grow. **(b)** (fig) (of children) to grow taller.

spruce /spruːs/ adj neat and smart in dress and appearance. □ vt **spruce oneself/sb up** to make oneself, a person look smart: *Go and spruce yourself up.*
spruce·ly adv

sprung /sprʌŋ/ pp of spring³.

spry /spraɪ/ adj (—er, —est) lively: *still spry at eighty.* **look spry** to do something quickly.

spud /spʌd/ nc (sl) potato.

spue /spjuː/ vt,vi = spew.

spun /spʌn/ pt,pp of spin.

spunk /spʌŋk/ nu (informal) courage: *a boy with plenty of spunk.*

spur¹ /spɜː(r)/ nc **1** one of a pair of sharp-toothed wheels on the heels of a rider's boots, used to make the horse go faster. **2** (fig) something that encourages a person to do more: *the spur of poverty.* **on the spur of the moment** suddenly and without thinking: *I bought it on the spur of the moment and later discovered that it was too big.* **3** a ridge extending from a mountain or hill.

spur² /spɜː(r)/ vt (-rr-) **spur oneself/sb/sth (on)** to encourage oneself, a person, a horse etc to move quickly, do something, make more effort etc: *He was spurred (on) by ambition.*

spu·ri·ous /'spjʊərɪəs/ adj (formal) false; not genuine: *a spurious claim to the money.* Compare specious.
spu·ri·ous·ly adv

spurn /spɜːn/ vt to refuse (an offer etc) because of anger, pride etc: *spurn an offer of help.*

spurt¹ /spɜːt/ nc **1** a sudden rush (of liquid): *a spurt of blood.* **2** a sudden use: *a spurt of energy/effort.* **put on a spurt** to increase one's effort or speed suddenly, e.g. in a race.

spurt² /spɜːt/ *vi* **1** (of liquid etc) to come out in a sudden rush: *Blood spurted (out) from the wound.* **2** to make a sudden, short effort, esp in a race or other contest: *The runner spurted as she approached the winning-post.*

sput·ter /'spʌtə(r)/ *v* **1** *vi* to make a series of spitting sounds: *The sausages were sputtering in the frying-pan.* **2** *vi, vt* to say (something) in a quick, angry voice.

spu·tum /'spjuːtəm/ *nu* (*tech*) the semi-liquid coughed up from the throat.

spy¹ /spaɪ/ *nc* (*pl* **spies**) **1** a person who tries to get secret information, esp about the military affairs of other countries. **2** a person who keeps a secret watch on the movements of others: *industrial spies* (i.e. employed to learn about a rival business).

spy² /spaɪ/ *v* (*pt,pp* **spied**) **1** *vi* **spy (for sb/sth)** to be a spy (for a person, country, government, business etc). **2** *vi* **spy on sb/sth** to watch a person, activity, business etc secretly. **3** *vt* **spy sth out** to watch and get information about something: *spy out the land* (i.e. find out what is happening). **4** *vt* (usually *literary*) to see or notice (a person, thing): *I spied someone coming up the garden path.*

'spy·glass *nc* (*dated*) a small telescope.

Sq. *written abbr* Square.

sq *written abbr* (*maths*) square.

Sqn Ldr *written abbr* (*mil*) Squadron Leader.

squabble /'skwɒbl/ *vi, nc* (to take part in) a small or noisy quarrel: *Tom was squabbling with his sister about who should use the bicycle.*

squad /skwɒd/ *nc* a small group of people, e.g. of players, soldiers, police, working or being trained together: *England's football squad.*

'squad car *nc* (*US*) police patrol car.

squad·ron /'skwɒdrən/ *nc* a division of soldiers, warships, aircraft etc.

,squadron 'leader *nc* (abbr **Sqn Ldr**) (*mil*) an officer below a wing commander in the air force.

squal·id /'skwɒlɪd/ *adj* (*derog*) very dirty, poor, uncared for: *living in squalid conditions/houses.* ⇨ squalor.

squalid·ly *adv*

squall¹ /skwɔːl/ *nc* **1** a loud cry of pain or fear (esp from a baby or child). **2** a sudden violent wind, often with rain or snow.

squall² /skwɔːl/ *vi* to make squalls(1): *squalling babies.*

squal·or /'skwɒlə(r)/ *nu* a squalid state: *born in squalor; the squalor of the slums.*

squan·der /'skwɒndə(r)/ *vt* to use up (time, money, and property etc) carelessly.

square¹ /skweə(r)/ *adj* **1** having the shape of a square(1): *a square table.* ⇨ also peg¹(1). **2** (almost) forming a right angle: *a square corner; a square chin.* **3** (*maths*) (abbr **sq** or ² as in *5sq cm* or *5cm²*) having an area equal to that of a square(1) having a side with the length mentioned. **4** (*informal*) fair and honest: *Are you being square with me?* **a square deal** ⇨ deal²(1). **a square meal** ⇨ meal¹(1). **5** (*pred*) arranged in good order: *get one's papers square; get one's accounts square* (i.e. settled). **be (all) square (with sb)** (a) to have paid one's debts and received what one is owed: *I think we're all square*

now. **(b)** to have settled an argument, quarrel: *Now we're all square.* **(c)** to have scored the same number of points in a game or sport.

,square 'brackets *n pl* the symbols [ ] used to separate a section of writing. ⇨ parenthesis(2).

,square 'number *nc* (*maths*) any number that is the square³(3) of another number, e.g. 4 (2×2), 9 (3×3), 16 (4×4) etc.

,square 'root *nc* (*maths*) a number which equals another mentioned number when multiplied by itself: *The square root of 4 is 2/of 9 is 3/of 16 is 4.*

square² /skweə(r)/ *adv* **1** at a right angle: *sit square in one's seat.* **2** (*informal*) directly: *hit him square on the jaw.* **fair and square** ⇨ fair².

square³ /skweə(r)/ *nc* **1** a shape or area with four equal sides and four right angles (□). **back to square one** back to the starting-point and forced to start again: *With this new evidence, we shall have to go back to square one.* **2** (also S-; abbr Sq.) (the buildings along the edges of) an open area in a town: *listening to the band playing in the square. He lived at 95 Russell Square.* **3** (*maths*) the result when a number is multiplied by itself: *The square of 7 is 49.* **4** (*maths*) an L-shaped or T-shaped instrument for drawing or testing right angles.

square⁴ /skweə(r)/ *v* **1** *vt* to make (something) square; give a square shape to (something): *squaring wood.* **2** *vt* to make (something) straight or level: *square one's shoulders.* **3** *vt* (*maths*) to multiply (a number) by itself: *Three squared is nine.* **4** *vt, vi* (to cause something) to agree (with something): *Your explanation doesn't square with the facts.* **5** *vt* to pay (one's debts). ⇨ account¹(8). **6** *vi* **square up** (*informal*) to pay a bill, esp a long one: *Let me square up with you* (= pay what I owe you).

squash¹ /skwɒʃ/ *nu* (also *squash rackets*) an indoor game played with rackets and a small rubber ball in a walled court.

squash² /skwɒʃ/ *n* **1** *n sing* a crowd (of people) close together: *There was a squash (of people) at the gate.* **2** *nc,nu* (a portion of) a kind of drink made from fruit juice: *orange/lemon squash.*

squash³ /skwɒʃ/ *v* **1** *vt* to press (a person, thing) into a small space: *squash a fly; squash too many people into a bus.* **2** *vi* to become squashed or pressed out of shape: *Soft fruits squash easily.* **3** *vt* to defeat (an enemy, criticism etc) completely. **4** *vt* (*informal*) to make (a person) feel foolish by using a clever, sarcastic etc reply, statement: *He was/felt completely squashed.*

squat¹ /skwɒt/ *adj* short and fat: *a squat man.*

squat² /skwɒt/ *nc* **1** a squatting position. **2** (*informal*) a place used for squatting(2): *live in a squat.*

squat³ /skwɒt/ *vi* (-**tt**-) **1** to sit on one's heels, or on the ground with the legs drawn up under or close to the body: *The old man squatted in front of the fire.* **2** (*informal*) to use a building, land etc as a home without authority or permission: *poor families squatting in deserted buildings.*

squat·ter *nc* a person who squats(2).

squawk /skwɔːk/ *vi, nc* (esp of birds) (to make) a long, loud, harsh cry.

squeak¹ /skwiːk/ *nc* **1** a high sound: *a squeak of a mouse/a door.* **2 a narrow squeak** a lucky, almost unsuccessful, escape from danger or failure.

squeak² /skwiːk/ *vi* to make a high sound: *These new shoes squeak.*

squeaky *adj* (**-ier**, **-iest**) (*attrib*) squeaking: *squeaky shoes/a squeaky voice.*

squeal¹ /skwiːl/ *nc* a long, high sound: *the squeal of frightened animals; squeals of pain; squeals of laughter; the squeal of brakes.*

squeal² /skwiːl/ *vi* **1** to make a long, high sound: *He squealed like a pig.* **2** (*informal*) to report a person to the police.

squeam·ish /ˈskwiːmɪʃ/ *adj* (usually *derog*) **1** (*pred*) (too) easily made sick; feeling sick: *A nurse cannot be squeamish.* **2** (too) easily disgusted or shocked: *a squeamish woman.*

squeam·ish·ly *adv*

squeeze¹ /skwiːz/ *nc* **1** an act of squeezing(1): *She gave my arm a squeeze.* **a tight squeeze** (a) a crowd of people very close together. (b) a lucky escape or victory: *That was a tight squeeze!* **2** (*finance*) a situation when money (esp to borrow) is not easily obtained.

squeeze² /skwiːz/ *v* **1** *vt* to press on (something) from the opposite side or from all sides: *squeeze her hand; squeeze a sponge; squeeze one's fingers* (e.g. in a door). **2** *vt* **squeeze sth (out)** to get water, juice etc (out of something) by pressing hard: *squeeze (the juice out of) a lemon; squeeze the water out of clothes.* **3** *vt,vi* to fit in, get in, get past etc by pushing or forcing (oneself, a person) (through a narrow passage or small space): *squeeze (one's way) into a crowded bus; squeeze (oneself) through a gap in a hedge.* **4** *vt* to get (money, information etc) by using force etc: *squeeze more money out of the public* (e.g. by increasing taxes).

squeezer *nc* a device that squeezes (fruit): *a lemon-squeezer.*

squelch /skweltʃ/ *vi, nc* (to make) a sucking sound as when feet are lifted from stiff, sticky mud: *cows squelching through the mud.*

squid /skwɪd/ *nc* a kind of sea-animal with ten long arms round its mouth.

squiggle /ˈskwɪɡl/ *nc* a small twisted line: *Is this squiggle his signature?*

squint¹ /skwɪnt/ *nc* a condition in which the eyes look in different directions.

squint² /skwɪnt/ *vi* **1** to have eyes that look in different directions. **2** to look with half-shut eyes or through a narrow opening.

squire /skwaɪə(r)/ *nc* (*dated*) (in England) a main landowner in a country parish.

squirm /skwɜːm/ *vi* to twist the body (showing discomfort, shame or embarrassment).

squir·rel /ˈskwɪrəl/ *nc* a kind of small, tree-climbing, bushy-tailed animal with red, grey or black fur.

squirt¹ /skwɜːt/ *nc* **1** a thin stream (of liquid, powder etc). **2** (*informal; derog*) an unimportant, nasty person: *You little squirt!*

squirt² /skwɜːt/ *v* **1** *vi* (of liquid, powder) to be forced out in a thin stream or jet: *The water squirted all over me.* **2** *vt* to force (liquid, powder etc) onto (a person, thing) in a thin stream or jet: *They squirted me with soda water.*

Sr *written abbr* (also **Sen.**, **Snr**) Senior.

SRCN /ˌes ɑː siː ˈen/ *abbr* State Registered Children's Nurse.

SRN /ˌes ɑː ˈen/ *abbr* State Registered Nurse.

SSE *written abbr* south-south-east.

SSW *written abbr* south-south-west.

St *written abbr* **1** Street. **2** Saint. **3** Strait.

st *written abbr* **1** stone(s). **2** (used only after the number 1) first: *1st, 31st etc.*

stab¹ /stæb/ *nc* **1** a blow, wound, pain, caused by stabbing. **2** **have a stab at sth** (*informal*) to try to be successful at it: *have a stab at an exam question.*

stab² /stæb/ *vt,vi* (**-bb-**) to hit or wound (a person, animal) using something pointed: *She was stabbed in the back. I stabbed at the ice with a stick.*

stable¹ /ˈsteɪbl/ *adj* (**—r**, **—st**) firm; not likely to move or change: *What we need is a stable government. She has a stable character. He needs a stable job.* Opp **unstable**.

sta·bil·ity /stəˈbɪlətɪ/ *nu* the quality of being stable. Opp **instability**.

sta·bil·ize (also **-ise**) /ˈsteɪbəlaɪz/ *vt,vi* (to cause something) to become stable: *The banks must stabilize interest rates. Prices have stabilized.* Compare **destabilize**.

sta·bil·iz·er (also **-is·er**) *nc* a substance, apparatus, that stabilizes.

sta·bil·iz·ing *adj* making (esp a person) stable: *He's a stabilizing influence on my sister.*

stable² /ˈsteɪbl/ *nc* **1** a building in which horses are kept and fed. **2** a number of horses (esp racehorses) belonging to one particular owner.

stable³ /ˈsteɪbl/ *vt* to keep, put, (horses) in a stable: *Where do you stable your horse?*

stack¹ /stæk/ *nc* **1** a pile of (hay, straw etc) for storage in the open. **2** a pile or heap (of books, papers, wood etc). **3** (*informal*) a large amount: *I have a stack of work waiting to be done.* **4** (*computers*) a part of the memory where information is stored for a short time (and where only the last item can be looked at).

stack² /stæk/ *vt* **stack sth (up)** to make (things) into a stack: *stack (up) chairs; stack books on a shelf.*

sta·di·um /ˈsteɪdɪəm/ *nc* (*pl* **—s**) a building with seats round a sports field, used for games, athletic competitions: *design a new Olympic stadium.*

staff¹ /stɑːf/ *nc* **1** (also *attrib*) a group of professional workers in a business, school etc: *office staff; the teaching staff of a school. I'm a member of staff/am a staff member/am on the staff at the university.* **2** (*mil*) a group of officers in the army. **3** a strong stick used as a support, as a weapon or as a sign of office or authority: *a flagstaff.* **4** (*music*) (*pl* **staves** /steɪvz/) a set of five parallel lines on which notes are written.

staff² /stɑːf/ *vt* to provide (a business etc) with staff(1): *The office is staffed with experienced people.* ⇨ **over/understaffed.**

stag /stæɡ/ *nc* a male deer.

'stag-party *nc* (*informal*) a party for men only, usually for a man about to get married.

stage¹ /steɪdʒ/ *nc* **1** (in a theatre) the raised structure on which the actors appear. **2** (the **—**) the profession of acting in theatres. **be/go on the stage** to be/become an actor or actress. **3** (*fig*) a place where events occur: *a suitable stage for a battle.* **4** a point, period or step in development: *at an early stage in our history. The baby* has reached the talking stage. **5** a journey, distance, between two stopping-places along a road or route; such a stopping-place: *travel by easy stages* (= for only a short distance at a time). ⇨ also landing-stage.

'stage-coach *nc* a horse-drawn vehicle once used for carrying passengers (and often post) along a regular route.

'stage-craft *nu* skill or experience in writing or producing plays.

'stage fright *nu* nervousness felt when facing an audience.

,stage 'manager *nc* a person who organizes scenery and props etc in a theatre.

'stage-struck *adj* having a strong desire to become an actor or actress.

,stage 'whisper *nc* a whisper that is meant to be overheard.

stage² /steɪdʒ/ *vt* **1** to organize and produce (a play etc): *We're staging 'Hamlet'.* **2** to organize and carry out (an activity esp a protest): *stage a strike.*

stag·fla·tion /stæg'fleɪʃn/ *nu* (*economics*) inflation with a fall in productivity.

stag·ger¹ /'stægə(r)/ *n sing* an unsteady movement or walk.

stag·ger² /'stægə(r)/ *v* **1** *vi* to walk or move unsteadily (because of weakness, a heavy burden, drunkenness etc): *The man staggered along/to his feet/across the room/from side to side of the pavement.* **2** *vt* (often *passive*) (of news etc) to shock (a person) deeply: *I was staggered to hear/on hearing/when I heard that she had been arrested.* **3** *vt* to arrange (times of events) so that they do not all occur together: *stagger office hours.*

stag·ger·ed *adj* (*pred*) (*informal*) (of a person) shocked; amazed. ⇨ stagger(2).

stag·ger·ing *adj* (of an event, news effect, result etc) very surprising.

stag·ing /'steɪdʒɪŋ/ *nu* **1** a temporary structure, e.g. for a building. **2** the activity of producing (a play) in the theatre.

stag·nant /'stægnənt/ *adj* **1** (of water) not moving (and so not fresh): *water lying stagnant in ponds and ditches.* **2** (*fig*) inactive: *Business was stagnant last week.*

stag·nate /stæg'neɪt/ *vi* (*fig*) to be or become inactive and dull because of no opportunity, will, interest etc.

staid /steɪd/ *adj* (often *derog*) (of a person, appearance, behaviour etc) conservative, quiet and serious.

staid·ly *adv*

stain¹ /steɪn/ *n* **1** *nu* a liquid used for staining wood etc. **2** *nc* a dirty mark or patch of colour: *ink-/blood-stains.* **3** *nc* (*fig*) a moral defect: *a stain on your character.*

stain² /steɪn/ *v* **1** *vt,vi* (to cause something) to change colour, make coloured patches or dirty marks on (something): *blood-stained hands.* **2** *vt* to colour (wood, glass etc) with a substance that soaks into the material: *He stained the wood brown.*

stain·less *adj* (**a**) without a fault: *a stainless reputation.* (**b**) (*attrib*) (esp of a kind of steel alloy) that cannot rust or stain: *stainless steel cutlery.*

stair /steə(r)/ *nc* (usually *pl*) (one of) a series of steps leading from one floor inside a building to

another: *She always runs up/down the stairs. The child was sitting on the bottom stair.* **a flight of stairs** ⇨ flight¹(4). Compare step¹(6). ⇨ also downstairs, upstairs.

'stair·case *nc* a series of stairs (with banisters) inside a building.

stake¹ /steɪk/ *nc* **1** a pointed length of wood or metal (to be) hit into the ground as a post (for a fence) or as a support (for something, e.g. plants, young trees). **2** a sum of money risked when gambling. **at stake** to be risked, depending, on the result of something: *His reputation/His life itself was at stake.* **3** *stake (in sth)* a financial interest (in a business deal etc). **4** (in history) the post to which a person was tied before being burnt to death as a punishment: *be burned at the stake.*

stake² /steɪk/ *vt* **1** to support (plants etc) with a stake: *stake newly planted trees.* **2** *stake sth out* to mark an area using stakes: *stake out a claim* (to land etc). **3** *stake sth (on sth)* to put money, hopes etc (on a result, belief etc): *stake money on a race. I'd stake my life on it* (i.e. I am very confident about it).

stal·ac·tite /'stæləktaɪt/ *nc* a length of lime hanging from the roof of a cave as water drips from it.

stal·ag·mite /'stæləgmaɪt/ *nc* a length of lime going up from the floor of a cave as water drips from the roof.

stale /steɪl/ *adj* (**—r, —st**) **1** (of food) dry and unappetizing because not fresh: *stale bread.* **2** uninteresting because heard before: *stale news/ jokes.* **3** (of an athlete, musician etc) no longer able to perform well because of too much playing, training, practice etc: *become stale.*

stale·ness *nu*

stale·mate /'steɪlmeɪt/ *nc,nu* **1** (*chess*) a position of the pieces from which no further move is possible. **2** (*fig*) any stage of a dispute at which further action by either side seems to be impossible.

stalk¹ /stɔːk/ *nc* a part of a plant that supports flowers, leaves or fruit.

stalk² /stɔːk/ *v* **1** *vi* *stalk out (of a place)* to walk out in a proud, self-important or serious way: *stalk out of the room.* **2** *vt* to move quietly and cautiously towards (wild animals etc) in order to get near: *stalk deer.*

stall¹ /stɔːl/ *nc* **1** a compartment for one animal in a stable or cattle shed. **2** a table, small open shop etc, used by a trader in a market, on a street, in a railway-station etc: *a book-/flower-/coffee-stall.* **3** (*pl*) (the **—s**) the seats in the part of a theatre nearest to the stage.

stall² /stɔːl/ *v* **1** *vi* (of a car engine) to stop because of insufficient power or speed. **2** *vt* (of a driver) to cause an engine to stop in this way. **3** *vt,vi* to avoid giving (a person) a clear answer to a question, making a decision (in order to get more time): *stall for time.*

stal·lion /'stæliən/ *nc* a fully-grown male horse, esp one used for breeding.

stal·wart¹ /'stɔːlwət/ *adj* (*formal*) strong and determined: *stalwart supporters.*

stal·wart² /'stɔːlwət/ *nc* a loyal supporter.

sta·men /'steɪmən/ *nc* (*science*) the male part of a flower, bearing pollen.

stam·ina /'stæmɪnə/ *nu* energy and physical,

mental and moral strength, making it possible for a person or animal to work hard for a long time, to survive a serious illness, difficulty etc.

stam·mer[1] /'stæmə(r)/ *nc* an act, condition, of stammering.

stam·mer[2] /'stæmə(r)/ *vi,vt* to say (something), speak, with a tendency to repeat the same sound or syllable, as in 'G-g-give me that b-b-book': *stammer out a request.*

stam·mer·er *nc* a person who stammers.

stamp[1] /stæmp/ *nc* **1** (also *postage-stamp*) a piece of printed paper put on envelopes, parcels etc to show the postage paid. **2** a similar piece of paper put on documents etc to show money paid, agreement etc. **3** an act of stamping the foot: *a stamp of impatience.* **4** something used to make a mark or design on a surface: *a rubber stamp.* **5** (usually *sing*) a characteristic mark or quality: *He bears the stamp of genius.*

'**stamp-album** *nc* one for postage stamps.

'**stamp-collector** *nc* a person who collects postage stamps.

'**stamp-duty** *nc* a tax (to be) paid on certain kinds of legal documents.

stamp[2] /stæmp/ *v* **1** *vt* to put a stamp(1,2) on (an envelope, parcel etc): *I enclose a stamped, addressed envelope.* **2** *vt,vi* to put (one's foot) down with force (on something): *stamp one's foot; stamp on a spider; stamp about/out of the room.* **stamp sth out** to destroy, end, something using determined effort: *stamp out a fire in the grass/a rebellion/an epidemic disease.* **3** *vt* to print (a design, lettering, the date etc) (on paper, cloth or other surface): *The girl forgot to stamp my library books.* **4** *vt* to produce, give shape to, (something, e.g. pieces of metal) using a cutter. **5** *vt* (*fig*) to use (one's strong personality etc) to influence something strongly: *He stamped his authority/personality on the meeting.*

stam·pede[1] /stæm'pi:d/ *nc* a sudden rush of frightened people or animals.

stam·pede[2] /stæm'pi:d/ *v* **1** *vt,vi* (to cause animals etc) to take part in a stampede. **2** *vt* to force or frighten (a person) into action: *Don't be stampeded into buying the house.*

stance /stæns/ *nc* **1** a way of standing: *an athletic stance.* **2** a personal attitude or opinion: *What is your stance on nuclear weapons?*

stand[1] /stænd/ *nc* **1** a position: *He took his stand near the window.* ⇨ handstand. **make a stand (against sth)** to oppose something actively. **take a stand** to take a particular public position against or in favour: *take a stand against violence.* **2** a small support on which something can be placed: *a music-/hat-stand.* **3** a structure from which things are sold or exhibited: *a news-stand; stands at an exhibition.* **4** an open structure in a stadium etc where people may stand or sit to watch an event: *a seat in the stands.* ⇨ grandstand.

stand[2] /stænd/ *v* (*pt,pp* **stood** /stud/) Ⓝ Not usually used in continuous tenses, e.g. *is/was -ing*, in 3, 6 and 8 below. For uses of 'stand' in special phrases such as *stand a chance, stand trial*, ⇨ the noun entries as at *ceremony, chance, feet, ground, reason, trial.* **1** *vi* to rise to, keep, an upright position: *We stood as the speaker came in. I was standing by the door. He was too weak to stand. The surprising news*

made my hair stand on end! **stand firm** to refuse to change one's opinion, decision etc. **stand still** to stay upright and not move at all. **2** *vt* to put (a person, thing) in an upright position: *stand a child in the corner/on a chair; stand a ladder against a wall.* **3** *vi* to have the height mentioned when upright: *She/The ladder stands two metres tall. The building stands 100 metres high.* **4** *vi* to be in the position, place, mentioned: *The house stands on a hill/by the river/opposite the station.* **5** *vi* to be in the condition or position mentioned: *As affairs/things stand* (= As the situation, condition, is now), *I can't help you. My debts/savings stand at £100. He stands alone* (= has no equal) *as a politician. Where does Tom stand* (= What is his comparative position) *in class? I stand to lose/gain money on the deal. She stands high in the opinion of the staff. I stand corrected* (i.e. I accept that I was wrong). **6** *vi* (of an order, decision etc) to remain in force: *The rule will stand for another year.* **7** *vt* to survive (a trial etc): *stand the test of time.* **8** *vt* to put up with (a person, thing): *I can't stand much more of this noise! She won't be able to stand this hot weather. I've stood all I can of your nonsense! I can't stand you* (= I do not like you at all). Ⓝ Usually used with '*can/could*'. ⇨ stand for sth(c). **9** *vt* (*informal*) to buy (a person) a drink or meal: *I'll stand you a beer.*

stand about/around to do nothing (because one is lazy, not given orders etc): *Don't stand about doing nothing!*

stand apart (from sth) to keep oneself separate (from other people) (because one is shy, too proud etc).

stand aside (a) to move to one side (e.g. to let a person pass). **(b)** to watch and do nothing: *Why stand aside and let others decide for you?*

stand at sth to be at the amount, price, size, temperature etc mentioned: *The temperature stands at 30°C. The price stands at £50.*

stand back (from sth) (a) to move back (from an event etc): *The police asked the crowd to stand back (from the car crash).* **(b)** to be situated away (from something): *The house stands 50 metres back from the road.* **(c)** to cause one's thoughts to be separated (from something): *A judge must often stand back from the detail and look at the general picture of events.* **(d)** to refuse or agree not to decide, act, (on something): *This is one issue from which you mustn't stand back.*

stand between sb/sth (and sb/sth) to be an obstacle between one person, thing and another: *Only one more exam stands between me and a degree.*

stand by (a) to be ready for action: *The ambulances are standing by.* Hence '**stand-by** *nu* a state of readiness: *be on stand-by.* **(b)** to watch without doing anything: *How can you stand by and let the children suffer?* **stand by sb** to be ready to support, help a friend, colleague, relation etc: *I'll stand by you whatever happens.* **stand by sth** to be true to a promise, continue to support something etc: *I stand by everything I said.*

stand down (a) (of a candidate, a person in authority) to withdraw: *He stood down in favour of the younger person.* **(b)** (*legal*) (of a witness in a law court) to leave the witness box after giving evidence.

stand for sth (a) to be a candidate for a position: *stand for the city council* **(b)** to represent a word or words: *'BA' stands for 'British Airways'*. **(c)** *(informal)* to put up with nonsense, rudeness etc: *I won't stand for this bad behaviour*. ⓝ Usually negative with *'will not'*.

stand in (for sb) to take the place of a person who is ill, absent etc. Hence '**stand-in** *nc* a person who does this.

stand-offish ⇨ separate entry.

stand out to be obvious (e.g. because better): *The reason/cause/fact stands out above everything. His work stands out from all the others*. ⇨ mile(1). **stand out against sth (a)** to be firm in one's position against an employer, piece of legislation etc: *We shall stand out against such a policy*. **(b)** to be obvious against a background: *The mountains stood out against the clear blue sky*.

stand over sb to watch a worker, student etc closely: *I can't do it while you're standing over me*.

stand up to rise to an upright standing position. **stand sb up** *(informal)* to fail to keep an appointment with a boyfriend etc: *I've been stood up! She'll never stand me up again!* **stand sth up** to put an object in an upright position. **stand up for sb** to defend, take the side of, a person, esp in an argument. **stand up to sb** to (be ready to) resist an attacker. **stand up (to sth) (a)** to remain in a good condition after long or hard use: *metals that stand up well to high temperatures*. **(b)** to manage to survive a test: *Will this theory stand up to examination? This evidence would not stand up in any law court*.

stan·dard[1] /ˈstændəd/ *adj* (usually *attrib*) of the usual or accepted kind: *a standard size/method; standard English; standard authors* (i.e. those accepted as very good).

'**standard time** *nu* the time officially adopted for (part of) a country.

stan·dard[2] /ˈstændəd/ *nc* **1** something used as a test or measure of something: *You must set yourself high standards (of work/behaviour). What standard are you using to judge it by? They enjoy a high standard of living* (= a life with money, food, possessions, holidays etc). **be up to/below standard** to be equal to/not so good as normal etc: *Their work is not up to standard*. **2** a flag used to represent an important person, family etc: *the royal standard*.

stan·dard·ize (also **-ise**) /ˈstændədaɪz/ *vt* to make (something) the same size, shape, quality etc: *The parts of vehicles are usually standardized*. **stan·dard·iz·ation** (also **-is·ation**) /ˌstændədaɪˈzeɪʃn/ *nu*

stand-by /ˈstændbaɪ/ *nc* ⇨ stand by.

stand-in /ˈstændɪn/ *nc* ⇨ stand in (for sb).

stand·ing[1] /ˈstændɪŋ/ *adj* (*attrib*) established and in use: *a standing committee* (i.e. that meets regularly); *a standing order for milk* (i.e. for regular delivery); *a standing order* (for money to be paid from a bank regularly, e.g. for rent); *a standing invitation* (= a permanent one to come or go when one wants to).

stand·ing[2] /ˈstændɪŋ/ *nu* **1** duration: *a debt of long standing*. **2** a position or reputation: *people of high standing*.

stand-off·ish /ˌstænd ˈɒfɪʃ/ *adj* (*derog*) (of a person's character) unfriendly; arrogant and unwilling to speak, take part.

stank /stæŋk/ *pt* of stink[2].

stan·za /ˈstænzə/ *nc* (*pl* —s) (*literature*) a group of rhymed lines forming a division in some forms of poem.

staple[1] /ˈsteɪpl/ *adj* (*attrib*) forming the main part: *Their staple food is corn. Is coffee the staple export of Brazil?*

staple[2] /ˈsteɪpl/ *nc* **1** a main article or product for trading: *Cotton is one of the staples of India*. **2** a main kind of food in a diet: *Rice is a staple in China*.

staple[3] /ˈsteɪpl/ *nc* **1** a U-shaped metal pin hammered into a surface, used to hold something in position. **2** a U-shaped part of a padlock. **3** a piece of wire as pushed through sheets of paper and bent to hold them together.

staple[4] /ˈsteɪpl/ *vt* to fasten or fit (something) with a staple: *stapling papers together*.

sta·pler /ˈsteɪplə(r)/ *nc* a small device used for fastening papers together with staples(3).

star[1] /stɑː(r)/ *nc* **1** any one of the points of light seen in the sky at night. **see stars** to seem to see flashes of light, e.g. as the result of a hit on the head. **2** a shape or design with points round it, suggesting a star by its shape: *a five-star hotel* (= one of the highest standard). **3** a badge of rank (worn by officers on the shoulder-strap). **4** a planet or heavenly body regarded as influencing a person's fortune etc: *be born under a lucky star*. **5** a person who is famous as a singer, actor, actress etc: *film stars; pop stars; a tennis star*.

'**star·dom** /-dəm/ *nu* the state of being a star(5).

'**star·fish** *nc* a sea-animal shaped like a star.

'**star·less** *adj* (*attrib*) with no stars to be seen: *a starless sky/night*.

'**star·light** *nu* the light from the stars. Hence '**star·lit** *adj*

star[2] /stɑː(r)/ *v* (**-rr-**) **1** *vt* to mark (something) with a star shape: *I've starred the important articles to read*. **2** *vi* **star (in sth)** to be a star(5) (in a play, film etc). **3** *vt* (of a play, film etc) to present (a person) as a star(5).

star·board /ˈstɑːbəd/ *nu* the right-hand side of a ship or plane as one faces forward. Compare port[2].

starch[1] /stɑːtʃ/ *nu* **1** a white, tasteless substance as present in potatoes, grain etc. **2** this substance in powdered form, used to stiffen cloth etc.

starchy *adj* (**-ier, -iest**) of, like, containing, starch: *starchy foods*.

starch[2] /stɑːtʃ/ *vt* to make (cloth) stiff using starch(2).

stare[1] /steə(r)/ *nc* a staring look: *a rude stare*.

stare[2] /steə(r)/ *v* **1** *vi* **stare (at sb/sth)** to look (at a person, thing) with wide eyes and a fixed look: *Do you like being stared at? She was staring into the distance. They all stared with astonishment*. **2** *vt* **stare one in the face** (*fig*) to be obvious, be right in front of one: *The book I was looking for/The truth was staring me in the face*.

stark[1] /stɑːk/ *adj* **1** bare and harsh: *the stark facts; a stark landscape*. **2** (*attrib*) complete: *stark madness*.

stark[2] /stɑːk/ *adv* completely: *stark raving mad; stark naked*.

star·ling /ˈstɑːlɪŋ/ *nc* a kind of small bird often

seen in towns, black with a short tail.

star·ry /'stɑːrɪ/ adj (attrib) having light from, shining like, stars: a starry night.

,starry-'eyed adj (informal; usually derog) full of ideas but impractical: starry-eyed reformers.

start¹ /stɑːt/ n **1** nc the first part of a journey, activity etc: make an early start; the start of a race. The holdiay was fun from start to finish. Compare beginning. **for a start** (informal) = to begin with. **make a fresh start** to start again from the beginning. **2** n sing an amount of time or distance by which one person starts before others: They didn't give me much/any start. He got a good start (= a position of economic or social advantage) in life/business. **3** nc a sudden movement of surprise, fear etc: He sat up with a start. **by fits and starts** ⇨ fit²(3).

start² /stɑːt/ v **1** vt,vi (to cause a person, thing) to take the first action, go into operation: I start work at eight. The engine won't start. He can't start the car. It's starting to rain. It started raining. When can we start? When did the pain start? Don't start complaining yet. (N) For the differences between start, begin and commence, ⇨ begin(1). Opp stop²(1). **2** vt,vi to set out on (a journey): Let's start early. We started our trip last Friday. They've started their journey home. ⇨ start out. **3** vt to cause (something) to happen to (a person), exist: The smoke started her coughing. The news started me thinking. We've started a fund to help the poorer students. How did the fight start? What started the argument? **4** vi to make a sudden, uncontrolled movement (because of pain, surprise, fear etc): The bang made me start. ⇨ start at sth(b).

start at sth (a) to start(1) at the time mentioned: We started at 6 o'clock. **(b)** to start(5) because of something: They started at the sight of the old woman.

start back to start(2) to return: It's time we started back.

start for a place to leave one place to go to another: I try to start for school early.

start from a place to start(1) a journey from: The race starts from Paris. **start (sth) from scratch** ⇨ scratch²(3).

start off (informal) to start(1) to talk, show etc: He started off by describing the scenery/by pressing the switch. **start sb off (on sth)** to cause a person to start(1) talking, working etc: My coach started me off on short exercises. The photograph started her off on a boring account of a day in Vienna.

start out (on sth) to start(2): start out on a journey. **start out (to do sth)** to take the first steps: start out to write a novel.

start sth up (a) to make an engine begin to work: start up an old car. **(b)** to start(1) a conversation etc with a person: I started up a conversation with somebody on the bus this morning. **(c)** to set up a business: start up a business in Cornwall. **start (sb) up (in sth)** to set (oneself, a person) up (in a career): We need money to start ourselves up in computers/an interesting career.

to start with = to begin with.

start·er /'stɑːtə(r)/ n **1** a person who gives a signal for a race to start. **2** a device used to make an engine start to work. **3** (informal) the first course of a meal. **4** a person, animal etc taking part in a race: There are only four starters.

start·ing-block /'stɑːtɪŋ blɒk/ nc the place where runners start in a race.

start·ing-point /'stɑːtɪŋ pɔɪnt/ nc a place where an activity starts: several starting-points for the big race; a useful starting-point in one's career; read this book as a starting-point.

startle /'stɑːtl/ vt to cause (a person) to be suddenly surprised or to move in surprise: The noise startled me. I was startled by the light. It startled me out of my sleep. I was startled out of my wits (= made suddenly very afraid).

start·ling /'stɑːtlɪŋ/ adj very surprising: startling news; a startling sucess.

starve /stɑːv/ v **1** vt,vi (to cause a person, animal) to suffer or die from hunger: she starved to death. **be starved of sth** (fig) to be in great need of something: The children were starved of love. **2** vi (informal) to feel very hungry: What time's dinner? I'm starving!

star·va·tion /stɑː'veɪʃn/ nu suffering or death caused by having no food: die of starvation.

state¹ /steɪt/ adj (often S-) of, belonging to a state(2): state documents/ownership/secrets; State schools (i.e. paid for by a government); State affairs (i.e. matters concerning government.)

state² /steɪt/ n **1** n sing a condition in which a person or thing is (in appearance, mind, health etc): The house was in a dirty state. She's in a poor state of health. **state of affairs** general condition(s): The report described the bad state of affairs of the economy. **state of play** the position of people etc in an argument, contest etc as likely to be successful or not. **2** nc (often S-) an organized political community with a government; territory in which this exists: How many States are there in the United States of America? **affairs of State** (= matters concerning government of a State). **3** nu ceremonial formality: The President was received in state. **lie in state** (of the dead body of an important person) to be placed on view in a public place before burial.

state·less adj (of a person) not recognized as a citizen or national of any country.

state·ly adj (-ier, -iest) impressive; dignified: the stately homes of England (= those belonging to the aristocracy).

state³ /steɪt/ vt (formal) to express (an opinion etc) in words, esp carefully, fully and clearly: state one's views.

stated adj made known; announced: at stated times/intervals; at the time stated.

state·ment /'steɪtmənt/ n **1** nc something that is stated, esp a formal announcement: make a statement to the press about the affair. **2** nc (legal) a formal account of an event or set of facts: make a statement to the police. **3** nu the act of stating something formally. **4** nc a list of money spent, received, owed etc: a bank statement. **5** nc (gram) a form of sentence giving information, e.g. She's ill. The meeting starts at 8. I gave it to him. **6** nc (computers) an instruction or set of instructions in a program.

states·man /'steɪtsmən/ nc (pl **-men**) **1** a person taking an important part in politics. **2** a person with skill and ability in politics.

'states·man·like adj showing skill and ability in public affairs.

'states·man·ship /-ʃɪp/ *nu*

stat·ic¹ /'stætɪk/ *adj* not changing; in a state of balance: *Sales are static.*

,static elec'tricity *nu* the kind that builds up on the surface of some materials, e.g. nylon.

stat·ic² /'stætɪk/ *nu* (*tech*) interference in the signal received by a radio or TV.

sta·tion¹ /'steɪʃn/ *nc* **1** a place, building etc where a service is organized and provided: *a bus/ police station.* **2** a place where trains stop. **3** a system, company, providing radio or TV programmes. **4** a social position, rank: *people in all stations of life.* **5** a small military base: *a naval station.*

'station-master *nc* the person in charge of a railway station.

sta·tion² /'steɪʃn/ *vt* (usually *passive*) to put (people, things) in a certain place: *Police were stationed along the route.*

sta·tion·ary /'steɪʃnrɪ/ *adj* not moving or changing: *remain stationary; a stationary vehicle.*

sta·tion·er /'steɪʃənə(r)/ *nc* a shop selling stationery.

sta·tion·ery /'steɪʃnrɪ/ *nu* paper, envelopes, pens etc for writing.

stat·is·ti·cal /stə'tɪstɪkl/ *adj* of statistics: *The report included statistical evidence.*

stat·is·ti·cal·ly /-klɪ/ *adv*

stat·is·ti·cian /ˌstætɪ'stɪʃn/ *nc* a person who uses statistics to examine information and form opinions.

stat·is·tics /stə'tɪstɪks/ *n* **1** *n pl* information in the form of quantities that can be compared: *Statistics suggest that the population will double in ten years' time.* **2** *nu* the science of the types and uses of statistics.

sta·tive /'steɪtɪv/ *adj* (*gram*) of a stative verb.

'stative verb *nc* (*gram*) a verb describing a condition or state (and not an activity, event or action), as in 'Do you *believe* me?' 'I *know* that'. ⃝ A stative verb is not usually used in continuous tenses, e.g. *is/was -ing.* Compare dynamic verb, non-stative verb.

statue /'stætʃuː/ *nc* a representation of a person, animal etc in stone, metal, wood etc.

statu·ette /ˌstætʃʊ'et/ *nc* a small statue.

stat·ure /'stætʃə(r)/ *nu* **1** a person's natural height. **2** (*fig*) intellectual or moral quality: *the stature of a great writer.*

sta·tus /'steɪtəs/ *nu* or *sing* a person's legal, social or professional position in relation to others: *What is your status here?* (e.g. Are you a citizen?) *She achieved high status as a poet.*

'status symbol *nc* something thought to be evidence of success in one's career or in life, e.g. a large, expensive car.

stat·ute /'stætʃuːt/ *nc* a written law.

statu·tory /'stætʃʊtrɪ/ *adj* done, required, by a statute: *statutory control of incomes.*

staunch¹ /stɔːntʃ/ *adj* (of a friend, supporter etc) loyal; firm.

staunch·ly *adv*

staunch² /stɔːntʃ/ *vt* to stop the flow of (esp blood).

stave¹ /steɪv/ *nc* **1** (*music*) = staff¹(4). **2** (*poetry*) = stanza.

stave² /steɪv/ *vt* (*pt,pp* **—d** or **stove** /stəʊv/)
stave sth off to keep off, delay, hunger, disaster, bankruptcy etc.

stay¹ /steɪ/ *nc* **1** a short period living in a place: *a stay in hospital; leave after a short stay with friends.* **2** *a stay of execution* (a) a short delay ordered by a judge (e.g. while new evidence is considered). (b) any similar delay before a punishment or any unfortunate event.

stay² /steɪ/ *v* **1** *vi* to continue to be in a particular place: *stay in the house/at home/in bed/outside. I'm afraid I can't stay long — I'm very busy.* ⇨ stay in/on/out. **stay put** (*informal*) to refuse to leave a place: *I refuse to move — I'm staying put!* **2** *vi* to (continue to) live at a place: *I'm staying with friends in London. Have you anywhere to stay? I once stayed there for four weeks.* **come to stay** (a) to come and live at a place: *The Browns are coming to stay (with us) next month.* (b) to (seem to) become permanent: *I think high unemployment in Europe has come to stay.* **3** *vi* to continue to be in the condition mentioned: *stay asleep/ awake; stay single* (= not get married). **4** *vt* to stop or delay (an activity, condition): *stay the course of a disease* **5** *vt,vi* to be able to continue, finish, (the work): *Will they be able to stay the course of the race/training? That horse has no staying power* (i.e. gives up easily).

stay abreast of sth to keep oneself informed about the latest methods, machines etc.

stay ahead (of sb) to keep oneself in front (of rivals).

stay at a place to live for a short time at: *I'm staying at a hotel in Devon.*

stay away (from sb/sth) (a) to be absent (from school, work etc). (b) (often used as an order) to agree not to go near (a person, place etc one may wish to harm): *Stay away from my sister!*

stay behind to be in a place after others have left: *I stayed behind to finish my work.*

stay down (a) to keep oneself in a bent or low position (to avoid harm). (b) (of food) to (be able to) remain in the stomach.

stay for sth to continue to be at a person's home and eat a meal, at a meeting and hear the next speaker etc: *Can you stay for dinner?*

stay in (a) to not go outside: *I'm staying in tonight to wash my hair.* (b) (of a machine part, plug etc) to remain in position: *This pin won't stay in.* **stay in a place** to be a visitor in: *stay in Venice.*

stay off sth to avoid eating, drinking, smoking, something (because it is harmful): *You should stay off alcohol/cigarettes.*

stay on (at sth) to continue to live (at a place), study (at a college) etc for an extra length of time. ⇨ stop on at sth.

stay out (a) to continue to be outside or away from home: *Don't stay out after dark.* (b) to continue to be on strike: *How long have the miners stayed out this time?* **stay out of sth** to be where one cannot be involved in trouble or difficulty, or where one cannot be reached: *stay out of trouble/ debt/prison; stay out of sight/reach/earshot.*

stay up (a) to delay going to bed: *I stayed up reading until very late.* (b) to fail to fall or sink: *I can't stay up (in water) wearing shoes. This house has stayed up for 100 years.*

stay with sb (a) to be a guest at the home of a person: *I'm staying with my aunt.* (b) to keep at the same level as a competitor. *Stay with it!* (*informal*) Keep trying!

STD /ˌes tiː 'diː/ *abbr* **1** Subscriber Trunk Dialling (the code number that enables a person to telephone another city or area directly and not through an operator). **2** sexually transmitted diseases: *an STD clinic.* ⇨ sexually.

std *written abbr* standard.

stead·fast /'stedfɑːst/ *adj* (*formal*) **1** firmly fixed: *a steadfast look/gaze.* **2** loyal: *a steadfast supporter.*

stead·fast·ly *adv*

steady¹ /'stedɪ/ *adj* (**-ier, -iest**) **1** firmly fixed or supported; not likely to fall over: *make a table steady; a steady hand; not very steady on one's legs.* **2** not changing in amount, speed etc: *make a steady profit/income; a steady speed/rate of progress.* **3** (of a person, behaviour) having, keeping to, a regular (good) pattern: *a steady worker.* Opp unsteady.

stead·ily /'stedɪlɪ/ *adv* in a regular manner: *His health is getting steadily worse.*

steadi·ness *nu*

steady² /'stedɪ/ *adv* **go steady** (*informal*) to go out with one boyfriend or girlfriend regularly.

steady³ /'stedɪ/ *nc* (*pl* **-ies**) (*informal*) a regular boyfriend or girlfriend.

steady⁴ /'stedɪ/ *vt,vi* (*pt,pp* **-ied**) (to cause a person, thing) to become steady: *steady a boat; drink brandy to steady one's nerves; steady oneself by holding the rail.*

steak /steɪk/ *nc,nu* (also *attrib*) (a piece of) meat (or fish) for frying, grilling etc: *a steak sandwich.*

steal /stiːl/ *v* (*pt* **stole** /stəʊl/, *pp* **stolen** /'stəʊlən/) **1** *vt,vi* to take (a person's property) secretly and without right: *Someone has stolen my watch.* ⇨ show¹(4). **2** *vi* to move, come, go, secretly and quietly: *He stole out of the room.* **3** *vt* to do or get (something) secretly: *He stole a glance at her in the mirror.*

steam¹ /stiːm/ *nu* **1** the gas that rises from boiling water: *steam-covered windows.* **2** the power obtained from steam: *Ships and trains used to run on steam.* **3** (*fig*) (*informal*) energy. **let off steam** to release energy or emotion and become less excited: *I wrote an angry letter to the newspaper in order to let off steam.* **run out of steam** to become exhausted: *I wanted to finish the work last night but I ran out of steam.* **under one's own steam** without help from others: *It's OK—I can get to the meeting under my own steam.*

,steam·'roller *nc* a heavy engine with wide wheels, used to make roads flat. □ *vt* (*fig*) to use force to destroy opposition to (a plan etc).

'steam·ship *nc* a ship driven by steam.

steam·er (**a**) = steamship. (**b**) a kind of pot in which food is steamed.

steamy *adj* (**-ier, -iest**) of, like, full of, steam: *the steamy heat of the tropics.*

steam² /stiːm/ *v* **1** *vi* to give out steam: *This coffee is steaming.* **2** *vi* to move, work etc (as if) under the power of steam: *a ship steaming along the river.* **3** *vt* to cook (food) by the use of steam: *steam fish.* **4** *vt* to do (something) using steam: *steam open an envelope.* **5** *vi* **steam up** to become covered with steam changing to water: *The windows steamed up.*

,steaming 'hot *adj* (of a liquid, esp a drink)

extremely hot: *steaming hot coffee.*

steel¹ /stiːl/ *nu* iron mixed with carbon or other elements, used to make knives, tools etc.

,steel 'band *nc* a group of musicians who use old oil drums etc as instruments.

,steel 'wool *nu* fine steel lengths (used for scouring and polishing).

'steel·works *n sing* or *pl* a factory where steel is made.

steel² /stiːl/ *v reflex* to harden (oneself) in order to do something: *steel oneself/one's heart* (*against pity*).

steep¹ /stiːp/ *adj* (**—er, —est**) **1** (of a slope) rising or falling sharply: *a steep gradient/path/descent.* **2** (*informal*) (of a demand) unreasonable; excessive: *It's a bit steep that I should pay for all of your clothes!*

steep·ly *adv*

steep·ness *nu*

steep² /stiːp/ *v* **steep (sth) (in sth)** **1** *vt,vi* to soak (something) (in liquid): *steep sheets in bleach.* **2** *vt* (usually *passive*) (*fig*) to fill (a person) with (a mental quality); give (a person) thorough knowledge (of a subject): *steeped in ignorance; a scholar steeped in Greek history.*

steeple /'stiːpl/ *nc* a pointed church tower.

steeple·chase /'stiːpl,tʃeɪs/ *nc* a race with obstacles such as fences, hedges and ditches.

steer¹ /stɪə(r)/ *nc* a young ox raised for beef.

steer² /stɪə(r)/ *vt,vi* to direct the course of (a boat, ship, car etc): *steer a car through a narrow space; steer north; steer by the stars.* **2 steer clear of (sb/sth)** (*fig*) to avoid a bad person, trouble etc.

'steering-wheel *nc* the wheel used to control the direction of a car, boat etc.

stel·lar /'stelə(r)/ *adj* (*formal*) of stars: *stellar light.*

stem¹ /stem/ *nc* **1** a part of a plant coming up from the roots; part of a leaf, flower or fruit that joins it to the main stalk or twig. **2** a long, thin part like a stem, e.g. of a wineglass.

stem² /stem/ *vi* (**-mm-**) **stem from sb/sth** to have a person, thing as its origin: *His illness stems from the period he lived in the tropics.*

stem³ /stem/ *vt* (**-mm-**) to check, stop, (a flow) (of a liquid): *stem the flow* (*of blood*).

stench /stentʃ/ *nc* a strong, bad smell.

sten·cil¹ /'stensl/ *nc* a thin sheet of metal, cardboard etc with letters or designs cut through it.

sten·cil² /'stensl/ *vt* (**-ll-**, *US* also **-l-**) to produce (a pattern, word etc) by using a stencil.

step¹ /step/ *nc* **1** the act of stepping once; distance covered by doing this: *He was walking with slow steps.* **step by step** gradually: *Driving's not difficult if you take it step by step.* **in/out of step (with sb/sth)** (**a**) marching, dancing using/not using the same foot, rhythm etc as. (**b**) in/not in agreement (with): *He's out of step with the official view.* **watch one's step** (*informal*) to be careful, behave well. **2** the sound made by walking: *I recognize that step.* ⇨ footstep. **3** one of a series of movements for a particular dance, march etc. **4** one in a series of actions in order to do something: *take steps to prevent the spread of the disease; a false step* (= a mistaken action). *What's the next step?* (= What must I/we do next?) **be one step ahead (of sb)** to have an advantage (over a person). **5** one of a series of stages towards something: *It's a step towards better housing. When do you get your next step up?* (i.e. promotion?) **6** (one of) a series of raised levels used when going from one level to another, esp outside a building or door: *We walked up the steps to the entrance. The child was sitting on the bottom step.* Compare stair. **7** one of the parts of a ladder on which one puts one's feet. **8** (*pl*) (also *a pair of steps*) = stepladder.

step² /step/ *v* (**-pp-**) **1** *vi* to move by putting one's foot down and then moving the other one (esp in a careful way): *step across a puddle; step over a brick; step into a boat.* **2** *vt* to step(1) (the distance or direction mentioned): *step a metre. Step this way, please.* **3** *vt* to arrange a series of (instructions, pictures etc) so that they progress in a clear order.

step aside to move out of the way of a person, vehicle etc.

step back to move backwards (e.g. because surprised).

step down to give up a position of importance or authority.

step forward to come forward (to offer help, information etc).

step in to become involved (either to help or to interfere).

step off *a vehicle* to get off a bus, boat, train etc.

step on it! (*informal; usually imperative*) Hurry up! (esp used to a driver).

step outside (*informal*) (to ask a person) to leave a party, meeting etc, esp to have a fight.

step up sth to increase or improve something: *step up production/attendance.*

step- /step/ *prefix* (used to show a relationship not by blood but by a later marriage):

'**step·child**/**·son**/**·daughter** *nc* a child of an earlier marriage of one's wife or husband.

'**step·brother**/**·sister** *nc* a child of an earlier marriage of one's stepfather or stepmother.

'**step·father**/**·mother** *nc* one's parent's later husband or wife.

step·ladder /'step lædə(r)/ *nc* a folding ladder with steps(7).

ster·eo /'sterɪəʊ/ *n* (*pl* **—s**) (also *attrib*) **1** *nu* (*informal*) = stereophonic. *in stereo* using stereophonic sound. **2** *nc* a stereophonic record-player: *a stereo cassette(-player).*

ster·eo·phon·ic /ˌsterɪə'fɒnɪk/ *adj* (of a record(-player), radio or TV broadcast etc) giving sound from two places.

ster·eo·type¹ /'sterɪətaɪp/ *nc* **1** a fixed pattern of behaviour, thinking etc. **2** a typical example: *He's the stereotype of a male teacher.*

ster·eo·typed *adj* (of words, ideas etc) used and repeated (too) often: *There are many stereotyped greetings such as 'Hi' and 'How do you do?'*

ster·ile /'steraɪl/ *adj* **1** not able to produce offspring, fruit etc. Compare fertile(3). **2** (*fig*) without a productive purpose; producing nothing: *a sterile discussion.* Compare fertile(2). **3** free from living germs: *sterile bandages.*

ste·ril·ity /stə'rɪlətɪ/ *nu*

ster·il·iz·ation (also **-is·ation**) /ˌsterəlaɪ'zeɪʃn/ *nu*

ster·il·ize (also **-ise**) /'sterəlaɪz/ *vt* to make (a

person, bandage etc) sterile.

ster·ling¹ /'stɜːlɪŋ/ *adj* (*attrib*) **1** (of gold and silver) of standard value. **2** (*fig; attrib*) (of a person's character etc) deserving praise because good and genuine: *sterling qualities.*

ster·ling² /'stɜːlɪŋ/ *nu* British money: *payable in sterling.*

stern¹ /stɜːn/ *adj* (**—er, —est**) **1** demanding and enforcing obedience: *a stern teacher.* **2** severe; strict: *a stern face/look.*

stern·ly *adv*

stern·ness *nu*

stern² /stɜːn/ *nc* the back end (of a ship or boat).

ster·num /'stɜːnəm/ *nc* (*pl* **—s**) (*anat*) (also called *breastbone*) the narrow bone in the front of the chest connecting the collar-bone and the top ribs.

ster·oid /'stɪərɔɪd/ *nc* (*med*) a substance used in medicine (often with hormones) that directly affects the body organs.

stetho·scope /'steθəskəʊp/ *nc* (*med*) an instrument used for listening to the heart, lungs etc.

stew¹ /stuː/ *nc,nu* (a dish of) stewed meat with vegetables etc: *lamb stew.* **be in/get into a stew (about sb/sth)** to be/become very worried (about a person, money, promise etc).

stew² /stjuː/ *vt,vi* to cook (food), be cooked, in water or juice, slowly: *stewed chicken/fruit.* **stew in one's own juice** (to be left) to suffer the result of one's own bad actions.

stew·ard /'stjuːəd/ *nc* **1** a man who attends to the needs of passengers in a ship or plane. **2** a man who organizes a race-meeting, public meeting, etc: *The hecklers were thrown out by the stewards.*

stew·ard·ess /'stuːədɪs/ *nc* a woman steward(1).

stick¹ /stɪk/ *nc* **1** a thin branch broken, cut or fallen from a bush, tree etc. **be in a cleft stick** to be undecided about which (of two possibilities) to choose. **2** such a branch cut, shaped etc for a special purpose: *The old man cannot walk without a (walking-)stick.* ⇨ hockey stick. **have/get hold of the wrong end of the stick** to misunderstand things completely. **3** a long piece (of chalk, sealing-wax, celery etc).

stick² /stɪk/ *v* (*pt,pp* **stuck** /stʌk/) **1** *vt* to push (something pointed) (into, through etc): *stick a fork into a potato; stick a pin through the paper.* **2** *vi* (of something pointed) to be in something: *The needle has stuck in my finger.* **3** *vt,vi* (to cause something) to become fastened (as if) with glue, paste etc: *stick a stamp on a letter; stick a picture in a book; stick two pieces together; jam sticking the paper to the floor.* **4** *vi* to become fixed and not easily moved: *This drawer has stuck and I can't close it. I'm stuck and I can't get out. The key stuck in the lock.* **5** *vt* (*informal*) to put (a person, thing) in a place or position quickly or carelessly: *He stuck his pen behind his ear/his hands in his pockets/the papers in a drawer. Stick that box on the table for a minute.* ⇨ stick sth down(b). **6** *vt* (*informal*) to put up with (an uncomfortable or bad thing or situation): *I can't stick this job much longer.* ⇨ stick it out. **7** *vi* (*informal*) (of memories) to remain for a long time: *It stuck in my mind for ages.* **8** *vi* (*informal*) (of an accusation) to be believed: *You can say he stole it but can you make* *it stick?*

stick around (*informal*) to stay in or near a place: *Stick around—we may need you.*

stick at sth to work steadily at an activity: *She sticks at the work for hours.* **stick at nothing** ⇨ nothing².

stick by sb (*informal*) = stand by sb.

stick sth down (a) to fasten something (as if) with glue etc. (b) (*informal*) to put an object down: *Stick it down in the corner.* (c) (*informal*) to write something down quickly: *I'll stick your address down in my diary.*

stick sth on to fasten something on a surface (as if) with glue. **be stuck on sb/sth** (*informal*) to be very attracted to a person, idea etc: *I'm stuck on you/on the idea of buying a boat.*

stick out to stand out beyond the surface: *His ears stick out.* ⇨ mile(1). **stick sth out** to put one's tongue, head etc out: *He stuck his tongue/chest out.* ⇨ also neck¹(1). **stick it out** (*informal*) to put up with something unpleasant (until the end): *I hate this job but I'll have to stick it out for a while.* **stick out for sth** to refuse to give in until one gets something better: *stick out for higher wages.*

stick to sb to be loyal to a person. **stick to sth** (a) to refuse to change or abandon a decision, an agreement, the rules, a belief. (b) to refuse to move away from the facts, the subject or topic being discussed. ⇨ also gun¹.

stick together (*informal*) to remain loyal or friendly; give each other support; stay close to each other.

stick up to stand above the surface: *The building stuck up behind the older ones and looked completely out of place.* **stick sb/sth up** (*sl*) to use guns etc to steal from a person, bank etc. Hence **'stick-up** *nc* such a kind of robbery. **stick up for oneself/sb/sth** to give one's confident support to one's own ideas, a friend, a person's rights etc.

stick with sb/sth to remain loyal to, continue to support, a person, idea etc: *stick with a friend/socialism.* **be/get stuck with sb/sth** to be/become unable to stop using, owning, being involved with, a person, thing: *I'm stuck with this old bike/this boring work/my poor assistant.*

stick·er /'stɪkə(r)/ *nc* a label, sign, notice etc with glue on the back.

stick-in-the-mud /'stɪk ɪn ðə mʌd/ *nc* (*derog*) a conservative, stubborn person.

stick·up /'stɪkʌp/ *nc* ⇨ stick sb/sth up.

stick·ler /'stɪklə(r)/ *nc* **stickler for sth** a person who insists on the importance of something: *He's a stickler for being on time.*

sticky /'stɪkɪ/ *adj* 1 (**-ier, -iest**) that sticks or tends to stick to anything that touches it: *sticky fingers.* **come to a sticky end** ⇨ end¹(4). 2 (*informal*) making, likely to make, objections, be unhelpful etc: *My bank manager was very sticky about an overdraft.*

stiff¹ /stɪf/ *adj* (**—er, —est**) 1 not easily bent or changed in shape: *a sheet of stiff cardboard; have a stiff leg/back.* **keep a stiff upper lip** ⇨ upper. 2 hard to stir, work, move etc: *a stiff paste.* 3 difficult to do: *a stiff climb/examination.* 4 formal, unfriendly: *be stiff with the new neighbours.* 5 large in degree: *a stiff (= strong) breeze; a stiff*

(= strong) *drink; a stiff* (= high) *price.*

stiff·ly *adv*

stiff·ness *nu*

stiff² /stɪf/ *adv* thoroughly: *be bored/scared stiff.*

stiff³ /stɪf/ *nc* (*sl*) a dead body.

stiff·en /'stɪfn/ *vt,vi* (to cause a part of the body etc) to become stiff(1,2).

stifle /'staɪfəl/ *vt* to keep (a feeling etc) back: *stifling a yawn.*

sti·fling *adj* hot and heavy: *a stifling heat/atmosphere.*

sti·fling·ly *adv: stiflingly hot.*

stig·ma /'stɪgmə/ *nc* (*pl* **—s**) 1 (*fig*) a mark of shame or disgrace: *the stigma of imprisonment.* 2 (*science*) the part of a flower that receives pollen.

stile /staɪl/ *nc* a kind of step used to climb over a fence, gate etc.

still¹ /stɪl/ *adj* 1 (usually *pred*) without movement or sound: *Please keep/sit/stand still.* 2 (*attrib*) (of liquid) not having bubbles: *still wine/juice.*

still 'life *nc,nu* (*pl* **still lifes**) (a/the) painting of objects, flowers, fruit etc.

still·ness *nu*

still² /stɪl/ *adv* 1 (of an action, situation) continuing as in the past: *He's still busy. She still loves him/loves him still. Will you still be here when I return? Is your brother still here? It's still cold outside/raining/difficult to find work. She still believes he stole it. I still can't drive. He still wondered what had happened.* Ⓝ For the differences between *still*, *already* and *yet*, ⇨ already. 2 (used to make stronger comparisons): *Tom is tall, but Mary is still taller/taller still. It took still more of my time and money.* Ⓝ *'Even'* is also possible and is more usual. 3 (used to join sentences) in spite of that: *He behaved badly; still he is your brother so you must help him. I understand you were hungry, but still you could have asked.* Compare yet(5).

still³ /stɪl/ *n sing* (*poetic*) a quiet and calm atmosphere: *in the still of the night.*

still⁴ /stɪl/ *vt* (*formal*) to make (a person, group) quiet and calm: *I tried to still the anxious parents.*

still·born /'stɪlbɔːn/ *adj* 1 (of a child) dead when born. 2 (*fig*) (of an idea, plan) never used.

stilt·ed /'stɪltɪd/ *adj* (*derog*) (of written style, talk, behaviour etc) too formal and unnatural.

stilts /stɪlts/ *n pl* (also *a pair of stilts*) two poles with a high support for the foot, used to raise the user (e.g. a clown) from the ground: *walk on stilts.*

stimu·lant /'stɪmjʊlənt/ *nc* 1 a drink (e.g. coffee, brandy), drug etc that increases bodily or mental activity. 2 anything that encourages a person (e.g. praise, hope of gain).

stimu·late /'stɪmjʊleɪt/ *vt* to encourage (a person); make (a person) more determined: *stimulating him to make greater efforts.*

stimu·lat·ing *adj*

stimu·lus /'stɪmjʊləs/ *nc* (*pl* **-li** /-laɪ/) 1 something that encourages (a person to do something, an activity etc): *a stimulus to industrial growth.* 2 (*science*) something, e.g. light, heat, electricity etc that causes an animal or plant to do something.

sting¹ /stɪŋ/ *n* 1 *nc* a sharp, often poisonous, pointed organ of some insects (e.g. bees). 2 *nc* a substance on a plant causing pain when touched. 3 *nc* a sharp pain caused by the sting of an insect or plant. **4** *nc,nu* any sharp pain of body or mind: *feel the sting of a whip/of hunger.*

sting² /stɪŋ/ *v* (*pt,pp* **stung** /stʌŋ/) **1** *vt,vi* (to have the power) to injure (a person, animal) (as if) with a sting: *A bee stung me on the cheek. Do ants sting?* **2** *vt* to cause sudden, strong physical or mental pain to (a person): *He was stung by his enemy's insults.* **3** *vi* (of parts of the body) to feel strong pain: *His fingers were still stinging after touching the plants.* **4** *vt* (*informal*) to charge (a person) an excessive price: *He stung me for £5.*

stin·gy /'stɪndʒɪ/ *adj* (**-ier, -iest**) (*informal; derog*) (of a person) spending, using or giving something unwillingly: *Don't be so stingy with the sugar!*
stin·gi·ly /-əlɪ/ *adv*
stin·gi·ness *nu*

stink¹ /stɪŋk/ *nc* an unpleasant smell: *There's a terrible stink in the fridge.* **kick up a stink (about sth)** (*informal*) to complain angrily and noisily.

stink² /stɪŋk/ *v* (*pt* **stank** /stæŋk/ or **stunk** /stʌŋk/, *pp* **stunk**) **1** *vi* to have an unpleasant smell: *stink to high heaven* (= very much). *Her breath stank of garlic.* **2** *vt* to fill (a place) with a stink: *You'll stink the place out with your cheap cigars!* **3** *vi* (*fig; informal*) to be very bad, have a bad reputation: *Her name stinks in this town. That business deal stinks* (of deceit).

stint¹ /stɪnt/ *n* **1** *nc* a fixed amount (of work): *do one's daily stint.* **2** *nu* **without stint** without limit (of effort etc).

stint² /stɪnt/ *vt* (often *reflex*) to give (oneself, a person) a small amount or share: *Don't stint yourself—there's plenty of food.*

stipple /'stɪpl/ *vt* to draw, paint, (something) using dots.

stipu·late /'stɪpjʊleɪt/ *vt* **stipulate (that)** *sth* to state formally (something) as a necessary condition (that): *It was stipulated (that) the goods should be delivered within three days.*

stipu·la·tion /ˌstɪpjʊ'leɪʃn/ *nc* a condition stated: *The job is yours on the stipulation that you pass the test.*

stir¹ /stɜː(r)/ *n* **1** *n sing* an excited atmosphere: *The news caused quite a stir in the village.* **2** *nc* an act of stirring(2): *give the soup a stir.*

stir² /stɜː(r)/ *v* (**-rr-**) **1** *vt,vi* (to cause a person, thing) to move: *A breeze stirred the leaves. Nobody was stirring in the house* (i.e. everyone was resting, in bed). **2** *vt* to move a spoon etc round and round in (liquid etc) in order to mix it thoroughly: *stir one's tea.* **3** *vt* to excite (a person, mind etc): *The story stirred the boy's imagination.* **4** **stir sth up** (*fig*) to cause trouble, anger etc: *She's always stirring up trouble among the staff.*
stir·ring *adj* (*attrib; literary*) exciting: *stirring tales of adventure.*

stir·rup¹ /'stɪrəp/ *nc* a metal piece hanging down from a saddle, for a rider's foot.

stir·rup² /'stɪrəp/ *nc* (*anat*) a bone in the ear.

stitch¹ /stɪtʃ/ *nc* **1** one act of passing thread in and out of cloth etc to join or decorate. **a stitch in time saves nine** (*saying*) a small amount of work done now may save a lot of work later. **2** the thread etc seen after making a stitch(1). **3** one turn of wool over needles when knitting. **4** a particular kind of stitch: *a chain-stitch.* **5** *n sing* a

sharp pain in the side (as caused sometimes when running). **in stitches** (*informal*) laughing a lot: *The actor had me in stitches* (= made me laugh a lot).

stitch² /stɪtʃ/ *vi,vt* to sew (something) up: *stitch a dress; stitch a wound.*

stoat /stəʊt/ *nc* a kind of small, furry animal from Europe and Asia, called *ermine* when it has its white winter coat.

stock¹ /stɒk/ *n* **1** *nc,nu* a supply or store of goods available for sale, distribution or use, esp goods kept by a trader or shopkeeper: *We have large stocks of tinned peas.* **(be) in/out of stock** to be available/not available. **take stock of sth** (*fig*) to consider a situation etc (before deciding etc): *Let's take stock of the situation before we spend any more money on the project.* **2** *nc,nu* a supply (of anything): *a good stock of information; get in stocks of wood for the winter.* **3** *nu* = livestock. **4** *nc,nu* (a number of) shares in the capital of a business company. **5** *nu* a line of ancestry: *a woman of Irish/farming stock.* **6** *nu* liquid in which bones etc have been boiled, used for making soup etc.
'stock·broker *nc* a person, business that buys and sells shares for investors.
'stock exchange *nc* (often the —) (also *attrib*: *stock-exchange*) a place where shares are bought and sold: *stock-exchange practices.*
'stock market *nc* (often the —) (also *attrib*: *stock-market*) (business at) the stock exchange: *stock-market prices.*
'stock·pile *vt, nc* (to collect) a large amount of supplies.
'stock·room *nc* one for storing stock(1).
'stock-taking *nu* the act of counting and recording stock(1).

stock² /stɒk/ *vt* **1** to have supplies of (goods for sale): *We stock several different pens.* **2** to supply, equip, (a place) with stock(1): *stock shelves; stock a shop.*

stock·ist /-ɪst/ *nc* a business that stocks (particular goods) for sale: *Your nearest stockist is Smith's.*

stock·ade /stɒ'keɪd/ *nc* a wall of upright posts, built as a defence.

stock·ing /'stɒkɪŋ/ *n* a thin, tight covering, usually made of nylon, for a woman's leg.

stocky /'stɒkɪ/ *adj* (**-ier, -iest**) (of a person, animal, plant) short, strong and fat.
stock·ily /-əlɪ/ *adv*: *stockily built.*

stodge /stɒdʒ/ *nu* (*sl; derog*) heavy and tasteless food, e.g. boiled rice that has been cooked badly.
stodgy /'stɒdʒɪ/ *adj* (**-ier, -iest**) (*derog*) (a) (of food) heavy and tasteless. (b) (of writing style) heavy and dull.

sto·ic /'stəʊɪk/ *nc* a person with great self-control when suffering difficulties, pain etc.
sto·ic·al /-kl/ *adj* of, like, a stoic.
sto·ic·al·ly /-klɪ/ *adv*

stoke /stəʊk/ *vt* **stoke sth (up)** to put coal etc on the fire of an engine, furnace etc: *stoking (up) the furnace.*
stoker *nc* a workman who stokes a furnace etc.

stole¹ /stəʊl/ *nc* a long piece of material worn over the shoulders.

stole² /stəʊl/ *pt* of steal.

stolen /'stəʊlən/ *pp* of steal.

stol·id /'stɒlɪd/ *adj* not easily excited.

stom·ach¹ /ˈstʌmək/ n 1 nc the part of the body into which food passes to be digested: *Don't work on an empty stomach.* 2 nc (*formal*) = abdomen(1). 3 nu **have no stomach for sth** to dislike or disapprove of it: *I have no stomach for war.*
'**stomach-ache** nc,nu (a) pain in the abdomen.

stom·ach² /ˈstʌmək/ vt to put up with (something unpleasant): *How can you stomach the violence in so many films today?* Ⓝ Used with 'can/could' in questions or negative statements.

stomp /stɒmp/ vi to stamp or tread heavily: *stomp about the room in anger.*

stone¹ /stəʊn/ adj (*attrib*) made of stone: *a stone wall.*

stone² /stəʊn/ n 1 nu a solid mineral material that is not a metal: *a wall made of stone; sandstone; limestone.* **have a heart of stone** ⇨ heart(2). 2 nc a piece of stone (smaller than a rock): *a fall of stones down a hillside.* **leave no stone unturned** to try every possible means: *We'll leave no stone unturned until we find her.* **within a stone's throw (of sth)** very near (to a place, building): *She lives within a stone's throw of the school.* 3 nc (also **precious stone**) = jewel(1). 4 nc a piece of stone of a definite shape, for a special purpose: *a tombstone.* 5 nc a hard seed in some fruit: *a cherry/peach/plum/mango stone.* 6 nc any small hard piece: *a hailstone; gallstones.* 7 (*pl —*) a unit of measurement of mass, 14lb (or 6·35 kg), esp of a person: *I weigh 10 stone.*
'**Stone Age** n (the —) the period when people used weapons and tools made of stone (before the use of metals was known).
,**stone-'blind/-'cold/-'dead/-'deaf** adj completely blind etc.
'**stone·mason** nc a man who cuts, prepares and builds with stone.
'**stone·ware** nu (pots etc made of) clay mixed with pieces of stone.
'**stone·work** nu the part(s) of a building made of stone.

stoned /stəʊnd/ adj (*informal*) 1 under the influence of drugs(2). 2 drunk.

stony /ˈstəʊnɪ/ adj (**-ier, -iest**) 1 having, covered with, many stones: *stony soil/ground; a stony path/road.* 2 (usually *attrib; derog*) hard, cold and unsympathetic: *a stony stare.*
,**stony-'broke** adj (*informal*) completely without money.
ston·ily /-əlɪ/ adv in a stony(2) manner.

stood /stʊd/ pt,pp of stand².

stool /stuːl/ nc 1 a seat without a back or arms, usually for one person: *a piano-stool.* **fall between two stools** to fail because one cannot or did not decide between two possibilities. 2 (*pl*) (*med*) solid waste from the body.
'**stool-pigeon** nc (*fig*) a person used by the police to trap a criminal.

stoop¹ /stuːp/ nc (usually *sing*) a stooping position of the body.

stoop² /stuːp/ v 1 vt,vi to bend the body forwards and downwards: *He stooped (down) to pick up the stone.* 2 vi (*fig*) **stoop to (doing) sth** to lower oneself morally by doing something bad: *He's a man who would stoop to anything* (= who would not hesitate to do anything bad).

stop¹ /stɒp/ nc 1 an act of stopping or being

stopped: *The train came to a sudden stop. Traffic was brought to a complete stop.* **put a stop to sth** to cause it to stop or end: *I'll put a stop to their fight.* 2 a place at which buses etc stop: *Where's the nearest bus-stop?* 3 a device used to change a note on a musical instrument, e.g. a knob or lever that controls the pipes of an organ. **pull out all the stops** (*fig*) to make a great effort. ⇨ also full stop.

stop² /stɒp/ v (**-pp-**) 1 vt,vi (to cause a person, machine etc) to put an end to action, movement, progress etc: *Stop doing that! How do I stop this alarm clock? My watch has stopped. Stop (the car) at the next corner. You must ring the bell to stop the bus. Can't you stop biting your nails? We stop work/working at 6 o'clock. He never stops talking. It's stopped raining. The rain has stopped.* Opp start²(1). **stop dead** to stop suddenly: *The car stopped dead.* **stop at nothing** ⇨ nothing². **stop short of sth** ⇨ short²(1). 2 vt **stop sb/ sth ((from) doing sth)** to prevent a person, thing: *Nothing can stop the disease (from) spreading. What can stop us (from going if we want to)? You ought to stop the children making so much noise.* 3 vt to fill, close, (a hole etc) in a pipe etc: *stop a leak with a piece of cloth.* ⇨ stop sth up. 4 vi to stay in a place: *Can you stop for dinner? I'll stop with the baby while you go shopping.* ⇨ stop at a place. 5 vt to prevent payment of (a cheque, bill etc).

stop at a place = stay at a place. **stop at sth** to stop doing something: *She won't stop at stealing small things—soon she'll take big ones.*

stop behind = stay behind (which is more usual).

stop by to visit a person at home etc for a short time: *I'll stop by later for a chat.*

stop for sth = stay for sth.

stop sb/sth from doing sth ⇨ 2 above.

stop in to stay inside because one has been ordered to: *I have to stop in tonight.*

stop off (at/in a place) to stop a journey and stay (at or in a place) as a tourist: *We're stopping off at/in Delhi for a few days.*

stop on at sth to remain at school, university etc after one could have left or after others have left. ⇨ stay on (at sth).

stop out = stay out.

stop over to break one's journey (by air) and stay at a place for a very short time: *Let's stop over in Paris.* Hence '**stop·over** nc such a break.

stop up = stay up(a): *Don't stop up too late.* **stop sth up** to block a hole etc: *stop up a hole with a wooden stick.* ⇨ stopper.

stop·gap /ˈstɒpgæp/ nc something used as an alternative for a short time: *We can use this room as a stopgap until the other one has been painted.*

stop·over /ˈstɒpəʊvə(r)/ nc ⇨ stop over.

stop·page /ˈstɒpɪdʒ/ nc 1 a block (in a pipe etc). 2 an act of stopping work, payment etc: *The bad weather caused many stoppages, and the building work was seriously delayed.*

stop·per /ˈstɒpə(r)/ nc an object that closes an opening of a bottle, pipe etc.

stop-press /ˌstɒp ˈpres/ n (*GB*) items of news put in a newspaper after printing has begun.

stop·watch /ˈstɒpwɒtʃ/ nc a kind of watch used to time events such as races.

stor·age /'stɔːrɪdʒ/ *nu* (also *attrib*) (space used for, money paid for) the storing of goods: *put one's furniture in storage; storage tanks.*

'storage heater *nc* a kind of electric heater that stores heat.

store¹ /stɔː(r)/ *n* **1** *nc* an amount or supply (of something) kept for use when needed: *have a large store of tinned food in the house.* **2** *nc* a large shop selling many different goods: *the big department stores of London.* ⇨ also chain store. **3** *nu* **in store** (a) kept ready for (future) use: *That's a treat in store.* (b) about to happen; coming: *Who knows what the future has in store (for us)?* **lie in store** to be waiting to happen: *Who knows what lies in store for you if you move to London?* **4** (*pl*) goods etc of a particular kind: *naval and military stores.* **5** *nu* **set great/little/no/not much store by sth** to consider something to be of much/little etc value or importance.

store² /stɔː(r)/ *vt* **store sth (up) (in sth)** to collect and keep supplies, food, facts, information etc for future use (in a room, warehouse, computer, the mind etc).

storey (*US* = **story**) /'stɔːrɪ/ *n* (*pl* —**s**, *US* -**ies**) a floor or level in a building.

-storeyed (*US* = **-stor·ied**) /-'stɔːrɪd/ *suffix* having the number of storeys mentioned: *a six-storeyed building.*

stork /stɔːk/ *nc* a kind of large, long-legged, usually white bird that lives near water.

storm¹ /stɔːm/ *nc* **1** an occasion of violent weather conditions: *a thunder/rain/dust/sand-storm.* **a storm in a teacup** a lot of excitement about something unimportant: *Their complaints were a storm in a teacup because they were easy to deal with.* **ride out a storm** (*fig*) to survive problems, trouble, attack etc. **2** a violent outburst (of feeling): *a storm of protests/cheering/applause/abuse.* **take sth by storm** (a) to capture a town etc using a sudden, violent attack. (b) to win great approval from an audience: *The new group has taken the music world by storm.*

'storm-cloud *nc* a heavy, grey cloud as a sign of a storm.

stormy *adj* (-**ier**, -**iest**) (a) marked by a storm(1): *stormy weather; a stormy night.* (b) marked by strong, angry feeling: *a stormy meeting/discussion.*

storm² /stɔːm/ *v* **1** *vi* to use violence and anger; shout angrily. **2** *vt* to force (a way) into (a building etc); capture (a place) by sudden and violent attack: *The men stormed (their way) into the building/stormed the building.*

story¹ /'stɔːrɪ/ *nc* (*pl* -**ies**) **1** an account of (real or imaginary) events: *stories of ancient Greece.* **2** (esp used by and to children) an untrue statement: *Don't tell stories, Tom.* **a tall story** an obvious lie.

'story-book *nc* a child's book of stories. **a story-book ending** a happy end (to a situation).

'story-teller *nc* a person who tells stories.

story² /'stɔːrɪ/ *nc* (*US*) = storey.

stout¹ /staʊt/ *adj* (—**er**, —**est**) **1** strong and not easily broken or worn out: *stout boots for mountain-climbing.* **2** (*attrib*) determined and brave: *a stout supporter; a stout heart.* **3** (of a person) fat: *She's growing too stout to walk far.*

,stout-'hearted *adj* full of courage. Compare faint-hearted.

stout·ly *adv*

stout² /staʊt/ *nu* a kind of strong, dark beer.

stove¹ /stəʊv/ *nc* a closed apparatus burning wood, coal, gas, oil etc, used for cooking, heating etc. Compare cooker(1).

stove² /stəʊv/ *pt,pp* of stave².

stow /stəʊ/ *vt* **stow sth (away)** to pack things (away) for a time: *stow cargo in a ship's holds; stow things away in the attic.*

stow·away /'stəʊəweɪ/ *nc* a person who hides in a ship or plane (until after it starts) in order to make a journey without paying. □ *vi* to become a stowaway.

straddle /'strædl/ *vt* to sit or stand across (something) with the legs on either side: *straddle a horse/motorbike/fence.*

straggle /'strægl/ *vi* **1** to grow, spread, in an irregular or untidy manner: *roses straggling over the fences.* **2** to be (far) behind a group while moving forward.

strag·gler *nc* a person who straggles(2).

straight¹ /streɪt/ *adj* (—**er**, —**est**) **1** without a bend or curve: *a straight line/road; straight hair.* **2** level; even; upright: *put a picture straight.* **3** (*attrib*) continuous: *a straight path between both houses.* **4** (*pred*) in good order: *put a bed/room/the books straight.* **put the record straight** ⇨ record²(2). **5** (of a person, behaviour, performance) honest; serious: *a straight manner/answer.* **keep a straight face** ⇨ face¹(2). **6** (of a play, film etc) simple and serious (and not a musical, farce etc). **7** (*informal*) not owing or being owed money: *If you give me £2, we'll be straight.* **8** (*informal*) (of a person) heterosexual. **9** (of alcoholic drink) without anything added: *a straight whisky.*

straight·ness *nu* the quality of being straight(1).

straight² /streɪt/ *adv* **1** not bending or curving: *Keep straight on. Look straight ahead. Sit straight up in your chair.* **2** by a direct route; without stopping: *Come straight home. Go straight to the doctor.* **3** immediately: *Wash your hands and go straight to bed.* **straight away** immediately: *Let's get married straight away.* **straight out** without hesitating: *He came straight out with his opinion of my work.* **4** **go straight** (after a life as a criminal) to begin to live an honest life.

straight³ /streɪt/ *n sing* (the —) **1** the straight part of something, esp the final part of a track or race-course: *The two horses were together as they entered the final straight.* **2** **the straight and narrow** (*fig*) an honest and moral way of behaving.

straight·en /'streɪtn/ *v* **1** *vt,vi* (to cause something) to become straight(1,2,3): *straighten a picture.* **2** *vt* **straighten sb/sth out** (a) to remove bends or curves in something. (b) to remove doubt, ignorance, so that a person understands: *These books will soon straighten you out.* (c) to settle a misunderstanding etc: *straighten out a confused situation.* **3** *vi, v reflex* **straighten (oneself) up** to make oneself upright after bending.

straight·for·ward /ˌstreɪt'fɔːwəd/ *adj* **1** serious and honest; with nothing hidden or avoided: *a* *straightforward person/explanation.* **2** easy to understand or do: *written in straightforward language.*

straight·for·ward·ly *adv*

strain¹ /streɪn/ *n* **1** *nu* the condition of being stretched; the force used: *The rope broke under the strain.* **2** *nc,nu* something that tests one's mental strength; a great demand on one's strength etc: *Do you suffer from the strain of modern life? He has been under (a) severe strain. She's suffering from mental/nervous strain.* **3** *nc* a tendency in a person's character: *There is a strain of insanity in the family.* **4** *nc* a breed (of animals, plants etc): *strains of beans that can survive frost.*

strain² /streɪn/ *v* **1** *vt,vi* **strain ((at) sth)** to stretch (something) tightly by pulling: *a dog straining at its lead.* **2** *vt,vi* to make the greatest possible effort (using something): *I had to strain (my eyes) to see it.* **3** *vt* to injure (something) by straining(2): *strain a muscle; strain one's eyes.* **4** *vt* (*fig*) to force (a belief etc) beyond a limit or what is right: *strain the belief of one's listeners.* **5** *vt* to separate (a liquid) from solids by passing (it) through cloth, netting etc: *strain the vegetables; strain off the water.*

strain·ed *adj* (**a**) looking nervous and tired: *a strained face/expression; look strained.* (**b**) not natural: *a strained laugh.*

strain·er *nc* a device used for straining(5): *a tea-strainer.*

strait /streɪt/ *nc* **1** (S- in names) (often *pl*) a narrow passage of water connecting two seas: *the Straits of Gibraltar; the Magellan Strait.* **2** (*pl*) trouble; difficulty: *We seem to be in financial straits.*

strait-jacket¹ /'streɪt dʒækɪt/ *nc* a jacket with long sleeves, tied round a mentally ill or violent person to prevent movement.

strait-jacket² /'streɪt dʒækɪt/ *vt* **1** to use a straight-jacket on (a person). **2** (*fig*) to prevent the development of (a person, plan).

strait-laced /ˌstreɪt 'leɪsd/ *adj* (*derog*) (of a person) too strict, conservative, serious.

strand /strænd/ *nc* **1** any of the threads, hairs, wires etc twisted together into a rope, cable or cloth. **2** a hair. **3** (*fig*) a line of development (in a story etc).

strand·ed /'strændɪd/ *adj* in a helpless position, without money, friends etc: *be left stranded in a foreign country.*

strange /streɪndʒ/ *adj* (**—r, —st**) **1** difficult to accept; surprising because not known, seen, heard etc before: *I heard a strange noise. Truth is stranger than fiction.* **2 be strange to sth** to be fresh or new to a situation: *The village boy was strange to city life.*

strange·ly *adv* in a strange way: *behave/act strangely.* **strangely (enough) . . . ,** It's hard to believe, but . . .

strange·ness *nu*

stranger /'streɪndʒə(r)/ *nc* a person one does not know; person in a place where he or she is not known: *My dog always barks at strangers.*

strangle /'stræŋgl/ *vt* to kill (a person) by squeezing her or his throat.

'strangle·hold *nc* (usually *fig*) a tight hold: *The new laws have put a stranglehold on our imports.*

strap¹ /stræp/ *nc* a length of leather etc used to

fasten things together or to keep something (e.g. a wrist-watch) in place.

strap² /stræp/ *vt* (**-pp-**) to fasten or hold (a person, thing) in place with a strap: *strap on a wrist-watch. Is the baby strapped in?*

strata /'strɑːtə/ *n pl* ⇨ stratum.

strat·agem /'strætədʒəm/ *nc,nu* (*pl* **—s**) (the use of) a trick to deceive a person.

stra·te·gic /strə'tiːdʒɪk/ *also* **-gic·al** /-kl/) *adj* of, serving the purpose of, strategy: *a strategic retreat/answer.*

stra,tegic 'weapon *nc* a weapon aimed at the enemy's land. Compare tactical weapon.

stra·te·gi·cal·ly /-klɪ/ *adv*

strat·egy /'strætɪdʒɪ/ *n* **1** *nu* the art of planning an activity, e.g. a war. **2** *nc,nu* (*pl* **-ies**) (an instance of) skill in organizing and doing something: *What strategy will you use to persuade her?*

strat·ify /'strætɪfaɪ/ *vt,vi* (*pt,pp* **-ied**) (to cause rock etc) to be formed in layers: *stratified rock.*

strat·ifi·ca·tion /ˌstrætɪfɪ'keɪʃn/ *nu*

strato·sphere /'strætəsfɪə(r)/ *n* (the **—**) (*science*) the layer of atmospheric air between about 10 and 60 km above the earth's surface.

stra·tum /'strɑːtəm/ *nc* (*pl* **-ta** /-tə/) (*tech*) **1** a layer of rock etc in the ground. **2** a social class or division.

straw /strɔː/ *n* **1** *nu* dry cut stalks of wheat, barley, rice and other grains, used as material for making mats, bedding for cattle etc. **2** *nc* a single piece of straw. **not worth a straw** worth nothing. **the last straw** an addition to a series of bad acts, experiences etc that makes a situation no longer bearable: *He had missed the bus and forgotten his coat, so the rain was the last straw.* **3** *nc* a thin tube of paper or plastic, used for sucking up liquid: *suck lemonade through a straw.*

'straw-coloured *adj* pale yellow.

straw·ber·ry /'strɔːbrɪ/ *nc* (*pl* **-ies**) (also *attrib*) (a plant with) a soft red fruit with tiny yellow seeds on its surface: *strawberry jam.*

stray¹ /streɪ/ *adj* (*attrib*) **1** without a home: *a stray cat.* **2** not in the usual or expected place: *a stray taxi.*

stray² /streɪ/ *nc* an animal without a home.

stray³ /streɪ/ *vi* (*pt,pp* **—ed**) **stray (from sth)** **1** to move away (without realizing) (from the right path, from one's friends etc): *stray from the path.* **2** (*fig*) to lose one's line of thought: *Don't stray from the point.*

streak¹ /striːk/ *nc* **1** a long, thin line or band: *blue streaks in the pattern; streaks of cloud in the sky.* **2** a trace: *There's a streak of cruelty in his character.* **3** a brief period: *The gambler had a streak of good luck.*

streaky *adj* (**-ier, -iest**) marked with, having, streaks: *streaky bacon.*

streak² /striːk/ *v* **1** *vt* to mark (something) with streaks: *white fur streaked with brown.* **2** *vi* (*informal*) to move very fast: *He streaked past the winning-post.* **3** *vi* (*informal*) to run in a public place without wearing clothes.

stream¹ /striːm/ *nc* **1** a very small river. **2** a current (of a river): *go up/down stream.* **3** a steady flow (of liquid, people, things): *a stream of blood/abuse. Streams of people were coming out of the railway station.* **4** (a division of) a class of children in groups according to ability and intelligence:

The clever boys and girls are in the A-stream.

stream² /striːm/ *v* **1** *vi* to flow freely; move continuously and smoothly in one direction: *Tears were streaming down his face.* **2** *vi* to float or wave (in the air): *Her long hair was streaming in the wind.* **3** *vt* to place (children) in streams(4).

stream·er /'striːmə(r)/ *nc* a long, narrow piece of paper, flag etc used as a decoration.

stream·line /'striːmlaɪn/ *vt* to make (something) more efficient (by getting rid of slow or wasteful methods etc): *We must streamline production* (e.g. in a factory).

'stream·lined *adj* **(a)** having a shape that offers least resistance to the flow of air, water etc: *streamlined cars.* **(b)** designed to be efficient: *a streamlined factory/kitchen.*

street /striːt/ *nc* (S- in names; abbr St) a specially prepared way for the movement of vehicles, people etc in villages, towns and cities: *I met a friend in the street today. He lives just across the street. I work in Oxford Street. I live at 4 Summer St, York.* Compare road(1). **the man in the street** ⇨ **man¹**(1). **streets ahead of sb/sth** superior to or more advanced than another person, piece of work etc. **streets apart** very different: *Those two brothers are streets apart.* **(not/ right) up one's street** (not/exactly) what one knows or likes to do: *I'm sorry, but mending bikes is not up my street.*

strength /streŋθ/ **1** *nu* the quality of being strong: *She hasn't the strength to walk upstairs. What is the strength of the pound compared to the dollar? How is the strength of alcoholic liquors measured?* **on the strength of** encouraged by, relying on: *I employed him on the strength of your recommendation.* **go from strength to strength** to become even more successful: *During the year, the business/my daughter went from strength to strength.* **2** *nc* something that helps to make a person or thing strong: *Knowing that you love me is my strength.* **3** *nu* power measured by numbers of people who can be used: *The police force is 500 below strength* (= needs 500 more people). *We must bring the army up to strength.* **in strength** in large numbers: *The supporters turned out in strength.*

strength·en /'streŋθn/ *vt,vi* (to cause something) to become strong(er): *strengthen a rope by adding wire.* Opp weaken.

strenu·ous /'strenjʊəs/ *adj* using or needing great effort: *work that is strenuous; making strenuous efforts; lead a strenuous life.*

strenu·ous·ly *adv*

stress¹ /stres/ *n* **1** *nu* the condition causing depression, mental illness, worry etc: *times of stress; be under enormous stress at work; the stress of poverty/fear.* **2** *nc,nu* an emphasis: *a school that lays stress on foreign languages. In 'extra' the stress* (force used when speaking) *is on 'ex-'.* **3** *nc,nu* **(a)** force on something producing strain: *stress on the sides of a boat/on the walls of a house/ on the legs of a chair.*

'stress-mark *nc* (lang) a mark that shows the stress(2) on a syllable, esp in phonetics. Ⓝ In this dictionary, / ' / marks the strongest (or *primary*) stress and /ˌ/ marks the weaker (or *secondary*) stress, as in *interfere* /ˌɪntə'fɪə(r)/.

stress² /stres/ *vt* to give emphasis or importance

to (something): *He stressed the value of exercise. You must stress the first syllable of 'into'.*

stretch¹ /stretʃ/ *nc* **1** an act of stretching or being stretched: *The cat woke and gave a stretch.* **at full stretch** using maximum effort, speed etc: *The factory workers were at full stretch.* **by any stretch of the imagination** however much one may try (to imagine something). **2** a continuous period of time, extent of country etc: *a two-hour stretch; a beautiful stretch of land.* **at a stretch** without stopping: *work 12 hours at a stretch.*

stretch² /stretʃ/ *v* **1** *vt,vi* (to cause something) to become wider, longer: *stretch a rope across a path; stretch out one's arm for a book.* **stretch one's legs** ⇨ **leg¹**(1). **2** *vi* **stretch out (a)** to try to touch, hold etc a person, thing by putting one's arm etc out at full length. **(b)** to lie at full length: *They were stretched out on the lawn.* **3** *vt* to make (an account, law etc) include or cover more than is strictly right or true: *stretch the law/a story.* **stretch a point** ⇨ **point¹**(6). **4** *vi* **stretching for sth** to extend over an area: *forests stretching for many miles.* **5** *vi* **stretch over sth** to extend over a period of time mentioned: *a holiday stretching over several weeks.*

stretch·er /'stretʃə(r)/ *nc* an apparatus of cloth between poles, used for carrying a sick or injured person.

strew /struː/ *vt* (*pt* —**ed**, *pp* —**n** /struːn/ or —**ed**) to throw (things) over a surface; cover (something) with things: *strew flowers over a path; strew a path with flowers.*

strick·en /'strɪkn/ *adj* badly affected (with illness, by fear etc): *stricken with malaria; stricken by fear.*

strict /strɪkt/ *adj* (—**er**, —**est**) **1** very serious about good behaviour: *a strict father; be strict with children.* **2** (attrib) clear and exact: *using the strict sense of the word. I told her in strictest confidence.*

strict·ly *adv* in a strict manner. **strictly speaking** being exact in interpreting the rules or law: *Strictly speaking, you shouldn't park here.*

stride¹ /straɪd/ *nc* (a distance covered in) one long step. **make great strides** to make good and quick progress. **take sth in one's stride** to do work, suffer misfortune etc without too much difficulty or worry.

stride² /straɪd/ *v* (*pt* **strode** /strəʊd/, *pp* (rare) **stridden** /'strɪdn/) **1** *vi* to walk with long steps: *stride along the road; stride off/away.* **2** *vt,vi* to pass over (something) using one long step: *stride across/over a ditch.*

strife /straɪf/ *nu* an angry disagreement (between people or groups): *industrial strife* (between workers and employers).

strike¹ /straɪk/ *nc* **1** (often **on strike**) an act of striking(8): *a strike of bus-drivers. They came out on strike yesterday. We've been* (out) *on strike for six weeks.* **call a strike** to order workers to begin a strike. ⇨ **general strike**. **2** an act of finding oil etc in the ground. **a lucky strike** (fig) a fortunate discovery.

'strike pay *nu* money paid to strikers from trade-union funds.

strike² /straɪk/ *v* (*pt,pp* **struck** /strʌk/) **1** *vt,vi* to hit, aim a blow at, (a person, thing): *He struck me on the chin. She struck the table with her fist. You* *struck first! **strike a blow for sth** ⇨ blow¹(1).* **strike at the root of sth** ⇨ root¹(3). **strike while the iron is hot** ⇨ iron¹(2). **be within striking distance** ⇨ distance. **2** *vt* to hit (something) with force: *The ship struck a rock. The tree was struck by lightning.* **3** *vt,vi* (to cause something) to be active by hitting etc: *strike a match. The clock struck (four).* **strike a note of sth; strike the right note** ⇨ note¹(5). **4** *vt* **strike sb (as sth)** to seem to a person to have an effect or quality mentioned: *Doesn't she strike you as odd! The room strikes you as warm when you enter it. It struck me as strange that she didn't telephone. How does the idea strike you?* (= What do you think about it?) **5** *vt* (usually *passive;* always *pp*) to cause (a person) to be (the condition mentioned): *I was struck dumb by the news* (i.e. I could not speak). *The noise struck fear into us. He was struck blind by the disease.* **6** *vt* to find (something): *We've struck oil!* **strike it rich** to become rich suddenly and quickly. **7** *vt* to achieve (an agreement etc) by comparing things: *strike a balance between freedom and security.* **strike a bargain** ⇨ bargain¹(1). **8** *vi* to stop working for an employer (in order to get more pay, better conditons etc): *strike for higher wages.* **9** *vt* to take down (sails, tents etc): *strike a flag/the sails.* **strike camp** to take down and pack up tents and equipment.

strike sb as sth ⇨ 4 above.

strike at sth to (try to) harm or damage something: *This policy strikes at one of our basic rights as citizens.*

strike sb down (**a**) to hit a person so that he or she falls down. (**b**) to cause a person to become very ill (or die): *She was struck down by cancer.*

strike sb off (sth) to remove a person from a list, membership of a professional body (esp of doctors or lawyers): *He's been struck off the list.*

strike sth off sth to remove a part from something with one blow: *strike a branch off a tree.*

strike out (at sb) to aim violent blows (at a person). **strike out (for a place)** (*formal*) to move with determination (towards a place): *strike out for home.* **strike out (on one's own)** to begin a new independent career, way of life etc. **strike sth out** to remove a name, item etc from a list by drawing a line through it.

strike sth through = strike sth out.

strike up (sth) to begin to play (a tune). **strike up sth (with sb)** to begin a friendship etc with (a person): *I struck up a conversation with her at the party.*

striker /ˈstraɪkə(r)/ *nc* **1** a worker who strikes(8). **2** (*football*) a player in an attacking position.

strik·ing /ˈstraɪkɪŋ/ *adj* attracting attention or great interest: *a striking appearance.*

strik·ing·ly *adv*

string¹ /strɪŋ/ *n* **1** *nc,nu* (a piece or length of) narrow cord, used for tying things, keeping things in place etc: *a ball of string; a piece of string.* **the first/second etc string** the first etc person, plan etc relied on for achieving one's purpose. **2** *nc* a tightly stretched length of nylon, wire etc, used for producing musical sounds in a guitar etc. **3** (*pl*) (the —s) musical instruments (in an orchestra) using strings(2). **4** (*pl*) strings(1) used to make puppets move. **have/keep sb on a string** to have/keep a person under one's control. **pull strings** to use one's personal influence to gain something: *I need that job badly—can you pull any strings?* **no strings attached** (*informal*) (of help, esp of money) without conditions about how the help is to be used or repaid. **5** *nc* a series of things threaded on a string(1): *a string of beads.* **6** *nc* a repetition (of types of things): *a string of abuse/curses/lies.*

,string(ed) 'instrument *nc* a musical instrument with strings(2), e.g. *violin, guitar, harp.*

stringy *adj* (**-ier, -iest**) having tough fibres: *stringy meat.*

string² /strɪŋ/ *vt* (*pt,pp* **strung** /strʌŋ/) **1** to put a string or strings on (a violin, tennis racket etc). **2** to put, tie or hang (something) on a string etc: *string beads; string lamps across a street.*

string sb along (*informal*) to deceive a person into believing or doing something: *He doesn't intend to marry the girl—he's just stringing her along.* **string along with sb** (*informal*) to stay with a friend, colleague etc (esp one with more experience): *String along with me and you'll soon learn how to cope.*

string (sth) out (to cause animals, things) to become positioned at intervals: *The horses were strung out across the field.* **string sth out** (*informal*) to take a long time to tell or explain a story, account, excuse etc.

string sth together to put words etc together to make a meaningful statement: *Can you string together a few words in Chinese?*

string sth up to hang flags, decorations etc on a high string.

string bean /ˌstrɪŋ 'biːn/ *nc* = runner bean.

strin·gent /ˈstrɪndʒənt/ *adj* (*formal*) (of rules) strict, severe; that must be obeyed: *take stringent measures against smoking.*

strin·gent·ly *adv*

strip¹ /strɪp/ *nc* **1** a long narrow piece (of cloth, land etc): *a strip of garden behind the house; a strip of paper.* ⇨ also comic strip. **2** (*modern informal*) clothes worn by players in a team: *the colourful strip of football teams.*

,strip car'toon *nc* = comic strip.

strip² /strɪp/ *v* (**-pp-**) **1** *vt,vi* (often **strip (sth) off**) take off (coverings, clothes, parts etc): *They stripped the house of all its furnishings. They stripped (off) (their clothes) and jumped into the lake.* **strip sth down** to divide an engine etc into parts (for servicing etc). **2** *vt* to take possessions etc away from (a person): *strip a man of his possessions/titles.*

,strip-'tease, 'strip-show *nc* an entertainment in which a man or woman takes off his or her clothes one by one.

stripe /straɪp/ *nc* **1** a band on a surface that is different in colour, material, texture etc: *a tiger's stripes.* ⇨ pin-striped. **2** a badge (often V-shaped) worn on a uniform, showing rank: *How many stripes are there on the sleeve of a sergeant?*

striped /straɪpt/ *adj* having stripes(1).

strip·per /ˈstrɪpə(r)/ *nc* a person who performs a strip-tease.

strive /straɪv/ *vi* (*pt* **strove** /strəʊv/, *pp* **striven** /ˈstrɪvn/) **1** to struggle: *striving with/against poverty/opposition/the enemy.* **2** to make great efforts: *strive for power/to win.*

strode /strəʊd/ *pt* of stride².

stroke¹ /strəʊk/ *nc* **1** (an act of making) a blow: *the stroke of a sword; 20 strokes of the whip.* **2** one of a series of regularly repeated movements, esp as a way of swimming or rowing: *swimming with a slow stroke; the breast-/side-/back-stroke.* **3** a single movement of the upper part of the body and arm(s), esp in games, e.g. cricket, golf. **4** a single effort; result of this: *I haven't done a stroke of work today.* *a stroke of luck* a piece of good fortune: *Meeting you that night was a stroke of luck.* *at a/one stroke* with one effort and immediately: *By giving them each a new pen, he stopped their quarrel at a stroke.* **5** (a mark made by) a single movement of a pen or brush: *cross a name out with one stroke of the pen; use thin/thick strokes.* **6** a sound made by a large bell striking: *on the stroke of three* (= at three o'clock). **7** a sudden attack of illness in the brain, with loss of feeling, power to move etc. ⇨ also heatstroke, sunstroke.

stroke² /strəʊk/ *nc* an act of stroking an animal, hair.

stroke³ /strəʊk/ *vt* to pass the hand along (the/a surface of something): *stroke a cat/one's beard.*

stroll /strəʊl/ *vi, nc* (to go for) a quiet, unhurried walk: *Let's go for a stroll.*

stroll·er *nc* a person who strolls.

strong¹ /strɒŋ/ *adj* (**—er**, **—est**) **1** (of the body) having power, able to do things easily: *as strong as a horse/an ox* (= very strong); *feeling stronger after a holiday/rest.* Opp weak(1). **2** (of the mind) feeling confident, sure, determined: *feel strong about the exam/interview/one's opinions; a strong imagination/will.* Opp weak(2). ⇨ strong-minded/-willed. **3** not easily broken, damaged etc: *a strong stick/rope; strong cloth; a strong structure.* Opp weak(3). **4** not easily defeated or changed: *strong beliefs/arguments.* Opp weak(4). **5** not easily beaten or defeated: *a strong candidate/runner.* Opp weak(5). **6** having a large effect on the senses: *a strong taste/colour/smell; strong coffee/tea; strong curry.* Opp weak(6). *strong drink* the kind containing alcohol. **7** determined or rude: *strong words/language.* **8** (*pred*) having the number mentioned: *an army 50 000 strong.*

'strong form *nc* (*lang*) the way of saying a word carefully or with emphasis, such as *can* /kæn/, *must* /mʌst/, *shall* /ʃæl/. Compare weak form.

,strong-'minded *adj* having a mind that is determined and energetic. Opp weak-minded.

'strong verb *nc* (*gram*) one that forms tenses with a vowel change, e.g. *sing, sang, sung.* Compare weak verb.

,strong-'willed *adj* very determined. Opp weak-willed.

strong·ly *adv* (used for emphasis to express seriousness, determination): *I strongly advise you to go.*

strong² /strɒŋ/ *adv* *be going strong* (*informal*) to continue to be active: *He's 80 and still going strong.*

strove /strəʊv/ *pt* of strive.

struck /strʌk/ *pt,pp* of strike².

struc·tur·al /'strʌktʃərəl/ *adj* **1** of a structure(1): *structural alterations to a building.* **2** (*lang*) of, concerning, grammatical structure: *a structural language course; a structural approach to learning*

English.

struc·tur·al·ly /-rəlɪ/ *adv*

struc·ture¹ /'strʌktʃə(r)/ *n* **1** *nc* (an arrangement or parts of) a building: *The National Theatre is a fine structure.* **2** *nu* the way in which parts are put together: *the structure of society/a building/an exam/a course of study.* **3** *nu* (*gram*) the way words etc are put together to form meaningful statements etc: *grammatical structure.*

struc·ture² /'strʌktʃə(r)/ *vt* to arrange (parts) in an organized way: *structuring one's methods/argument/course of study.*

struggle /'strʌgl/ *vi, nc* (to make) a great effort, fight: *struggling against difficulties/with the accounts. The thief struggled to get free. Join our struggle for freedom.*

strum /strʌm/ *vi,vt* (**-mm-**) *strum (on) sth* to play music (on a stringed instrument) (and often without great skill): *strum (on) the guitar.*

strung /strʌŋ/ *pt,pp* of string². □ *adj* ⇨ highly strung.

strut¹ /strʌt/ *nc* a piece of wood or metal used in a building etc to strengthen it.

strut² /strʌt/ *vi* (**-tt-**) to walk in a proud, self-important way: *strut about/along.*

strych·nine /'strɪkniːn/ *nu* a kind of strong poison.

stub¹ /stʌb/ *nc* **1** a short remaining end of a pencil, cigarette or similar object: *a stub of a tail.* **2** a section (of a cheque etc) (to be) kept as a record.

stub² /stʌb/ *vt* (**-bb-**) **1** to hit (one's toe) against something accidentally. **2** *stub sth (out)* to put out a cigarette etc by pressing it against something hard: *stub out a cigar.*

stubble /'stʌbl/ *nu* short pieces of something stiff, e.g. wheat, a beard.

stub·born /'stʌbən/ *adj* **1** (usually *derog*) (of a person) having a strong, determined will: *as stubborn as a mule* (= very stubborn) **2** difficult to deal with: *a stubborn disease; stubborn soil.*

stub·born·ly *adv*

stub·born·ness *nu*

stub·by /'stʌbɪ/ *adj* (**-ier, -iest**) short and thick: *stubby fingers.*

stuck /stʌk/ *pt,pp* of stick².

stuck-up /,stʌk 'ʌp/ *adj* (*informal; derog*) conceited; too proud.

stud¹ /stʌd/ *nc* a number of horses kept by one owner for a special purpose (esp for breeding or racing).

'stud-farm *nc* a place where horses are bred.

stud² /stʌd/ *nc* **1** a small device (two pieces joined together) put through holes in a shirt etc to fasten a collar (*collar-stud*) etc. **2** a device used on roads to separate lanes (and reflecting light from headlamps at night).

stud³ /stʌd/ *vt* (**-dd-**) (usually *pp*) to have (something) set in or scattered on the surface: *a crown studded with jewels; a sea studded with islands.*

stu·dent /'stjuːdənt/ *nc* a person who is studying or training: *medical students; foreign students studying English in London.*

stu·dio /'stjuːdɪəʊ/ *nc* (*pl* **—s**) **1** a workroom of a painter, sculptor, photographer etc. **2** a place where films are made. **3** a room from which radio or TV programmes are broadcast or in which recordings are made.

stu·dio couch /'stjuːdɪəʊ kaʊtʃ/ *nc* a couch that

can be used as a bed.

stu·di·ous /'stjuːdɪəs/ adj **1** (formal) enjoying and wanting to study. **2** (formal) very careful: with studious politeness.
stu·di·ous·ly adv

study¹ /'stʌdɪ/ n (pl **-ies**) **1** nu the act of studying: be fond of study. **2** nc a room used for studying. **3** nc (often pl) work related to a particular subject or topic: social studies. **4** nc something produced after studying, esp a report or book. **5** nc a drawing etc made for practice or as an experiment. **6** nc a piece of music as a technical exercise.

study² /'stʌdɪ/ v (pt,pp **-ied**) **1** vt,vi to give attention and time to learning or discovering (something): study medicine; study to become a doctor; study until very late at night. **2** vt to examine (something) carefully: study a map. **3** vt to give careful thought to (something): study a situation and decide. **4** vt to read and (try to) remember (something): study one's part for a play.

stuff¹ /stʌf/ nu **1** (informal) material of which something is made or which may be used for some purpose: What stuff will you use to fill the cushions? ⇨ stuffing. **2** (fig) type: He is not the stuff heroes are made of. **3** (informal) a substance or collection: Where did I leave my stuff? (= my personal things?); Do you call this stuff beer? **4** (sl) **do one's stuff** to show what one is capable of. **know one's stuff** to be expert in what one claims to know.

stuff² /stʌf/ vt **1** to fill (something) with, push (a substance) into, something: stuff feathers into a bag; stuff oneself with food; a head stuffed with silly ideas. **2** to put chopped up and specially flavoured food into (a chicken etc) before cooking it. **3** to fill the body of (a dead animal) with material to give it its original shape: a stuffed bird.
stuff·ing nu (a) material used for stuffing cushions. (b) food used for stuffing chickens etc.

stuf·fy /'stʌfɪ/ adj (-ier, -iest) **1** (of a room) not having fresh air. **2** (informal; derog) (of a person) easily shocked or offended; too formal. **3** (derog) (of language etc) dull; formal: a stuffy book.
stuff·ily /-əlɪ/ adv
stuffi·ness nu

stul·ti·fy /'stʌltɪfaɪ/ vt (pt,pp **-ied**) (formal) to make (effort etc) useless: stultify efforts to reach agreement.

stumble¹ /'stʌmbl/ nc an act or instance of stumbling.

stumble² /'stʌmbl/ vi **1** to hit the foot against something and (almost) fall: stumble over the root of a tree. The child stumbled and fell. **stumble across/on sth** (fig) to find something by accident. **2** to speak with pauses and mistakes: He stumbled over his words.
'stumbling-block nc something that causes difficulties or prevents progress.

stump¹ /stʌmp/ nc **1** a part of a tree remaining in the ground when the trunk has fallen or has been cut down. **2** anything remaining after the main part has been cut or broken off or has worn off: the stump of a pencil. **3** (cricket) one of the three upright pieces of wood at which the ball is bowled.

stump² /stʌmp/ v **1** vi to walk with stiff, heavy movements: stumping along/about. **2** vt (infor-

mal) to be too difficult for (a person): All the candidates were stumped by the second question. **3** vt (cricket) to end the innings of (a batsman) by touching the stumps with the ball.

stumpy /'stʌmpɪ/ adj (-ier, -iest) short and thick: a stumpy little man; a stumpy umbrella.

stun /stʌn/ vt (-nn-) **1** to make (a person) unconscious by a blow, esp on the head. **2** to shock or surprise (a person): He was stunned by the news of his father's death.

stung /stʌŋ/ pt,pp of sting².

stunk /stʌŋk/ pp of stink².

stun·ning /'stʌnɪŋ/ adj (informal) splendid: a stunning performance/dress.

stunt¹ /stʌnt/ nc (informal) a dangerous act needing skill or daring (as in a film or circus).
'stunt·man nc a person who does stunts.

stunt² /stʌnt/ vt to slow down the growth or development of (a person, body): Smoking will stunt your growth.

stu·pe·fy /'stjuːpɪfaɪ/ vt (pt,pp **-ied**) (formal) to make (a person) unable to think clearly: stupefied with drink/amazement.

stu·pen·dous /stjuː'pendəs/ adj (formal) amazingly good: a stupendous achievement.
stu·pen·dous·ly adv

stu·pid /'stjuːpɪd/ adj unintelligent; foolish: Don't be stupid enough to believe that.
stu·pid·ly adv
stu·pid·ity /stjuː'pɪdətɪ/ nc,nu

stu·por /'stjuːpə(r)/ nc,nu an almost unconscious condition caused by shock, drugs, drink etc: in a drunken stupor.

stur·dy /'stɜːdɪ/ adj (-ier, -iest) strong and solid: sturdy children; offer a sturdy resistance.
stur·di·ly /-əlɪ/ adv: a sturdily built bicycle.

stut·ter /'stʌtə(r)/ vi,vt, nc = stammer.
stut·ter·er nc a person who stutters.

sty¹ /staɪ/ nc (pl sties) = pigsty.

sty² (also **stye**) /staɪ/ nc (pl sties, styes) an inflamed swelling on the edge of the eyelid.

style¹ /staɪl/ n **1** nc,nu (a kind of) manner of doing anything: written in a delightful style. What do you know about the styles of architecture? **2** nu the quality that marks something done or made as superior, fashionable or distinctive: live in (grand) style. Did they live in European style when they were in Japan? **3** nc,nu (a kind of) fashion in clothes, hair etc: the latest styles in shoes/in hairdressing. **4** nc a general appearance, form or design: made in all sizes and styles. **5** nc (science) the part of a flower that supports the stigma.

style² /staɪl/ vt to design, make, (something) in a particular shape: new handbags styled by Italians.

styl·ish /'staɪlɪʃ/ adj **1** having good style(2): stylish living. **2** fashionable: stylish clothes.
sty·lish·ly adv: stylishly dressed.

sty·list /'staɪlɪst/ nc a person who is concerned with creating styles(3): a hair-stylist.

sty·lis·tic /staɪ'lɪstɪk/ adj of style(1).
styl·is·ti·cal·ly /-klɪ/ adv

sty·lize (also **-ise**) /'staɪlaɪz/ vt to represent or treat (art forms etc) in a particular, conventional style.

sty·lus /'staɪləs/ nc (pl —es) a part like a needle in a record-player, used to reproduce sound from records.

suave /swɑːv/ adj (often derog) (esp of a man)

pleasant and gracious (often insincerely) in manner.

suave·ly *adv*

sub /sʌb/ (*informal*) *abbr* **1** submarine. **2** substitute. **3** subscription.

sub·com·mit·tee /'sʌb kəmɪtɪ/ *nc* a committee formed from members of a main committee.

sub·con·scious /ˌsʌb'kɒnʃəs/ *adj* of thoughts, feelings etc of which one is not (completely) aware: *subconscious guilt/love/desire*. □ *n* (the —) subconscious activities in the mind. Compare unconscious².

sub·con·scious·ly *adv*

sub·con·ti·nent /ˌsʌb'kɒntɪnənt/ *nc* a mass of land large enough to be regarded as a separate continent but forming part of a larger mass.

sub·cu·taneous /ˌsʌbkjuː'teɪnɪəs/ *adj* (*science*) under the skin: *subcutaneous tissue*.

sub·di·vide /ˌsʌbdɪ'vaɪd/ *vt,vi* to divide (something already divided) into more divisions.

sub·di·vi·sion /ˌsʌbdɪ'vɪʒn/ *nc,nu*

sub·due /səb'djuː/ *vt* to bring (an angry person, a strong feeling etc) under control: *subdue one's hatred*.

sub·dued *adj* (a) (of sound) quiet. (b) (of light) not bright. (c) (of a person) quiet (and perhaps sad).

sub·hu·man /ˌsʌb'hjuːmən/ *adj* (*derog*) more like an animal than a human being: *subhuman behaviour*.

sub·ject¹ /'sʌbdʒɪkt/ *adj* **subject to sth** (*formal*) **1** owing obedience to something: *We are subject to the law of the land*. **2** having a tendency to suffer something: *Are you subject to colds?* **3** dependent on something: *The plan is subject to confirmation*.

sub·ject² /'sʌbdʒɪkt/ *nc* **1** a person who is a member of a nation: *British subjects*. **2** something (to be) talked or written about or studied: *This is an interesting subject of conversation. What subject are you studying?* **change the subject** to talk about something different. **3** a person, animal or thing (to be) treated or dealt with: *a subject for experiment*. **4** (*gram*) a word or phrase in a sentence which does the action of the verb or is described, as in 'The *book* is green', '*This* is yours' 'Did *they* go?' '*One of us* is wrong.' ⇨ preparatory subject.

'subject matter *nu* the plot, topic etc of a book or speech (contrasted with style).

sub·ject³ /səb'dʒekt/ *vt* **subject sb/sth (to sth)** **1** to bring, get, a country, nation, person under control: *The Romans subjected most of Europe to their rule*. **2** to cause (a person) to experience something: *subject a man to torture*.

sub·jec·tion /səb'dʒekʃn/ *nu*

sub·jec·tive /səb'dʒektɪv/ *adj* from, influenced by, personal thoughts and emotions (and not actual fact): *give a subjective impression of what happened*. Compare objective.

sub'jective case *nc* (*gram*) the use of a word or phrase as the subject(4) in a sentence. Compare objective case.

sub'jective form *nc* (*gram*) the form of a word used as a subject(4): *The subjective form of 'me' is 'I'*. Compare objective form.

sub·jec·tive·ly *adv*

sub·jec·tiv·ity /ˌsʌbdʒek'tɪvətɪ/ *nu*

sub·ju·gate /'sʌbdʒʊgeɪt/ *vt* (*formal*) to conquer (people).

sub·ju·ga·tion /ˌsʌbdʒʊ'geɪʃn/ *nu*

sub·junc·tive /səb'dʒʌŋktɪv/ *adj, n* (*gram*) (of, concerning) a special form (*mood*) of a verb used to express condition, desire, what ought to be done etc, as in 'If I *were* you I'd take a coat.' 'I wish I *knew* what you're thinking.' 'He demanded that another meeting *be held* soon.' Ⓝ This form is used only in formal style except with *'wish (that)'*, *'If only'*, *'would rather/sooner'* etc, as in: 'You'll wish you'd *been* there.' 'If only she'd *arrived* sooner!' 'He'd rather you *paid* him now.'

sub·lease /ˌsʌb'liːs/ *vt,vi* to lease (a room etc one has leased) to another person.

sub·let /ˌsʌb'let/ *vt,vi* (**-tt-**) to rent (a room, house etc of which one is a tenant) to another person.

sub·lime /sə'blaɪm/ *adj* of the greatest and highest sort; causing wonder or admiration: *sublime heroism*. □ *n* (the —) something that fills one with wonder or admiration.

sub·lime·ly *adv*

sub·lim·inal /ˌsʌb'lɪmɪnl/ *adj* (*formal*) of which one is not consciously aware: *subliminal advertising on TV using pictures which last a very short time*.

sub·mar·ine /ˌsʌbmə'riːn/ *nc* a ship that can operate under water.

sub·merge /səb'mɜːdʒ/ *v* **1** *vt,vi* (to cause a ship etc) to go under water. **2** *vt* (usually *passive*) (*fig*) (of work etc) to be so much that one is working too hard, very tired etc: *be submerged by paper work/requests for help*.

sub·merged *adj* (a) under the surface of the sea etc: *submerged rocks*. (b) (*pred*) (*fig*) busy with work etc.

sub·mis·sion /səb'mɪʃn/ *n* **1** *nu* acceptance of another's power or authority; obedience: *The enemy were starved into submission*. **2** *nc,nu* (*legal*) a theory or suggestion: *My submission is that the rain weakened the soil*.

sub·miss·ive /səb'mɪsɪv/ *adj* giving in to the control or authority of another: *Marian is not a submissive wife*.

sub·miss·ive·ly *adv*

sub·mit /səb'mɪt/ *v* (**-tt-**) **1** *vi,vt* to put (oneself) under the control of another: *submit (oneself) to discipline*. **2** *vt* to put (an idea etc) forward for an opinion, decision etc: *submit plans/proposals to a committee*. **3** *vt* (*legal*) to suggest (something): *Counsel submitted that there was no case against his client*. **4** *vi* **submit (to sth)** (*formal*) to be forced to agree: *submit to separation from one's family*.

sub·nor·mal /ˌsʌb'nɔːml/ *adj* below normal (esp intelligence). Compare abnormal.

subord written *abbr* (*gram*) subordinating (conjunction) (as used in this dictionary).

sub·or·di·nate¹ /sə'bɔːdɪnət/ *nc, adj* (a person who is) lower in rank or position: *in a subordinate position*.

sub,ordinate 'clause *nc* (*gram*) a clause that cannot act as a separate sentence or is part of another clause (e.g. as the subject or object of a main clause), as in '*What you do* is your own decision.' 'Tell me *that you love me*.' '*Although it was raining*, we walked to the station.'

sub·ordinating con'junction *nc* (*gram*) one used to join a subordinating clause in a sentence, such as 'She's happy *because* it's Friday.' Ⓝ Marked *conj* (*subord*) in this dictionary. Compare coordinating conjunction.

sub·or·di·nate² /səˈbɔːdɪneɪt/ *vt* (*formal*) to consider or treat (a person, one's own wishes) as less important.

sub·scribe /səbˈskraɪb/ *v* **1** *vt,vi* to (agree to) pay (a sum of money) regularly (to a cause, for something): *He subscribes £100 each year to charities. Which magazines do you subscribe to now?* **2** *vi* **subscribe to sth** (*formal*) to agree with, share, an opinion, view etc: *I had been subscribing to the general view that the trains are dirty.*

sub·scriber *nc* (**a**) a person who subscribes(1). (**b**) a person, business etc paying for the use of a telephone etc.

sub·scrip·tion /səbˈskrɪpʃn/ *n* **1** *nu* an act of subscribing or being subscribed: *The sports centre was paid for by public subscription.* **2** *nc* a sum of money paid (to charity, for receiving a newspaper, magazine etc or for membership of a club).

sub·se·quent /ˈsʌbsɪkwənt/ *adj* later; following: *subsequent events; her actions subsequent to this event.*

sub·ser·vi·ent /səbˈsɜːvɪənt/ *adj* (*derog*) giving too much power or respect (to a senior person): *subservient junior staff; be subservient to one's boss.*

sub·ser·vi·ent·ly *adv*

sub·side /səbˈsaɪd/ *vi* **1** (of flood water) to sink to a lower or to the usual level. **2** (of land, buildings) to sink lower down in the ground. **3** (of winds, anger etc) to become less strong.

sub·sid·ence /səbˈsaɪdəns/ *nc,nu* (an instance of) subsiding(1,2).

sub·sidi·ary /səbˈsɪdɪərɪ/ *nc* (*pl* **-ies**), *adj* (a person, business etc) not as important, high in position etc as the main person, business etc: *We have our main offices in Rome with subsidiaries throughout Europe.*

sub·si·dize (also **-ise**) /ˈsʌbsɪdaɪz/ *vt* to give a subsidy to (farmers, a theatre etc).

sub·si·dy /ˈsʌbsədɪ/ *nc* (*pl* **-ies**) an amount of money granted, esp by a government or society, to an industry or other cause needing help or to keep prices down.

sub·sist /səbˈsɪst/ *vi* **subsist (on sth)** (*formal*) to exist (on): *subsist on a vegetable diet.*

sub·sis·tence /-təns/ *nu* (also *attrib*) (the means of) existing: *subsistence farming.*

sub'sistence crop *nc* a kind grown by people for themselves to eat. Compare cash crop.

sub·soil /ˈsʌbsɔɪl/ *nu* the layer of soil that lies immediately beneath the surface layer.

sub·stance /ˈsʌbstəns/ *n* **1** *nc,nu* (a particular kind of) matter: *Water, ice and snow are the same substance in different forms.* **2** *nu* the most important part; chief or real meaning of something: *I agree in substance with what you say but differ on some small points.*

sub·stan·dard /ˌsʌbˈstændəd/ *adj* (*derog*) below the usual, average or expected standard.

sub·stan·tial /səbˈstænʃl/ *adj* **1** solidly or strongly built or made. Compare insubstantial(1). **2** large; considerable: *a substantial meal/improvement/loan.* Compare insubstantial(2). **3**

of the main or most important part(s): *We are in substantial agreement.*

sub·stan·tial·ly /-ʃəlɪ/ *adv*: *Your efforts contributed substantially* (= a great deal) *to our success.*

sub·stan·ti·ate /səbˈstænʃɪeɪt/ *vt* (*formal*) to provide facts to support (a claim, statement, charge etc).

sub·sti·tute¹ /ˈsʌbstɪtjuːt/ *nc* **substitute (for sb/sth)** a person or thing taking the place of, acting for, another: *Substitutes for rubber can be made from petroleum.*

sub·sti·tute² /ˈsʌbstɪtjuːt/ *vi,vt* **substitute (sb/sth) (for sb/sth)** to act as, provide (a person, thing) as, a substitute: *substitute margarine for butter; substitute for a colleague who is ill; substitute pronouns for nouns in the following sentences.*

sub·sti·tu·tion /ˌsʌbstɪˈtjuːʃn/ *nu*

sub·sume /səbˈsjuːm/ *vt* (*formal*) to include (an example etc) in another (larger) class: *Whales, rats and humans are all subsumed under the term 'mammals'.*

sub·ter·fuge /ˈsʌbtəfjuːdʒ/ *nc,nu* (*formal*) (an instance of) deceitful activity or behaviour.

sub·ter·ra·ne·an /ˌsʌbtəˈreɪnɪən/ *adj* (*formal*) = underground¹(1): *subterranean rivers.*

sub·titles /ˈsʌbtaɪtlz/ *n pl* a translation of a film script printed on the film.

subtle /ˈsʌtl/ *adj* (**-r, —st**) **1** difficult to become aware of or describe because very small: *a subtle distinction. Avocados have a subtle taste.* **2** clever; complex: *a subtle argument.* Opp unsubtle.

subtle·ty *nc,nu* (*pl* **-ies**)

sub·tly /ˈsʌtlɪ/ *adv*

sub·tract /səbˈtrækt/ *vt* **subtract sth (from sth)** to take a number, amount etc away (from another number etc): *subtract 6 from 9.*

sub·trac·tion /səbˈtrækʃn/ *nc,nu*

sub·tropi·cal /ˌsʌbˈtrɒpɪkl/ *adj* almost tropical: *a subtropical climate/region.*

sub·urb /ˈsʌbɜːb/ *nc* (often the **—s**) a residential district round the outside of a town or city.

sub·ur·ban /səˈbɜːbən/ *adj* of or in a suburb: *suburban life.*

sub·ur·bia /səˈbɜːbɪə/ *nu* (often *derog*) (kind of dull life characteristic of people in) the suburbs.

sub·ver·sion /səbˈvɜːʃn/ *nu* an act of destroying or an attempt to destroy a government, system etc.

sub·vers·ive /səbˈvɜːsɪv/ *adj* tending to subvert: *subversive literature/speeches/policies.*

sub·vert /sʌbˈvɜːt/ *vt* to destroy (a government, religion etc) by weakening people's trust, confidence, belief.

sub·way /ˈsʌbweɪ/ *nc* an underground passage or tunnel, e.g. used to get from one side of a busy street to the other.

suc·ceed /səkˈsiːd/ *v* **1** *vi* **succeed (in sth)** to do well (in something one is trying to do): *succeed in passing an examination. The attack succeeded.* Opp fail²(1). **2** *vt* **succeed sb (as sb)** to come next after a person and take her or his place: *Who succeeded Kennedy as President?*

suc·cess /səkˈses/ *n* **1** *nu* the achievement of what one is trying to do: *Our plans met with success.* **2** *nc* a person or thing that succeeds: *The plan/play/lecturer was a great success.* Opp failure(1,2). *make a success (of sth)* to do it successfully.

suc·cess·ful /-fəl/ *adj* having succeeded(1): *successful candidates; a successful application.* Opp *unsuccessful.*

suc·cess·ful·ly /-fəlɪ/ *adv*

suc·ces·sion /sək'seʃn/ *n* **1** *nu* the coming of one thing after another in time or order: *the succession of the seasons.* **in succession** one after the other. **2** *nc* a number of things happening in succession: *a succession of defeats.* **3** *nu* (the right of) succeeding(2): *Who is first in succession to the throne?*

suc·cess·ive /sək'sesɪv/ *adj* coming one after the other in an uninterrupted sequence: *Liverpool won eleven successive games.*

suc·cess·ive·ly *adv*

suc·ces·sor /sək'sesə(r)/ *nc* a person or thing that succeeds(2) another: *appoint a successor to a headteacher.*

suc·cinct /sək'sɪŋkt/ *adj* expressed briefly and clearly: *a succinct report.*

suc·cinct·ly *adv*

suc·cour (*US* = **-cor**) /'sʌkə(r)/ *nu* (*formal*) help given in time of need.

suc·cu·lent¹ /'sʌkjulənt/ *adj* **1** (of fruit and meat) juicy; tasting good: *a succulent steak.* **2** (*science*) (of stems, leaves) thick and fleshy.

suc·cu·lent² /'sʌkjulənt/ *nc* (*science*) a succulent plant, e.g. *cactus.*

suc·cumb /sə'kʌm/ *vi* **succumb (to sb/sth)** (*formal*) to give in (to a ruler, death, temptation, flattery etc).

such /sʌtʃ/ *adj* or *det* Ⓝ 'Such' is used before 'a' or a noun. **1** (*attrib*) of the same kind (mentioned): *All such plants have long leaves. On such a night as this I stay at home. There's no such person working here. On such occasions we usually make a cake. I've never heard such nonsense before.* **such as** of the same kind as; for example: *Many countries are surrounded by sea, such as England, Australia, Cyprus and Japan.* **no such thing (as)** ⇨ thing(1). **2** **such a + noun** (used for emphasis) having the degree mentioned: *It's such a long way away. His room's such a mess! She made such a lot of mistakes. He's such a nice person.* Ⓝ 'Such a + noun' can be replaced by 'so + adj', as in *It's so far, His room's so messy, She made so many mistakes, He's so nice.* **3** (used to emphasize a feeling, opinion etc): *We had such a good time! That's such a good idea! It's given us such great pleasure.* **4** **such that** of the kind to have the result mentioned: *His behaviour was such that everyone disliked him. Such was the force of the explosion that the windows broke.*

such² /sʌtʃ/ *pron* the kind of person, thing, (already) mentioned: *Such were his words. We can only buy cabbage, lettuce, spinach and such. Such is life!* (= Life is like that!) **as such** (a) as that kind of person, thing: *He's a doctor and as such can be trusted.* (b) considered without other facts: *Money as such does not bring happiness—it's what you do with it.* **such as it is** (used to suggest that something is of poor quality): *You can use my bike, such as it is.* **such as there is/was** (used to suggest that an amount is/was small): *The meat, such as there was, was very good.*

'such·like *adj* (*attrib*), *nu* (*informal*) (people, things) of the same kind: *I have no time for pop concerts and suchlike.*

suck¹ /sʌk/ *nc* an act of sucking.

suck² /sʌk/ *vt,vi* **1** to draw (liquid) into the mouth by using the tongue and lip muscles: *suck the juice from an orange.* **2** hold (something) in the mouth and lick with the tongue: *suck at a sweet. He still sucks his thumb.*

suck at sth ⇨ 2 above.

suck sb/sth down (of a current etc) to pull a person, thing, below the surface of water: *The mud sucked him/the car down.*

suck sb/sth under = suck sb/sth down.

suck sth up to draw up liquid, dirt etc: *suck up lemonade through a straw; suck up dirt with a vacuum cleaner.* **suck up to sb** (*informal*) to try to please, praise, a person for one's own benefit.

suck·er /'sʌkə(r)/ *nc* **1** an organ of some animals that sticks to a surface by suction. **2** (*informal; derog*) a person foolish enough to be deceived by advertisements, a deceitful person etc.

suckle /'sʌkl/ *vt* (*tech*) to feed (a baby, young animal) with milk from the breast or udder.

suc·tion /'sʌkʃn/ *nu* **1** the action of sucking. **2** the process of removing air etc to produce a vacuum and to force in liquid or dust: *Vacuum cleaners work by suction.* **3** a similar process producing a vacuum that causes two surfaces to stick together.

sud·den¹ /'sʌdn/ *adj* happening unexpectedly, quickly, without warning: *a sudden shower.*

sud·den·ly *adv: Suddenly the door opened. The lights suddenly went off.*

sud·den² /'sʌdn/ *n* (only in) **all of a sudden** suddenly: *All of a sudden she screamed.*

suds /sʌdz/ *n pl* a mass of tiny bubbles on soapy water.

sue /su:/ *vt,vi* **sue (sb) (for sth)** to make a legal claim against a person (for something): *sue (a person) for damages.*

suede (also **suède**) /sweɪd/ *nu* a kind of soft leather without a shining surface.

su·et /'su:ɪt/ *nu* (also *attrib*) the hard fat round the kidneys of sheep and oxen, used in cooking: *suet pudding.*

suf·fer /'sʌfə(r)/ *v* **1** *vt,vi* **suffer (from sth)** to feel or experience pain, difficulty etc: *suffer pain; suffer from* (= often have) *headaches. The business suffered while he was ill* (= It did not do well). **2** *vt* to bear (something unpleasant): *How can you suffer such insolence?*

suf·fer·er *nc* a person who suffers.

suf·fer·ing *nc,nu* (an example of) an unpleasant experience, e.g. pain, unhappiness.

suf·fer·ance /'sʌfərəns/ *nu* **on sufferance** (*formal*) with agreement but not willingly: *He's here on sufferance.*

suf·fice /sə'faɪs/ *v* Ⓝ Not used in continuous tenses, e.g. *is/was -ing.* **1** *vi* **suffice (for sth)** to be enough (the more usual words): *Will £10 suffice (for your needs)?* **2** *vt* (*formal*) to meet the needs of (a person): *One meal a day won't suffice a growing boy.*

suf·fi·cien·cy /sə'fɪʃnsɪ/ *n sing* **sufficiency (of sth)** (*formal*) enough: *a sufficiency of fuel.*

suf·fi·cient /sə'fɪʃnt/ *adj* (*formal*) enough: *sufficient time/money. Have we sufficient food for ten* *people?* Opp insufficient.

suf·fi·cient·ly *adv*

suf·fix /'sʌfɪks/ *nc* (*lang*) letter(s), sounds or syllable(s) added at the end of a word to make another word, e.g. *-ly*, *-ment*. Compare prefix(1).

suf·fo·cate /'sʌfəkeɪt/ *vt,vi* (to cause a person, animal) to have great difficulty in breathing (and die): *The fumes were suffocating me.*

suf·fo·ca·tion /,sʌfə'keɪʃn/ *nu*

sug·ar¹ /'ʃʊgə(r)/ *nu* a sweet substance obtained from the juices of various plants, used in cooking and for sweetening drinks.

'sugar daddy *nc* (*informal*) a rich, elderly man who is generous to a young woman.

sugary *adj* (**a**) tasting of sugar. (**b**) (*fig; derog*) (of behaviour, music etc) too sweet or kind to be sincere.

sug·ar² /'ʃʊgə(r)/ *vt* to add sugar to (drink, food): *sugar coffee/cream.*

sug·gest /sə'dʒest/ *vt* **1** to put (an idea) forward for consideration, as a possibility: *I suggested a visit to/suggested going to/suggest that we should go to the theatre.* **2** to bring (an idea, possibility etc) into the mind: *That cloud suggests an old man.*

sug·ges·tion /sə'dʒestʃən/ *n* (**a**) *nu* an act of suggesting: *at the suggestion of my brother; on your suggestion.* (**b**) *nc* an idea, plan etc that is suggested: *What a silly suggestion!* (**c**) *nc* a small indication: *a suggestion of a French accent.*

sug·ges·tive /sə'dʒestɪv/ *adj* (*derog*) tending to suggest(2) something indecent: *suggestive jokes.*

sug·ges·tive·ly *adv*

sui·cid·al /,su:ɪ'saɪdl/ *adj* **1** of suicide: *feel suicidal.* **2** (*fig*) very harmful: *suicidal economic policies.*

sui·cide /'su:ɪsaɪd/ *n* **1** *nc,nu* (an instance of) killing oneself: *commit suicide; three suicides last week.* **2** *nu* (*fig*) any act that harms one's interests or welfare: *economic suicide* (e.g. supporting policies that will ruin the country's economy).

suit¹ /su:t/ *nc* **1** a set of articles of outer clothing of the same material: *a man's suit* (= jacket, (waistcoat) and trousers). **2** = lawsuit. **3** any of the four sets of playing-cards (*spades, hearts, diamonds, clubs*) used in many card-games. *follow suit* (*fig*) to do what another person has done.

suit² /su:t/ *v* **1** *vt,vi* to satisfy the needs of (a person, situation etc); be convenient to or right for (a person, thing): *Does the climate suit you/your health? Will Thursday suit (you)?* *suit oneself* to act according to one's own wishes. **2** *vt* (esp of clothes, hair-styles etc) to look well; be suitable for (a person, event): *Does this hat suit me?* **3** *vt* (*passive*) *be suited (for sb/sth; to (do) sth)* to have the right qualities: *That man is not suited for teaching/to be a teacher.*

suit·able /'su:təbl/ *adj* *suitable (as/for sb/ sth)* fit, right (for the person, purpose or occasion): *suitable as a nurse; suitable clothes for cold weather.* Opp unsuitable.

suit·ably /-əblɪ/ *adv: suitably dressed.*

suit·abil·ity /,su:tə'bɪlətɪ/ *nu*

suit·case /'su:tkeɪs/ *nc* a flat case used to hold clothes etc when travelling.

suite /swi:t/ *nc* **1** a complete set of matching articles of furniture: *a bedroom suite.* **2** a set of rooms (e.g. in a hotel): *the bridal suite.* ⇨ en

suite. **3** (*music*) an orchestral composition made up of three or more related parts.

suit·or /'su:tə(r)/ *nc* **1** (*legal*) a person bringing a lawsuit. **2** (*dated*) a man courting a woman.

sulk /sʌlk/ *vi* to be in a bad temper and show this by refusing to talk.

sulky *adj* (**-ier, -iest**)

sul·len /'sʌlən/ *adj* (*derog*) **1** silent and angry: *sullen looks.* **2** dark and gloomy: *a sullen sky.*

sul·len·ly *adv*

sul·phur (*US* **sul·fur**) /'sʌlfə(r)/ *nu* (*science*) a light-yellow non-metallic element (symbol S) that burns with a bright flame and a strong smell, used in medicine and industry.

sul·phu·ric (*US* = **sul·fu-**) /sʌl'fjʊərɪk/ *adj: sulphuric acid.*

sul·tan /'sʌltən/ *nc* a Muslim ruler.

sul·tana /sʌl'tɑːnə/ *nc* (*pl* **—s**) a kind of small seedless raisin, used in puddings and cakes.

sul·try /'sʌltrɪ/ *adj* (**-ier, -iest**) **1** (of the atmosphere, the weather) hot, heavy and uncomfortable. **2** (*formal*) (of a person's look etc) passionate.

sum¹ /sʌm/ *nc* **1** a total amount obtained by adding together items, numbers or amounts. **2** a problem in arithmetic: *be good at sums.* **3** an amount of money: *save a nice little sum each week.* *a lump sum* one payment for a number of separate sums that are owed.

sum² /sʌm/ *v* (**-mm-**) **1** *vt,vi* *sum (sth) up* to state the chief points of what has been said: *The judge summed up (the evidence).* **2** *vt* *sum sb/ sth up* to form a judgement or opinion of a person, situation etc: *He summed up the situation/ summed her up very quickly.*

sum·mar·ize (also **-ise**) /'sʌməraɪz/ *vt* to make a summary of (a report, speech, a person's character etc).

sum·mary¹ /'sʌmərɪ/ *adj* (*attrib*) (*formal*) **1** brief; giving the chief points only: *a summary account.* **2** done or given without delay or mercy: *summary justice.*

sum·mary² /'sʌmərɪ/ *nc* (*pl* **-ies**) a brief account giving the chief points. Compare abstract³.

sum·mer /'sʌmə(r)/ *nc* (often S-) (also *attrib*) the warmest season of the year; between spring and autumn: *a very hot summer; swim in the river in (the) summer; summer weather; the summer holidays.*

'summer-house *nc* a small building in a park or garden for relaxing in summer.

'summer school *nc* (a place with) a set of organized educational courses during the summer holidays of universities etc.

'sum·mer-time *nu* the season of summer.

sum·mery *adj* like, suitable for, summer: *a summery dress.*

sum·mit /'sʌmɪt/ *nc* **1** the top of a mountain: *reach the summit of Mont Blanc.* **2** (*fig*) the highest point: *the summit of his power.* **3** (also *attrib*) (*fig*) a meeting between heads of state: *a summit conference/meeting/talk.*

sum·mon /'sʌmən/ *vt* **1** (*formal*) to call or send for (a person) officially: *summon a person to court.* **2** *summon up sth* to build up a strong feeling etc inside oneself: *summon up courage.*

sum·mons¹ /'sʌmənz/ *nc* (*pl* **—es**) (*legal*) an official order to appear in a law court: *issue/*

receive a summons.

sum·mons² /'sʌmənz/ *vt (legal)* to give a summons to (a person).

sump·tu·ous /'sʌmptjʊəs/ *adj (formal)* looking expensive: *sumptuous clothes.*

sun¹ /sʌn/ *n* **1** (the —) the heavenly body from which the earth gets warmth and light. **2** (the —) light and warmth from the sun: *sit in the sun.* **under the sun** anywhere in the world: *the best apples under the sun.* **3** *nc* any fixed star with planets: *There are many suns larger than ours.*

'sun·baked *adj* made hard by the heat of the sun: *sunbaked fields.*

'sun·bathe *vi* to lie or sit in the sun to get brown.

'sun·beam *nc* a ray of sunshine.

'sun·burn *nc,nu* (a place where there is) a reddening and blistering caused by too much exposure to the sun. Hence **'sun·burnt** *adj*

'sun·dial *nc* an apparatus that shows the time by the sun producing a shadow on a marked surface.

'sun·down *nu* = sunset (which is more usual).

'sun·drenched *adj* exposed to great light and heat from the sun: *sun-drenched beaches.*

'sun·glasses *n pl* a kind with dark-coloured glass to protect the eyes from bright sunshine.

'sun·light *nu* the light of the sun.

'sun·lit *adj* bright with sunlight: *a sunlit room.*

'sun·rise *nu* (the time of) the sun's rising.

'sun·set *nu* (the time of) the sun's setting.

'sun·shine *nu* light from the sun.

'sun·spot *nc* **(a)** *(science)* a dark patch on the sun. **(b)** *(informal)* a place that has a sunny climate (e.g. for holidays).

'sun·stroke *nc,nu* an illness caused by too much exposure to the sun, esp on the head.

'sun·tan *nc* (also *attrib*) the browning of the skin from exposure to sunlight: *suntan lotion/oil.*

sun·less *adj* receiving little or no sunlight.

sun·ny *adj* (-**ier, -iest**) **(a)** bright with sunlight: *a sunny room.* **(b)** cheerful: *a sunny smile.*

sun² /sʌn/ *v reflex* (-**nn-**) to place (oneself) in the sun: *The cat was sunning itself on the path.*

Sun *written abbr* Sunday.

Sun·day /'sʌndɪ/ *nc* (also *attrib*) the first day of the week: *Let's meet on Sunday/next Sunday morning. On Sundays* (= Every Sunday) *I go for a walk.* **not in a month of Sundays** ⇨ month.

sun·dries /'sʌndrɪz/ *n pl* various small items.

sung /sʌŋ/ *pp* of sing¹.

sunk /sʌŋk/ *pt,pp* of sink².

sunk·en /'sʌŋkən/ *adj* **1** (that has sunk: *a sunken boat.* **2** (made) lower than the rest of the surface: *a sunken garden; sunken cheeks.*

su·per /'su:pə(r)/ *adj (informal)* extremely good; splendid: *a super holiday.*

su·per·an·nu·ation /,su:pər,ænjʊ'eɪʃn/ *nu* pension (the usual word).

su·perb /su:'pɜ:b/ *adj* excellent; first class: *a superb meal/swimmer/result; superb weather.* **su·perb·ly** *adv*

su·per·cili·ous /,su:pə'sɪlɪəs/ *adj (formal; derog)* snobbish and ignoring people: *with his nose high in the air, looking supercilious.* **su·per·cili·ous·ly** *adv*

su·per·fi·cial /,su:pə'fɪʃl/ *adj* **1** of or on the surface only: *a superficial wound.* **2** not thorough or deep: *have only a superficial knowledge of a subject.*

su·per·fi·cial·ly /-ʃəlɪ/ *adv*

su·per·flu·ous /su:'pɜ:flʊəs/ *adj* more than is needed or wanted: *superfluous staff/energy.* **su·per·flu·ous·ly** *adv*

su·per·hu·man /,su:pə'hju:mən/ *adj* much greater than ordinary human power, size, knowledge etc: *by a superhuman effort.*

su·per·im·pose /,su:pərɪm'pəʊz/ *vt* to put (one thing) on top of another one: *superimpose one set of wavy lines on another.*

su·per·in·tend /,su:pərɪn'tend/ *vt* to watch and direct (work etc).

super·in·ten·dence /-əns/ *nu*

super·in·ten·dent /-ənt/ *nc* **(a)** a person who watches and directs others. **(b)** a police officer above a chief inspector in rank.

su·per·ior¹ /su:'pɪərɪə(r)/ *adj* **superior (to sb/ sth)** **1** better than the average in quality: *superior intelligence; ability that is superior to his; superior grades of coffee.* Opp inferior¹(1). **2** larger in number: *The enemy attacked with superior forces.* **3** of higher position or rank: *a superior officer. She's superior to me in the office.* Opp inferior¹(2). **4** *(derog)* showing one to feel better than others: *a superior look; feeling superior.* Compare inferior¹(3).

su·per·ior·ity /sə,pɪərɪ'ɒrətɪ/ *nu*

su·per·ior² /su:'pɪərɪə(r)/ *nc* **1** a person of higher rank, importance etc than another: *Take me to your superior.* Compare inferior². **2** (S-) (the title of) a head of a monastery or nunnery: *the Father Superior; the Mother Superior.*

su·per·la·tive¹ /su:'pɜ:lətɪv/ *adj* **1** *(formal)* of the highest degree or quality: *superlative beauty.* **2** *(gram)* a form of an adjective or adverb expressing the highest degree (usually made by adding -*est* or with *most*), such as *happiest, longest, worst, most likely.* Compare comparative(3), positive(9).

su·per·la·tive² /su:'pɜ:lətɪv/ *nc (gram)* a superlative(2) form: *'Best' is the superlative of 'good'.*

su·per·mar·ket /'su:pəmɑ:kɪt/ *nc* a large self-service store selling food, household goods etc.

su·per·natu·ral /,su:pə'nætʃrəl/ *adj* of something that is not controlled or explained by physical laws: *supernatural beings.*

super·sede /,su:pə'si:d/ *vt* to take the place of (an earlier thing): *Motorways have superseded ordinary roads for long-distance travel.*

super·son·ic /,su:pə'sɒnɪk/ *adj (attrib)* **1** (of speed) faster than that of sound. **2** (of a plane) able to fly at supersonic speed.

super·sti·tion /,su:pə'stɪʃn/ *nc,nu* (an idea, practice etc based on) belief in the power of magic, witchcraft etc.

super·sti·tious /,su:pə'stɪʃəs/ *adj* of, showing, resulting from, believing in, superstitions: *superstitious beliefs/ideas/people.* **super·sti·tious·ly** *adv*

su·per·vise /'su:pəvaɪz/ *vt,vi* to watch and direct (work, workers, students, an organization).

super·vi·sion /,su:pə'vɪʒn/ *nu* an act of supervising: *done under the supervision of the teacher.*

super·vi·sor /-zə(r)/ *nc* a person who watches and directs (a worker, student etc).

sup·per /'sʌpə(r)/ *nc,nu* the last meal of the day.

sup·plant /sə'plɑ:nt/ *vt (formal)* to take the

place of (a person, machine, system etc): *The Prime Minister was supplanted by his rival.*

sup·ple /'sʌpl/ *adj* (—r, —st) easily bending, not stiff: *the supple limbs of a child.*

sup·ple·ment¹ /'sʌplɪmənt/ *nc* **1** something added later to improve or complete: *a supplement to his wages/the encyclopaedia.* **2** an extra and separate addition to a newspaper or magazine: *a colour supplement; The Times Literary Supplement.*

sup·ple·ment² /'sʌplɪmənt/ *vt* **supplement sth (by/with sth)** to make an addition or additions to something: *supplement one's ordinary income by writing books.*

sup·ple·men·tary /,sʌplɪ'mentrɪ/ *adj* **1** additional; extra: *a supplementary income.* **2** (*maths*) used to make up 180°: *Angles of 60° and 120° are supplementary.* ⇨ complementary(2).

sup·ply¹ /sə'plaɪ/ *n* (*pl* -ies) **1** *nu* an act, process, of supplying. **be in short supply** to be difficult to obtain or find. **supply and demand** to be the balance between goods available and goods needed. **2** *nc* something supplied; amount available: *Have you a good supply of clothes for the holiday?* **3** (*pl*) (*esp*) things necessary for a particular use: *medical supplies; office supplies.*

sup·pli·er *nc* a person or business that supplies goods, materials etc.

sup·ply² /sə'plaɪ/ *vt* **1** **supply sth to sb/sth** to give (what is wanted or needed) to a person, organization: *supply pencils to children.* **2** **supply sb/sth (with sth)** to give (a person, organization etc) what is wanted or needed: *supply children with pencils.*

sup·port¹ /sə'pɔːt/ *n* **1** *nu* the act of supporting or being supported(2): *I hope to have your support in the election. If you decide to oppose the decision, you have my full (= total) support. He spoke in support of the motion.* **2** *nc* something that supports(1) weight. **3** *nu* money etc to live on: *What are your means of support? The divorced wife claimed financial support* (i.e. a regular contribution) *for her children from her ex-husband.* **4** *nc* a person who provides support(3): *He's the main support of his family.*

sup·port² /sə'pɔːt/ *vt* **1** to bear the weight of (something); keep (something) in place: *Is this bridge strong enough to support heavy lorries?* **2** to provide (a person, thing) with what is necessary: *support a scheme with money. Your accusation is not supported by proof.* **3** to show one's loyalty or approval of (a player, team, belief, political group etc): *support a friend/football team/political party.* **4** to provide money etc for (a person, family etc): *He has a large family to support.*

sup·port·er *nc* a person who supports (esp 3): *a football supporter.*

sup·pose¹ /sə'pəʊz/ *conj* (*subord*) = supposing.

sup·pose² /sə'pəʊz/ *vt* Ⓝ Not used in continuous tenses, e.g. *is/was -ing.* **1** to think of (something) as likely: *Do you suppose she's telling the truth. What do you suppose he wanted? 'Will he come?'* — *'Yes, I suppose so'/'No, I suppose not'/'No, I don't suppose so'.* **2** to take (something) as a fact: *Let us suppose (that) the news is true.* **3** **be supposed to** + *verb* (a) to be expected or required to (by customs, duty etc): *Everyone's supposed to know the rules. Is he supposed to clean the outside of the windows or only the inside?* (**b**) (*informal*) (used with *not*) to be not allowed to: *We're not supposed to play football on Sundays.* (**c**) to be (generally) thought of as: *Is that supposed to be a table!*

sup·pos·ed·ly /sə'pəʊzɪdlɪ/ *adv* as seems likely; I suppose(1): *Supposedly, you'll wait for the others.*

sup·pos·ing /sə'pəʊzɪŋ/ *conj* (*subord*) if: *Supposing it rains, what shall we do?*

sup·po·si·tion /,sʌpə'zɪʃn/ *n* **1** *nu* the act of supposing something to be true but without proof: *This newspaper article is based on supposition.* **2** *nc* (*formal*) a guess: *Our suppositions were fully confirmed.*

sup·posi·tory /sə'pɒzɪtrɪ/ *nc* (*pl* -ies) a form of medicine in a container (to be) put into the rectum or vagina.

sup·press /sə'pres/ *vt* **1** to put an end to the activity or existence of (a revolt etc): *suppress a rebellion.* **2** to prevent (something) from being known or seen: *suppress the truth/a yawn/one's feelings.*

sup·pres·sion /sə'preʃn/ *nu*

sup·pres·sive *adj* tending to, designed to, suppress(1): *suppressive action by the police.*

su·prem·acy /sʊ'preməsɪ/ *nu* the state of being supreme; highest authority: *His supremacy was unchallenged.*

su·preme /sʊ'priːm/ *adj* **1** highest in rank or authority: *the Supreme Commander.* **2** (*formal*) most important; greatest: *supreme joy.*

su·preme·ly *adv* extremely: *supremely happy.*

Supt *written abbr* Superintendent.

sur·charge /'sɜːtʃɑːdʒ/ *nc* a payment demanded in addition to the usual charge, e.g. for a letter without enough postage paid on it.

surd /sɜːd/ *nc* (*maths*) a number (e.g. $\sqrt{17}$) or equation that cannot be expressed using ordinary numbers.

sure¹ /ʃʊə(r)/ *adj* (—r, —st) **1** (*pred*) having good reasons to believe something; free from doubt: *I think he's coming but I'm not sure. Are you sure (that) he said he'd come? I'm not sure why he wants it. She felt sure you'd like it. I think the answer's right but I'm not quite sure (about it).* Ⓝ *'Certain' is also possible.* Opp unsure(1). **make sure (of sth/that)** (**a**) to find out (about something) in order to have no doubts: *I think there's a train at ten but I'll ring and make sure (of it/that there is).* (**b**) to arrange things so that: *I made sure (that) he'd be there.* **2** (*pred*) **sure of sth/to** + *verb* certain to experience or to happen: *You'll be sure of a warm welcome. You're sure to enjoy your visit to Geneva.* ⇨ assure. **be sure to do sth** to remember and do something: *Be sure to write and give me all the news.* **3** (*attrib*) proved; reliable: *a sure cure for a cold; a sure sign of success.* **4** (*attrib*) (of a person) reliable: *a sure friend.*

sure² /ʃʊə(r)/ *adv* **1 for sure** without a doubt: *If you leave your coat, it will rain for sure.* **2** (esp US) (used to express willingness or agreement): *'Will you hold this a moment?'—'Sure (I will).'* **3 sure enough** (*informal*) (used to express confidence, satisfaction, about something that happened): *I said it would rain and sure enough it did.*

sure·ly /'ʃʊəlɪ/ *adv* **1** (used to express difficulty in believing) if experience or probability can be trusted: *Surely this rain cannot last much longer. You didn't say that, surely! 'He's in hospital'—'Surely not!* Compare certainly. **2** with certainty: *He was moving slowly but surely up the mountain.*

sure·ty /'ʃʊərəti/ *nc,nu* (*pl* **-ies**) (something given as a) guarantee.

surf¹ /sɜ:f/ *nu* the waves breaking in white foam on the seashore.

'surf·board *nc* a board used for surfing.

surf·ing, 'surf-riding *nu* the sport in which one balances on a long narrow board while being carried along by surf.

surf² /sɜ:f/ *vi* to take part in surfing.

sur·face¹ /'sɜ:fɪs/ *adj* (*attrib*) **1** (of post) sent by sea and land: *by surface mail.* **2** of the surface(3): *surface impressions.*

sur·face² /'sɜ:fɪs/ *nc* **1** the outside of any object etc: *Glass has a smooth surface.* **2** (the —) the top (of a liquid): *The submarine rose to the surface.* **3** (the —) the outward appearance; what is seen or learnt from a quick view or consideration: *His faults are all on the surface. When you get below the surface you find that he is generous.*

sur·face³ /'sɜ:fɪs/ *v* **1** *vt* to give a surface to (something): *surface a road with tarmac.* **2** *vi* (of a submarine, diver etc) to come to the surface.

sur·feit /'sɜ:fɪt/ *n sing* **surfeit (of sth)** too much of anything, esp food and drink: *have a surfeit of cakes while in Austria.*

surge¹ /sɜ:dʒ/ *nc* **1** a forward or upward movement: *the surge of the sea; a surge* (= quick rise) *in prices.* **2** (*fig*) (of feelings) sudden growth: *a surge of anger/pity.*

surge² /sɜ:dʒ/ *vi* **1** to move forward, like waves: *The crowds were surging out of the sports stadium.* **2** (of feeling) to grow suddenly: *Hatred surged in her heart.*

sur·geon /'sɜ:dʒən/ *nc* a doctor who performs medical operations.

sur·gery /'sɜ:dʒərɪ/ *n* (*pl* **-ies**) **1** *nu* the science and practice of treating injuries and disease by cutting the body open and removing or mending part of it: *She's qualified in both surgery and medicine.* **2** *nc* a doctor's or dentist's room where patients are checked, treated etc.

sur·gi·cal /'sɜ:dʒɪkl/ *adj* (*attrib*) of, by, for, surgery: *surgical instruments.*

sur·gi·cal·ly /-klɪ/ *adv*

sur·ly /'sɜ:lɪ/ *adj* (**-ier, -iest**) (*derog*) bad-tempered and unfriendly.

sur·mise /sə'maɪz/ *vt,vi* (*formal*) to guess (the usual word).

sur·mount /sə'maʊnt/ *vt* (*formal*) to overcome (difficulties).

sur·mount·able /-əbl/ *adj* (of difficulties) that can be overcome. Opp insurmountable.

sur·name /'sɜ:neɪm/ *nc* (also *family name*) the name used by the members of a family: *Smith is a very common English surname.* ⇨ first name.

sur·pass /sə'pɑ:s/ *vt* (*formal*) to do or be better than (a person, an earlier achievement): *surpass him in speed/skill.*

sur·pass·ing *adj* (*attrib*) (*formal*) excellent: *of surpassing beauty.*

sur·plus /'sɜ:pləs/ *nc* an amount (of money, goods etc) that remains after needs have been supplied: *a surplus of milk; a coffee surplus.* Compare deficit.

sur·prise¹ /sə'praɪz/ *adj* (*attrib*) done, happening, without warning: *a surprise visit/attack.*

sur·prise² /sə'praɪz/ *nc,nu* (the feeling caused by) something sudden or unexpected: *What a horrible/wonderful surprise! He looked up at me in surprise.* **take sb by surprise** to happen unexpectedly: *The news took me completely by surprise.*

sur·prise³ /sə'praɪz/ *vt* **1** to cause surprise to (a person, animal): *She was more surprised than frightened. We were surprised at the news/surprised to hear the news.* **2** to discover, see, (a person) suddenly or without warning: *surprise a burglar in a house.*

sur·pris·ing *adj* causing surprise.

sur·pris·ing·ly *adv*

sur·real·is·tic /sə,rɪə'lɪstɪk/ *adj* (*formal*) having the quality of a dream.

sur·ren·der /sə'rendə(r)/ *v* **1** *vt,vi* **surrender (sb/sth) to sb** to give up (oneself, a ship, a town etc) to the enemy, the police etc: *We shall never surrender.* **2** *vt* to give up possession of (something): *We shall never surrender our liberty.*

sur·rep·ti·tious /,sʌrəp'tɪʃəs/ *adj* (*formal*) (of actions) done secretly.

sur·ro·gate /'sʌrəgət/ *adj* (*attrib*) acting as a substitute: *a surrogate mother.*

sur·round¹ /sə'raʊnd/ *nc* an edge, e.g. of a floor: *paint the surrounds white.*

sur·round² /sə'raʊnd/ *vt* to be, go, all round (an area, thing): *a house surrounded by/with trees.*

sur·round·ing *adj* (*attrib*) that is around: *York and the surrounding countryside.*

sur·round·ings *n pl* everything around and in a place: *pleasant surroundings. Animals are not in their natural surroundings at a zoo.*

sur·veil·lance /sə'veɪləns/ *nu* a close watch kept on a place, a person suspected of doing wrong etc: *He/His house is under police surveillance.*

sur·vey¹ /'sɜ:veɪ/ *nc* **1** a mental or written report or review: *make a general survey of the situation/ of modern French poets.* **2** a detailed inspection: *a survey of a house one is thinking of buying.* **3** a detailed map (of an area).

sur·vey² /sə'veɪ/ *vt* **1** to take a general view of (something): *survey the countryside from the top of a hill.* **2** to examine the general condition of (something): *The Prime Minister surveyed the international situation.* **3** to examine the condition of (a building): *Have the house surveyed before you offer to buy it.* **4** to make a detailed map of (an area).

sur·vey·ing *nu* (**a**) the activity, profession, of measuring heights and distances for maps or for planning buildings. (**b**) the activity, profession, of surveying(3) buildings.

sur·vey·or /sə'veɪə(r)/ *nc* a person who surveys(3,4).

sur·viv·al /sə'vaɪvl/ *n* **1** *nu* the state of continuing to live or exist: *the survival of the fittest* (= the continuing existence of those animals and plants which are best adapted to their surroundings). **2** *nc* something that is surviving: *The custom is a survival from an earlier civilization.*

sur·vive /sə'vaɪv/ *vt,vi* to continue to live or exist (longer than): *survive an earthquake/shipwreck. The old lady has survived all her children/is still surviving.*

sur·viv·or /-vǝ(r)/ *nc* a person who has survived a disaster: *Help was sent to the survivors of the air crash.*

sus·cep·ti·ble /sǝ'septǝbl/ *adj* (*formal*) **1** easily influenced by feelings: *a susceptible nature.* **2** (*pred*) **susceptible to sth** easily affected, influenced, by something: *susceptible to pain.*
  sus·cep·ti·bil·ity /sǝ,septǝ'bɪlǝtɪ/ *nc,nu*

sus·pect¹ /'sʌspekt/ *adj* (*pred*) doubtful; possibly not true: *His motives/statements are suspect.*

sus·pect² /'sʌspekt/ *nc* a person suspected of doing wrong etc: *Are political suspects kept under police observation in your country?*

sus·pect³ /sǝ'spekt/ *vt* Ⓝ Not used in continuous tenses, e.g. *is/was -ing.* **1** to have an idea or feeling concerning the possibility or truth of (something): *She has more intelligence than we suspected.* **2** to feel doubt about the value of (something): *suspect a person's true motives.* **3** to have a feeling that (a person) may be guilty (of something): *He is suspected of telling lies.*

sus·pend /sǝ'spend/ *vt* **1** **suspend sth (from sth)** to hang something up (from): *lamps suspended from the ceiling.* **2** (usually *passive*) (of solid particles in the air, a liquid etc) to be or remain in place: *dust/smoke suspended in the air.* **3** to delay (a decision etc): *suspend judgement.* **4** to ban (a person) from being a member, playing etc for a time: *suspend a football player.*

sus·pense /sǝ'spens/ *nu* a state of (excited or worried) uncertainty: *We waited in suspense for the doctor's opinion.*

sus·pen·sion /sǝ'spenʃn/ *nu* the act of suspending or being suspended: *the suspension of a member of Parliament.*
  sus'pension bridge *nc* a kind of bridge hanging on steel cables supported from towers.

sus·pi·cion /sǝ'spɪʃn/ *n* **1** *nc,nu* the feeling that a person has when believing a person, idea etc is possibly right (or wrong): *I have a suspicion that he may be right/wrong. He was arrested on (the) suspicion of having stolen the money.* **above suspicion** (of a person) of such good reputation that suspicion is not possible. **under suspicion (of sth)** (of a person) being considered as possibly guilty (of the crime mentioned). **2** *n sing* a small suggestion: *There was a suspicion of sadness in her voice.*

sus·pi·cious /sǝ'spɪʃǝs/ *adj* having, showing, causing, a feeling of doubt (because a person, thing, cannot be trusted or believed): *The excuse is suspicious to me. He's a suspicious character.*
  sus·pi·cious·ly *adv*: *behave suspiciously.*

sus·tain /sǝ'steɪn/ *vt* **1** (*formal*) to keep (a person, thing) from falling or sinking: *Will this shelf sustain (the weight of) all these books?* **2** to keep (a person, health etc) strong: *eat to sustain oneself/one's energy.* **3** to keep (something) active, existing etc for a long period: *sustain a musical note; a sustained attempt/effort.* **4** (*formal*) to suffer, experience (something unpleasant): *sustain a defeat/an injury.*

sus·ten·ance /'sʌstɪnǝns/ *nu* (*formal*) (the nourishing quality of) food or drink: *There's more sustenance in cocoa than in tea.*

SW *written abb* **1** south-west. **2** (*radio*) short wave.

swab¹ (also **swob**) /swɒb/ *nc* **1** a piece of absorbent material etc for medical use. **2** a specimen taken with a swab: *take throat swabs.*

swab² (also **swob**) /swɒb/ *vt* (**-bb-**) to clean or wipe (something) with a swab: *swab an injury.*

swag·ger /'swægǝ(r)/ *vi, nc* (to walk in) a self-important or self-satisfied manner.

swal·low¹ /'swɒlǝʊ/ *nc* a kind of small bird with a forked tail.
  'swallow-dive *vi, nc* (to make) a type of diving with arms wide apart until entering the water.
  'swallow-tailed *adj* (of butterflies, birds) having a forked tail.

swal·low² /'swɒlǝʊ/ *nc* an act of swallowing; amount swallowed at one time.

swal·low³ /'swɒlǝʊ/ *v* **1** *vt* to cause (food) or allow to go down the throat: *swallow one's food.* **swallow sth whole** (*fig*) to believe an excuse etc without argument, doubt. **swallow one's words** ⇨ word¹(2). **2** *vi* to make this movement, e.g. as an expression of surprise, fear. **3** *vt* (*fig*) to accept (something unpleasant): *swallow an excuse; swallow an insult* (i.e. without complaining). **4** *vt* **swallow sth up** (*fig*) to use up supplies: *money swallowed up by bills.*

swam /swæm/ *pt* of swim².

swamp¹ /swɒmp/ *nc,nu* (an area of) soft, very wet land.
  swampy *adj* (**-ier, -iest**) having swamps.

swamp² /swɒmp/ *vt* **1** to flood, soak, (something) with water: *A big wave swamped the boat.* **2** **swamp sb (with sth)** to make a person very busy (with large amounts): *We are swamped with work. They swamped us with orders.*

swan¹ /swɒn/ *nc* a kind of large, long-necked, white waterbird.

swan² /swɒn/ *vi* (**-nn-**) (*informal*) to move, go, in a slow, often aimless manner: *swan around. I suppose you're swanning (off) to Paris for the weekend.*

swan song /'swɒn sɒŋ/ *nc* a last performance, appearance, work of a poet, musician etc.

swap /swɒp/ *vt, vi* (**-pp-**) = swop.

swarm¹ /swɔːm/ *nc* a large number of insects, birds etc moving about together: *a swarm of ants/locusts/bees.*

swarm² /swɔːm/ *vi* **1** (of insects etc) to move or go in large numbers. **2** **swarm with sb** (of places) to be crowded: *The beaches were swarming with people.* **3** **swarm into** a place to move into it in large numbers: *The crowds swarmed into the cinema.*

swat¹ /swɒt/ *nc* **1** an act of swatting. **2** an implement for swatting: *a fly-swat.*

swat² /swɒt/ *vt* (**-tt-**) to hit (an insect) with a flat object.

swathe /sweɪð/ *vt* (*literary*) to wrap (a body etc): *He was swathed in bandages.*

sway¹ /sweɪ/ *nu* **1** a swaying movement. **2** (*old use*) rule or control: *under the sway of the Romans.*

sway² /sweɪ/ *v* **1** *vt,vi* (to cause a person, thing) to move, first to one side and then to the other: *The branches of the trees were swaying in the wind.* **2** *vt* to influence (a person): *a speech that swayed the voters.*

swear /sweǝ(r)/ *v* (*pt* **swore** /swɔː(r)/, *pp* **sworn** /swɔːn/) **1** *vi* to use bad, obscene, language: *I don't like to hear children swear.* ⇨

swear at sb. **2** *vt* to state or promise (something) seriously and formally: *He swore to tell the truth/ that he would tell truth. She swore her allegiance to the organization.* ⇨ **sworn²**. **3** *vt* (usually *passive*) to make (a person) make a solemn promise: *I was sworn to secrecy.*

swear at sb to use bad language or curses to a person: *The captain swore at his crew. Don't you swear at me!*

swear by sth (a) (*informal*) to express great confidence in something as a cure: *He swears by this ointment.* **(b)** to appeal to a god, close relative etc as a witness of one's honesty: *I swear by all that is sacred that I didn't do it.*

swear sb in to make a person swear(3) in order to become a member, speak in a law court etc.

swear on sth = swear by sth(b): *I swear on my son's head that I'm innocent.*

swear to sth (*informal*) (used with *can/could*; usually used with *not* or in questions) to be certain that something is true or right: *It may have been Sally I saw but I can't swear to it.* **swear sb to secrecy** ⇨ secrecy.

swear·er *nc* a person who swears(1).

swear-word /'sweəwɜ:d/ *nc* a word used when swearing(1).

sweat¹ /swet/ *nu* the moisture that is given off by the body through the skin: *wipe the sweat off one's brow.*

'sweat-shirt *nc* a kind of thick cotton sweater with long sleeves, worn informally.

sweaty *adj* (-**ier**, -**iest**) (making a person) damp with sweat.

sweat² /swet/ *vi* to produce sweat: *The long hot climb made him sweat.*

sweat·er /'swetə(r)/ *nc* a knitted jersey, usually of thick wool.

swede /swi:d/ *nc,nu* a kind of turnip.

sweep¹ /swi:p/ *nc* **1** an act of sweeping (as if) with a broom: *Give the room a good sweep.* **make a clean sweep (of sth)** to get completely rid of what is unwanted: *They made a clean sweep of their old furniture/of the members of the committee.* **2** a sweeping movement: *with one sweep of his arm.* **3** (*formal*) an unbroken stretch: *a fine sweep of country.*

sweep² /swi:p/ *v* (*pt,pp* **swept** /swept/) **1** *vt* to clear (dust, dirt etc) away (as if) with a brush or broom: *sweep the carpets/the floor; sweep up the crumbs; sweep a room clean.* **2** *vt* (of wind, current etc) to move (a crowd, group, mass) easily and quickly: *The wind swept the leaves away.* **sweep the board** ⇨ board¹(7). **sweep sb off her/his feet** ⇨ foot¹(1). **3** *vi,vt* to pass over or along (something) powerfully and easily: *A huge wave swept over us. The searchlights swept (across) the sky. Her dress swept the ground. A huge wave swept over the deck.* **4** *vi* (of a person) to move in a proud or stately manner: *She swept out of the room.* **5** *vi* to extend: *The coast sweeps northwards in a wide curve.*

sweep·er *nc* **(a)** a person or thing that sweeps: *street-sweepers.* **(b)** (*football*) a defender who covers the backs, tackling any opponent who passes them.

sweep·ing /'swi:pɪŋ/ *adj* (*attrib*) **1** having an effect on many people: *sweeping changes/ reforms.* **2** too general (and so not accurate): *make sweeping statements about her ability.*

sweep·stake /'swi:psteɪk/ *nc* a system of gambling (on a horse race) in which the money paid is divided among the winners.

sweet¹ /swi:t/ *adj* (—**er**, —**est**) **1** tasting like sugar or honey: *It tastes sweet.* Opp sour¹(1), bitter¹(1) **have a sweet tooth** ⇨ tooth(1). **2** fresh and pure: *keep a room clean and sweet; sweet breath.* **3** having a pleasant smell: *Don't the roses smell sweet?* **4** pleasant or attractive: *a sweet face. Isn't the baby sweet!* ⇨ also short¹(3).

'sweet corn *nu* maize kernels, boiled and eaten as food.

'sweet·heart *nc* (*dated*) either of a pair of lovers: *David and his sweetheart.*

,sweet po'tato *nu* a kind of tropical climbing plant with thick edible roots, cooked as a vegetable.

sweet·ly *adv*

sweet·ness *nu*

sweet² /swi:t/ *nc* **1** a small piece of something sweet (boiled sugar etc). **2** a dish of sweet food (pudding, jelly etc) at the end of a meal.

sweet·en /'swi:tn/ *v* **1** *vt,vi* (to cause something) to become sweet: *sweeten one's tea with sugar.* **2** *vt* (*informal*) to use gifts, praise etc to make (a person) agree, be friendly etc.

sweet·en·er *n* **(a)** *nc,nu* something that sweetens food and drink. **(b)** *nc* (*fig*) an action, gift etc used to please a person, esp after he or she has been made to accept something unpleasant.

swell¹ /swel/ *n* **1** *nc* a gradual increase in size or sound. **2** *n sing* the slow rise and fall of the sea's surface after a storm: *There was a heavy swell after the storm.*

swell² /swel/ *vi,vt* (*pt* —**ed** /sweld/, *pp* **swollen** /'swəʊlən/) **1** *vi* to become greater in volume, thickness or force: *Wood often swells when wet. His face began to swell (up).* **2** *vt,vi* (to cause something) to have a curved surface: *The sails swelled out in the wind. The wind swelled the sails.*

swell·ing *nc* a swollen place on the body.

swel·ter /'sweltə(r)/ *vi* to be uncomfortably hot.

swel·ter·ing /'sweltərɪŋ/ *adj* uncomfortably hot: *a sweltering day. I'm sweltering in here!*

swept /swept/ *pt,pp* of sweep².

swerve¹ /swɜ:v/ *nc* a swerving act or movement.

swerve² /swɜ:v/ *vt,vi* (to cause a vehicle, cyclist etc) to change direction suddenly: *The car swerved to avoid knocking the boy down.*

swift¹ /swɪft/ *adj* (—**er**, —**est**) quick to happen; fast: *a swift revenge.*

swift·ly *adv*

swift·ness *nu*

swift² /swɪft/ *nc* a kind of small bird with long wings, similar to a swallow.

swill¹ /swɪl/ *n* **1** *nc* an act of swilling. **2** *nu* semiliquid pigs' food.

swill² /swɪl/ *vt* **1** **swill sth (out)** to wash something by pouring liquid into, over or through: *swill out a dirty tub.* **2** **swill sth (down)** (*informal*) to drink something greedily: *The students were swilling beer when they ought to have been working.*

swim¹ /swɪm/ *nc* **1** an act or period of swimming: *have/go for a swim.* **2** **be in/out of the swim** to be/not be taking part in, aware of, what is going on, the latest fashion etc.

swim² /swɪm/ v (pt **swam** /swæm/, pp **swum** /swʌm/; **-mm-**) **1** vi to move the body through water by using arms, legs, tail etc: *Fishes swim. Let's go swimming. He swam across the river.* **2** vt to cover (a distance), cross (a place), by swimming: *swim the English Channel; swim a race; swim two lengths of the pool.* **3** vi **swim in/with sth** to be covered with, full of, something: *The meat was swimming in gravy. Her eyes swam with tears.* **4** vi to seem to be moving round and round: *The room swam before his eyes. His head swam.*

swim·mer nc a person who swims.

swim·ming nu the sport, activity, of a person who swims.

'**swim·ming-bath/-pool** nc a place built for people to swim in.

'**swim·ming-costume**, '**swim-suit** nc one-piece clothing worn by girls and women for swimming. ⇨ bikini.

'**swim·ming-trunks** n pl shorts worn by boys and men for swimming.

swindle¹ /'swɪndl/ nc **1** an act of swindling. **2** something that is not as good as it was described to be: *This pen I bought is a swindle.*

swindle² /'swɪndl/ vt **swindle sb (out of sth)** to cheat a person (in order to get money etc): *swindling money out of a brother; swindle a child out of his money.*

swin·dler /'swɪndlə(r)/ nc (derog) a person who gets money etc by cheating.

swine /swaɪn/ nc **1** (pl —) pig. **2** (sl; derog) a cruel, unpleasant person.

swing¹ /swɪŋ/ nc **1** a swinging movement: *the swing of the pendulum.* **2** a seat held by ropes or chains for swinging on; act of swinging on such a seat: *have a swing.* **3** a change (in opinion, voting etc): *a swing to the Tories.* **4** **in full swing** (of a party, process, activity) fully active.

swing² /swɪŋ/ v (pt,pp **swung** /swʌŋ/) **1** vt,vi (to cause something having one end or one side fixed and the other free) to move forwards and backwards or in a curve: *His arms swung as he walked. The door swung shut/swung to.* **2** vi to turn quickly: *He swung round and faced his accusers. The car swung into the drive. Opinion is swinging away from the government.* **3** vi (dated informal) (of popular music or musicians) to produce an exciting rhythm.

swinge·ing /'swɪndʒɪŋ/ adj (usually attrib; informal) causing anxiety; severe: *swingeing criticism; a swingeing attack; a swingeing tax increase.*

swipe¹ /swaɪp/ nc a swinging hit (with a stick, bat or the hand).

swipe² /swaɪp/ vt (informal) **1** to hit (a person, thing) hard: *The batsman swiped the ball into the grandstand.* **2** to steal (something).

swirl¹ /swɜːl/ nc a swirling movement: *a swirl of dust/smoke.*

swirl² /swɜːl/ vi (of water, air etc) to move or flow with twists and turns: *dust swirling about the streets.*

swish¹ /swɪʃ/ nc a sound, act, of swishing.

swish² /swɪʃ/ v **1** vt,vi (to cause something) to move through the air with a hissing or brushing sound: *The horse swished its tail.* **2** vi to make, move with, a sound like that of something moving through the air: *Her long silk dress swished as she came in.*

switch¹ /swɪtʃ/ nc **1** an apparatus for making and breaking an electrical connection: *a light-switch.* **2** an abrupt change: *a switch from Liberal to Labour.*

switch² /swɪtʃ/ v **1** vt,vi to use a switch(1) to turn (electricity) off or on: *switch (a light) on/off.* **2** vt,vi to change; change (things) over: *switch seats; switch to another course.*

switch sb/sth around to change the positions of people, things, with each other: *Let's switch the chairs around.*

switch (from sth) to sth to change (from (doing) something) to something else: *switch from Democrat to Republican; switch from studying biology to mathematics.*

switch off (a) ⇨ 1 above. **(b)** (informal) to stop being interested or involved.

switch on ⇨ 1 above. **switch sb on** (dated informal) to make a person feel excited. Ⓝ 'Turn sb on' is more usual except when the passive 'switched on' is used as an adj.

switch over (to sth) to turn a knob or switch(1) (to another radio or TV station).

switch·board /'swɪtʃbɔːd/ nc an apparatus for operating several telephone connections, e.g. in an office.

swiv·el /'swɪvl/ vt,vi (**-ll-**, US also **-l-**) **swivel (sb/sth) (round)** (to cause a person, thing) to turn round: *He swivelled round in his chair.*

swob /swɒb/ nc, vt (**-bb-**) = swab.

swol·len /'swəʊlən/ **1** pp of swell². **2** adj larger (because of air or liquid inside): *a swollen ankle.*

'**swollen-'headed** adj (informal; derog) very conceited.

swoon /swuːn/ vi (dated) to faint. □ nc an act of fainting.

swoop¹ /swuːp/ nc a sudden, long downward attack (e.g. by a bird).

swoop² /swuːp/ vi **swoop (down)** to come down with a rush: *The eagle swooped (down) on the rabbit.*

swop¹ (also **swap**) /swɒp/ nc an act, result, of swopping.

swop² (also **swap**) /swɒp/ vt,vi (**-pp-**) (informal) to change ownership of (something) after bargaining: *swop foreign stamps.* **swop places (with sb)** ⇨ place¹(1).

sword /sɔːd/ nc a long steel blade fixed in a handle (hilt), used as a weapon.

sword·fish /'sɔːdfɪʃ/ nc a large sea-fish with a long upper jaw.

swore /swɔː(r)/ pt of swear.

sworn /swɔːn/ **1** pp of swear. **2** adj (attrib) **(a)** made by swearing(2): *a sworn statement.* **(b)** determined (and well-known): *sworn enemies.*

swot /swɒt/ vi (**-tt-**) **swot (up on sth)** to study a subject for an examination. □ nc (often derog) a person who swots (too much).

swum /swʌm/ pp of swim².

swung /swʌŋ/ pt,pp of swing².

syca·more /'sɪkəmɔː(r)/ nc,nu (the wood of) a large tree with wide leaves.

syl·lab·ic /sɪ'læbɪk/ adj of or in syllables.

syl·lable /'sɪləbl/ nc (lang) a part or word with one sound: *'Arithmetic' has four syllables.*

syl·la·bus /'sɪləbəs/ nc (pl —**es**) an outline or summary of a course of studies.

syl·lo·gism /'sɪlədʒɪzəm/ nc a form of reasoning

in which a conclusion is reached from two statements, e.g. *People must die; I am a person; therefore I must die.*

sym·bol /'sımbl/ *nc* a sign, mark, object, etc used to represent something: *Mathematical symbols include* ×, ÷, + *and* −. *The chemical symbol for sulphur is S.*

sym·bol·ic /sım'bɒlık/ *adj* of, using, used as, a symbol.

sym·boli·cal·ly /-klı/ *adv*

sym·bol·ism /'sımbəlızəm/ *nu* (*literature*) the use of an object, activity etc to represent a feeling, idea etc: *The storm is a symbolism of the anger caused by her murder.*

sym·bol·ize (also **-ise**) /'sımbəlaız/ *vt* to be a sign of (something); represent (something) by symbols: *The storm symbolizes the violence in the action of the drama.*

sym·met·ric /sı'metrık/ (also **sym·met·ri·cal** /-kl/) *adj* having symmetry.

sym·met·ri·cal·ly /-klı/ *adv*

sym·me·try /'sımətrı/ *nu* **1** (beauty resulting from) the exact shape, design, of opposite parts. **2** the quality of harmony or balance (in size, design etc) between different things.

sym·path·etic /ˌsımpə'θetık/ *adj* having or showing, caused by, sympathy: *sympathetic looks/words/smiles; be/feel sympathetic to/ towards someone.* Opp unsympathetic.

sym·path·eti·cal·ly /-klı/ *adv*

sym·path·ize (also **-ise**) /'sımpəθaız/ *vi* **sym·pathize (with sb/sth)** to feel or express sympathy (with a person, thing): *I sympathize (with you/your problem), but you must be more careful.*

sym·path·izer (also **-iser**) *nc* a person who sympathizes.

sym·pa·thy /'sımpəθı/ *n* (*pl* **-ies**) **1** *nu* (the capacity for) feeling pity and sadness: *send her a letter of sympathy; feel sympathy for her.* **2** *nc* a feeling of understanding or agreement: *There is a lot of sympathy for that particular theory. My sympathies are with the miners.*

sym·phon·ic /sım'fɒnık/ *adj* (*music*) of, like, a symphony.

sym·pho·ny /'sımfənı/ *nc* (*pl* **-ies**) (*music*) a (long) composition in (usually) three or four parts (called *movements*) for an orchestra.

symp·tom /'sımptəm/ *nc* **symptom (of sth) 1** a change in the body's condition that is a sign (of illness): *symptoms of measles.* **2** a sign of the existence (of something): *symptoms of political discontent.*

symp·to·mat·ic /ˌsımptə'mætık/ *adj* (*pred*) **symptomatic (of sth)** serving as a symptom: *Headaches may be symptomatic of many kinds of trouble.*

symp·to·mati·cal·ly /-klı/ *adv*

syna·gogue /'sınəgɒg/ *nc* a place where Jews meet to worship.

syn·chro·flash /'sıŋkrəυflæʃ/ *nu* (*tech*) a device in a camera that allows light from a flashlight to enter at the correct moment.

syn·chro·mesh /'sıŋkrəυmeʃ/ *adj* (*tech*) (of gears in a vehicle) having a system for relating the speed of the vehicle to the gears to prevent noise and wear.

syn·chro·nize (also **-ise**) /'sıŋkrənaız/ *vt, vi* (to cause things) to happen at the same time, agree in time, speeds etc: *synchronize the clocks in a building.*

syn·chro·ni·za·tion (also **-ni·sa·tion**) /ˌsıŋ-krənaı'zeıʃn/ *nu*

syn·co·pa·tion /ˌsıŋkə'peıʃn/ *nu* (*music*) an act of emphasizing the weak beat in a piece of music to create an unusual rhythm.

syn·co·pe /'sıŋkəpı/ *nu* (*lang*) an instance of leaving out part of the middle of a word, as in *e'er* (= ever). Compare elision.

syn·di·cate /'sındıkət/ *nc* **1** a business association that supplies articles, cartoons etc to magazines. **2** a group of businesses associated for a common purpose.

syn·drome /'sındrəυm/ *nc* **1** (*med*) a number of symptoms which indicate an illness etc. **2** a similar number of qualities, happenings etc describing a general condition.

syn·od /'sınɒd/ *nc* a meeting of church officers to discuss church matters.

syn·onym /'sınənım/ *nc* (*lang*) a word with the same meaning as another in the same language (but often with different associations): *'Small' and 'little' are synonyms.* Compare antonym.

syn·ony·mous /sı'nɒnıməs/ *adj*

syn·op·sis /sı'nɒpsıs/ *nc* (*pl* **-ses** /-si:z/) a summary or outline (of a book, play etc).

syn·op·tic /sı'nɒptık/ *adj*

syn·tac·tic /sın'tæktık/ *adj* (*lang*) of syntax.

syn·tac·ti·cal·ly /-klı/ *adv*

syn·tax /'sıntæks/ *nu* (*lang*) (grammatical rules for) forming sentences.

syn·the·sis /'sınθəsıs/ *nc, nu* (*pl* **-ses** /-si:z/) a combination of separate parts, elements, substances etc into a whole; that which results from this process: *produce rubber from petroleum by synthesis.*

syn·thet·ic /sın'θetık/ *adj* **1** produced by synthesis: *synthetic rubber.* **2** (*informal*) not made of natural substances: *Nylon is a synthetic material.*

syn·the·sizer /'sınθəsaızə(r)/ *nc* an electronic instrument with a keyboard and controls, able to reproduce a wide variety of musical sounds.

syph·ilis /'sıfəlıs/ *nu* a kind of sexually transmitted disease.

sy·phon /'saıfn/ *n* = siphon.

sy·ringe¹ /'sırındʒ/ *nc* a device for drawing in liquid by suction and forcing it out again, used for injecting liquids into the body etc: *a hypodermic syringe.*

sy·ringe² /sı'rındʒ/ *vt* to inject liquid into (something), apply (liquid) with, a syringe.

syr·up /'sırəp/ *nu* the thick sweet liquid made from sugar-cane juice or by boiling sugar with water.

sys·tem /'sıstəm/ *nc* **1** a group of related things or parts working together: *the nervous system; the computer system; a railway system.* **2** an organized set of ideas, theories, methods etc: *a system of government.*

sys·tem·at·ic /ˌsıstə'mætık/ *adj* based on, using, a system(2): *a systematic analysis.*

sys·tem·ati·cal·ly /-klı/ *adv*

sys·tem·atize (also **-ise**) /-ətaız/ *vt* to arrange (methods, ideas etc) in a system(2).

sys·tem·ic /sı'stemık/ *adj* (*science*) (of a disease, poison etc) affecting the whole of a body, plant.

Tt

T, t /tiː/ (*pl* **T's, t's** /tiːz/) the 20th letter of the English alphabet.

'**T-junction** *nc* a place where two roads, pipes, wires etc meet to form a T.

'**T-shirt** *nc* a short-sleeved, cotton shirt like a vest, worn informally.

'**T-square** *nc* a T-shaped instrument used for drawing right angles.

ta /tɑː/ *int* (*informal*) thank you.

tab /tæb/ *nc* **1** a small piece of cloth etc fixed to clothing etc as a badge or (as a loop) for hanging up a coat etc. **2** (*informal*) an account. **keep tabs on sb/sth** to watch a person, situation etc carefully.

tab·er·nacle /'tæbənækl/ *n* (the —) the movable structure formerly used by the Jews for worship.

table¹ /'teɪbl/ *nc* **1** a piece of furniture consisting of a flat top with (usually four) legs: *a dining-table; a kitchen-table*. **clear the table** to remove the plates etc after a meal. **lay the table** to put plates, knives, forks etc on it ready for a meal. **put one's cards on the table** ⇨ card(2). **set the table** = lay the table. **turn the tables on sb** to gain a position of superiority after having been defeated or in a lower position. **wait at/on tables** to be a waiter or waitress. **2** *n sing* people seated at a table: *jokes that amused the whole table*. **3** a list, arrangement, of facts, information etc: *a timetable; a table of contents* (= in a book). ⇨ tabular.

'**table·cloth** *nc* one (to be) spread on a table.

'**table-mat** *nc* a small mat (to be) placed under a hot dish or plate on a table.

'**table-napkin** *nc* = napkin.

'**table·spoon** *nc* a large spoon for serving food from a dish etc.

'**table·spoon·ful** /-fʊl/ *nc* as much as a table-spoon can hold.

table² /'teɪbl/ *vt* to present (a proposal etc) officially for discussion: *table a motion/bill*.

tab·let /'tæblɪt/ *nc* **1** a small piece of medicine: *an aspirin tablet*. **2** a flat surface with words cut or written on it.

table ten·nis /'teɪbl tenɪs/ *nu* a game played with round bats and a small ball on a table with a net across the centre.

tab·loid /'tæblɔɪd/ *nc* a newspaper with many pictures and without long or complicated news items.

ta·boo¹ /tə'buː/ *adj* forbidden: *Many words are taboo because they are offensive*.

ta·boo² /tə'buː/ *nc,nu* (an expression, word, object, act that is forbidden because of) a religious or social reason for strong disapproval: *a taboo against drinking alcohol in some countries*.

tabu·lar /'tæbjʊlə(r)/ *adj* arranged in tables(3).

tabu·late /'tæbjʊleɪt/ *vt* to arrange (facts, figures etc) in tables(3).

tabu·la·tion /ˌtæbjʊ'leɪʃn/ *nu*

ta·cit /'tæsɪt/ *adj* (*attrib*) understood without being put into words: *tacit consent/agreement*.

ta·cit·ly *adv*

taci·turn /'tæsɪtɜːn/ *adj* (*formal*) (in the habit of) saying very little.

tack¹ /tæk/ *nc* **1** a small, flat-headed nail: *They used tacks to fasten the carpet to the floor*. ⇨ also brass(1). **2** a long, loose stitch used to fasten pieces of cloth together loosely or temporarily. **3** a sailing-ship's direction described according to the direction of the wind and the position of the sails. **on the right/wrong tack** (*fig*) following a wise/unwise course of action.

tack² /tæk/ *v* **1** *vt* to fasten (something) using tacks(1): *tack down the carpet*. **2** *vt* to fasten (cloth) using tacks(2): *tack a hem*. **3** *vi* to change the direction of a sailing-ship so that the wind blows from the other side.

tackle¹ /'tækl/ *n* **1** *nc,nu* a set of ropes and pulleys for lifting weights etc. **2** *nu* equipment for doing something: *fishing tackle*. **3** *nc* (*sport*) (in rugby) an act of seizing and bringing down an opponent with the ball; (in soccer) an act of taking the ball from an opponent.

tackle² /'tækl/ *v* **1** *vt* to deal with (a problem, a piece of work): *I don't know how to tackle this problem*. **tackle sb (about/over sth)** to speak to a person frankly (about a problem etc). **2** *vt,vi* to (try to) get the ball from (a player) in football or rugby. **3** *vt* to (try to) hold and keep (a thief, attacker etc).

tact /tækt/ *nu* (the use of) skill and understanding shown by a person who handles people and situations successfully and without causing offence: *show/have great tact*.

tact·ful /-fəl/ *adj* having or showing tact.

tact·fully /-fəlɪ/ *adv*

tact·less *adj* without tact: *a tactless remark*.

tact·less·ly *adv*

tac·tic /'tæktɪk/ *nc* **1** a means of achieving an aim. **2** (*pl*) (*mil*) the art of placing or moving fighting forces for or during battle. **3** (*pl*) (*fig*) plan(s) or method(s) for carrying out a policy: *These tactics are unlikely to help your candidate*.

tac·ti·cal /'tæktɪkl/ *adj* of, serving the purpose of, tactics (esp 3): *a tactical error*.

'**tactical weapon** *nc* a weapon used on a battle-field. Compare strategic weapon.

tac·ti·cal·ly /-klɪ/ *adv*

tac·ti·cian /tæk'tɪʃn/ *nc* an expert in tactics.

tac·tile /'tæktaɪl/ *adj* (*formal*) of, experienced by, the sense of touch: *tactile greetings* (e.g. kissing).

tad·pole /'tædpəʊl/ *nc* a form of a frog or toad between the time it leaves the egg to the time when it takes its adult form.

tag¹ /tæg/ *n* **1** *nc* a metal or plastic point at the end of a shoelace, string etc. **2** *nc* a label (showing size, a price, an address etc) fastened to or stuck into something. **3** *nu* a game in which one child chases and tries to touch another. **4** *nc* (*gram*) a short phrase used at the end of a sentence for emphasis or to form questions, esp when asking for agreement, as in 'She's such a fool, *she is*', 'It's a lovely day, *isn't it*?'

tag² /tæg/ *v* (**-gg-**) **1** *vt* to fasten a tag(2) to (something). **2** *vi* **tag along/behind (sb)** to follow (a person) closely: *Tag along with us* (= Come with us) *if you like.*

tail¹ /teɪl/ *nc* **1** the long movable part at the end of the body of a bird, some animals, fish or reptiles: *Dogs wag their tails when they are pleased.* **turn tail** to run away. **2** something like a tail in position: *the tail of a kite/plane.* **3** (*pl*) the side of a coin opposite to that on which there is the head of a ruler etc. Compare head¹(7). **4** (*informal*) a person employed to follow and watch another person: *put a tail on him.*

,**tail·'end** *nc* (the —) the final part: *at the tail-end of the procession.*

'**tail-gate** *nc* a door or flap at the back of a vehicle that can be opened for loading and unloading.

'**tail-light** *nc* a light at the back of a car, bus etc.

'**tail wind** *nc* a wind blowing in the same direction as a plane, ship etc.

tail·less *adj* having no tail: *a tailless cat.*

tail² /teɪl/ *v* **1** *vt* (*informal*) to follow (a person) closely: *The police are tailing her.* **2** *vi* **tail back** (of a queue, line of vehicles etc) to extend back a long way. Hence '**tail-back** *nc* such a line. **3** *vi* **tail away/off** to become gradually smaller in amount, size, strength etc: *His voice tailed off into silence.*

tail·or¹ /'teɪlə(r)/ *nc* a person who makes coats, suits etc for a person.

,**tailor-'made** *adj* (**a**) made by a tailor for a particular person. (**b**) (*fig; usually pred*) highly appropriate, suitable: *He seems tailor-made for the job.*

tail·or² /'teɪlə(r)/ *vt* **1** to make (a coat, suit etc), esp for a particular individual. **2** (*fig*) to arrange and adapt (a system, method, machine) for a particular purpose or person: *tailor the computer system to meet the needs of a business.*

taint¹ /teɪnt/ *nc,nu* a very small indication of some bad smell, decay etc: *There was a taint of insanity in the family.*

taint² /teɪnt/ *vt* to make (food) bad; make (a person) morally bad: *tainted meat; be tainted by deceit.*

take¹ /teɪk/ *nc* **1** an act of taking. **2** (*informal*) an amount of money obtained for a show, sale etc. **3** a period of filming or recording without stopping: *That whole scene was recorded in only two takes.*

take² /teɪk/ *v* (*pt* **took** /tʊk/, *pp* **taken** /'teɪkən/) Ⓝ 'Take' is used with many nouns referring to activity where 'take + noun' has the same meaning as the verb form of the noun, as in *take a breath* (= breathe), *take a walk* (= walk). For other examples, ⇨ the *noun* entries as at *jump, run, rest* etc. 'Take' is also used with many nouns in special senses, as in *take charge, take a hand, take place.* For these special uses, ⇨ the *noun* entries as at *account, action, care, chair, chance, charge, control, cover, courage, effect, exception, fancy, floor, heart, hint, lead, leave, life, notice, offence, opportunity, part, place, risk, shape, side, trouble.* **1** *vt* to hold, get, (a person, thing) with the hand, or with another part of the body or a tool: *He took her hand. She took the spider between her finger and thumb. The dog took the rope in its teeth. He had taken her in his arms.* **2** *vt* to cause (a person, thing) to go to another place by carrying, driving, leading etc: *I'll take her some flowers. Please take these letters to the post. He's*

taken a friend home in his car. Let's take the dog for a walk. My job often takes me abroad. This bus will take you to the station. Compare bring(1), fetch(1), send(1). **3** *vt* to accept, have, use, (something): *I'll take £40 for my bike. Please take a seat. I won't take any more of your insults. May I take this opportunity to thank you. I'll take the next bus/train home. Whose advice did you take? She's taken her punishment well.* **can/can't take it** to be able/not able to bear suffering, punishment, criticism etc easily. **take it from me** to believe me: *Take it from me, she's dishonest.* **4** *vt* to catch, gain, win (something): *The soldiers took 50 prisoners/took the town. Chris took the first set of the match. He's taken first prize. The shop took over £1000 yesterday.* ⇨ takings. ⇨ also aback, ill¹(1), short²(2), surprise², unawares. **5** *vt* to use, gain possession of, (something) (by mistake, after being offered, by stealing etc): *Someone's taken my coat. John's taken a wife. The window was broken but nothing was taken. That quotation was taken from Shakespeare. Take the second road on the right. Take this dictionary, for example. I'll take* (= buy) *the vase over there, please.* **6** *vt* to eat, drink, (something): *Do you take milk? Take an aspirin before you go to bed.* **7** *vt* to be involved in (an activity): *take a bath/holiday/walk/look/rest.* **8** *vt* to experience (a feeling etc) personally: *take pleasure/pride/an interest in one's work; take offence.* **9** *vt* to have and pay for (something) regularly: *Which newspaper do you take?* **10** *vt* to make a record of (something), e.g. after measuring, using an instrument etc: *take notes; take the measurements of a room. The doctor took my temperature. She took a photograph of the flower.* **11** *vt* to have enough space for (people, things): *This car takes 5 people. The school can take 1000 children. Will this suitcase take all your clothes?* **12** *vt* to use up, need, (time): *The work took a whole year. She takes an hour to bath. It took ten minutes to drive to the station.* **13** *vt* to use up (energy, money etc): *The holiday has taken all my savings. It took every bit of strength to get to the top.* **14** *vt* to consider (a person, look, speech etc) to be the kind mentioned; suppose: *I took you to be an honest person. He took her expression as a sign of disappointment.* ⇨ take sb for sb. **15** *vt* to organize and be in charge of (people, a group etc): *take a lesson/class/meeting.* **16** *vt* to act (a role): *take the part of the hero in the play.* **17** *vt* to study (a subject) for an examination: *I'm taking physics at university.* **18** *vi* (of glue, a photograph, an injection etc) to be successful. **19** *vt* (*gram*) (of one kind of word or structure) to use (another): *An intransitive verb does not take a direct object.*

be taken aback ⇨ aback.

take after sb to have the same appearance or character as a relative: *I take after my mother.*

take sth apart to divide a machine, engine, instrument into its parts.

take sb around to take(2) a person with one while visiting, travelling etc: *He's taking his daughter around to teach her the business.*

take sb aside to lead a person away from a group in order to talk privately.

take sth away (**a**) to take(2) food or drink out of a restaurant to eat at home. Hence '**take-away** *adj* (*attrib*), *nc* (of) a meal that is taken in this way: *Chinese take-aways*. **(b)** (*maths*) to remove (one number etc) from (another): *5 take away 3 is 2*. **take sb/sth away (from sb/sth) (a)** to remove a person, thing, (from): *take a child away from home/its parents; take a knife away from a child*. **(b)** to cause a feeling, pain, emotion, to disappear: *I'll give you a pill to take away the pain. The worry took away all my enjoyment*.

take sb back to agree to have a person as one's girlfriend, boyfriend, employee etc again. **take sth back (a)** to agree to accept something after it has been sold: *Some shops refuse to take back anything they have sold*. **(b)** to withdraw an accusing remark, criticism, statement etc as a sign of error, an apology etc: *I take back everything I said about you*. **take sb back (to sth)** to cause a person to remember (an earlier event, place, situation): *The music took me back to that holiday in Paris*. **take sb/sth back (to a place)** to take(2) a person, thing to the place where he/she/it came from: *take a child back to school; take a book back to the library*.

take sb/sth by sth (a) to take(2) a person, thing, in a bus, taxi etc. **(b)** to hold a person, thing, using the part mentioned: *take a girl by the hand; take a cup by the handle*.

take sth down (a) to write something down: *take down instructions*. **(b)** to get something by lifting it from a higher place: *take down a book*. **(c)** to separate a structure into parts: *take down the poles supporting the wall*.

take sb for sb to think that a person is another or is the kind of person mentioned by mistake: *I took you for an English person. What do you take me for?* (e.g. Do you think I'm a fool?)

take sth from sb (*informal*) to suffer insults etc from a person: *I've taken all I can stand from her!* **take sb/sth from sb/sth** = take sb/sth away (from sb/sth).

take sb in (a) to allow a person to live in one's home for payment: *take in students*. **(b)** (*informal*; often *passive*) to deceive a person: *be taken in by his charm*. **take sth in (a)** to take(2) washing etc indoors. **(b)** to receive work to be done at home: *take in typing*. **(c)** to make clothes smaller in width by sewing. **(d)** to include something: *Our holiday took in six countries. The report takes in the various schemes. Biology takes in botany*. **(e)** to (see, hear, and) understand, or be interested in, something: *I listened but I wasn't taking in a word of the lesson*.

take sb into sth (a) to lead a person into a building etc. **(b)** to allow a person to live in one's home for payment.

take off (a) (of a plane, passengers) to leave the ground. **b)** (of a business) to begin to improve: *At last our company is taking off!* **take sb off** (*informal*) to copy a person's voice, expressions etc for amusement. Hence **'take-off** *nc* **(a)** (of a plane etc) an act of leaving the ground. **(b)** an act of copying a person for amusement. **take sth off (a)** to remove clothes: *Take your coat off*. Opp put sth on(b). **(b)** to remove a bus, train etc from service. **(c)** to remove an amount of weight mentioned: *I took off 10 kilos on that diet*. **(d)** to reduce a price by an amount mentioned: *take 10% off the marked prices*. **(e)** to have an amount of time mentioned away (from work): *take a few*

days off and go walking. **(f)** to remove a play from a theatre, a programme from TV, a meal from a menu etc.

take sb on (a) to accept a person as a worker: *take on five more staff*. **(b)** to accept a person as an opponent: *take him on at golf. You can't take on the whole world!* **(c)** (of a bus, train etc) to accept people as passengers: *The bus stopped to take on some children*. **take sth on (a)** to agree and start something: *take on more work/extra responsibility*. **(b)** to change in appearance, quality, meaning etc: *After that, her warning took on a new importance*. **take on so** (*informal*) (of a person) to express strong feelings: *You mustn't take on so; you'll become ill*.

take sb out (a) to take(2) a person outside: *take the children out for a walk*. **(b)** to invite and go with a person on a social outing: *Can I take you out for dinner? Who are you taking out these days?* **take sth out (a)** (usually *passive*) to remove a tooth etc: *have a tooth taken out*. **(b)** to get an official document after payment: *take out an insurance policy/a subscription/a licence*. **(c)** to make clothes wider by sewing. **take sth out (of sth) (a)** to remove something (from): *She took a pound out of her pocket*. **(b)** to remove money owed etc (from the source mentioned): *We can take the cost/fee straight out of your wages*. **take it out of sb** (*informal*) to make a person feel very tired: *Bringing up a family takes it out of you*. **take it out on sb** (*informal*) to show one's anger, disappointment etc by being unpleasant to a person: *He was angry at losing his job and took it out on his children*.

take sb over to accept responsibility for a person from another person: *I'm hoping she'll take me over and show me what to do*. **take sth over** to succeed to the control, ownership etc of a business: *When I retire my son will take over the company*. Hence **'take-over** *nc* a change of control or ownership of a business. **take (sth) over (from sb)** to accept duties, responsibilities, control etc (from a person): *John's ill and I have to take over (his job). Take over from me while I wash my hands*.

take sb through sth to read and explain something to a person: *I'll take you through this contract so that we both understand it clearly*.

take to sth (a) to adopt something as a habit, practice, pastime etc: *take to staying up late/to reading in one's free time/to smoking cigars*. **(b)** to go to something in order to escape or be sheltered: *take to the woods*. **take to sb/sth** to develop a liking for a person, design, game etc: *She'll never take to cricket. I've really taken to my mother-in-law*. **take sth to bits/pieces** = take sth apart.

take sth up (a) to pick something up: *take up one's pen/book*. **(b)** to absorb a liquid: *take up milk with a cloth*. **(c)** to begin to do something as a pastime: *take up photography*. **(d)** to continue a story left unfinished: *Harry took up the tale at the point where John left off*. **(e)** to mention, discuss, a topic: *There is a small detail I'd like to take up with you*. **(f)** to occupy, fill, time or space: *This bed takes up too much space. The afternoon was taken up with cooking and cleaning*. **(g)** to make clothes shorter by sewing. **take sth up with sb**

to speak, write, to a person about something: *I promise to take your problem up with the manager.*

take-away /'teɪk əweɪ/ *nc* ⇨ take sth away.

take-off /'teɪk ɒf/ *nc* ⇨ take sb off.

take-over /'teɪk əʊvə(r)/ *nc* ⇨ take sth over.

taker /'teɪkə(r)/ *nc* a person who accepts an offer from a person selling something.

tak·ings /'teɪkɪŋz/ *n pl* an amount of money received by a business, esp a shop.

tal·cum powder /'tælkəm paʊdə(r)/ *nu* a kind of perfumed powder for the skin.

tale /teɪl/ *nc* **1** a (usually short and simple) story: *tales of adventure.* **2** a report; account: *If you try that, you'll never live to tell the tale.* **tell tales** to tell something critical about a person to get her or him into trouble. ⇨ tell-tale.

tal·ent /'tælənt/ *nc,nu* **talent (for sth)** (an example of) natural ability (to do something well): *a person of many talents; have a talent for music/not much talent for painting.*

tal·ent·ed *adj* having talent.

tal·is·man /'tælɪsmən/ *nc* a lucky charm.

talk¹ /tɔːk/ *n* **1** *nc,nu* **talk (with sb)** a conversation; discussion: *I've had several talks with the head teacher about my boy.* ⇨ small talk. **2** *nu* gossip: *There's been a great deal of talk about my neighbours lately.* **the talk of the town** a person, thing, that everyone is gossiping about. **3** *nc* **talk (about/on sth)** an informal speech: *give a talk on a holiday in Kenya.*

talk² /tɔːk/ *v* **1** *vi* **talk (to sb) (about sb/sth)** to speak (to a person) in order to give information, have a discussion etc (about): *He was talking to a friend. He was talking about his new job. What are they talking about? I'll talk to her on the telephone tonight. Can I talk to you for a minute, please? They're not talking to each other* (i.e. because they have quarrelled.) Ⓝ For the difference between *talk* and *speak,* ⇨ speak(1). **You can/can't talk!** (*informal*) You have no right to be critical because you‚ are the same! **talking of sb/ sth, . . .** (*informal*) while he/she/it is being discussed I would like to mention: *Talking of travel, have you ever been to Peru?* **2** *vi* to have the power of speech; be able to use words: *She's very ill and cannot talk at the moment. Babies learn to talk around the first year.* **3** *vt* to have a conversation using (a language): *They're talking French.* Ⓝ 'Talk' is used with a language only when referring to a conversation, discussion etc. 'Speak' is used when referring to the ability to use a language or the way one uses a language, as in *She can speak Russian (well).* **4** *vt* to have a conversation about (a subject); say (the kind of thing mentioned): *We talked computers all evening. He talks sense/nonsense/rubbish.* **talk big** to say one has great ability, a lot of money etc. **talk shop** ⇨ shop¹(2). **5** *v reflex* to cause (oneself) to be in the condition mentioned: *talk oneself hoarse.* **6** *vi* to gossip: *I won't stay late—you know how people talk.* **7** *vi* (*fig*) to have influence: *Money/Power talks.* **8** *vi* to give information (after suffering threats, beatings etc): *Let him have no food for a few days and then he'll talk.*

talk about sb (a) ⇨ 1 above. (b) to discuss a possible course of action: *He's talking about going to live in America.* **be/get oneself talked**

about to become the subject of gossip: *If you go out late you'll get yourself talked about.*

talk back to reply (suggesting rudeness): *I wish my son wouldn't talk back each time I tell him he's done something wrong.*

talk down to sb to talk to a person as if that person is inferior.

talk in a language to have a discussion or conversation in: *We talked in Spanish.* ⇨ speak in a language.

talk sb into doing sth to discuss, argue, with a person and persuade her or him to do something: *Who talked you into buying this cassette player?*

talk of sb/sth to discuss a person, thing: *For days people talked of nothing else but the air crash.*

talk of doing sth to speak about the possibility of doing something: *She's talking of becoming an engineer.*

talk sb out of doing sth to discuss, argue with a person and persuade her or him not to do something: *He talked me out of buying it.*

talk sth over (with sb) to discuss a possibility, issue, plan etc fully (with a person): *I'll talk it over with my wife and tell you what we've decided.*

talk sb round to persuade a person to do something that he or she did not want to do: *I didn't want to go but she talked me round.* **talk round sth** to avoid mentioning a subject directly in a conversation (and so not reach a decision etc): *We talked round the problem all evening.*

talk sb through sth to describe the movements etc he or she must make in order to do something.

talk to sb (a) ⇨ 1 above. (b) to complain to a person. ⇨ talking-to.

talka·tive /'tɔːkətɪv/ *adj* fond of talking.

talk·er /'tɔːkə(r)/ *nc* a person who talks in the way mentioned: *a good/poor talker.*

talk·ing point /'tɔːkɪŋ pɔɪnt/ *nc* a topic for discussion.

talking-to /'tɔːkɪŋ tuː/ *nc* (*informal*) a speech in which one describes a person's faults or errors: *I'll have to give that boy a talking-to.*

tall /tɔːl/ *adj* (**—er, —est**) **1** (of a person, mountain etc) above the average or usual height: *a tall girl; a tall tower.* Opp short¹(2). Compare high¹(1). **2** (*pred*) having the height mentioned: *Tom is nearly two metres tall.* **3 a tall order** ⇨ order¹(6). **a tall story** ⇨ story¹(2).

tall·ish /-ɪʃ/ *adj* rather tall.

tall·ness *nu*

tal·ly /'tælɪ/ *vi* (*pt,pp* **-ied**) **tally (with sth)** (of stories, amounts etc) to agree: *The two lists do not tally. Does your total tally with mine?*

tal·on /'tælən/ *nc* a curved claw of a bird, e.g. an eagle.

tam·bour·ine /ˌtæmbə'riːn/ *nc* a musical instrument with a ring of metal discs, that is shaken or hit with the hand.

tame¹ /teɪm/ *adj* (**—r, —st**) **1** (of an animal) trained to live with people and obey orders: *a tame monkey.* Compare wild¹(1). **2** (*derog*) dull; not exciting: *The story/film has a tame ending.*

tame·ly *adv*

tame·ness *nu*

tame² /teɪm/ *vt* to make (an animal) tame: *tame a lion.*

tamer *nc* a person who tames animals: *a lion-*

tamer.

tam·per /'tæmpə(r)/ *vi* **tamper (with sth)** to interfere with something: *Someone has been tampering with the lock*.

tam·pon /'tæmpɒn/ *nc* a long piece of cotton-wool etc, used inside a woman to collect blood during her period(3).

tan¹ /tæn/ *adj, nc* yellowish-brown (colour); sun-tan: *tan leather gloves; get a good tan* (i.e. on one's skin).

tan² /tæn/ *v* (**-nn-**) **1** *vt,vi* (to cause a person) to become brown with sunburn: *Some people tan quickly*. **2** *vt* to make (animal skin) into leather. **tan sb's hide** (*sl*) to give a person a good beating.
tan·ner *nc* a person who tans skins.
tan·nery /'tænərɪ/ *nc* (*pl* **-ies**) a place where animal skins are tanned.

tan³ /tæn/ *abbr* (*maths*) tangent.

tan·dem /'tændəm/ *nc* a bicycle made for two people to ride on with pedals for both.

tang /tæŋ/ *nc* a strong, sharp taste or smell: *the salty tang of the sea air*.

tan·gent /'tændʒənt/ *nc* (*maths*) (abbr tan) a straight line touching a curve. **go/fly off at a tangent** (*fig*) to change suddenly from one line of thought, action etc to another.

tan·ger·ine /ˌtændʒə'riːn/ *nc* a kind of small, sweet orange.

tan·gible /'tændʒəbl/ *adj* **1** that can be known by touch. Compare intangible. **2** clear and definite: *tangible proof*.
tan·gibly /-əblɪ/ *adv*

tangle¹ /'tæŋgl/ *nc* **1** a confused mass (of string, hair etc): *brush the tangles out of a dog's hair*. **2** (*fig*) a confused state: *The traffic was in a tangle*.

tangle² /'tæŋgl/ *v* **1** *vt,vi* (to cause something) to become confused, disordered: *tangled hair*. **2** *vi* **tangle with sb** (*informal*) to become involved in a fight or quarrel with a person: *Don't tangle with Peter—he's bigger than you*.

tan·go /'tæŋgəʊ/ *nc* (*pl* **—s**) (music for) a kind of S American dance: *dance a/the tango*.

tank /tæŋk/ *nc* **1** a (usually large) container for liquid or gas: *the petrol-tank of a car; an oil-tank*. **2** an armoured fighting vehicle with guns, moving on belts instead of wheels.
tank·er *nc* a ship or heavy road vehicle, used for carrying liquid: *an oil-tanker*.
tank·ard /'tæŋkəd/ *nc* a large drinking mug, esp one for beer.
tan·ner, tan·nery ⇨ tan².

tan·ta·lize (also **-ise**) /'tæntəlaɪz/ *vt* to tease (a person) by raising hopes that cannot (yet) be realized.
tan·ta·liz·ing *adj* attractive: *a tantalizing smell of food*.

tan·ta·mount /'tæntəmaʊnt/ *adj* (*pred*) **tantamount to sth** equal in effect to: *Her request was tantamount to a command*.

tan·trum /'tæntrəm/ *nc* (*pl* **—s**) a fit of temper or anger: *He's in one of his tantrums again*.

tap¹ /tæp/ *nc* an apparatus used for controlling the flow of liquid or gas from a pipe, barrel etc: *Turn the tap on/off. Don't leave the tap running* (i.e. turn it off). **on tap** (*fig*) available immediately: *The figures you need for last month's sale are now on tap*.

tap² /tæp/ *nc* a quick, light touch or blow: *a tap on the window/at the door*.

tap³ /tæp/ *vt,vi* (**-pp-**) **tap (sb/sth) (at/on sth)** to give a quick, light touch (to a person, thing) (on something): *tap her on the shoulder; tap at/on a window*.

tap⁴ /tæp/ *vt* (**-pp-**) **1** to get (liquid) from (a container) by opening a tap: *tap beer from a barrel*. **2** to get (liquid called *sap*) from a tree by cutting the bark. **3** (*fig*) to get (something) gradually from (a person, thing): *tap a man for information; tap the wealth of the sea*. **4** to get information from (a telephone call) by listening secretly: *tap a conversation/telephone*.

tape¹ /teɪp/ *nc,nu* **1** (a length of) a narrow strip of material used for tying up parcels etc or in dressmaking: *three metres of tape*. ⇨ also insulating tape, red tape. **2** a length of tape between the winning-posts on a race-track (not now used in major competitions). **3** = magnetic tape or videotape.
'tape deck *nc* a tape recorder (without speakers or amplifiers) as part of a hi-fi system.
'tape-measure *nc* a length of metal or cloth marked for measuring distances, widths etc.
'tape-recorder *nc* an electrical apparatus for recording sound and playing sound back using magnetic tape.
ˌtape-to-'tape *adj, adv* from one recorded tape to another: *record tape-to-tape; a tape-to-tape recording*.

tape² /teɪp/ *vt* **1** **tape sth (up)** to fasten, tie, something together with tape. **2** to record (sound) on magnetic tape. **3** **have sb/sth taped** (*informal*) to understand a person, machine, method etc thoroughly.

ta·per¹ /'teɪpə(r)/ *nc* a length of string with a covering of wax, burnt to give a light.

ta·per² /'teɪpə(r)/ *vt,vi* **taper (sth) (off)** (to cause something) to become gradually narrower towards one end: *One end tapers/is tapered (off) to a point*.

tap·es·try /'tæpɪstrɪ/ *nc,nu* (*pl* **-ies**) (a piece of) cloth into which threads of coloured wool are woven by hand to make designs and pictures.

tape·worm /'teɪpwɜːm/ *nc* a kind of long, flat worm that lives inside people and animals.

tapi·oca /ˌtæpɪ'əʊkə/ *nu* (also *attrib*) a kind of food (hard, white grains) used to make a milk pudding: *tapioca pudding*.

tar¹ /tɑː(r)/ *nc* a black substance obtained from coal etc, used to preserve wood, make roads etc.
'tar·mac *nu,nc* (also *attrib*) (a mixture of tar and gravel, as used for) a road surface: *tarmac roads*.

tar² /tɑː(r)/ *vt* (**-rr-**) to cover (a road etc) with tar. **tar and feather sb** to put tar on a person and then cover her or him with feathers as a punishment. **tarred with the same brush** (*informal*) having the same faults.

ta·ran·tu·la /tə'ræntjʊlə/ *nc* a kind of large, hairy, poisonous spider.

tar·get /'tɑːgɪt/ *nc* (also *attrib*) **1** something (to be) aimed at when shooting etc: *the target area*. **2** anything (an amount, extent etc) which one wants to achieve: *My target is to swim 1000 metres a day/ to save £20 a week/to lose 5 kilos a month. That's my target figure*. **3** a thing, plan etc against which criticism is directed: *This book will be the target of* *a lot of criticism*.

tar·iff /'tærɪf/ *nc* **1** a list of fixed charges, esp for meals, rooms etc at a hotel. **2** a list of taxes on goods imported.

tar·mac /'tɑːmæk/ *nc,nu* ⇨ tar.

tarn /tɑːn/ *nc* a small mountain lake.

tar·nish¹ /'tɑːnɪʃ/ *nu* dullness (on metal) because the brightness has gone.

tar·nish² /'tɑːnɪʃ/ *vi,vt* **1** (to cause a metal) to lose brightness: *Brass tarnishes easily*. **2** (*fig*) to lessen the quality of (a person's reputation): *His reputation is tarnished*.

tar·pau·lin /tɑː'pɔːlɪn/ *nc,nu* (a sheet or cover of) heavy cloth made waterproof by being covered with tar.

tar·ra·gon /'tærəgən/ *nu* (also *attrib*) a kind of herb with sharp-tasting leaves: *tarragon vinegar*.

tart¹ /tɑːt/ *adj* **1** very sour: *a tart flavour*. **2** (*fig; derog*) unpleasant and hurting people's feelings: *tart humour*.

tart·ly *adv*

tart² /tɑːt/ *nc* a piece of pastry with fruit or jam on it: *apple tarts*.

tart³ /tɑːt/ *nc* (*sl; derog*) a girl or woman of immoral character.

tart⁴ /tɑːt/ *vt* **tart oneself/sb/sth up** (*informal*) to dress, decorate, oneself, a person, thing, (too) brightly.

tar·tan /'tɑːtən/ *nc,nu* (a particular kind of) Scottish woollen fabric woven with coloured crossing stripes.

tar·tar¹ /'tɑːtə(r)/ *nu* a hard substance formed on the teeth by food, salts etc. ⇨ plaque(2).

task /tɑːsk/ *nc* a particular piece of work (to be) done: *set a boy a task*. **take sb to task (about/ for sth)** to criticize a person.

'task-force *nc* an organized unit (of soldiers, police etc) for a special purpose.

'task-master/-mistress *nc* (*derog*) a person who decides on (unpleasant or difficult) work to be done: *a hard task-master*.

tas·sel /'tæsl/ *nc* a bunch of threads etc tied together at one end and hanging (from a lampshade etc) as an ornament.

taste¹ /teɪst/ *n* **1** *nu* the sense by which flavour is known: *sweet/sour to the taste*. **2** *nc,nu* the quality of a substance made known by this sense: *Sugar has a sweet taste*. **3** *nc* (usually *sing*) a small quantity (of something to eat or drink): *Won't you have a taste of this cake/wine?* **4** *nc,nu* (a) liking or preference: *She has expensive tastes in clothes*. **an acquired taste** a liking for a particular kind of food only after tasting it often: *Is beer an acquired taste?* **There's no accounting for tastes** (*saying*) It is not obvious why different people like different things. **5** *nu* the ability to enjoy beauty, to form judgements, to choose and use the best kind: *She's a woman of great musical/ literary/artistic taste*.

taste·ful /-fəl/ *adj* showing good taste(5). Compare distasteful.

taste·fully /-fəlɪ/ *adv*

taste·less *adj* (*derog*) **(a)** (of food) having no flavour. **(b)** without taste(5).

tasty *adj* (**-ier, -iest**) having a pleasant flavour.

taste² /teɪst/ *v* **1** *vi* **taste** + *adj*; **taste of sth** to have the taste(2) or flavour mentioned: *It tastes sour/bitter/sweet. This coffee tastes of soap!* Ⓝ

Not used in continuous tenses, e.g. *is/was* -*ing*. **2** *vt* to test the flavour of (something): *She tasted the soup to see if she had put enough salt in it*. **3** *vt* to experience the taste(2) of (something): *Can you taste anything strange in this ice-cream?* **4** *vt* (*fig*) to experience (something): *taste happiness/the joys of freedom*.

tat /tæt/ *n* ⇨ tit².

ta ta /ˌtɑː 'tɑː/ *int* (*informal*) goodbye.

tat·ters /'tætəz/ *n pl* (esp **in tatters**) pieces of cloth, paper etc torn off or hanging from something: *The book was in tatters*.

tat·too¹ /tæ'tuː/ *n* (*pl* —**s**) **1** *n sing* the beating of drum(s) to call soldiers back to quarters; hour at which this is sounded: *beat/sound the tattoo*. **2** *nc* a public entertainment, with music, marching etc by soldiers: *a military tattoo*.

tat·too² /tæ'tuː/ *nc* (*pl* —**s**) a design made by tattooing.

tat·too³ /tæ'tuː/ *vt* to mark (a person's skin) with permanent designs or patterns by pricking it and putting in dyes or stains: *The sailor had a ship tattooed on his arm*.

tat·ty /'tætɪ/ *adj* (**-ier, -iest**) (*informal; derog*) untidy and worn: *tatty clothes/furniture*.

taught /tɔːt/ *pt,pp* of teach.

taunt¹ /tɔːnt/ *nc* an unkind remark intended to hurt a person's feelings: *the taunts of a successful rival*.

taunt² /tɔːnt/ *vt* to attack (a person) with taunts: *They taunted the boy with being a coward*.

taunt·ing·ly *adv*

Tau·rus /'tɔːrəs/ *n* the Bull, second sign of the zodiac.

taut /tɔːt/ *adj* (—**er**, —**est**) (of ropes, the skin etc) tightly stretched: *pull a rope taut; a taut expression*.

tauto·logi·cal /ˌtɔːtə'lɒdʒɪkl/ *adj* of, containing, tautology.

taut·ol·ogy /tɔː'tɒlədʒɪ/ *nc,nu* (*lang*) (an instance of) saying the same thing in different ways, esp by using unnecessary words, as in '*a two-wheeled bicycle*' ('bicycle' means 'having two wheels'); '*modern fashions of today*' ('modern' means 'of today').

tav·ern /'tævən/ *nc* (*old use*) a pub.

taw·dry /'tɔːdrɪ/ *adj* (**-ier, -iest**) (*derog*) brightly coloured or decorated, but cheap or in bad taste: *tawdry jewellery/dresses*.

taw·dri·ly /-əlɪ/ *adv*

taw·ny /'tɔːnɪ/ *adj, nu* brownish-yellow (colour).

tax¹ /tæks/ *n* **1** *nc,nu* (an amount of) money (to be) paid by citizens to the government: *direct taxes* (i.e. on income)*; indirect taxes* (e.g. paid on goods bought). **2** *n sing* **tax on sth** something that is a burden or strain: *a tax on one's strength/ health/patience*.

'tax-collector *nc* an official who collects taxes.

ˌtax-'free *adj* free from tax: *tax-free earnings*.

'tax·payer *nc* a person who pays taxes.

'tax return *nc* a paper providing information about income and expenses, used to calculate tax.

tax·able /-əbl/ *adj* to be taxed: *taxable income*.

tax·ation /tæk'seɪʃn/ *nu* (the system of) raising money by taxes; taxes (to be) paid.

tax² /tæks/ *vt* **1** to charge a tax on (something): *tax luxuries/incomes/rich and poor alike*. **2** to be a burden or strain on (a person, feeling): *tax a* *person's patience.*

taxi[1] /ˈtæksɪ/ *nc* (*pl* **—s**) a car with a meter for payment, that may be hired for journeys.

ˈtaxi-cab *nc* (common abbr cab) = taxi.

ˈtaxi rank *nc* a place where taxis wait to be hired.

taxi[2] /ˈtæksɪ/ *vi* (of a plane) to move on wheels along the ground: *The plane taxied/was taxiing along the runway.*

TB /ˌtiː'biː/ *abbr* (*med*) tuberculosis.

tbs(p) *written abbr* tablespoon(ful).

tea /tiː/ *n* **1** *nu* (also *attrib*) (the dried leaves of) a kind of a small bush of eastern Asia, India etc, used to make a drink by pouring hot water on the leaves: *a packet of tea; Chinese tea; a cup of tea; tea leaves.* **not my cup of tea** (*fig*) not the sort of thing I like. **2** *nc* a cup etc of tea(1): *Two teas, please.* **3** *nc,nu* a meal, occasion (in the late afternoon) at which tea is drunk: *We have tea at half-past four.* ⇨ high tea.

ˈtea bag *nc* a small bag with enough tea leaves for one cup of tea.

ˈtea-break *nc* (in an office, factory etc) a short period when work is stopped for drinking tea.

ˈtea-caddy *nc* (*pl* **-ies**) a box for keeping tea leaves.

ˈtea-cloth *nc* a cloth used for drying cups etc when they are washed.

ˈtea-cosy *nc* (*pl* **-ies**) a cover for keeping the contents of a teapot warm.

ˈtea-cup *nc* a cup in which tea is served. *a storm in a teacup* ⇨ storm[1](1).

ˈtea-pot *nc* a pot in which tea is made.

ˈtea-room *nc* a restaurant which serves tea and light refreshments.

ˈtea-service/-set *nc* a set of cups, saucers, plates with a teapot, milk jug etc.

ˈtea-spoon *nc* a small spoon for stirring tea.

ˈtea-spoon·ful /-fʊl/ *nc* as much as a teaspoon can hold.

ˈtea-strainer *nc* a utensil for pouring tea through to stop tea leaves getting into the cup.

ˈtea-things *n pl* (the —) (*informal*) the things used for having tea: *Please wash up the tea-things.*

ˈtea-time *nu* the time when tea(3) is usually taken in the afternoon.

teach /tiːtʃ/ *vt,vi* (*pt,pp* **taught** /tɔːt/) **1** *vt,vi* to give (a person) instruction or training (in an area of knowledge, skill etc): *teach a child (how) to swim. My dad's teaching me to drive. I was taught that swearing is wrong. She teaches at a university/ school/college in Brazil. He teaches French/engineering/football/the piano.* Compare learn(1). **2** *vt* **teach sb (not) to** + *verb* to show (a person) why something should (not) be done: *That experience will teach her not to touch hot things.*

teach·er *nc* a person who teaches (for a living).

teach·ing (**a**) *nu* the work, profession of a teacher: *earn a living by teaching.* (**b**) (*pl*) ideas (esp religious) that are (to be) taught; *the teachings of Islam.*

teak /tiːk/ *nc,nu* (the hard wood of) a kind of tall, evergreen tree, used for making furniture etc.

team[1] /tiːm/ *nc* or *npl* **1** (also *attrib*) a number of people playing together and forming one side in a game or sport: *a football team; team games; team spirit. I'm a member of the school swimming team. Which team is winning/do you play for?* **2** a group

of people working together: *a team of surgeons in the operating theatre.* **3** two or more animals pulling a cart etc: *a team of horses.*

ˈteam-work *nu* organized cooperation; united effort: *good/poor team-work.*

ˈteam-mate *nc* a fellow member of a team(1).

ˌteam ˈspirit *nu* the loyal feeling between members of a team(1) helping each other to win.

team[2] /tiːm/ *vi* **team up (with sb)** to work, cooperate, (with a person): *team up with a friend to organize a party.*

tear[1] /tɪə(r)/ *nc* a drop of salty water coming from the eye: *Her eyes filled with tears.* **in tears** crying. **burst into tears** to begin to cry suddenly. **move sb to tears** (of a sad story, feeling etc) to make a person cry. **shed tears/a tear** to cry.

ˈtear-drop *nc* a single tear.

ˈtear-gas *nu* a kind of gas that causes severe watering of the eyes (as used by police etc).

tear·ful /-fəl/ *adj* crying; wet with tears: *a tearful face.*

tear·ful·ly /-fəlɪ/ *adv*

tear[2] /teə(r)/ *nc* a torn place: *a tear in his trousers.* **wear and tear** ⇨ wear[1](2).

tear[3] /teə(r)/ *v* (*pt* **tore** /tɔː(r)/, *pp* **torn** /tɔːn/) **1** *vt* to pull (something) into pieces or so that there is a hole: *I've torn my dress on a nail. She tore the paper in half/in two. She was tearing it to pieces/ bits. He tore the parcel open.* **that's torn it** (*informal*) that action, statement etc has created a difficulty: *'I've told my mother all about you.'— 'That's torn it—she'll never like me now'.* **2** *vt* to remove (a person, animal, thing) by pulling: *tear a page out of a book; tear the curtains down; tear a picture off a wall; tear a child away from the edge.* **3** *vi* to become torn: *Some cloth tears easily/is difficult to tear.* **4** *vi* to move in excitement or very fast (in the direction mentioned): *The children tore out of the gates/down the street/into the park/ across the road.*

tear oneself away (used with *can/could*) to make oneself leave a place, stop doing something: *The book/TV programme/game was so exciting I couldn't tear myself away. She could hardly tear herself away from the scene.*

be torn between sth and sth to be unable to choose between (opposing wishes, possibilities).

tear sth down to pull a building down: *They tore down several houses and built an office-block.* ⇨ also 2 above.

tear sth off (**a**) ⇨ 2 above. (**b**) to write or draw a letter, diagram etc quickly: *tear off a letter to the bank.* Ⓝ *'Toss something off'* is more usual.

tear sth up (into sth) to tear(1) (esp) paper into small pieces: *I found that letter and I tore it up. He tore up the note into tiny pieces.*

tear·away /ˈteərəweɪ/ *nc* (*derog*) an uncontrollable, ill-mannered or violent young person: *He's a young tearaway.*

tease /tiːz/ *vt* **1** to make fun of (a person) playfully or unkindly: *She teased her father about his bald head.* **2** to annoy (an animal): *Molly was teasing the cat* (e.g. by pulling its tail).

teas·er *nc* a person who often teases.

teaspoon /ˈtiːspuːn/ ⇨ tea.

teat /tiːt/ *nc* a plastic copy of a nipple, e.g. on a baby's bottle.

Tech /tek/ *abbr* Polytechnic; Technical (College).

tech·ni·cal /'teknɪkl/ adj **1** of, concerning, a practical, mechanical or industrial skill: *technical ability; go to a technical college. Engineering is a technical subject.* **2** of, concerning, a particular subject or activity: *the technical language of computers.* **3** according to a strict interpretation of a rule, law etc: *win a technical victory but gain nothing.*
  tech·ni·cal·ly /-klɪ/ adv
tech·ni·cal·ity /ˌteknɪ'kælətɪ/ nc (pl **-ies**) a technical(2) word, phrase, point etc: *The judge explained the legal technicalities of the case to the jury.*
tech·ni·cian /tek'nɪʃn/ nc a person with a practical, mechanical or industrial skill: *a laboratory technician.*
tech·nique /tek'ni:k/ n **1** nu practical skill in art, music etc: *He played the right notes but had poor technique.* **2** nc a practical method applied to a particular task: *the technique of painting water/ playing a guitar; a useful technique for removing stains/putting up a tent.*
tech·no·logi·cal /ˌteknə'lɒdʒɪkl/ adj of technology: *a technological society.*
tech·nol·ogist /tek'nɒlədʒɪst/ nc an expert in, student of, technology.
tech·nol·ogy /tek'nɒlədʒɪ/ nu **1** the use of technical skills in industry. **2** the scientific theory, methods, used in technical skills: *study engineering at a college of technology.* ⇨ polytechnic.
ted·dy bear /'tedɪ beə(r)/ (also **teddy,** pl **-dies**) nc a soft toy bear for children.
tedi·ous /'ti:dɪəs/ adj long, tiring and not interesting: *a tedious lecture/lecturer; tedious work.*
  tedi·ous·ly adv
te·di·um /'ti:dɪəm/ nu (formal) boredom.
tee¹ /ti:/ nc (golf) (a piece marking) a place from which a player starts at each hole. **to a tee** perfectly; exactly: *She suits him to a tee.*
tee² /ti:/ vi **tee off** to hit a golf ball from a tee.
teem /ti:m/ vi **1 teem (down) (with sth)** to fall heavily (with rain): *It was teeming (down) with rain.* **2 teem (with sth)** to be present, have, in large numbers: *Fish teem in this river. His head is teeming with bright ideas.*
teen·age /'ti:neɪdʒ/ adj (attrib) for, of, people in their teens: *teenage fashions/music.*
teen·ager /'ti:neɪdʒə(r)/ nc a person between about 13 and 19 years of age: *a club for teenagers.*
teens /ti:nz/ n pl the period between ages 13 and 19: *girls in their teens.*
tee-shirt /'ti: ʃɜ:t/ nc = T-shirt. ⇨ T, t.
tee·ter /'ti:tə(r)/ vi **1** to stand or move unsteadily: *teeter along a narrow pole.* **2 teeter on sth** to be about to suffer failure, disaster, death etc: *teetering on the edge of disaster.*
teeth /ti:θ/ pl of tooth.
teethe /ti:ð/ vi (of a baby) to get its first teeth.
  'teething troubles n pl (fig) problems which occur when something is first used.
tee·to·tal /ti:'təʊtl/ adj not drinking alcoholic liquor.
  tee·to·tal·ler (US also **tee·to·tal·er**) nc a person who does not drink alcoholic liquor.
TEFL /'tefl/ acronym teaching English as a foreign language.
tel. written abbr telephone.
tele·com·mu·ni·ca·tions /ˌtelɪkəˌmju:nɪ-

'keɪʃnz/ n pl communications by telegraph, telephone, radio or TV.
tele·fax /'telɪfæks/ nu (tech) a process of sending writing and pictures to another place using a computer-linked telephone system.
tele·gram /'telɪgræm/ nc a message sent by telegraph.
tele·graph /'telɪgrɑ:f/ nc an apparatus for sending messages by the use of electric current along wires or by radio. □ vi,vt to send (news etc) by telegraph.
  tele·graph·ic /ˌtelɪ'græfɪk/ adj
tel·egra·phy /tɪ'legrəfɪ/ nu the science, process, of sending and receiving messages by telegraph.
tel·epa·thy /tɪ'lepəθɪ/ nu the sending of thoughts or ideas from one mind to another without using speech, signs etc.
  tele·path·ic /ˌtelɪ'pæθɪk/ adj (esp) having the ability to receive or send thoughts without using speech or writing.
tele·phone¹ /'telɪfəʊn/ nc,nu (also attrib) (usually *phone,* esp in speech) an apparatus using electricity to send sound over long distances: *Can you let me know by (tele)phone as soon as possible. What's your (tele)phone number? He's on the phone* (i.e. using a telephone). *You're wanted on the phone* (i.e. Someone wishes to talk to you by telephone). **answer the (tele)phone** to pick up a receiver when the telephone has rung.
  'telephone booth nc (also *phone booth* or *call-box*) a small enclosure with a public telephone.
  'telephone directory nc (informal = *phone book*) a list of names with telephone numbers and addresses.
tele·phone² /'telɪfəʊn/ vt,vi (usually *phone,* esp in speech) **1** to give a message etc using a telephone: *Did my mother (tele)phone? If anyone (tele)phones, tell them I'm out. I'll (tele)phone my wife/boss/the office/home.* **2** to be able to use (a telephone), reach (a place), using a telephone: *Can I telephone Australia from this phone?*
tel·ephon·ist /tɪ'lefənɪst/ nc a person who makes telephone connections in an office or at the central office of a telephone company.
tele·pho·to lens /ˌtelɪfəʊtəʊ 'lenz/ nc (photography) an apparatus that increases the ability of a camera to make distant objects larger.
tele·scope¹ /'telɪskəʊp/ nc a long instrument with lenses, used to make distant objects appear nearer and larger.
tele·scope² /'telɪskəʊp/ vt,vi (to cause something) to become come shorter by having sections that slide into each other: *The camera telescopes to fit into a bag.*
tele·scop·ic /ˌtelɪ'skɒpɪk/ adj **1** of, able to be seen with, a telescope: *a telescopic view of the moon.* **2** having sections which slide into each other: *a telescopic aerial.*
tele·vise /'telɪvaɪz/ vt to send a report and picture of (something) by television: *The Olympic Games were televised.*
tele·vi·sion /'telɪvɪʒn/ n (abbr TV) **1** nu the process of sending pictures, usually with sound, using electrical waves: *Did you see the news on (the) television?* **2** nc (also *television set*) an apparatus for receiving and showing these pictures.
tel·ex¹ /'teleks/ nc,nu (also attrib) (an instance

of) sending messages very long distances by a system that changes signals into typed words: *send a message by telex; a telex machine.*

tel·ex² /'teleks/ *vt,vi* to send a message (to a person) using a telex machine: *I've telexed her.*

tell /tel/ *v* (*pt,pp* **told** /təʊld/) **1** *vt* to make (something) known (to a person) using words: *I told him my name/that I couldn't come. I'd like you to tell that to my father. I can't tell you* (= It is difficult to express) *how happy I am. He told a lie. Always try to tell the truth.* Ⓝ For a comparison of *tell* and *say*, ⇨ say²(1). **I told you so** I warned you it would happen (and I was right): *'I've failed the exam.'—'I told you so!'* ⇨ also fortune(1), tale(2). **2** *vt* to give an order to (a person): *We told you not to do that. Tell him to wait. Please do as you're told.* **3** *vt* to give (a person) an account or report of (something): *She's told me (about) her difficulties. He was telling us of his problems finding a place to live.* **4** *vt,vi* to make a secret known (to a person): *Please don't tell (anyone). You promised not to tell but everyone knows.* ⇨ tell (on sb) (b). **5** *vt* to say something firmly to (a person): *I'm telling you I'm not giving you any more money.* **6** *vt* to give information to (a person): *That red light tells you the bag is full.* **7** *vt* to know or recognize (something) by looking, feeling etc: *How do you tell which key to use? Can you tell which glove is yours?* **there is/was no telling** it is/was impossible to know: *There's no telling where she's gone/what he's doing.* **8** *vt* (used with *can/could* etc) to discover, identify (a person, thing): *How can you tell which twin is which? Can you tell butter from margarine? 'Who'll win the competition?'—'Who can tell?'* **9** *vt* **tell (sb) the time** ⇨ time¹(3).

tell sb about sb/sth to give a person information about a person, thing: *Tell me about your holiday.*

tell against sb (of age, size, experience etc) to be something that prevents a person from being accepted, successful etc: *His behaviour is sure to tell against him.*

tell sb/sth apart to be able to identify the particular features of two similar people or things. ⇨ also difference(2).

tell by sth to judge, identify, something by looking etc: *I can tell by your face that you're lying.*

tell from sth = tell by sth. **tell sb/sth from sb/sth** = tell sb/sth apart.

tell sb off (for (doing) sth) (*informal*) to blame, criticize, a person using angry words: *He told me off for being late. I got told off* (= was told off) *for being late.* Hence **,telling-'off** *nc* such an act.

tell on sb (a) to have an effect on the health etc of a person: *The long hours/pressures/responsibilities are beginning to tell (on her).* (b) (*informal*) (used esp by children) to report what a person has done wrong in order to get her or him into trouble: *Do you promise not to tell on me?*

tell·er /'telə(r)/ *nc* **1** a person who receives and pays out money in a bank. **2** a person who counts votes.

tell·ing /'telɪŋ/ *adj* effective: *a telling argument/ blow.*

tell·ing-off /,telɪŋ 'ɒf/ *nc* ⇨ tell sb off.

tell-tale¹ /'telteɪl/ *adj* (*attrib*) that causes something to be known: *a tell-tale mark/blush/look.*

tell-tale² /'telteɪl/ *nc* a person who tells about another's private affairs, makes known a secret etc.

tel·ly /'telɪ/ *nc,nu* (*pl* **-ies**) (*informal*) = television: *I saw it on (the) telly.*

te·mer·ity /tɪ'merətɪ/ *nu* (*formal*) foolishly rude speech or action: *They had the temerity to leave the meeting early after arriving late.*

temp /temp/ *abbr* **1** temperature. **2** (a) temporary (worker).

tem·per¹ /'tempə(r)/ *nc,nu* a (mentioned) state or condition of the mind: *in a good temper* (i.e. calm and pleasant); *in a bad temper* (also *in a temper*) (i.e. angry, impatient etc). **fly/get into a temper** to become very angry. **have a short temper** to be easily or quickly made angry. Hence **,short-'tempered** *adj* (*derog*). **keep/ lose one's temper** to keep/fail to keep one's temper under control.

tem·per² /'tempə(r)/ *vt* **1** to harden (metal) by heating and cooling. **2** (*fig; formal*) to make (a judgement etc) less severe: *temper justice with mercy.*

tem·pera·ment /'tempərəmənt/ *nc,nu* a person's personality or nature, esp as this affects her or his way of thinking, feeling and behaving: *a girl with a nervous/an artistic temperament.*

tem·pera·men·tal /,temprə'mentl/ *adj* (a) caused by temperament: *a temperamental dislike for study.* (b) (*derog*) quickly changing one's mood: *a temperamental tennis player.*

tem·pera·men·tal·ly /-təlɪ/ *adv*

tem·per·ance /'tempərəns/ *nu* (*formal*) **1** self-control in speech, behaviour and (esp) in the use of alcoholic drinks. **2** the state of not drinking any alcoholic drink.

tem·per·ate /'tempərət/ *adj* (*attrib*) **1** (*formal*) showing, behaving with, self-control: *Be more temperate in your language, please.* **2** (of parts of the world) free from extremes of heat and cold: *a temperate climate.*

tem·per·ate·ly *adv*

tem·pera·ture /'temprətʃə(r)/ *nc,nu* the degree of heat and cold: *The temperature of the oven must be low. What's the temperature outside today?* **have/run a temperature** to have a fever. **take sb's temperature** to measure a person's body temperature using a thermometer: *The nurse took the temperatures of all the patients.*

tem·pest /'tempɪst/ *nc* a violent storm.

tem·pes·tu·ous /tem'pestjʊəs/ *adj* (a) (of the weather) stormy. (b) (of behaviour) violent.

temple¹ /'templ/ *nc* a building used for the worship of a god in some religions.

temple² /'templ/ *nc* the flat part of either side of the forehead.

tem·po /'tempəʊ/ *nc* (*pl* **—s** or, in music, **tempi** /-pɪ/) (*It*) **1** the rate of movement or activity: *the tiring tempo of city life.* **2** (*music*) the speed at which music is (to be) played.

tem·po·ral /'tempərəl/ *adj* (*formal*) **1** of earthly human life; of this physical life only: *temporal needs.* **2** (*gram*) of, concerning, time.

,temporal 'adverb *nc* (*gram*) one concerning time, e.g. *when.*

tem·po·rary /'tempərɪ/ *adj* lasting for, designed

to be used for, a limited time only: *temporary employment; a temporary bridge*. Compare permanent.

tem·po·rar·ily /'tempərəlɪ/ *adv*

tempt /tempt/ *vt* **1** to (try to) persuade (a person) to do something wrong or foolish: *Nothing could tempt him to agree that torture is a necessary evil.* **2** to attract (a person) to have or do something: *The warm weather tempted us to go for a swim.*

tempt·er *nc* a person who tempts.

tempt·ing *adj* attractive: *a tempting offer.*

temp·ta·tion /temp'teɪʃn/ *n* **1** *nu* the act of tempting or being tempted: *give way to temptation. Don't put temptation in my way.* **2** *nc* something that tempts or attracts: *Clever advertisements are temptations to spend money.*

ten /ten/ *adj* or *det, nc* (of) 10. **ten to one** very probably: *Ten to one he will arrive late.*

'ten·fold *adj, adv* ten times as many or as much.

'ten·pence *nu* the value of 10 pence.

,ten·pence 'piece *nc* (*pl* **ten-pence pieces**) a GB coin worth 10 pence.

tenth /tenθ/ *adj* or *det, nc* (abbr 10th) (of) the next after 9 or one of 10 equal parts.

tenth·ly *adv* as the next after the ninth.

ten·able /'tenəbl/ *adj* (*formal*) **1** that can be defended successfully: *His theory is hardly tenable.* Opp untenable. **2** (*pred*) (of an office or position) that can be held by a person: *The lectureship is tenable for a period of three years.*

te·na·cious /tɪ'neɪʃəs/ *adj* (*formal; usually attrib*) **1** holding tightly: *a tenacious hold on the branch.* **2** very determined to get or keep something, be successful in winning an argument etc: *a tenacious lawyer; be tenacious of one's basic rights.*

te·na·cious·ly *adv*

te·na·city /tɪ'næsətɪ/ *nu*

ten·an·cy /'tenənsɪ/ *n* **1** *nu* the use of a building, land etc as a tenant: *during his tenancy of the farm.* **2** *n sing* the length of time during which a tenant can use a building etc: *hold a life tenancy of a house.*

ten·ant /'tenənt/ *nc* a person who pays rent for the use of a building, land etc.

tend¹ /tend/ *vt* to look after (animals): *shepherds tending their flocks.* ⇨ attend(3).

tend² /tend/ *vi* **tend to do sth** to be likely to; have as a characteristic or direction: *Vegetables tend to be more expensive in winter. He tends to make too many mistakes.* Ⓝ Not used in continuous tenses, e.g. *is/was -ing.*

ten·den·cy /'tendənsɪ/ *nc* (*pl* **-ies**) **tendency (to do sth)** a probable change (to another condition or activity): *Business is showing a tendency to improve.*

ten·der¹ /'tendə(r)/ *adj* (**—er, —est**) **1** (of meat) easily chewed: *a tender steak.* **2** (*attrib*) kind, loving: *tender looks; tender parents; a tender heart* (= one easily moved to pity). **3** easily damaged: *tender blossoms.* **4** feeling painful: *a tender muscle.*

,tender-'hearted *adj* kind, loving.

ten·der·ly *adv*

ten·der·ness *nu*

ten·der² /'tendə(r)/ *nc* a statement of the price at which one offers to supply goods or services, or to do something: *invite tenders for a new bridge.* ⇨ legal tender.

ten·der³ /'tendə(r)/ *v* **1** *vt* to make a formal offer about (something): *He tendered his resignation to the Prime Minister.* **2** *vi* **tender (for sth)** to make an offer (to do a job) at a stated price: *We've tendered for the building of a new motorway.*

ten·der·loin /'tendəlɔɪn/ *nc* (also *attrib*) a piece of meat from (the side of) beef or pork that is very tender(1): *tenderloin steak.*

ten·don /'tendən/ *nc* (*anat*) a tough, thick part like string that joins muscle to bone.

ten·dril /'tendrɪl/ *nc* (*science*) a part of a plant like a thread, used to twist round any support.

ten·ement /'tenɪmənt/ *nc* a large house for the use of many families at low rents.

ten·et /'tenɪt/ *nc* (*formal*) principle; belief.

ten·nis /'tenɪs/ *nu* (also *attrib*) a game for two or four players who hit a ball with a racket backwards and forwards across a net: *tennis players.*

'tennis-court *nc* a marked area on which tennis is played.

,tennis 'elbow *nu* inflammation of the elbow caused by playing tennis.

ten·or /'tenə(r)/ *nc* (also *attrib*) **1** (music for, a singer with) the highest normal adult male voice: *a tenor voice; the tenor part.* **2** (of instruments) with a range like that of the tenor voice: *a tenor saxophone.*

tense¹ /tens/ *adj* (**—r, —st**) **1** tightly stretched or strained: *tense ropes; tense nerves.* **2** very nervous or excited: *a moment of tense excitement/a tense moment; look tense.*

tense·ly *adv*

tense·ness *nu*

tense² /tens/ *nc, nu* (*gram*) a verb form that shows time. ⇨ future/past/present tense.

tense³ /tens/ *vt, vi* (to cause something) to become tense: *tense one's muscles.*

ten·sion /'tenʃn/ *nu* **1** the state, degree, of being tight: *If you increase the tension of the rope, it will break.* **2** *nc, nu* (a feeling, condition of) mental, emotional or nervous strain between people, groups, states etc: *political tension.*

tent /tent/ *nc* a shelter made of a strong cloth supported by poles and ropes, esp as used by campers. ⇨ also oxygen tent.

ten·tacle /'tentəkl/ *nc* a long, boneless growth on certain animals, such as an octopus, used for touching, feeling, holding, moving etc.

ten·ta·tive /'tentətɪv/ *adj* made or done as a trial, to test the effect: *make a tentative offer.*

ten·ta·tive·ly *adv*

tenth /tenθ/ *adj* or *det, nc* ⇨ ten.

tenu·ous /'tenjʊəs/ *adj* (*formal*) **1** thin and weak: *the tenuous web of a spider.* **2** (of connections, e.g. between ideas) weak; without much meaning or value.

ten·ure /'tenjʊə(r)/ *nc, nu* (the period, right etc of) holding (e.g. political office) or using (land): *The farmers want security of tenure.*

tep·id /'tepɪd/ *adj* (of water etc) a little warm.

Ter., Terr. *written abbr* **1** Territory. **2** (in addresses) Terrace.

term¹ /tɜːm/ *nc* **1** a fixed or limited period of time: *a long term of imprisonment; during his term of office as President.* **in the long/short term** for a long/short period: *I'm prepared to help you in the short term but you'll need to find another* *place to live in the long term.* ⇨ long-/short-term. **2** (also *attrib*) (of schools, universities etc) one of the periods into which the academic year is divided: *the summer term; end-of-term examinations; during term-time.* **3** (*legal*) a period during which a law court considers cases. **4** a word, meaning, expression etc used in a particular profession, activity etc: *technical/scientific/legal terms.* ⇨ terminology. **5** (*maths*) a part of an expression joined to the rest by + or −: *The expression $a^2+2ab+b^2$ has three terms.*

term² /tɜːm/ *vt* to give (a person, thing) a title, name, quality etc: *He has no right to term himself a professor.*

ter·min·able /'tɜːmɪnəbl/ *adj* (*formal*) that can be terminated. Compare interminable.

ter·mi·nal¹ /'tɜːmɪnl/ *adj* **1** of, taking place, each term: *terminal examinations/accounts.* **2** (of a disease) causing death: *terminal cancer.*

ter·mi·nal·ly *adv*: *be terminally ill.*

ter·mi·nal² /'tɜːmɪnl/ *nc* **1** an end of a railway line, bus route etc. **2** a place used by passengers in an airport. **3** (*electricity*) a point of connection in an electric circuit: *the terminals of a battery.*

ter·min·ate /'tɜːmɪneɪt/ *vt,vi* (to cause something) to come to an end: *terminate his contract/a discussion.*

ter·mi·na·tion /ˌtɜːmɪ'neɪʃn/ *nc,nu*

ter·mi·nol·ogy /ˌtɜːmɪ'nɒlədʒɪ/ *nu* (*pl* -ies) (a system of) the words, meanings, expressions etc used in a particular profession, activity: *computer/legal/medical terminology.*

ter·mi·no·logi·cal /ˌtɜːmɪnə'lɒdʒɪkl/ *adj*

ter·mi·nus /'tɜːmɪnəs/ *nc* (*pl* -**ni** /-naɪ/ or —**es**) a station at the end of a railway line, bus route etc.

ter·mite /'tɜːmaɪt/ *nc* an insect (popularly called *white ant*) that makes large hills of hard earth.

terms /tɜːmz/ *n pl* **1** the conditions of an agreement: *the terms in a contract; terms of surrender.* **come to terms with sb** to reach agreement. **come to terms with sth** to agree finally to accept something unpleasant as existing or having happened: *come to terms with the fact that you'll never be rich.* **terms of reference** the purposes, range of power etc given to a committee, enquiry etc: *That problem is outside our terms of reference.* **2** (used with an *adj* describing) the kind of language used: *explain in vague terms.* **in no uncertain terms** leaving no room for doubt: *I was told in no uncertain terms that my work isn't good enough.* **3** **be on bad/good etc terms (with sb)** to have (the mentioned kind of) relationship (with): *be on bad/friendly/good terms with the neighbours.* **be (not) on speaking terms** to be (not) talking to each other.

ter·race /'terəs/ *nc* **1** a level(led) area of ground; a series of these separated by sloping banks as a method of irrigation on a hillside. **2** (T- in names; abbr Ter. or Terr.) a row of houses joined together. **3** a set of wide, shallow steps for spectators in a sports stadium.

ter·rain /te'reɪn/ *nc* a stretch of land, esp regarding its natural features: *difficult terrain for walking.*

ter·res·tri·al /tə'restrɪəl/ *adj* **1** of, on, living on, the earth or land: *terrestrial animals.* **2** of the earth. Compare celestial.

ter·rible /'terəbl/ *adj* **1** causing great fear or

horror: *a terrible war/accident.* **2** causing great discomfort; extreme: *The heat is terrible in Baghdad during the summer.* **3** (*informal*) extremely bad: *What terrible food they gave us!*

ter·ribly /-əblɪ/ *adv* (*informal*) **1** much: *It hurts terribly.* **2** extremely: *How terribly boring/kind he is! I'm terribly sorry.*

ter·ri·er /'terɪə(r)/ *nc* a kind of small, lively dog.

ter·rif·ic /tə'rɪfɪk/ *adj* (*informal*) **1** very good: *a terrific film/response/view.* **2** very great; extreme: *driving at a terrific pace.*

ter·rifi·cal·ly /-klɪ/ *adv* extremely: *It was terrifically exciting.*

ter·ri·fy /'terɪfaɪ/ *vt* (*pt,pp* -**ied**) to fill (a person) with fear: *The idea of another war terrifies me.*

ter·ri·fied *adj* very afraid: *terrified children.*

ter·ri·fy·ing *adj* causing fear: *a terrifying experience.*

ter·ri·tor·ial /ˌterɪ'tɔːrɪəl/ *adj* of land, esp land forming a division of a country: *territorial possessions.*

ˌterritorial 'waters *n pl* the sea near a country's coast over which special rights are claimed, e.g. for fishing.

ter·ri·tory /'terɪtrɪ/ *n* (*pl* -**ies**) **1** *nc,nu* (an area of) land under one ruler or government: *Is this American territory?* **2** *nu* an area of land: *How much territory can he cover* (= travel across) *in a day?* **3** *nc,nu* (*fig*) an area of knowledge, interest, responsibility: *Computer science is outside my territory/is unknown territory to me.*

ter·ror /'terə(r)/ *n* **1** *nc,nu* (a cause of) great fear: *run away in terror; have a terror of fire.* **2** *nc* (*informal; derog*) a child who is annoying: *He's a little terror!*

ter·ror·ism /'terərɪzəm/ *nu* the use of (threats of) violence, esp for political purposes.

'ter·ror·ist /-ɪst/ *nc* a supporter of, person involved in, terrorism.

ter·ror·ize (also -**ise**) /'terəraɪz/ *vt* to fill (people) with terror by threats or acts of violence.

terse /tɜːs/ *adj* (of speech, style, speakers) brief and exact.

terse·ly *adv*

ter·tiary /'tɜːʃərɪ/ *adj* third in order, occurrence: *tertiary education* (i.e. after secondary school).

TESL /'tesl/ *acronym* teaching English as a second language.

test¹ /test/ *nc* **1** a set of questions, tasks etc used to measure a person's knowledge or ability: *a maths test; a driving test.* **2** an examination or trial (of something) to find its quality, value, composition etc: *a blood test. Let's ban tests on nuclear bombs;* **put sb/sth to the test** to find out if a person, thing, is suitable, strong enough etc. **stand the test of time** to be shown to be useful, correct etc for a long period of time: *methods that have stood the test of time.*

'test case *nc* (*legal*) one that shows the principle involved (even though it may not be important in itself).

'test drive *nc* a drive in a car one thinks of buying, to judge its qualities, worth etc. Hence **'test-drive** *vt*

'test flight *nc* a flight to judge the performance of a new plane.

'test match *nc* one of a series of international (cricket, rugby) matches.

'test pilot *nc* a pilot who performs test flights.

'test-tube *nc* (*science*) a long glass tube, closed at one end, used in chemical experiments.

'test-tube baby *nc* a baby who was artificially conceived outside the mother's body.

test² /test/ *vt* **1** to examine the quality of (something) using a test: *have one's eye-sight tested.* **2** to be a difficult trial of (a person, energy etc): *The long climb tested our strength.*

tes·ta·ment /'testəmənt/ *nc* **1** (often *last Will and Testament*) ⇨ will¹(4). **2** (Old T-, New T-) the two main divisions of the Bible.

tes·ti·cle /'testɪkl/ *nc* (*anat*) each of the two male sex organs that produce sperm.

tes·ti·fy /'testɪfaɪ/ *v* (*pt,pp* **-ied**) (*formal* or *legal*) **1** *vt,vi* to give evidence: *He testified that he had not stolen the bike. The teacher testified to the boy's ability. She testified against me in the court.* **2** *vt* to be evidence of (something): *Her tears testified her grief.*

tes·ti·mo·ni·al /ˌtestɪ'məʊnɪəl/ *nc* **1** a written statement describing a person's merits, abilities, qualifications etc. **2** (also *attrib*) something given to a person to show appreciation of services: *a testimonial match* (e.g. for a football player).

tes·ti·mony /'testɪmənɪ/ *nu,nc* (*pl* **-ies**) (*formal* or *legal*) a formal statement esp in a law court, that something is true: *The witness's testimony is false. According to the testimony of the medical profession, the health of the nation is improving.*

tes·tis /'testɪs/ *nc* (*pl* **-tes** /-tiːz/) = testicle.

teta·nus /'tetənəs/ *nu* a serious disease from an infected cut, causing muscles to become stiff.

tête-à-tête /ˌtet ɑː 'tet/ *nc, adv* (*Fr*) (a conversation) in private: *talk tête-à-tête; have a tête-à-tête in the kitchen.*

teth·er /'teðə(r)/ *nc* a rope or chain to which an animal is fastened while grazing. **at the end of one's tether** (*fig*) at the end of one's patience etc. □ *vt* to fasten (an animal) (to something) using a rope: *He tethered his horse to the fence.*

text /tekst/ *n* **1** *nu* the printed words in a book. **2** *nc* the original words of an author, apart from anything else in a book. **3** *nc* a short piece of writing, esp from the Bible, as the subject of a sermon or discussion.

'text·book *nc* a book used to learn a subject: *a physics textbook; a textbook on grammar.*

tex·tu·al /'tekstjʊəl/ *adj* of, in, a text: *textual errors.*

tex·tile /'tekstaɪl/ *adj* of, concerning, the making of cloth: *the textile industry.* □ *nc* (*commerce*) a cloth.

tex·ture /'tekstʃə(r)/ *nc,nu* **1** the arrangement of the threads in a cloth: *cloth with a loose/close texture.* **2** the arrangement of the parts that make up something: *the texture of a mineral.*

Th *written abbr* Thursday.

th *written abbr* (used after numbers (except 1, 2, 3)), e.g. *4th, 15th, 20th, 26th* etc for the sound '-(e)th', e.g. 'fourth', 'twentieth'.)

than /ðən *strong form:* ðæn/ *conj* (*coord*) (used to introduce the second part of a comparison: *taller than you; better than all of you; ran faster than the dog; is more beautiful than mine; has many more books than you have.* Compare *as + adj + as* . . . at as²(1). *other than* ⇨ other². *(no) sooner than* ⇨ soon(2).

thank /θæŋk/ *vt* **1** to say to (a person) that one feels pleased etc to receive something, be helped etc: *She thanked him for the present. I must thank you for your kind help. There's no need to thank me.* **thank you** (*informal* **thanks**) (used when accepting something or expressing thanks): *'Here's your coat.' 'Thank you'. 'Thank you'. Thanks for the present.* Ⓝ 'Thank you' is not used to accept an invitation, e.g. *Would you like . . . ?* Use 'Yes, please'. **no, thank you** (*informal* **no, thanks**) (used to refuse an offer politely): *'Would you like another cake?'—'No, thank you'.* **2** to accept (a person) as responsible (for something): *You've your mother to thank for your health.* **3** (used in many expressions of relief): *Thank goodness! Thank heaven!*

thank·ful /-fəl/ *adj* (usually *pred*) grateful: *You should be thankful that we waited for you.*

thank·ful·ly /-fəlɪ/ *adv*

thank·less *adj* not feeling or expressing gratitude or winning appreciation: *a thankless task* (= one with no expected appreciation or reward).

thanks /θæŋks/ *n pl* **1** an expression thanking a person: *June sends her thanks for the book.* ⇨ vote¹(1). **thanks to sb** because of a person's help, generosity: *Thanks to you, we were successful.* **2** (*informal*) thank you. ⇨ thank(1).

that¹ /ðæt/ *adj* or *det* (used with a *sing noun*) **1** of, concerning, the person, thing etc mentioned, known or understood: *What was that noise? Please explain that plan you mentioned. I don't like that new secretary of his.* Compare those¹(1), this¹(1). *in that case* ⇨ case¹(1). **2** of, concerning, the person or thing farther in space: *That book is much better than this* (nearby) *one. Let us try that restaurant across the street. Look at that man over there!* Compare those¹(2), this¹(2). ⇨ also that⁴(1,2). **3** of, concerning, a particular time or occasion in the past: *That night she was at home. I was successful that time/on that occasion.*

that² /ðæt/ *adv* (*informal*) as much as the extent etc mentioned or understood: *I can't walk that far. It's about that high. The play wasn't all that good.* Compare this².

that³ /ðət/ *conj* (*subord*) Ⓝ 'That' can be left out without changing the meaning in 1,2 below. **1** (used to introduce a noun clause): *She said (that) she was sorry/she couldn't come. The problem is (that) we've no money. It's not certain (that) she'll come. Is it true (that) cats can't swim?* **2** (used to introduce clauses of result) and the result was: *He was so badly behaved (that) I sent him to bed. She was so rude (that) I walked out.* **3** (used to introduce clauses of purpose, condition): *Bring it here so that I can see it. I came early in order that I could speak to you privately. I'll agree on condition that you drive.*

that⁴ /ðət *strong form:* ðæt/ *pron* **1** (usually /ðæt/) the person, thing etc mentioned, known or understood: *What noise was that? Can you explain that? He's often like that* (i.e. that kind of person). *That's more like it* (= is an improvement, a better example etc). *Did he really say that! I watched TV and after that I went to bed. Her face isn't at all like that.* **that's that** (*informal*) there is nothing more to say, do: *I'm not coming with you and that's that!* Compare these², this³(2). **2** (usually /ðæt/) the person, thing, farther in space:

That's my car over there. That's much nicer than this. What's that (on the ceiling)? Compare those², this³(2). **3** (usually /ðət/) **(a)** (used as the subject with a sing or pl verb): *The letters that came this morning were from the bank. Mozart was one of the greatest composers that ever lived. You're the only person that can help me.* Ⓝ *'Who'* is usually preferred for a person, as in *Is he the man who stole your watch? 'That'* is used for animals and things. *'That'* is also used for a person with a superlative (such as *tallest, most intelligent*) and with words such as *all, every, only,* as in *'the best teacher that we've had', 'She was all that he ever wished for'. 'That'* is also used for groups of people and animals or things, as in *'the people and animals that live on the farm'; 'the staff and equipment that will be needed'.* **(b)** (used as the object with a sing or pl verb): *The pen (that) you gave me is very nice. Is this the best (that) you can do? Those are the ones (that) I was describing.* Ⓝ *'That'* can be left out in (b) without changing the meaning. ⇨ which²(2).

thatch /θætʃ/ *nc,nu* a roof (made of) dried straw, reeds etc. □ *vt* to cover (a roof) with thatch.

thaw¹ /θɔː/ *n sing* the state of the weather causing thawing: *Let's go skating before a thaw sets in.*

thaw² /θɔː/ *v* **1** *vi* (of snow and ice) to begin to melt. Compare freeze. **2** *vt,vi* (to cause anything frozen) to become liquid or soft again: *leave frozen food to thaw before cooking it.* **3** *vt,vi* (fig) (to cause a person, behaviour) to become less formal, more friendly: *After a good dinner he began to thaw.*

the¹ /ðə/ *adv* **the** + *comp* . . . , **the** + *comp* . . . (used to show a connection between two actions or conditions) by the same amount: *The more I read, the less I understand. The sooner he leaves, the better it will be for all of us.*

the² /ðə/ *strong form:* ðiː/ *definite article or det* **1** (used with sing, pl or uncountable nouns) a particular person, animal, thing, idea etc (known, mentioned, understood etc): *Please close the door. The meal is ready. I saw her in the High Street. The plan seems a good one. That's the person I meant. I fell in the water. I telephoned the moment I knew. I stayed in during the last week. Can I see the ones next to it? I always listen to the 7 o'clock news. All the children laughed. The result was that no-one came. The point is that you were wrong. You've got the right idea. He's gone to the hospital/doctor* Ⓝ When referring to people, animals or things in general (i.e. to all of them), 'the' is not used, as in *Lions are dangerous. Beer tastes nice.* When referring to a particular one, 'the' is used, as in *The lion escaped, The beer was too sweet.* Compare a(1). **2** (used to refer to a particular kind or class as a group): *the rich/poor/dead; the Italians/English/Europeans; the Smiths* (i.e. the Smith family); *the arts/sciences. The crab is a crustacean. Who invented the microphone?* **3** (used to refer to a particular profession or service): *the law/civil service/government/postal service/railway; the theatre/cinema.* **4** (used to refer to a particular one existing now, in one area etc): *the president/chairman/manager; the population of Africa; the weather in New York.* **5** (used before something that is unique): *the sun/moon/sky; the earth/universe; in the year 1991; the Bible; the River Nile; the Alps; the Sahara Desert.* **6** (used with

musical instruments): *playing the piano/guitar/drums.* **7** /ðiː/ (used to emphasize the best or most important one): *Paris is the place to be in spring.* **8 by the sth; in the sth; to the sth** (used to refer to a particular amount): *I'm paid by the hour. You can buy it by the metre. I pay 30p in the pound as tax. This car does 50 miles to the gallon.* Compare a(4).

the·atre (*US* = **the·ater**) /'θɪətə(r)/ *nc* **1** a building etc for the performance of plays, for dramatic events etc: *go to the theatre to see a play by Shakespeare.* **2** a room with seats in rows rising one behind another for lectures, scientific demonstrations etc. **3** = operating theatre. **4** a scene of important events: *a theatre of war.* **5** *n sing* (the —) the writing and acting of plays, esp when connected with one author, country, period etc: *a book about the Greek theatre.*

'theatre-goer *nc* a person who (often) visits theatres.

the·atri·cal /θɪˈætrɪkl/ *adj* **(a)** (*attrib*) of, for, the theatre: *theatrical costumes.* **(b)** (usually *pred; derog*) (of behaviour, a person's manner, a way of speaking etc) (not genuine and) exaggerated in order to gain attention, sympathy.

the·atri·cal·ly /-klɪ/ *adv*

theft /θeft/ *nc,nu* (the act of, an instance of) stealing.

their /ðeə(r)/ *possessive adj or det* belonging to them: *They have lost their dog. They have a house of their own. It's their house, not yours.*

theirs /ðeəz/ *possessive pron* (the one or ones) belonging to them: *That dog is theirs, not ours. I'm a friend of theirs.*

them /ðəm *strong form:* ðem/ *personal pron* (used as the object form of *they*) more than one person, animal or thing: *Give them to me. It was kind of them.*

theme /θiːm/ *nc* **1** a subject of a talk or a piece of writing. **2** (*music*) a short tune used in a piece of music.

'theme song *nc* one that is often repeated in a musical play, film etc.

them·selves /ðəmˈselvz/ *pron* **1** (used as the reflexive form of *them*): *They hurt themselves. They kept some for themselves.* **(all) by themselves** ⇨ by²(1). **2** (used for emphasis): *They themselves have often made that mistake.* **3** their usual selves: *They don't look themselves today.*

then¹ /ðen/ *adj* (*attrib*) existing at that time: *the then prime minister.*

then² /ðen/ *adv* **1** at the/that time (past or future): *I was still unmarried then. He'll still be too young then.* Compare now¹(1). **(every) now and then** ⇨ now¹(1). **then and there** (also **there and then**) immediately and in that place: *I'll meet you at 6 and I want my money then and there.* **2** next; after that; afterwards: *We spent a week in Rome and then we went to Naples.* **then again** also: *And then again there's the problem of the climate.* **3** in that case; that being so: *'It isn't here.'—'Then it must be in the next room.'*

theo·lo·gi·an /ˌθiːəˈləʊdʒən/ *nc* an advanced student of theology.

theo·logi·cal /ˌθiːəˈlɒdʒɪkl/ *adj* of theology.

theo·logi·cal·ly /-klɪ/ *adv*

the·ol·ogy /θiːˈɒlədʒɪ/ *nu* the study of the nature of God and of religious belief.

the·orem /'θɪərəm/ nc (pl **—s**) (tech) a statement which logical or mathematical reasoning shows to be true.

the·or·eti·cal /ˌθɪə'retɪkl/ (also **the·oret·ic**) adj based on theory, not on practice or experience; not tested yet. Compare practical(1).
   the·or·eti·cal·ly /-klɪ/ adv

the·ory /'θɪərɪ/ n (pl **-ies**) 1 nc,nu (an explanation of) the general principles of an art or science: scientific theory. 2 nc a reasoned account offered to explain facts or events: Darwin's theory of evolution. 3 nc,nu an opinion or idea that is not necessarily based on known facts or reasoning: He has a theory that wearing hats makes men bald. **in theory** as a theory(3): Your plan is excellent in theory, but would it succeed in practice?
   the·or·ist /-ɪst/ nc a person who forms theories.
   the·or·ize (also **-ise**) /'θɪəraɪz/ vi **theorize (about sth)** to form theories (about something).

thera·peu·tic /ˌθerə'pjuːtɪk/ adj (tech) connected with treating and curing an illness.

thera·pist /'θerəpɪst/ nc 1 a specialist in therapy. 2 = psychotherapist.

ther·apy /'θerəpɪ/ nu the treatment of mental or physical illness (without an operation or drugs) (with the kind shown by the word in front): occupational therapy (one using activity as treatment). ⇨ physiotherapy, psychotherapy, speech therapy.

there¹ /ðeə(r)/ adj (pred) that, who, is in that place: That dress/man there is the one I like.

there² /ðeə(r)/ adv 1 in, at, to, towards, that place: I live in that house over there. I went to see if Ben was next door but he's not there. Go and sit there by the window. I've never been to Rome but I hope to go there next year. We can get there and back in one day. Compare here(1). **here and there** ⇨ here(4). **there and then** ⇨ then²(1). 2 at that point (in a series of events, during a process etc): Answer the first five questions and then stop there. There is where I'd like you to check your figures. Compare here(2). 3 (used to call attention to a person, thing): There goes the last bus! There they go! There's the bell for lunch. **there you are** (a) (used when giving something to a person). (b) I said that this would happen and I was right: There you are, I knew it would be sunny today.

there³ /ðeə(r)/ int 1 (used to give comfort, esp to a child): There! There! You'll soon feel better. 2 (used to express success, slight anger etc): There, I've finished it! There, you've broken it!

there⁴ /ðeə(r)/ pron (used as the subject of verbs such as be, seem etc to show that a person, thing, state etc exists, is happening etc): There's a man at the door. There's a fly in my soup. There's snow in the north. There was no truth in her account. There seems to be a mistake. There doesn't appear to be any problem. There happens to be enough food.

there·abouts /'ðeərəbauts/ adv or **thereabouts** near a place, number, time, degree etc: in March 1978 or thereabouts; £5/15 metres/3 o'clock or thereabouts.

there·after /ðeər'ɑːftə(r)/ adv (formal) = afterwards.

there·by /ðeə'baɪ/ adv (formal) by that means; because of that: She paid the rent, thereby having the right to stay.

there·fore /'ðeəfɔː(r)/ adv 1 as a result; for that reason: I was late and therefore I missed the bus. He's busy, therefore he can't see you today. 2 (used to express one's decision or opinion based on evidence): It's moving; therefore it must be alive.

there·in /ðeə'rɪn/ adv (formal) in that statement, document, situation etc: Therein lies the cause of the quarrel.

there·up·on /ˌðeərə'pɒn/ adv (formal) immediately; because of that; then: He gave the signal and thereupon everyone stood up.

therm /θɜːm/ nc (tech) a unit of measurement of heat, esp used for measuring the amount of gas used.

ther·mal /'θɜːml/ adj (attrib) of heat: thermal springs (of naturally warm or hot water); thermal underwear (made of a substance that helps a person to stay warm).

ther·mo·dy·nam·ics /ˌθɜːməudaɪ'næmɪks/ n pl the scientific study of the relation between different forms of energy.

ther·mom·eter /θə'mɒmɪtə(r)/ nc an instrument for measuring temperature.

ther·mos /'θɜːmɒs/ nc (pl **—es**) (P) (also thermos flask) = vacuum flask.

ther·mo·stat /'θɜːməstæt/ nc an apparatus that controls temperature in a building, tank etc.

the·sau·rus /θɪ'sɔːrəs/ nc (pl **—es**) a book or collection or words, phrases etc grouped together according to similarities in their meanings. Compare dictionary.

these¹ /ðiːz/ adj or det (used with a pl noun) 1 of or concerning people, things, events etc mentioned, known etc now or for the future: What are these plans you have? Compare this¹(1), those¹(1). 2 of, concerning, people or things nearer in space: Put them in these boxes. These pens are nicer than those (farther away) ones. Compare this¹(2), those¹(2). 3 (used for emphasis in a story or account) some: Then these strange men appeared.

these² /ðiːz/ pron (pl of this) people, things etc nearer in space or time: These are my drawings here. These are much more tasty than those. What are these? Compare this¹(2), those².

the·sis /'θiːsɪs/ nc (pl theses /-siːz/) a long, detailed piece of writing explaining, supporting or criticizing something, esp as part of an academic course.

they /ðeɪ/ pron 1 (pl form of he, she, it) the people, animals, things, events etc already mentioned: They are always watching TV. They're part of a series. ⇨ them. 2 people in general: They say the prime minister will resign. What a lot of questions they ask in these application forms. Compare one³(2), you(2).

they'd /ðeɪd/ = they had; they would.

they'll /ðeɪl/ = they will; they shall.

they're /ðeə(r)/ = they are.

they've /ðeɪv/ = they have.

thick¹ /θɪk/ adj (**—er, —est**) 1 having a large extent from one side to the other: a thick line/ book; ice three metres thick. Opp thin¹(1). 2 having a large number of units close together: thick hair; a thick forest. Opp thin¹(2). 3 (pred) **thick with sth** full of or packed with something: The air was thick with dust. 4 (of liquids) semi-solid:

thick soup. Opp thin¹(4). ⇨ also blood(2). **5** (*informal; derog*) (of a person) stupid. **6 as thick as thieves** very friendly. **7** (*informal*) *a bit thick* more than what is reasonable or acceptable: *Three weeks of rain is a bit thick.*

thick-'headed *adj* (*informal; derog*) (of a person) stupid; not able to think clearly.

thick-'set *adj* (of a person) short and solid.

thick-'skinned *adj* (*fig*) not worried about criticism, insults etc. Opp thin-skinned.

thick·ly *adv: a thickly planted forest.*

thick·ness (a) *nu* the quality or degree of being thick: *four centimetres in thickness.* **(b)** *nc* a layer: *two thicknesses of woollen cloth.*

thick² /θɪk/ *nu* **the thick (of sth) 1** the most crowded part; part where there is greatest activity: *We were in the thick of the crowd.* **through thick and thin** under any kind of conditions, good or bad: *I'll stay with you through thick and thin.* **2** the thick part of anything: *the thick of the thumb.*

thick·en /'θɪkən/ *vt,vi* (to cause a liquid etc) to become thick: *Thicken the gravy with flour.*

thick·et /'θɪkɪt/ *nc* a group of small trees and bushes, growing close together.

thief /θiːf/ *nc* (*pl* **thieves** /θiːvz/) a person who steals, esp secretly and without violence. ⇨ burglar, robber.

thieve /θiːv/ *vi,vt* to steal (the usual word): *He does not seem able to stop thieving.*

thigh /θaɪ/ *nc* **1** the part of the human leg between the knee and the hip. **2** the similar part of the back legs of other animals.

thimble /'θɪmbl/ *nc* a cap put on the end of the finger when sewing.

thin¹ /θɪn/ *adj* (**—ner, —nest**) **1** having a small extent from one side to the other: *a thin sheet of paper; thin string.* Opp thick¹(1). **2** not having a large number of units close together: *thin hair; a thin audience* (= with more seats empty than occupied). Opp thick¹(2). *into thin air* ⇨ air¹(1). *thin on the ground* (of people) few in number. **3** having not much flesh: *looking thin in the face.* Opp fat¹(1). **4** (of a liquid) not having many solids: *thin soup.* Opp thick¹(4). **5** not having some important quality: *a thin excuse* (= not very convincing); *a thin disguise.*

thin-'skinned *adj* (*fig, derog*) easily worried about criticism, insults etc. Opp thick-skinned.

thin·ly *adv*

thin·ness /'θɪnnɪs/ *nu*

thin² /θɪn/ *vt,vi* (**-nn-**) **thin (sth) (out)** (to cause something) to become thin: *Let's wait until the fog thins. At last the crowd thinned (out).*

thing /θɪŋ/ *nc* **1** any object: *What are those things on the table? I went shopping but I didn't buy a thing. There's no such thing* (as a ghost). *What's this thing made of?* **be seeing things** to be imagining one can see objects that do not exist: *You must be seeing things—there's no-one there.* ⇨ also anything, something. **2** (*pl*) personal possessions; necessary equipment: *Bring your swimming things. Have you packed your things for the holiday? I've got the things to mend the roof.* **3** a subject; fact: *There's another thing I wanted to ask you. What things do I need to know?* *for one thing* (used to introduce the first part of a reason): *For one thing, I've no money and for*

another *I'm too busy.* **all things considered** having thought about all the facts: *All things considered, she's a good manager.* **the next best thing** the second choice (if the first fails): *If the train is full, the next best thing is to take a taxi.* **the thing is** the problem is: *The thing is—can we get there in time?* **be a good thing (a)** to be fortunate: *It's a good thing she doesn't know.* **(b)** to be a good idea: *Do you think free university education would be a good thing?* **have a thing about sb/sth** (*informal*) to take a person, effect, fact etc very seriously: *I've got a thing about eating uncooked meat* (i.e. I prefer not to). **know a thing or two** to have some detailed knowledge. **be/amount to/come to the same thing** to be basically the same. **4** an act; task: *What's the next thing to do? I do so many things for you.* **a close/near thing** a lucky, almost unsuccessful escape or victory. **first thing** (*informal*) as soon as possible, esp on a particular day: *I'll do it first thing tomorrow.* **5** (*informal*) (used of a person, animal, plant expressing a feeling): *Poor thing, he's been ill all winter. You silly thing!* **6** (the —) something needed, wanted or suitable: *a holiday will be the very thing for you. He always says the right/wrong thing. This shirt is the latest thing* (= the latest fashion).

think¹ /θɪŋk/ *n sing* (*informal*) an occasion of careful thought: *Let me have a think. He's got another think coming* (= will need to think again, e.g. because I refuse).

think² /θɪŋk/ (*pt,pp* **thought** /θɔːt/) **1** *vi* to use the mind in order to consider, form opinions, decide: *What she said made me think. You should think carefully before you do anything. Do you think in English when you speak English? Is a human the only animal that can think?* **think again** to reconsider one's decision. **think aloud** to speak one's thoughts. **think twice** to think (again) very carefully before deciding. **2** *vt* to consider, believe, (something): *Do you think it will rain? Yes, I think so. I thought (that) you'd be here. I can't think* (= have no idea) *why he came/ how it happened.* **3** *vt,vi* to expect (something): *I never thought (that) she'd do that! I thought as much* (= That is what I expected.) ℕ Not used in continuous tenses, e.g. *is/was -ing.* **4** *vi* to use the mind in the way mentioned: *think big* (i.e. believe big profits, gains, successes are possible).

think about sb/sth (a) to think(1) on the subject of a person, thing: *I'm thinking about you/my childhood.* **(b)** to consider something as a practical, desirable etc idea: *I'm thinking about going to live in Germany.*

think ahead to plan for the future.

think back (to sth) to consider an event, period, situation etc from the past: *Can you think back a few years to the time when food was cheap?*

think of sth (a) to take something into account: *We have so many things to think of before we can decide.* **(b)** (usually *be thinking of*) to consider something (without finally deciding or acting): *We're thinking of going to Venice for Easter.* **(c)** to imagine something: *Think of the cost/danger!* **(d)** to remember something: *I can't think of his name.* **(e)** to invent, suggest, something: *We're trying to think of a suitable title. Can you think of a good* *place to go for the weekend?* **think** + *adv* + *of sb/sth* to have the opinion mentioned: *They think highly/well of her/her work. He's highly/well thought of.* ⇨ *also* nothing², world²(5).

think sth out to consider a situation carefully and plan: *Have you thought out the long-term effects? It's a well-thought-out scheme.*

think sth over to consider carefully something that will affect the future before deciding or acting: *Please think over what I've said.*

think sth up to invent a plan, excuse, story, name etc.

think·er /'θɪŋkə(r)/ *nc* a person who thinks (in the way mentioned): *a great thinker.*

think·ing¹ /'θɪŋkɪŋ/ *adj* (*attrib*) who are capable of intelligent thought: *All thinking people would agree.*

think·ing² /'θɪŋkɪŋ/ *nu* thought; way of reasoning: *do some hard thinking* (= think deeply).

third¹ /θɜːd/ *adj or det* (abbr **3rd**) **the/my/its** etc *third* + *noun* coming after the second in order, time, importance etc: *March is the third month of the year. The third prize is £100. I need to buy petrol every third day.*

,**third 'class** *nu* the standard of accommodation in a hotel, train etc next to second. □ **'third-class** *adj* of a third or average standard: *third-class travel.* □ *adv* in the third standard in a train etc: *travel third-class.*

,**third-de'gree** *adj* (*attrib*) of the most serious kind: *third-degree burns.*

,**third 'party** *nc* (also *attrib*) a person other than the two main people involved: *third-party insurance* (i.e. covering costs for damage, injury etc to another person or her or his property).

,**third 'person** *nu* (*gram*) the pronouns *he, she, it, they* etc (and the verb forms used with them), used to show the person etc being spoken about. ⇨ first/second person.

,**third-'rate** *adj* of poor quality.

,**Third 'World** *n* (the —) the developing countries of the world in Africa, Asia and S America.

third·ly *adv*

third² /θɜːd/ *adv* after the second: *If you lock the door and turn off the lights, what will you do third?*

third³ /θɜːd/ *nc* (abbr **3rd**) **1** one of 3 equal parts: *own a third of the business; eat one third (of the cake).* **2** (the —) the next after the second person, thing, date etc: *It's 3 June* (spoken as 'the third of June' or 'June the third'). *I was the third to arrive.* **3** (in examinations) an average standard: *She got a third in maths.* ⇨ third class.

thirst¹ /θɜːst/ *n* **1** *nu* the feeling caused by a need to drink; suffering caused by this: *They lost their way in the desert and died of thirst.* **2** *n sing* **a thirst for sth** (*fig*) a strong wish for: *a thirst for knowledge.*

thirst² /θɜːst/ *vi* **thirst after/for sth** to have a very strong wish for something: *thirsting for revenge.*

thirsty /'θɜːstɪ/ *adj* (**-ier, -iest**) having or causing thirst: *be/feel thirsty; thirsty work.*

thir·teen /ˌθɜːˈtiːn/ *adj or det, nc* (of) 13.

thir·teenth /ˌθɜːˈtiːnθ/ *adj or det, nc* (abbr **13th**) (of) the next after 12 or one of 13 equal parts.

thirty /'θɜːtɪ/ *adj or det, nc* (of) 30. **in the thirties** (**a**) (of temperature, speed etc) between

30 and 39. (**b**) between '30 and '39 in a century.

thir·ti·eth /'θɜːtɪɪθ/ *adj or det, nc* (abbr **30th**) (of) the next after 29 or one of 30 equal parts.

this¹ /ðɪs/ *adj or det* (used with a *sing noun*) **1** of or concerning the person, thing, event etc mentioned, known etc now or for the future: *This pain is a nuisance. Please tell me about this idea you have for a new product.* Compare these¹(1), that¹(1). **2** of, concerning, the person or thing nearer in space: *Put it in this box. Let's stay in this hotel here. This chair is nicer than that* (farther away) *one. Look at this car I'm drawing.* Compare these¹(2), that¹(2). **3** of, concerning, the present time: *this week/year; this morning/after-noon/evening.* Compare next¹(2). **4** (used for emphasis in a story or account) a, an: *Suddenly this strange man appeared.*

this² /ðɪs/ *adv* (*informal*) as much as this extent, amount etc: *It's about this high/long. Now that we've come this far we might as well finish.* Compare that².

this³ /ðɪs/ *pron* **1** the person, thing, event etc mentioned, known etc now or for the future: *This I must see! Will you be able to do this? She's often like this* (i.e. this kind of person). **2** (*pl* these) the person, thing, nearer in space: *This is my house here. This is much heavier than that. What's this doing in here?* ⇨ these².

thistle /'θɪsl/ *nc* a wild plant with prickly leaves and yellow, white or purple flowers.

tho' /ðəʊ/ *adv, conj* = though.

thong /θɒŋ/ *nc* a narrow strip of leather, used as a fastening, a whip etc.

tho·rax /'θɔːræks/ *nc* (*science*) **1** the part of the body between the neck and the abdomen. **2** the middle of the three main sections of an insect (with the legs and wings).

thorn /θɔːn/ *n* **1** *nc* a pointed growth on the stem of a plant. **a thorn in one's flesh/side** (*fig*) a person, situation etc that often annoys. **2** *nc,nu* a kind of bush or tree with thorns.

thorny *adj* (**-ier, -iest**) (**a**) having thorns. (**b**) (*fig*) full of trouble and difficulty: *a thorny problem.*

thor·ough /'θʌrə/ *adj* **1** complete in every way; not forgetting or ignoring anything; detailed: *a thorough search/worker; be thorough in one's work.* **2** (*attrib*) (*informal*) complete: *She's a thorough nuisance/bore.*

thor·ough·ly *adv*: *work thoroughly; be thoroughly bad.*

thor·ough·ness *nu*

thor·ough·bred /'θʌrəbred/ *nc, adj* (an animal, esp a horse) of pure breed.

thor·ough·fare /'θʌrəfeə(r)/ *nc* a road or street used by many vehicles and people: *Broadway is New York's most famous thoroughfare.*

those¹ /ðəʊz/ *adj or det* (used with a *pl noun*) **1** of or concerning people, things, events etc mentioned, known etc: *Do you still have those receipts? All those holidays were exciting. What were those names you mentioned?* Compare that¹(1), these¹(1). **2** of, concerning, people or things farther in space: *Put them up on those shelves. These pens are cheaper than those.* Compare that¹(2), these¹(2).

those² /ðəʊz/ *pron* (*pl* of *that*) people, things etc farther in space or time: *Those are my clothes over*

there. *These are much bigger than those*. Compare that[4](2), these[2].

though /ðəʊ/ *conj* (*subord*) **1** (often **even though**) regardless of the fact that: *Though they're poor, they're always clean. I like her even though she can be rude.* **2** but continuing to be: *She's poor though honest.* **3** and yet; but: *I'll try, though I don't think I'll win.* Ⓝ For a comparison of *though* and *although*, ⇨ the note at although. **as though** ⇨ as[2].

thought[1] /θɔːt/ *n* **1** *nu* the act, process, of thinking: *He was deep/lost in thought.* **food for thought** ⇨ food(1). **2** *nc* an idea, opinion, intention etc formed by thinking: *I wish I could read your thoughts. He hasn't a thought in his head. I had no thought of harming you.* **on second thoughts** after thinking again: *On second thoughts, I'll wait here.* **spare a thought for sb/sth** to consider a person, situation when deciding. **3** *nu* ideas, ways of thinking, characteristic of a period, nation: *classical/scientific/Greek thought.* **4** *nu* consideration; mental attention: *He often acts without thought. I promise to give the matter a lot of thought.*

thought·ful /-fəl/ *adj* (**a**) full of, showing, thought: *thoughtful looks.* (**b**) thinking of the needs of others: *It was thoughtful of you to warn me of your arrival.*

thought·ful·ly /-fəlɪ/ *adv*

thought·less *adj* (**a**) not thinking: *Young people are often thoughtless for the future.* (**b**) (*derog*) selfish; inconsiderate: *a thoughtless action/person.*

thought·less·ly *adv*

thought[2] /θɔːt/ *pt,pp* of think[2].

thou·sand /'θaʊzənd/ *adj* or *det, nc* (of) 1000: *two thousand, six hundred and ten* (2610). Ⓝ The plural of *'thousand'* is *thousand* in spoken numbers. **thousands of sb/sth** a very large number of people, things: *thousands of insects.* **a thousand to one (chance)** a very small possibility. **one in a thousand** a rare exception.

thousand·fold /-fəʊld/ *adj, adv* a thousand times as many or as much.

thou·sandth /'θaʊzənθ/ *adj* or *det, nc* (abbr 1000th) (of) the next after 999 or one of 1000 equal parts.

thrash /θræʃ/ *v* **1** *vt* to beat (a person) with a stick, whip etc. **2** *vt* (*informal*) to defeat (a person, team etc) in a contest. **3** *vi* **thrash about** to toss, move, violently: *The swimmer thrashed about in the water.* **4** *vt* **thrash sth out** to arrive at a decision or agreement after a lot of discussion.

thrash·ing *nc* (**a**) a beating: *give/get a good thrashing.* (**b**) (*fig*) a defeat, e.g. in games.

thread[1] /θred/ *n* **1** *nc,nu* (a length of) cotton, silk, wool etc, esp for use in sewing and weaving: *a needle and thread.* **2** *nc* something long and thin like a thread: *A thread of light came through the keyhole.* **3** *nc* a line of thought or action (connecting parts of a story etc): *lose the thread of one's argument.* **4** *nc* the spiral ridge round a screw or bolt.

thread·bare /-beə(r)/ *adj* (of cloth) very worn.

thread[2] /θred/ *vt* **1** to pass a thread through the eye of (a needle); put (beads etc) on a thread. **2 thread one's way through (sth)** to make one's way through (a crowd etc).

threat /θret/ *nc* **1** a statement of an intention to punish or hurt a person, esp if he or she does not do as one wishes: *carry out a threat; be under the threat of severe punishment.* **2** a sign or warning of possible trouble, danger etc: *There was a threat of rain in the dark sky.*

threat·en /'θretn/ *v* **1** *vt* to use threats against (a person): *threaten an employee with dismissal.* **2** *vt* to warn of (something bad): *The clouds threatened rain.* **3** *vi* to seem likely to occur or come: *Knowing that danger threatened, I kept an extra careful watch.*

threat·en·ing *adj: a threatening sky.*

threat·en·ing·ly *adv*

three /θriː/ *adj* or *det, nc* (of) 3. ⇨ third.

three-'cornered *adj* involving three parts: *a three-cornered contest/fight* (= one with three contestants or competitors).

three-di'mensional *adj* (abbr three-D or 3-D) having, or appearing to have, three dimensions (length, breadth and depth).

three-'figure *adj* (of numbers, amounts) between 100 and 999: *a three-figure weekly wage.*

'three·fold *adj, adv* three times as many or as much.

three-'piece *adj* (*attrib*) (**a**) a set of three articles of clothing: *a three-piece suit.* (**b**) a set of furniture (a sofa and two armchairs): *a three-piece suite.*

three-'ply *adj* (of wool, thread) having three strands.

three'quarter(s) *adj, nc* (¾) three fourths (of the size, amount, length, area etc).

three'score *adj* or *det* (*old use*) sixty.

'three·some /-səm/ *nc* (a game, dance, for) three people.

thresh /θreʃ/ *vt,vi* to beat (the grain out of) wheat etc: *thresh corn by hand.*

'thresh·ing-machine *nc* one used for threshing grain.

thresh·er *nc* a person, machine, that threshes.

thresh·old /'θreʃhəʊld/ *nc* **1** a stone or piece of wood under a doorway: *cross the threshold.* **2** (*fig*) a beginning: *He was on the threshold of his career.*

threw /θruː/ *pt* of throw[2].

thrice /θraɪs/ *adv* (*old use*) three times.

thrift /θrɪft/ *nu* care, economy, in the use of money of goods.

thrifty *adj* (**-ier, -iest**) economical (the usual word).

thrill[1] /θrɪl/ *nc* (an experience causing) an excited feeling passing like a wave along the nerves: *a thrill of joy/pleasure/horror.*

thrill[2] /θrɪl/ *vt,vi* (to cause a person) to feel a thrill: *The film thrilled the audience. We're thrilled at/by the good news. We were thrilled to see her.*

thrill·er *nc* (*literature*) a novel, play or film in which excitement and emotional appeal are the essential elements, esp one involving crime.

thrive /θraɪv/ *vi* (*pt* **—d** or **throve** /θrəʊv/, *pp* **—d** or **—n** /'θrɪvn/) **thrive (on sth)** to develop well, grow strong and healthy, (because of something): *Children thrive on good food.*

thriv·ing *adj* developing well; very healthy: *a thriving business/child.*

throat /θrəʊt/ *nc* **1** the front part of the neck: *I gripped him by the throat.* ⇨ throttle[2]. **2** the passage in the neck through which food passes to the stomach and air to the lungs: *A bone has stuck in my throat.* **clear one's throat** to cause one's throat to empty by coughing etc. **cut one's own throat** (*fig*) to cause one's own defeat. **force/ thrust sth down sb's throat** to try to make a person accept one's views, beliefs etc. **jump down sb's throat** to become suddenly angry with a person. **stick in one's throat** (*fig*) to be unable to be accepted: *His criticism stuck in my throat.*

throb¹ /θrɒb/ *nc* an act, feeling, of throbbing or vibration: *throbs of joy.* ⇨ also heart-throb.

throb² /θrɒb/ *vi* (-bb-) (of the heart, pulse etc) to beat, esp strongly.

  throb·bing *adj* that throbs: *a throbbing pain/ sound.*

throes /θrəʊz/ *n pl* **in the throes of sth** involved in a struggle etc: *in the throes of war.*

throm·bo·sis /θrɒm'bəʊsɪs/ *nc,nu* ⇨ coronary.

throne /θrəʊn/ *nc* **1** the ceremonial chair of a king, queen, bishop etc. **2** (the —) royal rank or authority: *come to the throne* (= become king/ queen).

throng¹ /θrɒŋ/ *nc* a large crowd.

throng² /θrɒŋ/ *vt,vi* to form a large crowd: *People thronged to see the new play.*

throttle¹ /'θrɒtl/ *nc* (*tech*) a valve controlling the flow of steam etc in an engine.

throttle² /'θrɒtl/ *vt* to seize (a person) by the throat and stop her or his breathing: *He throttled the guard and then robbed the bank.*

through¹ /θruː/ *adj* **1** (*attrib*) going all the way (often without stopping): *a through train to Chicago; a road for through traffic.* **2** (*pred*) connected by telephone: *You're through now.* **3** (*pred*) (*informal*) (of a person) not able to continue, make progress, in some activity: *He's through as a teacher.*

through² /θruː/ *adv* Ⓝ For uses of 'through' with verbs such as *be, come, get, go, pull, put, see* etc, ⇨ the *verb* entries. **1** from end to end, beginning to end, side to side: *He slept the whole night through. They wouldn't let us through* (e.g. pass the gates). *The nail won't go through easily.* **2** to the end: *I read the letter through.* **through and through** completely: *He's an honest person through and through.* **3** all the way (to): *Does this train go through to Paris? The stain went right through to the floor.* ⇨ through¹(1). **4** (*telephoning*) connected: *I'll put you through (to the manager).* ⇨ through¹(2). **5** **through with sb/sth** (*informal*) finished with: *I'm through with lying/smoking/you.*

through³ /θruː/ *prep* **1** in at one side, part etc and out at the other: *We drove through London. There's a path through the field. She looked through the telescope.* **2** over all the parts of: *search through the files; look through a book; go through the accounts.* **3** from the beginning to the end of (a period): *sleep through the night; live through a difficult time.* **4** by means of; using: *I bought it through an advertisement in the newspaper. I heard of it through a friend.* **5** because of: *She failed through not working hard. It happened through no fault of yours.*

through·out¹ /θruː'aʊt/ *adv* right through; in every part; in all ways or respects: *The house*

needs painting throughout.

through·out² /θruː'aʊt/ *prep* in every part of; from end to end of: *throughout the country; throughout the war; throughout the year.*

throve /θrəʊv/ *pt* of thrive.

throw¹ /θrəʊ/ *nc* an act of throwing; the distance something is thrown: *a throw of 70 metres.* ⇨ stone²(2).

throw² /θrəʊ/ *vt* (*pt* **threw** /θruː/, *pp* **thrown** /θrəʊn/) Ⓝ For uses of 'throw' with nouns such as *throw a party, throw light on sth,* ⇨ the noun entries, as at *doubt, fit, gauntlet, light, money, party, towel, weight.* **1** to cause (something) to go through the air by a strong movement of the arm etc: *He threw the ball to his sister. Don't throw stones at the birds! She threw her hat in the air.* **2** to put (something) suddenly and carelessly in a place or position: *He threw down his coat/threw it on the bed/ onto the floor/over his shoulder.* **3** to move (part of the body) with energy: *throw one's head back/ one's chest out/one's arms about.* **4** to send (a person) to the ground: *The horse threw its rider. She threw me to the floor.* **5** to move (a switch etc) to the opposite position. **6** to make (one side of) a dice fall on a surface: *throw a six.* **7** to direct, send, (a shadow, light): *throw a shadow/beam on a wall.* **8** to cause (an expression) to be suddenly noticed: *He threw me an angry look.* **9** to cause (a person) to be suddenly in an excited state: *The whole class was thrown into a panic.* **10** to confuse, be too difficult for, (a person): *The question on evolution threw me completely.*

  throw sth around sth = throw sth round sth.

  throw sth away (a) to get rid of something unwanted permanently. (b) to lose an opportunity etc by foolishness or neglect: *throw away a chance of winning.* (c) (of an actor) to speak words in a way that makes them seem unimportant: *Don't throw away your best lines.*

  throw sth back (a) to return something by throwing(1) it: *Please throw it back to me.* (b) to fold or remove a covering etc suddenly: *She threw back the bedclothes.* **throw sth back at sb** to remind a person unkindly about something he or she has done wrong: *You've no right to throw my faults back at me when you are so bad yourself.* ⇨ also throw-back below.

  throw sth in (a) (in sports such as football) to put the ball back into play using a throw. Hence **'throw-in** *nc* such an act. (b) (*informal*) to include something as an extra: *If you buy the house, we'll throw in the carpets.* (c) to add something: *I thought I'd throw in a reminder that fees must be paid by Friday.*

  throw oneself into sth to become involved in an activity with enthusiasm: *I threw myself into my work.*

  throw sb off to get rid of a person who is following one. **throw sth off** (a) to remove clothing etc with a quick, careless, movement. (b) to get rid of something that is troublesome: *throw off a cold.* (c) (*informal*) to produce a piece of writing, music etc quickly: *throw off an essay.*

  throw oneself on sb/sth to put one's trust in a person, thing: *throw oneself on the mercy of the court.* **throw sth on** to put on clothing etc with a quick, careless movement.

  throw sb out (of a place) to force a person to

leave (one's home etc). ***throw sth out*** (**a**) =
throw sth away. (**b**) to reject an idea etc: *throw
out a new plan.* (**c**) to mention a hint, suggestion:
He threw out the possibility that he would resign.
(**d**) to be the source of something: *This fire throws
out a lot of heat.*

throw sb over (*informal*) to end a relationship
with a person: *I've been thrown over for a younger
man.*

throw sth round sth to put a rope, ring of
police etc round an area, building, crowd etc.

throw sth together (*informal*) to produce
clothes, a meal, building, essay etc quickly and
carelessly: *This dress has been thrown together.*

throw (sth) up to send up food from the
stomach. ***throw sth up*** (**a**) to produce something unexpectedly: *How does Britain manage to
throw up so many good runners?* (**b**) to resign
from a position: *I've thrown up my job.*

throw oneself upon sb/sth (*formal*) = throw
oneself on sb/sth.

throw-back /'θrəʊbæk/ *nc* a person, animal or
plant with the characteristics of an earlier form.

throw-in /'θrəʊ ɪn/ *nc* ⇨ throw sth in(a).

thru /θru:/ (*US*) = through.

thrush /θrʌʃ/ *nc* a kind of songbird.

thrust¹ /θrʌst/ *n* **1** *nc,nu* (an act of) thrusting. **2**
nu the force in a jet engine that moves a plane. **3**
nu (*science*) pressure by one part of a structure on
another.

thrust² /θrʌst/ *v* (*pt,pp* —) **1** *vt* to push or put
(something) suddenly and with force: *He thrust
his hands into his pockets/a coin into my hand.* **2**
vi **thrust at sb/sth** to make a forward stroke
with a knife, sword etc at a person, thing. **3** *vt*
thrust oneself/sb on sb (*informal*) to force a
person to accept one's, a person's, company.

thud /θʌd/ *vi* (**-dd-**), *nc* (to make) a low sound as
of a knock on something heavy but soft: *He fell
with a thud to the carpet.*

thug /θʌg/ *nc* (*derog*) a violent and dangerous
person.

thumb¹ /θʌm/ *nc* the short, thick finger set apart
from the other four. ***under sb's thumb*** under a
person's influence and control.

thumb² /θʌm/ *vt* **1** **thumb (through) sth** to
turn over pages etc: *thumb (through) the pages of
a dictionary.* **2 thumb a lift** = hitch-hike.

thump¹ /θʌmp/ *nc* (a noise (as if) of) a heavy
blow: *Give him a friendly thump on the back.*

thump² /θʌmp/ *v* **1** *vt* to strike (a person, thing)
heavily or hard: *He thumped (on) the door. The
two boys began to thump each other. He was
thumping out a tune on the piano.* **2** *vi* to beat(5)
strongly: *His heart thumped with excitement.*

thun·der¹ /'θʌndə(r)/ *nu* the noise which usually
follows a flash of lightning: *a loud crash/a long
roll of thunder.*

'**thunder·bolt** *nc* a flash of lightning with a crash
of thunder.

'**thunder·clap** *nc* a sudden noise of thunder.

'**thunder·storm** *nc* a storm with thunder and
lightning.

'**thunder·struck** *adj* (*fig*) amazed.

thun·der·ous /-əs/ *adj* making a noise like
thunder: *thunderous applause.*

thun·der² /'θʌndə(r)/ *v* **1** *vi* to produce thunder:
It was thundering and lightening. **2** *vt* to say

(something) in a loud, serious voice: *'Who are
you?' he thundered.*

Thur(s) *written abbr* Thursday.

Thurs·day /'θɜ:zdɪ/ *nc* (also *attrib*) the fifth day
of the week: *We'll meet on Thursday/next Thursday morning. On Thursdays* (= Every Thursday)
I play tennis.

thus /ðʌs/ *adv* (*formal*) **1** in this way: *do it thus.* **2**
to this extent: *thus far.* **3** therefore: *The bee has
six legs; thus it is an insect.*

thwack /θwæk/ *vt, nc* = whack.

thwart /θwɔ:t/ *vt* (*formal*) to oppose or prevent
(something) successfully: *be thwarted in one's
ambitions/aims.*

thyme /taɪm/ *nu* a kind of herb.

thy·roid /'θaɪrɔɪd/ *nc* (also *thyroid gland*) the
gland in the front part of the neck, producing a
substance which affects the body's growth and
activity.

ti·ara /tɪ'ɑ:rə/ *nc* (*pl* —**s**) a small crown for a
woman.

tib·ia /'tɪbɪə/ *nc* (*pl* —**e** /-bɪiː/) (*anat*) the inner
and thicker of the two bones between the knee
and the foot.

tic /tɪk/ *nc* an involuntary twitching of the muscles
(esp the face).

tick¹ /tɪk/ *nc* a small creature that fastens itself on
the skin and sucks blood.

tick² /tɪk/ *nc* **1** a light, regularly repeated sound,
esp of a clock or watch. **2** (*informal*) a moment:
I'll be with you in a couple of ticks. **3** a small mark
(often √) to show that something is correct.

tick³ /tɪk/ *v* **1** *vi* (of a clock etc) to make ticks(1):
*The child put the watch to its ear and listened to it
ticking.* **what makes sb/sth tick** (*informal*)
what gives energy, life, to a person, business etc.
2 *vt* to put a tick(3) against (something): *tick a
name on a list.*

tick away (of a clock, watch) to tick(1).

tick sb off (**a**) to put a tick(3) against a person's
name on a list. (**b**) (*informal*) to complain to a
person with slightly angry words. Hence **tick-
ing-'off** *nc* such an act: *get a good ticking-off.*
Compare tell sb off. **tick sth off** to put a tick(3)
against an item on a list.

tick over (**a**) (of an engine) ⇨ idle²(2). (**b**) (of a
business etc) to be profitable but only by a small
amount.

tick·er /'tɪkə(r)/ *nc* (*sl*) the heart.

tick·et /'tɪkɪt/ *nc* **1** a piece of card or paper giving
the holder the right to travel in a train, bus etc or
to a seat in a cinema etc: *a bus/cinema ticket. Do
you want a single or a return ticket?* **2** a piece of
card or paper, label, attached to something and
giving information, e.g. about the price, size etc.
3 a printed notice of an offence against traffic
regulations: *get a parking ticket.*

'**ticket-collector** *nc* a person who collects (railway) tickets.

tickle¹ /'tɪkl/ *nc* an act, feeling, of tickling.

tickle² /'tɪkl/ *v* **1** *vt* to excite the nerves of the skin
by touching (a person) lightly, often to cause
laughter: *tickle him in the ribs.* **be tickled pink/
to death** to be very pleased, amused: *I was
tickled pink at the praise given to me.* **2** *vi* to have,
feel, cause, an itching or tingling sensation: *My
nose tickles.*

tick·lish /'tɪklɪʃ/ *adj* (**a**) (of a person) easily

made to laugh when tickled. **(b)** (of a problem etc) needing care or attention: *I'm in a ticklish situation.*

ti·dal /'taɪdl/ *adj* of a tide or tides.

'tidal wave *nc* a large ocean wave.

tid·dler /'tɪdlə(r)/ *nc* (*informal*) **1** a very small fish. **2** a small, young child.

tide¹ /taɪd/ *n* **1** *nc,nu* the regular rise and fall in the level of the sea, caused by the attraction of the moon: *at high/low tide.* **2** *nc* a change in opinion (of public opinion, feeling etc): *The Liberals hoped for a turn of the tide.*

tide² /taɪd/ *vt* **tide sb over (sth)** to help a person to get through or survive (a period of difficulty etc): *Will £5 tide you over until you're paid?*

tid·ings /'taɪdɪŋz/ *n pl* (*literary*) news: *He's full of glad tidings.*

ti·dy¹ /'taɪdɪ/ *adj* (**-ier, -iest**) **1** arranged neatly and in order; having the habit of placing and keeping everything in its right place: *a tidy room/ boy.* Opp untidy. **2** (*attrib*) (*informal*) fairly large (esp of money): *a tidy sum of money.*

ti·di·ly /'taɪdəlɪ/ *adv*

ti·di·ness *nu*

ti·dy² /'taɪdɪ/ *vt,vi* (*pt,pp* **-ied**) **tidy (sb/sth) (up)** to make (oneself, a person, place) neat: *tidy (up) one's room; tidy one's hair. Please tidy up.*

tie¹ /taɪ/ *nc* **1** (also *necktie*) a band of material worn under the collar of a shirt and knotted in front. **2** a long piece of rope etc used for fastening. **3** (*fig*) something that keeps people united: *the ties of friendship; family ties.* **4** something that takes up one's attention and limits one's freedom of action: *Mothers often find their small children a tie.* **5** an equal score in a game etc: *The game ended in a tie, 2—2.*

tie² /taɪ/ *v* (*pres p* **tying**, *pt,pp* **tied**) Opp untie (except **5** below). **1** *vt* to fasten (a person, thing) with string, rope etc: *tie a man's feet together; tie a parcel.* **2** *vt* to arrange (a ribbon etc) in the form of a bow or knot: *tie one's shoelaces; tie a ribbon/ scarf; tie the ribbon in(to) a bow.* **3** *vt* to make (a bow, knot etc) by tying: *tie a knot in a piece of string.* **4** *vi* to be fastened: *Does this dress tie in front or at the back?* **5** *vi* (of players, teams, candidates in a competitive examination) to make the same score: *The two teams tied. They tied for first place (in the examination).*

tie sb down to limit a person's freedom: *He's not in a hurry to get married; he doesn't want to get tied down.* **tie sb down to sth** to limit a person to a certain amount, the terms of a contract etc.

tie in with sth to link, agree, with something: *Doesn't this tie in with what we were told last week?*

tie sth up (a) to tie(1) something: *tie up a parcel/ thief/dog.* **(b)** to use methods to limit the use of money, property: *My money is tied up in a savings account.* **be/get tied up (with sb/sth) (a)** to be, get, involved (with a person, situation) so that one has no time for other things: *I'm afraid I can't help you now—I'm too tied up with other things.* **(b)** to be, become, linked with a person, thing: *Isn't this company tied up with United Oil?*

tier /tɪə(r)/ *nc* one of a set of rows (esp of seats) parallel to and rising one above another, e.g. in a theatre or stadium.

tiff /tɪf/ *nc* (*informal*) a slight quarrel.

ti·ger /'taɪgə(r)/ *nc* a large, fierce animal of the cat family from Asia, yellow with black stripes. ⇨ paper tiger.

ti·ger·ish /-ɪʃ/ *adj* like, cruel as, a tiger.

ti·gress /'taɪgrɪs/ *nc* a female tiger.

tight¹ /taɪt/ *adj* (**—er, —est**) **1** fastened, fixed, fitting or held closely: *a tight knot. The drawer is so tight that I can't open it.* Opp loose¹(2). **2** stretched fully: *a tight rope.* Opp loose¹(3). **3** (esp in compounds) made so that something cannot get out or in: *water-/air-tight.* **4** packed so as to occupy the smallest possible space or to get in as much as possible: *Make sure that the bags are filled/packed tight.* Opp loose¹(7). **in a tight spot** ⇨ spot¹(5). **a tight schedule** ⇨ schedule¹. **a tight squeeze** ⇨ squeeze¹(1). **5** (*informal*) drunk; affected by alcoholic drink: *He gets tight every pay-day.* **6** (of money) not easily obtainable, e.g. on loan from banks: *Money is tight.*

,tight-'fisted *adj* (*derog*) unwilling to lend or spend money.

,tight-'lipped *adj* (*fig*) saying little or nothing.

'tight·rope *nc* one on which acrobats perform.

tight·ly *adv*

tight·ness *nu*

tight² /taɪt/ *adv* tightly: *hold it tight; packed tight.* **sit tight** ⇨ sit(1).

tight·en /'taɪtn/ *vt,vi* (to cause something) to become tight(er): *tighten (up) the screws; tighten the ropes of the tent.* Opp loosen.

tights /taɪts/ *n pl* (also *a pair of tights*) **1** a very thin close-fitting (usually nylon) covering for the hips, legs and feet, as worn by girls and women. **2** a similar clothing covering the legs and body, worn by acrobats, ballet-dancers etc.

tile /taɪl/ *nc* a (usually square or oblong) piece of baked clay, used for covering roofs, walls etc. **be (out) on the tiles** (*sl*) to be out having fun. □ *vt* to cover (a roof, wall etc) with tiles.

till¹ /tɪl/ *conj, prep* = until.

till² /tɪl/ *nc* a drawer for money in a shop.

till³ /tɪl/ *vt* to cultivate (land).

till·er /'tɪlə(r)/ *nc* that moves the rudder and is a long handle used to turn a small boat.

tilt¹ /tɪlt/ *nc* a sloping position.

tilt² /tɪlt/ *vt,vi* (to cause something) to come into a sloping position (as if) by lifting one end: *don't tilt the table.*

tim·ber /'tɪmbə(r)/ *n* **1** *nu* wood prepared for use in building etc. **2** *nu* trees that are growing and have wood suitable for building, carpentry etc: *The fire destroyed thousands of acres of timber.* **3** *nc* a piece of shaped wood forming a support.

time¹ /taɪm/ *n* **1** *nu* (the passing of) all the days, years etc of the past, present or future: *The world exists in space and time. Only time will prove/tell who was right. Time can be a marvellous healer.* **for all time** for ever. **time flies** (*informal*) time passes very quickly (when one is busy). **2** *nu* or *sing* an amount of time: *Six minutes is a short (period of) time to wait. What a long time you're taking! Take as much time as you like. I could have done the job in half the time. I need time to think about it. How much time will you need? You can save a lot of time if you drive. The winner's time was exactly 11 seconds.* **ahead of time** before the agreed amount of time: *We finished* *ahead of time*. **all the time** (a) during the whole period: *I had the letter in my pocket all the time.* (b) very often: *He's at discos all the time.* **for the time being** now until another arrangement is agreed: *You can stay with us for the time being.* **in time** (a) during a period of future time: *You'll learn how to do it in time.* (b) early enough: *We'll be in time to catch the train.* **in good time** well before the expected or agreed time for something to happen or begin: *He arrived in good time for the meeting.* **in (less than) no time; in no time at all** very soon; very quickly: *The ambulance arrived in no time.* **(all) in one's own good time** at a rate decided oneself: *I'll finish in my own good time.* **time off** a period of rest from an activity: *take time off to eat.* **time out** a short period of rest, esp during a game. **a race against time** ⇨ race[2]. **do time** (*informal*) to spend a period of time in prison. **gain time** to obtain an extra amount of time (e.g. by delaying something) in order to improve one's chances of success. **have a good time** to enjoy oneself. **have a hard/rough time** to experience difficulties, suffer, for a period of time. **have the time for sth** to be able to use a period of time doing it. **have the time of one's life** to enjoy a period of particularly good pleasure. **have no time for sb/sth** to have no patience with, be unable to put up with, a person, thing: *I've no time for lazy students.* **have time on one's hands** to have a long period of free time. **kill time** to find ways to use time while waiting. **lose no time** to act immediately. **make time** to organize oneself in order to have a period of time available. **make up for lost time** to hurry, work harder etc after starting late. **pass the time** to use up free time (e.g. while waiting): *What shall we do to pass the time?* **pass the time of day with sb** to have an informal conversation with a friend etc. **play for time** to cause delays and interruptions in order to obtain more time. **take one's time (over sth)** to use as much time as one needs or wants to (in order to finish a task): *Take your time, there's no need to hurry.* **3** *nu* or *sing* a point of time stated in hours, minutes and seconds: *What's the time? What time is it? What do you make the time? Have you got the right time? The time's/It's 6 o'clock. Is that the right time? What time does that clock/your watch say? What time do you call this?* (i.e. You're very late.) **tell sb the time** to give (a person) the correct time: *Could you tell me the time, please?* **tell the time** to be able to recognize the time on a watch or clock: *My little boy can tell the time now.* **4** *nc,nu* an exact point of time or period related to, suitable for, a particular activity, event, occasion, purpose etc: *I forgive you this time. Next time you can pay. We met for the first/last time. It's lunch time. It's time I was going/time for me to go. By the time I arrived, the food was eaten. It's well past your bedtime. It's time for bed/ school. How many times do the buses pass your house? We play football six times a week. She had a difficult/easy time as a child. He had a hard/ rough time at school.* **at a time** in a group; together: *We were allowed in two at a time.* **at one time** during one period in the past: *At one time there were six of us living here.* **at times**

occasionally: *At times she is so unpleasant.* **at all times** (*formal*) always: *Keep your driving licence with you at all times.* **at the same time** (a) together: *laughing and crying at the same time.* (b) (used to introduce another fact to be considered) (but) I must also mention: *He broke it, (but) at the same time he did try to mend it.* **between times** occasionally; between other activities. **each time** on each individual occasion: *Each time I see him he's wearing something new.* **every time** on all the occasions: *It happens to me every time I try.* **from time to time** = at times. **in the nick of time** ⇨ nick[1](2). **many a time** on many occasions: *I've warned you many a time to try harder.* **on time** at the agreed or expected point of time: *I hope the bus arrives on time.* **time after time; time and (time) again** very often. **be high time (sb + pt)** to be (almost past) the point of time (when something ought to be done): *It's high time you cleaned the car.* **5** *nc* (often *pl*) a period of time associated with particular conditions of life, circumstances etc: *ancient/ modern times. We lived through terrible times when we were poor. Times are getting better/ worse.* **ahead of one's time** in advance of contemporary fashion, ideas etc. **before one's time** before the period of one's lifetime. **behind the times** not up to date with contemporary fashion, ideas, ways of living etc. **keep up with the times** to keep up to date with contemporary fashions, ideas etc. **6** (*pl*) (*maths*) multiplied by: *Three times five is/are fifteen.* **7** *nu* (*music*) the rate of (playing) a piece of music.

'**time-consuming** *adj* using, needing, a lot of time: *time-consuming work.*

'**time-honoured** (*US* = **-honored**) *adj* (*attrib*) respected because of its age: *time-honoured traditions.*

'**time-keeper** *nc* (a) a person, machine, that records the time spent by workers at their work. (b) (of a watch etc) one that keeps time (in the way mentioned): *a good/bad timekeeper.*

'**time-lag** *nc* an interval of time between two connected events: *a 5-minute time-lag between the arrival of the two trains.*

'**time-limit** *nc* a limited period of time; last moment of this: *set a time-limit for the completion of a job.*

'**time-saving** *adj* (*attrib*) used to save time: *a time-saving idea.*

'**time-scale** *nc* a series of events used to measure the length of a period of time.

'**time-switch** *nc* a switch set to operate at a desired time (e.g. to turn a light on or off).

'**time-table** *nc* a list showing the days or hours at which events will take place, work will be done etc, e.g. a list showing the times at which trains etc will arrive and depart.

'**time-worn** *adj* (usually *attrib*) used often (and so lacking value etc): *time-worn traditions; time-worn reasons for not being able to help.*

'**time-zone** *nc* a region of the world where the same time(3) is used.

time[2] /taɪm/ *vt* **1** to choose or arrange the time or moment for (something): *He timed his journey so that he arrived before dark.* **2** to measure the time taken by or for (a race, runner, an action or event).

tim·ing *nu* the act of regulating the (order of) events etc to achieve the desired results: *The timing of last night's performance was excellent.*

time·ly /'taɪmlɪ/ *adj* (**-ier, -iest**) happening at just the right time: *a timely arrival.*

timer /'taɪmə(r)/ *nc* a device that measures a period of time: *an egg-timer.*

tim·id /'tɪmɪd/ *adj* easily frightened: *He's as timid as a mouse* (= very timid).

tim·id·ity /tɪ'mɪdətɪ/ *nu*

timid·ly *adv*

tim·or·ous /'tɪmərəs/ *adj* (*formal*) afraid.

tim·or·ous·ly *adv*

tim·pani /'tɪmpənɪ/ *n pl* (*music*) a set of kettle-drums (e.g. of an orchestra).

tim·pan·ist /'tɪmpənɪst/ *nc* a person who plays timpani.

tin¹ /tɪn/ *n* **1** *nu* a soft, white metal (symbol Sn) used in alloys and for coating iron sheets. **2** *nc* a tin-plated airtight container for food: *a tin of sardines/beans.* ⇨ **can**(2).

'tin·foil *nu* tin in very thin sheets, used for wrapping and packing cigarettes etc.

'tin-opener *nc* a utensil for opening tins.

tin² /tɪn/ *vt* (**-nn-**) to put (food etc) in tins(2): *tinned peaches.*

tinge¹ /tɪndʒ/ *nc* **1** a slight colour: *a tinge of pink.* **2** (*fig*) a slight sign: *a tinge of sadness in her voice.*

tinge² /tɪndʒ/ *vt* **tinge sth (with sth) 1** to colour (something) slightly. **2** (*fig*) (esp in *pp*) to affect (something) slightly: *admiration tinged with envy.*

tingle /'tɪŋgl/ *vi, nc* (to have) a pricking or stinging feeling in the skin: *His fingers tingled with the cold. The children were tingling with excitement.*

tin·ker¹ /'tɪŋkə(r)/ *nc* **1** (*old use*) a worker who repairs kettles, pans etc. **2** (*informal*) an attempt to repair (an apparatus): *have an hour's tinker with the radio.*

tin·ker² /'tɪŋkə(r)/ *vi* **tinker (with sth)** to try to repair something without knowledge or skill: *Please don't tinker with my car engine.*

tinkle /'tɪŋkl/ *vt,vi* (to cause something) to make a series of light, ringing sounds, e.g. of a small bell. □ *n sing* a series of such sounds: *the tinkle of a bell.*

tin·ny /'tɪnɪ/ *adj* (**-ier, -iest**) (*derog*) **1** (of something made of metal) of poor quality: *a tinny car.* **2** having a thin sound: *a tinny piano.*

tin·sel /'tɪnsl/ *nu* a glittering metallic substance, used for decoration: *trim a Christmas tree with tinsel.*

tint /tɪnt/ *nc* a (pale or delicate) shade or variety of colour: *tints of green in the sky at dawn.* □ *vt* to give a tint to (something): *tint one's hair.*

ti·ny /'taɪnɪ/ *adj* (**-ier, -iest**) very small.

tip¹ /tɪp/ *nc* **1** a pointed or thin end of something: *the tips of one's fingers/the finger-tips.* **on the tip of one's tongue** about to be spoken or remembered: *Her name is/I have her name on the tip of my tongue.* **2** a small piece put at the end of something: *cigarettes with filter-tips.*

'tip·toe *adv* **on tiptoe** on the tips of one's toes: *be on tiptoe with excitement.* □ *vi* to walk on tiptoe: *She tiptoed out of the bedroom.*

‚tip'top *adj* (*attrib*), *adv* (*informal*) first-rate: *in tiptop condition.*

tip² /tɪp/ *nc* **1** a public place where rubbish is (to

be) put. **2** a hill of waste material from a mine. **3** (*informal; derog*) an untidy place: *Your room is a tip!*

tip³ /tɪp/ *nc* **1** a gift of money to a waiter, porter etc. **2** a small piece of advice: *If you'll take my tip you'll say you're sorry.*

tip⁴ /tɪp/ *v* (**-pp-**) **1** *vt,vi* (to cause something) to rise, lean or tilt on one side or at one end: *He tipped the table and the glass fell over.* **2** *vt,vi* **tip (sth) over/up** (to cause something) to fall or turn over: *She tipped the chair up/the canoe over. The bottle tipped over.* **3** *vt* to empty (the contents of something): *No rubbish can be tipped here. She tipped the water (out of the bowl) into the sink.*

tip⁵ /tɪp/ *vt* (**-pp-**) **1** to touch or hit (something) lightly: *His bat just tipped the ball.* **2** to give a **tip³**(1) to (a person): *tip the waiter.* **3 tip sb off** (*informal*) to give secret information to a person as a warning. Hence **'tip-off** *nc: give the police a tip-off.*

tipple /'tɪpl/ *nc* (*informal*) alcoholic drink: *My favourite tipple is sherry.*

tip·ster /'tɪpstə(r)/ *nc* a person who gives advice about who will win races.

tip·sy /'tɪpsɪ/ *adj* (**-ier, -iest**) (*informal*) slightly drunk.

tip·toe /'tɪptəʊ/ *adv, vi* ⇨ **tip¹**.

ti·rade /taɪ'reɪd/ *nc* a long, angry complaint or accusation.

tire /taɪə(r)/ *vt,vi* (to cause a person, animal) to become weary, in need of rest etc: *The long walk tired the child/tired him out/made him tired.* **be tired of sb/sth** to be unable to put up with a person, thing any longer: *be tired of boiled eggs.*

tired /'taɪəd/ *adj* weary in body or mind; sleepy: *feel tired after a long climb.* **be tired out** to be completely exhausted.

tired·ness *nu*

tire·less *adj* (**a**) not easily made tired: *a tireless worker.* (**b**) continuing a long time: *tireless energy.*

tire·some /'taɪəsəm/ *adj* annoying: *a tiresome boy.*

tis·sue /'tɪʃu:/ *n* **1** *nu* a mass of cells and cell-products in an animal body: *muscle tissue.* **2** *nc,nu* (also **tissue paper**) (a piece of) thin, soft paper for wrapping things etc. **3** *nc* (*fig*) a series: *a tissue of lies.*

tit¹ /tɪt/ *nc* a kind of small bird.

tit² /tɪt/ *n* (only in) **tit for tat** an act of repaying an insult, injury etc by doing something similar back.

tit³ /tɪt/ *nc* (*vulgar sl*) a woman's breast.

tit·bit /'tɪtbɪt/ *nc* **titbit (of sth)** an attractive piece (of food, news, gossip etc).

tit·il·late /'tɪtɪleɪt/ *vt* (*formal*) to excite (a person) pleasantly (esp sexually).

tit·il·la·tion /‚tɪtɪ'leɪʃn/ *nu*

titi·vate /'tɪtɪveɪt/ *v reflex* (*informal*) to make (oneself) smart: *She was titivating herself in front of the mirror.*

title /'taɪtl/ *n* **1** *nc* a name of a book, poem, picture etc. **2** *nc* a word used to show a person's rank, occupation, status etc, e.g. *Lord, Princess, Professor, Dr.* **3** *nc,nu* (*legal*) a right, esp to possess a property: *Have we any title to the land?* **4** (*pl*) = credit titles. ⇨ **credit¹**(11).

'title-deed *nc* (*legal*) a document proving a

title(3) to property.

'title-role *nc* a part in a play that gives the play its name: *a great production of 'Othello' with Olivier in the title-role* (i.e. with Olivier as Othello).

tit·ter /'tɪtə(r)/ *vi, nc* (to give) a silly little laugh.

titu·lar /'tɪtjʊlə(r)/ *adj* existing in name but not having authority or duties: *the titular ruler.*

tiz·zy /'tɪzɪ/ *n sing* **be in a tizzy** (*informal*) to be in a nervous state.

T-junction /'ti: dʒʌŋkʃn/ *nc* ⇨ T, t.

TNT /,ti: en 'ti:/ *abbr* **tri**nitro**t**oluene (a powerful explosive).

to¹ /tu:/ *adverbial particle* Ⓝ For the use of 'to' with verbs as in *come to, set to, turn to* ⇨ the *verb* entries. **1** towards the position wanted (esp a closed one): *push the door to.* **2 to and fro** in one direction and then the opposite one: *travel to and fro between London and Paris.*

to² /tə *strong form:* tu:/ *participle* Ⓝ 'To' is used to mark the infinitive form of a verb, as in *to run, to sleep, to exist.* Some verbs, e.g. *can, may, must, ought, shall, will, would,* do not have an infinitive form and (except for *ought*) are always followed by an infinitive without 'to', e.g. *I can/may/must/will go.* **(a)** (used after many verbs to make sentences etc): *He wants to go. I love to swim.* **(b)** (used when limiting the meaning of adjectives or adverbs): *easy to understand; old enough to get married; sure to succeed.* **(c)** (used to express purpose, result etc): *I wrote so as to warn you. They came to apologize. We did it in order to help. He lived to be a hundred. Do try to join us.* Ⓝ 'And' is now often used to replace *to* meaning 'in order to', as in *Please try and come,* but 'to' is more formal and often considered to be the correct word. **(d)** (used after *how, what, when, where, whether, which, who* etc with verbs such as *know, understand, explain* etc): *I know how to do it. Did she explain where to go? I can't decide who to ask.* **(e)** (used when using a verb as a noun): *To steal is a crime. To forgive was difficult.* **(f)** (used to replace an infinitive to avoid repetition): *I don't want to go but I have to* (i.e. I have to go). *'Will you come?'—'I hope to'* (i.e. I hope to come). *He wants to/would like to/was planning to.*

to³ /tə *strong form:* tu:/ *prep* Ⓝ For the use of 'to' with verbs as in *go to sth, keep to sth, put sth to sb, run to sth* etc, ⇨ the *verb* entries. **1** in the direction of; towards: *walk to work; point to it; hold it up to the light; climb to the top.* **2** towards a condition, quality, state etc: *starved to death; torn to pieces; slow to anger.* **3** (used to introduce an indirect object): *I have posted the letter to you. The man I gave it to has left. Who did you give it to? Don't send it to her.* **4** as far as; until: *from beginning to end; from morning to night; count to ten.* **5** (used when telling the time) before the hour mentioned: *It's five (minutes) to nine.* Compare *past*⁴(2). **6** accompanied by: *sing to the piano; dance to pop music.* **7** as compared with: *I prefer walking to climbing. We won by 6 goals to 3.* **to the sth** in each part: *There are 100 centimetres to the metre. The music has 8 beats to the bar.*

toad /təʊd/ *nc* an animal like a frog that lives on land except when breeding.

toad·stool /'təʊdstu:l/ *nc* a kind of plant (*fungus*) like a mushroom and often poisonous.

toast¹ /təʊst/ *n* **1** *nu* bread made brown and crisp by heating: *two slices of toast.* **2** *nc* an act of toasting(3): *Let's drink a toast to their happiness.*

toast² /təʊst/ *v* **1** *vt, vi* (to cause bread) to become brown and crisp by heating: *toasted sandwiches.* **2** *vt* to warm (oneself, one's feet etc) near a fire. **3** *vt* to wish happiness, success etc to (a person, thing) while raising a glass of wine: *Let's toast the bride and bridegroom.*

toast·er *nc* an electrical apparatus used for toasting bread.

to·bac·co /tə'bækəʊ/ *nu,nc* (a plant having) leaves which are used for smoking in pipes, cigars, cigarettes: *This is a mixture of the best tobaccos.*

to·bac·co·nist /tə'bækənɪst/ *nc* a shop, person, that sells tobacco, cigarettes etc.

-to-be /tə 'bi:/ ⇨ be²(2).

to·bog·gan /tə'bɒgən/ *nc* a long, narrow board used for sliding on ice. □ *vi* to use a toboggan.

to·day /tə'deɪ/ *adv, nu* **1** (on) this day: *Today is Sunday. Have you seen today's newspaper? We're leaving today week/a week today* (= on this day next week). **2** (at) this present age or period: *the writers/the young people (of) today.*

toddle /'tɒdl/ *vi* to walk with short, uncertain steps as a baby does.

tod·dler /'tɒdlə(r)/ *nc* a baby who can toddle.

toe¹ /təʊ/ *nc* **1** each of the five divisions of the front part of the foot. **step/tread on sb's toes** (*fig*) to offend a person. **from top to toe** ⇨ top³(1). **on one's toes** (*fig*) ready to act immediately. **on tiptoe** ⇨ tiptoe. **2** a part of a sock, shoe etc covering the toes.

'toe-nail *nc* a nail on a toe.

toe² /təʊ/ *vt* **toe the line** ⇨ line¹(10).

tof·fee /'tɒfɪ/ *nc,nu* (a piece of) hard, brown sticky sweet made by boiling sugar, butter etc.

to·geth·er /tə'geðə(r)/ *adv* Ⓝ For uses with verbs such as *come, get, go, pull* etc, ⇨ the *verb* entries. **1** with each other or the others: *They went for a walk together.* **together with** in addition to; and also: *These new facts, together with the evidence you have already heard, prove the prisoner's innocence.* **2** so as to be joined: *Tie the ends together.* **3** in, to, the same place: *The leader called his men together. Are the children all together?* **4** at the same time: *All his troubles seemed to come together. The bills arrived all together.* Ⓝ For the difference between 'altogether' and 'all together', ⇨ the note at 'altogether'. **5** (*informal*) organized; thinking clearly: *He's trying to get things together. She's not very together early in the morning.*

toil¹ /tɔɪl/ *nu* hard and long work.

toil² /tɔɪl/ *vi* **1** to work long or hard (at a task). **2** to move with difficulty and trouble: *toil up a steep hill.*

toi·let /'tɔɪlɪt/ *n* **1** *nc* (a room with) a lavatory: *He's gone to the toilet. May I use your toilet? Where's the ladies' toilet, please?* ⇨ lavatory, loo. **2** *nu* (*formal*) the process of dressing, arranging the hair etc: *She spent only a few minutes doing her toilet.*

'toilet-paper *nu* paper for use in a toilet.

'toilet-roll *nc* a roll of toilet-paper.

toi·let·ries /'tɔɪlɪtrɪz/ *n pl* (*commerce*) articles used for washing, dressing, oneself.

to·ken¹ /'təʊkən/ adj (attrib) small: *The enemy offered only token resistance.*

‚token 'payment nc a payment of a small part of what is owed, made to show that the debt is recognized.

‚token 'strike nc one for a few hours only (as a warning that a long strike may follow).

to·ken² /'təʊkən/ nc a sign, evidence or mark: *I was given this watch as a token of his affection.*

told /təʊld/ pt,pp of tell.

tol·er·able /'tɒlərəbl/ adj (formal) fairly good: *tolerable weather.* Compare intolerable.

tol·er·ance /'tɒlərəns/ nu the ability, willingness, to allow and accept opinions, beliefs, customs, physical types, behaviour etc different from one's own: *religious/racial tolerance; behave with tolerance towards others.* Opp intolerance.

tol·er·ant /'tɒlərənt/ adj having or showing tolerance: *tolerant parents. He's not very tolerant (of criticism).* Opp intolerant.

tol·er·ant·ly adv

tol·er·ate /'tɒləreɪt/ vt to put up with, allow, (something unwanted or unpleasant) without protest: *I won't tolerate your rudeness/your doing that. I can tolerate pop music for about ten minutes only.*

tol·er·ation /,tɒlə'reɪʃn/ nu = tolerance.

toll¹ /təʊl/ nc **1** a payment required for the use of a road, bridge, harbour etc. **2** (fig) the costs suffered as a result of a war, disease, famine etc: *The war took a heavy toll of the nation's men.*

'toll-gate nc one across a road at which a toll is payable.

toll² /təʊl/ vt,vi (to cause a bell) to ring with slow, regular sounds: *The funeral bell tolled.* Compare peal². □ n sing a sound of a bell.

tom·ato /tə'mɑːtəʊ/ nc (pl —es) (also attrib) (a plant with) a soft, juicy, red fruit: *tomato juice.*

tomb /tuːm/ nc a place for a dead body, esp one with a monument over it.

'tomb·stone nc = gravestone.

tom·boy /'tɒmbɔɪ/ nc a girl who likes rough, noisy games and play.

tom·cat /'tɒmkæt/ nc a male cat.

tome /təʊm/ nc (formal) a large book.

to·mor·row /tə'mɒrəʊ/ adv, nc,nu (on) the day after today: *If today is Monday, tomorrow will be Tuesday and the day after tomorrow will be Wednesday. Let's meet tomorrow. The announcement will appear in tomorrow's newspapers.*

ton /tʌn/ nc **1** a unit of measurement of weight (2240 lb or 1016 kg). ⇨ tonne. **2** (informal) a large weight or quantity: *He has tons of money.* **weigh a ton** to be extremely heavy.

tone¹ /təʊn/ n **1** nc a sound, esp with reference to its quality: *the sweet tone(s) of a violin; a serious tone of voice.* **2** nc a quality of the voice in speaking: *In 'Are you ill?' there is a rising tone on 'ill.'* **3** n sing a general spirit, character, of a community etc: *The tone of the school is excellent.* **4** nc shade (of colour); degree (of light): *a carpet in tones of brown.* **5** nc (music) any one of the five larger intervals between one note and the next.

‚tone-'deaf adj not able to (hear the differences in musical pitch and) sing in tune.

tone·less adj (derog) not having spirit etc; dull: *answer in a toneless voice.*

tone·less·ly adv

tone² /təʊn/ vt to give a particular tone of sound or colour to (something): *tone a photograph.*

tone sth down (**a**) to make colour etc less strong. (**b**) to make criticism, a style of writing, an opinion etc less extreme: *You should tone down some of the severe criticism in your article.*

tone in (with sth) (esp of colours) to be in harmony: *The curtains tone in well with the carpet.*

tone sth up (of exercise etc) to make muscles, a person etc stronger, more lively.

tone with sth = tone in (with sth).

tongs /tɒŋz/ n pl (also *a pair of tongs*) one of various kinds of U-shaped tool for taking up and holding something: *sugar tongs.* **be/go at it hammer and tongs** ⇨ hammer¹(1).

tongue /tʌŋ/ n **1** nc the movable organ in the mouth, used in talking, tasting, licking etc: *A white layer on your tongue can be a sign that you are ill.* **have a rough tongue** to have a habit of being rude or bad-tempered. **on the tip of one's tongue** ⇨ tip¹(1). **have one's tongue in one's cheek** to say something that one does not intend to be taken seriously. **have lost one's tongue** to be too shy to speak. **have a sharp tongue** to be easily angered, critical etc. **hold one's tongue** to be silent, stop talking. **put one's tongue out (at sb)** to do this as a rude sign. **2** nc,nu (also attrib) an animal's tongue, cooked and eaten: *tongue sandwiches.* **3** nc something like a tongue in shape or use, e.g. a flame or the strip of leather under the laces of a shoe. **4** nc a language: *one's mother tongue* (i.e. the language of one's parents).

'tongue-tied adj unable or unwilling to speak because of shyness, fear etc.

'tongue-twister nc a word or succession of words difficult to say quickly and correctly, e.g. 'sixty three thousand thrushes flew through the thunderstorm.'

ton·ic /'tɒnɪk/ nc,nu something, e.g. medicine, giving strength or energy: *get a bottle of tonic from the doctor. Praise can be a useful mental tonic.*

'tonic water nu (bottled) water with quinine, used to (mix with an alcoholic) drink: *a gin and tonic.*

to·night /tə'naɪt/ adv, nu (on) the night of today: *last night, tonight, and tomorrow night; tonight's television news.*

ton·nage /'tʌnɪdʒ/ nu (commerce) **1** the measurement of the amount a ship can carry: (1 ton = 100 cu ft). **2** the total tonnage(1) of a country's shipping.

tonne /tʌn/ nc (tech) a metric ton (1000 kg).

ton·sil /'tɒnsɪl/ nc either of two small oval masses of tissue at the sides of the throat, near the root of the tongue.

ton·sil·li·tis /,tɒnsɪ'laɪtɪs/ nu inflammation of the tonsils.

too /tuː/ adv **1** in addition: *I, too, have been to Madrid* (i.e. in addition to other people). Ⓝ Be careful because the position of *'too'* can change the meaning. Compare *She, too,* (i.e. She is another person who) *understands Greek* and *She understands Greek, too* (i.e. in addition to another language). For the differences between *too, also* and *as well* ⇨ also(1). **2** more than is allowed, needed etc: *We've had too much rain. You're driving too fast. These shoes are too small/big. You eat too much (food).*

I've eaten too many (chips). It's too cold to go swimming. It's far too cold outside. She's much too sensible. If you don't hurry, you'll be too late. **only too** ⇨ only²(1).

took /tʊk/ *pt of* take².

tool /tuːl/ *nc* **1** an object held in the hand(s) and used to do or make something, e.g. a *hammer*, *screwdriver*. **to down tools** to stop working (i.e. to strike). **2** (*derog*) a weak person used by another: *He was a tool in the hands of the director.*

toot /tuːt/ *vt,vi, nc* (to make) a short, sharp warning sound from (a horn, whistle, trumpet etc).

tooth /tuːθ/ *nc* (*pl* **teeth** /tiːθ/) **1** one of the hard, white structures in the mouth, used for biting and chewing: *clean one's teeth; have a tooth filled/out.* **armed to the teeth** having (too) many weapons. **by the skin of one's teeth** ⇨ skin¹(1). **in the teeth of sth** against the full strength, effect, of something: *in the teeth of danger.* **bare one's teeth** = show one's teeth. **be long in the tooth** to be rather old. **fight tooth and nail** to make every possible effort to win. **get one's teeth into sth** to attack a task with energy and determination. **grit one's teeth** (to hold one's teeth together) to show determination. **have a sweet tooth** to enjoy eating sweet food. **set one's/sb's teeth on edge** to upset one's, a person's, nerves, esp by using a scraping noise. **show one's teeth** to produce a threatening expression. **smile through one's teeth** to smile insincerely. **2** any pointed part of a comb, saw, rake etc like a tooth. **3** (*pl*) (*informal*) the strength or ability to have an effect: *Does that committee have any teeth?*

'tooth·ache *nc,nu* (a) pain in a tooth or teeth.
'tooth·brush *nc* one used for cleaning the teeth.
'tooth·paste/-powder *nu* the kind used for cleaning the teeth.
'tooth·pick *nc* a short, pointed piece of wood etc for removing small pieces of food from between the teeth.
tooth·less *adj* without teeth: *a toothless grin.*

tootle /'tuːtl/ *vi, nc* (to make) a toot softly or continuously, as on a car horn.

top¹ /tɒp/ *adj* **1** first or best: *He's top of the class. We're sending you our top engineer.* **2** (*attrib*) in the highest, first, position: *the top floor/window; on the top shelf.* Opp bottom(5). **3** (*attrib*) most in extent, degree: *pay top rates; at top speed; charge top prices.* Opp lowest.

top² /tɒp/ *nc* a toy that turns and balances on a point. **sleep like a top** to sleep deeply.

top³ /tɒp/ *n* **1** *nc* the highest physical position or part: *at the top of the hill; the top of the table; mountain tops covered in snow.* Opp bottom(1). **from top to bottom** throughout: *clean the house from top to bottom.* **from top to toe** all over one's body: *I was aching from top to toe.* **on top** on the top: *The blue book is at the bottom with the red ones on top.* **on (the) top of sth** (a) over and resting on something: *put it on (the) top of those.* (b) in addition to something: *He borrowed £5 and on top of that asked to borrow the car.* **on top of the world** very confident, healthy, happy: *I'm feeling on top of the world this morning.* **on top of things/one's work** able

to cope. **blow one's top** (*informal*) to become suddenly very angry. **2** *n sing* (the —), the highest or best place, rank, quantity etc: *She's reached the top of her profession. You'll only get to the top by working hard. He shouted at the top of his voice* (= loudly). *He came top in the exam.* ⇨ bottom(5). **over the top** beyond the limit, esp of one's patience: *His loud drumming sent me over the top and I screamed with anger.* ⇨ OTT. **3** *nc* a cover for a container: *the top of a bottle.* **4** *nc* an article of clothing worn over the upper part of the body: *She was wearing a red top and blue trousers.*

,**top 'brass** *nu* (*informal*) senior management.
,**top 'dog** *nc* (*sl*) a person in the senior position.
,**top 'hat** *nc* a tall silk hat for formal occasions.
,**top-'heavy** *adj* too heavy at the top so as to be in danger of falling.
'**top-level** *adj* (*attrib*) involving the most important or highest-ranking officials: *top-level talks.*
'**top·most** /-məʊst/ *adj* (*attrib*) highest.
,**top-'ranking** *adj* (*attrib*) of the highest rank.
,**top 'secret** *adj* (usually *pred*) needing to be secret because very important.
'**top·soil** *nu* the soil on the surface.
top·less *adj* (esp of a woman's clothes) leaving the breasts bare: *a topless swimsuit; topless bathing.*

top⁴ /tɒp/ *vt* (**-pp-**) **1** to provide, be, a top for (something): *a cake topped with icing.* **2** **top sth up** to fill up a partly empty container: *top up a drink* (= fill a partly filled glass). **3** to be more than (an amount mentioned): *Our exports have just topped the £80 000 mark.* **to top it all . . . ,** the last (and surprising etc) fact is . . . . **4** to cut the tops off (plants): *top carrots.*

to·paz /'təʊpæz/ *nc,nu* (a gem from) a kind of transparent yellow mineral.

top·ic /'tɒpɪk/ *nc* a subject (for discussion, writing etc).
topi·cal /-kl/ *adj* of interest now: *topical news.*
topi·cal·ly /-klɪ/ *adv*

top·og·ra·phy /tə'pɒgrəfɪ/ *nu* (description of) the features, e.g. rivers, valleys, roads, of a place.
topo·graphi·cal /,tɒpə'græfɪkl/ *adj*
topo·graphi·cal·ly /-klɪ/ *adv*

topple /'tɒpl/ *vt,vi* (to cause a person, thing, pile etc) to be unsteady and fall (over): *The pile of books toppled over/down. The dictator was finally toppled from power.*

tor /tɔː(r)/ *nc* a small hill; rocky peak.

torch /tɔːtʃ/ *nc* **1** an electric light held in the hand. **2** a piece of wood etc soaked in oil etc, used as a flaming light.
'**torch·light** *nu* (also *attrib*) light from a torch: *a torchlight procession.*

tore /tɔː(r)/ *pt of* tear³.

tor·ea·dor /'tɒrɪədɔː(r)/ *nc* a bullfighter on a horse.

tor·ment¹ /'tɔːment/ *nc,nu* (something that causes) severe bodily or mental pain or suffering: *be in torment; suffer torment(s) from an aching tooth.*

tor·ment² /tɔː'ment/ *vt* to cause severe suffering to (a person): *be tormented with pain/hunger.*
tor·men·tor /-tə(r)/ *nc* (*derog*) a person who torments.

torn /tɔːn/ *pp of* tear³.

tor·na·do /tɔː'neɪdəʊ/ *nc* (*pl* **—es**) a violent and

tor·pe·do¹ /tɔːˈpiːdəʊ/ *nc* (*pl* **—es**) a long self-propelled weapon filled with explosives, travelling below the surface of the sea.

tor·pe·do² /tɔːˈpiːdəʊ/ *vt* **1** to attack or destroy (a ship etc) with a torpedo. **2** (*fig*) to attack (a policy, institution etc) and make it ineffective: *Who torpedoed the disarmament talks?*

tor·rent /ˈtɒrənt/ *nc* **1** a strong rush of liquid (esp water): *mountain torrents; torrents of rain.* **2** (*fig*) a violent outpouring: *a torrent of abuse/insults.*

tor·ren·tial /təˈrenʃl/ *adj* (*attrib*) of, like, caused by, a torrent: *torrential rain.*

tor·so /ˈtɔːsəʊ/ *nc* (*pl* **—s**) (a statue of) a human body without the head, arms and legs.

tor·toise /ˈtɔːtəs/ *nc* a kind of slow-moving, four-legged land animal with a hard shell.

tor·tu·ous /ˈtɔːtjʊəs/ *adj* **1** full of twists and bends: *a tortuous path.* **2** (*fig*) not straightforward: *a tortuous argument/method.*

tor·tu·ous·ly *adv*

tor·ture¹ /ˈtɔːtʃə(r)/ *n* **1** *nu* the causing of mental or physical suffering, esp to get information. **2** *nc,nu* (a) pain caused or suffered: *suffer torture from the secret police.*

tor·ture² /ˈtɔːtʃə(r)/ *vt* to cause severe mental or physical suffering to (a person): *torture a man to make him confess; be tortured with anxiety.*

tor·tur·er *nc* a person who tortures.

Tory /ˈtɔːrɪ/ *adj, nc* (*pl* **-ies**) = Conservative²(2).

toss¹ /tɒs/ *n* **1** *nc* an act of tossing: *a toss of a coin/ ball; with a toss of the head* (= moving the head quickly e.g. to express refusal). **2** *n sing* the result of tossing a coin: *Our team lost/won the toss.*

toss² /tɒs/ *v* **1** *vt* to throw (something): *toss a ball into the air; toss a coin to a beggar.* **2** *vt* to move (the head, tail etc) quickly: *The horse tossed its head.* **3** *vt,vi* (to cause a person, thing) to move restlessly from side to side or up and down: *The ship (was) tossed about on the waves.* **toss and turn** to be very restless: *She tossed and turned in bed.* **4** *vt,vi* to throw (a coin) up to decide something according to which side it falls on: *They tossed (a coin) to decide who would pay.*

toss (sb) for sth to toss(1) a coin (with a person) to decide something: 'Who's to pay?'—'Let's toss for it/I'll toss you for it'.

toss sth off to produce a piece of writing, drawing etc quickly: *toss off a letter to a friend.*

toss up to toss(1) a coin. Hence **'toss-up** *nc* (*informal*) something about which there is doubt: *It's a toss-up whether he'll get here in time.*

tot¹ /tɒt/ *nc* **1** (often *tiny tot*) a very small child. **2** (*informal*) a small glass of alcoholic drink.

tot² /tɒt/ *vt,vi* (**-tt-**) *tot (sth) up* (*informal*) to add (something) up: *tot up a column of figures.*

to·tal¹ /ˈtəʊtl/ *adj* complete; entire: *total silence.*

to·tal·ly /ˈtəʊtəlɪ/ *adv* completely: *totally blind.*

to·tal·ity /təʊˈtælətɪ/ *nu*

to·tal² /ˈtəʊtl/ *nc* a total amount (of the size mentioned): *Our costs reached a total of £20.*

to·tal³ /ˈtəʊtl/ *vt,vi* (**-ll-**, *US* also **-l-**) to add (something) up to (an amount mentioned): *The number of visitors totalled 15 000. Have you totalled all the costs?*

to·tali·tar·ian /ˌtəʊtælɪˈteərɪən/ *adj* of, concerning, a political system with only one political party allowed: *a totalitarian regime.*

tot·ter /ˈtɒtə(r)/ *vi* **1** to stand, walk, with weak, unsteady steps: *The wounded man tottered to his feet.* **2** to be almost falling; seem to be about to collapse: *The tree tottered and then fell.*

tou·can /ˈtuːkən/ *nc* a kind of tropical American bird with brightly coloured feathers and a large beak.

touch¹ /tʌtʃ/ *n* **1** *nc* an act of touching: *I felt a touch on my arm.* ⇨ tactile. **2** *nu* (the sense giving) feeling by touching: *soft/rough to the touch* (= when touched). **3** *nc* a stroke made with a brush, pen etc: *add a few finishing touches.* **4** *nc* a slight amount: *a touch of frost in the air; a touch of sadness in his voice.* **5** *nc* a style or manner of playing a musical instrument, painting, typing etc: *have a light touch* (e.g. on a piano, a typewriter). **6** *nu* **in/out of touch (with sb/sth)** in/ not in (regular) communication (with); having/ not having information (about): *get in touch with* (= contact) *her parents; keep in touch with old friends; be out of touch with the political situation.*

lose touch to lose contact with a person, each other: *If we correspond regularly we shan't lose touch.* **7** *nu* (in football, rugby) part of the field outside the side-lines: *The ball is in/out of touch.*

,touch-and-'go *adj* (*pred*) very uncertain: *It was touch-and-go whether the doctor would arrive in time.*

touch² /tʌtʃ/ *v* **1** *vt,vi* (to cause a person, thing) to come into contact with another: *One of the branches is touching the water. Can you touch your toes with your legs straight? Make sure the two edges are touching. Please do not touch the fruit.* **touch wood** ⇨ wood(1). **2** *vt* to press (a person, thing) lightly, usually with the hand: *He touched the bell. I touched her on the shoulder.* **3** *vt* to touch(2) and change the position of (something): *Who's touched my things?* **4** *vt* (usually with *not*) to eat or drink (food): *I haven't touched a thing all day.* **5** *vt* to produce an emotion in (a person): *Her sad story touched us all. I was so touched by your kind letter. The severe criticism has touched him deeply.* ⇨ touched(1), touching¹. **6** *vt* (usually with *not*) to have anything to do with: *As a pacifist I won't touch shares in the weapons industries.* **7** *vt* to damage, harm, (a person, thing) slightly: *Luckily the carpet wasn't touched by the fire.* **8** *vt* (usually with *not*) to be equal to (another person): *He cannot be touched/ No-one can touch him as an actor.* **9** *vt* (usually with *not*) to deal with (something) successfully; cope with: *I couldn't touch the first two questions in the exam. Nothing seems to touch these grease spots.*

touch down (of a plane) to come down to the ground. Hence **'touchdown** *nc.* **touch (sth) down** (*rugby*) to put the ball on the ground to score a try. Hence **'touch-down** *nc.*

touch sb for sth (*sl*) to borrow money from a person (without intending to return it): *He touched me for £5.*

touch sth in to add a few details to a painting.

touch sth off to cause the start of an argument etc: *The news of the arrests touched off a riot.*

touch on sth to mention something briefly.

touch sth up to add a few details to a painting.

touch upon sth (*formal*) = touch on sth.

touch·down /ˈtʌtʃ daʊn/ *nc* ⇨ touch down.

touch·ed /'tʌtʃt/ *adj* (*pred*) **1** feeling pleased and thankful: *She was so touched by the flowers.* **2** (*informal; derog*) mad: *Is he touched?*

touch·ing[1] /'tʌtʃɪŋ/ *adj* causing a feeling of gratitude, sympathy etc: *a touching request for help.*
touch·ing·ly *adv*

touch·ing[2] /'tʌtʃɪŋ/ *prep* (*formal*) on the subject of: *Touching your earlier question, I've decided not to go.*

touchy /'tʌtʃɪ/ *adj* (**-ier, -iest**) (*derog*) easily or quickly offended: *Don't be so touchy!*

tough /tʌf/ *adj* (**—er, —est**) **1** (of meat) hard to cut or get one's teeth into. **2** not easily cut, broken or worn out: *This cloth is as tough as leather.* **3** (of a person) strong; able to endure hardships: *tough soldiers.* **4** (of a person) rough and violent: *a tough criminal.* **5** (of a person, group) determined and severe: *a tough boss. The government got tough with the unions.* **6** hard to carry out, solve etc: *a tough job/problem.* **7** **tough (on sb)** (*informal*) unfortunate (for a person): *It will be tough on her if he goes. What tough luck!*
tough·ly *adv*
tough·ness *nu*

tough·en /'tʌfn/ *vt,vi* (to cause a person, meat) to become tough.

tou·pee /'tu:peɪ/ *nc* a piece of false hair worn to cover a bald patch.

tour[1] /tʊə(r)/ *nc* **1** a journey out and home again during which several or many places are visited: *a tour round Europe; a round-the-world tour; go on a conducted tour* (i.e. one with a guide). **2** a short visit to or through: *a tour of the palace.* **3** a period of duty or employment (overseas): *a tour of two years as a lecturer in Nigeria.* **4** a series of (official) visits: *The Director leaves tomorrow on a tour of overseas branches.* **5** a number of visits to places made by a theatrical company etc. **on tour** touring: *The Royal Ballet is now on tour in America.*

tour[2] /tʊə(r)/ *vt,vi* **1** to make a tour (of a place): *They'll tour western Europe.* **2** to go on a tour(5): *The play will tour the provinces in the autumn.*

tour·ism /'tʊərɪzəm/ *nu* **1** the business of providing travel and services for tourists: *Tourism is Greece's biggest industry.* **2** the practice of having a holiday as a tourist.

tour·ist[1] /'tʊərɪst/ *adj* (*attrib*) of, for, tourism: *the tourist industry; a tourist agency; tourist class* (the cheapest class of travel, e.g. on a plane or ship).

tour·ist[2] /'tʊərɪst/ *nc* a person making a tour for pleasure: *London is full of tourists in summer.*

tour·na·ment /'tʊənəmənt/ *nc* a series of competitions of skill between a number of players: *a tennis/chess tournament.*

tour·ni·quet /'tʊənɪkeɪ/ *nc* any device (e.g. a piece of rope) used for stopping a flow of blood through an artery.

tousle /'taʊzl/ *vt* (*formal*) to make (esp the hair) untidy: *a girl with tousled hair.*

tout[1] /taʊt/ *nc* a person who encourages others to buy something: *a ticket tout.*

tout[2] /taʊt/ *vi* **tout (for sth)** to act as a tout: *men outside the station touting for the hotels.*

tow[1] /təʊ/ *nc* an act of towing: *Can we give you a tow? in tow* (*informal*) also with (a person): *She arrived with her mother in tow.* **on tow** (of a vehicle) being towed.

tow[2] /təʊ/ *vt* to pull (something, esp a vehicle) along by using a rope or chain: *tow a damaged car to the nearest garage.*

to·wards /tə'wɔːdz/ *prep* **1** in the direction of: *walking towards the sea; first steps towards the abolition of armaments.* **2** regarding; in relation to: *What will the Government's attitude be towards the plan?* **3** for the purpose of (helping): *We must save money towards her education. That can go towards the cost of the fare.* **4** (of time) a little before: *towards the end of the century.*

tow·el[1] /'taʊəl/ *nc* a piece of cloth etc used for drying or wiping something wet (e.g. one's hands or body): *a bath-towel; a paper towel.* **throw in the towel** (*informal*) to admit defeat.
towel·ling (*US* = **towel·ing**) *nu* a kind of cloth used for towels.

tow·el[2] /'taʊəl/ *vt* (**-ll-**, *US* **-l-**) **towel oneself/ sb (down)** to dry or rub oneself, a person, with a towel.

tow·er[1] /'taʊə(r)/ *nc* **1** a tall building, either standing alone or forming part of a church or other large building: *an office tower.* **2** **a tower of strength** (*fig*) a person who can be relied on for protection, strength or comfort in time of trouble.
'tower-block *nc* a tall building with flats or offices.

tow·er[2] /'taʊə(r)/ *vi* **1** to rise to a great height, be very tall, esp in relation to the height of the surroundings: *the skyscrapers that tower over New York.* **tower above sb** (*fig*) (of a person) to have much more ability, intelligence, courage etc than another or others: *a man who towers above his contemporaries.*

town /taʊn/ *n* **1** *nc* a large group of buildings and streets where people live and work. *Would you rather live in a town or in the country?* Compare city(1), village. **paint the town red** (*informal*) to go out and have a lively, exciting time, especially when celebrating. **the talk of the town** ⇨ talk¹(2). **2** *n sing* (used without *a, an*) the business, shopping etc part of a town: *go to town to shop. He's in town today.* **out on the town** out enjoying the entertainment facilities of a town, esp at night. **go to town** (*informal*) to act, behave, freely, e.g. by spending lots of money in town. **3** *n sing* (the —) the people of a town: *The whole town was talking about it.* **4** *n sing* (the —) towns in general; life in a town: *There are so many problems caused by people moving from the countryside to the town.*

,town 'centre *nc* the central area with the town hall, public library, main shops etc.

,town 'clerk *nc* an official who keeps town or city records and advises on certain legal matters.

,town 'council *nc* (in England) the governing body of (a district in) a town.

,town 'councillor *nc* an elected member of a town council.

,town 'hall *nc* a building containing local government offices.

tox·ic /'tɒksɪk/ *adj* (*tech*) poisonous (the usual word): *toxic gases.*

tox·in /'tɒksɪn/ *nc* (*tech*) a poisonous substance.

toy[1] /tɔɪ/ *adj* (*attrib*) **1** used as a toy: *a toy soldier/ car.* **2** (of a dog) very small: *a toy poodle.*

toy² /tɔɪ/ nc something, e.g. a doll, used for a child to play with.

'toy·shop nc a shop where toys are sold.

toy³ /tɔɪ/ vi **toy with sth 1** to think not very seriously about a possibility etc: *He's toying with the idea of buying a new car.* **2** to play idly with something: *toying with a pencil.* **3** to treat a person's feelings too lightly: *Stop toying with her affections.*

trace¹ /treɪs/ nc **1** a mark, sign etc showing that a person or thing has been present, that something has existed or happened: *traces of an ancient civilization. We've lost all trace of them.* **2** a very small amount: *There were traces of poison in his blood.*

trace² /treɪs/ vt **1** to draw along, follow, the course, outline etc of (something): *tracing (out) one's route on a map.* **2** to copy (something) by drawing on transparent paper. **3** to discover (a person or thing) by looking at marks, evidence etc: *I cannot trace* (= cannot find) *any letter from you dated 1 June.* **trace sth/sb back (to sth)** (a) to find the origin of a person, thing by going back in time: *He traces his ancestors back to an old Scottish family.* (b) to find the person responsible, the origin of a fault etc, by going back through evidence: *The rumour was traced back to a journalist.*

trac·ing nc a reproduction (of a map, design etc) made by tracing(2).

tra·chea /trə'kɪə/ nc (pl **tracheae** /-kɪːɪ/) (anat) = windpipe.

track¹ /træk/ nc **1** a line or series of marks left by a vehicle, person, animal etc passing along: *tracks in the snow.* **off the track** (fig) following a wrong line of action. **go off the beaten track** to do something unusual. **be on sb's track/on the track of sb** to be following the tracks of a person: *The police are on the track of the thief.* **cover up one's tracks** to hide one's movements or activities. **have a one-track mind** to give all one's attention to one topic or thought (esp sex). **keep/lose track of sb/sth** to follow/ fail to follow the course or development of: *read the newspapers to keep track of current events.* **2** a rough path. **3** a path prepared for racing: *a motor-racing/cycling/running track.* **4** a set of rails for trains etc: *The train hit a tree and left the track.* **5** a course (marked or not) taken by something: *the track of a storm/spacecraft.* **6** a section of music etc recorded on a record or tape: *The first track is a beautiful song.*

'track event nc any running event in an athletic contest, done on a track(3).

'track record nc (fig) an individual's known personal achievements: *He has a good/bad track record.*

'track shoe nc a spiked shoe worn by a runner.

'track suit nc a loose-fitting warm suit as worn by an athlete.

track² /træk/ vt to follow the track of (a person, thing): *track an animal.* **track sb/sth down** to find a person, thing, by searching: *track down a fox/a reference.*

track·er nc a person who tracks wild animals.

'track·ing station nc one which, by radar or radio, maintains contact with spacecraft etc.

tract¹ /trækt/ nc **1** a stretch or area (of forest, farmland etc): *the wide tracts of desert in N Africa.*

2 (anat) a system of related parts in an animal body: *the digestive/respiratory tract.*

tract² /trækt/ nc a short printed essay, esp on a moral or religious subject.

tract·able /'træktəbl/ adj (formal) easily controlled or guided.

trac·tor /'træktə(r)/ nc a kind of vehicle used for pulling agricultural machinery or other heavy equipment over rough ground.

trade¹ /treɪd/ n **1** nu the business of buying and selling of goods: *Trade was good last year.* **2** nc a particular branch of buying and selling: *He's in the furniture/book trade.* **3** nc,nu an occupation; way of making a living, esp a handicraft: *He's a carpenter/tailor by trade.* ⇨ also Jack of all trades.

,trade 'deficit nc an amount by which imports cost more than exports.

,trade 'discount nc an amount taken off the usual price by a manufacturer or supplier.

'trade gap nc an unfavourable difference between exports and imports.

'trade·mark nc (a) a design, special name etc used to distinguish a manufacturer's goods from others. (b) (fig) a distinguishing characteristic: *He leaves his trademark on all his activities.*

'trade name nc a name given to a manufactured product. Ⓝ Marked (P) in this dictionary.

'trade price nc the price charged by a manufacturer or wholesaler to a retailer.

'trades·man nc a shopkeeper (the usual word).

,trade 'secret nc a technique etc used by an industry that is not known by its competitors.

,trade 'surplus nc an amount by which exports produced more money than the cost of imports.

,trade 'union nc an organized association of workers in a trade formed to protect their interests, improve their working conditions etc. Ⓝ The use of *'trades union'* is now considered to be very formal or dated.

,trade 'unionist nc a member of a trade union.

'trade wind nc a strong wind blowing always towards the equator from the SE and NE.

trade² /treɪd/ v **1** vi to engage in trade(1); buy and sell: *Britain trades with most overseas countries.* **2** vt to exchange (things): *The boy traded his skates for a cricket bat.* **3** vt **trade sth in** to give (a used article) in part payment when buying a new one: *He traded in his car for a new one.* Hence **'trade-in** nc. **4** vi **trade on sth** to use a person's misfortune, generosity etc in a way that gives advantage to oneself: *He was trading on her sympathy.*

trad·er nc a person who trades(1).

tra·di·tion /trə'dɪʃn/ n **1** nu (the passing on from generation to generation of) opinions, beliefs, customs etc: *Country life in Wales is full of tradition.* **2** nc a habit, custom, belief etc that is passed to the next generation: *It's a tradition to send greeting cards at Christmas.*

tra·di·tion·al /-ʃənl/ adj

tra·di·tion·al·ly /-nəli/ adv

traf·fic¹ /'træfɪk/ nu **1** the movement of vehicles etc along roads and streets, of planes in the sky: *There was a lot of/not much traffic on the roads yesterday.* **2** illegal trading: *the drug traffic.*

'traffic indicator nc = trafficator.

'traffic island nc a platform in the centre of a busy road, for people when walking across it.

'traffic jam nc a number of vehicles close

together so that movement is difficult or impossible.

'traffic-lights *n pl* coloured lights by the roadside controlling traffic.

'traffic warden *nc* an official controlling the parking of cars and the use of parking-meters.

traf·fic² /'træfɪk/ *vi* (**-ck-**) *traffic in sth (with sb/sth)* to trade(1) in illegal goods: *He was arrested for trafficking in drugs.*

traf·fi·ca·tor /'træfɪkeɪtə(r)/ *nc* a yellow pointer on a vehicle, formerly used to show the direction in which it is about to turn.

tra·gedy /'trædʒədɪ/ *n* (*pl* **-ies**) *nc,nu* **1** (*literature*) (an example of) a form of drama in which there is conflict and suffering and a sad ending. Compare comedy. **2** (an instance of) a very sad event, experience etc in real life.

tra·gic /'trædʒɪk/ *adj* **1** (*attrib*) of tragedy(1): *a tragic actor.* **2** very sad or unfortunate: *It's tragic that his wife died.*

 tragi·cal·ly /-klɪ/ *adv*

trail¹ /treɪl/ *nc* **1** a mark or series of marks left by a person or thing that has passed by: *a trail of mud/smoke.* **2** a track or smell left by an animal or person. **3** a path through rough country.

trail² /treɪl/ *v* **1** *vt,vi* (to cause something) to be pulled behind (through the air or over a surface): *Her scarf was trailing in the wind/along the floor. He trailed his bag through the mud.* **2** *vt* to follow the marks or signs of (a person): *trail a thief.* **3** *vi* (of plants) to grow over or along the surface: *roses trailing over the walls.*

trail·er /'treɪlə(r)/ *nc* **1** a wheeled carrier pulled by a tractor or lorry. **2** a caravan pulled by a vehicle. **3** a trailing plant. **4** a series of short extracts from a film, used to advertise it.

train¹ /treɪn/ *n* **1** *nc* a number of railway coaches etc joined together: *passenger/goods/freight trains; go/travel by train; get on/off a train.* **2** a number of people, animals, vehicles etc moving in a line: *a train of camels.* **3** a series (of events etc): *A knock at the door interrupted my train of thought.* **4** a part of a long, formal dress that trails on the ground.

train² /treɪn/ *v* **1** *vt* to give (a person, animal) teaching and practice in a skill or profession: *train a horse for a race/circus. There is a shortage of trained nurses.* **2** *vi* *train (for sth/to be sb)* to attend a course, practise etc to qualify or to achieve something: *I'm training to be a vet/training for the Olympic Games.* **3** *vt* to cause (a plant) to grow in a required direction: *train roses against/over a wall.* **4** *vt* to point, aim, (a weapon, light from a torch etc): *train a gun on the enemy.*

train·ee /treɪ'niː/ *nc* a person being trained.

train·er *nc* a person who trains (esp athletes, race-horses etc).

train·ing *nu* **in/out of training** in/not in good physical condition for a sport etc.

traipse /treɪps/ *vi* to walk in a tired way: *traipsing round the shops.*

trait /treɪt/ *nc* a particular quality or characteristic: *Two good traits in the American character are generosity and energy.*

trai·tor /'treɪtə(r)/ *nc* (*derog*) a person who betrays a friend, is disloyal to his country etc.

 trai·tor·ous /-əs/ *adj* = treacherous(1) (the usual word).

tram /træm/ *nc* (also *tramcar*) a form of public transport powered by electricity on rails in the road surface (*US = street-car*).

tramp¹ /træmp/ *n* **1** *nc* a poor person with no home, job etc. **2** *n sing* a sound of heavy footsteps: *the tramp of marching soldiers.* **3** *nc* a long, tiring walk: *a tramp up a hill.*

tramp² /træmp/ *v* **1** *vi* to walk with heavy steps: *He tramped up and down the platform waiting for the train.* **2** *vt,vi* to walk through or over (a place) (esp for a long distance): *tramp through the mountains; tramp over the hills. They tramped (for) miles and miles.*

trample /'træmpl/ *v* **1** *vt,vi* to tread heavily on (something): *The children have trampled (down) the flowers/trampled the grass flat.* **2** *vi* **trample on sth** (*fig*) to affect a person's feelings badly and thoughtlessly: *trample on his feelings.*

tram·po·line /'træmpəliːn/ *nc* an apparatus made of very strong cloth on a spring frame, used by gymnasts for acrobatic leaps.

trance /trɑːns/ *nc* a condition like a deep sleep: *be/fall/go into a trance; send her into a trance.*

tran·quil /'træŋkwɪl/ *adj* (*formal*) calm; quiet: *live a tranquil life in the country.*

 tran·quil·ly /-wɪlɪ/ *adv*

 tran·quil·li·ty (*US* also **tran·quil·ity**) /træŋ'kwɪlətɪ/ *nu* a calm, quiet state.

tran·quil·lize (also **-ise**) (*US* also **tranquil·ize**) /'træŋkwɪlaɪz/ *vt* to make (a person, animal) calm, quiet (esp by using drugs).

 tran·quil·lizer (also **-li·ser**) (*US* also **tran·quil·izer**) *nc* a drug that produces a calm mental state.

trans. written *abbr* translated (by).

trans·act /træn'zækt/ *vt* (*formal*) to carry out (business etc).

trans·ac·tion /træn'zækʃn/ *n* **1** *nu* the act of transacting: *the transaction of business.* **2** *nc* a piece of business: *cash transactions.* **3** (*pl*) the records of the meetings etc of a learned society: *the transactions of the Royal Archaeological Society.*

trans·at·lan·tic /ˌtrænzət'læntɪk/ *adj* (*attrib*) **1** across the Atlantic: *a transatlantic voyage/flight.* **2** concerning countries on both sides of the Atlantic: *a transatlantic treaty.*

tran·scend /træn'send/ *vt* to go or be beyond or outside the range of (human experience, reason, belief, imagination etc).

tran·scen·den·tal /ˌtrænsən'dentl/ *adj* not based on experience, human knowledge etc: *transcendental meditation* (= a technique (using concentration and silent repetition) for relaxing the mind and body).

 tran·scen·den·tal·ly /-təlɪ/ *adv*

trans·con·ti·nen·tal /ˌtrænz‚kɒntɪ'nentl/ *adj* crossing a continent: *a transcontinental railway.*

tran·scribe /træn'skraɪb/ *vt* **1** to copy (something) in ordinary writing, esp from shorthand notes or from recorded tape. **2** to write (words) in a special form: *words transcribed into phonetics.*

tran·script /'trænskrɪpt/ *nc* a written form of something transcribed.

trans·fer /'trænsfɜː(r)/ *n* **1** *nc,nu* (an instance of) transferring or being transferred: *Your transfer to the office in Tokyo has arrived.* **2** *nc* a drawing etc transferred from one surface to another.

trans·fer² /træns'fɜː(r)/ v (**-rr-**) **1** vt,vi (to cause a person, office etc) to change position, job etc: *He has been transferred to the Sales Department. The head office has been transferred from York to London.* **2** vt to hand over the possession of (property etc) (to a person): *transfer rights to the new tenant.* **3** vt to press or rub and move (a drawing etc) from one surface to another. **4** vt,vi (to cause a person) to change from one train, bus etc to another.

trans·fer·able /-əbl/ adj that can be transferred: *These tickets are not transferable* (i.e. cannot be given to anyone else).

trans·fer·ence /'trænsfərəns/ nu

trans·fix /træns'fiks/ vt (*formal*) (often *passive*) to cause (a person) to be unable to move, speak, think etc: *He stood transfixed with horror.*

trans·form /træns'fɔːm/ vt **transform sth (into sth)** to change the shape, appearance, quality or nature of a person, thing: *Success and wealth transformed his character. A steam-engine transforms heat into energy.*

trans·for·ma·tion /ˌtræsfə'meiʃn/ nc,nu

trans·for·mer nc (*electricity*) an apparatus that increases or decreases the voltage of an electric power supply.

trans·fuse /træns'fjuːz/ vt (esp) to transfer (the blood of one person) to another.

trans·fu·sion /træns'fjuːʒn/ nc,nu (an instance of) the process of transfusing: *The injured man was given a blood transfusion.*

trans·gress /trænz'gres/ vt (*formal*) **1** to go beyond (a moral limit): *transgress the limits of decency.* **2** to break (a law, agreement).

trans·gres·sion /trænz'greʃn/ nc,nu

trans·gres·sor /-sə(r)/ nc (*formal*) a person who transgresses.

tran·si·ent /'trænziənt/ adj (*formal*) lasting for a short time only: *transient happiness.*

tran·sis·tor /træn'zɪstə(r)/ n (*tech*) a small electronic device, used in radios, hearing aids and other kinds of electronic apparatus.

tran,sistor ('radio) nc one using transistors.

tran·sit /'trænsɪt/ nu the act of sending, carrying or being sent, across, over or through. **in transit** (while) being carried or sent from one place to another: *lost in transit.*

'transit visa nc one allowing a traveller to pass through (but not a stay in) a country.

tran·si·tion /træn'zɪʃn/ nc,nu (an act of) changing, from one condition or set of circumstances to another: *Adolescence is the period of transition between childhood and adulthood.*

tran·si·tion·al /-ʃənl/ adj

tran·si·tive /'trænsətɪv/ adj (*gram*) of, concerning, a transitive verb.

'transitive verb nc (*gram*) a verb used with a direct object, as in 'She *wrote* a letter', 'I *love* you', 'Don't *eat* it'. Ⓝ Marked vt in this dictionary. Compare intransitive verb.

tran·si·tory /'trænsɪtrɪ/ adj = transient.

trans·late /trænz'leɪt/ vt **translate (sth) (from sth into sth)** to give the meaning of (something said or written) in another language: *translate a book from English into French.*

trans·la·tor /-tə(r)/ nc a person who translates.

trans·la·tion /ˌtrænz'leɪʃn/ nc,nu

trans·lu·cent /trænz'luːsnt/ adj (*tech*) allowing light to pass through but not transparent: *Frosted glass is translucent.*

trans·mis·sion /trænz'mɪʃn/ n **1** nu an act, process, of transmitting or being transmitted: *the transmission of news/a TV programme.* **2** nc the clutch, gears etc that help to send power from the engine to the wheels (of a vehicle).

trans·mit /trænz'mɪt/ v (**-tt-**) **1** vt,vi to send out, pass on (something): *transmit a message by radio; transmit a disease.* **2** vt (*science*) to allow (something) through or along: *Iron transmits heat.*

trans·mit·ter nc (**a**) a person who passes on a message, disease. (**b**) an apparatus for sending out radio or TV signals.

trans·par·en·cy /træn'spærənsɪ/ n (pl **-ies**) **1** nu the state of being transparent. **2** nc a framed diagram, picture etc on photographic film (to be seen on a screen).

trans·par·ent /træn'spærənt/ adj **1** allowing light to pass through so that objects (or at least their outlines) behind can be seen: *Ordinary glass is transparent.* **2** (*informal; derog*) (of a person, behaviour) obviously insincere etc. **3** (*formal*) easily understood: *a transparent meaning.*

tran·spire /træn'spaɪə(r)/ vi (*formal*) **1** **transpire (that . . .)** (of an event, a secret) to come to be known: *It transpired that the President had spent the weekend playing golf.* **2** (*dated*) to happen: *Let's wait and see what transpires.*

trans·plant¹ /'trænsplɑːnt/ nc **1** an act, instance of transplanting(2): *a kidney transplant.* **2** something transplanted.

trans·plant² /'trænsplɑːnt/ vt **1** to take up (plants etc) with their roots and plant in another place. **2** to transfer (skin or an organ, e.g. a heart or kidney) from one place on the body or from one person to another.

trans·port¹ /'trænspɔːt/ nu (also *attrib*) (the means of) carrying (to another place) or being carried: *the transport of goods by air; road transport; public transport* (e.g. buses, trains); *transport vehicles; the transport industry.*

trans·port² /træn'spɔːt/ vt **1** to carry (goods, people) from one place to another (using a vehicle etc): *transport goods by rail/road/train/lorry.* **2** (in history) to send (a criminal) to a distant place as a punishment: *be transported to Australia.*

trans·port·able /-əbl/ adj

trans·por·ta·tion /ˌtrænspɔː'teɪʃn/ nu

trans·port·er /træn'spɔːtə(r)/ nc a kind of long vehicle used for carrying vehicles from a factory.

trans·pose /træn'spəʊz/ vt **1** to cause (two or more people, things) to change places. **2** (*music*) to put (a piece of music) into another key.

trans·po·si·tion /ˌtrænspə'zɪʃn/ nc,nu

trans·verse /'trænzvɜːs/ adj lying or placed across: *a transverse engine in a car.*

trans·verse·ly adv

trans·ves·tite /trænz'vestaɪt/ nc a person who enjoys wearing clothes worn by the opposite sex.

trap¹ /træp/ nc **1** an apparatus used for catching animals etc: *a mousetrap.* **2** (*fig*) a plan for deceiving a person or making a person say or do something: *The employer set a trap for the man by putting marked money in the till.* **3** a light, two-wheeled vehicle pulled by a horse or pony. **4** (*sl*) a mouth: *Shut your trap!* (= Be quiet!)

trap² /træp/ *vt* (**-pp-**) **1** to catch (animals etc) in a trap(1). **2** *trap sb (into doing sth)* to cause a person to say, do, something by using a trick.

trap·per *nc* a person who catches animals for their fur.

tra·peze /trə'pi:z/ *nc* a horizontal bar supported by two ropes, used by acrobats and for gymnastic exercises.

tra·pezi·um /trə'pi:zɪəm/ *nc* (*pl* **—s**) (*maths; GB*) a four-sided figure having two sides which are parallel.

trap·ezoid /'træpɪzɔɪd/ *nc* (*maths; GB*) a four-sided figure having no sides parallel.

trap·pings /'træpɪŋz/ *n pl* uniforms or decorations, esp as a sign of public office: *He had all the trappings of high office but very little power.*

trash /træʃ/ *nu* (*derog*) **1** worthless material or writing. **2** (*US*) rubbish; refuse. **3** worthless people.

'trash-can *nc* (*US*) = dustbin.

trashy *adj* (*informal; derog*) worthless: *trashy novels.*

trau·ma /'trɔ:mə/ *nc,nu* (*pl* **—s** or **-mata** /-mətə/) **1** (*med*) a diseased condition of the body produced by a wound or injury. **2** a severe emotional shock.

trau·mat·ic /trɔ:'mætɪk/ *adj*

trav·el¹ /'trævl/ *n* **1** *nu* the act of travelling: *He is fond of travel.* **2** (*pl*) journeys, esp abroad: *write a book about one's travels.*

trav·el² /'trævl/ *v* (**-ll-**, *US* **-l-**) **1** *vt,vi* to make (esp long) journeys: *travel round the world; travel (for) thousands of miles; travel (over) the whole world.* **2** *vt,vi* to move through a space: *Light travels faster than sound.*

'travel agent *nc* a person, business, that makes arrangements for travel, by selling tickets, reserving accommodation etc. Hence **'travel agency/bureau** *nc*

trav·el·led (*US* = **-eled**) *adj* (*attrib*) (**a**) having made many long journeys: *a travelled man.* (**b**) used by people who travel: *a much travelled part of the country.*

trav·el·ler (*US* = **-el·er**) /'trævlə(r)/ *nc* a person on a journey.

'traveller's cheque (*US* = **'traveler's check**) *nc* one issued by a bank or tourist agency for the use of travellers in a foreign country.

tra·verse /'trævəs/ *vt* (*formal*) to pass across, over (an area): *Searchlights traversed the sky.*

trav·es·ty /'trævɪstɪ/ *nc* (*pl* **-ies**) *travesty (of sth)* a copy or description (of something) that is a very poor example of or much worse than the real thing: *His trial was a travesty of justice.*

trawl /trɔ:l/ *vi,vt* to fish with a large net.

traw·ler *nc* a kind of boat used for trawling.

tray /treɪ/ *nc* a flat piece of wood, metal etc with raised edges, used for carrying things.

treach·er·ous /'tretʃərəs/ *adj* **1** (*derog*) false or disloyal (to a friend, cause etc). **2** dangerous, severe: *treacherous weather.*

treach·er·ous·ly *adv*

treach·ery /'tretʃərɪ/ *n* (*pl* **-ies**) (**a**) *nu* the act, result, of being treacherous. (**b**) (*pl*) treacherous acts.

treacle /'tri:kl/ *nu* a thick, sticky, dark liquid produced while sugar is being refined.

tread¹ /tred/ *nc* **1** a way, sound, of walking: *with a heavy/loud tread.* **2** a part of a step or stair on which the foot is placed. **3** the grooved part of a tyre which touches the ground.

tread² /tred/ *v* (*pt* **trod** /trɒd/, *pp* **trodden** /'trɒdn/) **1** *vi* *tread on sb/sth* to put the foot or feet down on a person, thing: *Don't tread on the flowers.* **tread on sb's toes** ⇨ toe¹(1). **2** *vt* to push (something) down with the feet: *tread grapes.* **tread water** ⇨ water¹(1). **3** *vt* to walk along, over (a path etc): *tread the same route to work each day.*

treadle /'tredl/ *vi, nc* (to use) a pedal or lever that drives a machine (e.g. a sewing-machine) worked by pressure of the foot or feet.

trea·son /'tri:zn/ *nu* (the serious crime of) betrayal of one's country or ruler. ⇨ traitor.

trea·son·able /-əbl/ *adj* involving treason.

treas·ure¹ /'treʒə(r)/ *n* **1** *nc,nu* (a store of) gold, silver, jewels etc: *buried treasure.* **2** *nc* a highly valued object or person: *The National Gallery has many priceless art treasures. She says her new secretary is a perfect treasure.*

treas·ure² /'treʒə(r)/ *vt* to (keep and) value (something) highly: *treasure memories of one's youth. He treasures the watch she gave him.*

treas·ur·er /'treʒərə(r)/ *nc* a person in charge of money etc belonging to a club or society.

treas·ury /'treʒərɪ/ *n* (*pl* **-ies**) **1** (the T-) (in *GB*) the government department controlling public revenue. **2** *nc* (a place for) the funds of a society, organization etc: *The treasury of our tennis club is almost empty.*

treat¹ /tri:t/ *nc* **1** something that gives pleasure, esp not often enjoyed or unexpected: *It's a great treat for her to go to the cinema.* **2** an act of treating(6): *This is to be my treat* (= I'm going to pay).

treat² /tri:t/ *vt* **1** to act or behave towards (a person) in the way mentioned: *He treats his wife badly.* **2** *treat sb/sth as sb/sth* to consider a person, thing, to be: *We had better treat it as a joke.* **3** to deal with (a subject) in the way mentioned: *The lecturer treated his subject thoroughly.* **4** to give medical or surgical care to (a person, animal): *Which doctors are treating her for her illness?* **5** to put (a substance) through a process (in manufacture etc): *treat metal against rust.* **6** *treat sb (to sth)* to give a person food, drink, entertainment etc at one's own expense: *I shall treat myself/you to a good weekend holiday.*

treat·ise /'tri:tɪz/ *nc* an academic book that deals with one subject in detail.

treat·ment /'tri:tmənt/ *nc,nu* (a particular way of) treating a person or thing: *Is the treatment of prisoners worse than it used to be? They are trying a new treatment for cancer.*

treaty /'tri:tɪ/ *n* (*pl* **-ies**) **1** *nc* (*formal*) an official agreement made and signed between nations: *a peace treaty.* **2** *nu* an agreement or negotiation between people: *sell a house by private treaty.*

treble¹ /'trebl/ *adj, adv* three times as much or as many: *He earns treble my salary.*

treble² /'trebl/ *nc* (a boy's voice with, instrument that makes) the highest part in a piece of music.

treble³ /'trebl/ *vt,vi* (to cause an amount) to become three times as large: *He has trebled his earnings/His earnings have trebled during the last few years.*

tree /triː/ *nc* a kind of tall plant with a strong, thick, wooden stem (*trunk*): *cut down trees for timber*. ⇨ family tree.

tree·less *adj* without trees.

tre·foil /'treːfɔɪl/ *nc* 1 a three-leaved plant, e.g. clover. 2 a similar ornament or design.

trek /trek/ *vi* (**-kk-**), *nc* (to make) a long journey on foot or by pony etc: *trekking across the mountains*. Compare safari.

trel·lis /'trelɪs/ *nc* a light, upright structure of strips of wood, used for supporting plants etc.

tremble¹ /'trembl/ *nc* an act, sound, of uncontrollable shaking: *a tremble in his voice*.

tremble² /'trembl/ *vi* 1 to shake uncontrollably (from fear, anger, cold, physical weakness etc): *His voice trembled with anger. We were trembling with cold/excitement. The bridge trembled as the heavy lorry crossed it.* 2 to be in a state of anxiety: *I tremble to think what has happened to him.*

tre·men·dous /trɪ'mendəs/ *adj* 1 extremely large, great, powerful: *a tremendous explosion/ victory; travelling at a tremendous speed.* 2 (*informal*) excellent: *a tremendous concert/performance/meal.*

tre·men·dous·ly *adv* (*informal*) extremely: *You've pleased me tremendously.*

trem·or /'tremə(r)/ *nc* a shaking or trembling movement: *earth tremors; a tremor of fear.*

trench /trentʃ/ *nc* a deep ditch dug in the ground, e.g. for the draining of water.

trend /trend/ *nc* a general direction; tendency: *The trend of the coastline is to the south. The trend of prices is still upwards.* **set the trend** to start a fashion etc which others follow. Hence **'trend-setter** *nc* a person who does this. **'trend-set-ting** *adj, nu*

trendy *adj* (**-ier, -iest**) (*informal*) following the latest fashion: *a trendy hairstyle.*

trepi·da·tion /ˌtrepɪ'deɪʃn/ *nu* (*formal*) a state of anxiety: *in fear and trepidation.*

tres·pass¹ /'trespəs/ *nc,nu* (an instance of) trespassing(1).

tres·pass² /'trespəs/ *vi* **trespass (on sth)** 1 (*formal* or *legal*) to go onto privately owned land without right or permission: *trespass on someone's (private) property.* 2 (*formal*) to make too much use of something: *trespass on my time/ hospitality/privacy.*

tres·pas·ser *nc* a person who trespasses(1): *Trespassers will be prosecuted.*

tress·es /'tresɪz/ *n pl* (*dated*) a woman's hair.

trestle /'tresl/ *nc* (also *attrib*) a horizontal beam of wood fixed to a pair of crossed legs, used to support a table top, bench etc: *a trestle table.*

tri·al /'traɪəl/ *n* 1 *nc,nu* (an instance of) testing, trying, proving: *Why not give this new tool a trial? **trial and error** a method of solving a problem by making tests until there are no more errors. 2 *nc,nu* (an instance of) examination in a law court before a judge (and jury): *The trial lasted a week.* **be/go/be put on trial (for sth)** to be tried in a law court (for an offence). **bring sb to trial; put sb on trial** to cause a person to be tried in a law court. **stand (one's) trial** to be put on trial. 3 *nc* a troublesome or annoying person or thing, esp thought of as a test of one's patience: *Life is full of little trials.*

tri·angle /'traɪæŋgl/ *nc* 1 (*maths*) any flat figure

that has three straight sides. 2 **the eternal triangle** a situation when two people are in love with the same person.

tri·an·gu·lar /traɪ'æŋgjʊlə(r)/ *adj* (a) in the shape of a triangle. (b) in which there are three people etc: *a triangular contest.*

tri·bal /'traɪbl/ *adj* of a tribe or tribes: *tribal dances.*

tri·bal·ism /-ɪzəm/ *nu* the organization of a group of people in tribes.

tribe /traɪb/ *nc* a group of people united by language and customs, living as a community under one or more chiefs: *the Indian tribes of America.*

tribu·la·tion /ˌtrɪbjʊ'leɪʃn/ *nc,nu* (*formal*) (a cause of) trouble, grief: *trials and tribulations.*

tri·bu·nal /traɪ'bjuːnl/ *nc* a group of officials or judges appointed for special duty, e.g. to hear appeals against high rents.

tribu·tary /'trɪbjʊtrɪ/ *nc* (*pl* **-ies**) a river flowing into a larger one.

trib·ute /'trɪbjuːt/ *nc,nu* 1 something done, said or given to show respect or admiration: *The actress received numerous tributes.* 2 a (regular) payment which one government or ruler demands from another: *Many conquered nations had to pay tribute to the rulers of ancient Rome.*

trice /traɪs/ *n* (only in) **in a trice** instantly.

trick¹ /trɪk/ *nc* 1 something done in order to deceive or done to make a person appear ridiculous: *He got the money from me by a trick.* **the tricks of the trade** the ways of attracting customers, gaining advantages over rivals etc in a particular business. 2 a practical joke: *The children are always up to amusing tricks.* **play a trick on sb** to deceive a person for fun. 3 a feat of skill with the hands etc: *conjuring tricks. Are you clever at card tricks?* **do the trick** (*sl*) to make it possible to get something done, finished: *One more turn of the screwdriver should do the trick* (i.e. fasten the screw securely). 4 a strange or characteristic habit etc: *He has a trick of pulling his left ear when he is thinking out a problem.* 5 the cards played in one turn in many card-games: *win/lose a trick.*

trick² /trɪk/ *vt* **trick sb (into doing sth/out of sth)** to deceive a person: *He tricked the poor girl into marrying him/tricked her out of her money.*

trick·ery /-ərɪ/ *nu*

trickle¹ /'trɪkl/ *nc* a small, weak flow (of a liquid): *a trickle of blood.*

trickle² /'trɪkl/ *vi* to flow in small drops or in a thin stream: *The tears trickled down her cheeks.*

tricky /'trɪkɪ/ *adj* (**-ier, -iest**) 1 (*derog*) (of a person, action) deceptive: *a tricky politician.* 2 (of work etc) having hidden or unexpected difficulties: *a tricky problem/job.*

tri·cycle /'traɪsɪkl/ *nc* a three-wheeled cycle.

tried /traɪd/ *pt,pp* of try².

tri·en·ni·al /traɪ'enɪəl/ *nc, adj* (something) lasting for, happening or done, every three years.

tri·er /'traɪə(r)/ *nc* a person who tries(1).

trifle¹ /'traɪfl/ *n* 1 *nc* a thing, event, of little value or importance: *It's silly to quarrel over trifles.* 2 *nc* a small amount of money: *The carpet cost me only a trifle.* **a trifle + adj** a little: *a trifle small/ unhappy/annoyed.* 3 *nc,nu* (a portion of) a sweet dish made of cake with jam, jelly, cream etc.

trifle² /'traɪfl/ vt **trifle with sb/sth** to treat a person, feelings lightly or insincerely: *trifling with the girl's affections.*

trig·ger¹ /'trɪgə(r)/ nc a lever used for releasing a spring, esp of a gun.

trig·ger² /'trɪgə(r)/ vt **trigger sth (off)** to be the immediate cause of something serious or violent: *Who/What triggered (off) the rebellion?*

trig·on·om·etry /ˌtrɪgə'nɒmətri/ nu (*maths*) the branch of mathematics that deals with the relations between the sides and angles of triangles.

trill /trɪl/ nc **1** a vibrating sound as made in bird song. **2** (*music*) a quick alternation of two notes. **3** a vibrating speech sound (e.g. Spanish 'r').

tril·lion /'trɪljən/ adj or det, nc **1** (*GB*) one million million million. **2** (*US*) one million million.

tril·ogy /'trɪlədʒi/ nc (pl **-ies**) (*literature*) a group of three related plays, novels etc.

trim¹ /trɪm/ adj (**—mer, —mest**) in good order; neat and tidy: *a trim little garden.*

trim² /trɪm/ nu a trim state: *Everything was in good/proper trim.*

trim³ /trɪm/ vt (**-mm-**) **1** to make (something) neat and tidy, esp by taking or cutting away uneven, irregular or unwanted parts: *trim one's beard.* **2** to decorate or ornament (a dress etc): *a hat trimmed with fur.* **3** to set (the sails of a boat) to suit the wind.

trim·mings /'trɪmɪŋz/ n pl things used for trimming(2): *lace trimmings.*

Trin·ity /'trɪnəti/ n (the T-) (*Christianity*) the Father, Son and Holy Ghost as one God.

trin·ket /'trɪŋkɪt/ nc an ornament or jewel of small value.

trio /'triːəʊ/ nc (pl **—s**) **1** a group of three. **2** (a musical composition for) a group of three singers or players.

trip¹ /trɪp/ nc **1** a journey for pleasure: *a trip to the seaside.* **2** an act of falling. **3** (*informal*) an excited mental experience as a result of taking certain drugs.

trip² /trɪp/ v (**-pp-**) **1** vt,vi to catch one's foot etc in an obstacle and fall: *He tripped over the root of a tree.* **trip (sb) up** (**a**) (to cause a person) to fall or make a false step: *He tripped up and nearly fell.* (**b**) (*fig*) (to cause a person) to make an error: *The barrister's next question tripped the witness up.* **2** vi (*poetic*) to walk, run or dance with quick, light steps: *She came tripping down the garden path.* **3** vi to experience a trip(3).

trip·per nc a person making a short journey for pleasure: *weekend trippers.*

tri·par·tite /ˌtraɪ'pɑːtaɪt/ adj (usually *attrib*) (of an agreement) in which three groups etc have a share: *a tripartite agreement.*

tripe /traɪp/ nu **1** the part of the wall of the stomach of an ox or cow used as food: *a dish of stewed tripe and onions.* **2** (*sl; derog*) useless talk, writing, ideas etc: *Stop talking tripe!*

triple¹ /'trɪpl/ adj made up of three (parts or parties): *a triple sherry; a triple-layered cake.*

'triple jump nc (the —) an athletic contest consisting of a hop, a step and then a jump.

triple² /'trɪpl/ vt,vi (to cause something) to become three times as many or as much: *triple the dose.*

trip·let /'trɪplɪt/ nc one of three children born at one birth: *One of the triplets is ill.* Ⓝ Usually used in the plural, i.e. 'one of the triplets', not 'a triplet'.

tri·li·cate /'trɪplɪkət/ nc one of three copies. **in triplicate** (**a**) three times: *signed in triplicate.* (**b**) one original and two copies: *written in triplicate.*

tri·pod /'traɪpɒd/ nc a three-legged support, e.g. for a camera.

trip·per /'trɪpə(r)/ n ⇨ trip.

trite /traɪt/ adj (*derog*) (of remarks, ideas, opinions) ordinary and dull.

tri·umph¹ /'traɪəmf/ nc,nu (the joy or satisfaction at) a success or victory: *return home in triumph; shouts of triumph.*

tri·um·phant adj

tri·um·phant·ly adv

tri·umph² /'traɪəmf/ vi **triumph (over sb/sth)** to win a victory (over a person, army etc).

tri·um·phal /traɪ'ʌmfl/ adj (*attrib*) of, for, in memory of, a victory: *a triumphal arch.*

triv·ial /'trɪvɪəl/ adj **1** of little value or importance: *a trivial offence.* **2** (*derog*) ordinary (and so dull): *a trivial speech.*

triv·ial·ly /-ɪəlɪ/ adv

triv·ial·ity /ˌtrɪvɪ'æləti/ nc,nu

trod /trɒd/ pt of tread².

trod·den /'trɒdn/ pp of tread².

trol·ley /'trɒli/ nc (pl **—s**) a basket or small table on wheels.

trol·lop /'trɒləp/ nc (*dated; derog*) a prostitute.

trom·bone /trɒm'bəʊn/ nc a kind of large brass musical instrument with a sliding tube.

trom·bon·ist /-ɪst/ nc a person who plays a trombone.

troop¹ /truːp/ nc **1** a group of people or animals, esp when moving: *a troop of Scouts.* **2** (pl) soldiers.

troop² /truːp/ vi to move as a group: *troop in/out.*

troop·er /'truːpə(r)/ nc a soldier, esp in a cavalry regiment.

tro·phy /'trəʊfɪ/ nc (pl **-ies**) **1** something kept in memory of a victory or success. **2** a prize, e.g. for winning a tournament: *tennis trophies.*

trop·ic /'trɒpɪk/ n (also T-) **1** nc a line of latitude 23°27' north (*Tropic of Cancer*) or south (*Tropic of Capricorn*) of the equator. **2** (pl) (the —s, T-s) the parts of the world between these two latitudes.

tropi·cal /-kl/ adj of, in, like, the tropics: *a tropical climate.*

tropi·cal·ly /-klɪ/ adv

trot¹ /trɒt/ n sing **1** a trotting pace: *go at a steady trot.* **on the trot** (*sl*) one after the other: *She drank five whiskies on the trot.* **2** a period of trotting: *go for a trot.*

trot² /trɒt/ v (**-tt-**) **1** vi (of horses etc) to go at a pace faster than a walk but not so fast as a canter or gallop. **2** vt **trot sth out** to say something without real feeling or sincerity: *trot out an excuse.*

trot·ter /'trɒtə(r)/ nc a pig's foot eaten as food.

trouble¹ /'trʌbl/ n **1** nc,nu (an example of) worry; unhappiness; difficulty: *She's always making trouble for her friends. He has been through much trouble/has had many troubles. The trouble is* (= The problem is) *that I've no money left.* **in trouble** suffering, or likely to suffer, anxiety, punishment etc: *I think William is in (financial) trouble.* **be asking/looking for**

trouble (*informal*) to behave in such a way that trouble is likely: *It's asking for trouble to associate with criminals.* **get into trouble** to do something deserving punishment etc. **get sb into trouble** to cause a person to be in trouble. **get a girl into trouble** (*informal*) to make her pregnant. **2** *nc* a nuisance: *I don't want to be any trouble to you.* **take the trouble (to do sth)** to be willing to and do it: *Thank you for all the trouble you've taken to help my son.* **3** *nc,nu* (often *pl*) (an instance of) political unrest: *the troubles in Northern Ireland.* **4** *nc,nu* (an) illness: *liver trouble.*

'**trouble-maker** *nc* (*derog*) a person who causes difficulties or problems for other people.

'**trouble-shooter** *nc* (*informal*) a person employed to identify and solve an industrial problem.

'**trouble-spot** *nc* a place where trouble(3) often occurs.

trouble·some /-səm/ *adj* causing worry, unhappiness, difficulty: *a troublesome child/headache/problem.*

trouble² /'trʌbl/ *v* **1** *vt* to cause (a person) to be worried, unhappy, in difficulties etc: *be troubled by bad news.* **2** *vt,vi* (used to make polite requests or suggestions about something inconvenient): *May I trouble you for a match? I'm sorry to trouble you but I think that's my seat. Don't trouble to meet me at the station.* **3** *vt* to cause (a person) pain, anxiety etc: *be troubled by a severe cold.*

trough /trɒf/ *nc* **1** a kind of long, open box used for animals to feed or drink from. **2** (*science*) a region of lower atmospheric pressure between two regions of higher pressure.

trounce /traʊns/ *vt* (*dated*) to defeat (a person, team etc) heavily: *Our team was trounced on Saturday.*

troupe /truːp/ *nc* a company of actors, members of a circus etc.

troup·er *nc* a member of a theatrical troupe: *She's a good trouper* (= a loyal and uncomplaining colleague).

trou·ser /'traʊzə(r)/ *adj* (*attrib*) of, for, trousers: *a trouser leg/pocket.*

trou·sers /'traʊzəz/ *n pl* (also *a pair of trousers*) two-legged outer clothing reaching from the waist to the ankles.

trous·seau /'truːsəʊ/ *nc* (*pl* **—s**) an outfit of clothing etc for a bride.

trout /traʊt/ *nc* (*pl* **—**) (also *attrib*) a freshwater fish valued as food and for the sport of catching it: *a trout farm.*

trow·el /'traʊəl/ *nc* **1** a kind of small flat-bladed tool, used for spreading cement etc. **2** a small tool with a curved blade, used for lifting plants etc.

tru·ant /'truːənt/ *nc* a child who stays away from school without permission. **play truant** to be a truant.

tru·an·cy /'truːənsɪ/ *nu*

truce /truːs/ *nc* (an agreement for) the act of stopping of fighting for a time.

truck /trʌk/ *nc* **1** an open railway wagon for heavy goods. **2** (esp *US*) a lorry.

trudge /trʌdʒ/ *vi* to walk wearily or heavily: *trudging through the deep snow.*

true¹ /truː/ *adj* (**—r**, **—st**) **1** (*pred*) according to, in agreement with, fact: *Is the news true?* Opp untrue. **true to life** (of a story, play etc) giving an accurate description of how people live. **true to type** being, behaving etc as expected. **come true** (of a hope, dream) to really happen. **2** (*pred*) loyal, faithful: *be true to one's word/promise.* Opp false(2). **3** (*attrib*) genuine: *True friendship should last for ever.* **ring true** to seem genuine, sincere: *Her explanation rang true.* **4** (*pred*) accurately fitted or placed: *Is the wheel true?*

true² /truː/ *adv* honestly: *tell me true.*

true·love /'truː lʌv/ *nc* (*dated*) a boyfriend or girlfriend.

tru·ism /'truːɪzəm/ *nc* a statement that is obviously true and need not have been made: *It's a truism to say that you are alive.*

tru·ly /'truːlɪ/ *adv* **1** sincerely: *feel truly grateful.* **Yours truly** (a formula used at the end of a formal letter). **2** genuinely; certainly: *a truly brave action.*

trump¹ /trʌmp/ *nc* (in card-games) each card of a suit that has been declared as having higher value than the other three suits: *Hearts are trumps.* **turn up trumps** (*informal*) (of a person) to behave better, be more successful etc than expected.

trump² /trʌmp/ *vt* to play a trump on (another card): *trump the ace of clubs.*

trumped-up /'trʌmpt ʌp/ *adj* (usually *attrib*) not genuine or true: *be arrested on trumped-up charges.*

trum·pet¹ /'trʌmpɪt/ *nc* **1** a kind of brass musical instrument played by blowing into it. **blow one's own trumpet** to praise oneself, one's own abilities. **2** a sound (as if) of a trumpet: *the trumpet of an elephant.* **3** something like a trumpet in shape (e.g. a flower that is long and round). **trum·pet·er** *nc* a person who plays a trumpet.

trum·pet² /'trʌmpɪt/ *vi* **1** to play a trumpet. **2** (of an elephant) to make loud sounds.

trun·cheon /'trʌntʃən/ *nc* a short thick stick (as carried by the police).

trunk /trʌŋk/ *nc* **1** the main stem of a tree. **2** the human body (not the head, arms or legs). **3** a large box with a hinged lid. **4** the long nose of an elephant. **5** (*US*) = boot¹(2).

'**trunk call** *nc* a telephone call to a distant place.

'**trunk road** *nc* a main road.

trunks /trʌŋks/ *n pl* (also *a pair of trunks; swimming trunks*) a piece of clothing for the lower part of the body, worn by boys and men for swimming.

truss¹ /trʌs/ *nc* **1** a bundle of hay, straw. **2** a framework supporting a roof, bridge etc. **3** a padded belt worn by a person suffering from hernia.

truss² /trʌs/ *vt* **1** **truss sb/sth (up)** to tie or fasten a person, animal, hay etc (up): *truss (up) a chicken before cooking it.* **2** to support (a roof, bridge etc) with a truss(2).

trust¹ /trʌst/ *n* **1** *nu* **trust (in sb/sth)** a feeling of confidence, strong belief, (in the goodness, strength, reliability of a person or thing): *A child usually has perfect trust in its mother.* **on trust** being confident without proof: *You'll have to take my statement on trust.* **2** *nu* personal responsibility: *a position of great trust.* **3** *nc,nu* (*legal*) (an arrangement for) money or property held and managed by one or more people (*trustees*) for the benefit of another or others: *By his will he created* *trusts for his children.*

trus·tee /trʌs'tiː/ *nc* a person who manages a trust(3).

trust·ful /-fəl/ (also **trust·ing**) *adj* ready to have trust in others. Compare trustworthy.

trust·ful·ly /-fəlɪ/ (also **trust·ing·ly**) *adv*

trust² /trʌst/ *v* **1** *vt* to believe in the honesty and reliability of (a person): *He's not the sort of man to be trusted/not a man I would trust. I trust her to pay the loan back on time.* **2** *vt* to have confidence in (something): *trust your instincts.* **3** *vt* to allow (a person) to do something knowing that he or she will act sensibly etc: *Do you trust your daughter to go to discos with any man?* **4** *vt,vi* (*formal*) to hope (something) sincerely: *I trust you're happy.*

trust·ee /trʌs'tiː/ ⇒ trust¹.

trust·worthy /'trʌstwɜːðɪ/ *adj* dependable; reliable: *Is she trustworthy?* Opp untrustworthy.

truth /truːθ/ *n* (*pl* —s /truːðz/) **1** *nu* the quality or state of being true: *There's no truth/not a word of truth in what he says.* **2** *nu* something that is true: *tell the truth.* **to tell the truth, . . .** (formula used when making a confession): *To tell the truth, I forgot all about it.* **the naked truth** a complete confession. **3** *nc* a fact, belief etc accepted as true: *scientific truths.*

truth·ful /-fəl/ *adj* (**a**) (of a person) in the habit of telling the truth. Opp untruthful. (**b**) (of a statement) true.

truth·ful·ly /-fəlɪ/ *adv*

truth·ful·ness *nu*

try¹ /traɪ/ *nc* (*pl* **tries**) **1** an attempt: *Let me have a try.* **be worth a try** to be worth attempting (even though there is only a slight chance of success). **2** (*rugby*) a score made by putting the ball down behind the opponent's goal.

try² /traɪ/ *v* (*pt,pp* **tried**) **1** *vi* to make an attempt or effort: *I don't think I can do it but I'll try. I'll try to ring you later. He tried and tried* (= tried a great deal) *but he couldn't open it. She tried her hardest* (= made a big attempt). **2** *vt* to test, use or do (something) as an experiment: *Have you tried getting up earlier? Why not try this new glue?* ⇒ try sth on/out. **3** *vt* (*legal*) to examine (evidence about) (a person) in a law court: *He was tried and found guilty of murder. The case was tried in the criminal court.* **4** *vt* to cause (a person's feelings) to become tired, strained: *That woman tries my patience.* ⇒ trying.

try for sth to attempt to get, win etc something: *try for a place at university; try for the world record; try for a job overseas.*

try sth on (**a**) to put on clothes to see if they fit, look nice etc. (**b**) (*informal*) to behave in order to deceive: *You needn't think you can try anything on with me.*

try sb out to test the ability, character of a player, applicant, candidate etc. **try sth out** to use, experiment with, a car, machine etc in order to test it: *The idea seems good but it needs to be tried out.* Hence '**try-out** *nc* such a test. **try sth out (on sb)** to test the effect, success, of a song, joke, tool etc (on a person): *We need to try out the new soup on a group of children.*

try·ing /'traɪɪŋ/ *adj* causing tiredness, exhaustion, impatience etc: *have a trying day; because he's very trying.*

try-out /'traɪ aʊt/ *nc* ⇒ try sth out.

tsar /zɑː(r)/ *nc* (also **czar, tzar**) the title of the emperor of Russia (until 1917).

tsar·ina /zɑː'riːnə/ *nc* (also **czarina, tzarina**) the title of the empress of Russia (until 1917).

tset·se /'tetsɪ/ *nc* (also *tsetse-fly*) a kind of blood-sucking fly (in tropical Africa) causing a serious disease in cattle, horses etc.

tsp *written abbr* teaspoon(ful).

T-shirt /'tiː ʃɜːt/ *nc* ⇒ T, t.

T-square /'tiː skweə(r)/ *nc* ⇒ T, t.

TT *written abbr* teetotaller.

Tu *written abbr* Tuesday.

TU *written abbr* Trade Union.

tub /tʌb/ *nc* **1** a large, open container, used for washing clothes, holding liquids, growing plants in etc. **2** a plastic container for food: *a tub of ice-cream/margarine.* **3** (*informal*) a bathtub.

tub·ful /-fʊl/ *nc* as much as a tub can hold.

tu·ba /'tjuːbə/ *nc* (*pl* —s) *nc* a kind of large, brass musical instrument playing deep notes.

tub·by /'tʌbɪ/ *adj* (**-ier, -iest**) (*informal*) fat and round: *a tubby little man.*

tube /tjuːb/ *nc* **1** a long, hollow pipe of metal, glass or rubber, esp for holding or carrying air, liquids etc: *the inner tube of a bicycle/car tyre.* ⇒ tubular. **2** a soft metal container with a screw-cap: *a tube of toothpaste.* **3** ((the) T-) (in London) underground railway: *travel to the office by (the) Tube every morning.* **4** (*science*) a long, hollow organ in the body: *the bronchial tubes.*

tub·ing *nu* material in the form of a tube: *copper tubing.* ⇒ tubular.

tube·less *adj* having no inner tube: *tubeless tyres.*

tu·ber /'tjuːbə(r)/ *nc* an enlarged part of an underground stem, e.g. a potato.

tu·ber·cu·lar /tjuː'bɜːkjʊlə(r)/ *adj* of, affected by, tuberculosis.

tu·ber·cu·lo·sis /tjuːˌbɜːkjʊ'ləʊsɪs/ *nu* (common abbr **TB**) a kind of serious disease affecting various parts of the body's tissues, esp the lungs.

tu·bu·lar /'tjuːbjʊlə(r)/ *adj* having, consisting of, tubes or tubing: *tubular furniture.*

TUC /ˌtiː juː 'siː/ *abbr* (the —) the Trades Union Congress (the central organization for trade unions in Britain).

tuck¹ /tʌk/ *n* **1** *nc* a flat, stitched fold of cloth. **2** *nu* (also *attrib*) (*GB informal*) food, esp the cakes, pastry etc that children enjoy: *a tuck shop.* ⇒ tuck in.

tuck² /tʌk/ *vt* **1** to push, fold, (something) into a small space: *He sat with his legs tucked up under him.* **2** to put (something) into a desired position, place: *She tucked her blouse into her skirt. He tucked his clothes into a drawer.*

tuck sth away to put something into a box, drawer etc because it is no longer wanted: *She tucked the map away in her pocket.* **tucked away** hidden, difficult to find: *The house was tucked away behind a hill.*

tuck in (*dated*) to eat a lot of food quickly. **tuck sb in** to settle a person in bed by pushing the covers under the mattress. **tuck sth in** to push clothes into a belt, narrow space. *Tuck your shirt in!* (i.e. put it into your trousers).

tuck into sth ⇒ tuck in. **tuck sth into sth** ⇒ 2 above.

tuck sb up (in bed) = tuck sb in. **tuck sth up**

to fold a loose part of clothing round itself: *tuck up one's sleeves/trouser bottoms.*

Tues *written abbr* Tuesday.

Tues·day /'tju:zdɪ/ *nc* (also *attrib*) the third day of the week, next after Monday: *Let's meet on Tuesday/next Tuesday evening. On Tuesdays* (= Every Tuesday) *I visit my grandmother.*

tuft /tʌft/ *nc* a bunch of feathers, grass etc growing or held together at the base.

tuft·ed *adj* having, growing in, tufts.

tug¹ /tʌg/ *nc* **1** a sudden hard pull: *I felt a tug at my sleeve.* **2** (also *tug-boat*) a kind of small powerful boat, used for guiding or pulling ships.

tug² /tʌg/ *vt,vi* (**-gg-**) *tug (at/on sth)* to pull hard: *We tugged so hard that the rope broke.*

,tug of 'war *nc,nu* a contest in which two teams pull against each other on a rope: *play tug of war.*

tu·ition /tju:'ɪʃn/ *nu* (*formal*) (a fee for) teaching a person, esp on her or his own: *have private tuition in mathematics.* ⇨ tutor(1).

tu·lip /'tju:lɪp/ *nc* a kind of bulb plant with a large bell-shaped flower on a tall stem.

tumble¹ /'tʌmbl/ *nc* a fall: *I had a nasty tumble and hurt my knee.*

tumble² /'tʌmbl/ *vi* **1** to fall, esp quickly: *tumbling down the stairs.* **2** to move in a restless or disorderly way: *The puppies were tumbling about on the floor.* **3** *tumble down* to collapse: *The old barn is tumbling down.* **4** *tumble to sth* (*informal*) to realize the truth etc suddenly: *At last he tumbled to what I was hinting at.*

'tumble-drier (also **-dryer**) *nc* an electrical machine used for drying wet clothes etc by turning them in warm air.

tum·bler /'tʌmblə(r)/ *nc* a kind of drinking glass without a handle or stem.

tu·mes·cent /tju:'mesnt/ *adj* (*formal; med*) swelling; swollen.

tum·my /'tʌmɪ/ *nc* (*pl* **-ies**) (*informal*) (used by and to children) stomach; belly.

'tummy-ache *nc,nu* (a) pain in the stomach.

tu·mour (*US* = **tu·mor**) /'tju:mə(r)/ *nc* (*med*) a diseased growth in some part of the body.

tu·mult /'tju:mʌlt/ *nc,nu* (*formal*) **1** (a) large disturbance: *the tumult of battle.* **2** a confused and excited state of mind: *be in a tumult.*

tu·mul·tu·ous /tju:'mʌltʃʊəs/ *adj* (*formal*) noisy and energetic: *a tumultuous welcome.*

tu·mul·tu·ous·ly *adv*

tu·na /'tju:nə/ *nc* (*pl* — or **—s**) (also *attrib*) a kind of large seafish used as food: *tuna-fish salad.*

tune¹ /tju:n/ *n* **1** a series of notes forming a melody (of a song etc). *to the tune of an amount* involving the amount of money mentioned: *We were robbed to the tune of £30.* *change one's tune* to change one's bad behaviour, decision or opinion. **2** *nu* a quality of having a strong melody: *music with very little tune in it.* **3** *nu* *in/out of tune* (a) at/not at the correct musical pitch: *sing/play in tune.* (b) (*fig*) in/not in harmony: *be in/out of tune with one's surroundings/ companions.*

tune·ful /-fəl/ *adj* having a pleasing tune.

tune·ful·ly /-fəlɪ/ *adv*

tune² /tju:n/ *v* **1** *vt* to adjust (a musical instrument) to the right pitch: *tune a guitar.* **2** *vt* to adjust or adapt (the engine of a vehicle) so that it gives its best performance. **3** *vi* *tune in (to sth)*

(a) to adjust the controls of a radio or television to a particular frequency/station: *tune in to the BBC.* **(b)** (*fig*) to be aware of what other people are saying, feeling etc: *He's not very well tuned into his surroundings.*

tun·ing fork /'tju:nɪŋ fɔ:k/ *nc* a steel instrument like a fork which produces a musical note when struck.

tuner /'tju:nə(r)/ *nc* **1** a person who tunes musical instruments: *a piano-tuner.* **2** (a part of) a radio or TV that receives the signals.

tu·nic /'tju:nɪk/ *nc* **1** a close-fitting jacket as worn by policemen, soldiers etc. **2** (*dated*) a loose, pleated dress gathered at the waist with a belt.

tun·nel¹ /'tʌnl/ *nc* an underground passage, esp through a hill or mountain, used for a road, railway etc.

tun·nel² /'tʌnl/ *vi* (**-ll-**, *US* also **-l-**) to dig a tunnel (through/into something).

tun·ny /'tʌnɪ/ *nc* (*pl* **-ies** or unchanged) = tuna.

tur·ban /'tɜ:bən/ *nc* **1** a length of cloth wound round the head by Muslim, Hindu or Sikh men. **2** a woman's similar close-fitting hat.

tur·bine /'tɜ:baɪn/ *nc* (*tech*) an engine or motor whose driving-wheel is turned by a current of water or gas.

tur·bu·lence /'tɜ:bjʊləns/ *nc,nu* the state of irregular or confused movement, esp of air: *Turbulence in the air is sometimes felt during a journey in a plane.*

tur·bu·lent /'tɜ:bjʊlənt/ *adj* **1** violent and irregular: *turbulent waves/weather.* **2** (*fig*) very disturbed, confused etc: *turbulent times during a war.*

tur·bu·lent·ly *adv*

tur·een /tjʊ'ri:n/ *nc* a kind of large, deep container with a lid, used for food: *a soup tureen.*

turf¹ /tɜ:f/ *n* (*pl* **turves**) **1** *nu* the soil with grass growing in it. **2** *nc* a piece of turf. **3** (the —) horse-racing as a sport.

turf² /tɜ:f/ *vt* **1** to cover or lay (an area of land) with turf. **2** *turf sb/sth out* (*GB sl*) to throw a person, thing, out: *turf out an old cupboard.*

tur·key /'tɜ:kɪ/ *nc,nu* (the flesh of) a kind of large bird, eaten as food. *talk turkey* (*informal*) to be honest, realistic, frank.

Tur·kish bath /,tɜ:kɪʃ 'bɑ:θ/ *nc* a bath of hot air or steam, followed by a shower and massage.

tur·moil /'tɜ:mɔɪl/ *nc,nu* (an instance of) serious trouble, confusion: *The town was in (a) turmoil during the heavy rains.*

turn¹ /tɜ:n/ *nc* **1** an act of turning; turning movement: *a few turns of the handle.* *done to a turn* (of meat) cooked just enough. **2** a change of direction: *sudden turns in the road; the turn of the tide. Take the next turn on the left/the next left turn.* ⇨ turning. *at every turn* (*fig*) very often: *I've been noticing her at every turn.* **3** a change in condition: *The sick man/My business/The economy has taken a turn for the better/worse.* **4** the point in time when a change (from one unit to another) happens: *at the turn of the century; on the turn of 2 o'clock.* **5** a short (period of) activity: *I'll take a turn at the wheel* (= drive) *for a while. Come for a turn* (= walk) *round the lake with me. do sb a good turn* to be helpful or useful to a person. **6** an occasion, opportunity for doing something, esp in the correct order: *It's your turn* *to wash up.* **in turn** (a) (of two people etc) one after the other: *Take it in turns to do the shopping.* (b) (of many people etc) in succession: *We were asked in turn to see the manager.* **out of turn** before or after the permitted or agreed time: *Don't speak out of turn.* **serve its turn** (of an article) to be useful, do what is needed. **take turns (at sth)** to do (an activity) one after another: *Mary and Helen took turns at cooking.* **turn and turn about** alternately. **7** a shock; feeling of being unsteady: *The news gave her a nasty turn.* **8** a natural tendency: *He has a mechanical turn of mind.* **9** (a person giving) a short performance: *a comical turn.* **10 turn of phrase** a way of expressing something: *a clever/ original turn of phrase.*

turn² /tɜːn/ v Ⓝ For uses of 'turn' with nouns in phrases such as *turn the corner, turn sb's head, turn up one's nose at sth etc*, ⇨ the noun entries, as at *clock, corner, ear, hair, hand, head, leaf, mind, nose, table, tail.* **1** vt,vi (to cause something) to move round a point: *The earth turns round the sun. I turned the knob and opened the door.* **2** vt,vi (to cause a person, thing) to change position or direction by moving round: *He turned to look at me. Don't turn away. When does the tide turn? Turn left at the next traffic lights. There's a cyclist turning the corner. The path turns sharply after about 100 metres.* **3** vt,vi (to cause something) to change in nature, quality, condition, shape etc: *His hair turned grey. She turned angry at the news. The sky is turning blue. The clouds have turned the day cold. The warm weather has turned the milk (sour)* (i.e. made it go bad). *The sight turned my stomach* (= made me feel sick). ⇨ turn sb/sth into sb/sth. **4** vt to reach and pass (the age, time etc mentioned): *It's turned 2 o'clock. She's turning 40.* **5** vt to shape (something) on a wheel, lathe etc: *turn a chair leg; turn a bowl.*

turn (sb) against sb to (cause a person to) become an enemy of a person: *Why did you turn her against me?*

turn around = turn round.

turn away (from sb/sth) to stop facing or looking (at a person): *She turned away in disgust.*

turn sb away (from a place) to refuse entry, help etc to a person: *We had to turn away hundreds of fans from the football stadium.*

turn back to go back in the direction one had come. **turn sth back** to fold one part of something over another part: *She turned back the bed-clothes.*

turn sb down to refuse to accept a person who has applied for a job, a place at a college etc. **turn sth down** (a) to refuse to accept an offer, application, manuscript etc. (b) to reduce the light or sound from a lamp, radio, TV etc: *Turn that radio down!* (c) to fold one part of something over another: *turn down the corner of a page/one's collar/the bedclothes/the brim of a hat.*

turn in (a) (*informal*) to go to bed: *I think I'll turn in.* (b) to face, bend, inwards: *His feet turn in at the toes.* **turn sb in** (*informal*) to hand a person over to the police. **turn sth in** (a) to give back a machine, uniform, equipment etc because it is no longer needed, useful etc. (b) (*informal*) to give up a job etc: *I'll have to turn in that evening work because I'm too busy.* (c) to hand in a piece of work: *That was a good report you turned in yesterday.* (d) (*informal*) to carry out work: *You've turned in a good day's work.* **turn it in** (sl; *imperative*) stop doing that.

turn into sth to change completely into something: *Caterpillars turn into butterflies.* **turn sb/ sth into sb/sth** to cause a person, thing, situation etc to become the kind mentioned: *She's turned him into a miserable man. He's turned the garage into another bedroom. That quarrel turned the party into a riot. No-one has ever been able to turn tin into gold.*

turn off (sth) to leave one road (for another): *Turn off at the next exit.* Hence '**turn-off** nc the place one turns off a road. **turn sb off** (*informal*) to make a person lose interest or appetite: *That music/He really turns me off!* **turn sth off** (a) to stop the flow of water, electricity etc by using a tap, switch etc: *turn off the tap/switch; turn off the gas/water/electricity/light.* (b) to use a switch, knob etc to stop a machine, engine etc from operating: *turn off the radio/TV/engine.*

turn on sb to become hostile towards a person: *Don't turn on me just because I made a small mistake!* **turn sb on** (*informal*) to give a person much pleasure, excitement: *That music/He really turns me on! He was turned on by the drug.* **turn on sth** to depend on something: *The success turns on how many people vote.* **turn sth on** (a) to start the flow of water, electricity etc by using a tap, switch etc: *turn on the tap/switch; turn on the gas/water/electricity/light.* (b) to use a switch, knob etc to start a machine, engine etc: *turn on the radio/TV/engine.*

turn out (a) to face, bend, outwards: *His feet turn out at the toes.* (b) (of people) to come out in large numbers: *Not many people turned out to watch the match.* Hence '**turn-out** nc the number of people present: *a small/huge turn-out.* (c) to develop, progress, (in the way mentioned): *The holiday is turning out well. As it/things turned out* (= Because of the way things happened) *we never did see the exhibition. It turns out (that)* (= It is now known (that)) *they got married a month ago. The spot turned out to be* (= proved eventually to be) *the start of a serious illness.* **turn out sb** (a) to produce the kind of person mentioned: *The polytechnic has turned out some first-class mechanics.* (b) to force a person to leave a home, disco, pub etc: *Everyone is turned out at midnight.* (c) to dress a person in the way mentioned: *She always turns her children out smartly.* Hence '**turn-out** nc a set of clothes: *a smart turn-out.* **turn sth out** (a) to stop a source of light or heat by using a switch or knob: *turn out the lights/an electric or gas fire.* (b) to empty a drawer, pocket, cupboard etc, esp to look for something: *I turned out my desk but I couldn't find the letter. Turn out your pockets.*

turn (sb) over to change one's position (to face another way): *Turn over so that I can examine your back. The nurse turned the patient over onto his side. Turn over and face the other way.* **turn (sth) over** to change the position (of something) to face another way: *He turned the stone over. Don't turn my egg over. The car turned over and over as it rolled down the hill.* **turn over sth** (a) to do business to the amount mentioned: *The*

company/shop turns over about £5000 a month.
Hence **'turn·over** *nc* an amount of money a business gets: *We make a profit of £1500 on a turnover of £10 000.* (**b**) to use and replace stock, staff etc: *A fruit shop must turn over its stock quickly.* Hence **'turn·over** *nc* a rate of putting in new stock or staff: *a high turnover of staff.* **turn sb/ sth over (to sb/sth)** (**a**) to pass the control, organization of a business etc to another person. (**b**) to hand a person, evidence etc to the police, authorities etc.

turn (sb/sth) round (to cause a person, thing) to face the opposite way: *Turn round and face the wall.* **turn sth round** (*commerce*) (to cause business etc) to begin to show an improvement: *She's really turned this badly managed business round.* *The price of the pound is turning round.* Hence **'turn·round** *nc* such an improvement

turn to to become busy: *The staff turned to and finished the job in an hour.* **turn to sb (for sth)** to go to a person (for help, advice, sympathy etc): *Who can I turn to?* **turn (sb/sth) to sth** (to cause a person, thing) to become another substance: *The water turned to ice.*

turn up (**a**) (of a person) to appear, arrive: *He promised to come but he hasn't turned up yet.* (**b**) (of a person, thing) to be found: *It's lost but it will turn up one of these days.* (**c**) (of an opportunity etc) to happen: *I'm still waiting for something (e.g. a job, offer) to turn up.* Hence **'turn-up (for the book)** *nc* (*informal*) an unexpected event. (**d**) (*commerce*) to improve: *The economy/ Business is turning up.* Hence **'upturn** *nc* such an improvement. **turn sth up** (**a**) to discover something by uncovering it: *He turned up some valuable stones on the beach.* (**b**) to fold or roll up cloth, paper etc: *turn up one's sleeves/trouser legs.* Hence **'turn-up** *nc* a fold at the bottom of a trouser leg.

turn·coat /'tɜ:nkəʊt/ *nc* (*derog*) a person who leaves one group and joins another.

turn·er /'tɜ:ne(r)/ *nc* a person who works a lathe.

turn·ing /'tɜ:nɪŋ/ *nc* a place where a road turns, esp where one road branches off from another: *Take the first turning on/to the right.*

'turning-point *nc* (*fig*) a point in place, time, development etc when there is a major change: *reach a turning-point in history/in one's life.*

tur·nip /'tɜ:nɪp/ *nc* (a kind of plant with) a large round root, used as food, esp for cattle.

turn-off /'tɜ:n ɒf/ *nc* ⇒ turn off.

turn-out /'tɜ:n aʊt/ *nc* ⇒ turn out.

turn·over /'tɜ:n əʊvə(r)/ *nc* ⇒ turn sth over.

turn-round /'tɜ:n raʊnd/ *nc* ⇒ turn sth round.

turn·stile /'tɜ:nstaɪl/ *nc* a revolving gate that allows one person through at a time.

turn·table /'tɜ:nteɪbl/ *nc* the round flat part that a record rests on in a record-player.

turn-up /'tɜ:n ʌp/ *nc* ⇒ turn up.

tur·quoise /'tɜ:kwɔɪz/ *adj, nc,nu* (of) (the colour of) a greenish-blue precious stone.

tur·ret /'tʌrɪt/ *nc* a small tower, esp at a corner of a building or wall.

turtle /'tɜ:tl/ *nc* a kind of sea-animal like a tortoise but with feet like flippers.

turves /tɜ:vz/ *n pl* ⇒ turf.

tusk /tʌsk/ *nc* a long-pointed tooth coming out near the mouth of an elephant, walrus etc.

tussle /'tʌsl/ *vi, nc* **tussle (with sb) (over sb/ sth)** (to have) a difficult fight or struggle: *tussling with one's neighbours over a piece of land.*

tut /tʌt/ (also **tut-tut** /ˌtʌt 'tʌt/) *int* (used to express impatience).

tu·te·lage /'tju:tɪlɪdʒ/ *nu* (*formal*) guardianship.

tu·tor¹ /'tju:tə(r)/ *nc* **1** a private teacher of a single pupil or a very small class. **2** (*GB*) a university teacher who advises and guides a student.

tu·tor² /'tju:tə(r)/ *vt,vi* to act, teach, as a tutor. ⇒ tuition.

tu·tor·ial /tju:'tɔ:rɪəl/ *nc* a teaching period for a small group of university students.

TV /ˌti: 'vi:/ *abbr* television: *What's on TV?*

tux·edo /tʌk'si:dəʊ/ *nc* (*pl* **—s**) (*US*) = dinner-jacket.

twaddle /'twɒdl/ *nu* (*derog*) foolish talk.

twang¹ /twæŋ/ *nc* **1** a sound of a tight string or wire being pulled and released: *the twang of a guitar.* **2** a harsh, nasal tone of voice: *speak with a twang.*

twang² /twæŋ/ *vt,vi* (to cause a musical instrument) to make a twang: *He was twanging a banjo.*

'twas /twəz *strong form:* twɒz/ (*old use*) = it was.

tweak /twi:k/ *vt* to pinch and twist (something): *tweak a child's nose.* □ *nc* an act of tweaking.

tweed /twi:d/ *n* **1** *nu* (also *attrib*) a thick, woollen cloth of mixed colours: *a tweed coat.* **2** (*pl*) clothes made of tweed: *dressed in tweeds.*

tweet /twi:t/ *vi, nc* (of a bird) (to make) a short, high cry.

tweez·ers /'twi:zəz/ *n pl* (also *a pair of tweezers*) a small pair of tongs for picking up or pulling out very small things, e.g. hairs.

twelfth /twelfθ/ *adj or det, nc* (*abbr* 12th) (of) the next after the 11 or one of 12 equal parts. **,Twelfth 'Night** *n* the evening of 5 January.

twelve /twelv/ *adj or det, nc* (of) 12.

twen·ti·eth /'twentɪəθ/ *adj or det, nc* (*abbr* 20th) (of) the next after 19 or one of 20 equal parts.

twenty /'twentɪ/ *adj or det, nc* (of) 20. **in the twenties** (**a**) (of temperature, speed etc) between 20 and 29. (**b**) between '20 and '29 in a century.

twice /twaɪs/ *adv* two times: *twice as much/as many. He's twice the man he was* (e.g. much more healthy, strong, confident, capable etc than before). **think twice about/before doing sth** to hesitate, think carefully, before deciding whether to do something.

twiddle /'twɪdl/ *vt,vi* (to cause something) to twist or turn idly: *twiddle one's thumbs; twiddling a ring on one's finger.*

twig¹ /twɪg/ *nc* a small shoot on a branch.

twig² /twɪg/ *vt,vi* (-gg-) (*GB informal*) to notice, realize, (something): *I soon twigged (what he was up to).*

twi·light /'twaɪlaɪt/ *nu* the faint light before sunrise or after sunset: *go for a walk in the twilight.*

twin /twɪn/ *nc* (also *attrib*) either of two children or animals born together of the same mother: *She's had twins. We're twin brothers.* (N) Usually used in the plural, i.e. *'one of the twins',* not *'a twin'.* ⇒ twinned.

'twin deck *nc* (also *twin cassette deck*) a music centre with two cassette tape-recorders in it.

'twin pack *nc* a packet containing two.

'twin set *nc* a woman's jumper and cardigan of the same colour and style.

twine¹ /twaɪn/ *nu* thin string made by twisting two or more threads together.

twine² /twaɪn/ *vt, vi* (to cause something) to twist; wind: *vines twining round a tree.*

twinge /twɪndʒ/ *vi, nc* (to produce) a sudden, sharp pain: *a twinge of toothache.*

twinkle¹ /'twɪŋkl/ *n* **1** *nu* twinkling light: *the twinkle of the stars.* **2** *n sing* a sparkle: *There was a mischievous twinkle in her eyes.*

twinkle² /'twɪŋkl/ *vi* **1** to shine with an unsteady light: *stars that twinkle in the sky.* **2** (of eyes) to sparkle: *Her eyes twinkled with pleasure.*

twink·ling /'twɪŋklɪŋ/ *nc* **in a twinkling (of an eye)** very quickly: *In a twinkling of an eye she jumped out of the car.*

twin·ned /twɪnd/ *adj* paired (with): *a town in England twinned with a town in France* (i.e. for cultural, educational etc exchanges).

twirl¹ /twɜ:l/ *nc* a quick circular motion.

twirl² /twɜ:l/ *vt, vi* **1** (to cause a person, thing) to turn round and round quickly: *He sat twirling his thumbs.* **2** (to cause hair etc) to curl: *He twirled his moustache.*

twist¹ /twɪst/ *nc* **1** an act of turning or being turned: *Give the rope a few more twists.* **2** a sharp bend: *a road/rope full of twists. There are many twists in the road.* **3** string, rope etc made by twisting together two or more threads: *a twist of cotton.* **4** a peculiar type or tendency of mind or character: *He has a criminal twist in him.* **5** a dance (popular in the 1960's) with twisting of the arms and hips.

twist² /twɪst/ *v* **1** *vt* to wind or turn (threads etc) one around the other: *twist pieces of straw into a rope.* **2** *vt* to turn (something), esp by the use of force: *twist the cap off a tube of toothpaste. He fell and twisted his ankle.* **twist sb's arm** ⇨ arm¹(1). **twist sb round one's little finger** ⇨ finger¹. **3** *vt* to use force to change the meaning of (a person's words): *The police tried to twist his words into a confession of guilt.* **4** *vt, vi* (to cause something) to turn and curve in different directions; change position or direction: *The road twists and turns up the side of the mountain. I twisted (my head) round and saw a man behind me.* **5** *vi* to dance the twist(5).

twit /twɪt/ *nc* (*sl; derog*) a foolish person.

twitch¹ /twɪtʃ/ *nc* a sudden, quick, usually uncontrollable movement of a muscle, tail etc.

twitch² /twɪtʃ/ *vt, vi* (to cause a tail etc) to move in twitches: *The horse twitched its ears.*

twit·ter¹ /'twɪtə(r)/ *nc* a sound of twittering: *the twitter of sparrows.*

twit·ter² /'twɪtə(r)/ *vi* **1** (of a bird) to make a series of soft, short sounds. **2** (of a person) to talk quickly because excited, nervous etc.

two /tu:/ *adj* or *det, nc* (of) 2. ⇨ second¹(1), twice. **break/cut sth in two** to divide it into two parts. **put two and two together** to realize or understand something from what one sees, hears, learns etc. ⇨ also mind¹(3).

two-'faced *adj* (*fig; derog*) insincere.

'two·fold *adj, adv* two times as many or as much.

two·pence /'tʌpens/ *nu* the value of 2 pence. **not care twopence** to not care at all.

,two-pence 'piece *nc* (*pl* **two-pence pieces**) a GB coin worth 2 pence.

'two-piece *nc* (also *attrib*) a set of clothes of similar or matching material, e.g. a skirt and jacket, trousers and a jacket: *a two-piece bathing-suit.*

,two-'ply *adj* having two threads or layers: *two-ply wool/wood.*

,two-'seater *nc* a car, plane etc with seats for two people.

,two-'time *vt* (*sl*) to deceive (a person).

'two-timing *adj* (*sl; derog*) deceitful.

two-way /'tu: weɪ/ *adj* (*attrib*) **(a)** (of a street) in which traffic can move in both directions. **(b)** (of a radio) for both sending and receiving sound.

ty·coon /taɪ'ku:n/ *nc* (*informal*) a wealthy and powerful business man or industrialist: *oil tycoons.*

ty·ing /'taɪɪŋ/ *pres p* of tie².

type¹ /taɪp/ *n* **1** *nc* a particular group, class, variety etc with the same characteristics or features: *A whale is a type of mammal. These flowers are the same type. Some types of cattle are brown.* Ⓝ For the differences between *type*, *kind*, and *sort*, ⇨ kind²(1). **2** *nc* a group considered to have similar characteristics: *men of this type.* **true to type** behaving as expected: *The young nurse was true to type and did much more than she was asked.* **3** *nc, nu* (one of the) letters used in printing.

'type·script *nc* a typewritten copy (prepared for printing etc).

'type·writer *nc* a machine for producing printed letters by pressing keys. ⇨ word processor.

'type·written *adj* typed: *a typewritten letter.*

type² /taɪp/ *vt, vi* to use, write (letters etc) with, a typewriter: *type a letter. She types well. Please type out/up this report.*

typ·ing *nu* the act, job, of using a typewriter.

ty·pist /'taɪpɪst/ *nc* a person who types.

type·cast /'taɪpkɑ:st/ *vt* (*pt, pp* **typecast**) to give (a person) a part in a play etc which seems to fit her or his personality.

ty·phoid /'taɪfɔɪd/ *nu* (also *typhoid fever*) a kind of serious disease from infected water or food.

ty·phoon /taɪ'fu:n/ *nc* a very strong hurricane.

ty·phus /'taɪfəs/ *nu* a kind of serious disease with fever and purple spots on the body.

typi·cal /'tɪpɪkl/ *adj* **typical (of sb/sth)** being a good representative example (of a particular kind of person, thing).

typi·cal·ly /-klɪ/ *adv*

typ·ify /'tɪpɪfaɪ/ *vt* (*pt, pp* **-ied**) (*formal*) to be a typical example of (a person, thing): *He typifies the young, ambitious worker.*

ty·pist /'taɪpɪst/ *nc* ⇨ type².

ty·ran·ni·cal /tɪ'rænɪkl/ *adj* (*derog*) of, like, a tyrant.

tyr·an·nize (also **-ise**) /'tɪrənaɪz/ *vi, vt* to rule (people) cruelly and unjustly: *tyrannize the weak.*

tyr·an·nous /'tɪrənəs/ *adj* = tyrannical.

tyr·an·ny /'tɪrənɪ/ *n* (*pl* **-ies**) **1** *nc, nu* (an instance of) the cruel or unjust use of power. **2** *nc, nu* (an instance of, country with) the kind of government existing when a ruler has complete power, esp power obtained by force and used unjustly: *live under a tyranny.*

ty·rant /'taɪrənt/ *nc* (*derog*) a cruel or unjust

ruler, esp one who has obtained complete power by force.

tyre (*US* = **tire**) /taɪə(r)/ *nc* a band of rubber used on the rim of a bicycle or car wheel.

tzar, tzarina /zɑː(r), zɑːˈriːnə/ = tsar, tsarina.

Uu

U, u /juː/ (*pl* **U's, u's** /juːz/) the 21st letter of the English alphabet.

  'U-turn *nc* (**a**) a turn made by a vehicle in order to face in the opposite direction: *U-turns are not allowed on motorways.* (**b**) (*fig*) a complete change in government policy, health, an earlier decision etc: *Her health suffered a U-turn.*

U *written abbr* (*films*) universal (used to identify a film that is suitable for young children).

ubi·qui·tous /juːˈbɪkwɪtəs/ *adj* (*formal*) (seeming to be) present everywhere or in several places at the same time: *an ubiquitous politician.*

UCCA /ˈʌkə/ *acronym* Universities Central Council on Admissions (an organization that deals with applications to become a student at a university in Britain).

ud·der /ˈʌdə(r)/ *nc* the part of a cow, goat etc from which milk comes.

UEFA /juːˈeɪfə/ *acronym* Union of European Football Associations.

UFO /juː efˈəʊ/ *abbr* unidentified flying object.

ugh /ɜː *made with an expression of disgust*/ *int* (used to show an unpleasant taste, disgust etc).

ug·ly /ˈʌɡlɪ/ *adj* (**-ier, -iest**) **1** unpleasant to look at: *ugly men/furniture.* **2** dangerous; unpleasant: *The situation looks ugly.*

  ug·li·ness *nu*

UHF /juː eɪtʃ ˈef/ *abbr* (*radio*) ultra-high frequency. ⇨ VHF.

UK /juː ˈkeɪ/ *abbr* (the —) the United Kingdom.

ul·cer /ˈʌlsə(r)/ *nc* an open sore forming poisonous matter (on the outside or inside surface of the body).

  ul·cer·ous /-əs/ *adj*

ul·na /ˈʌlnə/ *nc* (*pl* — e /-niː/) (*anat*) the inner of the two bones of the forearm.

ul·ter·ior /ʌlˈtɪərɪə(r)/ *adj* (*formal*) beyond what is first seen or said: *an ulterior cause.*

  ul,terior 'motive *nc* a (bad) motive other than what is expressed or admitted.

ul·ti·mate /ˈʌltɪmət/ *adj* (*attrib*) last, final: *the ultimate truth; the ultimate deterrent* (i.e. nuclear weapons). ⇨ penultimate.

  ul·ti·mate·ly *adv* finally; in the end.

ul·ti·ma·tum /ˌʌltɪˈmeɪtəm/ *nc* (*pl* —**s** or **-ta** /-tə/) a final demand (as a threat or warning): *issue an ultimatum to return the money.*

ul·tra-mod·ern /ˌʌltrə ˈmɒdn/ *adj* (*informal*) completely up to date: *ultra-modern computers.*

ul·tra·son·ic /ˌʌltrəˈsɒnɪk/ *adj* (*tech*) (of sound waves) above normal human hearing.

ul·tra·vio·let /ˌʌltrəˈvaɪələt/ *adj* (*tech*) of the invisible part of the spectrum beyond the violet: *ultraviolet light.*

um·bili·cal cord /ʌmˌbɪlɪkl ˈkɔːd/ *nc* (*science*) the cord connecting an unborn baby to its mother (at her *placenta*).

um·brel·la /ʌmˈbrelə/ *nc* (*pl* —**s**) **1** a folding frame covered with cloth, used to shelter the person holding it from rain. **2** (*fig*) any protection: *under the umbrella of the UN.*

um·pire¹ /ˈʌmpaɪə(r)/ *nc* a person who controls games and competitions. Ⓝ *'Umpire'* is used for athletics, badminton, baseball, cricket, squash, swimming, tennis, volleyball etc. Compare referee¹(1).

um·pire² /ˈʌmpaɪə(r)/ *vt,vi* to act as an umpire of (a game): *umpiring a tennis match.*

ump·teen /ˈʌmptiːn/ *adj* (*attrib*) (*sl*) many: *I've warned you umpteen times.*

  ump·teenth /ˈʌmptiːnθ/ *adj* or *det*: *For the umpteenth time* (= I don't know how many times I have told you), *stop that noise.*

UN /ˌjuː ˈen/ *abbr* (the —) the United Nations.

un·abash·ed /ˌʌnəˈbæʃt/ *adj* not abashed.

un·abated /ˌʌnəˈbeɪtɪd/ *adj* (*pred*) (of a storm etc) (continuing) without a decrease in strength.

un·able /ʌnˈeɪbl/ *adj* (*pred*) **unable to (do sth)** not able to: *He wants to come but he's unable to.*

un·abridged /ˌʌnəˈbrɪdʒd/ *adj* not abridged.

un·ac·cept·able /ˌʌnəkˈseptəbl/ *adj* not acceptable.

un·ac·com·pan·ied /ˌʌnəˈkʌmpənɪd/ *adj* **1** without a companion: *unaccompanied luggage* (i.e. sent separately). **2** (*music*) performed without an accompaniment.

un·ac·count·able /ˌʌnəˈkaʊntəbl/ *adj* in a way that cannot be accounted for or explained.

  un·ac·count·ably /-əblɪ/ *adv*

un·ac·count·ed for /ˌʌnəˈkaʊntɪd fɔː(r)/ *adj* (*pred*) not explained, taken into consideration: *There is still some money unaccounted for* (e.g. costs or receipts not explained).

un·ac·cus·tom·ed /ˌʌnəˈkʌstəmd/ *adj* **1** not accustomed to: *unaccustomed to pain; unaccustomed as I am to speaking in public.* **2** not usual: *his unaccustomed silence.*

un·af·fec·ted /ˌʌnəˈfektɪd/ *adj* **1** (*formal*) sincere; frank: *an unaffected personality.* **2** (*pred*) not affected: *be unaffected by the storm.*

un·afraid /ˌʌnəˈfreɪd/ *adj* (*pred*) not afraid.

una·nim·ity /ˌjuːnəˈnɪmətɪ/ *nu* complete agreement or unity.

unani·mous /juːˈnænɪməs/ *adj* in, showing, complete agreement: *He was elected by a unanimous vote/with unanimous approval.*

  unani·mous·ly *adv*

un·an·swer·ed /ˌʌnˈɑːnsəd/ *adj* not replied to: *unanswered letters.*

un·ap·peal·ing /ˌʌnəˈpiːlɪŋ/ *adj* not attractive or interesting.

un·ap·pe·tiz·ing /ʌnˈæpɪtaɪzɪŋ/ *adj* not appetizing.

un·ap·preci·ative /ˌʌnəˈpriːʃɪətɪv/ *adj* not appreciative.

un·ap·proach·able /ˌʌnəˈprəʊtʃəbl/ *adj* (*derog*) (esp of a person) difficult to talk to (because too formal).

un·ar·gu·able /ʌnˈɑːɡjʊəbl/ *adj* that cannot be disagreed with: *It is unarguable that pigs can't fly.*

un·arm·ed /ˌʌnˈɑːmd/ *adj* without weapons.

un·as·sail·able /ˌʌnəˈseɪləbl/ *adj* that cannot be attacked and defeated.

un·as·sum·ing /ˌʌnəˈsjuːmɪn/ *adj* not drawing attention to oneself; modest.

un·as·sum·ing·ly *adv*

un·at·tach·ed /ˌʌnəˈtætʃt/ *adj* **1** not connected or associated with a particular person, group, organization etc; independent. Compare detached. **2** not married or engaged to be married.

un·at·tain·able /ˌʌnəˈteɪnəbl/ *adj* that cannot be achieved.

un·at·tend·ed /ˌʌnəˈtendɪd/ *adj* with no-one to give care or attention: *Would you leave small children at home unattended while you went to the cinema?*

un·at·trac·tive /ˌʌnəˈtræktɪv/ *adj* not attractive.

un·au·then·tic /ˌʌnɔːˈθentɪk/ *adj* not authentic.

un·auth·or·ized (also **-ised**) /ˌʌnˈɔːθəraɪzd/ *adj* not authorized.

un·avail·able /ˌʌnəˈveɪləbl/ *adj* not available.

un·avail·ing /ˌʌnəˈveɪlɪŋ/ *adj* without effect or success.

un·avoid·able /ˌʌnəˈvɔɪdəbl/ *adj* that cannot be avoided.

un·a·void·ably /-əblɪ/ *adv*

un·aware /ˌʌnəˈweə(r)/ *adj* (*pred*) not aware.

un·awares /-ˈweəz/ *adv* **be caught/taken unawares** to be suddenly discovered doing something (usually bad).

un·bal·anced /ˌʌnˈbælənst/ *adj* (*derog*) (esp of a person, the mind) not sane or normal.

un·bear·able /ˌʌnˈbeərəbl/ *adj* that cannot be borne or tolerated: *I find his rudeness unbearable.*

un·bear·ably /-əblɪ/ *adv* in a way that cannot be borne: *unbearably hot/rude.*

un·beat·able /ˌʌnˈbiːtəbl/ *adj* that cannot be improved on: *unbeatable prices.*

un·beat·en /ˌʌnˈbiːtn/ *adj* (esp) not having been defeated or surpassed: *an unbeaten record for the 3000 metres race.*

un·be·com·ing /ˌʌnbɪˈkʌmɪŋ/ *adj* (*formal*) not suitable: *behaviour that is unbecoming to a woman.*

un·bend /ˌʌnˈbend/ *vi,* (*pt,pp* **unbent** /-ˈbent/) to behave in a way free from strain or formality: *After teaching I unbend.* Ⓝ *'Unwind'* is more usual.

un·bi·as·sed (also **un·bi·as·ed**) /ˌʌnˈbaɪəst/ *adj* not biassed.

un·block /ˌʌnˈblɒk/ *vt* to remove an obstruction from (a drain etc).

un·born /ˌʌnˈbɔːn/ *adj* (usually *attrib*) not yet born; future: *unborn generations.*

un·bound /ˌʌnˈbaʊnd/ *adj* **1** (of hair) loose, not tied. **2** (of a book) without a cover.

un·break·able /ˌʌnˈbreɪkəbl/ *adj* that cannot be broken.

un·bro·ken /ˌʌnˈbrəʊkn/ *adj* (esp) **1** (e.g. of a horse) not tamed. **2** (*attrib*) not interrupted: *six hours of unbroken sleep.* **3** (of a record etc) not beaten.

un·buckle /ˌʌnˈbʌkl/ *vt* to undo the buckle(s) of (something): *unbuckle one's shoes/belt.*

un·built /ˌʌnˈbɪlt/ *adj* not (yet) built.

un·bur·den /ˌʌnˈbɜːdn/ *vt* to relieve (oneself, one's mind) by talking or writing about one's troubles, anxiety, guilt etc: *unburden one's conscience.*

un·called-for /ˌʌnˈkɔːld fɔː(r)/ *adj* (*pred*) not justified, desirable or necessary: *Such rude comments are uncalled-for.*

un·can·ny /ˌʌnˈkænɪ/ *adj* not natural, mysterious: *an uncanny ability to predict disaster.*

un·cared-for /ˌʌnˈkeəd fɔː(r)/ *adj* neglected: *uncared-for children.*

un·ceas·ing /ˌʌnˈsiːsɪŋ/ *adj* (*formal*) going on, happening, all the time: *unceasing pain.*

un·ceas·ing·ly *adv*

un·cer·e·mo·ni·ous /ˌʌnˌserɪˈməʊnɪəs/ *adj* (*formal*) **1** informal. **2** lacking in courtesy.

un·cer·e·mo·ni·ous·ly *adv*

un·cer·tain /ˌʌnˈsɜːtn/ *adj* **1** not reliable: *uncertain weather; a man with an uncertain temper.* **2** (*pred*) not certainly knowing or known: *be/feel uncertain (about) what to do next; be uncertain of/about/as to plans for the future.*

un·cer·tain·ly *adv*

un·cer·tain·ty /ˌʌnˈsɜːtntɪ/ *n* (*pl* **-ies**) **1** *nu* state of being uncertain. **2** *nc* something which is uncertain: *the uncertainties of employment in many countries.*

un·changed /ˌʌnˈtʃeɪndʒd/ *adj* staying, having stayed, the same: *unchanged weather.*

un·chari·table /ˌʌnˈtʃærɪtəbl/ *adj* (*derog*) (esp) severe or harsh (in judging the conduct of others).

un·check·ed /ˌʌnˈtʃəkt/ *adj* not kept under control: *unchecked anger.*

un·civ·il /ˌʌnˈsɪvl/ *adj* (*derog*) impolite (the usual word).

un·civ·il·ized (also **-ised**) /ˌʌnˈsɪvəlaɪzd/ *adj* **1** not (yet) civilized. **2** (*informal; derog*) (of behaviour) bad, thoughtless.

un·claim·ed /ˌʌnˈkleɪmd/ *adj* that has or have not been claimed: *unclaimed letters/parcels.*

un·clas·si·fied /ˌʌnˈklæsɪfaɪd/ *adj* **1** not arranged in a particular order. **2** (of information) not officially secret.

uncle /ˈʌŋkl/ *nc* **1** the brother of one's father or mother. **2** the husband of one's aunt.

un·clear /ʌnˈklɪə(r)/ *adj* not clear(6,7).

un·com·fort·able /ʌnˈkʌmftəbl/ *adj* not comfortable.

un·com·mit·ted /ˌʌnkəˈmɪtɪd/ *adj* not committed; free, independent.

un·com·mon /ʌnˈkɒmən/ *adj* unusual (and so interesting).

un·com·mon·ly *adv* (*formal*) (esp) exceptionally: *an uncommonly intelligent boy.*

un·com·muni·ca·tive /ˌʌnkəˈmjuːnɪkətɪv/ *adj* not communicative.

un·com·peti·tive /ˌʌnkəmˈpetətɪv/ *adj* not competitive(2).

un·com·pli·men·tary /ˌʌnkɒmplɪˈmentrɪ/ *adj* not complimentary(1).

un·com·pro·mis·ing /ʌnˈkɒmprəmaɪzɪŋ/ *adj* (*derog*) not prepared to make any compromise: *an uncompromising member of the committee.*

un·con·cern·ed /ˌʌnkənˈsɜːnd/ *adj* **1** **unconcerned (about sb/sth)** not anxious (about). **2** **unconcerned (with sb/sth)** not (emotionally) concerned (with).

un·con·di·tion·al /ˌʌnkənˈdɪʃənl/ *adj* not involving conditions: *We demanded unconditional surrender.*

un·con·di·tion·al·ly /-nəlɪ/ *adv*

un·con·gen·ial /ˌʌnkənˈdʒiːnɪəl/ *adj* not congenial.

un·con·nect·ed /ˌʌnkəˈnektɪd/ *adj* not linked: *two unconnected incidents.* Compare disconnected.

un·con·scious¹ /ˌʌnˈkɒnʃəs/ adj not conscious (all senses).

un·con·scious² /ˌʌnˈkɒnʃəs/ nu (the —) that part of one's mental activity of which one is not aware, but which can be detected and understood through the skilled analysis of dreams, behaviour etc. Compare subconscious.

un·con·scious·ly adv

un·con·sid·er·ed /ˌʌnkənˈsɪdəd/ adj (of words, remarks) spoken thoughtlessly.

un·con·sti·tu·tion·al /ˌʌnkɒnstɪˈtjuːʃənl/ adj not according to or allowed by a country's constitution.

un·con·trol·lable /ˌʌnkənˈtrəʊləbl/ adj unable to be controlled: *uncontrollable laughter/children.*

un·con·tro·ver·sial /ˌʌnkɒntrəˈvɜːʃl/ adj not controversial.

un·con·vinc·ing /ˌʌnkənˈvɪnsɪŋ/ adj not convincing.

un·co·op·er·ative /ˌʌnkəʊˈɒprətɪv/ adj not cooperative(1).

un·cork /ˌʌnˈkɔːk/ vt to take the cork from (a bottle).

→ **un·count·able** /ˌʌnˈkaʊntəbl/ adj that cannot be counted.

un‚countable 'noun nc (gram) one that can be used with *some, enough, a lot of* etc and that has no plural form, as in 'some *bread*', 'enough *heat*', 'a lot of *laughter*'. Ⓝ Marked nu in this dictionary. Compare countable noun.

un·couth /ʌnˈkuːθ/ adj (derog) (of a person, behaviour) rough, awkward, uncultured.

un·couth·ly adv

un·cov·er /ʌnˈkʌvə(r)/ vt **1** to remove a cover or covering from (something). **2** (fig) to find out (information about a plan etc): *The police uncovered a plot against the President.*

un·cros·sed /ʌnˈkrɒst/ adj (of a cheque) not crossed.

un·cul·tured /ʌnˈkʌltʃəd/ adj not cultured(1).

un·daunt·ed /ʌnˈdɔːntɪd/ adj (formal) fearless.

un·de·cided /ˌʌndɪˈsaɪdɪd/ adj not yet having made up one's mind.

un·de·feat·ed /ˌʌndɪˈfiːtɪd/ adj not defeated.

un·demo·crat·ic /ˌʌnˌdeməˈkrætɪk/ adj not democratic.

un·de·mon·stra·tive /ˌʌndɪˈmɒnstrətɪv/ adj not showing one's true affection, interest etc.

un·de·ni·able /ˌʌndɪˈnaɪəbl/ adj undoubtedly true: *of undeniable value.*

un·de·ni·ably /-əblɪ/ adv: *undeniably true.*

un·der¹ /ˈʌndə(r)/ adv **1** in or to a lower place, position etc: *The ship went under* (= sank). **down under** (informal) in or to Australia or New Zealand: *travel down under.* **2** less: *costing £10 and under.* Opp over²(9).

un·der² /ˈʌndə(r)/ prep **1** directly below; in, to, a position lower than: *The cat was under the table. Write the numbers in columns, one under the other. Put a mat under that hot plate.* Compare below², above²(1). **2** in and covered by: *under the ground/blankets. He's hiding something under his coat.* **3** less than (in quantity, age, rank, speed, mass etc): *children under 16 years of age; incomes under £8000 a year; run 100 metres in under 10 seconds; under 20 miles per gallon; costing (well) under £20 each.* Ⓝ *'Below'* is more usual with

numbers, as in *below 30 people, below 16 years of age.* Compare above²(2), over⁴(10). **4** lower in rank, position etc: *no-one under the rank of captain. Who is under you in the office?* Compare above²(4). **5** (used to show various conditions; ⇨ the *noun* for explanations): *under age/consideration/discussion/repair/suspicion.* **6** during the rule of: *Greece under the Romans.*

un·der·achieve /ˌʌndərəˈtʃiːv/ vi to fail to achieve the expected or possible standard or result: *Many children underachieve at school.*

un·der·act /ˌʌndərˈækt/ vt,vi to act (a part in a play) with too little energy, enthusiasm.

un·der·arm /ˈʌndərɑːm/ adj, adv (hitting or throwing a ball) with the hand kept below the level of the elbow.

un·der·car·riage /ˈʌndəkærɪdʒ/ nc (usually the —) the landing gear of an aircraft.

un·der·charge /ˌʌndəˈtʃɑːdʒ/ vi,vt to charge (a person) too little for something. Compare overcharge(1).

un·der·clothes /ˈʌndəkləʊðz/ n pl underwear (the usual word).

un·der·cov·er /ˌʌndəˈkʌvə(r)/ adj (attrib) acting secretly: *an undercover agent.*

un·der·cur·rent /ˈʌndəkʌrənt/ nu **1** a current of water flowing beneath the surface. **2** (fig) a tendency (of thought or feeling) below what is apparent: *an undercurrent of hatred.*

un·der·cut /ˌʌndəˈkʌt/ vt (pt,pp —; -tt-) to offer goods, services, at a lower price than (competitors).

un·der·de·vel·op·ed /ˌʌndədɪˈveləpt/ adj not yet fully developed: *underdeveloped muscles.*

un·der·dog /ˈʌndədɒg/ nc (usually the —) (fig) a person who is considered the poorest, weakest, the probable loser in a competition etc.

un·der·done /ˌʌndəˈdʌn/ adj (of meat) not completely cooked throughout.

un·der·esti·mate /ˌʌndərˈestɪmeɪt/ vt to have too low an estimate or opinion of (a person, ability etc): *underestimate the enemy's strength.*

un·der·fed /ˌʌndəˈfed/ adj having had too little food.

un·der·foot /ˌʌndəˈfʊt/ adv under one's feet: *It is very stony underfoot.*

un·der·go /ˌʌndəˈgəʊ/ vt (pt -went /-ˈwent/, pp -gone /-ˈgɒn/) to experience (difficulty): *The explorers had to undergo much suffering.*

un·der·grad·uate /ˌʌndəˈgrædjuət/ nc (also attrib) a university student working for a first degree: *an undergraduate course.*

un·der·ground¹ /ˈʌndəgraʊnd/ adj (usually attrib) **1** under the surface of the ground: *underground passages/caves.* **2** acting secretly (esp of a movement for resisting the enemy): *underground workers.*

un·der·ground² /ˌʌndəˈgraʊnd/ adv **1** under the surface: *flow underground.* **2** in, to, a secret place, situation: *He went underground when the police came to arrest him.*

un·der·ground³ /ˈʌndəgraʊnd/ nc **1** (the U-) the underground railway system in London. **2** (the —) a secret movement to oppose an enemy ruling one's country: *join the French underground.*

un·der·growth /ˈʌndəgrəʊθ/ nu shrubs, bushes, low trees, growing among taller trees.

un·der·hand /ˌʌndəˈhænd/ *adj, adv* deceitful(ly).

un·der·lay¹ /ˈʌndəleɪ/ *nu* material (felt, rubber etc) (to be) laid under a carpet.

un·der·lay² /ˌʌndəˈleɪ/ *pt* of underlie.

un·der·lie /ˌʌndəˈlaɪ/ *vt* (*pt* **-lay** /-ˈleɪ/, *pp* **-lain** /-ˈleɪn/) (*formal*) to form the basis of (a theory, a person's behaviour etc).

un·der·line¹ /ˈʌndəlaɪn/ *nc* a line drawn under a word or words.

un·der·line² /ˌʌndəˈlaɪn/ *vt* **1** to draw a line under (a word etc). **2** (*fig*) to emphasize (a remark, warning etc).

un·der·ling /ˈʌndəlɪŋ/ *nc* (*derog*) a person in an unimportant position compared to others.

un·der·ly·ing /ˈʌndəlaɪɪŋ/ *adj* basic; hidden but able to be found: *the underlying cause.*

un·der·man·ned /ˌʌndəˈmænd/ *adj* not having enough workers to do the work.

un·der·men·tion·ed /ˌʌndəˈmenʃənd/ *adj* mentioned below or later (in a piece of writing).

un·der·mine /ˌʌndəˈmaɪn/ *vt* **1** to make a hollow or tunnel under (an area of ground): *cliffs undermined by the sea.* **2** to weaken (health, confidence etc) gradually: *His health was undermined by drink.*

un·der·neath¹ /ˌʌndəˈniːθ/ *adv, prep* **1** at, to, a lower place: *She was wearing a sweater underneath her jacket. What have you got on underneath? The pen is underneath the book.* **2** below the surface: *swimming underneath the water. She seems happy but underneath she's extremely sad.*

un·der·neath² /ˌʌndəˈniːθ/ *nu* (the —) the lower or bottom surface: *Has the underneath of the car been damaged?*

un·der·nour·ish·ed /ˌʌndəˈnʌrɪʃt/ *adj* not provided with sufficient food for good health and normal growth.

un·der·paid /ˌʌndəˈpeɪd/ *pt,pp* of underpay.

un·der·pants /ˈʌndəpænts/ *n pl* male underwear covering the lower part of the body.

un·der·pass /ˈʌndəpɑːs/ *nc* a section of a road that goes under another road or railway.

un·der·pay /ˌʌndəˈpeɪ/ *vt* (*pt,pp* **-paid** /-ˈpeɪd/) to pay (workers) too little.

un·der·pay·ment *nc,nu*

un·der·privi·leged /ˌʌndəˈprɪvɪlɪdʒd/ *adj* not having had the educational and social advantages enjoyed by more fortunate people. Compare privileged.

un·der·rate /ˌʌndəˈreɪt/ *vt* to place too low a value or estimate on (a person, influence etc): *underrate an opponent.*

un·der·sell /ˌʌndəˈsel/ *vt* (*pt,pp* **-sold** /-ˈsəʊld/) to sell (goods) at a lower price than competitors.

un·der·sign·ed /ˌʌndəˈsaɪnd/ *n* (the —) (*formal*) the person or people who have signed below.

un·der·sized /ˌʌndəˈsaɪzd/ *adj* of less than the usual size: *an undersized boy.*

un·der·skirt /ˈʌndəskɜːt/ *nc* a petticoat.

un·der·sold /ˌʌndəˈsəʊld/ *pt,pp* of undersell.

un·der·staff·ed /ˌʌndəˈstɑːft/ *adj* not having enough staff to do the work.

under·stand /ˌʌndəˈstænd/ *v* (*pt,pp* **-stood** /-ˈstʊd/) **1** *vt,vi* to know the meaning, nature, explanation, of (something): *understand him/ French/a problem. He didn't understand me/what*

I said. Do you understand what to do? I understand how you feel/how much she means to you. Compare misunderstand. **2** *vt* to know (something) from a conversation, remark etc: *I understand that you are now married.* **3** *vt* to accept a word, statement, as meaning (something): *By 'management' do I understand you to include me? It's understood that the profit will be shared equally.*

under·stand·able /ˌʌndəˈstændəbl/ *adj* (*pred*) reasonable; acceptable; that can be understood: *His refusal to agree is understandable.*

under·stand·ing¹ /ˌʌndəˈstændɪŋ/ *adj* (good at) realizing other person's feelings or points of view: *with an understanding smile. When I told her why I was late she was very understanding.*

under·stand·ing² /ˌʌndəˈstændɪŋ/ *n* **1** *nu* the ability to see something from another's point of view etc: *show understanding.* Compare misunderstanding. **2** *n sing* an agreement: *reach/come to an understanding with the bank manager.* **on the understanding that . . .** on condition that . . . : *I lent her the book on the understanding that I could have it back at the weekend.*

un·der·state /ˌʌndəˈsteɪt/ *vt* to fail to state (something) fully or adequately: *They exaggerated the enemy's losses and understated their own.*

under·state·ment /ˈʌndəsteɪtmənt/ *nc,nu*

un·der·stock /ˌʌndəˈstɒk/ *vt* to equip (a shop etc) with less stock than is needed.

under·stood /ˌʌndəˈstʊd/ *pt,pp* of understand.

un·der·study /ˈʌndəstʌdɪ/ *nc* (*pl* **-ies**) a person learning to, able to, take the place of another (esp an actor).

un·der·take /ˌʌndəˈteɪk/ *vt* (*pt* **-took** /-ˈtʊk/, *pp* **-taken** /-ˈteɪkən/) **1** to make oneself responsible for (something); agree, promise, (to do something): *He undertook to finish the job by Friday.* **2** to start (a piece of work).

under·tak·ing /ˌʌndəˈteɪkɪŋ/ *nc* (**a**) a piece of work that one has promised or agreed to do. (**b**) (*formal*) a promise; guarantee.

un·der·taker /ˈʌndəteɪkə(r)/ *nc* a person whose business is to organize funerals.

un·der·tone /ˈʌndətəʊn/ *nc* (*formal*) **1** (usually *pl*) a low, quiet tone: *talk in undertones.* **2** an underlying quality: *an undertone of sadness.*

un·der·took /ˌʌndəˈtʊk/ *pt* of undertake.

un·der·val·ue /ˌʌndəˈvæljuː/ *vt* to value (something, work, a person) at less than the true worth.

un·der·wa·ter /ˈʌndəwɔːtə(r)/ *adj, adv* below the surface of the water: *underwater swimming; swim underwater.*

un·der·wear /ˈʌndəweə(r)/ *nu* clothing worn next to the skin.

un·der·went /ˌʌndəˈwent/ *pt* of undergo.

un·der·world /ˈʌndəwɜːld/ *nc* (the —) **1** (in stories) the place where the spirits of the dead exist. **2** the part of society that lives by vice and crime.

un·der·write /ˌʌndəˈraɪt/ *vt* (*pt* **-wrote** /-ˈrəʊt/, *pp* **-written** /-ˈrɪtn/) (esp *legal*) to agree to take responsibility for all or part of possible loss (by signing an agreement about insurance).

un·de·serv·ed·ly /ˌʌndɪˈzɜːvɪdlɪ/ *adv* not according to what is deserved; wrongly. Opp deservedly.

un·de·sir·able /ˌʌndɪˈzaɪərəbl/ *adj* (*derog*) (of a

person) not welcome, liked. □ *nc* (*derog*) an undesirable person.

un·de·ter·red /ˌʌndɪ'tɜːd/ *adj* (*pred*) **undeterred (by sth)** not discouraged: *undeterred by the bad weather/by failure.*

un·de·vel·op·ed /ˌʌndɪ'veləpt/ *adj* not used or developed: *undeveloped land.*

un·did /ˌʌn'dɪd/ *pt* of undo.

un·dies /'ʌndɪz/ *n pl* (*informal*) women's underwear.

un·dip·lo·mat·ic /ˌʌn,dɪplə'mætɪk/ *adj* not diplomatic(2).

un·dis·charged /ˌʌndɪs'tʃɑːdʒd/ *adj* (*commerce*) **1** (of a cargo) not unloaded. **2** (of a debt) not paid.

un·dis·ci·plined /ˌʌn'dɪsɪplɪnd/ *adj* not disciplined.

un·dis·tin·guish·ed /ˌʌndɪ'stɪŋgwɪʃt/ *adj* not distinguished.

un·do /ˌʌn'duː/ *vt* (*pt* **undid** /ˌʌn'dɪd/, *pp* **undone** /ˌʌn'dʌn/) **1** to untie, unfasten, loosen (knots, buttons etc): *My shoelace has come undone.* **2** to destroy (something good) and bring back the (bad) state of affairs that existed before: *He has undone the good work of his predecessor.*

un·do·ing /ˌʌn'duːɪŋ/ *nu* the cause of (a person's) ruin: *Drink was his undoing.*

un·do·mes·ti·cated /ˌʌndə'mestɪkeɪtɪd/ *adj* not domesticated(1).

un·done /ˌʌn'dʌn/ **1** *pp* of undo. **2** *adj* (*pred*) not finished: *leave one's work undone.*

un·doubt·ed /ˌʌn'daʊtɪd/ *adj* (*attrib*) certain; accepted as true: *show an undoubted improvement in health.*

un·doubt·ed·ly *adv*

un·dreamt-of /ˌʌn'dremt əv/ *adj* not imagined: *undreamt-of wealth.*

un·dress¹ /ˌʌn'dres/ *nu* **in a state of undress** naked.

un·dress² /ˌʌn'dres/ *v* **1** *vt* to remove the clothes of (a person, toy): *Jane undressed her doll.* **2** *vi* to take off one's clothes: *undress and get into bed/get undressed and go to bed.*

un·drink·able /ˌʌn'drɪŋkəbl/ *adj* not drinkable.

un·due /ˌʌn'djuː/ *adj* (*attrib*) too much: *with undue haste.*

un·du·ly /ˌʌn'djuːlɪ/ *adv* too: *unduly pessimistic.*

un·du·late /'ʌndjʊleɪt/ *vi* (*formal*) (of surfaces) to rise and fall in gentle slopes: *undulating land.*

un·du·la·tion /ˌʌndjʊleɪʃn/ *nc,nu*

un·dy·ing /ˌʌn'daɪɪŋ/ *adj* (*attrib*) everlasting: *undying love.*

un·earn·ed /ˌʌn'ɜːnd/ *adj* **1** not gained by work or service: *unearned income* (e.g. inherited). **2** not deserved: *unearned praise.*

un·earth /ˌʌn'ɜːθ/ *vt* to discover and cause (something) to be known: *unearth new evidence.*

un·earth·ly /ˌʌn'ɜːθlɪ/ *adj* (*attrib*) **1** mysterious; ghostly: *unearthly screams.* **2** (*informal*) unreasonable: *Why do you wake me up at this unearthly hour?*

un·easy /ˌʌn'iːzɪ/ *adj* (**-ier, -iest**) uncomfortable in body or mind: *have an uneasy conscience; feel uneasy about it.* Compare easy¹(3).

un·easi·ness *nu*

un·econ·omi·cal /ˌʌni:kə'nɒmɪkl/ *adj* not economical.

un·em·ploy·ed¹ /ˌʌnɪm'plɔɪd/ *adj* **1** not work-

ing, not able to get work: *unemployed people.* **2** not being used: *unemployed capital.*

un·em·ploy·ed² /ˌʌnɪm'plɔɪd/ *n pl* (**the —**) people who are without jobs.

un·em·ploy·ment /ˌʌnɪm'plɔɪmənt/ *nu* **1** the state of being unemployed: *Unemployment is a serious social evil.* **2** the number of unemployed people: *There is more unemployment now than there was six years ago.*

unem'ployment pay/benefit *nu* money paid to a worker who cannot get a job.

un·end·ing /ˌʌn'endɪŋ/ *adj* everlasting; continuous: *unending pain/efforts.*

un·en·dur·able /ˌʌnɪn'djʊərəbl/ *adj* (*formal*) not endurable.

un·en·joy·able /ˌʌnɪn'dʒɔɪəbl/ *adj* not enjoyable.

un·en·light·en·ed /ˌʌnɪn'laɪtnd/ *adj* (*derog*) not well-informed.

un·en·ter·pris·ing /ˌʌn'entəpraɪzɪŋ/ *adj* not enterprising.

un·en·ter·tain·ing /ˌʌn,entə'teɪnɪŋ/ *adj* (*derog*) not entertaining.

un·en·thu·si·as·tic /ˌʌnɪn,θjuːzɪ'æstɪk/ *adj* not enthusiastic.

un·en·vi·able /ˌʌn'envɪəbl/ *adj* (*formal*) not enviable.

un·equal /ˌʌn'iːkwl/ *adj* **1** not equal: *unequal portions.* **2** (esp of work such as writing) variable in quality. **3** (*pred*) **unequal to sth** not capable, strong etc enough: *I feel unequal to the task.*

un·equal·ly /-kwəlɪ/ *adv*

un·equal·led /ˌʌn'iːkwəld/ *adj* (*formal*) without an equal: *be unequalled as a musician.*

un·equivo·cal /ˌʌnɪ'kwɪvəkl/ *adj* (*formal*) having only one possible meaning.

un·err·ing /ˌʌn'ɜːrɪŋ/ *adj* (*formal*) accurate: *fire with unerring aim.*

UNESCO /juː'neskəʊ/ *acronym* United Nations Educational, Scientific and Cultural Organization.

un·ethi·cal /ˌʌn'eθɪkl/ *adj* not ethical.

un·even /ˌʌn'iːvn/ *adj* **1** not similar in size, quality etc: *an uneven contest between a small boy and a youth.* Opp even¹(2). **2** (of a surface) not level, not smooth: *an uneven road surface.* Opp even¹(1).

un·even·ly *adv*

un·event·ful /ˌʌnɪ'ventfəl/ *adj* ordinary; with no surprises: *an uneventful journey.*

un·ex·cep·tion·able /ˌʌnɪk'sepʃənəbl/ *adj* (*formal*) beyond criticism.

un·ex·cep·tion·al /ˌʌnɪk'sepʃənl/ *adj* of ordinary ability, standard: *an unexceptional student.*

un·ex·cit·ing /ˌʌnɪk'saɪtɪŋ/ *adj* not exciting.

un·ex·pec·ted /ˌʌnɪkspektɪd/ *adj* surprising because not expected.

un·fail·ing /ˌʌn'feɪlɪŋ/ *adj* never coming to an end: *unfailing trust/support.*

un·fail·ing·ly *adv* at all times: *unfailingly honest.*

un·fair /ˌʌn'feə(r)/ *adj* not fair or just: *unfair criticism/competition.*

un·fair·ly *adv*

un·fair·ness *nu*

un·faith·ful /ˌʌn'feɪθfəl/ *adj* **unfaithful (to sb/sth)** **1** not true (to one's duty, a promise etc). **2** committing adultery: *Her husband is unfaithful*

un·faith·ful·ly /-fəli/ adv
un·faith·ful·ness nu
un·fal·ter·ing /ˌʌn'fɔːltərɪŋ/ adj (formal) not hesitating: with unfaltering courage.
un·fam·il·iar /ˌʌnfə'mɪlɪə(r)/ adj 1 **unfamiliar (to sb)** not well known: That face is not unfamiliar to me/is an unfamiliar face. 2 (pred) **unfamiliar (with sth)** not knowing (about) something: He is still unfamiliar with this district.
un·fash·ion·able /ʌn'fæʃənəbl/ adj not fashionable.
un·fath·om·able /ʌn'fæðəməbl/ adj (formal) 1 so deep that the bottom cannot be reached. 2 (fig) too strange or difficult to be understood.
un·fav·our·able /ˌʌn'feɪvrəbl/ adj not favourable: unfavourable weather.
un·fit /ˌʌn'fɪt/ adj 1 not suitable or good enough: He is unfit for driving/unfit to be a doctor. Opp fit¹(1). 2 not healthy, strong: medically unfit. Opp fit¹(2).
un·flap·pable /ˌʌn'flæpəbl/ adj (of a person, behaviour) not becoming excited or nervous during a crisis.
un·flinch·ing /ˌʌn'flɪntʃɪŋ/ adj (formal) fearless; not avoiding danger or difficulty.
un·fold /ʌn'fəʊld/ v 1 vt to open out (cloth etc): unfold a newspaper. 2 vt,vi (to cause something) to become known or visible: as the story unfolds (itself).
un·fore·see·able /ˌʌnfɔː'siːəbl/ adj not foreseeable.
un·fore·seen /ˌʌnfɔː'siːn/ adj unexpected (the usual word).
un·for·get·table /ˌʌnfə'getəbl/ adj that cannot be forgotten: an unforgettable experience.
un·for·giv·able /ˌʌnfə'gɪvəbl/ adj too bad to be forgiven: an unforgivable lie.
un·for·giv·ing /ˌʌnfə'gɪvɪŋ/ adj not ready, willing, to forgive.
un·for·tu·nate /ʌn'fɔːtʃʊnət/ adj 1 unlucky: an unfortunate result/accident. Opp fortunate. 2 causing a person to feel sorry or bad: an unfortunate remark.
un·for·tu·nate·ly adv (used as a polite way of expressing something unwelcome): Unfortunately I can't come with you tomorrow.
un·found·ed /ˌʌn'faʊndɪd/ adj (no comp) without proof: unfounded rumours.
un·freeze /ˌʌn'friːz/ v (pt -froze /-frəʊz/, pp -frozen /-'frəʊzn/) 1 vt,vi (to cause something) to thaw: Slowly my fingers began to unfreeze. Compare defreeze. 2 vt to remove government restrictions on (wages, prices etc).
un·fre·quent·ed /ˌʌnfrɪ'kwentɪd/ adj visited rarely: unfrequented places.
un·friend·ly /ˌʌn'frendlɪ/ adj (derog) not friendly.
un·froze /ˌʌnˌfrəʊz/ pt of unfreeze.
un·frozen /ˌʌn'frəʊzn/ pp of unfreeze.
un·fruit·ful /ˌʌn'fruːtfəl/ adj (fig) without success: unfruitful discussions.
un·furl /ʌn'fɜːl/ vt,vi (to cause something) to unroll, spread out: unfurl a flag/the sails.
un·fur·nish·ed /ˌʌn'fɜːnɪʃt/ adj without furniture: a house to let unfurnished.
un·gain·ly /ʌn'geɪnlɪ/ adj clumsy; awkward.
un·gen·er·ous /ʌn'dʒenərəs/ adj (derog) not generous.

un·god·ly /ˌʌn'gɒdlɪ/ adj 1 not religious. 2 (attrib; informal) unreasonable: Why did you phone me at this ungodly hour?
un·gov·ern·able /ˌʌn'gʌvənəbl/ adj that cannot be controlled: an ungovernable temper.
un·gram·mati·cal /ˌʌngrə'mætɪkl/ adj not grammatical.
un·grate·ful /ʌn'greɪtfəl/ adj not showing gratitude.
un·guard·ed /ˌʌn'gɑːdɪd/ adj (formal) careless; indiscreet: say something critical in an unguarded moment.
un·hap·py /ˌʌn'hæpɪ/ adj (-ier, -iest) not happy.
un·hap·pi·ly adv
un·hap·pi·ness nu
un·healthy /ʌn'helθɪ/ adj harmful to bodily or mental health.
un·heard /ˌʌn'hɜːd/ adj **go unheard** (esp) to have no-one willing to listen: Her request for help went unheard.
un·heard-of /ʌn'hɜːd əv/ adj without an equal: unheard-of wealth.
un·hinged /ˌʌn'hɪndʒd/ adj (informal) stupid; silly.
un·hook /ˌʌn'hʊk/ vt to undo the hooks of (a dress etc): Please unhook my dress.
un·hoped-for /ˌʌn'həʊpt fɔː(r)/ adj unexpected: unhoped-for luck.
un·hur·ried /ˌʌn'hʌrɪd/ adj (done) without hurrying: a unhurried drive.
un·hurt /ˌʌn'hɜːt/ adj (usually pred) not injured.
un·hy·gien·ic /ˌʌnhaɪ'dʒiːnɪk/ adj not hygienic.
UNICEF /'juːnɪsef/ acronym United Nations Children's Fund.
uni·corn /'juːnɪkɔːn/ nc (in stories) an animal like a small horse with one long horn.
un·iden·ti·fied /ˌʌnaɪ'dentɪfaɪd/ adj not identified: The victim is still unidentified.
uni,dentified ,flying 'object nc (abbr UFO) an object seen in the sky that is (claimed to have been) sent from another planet.
uni·form¹ /'juːnɪfɔːm/ adj not varying in form, quality etc: uniform temperature.
uni·form·ly adv without varying in quality, timing etc.
uni·form² /'juːnɪfɔːm/ nc,nu (a style of) clothes worn by all members of an organization, e.g. the police, the armed forces. **in uniform** wearing such clothes: He looks smart in (his) uniform.
uni·form·ity /ˌjuːnɪ'fɔːmətɪ/ nu the condition of being the same throughout.
uni·fy /'juːnɪfaɪ/ vt (pt,pp -ied) to form (parts) into one; unite.
uni·fi·ca·tion /ˌjuːnɪfɪ'keɪʃn/ nu
uni·lat·er·al /ˌjuːnɪ'lætərəl/ adj affecting, done by, one side or party only: unilateral nuclear disarmament.
uni·lat·er·al·ly /-rəlɪ/ adv
un·im·agin·able /ˌʌnɪ'mædʒɪnəbl/ adj that cannot be imagined.
un·im·agin·ative /ˌʌnɪ'mædʒɪnətɪv/ adj (formal; derog) not having, using, imagination.
un·im·peach·able /ˌʌnɪm'piːtʃəbl/ adj (no comp) that cannot be questioned or doubted: news from an unimpeachable source.
un·im·port·ant /ˌʌnɪm'pɔːtənt/ adj not important.

un·im·pres·sive /ˌʌnɪmˈpresɪv/ *adj* not impressive: *an unimpressive speech.*

un·in·form·ed /ˌʌnɪnˈfɔːmd/ *adj* (esp) not having, made without, adequate information: *uninformed criticism.*

un·in·hab·it·able /ˌʌnɪnˈhæbɪtəbl/ *adj* not habitable.

un·in·hib·it·ed /ˌʌnɪnˈhɪbɪtɪd/ *adj* without inhibitions; unconventional.

un·in·spired /ˌʌnɪnˈspaɪəd/ *adj* (*derog*) dull; ordinary: *uninspired singing.*

un·in·tel·li·gible /ˌʌnɪnˈtelɪdʒəbl/ *adj* not intelligible.

un·in·ten·tion·al /ˌʌnɪnˈtenʃənl/ *adj* not intentional.

un·in·ter·est·ed /ˌʌnˈɪntrɪstɪd/ *adj* 1 having, showing, no interest. 2 having no personal concern in something: *an uninterested observer.* Compare disinterested.

un·in·vit·ing /ˌʌnɪnˈvaɪtɪŋ/ *adj* (*derog*) not attractive or tempting: *an uninviting meal/offer.*

uni·on /ˈjuːnɪən/ *n* 1 *nc,nu* (an instance of) joining or uniting and being joined: *the union of three states.* 2 *nc* (U-) a nation formed by joining a group of countries or states: *the Union of Soviet Socialist Republics.* 3 *nc* = trade union.

ˌUnion ˈJack *n* (the —) the British national flag.

uni·on·ize (also **-ise**) /ˈjuːnɪənaɪz/ *vt* to organize (workers) into a trade union.

unique /juːˈniːk/ *adj* (*no comp*) being the only one of its kind or standard.

unique·ly *adv*

uni·sex /ˈjuːnɪseks/ *adj* (of clothes) of a style designed for, to be worn by, both sexes.

uni·son /ˈjuːnɪsn/ *nu* **in unison** together; in the same pitch: *sing in unison.*

unit /ˈjuːnɪt/ *nc* 1 a single person, thing or group regarded as complete. 2 an amount used as a standard of measurement: *The metre is a unit of length.*

unite /juːˈnaɪt/ *v* 1 *vt,vi* (to cause people, groups, things) to become one; join: *the interests that unite our two countries.* 2 *vi* to act or work together: *Let's unite to fight for human rights.*

unit·ed *adj* (a) joined by love and sympathy: *a united family.* (b) (*attrib*) resulting from association for a common purpose: *make a united effort.* (c) (*attrib*) joined politically: *the United Kingdom.*

Uˌnited ˈKingdom *n* (the —) (abbr UK) Great Britain and Northern Ireland.

Uˌnited ˈNations *n* (the —) (abbr UN) (also *United Nations Organization*) since 1945, the international organization for peace and mutual aid.

uni·ty /ˈjuːnətɪ/ *n* (*pl* **-ies**) 1 *nc,nu* (the result of) the state of being united: *The figure on the left spoils the unity* (= balanced relationship) *of the painting.* 2 *nu* agreement (of aims, feelings etc): *political unity.*

Univ. *written abbr* University.

uni·ver·sal /ˌjuːnɪˈvɜːsl/ *adj* of, belonging to, done by, affecting, all: *War causes universal misery.*

uni·ver·sal·ly /-səlɪ/ *adv*

uni·verse /ˈjuːnɪvɜːs/ *n* (the U-) everything that exists everywhere; all the stars, planets etc.

uni·ver·sity /ˌjuːnɪˈvɜːsətɪ/ *nc* (*pl* **-ies**) (U- in names) **1** (the colleges, buildings etc of) an institution for advanced teaching, conferring degrees and engaging in academic research. **2** members of such an institution collectively.

un·just /ˌʌnˈdʒʌst/ *adj* not just; unfair: *unjust criticism.*

un·just·ly *adv*: *behave unjustly.*

un·jus·ti·fi·able /ˌʌndʒʌstɪˈfaɪəbl/ *adj* that cannot be justified.

un·jus·ti·fied /ˌʌnˈdʒʌstɪfaɪd/ *adj* not justified.

un·kempt /ˌʌnˈkempt/ *adj* = untidy (the usual word).

un·kind /ˌʌnˈkaɪnd/ *adj* (*derog*) not showing kindness: *an unkind remark.*

un·kind·ly *adv* in an unkind manner.

un·known /ˌʌnˈnəʊn/ *adj* not known or identified: *living at an unknown address.* ⇨ also quantity(4).

un·law·ful /ˌʌnˈlɔːfəl/ *adj* illegal. Ⓝ *'Illegal'* is now the usual word but *'unlawful'* is sometimes preferred when referring to international law or basic legal or moral issues. Compare illegal, illicit.

un·leash /ˌʌnˈliːʃ/ *vt* (*fig*) to set (one's anger etc) free to attack: *unleash one's temper.*

un·leav·en·ed /ˌʌnˈlevnd/ *adj* (of bread) made without yeast and so flat.

un·less /ənˈles/ *conj* (*subord*) 1 if . . . not: *You will fail unless you* (= if you do not) *work harder. Unless you* (= if you do not) *work harder, you will fail.* 2 except on the condition that: *He refuses to go unless you apologize.*

un·lik·able (also **-like-**) /ʌnˈlaɪkəbl/ *adj* not likable.

un·like /ˌʌnˈlaɪk/ *adj*, *prep* not like; different from: *It's unlike anything I've seen before. Unlike you, I need to lose weight.*

un·like·ly /ˌʌnˈlaɪklɪ/ *adj* not likely to happen or be true: *an unlikely event/story.*

un·list·ed /ˌʌnˈlɪstɪd/ *adj* (of a telephone number) not in the directory (because a person wants privacy).

un·load /ˌʌnˈləʊd/ *v* 1 *vt,vi* to remove a load, cargo from (a lorry, ship etc): *unload a ship. The ship is unloading.* 2 *vt* to get rid of (a person, thing, not wanted): *Don't try to unload all your boring girlfriends on me!*

un·lock /ˌʌnˈlɒk/ *vt* to use a key to open a lock on (a door, cupboard etc).

un·looked-for /ˌʌnˈlʊkt fɔː(r)/ *adj* unexpected (the usual word): *unlooked-for financial help.*

un·lucky /ˌʌnˈlʌkɪ/ *adj* (**-ier, -iest**) not lucky.

un·luck·ily /-əlɪ/ *adv* unfortunately.

un·made /ˌʌnˈmeɪd/ *adj* (of a bed) not tidy.

un·made-up *adj* (of a bed) not prepared (for a visitor).

un·man·age·able /ˌʌnˈmænɪdʒəbl/ *adj* not manageable.

un·man·ly /ˌʌnˈmænlɪ/ *adj* weak; cowardly.

un·manned /ˌʌnˈmænd/ *adj* having no crew: *send an unmanned spacecraft to Mars.*

un·ma·noeu·vrable /ˌʌnməˈnuːvrəbl/ *adj* not manoeuvrable.

un·mar·ried /ˌʌnˈmærɪd/ *adj* not married.

un·mask /ˌʌnˈmɑːsk/ *vt* (*fig*) to show the true character or intentions of (a person): *unmask a traitor.*

un·meant /ˌʌnˈment/ *adj* (*pred*) not intentional.

un·men·tion·able /ˌʌnˈmenʃnəbl/ *adj* so bad

etc that it must not be spoken of.

un·mind·ful /ˌʌnˈmaɪndfəl/ *adj* (*pred*) **unmindful of sth** (*formal*) unaware of something: *unmindful of the time.*

un·mis·tak·able /ˌʌnmɪˈsteɪkəbl/ *adj* about which no mistake or doubt is possible: *Are black clouds an unmistakable sign of rain?*

un·mis·tak·ably /-əblɪ/ *adv*

un·miti·gated /ˌʌnˈmɪtɪɡeɪtɪd/ *adj* (*formal*; usually *attrib*) complete; absolute: *an unmitigated rascal.*

un·moved /ˌʌnˈmuːvd/ *adj* (*pred*) (esp) not showing pity or sympathy.

un·named /ˌʌnˈneɪmd/ *adj* **1** not yet named. **2** not identified publicly.

un·natu·ral /ˌʌnˈnætʃərəl/ *adj* not natural or normal: *unnatural behaviour/requests.*

un·nec·es·sary /ˌʌnˈnesəsrɪ/ *adj* **1** (*pred*) not necessary: *It's unnecessary to apologize.* **2** (*attrib*) that could have been avoided: *unnecessary errors.*

un·nec·es·sar·ily /ˌʌnˈnesəserəlɪ/ *adv*

un·nerve /ˌʌnˈnɜːv/ *vt* to cause (a person) to lose self-control, power of decision, courage.

un·no·tice·able /ˌʌnˈnəʊtɪsəbl/ *adj* not easily seen or noticed.

un·noticed /ˌʌnˈnəʊtɪst/ *adj* (*pred*) not observed or noticed: *Her sadness went unnoticed.*

un·num·ber·ed /ˌʌnˈnʌmbəd/ *adj* **1** more than can be counted. **2** having no number(s): *unnumbered tickets.*

UNO /ˌjuː en ˈəʊ/ *abbr* United Nations Organization. ⇨ United Nations.

un·ob·serv·ant /ˌʌnəbˈzɜːvnt/ *adj* not quick at noticing things.

un·ob·tain·able /ˌʌnəbˈteɪnəbl/ *adj* not obtainable.

un·ob·trus·ive /ˌʌnəbˈtruːsɪv/ *adj* (*formal*) not too obvious or easily noticeable.

un·of·fi·cial /ˌʌnəˈfɪʃl/ *adj* not official²(2).: *an unofficial strike.*

un·of·fi·cial·ly *adv*

un·or·tho·dox /ˌʌnˈɔːθədɒks/ *adj* not in accordance with what is orthodox, conventional, traditional: *unorthodox teaching methods.*

un·pack /ˌʌnˈpæk/ *vt,vi* to take out (things) already packed: *unpack one's clothes/a suitcase.*

un·paid /ˌʌnˈpeɪd/ *adj* (of a bill, debt etc) not yet paid.

un·pal·at·able /ˌʌnˈpælətəbl/ *adj* not palatable.

un·par·al·lel·ed /ˌʌnˈpærəleld/ *adj* having no equal: *an unparalleled disaster.*

un·pa·tri·ot·ic /ˌʌnpætrɪˈɒtɪk/ *adj* not patriotic.

un·pick /ˌʌnˈpɪk/ *vt* to loosen and remove (stitches).

un·pleas·ant /ˌʌnˈplezənt/ *adj* not pleasant.

un·pleas·ant·ness *nc,nu*

un·plug /ˌʌnˈplʌg/ *vt* to take a plug out and so stop the supply of electricity to (an electrical apparatus): *unplug a TV.*

un·popu·lar /ˌʌnˈpɒpjʊlə(r)/ *adj* not popular(1).

un·prac·ti·cal /ˌʌnˈpræktɪkl/ *adj* (usually *pred*; *derog*) (of a person) not able to do practical things well. Compare **impractical.**

un·prece·dent·ed /ˌʌnˈpresɪdentɪd/ *adj* never done or known before.

un·pre·dict·able /ˌʌnprɪˈdɪktəbl/ *adj* not predictable.

un·preju·diced /ˌʌnˈpredjʊdɪst/ *adj* free from prejudice.

un·pre·par·ed /ˌʌnprɪˈpeəd/ *adj* (*pred*) **unprepared (for sb/sth)** not prepared or ready.

un·pre·pos·sess·ing /ˌʌnpriːpəˈzesɪŋ/ *adj* (*formal*) unattractive (the usual word).

un·pre·ten·tious /ˌʌnprɪˈtenʃəs/ *adj* not trying to seem important, rich etc.

un·prin·ci·pled /ˌʌnˈprɪnsəpld/ *adj* (*derog*) without moral principles; dishonest.

un·print·able /ˌʌnˈprɪntəbl/ *adj* not printable.

un·pro·duc·tive /ˌʌnprəˈdʌktɪv/ *adj* not productive.

un·pro·fes·sion·al /ˌʌnprəˈfeʃnl/ *adj* (*derog*) (esp of behaviour) bad because not obeying the rules or customs of a profession.

un·prompt·ed /ˌʌnˈprɒmptɪd/ *adj* (of an answer, action) not said, done etc as the result of a hint, suggestion etc.

un·pro·voked /ˌʌnprəˈvəʊkt/ *adj* without provocation: *unprovoked aggression/attacks.*

un·quali·fied /ˌʌnˈkwɒlɪfaɪd/ *adj* **1** not limited or restricted; absolute: *unqualified praise.* **2** not qualified: *unqualified to speak on the subject.*

un·ques·tion·able /ˌʌnˈkwestʃənəbl/ *adj* beyond doubt; certain.

un·ques·tion·ably /-əblɪ/ *adv*

un·quote /ˌʌnˈkwəʊt/ *int* (used to state the end of a quotation): *The rebel leader said (quote) 'We shall never surrender!' (unquote).*

un·rav·el /ˌʌnˈrævl/ *v* (**-ll-**, US **-l-**) **1** *vt,vi* (to cause threads) to become separate: *The cat has unravelled the knitting.* **2** *vt* to solve (a mystery): *unravel a mystery.*

un·read·able /ˌʌnˈriːdəbl/ *adj* that is difficult or unpleasant to read.

un·real /ˌʌnˈrɪəl/ *adj* imaginary; not real.

un·reas·on·able /ˌʌnˈriːzənəbl/ *adj* **1** not reasonable: *unreasonable behaviour.* **2** excessive: *unreasonable prices.*

un·rec·og·niz·able (also **-is-**) /ˌʌnˈrekəɡnaɪzbl/ *adj* impossible to recognize.

un·rec·og·nized (also **-is·ed**) /ˌʌnˈrekəɡnaɪzd/ *adj* not publicly acknowledged.

un·re·lated /ˌʌnrɪˈleɪtɪd/ *adj* not of the same kind; not connected.

un·re·lent·ing /ˌʌnrɪˈlentɪŋ/ *adj* not becoming less in force, degree: *unrelenting pressure/attacks.*

un·re·li·able /ˌʌnrɪˈlaɪəbl/ *adj* (*derog*) cannot be relied on; not to be trusted: *unreliable people/evidence.*

un·re·mark·able /ˌʌnrɪˈmɑːkəbl/ *adj* not special or worth noting.

un·re·mit·ting /ˌʌnrɪˈmɪtɪŋ/ *adj* (*formal*) not stopping: *unremitting efforts.*

un·rep·re·sen·ta·tive /ˌʌnreprɪˈzentətɪv/ *adj* not representative.

un·re·quit·ed /ˌʌnrɪˈkwaɪtɪd/ *adj* not returned or rewarded: *unrequited love.*

un·re·serv·ed·ly /ˌʌnrɪˈzɜːvɪdlɪ/ *adv* without reservation or restriction: *speak unreservedly.*

un·rest /ˌʌnˈrest/ *nu* (esp) disturbed social condition(s): *political unrest.*

un·re·strain·ed /ˌʌnrɪˈstreɪnd/ *adj* not kept under control: *unrestrained hatred/laughter.*

un·ripe /ˌʌnˈraɪp/ *adj* not ripe.

un·ri·val·led (*US* = **-ri·val·ed**) /ˌʌnˈraɪvld/ *adj* having no rival: *unrivalled in courage.*

un·ruf·fled /ˌʌnˈrʌfld/ *adj* calm; not upset or

agitated: *He was unruffled by all the criticisms.*

un·ru·ly /ˌʌn'ru:lɪ/ *adj* (**-ier, -iest**) (*derog*) not easily controlled; naughty: *an unruly child.*

un·safe /ˌʌn'seɪf/ *adj* not safe(3,4).

un·said /ˌʌn'sed/ *adj* (*pred*) not expressed: *Some things* (e.g. opinions) *are better left unsaid.*

un·sat·is·fied /ˌʌn'sætɪsfaɪd/ *adj* not having been given enough (food, evidence etc). ⇨ satisfy. Compare dissatisfied.

un·sat·is·fac·tory /ˌʌnsætɪs'fæktrɪ/ *adj* not satisfactory.

un·sa·voury (*US* = **-sa·vory**) /ˌʌn'seɪvərɪ/ *adj* (*derog*) (esp) unpleasant; disgusting: *unsavoury stories/scandals.*

un·scathed /ˌʌn'skeɪðd/ *adj* (*formal*) not harmed.

un·scien·ti·fic /ˌʌnˌsaɪən'tɪfɪk/ *adj* (often *derog*) not following or using the principles or rules of science.

un·screw /ˌʌn'skru:/ *vt* to remove a screw or screws from (something).

un·scru·pu·lous /ˌʌn'skru:pjʊləs/ *adj* (*derog*) not caring about being honest or doing wrong.

un·scru·pu·lous·ly *adv*

un·seas·on·ed /ˌʌn'si:znd/ *adj* **1** (of wood) not matured. **2** (of food) not flavoured with seasoning.

un·seal·ed /ˌʌn'si:ld/ *adj* not sealed.

un·seat /ˌʌn'si:t/ *vt* to remove (a person) from office: *Mr Green was unseated at the last General Election.*

un·seed·ed /ˌʌn'si:dɪd/ *adj* (*sport*) (of a player) not seeded.

un·seem·ly /ˌʌn'si:mlɪ/ *adj* (*formal*) (of behaviour) not correct or good.

un·seen /ˌʌn'si:n/ *adj* not seen.

un·self·ish /ˌʌn'selfɪʃ/ *adj* not selfish.

un·settle /ˌʌn'setl/ *vt* to cause (a person) to become troubled, anxious or uncertain.

un·set·tled /ˌʌn'setld/ *adj* not settled.

un·sight·ly /ˌʌn'saɪtlɪ/ *adj* unpleasant to look at: *unsightly litter.*

un·skill·ed /ˌʌn'skɪld/ *adj* **1** (of work) not needing special skill. **2** (of a worker) not having special skill or special training. Compare semi-skilled, skilled.

un·so·ciable /ˌʌn'səʊʃəbl/ *adj* not willing to be with others.

un·so·cial /ˌʌn'səʊʃəl/ *adj* **1** not social. **2** outside the usual working day: *work unsocial hours.* Compare antisocial.

un·soph·is·ti·cated /ˌʌnsə'fɪstɪkeɪtɪd/ *adj* not sophisticated(1).

un·sound /ˌʌn'saʊnd/ *adj* not sound¹(2): *an unsound argument/building.* **of unsound mind** ⇨ mind¹(2).

un·spar·ing /ˌʌn'speərɪŋ/ *adj* (usually *pred; formal*) holding nothing back: *be unsparing in one's efforts; unsparing of praise.*

un·speak·able /ˌʌn'spi:kəbl/ *adj* that cannot be expressed or described in words: *unspeakable joy/sadness.*

un·sport·ing /ˌʌn'spɔ:tɪŋ/ *adj* not fair; not sporting(2).

un·stable /ˌʌn'steɪbl/ *adj* (of a person, conditions) not stable. ⇨ instability.

un·steady /ˌʌn'stedɪ/ *adj* **1** not firmly fixed or supported; likely to fall over: *an unsteady chair;*

an unsteady hand/person; an unsteady walk. **2** often changing in amount etc: *unsteady profits/ prices.* **3** (of behaviour etc) not having a regular pattern. Opp steady.

un·stress·ed /ˌʌn'strest/ *adj* (*lang*) of, concerning, a part of a word that is not emphasized when speaking.

un·stuck /ˌʌn'stʌk/ *adj* (*pred*) (esp **come unstuck**) **1** not stuck or fastened: *The flap of the envelope has come unstuck.* **2** not happening according to plan: *Our plan has come unstuck.*

un·subtle /ˌʌn'sʌtl/ *adj* not subtle(2).

un·suc·cess·ful /ˌʌnsək'sesfəl/ *adj* not successful.

un·suit·able /ˌʌn'su:təbl/ *adj* not suitable.

un·sung /ʌn'sʌŋ/ *adj* (of a person, ability) not recognized and praised.

un·sure /ˌʌn'ʃʊə(r)/ *adj* (usually *pred*) **1** not confident: *I feel unsure about appointing her.* Opp sure¹(1). **2** not certain or reliable: *The hotel arrangements are still unsure.*

un·sus·pect·ed /ˌʌnsə'spektɪd/ *adj* (usually *attrib*) not known or imagined: *unsuspected ability.*

un·sus·pect·ing /ˌʌnsə'spektɪŋ/ *adj* (*attrib*) not aware of, feeling the possibility of, deceit or danger: *sell stale bread to unsuspecting customers.*

un·swerv·ing /ˌʌn'swɜ:vɪŋ/ *adj* (usually *attrib*) (esp of aims, purposes) not changing: *unswerving loyalty.*

un·sym·path·etic /ˌʌnsɪmpə'θetɪk/ *adj* not sympathetic.

un·tap·ped /ˌʌn'tæpt/ *adj* not used: *untapped mineral resources.*

un·ten·able /ˌʌn'tenəbl/ *adj* that cannot be defended.

un·think·able /ˌʌn'θɪŋkəbl/ *adj* not to be considered: *Such a possibility is unthinkable!*

un·thought-of /ˌʌn'θɔ:t əv/ *adj* that could not have been imagined: *unthought-of wealth.*

un·ti·dy /ˌʌn'taɪdɪ/ *adj* (**-ier, -iest**) (of a room, person etc) not tidy(1).

un·tie /ˌʌn'taɪ/ *vt* (*present participle* **untying**, *pt,pp* **untied**) to unfasten (a knot etc).

un·til¹ /ən'tɪl/ *conj* (*subord*) (also **till**) **1** up to (the time) that: *Go straight on until you come to the post office, then turn left. She laughed until she cried.* **2** except on the condition or before the time that: *She won't leave until you apologize.*

un·til² /ən'tɪl/ *prep* (also **till**) during the period of time before: *I'll wait until 8 o'clock. No-one will arrive until Friday.* Compare by²(12).

un·time·ly /ˌʌn'taɪmlɪ/ *adj* happening before the expected time: *her untimely death* (e.g. when she was still young).

un·tir·ing /ˌʌn'taɪərɪŋ/ *adj* (*formal*) never wanting to stop: *an untiring worker. She was untiring in her efforts.*

un·told /ˌʌn'təʊld/ *adj* (*attrib*) (esp) too many or too much to be measured etc: *untold wealth.*

un·tried /ˌʌn'traɪd/ *adj* not tested: *untried methods.*

un·true /ˌʌn'tru:/ *adj* **1** false: *an untrue story.* Opp true¹(1). **2** (*dated; usually pred*) disloyal: *be untrue to one's mother.* Compare true¹(2), false(2).

un·trust·wor·thy /ˌʌn'trʌstwɜ:ðɪ/ *adj* (*derog*) not trustworthy.

un·truth·ful /ˌʌn'truːθfəl/ adj (derog) not truth-ful(a).

un·tu·tor·ed /ˌʌn'tjuːtəd/ adj (formal) **untu-tored (in sth)** uneducated (the usual word).

un·used /ˌʌn'juːzd/ adj never having been used: unused paper.

un·used to /ˌʌn'juːst tə before vowel sounds: tu:/ adj (pred) not having become familiar with: I'm unused to city life/hot weather. Opp used to[1].

un·usu·al /ˌʌn'juːʒʊəl/ adj not usual; strange. **un·usu·al·ly** adv: unusually hot.

un·veil /ˌʌn'veɪl/ v **1** vt, vi to remove a veil (from a face etc). **2** vt to allow (something) to be seen for the first time: unveil a new car design.

un·waged /ˌʌn'weɪdʒd/ adj unemployed.

un·war·rant·ed /ˌʌn'wɒrəntɪd/ adj (done) without a suitable reason or cause: unwarranted criti-cism.

un·wel·come /ˌʌn'welkəm/ adj **1** (of a person) not welcome. **2** (of weather, criticism, behaviour) not liked because bad, inappropriate etc.

un·well /ˌʌn'wel/ adj (pred) not well; ill: feeling unwell.

un·whole·some /ˌʌn'hɒlsəm/ adj **1** (of food) not good for one's health. Opp wholesome. **2** (formal) harmful: an unwholesome climate.

un·wieldy /ˌʌn'wiːldɪ/ adj awkward to move or control because of shape, size or weight.

un·will·ing /ˌʌn'wɪlɪŋ/ adj not willing (to do something). **un·will·ing·ly** adv

un·wind /ˌʌn'waɪnd/ vt, vi (pt, pp **-wound** /-'waʊnd/) **1** vt, vi (to cause a ball of wool, a knot etc) to become a straight piece, without twists. Opp wind[4](2). **2** vi (informal) (of a person) to relax after a period of tension, exhausting work etc.

un·wit·ting·ly /ˌʌn'wɪtɪŋlɪ/ adv not intention-ally.

un·work·able /ʌn'wɜːkəbl/ adj not practicable.

un·wor·thy /ˌʌn'wɜːðɪ/ adj **unworthy (of sb/sth)** not worthy.

un·wound /ˌʌn'waʊnd/ pt, pp of unwind.

un·wrap /ˌʌn'ræp/ vt (**-pp-**) to remove the wrap-ping or cover of (a parcel etc).

un·writ·ten /ˌʌn'rɪtn/ adj not written down; understood but not stated: Great Britain has an unwritten constitution. It is an unwritten rule of the club that men wear ties.

un·zip /ˌʌn'zɪp/ vt (**-pp-**) to unfasten or open (clothes etc) by pulling a zip.

up¹ /ʌp/ adverbial particle (N) For uses of 'up' with verbs such as bring, come, get, go, hold, keep, let, put, run, take, wind etc, ⇨ the verb entries. Compare down². **1** from a low(er) level or position to a high(er) one: jump/sit/stand up; look up and see the sky; watch the sun coming up; get/stay up (= out of bed). Opp down²(1). **be up and about** to be out of bed and active (e.g. after being ill). **2** in a high(er) place: up on a shelf; up above the ground. The flap is up. Has Ben come up (= upstairs) yet? **up above** us in the sky or in space. Compare down²(4). **3** to a large(r) volume, size, grade, standard etc: His temperature is up. Please blow up this balloon. Prices/Costs are up. Busi-ness is up. We are £100/10% up on last week's profits. We must all work hard, from the most junior assistant up. Opp down²(5). **4** from a less

active, loud etc level to a high(er) one: Could you speak up (= louder), please? Turn the music/sound/TV up, I can't hear it. Opp down²(6). **5** towards: A man came/walked/ran up to me. **6** from south to north; from the country to the town; from a (less important) place to another: travel up from Cornwall; drive up to Scotland; live up north; shopping up in town; go up to university; work up in London. Opp down²(8). **7** so as to be together, tight etc: tie up a parcel; do up a shoe-lace; fold up a newspaper; collect up the pens; shut up a box. **8** so as to be in pieces: break/divide it up. **9** so as to be finished: eat up/finish up (your soup); because the matches are used up. **10** wrong[1](4): What's up (with you)? Something's up.

up against sth upright and touching: up against a wall. **up against it** experiencing difficulties.

up before sth in court and standing in front of (a judge etc).

up and down (a) in a particular direction and back again: walking up and down. (b) rising and falling: a boat moving up and down in the water. ⇨ also ups and downs at up²(2).

up for sth (a) being considered for: The house is up for sale. She's up for the job as supervisor. (b) being tried in a court for: He's up for stealing.

up to sb the responsibility of a person: It's up to you to help/decide. **up to sth** (a) busy doing something: He's up to mischief/no good. What are they up to now? (b) capable of doing something: I don't feel up to going to work today. (c) as far as something: I read up to page 16. Up to now I believed you. **up to date** ⇨ date²(2).

up² /ʌp/ n **1 on the up and up** (informal) (of a business etc) making good progress. **2** (pl) **ups and downs** (informal) good or bad fortune.

up³ /ʌp/ prep (⇨ up¹) **1** at, to, a high(er) level or place: climb up a mountain; walk up the stairs. The farm is situated farther up the river. Opp down⁴(1). **2** along: walking up the street; sail up and down the river. Compare down⁴(2).

up-and-coming /ˌʌp ən 'kʌmɪŋ/ adj (attrib) (of a person) likely to succeed in a profession, career etc: an up-and-coming artist.

up·bring·ing /'ʌpbrɪŋɪŋ/ n sing (a method of) training and education during childhood, esp in a family: a good upbringing.

up·coun·try /ˌʌp'kʌntrɪ/ adj, adv (esp in a large thinly populated country) in or towards the inter-ior; inland: travel upcountry.

up·date /ˌʌp'deɪt/ vt to bring (a book, report etc) up to date: update a dictionary.

up·end /ˌʌp'end/ vt (informal) to cause (a person, large package etc) to be upside down.

up·grade /ˌʌp'greɪd/ vt to raise (an exam result, the quality of a product etc) to a higher grade. Compare downgrade.

up·heav·al /ˌʌp'hiːvl/ nc, nu a great and sudden change: political/social upheavals.

up·held /ˌʌp'held/ pt, pp of uphold.

up·hill /ˌʌp'hɪl/ adj (attrib) **1** sloping upward: an uphill road. **2** (fig) difficult; needing effort: an uphill task. □ adv up a slope: walk uphill.

up·hold /ˌʌp'həʊld/ vt (pt, pp **upheld** /-'held/) (formal) **1** to support or approve of (a person's behaviour, action etc): I cannot uphold such con-duct. **2** to confirm (a decision, a verdict) as cor-rect.

up·hol·ster /ˌʌpˈhəʊlstə(r)/ vt to provide (seats etc) with padding, springs, covering material etc. **up·hol·ster·er** nc a person who upholsters. **up·hol·stery** /-strɪ/ nu (materials used in, the business of) upholstering.

up·keep /ˈʌpkiːp/ nu (the cost of) keeping something in good order and repair: *I can't afford the upkeep of this large garden.*

up·lands /ˈʌpləndz/ n pl higher parts of a region or country.

up·lift¹ /ˈʌplɪft/ nu (formal) spiritual or emotional inspiration.

up·lift² /ˌʌpˈlɪft/ vt (formal) to raise (a person's spirits etc) spiritually or emotionally: *His soul was uplifted by Bach's music.*

up·mar·ket /ˌʌpˈmɑːkɪt/ adj (of goods, an address, shops etc) of a high standard.

up·most /ˈʌpməʊst/ adj = uppermost.

up·on /əˈpɒn/ prep = on³(1) (which is more usual and considered less formal).

up·per /ˈʌpə(r)/ adj higher in place; situated above: *the upper lip; the upper arm.* Opp lower¹. **gain/get/have the upper hand** to have/get control or an advantage. **keep a stiff upper lip** to manage not to complain (when upset, in pain etc).
'**upper case** nu (in printing) capital letters.
'**upper class(es)** nu or pl (the —) (also attrib) the top levels of society.
ˌUpper 'House n (the —) (in Parliament) the House of Lords.

up·per·most /ˈʌpəməʊst/ adj highest: *Thoughts of the holidays were uppermost in their minds.* □ adv on, to, at, the top or surface: *say whatever comes uppermost.*

up·pi·ty /ˈʌpətɪ/ adj (informal; derog) snobbish.

up·right¹ /ˈʌpraɪt/ adj, adv 1 placed vertically (at an angle of 90° to the ground): *sit bolt upright* (= sit with one's back straight suddenly); *an upright post.* 2 (attrib) honourable; straightforward in behaviour: *an upright man/judge.*

up·right² /ˈʌpraɪt/ nc an upright(1) support in a structure.
ˌupright pi'ano nc one with vertical strings.

up·ris·ing /ˈʌpraɪzɪŋ/ nc a revolt; rebellion.

up·roar /ˈʌprɔː(r)/ nu or sing (an outburst of) noise and excitement: *The meeting ended in (an) uproar.*

up·root /ˌʌpˈruːt/ vt 1 to pull up with the roots: *The gale uprooted numerous trees.* 2 (often passive) to take a person out of one place to work or settle in another.

up·set¹ /ˈʌpset/ nc 1 a condition of being ill: *a stomach upset.* 2 (sport) an unexpected result.

up·set² /ˌʌpˈset/ v (pt,pp —; -tt-) 1 to knock over; overturn: *I've upset some tea on your carpet. Don't upset the boat.* 2 to cause (a person or thing) to be disturbed: *The weather upset our plans. I upset my stomach by eating too much rich food. She is easily upset emotionally.*

up·shot /ˈʌpʃɒt/ n **the upshot (of sth)** the result: *What will be the upshot of it all?*

up·side-down /ˌʌpsaɪd ˈdaʊn/ adv 1 with the upper side underneath or at the bottom: *hanging upside-down in the tree.* 2 (fig) in disorder: *The house was turned upside-down by the burglars.*

up·stairs /ˌʌpˈsteəz/ adj, adv to, on, a higher floor: *an upstairs room; go/walk upstairs.*

up·stand·ing /ˌʌpˈstændɪŋ/ adj (formal) 1 (attrib) strong and healthy: *fine upstanding children.* 2 honest: *an upstanding witness.*

up·start /ˈʌpstɑːt/ nc (derog) a person who has suddenly risen to wealth, power or higher social position, esp one who is arrogant.

up·stream /ˌʌpˈstriːm/ adv (moving) in the opposite direction to the stream or current.

up·surge /ˈʌpsɜːdʒ/ nc a sudden increase (in emotion): *an upsurge of anger/indignation.*

up·tight /ˌʌpˈtaɪt/ adj (informal) extremely tense or nervous: *feel uptight about an interview.*

up-to-date /ˌʌp tə ˈdeɪt/ adj (attrib) (up to date when pred) of the present time; of the newest sort: *up-to-date methods.*

up-to-the-minute /ˌʌp tə ðə ˈmɪnɪt/ adj (attrib) very modern; latest: *up-to-the-minute information.*

up·turn /ˈʌptɜːn/ nc 1 an upward turn. 2 (fig) an improvement: *an upturn in profits.* ⇨ turn up(d).

up·ward /ˈʌpwəd/ adj moving or directed up: *an upward glance.*

up·wards /ˈʌpwədz/ adv towards a higher place, level etc: *looking upwards.*

ura·nium /jʊˈreɪnɪəm/ nu (science) a heavy white metal (symbol U) with radioactive properties, a source of atomic energy.

Ura·nus /jʊˈreɪnəs or ˈjʊərənəs/ n (astron) the planet seventh in order from the sun.

ur·ban /ˈɜːbən/ adj of, in, a town: *urban development.* Compare rural.
ˌurban guer'rilla nc a member of an armed political group fighting in towns.

ur·bane /ɜːˈbeɪn/ adj (formal) (of behaviour) polite and (sometimes too) well-mannered.
ur·bane·ly adv

ur·chin /ˈɜːtʃɪn/ nc 1 a mischievous small boy. 2 a poor, untidy child.

urge¹ /ɜːdʒ/ nc a strong wish: *have/feel an urge to travel.*

urge² /ɜːdʒ/ vt 1 to request (something) earnestly; try to persuade (a person): *I urge you to go. 'Buy it now,' he urged.* 2 **urge sb (on)** to encourage a person to try: *The crowd was urging the tennis star on.* 3 **urge sth on sb** to stress to a person (the importance of) requests and arguments: *He urged on his students the importance of hard work.*

ur·gen·cy /ˈɜːdʒənsɪ/ nu the importance of, need for, haste or quick action: *a matter of great urgency.*

ur·gent /ˈɜːdʒənt/ adj 1 important and so needing a quick decision or action: *It is most urgent that the patient should get to hospital.* 2 (of a person, voice etc) showing that something is urgent: *an urgent tone of voice.*
ur·gent·ly adv

uri·nary /ˈjʊərɪnrɪ/ adj (med) of urine: *urinary infection.*

uri·nate /ˈjʊərɪneɪt/ vi (formal) to pass urine.

urine /ˈjʊərɪn/ nu (science) the waste liquid which collects in the bladder and is discharged from the body.

urn /ɜːn/ nc 1 a large metal container in which tea or coffee is kept hot. 2 a container used for holding the ashes of a person whose body has been cremated.

US /ˌjuː ˈes/ abbr (the —) the United States (of

America).

us /əs *strong form:* ʌs/ *personal pron* (used as the object form of *we*) a group including the speaker: *We hope you'll soon visit us. One of us must remember the key. It's the responsibility of all of us. Please write to us soon.*

USA /ˌjuː es 'eɪ/ *abbr* (the —) the United States of America.

us·age /'juːsɪdʒ/ *n* **1** *nu* the way of using something; amount of use: *Machines soon wear out under rough usage.* **2** *nc,nu* (an instance of) the way of using a language (esp not governed by grammatical rules): *Such usages are not typical of educated speakers.*

USAID /ˌjuːesˈeɪd/ *acronym* United States Agency for International Development (an organization offering aid to developing countries).

use¹ /juːs/ *n* **1** *nu* the act, condition, of using or being used: *the use of electricity for cooking.* **in use** being used. **come into use** to begin to be used: *When did the words 'silicon chip' come into common use?* **2** *nc,nu* the purpose, reason, for using a person or thing: *a tool with many uses; find a use for it; have no further use for it.* **3** *nu* **be of use (to sb)** to be of value for a purpose: *Is this paper of any use to you?* **be no (earthly)** *use* to be of no value for doing anything. **4** *nu* the ability to use something: *lose the use of one's legs.* **5** *nu* (the —) the right or opportunity to use: *You can have the use of my car.*

use² /juːz/ *vt* (*pt,pp* used /juːzd/) **1** to cause (something) to act or serve for a purpose: *May I use your car? You can use my room if you like.* **2** **use sth (up)** to have the use of a supply (until nothing is left): *How much coal did we use last winter? He has used up all his strength.* **3** to behave towards (a person): *Use others as you would like them to use you.*

use to /'juːs tə/ (forms the negative or question form of *used to*). ⇨ used¹.

used¹ /juːst/ *auxiliary verb* Ⓝ *'Used'* is put with another verb to express a past situation or habit. *'Used'* is always followed by an infinitive with *'to'* and is often referred to as *'used to'*. (*pt* **used to** (all persons), *negative* **used not to**, **usedn't to** /'juːsnt tə/ or **didn't use to**; *question form* **used sb/ sth to** or **did sb/sth use to**; *negative question form* **usedn't sb/sth to** or **didn't sb/sth use to**) **1** (used to express a past habit or situation that no longer exists): *I used to smoke but I've stopped now. There used to be a good pub near here. Didn't you use to smoke? She used not to/ usedn't to like beer/didn't use to like beer when she was a student. Did he use to ride a motorbike when you knew him? I used to like you once. Life isn't as easy as it used to be.* ⇨ used to¹. **2** (used to express a routine during a period in the past): *Every morning I used to get up early and go for a walk. He always used to bring me flowers on Fridays.* Compare would(2).

used² /juːzd/ **1** *pt,pp* of use². **2** *adj* (usually *attrib*) no longer new: *used cars/clothes.*

usedn't to /'juːsnt tə/ = *used not to*. ⇨ used¹.

used to¹ /'juːst tə *before vowel sounds:* tuː/ *adj* (*pred*) having become familiar to (something) by habit or custom: *You will soon be/get used to it.*

I'm not used to such hot weather. Opp unused to.

used to² /'juːzt tə/ *auxiliary verb* ⇨ used¹.

use·ful /'juːsfəl/ *adj* **1** having a use: *a useful tool/ idea.* **2** helpful: *a useful son.*

use·ful·ly *adv*: *usefully employed.*

use·ful·ness *nu*

use·less /'juːslɪs/ *adj* **1** having no use; not able to do what is intended: *a useless gadget. A car is useless without petrol.* **2** having no result: *It's useless to argue with him.*

use·less·ness *nu*

user /'juːzə(r)/ *nc* a person, thing, that uses something: *telephone users; a car that is a heavy user of petrol.*

,user-'friendly *adj* (*pred*) (of a machine, set of instructions etc) simple and pleasant to use.

ush·er¹ /'ʌʃə(r)/ *nc* a person who shows people to their seats in theatres, cinemas etc.

ush·er·ette /ˌʌʃə'ret/ *nc* a woman usher.

ush·er² /'ʌʃə(r)/ *vt* **1** to show (a person) the way (to): *The girl ushered me to my seat.* **2** **usher sth in** to produce something as a result: *The change of government ushered in a period of prosperity.*

USSR /ˌjuː es es 'ɑː(r)/ *abbr* (the —) the Union of Soviet Socialist Republics.

usu·al /'juːʒʊəl/ *adj* happening often; ordinary, expected: *Is the weather usual for this time of year? He arrived later than usual.* Compare unusual. **as usual** as is/was generally expected: *She's late as usual.*

usu·al·ly *adv* (**a**) in the ordinary way: *What do you usually do on Sundays?* (**b**) more often than not: *She's usually late.*

usurp /juː'zɜːp/ *vt* to take (a person's power, authority, position) without right: *usurp the chairman's authority.*

usurp·er *nc* (*derog*) a person who usurps.

uten·sil /juː'tensl/ *nc* a simple instrument, tool etc for use in the home: *household utensils.*

uter·us /'juːtərəs/ *nc* (*pl* —es) (*anat*) = womb.

utili·tar·ian /juːˌtɪlɪ'teərɪən/ *adj* designed for use rather than beauty.

util·ity /juː'tɪlətɪ/ *n* (*pl* -ies) **1** *nu* (*formal*) the quality of being useful. **2** *nc* a public service such as the supply of water or a bus service.

util·ize (also **-ise**) /'juːtɪlaɪz/ *vt* (*formal*) to make use of, find a use for, (something): *Is the sports centre being fully utilized? We'll utilize the extra money to buy another machine.*

util·iz·ation (also **-is·ation**) /ˌjuːtɪlaɪ'zeɪʃn/ *nu*

ut·most /'ʌtməʊst/ *adj* (*attrib*), *n sing* (the) most extreme; greatest possible: *with the utmost care. I shall do my utmost* (= do all I can) *to see that justice is done.*

ut·ter¹ /'ʌtə(r)/ *adj* (*attrib*) complete; total: *utter darkness/disbelief.*

ut·ter·ly *adv* completely: *She's utterly bored with him.*

ut·ter² /'ʌtə(r)/ *vt* **1** to make (a sound or sounds) with the mouth: *utter a sigh/a cry of pain.* **2** to say (something): *the last words he uttered.*

ut·ter·ance /'ʌtərəns/ *n* **1** *n sing* (*formal*) a way of speaking: *a clear utterance.* **2** *nc* a spoken word or words. **give utterance to one's feelings** (*formal*) to express one's feelings in words.

ut·ter·most /'ʌtəməʊst/ *adj, n sing* = utmost.

U-turn /'juː tɜːn/ *nc* ⇨ U, u.

692

Vv

V, v /viː/ (*pl* **V's, v's** /viːz/) the 22nd letter of the English alphabet.

V *symbol* **1** (also **v**) the Roman numeral 5. **2** Victory. **3** (*electricity*) volt(s).

v *written abbr* **1** verb. **2** (*legal* and *sport*) versus.

vac /væk/ *nc* (*informal*) = vacation.

va·can·cy /ˈveɪkənsɪ/ *n* (*pl* **-ies**) **1** *nc* a job in a business, factory etc for which a person is needed: *There is a vacancy for a qualified electrician.* **2** *nc* a place available for a person to join a university as a student, a team as a player etc: *I promise that you can have the next vacancy.* **3** *nc* a place available in a hotel etc: *Sorry, no vacancies* (i.e. the hotel is full). **4** *nu* (*formal*) the state of lacking ideas, concentration etc.

va·cant /ˈveɪkənt/ *adj* **1** (of a hotel, room, seat, space, job etc) not occupied by any person: *apply for a vacant position in an office; ask if there are any double rooms vacant.* **2** (*attrib; formal*) empty: *gazing into vacant space.* **3** showing a lack of ideas, thought or concentration: *a vacant expression.*

va·cant·ly *adv*

va·cate /veɪˈkeɪt/ *vt* **1** to give up living in (a building etc): *vacate a house.* **2** to stop occupying (a place): *vacate one's seat.*

va·ca·tion /vəˈkeɪʃn/ *nc* **1** the period during which universities and law courts stop work: *the summer vacation.* **2** (esp *US*) = holiday.

vac·ci·nate /ˈvæksɪneɪt/ *vt* **vaccinate sb (against sth)** (*formal*) to protect a person (against a disease) by giving vaccine.

vac·ci·na·tion /ˌvæksɪˈneɪʃn/ *nc,nu*

vac·cine /ˈvæksiːn/ *nc,nu* a substance containing a virus or bacteria, used to protect a person from a disease by encouraging antibodies.

vac·il·late /ˈvæsɪleɪt/ *vi* **vacillate (between/ over sth)** (*formal*) to change one's mind often; be uncertain (in opinion etc): *vacillate between hope and fear.*

vac·il·la·tion /ˌvæsɪˈleɪʃn/ *nc,nu*

vac·uum¹ /ˈvækjʊəm/ *nc* **1** a space completely empty of substance or gas(es). **2** a space in a container from which (almost all) the air has been pumped out.

ˈvacuum cleaner *nc* an electrical apparatus which takes up dust, dirt etc by sucking air.

ˈvacuum flask *nc* one having a vacuum between its inner and outer walls, to keep the contents hot or cold.

ˈvacuum-packed *adj* (of food etc) sealed in airtight packets or tins in order to maintain freshness.

vac·uum² /ˈvækjʊəm/ *vt,vi* to use a vacuum cleaner to clean (a carpet etc).

vaga·bond /ˈvægəbɒnd/ *nc* (*dated*) a poor person having no fixed home.

va·gary /ˈveɪgərɪ/ *nc* (*pl* **-ies**) (*formal*) a strange, unusual act or idea, esp one for which there seems to be no good reason: *the vagaries of fashion.*

va·gi·na /vəˈdʒaɪnə/ *nc* (*pl* **-s**) (*anat*) the passage in a female mammal from the external genital organs to the womb.

va·gi·nal /vəˈdʒaɪnl/ *adj*

va·gran·cy /ˈveɪgrənsɪ/ *nu* the state of being a vagrant.

va·grant /ˈveɪgrənt/ *nc* (often *derog*) a person who wanders from place to place and has no home.

vague /veɪg/ *adj* (**—r, —st**) **1** not clear or distinct; slight: *I haven't the vaguest idea what they want.* **2** (of a person, expression, behaviour) uncertain, esp about details: *He was a little vague when I asked what had happened.*

vague·ly *adv*

vague·ness *nu*

vain /veɪn/ *adj* (**—er, —est**) **1** without use, value, meaning or result: *a vain attempt; vain hopes.* **in vain** (**a**) not having the desired result: *All our work was in vain.* (**b**) without due honour or respect. ⇨ name¹(1). **2** (*derog*) having too high an opinion of one's looks, abilities etc: *as vain as a peacock* (= very vain). ⇨ vanity.

vain·ly *adv*

vale /veɪl/ *nc* (*literary*) = valley.

val·en·tine /ˈvæləntaɪn/ *nc* (often V-) (a letter, card etc sent on St Valentine's Day, 14 February to) a sweetheart: *Will you be my Valentine? I sent her a valentine card.*

val·et /ˈvælɪt/ *nc* **1** a member of (hotel) staff employed to dry-clean or press clothes. **2** a rich man's personal servant who looks after his clothes, meals etc.

val·iant /ˈvælɪənt/ *adj* (*formal*) brave (the usual word).

val·iant·ly *adv*

val·id /ˈvælɪd/ *adj* **1** (*legal*) genuine and acceptable because made or done with the correct formalities: *a valid claim/marriage.* **2** that can be legally used: *a ticket that is valid for three months.* **3** (of arguments, reasons etc) acceptable: *raise valid objections to a plan.* Opp invalid¹.

val·id·ly *adv*

val·id·ity /vəˈlɪdətɪ/ *nu*

vali·date /ˈvælɪdeɪt/ *vt* (*formal* or *legal*) to make (something) valid: *validate a claim.* Opp invalidate.

va·lise /vəˈliːz/ *nc* (*dated*) a small bag used for clothes etc during a journey.

val·ley /ˈvælɪ/ *nc* (*pl* **-s**) the low land between hills or mountains, often with a river flowing through it.

val·our (*US* = **val·or**) /ˈvælə(r)/ *nu* (*formal*) bravery, esp in war.

valu·able /ˈvæljʊbl/ *adj* **1** of great value, worth or use: *a valuable discovery.* Opp valueless. **2** very useful: *valuable advice.* Compare invaluable.

valu·ables /ˈvæljʊblz/ *n pl* possessions (e.g. jewelry) of great value.

valu·ation /ˌvæljʊˈeɪʃn/ *n* **1** *nu* the process of deciding the value of a person or thing. **2** *nc* the value that is decided: *Will you accept the agent's valuation for the house?*

val·ue¹ /ˈvæljuː/ *n* **1** *nu* the quality of being useful or desirable: *the value of walking as an exercise.* **2** *nu* the worth of something when compared with something else: *This book will be of great/little/ some/no value to him in his studies.* **3** *nc,nu* the worth of something in terms of money or other goods for which it can be exchanged: *Is the value of the dollar likely to fall?* **4** *nu* what something is considered to be worth (contrasted with the price obtainable): *I've been offered £350 for my old car, but its value is much higher.* **5** (*pl*) standards: *moral/ethical values.*

val·ue² /'vælju:/ *vt* **1** to decide the price or worth of (something): *He valued the house for me at £60 500.* **2** to have a high opinion of (a person): *Do you value her as a secretary?*

value-'added-tax *nu* (*abbr* VAT) tax paid by the buyer on something bought, or for a service, that is then paid to the government.

val·ue·less *adj* worthless. Opp valuable(1).

valu·er *nc* a person whose profession is to estimate the money value of property, land etc.

valve /vælv/ *nc* **1** a mechanical device used for controlling the flow of air, liquid, gas etc in one direction only. **2** (*science*) a structure in the heart or in a blood-vessel allowing the blood to flow in one direction only. **3** (*tech*) a closed, airless tube used to control electricity (now replaced with transistors).

val·vu·lar /'vælvjulə(r)/ *adj* of valves(2).

vamp·ire /'væmpaɪə(r)/ *nc* (in stories) a dead body that comes to life at night and sucks the blood of sleeping people.

'vampire bat *nc* a kind of blood-sucking bat.

van¹ /væn/ *nc* **1** a roofed vehicle used for carrying and delivering goods: *a furniture van.* **2** (*GB*) a railway carriage for goods: *the luggage van.*

van² /væn/ *nc* **1** the front or leading part of an army or fleet in battle. **2** those people who lead a procession or (*fig*) an activity: *in the van of scientific progress.*

'van·guard *nc* an advance group of an army etc sent as a guard against surprise attack.

van·dal /'vændl/ *nc* (*derog*) a person who deliberately destroys public and private property.

van·dal·ism /-ɪzəm/ *nu* destruction by vandals.

vane /veɪn/ *nc* **1** an arrow or pointer on the top of a building, turning to show the direction of the wind: *a weather vane.* **2** a blade of a propeller, or any other flat surface acted on by wind or water.

van·guard /'vænga:d/ *nc* ⇨ van².

va·nil·la /və'nɪlə/ *nu* (also *attrib*) a substance made from the beans of a tropical plant, used for flavouring sweet things: *vanilla ice-cream/cakes.*

van·ish /'vænɪʃ/ *vi* to disappear or fade away suddenly: *The thief ran into the crowd and vanished.*

van·ity /'vænətɪ/ *n* (*pl* **-ies**) *nu* the state of having too high an opinion of one's looks, abilities etc: *do something out of vanity.*

van·quish /'væŋkwɪʃ/ *vt* (*formal*) to defeat (the usual word).

va·por·ize (also **-ise**) /'veɪpəraɪz/ *vt,vi* (to cause liquid) to be changed into vapour.

va·pour (*US =* **va·por**) /'veɪpə(r)/ *nu* the wet, gassy form of water or other liquids: *Clouds are formed by water vapour.*

vari·able¹ /'veərɪəbl/ *adj* varying; changeable: *variable winds; variable standards.* Opp invariable.

'variable cost *nc* (*finance*) a cost that changes according to the number of things being produced, such as the cost of materials. Compare fixed cost.

vari·ably /-əblɪ/ *adv*

vari·able² /'veərɪəbl/ *nc* a quantity or thing (e.g. cost, temperature) that can change according to conditions. Opp invariable.

vari·abil·ity /ˌveərɪə'bɪlətɪ/ *nu*

vari·ant¹ /'veərɪənt/ *adj* (*attrib*) different or alternative: *variant spellings of a word* (e.g. 'programme' and 'program').

vari·ant² /'veərɪənt/ *nc* a variant form (e.g. of spelling): *American English variants.*

vari·ation /ˌveərɪ'eɪʃn/ *nc,nu* (an instance, amount, of) the act of varying: *variations in temperature/prices/colour.*

vari·cose vein /ˌværɪkəʊs 'veɪn/ *nc* a vein that has become permanently swollen or enlarged.

var·ied /'veərɪd/ *adj* **1** having different sorts: *varied colours.* **2** full of changes or variety: *a varied career.*

var·ie·gat·ed /'veərɪgeɪtɪd/ *adj* marked irregularly with differently coloured patches: *Flowers are often variegated.*

varie·ga·tion /ˌveərɪ'geɪʃn/ *nu*

va·ri·ety /və'raɪətɪ/ *n* (*pl* **-ies**) **1** *nu* the state of not being the same, or not being the same at all times: *a life full of variety.* **2** *n sing* a number or range of different things: *for a variety of reasons.* **3** *nc* (*science*) a subdivision of a species. **4** *nc* a sort that differs from others of the larger group of which it is a part: *rare varieties of early postage stamps.* **5** *nu* (also *attrib*) a kind of entertainment consisting of singing, dancing, comedy etc: *a variety act.*

vari·ous /'veərɪəs/ *adj* (*attrib*) **1** different: *for various reasons.* **2** a number of different kinds: *Various animals have fur.*

vari·ous·ly *adv*

var·nish¹ /'vɑːnɪʃ/ *nc,nu* (a particular kind of) (liquid used to give) a hard, shiny, transparent coating on a surface.

var·nish² /'vɑːnɪʃ/ *vt* to put varnish on (something): *Some women varnish their toe-nails.*

vars·ity /'vɑːsətɪ/ *nc* (*pl* **-ies**) (*dated; informal*) = university.

vary /'veərɪ/ *vi,vt* (*pt,pp* **-ied**) (to cause something) to be, become, different: *They vary in weight between 3 and 5 kilos/from 3 to 5 kilos.*

vas·cu·lar /'væskjʊlə(r)/ *adj* (*anat*) of, made up of, containing, vessels or ducts through which blood, lymph flows: *vascular tissue.*

vase /vɑːz/ *nc* a container of glass, pottery etc used for cut flowers or as an ornament.

va·sec·to·my /və'sektəmɪ/ *nc,nu* (*pl* **-ies**) a surgical operation to make a man sterile.

vast /vɑːst/ *adj* immense; extensive: *vast sums of money; a vast expanse of desert.*

vast·ly *adv*: *vastly* (= greatly) *improved.*

vast·ness *nu*

vat /væt/ *nc* a very large container for liquids, esp in brewing, dyeing.

VAT /ˌvi: eɪ 'ti:/ *abbr* value-added tax.

vault¹ /vɔːlt/ *nc* **1** an arched roof; series of arches forming a roof. **2** an underground room used for storing things (e.g. a *wine vault*) or for keeping valuables (a *bank vault*) or for dead bodies (e.g. under a church).

vault² /vɔːlt/ *nc* a jump made by vaulting. ⇨ pole vault.

vault³ /vɔːlt/ *vi,vt* to jump in a single movement,

with the hand(s) resting on something, or with the help of a pole: *vault (over) a fence*.

'vaul·ting-horse *nc* an apparatus for practice in vaulting.

vault·er *nc* a person who vaults: *a pole-vaulter*.

VC /,vi: 'si:/ *abbr* **1** vice-chairman. **2** vice-chancellor. **3** Victoria Cross (a GB award for bravery).

VD /,vi: 'di:/ *abbr* venereal disease (now referred to as STD).

VDU /,vi: di: 'ju:/ *abbr* (*computers*) Visual Display Unit.

've /-v/ = have, as in *I've, We've, They've.*

veal /vi:l/ *nu* the flesh of a calf eaten as food.

veer /vɪə(r)/ *vi* to change direction: *The wind veered round to the north. Opinion veered in our favour.*

ve·gan /'vi:gən/ *adj, nc* (of) a person who eats no meat or any produce from animals such as milk, eggs (and who does not wear or use animal products such as leather).

veg·et·able¹ /'vedʒtəbl/ *adj* (*attrib*) of, from, relating to, plants or plant life: *vegetable oils.*
  'vegetable kingdom *n* (the—) all plant life.

veg·et·able² /'vedʒtəbl/ *nc* (a part of) a plant used for food, e.g. potatoes, cabbage, carrots, beans.

veg·etar·ian /,vedʒɪ'teərɪən/ *adj, nc* (of) a person who eats no meat: *a vegetarian diet.*

veg·etate /'vedʒɪteɪt/ *vi* to lead a dull life with little activity, thought or interest.

veg·eta·tion /,vedʒɪ'teɪʃn/ *nu* plants generally and collectively: *a desert with no sign of vegetation anywhere.*

ve·he·ment /'vi:əmənt/ *adj* (*formal*) **1** (of feelings) strong: *vehement anger.* **2** (of a person, speech, behaviour etc) filled with, showing, strong or eager feeling: *vehement requests for aid.*
  ve·he·ment·ly *adv*

ve·hicle /'vi:ɪkl/ *nc* **1** (also *motor vehicle*) something with wheels and an engine, e.g. a car, lorry, van, bus etc, used for carrying things or people on land. ⇨ space-vehicle. **2** something with wheels but no engine, e.g. a cart, carriage, caravan etc, used for carrying things or people. **3** a means by which thought, feeling etc can be carried: *She used the meeting as a vehicle for introducing her theories. Newspapers can be a useful vehicle for becoming famous.*

ve·hicu·lar /vi:'hɪkjʊlə(r)/ *adj* (*formal*) **1** related to, consisting of, carried by, vehicles: *The road is closed to vehicular traffic.* **2** (*attrib*) (of a language) used as a means of communication between people with different first languages, e.g. English in Nigeria.

veil¹ /veɪl/ *nc* **1** a covering of fine net or other material used to protect or hide a woman's face: *She lowered her veil.* **2** (*fig*) something that hides or disguises something: *a veil of mist.*

veil² /veɪl/ *vt* **1** to put a veil over (one's face etc): *Not all Muslim women are veiled.* **2** (*fig*) to hide (something): *He could not veil his distrust.*

vein /veɪn/ *nc* **1** a blood-vessel along which blood flows from all parts of the body to the heart. Compare artery(1). **2** one of the lines in some leaves or in the wings of some insects. ⇨ venous. **3** a coloured line or streak in some kinds of stone. **4** (*fig*) a particular characteristic: *There is a vein of madness in him.* **5** a crack in rock, filled with min-

eral or ore: *a vein of gold.* **6** a way of thinking: *in an imaginative vein.*

vel·oc·ity /vɪ'lɒsətɪ/ *nu* (*formal*) = speed¹(1).

ve·lours (also **ve·lour**) /və'lʊə(r)/ *nu* a kind of cloth like velvet.

vel·vet /'velvɪt/ *nu* a kind of cloth wholly or partly made of silk with a thick soft pile on one side.
  vel·vety *adj* smooth and soft (like velvet).

ve·nal /'vi:nl/ *adj* (*derog*) **1** (of a person) ready to do something dishonest (e.g. using influence or position) for money: *venal politicians.* **2** (of behaviour) influenced by, done for, (possible) payment: *venal practices.*
  ve·nal·ly /-nəlɪ/ *adv*

ven·det·ta /ven'detə/ *nc* a long quarrel or disagreement (between families).

vend·ing machine /'vendɪŋ məʃi:n/ *nc* a machine that provides food, cigarettes etc when money is put in it.

ve·neer /vɪ'nɪə(r)/ *n* **1** *nc,nu* (a thin layer of) fine quality wood glued to the surface of cheaper wood (for making furniture etc). **2** *n sing* (*fig*) a surface appearance (of politeness etc) covering the true nature: *a veneer of kindness.*

ven·er·able /'venərəbl/ *adj* (of a person) deserving respect because of age, character, religious importance etc.

ven·er·ate /'venəreɪt/ *vt* (*formal*) to regard (a person, a memory etc) with great honour or respect: *They venerate the old man's memory.*
  ven·er·ation /,venə'reɪʃn/ *nu*

ve·nere·al dis·ease /vɪ,nɪərɪəl dɪ'zi:z/ *nc* (*abbr* VD) (*dated*) = sexually transmitted disease.

Ve·ne·tian blind /vɪ,ni:ʃn 'blaɪnd/ *nc* a kind of covering for a window made up of series of horizontal pieces that can be moved to allow light to enter.

venge·ance /'vendʒəns/ *n* **1** *nu* revenge; the return of injury for injury: *take vengeance on an enemy.* **2** *n sing* (*informal*) a greater degree than is normal, expected or desired: *The rain came down with a vengeance.*

venge·ful /'vendʒfəl/ *adj* showing a desire for revenge.

ve·ni·al /'vi:nɪəl/ *adj* (*formal*) (of a sin, error, fault) that can be forgiven or excused.

ven·ison /'venɪsn/ *nu* the flesh of a deer eaten as food.

ven·om /'venəm/ *nu* **1** the poisonous fluid of certain snakes. **2** (*fig*) hate; spite.
  ven·om·ous /'venəməs/ *adj* deadly; spiteful: *venomous snakes/criticism.*
  ven·om·ous·ly *adv*

ve·nous /'vi:nəs/ *adj* **1** (*anat*) of the veins: *venous blood.* **2** (*science*) having veins: *a venous leaf/wing.*

vent¹ /vent/ *nc* **1** a hole serving as an inlet or outlet for air, gas, liquid etc. **2** a means of escape: *The floods found a vent through the walls.* **3** *n sing* an outlet for one's feelings: *a vent for my anger.*
  give vent to sth to give free expression to (feelings): *He gave vent to his anger in an impassioned speech.*

vent² /vent/ *vt* to find or provide an expression for (feelings): *He vented his anger on his long-suffering wife.*

ven·ti·late /'ventɪleɪt/ *vt* to cause air to move in and out of (a place) freely: *ventilate a room.*

ven·ti·la·tion /ˌventɪˈleɪʃn/ *nu*

ven·ti·la·tor /ˈventɪleɪtə(r)/ *nc* an apparatus used for ventilating a room, e.g. in a kitchen or bathroom.

ven·ture¹ /ˈventʃə(r)/ *nc* an undertaking in which there is risk: *a business venture.*

'venture capital *nu* (*finance*) money used to start a new business.

ven·ture² /ˈventʃə(r)/ *v* 1 *vi* to take the risk of danger or loss: *venture too near the edge of a cliff; venture out of doors on a cold day.* 2 *vt* (*formal*) to dare (to do, say, (something): *venture* (*to put forward*) *an opinion; venture a guess.*

Ve·nus /ˈviːnəs/ *n* (*astron*) the planet second in order from the sun.

ve·ran·da (also **-dah**) /vəˈrændə/ *nc* a roofed and floored open space along the side(s) of a house, sports pavilion etc.

verb /vɜːb/ *nc* (*gram*) a word showing the performance or occurrence of an action, the existence of a state or condition etc; as in 'I *laugh*', 'You *can*', 'He *got up*', 'It *is raining*', '*Hurry up!*' ⇨ auxiliary/intransitive/irregular/main/modal auxiliary/phrasal/stative/nonstative/transitive verb. ⇨ also copula, finite(2), non-finite.

ver·bal /ˈvɜːbl/ *adj* 1 of or in words: *have a good verbal memory* (i.e. be able to remember well the exact words of a statement etc). 2 (*attrib*) spoken, not written: *a verbal agreement.* Opp non-verbal. 3 (*gram*) of verbs.

ˌverbal 'noun *nc* (*gram*) = gerund.

ˌverbal 'phrase (*gram*) a verb with many parts, as in 'She *would have been thrown out*'.

ver·bal·ly /ˈvɜːbəlɪ/ *adv* in spoken words, not in writing.

ver·bal·ize (also **-ise**) /ˈvɜːbəlaɪz/ *vt* to put (ideas, thoughts) into words.

ver·ba·tim /vɜːˈbeɪtɪm/ *adj* (*attrib*), *adv* exactly as spoken or written: *report a speech verbatim.*

ver·bi·age /ˈvɜːbɪdʒ/ *nu* (*formal*) (the use of) unnecessary words to express an idea etc.

ver·bose /vɜːˈbəʊs/ *adj* (*derog*) using, contain·ing, more words than are needed: *a verbose speech/speaker.*

ver·bose·ly *adv*

ver·bos·ity /vɜːˈbɒsətɪ/ *nu*

ver·dict /ˈvɜːdɪkt/ *nc* 1 (*legal*) a decision reached by a jury on a question of fact in a law case. **bring in a verdict** (of a jury) to tell the court its decision: *The jury brought in a verdict of* (*not*) *guilty.* ⇨ open verdict. 2 a decision or opinion given after testing, examining or experiencing something: *The popular verdict* (= The opinion of people in general) *was against the strike.*

verge¹ /vɜːdʒ/ *n* 1 *nc* a border (e.g. strip of grass at the side of a road). 2 **be on the verge of (doing) sth** to be very close to (doing) it: *The country is on the verge of disaster.*

verge² /vɜːdʒ/ *vi* **verge on sth** to be almost the kind mentioned: *Such ideas verge on stupidity.*

ver·ify /ˈverɪfaɪ/ *vt* (*pt, pp* **-ied**) 1 to test the truth or accuracy of (a report etc): *verify a report/statement.* 2 (of an event etc) to prove, show, the truth of (something): *Subsequent events verified my suspicions.*

veri·fi·able /ˈverɪfaɪəbl/ *adj* that can be verified.

veri·fi·ca·tion /ˌverɪfɪˈkeɪʃn/ *nu*

veri·table /ˈverɪtəbl/ *adj* (*attrib*) rightly named:

She's a veritable liar.

ver·mil·ion /vəˈmɪlɪən/ *adj, nu* bright red (colour).

ver·min /ˈvɜːmɪn/ *nu* (usually used with a *pl verb*) 1 wild animals (e.g. rats, foxes) harmful to plants, birds and other animals. 2 kinds of insect (e.g. *lice*) living on the bodies of human beings and other animals.

ver·min·ous /ˈvɜːmɪnəs/ *adj*

ver·nacu·lar /vəˈnækjʊlə(r)/ *adj, nc* (of) a word, language of a particular country: *a vernacular language; speak in the vernacular.*

ver·sa·tile /ˈvɜːsətaɪl/ *adj* interested in, clever at doing, many different things; having various uses: *a versatile mind/invention/machine.*

ver·sa·til·ity /ˌvɜːsəˈtɪlətɪ/ *nu*

verse /vɜːs/ *n* (*literature*) 1 *nu* (a form of) writing arranged in lines, each with a pattern of stressed and unstressed syllables: *prose and verse.* ⇨ blank verse. 2 *nc* a group of lines of this kind forming a unit: *a poem/hymn of five verses.* 3 *nc* one of the short numbered divisions of a chapter in the Bible. **chapter and verse** ⇨ chapter(1).

versed /vɜːst/ *adj* (*pred*) **versed in sth** skilled or experienced in something: *well versed in mathematics/the arts.*

ver·sion /ˈvɜːʃn/ *nc* 1 an account of an event etc from the point of view of one person: *There were three versions of what happened/of what the Prime Minister said.* 2 a different form or style: *a new version of the Bible.*

ver·sus /ˈvɜːsəs/ *prep* (*Latin*) (*legal* and *sport*; *abbr* v) against: *Robinson v Brown; England v Brazil.*

ver·te·bra /ˈvɜːtɪbrə/ *nc* (*pl* **—e** /-briː/) (*anat*) any one of the small bones forming the backbone.

ver·te·brate /ˈvɜːtɪbrət/ *adj, nc* (*science*) (of) an animal, having a backbone, e.g. a monkey, cow, fish. Compare invertebrate.

ver·ti·cal /ˈvɜːtɪkl/ *adj* (of a line or plane) at a right angle to the earth's surface or to another line or surface. □ *nc* a vertical line. Compare horizontal.

ver·ti·cal·ly /-klɪ/ *adv*

verve /vɜːv/ *nu* enthusiasm, spirit, vigour (esp in artistic or literary work).

very¹ /ˈverɪ/ *adj* (*attrib*) 1 itself and no other; truly such: *At that very moment the phone rang. You're the very man I want to see.* 2 extreme: *at the very end/beginning; the letter at the very top of the pile.*

very² /ˈverɪ/ *adv* 1 (used to emphasize an adv or adj): *very quickly/little/hot/big/important. There were very many people. Thank you very much.* **very well** (often used to show agreement after persuasion or argument, or agreement to a command, request etc): *Very well, doctor, I'll give up smoking.* 2 (used to emphasize a superlative or similar word such as *last, same, first* etc) in the greatest possible degree: *at the very latest; the very best example; for the very first/last time; my very own car.* Ⓝ *'Very'* cannot be used with comparatives. Use *'far'* or *'much'*, as in *far/much better; far/much easier.*

ves·sel /ˈvesl/ *nc* 1 (*formal*) a hollow container, esp for a liquid, e.g. a bucket, bowl, cup ⇨ also blood-vessel. 2 a ship or large boat.

vest¹ /vest/ *nc* 1 (*GB*) an article of underwear worn on the upper part of the body next to the skin (US = undershirt). **2** (US) a waistcoat.

vest² /vest/ vt (formal) to give (a person) (something) as a fixed right: vest a man with authority/ rights in an estate.

‚vested 'interest nc a personal reason for doing something, e.g. for personal gain: He has a vested interest in your decision not to accept the job (e.g. because he wants it himself).

ves·tige /'vestɪdʒ/ nc **1** a trace or sign; small remaining bit of what once existed: There is not a vestige of truth in the report. **2** (science) an organ, or part of one, which is a survival of something that once existed: A human being has the vestige of a tail.

ves·tigi·al /ve'stɪdʒɪəl/ adj (science) surviving (in reduced size etc) from an earlier form: the vestigial legs on some snakes.

vest·ment /'vestmənt/ nc a ceremonial robe as worn by a priest in church.

ves·try /'vestrɪ/ nc (pl -ies) **1** a part of a church where vestments are kept. **2** a room in some churches used for prayer meetings etc.

vet¹ /vet/ nc (informal) = veterinary surgeon.

vet² /vet/ vt (-tt-) (informal) to examine (a person, plan etc) closely and critically: He must be thoroughly vetted before he's given the job.

vet·er·an /'vetərən/ nc (also attrib) **1** a person who has a lot of experience: a veteran teacher. **2** a car built before 1916, esp before 1905: a veteran Rolls Royce. Compare vintage. **3** (US) a person who has been in the armed forces.

vet·eri·nary /'vetrɪnərɪ/ adj (attrib) of, concerned with, the diseases and injuries of (esp farm and domestic) animals: a veterinary surgeon/college.

ve·to¹ /'vi:təʊ/ nc (pl —es) a constitutional right of a sovereign, president, legislative assembly or other body, or a member of the United Nations Security Council, to reject or forbid something; statement that rejects or prohibits something: exercise one's (power of) veto.

ve·to² /'vi:təʊ/ vt to put a veto on (something): The police vetoed the demonstration that the workers wanted.

vex /veks/ vt (often passive) (formal) to annoy, cause distress in, (a person): He was vexed at his failure.

vex·ation /vek'seɪʃn/ nc,nu.

v.g. written abbr very good.

VHF /ˌvi: eɪtʃ 'ef/ abbr (radio) very high frequency. ⇨ UHF.

via /vaɪə/ prep (Latin) by way of: travel from London to Paris via Dover.

vi·able /'vaɪəbl/ adj capable of existing, developing and surviving. Opp non-viable.

vi·abil·ity /ˌvaɪə'bɪlətɪ/ nu.

vi·aduct /'vaɪədʌkt/ nc a long bridge (usually with many arches) carrying a road, railway or canal across a valley.

vi·al /vaɪl/ nc a small bottle (for medicine).

vibe /vaɪb/ nc (informal) a strong feeling or reaction: get good vibes from a new house.

vi·brant /'vaɪbrənt/ adj **1** vibrating: the vibrant notes of a cello. **2** (of colour, light) strong. **3** exciting and busy: the vibrant atmosphere during the ceremony.

vi·brate /vaɪ'breɪt/ vt,vi (to cause something) to move quickly and continuously backwards and

forwards: The house vibrates whenever a heavy lorry passes. The strings of a piano vibrate when the keys are struck.

vi·bra·tion /vaɪ'breɪʃn/ nc,nu.

vic·ar /'vɪkə(r)/ nc a priest of the Church of England in charge of a parish.

vicar·age /'vɪkərɪdʒ/ nc a vicar's home.

vi·cari·ous /vɪ'keərɪəs/ adj (formal) **1** experienced by watching or reading about other people doing it: vicarious pleasure from looking at sexy photographs. **2** experienced as a substitute for another person: vicarious punishment.

vi·cari·ous·ly adv

vice¹ /vaɪs/ nc,nu (a particular kind of) evil conduct or practice: Torture is a vice.

vice² (US = **vise**) /vaɪs/ nc an apparatus with strong clamps in which things can be held tightly while being cut, shaped etc.

vice- /vaɪs-/ prefix second in authority; deputy: the vice-chairperson; the Vice-President.

vice versa /ˌvaɪsə 'vɜːsə/ adj (Latin) the other way round; with the terms or conditions reversed: We gossip about them and vice versa (= and they gossip about us).

vi·cin·ity /vɪ'sɪnətɪ/ n (pl -ies) **1** nu (formal) nearness in space: in close vicinity to the church. **2** nc (usually the —) a neighbourhood: There isn't a good school in the vicinity.

vi·cious /'vɪʃəs/ adj (derog) given or done with evil or cruel intent: a vicious kick/look.

‚vicious 'circle nc a state of affairs in which a cause produces an effect which itself produces the original cause.

vi·cious·ly adv

vic·tim /'vɪktɪm/ nc a person, animal etc suffering injury, pain, loss etc because of circumstances, an event, war, an accident etc: the victims of the earthquake.

vic·tim·ize (also **-ise**) /-aɪz/ vt to cause (a person) to suffer ill-treatment unfairly: Trade union leaders claimed that some of their members had been victimized (e.g. by being dismissed).

vic·tim·iz·ation (also **-is·ation**) /ˌvɪktɪmaɪ'zeɪʃn/ nu

vic·tor /'vɪktə(r)/ nc (formal) a person who conquers or wins.

vic·tori·ous /vɪk'tɔːrɪəs/ adj having gained the victory.

vic·tori·ous·ly adv

vic·tory /'vɪktərɪ/ nc,nu (pl -ies) (an instance, occasion, of) success (in war, a contest, game etc): gain/win a victory over the enemy; a victory in a tennis competition. Opp defeat¹.

vid·eo /'vɪdɪəʊ/ adj (attrib) connected with (a) use on a TV screen etc: a video display unit; (b) reproducing vision using videotape: a video camera.

‚video cas'sette nc a cassette containing videotape (used in a video recorder).

'video (machine/recorder) nc an electrical apparatus that records and reproduces vision and sound using videotape.

'video·tape nc,nu (also attrib) a kind of magnetic tape used for recording sound and vision, e.g. of television programmes: a videotape recorder. □ vt (also video) to record (a TV programme) using a video recorder.

vie /vaɪ/ vi (pres p **vying**; pt,pp **vied**) **vie with sb/for sth** to compete (the usual word): The two *boys vied with one another for the first place.*

view¹ /vju:/ *n* **1** *nu* the ability to see or be seen: *Their view of the stage was blocked by her hat. The speaker stood in full view of the crowd. As they drove round the corner the house came into view/ the mountain went out of view.* **on view** being shown or exhibited: *Liz's photographs are on view at the local art gallery.* **2** *nc* (a picture, photograph etc of) an area seen from a particular position or place: *a house with a fine view of the mountains/a fine mountain view. We took* (i.e. photographed) *some superb views from the top of the hill.* **3** *nc* a special opportunity to see something: *a private view* (e.g. of paintings). **4** *nc* a personal opinion, thought or observation: *She has strong/no views on the subject. What are your views on marriage? In my view university education should be free.* **point of view** ⇨ point¹(2). **take a dim view of sb/sth** to consider a person, plan etc to be bad, hopeless. **5** *n sing* **with a view to doing sth** with a desired aim, intention: *He is studying maths with a view to becoming an engineer.* **6** **in view of sth** taking something into account: *In view of the weather, it seems silly to try. I'll be kind in view of her age.*
'view·finder *nc* a device in a camera showing the area etc that will be photographed.
'view·point *nc* = point of view.
view² /vju:/ *vt* **1** to look at, examine, (something): *view a situation/property.* **2** to consider (something): *The subject may be viewed in various ways. How do you view the situation?* (= What do you think about it?)
view·er *nc* (also *television viewer*) a person watching a television programme. Compare listener.

vig·il /'vɪdʒɪl/ *nc,nu* (an act of) staying awake to keep watch or to pray: *keep vigil over a sick child.*
vigi·lance /'vɪdʒɪləns/ *nu* (formal) the act of keeping watch: *use vigilance.*
vigi·lant /'vɪdʒɪlənt/ *adj* (formal) keeping careful watch.

vi·gnette /vɪ'njet/ *nc* (formal) a small illustration, short essay etc.
vi,gnette per'formance *nc* a good performance of a minor part in a drama.

vig·our (*US* = **vig·or**) /'vɪgə(r)/ *nu* mental or physical strength; energy.
vig·or·ous /'vɪgərəs/ *adj* strong; energetic.
vig·or·ous·ly *adv*

vile /vaɪl/ *adj* (**—r**, **—st**) **1** (derog) shameful and disgusting: *a vile person; vile habits/language.* **2** (informal) very bad: *vile weather.*
vile·ly /'vaɪllɪ/ *adv*

vil·ify /'vɪlɪfaɪ/ *vt* (*pt,pp* **-ied**) (formal) to say evil things about (a person).
vil·ifi·ca·tion /,vɪlɪfɪ'keɪʃn/ *nu*

vil·la /'vɪlə/ *nc* (*pl* **—s**) (V- in names) **1** a detached or semi-detached house: *No 13 Laburnum Villas.* **2** a country house with a large garden, esp in a place with a warm climate.

vil·lage /'vɪlɪdʒ/ *nc* (also *attrib*) an area of houses and streets, smaller than a town: *the village post office.*
vil·lager /'vɪlɪdʒə(r)/ *nc* a person who lives in a village.

vil·lain /'vɪlən/ *nc* (derog) (esp in stories and plays) a wicked person.

vil·lain·ous /'vɪlənəs/ *adj* (derog) wicked.
vil·lainy *nu* wicked behaviour.

vin·ai·grette /,vɪnɪ'gret/ *nu* a sauce made of oil, vinegar etc, used on salads.

vin·di·cate /'vɪndɪkeɪt/ *vt* (formal) to show or prove the truth, justice, validity etc of (something that has been attacked or disputed): *vindicate a claim. Events have vindicated his judgement/ actions.*
vin·di·ca·tion /,vɪndɪ'keɪʃn/ *nc,nu*
vin·dic·tive /vɪn'dɪktɪv/ *adj* (derog) wanting to hurt a person or have revenge.
vin·dic·tive·ly *adv*

vine /vaɪn/ *nc* **1** a kind of climbing plant producing grapes. **2** any plant that trails or climbs (e.g. ivy).
vine·yard /'vɪnjəd/ *nc* an area of land planted with vines for grapes.

vin·egar /'vɪnɪgə(r)/ *nu* an acid liquid used to flavour food and for pickling.
vin·egary /'vɪnɪgrɪ/ *adj* (tasting) like vinegar.

vin·tage¹ /'vɪntɪdʒ/ *adj* (attrib) of a period in the past and having a reputation for high quality: *a vintage car* (= one built between 1917 (or 1905) and 1930); *a vintage year* (= one in which good wine was made). Compare veteran(2).
vin·tage² /'vɪntɪdʒ/ *nc* (wine from) grapes of a particular year: *of the vintage of 1983.*

vi·nyl /'vaɪnɪl/ *nc,nu* (a kind of) tough flexible plastic, used for coverings, clothing etc.

vi·ola /vɪ'əʊlə/ *nc* a kind of stringed musical instrument larger than the violin.

vi·o·late /'vaɪəleɪt/ *vt* (formal) **1** to break (an oath, law, treaty etc). **2** to act towards (something) without proper respect: *violate a person's privacy.* **3** (old use) to rape (a person).
vi·o·la·tion /,vaɪə'leɪʃn/ *nc,nu*

vi·o·lence /'vaɪələns/ *nu* **1** the state of being violent: *the violence of the storm* **2** cruel and harmful behaviour or actions: *robbery with violence.*
vi·o·lent /'vaɪələnt/ *adj* **1** (attrib) using, showing, accompanied by, great force: *a violent wind/pain/ temper.* **2** (derog) using, caused by, violent behaviour: *a violent man; meet a violent death.*
vi·olent·ly *adv*

vi·olet /'vaɪələt/ *n* **1** *nc* a kind of small wild or garden plant with sweet-smelling flowers. **2** *nu* the bluish-purple colour (of wild violets).

vi·olin /,vaɪə'lɪn/ *nc* a four-stringed musical instrument played with a bow.
vi·ol·in·ist /-ɪst/ *nc* a person who plays a violin.

vi·ol·on·cello /,vaɪələn'tʃeləʊ/ *nc* (*pl* **—s**) (formal) = cello.

VIP /,vi: aɪ 'pi:/ *abbr* very important person.

vi·per /'vaɪpə(r)/ *nc* a kind of small poisonous snake.

vir·gin¹ /'vɜ:dʒɪn/ *adj* **1** (of a girl or woman) being a virgin. **2** pure and untouched: *virgin snow; virgin soil.*

vir·gin² /'vɜ:dʒɪn/ *nc* a person, esp a girl or woman, who has not experienced sexual intercourse.
vir·gin·ity /və'dʒɪnətɪ/ *nu* state of being a virgin.
Vir·go /'vɜ:gəʊ/ *n* the Virgin, sixth sign of the zodiac.

vir·ile /'vɪraɪl/ *adj* **1** having or showing strength, energy: *a virile style* (of writing). **2** (of a man) able to have sexual intercourse.

vir·il·ity /vɪ'rɪlətɪ/ *nu* masculine strength and vigour or sexual power.

vir·tu·al /'vɜ:tʃʊəl/ *adj* (*attrib*) (almost) as described but not accepted or stated openly: *a virtual defeat/confession*.

vir·tu·al·ly /-tʃʊlɪ/ *adv*

vir·tue /'vɜ:tʃu:/ *n* **1** *nc,nu* (any particular kind of) goodness or excellence: *Patience is a virtue.* **2** *nu* the ability to produce a definite result: *Have you any faith in the virtue of herbs to heal sickness?* **3** *nc,nu* (an) advantage: *The great virtue of the scheme is that it costs very little.* **4** *by/in virtue of sth* by reason of, because of, something: *He claims a pension by virtue of his age.*

vir·tu·ous /'vɜ:tʃʊəs/ *adj* morally good: *a virtuous wife.*

vir·tu·ous·ly *adv*

vir·tu·os·ity /,vɜ:tʃʊ'ɒsətɪ/ *nu* (*formal*) a special artistic or musical skill.

viru·lent /'vɪrʊlənt/ *adj* (*formal*) **1** (of poison) strong; deadly. **2** (of ill-feeling, hatred) very strong. **3** (of words etc) full of hatred. **4** (*attrib*) (of a disease etc) very dangerous.

viru·lent·ly *adv*

vi·rus /'vaɪrəs/ *nc* (*pl* **—es**) any of various poisonous living things, smaller than bacteria, causing the spread of infectious disease.

vi·sa /'vi:zə/ *nc* (*pl* **—s**) an official stamp or paper used to show that a person may visit a foreign country: *an entry/exit visa.*

vis·count /'vaɪkaʊnt/ *nc* a nobleman between an earl and a baron in rank.

vis·count·ess /-ɪs/ *nc* (**a**) the wife of a viscount; (**b**) a woman viscount.

vis·ible /'vɪzəbl/ *adj* that can be seen; that is in sight: *The eclipse will be visible to observers in western Europe.* Opp invisible.

'visible earnings *n pl* (*finance*) earnings from trade in goods. Compare invisible earnings.

vis·ibly /-əblɪ/ *adv* in a way that is obvious: *She was visibly annoyed.*

vis·ibil·ity /,vɪzə'bɪlətɪ/ *nu* (esp) the condition of the atmosphere for seeing things at a distance: *The plane returned because of poor visibility.*

vi·sion /'vɪʒn/ *n* **1** *nu* the ability to see: *his field of vision* (= all that he could see from a certain point). **2** *nu* the ability to imagine, think ahead etc: *A man or woman of vision is needed to run this company.* **3** *nc* something seen or imagined, dreamt etc: *visions of life in the future/of becoming a popstar/of missing the train. Have you ever had visions of great wealth?*

vi·sion·ary /'vɪʒənrɪ/ *adj* (*formal*) **1** existing only in the imagination and unlikely to happen: *visionary schemes.* **2** (of a person) having grand (and often impossible) ideas. □ *nc* (*pl* **-ies**) a visionary(2) person.

vis·it¹ /'vɪzɪt/ *nc* an act, time, of visiting: *pay a visit to a friend/a patient; a visit of several hours.*

vis·it² /'vɪzɪt/ *v* **1** *vt,vi* to go to see (a person); go to (a place) for a time: *visit a friend; visit Rome.* **2** *vt* to go to (a place) in order to inspect or examine it officially: *Restaurant and hotel kitchens are visited regularly by public health inspectors.*

visi·tor /'vɪzɪtə(r)/ *nc* a person who visits: *visitors to Paris; a visitor in a hotel; summer visitors to Greece. A mysterious visitor called at the house*

last night.

visi·ta·tion /,vɪzɪ'teɪʃn/ *nc* (*formal*) an official visit.

vi·sor /'vaɪzə(r)/ *nc* **1** the front part of a helmet or cap protecting the face or eyes.

vis·ta /'vɪstə/ *nc* (*pl* **—s**) **1** a distant view: *a vista of the church at the end of an avenue of trees.* **2** (*fig*) a series of scenes, events etc that one can look back on or forward to: *new vistas of scientific discoveries.*

vis·ual /'vɪʒʊəl/ *adj* concerned with, used in, seeing: *She has a visual memory* (= is able to remember well the things she sees).

,visual 'aids *n pl* (e.g. in teaching) pictures, filmstrips, films, video etc.

,visual dis'play unit *nc* (*computers*) (abbr VDU) an apparatus used to show information on a screen.

vis·ual·ly /'vɪʒʊəlɪ/ *adv*

vis·ual·ize (also **-ise**) /'vɪ:ʒʊəlaɪz/ *vt* to imagine (something) as a picture: *I remember meeting the man two years ago but I can't visualize him.*

vi·tal /'vaɪtl/ *adj* **1** (*tech*) of, connected with, necessary for, living: *Air is vital for all animals. It is a vital substance. The heart is a vital organ.* **2** greatest; indispensable: *be of vital importance; be vital to the enquiry.*

,vital sta'tistics *n pl* (**a**) the figures relating to the duration of life, and to births, marriages and deaths. (**b**) (*informal*) a woman's measurements at bust, waist and hips.

vi·tal·ly /'vaɪtəlɪ/ *adv: vitally important.*

vi·tal·ity /vaɪ'tælətɪ/ *nu* (*formal*) **1** capacity to endure, survive, perform functions: *Can an artificial language have any vitality?* **2** energy, liveliness: *the vitality of young children.*

vi·tal·ize (also **-ise**) /'vaɪtəlaɪz/ *vt* to put energy, strength, into (workers, a scheme etc).

vit·amin /'vɪtəmɪn/ *nc* any of a number of organic substances which are present in certain foods and are essential to the health of people and animals.

vit·reous /'vɪtrɪəs/ *adj* (*attrib; science*) of or like glass: *vitreous rocks.*

vit·ri·ol·ic /,vɪtrɪ'ɒlɪk/ *adj* (*derog*) (of words, feelings) full of abuse: *vitriolic language.*

vi·va·cious /vɪ'veɪʃəs/ *adj* lively; high-spirited: *a vivacious girl.*

vi·va·cious·ly *adv*

vi·vac·ity /vɪ'væsətɪ/ *nu*

viv·id /'vɪvɪd/ *adj* **1** (of colours etc) strong and bright: *a vivid flash of lightning.* **2** lively; active: *a vivid imagination.* **3** clear and distinct: *have vivid recollections of a holiday in Italy.*

viv·id·ly *adv*

vivi·sect /,vɪvɪ'sekt/ *vt* (*science*) to operate or experiment on (living animals) for scientific research.

vivi·sec·tion /,vɪvɪ'sekʃn/ *nc,nu*

vivi·sec·tion·ist /-ɪst/ *nc* a person who vivisects or considers vivisection to be justifiable.

vix·en /'vɪksn/ *nc* **1** a female fox. **2** (*derog*) a bad-tempered woman.

viz. /vɪz/ *adv* that is to say; namely: *There are two possibilities, viz. to wait for rain or look for water.*

vo·cabu·lary /və'kæbjʊlərɪ/ *n* (*pl* **-ies**) **1** *nu* the total number of words that make up a language: *No dictionary could list all the vocabulary of a language.* **2** *nc,nu* (the range of) words known to, or used by, a person, profession etc: *a writer with a large vocabulary; scientific vocabulary*.

vo·cal /'vəʊkl/ *adj* **1** (*attrib*) of, for, with or using, the voice: *the vocal organs* (e.g. the lips, tongue). **2** expressing feelings freely: *a vocal participant*.

ˌvocal 'cords *nc* (*anat*) a pair of folds of skin-like tissue in the throat, used to produce vocal sounds.

vo·cal·ly /-əlɪ/ *adv*

vo·cal·ist /'vəʊkəlɪst/ *nc* a singer.

vo·cal·ize (also **-ise**) /-aɪz/ *vt* to say or sing (something).

vo·ca·tion /vəʊ'keɪʃn/ *n* **1** *n sing* the feeling that one is called to (and qualified for) a certain kind of work (esp social or religious): *Nursing, said Florence Nightingale, is a vocation as well as a profession*. **2** *nu* a special ability (for something): *He has little or no vocation for teaching*. **3** *nc* a person's trade or profession.

vo·ca·tion·al /-ʃənl/ *adj* of or for a vocation(3): *vocational courses*.

vo·cif·er·ous /və'sɪfərəs/ *adj* (*formal*) making a loud, strong noise (of protest): *a vociferous reply/mob*.

vod·ka /'vɒdkə/ *nc,nu* (a portion of) a kind of strong alcoholic drink distilled from rye etc.

vogue /vəʊg/ *nc* (usually *sing*) **1** the current fashion; something currently being done or used: *Are personal computers the vogue?* **2** a popular use or acceptance: *The Beatles had a great vogue many years ago. When did pointed shoes come into/go out of vogue?* (= become popular/unpopular?)

voice¹ /vɔɪs/ *n* **1** *nc,nu* (the ability to produce) the sounds made when speaking or singing: *He lost his voice when he had a bad cold. Please lower your voice in the library. He spoke in a loud/soft voice*. **lose one's voice** to be unable to speak, e.g. because of illness. **raise one's voice** to shout. **shout at the top of one's voice** to shout as loudly as one can. **2** *nu* an act of expressing an opinion etc: *They gave voice to their anger*. **have/demand a voice in sth** to have/demand a right to express an opinion on it: *I have no voice in the matter*. **3** *nc* (*fig*) something expressing ideas, feelings etc: *the voice of experience*. **4** *nu* (*gram*) the form of the verb showing the relation between the subject and the verb. ⇨ active/passive (voice).

voice² /vɔɪs/ *vt* to put (an opinion, feeling etc) into words: *The spokesman voiced the feelings of the crowd*.

void¹ /vɔɪd/ *adj* (*pred*) **1** **void of sth** (*formal*) without something: *a subject void of interest*. **2** **null and void** ⇨ null.

void² /vɔɪd/ *n sing* (*formal*) an empty space: *There was an aching void in his heart* (= a strong feeling of sadness).

vol *written abbr* volume(3).

vol·atile /'vɒlətaɪl/ *adj* **1** (*science*) (of a liquid) that easily changes into gas or vapour. **2** (*formal; usually derog*) (of a person, mood) changing quickly or easily from one mood or interest to another.

vol·atil·ity /ˌvɒlə'tɪlətɪ/ *nu*

vol·ca·no /vɒl'keɪnəʊ/ *nc* (*pl* **—es**) a hill or mountain with an opening (*crater*) through which very hot gases, ashes, liquid 'rock' (*lava*) etc come

up from below.

vol·can·ic /vɒl'kænɪk/ *adj* of, from, like, a volcano.

vole /vəʊl/ *nc* a kind of animal like a mouse with a short tail.

vo·li·tion /və'lɪʃn/ *nu* (*formal*) the act of using one's own will, of choosing, making a decision etc: *do something of one's own volition*.

vol·ley¹ /'vɒlɪ/ *nc* **1** the throwing or shooting of a number of (stones, arrows, bullets etc) together. **2** a succession (of oaths, curses, questions). **3** (in tennis etc) a stroke which returns the ball before it touches the ground.

vol·ley² /'vɒlɪ/ *vt,vi* (in tennis etc) to return (a ball) before it touches the ground.

'volley·ball *nu* a game in which players on each side of a high net try hit a large ball with their hands over it without letting the ball touch the ground.

volt /vəʊlt/ *nc* (symbol V) (*electricity*) a unit of measurement of electrical force.

volt·age /'vəʊltɪdʒ/ *nc,nu* (an amount of) electrical force measured in volts.

vol·uble /'vɒljʊbl/ *adj* (*formal*) talking very quickly and easily

vol·ubly /-jʊblɪ/ *adv*

vol·ubil·ity /ˌvɒljʊ'bɪlətɪ/ *nu*

vol·ume /'vɒljuːm/ *n* **1** *nc* a book, esp one of a set of books: *an encyclopedia in 20 volumes*. **speak volumes for sb/sth** to give much significant information about a person, thing. **2** *nu* the power, amount (of sound): *turn the volume down*. **3** *nu* (abbr vol) an amount of space occupied by a substance, liquid or gas: *the volume of water in a tank*. Compare area(3). **4** *nc* a large mass, amount: *a volume of business/work*. **5** (*pl*) a large mass (of steam or smoke): *volumes of black smoke*.

vol·umi·nous /və'luːmɪnəs/ *adj* (*formal*) **1** having a large size, amount, extent: *voluminous skirts; a voluminous history of Europe*. **2** (of a person) producing many speeches or writings.

vol·un·tary /'vɒləntrɪ/ *adj* **1** doing or ready to do things willingly, without being forced; (something) done in this matter: *voluntary work/helpers; a voluntary confession*. **2** carried on, supported by people without payment: *overseas aid supported by voluntary organizations*. **3** (*science*) (of bodily, muscular, movements) done consciously or intentionally. Compare involuntary(2).

vol·un·tar·ily /'vɒləntrəlɪ/ *adv*

vol·un·teer¹ /ˌvɒlən'tɪə(r)/ *nc* a person who offers to do something (esp unpleasant or dangerous, or without being paid).

vol·un·teer² /ˌvɒlən'tɪə(r)/ *v* **1** *vi* to offer one's services as a volunteer: *volunteer to do the washing-up*. **2** *vt* to report (something) without being asked: *She volunteered some information*.

vo·lup·tu·ous /və'lʌptjʊəs/ *adj* of, for, causing or expressing sensual or sexual pleasure: *voluptuous beauty*.

vo·lup·tu·ous·ly *adv*

vom·it /'vɒmɪt/ *vt,vi* to throw up (food) from the stomach through the mouth: *He vomited everything he had eaten. He was vomiting blood*.

vomit *nu*

voo·doo /'vuːduː/ *nu* a form of religion, with

magic and witchcraft, practised in the Caribbean, esp Haiti.

vo·ra·cious /vəˈreɪʃəs/ *adj* (*formal*) very hungry or greedy: *a voracious appetite.*
vo·ra·cious·ly *adv*
vo·rac·ity /vəˈræsətɪ/ *nu*

vor·tex /ˈvɔːteks/ *nc* (*pl* **—es** or **vortices** /-tɪsiːz/) (*formal*) **1** a whirlpool. **2** any (esp violent) activity or situation considered as involving people's lives generally: *the vortex of war.*

vote¹ /vəʊt/ *nc* **1** (a right to give) an expression of opinion or will by a person for or against a person or thing, esp by ballot or by putting up of hands. ***cast one's vote*** to vote. ***vote of confidence*** a public expression of support. ***vote of thanks*** a public expression of thanking: *The chairperson proposed a vote of thanks to the speaker.* **2** the total numbers of votes (to be) given (e.g. at a political election): *Will the Labour vote increase or decrease at the next election?*

vote² /vəʊt/ *v* **1** *vi* **vote (for/against sb/sth)** to support/oppose (a person, idea etc) by voting: *voting for the motion/the Tories.* **vote on sth** to express an opinion about something by voting: *vote on nuclear disarmament.* **2** *vt* to agree to grant (money) (to): *voting a sum of money to the universities for equipment.* **3** *vt* (*informal*) to give an opinion of (a person): *He was voted a fine teacher.* **4** *vt* to suggest (something): *I vote (that) we avoid him in future.*
voter *nc* a person who votes(1).

vouch /vaʊtʃ/ *vi* **vouch for sb/sth** to be responsible for, express confidence in, a person, a person's character: *vouch for him/his ability.*
vouch·er /ˈvaʊtʃə(r)/ *nc* a receipt or document used instead of money. ⇨ gift voucher.
vouch·safe /vaʊtʃˈseɪf/ *vt* (*formal*) to be kind enough to give, do, (something): *He vouchsafed to help.*

vow¹ /vaʊ/ *nc* a solemn promise or undertaking: *marriage vows; a vow of chastity; break a vow.*
vow² /vaʊ/ *vt* **vow sth/to do sth/that** to promise or declare (something) solemnly: *He vowed to avenge/that he would avenge the insult.*
vow·el /ˈvaʊəl/ *nc* **1** a vocal sound made without audible stopping of the breath. **2** a letter or symbol used to represent such a sound (e.g. the letters *a, e, i, o, u*; the phonetic symbols /iː, ɪ, e, æ, ɑː, ɒ, ɔː, ʊ, uː, ʌ, ɜː, ə/). Compare consonant.

voy·age¹ /ˈvɔɪɪdʒ/ *nc* a journey, esp a long one, in a ship or boat (or a spacecraft): *a voyage from London to Australia; during the voyage out/home; on the outward/ homeward voyage.*
voy·age² /ˈvɔɪɪdʒ/ *vi* (*formal*) to go on a voyage: *voyaging through the South Seas.*
voy·ager /ˈvɔɪɪdʒə(r)/ *nc* a person who makes a voyage (esp a person who in former times explored unknown seas).

vs *written abbr* (*legal*) versus.
VSO /ˌviː es ˈəʊ/ *abbr* Voluntary Service Overseas (a British government organization sending qualified volunteers to work in developing countries).
vul·gar /ˈvʌlgə(r)/ *adj* (*derog*) **1** very rude; showing bad manners: *vulgar language/behaviour/ ideas; a vulgar person.* **2** showing the absence of taste¹(5): *vulgar patterns on the carpets.*
vulgar 'fraction *nc* (*maths*) (also called *simple fraction*) one written in the form ¾. Compare decimal fraction.

vul·gar·ity /vʌlˈgærətɪ/ *n* (*pl* **-ies**) (**a**) *nu* vulgar behaviour, language or taste¹(5). (**b**) (*pl*) vulgar acts, words etc.
vul·gar·ly *adv*

vul·ner·able /ˈvʌlnrəbl/ *adj* **vulnerable (to sth)** easily harmed or damaged; not protected against attack: *a vulnerable position; people who are vulnerable to criticism.* Opp invulnerable.
vul·ner·abil·ity /ˌvʌlnrəˈbɪlətɪ/ *nu*

vul·ture /ˈvʌltʃə(r)/ *nc* **1** a kind of large bird that lives on the flesh of dead animals. **2** (*fig; derog*) a greedy person who profits from the misfortunes of others.

vy·ing /ˈvaɪɪŋ/ *pres p* of vie.

Ww

W, w /ˈdʌblju:/ (*pl* **W's, w's** /ˈdʌblju:z/) the 23rd letter of the English alphabet.
W *symbol* **1** West. **2** (*commerce*) women's size (of clothes). **3** (*electricity*) watt(s).
w. *written abbr* **1** week. **2** width. **3** weight.
wad /wɒd/ *nc* **1** a lump of soft material used to keep things apart or in place, or to stop up a hole: *wads of cotton-wool.* **2** a collection (of banknotes, documents etc) folded or rolled together.
waddle /ˈwɒdl/ *vi, n sing* to/a walk with slow, wide steps like a duck's: *The baby waddled across the room.*
wade /weɪd/ *vi, vt* to walk with an effort (across a stream, through water, mud or anything that makes progress difficult): *He waded through the water.*
wade in (*informal*) to make a strong physical or verbal attack.
wade into sb/sth (*informal*) to attack a person, task etc with energy.
wade through sth (**a**) ⇨ above. (**b**) (*fig; informal*) to carry out a long task: *wading through the accounts/the paperwork.*
wa·fer /ˈweɪfə(r)/ *nc* a kind of thin, flat biscuit (as eaten with ice-cream).
waffle¹ /ˈwɒfəl/ *nc* a kind of sweet cake made of batter.
waffle² /ˈwɒfəl/ *nu* (*derog*) talk or writing which (even when it sounds impressive) means little or nothing.
waffle³ /ˈwɒfəl/ *vi* (*informal; derog*) to talk about something without giving any information, esp because one lacks any knowledge about the subject: *What's she waffling (on) about now?*
waft¹ /wɒft/ *nc* a light breeze, smell: *wafts of fresh air through the window.*
waft² /wɒft/ *vt* (of a breeze, light smell etc) to carry lightly and smoothly through the air or over water: *The scent of the flowers was wafted to us by the breeze.*
wag¹ /wæg/ *nc* a wagging movement: *with a wag of the tail.*
wag² /wæg/ *vt, vi* (**-gg-**) (to cause something) to move from side to side or up and down: *The dog wagged its tail.*
wage¹ /weɪdʒ/ *nc* (also *attrib*) a payment made or

received for work or services: *His wages are £50 a week. The postal workers have asked for a wage increase/rise of £25 a week.* Ⓝ *'Wage' is usually plural except when it is attrib, as in a wage freeze.* Compare fee(1), pay¹, salary.

waged *adj* employed. Opp unwaged.

'wage-earner *nc* a person who works for wages (contrasted with salaried staff.)

'wage freeze *nc* an official control of wage increases.

wage² /weɪdʒ/ *vt* to engage in (war etc).

wa·ger /'weɪdʒə(r)/ *nc, vt, vi* (to offer (something) as) a bet (the usual word): *I'll wager £5 that the horse wins.*

waggle /'wægl/ *vt, vi* = wag².

wag·gon (*US* usually **wag·on**) /'wægən/ *nc* **1** a four-wheeled vehicle used for carrying goods, pulled by horses or oxen. Compare cart¹. **2** an open railway truck (e.g. for coal) (*US = freight car*).

wa·gon-lit /ˌvægɒn 'liː/ *nc* (*pl* **wagons-lit**) a carriage for sleeping in a train (as on European railways).

waif /weɪf/ *nc* a poor, homeless child: *waifs and strays* (= homeless and abandoned children).

wail¹ /weɪl/ *nc* a wailing sound.

wail² /weɪl/ *vi* **1** to cry or complain about something in a loud voice: *babies who wail at night.* **2** to make a similar sound (e.g. of a siren): *an ambulance racing through the streets with sirens wailing.* **3** (of the wind) to make similar sounds.

wain·scot /'weɪnskət/ *nc* a wooden structure along the bottom of the walls of a room.

waist /weɪst/ *nc* **1** the part of the body between the ribs and the hips: *He measures 60 centimetres round the waist.* **2** that part of clothing that goes round the waist. **3** the middle and narrow part: *the waist of a violin.*

'waist·band *nc* a part of a skirt etc that fits round the waist.

ˌwaist-'deep *adj, adv* up to the waist: *waist-deep in the mud.*

ˌwaist-'high *adj, adv* high enough to reach the waist: *The wheat was waist-high.*

'waist·line *nc* the part of the body, a dress etc at the smallest part of the waist: *a dress with a narrow waistline.*

waist·coat /'weɪskəʊt/ *nc* a close-fitting, sleeveless article of clothing worn under a jacket, esp as part of a man's suit.

wait¹ /weɪt/ *n* **1** *nc* an act or time of waiting: *We had a long wait for the bus.* **2** *nu* **lie in wait for sb/sth** to be hiding in order to attack etc: *The cat lay in wait for the bird to fly down.*

wait² /weɪt/ *vi* to stay in one place or position, delay acting, (until a person arrives, something happens etc): *Please wait a minute. How long have you been waiting? We're waiting for an answer/until he arrives/for her to come/(in order) to see what will happen. Wait a bit/moment/while, I'll soon be ready.* **keep sb waiting** to prevent a person from doing something by not arriving at the agreed time, by doing something else that takes time etc: *He kept me waiting for an hour while he had a bath.* **wait and see** (esp *imperative*) to do nothing and watch the progress of events. **sb can't wait** (*informal*) a person is too excited etc to be patient: *He says he'll bring it*

tomorrow and I can't wait (to see it). **sth can wait** a task can be delayed because it is not important: *That job can wait until tomorrow.* **(just) you wait** (used to express an angry threat of revenge): *You wait—I'll get my revenge!*

wait about/around to stay in a place because a person has not arrived etc.

wait at tables ⇨ table¹(1).

wait behind to stay in a room etc after others have left: *Some students waited behind to talk to the teacher after the lesson.*

wait for sb/sth ⇨ 1 above. **wait for it** (*informal; imperative*) to delay beginning until the correct moment. **wait for me** (*imperative*) go more slowly so that I am not left behind.

wait on sb to do things, bring and take things for a person: *She waits on her husband far too much.* ⇨ also hand¹(1). **wait on tables** ⇨ table¹(1).

wait sth out to wait calmly until an unpleasant period is finished: *wait out a storm.*

wait up (for sb) to stay out of bed (until a person comes home).

wait·er /'weɪtə(r)/ *nc* a man who serves food etc in a restaurant. ⇨ waitress.

wait·ing list /'weɪtɪŋ lɪst/ *nc* a list of people who want something, e.g. medical treatment, tickets.

wait·ing-room /'weɪtɪŋ rʊm/ *nc* a room for people to wait, e.g. to see a doctor, to catch a train etc.

wait·ress /'weɪtrɪs/ *nc* a woman who serves food etc in a restaurant. ⇨ waiter.

waive /weɪv/ *vt* to (say that one will) give up (a right or claim): *waive the age-limit.*

wake¹ /weɪk/ *nc* (esp in Ireland) an all-night watch with a dead body before burial.

wake² /weɪk/ *nc* a track left by a ship on smooth water. **in the wake of sth** after; following: *Traders arrived in the wake of the explorers.*

wake³ /weɪk/ *v* (*pt* **woke** /wəʊk/, *pp* **woken** /'wəʊkən/) **1** *vi* **wake (up)** to stop sleeping: *What time do you usually wake (up)? He woke (up) with a start* (= suddenly). **2** *vt* **wake sb (up)** (**a**) to cause a person to stop sleeping: *Don't wake the baby. The noise woke me (up).* (**b**) (*fig*) to cause a person to become active, interested etc: *He needs someone to wake him up/needs waking up.* ⇨ awake.

wak·ing *adj* (*attrib*) not being asleep: *one's waking hours* (= the time when one is not asleep); *waking or sleeping* (= while awake or asleep). ⇨ awake.

wak·en /'weɪkən/ *vt, vi* (to cause a person) to stop sleeping. ⇨ awake, awakening. Ⓝ *'Wake (sb) (up)'* is much more usual than *'waken (sb)'*.

walk¹ /wɔːk/ *nc* **1** a journey on foot, esp for pleasure or exercise: *go for a walk. The station is ten minutes' walk from my house.* **2** a manner or style of walking: *I recognized him at once by his walk.* **3** a path or route for a walk(1): *my favourite walks in the neighbourhood.* **4** **walk of life** (usually *pl*) a profession, occupation: *They interviewed people from all walks of life.*

walk² /wɔːk/ *v* **1** *vt, vi* (to cause a person, animal) to move by putting forward each foot in turn: *We walked five miles. He walked up and down the station platform. She's walking the dog in the park. Do you walk to work? Can I walk with you?*

We like to walk while we're on holiday. **2** *vt* to go over, through etc (a place) on foot: *We walked everywhere looking for a room. I've walked all these mountains.* **3** *vt* to go with (a person) on foot: *Can I walk you home?*

walk about to walk in various directions, e.g. as a tourist. Hence **'walk·about** *nc* a walk among spectators in the streets (as a politician etc does).

walk away with sth to win a competition, prize etc easily: *The Russian team walked away with the gymnastics competition.*

walk by (sb/sth) to pass a person, place, while walking.

walk in to enter a room etc: *Look who's walked in!*

walk into sb/sth to meet with a person, group, something unpleasant, by accident: *walk into an ambush.*

walk off with sth to take something (either on purpose or by accident): *Someone has walked off with my umbrella.* **walk sb off her/his feet** ⇨ **foot¹**(1).

walk out to leave a place of work and go on strike: *The workers walked out yesterday.* Hence **'walk-out** *nc.* **walk out (on sb)** *(informal)* to abandon a person (e.g. at a time when he or she is expecting help etc).

walk (all) over sb *(informal)* to defeat a person easily: *She walked all over the other competitors.* Hence **'walk-over** *nc* an easy victory.

walk up (sth) (a) *(imperative)* (used as an invitation to enter a circus, show etc). **(b)** to walk along: *walk up the High Street.* **(c)** to walk upstairs. **walk up (to sb)** to approach: *A stranger walked up (to me) and asked me the time.*

walk·about /'wɔːkəbaʊt/ *nc* ⇨ walk about.

walk-out /'wɔːk aʊt/ *nc* ⇨ walk out.

walk-over /'wɔːk əʊvə(r)/ *nc* ⇨ walk (all) over sb.

wall¹ /wɔːl/ *nc* **1** an upright solid structure of stone, brick etc forming one of the sides of a building or room, or used to enclose, divide or protect something (including land): *Hang the picture on that wall. Some old towns have walls right round them.* **walls have ears** a person who should not hear may be listening. **be/go up the wall** *(sl)* to be/become very angry. **go to the wall** to be defeated, especially financially. **2** *(fig)* something like a wall: *a wall of fire; the abdominal wall.*

'wall·paper *nc,nu* paper with a coloured design, used for covering the walls of rooms.

,wall-to-'wall *adj (attrib)* covering the whole floor: *wall-to-wall carpets.*

wall² /wɔːl/ *vt* **1** (usually *pp*) to surround (something) with walls: *a walled garden.* **2** **wall sth in/off/up** to fill or close up an empty space with bricks etc: *wall up a window.*

wal·la·by /'wɒləbɪ/ *nc (pl* **-ies)** a kind of small animal like a kangaroo.

wal·let /'wɒlɪt/ *nc* a folding case of leather etc, used for banknotes, credit cards etc.

wal·lop¹ /'wɒləp/ *n sing (informal)* a heavy blow or fall: *Down he went with a wallop!*

wal·lop² /'wɒləp/ *vt (informal)* to beat (a person) severely; hit (a person) hard.

wal·low /'wɒləʊ/ *vi* **wallow (in sth) 1** to roll about (in mud, dirty water etc): *pigs wallowing in*

the mud. **2** *(fig)* to take great delight in something: *wallowing in her success.*

wal·nut /'wɔːlnʌt/ *n* **1** *nc* (a kind of tree producing) a large nut with a wrinkled seed that can be eaten. **2** *nu* the wood, used for making furniture.

wal·rus /'wɔːlrəs/ *nc (pl* **—es)** a sea-animal like a large seal, with two long tusks.

waltz¹ /wɔːls/ *nc* (the music for) a slow ballroom dance.

waltz² /wɔːls/ *vt,vi* (to accompany a person) to dance a waltz: *She waltzes well.* **waltz off with sth** *(informal)* to gain a prize etc by defeating others easily.

wan /wɒn/ *adj* **1** (of a person, expression) looking ill, sad, tired, anxious: *a wan smile.* **2** (of light, the sky) pale; not bright.

wan·ly *adv*

wand /wɒnd/ *nc* a stick used by a conjurer, fairy or magician.

wan·der /'wɒndə(r)/ *v* **1** *vi,vt* to go from place to place without any special purpose or destination: *wander about; wander up and down the road; wander (through/over) the world. Some of the sheep have wandered away. We wandered (for) miles and miles in the mist.* **2** *vi* to allow one's thoughts to go from subject to subject: *Don't wander off the subject/point. His mind is wandering.*

wan·der·er *nc* a person or animal that wanders.

wan·der·ings *n pl* **(a)** long travels; journeys: *tell the story of one's wanderings.* **(b)** a confused speech during illness (esp high fever).

wan·der·lust /'wɒndəlʌst/ *nu* the strong desire to travel.

wane¹ /weɪn/ *n* (esp) **on the wane** becoming less: *Her popularity is on the wane.*

wane² /weɪn/ *vi* **1** (of the moon) to show a decreasing bright area after a full moon. Opp wax³. **2** to become less or weaker: *His strength/reputation is waning.*

wangle /'wæŋgl/ *vt (sl)* to get, arrange, (something) by using unfair influence, trickery, persuasion etc: *wangle an extra week's holiday.*

want¹ /wɒnt/ *n* **1** *nu* the state of being absent: *The plants died from want of water. Your work shows want of thought/care.* **2** *nu* need: *The house is in want of repair.* **3** *nc* (usually *pl*) a desire for something as necessary to life, happiness etc; thing to be desired: *We can supply all your wants.*

want² /wɒnt/ *v* Ⓝ Not usually used in continuous tenses, e.g. *is/was -ing.* **1** *vt* to feel a desire or need for (a person, thing): *I want a better job. She wants to go to Italy. Do you want me to go with you? I want you near me during the trial. What do you want for your birthday? I don't want him to come. I've been wanting to do that for a long time.* ⇨ **badly**(7). Ⓝ *'Want'* is used when referring to something that is possible to have or get. *'Wish'* is used when referring to something impossible or unlikely, e.g. *I wish I had more money.* **2** *vt* to need (something to be done): *Your hair wants cutting. This car wants a good clean.* **3** *vi,vt* (used to make a polite suggestion, question, reply etc about what a person should like to happen): *Do you want me to stay? If you want to.* **4** *vt* **want to do sth** ought to do something: *You want to see your teacher about that problem.* **5** *vt (passive)* being looked for, sought, (by officials) for a reason:

He's wanted by the police for murder. **6** *vi* to be without enough food, money etc: *He'll never want while his mother is alive.* **want for nothing** to have all one needs. **7** *vi* **want in/out** (*informal*) to desire to be included/not included in a scheme etc. **8** **be (found) wanting (in sth)** to be considered to be lacking strength, personality, training etc: *He was tested and found wanting.*

want ad /'wɒnt æd/ *nc* (*informal*) a small advertisement in a newspaper or magazine for something needed or desired.

wan·ton /'wɒntən/ *adj* (*attrib*) deliberate, bad and without any reason: *wanton destruction/ damage.*

wan·ton·ly *adv*

war¹ /wɔː(r)/ *n* **1** *nc,nu* (a state, period, of) the use of weapons when fighting between countries or rival groups in a nation: *We have had two world wars in this century.* **at war** in a state of war. **declare war (against/on sth)** to announce that a state of war exists (with another state). **have been in the wars** (*informal*) to have suffered injury, bad luck etc. **2** *nu* the science or art of fighting, using weapons etc: *the art of war.* **3** *nc* (*fig*) any kind of struggle or conflict: *the war against disease/poverty; a war of nerves/words.*

war·fare /'wɔːfeə(r)/ *nu* (the condition of) being at war: *the horrors of modern warfare.*

'war·head *nc* (of a torpedo, shell etc) an explosive head.

'war·like *adj* (**a**) ready for, suggesting, war: *warlike preparations.* (**b**) (*derog*) fond of war: *a cruel, warlike people.*

'war·monger *nc* (*derog*) a person who encourages war.

'war·path *n* (only in) **on the warpath** ready for a fight or quarrel; very angry.

'war·ship *nc* a ship for use in war.

'war·time *nu* the period when there is war.

war² /wɔː(r)/ *vi* (**-rr-**) to take part in a war.

warble /'wɔːbl/ *vi, nc* (esp of birds) (to sing with) a gentle trilling note: *a blackbird warbling in a tree.*

war·bler *nc* a kind of bird that warbles.

ward¹ /wɔːd/ *nc* **1** a division, separate room, of a hospital: *the children's ward.* **2** a division of a local government area, each division being represented by one councillor. **3** a person under the guardianship of an older person or of law authorities.

ward² /wɔːd/ *vt* **ward sth off** to keep something away, avoid something: *ward off a blow/danger/ an illness.*

war·den /'wɔːdn/ *nc* **1** a person having control or authority: *the warden of a youth hostel; a game warden* (who guards wild animals in a park). ⇨ also *traffic warden.* **2** (*US*) = warder.

war·der /'wɔːdə(r)/ *nc* (*GB*) a person who guards prisoners.

ward·robe /'wɔːdrəʊb/ *nc* **1** a tall cupboard with pegs, shelves etc for clothes. **2** a stock of clothes: *My wardrobe needs to be renewed.*

ware·house /'weəhaʊs/ *nc* a building for storing goods before distribution to retailers. □ *vt* /-haʊz/ to store (goods) in a warehouse.

wares /weəz/ *n pl* (*commerce*) articles offered for sale: *advertise one's wares.*

war·fare /'wɔːfeə(r)/ *nu* ⇨ war¹.

warm¹ /wɔːm/ *adj* (**—er, —est**) **1** having a medium degree of heat (between *cool* and *hot*): *Come and get warm by the fire.* **2** (of clothing) used to keep the body warm: *Put your warmest coat on.* **3** (of colours) bright; suggesting heat: *Red and yellow are warm colours.* **4** (*attrib*) enthusiastic, hearty: *give a speaker a warm welcome.* **5** sympathetic; affectionate: *He has a warm heart.* Compare cold¹, cool¹.

,warm-'blooded *adj* (of an animal) having a body temperature that is controlled by itself, usually higher than its surroundings. Compare cold-blooded.

,warm-'hearted *adj* kind and sympathetic. Opp cold-hearted.

warm·ly *adv* in a warm manner: *warmly dressed; thank them warmly.*

warm² /wɔːm/ *n sing* **1** an act of warming: *Come near the fire and have a warm.* **2** a warm place: *stay in the warm.*

warm³ /wɔːm/ *vt,vi* (to cause a person, thing) to become warm or warmer: *warm oneself/one's hands by the fire. Please warm* (*up*) *this milk.* **warm to/towards sb/sth** to become more interested and involved in a person, idea etc. **warm up** (of an athlete, player etc) to exercise as a preparation for an event.

warmth /wɔːmθ/ *nu* the state of being warm: *He was pleased with the warmth of his welcome.*

warn /wɔːn/ *vt* to inform (a person) of possible danger or unpleasant consequences; inform in advance of what may happen: *He was warned of the danger. He often warned me that there were pickpockets in the crowd/warned me against* (i.e. about) *pickpockets.*

warn·ing¹ /'wɔːnɪŋ/ *adj* (*attrib*) that warns: *They fired some warning shots.*

warn·ing² /'wɔːnɪŋ/ *n* **1** *nc* something that warns or serves to warn: *Let this be a warning to you.* **2** *nu* the state of being warned: *The speaker sounded a note of warning* (= spoke of possible danger).

warp¹ /wɔːp/ *nc* **1** a twisted or bent condition in a piece of wood etc caused by shrinking or expansion. **2** (usually the —) the threads over and under which other threads (the *weft*) are passed when cloth is woven.

warp² /wɔːp/ *vt,vi* **1** (to cause something) to become bent or twisted from the usual or natural shape: *Some metals warp in very hot weather.* **2** (*fig*) (to cause a person, character etc) to become evil: *warp a child's mind.*

warp·ed *adj* (**a**) bent or twisted: *warped wood.* (**b**) (*fig*) evil; cruel: *He has a warped sense of humour.*

war·rant¹ /'wɒrənt/ *nc* a written order giving official authority: *a warrant for his arrest.*

war·rant² /'wɒrənt/ *vt* to make (something) seem justified: *His interference was certainly not warranted. His anger is not warranted.*

war·ran·ty /'wɒrəntɪ/ *nc* (*pl* **-ies**) a (written or printed) guarantee (e.g. to repair or replace defective goods): *The car is still under warranty.*

war·ren /'wɒrən/ *nc* **1** an area of land in which there are many burrows in which rabbits live and breed. **2** (*fig*) a building or district in which it is difficult to find one's way about: *lose oneself in a warren of narrow streets.*

war·rior /'wɒrɪə(r)/ nc (formal or literary) a soldier; fighter.

wart /wɔ:t/ nc a kind of small, hard, dry growth on the skin.

wart-hog /'wɔ:thɒg/ nc a kind of African pig with two large tusks and growths like warts on the face.

wary /'weərɪ/ adj (-ier, -iest) **wary (about/of sb/sth)** careful about possible danger or trouble: be wary of giving offence/of strangers.
war·ily /-əlɪ/ adv

was /wəz strong form: wɒz/ ⇨ be.

wash¹ /wɒʃ/ n sing **1** an act of washing or being washed: Will you give the car a wash, please? **2** (the —) (also the washing) clothing, sheets etc (to be) washed: When does the wash come back from the laundry? **3** (the —) the movement or flow of water: the wash of the waves.

wash² /wɒʃ/ v **1** vi,vt to make (oneself, a person, thing) clean using water or another liquid: wash one's hands/face; wash the baby. Have you washed? He never washes in cold water. This soap will wash the dirt out/away/off. **2** vi (of materials) to be able to be washed without damage, loss of colour etc: Does the cloth wash well? **3** vi (fig) to be acceptable: That argument/excuse won't wash (with me). **4** vt,vi (of waves etc) to flow over or against: The sea washes the base of the cliffs. The waves were washing against the boat/over the stones. **5** vt (of a mass of water) to carry (a person, thing) in the direction mentioned: He was washed overboard by a huge wave/washed under by the current.

wash sb/sth away to remove a person, object etc by washing(4): The cliffs are being washed away by the tide.

wash sth down (with sth) (a) to clean something (using a flow of water e.g. from a hosepipe): wash down a car; wash the sides of a boat down. (b) to eat or drink something and then swallow (liquid): bread and cheese washed down with beer.

wash sth off ⇨ 1 above.

wash sth out to clean (the inside of) something: wash out a saucepan. **be washed out** (a) (of a game, sport) to be cancelled because of heavy rain. (b) (of roads etc) to be flooded. (c) (fig) (of a person) to be exhausted. Hence **'wash-out** nc (informal) (a) a cancelled game or sport. (b) a useless person.

wash over sb (of noise, tension, quarrelling) to happen near a person who ignores it and is not affected: The sound of the children fighting seemed to wash over her.

wash (sth) up to clean plates, knives, forks, pans etc: wash up the breakfast things. It's your turn to wash up. Hence **,washing-'up** n (the —) such an activity: do the washing-up. **be (all) washed up** to be ruined, at an end: Their marriage is washed up. **be washed up (on sth)** to be carried onto the beach etc by the waves.

wash·able /'wɒʃəbl/ adj (of clothes etc) that can be washed without being spoiled.

wash-basin /'wɒʃ beɪsn/ nc a basin fixed in a bathroom etc, used to wash one's hands and face etc.

wash·er /'wɒʃə(r)/ nc **1** = washing-machine. **2** = dishwasher. **3** a small flat ring of metal, plastic etc, used for making a joint or screw tight.

wash·ing /'wɒʃɪŋ/ nu **1** the act of washing or being washed. **2** (the —) clothes etc (to be) washed: put out the washing on the line to dry.

'wash·ing-machine nc an electrical apparatus used for washing clothes.

'washing-line nc a length of rope etc used to hang up wet washing.

'washing-powder nc,nu a kind of powdered soap or detergent used for washing clothes etc.

,washing-'up ⇨ wash (sth) up.

,washing-'up liquid nc.nu a liquid detergent used for washing dishes, cutlery etc.

,washing-'up machine nc = dishwasher (which is more usual).

wash-out /'wɒʃ aʊt/ nc ⇨ be washed out.

wash·room /'wɒʃrʊm/ nc (esp US) a toilet.

wasn't /'wɒznt/ = was not. ⇨ be.

wasp /wɒsp/ nc a kind of flying insect with a powerful sting in its tail.

wast·age /'weɪstɪdʒ/ nu the amount wasted; loss by waste.

waste¹ /weɪst/ adj (attrib) **1** (of land) that is not or cannot be used; no longer of use. **laid waste** (of land) destroyed, badly damaged. **2** useless; thrown away because not wanted: waste paper.

waste² /weɪst/ n **1** nu or sing an act of wasting or being wasted: It's a waste of time to wait any longer. **go to waste** to be wasted: What a pity to see so many ideas going to waste! **2** nu waste material; refuse. **3** nc an area of unused or unusable land etc: the wastes of the Sahara.

waste³ /weɪst/ **1** vt to make no use of (something); use without a good purpose; use more of (something) than is necessary: waste one's time and money on silly things. All his efforts were wasted. **2** vt, vi (to cause a person) to lose strength gradually: He's wasting away.

waste·ful /'weɪstfəl/ adj causing waste; using more than is needed: wasteful habits/processes.
waste·ful·ly /-fəlɪ/ adv

waste(-pa·per) bas·ket /,weɪst 'peɪpə bɑ:skɪt, 'weɪst bɑ:skɪt/ nc a container used in a room, office etc for unwanted paper.

waste-pipe /'weɪspaɪp/ nc a pipe used for carrying away used water.

watch¹ /wɒtʃ/ n **1** nc a small instrument used for telling the time, worn on the wrist or carried in a pocket: a wrist-watch; a pocket-watch. My watch is slow/fast/has stopped. **2** nu an act of watching or being watched. **keep watch (on sb/sth)** to be watching a person, thing carefully: keep a close watch on her. **3** (the —) people employed or used to guard a place. **4** (the —) (sailors on duty during) a period of two or four hours at sea.

'watch-strap nc a small strip of metal etc, used to fasten a watch(1) to the wrist.

watch² /wɒtʃ/ v **1** vi,vt to look at (a person, thing) for a period: Watch me carefully. Watch how I do it. We sat watching the TV/the football game. If you hate the sight of blood, don't watch. **2** vt to pay attention to (something): Watch that step. Please watch the baby while I'm out. Watch what you say in the interview. **watch it** (informal; imperative) be careful. **watch one's step** ⇨ step¹(1).

watch out (often imperative) to be careful (about a possible danger): You'd better watch out or you'll be sacked. **watch out (for sb/sth)** to look carefully and be ready (for an important person or thing): *You must watch out for any signs of the infection.*

watch over sb to be responsible for health, safety, happiness etc of a person: *A teacher watches over all the students.*

watch·dog /'wɒtʃdɒg/ *nc* a dog used to guard property.

watch·er /'wɒtʃə(r)/ *nc* a person who watches.

watch·man /'wɒtʃmən/ *nc* (*pl* **-men**) a man who guards property, esp at night: *He has a job as a night-watchman.*

wa·ter¹ /'wɔ:tə(r)/ *n* (*pl* only as shown in examples below) **1** *nu* the liquid in rivers, lakes, seas etc: *Fish live in water.* **by water** by boat, ship etc: *travel by water.* **blood is thicker than water** ⇨ blood(2). **be in deep water** to be in serious trouble or difficulty. **under water** flooded: *The fields were under water after the heavy rain.* **(take to sth) like a duck to water** ⇨ duck¹(1). **like water off a duck's back** without having any obvious effect: *Her criticism was like water off a duck's back—I ignored it.* **like a fish out of water** ⇨ fish¹(1). **be in/get into hot water** to have/get into trouble (esp because of foolish behaviour etc). **hold water** (of a theory, excuse etc) to be believed when tested. **keep one's head above water** ⇨ head¹(1). **pass water** to urinate. **spend (money) like water** to spend money extravagantly. **throw cold water on sth** to discourage a plan etc. **tread water** to keep oneself at the surface in deep water by moving the feet up and down. **2** *nu* the state of the tide: *at high/low water.* **3** (*pl*) seas (as described): *home waters* (= the seas near the country to which a ship belongs). **4** *nu* a solution of a substance in water: *rose-water.*

'water·bird *nc* any kind of bird that swims or wades in water.

'water-biscuit *nc* a kind of thin, hard biscuit eaten with butter and cheese.

'water-borne *adj* **(a)** (of goods) carried by water. **(b)** (of diseases) passed on by infected water.

'water-buffalo *nc* the common domestic buffalo of India, Indonesia etc.

'water-closet *nc* (abbr WC) (*dated*) a small room with a lavatory.

'water-colour (*US* = **-color**) **(a)** (*pl*) paints (to be) mixed with water, not oil. **(b)** a picture painted with water-colours. **(c)** (*pl* or *sing*) the art of painting such pictures.

'water·cress *nu* a creeping plant that grows in running water with hot-tasting leaves, used in salads.

'water·fall *nc* a long fall of water, esp where a river falls over rocks or a cliff.

'water·front *nc* the land at the water's edge, esp the part of a town facing the harbour etc.

'water-hole *nc* a shallow place in which water collects (esp in a dry river bed, and to which animals go to drink).

'water-ice *nc,nu* frozen, flavoured water.

'water-lily *nc* (*pl* **-ies**) a kind of plant with round leaves floating on the surface of water.

'water-logged *adj* thoroughly soaked or filled with water.

'water-main *nc* the main pipe in a system of water-supply.

'water·mark *nc* **(a)** a manufacturer's design in some kinds of paper. **(b)** a mark that shows how high water (e.g. the tide, a river) has risen or how low it has fallen.

'water·melon *nc* (a plant with) a large, smooth-skinned melon with juicy pink or red flesh.

'water-pipe *nc* a pipe for carrying water.

'water polo *nu* a game played by two teams of swimmers who try to throw a ball into a goal.

'water-power *nu* the power obtained from flowing or falling water, used to drive machinery or produce electricity.

'water·proof *adj* that does not let water in or through: *a waterproof watch; waterproof material.* □ *vt* to make (cloth etc) waterproof.

'water-ski *nc, vi* (one of a pair of skis used) to ski on water while being towed by a fast motor-boat. Hence **'water-skiing** *nu*

'water-supply *nc* (*pl* **-ies**) the system of providing and storing water for a town, building etc.

'water-table *nc* the level below which the ground is filled with water: *The water-table has been lowered by drought.*

'water·tight *adj* **(a)** so that water cannot get in or out: *watertight boots.* **(b)** (*fig*) (of an agreement etc) so that there can be no escape from any part of it; leaving no possibility of misunderstanding.

'water·works *nu* or *pl* **(a)** a system of reservoirs, pumping stations, for supplying water. **(b)** (*informal*) the working of the bladder: *Are your waterworks all right?* (= Can you pass urine normally?)

wa·ter² /'wɔ:tə(r)/ *v* **1** *vt* to put water on (plants): *water the lawn/the plants.* **2** *vt* to give water to (an animal): *water the horses.* **3** *vi* (of the eyes or mouth) to fill with water: *The smoke made my eyes water.* ⇨ mouth¹(1). **4** **water sth down (a)** to add water to a drink: *This whisky has been watered down.* **(b)** (*fig*) to weaken a report: *The story was watered down.*

'watering-can *nc* a container with a long spout, used for watering plants.

'watering-place *nc* **(a)** a water-hole. **(b)** a spa.

wa·tery /'wɔ:tərɪ/ *adj* (**-ier**, **-iest**) **1** of or like water; containing, cooked in, too much water: *watery soup.* **2** (of colour) pale. **3** (of the eyes etc) filled with water.

watt /wɒt/ *nc* (symbol W) (*electricity*) a unit of measurement of electrical power: *a 60-watt light-bulb.*

wave¹ /weɪv/ *nc* **1** a long ridge of water, esp on the sea, curling over and breaking on the shore. ⇨ crest(4). **in waves** in successive lines like waves: *The infantry attacked in waves.* **2** an act of waving(2); waving movement: *with a wave of his hand.* **3** a curve like a wave of the sea: *the waves in her hair.* **4** a steady increase and spread: *a wave of enthusiasm/hatred.* ⇨ also crime wave, heatwave. **5** (*science*) a motion like a wave by which heat, light, sound or electricity is spread or carried. **6** (also *waveband*) (*radio*) a group of wavelengths used for radio broadcasts: *This radio has short wave and long wave. Which waveband is the station on?*

wave² /weɪv/ *v* **1** *vi* to move to and fro, up and down: *flags/branches waving in the wind.* **2** *vt,vi* (to cause something) to move in this way (e.g. to make a signal or request, to give a greeting etc): *wave one's hand/a flag. He waved at us. She waved (goodbye) to us.* **3** *vt* to cause (a person) to move in a certain direction by waving: *He waved us away/on.* **wave sth aside** (*fig*) to show that something is not at all important: *My objections were waved aside.* **4** *vi* (of a line or surface, of hair) to be in a series of curves: *Her hair waves beautifully.* **5** *vt* to cause (hair) to be in a series of curves: *She's had her hair permanently waved.*

wave·band /'weɪvbænd/ *nc* ⇨ wave¹(6).

wave·length /'weɪvleŋθ/ *nc* (*science*, esp *radio*) the distance between the highest point of one wave(5) and that of the next. **(not) on the same wavelength** (*fig*) (not) in agreement.

wa·ver /'weɪvə(r)/ *vi* **1** to move uncertainly or unsteadily: *wavering shadows/flames.* **2** to be or become unsteady: *His courage wavered.* **3** to hesitate: *waver between two opinions.*

wa·ver·er *nc* a person who hesitates.

wavy /'weɪvɪ/ *adj* (**-ier, -iest**) having curves: *a wavy line; wavy hair.*

wax¹ /wæks/ *nu* **1** the soft yellow substance produced by bees and used for making honeycomb cells: *beeswax.* **2** a kind of substance similar to beeswax, used for making candles etc: *a wax candle.* ⇨ sealing-wax. **3** the soft brown substance produced in the ear.

waxy *adj* (**-ier, -iest**) of, like, wax.

wax² /wæks/ *vt* to cover, polish or treat (furniture, wood etc) with wax: *wax furniture/a wooden floor.*

wax³ /wæks/ *vi* (of the moon) to show an increasing bright area. Opp wane²(1).

way¹ /weɪ/ *adv* (*informal*) at a considerable distance: *They must be way past Stratford by now.*

way² /weɪ/ *n* **1** *nc* a path, road or route etc: *a way across the fields. Can you tell me the way to the library, please? Which is the quickest/shortest way there? I can't find my way home. Which is the way in/out? Don't stand in my/the way. It's a long way* (= far) *from here.* **by way of** (**a**) using a route through: *travel to Cambridge by way of London.* (**b**) as a substitute for: *say a few words by way of an introduction.* **by the way** (often used to introduce a related remark or a sudden thought): *By the way, what happened to your sister?* **on the way; on her/their etc way** coming (or going): *The police are on their way.* **be on the way out** (*fig*) to be going out of fashion. **out of harm's way** in a safe place: *put the knife/be out of harm's way.* **cut both ways** (of an action, argument) to have an effect both in favour and against. **feel one's way** (**a**) to go forward carefully using touch as if in the dark. (**b**) (*fig*) to make careful progress: *feel one's way towards an agreement.* **get sth out of the way** to settle a difficulty. **give way (to sb/sth)** (**a**) to allow a person, vehicle etc to pass first: *Give way to traffic on your right.* (**b**) to be replaced by something: *Tears gave way to smiles.* (**c**) to agree to the demands of a person, organization: *We won't give way to terrorists.* (**d**) (*formal*) to abandon oneself to a feeling: *give way to despair.* **go one's own way** to act as one wants to. **go a long way (towards sth)** to be a helpful contribution: *This will go a long way to meeting expenses.* **go one's way** to leave. **go**

out of one's way (to do sth) to make a particular effort: *He went out of his way to be rude to me.* **lead the way** (**a**) to go ahead as a leader. (**b**) to show by example how something can be achieved. **make way (for sb/sth)** to allow enough space (for a person, vehicle etc to pass): *All traffic must make way for an ambulance.* **pave the way for sth** (*fig*) to prepare people in order that ideas, changes etc will be accepted. **pay one's way** to provide one's share of the expenses. **make one's way in life/the world** to succeed. **show sb the way** to show how something should be done by doing it as an example. **2** *nc* a method, plan; course of action: *Which is the best/right way to do it/of doing it? You'll be successful whichever way you choose. This work must be finished (in) one way or another. One way to do it is to jump straight in. She has a peculiar way of dressing.* **ways and means** methods, esp of providing money. **get/ have one's own way** to do what one wants to do. **learn sth the hard way** to learn by suffering, having to make an extra effort etc. **take the easy way out** to do what is easier (but often not as useful or productive). **3** *nc* a way of behaving; habit; custom: *English/Chinese ways of living. I didn't like the way he looked at me. What way do they dress in Nigeria?* **to my way of thinking** in my opinion: *To my way of thinking, the green one is best.* **mend one's ways** to improve one's behaviour, manners: *I've warned her to mend her ways.* **the way of the world** what people do generally: *There will always be things that succeed and things that fail—that's the way of the world.* **4** *nc* a direction: *He went this/that way. Look both ways before you cross the road.* **come one's/ sb's way** to happen to oneself, a person: *Such a fine opportunity never came my way before.* **be set in one's ways** to be unwilling to change one's ideas or habits. **5** *nc* a detail, degree; condition: *He's a clever man in some ways. She's a pleasant person in her own way. In a way I agree with you but not altogether. Things are/She's in a bad way. You can't have it both ways, you must either spend the money on a ticket or walk.* **in a small way** to a small but important degree: *This book should help in a small way to improve your English.* **in every way** in all details or aspects: *This is better than other books in every way.* **6** *nu* forward movement; progress. **be/get (sth) under way** (of a ship or a project, scheme etc) to be making progress/start to make progress: *Let's get this new sales plan under way.*

way·farer /'weɪfeərə(r)/ *nc* (*literary*) a traveller, esp one who is walking.

way·lay /ˌweɪ'leɪ/ *vt* (*pt,pp* **-laid** /-'leɪd/) to stop (a person) unexpectedly in order to attack, make a request etc: *He waylaid me with a request for a loan.*

way-out /ˌweɪ 'aʊt/ *adj* (*informal*) extremely modern or strange: *way-out clothes.*

way·side /'weɪsaɪd/ *n sing* (also *attrib*) the side of a road: *by the wayside; wayside flowers.*

way·ward /'weɪwəd/ *adj* not easily controlled or guided: *a wayward child.*

WC /ˌdʌblju: 'si:/ *abbr* water closet (the toilet).

we /wi:/ *pron* (used by a speaker or writer referring to herself or himself and another or others):

Can we all come to visit you? We're late. We've already seen it. ⇨ **us.**

WEA /ˌdʌblju: i: 'eɪ/ *abbr* Workers' Educational Association (a government organization for adult education).

weak /wiːk/ *adj* (**—er, —est**) **1** (of the body) having little power or energy: *have a weak heart; feeling weak after a long illness.* Opp strong(1). **2** (of the mind) not confident, sure or determined: *have a weak will/imagination.* Opp strong(2). ⇨ **weak-minded/-willed.** ⇨ also **head¹**(2). **3** easily broken, damaged etc: *a weak material/structure.* Opp strong(3). **4** easily defeated or changed: *a weak theory/argument.* Opp strong(4). **5** easily beaten or defeated: *a weak candidate/player.* Opp strong(5). **6** having little effect on the senses: *weak soup/tea; a weak colour/smell/taste.* Opp strong(6). **7** (*pred*) **weak (in sth)** not having a high standard: *weak in spelling/grammar. His vocabulary is weak.*

'**weak form** *nc* (*lang*) the way of saying a word when it is not emphasized, such as *can* /kən/, *must* /məst/, *shall* /ʃəl/. Compare strong form.

,**weak-'minded** *adj* (*derog*) having a mind that is not determined or energetic. Opp strong-minded.

'**weak verb** *nc* (*gram*) a verb that forms tenses by additions to the stem, not by vowel changes (e.g. *walk, walks, walked*). Compare strong verb.

,**weak-'willed** *adj* (*derog*) not at all determined. Opp strong-willed.

weak·ly *adv* in a weak manner.

weak·ness *n* (**a**) *nu* the state of being weak: *the weakness of old age.* (**b**) *nc* a fault or defect of character: *We all have our little weaknesses.* (**c**) **have a weakness for sb/sth** to have a special or foolish liking for a person, thing: *He has a weakness for ice-cream.*

weak·en /'wiːkən/ *vt,vi* (to cause a person, liquid, determination etc) to be or become weak(er). Opp strengthen.

weak·ling /'wiːklɪŋ/ *nc* (often *derog*) a physically weak person or animal.

weal /wiːl/ *nc* a mark on the skin made by a blow from a whip etc.

wealth /welθ/ *n* **1** *nu* (the possession of) a large amount of property, money etc: *a man of wealth.* **2** *n sing* a large amount of number of: *a book with a wealth of illustrations; the wealth of phrases and sentences to illustrate meanings in this dictionary.*

wealthy *adj* (**-ier, -iest**) (of a person) rich.

wean /wiːn/ *vt* **1** to accustom (a baby, a young animal) to food other than its mother's milk. **2** (*fig*) to cause (a person) to turn away (from a bad habit etc): *wean a person off/away from drugs.*

weap·on /'wepən/ *nc* something designed for, or used in, fighting or struggling (e.g. swords, guns, bombs, fists, a strike by workers).

weap·on·ry *nu* weapons collectively.

wear¹ /weə(r)/ *nu* **1** wearing or being worn; use as clothing: *This coat is beginning to look the worse for wear.* **2** the loss of quality from use: *The carpet is showing signs of wear.* **wear and tear** damage, loss in value, because used. **3** the capacity for keeping in good condition: *There's not much wear left in these tyres.*

wear² /weə(r)/ *nu* (*commerce*) clothes: *children's/sports/men's wear.*

wear³ /weə(r)/ *vt,vi* (*pt* **wore** /wɔː(r)/, *pp* **worn** /wɔːn/) **1** *vt* to have (something) on the body or on some part of it: *He was wearing a coat/glasses/heavy shoes/a ring on his finger. She never wears green* (i.e. green clothes). *She used to wear her hair long* (= used to have long hair). **2** *vt* to have (an expression) on the face: *wear a smile.* **3** *vt,vi* (to cause something) to become less useful or be in the condition mentioned by being used: *I have worn my socks into holes. This material has worn thin. The stones were worn by the constant flow of water.* **4** *vt* to make (a hole, groove etc) in (something) by rubbing or use etc: *wear holes in a rug/one's socks. In time a path was worn across the field.* **5** *vi* to remain in the condition mentioned (after use): *Good leather will wear for years. This cloth has worn well/badly. Old Mr Smith is wearing well* (= looks well in spite of being old).

wear away (**a**) to become broken, thin, weak, as the result of use: *The inscription on the stone had worn away.* (**b**) (of time) to pass slowly: *as the evening wore away.* **wear sth away** to use up or damage something by constant use etc: *The footsteps of thousands of visitors had worn away the stones.*

wear (sth) down (to cause something) to become gradually shorter, lower etc: *The heels of these shoes are wearing down.* **wear sb down** to weaken a person, thing, by constant attack, nervous strain etc: *These noisy children do wear me down!*

wear off to disappear gradually: *The excitement will soon wear off.*

wear on (of time) to pass: *as the evening wore on.*

wear (sth) out (to cause something) to become useless, worn thin, exhausted: *Cheap shoes soon wear out. His patience had/was at last worn out.* **wear sb out** to exhaust, tire out a person: *I'm worn out by all this hard work.*

wear·able /'weərəbl/ *adj* that can be, is fit to be, worn.

wear·ing /'weərɪŋ/ *adj* tiring (the usual word): *This is a wearing task.* ⇨ also hardwearing.

weari·some /'wɪərɪsəm/ *adj* tiring; long and dull: *a wearisome journey.*

weary¹ /'wɪərɪ/ *adj* (**-ier, -iest**) **1** physically tired: *feel weary.* **2** (usually *pred*) mentally tired: *weary of all her complaints.* **3** (*attrib*) causing tiredness: *a weary journey.* **4** (*attrib*) showing tiredness: *a weary sigh.*

weary² /'wɪərɪ/ *vi,vt* **weary (of sth); weary sb (with sth)** (to cause a person) to become weary: *weary of living alone; wearying me with her problems.*

wear·ily /-əlɪ/ *adv*
weari·ness *nu*

wea·sel /'wiːzl/ *nc* a kind of small, fierce animal with red-brown fur.

weath·er¹ /'weðə(r)/ *nu* (also the **—**) the conditions of temperature, wind, rain etc in a place at a certain time: *He stays indoors in wet weather. What's the weather like outside?* Ⓝ *'Climate'* is used when referring to a long period of time. **in all weathers** in all kinds of weather: *She goes out in all weathers.* **be/feel under the weather** (*informal*) to be/feel unwell. **make heavy weather of sth** to make a task (seem to be) difficult.

'weather-beaten *adj* showing signs of being in the sun, wind, rain etc: *a weather-beaten face.*

'weather-bound *adj* unable to make or continue a journey because of bad weather.

'weather-chart/-map *nc* a diagram showing details of the weather over an area.

'weather forecast *nc* one giving details of weather expected in an area.

'weather-station *nc* a building where the weather is observed.

'weather-vane *nc* = vane(1).

weath·er² /'weðə(r)/ *v* **1** *vt* (*literally* and *fig*) to come through (something difficult) safely or successfully: *weather a storm/crisis.* **2** *vt, vi* (to cause something) to discolour, become worn, by the weather: *rocks weathered by wind and rain.*

weave¹ /wi:v/ *nc* a style of weaving.

weave² /wi:v/ *v* (*pt* **wove** /wəʊv/, *pp* **woven** /'wəʊvən/) **1** *vi, vt* to make (threads) into cloth etc; make (cloth etc) from threads: *weave cotton thread into cloth.* **2** *vt* to make (garlands, baskets etc) by a similar process: *weave flowers into a wreath; weave a garland of flowers.* **3** *vt, vi* (*fig*) to put together, compose (a story etc): *weave a plot.* **get weaving (on sth)** (*informal*) to make an energetic start (on a task etc). **4** *vi, vt* to twist and turn: *The driver was weaving* (*his way*) *through the traffic.*

weaver *nc* person who weaves cloth.

web /web/ *nc* **1** a net made of threads by a spider. ⇨ cobweb. **2** (*fig*) an arrangement as a trap or barrier: *a web of* (= many) *lies.* **3** the skin joining the toes of some waterbirds and animals. Hence ,**web-'footed** *adj.*

wed /wed/ *vt, vi* (*pt, pp* **-ded** or —; **-dd-**) to marry (the usual word). **be wedded to sth** to be devoted to, unable to give up, a sport, idea etc: *He is wedded to his own opinions and nothing can change him.*

Wed written *abbr* Wednesday.

we'd /wi:d/ = *we had; we would.*

wed·ding /'wedɪŋ/ *nc* (also *attrib*) a marriage ceremony (and festivities connected with it): *attend/invite one's friends to a wedding; the wedding dress.*

'wedding breakfast *nc* a meal for the bride and bridegroom, their relatives, friends etc after a wedding.

'wedding-ring *nc* a ring placed on the bride's or groom's finger at a wedding.

wedge¹ /wedʒ/ *nc* **1** a V-shaped piece of wood or metal, used to split wood or rock (by being hammered), to widen an opening or to keep two things separate. **the thin end of the wedge** (*fig*) a small change or demand likely to lead to big changes or demands: *Closing one department is the thin end of the wedge—the whole factory may be closed soon.* **2** (also *attrib*) something shaped like or used like a wedge: *wedge heels* (*on shoes*).

wedge² /wedʒ/ *vt* to fix (something) tightly (as if) with a wedge: *wedge a door open* (= by placing a wedge under it*); be tightly wedged between two fat women on the bus; be wedged in.*

wed·lock /'wedlɒk/ *nu* (*formal*) the condition of being married: *born out of wedlock* (of unmarried parents).

Wed·nes·day /'wenzdɪ/ *nc* (also *attrib*) the

fourth day of the week: *I'll see you on Wednesday/next Wednesday afternoon. On Wednesdays* (= Every Wednesday) *I go swimming.*

wee¹ /wi:/ *adj* (usually *attrib*) very small: *I'll have a wee drop of brandy in my coffee.*

wee², wee-wee /'wi:/ wi:/ *nu* (as used by and to small children) urine. □ *vi* to pass urine.

weed¹ /wi:d/ *nc* **1** a wild plant growing where it is not wanted (e.g. in a garden). **2** (*fig; derog*) a thin or timid person.

weedy *adj* (**-ier, -iest**) (**a**) full of, overgrown with, weeds. (**b**) (*derog*) tall, thin, weak: *a weedy young man.*

weed² /wi:d/ *vt, vi* **1** to take weeds out of (the ground): *weed the garden.* **2** to remove, get rid of, (what is unwanted or of lower value than the rest): *weed out the lazy students.*

weeds /wi:dz/ *n pl* (also *widow's weeds*) black clothes as (formerly) worn by a widow for mourning.

week /wi:k/ *nc* **1** any period of seven days (esp seven days from Saturday midnight to Saturday midnight): *I'm on duty this/next week. I saw her last week. Let's meet this day week* (= one week from today)*/on Monday week* (= one week from next Monday)*; for the last/next six weeks; a six weeks' holiday; a week tomorrow/tomorrow week* (i.e eight days from today); *for weeks* (= for a long time); *all week* (through) (= during the whole week). **week in, week out** for weeks in succession. **2** the working days of the week: *work a 5-day week; the working week* (usually Monday to Friday).

'week·day *nc* any day except Sunday: *I'm always busy on weekdays.*

,**week·'end** *nc* Saturday and Sunday (as a period of rest or holiday): *spend the weekend with friends; a weekend holiday.* **a long weekend** one (for a holiday etc) including Friday or Monday. □ *vi* to spend a weekend: *I'm weekending at Brighton.*

week·ly *adj, adv* (happening) once a week, every week; of, for or lasting a week: *a weekly wage of £120; weekly visits.* □ *nc* (*pl* **-ies**) a magazine etc published once a week.

weep /wi:p/ *vi, vt* (*pt, pp* **wept** /wept/) to cry: *weep for joy. She wept to see him so ill. She wept over her sad fate. She wept bitter tears.*

weep·ing /'wi:pɪŋ/ *adj* (*attrib*) (of a tree) having drooping branches.

wee·vil /'wi:vl/ *nc* a kind of small beetle with a hard shell, feeding on stores of grain, nuts and other seeds.

weft /weft/ *nc* (usually the —) threads over and under which other threads (the *warp*) are passed when cloth is made.

weigh /weɪ/ *vt* **1** to measure (by means of a scale, balance etc) how heavy something is: *He weighed himself on the scales.* **2** to show a certain measure when put on a scale etc: *weigh 10 kilos/a ton/ nothing.* **weigh a ton** ⇨ ton(2). **3** to compare the importance, value etc of (one thing and another): *weigh one plan against/with another.*

weigh against sb (of age, lack of experience etc) to cause a person to be unsuccessful or not accepted for a job. ⇨ also **3** above.

weigh sb down to make a person tired, depressed, troubled etc: *weighed down with sor-*

row/cares/anxieties. **weigh sth down** to pull or bring something down: *The fruit weighed the branches down.*

weigh in (at sth) (of a boxer, jockey etc) to weigh (an amount mentioned) before a fight, race etc. **weigh in (with sth)** (*informal*) to produce (strong arguments, facts) in a discussion; to give one's skills, influence etc to: *We all weighed in with offers of help.*

weigh on sb/sth to cause a person, one's mind etc concern or anxiety (because of importance, seriousness): *The problem/responsibility weighs heavily on him/his mind.*

weigh sth out to measure an amount of something by weight: *weigh out a kilo of apples.*

weigh sth up to consider the possibilities, evidence etc before deciding.

weigh with sb to influence a person: *evidence that did not weigh with the judges.*

weight¹ /weɪt/ *n* **1** *nu* how heavy a person or thing is as measured by a system such as kilos: *That man is twice my weight. My weight is 70 kilos/I'm 70 kilos in weight. I'm over/under weight* (= weigh too much/too little). Ⓝ Scientists now use *'mass'.* **pull one's weight** to do one's fair share of the work. **put on/lose weight** (of a person) to become heavier/lighter. **throw one's weight about** to try to make people obey one's orders, accept one's ideas etc because one considers oneself to be more important. **2** *nc* a metal object of an exact weight used to measure the weight (*mass*) of another thing. **3** *nc* a heavy object (as used to keep something in position): *a paper weight. My shopping bag is such a weight!* **4** *n sing* a load to be supported: *The walls have to support the weight of the roof. That's a great weight* (= anxiety, problem etc) *off my mind.* **5** *nu* (a degree of) importance or influence. **carry weight** to have influence or value: *Her opinions don't carry a lot of weight.*

weight² /weɪt/ *vt* **1** to put a weight(2) on (something): *weight a fishing line.* **2** **weight sb down (with sth)** (usually *passive*) to burden a person (using): *He was weighted down with suitcases.*

weight·ed /'weɪtɪd/ *adj* (*pred*) giving advantage: *The system is weighted towards the richer countries.*

weight·less /'weɪtlɪs/ *adj* having no weight (e.g. as in space).

weight-lift·ing /'weɪtlɪftɪŋ/ *nu* the sport of picking up heavy weights for exercise or competition.

weight-watch·er /'weɪt wɒtʃə(r)/ *nc* a person trying to become lighter using a diet.

weighty /'weɪtɪ/ *adj* (-**ier**, -**iest**) **1** very heavy: *a weighty bag.* **2** (*fig*) having strong influence; important: *weighty arguments/considerations.*

weir /wɪə(r)/ *nc* a wall or barrier across a river or canal used to control the flow of water.

weird /wɪəd/ *adj* **1** unnatural; strange: *weird shrieks from the ruined castle.* **2** (*informal*) very unusual: *Have you seen the weird make-up some people use?*

weird·ly *adv*

weird·ness *nu*

wel·come¹ /'welkəm/ *adj* **1** wanted; received with, giving, pleasure: *a welcome visitor/rest; welcome news.* Compare unwelcome. **make sb welcome** to be friendly and pleased to see a

guest etc. **2** (*pred*) **welcome (to sth)** (a) allowed with pleasure to do something: *You are welcome to borrow my bicycle.* (b) (*ironic*) allowed to have something burdensome or unwanted: *If anyone thinks he can do this job any better, he's welcome (to it)/welcome to try!* **3** (used as an *int*): *Welcome home! Welcome to England!*

wel·come² /'welkəm/ *nc* a greeting, response by word or action, when a person arrives, when an offer is received etc: *They gave us/We received a very warm/cold/enthusiastic welcome.* **outstay one's welcome** to stay until one is no longer a wanted guest.

wel·come³ /'welkəm/ *vt* to show pleasure or satisfaction at (something), at the arrival of (a person or thing): *welcome a friend to one's home; welcome a suggestion.*

weld¹ /weld/ *nc* a welded join.

weld² /weld/ *v* **1** *vt* to join (pieces of metal) by hammering or pressure (usually when the metal is softened by heat) or fusing; make by doing this: *weld the pieces of a broken axle; weld parts together.* **2** *vi* (of iron etc) to be capable of being welded: *Some metals weld better than others.*

wel·der *nc* a person who welds metal parts.

wel·fare /'welfeə(r)/ *nu* (also *attrib*) the condition of having good health, comfortable living and working conditions etc: *work for the welfare of the nation; child/infant/social welfare; be concerned about the welfare of the family; welfare workers.*

,Welfare 'State *nc* (or the —) (a country with) State-financed social services, e.g. health, insurance, pensions.

well¹ /wel/ *adj* (*pred*) (**better**, **best**) **1** in good health: *be/look/feel well. I'm quite well, thank you.* **get well** to recover from an illness etc: *I hope you get well soon.* Compare ill¹(1). **2** in a satisfactory condition: *All's well that ends well.* ⇨ all³(1). **It's all very well . . .** (used ironically to show discontent, dissatisfaction, disagreement etc): *It's all very well (for you) to suggest a holiday in Italy, but how am I to find the money?* **3** advisable; desirable: *It would be well to start early.*

well² /wel/ *adv* (*comp* **better**, *superl* **best**) **1** in a good, right or satisfactory manner: *The children behaved well. They are well-behaved children. I hope everything's going well with you/the business. Does this colour go well with* (= suit) *that colour?* **do well** to make good progress; succeed: *Simon did well at school last year.* **be doing well** (used in the continuous tenses only) to be making a good recovery after being ill etc. **do well out of sth** to make a good profit from a sale, agreement etc. **get well (soon)** to recover from an illness (quickly): *I hope you get well soon.* **Well done!** (used to express congratulations). **2** with good reason; fairly; advisably: *You may well be surprised. I couldn't very well refuse to help. It's just as well* (= There's no need for regret, no harm done after all) *I didn't lend him the money. It may well be* (= It is possible) *that I can help you. You may well be right.* **may as well** ⇨ may(3). **3** thoroughly; completely: *Examine it well before you buy it. Clean it well before you eat it.* **well and truly** + *adj* completely: *She's well and truly defeated this time.* **4** very much: *He must be well past 40/well over 40 years old. It's well past mid-*

night. Your name is well up the list. This is well below the minimum standard. **well off** wealthy: *They're extremely well off.* **be well out of sth** to be fortunate to be free from a commitment etc: *The project is going badly—you're well out of it.* **pretty well** ⇨ pretty². **5 as well (as)** in addition (to): *He gave me money as well as advice. Give me those as well* (= also). Ⓝ For a comparison of *as well, also* and *too,* ⇨ also(1).

well³ /wel/ *int* **1** (expressing astonishment): *Well, who would have thought he'd do that? Well, well!* **2** (expressing relief): *Well, here we are at last!* **3** (expressing resignation): *Well, there's nothing we can do about it.* **4** (expressing understanding or agreement): *'Can I borrow your bike?' 'Very well, but bring it back by 7 o'clock.'* **5** (expressing hesitation etc): *Well, I'll think about it.* **6** (used to resume a story etc): *Well, as I was saying, . . .*

well⁴ /wel/ *nu* good fortune, success, etc: *I wish him well.* **let well alone** to decide not to change what is already satisfactory.

well⁵ /wel/ *nc* **1** a place for obtaining water from an underground source: *drive/sink a well.* **2** a hole bored for mineral oil: *oil wells.* **3** a tall space in a building for a staircase or lift: *a stair well.*

well⁶ /wel/ *vi* to flow like water from a well: *The blood was welling out (from the wound). Tears welled (up) in her eyes.*

we'll /wiːl/ = *we shall; we will.*

well-ad·vised /ˌwel ədˈvaɪzd/ *adj* wise: *You'd be well-advised to apologize.*

well-bal·anced /ˌwel ˈbælənst/ *adj* sane, sensible.

well-be·haved /ˌwel bɪˈheɪvd/ *adj* behaving well: *well-behaved children.*

'well-be·ing /ˈwel biːɪŋ/ *nu* welfare; health, happiness and prosperity: *the well-being of the nation.*

well-bred /ˌwel ˈbred/ *adj* of good upbringing.

well-earn·ed /ˌwel ˈɜːnd/ *adj* fully deserved: *well-earned praise; a well-earned rest.*

well-found·ed /ˌwel ˈfaʊndɪd/ *adj* based on good evidence: *well-founded suspicions.*

well-heel·ed /ˌwel ˈhiːld/ *adj* (*informal*) rich.

well-in·form·ed /ˌwel ɪnˈfɔːmd/ *adj* having much knowledge about something: *well-informed sources.*

wel·ling·ton /ˈwelɪŋtən/ *nc* (also *wellington boot*) a kind of tall rubber boot: *a pair of wellingtons.*

well-in·ten·tion·ed /ˌwel ɪnˈtenʃnd/ *adj* showing good intentions.

well-known /ˌwel ˈnəʊn/ *adj* (*attrib*) (*well known* when *pred*) known by many.

well-man·ner·ed /ˌwel ˈmænəd/ *adj* having good social manners. Opp ill-mannered.

well-mean·ing /ˌwel ˈmiːnɪŋ/ *adj* = well-intentioned.

well-meant /ˌwel ˈment/ *adj* done, said etc with good intentions.

well-nigh /ˈwel naɪ/ *adv* almost: *It's well-nigh impossible.*

well-off /ˌwel ˈɒf/ *adj* rich: *well-off students.*

well-read /ˌwel ˈred/ *adj* having a mind full of ideas, information, as the result of reading much.

well-spoken /ˌwel ˈspəʊkən/ *adj* speaking well, politely.

well-thought-of /ˌwel ˈθɔːt əv/ *adj* having a good reputation.

well-timed /ˌwel ˈtaɪmd/ *adj* done, said, at the right or a suitable time.

well-to-do /ˌwel tə ˈduː/ *adj* wealthy; from a high social class.

well-tried /ˌwel ˈtraɪd/ *adj* (of methods, remedies) tested and proved useful.

'well-wish·er /ˈwel wɪʃə(r)/ *nc* a person who wishes another person good luck.

well-worn /ˌwel ˈwɔːn/ *adj* (*fig; derog*) used, heard, often (and so dull): *well-worn expressions.*

wel·ter /ˈweltə(r)/ *n sing* a confusing mixture: *the welter of political beliefs.*

wel·terweight /ˈweltəweɪt/ *nc* (also *attrib*) a boxer weighing between 135 and 147 lb (61 and 66·6 kg).

went /went/ *pt* of go².

wept /wept/ *pt,pp* of weep.

were /wɜː(r)/ *pt* of be¹.

we're /wɪə(r)/ = *we are.*

weren't /wɜːnt/ = *were not.*

were-wolf /ˈwɪəwʊlf/ *nc* (*pl* -wolves /-wʊlvz/) (in stories) a human being turned into a wolf.

west¹ /west/ *adj* (*attrib*) from, in, towards, the west: *a west wind; living on the west side of the river.* ⇨ western.

west² /west/ *adv* towards the west: *to travel/face west.* **west of (a place)** farther west than a place.

west³ /west/ *n* **1** (the —) the direction, point, where the sun goes down. **2** that part of a country, the world etc in this direction: *the west of Europe; life in the West* (i.e. in Europe or N America).

,West 'End *n* (the —) the part of London with theatres, large, fashionable shops etc.

west·er·ly /ˈwestəlɪ/ *adj, adv* in a western position or direction.

west·ern¹ /ˈwestən/ *adj* (*attrib*) of, from, in, the west part of a country, continent, the world etc: *western religions; western dress; western Europe.*

,Western 'Hemisphere *n* (the —) N and S America.

west·ern·ize (also **-ise**) /-aɪz/ *vt* to introduce western civilization into (a population).

west·ern·most /-məʊst/ *adj* farthest west.

west·ern² /ˈwestən/ *nc* a film, story etc dealing with the life of settlers and cowboys in the western part of the USA esp during the time of the wars with the American Indians.

west·ward /ˈwestwəd/ *adj* towards the west: *in a westward direction.*

west·wards /-wədz/ *adv*: *travel westwards.*

wet¹ /wet/ *adj* (**—ter**, **—test**) **1** covered or soaked with water or other liquid: *wet clothes/roads. Did you get wet?* (e.g. in the rain?) *You're dripping/ soaking/wringing wet* (= very wet). **wet through** soaked: *Your coat is wet through.* Opp dry(1). **2** rainy: *wet weather.* Opp dry(2). **3** (*sl; derog*) (of a person) without courage, strong personality etc.

,wet 'blanket *nc* (*informal; derog*) a person who prevents others from enjoying themselves by being gloomy or bad-tempered.

wet² /wet/ *n* **1** (the —) rain: *Come in out of the wet.* **2** *nu* moisture.

wet³ /wet/ *vt* (*pt,pp* **wet** or **—ted**; **-tt-**) to make (something) wet: *The baby has wet its bed again.*

we've /wiːv/ = *we have.*

whack¹ /wæk/ nc **1** (a sound of) a hard blow. **2** (sl) share: *You'll get your fair whack.*

whack² /wæk/ vt to hit (a person, thing) with a hard blow, object.

whack·ed /wækt/ adj (pred) (informal) (of a person) worn out; very tired: *I feel whacked.*

whack·ing¹ /'wækɪŋ/ adj, adv (informal) very big of its kind; very: *a whacking lie; a whacking great lie.*

whack·ing² /'wækɪŋ/ nc a beating: *give a child a whacking.*

whale /weɪl/ nc **1** a kind of very large sea animal. **2 have a whale of a (good) time** (informal) to have a very enjoyable time.

wharf /wɔːf/ nc (pl —s or **wharves** /wɔːvz/) a wooden or stone structure at which ships (un)load cargo.

what¹ /wɒt/ adj or det **1** (used with a noun asking information about identity, type, characteristics etc): *What books have you read about it? Tell me what films you've seen. What kind of fish is it? What colour/size/shape is it? What time is it?* **2** (used for emphasis): *What a good idea! What big teeth you have! 3* the, those: *Give me what money you can afford. What few friends she had were very kind to her.*

what² /wɒt/ pron **1** (used when asking for information): *What's her name? What do you want? What can I say? Tell me what happened. What is the time? What's the weather like outside? What's it like being a popstar? What about* ⇨ about²(5). *what for* (a) for what occasion or purpose: *What did you do that for? What's this handle for?* (b) (informal) why: *'Come here a minute.' 'What for?' what if* what would happen if: *What if it rains while we're out? what with* (informal) because of (something unpleasant): *I'll never be rich what with all my expenses.* **2** the thing(s) which: *I don't know what to do. Do what you think best. Show me what he wrote. What he says is not important. what is more* in addition: *It's a useful book and what is more it's not expensive. What on earth/what the* ... ? (used to express surprise): *What on earth/what the devil are you doing? what's what* (informal) the real or true state of affairs: *Please explain what's what.*

what·e'er /wɒt'eə(r)/ adj or det, pron (poetic) = whatever.

what·ever¹ /wɒt'evə(r)/ adj or det (an emphatic form of *what*) of any sort, degree etc: *Whatever nonsense the newspapers print, some people always believe it. There can be no doubt whatever about it.*

what·ever² /wɒt'evə(r)/ pron **1** no matter what: *You are certainly right, whatever others may say. Keep calm, whatever happens.* **2** anything or everything that: *Do whatever you like.*

what·so·e'er /ˌwɒtsəʊ'eə(r)/ adj or det, pron (poetic) = whatsoever.

what·so·ever /ˌwɒtsəʊ'evə(r)/ adj or det, pron = whatever.

wheat /wiːt/ nu (also attrib) (a kind of plant producing) grain from which flour (as used for bread) is made: *a field of wheat; wheat fields.*

wheedle /'wiːdl/ vt to be pleasant to (a person) to get (something) one wants: *She wheedled a pound out of her father/wheedled her father into buying her a bicycle.*

wheel¹ /wiːl/ nc **1** a circular object that turns (as on carts, cars, bicycles etc and machines). **2** = steering wheel. *at the wheel* driving.

wheel² /wiːl/ v **1** vt to push or pull (something using) (a vehicle with wheels): *wheel a bike up the hill; wheel a barrow; wheel the rubbish out to the dump.* **2** vi to turn in a curve or circle: *The birds were wheeling in the air above me. He wheeled round and hit the man.*

wheel·bar·row /'wiːlbærəʊ/ nc a small cart with one wheel and two handles, used for moving small loads.

wheel·chair /'wiːltʃeə(r)/ nc a chair with large wheels, used by a handicapped person.

wheeze /wiːz/ vi to breathe noisily, esp with a whistling sound in the chest. □ nc a sound of wheezing.

wheezy adj (-ier, -iest)

whelk /welk/ nc a kind of sea-animal with a shell, used as food.

when¹ /wen/ adv **1** (used esp to form questions) at what time; on what occasion; during what period: *When can you come? When did that happen? When was he living in Madrid? Tell me when to start. I don't know when that happened. Since when has he been missing?* **2** (used as a pron): *Sunday is the day when I'm least busy. There are times when I wish I was back in Brazil.* Ⓝ 'When' as a pronoun can be left out without changing the meaning.

when² /wen/ conj (subord) **1** at or during the time that: *It was raining when we arrived. When he spoke there was silence.* **2** although: *He walks when he could take a taxi.* **3** considering that: *How can I help you when you won't listen to me? Why do you think you'll succeed when you've not done any work?* **4** during which time: *The manager will visit the factory in April, when she'll talk to all the staff.*

whence /wens/ adv (old use) **1** (used in questions) from what place or cause: *Do you know whence she came?* **2** (used in statements) from which place: *the land whence they are come.* **3** to the place from which: *Return whence you came.*

when·ev·er¹ /wen'evə(r)/ adv no matter when: *I'll discuss it with you whenever you like.* **or whenever** (informal) or at any time: *He'll arrive on Monday, Tuesday or whenever and expect to be given a meal.*

when·ev·er² /wen'evə(r)/ conj (subord) every time that: *I remember Austria whenever I think of you. Whenever that man says 'To tell the truth', he's about to tell a lie.*

where¹ /weə(r)/ adv **1** (used esp in questions) at, in, to, what place or position: *Where does he live? I wonder where he lives. I can't decide where to put it. Tell me where she is. Where are you going? 'I've lost it.'—'Where?'* **2** at which, to which: *This is the spot where the accident happened.*

where² /weə(r)/ conj (subord) **1** at, in, to, the place that: *It's hot where I live. Where you find good food you'll find my mother.* **2** in, to, any place at all: *Sit where you prefer.* Ⓝ 'Wherever' is more usual.

where³ /weə(r)/ pron the place that: *This is where I found it. That's where (= the issue about which) you are mistaken.*

where·abouts¹ /'weərəbaʊts/ adv in, near,

what place: *Whereabouts did you find it?*

where·abouts² /'weərəbaʊts/ *n sing* or *pl* the place (near to) where a person or thing is: *Her whereabouts is/are still unknown.*

where·as /weər'æz/ *conj* (*coord*) but (on the other hand): *Some people like spinach whereas others hate it.*

where·by /weə'baɪ/ *adv* (*formal*) by which: *He thought of a plan whereby he might escape.*

where·in /weər'ɪn/ *adv* (*formal*) in what; in which; in what respect: *Wherein am I mistaken?*

where·so·ever /,weərsəʊ'evə(r)/ *adv* (*old use*) (emphatic for) wherever.

wher·ever /weər'evə(r)/ *adv* in, to, at, any place at all: *Sit wherever you like. Wherever you go, I'll follow you.*

where·with·al /'weərwɪðɔːl/ *nu* (the —) (*informal*) the money needed for a purpose: *I'd like to buy a car but haven't got the wherewithal.*

whet /wet/ *vt* (**-tt-**) **1** to sharpen (the usual word): *whetting an axe on a stone.* **2** (*fig*) to excite (the appetite).

'whet·stone *nc* one used for sharpening tools.

wheth·er /'weðə(r)/ *conj* (*subord*) (used to introduce an indirect question, to suggest doubt or to express choice): *I wonder whether it will be big enough. I'm not sure whether we should take a bus or whether we should walk. I don't know whether to accept or not. I'm not interested in whether you like me or not. She asked whether, if Paul had no money, he would sell his car.* **(N)** For the differences between *if* and *whether*, ⇨ if(2).

whew /hwu:/ *int* = phew.

which¹ /wɪtʃ/ *adj* or *det* **1** (used in questions etc concerning choice): *Which way shall we go? Which languages do you speak? Tell me which one is yours.* **2** concerning, referring to, the particular one: *Don't phone me between 6 and 8, at which time I'm usually eating. I can't come unless it's next week, in which case I can join you. They met in the park, on which occasion they agreed to the plan.*

which² /wɪtʃ/ *pron* **1** (used in situations concerning choice) which person, thing etc: *Which is yours? Which of the bicycles is yours? Which boy is the tallest? I can't decide which to buy. I can't tell which is which* (= I can't see the difference between them). **2 (a)** (used as the subject, *sing* or *pl*): *Take the book which is lying on the table. The tools which are in this box belong to me.* **(b)** (used as the object, *sing* or *pl*): *Was the book which you were reading a novel?* **(N)** 'Which' is only used of things, not people. For people use *'who'. 'That'* is also possible for *which(2).* ⇨ that⁴(3). In (b), *'which'* is often left out without changing the meaning. **3** (used as the object of a prep): *the time at which he arrived; the occasion on which she wore the hat; the night during which he died; the reason for which the money was given; the disagreement over which the quarrel took place.* **4** (used to add further information): *The meeting, which was held in the park, was a big one. The car, which is still in the garage, has no tyres. The computer, for which she paid £400, can do many things.* **5** (used to refer to the first part of a statement): *He said he'd lost the book, which was untrue.*

which·ev·er¹ /wɪtʃ'evə(r)/ *adj* or *det* **1** any thing(s), idea(s) etc which: *Take whichever one you like.* **2** no matter which: *Whichever career*

you choose, you'll be successful.

which·ev·er² /wɪtʃ'evə(r)/ *pron* **1** any thing(s), idea(s) etc which: *Take whichever you want.* **2** any, no matter which: *Whichever (of you/them) wins will receive a prize.*

whiff¹ /wɪf/ *nc* **whiff (of sth)** a slight puff or smell (of): *a whiff of fresh air; the whiff of a cigar.*

whiff² /wɪf/ *vt* to get a slight smell of (something).

while¹ /waɪl/ *conj* **1** (*subord*) during the time that: *He fell asleep while he was reading a book. We stayed in while it was raining.* **2** (*subord*) although: *While I admit that the problem is difficult, I think we can solve it.* **3** (*coord*) but (in contrast): *Jane was wearing brown while Mary was dressed in red.*

while² /waɪl/ *n sing* a period of time: *Where have you been all this while? He'll be here in a* (little) *while. We hadn't met in a long while. I haven't seen you for some while.* **(every) once in a while** ⇨ once¹(1). **worth sb's while** to a person's advantage, benefit: *If you help me, I'll make it worth your while.* ⇨ worthwhile.

while³ /waɪl/ *vt* **while away sth** to pass time etc in a lazy way: *while away the time/hours/evening listening to music.*

whilst /waɪlst/ *conj* = while (which is much more usual).

whim /wɪm/ *nc* a sudden desire or idea, often something unusual or unreasonable: *full of whims.*

whim·per¹ /'wɪmpə(r)/ *nc* a sobbing sound.

whim·per² /'wɪmpə(r)/ *vi* to make weak, frightened or complaining sounds, e.g. like a baby when ill, a dog when frightened or hurt.

whim·si·cal /'wɪmzɪkl/ *adj* (*formal*) strange and playful: *be in a whimsical mood.*

whim·si·cal·ly /-klɪ/ *adv*

whine¹ /waɪn/ *nc* a long complaining cry or high-pitched sound (e.g. as made by a miserable dog, a child, an engine).

whine² /waɪn/ *vi* **1** to make whines: *The dog was whining to come into the room.* **2** to complain, esp about unimportant things: *a child who never stops whining.*

whin·ny /'wɪnɪ/ *vi* (*pt,pp* **-ied**), *nc* (*pl* **-ies**) (to make) a pleased cry of a horse.

whip¹ /wɪp/ *nc* **1** a long piece of cord, leather etc fastened to a handle, used for urging a horse on etc. **2** an organizing secretary of a political party with authority over its members to maintain discipline. **3** a sweet dish of beaten eggs, cream etc: *strawberry whip.*

whip² /wɪp/ *v* (**-pp-**) **1** *vt* to beat (an animal etc) with a whip: *whip a horse.* **2** *vt* to beat (eggs, cream etc) with a fork or other utensil to mix it thoroughly or to make it stiff: *whipped cream.* **3** *vt* (*informal*) to defeat (a person) in a competition. **4** *vt,vi* to take out (something), be taken, move, be moved, suddenly: *He whipped out a knife. The waves whipped against the cliff.*

whip·ping *nc* a beating with a whip as a punishment.

'whip·ping-boy *nc* (*informal*) a person (being) punished for another's offence.

whir /wɜ:(r)/ = whirr.

whirl¹ /wɜ:l/ *n sing* **1** a whirling movement: *a whirl of dust/of dead leaves.* **2** a quick succession of activities etc: *the whirl of modern life in a big city*.

whirl² /wɜ:l/ *v* **1** *vt,vi* (to cause a person, thing) to move quickly round and round: *The wind whirled us/the dead leaves about*. **2** *vt,vi* (to cause a person) to move or travel quickly: *Our friends were whirled away in Jack's sports car*. **3** *vi* (of the brain, thoughts etc) to seem to go round and round: *His head whirled*.

whirl·pool /'wɜ:lpu:l/ *nc* a place where there are circular currents in the sea etc (pulling floating objects towards its centre).

whirl·wind /'wɜ:lwɪnd/ *nc* a fast, circling current of air: *The trees were destroyed in the whirlwind*.

whirr¹ /wɜ:(r)/ *n sing* a sound (as if) of a bird's wings moving quickly or of wheels etc turning fast: *the whirr of a helicopter's propellers*.

whirr² /wɜ:(r)/ *vi* (**-rr-**) to make whirring sounds.

whisk¹ /wɪsk/ *nc* **1** a utensil (e.g. coiled wire) used for whipping eggs, cream etc. **2** a light brushing movement (e.g. of a horse's tail).

whisk² /wɪsk/ *v* **1** *vt,vi* to beat (food) with a whisk(1): *whisk eggs*. **2** *vt* to move (a tail etc) with a whisk(2). **3** *vt* **whisk sth off/away** to brush away an insect, piece of dirt etc quickly and lightly: *whisk the flies off*. **whisk sb away/off (to a place)** to take a person quickly and suddenly: *They whisked him off to prison*.

whisk·er /'wɪskə(r)/ *nc* one of the long, stiff hairs growing near the mouth of a cat, rat etc.

whisk·ers /'wɪskəz/ *n pl* (also *side-whiskers*) hair growing on the sides of a man's face.

whis·key /'wɪskɪ/ *nc,nu* (*pl* **—s**) US and Irish spelling of whisky.

whis·ky /'wɪskɪ/ *nc,nu* (*pl* **-ies**) (a portion of) strong alcoholic drink made from malted grain (esp barley or rye).

whis·per¹ /'wɪspə(r)/ *nc* **1** a whispering sound or speech: *He answered in a whisper*. **2** a whispered remark: *There are whispers that the firm is going bankrupt*.

whis·per² /'wɪspə(r)/ *v* **1** *vi,vt* to speak, say (something), using the breath but no sound from the voice: *whisper (a word) to a person*. **2** *vt* to tell (something) privately or secretly: *It is whispered that he is heavily in debt*. **3** *vi* (of leaves, the wind etc) to make soft sounds: *The wind was whispering in the trees*.

whistle¹ /'wɪsl/ *nc* **1** a (usually long) tuneful sound made by forcing air or steam through a small opening (e.g. the mouth, a bird's beak) or made by the wind. **2** a simple instrument making a similar sound as used by a referee in games and sports.

whistle² /'wɪsl/ *v* **1** *vi* to make a whistle(1) (e.g. by blowing through rounded lips or by using a whistle(2)): *whistling at the girls*. ⇨ wolf-whistle. **whistle for sth** (*informal*) to wish for it but not get it: *I owe him £10 but he can whistle for it*. **2** *vt* to produce (a tune) by whistling(1): *whistle a tune*. **3** *vi* to move through the air with a whistling(1) sound: *The bullets whistled past our ears*.

white¹ /waɪt/ *adj* (**—r, —st**) of the colour of fresh snow or common salt: *as white as snow/a sheet* (= very white). *His hair has turned white. Her face went white* (= pale). Compare black¹(1).

'white ant *nc* a termite.

'white·bait *nc,nu* (a) small young fish (to be) eaten fried.

,white-'collar *adj* (*attrib*) of a person who works in an office etc: *white-collar jobs/workers*. Compare blue-collar.

,white 'elephant *nc* a useless possession.

,white 'lie *nc* a small lie considered to be harmless.

,white 'meat *nu* poultry, veal, pork. Compare red meat.

white² /waɪt/ *n* **1** *nu* the white colour: *dressed in white*. **2** *nc,nu* a colourless part, e.g. round the yolk of an egg.

white·ness *nu*

white·wash¹ /'waɪtwɒʃ/ *nu* **1** a mixture of powdered lime or chalk and water, used for coating walls, ceilings etc. **2** (*fig*) a means used to cover or hide errors, faults etc: *The report was a whitewash*. **3** (*fig*) a game or competition in which the loser does not win any points, games etc.

white·wash² /'waɪtwɒʃ/ *vt* **1** to put whitewash on (a wall etc). **2** (*fig*) to try to make (a person, reputation etc) appear blameless by covering up faults etc.

Whit·sun /'wɪtsn/ *n* (also *Whit Sunday*) the seventh Sunday after Easter.

whittle /'wɪtl/ *vt* **whittle sth away/down** **1** to reduce the size of something by cutting away parts etc. **2** (*fig*) to reduce the size of something gradually: *Our membership was slowly whittled away/down*.

whiz /wɪz/ *vi* (**-zz-**), *nc* (to make) the sound of something rushing through the air: *The bullets whizzed past*.

whiz-kid /'wɪz kɪd/ *nc* (*informal; sometimes derog*) a clever young person with progressive ideas who achieves success (too) quickly.

who /hu:/ *pron* (used only of people) **1** (used in questions) which person or group: *Who is that man/are those men? Who told you that? I don't know who to ask. Who do you think you are? Tell me who told you. Who in this team is likely to win?* **2** (used to show which person or group is being referred to): *This is the man who asked to see you. Surgeons are people who perform medical operations. I want you to find the person who stole my bike*. Compare whom. ⇨ whose. Ⓝ *'That'* is also possible but is considered to be less acceptable. For the differences between *who, that* and *which*, ⇨ that⁴(3). **3** (used to add further information): *The singers, who arrived earlier this morning, are resting in the hotel*.

WHO /ˌdʌblju: eɪtʃ 'əʊ; *also* hu:/ *abbr* World Health Organization.

whoa /wəʊ/ *int* (used to stop a horse).

who'd /hu:d/ = *who had; who would*.

who·ever /hu:'evə(r)/ *pron* **1** any person who; the person who: *Whoever said that is wrong*. **2** no matter who: *Whoever you are, I'm not answering the door*.

whole¹ /həʊl/ *adj* **1** not damaged, divided or broken: *She swallowed the sweet whole*. **2** (*attrib*) entire; complete: *I waited for her a whole hour. It rained for three whole days*. **3** (*attrib*) **the whole sth** all that there is/was of; all the members of: *I want to know the whole truth about this matter. He ate the whole loaf. The whole country was anxious for peace*.

whol·ly /'həʊllɪ/ *adv* completely; entirely: *I*

wholly agree with you.

whole² /həʊl/ *n sing* **1 the whole (of sth)** the complete amount; all that there is of something: *He spent the whole of the year in Poland.* **2** the total of the parts: *Four quarters make a whole.* **as a whole** considered together: *I'd prefer to deal with the staff as a whole, not individually.* **on the whole** having considered all the facts (and decided); for the most part: *On the whole I agree with you.*

whole·heart·ed /ˌhəʊl ˈhɑːtɪd/ *adj* with complete commitment, sympathy etc: *I'll give it my whole-hearted support.* Compare half-hearted. **whole·heart·ed·ly** *adv*

whole·meal /ˈhəʊlmiːl/ *nu* flour with all the parts of the grain.

whole·sale /ˈhəʊlseɪl/ *adj, adv* **1** concerning selling in large amounts (esp to shops etc): *Our business is wholesale only.* Compare retail¹,²,³,⁴. **2** *(fig)* on a large scale: *There was a wholesale slaughter when the police opened fire.*

'whole·saler *nc* a person, business, that sells wholesale goods.

whole·some /ˈhəʊlsəm/ *adj* making a person healthy: *wholesome food.* Opp unwholesome(1).

who'll /huːl/ = who shall; who will.

whom /huːm/ *pron (formal)* (used as the object form of *who*): *Whom did you give it to? The person to whom I gave money* (or 'who I gave the money to', which is more usual) *has left the country.* Ⓝ *'Whom'* is now only used in very formal writing.

whoop¹ /huːp/ *nc* **1** a loud cry: *whoops of joy.* **2** a gasping sound heard during a fit of coughing.

whoop² /huːp/ *vi* to make a loud cry or yell: *whooping with joy.*

'whoop·ing cough *nu* a children's disease with gasping coughs and long, noisy breaths.

who're /ˈhuːə(r)/ = who are.

whore /hɔː(r)/ *nc* a prostitute.

whorl /wɜːl/ *nc* **1** a ring of leaves, petals etc round a stem of a plant. **2** one turn of a spiral, e.g. as seen on the shell of a snail or on a fingerprint.

who's /huːz/ = who is; who has.

whose /huːz/ *adj* or *det*, possessive *pron* belonging to who; of which: *Whose house is that? I wonder whose house that is. Is that the man whose house was burnt down last week? Firemen, whose work is often dangerous, are paid less than the police. That's the house whose roof collapsed. Whose is that bike?*

who·so·ever /ˌhuːsəʊˈevə(r)/ *pron (old use)* = whoever.

who've /huːv/ = who have.

why¹ /waɪ/ *adv* for what reason or purpose: *Why was he late? Tell me why you did it. Did you find out why he was late? That's why I left. 'I'm leaving you'—'Why?' 'She won't come'—'Why not?' 'Will you help me?'—'Why not, you'd do the same for me.'*

why² /waɪ/ *pron* because of which: *That's the reason why I left.*

wick /wɪk/ *nc* **1** (a length of) string through a candle. **2** (a strip of) woven material by which oil is drawn up in some cigarette lighters, oil-lamps etc.

wick·ed /ˈwɪkɪd/ *adj (derog)* **1** (of a person, behaviour) wrong; immoral; very bad: *It was*

wicked of you to hit the old woman. That was a wicked lie! **2** mischievous: *She gave me a wicked look/smile.*

wick·ed·ly *adv*
wick·ed·ness *nu*

wick·er /ˈwɪkə(r)/ *adj (attrib)* made of twigs or canes woven together: *a wicker chair.*

wick·et /ˈwɪkɪt/ *nc (cricket)* either of the two pairs of three sticks at which the ball is bowled; area of grass between two wickets.

'wicket-keeper *nc* a player who stands behind the wicket.

wide¹ /waɪd/ *adj (—r, —st)* **1** measuring much from side to side: *a wide river; a road twelve metres wide.* Opp narrow¹(1). **2** *(fig)* large, unlimited; of great extent: *a man with wide interests; a wide selection of new books/circle of friends; in the widest sense of the word.* Compare narrow¹(2,3). ⇨ the notes at broad¹.

wide·ly *adv* **(a)** over a large area: *widely distributed.* **(b)** to a large extent or degree: *widely different.* **(c)** by many people: *It is widely known that she did it.*

wide² /waɪd/ *adv* **1** fully: *The window was wide open.* **wide apart** with a large space in between: *Stand with your legs wide apart.* **wide awake** not at all sleepy. **2** over a large area: *travel far and wide.*

wide-angle lens /ˌwaɪd æŋgl ˈlenz/ *nc (photography)* a system in a camera that allows a wide area to be photographed.

wide-eyed /ˌwaɪdˈaɪd/ *adj* foolishly trusting.

wid·en /ˈwaɪdn/ *vt,vi* (to cause something) to become wide(r): *They're widening the road.*

wide·spread /ˈwaɪdspred/ *adj* found, distributed, over a wide area: *widespread poverty.*

wid·ow /ˈwɪdəʊ/ *nc* a woman who has not married again after her husband's death.

wid·ow·er /ˈwɪdəʊə(r)/ *nc* a man who has not married again after his wife's death.

width /wɪtθ/ *n* **1** *nu* the quality or state of being wide: *a road of great width.* **2** *nc* the measurement from side to side: *a width of 10 metres; 10 metres in width.* **3** *nc* a piece of material of a certain width: *silk of various widths.*

wield /wiːld/ *vt (esp fig)* to have and use (power etc): *wield power/influence.*

wife /waɪf/ *nc (pl* **wives** /waɪvz/) a woman who a man is married to. Compare husband. ⇨ housewife, midwife.

wife·ly *adj (dated)* of, like, suitable for, a wife: *wifely duties.*

wig /wɪg/ *nc* a head-covering of false hair.

wiggle¹ /ˈwɪgl/ *nc* a wiggling movement.

wiggle² /ˈwɪgl/ *vt,vi* (to cause one's body etc) to move with quick, short, side-to-side movements: *The baby was wiggling its toes.*

wig·gly /ˈwɪgli/ *adj (attrib)* wavy: *a wiggly line.*

wild¹ /waɪld/ *adj (—er, —est)* **1** (of an animal, plant) living or growing in natural conditions: *wild flowers/birds.* Compare tame¹(1), domestic¹(3). **2** (of a person, group of people) uncivilized. **3** excited: *There were sounds of wild laughter. He was wild with anger.* **be wild about sb/sth** *(informal)* to have a strong desire for, be madly enthusiastic about, a person, thing: *I'm still wild about the Beatles.* **drive sb wild** to make a person angry, mad. **4** (of scenery, areas of land etc) not lived in and perhaps dangerous: *wild mountainous areas*. **5** stormy: *You'd better stay indoors on a wild night like this*. **6** disorderly; out of control: *a state of wild confusion; settle down after a wild youth*. **7** done, said etc without thought or knowledge: *a wild remark/guess/hope*.

,wild '**boar** *nc* a kind of wild pig with tusks.

,wild '**cat** *nc* a kind of wild European cat.

'**wild·cat** *adj* (*attrib*) (of a strike) sudden and unofficial: *a wildcat strike*.

'**wild·fire** *nu* **spread like wildfire** (of rumours etc) to spread very quickly.

,wild-'**goose chase** *n sing* a hopeless and foolish search etc.

'**wild·life** *nu* all wild animals, birds, insects etc collectively.

wild·ly *adv* in a wild manner: *rush about wildly; a wildly* (= greatly) *exaggerated story*.

wild·ness *nu*

wild² /waɪld/ *adv* in a wild(6) way: *shoot wild*. **run wild** to be without control or discipline: *She lets her children run wild*.

wild³ /waɪld/ *n* (the — or *the wilds of a region*) wild(4) areas: *elephants living in the wild/in the wilds of Africa*.

wil·der·ness /'wɪldənɪs/ *n* **1** (the —) a wild, uncultivated area of land. **2** *n sing* an empty expanse: *a wilderness of deserted streets*.

wiles /waɪlz/ *n pl* tricks used to get something one wants: *the wiles of a small boy*.

wil·ful (*US* also **will-**) /'wɪlfəl/ *adj* **1** (*derog*) (of a person) determined to have one's own way: *a wilful child*. **2** intentional: *wilful murder/negligence*.

wil·ful·ly /-fəlɪ/ *adv*

will¹ /wɪl/ *n* **1** (the —) the mental power by which a person can direct thoughts and actions, and influence those of others: *the freedom of the will*. **2** *nc,nu* the control exercised over oneself, one's desires etc; determination: *He has no will of his own* (= is easily influenced by others). *She has a strong/weak will. The will to live helps a patient to recover*. **of one's own free will** without being forced to: *You did it of your own free will*. **with the best will in the world** however hard one tries (not) to: *With the best will in the world we cannot please everyone*. **3** *n sing* energy; enthusiasm: *work with a will*. **where there's a will there's a way** (*saying*) if one really wishes to succeed, a method will be found. **4** *nc* (also *last will and testament*) a statement of how a person's property is to be owned after death. ⇨ will³(2).

will² /wɪl/ *auxiliary verb* Ⓝ *'Will' is a* (modal) *auxiliary verb* used with another verb to form the future tense, to ask questions and to express willingness and intention. *'Will'* has no infinitive form, no imperative form and no participles. *'Will'* is always followed by an infinitive without *'to'*. Compare **shall**, **would**. (*present tense* (all persons) **will**; *I will* often shortened to **I'll** /aɪl/, *he will*; she will to **he'll**, **she'll** /hi:l, ʃi:l/, *it will* to **it'll** /'ɪtl/, *we will* to **we'll** /wi:l/, *you will* to **you'll** /jəl, jʊl/ and *they will* to **they'll** /ðeɪl/; *negative* **will not** or **won't** /wəʊnt/; *pt conditional* **would** /wəd *strong form:* wʊd/, *negative* **would not** or **wouldn't** /'wʊdnt/) **1** (used as an auxiliary to form the future tense): *He will come as soon as he can. They'll arrive next Friday. It'll be ready by tomorrow. We'll be visiting her tonight. They will have*

caught the train by now. Compare **shall**(1). **2** (used with *you, he, she, it, they* and also *we* to ask questions): *Will you come in? Won't you stay a little longer? Close the window, will you? Will we* (= Do you think we will) *get there in time?* Compare **shall**(2). **3** **will have to** + *verb* (used to express future obligation): *They'll have to pay if they break it*. Compare **shall**(3). **4** (used with *I* and *we* to express willingness, agreement etc): *All right, I/we will be there. I will go whether you want me to or not. We won't do it again, we promise. 'Who'll light the fire for me?' 'I will.'* **5** (used in the negative to express refusal): *He won't let me in. She wouldn't help me. This box won't open. The car wouldn't start this morning*. **6** (used to express insistence or probability): *He 'will interrupt when I'm talking. She 'will have her own way. Accidents 'will happen. This'll be the book you wanted*. **7** (used to refer to expected or regular behaviour): *She'll do nothing for months and then suddenly she'll ring me. The dog will go for days without food*. Compare **would**(2).

will³ /wɪl/ *vt* **1** to use one's mental powers in an attempt to do or get (something): *We cannot be successful simply by willing it. He willed the horse to win. I'm willing you to get well.* ⇨ will-power. **2** to leave (property, money etc) to a person in a will¹(4): *She willed her money to charity*.

will⁴ /wɪl/ *vt* (*pt* **would**) (*old use*) to wish (something): *Let him do what he will*.

will·ing /'wɪlɪŋ/ *adj* **1** **willing (to do sth)** ready, agreeing, (to help, do what is needed, asked etc): *willing workers; willing to work late*. Opp **unwilling**. **2** (*attrib*) given etc without hesitation: *willing obedience*.

will·ing·ly *adv*

will·ing·ness *nu*

wil·low /'wɪləʊ/ *nc,nu* (the wood of) a kind of tree with thin, easily bent branches, used for weaving into baskets etc.

will-pow·er /'wɪlpaʊə(r)/ *nu* strength or firmness of will¹(1): *She has no will-power*.

wilt /wɪlt/ *vt,vi* **1** (to cause plants, flowers) to droop, lose freshness. **2** (*fig*) (to cause a person) to lose energy: *wilt in the hot weather*.

wily /'waɪlɪ/ *adj* (**-ier**, **-iest**) (*derog*) cunning (the usual word).

wimp /wɪmp/ *nc* (*sl; derog*) a person without courage, determination etc.

win¹ /wɪn/ *nc* (in a game, sport, election etc) an act of winning(1): *The parliamentary seat of Oxford East was an important win for Labour. Our team managed only three wins last year*.

win² /wɪn/ *v* (*pt,pp* **won** /wʌn/; **-nn-**) **1** *vi,vt* to be the best, first etc as the result of hard work, effort, determination etc: *win a race/competition/election*. **2** *vt* to get (a prize etc) by winning(1): *win a prize/£20/a scholarship/a large order/fame and fortune*. **3** *vt* to get (something) by effort: *win the summit/the shore/a place in the team*.

win sb/sth back to get a girlfriend, market, sports record etc back after a struggle.

win sb over (to sth) to persuade a person to agree (to something): *We've won them over to our point of view*.

win sb round to gain a person's friendship or favour.

win through (*informal*) to deal with a difficult

period successfully: *With your help we'll win through.*

wince /wɪns/ *vi* to show pain or distress by a movement, sound or by loss of control: *He winced at the insult.*

winch /wɪntʃ/ *vt, nc* (to move something using) a kind of machine for hoisting or pulling heavy objects.

wind¹ /wɪnd/ *n* **1** *nc,nu* air moving as the result of natural forces: *a light/strong/north wind; a little/too much wind. The wind blew my hat off.* **put the wind up sb** (*sl*) to cause a person to feel frightened. **see how the wind blows** to wait to find out what people are thinking, what is likely to happen etc before deciding or acting. **2** *nu* breath needed for running or continuous exercise: *The runner soon lost his wind.* ⇨ second wind. **3** *nu* a smell carried by the wind (showing where something is). **get wind of sth** (*fig*) to learn about something, esp accidentally: *How did you get wind of what happened?* **4** *nu* meaningless or useless talk: *Don't listen to the politicians—they're all wind.* **5** *nu* gas formed in the bowels and causing discomfort: *The baby is suffering from wind.* **break wind** to send out wind from the anus.

'wind·bag *nc* (*informal; derog*) a person who talks a lot but says nothing important.

'wind·break *nc* a hedge, fence, line of trees etc used to give protection from the wind.

'wind·cheater *nc* a jacket designed to give protection against the wind.

'wind·fall *nc* (**a**) a fruit (e.g. an apple) blown off a tree by the wind. (**b**) (*fig*) an unexplained piece of good fortune, esp unexpected money.

'wind instrument *nc* a musical instrument in which sound is produced by blowing air into it (e.g. a flute).

'wind·mill *nc* one worked by the action of the wind on sails(2) which revolve.

'wind·pipe *nc* the passage for air from the throat to the lungs.

'wind·screen (*US* = **-shield**) *nc* a screen of glass in front of a car etc.

'wind·screen-wiper *nc* an apparatus used for wiping rain from a windscreen.

'wind-swept *adj* exposed to (and blown bare by) strong winds: *a wind-swept hillside.*

wind·less *adj* without wind: *a windless day.*

windy *adj* (**-ier, -iest**) with a lot of wind: *a windy day; windy weather.*

wind² /waɪnd/ *nc* one turn when winding⁴.

wind³ /wɪnd/ *vt* to cause (a person) to have no breath: *be winded by a long climb.*

wind⁴ /waɪnd/ *v* (*pt,pp* **wound** /waʊnd/) **1** *vt,vi* (to cause an animal, plant, river, path etc) to move or grow in a bending, twisting or wavy path: *The river winds (its way) to the sea.* **2** *vt,vi* (to cause something) to be turned, twisted etc round (an object or itself): *wind a ball of string; wind the wool round her hands; wind a scarf round his neck.* Opp unwind. **3** *vt* to turn (a handle etc) (and move something): *wind a handle; wind up a bucket; wind down a window.* **4** *vt* to tighten the working parts of (a machine) by winding(2): *wind a watch/clock.*

wind sth back to return a film or tape to an earlier place by winding(2) the spool.

wind (sth) down (**a**) ⇨ 3 above. (**b**) (to cause a business, effort etc) to have less energy, to produce less etc: *wind a branch office down. The discussion is winding down.*

wind sth in to shorten a measuring tape, fishing line etc by winding(2).

wind sth on to send a film or tape to a later place by winding(2) the spool.

wind sth round sth ⇨ 2 above.

wind sb up (often *passive*) to cause a person to become very excited, anxious etc: *His speech wound up the crowd. She was wound up to a high pitch of excitement.* Compare unwind(2). **wind sth up** (**a**) to tighten the working parts of something: *wind up a clock.* (**b**) to bring a speech, meeting, discussion etc to an end. (**c**) to cause a business, club, department etc to stop operating: *We've wound up the office in Hong Kong.* **wind up (with) sth** (*informal*) to get or experience a serious condition as a result: *If you drive that fast you'll wind up dead/in hospital. If you work so hard you'll wind up with a serious illness.*

wind·er /'waɪndə(r)/ *nc* a part on a clock or similar instrument used to wind it up.

win·dow /'wɪndəʊ/ *nc* an opening covered with glass in a wall or roof of a building, car etc, used to let in light and air: *look out of the window; break a window.*

'window-box *nc* a box fixed to a window-sill, used for plants.

'window-dresser *nc* a person whose profession is designing shop-window displays.

'window-pane *nc* a piece of glass (to be) put in a window.

'window-shopping *nu* the activity of looking at goods displayed in shop windows.

'window-sill *nc* the flat shelf at the base of a window, esp outside.

windy /'wɪndɪ/ ⇨ wind¹.

wine¹ /waɪn/ *nc,nu* (a particular kind of) alcoholic drink made from the juice of grapes (or other fruit, vegetables): *a bottle/glass of wine; French wines.*

'wine-glass *nc* a glass for drinking wine.

wine² /waɪn/ *vt* (esp) **wine and dine sb** to entertain a person to a meal: *We were wined and dined at the firm's expense.*

wing¹ /wɪŋ/ *nc* **1** either of the two limbs by which a bird, insect or plane flies. **take sb under one's wing** to give a person care and protection. **2** a part of a building etc which is extended from one of its sides: *add a new wing to a hospital.* **3** the part of a vehicle covering the wheel. **4** those members of a political party holding more extreme views than those of the majority: *the left/right wing.* **5** (*sport*) (a player on) the extreme left or right of a sports field. **6** (*pl*) the unseen areas to the right and left of the stage of a theatre. **7** something like a wing(1) in appearance or position, e.g. certain types of seeds (esp of the maple and the sycamore).

wing² /wɪŋ/ *v* **1** *vt,vi* (*formal*) to fly: *The planes winged (their way) over the Alps.* **2** *vt* to injure (a bird) in flight.

wing com·mand·er /'wɪŋ kəmɑːndə(r)/ *nc* (also W- C-) an officer in the air force.

wing·span /'wɪŋspæn/ *nc* a measurement from one end of a wing across to the end of the opposite one.

wink¹ /wɪŋk/ *nc* **1** an act of winking, esp as a signal or hint. **2** a very short time: *I didn't sleep a wink/didn't have a wink of sleep last night* (i.e. I didn't sleep at all). ⇨ **forty winks**.

wink² /wɪŋk/ *vi* **1 wink (at sb)** to close and open one eye as a signal: *She winked at me.* **2** (of a star, light etc) to shine or flash at very short intervals: *A lighthouse was winking in the far distance.*

winkle¹ /'wɪŋkl/ *nc* a kind of sea-animal with a spiral shell, used as food.

winkle² /'wɪŋkl/ *vt* **winkle sth out (of sb)** to get, things, statements etc (from a person) by force: *winkling the truth out of him.*

win·ner /'wɪnə(r)/ *nc* a person, animal, suggestion, political party etc that wins. Opp **loser**.

win·ning /'wɪnɪŋ/ *adj* (*attrib*) **1** that wins: *the winning horse.* **2** attracting confidence and friendship: *a winning smile; winning ways.*

win·nings /'wɪnɪŋz/ *n pl* money won as a result of gambling.

win·some /'wɪnsəm/ *adj* (*formal*) (of a person, appearance) attractive; pleasing.

win·ter /'wɪntə(r)/ *nc,nu* (also *attrib*) the cold season between autumn and spring: *a cold winter; have snow in winter; winter weather/clothes.*

winter 'sports *n pl* sports such as skiing, ice-skating, tobogganing.

win·try /'wɪntrɪ/ *adj* of, like, winter: *a wintry sky/day.*

wipe¹ /waɪp/ *nc* **1** an act of wiping. **2** (*med*) something used for cleaning wounds etc.

wipe² /waɪp/ *vt* **1** to clean or dry (something) by rubbing with a cloth, paper, the hands etc: *wipe one's hands on a towel; wipe plates dry.* **wipe the floor with sb** ⇨ **floor¹(1)**. **2** to remove sound from a (tape), information from (a computer disk etc).

wipe sth away to remove, e.g. tears, by wiping.

wipe sth off (a) to remove something by wiping: *wipe off a drawing from the blackboard.* **(b)** to get rid of something owed: *wipe off a debt.*

wipe sb out (a) (*informal*) to use up all of a person's money: *The holiday has wiped me out.* **(b)** (*sl*) to murder a person. **wipe sth out (a)** to clean the inside of something: *wipe out a jug.* **(b)** to get rid of something bad: *wipe out a debt/an insult.* **(c)** to destroy a business, a group etc completely: *a disease that almost wiped out the population.*

wipe sth over to clean the surface of something by wiping it.

wipe sth up (a) to wipe plates, dishes, knives and forks etc dry. **(b)** to take up liquid etc by wiping: *wipe up spilt milk; wipe up a mess.*

wiper /'waɪpə(r)/ *nc* = windscreen-wiper.

wire¹ /'waɪə(r)/ *n* **1** *nc,nu* (also *attrib*) (a piece or length of) metal in the form of a thread: *telephone wire(s); a wire fence. Fasten the bag with a piece of wire.* ⇨ also **barbed wire**. **2** *nc* (*informal*, esp *US*) = telegram: *send off a wire.*

'wire-cutters *n pl* a kind of tool used for cutting wire.

'wire-haired *adj* made with, having, stiff, wiry hair: *a wire-haired brush; a wire-haired dog.*

,wire 'wool *nu* fine wire used for cleaning.

wir·ing *n* (the —) (esp) the system of wires (in a building) for electric current.

wire² /waɪə(r)/ *vt* **1** to fasten (something) with wire: *wiring two things together.* **2** to put electrical circuits in (a building): *Has the house been wired for electricity yet?* **3** (*informal*, esp *US*) to send a telegram to (a person): *He wired me that he would be delayed.*

wire·less /'waɪəlɪs/ *nc* (*old use*) = radio.

wiry /'waɪərɪ/ *adj* (**-ier, -iest**) **1** looking like wire: *wiry hair.* **2** (of a person) thin but strong.

wis·dom /'wɪzdəm/ *nu* the quality of being wise: *the wisdom of experience.*

'wisdom tooth *nc* a back tooth, usually coming through at about 20 years of age.

wise /waɪz/ *adj* (**—r, —st**) having or showing experience, knowledge, good judgement etc: *wise men/acts. He was wise enough not to drive when he was feeling ill.* **be none the wiser** to know no more than before: *After the lecture he was none the wiser.*

wise·ly *adv*

wish¹ /wɪʃ/ *nc* **1** a feeling of desiring something (esp impossible or unlikely): *a wish for peace and prosperity for all; a wish to travel across the Andes mountains.* **2** something that is wished for: *She got her wish.* **best wishes** (used, e.g. at the end of a letter, to express one's hope that a person will get what he or she wants, be happy and healthy etc). **3** an attempt to make something wanted to happen, become a reality etc, esp by using magic: *If you see a rainbow you can have three wishes/make a wish.*

wish² /wɪʃ/ *v* Ⓝ Not used in continuous tenses, e.g. *is/was -ing.* **1** *vt* to feel a desire or need for (something impossible or unlikely): *I wish (that) he would give me his car. I wish I knew what is happening. She wishes she were rich.* Ⓝ For a comparison of *wish* and *want*, ⇨ **want²(1)**. **2** *vt* to say that one hopes for (something): *I wish you a pleasant journey. I wished him good morning.* **wish sb ill/well** to hope that a person will have bad/good fortune: *He wishes me well. I wish nobody ill.* **3** *vt,vi* (*formal*) (used to make a polite suggestion, question, reply etc about what a person would like): *Do you wish her to work late tomorrow? 'May I go now?' 'If you wish'.* Ⓝ *'Want to'* is more usual.

wish for sth to have a strong desire for something impossible or unlikely: *He wished for an opportunity to go abroad. What more could you wish for? I couldn't wish for a better wife.* Compare **hope for sth**.

wish sb/sth on sb (*informal*) to send, give, a difficult or unpleasant person or thing to a person: *Why must we have that rude cousin wished on us for the summer holidays?*

wish·ful /'wɪʃfəl/ *adj* having, expressing, a wish. **wishful thinking** acting as if something were true because one now wishes it were true.

wisp /wɪsp/ *nc* a small mass or amount: *a wisp of straw/hair/smoke.*

wispy *adj* (**-ier, -iest**) small; vague; slight.

wist·ful /'wɪstfəl/ *adj* sad and wishing for something; having, showing disappointment: *a wistful expression.*

wist·ful·ly /-fəlɪ/ *adv* in a wistful manner: *She looked wistfully at the photographs of herself when she was young and beautiful.*

wit /wɪt/ n 1 n sing (or pl) intelligence; under-standing; quickness of mind: *He hadn't the wits/ hadn't wit enough to realize what to do in the emer-gency.* **be at one's wit's end** to be unable to decide, not know, what to do or say after trying often, because of worry etc. **have/keep one's wits about one** to be ready to think quickly and act. **live by one's wits** to live by clever, not always honest, methods. **scare sb out of her/ his wits** to make a person extremely frightened. **2** nu a clever and humorous expression of ideas; liveliness of spirit: *His writings sparkle with wit.* **3** nc a person noted for her or his wit(2).

wit·ti·cism /'wɪtɪsɪzəm/ nc a witty remark.

wit·ti·ly /-əlɪ/ adv

wit·ty adj (-ier, -iest) having, full of, wit(2): *a witty girl/remark.*

witch /wɪtʃ/ nc a woman said to use magic, esp to do evil things.

'witch·craft nu the use of magic.

'witch-hunt nc (modern informal) a search for people with political views that are considered unacceptable, esp in order to make them suffer.

with /wɪð/ prep **1** using; by means of: *killed with a knife; pay for it with a credit card; carry it with both hands; see it with one's own eyes; manage it with your help; write with a pen. With your sup-port, I'm sure to win. With all this rain, the vege-tables ought to grow.* Compare by²(8). **2** possessing; having; characterized by: *a coat with two pockets; a girl with green eyes; a child with intelligence.* **3** having inside or as a cover: *a box filled with sand; hills covered with snow; a car fit-ted with a radio.* **4** in the company of: *live with your parents; travelling with friends; going out with one's boyfriend; eat chips with vinegar; cur-tains that are sold with the house. Is anyone with you or are you alone?* **in with sb** involved with a person or group: *She's in with the rich set/the wrong crowd.* **together with sb/sth** ⇨ together(1). **5** at the same time as: *a headache with fever; a storm with strong winds.* **6** (used to express an action, situation, state, affecting both sides): *(dis)agree with you; playing with her; has broken with her best friend.* **7** in favour of: *vote with the government. He who is not with me is against me.* **8** against: *fight/argue/quarrel/ struggle with them.* **9** in a manner showing: *did it with effort; fought with courage.* **10** concerning: *angry/pleased with me; good with one's hands; sympathize with her. What do you want with me? What's the matter with it? I can't do anything with my hair/that child* (= It/He cannot be controlled). **11** because of: *trembling with fear; shaking with cold; green with envy; smiling with delight; faint-ing with hunger.* **12** in spite of: *With all her faults, I love her still.* **13 I'm not with you** I don't understand what you are saying. **with it** (infor-mal) **(a)** up to date; fashionable: *Her clothes are with it.* **(b)** understanding what is happening: *I'm sorry but I'm not quite with it this morning.* **14 with that** having done, said, that: *With that he left the room.*

with·draw /wɪð'drɔː/ v (pt -drew /-'druː/, pt -drawn /-'drɔːn/) **1** vt to take (something) out or away: *withdraw money from the bank. The workers threatened to withdraw their labour* (i.e. to go on strike). **2** vi,vt to take back (a statement, an offer): *He refused to withdraw (the accusation/ remark).* **3** vt,vi (to cause a person, animal, claw etc) to move back or away: *withdraw soldiers from the town; withdraw from society. The lion withdrew. That cat withdrew its claws.*

with·draw·al /wɪð'drɔːəl/ nc,nu (an instance of) taking a person, thing, out or away: *a withdrawal of money; withdrawal from the race.*

with·drawn /wɪð'drɔːn/ adj (of a person) unusually quiet and shy.

with·er /'wɪðə(r)/ vt,vi **1** (to cause a plant etc) to become dry, faded or dead: *The hot summer with-ered (up) the grass.* **2** (fig) (to cause a hope etc) to become less strong (and stop): *Her hopes with-ered (away).*

with·hold /wɪð'həʊld/ vt (pt,pp -held /-'held/) **withhold sth (from sb)** to keep back, refuse to give, information, permission etc: *He tried to withhold the truth from us. I shall withhold my consent.*

with·in /wɪð'ɪn/ prep **1** in; inside: *within the room.* **2** not beyond the limits of: *within the law; be within reach; live within one's income* (= not spend more than one earns); *within an hour* (= in less than an hour); *within a mile of the station; within my experience.* ⇨ outside⁴(3).

with·out /wɪð'aʊt/ prep **1** not having: *You can't buy things without money. He was trying without any hope of success.* **without doubt** ⇨ doubt¹. **without end** ⇨ end¹(2). **without fail** ⇨ fail¹. ⇨ also do without, go without. **2** not using or needing: *Can you open it without a tool? I can't do it without your help. She won't sleep without a pil-low.* **3** not in the company of: *travelling without companions; went to the party without a girlfriend.* **4** (used with the -ing form of a verb) while not: *She can't go anywhere without complaining. He speaks Russian without making any mistakes.* **go without saying** ⇨ say²(1).

with·stand /wɪð'stænd/ vt (pt,pp -stood /-'stʊd/) to resist (something) successfully; hold out against (pressure, attack): *withstand an attack; shoes that will withstand hard wear.*

wit·ness¹ /'wɪtnɪs/ n **1** nc (often eye-witness) a person who was actually present at an event and should, for this reason, be able to describe it. **2** nc (legal) a person who gives evidence under oath in a law court. **3** nc a person who adds her or his sig-nature to a document to prove that another per-son's signature on it is genuine. **4** nc,nu evidence, proof, about what is said regarding a person, event etc: *Her clothes are a witness to her poverty.* **bear witness to sth** to be proof of something: *acts that bear witness to her courage.*

'witness-box nc the enclosure in a law court in which a witness stands while giving evidence.

wit·ness² /'wɪtnɪs/ v **1** vt to be present at and see (an event): *witness an accident.* **2** vi **witness to sth** (legal) to give evidence about (something) in a law court: *witness to the truth of a statement.* **3** vt to be a witness(3) to (something): *witness a signa-ture.* **4** vt to give evidence of (something): *Her pale face witnessed the pain she felt.*

wit·ti·cism /'wɪtɪsɪzəm/ nc ⇨ wit.

wit·ting·ly /'wɪtɪŋlɪ/ adv knowingly; intention-ally: *I didn't hurt her wittingly.* Opp unwittingly.

wives /waɪvz/ pl of wife.

wiz·ard /'wɪzəd/ nc **1** (in stories) a magician. **2**

(*informal*) a person with amazing abilities: *a financial wizard.*

wiz·en·ed /'wɪznd/ *adj* old and dried: *a wizened tree/apple/face.*

wk *written abbr* **1** week. **2** work.

WNW *written abbr* west-north-west.

w/o *written abbr* (*commerce*) **1** without. **2** (of debts) written off.

wobble /'wɒbl/ *vi* (to cause something) to move unsteadily from side to side: *Jellies wobble.*

wob·bly /'wɒblɪ/ *adj* (**-ier, -iest**) not firm or steady: *He's still a little wobbly on his legs after his long illness.*

woe /wəʊ/ *n* (*poetic*) **1** *nu* great sadness; distress: *a tale of woe.* **2** (*pl*) causes of woe; troubles: *poverty, illness and other woes.*

woe·ful /-fəl/ *adj* (**a**) very sad: *a woeful expression.* (**b**) extreme and bad: *woeful ignorance.*

woe·ful·ly /-fəlɪ/ *adv*

woke /wəʊk/ *pt* of wake³.

woken /'wəʊkən/ *pp* of wake³.

wolf¹ /wʊlf/ *nc* (*pl* **wolves** /wʊlvz/) a kind of wild, flesh-eating animal of the dog family. **cry wolf** to raise false alarms: *David has cried wolf so often that no-one believes him now.*

wolf² /wʊlf/ *vt* **wolf sth (down)** to eat food quickly and greedily: *He wolfed (down) his dinner.*

wolf-whistle /'wʊlfwɪsl/ *vi, nc* (of a man) (to make) a whistle or other sound expressing admiration of a woman's beauty.

wom·an /'wʊmən/ *n* (*pl* **women** /'wɪmɪn/) **1** (also *attrib*) an adult female human being: *men, women and children. a woman driver/doctor.* **a woman of the world** one with wide experience of business and society. **2** *n sing* used without *a, an* or *the*) the female sex; any woman: *Woman is as capable as man.*

'woman·hood /-hʊd/ *nu* (**a**) the state of being a woman: *She had now grown to/reached womanhood.* (**b**) women in general.

woman·kind /'wʊmənkaɪnd/ *nu* the female sex; all women. Compare mankind.

'woman·ize (also **-ise**) /-aɪz/ *vi* to try to get a woman's friendship (esp for a sexual relationship).

,women's 'lib *nu* the movement begun in the early 1970's for women to have equal social, educational and economic opportunities.

womb /wuːm/ *nc* (*anat*) the organ in a female mammal in which offspring are carried and nourished while developing before birth.

wom·en·folk /'wɪmɪnfəʊk/ *n pl* (*old use*) women, esp of one's own family.

won /wʌn/ *pt,pp* of win².

won·der¹ /'wʌndə(r)/ *adj* (*attrib*) (*informal*) surprisingly good: *a wonder cook/cure/drug.*

won·der² /'wʌndə(r)/ *n* **1** *nu* the feeling caused by something unusual, surprising or that cannot be explained; surprise combined with admiration, etc: *They were filled with wonder.* **be a/no wonder (that)** to be a/no surprise (that): *It's no wonder (that) you lost your way in the dark.* **no/ little/small wonder** it is not surprising: *No/ Small wonder you were so late.* **2** *nc* something that causes a feeling of wonder(1): *Walking on the moon is one of the wonders of our times.* **work**

wonders to have remarkable results.

won·der³ /'wʌndə(r)/ *v* **1** *vi* to feel or express curiosity: *I wonder why she didn't come. I was wondering about that. I wonder who he is. He was wondering where she lived.* **2** *vi,vt* to feel surprise (and a desire to know something): *We wondered at her refusal to accept the job. I wonder that you weren't told sooner.*

won·der·ful /'wʌndəfəl/ *adj* surprisingly good: *wonderful weather/scenery.*

won·der·ful·ly /-fəlɪ/ *adv*

won·der·ment /'wʌndəmənt/ *nu* (*formal*) = surprise.

won·ky /'wɒŋkɪ/ *adj* (**-ier, -iest**) (*informal*) not steady: *a wonky chair.*

wont /wəʊnt/ *n sing* (*dated*) what a person is accustomed to doing: *He went to bed much earlier than was his wont.*

won't /wəʊnt/ = will not.

woo /wuː/ *vt* (*pt,pp* **—ed**) **1** (*old use*) to try to get the love of (a woman), esp and marry her. **2** (*modern use*) to try to win (fame, support): *woo voters/votes.*

woo·er *nc* a person who woos.

wood /wʊd/ *n* **1** *nc,nu* (a particular kind of) the hard solid substance of a tree below the bark: *Tables are usually made of wood. Put some more wood on the fire. Teak is a hard (kind of) wood and pine is a soft (kind of) wood.* **touch wood** to touch something made of wood and so avoid bad luck: *I've never been in a road accident—touch wood!* **2** *nc* (often *pl*) an area of land covered with trees (not as big as a forest): *a house in the middle of a wood; go for a walk in the wood(s).* ⇨ **wooded. out of the wood** (*fig*) free from (esp financial) troubles or difficulties: *We're not yet out of the wood.* **unable to see the wood for the trees** (*fig*) unable to get a general view because of too many details.

'wood·land *nu* land covered with trees.

'wood·work *nu* (**a**) carpentry. (**b**) things made using wood.

wood·ed /'wʊdɪd/ *adj* (usually *attrib*) covered with trees: *a thickly wooded country.*

wood·en /'wʊdn/ *adj* **1** made of wood: *a wooden leg.* **2** stiff, clumsy, awkward (and insincere): *a wooden smile.*

wood·peck·er /'wʊdpekə(r)/ *nc* a kind of bird that clings to a tree and makes holes in it with its long beak.

wood·wind /'wʊdwɪnd/ *nu* (the —) (also *attrib*) (used with a *sing* or *pl* verb) the musical wind instruments made of wood, e.g. the flute.

wood·worm /'wʊdwɜːm/ *nc,nu* (damage caused by) a kind of wood-eating larva of an insect.

woody /'wʊdɪ/ *adj* (**-ier, -iest**) **1** (*attrib*) wooded: *a woody hillside.* **2** of, like, wood: *the woody stems of a plant.*

woo·er /'wuːə(r)/ *nc* ⇨ woo.

woof /wʊf/ *vi, nc* (to make) the cry of a dog.

wool /wʊl/ *nu* **1** the soft hair of sheep, goats and some other animals. **2** the thread, cloth made from this; *knitting-wool.* **pull the wool over sb's eyes** to deceive or trick a person. **3** a material similar in appearance or texture to wool: *cotton-wool.*

wool·len (*US* = **wool·en**) /'wʊlən/ *adj* made of wool: *woollen cloth/blankets.*

wool·lens (*US* = **wool·ens**) *n pl* woollen sweaters, cardigans etc.

wool·ly (*US* also **wooly**) /'wʊlɪ/ *adj* (**-ier, -iest**) (**a**) covered with, made of, looking like, wool: *woolly hair; a woolly coat; woolly sheep.* (**b**) (*fig*) (of the mind, ideas, decisions) confused; not clear. □ *nc* (*pl* **-ies**) (*informal*) an article of clothing made of wool, esp a sweater: *Put an extra woolly on when you go out.*

word¹ /wɜːd/ *n* **1** *nc* a sound or combination of sounds (or the written symbols) forming a unit expressing an object, action, idea etc in a language: *When we speak we put our thoughts into words. What is the word for 'sympathy' in Spanish? Do you know the words of this song? There are no words to express how happy I feel.* **a four-letter(ed) word** any of the obscene or vulgar words used in swearing. **a play on words** ⇨ play¹(2). **by word of mouth** using spoken words, not in writing. **from the word go** from the very beginning: *I knew from the word go that she'd refuse.* **in a word** using as few words as possible: *It's big, colourful, exciting—in a word, I love it!* **not a word** no information to be given: *I've got £20 but not a word to anyone about it.* **not believe a word (of it)** to believe no part of what is said or written. **the last word (in sth)** a person, thing, fashion, home etc that is so good etc that it cannot be improved on: *This bed is the last word in comfort.* **2** *nc* a statement, remark; conversation: *We exchanged a few words this afternoon. He hasn't said a word about it.* **famous last words** (**a**) the final statement made by a famous person who is dying. (**b**) (used to or about a person who made a foolishly optimistic remark before failing). **in other words** or to use other words: *A whale is a mammal; in other words it feeds milk to its young.* **eat one's words** to admit that one was wrong. **not get a word in (edgeways)** to be unable to say anything because another person will not stop speaking. **have a word with sb** to speak to a person: *Can I have a word with you privately?* **have the last word** to make the final remark in an argument. **(you) mark my words** (*imperative*) listen to what I say and later you will learn that I was right. **mean every word (of sth)** to be speaking sincerely or honestly. **put in/say a good word for sb** to say something in support of a person or a person's character. **put words into sb's mouth** to suggest falsely that he or she said or believes something. **say a few words** to make a short speech. **send word** to send a message or order: *If it arrives, send word with John.* **swallow one's words** to say that one was wrong and is sorry. **take the words out of sb's mouth** to say what another person was about to say. **3** *n sing* a promise. **as good as one's word** completely reliable; able to be trusted. **give sb one's word (of honour) (that)** to promise (that): *I give you my word that I won't tell anyone.* **go back on one's word** to fail to keep a promise. **take sb's word for it; take sb at her/his word** to believe that a person is telling the truth, will keep a promise. **4** *n sing* a command; order: *The officer gave the word to fire. His word is law* (i.e. He must be obeyed). **say the word** to ask; give the order: *If you need*

help, say the word and I'll be there. ⇨ also password.

word² /wɜːd/ *vt* to state (something) in (particular) words: *How should I word this application?*

word·ing /'wɜːdɪŋ/ *n sing* the way in which something is expressed; choice of words to express meaning: *A different wording might make the meaning clearer.*

word-per·fect /,wɜːd 'pɜːfɪkt/ *adj* (*no comp*) knowing, able to repeat, a poem, a part in a play etc without reading it.

word-pow·er /'wɜːd paʊə(r)/ *nu* the ability to express oneself well.

word pro·ces·sor /'wɜːd prəʊsesə(r)/ *nc* an electronic apparatus using computer software to write, correct and print text. **'word pro·ces·sing** *nu*

wore /wɔː(r)/ *pt* of wear³.

work¹ /wɜːk/ *n* **1** *nu* the use of the body or mind to do or make something (esp contrasted with play or recreation): *Are you fond of hard work? The work of building the garage took six months. It was hard work getting to the top of the mountain.* **at work (on sth)** busy or occupied (with a task). **set/get to work (on sth/to do sth)** to begin; make a start. **2** *nu* what a person does to earn a living; employment: *What work do you do? What time do you get to work every day? The men were on their way to work.* **at work** at one's place of employment: *She's at work now but she'll be back at six.* **in/out of work** employed/unemployed. **3** *nu* something to be done that is not connected with a trade or occupation, not necessarily for payment: *I always find plenty of work that needs doing in my garden.* **4** *nu* things needed or used for work: *She took her work* (e.g. her sewing materials) *into the garden.* **5** *nc* (often *pl*) something produced by using intelligence, imagination, physical skill: *the works of Shakespeare/ Beethoven. The work of famous sculptors can be seen in museums.* ⇨ stonework, woodwork. **6** *nu* the use of energy supplied by electricity etc: *Many machines now do the work of men.* **7** (*pl*) the moving parts (of a machine): *the works of a clock or watch. There's something wrong with the works.*

,work of 'art *nc* a (good) painting, piece of sculpture etc.

'work-bench *nc* a table at which a person works with tools.

'work·book *nc* a book with questions to be answered (in spaces provided), for notes etc.

'work·day *nc* a day which is not a Sunday or a holiday.

'work-force *nc* a total number of people working in a factory etc.

'work·man *nc* a person who works in a specified way: *a skilled workman.* Compare worker.

'work·man·like *adj* characteristic of a good workman.

'work·man·ship /-mənʃɪp/ *nu* the quality as seen in something made: *articles of poor/excellent workmanship.*

'work·room *nc* a room in which work is done.

'work·shop *nc* room or building in which things (esp machines) are made or repaired.

'work-shy *adj* (*derog*) lazy.

work² /wɜːk/ *v* **1** *vt,vi* (to cause a person) to do work; engage in physical or mental activity: *I've* been working hard all day. *The men in this factory work 40 hours a week. She works too hard. He works his assistant too hard.* **2** *vt* to do work(2) to pay for (something): *He's working his way through university.* **3** *vi* to do what it is designed to do, have the desired result: *The lift/telephone is not working. This machine works by electricity. My brain doesn't seem to be working well today. Will this new plan/method work?* **4** *vt* to produce or obtain (the effect mentioned) as the result of effort: *work wonders/miracles.* **5** *vt,vi* (to cause a person, thing) to move into, reach, a new state or position, using small movements: *One of the screws has worked loose. She's working her way to the front of the queue. You'll work yourself into a bad state of health.* **6** *vt* to make or shape (a mass or mixture) by mixing, squeezing, pressure etc: *work clay* (when making pots)*; work dough* (when making bread).

work against sb/sth to have a negative effect on, prevent the progress of, a person, plan etc: *His poor education will work against him/his ambitions.*

work at sth to give effort, thought etc to a difficulty, task etc: *I can't find the answer to this problem—I'll have to work at it longer.*

work away (at sth) to continue to work: *He's been working away at this job since breakfast.*

work sth in; work sth/into sth to include, find a place for, something: *Can't you work in a few jokes/work a few jokes into your lecture?*

work sth off to get rid of something by exercise or effort: *work off extra energy/excess weight/a debt.*

work on sb (a) to have an effect on a person: *That new drug didn't work on her.* **(b)** to use one's effort to try to persuade a person: *She hasn't agreed to come but I'm working on her.* **work on sth (a)** to have an effect on something: *That dye didn't work on my hair.* **(b)** to give effort, thought, to something: *I'm working on a new book/a way to improve efficiency.* **(c)** to excite, influence something: *The information about the treatment of prisoners worked on the consciences of the United Nations representatives.*

work out (a) to be capable of being solved: *This sum/problem will not work out.* **(b)** to be, turn out, in the end: *The situation worked out quite well.* **(c)** (of life) to develop (well/badly): *I'm glad life is working out (well) for them in India.* **(d)** to come out by small movements: *Your shirt has worked out.* **(e)** to exercise, train (for a contest): *The champion is working out in the gym this morning.* Hence, '**work-out** *nc* a period, form, of exercise or training. **work sth out (a)** to calculate a cost etc: *I've worked out your share of the expenses at £5.* **(b)** to solve a problem: *I can't work out these maths problems.* **(c)** to think of, invent, a method etc: *They've worked out a way of sending a spacecraft to Mars.* **(d)** to solve problems in a relationship, marriage: *We can work it out.* **(e)** to exhaust supplies in a mine etc: *That silver-mine is now worked out* (= has no more ore). **work out at sth** to be calculated as the amount mentioned: *Her expenses work out at £30 a week.*

work sb over (*sl*) to hit a person many times.

work to sth to be guided by, controlled by, a budget, plan, timetable etc. **work to rule** ⇨

rule¹(1).

work towards sth to make efforts to achieve an agreement or settlement.

work under sb to be an assistant to a person, do a job under a person's directions.

work sth up (a) to encourage, excite, something: *work up an appetite; work up interest; work up the feelings of an audience.* **(b)** to develop something gradually: *work up trade/a market/ business.* **(c)** to encourage an increase in amount or strength of support etc: *work up support for an idea.* **work oneself/sb up (into sth)** to encourage oneself, a person, to a high point of excitement, anger etc: *He worked himself/everyone up into a rage. Don't get so worked up.* **work up to sth** to develop what one is doing or saying to a climax, crescendo.

work·able /'wɜːkəbl/ *adj* that will work; practicable: *Is the proposed scheme workable?* Opp unworkable.

work·ahol·ic /ˌwɜːkəˈhɒlɪk/ *nc* (*informal*) a person who finds it difficult to stop working, e.g. a business person, writer, researcher.

work·er /'wɜːkə(r)/ *nc* **1** a person who works in a factory or in a semi-skilled way, esp people in the working class. **2** a person who works in the way mentioned or at the job mentioned: *a good/poor worker; a research worker.*

work-in /'wɜːk ɪn/ *nc* an occasion when workers continue to work in a factory etc that is threatened with closure.

work·ing¹ /'wɜːkɪŋ/ *adj* (*attrib*) **1** concerning a person, machine etc that works: *a working man; a working lunch* (i.e. during which one works)*; a working day* (i.e. the hours a person works)*; a working wife* (i.e. a wife with a job outside the home). **2** suitable for work: *working clothes.* **3** able to be used: *a working model; a working knowledge of English.*

'**working-class** *adj, n sing* or *pl* (of) people who work in a factory or in semi-skilled jobs: *The working-class is/are worried about unemployment. The working-classes are watching traditional jobs disappear because of computers and robots.*

'**working party** *nc* a committee appointed to examine and report on a subject.

work·ings /'wɜːkɪŋz/ *n pl* **1** (part of) a mine or quarry. **2** the way that something works or the result from this: *the workings of the mind/of a washing-machine.*

work-out /'wɜːk aʊt/ ⇨ work out (d).

world¹ /wɜːld/ *adj* (*attrib*) concerning, intended for, extending over, the world(1): *a world tour; a world champion/record; world affairs; world wars; the World Games* (an international athletic meeting by individuals to find world champions)*; world-famous* (= known throughout the world).

world² /wɜːld/ *n* **1** (the —) the earth, its countries and the people in it: *sail round the world; all the countries/people of the world; see the world from a spacecraft.* **it's a small world** (*saying*) one will probably meet or hear about a person one knows wherever one travels in the world. **the (whole) world over** everywhere. **2** a particular part of the world(1): *the developing world; the western world.* **the outside world** places, people, activities etc that are not shut off from others:

We were cut off from the outside world for weeks when the bridge collapsed. **worlds apart** very different (in character): *Their lives are worlds apart since one of them went to university.* **3** (the —) human or social life: *come down in the world* to lose one's social position by becoming poor. *dead to the world* (fig) fast asleep. *a man/woman of the world* ⇨ man/woman. *set the world on fire* to be extremely successful in life. *the way of the world* ⇨ way²(3). **4** *nc* a period, state, of existing: *in this world and the next* (i.e. during existence now and after death). *not long for this world* dying. *bring sb into the world* to give birth to a child. **5** *nc* the universe; everything that exists: *Is this the best of all possible worlds?* *for all the world (as if/ like)* in every way (often suggesting surprise): *The old man walked in the rain for all the world as if the sun was shining brightly.* *not for (all) the world* not on any account (whatever the method of persuasion): *I wouldn't give up my house for all the world.* *in the world* in existence: *Nothing in the world would please me more.* *out of this world* (*informal*) excellent: *The cake is out of this world!* *on top of the world* (*informal*) extremely happy. *think the world of sb* to be extremely fond of, have a very high opinion of, a person. **6** *nc* the people, institutions, kinds etc connected with a particular interest, activity, group etc: *the insect/animal/plant worlds; the world of sport; the art/scientific world.* **7** *n sing* *a world of sth* a large amount or number of something: *My holiday did me a world of good. There's a world of difference between promising to do something and doing it.*

world·ly /'wɜːldlɪ/ *adj* (**-ier, -iest**) **1** (*attrib*) material: *my worldly goods* (= my possessions). **2** concerning the affairs of life, esp social life: *worldly-wise.*

world·li·ness *nu*

world pow·er /ˌwɜːld 'paʊə(r)/ *nc* a country influencing international economics and politics.

world·wide /ˌwɜːld'waɪd/ *adj* concerning, in, the whole world(1).

worm¹ /wɜːm/ *nc* **1** a kind of small, boneless, limbless, creeping creature. ⇨ earthworm, hookworm, tapeworm. **2** (used in compounds) a kind of larva, insect etc: *silkworm; glowworm.* **3** (fig; derog) a person who is a coward, cannot be trusted, has no moral strength etc.

worm² /wɜːm/ *vt* **1** to move (oneself) slowly, patiently or with difficulty: *He wormed himself/ his way through the undergrowth. He wormed himself into her confidence.* **2** *worm sth out of sb* to get information from a person by using repeated questions, flattery etc: *He wormed the secret out of me.* **3** to rid (an animal) of worms: *I think we'd better worm the cat.*

worn /wɔːn/ *pp* of wear³.

wor·ri·some /'wʌrɪsəm/ *adj* causing worry.

wor·ry¹ /'wʌrɪ/ *nc,nu* (*pl* **-ies**) (something that causes) the state of feeling anxious or troubled: *show signs of worry. Her son has always been a worry to her. He's full of worries about his future.*

wor·ry² /'wʌrɪ/ *v* (*pt,pp* **-ied**) **1** *vt,vi* (to cause a person) to be, become, anxious or troubled: *The noise of the traffic worried her. What's worrying you? I'm worried about Ben/the exams. He's not*

worth worrying over. *You have no need to worry. What's the use of worrying?* *not to worry* (*informal; imperative*) do not worry: *He's lost his pen but not to worry, I'll lend him this one.* **2** *vt* (esp of dogs) to seize (an animal etc) with the teeth and shake: *The dog was worrying a rat.*

wor·ried *adj* troubled; anxious: *a worried look.*

wor·ry·ing *adj* full of, causing, worry: *have a worrying time. Her lateness is worrying.*

worse¹ /wɜːs/ *adj* **1** (used as the comparative form of *bad*): *Your work is bad but mine is much worse. My eyesight is getting worse. I'm bad at biology but I'm worse at physics.* **2** (*pred*) more ill: *The doctor says she's much worse today.* **3** more unpleasant: *Having to wear a suit and tie is worse than going to the dentist.* *worse luck!* (*informal*) unfortunately: *I have to work all this weekend, worse luck!*

worse² /wɜːs/ *adv* **worse (than . . .)** **1** (used as the comparative form of *badly*): *He's behaving worse than ever. She cooks badly but I cook worse!* *be worse off* to be in a more unfortunate (financial) condition: *You're no worse off without him.* Compare better²(1). **2** (used to make a state or condition more extreme): *It's raining/hurting worse than before.*

worse³ /wɜːs/ *nu* something that is worse: *I have worse to report. The first reports were bad but worse followed.* *for better or (for) worse* ⇨ better³(1). *none the worse (for sth)* not harmed or badly affected (by a bad event or situation): *The boy got lost on the mountain overnight, but luckily he was none the worse for it when we found him.* *the worse for wear* (*fig*) exhausted (and untidy etc): *He looks the worse for wear after only a year as prime minister.* *go from bad to worse* ⇨ bad¹(2). Compare better³.

wors·en /'wɜːsn/ *vt,vi* (to cause health, a situation etc) to become worse: *Her health/The economy has worsened.*

wor·ship¹ /'wɜːʃɪp/ *nu* **1** the act of showing religious respect and devotion to God: *places of worship* (e.g. churches). **2** admiration and respect shown to or felt for a person or thing: *the worship of success; hero worship.*

wor·ship² /'wɜːʃɪp/ *vt,vi* (**-pp-**, *US* **-p-**) to give great admiration and respect to (God, a person): *worship God. She worships her husband.*

wor·ship·per (*US* = **wor·ship·er**) *nc* a person who worships.

worst¹ /wɜːst/ *adj* (*attrib*) (used as the superlative of *bad*): *the worst storm for five years; the worst behaviour; the worst condition.* Compare best¹.

worst² /wɜːst/ *adv* (used as the superlative of *badly*): most badly: *Tom played badly, Harry played worse and I played worst.* Compare best².

worst³ /wɜːst/ *n* (the —) a condition, event, part etc that is the most bad: *I've eaten bad meals but this is the worst. You must be prepared for the worst* (i.e. the worst possible news, result etc). *at worst* if one considers a situation etc in the most unfavourable way: *At worst she's a liar but she's never really unkind.* *if the worst comes to the worst* if the worst possible thing happens: *He's applied for a job in London, and if the worst comes to the worst he'll go back to college.* *come off worst; get the worst of sth* to get the smallest benefit or be defeated. **fear the worst** to think that something very sad etc will happen, e.g. a person who is ill will die soon. Compare best³.

worth¹ /wɜ:θ/ *adj* (*pred*) as a *prep* **1** giving a satisfactory or rewarding return for; good enough for: *The book is well worth reading. It's hardly worth worrying about. She's not worth the trouble.* **2** having property to the value of: *What's the old man worth? He's worth £50 000.* **for all one is worth** (*informal*) making every effort: *He was running for all he was worth.* **be worth a try** ⇨ try¹(1). **3** of value, equal to: *It's not worth more than £2. The car is worth much more than that.* **for what it's worth** (used to suggest that one doubts the truth or value of the information one is offering): *For what it's worth, she asked me to say that she's sorry.* **worth one's while** ⇨ while².

worth·less *adj* **1** having no value: *a worthless piece of stone.* **2** that is not worth the time, trouble etc needed: *a worthless attempt.* Compare worthwhile.

worth² /wɜ:θ/ *nu* **1** value: *know a friend's worth.* **2** (usually /wəθ/) an amount of something of the value or quantity mentioned: *a pound's worth of apples.*

worth·while /ˌwɜ:θ'waɪl/ *adj* that is worth the time, trouble etc needed: *a worthwhile experiment; worthwhile waiting for.* Compare worthless(2).

wor·thy /'wɜ:ðɪ/ *adj* (**-ier, -iest**) **1** (*pred*) **worthy of sth** deserving something: *a cause worthy of support; a man who is worthy of a place in the team/to be in the team.* **2** (often *ironic*) deserving respect: *a worthy gentleman.* Opp unworthy.
wor·thi·ly /-əlɪ/ *adv*
wor·thi·ness *nu*

would /wəd *strong form* wʊd/ Ⓝ 'Would' is a (*modal*) *auxiliary verb* used with another verb to form the past tense of 'will' and to form conditional statements. 'Would' has no infinitive or imperative form and no participles. 'Would' is always followed by an infinitive without 'to'. Compare will², shall. (*all persons* **would**, *negative* **would not** or **wouldn't** /'wʊdnt/; *would have* can be shortened to **would've** /'wʊdəv/; *would* is often shortened to '**d**, esp after *I, he, she, you, we, they.*) **1** (used as the past tense form of *will* esp in reported speech and to express refusal): *She realized she would fail. He promised that he would telephone me next Friday. Peter said he'd feed the cat. She wouldn't pay me. The machine wouldn't work so I had to wash the clothes myself. He knew he would have to try again.* **2** (used to report regular or usual behaviour in the past): *He would often sit and watch the birds. We'd nearly always eat with my mother on Fridays.* Compare will²(7), used¹(2). **3** (used to express the conditional): *If you hadn't come, we would have starved. I would/I'd apologize if I were you. If he were to apologize, would you forgive him? If you'd (= you had) listened carefully, you'd (= you would) know what to do. If she had asked sooner, this wouldn't have happened. I would've stayed if you had been there. I would have been late if you hadn't fetched me. You would be wrong if you thought that. It would be wrong to take it without asking.* **4** (used to make polite offers and requests): *Would you like to see*

my paintings? Would you like another cup of tea? Would she care to join us? Would you please ask her to wait? She asked if you would wait. I'd be very pleased if you would show me the way out. If you'd sign here, I'll bring your key. Close the door, would you? **5** (used to express preference): *I would rather walk than go in that car. She'd sooner die than wear this dress. We'd prefer to go by bus.* **6** (used to express wishes): *I wish you would wear warmer clothes. She wished he would ring her more often. I wish it would stop raining. We wish Ben would help us more. If only he would help us.* **7** (used to express annoyance): *Jane would be late just when we asked her to come early. 'I'll go alone'—'You would!'* Compare will²(6).

would-be /'wʊd bi:/ *adj* (*attrib*) wanting or claiming to be (often unjustly): *would-be authors.*

wouldn't /'wʊdnt/ = would not.

would've /'wʊdəv/ = would have.

wound¹ /wu:nd/ *nc* **1** a hurt or damage to the body, caused by cutting, shooting, tearing etc, esp as the result of attack: *a bullet/knife wound.* Ⓝ *'Injury'* is more usual for the result of an accident. **2** an instance of damage to a person's feelings: *a wound to his pride/vanity.*

wound² /wu:nd/ *vt* to give a wound to (a person): *Ten soldiers were killed and thirty wounded.*

wound³ /waʊnd/ *pt,pp* of wind⁴.

wove /wəʊv/ *pt* of weave².

woven /'wəʊvən/ *pp* of weave².

wow /waʊ/ *nc* (*sl*) a great success: *The new play at the National Theatre's a wow.* □ *int* (used to express wonder, admiration etc): *Wow, what a good play!*

wpm *written abbr* words per minute (e.g. in typing). ⇨ cps(2).

wrangle /'ræŋgl/ *vi, nc* (to take part in) a noisy or angry argument.

wrap¹ /ræp/ *nc* (*dated*) an outer article of clothing or covering, e.g. a cloak, wide scarf etc.

wrap² /ræp/ *vt* (**-pp-**) **1 wrap sb/sth (up) (in sth)** to put something round a person, thing; cover or roll up a person, thing in it: *wrap a child in a shawl; wrap up a present in tissue paper; wrap oneself (up) in a blanket.* **be wrapped up in sb/ sth** (**a**) (*fig*) to be hidden in something: *The affair is wrapped (up) in mystery.* (**b**) to be deeply interested in something: *He is wrapped up in his work/ studies.* (**c**) to be deeply devoted to a person, thing: *She is wrapped up in her children.* **2** to wind or fold (something) round as a covering or protection: *Wrap plenty of paper round it.*

wrap·per /'ræpə(r)/ *nc* **1** a loose paper cover for a book. **2** a cloth (to be) tied round the body as a long skirt.

wrap·ping /'ræpɪŋ/ *n* **1** *nc* something used for covering or packing: *sweet wrappings.* **2** *nu* material used for covering or packing something: *Put plenty of wrapping round the cups.*

WRAC *written abbr* (the —) (*GB*) the Women's Royal Army Corps.

WRAF *written abbr* (the —) (*GB*) the Women's Royal Air Force.

wrath /rɒθ/ *nu* (*formal*) great anger (esp caused by injustice).

wreak /ri:k/ *vt* (*formal*) to cause (a bad condition): *wreak havoc.*

wreath /riːθ/ *nc* (*pl* —**s** /riːðz/) **1** a woven circle of flowers or leaves (as placed on a coffin, a grave, a memorial to the dead etc). **2** *wreath of sth* a twisting line of smoke, mist etc.

wreathe /riːð/ *vt* to go round and cover (something): *wreathe a head with flowers; hills wreathed in mist; a face wreathed in smiles.*

wreck[1] /rek/ *n* **1** *nc* a ship that has been damaged or destroyed at sea: *Robinson Crusoe obtained food and supplies from the wreck.* **2** *nc,nu* (a thing, building, car etc in) a badly damaged state: *The car was a worthless wreck after the accident.* **3** *nc* a person whose health has been destroyed: *If you worry too much, you'll become a nervous wreck.*

wreck[2] /rek/ *vt* to destroy (something): *The ship/ train was wrecked. Their marriage was wrecked by disagreements.*

wreck·age /'rekɪdʒ/ *nu* a wrecked object; pieces left after something has been destroyed: *The wreckage (of the plane) was scattered over a wide area.*

wren /ren/ *nc* a kind of small songbird.

Wren /ren/ *abbr* (*GB*) (a member of) the Women's Royal Naval Service (*the Wrens*).

wrench[1] /rentʃ/ *nc* **1** a sudden and violent twist or pull: *He gave his ankle a wrench.* **2** (a pain caused by) a sad parting or separation: *Separation from her children was a terrible wrench.* **3** a kind of tool for gripping and turning nuts, bolts etc.

wrench[2] /rentʃ/ *vt* **1** to twist or pull (something) violently: *wrench the door open; wrench a door off its hinges.* **2** to injure (e.g. one's ankle) by twisting.

wrest /rest/ *vt* (*formal*) **1** to take (something) away with force: *wrest a knife from him/wrest it out of his hands.* **2** to get (agreement etc) by force: *wrest a confession of guilt from a person.*

wrestle /'resl/ *vi* *wrestle (with sb/sth)* **1** to struggle (with a person) and try to throw her or him to the ground. **2** to wrestle(1) as a sport. **3** (*fig*) to struggle (with something): *wrestle with a problem/one's conscience.*

wres·tler /'reslə(r)/ *nc* a person who wrestles(2).

wretch /retʃ/ *nc* **1** a very poor and sad person. **2** (*derog*) a mean, unwilling person.

wretch·ed /'retʃɪd/ *adj* **1** very bad. sad etc: *living in wretched poverty.* **2** (*informal; derog*) of poor quality: *wretched weather/food.*

wretch·ed·ly *adv*

wriggle[1] /'rɪgl/ *nc* a wriggling movement.

wriggle[2] /'rɪgl/ *v* **1** *vi* to move with quick, short, twistings; move along in this way: *Small children wriggle in their seats when they are bored. The eel wriggled out of my fingers.* **2** *vt* to make (a route) by using a wriggling motion: *wriggle one's way out.*

wring[1] /rɪŋ/ *nc* an act of wringing wet clothes etc: *Give it another wring.*

wring[2] /rɪŋ/ *vt* (*pt,pp* **wrung** /rʌŋ/) **1** to twist, squeeze, (something): *wring clothes* (to force water out); *wring a hen's neck* (i.e. to kill it). **be wringing wet** to be very wet. *wring one's hands* to squeeze them together (to show sorrow etc). **2** *wring sth (out)* **(a)** to twist and squeeze something tightly (to force out water): *wring out wet clothes.* **(b)** (*fig*) to force a person to confess (something) using persuasion, threats etc:

wring the truth out of him.

wrinkle[1] /'rɪŋkl/ *nc* a small fold or line in the skin (esp of the kind produced by age) or on the surface of something: *She's beginning to get wrinkles round her eyes. She ironed out the wrinkles in her dress.*

wrin·kly /'rɪŋklɪ/ *adj*

wrinkle[2] /'rɪŋkl/ *vt,vi* (to cause something) to have, get, wrinkles: *wrinkle up one's forehead; wrinkled with age.*

wrist /rɪst/ *nc* the joint between the hand and the arm: *He took me by the wrist.*

'wrist·band *nc* a band of cloth worn round the wrist, e.g. by tennis-players.

'wrist-watch *nc* a watch worn on the wrist.

writ /rɪt/ *nc* (*legal*) a written order issued in the name of an official to do or not to do something: *a writ for the arrest of a suspected criminal.*

write /raɪt/ *v* (*pt* **wrote** /rəʊt/, *pp* **written** /'rɪtn/) **1** *vi* to make letters or other symbols on a surface, esp with a pen or pencil on paper: *learn to read and write. I've been writing (for) three hours. Are we to write in ink or (in) pencil?* ⇒ **writing**. **2** *vt* to put (something) down (on paper) by means of words etc: *write words/a letter/Chinese characters/shorthand; write one's name and address; write a cheque/a book. Please write your name in full* (i.e. in words, without abbreviations). **3** *vt,vi* to do the work of an author: *write a novel/a play; write for the newspapers; make a living by writing.* **4** *vi,vt* *write (to sb) (that)* to write and send a letter: *He promised to write to me every week. He writes home/writes to his parents regularly. She wrote that the cat was ill. Write her a reply as soon as you can.* **5** *vt* (usually *passive*) (*fig*) to show clear signs of (something): *He had pain/honesty written on his face.*

write about sth to produce a book, letter etc about a subject.

write away for sth to send an order by post for something.

write back (to sb) to write and send a letter in reply (to a person).

write sth down to put something down on paper in words: *You'd better write the address down before you forget it.*

write in (for sth) to apply by letter for something. *write in (to sth)* to send a letter asking for or giving information (to a radio/TV programme etc). *write sth in* to write one's name, address etc in spaces in an application form etc.

write off (for sth) to send an order by post: *write off for an application form.* *write sth off* **(a)** to recognize that something is a loss or failure: *write off a debt.* **(b)** to destroy something completely: *He has just written off a new car.* Hence **'write-off** *nc*: *The burnt-out plane was a complete write-off* (= had no value whatever).

write on sth = write about sth.

write sth out to write (the whole of) something in full: *write out a copy of an agreement; write out a cheque for £100.*

write sth up to write something in detail: *write up one's diary. I must write up my notes of the lecture.* Hence **'write-up** *nc* a written account of an event.

writer /'raɪtə(r)/ *nc* **1** a person who writes: *the* *writer of this letter.* **2** an author.

write-off /'raɪt ɒf/ *nc* ⇨ write sth off(b).

write-up /'raɪt ʌp/ *nc* ⇨ write sth up.

writhe /raɪð/ *vi* to twist or roll about (because of physical or mental pain): *writhing under insults.*

writ·ing /'raɪtɪŋ/ *n* **1** *nu* the act of writing something, esp books: *He's busy with his writing.* **put sth down in writing** = write sth down. **2** = handwriting. **3** (*pl*) literary work: *the writings of Swift.*

'writing-paper *nu* a kind of paper for letters.

writ·ten /'rɪtn/ *pp* of write.

WRNS *abbr* (the —) (*GB*) the Women's Royal Naval Service.

wrong¹ /rɒŋ/ *adj* **1** (*pred*) (of behaviour etc) morally bad, illegal, unjust: *It's wrong to steal. He was quite wrong to stop her. It would be wrong to refuse to help.* Opp right²(1). **2** (of facts, reasons, time etc) not correct; untrue: *Your calculations are wrong. This clock shows the wrong time. You've given me the wrong change. She's dialled the wrong number. They've gone the wrong way.* Opp right²(2). **3** not at all suitable: *The conditions are wrong for an attempt at the world record. It's the wrong time to sell your house. He is obviously the wrong man for the job.* Opp right²(3). **4** (*pred*) **wrong (with sth)** in a bad condition: *There's nothing/something wrong with you/the car. What's wrong with your bike?* Compare right²(4).

wrong² /rɒŋ/ *adv* not correctly: *guess wrong. You've spelt my name wrong. You've got the sum wrong.* Opp right⁴(1). **go wrong (a)** to take the wrong path or road. (**b**) to have a bad result: *All our plans went wrong.* (**c**) (of a machine) to fail to work correctly. (**d**) (of a person) to do the wrong things, take the wrong decisions: *My son is so lazy—where did I go wrong?*

wrong³ /rɒŋ/ *nc,nu* what is morally bad, illegal, unjust: *She knows the difference between right and wrong. You've done her a great wrong. Two wrongs don't make a right.* **be in the wrong** to have behaved or acted incorrectly; be responsible for an error: *He admitted that he was in the wrong.* Opp right⁶(1).

wrong⁴ /rɒŋ/ *vt* to treat (a person) unfairly or unjustly: *He wronged me when he said that I was greedy.*

wrong·do·er /'rɒŋduːə(r)/ *nc* a person who does something bad or illegal.

wrong·do·ing *nc,nu* (an instance of) bad or illegal behaviour.

wrong·ful /'rɒŋfəl/ *adj* unjust; unlawful: *wrongful dismissal (from a job); wrongful arrest.*

wrong·ful·ly /-fəlɪ/ *adv*

wrong·ly /'rɒŋlɪ/ *adv* incorrectly (esp before a *pp*): *wrongly informed/accused.* Compare rightly.

wrote /rəʊt/ *pt* of write.

wrought /rɔːt/ *adj* (*attrib*) (of metal) beaten into shape: *wrought iron.*

wrung /rʌŋ/ *pt,pp* of wring².

wry /raɪ/ *adj* (**wrier, wriest**) showing dislike, a humorous thought etc: *a wry smile.*

wry·ly *adv*

WSW *written abbr* west-south-west.

wt *written abbr* weight.

Xx

X, x /eks/ (*pl* **X's, x's** / 'eksɪz/) the 24th letter of the English alphabet.

x *symbol* (*maths*) **1** the horizontal axis in a graph. **2** an unknown quantity.

X *symbol* **1** (also *x*) the Roman numeral 10. **2** (*old use*) identifying a cinema film that may not be shown to people under 18. **3** showing an answer (e.g. in an exam) that is wrong. **4** showing a person's choice or preference (on an official form, a voting card etc).

xeno·pho·bia /ˌzenəˈfəʊbɪə/ *nu* (*formal*) an extreme hatred or fear of strangers or foreigners.

xeno·pho·bic /ˌzenəˈfəʊbɪk/ *adj*

XL *symbol* (*commerce*) extra large size (clothing).

Xmas /'krɪsməs, 'eksməs/ *n* (*informal*) = Christmas.

X-ray¹ /'eks reɪ/ *nc* (also *attrib*) (a special photograph made using) a form of short-wave rays that makes it possible to see into or through objects: *X-ray photos/examinations of bones in the body.*

X-ray² /'eks reɪ/ *vt* to examine, treat, photograph, (a part of the body) using X-rays.

XS *symbol* (*commerce*) extra small size (clothing).

xylo·phone /'zaɪləfəʊn/ *nc* (also *attrib*) a kind of musical instrument with wooden bars that produce different notes when hit: *a xylophone player.*

Yy

Y, y /waɪ/ (*pl* **Y's, y's** /waɪz/) the 25th letter of the English alphabet.

y *symbol* (*maths*) **1** the vertical axis in a graph. **2** a second unknown quantity.

yacht /jɒt/ *nc* **1** a light sailing-boat built specially for racing. **2** a large (usually motor-driven) boat for pleasure-cruising.

yacht·ing *nu* the art, sport, of sailing yachts.

yak /jæk/ *nc* a kind of long-haired ox of Central Asia.

yam /jæm/ *nc,nu* (an edible white tuber of) a kind of tropical climbing plant.

yank /jæŋk/ *vi,vt, nc* (to give) a sudden sharp pull to (something): *yank (out) a tooth.*

yap /jæp/ *vi* (**-pp-**), *nc* (esp of dogs) (to make) a short, sharp bark.

yard¹ /jɑːd/ *nc* **1** an enclosed or partly enclosed space near or round a building or group of buildings: *a farmyard. Come and play in our back yard.* **2** (usually in compounds) an enclosure for a particular purpose: *the railway yard; a dockyard.* **3** (*US*) = garden.

yard² /jɑːd/ *nc* (abbr yd) a unit of measurement of length, 3 feet (or 0·914m): *Can you still buy cloth by the yard in Britain?*

yard·stick /'jɑːdstɪk/ *nc* a standard used for comparison: *Do you judge other children by the* *same yardstick as your own?*

yarn /jɑ:n/ *n* **1** *nu* thread (cotton or wool etc). **2** *nc* (*informal*) a long story. **spin a yarn** to tell a story (often one that is untrue).

yash·mak /ˈjæʃmæk/ *nc* a veil worn in public by some Muslim women.

yawn¹ /jɔ:n/ *nc* an act of yawning.

yawn² /jɔ:n/ *vi* to open the mouth wide and breathe in, as when sleepy or bored.

yawn·ing *adj* (*attrib*) wide open: *a yawning gap.*

yaws /jɔ:z/ *nu* a kind of infectious tropical skin disease.

yd(s) *written abbr* yard(s) (⇨ yard²).

yeah /je/ *int* (*informal*) yes.

year /jɪə(r)/ *nc* **1** the time taken by the earth to go round the sun, about 365¼ days. **2** (also called the *calendar year*) the period from 1 January to 31 December: *in the year 1865; last year; this year; next year; the year after next; next year's holiday.* **year after year; year in year out** for a very long time: *We have visited this island year in year out and we never get bored.* **all the year round** at all times of the year. **for years** for a long time: *We've been friends for years.* **3** any period of 365 consecutive days: *It is just a year since I arrived here. He's twenty years of age/twenty years old.* **4** a period of one year associated with something: *the academic year; the financial year.*

year·ly *adj, adv* (taking place) every year; once a year.

year·ling /ˈjɪəlɪŋ/ *nc* an animal between one and two years old.

yearn /jɜ:n/ *vi* **yearn (for sth/to do sth)** to long (for something, to do something) with great, tender feeling, affection etc: *He yearned for home/to see his family again.*

yearn·ing *nu* (also *pl*) a strong desire.

yeast /ji:st/ *nc,nu* a substance used to make bread rise and used to make beer, wine etc.

yell¹ /jel/ *nc* a loud, sharp cry: *yells of pain/terror.*

yell² /jel/ *v* **1** *vi* **yell (with sth)** to make a loud sharp cry or cries (of pain, excitement etc): *yell with fright/laughter.* **2** *vt* to say (something) in a loud voice: *yell (out) an order.*

yel·low¹ /ˈjeləʊ/ *adj, nu* **1** (of) the colour of gold or the yolk of a hen's egg. **2** (*informal*) cowardly: *He has a yellow streak in him.*

‚yellow 'fever *nu* a kind of infectious tropical disease causing the skin to turn yellow.

‚yellow 'pages *n pl* (the —) (a section of) a telephone directory listing businesses, professions and services.

yellow·ish /-ɪʃ/ *adj* a little yellow.

yellow·ness *nu*

yel·low² /ˈjeləʊ/ *vt,vi* (to cause something) to become yellow: *The leaves of the book were yellowed/had yellowed with age.*

yelp /jelp/ *vi, nc* (to make) a short, sharp cry (of pain, anger, excitement etc).

yep /jep/ *int* (*informal*) yes.

yes /jes/ *int* (used as a short addition or in short answers to express agreement, approval, consent etc): *'Is it raining?'—'Yes, it is.' 'Do you like carrots?'—'Yes, I do.' 'Can I have it?'—'Yes, you can.' 'Would you like some?'—'Yes, please.' 'Did you enjoy the film?'—'Yes, but I didn't like the music.'* **Yes and no** partly: *'Was it a good*

party?'—'Yes and no.' **yes or no** (used when asking for a plain answer, esp when angry): *Do you want it—yes or no?* Compare no³.

yes·ter·day /ˈjestədɪ/ *adv, nc* (on) the day just past; (on) the day before today: *He arrived yesterday. Yesterday was Sunday. The day before yesterday was Saturday. Where's yesterday's newspaper?*

yes·ter·year /ˈjestəjɪə(r)/ *nu* **of yesteryear** (*formal*) (of) the past: *fashions of yesteryear.*

yet /jet/ *adv* **1** by this/that time: *They're not here yet. Has the postman been yet?* **2** before now: *I haven't been to Brazil yet.* **as yet** up to now: *As yet we've made no plans for the holidays. She has no job as yet.* Ⓝ 'Yet' is only used in questions and negative statements. For the differences between yet, already and still, ⇨ already(3). **3** at some future time: *He may surprise us all yet.* **just yet** in the immediate future: *You needn't pay me just yet.* **4** (often used to emphasize an amount): *yet another war; yet more problems.* **5** (used to join sentences) but at the same time: *He worked hard, yet he failed.* Compare still²(3).

yew /ju:/ *nc,nu* (the wood of) a kind of tree with dark-green leaves and red berries, often used for garden hedges.

YHA /ˌwaɪ eɪtʃ ˈeɪ/ *abbr* (the —) the Youth Hostels Association.

yield¹ /ji:ld/ *nc,nu* (*formal*) an amount produced: *a good yield of wheat.*

yield² /ji:ld/ *vt,vi* (*formal*) **1** to give (a natural product, result or profit): *trees that yield fruit.* **2** to give in (to): *We will never yield to force. He yielded to temptation.*

yip·pee /ˈjɪpi/ *int* (used to express joy).

YMCA /ˌwaɪ em si: ˈeɪ/ *abbr* (the —) the Young Men's Christian Association. ⇨ YWCA.

yo·del /ˈjəʊdl/ *vt,vi* (-ll-, US also -l-) to sing (a song), make a musical call, with frequent changes from the normal voice to high (*falsetto*) notes (like Swiss mountaineers). □ *nc* such a song or call.

yo·del·ler (*US* also **yo·del·er**) *nc* a person who yodels.

yo·ga /ˈjəʊɡə/ *nu* (also *attrib*) a Hindu system of mental and physical exercises to produce mystical experience and the union of the individual soul with the universal spirit: *yoga lessons.* ⇨ yogi.

yo·ghurt (also **yo·gurt, yo·ghourt**) /ˈjɒɡət/ *nu* a semi-solid food made from fermented milk.

yo·gi /ˈjəʊɡi/ *nc* (*pl* —s) a teacher of, expert in, yoga.

yoke¹ /jəʊk/ *nc* **1** a shaped piece of wood placed across the necks of oxen pulling a cart etc. **2** a shaped piece of wood to fit a person's shoulders and support a pail at each end. **3** a part of a dress etc fitting round the shoulders from which the rest hangs. **4** (*fig*) a symbol of defeat etc: *the yoke of oppression.*

yoke² /jəʊk/ *vt* to put a yoke on (oxen).

yo·kel /ˈjəʊkl/ *nc* a simple countryman.

yolk /jəʊk/ *nc,nu* the yellow part of an egg: *Beat up the yolks of three eggs.*

yon·der /ˈjɒndə(r)/ *adj, adv* (*formal*) (that is, that can be seen) over there.

yoo-hoo /ˈju: hu:/ *int* (*informal*) (used to call a

greeting to a friend etc).

you /ju:/ *personal pron* **1** the person(s) addressed: *You are my friend/friends. Does he know you? Who gave it to you?* **2** (*impersonal pron*) any person but no particular individual; anybody: *It is much easier to cycle with the wind behind you.* Compare one³(2).

you'd /ju:d/ = *you had; you would.*

you'll /ju:l/ = *you will.*

young¹ /jʌŋ/ *adj* (**—er, —est**) **1** having lived a short time: *a young woman/tree/animal. Is she too young for the job?* Compare old¹(2). **2** having existed for a short time: *a young nation.* Compare old¹(3). **3** still near its beginning: *The evening/century is still young.* **4** (*attrib*) (used before a person's name to distinguish, esp a son from his father): *Young Jones is always ready to help his parents.* **5** (*attrib*) (used as a form of address): *Now listen to me, young man/my young lady!* **6** having little practice or experience (in something): *young councillors; young in experience.*

young² /jʌŋ/ *n* **1** *n pl* (the —) young people; children: *books for the young.* **(the) young and old** everyone. **2** *nu* young animals, birds: *The cat fought to defend its young.*

young·ish /'jʌŋgɪʃ/ *adj* fairly young.

young·ster /'jʌŋstə(r)/ *nc* a young person, esp a boy. ⇨ youth(2).

your /jɔ:(r)/ *possessive adj* or *det* belonging to you: *Show me your hands. You'll see the post office on your right* (i.e. on the right side).

you're /jɔ:(r)/ = *you are.*

yours /jɔ:z/ *possessive pron* **1** of, belonging to, you: *Is that book yours? I borrowed a book of yours.* **2** (used to end a letter): *Yours, Jim.* ⇨ affectionately, faithfully, sincerely, truly.

your·self /jɔ:'self/ *pron* (*pl* **-selves** /-'selvz/) **1** (used as the *reflex* of *you*): *Did you hurt yourself? Please look after yourself.* **(all) by yourself** ⇨ by²(1). **2** (used for emphasis): *You said so yourself.* **3** your usual self: *You don't seem yourself today.*

youth /ju:θ/ *n* (*pl* **—s** /ju:ðz/) **1** *nu* the period of being young: *the friends of one's youth; in my youth.* **2** *nc* a young man: *Half a dozen youths were standing at the street corner.* **3** *nu* young men and women in general: *the youth of today.*

'youth club *nc* a club for the leisure activities of young people.

'youth hostel *nc* a place where people can stay cheaply while walking or cycling in the countryside. ⇨ YHA.

youth·ful /-fəl/ *adj* young; having the qualities etc of young people: *a youthful appearance.*

youth·ful·ly /-fəlɪ/ *adv*

youth·ful·ness *nu*

you've /ju:v/ = *you have.*

yr(s) *written abbr* **1** year(s). **2** (*commerce*) your(s).

yule /ju:l/ *n* (*dated*) (also Y-) Christmas.

yup·pie /'jʌpɪ/ *nc* (*informal*) a young professional person, esp who is becoming more successful and earns a lot of money.

YWCA /ˌwaɪ dʌblju: si: 'eɪ/ *abbr* (the —) the Young Women's Christian Association. ⇨ YMCA.

Zz

Z, z /zed/ (*pl* **Z's, z's** /zeds/) the 26th and last letter of the English alphabet.

z *symbol* (*maths*) a third unknown quantity.

za·ny /'zeɪnɪ/ *adj* (**-ier, -iest**) (*informal*) (of a person, action) pleasantly foolish; odd.

zeal /zi:l/ *nu* great interest and effort: *work with great zeal.*

zeal·ous /'zeləs/ *adj* enthusiastic; keen (the usual words): *a zealous worker.*

ze·bra /'zebrə/ *nc* (*pl* **—s**) a wild animal of Africa like a horse, with dark stripes on its body.

ˌzebra 'crossing *nc* a street-crossing marked with broad white stripes, where people have priority over traffic.

Zen /zen/ *nu* a form of Buddhism teaching that enlightenment comes from meditation.

zen·ith /'zenɪθ/ *n sing* **1** the part of the sky directly overhead. **2** (*fig*) the highest point of one's fame, fortunes etc): *at the zenith of his career.* Compare nadir.

ze·ro¹ /'zɪərəʊ/ *nc* (*pl* **—s**) **1** the figure 0. Ⓝ /əʊ/ is the spoken form of 0 when speaking numbers, e.g. when telephoning, and 'nil' is usually used in scores for games, as in 'We won, five-nil'. 'Zero' is mainly used in scientific contexts. **2** the point between the positive (+) and negative (−) on a scale, esp on a thermometer: *The thermometer fell to zero last night. It was ten degrees below zero* (e.g. −10°C or −10°F). ⇨ absolute zero.

ˌzero 'gravity *nu* (*science*) the state of having no gravity.

ˌzero 'plural *nc* (*gram*) a plural form of a word that is the same as the singular form, e.g. *fish, fruit, sheep.*

'zero-rated *adj* (*finance*) (of goods) for which value added tax need not be paid, e.g. books.

ze·ro² /'zɪərəʊ/ *vi* **zero in (on sb/sth)** **1** (*photography*) to direct a camera lens towards: *zero in on a child's face.* **2** (*fig*) to get near to a point: *He's never slow to zero in on an opportunity to make a profit. The police are zeroing in on the thief.*

zest /zest/ *n* **1** *nu* extreme interest or pleasure: *He entered into our plans with zest.* **2** *nu* or *sing* a pleasing or stimulating quality or flavour: *Garlic adds* (*a*) *zest to a stew.*

zig·zag¹ /'zɪgzæg/ *nc* (also *attrib*) a line or path which turns right and left alternately at sharp (equal or unequal) angles: *a zigzag path up the hillside.*

zig·zag² /'zɪgzæg/ *vi* (**-gg-**) to move, go, in a zigzag: *The drunken man zigzagged down the street.*

zil·lions /'zɪlɪənz/ *n pl* (*informal*) an extremely large quantity: *zillions of stars/insects.*

zinc /zɪŋk/ *nu* (*science*) a hard, bluish-white metal (symbol Zn) used to produce alloys and to protect against rust.

zip¹ /zɪp/ *nc* **1** a sound as of a bullet going through the air, or of the sudden tearing of cloth. **2** (also *zipper, zip-fastener*) a device with two toothed metal or plastic edges fastened together by means of a sliding tab, used for fastening articles of clothing, bags etc.

zip² /zɪp/ *vt* (-pp-) *zip sth (open/up/shut)* to open or close a coat, bag etc using a zip(2): *Zip (up) your coat—it's cold.* Opp unzip.

zip code /ˈzɪp kəʊd/ *nc* (*US*) = postcode.

zip-fastener /ˌzɪp ˈfɑːsnə(r)/ *nc* ⇨ zip¹(2).

zip·per /ˈzɪpə(r)/ *nc* ⇨ zip¹(2).

zith·er /ˈzɪðə(r)/ *nc* a kind of musical instrument with many strings on a flat board.

zo·di·ac /ˈzəʊdɪæk/ *n* **1** (the —) the band of space extending about 8° on each side of the path followed by the sun and containing the path of the planets. **2** (the Z—) this region divided into 12 equal parts (called *the signs of the Zodiac*) named after 12 groups of stars.

zone /zəʊn/ *nc* an area with the features, purpose or use mentioned: *the war zone; the danger zone; a tropical zone; a smokeless zone* (= an area where only smokeless fuels may be used).

zon·al /-nl/ *adj* relating to, arranged in, zones.

zonk /zɒŋk/ *vi* **zonk** *(out)* (*informal*) to (sit in a chair and) fall asleep because very tired.

zonked *adj* **zonked** *(out)* extremely tired.

zoo /zuː/ *nc* (*pl* —s) a place where many kinds of animals are kept for exhibition.

zo·ologi·cal /ˌzəʊəˈlɒdʒɪkl/ *adj* of zoology: *zoological gardens*.

zo·ol·ogist /zəʊˈɒlədʒɪst/ *nc* a student of, expert in, zoology.

zo·ol·ogy /zəʊˈɒlədʒɪ/ *nu* the scientific study of the structure, forms and distribution of animals.

zoom¹ /zuːm/ *nu* (the low, deep humming sound of) the sudden upward flight of a plane.

zoom² /zuːm/ *vi* **1** (of a vehicle) to move quickly: *The sports car zoomed past.* **2** (of a plane) to move upwards quickly. **3** *zoom in (on sb/sth)* (*photography*) (of a camera with a *zoom lens*) to move quickly from a person, thing that is far away to one closer: *zoom in on a flower.* ⇨ zero²(1).

'zoom lens *nc* (*photography*) (on a camera) one able to move quickly between distant and close objects. ⇨ macro-zoom.

zuc·chi·ni /zuːˈkiːnɪ/ (*pl* —s or —) (esp *US*) = courgette.

Appendix 1

Spelling

It is sometimes difficult to find a word in the dictionary if you do not know how the first sound is written. Here are the most common difficulties:

The first letter is silent

wh- is sometimes spoken as /h-/ as in *who, whole*.
wr- is spoken as /r-/ as in *write, wrist*.
kn- is spoken as /n-/ as in *knife, know*.

Also
ho- is sometimes spoken as /ɒ-/ as in *honest, honour*.
ps- is spoken as /s-/ as in *psychology*.
pn- is spoken as /n-/ as in *pneumonia*.

The second letter is silent

wh- is sometimes spoken as /w-/ as in *which, whether*.
gu- is sometimes spoken as /g-/ as in *guest, guess*.
gh- is spoken as /g-/ as in *ghastly, ghost*.

Also
bu- is sometimes spoken as /b-/ as in *build, buoy*.

The first two letters have a special sound

ph- is spoken as /f-/ as in *photo*.
qu- is nearly always spoken as /kw-/ as in *quick*.
ch- is sometimes spoken as /k-/ as in *chorus*.

Remember

c- can be /k-/ as in *call* or /s-/ as in *centre*.
g- can be /g-/ as in *good* or /dʒ-/ as in *general*.

If you have looked for a word in the dictionary and cannot find it, here is a list for you to use as a guide:

If the sound is:	look at this possible spelling:	
f-	**ph-**	(as in *photo*)
g-	**gh-**	(as in *ghost*) or
	gu-	(as in *guest*)
h-	**wh-**	(as in *who, whole*)
k-	**ch-**	(as in *character*)
kw-	**qu-**	(as in *quick*)
n-	**kn-**	(as in *knife*) or
	pn-	(as in *pneumonia*)
r-	**wr-**	(as in *write*)
s-	**c-**	(as in *centre*) or
	ps-	(as in *psychology*)
dʒ-	**j-**	(as in *job*) or
	g-	(as in *general*)
ʃ-	**sh-**	(as in *shop*) or
	ch-	(as in *chalet*)
iː	**ea-**	(as in *each*)
ɪ	**e-**	(as in *enjoy*)
e	**a-**	(as in *any*)
ɑː	**au-**	(as in *aunt*)
ɒ	**ho-**	(as in *honest*)
ɔː	**au-**	(as in *author*) or
	oa-	(as in *oar*)
ə	**a-**	(as in *awake*) or
	o-	(as in *obey*)
ɜː	**ear-**	(as in *early*) or
	ir-	(as in *irk*)
eɪ	**ai-**	(as in *aim*) or
	ei-	(as in *eight*)
əʊ	**oa-**	(as in *oath*)
aɪ	**ei-**	(as in *either*)
juː	**eu-**	(as in *Europe*)

Verbs: spelling

Look at the section on spelling in Appendix 2.

Nouns: spelling

Plurals

Add **-s** to the noun (e.g. *hands, cooks, hotels, apples, trees, storeys*).

EXCEPTIONS:

For nouns ending in *-sh* (e.g. *dish*), *-ss* (e.g. *class*), *-ch* (e.g. *watch*), *-x* (e.g. *box*) and *-o* (e.g. *tomato*),

add *-es* to the noun (e.g. *dishes, classes, watches, boxes, tomatoes*).

For nouns ending in a consonant + *-y* (e.g. *story, fly*),

change the *-y* to *-ies* (e.g. *stories, flies*).

⇨ the notes below on doubling the last letter.

There are many nouns that do not form the plural in any of these ways (e.g. *child/children*). These irregular plurals are given in the entries for the nouns in the dictionary.

The *-ing* form

A special group of nouns is made by using the *-ing* form of a verb as a noun (e.g. '*Dancing* is fun'). To make this *-ing* form,

add *-ing* to the verb (e.g. *cooking, washing, marrying, seeing, trying*).

EXCEPTIONS:

For verbs ending in a consonant + *-e* (e.g. *love, make, change*),

change the *-e* to *-ing* (e.g. *loving, making, changing*).

For verbs ending in *-ie* (e.g. *lie, tie*),

change the *-ie* to *-ying* (e.g. *lying, tying*).

⇨ the notes below on doubling the last letter.

Adjectives: spelling

Comparative and superlative forms

Add *-er, -est* to the adjective if it ends in a consonant (e.g. *greater, greatest; narrower, narrowest; nearer, nearest; smaller, smallest; greyer, greyest*).

Add *-r, -st* to the adjective if it ends in *-e* (e.g. *wider, widest; freer, freest; bluer, bluest*).

EXCEPTIONS:

For adjectives ending in a consonant + *-y* (e.g. *happy, lovely*),

change the *-y* to *-ier, -iest* (e.g. *happier, happiest; lovelier, loveliest*).

⇨ the notes below on doubling the last letter.

There are many adjectives that do not form the comparative and superlative in any of these ways (e.g. *bad: worse, worst*). These irregular forms are given in the entries for the adjectives (e.g. *bad*) in the dictionary.

Longer adjectives do not change their spelling to form the comparative or superlative. Use *more . . ., most . . .* (e.g. *more beautiful, most beautiful*).

Doubling the last letter

For verbs, look at the section in Appendix 2.
Nouns do not have the last letter doubled in their plural forms.

The -ing form used as a noun (e.g. 'Cooking is easy') follows the same
rules for doubling the last letter as the verb, e.g. *knitting, shopping,
forgetting, travelling*).

The comparative and superlative forms of adjectives have the last letter
doubled if the word is short with one written vowel (*a, e, i, o, u*) followed

---

Appendix 2

Verbs

Tenses

The following table will show you how to identify a particular tense in English.
Look at the entry for each tense in the dictionary (e.g. **present continuous**)

Time	Name of tense
PAST (referring to an even earlier time)	**past perfect** **past perfect continuous***
PAST	**past (simple)** **past continuous***
PRESENT (referring to the past)	**present perfect** **present perfect continuous***
PRESENT	**present (simple)** **present continuous***
FUTURE	**future (simple)** **future continuous***
FUTURE (referring to a time between now and then)	**future perfect** **future perfect continuous***

* Some verbs, e.g. *hear, know,
love, mean, own, prefer, seem,
want, wish*, cannot be used in
the continuous tenses. This is
marked at the entries for these
verbs in the dictionary.

by one consonant on the end (e.g. *d, t* etc), e.g. *bigger, biggest; hotter, hottest*.

EXCEPTIONS:

Adjectives ending in *-w* or *-y* (e.g. *new, grey*) do not have the last letter doubled.

Adjectives with the vowel sound written using two letters, e.g. *-ee-* (*sweet*), *-ea-* (*near*), *-oo-* (*poor*), do not have the last letter doubled.

---

where you will find an explanation with examples. For more detailed information, look at a good grammar book such as *A Basic English Grammar* (Oxford University Press).

Example (active)	Example (passive)
It *had grown* It *had been growing*	It *had been grown* It *had been being grown*
It *grew* It *was growing*	It *was grown* It *was being grown*
It *has grown* It *has been growing*	It *has been grown* It *has been being grown*
It *grows* It *is growing*	It *is grown* It *is being grown*
It *will grow* It *will be growing*	It *will be grown* It *will be being grown*
It *will have grown* It *will have been growing*	It *will have been grown* It *will have been being grown*

The auxiliary verbs *be, have* (and *do*) are used to help form verb tenses. For details, ⇨ the entries for these verbs.

For tenses with *if* which express the *conditional*, ⇨ the detailed information at **if** (**1a–g**).

The *passive* is formed using forms of the verb 'be' (*is/are; was/were; has/have been; will be; is/was going to be* etc) and a *past participle* (e.g. *grown, heard, given*), as in 'Oranges *are grown* in Spain', 'A noise *was heard* outside', 'The speech *is going to be given* by the President'.

Verb endings: spelling

Present tense (3rd person singular)

Add **-s** to the verb (e.g. *needs, loves, sighs, plays, ties*).

EXCEPTIONS:

For verbs ending in *-sh* (e.g. *wish*), *-ss* (e.g. *miss*), *-ch* (e.g. *catch*), *-x* (e.g. *mix*) and *-o* (e.g. *echo*),
    add **-es** to the verb (e.g. *wishes, misses, catches, mixes, echoes*).
For verbs ending in a consonant + *-y* (e.g. *try, marry*),
    change the *-y* to **-ies** (e.g. *tries, marries*).

Present participle (used in continuous tenses)

Add **-ing** to the verb (e.g. *needing, sighing, playing, trying, missing, echoing, agreeing, seeing, pleading*).

EXCEPTIONS:

For verbs ending in a consonant + *-e* (e.g. *love, care, take*),
    change the *-e* to **-ing** (e.g. *loving, caring, taking*).
For verbs ending in *-ie* (e.g. *lie, tie*),
    change the *-ie* to **-ying** (e.g. *lying, tying*).

⇨ the notes below on doubling the last letter.

Past tense

Add **-ed** to the verb (e.g. *needed, sighed, played, wished, mixed, echoed*).

EXCEPTIONS:

For verbs ending in *-e* (e.g. *love, care, lie, tie, agree*),
    add **-d** (e.g. *loved, cared, lied, tied, agreed*).
For verbs ending in a consonant + *-y* (e.g. *try, marry*),
    change the *-y* to **-ied** (e.g. *tried, married*).

⇨ the notes below on doubling the last letter.

Doubling the last letter

If a verb is a short word with one written vowel (*a, e, i, o, u*) followed by one consonant on the end (*b, d, f* etc), the last letter is doubled in the present participle (*-ing*) and the past tense (*-ed*), e.g. *rubbing, knitting, shopping; rubbed, knitted, shopped*).

EXCEPTIONS:

Verbs ending in *-w* or *-y* (e.g. *flow, stay*) do not have the last letter doubled.

Verbs with the vowel sound written using two letters, e.g. *-ea-* (*beat*), *-ee-* (*seem*), *-ai-* (*fail*), *-oo-* (*look*), do not have the last letter doubled.

The last letter is also doubled if a verb is longer and ends with one written vowel (e.g. *i, o*) + one consonant (e.g. *n, t*) but *only* if this last vowel is stressed (e.g. *be'ginning, for'getting*) and not if the stress comes earlier in the word (e.g. *de'veloping, 'profiting*).

EXCEPTION:

The exception to this last rule is that, in British spelling, verbs ending in *-el* (e.g. *travel*, *model*) have the last letter doubled (e.g. 'travelling, 'travelled; 'modelling, 'modelled*) even though the stress is on the first part of the word.

Irregular verbs

There are many verbs that do not form the past tense and past participle in the usual way (i.e. by adding *-ed* or *-d* or by changing *-y* to *-ied*). These are listed below. Full phonetic information is given in the entry for each verb.

If a verb has two or three different past tenses or past participles (e.g.

| hang | hung, hanged | hung, hanged), |

look at the entry for the verb to find out which form you need.

Infinitive	Past Tense	Past Participle
arise	arose	arisen
awake	awoke	awoken
be	was, were	been
bear	bore	borne
beat	beat	beaten
become	became	become
begin	began	begun
behold	beheld	beheld
bend	bent	bent
beseech	besought	besought
beset	beset	beset
bet	bet, betted	bet, betted
bid	bid, bade	bid, bidden
bind	bound	bound
bite	bit	bitten
bleed	bled	bled
bless	blessed, blest	blessed, blest
blow	blew	blown
break	broke	broken
breed	bred	bred
bring	brought	brought
broadcast	broadcast	broadcast
build	built	built
burn	burnt, burned	burnt, burned
burst	burst	burst
buy	bought	bought
cast	cast	cast
catch	caught	caught
chide	chided, chid	chided, chidden
choose	chose	chosen
cleave	clove, cleft, cleaved	cleft, cloven
cling	clung	clung
come	came	come
cost	cost, costed	cost, costed
creep	crept	crept
cut	cut	cut
deal	dealt	dealt
defreeze	defroze	defrozen
dig	dug	dug

do	did	done
draw	drew	drawn
dream	dreamed, dreamt	dreamed, dreamt
drink	drank	drunk
drive	drove	driven
dwell	dwelt	dwelt
eat	ate	eaten
fall	fell	fallen
feed	fed	fed
feel	felt	felt
fight	fought	fought
find	found	found
flee	fled	fled
fling	flung	flung
fly	flew	flown
forbear	forbore	forborne
forbid	forbad, forbade	forbidden
forecast	forecast, forecasted	forecast, forecasted
foresee	foresaw	foreseen
foretell	foretold	foretold
forget	forgot	forgotten
forgive	forgave	forgiven
forsake	forsook	forsaken
forswear	forswore	forsworn
freeze	froze	frozen
get	got	got
gild	gilded, gilt	gilded, gilt
give	gave	given
go	went	gone
grind	ground	ground
grow	grew	grown
hamstring	hamstrung	hamstrung
hang	hung, hanged	hung, hanged
have	had	had
hear	heard	heard
hew	hewed	hewed, hewn
hide	hid	hidden
hit	hit	hit
hold	held	held
hurt	hurt	hurt
inlay	inlaid	inlaid
interweave	interwove	interwoven
keep	kept	kept
kneel	knelt	knelt
knit	knitted, knit	knitted, knit
know	knew	known
lay	laid	laid
lead	led	led
leap	leaped, leapt	leaped, leapt
learn	learned, learnt	learned, learnt
leave	left	left
lend	lent	lent
let	let	let
lie	lay	lain
light	lit, lighted	lit, lighted
lose	lost	lost

make	made	made
mean	meant	meant
meet	met	met
miscast	miscast	miscast
mislay	mislaid	mislaid
mislead	misled	misled
misread	misread	misread
misspell	misspelled, mispelt	misspelled, misspelt
mistake	mistook	mistaken
misunderstand	misunderstood	misunderstood
mow	mowed	mown
outdo	outdid	outdone
outgrow	outgrew	outgrown
outrun	outrun	outrun
outsell	outsold	outsold
outshine	outshone	outshone
outwear	outwore	outworn
overcome	overcame	overcome
overdo	overdid	overdone
overhang	overhung	overhung
overhear	overheard	overheard
overpay	overpaid	overpaid
override	overrode	overridden
overrun	overran	overran
oversee	oversaw	overseen
overshoot	overshot	overshot
oversleep	overslept	overslept
overtake	overtook	overtaken
overthrow	overthrew	overthrown
partake	partook	partaken
pay	paid	paid
put	put	put
read	read	read
rebuild	rebuilt	rebuilt
redo	redid	redone
relay	relayed, relaid	relayed, relaid
remake	remade	remade
rend	rent	rent
repay	repaid	repaid
retake	retook	retaken
retell	retold	retold
rewrite	rewrote	rewritten
rid	rid	rid
ride	rode	ridden
ring	ringed, rang	ringed, rung
rise	rose	risen
run	ran	run
saw	sawed	sawn
say	said	said
see	saw	seen
seek	sought	sought
sell	sold	sold
send	sent	sent
set	set	set
sew	sewed	sewn
shake	shook	shaken

shear	sheared	shorn, sheared
shed	shed	shed
shine	shone, shined	shone, shined
shoe	shod	shod
shoot	shot	shot
show	showed	shown, showed
shrink	shrank, shrunk	shrunk
shut	shut	shut
sing	sang	sung
sink	sank, sunk	sunk
sit	sat	sat
slay	slew	slain
sleep	slept	slept
slide	slid	slid
sling	slung	slung
slit	slit	slit
smell	smelt	smelt
smite	smote	smitten
sow	sowed	sown, sowed
speak	spoke	spoken
speed	sped, speeded	sped, speeded
spell	spelt, spelled	spelt, spelled
spend	spent	spent
spill	spilt, spilled	spilt, spilled
spin	spun	spun
spit	spat	spat
split	split	split
spoil	spoilt, spoiled	spoilt, spoiled
spread	spread	spread
spring	sprang	sprung
stand	stood	stood
stave	staved, stove	staved, stove
steal	stole	stolen
stick	stuck	stuck
stink	stank, stunk	stunk
strew	strewed	strewn, strewed
stride	strode	stridden
strike	struck	struck
string	strung	strung
strive	strove	striven
swear	swore	sworn
sweep	swept	swept
swell	swelled	swollen, swelled
swim	swam	swum
swing	swung	swung
take	took	taken
teach	taught	taught
tear	tore	torn
tell	told	told
think	thought	thought
thrive	throve, thrived	thriven, thrived
throw	threw	thrown
thrust	thrust	thrust
tread	trod	trodden
unbend	unbent	unbent
undercut	undercut	undercut

undergo	underwent	undergone
underlie	underlay	underlain
underpay	underpaid	underpaid
undersell	undersold	undersold
understand	understood	understood
undertake	undertook	undertaken
underwrite	underwrote	underwritten
undo	undid	undone
unfreeze	unfroze	unfrozen
unwind	unwound	unwound
upset	upset	upset
wake	woke	woken
waylay	waylaid	waylaid
wear	wore	worn
weave	wove	woven
wed	wedded, wed	wedded, wed
weep	wept	wept
win	won	won
wind	winded, wound	winded, wound
withdraw	withdrew	withdrawn
withhold	withheld	withheld
withstand	withstood	withstood
wring	wrung	wrung
write	wrote	written

Appendix 3

Geographical names

This list will help you to read and say geographical names and the adjectives for them.

The word for a person from a country or state is given when it is different from the adjective, e.g. Poland (*person* Pole).

The plural of the word for a person from a country is formed by adding -*s*, except for *Swiss* and words ending in -*ese*, which do not change (e.g. *two Swiss, several Chinese*), and words ending in -*man* and -*woman*, which change to -*men* and -*women* (e.g. *three Frenchmen, all Englishwomen*).

The word for all the people of a country is given when it is different from the plural of one person, e.g. ⇨ France, Great Britain. *Five Frenchmen* or *many Britons* is possible, but the way to describe all French or British people is *the French* or *the British*.

Countries and states

Name	Adjective
Afghanistan /æf'gænɪstɑːn/	Afghan /'æfgæn/, Afghani /æf'gæni/, Afghanistani /æf,gænɪ'stɑːni/
Albania /æl'beɪnɪə/	Albanian /æl'beɪnɪən/
Algeria /æl'dʒɪərɪə/	Algerian /æl'dʒɪərɪən/
Angola /æŋ'gəʊlə/	Angolan /æŋ'gəʊlən/
Argentina /ˌɑːdʒən'tiːnə/, the **Argentine** /'ɑːdʒəntaɪn/	Argentinian /ˌɑːdʒən'tɪnɪən/, Argentine /'ɑːdʒəntaɪn/
Armenia ɑː'miːnɪə	Armenian /ɑː'miːnɪən/
Australia /ɒ'streɪlɪə/	Australian /ɒ'streɪlɪən/
Austria /'ɒstrɪə/	Austrian /'ɒstrɪən/
Azerbaijan /ˌæzəbaɪ'dʒɑːn/	Azerbaijani /ˌæzəbaɪ'dʒɑːni
the **Bahamas** /bə'hɑːməz/	Bahamian /bə'heɪmɪən/
✳ **Bahrain, Bahrein** /bɑː'reɪn/	Bahraini, Bahreini /bɑː'reɪni/
Bangladesh /ˌbæŋglə'deʃ/	Bangladeshi /ˌbæŋglə'deʃi/
Barbados /bɑː'beɪdɒs/	Barbadian /bɑː'beɪdɪən/
Belarus /'belərʊs/	Belorussian /belə'rʌʃn/
Belgium /'beldʒəm/	Belgian /'beldʒən/
Belize /be'liːz/	Belizean /be'liːzɪən/
Benin /be'niːn/	Beninese /be,niː'niːz/
Bermuda, /bə'mjuːdə/	Bermudan /bə'mjuːdn/
Bhutan /buː'tɑːn/	Bhutanese /ˌbuː'tɑː'niːz/
Bolivia /bə'lɪvɪə/	Bolivian /bə'lɪvɪən/
Bosnia-Herzegovina /ˌbɒznɪə ˌhɜːtsə'gɒvɪnə/	Bosnian /'bɒznɪən/
Botswana /bɒt'swɑːnə/	Botswanan /bɒt'swɑːnən/ (*person* Motswana/ mɒt'swɑːnə/, people Ba-tswana /baet'swɑːnə/)

Brazil /brə'zɪl/

Brazilian /brə'zɪlɪən/

Britain = Great Britain

Brunei /bru:'naɪ/

Brunei, Bruneian /bru:'naɪ(ən)/

Bulgaria /bʌl'geərɪə/

Bulgarian /bʌl'geərɪən/

Burkina /bɜ:'ki:nə/

Burkinese /ˌbɜ:kɪ'ni:z/

Burundi /bə'rʊndɪ/

Burundian /bə'rʊndɪən/

Cambodia /kæm'bəʊdɪə/

Cambodian /kæm'bəʊdɪən/

Cameroon /ˌkæmə'ru:n/

Cameroonian /ˌkæmə'ru:nɪən/

Canada /'kænədə/

Canadian /kə'neɪdɪən/

the ˌCentral ˌAfrican Re'public

Chad /tʃæd/

Chadian /'tʃædɪən/

Chile /'tʃɪlɪ/

Chilean /'tʃɪlɪən/

China /'tʃaɪnə/

Chinese /tʃaɪ'ni:z/

Colombia /kə'lɒmbɪə/

Colombian /kə'lɒmbɪən/

the Congo /'kɒŋgəʊ/

Congolese /ˌkɒŋgə'li:z/

Costa Rica /ˌkɒstə 'ri:kə/

Costa Rican /ˌkɒstə 'ri:kən/

Côte d'Ivoire /ˌkəʊt di:'vwɑ:/

Croatia /krəʊ'eɪʃə/

Croatian /krəʊ'eɪʃən/,
Croat /'krəʊæt/

Cuba /'kju:bə/

Cuban /'kju:bən/

Cyprus /'saɪprəs/

Cypriot /'sɪprɪət/

Czech Republic /ˌtʃek rɪˌpʌblɪk/

Czech /tʃek/

Denmark /'denmɑ:k/

Danish /'deɪnɪʃ/ (person Dane /deɪn/)

Djibouti /dʒɪ'bu:tɪ/

Djiboutian /dʒɪ'bu:tɪən/

Dominica /də'mɪnɪkə/

Dominican /də'mɪnɪkən/

the Do,minican Re'public

Dominican /də'mɪnɪkən/

Ecuador /'ekwədɔ:(r)/

Ecuadorian /ˌekwə'dɔ:rɪən/

Egypt /'i:dʒɪpt/

Egyptian /ɪ'dʒɪpʃən/

El Salvador /el 'sælvədɔ:(r)/

Salvadorian /ˌsælvə'dɔ:rɪən/

England /'ɪŋglənd/

English /'ɪŋglɪʃ/ (person 'Englishman,
-woman; people the English)

Equatorial Guinea /ˌekwəˌtɔ:rɪəl 'gɪnɪ/

Equatorial Guinean /ˌekwəˌtɔ:rɪəl
'gɪnɪən/

Eritrea /ˌerɪˌtreɪə/

Eritrean /ˌerɪ'treɪən/

Estonia /e'stəʊnɪə/

Estonian /e'stəʊnɪən/

Ethiopia /ˌi:θɪ'əʊpɪə/

Ethiopian /ˌi:θɪ'əʊpɪən/

Fiji /'fi:dʒɪ/

Fijian /fɪ'dʒi:ən/

Finland /'fɪnlənd/

Finnish /'fɪnɪʃ/ (person Finn /fɪn/)

France /frɑ:ns/

French /frentʃ/ (person 'Frenchman,
-woman; people the French)

Gabon /gæ'bɒn/

Gabonese /ˌgæbə'ni:z/

the Gambia /'gæmbɪə/

Gambian /'gæmbɪən/

Georgia /'dʒɔ:dʒə/

Georgian /'dʒɔ:dʒən/

Germany /'dʒɜ:mənɪ/

German /'dʒɜ:mən/

Ghana /'gɑ:nə/

Ghanaian /gɑ:'neɪən/

Gibraltar /dʒɪ'brɔ:ltə(r)/

Gibraltarian /ˌdʒɪbrɔ:l'teərɪən/

Great Britain /ˌgreɪt 'brɪtn/

British /'brɪtɪʃ/ (person Briton /'brɪtn/;
people the British)

Greece /gri:s/

Greek /gri:k/

Grenada /grə'neɪdə/

Grenadian /grə'neɪdɪən/

Guatemala /ˌgwɑ:tə'mɑ:lə/

Guatemalan /ˌgwɑ:tə'mɑ:lən/

Guinea /'gɪnɪ/

Guinean /'gɪnɪən/

Guinea Bissau /ˌgɪnɪbɪ'saʊ/

Guyana /gaɪ'ænə/

Guyanese /ˌgaɪə'ni:z /, Guyanan
/ˌgaɪə'ænən/

Haiti /'heɪtɪ/

Haitian /'heɪʃən/

Holland /'hɒlənd/ = the Netherlands
Honduras /hɒn'djʊərəs/ — Honduran /hɒn'djʊərən/
Hong Kong /ˌhɒŋ 'kɒŋ/
Hungary /'hʌŋgərɪ/ — Hungarian /hʌŋ'geərɪən/
Iceland /'aɪslənd/ — Icelandic /aɪs'lændɪk/ (*person* Icelander /'aɪsləndə(r)/)
India /'ɪndɪə/ — Indian /'ɪndɪən/
Indonesia /ˌɪndə'ni:zɪə/ — Indonesian /ˌɪndə'ni:zɪən/
Iran /ɪ'rɑ:n/ — Iranian /ɪ'reɪnɪən/
Iraq /ɪ'rɑ:k/ — Iraqi /ɪ'rɑ:kɪ/
(the Republic of) Ireland /'aɪələnd/ — Irish /'aɪrɪʃ/ (*person* 'Irishman,-woman; *people* the Irish)
Israel /'ɪzreɪl/ — Israeli /ɪz'reɪlɪ/
Italy /'ɪtəlɪ/ — Italian /ɪ'tælɪən/
Jamaica /dʒə'meɪkə/ — Jamaican /dʒə'meɪkən/
Japan /dʒə'pæn/ — Japanese /ˌdʒæpə'ni:z/
Jordan /'dʒɔ:dn/ — Jordanian /dʒɔ:'deɪnɪən/
Kazakhstan /ˌkæzæk 'stɑ:n/ — Kazakh /kæ'zæk/
Kenya /'kenjə/ — Kenyan /'kenjən/
Kirgyzstan /ˌkɪəgɪ'stɑ:n/ — Kirgyz /kɪə'gi:z/
Korea /kə'rɪə/
  ˌSouth Ko'rea — South Korean /ˌsaʊθ kə'rɪən/
  ˌNorth Ko'rea — North Korean /ˌnɔ:θ kə'rɪən/
Kuwait /kjʊ'weɪt/ — Kuwaiti /kjʊ'weɪtɪ/
Laos /laʊs/ — Laotian /'laʊʃən/
Latvia /'lætvɪə/ — Latvian 'lætvɪən/
Lebanon /'lebənən/ — Lebanese /ˌlebə'ni:z/
Lesotho /lɪ'su:tu:/ — Sotho /'su:tu:/ (*person* Mosotho /mə'su:tu:/, *people* Basotho /bə'su:tu:/)
Liberia /laɪ'bɪərɪə/ — Liberian /laɪ'bɪərɪən/
Libya /'lɪbɪə/ — Libyan /'lɪbɪən/
Lithuania /ˌlɪθjʊ'eɪnɪə/ — Lithuanian /ˌlɪθjʊ'eɪnɪən/
Luxemburg /'lʌksəmbɜ:g/ — Luxemburg (*person* 'Luxemburger)
Macedonia /ˌmæsɪ'dəʊnɪə/ — Macedonian /ˌmæsɪ'dəʊnɪən/
Madagascar /ˌmædə'gæskə(r)/ — Malagasy /'mælə'gæsɪ/, Madagascan /ˌmædə'gæskən/
Malawi /mə'lɑ:wɪ/ — Malawian /mə'lɑ:wɪən/
Malaysia /mə'leɪzɪə/ — Malaysian /mə'leɪzɪən/
Mali /'mɑ:lɪ/ — Malian /'mɑ:lɪən/
Malta /'mɔ:ltə/ — Maltese /mɔ:l'ti:z/
Mauritania /ˌmɒrɪ'teɪnɪə/ — Mauritanian /ˌmɒrɪ'teɪnɪən/
Mauritius /mə'rɪʃəs/ — Mauritian /mə'rɪʃn/
Mexico /'meksɪkəʊ/ — Mexican /'meksɪkən/
Moldova /mol'dəʊvə/ — Moldovan /mol'dəʊvən/
Monaco /'mɒnəkəʊ/ — Monegasque /ˌmɒnɪ'gæsk/
Mongolia /mɒŋ'gəʊlɪə/ — Mongolian /mɒŋ'gəʊlɪən/
Morocco /mə'rɒkəʊ/ — Moroccan /mə'rɒkən/
Mozambique /ˌməʊzæm'bi:k/ — Mozambiquean /ˌməʊzæm'bi:kən/
Myanmar /'mɪənmɑ:(r)/ — Myanmar /'mɪənmɑ:(r)/
Namibia /nə'mɪbɪə/ — Namibian /nə'mɪbɪən/
Nepal /nɪ'pɔ:l/ — Nepalese /ˌnepə'li:z/
the Netherlands /'neðələndz/ — Dutch /dʌtʃ/ (*person* 'Dutchman, -woman; *people* the Dutch)
New Zealand /ˌnju: 'zi:lənd/ — New Zealand (*person* ˌNew 'Zealander)

Nicaragua /ˌnɪkəˈrægjʊə/
Niger /ˈnaɪdʒə(r), niːˈʒeə(r)/

Nigeria /naɪˈdʒɪərɪə/
Northern Ireland /ˌnɔːðən ˈaɪələnd/
North Korea ⇨ Korea
Norway /ˈnɔːweɪ/
Oman /əʊˈmɑːn/
Pakistan /ˌpɑːkɪˈstɑːn/
Palestine /ˈpælɪstaɪn/
Panama /ˈpænəmɑː/
Papua New Guinea /ˌpæpjʊə ˌnjuːˈgɪnɪ/
Paraguay /ˈpærəgwaɪ/
Peru /pəˈruː/
the **Philippines** /ˈfɪlɪpiːnz/

Poland /ˈpəʊlənd/
Portugal /ˈpɔːtʃʊgəl/
Puerto Rico /ˌpwɜːtəʊ ˈriːkəʊ/
Qatar /kʌˈtɑː(r)/
Romania, /ruːˈmeɪnɪə/
Russia /ˈrʌʃə/
Rwanda /rʊˈændə/
Samoa = Western Samoa
Saudi Arabia /ˌsaʊdɪ əˈreɪbɪə/

Scotland /ˈskɒtlənd/

Senegal /ˌsenɪˈgɔːl/
the **Seychelles** /seɪˈʃelz/
Sierra Leone /sɪˌerə lɪˈəʊn/
Singapore /ˌsɪŋəˈpɔː(r)/
Slovakia /sləʊˈvækɪə/
Slovenia /sləʊˈviːnɪə/

Somalia /səˈmɑːlɪə/
South Africa /ˌsaʊθ ˈæfrɪkə/
South Korea ⇨ Korea
Spain /speɪn/

Sri Lanka /ˌsriːˈlæŋkə/
Sudan /suːˈdɑːn/
Surinam /ˌsʊərɪˈnæm/
Swaziland /ˈswɑːzɪlænd/
Sweden /ˈswiːdn/

Switzerland /ˈswɪtsələnd/

Syria /ˈsɪrɪə/
Tahiti /təˈhiːtɪ/
Taiwan /taɪˈwɑːn/
Tajikistan /tæˌdʒiːkɪˈstɑːn/
Tanzania /ˌtænzəˈnɪə/
Thailand /ˈtaɪlənd/
Tibet /tɪˈbet/

Nicaraguan /ˌnɪkəˈrægjʊən/
Nigerien /niːˈʒeərɪən/ (*person*
   Nigerien, -ienne /niːˌʒeərɪˈen/)
Nigerian /naɪˈdʒɪərɪən/
Northern Irish /ˌnɔːðən ˈaɪrɪʃ/

Norwegian /nɔːˈwiːdʒən/
Omani /əʊˈmɑːnɪ/
Pakistani /ˌpɑːkɪˈstɑːnɪ/
Palestinian /ˌpælɪˈstɪnɪən/
Panamanian /ˌpænəˈmeɪnɪən/
Papuan /ˈpæpjʊən/
Paraguayan /ˌpærəˈgwaɪən/
Peruvian /pəˈruːvɪən/
Philippine /ˈfɪlɪpiːn/ (*person* Filipino
   /ˌfɪlɪˈpiːnəʊ/)
Polish /ˈpəʊlɪʃ/ (person Pole /pəʊl/)
Portuguese /ˌpɔːtʃʊˈgiːz/
Puerto Rican /ˌpwɜːtəʊ ˈriːkən/
Qatari /kʌˈtɑːrɪ/
Romanian, /ruːˈmeɪnɪən/
Russian /ˈrʌʃən/
Rwandan /rʊˈændn/

Saudi /ˈsaʊdɪ/, Saudi Arabian
   /ˌsaʊdɪ əˈreɪbɪən/
Scottish /ˈskɒtɪʃ/, Scots /skɒts/
   (*person* Scot /skɒt/, ˈScotsman,
   -woman; *people* the Scots)
Senegalese /ˌsenɪgəˈliːz/
Seychellois /ˌseɪʃelˈwɑː/
Sierra Leonean /sɪˌerə lɪˈəʊnɪən/
Singaporean /ˌsɪŋəˈpɔːrɪən/
Slovak /ˈsləʊvæk/
Slovene /ˈsləʊviːn/, Slovenian
   /sləʊˈviːnɪən/
Somali /səˈmɑːlɪ/
South African /ˌsaʊθ ˈæfrɪkən/

Spanish /ˈspænɪʃ/ (*person* Spaniard
   /ˈspænjəd/; *people* the Spanish)
Sri Lankan /ˌsriːˈlæŋkən/
Sudanese /ˌsuːdəˈniːz/
Surinamese /ˌsʊərɪnəˈmiːz/
Swazi /ˈswɑːzɪ/
Swedish /ˈswiːdɪʃ/ (person
   Swede /swiːd/)
Swiss /swɪs/ (*person* Swiss; *people* the
   Swiss)
Syrian /ˈsɪrɪən/
Tahitian /təˈhiːʃən/
Taiwanese /ˌtaɪwəˈniːz/
Tajik /tæˈdʒɪk/
Tanzanian /ˌtænzəˈnɪən/
Thai /taɪ/
Tibetan /tɪˈbetn/

Togo /ˈtəʊgəʊ/   Togolese /ˌtəʊgəˈliːz/
Tonga /ˈtɒŋgə/   Tongan /ˈtɒŋgən/
Trinidad /ˈtrɪnɪdæd/ **and Tobago**   Trinidadian /ˌtrɪnɪˈdædɪən/, Tobagan
/təˈbeɪgəʊ/   /təˈbeɪgən/,
         Tobagonian /ˌtəʊbəˈgəʊnɪən/

Tunisia /tjuːˈnɪzɪə/   Tunisian /tjuːˈnɪzɪən/
Turkey /ˈtɜːkɪ/   Turkish /ˈtɜːkɪʃ/ (*person* Turk /tɜːk/)
Turkmenistan /ˌtɜːkmenɪˈstɑːn/   Turkmen /ˈtɜːkmen/
Uganda /juːˈgændə/   Ugandan /juːˈgændən/
the **United Kingdom** /jʊˌnaɪtɪd ˈkɪŋdəm/   British /ˈbrɪtɪʃ/ (*person* Briton /ˈbrɪtn/;
         people the British)

the **U‚nited ‚States of A'merica**   American /əˈmerɪkən/
   /əˈmerɪkə/
Uruguay /ˈjʊərəgwaɪ/   Uruguayan /ˌjʊərəˈgwaɪən/
Uzbekistan /ˌʊzbekɪˈstɑːn/   Uzbek /ˈʊzbek/
Venezuela /ˌvenəˈzweɪlə/   Venezuelan /ˌvenəˈzweɪlən/
Vietnam /ˌvɪətˈnæm/   Vietnamese /vɪˌetnəˈmiːz/
Wales /weɪlz/   Welsh /welʃ/ (*person* ˈWelshman,
         -woman; *people* the Welsh)

Western Samoa /ˌwestən seˈməʊə/   Samoan /səˈməʊən/
Yemen Republic /ˈjemən rɪˈpʌblɪk/   Yemeni /ˈjemənɪ/
Yugoslavia /ˌjuːgəˈslɑːvɪə/   Yugoslavian /ˌjuːgəˈslɑːvɪən/
         (*person* Yugoslav /ˈjuːgəslɑːv/)

Zaire /zaɪˈɪə(r)/   Zairean /ˌzaɪˈɪərɪən/
Zambia /ˈzæmbɪə/   Zambian /ˈzæmbɪən/
Zimbabwe /zɪmˈbɑːbweɪ/   Zimbabwean /zɪmˈbɑːbwɪən/

Other geographical regions

Name	Adjective
Africa /ˈæfrɪkə/	African /ˈæfrɪkən/
the **Atlantic** /ətˈlæntɪk/	Atlantic /ətˈlæntɪk/
America /əˈmerɪkə/	American /əˈmerɪkən/
the **Antarctic** /ænˈtɑːktɪk/	Antarctic /ænˈtɑːktɪk/
Antarctica /ænˈtɑːktɪkə/	Antarctic /ænˈtɑːktɪk/
the **Arctic** /ˈɑːktɪk/	Arctic /ˈɑːktɪk/
Asia /ˈeɪʃə/	Asian /ˈeɪʃən/
Australasia /ˌɒstrəˈleɪʃə, -ˈleɪzɪə/	Australasian /ˌɒstrəˈleɪʃən, -ˈleɪzɪən/
the **Baltic** /ˈbɔːltɪk/	Baltic /ˈbɔːltɪk/
the **Caribbean** /ˌkærɪˈbiːən/	Caribbean /ˌkærɪˈbiːən/
Europe /ˈjʊərəp/	European /ˌjʊərəˈpiːən/
the **Far East** /ˌfɑːr ˈiːst/	Far Eastern /ˌfɑːr ˈiːstn/
the **Mediterranean** /ˌmedɪtəˈreɪnɪən/	Mediterranean /ˌmedɪtəˈreɪnɪən/
the **Middle East** /ˌmɪdl ˈiːst/	Middle Eastern /ˌmɪdl ˈiːstn/
the **Pacific** /pəˈsɪfɪk/	Pacific /pəˈsɪfɪk/
Polynesia /ˌpɒlɪˈniːʒə/	Polynesian /ˌpɒlɪˈniːʒən/
the **Soviet Union** /ˌsəʊvɪət ˈjuːnɪən/	Soviet /ˈsəʊvɪət/
the **West Indies** /ˌwest ˈɪndɪz/	West Indian /ˈwestˈɪndɪən/

Appendix 4   Numbers, weights and measures

'*A/an*', as in *a hundred, an eighth* etc., is less formal than '*one*'.

Numbers

Cardinal

1 one /wʌn/
2 two /tu:/
3 three /θri:/
4 four /fɔ:(r)/
5 five /faɪv/
6 six /sɪks/
7 seven /'sevn/
8 eight /eɪt/
9 nine /naɪn/
10 ten /ten/
11 eleven /ɪ'levn/
12 twelve /twelv/
13 thirteen /ˌθɜ:'ti:n/
14 fourteen /ˌfɔ:'ti:n/
15 fifteen /ˌfɪf'ti:n/
16 sixteen /ˌsɪk'sti:n/
17 seventeen /ˌsevn'ti:n/
18 eighteen /ˌeɪ'ti:n/
19 nineteen /ˌnaɪn'ti:n/
20 twenty /'twentɪ/
21 twenty-one /ˌtwentɪ 'wʌn/
22 twenty-two /ˌtwentɪ 'tu:/
23 twenty-three /ˌtwentɪ 'θri:/
30 thirty /'θɜ:tɪ/
38 thirty-eight /ˌθɜ:tɪ 'eɪt/
40 forty /'fɔ:tɪ/
50 fifty /'fɪftɪ/
60 sixty /'sɪkstɪ/
70 seventy /'sevntɪ/
80 eighty /'eɪtɪ/
90 ninety /'naɪntɪ/
100 a/one hundred /ə, wʌn 'hʌndrəd/
1000 a/one thousand /ə, wʌn 'θaʊznd/
10 000 ten thousand /ˌten 'θaʊznd/
100 000 a/one hundred thousand /ə, wʌn ˌhʌndrəd 'θaʊznd/
1 000 000 a/one million /ə, wʌn 'mɪlɪən/

Ordinal

1st first /fɜ:st/
2nd second /'sekənd/
3rd third /θɜ:d/
4th fourth /fɔ:θ/
5th fifth /fɪfθ/
6th sixth /sɪksθ/
7th seventh /'sevnθ/
8th eighth /eɪtθ/
9th ninth /naɪnθ/
10th tenth /tenθ/
11th eleventh /ɪ'levnθ/
12th twelfth /twelfθ/
13th thirteenth /ˌθɜ:'ti:nθ/
14th fourteenth /ˌfɔ:'ti:nθ/
15th fifteenth /ˌfɪf'ti:nθ/
16th sixteenth /ˌsɪk'sti:nθ/
17th seventeenth /ˌsevn'ti:nθ/
18th eighteenth /ˌeɪ'ti:nθ/
19th nineteenth /ˌnaɪn'ti:nθ/
20th twentieth /'twentɪəθ/
21st twenty-first /ˌtwentɪ 'fɜ:st/
22nd twenty-second /ˌtwentɪ 'sekənd/
23rd twenty-third /ˌtwentɪ 'θɜ:d/
30th thirtieth /'θɜ:tɪəθ/
38th thirty-eighth /ˌθɜ:tɪ 'eɪtθ/
40th fortieth /'fɔ:tɪəθ/
50th fiftieth /'fɪftɪəθ/
60th sixtieth /'sɪkstɪəθ/
70th seventieth /'sevntɪəθ/
80th eightieth /'eɪtɪəθ/
90th ninetieth /'naɪntɪəθ/
100th hundredth /'hʌndrədθ/
1000th thousandth /'θaʊznθ/
10 000th ten thousandth /ˌten 'θaʊznθ/
100 000th hundred thousandth /ˌhʌndrəd 'θaʊznθ/
1 000 000th millionth /'mɪlɪənθ/

Vulgar Fractions

⅛ an/one-eighth /ən, wʌn 'eɪtθ/
¼ a/one quarter /ə, wʌn 'kwɔ:tə(r)/
⅓ a/one third /ə, wʌn 'θɜ:d/
½ a/one half /ə, wʌn 'hɑ:f/
¾ three-quarters /ˌθri: 'kwɔ:təz/

Decimal Fractions

0·125 (ˌnought) point ˌone two 'five
0·25 (ˌnought) point ˌtwo 'five
0·33 (ˌnought) point ˌthree 'three
0·5 (ˌnought) point 'five
0·75 (ˌnought) point ˌseven 'five

Collective Numbers

6 a half dozen/half a dozen

12 a/one dozen (*pl* dozen): *two dozen*

20 a/one score (*pl* score): *Three score and ten equals seventy.*

144 a/one gross /grəʊs/ (*pl* gross): *six gross.*

Time of day

GB

US

7.00 *seven o'clock* or
seven am /ˌeɪ 'em/ or
seven pm /ˌpiː 'em/

After is usual where *GB* has *past*;
of is common where *GB* has *to*, e.g.:

8.15 *a quarter past eight* or
eight fifteen

a quarter after eight

9.45 *a quarter to ten* or
nine forty-five

a quarter of ten

4.30 *half past four* or
four thirty or
(*informal*) *half four*

four thirty

2.03 *three minutes past two* or
two oh three

5.10 *ten (minutes) past five* or
five ten

ten after five

6.25 *twenty-five (minutes) past six* or
five and twenty (minutes) past six
or *six twenty-five*

6.35 *twenty-five (minutes) to seven* or
five and twenty (minutes) to seven
or *six thirty-five*

5.40 *twenty (minutes) to six* or
five forty

3.50 *ten (minutes) to four* or
three fifty

7.55 *five (minutes) to eight* or
seven fifty-five

five of eight

9.57 *three minutes to ten* or
nine fifty-seven

Twenty-four-hour clock

07.00 (ˌoh) ˌseven 'hundred hours
= 7.00 am

12.00 ˌtwelve 'hundred hours
= midday/noon

13.45 ˌthirteen ˌforty-'five
= 1.45 pm

19.00 ˌnineteen 'hundred hours
= 7.00 pm

24.00 ˌtwenty-ˌfour 'hundred hours
= midnight

Dates

55 BC *fifty-five BC* /ˌbiː 'siː/
AD 55 *AD* /ˌeɪ 'diː/ *fifty-five*

GB

23(rd) January 1991
23 Jan 1991
23/1/91

US

January 23(rd) 1991
Jan 23, 1991
1/23/91

International

1991–01–23

The Metric system

Length

		GB and US
10 millimetres (mm)	= 1 centimetre (cm)	= 0·3937 inch (in)
100 centimetres	= 1 metre (m)	= 39·37 inches or 1·094 yards (yd)
1000 metres	= 1 kilometre (km)	= 0·62137 mile or about ⅝ mile

Area

		GB and US
100 square metres (sq m)	= 1 are (a)	= 0·0247 acre
100 ares	= 1 hectare (ha)	= 2·471 acres
100 hectares	= 1 square kilometre (km²)	= 0·386 square mile

Weight

		GB and US
10 milligrams (gm)	= 1 centigram (cg)	= 0·1543 grain
100 centigrams	= 1 gram (g)	= 15·4323 grains
1000 grams	= 1 kilogram (kg)	= 2·2046 pounds
1000 kilograms	= 1 tonne	= 19·684 cwt

Capacity

		GB and US
1000 millilitres (ml)	= 1 litre (l)	= 1·75 GB pints = 2·101 US pints
10 litres	= 1 dekalitre (dl)	= 2·1997 GB gallons = 2.63 US gallons

The Imperial system (GB and US)

Length

		Metric
	1 inch (in)	= 25·3995 millimetres (mm)
12 inches	= 1 foot (ft)	= 30·479 centimetres (cm)
3 feet	= 1 yard (yd)	= 0·9144 metre (m)
220 yards	= 1 furlong (fur)	= 201·168 metres
8 furlongs	= 1 mile	= 1·6093 kilometres (km)
1760 yards	= 1 mile	= 1·6093 kilometres

Avoirdupois weight

		Metric
	1 grain (gr)	= 0·0648 gram (gm)
437½ grains	= 1 ounce (oz)	= 28·35 grams
16 drams (dr)	= 1 ounce	= 28·35 grams
16 ounces	= 1 pound (lb)	= 0·454 kilogram (kg)
14 pounds	= 1 stone	= 6·356 kilograms
112 pounds	= 1 hundredweight (cwt)	= 50·8 kilograms
20 cwt	= 1 ton	= 1016·04 kilograms
2000 pounds	= 1 short ton	= 0·907 tonne
2240 pounds	= 1 long ton	= 1·016 tonnes

Capacity

GB

20 fluid ounces (fl oz)	= 1 pint (pt)	= 0·568 litre
2 pints	= 1 quart (qt)	= 1.136 litres
8 pints	= 1 gallon (gall)	= 4·546 litres

US

16 fluid ounces	= 1 pint	= 0·473 litre
2 pints	= 1 quart	= 0·946 litre
8 pints	= 1 gallon	= 3·785 litres

Time

60 seconds	= 1 minute	28/29/30/31 days	= 1 calendar month
60 minutes	= 1 hour	12 calendar months	= 1 year
24 hours	= 1 day	365 days	= 1 year
7 days	= 1 week	366 days	= 1 leap year

GB Money

£ p (pounds and pence)   100 pence (100p) = 1 pound (£1)

	Amount	**Coin**
1p	a penny, (*informal* one p /piː/)	a penny
2p	twopence /ˈtʌpəns/, two pence, (*informal* two p)	a two-pence piece, (*informal* a two-p (piece))
5p	five pence, (*informal* five p)	a five-pence piece, (*informal* a five-p (piece))
10p	ten pence, (*informal* ten p)	a ten-pence piece, (*informal* a ten-p (piece))
20p	twenty pence, (*informal* twenty p)	a twenty-pence piece, (*informal* a twenty-p (piece))
50p	fifty pence, (*informal* fifty p)	a fifty-pence piece, (*informal* a fifty-p (piece))
£1	a pound, (*sl* a quid)	a pound (coin)

Note

£5, £10, £20, £50	five/ten/twenty/fifty pounds (*sl* quid)	a five-/ten-/twenty-/fifty-pound note; (*sl* a fiver/a tenner)
£3.82	three pounds eighty-two (pence)	